WALFORD'S GUIDE TO REFERENCE MATERIAL

EIGHTH EDITION

WALFORD'S GUIDE TO REFERENCE MATERIAL

Volume 2

Social and Historical Sciences, Philosophy and Religion

Edited by

Alan Day MA MPhil PhD DipLib FRGS FLA

and

Michael Walsh STL MA DipLib
Librarian, Heythrop College, University of London

LIBRARY ASSOCIATION PUBLISHING
LONDON

Published by
Library Association Publishing
7 Ridgmount Street
London WC1E 7AE

Library Association Publishing is wholly owned by The Library Association.

First published 1959
Supplement 1963
Second edition 1968
Third edition 1975
Fourth edition 1982
Fifth edition 1990
Sixth edition 1994
Seventh edition 1998
This eighth edition 2000

British Library Cataloguing in Publication Data
A catalogue record for this book is available from
The British Library

ISBN 1-85604-369-X

Computer production software and typesetting by LIBPAC (Computer Services) Ltd, Whittle le Woods, Lancs.
Printed and made in Great Britain by MPG Books Ltd, Bodmin, Cornwall.

This volume is dedicated
to the memory of

John Walford

MBE MA PhD FRHistS HonFLA FLA DipLib

1906–2000

Contents

Contents

Introduction

Background and compilation

From its first edition the purpose of *Walford* has been to identify and evaluate the widest possible range of reference materials. In addition to the expected bibliographies, indexes, dictionaries, encyclopaedias, directories, etc, a number of important textbooks and manuals of general practice are included. While the majority of items are reference 'books', *Walford* is a guide to reference 'material'. Thus periodical articles, microforms, online, CD-ROM and Internet sources are all represented. The objective is for *Walford* to provide a 'one-stop' source of information on all types of reference material, regardless of form. Targeted users include librarians developing and revising reference collections, staff on enquiry desks needing advice on further sources when local stock has been checked, research workers in the preliminary stages of projects, and students of library and information studies.

To be of manageable proportions a guide such as this must inevitably be selective. Most major reference tools are included, whenever originally published, provided they remain useful. Geographic scope is international, but with an emphasis on English-language material. A special effort has been made to ensure that the output of small and specialist publishers is not neglected. A special effort has also been made to include a selection of websites and electronic reference sources throughout. All URLs were checked and correct at the time of compilation.

Individual entries in *Walford* are wherever possible based on examination of the actual item and include full bibliographical details, ISBN, ISSN and, if in print, the price when it can be ascertained. Brief critical annotations are provided in most cases, giving summary publishing history, outline of contents, comparison with other works, especially notable features and a brief general assessment of overall value, often illustrated by quotations from or references to reviews. The example overleaf shows the general layout of entries.

Work on this volume was completed in mid-2000. Although no cut-off date for new material was specified, the aim has been to include as many 1999 publications as possible, together with some items published early in 2000. Intimation of planned new and revised editions is also given where possible.

A note from the compilers of this edition

This volume is divided, for the purposes of compilation, into two roughly equal parts. A number of members of staff of the Heythrop College Library, University of London (Michael Morgan, Brenda Weeden and Galina Bradley, under the overall supervision of Michael Walsh) are responsible for Classes 1, 2, 3 and 65. Alan Day is responsible for Class 9.

The 1990s saw a huge increase in the production of titles in almost every area and nowhere more so than in the publishing of reference materials. In the fields of philosophy and religion in particular, 'Companions', 'Guides', and 'Handbooks' flourished, the format of one series hardly distinguishable from another, save by the name of the publisher put proudly before the title. Within the historical sciences field this phenomenon is most visible in the superabundance of travel guides and handbooks, and in the continually burgeoning interest in genealogy and family history, but it is also evident across a wide range of subjects. In fact, there is now scarcely a topic not covered by a massive encyclopaedia, sometimes two or three, each offering a slightly different slant in order to find a niche in an increasingly competitive market.

A number of impressive new reference works have been published in the three years since the seventh edition of this volume was published. Routledge's ten-volume *Encyclopedia of philosophy* has apparently carried all before it, being an impressive commercial success as well as being enthusiastically received within the scholarly community. The *Biographisch-bibliographisches Kirchenlexikon* began in modest style in 1975 – the first volume reached 'Faustus' – but the publishers have realized its potential and are busily filling in the gaps, so that there are now sixteen volumes available making it by far the

37 Education

— Broad subject class

Further & Higher Education

— First level subheading

Form subheading ———————— *Bibliographies*

[3892] —— Running number used for index reference

The International encyclopedia of higher education. Knowles, A.S., *ed.* Washington, Jossey-Bass Publishers, 1977. 10v. (5208p.). $700 the set. ISBN: 0875893236.

V.1. *Contents. Contributors, Acronyms. Glossary.* v.2-9. *A-Z entries.* v.10 *Index.* About 500 named contributors. Appended to each substantial article are lists of (a) major international and national organizations; (b) principal information sources. 'Adult education': v.2. p.120-73: 7 sections, plus two appendices (p.168-73). Country entries are a feature. V.9 concludes with 'International directory' (p.4477-4588). V.10: *Index* comprises a name index and a subject index (p.4633-5208). Somewhat elaborate layout. For the very large reference library. 'A unique source for state-of-the-art surveys, and particularly for comparative studies ... (*Library journal*, 15th April 1979, p. 886). *Class No:* 378(031)

— Explanatory detail of contents

— Evaluative comment from compiler

— Subject arrangement by UDC

Evaluative comment from review ——

— ALTBACH, P.G. International higher education: an encyclopedia. New York, Garland, 1991. 2v.(1165p.) $150. £110. ISBN: 0824048474, US; 1558621520, UK.

Secondary entry ——

52 country and regional profiles (mainly underdeveloped areas) arranged by countries, blend description and analysis into short overviews of 10 to 20 pages, covering historical developments, current trends, structure and governance, higher education's relationship with political systems and labour markets, etc. Also included are 15 cross-cultural topics, including foreign education, graduate education, private higher education, and academic freedom. Updates, in part, the above aging encyclopedia. *Class No:* 378(031)

most satisfactory source for biographical information in Christianity. In the 900s the pre-eminent title is without doubt the American Council of Learned Societies' 24-volume *American national biography*, a completely new work to replace the venerable *Dictionary of American biography*. Another American title that cannot possibly be overlooked is the exuberant *Encyclopaedia of the Renaissance* in six volumes. Both these titles exemplify American scholarship at its very best. In the UK, a new edition of *Burke's Peerage* was published, the first for 30 years, which attracted some notoriety for its inclusion of illegitimate offspring. Monopolizing for a time the display windows of the Belfast bookshops, *Lost lives: the stories of the men, women and children who died as a result of the Northern Ireland troubles* chronicling 3,637 fatalities, in the period 1 June 1966 to 29 July 1999, is surely the saddest title ever entered.

In the first part of this volume, some 450 new titles have been added, and a similar number updated. In the 900s, some 650 titles are new to this edition and over 500 existing entries have been updated. Space is always

at a premium, and to make way for the new titles an equal number of old entries have been discarded. This might appear wholesale butchery, but the opportunity has been taken to remove some titles, useful in their day, but now very much showing their age. This process was eased by the lengthening lists of two publishers. Scarecrow Press's expanding Historical Dictionaries series, including not only new titles, but also many updated editions, all of which provide factual content, extensive bibliographies, and a chronological framework, considerably improve the reference coverage of regions and countries overseas, for which there was previously scant English-language reference provision. Equally active in revising and updating its titles, Clio Press's World Bibliographical Series also offers solid and dependable support to reference librarians and information officers. Nothing of a similar nature exists for the – admittedly more disparate – subject areas of Classes 1, 2, 3 and 65, but the proliferating 'Companions', 'Guides' and 'Handbooks' mentioned above commonly carry extensive and up-to-date bibliographical information and guidance for research. In its role as a first-stop reference work, *Walford's guide* has traditionally noted bibliographies subsumed in other publications, a practice conspicuously apparent and effective in regard to these two series.

Subject arrangement and indexing

Entries in *Walford* follow a subject arrangement based on the Universal Decimal Classification International Medium Edition of 1985 (BS1000M). Subject access for users unfamiliar with UDC can be gained either by checking the contents page to find the relevant section and then browsing through the entries, which are subdivided by form, place, etc, or by using the subject index. The first level of subheading within each broad subject class is typographically highlighted by the use of rules (see sample entry overleaf).

Terms in the subject index are generated by the classification numbers given to the entries. Each entry has been allocated a running serial number in the text to provide easy access from both the subject and author/title indexes. There is an index of online, Internet and database services. Full instruction on the structure and use of the indexes can be found in their introductions.

Acknowledgments

This volume is the first to appear since the death of its founder, John Walford. Tributes to his illustrious professional career, and the part played by his *Guide to reference material* in the development of reference work have appeared elsewhere, but it would be unthinkable not to remember his contribution to successive issues of this *Guide* since he 'retired'. The compilers were delighted to receive at intervals batches of dustwrappers and review clippings that had caught his ever-vigilant eye. It was not always possible to enter them all, but many deserving titles came to our notice, which otherwise might well have escaped our attention. We shall miss his input. In later years he was assisted in this work by his wife, Mrs Jean Walford and the compilers are grateful that she has indicated her willingness to continue this rôle.

The whole project was overseen by Kathryn Beecroft of Library Association Publishing. Joan Bibby ably constructed a thesaurus based on the UDC classification scheme. Martin Harrison of LIBPAC Computer Services automated the data capture, indexing and typesetting.

Libraries consulted

General libraries
The British Library (Humanities; Map Library; Oriental and India Office Collections; Manuscripts)

Academic libraries
Advanced Legal Studies (School of Advanced Study, University of London)
British Library of Political and Economic Science (LSE Library)
Heythrop College Library, University of London
Manchester Metropolitan University
University College London (Institute of Archaeology)
University of London (Institute of Historical Research; School of Oriental and African Studies; School of Slavonic Studies)
University of London Library
University of Manchester

Public libraries
Birmingham
Bradford
Cardiff
Cheshire (Congleton; Crewe; Macclesfield; Nantwich; Sandbach; Wilmslow)
Edinburgh
Hammersmith and Fulham
Herefordshire (Hereford)
Highland Council (Inverness)
Kensington and Chelsea
Lancashire (Preston)
Leeds
Liverpool
Manchester
Shropshire Information Service, Shrewsbury
Stockport
Trafford (Altrincham)
York

Special libraries
Goethe Institute Manchester
Royal Geographical Society

E-mail discussion lists and Internet sites too numerous to mention have also been used.

Alan Day
Michael Walsh

Abbreviations

Listed below are the chief bibliographical abbreviations used in the *Guide*. Generally accepted abbreviations such as Co., Corpn. e.g., i.e., Inc., Ltd. and q.v. are not included.

AG [German] – Aktiengesellschaft: Co.
ALA – American Library Association
Abt. [German] – Abteiling: part
ampl. [Italian] – ampliata: enlarged
ampl. [Spanish] – ampliado: enlarged
Aufl. [German] – Auflage: edition
augm. [French] – augmenté: enlarged
aum. [Portuguese] – aumentada: enlarged
aum. [Spanish] – aumentado: enlarged
Ausg. [German] – Ausgabe: printing, edition

BS – British Standard
Bd [German] – Band: volume
BFr – Belgian francs
bearb. [German] – bearbeitet: compiled, edited
Belg. – Belgian

c – copyright date
C. Cd. Cmd. Cmnd. – Command papers
ch. – chapter(s)
chron. – chronology
col. – colour, coloured
cols. – columns
comp. – compiler
corr. – corrected
corr. – [French] – corrigé: corrected
corr. – [Spanish] – corregido: corrected
corr. – [Portuguese] – corrigida: corrected

DFI – Dutch florins
Dan. – Danish
diagrs. – diagrams
distr. – distributed
DM [German] – Deutschmark
druk [Dutch] – edition

ea. – each

ed. – edition, editor(s)
ed. – [Italian] – edizione
ed. – [Spanish] – edición
ed. – [French] – édition
ed. – [Portuguese] – edição: edition
enl. – enlarged
erw., erweit. [German] – erweiterte: enlarged
exp. – expanded

FID – Fédération Internationale de Documentation
facsim(s) – facsimile(s)
fasc(s) – fascicule(s)
fig. – figures
fldg. – folding
FFr – French francs
front. – frontispiece

ganz. [German] – gänzlich: complete
glav.red. [Russian] – glavnyi redaktor: editor-in-chief
Gld. [Dutch] – guilders
GmbH [German] – Gesellschaft mit beschränkter Haftung: Ltd
Gosud. [Russian] – Gosudarstvo: State

HMSO – Her Majesty's Stationery Office
Hft [German] – Heft: part number
hrsg. [German] – herausgegeben: edited, published

illus. – illustrations, illustrated
imp. [French] – imprimé, imprimerie: printed, printing firm
izd. [Russian] – izdanie: edition
izd. [Serbo-Croat] – izdanje: edition
Izdat. [Russian] – Izdatel': publisher

Jahrg. [German] – Jahrgang: annual publication

kiad. [Hungarian] – kiadás: edition

Kr [Danish, Norwegian, Swedish] – kroner

L. [Italian] – lire
l. – leaves
Lfg. [German] – Lieferung: number, part

m. fl. [Danish] – med flere: and others

n.d. – no date
neubearb. [German] – neubearbeitet:: revised
no. – number
Nor. – Norwegian
nouv. [French] – nouvelle: new (edition)
n.p. – no place of publication
Nr [Danish, German] – Nummer: number
n.s. – new series
NV [Dutch] – naamloze vennootschap: limited company

o.p. – out of print
omarb. [Swedish] – omarbetad: revised
opl. [Danish] – oplag: edition

p. – page(s)
pl. – plate(s)
port. – portrait(s)
pt(s) – part(s)
pub. – publisher
pubn. – publication

réd. [French] – rédigé: edited, compiled
repr. – reprinted
rev. – revised, revision
rev. – [French] – révisé: revised
rev. – [Portuguese] – revistada: revised
riv. [Italian] – riveduto: revised
R. [South Africa] – rands

Rs – rupees

Sch – Schillings
ser. – series
sér. [French] – série: series
SFr – Swiss francs
supp. – supplementary, supplement(s)
Sw. – Swiss
Swed. – Swedish

t. [French] – tome(s): volume(s)
T. [German] – Teil(e): part(s)

u. [German] – und: and
UDC – Universal Decimal Classification
udg. [Danish] – udgave: edition
uit. [Dutch] – uitgaaf: publication
uitg. [Dutch] – uitgegeven: published
umgearb. [German] – umbearbeitete: revised
Univ. – University
unveränd. [German] – unverändert: unaltered
uppl. [Swedish] – upplaga: edition
utg. [Norwegian] – utgave: edition

v. – volume(s)
v. p. – various pagings
VEB [German] – Volkseigener Betrieb: People's
    Concern
verand. [German] – verandert: revised
verb. [German] – verbesserte: improved
verm [German] – vermehrte: enlarged
vyd. [Czech] – vydání: edition
vyd. [Slovak] – vydanie: edition

wyd. [Polish] – wydanie: edition

1 Philosophy & Psychology

Philosophy

[1]
SPARKES, A.W. **Talking philosophy: a wordbook.** London, Routledge, 1991. [v],307p. £40. ISBN: 0415042224.

Attempts to give an account of the more important components of the vocabulary of philosophy in 10 chapters: 1. Saying things - 2. Meaning - 3. Nonsense, necessity, and possibility - 4. Inferring, implying, arguing, and 'if' - 5. Investigating - 6. Symbols: basic propositional forms; basic argumental forms - 7. of isms, ists, and ologies - 8. Arguing and investigating again - 9. Doing - 10. Relations. Notes (p.262-3). Bibliography (p.264-291). Index (p.292-307). 'A wonderful book to read' (*Choice,* v.28(10), June 1991, p.1624).
Class No: 101

Bibliographies of Bibliographies

[2]
A Bibliography of philosophical bibliographies, edited and compiled by H. Guerry. Westport, Conn. & London, Greenwood Press, 1977. xiii, [1], 332p. £58.50. ISBN: 083719542x.

2,353 numbered entries, covering the period *c.*1450-1974. Two main sections: 1. Bibliographies of individual philosophers (1-1395); 2. Subject bibliographies (subjects, A-Z; items 1396-2353). Some entries have brief annotations. 'J.J. Rousseau': entries 1120-35, including articles. 'Logic': entries 1994-2025. Author index. Interprets the scope of philosophy in a wide sense. *Class No:* 101(009)

Bibliographies

[3]
Bibliographie de la philosophie/Bibliography of philosophy. Paris, J. Vrin, 1937-. Quarterly. ISSN: 00061352.

Published by Institut International de Philosophie with the aid of Unesco.

Each issue has *c.*250 entries for books, arranged in 10 subject sections (1. Philosophy in general. Metaphysics. Phenomenology - 2. Logic. Semantics. Philosophy of science - 3. Philosophical psychology - 4. Philosophy of art. Aesthetics - 5. Ethics. Philosophy of values - 6. Social philosophy, Philosophy of law and politics - 7. Philosophy of history, of culture, of education - 8. Philosophy of religion - 9. History of philosophy - 10. Annuals. Reference books, Miscellanea. Annotations in language of the original for books in English, French, German, Italian and Spanish; in English or French for books in other languages. Annual indexes of books, names, and publishers.
Class No: 101(01)

[4]
BYNAGLE, H.E. **Philosophy,** a guide to the reference literature. Littleton, Col., Libraries Unlimited, 1986. x, 170p. $35. ISBN: 0872874648.

An annotated listing of general and specialized, mainly English-language, reference works in philosophy and related areas. Arranged in 14 numbered sections by type of reference work (indexing, abstracting and reviewing publications; directories and biographical sources; concordances: indexes; works of individual philosophers; computer databases), with general sources preceding specialized works. Author/title and subject indexes. '... detailed and judicious guide ...' (*Bulletin of the ABTPL,* no. 40, November 1987, p.2). DeGeorge's '*The philosophers' guide*' Lawrence, Kans, Regents Press of Kansas, 1980 (qv), is more comprehensive but less up-to-date.
Class No: 101(01)

[5]
D'ANGELO, E. **Developing a basic philosophy collection** - for reference and research. In *The Reference librarian,*v.40, 1993, p.169-188.

Recommendations for philosophy collections. In 6 sections: 1. General bibliographies - 2. Bibliographies of fields, schools or traditions - 3. Bibliographies of writings by and about philosophers - 4. Indexes and abstracts - 5. Journals for reviews - 6. General review media. Most entries have short annotations. *Class No:* 101(01)

[6]
DEGEORGE, R.T. **A Guide to philosophical bibliography and research.** New York, Appleton-Century-Crofts: Meredith Corporation, 1971. vii,141p.

About 1500 entries, briefly annotated, for sources, bibliographies and other reference tools, both general and special. 9 sections: 1. Dictionaries - 2. Encyclopedias - 3. Histories of philosophy - 4. Sources: bibliographies, standard editions and collected works of individual philosophers - 5. Bibliographies - 6. Library catalogues, trade bibliographies and American doctoral dissertations - 7. Philosophical serials - 8. Philosophical research, reports and publishing - 9. Biographies - 10. Philosophical professional life. Detailed subject, author and anonymous title index. Graduate and research level.
Class No: 101(01)

[7]
GAYGILL, H. **A Kant dictionary** Oxford, Blackwell, 1995 ix, 453p. £15.99 ISBN: 0631175350.

An opening essay traces Kant's publishing career and sets the tone for a dictionary which not only defines the terms Kant uses but also relates them to their (philosophically) historical context. It is admirably comprehensive and scholarly, but it is nonetheless written with a skill which will not daunt readers coming to Kant for the first time.
Class No: 101(01)KAN

[8]
LUCAS, G.R. **The Genesis of modern process thought:** historical outline, with bibliography. Metuchen, N.J., Scarecrow Press, 1983. 245p. $18.50, £16.50. (*ATLA bibliography series,* 7.) ISBN: 0810815893.

Essays precede annotated lists of articles and monographs. Arranged in 6 sections: Process rationalism - The Whiteheadian School - Evolutionary cosmology - Hegelian idealism - Pragmatism and realism - Bridge movements (personalism and English Hegelianism) - Concluding comments: The 'Heuristic Fallacy' in process metaphysics. Each section is subdivided by sub-topics. Bibliography of sources. Author index. '... balanced and much-needed volume ...' (*Choice,* October 1983. p.253). *Class No:* 101(01)

[9]
Philosophical books. 1960- Quarterly. Ellis, A., *ed.* Oxford, Basil Blackwell (previously Leicester University Press), 1960-. Institutions: £104. $216. Individuals: £38. $74 pa. ISSN: 00318051.

Aims to provide prompt scholarly reviews to assist both the librarian and individuals in the choice of professional works of philosophy, with both short one-page reviews to lengthy critical notices and regular subject surveys. Arranged in subject sections, including History of philosophy, General philosophy, Metaphysics, Philosophy of mind, Ethics, Philosophy of religion, Aesthetics, Philosophy of science, Political philosophy, Philosophy of social science, and Legal philosophy, preceded by sections of new journals and critical notices.
Class No: 101(01)

[10]
—The Philosophical quarterly. Fife, University of St. Andrews, for the Scots Philosophical Club, 1950-. £33pa. ISSN: 00318094.

Each issue carries several articles and a number of lengthy book reviews of 1-2 pages. Also lists books received. *Class No:* 101(01)

[11]
—Philosophischer Literaturanzeiger. Klostermann, 1945/50-. Quarterly (previously 8pa). ISSN: 00318175.

A reviewing journal on an international scale, reviewing *c.*100 items pa and listing others. Author index. *Class No:* 101(01)

[12]
Répertoire bibliographique de la philosophie. Louvain, Peeters, 1949-. v.1-. Quarterly. ISSN: 00344567.

Over 10,000 references a year. Issues 1-3 cover books and periodical articles; issue 4 includes list of review articles and a general index of names. Arranged in subject sections. Claims to have complete coverage of monographs in Western languages. *Class No:* 101(01)

[13]
Resources in ancient philosophy an annotated bibliography of scholarship in English. Bell, A.A. *and* Allis, J.B., *comps.* Metuchen, N.J., Scarecrow, 1991 xvii,799p. $79.50 ISBN: 0810825201.

An immense bibliography (over 7,000 entries) from the earliest philosophers down to St Augustine. Entries are annotated. The volume is, however, not very well organized, and there are no author indexes. *Class No:* 101(01)

[14]
TICE, T.N. *and* SLAVENS, T.P. **Research guide to philosophy.** Chicago, American Library Association, 1983. xii, 608p. $40. £39.95. (*Sources of information in the humanities, no.3.*) ISBN: 0838903339.

In 3 parts: a historical survey (p.3-301): 17 areas of philosophy p.305-500); reference works, classified, annotated (p.503-519). Author/title and subject indexes (p.517-608). 'An excellent work; the best in the field. It does not exactly replace R.T. DeGeorge's *The philosophers' guide* but it will be of greater help to reference librarians assisting advanced students in philosophy ...' (*RQ*, Summer 1984, p.479). *Class No:* 101(01)

Ancient Greece & Rome

[15]
'**The Classical world' bibliography of philosophy, religion and rhetoric.** New York & London, Garland Publishing Inc., 1978. 396p. (Garland reference library of the humanities, v.95). $51. ISBN: 0824098781.

19 bibliographical essays (some with critical comments) on Greek and Roman philosophy, Roman religion and ancient rhetoric (*e.g.* 'A bibliography of works on Lucretius, 1945-1972', p.139-226 (822 items in 15 sections);'Early Roman religion, 1945-1972', p.227-42. Reprinted from the monthly *Classical world* (Classical Association of the Atlantic States. Duquesne University, Department of Classics, Pittsburgh, Pa.). 'This book will be of great use to the researcher as well as the teacher and students' (*American reference books annual*, v.10, 1979, item 1080). *Class No:* 101(01)(37/38)

Aristotle

[16]
ARISTOTELIAN SOCIETY. **A Synoptic index to the 'Proceedings of the Aristotelian Society...'** Scott, J.W., *ed.* V.1 Oxford, Blackwell, 1954. v.2-3. London, Methuen, 1961, 1975. 3v.

V.1: 1900-1949; v.2: 1950-1959; v.3: 1960-1969.

Pt.1 of the 1900-1949 volume consists of entries, arranged by authors of papers, A-Z. Synopses of arguments for all the papers listed. Synopses are asterisked if the contributor has not collaborated in making them. Pt.2 is an index of subjects, with cross-references to pt.1. An appendix gives contents lists of separate volumes of the 'Proceedings' for the pre-1900 period (*i.e.* 1887-96), for 1900-49, and for 1950-53. Covers a wide range of aspects of philosophy. Considered 'a major new tool for the subject, an indexing and abstracting service' (Stavely, R. *Notes on subject bibliography* (1959), p.34). *Class No:* 101(01)ARI

[17]
—BARNES, J., *and others.* Aristotle: a bibliography. Rev. ed. Oxford, University of Oxford, Sub-Faculty of Philosophy, 1981. [vii], 88p. (*Study aids, v.7.*)

10 sections: 1. Introductory (tests, etc.; biography; Aristotle; general studies; collections) - 2. Juvenilia - 3. Logic - 4. Metaphysics - 5. Philosophy of science - 6. Science - 7. Psychology - 8. Ethics - 9. Politics - 10. Poetics. About 1000 references. No index. 'Designed primarily to suit the interests of English-speaking philosophers' (*Preface*). *Class No:* 101(01)ARI

Augustine

[18]
INSTITUT DES ÉTUDES AUGUSTINIENNES, PARIS. **Fichier Augustinien/Augustine bibliography.** Boston, Mass., G.K. Hall, 1972. 4v. (2,675p.). $355 the set. ISBN: 0816109478.

60,000 photolithographed cards. Author and subject catalogues. Based on the bibliographies appearing in the quarterly *Augustiniana*. A supplement was published in 1981 ($125. 0816103658).

T.J. van Bavel's *Répertoire bibliographique de Saint Augustin, 1950-1960* (Steenbergen, Abbatia Santi Petri, 1963. 991p.) has author and name indexes. *Class No:* 101(01)AUG

[19]
MIETHE, T.L. **Augustinian bibliography, 1970-1980,** with essays on the fundamentals of Augustinian scholarship. Westport, CT., Greenwood Press, 1982. 218p. $35. ISBN: 0313226295.

A listing of 1400 (mostly secondary) books, parts of books, and periodical articles published worldwide during the 1970s and of American dissertations from the 1890s to the present. An elaborate subject arrangement within 4 main chapters covering the life and works, philosophical issues, and historical and doctrinal relations. Name index but no subject index. 'Need time to use the bibliography - not for rapid access' (*Bulletin of ABTAPL*, no.28, November 1983, p.6-7). *Class No:* 101(01)AUG

Buber

[20]
MOONAN, W. **Martin Buber and his critics:** an annotated bibliography of writings in English through 1978. New York, Garland, 1981. 240p. $39.50.

Compiled as a retrospective contribution to Buber's 1978 centenary. Over 1000 items noted, including 378 of Buber's in their English version. Many entries substantially annotated. Comprehensive subject index, index of translated titles, index of translators, and index of authors of secondary works. ' ... a model of reliable and cogent presentation'. (*Bulletin* of ABTAPL, No.28. November 1983. p.6). *Class No:* 101(01)BUB

Descartes

[21]
The Cambridge companion to Descartes. Cottingham, J., *ed.* Cambridge, Cambridge University Press, 1992. 624p. £45. (*Cambridge companions to philosophy.*) ISBN: 0521366232.

An account of his life, development of his thought, intellectual background and reception of his work. A central section is on Cartesian metaphysics. *Class No:* 101(01)DES

[22]
SEBBA, G. **Bibliographia Cartesiana:** a critical guide to the Descartes literature, 1800-1960. The Hague, Nijhoff, 1964.

3612 numbered entries. In 3 pts.: (1) bibliographical and biographical studies of Descartes (11 subheadings); (2) an exhaustive bibliography of Descartes's writings; (3) a bibliography of all works devoted to Descartes (excluding items in (1), published 1800-1960, classified and A-Z subect indexes. *Class No:* 101(01)DES

Freud

[23]
The Cambridge companion to Freud. Neu, J., *ed.* Cambridge, Cambridge University Press, 1992. 368p. £50. (*Cambridge companions to philosophy.*) ISBN: 0521374243.

Approaches Freud from the philosophical, historical, psychoanalytical, anthropological and sociological perspectives, showing how he gave new and powerful way to think about human thought and action. 14 contributors. *Class No:* 101(01)FRE

Hegel

[24]
INWOOD, M. **A Hegel dictionary.** Oxford, Blackwell, 1992. 260p. £37.50. ISBN: 0631175326.

Two chapters (*Hegel and his language*; *Introducing Hegel*) precede the dictionary of c.100 key terms used by Hegel, covering German words and their English, Greek and Latin equivalents. Annotated bibliography of c.300 items. Index of foreign-language terms. General index, p.251-60. '... helpfully arranged, thorough, beautifully produced ...' (*Choice*, v.30(6), February 1993, p.941). *Class No:* 101(01)HEG

[25]
STEINHAUER, K., *comp.* **Hegel bibliography:** background material on the international recognition of Hegel within the context of the history of philosophy/Hegel Bibliographie... Munich, K.G. Saur, 1980. xvi,894p. DM248. ISBN: 059803184x.

Over 13,000 entries. Sections: Bibliographies (complete works; selected works; single editions & correspondence) - Bibliography of secondary sources (including disserations, theses and articles) on Hegel's philosophy and the philosophy of his period, arranged chronologically. 1802-1975 (18 periods; items 871-12,032). Annex: Index of articles on Hegel, p.669-76. List of most significant periodicals and series. Index of authors, editors and translators. 'This work replaces all other Hegel bibliographies' (*Choice*, v.18, no.10, June 1981, p.1394). *Class No:* 101(01)HEG

Hume

[26]

HALL, R. **Fifty years of Hume scholarship:** a bibliographical guide. Edinburgh, Edinburgh University Press, 1978. 166p.

Aims at completeness for the 50 years, 1925-76, and also lists titles of main contributions, 1900-24. Author and subject indexes. 'An extremely useful book' (*Library journal*, v.104(6), 15 March 1979, p.717). *Class No:* 101(01)HUM

[27]

—JESSOP, T.E. A Bibliography of David Hume, and of Scottish philosophy, from Francis Hutcheson to Lord Balfour. London, Brown, 1938. xiv,201p.

Hume (p.3-71): Collected works - Works published by Hume and translations of these - Posthumously published works - Spuria - Works on Hume.

Scottish philosophy: chronological list of authors; general; philosophers, A-Z. An appendix on the Gifford Lectures gives a complete list of the lectures published. Index of names. *Class No:* 101(01)HUM

Kant

[28]

The Cambridge companion to Kant. Guyer, P., *ed.* Cambridge, Cambridge University Press, 1992. 496p. £50. (*Cambridge companions to philosophy*.) ISBN: 0521365872.

A systematic and comprehensive account of the full range of Kant's writings available. 14 contributors. *Class No:* 101(01)KAN

[29]

WALKER, R.C.S. **A Selective bibliography on Kant.** 2nd. ed. Oxford, Sub-Faculty of Philosophy, 1978. vi, 68p. Mimeographed. (*Study aids, v.5*.)

9 sections: 1. Works by Kant and their English translations - 2. Books - 3. Development up to 1781 - 4. *Critique of pure reason* and *Prolegomena* - 5. *Critique of practical reason* and *Grundlegung* - 6. *Critique of judgement* - 7. *Metaphysical foundations of natural science* - 8. *Metaphysics of morals* - 9. Opus postumum. List A: 'Compulsory reading'; B; 'Slightly less compulsory reading'. Aims at being 'a bibliography which may be of some use to graduate students'. *Class No:* 101(01)KAN

[30]

—EISLER, R. Kant-Lexikon. Nachschlagewerk zu Kants sämlichen Schriften, Briefen und handschriftlichen Nachlass. Berlin, Mittler, 1930 (reprinted 1964). viii,642 p.

Compiled with the co-operation of the Kantgessellschaft.

A dictionary-index to keywords in Kant's writings, with numerous cross-references. List of Kant's works, p.640-2. *Class No:* 101KAN(01)

Kierkegaard

[31]

EVANS, C.D. Søren Kierkegaard bibliographies: remnants, 1944-80, and multi-media, 1929-1991. Montreal, Quebec, McGill University Library, 1993. 185p. $25. (*(Fontanus monograph series, ll)*.) ISBN: 0771702728.

475 unique items, supplementing and continuing J. Himmelstrup's *Søren Kierkegaard: international bibliography* (1962) and F.H.Lapointe's *Søren Kierkegaard and his critics* (1981) (*qv*). Entries arranged A-Z under each grouping. No annotations or index. All items included in the International Kierkegaard Bibliographic Database at the University of Toronto. *Class No:* 101(01)KIE

[32]

HIMMELSTRUP, J. *and* BIRKET-SMITH, K., *eds.* Søren Kierkegaard: international bibliografi. København, Nyt Nordisk Forlag, 1962. 216p.

6,995 entries, in 2 sections: 1. Works by Kierkegaard; 2. Literature on Kierkegaard, citing important reviews. *Class No:* 101(01)KIE

[33]

—JØRGENSEN, A. Søren Kierkegaard-Literatur, 1961-1970. Aarhus, Akademisk Boghandel, 1971. 99p. *Class No:* 101(01)KIE

[34]

—JØRGENSEN, R. Søren Kierkegaard-Literatur, 1971-1980: en bibliografi. Aarhus, Akademisk Boghandel, 1983, 112p. ISBN: 9798017209.

Both Jørgensen's volumes update the earlier title. Introductions and notes are in Danish. *Class No:* 101(01)KIE

[35]

LAPOINTE, F.H., *comp.* Søren Kierkegaard and his critics: an international bibliography of criticism. Westport, CT., Greenwood Press, 1980. viii,430p. ISBN: 0313223335.

In 2 parts: Bibliography of Søren Kierkegaard - Bibliography on Søren Kierkegaard. Part 2 has 8 chapters: 1. Books and reviews - 2. Dissertations - 3. General discussion of ... work and life - 4. Studies of individual works - 5. Entries arranged by proper names - 6. Entries arranged by subject - 7. Memoirs, portraits, personal - 8. Anniversary and commemoration. Items are numbered. No annotations. Appendix: Kierkegaard bibliographies. Index of authors and editors, p.389-430. *Class No:* 101(01)KIE

Leibniz

[36]

MÜLLER, K. Leibniz-Bibliographie: der Literatur über Leibniz bis 1980. Neue Aufl. Frankfurt am Main, Klostermann, 1982. xxiii,742p. ISBN: 3465015827.

First published 1967.

6796 items on Leibniz. 7 main sections: 1. General - 2. Leibniz' life - 3. General characteristics - 4. Special characteristics - 5. Leibniz' work (p.83-208) - 6. Philosophy - 7. Connections, activities. *Class No:* 101(01)LEI

[37]

—MÜLLER, K. Leibniz-Bibliographie Bd. 2. die Literatur uber Leibniz 1981-1990. Frankfurt-am-Main, Klosterman, 1991. 267p. (*Veroffentlichungen des Leibniz-Archivs; 12.*.) ISBN: 3465028090. *Class No:* 101(01)LIE

[38]

—RAVIER, E. Bibliographie des oeuvres de Leibniz. Paris, Alcan, 1937 (facsimile reprint, Hildesheim, G. Olms Verlagsbuchhandlung, 1966). v.703p.

Complementary to the above. *Class No:* 101(01)LEI

Locke

[39]

YOLTON, J.S. *and* YOLTON, J.W. John Locke: a reference guide. Boston, Mass., G.K. Hall, 1985. 294p. $49.50. £49. (*A reference guide to literature*.) ISBN: 0816182361.

Over 1800 entries, with resumés, of secondary works published from 1689 to 1982. Arranged chronologically by publication date subdivided by author, A-Z. Name and subject indexes. Supercedes Christopherson's *Bibliographical notes to the study of John Locke* (1930). Some large blocks of numbers in the index under one heading (*e.g.* 140 under 'Education, some thoughts concerning') 'but despite flaws, high recommended' (*Choice*, v.22(11/12), July/August 1985, p.1622). *Class No:* 101(01)LOC

Marx

[40]

The Cambridge companion to Marx. Carver, T., *ed.* Cambridge, Cambridge University Press, 1992. 373p. £50. (*Cambridge companions to philosophy*.) ISBN: 0521366259.

Aims to place Marx's writings in their historical context and to separate what he actually said from what others (Engels, etc.) interpreted him as saying. Covers all the major areas in which he made significant contributions. 13 contributors. *Class No:* 101(01)MAR

Mill

[41]

LAINE, M. Bibliography of works on John Stuart Mill. Toronto, University of Toronto Press, 1981. 173p. $31.25; £26.50. ISBN: 0802024149. *Class No:* 101(01)MIL

Nietzsche

[42]

REICHERT, H.W. *and* SCHLECTA, K., *comps. & eds.* International Nietzsche bibliography. Rev. & expanded ed. Chapel Hill, University of North Carolina Press, 1969. 162p.

First published 1960.

Updated to 1967, identifying some 566 new publications. 4566 numbered entries, 'omitting most of the purely popular accounts' (*Library journal*, v.94(22), 15 December 1969, p.4514). *Class No:* 101(01)NIE

Plato

[43]
McKIRAHAN, R.D. **Plato and Socrates:** a comprehensive bibliography, 1958-1973. New York, Garland, 1978. 592p. (Garland reference library of the humanities, v.78). $75. ISBN: 0824098951.
Continues 'Plato (1950-1957)' by Harold Cherniss, in *Lustrum*, v.4 (1959) & 5 (1960). Over 4,600 unannotated entries under detailed topics, with full cross-references. Lists book reviews. Author index. ' ... an essential tool in graduate and advanced undergraduate collections'. (*Choice*, September 1978, p.843). *Class No:* 101(01)PLA

[44]
PLATO. Complete works. Cooper, J. M. *and* Hutchinson, D.S., *eds.* Indianapolis, Ind., Hackett Publishing, 1997 xxx,1808p. $29.95 ISBN: 0872203492.
An extraordinarily cheap edition of all the dialogues, translated by several different hands, most if not all of them very capable interpreters of Plato. *Class No:* 101(01)PLA

Rousseau

[45]
DENT, N.J.H. **The Rousseau dictionary** Oxford, Blackwell, 1992. 260p. £37.50. (*(Blackwell philosopher dictionaries)*.) ISBN: 0631175687.
Over 100 entries A-Z on the principal philosophical, social and political works of Rousseau, and his life. *Class No:* 101(01)ROU

Russell

[46]
A **Bibliography of Bertrand Russell** Blackwell, K. *and* Ruja, H., *ed.* London, Routledge, 1994 £250.00
Published in three volumes.
Volume I covers separate publications from 1896 to 1990. Volume II covers serial publications from 1890 to 1990. Volume III gives indexes for the two previous volumes.
An exhaustive bibliography of Russell's writings, serving as the final volumes of the Lee Mest University edition of his collected works. Very detailed bibliographic information. It even lists a few pieces erronously attributed to him. *Class No:* 101(01)RUS

[47]
MARTIN, W., *comp.* **Bertrand Russell:** a bibliography of his writings ... 1895-1976. New York, K.G. Saur, 1981. xlv, 332p. $27. ISBN: 3598103484.
The bibliography is arranged chronologically, and supported by several indexes (p.261-332), a chronological index of main works; a synopsis; secondary literature; index of works; and list of sources. In English and German. *Class No:* 101(01)RUS

Sartre

[48]
BELKIND, A. **Jean-Paul Sartre:** Sartre and existentialism in English; a bibliographical guide. Kent, Ohio, Kent State University Press, 1970 (available from Books on Demand UMI). 234p. $63.50. ISBN: 0835793672.
Lists English translations of Sartre's works, English books on Sartre, periodical reviews of Sartre's works, etc. List of sources; index, p.217-34. *Library journal* (v.95(12), 15 June 1970, p.2247) praises tracing of pamphlets, periodical material, unpublished theses and dissertations. *Class No:* 101(01)SAR

[49]
—Les Écrits de Sartre. Chronologie, bibliographie commentée. Contat, M. *and* Rybalka, M., *comps.* Paris, Gallimard, 1970. 788p.
An annotated bibliography (7 sections, p.45-482), preceded by a detailed chronology. Index of titles; index of periodicals; index of names and subjects. *Class No:* 101(01)SAR

[50]
The **Cambridge companion to Sartre.** Howells, C., *ed.* Cambridge, Cambridge University Press, 1992. 400p. £45. (*Cambridge companions to philosophy.*) ISBN: 0521381142.
Essays cover Sartre's writings on ontology, phenomenology, psychology, ethics, and aesthetics, as well as his work on history, commitment and progress. Special feature is the treatment of recently published posthumous works. 11 contributors. *Class No:* 101(01)SAR

[51]
LAPOINTE, F.H. *and* LAPOINTE, C., *comps.* **Jean-Paul Sartre and his critics:** an international bibliography (1938-1980): annotated and revised. 2nd ed. Bowling Green, Ohio, Philosophy Documentation Centre, 1981. 697p. $39.25. ISBN: 0912632445.
Class No: 101(01)SAR

Schopenhauer

[52]
HÜBSCHER, A. **Schopenhauer-Bibliographie.** Stuttgart-Bad Cannstatt, Frommann-Holzhoog, 1981. 331p. DM.98. ISBN: 3772807925.
Includes both primary and secondary sources, in German and in the other languages. Detailed subject arrangement includes sections on philosophers and their contemporaries. Author index and detailed list of contents, but no subject index. *Class No:* 101(01)SCH

Spinoza

[53]
OKO, A.S., *comp.* **The Spinoza bibliography.** Boston, Mass., G.K. Hall, under the auspices of the Columbia University Libraries, 1970. xxiii,700p. $85. ISBN: 0816106991.
A photolithographed reproduction of about 7000 cards (10 per page). Classified arrangement in main sections A-M. No index. *Class No:* 101(01)SPI

St. Thomas

[54]
MIETHE, T.L. *and* BOURKE, V.J. **Thomistic bibliography, 1940-1978.** Westport, CT., Greenwood Press, 1980. 318p. $46.95; $23.95. ISBN: 0313219915.
Continues V.J. Bourke's *Thomistic bibliography, 1920-1940*, listing 4746 titles, which appeared as a supplement to v.21 (1945) of *The Modern schoolman* (St. Louis, Missouri, 1945, viii,312p. (Reprinted by Hackett Publishers)).
Includes 4097 entries for editions and translations of St. Thomas's writings, and books and periodical articles on his life, teachings and influence. *Class No:* 101(01)THO

Teilhard de Chardin

[55]
JARQUE, J.E. **Bibliographie générale des oeuvres et articles sur Pierre Teilhard de Chardin.** Fribourg, Éditions Universitaires Fribourg, 1970. 206p.
2228 unannotated entries (with many interpolations) on Teilhard de Chardin, under authors, A-Z. Appended list of items not in French, of reviews and publishers. Subject and name indexes. *Class No:* 101(01)TEI

[56]
—BAUDRY, G.-H. **Pierre Teilhard de Chardin:** bibliographie (1881-1972). Lille, Facultés Catholiques, 1972. 113,[1]p. (*Mémoires et travaux, fasc.61.*)
Devotes part 1 to listing editions of works and corespondence, and part 2 to works and articles on Teilhard de Chardin (p.25-100; 1855 entries). Appendix of theses in French. Index of authors, persons cited and subjects. *Class No:* 101(01)TEI

[57]
—McCARTHY, J.M. **Pierre Teilhard de Chardin:** a comprehensive bibliography. New York, Garland, 1981. 438p. $40. (*Garland reference library of the humanities, v.158.*) *Class No:* 101(01)TEI

Wittgenstein

[58]
LAPOINTE, F.H. **Ludwig Wittgenstein:** a comprehensive bibliography. Westport, CT., Greenwood Press, 1980. ix,297p. $46.95; £22.95. ISBN: 0313221278.
An unannotated bibliography of Wittgenstein's writings and writings on Wittgenstein, the second section including books and reviews, dissertations, studies of individual works, and a general discussion of the works of Wittgenstein. Entries arranged by proper names, p.134-158; entries arranged by subjects, p.159-258. Index, p.269-297. *Class No:* 101(01)WIT

Encyclopaedias & Dictionaries

[59]
INWOOD, M. **A Heidegger dictionary** Oxford, Blackwell, 1999 xvi, 283p. £50.00 ISBN: 0631190945.
Inwood is a highly competent interpreter of Heidegger, and renders as clearly as possible with a difficult thinker the philosophy of Heidegger in a series of brief essays. There is an excellent bibliography of Heidegger's own writings, a rather brief one on secondary publications. The listing of philosophical terms is in English - rather than the German which some users might have expected. *Class No:* 101(03)HEI

[60]

JAMIESON, D., *ed*. **Singer and his critics** Oxford, Blackwell, 1999. x, 368p. £55.00. (*Philosophers and their critics*.) ISBN: 155786909x.

Thirteen essays, together with a final response from Singer himself, on the whole range of Singer's ethical views, including the issue of animal rights for which he is perhaps best known.
Class No: 101(03)SIN

Encyclopaedias

[61]

CRAIG, E., *ed*. **Routledge encyclopedia of philosophy** London, Routledge, 1998. 10 vols. £1995.00 (includng CDRom) ISBN: 0415169178.

An extremely important and thorough publication. It has been geared both to the expert and, at least to some extent to the non-expert, for each main article opens with a paragraph giving an overview of the subject, before detailed, and highly competent, academic discussion. Articles can be extremely long: that on Aristotle, for example, runs to nearly 40 columns, with another six of bibliography. An important aspect of this work of reference is the attention which has been paid to non-Western philosophy. The final volume is an index volume.
Class No: 101(031)

[62]

Enciclopedia filosofica. Centro di Studi Filosofici di Gallarate. 2nd ed. Novara, Edipem, 1979. 8v.

First published 1957 (4v).

A scholarly encyclopedia, with signed and well documented articles. Range extends to literary, scientific and legal concepts. Features biographical articles (*eg*. on Coleridge), emphasizing philosophical thinking or contributions. V.8 includes two classified indexes, one arranged by branches of philosophy, the other by periods and regions. 'For layman and scholar alike'. (Entry based on Swidan, F.A. *Reference courses* (6th ed., 1988, p.63) and Sheehy's *Guide to reference books* (10th ed. 1986), entry BA 73). *Class No:* 101(031)

[63]

Encyclopedia of phenomenology. Embree, L., *ed*. Dordrecht, Germany, Kluwer Academic, 1997 £295.00 ISBN: 0792329562.
Class No: 101(031)

[64]

GARRETT, D. *and* BARBANELL, E., *eds*. **Encyclopedia of empiricism**. Greenwood, 1997. 455 p. $99.50. ISBN: 0313289328.

Covers empiricism as the term refers to: 1. a philosophical emphasis on the relative importance of experience and processes grounded in experience; and 2. the tendency in 17th and 18th century thought usually identified with British philosophers such as Locke and Hume. Entries have bibliographies. *Class No:* 101(031)

[65]

PARKINSON, G.H.R., *ed*. **An Encyclopaedia of philosophy**. London, Routledge, 1990.$bxi, 950p.$c£90. ISBN: 0415603237.

Designed to provide a survey of current philosophical thought which will not merely provide information but will also help the reader to understand the nature of the subject (*Preface*). 37 self-contained articles are grouped in 6 sections (A: Meaning and truth - B: Theory of knowledge - C: Metaphysics - D: Philosophy of mind - E: Moral philosophy - F. Society, art and religion). Each section includes notes and a bibliography for further reading. The work is prefaced by a survey of various views of the nature of philosophy, and completed by a glossary of philosophical terms (p.885-908); a chronological survey, 1600-1960; an index of names (p.921-925); and an analytical subject index (p.926-935). *Class No:* 101(031)

English

[66]

Dictionary of the history of ideas: studies of selected pivotal ideas. Wiener, P.P., *ed*. New York, Scribner's, 1968-73. 4v. & index. (3066p.). 5v. boxed set issued 1980, $67.50. ISBN: 0684164183.

V.1: Abstraction in the form of concepts - design argument; v.2: Despotism - Law, Common; v.3: Law, Concept of - Protest movements; v.4: Psychological ideas - Zeitgeist; v.5: Index.

About 250 contributors . Preface outlines 'domains and disciplines' involved in the history of ideas: the external order of nature, anthropology, psychology, religion and philosophy, literature and the arts; historical criticism; economics, law and politics; mathematics, logic, linguistics. Articles A-Z on 311 selected 'pivotal ideas' ('Cosmology from antiquity to 1850': v.1. p.535-54, with 1 col. of bibliography). Other articles, at random, on 'Baroque in literature'. 'Buddhism', 'China on Western thought and culture'. 'Faith, hope and charity', 'Welfare state', 'Space', 'Balance of power', 'Moral sense', 'Relativity', 'Game theory'. Index ([lx], 479p.) is fully analytical (*e.g.* 'Evil'; over 5 columns). *Class No:* 101(031)=20

[67]

The Encyclopedia of philosophy. Edwards, P., *ed*. New York, Collier-Macmillan, 1973. 4v. (2400p.). $200. £250. ISBN: 0028949501.

First published in 1967 in 8v.

1450 comprehensive signed articles (over 900 on individual thinkers). 500 contributors from 24 countries; international editorial board of 153. Some Western slant. Systematic bibliographical coverage is a feature. Copious cross-references. Detailed subject index with 38,000 entries. Articles are scholarly but readable. 'A valuable, definitive encyclopedia' (*ARBA*, 1975, item 1287).
Class No: 101(031)=20

[68]

REESE, W.L. **Dictionary of philosophy and religion:** Eastern and Western thought. 2nd ed. Atlantic Highlands, N.J., 1996. xiv, 856p. diagrs. ISBN: 0391038648.

First published 1980.

'Has many encyclopedic features, including analysis of the thought of all major philosophers and religious leaders' (*Preface*). A key feature; numerous cross-references from concepts to the thinkers concerned. Major emphasis is on explication of terms. 'Santayana'; 2½ cols. (11 sections), listing principal writings and noting concepts. Sometimes there is main entry under the term (*e.g.* 'Ontology': 2 cols., 13 sections - 1 per philosopher's concept). Expensive. 'Not an essential purchase for most reference collections. It could be very useful for personal collections or for a small library'. (*Choice*, v.17, no 5/6, July/August 1980, p.656). *Class No:* 101(031)=20

German

[69]

RITTER, J., *ed*. **Historisches Wörterbuch der Philosophie**, unter Mitwirkung von mehr als 700 Fachgelehrten in Verbindung mit Guenther Bien [and others]. Völlig neubearb. Basel & Stuttgart, Schwabe & Co., AG., 1971- v.1-8 (1971-92) A-Sc.

Revision of Rudolf Eisler's *Wörterbuch der philosphischen Begriffe* (4. Aufl. 1927-30, 3v.).

Planned to be in 10v. (*c*.5500 articles), plus an index volume. Almost 1000 contributors. Unsigned articles, often lengthy. Appended to each volume are a list of articles in that volume, a list of contributors, and abbreviations for sources and for periodicals. No biographies, but 'isms' are included. *Class No:* 101(031)=30

Handbooks & Manuals

[70]

The Cambridge companion to Aristotle. Barnes, J., *ed*. Cambridge, Cambridge University Press, 1995 xix,404p. £40.00 (*Cambridge Companions to Philosophy*.) ISBN: 0521411335.

An excellent volume by which to introduce students to the main topics of Aristotle's thought. There is a particularly good bibliography.
Class No: 101(035)

[71]

A Companion to philosophy of language. Wright, C. *and* Hale, B., *eds*. Oxford, Blackwells, 1997 xiii,721p. £70.00 (*Blackwells companions to philosophy*.) ISBN: 0631167579.

There is, say the editors in their preface, "no shortage of companionship for the philosophical tourist whose desire is merely for a short excursion. Our *Companion* is intended for the more determined and ambitious explorer". There are 25 "state-of-the-art" articles in three sections: I Meaning and theories of meaning (11 articles); II Language, truth and reality (7 articles); III Reference, identity and necessity. *Class No:* 101(035)

[72]

A Companion to the philosophy of mind. Guttenplan, S., *ed*. Oxford, Blackwell, 1994 xiv,642p. £60.00 (*Blackwell companion to Philosophy*.)

A particularly valuable aspect of this volume as one of the growth areas in Philosophy, is having major philosophers contributing essays on their own work. *Class No:* 101(035)

[73]

FLEW, A. **An Introduction to Western philosophy:** ideas and arguments from Plato to Popper. New rev. ed. London, Thames & Hudson, 1989. 512p. £10.95. ISBN: 0500275475.

First published 1971, subtitled 'ideas and arguments from Plato to Sartre'.

An introduction and textbook. Begins with Plato's Theory of Forms and ends with existentialism, linguistic philosophy and Karl Popper's radical integration of philosophy with the scientific method. Analytical index. *Class No:* 101(035)

[74]

PARKINSON, G.H.R., *and others, eds*. **The Handbook of Western philosophy.** New York, Macmillan, 1988. 935p. $90. ISBN: 0029495938.

Aims to give an account of the present state of philosophical thinking, mainly in British philosophy, European philosophy being treated only as necessary. 37 scholarly articles are grouped in 6 sections (Meaning and truth - Theory of knowledge - Metaphysics - Philosophy of mind - Moral philosophy - Society, art and religion). Each section has an introduction; each article has endnotes and an annotated bibliography. Several appendices, including a glossary of philosophical terms and a chronological chart. Subject and name indexes. 'The handbook will become a standard source of reference ... complementing the bibliographic essays in Tice and Slaven's *Research guide to philosophy* (1984)' (*Choice*, v.26(5), January 1989, p.782). *Class No:* 101(035)

[75]

Philosophy a guide through the subject. Grayling, A.C., *ed*. Oxford, Oxford University Press, 1995 viii,677p. ISBN: 0198751567.

Prepared by London University lecturers for London University students, this extremely thorough volume has seven essays on the major philosophical disciplines from Epistemology (distinguished here from Philosophy of Mind) to Aesthetics and four articles on the history of philosophy. A bibliography is appended to each contribution, and there is a particularly detailed index. *Class No:* 101(035)

Dictionaries

[76]

AUDI, R. **The Cambridge dictionary of philosophy.** Cambridge, Cambridge University Press, 1995 xxviii,882p. ISBN: 0521402247.

Described by one admirer as "not merely the best available dictionary of philosophy, but the best ever", it includes people as well as concepts. Its value, however, is diminished by an absence of bibliographies. *Class No:* 101(038)

[77]

BLACKBURN, S. **The Oxford dictionary of philosophy.** Oxford, Oxford University Press, 1994 vii,408p. £19.99 ISBN: 0192116940.

Circa 2,500 entries, most very brief on people and topics. No bibliographies. *Class No:* 101(038)

[78]

A **Dictionary of philosophy.** Mountner, T., *ed*. Oxford, Blackwells, 1996 xiv,482p. ISBN: 0631184597.

Features what the preface calls "philosophical self-portraits" by a number of eminent thinkers. Limited to Western traditions in philosophy. There is a "short list of books in print" which offers guidance to the available texts of major philosophers. *Class No:* 101(038)

[79]

Dictionary of the history of ideas: studies of selected pivotal ideas. P.P. Weiner, editor-in-chief. New York, Scribner's, 1968-73. 4v. & index. 5v. boxed set issued 1980, $67.50. ISBN: 0684164183.

V.1. Abstraction in the form of concepts - Design argument; 2. Despotism - Law, Common; 3. Law, Concept of - Protest movements; 4. Psychological ideas - Zeitgeist; 5. Index. About 250 contributors. Preface outlines 'domains and disciplines' involved in the history of ideas: the external order of nature, anthropology, psychology, religion and philosophy; literature and the arts; historical criticism; economics, law and politics; mathematics, logic, linguistics. Articles A-Z on 311 selected 'pivotal ideas' (*e.g.* 'Baroque in literature', 'Buddhism', 'Cosmology from antiquity to 1850', 'Faith, hope and charity', 'Welfare state', 'Relativity', 'Game theory'). Index ([lx], 479p.) is fully analytical (*e.g.* 'Evil'; over 5 columns). *Class No:* 101(038)

[80]

DURBIN, P.T. **Dictionary of concepts in the philosophy of science.** Westport, CT., Greenwood Press, 1988. 362p. $59.95. (*Reference sources for the social sciences and humanities, 6*.) ISBN: 0313229791.

About 100 terms from the natural and social sciences are included. Entries average about 4 pages in length and contain extended definitions and discussions of related philosophic issues, followed by a bibliography of up to 12 sources. Good index of subjects and persons. '... an excellent source for an entree to scholarly literature on basic topics (*e.g.* chance, gender, history, indeterminism, instrumentalism, paradigm, vitalism)' (*Choice*, v.26(6), February 1989, p.918). *Class No:* 101(038)

[81]

GRASSL, W., *ed*. **Dictionary of conservative thought.** London, Routledge & Kegan Paul, 1988. 300p. £27.50. ISBN: 0415003024.

About 100 lengthy articles arranged A-Z by topic, the aim being to map the range of the philosophic, economic and political ideas developed under general heading of conservatism. (Anarchism, Aristocracy, Art ... Democracy, Deviance, Duty ... Marxism ... War, Welfare). *Class No:* 101(038)

[82]

—ASHFORD, N. *and* DAVIES, S. A Dictionary of conservative and libertarian thought. London & New York, Routledge, 1991. 320p. £35; $49.95. ISBN: 0415003024.

Examines the ideas and arguments produced by the intellectual traditions of both conservatism and classical liberalism. 11 signed sections, each with brief bibliographies. An important supplement to the above. *Class No:* 101(038)

English

[83]

ANGELES, P.A. **A Dictionary of philosophy.** 2nd ed. London, HarperCollins, 1992. ix, 326p. £7.99. ISBN: 0064610268.

First published 1981.

Intended for students, laypersons and teachers, 'the emphasis is on areas most commonly covered by philosophy courses, including epistemology, metaphysics, logic, ethics, aesthetics and the philosophies of religion and politics' (*Preface*). Entries vary in length from *c*.20 to *c*.200 words. Cross-references. Index of philosophers, referring to page numbers of entries in which they are mentioned. *Class No:* 101(038)=20

[84]

BALDWIN, J.M., *ed*. **Dictionary of philosophy and psychology,** including many of the principal conceptions of ethics, logic, aesthetics, philosophy of religion, mental pathology, anthropology, political and social philosophy, philology, physical science and education, and giving a terminology in English, French, German and Italian. New York, Macmillan, 1901-05 (Reprinted New York, Gordon Press, 1977). 3v. in 4. $395 the set. ISBN: 0849017211.

The editor was assisted by 17 consulting editors from various countries and 50 contributing subject-specialists. Mainly concerned with philosophical subjects; articles on psychology are hopelessly dated and biography is treated very summarily. 'Antiquated' (*Times literary supplement* no.3, 420, 14 September 1967. p.809). Signed articles by experts, chiefly American and British. Thus the 3-column article 'Scepticism', by John Dewey, states etymology and discusses philosophical, ethical and religious aspects, with ten references. But the article on 'Plato' is 20 lines only, with cross-references. Appended to v.2 are indexes of Greek, Latin, German, French and Italian terms. *Class No:* 101(038)=20

[85]

BULLOCK, A., *and others*. **The new Fontana dictionary of modern thought.** 3rd ed. completely rev., expanded & updated. London, HarperCollins, 1999. xxiv,933p. £29.99. ISBN: 0006861296.

First published 1977, ed. by A. Bullock & O. Stallybrass. Published in New York by Norton as *The Norton dictionary of modern thought*.

In this latest edition of what has become something of a standard work, there are 3764 entries, contributed by 326 different scholars, Anglo-American, but mainly British. 711 entries have been deleted from the 2nd edition of 1988, and 984 new ones added. The majority of the remainder have been revised, or in some cases re-commissioned. The articles are signed (actually, initialled, but authors are identified). It is better on philosophy, psychology and politics than it is in its treatment of religion - which is weak, and sometimes even misleading. *Class No:* 101(038)=20

[86]

LACEY, A.R. **A Dictionary of philosophy.** 3rd ed. London, Routledge, 1996. ix, 386p. ISBN: 0415133327.

First published 1976.

Aims 'to give the layman or student a pocket encyclopaedia of philosophy, one with a bias towards explaining terminology' (*Preface*). 'Epistemology and logic occupy far more space than, say, either politics or aesthetics' (*Preface*). Longer articles have briefly annotated references (*e.g.* 'Naturalism': 3p., including 1p. of bibliography, 'Ought, obligation, duty': 2½p. 14 references). Potted biographies. Entries well-written, but too small to be useful and 'can in no way compete with Paul Edwards' 'The Encyclopaedia of philosophy' (8v. 1967). (*Choice*, October 1987, p.286). *Class No:* 101(038)=20

[87]

LAWRENCE URDANG ASSOCIATES LTD. **A Dictionary of philosophy,** prepared by Lawrence Urdang Associates Ltd. (A. Flew, editorial consultant; J. Speake, editor). 2nd rev. ed. London, Macmillan; New York, St. Martin's Press, 1984. xiii, 380p. £25; $22.50. ISBN: 0333369777.

1st ed. 1979.

Majority of items are accounts of keywords and phrases, but also includes some biographical entries (as much as 3000/4000 words for the greatest philosophers). Double column. Heavily cross-referenced. *Class No:* 101(038)=20

Russian

[88]

BALLESTREM, K.G. Russian philosophical terminology. Dordrecht, Netherlands, D. Reidel Publishing Company, 1964. viii, 117p. $18.50. (*Sovietica series no. 19.*) ISBN: 9027700362.

Glossary of *c*.1000 Russian philosophical terms, arranged in Russian alphabetical order, numbered, and followed by English, German and French equivalents. English, German and French indexes.
Class No: 101(038)=82

Reviews & Abstracts

[89]

FRANCIS. 519. Bulletin signalétique. 519. Philosophie. Paris, INIST Diffusion, 1947-. Quarterly. ISSN: 11573694.

Formerly *Bulletin analytique, Philosophie* (v.1-9, 1947-55), then *Bulletin signalétique. 519. Philosophie*

Since 1995 on CD-ROM; paper version no longer published.

Sections: 01. Études historiques - 02. Philosophie générale. Metaphysique - 03. Théorie des valeurs et philosophie morale. Philosophie de l'action - 04. Philosophie de l'histoire. Philosophie politique et sociale. Philosophie du droit - 05. Philosophie de la religion - 06. Philosophie de l'art. Esthétique - 07. Esprit et corps. Identité personnelle - 08. Philosophie de la culture. Anthropologie philosophique - 09. Économie. Civilization. Éducation - 10. Logique philosophie. Philosophie du langage - 11. Épistemologic. Philosophie des sciences. Théorie de la connaissance - 12. Dictionnaires. Encyclopédies. Bibliographies. Sociétés. Divers. Each issue has a list of periodicals processed. Index of concepts (analytical); index of authors. Available online. *Class No:* 101(048)

[90]

The Philosopher's index: an international index to philosophical periodicals and books. Bowling Green, Ohio, Bowling Green University, 1967-.v.1,no.1-, Quarterly. Institutions $209. Individuals $62. ISSN: 00317993.

c.2000 indicative and informative abstracts each year of articles in *c*.300 major journals in English, French, German, Spanish and Italian. Subject index. Arrangement is under authors. Includes books and dissertations as well as journal articles. *The philosopher's index: a retrospective index to US publications from 1940* (1978. 3v.) includes entries for *c*.15,000 articles and *c*.6000 books, 1940-76. 'Philosopher's index' database covers international philosophical periodicals, 1967-, and US philosophical periodicals, 1940-. Also available online (DIALOG) and CD-ROM. *Class No:* 101(048)

[91]

World philosophy: essay reviews of 225 major works. Magill, F.N. *and* McGreal, I.P., *eds.* Englewood Cliffs, N.J., Salem Press, 1982. 5v.

An expansion of *Master pieces of world philosophy in summary form* (1961. 2v.).

A chronological series of essay-digests of major philosophical treatises, explaining basic themes. Each essay carries further readings (briefly annotated). Western philosophical works preponderate.
Class No: 101(048)

Periodicals & Progress Reports

[92]

RUBEN, D.H., *comp.* Philosophy journals and serials: an analytical guide. Westport, CT., Greenwood Press, 1985. 147p. $35; £40.95. (*Annotated bibliographies of serials, no.2.*) ISBN: 0313239584.

An evaluative guide to 335 English-language serials, 38 of which are British, arranged A-Z by title. Each entry includes detailed information about publisher, price, circulation, MS selection, indexes and abstracts, target audience, acceptance rates, and critical annotation. 'This will be a valuable research tool for scholars and a selection tool for librarians' (*Journal of academic librarianship*, v.11(5), November 1985, p.321). *Class No:* 101(05)

Quotations

[93]

ADLER, M.J. *and* VAN DORAN, C., *eds.* Great treasury of Western thought: comments on man and his institutions by the great thinkers in Western history. New York, Bowker, 1977. 1771p. $49.50. £41. ISBN: 0835208338.

Nearly 50,000 entries, arranged chronologically in 20 chapters (127 subdivisions). Coverage extends to political as well as philosophical, ethical and religious topics. Author and subject indexes. Very favourably reviewed in *RQ*, v.17(3), September 1978, p.268-9.
Class No: 101(082.2)

Histories

[94]

BALES, E.F. A Ready reference to philosophy East and West. Lanham, MD., University Press of America, 1988. 289p. $24.50. ISBN: 0819166404.

A concise manual of the history of Western, Indian and Chinese philosophy. A summary chapter compares Western, Indian and Chinese thought, and bibliographies of selected works are appended to each entry. Index of philosophers. *Choice* (v.25(9), May 1988, p.1378) considers it surpasses recent philosophy reference books.
Class No: 101(091)

[95]

BRÉHIER, É. The History of philosophy. Translated from French by W. Baskin. Baskin, W., *trans.* Chicago & London, University of Chicago Press, 1963-69. 7v.

Translated from *Histoire de la philosophie* (Paris, Presses Universitaires de France. 1st ed. 1928-38. 6v.: 9th ed. 1967-68. 1: *The Hellenic age.* 1963. 2.: *The Hellenistic and Roman age.* 1965. 3: *The Middle Ages and the Renaissance.* New ed. 1966. 4: *The seventeenth century.* 1966. New ed. 1969. 5: *The eighteenth century.* 1967. New ed,. 1971. 6: *The nineteenth century: period of systems.* 1800-50. 1968. 7.: *Contemporary philosophy since 1850.* 1969.

A clear and comprehensive study of the development of philosophical thought, with chapter bibliographies. The author, Professor of Philosophy of the Sorbonne.

The French original has two supplementary fascicules: *La Philosophie en Orient*, by P. Masson-Oursel (1948), and *La philosophie byzantine*, by B. Tatakis (1949). *Class No:* 101(091)

[96]

CAVALIER, R., *and others.* Ethics in the history of Western philosophy. London, Macmillan Press, 1989. 336p. £35. ISBN: 0333452437.

A series of 13 studies of selected ethical theories of major figures in the history of philosophy, seeking to uncover their original context. 16 contributors. A basic work in the field. *Class No:* 101(091)

[97]

COPLESTON, F.C. A History of philosophy. Tunbridge Wells, Kent, Search Press Ltd. (previously Burns & Oates), 1947-1975. 9v. £12.50 each vol. £105 for 9 vols. ISBN: 0855324384, the set.

A lucid, scholarly work, written from the standpoint of the scholastic philosopher. Volume titles are: 1. Greece and Rome - 2. Augustine to Scotus - 3. Ockham to Suárez - 4. Descartes to Leibniz - 5. Hobbes to Hume - 6. Wolff to Kant - 7. Fichte to Nietzsche - 8. Bentham to Russell - 9. Maine de Biran to Sartre. Each volume has a substantial bibliography (*e.g.* v.9: p.419-68), many footnote references and a detailed, partly analytical index. Father Copleston, S.J., was Professor of the History of Philosophy at Heythrop College, Oxford, 1939-70.
Class No: 101(091)

[98]

—COPLESTON, F.C. Philosophy in Russia: from Herzen to Lenin and Berdyaev. Tunbridge Wells, Kent, Search Press Ltd. 1986. 480p. £25. ISBN: 0855325771.

Complements the above, covering the subject broadly and in detail from the eighteenth century to Lenin and into post-Stalin period.
Class No: 101(091)

[99]

GUTHRIE, W.K.C. A History of Greek philosophy. Cambridge, Cambridge University Press, 1962-81. 6v. £60.00 each vol. ISBN: 0521051592 V.1; 0521051606 V.2; 0521075661 V.3; 0521200024 V.4; 0521200032 V.5; 0521235731 V.6.

V.1: *The earlier Presocratics and the Pythagoreans*(1962); V.2: *The Presocratic tradition, from Parmenides to Democritus*(1965); V.3: *The fifth-century enlightenment*(1969); 4: *Plato. The man and his Dialogues: earlier period* (1975); 5: *The later Plato and the Academy*(1978); 6: *Aristotle: an encounter*(1981). The study of Anaxagoras in v.2.(p.266-344) provides a detailed analysis of his writings, with citations and footnote references. Each volume has an index of passages quoted or referred to, and a general, analytical index, plus a bibliography (unhelpfully arranged A-Z by authors; *e.g.* v.5,p.493-514). The section on Plato's *Apology* (v.5. p.70-93) gives date, historicity, summary and comment, with 30 footnotes. V.3. deals fully with the Sophists, their contemporaries, and Socrates. One reviewer (*Philosophy* v.39.no.148, April 1964, p.184-5) notes the paucity of Greek quotations, confined to footnotes and appendices. A scholarly survey, by the Professor of Ancient Philosophy in Cambridge University. 'Indispensable' (*British book news*, December 1976, p.892). *Class No:* 101(091)

[100]

A History of Western philosophy. Oxford, Oxford University Press, 1985-.

A comprehensive and up-to-date survey of philosophical ideas from earliest times to the present day, for students of philosophy and the general reader. 8 volumes are planned: No.1. Classical thought, by T. Irwin (1989 ISBN 0192191969). No.2. Medieval thought, by D. Luscombe (1997 ISBN 0192891790). No.3. Renaissance philosophy, by B. P. Copenhaver and C. Schmitt (1988. ISBN 0521251044). No.4. The Rationalists, by J. Cottingham (1988. ISBN 0192192094). No.5. The Empiricists, by R.S. Woolhouse (1988. ISBN 0192192075). No.6. English-language philosophy, 1750 - 1945, by J. Skorupski 1993 (ISBN 0192192116). No.7. Continental philosophy since 1750, by R. Solomon (1985. ISBN 0192192167) No.8. English-language philosophy since 1945, by D. Stroud. *Class No:* 101(091)

[101]

MARENBON, J. **Later medieval philosophy (1150-1350):** an introduction. London, Routledge & Kegan Paul, 1987. xi, 230p. £18.95. ISBN: 0710202865.

Aims to provide some of the important information without which medieval philosophical texts tend to baffle or mislead, and to give some detailed examples of how later medieval thinkers argued. 11 chapters in 2 parts: pt.1 examines the organization of studies in medieval universities; pt.2 examines in detail the way in which some important later medieval thinkers discussed a difficult and central question, the nature of intellectual knowledge. Bibliography, by chapter, p.194-224. Index, p.225-230. *Class No:* 101(091)

[102]

—MARENBON, J. **Early medieval philosophy (480-1150):** an introduction. Rev. ed. London, Routledge & Kegan Paul, 1988. xiv,197p. £8.95. ISBN: 041500070x.

First published 1983.

A companion volume to the above. *Class No:* 101(091)

[103]

PASSMORE, J.A. **A Hundred years of philosophy.** 2nd ed. London, Duckworth, 1966 (Reprinted Harmondsworth, Penguin Books, 1970). 574p. £5.95. ISBN: 0140209271.

First published 1957.

Author was Professor of Philosophy at the Australian National University. An excellent survey of 19th century and contemporary philosophers (starting with J.S. Mill and ending with Nagel and Feyerabend). The 2nd ed. adds considerably to accounts of Ayer, Popper, Wittgenstein and Sartre, completely rewritten and much enlarged sections on Austin, Jaspers and Heidegger, and a new section on Merleu-Ponty, etc. Extensive footnote references and notes; 'Further reading', p.147-9. Index of names; index (non-analytical) of subjects. 'One of the best handbooks on modern thought, as it is certainly one of the most readable' (*British book news,* no.338, October 1968, p.731). *Class No:* 101(091)

[104]

—PASSMORE, J.A. **Recent philosophers:** a supplement to *A Hundred years of philosophy.* London, Duckworth, 1985. 173p. £19.50; $21.95. ISBN: 0715618962.

Sketches recent happenings in the field and supplies a point of entry for those who wish to explore more deeply. 5 chapters (1. Introduction; change and continuity - 2. Structure and syntax - 3. From syntax to semantics - 4. Davidson and Dummett - 5. Realism and relativism). Notes, p.123-164. Index, p.165-173. *Class No:* 101(091)

[105]

RUSSELL, B. **History of Western philosophy** and its connection with political and social circumstances from the earliest times to the present day. 2nd ed., 1960, new impression of 2nd ed. 1992. London, Allen and Unwin, 1992. 916p. £30. ISBN: 0415090733.

First published 1946.

In 3 sections, each subdivided: Book 1. Ancient philosophy (part 1. The Pre-Socratics; pt.2. Socrates, Plato and Aristotle; pt.3. Ancient philosophy after Aristotle; Book 2. Catholic philosophy (pt.1. The fathers; pt.2. The schoolmen); Book 3. Modern philosophy (pt.1. From the Renaissance to Hume; 2. From Rousseau to the present day). Detailed index. ' ... brilliantly written exposé of changing philosophical doctrines ... ' (*Sir Julian Huxley*). ' ... monument of learning ... flashes of humour ... touches of malicious wit ... (C.E.M. Joad). *Class No:* 101(091)

[106]

WEDBERG, A. **A History of philosophy.** Oxford, Oxford University Press, 1982-84. 3v. illus., fig. v.1: £10.50;v.2: £12.50; v.3: £17.50. ISBN: 0198246390, v.1; 0198246404, v.2; 0198246412, v.3.

Originally published in Swedish in 1958 under the title 'Filosofins historia' and translated into English by Wedberg himself.

V.1. Antiquity and the Middle Ages; v.2 The Modern Age to Romanticism; v.3. From Bolzano to Wittgenstein. Aims to give an insight into the nature of problems, themes, and theories which are of present day, and possibly permanent, philosophical interest. Emphasis

....(contd.)

is on intellectual problems, and the content of theories, rather than on the personalities of the philosophers. Separate indexes to each volume. *Class No:* 101(091)

Ancient Greece & Rome

[107]

The Cambridge history of later Greek and early medieval philosophy, ed. by A.H. Armstrong. Cambridge, University Press, 1967. xiv, 710 [1]p. £80; ISBN: 0521226058.

'Originally planned in connection with W.K.C. Guthrie's *History of Greek philosophy,* but has developed on rather different lines ... It is an independent survey designed to show how Greek philosophy took the form which it was known to and influenced the Jews, the Christians of East and West and the Moslems, and what these inheritors of Greek thought did with their heritage during, especially the first millennium' (*Preface*). Coverage: from the Old Academy (4th century B.C.) to St. Anselm (beginning of 12th century A.D.). Final chapter 8: 'Early Islamic philosophy'. Select bibliography, by chapters, p.670-91. Index of ancient and medieval books referred to in the text; general, analytical index; index of Greek terms. *Class No:* 101(091)(37/38)

[108]

GOULET, R., ed. **Dictionnaire des philosophies antiques.** Paris, Centre National de la Recherche Scientifique, 1989-.

V.1: Abam(m)on à Axiothá. 838p. F.425. ISBN 2222040426.

Concerned primarily with Greek philosophers from earliest times to about the 6th century. 'Aristotle': over 150p. Citation to articles in Pauly-Wissowa. Well documented, with lists of standard editions, translations. Outline form for longer articles. Lengthy appendix on the Academy in Athens, plus maps and illustrations. Name, keyword and Greek keyword indexes. 'Recommended for all libraries with extensive collections in classics or philosophy.'(*College and research libraries,* v.52(2), March 1991, p.177). *Class No:* 101(091)(37/38)

Austria

[109]

SMITH, B. **Austrian philosophy** the legacy of Franz Brentano. Chicago, Ill., Open Court, 1994 xii,381p. $36.95 ISBN: 081269256x.

A history of Austrian philosophy from the 1870's down to the 1938 Anschluss from the perspective of the impact made by Brentano not only on philosophy proper but on psychology and linguistics. The author's concerns stretch beyond Austria to the surrounding countries, Germany, Poland, and (the then) Czechoslovakia in particular. *Class No:* 101(091)(436)

Middle Ages

[110]

The Cambridge history of later medieval philosophy, from the rediscovery of Aristotle to the disintegration of Scholasticism, 1100-1600. Kretzmann, N., *and others, eds.* Cambridge, Cambridge University Press, 1982. xiv, 1035p. £32.50. ISBN: 0521369339.

11 sections, each subdivided (1. Medieval philosophical literature; 2. Aristotle in the Middle Ages; 3. The old logic; 4. Logic in the Middle Ages: semantic theory; 5. Logic in the Middle Ages: propositions and modalities; 6. Metaphysics & epistemology; 7. Natural philosophy; 8. Philosophy of mind and action; 9. Ethics; 10. Politics; 11. The defeat, neglect and revival of Scholasticism). 41 academic contributors. Brief biographies, arranged A-Z by first name, p.853-892. Bibliography, p.893-975. Index nominum (name index with 'see' references), p.979-994. Index regum (subject index), p.995-1035.

Class No: 101(091)"01/14"

[111]

GILSON, É. **History of Christian philosophy in the Middle Ages.** 2nd ed. London, Sheed & Ward, 1972 (reprinted 1980). xvii,829p. £27.50. ISBN: 0722041144.

Based on the French *La philosophie au moyen âge, des origines patristiques à la fin du XIVe siècle* (Paris, Payot, 1922; 2nd ed. 1944), being not a translation but a 'reworking' of the material.

Arranged in 11 parts, covering 14 centuries. Bibliographical and other notes (p.549-804) on each of the leading philosophers. Indexes of authors and historians. The work of a leading expert in the field. Roman Catholic viewpoint. *Class No:* 101(091)"01/14"

[112]

—STEENBERGHEN, F. van. **Histoire de la philosophie.** Périod chrétienne. Louvain, Publications Universitaires, 1964. 196p.

Period covered ranges from the end of the 5th century to the end of the 12th; pt.3 deals with Arabic philosophy. The bibliography (p.181-6) notes both sources for research work and items for further reading. *Class No:* 101(091)"01/14"

[113]
—WEINBERG, J.R. A Short history of medieval philosophy. Princeton, N.J., Princeton University Press, 1964. ix,304p.

Considered by *Philosophical review* (v.75(3), July 1966, p.407-9) to be a work of first-rate scholarship and something of a classic. Selective bibliography, p.295-300. *Class No:* 101(091)"01/14"

Renaissance

[114]
The Cambridge history of renaissance philosophy. Schmitt, C.B., *and others*. Cambridge, Cambridge University Press, 1988. xiii,968p. £50. ISBN: 0521251044.

Aims to offer a balanced and comprehensive account of philosophical thought from the middle of the 14th century to the emergence of modern philosophy at the turn of the 17th century. 23 chapters arranged in 13 sections in 3 parts: Part 1 (I. Conditions of enquiry - II. The renaissance concept of philosophy - III. Translations, terminology and style in philosophical discourse - IV. Humanism). Part 2. (V. Logic and language - VI. Natural philosophy - VII. Moral philosophy - VIII. Political philosophy - IX. Psychology - X. Metaphysics - XI. Problems of knowledge and action - XII. Philosophy and humanistic disciplines). Part 3 (XIII. Appendices: The availability of ancient works. The rise of the philosophical textbook). Footnotes throughout. Biobibliographies, p.805-941. Bibliography, p.842-930, divided into primary and secondary sources, each A-Z. Index nominum, p.931-947. Index rerum, p.948-968.
Class No: 101(091)"1095-1300"

Modern Times

[115]
SCRUTON, R. A Short history of modern philosophy from Descartes to Wittgenstein. 2nd ed. (rev. and enl.) London, Routledge, 1995. xi,302p. ISBN: 0415130352.

A survey of modern philosophy in 5 chapters (1. Rationalism - 2. Empiricism - 3. Kant and idealism - 4. The political transformation - 5. Recent philosophy). Bibliography (p.285-293). Index (p.294-298).
Class No: 101(091)"15/19"

20th Century

[116]
AYER, A.J. Philosophy in the twentieth century. London, Weidenfeld & Nicolson, 1982. x, 283p. £12.50. ISBN: 0297781790.

Conceived as a sequel to B. Russell's *History of Western philosophy*, the major part of the book is devoted to representatives of two major schools, the American pragmatists and the analytic movement, dealing in depth with a relatively small number of outstanding individuals. Chapter I. Philosophical inheritance; II. The revolt from Hegel; III. Pragmatism; IV. Wittgenstein, Popper and the Vienna Circle; V. Wittgenstein, Carnap and Ryle; VI. Physicalism; VII. The philosophy of R.G. Collingwood; VIII. Phenomenology and Existentialism; IX. Later developments. Index p.271-83 in double column.
Class No: 101(091)"19"

Biographies

[117]
Bibliographic dictionary of twentieth-century philosophers. Brown, S. *and* Collinson, D. *and* Wilkinson, R., *eds*. London, Routledge, 1996 xxi,947p. ISBN: 0415060435.

Nearly 900 pages of A-Z entries, usually fairly brief, but with some bibliography in each case. This is followed by a 25 page "Guide to schools and movements", a nationality index for the circa 1,000 philosophers surveyed, a category index, defining them by their "type" of philosophy, an index of influences (who was important to whom), an index of people and of subjects. The definition of "philosophers" is fairly broad. *Class No:* 101(092)

[118]
BULLOCK, A. *and* WOODINGS, R.B., *eds*. The Fontana biographical companion to modern thought. London, Collins, 1983. xxv,867p. ISBN: 0002163292.

Cover title: *The Fontana dictionary of modern thinkers*.

Over 1500 entries, each by an authority on the subject, giving biographical details and an assessment of career and work. A list of contributors precedes the biography (AALTO ... ZWICKY); entries include subject, details of birth and death, subject's category, publications, bibliography (restricted to critical studies relating to subject's life and work and limited to 2 titles. Details of the subject's own publications are included in the entry itself. Entries average about a column in length. Cross-references. *Class No:* 101(092)

[119]
COLLINSON, D. Fifty major philosophers: a reference guide. London, Croom Helm, 1987. [4],170p. £22.50; $29.50. ISBN: 0709934661.

The philosophers included are all Western, all deceased, and range from Thrale to Sartre, in chronological order. Easy-to-read essays, describing the main thrust of the philosopher's thinking, information about his life, and concise expositions of one or two aspects of his thought, along with mention, where appropriate, of its connection with the thought of other philosophers. Notes and lists for further reading attached to each entry. Cross-references. Glossary of philosophical terms, p.164-170. *Class No:* 101(092)

[120]
Thinkers of the twentieth century: a biographical, bibliographical and critical dictionary. Turner, R.W. 2nd ed. New York, St. James' Press, 1987. 977p. $85; £64. ISBN: 091228983x.

First published in 1983.

A selection of 500 individuals representing a wide range of thinkers in the fields of philosophy, theology, social thought, psychology, economics, law, mathematics, and the biological and physical sciences. Entries include a biographical sketch, an extensive bibliography, a reading list, and a critical essay (of up to 3000 words) written by a noted expert on the individual. *Class No:* 101(092)

[121]
VESEY, G., *ed*. Philosophers ancient and modern. Cambridge, Cambridge University Press, 1986. v.313p. £8.95. ISBN: 0521337992.

Royal Institute of Philosophy lecture series 20. Published as a supplement to *Philosophy* (1986).

Chapters on Plato, Aristotle, Descartes, Hume, Marx, J.S. Mill, Nietzsche, Russell, Ayer and Sartre. Name index, p.309-312; subject index, p.313. Intended for examinations. *Class No:* 101(092)

Europe

Encyclopaedias

[122]
Great thinkers of the Western world the major ideas and classic works of more then 100 outstanding Western philosophers, physical and social scientists, psychologists, religious writers and theologians. McGreal, I.P., *ed*. New York, HarperCollins, 1992. 592p. $40. ISBN: 006270026x.

116 essays by 35 contributors, each with a brief annotated bibliography. Non-political expositions. Wider in range than Urmson's *Concise encyclopedia*. *Class No:* 101(4)(031)

[123]
URMSON, J.O. *and* RÉE, J., *eds*. The Concise encyclopedia of Western philosophy and philosophers. New ed. [3rd], completely revised. London, Unwin Hyman, 1989. xiii,331p. £25. ISBN: 0044453795.

First published 1960, by Hutchinson.

79 contributors. Signed articles (Hobbes: 6½ columns). Cross-references indicated in bold in the text. 80 new articles added to this edition, but bibliography omitted. *Class No:* 101(4)(031)

Histories

[124]
HIRSCHBERGER, J. A Short history of Western philosophy. Guildford, Lutterworth Press, 1976. xi,218p. £4.50. ISBN: 071882279x.

A translation from the German by Jeremy Moiser of *Geschichte der Philosophie* (9th ed., Freiburg, Herder, 1971).

In 4 parts, each subdivided: 1. The philosophy of antiquity - 2. The philosophy of the Middle Ages - 3. The philosophy of modern times - 4. The philosophy of the 19th and 20th centuries. No bibliography but works are referred to in the text. Indexes of names and subjects. *Class No:* 101(4)(091)

[125]
O'CONNOR, D.J., *ed*. A Critical history of Western philosophy. 2nd ed. London, Macmillan Educational, 1985. viii,600p. £12.95. ISBN: 033339366x.

First published 1964.

'... designed for use of undergraduate students of philosophy and for the intelligent general reader ...' (*Preface*). 21 chapters, most of which are devoted to one particular philosopher: (1. Early Greek philosophy - 2. Socrates and Plato ... 18. Bertrand Russell - 19. Logical positivism - 20. Existentialism - 21. Contemporary British philosophers). Notes, p 557-575, by chapter and page. Bibliography, p.576-789, by chapter, updated and simplified with this edition. Analytical index, p.591-600. *Class No:* 101(4)(091)

Renaissance

[126]

DRONKE, P., *ed*. **A History of twelfth-century Western philosophy.**
Cambridge, Cambridge University Press, 1988. xi,495p. £37.50.
ISBN: 0521258960.

'15 scholars from 8 different countries have collaborated to make the
first detailed survey of the subject' (Book jacket). 16 chapters arranged
in 4 parts: 1. Background - 2. New perspectives - 3. Innovations - 4.
The entry of the 'new' Aristotle. Biobibliographies of important
persons, p.443-457. General bibliography, p.459-486, arranged A-Z.
Index of manuscripts, p.487. General analytical index, p.488-495.
Class No: 101(4)(091)"1095-1300"

Contemporary

[127]

BOCHÉNSKI, I.M. **Contemporary European philosophy.** Translated
from the German by Donald Nicholl and Karl Aschenbrennen.
Nicholl, D. *and* Aschenbrenner, *trans*. Berkeley, Los Angeles &
London, University of California Press, 1956. (Reprinted by
Greenwood, 1982). xviii, 326p. $38.50; £26.75. ISBN: 0313234906.

7 chapters, 26 sections (separate sections for Croce, Bergson,
Heidegger, etc.). Appendix: Mathematical logic. International
organizations. Bibliography, p.265-321 (by chapters and sections).
Index. *Class No:* 101(4)"312"

Great Britain

[128]

SORLEY, W.R. **A History of British philosophy, to 1900.** Cambridge,
University Press, 1965 (Reprinted Westport, Conn., Greenwood Press,
1973. xx, 386p. $35; £22.95. ISBN: 0837167183.

First published 1920.

The text is based upon a series of chapters contributed to *The
Cambridge history of English literature* and is ably written. The
lengthy chapter-bibliographies in the 1st ed. (p.323-73) have been
revised and brought up to date. *Class No:* 101(410)

Germany

[129]

BUBNER, R. **Modern German philosophy.** Cambridge, Cambridge
University Press, 1981. xi,223p. £25. ISBN: 0521229081.

Translated from the German by E. Matthews.

Structured thematically to demonstrate the different active strains of
philosophy. Deals with individual philosophers as well as the schools
of the period. Introduction, 'On the historicity of philosophy' is
followed by 3 sections, all subdivided: (1. Phenomenology and
hermeneutics - 2. Philosophy of language and theory of science - 3.
Dialectic and philosophy of practice) and concluding remarks. Index of
names, p.221-223. *Class No:* 101(430)

[130]

Contemporary German philosophy, v.1-6, 1982-87.
Christensen, D.E., *and others*. University Park, PA., Pennsylvania
University Press, 1982-87. 6v. $26.50 each vol.

Each volume contains several articles, book reviews and review
articles. Devoted principally to making available in English,
contributions to philosophical comprehension originally published in
German. *Class No:* 101(430)

[131]

SCHNÄDELBACH, H. **Philosophy in Germany, 1831-1933.**
Cambridge, Cambridge University Press, 1984. x,265p. £25. ISBN:
0521227933.

Translated from the German by E. Matthews.

'... an attempt to give an account of the history of German
philosophy between the end of the Idealist period and the first stirrings
of the philosophy of our own time' (*Introduction*). 8 chapters: 1.
Sketch of an age - 2. History - 3. Science - 4. Understanding - 5. Life
- 6. Values - 7. Being - 8. Epilogue: Man. Notes, by chapter, p.235-
256. Select bibliography, by chapter, p.257-259. Index, p.260-65.
Class No: 101(430)

France

[132]

DESCOMBES, V. **Modern French philosophy.** Cambridge, Cambridge
University Press, 1981. xii,192p. £22.50. ISBN: 0521228379.

Translated from the French original, *Le Même de l'autre,* by L.
Scott-Fox and J.M. Harding.

An introduction, *Philosophy in France,* is followed by 6 sections, all
subdivided: 1. The humanisation of nothingness - 2. The human origin
of truth - 3. Semiology - 4. The critique of history - 5. Difference - 6.
The end of time. Footnotes throughout. Index, p.191-192.
Class No: 101(44)

Asia

[133]

NAUMANN, St. E., *jr*. **Dictionary of Asian philosophies.** New ed.
London, Routledge & Kegan Paul, 1990. xxi,394p. tables. £17.99.
ISBN: 0415039711.

Abhidharma ... Zoroastrianism. Entries for terms (giving
pronunciation), philosophies and thinkers. Sufism: p.316-21; Mao Tse-
tung: p.248-59; Indian philosophy (p.171-93: 7 sections). Text
interspersed with quotations. Cross-references. Preliminaries include
'Chronology of Asian philosophers', p.xiii-xvii. 'No doubt it could be
better, but in any case, it is the best there is' (*American reference
books annual,* v.10, 1979, item 1082). 'The best source [for Eastern
philosophers] is still the *Encyclopedia of philosophy,* edited by Paul
Edwards' (*Choice,* v.16, no.1, March 1979, p.57). *Class No:* 101(5)

Encyclopaedias

[134]

Companion encyclopedia of Asian philosophy. Carr, Brian *and*
Mahalingham, I., *eds*. London, Routledge, 1997 xxiii,1139p. ISBN:
041503535x.

48 articles, each with a bibliography, divided into six sections
(Russian, Indian, Buddhist, Chinese, Japanese, and Islamic). There is a
substantial glossary and a very thorough index. *Class No:* 101(5)(031)

China

[135]

ADELMANN, F.J., *ed*. **Contemporary Chinese philosophy.** The
Hague, Martinus Nijhoff, 1982. xx,219p. £44.75. (*Martinus Nijhoff
philosophy library, v.9. Boston College studies in philosophy, VI.*)
ISBN: 9024730570.

An introduction by the editor is followed by 8 chapters by 8
contributors. 76 references are given at the end of the book.
Class No: 101(510)

[136]

CHAN, W.-T. **An Outline and an annotated bibliography of Chinese
philosophy.** Rev. ed. New Haven, CT., Far Eastern Publications, Yale
University, 1969. vii,220p. $7.50. ISBN: 0887100554.

Previous editions as *An outline and bibliography of Chinese
philosophy.*

The same author's *A source book in Chinese philosophy,* (Princeton,
N.J., Princeton University Press, 1963) has chapter bibliographies and
a list of works in European languages referred to, p.793-811.
Class No: 101(510)

[137]

FU, C.W. *and* CHANG, W. **Guide to Chinese philosophy.** London, C.
Prior; Boston, Mass., G.K. Hall, 1978. xxxi,362p. (*The Asian
philosophies and religious resources guides.*)

About 1500 entries, with evaluative annotations. 16 closely divided
chapters (*e.g.* 1. Confucius and Lao-Tza; 14. Companion with
Western philosophy; 16. Authoritative texts and their philosophical
significance). English translations of original Chinese classics, plus
secondary books and articles about Chinese philosophy, with some
important French and German items. Numerous cross-references. 'An
indispensible guide' (*RQ,* v.18(3), Spring 1979, p.306).
Class No: 101(510)

[138]

FUNG, Y.L. **A History of Chinese philosophy.** London, Allen &
Unwin, 1937-53. 2v.

Translated by D. Bodde.

1. *The period of the philosophers* (from the beginnings to *c.*100
B.C.); 2. *The period of classical learning* (from the 2nd century B.C.
to the 20th century A.D.). A thorough and scholarly presentation of a
subject hardly covered (especially as regards the period of v.2.) in
Western writings. Well translated. Detailed chronological tables,
bibliographies, (v.1. p.xxiii-xxvi, 410-22; v.2. p.726-54) and indexes
at the end of each volume. A shortened version, titled *A short history
of Chinese philosophy* was published in 1966 (Free Press, £13.95).
Class No: 101(510)

India

[139]

DASGUPTA, S. **A History of Indian philosophy.** Cambridge,
Cambridge University Press, 1922-25. (Available from Oriental Bk.
Dist.). 5v. $56 the set. ISBN: 0842609636.

Mainly intended as an exposition of Indian thought, strictly on the
basis of the original texts and commentaries. Often the ground covered
is wholly new and the materials have been obtained by a direct and
first-hand study of all available texts and mansucripts. No attempt has
been made to draw any comparison or contrasts with Western
philosophy (*Preface to v.2*). Each volume has footnotes and an
analytical index. *Class No:* 101(540)

[140]

GRIMES, J. A Concise dictionary of Indian philosophy: Sanscrit terms defined in English. New York, State University of New York, 1989. 440p. $39.50. ISBN: 0791401006.

'It is basic in that (i) it includes virtually all the words basic to the various Indian philosophical systems, and (ii) it defines those terms, in their dictionary or common and literal meanings. The book is comprehensive in that it defines many of its terms with the specific meaning that a word has for a specific school' (*Preface*). Sanscrit terms are given in Devanagari script and transliterated. '... a kind of "ready reference" which will be found useful both by scholars and generalists' (*Choice*, v.27(5), January 1990, p.768). *Class No:* 101(540)

[141]

LAL, B.K. Contemporary Indian philosophy. New ed. Delhi, Motilal Banarsidass, India, 1987. xxi,346p. Rs.50; £9. ISBN: 8120802608.

First published 1973.

An introduction, 'Characteristics of contemporary Indian philosophy' precedes 7 chapters devoted to Indian philosophers (1. Swami Vivekanande - 2. Rabindranath Tagore - 3. Mahatma Gandhi... 7. Sir Mohammad Iqbal. Footnotes. Bibliography, p.335-341, arranged by chapters. Index, p.342-345. *Class No:* 101(540)

[142]

POTTER, K.H., *and others*. Guide to Indian philosophy. Boston, Mass., G.K. Hall & Co., 1988. xviii,159p. $37.50. (*The Asian philosophies and religions resource guides*.) ISBN: 0816179042.

'Indian philosophy' defined as thought originating in India and concerning the subject of bondage and liberation. 884 books and journal articles are listed and briefly annotated. Material selected was published between 1975 and 1985 and covers standard philosophical topics such as epistemology; logic; metaphysics and ethics; plus aesthetics; philosophy of religion; social, legal and political philosophy; philosophy of history; and philosophy of education. Name index, p.133-146; subject index, p.147-159. *Class No:* 101(540)

Islamic World

[143]

FAKHRY, M. A History of Islamic philosophy. 2nd ed. New York, Columbia University Press; Harlow, Essex, Longman Group, 1983. xxx,394p. $29.50; £23. (*Columbia studies in oriental culture*.) ISBN: 0231055323, US; 0582783240, UK.

First published 1970.

A detailed survey, in chronological order, from the 7th century to the present. 'Fakhry's book should now be considered the best comprehensive book ever written on the history of Arabic philosophy' (*Journal of the history of philosophy*, v.10(2), April 1972, p.223, of the first edition). *Class No:* 101(5.297)

[144]

LEAMAN, O. An Introduction to medieval Islamic philosophy. Cambridge, Cambridge University Press, 1985. xii,208p. £20. ISBN: 0521247071.

An introduction to debates on philosophy within the medieval Islamic world. 6 chapters in 2 parts: 1. Ghazali's attack on philosophy - 2. Reason v. revelation in practical reasoning. Further reading, p.202-203. Glossary, p.204. Index of passages, p.205-206. General index, p.207-208. *Class No:* 101(5.297)

USA

[145]

Directory of American philosophers, 1998-1999. Bahm, A.J., *ed*. Bowling Green, OH, Philosophy Documentation Center, Bowling Green State University, 1998. Biennial. 545p. tables. $129. ISBN: 091263295x.

First published 1970 for 1970-71.

Arrangement is by universities, A-Z for US and separately for Canada. Information on faculties of philosophy, with names and addresses; specialities of philosophers; data on colleges and universities; philosophical societies; philosophical centres and institutes; philosophical journals; publishers of philosophical works; data on fellowships, etc., available in philosophy. Indexes of philosophers (names and addresses); universities, centres and institutes; societies; journals; and publishers. *Class No:* 101(73)

Jews

[146]

SIRAT, C. A History of Jewish philosophy in the Middle Ages. Cambridge, Cambridge University Press; Paris, Editions de la Maison des Sciences de l'Homme, 1985. x, 477p. £45. ISBN: 0521260876, UK; 2735101037, France.

An introduction to the study of Jewish medieval philosophy, based on the texts themselves, printed or in manuscript. 9 chapters: 1. Introduction - 2. The Mutakallimŭn and other Jewish thinkers inspired by Muslim theological movements - 3. The Neoplatonists - 4. Judah

....(contd.)

Halevi and Abu-l-Barakăt - 5. Aristotelianism - 6. Maimonides - 7. The thirteenth century - 8. The fourteenth century - 9. The fifteenth century. Bibliography, p.413-457, relates to pages of text. Analytical index, p.459-475. Index of ancient works quoted in the text, p.476-477. *Class No:* 101(=924)

Conferences

[147]

GELDSETZER, L. Bibliography of the international congresses of philosophy/Bibliographie der internationalen Philosophie Kongress, 1900-1978... Munich, etc., K.G. Saur, 1981. 209p. DM.98.

Full listing of papers presented at 16 international philosophy congresses (arranged chronologically). Detailed name and subject indexes, p.158-208. *Class No:* 101:061:061.3

Wittgenstein

[148]

FRONGIA, G. *and* McGUINNESS, B. Wittgenstein: a bibliographic guide. Oxford, Blackwell, 1990. x,438p. £65. ISBN: 0631137653.

Part I: History of the reception of Wittgenstein's work; Pt.II: Lists and indexes. Publications of writings by Wittgenstein. Writings *on* Wittgenstein. Reviews of Wittgenstein's own writings. Entries are annotated and numbered. Indexes of subjects, of thinkers referred to in the literature, and of authors of items. *Class No:* 101WIT

Metaphysics

Encyclopaedias

[149]

KELLY, M., *ed*. Encyclopedia of aesthetics. New York, Oxford University Press, 1998. 4v. £300. $495. ISBN: 0195113071.

Critical reflections on art, culture and nature. Over 500 contributors and around 600 articles, with bibliographies. There is a comprehensive 65-page index. Includes biographical entries on philosophers, psychologists and creative artists. *Class No:* 11(031)

Handbooks & Manuals

[150]

A Companion to metaphysics. Jaegwon, K. *and* Sosa, E., *eds*. Oxford, Blackwell, 1995 xiv,540p. £60.00 (*Blackwell companions to philosophy*.) ISBN: 0631172726.

As with other volumes in this excellent series, the entries include long treatments of topics as well as the briefer definition of terms. There is some coverage of the non-Western Traditions. *Class No:* 11(035)

Death

Bibliographies

[151]

FULTON, R., *and others*. Death, grief and bereavement II: a bibliography, 1975-1980. ARNO, 1981. 230p. $25. ISBN: 0405142129.

Continues the author's *Death, grief and bereavement: a bibliography, 1845-1975* (Ayer Co. Publications, 1976, $27.50. 0405095708), which had 3800 entries.

2300 entries arranged A-Z by author and numbered. Broad subject index of terms refers to the numbered entries. An addendum, J.C. Santora's *Guide to doctoral dissertations on death and dying, 1970-1978* duplicates some of the entries in the main section. *Class No:* 128(01)

[152]

SIMPSON, M.A. Dying, death and grief: a critical bibliography. Pittsburgh, Pa., University of Pittsburgh (distributed by Harper), 1987. xv, 259p. $27.95. (*Contemporary community health series*.) ISBN: 0822935619.

First published in 1979 by Plenum Press.

1,700 non-fiction and fiction books published, mainly, since 1979, on subjects such as grief, suicide, murder, war, counselling, loneliness, death customs of different peoples, hospices, genocide, and the death penalty. Arranged A-Z by title, most entries having an evaluative annotation. Ratings given for recommendation, 1-5. Subject and author indexes. *Class No:* 128(01)

Handbooks & Manuals

[153]

RAPHAEL, B. **When disaster strikes:** a handbook for the caring professions. London, Hutchinson Ltd., 1986. x,342p. £19.95. ISBN: 009165470x.

In two parts: the 1st part, 'The disaster experience', has 7 chapters on reactions to disasters; the 2nd part has 5 chapters on psychosocial care, mental health and adjustment, victims and helpers. Each part has substantial reference, subject and name indexes. Presentation is excellent. *Class No:* 128(035)

Occultism & Parapsychology

---

[154]

GORDON, S. **The Paranormal:** an illustrated encyclopedia. Headland, Cleveland, Headline, 1992. 736p. 40 illus. £18.99. ISBN: 0747203563.

'Looks at every conceivable phenomenon and idea that strays outside what is perceived as normal'. (*British book news*, April 1992, p.298). *Class No:* 133

Bibliographies

[155]

CLARIE, T.C. **Occult/paranormal bibliography:** an annotated list of books published in English, 1976 through 1981. Metuchen, N.J., Scarecrow Press, 1984. 579p. $37.50; £29.65. ISBN: 0810816741.

Continues the same author's '*Occult bibliography: an annotated list of books published in English, 1971 through 1975*' (482p. $32.50. £24.35. ISBN 0810811529). *Class No:* 133(01)

[156]

KIES, C. **The Occult in the Western world:** an annotated bibliography. Hamden, C.T., Shoe String Press, 1986. 233p. $29.50. ISBN: 0208021132.

Intended to be a source book for beginners and casual readers needing a general overview of occult topics, the bibliography contains nearly 900 important English-language monographs on witchcraft, magic, mysticism, parapsychology, U.F.O.'s, mythical creatures, prophesy and astrology. Emphasis is given to books useful as reference works. Includes a glossary, name and title indexes. 'Excellent and well-written introductory material ... entries well organized' (*Choice*, January 1987, p.744). *Class No:* 133(01)

[157]

SOCIETY FOR PSYCHICAL RESEARCH. **Catalogue of the Library of the Society for Psychical Research.** Boston, Mass., G.K. Hall, 1976. 341p. $75. ISBN: 081610008x.

Author-title catalogue; 7,100 photolithographically reproduced cards. Coverage includes telepathy, paranormal cognition, mediumship, psychology, philosophy, mysticism, hypnotism. *Class No:* 133(01)

Encyclopaedias

[158]

CAVENDISH, R., *ed.* **Encyclopedia of the unexplained:** the ultimate guide to the unknown, the esoteric and the unproven. 2nd ed. London, Penguin Books, 1990. 304p. illus. ISBN: 0140191909.

First published 1974.

Highly readable entries, A-Z, covering terms, persons, organizations and movements. Longer articles are signed and documented. Embraces spiritualism, astrology, ESP, the mystery religions, Eastern beliefs, divinations and the like. Updates significantly Fodor's *Encyclopaedia of psychic science* (1933) and Spence's *Encyclopaedia of occultism* (1920), states *Library journal* (August 1974, p.1925). *Class No:* 133(031)

[159]

CAVENDISH, R., *ed.* **Man, myth and magic:** the illustrated encyclopaedia of mythology, religion and the unknown. 2nd ed. Freeport, N.Y., Marshall Cavendish, 1983. 12v. (3268p.). $399.95; £313.50. ISBN: 0863070418.

First published 1970 in 24 vols.

Heavily illustrated articles, treating their subjects in an objective, reportorial manner, Nearly all the revision is in the bibliographies (appended to articles) and subject bibliographies. 'For a popular audience. Libraries lacking the 1970 ed. should fill that void'. (*Wilson library bulletin*, November 1983, p.228-9). *Class No:* 133(031)

[160]

Harper's encyclopedia of mystical & paranormal experiences. Guiley, R.E., *ed.* New York & London, HarperCollins, 1991. 666p. illus. 35.95. £15.99. ISBN: 0062503659.

500 entries, arranged A-Z and cross-referenced. Emphasis is on major personalities, mystical techniques and traditions, locations of interest, original and paranormal phenomena.All articles list bibliographical references. *Class No:* 133(031)

[161]

SHEPARD, L.A., *ed.* **Encyclopedia of occultism and parapsychology.** 3rd ed. Detroit, Mich., Gale Research Co., 1991. 2v. (2008p.). ISBN: 0810349078.

First published in 1978, 2nd ed. 1984-85. Adapted from L. Spence's *Encyclopaedia of the occult* (1920) and N. Fodor's *Encyclopaedia of psychic science* (1934).

Over 5000 entries, varying from 1 sentence to many pages in length in one A-Z sequence. Scope includes the occult, magic, miracles and witchcraft, as well as numerous paranormal events previously regarded as supernatural. Prominent individuals in the field are covered. Many entries include a wide range of bibliographical references. Comprehensive general index and 9 topical indexes. 'Can be faulted in many cases by its ignoring of evidence and conclusions ... Would be a valuable resource if supplemented by the use of critical studies' (*Choice*, v.28(10), June 1991, p.1615). *Class No:* 133(031)

Handbooks & Manuals

[162]

LITVINOFF, S., *ed.* **The Illustrated guide to the supernatural.** Boston, Mass., G.K. Hall, 1986. iv,156p. illus. $25. (*Hall reference.*) ISBN: 0816189048.

145 articles, arranged A-Z by subject, covering popular occult areas such as magical beliefs, fortune-telling and divination, psychic phenomena, and biographies from ancient times to the present. Introductory level, not for the specialist. Entries vary in length from a paragraph to 3 pages, with references to other entries at the end of each article. Table of contents. Bibliography. '... entertaining, profusely illustrated guide...' (*Reference books bulletin*, 1986/87, p.50). *Class No:* 133(035)

[163]

WILSON, D. *and* WILSON, C. **Unsolved mysteries past and present.** London, Headline, 1993. 448p. £19.99. ISBN: 0747208379.

Attempts to explain historical enigma, voices from the grave, and psychic and supernatural occurrences. *Class No:* 133(035)

Dictionaries

[164]

DRURY, N. **Dictionary of mysticism and the esoteric traditions.** Rev. ed. New York, ABC-Clio, 1992. 328p. $49.50. ISBN: 0874366992.

First published 1985 by Harper & Row as Dictionary of mysticism and the occult

Nearly 3000 names and terms from the fields of magic, mysticism, parapsychology and spiritualism. Includes brief biographies of prominent occult figures. Entries are short, but clear. 'No substitute for Shepard's *Encyclopedia of occultism and parapsychology*' (*qv*) but a good, inexpensive ready-reference tool (*Choice*, v.23(2), October 1985, p.270) of the 1st ed. *Class No:* 133(038)

[165]

GETTINGS, F. **Dictionary of occult, hermetic and alchemical sigils.** London, Routledge & Kegan Paul, 1981. 410p. £15.95. ISBN: 0710000952.

Designed as a reference, guide and sourcebook for those involved in general occult studies. 1500 headings. Meanings of over 9000 sigils (line patterns with magical significance) which appear in European alchemical, astrological, geomatic and related hermetic sources, plus a unique graphic index of sigils by number of strokes, p.323-410. Bibliography, p.293-312. Dating of sigils, p.239-291. 7 appendices (7, 'standard' sigils in modern astrology from Deutsche [*Die Deutsche Ephemeride*, 1980). *Class No:* 133(038)

[166]

PICKNETT, L. **The Encyclopedia of the paranormal:** a complete guide to the unexplained. London, Macmillan, 1990. [5],296p. 196 illus (16 col). £19.95. ISBN: 0333491009.

Deals comprehensively and objectively with all the main documented instances of phenomena that cannot be explained. Claims to be about the paranormal, not the "occult". 8 chapters: 1. The power of belief - 2. Secrets of the mind - 3. Extraordinary people - 4. The unpredictable world - 5. The UFO enigma - 6. Psi research - 7. Frontiers of science - 8. Life after death. Index, p.288-296. *Class No:* 133(038)

[167]

WATSON, D., *ed*. **A Dictionary of mind and spirit.** London, Deutsch, 1991. 406p. £15.99. ISBN: 0233986715.

Over 500 terms related to paranormal phenomena. esoteric and parapsychology. 'An instructive and entertaining attempt to draw together science and the spiritual tradition.'*(The good book guide*, v.56, March/April 1992, p.11). *Class No:* 133(038)

Histories

[168]

HAYNES, R. **The Society for Psychical Research, 1882-1982: a** history. London, Macdonald & Co., 1982. 256p. £7.95. ISBN: 0356078752.

'Any serious research into "the unknown", whether it be apparitions or mediumship, precognition or electro-voice phenomena, out-of-body experiences or poltergeists, would not only find this work of considerable value but also, because of the "behind-the-scenes" detail, of great interest' (*British book news,* November 1982, p.667). *Class No:* 133(091)

[169]

INGLIS, B. **Natural and supernatural:** a history of the paranormal. Bridport, Dorset, Prism Press, 1992. 508p. £9.95. ISBN: 1853270741.

First published 1977.

A history of the paranormal from early times to 1944, together with the careers of people associated with such phenomena. Sources, p.454-72. Bibliography, p.473-94. Index, p.495-500. *Class No:* 133(091)

Research Projects

[170]

OPPENHEIM, J. **The Other world:** spiritualism and psychical research in England, 1850-1914. Cambridge, Cambridge University Press, 1985. xii, 503p. plus 16 unnumbered pages of illustrations. £40. ISBN: 0521265053.

Examines the public fascination with spiritualism in Britain from the mid-19th to early 20th century. Based on extensive research of manuscripts, pamphlets, newspapers and books by and about Victorian spiritualists and psychical researchers. 8 chapters in 3 parts: Part I. The setting (1. Mediums - 2. Membership); II. A surrogate faith (3. Spiritualism and Christianity - 4. Psychical research and agnosticism - 5. Theosophy and the occult); III. A pseudoscience (6. Concepts of mind - 7. The problem of evolution - 8. Physics and psychic phenomena). A conclusion is followed by section of notes relating to the various chapters (1162 references, p.399-486) and a detailed index (p.487-503) with cross-references. 'An altogether superior study' (*Nature,* 4 July 1985, p.25). *Class No:* 133:061:061.62.005

Occultism

[171]

WOLMAN, B.B., *ed*. **Handbook of parapsychology.** New York, Van Nostrand, Reinhold, 1977 (reprinted by McFarland & Co., 1986). xxiv, 1007p. illus. $49.95. ISBN: 0899501869.

31 contributors. 11 parts: 1. History of parapsychology - 2. Research methods - 3. Perception, communication, and parapsychology - 4. Parapsychology and physical systems - 5. Parapsychology and altered states of consciousness - 6. Parapsychology and healing - 7. Survival of bodily death - 8. Parapsychology and other fields (*e.g.* anthropology) - 9. Parapsychologic models and theories - 10. Social research in parapsychology - 11. Suggested readings (annotated bibliography, p.907-20). Glossary, p.921-36. Parts 1-10 each have appended bibliogaphies. Name and subject indexes. *Class No:* 133.2

Encyclopaedias

[172]

GUILEY, R.E. **The Encyclopedia of ghosts and spirits.** New York, Facts on File, 1992. 374p. illus. $40. £21.95. ISBN: 0816021406.

Aims to present both sceptical and believing viewpoints. Very thorough coverage, with concise, clear entries. Includes sources for further reading. 'A useful addition to reference shelves'(*Library journal,* 1 September 1992, p.168). *Class No:* 133.2(031)

[173]

—SPENCER, J *and* SPENCER, A. **The Encyclopedia of ghosts and** spirits. London, Headline, 1992. 416p. 16 illus. £18.99. $39.95. ISBN: 0747205086. *Class No:* 133.2(031)

Dictionaries

[174]

BLETZER, J.G. **The Donning international encyclopedic psychic** dictionary. Norfolk, VA., Donning, 1986. 888p. $29.95. ISBN: 089865372x.

Includes over 9000 terms taken from popular occultism. Entries are brief, with no etymology. Extensive cross-references. *Class No:* 133.2(038)

[175]

HAINING, P. **A Dictionary of ghosts.** London, Robert Hale, 1982. 271p. 136 illus. £9.50. ISBN: 0709196229.

'... does not claim to be exhaustive ... but it *is* representative and does ... give a very fair coverage of the topic ...' (Foreword). Entries vary in length from 5 or 6 lines to a page and cover the various different types of ghosts throughout the world, detailing the most famous hauntings, and including information on all the people and phenomena associated with the topic. *Class No:* 133.2(038)

[176]

SPENCE, L. **An Encyclopaedia of occultism:** a compendium of information on the occult sciences, occult personalities, psychic science, magic, demonology, spiritualism and mysticism. London, Routledge, 1920 (Reprinted Citadel Press, 1985). 464p. illus. $12.95; £11.95. ISBN: 0806509058.

'This is perhaps the finest source book on the subject' (*RQ,* v.11(1), Fall, 1971, p.12). Articles, A-Z, are supported by references. 'Banshee' : 1¾ cols.; 'Paracelsus': 5½ cols. Select bibliography. Index. *Class No:* 133.2(038)

Histories

[177]

BARROW, L. **Independent spirits:** spiritualism and English plebeians, 1850-1910. London, Routledge & Kegan Paul, 1986. xiii, 338p. 21 illus. £20. (*History workshop series*.) ISBN: 0710098839.

'Concerning the intellectual world of the humbly-born in late 19th and early 20th century Britain, focusing on plebeian, or working- and lower middle-class spiritualists. Chapter 1. Germination - 2. Owenism and the millennium - 3. Nottingham and cabala - 4. The problematic and imponderables - 5. Plebeians and others - 6. Presence and problems of democratic epistemology - 7. Healing - 8. Bridging the great divide. Notes (p.281-329) are arranged by chapter. Index (p.300-332). *Class No:* 133.2(091)

Parapsychology

[178]

BERGER, A.S. *and* BERGER, J. **The Encyclopedia of** parapsychology and psychical research. New York, Paragon House, 1991. 554p. $45. ISBN: 1557780439.

1400 entries, A-Z, relating to both areas of the paranormal - concepts, methods, phenomena, research organizations, publications and biographies. Short bibliographies after each entry. Cross-references. 3 appendices, including a country index and a 39-page bibliography. Intended for the general public, science writers and journalists. '... an authoritative and unbiased reference source...'(*Booklist,* v.87(12), 15 February 1991, p.1248). *Class No:* 133.3

Bibliographies

[179]

WHITE, R.A. *and* DALE, L.A. **Parapsychology:** sources of information. Compiled under the auspices of the American Society of Psychical Research. Metuchen, N.J. Scarecrow Press, 1973. 303p. $19. ISBN: 0810806177.

Annotated bibliography of 282 books, under 24 subject headings. Short introduction to each subject section. Annotations indicate level of readership; type of library; notes inclusion of glossaries, illustrations and bibliographies; and gives citations to book reviews. 'The authors have produced the "Winchell" of parapsychology' (*Library journal,* v.99(2), 15 January 1974, p.126). *Class No:* 133.3(01)

[180]

—WHITE, R. **New sources of information, 1973-1989.** Metuchen, NJ, Scarecrow Press, 1990. 699p. $67.50. ISBN: 0810823853.

Chronological continuation of the above, with *c.*480 books, with descriptive annotations, arranged in 27 topical categories, each category prefaced by a brief bibliographical essay. Also includes chapters on the field's journals, organizations and graduate theses. '... a carefully crafted guide to the recent literature.'(*Wilson library bulletin,* v.65(9), p.141). *Class No:* 133.3(01)

Reviews & Abstracts

[181]

Exceptional human experience: studies of the psychic-spontaneous - intangible, 1983- 2pa. Dix Hills, N.Y., Parapsychology Sources of Information, 1983-. $50 pa. ISSN: 07407629.

Prior to 1990 title was *Parapsychology abstracts international*

*c.*250 abstracts in each issue, each abstract containing 200-300 words or more, arranged in 9 subject sections. About 100 current parapsychological journals are analysed, together with material of interest found in non-parapsychological journals, books, etc., mainly in English although some non-English material is included. Author and detailed subject index in each issue. '... a model of its kind ...' (*Library journal*, v.109(20), December 1984, p.2252). Also available online. *Class No:* 133.3(048)

USA

[182]

BERGER, A.S. Lives and letters in American parapsychology: a biographical history, 1850-1987. Jefferson, N.C., McFarland, 1988. 381p. illus. $39.95; £29.95. ISBN: 0899503454.

An overview, outlining significant events in American parapsychology and providing biographies of predominant figures. Divided into 5 periods, each with short introduction followed by highlights of the history of parapsychology, chronologically arranged, and with emphasis on the persons who contributed. Many quotations included. Footnotes. 54 pages of references but no comprehensive bibliography. Index of persons, topics and titles. *Class No:* 133.3(73)

Witchcraft & Magic

[183]

Early modern European witchcraft: centres and peripheries. Ankarloo, B. and Henningsen, G., *eds.* Oxford, Clarendon Press, 1990. [9],477p. 5 figs., maps. £45. ISBN: 019821989x.

First published by Olin Foundation in Swedish.

18 chapters in 4 sections: 1. Witchcraft, law and theology; 2. Origins of the witch's sabbath; 3. Witch-hunting in Scandinavia and other peripheries; 4. Conclusions. 19 contributors. Footnotes. Bibliography of secondary works, p.446. Index. *Class No:* 133.4

[184]

GUILEY, R.E. The Encyclopedia of witches and witchcraft. New York, Facts on File, 1989. 421p. illus. $45. ISBN: 081601793x.

Arranged A-Z by subjects and covering the history of witchhunts, beliefs of witches, their organizations, folk magic, pagan deities, sorcery, occultism, shamanism, etc. Includes biographies. The length of citations varies from a paragraph to several pages. 100 black-and-white illus. Bibliography of 355 items, and also a list of works mentioned in the text. Cross-references. '... comprehensive coverage of terminology, biography and history make this work an important addition to the reference works available on the topic' (*Reference books bulletin*, November 1989, p.604). '... fills a unique niche. While covering the history of witchcraft in a serviceable and accurate way, it also includes a large amount of material, mostly biographical, on modern witches' (*Choice*, v.27(5), January 1990, p.768). *Class No:* 133.4

Histories

[185]

RUSSELL, J.B. A History of witchcraft throughout the ages. London, Thames and Hudson, 1981. 192p. illus. £5.95. ISBN: 0580272425.

A critical study of witchcraft throughout the ages. Following an introduction ('What is a witch?'), 10 chapters are arranged in 2 parts: 1. Sorcery and historical witchcraft (Sorcery - The roots of European witchcraft - Witchcraft, heresy, and inquisition - The witch-craze on the continent of Europe - Witchcraft in Britain and America - Witchcraft and society - The decline of Witchcraft) and 2. Modern witchcraft (Survivals and revivals - The religion of the witches - The role of witchcraft). The study concludes with a section of 74 reference notes on the text, a bibliography (p.180-183) arranged A-Z by author, and a detailed subject index (p.188-192). *Class No:* 133.4(091)

[186]

THORNDIKE, L. History of magic and experimental science. New York, Columbia University Press, 1923-58. 8v.

V.1-2: First 13 centuries; 3-4; 14 & 15 centuries; 5-6: 16 century; 7-8: 17 century.

'Based on an examination of the original MSS and documents of the early writers, scientists and historians in library collections all over the world'. The word 'magic' as used in the title 'is understood in its broadest sense as including all occult arts and sciences, superstitions and folklore' (Hawkins, R.R. *Scientific, medical and technical books ... 1930-44*, p.4). Well documented. V.1-2 include a general index, bibliographical index, and index of MSS; v.3-4 & 5-6, general index, index of MSS and index of incipits; v.7-8, general index and index of MSS. A monumental survey. *Class No:* 133.4(091)

Alchemy

[187]

Alchemy: a comprehensive bibliography of the Manly P. Hall Collection of books and manuscripts. Hogart, R.C., *ed.* Los Angeles, CA., Philos Research, 1985. xiv,[1],314p. illus. (incl.pl.), facsims. $125. ISBN: 0893145424. *Class No:* 133.5

[188]

PRITCHARD, A. Alchemy: a bibliography of English-language writings. London, Routledge & Kegan Paul, jointly with The Library Association, 1980. [vii], 439p. ISBN: 0710004729.

Originally as a bibliography approved for the L.A. diploma. 3,188 entries for items written 1597-1978: A. Alchemical texts (16 sections: Greek and hermetic texts) - B. Works about alchemy: countries (19 sections: Ancient Middle East ... U.S.A.) - C. Works about alchemy: subjects (Alchemy, general - Bibliography and libraries ... Symbols and yearbooks ... Science - Chemistry - Art - Literature and fiction - Biographies - Unclassified). Section A items are often annotated. Items not examined are asterisked. Appendix: 'Major sources searched', p.402-6. Index of 'all personal names occurring in the bibliography, together with subjects', p.407-39. Preface: 'On alchemy and its bibliography', p.1-9. Includes theses. 'An outstanding contribution to works on alchemy in English ...' (*British book news*, October 1980, p.588-9). Awarded the Library Association's Besterman Medal for 1980. *Class No:* 133.5

[189]

—**HAEFFNER, M. The Dictionary of alchemy: from Maria Prophetinsa to Isaac Newton.** London, Aquarium Press, 1991. 272p. illus. £12.99. ISBN: 1855380854.

A glossary of alchemical terms, concepts and symbols, and main practitioners. Includes Western, Indo-Tibetan and Chinese Taoist traditions. *Class No:* 133.5

Astrology

[190]

FILBY, J. and **FILBY, P. Astronomy for astrologers.** Wellingborough, Northants., The Aquarian Press, 1984. 255p. tables, charts. £6.55. ISBN: 0850303931.

An introduction to the astronomical basis of astrology. 11 chapters: 1. An outline of the history of astronomy - 2. The development of modern astronomy ... 4. The calendar - 5. Time - 6. The astrological ephemeris ... 10. The universe: stars and galaxies - 11. Cosmic cycles and mundane events. Glossary, p.193-202. 5 appendices: 3. Calculation tables; 5. Star charts. Bibliography, p.246-250. Index, p.251-255. *Class No:* 133.52

[191]

PARKER, D. and **PARKER, J. Parker's astrology.** London, Dorling Kindersley, 1991. 415p. illus. charts. £19.95. ISBN: 0863186017.

A practical guide to astrology. A foreword on the craft of the astrologer and 'How to use this book' are followed by 5 chapters: 1. Astrological techniques; 2. Understanding the Sun signs; 3. Astrology in action; 4. The planets at work; 5. Astrological tables. Profusely illustrated. 'Coffee table' size. Analytical index, p.412-6. *Class No:* 133.52

[192]

WHITE, S. The New astrology. London, Macmillan, 1986. [2], 682, [5]p. £10.95. ISBN: 0333434919.

First published in France by Editions Robert Laffont, S.A., under the title *La double astrologie*.

Claims to be a unique synthesis of the world's two great astrological systems: The Chinese and Western. *Class No:* 133.52

Bibliographies

[193]

GARDNER, F.L. Bibliotheca astrologica: catalog of astrological publications of the 15th through the 19th centuries ... with a sketch of the history of astrology by Dr. William Wynn Westcott. North Hollywood, CA., Symbols and Signs, 1977. xx, 164p. $12.50. ISBN: 0912504382.

Reprint of the 1911 edition.

1340 items arranged A-Z by author (or title in some cases) subdivided chronologically. Some entries annotated. Items 944-1003 are periodical titles indexed A-Z and inserted in the main sequence between P and Q. Some cross-references. Index, which includes important persons (*e.g.* William Lilly). *Class No:* 133.52(01)

[194]

PATTIE, T.S. **Astrology,** as illustrated in the collections of the British Library and the British Museum: an historical account of the subject which includes the author's 'Horoscope for the British Library'. London, British Library, Reference Division, 1981. 36p. illus. £1.95. ISBN: 0904654494.

Includes 4 plates and 16 black-and-white illus.
Class No: 133.52(01)

Handbooks & Manuals

[195]

FREEMAN, M. **How to interpret a birth chart:** a guide to the analysis and synthesis of astrological charts. Wellingborough, Northants, Aquarian Press, 1981. [128]p. illus. £3.99. ISBN: 0850302498.
Class No: 133.52(035)

[196]

LYNDOE, E. **Everyman's astrology.** Rev. ed. Sudbury, Suffolk, Neville Spearman Ltd., 1970 (reprinted 1972 and 1977). xi, 236p. illus. £3.95. ISBN: 0854352848.

First published 1959.

A simple how-to-do-it guide to making astrological maps and reading them. In 5 parts: Drawing the map - Meaning in the map - Judgement of the map - Tertiary directions - Tabulations (p.101-236) include planetary tables 1900-1999 inclusive. *Class No:* 133.52(035)

[197]

SAKOIAN, F. *and* ACKER, L.S. **Astrologer's handbook.** New ed. Harmondsworth, Herts., Penguin Books Ltd., 1981. xiv,461p. £7.99. ISBN: 0140053360.

Originally published by Harper & Row, 1973, and P. Davies, 1984.

16 chapters in two parts: I. Basic astrology; II. Interpreting the aspects. '... designed to provide the layman, the astrological student, and the practitioner of astrology with the information necessary for interpreting horoscopes'. (Section on 'How to read this book'). Glossary, p.441-442. General index, p.443-449. Cross index of aspects, p.450-461. *Class No:* 133.52(035)

Dictionaries

[198]

GETTINGS, F. **Dictionary of astrology.** London, Routledge & Kegan Paul, 1985. x, 365p. £25. ISBN: 0710096720.

Aimed at the non-specialist and the practical astrologer, and 'designed to form a reference guide and sourcebook' (*Introduction*). Over 3000 headings, including terms derived from the major post-medieval sources up to the present. Entries vary in length from one or two lines to 2 pages. Many 'see' references. Bibliography (p.359-365) A-Z by author. '... a fit companion for *Larousse encyclopedia of astrology*' (1980) (*Choice,* v.23 (10), June 1986, p.1520). *Class No:* 133.52(038)

Histories

[199]

PARKER, D. *and* PARKER, J. **A History of astrology.** London, André Deutsch Ltd., 1983. 192p. 111 illus. (36 col.). ISBN: 0233975764.

Following an introduction, the work is divided into 11 chapters (1. Distant beginnings - 2. The prestigious planets - 3. Through the doors of Greece - 4. The imperial planets - 5. The pervasive planets - 6. The coming of Christianity - 7. Astrology in medieval Europe - 8. 'First cause of motion, cruel firmament' - 9. Success - and the beginning of failure - 10. Towards the dark - 11. Into the twentieth century). A brief glossary (p.189) and bibliography (p.190) are followed by an index (p.191-2). *Class No:* 133.52(091)

[200]

TESTER, J. **A History of Western astrology.** Woodbridge, Suffolk, Boydell Press, 1987. 256p. illus. £19.95. ISBN: 0851154468.

A history of astrological ideas and practices from their shadowy beginnings in Mesopotamia and subsequent scientific establishment in Greece in about the 5th century, up to today's surviving popular almanacs and astrological magazines, showing how little has changed. Lucid and concise. *Class No:* 133.52(091)

Palmistry

[201]

BROEKMAN, M. **Complete encyclopaedia of practical palmistry.** London, Souvenir Press, 1986. [6], 187p. illus. £6.95. ISBN: 0285627767.

Reissue of the 1st, 1972 ed.

Aims to be a comprehensive straightforward introduction to the

....(contd.)
ancient art of palmistry. In 4 sections: 1. Event markings - 2. Character markings - 3. Analysis - 4. Sample readings.
Class No: 133.6

[202]

FITZHERBERT, A. **The Palmist's companion:** a history and bibliography of palmistry. Metuchen, NJ, Scarecrow Press, 1992. 236p. $27.60. ISBN: 0810825244.

Choice (December 1992) considers it to be haphazard, with errors, and that it succeeds only because information is difficult to find elsewhere. Partly a bibliography, partly a history of palmistry, and partly biographies of palmists. Title index. *Class No:* 133.6

Philosophical Systems

[203]

DUNN, J., *and others.* **The British Empiricists:** Locke, Berkeley, Hume. Oxford, Oxford University Press, 1992. 304p. £8.99. ISBN: 0192830686.

Concise introductions to Locke's theory of knowledge, Berkeley's philosophy in relation to the thought of Newton, and Hume's ideas on perception and self-identity. *Class No:* 14

[204]

EBENSTEIN, W. **Today's isms:** Communism, Fascism, Capitalism, Socialism. 9th ed. Englewood Cliffs, N.J., Prentice-Hall, 1985. x,229p. illus. $29. ISBN: 0139244735.

Arranged in 4 sections, each subdivided. 1. Communism - 2. Fascism - 3. Capitalism - 4. Socialism. A discussion of the main representations on each side. Lists of further reading are appended to each section. Index, p.221-229.

A 10th rev. ed. by A.O.Ebenstein and others was issued in 1993 (ISBN 013138595x). *Class No:* 14

Encyclopaedias & Dictionaries

[205]

GLENDINNING, S., *ed.* **The Edinburgh encyclopedia of continental philosophy** Edinburgh, Edinburgh University Press, 1999. xiii, 685. £80.00. ISBN: 0748607838.

Not really an encyclopedia but a collection of 57 essays by 48 Anglo-American academics, the essays arranged in 8 sections. The essays are at a fairly introductory level, but are accompanied by sources, both in the original and in translation. Topics include individual philosophers, and modern trends - French feminism, for example, and the Frankfurt School. *Class No:* 14(03)

[206]

GORDON, H., *ed.* **Dictionary of existentialism** London, Fitzroy Dearborn, 1999. xii, 539p. £65.00. ISBN: 1579581676.

Entries vary in length from half a page to several pages. This reference work has been written by experts - the entries are all signed - and has an impressive array of references and cross-references. It covers the existentialist thinkers themselves, the terms and ideas they employed - and indicates their lasting influence. *Class No:* 14(03)

Scholasticism

Handbooks & Manuals

[207]

The Cambridge companion to Aquinas. Kretzmann, N. *and* Stump, E., *ed.* Cambridge, Cambridge University Press, 1993 viii,303p. (*Cambridge companions to Philosophy.*) ISBN: 0521437695.

This, it has to be stressed, is an introduction to Aquinas the philosopher and his relationship to other philosophers, including non-Christian ones. It does not treat of Aquinas as a theologian. *Class No:* 141.31(035)

Mysticism

Bibliographies

[208]

GRANT, P. **Literature of mysticism in Western tradition.** London, Macmillan Press, 1983. x,179p. £35. ISBN: 0333287983.

7 essays claiming that mysticism cannot be well discussed separately from a framework of faith: 1. Mysticism, faith and culture - 2. Imagination and mystery - 3. Historical crises: from incarnation to imagination - 4. Self and ego - 5. The Cross - 6. The Way - 7. Conclusion. Notes, p.156-167, by chapter. Bibliographical guide to texts, without comment, p.168-174, by chapter. Index, p.175-179. *Class No:* 141.33(01)

Socialist Systems

[209]

SCRUTON, R. **Thinkers of the new Left.** Harlow, Essex, Longman Group UK Ltd., 1985. [5],227p. £15. ISBN: 0582902738.

An analysis of 14 of the thinkers most influential on the attitudes of the post-1960 new Left. Chapter 1. What is Left?; ch.2-15 on individuals; ch.16 What is right?. Appendix: Biographical and bibliographical data (p.212-233) summarizes their careers and most important writings. Index of names (p.225-227). Originally appeared as separate essays in *The Salisbury review*. *Class No:* 141.8

Histories

[210]

COLE, G.D.H. **A History of Socialist thought.** London, Macmillan, 1953-60 (Reprinted 1961-63). 5v. (7v. in reprint).
    1. *Socialist thought: the forerunners. 1789-1850.*
    2. *Socialist thought: Marxism and Anarchism, 1850-1890.*
    3. *The Second International, 1889-1914* (forms v.3-4 of reprint).
    4. *Communism and social democracy, 1914-1931* (v.5-6 of reprint).
    5. *Socialism and Fascism, 1931-1939* (v.7 of reprint).
Not a history of Socialism but of Socialist thought. Cole originally intended his history to go up to 1945, but he died in 1959 with this objective uncompleted. V.1 has 26 chapters, a select bibliography (p.317-32: chapter bibliographies preceded by general references), index of names and subject index. *Class No:* 141.8(091)

[211]

DROZ, J., *ed*. **Histoire générale du socialisme.** Paris, Presses Universitaires de France, 1972-78. 4v. illus.

V.1. From the origins to 1875 (1972. 600p.); v.2. From 1875 to 1919 (1974. 676p.); v.3. From 1919 to 1945 (1977. 762p.); v.4. From 1945 to the present (1978. 705,48p.). A comprehensive study of the general history of socialism in the French language. Includes notes, bibliographies and indexes in all 4v. *Class No:* 141.8(091)

[212]

YOUNG, J.D. **Socialism since 1889:** a biographical history. London, Pinter Publishers, 1988. viii,269p. £29.50. ISBN: 0861879856.

Describes the history of the labour movement, 1889-1986, through portraits of 18 men and women, varying from Hyndman and De Leon, through Lenin and Zetkin to Kolakowski and Fanon. 11 chapters: 1. The history of socialism; an overview, 1889-1939; 2-10. devotes each chapter to two socialists; 11. Contemporary socialism: tragedies and crises, 1939-86. Includes many quotations. 768 notes, p.237-262. Index, p.263-269. *Class No:* 141.8(091)

Great Britain

[213]

BEER, M. **History of British Socialism.** Nottingham, Spokesman Books, 1984. xiii,271p. illus., ports. £11.95. ISBN: 0851244084.

First published 1919.

Introduction to this ed. by R.H. Tawney. 18 chapters, each subdivided, in two parts: 1. Primitive Christian influences - 2. The English Schoolmen - 3. Early English Communism ... 7. The economic revolution ... 11. The economists - 12. Robert Owen - 13. The Co-operative Socialists ... 16. The birth of Chartism - 17. The alliance between the working class and the middle class - 18. Separation of the middle and working classes. Includes 300 illus. *Class No:* 141.8(091)(410)

Russia

[214]

WALICKI, A. **A History of Russian thought:** from the enlightenment to Marxism. Oxford, Clarendon Press, 1980 (reprinted as a paperback, 1988). xvii,456p. £14.95. ISBN: 0198277040.

First published in Polish in 1973 as *Rosyjska filozofia i myśl społeczna od oświecenia do marksizmu.* First published in English, translated by H. Andrews-Rusiecka, by Oxford University Press in 1980.

18 chapters (1. Trends in enlightenment thought ... 6. The Slavophiles - 7. The Russian Hegelians ... 10. The origins of Russian socialism ... 12. Populist ideologies - 13. Anarchism ... 18. From populism to Marxism). Footnotes. Index of names, p.449-456. '... excellent and brilliant work' (*Political studies*, September 1989, p.476-7). *Class No:* 141.8 (091)(47)

Utopian Socialism

[215]

CLARK, I.F., *Comp*. **Tale of the future**, from the beginning to the present day: an annotated bibliography of those satires, ideal states, imaginary wars and invasions, coming catastrophies and end-of-the-world stories, political warnings and forecasts, inter-planetary voyages and scientific romances - all located in an imaginary future period - that have been published in the United Kingdon between 1644-1976. 3rd ed. London, Library Association, 1978. xvii, 357p.

....(contd.)

First published 1961.

Over 4000 concisely annotated entries. 5 parts: 1. Chronological list, with annotations - 2. Short-title index - 3. Author index - 4. Notes - 5. Bibliography (p.356-7). Annotations 'now include the date of publication for American and British titles that were first published in the United States and the original titles of foreign works published in English translation ...' (*The arrangement of this bibliography*). Fills a gap. *Class No:* 141.81

[216]

FOGARTY, R.S. **Dictionary of American communal and utopian history.** Westport, CT., Greenwood Press, 1980. 320p. $40.95. ISBN: 031321347x.

Over 140 short biographies of major figures, 'biographies' of 59 communities, and a chronological list of 270 settlements founded before 1919 compiled by O. Okugawa. A review in *Library journal* (1 June 1980) deplores the lack of volume and page numbers for articles cited but 'even so, in a field of great interest and few general references, this would be an essential tool in most libraries'.

An update of the author's bibliographical essay published in *Choice* in 1973. *Class No:* 141.81

[217]

NEGLEY, G.R. **Utopian literature:** a bibliography. Lawrence, University Press of Kansas, 1978. 288p. $25. ISBN: 0700601643.

A list of utopias and dystopias, mostly European and American, ranging from Thomas More's to the present, arranged under authors, A-Z. Major locations given. Short titles and chronological indexes. *Class No:* 141.81

Chartism. Owenism

Chartism

[218]

HAMBRICK, M. **A Chartist's library.** London, Mansell Publishing Ltd., 1986. [iii], 266p. £30.00. ISBN: 072011831x.

A catalogue of some 1634 titles, of which *c*.1400 were owned by the Chartist, George Julian Harney. Arranged A-Z by author (anonymous works by title). Cross-references for editors, pseudonyms and some translators. Each entry includes name of author, complete title, place and year of publication, pagination, and the Vanderbilt University library accession number. Also includes descriptive notes about the book; full text of annotations, enclosures, dedications, autographs and inscriptions; and bibliographic information about the newspaper clippings found in the books. The introduction includes a short biography of Harney. *Class No:* 141.814CHA

[219]

HARRISON, J.F.C. *and* THOMPSON, D. **Bibliography of the Chartist movement, 1837-1976.** Hassocks, Sussex, Harvester Press; Atlantic Highlands, N.J., Humanities Press Inc., 1978. xvi, 214p.

'Intended as a modest tool for working scholars and a survey of the state of Chartist scholarship to date' (*Introduction*). Lists the major manuscript collections; pamphlets, serials and other printed materials by Chartists and their contemporaries: relevant parliamentary papers; and secondary source books and articles on the movement, the aim being to include all known items in local and national libraries and archives, including certain libraries abroad. Contains about 2,000 items. Index principally of names and titles, but includes some topical entries. Very favourably reviewed when first published. *Class No:* 141.814CHA

Communism. Marxism. Leninism

[220]

A Dictionary of Marxist thought. Bottomore, T., *ed*. 2nd ed. Oxford, Basil Blackwell Publishers Ltd.; Cambridge, Mass., Harvard University Press, 1992. 672p. £50; $64.95. ISBN: 0631164812, UK. lst ed. 1983.

Provides clear accounts of concepts, schools of thought and individual Thinkers by *c*.80 eminent scholars of Marxism, taking account of different interpretations and criticisms. Each entry is a short essay, followed by a short bibliography or guide to further reading. Includes an editorial article on critics of Marxism. Also includes a list of contributors, with affiliations; a consolidated bibliography, A-Z by author (p.593-633); a chronological list of writings by Marx and Engels; and a subject index (p.567-87). Lists 49 entries new to the 2nd ed. '... an excellent guide'. (*College and research libraries*, v.45(4), July 1984, p.293). 'Definitely supersedes Russell's *Marx-Engel's dictionary*' (1981) (*Library journal*, 15 October 1983, p.1955). *Class No:* 141.82

Bibliographies

[221]

HAYNES, J.E. **Communism and anti-Communism in the United States:** an annotated guide to historical writings. New York, Garland, 1987. 321p. $47. ISBN: 0824085205.

Author is editor of the Newsletter of the Historians of American Communism and entries are drawn from the newsletter's annual bibliography. Includes books, journal articles and dissertations. Concerned with the period from the Bolshevik Revolution through McCarthyism of the 1950s, the emphasis is on scholarly examinations of the history and influence of Communism in American life, and includes some primary materials. Structured into 37 time-periods and issues (labour, literature, women, etc.). Author index but no subject index (table of contents) '... otherwise a unique and useful volume' (*College and research libraries*, January 1988, p.62).
Class No: 141.82(01)

[222]

KINNELL, S.K., *ed*. **Communism in the world since 1945:** an annotated bibliography. Santa Barbara, CA., ABC-Clio, 1987. 415p. $85. (*Clio bibliography series, 25*.) ISBN: 0874361699.

4151 entries, half of them on the Soviet Union and Eastern Europe, published between 1974 and 1985. Non-English-language titles are given English sub-titles. Cross-references. Author and subject indexes. Scholarly. Complements Charles Hobday's *Communist and Marxist parties of the world* (1986). *Class No:* 141.82(01)

[223]

LUBITZ, W. **Trotsky bibliography:** a classified list of published items about Leon Trotsky and Trotskyism. 2nd ed. rev. & expanded. New York, K.G. Saur, 1988. 581p. $120. ISBN: 3598107544.

First published 1982.

A classified bibliography of 5009 items, including monographs, journal articles, symposia, masters' theses and doctoral dissertations, published speeches, review articles, introductions and prefaces to Trotsky's works, etc. Arranged in 8 topical sections, each section subdivided. Several indexes. Complements Louis Sinclair's *Leon Trotsky* (1972; supplements 1977 & 1980). *Class No:* 141.82(01)

[224]

NARKIEWICZ, O. **Eurocommunism, 1968-1986:** a select bibliography. London, Mansell Publishing Ltd.; New York, H.W. Wilson, 1987. xxi,188p. £25; $56. ISBN: 0720118018.

1425 items arranged in 2 parts: 1. Bibliography of monographs, studies and selected essays - 2. Bibliography of published sources (journals and newspapers). Entries listed A-Z in each part, with very brief annotations. Includes a lengthy introductory essay on the subject, p.vii-xxi, which states that the volume was compiled with a view to documenting new and interesting political phenomenon, both for the specialist and for the student of politics. No indexes.
Class No: 141.82(01)

[225]

SINCLAIR, L. **Trotsky: a bibliography.** Aldershot, Hants, Scolar Press, 1989. 2v.(1384p). £95. ISBN: 0859678202.

Earlier ed. published 1972 as *Leon Trotsky: a bibliography*.

*c.*5200 items listed chronologically, with references to later reprints, translations, etc. Also lists a further *c.*7200 unpublished items. '... a valuable and useful approach ...'(*International review of social history*, v.36(1), 1991,p.113). *Class No:* 141.82(01)

Dictionaries

French

[226]

LABICA, G. *and* BENSUSSAN, G., *eds*. **Dictionnaire critique du Marxisme.** 2e. refondue et augmentée. Paris, Presses Universitaire de Paris, 1985. xvi,1240p. ISBN: 213038739x.

First published 1982.

Lengthy entries of between 2 to 10 pages each, followed by bibliographies and lists of alternative or related terms. Cross-references. Notes. A list of contributors precedes.
Class No: 141.82(038)=40

Chinese

[227]

DOOLIN, D. *and* RIDLEY, C. **A Chinese-English dictionary of Communist Chinese terminology.** Stanford, CA., Hoover Institution Press, 1973. 569p. $30. ISBN: 0817962417.
Class No: 141.82(038)=951

Periodicals

[228]

The Left index: a quarterly index to periodicals of the Left. Political Research Inc., 1982-. Quarterly. ISSN: 07332998.

Covers journals representing a Marxist, radical, or Left perspective, and includes topics on anthropology, black studies, economics, education, philosophy, political science, psychology, science, sociology, and women's studies. *c.*80 journals are indexed regularly, including 22 foreign titles. *c.*500 numbered entries in each issue, arranged A-Z by author. Cross-references. Book review index (arranged A-Z by author); cumulated subject index (based on Library of Congress subject headings); journal index (analysing contents).
Class No: 141.82(051)

Quotations

[229]

WEEKS, A.L., *comp*. & *ed*. **Brassey's Soviet and communist quotations.** Washington, D.C., Pergamon-Brassey's; International Defence Publishers, 1987. xxii,387p. $50. ISBN: 0080344887.

Statements rather than mere quotations. 2117 numbered items arranged by subject in 17 chapters: 1. Capitalism and socialism - 2. Class and class warfare - 3. Communism - 4. Communist party ... 9. Marxist-Leninist ideologies ... 12. Religion and ethics - 13. Revolution ... 15. Terrorism/guerrilla warfare ... 17. War preparation. Quotations are followed by the source (person, and where published). Index, by chapter, p.369-386. 'A useful and unique reference source, it would be vastly improved by a more utilitarian index' (*College & research libraries*, v.49(1), January 1988, p.62). *Class No:* 141.82(082.2)

Histories

[230]

STERN, G. **Atlas of Communism.** New York, Macmillan, 1991. 256p. illus. 48 maps. $95. ISBN: 0028972651.

A descriptive, historical essay, with maps, on the origins, development and recent decline of Communism, and some movements that had viewpoints in common with Communism. 5 main sections, each subdivided: The roots of Communism, 1848-1917 - The Soviet experience, 1917-1945 - Cold War Communism, 1945-62 - New perspectives, 1962-85 - Reform and revolution, 1985 to the present. Index. 'The book's main strength is that it is comprehensive ... coverage, combined with an excellent index, gives it considerable value as a reference tool.'(*Choice*, v.29(1), September 1991, p.51).
Class No: 141.82(091)

Biographies

[231]

GORMAN, R.A., *ed*. **Biographical dictionary of Marxism.** London, Mansell Publishing; Westport, CT., Greenwood Press, 1986. x, 389p. £45. $55. ISBN: 0720118190, UK; 0313248516, US.

Focuses on materialist or orthodox Marxism. Selective biographies of over 210 major twentieth-century philosophers throughout the world. Each entry, ranging from ½-page to 3 pages in length, has biographical data on the individual, a summary of his/her significant contributions to Marxist theory and practice, and a bibliography of primary and secondary sources for research. Appendix: Entrants by nationality contribution. Index (p.371-388, double-column).' ... eminently readable ...' (*Library journal*, 1 February 1986, p.73). '... clearly written and concise entries ...' (*Choice*, July/August 1986, p.1651). *Class No:* 141.82(092)

[232]

GORMAN, R.A., *ed*. **Biographical dictionary of Neo-Marxism.** London, Mansell Publishing Ltd.; Westport, CT., Greenwood Press, 1986. x, 464p. £45. $55. ISBN: 0720118204, UK; 0313235139, US.

Companion volume to the author's '*Biographical dictionary of Marxism*' (qv).

A useful introduction, outlining the origins and several key components of Neo-Marxist thought and action, precedes more than 205 biographical entries and 10 entries describing important groups, movements and journals. Cross-references. Selective bibliography of primary and secondary sources. Two appendices: Entrants by nationality; List of contributors. Good subject index (p.447-463 double-column). '... a valuable reference for the study of Neo-Marxism'. (*Choice*, v.23(9), May 1986, p.1368).
Class No: 141.82(092)

Psychology

[233]

BECHTEL, W. *and* GRAHAM, G, *eds.* **Companion to cognitive science** Oxford, Blackwell, 1998. xvii, 600p. £75.00. (*Blackwell Companions to Philosophy.*.) ISBN: 1557865426.

This is an unusually thorough addition to the series of which it forms a part. The volume opens with a long account of congitive science's relatively short history. This constitutes Part I: "The life of cognitive science". The 60 essays, each of 9-10 pages are divided thereafter into Part II: "Areas of study"; Part III: "Methodologies"; Part IV: "Stances in cognitive science"; Part V: "Controversies" and Part VI: "Cognitive science in the real world" - treating its relationship to, for example, education and law. Within each part the essays are in alphabetical order and, where necessary, are illustrated. These sections are followed by some 25 pages of brief biographies of significant researchers in this field. Each essay provides its own "references and recommended reading" section, though these are not extensive. There is no general bibliography. There is an index of persons, and a fairly brief one of subjects. *Class No:* 159.9

[234]

The Blackwell dictionary of cognitive psychology. Eysenck, M.W. Oxford, Blackwell, 1991. xvi,390p. £60. ISBN: 0651156828.

One of the main aims of the book is to 'provide the reader with the scope and diversity of contemporary cognitive psychology' (*Introduction*). Arranged A-Z, 140 terms are defined at length. Each essay-length entry includes a well-balanced bibliography with details of the key publications relating to the particular topic. 'an outstanding publication of high quality content matched by thoughtful editing, arrangement and indexing ... good value ...'(*Reference reviews*, v.5(2), 1991, p.8. *Class No:* 159.9

[235]

BORCHARDT, D.H. *and* FRANCIS, R.D. **How to find out in psychology:** a guide to the literature and methods of research. Oxford, Pergamon Press, 1986. xi,189p. 17 illus. £14.75. ISBN: 0080312802.

First published in 1968 as *How to find out in philosophy and psychology*, by D.H. Borchardt.

'... eleven chapters. The first two deal with what psychology is about and its major theories, and chapters III-VI deal with the bibliographic aids used by psychologists ... How one gathers and presents such material is the subject of chapters VIII-X ... Chapter XI is concerned with professional matters and includes information on psychological organizations ...' (*Preface*). 5 appendices A. A guide to library searches ... E. Psychological societies). Bibliography, p.175-186. A-Z by author; journals A-Z by title. Subject index, p.187-189. *Class No:* 159.9

[236]

COADY, C.A.J. **Testimony** a philosophical study. Oxford, Clarendon Press, 1994 x,315p.

A major philosophical study, possibly the first of its kind, on the philosophical basis for our trust in the testimony of others. *Class No:* 159.9

[237]

Concordance to the standard edition of the complete psychological works of Sigmund Freud. Guttman, Samuel *and* Jones, Randall L. *and* Parrish, S.M., *eds.* Boston, Mass., GK Hall, 1980 ISBN: 081618383x, US.

Published in six volumes, and alphabetically arranged

Index of words in order of frequency down to 100. Has a pagination converter which tells the reader the page on which the phrase occurs in the Gesammelte Werke. *Class No:* 159.9

[238]

MORRIS, B. **Western concepts of the individual.** New York, Berg, 1991 ix,505p. $74.00 ISBN: 0854966986.

An historical approach to the concept of what it is to be human, from Descartes down to the present day. The approach is mainly anthropological. *Class No:* 159.9

[239]

STRATTON, P. *and* HAYES, N. **A Student's dictionary of psychology.** 2nd ed. London, Edward Arnold; New York, Routledge, Chapman & Hall, 1993. 240p. illus. £10.99. ISBN: 0340569263.

First published in 1988.

An explaining, rather than a defining dictionary. Includes definitions of basic terms used in contemporary psychology; brief notes on famous psychologists; explanations of statistical and methodological terms; and longer entries on topics representing significant areas within modern psychology. Uses illustrations to clarify difficult points. *Class No:* 159.9

Databases

[240]

BRAND, A.A. *and* KINZIE, L.A. 'A Comparison of online access to psychoanalytic literature'. In *Database*, v.7(1), February 1984, p.54-55, 58-63.

Includes evaluation of PSYCINFO, MEDLINE, and NIMH. 6 appendices: 1. Major mental health databases - 2. Comparison of psychoanalytic journal coverage by selected databases - 3-6. other comparisons. *Class No:* 159.9(003.4)

[241]

PsycINFO database. Arlington, VA., American Psychological Association, 1974 -. Quarterly.

Includes references to all relevant original research and other significant published material drawn from over 1400 periodicals, dissertations, technical reports, etc. Includes over 340,000 citations.

See *The Reference librarian*, v.40, 1993, p.144-5, for a discussion on search differences between PsycINFO and Silverplatter's PsycLIT. *Class No:* 159.9(003.4)

Bibliographies

[242]

BAXTER, P.M. **Psychology:** a guide to reference and information sources. Littleton, Col., Libraries Unlimited, 1993. 219p. $36.50. ((*Reference sources in the social sciences*).) ISBN: 0872877086.

In 4 parts: part 1 lists general social science reference sources; pt 2 'Social science disciplines', covers materials relative to psychology; pt 3 has general psychology reference sources (guides, bibliographies, indexing and abstracting tools, online databases, handbooks and yearbooks, dictionaries and encyclopedias, biographies, journals, organizations, publishers, and directories); and pt 4, with well over half the entries, is divided among 24 subtopics (history, theory, test construction, intelligence, personality, etc.). Entries are annotated. Author, title and subject indexes. *Class No:* 159.9(01)

[243]

Bibliographic guide to psychology. The Research Libraries of the New York Public Library and the Library of Congress. Boston, Mass., G.K. Hall, 1974-. Annual. prices vary; c.£200. ISSN: 0360277x.

Formerly *Psychology book guide*.

Each annual volume lists all materials catalogued during the previous year by the N.Y.P.L. Research Libraries, with additions from Library of Congress MARC tapes. Covers all aspects of psychology, as well as parapsychology and the occult sciences. *Class No:* 159.9(01)

[244]

Female psychology: a partially annotated bibliography, edited by C. Dilling and B.L. Claster. New York, New York City Coalition for Women's Mental Health, 1985. 326p. $25. ISBN: 0961602805.

Lists recent and historically important articles and books in areas of female developmental theory, psychoanalytic theory and practice, psychopathology, gender and sex roles, and special issues relevant to women and their mental health needs in a psychological, sociological and political context. *Class No:* 159.9(01)

[245]

GILMORE, W.J. **Psychological enquiry:** a comprehensive research bibliography. New York, Garland, 1984. 317p. $40. (*Garland reference library of social science, 156.*) ISBN: 0824091671.

c.5000 entries arranged in two parts: the first part methodology; the second part studies arranged by geographical area and subject, concentrating on Europe and the US. About 20% of the entries are annotated. 'Informative introduction and helpful author index' (*Choice*, v.22(2), October 1984, p.248). *Class No:* 159.9(01)

[246]

HOWELLS, J.G. *and* OSBORN, M.L. **A Reference companion to the history of abnormal psychology.** Westport, CT., Greenwood Press, 1984. 2v. (1141p.) illus. $95 the set. ISBN: 0313221839.

4000 entries, arranged A-Z, referring to persons, institutions, beliefs, terminology, groups, books, etc. that have figured in the history of psychopathology from antiquity to the present time. References are connected by the use of 'q.v.'. General index. '... serves a need not apparently met by any existing library resource for a combined biographical dictionary and brief encyclopedia for the field ...' (*RQ*, Fall 1984, p.109). 'A unique contribution' (*Library journal*, 15 December 1983, p.2324). *Class No:* 159.9(01)

[247]

KIELL, N. **Psychoanalysis, psychology and literature:** a bibliography. 2nd ed. Metuchen, N.J., Scarecrow Press, 1982. 2v. (1269p.). $65. £58.10. ISBN: 0810814218.

First published 1963.

19,764 unannotated entries for books, journal articles and dissertations published between 1900 and 1980, arranged in 14 categories. Author, title and subject indexes. A supplement was issued in 1990 ($67.50. ISBN 0810821788 *Class No:* 159.9(01)

[248]
McINNIS, R.G. **Research guide for psychology.** Westport, CT.,
Greenwood Press, 1982. xxvi, 604p. illus. $50.95. (*Reference sources
for social science and humanities, 1.*) ISBN: 0313213992.
17 chapters are each bibliographic essays on a different sub-division
of psychology, with general commentary and annotations about
specific sources. Covers indexes and abstracts, literature reviews,
current and retrospective bibliographies, encyclopedias and handbooks,
etc. Combined author, subject and title index. 'An ambitious guide of
slightly uneven quality' (*RQ*, Winter 1982, p.205-6). 'Arrangement is
logical and analytical, enhanced by ... index' (*Choice*, v.20(4),
December 1982, p.562). *Class No:* 159.9(01)

[249]
NATOLI, J. *and* RUSCH, F.L. **Psychocriticism:** an annotated
bibliography. Westport, CT, Greenwood Press, [1984]. 267p.
(Bibliographies and indexes in world literature, 1). $35. ISBN:
0313236410.
Long introductory essay, followed by entries for 1435 English-
language books, articles and essays selected from critical and scholarly
secondary works published between 1969 and 1982. Each chapter
begins with a list of general items, followed by items by specific
authors. Annotations of one or two sentences. Subject and author
indexes. *Class No:* 159.9(01)

[250]
Psychological index: an annual bibliography of the literature of
psychology and cognate subjects, 1894-1935, v.1-42. Princeton, N.J.,
Psychological Review Co., 1895-1936. 42v.
Continued Section G of v.3 ('*Bibliography of philosophy*'), by B.
*Rand (1905), of J.M. Baldwin's Dictionary of philosophy and
psychology.* A classified index to 150,844 books and periodical articles
published during the period. Author indexes but no subject index.
*Cumulative author index to 'Psychological index,' 1894 to 1935, and
'Psychological abstracts,' 1927 to 1958,* compiled by Columbia
University, New York (Boston, Mass., G.K. Hall, 1960. 5v. (4286p.))
has *c.*320,000 entries. *Class No:* 159.9(01)

[251]
TAVISTOCK JOINT LIBRARY. London. **Catalogue of the Tavistock
Joint Library.** Boston, Mass., G.K. Hall, 1975. 2v.(1085p.). $145.
ISBN: 0816111677.
Covers the combined holdings of the Tavistock Clinic and the
Tavistock Institute of Human Relations - *c.*15,000 books and
pamphlets. Extensive analyticals. A list of the Library's periodical
holdings (230 periodicals in psychology are currently received) is
appended. Main strength: psychology, psychiatry, psychoanalysis and
the study of organizations. *Class No:* 159.9(01)

[252]
VANDE KEMP, H. **Psychology and theology in Western thought,
1672-1965:** a historical and annotated bibliography. Millwood, N.Y.,
Kraus International Publications, [1984]. 367p. (Bibliographies in the
history of psychology and psychiatry). $65. ISBN: 0527927791.
Concerned with the movement leading towards 'psychotheological
integration', hence the dates 1672-1965. Covers books, monographs,
pamphlets and journal titles. Arranged by topic, then chronological by
date of publication. Particular attention given to 'schools' or traditions.
Final section on major journals, institutions, and special book series.
Separate name, institution, title and subject indexes.
Class No: 159.9(01)

[253]
WERTHEIMER, M.L. 'Psychology'. In Webb, W.H. *Sources of
information in the social sciences* (3rd ed. American Library
Association, 1986, p.403-54).
The late Robert I. Wilson, Sr., who completed his draft of this
chapter shortly before he died, provided an overview of the most
significant literature in psychology as a social science up to the middle
of 1980. M.L. Wertheimer has appended a small number of more
recent works in each of the subdivisions. In two parts, survey of the
field and survey of the reference works (guides to the literature,
reviews, abstracts and summaries, bibliographies of bibliographies,
current bibliographies, retrospective bibliographies, periodicals,
directories and biographical information, dictionaries, encyclopedias,
handbooks, audiovisual materials, sources of scholarly contributions,
sources of current information, and computerized databases. *c.*300
references. *Class No:* 159.9(01)

Encyclopaedias & Dictionaries
[254]
WILSON SH R. A. *and* KEIL, F. C., *eds.* **The MIT encyclopedia of
the cognitive sciences** Cambridge MA, MIT Press, 1999. cxxxii,
964p. $105.00 ISBN: 0262232006.
This magisterial publication covers neuroscience and linguistics as
well as psychology and philosophy. It contains 471 entries in
alphabetical order, and its usefulness is much increased by the
provision not only of a CD Rom but also of free access for purchasers
to an on-line version. *Class No:* 159.9(03)

Encyclopaedias
[255]
Companion encyclopedia of psychology. Colman, Andrew M., *ed.*
London, Routledge, 1994
Includes bibliography and index.
Contains over sixty contributions from more than seventy authors.
Arrangement of contents is arbitrary. Work not aimed at a specialist
readership. Thematic arrangement of contents, with each section
beginning with a brief introduction. Contains cross-references to other
sections and chapters of the encyclopedia *Class No:* 159.9(031)

[256]
CORSINI, R.J., *ed.* **Encyclopedia of psychology.** 2nd ed New York,
John Wiley & Sons, 1994 4v. tables, charts ISBN: 0471558192.
Includes bibliographical entries with references at the end of some
entries. The size of entries varies as does the number of cross
references. This edition cuts out many of the bibliographical entries in
the "Concise Encyclopedia of Psychology" *Class No:* 159.9(031)

[257]
EYSENCK, H.J., *and others.* **Encyclopedia of psychology.** 2nd ed.
London, Search Press, 1979. 3v. illus. ISBN: 0855324392.
First published 1972.
Covers all aspects of modern psychology. *c.*5000 entries; 300 major
articles, some attaining 4000 words, with bibliographies. Some
biographies are included. *Class No:* 159.9(031)

[258]
WOLMAN, B.B., *ed.* **International encyclopedia of psychiatry,
psychology, psychoanalysis & neurology.** New York, Van Nostrand
Reinhold, for Aesculapius Publishers Inc., 1977. 12v. diagrs. $675 the
set. ISBN: 0918228018.
1500 authors: nearly 300 editors and consultants. Nearly 2000
survey-articles, each documented. 305 biographies (*e.g.* Adler: v.1,
p.235-40; ½ column of biography); 1605 articles on concepts and
issues (*e.g.* 'Aggression in children': v.1, p.348-53; 11/3 cols. of
bibliography); v.12 (410p.): Author and subject indexes. (The non-
analytical subject index has *c.*200 unspecified entries under
'Transference'). 'This eminently readable and impressive
encyclopedia' (*Library journal*, 15 April 1978, p.817).
Progress volume 1 (New York, Aesculapius Publishers Inc., 1983.
xxxiv, 599p. $89. ISBN 091822828x) is the first supplement to the
basic 12 volumes. *Class No:* 159.9(031)

Handbooks & Manuals
[259]
GROTH-MARNAT, G. **Handbook of psychological assessments.** 2nd
ed. Chichester, New York, Wiley-Interscience, 1990. xiii,594p. tables,
diagrs. £36. ISBN: 0471510343.
1st published 1984.
12 chapters: 1. Introduction; 2. The context of clinical assessments;
3. The assessment interview; 4. Behavioral assessment; 5. Wechsler
intelligence scales ... 11. Projective drawings; 12. The psychological
report. Includes appendices A to T. Bibliography, p.499-563. Author
and subject indexes. *Class No:* 159.9(035)

[260]
Handbook of developmental psychology. Wolman, J.B., *ed.*
Englewood Cliffs, NJ., Prentice Hall, 1987. xv,953p. $132. ISBN:
0133725995.
In 6 parts, each subdivided: 1. Research methods and theories - 2.
Infancy - 3. Childhood - 4. Adolescence - 5. Adulthood - 6. Aging.
*c.*75 contributors. Deals with fundamental concepts and research
findings. Author index, p.937-953 (*c.*7000 entries).
Class No: 159.9(035)

[261]
LINDZEY, G. *and* ARONSON, E., *eds.* **Handbook of social
psychology.** 3rd ed. New York, Newbery Award Records/Random
House, 1985. 2v. v.1: $50. v.2: $45. set: $95. ISBN: 0394350499,
v.1; 0394350502, v.2.
First published 1954.
V.1: *Theory and method;* v.2: *Special fields and applications.* 30
chapters in all. The authors hoped to provide an affordable
compendium that would be widely read by professionals and graduate
students and not treated merely as a reference work. Each volume has
a list of references and a subject and name index.
Class No: 159.9(035)

[262]
The Oxford companion to the mind. Gregory, R.L. *and* Zangwill, O.L.
Oxford, Oxford University Press, 1987. xvii,856p. illus (200 half-
tone & line-drawings). £25; $49.95. ISBN: 019866124x.
Wide-ranging reference book written for a non-specialist readership,
with 1001 articles in the fields of psychology, philosophy of mind, and
physiology of the brain and nervous system, by a team of over 100
authorities and scholars. Entries range from brief definitions to
substantial essays. Predominantly, but not exclusively, Anglo-
American. Cross-references. Includes biographies of deceased persons.

....*(contd.)*

'... fun to browse through ...' (*Choice*, v.25(7), March 1988, p.1068). '... overanxious to avoid being stuffy ...' (*Philosophy*, April 1988, p.289-90). *Class No:* 159.9(035)

Dictionaries

[263]
GOLDENSON, Robert M., *editor-in-chief*. Longman dictionary of psychology and psychiatry. New York & London, Longman, 1984. xvi, 816p. $39.95; £29.50. ISBN: 0582282578.

Aims were to present a comprehensive lexicon on all phases of the two vast areas; to place heavy emphasis on current terms the reader is likely to encounter in the professional literature and professional practice today, without overlooking older terms that have special historical value; and to avoid the limitations of a one-dimensional glossary by giving a maximum amount of information in a minimum number of words. Comprises 21,164 entries, including 488 kinds of tests, 216 therapy entries, 70 entries treating Piaget's work and ideas, 100 treating Jung's etc. *Class No:* 159.9(038)

[264]
JUNG, C.G. Dictionary of analytical psychology. London, Routledge, 1987. [4], 183p. £4.50. ISBN: 0744800773.

Sums up Jung's ideas (types) in his own words, providing an introduction for anyone who wants to understand his typology and his ideas about human personality. General descriptions of introverted and extroverted types precede the dictionary proper. Bibliography, p.167-172. Index, p.173-180. *Class No:* 159.9(038)

[265]
KRISTAL, L., *ed*. ABC of psychology. New ed. London, Michael Joseph; New York, Facts on File, 1982. 250p. 60 illus. £7.95; $16.95. ISBN: 0871968444.

First published 1981 by Murray.

A layman's encyclopedia of concepts in modern psychology. *Class No:* 159.9(038)

[266]
POPPLESTONE, J.A. *and* McPHERSON, M.W. Dictionary of concepts in general psychology. Westport, CT., Greenwood Press, 1988. xi,380p. $65. (*Reference sources for the social sciences and humanities, 7.*) ISBN: 0313231907.

Includes *c.*50 concepts and *c.*50 cross-references. Entries all lengthy and include references and sources of additional information (*e.g.* 'Anger': 3½ pages of definition; 12 references and sources - nearly 5p. in all; 'Intelligence': 4 definitions in 4½ pages of text; 18 references and sources - nearly 6p. in all). Author index, p.357-372;p analytical subject index, p.373-380. *Class No:* 159.9(038)

[267]
Psychoanalytic terms and concepts. Moore, B.E. *and* Fine, B.D., *eds*. 3rd ed. New Haven, Co., American Psychoanalytic Association/Yale University Press, 1990. xxv,210p. £35. ISBN: 0300045778.

First published 1967; revised ed. 1968 as *A glossary of psychological terms and concepts.*

Nearly 300 concepts defined, the long definitions containing both historical and current aspects of many of the terms. Includes references to cited works. 'See' references. *c.*200 experts contributed. 'This is a fine reference tool' (*Choice*, v.27(11/12), July/August 1990, p.1810). *Class No:* 159.9(038)

[268]
STUART-HAMILTON, I. Dictionary of developmental psychology. London, Jessica Kingsley Publishers, 1995 viii,163p.

Author attempts to avoid technical terms. The material is arranged alphabetically with an emphisis on easily read definitions. The book focuses on those terms frequently used in textbooks. *Class No:* 159.9(038)

[269]
SUTHERLAND, S. Macmillan dictionary of psychology. 2nd ed Basingstoke, Macmillan, 1995 ix, 515p. diagrs. ISBN: 0333623231.

Published in the US by Crossroad/Continuum in 1989 with the title *The International dictionary of psychology* (ISBN 0826404405).

Intended as a dictionary for psychologists, including terms from neurology, linguistics, artificial intelligence, sociology, anthropology, statistics and philosophy. Liberal cross-references. Examples are given in many cases. *Class No:* 159.9(038)

[270]
WOLMAN, B.B., *comp. and ed*. Dictionary of behavioral science. 2nd ed. London, Academic Press; New York, Van Nostrand Reinhold, 1989. 720p. $59. ISBN: 0127624554.

First ed. published 1973.

*c.*10,000 terms in all areas of theoretical, experimental and applied psychology and psychiatry. Includes biographical notes. *Class No:* 159.9(038)

[271]
ZUSNE, L. Eponyms in psychology: a dictionary and biographical sourcebook. Westport, CT., Greenwood Press, 1987. 339p. $85. ISBN: 0313257507.

*c.*850 terms in the field of psychology and selected related fields are defined, their origins discussed, and short bibliographies included. *Class No:* 159.9(038)

English

[272]
BRUNO, F.J. Dictionary of key words in psychology. London, Routledge & Kegan Paul, 1986. xi, 275p. £16.95. ISBN: 0710201907.

'This book does not seek to present an exhaustive catalogue of psychological terms, but a selective list of key terms - terms that are used with very high levels of frequency' (*Preface*). A tripartite form of presentation (Abnormal behaviour - Zen): 1. Definition; 2. Example; 3. Connections. Bibliography (p.259-262) is a selective listing, A-Z by author. Analytical topical index, name index and subject index (p.263-275). *Class No:* 159.9(038)=20

[273]
ENGLISH, H.B. *and* ENGLISH, A.C. A Comprehensive dictionary of psychological and psychoanalytical terms: a guide to usage. New York, Longmans Green, 1958 (reprinted by Mackay). xiv. 594p. diagrs. ISBN: 0679300333.

More than 13,000 terms and abbreviations are explained. The aim (*Preface*) is to include all terms frequently used in a special or technical sense by psychologists, with one set of definitions for the comparative layman and another set for the person working in the field of psychology. Pronunciation is given for unusual or difficult words. The inclusion of compound-word terms is a feature (*e.g.* 'Reinforcement' and its compounds occupy 5 pages). Extensive cross-references. *Class No:* 159.9(038)=20

[274]
HARRÉ, R. *and* LAMB, R., *eds*. The Dictionary of personality and social psychology. Oxford, Basil Blackwell, 1986. 416p. illus. £29.50. ISBN: 0631146016.

Over 300 entries on the theories of personality development and organization, and the topics and approaches which make up social psychology. *Class No:* 159.9(038)=20

[275]
REBER, R.S. The Penguin dictionary of psychology. ed London, Penguin Books; New York, Viking/Penguin Inc., 1995. xvii, 800p. ISBN: 0140512802, UK.

c. Terms from psychology, psychiatry and related fields. Entries vary in length. Excludes biographies except for those who have given their names to a subject (*e.g.* Freudian, Pavlovian, Adlerian). Cross-references. The dictionary proper is preceded by a list of terms which are given extensive coverage, and ends with a list of authorities cited. *Class No:* 159.9(038)=20

Reviews & Abstracts

[276]
L'Année psychologique. 1894-. Paris, Presses Universitaire de France, 1895-. v.1-. Quarterly (previously 2pa., annual until 1951 (1952). ISSN: 00035033.

Published with the assistance of the Centre National des Lettres, previously the Centre National de la Recherche Scientifique.

Each issue has 3 main sections: Memoires originaux' (original contributions, in French but with abstracts in English) - 'Revues critiques' - 'Analyses bibliographiques' (signed abstracts of periodical articles, and book reviews). International coverage. *Class No:* 159.9(048)

[277]
The Annual review of psychology. Stanford, CA., Annual Reviews Inc., 1950-.v.1-. Annual. ISSN: 00664308.

A systematic critical, well-documented review of developments in various fields of psychology, so arranged that the fields are surveyed at regular intervals. Author and subject indexes; cumulative indexes of authors and chapter titles. *Class No:* 159.9(048)

[278]
Contemporary psychology: a journal of reviews. Washington, D.C., American Psychological Association, 1956-. v.1, no.1-. Monthly. ISSN: 00107549.

Each issue consists of some 23 sections, with *c.*55 extended critical reviews of books and films; short notices; and a list of books received. Apparently confined to English-language material published in the US. A feature is the inclusion in longer reviews of the detailed qualifications of both reviewer and author/editor. Coverage extends to psychiatry, public opinion and animal behaviour. Annual author and reviewer index. *Class No:* 159.9(048)

[279]

PsycBooks: books and chapters in psychology, 1987-. Arlington, VA., American Psychological Association. Annual. 5v. each year. ISSN: 10441514.

Psychological abstracts ceased to include books in 1980. In 1984 an effort was made to rectify this deficiency, resulting in this title.

Gives access to the latest books and chapters in psychology. V.I. Experimental psychology: basic and applied - II. Developmental, personality, social psychology - III. Professional psychology, disorders and treatment - IV. Educational psychology and health psychology - V. Author and subject indexes. *Class No:* 159.9(048)

[280]

Psychological abstracts: non-evaluative summaries of the serial literature in psychology and related disciplines. Arlington, VA., The American Psychological Association Inc., 1927-. Monthly. ISSN: 00332887.

Over 3000 entries in each issue, from over 1400 journals, arranged in a classified order: General psychology - Psychometrics - Human experimental psychology - Animal experimental and comparative psychology - Psychological psychology - Psychological intervention - Communication systems - Developmental psychology - Social processes and social issues - Social psychology - Personality - Physical and psychological disorders - Treatment and prevention - Professional personnel and professional issues - Educational psychology - Applied psychology - Sport psychology and leisure. Brief subject index; author index. Available online and also on CD-ROM (American Psychological Association, Silver Platter (PsyclLIT). *Class No:* 159.9(048)

[281]

Psychological bulletin. Washington DC., American Psychological Association, 1904-. v.1-. Bi-monthly.

Features review articles with bibliographies. An important aid to bibliographical research. *Class No:* 159.9(048)

Periodicals & Progress Reports

[282]

MARKLE, A. and RINN, R. Author's guide to journals in psychology, psychiatry & social work. New York, Haworth Press, 1977. 256p. $29.95; £25.90. ISBN: 0917724003.

Profiles of more than 400 journals, based on replies to questionnaires. Data include topic coverage, time lag in publishing, style requirements, circulation, price and coverage by indexing/abstracting services. Subject, title and keyword index. *Class No:* 159.9(05)

[283]

OSIER, D.V. and WOZNIAK, R.H. A Century of serial publications in psychology, 1850-1950; an international bibliography. Millwood, N.Y., Kraus International, 1984. 805p. $100. (*Bibliographies in the history of psychology and psychiatry.*) ISBN: 0527981966.

1107 serial titles arranged chronologically by inaugural year of publication, with titles published in the same year arranged A-Z. Also included are 41 entries for titles that first appeared between 1783 and 1849. Titles that began since 1950 are excluded. Each entry contains title, name of sponsoring organization, variations of title, publication date, frequency, numbering variations, publisher, primary editors, associated editors, and editorial board members. Title and name indexes, with cross-references. An appendix lists titles, with dates of publication, of serials in allied fields. *Class No:* 159.9(05)

Yearbooks & Directories

[284]

The Register of chartered psychologists. Leicester, The British Psychological Society, 1993 262p. ISBN: 1854331116.

Includes indexes.

Covers the British Isles. Gives the society's code of conduct, criteria for inclusion, and the procedure whereby a complaint may be lodged against a practioner. *Class No:* 159.9(058)

[285]

WOLMAN, B.B. International directory of psychology: a guide to people, places and policies. New York & London, Plenum Press, 1979. xxxiv, 279p. tables. $45. ISBN: 0306402092.

Describes the structure and functions of nearly 70 national psychological organizations. Under countries, A-Z, data on educational and research facilities, legal status and occupations of psychologists, and the major publications (journals and books) in the field. *Class No:* 159.9(058)

Histories

[286]

SCHULTZ, D.P. and SCHULTZ, S.E. History of modern psychology. 6th ed. Fort Worth, Harcourt Brace College Publishers, 1996. xvi,511p. $27. ISBN: 0155025600.

First published 1969. A 5th ed. was published in 1992 (xv,416p. $45.25. ISBN 0155374672).

Arranged in sections, all subdivided: 1. The study of the history of psychology - 2. Philosophical influences on psychology - 3. Physiological influences on psychology - 4. The new psychology - 5. Structuralism - 6.7.8. Functionalism - 9.10.11. Behaviorism - 12. Gestalt psychology - 13.14. Psychoanalysis - 14. Beyond the schools of thought: more recent developments. Suggested readings are given at the end of each section. Includes references and index *Class No:* 159.9(091)

[287]

WERTHEIMER, M. A Brief history of psychology. 3rd ed. New York, Holt, Rinehart & Winston, 1987. 175p. $19. ISBN: 0030095042.

Previous ed. 1979.

An encapsulated overview of a select set of individuals and ideas, from Plato to major psychologists of the 20th century, who have played a significant role in psychology's history. 'A clear exposition...' (*Contemporary psychology,* v.33(5), May 1988, p.419). *Class No:* 159.9(091)

Bibliographies

[288]

PEETERS, H., and others. Historical behavioural sciences. A guide to the literature. Tilburg, Netherlands, Tilburg University Press, 1988. xx.311p. Dfl.49.50. ISBN: 9036195225.

In 2 parts. Pt.1 discusses 40 journals relevant to the study of the historical sciences. Pt.2 has *c*.5500 bibliographical entries for articles, books, collections, essays, all thematically arranged (Theory - Methods and techniques - Psychological functions - Psychological development - Personality - Ecology - Mentalities and culture - Family and kinship - Deviant behaviour and social control - Women's history. Author index. *Class No:* 159.9(091)(01)

Biographies

[289]

ZUSNE, L. Biographical dictionary of psychology. Westport, CT., Greenwood Press; London, Aldwych Press, 1984. xxi,563p. $49.95; £47.50. ISBN: 0313240272.

544 brief biographies of deceased psychologists, A-Z. 3 appendices: A. Chronological list; B: List by degree of eminence; C: Academic and research institutions by country. *Class No:* 159.9(092)

Worldwide

Encyclopaedias

[290]

International encyclopedia of psychology. Magill, F.N., *ed.* 2nd ed. London, Fitzroy Dearborn Publishers, 1996 ISBN: 1884964605.

Designed to provide the general reader with insight into topics often only accessible to academics. There are 410 articles, each beginning with a ready reference section, and a brief summary of the topic. The main section on the topic is divided into; - 1. Overview - 2. Application and context - 3. Bibliography. This is not an easy read for the layperson. *Class No:* 159.9(100)(031)

Great Britain

Histories

[291]

HEARNSHAW, L.S. A Short history of British psychology, 1804-1940. London, Methuen, 1964 (reprinted by Greenwood Press, 1986). 344p. £59.40 $62.50. (*Methuen's manuals of modern psychology series.*) ISBN: 0313252785.

'Likely to be a standard work on its subject for many years to come. It will encourage students to attain what is necessary in a human science - a sense of historical and social process ... ' (*The British journal of psychology,* v.56 pts.2 & 3, August 1965. p.321-2). 'Select bibliography', p.298-316 (arranged by chapters). *Class No:* 159.9(410)(091)

Counselling

[292]

DRYDEN, W., *and others*. **Handbook of counselling in Britain.** London, Tavistock/Routledge, in association with the British Association for Counselling, 1989. xvi,454p. tables. £30. ISBN: 0415013275.

A review of the main fields of counselling activity in Britain, a source of information for professional counsellors, students, and voluntary organisers. 25 chapters in 5 parts: 1. Introduction - 2. Areas - 3. Settings - 4. Themes - 5. Issues. Appendices on codes of ethics. Author and subject indexes. *Class No:* 159.9(410)COU

Russia

[293]

JORAVSKY, D. **Russian psychology:** a critical history. Oxford. Basil Blackwell Ltd., 1989. 624p. £45. ISBN: 0631163379.

Assesses the familiar and less familiar, the political and the cultural expressions of Russian psychology. *Class No:* 159.9(47)

America—North & Central

Libraries

[294]

EPSTEIN, B.A. and DETLEFSEN, E.G., eds. **Directory of mental health libraries and information centers.** Washington, D.C., American Psychiatric Press Inc., 1984. vii,297,[4]p. $20. ISBN: 0880480475.

Compiled under the auspices of the Association of Mental Health Libraries.

Geographical arrangement, A-Z by State for the US, then Canada. Information includes name and address, telephone number, parent institute, funding, staff, specialized services, stock of publications, access, and publications of the organization. 1 page per library or information centre. Personnel, institution and subject indexes. *Class No:* 159.9(71/73):061:026/027

USA

[295]

BENJAMIN, L.T., *and others*. **A History of American psychology in notes and news, 1883-1945:** an index to journal sources. White Plains, NY, Kraus International Publications, 1988. 896p. $125. ISBN: 0527066265.

Indexes the 'notes and news' sections from the six major journals in the development time period of American psychology in one cross-referenced A-Z listing. Over 50,000 citations to individuals, institutions, awards, special meetings, apparatus, etc., relating to psychology and associated fields. *Class No:* 159.9(73)

[296]

Directory of the American Psychological Association. 1989 ed. Washington, DC., the Association, 1989. 1792p. $70. ISBN: 1557980586. ISSN: 01966545.

First published 1918. Quadrennial. Early title was *Biographical directory*.

Lists *c*.47,000 members, with geographical index. *Class No:* 159.9(73)

English

Handbooks & Manuals

[297]

ROBERTS, J. **Making sense of English in psychology.** Edinburgh, Chambers, 1993 vii,151p. ISBN: 0550180486.

Aimed at helping lay people to come to grips with terminology. Not written as a dictionary of psychology. Cross references included to refer to other articles. A pronunciation guide is included. An easy book to use. *Class No:* 159.9=20(035)

Thesauri

[298]

AMERICAN PSYCHOLOGICAL ASSOCIATION. **Thesaurus of psychological index terms.** Staff of the Retrieval Service Unit, Psycinfo Dept. 8th ed. Arlington, Va., the Association, 1997. xxix 378p. ISBN: 1557984026.

First published 1974.

A-Z ('Abdomen' ... 'Zungs self rating depression scale'). Relationships noted are use/used for/broader/narrower/related. Rotated alphabetical terms section (preferred *Thesaurus* terms are listed in alphabetical order by each word contained in them). Generated from file of *Psychological abstracts*. *Class No:* 159.9:025.43

Experimental Psychology

[299]

BORING, E.G. **A History of experimental psychology.** 2nd ed. New York, Appleton-Century-Crofts, 1950. xxi, 771p. $48. ISBN: 0133900398.

First published 1929.

Ranges from the time of Copernicus up to 1950. Particularly valuable for its bio-bibliographical data (*e.g.* Wundt, p.316-27). 26 chapters, each with notes and references appended. Chapter 27: 'Retrospect'. Index of names and analytical index of subjects. *Class No:* 159.9.07

Child Psychology

[300]

BRUNO, F.J. **The Family encyclopedia of child psychology** and child development: an easy to understand parents' guide. New York, Wiley, 1992. 432p. $30. ISBN: 0477827939. *Class No:* 159.922.7

[301]

Child development abstracts and bibliography. Chicago, Ill., University of Chicago Press, for the Society for Research in Child Development, 1927-. 3 p.a. ISSN: 00093939.

Over 2000 abstracts and references a year. Main sections: Biology, health medicine - Cognition, learning, perception - Social, psychological, cultural and personality studies - Educational processes - Psychiatry, clinical psychology - History, theory and methodology. Book notices. Books received. Author and subject indexes per issue, cumulated annually. List of journals regularly searched. *Class No:* 159.922.7

[302]

JOHNSON, R.C. and MEDINNUS, G.R. **Child psychology: behavior and development.** 3rd ed. New York, London, etc., Wiley, 1974. xiv, 562p. illus, tables. $26.95. ISBN: 0471446246.

First published 1965.

17 chapters, in 5 sections: 1. Introduction - 2. Basic factors in development - 3. The family and its influence on development - 4. Societal influence on socialization - 5. The emerging self. Extensive chapter references (*e.g.* 15: Personality development: 9½p. of references). Author and subject indexes. Data are 'directed towards presenting a solid body of information rather than defending a specific theoretical position' (*Preface to the second edition*. 1968). *Class No:* 159.922.7

[303]

SATTLER, J.M. **Assessment of children's intelligence and special abilities.** 2nd ed. Boston, Mass., Allyn & Bacon, 1981. xxiv,722,[2]p. ISBN: 020507362x.

First published 1974 as *Assessment of children's intelligence*.

'Designed to teach clinical assessment skills to students in clinical, school, and counselling psychology and to enable students in special education to understand the assessment process. It also serves as a reference book for practicing professionals in these areas'(*Preface*). Arranged in 25 chapters, all subdivided. Notes, p.534-540, include references; 5 appendices (A. Publishers of tests reviewed; C. Miscellaneous tables); extensive glossary (p.630-646); over 1800 references, A-Z (647-699); name index (p.700-712); subject index (p.713-722). *Class No:* 159.922.7

Personality

[304]

BUROS, O.K., ed. **Personality tests and reviews...** Highland Park, N.J., Gryphon Press, University of Nebraska Press, 1970-1975. 2v. (xxxi,1659p. 841p.). v.I. $50; v.II. $55. ISBN: 0910674108, v.1; 0910674191, v.2.

Sub-title to v.I is 'including an index to *The mental measurement yearbooks*'.

V.I has Personality test index, p.1-241; Personality test reviews, p.242-1345; a classified index to 'TIMMY', p.1346-1427; 'MMY' book review index, p.1428-77. Index of titles; index of names; scanning index to tests. 'Invaluable for users who want published names, prices, descriptions and a critical evaluation of these testing instruments' (*Wilson library bulletin*, v. 44(8), April 1970. p.879). *Class No:* 159.923

[305]

HARGREAVES, G. and WILSON, P. **Dictionary of graphology:** the A-Z of your personality. London, Peter Owen, 1983. 215p. £10.95. ISBN: 0720605938.

A-Z listing of the various ways of writing, capitals and small letters - descriptions - character qualities revealed; Character traits - type of writing described; Glossary - Recommended reading (1p.). *Class No:* 159.923

[306]

MOSAK, H.H. *and* MOSAK, B. A Bibliography of Adlerian psychology. New York, Halstead Press: Wiley, 1975 (for v.1.); New York, Hemisphere Publishing Corp., 1985 (for v.2). 2v. ([xv],320p.; 403p.). V.2: $49.95. ISBN: 0891162968, v.2:.

Sponsored by The International Association of Individual Psychology and The North American Society of Adlerian Psychology.

V.1 has nearly 10,000 references under authors, A-Z (Adler: nos.125-579), and covers books, chapters of books, dissertations, journal and newspaper articles, with a non-analytical subject index (p.283-320). In v.2 the listings are expanded from 1973 through 1977, adding 3635 references and numerous corrections to the original volume. Entries are unannotated, arranged A-Z by author, and numbered. *Choice*, (v.24(1), September 1986, p.90) says '... numbering system ... can be confusing in utilization'. It is necessary to use both volumes together. *Class No:* 159.923

Encyclopaedias & Dictionaries

[307]

LEVINSON, D., *et al., eds*. Encyclopedia of the human emotions New York, Macmillan, 1999 2 vols. £135.00 ISBN: 0028647661.

On the emotions, and the role of the emotions. Each of the entries has a bibliography. The main emphasis is psychological, but there is some philosophical input (e.g., biographies of Kant and Descartes alongside those of Erikson and Freud). The scientific aspects of the emotions, such as biochemistry and neurobiology, are, however, not covered. While it is thoroughly academic in its approach, incorporating recent research, an attempt has been made to ensure that non-technical readers will be able to find their way around the volunes. *Class No:* 159.923(03)

Intelligence

[308]

BOFF, K.R., *and others, eds*. Handbook of perception and human performance. New York, Wiley, 1986. 2v. (xxi,1568p.;xxi,1358p.). v.1 $125; v.2 $145.95. ISBN: 0471885444, v.1; 0471829579, v.2; 0471829560, set.

V.1. *Sensory processes and perception;* v.2. *Cognitive processes and performance.* 45 essays by 166 contributors and arranged in 7 sections in the 2 vols. (Sections 1-4 in v.1, 5-7 in v.2): 1. Theory and method - 2.-3. Basic sensory processes - 4. Space and motion perception - 5. Information processing - 6. Perceptual organization and cognition - 7. Human performance. Author index. Cumulative subject index of 99p. *Class No:* 159.928

Dreams

[309]

JUNG, C.G. Dreams. London, Routledge/Ark paperback, 1985. xix,337p. illus. £5.50. ISBN: 0744800323.

First published in the UK 1982. Translated by R.F.C. Hull.

8 chapters in 4 parts: 1. Dreams and psychoanalysis - 2. Dreams and psychic energy - 3. The practical use of dream-analysis - 4. Individual dream symbolism in relation to alchemy. A bibliography (p.299-311) is in 2 sections: A. Volumes containing collections of alchemical works by various authors; B. General bibliography. Analytical index, p.313-337. *Class No:* 159.963.3

[310]

The Oxford book of dreams. Brook, S., *comp*. Oxford, Oxford University Press, 1983. xii,268p. £8.95. ISBN: 0192141309.

An anthology, mostly of instances of the literary exploitation of the dream experience, with some examples of dream interpretation. Arranged in 3 sections: I. From birth to death - II. Earthly things - III. The dream world. Index (of names), p.266-268. *Class No:* 159.963.3

[311]

WHITMORE, E.C. *and* PERERA, S.B. Dreams: a portal to the source: a guide to dream interpretation. London, Routledge, 1989. 200p. £19.95. ISBN: 0415010705.

An introductory guidebook to the interpretation of dreams. *Class No:* 159.963.3

Encyclopaedias

[312]

Encyclopedia of sleep and dreaming. Carskadon, M.A., *ed*. New York, Macmillan, 1993. 704p. illus. diagrs, tables, graphs. $105. ISBN: 0028970853.

Summarizes the findings on the medical, biological and psychological facets of sleep and dreaming. Aimed at the public, the

....(contd.)

student and the researcher. Entries are half to a page in length, signed, and most have current bibliographies attached. Detailed analytical index. *Class No:* 159.963.3(031)

[313]

FORARI, A.M. Illustrated encyclopedia of dreams. London, Hamlyn Publishing Group, 1989. 192p. 282 col.illus. £12.95. ISBN: 0600567060.

An introduction, 'sleep: the pattern of your dreams' precedes the dictionary, which has short descriptions of dreams and what they mean, arranged A-Z (Abandonment ... Zebra). A dictionary rather than an encyclopedia. *Class No:* 159.963.3(031)

[314]

GUILEY, R.E. The Encyclopedia of dreams: symbols and interpretations. New York, Crossroad, 1993. 176p. $27.50. ISBN: 0824512405.

Essays on the science of dreams, cross-cultural beliefs, nightmares, dreams and the paranormal, dreams and alchemy, working with dreams. Lists *c*.1000 entries, A-Z, of dream symbols and their interpretations. Cross-references. Bibliography of 125 titles. 'The result is a do-it-yourself dream manual anchored in symbols primarily from the Western tradition.'(*Booklist*, v.90(4), 15 October 1993, p.470). *Class No:* 159.963.3(031)

Psychoanalysis

[315]

BADCOCK, C. Essential Freud. 2nd ed. Oxford, Blackwell, 1991. 192p. £12.95. ISBN: 0631177744.

An introduction to the topics that most crucially characterize the contribution Freud's thinking has made. This edition takes account of recent developments in evolutionary science and examines fresh evidence. *Class No:* 159.964.2

[316]

BEIT-HALLAHMI, B. Psychoanalytic studies of religion a critical assessment and annotated bibliography. Westport, Conn., Greenwood Press, 1996 xv,188p. (*Bibliograpies and indexes in relgious studies ; no. 39.*) ISBN: 0313273626, US.

In part one "the critical assessment" Beit-Hallahmi presents a record of the scholarship on psychoanalysis and religion and offers a summary of the lay literature as an aid to further study. In the second part, his annotated bibliography, he uses clear and to the point language in describing the literature. *Class No:* 159.964.2

[317]

Feminism and psychoanalysis: a critical dictionary. Wright, E., *ed*. Oxford, Blackwell, 1992. xix,485p. £40. ISBN: 0631173129.

'... not a dictionary in the conventional sense, for it does not merely define terms, but explores, historizes and politicizes them ...'(Introduction). Entries are signed by the 73 contributors, and include phrases as well as words, and also people. They are often lengthy and subdivided (Sigmond Freud: 6p.; Freud's female patients: 6p.). Each entry ends with a substantial bibliography. Cross-references. Analytical index, p.462-85. *Class No:* 159.964.2

[318]

HINSHELWOOD, R.D. A Dictionary of Kleinian thought. 2nd ed. Northvale, NJ, J. Aronson, 1991. xii, 503p ISBN: 0876685564.

. Main entries with lengthy paragraphs for fundamentals of Kleinian thought in chronological order. General entries, of words, phrases and proper names associated with Kleinian thought. *Class No:* 159.964.2

[319]

HOPCKE, R.H. A Guided tour of the collected works of Jung. Shambala, 1992. 208p. £8.99. ISBN: 0877735824.

A guide to Jung's 19-volume *Collected works*. *Class No:* 159.964.2

Bibliographies

[320]

GRINSTEIN, A., *comp. and ed*. The Index of psychoanalytic writings. New York, International Universities Press Inc. (distributed by Academic Press), 1956-75. 14v. v.1-5, 6-9, v.10-14, $150 each of the 3 sets. ISBN: 0823684008, v.1-5; 0823684016, v.6-9.

A revision and updating of J. Rickman's *Index psychoanalyticus* (covering 1893-1926).

Covers psychoanalytic literature up to the end of 1969, well over 100,000 items. V.1-5 set (1956-60) indexes the literature to the end of 1952 - 37,121 numbered items under authors A-Z, followed by anonymous items and reports. All of Freud's writings that are known or currently available are listed at nos. 10,350-10,714. V.5, the subject index to v.1-4, covers *c*.25,000 conceptual categories and notes additions and corrections. The v.6-9 and v.10-14 sets, similarly arranged, list supplementary items. *Class No:* 159.964.2(01)

[321]

—GRINSTEIN, A., *comp and ed*. Sigmund Freud's writings: a comprehensive bibliography. New York, International Universities Press Inc., 1977. 181p. $22.50. ISBN: 0823660761.

Includes Freud's early non-psychological writings not included in the Standard edition, and also a bibliography of Freud's letters. *Class No:* 159.964.2(01)

[322]

—GUTTMAN, S.A., *ed*. The Concordance to the Standard edition of the complete psychological works of Sigmund Freud. ed Boston, Mass., G.K. Hall, 1980. 6v. ISBN: 0823610756.

Published in six volumes and alphabetically arranged. Index of words in order of frequency. Has a pagination converter which tells the reader the page on which the phrase occurs in the Gesammelte Werke. *Class No:* 159.964.2(01)

[323]

VINCIE, J.F. *and* RATHBAUER-VINCIE, M. C.G. Jung and analytical psychology: a comprehensive bibliography. New York, Garland Publishing Co., 1977. xiv,[1],297p.

'Works on Jung and analytical psychology', p.1-236 (3687 entries, arranged chronologically by years, pre 1916 to 1976). Book reviews of works by Jung (1942-75). Subject and author indexes. *Class No:* 159.964.2(01)

Handbooks & Manuals

[324]

KLAMPNER, G.H. A Guide to the language of psychoanalysis an emprical study of the relationship among psychoanalytic terms and concepts. International Universities Press, 1992 xvii,199p. ISBN: 0823622770.

Includes bibliography and index.

Originally intended to improve the usefullness of psychoanalytic indexes. Sets out to show that psychoanalysis is a set of continual interrelated concepts. Not an easy guide to use. *Class No:* 159.964.2(035)

Dictionaries

[325]

LAPLANCHE, J. *and* PONTALIS, J.-B. The Language of psychoanalysis. Translated by Donald Nicholas-Smith. London, Hogarth Press and the Institute of Psychoanalysis, 1973. xv, 510p. £17.50. ISBN: 0701203439.

Originally as *Vocabulaire de la psychoanalyse* (Paris, Presses Universitaires de France, 1967; 5 éd. 1976). Paperback published in 1988 (London, Karnac House. 510p. ISBN 0946439494).

Entries (Abreaction ... Working-through) give German, Spanish, French, Italian and Portuguese equivalents of terms, plus definitions, discussion and references. 'Unconscious': 3p.: 3 main definitions, plus sub-entries: 4 references: 4 cross-references. Bibliography, p.491-7 (works by Freud cited: other authors: journals). Indexes of German and English terms. Intended for readers of Freud's writings. *Class No:* 159.964.2(038)

[326]

MOORE, B.E. *and* FINE, B.D., *eds*. Psychoanalystic terms and concepts Newhaven, CT, Yale University Press, 1990. 210p. $35. ISBN: 0300045778.

Produced by the American Psychological Association. Arranged A-Z but some terms are grouped *eg*'Collective unconsciousness'). Solid and up-to-date. Entry devised from review in *Science & technology libraries*,v.12(1), Fall 1991, p.138. *Class No:* 159.964.2(038)

[327]

RYCROFT, C. A Critical dictionary of psychoanalysis. 2nd ed London, Penguin Books, 1995. xxix, 213p. ISBN: 0140513108.

Entries are listed A-Z. Includes an introductory reading list. There are referecnes and cross references and a comprehensive bibliography. Clear definitions. *Class No:* 159.964.2(038)

[328]

SAMUELS, A., *and others*. A Critical dictionary of Jungian analysis. London, Routledge & Kegan Paul, 1986. [4],171p. £18.95; $36. ISBN: 0710204108.

In A-Z dictionary format, consisting of 'Jargon' words usually associated with Jung, words and concepts originated by him, and terms that have a special meaning in the context of Jung's understanding of the nature of psychic life. References, p.163-168, A-Z. List of entries, p.169-171. '... a useful, practical reference to Jungian terminology and ideas ...' (*Contemporary psychology*, v.33(2), February 1988, p.166). *Class No:* 159.964.2(038)

Histories

[329]

FINE, R. A History of psychoanalysis. New York, Columbia University Press, 1979. xii, [1], 686p. (Reprinted 1990. 784p. $50.) ISBN: 0876687915.

20 chapters: 1. The need for historical perspective ... 4/5. Organizational vicissitudes ... 9/10. The unconscious - 11/12. Ego psychology ... 19. The advance of psychoanalysis to a unifying theory of human behaviour - 20. Observations, hopes and dreams. Notes, p.581-600. Bibliography (A-Z authors), p.601-49. Analytical index (p.651-86). *Class No:* 159.964.2(091)

Mental Disorders & Deficiencies

[330]

GREENBERT, B. How to find out in psychiatry: a guide to sources of mental health information. Oxford, Pergamon Press, 1978. . xii[1],112,[1]p. facsims., tables. £16. ISBN: 0080218601.

12 chapters: 1. Introduction to the literature of psychiatry - 2. Guides to libraries & the psychiatric literature - 3. Primary sources of information; periodicals and books - 4. Secondary sources of information: bibliographies, indexes, abstracts & reviews - 5. Dictionaries, glossaries, encyclopedias & handbooks - 6. Directories - 7. Nomenclature & classification - 8. Education - 9. Mental health statistics - 10. Drugs and drug therapy - 11. Tests and measurements - 12. Nonprint materials. References (9). p.83. Appendix A: Classics in psychiatric literature (chronologically arranged, p.87-97). Index of titles, authors. 'Highly recommended' (*Choice* v.16. no.5/6, July/ August 1979. p.648). *Class No:* 159.972/.973

[331]

THAKURDAS, H. *and* THAKURDAS, L. Dictionary of psychiatry. Revised by Betty Thakurdas. Lancaster, MTP., 1979. vii, 111p. diagrs. £13.75. ISBN: 0852002351.

About 900 definitions, designed as a ready reference for doctors, medical-students, psychiatric nurses, social workers 'or anybody involved with psychiatric patients' (*Introductory note*). Appendix A: International Standard classification of mental disorders - B. List of abbreviations - C. A guide to prefixes and suffixes - D. Common phobias - E. Normal values in the body - F. Essential statistical formulae - H. Symbols of the Mental Health Act, 1959. *Class No:* 159.972/.973

Mental Tests

[332]

HERSEN, M. *and* BELLACK, A.S., *eds*. Dictionary of behavioral assessment techniques. London & New York, Pergamon Press, 1988. 519p. $85; £67. ISBN: 0080319750.

Surveys *c*.300 behavioural assessment techniques used by psychiatrists and counsellers to deal with psychological problems ranging from depression and marital distress to eating disorders and unassertiveness. Arranged A-Z by name of technique, experts examine their purpose, reliability and usefulness. References to the reviews from the literature follow each entry. '... users guide is an inadequate substitute for a detailed subject index'. (*Choice*, v.26(7), March 1989, p.1120). *Class No:* 159.98

[333]

KRUG, S.E., *comp. and ed*. Psychware sourcebook. 4th ed Champaign, Ill, MetriTech Inc. 1993 b xvi, 535p ISBN: 0963589512.

First published 1984 as *Psychware*.

A guide to computer-based products for assessment in psychology, education, and business. Lists about 400 products in numeric order by product code and also in alphabetical order by title. Information given includes product number, name, supplier, category, application, sale restrictions, pricing, and product description. 5 indexes (product title, product category, product application, service, and supplier). *Class No:* 159.98

Tables & Data Books

[334]

ANASTASI, A. Psychological testing. 6th ed. London, Collin Macmillan, 1988. xiv,817p. tables. £16.95. ISBN: 0029775108.

First published 1954.

20 chapters in 5 parts: 1. Context of psychological testing - 2. Technical and methodological principles - 3. Tests of general intellectual level - 4. Tests of separate abilities - 5. Personality tests. 4 appendices (A. Ethical principles of psychologists; B. A suggested

....*(contd.)*

outline for test evaluation; C. Test publishers; D. Classified list of representative tests). Name and subject indexes. *Class No:* 159.98(083)

[335]

MADDOX, T. Tests: a comprehensive reference... Sweetland, R. C. *and* Keyser, D.J., *eds.* 4th ed. Austin, TEX, Pro-Ed, 1997 xi, 809p ISBN: 0890797072.

First published, 1983.

Arranged in 3 broad categories: (Psychology, Education, Business) and many specific subject subheadings. Cross-references. Entries provide statements of test's purpose, description of test, relevant cost and availability information, a set of coded visual keys, intended age level, and name of publisher. Includes indexes and bibliography *Class No:* 159.98(083)

[336]

Test critiques. Keyser, D.J. *and* Sweetland, R. C., *eds.* Kansas City, Test Corporation of America, 1985-. $97.75 each vol.

A continuing project.

In each volume noted experts evaluate the validity of more than 100 tests for psychology, education and business. These in-depth analyses range from 5-15 pages each. *Class No:* 159.98(083)

[337]

Tests in print V: an index to tests, test reviews and the literature on specific tests. Murphy, L.L. *and* Impara, J.C. *and* Plake, B., *eds.* Lincoln, NE., University of Nebraska Press, 1999. 2v. ISBN: 0910674515.

A bibliography of tests, arranged A-Z by test name/use of specific tests, test title index, classified subject index, a publishers directory and index that includes addresses, and a name index of all test authors and reviewers. *Class No:* 159.98(083)

Logic

[338]

GREENSTEIN, C.H., *ed.* **Dictionary of logical terms and symbols.** Rev. ed. New York, Van Nostrand Reinhold, 1982. 188p. $9.95; £8.45. ISBN: 0442228341.

First published 1978.

Aims 'to present compactly, concisely and side by side a variety of alternative notational systems currently used by logicians, computer scientists, and engineers' (*Preface*). Glossary of logical terms, p.111-177. Bibliography, p.179-188. *Class No:* 164

Bibliographies

[339]

PEACOCKE, C.A.B. *and* **SCOTT, D.,** *eds.* **A Selective bibliography of philosophical logic.** 3rd ed. rev. by M. Davies and G. Forbes. Oxford, Sub-Faculty at Philosophy, 1978. [v],125p. mimeographed. (*Study aids, v.1.*)

First published 1975.

6 main sections: 0. Books (collected works; monographs) - 1. References (proper names; definitive descriptions; pronouns and relative pronouns; demonstratives; eliminability of singular terms; ontological commitment; abstract objects) - 2. Predication - 3. Composition - 4. Interference - 5. Meaning. Further subdivisions; final chronological order. No index. *Class No:* 164(01)

[340]

RISSE, W. Bibliographia logica. Hildesheim, G. Olms Verlagsbuchhandlung, 1965-79. 4v.

V.1. 1472 - 1800 (1965); 2. 1800 bis zu Gegenwart (1973); 3. Zeitschriftenartikel (1979); 4. Handschriften zur logic (1979) V.1. contains *c.*6000 entries, arranged chronologically by year, locations in 171 libraries (65 of them German). Four indexes of authors, anonymous works and commentators, and a systematic index. *Class No:* 164(01)

[341]

—Notre Dame journal of formal logic: devoted to symbolic logic. Notre Dame, Indiana, University of Notre Dame Press, 1960-. Quarterly. $40pa. ISSN: 00294527.

Focuses on foundations of mathematical logic. *Class No:* 164(01)

[342]

BASTABLE, P.K. Logic: depth grammar of rationality. A textbook of the science and history of logic. Dublin, Gill and Macmillan, 1975. [vii],429p.

Sections A-F: A. Preparatory section - B. Formal logic - C. Metalogic - D. Philosophy of logic - E. Applied logic - F. A bibliography of logic (p.389-420). Indexes of proper names and subjects. *Class No:* 164(035)

[343]

Handbook of philosophical logic. Gabbay, D. *and* Guenthner, F., *eds.* Dordrecht, D. Reidel Publishing Co., 1983-86. 4v. v.1 £77.50; v.2 £95.50; v.3 £71.75; v.4 £112.00. ISBN: 9027715424, v.1; 9027716048, v.2; 9027716056, v.3; 9027716064, v.4.

V.1: Elements of classical logic (6 essays); v.2: Extensions of classical logic (12 essays); v.3: Alternatives to classical logic (8 essays); v.4: Topics in the philosophy of language (14 essays). References are appended to each essay. Name and subject indexes in each volume. *Class No:* 164(035)

Histories

[344]

DUMITRIU, A. History of logic. New York, Abacus Press, 1977. 4v. ISBN: 0856261394, set; 0856261408, v.1; 0856261416, v.2; 0856261424, v.3; 0856261432, v.4.

A summary by the author of his *Istoria logicii.*

Attempts to deal exhaustively with the whole range of the discipline, covering methodology of science, the problem of categories, the dialectics, the philosophy of logic, etc. Includes many quotations to supplement and explain his argument. *Class No:* 164(091)

[345]

KNEALE, W. *and* **KNEALE, M. The Development of logic.** Oxford, Clarendon Press, 1975 (reprinted by Oxford University Press, 1984). 790p. £12.95. ISBN: 0198247737.

The 1975 ed. was a corrected reprint of the first ed., 1962.

Development of formal logic from its origin with the Greeks to the present day. 12 chapters: 2. Aristotle's *Organon* - 3. The Megarians and the Stoics - 4. Roman and medieval logic - 5. Logic after the Renaissance - 6. Mathematical abstraction - 7. Numbers, sets and series - 8. Frege's general logic - 9. Formal developments after Frege - 10. The philosophy of logic after Frege - 11. The philosophy of mathematics after Frege - 12. The theory of deductive systems. Appendix (translations from Latin quotations in chapter 4). Selective bibliography, p.765-73 (A-Z authors). Analytical index. *Class No:* 164(091)

Knowledge Theories & Beliefs

[346]

A Companion to epistemology. Dancy, J. *and* Sosa, E., *eds.* Oxford, Blackwell, 1992. xv,541p. £65. $74.95. ((*Blackwell companions to philosophy*).) ISBN: 0631172041.

*c.*250 original articles on topics of Anglo-American epistemology, by 130 scholars. Articles are 250-3500 words in length, often with selected bibliographies, on subjects which includes people, terms and phrases. Cross-references. Detailed index. *Class No:* 165

[347]

GRECO, J. *and* **SOSA, E.,** *eds.* **The Blackwell guide to epistemology.** Oxford, Blackwell, 1999. ix, 464p. £60.00. (*Blackwell philosophy guides*..) ISBN: 0631202900.

Seven essays cover the standard topics in the theory of knowledge, but also include religious epistemology and feminist epistemology. *Class No:* 165

Utopias

[348]

SARGENT, L.T. British and American utopian literature, 1516-1985: an annotated, chronological bibliography. New edition. New York, Garland, 1988. 559p. $75. (*Garland reference library in the humanities.*) ISBN: 0824006941.

First published 1979, by G.K. Hall.

Lists science fiction works with utopian dimensions, arranged chronologically. Annotations are brief. US library locations indicated for every book title. ' ... magisterial bibliography ... Introduction is a model of clarity as to intention, definition of terms, and rationale for inclusion or exclusion (*Choice*, October 1988, p.296). *Class No:* 167.5

Ethics

[349]

A Companion to ethics. Singer, P., *ed.* Oxford, Blackwell, 1991. xxii,565p. (*Blackwell companion to philosophy.*) ISBN: 0631162119.

47 original essays, arranged in 7 parts, dealing 'with the origins of ethics, with the great ethical traditions, with theories about how we ought to live, with arguments about specific ethical issues, and with the nature of ethics itself' (*Intro.*). Detailed analytical index, p.547-565. *Class No:* 17

[350]

LAFOLLETTE, H., *ed.* The Blackwell guide to ethical theory Oxford, Blackwell, 2000. x, 446p. £60.00. (*Blackwell philosophy guides..*) ISBN: 0631201181.

The volume is in two parts. The first covers general questions ("Meta-Ethics" is the jargon), the second normative ethics - consequentialism, intuitionism and the like. There is also a section entitled "Alternative views" which includes virtue ethics, feminist ethics, continental ethics, none of which are "alternative" in the way that term is usually employed. Despite that very minor cavil, this is a particularly helpful guide for philosophy students as they embark on ethics. *Class No:* 17

Bibliographies

[351]

A Bibliographic guide to the comparative study of ethics. Carman, J. *and* Juergensmeyer, M., *eds.* Cambridge, Mass., Harvard University Press, 1991. 811p. $100. ISBN: 0521344484.

15 bibliographical essays by scholars who participated in the Berkeley-Harvard Program in Comparative Religion. Essays follow a standard format and each is devoted to a particular tradition (*e.g.*,Islam, Taoism). *Class No:* 17(01)

[352]

HERRING, M.Y. Ethics and the professor: an annotated bibliography, 1970-1985. New York, Garland, 1988. 576p. $77. (*Garland reference library of the humanities, 742.*) ISBN: 0824084919.

1905 informative, sometimes also evaluative, entries dealing with professional ethics, ethics and government, personal values, moral and religious education, professional moral conduct, justice, science and ethics, etc. Brief introductory essays precede subject sections. Name, title and brief subject indexes. *Class No:* 17(01)

Encyclopaedias

[353]

Encyclopedia of applied ethics Chadwick, R., *ed.* San Diego, Calif., Academic Press, 1997. 4v. (3328p.) $695. ISBN: 0122270657.

With nearly 300 major entries from high quality contributors, it seems set to become a major reference work in its field. *Class No:* 17(031)

[354]

Encyclopedia of ethics. Becker, L. *and* Becker, C., *eds.* Hamden, CT, Garland; London, St. James Press, 1992. 2v.(1462p.) $150. £140. ((*Garland reference library of the humanities, v.925*).) ISBN: 081530403x, US; 1558621539, UK.

435 signed articles, of 1000-3000 words each, on concepts, issues, principles, theories, major figures and history of philosophical ethics. Each article carries its own bibliography. Analytical index of names and subjects. Some omissions, but generally well-written and well-edited, according to *Library journal*, 15 June 1992, p.88. '... a well-organized, scholarly achievement.'(*Choice*, v.30(3), November 1992, p.440). *Class No:* 17(031)

[355]

Encyclopedia of religion and ethics. Hastings, J, *and others.* Edinburgh, T & T. Clarke Ltd.; New York, Scribner, 1908-26. 12v. and index. £450; $650 for 13v. set. ISBN: 0567094898 UK; 0567065146 US.

Aims to include articles on every religious belief or custom, every ethical movement, every philosophical idea, and every moral practice. Includes persons and places famous in history of religion and morals. Particularly valuable for its comparative approach. Extensive articles by leading experts on philosophers and ethical and philosophical subjects are included, with bibliographical references. Thus, the article 'Ethics and morality' (v.5. p.436-522) has 18 sections ('American', 'Australian', 'Babylonian' ...), each by a specialist; 'Drunkenness': 6 sections (11 columns), with 54½ lines of bibliography. Extensive quotations, in very small type. Analytical subject index in v.13. *Class No:* 17(031)

Histories

[356]

BOURNE, V.I. History of ethics. Garden City, N.Y., Doubleday, 1968. 432p.

5 parts (18 chapters): 1. Graeco-Roman ethics - 2. Patristic and medieval theories - 3. Early modern ethics, 1450-1750 - 4. Modern theories - 5. Contemporary ethics. Notes (by chapters), p.311-51; bibliography (by chapters), p.353-417). Detailed index, p.419-32. *Class No:* 17(091)

Social Ethics

[357]

LENDER, H.E. Dictionary of American temperance biography: from temperance reform to alcohol research, the 1600s to the 1980s. Westport, CT., Greenwood Press, 1984. 572p. $95. ISBN: 0313223351.

Short biographies of 373 men and women who have attempted to understand and 'come to grips' with the human and social problems associated with alcohol abuse. Each entry includes basic biography and career information of about 2 paragraphs in length, followed by up to a dozen bibliographical references by or about the person. Somewhat arbitrary selection of names for inclusion, but 'on the whole there is much accurate and useful information presented ...' (*Choice*, v.22(2), October 1984, p.250). *Class No:* 172

Business Ethics

[358]

Business ethics. Drummond, J., *ed.* London, Butterworth-Heinemann, 1993. 200p. £16.95. ISBN: 0750606630.

Essays and extracts contributed by leading figures in business ethics worldwide. Covers marketing, advertising, investment, strategic business and ethics. *Class No:* 174.4

[359]

McHUGH, F.P. Keyguide to information sources in business ethics. London, Mansell Publishing Ltd.; New York, Nichols Publishing, 1988. viii,173p. £28; $34.50. ISBN: 0720118492, UK; 0893973270, US.

An overview and survey in 3 parts: 1. Review of business ethics and its literature - 2. Bibliographical listing of sources - 3. Directory of selected organizations. Part 1 is a narrative account of the historical development of the subject in 5 chapters. Part 2 has 685 items, unannotated, of books and journal articles in a classified arrangement, and with an emphasis on contemporary literature. Part 3 (items 686-922) lists academic centres, business organizations, centres and organizations for professional ethics, and libraries, all subdivided by country, A-Z. Index, p.151-173. *Class No:* 174.4

Bibliographies

[360]

Bibliography of business ethics. Jones, D.G., *and others, eds.* University of Virginia, 1977-86. 3v.

The bibliography covering 1971-75 was published in 1977 (207p. $14.95. ISBN 081390711x); that for 1976-80 in 1982 (220p. $14.95. ISBN 081390921x); and the latest for 1981-85 (304p. $69.95. ISBN 0889461546) in 1986. *Class No:* 174.4(01)

[361]

BICK, P.A. Business ethics and responsibility: an information sourcebook. Phoenix, AZ., Oryx, 1988. 204p. £34.95. (*Oryx series in business and management, 11.*) ISBN: 0897742966.

1018 annotated entries arranged in 13 subject sections, each section including a core collection. Journal articles selected from business publications and dissertations published between 1980 and 1986. '... a solid work ...' (*Choice*, October 1988, p.284). *Class No:* 174.4(01)

Recreational Ethics

Bibliographies

[362]

COOPER, T.W., *and others, eds.* Television and ethics: a bibliography. Boston, Mass., G.K. Hall, 1988. 203p. $45. ISBN: 0816189668.

Includes over 1000 items, nearly half of which are annotated, of books, journal articles, conference papers and dissertations. The first part contains items on classical ethics; professional ethics; business, legal, medical, governmental, science and engineering, communications and mass media ethics. The second part deals with advertising, children and T.V., T.V. news, politics and government, law and court-room coverage, public T.V., etc. Author and subject indexes. *Class No:* 175(01)

2 Religion

[363]

ELIADE, M. **A History of religious ideas.** Translated from the French. Chicago, Ill., 1979-83. 3v. (c.1500p.). $27.50 each vol. ISBN: 0226204006, v.1; 0226204022, v.2; 0226204049, v.3.

Translated from *Histoire des croyances et des idéas religieuses* (Paris, Payot).
V.1. *From the Stone Age to the Eleusinian mysteries* (1979) 15 footnoted chapters on Sumerian, ancient Egyptian, Hittite and Canaanite, Vedic and Indian religions before Buddha, with several chapters on Greek religion. 125 sections, each with bibliography. V.2. *From Gautama Buddha to the triumph of Christianity* (1985) progresses through the history of religious ideas, covering the religions of ancient China, Brahminism and Hinduism, Buddha and his contemporaries, Roman religion, Celtic and German religion, Judaism, the Hellenistic period, the Iranian syntheses, and the birth of Christianity. V.3 *From Muhammed to the age of reforms* (1986) examines the movement of Jewish thought out of ancient Eurasia, the Christian transformation to the Mediterranean area and Europe, and the rise and diffusion of Islam from approximately the sixth century through the 17th century. Each volume has a bibliography and index. *Class No: 20*

[364]

PETERS, F.E. **Judaism, Christianity and Islam:** the classical texts and their interpretation. Princeton, NJ, Princeton University Press, 1990. 3v.(1216p). $85. ISBN: 0691020442, v.1; 069102054x, v.2; 0691020558, v.3; 0691073562, set.

Selects and compiles quotations from the religions' classical period plus connective commentary with explanatory and factual data. V.1: From covenant to community; v.2: The word and the law and the people of God; v.3: The works of the spirit. Short titles index at the end of each volume. *Class No: 20*

[365]

SUTHERLAND, S., *ed*. **The World's religions.** London, Routledge & Kegan Paul; Boston, Mass., G.K. Hall, 1988. 995p. £50; $75. ISBN: 0413003245, UK; 0816189781, US.

An introduction, giving an account of the history, the theological basis and the practice of religion and religions, and also of the current state of the study of religion and religions. The chapters are organized into 6 parts: 1. Religion and the study of religions - 2. Judaism and Christianity - 3. Islam - 4. The religions of Asia - 5. Traditional religions - 6. New religious movements. Each chapter includes a select bibliography. 'This volume is clearly a major contribution to the field, forming an invaluable one-volume reference work for students studying comparative and world religions' (*Bulletin of the ABTPL*, v.2(10), March 1991, p.21). *Class No: 20*

[366]

WHALING, F., *ed*. **Religion in today's world:** the religious situation of the world from 1945 to the present day. Edinburgh, T. & T. Clark, 1987. viii,383p. £16.95. ISBN: 0567094529.

13 essays by 11 experts from 10 different universities around the world. Attempts to look in breadth and in depth at the religious situation of the world as a whole in the latter part of the 20th century. In addition to focusing on the 5 major religious traditions (Buddhist, Christian, Hindu, Jewish and Muslim) and the present religious situations in China and Japan, the authors also look at civil religion, cults and new religious movements, secular world-views, spirituality, and the study of religion in today's world. Analytical index, p.370-383. *Class No: 20*

Abbreviations & Symbols

[367]

SCHWERTNER, S.M., *ed*. IATG2 Internationales Abkürzungsverzeichnis für Theologie und Grenzgebiete. 2nd revised and expanded edition. Berlin & New York, de Gruyter, 1992. xli, 488p. ISBN: 3110111179.

First edition 1974.
Approximately 12,250 entries in two sequences. The first lists standard abbreviations for, as the subtitle puts it, "periodicals, series, encyclopaedias, sources". This runs from AA to ZZ.B. The second, and much larger, section lists the names of these periodicals etc. in alphabetical order from AFER to Zygon, giving basic bibliographic details (publisher, dates, whether entry is a continuation of, or is

....(contd.)
continued by, another entry) and abbreviation.
In the introduction (printed in five languages) are listed standard abbreviations as used in the volume itself, for biblical books, biblical sources and versions, for deutero-canonical books, NT apocrypha and patristic texts, and for Qumran texts. It should be noted that this volume appears as a supplement to the *Theologische Realenzyklopadie*. *Class No: 20(003)*

Bibliographies

[368]

ADAMS, C.J., *ed*. **A Reader's guide to the great religions.** 2nd ed. New York, Collier Macmillan, 1977. xvii, 521p. $24.95. ISBN: 0029002400.

First published 1965.
14 contributors (13 of them North American). 13 chapters: 1. Primitive religion - 2. The ancient world - 3. The religions of Mexico and of Central and South America - 4. The religions of China - 5. Hinduism - 6. Buddhism - 7. The Sikhs - 8. The Jainas - 9. The religions of Japan - 10. Early and Classical Judaism - 11. Medieval and modern Judaism - 12. Christianity (p.345-406) - 13. Islam. Appendix: 'The history of religions'. Running commentary. Chapter 9 (p.247-82) has appended lists: 1. Reference books relevant to religions of Japan - 2. Published bibliographies (5 sections) - 3. Periodicals relevant to religions of Japan. Author index; analytical subject index (p.494-521). 'It is hard to fault such an excellent work' (*American reference books annual*. 1978, v.9, entry no.969). *Class No: 20(01)*

[369]

'A Basic stock of religious books' In *The bookseller*, October 20th, 1984, p.1701-2.

50 titles, arrranged in four sections: General guides to world religions and their texts - Books of synthesis and dialogue - Books on individual world religions - Philosophical, scientific and psychological approaches. *Class No: 20(01)*

[370]

Bibliographies of books printed before 1800. Careless, G.C. *and* Morris, P., *eds*. Deeside, Clwyd, St Deiniol's Library, 1980 - 81. 9v. £1.20 to £2.60 each vol.

V.1. Biblical studies and patristics; v.2. Philosophy and Christian doctrine; v.3. Life in the Church - spirituality, morality, and homiletics; v.4. Liturgical studies; v. 5-6. Church history; v.7. European history; v.8. Language and literature; v.9. Miscellaneous. A complete listing of the library's main pre-1800 collection. *Class No: 20(01)*

[371]

Contemporary religious ideas bibliographic essays. Lundin, G.E. *and* Lundin, Anne H., *eds*. Littleton, Col., Libraries Unlimited, 1996 $75.00 ISBN: 0872876799.

Essays arranged in three sections, by 14 academics and clergy, text books in world religions, followed by articles on Jewish Literature, Catholic Spirituality, Islam, and so on. Essays well written and informative, but target audience is non-academic (*Choice* Feb 1997 p. 940). *Class No: 20(01)*

[372]

DR. WILLIAMS'S LIBRARY, London. Catalogue ... the Library, 1841-.

Volumes so far are: *Catalogue of the Library* (1841. 2v. (v.2: Tracts and pamphlet material)); *Catalogue of the Library*. v.3 [1842-1885] (1885. 3 pts); *Author catalogue of additions*, 1900-1932 [with supplement of publications of learned societies, connected series, etc.]. (1933. 3 pts.); *Catalogue of accessions*, 1900-1950; being a catalogue of books published and added to the Library during that period [with supplement of titles of periodicals, publications of learned societies, connected series, etc.]. (1955. viii,776,cxlvp.); *Catalogue of accessions*, v.2; being a catalogue of books published in the twentieth century and added to the Library, 1951-1960 (1961. xi,181,xxxvp.); *Catalogue of accessions*, v.3: being a catalogue of books published in the twentieth century and added to the Library, 1961-1970 (1973. x,261,xlvp.); *Catalogue of accessions*, v.4; books added 1971-1980 (1983. ix,165,xxxviiip.).

A catalogue, by authors, of a library founded in 1715 and now possessing some 100,000v. covering all aspects of religion, philosophy and kindred subjects; especially strong in early Nonconformist material. Each volume has a supplement listing serials, periodicals and other regularly taken titles. No printed catalogue exits for the years 1886-99. *Class No: 20(01)*

[373]

FRANCIS. 527. Bulletin signalétique. 527. Histoire et sciences des religions. Paris, Centre National de la Recherche Scientifique, Centre de Documentation. Sciences Humaines, 1947-. Quarterly. ISSN: 01809296.

Formerly part of *Bulletin signalétique. Philosophie* (v.1-9, 1947-55), then of *Bulletin signalétique. 19. Philosophie. Sciences humaines* (1956-60), later =2Bulletin signalétique. 527

9 main sections: 01. Studies in religion - 02. Ancient religions - 03. Israel - 04. Christianity - 05. Exegisis and Biblical criticism - 06. Islam - 07. African religions - 08. Religions in America, Arctic and Oceania - 09. Asian religions. List of periodicals scanned. Subject indexes (01 ... 09) and author index per issue. Available online and on CD-ROM. *Class No:* 20(01)

[374]

GORMAN, G.E. *and* GORMAN, L. **Theological and religious reference materials.** Westport, CT., Greenwood Press, 1984-. To be in 4 vols. v.1 $58.95; v.2 $59.95; v.3 $50.95. (*Bibliographies and indexes in religious studies, 1, 2, & 7.*) ISBN: 0313209243, v.1; 031324779x, v.2; 0313253978, v.3.

Aim was to provide a work introducing students to the full range of reference materials likely to be required in theological or religious studies and available in academic libraries. 5845 titles have been listed in the 3 vols. published, almost all titles having evaluative annotations and references to related titles. Volumes are: 1. General resources and biblical studies - 2. Systematic theology and church history - 3. Practical theology. V.4 will deal with comparative and non-Christian religions. There is a tentative promise of a supplement to incorporate new material. Scope is both international and interdenominational. Periodical articles are omitted. Each volume is self-contained with author, title and subject indexes. 'Will not replace Kepple ... but a must for all academic and theological libraries (*Journal of academic librarianship*, July, 1985, p.4873). 'Planned work greatly exceeds scope of Kepple or McCabe, tho' less convenient to use' (*Wilson library bulletin*, November 1984, p.228-9). 'A new standard work' (*Bulletin of ABTAPL*, no.39, June 1987, p.4). *Class No:* 20(01)

[375]

HOMAN, R., *comp.* **The Sociology of religion:** a bibliographical survey. Westport, CT., Greenwood Press, 1986. 309p. $45. £39.95. (*Bibliographies and indexes in religious studies, 9.*) ISBN: 0313247102.

Introductory essay examines the foundations of the sociology of religion, and is followed by 1013 annotated entries to books on the subject. Annotations are clearly written and often evaluative as well as descriptive. Mainly material in English published in the last 20 years. Arranged in 20 subject areas. Author, title and subject indexes. 'A well-realized bibliography of lasting value' (*Choice*, March 1987, p.1032), but *RQ* (v.26(4) p.524) considers Blasi and Cuneo's *Issue in sociology ...* better. *Class No:* 20(01)

[376]

KARPINSKI, L.M., *comp.* **The Religious life of man:** guide to basic literature. Metuchen, N.J., & London, Scarecrow Press, 1978. xx,399p. $27.50; £18.95. ISBN: 0810811103.

2032 numbered, unannotated entries for books and periodical articles. 6 parts (further divided): 1. Religions of mankind (general) - 2. Religions of the past - 3. Judaism, Christianity, Islam - 4. Asian religions (Hinduism, Buddhism, Confucianism, Taoism, etc.; items 1199-1688) - 5. The beliefs of native peoples - 6. The occult. Author title and subject index. *Class No:* 20(01)

[377]

LAMBE, D. **Reference works on world religions.** In *Bulletin of the Association of British theological and philosophical libraries*, v.2(10), March 1991, p.20-24.

10 major reference works are given comparative evaluation. *Class No:* 20(01)

[378]

Library research guide to religion and theology: illustrated search strategy and sources. Kennedy, J.R. 2nd rev. ed. Ann Arbor, Mich., Pierian Press, 1984. $25. ISBN: 0876501854.

First published 1974.

Aims to instruct students in religious studies how to use books and libraries as part of the research process. 'A reliable technique and an adequate resource guide for research in the general area of religious studies' (*RQ*, v.14(4), Summer 1975, p.356-7, of the 1st ed.). *Class No:* 20(01)

[379]

MITROS, J.F. **Religions:** a select, classified bibliography. New York, Learned Publications, 1973. 435p. $45. (*Philosophical questions, 8.*) ISBN: 0912116080.

Aims 'to provide a student of religion with a handy guide in his research while he is preparing a paper, an examination, a lecture, a course, writing a book or conducting a seminar' (*Introduction*). Annotated entries in 7 sections, including general reference books and relevant journals, Christianity (with special reference to Patristic studies), the Scriptures, and non-Christian religions. 'An excellent

....(contd.)

bibliography ... for the advanced student in Western religious history' (*College & research libraries*, v.30, January 1975, p.64). *Class No:* 20(01)

[380]

Religion index one: periodicals: a subject index to periodical literature, including an author/editor index and Scripture index. Evanston, Ill., American Theological Library Association, v.13(1977-78)-. ISSN: 01498428.

Previously *Index to religious periodical literature*, v.1-12, 1949-76. Annually indexes some 15,000 articles from 550 journals. Bibliographic access is by subject heading, author/editor name, and scriptural citation. Available also in a CD-ROM version together with Religion index two. *Class No:* 20(01)

[381]

—Religion index two: multi-author works, 1976-. Evanston, Ill., American Theological Library Association, 1978-. Annual. ISSN: 01498436.

This work annually indexes over 500 books and the 8,000 articles/ parts they contain. In addition festschriften and collections of conference proceedings are indexed at book level. Contents: List of titles indexed; Subject index; Author/editor index; Scripture index.

Both series are available on CD-ROM in the ATLA Religion database. *Class No:* 20(01)

[382]

Religious books in print: a reference catalogue, 1999. London, Whitaker, 1999. 1280p. £65. ISBN: 0850212642. ISSN: 0305960x.

First published 1974. Annual.

Lists over 40,000 in-print titles plus a directory of their publishers and distributors. Author, title and keyword index. Classified index of principal subjects and subsidiaries. *Class No:* 20(01)

[383]

Religious information sources: a worldwide guide. Melton, J.G. *and* Köszegi, M.A., *comps.* New York, Garland, 1992. xxiii,569p. $75. ((*Garland reference library of the humanities, v.1593*). (*Religious information systems series, v.2*).) ISBN: 0815308590.

A comprehensive guide to the many sources of information in the broad field of religion. An introduction to non-print sources in religion is followed by 7 sections: 1. Religion: general and theoretical considerations; 2. The religions of the world (General - Eastern - Africa and the Middle East - The Americas, Europe and Oceania); 3. Issues in comparative religion; 4. Christianity; 5. Christianity: issues in Christian studies; 6. Christian historical studies; 7. Christian denominational family traditions. Indexes of titles, authors, organizations and subjects. *Class No:* 20(01)

[384]

SHERMIS, M. **Jewish-Christian relations: an annotated bibliography and resource guide.** Indiana University Press, 1988. 291p. $29.95. ISBN: 0253331536.

Includes entries, many annotated, for books, pamphlets, journal articles, journal issues and special publications, and non-print media, arranged by broad subject areas. Includes examples of syllabi for study of Jewish-Christian relations, and lists organizations and speakers on the subject. '...valuable addition to the growing body of literature ...' (*Choice*, v.26(6), February 1989, p.926). *Class No:* 20(01)

[385]

Theological and religious bibliographies. Harrogate, North Yorks., Theological Abstracting and Bibliographical Services, (T.A.B.S), 1979-81. Irregular.

Continued *Theological and religious index*, 1972-1978. (ISSN 0306087x).

About 1000 index entries per issue, arranged in subject sections. *Class No:* 20(01)

Encyclopaedias

[386]

ELIADE, M. *and* COULLARDO, A.P. **The Eliade guide to world religions:** the authoritative compendium of the 33 major religious traditions. New York, HarperCollins, 1991. 301p. $22.95. ISBN: 0060621481.

A one-volume compendium. Brief and unbiassed. Scholarly, but accessible to the informed lay reader. (Eliade died in May, 1991). *Class No:* 20(031)

[387]

FISHER, M.P. *and* LUYSTER, R.W. **Living religions:** an encyclopedia of the world's faiths. London, I.B.Taurus, 1990. 367p. 200 illus. £19.95. ISBN: 1850432996.

13 chapters, all subdivided: 1. The religious response; 2. Indigenous sacred ways; 3. Hinduism; 4. Jainism; 5. Buddhism; 6. Taoism and Confucianism; 7. Shinto; 8. Zoroastrianism; 9. Judaism; 10. Christianity; 11. Islam; 12. Sikhism; 13. New religious movements. A feature is interviews with believers. 'Suggested reading' after each subdivision. Notes (by chapters), p.349-56. Glossary, p.357-61.

....(contd.)

Index, p.362-67. '... this is the best for the general reader who wants a clear, attractive and accurate introduction to world religions ...' (*Bulletin of the Association of British Theological and Philosophical Libraries*, v.2(10), March 1991, p.22). *Class No:* 20(031)

[388]

MELTON, J.G. **Encyclopedia of American religions.** 4th ed. Detroit, Mich., Gale Research Co., 1993. 3v. $175. ISBN: 089243497x.

First published 1980.

Detailed information on individual churches, religious bodies and spiritual groups, ranging from Adventists to Zen Buddhism, organized into religious families of churches related to one another through similarities of creed. Includes essays on the historical development of the American religions and on each religious group, including information on beliefs and practices of the religion, publications produced, headquarters or contact address, number of congregations and membership, and list of sources for further information. There are various indexes. 'Especially valuable for its exhaustive coverage of religious bodies outside the main stream' (*Reference books bulletin*, 1986/87, p.53-4). Complemented by the author's *Encyclopedia of American religions: religious creeds.* (*qv*). *Class No:* 20(031)

[389]

MELTON, J.G. **Encyclopedia of American religions:** religious creeds. Detroit, Mich., Gale Research Co., 1988. 838p. $125. ISBN: 0810321327.

A collection of over 450 creeds, confessions, and statements of belief of America's religious groups (not only Christian, but also Jewish, Islamic, Scientology, Wiccan (witches), etc., and even 'Flying saucer' groups), arranged in 23 chapters, representing religious families, each sub-divided by names of religious groups. Information for each group includes historical notes and comments as well as the texts of the creeds, etc. Detailed table of contents, name and keyword index. Complements the author's *Encyclopedia of American religions* (*q.v.*).

A new ed. was issued in 1993 ($135. ISBN 0810354918).

Class No: 20(031)

[390]

WUTHNOW, R., *ed.* **The Encyclopedia of politics and religion** London, Routledge, 1998. 2 v. (xxxvi, 875, 34p). £160. ISBN: 0415187400.

index, illus., bibliogs.

There is a slight US bias in this encyclopedia (all but one of the editorial board works in the States) but coverage from "Abolitionism" to "Zionism" is international - documents cited at the end of volume 2 range from Luther's 95 theses to the 1998 Irish peace accord. Similarly excerpts from national constitutions on religion and society range from the Constitution of Cambodia to that of Zambia. There are entries on most countries in the world, on places, institutions, even devotions (there is an article on saints and their political significance). The contributions are well done, and each is provided with bibliography and see references. It is, however, rather difficult to categorize the precise scope of these volumes. *Class No:* 20(031)

[391]

YOUNG, S., *ed.* **Encyclopedia of women and world religion.** Macmillan, 1999. 2v. (1152p.) $225. ISBN: 0028646088.

Entries are signed, arranged alphabetically, and have bibliographies. Index. *Class No:* 20(031)

English

[392]

ELIADE, M., *ed.* **The Encyclopedia of religion.** New York, Collier Macmillan, 1987. 16v. (8000p.). £950.00; $1400.00 the set. ISBN: 0029094801.

*c.*2750 signed articles, plus a further 150 articles featuring biographies of scholars of religion, arranged A-Z through vols. 1-15, written by 1400 international scholars. Articles vary in length from *c.*300 to *c.*15000 words, and each article is followed by a bibliography. Covers 'the history of religious traditions past and present, large and small, Western and non-Western; cross-cultural themes, symbols, legends, rituals and motifs; religious beliefs, doctrines, literature and practices; religious institutions, organizations and communities; the major figures in religion; the history, theories, terms, concepts, methods and leading authorities in the study of religion; the place of religion in culture and society, including the arts, philosophy, science, politics, law and social organizations' (*Publicity document no. 19*). V.16, *Index* (352p.), includes a directory of contributors; an alphabetical list of entries; and synoptic outline of contents (p.97-127), as well as a detailed index (p.129-470) and corrigenda. 'Major event in encyclopaedia publishing ... two strengths ... are its organization and its bibliographies'. (*Choice*, v.25(10), June 1988, p.1517-8). 'Improvements could doubtless have been made in the selection of topics, the balance of the articles, the correspondence between theory and practice, and the accessibility of relevance of the

....(contd.)

data to the "nonspecialist educated reader". With all its defects and inbalances ... remains a good achievement'. (*Bulletin of ABTPL* (no. 40, November 1987, p.13). *Class No:* 20(031)=20

[393]

Encyclopaedia of religion and ethics: edited by J. Hastings, with the assistance of J.A. Selbie and other scholars. Edinburgh, T. & T. Clark Ltd; New York, Scribner, 1908-26. 12v. & index. £450; $650 for 13v. set. ISBN: 0567094898, UK; 0567065146, US.

Aims to include articles on every religious belief or custom, every ethical movement, every philosophical idea, and every moral practice. Includes persons and places famous in history of religion and morals. Particularly valuable for its comparative approach (*e.g.* the series of articles: Faith, Buddhist; Faith, Christian; Faith, Greek; Faith, Hindu; Faith, Muslim ...). Articles are signed and well documented; systematic treatment of major subjects (*e.g.* 'Architecture' (v.1. p.677-733) has 24 sections., from 'Aegean' to 'Shinto'). The index volume comprises a general, analytical index (p.1-660), an index to foreign words, an index to Scripture passages, and an index to authors or articles. Diacritical markings are given. *Class No:* 20(031)=20

[394]

The Encyclopedia of world faiths: an illustrated survey of the world's living religions. Bishop, P. *and* Darton, M., *eds.* New York, Facts on File, 1988; London, Macdonald & Co. (Publishers) Ltd., 1987. 352p. illus., maps (some col.), charts, diagrs. $40. £19.95. ISBN: 081601860x, US; 0356140628, UK.

Introduction on the nature of religion is followed by information on 12 major religions, covering the history, beliefs, writings, ethics, rituals and worship, subgroups, and present day organization. The religions are Judaism, Zoroastrianism, Christianity, Islam, Baha'i, Hinduism, Jainism, Buddhism, Sikhism, Confucianism, Taoism, and Shinto. Concluding chapters are on new religious movements in modern Western society, new religious movements among pastoral peoples, and conclusions. Further reading (p.324-326) is arranged by chapter, subdivided by authors. Glossary, p.327-345. Index, p.346-352. *Class No:* 20(031)=20

German

[395]

Die Religion in Geschichte und Gegenwart: Handwörterbuch für Theologie und Religionswissenschaft. 3.völlig. neu bearb. Aufl. in Gemeinschaft mit Hans Freiherr v. Campenhausen u.a.; hrsg. von Kurt Galling. Tübingen, Mohr, 1957-65. 7v. illus., maps.

First published 1909-13. 5v.; 2nd ed. 1927-32. 5v.

A scholarly work; all articles signed, with bibliographies. A feature is the lengthy systematic treatment of subjects. 'Kirchenbau' (v.3) covers columns 1347-1411, including 58 plans, 16 pages of plates, and treats the subject in terms of its major periods. 10p. on Buddhism; 18p. on Islam. Valuable, too, for its articles on marginal topics and appropriate men of letters (*e.g.* articles on the ikon, Existentialism, the film, and Franz Kafka). V.7, the index, comprises bibliographical notes on the *c.*3000 contributors, a subject index (p.272-1102); and errata. German Protestant standpoint. *Class No:* 20(031)=30

Handbooks & Manuals

[396]

CARMODY, D.L. *and* CARMODY, J.T. **Mysticism:** holiness east and west. Oxford, Oxford University Press, 1995 312p. $25.00 ISBN: 0195088182.

A fairly straightforward guide to mysticism and holiness as it is understood in the world's main religions. *Class No:* 20(035)

[397]

A New handbook of living religions. Hinnells, J.R., *ed.* 2nd ed. Oxford, Blackwells, 1997 xi,902p £65.00 ISBN: 0631182756.

A through revision of Hinnell's 1984 *Handbook* published by Penguin. It is divided into two sections - the religions (sometimes groups of religions) themselves, and what are entitled "cross-cultural issues", eg religion and gender, and the effects of migration. *Class No:* 20(035)

[398]

QUINN, P.L. *and* TALIAFERRO, C., *eds.* **A Companion to the philosophy of religion.** Oxford, Blackwell, 1997. xvi,639p. (*Blackwell companions to philosophy.*) ISBN: 0631191534.

78 essays divided into 11 sections: I. 'Philosophical issues in the religions of the world' which deals with each of the main religions separately, apart from a chapter on African religions as a group; II. 'Philosophical Theology and Philosophy of Religion in Western history', which discusses ancient, early modern and modern philosophy of religion, with three essays on Christian, Jewish and Islamic contributions in the Middle Ages; III. 'some currents in Twentieth-Century Philosophy of Religion'; IV. 'Theism and the linguistic turn'; V. 'The Theistic conception of God'; VI. 'The justification of theistic belief'; VII. 'Challenges to the rationality of theistic belief'; VIII. 'Theism and modern science'; IX. 'Theism and

....(contd.)

values'; X. 'Philosophical reflection on Christian faith'; XI. 'New directions in philosophy and religion'. Bibliographies accompany each article. *Class No:* 20(035)

Dictionaries

[399]

The HarperCollins dictionary of religion. Smith, J.Z. *and* Green, W.S., *eds.* San Francisco, Calif., HarperSanFrancisco, 1996 xxviii,1154p. £40.00 ISBN: 0006279678.

Well-illustrated A-Z dictionary of terms used by all the world's major religions. It comes with the backing of the prestigious American Academy of Religion. *Class No:* 20(038)

[400]

A New dictionary of religions. Hinnells, J.R., *ed.* 2nd ed. Oxford, Blackwells, 1995 xxxvii,760p. £60.00

A revision of Hinnell's 1984 *Penguin Dictionary*. It has clear guides to the subject areas, a substantial bibliography (also by subject areas), and a thorough index. *Class No:* 20(038)

English

[401]

Abingdon dictionary of living religions. Crim, K., *ed.* Nashville, Tenn., Abingdon Press, 1981. 864p. illus. $39.95. £25. ISBN: 0687004098.

1600 keywords and phrases. Concentrates on religions currently practiced in the world today. Over 150 American scholars contributed, providing comprehensive articles on the historical development and current status of the religions, describing the doctrines, sects, movements, significant personalities, sacred writings, religious practices, and holy sites and objects. Pronunciations given where not in general English usage. Complements Brandon's *Dictionary of comparative religion* (1970), which has fewer non-Christian religion entries. 'A good buy' (*RQ, v.21(3),* Spring 1982, p.296). *Class No:* 20(038)=20

[402]

BRANDON, S.G.F., *ed.* A Dictionary of comparative religion. London, Weidenfeld & Nicolson; New York, Scribner, 1978. viii, 704p. $60. ISBN: 0684155613.

4 section editors; 28 contributors. About 4000 concise signed articles (*e.g.* 'Scandinavian religion': p.159-64; 25 lines of bibliography. 'Buddhism. General survey', p.157-60). Adequate cross-references. General index, p.680-704. List of main sources, p.9-15. A standard dictionary to update Hastings' *Encyclopaedia of religion and ethics* (Edinburgh, T.& T. Clark Ltd; New York, Scribner, 1908-26) in this field. *Class No:* 20(038)=20

[403]

—GASKELL, G.A. Dictionary of all Scriptures and myths. New York, Julian Press, 1960 (Reprinted Dorset Press, 1989). 842p. $29.95. ISBN: 0880292695.

Over 5000 entries, stressing symbolism of religious terms and how symbols vary from religion to religion. Many quotations and cross references. *Class No:* 20(038)=20

[404]

Chambers dictionary of beliefs and religions. Goring, R., *ed.* London, Chambers, 1992. 672p. 100 illus. £25. ISBN: 0550150005.

Over 3000 entries, A-Z. Subject coverage is wide-ranging and includes scientology, pantheism and witchcraft. *Class No:* 20(038)=20

[405]

HINNELLS, J.R., *ed.* The Penguin dictionary of religions. London, Allan Lane/Penguin Books; New York, Facts on File, 1984. 550p. illus., diagrs., maps. £14.75. $27.95. ISBN: 0713915145, UK; 0871968622, US.

Mainly concerned with 'living' religions, including new religious movements, astrology, magic, the occult, as well as secular alternatives to religion, such as Marxism and humanism. A-Z arrangement and ample cross-references. The 29 international contributors have written entries ranging from *c.*40 to *c.*1500 words in length. Valuable scholarly bibliography is arranged under 30 broad subject headings and keyed to the dictionary entries (p.382-446). Also includes maps (p.366-381); a general index (p.465-550); and a synoptic index (p.447-464). Flowing, readable text, and the work's strength is in its coverage of Eastern religions and concepts. *Class No:* 20(038)=20

[406]

PYE, M. Macmillan dictionary of religion. London, Macmillan, 1993. 500p. £29.50. ISBN: 033345409x.

Based on 'concepts drawn partly from the various religious traditions and partly from the historical and reflective study of religion as a modern academic discipline'. Gives concise explanations of nearly 6000 terms covering all aspects of the subject, and distinguishing between religious and theological terminology. Subject arrangement (Extinct and ancient religions - Israelite religion and Judaism - Islam - Christianity - Indian religions ... Sociology of religion - Psychology of religion ... Religions in various cultural disciplines). *Class No:* 20(038)=20

[407]

REESE, W.L. Dictionary of philosophy and religion: Eastern and Western thought. 2nd ed. Atlantic Highlands, N.J., Humanities Press; Hassocks, West Sussex, Harvester Press, 1996. xiv, 856p. illus. ISBN: 0391038648.

First published 1980.

'Has many encyclopedic features, including analysis of the thought of all major philosophers and religious leaders' (*Preface*). A key feature is numerous cross-references from concepts to the thinkers concerned. Major emphasis is on explication terms. Expensive. *Class No:* 20(038)=20

Reviews & Abstracts

[408]

Religious and theological abstracts. 1958-. v.1-. 4pa. Myerstown, Pa., Religious and Theological Abstracts Inc., 1958-. ISSN: 00344044.

Abstracts of articles from more than 300 scholarly periodicals in religion, including Christian, Jewish and other world religions. Four main classes: 1. Biblical - 2. Theological - 3. Historical - 4. Practical. Subject index and author index. Addresses of journals. Annual subject, author and Scripture indexes in 4th volume each year. Also available as CD-ROM. *Class No:* 20(048)

[409]

Religious studies review: a quarterly review of publications in the field of religion and related disciplines. 1975-. Valparaiso, IN, Council of Societies for the Study of Religion, 1975-. $36 (institutions); $30 (individuals) pa. ISSN: 0319485x.

Each issue contains *c.* 12 reviews of 3-4 double column pages; *c.* 250 notices of recent publications (*c.*1/3 col. each); and notices of recent dissertations in religion. *Class No:* 20(048)

[410]

—WALSH, M.J., *and others.* Religious bibliographies in serial literature: a guide. London, Mansell, 1981. 240p. £20. ISBN: 0720115930.

Describes *c.*175 current serials that include bibliographical coverage of religious study. *Class No:* 20(048)

Periodicals

[411]

BURNS, E. Religious periodicals: a recommended collection. In *Serials review,* v.7 January-March 1981, p.9-32.

Reviews of 77 English-language serial titles, mostly published in US. Separate sections, each with an introduction, on charismatic Christianity (2 entries); bibliographic aids (3); 36 best known titles selected from many religious traditions, academic disciplines and ecclesiastical slants; Catholic periodicals (12); Judaic theological journals (6); and Mormon periodicals (18); the last three sections being by other contributors. Some duplication of titles. *Class No:* 20(051)

[412]

CORNELL, E., *ed.* ABTAPL union list of periodicals London, ABTAPL, 2000 252p. £15.00

ABTAPL stands for The Assocation of Theological and Phiosophical Libraries. This publication records the periodical holdings of 41 such libraries, all but four of them in England (the remaining four are in Scotland). Each entry includes the postal address, names of contact persons, telephone and fax numbers, e-mail addresses, with a brief indication of the library's lending/photocopying policy. The periodicals - some 4,500 of them it would seem - are listed alphabetically, with a modicum of information about each and then the holdings of each library. Libraries included range from large, university-affiliated, institutions to seminary and cathedral collections and even smaller bodies such as pastoral centres. The journals represented, both current and deceased, range from children's magazines within a single institution, to the heavy-weights such as the Journal of Ecclesiastical History or the Journal of Theological Studies with multiple holdings. There would seem to be some disagreement about what constitutes a periodical, but this should cause little problem. It is an extremely useful finding list for the United Kingdom, and it is a pity more libraries did not contribute. Oddly, for a publication produced by and for librarians, there is no ISBN. *Class No:* 20(051)

[413]

CORNISH, G.P., *ed*. **Religious periodicals directory**. Santa Barbara, CA., ABC-Clio, 1986. xii, 330p. $89. £77.95. ISBN: 0874363659.

Claims to be a 'comprehensive source of information about periodicals and other serials in the field of religion and theology in the broadest sense of those terms' (*Preface*), and coverage extends to journals in the fields of anthropology, linguistics, sociology, archeology, art and literature. 1800 periodicals are listed by title within country sections, that are arranged A-Z within broad geographical regions. Entries include information on frequency, publisher with address, sponsoring body, statement of purpose or subject content, language of publication, sources in which indexed, variant titles, and special features. Title and subject/geographic indexes. *Class No:* 20(051)

[414]

FIEG, E.C., *comp*. **Religion journals and serials: an analytical guide**. Westport, CT., Greenwood Press, 1988. 218p. $45. (*Annotated bibliographies of serials: a subject approach, 13*.) ISBN: 0313245134.

Primary aim is to help libraries in the selection of scholarly journals, and 328 titles have been selected from about 2000 English-language serials in religion. Titles arranged under broad subject headings. Entries include title, date founded, frequency, publisher, etc., and descriptive annotations. *Class No:* 20(051)

[415]

KASTEN, S. 'Religion periodical indexes': a basic list. in *RSR*, v.9(1); January-March 1981, p.53-55.

One reference librarian's selection of significant titles among the currently-published religion periodical indexes. Brief descriptions included suggest how the tools might be useful. *Class No:* 20(051)

[416]

LIPPY, C.H., *ed*. **Religious periodicals of the United States**: academic and scholarly journals. London, Greenwood Press, 1986. xxi,607p. £46.95; $67.95. (*Historical guides to the world's periodicals and newspapers*.) ISBN: 0313234205.

A selection of c.100 American academic religious and theological journals. Represents academic, scholarly and professional societies; religious groups and denominations; institutions such as theological seminaries and universities. Articles on each title are 3-4 pages in length. 2 appendices (A. Chronological capsule; B. Listing by sponsoring organization or religious orientation). Index, p.563-600. *Class No:* 20(051)

[417]

REGAZZI, J.J. and HINES, T.C. **A Guide to indexed periodicals in religion**. Metuchen, N.J., Scarecrow Press, 1975. 328p. $22.50. £15. ISBN: 0810808684.

Lists over 2700 periodicals (A-Z by title and also by keyword in context), indicating which of 17 indexing or abstracting services cover them. The 17 services are then listed (no details), sub-arranged by titles of periodicals served. 'A significant addition to the bibliographic control in the fields of religion and theology' (*Library journal*, v.101(3), 1 March 1976,. p.705). *Class No:* 20(051)

Quotations

[418]

MEAD, F.S., *ed. & comp*. **Encyclopaedia of religious quotations**. London, Peter Davies, 1965. [vii],534p.

More than 10,000 quotations, arranged A-Z by topics, from 'Advertising' (19 entries, authors A-Z, anonymous preceding) to 'Zeal' (16 entries). 170 subject headings. Covers verse and prose, and draws on non-Christian as well as Christian (including Biblical) sources. Quotations are sometimes lengthy, but there are obvious omissions. Indexes of authors and topics, but no first-line index. *Class No:* 20(082.2)

[419]

—NEIL, W., *comp*. **Concise dictionary of religious quotations**. London, Mowbrays, 1975. vii,214p.

Includes c. 2500 quotations, many from the Bible. Source index; keyword subject index. Prefers the 'eminently forgettable New English Bible every time to the King James Version' (*TLS*, no.3821, 30 May 1975, p.604). *Class No:* 20(082.2)

[420]

—WOODS, R.L., *comp. & ed*. **The World treasury of religious quotations**. New York, Hawthorn, 1966. 1106p.

10,000 quotations, chronologically under 1500 subject headings. Universal coverage; no poetry and only 2 Bible verses. Author, title and date of publication for each quotation. Author index, but no keyword index. *Class No:* 20(082.2)

[421]

PARRINDER, E.G., *comp*. **A Dictionary of religious and spiritual quotations**. London, Routledge; New York, Simon & Schuster, 1990. xi,218p. £14.99; $40. ISBN: 0132101211, US; 0415041287, UK.

Over 3000 quotations, arranged under 18 broad headings, with 177 subdivisions. Author and title index. Subject index. Eastern religions are well represented. Wider in scope than Pepper. *Class No:* 20(082.2)

[422]

PEPPER, M., *comp*. **Dictionary of religious quotations**. London, André Deutsch, 1989. 496p. ISBN: 0233983732.

Paperback ed. as *The Pan dictionary of religious quotations* (London, Pan Books, 1991. ISBN 0330315005). American ed. as *The Harper religious and inspirational quotation companion* (Harper, 1989. ISBN 0060161795).

Over 4000 quotations under topics, A-Z, with two or more quotations for each subject, spanning the world's major religions from classical times to the present. Includes unusual and entertaining quotations. Subject index, p.461-468. Index of authors and major works, p.469-496. *Class No:* 20(082.2)

Tables & Data Books

[423]

Reviews of United Kingdom statistical sources: v.20: Religion. Oxford, Pergamon Press for the Royal Statistical Society and the Economic and Social Research Council, 1987. 635p. £97. ISBN: 0080347789.

Four reviews (nos. 33, 34, 35, & 36), each review standing alone: Recurrent Christian sources - Non-recurrent Christian data - Judaism - Other religions. *c*.500 pages of the 635p. given to Christian sources. Each review starts with a general introductory section of background information, specific problems and topics. This is followed by the 'Quick reference list', arranged by subject or denomination, including types of data, geographical area covered, date, publications details, etc. The 'Key' to sources listed has full bibliographical details. There is then a second bibliography listing workings of wider scope, and a subject index. *Class No:* 20(083)

Maps & Atlases

[424]

SMART, N., *ed*. **Atlas of the world religions** Oxford, Oxford University Press, 1999 240p. £30.00 ISBN: 0198662351.

After introductory essays on "Religion today" and "The historical geography of religion", the text of this atlas is divided into ten sections under the general heading of "The world's religions": 1. The Hindu world; 2. Buddhism; 3. East Asian traditions; 4. The Pacific; 5. The ancient Near East and Europe; 6. Judaism; 7. Christianity (easily the longest section); 8. Islam; 9. Africa and 10. Indigenous religions. There is a glossary, plus bibliography and index. The maps are clear and attractively produced in full colour, and illustrated. The basic approach is historical, though there is some, not wholly successful, effort to map ideas. The approach is academic, but the scale is too all-embracing for detailed treatment of any one of the faiths. *Class No:* 20(084.3)

Histories

[425]

BLEEKER, C.J. and WIDENGREN, G. **Historia religionum**: handbook for the history of religions. Leiden, E.J. Brill, 1969-71. 2v. (viii, 691 & vi, 715p.). V.1 Gld.144. $72. V.2 Gld.166. $83. ISBN: 9004089284, v.1; 9004025987, v.2.

A second impression of v.1 was made in 1988; v.2 is still the 1971 edition.

V.1: *Religions of the past*, includes a section on prehistoric religion, and on Israelite-Jewish religion (p.222-317); bibliography (p.313-7). V.2: *Religions of the present*, has sections on Christianity (p.49-124), with bibliography) and Buddhism (p.372-464; bibliography of 91 items). It also has indexes of authors and subjects. *Class No:* 20(091)

[426]

International bibliography of the history of religions/ Bibliographie internationale de l'histoire des religions ... 1952-73. Leiden, E.J. Brill, 1954-1979. ISSN: 05385105.

The 1973 volume (the last to be published) has c.3000 unannotated entries for books, periodical articles and reviews. 11 sections: 1. General works - 2. Prehistorical and primitive religions - 3. Religions of antiquity - 4. Judaism - 5. Christianity - 6. Islam - 7. Hinduism - 8. Buddhism - 9. Chinese religions - 10. Japanese religions - 11. Minor religions. About 500 journals in theory, archaeology and antiquities were scanned. Name index. *Class No:* 20(091)

Biographies

[427]

HINNELLS, J.R. **Who's who of religions.** London, Macmillan; New York, Simon & Schuster, 1991. 450p. illus. £29.95. $75. ISBN: 0333440994, UK; 0139529462, US.

Biographical studies of *c.*1500 prominent religious leaders throughout the world. *c.*60 contributors. The longer entries are for lesser-known people. 'Objective and authoritative information, some of which is difficult to obtain elsewhere.' (*Library journal*, 1 February 1992, p.82). *Class No:* 20(092)

[428]

LIPPY, C.H., *ed.* **Twentieth-century shapers of American popular religion.** Westport CT., Greenwood Press, 1989. 494p. $65. ISBN: 0313253560.

Biographical and bibliographical information on more than 60 individuals who have influenced popular religion in North America during the 20th century. Arranged A-Z by name (William Aberhart ... Wovoka). Supplements Peter. W. Williams' *Popular religion in America* (1980) ' ... this engaging volume' (*Choice* v.27(1) September 1989, p.96). *Class No:* 20(092)

Worldwide

[429]

SMART, N. **The World's religions:** old traditions and modern transformations. Cambridge, Cambridge University Press, 1989. 576p. illus., maps. £25. ISBN: 0521340055.

Looks at the world's religions in terms of world history and as constantly developing systems of belief, each religion being analysed in its main aspects - practical or ritual, emotional, narrative or mythic, doctrinal, ethical or legal, social or institutional. Part I traces the development of religions, region by region, as they evolved; Part II examines the changes to faiths and cultures. Richly illustrated with 200 half-tones and maps, 48 col.photos. *Class No:* 20(100)

[430]

SMART, Ninian. **Dimensions of the sacred** an anatomy of the world's religions. Berkeley, Calif., University of California Press, 1996 331p. $29.95 ISBN: 0520207777.

Contains bibliography and index.

A comparative study of all the world's great religions, including the political effect of religion. *Class No:* 20(100)

USA

Periodicals

[431]

FACKLER, P.M. *and* LIPPY, C.H., *eds.* **Popular religious magazines of the United States** Westport, CT, Greenwood Press, 1994. xvii,595p. $125.00 (*Historical guides to the world's periodicals and newspapers.*.) ISBN: 0313285330.

According to the editors there are some ten thousand titles falling into the category of popular magazines published in the United States. Only a representative 100 are examined here, by some 60 different scholars. Articles average at five pages in length. Locations are given for the best collections of each title. *Class No:* 20(73)(051)

Histories

[432]

LIPPY, C. **Being religious, American style** a history of popular religiosity in the United States. Westport, Conn., Greenwood Press, 1994 284p. $65.00 ISBN: 0313278954.

An encyclopedic (despite its comparatively short length) study of popular religion in the U.S., embodying everything from television evangelists to prayer books. There is a thorough bibliography and excellent index. *Class No:* 20(73)(091)

Libraries

[433]

A **Guide to theological and religious studies collections of Great Britain and Ireland.** Kerry, D.A. *and* Cornell, E., *comp. & ed.* Cambridge, ABTAPL Publishing, 1999. iv,275p. £10. ISBN: 094894501x.

Aim was a comprehensive survey of library resources in the field. Lists 389 'significant' collections, A-Z by place, subdivided by library. Information includes name and address, function, coverage, special collections, librarian, governing body, history, stock, catalogues, access, staff, publications (except for those libraries which did not reply to the questionnaire). *Class No:* 20:061:026/027

Psychology of Religion

[434]

CAPPS, D., *and others.* **Psychology of religion:** a guide to information sources. Detroit, Mich., Gale Research Co., 1976. xii, 352p. $68. (*Philosophy and religion information guide series.*) ISBN: 0810313561.

About 4000 briefly annotated entries. Sections A-G (A: General works on psychology of religion; B-G: mythological, ritual, experimental, dispositional, social and directional dimensions of religion). Author, title and subject indexes. Limited to material published 1950-74. *Class No:* 20:159.9

[435]

SALIBA, J.A. **Psychiatry and the cults:** an annotated bibliography. New York, Garland, 1987. 601p. $60.00. (*Sects and cults in America. Bibliographical guides, 10. Garland reference library of social sciences, 349.*) ISBN: 0824085868.

1916 annotated entries, with author and subject indexes. '... balanced bibliography ... reflects all professional and academic viewpoints, including those with which [the author] disagrees'. (*Choice*, v.25 (7), March 1988, p.1070).

Complements D. Capp's *Psychology of religion: a guide to information sources* (q.v.). *Class No:* 20:159.9

Rationalism

Bibliographies

[436]

STEIN, G. **Freethought in the United Kingdom and the Commonwealth:** a descriptive bibliography. Westport, CT., Greenwood Press, [1981]. xxiii, 193p. $76.95. ISBN: 0313208697.

Arranged by historical periods (1624-1760, 1760-1860, 1860-1915, 1915 to the present). Each section has a detailed essay, followed by a bibliography of the publications cited. Appendices on the freethought movement in New Zealand, Canada, Australia and India, giving brief information on the same lines as the main text. Other appendices indicate libraries with major holdings in the field, and a list of master's theses and dissertations. Glossary of terms. Author, title and subject indexes. *Class No:* 211.5(01)

[437]

STEIN, G. **God pro and con:** a bibliography of Atheism. New York, Garland, 1990. xv,531p. $65. ((*Garland reference library of social science, 588*).) ISBN: 0824070410.

Pseudonyms of Atheist/Freethought authors precedes the main 3 sections: I.A. Atheist books and pamphlets; B. Historical/philosophical studies of Atheism. II.A. Atheist periodicals; B. Important articles about Atheism (pro & con). III. Anti-Atheist books and pamphlets. Title index, p.393-531. *Class No:* 211.5(01)

Encyclopaedias

[438]

STEIN, G., *ed.* **The Encyclopedia of unbelief.** Buffalo, NY, Prometheus Books, 1986. 2v. (819p.). $99.95 the set. ISBN: 0879753072.

Over 100 articles, including short bibliographies, covering philosophy, history and biography of the various branches of unbelief from scepticism to atheism. Cross-references. 5 appendices include 'Periodicals of unbelief' with nearly 500 periodical and newspaper titles. 'There is no comparable work' (*Library journal*, 1 November 1985, p.87). *Class No:* 211.5 (031)

Histories

[439]

BERMAN, D. **A History of atheism in Britain:** from Hobbes to Russell. London, Croom Helm, 1987. 242p. £30. ISBN: 0709932715.

10 chapters: 1. The repression of atheism - 2. Restoration atheists: founding followers of Hobbes ... 5. The birth of avowed atheism, 1782-1979... 9. The atheists: 1822-1842 - 10. Militant and academic atheism. Epilogue: The ethics of unbelief. Index. *Class No:* 211.5(091)

[440]

POSPIELOVSKY, D.V. **A History of Soviet atheism in theory and practice,** and the believer. London, Macmillan Press, 1987-88. 3v. (856p.). V.1: £29.50; v.2: £29.50; v.3: £35. ISBN: 0333423267, v.1; 0333423275, v.2; 0333423283, v.3.

Outlines the theoretical and ideological foundations of Soviet atheism from Feuerbach and Marx to Khrushchev and Adropov. V.1: *A history of the Marxist-Leninist atheism and Soviet anti-religious policies,* deals with the theory of Marxism and with the offical Soviet policy declarations regarding 'the struggle' against religion through history. V.2: *Soviet anti-religious campaigns and persecutions,* exposes and analyses the strategy and tactics of the anti-religious propaganda and persecutions in day-to-day practice, from 1917 to 1986. V.3: *Soviet studies on the Church and the believer's response to atheism,* presents

....(contd.)
a picture of how the Church and believers actually live in a society of militant atheism. Each volume has appendices ('Annotated texts of Soviet laws on religion' is in v.1.), bibliographies, and indexes. (*Theology*, v.42, no.747, May 1989, p.225-227) remarks that it is expensive and has too many misprints 'but brings together an immense quantity of detailed information about policies and events which is relevant to any attempt to evaluate the changes now taking place'. *Class No: 211.5(091)*

Science & Religion

[441]
EISEN, S. *and* LIGHTMAN, B.V. **Victorian science and religion:** bibliography of works and ideas and institutions with emphasis on revolution, belief and unbelief, comprised of works published from *c.*1900-1975. Santa Barbara, CA., ABC-Clio, 1985. xix, 696p. $55. ISBN: 0208020101.
6267 items of work about science, religion and their interrelationship during the Victorian era (*c.*1830 to 1900). Includes articles, books and dissertations, focusing mainly on England and almost exclusively on the Christian religion. Organized topically in 3 sections: Main currents - National theology, geology and evolution - Religion: ideas and institutions. Each section subdivided by subjects or persons. Unannotated. Author and subject indexes. 'Citations clear and consistant' (*Choice*, v.22(9), May 1985, p.1304). *Class No: 215*

[442]
McIVOR, T. **Anti-evolution:** an annotated bibliography. 385p. $39.95. ISBN: 0899503135.
Entries are arranged A-Z by author, with descriptive annotations varying from one line to ½-page in length. Focuses on books, tracts and pamphlets, and includes Islamic and Jewish as well as Protestant sources; also anti-Darwinian material. Name, title and subject indexes keyed to numbered entries, the name index including both authors and important individuals mentioned in the annotations. Comparable publications are E. Lazar's *The creation/evolution bibliography & directory* (privately printed. 3rd. ed. 1987) and the CREVO/IMS database, maintained since 1982 by creationist students. 'This unique bibliography provides an invaluable tool for scholars ...' (*Choice*, v.26(7), March 1989, p.1126). *Class No: 215*

Histories

[443]
BROOK, J.H. **Science and Religion** some historical perspectives. Cambridge, Cambridge University Press, 1991 x,422p. $44.50 (*Cambridge History of Science*.) ISBN: 0521239613.
Not so much a history as a discussion of the issues involved in the interaction of science and religion, mainly in the Post-reformation to modern period. *Class No: 215(091)*

Worship & Meditation

[444]
WHITAKER, S. **The good retreat guide.** London, Rider, 1998. 316p. £12.99. ISBN: 0712671277.
1st published 1991.
Explains the nature of retreats and lists more than 300 places 'to find peace and spiritual renewal' in Britain, Ireland, France and Spain. *Class No: 217*

Encyclopaedias

[445]
Encyclopedia of Transcendentalism. Mott, W.T., *ed.* Westport, Conn., Greenwood Press, 1996 280p. $75.00 ISBN: 0313299242.
Seventy contributors, entirely US in focus. *Class No: 217(031)*

Maps & Atlases

[446]
WILSON, Colin. **The Atlas of holy places and sacred sites.** London, Dorling Kindersley, 1996 192p. £19.99 ISBN: 0751303372.
Fairly popular level atlas of 1,000 sites sacred to the world's religions. *Class No: 217(084.3)*

Bible

Databases

[447]
The Bible in English [full-text database on CD-Rom]. London, Chadwyck-Healy, 1996. £1,250. ISBN: 0859643131.
21 different versions of the Bible. Requires IBM-compatible 486 PC with at least 8MB of RAM, running Windows 3.1. *Class No: 22(003.4)*

Bibliographies

[448]
Elenchus of biblica. Rome, Pontificio Istituto Biblico. 1985-. v.1-. Annual. L.150000; $140.
Continues *Elenchus bibliographicus biblicus* (1920-1984, v.1-65), issued as part of the periodical *Biblica* from 1920 to 1967.
A bibliography covering all areas of Biblical research, including the scientific study of the Bible. Arranged in 20 sections, with subdivisions (I. Bibliographia ... V. Exegesis totius VT vel cum NT ... IX. NT exegesis generalis ... XII. Actus Apostolorum ... XVI. Philologia biblica ... XX. Historia scientiae biblicae). Indexes of authors, Greek words, Hebrew words, scriptural references. C. 17,000 items listed. Mainly in Latin. Roman Catholic viewpoint. *Class No: 22(01)*

Encyclopaedias

[449]
BAUER, J.B., *ed.* **Encyclopedia of Biblical theology.** London & Sydney, Sheed & Ward, 1970 (reprinted 1982). 3v. (xxxiii, 1141p.). illus. £22.50 the set. ISBN: 0722034202.
Originally as *Bibeltheologisches Wörterbuch* (Graz, Verlag Styria, 1959). Translated from the 1967. 3rd. rev. and enl. German ed.
53 contributors. Signed and documented articles (*e.g.* 'Eucharist': v.1, p.227-41: ½col. of bibliography). V.3 (p.797-1141) carries a supplementary bibliography (subjects A-Z, p.1015-25) and appendices: analytical index of articles and cross-references: index of Biblical references; index of Hebrew and Greek words. 'An outstanding example of the renewal of Catholic biblical scholarship' (*Library journal*, v.96 no.2, 15 January 1971, p.102). *Class No: 22(031)*

[450]
The International standard Bible encyclopedia. Bromiley, G.W., *ed.* 3rd ed. Grand Rapids, Mich., Eerdmans, 1984-1988. 4v. illus., maps. $159.80 the set. ISBN: 0802881610, v.1; 0802881629, v.2; 0802881637, v.3; 0802881645, v.4; 0802881602, set.
First published 1915. 2nd ed. 1929.
Presents the Protestant evangelical viewpoint. RSV texts used. Original Hebrew, Aramaic and Greek words are transliterated. Includes entries for every person or place mentioned in the Bible, and also articles dealing with the Bible itself. Longer articles are signed and include bibliographies. Highly recommended by *Choice*, (v.16(12), February 1980, p.1562). *Class No: 22(031)*

[451]
MILLER, M.S. *and* MILLER, J.L. **Harper's encyclopedia of Bible life.** Bennett, B.M. *and* Scott, D.H., *eds.* 3rd rev. ed. London, A. & C. Black , 1979. xviii,423p. illus., maps. ISBN: 0713619139.
First published 1944.
4 contributors. 3 main sections (closely subdivided): 1. The world of the Bible - 2. How the people of the Bible lived - 3. How the people of the Bible worked. 'Suggestions for further reading' (p.390-5; subdivided). Index of scriptural references, p.397-410; Index of names and subjects, p.411-23. 150 illus., with descriptive captions. 'A recently-revised work that should prove very useful' (Rogers, A.R. *The humanities.* 2nd ed., 1979. entry 176). *Class No: 22(031)*

[452]
The Zondervan pictorial encyclopedia of the Bible. Tenney, M. *and* Barabas, S., *eds.* New York, Zondervan Press, 1977. 5v. illus (some col.). $149.95 the set. ISBN: 0310331889.
7500 signed articles, contributed by 238 scholars - an international team. 32p. of full-colour maps (with index in v.5); 48p. of colour plates, unfortunately unnumbered and lacking text cross-references. Truly pictorial. Conservative standpoint. Compared with *The interpreter's dictionary of the Bible (qv)* in *American reference books annual 1976* (entry 1104) and considered 'particularly valuable for its supplementary information and alternative viewpoints'. *Class No: 22(031)*

Handbooks & Manuals

[453]

ALTER, R. *and* KERMODE, F., *eds*. **The Literary guide to the Bible.** London, Collins, 1987. [6], 678p. £20. ISBN: 0002174391.

International team of contributors. Includes a general introduction and introductions to the Old and New Testaments. The main part of the publication is a book-by-book discussion from Genesis to Revelation, followed by essays on various aspects of Biblical literature, including one on English translations of the Bible. Glossary of Biblical and literary terms (p.668-670). Analytical index (p.673-678). *Class No:* 22(035)

[454]

Marshall's Bible handbook. Packer, J.I., *and others*. London, Marshall, Morgan & Scott, 1980. 765p. illus. ISBN: 0551008342.

Arranged in 46 chapters: 1. The ancient world - 2. Bible history - 3. Bible chronology - 4. Text and translations - 5. Archaeology - 6. Pagan religions and cultures ... 14. Minerals and gems ... 17. Agriculture ... 44. Outline of the books of the Bible - 45. All the people of the Bible (p.602-677, A-Z) - 46. All the places of the Bible (p.678-726, A-Z). Index to proper names and other significant topics, p.729-765. *Class No:* 22(035)

[455]

METZGER, B.M. *and* COOGAN, M.D. **The Oxford companion to the Bible.** Oxford, Oxford University Press, 1993. xxi,874p. ISBN: 0195046455.

Signed articles, from a distinguished international team of contributors, arranged in alphabetical order. Covers people, places, events, books and religious beliefs of the Bible, as well as the influence of the Bible on secular culture. Extensive cross-references. Index and bibliography. Contains maps. *Class No:* 22(035)

Dictionaries

[456]

BLAIKLOCK, E.M. *and* HARRISON, R.K., *eds*. **The New international dictionary of Biblical archaeology.** Grand Rapids, Mich., Regency Reference Library, Zondervan Publishing House, 1983. 485p. illus. 33 col. maps. $30.95. ISBN: 0310212502.

Brief definitions of terms and concise signed articles on persons, places, deities relevant to the study of Biblical archaeology. Most articles are followed by bibliographies. Citations to the Bible, classical sources, etc. are frequently included in the text. Pronunciations given for entry words other than English. Cross-references from alternative terms and variant spellings. *Class No:* 22(038)

[457]

BROWNING, W.R.F. **A Dictionary of the Bible.** Oxford, Oxford University Press, 1996. xv,423p. £16.99. ISBN: 0192116916.

Includes maps and bibliography.

Over 2,000 entries on themes and doctrines of the Bible, its books, people and places. There are also notes on leading biblical scholars and their contributions. There is comprehensive cross-referencing. 'The dictionary is intended for students whether at school or university, and for a more general public consisting of those who may be reading or studying the Bible.' - Introduction. A good general Bible dictionary which acknowledges the achievements of modern critical scholarship. *Class No:* 22(038)

[458]

The Eerdmans Bible dictionary. Myers, Allen C., *and others, eds*. Grand Rapids, Missouri, W. Eerdmans, 1987. 1094p. maps. $29.85. ISBN: 0802824021.

Based on the highly respected Dutch *Bijbelse encyclopedie* (rev. ed. 1975).

About 5,000 entries and many cross-references. Uses the Revised Standard Version of the Bible as authority for quoted passages and forms of names. This American edition adds about 300 new articles and revises many others, but retains the Protestant evangelical flavour of the earlier work. Includes basic information concerning people, places and things of the Bible; surveys all the books of the Bible; includes articles on the animals, jewels, birds, etc., mentioned; and investigates the chief themes and ideas. Bibliographies are somewhat sketchy. 'Entries reflect modern biblical scholarship and archaeological research. An excellent and inexpensive study aid ...' (*Library journal*, August 1987, p.115). *Class No:* 22(038)

[459]

GEHMAN, H.S., *ed*. **The New Westminster dictionary of the Bible.** 1982 thumb-indexed ed. Philadelphia, Pa., Westminster Press, 1982. 1064p. illus. $25.95. ISBN: 066421388x.

First published 1944 as *The Westminster dictionary of the Bible*, revised ed. by J.D. Davis, 1970.

c.4000 entries, with brief biographies of Biblical characters, outlines of Biblical books and entries for flora, fauna, etc., mentioned in the Bible. Pronunciations shown; numerous references to the Revised Standard Version. 'Nineveh': 3 columns, 1 illus.; 'Romans, the Epistle ...': 3½ cols. 16 full-colour maps, taken from *Westminster historical atlas to the Bible*. Incorporates results of recent archaeological finds.

....(contd.)

'One of the best and most useful 1-volume Bible dictionaries' (*Library journal*, v.95, no.15, 1 April 1970, p.2758). Protestant viewpoint. *Class No:* 22(038)

[460]

Harper's Bible dictionary. Achtermeier, P.J., *ed* and Society of Biblical Literature. New ed. New York, Harper & Row, 1985. 1178p. illus (some col.), maps. $29.95. £23.95. ISBN: 0060698624.

First published 1952. Published in the UK as *Black's Bible dictionary*, 1st ed., 1954; 8th ed. 1973, compiled by M.S. & J.L. Miller.

A one-volume dictionary intended to embody recent discoveries in archaeology, geography, chronology, textual criticism and other fields of contemporary Biblical investigation. Over 3700 commissioned articles by 179 Christian and Jewish scholars are included in this non-sectarian source which can be used with any Bible translation. A-Z arrangement of entries which deal with all important persons and places in the Bible, together with theological terms. Written in non-technical language. 92 maps (76 in black & white, 16 in colour). '... this splendid volume presents a balanced summary of current Biblical scholarship accessible to the general reader ...' (*Library journal*, v.111(1), January 1986, p.72). 'It is likely to become an indispensable vade-mecum for serious students of the Bible' (*Church times*, 10 October 1986, p.7). *Class No:* 22(038)

[461]

HASTINGS, J., *ed*. **A Dictionary of the Bible,** dealing with its language, literature, and contents, including Biblical theology. Edinburgh, T. & T. Clark Ltd., 1898-1904. 5v.

The standard dictionary, containing articles, some of considerable length and sectionalized, by Biblical scholars, on persons, places, antiquities, archaeology, ethnology, geology, natural history, Biblical theology and ethnics. Etymology given. The article 'Jerusalem' (34½ large columns; 1 plan) has 8 sections, the last, 'Literature' (34 lines), being an evaluative survey. The fifth, 'extra' volume contains supplementary articles, with maps and indexes. Protestant standpoint.

The one-volume *Dictionary of the Bible*, edited by J. Hastings, with the co-operation of J.A. Selbie (Edinburgh, T. & T. Clark Ltd., 1909) is an independent work. A 2nd ed., revised by F.C. Grant and H.H. Rowley (1963. xvi, 1059, 16p. £14.95. ISBN 0567062015) is a thorough overhaul, based on the Revised Standard Version, with cross-references from both A.V. and R.V. forms; 148 contributions; sectionalized longer articles. No appended bibliographies, but abbreviated references in text. 16 coloured maps. For clergy. Protestant standpoint. *Class No:* 22(038)

[462]

HILLYER, N., *ed*. **The New Bible dictionary.** 2nd ed. Leicester, Inter-Varsity Press; Wheaton, Ill., Tyndale House, 1982. xviii, 1326p. 43 illus., 52 diagr., 76 maps. £21.95. ISBN: 0851106307.

First published in 1962, edited by J.D. Douglas.

'... a major product of the Tyndale Fellowship for Biblical Research' (*Preface*). c.2300 signed articles, with short bibliographies, by more than 150 contributors. Longer articles (*e.g.* 'Messiah', over 12 columns, bibliography of 11 items) are sectionalized. Each book of the Bible is analysed; Biblical references. Strong in archaeology (*e.g.* 'Palestine': p.865-71; 3 maps; 3 diagrams; bibliography of 9 items). Better layout than McKenzie (*q.v.*). Protestant viewpoint. *Class No:* 22(038)

[463]

The Interpreter's dictionary of the Bible: an illustrated encyclopedia, identifying and explaining all proper names and significant terms and subjects in the Holy Scriptures, including the Apocrypha, with attention to archaeological discussions and researches into the life and faith of ancient times. New York, Abingdon Press, 1962 (Supplement 1977). (Reprinted 1979). 4v. & supplement. illus (inc. col. plates). maps. $119 the set of 4 vols; $24.95 for supplement. ISBN: 0687192684.

About 250 contributors, mostly American. Signed longer articles with brief bibliographies (*e.g.* 'Daniel': I. The man - II. The book; nearly 8p.; bibliography of 26 lines; 'Jerusalem': p.843-66; 4 illus., 5 maps; 6 references). V.1 has 24p. of coloured maps. In all nearly 1000 illus. and 32 col. plates. Scholarly; gives etymology. Intended as companion to the 12v. *Interpreter's Bible*. Protestant approach. *Class No:* 22(038)

[464]

—Anchor Bible dictionary. Freedman, D.N., *ed*. New York, Bantam Doubleday, 1992. 6v. $60 each vol. ISBN: 0385193513, v.1(A-C); 0385193602, v.2(D-G); 0385193610, v.3(H-J); 0385193629, v.4(K-N); 0385193637, v.5(O-Sh); 038526190x, v.6(Si-Z).

Supersedes the 'Interpreter's dictionary of the Bible', but that should be kept for more complete coverage of Biblical words.

More than 6000 entries from nearly 1000 contributors. A virtual encyclopedia, most articles having substantial bibliographies. Cross-references. *Class No:* 22(038)

[465]

—DOUGLAS, J.D., *ed*. The Illustrated Bible dictionary. Leicester, Inter-Varsity Press, 1980. 3v. (each 592p.).

An extensive revision of *The new Bible dictionary* (1962).

More than 160 contributors. Over 2000 articles, *c*.1600 illus., mostly in colour, 200 maps and 250 charts. Quotations use the Revised Standard Version. 'It will be invaluable to every minister, teacher or student fortunate enough to own it' (*British book news*, April 1981, p.264). *Class No: 22(038)*

[466]

LÉON-DUFOUR, K., *ed*. Dictionary of Biblical theology. 2nd ed. London & Dublin, Geoffrey Chapman, 1973 (Reprinted 1982). xxxii,712p. £17.95. ISBN: 0225660083.

Translated by P.J. Cahill from *Vocabulaire de théologie biblique* (Paris, Les Éditions du Cerf, 1962, 2 éd., 1970). First English edition 1969.

70 contributions. Arranged under broad subject headings (*e.g.* Creation; Faith; Salvation), with extended discussion based closely on Biblical teaching, plus appropriate Bible references. Numerous cross-references. Analytical table of subject headings. Intended primarily for Roman Catholic Clergy and laity. 'A first-rate work of Roman Catholic scholarship (*The Church times*, 14 December 1973, p.7). *Class No: 22(038)*

[467]

MEYERS, C., *ed*. Women and scripture: a dictionary of named and unnamed women in the Hebrew Bible, the Apocryphal/Deuterocanonical books, and the New Testament. New York, Houghton Mifflin, 2000. 720p. $45. ISBN: 0395709369. *Class No: 22(038)*

[468]

ODELAIN, O. *and* SÉGUINEAU, R. Dictionary of proper names and places in the Bible. New ed. London, Robert Hale, 1991. 528p. 12p. of maps. £10.95. ISBN: 0709044003.

First published 1982.

Over 3500 proper names and places found in the Old and New Testaments arranged A-Z. Each entry cites the number of times a name occurs in the Bible, provides a transcription of the name from the original language or one of the other ancient languages, gives its meaning and its etymological kinship with other names. Cross-references. An appendix gathers together the most-used information from the Bible into one section for handy reference (*e.g.* the Tribes of Israel; the sons of David; the descendents of Levi). Also a general chronology, dynastic chart, and 12 pages of full-colour maps. *Class No: 22(038)*

[469]

RICHARDSON, A., *ed*. A Theological word book of the Bible. London, S.C.M. Press, 1950 (14th impression 1977). 288p. £12.50. ISBN: 0334016207.

A work on the lines of Kittel's *Theologisches Wörterbuch* (*qv*), by a team of English-speaking scholars, elucidating the distinctly theological meanings of the main Bible keywords, and based on the Revised Version. All Hebrew and Greek words are transliterated and historical details are included where necessary for theological understanding. *Class No: 22(038)*

[470]

RYKEN, L. *and* WILHOIT, J. C. *and* LONGMAN III, T., *eds*. Dictionary of biblical imagery Downers Grove IL and Leicester, Intervarsity Press, 1998. xxi, 1058. £29.99. ISBN: 0851117538.

The compass of this volume is defined on its cover: "an encyclopedic exploration of the images, symbols, motifs, metaphors, figures of speech and literary patterns of the bible". Thus the article "Deaf" points out that while actual deafness is very rarely mentioned in the bible, deafness is regularly used as a symbol of stubbornness - and this symbolic usage is then discussed. The c. 850 articles are unsigned (there is a list of the 150+ contributors, but no mention of which entries are whose) and for the most part without bibliographies. Even when very brief bibliographies are added, they have a tendency to include only works in sympathy with the generally rather Evangelical tone of the whole volume. There is a scripture index and a subject index though, with regard to the latter, the value of, for example, nearly 150 undifferentiated page references to "bear, bears" is not immediately obvious. *Class No: 22(038)*

[471]

TOORN, K. van der *and* BECKING, B. *and* HORST, P.W. van der, *eds*. Dictionary of deities and demons in the Bible. 2nd rev. ed. Grand Rapids, MI, Wm. B. Eerdmans, 1999. 960p. $120. £70. ISBN: 0802824919.

Over 400 entries on gods, demons and heroes mentioned in the Bible. Entries provide etymology, historical background and cultural context. Extensive indexes, cross-references and bibliography. *Class No: 22(038)*

[472]

TURNER, N. Handbook for Biblical studies. Oxford, Basil Blackwell Ltd.; Philadelphia, Pa., Westminster Press, 1982. 156p. maps. £6.95. $6.95. ISBN: 063113025x, UK; 066424436x, US.

Contains short definitions from the jargon of the scholar in religious and Biblical studies. Primarily aimed as an introduction to unfamiliar words for the seminary students, but is also useful to laypeople. Includes a *Theological who's who* of scholars, past and present. 'Most definitions too brief to be more than cursory explanations of words ... Handy source for quick answers to questions' (*Choice*, v.20(9), May 1983, p.1272). *Class No: 22(038)*

[473]

WIGODER, G., *and others*, *eds*. Illustrated dictionary and concordance of the Bible. New York, Collier-Macmillan, 1987. 1970p. illus (some col.), maps. $100. £90. ISBN: 0029163803.

More than 4000 entries, ranging from one-line definitions to long articles on major figures, places and concepts. Based on the new King James Version English translation. Identifies and describes all the persons and places mentioned in the Bible; also fundamental concepts; tribes; civilizations; plants, animals and food; and objects such as coins and glass. Outstanding illustrations. 'Although some may prefer a plain concordance ... the dictionary portion by itself is excellent enough to recommend the work' (*Choice*, April 1987, p.1200). *Reference books bulletin* (1986/87, p.51-52) prefers Harper's Bible dictionary but 'outstanding illustrations and reliable scholarship make this a desirable secondary purchase ...'. *Class No: 22(038)*

Periodicals

[474]

HUPPER, W.G., *comp. and ed*. An Index to English periodical literature on the Old Testament and ancient Near Eastern studies. V.I. Metuchen, N.J., American Theological Library Association and Scarecrow Press, 1987. 516p. $47.50. (*ATLA bibliography series, 21*.) ISBN: 0810819848.

An analytical index to periodical literature on the Old Testament and ancient Near Eastern studies. Over 600 journals of archaeology, history, language, science and theology, covering English-language articles from 1793 to 1969/70 are indexed. Articles arranged chronologically under specific sections, this first volume containing 138 sections on bibliographical, biographical and historical material, etc. (V.II was published in 1988 (544p. $45. ISBN 0810821265); V.III in 1990 (823p. $79.50. ISBN 0810823195); V.IV in 1990 (594p. $62.50. ISBN 0810823934); V.V in 1992 (797p. $72.50. ISBN 0810826186). *Class No: 22(051)*

Quotations

[475]

CASTAGNO, A.J., *ed*. Book of Biblical quotations. London & Glasgow, Pickering & Inglis, 1981. 271p. £3.95. ISBN: 072080485x.

Published in the US by Lawrence Urdang Inc., as *A Treasury of Biblical quotations*.

4000 Scripture quotations arranged A-Z under 1150 topic headings. Several quotations are given for each topic (*e.g.* 'Friendship' has 11; 'Scorn' has 8). Sources are given. '... a topical anthology of better-known verses designed for use by Bible students, pastors, Bible teachers, professional speakers and writers and lay persons ...' (*Introduction*). *Class No: 22(082.2)*

[476]

LEVINE, M.L. *and* RACHLIS, E., *eds*. The Complete book of Bible quotations. New York, Peter Bedrick Books, 1986; London, Robert Hale Ltd., 1987. xxi,568p. $12.95; £14.95. ISBN: 0671498649, US; 0709031610, UK.

c.5000 quotations from the Old and New Testaments in the King James version of the Bible, arranged under about 800 subject headings. Cross-references. An appendix has reprints from famous Bible passages. Full keyword index to significant words. 'Judiciously selected quotations' (*Reference books bulletin*, 1986/87, p.51). *Class No: 22(082.2)*

[477]

McLEISH, K. *and* McLEISH, V. Longman guide to Bible quotations. Harlow, Essex, Longman Group, 1986. vi,415p. £11.95. ISBN: 0582555736.

Arranged in 3 sections (Old Testament - Apocrypha - New Testament) each subdivided by the Books (Genesis ... Revelation). *c*.2000 quotations, each identified by verse-numbers in the Authorized Version. Keyword index, p.371-415. *Class No: 22(082.2)*

[478]

SPEAKE, J. **Biblical quotations.** New York, Facts on File, 1983. 203p. $22.95. ISBN: 0871962411.

Arranged by the books of the Old and New Testaments and the Apocrypha, and employing the text of the King James Version of 1611, except for the Book of Psalms, which employs Coverdale's translation. '... may be regarded more as a highly selective miniconcordance ...' '... a very useful addition to any reference collection'. (*RQ*, v.24(1), Fall 1984, p.99). *Class No:* 22(082.2)

[479]

—VICHAS, B.P. Annotated handbook of biblical quotations, verses and parables. Englewood Cliffs, N.J., Prentice-Hall, 1986. xviii,411p. $29.95. ISBN: 0130378704.

Cites *c.*1600 verses, grouped in 200 contemporary topics, reflecting a conservative point of view. Extensive cross-references. Does not claim to be a theological work or a concordance. *Class No:* 22(082.2)

Gazetteers

[480]

ROWLEY, H.H. **Dictionary of Bible place names.** London, Oliphants, 1970. [vii],173p. maps.

About 2000 concise entries for every place name mentioned in the Revised Standard Version, including the Apocrypha. States meaning of place name and modern name (if any), plus Biblical references. 8p. of black-and-white maps. *Class No:* 22(083.86)

Maps & Atlases

[481]

GROLLENBERG, L.H. **Atlas of the Bible.** Reid, J.M.H. *and* Rowley, H.H., *trans. and eds.* London, Nelson, 1956. 166p. illus., maps.

First published as *Atlas van den Bibjel* (Amsterdam, 1954).

Contains 37 excellent maps in colour and 408 photogravure illus. The three media (maps, photographs & text) are independent. The illus., which include aerial views, cover ancient monuments and sites, landscapes and localities in the Holy Land. 26-page index of places and persons aims 'to catalogue and describe all the "Geographical indications" provided by the Bible ... Non-Biblical place-names and personal names are included where their mention on the maps or in the text appear to require further elucidation'. Index entries give etymology, map reference and Biblical reference. 'Absolutely essential to any intelligent study of the Bible ...' (*Times literary supplement*, no.2859, 14 December 1956, p.753). Page size: 35 x 26cm. *Class No:* 22(084.3)

[482]

—GROLLENBERG, L.H. **Penguin shorter atlas of the Bible.** Hudland, M.F., *trans.* Harmondsworth, Mddx., Penguin Books, 1978. 284p. illus., maps. £4.50. ISBN: 0140510567.

A popular edition of the atlas, in smaller format. Over 100 plates and maps. Page size: 19.8 x 12.9cm. *Class No:* 22(084.3)

[483]

MAY, H.G., *with others, eds.* **Oxford Bible atlas.** Day, J., *ed.* 3rd ed. rev. New York & Toronto, Oxford University Press, 1984. 144p. illus. $18.95. £8.50. ISBN: 0191434523.

First published 1962. 3rd ed. revised by John Day.

The 26 coloured maps and plans well reflect archaeological advances since the earlier editions. Illus. are admirably diverse, and some new ones have been inserted in the 3rd ed. Also map colours changed or shadings intensified to provide greater clarity, but not redrawn. Textual changes have not involved resetting. Combined gazetteer and index. 'It can form an exciting and valuable starting point for more detailed study by the student of Bible history and of the supporting evidence for modern archaeological work' (*Geographical journal*, v.140, 1974, p.515, of the 2nd ed.). *Class No:* 22(084.3)

[484]

Reader's Digest atlas of the Bible: an illustrated guide to the Holy Land. Gardner, J.L., *ed.* Rev.ed. New York, Rand McNally, 1992. 239p. illus., maps. $39.95. ISBN: 0528835394.

Profusely illustrated, some in colour. A popular guide. Sections: 'In the beginning... ' - People of the Bible - Animals of the Bible - Plants of the Bible - Weights and measures, currency - History of the Bible ... Historical atlas of Biblical times, with text. Gazetteer of the Bible world. Chronology of Biblical times. Biblical citations. Detailed index. *Class No:* 22(084.3)

[485]

RHYMER, J. **Atlas of the Biblical world.** London, Hamlyn, 1983. 224p. illus. (incl. col.), maps, charts. £8.95. ISBN: 0600384861.

Aims to provide a bridge between the world of the Bible and the world of the present day and, as such, is not really an atlas - includes small maps but mainly text and pictures. In 5 parts: 1. God's chosen people - 2. The birth of Palestine - 3. The fall of the kingdom - 4. Rebuilding the Hebrew nation - 5. The origins of Christianity. Appendices include a chronology, a glossary (p.218-219), and an index (p.220-224). *Class No:* 22(084.3)

[486]

ROGERSON, J. **The New atlas of the Bible.** London, Macdonald; New York, Facts on File, 1985. 240p. 400 illus (300 col.). £14.95. $35. ISBN: 035610706x.

Arranged in 12 geographical sections (as opposed to the more usual historical orientation). Clear, detailed and colourful maps and also many aerial photographs, Gazetteer and index. '... collection of Biblical art is superfluous and picture captions include redundancies between picture captions and text ... On the whole, though, enthusiastically recommended' (*Wilson library bulletin*, November 1985, p.59). *Class No:* 22(084.3)

[487]

The Times atlas of the Bible. Pritchard, J.B., *ed.* London, Times Books, 1987; New York, Harper & Row, 1988. 254p. illus. maps. £25; $49.95. ISBN: 0723002959, UK; 0061818836, US.

Published in the US as *The Harper atlas of the Bible*.

Based on the latest archaeological research. Arranged chronologically: Old Testament (In the beginning - Emergence of Israel: patriarchal traditions - Between Genesis and Exodus: 400 years of Egyptian supremacy - From Egyptian bondage to settlement in Canaan - The institution of the monarchy - The imperial age of Solomon - The divided kingdom: Israel - The divided kingdom; Judah - Judah under Babylon); Inter-Testamental period (The Persian period - Judah in the Hellenistic era); New Testament (Palestine under the Romans - The Christian era). Chronology, p.15-23. People of the Bible, p.195-208. Gazetteer. Over 600 coloured maps and illustrations. '... a visually stunning and almost perfectly integrated work combining text, illustrations and maps with such clarity and scholarly weight as to make this a standard reference work ...' (*Bulletin of ABTPL*, v.2(2), June 1988). *Class No:* 22(084.3)

Histories

[488]

The Cambridge history of the Bible. new ed. Cambridge, Cambridge University Press, 1963-70. 3v. £27.50 each vol,; £50 the set. ISBN: 0521099730, v.1; 0521290171, v.2; 0521290163, v.3; 052129018x, Set.

First published 1963-70 in 3v.

Contents: V.1. *From the beginnings to Jerome* (xv,649p. illus.); v.2 *The West, from the Fathers to the Reformation* (x,566p. 48 illus.); v.3. *The West, from the Reformation to the present day* (x,590p.). 'Deals with the history of the Bible in the West, that is, in Western Europe and America' (*Preface* to 1st ed.), *i.e.*, 'accounts of the texts and versions of the Bible used in the West, of its multiplication of manuscripts and exegesis; and of its place in the life of Western Church'. *Class No:* 22(091)

Biographies

[489]

CALVOCORESSI, P. **Who's who in the Bible.** New York, Viking, 1987. 269p. maps. $19.95. £10.95. ISBN: 0670811882.

Biographies of *c.*450 major and minor Biblical characters (Aaron ... Zophar) from Old and New Testaments and Apocrypha with, in addition lists of art and literature where these characters have appeared. Cross-references and bibliographical references for most entries. Genealogical appendix (p.241-247). Index (mainly names) (p.249-269). '... not an essential reference work, but it may appeal to browsers searching for an entertaining perspective on Bible figures' (*Reference books bulletin*, 1 April 1988, p.1327). *Class No:* 22(092)

[490]

The Complete who's who in the Bible. Gardner, P., *ed.* London, Marshall Pickering, 1995 xiii,688p. ISBN: 0551025751.

Contains over 2,000 entries by a team of evangelical scholars; it is based on the NIV translation of the Bible. Major characters, such as Moses, David and Mary, are treated in extended essays. There are also thematic entries on topics such as Angels, the Covenant, Theophanies, etc. *Class No:* 22(092)

[491]

LOCKYER, H. **All the men of the Bible:** a portrait gallery and reference library of more than 3000 Biblical characters. Grand Rapids, MI., Zondervan, 1983. 381p. $14.95. ISBN: 031028080x.

First published in London by Pickering & Inglis, 1958.

Most entries are short; longer ones appear to be somewhat imaginatively extended. Occasionally supplements Hastings' *Dictionary of the Bible. Class No:* 22(092)

[492]

—LOCKYER, H. **All the women of the Bible.** Grand Rapids, MI., Zondervan, 1983. 321p. $12.95; £10.25. ISBN: 0310281504.

Supersedes Edith Deen's *All the women of the Bible* (1959). Complementary to the above. *Class No:* 22(092)

Natural History

[493]

MOLLER-CHRISTENSEN, V. *and* JORGENSEN, K.E.J. **Encyclopedia of Bible creatures.** Heinecken, M.T., *ed.* Philadelphia, Pa., Fortress Press, 1965. 302p. illus.

Translated from the Danish by Carol Wilde.

Gives scientific and popular names, dictionary definition, Greek and Hebrew names, and habitat of every known creature in the Bible; explanations of Bible references. Editor has added footnotes based on the Revised Standard Version and current Biblical research. 3 indexes: Latin and common names; Biblical names and places; Scriptural index. *Class No:* 22:59

[494]

—MOLDENKE, H.N. *and* MOLDENKE, A.L. **Plants of the Bible.** Waltham, Mass., Chronica Botanica, 1952 (reprinted Dover, 1986). xix,328p. illus., facsims. $8.95. ISBN: 0486250695.

Includes a bibliography, p.259-74. *Class No:* 22:59

[495]

ZOHARY, M. **Plants of the Bible:** a complete handbook to all the plants, with 200 full-colour plates taken in the natural habitat. Cambridge, Cambridge University Press, 1982. 224p. illus.(col.), maps. £12.95. ISBN: 0521249260.

Bibliography, p.211-212. Index. *Class No:* 22:59

Introductions

[496]

MANSON, T.W. **A Companion to the Bible.** Rowley, H.H., *ed.* New ed. Edinburgh, T. & T. Clark Ltd., 1963. xii, 628p. 6 maps. £9.95. ISBN: 0567021971.

First published in 1959.

Main parts: 1. The book (chapters 1-7) - 2. The land and its people (8-11) - 3. The religion of the Bible (12-18). Each chapter has an appended bibliography. Six folding maps and plans. Four indexes: Scripture references; authors; general; Latin, Greek and Oriental works. Retains the original high level of scholarship. 'Invaluable for systematic accounts of the revelation against the historical and geographical background'. (*British book news*, no.283, March 1964, p.176). *Class No:* 22.01

Dictionaries

[497]

HAYES, J.H., *ed.* **Dictionary of biblical interpretation.** Nashville, TN, Abingdon, 1999. 2v. (xlix,653p.,xxxii,675p. $195. ISBN: 0687055318.

Covers the history of interpretation of the Christian Bible, gives biographies of many Bible interpreters, and examines interpretative methods and movements. *Class No:* 22.01(038)

Versions

[498]

The New Jerusalem Bible: standard edition. London, Darton, Longman & Todd; New York, Doubleday & Company, 1985. xv,2108p. 7 maps, plus index to maps 8p.). £25. ISBN: 0232516502.

First published 1966. This ed. is translation of *Bible de Jerusalem*, 1973 revision, translated by the staff of the École Biblique, Jerusalem, the originators.

One-volume Bible, together with the means of studying it. 'A comprehensive revision of text, notes and other materials; (Dust jacket). Old and New Testaments are followed by supplementary tables - Chronological table; Geneological table; Calendar; Table of measures and money; Alphabetical table of the major footnotes; Index of persons; Index of original collaborators. Cross-references. On Indian paper. *Class No:* 22.014

Prophecies

[499]

PAYNE, J.B. **Encyclopedia of Biblical prophecy:** the complete guide to Scriptural predictions and their fulfillment. New York, Harper & Row, 1973 (Reprinted Grand Rapids, Mich., Baker Books, 1980). xxv, 753p. $21.95. ISBN: 0801070511.

Lengthy introduction, p.3-150 (356 footnotes). Entries are arranged in the order of the books of Old and New Testaments. Summaries are appended. Bibliography, p.685-92. 5 indexes, including 1. 'The Biblical predictions'; 3. 'subjects'. Evangelical Christian viewpoint. *Class No:* 22.016

Concordances

[500]

A Concordance to the Apocrypha/Deuterocanonical books of the Revised Standard Version, derived from the Bible Data Bank of the Centre Informatique et Bible (Abbey of Maredsous). New York, Eerdmans, 1983. 479p. $35. ISBN: 0802823122.

Includes all the words in the 1977 edition of the Revised Standard Version Apocrypha, except 77 words of very high frequency, along with the exact frequency count. All different forms of the same word are grouped in one entry (*e.g.* men, man, etc., under Man). Easy-to-read double column pages. 'Clearly a must for any library aspiring to maintain a decent collection in Biblical studies' (*Choice*, v.21(1), September 1983, p.60). *Class No:* 22.03

[501]

CRUDEN, A.A. **A Complete concordance to the Old and New Testament ... with ... a concordance to the Apocrypha.** 3rd ed. London, Warne, 1769 (frequently reprinted: *e.g.* Lutterworth Press. £25; Warne. £16.95; Zondervan. $10.95. 944¹p. ISBN: 0718802055, UK; 0723202605, UK; 0310229219, US.

First published 1737, forming the basis for modern concordances.

*c.*250,000 entries in all, A-Z by English word (Authorized Version), with appendices of proper names and the Apocrypha concordance. 'Cruden's work is accurate and full, and later concordances only supersede him by combining an English with a Greek and Hebrew concordance' (*Encyclopaedia Britannica*, 11th ed., v.6, p.832). Particularly valuable for inclusion of the Apocrypha. *Class No:* 22.03

[502]

GOODRICK, E.W. *and* KOHLENBERGER, J.P. **The NIV complete concordance.** Grand Rapids, MI., Zondervan, 1981. 1056p. $29.95. ISBN: 0310436508.

This concordance of the New International Version of the Bible has 250,000 entries, the index words arranged in dictionary format and in bold type. Cross-references are given in parentheses. The contexts of the key words are comparatively long and useful. Small print, but easy to read. *Class No:* 22.03

[503]

JOY, C.R., *comp.* **Harper's topical concordance.** Rev. & enl. ed., 1961 (Reprinted 1976). New York, Harper & Row, 1976. 640p. $10.95. ISBN: 0060642297.

First published as *Harper's topical concordance* (1940); reprinted as *A concordance of subjects* (London, Black, 1952); and *Lutterworth's topical concordance* (2nd ed. London, Lutterworth, 1961).

A new type of Bible concordance, enabling texts and quotations to be easily found. Verses are arranged under 2775 topics, and a fairly complete list of texts specifically connected with these topics is given. Appended list of cross-references. *Class No:* 22.03

[504]

KOHLENBERGER, J.R. **The NRSV concordance unabridged** including the apocryphal/deuterocanonical books. Grand Rapids, Mich., Zondervan, 1991 xiv,1483p. ISBN: 0310539102.

Covers all 84 books of the New Revised Standard Version of the Bible (published 1990), including the deuterocanonical books. All 906,953 words of the NRSV are indexed and arranged in dictionary format in bold type. At the back of the book are useful indexes, including a topical index. *Class No:* 22.03

[505]

STRONG, J. **Abingdon's Strong's exhaustive concordance of the Bible,** with exclusive key-word comparison: words of Jesus in red. Nashville, Tenn., Abingdon Press; London, S.P.C.K., 1986 (44th printing of the 1894 edition). 2336p. $26.95. £26.95. ISBN: 0687400325.

Originally published by Hodder in London, 1894., with various printings since then.

About 400,000 entries. Contains key-words and phrases from the Authorized Version, set out for comparison with the five leading translations. Easy-to-read print. The most complete Bible concordance. *Class No:* 22.03

[506]

THOMPSON, N.W. *and* STOCK, R. **Complete concordance to the Bible (Douay Version).** 4th rev. and enl. ed. St. Louis, Mo., Herder, 1945. 2, [1], 1914p.

First published 1942.

Uses the text of the Roman Catholic Bible, which differs in several ways from the AV, in being translated from the Latin Vulgate. The Old Testament in this version has 46 books, as opposed to 39 in the AV, although the additional books appear in the Protestant Apocrypha. *Class No:* 22.03

[507]

WHITAKER, R.E., *comp.* **The Eerdmans analytical concordance to the Revised Standard Version of the Bible.** New York, Wm. B. Eerdmans Publishing Co., 1988. 1548p. $49.95. ISBN: 080282403x.

Claims to be the only analytical concordance to the RSV of the entire Bible and the Apocrypha. Entries are listed in dictionary form (A-Z), followed by every context in which any form of the word is found, and all forms of the word are under the same heading. All uses of each word are given in one list, not separated by language (Hebrew, Greek, Latin, etc.). Proper names and numbers are listed separately. Indexes of all Hebrew, Aramaic, Latin and Greek words translated in the RSV, with their English equivalents. Highly recommended by *Choice* (v.26(5), January 1989, p.790). *Class No:* 22.03

[508]

YOUNG, R. **Young's analytical concordance to the Bible** including the universal subject guide to the Bible, index-lexicons to the Old and New Testaments. Newly rev. and corrected. Nashville, Tenn., T. Nelson, c1982. [19],1090,93,23,219p. ISBN: 0840749716.

Based on the Authorised Version. Includes index lexicon to the Old and New Testaments, and a complete list of Scripture proper names, etc. *Class No:* 22.03

Commentaries

[509]

The Abingdon Bible commentary. Eiselen, F.C., *ed. and others.* London, Epworth Press, 1932. (Nashville, Tenn., Abingdon Press; London, S.P.C.K., 1981. Doubleday, $17.95). xvi, 1452p. ISBN: 0385148771, US.

First published 1929 by Abingdon Press.

Probably the best of the single-volume Bible commentaries. 66 scholarly contributors. Chapter-by-chapter commentary on the various books, plus more general treatment. Includes bibliogaphies. *Class No:* 22.07

[510]

—FULLER, R.C., *ed.* **A New Catholic commentary on Holy Scripture.** Rev. & updated ed. London, Nelson, 1981. xix, 1363p. £50. ISBN: 0840750170.

First published in 1953 as *A Catholic commentary on Holy Scripture.*

It has 64 contributors and reflects international scholarship. Commentary is paragraph by paragraph, according to the sense, rather than verse by verse. Includes maps and an index *Class No:* 22.07

[511]

—The New Jerome Biblical commentary. Poole, Dorset, Cassell; Englewood Cliffs, Prentice-Hall, 1989. 1478p. £60. $69.95. ISBN: 0225665883, UK; 0136149340, US.

First published in 1968 as *The Jerome Biblical commentary.*

The work of Roman Catholic scholars. In addition to book-by-book commentary, topical articles take up about a third of the text, many of which present other points of view in addition to the RC interpretation. Bibliographies are appended to each chapter and for major divisions within chapters. Analytical index. *Class No:* 22.07

[512]

—Peake's commentary on the Bible. Black, M. *and* Rowley, H.H., *eds.* New ed. London, Nelson, 1962. xv, 1162p. illus., maps. $39.95. ISBN: 0840750196.

First published 1919.

Based on the Revised Standard Version, with 62 distinguished contributors; bibliographies; detailed index. *Class No:* 22.07

[513]

The Cambridge Bible commentary on the New English Bible. London, Cambridge University Press, 1963-1977.

Old Testament (including *Making of the Old Testament* (1972), *Old Testament illustrations* (1971) and *Understanding the Old Testament* (1971-77. 31v.).

Apocrypha (1972-74. 4v.).

New Testament (including *New Testament illustrations* (1966) and *Understanding the New Testament* (1965). (1963-67. 17v.).

Full text of the New English Bible, with simple and brief commentary, dispensing with Hebrew or Greek words and strings of biblical references. Aimed at school user. *Class No:* 22.07

[514]

Harper's Bible commentary. Mays, J.L., *ed.* New York, Harper & Row, 1988. xviii,1328p. illus. (mostly coloured). $37.95. ISBN: 0060655410.

Introductory matter (p.1-84) is followed by the Books of the Bible, Genesis ... Revelations, including the Apocrypha, each with an introduction, commentary and bibliography. 4p. index precedes an appendix of coloured maps (16p.) *c.*70 contributors. *Class No:* 22.07

[515]

International critical commentary on the Holy Scriptures. Driver, S.R., *ed. and others.* 2nd ed. Edinburgh, T. & T. Clark Ltd., 1930 (1963 reprint). 43v. in 46.

A scholarly series of commentaries on individual books of the Bible, contributed by specialists and bringing modern research and criticism to bear on questions of authorship, etc. Each volume, which is complete in itself, carries a bibliography.

The series is being extended and renewed. Under the editorship of Professors J.A. Emerton, C.E.B. Cranfield, and the editor-elect, G.N. Stanton, commentaries on books of the Bible which have not appeared in the I.C.C. before are now in preparation and new editions of all existing volumes are being commissioned. (T. & T. Clark Ltd., 1989). *Class No:* 22.07

[516]

The Interpreter's Bible: the Holy Scriptures in the King James and Revised Standard Versions, with general articles and introduction, exegesis, exposition for each book of the Bible. Harmon, N.B., *ed.* New York, Abingdon-Cokesbury Press, 1952-57. (Reprinted by Abingdon Press, 1984). Originally in 12 vols. Reprint in 8 vols. £45 the set; £5.95 each vol. ISBN: 0687192315, set.

V.1. The Pentateuch ... - 2. Old Testament history ... - 3. Wisdom, literature and poetry - 4. The major prophets - 5. The minor prophets and the Apocrypha ... 6. The Gospels - 7. Acts and Paul's letters ... - 8. Revelation and the general Epistles. Contributors (including eminent British theologians and Biblical scholars) represent almost every branch of the Christian Church; consulting editors are from larger Protestant groups. Each page has text of A.V. and R.S.V. in parallel columns, with exegesis and exposition below. Aimed at the general reader, teacher and preacher of the Bible. Indispensible, although some volumes are now dated. *Class No:* 22.07

[517]

—The Interpreter's one-volume commentary on the Bible, including all the books of the Old and New Testament and the Apocrypha, together with forty-three general articles. Layamon, C.M., *ed.* Nashville, Tenn., Abingdon Press, 1983. 1412p. illus., diagrs., 16 maps. $24.95; £30. ISBN: 0687192994.

First published 1971.

Provides a verse-by-verse commentary aimed at layman and teacher. The work of *c.*70 contributors (mostly American; Protestant, Catholic and Jewish). Analytical subject index. *Class No:* 22.07

Bible. Old Testament

Bibliographies

[518]

FITZMEYER, J.A. **The Dead Sea Scrolls:** major publications and tools for study. Rev. ed. Atlanta, Ga, Scholars Press, 1990. xvi,246p. ISBN: 155540510x.

Records lists of surveys, bibliographies of scrolls, and aids *e.g.* dictionaries and concordances. *Class No:* 222(01)

Encyclopaedias

[519]

BOTTERWECK, G.J. *and* RINGGREN, H., *eds.* **Theologisches Wörterbuch zum Alten Testament.** Stuttgart, Kohlhammer, 1970- ,v.1-. To be in 12v. (10v. published so far).

Will provide for the Old Testament a counterpart to Kittel's Theologisches Wörterbuch zum Neuen Testament (*q.v.,*).

V.1-3: A-HARAS. V.2 (xc p., 574 cols.) has *c.*130 entries for Hebrew words, by 64 contributors. Appended list of German catchwords, bibliography of sources, and journal, etc. sources. *Class No:* 222(031)

[520]

—BOTTERWECK, G.J. *and* RINGGREN, H., *eds*. Theological dictionary of the Old Testament. Grand Rapids, Mich., Eerdmans; London, SCM Press, 1974-.v.1-. To be in 12v. (10v. published so far). ISBN: 0802823300.

Translated from the German edition (above) by J.T. Willis.

The intention is to concentrate on meaning, starting from narrower everyday senses of the words and building to an understanding of theologically significant concepts. Articles are by international scholars of various traditions. Entries are arranged under Hebrew terms, in order of the Hebrew alphabet *Class No:* 222(031)

Reviews & Abstracts

[521]

Old Testament abstracts. Cambridge, Mass., Weston School of Theology, 1978-. 3pa. ISSN: 03648591.

Abstracts of books and also articles from about 350 Catholic, Protestant and Jewish periodicals. V.22(3), October 1999 has *c*.500 abstracts and also over 40 pages of book notices and 'books received'. Author index; index of scripture texts; index of words in Hebrew, etc.; and List of periodicals abstracted. Intended for the lay persons as well as the scholar. *Class No:* 222(048)

Biographies

[522]

COMAY, J. Who's who in the Old Testament, together with the Apocrypha. London, Weidenfeld & Nicolson, 1971. 448p. illus. £8.95. ISBN: 0297004093.

Over 3,000 entries, covering all characters in the O.T. and Apocrypha - the history of the Jewish people up to the end of the First Book of Maccabees, *i.e.,* 135 B.C. The chief feature - the profusion and variety of illustrations. (450 black-and-white, plus 16 in colour). Favourably reviewed, with minor reservations, in T.L.S., 25 February, 1972. p.225. *Class No:* 222(092)

Bible. New Testament

Bibliographies

[523]

ELLIOTT, J.K. A Bibliography of Greek New Testament manuscripts. Cambridge, Cambridge University Press, 1989. 168p. £30. (*Society for New Testament Studies monograph series v.62.*) ISBN: 052135479x.

Includes references to every recognised Greek New Testament manuscript for which there exists an *editio princeps*, printed editions, facsimiles, photographic plates, collations, and major studies, *c*.5000 in all. Intended to assist those who wish to investigate the readings in a manuscript by directing them to primary sources. *Class No:* 225(01)

[524]

FRANCE, R.T., *ed*. A Bibliographical guide to New Testament research. 3rd ed. Sheffield, Journal for the Study of the Old Testament/JSOT Press, 1979. 56p. £2.25. ISBN: 0905774191.

First published in 1968 by the Tyndale Fellowship for Biblical Research.

Briefly annotated entries in 27 sections (1. Library facilities - 2. Bibliographical aids - 3. Periodicals - 4. Texts of the New Testament ... 10. Dictionaries and encyclopaedias ... 14. New Testament archaeology ... 24. Judaism and Rabbinical literature - 25. Early Christian and Gnostic literature ... 27. Modern languages. *Class No:* 225(01)

[525]

HULTGREN, A.J., *comp*. New Testament Christology: a critical assessment and annotated bibliography. Westport, CT., Greenwood Press, 1988. 485p. $65. (*Bibliographies and indexes in religious studies, 12.*) ISBN: 0313251886.

The introductory critical assessment is followed by the bibliography of 1917 items, arranged in 4 sections (Orientation and Christological foundations; Christological titles; Christologies of New Testament writers; Christological themes), each section subdivided and arranged A-Z by author within each subdivision. Includes books and periodical articles. The clear and concise annotations are descriptive rather than evaluative. Material included mainly published from the 1950s onwards. Author, editor and compiler index; title index; and subject index. 'The strength and particular value of this bibliography is that Hultgren keeps his focus on the doctrine of Christology and does not introduce extraneous material ...' (*Choice,*v.26(9), May 1989, p.1494). *Class No:* 225(01)

[526]

WAGNER, G. An Exegetical bibliography of the New Testament. Macon, GA., Mercer University, 1983. 667p. $35. ISBN: 0865540136.

A bibliography of critical books and journal articles on the Gospels of Matthew and Mark, arranged by verse of scripture. Includes foreign language works. No subject or author indexes. 'This work would nicely supplement any theological or university religion reference section' (*Choice,* v.21(1), September 1983, p.60). *Class No:* 225(01)

Encyclopaedias

[527]

BALZ, H. Exegetical dictionary of the New Testament. Schneider, G., *eds*. Grand Rapids, Mich., Eerdmans Publishing, 1990. ISBN: 0802824099.

3v.

Attempts to provide definitions of every significant word in the New Testament. Over 100 contributors, primarily from Germany, Austria and Switzerland. Arranged A-Z by Greek word, with transliteration and English translation. For major concepts, a bibliography of scholarly references. V.3 includes an index of English keywords. *Theological dictionary of the New Testament* (Eerdman, 1964-76) is more comprehensive, but is more dated and less accessible to readers without Greek. *Class No:* 225(031)

[528]

KITTEL, G. *and* FRIEDRICH, G., *eds*. Theologisches Wörterbuch zum Neuen Testament. Stuttgart, Kohlhammer, 1932-79. 10v.

V.1-9: ALPHA-OMEGA, v.10: Index & literature supplement (1978-79). An important work, planned by a distinguished Rabbinist with special collaborators, on a scale comparable with the new Liddell and Scott. It defines specific meanings which Greek terms have come to possess within Christian thought as a whole, and many articles amount to complete monographs. *Class No:* 225(031)

[529]

—Theological dictionary of the New Testament. Bromiley, G.W., *ed*. Grand Rapids, Mich., Eerdmans; Exeter, Devon, Paternoster Press, 1964-77. 10v. $399.50. ISBN: 0802823246.

Fully authorized English translation of G. Kittel's *Theologisches Wörterbuch zum Neuen Testament* (above) 'Indispensable for those seeking to do depth study in New Testament literature' (*Choice,* v.10(1), March 1973, p.62).

A one-volume abridgement, by G.W. Bromiley has been published by Paternoster Press (1985. £44.95. xxxvi,1356p.). *Class No:* 225(031)

Dictionaries

[530]

BROWN, C. The New international dictionary of New Testament theology. Exeter, Devon, Paternoster Press, 1975-86. 4v. & addenda. v.1: £24.95; v.2: £26.95; v.3: £39.95; v.4: £29.95; Addenda: £0.80. ISBN: 085364425x, v.1; 0853644268, v.2; 0853641803, v.3; 0853644284, v.4; 0853643601, Addenda.

Translated, with additions and revisions, from the German *Theologisches Begriffslexikon zum neuen Testament*. edited by Luther Coenen and others.

V.1 has 88 contributors, 'Bishop, Presbyter, Elder' (p.188-201), with Greek word boxed, has 2/3 column of bibliography. 'Word' (v.3, p.1081-1146) has 3p. of bibliography. Cross-references. Index of Hebrew and Aramaic words; index of Greek words; general index. Protestant standpoint. 'Expressly theologian in intension' (*Introduction,* v.1). *Class No:* 225(038)

Reviews & Abstracts

[531]

New Testament abstracts: a record of current literature. 1956-. v.10. no.1-. 3pa. Cambridge, Mass., Weston School of Theology, in co-operation with The Catholic Biblical Association of America, 1956-. ISSN: 00286877.

Each issue has *c*.750 concise and readable signed, 150-word abstracts of articles from more than 200 periodicals in ten languages. Sections: New Testament general - Gospels - Acts - Epistles - Revelation - Biblical theology - New Testament world. 'Book notices' is a *c*.50-page list of recent publications with short descriptions of contents, and is followed by a short list of 'Additional books received'. Annual indexes to principal Scriptural texts; authors; 'Book notices'. Annual list of journals abstracted. A cumulative index to v.1-15 (1956-11970) has been issued. *Class No:* 225(048)

[532]

—Zeitschrift für die neutestamentliche Wissenschaft. Berlin, Töpelmann (later Walter de Gruyter und Co), 1900- 2pa. $86pa. ISSN: 00442615.

Has a systematically arranged bibliography of periodical articles ('Zeitschrift - Bibliographie'), citing *c*.50 journals in each issue. *Class No:* 225(01)

Histories

[533]
FINEGAN, J. **The Archaeology of the New Testament:** the Mediterranean world of the early Christian Apostles. Boulder, Col., Westview Press; London, Croom Helm, 1981. xxxii,250p. illus., 13 maps, 22 plans. £19.95.

Alphabetical list of ancient sources (p.xxi-xxx) precedes the 8 chapters: 1. Sources - 2. Chronological history - 3. Beginnings... 8. In Rome; which trace the 15,000 mile travels of Paul. Lavishly illustrated with photographs of archaeological sites and museum artifices, plus maps and site places. Notes, p.235-244. Index of Biblical references, p.245-246. General index, p.247-250. Companion volume to the author's *The archaeology of the New Testament: the life of Jesus and the beginnings of the early Church* (Princeton University Press, 1972). *Class No:* 225(091)

Biographies

[534]
BROWNRIGG, R. **Who's who in the New Testament.** London, Weidenfeld & Nicolson, 1971. 448p. illus., facsims.

Companion volume to Joan Comay's *Who's who in the Old Testament, together with the Apocrypha* and, similarly, noted for its profusion and variety of illus. Favourably reviewed, with minor reservations, in *T.L.S.,* 25 February 1972, p.225. *Class No:* 225(092)

Concordances

[535]
BULLINGER, E.W. **A Critical lexicon and concordance to the English and Greek New Testament,** together with an index of Greek words, and several appendices. 9th ed. London, Bagster, Grand Rapids, MI., Zondervan, 1975. 1040p. £10.95; $30.95. ISBN: 0851501222, UK; 0310203104, US.

First published 1877.

Gives every word in alphabetical order, and under each the Greek word or words so translated, with variants; thus a Greek word with its literal and derivative meanings may be found for every word in the English N.T. The index is of Greek words in A-Z order, with the English translation following. A helpful and handy work. *Class No:* 225.03

[536]
—ARNDT, W.F. *and* GINGRICH, F.W. **A Greek-English lexikon of the New Testament and other early Christian literature.** 2nd ed. Chicago University Press, 1979. xl,900p. $47.50.

A translation and adaptation of Walter Bauer's *Griechisch-deutsches Wörterbuch zu den Schriften des Neuen Testaments* ... (5th rev. ed. 1981 reprint. $43.20. De Gruyter. ISBN 3110020734). The English work was first published by Oxford University Press in 1964.

A comparable work to the above, but with wider scope. 'The results cannot be praised too highly' (*Heythrop journal*, July, 1980, p.329). A condensed version is F.W. Gingrich's *Shorter lexicon of the Greek New Testament* (Chicago, University of Chicago Press, 1965, 304p.). *Class No:* 225.03

[537]
GORMAN, G.E. **'Concordances for Biblical studies'.** In *Bulletin of ABTAPL,* no. 28, November 1983, p.12-16.

Introduction is followed by a bibliographical list of 7 concordances (General - Latin - Hebrew - Greek - English). *Class No:* 225.03

[538]
MORRISON, C. **An Analytical concordance to the Revised Standard Version of the New Testament.** Philadelphia, Pa., 1979. xxv, 770p. $19.95. ISBN: 0664207731.

About 100,000 entries, 'Based on an analysis of the RSV New Testament that relates the RSV English to the original Greek' (*Explanatory notes*). Omits the most common Greek words in the New Testament for 'the', 'and', 'self', etc. 'Index-lexicon' (p.661-754) is an index to the analytical concordance and a lexicon of New Testament Greek. 2 appendices (1. Notes on the analysis of RSV New Testament). 'Will be an important tool for New Testament studies' (*Library journal*, v.104, no.14, August 1979, p.1551-2). *Class No:* 225.03

[539]
MOULTON, W.F. *and* GEDEN, A.S., *eds.* **A Concordance to the Greek Testament.** 5th ed. Edinburgh, T. & T. Clark Ltd., New York, Attic Press, 1978. 1120p. £28.95; $59.95. ISBN: 056701021x.

First published 1897.

The standard and complete concordance, following the text of Westcott and Hort, but equally available for Tischendorf and the 'revisers' text. Marginal readings are included in all cases, and Hebrew text is given beneath the Greek in all direct quotations from the Old Testament. *Class No:* 225.03

Bible. New Testament. Acts of the Apostles

[540]
MATTILL, A.J. *and* MATTILL, M.B. **A Classified bibliography of literature on the Acts of the Apostles.** Leiden, E.J. Brill, 1966. xviii, 513p. Gld.97. (*New Testament tools and studies, v.7.*) ISBN: 9004015531.

6646 numbered items, drawn from *c.*200 journals. 9 main sections: 1. Bibliographical studies - 2. General studies - 3. Textual studies - 4. Philological studies - 5. Literary studies - 6. Form-critical studies - 7. Historical studies (p.181-265) - 8. Theological studies - 9. Exegetical studies of individual passages. Entries date from the period of the Church Fathers up to 1961. Index of authors ('Anonymous' at end) only. A.J. Mattill was Professor of New Testament Language and Literature, Winebrenner Theological Seminary. *Class No:* 226.6

Bible. Apocrypha

[541]
CHARLES, R.H., *ed.* **The Apocrypha and Pseudepigrapha of the Old Testament in English** ..., edited, in conjunction with many scholars, by R.H. Charles. Oxford, Clarendon Press, 1913, Reissued by Oxford University Press, 1963. 2v. (696 + 886p.). v.1: £50; v.2 £45. ISBN: 0198261551, v.1; 0198261527, v.2.

The most important collection in English of all the non-canonical Jewish literature from 200 B.C.-A.D.. 100. Each book is translated from the best critical text, with an introduction giving detailed textual and bibliographical information, plus critical and explanatory notes. General index in v.2 (*The Pseudepigrapha*). *Class No:* 229

[542]
CHARLESWORTH, J.H. **The New Testament Apocrypha and Pseudepigrapha:** a guide to publications, with excursuses on Apocalypses. Metuchen, NY, Scarecrow Press, 1987. 450p. $42.50; £31.85. (*ATLA bibliography series, no. 17.*) ISBN: 0810818450.

More than 5000 citations to the primary and secondary literature concerning the extracanonical writings, being a companion volume to Charlesworth's '*The Pseudepigrapha and modern research with a supplement*'. Arranged in five broad sections: General studies (562 citations); apocalyptic literature (77); apocryphical acts (84); canon (168); agrapha, fragments of unknown works (284), followed by a list of citations under names of 99 major writings or cycles of writings. Entries arranged A-Z giving basic information, with occasional brief annotations. 3 introductory chapters report research and give overviews. Author index. '... an indispensible bibliography for anyone doing research on the Christian literature of the first few centuries of the Common Era' (*College and research libraries*, v.49(4), July 1988, p.344). *Class No:* 229

[543]
CHARLESWORTH, J.H. **The Pseudepigraphia and modern research, with a supplement.** Chicago, CA., Scholars Press, 1981. 344p. $13.95; £11.95. (*Society biblical literature septuagint and cognate studies.*) ISBN: 0891304404.

Covers writings related to Jewish intertestamental writings. *Class No:* 229

Christianity

Bibliographies of Bibliographies

[544]

KARI, Daven Michael. A Bibliography of sources in Christianity and the arts. Lewiston, New York, The Edwin Mellen Press, 1995 x,764p. (*Studies in Art and Religious Interpretation; 16.*) ISBN: 0773490949.

The interpretation of "Art" is wide. The Bibliography is divided into chapters (Aesthetics, Architecture, Cinema, etc), then into general bibliographies on the topic, "key works" in it, and finally in most cases into key works on the topic and religion (eg. "Wit and humour and religion"). Most entries are of a fairly recent date. There is an index of authors and one of titles. *Class No:* 230(009)

Bibliographies

[545]

BRANSON, M.L. The Reader's guide to the best evangelical books. New York, Harper & Row, 1982. 208p. $5.95. ISBN: 0060610468.

Focuses on books written by and for evangelicals within the parameters of classical orthodox thought. Arranged in subject areas: Popular treatments of the broad area of Christian life - Biblical materials - Church history - Christian ethics - The Church - The Christian in the world. Brief introductory essays to each area broadly evaluating the available literature, followed by the bibliographical entries with one-line annotations. Only includes books published between 1950 and 1980. '... invaluable for its intended audience' (*Library journal*, 13 September 1982, p.743). *Class No:* 230(01)

[546]

NICHOLS, A. 'Bibliography of current books on Christianity and politics, Christianity and the social order'. In *Bulletin of the Association of British Theological and Philosophical Libraries*, v.2(3), November 1988, p.8-10.

21 items listed with brief descriptive annotations. *Class No:* 230(01)

Encyclopaedias & Dictionaries

[547]

FAHLBUSCH, E., *et al*. Evangelisches Kirchenlexikon. [The Encyclopedia of Christianity.] Bromiley,, G.W, ed. Leiden, Brill, 1999. xxxviii, 893p. £50.00. ISBN: 9004113169.

Only the first volume (A-D) has so far appeared in the English version, translated from the third edition of the German. As its German title indicates, the perspective of the publication is specifically Protestant, though not overwhelmingly so. The majority of the contributors are German, and the otherwise excellent bibliographies show a strong German-language bias. The strength of this work lies in its theological articles, and in its articles on Christianity in each of 170 countries, compiled by David Barrett. One of its most striking weaknesses is the absence of biographies, even though more have been added to the English version than appeared in the German. This is clearly not intended as a quick refence work; on the other hand none of the articles (all signed) are of enormous length. *Class No:* 230(03)

Encyclopaedias

[548]

BARRETT, D.B., *ed*. World Christian encyclopedia: a comparative survey of churches and religions in the modern world, AD 1900-2000. Nairobi, Oxford University Press, 1982. [12], 1010p. illus., maps., tables. £110. ISBN: 0195724356.

Covers 20800 denominations. 14 parts (1. Status - 2. Chronology - 3. Methodology - 4. Culture - 5. Evangelization - 6. Codebook - 7. Survey (a survey of Christianity and religions in 223 countries, A-Z by country, p.131-771) - 8. Statistics - 9. Dictionary - 10. Bibliography (selective listing, p.839-861) - 11. Atlas - 12. Who's who - 13. Directory - 14. Indexes (polyglot glossary of religious terminology; names of countries in 6 languages; names of God in 900 languages; index of people and languages; Christian abbreviations, acronyms and initials; photographic index; standard and definitive locations index). *Class No:* 230(031)

[549]

COLLINS, J.J. *and* McGINN, B. *and* STEIN, S., *eds*. The Encyclopedia of apocalypticism. New York, Continuum Publishing, 1998. 3v. (1500p.) $285. £175. ISBN: 0826410871.

Covers Judaism, Christianity and Islam, with some coverage of Persian, Greek and Roman mythology. Vol.1 covers beginnings of apocalypticism in early Christian theology. Vol.2 discusses apocalyptic in medieval and renaissance literature. Vol.33 focuses on the influences of apocalypticism on modern thought, science, politics, art and popular culture. *Class No:* 230(031)

[550]

Encyclopedia of early Christianity. Ferguson, E., *and others, eds*. 2nd ed. New York, Garland, 1997. xxvii,1213p. illus. £125. (*Garland reference library of the humanities, 846.*) ISBN: 0819316631.

1245 entries by 167 scholars, covering persons, places, doctrines, practices, art, liturgy, heresies, and schisms of the first 600 years of Christianity. Entries vary in length from a few lines to c.4000 words. Cross-references. Bibliographies appended to most entries. *Class No:* 230(031)

Handbooks & Manuals

[551]

The Lion handbook of Christian belief. Organising editor: Robin Keeley. Tring, Herts., Lion Publishing; Sutherland, N.S.W., Albatross Books, 1982. 480p. 212 illus (15 col.), charts, diagr. £11.95; A$19.95. ISBN: 0856483214, UK; 0867604190, Australia.

Covers the whole sweep of Christian beliefs and their development down the centuries. Orthodox standpoint. 100 authors have contributed articles on the key beliefs. 6 parts: 1. How can we know? - 2. Jesus Christ - 3. God - 4. Creation: humanity and the world - 5. A new creation - 6. Christian belief in the making. Glossary (p.463-475). Detailed index (p.476-480). User-oriented and colourful presentation. *Class No:* 230(035)

[552]

NOLAN, M.L. *and* NOLAN, S. Christian pilgrimage in modern Western Europe. Chapel Hill, N.C., The University of North Carolina Press, 1989. xix,422p. illus., tables. $34.95. ISBN: 0807818143.

7 sections: Shrines of Western Europe - Pilgrimage in the European tradition - Periods of pilgrimage shrine formation - Holy persons: the subjects of devotion - Sacred objects: focal points for veneration - Wondrous events, miracles, and legends: original stories examined - Location and environment: shrines as holy places. Notes, p.339-380. Bibliography, p.381-402. Index, p.403-422. *Class No:* 230(035)

Dictionaries

[553]

The Blackwell encyclopedia of modern Christian thought. McGrath, A.E., *ed*. Oxford, Blackwells, 1993 xiii,701p. ISBN: 0631168966.

"Modern" is a somewhat vague term, though the editor defines it as from the Enlightenment onwards, roughly from 1700 to the present day. The entries are for the most part fairly long, some more central topics are given major essay treatment, occasionally by various hands. It is well cross-referenced and bibliographies are supplied. *Class No:* 230(038)

English

[554]

METFORD, J.C.J. Dictionary of Christian lore and legend. London, Thames & Hudson, 1983. 283p. illus. £12.50. ISBN: 0500110204.

Over 1700 articles spanning the whole field of Christian lore ('the learning and background knowledge which under-pins Christian culture') and legend ('the historical, traditional or symbolic content of Christianity without prejudging its veracity'). Entries vary in length from 2-3 lines to a column (*e.g.* 'Immaculate conception': 13 lines; 'Eden, Garden of': 16 lines; 'David, King': 37 lines). *Class No:* 230(038)=20

Reviews & Abstracts

[555]

ASSOCIATION OF BRITISH THEOLOGICAL AND PHILSOPHICAL LIBRARIES. Bulletin ... Birmingham Central Library, for the Association, 1956-66; New series, 1974- 3pa. £12pa; $20pa. ISSN: 0305781x.

A forum for professional exchange and development in the fields of theological and philosophical librarianship. Most issues include a review section (*i.e.* v.2(5), June 1997 has 4 reviews, p.20-24), and a list of significant web sites. *Class No:* 230(048)

[556]

Theologische Literaturzeitung. Monatsschrift für das gesamte Gebiet der Theologie und Religionswissenschaft. Berlin, Evangelische Verlagsanstalt GmbH, 1876-. Monthly. DM.198pa. ISSN: 00405671.

The leading Protestant Evangelical reviewing journal, with *Bibliographisches Beiblatt*, 1921 to 1942 (1922-43). 'Nearly indispensible'. (*Library trends*, v.15(3), January 1967, p.474). *Class No:* 230(048)

Quotations

[557]

CASTLE, T., *comp.* The Hodder book of Christian quotations. London, Hodder & Stoughton, 1982. [4], 293p.. £8.95. ISBN: 0340323396.

4115 quotations culled from a wide variety of sources, ancient and modern, English and American, Protestant and Catholic, by over 1000 authors. Grouped by 450 theme headings, A-Z (Abandonment ... Zeal), with several quotes under each heading. Each entry indicates author. Cross-references. Author index, p.267-293. *Class No:* 230(082.2)

[558]

CASTLE, T.C., *comp.* The New book of Christian quotations. New York, Crossroad, 1983. 272p. $10.95. ISBN: 08245005514.

4110 quotations by 1200 authors, arranged under 450 topics. 'See also' references. Lacks a keyword index. *Class No:* 230(082.2)

Histories

[559]

LATOURETTE, K.S. Christianity in a revolutionary age: a history of Christianity in the nineteenth and twentieth centuries. London, Eyre & Spottiswood, 1959-63. (Reprinted Greenwood Press, 1973). 5v. £144.50 the set. ISBN: 0837157005.

1: *The nineteenth century in Europe: background and the Roman Catholic phase* (xiv, 498p.); 2. *The nineteenth century in Europe: the Protestant and Eastern churches* [1], [1], 532p.); 3: *The nineteenth century outside Europe: the Americas, the Pacific, Asia and Africa* (viii, [1], 527p.); 4: *The twentieth century in Europe: the Roman Catholic, Protestant and Eastern churches* (viii, 568p.); 5: *The twentieth century outside Europe: the Americas, the Pacific, Asia and Africa; the emerging world Christian community* (viii, 568p.).

Discusses all aspects of Christianity throughout the world since 1815 - theology, organization, devotional life and influence on the social, political and education scene. Well documented (*e.g.* the chapter on Latin America in v.3 has 187 footnotes); each volume carries an annotated bibliography of *c.*17 pages of works cited more than once. Analytical index. *Class No:* 230(091)

[560]

LATOURETTE, K.S. A History of Christianity. New York, Harper & Row, 1975. 2v. (1552p.). $20 each volume. ISBN: 0060649526, v.1; 0060649534, v.2.

First published 1954 (xxviii, 1516p.).

62 chapters, each with a selected bibliography. Each volume has supplemented bibliography of books since 1950 (v.1, p.684-6; v.2, p.1507-14). 19 maps. Index to each volume. A tracing of the development of Christianity in the setting of human history. *Class No:* 230(091)

[561]

MANSCHRECK, C.L. History of Christianity in the world. 2nd ed. Englewood Cliffs, N.J., Prentice-Hall, 1985. viii,357p.illus. $38; £26.70. ISBN: 0133893545.

First published 1974.

21 chapters, arranged chronologically: 1. Presuppositions in the beginning of Christianity - 2. Conflict with Rome ... - 8. Eastern orthodoxy... 13. Reformation ... 18. The age of reason and piety ... 21. Retrenchment, outreach, reappraisal and uncertainty. General bibliography, p.336-344. Index, p.345-357. *Class No:* 230(091)

[562]

The Oxford illustrated history of Christianity. McManners, J., *ed.* Oxford, Oxford University Press, 1990. xi,726p. illus., maps. £25. ISBN: 0198229283.

19 chapters arranged in 3 parts: From the origins to 1800; Christianity since 1800; Christianity today and tomorrow. Contributions, by a team of 18 leading scholars, based on latest research. Further readings, p.667-685 (by chapter). Chronology, p.680-705. 150 illustrations, 32 colour plates, and 12 maps. Sources are given. Detailed analytical index, p.707-724. Editor was Regius Professor of Ecclesiastical History, Oxford University. *Class No:* 230(091)

Europe—Western

[563]

Religion and society in early modern Europe, 1500-1800. Greyerz, K. von, *and others.* London, George Allen & Unwin, for the German Historical Institute, 1985. x,281p. £35. ISBN: 0049400789.

17 chapters in 5 parts: 1. Religion as a cultural phenomenon - 2. The reform of popular culture and religion - 3. Religion and social control - 4. Religion and the community - 5. Historiography, sacred or profane?. Appendix: German, French and Italian works cited above available in English translation. 17 contributors. Many notes, including references, after each chapter. Index, p.275-281. *Class No:* 230(400)

England

[564]

DAVIES, H. Worship and theology in England. Grand Rapids, MI, Eerdmans, 1996. 3v. illus., facsims.

Bk.1 [pt.1]: *From Cranmer to Hooker, 1534-1603* - [pt.2]: *From Andrewes to Baxter, 1603-1690* - Bk.2 [pt.3]: *From Watts and Wesley to Maurice, 1690-1850* - [pt.4]: *From Newman to Martineau, 1850-1900* - Bk.3 [pt.5]: *The ecumenical century, 1900-1965.* - [pt.6]: *Crisis and creativity, 1965-present.* *Class No:* 230(420)

[565]

HASTINGS, A. A History of English Christianity, 1920-1985. London, SCM, 1991. xxix, 720p. ISBN: 0002152118.

42 chapters in 7 parts: I. 1920 and before - II. The 1920s - III. The 1930s - IV. 1939-1945 - V. 1945-1960 - VI. The 1960s - VII. 1970-1990. Includes many portraits of personalities. Notes (p.673-703) are mainly references and arranged in chapter order. Index (p.704-720) includes 'see' references. '... this finely printed, vigorously written, industrially researched, sensibly opinionated yet cosmically fair survey of a very complex and hard-to-judge phenomenon... ' (*Church times*, 3 October 1986, p.6). *Class No:* 230(420)

India

[566]

NEILL, S. A History of Christianity in India. Cambridge, Cambridge University Press, 1984-85. 2v. (xxi,583; xvii,578p.). £45 each vol. ISBN: 0521243513, v.1; 0521303761, v.2.

V.1 is subtitled *the beginnings to A.D. 1707*, v.2 *1707-1858.* Aims to be comprehensive, with 15 chapters in v.1 and 18 in v.2, all subdivided. Over 160 pages of notes, arranged by chapter, include a wealth of bibliographical detail of writings in many languages. Each volume has appendices, select bibliographies, and indexes. *Class No:* 230(540)

Africa

[567]

OFORI, P.E. Christianity in tropical Africa: a selective, annotated bibliography. Nendeln, Netherlands, KTO Press, 1977; Westport, CT., Greenwood Press, 1982. [5],461p. ISBN: 3262006027.

The 2nd vol. of a 3-volume work. V.1 was titled *Black African traditional religions and philosophy* and the 3rd vol. will be on Islamic religion in Africa.

2859 numbered, unannotated entries arranged by countries, A-Z, preceded by sections on reference and bibliographical works, general works, and Africa (general). Includes a list of journals and periodicals on Christianity in Africa. Name index, p.426-461. *Class No:* 230(6)

South Africa

[568]

CHICHESTER, D. *and* TOBLER, J., *eds.* Christianity in South Africa an annotated bibliography. Greenwood Press, 1997. 504p. £75.95. (*Bibliographies and indexes in religious studies 43.*.) ISBN: 0313304734.

Detailed reviews of 600+ works on the significance of Christianity in the development of South Africa. *Class No:* 230(680)

Theology

Bibliographies

[569]

Bibliography of British theological literature, 1850-1940. Hadidian, D.Y., comp. Pittsburgh, Pa., Barbour Library of Pittsburgh Theological Seminary, 1985. xxix, 453p. $34. (*Bibliographia Tripotamopolitana*.) ISBN: 0931222117.

18-page introduction to the British theological scene, followed by an A-Z list of c.3000 authors, subdivided by their main works, also arranged A-Z, with place and date of publication. Few annotations. Spacious layout to enable the addition of more titles. '... undoubtedly a major contribution to the librarianship of British theology but ... with more care ... could have produced an even more useful publication ...' (*Bulletin of ABTAPL*, no. 37, November 1986, p.8). *Class No:* 230.1(01)

[570]

BOLLIER, J.A. The Literature of theology: a guide for students and pastors. Philadelphia, Pa., Westminster Press, 1979. 208p. $5.95. ISBN: 0664242257.

Annotated entries for 543 reference tools, primarily English-language and recent (bibliographies, encyclopedias, dictionaries, indexing and abstracting services, guides and manuals, catalogues, commentaries and a few monographs with extensive bibliographies). General section (with biographies, almanacs, directories, yearbooks, quotation and poetry indexes, style manuals) is followed by coverage of Biblical studies, systematic theology, historical studies and practical theology. Primary coverage: the Judeo-Christian tradition, including both Protestant and Catholic approaches. 'The kind of book all Bible students and pastors should have in their personal libraries' (*Choice*, v.16(9), November 1979, p.1148). *Class No:* 230.1(01)

[571]

KEPPLE, R.J. Reference works for theological research: an annotated selective bibliographical guide. 2nd ed. Washington, University Press of America, 1981. xiv, 283p. $32.25. ISBN: 0819116793.

First published 1978.

About 800 entries, with concise, evaluative annotations. 39 chapters in 2 parts: 1. The general & general/religious/theological lists - 2. The subject area lists. Index to authors/editors and joint authors/editors, titles and alternative titles. A distinct drawback is the lack of a subject index. Some US slant, with special chapters on US bibliography and American church history. 'Because of the existance of James McCabe's useful work, *A critical guide to Catholic reference books* (2nd ed., 1980), this guide has been highly restrictive in including works about the Roman Catholic Church or produced under its auspices' (*General introduction*). 50% more entries than Bollier and generally more evaluative in its annotations. *Class No:* 230.1(01)

[572]

LONGSTAFF, T.R.W. and THOMAS, P.A., comps. and eds. The Synoptic problems: a bibliography, 1716-1988. Macon, GA., Mercer University, 1989. 235p. $35. (*New gospel studies, 4*.) ISBN: 0865543216.

A comprehensive bibliography covering the entire history of the so-called 'synoptic problems'. The author and title index includes a full bibliographical information as well as a printing and translation history of each item. Also a keyword index. *Class No:* 230.1(01)

[573]

Rediscovery of creation a bibliographical study of the Church's response to the environmental crisis. Sheldon, Joseph K., comp. Metuchen, N.J., Scarecrow Press, 1992 282p. $35.00 (*ATLA Bibliographic Series: 29*.) ISBN: 0810825392.

English language works only, and biased towards Protestant Theology. *Class No:* 230.1(01)

Encyclopaedias

[574]

Companion encyclopedia of theology. Byrne, P. and Houlden, L., eds. London, Routledge, 1995 xxiv,1092p. £85.00 ISBN: 0415064473.

48 state-of-the-art essays, by 47 well-known theologians, biblical scholars and historians. It is divided into six sections as follows: I The Bible; II The Tradition (largely an historical survey); III Philosophy; IV Spirituality; V Practical Theology (eight essays) and VI Christian Theology: Scene and Prospect, which discusses the contemporary theological landscape and makes suggestions as to possible future lines of development. Not an "encyclopedia" in the usual sense, the volume offers relatively in-depth surveys of major areas of research. Bibliographies, varying in size, are appended to the articles and there is a good index. *Class No:* 230.1(031)

[575]

O'DONNELL, C. Ecclesia a theological encyclopedia of the Church. Collegeville, Minn., The Liturgical Press, 1996 xxii,520p. $65.00 (*"A Michael Glazier book"*.) ISBN: 0814658326.

A remarkable achievement for a single author, this encyclopedia presents topics directly to do with the theory of the Christian Church, largely from a Roman Catholic perspective. There are particulary good bibliographies. *Class No:* 230.1(031)

[576]

Theologische Realenzyklopädie. [Encyclopedia of theology.] Krause, G. and Müller, G., eds. Series started in 1976 Berlin, Walter de Gruyter, 1977- ISBN: 311006944x.

Volume 29 (1998) covers Religionspsychologie to Samaritaner. This is the most thorough theological encycopedia available in any language. The entries themselves are sometimes of small-book length, and excellent bibliographies are appended. There is, not surprisingly, a distinctly German emphasis, however. *Class No:* 230.1(031)

Dictionaries

[577]

ANGELES, P.A. Dictionary of Christian theology. New York, Harper & Row, 1985. 211p. $17.95. £16.25. ISBN: 0060602376.

Follows the format of the author's *Dictionary of philosophy* (*qv*) with etymologies and frequent cross-references. Brief definitions for a wide range of Christian concepts, some rather remotely connected with theology. Terms mainly primarily of interest to Roman Catholics. Typical length of definitions is 30 to 50 words, but some are much longer (*e.g.* 'Christology' and 'Eucharist' have 3 pages each). Useful for ready reference. *Library journal* (15 April 1985, p.66) considers Rahner & Vorgrimler's *Dictionary of theology* (*qv*) more narrowly focused, scholarly, and thorough. *Class No:* 230.1(038)

[578]

The Collegeville pastoral dictionary of biblical theology. Stuhlmueller, C., ed. Collegeville, Minn., Liturgical Press, 1996 1120p. ISBN: 0814619967. *Class No:* 230.1(038)

[579]

Dictionary of Fundamental Theology. Latourelle, R. and Fisichella, R., eds. Slough, St Pauls, 1994 xxxix,1222p. ISBN: 0854393951.

"Fundamental theology" used to be a scholarly way of talking about apologetics. It treats of the notion of revelation, of the credibility of the Christian Faith and its relationship with other faiths. This is a sharply-focused encyclopedia, written from a Roman Catholic perspective (both the editors lecture at the Jesuit University in Rome, The Gregorianum), but is well done, with major essays (with bibliographies) on central topics. There is a detailed analytical index. *Class No:* 230.1(038)

[580]

Evangelical dictionary of biblical theology. Elwell, W.A., ed. Paternoster Press, 1996 993p $44.99 ISBN: 0801020492.

Includes bibliographic index.

Most entries have bibliographies. Plenty of cross-references provided. Written from an Evangelical outlook. "An excellent source for general readers" *Choice* v.34,4 Dec. 1996. *Class No:* 230.1(038)

[581]

Evangelical dictionary of theology. Elwell, W.A., ed. Grand Rapids, Mich., Baker Book House, 1984; Basingstoke, Hants., Marshall Pickering, 1985. xxii,1204p. $29.95; £24.95. ISBN: 0801034132, US; 0551012722, UK.

Designed to succeed *Baker's Dictionary of Theology* (1960).

1200 entries, written in popular language, encompassing the whole spectrum of theological discussion - dogmatic; historical philosophical; biblical moral-including current movements with broader implications, and historically significant personages. Scholarly entries are usual comprehensive and balanced handbook' (*Library journal*, January 1985, p.74). *Class No:* 230.1(038)

[582]

KOMONCHAK, J.A., and others, eds. The New dictionary of theology. Dublin, Gill & Macmillan; Wilmington, DE., Michael Glazier, 1987. viii,1112p. I£50; $59.95. ISBN: 0717115526, Ireland; 0894536095, US.

Articles ranging in length from a single paragraph to 15 double-columned pages, by distinguished scholars. Written from the point of view of the Roman Catholic Church. Articles includes 'see' references and bibliographies. 'Its purpose is to present Roman Catholic theology in the light of the teaching of the Second Vatican Council ... It particularly notes the decisions made by the American bishops in the light of the Vatican Council' (*Church times*, no.6531, 15 April 1988). *Class No:* 230.1(038)

[583]

RAHNER, K. *and* VORGRIMLER, H., *eds*. **Concise theological dictionary.** 2nd ed. Tunbridge Wells, Kent, Burns & Oates, 1983. [8], 541p. £15. ISBN: 0860121097.

First English edition 1965. Translated from *Kleines Theologisches Wörterbuch* (10th ed. Verlag Herder, Freiburg, 1976).

A revised and amplified edition, containing brief explanations (6 or 7 lines to 2p.) of the most important concepts of modern Catholic dogmatic theology. Entries arranged A-Z (Absolute ... Yahweh), with 'see' references. *Class No:* 230.1(038)

[584]

RICHARDSON, A. *and* BOWDEN, J., *eds*. **A New dictionary of Christian theology.** New ed. London, S.C.M. Press; Philadelphia, Pa., Westminster Press, 1989. 632p. £15. $24.95. ISBN: 0334022088, UK.

First published 1969. Title of both editions in US is *Westminster dictionary of Christian theology*.

About 800 signed entries by 175 contributors from many denominations. Short bibliographies for lengthier articles. Cross-references. A thorough revision and reworking of the first edition, with a nice balance between information and analyses. Drops biographical entries, 'focusing instead on theological thinking against a historical background rather than on historical events or figures (*Preface*). *Class No:* 230.1(038)

Reviews & Abstracts

[585]

Theological book review. October 1988-. Guildford, Surrey, Feed the Mind, 1988-. 3pa. ISSN: 09542191.

Claims to cover about 250 books from the UK, US and Third World in each issue. Subject arrangement. Author index and list of publishers in each issue. Michael Walsh found the entries in v.1(1) 'rather too uniformly fulsome' (*Bulletin of the ABTPL*, v.2(5), June 1989, p.35). *Class No:* 230.1(048)

Histories

[586]

LANE, T. **The Lion concise book of Christian thought.** Tring, Herts, Lion Publishing; Sutherland, N.S.W., Albatross Books, 1984. 240p. illus. (line drawings). £5.95. Aus. $11.95. ISBN: 0856485055, UK; 0867604972, AUS.

'... primary purpose of this book is to introduce leading thinkers from the past (and present) and to whet the appetite by giving abstracts from their writings' (*Introduction*). Contains brief introductions to 90 of the most formative thinkers, together with extensive quotations, and 25 important creeds and confessions, etc. summarized. 5 sections: The Church of the Fathers to AD 500 - The Eastern tradition from AD 500 - The medieval West, 500-1500 - Reformation and reaction, 1500-1800 - Christian thought in the modern world, 1800 onwards. Bibliography (p.233-235) arranged A-Z by author. Index (p.237-238). *Class No:* 230.1(091)

[587]

PELIKAN, J. **The Christian tradition:** a history of the development of doctrine. Chicago, University of Chicago Press, 1971-1989. 5v. v.1: $12.95; v.2: $10.95; v.3 & 4: $27.50 each; v.5: $29.95. v.1 & 2: £19.95 each; v.3 & 4: £21.95 each. ISBN: 0226653706, v.1; 0226653722, v.2; 0226653749, v.3; 0226653765, v.4; 0226653781, v.5.

V.1: *The emergence of the Catholic tradition (100-600);* v.2: *The spirit of eastern Christendom (600-1700);* v.3: *The growth of medieval theology (600-1300);* v.4: *Reformation of church and dogma (1300-1700);* v.5: *Christian doctrine and modern culture (since 1700).* Each volume starts with a list of primary sources and ends with a Biblical and general index (analytical). Early references are given in the left-hand margin of the text. *Class No:* 230.1(091)

19th Century

[588]

SMART, N., *and others, eds*. **Nineteenth-century religious thought in the West.** Cambridge, Cambridge University Press, 1985. 3v. (1038p.). £35 each volume. ISBN: 052122831x, v.1; 0521228328, v.2; 0212011149, v.3.

V.1: *Theology - 19th century* (Immanual Kant - Ludwig Feuerbach and Karl Marx); v.2: *Theology, doctrinal - history - 19th century* (Samuel Taylor Coleridge - William James and Josiah Royce); v.3: *Religion - history - 19th century* (Religion and science - Ernst Troeltsch). Each essay ends with a long list of notes, including references, and a bibliographical essay. Index to each volume. *Class No:* 230.1(091)"18"

Biographies

[589]

BOWDEN, J. **Who's who in theology.** London, SCM Press, 1990. 152p. £5.95. ISBN: 0334024641.

An A-Z guide for students and the general reader to the names that appear in theological works. Not a substitute for weightier works, of which there is a list at the beginning of the book. Entries vary in length, averaging about 6 to a page, and a typical entry includes person's dates, biographical details, and account of his or her works. No value judgements. Appendix on the Popes of Rome, in chronological order. 1-page alphabetical index. '... compact, concise, well-balanced and clear (both in form and content) ...'(*Reference reviews*,v.5(2),1991, p.9). *Class No:* 230.1(092)

South Africa

[590]

BORCHARDT, C.F.A. *and* VORSTER, W.S., *eds*. **South African theological bibliography...** Pretoria, University of South Africa, 1980. xxvii, 398p. ISBN: 0869811851.

'The aim ... is to index all Festschrifts and periodical literature published in South Africa covering the field (*Preface*). 6088 unannotated entries, arranged in 8 sections: Bibliological subjects - Systematic theology - Historical subjects - Practical theology - Science of religion - Science of missions - Apologetics - Sects - and an addendum. Author index, p.370-398. *Class No:* 230.1(680)

20th Century

Handbooks & Manuals

[591]

The Modern theologians an introduction to Christian theology in the twentieth century. Ford, D.F., *ed*. 2nd ed. Oxford, Blackwell, 1997 xviii,772p. £65.00 ISBN: 0631195912.

A much expanded new edition of a work originally published in 1989. It begins with discussions of major theologians of this century, then assesses theological trends. An excellent guide to modern Christian thought from a variety of perspectives. *Class No:* 230.1"19"(035)

Miracles

[592]

BREWER, E.C. **A Dictionary of miracles, imitative, realistic and dogmatic.** London, Chatto & Windus, 1884 (Reprinted Detroit, Mich., Gale Research Co., 1966). 632p. ISBN: 0810343533.

The only reference book of its kind, intended to reproduce in a handy form impartial information about a mode of religious thought. Three parts: miracles of saints, relating to Scripture miracles or secular stories; realistic miracles, founded on literal interpretation of Scripture; and dogmatic miracles, to prove ecclesiastical dogmas. Full index. *Class No:* 231.73

Mariology (Virgin Mary)

Dictionaries

[593]

ATTWATER, D., *comp*. **A Dictionary of Mary.** London, Longmans, Green, 1957. vii,312p.

Originally published 1956 (New York, Kennedy).

The aim is 'to provide the reader, whether a member of the Catholic Church or not, with a quick reference to matters connected with the many aspects of the life, significance and veneration of the Blessed Virgin Mary in ordinary non-technical language' (*Preface*). *Class No:* 232.931(038)

[594]

DE FIORES, S. *and* MEO, S. **Nuovo dizionaria di Mariologia.** 2nd ed. Milano, Edizioni Paoline, 1986. xxvii,1561p. ISBN: 8821509885.

First published 1985.

Lengthy signed essays commence with a summary and end with notes and bibliography. 65 contributors. Italian only. *Class No:* 232.931(038)

Angels

[595]

DAVIDSON, G. **A Dictionary of angels,** including the fallen angels. New ed. New York, Free Press, 1972. xxxii,387p. illus., facsims., charts. $22.95. ISBN: 0029069408.

First published 1967.

About 7,000 very brief entries (A'albiel ... Zuriel), with many references to angels in literature, art and mythology. Well documented, Many cross-references from alternatives names. Lengthy introduction

....*(contd.)*
(p.xi-xxix) has 46 footnote references. Many appendices, p.335-62 (*e.g.* 'The orders of the celestial hierarchy'). Bibliography, p.363-87. *Class No:* 235

Demonology

Dictionaries

[596]
GETTINGS, F. **Dictionary of demons:** a guide to demons and demonologists in occult lore. North Pomfret, VT., Trafalgar Square Publishing, 1988. 255p. illus., tables. $24.95. ISBN: 094395505x.

A compendium of historical, biographical and factual information. An introduction explains the historical evolution of demonological traditions. Arranged A-Z, the dictionary includes pagan, occult, pre-Christian, and Christian evil spirits and devils, explaining the origin of each and its representation in different traditions. Entries vary in length from a line to several pages. 'See' references connect name variants. Bibliography listing titles referred to in the text. Considered 'More scholarly than *Man, myth and magic* (1984)' (*Reference books bulletin*, 15th December 1988, p.689). *Class No:* 235.1(038)

Saints

[597]
METFORD, J.C.J. **The Christian year.** London, Thames & Hudson, 1991. 144p. £12.95. ISBN: 0500110212.

A companion to the holy days, festivals and seasons of the ecclesiastical year. Select bibliography, with some comment, p.129-30. Glossary, p.131-40. Detailed index. Scholarly discussion of origins, reasons and theological background. A calendar of saints' days would have been a helpful addition! *Class No:* 235.3

[598]
ROEDER, H. **Saints and their attributes:** with a guide to localities and patronage. London, Longmans, Green, 1955. xxviii, 391p.

Saints' emblems and symbols as depicted in pictorial representations and statuary, arranged by subjects A-Z. Sub-arranged under saints' names (giving date of death; religious order). Indexes of saints, patronage and localities; short bibliography, p.xiv. *Class No:* 235.3

Bibliographies

[599]
Analecta Bollandiana: revue critique d'hagiographie. Brussels, Société des Bollandistes, 1882-. 2pa (previously quarterly). EUR 85 pa. ISSN: 00032468.

Contains criticisms of recent works on questions relating to the lives of the saints. The work of a group of Belgian Jesuits. Also has commentaries, texts, etc., supplementary to the monumental *Acta sanctorum quotquot toto orbe coluntur* (1643-; Paris ed., 1863-1940, 85v. in 67, and supplements), a collection of biographies and legends of the saints, in calendar order. Inventories of the collection appear in: *Bibliotheca hagiographica graeca* (Brussels, 1895; 3rd ed. 1957. 3v.), *Bibliotheca hagiographica latina* (Brussels, 1898-1901. 2v.), and *Bibliotheca hagiographica orientalis* (Brussels, 1910). More recent is Analecta Bollandiana's *Inventaire hagiographique des tomes 1 à 100 (1882-1982)* (Brussels, Société des Bollandistes, 1983. 443p.). *Class No:* 235.3(01)

[600]
METZGER, B.M., *comp.* **Index to periodical literature on the Apostle Paul.** 2nd ed. Leiden, E.J. Brill, 1970. xvi,184p. Gld.41. ISBN: 9004015477.

First published 1960.

*c.*3000 entries in 6 sections: 1. Bibliographical articles on Paul - 2. Historical studies on the life of Paul - 3. Critical studies of the Pauline literature - 4. Pauline Apocrypha - 5. Theological studies - 6. The history of the interpretation of Paul and his work. Includes articles from *c.*135 journals in many languages. Author index. *Class No:* 235.3(01)

Encyclopaedias

[601]
Bibliotheca Sanctorum Rome, Instituto Giovanni XXIII, 1961-1970 Published in 13 volumes.

Written in Italian, rather than, as the title might indicate, in Latin, this is by far the best guide to the lives of the saints. The major figures have full scale scholarly treatment, discussing sources, biography, cult and iconography. All entries are signed and provided with bibliographies. It is abundantly illustrated and extremely well indexed (in volume 13). A supplement has been published ("Prima Appendice", 1987) covering individuals whose canonization processes have recently begun, and others whose status has changed (e.g. a "venerable" has become a "saint"). *Class No:* 235.3(031)

Dictionaries

[602]
The Book of Saints: a dictionary of servants of God canonized by the Catholic Church. Benedictine monks of St. Augustine's Abbey, Ramsgate, *comps.* 6th ed. rev. & updated. London, A. & C. Black, 1989. 624p. 135 black-and-white illus. £19.95. ISBN: 071363006x.

5th ed. published *c.*1966.

Brief biographical details, achievements, feast days, and emblems of *c.*10,000 saints of the Catholic Church, revised according to the recommendations of the Church. Includes many modern saints. Arranged A-Z. Also lists patron saints and a list of emblems, relating them to the saints. *Class No:* 235.3(038)

Quotations

[603]
ADELS, J.H. **The Wisdom of the saints:** an anthology. New York, Oxford University Press, 1987. 233p. $21.95. ISBN: 0195041526.

A collection of the saints' own words, thematically arranged. 60 items (Saints - God ... Mystic Union) with brief entries. Biographical notes, p.205-233. *Class No:* 235.3(082.2)

Biographies

[604]
BUTLER, A. **Butler's lives of the saints.** Burns, P., *ed.* New full ed. Tunbridge Wells, Burns and Oates, 1995 £16.95 each
Published in 12 volumes.

Each volume of this revision of the standard work in English of the lives of the saints has a different editor, and some variation of approach can be noted. In general lives have been up-dated from the Thurston-Attwater edition of the 1930s, rather than rewritten. New saints have been added, and the calendar brought into line with that currently in force in the Roman Catholic Church. *Class No:* 235.3(092)

[605]
BUTLER, A. **The Lives of the saints.** New ed., rev. and copiously supplemented by H. Thurston *and others*. London, Burns, Oates, 1926-38. 12v. & supplement.

A greatly expanded edition of a work published 1756-9, intended for the general reader. Lives of *c.*2500 saints. 1 volume per month, biographies being arranged according to the saint's day. Short bibliographies are appended. A general index to the rev. ed. (giving date for each saint) is published as *A dictionary of saints ... compiled by D. Attwater.* (New ed. London, Burns & Oates, 1958, vii, 280p.). *Class No:* 235.3(092)

[606]
—BUTLER, A. **Butler's lives of the saints:** edited, revised and supplemented by H. Thurston and D. Attwater. 3rd ed. London, Burns & Oates, 1981. 4v. (700p.). ISBN: 0860121127.

In this edition certain abbreviations have been made to the 1926-38 text (*e.g.* Butler's daily exhortations have been discarded). Each volume has an index, v.4 including a cumulated index. *Class No:* 235.3(092)

[607]
—WALSH, M., *ed.* **Butler's lives of the saints:** concise edition. London, Burns & Oates, 1985. 484p. £12.95. ISBN: 0860121402.

One-volume abridgement of the above. For each day of the year one saint is given, suitable for devotional reading as well as for historical background to Church history. Also reproduces full index from complete edition, with saints included in this volume highlighted in bold type. Contains the most recent canonizations as well as revised dating. *Class No:* 235.3(092)

[608]
—WALSH, M., *ed.* **Butler's lives of patron saints.** Rev. ed. London, Burns & Oates, 1987. xvi, 476p. illus. £14.95. ISBN: 0860121577.

Over 250 saints from legendary to modern times, showing how their patronages have become both popularly accepted and officially recognized. Arranged A-Z, giving a short biography of the patron saint, preceded by the history of each patronage. 3 indexes: by country, place, profession, occupation, and social or medical condition; a list of saints and their feast days; and an index of the saints and their patronages listed by the dates of their feast days. *Class No:* 235.3(092)

[609]
COULSON, J., *ed.* **The Saints:** a concise biographical dictionary. London, Burns & Oates, 1958. 496p. illus. (inc. 16 col. plates).

About 2500 entries arranged A-Z by anglicized form of Christian name. Entries vary in length from 3-4 lines to 3 columns (*e.g.* St. Thomas Aquinas: 2½ columns; St. Teresa of Avila: 2¼ columns, plus an illustration). Many cross-references. 'Calendar of feast days', p.473-85: 'For further reading', p.489-91. Articles unsigned; the impressive list of some 65 contributors does not indicate the specific contributions. *Class No:* 235.3(092)

[610]

—ATTWATER, D. *and* JOHN, R.J. Dictionary of saints. 3rd ed. Harmondsworth, Mddx., Penguin Books, 1995. 382p. £6.99. ISBN: 0140513124.

First published 1965.

Identifies more than 750 saints, especially those of Great Britain and Ireland. Many other individuals are mentioned in the biographical sketches, with cross-references. Contains a short general bibliography and a glossary. *Class No:* 235.3(092)

[611]

The Oxford dictionary of saints. Farmer, D.H. 4th ed. Oxford, Oxford University Press, 1997. 530p. £7.99. $14.95. ISBN: 0192800582.

First published 1978.

Concise accounts of the lives, cults, and artistic associations of *c.*1250 saints who lived or died or have been venerated in Great Britain and Ireland. Increased coverage of Greek and Russian saints in the 2nd ed. Arranged A-Z ('Joan of Arc': 3 columns; 10 references). 3 appendices (I. Some unsuccessful English candidates for canonization; II. Principal patronages; III. Principal iconographical problems). Index of places in Great Britain and Ireland associated with particular saints. Calendar of feasts. Valuable introduction refers to the 1969 reform of the Roman Calendar. 'Excellent value and as a single volume work based on critical principles is unlikely to be rivalled' (*Heythrop journal,* v.20, 1979, p.466, on the first edition). *Class No:* 235.3(092)

Europe

[612]

SHARP, M. A Traveller's guide to saints in Europe. London, Evelyn, 1964. xv, 251p.

Identifies more than 400 European saints, arranged A-Z, with chronological list of saints (by century and then date of death). Entries give names, dates, attributes in art, and patron. Bibliography (p.vii); glossary of terms (p.viii); index of churches containing relics (by countries, p.241-51). The *Times literary supplement,* no. 3241, 9 April, 1964, p.297, notes some omissions and misspellings. *Class No:* 235.3(4)

Wales

[613]

HENKEN, E.R. Traditions of the Welsh saints. Woodbridge, Suffolk, Boydell & Brewer, 1987. vii,368p. £29.50; $53. ISBN: 0859912213.

'... a survey of narrative traditions concerning the lives of the Welsh saints ... examines Welsh hagiographical traditions rooted in local lore as represented by a variety of sources, both written and oral' (*Introduction*). Deals with 47 Welsh saints, mainly real men and women of the 5th and 6th centuries. Extensive footnotes. Bibliography, p.311-320, A-Z by author. Index of saints' traditions, p.321-368. *Class No:* 235.3(429)

Middle Ages

[614]

VAUCHEZ, André. Sainthood in the middle ages. Cambridge, Cambridge University Press, 1997 £65.00 ISBN: 0521445590.

The standard work on medieval saints, originally published in French in 1981. The English edition has not been updated. *Class No:* 235.3"01/14"

Creeds

Histories

[615]

CURTIS, W.A. A History of creeds and confessions of faith in Christendom and beyond. Edinburgh, Clark, 1911. xx, 502p.

An admirable survey of religious creeds throughout the ages, with extensive and representative quotations from the authoritative documents, bibliographies, and appendices of historical tables. Index.

The 3rd ed. of J.N.D. Kelly's *Early Christian creeds* was issued in a new edition in 1982 (Longman, 460p. 058249219x). *Class No:* 238(091)

Ethics

[616]

CAMPBELL, A.V., *ed.* A Dictionary of pastoral care. London, SPCK Ltd., 1987. xi,300p. £20. ISBN: 0281042608.

'... a concise but comprehensive guide to the concepts and problems most likely to be encountered in pastoral care and counselling' (Book jacket). 300 entries by *c.*185 contributors, experts in their fields, arranged A-Z by subject (Abortion and abortion counselling ... Worship and pastoral care). Bibliographies are appended to each entry. Cross-references. *Class No:* 241

[617]

MACQUARRIE, J. *and* CHILDERS, J.F., *eds.* A New dictionary of Christian ethics. London, S.C.M. Press; Philadelphia, Pa., Westminster Press, 1990. 698p. £17.50. $34.95. ISBN: 0334022045, UK; 0664209408, US.

First published 1967 as *A dictionary of Christian ethics* in the UK and as *Westminster dictionary of Christian ethics* in US.

167 contributors, representing Protestant, Anglican, Roman Catholic, Orthodox and Jewish faiths. Signed articles and brief follow-up bibliographies for longer items (*e.g.* 'Jesus, Ethical teachings of': 7½ cols; 4 references). Wide range of subjects (*e.g.* Pride; Prison reform; Hippocratic oath; Industrial relations; Neoplatonism), including entries under moralists (*e.g.* Schleiermacher). Many additional entries in the new edition; articles updated; bibliographies revised; more cross-references. '... major contribution that reflects contemporary ideas on Christian ethics and moral theology ... distinguished reference work'. (*Reference books bulletin,* 1986/87, p.52-53). 'Major omission is biographical entries, though movements associated with individuals remain' (*Library journal,* 15 March 1986, p.62). *Class No:* 241

Dictionaries

[618]

Dictionary of ethics, theology, and society. Clarke, P. B. *and* Linzey, Andrew, *eds.* London, Routledge, 1996 xxxiii,926p £85.00 ISBN: 0415062128.

The editors describe this volume as an attempt to map out "the major ethical, theological, and political influences which have come to form Western Society". The result is a rather disparate collection of entries, from Abortion to Zoos. There are bibliographies appended to the over 200 entries, and a useful index. *Class No:* 241(038)

[619]

Dictionary of pastoral care and counselling. Hunter, Rodney J., *ed.* Nashville, Tenn., Abingdon Press, 1990 xxvii,1346p. £48.00 ISBN: 068710761x.

The target audience is defined as "religious caregivers" - priests and rabbis, pastoral counsellers and psychotherapists as well as students of theology and theologians. Though many articles are little different from those to be found in general theological reference works, there is an emphasis on phychological topics and on counselling. Bibliographies are supplied. *Class No:* 241(038)

[620]

New dictionary of Christian ethics and pastoral theology. Atkinson, D.J. *and* Field, D.H., *eds.* Leicester, Intervarsity Press, 1995 xxiii,918p. ISBN: 0851106501.

The first 127 pages consist of articles of some length arranged (say the editors) "in theological order" (ie beginning with "God" and ending with "Christian moral reasoning"). The remainder are in alphabetical order. They are written for the most part by authors in the Protestant evangelical tradition. The content of the volumes is sharply focused. There is an index of names. *Class No:* 241(038)

Christian Art & Symbols

Indexes

[621]

ROCHELLE, M. Post-biblical saints art index. Jefferson, N.C., McFarland, 1994 ix,357p. $65.00 ISBN: 0899509428.

The subtitle of this book indicates precisely its scope: "A location of paintings, scupltures, mosaics, icons, frescos, manuscript illuminations, sketches, woodcuts, and engravings created from the 4th century to 1950, with a directory of the institutions holding them". The paintings of the saints, arranged in alphabetica! order, from, rather oddly "Abba Macarius" to (Pope) "Zosimus", are all briefly described, and a bibliographical reference given. There is an index of artists, of "attributes and events" (by means of which saints may be indentified), a directory of museums and other collections holding these works, with (usually) a full address, and a bibliography. This is a very useful work indeed for students of the iconography of saints as well as for art historians (and picture researchers) in general. *Class No:* 246(014)

Handbooks & Manuals

[622]

CHILD, H. *and* COLLES, D. Christian symbols, ancient and modern: a handbook for students. London, Bell, 1971. xxi, 269p. illus. (incl. pl.). £17.50. ISBN: 0713519606.

18 sections: Symbolism - The Cross - The Trinity - Images of Christ - The Virgin Mary: her place in art - The nativity of Jesus Christ - Living water - The Holy Spirit - The Eucharist - Angels - Good and evil - Forerunners and followers - The four living creatures - The Evangelists - Benedicite omnia opera - The Church in work and time - Categories (*e.g.* The seven virtues and the seven vices) - The liturgy

....(contd.)
and the crafts. 'List of books', p.256-9. Non-analytical index. Excellent illus. (33 pl., 114 line-drawings, with descriptive captions). *Class No:* 246(035)

[623]
RÉAU, L. **Iconographie de l'art chrétien.** Paris, Presses Universitaire de France, 1955-59 (Reprinted Nendeln, Kraus-Thomson, 1974). 3v.
V.1: *Introduction générale*; v.2: *Iconographie de la Bible* (2 parts: Ancien Testament. Nouveau Testament); v.3: *Iconographie des saints* (3 pts. A-F, G-O, P-Z). A detailed survey, with section bibliographies. V.3 includes 80 plates and a general bibliography of hagiographies, etc. (p.1382-4), as well as sections: 'Les noms des saints'; 'Les patronages'; 'Les attributs', and a general index. Indispensible for research on Christian iconography. *Class No:* 246(035)

[624]
SILL, G.G. **A Handbook of symbols in Christian art.** New York, Macmillan, 1975. xii,241p. illus.
50 categories, A-Z (Angel ... Zodiac), follow a short introductory essay. Clear illustrations of 162 works of art, with captions. Select bibliography, with a long list of sources and credits. Copious cross-references. 'An indispensable reference work, especially for public collections' (*ARLIS/NA Newsletter*, v.4(1), December 1975, p.14, a review on which this annotation is based. *Class No:* 246(035)

Dictionaries

[625]
BOTTOMLEY, F. **The Church explorer's guide to symbols and their meaning.** London, Kaye & Ward, 1978. xvi, 176p., 320 illus. £1.95. ISBN: 0718211871.
A-Z entries on the symbolism of decorations, furniture and fabrics of churches, in terms of the Church's history and teaching. Further reading, p.161. Marginal illus., 2 or more per page. Index. 'The result of many years exploring churches in all parts of the country' (Note). *Class No:* 246(038)

[626]
Lexikon der christlichen Ikonographie. Kirschbaum, E., *and others.* Freiburg, Herder, 1968-1975,. 9v. illus.
V.1-4: Allgemeine Ikonographie (on Biblical concepts and persons, A-Z); v.5-9: Ikonographie der Heiligen (saints, A-Z, plus indexes of attributes, localities and artists in v.9). *Class No:* 246(038)

Spirituality

Bibliographies

[627]
CARSON, A. **Feminist spirituality and the feminine divine: an annotated bibliography.** Crossing Press, 1986. 125p. $39.95. ISBN: 0895942003.
Aimed at both lay and scholarly audiences. Over 700 entries, mainly books, for works produced by the women's spirituality movement and inspired by it. Wide subject field (history, folklore, mythology, religion, psychology, witchcraft, occult sciences, lesbian feminism, etc.). Arrangement is A-Z by author (periodicals by title). Average length of annotations is 40 words. Excellent subject index, but no title index. *Class No:* 248(01)

Dictionaries

[628]
VILLER, M., *and others, eds.* **Dictionnaire de spiritualité, ascétique et mystique, doctrine et histoire.** Paris, Beauchesne, 1937-1994. v.1-16.
A scholarly work, with long signed articles; rich in biographies. Bibliographies appended to articles include references to sources. The article on St. Bernard of Clairvaux, for instance, occupies p.1454-99 of v.1 and is in 5 sections (life; spiritual works; source of teaching; doctrine (20 pages); influence on spirituality) and has 1½ columns of bibliography. That on Jakob Boehme runs to 6 columns (life and work; doctrine) and has ½ column of bibliography (works; literature on). A further index volume was published in 1995. In addition to the index of subjects, a list of contributors indicates the entries for which each has been responsible *Class No:* 248(038)

[629]
WAKEFIELD,, G.S., *ed.* **A Dictionary of Christian spirituality.** New ed. London, SCM Press, 1983 (reprinted in paperback, 1988). xvi.400p. £15; $22.95. ISBN: 0334019672.
First published 1971. Published by Westminster Press in the US as *Westminster dictionary of Christian spirituality.*
The standard reference work on the subject. Includes 358 articles, written by a team of 153. Entries are signed, include bibliographical references, and are often lengthy (*e.g.* 'Asceticism': 6 cols., 5 references; 'Penitence': 2 cols., 6 references; 'Ecstasy': 1¼ cols., 4 references). Includes biographies. Cross-references. Clearly and

....(contd.)
concisely written, defining spiritual concepts, practices, schools and important persons. 'A fascinating exposition ... ' (Theology, v.87(717), May 1984. p.207-9). *Class No:* 248(038)

Histories

[630]
BOUYER, L., *and others.* **A History of Christian spirituality.** Burns & Oates, 1968. Tunbridge Wells, Kent (Reprinted 1982). 3v. (1404p.). £39.50 the set. V.1 & 2: £16 each; v.3: £10. ISBN: 0860121135, v.1; 0860121143, v.2; 0860121151, v.3; 0860121259, set.
Translated from the French 1960-65 ed.
V.I: *The Spirituality of the New Testament and the Fathers* has 19 chapters, an index of subjects, and a biblical index (p.534-541) divided into ancient authors and modern authors. V.II: *The spirituality of the Middle Ages* has 18 chapters, an appendix on Byzantine spirituality, and an index of names (persons and places). V.III: *Orthodox spirituality and Protestant and Anglican spirituality* has 6 chapters, Conclusion, and list of names. *Class No:* 248(091)

Meditation

[631]
JARRELL, H.R. **International meditation bibliography, 1950-1982.** Metuchen, N.J. Scarecrow Press, and The American Theological Library Association, 1985. x,432p. $32.50. (*ATLA bibliography series, no.12.*) ISBN: 0810817594.
Entries for about 1000 books, 900 journal and magazine articles, and over 200 dissertations and masters' theses, arranged A-Z, for items published between 1950 and 1982 with some 1983 references. Brief annotations are included for the articles. Articles are in English, some books in other Western languages; dissertations and theses in English and German. Also includes 32 motion pictures, 93 recordings, and 32 societies and associations. Subjects include Christian meditation, Zen-Buddhist meditation, relaxation techniques, Yoga meditation, and transcendental meditation. Author, title and subject indexes. *Class No:* 248MED

Pilgrimage

[632]
BARBER, R. **Pilgrimages.** Woodbridge, Suffolk & Rochester, NY, Boydell & Brewer Ltd., 1991. 160p. 12 plates. £16.95; $29.95. ISBN: 0851155197.
A survey of the major pilgrimage traditions of all the great religions of the world, outlining the history and nature of the different ideas and rites of pilgrimage. *Class No:* 248.1

[633]
DAVIDSON, L.K. *and* DUNN-WOOD, M. **Pilgrimages in the Middle Ages:** a research guide. New York, Garland, 1993. 480p. $74. ((*Garland medieval bibliographies,16*).) ISBN: 0824072219.
Topically organized bibliographical essays; a research guide; and an annotated, descriptive bibliography of over 1000 entries. No indexes. *Class No:* 248.1

Christian Church

Encyclopaedias

16th Century

[634]
The Oxford encyclopedia of the Reformation. Hillerbrand, H.J., *ed.* Oxford, Oxford University Press, 1996 2112p. £260.00 ISBN: 0195064933.
Published in four volumes.
Over 450 academic contributors. 1,200 cross-references alphabetical entries ranging from brief bibliographical sketches to authoritative essays on major topics. It focuses "on the entire range of social change wrought by the Reformation, including not only issues of church polity and theology, but also related developments in politics, demographics, art and literature". *Class No:* 26/28(031)"15"

Dictionaries

[635]
DOUGLAS, J.D., *General editor.* **The New international dictionary of the Christian Church.** Exeter, Devon, Paternoster Press, 1978. xiv, 1074p. £21.95. ISBN: 0310238307.
First published 1974.
Nearly 200 contributors. 5000 articles, nearly all signed. 'Aachen, Synod of' ... 'Zwingli'. Many biographies, with references appended (*e.g.* Ignatius of Loyola: 1 col., 6 references; John Wesley: nearly 2

....(contd.)

cols., 21 lines of references). 'Music, Christian': 7 cols., ½ col. of bibliography; 'Epistles, Pauline': 4 cols., ½ col. of bibliography; 'Mormonism': 1½ cols., 11 lines of references. Ample cross-references. Aims at impartiality, and a 'middle path between academic textbook and popular introduction' (*Preface*). *Class No:* 26/28(038)

[636]
The Oxford dictionary of the Christian Church. Cross, F.L. *and* Livingstone, E.A., *eds.* 3rd ed. Oxford, Oxford University Press, 1997 xxxvii,1786p. £70.00 ISBN: 019211655x.

First published 1957.

Hitherto the most complete, and successful, dictionary of its kind, far bigger than any of its one-volume competitors. Excellent for brief biographies of churchmen of all kinds, bibliographies (scholarly) appended to almost all articles - which are unsigned. The new entries to the 1997 edition, however, are somewhat different in style to the rather positivistic and heavily historical approach of earlier editions, and point up the the distinctly Anglican context from which it came. Nevertheless, still the volume which most theologians keep closest to hand. *Class No:* 26/28(038)

Yearbooks & Directories

[637]
WORLD COUNCIL OF CHURCHES. Directory of Christian Councils. 4th ed. Geneva, the Council, 1985. xii, 244p. ISBN: 2825408468.

Arranged by continent or region, subdivided by country A-Z, and then arranged A-Z by name. Information given : name and address; telephone number, cable, telex; general secretary, other full-time executive staff, part-time and honorary staff; president; membership (list of affiliated and associate members); date of foundation; basis of membership; aims and functions, main concerns and activities; organization of the council; sources of budget; ecumenical relationships. List of regional and inter-regional conferences. No index. *Class No:* 26/28(058)

Biographies

Bibliographies

Dictionaries

[638]
Biographisch-Bibliographisches Kirchenlexikon. [Biographical and bibliographical dictionary of the Christian Church.] Bautz, F.W. *and* Bautz, T., *eds.* Series started in 1975 Herzberg, Verlag Traugott Bautz, 1975- ISBN: 388309062x.

This bibliographical dictionary of church history has reached the 15th vol. It has considerably expanded since vol. I (Aalders to Faustus of Byzantium). Each signed entry has a bibliography, sometimes a quite substantial listing. A major reference work for theologians, biblical scholars, and church historians. The coverage is from earliest Christian times to the present day. *Class No:* 26/28(092)(01)(038)

England

[639]
EDWARDS, D.L. Christian England. London, Collins, 1981-1984. 3v. (1249p.). (Reprinted by Fount Publications, 1989). £10.95. ISBN: 0006274048.

A survey of Christian England to the end of the first world war. V.1. Its story to the Reformation (pt.1. The first England; pt.2. The Middle Ages): v.2 From the Reformation to the eighteenth century (pt.1. Christians under the Tudors; pt.2. A war between believers; pt.3. Religions in the age of reason. Outline of events); v.3. From the eighteenth century to the first world war (pt.1. Revival; pt.2. The Victorian Christians. Outline of events). Copious footnotes throughout; Lists for further reading after each part; and an 8-page index to each volume. '... an enthralling story told with lucidity, vividness and the most judicious discernment'. (*Church times*, August 17, 1984, p.6). *Class No:* 26/28(420)

Ecumenical Movement

[640]
EVANS, G.R. Method in ecumenical theology the lessons so far. Cambridge, Cambridge University Press, 1996 233p. $54.95 ISBN: 0521553040.

Contains index.

A wide-ranging survey of ecumenical dialogue over the course of this century, but especially in the aftermath of Vatican II. *Class No:* 261.8

Bibliographies

[641]
WORLD COUNCIL OF CHURCHES. Geneva. Library. **Classified catalog of the ecumenical movement.** Boston, Mass., G.K. Hall, 1972. 1st supplement, 1981. 2v. and supplement. $185 for 2v.; $105 for supplement. ISBN: 0816109257; 0816103607, Supplement.

20,200 photolithographed catalogue cards covering *c.*11,000 titles on the ecumenical movement in the Library. Arranged according to a modified Dewey Decimal scheme. *Class No:* 261.8(01)

Dictionaries

[642]
Dictionary of the Ecumenical Movement. Lossky, N., *and others, eds.* London, Council of Churches for Britain and Ireland, 1991 xvi,1196p. £44.95 ISBN: 0851692257.

Over 600 entries, with bibliographies, and illustrated. There is an index of names and one of subjects. Covers ecumenical themes, events, organizations and personalities, as well as theological issues, and the history of ecumenism around the globe. *Class No:* 261.8(038)

Histories

[643]
ROUSE, R. *and* NEILL, S.C., *eds.* A History of the ecumenical movement. London, S.P.C.K., on behalf of the Committee on Ecumenical History, Geneva, 1954-70. 2v.

1: *1517-1948* (1954. 3rd rev. ed 1986. 864p.). 2: *The ecumenical advance ... 1948-1968*, edited by H.E. Fey. (1970. 544p.). V.1 stresses the influence of evangelical revivals; bibliography, p.745-801. V.2 has chapter bibliographies (p.449-508), with index of authors cited; analytical general index. *Class No:* 261.8(091)

Liturgy & Worship

Bibliographies

[644]
A Bibliography of Christian worship. Thompson, B., *ed.* Metuchen, N.J. and London, American Theological Association and Scarecrow Press, 1989. xiii,786p. $79.50. (*ATLA bibliography series, 25.*) ISBN: 0810821540.

51 sections arranged in 6 parts: 1. Reference works and general works - 2. Worship and the liturgy in the Christian tradition (covering more than half the book) - 3. Word and sacraments: theology, liturgy and spirituality - 4. The daily office and the church year - 5. Worship and the arts - 6. Church music and hymnology. Includes periodical articles as well as books. Author/editor, p.741-782. Church bodies/ conference/organizations index, p.783-786. 'International in scope, its comprehensiveness and depth make this a truly outstanding work' (*Choice*, v.27(10), January 1990, p.1645). *Class No:* 264(01)

[645]
GRIMES, R.L. Research in ritual studies: a programmatic essay and bibliography. Metuchen, N.J., Scarecrow Press; The American Theological Library Association, 1985. 165p. $15. (*ATLA bibliography series, 14.*) ISBN: 0810817624.

Over 1600 entries for books and journal articles on ritual (in the disciplines covered by religion, anthropology, sociology, psychology and literary criticism) grouped in 4 sections: Ritual components - Ritual types - Ritual descriptions - General works. Includes festivals, pilgrimages, ritual objects, rituals of exchange, and civil ceremonies. An overview of the current state of the study precedes. '... unique because it does not classify rituals by particular group ...' (*Choice*, v.23(1), September 1985, p.81). *Class No:* 264(01)

Dictionaries

[646]
DAVIES, J.G. A New dictionary of liturgy and worship. Rev. & expanded ed. London, S.C.M. Press; Philadelphia, Pa., Westminster Press, 1986. xv, [1], 544p. £19.50. $29.95. ISBN: 033402207x, UK; 0664212700, US.

First published 1972. Title in US is *The new Westminster dictionary of liturgy and worship.*

Over 100 contributors, Emphasis is on Christian worship (baptism, eucharist, etc.), with brief treatment of other religions. 'The separate articles are not confined to simple definitions but give the historical background to the subject treated and seek to relate this to the contemporary scene' (*Preface* to 1st ed.). Signed articles; references in text and/or appended. It strikes a more ecumenical note than the *Oxford dictionary of the Christian church.* 'Students will come to find it extremely useful (especially in revision), both for its factual material and for the stimulation of faith' (*Heythrop journal*, v.15, 1976, p.240). '... will prove invaluable ...' (*British book news*, April 1986, p.211). *Class No:* 264(038)

Vestments

[647]

MAYO, J. A History of ecclesiastical dress. London, Batsford, 1984. 192p. 112 illus. (6 in colour). £20. ISBN: 0713437642.

Traces the origins and development of ecclesiastical dress (liturgical vestments, choir dress, and outdoor or general dress where it differs from contemporary fashionable dress). A chronological account is followed by a detailed and illustrated glossary in which individual items and their origins are described. *Class No:* 264-03

[648]

NORRIS, H. Church vestments: their origin & development. London, Dent, 1949. xv, 190p. illus.

A work which grew out of the author's *Costume and fashion* (1927-38), dealing with classical garments that were the ancestors of church vestments. Attention given to accurate dating; coloured, and black-and-white illustrations; brief historical data; index. *Class No:* 264-03

Hymns

Bibliographies

[649]

PARKS, E.D. Early English hymns. Metuchen, N.J., Scarecrow Press, 1972. 168p.

Lists and locates over 900 hymns written in English before Isaac Watts. Many of the titles do not appear in Julian's *Dictionary*. Data: metre, number of stanzas, author, date published, number and/or page where hymn located; and on tune and composer. Author, composer and tune indexes. *Class No:* 264-068(01)

[650]

—DIEHL, K.S. Hymns and tunes - an index. Metuchen, N.J., Scarecrow Press, 1966. lv, 1185p. $70. £52.50. ISBN: 0810800624.

An index to songs found in 78 hymnals, chiefly in English and representing British and North American Jewish-Christian institutions. Part 1: The hymns; part 2: The tunes. *Class No:* 264-068(01)

[651]

—McDORMAND, T.B. *and* CROSSMAN, F.S. Judson concordance to hymns. Valley Forge, Pa., Judson Press, 1965. 375p.

Indexes nearly 2400 hymns from 26 hymnals of major US and Canadian denominations. The user is referred from the keyword in any line to the 'Line index' and thence to the first line of the hymn. *Class No:* 264-068(01)

[652]

PERRY, D.W. Hymns and tunes indexed, the first lines, tune names and metres. Compiled from current English hymnbooks. Croydon, The Hymn Society of Great Britain and Ireland, and the Royal School of Church Music, 1980. ix,306p.

Indexes 37 hymnals (listed p.vii-viii). Index of first lines, p.121; index of tunes, p.123-229; index of metres, p.230-306. 'Intended as a comprehensive reference book for all who deal in hymns, whether as 'amateurs' or 'professionals' and will be especially valuable for those working with members of other denominations' (*The Church times*, 28 November, 1980, p.viii). *Class No:* 264-068(01)

[653]

TURNER-EVANS, H. A Bibliography of Welsh hymnology. Caernarfon, Arfon/Dwyfor Library HQ., 1977. [ii], 206p. £4.

Based on the author's Library Association thesis, *Bibliography of Welsh hymnology to 1960* (1964). About 200 entries for individual hymn-writers (Adams, David ... Wynne, Ellis; p.15-206). Data include: biographical sketch; works; hymn(s) in Welsh. No index of hymns. Prefixed list of Bardic names and pseudonyms; bibliography of books, periodical articles and manuscripts in hymnology. Mimeographed. *Class No:* 264-068(01)

Dictionaries

[654]

JULIAN, J. A Dictionary of hymnology, setting forth the origin and history of Christian hymns of all ages and nations ... Rev. 2nd ed., with new supplement. London, Murray, 1907 (Reprinted, 1958, 2v.; Gordon Press, 4v. 1977). $600 the set. ISBN: 884901719x.

First published 1892.

Includes biographical and critical notices of authors and translators, historical articles on national and denominational hymnody, breviaries, etc., the English language being the keynote. Lists of contributors, MSS., abbreviations; indexes of first lines and names. Still the standard work. *Class No:* 264-068(038)

[655]

TEMPERLEY, N. The hymn tune index: a census of English language hymn tunes in printed sources from 1535 to 1820. Manns, C. S. *and* Hal, J. Oxford, Oxford University Press, 1998. 4 vols. £300.00. ISBN: 0193111500.

extraordinary piece of work: a guide to narly three centuries of hymn tunes from Britain and North America - some 18,000 in all. The entry on each has, usually, the following elements: the name of the composer, where known; the date when it first appeared in print; the words which may be set to it. Each tune is provided with its own history. It is indispensable for the study of hymnology, and is an invaluable addition to Julian's *Dictionary of hymnology*. *Class No:* 264-068(038)

Biographies

[656]

HAYDEN, A.J. *and* NEWTON, R.F., *eds.* British hymn writers and composers: a check-list, giving their dates and places of birth and death. Guildford, Hymn Society of Great Britain & Ireland, 1977. [94]p. £3. ISBN: 0950558907.

Lists *c.*2,500 names, A-Z, includes 'the names of those who were born or died in a known year in the British Isles and who wrote or shared in the making of a hymn in English or a tune (*not* a harmonisation or a descant-setting only) included in a major British hymn-book published between January 1901 and December 1975' (*Compilers' Preface*). 35 hymn-books were consulted. *Class No:* 264-068(092)

Prayer Books

[657]

The Oxford book of prayer. Appleton, G., *ed.* Oxford, Oxford University Press, 1985. 399p. £10. ISBN: 0192132229.

Aims to be a reasonably representative collection of prayers. 7 sections: I. Prayers of adoration - II. Prayers from the scriptures - III. Prayers of Christians: personal and occasional - IV. Prayers of the Church - V. Prayer as listening - VI. Prayer from other traditions of faith (Jewish, Indian, etc., 10 in all) - VII. Prayer towards the unity of mankind. Appendix: Notes on the development of Eucharistic prayer. Index of authors and sources, p.391-396; index of subjects, p.397-399. *Class No:* 264-1

Missionary Work (Christian Church)

Bibliographies

[658]

International review of mission. Geneva, Commission on World Mission and Evangelism of the World Council of Churches (previously London, International Missionary Council). 1911-. v.1, no.1-. Quarterly. S.Fr.47.50. $35. £23.50. pa. ISSN: 00208582.

V.89, no. 352, January 2000 has the regular 'Bibliography on mission studies' on p.121-144. 12 sections: 1. Bibliographies and study of mission; 2. Surveys of the Christian situation; 3. History of theology of mission; 4. Religion, religions and dialogue; 5. The context of mission - environment and society; 6. The structure of mission - churches and mission; 7. The practice of mission - forms of ministry and witness; 8. Africa; 9. The Americas; 10. Asia; 11. Europe; 12. Oceania. *Class No:* 266(01)

Dictionaries

[659]

NEILL, S., *and others, eds.* Concise dictionary of the Christian world missions. London, United Society for Christian literature, Lutterworth Press, 1970. xv,682p.

Covers Protestant and Catholic missionary activities throughout the world. About 250 contributors. Many of the signed articles have brief bibliographies, Includes biographies (*e.g.* Livingstone: 2½ cols.; 2 references), countries (*e.g.* Pacific Islands; p.459-65; 20 lines of bibliography), forms (*e.g.* missionary atlases, dictionaries and journals), events, etc. Includes entries for 'Islam' and 'Buddhism'. Many cross-references. 'There is no comparable tool available in the field' (*Library journal*, v.96(13), July 1971, p.2296). *Class No:* 266(038)

Histories

[660]

LATOURETTE, K.J. A History of the expansion of Christianity. London, Eyre & Spottiswoode, 1938-47. 7v.maps.

1. *The first five centuries, to 500 A.D.* 2. *Thousand years of uncertainty, 500-1500 A.D.* 3. *Three centuries of advance, 1500-1800 A.D.* 4. *The Great Century: Europe and the U.S.* 5. *The Americas, Australasia and Africa.* 6. *North Africa and Asia.* 7. *Advance through storm, 1914 and after.*

A work of encyclopaedic range, by a well-known authority on

....(contd.)

Christian missions, likely to remain the standard history for many years to come, on the missionary enterprise of Christianity from its earliest times up to the present day. Each volume has its own index, full bibliography, and maps. 'Latourette handles temperately, charitably and with immense erudition every part of Christian expansion - Roman Catholic, Protestant, and Orthodox' (Neill, S. *A History of Christian missions* (1965), p.579). *Class No:* 266(091)

Religious Associations & Societies

Bibliographies

[661]

CRUMB, L.N. **The Oxford movement and its leaders:** a bibliography of secondary and lesser primary sources. New York, American Theological Library Association and Scarecrow Press, 1988. 706p. $66. (*ATLA bibliography series, 24.*) ISBN: 0810821419.

Lists over 500 titles in chronological order to the end of 1987. Author and subject indexes. *Class No:* 267(01)

Yearbooks & Directories

[662]

NATIONAL CENTRE FOR CHRISTIAN COMMUNITIES AND NETWORKS. **Directory of Christian groups, communities and networks.** London, the Centre, 1993. £5. ISBN: 0946185115.

First published in 1980, as *A directory of Christian communities and groups.*

A selective list of groups, arranged A-Z by name in two sections - More recently established groups - Religious orders and congregations. Information includes name and address, telephone number, ecumenical date, numbers of staff and residents, brief description of denominational allegiance, aims, etc. Geographical index (by country, A-Z). Subject index. *Class No:* 267(058)

Benedictines

[663]

A **Benedictine bibliography:** an author-subject union list. Kapsner, O.L., *ed.* 2nd ed. Collegeville, MN., St. John's Abbey Press, at the American Benedictine Academy, 1962. 2v. ([11],664p.;[10],479p.).

First published in 1952. Compiled for the Library Science Section of the American Benedictine Academy.

V.1 has 13,428 unannotated items arranged A-Z; v.2 is a subject and author index. A 1st *Supplement* was published in 1982 (Collegeville, MN., Liturgical Press. 832p. $20. £29.95. ISBN 081461258x. *Class No:* 267BEN

Salvation Army

[664]

MOYLES, R.G. **A Bibliography of Salvation Army literature in English (1865-1987).** Lewiston, N.Y., E. Mellen, 1988. 209p. $49.95. (*Texts and studies in religion, 38.*) ISBN: 0889468273.

Aims to be comprehensive, including both primary and secondary sources (books, periodical articles, novels, plays, poetry) about the Salvation Army. Omits personal ephemera. 9 subject sections, 3 of which are subdivided by specific topic, and all subdivided chronologically. No annotations, but each section has a brief overview of the topic. Author index. *Class No:* 267.12

[665]

The **Salvation Army year book.** London, International Headquarters of the Salvation Army. Annual. ISSN: 0080567x.

First published 1906.

Part 1 has articles of special interest; pt.2. Facts and figures; pt.3 Reports, staff lists and addresses; 4. Rolls of Honour; Who's who in The Salvation Army. Index. *Class No:* 267.12

[666]

—The History of the Salvation Army. Sandall, R. *and* Wiggins, A.R. *and* Coutts, F. London, Nelson/Hodder & Stoughton, 1947-88. 7v. v.7: £12.95. ISBN: 0340390875, v.7.

A detailed official account of the organization. V.1-2, 4 carry the narrative from 1865 to 1904; v.3 is subtitled '1883-1953: Social work and reform'; v.5 covers 1904-1914; v.6: 1914-1946; and v.7: 1944-1977. Each v. has a bibliography and an analytical index. *Class No:* 267.12

Church History

[667]

CHADWICK, O. **The Pelican history of the Church.** Later volumes are titled *The Penguin history of the Church*. Harmondsworth, Middlesex, Penguin Books, 1964-93. 7v.

1. *The early Church*, by Henry Chadwick. 1968.
2. *Western Society and the Church in the Middle Ages*, by R.W. Southern. 1970.
3. *The Reformation*, by O. Chadwick. 1964.
4. *The Church and the Age of Reason, 1648-1789*, by G.R. Cragg. 1972.
5. *The Church in an age of Revolution, 1789 to the present day*, by A.R. Vidler, 1971.
6. *History of Christian missions*, by S. Neill. 1964.
7. *The Christian Church in the Cold War*, by O.Chadwick, 1993.

V.3 (463p.) has 3 parts: 1. The protest - 2. The Counter Reformation - 3. The Reformation and the life of the Church. 'Suggestions for further readings', p.466-9. V.7 is the final volume, dealing with organized Christianity since the early 1970s, from survival of the Church in Communist Poland to the decline of the mainstream churches in Western Europe. 'It will certainly be one of the largest and most comprehensive Church histories of our time' (*The Church times*, 20 March 1981, p.6). *Class No:* 27

[668]

Conciliorum Oecumenicorum decreta. [Decrees of the Ecumenical Councils] Tanner, N., *ed.* London, Sheed & Ward, 1992 xxv,1342p. ISBN: 072203010x.

Published in two volumes.

The full text of the Ecumenical Councils, Latin (or Greek) and English on facing pages. Ten indexes, including biblical citations, authors and subjects. The text and facing translation have the same page numbers. All texts have been newly translated for this edition. *Class No:* 27

[669]

Oxford history of the Christian Church. Chadwick, H. *and* Chadwick, O., eds. Oxford, Clarendon Press, 1976-.

To be in some 20 volumes, published over several years. 'It will certainly be one of the largest and most comprehensive church histories of our time' (*The Church times*, 20 March 1981, p.6.).

Intended to provide a full survey of the Christian Churches and their part in the religious heritage of humanity, particular attention being paid to the place of the churches in surrounding society, the institutions of church life and the manifestations of popular religion, the link with forms of national culture, and the intellectual tradition within and beyond Europe. So far published are: *A history of the churches in the United States and Canada*, by R. Handy (1976. 486p. maps. £40. ISBN 0198269102); *The Frankish church*, by J.M. Wallace-Hadrill (1983. 472p. map. £45. ISBN 0108269064); *Religion in England, 1688-1791*, by Gordon Rupp (1986. 596p. £45. ISBN 0198269188); *The Orthodox Church in the Byzantine Empire*, by J.M. Hussey (1986. 428p. £45. ISBN 0198269013); *The Popes and European revolution*, by Owen Chadwick (1981. 656p. £40. ISBN 0198269196); *The Papal monarchy: the Western Church from 1050 to 1250*, by Colin Morris (1989. 688p. £55. ISBN 0198269072). *The Church in Africa 1450-1950* by Adrian Hastings (1994, xiv, 706p. maps. ISBN 0198209218); *German and Scandinavian Protestantism 1700-1918* by Nicholas Hope (1995, xiii, 685p. maps. ISBN 0198269234). *A history of the popes 1830-1914*, by Owen Chadwick (1998, x,614p. ISBN 0198269226) and *Church and society in eighteenth-century France*, by John McManners (1998, 2 vols.). *Class No:* 27

Bibliographies

[670]

BAKER, D., *ed.* The Materials, sources and methods of ecclesiastical history. Oxford, Blackwell, for the Ecclesiastical History Society, 1975. xii,370p. (*Studies in Church history, 11.*)

Papers read at the 12th Summer meeting and the 13th Winter meeting of the Society. Topics: particular documents or types of document; methodology and historiography: the contribution to church history of archaeological socio-linguistic and socio-cultural techniques. 3 major papers, including the presidential address, 'attempt to assess the place and role of the contemporary church historian, his problems and opportunities' (*Heythrop journal* v.19, 1978, p.205-6). *Class No:* 27(01)

[671]

Revue d'histoire ecclésiastique. Louvain, Université Catholique de Louvain, 1900-. v.1, no.1-. Quarterly. ISSN: 00352381.

V.94, no.3-4 Jul-Dec 1999, contains 6 articles; Comptes rendus ...; Chronique (country surveys); and Bibliographie (p.325*-503* with nearly 3000 items). Essential reading for the serious ecclesiastical historian. *Class No:* 27(01)

Handbooks & Manuals

[672]

BRADLEY, J.E. *and* MULLER, R.A. **Church history** an introduction to research, reference works, and authors Grand Rapids, MI, Eerdmans, 1995. xv,236p. £19.00. ISBN: 0802808263.

A handbook for doctoral students "characterized by an almost evangelical fervour for the computer age" (*Theologischer Literaturzeitung* 1997 nr. 7/8 p.673). Contains guidance on choosing research topics and is particularly strong on bibliographical tools, especially databases, available for research. About a quarter of the book is devoted to a bibliographical listing of reference material. Strong Anglo-American bias. *Class No:* 27(035)

Dictionaries

[673]

BRAUER, J.C. **The Westminster dictionary of church history.** Philadelphia, PA., Westminster Press, 1971. xii,887p. $27.50. ISBN: 0664212859.

'... purpose is to give an immediate, accurate introductory definition and explanation concerning the major men, events, facts, and movements in the history of Christianity' (*Preface*). Covers the early church (to A.D.600), the medieval church (600-1300), the Reformation church (1300-1700), and the modern church (1700 to present), giving greatest emphasis on the modern period. Over 140 contributors. Includes biographies. Entries vary in length from brief identifications to short articles with bibliographies (*e.g.* 'Canon law': 1½ cols.; 5 references; 'Cluny': 3 cols.; 5 references; 'Holy Roman Empire': 4¼ cols.; 7 references). Cross references.
Class No: 27(038)

Maps & Atlases

[674]

Atlas of the Christian church. Chadwick, H., *ed.* 2nd rev. ed. Oxford, Phaidon, 1990. 240p. £19.50.

First published 1987.

In 6 parts: 1. The early church ... 6. The Christian church today. 302 illus (236 col.): 42 highly coloured maps: chronological table: gazetteer (tiny print). Bibliography, p.229-31. Index, p.237-40.
Class No: 27(084.3)

Biographies

[675]

BARKER, W.P. **Who's who in Church history.** Grand Rapids, Mich., Baker Book House, 1977. 319p.

Biographies of over 1500 men and women who left an imprint on the history of the Christian Church. Excludes living persons. 'Provides a concise, inexpensive reference tool recommended for libraries for the churchman and layman'. (*American reference books annual*, 1979, item 1076). *Class No:* 27(092)

Scotland

[676]

Dictionary of Scottish church history and theology. Cameron, R., *ed.* London, Marshall Pickering, 1992. 800p. £35. ISBN: 0551022930.

Aims to provide a single source of reference for the history and theology of the Scottish church, with major coverage of biographies, missions, the development of Scottish theology, ecclesiastical history, art and architecture. *Class No:* 27(411)

[677]

DONALDSON, G. **Scottish church history.** Edinburgh, Scottish Academic Press, 1985. xii,250p. 25 illus. (incl. 14 pl.). £18.75. ISBN: 0707303613.

17 chapters dealing with various topics from the Dark Ages to the 20th century drawing on material ranging from archaeological and linguistic evidence, through record sources, to some lessons drawn from Inter-Church Discussions in which the author took part: 1. Scotland's earliest church buildings - 2. Bishops' Sees before the reign of David I ... 5. The Church Courts ... 8. The Parish Clergy and the Reformation ... 12. The foundations of Anglo-Scottish union ... 16. The emergence of schism in seventeenth-century Scotland - 17. Church and community. Index, p.239-245. *Class No:* 27(411)

USA

[678]

Religion and society in North America: an annotated bibliography. Brunkow, R. de V., *ed.* Santa Barbara, CA., ABC-Clio Press, 1983. xi,515p. $65; £58.25. (*Clio bibliographical series, no.12.*) ISBN: 0874360420.

4304 annotated entries selected from v.11-18 of *America: history and life,* arranged in 21 sections: 1. United States and Canada - 2. Americanizations of institutions - 3. Business (including Protestant ethic) - 4. Communal movements and utopian thought - 5. Ecumenism

....(contd.)
and intergroup relations - 6. Education - 7. Family - 8. Government and politics - 9. Health - 10. Labour - 11. Missionary impulse ... 21. Religious groups (37 + anti-religious movements). Annotations between 50 to 100 words in length. Subject index, p.323-501; author index, p.502-510; list of periodicals, p.511-513. *Class No:* 27(73)

Ancient Times

Manuscripts & Incunabula

[679]

BARDENHEWER, O. **Geschichte der altkirchlichen Literatur.** Darmstadt, Wissenschaftliche Buchgesellschaft, 1962. 5v.

V.1 covers the period from the end of the Apostolic era to the close of the 2nd century (xii, 633p.). V.5 (ix,423p.) includes a section on the oldest Armenian document. Arrangement is by authors, with biographical data and quotations. Thus 'Boethius' (p.250-64) is dealt with under five headings, each with a bibliography; 'De consolations philosphiae' has ¾p, listing editions, translations, commentaries and studies on it. Semi-analytical name index to each volume.
Class No: 27"-"(093)

Tudor & Stuart Times

Bibliographies

[680]

BAINTON, R.H. *and* GRITSCH, E.W. **Bibliography of the Continental Reformation:** materials available in English. 2nd ed., rev. & enl. Hamden, CT., Archon Books: Shoe String Press, 1972. xix,220p. $24.50; £19.60. ISBN: 0208012192.

First published 1935.

About 3,000 references (Bibliographies - Encyclopedia articles - Collected essays on the Reformation - Sources in translation - General histories of the Reformation - Special phrases of Reformation history - Roman Catholic reform - Martin Luther ... Doctrinal settlements, including the Augsburg Confession ... Zwingli ... Anabaptists ... Calvin (p.163-84) ... The Reformation in France - The Italian Reformers ... Erasmus ... The Reformation in Norway and Sweden ... The Reformation in Hungary and Poland). Many periodical articles. No indexes. *Class No:* 27"1485-1760"(01)

[681]

COMMISSION INTERNATIONALE D'HISTOIRE ECCLÉSIASTIQUE COMPARÉE. **Bibliographie de la Réforme, 1450-1648:** ouvrages parus de 1940 a 1955. Leiden, E.J. Brill, 1958-. fasc.1-.

fasc.1: Allemagne, Pays-Bas. (1958. 2nd ed. 1961. Gld.32. $16. ISBN 9004002057).

fasc.2: Belgique, Suède, Norvege, Danemark, Ireland, États-Unis. (1960. Gld.37. $18.50. ISBN 9004002065).

fasc.3: Italie, Espagne, Portugal. (1961. Gld.41. $20.50. ISBN 9004026541).

fasc.4: France, Angleterre, Suisse. (1963. Reprint under consideration).

fasc.5: Pologne, Hongrie, Tchécoslovaquie, Finlande (1965. Gld.41. $20.50. ISBN 9004002081).

fasc.6: Autriche. (1967. Gld.18. $9. ISBN 9004002103).

fasc.7: Écosse. (1970. Gld.69. $34.50. ISBN 9004067639).

Sponsored by the International Commission of Ecclesiastical History, part of the International Committee of Historical Sciences. The section on Germany, by G. Franz, in fasc.1, comprises 1745 unannotated entries plus 4 indexes (1. Begriffe und Institutionen - 2. Deutsche Länder und Städte - 3. Ausland - 4. Biographien); 38 journals are cited. *Class No:* 27"1485-1760"(01)

[682]

—COMMISSION INTERNATIONALE D'HISTOIRE ECCLÉSIASTIQUE COMPARÉE. **The Bibliography of the Reform, 1450-1648,** relating to the United Kingdom and Ireland for the years 1955-70. Baker, D., *ed.* Oxford, Blackwell, 1975. [x], 242p.

Compiled for the British Sub-Commission of the Commision.

2579 entries for England and Wales, 498 entries for Scotland, and 260 for Ireland (plus interpolations) in A-Z author order in each case. Supplements the entries in fascs, 4 & 7 (above). *Class No:* 27"1485-1760"(01)

Religious Orders & Communities

[683]

CONSTABLE, G. **Medieval monasticism:** a select bibliography. Toronto, University of Toronto Press, 1976. [xxi], 171p. (*Toronto medieval bibliographies, 6.*)

1036 references. Parts: 1. Reference - 2. Monastic history - 3. Monastic life and institutions. Closely subdivided. Includes a section on women in religious life. 'A standard reference tool for the study of many aspects of medieval culture' (*Library journal*, v.101(12), 15 June, p.1406). *Class No:* 271

[684]

GREENE, J.P. Medieval monasteries. Leicester, Leicester University Press (distributed in USA & Canada by St. Martins Press, New York), 1992. xiii,255p. illus. £47.50 (Archaeology of medieval Britain)

Covers the application of new archaeological techniques, describing the methods and resulting information about monastic life in 9 chapters. Postscript: 'The future of monastic archaeology'. Glossary, p.233-5. Bibliography, p.236-44. Index, p.245-55. *Class No:* 271

Encyclopaedias & Dictionaries

[685]

KAPSNER, O.L. Catholic religious orders, listing conventional and full names in English, foreign languages and Latin; also, abbreviations, date and country of origin, and founders. 2nd ed., enl. Collegeville, Minn., St. John's Abbey Press, 1957. xxxviii, 594p.

First published 1948.

Sponsored by the Catholic Library Association and 'Primarily ... intended for the use of library cataloguers' (*Preface*). 1777 main entries; abbreviations are cross-referred to full names. Glossary, p.xiii-xxvi; list of authorities consulted, p.xxvii-xxxvii. *Class No:* 271(03)

Dictionaries

[686]

Dizionario degli istituti di perfezione. [Dictionary of religious orders and congregations.] Pelliccia, G. *and* Rocca, G., *eds.* Rome, Edizioni Paoline, 1974-

Published in 9 volumes?

At the time of writing (October 1997) what was said to be the final volume has just appeared after a decade's delay. It covers, however, only "Spi-Ve", which suggests another volume is to be expected, especially as there are no general indexes. A major source, nonetheless, for the history and spirituality of the religious orders and congregations and their founders, mainly, but not only, within the Roman Catholic Church. Well illustrated, bibliographies attached to entries, which are signed. *Class No:* 271(038)

Histories

Bibliographies

[687]

POLGÁR, L. Bibliographie sur l'histoire de la Compagnie de Jésus. Rome, Institutm Historicum S.I., 1981-90. 3 vols. in 6. ISBN: 8870416062.

Volume I ('Toute le Compagnie') covers general works on the Jesuits, and works on or by Ignatius of Loyola; Volume II provides bibliographies by countries, part 1 being Europe, part 2 the rest of the world; Volume III 'Les personnes' (in three parts) lists individual Jesuits in alphabetical order, but only provides entries about them: their own writings are not listed. There is no general index and the volumes, though immensely thorough, are not easy to use. *Class No:* 271(091)(01)

Scotland

[688]

COWAN, I.B. *and* EASSON, D.E. Medieval religious houses: Scotland, with an appendix on the houses in the Isle of Man. 2nd ed. London & New York, Longman, 1976. xxviii, 246, [6]p. £15. ISBN: 0582120691.

First published 1957.

2nd ed. is the result of 'further research, particularly in the Vatican Archives, into the history of the Medieval Church in Scotland' (*Preface*). 10 Sections: Early Christian foundations - Houses of monks - Houses of regular canons - Houses of the mendicant orders - Houses of nuns - Houses of the military orders - Hospitals - Cathedral (secular; monastic) - Secular colleges - Academic secular colleges. Sources. p.32-45 (*c.* 400 items). Appendices: 1. The religious houses of the Isle of Man; 3. The incomes of the Scottish religious houses: sources. A closely documented study. *Class No:* 271(411)

Eire

[689]

GWYNN, A. *and* HADCOCK, R.N. Medieval religious houses: Ireland; with an appendix to early sites. New ed. Blackrock, Co. Dublin., Irish Academic Press, 1988. 492p. map. £27.50. ISBN: 0716524163.

Identifies and locates over a thousand religious foundations from the 5th to the 17th century. 22 sections, plus 'Unclassified'. A detailed bibliography of books on Irish monasteries precedes. O.S. map of monastic Ireland. *Class No:* 271(417)

England & Wales

[690]

KNOWLES, D. *and* HADCOCK, R.N. Medieval religious houses: England and Wales. 2nd ed. London, Longmans, 1971. xv, 565p. tables, maps.

First published 1953 (a much-expanded revision of D. Knowles' *Religious houses of medieval England* (1940).

Arranged by orders (Benedictines, etc.), then A-Z by name of house. Details for each house: county; rank (*e.g.* abbey; priory); income in 1535; date of foundation and dissolution; parent house. Appendices: 1. Religious houses existing at periods before 1066 - 2. Tables showing increase and decrease in various orders. 'A very stimulating inventory to handle' (*Journal of ecclesiastical history,* v.23, no.3, July 1972, p.276-7). A basic list of religious and secular communities. *Class No:* 271(42)

[691]

—KNOWLES, D., *and others.* The Heads of religious houses: England and Wales, 940-1216. Cambridge, Cambridge University Press, 1972. xlvii, 278p.

Gives the names under the various orders (The Benedictine houses ... The Gilbertine canons and nuns), with dates of accession and death, the details of careers. List of MSS referred to, and list of printed books and authors cited precede. Appendix 3: List of pre-Conquest charters used. Index of heads; index of religious houses.

Modern religious houses are listed and described in P.F. Anson's *The religious orders and congregations of Great Britain and Ireland* (Worcester, Stanbrook Abbey Press, 1949, 423p.). *Class No:* 271(42)

England

[692]

KNOWLES, D. The Monastic order in England: a history of its development from the times of St. Dunstan to the Fourth Lateran Council, 940-1216. 2nd ed. Cambridge, Cambridge University Press, 1963. xxii, 780p. £55. ISBN: 0521054796.

First published 1940.

An account, historical rather than antiquarian, of English monastic life during an important period of religious history; based on contemporary sources, quoted in full where space allows. Detailed bibliography and notes. Continued in: *Class No:* 271(420)

[693]

—Monasticon Anglicanum. Dugdale, Sir W. London, Bested, 1817-30 (Reprinted Gregg International, 1970). 8v. £950. ISBN: 0576785377.

First published in 1693.

Assessed by J.L. Hobbs (*Local history and the library,* p.200) as an essential source book; it 'details the charters of foundation and other deeds of monasteries and religious houses, with a historical summary of each'. *Class No:* 271(420)

[694]

KNOWLES, D. The Religious orders in England. Cambridge, Cambridge University Press, 1948-59. 3v.

The old orders, 1216-1314. 2. The end of the Middle Ages. 3. The Tudor age. Includes the history of the Friars of England. V.3 has a bibliography and detailed index, plus valuable appendices (*e.g.* 2. Religious houses suppressed by Wolsey; 10. Regulars as bishops (a list). *Bare ruined choirs: the dissolution of the English monasteries,* by D. Knowles (C.U.P. 1976. illus. ISBN 0521707126) is an abridged and illustrated edition of v.3.

The standard work, making use of many published records of episcopal visitations. *Class No:* 271(420)

Persecution

[695]

VEKENÉ, E. van der. Bibliographie der Inquisition: ein Versuch. Hildesheim, Olms, 1963. viii,323p.

1963 entries in all, arranged chronologically, 1483-1961, including periodical articles and sections/chapters of books (*e.g. Cambridge medieval history*). 26 European library locations. Index of journals. Sources, p.297-301. Index of authors and titles. *Class No:* 272

Patrology (Church Fathers)

Bibliographies

[696]

ALTANER, B. Patrology. Freiberg, Herder; Edinburgh & London, Nelson, 1960. xxiv,660p.

A translation by Hilda C. Graef, based on the 5th German edition of *Patrologie* (1958), revised and augumented.

Not a 'mere bibliography of patrology', but rather a literary history, with brief biographies and extensive bibliographical references. The section of St. Jerome, for example, covers p.462-77. Index. 'This indispensable manual for patristic studies is notable for the

....*(contd.)*

completeness of coverage and for its separate bibliographies for individual writers and subjects' (*Heythrop journal*, v.1(3), October 1960, p.359). *Class No:* 276(01)

[697]

Bibliographia patristica: Internationale patristische Bibliographie, 1956-. Berlin, de Gruyter, 1959-. v.1-. Annual. ISSN: 05232252.

V.33-35 lists 6516 articles, etc. with a separate section for reviews (1306 of them are referenced) on the early Church Fathers for 1988-90 (published 1997). The period covered is for the Eastern Church roughly to the end of the eighth century, and for the Western Church to the death of Ildephonsus of Toledo (667). Entries subdivided: 1. Generalia - 2. Novum Testamentum atque Apocrypha - 3. Auctores - 4. Liturgica - 5. Iuridica, symbola - 6. Doctrina auctorum et historia dogmatum - 7. Gnostica - 8. Patrum exegesis Veteris et Novi Testamenti - 9. Recensiones. Author index, and one of reviews. *Class No:* 276(01)

[698]

QUASTEN, J. Patrology. Westminster, MD, Newman Press; Utrecht, Spectrum, 1950-60 (reprinted 1983 by Christian Classics, Westminster, MD). 3v. in 4. $93.95. ISBN: 0870611410.

1: *The beginnings of Patristic literature.* (1950). 2: *The ante-Nicene literature after Irenaeus.* (1953). 3: *The golden age of Greek Patristic literature, from the Council of Nicaea to the Council of Chalcedon.* (1960). An important bibliography, designed to inform both specialist and student on the literature of the subject; the latter comprises (1) critical editions (2) translations, especially into English, and (3) articles and monographs. The fullest collection of Patristic texts is that produced by J.-P. Migne - *Patrologiae cursus completus* (Latin series. Paris, 1844-64, 221v. : Greek series (Greek text with Latin translation). Paris, 1857-66. 166v. Index. 1912. Index locupletissimus. 1928-45. 2v.; Latin texts of Greek authors. Paris, 1856-67. 81v. 'Its vast scope leaves it still unique and valuable, where other editions of special works do not exist' (*Encyclopaedia Britannica* (11th ed.), v.18p.426). *Class No:* 276(01)

[699]

—Corpus Christianorum. Series Latina. Turnhout, Brépols, 1954-.
To be published in 175v. and to cover all Patristic texts in Latin. *Class No:* 276(01)

Encyclopaedias & Dictionaries

[700]

Encyclopedia of the Early Church. Berardino, Angelo di, *ed.* Cambridge, James Clarke, 1992 xxv,1130p. ISBN: 0227678958.

Published in two volumes.

Period of encyclopedia covers from immediate post-New Testament times to circa 750 AD across the whole of the (by then) Christian World. Immensely scholarly, its strength lies particularly in the entries on churchmen (and some women) of the period. Entries vary in length according to the importance of the topic, and each is provided with a bibliography. The alphabetical entries are followed by a "Synoptic Table" (i.e. a chronology), a section of very detailed maps, some 320 illustrations, and a thorough index. *Class No:* 276(03)

Dictionaries

Greek

[701]

LAMPE, G.W.H., *ed.* **A Patristic Greek lexicon.** Oxford, Clarendon Press, 1961-67. (Reprinted in one volume by Oxford University Press, 1969). 5 fasc. in 1v. £125. ISBN: 019864213x.

A summary history of the use of all theologically important words by the Greek Christian writers of the period from the Apostolic Fathers to A.D.800. Each fascicule has *c.*300 pages. 'Basic and unique lexicon for patristic study' (*Religion & theology*, (1981), p.86). *Class No:* 276(038)=77

Christian Churches

Dictionaries

[702]

BURGESS, S.M., *and others, eds.* **Dictionary of Pentecostal and charismatic movements.** Grand Rapids, MI., Zondervan, 1989. 914p. illus. $29.95. ISBN: 0310441005.

Some 800 entries by 66 contributors focusing on movements in North America and, to some extent, in Europe. Includes biographies of people and descriptions of specific denominations with over 2000 members. Lengthy articles are prefaced by outlines of the text. All entries have bibliographies. Cross-references, but no index. *c.*200 black-and-white photographs, mainly portraits. '... successful both as a

....*(contd.)*

reference source ... and as a broadly based introduction to a religous movement ...' (*Reference books bulletin*, September 1989, v.86(1), p.102-3). *Class No:* 28(038)

Archives

Handbooks & Manuals

[703]

A Guide to church records. Belfast, Ulster Historical Foundation on behalf of the Public Records Office of Northern Ireland, 1994 xix,279p. ISBN: 0901905593.

Contains bibliography.

Arranged alphabetically by civil parish. Churches are indexed by denomination. Appendices 1. Key to abbreviations - 2. Places not arranged under civil parish - 3. PRO of Northern Ireland codes - 4. Indexes to church records - 5. Bibliography (pp. xvii-xviii) - 6. Useful addresses. Introduction includes information on baptism, marriage and burial records as well as notes on the records of various denominations. *Class No:* 28(093.20)(035)

Great Britain

[704]

UK Christian handbook, 2000-2001. London, Marshall Pickering, 1999. 686p. tables, maps. £25. ISSN: 09476971.

First published 1964. Bi-annual.

Sections on: Accommodation - Books - Churches - Evangelism - Media - Overseas - Services - Training - Other useful information and addresses. There is a section for late entries. There is a Location index, which lists places, and a Main index for all other types of entry. *Class No:* 28(410)

Scotland

[705]

BURLEIGH, J.H.S. A Church history of Scotland. London, Oxford University Press, 1960. x,456p. maps.

A survey from the coming of Christianity down to 1957. Addressed to the general reader and not to the specialist (*Preface*). The selective bibliography (p.423-4) is a guide to the more important literature available for consultation. Includes a very useful diagram showing the Church's divisions and reunions, 1690-1929. Detailed index, p.427-456. *Class No:* 28(411)

Ireland

[706]

KENNEY, J.F. The Sources for the early history of Ireland: an introduction and guide. Vol.1. Ecclesiastical. New York, Columbia University Press, 1929. (Reprinted New York, Octagon, 1966). xvi, 807p. maps. $57.50. ISBN: 0374945608.

659 numbered, annotated items in 8 chapters, arranged chronologically up to the 12th century. Many footnotes. References to manuscripts and to printed editions and commentaries, plus notes. General bibliography, p.91-109. Analytical index. No more published. *Class No:* 28(415)

England

Histories

[707]

OWEN, D.M. 'What to read in English religious history'. In *The local historian*, v.16(3), August 1984, p.151-155.

Lists 50 items, and follows an earlier bibliography by the author in *The local historian* (v.8(7), 1969). Author is Keeper of the Archives at the Library of the University of Cambridge. *Class No:* 28(420)(091)

America—North & Central

Encyclopaedias

[708]

LIPPY, C.H. *and* **WILLIAMS, P.W.,** *eds.* **Encyclopedia of the American religious experience:** studies of traditions and movements. New York, Macmillan/Charles Scribner's Sons, 1988. 3v. (xvli, 1872p.). $225 the set. ISBN: 0684180626.

105 commissioned essays on topics dealing with all aspects of the religious experience in the US (and to a limited extent in Canada), both historical and current, and including all denominations, faiths and sects. Arranged in 9 sections organized by broad topic and theme. Essays are lengthy, averaging 12-pages long and include excellent bibliographies. Good cross-references. Exhaustive index. '... valuable as a reference source for information about religious leaders, churches and sects.' (*Reference books bulletin*, 15 May 1988, p.1579-80). 'An

....(contd.)

outstanding achievement ... will become the standard reference tool in American religion'. (*Choice*, v.25(9), May 1988, p.1380). *Class No:* 28(71/73)(031)

Histories

[709]
HANDY, R. A History of the churches in the United States and Canada. Oxford, Clarendon Press, 1976. ix, [1], [1], 471p. maps. £45. (*Oxford history of the Christian Church.*) ISBN: 0198269102.

12 chapters (2. Conflict and diversity in Colonial Christianity (1650-1720) - 3. The era of the Great Awakening in Colonial America ... 10. Roman Catholic, Lutheran, Eastern Orthodox and other churches in America (1860-1920) - 11. Alternative visions of a Christian Canada (1867-1925) - 12. North American churches and the decline of Christendom (with 49 footnotes). Bibliography, p.429-49 (running commentary). Detailed index, p.455-71. *Class No:* 28(71/73)(091)

USA

[710]
MELTON, J.G. *and* **GEISENDORFER, J.V. Religious bodies in the United States.** 2nd ed. New York, Garland, 1992. 312p. $55. (*Religious information systems series, v.1).*.) ISBN: 081530806x.

First published in 1977 as *A Directory of religious bodies...*

Compiled from the files of the Institute for the Study of American Religion. Lists groups active in the Summer of 1991, giving addresses and major publications. A-Z index includes alternative names. *Class No:* 28(73)

Biographies

[711]
BOWDEN, H.W. Dictionary of American religious biography. 2nd ed, rev & enl. Westport, CT., Greenwood Press, 1993. 720p. $75. ISBN: 0313278253.

First published in 1977.

550 biographies of deceased persons 'drawn from three centuries of American religious life, each profile containing capsule summary of figure's life, discussion of historical content of contribution, bibliography of works by and about. Appended bibliographies of material on and by the biographee. 'An excellent acquisition for reference collections' (*Library journal*, v.102(10), 15 May 1977, p.1167.) of the first edition. *Class No:* 28(73)(092)

[712]
—**Who's who in religion.** 3rd ed. Chicago, Ill., Marquis Who's Who Inc., 1985. 439p. $99.50.

Instead of increasing the size for a 3rd ed. a more rigorous selection criteria has been used (2nd ed. covered 18,000 persons). New ed. includes 7000, only those who have 'attained conspicuous achievement' or who hold significant positions in major church or religious organizations. Brief entries indicate name, title, denomination, birthdate, parentage, marriage, children, education and ceritification, professional career, related activities, writings, political affiliations, etc. Also home and office address.

A 4th ed. for 1992-93 was issued in 1992 (768p. $129. ISBN 0837916046). *Class No:* 28(73)(092)

[713]
MELTON, J.G. Biographical dictionary of American cults and sect leaders. New York, Garland, 1986. xii,354p. $39.95. (*Garland reference library of social science, 212.*) ISBN: 0824090373.

Sketches of over 200 individuals, mainly 19th and 20th century (deceased before 1983) who were founders or outstanding leaders of religious group that can be defined as a cult or sect. Well-written entries of about 1½ pages, summarising the person's life and career and including a bibliography of works by and about him/her. General index, and list of leaders by religions, family traditions, birthplace and religious background. *Class No:* 28(73)(092)

Eastern Churches

[714]
The Coptic encyclopedia. Atiya, A.S., *ed. in chief.* New York, Macmillan, 1991. 8v.(2372+371p). $800. ISBN: 002897025x.

2500 signed entries by over 299 contributors. V.1 has a general bibliography. V.8 includes 12 maps and lengthy appendix on the Coptic language. '... its unique focus and depth will fill a real lacuna to reference publishing.'(*College & research libraries*, v.33(5),September 1992, p.418). *Class No:* 281

[715]
FITZGERALD, T.E. The Orthodox Church. Westport, Conn., Greenwood Press, 1995 xiii,240p. £58.50 (*Denominations in America: 7.*) ISBN: 0313262810. ISSN: 01936883.

This volume has to be understood in the light of the series title. Fitzgerald writes only about Orthodoxy in North America, starting with the Alaskan mission of 1794. Approximately half the volume contains biographical information on the Orthodox Church leaders. *Class No:* 281

[716]
KING, A.A. The Rites of Eastern Christendom. London, Burns & Oates, 1950. 2v. illus., map.

Intended as a manual for those (other than the expert liturgical scholar) who want information on the rites of the Eastern Orthodox Church, including the separated Churches. Historical, ritual and ceremonial detail is given, with liturgical tests, bibliography and index to each volume. *Class No:* 281

[717]
—**WARE, T. The Orthodox Church.** Harmondsworth, Mddx, Penguin Books, 1963 (latest of many reprints with revisions, 1983). 352p. illus. map. £3.50; $4.95. ISBN: 0140205926.

16 chapters on history, faith and worship. 'Further reading', p.335-340. Index, p.341-352. 'Clear and factual account by a convert' (*Religion and theology 4.* (S.C.M. Press, 1979, p.33). *Class No:* 281(035)

Dictionaries

[718]
PROKURAT, M. *and* **GOLITZIN, A.** *and* **PETERSON, M.D. Historical dictionary of the Orthodox Church.** Lanham, Md., Scarecrow, 1996 xvii,439p. $89.00 (*Historical dictionaries of religion, philosophy and movements: 9.*) ISBN: 0810830817.

This covers Orthodoxy world-wide and is especially valuable for its nearly 200 page bibliography, arranged by topic. *Class No:* 281(038)

Histories

[719]
ELLIS, J. The Russian Orthodox Church: a contemporary history. London, Croom Helm, 1986. [4],531p. £27.50. (*Keston book, 22.*) ISBN: 0709915675.

13 chapters in 2 parts: part 1 (1. Churches and dioceses - 2. Parish life - 3. The clergy - 4. Theological education - 5. Monasticism - 6. Publications - 7. The laity - 8. The episcopate - 9. Church and state relations). Part 2 (Prologue - 10. The rise of orthodox dissent: up to 1974 - 11. The growth of orthodox dissent, 1974-6 - 12. The flowering of orthodox dissent, 1976-9 - 13. The repression of orthodox dissent, 1976-80. Concluding summary: up to 1985). Notes, p.455-507, by chapter. Bibliography, p.508-539, of books, periodicals, samizdat (selected), legislation, and archives. Analytical index, p.520-531. A new ed. was published by Routledge in 1990. (544p. ISBN 0415034671). *Class No:* 281(091)

Roman Catholic

[720]
Catechism of the Catholic Church. London, Geoffrey Chapman, 1994 xix,691p. ISBN: 022566691x.

The offical statement of Roman Catholic belief, produced by a Vatican Commission and expressed in 2,865 numbered paragraphs. There are citation and subject indexes. *Class No:* 282

[721]
Catholic almanac, 1971-. Huntingdon, Indiana, Our Sunday Visitor, 1969-. Annual. ISBN: 0879732679. ISSN: 00691208.

Previously as *National Catholic almanac* (1904-1970).

Although primarily for the US, it covers the Catholic church worldwide. Includes a chronology and glossary, list of periodicals and encyclicals, statistics, and patron saints, popes, etc. Extensive index precedes. *Class No:* 282

[722]
DEEDY, J. The Catholic fact book. T. More, 1986. 412p. $23.95. ISBN: 0883471868.

Brings together facts from several annual editions of the *Catholic almanac* (formerly *National Catholic almanac* 1904-. Huntingdon, IN, Our Sunday Visitor Inc). 'A potpourri of information about the Roman Catholic Church arranged under various headings, according to history, tenets, saints, famous Catholics and several miscellanies' (*Choice* v.24(5) January 1987, p.739). *Class No:* 282

Bibliographies

[723]

Catholic periodical and literature index. Haverford, Pa., Catholic Library Association, 1930-. 6pa; cumulated 2-yearly. ISSN: 00088285.

Takes over from *Catholic periodical index* (covering 1930-67) and the *Guide to Catholic literature* (covering 1888-1940).

Author and subject indexes to *c.*160 Catholic periodicals, mostly American. Indexes also book and film reviews, conciliar and papal documents. *Class No:* 282(01)

[724]

McCABE, J.P. Critical guide to Catholic reference books. 3rd ed. Englewood, Co., Libraries Unlimited, 1989. xiv,323p. $47.00. (*Research studies in library science, no.20.*) ISBN: 0872876217.

First published 1971; 2nd ed. 1980.

Over 1500 main entries for publications on the teaching, history and mission of the Roman Catholic Church. 5 chapters, each closely subdivided: General; Theology; Humanities; Social science; History. Most entries are annotated, all are in European languages and available in North America. '...continues to be a mainstay for libraries supporting scholarly research on Catholicism' (*Reference books bulletin*, 1989-1990, p.37). *Class No:* 282(01)

[725]

MUSTO, R.G. The Peace tradition of the Catholic Church: an annotated bibliography. New York, Garland, 1987. 590p. $67. (*Garland reference library of social science, v.339.*) ISBN: 0824088841.

The 2nd vol. of the author's 'three-part study that hopes to document the history of the peace tradition in the Roman Catholic Church from the Gospels to the twentieth century' (*Preface*). The 1st part was *The Catholic peace tradition* (Orbis, 1986), a narrative history. The 3rd part is to be an anthology of texts.

1485 entries, mostly annotated, the annotations varying in length from a few sentences to several paragraphs. Covers the tradition from biblical concepts of peace and peacemaking from the Gospels and early church, the Middle Ages, the Renaissance, the age of colonization, and the modern period into the era of Vatican II in Europe, the US and the Third World. Includes items published through November 1986 in English, French, German, Italian, Spanish, Portuguese and Latin. Classified arrangement. Author, personal name, and title indexes. 'Not another source has the scope and depth of Musto's work' (*R.Q.,* v.27(4), Summer 1988, p.576). *Class No:* 282(01)

Encyclopaedias

[726]

COPPA, F.J., *ed*. Encyclopedia of the Vatican and papacy. London, Aldwych Press, 1999. viii, 484p. £70. ISBN: 0861721101.

Attractively produced, but very little else to recommend this volume. With a few exceptions, the signed entries are distinctly pedestrian, bibliographical references are provided, but all too frequently they are to out-of-date books (cf., for example, the entry on Adrian III). Some papal secretaries of state have been included, other, equally significant, cardinals have not. Topics such as "abortion and the papacy", "euthanasia and the papacy" are not notable contributions to the debate, and tend to be rather uncritical. Historical entries include Holocaust and the papacy. There are useful definitions, such as infallibility, papal bulls and encyclicals. There are biographical entries for all popes and antipopes and entries on all the church councils. Entries are signed. *Class No:* 282(031)

[727]

McBRIEN, R. P. The HarperCollins encyclopedia of Catholicism. New York, HarperCollins, 1995 xxxviii,1349p. £40.00 ISBN: 0006279317.

Contains a massive number of fairly brief entries (all apart from the shortest signed) with a number of full-length articles on, for example, the Bible, the Papacy, religious orders etc. The longer articles have a bibliography appended. *Class No:* 282(031)

[728]

MEAGHER, P.K., *ed*. Encyclopedic dictionary of religion. Palatine, Ill., Corpus Publications, 1978. 3v. $69.95 the set. ISBN: 0960257233.

Over 500 contributors. About 25,000 signed articles, primarily concerning Roman Catholicism, but also covering Protestant denominations, Judaism, philosophy, psychology, sociology, archaeology. 'Will be one of the most comprehensive and up-to-date references in the field of religious knowledge. It should be particularly useful for those libraries that cannot afford the *New Catholic encyclopedia* (1967)' (*RSR*, v.6(2), April/June 1978, p.18). *Class No:* 282(031)

[729]

New Catholic encyclopedia: an international work of reference on the teachings, history, organization and activities of the Catholic Church, and on all institutions, religions, philosophies, and scientific and cultural developments affecting the Catholic Church from its beginning to the present. Catholic University of America, editorial staff. New York, McGraw-Hill, 1967; supplements, 1974-79 (Reprinted Palatine, Ill., Publishers Guild, 1981). 15v. (15,350p.), illus., maps. Plus 3 supplementary vols. $875 for 18v. ISBN: 007010235x.

About 17,000 articles by *c.*4,800 contributors; 7,400 illus. (32 col.pl.) and 300 maps. V.15 is an index of 300,000 entries (including entries for maps and illus.). All articles carry select bibliographies, some briefly annotated. 'St. Anselm of Canterbury': 51/3 cols,; 2 illus.; 15 lines of bibliography. Wide coverage (*e.g.* 'Psychiatry': 13 cols.; 'Zionism': 3 cols.; 'Hungarian art': 6p.; 20 lines of bibliography). Some unusual articles (*e.g.* 'Translation literature, Greek and Arabic'). No biographies of living persons. Especially valuable on scholastic philosophy and theological writers. Excellently produced and illustrated. V.16-18 update and supplement. *Class No:* 282(031)

[730]

—**The Catholic encyclopedia.** New York, Encyclopedia Press, 1907-22; Gilmore Society, 1950-59. 18v.

Superseded by the above, but this title is still of value to the student of the Middle Ages as well as Catholic doctrine and history. *Class No:* 282(031)

[731]

—**CLIFTON, C.S. Encyclopedia of heresies and heretics.** Santa Barbara, CA, ABC-Clio, 1992. 156p. $50. ISBN: 0874366003.

Focuses on Christian heretics from the beginnings of the Church to the Reformation, distinguishing between heretics and reformers. Includes many individuals not in *New Catholic encyclopedia* (*qv*), which it supplements. Literate articles. Biographies. Ample illustrations. Cross-references. *Class No:* 272

[732]

Sacramentum mundi: an encyclopaedia of theology. Rahner, K., *ed. and others*. New York, Herder & Herder; London, Burns & Oates, 1968-70. 6v.

About 1000 signed articles, A-Z, on the central themes of modern religious thought, by over 600 specialists. Bibliographies are appended (*e.g.* 'Zionism': v.6, p.393-6; ½ col. of bibliography; 'Islam;': v.3, p.165-70, 5 sections; ½ col. of bibliography). Short general index in v.6. An international theological dictionary, published in English, Dutch, French, German, Italian and Spanish. A significant contribution to the field of Roman Catholic lexicography. *Class No:* 282(031)

[733]

—**Encyclopedia of theology:** the concise '*Sacramentum mundi*'. Rahner, K., *ed*. London, Burns & Oates, 1975. xiv, 1850p. £35. ISBN: 0860120066.

Contains revised versions of the major articles on theology, Biblical science and related topics from *Sacramentum mundi*, together with a large number of articles from the major German works, *Lexikon für Theologie und Kirche* and *Theologisches Taschenlexikon*, 'and entirely new articles on topics of major importance written for the occasion ...' (*Prefatory note*). Nearly 500 signed articles, 'Afterlife' ... 'Worship'. Biblical and other references in text. Non-Biblical sources listed, p.xiii-xiv. 'Recommended to all who wish to have a handy compendium of theology on their desks' (*Heythrop journal*, v.17, 1976, p.240). *Class No:* 282(031)

Dictionaries

[734]

COLLINGE, W.J. Historical dictionary of Catholicism Lanham, Md., The Scarecrow Press, 1996 xx,551p. (*Historical dictionaries of religions, philosophies and movements: 12.*) ISBN: 081083233x.

Some 500+ short articles for non-professional use. There is a particularly thorough bibliography though with a strong US bias. *Class No:* 282(038)

[735]

HARDON, J.A., *S.J.* Modern Catholic dictionary. London, Robert Hale, 1981. xiii, 619p. £12.50. ISBN: 0709193815.

An abbreviated ed., *Pocket Catholic dictionary* was issued in 1985 by Doubleday Image. (ISBN 038523281).

In two parts; part 1 is a dictionary of 5000 terms, directly or indirectly dealing with Catholic faith, worship, morals, history, canon law, and spirituality. The terms, even those from psychology and the social sciences, are described from the Roman Catholic point of view. Includes biographies, some 50 organizations and societies. Cross-references. Entries vary in length from 2-3 lines to a column or more. Part 2 is an appendix, containing the Credo of the People of God; a listing of popes from Peter to John Paul II; updated ecclesiastical calendars of both the Roman and Byzantine rites with saints for each day of the year; and a listing of religious communities and secular institutes in the United States and Canada. *Class No:* 282(038)

Quotations

[736]

CHAPIN, J., *ed.* **The Book of Catholic quotations,** compiled from approved sources, ancient, medieval and modern. London, J. Calder, 1957. xi, 1073, [1]p. £6.95. ISBN: 0714501360.

More than 10,400 quotations, arranged alphabetically by subject. Quotations, p.1-932; detailed analytical index of subjects, p.933-1056; index of sources, p.1057-73; corrigenda appended. *Class No:* 282(082.2)

Histories

[737]

HOLMES, J.D. *and* BICKERS, B.W. **A Short history of the Catholic Church.** Tunbridge Wells, Kent, Burns & Oates, 1983. 315p. £6.95. ISBN: 0860121267.

Replaces a book with the same title by Philip Hughes first published in 1964.

A one-volume history of the church from the origins of the church in the New Testament to the accession of Pope John Paul II in 1978. Divided into 7 broad chapters (1. The origins and early history of the Christian church to 461-2; 2. The development of the Western church and its final separation from the East, 461-1198; 3. Papalism and Conciliarism, 1198-1455; 4. The Protestant Reformation and the progress of Catholic reform, 1455-1648; 5. The age of rationalism and absolutism, 1648-1789; 6. The church, revolution and reaction, 1789-1914; 7. The church and the modern world, 1914-1978). There follows a table of major events in church history; a table of Popes and their reigns; notes for further reading (p.300-306); and a name index (p.307-315). *Class No:* 282(091)

Biographies

[738]

DELANEY, J.J. *and* TOBIN, J.E. **Dictionary of Catholic biography.** Garden City, N.Y., Doubleday, 1961; London, Hale, 1962. xi, 1245p.

Biographies of *c.*13,000 leading Roman Catholics (churchmen and laymen), from the founding of the Church to the present day. Bibliographies appended; numerous cross-references. Appendices: the saints as patrons of vocations; the saints as patrons of places; symbols of the saints in art; 12-page chart correlating papal and secular reigns. *Class No:* 282(092)

Archives

[739]

VATICAN. **Miscellanea bibliothecae Vaticanae** Vatican, Bibliotheca Apostolica Vaticana, 1987-. (*Studi e testi 329..*)

Articles on both the collections and those who had looked after them. *Class No:* 282(093.20)

Great Britain

[740]

GILLOW, J. **A Literary and biographical history,** or bibliographical dictionary, of the English Catholics, from the breach with Rome, in 1534, to the present time. London, Burns & Oates, 1885-1902. Reprinted New York, Franklin, 1961. 5v.

'The object ... is to present ... a concise record of the literary efforts, educational struggles and the sufferings for religion's sake of the Catholics in England down to the present time'. (*Preface,* v.1). A good example of biobibliography. Following the biographical sketch are given brief references to biographical dictionaries, histories, etc. for further material and then a full numbered list of works (*c.*15,000 items). *Index to Gillow's bibliographical dictionary of the English Catholics,* edited and published by J. Bevan, Ross-on-Wye, was issued in 1985 (£20. ISBN 0951090801). *Class No:* 282(410)

[741]

—BOSSY, J. **The English Catholic Community,** 1570-1850. London, Darton, Longman & Todd, 1975 (Reprinted 1979). 464p. tables, maps. £6.95. ISBN: 0232514402.

In 4 parts, with footnoted chapters (*e.g.* 10: Missionary questions, p.205-49; 103 footnotes). Sources, p.432-4. Detailed, non-analytical index. *Class No:* 282(410)

Scotland

[742]

The Catholic directory for Scotland. Glasgow, John S. Burns & Sons.
First published 1829. Annual.

Contents: Liturgical calendar - The hierarchy - The Church of Scotland - The dioceses in Scotland - The clergy of Scotland - Catholic societies and institutions - Diocesan statistics. Index of places. *Class No:* 282(411)

Ireland

[743]

Irish Catholic directory. Dublin, Veritas Publications for the Hierarchy. First published 1838. Annual

Contents: Hierarchy of Ireland - Episcopal commissions and advisory bodies - Dioceses of Ireland - Religious orders and congregations - Organizations and societies - Other Christian churches in Ireland - Religious periodicals - Clergy of Ireland, alphabetical list - Main towns index - Parish index - General index. *Class No:* 282(415)

England & Wales

[744]

ANSTRUTHER, G. **The Seminary priests:** a dictionary of the secular clergy of England and Wales, 1558-1850. Greenwood, SC., Attic Press, 1968-77. 4v. $18.50 each vol. ISBN: 0879210591, v.1; 0855970820, v.2; 0855971169, v.3; 0855971185, v.4.

Contents: v.1 Elizabethan, 1558-1608 (1968. 422p.); 2. 1603-59 (1975. 424p.); 3. 1660-1705 (1976. 318p.); 4. 1716-1800 (1977. 368p.). *Class No:* 282(42)

[745]

The Catholic directory of England and Wales. Manchester, Gabriel Communications. £25. ISSN: 00691224.
First published 1838.

Chief sections: Dioceses and provinces ...Welfare, caring services and institutions, Religious Orders, Congregations and Societies, Catholic Societies in England and Wales ... Clergy in England and Wales ... Statistical section. General index and index of places. *Class No:* 282(42)

USA

[746]

DELANEY, J.J. **Dictionary of American Catholic biography.** Garden City, New York, Doubleday, 1984. 624p. $24.95. ISBN: 0385178786.

A compendium of factual information about 1500 Roman Catholic lay people and clergy who have made a 'significant' contribution to the Church and nation. All entrants are deceased and mainly clergy. Arranged A-Z by name, with some cross-references. Succinct entries. '... unique biographical source'. (*Library journal,* 15th November 1984, p.2142). *Class No:* 282(73)

[747]

ELLIS, J.T. *and* TRISCO, R. **A Guide to American Catholic history.** 2nd rev. ed. Santa Barbara, CA., ABC-Clio Press, 1982. xiii,265p. $31. ISBN: 0874363187.
First published 1959.

1258 annotated entries arranged in 9 sections: 1. Guides - 2. General works - 3. Studies in diocesan, sectional, and parish history - 4. Biographies, correspondence, and memoirs - 5. Religious communities - 6. Education - 7. Special studies - 8. Periodicals - 9. Historical societies. Index, p.205-265. Omits section on manuscript repositories, which was in 1st ed. Heavily clerical. '... an excellent compilation which will prove invaluable to scholars' (*Bulletin of ABTAPL,* no.28, November 1983, p.11). *Class No:* 282(73)

The Popes

Biographies

[748]

KELLY, J.N.D. **The Oxford dictionary of Popes.** Oxford, Oxford University Press, 1986. xiii,347p. £12.95. ISBN: 0192139649.

'A Papal who's who' (*Preface*) precedes short biographies of 266 officially recognised Popes and 39 antipopes, arranged in chronological order (St. Peter ... John Paul II). Entries include birth and death dates, details of family background, pre-Papal career and activities in office, plus bibliographical sources. There is an appendix on Pope Joan. Extensive index, p.331-347, has cross-reference. 'The entries themselves are little gems of concise and pungent scholarship' (*British book news,* May 1986, p.283-4). *Class No:* 282POP(092)

[749]

—MANN, H.K. **The Lives of the Popes in the early Middle Ages.** London, Kegan Paul, 1903-32. 18v. in 19.

Deals with the period 590-1305, but the work is 'disfigured by complete lack of impartiality' (Sonnenschein, W.S. *The best books.* 3rd ed., 1910. v.1, p.252). *Class No:* 282POP(092)

[750]

—PASTOR, Freiherr von L. The History of the Popes, from the close of the Middle Ages. London, Hodges; Kegan Paul; Routledge & Kegan Paul, 1891-1953. 40v.

Translated from the German and edited by F.I. Autrobus and others.

A monumental history, drawn from the secret archives of the Vatican and other original sources. Commences with Clement V (1305-14); v.40 deals with Pius VI (1775-99). 2v. are devoted to some popes (*e.g.* Leo X, Paul III, Clement VIII, Pius VI). Each volume carries a list of most cited works; each is heavily footnoted and has an index of names, 'Unlikely ever to be superseded' (John E. *The Popes*, p.482). *Class No: 282POP(092)*

Protestant

[751]

The Church of England year book, 1997. The official year book of the General Synod of the Church of England. 113th ed. London, Church House Publishing, 1997. Annual. xlv, 486p. £21. ISBN: 0715180916. ISSN: 00693987.

8 parts. 1. Central structure - 2. Dioceses- 3. General - 4. Organizations - 5. Anglican and Porvoo communions - 6. Ecumenical - 7. Who's who - 8. Index. *Class No: 283/289*

Bibliographies

[752]

Christian periodical index: an index to subjects and authors and to book reviews and media reviews, 1959-. West Seneca, NY., Cedarville, Ohio, Association of Christian Librarians Inc., 1959-. 3 pa.including annual. $95 pa. ISSN: 00693871.

Indexes 85 conservative evangelical periodicals. Includes a periodical index and an index to reviews. *Class No: 283/289(01)*

Encyclopaedias

[753]

Encyclopédie du protestantisme. Gisel, P., *ed*. Paris, Éditions du Cerf, 1995 1710p. ISBN: 2204052434.

Around 1,320 shorter entries, 44 longer essays (on, for example, Communication, Europe, Church) written from a non-Roman Catholic perspective, but not polemically so. Strong on Protestant biography, and not only of churchmen, and on art history- there is a table of Protestant artists, and many of them are represented among the volume's illustrations. According to the chronological table, "Protestantism" appears to begin with the Waldensians in the late twelfth century. *Class No: 283/289(031)*

Biographies

Dictionaries

[754]

LEWIS, D.M. The Blackwell dictionary of Evangelical biography 1730-1860 Oxford, Blackwell, 1995 xxviii,1259p. ISBN: 0631173846.

Published in two volumes.

Some 3,500 entries written by circa 360 scholars. Each entry is signed and provided with a bibliography. Not all churchmen (and women) are included, but evangelicals of historical or literary significance. The chief problem lies in the definition of evangelical, which in practise embraces most Protestant denominations, but not all of their members. *Class No: 283/289(092)(038)*

Anglican

Histories

[755]

WELSBY, P.A. A History of the Church of England, 1945-1980. Oxford, Oxford University Press, 1984. xii, 300p. £27.50. ISBN: 0192132318.

A comparatively brief account of the many changes in the Church's structure and attitude to doctrine. Contents: Part 1: 1945-1959 (Reconstruction - Putting the house in order - Theology, worship, and morals - Church relations); part 2: The sixties (The bewilderment of the sixties - Theological and moral radicalism - Parishes, priests, and people - Liturgies, music, and cathedrals - The continuing search for unity); part 3: The seventies (Church and nation - Government by Synod - Church and State - Doctrine, worship, and the life of the spirit - Ministry and mission - One Church, one mission, one world); Epilogue. Bibliography (p.293-296) arranged in 3 parts. Index (p.297-300). *Class No: 283(091)*

Great Britain

[756]

Crockford's clerical directory: a directory of the clergy of the Church of England, the Church in Wales, the Scottish Episcopal Church, the Church of Ireland. London, Church House Publishing (early editions published by Oxford University Press), for the Church Commissioners for England and the Central Board of Finance of the Church of England.

First published 1858. Preceded by *Clerical guide*, 1817-36, and *Clergy list* (1840?-).

Biographical notes under clergy (*c.*22,000), A-Z. Index of English benefices and churches; Index of Welsh benefices; of Scottish incumbencies; Irish benefices. Index of cathedrals and collegiate churches. Service, prison and hospital chaplains. Bishops of Anglican dioceses overseas. Addresses of provincial offices, Episcopal succession lists. An essential source on all matters relating to Anglican clergy; primarily concerned with those ordained in the British Isles. *Class No: 283(410)*

[757]

—Guide to bishops' registers of England and Wales: a survey from the Middle Ages to the abolition of episcopy in 1646. Smith, D.M., *ed*. London, Royal Historical Society, 1981. 448p. £15. *Class No: 283(410)(058)*

[758]

Directory of orthodox parishes and clergy in the British Isles. Welshpool, Powys, Stylite Publishing Ltd. and the Orthodox Fellowship of St. John the Baptist, 1984. 68p. maps. £2.50. ISBN: 0947805087.

Arranged A-Z by town/city and jurisdiction, listing names and addresses of parish/church/community; names and addresses of clergy; names and addresses of persons to contact for details of services (times of services/languages/additional information). Index to clergy; index to towns/cities. *Class No: 283(410)*

England & Wales

Histories

[759]

STEPHENS, W.R.W. *and* HUNT, W., *eds*. A History of the English Church. London, Macmillan Press, 1899-1910 (and reprints). 8v. in 9. maps.

The standard history, based on a careful study of original authorities, and the best ancient and modern writers, in moderate-sized volumes. Goes beyond purely ecclesiastical history (*e.g.* v.2, chapter 16: 'Popular religion, learning and art'). Each volume is by a specialist in the period covered, with its own analytical index, chronological tables and maps. A list of sources is appended to each chapter. *Class No: 283(42)(091)*

England

Biographies

[760]

LE NEVE, J. Fasti Ecclesiae Anglicanae, 1066-1300. London, University of London, Institute of Historical Research, Athlone Press, 1968-77. 3v.

V.1: St. Paul's, London, 1066-1300. (1968. xx,115p.). v.2: Monastic cathedrals. (1971. 136p.). v.3: Lincoln. (1977). v. 4: Salisbury (1991). v. 5: Chichester (1996). *Class No: 283(420)(092)*

[761]

—LE NEVE, J. Fasti Ecclesiae Anglicanae, 1300-1541. New and expanded ed. London, University of London, Institute of Historical Research, Athlone Press, 1962-67. 12v.

First published 1716; rev.ed. by T.D. Hardy (covering the period from the earliest times to *c.*1850, 1854 (3v.).

A diocese-by-diocese list of every known bishop, canon and dignitary for the periods covered. 1. *Lincoln diocese* 2. *Hereford diocese* - 3. *Salisbury diocese* - 4. *Monastic cathedrals (Southern Province)* - 5. *St. Paul's London,* - 6. *Monastic Cathedrals (Northern Province: York, Carlisle, Durham* - 7. *Chichester diocese* - 8. *Bath and Wells diocese* - 9. *Exeter diocese* - 10. *Coventry and Lichfield diocese* - 11. *The Welsh dioceses* - 12. *Introduction, errata and index.* V.3, *Salisbury diocese* (x,117p.) has a list of references (words in print; manuscript) preceding the calendar (bishops, deans, subdeans, archdeacons, precentors, chancellors, treasurers, prebendaries, with dates of collation, election and death, and sometimes fuller notes; detailed indexes of persons and places. *Class No: 283(420)(092)*

[762]

—LE NEVE, J. Fasti Ecclesiae Anglicanae, 1541-1857. London, University of London, Institute of Historical Research, Athlone Press, 1969-.

1. St. Paul's, London, 1541-1857 (1968) - 2. Chichester diocese (1971) - 3. Canterbury, Rochester and Winchester diocese (1974) - 4. York diocese. Rev. ed. (1975) - 5. Bath and Wells diocese (1979) - 6. Salisbury diocese (1986) - 7. Ely, Norwich, Westminster and Worcester dioceses (1992) - 8. Bristol, Gloucester. Oxford and Peterborough dioceses (1996) - 9. Lincoln diocese (1999). *Class No:* 283(420)(092)

[763]

—STUBBS, W. Registrum sacrum Anglicanum: an attempt to exhibit the course of episcopal succession in England from the records and chronicles of the Church. 2nd ed., with an appendix of Indian, Colonial and missionary consecrations; collected and arranged by E.E. Holmes. Oxford, Clarendon Press, 1897. xvi,248p. *Class No:* 283(420)(092)

Official Records

[764]

Councils and synods, with other documents relating to the English Church. Oxford, Oxford University Press, 1964-1981. 2v. in 3. (1151p.1200p.). ISBN: 0198223943, v.2.

Planned under the general editorship of F.W. Powicke, in continuation of A.W. Haddan and W. Stubbs' *Councils and ecclesiastical documents of Great Britain and Ireland* (Oxford, Clarendon Press, 1969-78. 3v.).

V.1: *AD871-1204*, ed. by D. Whitelock and others (1981) is in 2v.; pt.1. 871-1066; pt.2. 1066-1204. V.2: *AD1205-1313*, ed. by Sir. F.M. Powicke and C.R. Cheney (1964) is in 2 parts. Pt.1 covers AD1205-1265; pt.2 the later years and including an index of manuscripts and a general analytical index. *Class No:* 283(420)(093.2)

[765]

—PURVIS, Canon J.S. An Introduction to ecclesiastical records. London, St. Anthony's Press, [1953]. 96p.

Deals fully with the records to be found in diocesan record offices - archbishops' and bishops' registers; visitations; records of ecclesiastical courts, etc. *Class No:* 283(420)(093.2)

[766]

OWEN, D.M. The Records of the Established Church in England, excluding parochial records. London, British Records Association, 1970. 64p. £2. (*Archives and their use, no.1.*) ISBN: 0900222018.

The Records: Description ((a) The Diocese, the archdeaconry and the peculiar jurisdictions; (b) The province; (c) The National church; (d) Capitular bodies) - Location of records. Index of terms used. *Class No:* 283(420)(093.2)

16th & 17th Centuries

Bibliographies

[767]

Cathedral libraries catalogue: books printed before 1701 in the libraries of the Anglican cathedrals of England and Wales. v.1. Books printed in the British Isles and British America and English books printed elsewhere. London, British Library, in association with the Bibliographical Society, 1985. (Limited edition). xxi, 442p. £30. ISBN: 0712300384.

In 6 sections: Locations of English books to 1640 as enumerated in Pollard & Redgrave's *Short-list catalogue;* ... 1641-1700 as enumerated in Wing's *STC;* English books to 1640 not in Pollard & Redgrave; ... from 1641-1700 not in Wing; Locations of periodicals published 1641-1700; Locations of Statutes published 1641-1700. Brief references are given for titles in Pollard & Redgrave and Wing; full bibliographical references for those not in those volumes. *Class No:* 283"15/16"(01)

Lutheran

Encyclopaedias

[768]

BODENSIECK, J.H., *ed*. The Encyclopedia of the Lutheran Church. Minneapolis, MN., Augsburg Publishing House, 1965. 3v.

Published under the auspices of the Lutheran World Federation.

*c.*3000 entries (A-E,F-M,N-Z), contributed by 723 Lutheran scholars and specialists from 34 countries. Includes 1000 biographical sketches and articles on places, etc., pertinent to Lutherism. Bibliographies. *Class No:* 284.1(031)

[769]

—BENZING, J. Lutherbibliographie. Verzeichnis der gedruckten Schriften Martin Luthers bis zu dessen Tod... Baden-Baden, Heiz, 1965-66. xi,512p.

A chronological list of Luther's writings, with locations. A supplement was published in 1982 (Gotha, 1982. 226p.). *Class No:* 284.1(01)

[770]

—Lutheran cyclopedia. Lueker, E.L., *ed*. Rev. ed. St. Louis, Miss., Concordia, 1975 (reprinted 1987). 845p. $22.95. ISBN: 0317604880.

First published 1954.

Has over 12,000 short articles, not confined to Lutherism. 246 contributors. *Class No:* 284.1(031)

Non-Conformist

[771]

The Church of Scotland year-book. Edinburgh, Saint Andrew Press for the Church of Scotland. Annual. illus. ISSN: 00693995.

First published 1884.

Directory information on synods, presbyteries and parishes; alphabetical list of ministers, probationers and lay missionaries. Index of personnel; index of places; index of subjects.

The United Free Church of Scotland issues *The handbook* biennially (Glasgow, United Free Church of Scotland, 1930-. *Class No:* 285/288

Bibliographies

[772]

DEXTER, H.M. **The Congregationalism of the last 300 years,** as seen in its literature. New York, Harper, 1880. (Reprinted 1988 by Gregg International Publications). 1072p. £120. $240.00. ISBN: 0685140989.

Consists of 12 lectures, with a bibliographical appendix (326p.): 'Collections toward a bibliography of Congregationalism'. *Class No:* 285/288(01)

[773]

DR. WILLIAMS'S LIBRARY, London. **Early Nonconformity, 1566-1800:** a catalogue of the books in Dr. Williams's Library. Boston, Mass., G.K. Hall, 1968. 12v. $495 the set. ISBN: 0816107971.

31,000 author cards, 33,000 subject cards and 14,000 chronological cards. Concerned with early Nonconformity in England and Elizabethan Puritanism to the end of the 18th century, and books and pamphlets printed 1566-1800. *Class No:* 285/288(01)

[774]

—Nonconformist congregations in Great Britain: a list of histories and other material in Dr. Williams's Library. London, Dr. Williams's Trust, 1973. vii,[1],151p.

*c.*2000 entries, including periodical articles as well as books. Geographical arrangement. *Class No:* 285/288(01)

Dictionaries

[775]

BENEDETTO, R. *and* GUDER, D.L. *and* McKIM, D.K. Historical dictionary of the reformed churches. Lanham, Scarecrow, 1999. 544p. £50. (*Religions, philosophies, and movements series, no. 24.*) ISBN: 0810836289.

Includes a detailed chronology followed by specific entries on geographical regions. Other entries are devoted to outstanding figures of the reformed tradition from the Reformation to the present. Includes a comprehensive bibliography and useful appendices. *Class No:* 285/288(038)

Histories

[776]

BROWN, K.D. A Social history of the Nonconformist Ministry in England and Wales, 1800-1930. Oxford, Clarendon Press, 1988. xi, 244p. tables. £25. ISBN: 0198227639.

An investigation into the private and professional lives of protestant nonconformist ministers, based on the statistical analysis of a sample of several thousand ministers of 5 denominations (Baptist, Congregational, Wesleyan, Primitive and United Methodist). 7 chapters: 1. Origins - 2. Training, 1800-c.1860 - 3. Training, c.1860-1914 - 4. An unsettled ministry? - 5. Private lives - 6. Public lives - 7. Postscript. Footnotes throughout. Select bibliography, p.235-241, by chapter. Index, p.241-244. '...an important contribution to British social and religous history ... most fascinating and scholarly study of a group of individuals who at one time wielded immense influence in society' (*Economic history review,* v.42(3), August 1989, p.411-2). *Class No:* 285/288(091)

United Reformed Church

[777]

The United Reformed Church year book. London, United Reformed Church in the United Kingdom. Annual. ISSN: 00698849.

First published 1973.

Includes sections: Assembly officers, committees and departments - Provincial moderators, past moderators, recognised colleges and affiliations - List of churches in provinces and districts - Summary of statistics - Roll of Ministers - Deaconesses - U.R.C. personnel serving overseas - Deceased Ministers and obituaries - Index of churches. *Class No:* 285.42

Baptist

[778]

BRACKNEY, W.H. **The Baptists.** Westport, CT., Greenwood Press, 1988. 352p. $49.95. (*Denominations in America series, 2.*) ISBN: 0313238227.

Focuses primarily on American Baptists. 2 sections: 1. Overview of the Baptist tradition - 2. Biographical sketches of over 100 prominent Baptist leaders, A-Z, describing events in their lives and careers, and including short bibliographies of works on and by the person. Other inclusions are a chronology; statistical data on Baptist Church membership; a bibliographical essay; and an index to persons and organizations. *Class No:* 286

Bibliographies

[779]

STARR, E.C. **A Baptist bibliography**; being a register of printed material by and about Baptists; including works written against Baptists. Philadelphia, Pa., Judson Press; subsequently Rochester, N.Y., American Baptist Historical Society, 1947-76. 25v. $400 the set.

About 125,000 entries in all, under authors A-Z. Each volume has an index of joint authors, translators, Baptist publishers, distinctive titles, and subjects. Location of copies. *Class No:* 286(01)

[780]

WHITLY, W.T. **Baptist bibliography**; being a register of the chief materials for Baptist history, whether in manuscript or in print, preserved in Great Britain, Ireland and the Colonies ... ; compiled for the Baptist Union of Great Britain and Ireland. London, Kingsgate Press, 1916-22 (Reprinted in 1984 by George Olms Verlag, Hildesheim, Zürich & New York). 2v. in 1. £66.25. ISBN: 3487074567.

V.1: 1526-1776; v.2: 1777-1837, and addenda for 1613-53. Chronological arrangement, with indexes of anonymous pamphlets, authors, places and subjects. Locations are given for 30 libraries in England and Wales, and one library in US. *Class No:* 286(01)

Dictionaries

[781]

BRACKNEY, W.H. **Historical dictionary of the Baptists.** Lanham, Scarecrow, 1999. 552 p. £43.70. (*Religions, philosophies, and movements series, no. 25.*) ISBN: 0810836521.

Covers Baptists worldwide. Cross-referenced entries include biographical, geographical, ecclesiastical, theological, and thematic discussions. *Class No:* 286(038)

Yearbooks & Directories

[782]

Baptist Missionary Society: directory of missionaries and other information relating to current work of the Society. London, the Society, 1986. 56p.

The directory (p.8-13) is an A-Z listing, with UK addresses, postings, etc. Very brief. *Class No:* 286(058)

[783]

The Baptist Union directory. Council of the Baptist Union of Great Britain, *ed.* London, Baptist Church House. Annual. ISSN: 03023184.

Directory information on the Baptist Union of Great Britain, with list of associations and churches; Baptist Missionary Society; Lay pastors and preachers. Index of churches (England, Scotland, Wales) etc. *Class No:* 286(058)

Church of God, Seventh Day

Bibliographies

[784]

BJORLING, J. **The Church of God, Seventh Day: a bibliography.** New York, Garland, 1987. xix, 296p. $48. (*Sects and cults in America, bibliographic guide 8.*) ISBN: 082408537x.

1627 unannotated entries arranged in 8 subject chapters, all

....(contd.)

subdivided. Each chapter has historical and biographical background information followed by listings of primary and secondary material. Footnotes. A highly specialized bibliography. Author index, p.291-296. *Class No:* 286CHU(01)

Methodist

[785]

GARLICK, K.B., *ed.* **Garlick's Methodist registry, 1983.** London, B. Edsall & Co. Ltd., 1983. 373, [2], xiii, [1], xvi, [1], vip. £17.50. ISBN: 090262332x.

Contents: Exortium - A brief survey of Methodist history - Methodist ministers (biographical notes presented by the ministers themselves) (p.43-371) - Abbreviations. 3 appendices: 1. Presidents, Secretaries, etc., of the Wesleyan Methodist Conference, 1744-1932; 2. Presidents, Vice-presidents, Secretaries, divisions, lectures, etc., of the Methodist Conference, 1932-1982; 3. The Independent Methodist Church, The Wesleyan Reform Union ... Glossary. *Class No:* 287

Bibliographies

[786]

Methodist Union catalog: pre-1976 imprints. Rowe, K.E., *ed.* Metuchen, N.J., Scarecrow Press, 1975-. v.1-. £21.75. $29 each volume, for v.1-6. ISBN: 0810808803, v.1; 0810809206, v.2; 0810810670, v.3; 0810812258, v.4; 0810814544, v.5; 081081725x, v.6.

V.1-6 (1975-1985); A-I. To be in 20 vols.

A repertory of the catalogued holdings (under author/anonymous title) of more than 200 libraries in the US, Canada, Great Britain and serveral other European countries. Includes works on Methodist history, biography, doctrine, polity, missions, education and sermons. Confined to books, pamphlets and theses, excluding manuscripts, periodicals and serials (for which see Batsel, J. and L. *Union list of United Methodist serials, 1773-1973.* 1974). A preliminary edition, *Methodist Union catalog of history, biography, disciplines and hymnals,* edited by B.B. Little, was issued in 1967 (Lake Junaluska, N.C., Association of Methodist Historical Society. xxl. 478p.). *Class No:* 287(01)

Dictionaries

[787]

Historical dictionary of Methodism. Yrigoyen, C. *and* Warrick, S.G., *eds.* Lanham, Md., Scarecrow, 1996 299p. $47.00 (*Historical dictionaries of religions, philosophies and movements: 8.*) ISBN: 0810831406.

Contains bibliographies.

From the birth of Wesley to the 1996 World Methodist Conference, lists persons, organizations and activities. Bibliography is particularly useful. Emphasis is on the USA, from which most of the contributors come. *Class No:* 287(038)

Histories

[788]

DAVIES, R. *and* RUPP, G., *eds.* **A History of the Methodist Church in Great Britain.** London, Epworth Press, 1965-1988. 4v. (c.2000p.). ISBN: 0716203960, v.1; 0716209014, v.2; 0716203871, v.3; 0716204444, v.4.

V.1 has 10 contributors and covers the 18th century in 9 chapters; bibliography of primary and secondary sources, p.317-9. Indexes of subjects, names and places. V.2 has 7 contributors and covers the first half of the 19th century; ample footnote references, but no bibliography. Analytical index. V.3 covers in depth the years from the middle of the 19th century to 1932 and the coming into operation of the Methodist Church Act in 1976. V.4 assembles primary documents of Methodist history from its beginnings, sections arranged chronologically; and includes a bibliography (p.650-800) arranged in 7 subject sections, all subdivided. Two appendices: 1. Chapter conversion table; 2. Index of authors and editors (p.803-830). Index of documents and source material (p.831-838). *Class No:* 287(091)

[789]

—The Encyclopedia of world Methodism. Harmon, N.B., *ed.* Rev. ed. Nashville, United Methodist Publishing House, 1974. 2v. (2814p.). illus. $89.50. ISBN: 0687117844.

Sponsored by the World Methodist Council and the Commission on Archives and History of the United Methodist Church.

Includes a bibliography, p.2721-66. *Class No:* 287(091)

The Brethren

Encyclopaedias

[790]

The Brethren encyclopedia. Dumbaugh, D.F. Ambler, PA., Brethren Encyclopedia, 1984. 3v. (2126p.). illus., tables, maps. $130 the set; $75 each vol. ISBN: 0318004878.

Comprehensive coverage of all aspects of Brethren life, practice, belief and history. *c.*6000 articles in v.1 & 2, as well as illustrations (including historic photographs), and each article is supported by a bibliography. V.3 has lists, maps, statistics, etc., including a 256-page bibliography of books, articles, theses and unpublished material about the Brethren; 'impossible to find' information (lists of congregations, Annual meetings, institutions, ministries); and statistics from 1770 to the 1980 US census. Thorough and carefully researched. *Class No:* 287BRE(031)

Unitarian

[791]

GENERAL ASSEMBLY OF UNITARIAN AND FREE CHRISTIAN CHURCHES. Directory. London, The Assembly.

6 sections, including: Directory of congregations [in England (inc. Isle of Man), Wales, Scotland, non-subscribing Presbyterian Church of Ireland, overseas]; Directory of ministers - Ministry students - Lay preachers - Affiliated societies - Obituaries. *Class No:* 288

Other Churches & Sects

Shakers

[792]

McKINSTRY, E.R., *comp.* **The Edward Deming Andrews Memorial Shaker collection.** New York, Garland, 1987. 357p. $67. ISBN: 0824094301.

The major collection of Shaker material. Arranged in 5 divisions: Printed material, including bibliographic description of 468 items written or published by the Shakers and 246 secondary works, A-Z by author - Manuscript material, including 497 individual manuscripts, collections of letters, etc. - Photographic material - Artifacts - Andrews archives. 'This excellent guide to an important research collection ... is also a useful reference tool' (*College & research libraries,* v.49(1), January 1988, p.59-60, on which this entry is based). *Class No:* 289SHA

Unification Church

[793]

MICKLER, M.L. The Unification Church in America: a bibliography and research guide... New York, Garland, 1987. 227p. $36. (*Sects and cults in America, bibliographic guides, 9. Garland reference library of social science, 201.*) ISBN: 0824090403.

Includes bibliographies and background essays. The bibliographies include materials of all kinds (pamphlets, speeches, theses, popular magazine articles, and critical materials). Items, original documents, scholarly books and articles) published between 1960 and 1985 in the US. No annotations. Author index to the bibliographies. *Class No:* 289UNI

Church of Jesus Christ of the Latter-Day Saints (Mormons)

[794]

BROOKE, J.L. The Refiner's fire. The making of Mormon cosmology, 1644-1844. Cambridge, Cambridge University Press, 1994 xix,421p. ISBN: 0521345456.

John Smith was born in 1805, his "Book of Mormon" appeared a quarter of a century later. This book is concerned therefore, with the occult traditions which influenced his thinking at least as much as with the world-view of Mormonism itself. It is however, an essential volume for the understanding of Mormonism. *Class No:* 289.3

Bibliographies

[795]

FALES, S.L. *and* **FLAKE, C.J.,** *comps.* **Mormons and mormonism in the US government documents:** a bibliography. Utah, 1989. 357p. $30. ISBN: 0874803128.

1467 annotated entries for items published between 1830 and 1930, the years of persecution by the Federal Government. Arrangement is chronological. Subject, title and series indexes. 'This excellent bibliography demonstrates the contribution such a work can make to scholarship' (*Choice,* v.27(3), November 1989, o.460). *Class No:* 289.3(01)

[796]

FLAKE, C.J., *ed.* **A Mormon bibliography, 1830-1930:** books, pamphlets, periodicals and broadsheets relating to the first century of Mormonism. Salt Lake City, University of Utah Press, 1978. xxxi,[i],825p. illus. $80. ISBN: 0874800161.

The standard source, 10,145 numbered items (plus 56 in addenda) arranged A-Z by author, with brief descriptions for some entries and also locations. Index by date (year) refers to item numbers. A ten-year supplement by Flake and L.W. Draper (426p. $30. ISBN 0874803381) was issued in 1990. *Class No:* 289.3(01)

[797]

—**SHIELDS, S.L. The Latter Day Saint churches:** an annotated bibliography. New York, Garland, 1987. 281p. $45. (*Bibliography on sects and cults in America, 11. Garland reference library of social science, 337.*) ISBN: 0824085825.

1538 citations to literature relating to the Mormon Church and splinter groups. Selective coverage of works by and about the Church of Jesus Christ of Latter Day Saints (Mormon Church) and the Reorganized Church of Jesus Christ of Latter Day Saints (RLDS Church); comprehensive coverage of the writings relating to over 60 smaller existing churches or movements within a similar religious origin. Author index, but no subject index. Intended to supplement the above. *Class No:* 289.3(01)

Encyclopaedias

[798]

Encyclopedia of Mormonism: the history, scripture, doctrine and procedure of the Church of Christ of Latter-day Saints. Ludlow, D.H., *ed.* New York, Macmillan, 1992. 5v..(2333p). illus, tables. $340. ISBN: 002904040x.

Presents research efforts of committed believers on a host of topics relating to the founding and growth of the Church. V.1-4 contain *c.*1500 articles by over 730 contributors. A synoptic outline organizes entries under 5 major headings. Cross-references. Detailed subject index in v.4. 13 appendices and a glossary. V.5 reproduces the standard works of the Church. The apologia approach 'in no way negates the overall values of the encyclopedia'(*Library journal,* 15 February 1992, p.158). *Class No:* 289.3(031)

Histories

[799]

SHIPPS, J. Mormonism: the story of a new religious tradition. Urbana & Chicago, University of Chicago Press, 1987. xviii,212p. illus. $22.95. ISBN: 0252011597.

Reconstructs the signal events of early Mormonism as perceived from inside the faith. 8 chapters: 1: Prologue - 2-7 are historical - 8: A chronology of 19th century Mormonism. Extensive notes, p.169-192. Bibliography, p.193-202. Index, p.203-212. *Class No:* 289.3(091)

Quakers (Society of Friends)

Bibliographies

[800]

SMITH, J. A Descriptive catalogue of Friends' books, or books written by members of the Society of Friends... London, J. Smith, 1867. Supplement published by Hicks, 1893. 2v.

An author catalogue, covering broadsheets as well as books. The heading 'Periodical publications' is followed by a list of contents of issues of various periodicals. Editions and reprints are recorded. Analytical notes are provided as necessary, as well as very brief biographical data. *Class No:* 289.6(01)

[801]

—**TURNER, A. A Bibliography of Quaker literature, 1893-1967.** 2v. (792p.,247p.).

A thesis accepted for L.A. Fellowship in 1974. 5700 entries, many with brief bibliographical or explanatory notes, in 14 classes. Excludes all Society of Friends publications. Index of authors and subjects. *Class No:* 289.6(01)

Yearbooks & Directories

[802]

RELIGIOUS SOCIETY OF FRIENDS. Handbook of the Religious Society of Friends. London, Friends World Committee for Consultation.

First published 1955. Issued 5-yearly since 1962.

Subtitled 'Finding friends around the world'. Lists Societies of Friends around the world, arranged geographically. Data on meetings, lists of Quaker schools, study centres, publications, libraries. *Class No:* 289.6(058)

Jehovah Witnesses

[803]

BERGMAN, J. **Jehovah's Witnesses and kindred groups:** a historical compendium and bibliography. New York, Garland, 1984. xli,[i],370p. $58. (*Sects and cults in America. Bibliographical guides, 4. Garland reference library of social science, 180.*) ISBN: 0824091094.

Arranged in 5 sections: 1. Official Watchtower Bible and Tract Society literature (A. Books; B. Song, hymn and poem books ... M. Indexes; N. Convention reports; O-R. articles) - 2. Material associated with the Russell Movement (subdivided A-H) - 3. Material about Jehovah's Witnesses (subdivided A-J) - 4. Offshoots of the Watchtower Bible and Tract Society (subdivided A-K) - 5. Non-American Bible student groups (Britain; Europe; Canada; Australia). An appendix gives addresses for Jehovah's Witnesss and their offshoots. Author index, p.353-369. '... important and unique bibliography of the religious sect ...' (*Choice*, v.22(5), January 1985, p.658).
Class No: 289.954

29 Non-Christian Religions

Encyclopaedias

[804]

JORDAN, M. **Encyclopedia of gods:** over 2500 deities of the world. New York, Facts on File, 1993. 448p. £18.99. $40. ISBN: 0816029091.

Entries arranged A-Z, giving the relevant cult, role and characteristics or symbols of the gods and goddesses. Subject index listing deities by religion and function, and civilization index by region. *Class No:* 29(031)

Non-Christian Religions

[805]

PARRINDER, G., *ed.* **An Illustrated history of the world's religions.** London, Newnes, 1983. 528p. illus. ISBN: 0600337982.

21 chapters (1. Prehistoric religions ... 21. Islam. Conclusion). 20 specialist contributors. Bibliography, by chapters, p.516-9. Marginal text references to illustrations. Index (tiny print). Comparative religion for the newcomer as well as the scholar. *Class No:* 29.0

Dictionaries

[806]

The Oxford dictionary of world religions. Bowker, J., *ed.* Oxford, Oxford University Press, 1997. xxiv,1111p. £30.00. ISBN: 0192139657.

The alphabetically-arranged, mostly brief, entries are followed by a useful topic index and an index of Chinese headwords. The central documents of each religion have their own entries, as well as the biographies of founders and leaders, pilgrimage sites etc. Brief bibliographies are occasionally appended. The entries are thoroughly cross-referenced. *Class No:* 29.0(038)

[807]

PARRINDER, G. **Dictionary of non-Christian religions.** 2nd ed. Amersham, Bucks, Hulton Educational Publications Ltd., 1981. 320p. illus. £7.95. ISBN: 0717509729.

First published 1971.

'This dictionary covers the whole field of the religions of the world, with the exception of Christianity and the Bible' (*Introduction*). About 3000 brief entries, including biographies. Special attention is paid to Hinduism, Buddhism and Islam, and other Far Eastern religions; also Near Eastern, Celtic, Teutonic and Scandinavian religions, the beliefs and customs of ancient American culture, Mayas, Aztecs and Incas, plus those of Australasia and Africa. Judaism is referred to in detail in the post-Biblical period. Ample cross-references. Over 300 drawings and photographs. No references to authorities consulted. Further reading list, p.318-9. Well produced. For undergraduates and the general reader. *Class No:* 29.0(038)

Almanacs

[808]

New Age almanac. Melton, J.G. and Clark, J. and Kelly, A.A., *eds.* London, Visible Ink Press, 1991. 479p. £16.95. ISBN: 0810394022.

The distinguished name of Gordon Melton is enough to guarantee the impartiality and academic respectability of this survey of the New Age Movement. There is a considerable bibliography but indexing is unsatisfactory. *Class No:* 29.0(059)

Great Britain

[809]

HUTTON, R. **The Pagan religions** of the ancient British Isles: their nature and legacy. Oxford & Cambridge, Mass., Blackwell, 1991. 288p. 150 illus. £20. $29.95. ISBN: 0631172882.

Claims to be the first survey of religious beliefs in the British Isles from the Old Stone Age to the coming of Christianity. *Class No:* 29.0(410)

America—North

Encyclopaedias

[810]

HIRSCHFOLDER, A. *and* MORIN, P. **The Encyclopedia of native American religions.** New York, Facts on File, 1992. 367p. illus. Maps. $40. ISBN: 0816020175.

Claims to be the first encyclopedia of native *North* American religions. Wide range. Entries A-Z, each 1-2 paragraphs, and including biographies of religious leaders and Christian missionaries. Extensive bibliography of popular and scholarly books, government publications and periodical articles. A unique compendium. *Class No:* 29.0(71+73)(031)

Handbooks & Manuals

[811]

MELTON, J.G. **Encyclopedic handbook of cults in America.** 2nd rev. ed. New York, Garland Publishing Inc., 1992. 424p. $65.00. (*Garland reference library of social science, 213.*) ISBN: 0815305028.

Aims to be a concise summary of the most accurate information available on the more important of the alternative or non-conventional religious movements. 6 sections, each having an appended short bibliography (1. What is a cult? [surveys the broad range of issues surrounding the topic] - 2. The established cults - 3. The new age movement - 4. The newer cults - 5. Counter-cult groups - 6. Violence and the cults) Index, p.265-272. *Class No:* 29.0(71+73)(035)

Comparative Studies

Encyclopaedias

[812]

KLAUSER, T., *ed.* **Reallexikon für Antike und Christentum.** Sachwörterbuch zur Auseinandersetzung des Christentums mit der antiken Welt. Leipzig (subsequently Stuttgart), Anton Hiersemann, 1950-. v.1-. illus.

V.1-15 (1950-1998): A-ITALIA II. An encyclopedia of the classical world and its relationship to early Christianity. Scholarly, signed articles, sometimes lengthy, with bibliographies (*e.g.* Constantine the Great is subject of a monograph (v.3, p.306-79), sectionalised A-G, with subdivisions, nearly two columns of bibliography, apart from references in the text). Occasional line-drawings. Each vol. has c.1280p. *Class No:* 291(031)

Handbooks & Manuals

[813]

FRAZER, J.G. **The Golden bough:** a study in magic and religion. 3rd ed. rev. & enl. London, Macmillan Press, 1911-15 (Reprinted in 13v., 1980). 13v. (5380p.). $250 the set. ISBN: 0333012828.

1st ed. 1890; 2nd ed. 1900.

1: *The magic art and the evolution of kings* (1911. 2v.); 2: *Taboo and the perils of the soul* (1911); 3: *The dying God* (1911); 4. *Adonis, Attis, Osiris* (1914. 2v.); 5: *Spirits of the corn and of the wild* (1912. 2v.); 6: *The scapegoat* (1913); 7. *Balder the beautiful. The fire-festivals of Europe and the doctrine of the external soul (1913. 2v.);* 8: *Bibliography and general index* (1915); *Aftermath: a supplement to the 'Golden bough'* (1936). A monumental contribution on primitive beliefs and customs, and their place in the comparative history of religion. The general index provides an adequate key to the many examples and analogies. Much of what is called 'primitive religion' is classified as magic by Frazer, and his views have accordingly been attacked as unscientific.

The Making of 'The Golden bough' was issued in 1990 (Macmillan. 256p. 5 illus. £45. ISBN 0333496310) *Class No:* 291(035)

[814]

—FRAZER, J.G. **The New golden bough:** a new abridgment of the classic work. Gaister, T.H., *ed.* New York, Criterion, [1959]. 758p. $39.95. ISBN: 0875990363.

Updates the original in the light of recent discoveries, plus further notes. Comprehensive index. *Class No:* 291(035)

Mythology

[815]
COTTERELL, A. **The Illustrated encyclopedia of myths and legends.** London, Cassell, 1992. 260p. illus. £14.95. ISBN: 0304341819.

An anthology, covering the popular myths and legends of 20 world cultures. Micropedia (p.180-248). Further reading (p.249-50). Index (p.251-259). *Class No: 292/293*

Bibliographies

[816]
'The Classical world' **bibliography of philosophy, religion and rhetoric.** New York, Garland Publishing Inc. 1978. 396p. $51. (*Garland reference library of the humanities, v.95.*) ISBN: 0824098781.

19 bibliographic essays (some with critical comments) on Greek and Roman philosophy, Roman religion and ancient rhetoric (*e.g.* 'Early Roman religion ...' reprinted from the monthly *Classical world* (Classical Association of the Atlantic States, Pittsburgh, Pa.). 'This book will be of great use to the researcher as well as the teacher and students' (American reference books annual, v.10, 1979. item 1080). *Class No: 292/293(01)*

[817]
SMITH, R. **Mythologies of the world:** a guide to sources. Urbana, Ill., National Council of Teachers of English, 1981. 347p. $13.95. ISBN: 0814132227.

The bibliographical essays are arranged in 6 broad geographical categories, subdivided by ethnic groups and further subdivided by types of material. Emphasis is on the myth as a tale, and only material in English is included. No indexes. Light-hearted. *Class No: 292/293(01)*

[818]
SOUTH, M., *ed.* **Mythical and fabulous creatures:** a source book and research guide. New York, Greenwood Press, 1987. xxxv, 393p. illus. $49.95. ISBN: 0313243387.

The editor's introduction, which includes a bibliographic essay, is followed by 20 chapters on individual creatures arranged in 4 sections: Birds and beasts - Human-animal composites - Creatures of the night - Giants and fairies. The chapters are written as bibliographic essays. The second part of the book includes 'A Miscellany' and 'A Taxonomy' which have information on another 43 creatures. Glossary. General bibliography. Index with 'see' references. '... a breadth of coverage that is both impressive and delightful' (*Choice*, v.24(11/12), July/August 1987, p.1678). *Class No: 292/293(01)*

Encyclopaedias

[819]
GORDON, S. **The Encyclopedia of myths and legends.** London, Headline, 1993. 512p. 32 illus. £19.99. ISBN: 0747206236.

A compilation of world folklore from 'Aboriginal myths' to 'Zodiac'. *Class No: 292/293(031)*

[820]
JORDAN, M. **Encyclopedia of gods:** over 2500 deities from both ancient and modern cultures. New York, Facts on File, 1993. 337p. $40. ISBN: 0816029091.

Brief sketches of gods and goddesses from both ancient and modern cultures. Arranged A-Z by name of deity. Subject index lists deities by function and type. Civilization index lists deities by specific culture. *Class No: 292/293(031)*

[821]
MERCATANTI, A.S., *ed.* **The Facts on File encyclopedia of world mythology and legend.** New York, Facts on File, 1988. xviii,807p. illus. $95; £55. ISBN: 0816010498.

Aim is to provide a quick reference to world myth, fairy tale, and legend, thus giving a better understanding of 'the thematic contents of the world's masterpieces of art, music and literature'. Over 3000 entries with concise definitions and background information, arranged A-Z by the most common English spelling. Annotated bibliography, p.699-716; Key to variant spellings, p.717-722; Cultural and ethnic index, p.723-740; General index, p.741-807. Includes 450 illustrations. *Class No: 292/293(031)*

Handbooks & Manuals

[822]
GRAY, I.H., *ed.* **Mythology of all races.** Boston, Mass., Archaeological Institute of America, Marshall Jones Co., 1916-32. (Reprinted New York, Cooper Square Publishers, 1964. 13v. illus.

Contents: V.1: *Greek and Roman*, by W.S. Fox (1916); 2: *Eddic*, by J.A. McCulloch (1930); 3: *Celtic*, by J.A. McCulloch; *Slavic*, by J. Machal (1918); 4: *Finno-Ugric. Siberian*, by U. Holmberg (1927); 5:

....(contd.)
Semitic, by S.H. Langdon (1931); 6: *Indian*, by A.B. Keith; *Iranian*, by A.J. Carnoy (1917); 7: *Armenian*, by M.H. Ananikian; *African*, by A. Werner (1925); 8: *Chinese*, by J.C. Ferguson; *Japanese*, by M. Anesaki (1928); 9: *Oceanic*, by R.B. Dixon (1916); 10: *North American*, by H.B. Alexander (1916); 11: *Latin American*, by H.B. Alexander (1920); 12. *Egyptian*, by W.M. Müller; *Indo-Chinese*, by J.G. Scott (1918); 13. Complete index to v.1-12 (1932). Each volume carries some 20-50 plates, in addition to figures in the text; also some 20 pages of bibliography. The detailed index runs to 477 pages. Valuable for its truly extensive geographical coverage, backed by a full index. *Class No: 292/293(035)*

[823]
Larousse world mythology. Grimal, P., *ed.* Rev. ed. London, Hamlyn, 1982. 569p. illus., (incl.col.pl.). £7.95.

Translated from the French by G.P. Beardmore. Originally published as *Mythologies* (Paris, Larousse, 1963).

23 specialist contributions (Prehistory - Egypt - Sumer - Babylon - The Hittites - Greece - Rome - Persia - India - The Celts - Germans - Slavs - Ugric Finns - China - Japan - North America - Siberia). Profusely illustrated with 40p. of colour plates and 600 black-and-white illus. Bibliography of selected readings, p.546-7. Index. Lacks maps. *Class No: 292/293(035)*

[824]
LEACH, M. **Guide to the gods.** Andover, Hants, Gale Research International, 1993. 1008p. £95. ISBN: 1873477856.

Originally published in US in 1992 by ABC-Clio.

A guide to more than 20,000 gods, from pre-history to the present, arranged by function or other attribute under 8 major headings (Cosmogonical deities - Celestial deities - Atmospheric deities - Terrestrial deities - Life/death cycle deities - Economic activities - Socio-cultural concepts - Religion) each subdivided. Each short entry has information under some or all of the headings: Primary or secondary functions of the deity; aspects and attributes; alternative names and spellings; relationships with other mythical figures; culture and country of origin; bibliographical references. Bibliography of 1600 works, and separate list of 45 learned journals. *Class No: 292/293(035)*

[825]
MONAGHAN, P. **The Book of goddesses and heroines.** Rev. ed. New York, Dutton, 1990. 456p. $17.95. ISBN: 0875425739.

A helpful list of goddesses by family and geographic location precedes the main part of the work, which is arranged A-Z by name (A ... Zuleika). A thorough bibliography follows. 'An excellent source for collections of comparative religions and women's studies' (*Library journal*, July 1981, p.1405) on the first edition. *Class No: 292/293(035)*

Dictionaries

[826]
COTTERELL, A., *ed.* **A Dictionary of world mythology.** Originally published by Windward, imprint of W.H. Smith, Reprinted 1986 by OUP in Oxford paperback series. [2], 320p. illus. maps. £4.95. ISBN: 0192177478.

Arranged in 7 main sections: West Asia; South and Central Asia; East Asia; Europe; America; Africa; and Oceania. Introduction to each section highlights history, lifestyle, and ideology of an ancient people, and the landscape in which they lived. In each section myths and mythologies are A-Z, entries ranging from 100 to 500 words. 'Further reading' is included for the introduction and each section. Cross-references. Double column index, p.303-14. *Class No: 292/293(038)*

[827]
JOBES, G. **Dictionary of mythology, folklore and symbols.** New York, Scarecrow Press, 1961-62. 3v. (1759p.+482p.). ISBN: 0810820366.

Vols. 1 and 2 are the dictionary: 1. A-Jephthah; 2. Jephuneh - ZZZ, and also a bibliography (p.1736-1759), A-Z by author. V.3 is the index, in 2 parts: A. Table of deities, heroes and personalities; B. Table of mythological affiliates. *Class No: 292/293(038)*

[828]
LURKER, M. **Dictionary of gods and goddesses, devils and demons.** New York, Routledge & Kegan Paul, 1987. 451p. $45; £16.95. ISBN: 0710208774.

First published in Stuttgart in 1984 as *Lexikon der Götter und Däomen: Namen, Funktionen, Symbole/Attribute*.

*c.*1800 articles, their length proportionate to their importance, on the gods, and other supernatural persons from all the world's religions. Followed by indexes of varient names, secondary names, and by-names; of functions, aspects and areas of influence; and of symbols, attributes and motives; and a select bibliography. *Class No: 292/293(038)*

[829]
SYKES, E., *comp.* Everyman's dictionary of non-classicial mythology. 3rd ed. London, J.M. Dent, 1961 (Reprinted Biblio. Dist., 1977). 298p. illus. $13.50. (*Everyman's reference library.*) ISBN: 0460030108.
Previous edition 1952.
Comprises *c.*2000 short articles, with cross-references and a brief general bibliography. Covers Chinese, Japanese and American mythology, as well as Scandinavian, Teutonic and Near Eastern, but omits *One thousand and one nights* as a source.
Class No: 292/293(038)

Biographies
[830]
SENIOR, M. The Illustrated who's who in mythology. London, Macdonald Illustrated, 1985 (reprinted 1990). 224p. illus. £12.95. ISBN: 0356197298.
Short entries arranged A-Z featuring more than 1200 figures from the world's myths, with more than 240 black and white and coloured illustrations. Main sources are given. Index of themes, p.219-223.
Class No: 292/293(092)

Ancient Egypt
[831]
LESKO, B.S. The Great goddesses of Egypt University of Oklahoma Press, 1999. 336p. illus. $19.95. ISBN: 0806132027.
Straightforward account of the goddesses of Egypt, their myths and their rituals, clearly presented. *Class No:* 292/293(32)

Biographies
[832]
HART, G. Dictionary of Egyptian gods and goddesses. London, Routledge & Kegan Paul, 1986. A paperback ed. was issued in 1990. ISBN 0415059097. 229p. illus. £12.95. ISBN: 0710209657.
An outline time-chart and 2 maps precede the dictionary, arranged by name A-Z (Aken ... Yamm). The author has 'tried to include all the important deities that figure in magical medicine and daily life' (*Preface*). Entries are detailed and clearly written; some lengthy. (e.g., 'Aten': 10 pages; 'Osiris': 15 pages) but others only 2 or 3 lines. Short 'Select further reading' (p.227) and 'Alternative renderings of divine names' (p.229) complete the book. *Class No:* 292/293(32)(092)

Great Britain
[833]
ASHE, G. Mythology of the British Isles. London, Methuen, 1990. 304p. 153 illus (50 col.). £17.99. ISBN: 0413629902.
Each section deals with topic first as presented in legend or story-telling or speculation; then a commentary discusses sources, facts, underlying ideas, etc. Sections: The peoples and their origins - Mysteries of early Britain - Dynasties - Magic and secret lore - The Roman era - Transition - Arthurian Britain - The birth of Scotland — The English inheritance. Epilogue. Bibliography, p.294-297. Index, p.298-304. *Class No:* 292/293(410)

Ireland
[834]
ELLIS, P.B. A Dictionary of Irish mythology. Santa Barbara, CA., ABC Clio, Oxford, University Press, 1989. 240p. $34.95. ISBN: 0874365538, US; 0192828711, UK.
Aimed at the enthusiast and the lay reader, but academics could find it useful. A lengthy introductory essay on the history of the Celts, the sources of their sagas and romances, precedes the dictionary, which covers gods, human heroes, titles, sites, objects, etc. A select bibliography is appended. *Choice* (v.27(2), October 1989, p.285) suggests an indication of pronunciations should be considered for a later edition. *Class No:* 292/293(415)

[835]
SMYTH, D. Guide to Irish mythology. Blackrock, Co. Dublin, Irish Academic Press, 1988. 176p. 98 illus. £6.95. ISBN: 0716524341.
A guide arranged A-Z (Aed ... Uisneach) to mythological places and things. Includes a list of 67 items of source material; special notes; p.158-163; and index, p.167-176. *Class No:* 292/293(415)

Scandinavia
[836]
LINDON, J. Scandinavian mythology: an annotated bibliography. New York, Garland, 1988. 593p. $25. ((*Garland folklore bibliographies, no.13).*) ISBN: 0824081736.
Lists over 3000 books and periodical articles published between the 1830s and 1982. Most items are in German or one of the Scandinavian languages. *Class No:* 292/293(48)

Asia
[837]
HACKIN, J., *and others.* Asiatic mythology: a detailed description and explanation of the mythologies of all the great nations of Asia. London, Harrap, 1832. (Reprinted 1963). 459, [1]p. illus (incl.pl.).
Deals in turn with the mythologies of Persia, the Kafirs, Buddhism in India, Brahmanic mythology (p.100-146), the mythology of Lamaism, of Indo-China and Java, Buddhist mythology in Central Asia, mythology of modern China (p.252-384), the mythology of Japan (p.385-448). Some footnote bibliographical references. Detailed analytical index. 16 col.pl. and 354 other illus. *Class No:* 292/293(5)

China
[838]
WALTERS, D. Chinese mythology: an encyclopedia of myth and legend. Aquarian Press, 1992. 240p. illus. £7.99. ISBN: 1855380803.
Covers the most prominent human, animal and supernatural figures of Chinese legend, folklore and religious beliefs.
Class No: 292/293(510)

[839]
WERNER, E.T.C. Dictionary of Chinese mythology. Shanghai, Kelly, 1932 (Reprinted Longwood Press, 1976). xvii,[i],627p. $60. ISBN: 0893410349.
'A who's who of the Chinese other world, compiled from the Chinese and foreign works named in the bibliography (p.625-27) from personal observations in Chinese temples, houses and streets, and conversations with Chinese scholars, priests and peasants' (*Preface*) Gives Chinese characters, following English head-word. Numerous cross-references. Index to myths. Bibliography, p.625-7.
Class No: 292/293(510)

India
[840]
Indian mythology: an encyclopedia of myths and legends. Knappert, J. London, Aquarium Press, 1991. 287p. illus. £8.99. (*World mythology.*) ISBN: 1855380404.
Draws on a 5,000 year history of Indian culture, looking at mythology in both the Hindu and Buddhist traditions. Includes the deities, epic heroes, prophets and saints; the creation of the world; and religious concepts of the afterlife. The encyclopedia, arranged A-Z, is preceded by 7 introductory sections (p.9-27): The myths - The language - Prehistory - The peoples - Literature - The sources - History - Further reading - A guide to pronunciation.
Class No: 292/293(540)

Australasia & Oceania
[841]
CRAIG, R.D. Dictionary of Polynesian mythology. New York, Greenwood Press, 1989. 456p. map. $55. ISBN: 0313258902.
Covers an area from Hawaii in the north to New Zealand in the south and Easter Island in the east. A nearly comprehensive listing of the goddesses, gods and ancient heroes chronicled in the legends of the Polynesians. Bibliography of almost 300 sources. Highly recommended as a 'significant new work ... for Pacific studies and comparative mythology collections' (*RQ,* v.30|(1), Fall 1990, p.112.
Class No: 292/293(9)

[842]
KNAPPERT, J. Pacific mythology: an encyclopedia of myth and legend. London, Aquarian/Thorsons, 1992. 336p. illus. Map. £8.99. $17. ISBN: 1855381338.
An A-Z guide (Abang Salamat ... Yusup), with entries from a few lines to a page. 'See' references. Bibliography, p.333-336. Capitalising on the growing interest in the Pacific. *Class No:* 292/293(9)

Classical Mythology
[843]
BULFINCH, T. Myths of Greece and Rome. Holme, B., *ed.* London, Allen Lane/Penguin Books Ltd., 1980. 308p. illus. (some col.). ISBN: 0713912901.
In 1855 Thomas Bulfinch wrote *The Age of fable* to instruct readers in classical mythology, and this is a new edition. 33 chapters: (1. Stories of the gods and heroes - 2. Prometheus and Pandora ... 11. Cupid and Psyche ... 21. Bacchus and Ariadne ... 32. The infernal regions. The Sibyl - 33. Aeneas in Italy ...) followed by a chart, The Descent of the gods, and a name index, p.305-308. *Class No:* 292

[844]

FERGUSON, J. The Religions of the Roman Empire. London, Thames & Hudson, 1970 (Reprinted 1982 in paperback). 296p. illus., chron, table. £5.95. (*Aspects of Greek and Roman life, 5.*) ISBN: 050027276x.

12 chapters (1. The Great Mother - 2. The Sky-father - 3. The Sun-god (56 references; 8 illus) - 4. The divine functionaries ... 7. Personal religion - 8. Beyond death ... 11. Philosophers and gods - 12. Syncretism and confrontation. Various quotations. 'Bibliography and references', p.244-74. 87 illus. in all. Chronological table. 800 B.C. - 461 A.D. *Class No: 292*

Encyclopaedias

[845]

ROSCHER, W.H. Ausführliches Lexikon der griechischen und römischen Mythologie. Leipzig & Berlin,. Teubner, 1884-1937 (reprinted Hildeshein, Verlagshandlung Olms, 1965. 6v. & 4 supplements, illus.

A scholarly work, the most detailed of its kind (7647p.); for the large library. Signed articles, with extensive references to sources as well as to secondary material. Many illustrations. *Class No: 292(031)*

[846]

STONEMAN, R. Greek mythology: an encyclopedia of myth and legend. London, HarperCollins, 1991. 192p. illus. Maps. £7.99. $13.95. ISBN: 0850309344.

Claims to include all major figures of Greek mythology. Black and white line drawings. Short entries making a handy but comprehensive guide for newcomers to the subject. Bibliography, p.187-92. *Class No: 292(031)*

Handbooks & Manuals

[847]

BURKERT, W. Greek religion in the archaic and classical periods. Oxford, Basil Blackwell, 1985. 512p. £29.50. ISBN: 0631112413.

A survey intended for classical scholars and students, drawing upon literature and myth, vase paintings and archaeology, and building up a picture of the current state of knowledge about the religions of the ancient Greeks. 7 chapters, followed by notes, a bibliography, and indexes. *Class No: 292(035)*

[848]

LYTTELTON, M. and FORMAN, W. The Romans, their gods and their beliefs. London, Orbis Publishing Ltd., 1984. 128p. 120 col. illus. £15. ISBN: 0856134732.

Concerned with Roman life and religion from *c.*100 B.C. to A.D. 100. 6 chapters: The changing image of the city - The traditional gods of Rome - Rites of sacrifice and divination - Augustus's religious revival - Private life and personal religion - The mystery religions. Suggestions for further reading (10 books). Index, p.126-128. *Class No: 292(035)*

[849]

MORFORD, M.P.O. and LENARDON, R.J. Classical mythology. 4th ed. New York, Longman Group Ltd., 1991. xxi, 703p. illus. maps. $28.95; £15.99. ISBN: 0801304652.

First published 1971.

3 parts (26 chapters): 1. The myths of creation; The Gods - 2. The Greek sagas; Greek local legends - 3. The survival of classical mythology (*e.g.* 26. Classical mythology in music and film). Select bibliography, p.671-674; also bibliographies at the end of the introduction (p.35-38) and appended to chapters. Indexes: A. Mythological and historical persons, subjects and placenames; B. Authors, artists, composers, subjects and titles. *Class No: 292(035)*

[850]

ROSE, H.J. A Handbook of Greek mythology, including its extension to Rome. 6th ed. London, Methuen, 1958. ix, 363p. £9.95 (paperback edition issued in 1964). ISBN: 0416682006.

First published 1928.

A standard, scholarly manual by the then Professor of Greek in the United College of St. Salvator and St. Leonard, St. Andrews. Chapter footnotes and bibliographical references (*e.g.* chapter 9, 'The legends of Greek lands', has 82 references); bibliography, p.335-9. Index of mythological names; index of real names. *Class No: 292(035)*

Dictionaries

[851]

BELL, R.E. Place-names in classical mythology: Greece. Santa Barbara, CA., ABC-Clio, 1988. 350p. $48.50. ISBN: 0874365074.

Companion volume to the above.

About 1000 entries for ancient names, listed in their Latin spellings with modern name in parenthesis. Cites specific references to standard sources. Includes a list of modern place-names associated with ancient locations; a guide to personae; and a brief bibliography. Some of the entries are lengthy (*e.g.* 'Athens' has 18 pages). *Class No: 292(038)*

[852]

GRIMAL, P., ed. The Dictionary of classical mythology. Oxford, Basil Blackwell Ltd., 1986. 603p. illus. £22.50. $34.95. ISBN: 0631132090.

First published as *Dictionnaire de la mythologie grecque et romaine* (Paris, Presses Universitaires de France. 6th ed., 1979).

Identifies the gods, goddesses, heroes and mortals of Greek and Roman mythology. Entries are arranged by the form of name commonly used in English, with the Greek (in Greek characters) and Latin names in parenthesis. Entries range in length from a paragraph to 14 pages, and each entry explains its subject's genealogy and summarizes the legends about it. Footnote references to sources. Cross-references, and an index. 40 genealogical tables included in an appendix. Scholarly. *Class No: 292(038)*

[853]

—GRIMAL, P., ed. A Concise dictionary of classical mythology. Oxford, Blackwell, 1990. 456p. £19.95; $34.95. ISBN: 0631166963.

A concise version of the above, translated by A.R. Maxwell-Hyslop, with entries concentrated on the principal versions of the myths and including only major variations. *Class No: 292(038)*

[854]

TRIPP, E. Dictionary of classical mythology. Rev. ed. London, Collins, Publishers, 1988. [14], 631p. maps & geneological charts. £4.95. ISBN: 0004343808.

First published 1970.

Over 2000 entries, A-Z, varying in length from 2 or 3 lines to 5 pages. Includes names of people and places as well as terms. Includes stories telling of the myths of Greece and Rome in readable and convenient form (*e.g.* 'Oedipus': 2½p.; 'Pan': 1¼p.; 'Media': 4¼p.; 'Zeus': 5p.). 'See' references. Pronouncing index. 5 maps of the classical world. 5 genealogical charts of great royal lines. *Class No: 292(038)*

Biographies

[855]

BELL, R.E. Women in classical mythology: a biographical dictionary. Santa Barbara, CA, ABC-Clio, 1991. 462p. $49. ISBN: 0874365813.

2600 entries, arranged A-Z by most standard name and spelling, of mortal, immortal and divine beings, monsters, hermaphrodites and transexuals. Entries vary in length from a sentence or paragraph to 4 pages (*e.g.* Athena, Helen). Cross-references. Special index: 'The men in their lives'. 'Because there is little written on women in classical literature, this will be a useful addition to the reference collection ... (*Booklist*, v.88(6), 15 November 1991,p.652). *Class No: 292(092)*

[856]

GRANT, M, and HAZEL, J. Who's who in classical mythology. London, Weidenfeld & Nicolson, 1973. 447p. illus., maps.

Fairly lengthy entries (*e.g.* Odysseus; Theseus; - each 10p.). Many cross-references. 400 illus. (16 in colour). Greek and Latin writers referred to. 'Handsome as well as scholarly' (*Financial times*. 25 October, 1973, p.33). No bibliographies, but indebtedness to Tripp and Rose is acknowledged. *Class No: 292(092)*

Africa

Dictionaries

[857]

SCHEUB, H. A Dictionary of African mythology: the mythmaker as storyteller. Oxford, Oxford University Press, 2000. 384p. $30. £190.06. ISBN: 0195124561.

Brief entries on 400 African myths. Full bibliography, indexes with cross-references. *Class No: 292(6)(038)*

Eastern Religions

[858]

The Rider encyclopedia of Eastern philosophy and religion: Buddhism, Hinduism, Taoism, Zen. Schumacher, S. and Woerner, G., eds. London, Rider Books, 1989. xv,[i],468p. illus., tables. ISBN: 0712611924.

Originally published in German by Otto-Wilhelm-Barth Verlag in 1986.

The A-Z encyclopedia (p.1-444) has over 4000 entries and over 100 illustrations (*e.g.* 'Nirvana': 3¼ columns. illus.). Appendix: Ch'an/Zen lineage chart; bibliography, p.457-468 (grouped: Buddhism-Zen; subdivided into primary and secondary sources). 4 contributors: I. Fischer-Schreiber (Buddhism & Taoism); F.K. Ehrhard (Tibetan Buddhism); K. Friedrichs (Hinduism); M.S. Diener (Zen). A scholarly survey of the teachers, traditions and literature of Asian writers. *Class No: 294/299*

[859]

The Sacred books of the East. Translated by various Oriental scholars and edited by F. Max Müller. Oxford, Clarendon Press, 1879-1910. (Reprinted by Chronica Botanica India (State Mutual), 1988). 50v. $2000 the set.

A major collection of translated Eastern religious literature, including the Upanishads, Sacred Laws of the Aryans, Texts of Confucianism, Zend-Avesta, Pahlavi Texts, Qur'an and Institutes of Vishnu. V.50 is the general index to the series by M. Winternitz.

Another important collection is the *Harvard Oriental series,* edited by C.R. Lanman and others (Cambridge, Mass., Harvard University Press, 1891-1950. 44v.). *Class No: 294/299*

[860]

WINTERNITZ, M., *comp.* **A Concise dictionary of Eastern religion:** being the index volume to The sacred books of the East. Oxford, Clarendon Press, 1910, (reprinted 1925). xvi, 683p.

Forms V.50 of *The Sacred books of the East (q.v.).* A remarkably detailed analytical index (*e.g.* 'Prayers': 15 columns, set solid). Many cross-references. Designed on the basis of a 'scientific classification of religious phenomena'. *Class No: 294/299*

Hinduism

[861]

The Sacred books of the Hindus. Allahabad, The Panini Office, 1909-37 (Reprinted by Baman Das Basu). Originally in 32v.; reprinted in 47v. $1575.50. ISBN: 0404195482.

In this valuable collection, as in Müller's *Sacred books of the east,* the most notable Hindu scriptures appear as complete documents. Some 30 extensive works have been translated and published in the two collections. (*A reader's guide to great religions,* ed. C.J. Adams (1965), p.47). *Class No: 294*

Bibliographies

[862]

DANDEKAR, R.N. Vedic bibliography: an up-to-date, comprehensive and analytically arranged register of all important work done since 1930. in the field of Veda and allied antiquities, including Indus Valley civilisation. Bombay, Karnatak Publishing House (Rater Poona, University of Poona), 1946-73, v.1-3.

Sequel to *Bibliographie védique,* by L. Renou (Paris, Adrien-Maisonneuve, 1931. v.339p.), with its 6750 items.

V.1 lists *c.*3500 books and periodical articles in Western and Indian languages. Some entries are annotated. Subject arrangement. Index to titles and subjects. V.2 (Poona, 1961) has 6500 entries, mostly annotated, for books and periodical articles published 1946-60. V.3 has over 700 entries. *Class No: 294(01)*

[863]

DELL, D.J., *and others.* **Guide to Hindu religion.** Boston, Mass., G.K. Hall, 1981. 434p. $47. ISBN: 0816179034.

Subject bibliography. Categories: Hindu history; religious thought and practice; sacred scriptures and rituals; popular practices; arts; mythology; Hinduism in social and political life; research aids. *Class No: 294(01)*

Encyclopaedias

[864]

Encyclopaedia of the Upanishads. Subrahmanian, N.S. London, Oriental Group, 1986. xii,564p. £35. ISBN: 074650005x.

Prints, describes and explains each of the 108 Upanishads now extant. Part 1 has the 10 major ones, pt.2 the lesser ones. Appendices: 1. On creation; 2. Yoga; 3. The Mudrās; 4-13. List of 108 upanishads. Index, p.547-564. *Class No: 294(031)*

Handbooks & Manuals

[865]

OXTOBY, W.G., *ed.* **World religions:** Eastern traditions 3rd ed. Toronto, Oxford, Oxford University Press, 1997. 554p. illus. $27.95. ISBN: 0195407504.

A companion to *World religions : Western traditions,* this volume covers Hinduism and Jainism, Buddhism, East Asian religions, aboriginal and Pacific religions. In a final chapter Oxtoby examines the problem of discussing non-Western religious traditions through Western categories. *Class No: 294(035)*

[866]

World religions: Western traditions. Oxtoby, W.G., *ed.* 3rd ed. Oxford, Oxford University Press, 1996. 597p. $27.95. ISBN: 0195407512.

This volume contains survey articles by A. Segal (Judaism), W. Oxtoby (Zorastorianism and Christianity), M. Ayoub (Islam), with a final chapter, also by Oxtoby, entitled "Rivals, Survivals, Revivals", the first including, eg the Baha'i faith as a rival to Islam, African religions as "survivals" and New Age Movements as "revivals". *Class No: 294(035)*

Dictionaries

[867]

STUTLEY, M. and STUTLEY, J. A Dictionary of Hinduism: its mythology, folklore and development, 1500 B.C. - A.D. 1500. London, Routledge & Kegan Paul, 1977 (Paperback ed. published 1985). xvii,372p. map. £25. ISBN: 0710205872.

Published by Harper & Row in the US as *Harper's dictionary of Hinduism.*

*c.*2500 subject entries ('Jaina': 2 cols., 10 references). Bibliography, p.353-68. Diacriticals are shown. 'This outstanding work will be a standard reference tool in libraries for many years to come' (*American reference books annual,* 1978, entry no. 983). *Class No: 294(038)*

[868]

—**WALKER, B. The Hindu world:** an encyclopedic survey of Hinduism. London, Allen & Unwin, 1968. 2v. (xiii,609p.;xi,696p.).

A-L, M-Z. About 600 articles, documented (*e.g.* 'Suttee'; over 9p.; 6 references; 'Jainism': v.1. p.492-6; 9 references; 'Buddhism': v.1. p.183-7; 16 references). Includes bibliographies (*e.g.* 'Ganésa': 2p.; 2 references). V.2 has a detailed index of articles and subjects. Cross-references. Articles are unsigned. 'The substance of this book is derived largely from the standard works of recognised authorities, supplemented by material drawn from traditional Indian sources'. *Class No: 294(038)*

[869]

—**WILKINS, W.J.** Hindu mythology: Vedic and Puranic. 2nd ed. London, Curzon Press, 1973. xviii,500p. illus.

Facsimile reprint of 2nd ed. (Calcutta, London, Thacker, Spink, 1901).

Part 1 discusses the Vedic deities; pt.2 the Puranic deities; pt.3, the inferior deities. Many illustrations. Detailed index. Supplements Stutley pictorially. *Class No: 294(038)*

[870]

SULLIVAN, B.M. Historical dictionary of Hinduism. Lanham, Scarecrow, 1997. 368p. $49. (*Religions, philosophies, and movements series, no. 13.*) ISBN: 0810833271.

Presents Hinduism's major events, individuals, texts, sects, and concepts in the context of its historical development. *Class No: 294(038)*

Indian Religions

[871]

CHOPRA, P.M., *ed.* **Religions and communities of India.** London, East-West Publications (UK), 1982. 316p. illus (photographs). £12.50. ISBN: 0856920819.

9 chapters, all divided and subdivided: 1. Hinduism - 2. Jainism - 3. Buddhism in India - 4. Sikhism - 5. Islam - 6. Christianity in India - 7. Zoroastrianism - 8. The Armenian community - 9. Judaism and the Jewish community. Glossary, p.270-291. Bibliography, p.292-297, by religion. Index, p.303-316. *Class No: 294.0/295*

Buddhism

[872]

BROWN, K. and O'BRIEN, J., eds. The Essential teachings of Buddhism: daily readings from the Sacred texts. London, Rider, 1988. 304p. £8.95. ISBN: 0712616748.

An anthology of daily readings from Buddhist texts and commentaries which explain fundamental ideas behind Buddhism for the non-Buddhist. Clear explanation of history, theology and spirtualism of Buddhism. *Class No: 294.3*

[873]

HARVEY, B.P. An Introduction to Buddhism: teachings, history and practices. Cambridge, Cambridge University Press, 1990. 350p. illus, diagrs. £55. $64.95. ISBN: 0521308151.

Aims to be a comprehensive introduction to Buddhist tradition as it has developed in three major cultural areas in Asia, and as it is now developing in the West. Primarily intended for students. *Class No: 294.3*

[874]

Sacred books of the Buddhists, translated by various Oriental scholars ... London, H. Frowde. Oxford University Press, 1895-1974. 30v. Previous edition, 1942. *Class No: 294.3*

[875]

—GODDARD, D., *ed*. A Buddhist Bible. 2nd ed., rev. & enl. Thetford, Vermont, D. Goddard, 1938 (Reprinted Beacon Press, 1991). viii,677p. $14.95. ISBN: 080705951x.

First published 1932.

A collection of translations of texts from Pali, Sanscrit, Chinese and Tibetan sources and from Japanese modern collections. Appendix of bibliographical and other notes. The 2nd ed. adds the work of Bhikshu Wai-tao and other Buddhist scholars. *Class No: 294.3*

Bibliographies

[876]

REYNOLDS, F.E., *and others*. Guide to Buddhist religion. Boston, Mass., G.K. Hall, 1981. 440p. $57.50. ISBN: 081617900x.

Subject bibliography. Categories: Historical development; religious thought; authoritative texts; popular beliefs and literature; the arts; social, economic and political aspects; religious practices and rituals; ideal beings; hagiography and biography; mythology (including sacred history), cosmology and basic symbols; sacred places; soteriological experience and processes; path and goal; research aids. *Class No: 294.3(01)*

[877]

VESSIE, P.A. Zen Buddhism: a bibliography of books and articles in English, 1892-1975. Ann Arbor, Mich., University Microfilms International, under the aegis of the East Asia Library, University of Washington, 1976. xiv, 81 leaves. $12.75. ISBN: 0835701735.

762 numbered entries, with occasional brief annotations. 2 parts. 1: General works ... Zen sects: Rinzai and Solo - 2. Zen and archery; Zen and the arts; Zen and Christianity ... Zen training; Zen and the West; Miscellaneous; Zen periodicals. *Class No: 294.3(01)*

[878]

YOO, Y. Buddhism: a subject index to periodical articles in English, 1728-1971. Metuchen, N.J., Scarecrow Press, 1973. 184p.

1261 numbered items from over 200 periodicals; author and title indexes. Appended list of Buddhist societies and associations. *Class No: 294.3(01)*

[879]

—YOO, Y. Books on Buddhism: an annotated subject guide. Metuchen, N.J., Scarecrow Press, 1977. 251p.

A companion volume to the above, with 1300 entries under 38 headings. All items are in English. *Class No: 294.3(01)*

Dictionaries

[880]

HUMPHREYS, C.A. A Popular dictionary of Buddhism. Rev. ed. London, Curzon Press, 1976. (Reprint 1984). 224p. £3.50. ISBN: 0700701842.

First published 1962.

Gives definitions and brief explanations of *c*.1000 terms (*e.g.* 'Four Paths': ½p.). Includes brief biographies; references to the literature. Modified diacriticals. Author was Founder-President of the Buddhist Society. *Class No: 294.3(038)*

[881]

—LING, T.O. A Dictionary of Buddhism: India and South-East Asia. New ed. Calcutta, K.P. Bagchi (South Asia Books), 1986. [4],202p. $15. (*Bagchi Indological series, 2.*) ISBN: 0836414365.

First published 1972.

Complementary to Humphreys, defining fewer terms more extensively; bibliographical references. Terms were the author's contribution to S.G.F. Brandon's *A dictionary of comparative religion* (1970). *Class No: 294.3(038)*

[882]

PREBISH, C.S. Historical dictionary of Buddhism. Metuchen, NJ,Scarecrow Press, 1993. 387p. $42.50. ((*Historical dictionaries of religions, philosophies, and movements, 1*).) ISBN: 0810826984.

Preliminaries include preface, pronunciation guide, overview of Buddhist scriptures, chronology and map of Asia showing Buddhist sites. The dictionary (p.36-288) has A-Z arangement of persons, places, events, texts, doctrines, practices, institutions and movements. A bibliography of nearly 100 pages is especially valuable. *Class No: 294.3(038)*

Yearbooks & Directories

[883]

BUDDHIST SOCIETY. The Buddhist directory: a directory of Buddhist groups and centres in the United Kingdom and Ireland and elsewhere. London, the Society, 1981- ISSN: 02652595.

Details of societies and organizations (subdivided England, Ireland, Scotland, Wales, and again by counties, A-Z, giving names, descriptions, addresses and telephone numbers); Other related organizations; the Buddhist Union of Europe (representatives names and addresses); Libraries; Buddhist literature - some retailers. Index of organizations. *Class No: 294.3(058)*

China

[884]

SOOTHILL, W.E. *and* HODOUS, L. A Dictionary of Chinese Buddhist terms, with Sanscrit and English equivalents. New ed. Delhi, Motilal Banarsidass, 1987. 510p. £20. ISBN: 8120803193.

First published 1937, London, Kegan Paul.

'Indexed by the number of strokes in the Chinese symbol, with definitions in clear and concise English' (Diehl, K.S. *Religions, mythologies, folklores* (2nd ed., 1962), item no. 931). *Class No: 294.3(510)*

Japan

[885]

NAKAMURA, H., *and others, comps. & eds*. Japanese-English Buddhist dictionary. Tokyo, 1965. xv,383p.

Over 5000 terms, arranged in order of Japanese syllabary. *Class No: 294.3(52)*

Sikhism

[886]

COLE, W.O. *and* SAMBHI, P.S. A Popular dictionary of Sikhism. London, Curzon Press, 1990. 174p. £4.50.$14.95. ISBN: 0700702026.

30-page introduction includes a historical sketch of Sikhism, with time charts and maps, and a bibliography for further reading. Entries go beyond mere definitions. '... concise, inexpensive but authoritative and well-written...'(*Choice*, v.28(5),January 1991). *Class No: 294.51*

[887]

COLE, W.O. *and* SAMBHI, P.S. The Sikhs: their religious beliefs and practices. Brighton, Sussex Academic Press, 1995. xxi, 232p. illus., maps. ISBN: 1898723133.

Useful handbook on Sikhism, with information on the place of the Ten Gurus in the Sikh religion; daily life, ceremonies and festivals; the attitude of Sikhism towards other religions. There is a list of primary sources for the study of Sikhism, secondary sources and an additional bibliography. Includes a glossary. Detailed index. *Class No: 294.51*

[888]

RAI, P.M., *comp*. Sikhism and the Sikhs: an annotated bibliography. Westport, CT., Greenwood Press, 1989. xv,257p. $69.95. (*Bibliographies and indexes in religious studies, 13.*) ISBN: 031326130x.

1150 numbered and annotated entries arranged in 7 chapters: 1. General works - 2. Sikh history - 3. Sikh gurus - 4. Sikh sculptures and philosophy - 5. Sikh politics and social-economic conditions - 6. Sikhs abroad - 7. Source materials. Author, title and subject indexes. *Class No: 294.51*

Yoga

[889]

ELIADE, M. Yoga: immortality and freedom. Trask, W.R., *translator*. 2nd ed. Princeton, N.J., Princeton University Press, 1970 (Reprinted 1991); London, Arkana (Penguin Group), 1989. xxii,536p. (*Bollinger series, v.56*.) ISBN: 0691017646, (US); 0140191585, (UK).

First published in US in 1958; 2nd ed. in 1969.

'A scholarly treatment of yoga philosophy, which gives an exhaustive survey of the history and main schools of thought' (Thompson, I. *Alternative medicine* (1981)). List of works cited, p.433-480. Index p.481-536. *Class No:* 294.527

[890]

FEUERSTEIN, G. Encyclopedic dictionary of Yoga. New York, Paragon House, 1990. 430p. illus. (90 black & white photographs). $24.95. (*Living traditions series*.) ISBN: 155778244x.

Defines more than 2000 words, expressions and concepts found in the study of Yoga, arranged in English A-Z order. Entries range in length from a few lines to several pages. English keywords refer to Sanscrit equivalents. Includes brief biographies. Bibliography (p.427-430) is in two parts: 1. Reference; 2. Recommended reading. *Class No:* 294.527

[891]

JARRELL, H.R. International yoga bibliography, 1950-1980. Metuchen, N.J., Scarecrow Press, 1981. ix,221p. $22.50; £13.85. ISBN: 0810814722.

Numbered entries of books, journal articles, magazine articles, and yoga periodicals, arranged A-Z in each of the four sections. Includes works published in English, French, German, Spanish, Portuguese, Italian and Dutch over the last 31 years, and also reprints, new editions, etc., of books originally printed before that time. No annotations. Author index, p.155-174; title index, p.175-211; subject index, p.212-221. *Class No:* 294.527

[892]

WOOD, E.E. Yoga dictionary. New ed. Harmondsworth, Mddx., Penguin Books, 1977. 328p. (*Pelican books*.)

Originally published in New York, by Philosophical Library, in 1956.

Includes both definitions and longer notes. All technical terminology taken from Sanscrit words. *Class No:* 294.527

Zoroastrianism

[893]

BOYCE, M. A History of Zoroastrianism. Leiden, E.J. Brill, 1975-. To be in 4v. v.1. Gld.165; $94.50. v.2. Gld.144; $82.50. v.3. Gld.380; $217.25. ISBN: 9004088474, v.1; 9004065067, v.2; 9004092714, v.3 505.00/00$aV.1: *The early period* (1975. xvi,349p. Rev. ed. 1988); v.2: *Under the Achaemenians* (1982. xvi,306p.); v.3: *Zoroastrianism under Macedonian and Roman rule* ; v.4: *Zoroastrianism under the Parthians and early Sasamans* (in preparation). *Class No:* 295

[894]

BOYCE, M. Zoroastrians: their religious beliefs and practices. London, Routledge & Kegan Paul, 1979. 252p. £10.50. (*Library of religious beliefs and practices*.) ISBN: 0710001215.

14 chapters (2. Zoroaster and his teaching - 3. The establishment of Mazda worship ... 5. Under the Achaemenians - 6. Under the Seleucids and Sassanids ... 10. Under the Caliphs ... 13. Under the Qajars and British - 14. In the twentieth century. Chapter bibliographies, p.229-36 (with some notes). Glossary, p.xv-xvii. *Class No:* 295

Jewish Religion (Judaism)

[895]

ELON, M. Jewish law: history, sources, principles. Philadephia, Jewish Publication Society, 1994. 2231p. ISBN: 0827603894.

Published in four volumes. Contains indexes.

Originally published as Ha-Mishpat ha-Ivri, and regarded as an essential resource in Israeli law schools and courses in Talmud and Jewish Thought.

The work provides a comprehensive overview of the entire field of Jewish Law. Part One outlines history and basic principles, Part Two looks at legal sources, Part Three surveys the literary sources of Jewish Law - pre-biblical, biblical and post-biblical literature, talmudic, post-talmudic commentaries, codes, responsa, as well as

.... (contd.)

scholarly and reference works. Part Four deals with Jewish law in the modern state of Israel.

There are extensive cross-references, a subject index, and index of sources. The comprehensive bibliography covers nearly 40 pages. *Class No:* 296

Bibliographies of Bibliographies

[896]

SHUNAMI, S. Bibliography of Jewish bibliographies. 2nd ed. enl. Jerusalem, The Magnes Press, The Hebrew University, 1965. xxiv,992,xxiip.

First published 1936.

4,727 numbered items, with very brief annotations, in 27 sections (including 1. Encyclopaedias - 2. Bibliography of bibliography - 3. General bibliographies - 4-5. Catalogues of public and private collections - 6. Booksellers' and publishers' catalogues (a selection) - 7. Bibliographical periodicals - 8. Lists of periodicals - 9-25. Subject sections - 26. Manuscripts - 27. Personal bibliographies). Index of names and subjects; index of Hebrew titles. The 2nd ed. has entries on the Dead Sea Scrolls and the Holocaust. A supplement (1975. xvii,464,xvip.) lists entries 4751-6859, also in 27 sections. *Class No:* 296(009)

Bibliographies

[897]

BRESLAUER, S.D. Contemporary Jewish ethics: a bibliographic survey. New York, Greenwood, 1985. xi,213p. (*Bibliographies and indexes in religious studies; number 6.*.) ISBN: 0313245940.

Contains indexes.

The introductory survey is a very useful look at the whole area of Jewish ethics. The bibliographical study has four chapters covering general works; history of jewish ethics; issues in Jewish ethics; theories in Jewish ethics; as well as Jewish and non-Jewish ethical theories. The entries are annotated, and indexed under author, title, and subject. *Class No:* 296(01)

[898]

BRESLAUER, S.D. Modern Jewish morality: a bibliographical survey. New York, Greenwood, 1986 x,239p. (*Bibliographies and indexes in relgious studies; Number 8.*) ISBN: 0313247005.

Contains indexes.

There is an introductory review of the most important moral questions discussed in the sources. This is followed by a major bibliographical survey with six chapters covering biomorality, sexuality and the family, selected problems evolving from sexuality and the family, ageing, death and mourning, interpersonal relationships, and aspects of political morality.

The bibliographic citations are annotated, and there are author, title and subject indexes. The work is a companion volume to the author's *Contemporary Jewish Ethics: a bibliographical survey* (1985). *Class No:* 296(01)

[899]

CUTTER, C. *and* OPPENHEIM, M.F. Jewish reference sources: a selective, annotated bibliographic guide. New York, Garland, 1982. 180p. $24. ISBN: 082409347x.

Supersedes H. Zafran's *Jewish reference books: a select list* (1970).

371 numbered items arranged in 2 sections: General reference-Subject reference. Arrangement is A-Z with some subdivisions. Short descriptive annotations. Hebrew titles transliterated. Cross-references. '... fills a unique need' (*Bulletin of ABTPL*, v.2(4), March 1989, p.21-22). *Class No:* 296(01)

[900]

FRANK, R.S. *and* WOLLHEIM, W. The Book of Jewish books: a reader's guide to Judaism. New York, Harper & Row, 1986. xiv,320p. illus. $15.95. ISBN: 0060630086.

c.500 annotated entries listing books on the Bible, Jewish thought, Jewish history, the Holocaust, the arts, Israel, prayer books, etc. Essays precede each section. List of Jewish periodicals; list of Jewish bookstores. Glossary. 'Despite the few questionable inclusions and omissions inevitable in undertakings of this nature, this collection is a fairly solid work' (*Library journal*, v.lll(18) November 1, 1986, p.87). *Class No:* 296(01)

[901]

LUBETSKI, E. *and* LUBETSKI, M. Building a Judaica library collection: a resource guide. Littleton, Col., Libraries Unlimited, 1983,. 185p. $30. ISBN: 0872873757.

Arranged in 2 parts: Selection - Acquisitions. The 1st part is non-evaluative bibliographic guide to selection aids for Judaica materials; the 2nd part is an annotated international directory of publishers, etc. in the field. Index. *Class No:* 296(01)

[902]

NEW YORK PUBLIC LIBRARY. Dictionary catalog of the Jewish collection of the New York Public Library, Reference Department. Boston, Mass., G.K. Hall, 1960. First supplement, 1975. 14v; supplement, 8v.

371,000 photolithographed catalogue cards in all, 'for publications in all European languages as well as in Hebrew and Yiddish, on the history and traditions of the Jewish people throughout the ages and in all lands. It covers archaeological and Biblical studies as well as *belles-lettres*, rabbinic and philosophic texts' (G.K. Hall & Co. *Catalog of publications*, 1979-80, p.32-33). *Class No: 296(01)*

[903]

ROTH, C. Magna bibliotheca anglo-judaica: a bibliographical guide to Anglo-Jewish history. New ed., rev. & enl. London, Jewish Historical Society of England, 1937. xiii,464p.

First published as *Bibliotheca anglo-judaica*, by J. Jacobs and L. Wulf (1888).

About 3000 items, 2 main parts: 1. Histories (sections A1-14, including biography and periodicals) - 2. Historical material (B1-22). Items in the Mocatta Library and allied collections in University College, London, are asterisked. Author index. *Class No: 296(01)*

[904]

—LEHMANN, R.P. Anglo-Jewish bibliography, 1937-1970. London, Jewish Historical Society of England, 1973. xi,364p.

27 sections(1. Bibliographies and works of reference - 2. Periodicals ... 25. Biography). Includes works in Hebrew and periodical articles. Analytical entries. Detailed analytical index, p.337-64. A volume covering 1971-90 was published in 1992 (£35. ISBN 0902528262. *Class No: 296(01)*

[905]

SPECTOR, S.A. Jewish mysticism: an annotated bibliography of the Kabbalah in English. New York, Garland, 1984. 399p. $45. (*Garland reference library of social science, 210.*) ISBN: 082409042x.

Lists English-language works, including festschrifts, reference books, serials, and monographs for the period 1659-1983, arranged by subject. Entries include quotations from the prefaces of cited works. 3-part index to primary materials, secondary materials and subjects. No title index. Only other published bibliography is G.G. Scholem's *Bibliographia Kabbalistica* (1927). *Class No: 296(01)*

Encyclopaedias

[906]

Encyclopaedia Judaica. Roth, C. *and* Wigoder, G., eds. Jerusalem, Keter Publishing House,1971; New York, Macmillan, 1972. 16v.(12,128p).illus. facsims. charts. maps.

The 16v. encyclopaedia has 25,000 entries. Major articles are signed. Over 1800 contributors. V.16: UR-Z, plus supplementary entries on ' Chronology', 'Migration', etc. The entry 'Hebrew language' (columns 1559-1662) has over 6 cols. of bibliography. V.1 carries the general index (249,580 references) with supplementary lists of newspapers and periodicals. Over 8000 illus., some in colour. Glossaries are appended to each volume. A well-printed, handsome set. 'The latest, most comprehensive and in many ways, most authoritative summary of research in all areas of Jewish scholarship.'(*Library journal*, August 1972, p.2582). It supplements but does not supersede the *Jewish encyclopedia* (12v. 1901-6), *Encyclopaedia Judaica* V,1-10, *c*.1928-34) or the 10v. *Universal Jewish encyclopaedia* (1939-43).

Encyclopaedia Judaica yearbook decennial book, 1973-1982 (1982). A CD-ROM version is also available. *Class No: 296(031)*

[907]

The Encyclopedia of Judaism. Wigoder, G., *ed.* New York, Macmillan, 1989. 768p. illus. $75. ISBN: 0026284103.

Articles (unsigned) vary in length according to significance (*e.g.* 'Torah', 2p.; 'Hillel' (the sage), 2p.). Hebrew translation/ transliteration is often given. *c*.300 illus.(including colour) and a 15-page index. 'It provides a concise introduction to many topics; at the same time, it is more comprehensive than older one-volume works on Judaism' (*Reference books bulletin*, 1989-90, p.60.). *Class No: 296(031)*

[908]

WIGODER, G., *ed.* Everyman's Judaica: an encyclopedic dictionary. London, W.H. Allen, 1975. xi,673p. illus. (incl. col. pl.). facsims, ports, tables, maps.

15,000 short entries. 'A guide to the Bible, to Israel old and new, to Jewish communities throughout the world, to famous Jews, to Jewish concepts and customs, to Jewish history and literature' (*Introduction*). 65 lists and tables (*e.g.* List of Kibbutz, p.339-40; Common Jewish abbreviations, p.3-5; Blessings and benedictions, p.73). Appendices include 'Hebrew-English basic vocabulary'; 'Daily calendar'. Many brief biographies. 200 illus. (many in colour). Planned as complimentary to the 16v. *Encyclopedia Judaica* and its *Yearbooks*. *Class No: 296(031)*

Handbooks & Manuals

[909]

JACOBS, L. The Jewish religion: a companion. Oxford, Oxford University Press, 1995. 641p. £25.00. ISBN: 0198264631.

Arranged alphabetically, covers most aspects of Jewish belief and practice, with entries also for Jewish thinkers and writers from biblical times to the present day. There are many cross-references and most entries have a short bibliography. There is also a very useful chapter on reference works at the end of the book. *Class No: 296(035)*

Dictionaries

[910]

Dictionary of Judaism in the biblical period: 450 B.C.E to 600 C.E. Neusner, J. *and* Green, W.S., *eds.* New York, Macmillan Library Reference, 1996. xxvi,693p. ISBN: 0028972929.

Published in two volumes. Contains maps. *Class No: 296(038)*

[911]

The Oxford dictionary of the Jewish religion. Werblowsky, R.J.Z *and* Wigoder, G., *eds.* Oxford, Oxford University Press, 1997. xviii,764p. ISBN: 0195086058.

2,400 alphabetically arranged entries, most of them fairly brief. The articles are by an impressive array of scholars from America, Europe and Israel, and are accompanied by short bibliographies. The work covers all aspects of Jewish practice, law and belief. There are also biographies of important personalities of Judaism. *Class No: 296(038)*

[912]

SOLOMON, N. Historical dictionary of Judaism. Lanham, Scarecrow, 1998. 528p. $60. (*Religions, philosophies, and movements series, no. 19.*) ISBN: 0810834979.

Includes excellent general bibliography as well as additional bibliographies on particular themes. Historical charts focus on special issues such as Jewish theology, philosophy, and religious law. *Class No: 296(038)*

Periodicals

Bibliographies

[913]

SINGERMAN, R. Jewish serials of the world: a research bibliography of secondary sources. New York, Greenwood, 1986. xxii,377p. ISBN: 0313244936.

Contains indexes.

This bibliographical guide covers the history of the Jewish Press, in any language, since the founding of the *Gazeta de Amsterdam* in 1675. The arrangement is geographical, with further subdivisions by language. There are over 3,000 citations, and the work includes references to dissertations and theses. Contains an author and subject index. *Class No: 296(051)(01)*

Yearbooks & Directories

[914]

The Jewish travel guide 2000. Zaidner, M., *ed.* London, Valentine Mitchell, 2000. £11.95. ISBN: 0853033846.

Contains index.

Organized by country, with short introductory notes on the Jewish Community in each country. Synagogues, Jewish bookstores, and kosher resturants are listed by town under each country. *Class No: 296(058)*

[915]

The Jewish yearbook 2000. Massil, S.W., *ed.* London, Valentine Mitchell, 2000. 448p. £26.00. ISBN: 0853033811.

Contains index.

Lists synagogues and Jewish communal organizations in Britain by place. There is also a who's who, a detailed Jewish calendar, and a calendar of religious festivals for the next 30 years. *Class No: 296(058)*

Quotations

[916]

KOLATCH, A.J. Great Jewish quotations. Jonathan David, 1996. 612p. $29.95. ISBN: 0824603699.

Contains indexes.

Ranges from biblical period to the present day. 5,000 quotations arranged by author, with sources given. There are also short biographical notes. *Class No: 296(082.2)*

Histories

[917]

BARON, S.W. **A Social and religious history of the Jews.** 2nd ed., rev. & enl. New York, Columbia University Press, 1952-80. 17v. $41.60 each vol.

First published 1937 in a 3-vol. ed.

Content: V.1: *To the beginning of the Christian era* (1952. vi,436p.); 2: *Christian era: the first five centuries* (1952. vi,436p.); 3: *Heirs of Rome and Persia* (1957. x,340p.); 4: *Meeting of east and west* (1957. 352p.); 5: *Religious controls and dissensions* (1957. 416p.); 6: *Laws, homilies and the Bible* (1958. 486p.); 7: *Hebrew languages and letters* (1958. 329p.); 8: *Philosophy and science* (1958. 405p.); 9: *Under Church and Empire* (1965. x,350p.); 10: *On the Empire's periphery* (1965. 432p.); 11. *Citizen or alien conjurer* (1967. 359p.); 12: *Economic catalyst* (1967. 359p.); 13: *Inquisition, Renaissance, and Reformation* (1969. vi,463p.); 14: *Catholic restoration and wars of religion* (1969. 412p.); 15: *Resettlement and exploration* (1973. 550p.); 16: *Poland - Lithuania, 1500-1650* (1976. 460p.); 17: *Byzantines, Mamelukes, and Maghribians* (1980. 450p.). Each volume has notes and references to sources. Index to v.1-8 (1960. xi,163p.). *Class No:* 296(091)

[918]

FRANK, D.H. *and* LEAMAN, O., *eds.* **History of Jewish philosophy.** London, Routledge, 1997. xii,934p. £104.50. (*Routledge history of world philosophies, v.2.*.) ISBN: 0415080649.

39 chapters by an impressive list of international contributors cover Jewish philosophy from biblical times to the present. There is an introductory chapter on 'What is Jewish philosophy?', with the rest of the book divided into four sections: Foundations and first principles, Medieval Jewish philosophy, Modern Jewish philosophy and Contemporary Jewish philosophy. Each chapter is accompanied by bibliographic notes, plus a bibliography divided into texts and studies. There is an index of names and an index of terms (including Hebrew terms, with translations). *Class No:* 296(091)

[919]

POLIAKOV, L. **The History of anti-Semitism.** London, Elek Books, 1966-85. 4v. v.2 £19.50; v.3 £25; v.4 £20. (*The Littman library of Jewish civilization.*) ISBN: 0197100260, v.2; 0197100279, v.3; 0197100384, v.4.

Translated from the French by Richard Howard.

Traces in detail the development of anti-Semitism in 4 chapters: 1. From the time of Christ to the court Jews; 2. From Mohammed to the Marranos; 3. From Voltaire to Wagner; 4. Suicidal Europe, 1870-1933. *Class No:* 296(091)

Bibliographies

[920]

EDELHEIT, A.J. *and* EDELHEIT, H. **Bibliography on Holocaust literature.** Boulder, Co., Westview, 1986. xxxvi,842p. ISBN: 0813308968.

Contains index

Comprehensive guide to nearly 15,000 books, pamphlets, periodicals and dissertations. The work is divided into sections, including Jewish Life in prewar Europe; antisemitism; fascism; the Nazis; Europe under National Socialism; the concentration camp system; haShoah; resistance and the bystanders. Especially useful are sections on historiography of the Holocaust, with a separate section on Holocaust diaries. *Class No:* 296(091)(01)

[921]

—EDELHEIT, A.J. *and* EDELHEIT, H. **Bibliography on Holocaust literature. Supplement.** Boulder, Co., Westview, 1990. xxx,684p. ISBN: 0813308968.

Contains indexes.

6,500 new entries supplementing the above, with new sections on Holocaust-related novels and short stories, and a useful introductory essay. Citations are cross-referenced. Author-title and subject indexes are included. *Class No:* 296(091)(01)

[922]

International bibliography of Jewish history and thought. Munich, K.G. Saur; Jerusalem, Magnes Press, Hebrew University, 1984. 483p. $41. ISBN: 3598075030.

First volume of a new bibliographical project sponsored by Rothberg School for Overseas Students of the Hebrew University.

Lists *c.*2000 major works in the field of Jewish studies published in Hebrew or various European languages. Arranged in 6 sections: General works; The Biblical period; The period of the Second Temple, the Mishnah and the Talmud; The medieval period; The modern period; Jewish Communities. Sections further divided by date, topic or geographic area, then A-Z by author. For each entry brief bibliographical information and brief note of contents. Cross-references. Index of authors, editors, translators, etc. *Class No:* 296(091)(01)

[923]

The Jewish world in modern times: a selected annotated bibliography. Edelheit, A.J. *and* Edelheit, H., *eds.* London, Mansell Publishing; Boulder, Col., Westview Press, 1988. xix, 569 p. £55. $ 85. ISBN: 072011988x, UK; 0813305721, US.

Aims to place Jewish history in both its universal and its local contexts, broadly covering modern Jewish life from the mid-17th century to the present. An introduction summarizing the most important events, people and places, precedes the annotated bibliography, which is in two parts. Part 1: *The Jewish World*, has surveys of Jewish history, social history, religious trends, culture trends, antisemitism, etc., arranged in 9 subject chapters. Part 2: *The Jewish Community* is arranged by geographical region. The final chapter 19 lists bibliographies and guides. 2170 entries in all. Glossary, p. 460 - 463, author, title and subject indexes, p. 464 - 569, complete the volume. ' ... an important work ... '. (*College and research libraries*, v.50 (1), January 1989, p.85). 'These biographies not only cover their subject thoroughly but provide succinct and critical annotations in a well-organized, amply cross-referenced and indexed volume' (*Choice*, v.26 (5), January 1989, p.780). *Class No:* 296(091)(01)

Encyclopaedias

[924]

Encyclopedia of the Holocaust. Gutman, I. *and* Wigoder, G., *eds.* New York, Macmillian, 1990. 1905p.

Published in four volumes. Contains illustrations, maps, tables and indexes.

Entries cover every aspect of the Holocaust - the background, geography (regions, cities, camps, sites of massacres), biographies, the postwar impact - including war crimes trials, reflections in literature etc. Over 200 contributors. Many cross-references. Detailed index in v.4. *Class No:* 296(091)(031)

Biographies

[925]

WIGODER, G. **Dictionary of Jewish biography.** New York, Simon and Schuster, 1991. 586p. ISBN: 013210105x.

Contains illustrations.

Nearly 1,000 entries covering Jews in all fields; writers, philosophers, politicians. The work has a coverage from biblical times to the present, including persons still living. Each entry has at least one bibliographic item listed. Many entries have boxed inserts providing quotations or anecdotes; *e.g,* under Maimonides his 13 principles of the Jewish faith are listed. *Class No:* 296(092)

USA

Bibliographies

[926]

SHERMAN, M.D. **Orthodox Judaism in America:** a bibliographical dictionary and sourcebook. Greenwood, 1996. 291p. $79.50. ISBN: 0313243166.

Contains bibliography and index.

Each entry has a list of publications by and about the subject; at the back of the book is a glossary and additional bibliographies. The work also has a useful survey of major Orthodox rabbinic organizations. "Highly recommended for all Judaica collections" *Choice* v.34, 3 Nov.1996. *Class No:* 296(73)(01)

Libraries

[927]

HOOGEWOUD, F.J., *and others.* **A Guide to libraries of Judaica and Hebraica in Europe.** Copenhagen, Det Kongelige Bibliotek, for the Association of Libraries of Judaica and Hebraica in Europe, 1986. 124 leaves, 15 of which are markers & only bear the name of the country. DKr.150. *c.*£13. ISBN: 8770235554.

Arranged A-Z by country, subdivided by city or town, A-Z. Information given: 1. Name, address, telephone number, librarian - 2. Size and contents - 3. Access to holdings - 4. Collection services - 5. Additional information. 3 appendices: 1. Hebrew manuscript collections in Europe on microfilm - 2. Hebrew incunabula in European libraries: a provisional list of bibliographical tools - 3. Names and addresses of national associations concerning Jewish studies. No pagination and no index; printed on one side of each leaf only. Correction sheets and additional information leaves to be supplied free of charge. *Class No:* 296:061:026/027

Talmud, Midrash etc.

[928]

The Babylonian Talmud; translated, with notes, glossary and indices. Epstein, I., *ed.* London, Soncino Press, 1935-52. 35v. (including index vol.).

The complete English translation of the Talmud. Comprehensive index; covering all cited Scriptural passages. Lists foreign-language glossaries and abbreviations and gives a complete list of Rabbis mentioned in the Talmud, with their sayings. *Class No:* 296.80

[929]

—Soncino books of the Bible. Cohen, A., *ed.* London, Soncino Press, 1945-52. (Reprinted by Bloch). 14v. $165 the set. ISBN: 0900689234.

Published in association with the Jewish Publication Society of America.

Hebrew text and English translation plus expositions based on the classical Jewish commentaries. Soncino Press has also published *The Midrash* (the classical Jewish commentaries), translated into English, with notes, glossary and indexes; and edited by H. Freedman and M. Simon (1951. 10v.). *Class No:* 296.80

[930]

Bar Ilan's Judaic Library [Tel Aviv], Torah Educational Software, 1994. CD-ROM + guide (89 p., ill., 23 cm.) $998.

Contains full text of the Hebrew Bible, Aggadic Midrashim, Talmud, classical commentaries (Rashi, Ibn Ezra etc.), and over 400 books of codifications and rabbinical writings covering a period from the 8th century to the present. Texts are in Hebrew, software in English. It is possible to do multiple database searches, copy and paste, print. Requires Windows 3.1 PC with at least 2MB RAM and 7MB free on the hard disk, plus CD-ROM drive. There is an online help feature. *Class No:* 296.80

[931]

STEINSALTZ, A. The Talmud: the Steinsaltz edition: a reference guide. Berman, I.V., *trans.* New York, Random House, 1989. 323p. maps. ISBN: 0679773673.

This book provides historical background, explanations of the Talmud page, a short introduction to Aramaic, methodology, terminology and hermeneutics, weights and measures. It also has a good general index and a list of abbreviations used in the Talmud. It is very useful in its own right as a reference tool for Talmud study, as well as an introductory volume to the Steinsaltz translation of the Talmud. *Class No:* 296.80

Dictionaries

Hebrew

[932]

JASTROW, M. Dictionary of the Targumin, the Talmud Babli and Yerushalmi, and the Midrashic literature. with an index of Scriptural quotations. London, Luzac, 1903 (Reprinted New York, Pardes Publishing House, 1950). 2v. (xx,1736p.).

First published 1886.

Includes many quotations, with exact references to sources and translation. A scholarly work; the standard Talmudic Hebrew-English dictionary. Well produced. *Class No:* 296.80(038)=924

Islam

[933]

Islam and Islamic groups: a worldwide reference guide. Shaikh, F., *ed.* Harlow, Longman, 1992. ix,316p. Map. £85;$155. ISBN: 0582091462.

105 signed entries by 11 contributors, arranged under country or region, and covering all politically significant national and international organizations. Bibliography. Short glossary. *Class No:* 297

[934]

KASSIS, H.E. A Concordance of the Qur'an. Berkeley, CA., University of California Press, 1984. 1440p. $115. ISBN: 0520043278.

The first concordance of the Koran in English. 2 sections: 1. All the verses in which the divine name appears (based on Arberry's *The Koran interpreted*) - 2. the remaining vocabulary. The vocabulary is arranged by root, subarranged grammatically. *Class No:* 297

Bibliographies

[935]

BINARK, L. and EREN, H. World bibliography of translations of the meanings of the Holy Qur'an: printed translations, 1515-1980. London, Routledge, 1988. 600p. £65. ISBN: 0710302290.

Contains details of every translation of the Qur'an from Arabic into every known language between 1515 and 1980. Full bibliographical entries of references and sources. *Class No:* 297(01)

[936]

GEDDES, C.L. Guide to reference books for Islamic studies. Denver, Col., American Institute of Islamic Studies, 1985. 429p. $45. (*American Institute of Islamic studies, no. 9.*) ISBN: 0933017006.

1069 annotated entries for reference books on the history, culture, society, and faith of Muslim peoples from the time of Muhammed to 1924. Includes some works in Western European and Asian languages as well as English. 79-page author, title and subject index. *Choice* (v.23(10), June 1986, p.1520) considers coverage of some subjects inadequate, many omissions, and no criteria for inclusion indicated. *Class No:* 297(01)

[937]

Guide to Islam. Ede, D., *ed.* Boston, Mass., G.K. Hall, 1983. 288p. $65.50. ISBN: 0816179050.

Annotated bibliography of primary and secondary materials on the Islamic faith and civilization from A.D. 600 to 1976. Includes translations, literary anthologies, travel accounts, biographies, ancient and modern histories, and theological and mystical writings. Arranged in 7 sections: Historical development, religious thought, religious practice, sacred places, institutions, art and architecture, and research aids. 'A particularly welcome feature is the inclusion of English-language translations of Muslim works' (*Library journal*, 15 November 1983, p.2151). *Class No:* 297(01)

Encyclopaedias

[938]

The Concise encyclopedia of Islam. Glassé, C. San Francisco, Calif., Harper, 1991 472p ISBN: 0060631260.

Contains illustrations, maps and a bibliography.

Comprehensive coverage of different aspects of Islamic culture. Well cross-referenced. *Class No:* 297(031)

[939]

The Encyclopaedia of Islam. New ed., prepared by a number of leading Orientalists, under the patronage of the International Union of Academies. Leiden, E.J. Brill, 1954-. v.1, fasc.1-. illus., plans, maps. To be in about 10v.

First published 1913-1936; reprinted 1987 in 9v. (5164p. illus., tables, 110 pl.) in view of the many years still needed to complete the new ed. (Gld.1500; $750. ISBN 9004082654).

Published primarily in double fascicules, then volumes. V.I - V (Fasc.1-98a): A - Mahi (1954-86); V.VI (Fasc.99-108) (1986-88) in 5 parts. Signed articles, with bibliographies. Many biographies and entries under localities (*e.g.* 'Afghanistan': has 5 sections: geography; ethnography; languages; religion; history - each with bibliography; folded black-and-white map). The article 'Crusades' has bibliography of 1¼ columns, with running commentary. A minor difficulty is the entry of articles under the appropriate Arabic word instead of the English (*e.g.* mosques - under 'Masdjid'). A definitive scholarly work. An index to the first five volumes and supplement has been published (1989. vii,295p. Gld.120. $60. ISBN 9004088490). *Class No:* 297(031)

[940]

The Shorter encyclopedia of Islam. Gibb, H.A.R. *and* Kramer, J.H., *eds.* Leyden, Brill, 1953 (Reprinted 1993). vii,671p. 7 pl., 2 plans. Gld.99; $63.00. ISBN: 9004006818.

Comprises all the articles in the 1st ed., and supplement of the *Encyclopaedia of Islam* (1913-33) relating particularly to the religion and law of Islam. Most of these articles have been reproduced without material alteration; some have been shortened or revised; a few new entries have been added. Bibliographies have been brought up-to-date. Included is a 'Register of subjects', which gives the English translation of Arabic words used as headings. A-Z index of articles, stating authors. Invaluable. *Class No:* 297(031)

Handbooks & Manuals

[941]

WEEKES, R.V. The World of Islam: a world ethnographic survey. 2nd rev. ed. Westport, CT., Greenwood Press, 1985. xii,546p. tables, maps. £85.50. ISBN: 0313233926.

1st ed., 1978, as *Muslim people*.

71 contributors. Articles A-Z, on the life and culture of all major ethnic groups (with Muslim population in excess of 100,000), 30 Muslim culture groups. 'Somali' (tribe), p.364-9 (bibliography, p.365-9). Appended bibliographies include periodical articles and theses. Maps show locations of ethnic groups. 3 appendices: 1. Muslim nationalities of the world; 2. Muslim ethnic groups within nations; 3.

....(contd.)

Major Muslim ethnic groups. 'A timely reference work for both public and academic libraries' (*Library journal*, 15 April 1979, p.587).
Class No: 297(035)

Dictionaries

[942]

NETTON, I.R. **A Popular dictionary of Islam**. London, Curzon Press; Atlantic Highlands, NJ, Humanities Press International, 1992. 279p. £9.99. ISBN: 0700702334, UK; 0391037560, US.

'Abasa'(Ar) ... al-Zumar (Ar). Includes people, places, parts of the Quran, etc. Length of entries varies (*eg* 'Muhommad' has over a page; 'Mecca' 12 lines). Guide to further reading, p.269-79.
Class No: 297(038)

[943]

PENRICE, J. **A Dictionary and glossary of the Koran**, with copious grammatical references and explanations of the text. London, Curzon Press, 1971. vi,168p. £7.50. ISBN: 0700700013.

'Using Penrice in conjunction with the reprinted Flügel text and Arberry's translation, many students with a basic foundation in Arabic grammar will discover for themselves the beauties and the profundities of the Koran' (*T.L.S.*, 14 July 1972, p.823). Sources, p.vi.
Class No: 297(038)

Arabic

[944]

MIR, M. **Dictionary of Qur'ānic terms and concepts**. New York, Garland, 1987. 244p. $40. (*Garland reference library of the humanities, 693*.) ISBN: 0824085469.

Lists over 500 terms found in the Qur'ān. English translations of the terms are arranged A-Z with cross-references from the transliterated Arabic. Definitions vary in length from several lines to 2 or more pages. Entries refer to specific passages in the Qur'ān where the term is used and explain its significance. A 20-page list of terms included follows the text. *Class No:* 297(038)=927

Histories

[945]

LAPIDUS, I.M. **A History of Islamic societies**. Cambridge, Cambridge University Press, 1988. xxxi,1002p. 30 illus., 37 maps. £35. ISBN: 0521225523.

A study of the civilization and patterns of life of Muslims throughout the world. Part 1 examines the formative era of Islamic civilization from the revelation of the Qu'ran to the 13th century; pt.2 traces the diffusion of the Middle Eastern Islamic paradigm from the 10th to the 19th centuries; and pt.3 treats the disruption of Islamic societies by economic decline, internal religious conflict, and the establishment of European domination in the 19th and 20th centuries. Glossary, p.918-928. Extensive bibliography, p.929-970. Index, p.971-1002.
Class No: 297(091)

[946]

RAHMAN, H.U. **A Chronology of Islamic history, 570-1000 C.E.** London, Mansell Publishing Ltd.; Boston, Mass., G.K. Hall, 1989. 256p. 3 maps. £25; $45. ISBN: 0720119820, UK; 0816190674, US.

Lists and describes the events that marked Islam's rise. Chronological entries are self-contained and there are frequent cross-references. Dates refer to the Gregorian calendar and formulas for transposing Gregorian into Muslim dates included. Footnotes. Index, p.169-181. *Class No:* 297(091)

Europe—Western

[947]

GERHOLM, T. *and* LITHMAN, Y.G., *eds*. **The New Islamic presence in Western Europe**. 2nd ed. London, Mansell Publishing Ltd., 1991. 304p. 8 illus. £19.99. ISBN: 0720120918.

Stems from a conference in Stockholm in 1986, organized by the Centre for Research in International Migration and Ethnicity at the University of Stockholm and the Royal Swedish Academy of Letters, History and Antiquities.

16 chapters arranged in 3 parts: 1. The institutionalization of Islam in various countries - 2. Migration and changes in the religious experience - 3. Additional themes for future research. Notes and references follow each chapter. Glossary, p.278-280. Subject index, p.281-288; name index, p.289-291; index of Muslim organizations, p.292-293. *Class No:* 297(400)

Russia

[948]

BENNINGSEN, A. *and* WIMBUSH, S.E. **Muslims of the Soviet empire**: a guide. Muskogee, OK., Indiana University Press, 1986. 294p. tables, 3 maps. $29.95. ISBN: 0253339588.

In 3 parts, part 1 discusses the historical roots of Islam; part 2 examines the history, culture, politics and demography of Soviet Muslims, grouped by religions; and part 3 is a selected bibliography of sources, English and Russian titles mostly. 'No comparable volume presents such a wealth of information in such a systematic, compact, and lucid form' (*Choice*, April, 1987, p.1194). *Class No:* 297(47)

Africa—North

Bibliographies

[949]

SHINAR, P. **Essai de bibliographie sélective et annotée sur l'Islam:** Maghrébin contemporain: Maroc, Algérie, Tunisie, Libye (1830-1978). Paris, Éditions du CNRS, 1983. 506p. F.280. ISBN: 2222027039.

2025 items, including 295 bibliographies and reference sources on 'Islam' in its broad cultural sense. Part I is basically an annotated list of source material used to compile the bibliography proper (Part II). Part II is arranged in 5 sections (General, and for each country), the sections being further divided by subject. Works in all formats (books, articles in journals, and congress proceedings) and in various languages (English, French, Arabic, Spanish, Italian and German) are included selectively. Each entry includes complete bibliographical information, annotation, and list of reviews. Library locations are also given for books. Author, detailed subject, cited personal name, geographical name, and Arabic or Berber term indexes.
Class No: 297(61/65)(01)

Babism

Handbooks & Manuals

[950]

SMITH, P. **The Babi and Baha'i religions:** from messianic Shi'ism to a world religion. Cambridge, Cambridge University Press, 1987. xiv,[3],243p. illus., diagrs., tables, maps. £25. ISBN: 0521301289.

10 chapters in 3 parts: 1. Babism - 2. The Baha's faith in the East, c. 1866-1921 - 3. The Baha's faith as a world religion. Chapter notes, p.296-299. Appendices: Glossary. Chronology. A note on the sources and a guide to further reading. Index, p.239-243.
Class No: 297BAB(035)

Celtic Cults

[951]

GREEN, M. **The Gods of the Celts**. Totowa, N.J., Barnes & Noble Books; Gloucester, A. Sutton Publishers, 1986. [8], 257p. 103 illus. $27.50. £14.95. ISBN: 0389206725, US; 0862992923, UK.

A guide to Celtic beliefs in Britain and Europe 'drawing on the latest research and covering all aspects of the gods' ritual customs, cult objects, and sacred places. 7 chapters: The Celts and religion - Cults of sun and sky - Fertility and the Mother-Goddesses - War, death and the underworld - Water-gods and healers - Animals and animism - Symbolism and imagery in Celtic cult expression. Notes/references (p.226-235), bibliography (p.236-249), Index (p.250-257).
Class No: 299.16

[952]

HUBERT, H. **The Greatness and decline of the Celts**. Rev.ed. London, Constable, 1987. xxii, 314p. 3 maps. £12.95. ISBN: 0094678006.

First published in French in 1932, as *Les Celtes depuis l'èpoque de la Tène*.

13 chapters arranged in 3 parts: 1. Celtic expansion in the La Tène period; 2. The end of the Celtic world; 3. The civilization of the Celts. Conclusion: The heritage of the Celts. Footnotes. Bibliography (p.281-299) in 13 sections (Sources - Inscriptions - Periodicals - Miscellaneous - Language - Literature - General works - and then by countries) each subdivided A-Z by author. Index (p.301-304). With the author's *The Rise of the Celts* (q.v.) a 2v. history of the Celts.
Class No: 299.16

[953]

—HUBERT, H. **The Rise of the Celts**. New ed. London, Constable, 1987. xxxiii,335p. 43 illus., 12 maps. £12.95. ISBN: 0094677905.

First published 1934.

10 chapters divided between 2 parts: pt.1: What the Celts were; pt.2: Movement of the Celtic peoples. Bibliography, p.303-322. Index, p.323-335. *Class No:* 299.16

[954]

NICHOLS, R. **The Book of Druidry:** history, sites and wisdom. Wellingborough, Northants, Aquarian Press, 1990. 320p. illus. £16.99. ISBN: 085030900x.

In 8 chapters, each subdivided: Stones, wood and culture - The Celts - Cymric takeover - How far underground: a study of aims and festivals in France and Britain - Nine groups of Druidic concepts - Greater sites of the Britannic Islands - Druidic wisdom - The eight-fold year-plan. Epitome. Bibliography, p.311-3. Index, p.315-9. *Class No: 299.16*

Dictionaries

[955]

ELLIS, P.B. **A Dictionary of Celtic mythology.** Santa Barbara, CA, ABC-Clio, 1992. 325p. 24 illus. $52. £44.95. ISBN: 0874366097.

Compares the Irish, Welsh, Manx, Scottish, Cornish and Breton cultures. Good introduction, followed by thorough and well-written entries. Selective bibliography.

Author also wrote *A Dictionary of Irish mythology* (ABC-Clio, 1991). *Class No: 299.16(038)*

[956]

GREEN, M.L. **Dictionary of Celtic myth and legend.** London, Thames & Hudson, 1992. 240p. 243 black & white illus. £16.95; $35. ISBN: 0500015163.

Over 400 entries, A-Z, on Celtic religious life, the Druids, animal and human sacrifice, and other aspects of the Celtic people, 500BC-400AD. Preceded by a 'Reader's guide': a lengthy introduction. Major sources are cited and full bibliographical references included. Subject index. 'An excellent source ...'(*Choice*, v.29(11/12), July/August 1992, p.1656). *Class No: 299.16(038)*

Chinese Religions

Bibliographies

[957]

YU, D.C. and THOMPSON, L.G. **Guide to Chinese religion.** Boston, Mass., G.K. Hall, 1985. 200p. $50. (*Asia philosophies and religious resource guide.*.) ISBN: 0816179026.

Deals with religions that originated on Chinese soil, and includes material from 1500B.C. to 1977. c.3000 short annotated entries, covering all aspects and periods of religion from folk beliefs to rituals to Maoism and to conflicts between religious institutions. Index. *Class No: 299.5(01)*

Dictionaries

[958]

PAS, J.F. **Historical dictionary of Taoism.** Lanham, Scarecrow, 1998. 400p. $64. (*Religions, philosophies, and movements series, no. 18.*.) ISBN: 0810833697.

A lengthy introduction looks at the historical development of Taoism, including its current situation in the world. It outlines the basic teachings, concepts and writings. The dictionary section has entries on concepts, persons, rituals, beliefs and events of Taoism in great detail. Also included is a chronology of Taoist history and notes on the romanization of Chinese. *Class No: 299.5(038)*

Japanese Religions

---

[959]

READER, I. **Religion in contemporary Japan.** London, Macmillan, 1991. xv,277p. £40. ISBN: 0333523210.

Aims to give the reader an overview of the contemporary nature of religion in Japan, in particular looking at religious behaviour and the ways in which religious themes are found in the lives of Japanese people. Notes (p.244-259); references cited (p.260-267); index (p.268-277). *Class No: 299.52*

Bibliographies

[960]

EARHART, H.B. **The New religions of Japan:** a bibliography of Western-language materials. 2nd ed. Ann Arbor, Mich., University of Michigan, Center for Japanese Studies, 1983; New York, Harper & Row, 1985. 158p. $7; £4.95. (*Michigan papers in Japanese studies, 9.*) ISBN: 0939512130.

First published 1970 (96p.).

1450 annotated entries arranged in 2 parts: General bibliography, A-Z by author; Bibliography of individual new religions, by name of

....(contd.)

religion. Many cross-references. Index of authors, translators and editors; topical index, Appendix on suggestions for locating Western-language materials. Highly recomended by *Choice*, November 1983, p.400. *Class No: 299.52(01)*

[961]

HOLZMAN, D., *and others*. **Japanese religion and philosophy:** a guide to Japanese reference and research material. Ann Arbor, Mich., Michigan University Press, 1959 (Reprinted 1975). vii, 142p. $22.50. (*Michigan University Center for Japanese Studies. Bibliographic series, no.7.*) ISBN: 0837179106.

992 numbered items, giving author and title in Japanese, with English translation. Limited to Japanese books on the doctrines and histories of the religions and philosophies of Japan published since the Meijiera. Most entries are annotated briefly. Sections: 1. General - 2. Shinto - 3. Buddhism - 4. Confucianism - 5. Bushidó, Kokugaku and Yogaku - 6. Christianity - 7. Meiji and after. Appendices: List of publishers; List of authors and editors; subject index. *Class No: 299.52(01)*

[962]

—Meiji taishô shôwa Shintô shoseki mokuroku. [A Bibliography of Shintoism of the Meiji, Taishô and Showâ eras.] Katô, G., *ed.* Tokyo, Meiji Jingû Shamusho, 1953. 707p.

Lists *c*.16,000 items. *Class No: 299.52(01)*

[963]

—Shintô shoseki mokuroku. [A Bibliography of Shintoism.] Katô, G., *ed.* 2nd ed. Tokyo, Meiji Seitoku Kinen Gakkai, 1943. 646p.

Lists *c*. 150,000 items up to 1940. *Class No: 299.52(01)*

Handbooks & Manuals

[964]

JAPAN. Agency of Cultural Affairs. **Japanese religion:** a survey. Tokyo & Palo Alto, Kodansha International Ltd., 1972 (reprinted 1981). 276p. illus. $12.95. ISBN: 0870111833.

9 contributors (all Japanese). Part 1: Description and interpretation (2. Shinto; 3. Buddhism; 4. Christianity; 5. New religious movements; 6. Confucianism; 7. Folk religion...) - Part 2: Specific religious organizations - Part 3: Statistical tables. Index, p.265-72, includes Japanese characters. A survey of major religious organizations, with particular reference to their present circumstances. *Class No: 299.52(035)*

African Religions

---

[965]

PARRINDER, G. **Africa's three religions.** 2nd ed. London, Sheldon Press, 1976. 256p. map. £3.95. ISBN: 0859690962.

First published 1969 as *Religion in Africa*.

4 parts (20 chapters): 1. Traditional religions - 2. Christianity - 3. Islam - 4. Conclusion (18. Other religions; 19. Relationship of Africa religions; 20. Characteristics of religion in Africa). Bibliography, p.239-42 (3 sections). Non-analytical index. *Class No: 299.6*

Bibliographies

[966]

MITCHELL, R.C. *and* TURNER, H.W. A Comprehensive **bibliography of modern African religious movements.** Evanston, Ill., Northwestern University Press, 1966. lxv,132p.

1313 items, many with annotations; arranged by countries (south of the Sahara), plus sections on 'Theory' and 'Africa, General'. Covers religious interpretations of such movements as Mau Mau, as well as Christian deviations. Omits Islamic movements. Author and ethnic indexes. Continued in periodic supplements in the *Journal of religion in Africa* (Leiden, E.J. Brill, ISSN 00224200). *Class No: 299.6(01)*

[967]

WILLIAMS, E.L. *and* BROWN, C.F. **The Howard University bibliography of African and Afro-American religious studies,** with locations in American libraries. Wilmington, Del., Scholarly Resources, [1977]. 525p. $55. ISBN: 0842020802.

Entries for over 13,000 books, periodical articles and parts of books. 5 main divisions: Africa heritage - Christianity and slavery in the New World - Black religious life in the Americas - The civil rights movement - The contemporary religious scene. At least one American library location per item; list of manuscripts and their locations. Appendix of biographies and autobiographies. Author index. Sources range from scholarly to popular accounts in national weeklies. *Class No: 299.6(01)*

Inca Religion

---

[968]

COBO, B. Inca religion and customs. Hamilton, R., *trans. & ed.*
Austin, Texas, University of Texas Press, 1990. 303p. $27.50. ISBN:
0292738544.
    Completed in 1653, Father Bernabe Cobo's *Historia del nuevo
mundo* is an important source of information on pre-conquest and
colonial Spanish America. This translation of part of Cobo's work
covers such topics as language, food and shelter, marriage and
childbearing, agriculture, warfare, medicine, practical crafts, games
and burial routines. *Class No:* 299.85

Oceanic Religions

---

[969]

POIGNANT, R. Oceanic mythology: the myths of Polynesia,
Micronesia, Melanesia, Australia. 2nd rev. ed. London, Newnes,
1985. 144p. illus. (incl.col.pl.). £7.95. ISBN: 0600342832.
    4 regional sections, as in title, with subdivisions. Many sub-sections.
148 illustrations, 48 in colour. 'Further reading list'. Index.
Class No: 299.9

[970]

SWAIN, T. Aboriginal religions in Australia: a bibliographical survey.
Westport, CT., Greenwood Press, 1991. 336p. $55. (*(Bibliographies
and indexes in religious studies, 18).*.) ISBN: 0313260443.
    Over 1000 references in Western languages. An encyclopedic,
interpretive survey of the literature is followed by a bibliography,
arranged in the 10 standard regions of Aboriginal habitats and
subdivided topically (*eg.* institutions, women, myth). Annotations are
evaluative and there are extensive 'see also' references. Author, title
and general subject indexes. '... easily the most comprehensive
bibliography on its topic.'(*Choice*, v.29(11/12), July/August 1992,
p.1662). *Class No:* 299.9

3 Social Sciences

Social Sciences

[971]
International current awareness services/ICAS. British Library of Political and Economic Science, at the London School of Economics, *comp.* London, Routledge, November 1991-. 4 series, each monthly. ISSN: 09601511, Anthropology; 0960152x, Economics; 09601538, Political science; 09601546, Sociology.

Aims to provide rapid international coverage of the world's most significant social science literature. Entries are drawn from a total of 13000 current serials, plus an extensive monograph collection. Coverage is worldwide, in 30 languages from over 60 countries. *Class No:* 30

Databases

[972]
RABEN, J. and MARKS, G., eds. Data bases in the humanities and social sciences: I.F.I.P. Working Conference proceedings. Oxford, North-Holland, 1980. xii, 330p. 36 illus., 8 tables. £37.54. ISBN: 0444854991.

58 short papers, mostly on specific databases. (Review in *Aslib information*, September 1981, p.211). *Class No:* 30(003.4)

Bibliographies of Bibliographies

[973]
Chicorel index to abstracting and indexing services: periodicals in the humanities and social sciences. 2nd ed. New York, American Library Publishing Co., 1978. 2v. (922p.).

c.33,000 entries from 135 services. Arranged A-Z by title of periodical, giving titles of indexing and abstracting services that cover them. List of addresses of services. List of inverted terms. International in scope. *Class No:* 30(009)

Bibliographies

[974]
APAIS: Australian public affairs information service: a subject index to current literature. Canberra, National Library of Australia, 1945-Monthly (except December), cumulated annually (since 1955). ISSN: 07278926.

'APAIS' is a current guide to material on Australian political, economic, social and cultural affairs. The March 1989 issue had over 500 items, arranged under subjects, A-Z, with sub-divisions. *c.*200 periodicals published both in Australia and overseas, indexed comprehensively. Some annual reports of government agencies and other important organizations are also indexed. *Class No:* 30(01)

[975]
COUNCIL OF PLANNING LIBRARIANS. CPL bibliographies. Chicago, Ill., the Council, 1958-. no.1-.

A series of subject bibliographies, mainly in the social sciences, compiled by individuals or groups of individuals in academic organizations. Recent bibliographies include: 180. *Community development resources: a selected and annotated bibliography* (1986. [2], 67p. $16. ISBN 0866021809). 181. *Congregate housing for the elderly: a selective and annotated bibliography* (1986. [4],27p. $12. ISBN 0866021817). 182. *Adaptive reuse of school buildings: a selective and annotated bibliography* (1986.[3],13p. $10. ISBN 0866021825). A comprehensive index to nos. 1-1565, 1958-July 1978, was published in 1979 in 3 vols. (subject, author and numerical listings). *Class No:* 30(01)

[976]
Current contents: social and behavioral sciences. Philadelphia, Pa., Institute for Scientific Information, 1969-, v.1, no.1-. Weekly. ISSN: 00926361.

Originally as *Current contents: behavioral, social and management sciences* and *Current contents: education.*

Reproduces tables of contents of several hundred domestic and foreign journals, *c.*150 journal issues covered in each weekly part. Coverage: Anthropology - Area studies - Business - Communications - Economics - Education - Geography - History - Information science - International relations - Law - Library science - Linguistics - Management - Planning and development - Political science - Psychology - Psychiatry - Public health - Rehabilitation - Social issues - Social medicine - Social work - Sociology - Special education.

....(contd.)
Weekly title word index; author index; address directory. Original Article Tear Sheet (OATS) service. Available online. *Class No:* 30(01)

[977]
FONDATION NATIONALE DES SCIENCES POLITIQUES. Bibliographie courante d'articles de périodiques postérieurs à 1944 sur les problemes politiques, économiques et sociaux. Boston, Mass., G.K. Hall, 1968-72. 17v. plus supplements. $1420. for 17v. Supplements, $225 for each set of 2v., Complete set: $1850.

Main bibliography reproduces 302,000 catalogue cards, arranged initially by countries or areas and then by a decimal classification. *Class No:* 30(01)

[978]
GABROVSKA, S., and others, comp. & eds. European guide to social science information and documentation services. Oxford, Pergamon Press, 1982. v, 234p. £31. ISBN: 0080289274.

Compiled and edited for European Cooperation in Social Science Information and Documentation.

An alphabetical list of countries precedes the list of 215 institutions providing social science information in 22 European countries. Arrangement is A-Z by country, subdivided A-Z by title of organization. Entries include address, date started, official status, telephone number, functions, subject coverage, library and publications. Indexes of institutions and subjects. *Class No:* 30(01)

[979]
GRANDIN, A. Bibliographie générale des sciences juridiques, politiques, économiques et sociales de 1800 à 1925/6. Paris, Recueil Sirey, 1926; Supplements 1-19, 1926-50. 1928-51. 3v. plus 19 supplements.

Systematic arrangement, with 16 subject groups. The bibliography is of books and only those in the French language, published in France or elsewhere. Includes theses and government publications. No annotations but frequent cross-references. Subject and author indexes. Aspects of law preponderate.

Continued, for economics, in Mossé, R. and Potier, M. (at 33(01)). *Class No:* 30(01)

[980]
International bibliography of the social sciences - political science. British Library of Political and Economic Science, *comp. and ed.* London, Routledge, 2000. ISBN: 0415221064. ISSN: 0076051x.

Continues: A London bibliography of the social sciences ... (1931/32-1990).

Lists important works in political science published during 1998. Covers over 2000 journals. *Class No:* 30(01)

[981]
LI, T-ch. Social science reference sources: a practical guide. 3rd ed. Westport, CT, Greenwood Press, 2000. 528p. $99.50. (*Contributions in librarianship and information science, 68.*)

Entries are extensive bibliographic essays and constitute the bulk of the book, each being devoted to one particular discipline. Comparisons are made between two or more titles covering much the same information. *Class No:* 30(01)

[982]
PAIS international in print: a selective list of the latest books, periodical articles, government documents, pamphlets, microfiche, and reports of public and private agencies relating to business, economic and social conditions, public policy and administration, and international relations, published in English, French, German, Italian, Portuguese and Spanish throughout the world. New York, Public Affairs Information Service, 1915-. v.1, no.1-. Monthly, with 3 quarterly and annual cumulations. CD-ROM. ISSN: 10514015.

Previously titled *Public affairs information service bulletin* and then *PAIS bulletin* and *PAIS foreign language index* until 1991.

Indexes *c.*3000 periodicals. The annual volume carries an author index. The main entry 'Directories' provides a handy check-list directory of publishers and organizations in cumulations. Because of its frequent cumulation and wide coverage of material, it is the major indexing service in the social sciences. PAIS on CD-ROM is available from 1972. Also online. *Class No:* 30(01)

[983]

—PAIS subject headings. Picon, A. *and* Sloan, G., *eds*. 2nd ed. New York, Public Affairs Information Service, 1990. $65. ISBN: 1877874019.

A listing of the controlled vocabulary terms used to index the other PAIS publications. *Class No:* 30(01)

[984]

Reader's guide to the social sciences. London, Fitzroy Dearborn, 2000. 2v. (2000p.) £175. ISBN: 1579580912.

A guide to key reading on a range of social science topics. The 1500 entries are arranged alphabetically. *Class No:* 30(01)

[985]

ROBERTS, N., *ed*. Use of social science literature. London, Butterworths, 1977. [x], 326p.

15 contributors (librarians and academics). 14 chapters: 1. Communication and bibliographical system of the social sciences - 2. The information needs and sources of economics - 3. The literature of sociology and the pattern of research and retrieval - 4. Politics, and data archives (largely on methodology) - 5. The literature and sources of social anthropology - 6. Management research - 7. The literature and sources of education - 8. Environmental planning information - 9. The literature and sources of public administration - 10. Criminology and its literature - 11. Exploiting social science journals - 12/14. Exploiting the official publications of the UK, foreign countries, and international organizations. Some chapters have selected references appended (that on 'Management research' has, exceptionally, 7½p. of references). Takes a narrow approach to the social sciences (omits law, business information). Brief index covers only subject fields, institutions and types of literature (*e.g.* abstracts, statistical sources). Noted: Burrington, F.A. *How to find out about the social sciences*. (Pergamon, 1975. vii, 144p. £11.75. ISBN 0080182895). *Class No:* 30(01)

[986]

The Social sciences: a cross-discipinary guide to selected sources. Herron, N.L., *ed*. Englewood Cliffs, CO, Libraries Unlimited, 1989. 287p. $36. (*(Library text series)*.) ISBN: 0872877256.

790 annotated entries in 12 disciplines (political science - economics and business - history - law - anthropology - sociology - education - psychology - communications - geography - statistics - demography). Lively, evaluative annotations. Author, title and subject indexes. '... a trustworthy textbook for library students ...' (*RQ*,v.30(1), Fall 1990, p.154). *Class No:* 30(01)

[987]

Social sciences citation index. Philadelphia, PA., Institute for Scientific Information, 1973-. 3pa. (3rd issue as bound annual cumulation; 5-year cumulations also available). ISSN: 00913707.

The annual cumulation, in 5v., comprises 3 indexes: *Citation index* (the main index, listing, A-Z, authors and titles of items cited in the *Source index*); *Source index* (listing, A-Z, authors and titles of citing articles); and *Permuterm subject index* (based on permuted words of titles of articles)., Titles are drawn from *c*.2,000 journals in the social sciences. Also available online and on CD-ROM. *Class No:* 30(01)

[988]

Social sciences index, New York, H.W. Wilson, 1974-. v.1-. Quarterly, with bound cumulation. Sold on a service basis. ISSN: 00944920.

One of two indexes superseding *Social sciences & humanities index* (1916-1974).

Author and subject entries to English-language periodicals in anthropology; area studies; community health and medical care; geography; gerontology; law & criminology; minority studies; planning and public administration; police science and corrections; policy sciences; psychiatry; psychology; social work and public welfare; sociology; urban studies, and related subjects. Author listing of citations to book reviews. 342 key periodicals currently indexed. Clear typography: good paper. Available online and CD-ROM. *Class No:* 30(01)

[989]

Social scisearch. Philadelphia, PA., Institute for Scientific Information, 1972-.

An online database, up-dated monthly, is a 'citation index of worldwide periodical literature covering all social science descriptions. *Class No:* 30(01)

[990]

UNITED NATIONS. Library. Geneva. Monthly bibliography. Part 1: Books, official documents, serials. Geneva, 1928-. Bi-monthly. ISSN: 02516616.

Formerly as *Monthly list of books catalogued in the Library of the United Nations*, 1946-77; originally ... *League of Nations*, 1928-45.

A subject compilation of newly acquired books, official documents and periodicals, which serves as the Library's monthly acquisition list as well as a current awareness list. Personal and corporate author index; a subject index which includes geographical terms; and a title index. *Class No:* 30(01)

[991]

UNITED NATIONS. Library. Geneva. Monthly bibliography. Part 2: Selected articles. Geneva, 1929-. Bi-monthly. ISSN: 02516624.

Up to 1977 as *Monthly list of selected articles*.

About 600 current-information items on periodical literature and contributions to collective works of interest to the United Nations and the international community. About 1000 titles regularly scanned. Excludes short news items and statistical notes. Subject arrangement: Political and legal affairs - economic affairs - natural resources - agriculture, forestry and fisheries - industry - transport - communications - trade - population - human settlements - health - employment - humanitarian aid - social affairs - cultural affairs - science and technology. A current awareness service. Author, subject and title indexes. *Class No:* 30(01)

[992]

—League of Nations and United Nations Monthly list of selected articles: cumulation, 1920-1970. Field, N.S., *ed*. Dobbs Ferry, N.Y., Oceana, 1971-5. 14v. $910 the set. ISBN: 0379411507.

Lists selected articles on international, constitutional and administrative law, politics and economics from *c*.3000 journals worldwide. Volumes have 3 broad subject groups: *Political questions* (v.1: 1920-1928; v.2: 1929-1945; v.3: 1946-1960; v.4: 1961-1970; v.5: Special problems, 1920-1970) - *Legal questions* (v.1: Public international law; private international law; v.2: National law - countries) - *Economic questions* (v.1: Economic conditions, 1920-1955; v.2: Economic conditions, 1956-1970; Economic conditions - food and agriculture, 1956-1970; Economic conditions - textiles, mining, coal, metals. 1920-1970; v.4: Economic conditions - petroleum, 1920-1970; Economic conditions - miscellaneous industries, 1920-1970; v.5: Commercial policy, 1920-1970; v.6: Economic policy, 1920-1970). *Class No:* 30(01)

[993]

WEBB, W., *and associates*. Sources of information in the social sciences: a guide to the literature. 3rd ed. Chicago, Ill., American Library Association, 1986. x, 777p. $70. £35. ISBN: 083890405x.

Supersedes C.M. White's *Sources of information in the social sciences* (Chicago, A.L.A., Preliminary ed. 1959; 1st ed. 1964; 2nd ed. 1973. xviii, 702p.).

A thorough updating of White's standard sources, describing the literature; some sections reworked, others merely updated. 8110 numbered entries (2nd ed. 4527), mostly annotated, in 9 main classes: 1. Social science literature - 2. History - 3. Geography - 4. Economics and business administration - 5. Sociology - 6. Anthropology - 7. Psychology - 8. Education - 9. Political science. 20 contributors. Each chapter commences with a survey of the field, followed by a survey of the reference works, subject grouped. Cross-references. Extensive index (p.585-776) has subject, author-title and title entries. 'Focuses on form rather than function' (*Choice*, v.24(5), January 1987, p.749). *Class No:* 30(01)

Encyclopaedias

[994]

Encyclopaedia of the social sciences. Seligman, E.R.A., *ed*. New York & London, Macmillan, 1930-35. (Reprinted 1951. 15v. in 8; Reprinted by Encyclopaedia Britannica Inc. in 5 vols. 5v. $129. ISBN: 0878273557.

A comprehensive work, projected under the auspices of 10 learned societies; signed articles by specialists. Some subject articles are lengthy and are provided with lists of contents (*e.g.* 'Agriculture'; 9 sections; 8 contributors); treatment is usually systematic (*e.g.* a subject will be introduced by giving historical background surveyed in various countries, and then discussed in terms of its problems). Although about one half of the articles are biographies, these are usually comparatively brief, being chiefly concerned with the person's achievements in the social sciences. Bibliographies, generally excellent, even if dated, are appended to articles. Includes an index and a classification of the articles in subject and biography groups. *Class No:* 30(031)

[995]

International encyclopedia of the social sciences. Sills, D.L., *ed*. New York, Macmillan Co. & The Free Press, 1968. (Reprinted by Collier-Macmillan, New York, 1977, in 8v. set, including Biographical supplement). Originally in 17v. plus v.18 (Biographical supplement). Reprint in 8v. including supplement. £495 the set. ISBN: 0028955404.

1900 articles by *c*.1500 contributors. 'First and foremost the work of social scientists' (*Preface*) and designed to complement, not to surplant its predecessor, *Encyclopaedia of the social sciences* (Macmillan, 1930-35). Emphasises theory and methodology, psychology and sociology. Historical topics are not plentiful; as against 4000 biographies in the earlier *Encyclopaedia,* here there are only a few hundred. No living person is included who was born after 1890.

Articles average 1500 words. 'Karl Marx': 7 columns of text plus 4 of bibliography; 'Urban revolution': 20p., each of the 3 sections having a bibliography of ½ column or more. Numerous cross-references. V.17, the index, has *c*.40,000 analytical entries, and a classified list of articles. A standard encyclopedia, with articles of lasting significance. *Class No:* 30(031)

[996]
KUPER, A. *and* KUPER, J., *eds*. **The Social science encyclopedia.** 2nd ed. London, Routledge, 1999. 952p. £24.99. ISBN: 0415207940.

Over 700 essays dealing with theories, issues and methods in the social sciences, and many others devoted to the life and work of individual scholars. Covers all the social sciences and related disciplines. Contributions by 500 international scholars in the field. Most entries followed by a list of references and suggestions for further reading. Some cross-references. *Class No:* 30(031)

Dictionaries

German

[997]
DIETL, E.-E., *and others*. **Wörterbuch für Recht, Wirtschaft und Politik. Dictionary of legal, commercial and political terms.** 2nd rev. ed. Munich, C.H. Beck; Albany, NY, Matthew Bender, 1988-90. 2v.

Rev. & enl. ed. of the dictionary by G. Erdsiek and C.-E. Dietl.

V.1: English-German (5th rev. ed., 1990. lxiv,937p. £133.75). v.2: German-English (3rd rev. ed., 1988. xxii,821p. £126.60). Terms illustrated by examples, explanations and commentaries. Incorporates American usage. *Class No:* 30(038)=30

[998]
—DIETL, E.-E., *and others*. Wirtschaftswörterbuch: Wörterbuch für den Wirtschafts-, Handels- und Rechtsverkehr .../Commercial dictionary: dictionary of commercial, business and legal terms - including the terminology of the European Communities. Wiesbaden, Gabler, 1985-87. 2v. (409 & 404p.). £39.60 each vol. ISBN: 3409199004, v.1; 3409198997, v.2.

Part 1: German-English; part 2: English-German.
Class No: 30(038)=30

[999]
KOSCHNICK, W.J. **Standard dictionary of the social sciences.** München, K.G. Saur, 1984-92. 3v. (x,664p.; ix,785.; x,780). DM.120-; £75 each vol.

V.1: English-German; v.2: German-English: Part 1: A-L; part 2: M-Z. *c.*20,000 terms from all areas of the social sciences, particularly sociology, psychology, statistics, communications research, psychiatry, anthropology, political science and research methodology. Definitions range in length from a few words to a paragraph or more. Identifies authors who originated or were closely associated with particular terms. Cross-references. '... likely to be the standard English-German social science dictionary for some time' (*Choice*, v.23(5), January 1986, p.728). *Class No:* 30(038)=30

[1000]
Market economy and planned economy: an encyclopaedic dictionary. Földi, T., *and others, eds*. London, K.G.Saur, 1991 (available from Bowker-Saur). xxxix,1045p. £105. ISBN: 3598110707.

Trilingual dictionary of 661 entries and over 1000 sub-entries for those interested in comparisons between very different economic systems, especially between capitalist and communist economies. Some terms are basic, but most refer to concepts revelant to the book's main purpose. Entries are arranged A-Z in German, with definitions and interpretation in German, English and Russian. Cross-references. Favourable review in *Reference reviews*, v.6(3), 1992.
Class No: 30(038)=30

French

[1001]
BRANCHIARD, M. **Dictionnaire économique et social: dictionnaire Thomas Suavet.** 11. éd., entièrement revue et corrigée. Paris, Économie et Humanisme, 1978. 582, 19p. ISBN: 270820209x.

First published 1961; 1st-10th eds. by T.H. Suavet.

Analyses *c.* 1600 key-words, definitions plus comment and usually a bibliography; (*e.g.* 'Malthusianisme': 2 cols., bibliography has anti-Malthusian items; 'Coopérative': 6 cols, including a ½-column bibliography). Appended chronology, 1830-1977. Numerous cross-references. No biographies, but a table of names of persons mentioned plus associated idea, theory, movement or group.
Class No: 30(038)=40

Arabic

[1002]
KHAN, M.A. **A Glossary of Islamic economics.** London, Mansell, 1990. 154p. $100. (*Mansell Islamic studies.*) ISBN: 072012042x.

*c.*850 terms, including legal and technical terms, mostly in Arabic but also in Urdu, Persian and Turkish, defined in English.
Class No: 30(038)=927

[1003]
SABIQ, J. **Majama'al-lughat:** qamus al-iqtiṣad, al-huquq, al tarbiya wal-ta'lim ... Beirut, the Author, 1971. 1189p.

Trilingual dictionary (Arabic-French-English; French-English-Arabic; English-French-Arabic) covering economics, law, sociology, statistics, political and diplomatic sciences. *Class No:* 30(038)=927

Chinese

[1004]
English-Chinese glossaries, v.1-5. Prepared by the Chinese Language Division of the Home Affairs Department. Hong Kong, 1981-1986. 5v.

V.1: Education (1981. 79p. *c.*2000 entries which are special terms used in government departments on subjects relating to education; v.2: Housing and land (rev. ed., 1986. 131p. Some 2700 entries ...); v.3: Finance (1983. 233p. *c.*4000 terms in finance and economy); v.4: Civil service (1985. 101p. 2000 terms); v.5: Internal transport, part 1 - Land transport. *Class No:* 30(038)=951

Theses

[1005]
BILBOUL, R.R. *and* KENT, F.L., *eds*. **Retrospective index to theses of Great Britain and Ireland, 1917-1950.** v.1: Social sciences and humanities. Santa Barbara, CA.; Oxford, ABC-Clio, 1977. [xviii], 393p. facsim. £78.

About 12000 entries. Subject index (subject; title; author; degree; date; university). Author index (author; title; degree; date; university). *Class No:* 30(043)

[1006]
Dissertation abstracts international: Section A. The humanities and social sciences. Ann Arbor, Mich., University Microfilms International, 1938-. Monthly. Cumulative author index. ISSN: 04194209.

Formerly *Dissertation abstracts*.

Sections on communications and the arts; education; language, literature, linguistics; philosophy, religion and theology; social sciences. Author-prepared abstracts are of doctoral dissertations and contain up to 350 words; they are submitted by nearly 500 participating institutions in North America and the world. Information for each entry includes title; author's name; degree; date awarded; institution granting degree; no. of pages; UMI order no. Author and keyword title indexes. Available online and on CD-ROM.
Class No: 30(043)

Reviews & Abstracts

[1007]
Book review index to social science periodicals. Ann Arbor, Pierian Press, 1978. 4v. $75 each vol.; $275 the set. ISBN: 0876500262, v.1; 0876501102, v.2; 0876500491, v.3; 0876501145, v.4; 0686770668, set.

Companion guide to *Book reviews in the humanities*.

Contains references to book reviews in more than 400 journals in the social sciences. V.1 - 1964-70; v.2. - 1971; v.3. - 1972; v.4 - 1973-74. Continued in *Social science index* (see at 3(01). *Class No:* 30(048)

[1008]
FONDATION NATIONALE DES SCIENCES POLITIQUES. **Bulletin analytique de documentation politique, économique et sociales contemporaines.** Paris, Fondation Nationale des Sciences Politiques (previously Presses Universitaires de France), 1946-. Monthly. ISSN: 00074171.

Preceded by *Bulletin bibliographique de documentation internationale contemporaine*.

Over 5000 indicative abstracts pa of periodicals and also official documents. An abstract sometimes has appended to it the titles of other articles on the same topic. Systematic arrangement: 1. Etudes nationales (subdivided by country/area) - 2. Etudes régionales - 3. Etudes générales mondiales ou internationales. Cross references. Annual subject index and list of periodicals scanned.
Class No: 30(048)

Periodicals

[1009]
Political and social science journals: a handbook for writers and reviewers. Santa Barbara, CA., ABC-Clio, 1983. xxx, 236p. $24.95. £17.50. (*Clio guides to publishing opportunities series, no.2.*) ISBN: 0874360269.

Entries describe editorial focus and list frequency, editor, address, circulation, readership characteristics, indexing, manuscript requirements, referee system, and book reviewing policies for both reviewers and publishers. Indexed by discipline and broad topics.
Class No: 30(051)

Bibliographies

[1010]

HARZFELD, L.A. **Periodical indexes in the social sciences and humanities:** a subject guide. Metuchen, N.J., Scarecrow Press, 1978. xiv, 174p. $16.50. £13.15. ISBN: 0810811332.

Succeeds J.A. Kujoth's *Subject guide to periodical indexes and review indexes* (Scarecrow Press, 1969).

Annotated entries for more than 200 abstracting and indexing services, contents - listing journals, plus periodic bibliographies in journals and elsewhere. Data: number of periodicals indexed; arrangement; availability of cumulations, or databases. 48 subject sections. Mostly English-language titles. Accurate and reasonably priced. 'Recommended for academic libraries' (*Library journal*, v.103(20), 15 April 1978, p. 2324). *Class No:* 30(051)(01)

Yearbooks & Directories

[1011]

WHITAKER, J. **An Almanack for the year of Our Lord ... 1868-** (Annual). 132nd, 2000. London, Whitaker, 1999. 1299p. illus., maps. £40. ISBN: 0117022527.

Includes British government and public offices (ministers and senior civil servants, with their salaries), lists of peers, baronets, knights, M.P.'s, judges, sheriffs (county and borough), holders of the V.C. and George Cross, societies. Data on churches, armed forces, education (public schools, universities, professional education), insurance companies and their rates, postal regulations, tide tables, income tax, national insurance, legal notes, conservation and heritage, etc. Detailed ndex at end of volume. Still no cross-references. *Class No:* 30(058)

[1012]

The World almanac & book of facts, 2000. New York, World Almanac, 1999. 1024p. illus. maps. Annual. $29.95 (hardback). $10.95 (paper). ISBN: 0886878489, hbk; 0886878470, pbk. ISSN: 00841382.

First published 1868.

Similar content to *Whitaker's almanack* and equally dependent on a detailed index. Includes a full annual chronology, memorable dates, US associations and institutions, US population statistics for places of 2500 or more, and has sections on noted personalities (not all US), foreign countries, A-Z, and sporting events. Quotes sources of statistics. 16p. of coloured flags and maps. The nearest approach to a general US yearbook. *Class No:* 30(058)

Quotations

[1013]

The Macmillan book of social science quotations: who said what, when and where. Sills, D.L. *and* Merton, R., *eds*. New York, Macmillan, 1992. 458p. $25; £19.95. ISBN: 0028973976.

Over 2500 quotations from *c*.1000 authors, mainly famous social scientists but also some literary figures. Arranged A-Z by names. Each entry includes nationality, discipline, date of birth and (where relevant) death, the quotation (often in longer paragraphs of text to show proper context) and its sources. Keyword subject index and 67-page bibliography. Adjunct to the 18v. *International encyclopedia of the social sciences* (1968-80. Macmillan and Free Press). *Class No:* 30(082.2)

Histories

[1014]

INTERNATIONAAL INSTITUUT VOOR SOCIALE GESCHIEDENIS, Amsterdam. **Alfabetische catalogus van de boeken en brochures. Alphabetical catalog of the books and pamphlets of the International Institute of Social History.** Boston, Mass., G.K. Hall, 1970. 1st supplement. 1975. 12v., plus 2v. supplement. $1220 & $250. ISBN: 0816108072, the set of 12v; 0816110336, supplement.

310,000 cards, photolithographically reproduced. One of the largest special collections of social history, the library has *c*.350,000v., of which 40,000 are Slavonic holdings. *Class No:* 30(091)

[1015]

International review of social history. Internationaal Instituut voor Sociale Geschiedenis, Amsterdam, *ed.* Assen, Netherlands, Van Gorcum Ltd., 1956-. v.1-. 3 pa. ISSN: 01650629.

Previously (1937-40, 1950-55) as *Bulletin of the International Institute of Social History*.

Each issue contains about 50 pages of bibliography, over 100 items, systematically arranged. (General issues (social theory and social science, history, contemporary issues); Continents and countries (subdivided by region, then country, A-Z. Annotations or abstracts average *c*.100 words. Annual author and geographical indexes. *Class No:* 30(091)

Biographies

[1016]

International encyclopedia of the social sciences. v.18: Biographical supplement. Sills, D.L., *ed*. New York, Free Press, 1979. xxxviii, [1], 820p. $90. ISBN: 0028955102.

The biographical supplement to the 17v. encyclopedia. The biographical supplement to the 8v. edition was published in 1989 (Free Press, $85. ISBN 0028956907). *See* 3(031)=20 for information on the encyclopedia.

Over 200 signed biographical sketches, 'placing' each biographee. 'Jean Piaget': 10½ columns (works by: 1 col.; supplementary biographies: 7 items). *Class No:* 30(092)

Official Records

[1017]

GREAT BRITAIN. Public Record Office. **Records of interest to social scientists, 1919 to 1939:** introduction. London, HMSO., 1971. viii, 282p. (*Public Record Office handbooks, no. 14.*)

Sections (each subdivided by Ministry, Office, etc.): Central direction - Finance - Foreign affairs - Industry and trade - Land - Social services - Law and order - Defence - Common services. Bibliography, p.281; glossary, p.282. *Class No:* 30(093.2)

Scotland

[1018]

People and society in Scotland. Edinburgh, John Donald Publishers Ltd. in association with The Economic and Social History Society of Scotland, 1988-1990. 3v. (900p.) illus. £12.50. ISBN: 0859762106, v.1; 0859762114, v.2; 0859762122, v.3.

Vol.I: 1760-1830, ed. by T.M. Devine & R. Mitchison; v.2: 1830=1914, ed. by W.H. Fraser & R.J. Morris; v.3: 1914 to the present day, ed. by A.R. Dickson & J.H. Treble. *Class No:* 30(411)

Russia

[1019]

A Researcher's guide to sources on Soviet social history in the 1930s. Fitzpatrick, S. *and* Armonk, L.V., *eds*. New York, M.E. Sharpe, 1992. 296p. illus. tables. $48.95. ISBN: 1563240785.

Western and Soviet specialists assess the potential of sources available for the Stalinist period in the USSR, with bibliographic essays on topics such as archives, laws, statistics, collectivization and industrialization. Subject index. *Class No:* 30(47)

Education Institutions

[1020]

RUBLE, B.A. *and* TEETER, M.J. **A Scholars' guide to humanities and social sciences in the Soviet Union and the Baltic States;** the Academies of Sciences of Russia, Ukraine, Belorussia, Moldova, and Transcaucasian and Central Asian republics, and Estonia, Latvia and Lithuania. 2nd ed. Harlow, Essex, Longman Group Ltd., 1992. 256p. £134. ISBN: 0582987008.

Jointly compiled by the American Council of Learned Societies and the Soviet Academy of Sciences' Commission on the Humanities and Social Sciences.

A guide to institutions belonging to the USSR Academy of Sciences which study the humanities and social sciences. Entries include name, address, telephone numbers, history, bibliographies, areas of research, staffing, contacts, and co-operation with other countries. *Class No:* 30(47):061:37

China

Tables & Data Books

[1021]

China's social statistics, 1986. New York, Praeger, 1989. 275p. $75. (*China statistics series*.) ISBN: 0275932737.

c. 300 statistical tables arranged by subject: General survey - Population and family - Labour - Income and consumption - Housing and services - Labour insurance and social welfare - Education - Scientific research - Health care - Environmental protection - Culture - Physical culture - Social order and security - Participation in political and social activities - Daily time allocation. *Class No:* 30(510)(083)

India

Maps & Atlases

[1022]

A Social and economic atlas of India. Oxford, Oxford University Press, 1988. 254p. £37.50; $65. ISBN: 0195620410.

Maps and information on land, physical features, urbanization, population, society, language, literacy, religion, employment, natural

....(contd.)

resources, climate, infrastructure (welfare, education, transport, communications, banking, irrigation and power), produce, tourism, and economy (including India's dependency on other nations and regions). Maps, on a relatively small scale, for each section. 'This is a no-nonsense, technically proficient volume, permitting at a glance a view of where India is now, and where its future lies' (*Choice*, v.26(5), January 1989, p.788). *Class No:* 30(540)(084.3)

Africa

Periodicals

[1023]

Index of African social science periodical articles. V.1-, 1989-. Dakar, CODESRIA (Council for the Development of Economic and Social Research in Africa), 1989-. ISSN: 08509379.

An abstracting service. V.2/3, 1990-1991, published in 1993, has 549 entries for articles from 49 journals. Author, title, description in English and French sequences. No meaningful order so indexes are important. Indexes of authors, English descriptions, French descriptions, periodicals, and titles of articles. *Class No:* 30(6)(051)

Latin America

Biographies

[1024]

Who's who in Latin America: government, politics, banking and industry. Corke, B., *ed.* 4th ed. New York, Clearwater Pub., 1997. 2v. $149. ISBN: 0883542250, set.

Biographies of contemporary leaders in 35 Latin American and Caribbean countries, arranged A-Z by country and then biographee. Name index indicates relevant country. No cross-references. Spanish and Portuguese names can cause difficulties in locating entries. *Class No:* 30(729.99)(092)

Writing & Lecturing

[1025]

MULLINS, C.J. A Guide to writing and publishing in the social and behavioral sciences. New York, Wiley, 1977 (Reprinted by Krieger, 1983). 448p. $29.50. ISBN: 0898746434.

'Written primarily for students and professionals in the social and behavioral sciences, but also for their typists, editors and publisher'. 4 parts: 1. Outlines, first drafts, revisions and resources - 2. Authors, articles and scholarly journals - 3. General instructions for preparing a book manuscript: monographs, textbooks and edited collections - 4. Publishers, prospectuses and contracts: the forthcoming book. Table 7.1: 'Characteristics of journals (540 in all) in the social and behavioral sciences', p.134-55. Bibliography, p.411-7. *Class No:* 30:001.81

Research Methods

[1026]

KANE, E. Doing your own research: basic descriptive research in the social sciences and humanities. London, M. Boyars, 1984 (Reprinted 1997). 220p. £10.95. ISBN: 0714528439.

Aimed at people with little or no experience in social research. Part 1: What do you want to know? - 2: How do you find it - 3: Preparing the results - 4: Counting the cost. References cited, p.215-217. Index (double column), p.218-220. *Class No:* 30:001.891

Dictionaries

[1027]

MILLER, P.M. *and* **WILSON, M.J. A Dictionary of social science methods.** Chichester, Wiley, 1983. 124p. illus. £18.55. $39.95. ISBN: 0471900354.

Aims to be a comprehensive dictionary of terms and methodologies used in all major social science disciplines. Explains and sets each term in its practical context in addition to providing simple definitions. Fully cross-referenced. 'Excludes concepts drawn from learning theory and behavior therapy or those used in the philosophy of science'. (*Choice*, v.21(3), November 1983, p.404). British orientation. *Class No:* 30:001.891(038)

Thesauri

[1028]

The Contemporary thesaurus of social science terms and synonyms: a guide to natural language computer searching. Knapp, S.D., *comp.* Oryx, 1993. xxi,401p. $95. ISBN: 0897745957.

Lists synonyms and related terms for more than 6000 concepts and terms in the social sciences, listing them logically, clearly and thoroughly with a large number of 'see' and 'see also' references.

....(contd.)

Appendix B: British spellings. Selected sources used to compile the thesaurus, p.399-400. Favourable review in *Choice*, v.30(10), June 1993, p.1606. *Class No:* 30:025.43

[1029]

Unesco thesaurus: a structured list of descriptors for indexing and retrieving literature in the fields of education, science, social and human science, culture, communication and information. Barsony, L. New ed. Paris, UNESCO, 1995. xxxix,705p. ISBN: 9231014692. *Class No:* 30:025.43

Libraries

[1030]

Subject directory of special libraries and information centers. v.1 Business, government and law libraries. Darnay, B.T. *and* DeMaggio, J., *eds.* 24th ed. Detroit, Mich., Gale Group, 1999. $350. ISBN: 0787621323.

Over 3000 entries for business and law libraries, including military libraries. Information includes name of library, sponsoring institution, address, name and title of person in charge and other professional personnel, collection statistics, description of subjects covered, policies regarding use of collection, services provided, special collections, automated operations, publications and special catalogues, and special indexes. Alphabetical title and alternative name index, and subject index. *Class No:* 30:061:026/027

Great Britain

[1031]

Aslib directory of information sources in the United Kingdom. Reynard, K.W. *and* Reynard, J.M.E. 10th ed. London, Aslib, 1998. 1506p.; CD-ROM. £295 (hardback); £360 (CD-ROM). ISBN: 085142418x, CDROM; 0851424090.

First published 1928.

Includes over 10,000 listings of associations, clubs, societies, companies, charities, educational establishments, government bodies and other information-providing organizations. Entries are listed alphabetically, and including name and contact details, with comprehensive cross-referenced subject index. The CD-ROM version has a keyword search facility, and also provides hotlinks to email addresses and websites. *Class No:* 30:061:026/027(410)

[1032]

LEVINE, H.M. *and* **OWEN, D.B. An American guide to British social science resources.** Metuchen, N.J., Scarecrow Press, 1976. xii, 281p. $18.50; £14.60. ISBN: 0810809508.

Basic information about important British social science library resources, designed to serve as a reference source for American social scientists conducting research in Britain. A general section on travel and living in Britain precedes a list of over 200 libraries with social science collections, with details of holdings, access requirements, hours of opening, facilities available. Also listed are 35 other organizations and universities. *Class No:* 30:061:026/027(410)

Institutions & Associations

[1033]

World directory of social science institutions, 1990: research, advanced training, documentation, professional bodies. 5th ed. Paris, Unesco, 1990. xv,1211p. £34. (*World social science information directories:* 2.) ISBN: 9230025526.

First consolidated ed., 1977, from basic loose-leaf index of 1970, plus updatings in the quarterly *International social science journal*. Now produced from Unesco's DARE BANK.

In 4 parts: - Section I is an alphabetical index of official names and acronyms of institutions, with the relevant entry number; Section II has full details of each institution, listed A-Z, preceded by international and regional organizations, with address, date of establishment, name of head, senior researchers, staff, subject coverage, type of organization, activities, finance, research facilities, method of data processing, and publications; Section III is an index, A-Z by name of head of institution; Section IV is an index by subject and geographic coverage, with indication of the host country of the institution. *Class No:* 30:061:061.2

Conferences

[1034]

Directory of published proceedings. Series SSH: Social sciences/ humanities. Harrison, N.Y. InterDoc Corporation, 1968-. v.1, no.1-. Quarterly. $335pa. ISSN: 00123307.

Chronological list of proceedings of conferences and meetings on social sciences and humanities. 4-year cumulations contain editor, location and subject/sponsor indexes. *Class No:* 30:061:061.3

[1035]

Index to social sciences and humanities proceedings. Philadelphia, PA., Institute for Scientific Information, 1978-. No.1-. 3 quarterly issues and annual cumulation. $625. pa. ISSN: 01910574.

Indexes over 21,000 individual papers a year from published proceedings of conferences throughout the world. A category index precedes the detailed contents of proceedings. 5 more indexes follow - author/editor; sponsor; meeting location; permutation subject; and corporate. *Class No: 30:061:061.3*

Research Establishments

[1036]

Directory of social research organisations in the United Kingdom. Sykes, W., *and others.* Poole, Dorset, Mansell Publishing, 1993. 448p. £35. ISBN: 0720121655.

11 short essays on aspects of social research precedes the directory proper, which lists, A-Z by name, over 1000 organizations currently carrying out social research in the United Kingdom. Includes those in central and local government, quangos, universities and other higher education establishments, independent research units, charities, market research companies, and management consultants. Data given for each is name, address, description of organization, director/head, number of researchers, fields and methods of research, details of a few recent projects, research services, training opportunities, and contact information. Also separate lists of freelance researchers, philanthropic funding bodies, professional associations, etc. There are various indexes, which could be unnecessarily time-consuming. *Class No: 30:061:061.62*

Research Projects

[1037]

BRITISH LIBRARY. Current research in Britain: social sciences. London, FT Media and Telecoms, 1996. 711p. £115. ISBN: 1860672116. ISSN: 02671964.

Supersedes *Research in British universities, polytechnics and colleges, government departments and other institutions,* v.3: *Social sciences,* which superseded the British Library's (and earlier the Department of Education and Science's) *Scientific research in British universities and colleges.* V.3 *Social sciences,* which in turn superseded in part Warren Spring Laboratory's *Register of research in the human sciences,* first published in 1967.

A register of current research in universities, colleges and other institutions. An introduction is followed by a Department index and an index of institutions. The main sequence, Research in progress, is arranged in subject groups, and is followed by name, study area, and keyword indexes. *Class No: 30:061:061.62.005*

[1038]

Comparative social research: an annual publication. Greenwich, CT., Jai Press, 1978-. Annual. Individually priced. V.10, 1987: $56.50.

Contributors mainly North American academics. V.1-5 (1978-82) did not have separate titles: v.6: *The welfare state, 1883-1983:* v.7: *Demography, development, dependency theory and policy;* v.8: *Deviance;* v.9: *Historical studies;* v.10: *Religion and belief systems* (1987. ISBN 0892327375) has 9 articles with copious references and notes, plus author and subject indexes for vols. 6-10. *Class No: 30:061:061.62.005*

[1039]

HEILIGER, W.S. Bibliography of the Soviet social sciences, 1965-1975. Troy, N.Y., Whitston, 1978. 2v. (v, 996p.). $65 the set. ISBN: 0878751114.

Comprises citations, in English translation, for publications of the 15 major research institutes in the social sciences affiliated to the Academy of Sciences, USSR. For each institution, a listing of the contents of its journal, arranged by year, precedes a listing of the other publications sponsored by that institute. Subject and author indexes. A critical review in *Soviet studies* (v.30(4), October 1978, p.596-8) complains of carelessness, translation errors, etc., but *Choice* (v.15, no.5/6, July/August 1978, p.668) welcomes 'the availability of Soviet social science literature to English readers for the extremely important period following the resolution of the 23rd party congress in 1966 that approved and initiated new directions in social science research'. *Class No: 30:061:061.62.005*

Sociology

Bibliographies

[1040]

ABY, S.H., *comp.* **Sociology:** a guide to reference and information sources. 2nd ed. Littleton, Col., Libraries Unlimited, 1997. 225p. $42. ISBN: 1563084228.

Covers general social science reference sources (guides,

....(contd.)

bibliographies, indexes and abstracts, handbooks and yearbooks, dictionaries and encyclopedias, statistics, directories, biographies); social science disciplines (education, economics, psychology, social work, anthropology and history; and sociology (*e.g.* clinical sociology, population and demography, race and ethnic relations, women's studies). Entries are annotated. Author/title index; subject index. First edition [ublished 1987: '... an excellent up-to-date guide to the major reference sources of sociology ...' (*Choice,* v.24(11/12), July/August, 1987. p.1671). *Class No: 301(01)*

[1041]

Alternatives in print: an international catalog of books, pamphlets, periodicals and audiovisual materials, compiled by the Task Force on Alternatives in Print, Social Responsibilities Round Table, American Library Association. 6th ed. New York, Neal-Schumann Publications, Inc; London, Mansell. xii, 668p. £35. ISBN: 0918212200, USA; 0720115191, UK.

First published in 1970.

Catalogue of publishers, A-Z by name of publisher, followed by address and titles of publications (p.1-330). Title index (books & pamphlets/periodicals/audiovisual recordings/films/slideshows/videotapes), author index, subject index and geographical index to publishers, key to publishers' abbreviations. *Class No: 301(01)*

[1042]

Combined retrospective index to journals in sociology, 1894-1974. Washington & Inverness, Carrollton Press; Reading, Berks., Newspaper Archive Developments Ltd., 1978. 6v. $615.

Includes over 105,000 articles and 87 catalogues. V.1 has journal codes; v.1-5 are arranged by subject; v.6 by author. Within each subject group the arrangement is Keyword - reference title - author - year/vol. - journal - page. Author index has Author - reference title - year - vol. - journal - page. *Class No: 301(01)*

[1043]

Current sociology ... the journal of the International Sociological Association. London, Newbury Park, CA., Sage Publications (previously UNESCO (1952-57) and then Blackwell), 1952-. 3pa. $87.; £53 pa. ISSN: 00113921.

An international bibliography of sociology. Each volume comprises a trend report plus supporting bibliography. V.36, no.1 Spring 1988: 'Cults, converts and charisma: the sociology of new religious movements'; by Thomas Robbins (trend report, p.1-207; bibliography (A-Z by author) of *c.*700 items, p.208-248); v.37, no.2, Summer 1989: 'The present state of sociology in Italy, 1', by Franco Ferrarotti (trend report, p.1-111; bibliography (A-Z by author) of *c.* 350 items, p.123-137). *Class No: 301(01)*

[1044]

Finding the source in sociology and anthropology: a thesaurus-index to the reference collection. Brown, S.R., *comp.* Westport, CT, Greenwood Press, 1987. xv,269p. $49.95. ((*Finding the source, no.1*).) ISBN: 0313252637.

In two sections: 'Bibliographic citations to selected reference books' has 586 citations (General sources - social science - anthropology - sociology - population and life style - racial, ethnic and social groups - sexuality - social issues - social forces - social welfare) all subdivided); 'Thesaurus-index to the contents of the books cited' has a title-subtitle index (p.55-67), an author index (p.69-75), and a thesaurus index (p.77-269). '...distinguished by its thesaurus-index' (*Choice,* v.24(11/12), July/August 1987, p.1672). *Class No: 301(01)*

[1045]

FRANCIS. 521. Sociologie. Paris, Centre National de la Recherche Scientifique. Sciences humaines, 1947-. Quarterly. ISSN: 07651465.

Formerly part of *Bulletin analytique. Philosophie (v.1-9, 1047-55), Bulletin signalétique. 19. Philosophie, Sciences humaines,* (1956-1960), then *Bulletin signalétique. 521.*

Over 5000 indicative abstracts and references a year, arranged in 16 subject sections: 1. History, theory and methodology - 2. Social psychology - 3. Social organization, social system, social structure ... 16. Social problems and social welfare, social work. Each issue has a list of journals abstracted; an index of 'concepts'; and a list of authors. Available online and on CD-ROM. *Class No: 301(01)*

[1046]

McMILLAN, P. *and* **KENNEDY, J.R. Library research guide to sociology:** illustrated research strategy sources. Ann Arbor, Mich., Pierian Press, 1981. x, 67p. facsims. $25. (*Library research guide series, no.5.*) ISBN: 0876501218.

Appendix 2 is 'Basic reference sources in sociology', p.51-65, in 18 sections. Items asterisked are those described in the text. *Class No: 301(01)*

[1047]

WEPSIEC, J. Sociology: an international bibliography of serial literature, 1880-1980. London, Mansell, 1983. 198p. £29; $55. ISBN: 072011652x.

Lists over 2300 serial publications from sociology and related fields, A-Z by title. Each entry has complete bibliographical description, and indications of where indexed or abstracted. International in scope, with romanization of foreign-language titles as necessary. Cross-references from varient titles. Subject index. *Class No:* 301(01)

Encyclopaedias & Dictionaries

[1048]

The Concise Oxford dictionary of sociology. Marshall, Gordon, *ed.* Oxford, Oxford University Press, 1994 viii,573p. ISBN: 019285237x.

2,500 entries, coverage of terms, methods and concepts. Bibliography of major figures deals with related themes from other disciplines and provides cross references. *Class No:* 301(03)

German

[1049]

Soziologie-Lexicon. [Dictionary of Sociology.] Reinhold, Gerd *and* Lamneck, S. *and* Recker, Helga, *eds.* München, Oldenbourg, 1991 xi,677p. ISBN: 3486212591, GE.

Includes bibliographic references.

German dictionary of sociological terms. *Class No:* 301(03)=30

Encyclopaedias

[1050]

Encyclopedia of sociology. Borgatta, E.F. *and* Borgatta, M.L., *eds.* New York, Macmillan, 1992. 4v.(2359p.) charts, tables. $340 the set. ISBN: 0028970519.

370 well-documented signed articles of 2 to 18 pages, by 337 academics (mostly American sociologists). Arranged A-Z, the articles reflect sociology in all its diverse manifestations and include titles for further study. Many cross-references. Excellent detailed subject/name index of 74 pages in v.4. Intellectual level 'somewhat challenging for undergraduates' (*Library journal*, July 1992, p.76). 'The field of sociology now has a current and authoritative standard encyclopedic work' (*Choice*, v,29(11/12). July/August 1992, p.1654). *Class No:* 301(031)

[1051]

Macmillan student encyclopedia of sociology; ed. by Michael Mann. London, Macmillan Press, 1983 (Reprinted 1987). xii, 434p. (Macmillan dictionary series). £25. (paperback ed. issued 1991. £9.95). ISBN: 0333281934.

Aimed at all students of social science, with over 2000 entries, A-Z, of all important sociological terms, theories, concepts, and proper names. Entries vary from 100 to 300 or more words. Cross-references. '...wide-ranging... in fact, encyclopedic'. (*The Times educational supplement,* 18 March, 1984, p.36). *Class No:* 301(031)

[1052]

MAGILL, F.N. International encyclopedia of sociology. Fitzroy Dearborn, 1999. 2v. (1800p.) £175. ISBN: 1884964451.

Includes bibliographies, glossaries, index. *Class No:* 301(031)

[1053]

Social sciences encyclopedia. Kuper, Adam *and* Kuper, J., *ed.* 2nd ed. London, Routledge, 1996 xxiv,923p. ISBN: 0415108292.

Covers central disciplines in social sciences; writers and their main theories, aspects of social studies, for example deviancy and the theories which have resulted from an interpretation of the data thereon. Covers practise, theory and the application of the social sciences to other areas. Over 500 contributers. Entries listed by discipline and subject, and are followed by references and/or further reading. *Class No:* 301(031)

Handbooks & Manuals

[1054]

COLLINS, Randall. Sociological insight an introduction to non-obvious sociology. 2nd ed. New York, Oxford University Press, 1992 viii,206p. $19.95. ISBN: 0195074424, US.

A basic and clearly written introduction to the major sociological theories, it seeks to outline these without resort to the use of jargon, and to relate them to the context in which people live. *Class No:* 301(035)

[1055]

Handbook for research students in the social sciences. Allan, G. *and* Skinner, C., *ed.* London, Falmer Press, 1991 xvi,283p. £14.95. ISBN: 1850009368.

Areas covered include the Nature of research, Degree Study, Skills including the use of online databases, libraries, offical publications, writing up, use of sources and references. Also covered are Research Strategies, quantitative and qualitative research, case studies, survey methods, secondary and statistical analysis. *Class No:* 301(035)

[1056]

Handbook of clinical sociology. Rebach, H.M. *and* Bruhn, J.J., *ed.* New York, Plenum Press, 1991 xxiv,410p. $92.50 hardback $49.50 paper. ISBN: 0306435594, hbk, US; 0306435799, pbk.

Contains illustrations.

A guide to sociology written for those involved in social work. It covers working with clients and the ethical framework needed therein, as well as dealing with issues in crime and health. *Class No:* 301(035)

[1057]

Handbook of sociology. Smelser, N. J., *ed.* Newbury Park, CA., Sage Publications Ltd., 1988. 824p. $89.95. ISBN: 0803926650.

Aims to supersede *Handbook of modern sociology* by R. E. L. Faris (1964).

22 Chapters arranged in 4 parts: 1. Theoretical and methodological issues - 2. Bases of inequality in society - 3. Major institutional and organizational settings - 4. Social process and change. Each chapter contains a lengthy, up-to-date bibliography. Subject index, p.775-791. Name index, p.792-824. US view of sociology. ' ... an excellent collection ... no better handbook of contemporary sociology' (*Choice* V.26 (7) March 1989, p.1122). ' ... uniformly high quality of contributions ... exceptionally rich in its coverage of fields of sociological specialisation, data sources, bibliographical material and theoretical expositions' (*The Sociological review*, v.37 (3), August 1989, p.551-3). *Class No:* 301(035)

[1058]

KURTZ, L.R. Evaluating Chicago sociology a guide to the literature, with an annotated bibliography. Chicago, Ilin., University of Chicago Press, 1984 x,303p. (*Heritage of Sociology*.) ISBN: 0226464768, US.

Includes index and bibliography.

Covers the main writers of this school, and gives an annotated bibliography of their work. *Class No:* 301(035)

[1059]

LAWSON, T. *and* GARROD, J. The Complete A-Z sociology handbook. 2nd ed. London, Hodder and Stoughton, 2000. 352p. illus. £9.99. ISBN: 0340077204.

An excellent guide to words and concepts found in sociological writings, it provides a guide to the buzz-words found in much political debate, and gives a brief synopsis of the main writers in social theory. Will appeal to both the general and academic reader. *Class No:* 301(035)

Dictionaries

[1060]

The Blackwell dictionary of twentieth-century social thought. Outhwaite, W. *and* Bottomore, T., *eds.* Oxford, Blackwell, 1992. 864p. £60 hardback, £20.99 paper. ISBN: 0631152628, hbk; 0631195750, pbk.

c.1000 entries, averaging 500-1000 words, on the main themes of social thought, broadly conceived, but including Western European thinkers only. Each entry includes a short reading list. A bibliography lists all books and articles referred to in the text. Biographical appendix. General index. *Class No:* 301(038)

[1061]

Collins dictionary of sociology. Jary, D. *and* Jary, J. 3rd ed. London, HarperCollins, 2000. 768p. illus. £10.99. ISBN: 0004725115.

Includes terms most likely to be met from associated disciplines (*e.g.* psychology, economics, anthropology and political science), and methodological terms and research techniques. Also biographical entries. Cross-references. *Class No:* 301(038)

Polyglot

[1062]

ENDRUWEIT, G. Dreisprachiges Wörterbuch der Soziologie (Deutsch/Englisch/Französisch): ... Trilingual dictionary of sociology (German/English/French). 2e, erw.Aufl. Königstein/Fs, Athenäum Verlag GmbH, 1982. 133p. £3.95. (*Athenäum Taschenbücher: 4065: Sozialwiss.*) ISBN: 3445011648.

First published 1975.

In three parts - German-English-French; English-French-German, and French-German-English. *Class No:* 301(038)=00

English

[1063]

ABERCROMBIE, N., *and others*. **The Penguin dictionary of sociology.** 4th ed. London, Penguin, 2000. 464p. £8.99. (*Penguin reference.*.) ISBN: 0140513809.

First published 1984.

Designed to appeal to students of the subject from O-level to undergraduates. Entries discuss the issues involved in, and alternative approaches to, the central concepts and theories of sociology. Includes entries for the principal writers in sociology. Bibliography. *Class No:* 301(038)=20

[1064]

SEYMOUR-SMITH, C. **Macmillan dictionary of anthropology.** London, Macmillan Press, 1986 reprinted 2000. vi,305p. £17.99. ISBN: 0333393341, pbk.

About 2000 entries, usually lengthy. Includes short biographies. Ample cross-references. 'intended to convey the critical spirit of anthropological enquiry to students of social and cultural anthropology and to the interested lay reader. Emphasis placed on theoretical and conceptual issues, as well as the clarification of technical terms ...' (*Foreword*). 'Selective bibliography for further reading' (authors, A-Z), p.293-305. *Class No:* 301(038)=20

French

[1065]

BOUDON, R. *and* BOURRICAUD, F. **Dictionnaire critique de sociologie.** Paris, Presses Universitaires de France, 1982. xv,651p.

93 terms and lengthy articles in French which include bibliographical references and cross-references to other terms. Includes names (*e.g.* 'De Tocqueville', 'Socialisme'). Bibliography. General thematic index, p.627-651. *Class No:* 301(038)=40

Reports Literature

[1066]

L'Année sociologique. Paris, Alcan, 1896-1925: Paris, Presses Universitaires de France, 1948-. Annual. ISSN: 00662399.

More than half of each annual is a selective survey of the significant literature of sociology, covering Political science - Sociology of science and technology - Sociology of crime - Sociology of education - Sociology of work. A-Z list of authors, periodicals and collective volumes; contents table. *Class No:* 301(047)

[1067]

—Annual review of sociology. Palo Alto, CA., Annual Reviews Inc., 1975-. v.1-. Annual. $31 pa. ISSN: 03600572.

Contains well-documented articles on topical subjects in each issue. V.14, 1988 (ix, 545p.) has 10 such articles. Subject indexes. Cumulative index of authors and chapter titles. *Class No:* 301(047)

Reviews & Abstracts

[1068]

Geographical abstracts: human geography. Norwich, Elsevier/Geo abstracts, 1966-. Monthly. £308pa. ISSN: 09539611.

*c.*800 abstracts in each issue of articles from over 1000 leading journals, books, conference proceedings, reports, and theses. Informative abstracts (author abstracts used where possible) arranged in subject groups (Methodology and theory - Techniques - Environment - Environmental resources - Historical - Population - People and regions - Rural studies - Urban studies - Regional and community planning - Exchange and development - Agriculture - Industry - Transport and communications - Recreational geography - Regional index). Also on line in GEOBASE. *Class No:* 301(048)

[1069]

Sociological abstracts. Brooklyn, N.Y., subsequently San Diego, CA., Sociological Abstracts, Inc., 1952-. v.1, no.1-. 5 issues pa. $475pa including cumulated index. ISSN: 00380202.

Sponsored by the International Sociological Association.

About 4000 indicative and informative abstracts pa. Main sections: 0100. Methodology and research technology - 0200. Sociology: history and theory - 0300. Social psychiatry ... 0800. Mass phenomena ... 1000. Social differentiation ... 1900. The family and socialization ... 2100. Social problems and social welfare ... 2400. Policy, planning, forecasting ... 2900. Feminist/gender studies - 3000. Marxist sociology - 9000. Papers presented at sociology meetings. Supplement section (International review of publications in sociology) contains book abstracts and a listing of book reviews that appear in the serials abstracted in the issue). Subject, author and periodical indexes. Also online from 1961, updated quarterly. (BRS(SOCA), DIMDI, DIALOG and CD-ROM. *Class No:* 301(048)

Quotations

[1070]

THOMPSON, K. **Key quotations in sociology.** London, Routledge, 1996 207p. ISBN: 0415135176.

A guide to the key quotations from the literature, indexed under subject and then by author. Somewhat puzzling that the latter is greater than the former. *Class No:* 301(082.2)

Histories

[1071]

SWINGEWOOD, A. **A Short history of sociological thought.** New ed. London, Macmillan Press, 2000. 288p. £45 hardback £14.99 paper. ISBN: 0333801989, hbk; 0333801997, pbk.

A selective history of sociological thought from its origins in eighteenth-century philosophy, history and political economy, an awareness of society as a distinctive object of study. Chapters are arranged in 3 parts: Part 1. Foundations; pt.2. Classical sociology; pt.3. Modern sociology. Further reading relates to chapters. Bibliography is A-Z by author. Index. *Class No:* 301(091)

Biographies

[1072]

Authors of their own lives Intellectual autobiographies by twenty American sociologists. Berger, B.M. *and* Bendix, R., *ed*. Berkley, Calif., University of California Press, 1990 xxviii,503p. ISBN: 0520065557, US.

A collection of autobiographical essays by a number of American sociologists, giving a synopsis of their academic careers, main theoretical stances and conclusions, and works published. A good overveiew of what is being published in American sociological literature. *Class No:* 301(092)

Great Britain

[1073]

WARDE, A., *et al*. **Contemporary British society.** 3rd ed. Oxford, Polity Press, 2000. 640p. illus., diagrs., graphs, tables, maps. £55; £14.99. ISBN: 0745622968.

Comprehensive coverage of all aspects of the social structure of modern Britain. Separate chapters look at the major areas of life in Britain - economic organization, employment, patterns of inequality, class, gender, ethnicity, family and households, education, health, media, deviance and politics. New in this edition are chapters on globalization, associations, and leisure. Extensive cross-references. *Class No:* 301(410)

Russia

[1074]

Contemporary Soviet society: a statistical handbook. Ryan, M., *comp. & translator*. Cheltenham, Edward Elgar Publishing, 1990. ix,283p. £45. ISBN: 1852783494.

Statistical tables for selected years to 1989 arranged in 13 subject sections. Sources are given. Data is by country, republic, town, etc.Index. *Class No:* 301(47)

China

French

[1075]

SCHMATZ, George-Marie. La sociologie de la Chine matériaux pour une histoire 1748-1989. [Chinese Sociology material for a history from 1748 to 1989.] Berne, Switzerland, P. Lang, 1993 xxiv,357p. (*Etudes asiatiques Suisses : monographies ; vol. 14*.) ISBN: 3906751139, SW.

Deals with the history of sociology in China, giving tables of information from over 600 sources. Covers European writing on China in the 18th and 19th centuries, as well as the Chinese school of sociology from 1900-1950. The author concentrates on four aspects of China; the social structure, ethical structure, role of the family and the future. It proposes an alternative way of understanding Eastern Cultures. *Class No:* 301(510)=40

Australia

[1076]

AUSTIN-BROOS, Diane J. **Australian sociologies.** Sydney, New South Wales, G. Allen and Unwin, 1984 viii,202p. ISBN: 0868615129, AUS.

Includes indexes.

Gives an analysis of Australian society in terms of class divisions, social mobility and elites. Covers issues of race and colour, as well as the role of the state. *Class No:* 301(94)

Writing & Lecturing

[1077]

DOBKIN, U.S. **Handbook for the teaching of social studies.** 2nd ed. Newton, Mass., Allyn & Bacon Inc., 1985. x, 323p. £26.75. ISBN: 0205081495.

First published 1977.

14 chapters (Goals and objectives - Planning - The art of questioning - Independent study - Dealing with values - Reading skills - Writing skills - Media - Simulation activities - Testing and evaluation - Electives and curriculum consideration - Mainstreaming - Professional growth - Professional evaluation. Examples are given in many chapters; end notes (including references) are added to all chapters. Index, p.317-323. *Class No:* 301:001.81

Research Methods

[1078]

New technology in sociology pratical applications in research and work. Blank, Grant *and* McCartney, James L. *and* Brent, Edward E., *ed.* New Brunswick, N.J., Transaction Publishers, 1989 185p. ISBN: 0887387691, US.

Includes bibliography and index.

Covers not only the practical difference which new technology makes to sociological research, but also how it changes the way sociology is done, and the theories by which people work. Deals with the emergence of a new way of imparting knowledge via hypertext as opposed to the printed page, where what the reader perceives is more a result of his or her own interests, and less under the control of the original writer. *Class No:* 301:001.891

Women

[1079]

CHAFETZ, J. S. **Handbook of the sociology of gender** Dordrecht, Kluwer/Plenum, 1999 630p. £84.50 ISBN: 0306459787.

Gender has to be interpreted in this book as heavily feminist, but Chafetz treats of the whole range of issues as they are affected by considerations of gender, and not just the obvious topics such as social roles and violence. Questions of migration and culture are addressed, for example, and the relationship between gender and social institutions is considered at length. Each chapter concludes with a bibliography. *Class No:* 301-0055.2

Social Change

Bibliographies

[1080]

SADLER, J.D. **Families in transition:** an annotated bibliography. Archon/Shoestring Press, 1988. 251p. $30. ISBN: 0208021809.

Topics include families of those in prison, surrogate parentage, and latchkey children, etc. Arrangement is by topical chapters, subdivided by books and articles, then A-Z by author. An appendix lists associations and organizations. Author, subject and title indexes. *Class No:* 301.15(01)

[1081]

The Social and economic impact of new technology, 1978-84: a select bibliography, compiled by L. Grayson. Letchworth, Herts, Technical Communications, 1984. [9]. 80p. ISBN: 0946655014.

*c.*700 references "... bringing together American, British and European literature on the social and economic effects on government, industry, business and the home" (Introduction). Subject arrangement: The overall picture - National and international initiatives, policies and political manifestos - Social impacts - Economic structure and policy - Impact of new technology on business, industry and communications - Administrative impact and industrial relations: impact of new technology. No index. This has been followed by a review publication with the same titles. First issue, June 1985, updated quarterly. *Class No:* 301.15(01)

Social Psychology

[1082]

Advances in experimental social psychology. San Diego, CA., Academic Press, 1964-.v.1-. Irregular. ISSN: 00652601.

Each issue has several articles by prominent scholars in the field, providing overviews and theoretical integrations of specialized areas of research. Extensive lists of references usually follow the articles. Subject index and contents lists of earlier volumes. *Class No:* 301.151

[1083]

European review of social psychology. No.1 issued 1990. Annual. New York, Wiley. ISSN: 10463283.

Aim is to reflect the dynamism of social psychology in Europe and the attention now being paid to European ideas and research. *Class No:* 301.151

Public Opinion

[1084]

Index to international opinion, 1998/1999. Westport, CT., Greenwood Press, 1980-. Annual. 692p. $350. ISBN: 0313311609. ISSN: 0193905x.

Prepared by Survey Research Consultants International Inc.

Single nation surveys (agriculture - business and industry ... crime and justice - economic affairs ... government ... marriage and family ... military affairs ... transportation); Multinational surveys. Bibliography. Indexes by topical categories, by countries and regions. Brings together many of the important surveys conducted by researchers throughout the world. *Class No:* 301.153

Bibliographies

[1085]

KRUGER, A.N. **Argumentation and debate:** a classified bibliography. 2nd ed. Metuchen, N.J., Scarecrow Press, 1975. 520p. $27.50. ISBN: 0810807491.

First published 1964.

Lists *c.*6,000 books, periodical articles and theses under 22 subject heads. Author and subject indexes. "The standard comprehensive bibliography in the field" (*Wilson library bulletin,* September 1975, p.76). *Class No:* 301.153(01)

[1086]

SMITH, B.L. *and* SMITH, C.M. **International communication and political opinion:** a guide to the literature. Prepared for the Rand Corporation by the Bureau of Social Science Research, Washington, D.C. Princeton, N.J., Princeton University Press, 1956 (Reprinted by Greenwood, 1972). xi, 325p. $22.50. ISBN: 0837160073.

2,563 numbered, annotated entries (annotations average *c.*100 words). 7 sections: 1. Theoretical and general writings relevant to international communication and censorship - 2. Political persuasion and propaganda activities (by country of origin) - 3. Specialists in political persuasion - 4. Channels ('Media') of international communication (to, from and in particular areas) - 5. Audience characteristics - 6. Methods of research and intelligence - 7. Bibliographies. Appendix A is a note on current sources, and B, a list of journals. Author and subject index. *Class No:* 301.153(01)

[1087]

WALDEN, G.R. **Public opinion polls and survey research** a selected annotated bibliography of US guides and studies from the 1990's New York, Garland Publishers, 1990 xxix,306p. (*Garland reference library of social sciences.*) ISBN: 0824057325.

Includes indexes. Originally published in 1988.

Introduction - Published polls (Gallup Organization, etc.) - Polling indexes and abstracts (journals) - Further readings (15 annotated titles) - Notes (27 items referring to the text). *Class No:* 301.153(01)

Handbooks & Manuals

[1088]

LAKE, C.C. *and* HARPER, P.C. **Public opinion polling:** a handbook for public interest and citizen advocacy groups. Washington, Island Press, [1987]. 166p. $29.95. ISBN: 0933280327.

How to plan, administer and analyse a poll. 10 chapters take the reader step-by-step through the polling process, each chapter including tips for success, warnings of potential problems, and checklists summarizing important points. Also, annotated bibliography, sample questionnaires, grids and tabulations, short glossary, and index. *Class No:* 301.153(035)

[1089]

Pros and cons: a debater's handbook. Sather, T. *and* Hutton, W., *eds.* 18th ed. London, Routledge, 1999. 280p. £35 hardback £11.99 paper. ISBN: 0415195470, hbk; 0415195489.

First published 1896.

Objective is to give debaters a useful guide to for-and-against arguments on a wide range of controversial issues. Topics A-Z ('Advertising, public control and taxation' ... 'Written constitution'). Pro and con points on each topic in adjacent columns per page. The index groups topics under 21 heads (Agriculture ... Women). *Class No:* 301.153(035)

Great Britain

[1090]

HEALD, G. *and* WYBROW, R.J. **The Gallup survey of Britain.** Beckenham, Kent, Croom Helm, 1986. [4], 303p. £19.95. ISBN: 0709938462.

8 chapters, mainly relating to 1985: 1. The year begins - 2. Domestic politics - 3. The economy - 4. The environment - 5. Law and order - 6. International affairs - 7. Social and other non-political issues - 8. Britain 20 years on. There follow 4 appendices (A. How scientific polls are conducted - B. Diary of events - C. Gallup's election record, 1945-1983 - D. Party fortunes, 1984-1985) and a 3-page index. Aims to be issued annually. *Class No:* 301.153(410)

[1091]

WYBROW, R.J. **Britain speaks out, 1937-87:** a social history as seen through the Gallup data. London, Macmillan Press, 1989. 224p. tables. £40. ISBN: 0333396634.

Based on a fraction of the available data, the author attempts to create a picture of British society over the 50-year period. 8 chapters are arranged chronologically and there is an appendix of tables. Author is Director of Gallup. 'This is a wonderful book - a real treasure trove of opinion poll results across a huge range of subjects ... ' (ESRC Data Archive. *Bulletin* No.45, Spring 1990, p.31). *Class No:* 301.153(410)

Adolescents

[1092]

Encyclopedia of adolescence. Lerner, R.M., *and others, eds.* New York, Garland, 1991. 2v. (*c.*1223p.). ISBN: 0824043782.

Over 200 articles (2 to 10 pages each) surveying the emotional upheaval and transformations that mark the passage from childhood to young adulthood. Bibliographies included at end of each article. Cross-references. Subject index. 'Highly recommended' (*Library Journal,,* 15 May 1991. p.77). *Class No:* 301.18-053.7

Aged People

Bibliographies

[1093]

ADAY, R.H., *comp.* **Crime and the elderly:** an annotated bibliography. Westport. CT., Greenwood Press, 1988. 118p. $35.95. (*Bibliographies and indexes in gerontology, 8.*) ISBN: 0313254702.

361 references arranged in 10 topical chapters (Criminal justice issues - The elderly as victims - Fear of crime - Elder abuse and neglect - Crime prevention problems - Old age and crime - Elderly crime patterns - Causes of criminal behavior - Aging prisoners - Rehabilitative programs. Includes books, journal articles, conference proceedings, research reports, Congressional hearings, unpublished MS, and dissertations. Annotations are short. Author and subject indexes. Highly recommended by *Choice* (v.26(10),June 1989). *Class No:* 301.18-053.9(01)

[1094]

BALKEMA, J.B., *ed.* **Aging:** a guide to resources. Syracuse, N.Y., Gaylord Professional Publications, 1983. 232p. $34.95. ISBN: 0915794489.

An annotated bibliography in a clear and logical arrangement. Annotations are brief and descriptive. Includes books, pamphlets and journal articles. Title, name and subject indexes. *Class No:* 301.18-053.9(01)

[1095]

New literature on old age: a guide to new publications, courses and conferences on aging, 1977- no. 1-. London, Centre for Policy on Aging. 6pa. £10 pa. ISSN: 01402447.

About 100 entries (often briefly annotated) per issue. Covers new books and periodical articles, central and local government reports and circulars, statistical reports, semi-published research documents, and informal publications issued by voluntary groups, Mainly British literature. Cross-references. Headings: General - Attitudes to aging - Women - Health - Physical disability - Falls - Nutrition - Psychology - Mental illness and services to the mentally ill - Alcohol and aging - Social characteristics - Retirement - Education in later life - Leisure - Services - Social work - Income maintenance - Housing - Residential care - Health services - Primary health care - Medications - Community care - Family care - Ethnic minorities - Crime/security/ abuse - Reference works - Annual reports. *Class No:* 301.18-053.9(01)

[1096]

ORIOL, W.E., *comp.* **Federal public policy on aging since 1960:** an annotated bibliography. Westport, CT., Greenwood Press, 1987. xiv, 127p. $52.95. (*Bibliographies and indexes in gerontology, no.5.*) ISBN: 0313252866.

750 briefly annotated references dating from 1960 to 1986. Part 1: Federal agency policy: general critiques, key themes; part 2: Specific programmes and issues (income and retirement policy - health and long-term care - housing ... minorities - research ... women). Appendix: Sources of information: Congressional committees and national organizations. Author index (p.115-122) and subject index (p.123-127). '... a well-executed bibliographical guide'. (*RQ,* v.27(4), Summer 1988, p.5734). *Class No:* 301.18-053.9(01)

[1097]

—GUTTMAN, D., *comp.* **European American elderly:** an annotated bibliography. Westport, CT., Greenwood Press, 1987. 122p. $42.95. (*Bibliographies and indexes in gerontology, 6.*) ISBN: 0313255830.

A bibliography of 310 English-language titles published in the United States in the past 15 years. Includes journal articles, chapters in monographs, and dissertations. Arranged in topical sections with subdivisions. Includes *c.*35 nationalities and ethnic groups. *Class No:* 301.18-053.9(01)

[1098]

Select bibliographies on aging. London, Centre for Policy on Aging, 1984-. ISSN: 02670348.

An occasional series designed to bring together a wide range of annotated references on a variety of topics. No.1: *Social planning for the elderly,* compiled by Barbara Meredith (1984. 44p. £3.50) has over 250 references on the services older people use at local government level, the final section listing government policy documents. No.2: *Education and older people,* compiled by Dianne Norton (1987. 50p. £4.50) explores the existing literature of ideas on aging and education, and catalogues the work that is being undertaken to make more opportunities available. *Class No:* 301.18-053.9(01)

Retirement

[1099]

MILETICH, J.J., *comp.* **Retirement:** an annotated bibliography. New York, Greenwood Press, 1986. xvii, 147p. $29.95. (*Bibliographies and indexes in gerontology, no.2.*) ISBN: 031324815x.

Selected references, annotated and numbered, dating from 1975 through 1985, that examine many aspects of retirement. Arranged in 9 topical sections: 1. Planning and counselling for retirement - 2. Retirement adjustment, health and leisure - 3. Financial aspects of retirement - 4. Housing and transportation for the retired - 5. Crime and the retired - 6. Executives, the professions and retirement - 7. Women and retirement - 8. Work after retirement - 9. Old age and death. Entries arranged A-Z by author within the subject sections. References are mainly to journal articles. Author index (p.125-131); subject index (p.132-147). 'Annotations are succinct and identify accompanying special features such as tables, figures, and references' (*Choice,* v.24(5), January 1987, p.746). *Class No:* 301.18-053.9(01)RET

Encyclopaedias

[1100]

MADDOX, G.L., *and others.* **The Encyclopedia of aging** a comprehensive resource in gerentology and geriatrics. 2nd ed. New York, Springer Publishing Co., 1995. xxxiv,1216p. ISBN: 0826148417.

Contains bibliographic references and indexes. First published in 1987.

Concise, descriptive articles on *c.*500 subjects in the field, including biological, psychological and sociological aging, life experience of the elderly. Written for the non-specialist, it lists references to classical and recent works. Over 200 contributors from academic, medicine and health-related agencies. Entries, arranged A-Z, vary in length from 1-7 pages. Cross-references. Bibliography of over 2000 references to sources cited in the text. Comprehensive index. '... an authoritative reference source ...' (*Library journal,* 15 April 1987, p.75). *Class No:* 301.18-053.9(031)

Handbooks & Manuals

[1101]

BINSTOCK, R.G., *and others.* **Handbook of aging and the social sciences.** 4th ed. San Diego, Calif., Academic Press, 1996. xxi,531p. (*The Handbooks of aging.*) ISBN: 0120991934.

First published 1977.

'Designed to provide comprehensive information and major reference sources and to suggest contemporary research issues'.'A necessary acquisition for all colleges and universities as a basic reference tool in the field' (*Choice,* September 1977, p.832, of the first ed.). Other volumes in the 'Handbooks of aging' series are: Schneider, E.L. and Rowe, J.W. *Handbook of the biology of aging*; and Birren, J.E. and Schaie, K.W. *Handbook of the psychology of aging (qv).* *Class No:* 301.18-053.9(035)

[1102]

BIRREN, J.E. *and* SCHAIE, K.W., *eds.* **Handbook of the psychology of aging.** 4th ed. San Diego, Calif., Academic Press, 1996. xx,416p. (*Handbooks of aging.*) ISBN: 0121012603.

Contains tables, bibliographic references and indexes.

Focuses on the psychology of adult development and aging. Summaries precede and extensive references follow each chapter. *Class No:* 301.18-053.9(035)

[1103]

PATMORE, E., *ed.* **International handbook of aging:** contemporary developments and research. Westport, CT., Greenwood Press, 1980. xviii, 529p. illus., tables. $50.95. ISBN: 0313208905.

The International Association of Gerontology requested scholars in 28 countries to submit evaluative essays on the gerontological work in their respective countries. Each essay discusses the roles and status of the aged in the given country, the history of gerontological research, programmes for the aged, and sources of further information. Bibliographies of major works end each essay. Two appendices - names and addresses of major organizations concerned with gerontological research and problems. Index. 'Articles informative and

....*(contd.)*

readable, enhanced by tables summarizing the statistical data'. (*College & research libraries,* July, 1981, p.354). *Class No:* 301.18-053.9(035)

Dictionaries

Polyglot

[1104]

GIBSON, J.S. *and* NUSBERG, C., *eds.* **International glossary of social gerontology.** New York, Van Nostrand Reinhold Co., 1985. $31.95. ISBN: 0442242824.

Published under the auspices of the International Federation of Aging.

Aim is to assist the international exchange of information and cross-national research on aging by assembling basic terms that are required to apply gerontological principles across national boundaries. *c.*40 contributors. Definitions in English, French, German and Spanish. *Class No:* 301.18-053.9(038)=00

Reviews & Abstracts

[1105]

Abstracts in social gerontology: current literature on aging. Newbury Park, Sage Publications (for the National Council on Aging). $126. ISSN: 10474862.

Prior to 1991 title was 'Current literature on aging'.

Indexes and abstracts selected books and journals on gerontology, including demography, economics, family relations, government policies and health. Books are a part of NCOA/s library; *c.*80 core journals are indexed cover-to-cover. Arrangement is A-Z by subject. Cumulated author and subject indexes included in last issue each year. *Class No:* 301.18-053.9(048)

Periodicals & Progress Reports

[1106]

HESSLEIN, S.B., *comp.* **Serials on aging:** an analytical guide. Westport, CT., Greenwood Press, 1986. 176p. $32.95. (*Annotated bibliographies of serials: a subject approach, 9.*) ISBN: 0313247099.

An exhaustive bibliography that identifies a broad range of serials, including newsletters and government publications, that have a substantial amount of information on aging. International, US State and regional English-language sources are cited. arranged by general disciplinary sources first and then by speciality areas. Descriptive annotations. 4 indexes - geographical, publisher and sponsoring organization, title, and subject. 'Hesslein has compiled the best source for serials on aging' (*Choice,* March 1987, p.1032). *Class No:* 301.18-053.9(05)

Yearbooks & Directories

[1107]

BROWN, R. **Retirement made easy** London, Kogan Page, 1994. xxviii,362p. ISBN: 074941099x.

First published 1987.

Topics include money management, budget planning, your home, leisure activities, starting your own business, looking for paid work, voluntary work, health, holidays, caring for elderly parents, wills, etc. Also a list of organizations that can help. Index. *Class No:* 301.18-053.9(058)

[1108]

CENTRE FOR POLICY ON AGING. **CPA world directory of old age.** Harlow, Longman, 1989. [8],208p. £35. ISBN: 0582044243.

In 2 parts: 1. International; 2. Country by country (Afghanistan ... Zimbabwe). For each country information is given on population, life-expectancy, socio-economic data, followed by organizations, A-Z by name of organization (and translation into English if necessary), address, telephone number, fax number, director, contact, formation, activities, international affiliates, publications). Index, p.201-8. *Class No:* 301.18-053.9(058)

[1109]

DARNBOROUGH, A. *and* KINRADE, D. **Directory for older people:** a handbook of information and opportunities for the over-55s. 2nd ed. New York, Harvester Wheatsheaf, 1992 xi,375p. £28.95 ISBN: 0745014429.

Lists organizations concerned with money, house/home, aids to daily living, welfare, bereavement, voluntary work, learning, etc. A-Z index. *Class No:* 301.18-053.9(058)

[1110]

Directory of resources for aging, gerontology, and retirement. 2nd ed. Mankate, MN., Minnesota Scholarly Press, 1987. 400p. $75. ISBN: 0933474415.

First published 1979.

Contains 6 directories: Reprint of *A directory of State and area agencies in aging* (4th ed. Washington, GPO, 1985), listing 57 State and 672 area agencies; and lists of 100 national associations, research centres, foundations, political action groups, and social service agencies; 100 local associations; 100 legal services; 150 colleges and universities offering degrees in gerontology and aging: and 55 international organizations. Glossary. Index. *Class No:* 301.18-053.9(058)

Research Methods

[1111]

ZITO, D.R. *and* ZITO, G.V. **A Guide to research in gerontology: strategies and resources.** Westport, CT., Greenwood Press, 1988. 144p. $35.95. ISBN: 0313259046.

Intended for information specialists and professionals concerned with gerontology in all its aspects - psychological, social and medical. Explains how to design a research strategy; how to evaluate different information sources; and the role of various kinds of reference sources in research. Examples are given. Also explains how to get information from other organizations, listing them. 4 appendices listing and annotating reference books, indexes and abstracts, databases, and journals. Subject index. 'A title index would have been a useful addition; (*Reference books bulletin,* July 1989, v.81(21), p.1883). *Class No:* 301.18-053.9:001.891

Race Relations

Bibliographies

[1112]

GILBERT, V.F. *and* TATLA, D.S. **Immigrants, minorities and race relations:** a bibliography of theses and dissertations presented at British and Irish universities, 1900-1981. London, Mansell, 1984. xxxiii, 153p. £20. ISBN: 0720116910.

Some 1700 entries, unannotated, arranged in two main sections: General theoretical and historical studies; and Theses relating to a particular region or country. Each section is divided into some 200 subject subdivisions. Time span ranges from ancient history, through medieval immigrant communities, slavery and the slave trade, to contemporary topics. An introductory essay by Colin Holmes surveys the history of immigrants in Great Britain, concentrating on immigration since World War II. Author index (p.138-153); subject index (p.105-137). *Class No:* 301.18-054(01)

[1113]

HALLMAN, C.N. *and* LISTER, L.F. **White supremacy and its associated groups:** an annotated bibliography. In *RSR,* v.17(4),1989, p.7-18,28.

55 annotated entries plus 32 listed books and reports. Includes sections on white supremacy, Aryan nations, Ku Klux Klan, skinheads, justice system/civil rights, media, and law enforcement. *Class No:* 301.18-054(01)

[1114]

PRUCHA, F.P. **A Bibliographical guide to the Indian-White relations in the United States.** Chicago, Ill., University of Chicago Press, 1977. $30. ISBN: 0226684768.

In two parts: part 1 is a guide to sources - national archives, government documents, manuscripts, newspapers, oral history, travel accounts and library catalogues. Part 2 cites published works, including periodical literature, under 12 major subject and numerous sub-sections. *Class No:* 301.18-054(01)

[1115]

—PRUCHA, F.P. **Indian-White relations in the United States:** a bibliography of works published, 1975-1980. Nebraska, 1982. 179p. $14.95. ISBN: 0803236654.

3400 unannotated citations, updating the above. Citations are arranged under 15 topical headings, including Guides to sources. Extensive index of subjects and names. 'These two volumes constitute the most comprehensive bibliographic treatment of the field.' (*Choice,* v.19(11/12), July/August 1982, p.1542). *Class No:* 301.18-054(01)

[1116]

World racism and related inhumanities: a country-by-country bibliography. Weinberg, M., *comp.* New York & Westport, CT, Greenwood Press, 1992. xiii,1048p. $99.50. (*Bibliographies and indexes in world history,26.*) ISBN: 0313281092.

Covers 135 countries, A-Z, plus a chapter for each continent, a short section on the ancient world, and a section of other related bibliographies. No annotations. Emphasis is on recent literature in English, French, German and Spanish. Author index, p.915-1020.

....(contd.)

Thematic subject index, p.1021-48. '... researchers concerned with racism will find no comparable compilation.'(*Choice*, v.30(3), November 1993, p.451). *Class No:* 301.18-054(01)

Handbooks & Manuals

[1117]

SIGLER, J., *ed*. **International handbook of race and race relations.** Westport, CT., Greenwood Press, 1987. 512p. $95; £56.95. ISBN: 0313247706.

Studies of the conditions which are extant in many of the world's societies and accounts of the movements in race and race relations throughout the world. *Class No:* 301.18-054(035)

Dictionaries

[1118]

CASHMORE, E.E., *and others*. **Dictionary of race and ethnic relations.** 4th ed. London, Routledge, 1996. xx,412p. £60; £17.99.

First published 1984.

A view of race and ethnic relations, including events and individuals significant to race relations as well as topics, theories and practices. Clearly written; long, signed articles, with reading lists appended. Cross-references. *Class No:* 301.18-054(038)

Reviews & Abstracts

[1119]

Sage race relations abstracts. London, Sage Publications, on behalf of the Institute of Race Relations, 1975-. v.1-,no.1-. Quarterly. £125pa. ISSN: 03079201.

Formerly *Race relations abstracts* (1968-74).

Over 1,000 indicative and informative abstracts pa, drawing on books and *c.*200 journals. 33 sections (Bibliographies - Adjustment and integration - Area studies ... Culture and identity ... Education (general, pre-school; further; higher; policy and planning; syllabuses) - Employment ... Housing ... Race relations (general; law and legislation; history and ideologies) ... Young people ... Ephemera. List of journals abstracted. Author and subject indexes. *Class No:* 301.18-054(048)

Great Britain

[1120]

GORDON, P. *and* **KLUG, F. Racism and discrimination in Britain:** a select bibliography, 1970-83. London, The Runnymede Trust, 1984. viii, 143p. £3.50. ISBN: 0902397508.

A basic unannotated guide to the material, books, pamphlets, official reports, journal articles published in Britain since 1970 and some important earlier material and material published abroad. 13 sections (1. Racism and discrimination; 2. Politics and race; 3. Immigration and nationality; 4. Women, race and racism; 5. Employment and unemployment; 6. Education, race and racism; 7. Housing and the inner city; 8. The Health Service; 9. Social and welfare services; 10. Policing and racial violence; 11. The criminal justice system; 12. The media; 13. Films and filmstrips. Finally an appendix listing organizations. *Class No:* 301.18-054(410)

[1121]

—**AMIN, K.**, *and others*. **Racism and discrimination in Britain:** a select bibliography, 1984-1987. London, Runnymede Trust, 1988. [3], 98p. £3.95. ISBN: 0902397753.

Lists books, pamphlets, offical reports and journal articles in 12 subject sections, each subdivided and subdivided again by form. Contents: 1. Racism and discrimination - 2. Politics and race - 3. Immigration and nationality - 4. Women, race and racism - 5. Employment and unemployment - 6. Education - 7. Housing and inner city - 8. The Health Service - 9. Social and welfare services - 10. Policing, racial violence and urban disorder - 11. Criminal justice and the legal system - 12. The media. Appendix lists addresses of publishing organizations. Supplements *Racism and discrimination in Britain: a select bibliography*, by P. Gordon and F. Klug, which covered 1970-83. No annotations and no index. *Class No:* 301.18-054(410)

South Africa

Bibliographies

[1122]

KALLEY, J.A. South Africa under Apartheid: a selected and annotated bibliography. Westport, CT., Meckler, 1989. 544p. $85. ISBN: 088736506x.

1123 references to books and articles produced over the last 30 years, with emphasis on the last decade. Good author index and useful subject index arranged in broad categories. Fuller than S.E. Pyatt's

....(contd.)

Apartheid: a selective annotated bibliography, 1979-1987 (Garland, 1990. 160p.), although the latter has an appendix on major South African laws and regulations. *Class No:* 301.18-054(680)(01)

[1123]

LIMB, P. The ANC and black workers in South Africa, 1912-1992: an annotated bibliography. London, Hans Zell, 1993. 380p. £48. ISBN: 1873836953.

Entries for circa 3000 books, pamphlets and periodical articles arranged A-Z by author (or title if no author), followed by circa 1000 entries for periodicals, newspapers, government publications, theses, conference papers, bibliographies and reference works. Subject index. *Class No:* 301.18-054(680)(01)

Histories

[1124]

HOLLAND, H. The Struggle: a history of the ANC. London, Grafton, 1989. 252p. illus., ports. (inc. 8p. of pl.). £4.50. ISBN: 0586206132.

A sympathetic and up-to-date history of the African National Congress, the political group fighting 'apartheid' inside and outside South Africa. *Class No:* 301.18-054(680)(091)

Latin America

[1125]

LEVINE, R.M. Race and ethnic relations in Latin America and the Caribbean: an historical dictionary and bibliography. Metuchen, N.J., Scarecrow Press, 1980. 260p. $17.50. ISBN: 0810813246.

Over 1200 terms with short definitions, and 1300 geographically arranged bibliographical citations, unannotated. Intended to facilitate the study of racial and ethnic issues in Latin American and Caribbean history. No index. *Class No:* 301.18-054(729.99)

USA

Bibliographies

[1126]

Black American families, 1965-1984: a classified, selectively annotated bibliography. Editor-in-chief: W.R. Allen. Westport, Conn., Greenwood, 1986. xxxi, 480p. (Bibliographies and indexes in Afro-American and African studies, no. 16). $45. ISBN: 0313256136.

More than 1100 entries, arranged A-Z, a quarter being annotated, published between 1965 and 1984, with a few issued in 1985. The majority of items are from scholarly journals, with some books, dissertations, government publications, etc. 'The strength of this work is its indexes which make up to 1/3rd of the book' (*Reference books bulletin*, 1986/87, p.59). A keyword index (150p.) based on titles cited, a classified subject index, and an author index. More comprehensive than '*The black family ...*'. *Class No:* 301.18-054(73)(01)

[1127]

DAVIS, L.G., *comp*. **The Black family in the United States:** a selected bibliography of annotated books, articles and dissertations on black families in America. Rev. ed. Westport, Conn., Greenwood, 1986. x, 234p. Bibliographies and indexes in Afro-American and African studies, no. 14). $ 39.95. ISBN: 0313252378.

First published 1978.

Lists 722 books, articles and dissertations, arranged by these forms subdivided by specific topics, most items dating from 1960 to 1985. Annotations are informative, with quotes from authors in many cases. All dissertations and the majority of the books and articles are American. Author and subject index. '... list of bibliographic sources searched would have been helpful'. (*Reference books bulletin*, 1986/87, p.58). *Class No:* 301.18-054(73)(01)

[1128]

DAVIS, N., *comp & ed*. **Afro-American reference:** an annotated bibliography of selected resources. Westport, CT, Greenwood Press, 1985. xiii, 288p. $49.95. (*Bibliographies & indexes in Afro-American and African studies, 9.*) ISBN: 031324930x.

An annotated guide to reference books useful in black studies. 105 general reference sources; 537 books in the topical chapters. 'A guide to the best of the field's vast monographic list'. (*Wilson library bulletin*. April 1986, p.62). *Class No:* 301.18-054(73)(01)

[1129]

MILLER, W.C. *and* **VOWELL, F.N.**, *and others*. **A Comprehensive bibliography for the study of American minorities.** New York, New York University Press, 1976. 2v. (xix, 690p.; xix, 691-1380). $150. ISBN: 0814753736.

29,300 entries. V.1: From Africa and the Middle East. From Europe (*e.g.* 'The Irish-American experience', p.381-422). From Eastern Europe and the Balkans. V.2: From Asia. From the Islands (*e.g.* Cuba). Typical subsections: Bibliographies; periodicals; history; sociology; economics; politics; education; religion, biography and autobiography; literary criticism; fiction; poetry and drama; music;

....(contd.)
English-language material; concise annotations; introductions to sections. Select list of general sources (p.969-70). V.2 includes author and title indexes. *Class No:* 301.18-054(73)(01)

[1130]
—Ethnic information sources in the United States: a guide to organizations, agencies, foundations, institutions, media, commercial and trade bodies, government programmes, research institutions, libraries and museums, etc. Wasserman, P. *and* Kennington, A.E., *eds.* 2nd ed. Detroit, Mich., Gale Research Co., 1983. 2v. (xix,1380p.). $165. ISBN: 0810303671.
First published 1976.
Arranged by ethnic group, A-Z, excluding Blacks, American Indians and Eskimos. Organizations and publications indexes. 'A primary source book ... on foreign nationalities [in the US]. (*RQ*, v.16(2), Winter 1976, p.181, of the 1st ed.).
A 3rd ed. is to be published in 1995. *Class No:* 301.18-054(73)(01)

Maps & Atlases

[1131]
ALLEN, J.P. and TURNER, E.J. We the people: an atlas of America's ethnic diversity. New York, Macmillan, 1988. 315p. $85. ISBN: 0029014204.
A comprehensive guide to the immigrant, ethnic, and racial groups in the US. 13 chapters on European, Asian, South American and African immigrants and native North Americans. Each chapter contains historical information, statistics, and maps depicting settlement patterns. An appendix lists the ancestries of state populations and ethnic populations for states and countries. Indexes of places and ethnic populations. More up-to-date and contains more detailed statistical data than the *Harvard encyclopedia of American ethnic groups* edited by S. Thermstron and others (Cambridge, Mass., Harvard University Press, 1980. 1076p. tables, maps, $90. 0674375122). *Class No:* 301.18-054(73)(084.3)

Jews

[1132]
LERMAN, A., *ed*. The Jewish communities of the world: a contemporary guide. 4th ed. London, Macmillan Press, in association with the Institute of Jewish Affairs, 1989. 224p. £35. ISBN: 0333480708.
3rd rev. ed. was published in 1971.
Based on material from the archives of the Institute and on detailed information from the communities obtained through the network of contacts of the World Jewish Congress. Provides up-to-date and comprehensive information on Jewish life and institutions in 98 national communities. Entries include a brief historical outline, the composition of the community, its legal status, communal organizations, religious life, education, cultural activities, libraries, museums, press, welfare and historical sites. Arranged by countries, A-Z. Table of world Jewish population. Glossary. *Class No:* 301.18-054(=924)

Black Races

[1133]
DIGGS, E.L. Black chronology, from 400 BC. to the abolition of the slave trade. Boston, Mass., G.K. Hall, 1983. 312p. $45. ISBN: 0816185433. *Class No:* 301.18-054(=96)

[1134]
Index to black periodicals. Boston, Mass. G. K. Hall, 1972-. Annual. $95.00. ISSN: 08996253.
Previously, from 1960 - *Index to periodical articles by and about blacks, Index to periodical articles by and about negroes,* and *Index to selected periodicals.*
An index to Afro-American periodicals of general and scholarly interest. Arrangement is A-Z by subject/author in the same sequence. Reviews are indicated. *Class No:* 301.18-054(=96)

Amerindians, North

[1135]
HUNTINGTON FREE LIBRARY AND READING ROOM. New York. Dictionary catalog of the American Indian collections. Boston, Mass., G.K. Hall, 1977. 4v. (2455p.). $435.00. ISBN: 0816100659.
51,500 photolithographed catalogue cards, covering 35,000 v. and pertinent periodical articles. Coverage includes anthropology, ethnology, art, archaeology, history and current affairs of the Indian in both North and South America. *Class No:* 301.18-054(=97)

[1136]
KLEIN, B.T. Reference encyclopedia of the American Indian. 9th ed. New York, Todd Publications, 2000. $125. ISBN: 0915344890.
First published 1967.
A series of directories relating to native Americans (USA and Canada) including government agencies; reservations; museums, monuments & parks; Indian health services, etc.; a list of shops dealing with Indian arts and crafts; a bibliography and a biographical dictionary. *Class No:* 301.18-054(=97)

Urban Communities

[1137]
MELVIN, P.M., ed. American community organizations: a historical dictionary. Westport, CT., Greenwood Press, 1986. xvi, 236p. $45. ISBN: 0313240531.
Relates to the subject over the past 100 years, from the settlement house movement in the 1880s to the present. Arranged A-Z is information on 59 significant community organizations, 8 federal laws that have affected organizing activities in urban areas, and 43 biographical sketches of key figures in the community organization movement. Ample cross-references. Subject and name indexes. 3 appendixes - chronological list of organizations, list of significant legislation, and list of prominent individuals. There is also a bibliographical essay on accessible published materials in the history of community organization. 'Should prove to be a valuable resource for those interested in neighborhood activism and its history' (*Reference books bulletin*, 1986/87, p.63). *Class No:* 301.185.2

Bibliographies

[1138]
DINER, H.R., *ed*. Women and urban society: a guide to information sources. Detroit, Mich., Gale Research Co., 1979. xii, 138p. $65. ISBN: 0810314258.
An annotated bibliography of articles and books on the effect of urbanization on women and the family situation, arranged in 6 sections: 1. Women and urbanization - 2. Women in urban families - 3. Urban fertility - 4. Employment and urban women - 5. Women's roles in urban societies: social and psychological implications - 6. Views of urban women. Appendices: A. Selected bibliography of books - B. Abstracts and indexes - C. Periodicals. Author, title and subject indexes. *Class No:* 301.185.2(01)

[1139]
FILIPOVITCH, A.J. *and* REEVES, E.J., *eds*. Urban community: a guide to information sources. Detroit, Mich., Gale. 1978. x, 286p. $65. ISBN: 0810314290.
Annotated bibliography of books and periodical articles, dealing primarily with recent American and British experience of urban community and research done since 1970. 5 major sections (each with a prefatory bibliographic essay) dealing in turn with theories of community, the community as a physical entity and as a social group, specific problems (*e.g.* safety, quality of life, physical design, and community power) and problems of community planning (*e.g.* citizen participation; new towns). Author, title and subject indexes. *Class No:* 301.185.2(01)

Dictionaries

[1140]
ROSENBERG, P.M. *and* DURR, W.T. The Urban information thesaurus: a vocabulary for social documentation. Westport, Conn., Greenwood, 1977. 374p. $45. ISBN: 0837194830.
A computer-based thesaurus developed by the Baltimore Region Institutional Studies Center as the subject authority list for the Center's archival collection. Based on HUD's 'Urban vocabulary' and the metropolitan Council of Government's 'Urban affairs and planning thesaurus'. Focuses on terms related to planning, urban development, human services, and social history. Main index includes scope notes and references, and there is also a KWOC index, a section of terms arranged in hierarchical order, a list of geographical codes, and a list of qualifiers. '... the most comprehensive and sophisticated source available and is highly recommended for appropriate reference collections. (*RQ*, v.18 no.2, Winter, 1978. p.214-5). *Class No:* 301.185.2(038)

China

[1141]
China urban statistics. State Statistical Bureau. People's Republic of China, *comp*. rev. ed. London, Longman Group and China Statistical Information and Consultancy Service Centre, 1988. 504p. tables. £75. ISBN: 0582997569.
First published 1985.
Part 1. has profiles of 34 major Chinese cities. Part 2: General surveys: statistics of 295 cities (demography, agriculture, industry, transport and telecommunications, urban development, trade and

....*(contd.)*

commerce, education and culture, public health, labour, public finance). Part 3. Appendix: Weights and measures. Glossary of city names in English and Chinese. *Class No:* 301.185.2(510)

India

[1142]

BOSE, A. **Bibliography on urbanization in India, 1947 - 1976.** New Delhi, Tata McGraw-Hill for the Institute of Economic Growth, New Delhi, 1977. xxxi, 179 p.

A by-product of continuous research in the field, the work lists 2,711 titles relating to important writings in the post-independence period, including books, monographs, reports, research papers, journal articles, a few selected newspaper articles, and important unpublished material. Sections on urban demography; urban economics; urban geography; urban history, politics and administration; urban housing, development and planning; a survey of literature, trend reports, etc; and an addenda. Author and subject indexes. *Class No:* 301.185.2(540)

Africa

[1143]

AJAEGBU, H.I. **African urbanization:** a bibliography. Edinburgh University, Centre for African Studies; London, International African Institute, 1972. (Reprint 1984). vi, 78p. £6.10.

Replaces Edinburgh University. Department of Social Anthropology's *African urbanization: a reading list ...* (1965).

Nearly 3000 items, intended as a guide to research into the process of urbanization and urban problems in African countries south of the Sahara; scope is mainly sociological, economic and demographic. An alphabetical index of towns cited and a list of abbreviations are followed by 25 other bibliographies, and then by the main bibliography, arranged A-Z by author under region, country and town sections. Author index. *Class No:* 301.185.2(6)

Rural Communities

Bibliographies of Bibliographies

[1144]

BERNDT, J. **Rural sociology:** a bibliography of bibliographies. Metuchen, N.J., Scarecrow Press, 1986. viii, 177p. $17.50; £17.50. ISBN: 0810818604.

Attempts to list and annotate, in about 100 words, all English-language bibliographies concerned exclusively with social aspects of rural life published since 1970. 454 numbered entries arranged in 15 subject divisions, then A-Z by author. Personal and corporate name index (p.153-9), title index (p.160-74), and geographical index (p.175-7). *Class No:* 301.185.20(009)

Bibliographies

[1145]

Village studies: data analysis and bibliography. Compiled by Mick Moore [and others]. Edited by Clare M. Lambert. London : Mansell, 1977-78. 2v.

Published originally by Bowker for the Institute of Development Studies, Univ. of Sussex. 1: *India, 1950-1975.* 1976. 351p. 2: *Africa, Middle East and North Africa, Asia (excluding India), Pacific Islands, Latin America, West Indies and the Caribbean, 1950-1075.* 1978. 346p. Aims to present information on studies of single villages, and especially to inform the researcher of the availability of primary data. Separate indexes of authors, institutions and topics. *Class No:* 301.185.20(01)

Plantations

[1146]

KIRK, C. **People in plantations:** a review of the literature and annotated bibliography. Brighton, Sussex, Institute of Development Studies, 1987. xxviii, 286p. £10.50. (*Research report 18.*) ISBN: 0903354780.

Part I has introductory pages, including a conclusion. Part II is a mainly annotated bibliography of 925 items, arranged A-Z by author. Annotations are descriptive and each entry has codes to indicate subject matter (14 subject codes). Index of subjects, countries, and commodities. *Class No:* 301.185.20(01)PAL

Hunger

[1147]

DRÈZE, J. *and* SEN, A. **The Political economy of hunger.** Oxford, Clarendon Press, 1991. 3v.(1277p). v.1 & 2: £40 each; v.3: £45. ISBN: 019823635x, v.1; 0198286368, v.2; 0198286376, v.3.

Essays addressing a wide range of policy isues relating to the role of public action in combating hunger and deprivation in the modern world. *Class No:* 304.9

[1148]

DRÈZE, J. *and* SEN, A. **The Political economy of hunger:** selected essays. Clarendon Press, Oxford, 1995 xiv,626p. (*WIDER studies in development economies*.) ISBN: 0198288832.

Volume consists of ten out of twenty-six papers and the general introduction to *The Political Economy of Hunger* qv. *Class No:* 304.9

[1149]

Hunger in history: food shortage, poverty and deprivation. Newman, L., *general ed.* Oxford, Blackwell, 1989. xiii,429p. 10 figures. 5 maps. £45. $29.95. ISBN: 1557860440.

Members of the World Hunger Program at Brown University have brought together 15 original and specially commissioned articles on the study of hunger. 15 chapters are arranged in 6 parts: 1. Introduction; 2. Hunger in prehistoric societies; 3. Hunger in complex societies; 4. Hunger in the emerging world system; 5. Hunger in the recent past; 6. Conclusions. Analytical index, p. 411-429. *Class No:* 304.9

Bibliographies

[1150]

BALL, N., *ed.* **World hunger:** a guide to the economic and political dimensions. Oxford, Clio Press; Santa Barbara, CA., ABC-Clio, 1981. xxii,386p. 6 charts. £39.30; $46.50. (*War/peace bibliography series, no. 15.*) ISBN: 087436308x.

Explains and chronicles the literature of food production and distribution from economic and political perspectives. Items mostly in English. Introductions to the chapters on the major elements of the topic, highlighting particular problems, 'Highly recommended...' (*RQ*, v.21(2), Winter 1981. p.207). *Class No:* 304.9(01)

[1151]

KUTZNER, P.L. **World hunger:** a reference handbook. Santa Barbara, CA, ABC-Clio, 1991. xii,359p. $39.50. ISBN: 0874365589.

An extensive analytical review of reference material for concerned people. 7 sections: 1. Overview; 2. Chronology (p.57-119); 3. Biographies (p.121-53); 4. Facts and data; 5. Organizations; 6. References in print; 7. Nonprint sources. Glossary, p.323-37. Index, p.339-59. '... researcher looking for a general guide would be well served.'*Choice*, v.29(3), November 1991, p.418). *Class No:* 304.9(01)

Social Climate

[1152]

KINLOCH, G.C. **Social stratification:** an annotated bibliography. New York, Garland, 1987. 357p. $55. (*Garland library of sociology, 11. Garland reference library of social science, 393.*) ISBN: 0824098056.

Over 1700 annotated and numbered entries arranged in broad categories. Most entries relate to journal articles published between the 1960s and the 1980s. Categories are general bibliographies and research trends; theoretical and conceptual issues; methodological issues; historical studies of stratification; stratification in the US; and stratification in other societies. Author and subject indexes. *Class No:* 308

Bibliographies

[1153]

SILIDAY, G.L., *ed.* **History of the family and kinship;** a select international bibliography. Millwood, N.Y., Kraus International Publications, 1980. 410p. $45. ISBN: 0527844519.

The published result of a special project of the *Journal of family history,* contains 6200 entries grouped by regional/national units published through 1976. World-wide and systematic coverage. Name index. *Class No:* 308(01)

[1154]

STREATFIELD, D. **Social work: an information sourcebook:** a guide to publications and other information sources. Edinburgh, Capital Planning Information Ltd., 1982. 165p. (CPI sourcebooks, no. 2). £17. ISBN: 0906011167.

Intended mainly for local authority social services staffs, voluntary agencies staff, and community workers. Part 1: Fieldworkers and their information world; part 2: Problems and information sources; part 3: Information workers; Appendix A: Organising a local information system; Appendix B: Some useful organisations. Author, title and subject index, p.148-162. *Class No:* 308(01)

Men's studies

[1155]

AUGUST, E.R. **Men's studies:** a selected and annotated interdisplinary bibliography. Littleton, Col., Libraries Unlimited, 1985. 232p. $36. £30. ISBN: 0872874818.

Describes nearly 600 English-language books in 10 topical chapters, including autobiographies, bibliographies and anthologies. Topics include men's awareness, divorce and custody, health and related matters, crime and sexual violence, women and men, masculine gender roles, sexuality, homosexuality, men in families, men in literature, art and religion. Works range from scholarly to popular. Cross-references at end of chapters. *Class No:* 308(01)MEN

Encyclopaedias & Dictionaries

[1156]

TIERNEY, H., *ed*. **Women's studies encyclopedia** 2nd edition. Westport CT, Greenwood; London, Aldwych, 1999. 3 vols. £250.00. ISBN: 086172111x.

This was originally published over three years, volume 1 (1989) being entitled "Views from the sciences", vol. 2 (1990) covering literature and the arts, and vol. 3 (1991) history, philosophy and religion. The three individual volumes have been considerably revised, new articles added, and combined into one publication, which is also available on CD Rom for the same price - the latter also includes URLs for relevant web sites. The CD Rom can be networked. All articles by the c. 400 contributors are signed, and constitute an excellent source of information on feminism in all its manifestations, as well as general social issues in which women are involved. *Class No:* 308(03)WOM

Encyclopaedias

[1157]

Encyclopedia of social inventions. Albery, N. *and* Yale, V., *eds*. London, The Institute of Social Inventions, 1991. 298p. £19.99.

New and imaginative solutions to social problems (*e.g.* pneumatic bicycle seats; using wild dolphins to help treat mental illness), 500 in all. The most worthwhile or controversial inventions are commented upon by experts in the field, and each entry has a contact name, address and telephone number. The Institute runs an annual £1000 prize competition for the best social inventions. (Entry taken from *The good book guide*, v.53, July/August 1991, p.17). *Class No:* 308(031)

Handbooks & Manuals

[1158]

THOMSON, A. *and* PLATT, R. **Help yourself:** an everyday survival handbook. 2nd ed. London, Impact Books, 1993. 192p £4.95 ISBN: 1874687110.

First published 1985.

Facts, tips and advice for young people about getting a job, working for a wage, beating unemployment, claiming benefit, managing money, education and training, rights and laws, having a say, mind and body, shelter, time out. Index. *Class No:* 308(035)

Reviews & Abstracts

[1159]

Geographical abstracts. D: Social and historical geography. Norwich, Geo Abstracts Ltd., 1974-?. 6pa. ISSN: 02687909.

Preceded by *Geographical abstracts. D: Social geography* (1966-7), thereafter *Geo abstracts. D. Social geography and cartography* (1968-73).

About 2500 indicative and informative abstracts pa. Sections: Social - Population distribution - Population change - Population migration - Population fertility - Man and environment - Natural hazards - Perception - Medical - Regional - Cultural - Historical: field evidence - Historical: documentary evidence - Historical: regional - Political - Urban - Rural - Methodology - Biography - Education. Author and regional indexes for each part appear in the last issue each year. *Class No:* 308(048)

[1160]

Sage family studies abstracts, 1979-. Newbury Park, CA. & London, Sage Publications Inc., 1979-. $232. £117 pa. ISSN: 01640283.

Sections: Trends in marriage, family and society - Gender roles - Issues concerning reproduction - Singlehood, mate selection & marriage - Early socialization: infancy & childhood - Childcare, problems & treatment = Late socialization: adolescence - Life cycles: adulthood, aging & the family - Family relations & problems - Family services, counselling & therapy - Divorce - Economics & the family - Minority & cross-cultural relations - Theory & method. Author and subject indexes. (V.15(3), August 1993, has 41 abstracts). *Class No:* 308(048)

Yearbooks & Directories

[1161]

WEEKS, G., *ed*. **Family directory:** information resources on the family. London, British Library, 1986. xii,183p. £12.50. (*BLIG 1*.) ISBN: 0712220755.

Part I: Organizations, databases and publications; part II: The family in perspective. The first part lists British organizations, non-British and international organizations, online databases, and publications relevant to family studies. The second part includes 4 essays, each with notes or references appended. *Class No:* 308(058)

Histories

[1162]

Encyclopedia of social history. Stearns, P.N., *ed*. New York, Garland, 1994 xxxvi,856p. (*Garland reference library of social science*.) ISBN: 0815303424, US.

Contains bibliographic references and indexes.

Deals with various aspects of social life from an historical perspective. Articles are signed and give references. Covers subjects such as slavery, apartheid, colonialism, missionary activity etc. *Class No:* 308(091)

Worldwide

[1163]

World quality of life indicators. O'Donnell, T.S., *ed*. 2nd ed. Santa Barbara, Calif., ABC-CLIO, 1991 vii,199p. ISBN: 0874366577, US.

Contains a compendium of current information, including bibliographic references .

For each political unit, gives the location, area, land use, population, statistics, health care, ethnic composton, religion, language, education, economic data, climate and travel notes, as well as a description of the form of goverment and constitution. This is a very useful guide, if somewhat out of date. It resembles a handbook for American businessmen going abroad. *Class No:* 308(100)

Developing Countries

[1164]

Third World resource directory 1994-1995 an annotated guide to print and audio-visual resources.. Fenton, T.P. *and* Heffron, M.J., *eds*. Maryknoll, N.Y., Orbis Books, 1995. xiv,785p.

Contains indexes.

A guide to organizations and publications. 'The book is a guide to resources about the Third World and the United States involvement in the affairs of the Third World nations and peoples' (*Preface*). *Class No:* 308(4/9-77)

Europe

Histories

[1165]

CASEY, J. **The History of the family.** Oxford, Basil Blackwell, 1989. 192p. £25. ISBN: 0631146687.

Concerns the changing interactions between family and social, political and religious structures over the last 1,000 years of European history. 7 Chapters: 1. The meaning of family - 2. The role of the ancestors - 3. The politics of family - 4. The arranged marriage - 5. The nature of passion - 6. The economics of the household - 7. The rise of domesticity. 'Suggestions for further reading'; 'Reference list of works cited in the text'; and glossary of kinship terms. *Class No:* 308(4)(091)

[1166]

A **History of private life.** Ariès, P. *and* Duby, G., *general eds*. Cambridge, Mass., & London, Harvard University Press, 1991. 5v.(3000p.). $39.95; £29.95 each vol. ISBN: 0317561685, v.1; 0674399765, v.2; 0674399773, v.3; 0674399781, v.4; 067439979x, v.5.

Contents: V.1: From pagan Rome to Byzantium; v.2: Revelations of the medieval world; v.3: Passions of the renaissance; v.4: From the fires of revolution to the Great War; v.5: Riddles of identity in modern times. *Class No:* 308(4)(091)

Great Britain

[1167]

Atlas of British social and economic history since *c*.1700. Pope, R., *ed*. London, Routledge, 1990. xiii,250p. diagrs., maps. £18.99. ISBN: 0415056330.

Maps and text illustrating historical development. 12 sections: 1. Agriculture - 2. The textile and chemical industries - 3. Metal, vehicle and engineering industries - 4. Coal, gas and electricity - 5. Transport and trade - 6. Demographic changes, 1901-1981 - 7. Employment and unemployment - 8. Urbanization and living conditions - 9. Labour movements - 10. Education - 11. Religion - 12. Leisure. Further

....(contd.)
reading, p.236-45 (by chapter). Detailed, analytical index ('Education': 1 column), p.246-50. 255 diagrs. and maps. A neat production. *Class No:* 308(410)

[1168]
The Cambridge social history of Britain, 1750-1950. Thompson, F.M.L., *and others, eds.* Cambridge, Cambridge University Press, 1991. 3v (1493p) £15.95 each vol.; £39.95 the set. ISBN: 0521257883, v.1; 0521257891, v.2; 0521257905, v.3; 0521438136, the set.
V.1 Regions and communities - v.2. People and their environment - v.3. Social agencies and institutions. Each volume has 6-8 contributions. V.3 includes chapters on education, health and medicine; crime, authority and the policemans work; religion; philanthropy; clubs, societies and associations. Each volume has bibliographies and an index. *Choice* (v.28(6), February 1991, p.982) considers it serves best as a reference work to be dipped into selectively. A comprehensive index to all three volumes is called for. *Class No:* 308(410)

[1169]
The General household survey: an inter-departmental survey ... 1993. Foster, K., *et al.* London, Stationery Office Books, 1995. 281p. tables. £18.50. (*GHS, vol. 24.*) ISBN: 0116916222.
First published 1971. Sponsored by the Central Statistical Office.
A continuous survey based each year on a sample of the general population resident in private households in Great Britain. Section 1: 'Introduction and main findings' precedes the report, which is in two main parts: Part 1, section 2. People, households and families - 3. Housing - 4. Health - 5. Sterilisation and infertility - 6. Entertainments, libraries, forests - 7. Occupational pension scheme coverage - 8. Share ownership. Part 2: Tables. 4 appendices (A. Definitions and terms - B. Household and individual interview schedules - C. Summary of main topics including a questionnaire - D. List of tables). *Class No:* 308(410)

[1170]
MITCHELL, A. **The New Penguin guide to personal finance:** make your money work for you. 3rd ed. London, Viking, 1992. 370p. illus. £17.99. ISBN: 0670847712.
Covers the whole spectrum of personal finance - savings and investment, tax, financing a family. 30 chapters in 3 parts: pt.1 has advice on building a capital sum by regular savings and investment; pt.2 is concerned with taxes; pt.3 has 18 chapters on family finance. Each chapter has a summary of contents, and cross-references to other chapters. *Class No:* 308(410)

Yearbooks & Directories
[1171]
Social policy review, 1999. London, Social Policy Association, 1999. 330p. £12. ISBN: 0951889583.
First published 1971 as *The Year book of social policy in Britain*; title changed in 1990.
The publication examines current issues and developments in social policy and social administration. No index. *Class No:* 308(410)(058)

Tables & Data Books
[1172]
Family spending. Office for National Statistics *and* Down, D. 1999 ed. London, Stationery Office Books, 1999. 193p. tables. £39.50. ISBN: 0116212519. ISSN: 09651403.
First published for 1957. Annual.
Based on a representative sample of about private households in the UK. Tables with data on household characteristics, household expenditure, household income, regional income and expenditure. Appendices: definitions; Index to tables. *Class No:* 308(410)(083)

[1173]
Social trends, 30, 2000. Office for National Statistics. London, Stationery Office Books, 2000. 244p. diagrs., graphs, tables, maps. £30. ISBN: 011621242x. ISSN: 03067742.
First published 1970. Annual.
Sections: Population - Households and families - Education - Employment - Income and wealth - Expenditure - Health and personal social services - Housing - Environment - Leisure - Participation - Crime and justice - Transport. Appendix: definitions and terms. Subject index. *Class No:* 308(410)(083)

Histories
[1174]
HALSEY, A.H., *ed.* **British social trends since 1900:** a guide to the changing structure of Britain. 2nd ed. London, Macmillan Press, 1988. xxviii,650p. tables. £80 (hardback) £21.50 (paperback). ISBN: 0333345215, hbk; 0333345223, pbk.
Updates Halsey's *Trends in British society since 1900...* (1972).
18 contributors, aiming to produce a volume which would complement *Social trends* by presenting longer time series and covering additional topics, drawing on both official and non-official statistics. 417 tables and graphs, providing an overview of trends since World War II. *Class No:* 308(410)(091)

[1175]
HALSEY, A.H. and WEBB, J., *eds.* **Twentieth-century British social trends.** 3rd ed. London, Macmillan, 2000. 760p. £95 hardback. £25 paper. ISBN: 0333721489, hbk; 0333721497, pbk.
A statistical record of Britain in the twentieth century. Each chapter gives explanations of the statistical trends - economic, social and political. *Class No:* 308(410)(091)

Institutions & Associations
[1176]
MOSS, L. **The Government Social Survey:** a history. London, HMSO, 1991. viii,297p. £16. ISBN: 0116913029.
A detailed study of how the Survey's work has evolved and developed over 40 years. Part 1 describes changes in the situations in government which provided the framework within which the Survey grew; pt.2 describes the main subject areas in which work was done and how changes and innovations in methods were developed. *Class No:* 308(410):061:061.2

Ireland
[1177]
MAC GRÉIL, Mícheal. **Prejudice and tolerance in Ireland** based on a survey of intergroup attitudes of Dublin adults and other sources. Dublin, Research Centre, College of Industrial Relations, 1997 xxiv,634p.
Contains index and bibliography.
Definitive guide to the social attitudes of Irish people, with particular regard to the in-groups and out-groups in society. Covers prejudice against those belonging to marginalized groups, such as members of the travelling community, or those precieved to be socialy or morally deviant. Of particular interest is the authors use of the Bogardus scale, in which tolerance of a paricular group is measured by the willingness or otherwise of a person to allow someone from that group to marry into his or her family. *Class No:* 308(415)

[1178]
MAC GRÉIL, Mícheal and O'KELLY, Caroline. **Prejudice in Ireland revisited** based on a national survey of intergroup attidudes in Ireland. Maynooth, Ireland, Research Unit, Department of Social Studies, St Patrick's College, 1996
A revision on a nationwide basis of the author's earlier work in 1977. *Class No:* 308(415)

[1179]
McGILVRAY, J. **Social statistics in Ireland:** guide to their sources and uses. Dublin, Institute of Public Administration, 1977. x, 204p. £3.50.
A guide to the main sources of social statistics published in Ireland, and the use of their statistics in social investigation and analysis. Contains chapters on basic demographic statistics; vital statistics; health; housing; education; social security; incomes, expenditures and the standard of living; other social statistics. The final two chapters explain some statistical concepts of statistical methods and sample survey techniques. *Class No:* 308(415)

[1180]
RYAN, Liam. **Social dimensions of Irish Catholicism.** Dublin, Columba Press, 1995 (*Maynooth Bicentenary Series.*)
Class No: 308(415)

20th Century
[1181]
PEILLON, Michel. **Contemporary Irish society** an introduction. Dublin, Gill and Macmillan, 1982
Contains indexes.
A study of social interaction in Ireland. Of particular interest is the study of politics, dealing with the absence of the normal right-wing left-wing division between political parties, and the phenomenon of clientalism as a form of political interaction. *Class No:* 308(415)"19"

London

[1182]

O'DAY, R. *and* ENGLANDER, D. Mr. Charles Booth's inquiry: life and labour of the people in London reconsidered. London, Hambledon Press, 1993. viii,246p. £40. ISBN: 1852850795.

20 chapters in 3 parts: 1. The poverty series; 2. The industry series; 3. The religious influence series. 6 appendices. A select bibliography. Index of names and places. Index of subjects. *Class No:* 308(421)

[1183]

SAWYER, P. *and* FRASER, J. Bridges: directory of African, Caribbean, Asian, Latin American and Mediterranean community groups in Greater London, 1988. London, London Voluntary Service Council, 1988. ISBN: 0901171638.

Over 800 groups and organizations were contacted for this first edition. Arrangement is first by area and then by name of organization, A-Z. Also lists Community Relations Councils and Councils for Voluntary Service. *Class No:* 308(421)

Wales

[1184]

Welsh social trends/Tueddiadau Cymdeithasol, 1991. Welsh Office. No.8. Cardiff, Welsh Office, 1991. £9.50. ISBN: 0750400501. ISSN: 01409018.

First published 1977. Biennial.

Statistics of population, vital statistics, social characteristics (*e.g.* household data and migration); economic characteristics; health and social security; social services; education; leisure; housing; justice and crime; finance. Appendices on sources and definitions. *Class No:* 308(429)

Germany

[1185]

MERRITT, A.J. *and* RICHARD, L. Politics, economics and society in the two Germanies, 1945-75: a bibliography of English-language works. Urbana, Ill., University of Illinois Press, 1978. xix, 268p. $24.95. ISBN: 0252006844.

A selective bibliography of 8548 items arranged according to primary focus in a number of discrete categories. Author index. *Class No:* 308(430)

France

[1186]

Histoire de la population française. Dupâquier, J., *Directeur*. Paris, Presses Universitaires de France, 1995. 559p. (*Collection Quadrige.*) ISBN: 2130468217.

Contains tables, graphs, bibliography and an index. *Class No:* 308(44)

[1187]

MAGRAW, R. A History of the French working-class. Oxford, Blackwell, 1992. 2v.(768p.). £80. ISBN: 063118046x.

V.1: 1815-70; v.2: 1871-1939. Surveys the changing structures and examines working-class politics and culture. *Class No:* 308(44)

Russia

[1188]

RYAN, M. *and* PRENTICE, R. Social trends in contemporary Russia a statistical sourcebook. New York, St Martin's Press, 1993 xiii,249p. $59.95.

Contains bibliography and index

Intended to provide easy access to a range of information about post-Soviet Russia, presented in tabulated form with accompanying text. Sections: Population change - The growth of towns - Migration - Patterns of child-bearing - The family and marriage - Ethnic composition - Education - Health care. List of abbreviated titles used in the tables. Notes and references. *Class No:* 308(47)

Asia—Middle & Near East

Bibliographies

[1189]

BANUAZIZI, A. *and* PROUCHESTIA, G. Social stratification in the Middle East and North Africa: a bibliographic survey. London, Mansell Publishing Ltd.,1984. xviii,248p. £25. ISBN: 0720117119.

A bibliography of sources published in English and French, 1946-82. An introduction is followed by a list of journals and periodicals consulted; the bibliography is arranged geographically (Middle East & North Africa: general and comparative studies - Afghanistan ... The Yemens). Subdivisions within each country are chronological. No annotations. Subject and author indexes. *Class No:* 308(53+56)(01)

Caribbean

[1190]

OBERG, L.R. Human services in postrevolutionary Cuba: an annotated international bibliography. Westport, Conn., Greenwood Press, 1984. 433p. $45. ISBN: 0313231257.

'Human services' includes education, public health, housing and sports, education being the main theme. Includes books, book chapters, pamphlets, journal articles, government and international agency publications, dissertations, and encyclopedia entries, also bibliographies. Annotations vary from brief descriptions to lengthy comments on intellectual content, bias, strengths and weaknesses. Author, title and detailed subject indexes. '... this significant bibliography...' (*College and research libraries,* July 1985, p.351-2). *Class No:* 308(729)

Latin America

[1191]

Welfare, poverty and development in Latin America. Abel, C. *and* Lewis, C.M., *eds.* London, Macmillan, 1993. 380p. £52.50. ISBN: 0333517377.

Describes the social consequences of recent development strategies in Latin America; social welfare and poverty during the 20th century. Issues are addressed from several different disciplines. *Class No:* 308(729.99)

31 Statistics

Statistics

[1192]

HUTCHINSON, T.P. *and* KE, Y. **An Index to corrections, addenda, and comments that were published in statistical journals, 1970-1991.** Sydney, NSW, Rumsby Scientific Publishing, 1992. AUS$55. £25.

78 major English-language journals were searched and 3200 items found. *Class No:* 310

Databases

[1193]

CD-ROM and online statistical databases. Brittin, M., *comp.* London, Aslib, 1993. 136p. £26. ISBN: 0851423000.

Lists 210 databases worldwide, including online, diskette, magnetic tape, and CD-ROM. A-Z arrangement, with information on format, content, language, countries covered, time span, frequency of update, hosts, producer or distributor, and costs. Subject index. *Class No:* 310(003.4)

Encyclopaedias

[1194]

International encyclopedia of statistics. Kruskal, W.H. *and* Tanur, J.M., *eds.* New York, Macmillan and Free Press, 1978. 2v. $80. each vol; $155. the set. ISBN: 002917970x, v.1; 0029179807, v.2; 0029179602, the set.

Includes articles from the *International encyclopedia of the social sciences* (*qv.*), such articles being revised, corrected and updated. 75 of the articles are on statistics proper, and of these 5 are new. Of the 57 biographies, 12 are new. Detailed, analytical index. 'This unique set will be used in undergraduate and graduate libraries' (*Library journal*, 1 May 1979, p.1044). 'This carefully edited compendium, useful to the student or researcher at any level'. (*College and research libraries*, v.40(4), July 1979, p.350-1). *Class No:* 310(031)

Dictionaries

[1195]

MARRIOTT, F.H.C. **A Dictionary of statistical terms.** 5th rev. ed. London, Longman Group, for the International Statistical Institute, 1990. xiii,222p. tables. £12.95. ISBN: 0582019052.

First published 1957. The first four eds. were compiled by M.G. Kendall and W.R. Buckland.

Defines over 3000 statistical terms. Entries range from 25 to 150 words. Author and date citations are given for more recent terms. Formulae and cross-references figure. As in the 3rd ed. (1971), the glossary of French, German, Italian and English terms in the 2nd ed. (1960) is omitted. 'Authoritative compilation of generally accepted definitions' (Webb, W.H. and others. *Sources of information in the social sciences* (3rd ed. 1986), entry A405) of the 4th ed. *Class No:* 310(038)

[1196]

MULHALL, M.G. **The Dictionary of statistics.** 4th ed., rev. to November 1898. London, Routledge, 1899 (Reprinted Gregg International). [vi], 853p. tables. $62.10. ISBN: 0576531847.

Arrangement is by subjects, A-Z; numerous tables. Period covered is from A.D. 300 to 1898. List of books of reference, p.822-25. Index of places and topics. Sources are sometimes quoted for the statistics cited, but their general omission is a serious drawback. Supplemented by Webb (q.v.). *Class No:* 310(038)

[1197]

WEBB, A.D. **The New dictionary of statistics: a complement to the fourth edition of Mulhall's** *Dictionary of statistics.* London, Routledge, 1911. (Reprinted Gale, 1971). xii, 682p. tables. $75. ISBN: 0810339889.

Covers the period 1899-1919. Similar in pattern to Mulhall, but does not give sources for all figures cited. On the other hand, Webb only cites data for which he can quote chapter and verse, thereby excluding a certain amount of useful information. The 325 sources cited are listed on p.648-54. *Class No:* 310(038)

Polyglot

[1198]

Dreisprachiges Verzeichnis statistischer Fachausdrücke Wiesbaden, Statistisches Bundesamt 1969 (Reprinted 1980) 201p. £.4.90.

Three-language index of statistical technical terms: German-English-French. *Class No:* 310(038)=00

French

[1199]

NIXON, J.W. **Glossary of terms in official statistics,** English-French, French-English. Edinburgh, Oliver & Boyd, for the International Statistical Institute, 1964. xiv,106p.

Pt.1. English-French (p.3-43); Pt.2. French-English (p.47-104); *c.* 3500 and 4500 specialised entry-words respectively, with equivalents. Appendix 1: 'List of principal sources consulted'; 2: 'Existing glossaries or dictionaries giving terms in English and French used in official statistics'. Clear layout; good use of bold type. *Class No:* 310(038)=40

Russian

[1200]

KOTZ, S. **Russian-English/English-Russian glossary of statistical terms.** Edinburgh & London, Oliver & Boyd for the International Statistical Institute, 1971. vii, 87p.

Selection of *c.*2,500 terms included in the 3rd edition of Kendall and Buckland's *Dictionary of statistical terms* (Oliver & Boyd, 1971). Some terms are given brief explanations. 'Not a book for the beginner, either in statistics or Russian' (*Nature*, v.239, 8 Sept. 1972, p.114-5). *Class No:* 310(038)=82

Worldwide

[1201]

'The Economist' book of vital world statistics... Smith-Morris, M., *ed.* London, Hutchinson Business Books Ltd., 1990. 256p. tables, map. £19.99. ISBN: 0091746523.

A view of how countries of the world compare on everything. Sections: Demography - Economic strength - Agriculture and food - Energy - Commodities - Transport and communications - Government finance - Inflation and finance - Trade and balance of payments - Debt and aid - Employment - Education - Health - Family life - Environment. Glossary, p.255. Sources, p.256. *Class No:* 310(100)

[1202]

The Economist pocket world in figures 00. The Economist, *comp.* New York, John Wiley, 2000. 224p. illus. $14.95. ISBN: 0471369551.

First published 1991.

Part 1 gives world rankings (natural facts; population; economic strength, economic growth, etc.) Part 2 has country profiles. *Class No:* 310(100)

[1203]

KURIAN, G.T. **New book of world rankings.** 3rd ed. updated by J. Marti. New York, Facts on File, 1991. xxi,324p. $40. ISBN: 0816019312.

First published 1979 as *The book of world rankings*.

Is 'designed as an international scorecard that compares & ranks over 190 nations of the world according to their performance in some 300 key areas' (*Introduction*). 23 subject chapters: Geography and climate - Vital statistics - Population dynamics and the family - Race and religion - Politics and international and international relations - Foreign aid - Military power - Economy - Finance and banking - Trade - Agriculture - Industry and mining - Energy - Labour - Transport and communications - Consumption - Housing - Health and food - Education - Crime rate - Media - World cities - Culture. Country profiles. Bibliography, p.319. Index, p.321-324. *Class No:* 310(100)

Bibliographies

[1204]

International directory of non-official statistical sources, 1990. London, Euromonitor Publications Ltd., 1990. x,155p. £135. ISBN: 0863383548.

*c.*1000 regularly produced titles arranged A-Z by organization or journal title name for countries outside Western Europe. Data includes title of the statistics, frequency, contents/coverage summary, information on availability, language, machine-readable version of

....(contd.)

source, price in currency of originating country, contact and address of department when available, telephone/telex/fax numbers where applicable. Subject index, p.135-146; geographical index of publishers, p.147-155. *Class No:* 310(100)(01)

[1205]

KURIAN, G.T. **Sourcebook of global statistics.** New York, Facts on File; Harlow, Essex, Longman Group, 1985. xi,413p. $85; £60. ISBN: 0582902665.

Information on 209 statistical publications, most of which are serials issued by international organizations (*e.g.* UN, OECD, EC). Arrangement is A-Z by title and includes year of publication, language, number of pages, edition, indexes, base period, updating, scope, sources of data, organization, contents, new features, graphs-tables-charts, evaluation, publisher, most recent price, availability on tape, database, etc. *International affairs* (v.63(1), Winter 1986/87, p.178) comments that the index is unsatisfactory and the format could be improved. *Class No:* 310(100)(01)

[1206]

World directory of non-offical statistical sources. 2nd ed. London, Euromonitor Publications Ltd, 1996 267p. $390.00 ISBN: 0863386555.

Contains indexes.

Revision of 1990 edition.

Extremely expensive listing of data for trade associations, financial institutions, and so on. The data, as the volume warns, varies in quality and reliability: half of it comes from the UK or USA. Details of the publishing body are given. *Class No:* 310(100)(01)

Yearbooks & Directories

[1207]

UNESCO. **Unesco statistical yearbook, 1999.** Paris, Unesco, 1999. [c.700p.], chiefly tables. $98.50. ISBN: 0890592454.

First published, 1964. Annual. Continues the biennial *Basic facts and figures* (Unesco, 1952-62).

Covers *c.*200 countries; computer-produced tables. Sections: Reference tables - Education - Education by level and by country - Educational expenditure - Science and technology - Culture and communications - Printed matter (Libraries - Book production - Newspapers and other periodicals - Cultural paper (*e.g.* newsprint) - Cultural heritage - Film and cinema - Broadcasting - International trade in printed matter. *Class No:* 310(100)(058)

[1208]

—Unesco statistical digest: a statistical summary of data on education, science and technology, culture and communication, by country. Paris, Unesco.

First published 1982. Annual.

Basic statistics on a country-by-country basis.

Class No: 310(100)(058)

[1209]

World facts and figures. Showers, V. 3rd ed. New York, John Wiley & Sons, 1989. xii, 721p. illus. tables. $74.95. ISBN: 0471857750.

First published in 1973 as *The World in figures*.

Mainly tabular data, allowing for comparisons to be made on 218 countries, 2664 of the largest and best-known cities, and nearly 3000 geographical and cultural features. 11 main chapters (chapter 1 has 11 tables on demography, economy, transport, communications and educational activities in all 218 countries; 2. City tables; 3. Country comparisons; 4. City comparisons - 5. Comparisons of cultural features; 6. Seas; 7. Islands; 8. Rivers; 9. Mountains; 10. Lakes; 11. Waterfalls). Selected bibliography of 258 items. Index, p.651-721. *Class No:* 310(100)(058)

Bibliographies

[1210]

WESTFALL, G. **Bibliography of official statistical yearbooks and bulletins.** Alexandria, VA., Chadwyck-Healey Inc., 1986. [18],247p. $75.£48. (*Government documents bibliographies*.) ISBN: 0859641244.

Supersedes P. C. Carter's *Statistical yearbooks; an annotated bibliography ...* and *Statistical bulletins: an annotated bibliography ...* (Washington, Library of Congress, 1953 and 1954).

374 titles, from more than 180 countries, arranged by continent, subdivided by country. Data includes title, translation of title where necessary, date first published, compiler language, history of changes, factual description of particular edition/issue, any other information, publisher, and price. Limited to statistical yearbooks and bulletins. *Class No:* 310(100)(058)(01)

Histories

[1211]

MITCHELL, B.R. **International historical statistics: the Americas, 1750-1993** . 4th ed. London, Macmillan, 1998. xv,830p. £225. ISBN: 0333726898, UK; 1561592358, US.

Covers the principal areas of economic and social activity in the Americas, each section having a short introductory commentary and extensive notes and footnotes. Contents: Introduction - Climate - Population - Labour force - Agriculture - Industry - External trade - Transport and communications - Finance - Prices - Education - National accounts. *Class No:* 310(100)(091)

[1212]

—MITCHELL, B.R. **International historical statistics: Africa, Asia and Oceania, 1750-1993.** London, Macmillan Reference, 1998. xix,1113p. £225. ISBN: 033372691x.

Includes data for all the principal areas of economic and social activity. *Class No:* 310(100)(091)

[1213]

MITCHELL, B.R. **International historical statistics: Europe, 1750-1993.** 4th ed. London, Macmillan Reference, 1998. xvii,959p. £253.15. ISBN: 0333726901.

Data for the last 250 years for all principal areas of economic and social activity in all countries of Western and Eastern Europe. *Class No:* 310(100)(091)

Developing Countries

[1214]

INSTITUTE OF DEVELOPING ECONOMIES. **Catalogue of statistical materials of developing countries.** 10th ed. Tokyo, Asia Economic Press, 1990. 607p.

First published in 1968 as *Bibliography of statistical materials ...*

Entries grouped by country, subdivided by general and 9 subject groups. Appendix 1 lists publications from international organizations and statistical institutes in developing countries; Appendix 2 is a directory of statistical organizations of developed countries. *Class No:* 310(4/9-77)

Europe

Bibliographies

[1215]

HARVEY, J.M. **Statistics Europe: sources for social, economic and market research.** 6th ed. Beckenham, Kent, CBD Research Ltd., 1997. 462p. £97.50. ISBN: 0900246669.

First published 1969.

Provides over 1200 different statistical sources for social, economic and market research in all European countries. Data include bibliographical information; time factor; price; pagination. Arranged in 9 subject groups for each country (general, production, external trade, internal distribution and service trades, population, social and political, finance, transport and communications, environment) many subdivided. Indexes of organizations, titles, and subjects. *Class No:* 310(4)(01)

Yearbooks & Directories

[1216]

The Economist pocket Europe. Butler, P., *ed.* London, Economist Books, 1992. 224p. £9.99 ISBN: 071269806x.

In 4 parts: 1. Country profiles (Albania ... Yugoslavia); 2. Country comparisons (area & population, economy, personal expenditure, life & leisure); 3. Country facts (statistics on the economy, structure of manufacturing, inflation & exchange rates, balance of payments & debt, government, people, society); 4. The organizations (The European Community, the institutions, aims and characteristics of other organizations). Notes on data and sources, p.214-7. Index, p.218-24. *Class No:* 310(4)(058)

Europe—Western

[1217]

MORT, D. **Western European statistics.** London, Pitman, 1992. 608p. £90. ISBN: 0273037366.

Evaluates and collates official and non-official sources of statistics and market information for EC countries and selected industries across the manufacturing and service sector. Each entry is evaluated in terms of ease of location, ease of use, strengths and weaknesses, time and cost factors. *Class No:* 310(400)

[1218]

RAMSEY, A., *comp*. **Eurostat index:** a detailed keyword subject index to the statistical series published by the Statistical Office of the European Communities with notes on the series. 5th rev.ed. Stamford, Capital Planning Information, 1992. 250p. £45.. ISBN: 0906011833.

First published 1981.

Lists the statistical series by subject (1. General statistics ... 9. Miscellaneous), followed by the keyword subject index. Bibliography, p.269-280. 7 appendices (4. Alphabetical list of Eurostat titles contained in the text). *Class No:* 310(400)

Periodicals

[1219]

Sigma: the bulletin of European statistics, no.1, Sept/Oct 1991-. Superseded *Eurostat news,* 1976-1991. Luxembourg, Eurostat, 1991-. 6pa. ISSN: 10185739.

Provides up-to-date information from a statistical viewpoint on the progress of measures taken in the run-up towards European integration. Supplemented by *Just published,* listing titles published during the month. *Class No:* 310(400)(051)

Histories

[1220]

FLORA, P., *ed*. **State, economy and society in Western Europe, 1815-1975.** London, Macmillan Press; New York, St. James Press; Frankfurt A.M., Campus Verlag, 1983-1987. 2v.(633, 758p.). £90 the set; $140 the set. ISBN: 0333359445, UK; 0912289066, US; 3593329107, Germany.

V.1: *The growth of mass democracies and welfare states; v.2: The growth of industrial societies and capitalist economies.* Includes statistical tables on population, suffrage, housing, labour disputes, bureaucracy, military personnel, education, public income and expenditure, gross national product, income distribution, etc. Has some advantages over Mitchell's *European historical statistics,* but 'Flora's presentation of data in reverse chronological order unnecessarily confusing' (*Choice,*v.25(4), December 1987, p.605). *Class No:* 310(400)(091)

Great Britain

Bibliographies

[1221]

GREAT BRITAIN. Central Statistical Office. **Guide to official statistics** 2000. London, HMSO, 2000. £32. ISBN: 011621161x.

First published 1976.

Meant to cover all official and significant non-official sources published in the last 5 years. Annotated entries; also running commentary. *Class No:* 310(410)(01)

[1222]

—GREAT BRITAIN. Government Statistical Service. **Government statistics:** a brief guide to sources. 1998 ed. London, HMSO, 1998. Annual. 50p. *Gratis.*

Short descriptions of the latest editions, arranged by subject: General background and reference - General digests - The economy - Defence - External trade - Transport, distribution and other services - Society - Environment - Overseas aid - Departmental responsibilities and contact points. *Class No:* 310(410)(01)

[1223]

GREAT BRITAIN. Interdepartmental Committee on Social and Economic Research. **Guides to official sources.** London., HMSO, 1948-61,nos.1-6.

1. *Labour statistics* (3rd ed., 1958) - 2. *Census reports of Great Britain, 1801-1931* (1051) - 3. *Local government statistics*(1953) - 4. *Agricultural and food statistics* (1961. Superseded by *Select list of reference books in agriculture, fisheries and food*) - 5. *Social security statistics* (1961) - 6. *Census of production reports*(1961) 'Intended to assist research workers, students and others who have occasion to use the extensive range of information on economic and social matters made available by government departments in official reports and papers'. *Class No:* 310(410)(01)

[1224]

MORT, D. *and* WILKINS, W. **Sources of unofficial UK statistics.** University of Warwick. Business Information Service, *ed.* 4th. Aldershot, Hants., Gower, 1999. 340p. £65. ISBN: 0566082365.

First published 1986, compiled by D. Mort and L. Siddell.

Gives details of almost 900 publications and services produced by trade associations, professional bodies, banks, forecasting agencies, etc. Titles and services are listed alphabetically by publisher. *Class No:* 310(410)(01)

[1225]

Reviews of United Kingdom statistical sources. Maunder, W.F., *(to 1987) and* Fleming, M.C, *(from 1985), eds.* London, Chapman & Hall (v.1-5 published by Heinemann Educational Books; v.6-21 by Pergamon Press), 1974- v.1-.

Succeeds M.G. Kendall's *Sources and nature of the statistics of the United Kingdom* (1952-1957. 2v.). Sponsored by The Royal Statistical Society and The Economic and Social Research Council.

1:1. Personal social services. 2. Voluntary organizations in the personal social service field. 1974.

2:3. Central government routine health statistics. 4. Social security statistics. 1974.

3:5. Housing in Great Britain. 6. Housing in Northern Ireland. 1974.

4:7. Leisure. 8. Tourism. 1975.

5:9. General sources of statistics, by G.F. Lock. 1976.

6:10 Wealth. 11. Personal incomes. 1978 (£35. ISBN 6080224504).

7:12. Road passenger transport. 13. Road goods transport. 1978.

8:14. Land use. 15. Town and country planning. 1978.

9. Health surveys and related studies. 1979. (£75. ISBN 0080224598).

10. Ports and inland waterways; and civil aviation. 1978.

11. Coal; gas; and electricity. 1979.

12. Construction and the related professions. 1980.

13. Wages and earnings. 1980. (£40. ISBN 0080240607).

14. Rail and sea transport. 1981. (£44. ISBN 0080261051).

15. Crime. 1981. (£52. ISBN 0080261043).

16. Iron and steel. 1984. (£23. ISBN 0080301916).

17. Weather and water. 1985. (£52. ISBN 0080318444).

18. Ports and telecommunications. 1986. (£29. ISBN 0080339670). 505.00/18$a19. Intellectual property. 1986.(ISBN 0080339026).

20. Religion. Recurrent Christian sources; Non-recurrent Christian data; Judaism; Other religions. 1987 (£97. ISBN 0080347789).

21. Financial data of banks and other institutions; Life assurance and pension funds. (ISBN 0080347800).

22. Printing and publishing. 1987. ISBN 0080347819)

23. Agriculture. 1988. (£35. ISBN 0412316706).

24. Local government. 1988. (£42.50. ISBN 0412316803).

25. Family planning. 1988. (£35. ISBN 0412316900).

26. International aspects of UK economic activities. 1991. (£49. ISBN 0412356503).

27. Research and development. 1993. (ISBN 0412356406)

28. The food industries. 1993. (ISBN 0412356600)

Class No: 310(410)(01)

[1226]

United Kingdom statistical sources: a selection guide for libraries. McShane, P., *ed.* 4th ed. London, Library Association's Information Services Group, for the Committee of Librarians and Statisticians, 1985. 24p. £5. ISBN: 0946347069.

'Basic minimum list' (10 annotated items), p.6-8. Extended list, (163 items), p.9-24. Subject sections: General statistical compilations - Agriculture, fishery and food ... Education, science and technology - Energy - Banking, insurance and finance - Foreign trade and balance of payments - Health , personal social services, social security - Housing, construction and property - Industrial production, distribution and other services - Justice and crime - Labour - Population, households and vital statistics - Public finance and taxation - Tourism, entertainment and leisure - Transport and communications. No index. *Class No:* 310(410)(01)

Periodicals

[1227]

Statistical news: developments in British official statistics. London, HMSO., 1968-. no.1-. Quarterly. £33pa; £8 single issue. ISSN: 00173630.

Each issue contains 2 or more articles dealing with a subject in depth. Shorter notes give news of latest developments in many fields, including international statistics. Cumulative analytical index. Lists recently available statistical series and publications. *Class No:* 310(410)(051)

Yearbooks & Directories

[1228]

Annual abstract of statistics, 1999. Central Statistical Office. No.135. London, HMSO, 1999. Annual. 461p. tables. £39.50. ISBN: 0116210680. ISSN: 00725730.

First published 1946. Continues *Statistical abstract,* 1st, 1840/53-83rd, 1924/38, compiled by the Board of Trade.

Covers: Area, Population and vital statistics, Social conditions, Law enforcement, Education, Employment, Defence, Production, Agriculture, fisheries and food, Transport and communications, Distributive trades, Research and development, External trade, Balance of payments, National income and expenditure, Personal income, expenditure and wealth, Home finance, Banking, insurance, etc., Prices. Sources appended to tables. Index of sources (by chapters). Index. Indispensable for British libraries. *Class No:* 310(410)(058)

[1229]

—Monthly digest of statistics. Central Statistical Office. London, HMSO, 1946-. £7.50 each; £85pa incl. supplement. ISSN: 03086666.

Supplements many of the tables in the *Annual abstract,* and its January issue carries a supplement: *Definitions and explanatory notes.* But the *Annual abstract* generally gives greater detail for comparable series and includes many other series that, by their nature, can only be included in an annual publication. *Class No:* 310(410)(058)

[1230]

Regional trends 30. Central Statistical Office. London, Stationery Office Books, 2000. Annual. 250p. maps, tables. £39.50. ISBN: 0116212713. ISSN: 02611783.

First published 1965. Nos. 1-17 were titled *Regional statistics.*

Provides a comprehensive source of official statistics about the regions of the UK. Regional profiles, statistics for the EU and sub-regional statistics are given, as well as data on each of the main topic areas, including population, education, the labour market and industry. *Class No:* 310(410)(058)

Histories

[1231]

MITCHELL, B.R. **British historical statistics.** Cambridge, Cambridge University Press, 1988. 886p. 322 tables. £80. ISBN: 0521330084.

Supplants the author's two previous volumes, *Abstract of British historical statistics* and *Second abstract of British historical statistics.*

Contains the major economic and social statistical series for the British Isles from the earliest available, in the 12th century to 1980/81. Tables are grouped under 16 subject headings: Population and vital statistics - Labour force (including wages) - Agriculture - Industry (5 sections) - External trade - Transport and communications - Public finance - Financial institutions - Consumption - Prices - Miscellaneous (inc. crime and education) - National accounts. Subject index. A standard reference work. *Class No:* 310(410)(091)

Scotland

[1232]

GREAT BRITAIN. Scottish Office. **Scottish abstract of statistics, 1998.** No.26. Edinburgh, HMSO, 1998. £25. ISBN: 0748071865.

First published 1971. Annual. Together with the *Scottish economic bulletin,* it replaces *Digest of Scottish statistics* (1953-71).

Data arranged in 16 subject sections (1. Population and vital statistics - 2. Social security - 3. Health services ... 9. Labour ... 12. Industrial activity ... 15. Finance - 16. Environment). Footnotes. *Class No:* 310(411)

[1233]

HORN, M. **Scottish Office statistical publications.** In *Statistical news,* no.1, Winter 1990, p.91.5-91.9.

Describes the statistical publications of the Scottish Office and advises how to obtain them. *Class No:* 310(411)

Northern Ireland

Yearbooks & Directories

[1234]

Digest of information on the Northern Ireland criminal justice system. Great Britain. Northern Ireland Office. Statistics and Research Branch. 3rd ed. Belfast, HMSO, 1998. xii,131p.,illus. £15.80. ISBN: 0337031010. *Class No:* 310(416)(058)

Eire

[1235]

GREAT BRITAIN. Northern Ireland Statistics and Research Agency. **The Northern Ireland annual abstract of statistics, 1999.** London, Stationery Office Books, 1999. £20. ISBN: 0114972710. ISSN: 02676044.

Divided into subject sections. Tables. Bibliography. *Class No:* 310(417)

Wales

[1236]

WILLIAMS, J. **Digest of Welsh historical statistics.** Department of Economic and Social History. University College of Wales, Aberystwyth. Cardiff, The Welsh Office, 1985. 2v. (x,359; x,356p.). maps. ISBN: 0863481205, v.1; 086348140x, v.2.

In English and Welsh. Data is arranged in 13 sections, all subdivided, covering various years. *Class No:* 310(429)

[1237]

—WILLIAMS, L.J. Digest of Welsh historical statistics, 1974-1996 Cardiff, Government Statistical Office, 1998. xiv,342p.,col.maps. *Class No:* 310(429)

Federal Republic of Germany

[1238]

GERMANY (FEDERAL REPUBLIC). Statistisches Bundesamt. **Statistisches Jahrbuch für die Bundesrepublik Deutschland.** Wiesbaden, Statistiches Bundesamt.

First published 1952-. Annual.

27 subject sections. Data is for several years. List of German official statistical publications. Subject index. In German only.

Supplemented by the monthly *Wirtschaft und Statistik* (1949-. ISSN 00436143) the second half of which consists of *Statistisches monatszahlen.* *Class No:* 310(430.1)

Luxembourg

[1239]

LUXEMBOURG. Service Central de la Statistique et des études Économiques. **Annuaire statistique.** Luxembourg, STATEC. various pagings. FLux ll00 ISSN: 00761575.

First published 1955. Annual.

Arranged in 22 subject sections and an international section. *Class No:* 310(435.9)

Austria

[1240]

AUSTRIA. Statistisches Zentralamt. **Statistisches Jahrbuch für die Republik Österreich.** New series. Vienna, the Office.

First published 1950. Annual.

Arranged in 36 subject chapters, plus an international chapter.

Supplemented by the monthly *Statistisches Nachrichten* (1946-). *Class No:* 310(436)

Poland

[1241]

POLAND. Glówny Ürzad Statystyczny. **Rocznik statystyczny.** Warsaw, the Central Statistical Office. ISSN: 00792780.

First published 1941. Annual.

Includes *c.*150 tables arranged in subject sections, with data for several years. Subject index. In Polish, but a translation of the text is available separately in English. Supplemented by the monthly *Biuletyn statystyczny.* *Class No:* 310(438)

Hungary

[1242]

HUNGARY. Központi Statisztikai Hivatal. **Magyar statisztikai evkönyv. Statistical yearbook.** Budapest, 'Kultura'. ISSN: 00734039.

First published in 1965. Annual.

Contains 27 subject sections, with statistical tables.

Supplemented by the monthly *Statisztikai havi közlemények* (ISSN 0018781x). There is also *Statistical pocket book for Hungary,* published annually. *Class No:* 310(439)

France

[1243]

FRANCE. Institut National de la Statistique et des Études économiques. **Annuaire statistique de la France.** Paris, the Institute.

First published 1978. Annual.

Data arranged in subject sections, all subdivided, with statistics for several years. A list of tables, an index, and sources (organizations) are printed on tinted paper.

Supplemented by the *Bulletin mensuel de statistique* (1950-. ISSN 00074713). *Class No:* 310(44)

Italy

[1244]

ITALY. Istituto Centrale di Statistica. **Annuario statistico italiano.** Roma, the Institute. ISSN: 00664545.

First published 1878. Annual.

Supplemented by the monthly *Bollettino mensile di statistica* (1926-. ISSN 00213136). *Compendio statistico italiano* (ISSN 00697958) is a shortened version of the yearbook.

Data arranged in subject sections, with a section of international statistics. Notes on methods. *Class No:* 310(450)

Malta
[1245]

MALTA. Central Office of Statistics. **Annual abstract of statistics.** Valletta, the Office.

First published 1947. Annual.

Data arranged in subject sections. Detailed contents list, but no index.

Supplemented by the Office's *Quarterly digest of statistics* (1960-).
Class No: 310(458.2)

Spain
[1246]

SPAIN. Instituto Nacional de Estadística. **Anuario estadístico de España.** Madrid, the Institute. maps. ISSN: 08930003.

First published 1913. Annual.

In two parts: part 1 has national statistics in subject sections, plus an international section; part 2 has regional data. Subject index.

Supplemented by the monthly *Boletín de estadística* (1918-. ISSN 00386391). *Class No:* 310(460)

Portugal
[1247]

PORTUGAL. Instituto Nacional de Estatística. **Anuário estatístico de Portugal = Statistical yearbook of Portugal.** Lisbon, the Institute. *c.*300p. ISSN: 00794112.

First published 1875. Annual. Prior to independence of the Portuguese colonies in 1974, the yearbook was in 2v., the second volume dealing with Portuguese territories overseas.

Data arranged in sections including one for international statistics, with data for Portugal, the Azores, and Madeira. Subject index. In Portuguese and French.

Supplemented by the *Boletín mensal de estatística* (1929. ISSN 00325082), which includes a list of publications of the institute.
Class No: 310(469)

Russia

Yearbooks & Directories
[1248]

Russia & Eurasia facts & figures annual (formerly *USSR facts and figures annual*). Karasik, T.W., *ed.* Gulf Breeze, FL, Academic International Press. tables, maps. ISBN: 0875691722. ISSN: 01487760.

First published 1972.

An annual review of developments in the countries of Russia and Eurasia, providing recent basic data on government, political parties, military and security, health and welfare, energy and environment, foreign trade and aid, or as much as is available.
Class No: 310(47)(058)

Scandinavia
[1249]

NORDIC STATISTICAL SECRETARIAT, *ed.* Yearbook of Nordic statistics. Copenhagen, Nordic Council of Ministers and the Nordic Statistical Secretariat. ISSN: 00781088.

First published 1962. Annual.

Statistical tables in sections, covering all the important economic and social statistics for Denmark, Finland, Iceland, Norway and Sweden. Tables are retrospective for 5-10 years. Explanatory footnotes; sources; bibliography; list of statistical reports; English/Swedish vocabulary; measures and weights. Introduction and headings in English and Swedish. *Class No:* 310(48)

Finland
[1250]

FINLAND. Tilastokeskus. **Suomen tilastollinen vuosikirja.** Helsinki, Tilastokeskus. ISSN: 00815063.

First published 1879.

The Finnish Central Statistical Office's statistical yearbook of Finland, has subject chapters plus an international section on yellow-tinted paper, with statistical tables for several years. Lists of official statistical publications. Subject index. In Finnish, Swedish and English. Supplemented by the monthly bulletin of statistics, *Tilastokatsauksia* (1924-. ISSN 00152390). *Class No:* 310(480)

Norway
[1251]

NORWAY. Statistisk Sentralbyra. **Statistisk årbok/Statistical yearbook of Norway.** Oslo, the Bureau. ISSN: 03778908.

First published 1880. Annual.

Arranged in 7 main sections, each subdivided: Survey of geography - Natural resources and environment - Socio-demographic subject matters - Industrial subject matters - General economic matters - Social organizations — International tables. In Norwegian and English.

Supplemented by the monthly *Statistisk månedshefte* (1882-. ISSN 00293636), also in Norwegian and English. *Class No:* 310(481)

Sweden
[1252]

SWEDEN. Statistiska Centralbyrån. **Statistisk arsbok för Sverige.** Stockholm, the Bureau, 1914-. Annual. ISSN: 00815381.

Subject sections, with *c.*450 tables, plus an international section. Detailed list of Swedish official statistical publications. Subject index. In Swedish and English.

Supplemented by the monthly *Allmän månadsstatistisk* (1963-.).
Class No: 310(485)

Denmark
[1253]

DENMARK. Danmarks Statistik. **Statistisk arbog:** Statistical yearbook. København, Danmarks Statistik, 1887-. Annual. ISSN: 00703567.

Sections on Denmark as a whole and 13 subject sections. Also sections for the Faroe Islands, Greenland, and international data. List of official statistical publications. Index of subjects (in English and Danish). Supplemented by the monthly *Statistisk månedsoverigt.* (ISSN 01085603). *Class No:* 310(489)

Netherlands
[1254]

NETHERLANDS. Centraal Bureau voor de Statistiek. **Statistical yearbook of the Netherlands.** Voorburg, the Bureau, 1881-. Annual. ISSN: 03036448.

Published only in English. Subject index. List of official statistical publications. *Class No:* 310(492)

Belgium
[1255]

BELGIUM. Institut National de Statistique. **Annuaire statistique de la Belgique.** Brussels, the Institute. ISSN: 07700415.

First published 1870. Annual.

29 subject chapters plus an international section. Subject index.

Supplemented by the monthly *Bulletin de statistique* (1909-) which includes some regional statistics. *Class No:* 310(493)

Switzerland
[1256]

SWITZERLAND. Eidgenössisches Statistisches Amt. **Statistisches Jahrbuch der Schweiz/Annuaire statistiques de la Suisse.** Berne, The Bureau. maps. ISSN: 00815330.

First published 1891. Annual.

The *Monatsbericht* (SwF.40pa) of the Schweizerische Nationalbank is a mainly statistical publication, and can be used to update the above.

20 main subject sections, with statistical tables for several years. Subject index. *Class No:* 310(494)

Liechtenstein
[1257]

LIECHTENSTEIN. Amt für Volkswirtschaft. **Statistisches Jahrbuch.** Vaduz, the Office. *Gratis.*

First published 1960. Annual.

Arranged in 22 subject sections, with data for several years.
Class No: 310(494.9)

Greece
[1258]

GREECE. Ethnike Statistike Yperesia. **Statistical yearbook of Greece.** Athens, National Printing Office. maps. diagrs.

First published 1930. Annual.

Title varies. In Greek and English. Subject chapters plus an international chapter, with data for various years.

Supplemented by the Bank of Greece's *Monthly statistical bulletin* (ISSN 11050519) in English and Greek, with tables and graphs.
Class No: 310(495)

Yugoslavia

[1259]

YUGOSLAVIA. Savezni Zavod za Statistiku. **Statisticki godisnjak FNRJ.** Beograd, the Office. maps. ISSN: 05851920.
First published 1954. Annual.
Subject sections plus an international review. Data after 1992 covers only Montenegro and Serbia. In Serbian.
Supplemented by the monthly *Indeks* (ISSN 00193585).
Class No: 310(497.1)

Bulgaria

Yearbooks & Directories

[1260]

BULGARIA. Natsionalen Statisticheski Institut. **Statisticheski godishnik = Statistical yearbook: Bulgaria.** Sofia, the Institute. ISSN: 02044838.
First published 1956. Annual.
A general overview with 22 subject sections, followed by a sectoral overview of 14 sections and 7 sections of international statistics. Detailed table of contents, but no subject index. In Bulgarian. Supplemented by the office's Statisticheski isvestia [statistical news] (quarterly ISSN 0204563x). *Class No:* 310(497.2)(058)

Romania

[1261]

ROMANIA. Comisa Nationala Pentru Statistica. **Anuarul statistic al României. Romanian statistical yearbook.** Bucharest, the Office.
Detailed chapter headings, but no index. Supplemented by the quarterly *Buletin statistic trimestrial* (1958-). *Class No:* 310(498)

Asia

Bibliographies

[1262]

HARVEY, J.M. **Statistics: Asia & Australia:** sources for social, economic and market research. 2nd ed. Beckenham, Kent, CBD Research Ltd., 1983. xiv, 440p. ISBN: 0900246413.
First published 1974.
2777 entries. Asia & Australasia (in general), nos. 1-420; then by countries, A-Z (Australia, nos. 449-674; Central Statistical Office; Libraries; Libraries and information services abroad; Bibliographies; Statistical publications, A-H (A. General; B. Production; C. External trade; D. Internal distribution and service trades; E. Population; F. Standard of living; G. Finance; H. Transport and communcation). Indexes of organizations, title and subjects. *Class No:* 310(5)(01)

Yearbooks & Directories

[1263]

UNITED NATIONS. Economic Commission for Asia and the Pacific. **Statistical yearbook for Asia and the Pacific, 1999.** Bangkok, the Commission, 1999. £65. ISBN: 9211198984. ISSN: 02523655.
First published 1970. Annual. Prior to 1974 the name of the Commission was Economic Commission for Asia and the Far East and of the publication *Statistical yearbook for Asia and the Far East.*
Covers 42 countries, arranged A-Z, with figures up to 1987. Each country entry is divided into sections (Population - Labour - National accounts - Agriculture, forestry, fishing - Industry - Energy - Transport and communications - External trade - Wages, prices and consumption - Finance - Social statistics). Updated by the *Quarterly bulletin of statistics for Asia and the Pacific* (1971-. ISSN 01250019). *Class No:* 310(5)(058)

China

[1264]

China: facts and figures annual, 1999 Friske, J.D., *ed.* v.24. Gulf Breeze, FL., Academic International Press, 1999. $90.
First published 1979. Annual.
Content varies each year. Sections cover: survey; summary of social and economic indicators; government; party; international relations; military; population; economy; resources; energy; industry; sports; society. *Class No:* 310(510)

[1265]

CHINA. State Statistical Bureau. **Statistical yearbook of China.** Beijing, Economic Information Agency. ISBN: 9627349186.
First published 1981. Annual.
Arranged in subject chapters, with national and provincial data for economic and social development. The English edition of the Chinese language *Zhongguo tongji nianjian.*
Supplemented by the State Statistical Bureau's *Monthly bulletin of statistics - China* (1986-). *Class No:* 310(510)

[1266]

China statistical abstract, 1990. New York, Praeger, 1991. 128p. £52.50. ISBN: 0275938697.
Data taken from statistical publications of the Statistical Bureau of the People's Republic of China.
Key statistics for principal sections of the national economy from 1978 to 1989. 9 sections: General survey - Population and labour force - Agriculture - Industry - Transportation, postal and telecommunications services - Investment in fixed assets - Finance, trade and prices - People's livelihood - Education, science and culture, public health and sports. *Class No:* 310(510)

Hong Kong

[1267]

HONG KONG. Census and Statistics Department. **Hong Kong monthly digest of statistics, 1978-.** Hong Kong, the Department. HK$48 each issue.
First published 1978, complementing *Hong Kong Statistics, 1947-1967* (1969).
Part 1: Regular tables in 11 subject sections, each subdivided; pt.2: Periodic tables; pt.3: special review articles, one in each of about five issues a year. *Class No:* 310(512.317)

Japan

[1268]

JAPAN. Statistics Bureau. Management and Coordination Agency. **Japan statistical yearbook.** Tokyo, the Bureau.
First published 1949. Annual.
Tables and charts in 23 chapters, plus an international chapter. In English and Japanese. 2 appendices (1. Key statistics - 2. Guide to sources (in Japanese only)). Index is in Japanese only.
Supplemented by *Monthly statistics of Japan* (1947-.).
Class No: 310(52)

[1269]

TSUNETA YANO MEMORIAL SOCIETY. **Nippon:** a charted survey of Japan. Tokyo, Kokusei-sha.
First published for 1936. Annual.
An English-language version of *Nihon Kokusai-Zue* (1927-). Data are mostly statistical. 45 chapters in 5 parts: 1. General aspects - 2. Economy in general - 3. Industries - 4. Social life and trends. Statistical sources. Index. *Class No:* 310(52)

India

[1270]

INDIA. Central Statistical Organisation. **Statistical abstract of the Indian Union.** New Delhi, Manager of Publications.
Contains tables and charts in subject sections. Sources are stated; includes footnotes and explanatory notes.
Supplemented by the *Monthly abstract of statistics* (1947-).
Class No: 310(540)

Bangladesh

[1271]

BANGLADESH. Bureau of Statistics. **Statistical yearbook of Bangladesh.** Dhaka, the Bureau.
First published 1975. Annual. Continues *Statistical digest,* published from 1966-1974.
Tables arranged in subject chapters. Updated by the *Statistical bulletin of Bangladesh* (monthly). An annual *Statistical pocket book of Bangladesh* (1978-) is also available. *Class No:* 310(549.3)

Turkey

[1272]

TURKEY. Devlet Istatistik Enstitüsü. **Türkiye istatistik yıllıgı. Statistical yearbook of Turkey.** Ankara, the Institute. maps. ISSN: 0082691x.
First published 1928. Annual.
Subject chapters, followed by a chapter of international statistics. Detailed list of contents but no subject index. In Turkish and English, Supplemented by the monthy bulletin, *Aylık istatistik bülteni.* (1952-. ISSN 00414263). *Class No:* 310(560)

Cyprus

[1273]

CYPRUS. Department of Statistics and Research. **Statistical abstract.** Nicosia, Printing Office of the Republic. maps. ISSN: 0253875x.
First published 1955. Annual.
Arranged in subject sections, with one being devoted to international statistics. Supplemented by *Monthly economic indicators* (ISSN 02538555). *Class No:* 310(564.3)

Israel

[1274]

ISRAEL. Central Bureau of Statistics. **Statistical abstract of Israel.** Jerusalem, the Bureau. ISSN: 00814679.

First published 1950. Annual.

In two parts, English and Hebrew. Subject chapters. Supplemented by the *Monthly bulletin of statistics* (ISSN 00211982). *Class No:* 310(569.4)

Thailand

[1275]

BANK OF THAILAND. **Quarterly bulletin.** Bangkok, the Bank, 1961-. B.650; $25. ISSN: 0125605x.

Includes a statistical section of 63 tables in each issue, on money and banking, public finance, foreign trade and payments, business capital, production and prices, rates of exchange, and the price of gold. Data is given for several years and quarters. *Class No:* 310(593)

[1276]

—WILSON, C.M. Thailand: a handbook of historical statistics. Boston, Mass., G.K. Hall, 1983. 360p. $80. ISBN: 0816181152.

Data collected between 1850 and 1979 is arranged under various chapter headings, including climate and land base, population, education, health, labour, transportation, communications, politics and government, money and banking, industry, and culture. *Class No:* 310(593)

Malaysia

[1277]

MALAYSIA. Department of Statistics. **Yearbook of statistics.** Kuala Lumpur, the Department, 1988. xxxi,334p. maps. Ringgit.12. ISSN: 01272624.

First published 1964. Early title was *Annual statistical bulletin, Malaysia.* Annual.

Brings together statistics for Sabah, Sarawak, and Peninsular Malaysia as well as data for Malaysia as a whole. Arranged in 19 subject sections with data for 4 or 5 years to 1985 or 1986. *Class No:* 310(595)

Africa

Bibliographies

[1278]

HARVEY, J.M. **Statistics Africa:** sources for social, economic and market research. 2nd ed. Beckenham, Kent, CBD Research Ltd., 1978. xii, 374p. £25. $80. ISBN: 090024626x.

First published 1970.

1461 entries covering the whole continent and adjacent islands. Sections: Africa, then countries A-Z. Data on central statistical offices, libraries with collections of statistical publications, principal bibliographies, and major statistical publications arranged in 8 subject groups (general, production, external trade, internal distribution and service trades, population, social, finance, transport and communication). *Class No:* 310(6)(01)

Egypt

[1279]

ARAB REPUBLIC OF EGYPT. Central Agency for Public Mobility and Statistics. **Statistical yearbook, 1952-91.** Cairo, the Agency, 1992. xvi,296p.

First published for 1952-64. Annual.

Sections: Population and consumption - Agriculture - Industry and petrol... Tourism - Economy - Useful information - International population information. *Class No:* 310(620)

Mali

[1280]

Mali: a handbook of historical statistics. Imperato, P.J. *and* Imperato, E.M. Boston, Mass., G.K. Hall, 1982. 364p. $86. ISBN: 0816181470.

Chapter headings include climate and landbase, population, education, labour, transportation, communications, politics and government, money and banking, industry and culture. *Class No:* 310(662.1)

Zimbabwe

[1281]

ZIMBABWE. Central Statistical Office. **Statistical yearbook of Zimbabwe,.** Harare, the Office.

First published 1986.

Statistical data arranged in subject chapters, each beginning with a list of the tables in that chapter. Supplemented by *Quarterly digest of statistics.* *Class No:* 310(689.1)

America

Bibliographies

[1282]

HARVEY, J.M. **Statistics America:** sources for social, economic and market research (North, Central and South America). 2nd ed., rev. & enl. Beckenham, Kent, CBD Research Ltd., 1980. xiv, 385p. £43.50. $185. ISBN: 0900246332.

First published 1973.

1592 entries. 'America', nos. 1-335: Some international organizations publishing statistics; Libraries and information services; Bibliographies; Statistical publications (A. General; B. Production; C. External trade; D. Internal distribution and service trades; E. Population; F. Social; G. Finance; H. Transport and communication). 56 countries, A-Z. Entries are annotated; prices given; language(s) of publication stated. Many cross-references. Indexes of organizations, titles and subjects. A basic source in this field. *Class No:* 310(7)(01)

America—North

Bibliographies

[1283]

Statistics sources, 2000. O'Brien, J.W. *and* Wasserman, S.R. 23th ed. Detroit, Mich., Gale Research Inc., 1999. 2v. $445. ISBN: 0787624624. ISSN: 0585198x.

First published 1962.

Citations arranged under 20,000 specific subject headings, including geographic headings for states and individual countries, in a single alphabetical sequence. Citations mainly to United States and Canadian publications, with a few publications of international organizations (*e.g.* the United Nations Statistical Office's *Statistical yearbook*). Directory of federal statistical telephone contacts, guiding users to experts within the federal government. *Class No:* 310(71+73)(01)

Canada

Bibliographies

[1284]

CANADA. Statistics Canada. **Statistics Canada: catalogue.** Ottawa, Statistics Canada. ISSN: 08384223.

Issued annually.

In 8 parts: 1. General - 2. Primary industries - 3. Manufacturing - 5. Transport, communications & utilities - 6. Commerce, construction, finance and prices - 7. Employment, unemployment and labour income - 8. Education, culture, health and welfare - 9. Census publications. Subject/title index. Brief annotations to the entries. *Class No:* 310(71)(01)

[1285]

Directory of statistics in Canada, 1985-. McClelland, R., *ed.* Toronto, Micromedia Ltd., 1986 - Annual. Can $190.

Formerly *Canadian statistics index.*

Initially included only English-language or bilingual material from Statistics Canada and other federal or provincial government bodies, but the scope is to be expanded. *Class No:* 310(71)(01)

Yearbooks & Directories

[1286]

CANADA. Statistics Canada. **Canada year book ... a review of economic, social and political developments in Canada, 1994.** Ottawa, Statistics Canada, 1994. various pagings, maps. ISBN: 0660151863.

First published 1905. Annual.

22 subject chapters, including many tables with the text. 6 appendices. Detailed analytical index. *Class No:* 310(71)(058)

Cuba

[1287]

CUBA. Dirección Central de Estadística. **Anuario estadístico de Cuba.** Habana, Comité Estatal de Estadística.

First published for 1966/67. Annual.

In Spanish. Supplemented by the quarterly *Boletín estadístico de Cuba.* *Class No:* 310(729.1)

Jamaica

[1288]

JAMAICA. Department of Statistics. **Statistical yearbook of Jamaica.** Kingston, the Department. maps.

First published 1973. Annual.

Arranged in subject chapters, with an introduction to each chapter. *Class No:* 310(729.2)

Latin America

[1289]

UNITED NATIONS. Economic Commission for Latin America and the Caribbean. **Anuario estadístico para América Latina y el Caribe ... Statistical year-book for Latin America and the Caribbean.** New York, United Nations. ISSN: 02519445.

First published for 1973. Annual.

An introduction, technical notes, and a list of sources precede the main part of the volume. Pt.1. Indicators of economic and social development ... (6 subject sections, with tables). Statistical series ... (11 sections with over 374 tables). Statistics are given for the area as a whole and for individual countries. *Class No:* 310(729.99)

USA

Databases

[1290]

EVINGER, W.R., *comp*. **Federal statistical data bases:** a comprehensive catalog of current machine-readable and on-line files. Phoenix, AZ., Oryx, 1988. 671p. $132.50. ISBN: 0897742559.

Updates US department of Commerce's *Directory of Federal statistical data files* (1981).

Files arranged by agency or department producing them. Entry for each file contains description of information in the file, and technical description of file characteristics (*e.g.* structure, size and tape format). Also A-Z listing of files by title. *Class No:* 310(73)(003.4)

Bibliographies

[1291]

American statistics index: a comprehensive guide and index to the statistical publications of the United States government. Washington, Congressional Information Service, 1973-, v.1-. Annual, with monthly and quarterly cumulations; bound annual supplements. price varies. ISSN: 00911658.

Each issue is in two parts: Index and Abstracts. The index volume has indexes by subjects and names, categories, titles, and agency report numbers; the abstracts volume has numbered abstracts arranged by government department, subdivided by division, service, etc., then by form (annuals & biennials, special & irregular publications, publications in series, reports, etc.); *c.*500 abstracts per issue. Database covers 1973- (DIALOG), also on CD-ROM (Statistical Masterfile). *Class No:* 310(73)(01)

[1292]

—**Statistical reference index:** to current American statistical publications from sources other than the US Government. Bethesda, MD., Congressional Information Service Inc., 1980-. v.1,no.1-. Monthly; quarterly and annual cumulations. (Also 5-year cumulated indexes). ISSN: 0278694x.

A companion serial to *American statistics index* (*qv*). Indexes and abstracts serial and monograph statistical publications of trade and professional associations, business organizations, commercial publishers, university and independent research centres, and state government agencies. Published in 2 parts: *Index,* providing access to the abstracts through 4 basic indexes (subjects and names, categories, issuing sources, and titles; and *Abstracts,* containing full bibliographical data and detailed descriptions of the items). Also available on CD-ROM (Statistical Masterfile). *Class No:* 310(73)(01)

[1293]

Guide to US government statistics. Andriot, D., *and others, eds*. 5th ed. McLean, VA., Documents Index, 1986. ix,686p. $215. ISSN: 04349067.

4th ed. published in 1973.

Identifies and annotates 11,945 recent monographic and serial publications reporting statistical data. Arranged by issuing agency in SuDocs order. Each agency has brief description of its creation and authority and address for further information. Each statistical publication, listed under its agency, has title, issuing agency, collation, item number, stock number, Library of Congress number, Dewey number, SuDocs number, price, ISSN, L.C. card number, OCLC number, and notes. Preferred to Wasserman's *Statistics sources* (10th ed. Gale, 1986) by *Reference books bulletin* (1986/87) who consider competitor is *American statistics index* (monthly). *Class No:* 310(73)(01)

[1294]

STRATFORD, J. *and* STRATFORD, J.S. **Guide to statistical materials produced by government and associations in the United States.** Alexandria, VA., Chadwyck-Healey Inc., 1987. 279p. £100. (*Government documents bibliographies.*) ISBN: 0859641279.

Intended as a bibliographical guide and acquisitions tool, the volume lists more than 700 statistical publications issued by US federal and state governments and membership associations. Includes only those publications that recur biennially or more frequently, and omits censuses. For each publication - citation, ISSN and LC card numbers, frequency, price, availability, annotation; for GPO publications also class number and depository item number. 5 appendixes, 3 on addresses of issuing sources, a glossary, and list of abbreviations used. Title and subject indexes (p.233-279). 'A useful supplement to existing statistical source books ...' (*Choice,* v.25(3), November 1987, p.460). *Class No:* 310(73)(01)

Yearbooks & Directories

[1295]

Statistical services directory: a guide to the organizations, corporations, professional and trade associations, research centers, universities, publishers, foundations and government agencies that provide statistical services. 2nd ed. Detroit, Mich., Gale Research Co., 1984. 461p. $150. ISBN: 0810306689. ISSN: 07326971.

First published 1982.

Over 2000 gatherers of statistical information are arranged A-Z by organization name, with address; telephone number; contact person; brief description of the organization, including subjects covered; methods of disseminating statistics; available formats; time period covered; dates of release and frequency; and cost of service. Over 500 subject areas covered. 4 indexes: subject index; geographic index; contact name index; and title index. *Class No:* 310(73)(058)

[1296]

UNITED STATES. Bureau of the Census. **Statistical abstract of the United States, 1999.** 119th ed. Washington, Hoovers Inc., 1999. £30.95. ISBN: 1573110604.

First published for 1878. Annual.

*c.*1500 tables and charts arranged in 31 sections: 1. Population ... 3. Health and nutrition ... 9. State and local government finances and employment ... 16. Banking, finance and insurance ... 19. Energy ... 25. Mining and mineral products ... 27. Manufactures - 28. Domestic trade and services - 29. Foreign commerce and aid ... 30. Outlying areas - 31. Comparative international statistics. 7 appendices: (1. Guide to sources of statistics ... 3. Statistical methodology and reliability). Detailed index, p.958-1009. A basic statistical tool. *Class No:* 310(73)(058)

[1297]

—UNITED STATES. Bureau of the Census. **Historical statistics of the United States: colonial times to 1970.** Washington, US Government Printing Office, 1976 (Reprinted 1989 by Kraus International Publications, White Plains, N.Y.). 2v. $58.50. ISBN: 0527917567.

Contains over 12,500 statistical time-series, largely annual, on American social, economic, political and geographic development, 1610 to 1970. Includes definitions of terms, descriptive text, specific source notes. Detailed subject index. *Class No:* 310(73)(058)

Brazil

[1298]

BRAZIL. Instituto Brasileiro de Geografia e Estatística. **Anuário estatístico do Brasil.** Rio de Janeiro, the Institute. ISSN: 01001299.

First published 1936. Annual.

Arranged in broad groups: Geographical area - Population - Agriculture and fisheries - Industry - Services, trade, transport and communications - Prices, wages, indices - Macroeconomics (money and finance). Text in Portuguese. *Class No:* 310(81)

Chile

[1299]

Historical statistics of Chile. Mamalakis, M.J., *comp*. Westport, CT, Greenwood Press, 1978-89. 6v. tables. $175. £125 each volume. ISBN: 0313206198, v.1; 0313208549, v.2; 0313208565, v.3; 0313208565, v.4; 0313251363, v.5; 0313265631, v.6.

V.1: National accounts; v.2: Demography and labour force; v.3: Forestry and related activities; v.4: Money, prices and credit services; v.5: Money, banking and financial services; v.6: Government services and public sector, and a theory of services. Mainly statistical tables, but also a number of brief essays. *Class No:* 310(83)

Indonesia

[1300]
INDONESIA. Biro Pusat Statistik. **Statistik Indonesia/Statistical yearbook of Indonesia**. Djakarta, the Central Bureau of Statistics. ISSN: 01262912.
First published for 1975. Annual.
*c.*400 tables arranged in subject chapters. In Indonesian and English.
Class No: 310(910)

New Zealand

[1301]
NEW ZEALAND. Department of Statistics. **Official yearbook.** Wellington, the Department. illus., tables, maps.
First published 1892.
Subject chapters. Appendices include a glossary of statistical terms; weights and measures; Department of Statistics publications; Index. Supplemented by *Key statistics: a monthly abstract of statistics* (1914-. NZ$295pa. ISSN 01142119). *Class No:* 310(931)

[1302]
—BLOOMFIELD, G.T. New Zealand a handbook of historical statistics. Boston, Mass., G.K. Hall, 1984. 252p. $65. ISBN: 0816181683.
Contains data from 1840 to the early 1980s, chronicling the nation's growth and development. *Class No:* 310(931)

Australia

Bibliographies

[1303]
HAGGER, A.J. A Guide to Australian economic and social statistics. Sydney, Pergamon Press, 1983. ix,116p. (*Guides to Australian information sources.*) ISBN: 0080298338.
7 sections: 1. Australian economic and social statistics: the broad picture - 2. Population - 3. Social statistics - 4. Economic accounts - 5. Labour and prices - 6. Public finance, industry and overseas trade - 7. Economic and social statistics produced outside the ABS. Index.
Class No: 310(94)(01)

Yearbooks & Directories

[1304]
AUSTRALIA. Bureau of Statistics. **Year book Australia.** Canberra, the Bureau. tables,maps. ISSN: 08108633.
First published 1908. Annual.
Subject chapters of text, with many maps and tables, and an appended statistical summary. Analytical index. List of special articles published in previous issues. Updated by *Monthly summary of statistics, Australia* (1912-. Early issues were quarterly. ISSN 07271689). *Class No:* 310(94)(058)

Statistical Theory

[1305]
CHAPMAN, M. *and* WYKES, C. **Plain figures.** Cabinet Office, Management and Personnel Office *and* Civil Service College. 2nd ed. London, Stationery Office Books, 1996. 150p. £29.95. ISBN: 0117020397.
'The aim of this book is to demonstrate and discuss ways of presenting numbers effectively so that their value can be realised in full. A subsidiary aim is to help the reader interpret all data more competently and confidently' (*Introduction*). Contents: 1. General principles for presenting data - 2. Summary of recommendations - 3. Structure and style of tables - 4. Demonstration tables - 5. Reference tables - 6. Charts - 7. Effective charts for general use - 8. Words. Appendices: A. Tables and charts as visual aids - B. Further reading - C. Research evidence - D. Bibliography. *Class No:* 311

Bibliographies

[1306]
Short book reviews. Voorburg, Netherlands, International Statistical Institute, 1981-. 3pa. $12 pa. ISSN: 02547694.
Prior to 1981 reviews were carried in the Institute's *Revue internationale de statistique* (1933-1971) and then *International statistical review*, 1972-.
Provides a rapid book review service for statisticians covering books on statistics and related subjects published throughout the world.
Class No: 311(01)

Dictionaries

Polyglot

[1307]
PAENSON, I. **Systematic glossary of the terminology of statistical methods.** Oxford, Permanon Press, 1970. xxxviii,517p. £96.
The glossary is in English-French-Spanish-Russian.
Class No: 311(038)=00

Histories

[1308]
STIGLER, S.M. **The History of statistics:** the measurement of uncertainty before 1900. Cambridge, Mass., Belknap Press of Harvard University Press, 1986. xvi,410p. illus., figs., tables. $27. ISBN: 0674403401.
10 chapters in 3 parts: 1. The development of mathematical statistics in astronomy and geodesy before 1827 - 2. The struggle to extend a calculus of probabilities to social sciences - 3. A breakthrough in studies of heredity. Appendices A & B are syllabuses. Suggested readings, p.370-373, by chapter. Bibliography p.374-398, A-Z, Index, p.399-410. '... an incredibly rich source of ideas ... (*Contemporary psychology*, v.33(4), April 1988, p.293-295). *Class No:* 311(091)

Population

Bibliographies

[1309]
Population index. Princeton, N.J., Office of Population Research (previously School of Public Affairs), for Population Association of America, 1935-. v.1-. Quarterly. charts, tables. $85pa. ISSN: 00324701.
Fall 1991 issue has 842 indicative, analytical abstracts. Contents include 'Current items' (documented), 'Bibliography': A. General population studies and theories - B. Regional population studies - C. Spatial distribution - D. Trends in population growth and size - E. Mortality - F. Fertility - G. Nuptiality and the family - H. Migration - I. Historical demography and demographic history - J. Characteristics - K. Demographic and economic interrelations and natural resources - L. Demographic and non-economic interrelations - M. Policies - N. Methods of research and analysis including models - O. The production of population statistics - P. Professional meetings and conferences - Q. Bibliographies, directories, and other information services - R. New periodicals - S. Official statistical publications - T. Machine-readable data files. Geographical and author indexes (cumulated annually). A first-class example of an annotated bibliography in a special field, covering periodical articles, monographs, statistical yearbooks and new journals. Available online (National Library of Medicine) and CD-ROM. *Class No:* 312(01)

[1310]
—'Population index' bibliography: cumulated 1969-1981, by authors and geographical areas ... Boston, Mass, G.K. Hall, 1984. 4v. $310.
Continues *'Population index' bibliography cumulated, 1935-1968, by authors and geographical areas* (Boston, Mass., G.K. Hall, 1971. 9v.).
V.1: author index; v.2: 1975-77; v.3/4: 1978-81.
Class No: 312(01)

[1311]
TEXAS UNIVERSITY. Population Research Center. **International population census bibliography.** Austin, Texas, Bureau of Business Research, University of Texas, 1965-67. 6v. Supplement, 1968.
V.1 Latin America and the Caribbean; v.2. Africa; v.3. Oceania; v.4. North America; v.5. Asia; v.6. Europe. Foreword to each volume mentions more general sources. V.5 deals with 47 countries, A-Z, with items in chronological order. Prefatory note on each country; parts of multi-volume works are detailed. Coverage of national, provincial, state and city censuses (India:102p.).
Updated in Goyer, D.S. *The international population census bibliography: revision and update, 1945-1977: Texas bibliography II* (New York, Academic Press, 1980. 20, 576p. (Studies in population, University of Wisconsin). *Class No:* 312(01)

[1312]
—DOMSCHKE, E. *and* GOYER, D.S. The Handbook of national population censuses. V.2: Africa and Asia. Westport, CT., Greenwood Press, 1986. xiii,[1],1032p. $195. £120. ISBN: 0313253617.
For each sovereign state or geographically separated area is provided a historical overview of the censuses conducted and a brief description of the content and geographic coverage of each specific national survey. No demographic data is included. Topographical index. *Class No:* 312(01)

[1313]

—DOMSCHKE, E. *and* GOYER, D.S. The Handbook of national population censuses. V.1: Latin America and the Caribbean, North America and Oceania. Westport, CT., Greenwood Press, 1983. xii,711p. $125.00. £69.96. ISBN: 0313213526.

A companion volume to the above. *Class No:* 312(01)

[1314]

—GOYER, D.S. *and* DRAAIJER, G.E. The Handbook of national population censuses. V.3: Europe. Westport, CT, Greenwood Press, 1992. 544p. $95. ISBN: 0313284261.

Includes all Europe, west of and including USSR, completing the series. 'A specialized but excellent guide ...'(*Choice*,v.30(6), February 1993, p.940). *Class No:* 312(01)

Encyclopaedias

[1315]

ROSS, J.A., *ed*. International encyclopedia of population. 2nd ed. New York, The Free Press; London, Collier Macmillan, 1982. 2v. (850p.). illus., tables, figs., maps. £116; $145. ISBN: 0029274400, v.1; 0029274609, v.2; 0029274303, set.

Concerned with the basic areas of population study (marriage, mortality, morbidity, migration, etc.) as well as interdisciplinary subjects (*e.g.* abortion). Includes corporate entries, which cover several related topics in the same article, and core entries, which define individual terms or concepts. Bibliographies follow all essays. Cross-references. '... should prove a basic reference source ...' (*Library journal,* 1 November 1982, p.2086). *Class No:* 312(031)

Handbooks & Manuals

[1316]

RHIND, D., *ed*. A Census user's handbook. London & New York, Methuen, 1983. xx,393p. £14.95. ISBN: 0416305105.

'Designed to be a guide to what is in and what can be obtained from the census; to what is good practice in analysing such data and what is definitely unwise' (*Introduction*). A list of tables, a list of figures, and a glossary of abbreviations precede 11 chapters (1. Censuses past and present - 2. The 1989 census and its results - 3. User needs: an overview - 4. Univariate analysis: presenting and summarizing single variables - 5. Creating new variables and new areas from the census - 6. Mapping census data ... 10. Linking census and other data - 11. Microdata from the British census). 8 appendices. Bibliography, p.375-388, A-Z by author. Name and subject indexes. *Class No:* 312(035)

Dictionaries

[1317]

PETERSEN, W. *and* PETERSEN, R. Dictionary of demography: terms, concepts and institutions. Westport, CT., Greenwood Press, 1984. 2v,. (c.1248p.). £125 for 2v. ISBN: 0313241341.

Relates to the past and present determinants and consequences of population trends throughout the world. The dictionary runs A-Z through the two volumes (A-M; N-Z), entries varying in length from a few lines to 2 or more pages. References, p.1015-6. Appendix: Classified list of institutes, organizations and associations. Index, p.1059-1154. *Class No:* 312(038)

[1318]

PRESSAT, R., *ed*. The Dictionary of demography. Wilson, C., *ed*. Oxford, Basil Blackwell Ltd., 1985. 368p. diagrs. £35. $60. ISBN: 0631127461.

First published in French (*Dictionnaire de démographie.* Paris, Presses Universitaires de France, 1979).

A dictionary of theories, concepts, techniques and technical terms relating to every aspect of contemporary and historical demography. The English edition has been adapted and includes many new entries from a team of some 30 international contributors. Entries range in length from 100 to 1000 words, illustrated where necessary with graphs and diagrams, and all but the shortest are followed by suggestions for further reading. Cross-references. British orientation; lacks some standard US concepts. Subject index. '... impressive, covers the subject well, and offers useful models, formulas, and graphs to illustrate specific points.' (*Choice,* February 1986, p.853). *Class No:* 312(038)

Polyglot

[1319]

LOGIE, G. Glossary of population and housing. Amsterdam, Elsevier, 1978. xxvii,266p. £89.90. (*International planning glossaries, v.1.*) ISBN: 0444417303.

Originally (1975) as 2v. in English, Dutch and German only.

825 English-base terms, with French, Italian, Dutch, German and Swedish equivalents. 17 subject sections (Demography - Migration - Statistics - Individuals - Populations - Age groups - Households - Family - Society - Housing policy - Slum area - Ownership -

....(contd.)

Housebuilding - Dwellings - Rooms - Density - Living climate). Signs denote terms that are only an approximate equivalent, and those officially recommended or disapproved. Bibliography (grouped). 6 language indexes. Favourably reviewed in *The Incorporated linguist,* v.18(4), Autumn 1979, p.118-9. *Class No:* 312(038)=00

[1320]

—COMMITTEE FOR INTERNATIONAL COORDINATION OF NATIONAL RESEARCH IN DEMOGRAPHY (CICRED). Population multilingual thesaurus ... Paris, CICRED/FNUAP, 1979. [3v.].

One volume is in English/French/Spanish; the other two have French and Spanish as the first language. *Class No:* 312(038)=00

[1321]

PETERSEN, W. *and* PETERSEN, R. Dictionary of demography: a multi-lingual glossary. New York, Greenwood Press, 1985. [2],260p. $100. ISBN: 0313251398.

Over 400 basic demography terms are listed A-Z in English, with translations into French, Spanish, Russian, Italian, German, Chinese and Japanese. The Russian is transliterated and the Japanese and Chinese terms are in European characters. Indexes refer from the other languages to English. *Class No:* 312(038)=00

Periodicals

[1322]

Population bulletin of the United Nations. United Nations. Department of International Economic and Social Affairs. New York, the Department, 1951-.no.1-. Bi-annual. ISSN: 04979133.

Publication was suspended from 1964 to 1975, recommencing in 1976 in a different format.

Presents brief articles on population which are aimed at research institutions and individuals who are engaged in social and economic research. (No.33. 1992, 125p. $9.00. ISBN 9211512425). *Class No:* 312(051)

Yearbooks & Directories

[1323]

TRZYNA, T.C., *ed*. Population: an international directory of organizations and information sources. Claremart, CA., Public Affairs Clearing House, 1976. xviii, 132p. $18.75. ISBN: 0912102225.

A 'user's guide to who's doing what' to over 600 governmental and non-governmental national and international organizations on population, family planning, abortion, and programmes, etc. Bibliography of other directories and published sources. Indexes of organizations, subjects, acronyms and initialisms. 'A valuable reference tool' (*Library journal,* v.102(5), 1 March 1977, p.594-5). *RQ* (v.17(3), Spring 1978, p.278) finds indexing inadequate and the price high. *Class No:* 312(058)

[1324]

UNITED NATIONS. Statistical Office. Demographic yearbook. New York, United Nations.

First published for 1949. Annual.

Returns from over 200 countries or areas. Tables published annually (tables 1-25); World summary - Population - Natality ... Infant and maternal mortality ... Subject matter index. *Class No:* 312(058)

Histories

[1325]

WRIGLEY, E.A. *and* SCHOFIELD, R.S. The Population history of England, 1541-1871: a reconstruction. New ed. Cambridge, Cambridge University Press, 1989. xxxvii,779,[2]p. tables. maps. £24.95. ISBN: 0521356881.

First published in 1981.

11 chapters in 2 parts: 1. From parish register to national vital series; 2. English population history. The first part of the book describes how statistics were assembled for three centuries (mid-16th to mid-19th); the second part is devoted to an analysis of the series to discover the course of population change in early modern England. 16 appendices. Bibliography, p.741-57 (Section 1: A-Z by author; Section 2 has statistical publications and county maps). Related publications are listed on p.xxxi-xxxiv. Analytical index, p.759-79. *Class No:* 312(091)

Worldwide

Histories

[1326]

ORGANISATION FOR ECONOMIC CO-OPERATION AND DEVELOPMENT. Demographic trends, 1950-1990. Paris, OECD, 1980. 145p. graphs, tables. £3.80. $8.50. ISBN: 9264120211.

Earlier volumes covered 1951-1971, 1956-1976, 1965-1980, &

....(contd.)
1970-1985.

A study containing projections for total population and active population in OECD countries. *Class No:* 312(100)(091)

Great Britain

Bibliographies

[1327]

BENJAMIN, B. **Population statistics:** a review of UK sources. Aldershot, Hants, Gower Publishing Co. Ltd., 1989. xi,355p. tables, maps. £45. ISBN: 056605731x.

A guide to sources of information over the whole field of demography relating to the population of the UK and including birth, death, marriage and divorce, migration, sickness, censuses and surveys (the position that obtained at the end of 1986). In 12 chapters, 10 of which describe the sources and include information on mode of collection, method of construction of standard indices, possible sources of error or bias, and guidance in the choice of information for particular purposes. Chapter 11 contains maps; chapter 12 is on desirable improvements; and there is a postscript. Index, p.351-355. Author is Emeritus Professor of Actuarial Science at the City University. *Class No:* 312(410)(01)

[1328]

GREAT BRITAIN. Office of Population Census and Surveys. **Government publications. Sectional list 56: Office of Population Censuses and Surveys.** Revised 1 September 1987. London, HMSO, 1987. 17p. Gratis.

Major sections are on: Census, 1981; Population trends; Reference series; OPCS monitors; Studies on medical and population subjects; Handbooks and survey reports. *Class No:* 312(410)(01)

[1329]

GREAT BRITAIN. Office of Population Census and Surveys *and* GENERAL REGISTER OFFICE FOR SCOTLAND. **Guide to census reports: Great Britain, 1801-1966.** London, HMSO, 1977. 7,279p.

Based on *Guides to official sources no.2., Census reports of Great Britain 1861 - 1931 (qv).* In 7 sections: 1. Introduction and list of reports. - 2. Significant developments in scope and organisation - 3. Questions and schedules for each census - 4. Selected subjects of census enquiry (showing the gradual elaboration and refinement of the various social measurements concerned in the 14 subject areas dealt with) - 5. Enumeration of special groups. - 6. Areas for which populations have been given - 7. Using census reports.. *Class No:* 312(410)(01)

[1330]

—HAKIM, C. **Census data and analysis:** a selected bibliography. London. Office of Population Censuses and Surveys, 1978. [ii],30p. *(OPCS occasional paper 6.)*

A selective annotated listing of 105 books and journal articles, arranged A-Z by author/institution. '... aimed at those who wish to make use of census data, whether to obtain a few tables or figures, or to analyse census statistics in some detail ... ' *(Preface).* No index. *Class No:* 312(410)(01)

[1331]

INTERDEPARTMENTAL COMMITTEE ON SOCIAL AND ECONOMIC RESEARCH. **Guide to official sources. No.2: Census reports of Great Britain, 1801-1931.** London, HMSO., 1951. iv, 119p. tables.

'The aim ... is to give a brief account for research workers and others of the development of the Census and of the wide range of information and analyses published in the long series of official reports'. Chapter 5: Selected subjects of census enquiry. Numerous tables and reproductions. *Class No:* 312(410)(01)

Periodicals

[1332]

Population trends. Office of Population Censuses and Surveys. London, HMSO, Autumn 1975-. v.1-. Quarterly. £50pa. ISSN: 03074463.

The journal of OPCS, with articles on a variety of population and medical subjects, and also regular series of tables on population, components of population change, vital statistics, live births, marriages, divorces, migration, deaths, and abortions.

Beginning with 1974 data, OPCS data are published in subject volumes: series FM: Family statistics (1-2) - DH: Deaths (1-5) - MB: Morbidity (1-5) - PP: Population estimate and projections (1-3) - AB: Abortion statistics - MN: International migration - VS: Vital statistics: local and health areas - EL Electoral statistics - DR: Demographic review - DS: Decennial supplement - LS: Longitudinal study - LFS: Labour force survey - GHS: General household survey. *Class No:* 312(410)(051)

Tables & Data Books

[1333]

GREAT BRITAIN. General Register Office for Scotland. **Census, 1991.** Edinburgh, HMSO, 1991-93.

Census publications include:.

Report for Scotland. 2v. (Part 1: £65. ISBN 0114951195); part 2: £33. ISBN 0114951209).

Report for new towns 2v. (£53. ISBN 0114952248).

Class No: 312(410)(083)

[1334]

GREAT BRITAIN. Office of Population Census and Surveys. **Census 1991** London, HMSO, 1992-94

A census has been taken every ten years since 1801

Census 1991 publications include:

Definitions (£13.80. ISBN 0116913614).

Users'guide (xvii,398p. £19,80. ISBN 0116915277).

Report for Great Britain (2 parts. £85 & £40) ISBN 0116915366 & 0116915269).

Historical tables (34p. £7.60. ISBN 0116915099).

Household composition (£27.40.ISBN 0116915609).

Ethnic group and country of birth (£45.40. ISBN 0116915188).

County reports (one for each county in England and Wales in 2 parts). *Class No:* 312(410)(083)

[1335]

GREAT BRITAIN. Office of Population Census and Surveys. **Population projections ... [1985 -2001. England].** London HMSO, 1988. iv.72p. tables. £7.40. *(Series PP3.)* ISBN: 0116912375.

First published for 1970-2010.

Data by area, sex and age, from mid-1985.

Class No: 312(410)(083)

[1336]

NORTHERN IRELAND. General Register Office. **Census of population, Northern Ireland, 1971.** Belfast, HMSO, 1971-76.

First census was taken in 1801.

The 1971 census publications include.

Summary tables.

County reports (7 reports).

Housing and household composition tables.

Religion tables, Northern Ireland.

Education tables. *Class No:* 312(410)(083)

Maps & Atlases

[1337]

DURHAM UNIVERSITY, *Department of Geography.* **Census Research Unit. People of Britain:** a census atlas. London, HMSO, 1981. 132p. tables, maps. £15. ISBN: 0116906189.

Prepared in collaboration with the Office of Population Censuses and Surveys and the General Register Office, Scotland.

Presents a unique and easy-to-grasp picture of the population of Great Britain, showing population distribution and information on major characteristics, bringing out national, regional and local patterns from the wealth of detail provided in the 1971 census of population. Pt.1 has 34 national maps on population, birthplace, demographic characteristics, socio-economic characteristics, travel to work, households and housing. Pt.2 is in 7 regional sections, each subdivided by population density, born outside UK, multi-car households, and bath-deficient households. Appendices give explanations; introduction explains computer mapping, etc. *Class No:* 312(410)(084.3)

Manuscripts & Incunabula

[1338]

HIGGS, E. **A clearer sense of the census :** the Victorian censuses and historical research. London, HMSO, 1996. 226p. *(Public Record Office handbooks ; no. 28..)* ISBN: 0114402574.

Based on *Making sense of the census,* 1989.

Class No: 312(410)(093)

[1339]

HIGGS, E. **Making sense of the census:** the manuscript returns for England and Wales, 1801-1901. Public Record Office. London, HMSO, 1989. 156p. £9.95. ISBN: 0114402191.

Provides researchers with a guide to the records. A general introduction and a means of reference when working on the records, which it describes in detail. Also comments on the nature and reliability of the information. *Class No:* 312(410)(093)

Ireland

Maps & Atlases

[1340]

HORNER, A.A., *and others*. **Population in Ireland:** a census atlas. Dublin, University College Dublin, Department of Geography, 1987. ix, 165p. tables, maps. IR£15. ISBN: 1870089103.

200 maps, together with text and tables, cover the Republic of Ireland and Northern Ireland. Using computer plotting techniques the volume displays the many spatial variations of population structure and distribution in Ireland in 1981. 'Most complete analysis of Irish census material yet to appear' (*The geographical journal*, March 1989, p.126-7). *Class No:* 312(415)(084.3)

Northern Ireland

Maps & Atlases

[1341]

COMPTON, P.A., *and others*. **Northern Ireland; a census atlas.** Dublin, Gill and Macmillan,1978. [2], 169p. diagrs, tables, maps.

A series of 115 computer-drawn maps summarizing the main spatial characteristics of the population of Northern Ireland and the urban area of Belfast in 1971, based on census data collected that year. Spans 3 broad themes - the demography of the province, the social and economic characteristics of the people, and household data. Short bibliography of 11 items. Detailed index. *Class No:* 312(416)(084.3)

Eire

[1342]

EIRE. Central Statistics Office. **Census of population of Ireland, 1991.** Dublin. Stationery Office, 1991-.

First census was taken in 1821. Excludes Northern Ireland.

Results of the 1991 census are n ow being published, including 'Preliminary results'; Local,population reports - 1st series (nos.1-28); 'Small area population statistics (SAPS).

A census was taken in 1986, and a preliminary report was issued in that year. The final report is in 8v. (V.1. Population classified by area (£10)). *Class No:* 312(417)

England & Wales

Bibliographies

[1343]

GIBSON, J.S.W., *comp*. **Census returns on microfilm. Directory to local holdings, 1841-1881.** Banbury, Oxfordshire, Federation of Family History Societies, 1982. 44p. £1.25. Paperback issued in 1987. ISBN: 090709919x.

First published 1979 as *Census returns, 1841, 1851, 1861, 1871, on microfilm ...*

Covers England and Wales, under counties A-Z. The holdings of the five census years are now released to the public under the '100 years' rule. *Class No:* 312(42)(01)

[1344]

GIBSON, J.S.W. *and* MEDLYCOTT, M. **Local census listings, 1522-1930 :** holdings in the British Isles Birmingham, Federation of Family History Societies, 1997. 60p. £3.10. ISBN: 1860060528. *Class No:* 312(42)(01)

Histories

[1345]

NISSEL, M. **People count:** a history of the General Register Office. London, HMSO, 1987. [4], 157p. illus. (col.). £5.75. ISBN: 0116911832.

11 chapters (Registration before 1837 - Establishing the General Register Office - The civil registration system - Social commentary - The population controversy and the first population census - The census: the first 100 years of the General Register Office - The census: the last 50 years - Social surveys - Health statistics: the early years of the General Register Office - Health statistics: later developments - Population). 4 appendices: Chronology of main events in the history of the Office; Registrars-General, 1837-1987; Some recent OPCS publications; Historical tables. Index, p.156-7. 'A potted history of social change in the past 150 years'. (*Library association record*, v.89(11), November 1987). *Class No:* 312(42)(091)

Biographies

[1346]

PETERSEN, W. *and* PETERSEN, R. **Dictionary of demography:** biographies. New York, Greenwood Press, 1985. 2v. (xx,1365p.). £142.50. ISBN: 0313214190.

Short biographies of 3363 nationals of 99 countries are arranged A-Z in the 2 volumes (A-L; M-Z). Average length of each biography is ½ page, including references. Appendix: classification of nationality. References, p.1187-1198. Index, p.1199-1365. *Class No:* 312(42)(092)

China

[1347]

New China's population. China. Financial & Economic Publishing House. New York, Collier Macmillan, 1988. xxiv,232p. tables, charts. $90. £82. ISBN: 0029054710.

A condensation in English of a 32v. survey in Chinese, summarizing the most important findings. 12 chapters: 1. Introduction - 2. The Chinese population: its size and growth - 3. Trend and differences in China's fertility rate - 4. The trend and difference of mortality of China's population - 5. Internal migration - 6. Urbanization - 7. Distribution of Chinese population - 8. Sex and age composition of China's population - 9. Marriage and family - 10. Working population - 11. Population of minority nationalities - 12. China's population policy and family planning. Data is based on the 1953, 1964 and 1982 censuses and the fertility sample survey of 1982. Extensive index. *Class No:* 312(510)

[1348]

The Population atlas of China. Population Census Office of the State Council of China *and* Institute of Geography of the Chinese Academy of Sciences. Hong Kong, Oxford University Press, 1988. 216p. 152 col. maps. £30. ISBN: 0195840925.

Based on the 1982 census of the People's Republic of China, the atlas covers population distribution and change, nationalities, sex and age, marriage and fertility, the level of education, and occupations. Hong Kong and Taiwan are included in so far as comparable data are available. *Class No:* 312(510)

Africa

Bibliographies

[1349]

PINFOLD, J.R., *comp. & ed*. **African population census reports:** a bibliography and check-list. München, K.G. Saur; Oxford, Hans Zell Publishers, on behalf of SCOLMA, 1985. xii, 100p. £15. DM60-. ISBN: 0905450191, UK; 3598105711, Germany.

Arranged A-Z by the names of African countries. Population censuses and other national demographic surveys are listed in chronological order. Regional and urban population censuses are included when there is no national survey. Covers a wide variety of sources, including statistical yearbooks, United Nations publications, periodicals, etc. Locations are given (25 libraries in Britain; 9 major collections in Europe). Cross-references between old and new names of countries. *Class No:* 312(6)(01)

[1350]

Union list of African censuses, development plans, and statistical abstracts. Evalds, V.K., *comp*. Oxford, Hans Zell; Munich, K.G. Saur, 1985. xiv,232p. £22.50; DM.88. ISBN: 0905450205, UK; 3598105762, Germany.

Lists the holdings of 13 major North American libraries, but not the Library of Congress, of government documents concerned with African censuses, development plans, and statistical abstracts from 1945 to 1983. *Class No:* 312(6)(01)

USA

[1351]

BOGUE, D.J. **The Population of the United States:** historical trends and future projections. New York, Free Press, 1985. 728p. tables. $70. ISBN: 0029047005.

An eminently readable portrait of the people of the United States from 1790 to 1980 in 20 chapters. Includes detailed bibliographies, clear definitions of terms, and a guide to obtaining further information. Hundreds of charts, graphs, pie charts, etc. are included. 'An excellent accompaniment to the *Statistical abstract* and *Historical statistics of the United States* (*Library journal*, 15 April 1986, p.36). *Class No:* 312(73)

[1352]

WELLS, R.V. **The Population of the British colonies in America before 1776:** a survey of census data. Princeton, Princeton, University Press, 1976. xii,342p. tables. $44. ISBN: 0691046166.

In 8 sections: 1. Subject, sources, methods - 2. The northern colonies - 3. New England - 4. The middle colonies - 5. The southern colonies - 6. The island colonies - 7. Colonial patterns - 8. Household size and composition. Includes 88 tables. References are give in footnotes. Analytical index. *Class No:* 312(73)

Bibliographies

[1353]

SCHULTZE, S. **Population information in nineteenth-century census volumes.** Phoenix, AZ., Oryx Press, 1983. 456p. illus., maps. $82. ISBN: 0897741226.

An index to tables containing population information in the first 11 federal censuses (1790-1890). For each census the bibliographical data and a table of contents are preceded by a short essay on its history and scope. *Class No:* 312(73)(01)

[1354]

—SCHULTZE, S. **Population information in twentieth-century census volumes...** Phoenix, AZ., Oryx Press, 1985-88. 2v. (289p.; 328p.), illus., maps. $82 each vol. ISBN: 0897741641; 0897744004.

Similar information to the above for 1900-1940 and 1950-1980. *Class No:* 312(73)(01)

Maps & Atlases

[1355]

Atlas of demographics: from the 1980 census. Boulder Co., Infomap Inc., 1982. 60p. 16 maps, tables. $175. ISBN: 0910471002.

Based on the 1980 census data, graphically presents socio-economic data at county level on population and housing. Data includes population density, age, race, housing. A table lists specific demographic data, A-Z, by State and counties within States. No. index. Recommended by *Choice,* (v.20(8), April 1983, p.1106). *Class No:* 312(73)(084.3)

Histories

[1356]

GERHAN, D. R. *and* WELLS, R.V., *comps.* **A Retrospective biography of American demographic history from colonial times to 1983.** Westport CT., Greenwood Press, 1989. 474p. $65. (*Bibliographies and indexes in American history.* 10.) ISBN: 0313231303.

Intended for user groups with more than a casual interest in the subject. 3840 entries are arranged in subject groupings corresponding to the author's earlier *Revolutions in Americans' lives* (1982). 6 chapters, all subdivided and with short introductions: 1. Introduction and general background - 2. Marriage and fertility - 3. Health and death - 4. Migration, pluralism and local patterns - 5. Family and demographic history - 6. Population, economics, politics and society. Author, place and subject indexes. A second volume is to cover material published since 1983. *Class No:* 312(73)(091)

Births & Deaths

[1357]

PRESTON, S.H., *and others.* **Causes of death:** life tables for national populations. San Diego, CA., Academic Press, 1972. xi, 787p. $49.50. £37. (*Studies in population.*) ISBN: 0127856641.

Sections (each with references): Method of calculation - Accuracy and comparability - Guide to life tables - Causes of death: life tables. 8 types of table per entry (age and sex). 180 populations. Australia ... Yugoslavia. Time series (*e.g.* Canada: 1921, 1931, 1941, 1951, 1960, 1964). Sources of data, p.54-65. *Class No:* 312.1/.2

[1358]

SINGER, R.B. *and* LEVINSON, L., *eds.* **Medical risks:** patterns of mortality and survival. A reference volume ... Lexington, Mass., Lexington Books, 1976. v.p., tables. $44. ISBN: 0669982288.

Sponsored by the Association of Life Insurance Medical Directors of America and the Society of Actuaries.

Part 1: Text (172p.): 16 chapters, with references (*e.g.* 5. Cancer: 8. Hypertension; 16. Endocrine and metabolic diseases). Part 2 (over 1000 tables, with text left, facing): Tabular abstracts: References - Subjects studied - Follow up - Results - Comment. Subject index to text and tables. *Class No:* 312.1/.2

Tables & Data Books

[1359]

ALDERSON, M. **International mortality statistics.** London, Macmillan; New York Facts on File, 1981. 524p. (380p. of tables). £45. $55. ISBN: 0871965143.

Comparative international data on causes of death during the 20th-century for 33 countries (US, Canada, Australia, New Zealand, Japan, Chile, Turkey, Europe, except Germany) and 178 causes of death. Mainly computer-produced serial mortality tables containing data in the form of age-standardized indexes. Each table devoted to a single cause of death for one sex. Preceded by explanatory material and state-of-the-art reviews on trends in mortality statistics, and on validity of data. Extensive bibliographical citations. *Class No:* 312.1/.2(083)

Marriage & Divorce

[1360]

DICANIO, M. **The Encyclopedia of marriage, divorce and the family.** New York, Facts on File, 1989. 607p. $45. ISBN: 081601695x.

Some 600 essays, A-Z, on specific topics (*eg,*Alcoholics; Cohabitation), their historical, legal, psychological and sociological aspects. Cross-references. 8 directory-type appendices. Index. US slanted. '... offers convenient access to short, objective explanations of the myriad phenomena pertaining to contemporary life.'(*Wilson library bulletin,* v.64(3), November 1989, p.115). *Class No:* 312.3

Bibliographies

[1361]

ALDOUS, J. *and* HILL, R. **International bibliography of research in marriage and the family, 1900-1964.** Minneapolis, University of Minnesota Press, 1967. 508p.

Nearly 13000 citations in 6 sections. KWIC index; classified index; author and periodical lists. 'Substantially valuable to social scientists' (*Library journal,* v.92(8), 15 April 1967, p.1001), noting that the compilers relied heavily on *International bibliography of sociology, Psychological abstracts* and *Sociological abstracts,* 'obviating the need for searching there'. 'Impressive, but poorish printing and layout' (*RQ,* v.6(4), Summer 1967, p.190-3). Continued in *International bibliography of research in marriage and the family, v.2: 1965-1972.* edited by J. Aldous and N. Dahl, then *Inventory of marriage and family literature* (qv). *Class No:* 312.3(01)

[1362]

Inventory of marriage and family literature. V.17, (published 1992). St. Paul, MN., National Council on Family Relations (previously Minnesota University Press; Minnesota University, Family Social Science Department; and Sage Publications), 1967-. v.1-. $129.95 pa. ISBN: 091617431x.

Earlier vols.: v.1. 1900-1964 (1967); v.2. 1965-1972 (1974); v.3. 1973-1974 (1975); v.4. 1975-1976 (1977) ...

A computer produced subject guide and subject index precedes the author index, which has full bibliographical references, a keyword-in-title index, and a periodical list. Over 600 journals are covered. *Class No:* 312.3(01)

[1363]

SELL, K.D. *and* SELL, B.H., *eds.* **Divorce in the United States, Canada and Great Britain:** a guide to information sources. Detroit, Mich., Gale, 1978. xvi, 298p. $66. ISBN: 0810313960.

Contains 13 chapters devoted to subject bibliographies, basic reference books, statistical sources, legal texts, etc. Author, title and subject indexes. 'A brilliantly organized compendium of published and unpublished, print and non-print, retrospective and current sources dealing with divorce and such related issues as child custody, alimony, re-marriage of divorced persons, and the like' (*RQ,* v.18(4), Summer 1979, p.410).

A similar book is M. McKenney's *Divorce: a selected annotated bibliography* (Metuchen, N.J., Scarecrow Press, 1975. 163p. ISBN 0810907777). *Class No:* 312.3(01)

[1364]

—SELL, K.D., *comp.* **Divorce in the 70s: a subject bibliography.** Phoenix, AZ., Oryx Press, 1981. viii,191p. $32.50; £25. ISBN: 0912700815.

Complements and to some extent supersedes the above. An unannotated bibliography of 4762 items published in the US in the 1970s, arranged in 7 sections (1. Social and behavioural science literature - 2. Legal literature - 3. Judeo-Christian literature - 4. Popular literature - 5. Non-print materials on divorce - 6. Addendum and appendix - 7. Indexes (author, geographical and analytical subject). *Class No:* 312.3(01)

32 Politics

Politics

[1365]

EVANS, G. *and* NEWNHAM, J. The Dictionary of world politics: a reference guide to concepts, ideas and institutions. Hemel Hempstead, Herts., Harvester Wheatsheaf; New York, Simon & Schuster, 1991. xiv,449p. £60; $25.50. ISBN: 0745002749, UK; 0132105276, US.

Over 600 entries, ranging from a few lines to 2 pages, providing information on concepts and institutions essential to an understanding of contemporary politics, including important terms likely to be found only in specialized texts or journals. Cross references. Omits South Africa, Iran and Cambodia. Well-designed and up-to-date. Usable in conjunction with Munro and Day's *A world record of major conflict areas* (qv). 'An essential purchase for most libraries' (*Library journal*, December 1990, p.116). *Class No:* 320

[1366]

The Oxford companion to politics of the world. Krieger, J., *and others, eds.* Oxford, Oxford University Press, 1993. xxxi,1056p. £35. $49.95. ISBN: 0195059344.

650 mini-essays from nearly 500 contributors from 40 countries (mostly US). Covers international relations and domestic politics worldwide, with emphasis on post-1945 events. Most articles conclude with cross-references and sources. '... will become indispensable for all academic libraries.' (*Library journal*, 15 March 1993, p.72). *Class No:* 320

[1367]

Political geography in the twentieth century: a global analysis. Taylor, P.J., *ed.* London, Belhaven Press; New York, Wiley, 1993. [11],269p. £35. ISBN: 1852931965, UK; 0470219661, US.

5 chapters: 1. Geopolitical world orders; 2. Political geography of war and peace; 3. The rise and decline of the corporate-welfare state; 4. Colonialism, post-colonialism and the political geography of the Third World; 5. The United States and American hegemony. Epilogue: *Fin de siècle* geopolitics. Towards a geographical dialogue. *Class No:* 320

Bibliographies

[1368]

ABC Pol Sci: a bibliography of contents: political science and government. Santa Barbara, CA., ABC-Clio, 1969-. v.1, no.1-. 5 pa plus annual index. Subscription based on service rate principal. ISSN: 00010456.

Current awareness service, reproducing table of contents pages of over 300 core journals (both foreign and domestic) on political science and government, law, sociology, and economics, etc. Arranged by journal titles, A-Z. 'Subject profile' and author indexes in each issue, cumulated annually and five-yearly, plus list of periodicals. *Class No:* 320(01)

[1369]

CRIS the combined retrospective index to journals in political science, 1886-1974. Wile, A.N., *ed.* Washington, Carrollton Press, 1977-78. 8v. $880. ISBN: 0840801866.

Indexes 115,000 articles from over 170 English-language periodicals under more than 130 subject headings in theoretical and applied political science, international relations, public administration and urban studies. Volumes are: 1. International affairs and organizations; 2. General studies and methodology; 3/6. Public administration; 7/8. Authors [index]. *Class No:* 320(01)

[1370]

ENGLEFIELD, D. *and* DREWRY, G., *eds.* Information sources in politics and political science: worldwide. London, Butterworths, 1984. xviii, 509p. £38. (*Butterworths guides to information sources.*) ISBN: 0408114703.

Aims to be a critical assessment of a large English library on both the study and the practice of the subject (*Preface*). In 4 parts: 1. Resources - 2. Approaches to the study of politics and government - 3. Politics and government: United Kingdom - 4. Politics and government: overseas. The 24 contributors are academics and librarians, and the chapters are essays covering the various aspects of political studies (*e.g.* political behaviour, political thought, comparative politics), of government, and of politics in the UK and the rest of the world by regions. Subject index, p.503-509. *Class No:* 320(01)

[1371]

FOUNDATION NATIONALE DES SCIENCES POLITIQUES. Bibliographie courante d'articles de périodiques postérieurs à 1944 sur les problèmes politiques, économiques et sociaux/Index to post-1944 periodical articles on political, economic and social problems. Boston, Mass., G.K. Hall, 1968. 17v. (14,391p.). *Supplements* (annual). 1-20.

Main volumes and supplements contain over 500,000 photolithographed catalogue-card entries. About 1500 periodicals (one-third in French) are currently received; over 20,000 new entries pa. Classified by countries or areas, with reverse-chronological sub-arrangement. *Class No:* 320(01)

[1372]

HARMON, R.B. Developing the library collection in political science. Metuchen, Scarecrow Press, 1976. x, 198p. $19.50. ISBN: 0810808986.

Aims primarily 'to provide librarians with a selection device for most types of materials in political science' (*Preface*), particularly for small to medium-sized libraries. 'Selected reference materials', p.122-54; 'The periodical literature', p.155-162. Author and title index. Very brief annotations. *Class No:* 320(01)

[1373]

HEROLD, J. 'Political science reference sources'. In *RSR*, v.10(3),Fall,1982,p 45-53.

A book survey including a bibliography of 46 books. *Class No:* 320(01)

[1374]

Information sources of political science. 5th ed. Santa Barbara, CA., ABC-Clio, 2001. $95. ISBN: 1576071049.

First published 1971.

Annotated citations of printed and computerized reference works in political science and related social sciences and humanities. Citations cover general references; the social sciences; American government, politics and public law; international relations and organizations; comparative government and area studies; political theory; and public administration. Citations are numbered and listed A-Z within the sections, containing bibliographical information and descriptive annotations of 1-2 paragraphs. Author, title, subject and typology indexes, the latter identifying reference sources by their genre (*e.g.* abstracts, bibliographies, directories, etc.). 'Every possible type of reference source is included, fully annotated, and easily located ... All in all, an indispensible volume for anyone doing political research'. (*College & research libraries,* v.48(1), January 1987, p.69). *Class No:* 320(01)

[1375]

International bibliography of political science. British Library of Political and Economic Science, *comp.* London and New York, Routledge 1954-. v.1-. Annual. ISSN: 00852058.

References to books, periodical articles, and documents, arranged in 6 subject sections, each subdivided: A. Political science. General studies and methods - B. Political thought - C. Political systems - D. Political life - E. Government policy - F. International life. Author and subject indexes. *Class No:* 320(01)

[1376]

A New handbook of political science. Goodin, R.E. *and* Klingemann, H.-D. Oxford, Oxford University Press, 1998. 864p. £19.99. ISBN: 0198294719. *Class No:* 320(01)

[1377]

WYNAR, L.R. Guide to reference materials in political science. Rochester, N.Y., Libraries Unlimited Inc., 1967-68. 2v. (318p., 342p.). (*Library science text series.*)

First published 1966.

Several thousand annotated entries. V.1 has 4 sections (Social science general reference sources; political science general reference sources; political theory; ideology). V.2, 6 main sections (International relations; public administration; political behavior, public opinion, political parties and electoral processes; comparative political systems; government documents; reference sources in law). Each volume has an index. Comparable in scope to Harmon (qv). *Class No:* 320(01)

[1378]

—BROCK, C. The Literature of political science: a guide for students, librarians and teachers. New York, Bowker, 1969. (Available from Books Demand, UMI). xii, 232p. illus., facsims. $46.40. ISBN: 0317103547.

About 500 brief annotated entries for bibliographies and other reference sources. Preliminary chapters on information sources and how to use them. Author-title index. US slanted. 'Does not supersede Harmon and Wynar (qqv), but it does supplement them' (*RQ*, Summer 1970, p.354-5). *Class No:* 320(01)

[1379]

YORK, H.E. **Political science:** a guide to reference and information sources. Englewood Cliffs, Co, Libraries Unlimited Inc., 1990. 249p. $38. (*Reference services in the social sciences, 4.*) ISBN: 0872877949.

650 evaluative as well as descriptive entries, 80-200 words each, arranged in 6 chapters. Sources include databases, periodicals and organizations. Author, title and subject indexes. 'This is an easily accessible, well-developed tool' (*Choice*, v.28(9), May 1991, p.1471) '... first choice guide for introducing students to political science reference literature and for evaluating political science reference collections' (*Wilson library bulletin*, v.65(8), April 1991, p.121). *Class No:* 320(01)

Encyclopaedias & Dictionaries

[1380]

DÉLURY, G. E. *and* KAPLE, D. A., *eds.* **The World encyclopedia of political systems and parties** 3rd edition New York, Facts on File, 1999. xxii, 1296p. in 3 vols. $225. ISBN: 0816028745.

Alphabetically arranged by each country's name in English (the "local" name is also supplied). Entries then follow a standard format: system of government (legislative, executive and judicial); statistical data (e.g., population, land mass, ethnicity). Where appropriate there are descriptions of the party system. Some entries have detailed information about other matters, such as religious adherence. There is a bibliography for each entry. The entries - all signed - naturally vary in length according to the size and importance of each country. *Class No:* 320(03)

[1381]

LENTZ, H. M. **Encyclopedia of heads of states and governments, 1900 through 1945.** McFarland, 1999. 508p. £67.50. ISBN: 0786405007.

This is a book which does just what the title says: it lists, alphabetically, all the countries of the world, providing for each biographies of its leaders, be they monarchs or elected presidents or prime ministers. Within each country's entry the biographies are arranged chronologically. A useful work of reference. *Class No:* 320(03)

Encyclopaedias

[1382]

SEGAL, G., *ed.* **Political and economic encyclopedia of the Pacific:** a world guide. Harlow, Essex, Longman, Group; Chicago, St. James Press, 1989. [6],293p. maps on endpapers. £65; $85.00. (*Longman international reference series.*) ISBN: 0582051614, UK; 1558620338, US.

Entries focus on terms and subject areas central to current affairs, covering all the countries of the Pacific and the Pacific Rim, including Japan, China, and the Pacific dimensions of the US and USSR. Arrangement is A-Z by name of person, place or subject (Akihoto, Emperor - Alitas, Ali - Aluminium - American Samoa - Andean Pact - Antarctic Treaty ... Yi Kun Mo). Length of entries ranges from a few lines to several columns (Vietnam, Socialist Republic of: 8½ cols.). General index, p.287-293. *Class No:* 320(031)

[1383]

WILCZYNSKI, J. **An encyclopedic dictionary of Marxism, socialism and Communism:** economic, philosophical, political and sociological theories, concepts, institutions and practices - classical and modern, east-west relations included. London, Macmillan, 1981. [4], 608p. £35. ISBN: 0333306899.

Over 2300 entries on theories, practices and institutions of left-wing ideologies. *Class No:* 320(031)

Handbooks & Manuals

[1384]

NAGEL, S. **Policy-studies handbook.** Lexington, Md., Lexington Books, 1981. 238p. diagrs., tables. $27. ISBN: 066903777x.

Identifies training programmes, research centres, publishing outlets and government agencies for policy-studies scholars. 28 tables. *Class No:* 320(035)

[1385]

Political handbook of the world, 1999: governments and intergovernmental organizations as of March 1, 1999. Banks, A.S. *and* Muller, T.C. *and* Overstreet, W., *eds.* Binghamton, N.Y., C.S.A., 2000. $125. ISBN: 0933199147. ISSN: 0193175x.

First published in 1927 as *Political handbook of Europe.* Title varies. Until recently, sponsored by the Council on Foreign Relations.

Covers government and intergovernmental organizations. Reports for each country include general data, the constitution, foreign relations, current issues, political parties, the legislature, the cabinet, news media, and inter-governmental representation of each country. A second part deals with intergovernmental organizations, including their history, structure, activities, official and/or working languages. Appendices: A chronology of major events, 1945-. Chart showing membership of the United Nations and agencies. A convenient source for quick reference. *Class No:* 320(035)

Dictionaries

[1386]

COMFORT, N. **Brewer's Politics** a phrase and fable dictionary. 2nd ed. London, Cassell, 1995. viii,693p. £25. £16.99 (pbk). ISBN: 0304346594; 0304348740, pbk.

First published in 1993.

A dictionary of political language from technical and procedural terms to cliches and insults. Over 5000 entries; includes nicknames, acronyms, places (ie rooms) etc. *Class No:* 320(038)

[1387]

A **New dictionary of political analysis.** Roberts, G. *and* Edwards, A., *eds.* London, Edward Arnold, 1991. [5],153p. £12.99. ISBN: 0340528605.

A guide to the current terminology of the subject, including concise definitions of basic terms and longer entries for more complex terms. 'Indicates subtle, but often significant differences in words which are sometimes misused.'(*British book news*, October 1991, p.682). *Class No:* 320(038)

[1388]

RAMIREZ FARIA, C. **The historical dictionary of world political geography.** London, Macmillan Reference, 2000. 288p. illus.,maps. £75. ISBN: 0333781775.

Very detailed coverage of world events, giving insight into areas of conflict such as the Balkans. *Class No:* 320(038)

[1389]

ROBERTSON, D. **A Dictionary of modern politics.** 2nd. ed. completely rev. & updated. London, Europa Publications, 1993. 500p. £35. ISBN: 0946653755.

First published in 1985.

A guide to the complex ideology and terminology which surrounds the world of politics. Over 500 extensive entries on political theories, dogmas, issues and institutions. 'Concise, straightforward definitions' (*British book news*, April 1993, p.251). *Class No:* 320(038)

[1390]

SAFIRE, W. **Safire's political dictionary:** an enlarged, up-to-date edition of *The new language of politics.* 3rd. ed. (A 4th ed., *Safire's new political dictionary* was published in 1993. $30.50. 0679420681). New York, Random House, 1978. 845p. $17.95. ISBN: 0394502612.

First published in 1968.

About 1200 entries, briefly defining over 1600 political terms or phrases, plus explanations placing source and period. Omits terms covered by ordinary dictionaries in favour of American catchwords, slogans and the like. 'A useful and amusing lexicon of political (not governmental) words and phrases' (*Wilson library bulletin*, v.47(3), November 1972, p.292, of earlier edition). *Class No:* 320(038)

[1391]

SPERBER, H. *and* TRITTSCHUH, T. **American political terms:** an historical dictionary. Detroit, Mich., Wayne State University, 1962. x, 516p. $29.95. ISBN: 0814311873.

On *OED* lines: definitions, different meanings; changes in usage, with quotations (*e.g.* 'loco foco'; 'egghead'). About 1000 entries. A few politically unimportant words are included solely because they did not appear in *OED* etc. *Class No:* 320(038)

Polyglot

[1392]

BACK, H., *and others.* **Polec: dictionary of politics and economics** ... 2. verbesserte und erw. Aufl. Berlin, de Gruyter, 1967. xvi,1037p. DM 61 £35.90.

16,000 English, French and German terms in one A-Z sequence, with definitions and frequently descriptive data, plus adequate cross-references. The definition and data are in the language of the entry-word, the equivalent of which is then given in the other two languages. Includes many abbreviations, also entries under the names of States and political parties. English entry-words are sometimes suspect (e.g.

....*(contd.)*
'sudden trip'; 'exceptional law') and English definitions can be awkwardly phrased (e.g. 'VVB' is translated as 'Society of people's owned industry'). *Class No:* 320(038)=00

French

[1393]
CHAUDESAIGUES-DEYSINE, A.E. *and* DREUILHE, A.E. **Dictionnaire anglais-français et lexique français-anglais des termes politiques, juridiques et économiques.** Paris, Flammarion, 1978,. 354p.
About 4-5,000 English entry-words, with French definitions, in the first and major part. Many idioms; numbered applications. US and British-English terms given. French-English index, p.291-354.
Class No: 320(038)=40

[1394]
—SANDAHL, P. *and* DEBEA, L. Dictionnaire politique et diplomatique. Paris, Libraires Techniques, 1976. x,193p.
Explains *c.*360 political and diplomatic terms in French. Appended list of principal international organizations, with data on origins, purpose, HQ, and number of member countries.
Class No: 320(038)=40

Chinese

[1395]
LAU, Y.-F., *and others.* **Glossary of Chinese political phrases.** Hong Kong, Union Research Institute, 1977. 590p.
'Contains over 2000 phrases in Chinese, with an English equivalent and explanation of political significance. Terms date from the beginning of the Communist period in China. Stroke-count index' (*RSR*, v.6(4), October/December 1978, p.66).
Class No: 320(038)=951

Reviews & Abstracts

[1396]
International political science abstracts. Documentation politique internationale. Paris, International Political Science Association, under the auspices of the International Social Science Council, in co-operation with the International Committee for Social Science Information & UNESCO. (previously Oxford, Blackwell), 1951-. 6pa (previously quarterly. F.1350 (institutions); F.400 (individuals) pa. ISSN: 00208345.
About 6000 indicative and informative, but not evaluative, abstracts of *c.*150 words, arranged in 6 main sections: 1. Political science: methods and theory - 2. Political thinkers and ideas - 3. Government and administrative institutions - 4. Political process: public opinion, attitudes, parties, forces, groups and elections - 5. International relations - 6. National and area studies. English abstracts of articles in English, otherwise French abstracts. Covers *c.*400 journals (listed in each issue). Subject index in each issue; annual author and cumulated subject index. Complementary to the *International bibliography of political science* (qv), in that it concentrates on periodical articles, is annotated, and is more frequent. *Class No:* 320(048)

[1397]
Neue politische Literatur: Berichte über das internationale Schriftum. Stuttgart, Franz Steiner Verlag, 1956-?. 3pa. ISSN: 00283320.
Contains long articles that are surveys of the international literature on a particular topic, and shorter reviews of new books. Reviews are in German, books reviewed mainly in German, but a few in English or French. V.34(1), 1989 has 5 articles and 56 book reviews. Annual index of authors of articles and books reviewed appears in the first issue the following year. *Class No:* 320(048)

Yearbooks & Directories

[1398]
The International yearbook and statesmen's who's who 1998. Fully revised and updated edition. London, Bowker Saur, 1997 1,400p. £175.00 ISBN: 1857392205.
Contains bibliographies on over 7,800 individuals active in international politics, business and world affairs. Entries include information on career history, educational background, awards, publications, associations, committees. Country profiles of national and international organisations *Class No:* 320(058)

[1399]
People in power. Harlow, Essex, Longman Group, 1987. 1v. loose-leaf. £90. $160. pa. (includes 2-monthly up-dates). ISBN: 0582017831.
A directory of the current political leadership in the sovereign countries of the world. Arranged by country, outlines the current political system, including details of the head of state, full composition of the cabinet or council of ministers, and, where relevant, the leadership of the ruling party, ruling council, or military junta. Name and address of each country's ambassador or high commission in the UK also included. *Class No:* 320(058)

Almanacs

[1400]
The Facts on file world political almanac. Cook, C., *comp.* 4th ed New York, Facts on File, 2000. 570p. tables. $60. ISBN: 0816042950.
First published 1989.
Key facts and figures on the major political developments since 1945. International political organizations and movements - Heads of State and governments - Legislatures and constitutions - Treaties, alliances and diplomatic agreements - Political parties (by country, A-Z) - Elections - The violent world (inc. conflicts, wars, civil strife, terrorism) The nuclear age - Populations and urbanization - Dictionary of political terms - Biographical dictionary. Analytical index. 'Unique in its specialized chronologies of international and civil conflicts, acts of terrorism, nuclear events and heads of state' (*Library journal*, 15 April; 1989, p.66), of the first ed. *Class No:* 320(059)

Quotations

[1401]
BAKER, D.B., *ed.* **Political quotations.** Detroit, Mich., Gale Research International Ltd, 1990. 508p. ISBN: 0810349205.
More than 5000 notable quotations on politics, from antiquity to the present, with emphasis on the 20th century. Author and keyword indexes. '... indisputably useful in its field ...' (*Wilson library bulletin*, v.65(4), December 1990. p.155). *Class No:* 320(082.2)

[1402]
The Macmillan dictionary of political quotations. Eigen, L.D. *and* Siegel, J.P. Macmillan, 1993. 785p. $40. £27.24. ISBN: 0026106507.
*c.*11000 quotations arranged A-Z by topic. Within each section entries arranged alphabetically by author. *Class No:* 320(082.2)

[1403]
MONTGOMERY, H. *and* CAMBRAY, P.G. **A Dictionary of political phrases and allusions.** London, Sonnenschein, 1906. (Reprinted Detroit, Mich., Gale, 1968). 406p. ISBN: 081033092x.
Mainly British political phrases and allusions, but includes some foreign and US. Short bibliography. *Class No:* 320(082.2)

[1404]
The Oxford dictionary of political quotations. Jay, A. Oxford, Oxford University Press, 1997. 576p. £15.99. $35. ISBN: 0198631588.
Class No: 320(082.2)

[1405]
RATHBONE, C. *and* STEPHENSON, M. **Guide to political quotations.** 2nd ed. Harlow, Essex, Longman Group Ltd., 1985. [4], 247p. £3.95. (*Longman pocket companion series.*) ISBN: 0582892090.
First published 1983.
Arranged in 19 sections (1. Some principles - 2. On the attack - 3. Historic phrases ... 8. On America ... 12. Women - 13. Wise words ... 18. In praise - 19. In memorium. Each entry begins with the quote, followed by the name of the person quoting and an explanation. Index, p.243-247. *Class No:* 320(082.2)

Tables & Data Books

[1406]
LANE, J.-E., *and others.* **Political data handbook: OECD countries.** New York, Oxford University Press, 1991. viii,257p. tables. £35. (*Comparative European politics.*) ISBN: 0198277180.
Statistics on 24 OECD countries' government and politics, plus social and economic background information. Data for a selection of years to 1985. Bibliographical references, p.255-7.
Class No: 320(083)

Histories

[1407]
BRACHER, K.D. **Age of ideologies:** history of political thought in the twentieth century. London, Weidenfeld & Nicolson, 1984. xii, 305p. £20. ISBN: 029778434x.
Translated from the German by Ewald Osers. Published in German by Deutsche Verlags-Anstalt GmbH, Stuttgart in 1982.

....(contd.)

21 chapters in 3 parts: I. The turn of the century - II the inter-war years - III. The present. Index of names, p.279-291. Analytical general index, p.293-305. *Class No:* 320(091)

[1408]

HAMPSHER-MONK, I. **A History of modern political thought:** major political thinkers from Hobbes to Marx. Oxford, Blackwell, 1992. xiii,609p. £45. ISBN: 1557861463.

A guide to the ideas and writings of major thinkers, plus background comment. 10 chapters: Thomas Hobbes - John Locke - David Hume - Jean-Jacques Rousseau - 'Publius': the Federalist - Edmund Burke - Jeremy Bentham - John Stuart Mill - G.W.F.Hegel - Karl Marx. Bibliography (p.563-92) by chapters, each in two parts: A. Original works; B. Subsidiary works. Analytical index, p.593-609. *Class No:* 320(091)

Biographies

[1409]

BLONDEL, J. *and* WALKER, C., *comps. & eds.* **Directory of European political scientists.** 4th rev. ed. Oxford, H. Zell, for the European Consortium for Political Research, University of Sussex, 1985. vi,640p. £48. ISBN: 0905450124.

3rd ed. published 1979.

*c.*3000 numbered entries, A-Z, covering academics working on a permanent or semi-permanent basis in Europe, including scholars who are not European citizens. Data includes information on careers, degrees, publications, and fields. Field index (African studies - American/Canadian studies ... Third world studies - Women's studies). *Class No:* 320(092)

[1410]

The Hutchinson encyclopedia of modern political biography. Helicon, 1999. 544p. £40. ISBN: 185986273x. *Class No:* 320(092)

[1411]

Who's who of women in world politics. London, Bowker-Saur, 1991. xxii,311p. tables. £55. $95. ISBN: 0862916275.

Over 1500 entries for women in world legislatures and other national and regional leadership roles in 115 countries. Arrangement is A-Z by name, and includes personal and professional achievements, biographical details in normal who's who format, and address. Biographies are followed by a statistical section showing the number of women elected to positions within the government, legislature, political parties and trade unions of each country. A biography index is arranged A-Z by country, subdivided by surnames, A-Z. *Class No:* 320(092)

Dictionaries

[1412]

LAW, C. **Women:** a modern political dictionary. London, I.B. Tauris, 2000. 304p. £24.95. ISBN: 186064502x.

Covers individuals involved in feminist political activism; highlights the "lost" period between 1914 and 1960. *Class No:* 320(092)(038)

Worldwide

[1413]

CALVOCORESSI, P. **World politics since 1945.** 7th ed. New York, Longman, 1996 xvii,878p. £19.99 ISBN: 0582277965, US.

Originally published in 1968. In six parts.

Covers all aspects of world politics over the last 50 years. Divided into six parts - 1. World power and world order - 2. Europe - 3. The Middle East - 4. Asia - 5. Africa - 6. America. The appendix includes a key to the United Nations Missions (acronyms and titles, and a history and analysis of the period from 1945. *Class No:* 320(100)

Dictionaries

[1414]

EVANS, Graham *and* NEWNHAM, Jeffrey. **The Dictionary of world politics** a reference guide to concepts, ideas and institutions. Rev. ed. London, Harvester Wheatsheaf, 1992 xii,364p. ISBN: 074501223x.

Contains bibliography.

Selection of entries governed by two main considerations; ideas considered essential to the understanding of world politics and terminology likely to be found in specialized texts or journals. Entries are made for individuals where their name is associated with particular ideas or policies. Entries are made for events only where they remain of current significance. *Class No:* 320(100)(038)

Almanacs

[1415]

QUAIN, A.J., *ed.* **The political reference almanac 1999-2000.** Pol. Sci. Books, 1999. 904p. $44.95. £28.56. ISBN: 0967028604.

In two parts: first, international information, dates and anniversaries; second, US government. Includes texts of the US Constitution, Monroe Doctrine. Includes index. *Class No:* 320(100)(059)

Developing Countries

[1416]

WILLIAMS, G. **Third World political organizations:** a review of developments. 2nd rev. ed. London, Macmillan Press, 1987. xiii,150p. tables. £29.50. ISBN: 0333362969.

First published 1981.

A review of organizations that help the Third-world. Includes UNCTAD conferences, the Non-aligned movement, special sessions of the United Nations, OPEC, and the Conference on International Economic Co-operation. An appendix is a data chart of the main events affecting the Third-world, 1944-1985. Notes, p.137-142, grouped by chapters. Select bibliography, p.143-44. Index, p.145-150. *Class No:* 320(4/9-77)

Europe

[1417]

COOK, C. *and* PUGH, G. **Sources in European political history.** London, Macmillan Press, 1987-90. 3v. (749p.). v.1. £38; v.2. £45; v.3. £35. ISBN: 0333239962, v.1; 0333277759, v.2; 0333423690, v.3.

V.1. *The European left;* v.2. *Diplomacy and international affairs;* v.3. *War and resistance* V.1. is a wide-ranging guide to the surviving personal papers of over 1000 individuals active on the European Left during the last century, including anarchists, syndicalists, pacifists, trade unionists, socialists and communists. Arrangement is A-Z (Abate ... Zyromsky), with brief information on the person and notes on the papers. V.2. provides a wide-ranging guide to the surviving private papers of over 1000 statesmen, politicians and diplomats who played a part in the shaping of modern Europe. Each volume includes a select bibliography. *Class No:* 320(4)

Encyclopaedias & Dictionaries

[1418]

Political and economic encyclopedia of Western Europe. Nicholson, F., *ed.* Harlow, Essex, Longman; Chicago, St. James Press, 1991. vii,411p. maps. £75. $85. ISBN: 0582068487, UK; 1558620729, US.

Data on the events, organizations and personalities shaping the future of Western Europe. 'The low price, generally high quality of the articles, and handbook format make this ... publication a useful purchase ...' (*Choice*, v.28(10), June 1991, p.1622). *Class No:* 320(4)(03)

Encyclopaedias

[1419]

ROSSI, E.E. *and* McCREA, B.P., *eds.* **The European political dictionary.** Santa Barbara, CA., ABC-Clio, 1986. xxii, 408p. 2 maps. $42.50. £37.40. (*Clio dictionaries in political science,* 7.) ISBN: 0874360463.

Preceded by a 'Guide to countries' the entries are grouped in 5 sections: 1. The United Kingdom - 2. France - 3. The Federal Republic of Germany - 4. Western European regionalism - 5. The Soviet Union. Sections on the major nations are divided into 'Historical perspectives', 'Social and economic background', 'Government institutions and processes', 'Political parties and elections', and 'Domestic and foreign politics'. Each of the 325 entries consists of 'Definition' and 'Significance' paragraphs. Cross-references follow the entries. Index, p.377-408. 'Useful for background information ... not complete enough for a real reference work' (*Parliamentary affairs*, v.41(2), April 1988, p.303). *Class No:* 320(4)(031)

Handbooks & Manuals

[1420]

COOK, C. *and* PAXTON, J. **European political facts of the twentieth century.** 5th ed. London, Macmillan, 2000. 458p. tables. £50. (*Macmillan historical and political facts.*) ISBN: 0333792033.

Contains statistical tables, annotated bibliographical lists, and brief summaries regarding governmental structure and political activity in each European country that has existed since 1900. Also documents the changes in European politics in recent years, including the fall of communism, the dissolution of the Soviet Union, and the conflict in the former Yugoslavia. *Class No:* 320(4)(035)

Yearbooks & Directories

[1421]

Who's who in European politics 3rd ed. London, Bowker-Saur, 1997 xxiv,873p. ISBN: 1857391632.

First issued for 1990/91

Section 1 contains over 8,000 biographies of active politicians arranged A-Z which focus on their political and professional life. Entries are checked by entrants themselves. Section 2 provides a country by country political directory and index, covering all members of the executive, the leaders of national and regional legislatures, and the main political parties and trade unions. *Class No:* 320(4)(058)

Almanacs

[1422]

COSSOLOTTO, M. The Almanac of European politics. Rev. ed. Washington D.C., Congressional Quarterly, 1995 321p. ISBN: 087187914x, US.

Previously published in 1991 under the title "The almanac of Transatlantic politics". The present edition has eliminated chapters on the the United States, Canada, NATO and Eastern Europe. The information is good, though the copy editing is poor.

Class No: 320(4)(059)

EU

Handbooks & Manuals

[1423]

The European union handbook. Barbour, P., *ed.* London, Fitzroy Dearbon, 1996 vi,349p. ISBN: 1884964281.

Covers politics and government in the European Union.

Class No: 320(40)(035)

Great Britain

[1424]

Biographical dictionary of British prime ministers. Eccleshall, R. *and* Walker, G., *eds.* London, Routledge, 1998. 448p. £65 hbk. £20.99 pbk. ISBN: 0415108306, hbk; 0415187214, pbk.

Written by some of the leading authorities on British politics, and a useful account of all British PMs from Walpole to Blair.

Class No: 320(410)

[1425]

COOK, C. Sources in British political history, 1900-1951. London, Macmillan Press, 1976-85. 6v. ISBN: 0333387899, set; 0333150368, v.1; 0333150376, v.2; 0333150384, v.3; 0333191609, v.4; 0333221249, v.5; 0333265688, v.6.

V.1. *A guide to the archives of selected organizations and societies*; v.2. *A guide to the papers of selected public servants*; v.3. *A guide to the private papers of Members of Parliament, A-K*; v.4. *...L-Z*; v.5. *A guide to the private papers of selected writers, intellectuals, and publicists*; v.6. *First consolidated supplement. Class No:* 320(410)

Handbooks & Manuals

[1426]

BUTLER, D. *and* BUTLER, G. Twentieth-century British political facts, 1900-2000. Basingstoke, Macmillan, 2000. 604p. tables. £25. (*Macmillan historical and political facts.*) ISBN: 0333772229.

First published 1963.

Ministers - Parties - Parliament - Elections - Political allusions - Civil Service - Royal Commissions, Committees of inquiry and tribunals - Administration of justice - Social conditions - Employment and trade unions - The economy - Nationalisation - Royalty - British Isles - Local government - The Commonwealth - International relations - Britain and Europe - Armed forces - The press - Broadcasting authorities - Religion - Bibliographical note. Analytical index. A valuable compendium of data. *Class No:* 320(410)(035)

Yearbooks & Directories

[1427]

The Directory of Westminster and Whitehall 1999/2000. Carlton, I., *ed.* Watford, Carlton, 1999 £88. ISBN: 1901581128. ISSN: 13601199.

Published annually.

A guide to the Civil Service and Parliament. Gives names of those to contact with regard to various issues in Government Departments, and contact points in their regional offices. Provides key data on Members of Parliament. *Class No:* 320(410)(058)

Almanacs

[1428]

WALLER, R. *and* CRIDDLE, B. The Almanac of British politics. 6th ed. London, Routledge, 1999. 992p. illus.,maps,tables. £90. £29.99 (pbk). ISBN: 0415185408.

Revised and updated following the 1997 general election. A comprehensive seat-by-seat analysis of all the parliamentary constituences, describing their social, economic and political character. Each profile also gives the seat's recent electoral history and looks forward to their prospects. *Class No:* 320(410)(059)

[1429]

—WALLER, R. Atlas of British politics. London, Croom Helm, 1985. ix.205p. 148 maps. £16.95. ISBN: 0709936087.

Complementary to the author's *Almanac of British Politics* and also a contribution in its own right.

Based on evidence provided by the 1983 General Election and the 1981 census of population. 13 geographical sections, all subdivided: 1. National maps - 2. South West - 3. South - 4. London ... 11. Wales - 12. Scotland - 13. Northern Ireland. Data include winners, Conservative support, Labour, Alliance, middle-class workers, professional and management workers, owner-occupied housing, local authority housing, non-white voters, unemployment, car ownership, educational qualifications, agricultural workers, coal mining.

Class No: 320(410)(059)

Chronologies

[1430]

FOOTE, G. A Chronology of post war British politics. London, Croom Helm, 1988. [3], 280p. £7.95. ISBN: 0709949227.

Covers from January 1945 to June 1987, and includes elections, government changes, significant legislation, internal party developments, social and economic developments, and international policies, documenting the major changes in British politics. No index. No introduction. A useful background reminder.

Class No: 320(410)(090)

Ireland

[1431]

MITCHELL, A. *and* Ó SNODAIGH, P., *eds.* Irish political documents, 1916-1949. Blackrock, Co. Dublin, Irish Academic Press, 1985. 254p. ISBN: 0716505886.

Lists 147 documents on political affairs, arranged chronologically.

Class No: 320(415)

[1432]

—MITCHELL, A. *and* Ó SNODAIGH, P., *eds.* Irish political documents, 1869-1916. Blackrock, Co. Dublin, Irish Academic Press, 1989. 195p. ISBN: 0716524228.

A companion volume to the above. 100 documents, chronologically arranged. '... traces the emergence of the Irish nation and responses to that development ... an effort to present a broad spectrum of political and constitutional issues' (*Introduction*). *Class No:* 320(415)

Quotations

[1433]

O'CLERY, C. Phrases make history here: political quotations in Ireland, 1886-1987. Rev.ed. O'Brien Press; Boston, Mass., G.K. Hall, 1987. 236p. £6.95; $25. ISBN: 0816189390, US.

First published in 1986, covering 1886-1986. Published in US as *The Dictionary of political quotations on Ireland, 1886-1987: phrases make history here.*

Over 1700 quotations, ranging from the significant to the trivial. Chronological arrangement. Attribution to each quotation.

Class No: 320(415)(082.2)

Northern Ireland

[1434]

FLACKES, W.D. *and* ELLIOTT, S. Conflict in Northern Ireland: an encyclopedia. 5th fully rev. & updated ed. Oxford, ABC-Clio, 1999. 750p. £37.50. ISBN: 0874369894.

First published 1980.

Entris are arranged alphabetically and cover events, people, parties and places from 1921 right down to July 1999. It has a very detailed chronology, but no bibliography. *Class No:* 320(416)

Commonwealth

[1435]

The Commonwealth. Larby, P.M. *and* Hannam, H., *comps.* Oxford, Clio Press; New York, Transaction, 1993. xxxvii,254p. Maps. $59.95 ISBN: 1560001100, US; 1851091866, UK.

Bibliographic guide arranged by topic, with wide coverage but political and economic concerns predominate. Includes bibliographies, archives and reference works. Author, subject and title index, p.223-54. *Class No:* 320(41-44)

Wales

[1436]

The Wales yearbook, 2000. Balsom, D., *ed.* Aberystwyth, HTV Cymru Wales, 1999. 700p. ports. £27.50. ISBN: 0953128725.

Critical review of the year in Wales and month-by-month chronology of principal news stories, cultural and linguistic profiles of all Parliamentary constituencies; guide to the Welsh Assembly and local government directory of over 800 organizations, pressure groups, public bodies, and Welsh media, etc. *Class No:* 320(429)

France

[1437]

BELL, D., *and others.* **A Biographical dictionary of French political leaders since 1870.** Hemel Hempstead, Herts, Harvester Wheatsheaf, 1989; New York, Simon & Schuster, 1990. 600p. £85. $85. ISBN: 0719810148; 0130846902.

Prepared under the auspices of the Association for the Study of Modern and Contemporary France.

Short, readable biographies of leading men and women in French politics since Napoleon III. Basic biographical data is combined with an explanation of why the figure is important to our understanding of French politics, and the shaping of modern France. Helpful appendices list presidents, prime ministers and important party leaders. Intended for students, the general reader and researchers. *Class No:* 320(44)

Spain

[1438]

DONAGHY, P.J. *and* **NEWTON, M.T. Spain: a guide to political and economic institutions.** Cambridge, Cambridge University Press, 1987. xiii,242p. £27.50. ISBN: 0521300320.

A guide to the major political and economic institutions established in Spain since the death of Franco. 14 chapters: 1. Introduction: political and economic background - 2. The Constitution of 1978 - 3. The monarchy - 4. Parliament - 5-8. Government and order - 9. Public sector enterprise - 10. Political parties - 11. Trade unions - 12. Business and professional organizations - 13. Financial organizations - 14. Geneal conclusions. All chapters are subdivided. 2 appendices (Chronological resumé of Spanish history since 1939; Elections since 1977). Select bibliography, p.229-232. Index of institutions, p.233-242. *Class No:* 320(460)

Russia

[1439]

McAULEY, M. Soviet politics, 1917-1991. New York, Oxford University Press, 1992. 160p. $21.95. ISBN: 0198780664.

An analysis of the developments which sustained, and then finally undermined, the Communist regime: revolution - state-building - party rule - terror - elections. *Class No:* 320(47)

[1440]

V.I. Lenin: an annotated bibliography of English-language sources to 1980. Egan, D.R., *and others, eds.* Metuchen, N.J., Scarecrow Press, 1982. 516p. $39.50; £29.65. ISBN: 0810815265.

Aims to include all English-language publications irrespective of place of publication or author's creed. Most entries have short annotations and the most important publications are marked with an asterisk. Book reviews are listed along with the works they review. Valuable for the study of 20th century Russian political science and history as well as for the study of Lenin. 'A quite extraordinarily detailed guide to the English end product' (*Library review,* Winter 1983, p.305). '... not only a welcome but even an indispensable contribution to Russian studies...' (*Choice,* v.20(7), March 1983, p.955). *Class No:* 320(47)

Asia

[1441]

KIM, E. *and* **ZIRING, L.,** *eds.* **The Asian political dictionary.** Santa Barbara, CA., ABC-Clio, 1986. xx, 438p. tables, maps. $40. £32.95. (*Clio dictionaries in political science 10.*) ISBN: 0874363683.

Focuses on south, southeastern and eastern Asia, including the Indian Ocean, 27 countries and territories in all. Over 3000 terms arranged in 8 chapters (political geography - political culture and ideology - political parties and movements - political institutions and

....(contd.)
processes - militarism and the armed forces - modernization and development - diplomacy - international relations and conflict). Maps, tables, index. *Class No:* 320(5)

[1442]

Who's who in Asian and Australasian politics. London, Bowker-Saur, 1991. xvii,475p. £99. $175. ISBN: 0862915937.

In 2 parts: part 1 has over 3000 biographies of politicians in the top and middle ranking levels, from over 25 countries; pt.2 is a political directory and index. *Class No:* 320(5)

Japan

[1443]

WARD, R.E. *and* **WATANABE, H. Japanese political science:** a guide to Japanese reference and research materials. Rev. ed. Ann Arbor, Mich., University of Michigan Press, 1961. (Reprinted Greenwood Press, 1978). xi, 210p. tables, maps. $59.75. ISBN: 0313204365.

1759 annotated items in 27 sections, each with an introduction (1. Bibliographies - 2. General reference works - 3. Periodicals - 4-27. Subject aspects (*e.g.* Constitutional law; National diet; Allied occupation of Japan). Author's name in entry is first given in romanized form, then in Japanese characters, and similarly with title. Cross-references. Index of authors and editors. *Class No:* 320(52)

Dictionaries

[1444]

STOCKWIN, A. Dictionary of the modern politics of Japan. London, Routledge, 2001. £45. ISBN: 0415151708. *Class No:* 320(52)(038)

Asia—Middle & Near East

[1445]

SHIMONI, Y., *ed.* **A Political dictionary of the Arab world.** Rev. ed. New York, Macmillan, 1988. 520p. illus., tables, charts, maps. $50; £40. ISBN: 0029164222.

Revised and updated version of *Political dictionary of the Middle East in the 20th century* (1972 & 1974).

600 entries prepared by a team of specialists from Tel Aviv University Centre for Middle Eastern and African Studies. Covers 21 Arab countries. Entries are arranged A-Z on a wide range of subjects from biographies to national political histories, movements and conflicts. 'Generally well researched and documented, the book is a useful tool for a wide ranging audience...' (*Library journal,* 15 February 1988p. p.161). *Class No:* 320(53+56)

[1446]

ZIRING, L. The Middle East political dictionary. Rev.ed. Santa Barbara, CA., ABC-Clio, 1992. 401p. tables, maps. $56.50. (*Clio dictionaries in political science, 5.*) ISBN: 0874366127.

Over 300 entries arranged in topical chapters (political geography - Islam - ethnicity - political parties and movements - the Arab-Israeli conflict - diplomacy and conflict). Cross-references.
Class No: 320(53+56)

Asia—South & South East

Dictionaries

[1447]

LEIFER, M. Dictionary of the modern politics of South-East Asia. 3rd ed. London, Routledge, 2001. £55.00. £18.99 (pbk). ISBN: 0415238757.

Contains bibliography and index.

Over 400 alphabetical cross-references covering the political history of the area. This work gives an extended narrative for each state and individual entries for the leading figures, political parties and organizations, major events and treaties found therein. Other documents are included. *Class No:* 320(54+59)(038)

Israel

Dictionaries

[1448]

REICH, B. *and* **GOLDBERG, D.H. The Political dictionary of Israel.** Woronoff, J., *ed.* Lanham, MD, Scarecrow Press, 2000. 528p. illus., tables. £56.25. $75. ISBN: 0810837781.

Comprehensive work of reference with detailed information on every aspect of the political life of modern-day Israel. It also aims at providing a guide through the complex political life of Israel, and covers biography of politicians and diplomats, institutions, organizations, events, concepts and documents.
Class No: 320(569.4)(038)

Africa

Bibliographies

[1449]

A Bibliography for the study of African politics. Waltham, Mass., Crossroads Press (new African Studies Association), 1977-. v.1-.

Published so far are:-

1, by R. Shaw and R.L. Sklar (1st published 1973 by University of California Press), 1977.

2, by A.C. Solomon, 1978.

3, by Eric Siegal, 1983. $18. ISBN 0918456479.

V.1 has 3951 entries for monographs and periodical articles, almost all in English and covering the period up to 1970. Complex arrangement: 2 main divisions - General works; Regions and states - with 90 sections. Extensive 30-page index. 'An excellent reference tool for anyone interested in African affairs' (RQ, v.13(2), Winter 1973, p.179).

V.2, also with over 300 entries and similarly arranged, is a supplement to v.1, covering the period 1971-75. V.3 is a second supplement. Class No: 320(6)(01)

Encyclopaedias & Dictionaries

[1450]

PHILLIPS, C.S. The African political dictionary. Santa Barbara, CA., ABC-Clio, 1984. xxvii,245p. $34; £25.25. (Clio dictionaries in political science, 6.) ISBN: 0874360366.

Over 225 terms grouped in chapters by subject, subdivided A-Z. Each term has a 'definition' and a 'significance' paragraph, highlighting the historical, geographical, economic, sociological, philosophical and religious characteristics. Cross-references. Index. Class No: 320(6)(03)

[1451]

Political and economic encyclopedia of Africa. Arnold, G., ed. Harlow, Longman, 1993. x,342p. £80. ISBN: 0582209951.

Four types of entry in A-Z order - country (54 countries and islands) - organizations - individuals (personalities and political parties) - general (problems or topics on more than one country). Cross-references. Cut-off point is early 1993. Index, p.323-342. Class No: 320(6)(03)

Handbooks & Manuals

[1452]

COOK, C. and KILLINGRAY, D. African political facts since 1945. 2nd ed. London, Macmillan; New York, Facts on File, 1990. 288p. £33. $35.00. £45. (Macmillan historical and political facts.) ISBN: 0333439856, UK; 0816024189, US.

First published 1983.

A chronology of key events is followed by sections on governors and heads of state - chief ministers - constitutions and parliaments - political parties - trade unions - armed forces and coups - foreign affairs and treaties - population and ethnic groups - basic economic statistics - biographies. Bibliography, p.257. Index, p.258-263. Class No: 320(6)(035)

Biographies

[1453]

WISEMAN, J.A. Political leaders in Black Africa: a biographical dictionary of the major politicians since Independence. Aldershot, Hants, Edward Elgar, 1991. xxiii,248p. £50. ISBN: 1852780479.

Alphabetical list of entries and list of abbreviations and acronyms precedes. Short biographical essays on 485 politicians who have shaped the development of Africa since Independence. Entries vary in length from ½p. to a page. Chronology of major events since 1960. Geographical index,p.247-8. Class No: 320(6)(092)

South Africa

[1454]

GASTROW, S, ed. Who's who in South African politics 5th ed. Johannesburg, Ravan Press, 1995. xxxiii,319p. illus. ISBN: 0869754580.

1st published 1985. Previous ed. Munich & London: H. Zell,1993

Over 100 profiles (1000-word essays) of people involved in South African politics on both the left and the right in and out of Parliament. Each profile ends with a list of sources. Includes list of politicians who appeared in previous editions but who no longer commanded a place. Class No: 320(680)

America—Central

[1455]

GUNSON, P., and others. The Dictionary of contemporary politics of Central America and the Caribbean. London, Routledge, 1991. vi,397p. illus. maps. £35. $45. ISBN: 0415024455.

A guide to the most important organizations, personalities, events and themes in the contemporary politics of the area. Countries covered are Mexico, Guatemala, Belize, British Honduras, El Salvador, Nicaragua, Costa Rica, Panama, Cuba, Dominican Republic, Haiti, Jamaica, Trinidad & Tobago, Barbados, Grenada, St. Vincent, St. Lucia, Dominica, St. Kitt's, Nevis, Antigua and Puerto Rico. 'This excellent reference work by three British journalists who specialize in Latin America' (Library journal, 15 April 1992, p.43-44). Class No: 320(728)

Latin America

Dictionaries

[1456]

ROSSI, E.E. and PLANO, J.C. Latin America: a political dictionary. Santa Barbara, CA., ABC-Clio, 1992. 242p. $56.50. ISBN: 0874366089.

Replaces The Latin American political dictionary.

10 chapters, each with entries A-Z (1. Geography, population and social structure - 2. Historical perspective - 3. Political culture and ideology - 4. Revolutionary and counter-revolutionary forces - 5. Political parties, pressure groups and elections - 6. The military - 7. Governmental institutions and processes - 8. Economic modernization and political development - 9. International law and organization - 10. United States-Latin American relations). Each entry is in two parts: definition, aim, etc. (plus cross-references); significance. Detailed analytical index. 'Entries are concise yet clearly written and convey essential introductory information' (Choice v.30 (10) June 1993 p.1608). Class No: 320(729.99)(038)

USA

Encyclopaedias

[1457]

BINNING, W.C. and ESTERLY, L.E. and STACIC, P.A. Encyclopedia of American parties, campaigns and elections. Westport, CT, Greenwood Press, 1999. 268p. $99.50. £78.50. ISBN: 0313303126.

Includes descriptions of modern political campaigns with attention to the structure of parties and electoral systems. Includes lists of presidents and vice-presidents. Bibliography. Class No: 320(73)(031)

Reviews & Abstracts

[1458]

United States political science documents. Pittsburgh, Pa., Industrial Applications Center, University of Pittsburgh, 1976-. v.1-. Annual. $395. ISSN: 01486063.

V.13 (published 1988) has over 3400 abstracts of political and social science articles from c.150 journals. Each issue is in two parts: Part 1 has a list of journals. Author/contributor index, rotated subject descriptor index, and subject index. Part 2 has the document description listing (abstracts). Also online from 1975-. Class No: 320(73)(048)

Almanacs

[1459]

JEE, S., ed. The World almanac of US politics, 1993-1995. New York, World Almanac (distributed by St. Martin's Press), 1993. 416p. $29.95. ISBN: 0886877091. ISSN: 10431535.

Designed to contain everything every citizen should know about who and what governs the country. Mainly a state-by-state directory of senators and representatives, with several lines of personal and political biography, committee memberships, voting data, as well as address and telephone number. '... a handy, inexpensive ready-reference guide to US government' (Reference books bulletin, 15 September 1989, v.86(2), p.211), of the 1989 ed. Class No: 320(73)(059)

Biographies

[1460]

American political scientists: a dictionary. Utter, G.H. and Lockhart, C., eds. Westport, CT, Greenwood Press, 1993. 362p. $85. ISBN: 0313278490.

Lists 171 political scientists who represent the origins and early years of the academic discipline, as well as the contemporary period. Entries arranged in A-Z order by name and are 2 to 3 pages each in length. Focus is on main themes, theories and major works of each

....*(contd.)*

scholar, and the most important publications by and about them are listed. Select bibliography. Appendices list the political scientists by university and by major field. *Class No:* 320(73)(092)

America—South

Encyclopaedias & Dictionaries

[1461]

GUNSON, P., *and others*. **The Dictionary of contemporary politics of South America.** London, Routledge, 1989. xi,314p. 14 maps. £19.95. *(Dictionaries of contemporary politics.)* ISBN: 0415028086.

A guide to the most important organizations, figures, events and themes in the contemporary politics of South America. Cross-references. Countries covered: Chile, Argentina, Paraguay, Colombia, Venezuela, Ecuador, Bolivia, Peru, Uruguay, Brazil, Surinam and Guyana. Includes list of entries by country, p.309-314.
Class No: 320(8)(03)

[1462]

Political and economic encyclopedia of South America and the Caribbean. Calvert, P., *ed.* New York, St. James Press, 1991. v,363p. Maps (on end papers). $85. *(Longman current affairs.)* ISBN: 1858621601, US; 0582085284, UK.

A chronology precedes the main A-Z listing. Includes countries and people. Length of entries varies (*eg* Brazilia (nearly 7 columns); Castro (3 columns); CARECOM (Caribbean Community and Common Market) (55 col.). General index, p.355-63. *Class No:* 320(8)(03)

Thesauri

[1463]

BECK, C., *and others, comps*. **Political science thesaurus II.** Rev. and expanded 2nd ed Pittsburgh, University Center for International Studies, University of Pittsburgh, in conjunction with the American Political Science Association. xviii, 696p. ISBN: 0916002470.

1st published under the title *Political science thesaurus*. Washington, Political Science Association, 1975

Main section records *c.*6000 terms, each followed by broader, narrower or related terms. 38 major concepts. Permuted and hierarchical indexes. 'An essential reference tool for academic and government libraries' *(Library journal,* v.100(21), 1 December 1975, p.2232). *Class No:* 320:025.43

Institutions & Associations

[1464]

BOGDANOR, V., *ed.* **The Blackwell encyclopedia of political institutions.** Oxford, Basil Blackwell Ltd., 1987. xvi, 667p. £45; $65. ISBN: 0631338412.

Contains 247 contributions from 13 Western industrialized countries. As well as political institutions, includes entries on many concepts and on deceased key political thinkers. Entries range from short paragraphs to 4-page articles (e.g., 'Civil rights': 3 cols.; 'European Community': 3 cols.; 'Monnet, Jean': 2 cols). Cross-references. Bibliographical references follow most entries. Contributors focus on their own world plus USSR and Eastern Europe. Index, p.647-667. '... the work is valuable because its main stream approach is more extensive and comprehensive than the various political science dictionaries available.' (*Choice,* v.26(1), September 1988, p.74). *Class No:* 320:061:061.2

Political Theory

[1465]

The Blackwell encyclopaedia of political thought. Miller, D., *ed.* Oxford, Blackwell, 1987. xiii,570p. ISBN: 0631140115.

350 entries, both substantial articles and brief definitions, analysing concepts in political thought that influence the contemporary world, and outlining the thought of leading political theorists, past and present. Mainly Western traditions. Cross-references. 134 contributors. '... a solid reference work' *(Reference books bulletin,* 1987/88, p.591). *Class No:* 320.001

[1466]

A Companion to contemporary political philosophy. Goodin, R.E. *and* Pettit, P., *eds.* Oxford, Blackwell, 1993. 679p. £60. *(Blackwell companions to philosophy.)* ISBN: 0631179933.

A guide to current thinking, focusing on normative issues. Explores the contribution that different disciplines have made to current debates, analyses political ideologies, and discusses major concepts.
Class No: 320.001

[1467]

PAREKH, B. **Contemporary political thinkers.** Oxford, Martin Robertson, 1982. x,219p. £17. ISBN: 0855203374.

'Explores the current state of political philosophy as reflected in the writings of some of its ablest practitioners' *(Preface)*. Chapters on 7 philosophers (Hannah Arendt - Isiah Berlin - C.B. Macpherson - Herbert Marcuse - Michael Oakeshott - Karl Popper - John Rawls) and a final chapter, 'Some reflections'. Notes (p.202-214) are arranged by chapter and include citations. Bibliography (p.215). Index (p.216-219). *Class No:* 320.001

[1468]

PLANT, R. **Modern political thought.** Oxford, Blackwell, 1991. 352p. £40. ISBN: 0631142231.

Reviews and analyses the major developments in political thought over the past 15 years (legitimacy of the state; rights, justice, power, welfare, equality, etc.). *Class No:* 320.001

Dictionaries

[1469]

Cassell dictionary of modern politics. London, Cassell, 1994 340p. ISBN: 030434432x.

Contains bibliographical index.

A dictionary of terms, abbreviations, concepts in political science, jargon words, key events, scandals, etc. Its coverage is world wide, dealing with the period from 1945 to 1994. The majority of terms are in English, but reference is made to some foreign terms in common use, such as Bundesbank and Perestroika. *Class No:* 320.001(038)

[1470]

The Concise Oxford dictionary of politics. McLean, I., *ed.* Oxford, Oxford University Press, 1996 559p. £7.99. ISBN: 0192852884.

Dictionary of concepts, people and institutions with an emphais on Britain and the United States. Coverage - Classical Greece to the present day. Includes a list of major political leaders by country. *Class No:* 320.001(038)

[1471]

PLANO, J., *and others*. **Dictionary of political analysis.** 2nd ed. Santa Barbara, CA., ABC-Clio, 1982. xvi, 197p. $17; £20.45. *(Clio dictionaries in political science, 3.)* ISBN: 0874363314.

First published 1973.

A-Z listing of terms, with cross-references. Each major entry is in two parts, a paragraph of definition, followed by a significance paragraph providing illustrations, examples, and applications for each defined concept. Selected bibliography, p.169-184. Index, p.185-197. *Class No:* 320.001(038)

[1472]

RIFF, M., *ed*. **Dictionary of modern political ideologies.** Manchester, Manchester University Press; New York, St. Martin's Press, 1987. xiv, 226p. £27.50; $37.60. ISBN: 071901882x, UK; 0312009283, US.

'... not a dictionary or encyclopedia of political concepts or doctrines ... an attempt to make clear how ideals and principles in fact lie at the heart of our political experience and aspirations.' *(Introduction)*. 42 essays arranged A-Z by subject (African nationalism - Anarchism - European integration - Fascism ... Keynesianism - Kuomintang ... Zionism). Short bibliographies of books (author & title only) conclude each essay. R. Scruton's *Dictionary of political thought* (1982) is considered to be better for simple explanations of political concepts and ideologies. *Class No:* 320.001(038)

[1473]

The Routledge dictionary of twentieth-century political thinkers. Benewick, R. *and* Green, P., *eds.* 2nd ed. London, Routledge, 1997. 296p. £50. ISBN: 0415158818.

Covers political theorists (and some practitioners, such as Lenin, Mao, Hitler). Articles vary in length from a sentence to several pages, and each is followed by cross-references and a selected bibliography of primary and secondary works. 'A useful, somewhat revisionist, supplement to other sources ...'(*Choice,* v.31(1), September 1993, p.88). *Class No:* 320.001(038)

[1474]

SCRUTON, R., *ed*. **A Dictionary of political thought.** 2nd ed. London, Macmillan Press Ltd., 1996. 592p. £9.99. ISBN: 0333337866.

1st published 1982

'... intention has been to extract, both from active debate, and from the theories and intuitions which surround it, the principle ideas through which modern political beliefs find expression. The emphasis of the dictionary is conceptual rather than factual ...' *(Preface)*. Includes over 1000 entries, ranging in length from 100 to 450 words. Includes biographies, but only when they cast light on intellectual conceptions. Cross-references. *Class No:* 320.001(038)

Histories

[1475]

Political thought since 1945: Philosophy, science, ideology. Tivey, L. *and* Wright, A., *eds*. Aldershot, Hants., Brookfield, Vt. :E. Elgar, distributed in the U.S. by Ashgate Publishing Co., 1992. x, 222p. £38.50. ISBN: 1852783117.

Accounts of the views of seven major thinkers - Arendt, Dahl, Habermas, Hayek, Macpherson, Oakeshott and Rawls. An introductory chapter sets out the ideas of other thinkers. *Class No:* 320.001(091)

[1476]

ROWE, C. *and* SCHOFIELD, M., *eds*. The Cambridge history of Greek and Roman political thought. Cambridge, Cambridge University Press, 2000. 766p. £75. ISBN: 0521481368. *Class No:* 320.001(091)

[1477]

SABINE, G.H. A History of political theory. 4th ed., rev. Hinsdale, Ill., Dryden Press, 1973. [xvii], 871p. $34.95. ISBN: 0030803055.
First published 1937.

3 parts: 1. The theory of the city state - 2. The theory of the universal community - 3. The theory of the national state (p.311-849). 36 chapters (35. Communism; 36. Fascism and National Socialism). Each chapter has footnotes and 'Selected bibliography'. Analytical index. Standard text-book, giving acceptable short analyses of major works concerned. *Class No:* 320.001(091)

Islamic Peoples

[1478]

ENAYAT, H. Modern Islamic political thought: the response of the Shi'i and Sunni Muslims in the twentieth century. London, Macmillan, 1982. 240p. £14. ISBN: 0333279689.

Aimed at those who wish to understand the often bewildering political situation in the Islamic world. Following a short introduction outlining how the traditional Islamic heritage has affected the development of modern intellectual currents, the author deals with an analysis of the differences and points of agreement between the two groups and also discusses the concept of the Islamic State. '... a lucid and detailed account of the most important religio-political movements in the Islamic world in the 20c. ... sheds valuable light on many of the problems which face the crucial area today.' (*British book news*, November 1982, p.670). *Class No:* 320.001(=95.297)

Middle Ages

[1479]

The Cambridge history of medieval political thought, c.350-1450. Burns, J.H., *ed*. Cambridge, Cambridge University Press, 1988. viii,808p. £60. ISBN: 0521243246.

Aims to be the contemporary successor to Gierke and Carlyle. 19 chapters in 5 parts: 1. Foundations; 2. Byzantium; 3. Beginnings: c.350-c.750; 4. Formation; c.750-c.1150; 5. Development: c.1150-1450; Conclusion. Within the parts treatment is largely thematic. Biographies (notes on medieval authors (p.690-777); index of names and persons (p.779-790); analytical subject index (p.791-808). '...quality of scholarship presentation uniformly high'. (*Political studies*, v.37(1). 1989. *Class No:* 320.001"01/14"

Tudor & Stuart Times

[1480]

The Cambridge history of political thought, 1450-1700. Burns, J.H., *ed*. Cambridge, Cambridge University Press, 1991. 800p. £70. ISBN: 0521247160.

A sequel and complement to the above. 21 chapters in 5 parts: 1. Renaissance and counter-renaissance; 2. Religion, civil government, and the debate on constitutions; 3. Absolutism and revolution in the sevemteenth century; 4. The end of Aristotelianism; 5. Natural law and utility. Conclusion. Biographies. Bibliography (for each part). Indexes of names of persons and of subjects. *Class No:* 320.001"1485-1760"

Government

[1481]

Federal systems of the world: a handbook of federal, confederal and autonomy arrangements. Elazar, D.J., *ed*. 2nd ed. (rev. and expanded) Harlow, Essex, Longman, 1994. xxi,364p. £99. ISBN: 0582236789.

Based on data collected by the Jerusalem Center for Public Affairs.

Main part is arranged A-Z by countries with federal, federacy/associated state and home rule arrangements (Basic introductory material, standard sections on government structure and the constitution, political dynamics/recent constitutional developments). Bibliography for each country. A second section examines confederal arrangements of ASEAN, Benelux, Caricom, the EC and the Nordic

....(contd.)
Council and Council of Ministers. '...useful addition to reference collections.'(*International affairs*, v.68(4), October 1992, p.721). *Class No:* 321

Encyclopaedias

[1482]

Encyclopedia of government and politics. Hawkesworth, M. *and* Kogan, M., *eds*. London, Routledge, 1992. 2v.(1404p.). £160 the set. ISBN: 0415030927.

84 detailed essays on theoretical and factual change of the last three decades, arranged under nine main headings (political theory - central concepts - contemporary ideologies - contemporary political systems - political institutions - political forces and political processes - centripetal and centrifugal forces in the nation-state - policy-making and policies - international relations - major issues in contemporary politics). Each topic includes extensive bibliographies and suggestions for further reading. Index of topics and people. 'This up-to-date and well-executed work provides a sound introduction to all aspects of political study' (*Choice*, v.30(7), March 1993, p.1110). *Class No:* 321(031)

[1483]

MAGILL, F.N., *ed*. International encyclopedia of government and politics. London, Fitzroy Dearborn, 1996. 2v. £175. ISBN: 188496463x.

Surveys 5000 years of politics and government. Topics covered include civil rights and liberties, and the functions of government. *Class No:* 321(031)

Yearbooks & Directories

[1484]

The International directory of government, 1995. 2nd ed. (rev. and extended) London, Europa Publications, 1995 830p. ISBN: 1857430042.
Originally published in 1990.

Guide to government ministries, departments, agencies and corporations for every country in the world. Each chapter provides details on Heads of State, legislative systems and a full list of ministries. Goverment organizations and affiliated groups are arranged by subject headings and include sections on agriculture, banking and the economy, defence, media and transport. Each entry includes the names of principal officers, with full address, telephone, fax and telex numbers, as well as an outline of activities. *Class No:* 321(058)

Biographies

[1485]

Regents of nations: a systematic chronology of states and their political representatives past and present; a biographical reference book. Truhart, P. München, K.G. Saur, 1984-88. 3v. in 4 (4258p.). Dm960; $525. ISBN: 359810491x.

Part 1. Africa/America; pt.2. Asia/Australia - Oceania; pt.3/1. Middle-, Eastern-, Northern-, Southern-, Southeastern Europe; pt.3/2. Western Europe. Bibliography, index, addenda to parts 103. Includes biographical information on c.30,000 heads of state and premiers from 1000 nations, along with information on territorial and provincial governors of nations back to the Middle Ages. Also includes information on the historical development of present nation states and a review of political structures of the past 5000 years. *Class No:* 321(092)

Worldwide

[1486]

DERBYSHIRE, J.D. *and* DERBYSHIRE, I. Political systems of the world. 2nd ed. (rev. and expanded) Oxford, Helicon Publishing, 1996 xii,684p. ISBN: 1859861148.
Originally published by W.R. Chambers, 1978. Contains bibliography.

Includes appendices, index, glossary of abbreviations and acronyms, regional maps and index of tables, including one of the leading political leaders in the world's leading states. Published in three parts; - 1. The comparative approach - 2. Political systems of the world's nation states - 3. Towards one world. *Class No:* 321(100)

Yearbooks & Directories

[1487]

DERBYSHIRE, J. Hutchinson political systems of the world. New ed. Oxford, Helicon, 1999. 480p. illus.,maps. £80. (*Helicon general encyclopedias.*) ISBN: 1859863035.

Comprehensive guide to world politics. *Class No:* 321(100)(058)

[1488]

Worldwide government directory 2000. London, Stationery Office Agencies/Keesing's Worldwide, 1996 $379. ISBN: 1886994277.

Current information on more than 26,000 appointed and elected officials. *Class No:* 321(100)(058)

Biographies

[1489]

Current leaders of nations CD Mossman, J., *ed.* Detroit, Mich., Gale, 1997 £99.00 (initial subscription for Windows stand-alone. Quarterly updates £42.00 per annum. LAN price (2-8 users) £130.00. Quarterly updates for LAN £60.50 ISBN: 0787616281, US.

Contains bibliographic references.

Recommended for second level students. Provides bibliographical data on world leaders. Coverage "- 1. Name of country and leader - 2. Leader's title, name pronunciation and portrait - 3. A thumbnail sketch of the country - 4. The nation's political background and recent political situation. - 5. Information about the leader's personal background, rise to power, domestic and foreign policies, successes and failures." *Class No:* 321(100)(092)

EU

Yearbooks & Directories

[1490]

Euro who's who: who is who in the institutions of the European Union and in the other European organizations. Seingry, G.-F., *ed.* 5th ed. Brussels, Éditions Delta, 1996 360p. £105.00 ISBN: 2802901109.

Title and text in English, French and German

Includes biographies of the senior civil servants currently working within the institutions of the European Union, and within 20 other European government organizations, members of the permanent representations, and the heads of mission accredited to the European Union, the chairman and secretaries of the main govermental organization, and of the trade and professional organizations set up at a European Level. *Class No:* 321(40)(058)

Great Britain

Handbooks & Manuals

[1491]

The Guide to public bodies: "Quangos" 1999. Carlton, I., *ed.* London, Carlton, 2000. 369p. £80.00. ISBN: 1901581187.

Published annually.

Contains details of over 1,000 public bodies. Details of each body include address, telephone, fax, email, website, functions, chairmen, chief executives and press officers. Arrangement is alphabetical within each Department, and there is an index of all the bodies. *Class No:* 321(410)(035)

[1492]

JELLINEK, D. Official UK: the essential guide to government web sites. 2nd ed. London, Stationery Office Books, 2000. 306p. £25. ISBN: 0117024465.

Lists hundreds of websites which give access to official information. Each major government website is reviewed, described and evaluated for its usefulness, and entries give a profile of the department or agency concerned. *Class No:* 321(410)(035)

EU

Handbooks & Manuals

[1493]

The Guide to the governance of Britain in Europe. Carlton, I., *ed.* London, Carlton, 1999. 300p. £95.00 ISBN: 1901581101. ISSN: 13642855.

Published annually.

Includes data and contact details of UK MEPs ; names of British Commitee members ; details of the Council of Ministers and data on European Commissioners and Directors General with contact details thereof. Good source of reference for information on the European Union and Britain's place therein. *Class No:* 321(410)(40)(035)

Scotland

Histories

[1494]

The Scots and Parliament Jones, C., *ed.* Edinburgh, Edinburgh University Press, 1996 147p. (*Parliamentary history*.) ISBN: 0748608230.

A collection of articles/essays on Scottish constituional history. Third volume in a series sponsored by the journal "Parliamentary History". *Class No:* 321(411)(091)

Russia

Yearbooks & Directories

[1495]

McCAULEY, M. Who's who in Russia from 1900. London, Routledge, 1997 296p. illus.,maps. £48 (hbk). £12.99 (pbk). ISBN: 0415138973; 0415138981, pbk.

Includes bibliographical references and index

Introductory chapter on Russian political history since 1917, with a chronological table of events. Entries are arranged alphabetically, and a glossary is placed at the end. *Class No:* 321(47)(058)

China

Yearbooks & Directories

[1496]

Directory of Chinese government and organizations. 2000 ed. Pacific Com Inc., 1999. 304p. $75. *Class No:* 321(510)(058)

Japan

Biographies

[1497]

Who's who in Japanese Government, 1988/89. Cloutier, M.M. *and* Nakazawa, M. 3rd ed. Tokyo, International Cultural Association, 1990. x,420p. ISBN: 4900477036.

Includes a profile of the Japanese political system, Lower House members, Upper House members, Committees of the Lower House, Committees of the Upper House, Political parties organizational charts. Political parties officials, and important addresses and telephone numbers. Index of personal names. *Class No:* 321(52)(092)

USA

[1498]

Congressional Quarterly's guide to the Presidency. Nelson, M., *ed.* 2nd ed. Washington D.C., Congressional Quarterly Inc., 1996 2 v. 1800p. illus. ports. ISBN: 156802018x, US.

First published in 1989 in 1 vol.

The second ed. has been extended to include all the Bush administration and the first 3 years of the Clinton presidency. Coverage - origin and development of the presidency; selection and removal of the president; powers of the presidency; the public and the parties; the White House and the executive branch; chief executive and federal government and biographies of the presidents and vice presidents. Two appendices contain documents and texts and tabular and graphical data with an index. '... the most complete and most up-to-date source on this office. Academic and public libraries will find the amount of revision certainly justifies purchase'. *Booklist*, v.93(11) 1 February 1997, p.963 *Class No:* 321(73)

[1499]

MOORE, J.L. Elections A to Z London, Fitzroy Dearborn, 1999. 560p. £65.00 ISBN: 1568022077.

Some 220 entries giving information about key concepts, issues and political parties in the United States. It has 25 appendices with electoral information not readily obtainable elsewhere, including web-sites. It is a useful aid to understand the US government system. "Too elementary foir researchers and faculty, this work is highly recommended for students and others in better understanding US elections" (*Choice*, December 1999). *Class No:* 321(73)

Bibliographies of Bibliographies

[1500]

SCHWARZKOPF, L. Government reference books 92/93: a biennial guide to US government publications; 8th biennial volume. Littleton, Col., Libraries Unlimited, 1994 400p. £72.95

Limited to print sources, essential for government depositories. *Class No:* 321(73)(009)

[1501]

—HARDY, G.J. *and* **ROBINSON, J.S. Subject guide to U.S. government reference sources.** 2nd ed. Littleton, Colo., Libraries Unlimited, 1996. 358p. ISBN: 156308189x, US.

"Includes both print and electronic sources. Entries range from atlases to indexes. Second edition adds 814 titles. Organized by four broad subject areas and arranged within catagories alphabetically by government agency". *Class No:* 321(73)(009)

Dictatorships

[1502]

Encyclopedia of nationalism. Motyl, A. Academic Press, 2000. £200. ISBN: 0122272307.

Scholarly and well-documented entries on movements, theories, proponents, scholars and goals. *Class No:* 321.6

Fascism

[1503]

LAQUEUR, W., *ed.* **Fascism: a reader's guide: analysis, interpretations, bibliography.** London, Wildwood House, 1978 (Reprinted by Wildwood House, 1988). x, 478p. £8.95. ISBN: 0704501902.

12 contributors. 6 parts: 1. Some notes towards a comparative study of Fascism in sociological historical perspective - 2. Italy and Germany - 3. Local Fascisms (E. Europe; Latin America; Western Europe) - 4. Fascist ideology - 5. Fascism and the economy - 6. Interpretations. Well documented (*e.g.* Italian Fascism; p.125-50; 77 references). Analytical index. 'The essays are thorough and analytical. They provide an excellent evaluation of the literature' (*Journal of politics*, v.40(2), May 1978, p.567). *Class No:* 321.64

[1504]

—REES, P. **Fascism in Britain.** Atlantic Highlands, N.Y., Humanities Press, 1980. 243p.

A bibliography of Fascism in Britain, 1923-77. 'An invaluable starting point for research digging, most likely to be used at university level' (*Choice*, v.18(8), April 1981, p.1077). *Class No:* 321.64

[1505]

REES, P. **Fascism and pre-Fascism:** a bibliography of the extreme right in Europe, 1890-1945. Brighton, Sussex., Harvester Press; Totawa, N.J. Barnes & Noble, 1984. xxii, 330p. £65. ISBN: 0710803729 (UK); 0389204722 (US).

A select bibliography on the ideology and practice of the extreme right, including books, journal articles and dissertations published since 1945. An introductory chapter precedes a chapter on Fascism generally and chapters on East and West European countries (*e.g.* Germany, p.233-315). Individual chapters focus on parties, movements and prominent figures, presented roughly in chronological order. Index of names, p.316-330. " ... the first useful general bibliography on European Fascism" (*Choice* v.22(6) February 1985 p.798). *Class No:* 321.64

Democracy

Dictionaries

[1506]

GREVE, B. **Historical dictionary of the welfare state.** Lanham, Scarecrow, 1998. 240 p. $44. (*Religions, philosophies, and movements series, no. 15.*.) ISBN: 0810833328.

Identifies, describes and defines the core concepts that are fundamental to an analysis of the welfare state. It aims to present the most relevant and important concepts and definitions. With chronology, listings of acronyms and abbreviations, and bibliography. *Class No:* 321.7(038)

Internal Relations

Jews

Bibliographies

[1507]

SINGERMAN, R. **Anti-semitic propaganda:** an annotated bibliography and research guide. New York, Garland, 1982. 448p. $60. (*Garland reference library of social science, 112.*) ISBN: 0824092708.

A major reference tool. Comprehensive, with informative but not evaluative annotations. Arranged in two unequal sections. The first section lists *c.*2000 English-language works (books, pamphlets, and dissertations) in chronological order from 1870 to the present. Includes one holding institution for each entry and reviews of major works. The second smaller section is a research guide of works on anti-semitism classified by subjects. 'An important acquisition for every college library'. (*Choice*, v.20(3), November 1982, p.412). *Class No:* 323(=924)(01)

Minorities

[1508]

ASHWORTH, G., *ed.* **World minorities.** Sunbury-on-Thames, Mddx., Quartermaine House Ltd., 1977-78. 2v. (167p. 192p.).

V.1 has 44 groups, A-Z: 1. The Adivasis: the 'scheduled tribes' of India - 2. The Afars and the Assas ... 8. The Bedouin ... 10. The Bretons ... 13. The Catalans ... 17. The Corsicans ... 28. The Kashmiri ... 31. The Maoris of New Zealand ... 34. Pakistan's Hindus

....(contd.)
... 43. The Ukrainians - 44. Yugoslav's minorities. Contributed by various hands; each contribution has selected bibliography. Index, p.163-167. *Class No:* 323.1

[1509]

—ASHWORTH, G., *ed.* World minorities in the eighties: a third volume in the series. Sunbury-on-Thames, Quartermain House Ltd., 1980. xvii, 174p. £4.25. ISBN: 0905878117.

37 groups, A-Z: (1. Aboriginal peoples of Siberia ... 10. Fiji ... 22. Migrant workers in the Gulf States ... 37. The Welsh in Argentina). Index, p.171-174. *Class No:* 323.1

[1510]

World directory of minorities. Anderson, B. *and* Minorities Rights Group, *ed.* London, Minority Rights Group, 1997 xvi,840p. maps. ISBN: 1873194366.

Previous ed. Harlow, Longman, 1990

Regional groupings. Within the groups, more than 150 ethnic or radical minorities are listed, A-Z, with a few salient facts (alternative names - location - population - percentage of population - religion - language) in 200-5000 words. Appendices are abstracts from original documents. Index. Essential for locating individual minority groups. *Class No:* 323.1

Almanacs

[1511]

MARTIN, M. **The Almanac of women and minorities in world politics.** Boulder, Co., Westview Press, 2000. 504p. £37.95. ISBN: 0813368057.

Gives political and biographical details on the achievements of women and minorities in the executive, legislative and judicial branches of every nation in the world. *Class No:* 323.1(059)

Europe—Eastern

Handbooks & Manuals

[1512]

HORAK, S.M., *and others.* **Eastern European national minorities, 1919-1980:** a handbook. Littleton, Col., Libraries Unlimited Inc., 1985. xv, 353p. tables. $47.50. ISBN: 0872874168.

Covers the treatment of national minorities; statistical data; the political, social, economic and educational aspects and changes that have occurred during the 3 periods: Interwar - World War II - Post-World War II. 10 chapters, the first 9 of which are each divided into 'Historical summary' and 'Bibliography', the bibliographies being annotated, selective, international, and representing different views and interpretations. Chapters: 1. Eastern Europe national minorities, 1919-1980 - 2. National minorities in Poland, 1919-1980 - 3/6 & 8/9 cover Czechoslovakia, Hungary, Romania, Yugoslavia, Bulgaria and Albania - 7. The Slovene and Croat minorities in Italy and Austria, 1945-1980 - 10. National research centers in Eastern European countries. Author/ short title index, p.331-353. *Class No:* 323.1(401)(035)

USA

Bibliographies

[1513]

COUTTS, B.E., *comp.* **Ethnics in American society.** In *Booklist*, v.80(21), July 1990, p.2109-2112.

A briefly annotated bibliography highlighting some of the best recent reference sources on ethnic minorities in American society, with special emphasis on African Americans, Asian Americans and Hispanic Americans. *Class No:* 323.1(73)(01)

[1514]

Minorities in America: the annual bibliography, 1976-. Miller, W.C., *ed.* Pennsylvania State University Press, 1985-?. Irregular. 1976 ed. published 1985, $100. ISSN: 07482302.

Follows Miller's *A comprehensive bibliography for the study of American minorities* (1977).

The 1976 ed. has *c.*7500 entries drawn from over 900 journals, and also including books, government publications and dissertations. Arrangement is in 41 subject groups, and includes people of European background as well as coloured people, indigenous and immigrant. Annotations of *c.*100 words. Author index. *Class No:* 323.1(73)(01)

[1515]

MOMENI, J.A. **Demography of racial and ethnic minorities in the United States:** an annotated bibliography with a review essay. Westport, CT. Greenwood Press, 1984. 293p. $35. (*Bibliographies and indexes in sociology, 2.*) ISBN: 0313239754.

688 entries for books, periodical articles, dissertations and master's theses. Except for Jewish Americans, white American ethnic groups are excluded. Includes a 40-page review essay giving an overview of historical, political and social events affecting minorities. Author and minority/subject index. *Class No:* 323.1(73)(01)

[1516]

—MOMENI, J.A. Housing and racial/ethnic minority status in the United States: an annotated bibliography with a review essay. Westport, CT., Greenwood Press, 1987. 310p. $45. (*Bibliographies and indexes in sociology, 8.*) ISBN: 0313248206.

1007 citations to monographs and journal articles on housing for minorities, with summaries or abstracts for each title.
Class No: 323.1(73)(01)

Yearbooks & Directories

[1517]

Minority organizations: a national directory. 4th ed. Garrett Park, MD., Garrett Park Press, 1992. 690p. $50. ISBN: 0912048301.

First published 1978.

The directory's real strength is in the large number of regional and local groups it lists, as well as the national ones. Includes 7700 active organizations and 2800 'lost' ones. *Class No:* 323.1(73)(058)

Resistance & Revolution

[1518]

DEGENHARDT, H.W., *ed.* Revolutionary and dissident movements: an international guide. 3rd ed. London, Longman Group, 1991 (Distributed in US and Canada by Gale Research Co.). 408p. £85. $145 (*A Keesing's reference publication.*) ISBN: 0582009863, UK; 0810320568, US.

First published 1983 as *Political dissent.*

Details of the activities, leadership, policy and affiliation of more than 1000 underground movements, national liberation or secessionist movements and human rights groups, arranged A-Z, by country (Afghanistan ... Zimbabwe - International revolutionary groupings). Coverage is through mid-1987. A brief introductory section to each country describes the political realities there, then details the various dissident groups. Select bibliography, p.427-430, arranged general, then by region, and A-Z by author. Detailed index of countries, individuals and revolutionary organizations, p.433-466. Aim is to update 5-yearly. 'Better country balance than *The Radical right ...*' (*Reference books bulletin*, 1 September 1988). *Class No:* 323.2

[1519]

JESSUP, J.E. A Chronology of conflict and revolution, 1945-1985. Westport, CT., Greenwood Press, 1989. x,943p. $85; £73.10. ISBN: 0313243085.

The chronology covers the period September 1945 to December 30, 1985. Brief information is given under the entries for each date. No cross-references. A glossary of abbreviations, and an index (p.847-942) complete the work. *Class No:* 323.2

[1520]

MUNRO, D. *and* DAY, A.J. A World record of major conflict areas. London, Edward Arnold Publishers Ltd.,; Chicago, Ill., St. James Press, 1990. [vi],374p. maps. £45. $85. ISBN: 0340522976, UK; 1558620664, US.

'The purpose is to describe and elucidate, in an easy reference format, some 28 current conflicts in different parts of the world' (*Preface*). Arranged in 5 regions (1. Africa - 2. Middle East - 3. Asia/ Far East - 4. Americas - 5. Europe), each subdivided by country. Chapters on specific conflicts follow a standard structure, beginning with a map and profile of the relevant country or territory, historical background, current status of conflict with chronology of events, followed by directory sections. General bibliography. p.374. *Class No:* 323.2

[1521]

SZAJKOWSKI, B. Encyclopedia of conflicts, disputes and flashpoints in Eastern Europe, Russia and the successor states. Harlow, Essex, Longman. 1993. 416p. illus. £85. (*Longman current affairs.*) ISBN: 058221002x. *Class No:* 323.2

Bibliographies

[1522]

BLACKEY, R. Modern revolutions and revolutionists: a comprehensive guide to the literature. Rev. ed. Santa Barbara, CA., ABC-Clio, 1982. 488p. $55.75. (*War/peace bibliography series, 17.*) ISBN: 0874363306.

First published 1976.

Aims to gather together the most important English-language writings on some 140 revolutions, most occurring in the 19th and 20th centuries. Following an introductory essay the chapters cite scholarly articles, books, collections of documents, and published primary sources. After the first chapter, 'Concepts and aspects', the arrangement of chapters is chronological order, the modern period being sub-divided geographically. Author/editor and subject indexes. Chronology of revolutions. '... a laudable accomplishment ...' (*Choice,* v.21(1), September 1983, p.58). *Class No:* 323.2(01)

[1523]

BOWMAN, J.S., *and others*. Professional dissent: an annotated bibliography. New York, Garland, 1984. 322p. $39. (*Public affairs and administration series, 2. Garland reference library of social science, 128.*) ISBN: 0824092171.

The subject is 'whistle-blowing' in government and business. The author's definition is 'an employee who reveals information about illegal, inefficient, or wasteful action that endangers the health, safety, or freedom of the public'. Nearly 1400 entries, covering books, periodical and newspaper articles, and government reports, are organized in chapters on business, government, science and engineering, selected professions, etc. Literature included is mainly US, and published during the past 15 years to 1982. More than half the entries are annotated. A resource section lists basic journals, directories, etc., and there are listings of works that offer personal guidance to employees, and relevant organizations.
Class No: 323.2(01)

[1524]

From radical left to extreme right: a bibliography of current periodicals of protest, controversy, advocacy, or dissent, with dispassionate content-summaries to guide librarians and other educators. Skidmore, G. *and* Spahn, T.J. 3rd ed., completely rev. Metuchen, N.J., Scarecrow Press, 1987. 503p. $59.50. ISBN: 0810819678.

First published 1967; 2nd ed. 1970-76.

280 annotated entries for periodicals with political content, grouped under 21 general chapter headings. Each chapter is introduced by a brief essay about the subject area and its publications. Content-summaries are preceded by such information as address, editor, price, frequency of publication and indexing. Geographical, subject, and title/ editor/publisher indexes. *Choice,* October 1987, p.290, reports that it has only 280 detailed entries as against 1200 in the 2nd ed. but many others are listed, and that it is 'A commendable attempt, but far from successful'. *Class No:* 323.2(01)

Encyclopaedias

[1525]

VAN CREVALD, M.L. Encyclopedia of revolutions and revolutionaries: from anarchism to Zhou Enlai. New York, Facts on File Publications, 1996. 496p. $75. ISBN: 081603236x.
Class No: 323.2(031)

Terrorism & Persecution

[1526]

WILKINSON, P. *and* STEWART, A.M., *eds.* Contemporary research on terrorism. Aberdeen, Aberdeen University Press, 1987. xx,634p. £45. ISBN: 0080350682.

The published proceedings of a conference held at Aberdeen University in April, 1986.

6 chapters, each subdivided: 1. Definitional and conceptional aspects - 2. Moral and religious aspects - 3. Trends and pattern in the history of terror - 4. Behavioural aspects - 5. Terrorism and the media - 6. National and international responses. A quarter of the book is devoted to chapter 3. 36 expert contributors. Selected English-language bibliography, p.599-623. Name index, p.625-631; index of terrorist movements and groups, p.633-634. ' .. wide coverage of facts and of sophisticated arguments; (*International affairs*, v.64(2), Spring 1988, p.274-275). *Class No:* 323.28

Bibliographies

[1527]

EL-SHERBINI, M. Terrorism: current readings. In *RSR*, v.18(4), 1990, p.49-63,48.

91 entries in sections: general works, psychological aspects, religious aspects, combating terrorism, periodicals, online batabases, and bibliographies. *Class No:* 323.28(01)

[1528]

LAKOS, A. International terrorism: a bibliography. London, Mansell; Boulder, Col., Westview, 1986. xii, 481p. £30. $37.50. ISBN: 072011862x, UK; 0813371570, US.

Claims to be the 'definitive bibliography of the literature of terrorism'. Includes over 5600 entries of English-language materials covering terrorist activities over the past two decades. No annotations. Arrangement of entries primarily by subject: 1. Reference works (subdivided by form) - 2. General works - 3. Theories of terrorism - 4. Psychological and social aspects of terrorism - 5. Strategies and tactics of terrorism - aspects - 6. Counter measures to terrorism - 7. Domestic and international law aspects - 8. Media and terrorism - 9. Nuclear terrorism threat - 10. Geographical, subdivided by regions and then countries. Author index, p.417-445; subject index, p.447-481. '... easy-to-read, handsome mixture of type faces and point sizes, and a modest purchase price.' (*Choice,* April 1987, p.1201).
Class No: 323.28(01)

[1529]

—LAKOS, A. Terrorism, 1980-1990: a bibliography. Boulder, CO, Westview Press, 1991. x,443p. $55. ISBN: 0813380359.

5850 entries in the same format as the above. Chapters 2-9 deal with broad subject categories; chapter 10: Geographical subdivision. *Class No:* 323.28(01)

[1530]

MICKOLUS, E., *comp*. The Literature of terrorism: a selectively annotated bibliography. Westport, CT., Greenwood Press, 1980. xi,553p. $67.95. ISBN: 0313222657.

3395 entries, mostly annotated. Sectionalised topics (*e.g.* the responses to terrorism; relationship between terrorism and the media and literature); also country sections. Some significant French, German and Italian titles included. Well indexed. 'Highly recommended for academic and large public libraries' (*Library journal*, 15 January 1981, p.136-7, on which the above annotation is partly based). Adversely reviewed in *Choice* (v.18(10), May 1981, p.1238), which finds the annotations sparse and of very little help, and the publication expensive. *Class No:* 323.28(01)

[1531]

MICKOLUS, E., *comp*. Terrorism, 1980-1987: a selectively annotated bibliography. Westport, CT., Greenwood Press, 1988. ix,314p. $55; £42.25. (*Bibliographies and indexes in law and political science, no.8.*) ISBN: 0313262489.

Concentrates on material written in the 1980s. 'In addition to surveying journalistic, social scientific and traditional historical studies in some dozen languages, the book also includes fictional literature of terrorism' (Advert.). *Class No:* 323.28(01)

[1532]

—MICKOLUS, E. Terrorism, 1988-1991: a chronology of events and a selectively annotated bibliography. Westport, CT., Greenwood Press, 1993. 916p. $125. ((*Bibliographies and indexes in military studies,6).*.) ISBN: 0313289700.

In 3 parts: Update on incidents between 1960 and 1987 - Review of the incidents, 1988-91 - Bibliography of books and journal articles (including fiction) in many languages. Highly commended in *Choice*(v.31(2), October 1993, p.270). *Class No:* 323.28(01)

[1533]

—MICKOLUS, E.F. *and* SIMMONS, S.L. Terrorism, 1992-1995. Westport, CT, Greenwood Press, 1998. 980p. £115. ISBN: 0313304688.

Includes bibliography of the most important literature on terrorism. *Class No:* 323.28(01)

[1534]

MILLER, R. 'The Literature of terrorism'. In *Terrorism*, v.11(1), 1988, p.63-87.

12 notes and 33 references, A-Z by author, follow the text of the literature review, dealing with traditional literature, historical studies, normative-judicial/legal studies, behaviourist literature, psychological studies, socio-economic studies, and public policy studies. *Class No:* 323.28(01)

[1535]

ONTIVEROS, S.R., *ed*. Global terrorism: a historical bibliography. Santa Barbara, CA., ABC-Clio, 1986. xiii, 168p. $49.50. (*ABC-Clio research guides, no. 16.*) ISBN: 0874364531.

598 abstracts of periodical articles published between 1965 and 1985, drawn from the publisher's history database. Includes some articles in foreign languages. Emphasis is on post-World War II terrorism generally. Arranged in 7 geographic chapters and including topics such as the use of terrorism as a means of political or economic coercion, terrorist groups, terrorist conspiracies by nations, and types and uses of terrorism. Lengthy, clearly written abstracts. Subject index, p.115-139; author index, p.141-144; chronology of terrorist events, p.145-168. 'Useful starting place for research on a timely topic'. (*Library journal*, v.111(15), 1 September 1986, p.190). *Class No:* 323.28(01)

Encyclopaedias

[1536]

HUNTER, T.B. The A to Z of international terrorist and counterterrorist organizations. Lanham, Scarecrow, 2000. 304p. $45. ISBN: 0810834286.

The book has detailed profiles of over 400 international terrorist, counterterrorist and militia groups. These are arranged alphabetically, with cross references. Appendices and bibliography included. *Class No:* 323.28(031)

[1537]

LENTZ, H. M. Assassinations and executions: an encyclopedia of political violence, 1865-1986. Jefferson, N.C., McFarland & Company, 1988. 275p. $29.95 £22.45. ISBN: 0899503128, US; 1558621008, UK.

Aims to present concise worldwide reference to political assassinations, political executions, and also unsuccessful attempts against major figures. Chronological arrangement. Entries detail the manner, the motive, the assailant (when known) brief biographical information on the victims, the immediate effects on the political climate of the day, and in some cases, the final fate of the assassin. Index to personal and country names. *Class No:* 323.28(031)

[1538]

THACKRAH, J.R. Encyclopedia of terrorism and political violence. London, Routledge & Kegan Paul, 1987. xi, 308p. £16.95. $35. ISBN: 0710206593.

Designed to provide information about theories and terms used in the rapidly growing academic study of terrorism and political violence. 200 entries of which about half focus on specific events, individuals, groups and nations. Virtually all entries relate to the post-World War II era, and vary in length from about 500 to 1000 words. Arranged A-Z (Abu Nidal ... Zimbabwe African People's Union (ZAPU). References and select bibliography of books and articles from the 1970s to 1986, p.290-294, with 'see also' references also after entries. Index, p.295-308. '... will be of use to researchers studying terrorism and to anyone trying to make some sense of terrorist activities reported in the daily press'. (*Reference books bulletin*, 1 March 1988, p.1119). *Class No:* 323.28(031)

Yearbooks & Directories

[1539]

JANKE, P. *and* SIM, R. Guerrilla and terrorist organisations: a world directory and bibliography. Brighton, Sussex, Harvester Press, 1983. 560p. £85. ISBN: 0710800134.

Brief descriptions of almost 600 violent intergovernmental organizations worldwide, grouped by region and country of origin. Introductions to the geographical sections also list the major analytical and historical works on the subjects, providing a useful bibliography. List of organizations cited, but no other index. 'This comprehensive work is to be praised for its thoroughness and detail and for the clarity of its organization'. (*Choice*, v.21(8), April 1984, p.1112, 1114). *Class No:* 323.28(058)

[1540]

ROSIE, G. The Directory of international terrorism. Edinburgh, Mainstream Publishing Co. (Edinburgh) Ltd., 1986. 310p. £14.95. ISBN: 1851580212.

Surveys more than a century of revolution, terror and counter-terror. A long introduction on terrorism (p.13-36) with 20 references, is followed by an A-Z listing of people (terrorists, people terrorized), operations, etc. Entries vary in length from a few lines to a page. Up-to-date basic information that is not easily available elsewhere. Select bibliography, p.307-310. 'A ready reference guide to the major events and players, but its lack of an index and sparse and inconsistent use of alphabetical cross-references diminish usefulness for this purpose'. (*Choice*, April 1987, p.1203). *Class No:* 323.28(058)

Almanacs

[1541]

SHAFRITZ, J.M., *and others*. Almanac of modern terrorism. New York, Facts on File, 1991. xiv,290p. £28. ISBN: 0816021236. *Class No:* 323.28(059)

Chronologies

[1542]

MICKOLUS, E.F., *and others*. International terrorism in the 1980s: a chronology of events. Iowa State University, 1989-. 2v.(v.1:541p.). V.1. $49.95. ISBN: 0813800242 V.1; 0813801729 v.2.

Continues the author's *Transnational terrorism: ... 1968-79* (1981).

V.1. covers 1980-1983; V.2. will cover 1984 - 1987. Comprehensive descriptions of terrorist incidents throughout the world, the length of the descriptions varying from a few lines to several pages. Sources are not indicated. 2 appendices to V.1. (I. lists terrorist groups; II. is a reprint of ITERATE 3 data codebook). *Class No:* 323.28(090)

Elections

[1543]

MACKIE, T.T. *and* ROSE, R. A Decade of election results updating the International Almanac. Glasgow, Centre for the Study of Public Policy, University of Strathclyde, 1997. 131p.,[5]p. (*Studies in public policy.*) *Class No:* 324

Bibliographies

[1544]

CATT, H. 'Diverse routes to electoral comprehension'. In *Parliamentary affairs*. v.42(1), January 1989, p.123-127.

A review article listing 8 items on electoral studies. *Class No:* 324(01)

Handbooks & Manuals

[1545]

ARMS, T.S. *and* RIDLEY, E., *eds*. **World elections on file.** New York, Facts on File, 1987. 2v.(loose-leaf), with quarterly up-date. $195 pa. ISBN: 0816017662.

A loose-leaf service of information on the latest election results and related political information for 165 nations. *Class No:* 324(035)

[1546]

Elections since 1945: a worldwide reference compendium. Gorvin, I., *ed*. Harlow, Essex, Longman; Chicago, St. James Press, 1989. ix,420p. £85. $150. ISBN: 0582036208, UK; 1558620176, US.

Arranged A-Z by country (Afghanistan ... Zimbabwe) and including all national presidential and legislative elections, in sovereign states, since 1945 or, in the case of former colonies, since accession to independence. Additional section covers elections to the European Parliament. Appendix describes principal systems of proportional representation. *Class No:* 324(035)

[1547]

INTER-PARLIAMENTARY UNION. **Chronicle of parliamentary elections and development; 1 July 1986/30 June 1987.** Geneva, International Centre for Parliamentary Documentation, 1987. 163p. SwF.30.

First published for July 1 1966/June 30, 1967.

Brief notes on developments in various countries, followed by information on 38 parliamentary elections (electoral systems and results), distribution of MPs by sex, profession, age, etc. *Class No:* 324(035)

Maps & Atlases

[1548]

LEONARD, D. *and* NATKIEL, R. **World atlas of elections:** voting patterns in 39 democracies. London, The Economist Publications Ltd., 1986 (distributed in North America by Gale Research Co.). [4] 160p. 197 maps 66 diagr & charts, all in col. £46; $85. ISBN: 0850580897.

Democracies covered were selected on the basis of size (minimum population: 500,000; independence: minimum five years; and freedom: minimum five years). For each country: short essay on government and elections, list of main political parties, election dates, map showing parliamentary seats. Entries vary in length from one to nine pages, mostly two to three pages. Includes brief bibliography of related materials and list of sources of country information (p.5-8). Intended to complement Mackie and Rose's *International almanac of electoral history* (qv). Mixed reviews; ' ... an excellent, easy-to-use handbook ...' (*Reference books bulletin, 1986/87, p.149*); ' ... doubtful whether there is a need for this book' (*Parliamentary affairs*, v.41(2), April 1988, p.302); ' ... difficult to assess the readership the work is aimed at. Specialists will feel the need to verify data' (*International affairs*, v.63(4), Autumn 1987, p.725). *Class No:* 324(084.3)

Worldwide

Yearbooks & Directories

[1549]

MACKIE, T.T. *and* ROSE, R. **The international almanac of electoral history** 3rd ed. (fully rev.) London, Macmillan, 1991 xv,511p. £27.50. ISBN: 0333452798.

Originally published in 1974. Contains bibliography.

A compilation of election results in Western nations since the beginning of competitive national elections. The study is confined to industrialised nations. It covers more than 600 elections in 25 countries and focuses on the elections for the lower houses of parliament ie. House of Commons, Congress etc, or Presidential Elections. Information given in two parts: 1) evolution of electoral system and franchise laws. 2) List of political parties with English equivalent. Four types of table are given; total number of votes, percentage share of each party, number of seats, percentage of seats. *Class No:* 324(100)(058)

Europe

[1550]

MACKIE, T.T. *and* CRAIG, F.W.S., *eds*. **Europe votes 3: European Parliamentary election results, 1989.** Aldershot, Hants. Dartmouth Publishing Co. Ltd., 1990. £37.50.

Full information about the 1989 elections, including brief outlines of the electoral system, notes on the less well-known parties, and results by constituencies. *Class No:* 324(4)

Maps & Atlases

[1551]

SALLNOW, J. *and* JOHN, A. **An Electoral atlas of Europe, 1968-1981:** a political geographic compendium including 76 maps. London, Butterworth Scientific, 1982. [8], 149p. maps, fig., tables. £22.50. ISBN: 0408108002.

Developed from a series of articles published by the authors in the *Geographical magazine* in 1977 and 1978, the book attempts to show the degree of electoral support in major administrative divisions of European countries. Chapter 1: Western and Southern Europe: a political overview; 2: Central Europe; 3: Maritime Europe; 4: Mediterranean Europe; 5: Nordic Europe; Appendix 1: Results of referendums in Denmark, Norway, Ireland and the United Kingdom on accession to the European Community; Appendix 2: The electoral systems of Europe. Index and index of political parties. *Class No:* 324(4)(084.3)

Europe—Western

Histories

[1552]

CARSTAIRS, A.McL. **A Short history of electoral systems in Western Europe.** London, Allen & Unwin, 1980. [5],236p. tables. £18. ISBN: 0043240062.

18 chapters in 6 parts: 1. Electoral systems - 2. Belgium and the Netherlands - 3. The Nordic countries - 4. Austria and Switzerland - 5. The great powers on the Continent [Italy, Federal German Republic, France] - 6. The United Kingdom and Ireland. An introduction (p.1-6), with references sets the scene from 1864. References also follow each chapter. Select bibliography, p.225-231, A-Z by author. Index, p.232-236. *Class No:* 324(400)(091)

Great Britain

[1553]

British electoral facts, 1832-2000. Rallings, C. *and* Thrasher, M. Aldershot, Hants., Ashgate Publishing, 2000. £45. ISBN: 1840140534.

First published 1968 as *British Parliamentary election statistics, 1918-70*; 2nd ed. 1976 as *British Parliamentary election facts, 1885-1975*, published by Parliamentary Research Services.

Facts and statistics on all of the general elections and by-elections that have taken place in the UK since the passing of the Reform Act in 1832. *Class No:* 324(410)

[1554]

British Parliamentary election results, 1983-1998. Rallings, C. *and* Thrasher, M. Aldershot, Hants, Ashgate Publishing, 1999. 432p. £65. ISBN: 1840140585.

Earlier editions are for 1832-1885 (2nd ed., 1989. 1st pub. 1977. 768p. £60. ISBN 0900178264); 1885-1918 (2nd ed., 1989. 1st pub. 1974. 704p. £60. ISBN 0900178272); 1918-1949 (3rd ed. 1983. 804p. ISBN 090017896x); 1950-1973 (2nd ed. 1983, 780p. £60. ISBN 0900178078) and 1974-1983.

Data is given for the 3 countries, counties, boroughs and universities. Indexes to candidates and constituencies. *Class No:* 324(410)

[1555]

—RALLINGS, C. *and* THRASHER, M. **Britain votes. 6: British Parliamentary election results 1997.** Aldershot, Hants., Ashgate Publishing, 1998. 238p. illus.,tables. £42. ISBN: 1840140542.

First published 1977.

Intended to provide an interim supplement to the series *British Parliamentary election results* (above). Gives the name and party of each candidate, the number of votes polled, the percentage of the total poll and the majority. Boundary changes and lost deposits indicated. Tables and appendices give details of total votes cast, turnout, etc. Index to candidates. *Class No:* 324(410)

[1556]

BUTLER, D. *and* KAVANAGH, D. **The British general election 1997.** London, Macmillan, 1997. 356p. illus., tables. £37.50 hbk. £19.50 pbk. ISBN: 0333647750, hbk; 0333647769, pbk.

First was for 1945.

Covers salient events of the Parliament, planning of the parties' campaign strategies, the election campaign itself, and the treatment of the campaign by the mass media and opinion polling agencies. Also provides extensive and analytical statistical appendix. *Class No:* 324(410)

[1557]

BUTLER, D. *and* TROTT, N. **British general elections since 1945.** New ed. Oxford, Blackwell, 2000. 160p. illus. tables. maps. £15.99. ISBN: 0745615767.

1st published 1990

Examines post-war elections, the mechanics of voting, timing of elections, cost, the media, local electioneering, etc. 2 appendices: 1. Election results, 1945-1997; 2. Election peaks and troughs. Bibliography and Index. *Class No:* 324(410)

[1558]

KINNEAR, M. **The British voter: an atlas and survey since 1885.** 2nd ed. New York, St. Martin's Press, 1981. 173p. maps. $40. ISBN: 0312105630.

First published 1968.

Comprehensive coverage of British general elections from 1885 to the 1970s, with special analyses of the effects of redistributions, of migrations of voters among parties, and of voting patterns by occupational and religious groups. Also the Common Market referenda and elections to the European Parliament. Special sections on Wales and Scotland and Northern Ireland. Excellent annotated bibliography. Maps somewhat overcrowded. '... a unique and valuable work ...' (*Choice,* March 1982, p.892). *Class No:* 324(410)

Scotland

[1559]

PARRY, R. **Scottish political facts.** Edinburgh, T. & T. Clark, 1988. 154p. £9.95. ISBN: 0567291235.

Contains parliamentary constituency results since 1945 and local election results since 1974; lists current Scottish Members of Parliament; and includes 100 key socio-economic indicators comparing Scotland and England. *Class No:* 324(411)

Ireland

[1560]

WALKER, B.M., *ed.* **Parliamentary elections results in Ireland, 1801-1922.** Dublin, Royal Irish Academy, 1978. xvi,438p. IR£8.10.

Fourth volume in the series of publications ancillary to *A New history of Ireland,* edited by T.W. Moody, and others (Oxford, Clarendon Press, 1976-), and conceived at the same time as the second volume, *Irish historical statistics, population, 1821-1971. Class No:* 324(415)

[1561]

—Parliamentary elections results in Ireland, 1918-1992: Irish elections to Parliaments and Parliamentary assemblies at Westminster and Belfast, Dublin, Strasbourg. Dublin, Royal Irish Academy; Belfast, The Institute of Irish Studies, Queen's University of Belfast, 1992. 358p. Maps. ISBN: 0901714968. *Class No:* 324(415)

Commonwealth

Bibliographies

[1562]

BLOOMFIELD, V. **Commonwealth elections, 1945-1970: a bibliography.** Westport, CT., Greenwood Press, 1977. xvi, 306p. $46.95. ISBN: 0837190673.

5654 numbered, unannotated entries, covering more than 760 elections and referenda held at national, state and provincial level in the Commonwealth countries and dependencies. 15 geographical areas (Commonwealth and general - Americas ... Pacific area). List of journals cited, p.267-74. Author and name index. 'A model of how such a work should be produced' (*African research & documentation,* no.14, 1977, p.36). *Class No:* 324(41-44)(01)

France

[1563]

COLE, A. *and* CAMPBELL, P. **French electoral systems and elections since 1789.** 3rd ed. Aldershot, Hants., Gower, 1989. xii,202p. tables. £25. ISBN: 0566056968.

9 chapters in 3 parts: I. Introduction; II. French electoral system and elections, 1789-1958; III. French electoral systems and elections in the Fifth Republic. Conclusion. 6 appendices: A. General surveys; B.

....(contd.)

Overseas deputies; C. Elections to Upper Chamber; D. Election of President; E. Local and regional elections; F. Tables of reference. Bibliography, p.193-97. Index, p.198-202. *Class No:* 324(44)

USA

[1564]

Presidential elections since 1789. 5th ed. Washington, D.C., Congressional Quarterly Inc., 1991. 235p. tables, maps. $19.95. ISBN: 0871876094.

First published 1975.

Consists largely of tables, maps, brief biographies of candidates. Deals with every presidential election since 1789 and every primary since 1912. *Class No:* 324(73)

[1565]

RENSTROM, P.G. *and* ROGERS, C.B. **The Electoral politics dictionary.** Santa Barbara, CA., ABC-Clio, 1989. 365p. $44.50. ISBN: 0874365171.

*c.*400 selected entries pertaining to electoral politics in the US, including words, concepts, organizations, court decisions, etc. grouped in chapters relating to political culture and public opinion, political participation, campaigns, elections, political parties, interest groups, and the media. Entries are lengthy and include 'significance' paragraphs. Cross-references. Considered to be a useful supplement to J.M. Shafritz's *The Dorsey dictionary of government and politics* (qv). *Class No:* 324(73)

[1566]

YOUNG, M.L. **The American dictionary of campaigns and elections.** Lanham, MD, Hamilton Press (distributed by University Press of America 1987). 246p. $24.95. ISBN: 0819154466.

Defines 725 terms used by US political campaigners. Clear, brief entries. Cross-references. Bibliography. Subject index. *Class No:* 324(73)

Migration

Tables & Data Books

[1567]

WILLCOX, W.F., *ed.* **International migrations.** New York, Gordon & Breach, 1929 (Reprinted 1969-70). 2v. (1112p., 715p.). tables, diagrs. v.1: $160. v.2: $188. ISBN: 0677022107.

V.1: Statistics: v.2: Interpretations. V.1 contains international migration statistics for 16 countries, from the beginning of the record of each country until 1924. Annotated tables, preceded by descriptive and historical commentary. *Class No:* 325(083)

Europe

[1568]

COUNCIL OF EUROPE. **People on the move:** new migration flows in Europe. Brussels, Council of Europe, 1992. 250p. ISBN: 9287120208.

Describes migration patterns, especially from east to west during the last five years; also national and United Nations policies. Includes bibliographical references. *Class No:* 325(4)

[1569]

The New geography of European migrations. King, R., *ed.* London & New York, Belhaven Press, 1993. 240p. 20 illus. £35. ISBN: 1852932910.

A study of population migrations following the collapse of the Soviet Bloc. Contributors are British, European and United States demographers. *Class No:* 325(4)

Biographies

[1570]

Biographisches Handbuch der deutschsprachigen Emigration nach 1933/International biographical dictionary of Central European emigrés, 1933-45. Institut f. Zeitgeschichte München/Research Foundation of Jewish Emigration Inc., New York., *comp.* Munich, K.G. Saur, 1980-83. 3v. (933p.; 1398p.; 301p.). DM.960.- the set. V.1 & 2: $175 each; v.3: $125. ISBN: 3598100876, set; 3598100884, v.1; 3598100892, v.2; 3598100906, v.3.

V.1 covers politics, economics, government and living; v.2 covers science, arts and literature; v.3 is the index. V.1 & 2 are in German; v.3 is in German and English. *Class No:* 325(4)(092)

USA

Bibliographies

[1571]

BUENKER, J.D. *and* BURCKEL, N.C., *eds*. **Immigration and ethnicity:** a guide to information sources. Detroit, Mich., Gale Research Co., 1977. xii, 305p. $68. (*American government and history information guide series*.) ISBN: 0810312026.

Nearly 1500 entries, mostly annotated, for primarily English-language items. 7 main sections: General accounts and miscellaneous - Old immigration - New immigration - Orientals - Recent ethnics - Post 1920s - Acculturation, assimilation, ethnicity and restrictions - Centers, repositories, societies, documents and journals (listing ethnic organizations and their publications). US-based.
Class No: 325(73)(01)

Histories

[1572]

Dictionary of American immigration history Cordasco, F., *ed*. Metuchen, NJ, Scarecrow Press, 1990. xxv,784p. $97.50. ISBN: 0810822415.

More than 2500 entries by *c*.100 contributors, mainly American social scientists. Arranged A-Z, entries range in length from a few lines to 7p. (*eg* White slave trade and immigrants). Includes information on most of the ethnic groups, important individuals, immigration societies, mutual aid societies, legislation and restrictions relating to immigrants. Cross-references. Appendix: Selected bibliography,p.776-84. *Class No:* 325(73)(091)

Black Races

Bibliographies

[1573]

Black immigration and ethnicity in the United States: an annotated bibliography. University of Michigan. Center for Afro-American & African Studies Staff, *comps*. Westport, CT., Greenwood Press, 1985. xi, 170p. $36.95. (*Bibliographies and indexes in Afro-American and African studies*, 2.) ISBN: 0313243662.

Entries for 1049 books, articles, government documents, dissertations, master's theses and chapter essays published through 1982, arranged in 6 topical main sections: Bibliographies and literature surveys - General works on immigration and ethnicity - United States immigration legislation and policies - Aspects of black immigration - Studies of individual groups - Selected list of works on black immigrants to Canada and Great Britain. About half the entries have descriptive annotations. Author and subject indexes. '... a useful bibliography'. (*College & research libraries*. January 1986, p.73). Highly recommended by *Choice*, (v.22(11/12), July/August 1985, p.1609). *Class No:* 325(73)(=96)(01)

Colonial Administration

[1574]

Colonialism in Africa, 1870-1960. Stanford, CA., Hoover Institution on War, Revolution and Peace, 1969-75. 5v. tables, maps. ISBN: 0521073731, v.1; 052107732x, v.2; 052107844x, v.3; 0521086418, v.4; 0521078598, v.5.

1: *The history and politics of colonialism. 1870-1914;* edited by L.H. Gann and P. Duignan. 1969. 532p. ($87.50). 2: *The history and politics of colonialism, 1914-1960;* edited by L.H. Gann and P. Duignan. 1970. 563p. ($84.50). 3: *Profiles of change: African society and colonial rule;* edited by V. Turner, 1971. 455p. ($74.50). 4: *The economics of colonialism;* edited by P. Duignan and L.H. Gann. 1975. 719p. ($99.50). 5: *A bibliographic guide to colonialism in sub-Saharan Africa,* by P. Duignan and L.H. Gann. 1973. 552p. ($84.50). V.5 (2,516 entries) ranges over anthropology, law, literature, medicine, natural science, politics and religion, as well as including *c.2,000* items, arranged by colonial power, region and colony. General introductory section (*c*.300 entries) on general reference material, bibliographies, etc. Index of authors, titles, organisations, agencies, colonies and main geographical areas. Includes an amount of non-English language material. 'In all this is a scholarly work which will be invaluable to anyone studying Africa over the last hundred years' (*International affairs*, v.50, no.3, July 1974, p.517). *Class No:* 325.3

[1575]

HENIGE, D.D. **Colonial governors,** from the fifteenth century to the present: a comprehensive list. Madison, University of Wisconsin Press, 1970. xx, 461p. $50. ISBN: 0299054403.

Under colonizing countries, A-Z (Belgium - Denmark - France (bibliography, p.63-65) -Germany - Great Britain (bibliography, p.191-195) - Italy - Japan - Netherlands - Portugal - Russia - Spain - Sweden - US (bibliography, p.359). General index; index of governors' names, p.375-461. *Class No:* 325.3

Bibliographies

[1576]

HALSTEAD, J.P. *and* PORCARI, S. **Modern European imperialism:** a bibliography of books and articles, 1815-1972. Boston, Mass. G. K. Hall, 1974. 2v. (xiv, 508p.; xiv, 501p.).

V.1. *General and British Empire;* V.2. *French and other empires. Regions.* V.1, divided geographically, has *c*.15,000 unannotated entries, including many periodical articles (*c*.100 journals cited: 20 English, 7 French, and 3 US journals searched comprehensively). 'British South Africa' (p.242-93) is closely subdivided (General; Atlases; Bibliographies; Documents and papers; Economic and financial; Federation and Union; Fiction and literary comment; Great Boer War; Historiography; Race relations and native policy; High Commission Territories ...). No index. *Class No:* 325.3(01)

Commonwealth

[1577]

MANSERGH, N. **The Commonwealth experience.** 2nd ed. London, Macmillan Press, 1982. 2v. (288p.; 308p.). £35 each vol. ISBN: 0333331583, v.1; 0333331605, v.2; 0333331680, set.

First published in one vol., 1969.

V.1 *The Durham report to the Anglo-Irish treaty;* v.2. *From British to multiracial Commonwealth.* V.1 has 7 chapters in 2 parts: 1. The foundation members and the nature of their association - 2. The British Commonwealth of Nations, 1914-21. V.2 has 7 chapters in 3 parts: 1. The British Commonwealth of Nations, 1921-47 - 2. The Commonwealth since 1947 - 3. Retrospect 1838-1981: the historical experience. Each volume has extensive notes by chapter and an analytical index. *Class No:* 325.3(41-44)

British Colonies

Bibliographies

[1578]

GREAT BRITAIN. Colonial Office. Library. **Catalogue of the Colonial Office Library, London.** Boston, Mass., G.K. Hall, 1964-79. 15v. + 7v. of supplements. $1490 the set of 15v. 1st. supplement: $140; 2nd ... $220; 3rd ... $545. ISBN: 0816106886, the set of 15v; 0816107297, 1st supplement; 0816108439, 2nd supplement; 0816100101, 3rd supplement.

187,000 photolithographed catalogue entries in v.1-15 (1-2: Author catalogue: pre-1950 accessions - 3-6: Author and title catalogue: post-1950 accessions - 7-8: Subject catalogue: pre-1950 accessions - 9-13: Subject catalogue: post-1950 accessions - 14-15: Classified catalogue: post-1950 accessions). *c*.100,000 entries in the 3 supplements (1st supplement: 1963-1967; 2nd supplement (1972. 2v.); 3rd supplement (1979. 4v.). No key to the classified catalogue (v.14-15), which follows the Library of Congress classification. 'All aspects of organization and development of those countries which form or have formed part of the Commonwealth, are covered by this catalogue, which reflects the changing interests and activities of the Colonial Office over the past 300 years' (*Introduction*). An invaluable catalogue of books, pamphlets, reports, official publications and periodical titles. *Class No:* 325.3(41-5)(01)

Handbooks & Manuals

[1579]

GREAT BRITAIN. Colonial Office. **The Corona Library.** London, HMSO, 1952-71. 13v. illus., maps.

A series of well-produced, illustrated volumes dealing with the United Kingdom's former dependent territories, the way their people live and how they were governed: Basutoland, Bechuanaland, British Guiana, British Honduras, Fiji, Hong Kong, Jamaica, North Borneo, Nyasaland, Sierra Leone, Swaziland, Uganda, Western Pacific Islands. Designed 'to fill the place between official Blue Books on the one hand and the writings of occasional visitors on the other, to be authoritative and readable' (Series note). *Class No:* 325.3(41-5)(035)

Histories

[1580]

MORGAN, D.J. **The Official history of colonial development.** London, Macmillan, 1980. 5v. tables, maps. each £33. ISBN: V. 1-5, 0333262247, 0333262301, 0333262328, 0333262336, 0333262344.

1. *The origins of British aid policy, 1924-1945.*
2. *Developing British colonial resources, 1945-1951.*
3. *A reassessment of British aid policy, 1951-1965.*
4. *Changes in British aid policy, 1951-1970.*
5. *Guidance towards self-government in British colonies, 1941-1971.*
V.5 (xvii, 382p.) has 11 chapters (8. 'Decolonialization, 1963-1966', p.207-50. 'Sources', 1-90). 5 appendices (1. Administrations and ministers concerned with colonial affairs, 1924-1974). Analytical index. Author is lecturer in Economics, Univ. of London. 'A valuable

....*(contd.)*
preview of unused evidence of a subject of great contemporary interest and importance' (*British book news*, December 1980, p.728). *Class No:* 325.3(41-5)(091)

Biographies

[1581]

KIRK-GREENE, A.H.M. **A Biographical dictionary of the British Colonial Service, 1939-1966.** Oxford, Hans Zell, 1990. ISBN: 0905450965.

Consisting of almost 10,000 entries, this is an A-Z register of all members of the Colonial Office whose names appeared in the *Colonial Office lists* in the period stated. It covers the Professional Services (education, forestry, medical, police, public works) as well as the Administrative Service, serving in all colonial territories. A substantial introduction assesses the annual *Colonial Office lists* as a primary biographical source for the social, administrative and career history of the Colonial Service. *Class No:* 325.3(41-5)(092)

Africa

[1582]

KIRK-GREENE, A.H.M. **Decolonization in British Africa.** In *History today*, v.42, January 1992, p.44-50.

A historiographical survey, which refers to important books on the subject in the text. *Class No:* 325.3(6)

[1583]

WESTFALL, G. **French colonial Africa:** a guide to official sources. London, Hans Zell, 1992. x,226p. ISBN: 1873836600.

Descriptive guide to guides and bibliographies; French colonial archives; publications of the Central Administration; semi-official publications; and colonial government publications. Bibliography of official publications of individual colonies,p.113-198. *Class No:* 325.3(6)

Slavery

[1584]

MILLER, J.C. **Slavery and slaving in world history:** a bibliography. 2nd ed. Armonk, NY, M.E. Sharpe, 1998. 2v. (828p.) £131.50. ISBN: 0765602814.

Updated and enl. ed. of *Slavery*, 1985.

Over 5000 consecutively numbered entries grouped in 11 sections (General and comparative; North America; Spanish mainland; Brazil; Caribbean; Africa; Muslim; Ancient; Medieval and early modern Europe; other areas; the slave trade). Includes books, chapters in books, journal articles, and doctoral dissertations, mainly in Western European languages. No annotations. Author index. Subject/keyword index. Annual supplements planned for publication in the journal *Slavery and abolition*. *Class No:* 326

Histories

[1585]

WALVIN, J. **Black ivory:** a history of British slavery. London, HarperCollins, 1992. 384p. illus. maps. £20. ISBN: 0246138912.

Using contemporary accounts, the author shows how British maritime trade and power were transformed by the Atlantic slave trade. Also describes the brutal conditions of the trade and its legacy of racism. *Class No:* 326(091)

Africa

[1586]

HOGG, P.C. **The African slave trade and its suppression:** a classified and annotated bibliography of books, pamphlets and periodical articles. London, Cass, 1973. xvii, 409p. £45. ISBN: 0714627755.

Originally as thesis for the L.A. fellowship, accepted 1970, with title 'A classified bibliography ... on the African slave trade'.

4,675 numbered entries. Part 1: 'Slave trade' (A. Collection of evidence - B. General accounts - C. West Africa - D. Sudan - E. East Africa - F. Slaving voyages - G. Medical conditions - H. Laws and official documents - I. Economic controversy - J. Economic history - K. Biographies of slaves - L. Ethnic origin of slaves). Part 2: 'Abolition and suppression' (M. Abolition controversies ... R. Laws and official documents - S. Naval blockade ... W. History of abolition ... Y. Biographies of abolitionists - Z. Imaginative literature. Appendix 1: Unpublished theses - 2. Addenda. Author, personal name, geographical name and anonymous title indexes.

The same author's *Slavery - the Afro-American experience* (British Library, 1979. 52p. illus. (incl. col.), map. £1.95) is an introduction - using British Library resources - 'to the history of slavery in the British colonies in America and the West Indies from the 17th century to the early 19th centuries' (*British library news*, no.48, December 1979, p.2). *Class No:* 326(6)

[1587]

MANNING, P. **Slavery and African life:** occidental, oriental, and African slave trades. Cambridge, Cambridge University Press, 1990. xi,236p. illus. tables, charts. Maps. ((*African studies series, 67*).) ISBN: 0521343968.

Prologue ('Tragedy and sacrifice in the history of slavery') is followed by 8 chapters: 1. The political economy of slavery in Africa; 2. Why Africans? The rise of the slave trade to 1700; 3. Slavery and the African population; 4. The quantitative aspect of the slave trade, 1700-1900; 5. The economics and morality of the slave supply; 6. Patterns of slave life; 7. Transformation of slavery and society, 1650-1900; 8. The end of slavery in the world and Africa. Appendices: 1. Slave prices; 2. The demographic simulation. Notes, p.182-211. Bibliography, p.212-26. Index, p.227-34. *Class No:* 326(6)

America

[1588]

SMITH, J.D., *comp.* **Black slavery in the Americas:** an interdisciplinary bibliography, 1865-1980. Westport, CT., Greenwood Press, 1982. 2v. (1847p.). $95 the set. ISBN: 0313231184.

15667 unannotated citations arranged in 25 chapters (*e.g.* African background, slave trade, geography, economics, Indian slave owners, conditions of slave life, family, religion, culture, resistance). Author and subject indexes (subject index weak: needs sub-divisions). 4394 cross-references. A massive bibliography, but computer-printout is difficult to read, however '... will surely be the most comprehensive compilation on slavery for a long time to come'. (*Choice*, v.20(10), June 1983, p.1438). *Class No:* 326(7)

USA

[1589]

MILLER, R.M. *and* SMITH, J.D., *eds.* **Dictionary of Afro-American slavery.** Updated ed. Westport, CT., London, Greenwood Press, 1997. xix, 892p. tables, maps. ISBN: 0275957993.

c.300 individual articles, A-Z, on people, places and themes during the first English settlement in America to the Reconstruction of the Civil War, over 200 written by recognized authorities on the subject of slavery. Emphasis is placed on the social, institutional, intellectual and political aspects of slavery. Each article includes a select bibliography for further reading. Helpful tables. Index. '... a magnificent reference compilation ...' (*Choice*, v.26(8), April 1989, p.1302). *Class No:* 326(73)

Foreign Relations

[1590]

HOLLIS, M. *and* SMITH, S. **Explaining and understanding international relations.** Oxford, Clarendon Press, 1990. v,226p. £25. ISBN: 0198275889.

An introduction to theoretical debates on international relations and as a contribution to those debates. 9 chapters in 3 parts: Growth of the discipline since 1918 - The international system, state, bureaucracies, decision-making individuals - Proposal for theoretical agenda. Short bibliographic essay as a guide to further reading. '... well-structured and clearly written ...'(*International affairs*,v.67(3), July 1991, p.565). *Class No:* 327

Bibliographies

[1591]

CONOVER, H.F., *comp.* **A Guide to bibliographic tools for research in foreign affairs.** 2nd ed., with supplement. Washington, D.C., Library of Congress, 1958 (reprinted Greenwood Press, 1970). iii, 145,15p. $250. ISBN: 0840191765.

351 main entries, with much other material referred to in annotations. Sorely needs updating. *Class No:* 327(01)

[1592]

COUNCIL ON FOREIGN RELATIONS, INC., New York City. **Catalog of the Foreign Relations Library.** Boston, Mass, G.K. Hall, 1969 (First supplement, 1979). 9v. + supplementary vol. $870. Supplement: $340. ISBN: 0816108404, (9v.); 0816103062, supplement.

148,000 lithographed catalogue cards in dictionary form, for books and pamphlets. Subject and bibliography analytics are a feature. *Class No:* 327(01)

[1593]

'Foreign affairs' 50-year index: volumes 1-50, 1922-1972. New York, Bowker, for the Council on Foreign Relations, 1973. 1282p.

Described (*Library Journal* 15 March 1974, p.744) as a work of 'extraordinary thoroughness'. *Class No:* 327(01)

[1594]

—The 'Foreign affairs' 50-year bibliography: new evaluations of significant books on international relations., 1920-1970. Dexter, B, *Ed.* New York, Bowker for the Council on Foreign Relations, 1972. xxvii, 936p.

A selection, by more than 400 specialists, of 2130 items, based on hindsight. Arrangement is as in the decennial volumes. 'A valuable reference tool useful for collection evaluation as well' (*Library journal* v.98(8), 15 April 1973, p.1246). *Class No:* 327(01)

[1595]

GREAT BRITAIN. Foreign Office. Library. **Catalogue of the Foreign Office Library, 1926-1968.** Boston, Mass., G.K. Hall, 1972. 8v. $790. ISBN: 0816109982.

About 135,000 photolithographed catalogue-cards, representing the complete collections of the Foreign Office and Commonwealth Office libraries for 1926-1968 (the two offices merged in 1968). 4 separate sequences: Author, Subject, Title, Class. Includes many British and foreign government publications. *Class No:* 327(01)

[1596]

GREAT BRITAIN. HM Stationery Office. **Government publications. Sectional list 69, revised April 1987. Overseas affairs.** London, HMSO, 1985. 29p. Gratis.

4 parts: 1. Classified list of subjects - 2. Country list (A-Z) - 3. Series (British Atlantic Survey ... Background briefs) - 4. Periodicals. Kraus reprints. *Class No:* 327(01)

[1597]

LAKOS, A. **International negotiations: a bibliography.** Boulder, CO, & London, Westview Press, 1989. xii,417p. $54.50. £43.95. ISBN: 0813375584.

Aims to identify and classify materials (books, journal articles, documents and reports) pertaining to the processes of diplomatic negotiation. 5419 entries arranged in 12 sections: Negotiations, processes and theories - Psychological and sociological aspects - Game theory - Mediation - Multilateral negotiations - Arms control negotiations - Summit meetings - International trade negotiations - Diplomacy - Soviet diplomacy & negotiating behavior - American diplomacy - Case studies. No annotations. Author and subject indexes. *Class No:* 327(01)

[1598]

PFALTZGRAFF, R. **The Study of international relations:** a guide to information sources. Detroit, Mich., Gale Research Co., 1977. 155p. $68. (*International relations information guide series, v.5. Gale information guide library.*) ISBN: 0810313316.

360 titles, mostly post-1945, and annotated. Topics: the nature and scope of international relations as a discipline; the international system; foreign policy and diplomacy; power and theory of conflict; military strategy; integration and alliance themes. *Class No:* 327(01)

[1599]

ROYAL INSTITUTE OF INTERNATIONAL AFFAIRS. Library. **The Classified catalogue of the Royal Institute of International Affairs for international relations, defence, diplomacy, international law, politics and economics...** Oxford, Oxford Microform Publications Ltd.

A catalogue of 170,000 catalogue cards on microfiche. In 2 parts: 1. International and general classification (8 major subjects with subdivisions); 2. Regional classification (11 major areas grouped into their regions, subdivided into countries and their parts). 26 microfiches in the first part and 163 in the second. There is a printed introduction and guide. *Class No:* 327(01)

[1600]

ROYAL INSTITUTE OF INTERNATIONAL AFFAIRS. Library. **Index to periodical articles, 1950-1964 ...** Boston, Mass., G.K. Hall, 1964. 2v. $225. ISBN: 0816107114.

The Library, now the leading specialist collection in Britain dealing with international affairs from 1918 onwards, currently receives *c.*600 periodicals. The *Index* is to *c.*31,500 articles taken from these, for the period January 1950 to October 1964. Arranged by the Chatham House scheme of classification (class A-H (general and subject), J-T (regions)). Preceding the index proper: list of principal periodicals indexed; guide to the classification scheme; geographic index; subject index. *Class No:* 327(01)

[1601]

—ROYAL INSTITUTE OF INTERNATIONAL AFFAIRS. Library. Index to periodical articles, 1965-1972 ... Boston, Mass., G.K. Hall, 1974. xxix, 879p. $120. ISBN: 081611062x.

Index to *c.*15000 articles from some 200 periodicals, on *c.*16400 photolithographed cards, 21 per page. Classified arrangement, as in the main volumes. List of 60 principal periodicals indexed. Subject index. *Class No:* 327(01)

[1602]

—ROYAL INSTITUTE OF INTERNATIONAL AFFAIRS. Library. Index to periodical articles, 1979-1989. Published at intervals - 1950/64; 1965/72; 1973/78... Boston, Mass., G.K. Hall, 1990. $250. ISBN: 0816117845.

The 1973/78 issue has index to *c.*15000 articles, similarly arranged. List of principal periodicals indexed (66). *Class No:* 327(01)

[1603]

WRIGHT, M., *and others.* **Essay collections in international relations:** a classified bibliography. New York, Garland, 1977. 172p. $29. (*Reference library of social science, v.45.*) ISBN: 0824098684.

Indexes essays in 'non-current multi-author works published between 1945 and 1975', listed under authors, subjects and into 22 groups. There is 'no comparable volume' (*Choice,* v.14(10), December 1977, p.1342). *Class No:* 327(01)

Encyclopaedias & Dictionaries

[1604]

EVANS, G. *and* NEWNHAM, J., *eds.* **The Penguin dictionary of international relations** London, Penguin, 1998. 623p. £8.99. ISBN: 0140513973.

Over 700 definitions on all aspects of international relations, including significant events, ideas and organizations. The focus is exclusively on the modern world - there is no historical dimension. *Class No:* 327(03)

Dictionaries

English

[1605]

WEIGALL, D. **Britain and the world, 1815-1986:** a dictionary of international relations. London, Batsford Ltd., 1987. 240p. + 12p. of maps. £17.95.505. ISBN: 0713447532.

A-Z entries on topics related to British foreign policy and international relations (Aberdeen - Abyssinian War ... Zinoviev letter - Zulu War). Cross-references. Entries range in length between 100 and 3000 words (*e.g.* Germany and Britain: 6½ cols. 10 references; 'Gladstone': 3 cols.; League of Nations': 2 cols.; 'Pearl Harbour' 1/3col.). Chronology of international relations, p.227-240. 12 maps. *Class No:* 327(038)=20

[1606]

ZIRING, L *and* PLANO, J.C. *and* OLTON, R. **International relations:** a political dictionary 5th ed. Santa Barbara, CA., ABC-Clio, 1995. x,458p. ISBN: 0874368979.

First published 1969 by Holt, Rinehart & Winston Inc., New York. 500.00/00$aPrevious ed. published as *The International relations dictionary* J. C. Plano, R. Olton. Harlow, Longman, 1988

A 'Guide to major concepts' precedes the 12 subject chapters of the dictionary: 1. Nature and role of foreign policy - 2. Nationalism, imperialism and colonization - 3. Ideology and communication - 4. Geography and population - 5. International economics - 6. War and military policy - 7. Arms control and disarmament - 8. Diplomacy - 9. International law - 10. International organizations - 11. American foreign policy - 12. Patterns of political organization. For each there is a paragraph of definitions and one headed 'significance'. Over 500 entries ranging in length from a half page to a page. Index. *Class No:* 327(038)=20

Arabic

[1607]

EL'ADAH, S.F. **A Dictionary of diplomacy and international affairs:** English-French-Arabic. New ed. Beirut, Librairie du Liban, 1979. 566p. £30. ISBN: 0948690569.

First published 1974.

About 5,000 English base-terms, with French and Arabic equivalents and indexes. Arabic equivalents/definitions are sometimes stated at length (*e.g.* 'Spying: Espionage: Arabic explanation of 1½ columns). *Class No:* 327(038)=927

Reviews & Abstracts

[1608]

International affairs. Cambridge. Cambridge University Press (previously Oxford University Press, then Butterworths) for the Royal Institute of International Affairs, 1922-. v.1, no.1-. Quarterly. ISSN: 00205850.

About a quarter in each issue comprises review articles, book reviews, 'Other books received' and an author index of books reviewed. V.69(4), October 1993 has 56 main articles, plus 115 signed book reviews (p.743-825) in sections: International relations and organizations - Security and arms control - Politics, social affairs and law - Political economy, economics and development - Energy and environment - History - Western Europe ... Latin America and the Caribbean - Bibliography and reference. 'Other books received'.

....(contd.)

Cumulative index, 1922-76 to *International affairs*, edited by L. Adolphus and F.L. Kent (Abingdon, Oxford, Learned Information (Europe), 1978. 78p. ISBN 0904933121) is noted.
Class No: 327(048)

Yearbooks & Directories

[1609]

Die Internationale Politik und Wirtschaft: Jahrbucher der Deutschen Gesellschaft für Auswärtige Politik. München, R. Oldenbourg Verlag.
First published 1955. Irregular.

The yearbook seeks to provide informed exposition and analysis of contemporary trends and developments in the global political system. Normally has 9 sections (global problems - world economy in crisis - superpowers and East-West relations) and 6 regional sections (the Western community - developments in Eastern and Southern Europe - conflicts in the Middle East and North Africa - development crises and unrest in Africa - continuity and change in Asia - democratization and conflict in Latin America). D.G.A.P. is one of the most prestigious and authoritative international affairs research institutes in Germany. *Class No:* 327(058)

Histories

[1610]

NORTHEDGE, F.S. *and* **GRIEVE, M.J. A Hundred years of international relations.** London, Duckworth, 1971. x, 397p. 7 maps. ISBN: 0715605755.

Assumes that there exists, and has existed for two or three centuries, the international system of sovereign states in continuous mutual interaction, and is a study of the development of that system over the past 100 years. 16 chapters, arranged chronologically, on the period since 1870. 1. The epoch of peace - 2. Growth of the European powers - 3. Early imperialism ... 12. Birth and death of the Cold War - 13. The United Nations and world economics - 15. The transcendence of sovereignty - 16. Conclusions. Chapter and footnote references. 'Further reading', p.371-380. Detailed, partly analytical index, p.381-97. *Class No:* 327(091)

[1611]

RENOUVIN, P., *ed.* **Histoire des relations internationales.** Paris, Hachette, 1994. 8v. in 3, maps. ISBN: 201235033x, v.1; 2012350348, v.2; 2012350356, v.3.

1. *Du moyen âge à 1789 : Le moyen âge, par F.-L Ganshof. Les Temps modernes I. De Christophe Colomb à Cromwell par G Zeller. Les temps modernes II. De Louis XIV à 1789 par G. Zeller. 2. De 1789-1871 : La révolution française et l'empire napoléonien. par A. Fugier. Le XIX siècle I. De 1815 à 1871 par P. Renouvin. Le XIXe siècle. II De 1871 à 1914 par P. Renouvin. 3. De 1871 à 1945 : Les crises du XXe siècle. I. De 1914 à 1929 Les crises du XXe siècle I. De 1929 à 1945 par P. Renouvin.* " La présente édition, en trois volumes, d'*Histoire des relations internationals*, reprend le texte de la dernière édition de huits tomes de la série ... seule la bibliographie générale de chaque tome a été conservée" ... T.p. verso. A standard work that does not confine itself to political and diplomatic history, but provides the economic, social and cultural setting. It also goes beyond European international relations. Chapter bibliographies. *Class No:* 327(091)

[1612]

ROYAL INSTITUTE OF INTERNATIONAL AFFAIRS. Survey of international affairs, 1920/23-66. London, Oxford University Press, for the Institute, 1925-77. tables, maps.

Pre-war series 1920-1938 by A.J. Toynbee, and others. 1925-53, 17v. *War-time series* 1939-1946 edited by A.J. Toynbee, 1952-58, 11v. *Post-war series* since 1947, by P. Calvocoressi, and others. 1952-77. Annual (1963 v. 1977) *Consolidated index to the 'Survey of international affairs' 1920-1938* compiled by E.M.R. Ditmas, 1967, 272p. (*Indexes, 1920-30* reprinted Johnson Reprint). Volumes in the war-time series deal with particular aspects over a period of years (*e.g. The Middle East, 1945-1950; The Far East, 1942-1946*). The Post-war series consist of annual surveys. That for 1961 was published in 1965. The surveys, by specialists in the various periods or regions, are characterised by their well-documented factual narratives and analytical indexes. *Class No:* 327(091)

Biographies

[1613]

Who's who in international affairs. 2nd ed. London, Euromonitor Publications, 1997. ISBN: 185743045x.

c,7000 biographies of key figures in international affairs, including diplomats, foreign ministers, heads of state, academics, and officials of international organizations. Entries give nationality; position; address; telephone, telex, & fax numbers; education and career progression; publications. Index by nationality. Index by organizations (over 600). '... rather expensive for a down-market edition of the *International who's who*, but useful nonetheless.' (*International affairs*, v.67(3), July 1991). *Class No:* 327(092)

Official Records

[1614]

ROYAL INSTITUTE OF INTERNATIONAL AFFAIRS. Documents on international affairs, 1928-1963. Wheeler-Bennett, J.W., *and others*. London, Oxford University Press for the Institute, 1929-73.

Intended to accompany and supplement the *Survey of international affairs* (qv), although it can now be used independently, thanks to the notes prefacing each section. A collection of available state papers, exchanges of notes, statements, speeches and other source material of a wide range of countries. The 1963v. (1973) was the last to be published by Chatham House.

Consolidated index to the 'Survey of international affairs'. 1920-1938, and 'Documents on international affairs', 1920-1938 (1967).
Class No: 327(093.2)

Worldwide

Laws

[1615]

The Major international treaties of the twentieth century. Grenville, J.A.S. *and* Wasserstein, B., *ed.* 3rd ed.(updated, rev. and expanded) London, Routledge, 1997 800p. £125.00 ISBN: 0415141257.

Covers from 1900 to the present. Provides key sources as well as guides to the documents and information on the role, form and vocabulary of treaties in general. Includes recent historical findings, developments, and the most authentic available treaty texts. Has sections on China, Germany, decolonization and the end of communism. A comprehensive guide to modern international history and politics. *Class No:* 327(100)(094.1)

[1616]

Treaties and alliances of the world. Rengger, N. 6th ed. London, Catermill, 1996. vi,538p. £99. ISBN: 1860670210.

First published 1968. H.W. Degenhardt edited the first four eds. Contains maps.

Compiled with the cooperation of the editorial team of Longman and *Keesing's Contemporary archives* (now *Keesing's Record of world events*). 5 parts: 1. The analysis of treaties and alliances in world politics - 2. International organizations - 3. Treaties and alliances of the Cold War - 4. Regional agreements - 5. Trans-regional and informal groupings. 13 maps. Grouped bibliography. p.567-70. Index. *Class No:* 327(100)(094.1)

Europe

[1617]

MESSICK, F.M., *comp.* **Primary sources in European diplomacy, 1914-45:** a bibliography of published memoirs and diaries. Westport, CT., Greenwood Press, 1987. xxii, 222p. map. $39.95. (*Bibliographies and indexes in world history series, no. 6.*) ISBN: 031324555x.

An introduction and list of frequently consulted sources are followed by a bibliography of 636 briefly annotated entries, arranged A-Z by author, which are sources of personal experience of those in the European arena from World War I to World War II. Predominantly English-language material. Appendix A: Authors by nationality; appendix B.i: Selected diplomatic events, 1914-1945; ii: Chronology. Cross-references. Subject index, p.202-221. *Class No:* 327(4)

Official Records

[1618]

THOMAS, D.H. *and* **CASE, L.M. The New guide to the diplomatic archives of Western Europe.** Philadelphia, Pa., University of Pennsylvania Press, 1975. 441p. $22.95. ISBN: 0812276973.

First published in 1959 as *Guide to the diplomatic archives of Western Europe*.

22 contributors. 'Western Europe' embraces Greece, Finland, the Vatican City, the UN, ILO, etc. A directory of archival repositories; data on each include history, organization and classification, availability, bibliography. 'Essential for all graduate libraries' (*Choice*, v.13(3), May 1976, p.351). *Class No:* 327(4)(093.2)

Europe—Eastern

[1619]

REMINGTON, R.A., *ed.* **The International relations of Eastern Europe:** a guide to information sources. Detroit, Mich., Gale Research Co., 1978. xvi, 273p. $68. (*International relations information guide series, v.8.*) ISBN: 0810313200.

An annotated bibliography. Part 1 covers sources that relate to Communist Eastern Europe as a region (bibliographies, references, basic texts ... The Warsaw Treaty Organization). Pt.2 provides specific country approach for Albania, Bulgaria, Czechoslovakia, East Germany, Hungary, Poland, Rumania, and Yugoslavia. Author, title

....(contd.)
and subject indexes. 'An indispensable ... tool for the subject librarian, despite many spelling errors and misprints' (*American reference book annual*, 1980, entry 515). *Class No:* 327(401)

Great Britain

Official Records

[1620]
TEMPERLEY, H. *and* PENSON, L.M., *eds*. **A Century of diplomatic blue books, 1814-1914.** London, Cambridge University Press, 1938 (reprinted by F. Cass, 1966). xvi, [2], 600p. £30. ISBN: 0714615196.
Lists titles of all Parliamentary papers published between 1814 and 1914, bearing directly on British foreign policy, with historical introduction. *Class No:* 327(410)(093.2)

[1621]
—TEMPERLEY, H. *and* PENSON, L.M., *eds*. A Century of diplomatic blue books, 1914-1936. London, Cambridge University Press, 1938 (reprinted by P.Cass, 1966). xviii,600p. £30. ISBN: 0714615196.
Continues the above. *Class No:* 327(410)(093.2)

[1622]
—VOGEL, R., *ed*. A Breviate of British diplomatic blue books, 1919-1939. Montreal, McGill University Press; Leicester, Leicester University Press, 1963. xxxv, 474p. $16.50. ISBN: 0773500057.
Continues the Temperley and Penson list. 1836 numbered items, chronologically arranged. Titles in full, with additional dates or notes, but no summary of contents. Analytical subject and country index, p.437-74. *Class No:* 327(410)(093.2)

19th Century

Histories

[1623]
The Cambridge history of British foreign policy, 1783-1919. Ward A.W., Sir *and* Gooch, G.P., *eds*. Cambridge, Cambridge University Press, 1922-23. 3v.
Modelled on the *Cambridge modern history*. A connected narrative based on official documents which gives the history of British foreign policy from the national point of view. Each volume has appendices of supporting documents and chapter bibliographies, and an index. Chapter 8 of v.3 deals with the history of the Foreign Office during the whole period. *Class No:* 327(410)"18"(091)

20th Century

[1624]
GREAT BRITAIN. Cabinet Office. **British foreign policy in the Second World War.** Woodward, Sir L. London, HMSO, 1970-76. 5v.
V.1. covers the period from the German invasion of Poland, on 1 September 1939, to the opening of the German attack on the U.S.S.R. on 22 June 1941. v.2-3 cover Anglo-Russian, Anglo-Japanese, Anglo-French, Anglo-Italian, etc., relations, Anglo-American relations, etc., V.4. covers British relations with Allied and neutral countries. V.5. deals mainly with British and Allied policy and planning for the post-war world, especially the treatment of Germany after her surrender. Also an abridged ed. in 1v. (HMSO, 1962. lv.592p).
Class No: 327(410)"19"

Official Records

[1625]
Documents on British policy overseas. Bullen, R. *and* Pelly, M.E. London, HMSO, 1984-.
A collection of documents from the archives of the Foreign and Commonwealth Office. Published so far are:- Series I (1945-1950).
V.I The Conference at Potsdam, July-August 1945 (1984. 1388p.+26 microfiches. £85. ISBN 0115916822).
V.II. Conferences and conversations, 1945: London, Washington and Moscow (1985, 1002p.+9 microfiches, £75. ISBN 0115916830).
V.III. Britain and America: negotiation of the United States loan, 3 August-7 December 1945. (1987. 453p.+microfiche. £35. ISBN 0115916849).
V.IV. Britain and America: atomic energy, bases and food, December 1945-July 1946. (1987.454p. £35. ISBN 0115916857).
V.V. Germany and Western Europe. ll August - 31 December l945 (1990. £55. ISBN 0115916865).
V.VI. Eastern Europe, 1945-1946.
Series II (1950-1955).
V.I The Schuman Plan, the Council of Europe and Western European integration, 1950-1952 (1986. 1096p. £70. ISBN 011591692x).
V.II The London conferences, 1950 (1987. 500p.+ microfiche. £35. ISBN 0115916938).
V.III. German rearmament, September-December 1950. (In

....(contd.)
preparation).
V.IV. Korea, 1950-1951. (ISBN 0115916954).
Class No: 327(410)"19"(093.2)

[1626]
GREAT BRITAIN. Foreign Office. **Documents on British foreign policy, 1919-1939.** London, HMSO, 1946-.
1st series: 1919-1939. (1949-. 37v. so far). 1st series A: 1925-1930 (1966-1976. 7v.). 2nd series: 1930-1938 (1946-1978.21v.). 3rd series: March 1938-September 1939 (1949-61.10v.). A more inclusive collection for the period than that provided by the Royal Institute of International Affairs' *Documents on international affairs*. 2nd series, v.9: *The Far Eastern crisis, 1931-1932* (lxv,713p.1965) reproduces 667 documents with a tabular summary-index preceding (p.xiii-xlv): number, name of sender, date, main subject, page.
Class No: 327(410)"19"(093.2)

[1627]
WATT, D.C. 'United States documentary resources for the study of British foreign policy, 1919-1939'. In *International affairs*. v.38(1), January 1962, p.63-72.
Describes diplomatic papers in Washington and elsewhere.
Class No: 327(410)"19"(093.2)

Research Methods

[1628]
ASTER, S., *comp*. **British foreign policy, 1918-1945: a guide to research and research materials.** Wilmington, DE., Scholarly Resources, 1984. 324p. $20. ISBN: 0842021760.
5 main chapters: I. Introduction (provides the historical background, including lists of Secretaries of State and Ambassadors to selected countries) - II. The Foreign Office and foreign policy - III. Research libraries and archives (A. Information and publications; B. General guides, directories, and union lists; C. Manuscript research) - IV. Bibliography of over 1600 selected references (A. General; B. Parliamentary and government; C. Memoirs, biographies; D. Secondary literature; E. Peacemaking and detente, 1918-1933; F. Diplomacy in crisis; G. The approach of war, 1937-1939; H. The Second World War, 1939-1945) - V. Index of authors, editors and compilers, p.301-324. Many entries are annotated. Mainly British publications, but some German and French. 'An important handbook ...' (*Choice*, v.22(5) January 1985, p.657). A revised ed. was published in 1991 (382p. ISBN 0842023100).
Class No: 327(410):001.891

Eire

Bibliographies

[1629]
MAGUIRE, M., *comp*. **Bibliography of published work on Irish foreign relations, 1921-78.** Dublin, Royal Irish Academy, 1981. viii,136p. IR£4.02. ISBN: 0901714151.
1314 unannotated entries arranged in 5 sections: 1. General works; 2. Foreign relations; 3. Defence; 4. Related areas; 5. Index of authors. Section 2: Foreign relations is subdivided A-H, geographically, and I-O by international organizations. *Class No:* 327(417)(01)

Germany

20th Century

Bibliographies

[1630]
CARLSON, A.R. **German foreign policy, 1890-1914, and colonial policy to 1914: a handbook and annotated bibliography.** Metuchen, N.J., Scarecrow Press, 1970. 333p. $19.80. £13.10. ISBN: 0810812961.
Over one-half of the volume consists of an extensive annotated bibliography. *Class No:* 327(430)"19"(01)

[1631]
—KIMMICH, C.M., *comp. & ed*. German foreign policy, 1918-1945: a guide to research and research materials. Rev. ed. Wilmington, DE., Scholarly Resources, 1991. 300p. $40. ISBN: 0842023119.
lst published 1981.
In 5 sections: 1. Introduction; 2. The foreign ministry and foreign policy; 3. Archives and libraries; 4. Bibliography (1025 entries arranged by subjects, p.97-280); 5. Index, p.281-293. 'This admirable research guide continues the bibliographic coverage ... begun by Andrew R. Carlson's *German foreign policy, 1890-1914 (College & research libraries*, January 1983, p.53). Bibliographies in footnotes and chapters have, in particular, been updated in the revised ed.
Class No: 327(430)"19"(01)

Official Records

[1632]

GREAT BRITAIN. Foreign Office. Documents on German foreign policy, 1918-1945. London, HMSO, 1950-.

Documents from the archives of the German Foreign Ministry. Series C: 1933-37, v.1-5 (1958-66): January 30th 1933-October 31st 1936; v.5-6: *The Third Reich: first phase.* 1966-83. Series D: 1937-45. v.1-13 (1950-64). *The War years begins with v.8.* V.13: The War years, June 23 1941-December 11, 1941 (1964).
Class No: 327(430)"19"(093.2)

[1633]

KENT, G.O. A Catalog of files and microfilm of the German Foreign Ministry archives, 1920-1945. Stanford, CA., Hoover Institution Press, 1962-72. 4v.

Prepared under the auspices of the US Department of State and the Hoover Institution.

'Analyses *c.*300 tons of records discovered by US and British troops in Germany' (*Library of Congress information bulletin.* 27 April 1973, p.152). *Class No:* 327(430)"19"(093.2)

France

Bibliographies

[1634]

YOUNG, R.J. French foreign policy, 1918-1945: a guide to research and research materials. Rev. ed. Wilmington, DE., Scholarly Resources, 1991. 280p. $40.00. ISBN: 0842023089.

First published 1981.

Intended as a handbook to help scholars plan their work to guide them on their visits to archives and libraries. Includes a bibliography of reference works, dissertations, documents, memoirs, biographical sources, journal articles and monographs. Also provides sketches of French archives and other depositories of primary source materials. Subject and name indexes. List of prominent officials, and organizational charts of the French Foreign Ministry. '... Young has provided a good introduction ...' (*Choice,* June 1982, p.1387).
Class No: 327(44)(01)

Italy

Bibliographies

[1635]

CASSELS, A. Italian foreign policy, 1918-1945: a guide to research and research materials. Rev.ed. Wilmington. Del.,Scholarly Resources, 1991. 261p. $40.00. (*Guides to European history research and research materials.*) ISBN: 0842023070.

3 main chapters: the first describes the structure and functions of the Foreign Ministry and includes list of prominent diplomats; the second lists archives, libraries and repositories in Italy and other countries, describing the various papers available in them; the third chapter is a bibliography of selected material (reference works, bibliographical aids, documents, memoirs, etc. in all major Western European languages. Index of authors, serials, and major document collections. 'A valuable guide ...' (*Choice,* v.19(11/12), July /August 1982, p.1534). *Class No:* 327(450)(01)

Spain

Bibliographies

[1636]

CORTADA, J.W., comp. A Bibliographic guide to Spanish diplomatic history, 1460-1977. Westport, CT., Greenwood Press, 1977. xii, 390p. ISBN: 083719685x.

About 5000 unannotated entries; over half of them for the period 1808-1977, and mostly in Spanish, French and English. 21 chapters (1: Archives and bibliographies; 2-21: Periods). Author index. No annotations. Includes theses. 'The highly uneven quality of the sources cited, the absence of annotations' - these limit the bibliography's value for undergraduate students (*Choice,* September 1978, p.838).
Class No: 327(460)(01)

Russia

Bibliographies

[1637]

HAMMOND, T.T., ed. Soviet foreign relations and world Communism: a selected annotated bibliography of 7,000 books in 30 languages. Princeton, N.J., Princeton University Press, 1965. xxiv, 1240p. $105. ISBN: 0691087148.

Three main sections: Soviet foreign relations since 1917 (subdivided into periods) - World Communism (regions and countries) - Special topics. Compiled by area and subject specialists. A judicious selection, with careful, frequently evaluative annotations. The leading ten items

....(contd.)

in each sub-section are marked 'A', and the next twenty 'B'. Detailed index of authors and anonymous titles. Well produced.
Class No: 327(47)(01)

[1638]

—**SWORAKOWSKI, W.S. The Communist International and its front organizations:** a research guide and checklist of holdings in American and European libraries. Stanford, CA., Hoover Institution on War, Revolution and Peace, 1965. 493p. $20. ISBN: 0817922113.
Class No: 327(47)(01)

Asia—South & South East

[1639]

KOZICKI, R.J., ed. International relations of South Asia, 1947-80: a guide to information sources. Detroit, Mich., Gale Research Co., 1981. xiv,166p. $68. ISBN: 0810313294.

A section on bibliographies and reference works (p.3-5) is followed by the 4 main sections: 1. South Asia as a region - 2. India - 3. Pakistan - 4. Bangladesh, Sri Lanka, Nepal, Bhutan, Afghanistan. Entries are annotated, and sections are subdivided (monographs - articles and essays). An appendix lists basic books, A-Z (p.145-153). Author and subject indexes. *Class No:* 327(54+59)

India

[1640]

Yearbook on India's foreign policy, 1984-85 and 1985-86. Kumar, S., ed. New Delhi & Newbury Park, CA., Sage Publications, 1987:1988. 246p. £30. ISBN: 8170361206, India; 0803995830, US.

First published for 1982/83. Annual.

Could be considered a successor to the defunct *Documents on India's foreign policy,* edited by S. Kumar. 4 sections: 1. India and the world (trends and events) - 2. The major issues (analysed by Indian academics) - 3. Country profiles (Nepal) - 4. Statistical and documentary profile. '... series is a handy starting point for information on and analysis of India's foreign relations, especially seen from the Indian point-of-view. More documents would, however, be welcome ... a useful addition to reference material on India' (*International affairs,* v.65(2), Spring 1989, p.395).
Class No: 327(540)

Asia—Near East

[1641]

SCHULZ, A., ed. International and regional politics in the Middle East and North Africa: a guide to information sources. Detroit, Mich., Gale Research Co., 1977. xiv, 244p. $68. (*International relations information guide series,* v.6.) ISBN: 081031326x.

Bibliographical essays in the form of 5 topical chapters (Regional issues - The foreign policies of Middle Eastern states - External powers in the Middle East - The Arab-Israeli conflict - Petroleum), followed by 2 chapters on reference materials (bibliographies and indexes, biographical indexes, chronologies, yearbooks and atlases) and on periodicals. Author, title and subject indexes. *Class No:* 327(56)

Africa

[1642]

Année africaine, 1963-. Paris, Editions A. Pedone, 1965-. Annual. ISSN: 05701937.

Deals mainly with external affairs of the territories of Africa south of the Sahara. *Class No:* 327(6)

[1643]

DELANCEY, M.W. African international relations: an annotated bibliography. 2nd ed. Boulder, Col., Westview Press, 1997. xxv, 677p. ISBN: 0813386535.

1st published 1981

Entries for books, journal articles, pamphlets and a few documents arranged in broad subject categories and sub-categories, and giving titles and brief annotations. 'See' references. Analytical subject index. *Class No:* 327(6)

America

[1644]

TRASK, D.F., and others, eds. A Bibliography of United States-Latin American relations since 1810: a selected list of eleven thousand published references. Lincoln, University of Nebraska Press, 1968. 441p. $32.50. ISBN: 0803201850.

Two main sections: a chronological survey, and a country-by-country survey. Books and periodical articles. Also specialised chapters, with lists of guides and aids, general studies, works on the Inter-American movements, etc.

M. C. Meyer edited a supplement to the above (University of Nebraska Press, 1979). *Class No:* 327(7)

America—North & Central

[1645]
SCHOOLEY, H. **Conflicts in Central America.** Harlow, Essex, Longman Group (UK) Ltd., 1987. xxiii,326p. maps. £25. (*Keesing's international studies.*) ISBN: 0582902746.

Covers Guatemala, Honduras, El Salvador, Nicaragua, Costa Rica, and Panama. In 6 main sections: 1. Political history (1.1: The region; 1.2-1.7 by region) - 2. Economic and social dimensions (subdivided by subjects, then country) - 3. Internal and cross-border conflict (subdivded as for above) - 4. Refugees, human rights and the Indian question (subdivided as before) - 5. Foreign involvement in Central America - 6. Central American peace initiatives. Includes a bibliography, p.316-317; name index, p.321-326; and subject index, p.319-320. *Class No:* 327(71/73)

Government Publications

[1646]
TURNER, C.A., *comp.* **Directory of foreign document collections.** Government Documents Round Table *and* American Library Association. White Plains, N.Y., Kraus Publications; UNIPUB, 1985. vii, 148p. $20. ISBN: 0890590451.

A list of major library collections in the United States and Canada containing publications of foreign governments and international agencies. Arranged A-Z by State (US) and Province (Canada). Includes information on the size and scope of the collection; access, loan and copying privileges; names of staff working with foreign publications; and National Union Catalog codes for each library. Indexed by country of origin. Libraries listed by State or Province, subdivided by name of institution, but no direct index to institutions or personal names. Overlaps with Kile & Taylor's *Directory of government documents collections and librarians* (4th ed., 1984). *Class No:* 327(71/73)(061.1)

Latin America

[1647]
FINAN, J.J. *and* CHILD, J. **Latin America: international relations:** a guide to information sources. Detroit, Mich., Gale Research Co., 1981. xviii, 236p. $38. (*International relations information guide series, v.11.*) ISBN: 0810313251.

Over 1400 items of interest to the general reader and the student arranged in 3 parts; 1. Bibliographies and aids - 2. General - 3. Countries (A-Z). Includes books and periodical articles only, mainly in the English language. Each item has a brief description of one or two lines. Author index, p.213-225; subject index, p.227-236. *Class No:* 327(729.99)

USA

Bibliographies

[1648]
PLISCHKE, E., *ed.* **US foreign relations:** a guide to information sources. Detroit, Mich., Gale Research Co., 1980. xviii, 715p. $68. (*Gale information guide library. American government and history information guide series, v.6.*) ISBN: 0810312042.

Annotated bibliography in 3 parts: 1. Diplomacy and diplomats-general - 2. Conduct of US foreign relations (15 chapters) - 3. Ready reference to Federal official sources, resources and guides, Presidential addresses and papers, publications of the Department of State, etc., Senate and House documents, journals and enactments, etc. *Class No:* 327(73)(01)

Histories

[1649]
FINDLING, J.E. **Dictionary of American diplomatic history.** 2nd rev. & expanded ed. Westport, CT., Greenwood Press, 1989. xviii,622p. £55.95. $79.95. ISBN: 0313260249.

First published 1980.

Attempts to provide 'basic factual information on over 500 persons associated with US foreign policy from the Revolution through 1978, and descriptions or definitions of more than 500 non-biographical items connected with American diplomacy, ranging from crises to catchwords' (*Preface*). Entries average ½p. in length. 5 appendices (A. Chronology of American diplomatic history - B. Key diplomatic personnel listed by presidential administration - C. Initiation, suspension, and termination of diplomatic relations - D. Place of birth - E. Locations of manuscript collections and oral histories). Index, p.591-622. *Class No:* 327(73)(091)

Bibliographies

[1650]
BEMIS, S.F. *and* GRIFFIN, G.G. **Guide to the diplomatic history of the United States, 1775-1921.** Washington, D.C., Government Printing Office, 1935. 979p.

Notes books and articles in many languages; source material, printed and manuscript; indexes collections of personal papers and authors. Also valuable for international relations as a whole. *Class No:* 327(73)(091)(01)

[1651]
—BRUNE, L.H. Chronological history of United States foreign relations, 1776-January 20 1981. New York, Garland, 1985. 2v. (1320p.), 24 maps. $150. ISBN: 082409056x. *Class No:* 327(73)(091)

[1652]
—BURNS, R.D., *ed.* Guide to American foreign relations since 1700. Santa Barbara, CA., ABC-Clio, 1983. xxvi,1311p. illus., map. $135. ISBN: 0874363233.

40 chapters, each with a contents list and introduction; 1. Reference aids 2. Overviews: diplomatic surveys, themes and theories - 3. Colonial and imperial diplomacy to 1774 - chapters 4-38 follow chronologically - 39. Economic issues and foreign policy - 40. The armed forces, strategy and foreign policy. Cross-references. 2 Appendices (I. Makers of American foreign policy; II. Secretaries of State, 1781-1982). Author and subject indexes. Designed to supplement the above guide. ' ... a worthy successor indeed' (*Library journal*, 1 February 1983, p.196). *Class No:* 327(73)(091)(01)

[1653]
—DE CONDE, A., *ed.* Encyclopedia of American foreign policy: studies of the principal movements and ideas. New York, Scribner's, 1978. 3v. (1202p.). $195. ISBN: 0684155036.

Has 1050 entries (about half of these biographical sketches) for the period from the American Revolution to 1978. *Class No:* 327(73)(091)(01)

Australia

[1654]
AUSTRALIA. Department of Foreign Affairs and Trade. **Documents on Australian foreign policy, 1937-1949.** Canberra, Australian Government Publishing Service.

V.III (1944) was published in 1988 (lvi,749p. ISBN 0644056657) with a chronological list of documents, followed by the documents. Appendices include: III. Bibliographical guide (p.727-32). Indexes of persons and subjects. *Class No:* 327(94)

Cold War

[1655]
BLACK, J.L. **Origins, evolution, and nature of the Cold War:** an annotated bibliographic guide,. Santa Barbara, California, and Oxford, ABC-Clio, 1986. xxviii,173p. indexes. $49. (*The War/peace bibliography series.*) ISBN: 0874363918.

13 separately contributed bibliographies totalling 1367 entries on all aspects of the Cold War: 1. History - 2. Origins - 3. Image of the enemy - 4. The actors - memoirs and biography - 5. Canada and the early Cold War - 6. American-Soviet relations - 7. The Soviet perspective - 8. Critical issues - 9. Critical issues - Policy - 10. Regional influences and developments - 11. Eastern Europe - 12. Institutions and alliances - 13. Collections, documents, and bibliographies. Author and subject indexes. *Class No:* 327.54

[1656]
The Cold War, 1945-1991. Frankel, B., *ed.* Detroit, Gale Research, 1992 3v. £199.00 ISBN: 0810389274, v.1; 0810389282, v.2; 0810389290, v.3.

1. *Leaders and other important figures in the United States and Western Europe* 2. *Leaders and other important figures in the Soviet Union and the Third World* 3. *Resources : chronology, history, concepts, events, organizations, bibliography, archives* "Covers people, places and events that shaped the post World War II period. 270 biographies on notable world and national figures. Defines terms and explains events. 300 photos, maps and diagrams, along with volume specific and cumulative subject indexes." *Class No:* 327.54

Handbooks & Manuals

[1657]
SCHWARTZ, R.A. **The Cold War reference guide:** a general history and annotated chronology with selected bibliographies. Jefferson, N.C, McFarland, 1997 vi,321p. £49.50 ISBN: 0786401737, US.

Includes bibliographical references and indexes

A historical account of the Cold War is followed by a throughly annotated chronology of Cold War events. Contains bibliographies of the major figures in American politics of the time. *Class No:* 327.54(035)

Espionage

Bibliographies

[1658]

BLACKSTOCK, P.W. *and* SCHAF, F.L. **Intelligence, espionage, counterespionage, and covert operations:** a guide to information sources. Detroit, Mich., Gale Research Co., 1978. xv, 255p. $68. (*International relations information guide series, v.2.*) ISBN: 0810313235.

Annotated bibliography of mainly English-language books, periodical articles and newspaper accounts. 4 parts (21 chapters): General bibliographic resources - Strategic intelligence - Espionage and counter espionage - Covert operations. International coverage. Appended 'Selected bibliography of fifty titles' for a personal library or core collection. Author and title indexes. 'A useful tool for large bibliographical service units faced with tracing fugitive materials' (*Library review*, v.28, Autumn 1979, p.187). *Class No:* 327.84(01)

[1659]

CALDER, J.D., *ed.* **Intelligence, espionage and related topics.** Westport, CT, Greenwood Press, 1999. 1388p. £112.50. (*Bibliographies and indexes in military studies, v. 11.*.) ISBN: 0313292906.

Annotated bibliography of *c* 9500 citations on intelligence and related subjects. Includes an introductory essay and indexes. *Class No:* 327.84(01)

[1660]

Scholar's guide to intelligence literature: bibliography of the Russell J. Bowen Collection in the Joseph Mark Lavinger Memorial Library, Georgetown University. Cline, M.W., *and others.* University Press of America, for the National Intelligence Study Center, 1983. 236p. $40. ISBN: 0890935408.

More than 5000 titles on topics concerning intelligence and related matters. Worldwide scope, coverage being from events B.C. to the 1980s. Includes entries for monographs, journals and journal articles, biographies, case histories, military field and technical manuals, fiction, etc., Author and title indexes. *Class No:* 327.84(01)

[1661]

SMITH, M.J. **The Secret wars:** a guide to sources in English. Santa Barbara. CA., ABC-Clio, 1980-1981. 3v. (938p.). $32.95 each vol. (*War-Peace bibliography series, nos. 12,13,14.*) ISBN: 0874362717 v.1; 0874363039 v.2; 0874363047 v.3; 0317588052 set.

V.1.*Intelligence, propaganda and psychological warfare, resistance movements and secret operations, 1939-1945.* (I. Reference works - II. Propaganda and psychological warfare - III. Intelligence: general works and secret services - IV. Military intelligence; land, sea and air - V. Selected military campaigns and battles influenced by intelligence operations - VI. Special forces - VII. Secret operations: resistance movements, special forces, intelligence agents and paramilitary units - VIII. Some personalities of the secret wars. V.2. deals with 1945-1980 (I. Reference works - II. Propaganda ... - III. Intelligence, espionage and covert operations - IV. Some personalities). V.3. *International terrorism 1968-1980* (I. Reference works - II. General works: violence and terrorism, 1968-1979 - III. Philosophy and psychology of terrorism - IV. Terrorist tactics - V. Terrorist armaments - VI. Domestic and international support for and countermeasures against terrorism. - VII. International law and terrorism - VIII,. Terrorism around the world, 1968-1980). Each chapter has an introduction and each volume a chronology. No annotations. Author and subject indexes. *Class No:* 327.84(01)

Encyclopaedias & Dictionaries

[1662]

BURANELLI, V. *and* BURANELLI, N. **Spy/counterspy:** an encyclopedia of espionage. New York, McGraw-Hill Book Company, 1982. 361p. $24.95; £18.95. ISBN: 0070089159.

Profiles of the major figures and organizations of international intelligence from the Renaissance to the present. Over 400 articles on espionage and related information, arranged A-Z, including biographical sketches of spymasters and spies, descriptions of intelligence organizations, indentification of networks and secret societies, explanations of historical events, clandestine techniques, and vocabulary. Information is authoritative, accurate, complete with dates. Many articles cite suggestions for further reading. Extensive index. *Class No:* 327.84(03)

[1663]

MINNICK, W.L. **Spies and provocateurs:** a worldwide encyclopedia of persons conducting espionage and covert action, 1946-1991. Jefferson, NJ, McFarland, 1992. 310p. £51.75. ISBN: 0899507468.

Short biographical dictionary aimed at providing quick information on the people involved in the post-World War II Soviet-Western spy wars. Numbered entries of varying lengths arranged A-Z. Emphasis is on personalities outside the Communist countries. Each entry ends with a list of books consulted, and there is an extensive bibliography of

....(contd.)

English-language reference books, monographs and periodical articles. Chronology of major Cold War espionage events. *Class No:* 327.84(03)

Dictionaries

[1664]

BECKET, H. **The Dictionary of espionage:** spookspeak into English. New York, Stein & Day, 1986. 203p. $17.95. ISBN: 0812830687.

Explains over 2000 cant terms used by the international spy community, those peculiar to the underground world of spies and also those that have surfaced into everyday language. Entries are enlivened by anecdotes explaining the terms' origins. '... this dictionary will be very useful to any serious student of espionage; it will also come in handy when readers of spy novels need an explanation of a technical term'. (*Wilson library bulletin,* April 1986, p.64). *Class No:* 327.84(038)

Biographies

[1665]

DOBSON, C. *and* PAYNE, R. **The Dictionary of espionage.** London, Harrap Limited, 1984. xiv, 234p. 30 illus. £10.95. ISBN: 0245542019.

Published in US as *Who's who in espionage* (New York, St. Martin's Press, 1985. $15.95. 0312874324.

A biographical dictionary with biographical sketches of more than 300 spies, spymasters and victims involved in spying or intelligence work since World War II. Supplemented by brief histories of intelligence organizations in 17 countries, a short glossary, and a bibliographical listing. '... a very esoteric style' (*International affairs,* v.61(1), Winter 1984/85, p.190). 'The bibliography provides a listing but no guidance on further reading' (*Library journal,* 1 June 1985, p.116). *Class No:* 327.84(092)

[1666]

MAHONEY, M.H. **Women in espionage:** a biographical dictionary. Santa Barbara, CA, ABC-Clio, 1993. 283p. illus. $65. ISBN: 0874367433.

150 essays on women, A-Z, varying in length from a few paragraphs to several pages. Cross-references and also 'see' references to alias. A few sources are given at the end of each entry. International in scope, but mostly American and European, and mainly 20th century. Black and white portraits. Personal name and subject index. Written for a lay audience. Author is a former CIA operative. *Class No:* 327.84(092)

Great Britain

Biographies

[1667]

DAVIES, P.H.J. **The British secret services.** Oxford, ABC-Clio, 1996 xxxix,147p. (*International Organizations Series : no. 12.*) ISBN: 1851092307.

"Each volume in the series contains a selective, annotated, critical bibliography of the organization concerned. Wide ranging in scope. British volume contains 518 citations". *Class No:* 327.84(410)(092)

Russia

[1668]

ROCCA, R.G. *and* DZIAK, J.J., *and others.* **Bibliography on Soviet intelligence and security services.** Boulder, Col., and London, Westview Press, 1985. xi, 203p. $16.00; £19.00. (*Westview special studies.*) ISBN: 0813370485.

A guide to Russian activities in intelligence, espionage, propaganda and psychological warfare. Includes 518 English-language sources, some translated Russian-language works, published since the Russian revolution. Sources grouped under 5 main headings (Selective bibliographies and other works; Russian/Soviet accounts; Defector/First-hand accounts; Secondary accounts; Congressional and other government documents). Each entry is numbered for reference from the indexes. Detailed annotations. Appendices. Glossary of abbreviations and terms; KGB and GRU leadership; and a chart depicting the growth of Soviet intelligence and security services. Author/source index, p.174-186. Title index, p.187-203. 'Strength lies not in its comprehensiveness ... but in extremely informative analysis provided in the extremely detailed annotations'. (*Choice,* v.23(2) October 1985, p.276). *Class No:* 327.84(47)

USA

[1669]

O'TOOLE, G.I.A. The Encyclopedia of American intelligence and espionage: from the Revolutionary War to the present. New York, Facts on File, 1988. 539p. $50. ISBN: 0816010110.

Nearly 700 articles arranged A-Z and cross-referenced. Some 70% of entries are biographical and include biographee's full name, birth and death dates, education, and intelligence and non-intelligence careers. Biographical and other sources appended. Remaining entries are on intelligence organizations, major events, techniques and devices, and the role of strategic/tactical intelligence and espionage in both peace and war. Longest article is an 18-page one on the CIA. Extensive subject index. 400-item unannotated bibliography of English-language books, articles and government documents. *Class No:* 327.84(73)

[1670]

RICHELSON, J.T. The U.S. intelligence community: organisation, operations and management 3rd ed. Boulder, Colo., Westview, 1995 xix,524p. ISBN: 0813323556.

First published in 1985. "Provides organizational diagrams, historical background and current issues in one volume. It is the bible for intelligence work for all research libraries and every intelligence course". *Class No:* 327.84(73)

Dictionaries

[1671]

WILSON, W. Dictionary of the United States intelligence services. Jefferson N.C., McFarland, 1996 vii,191p. ISBN: 078640180x, US.

Draws only on unclassified and public sources and includes over 1,500 terms, programs and agencies. It contains neither biographical nor historical entries. The information is organized into four sections; - 1. An Introduction - 2. A comprehensive list of abbreviations - 3. A dictionary of terms - 4. Bibliography. *Class No:* 327.84(73)(038)

Parliaments

Encyclopaedias

[1672]

KURIAN, G.T., *ed*. World encyclopedia of parliaments and legislatures. Chicago, IL, Fitzroy Dearborn, 1998. 2v. (xxxii, 878p.). £175. ISBN: 1579581218.

The range of contributors is international, and is a mix of political scientists and parliamentarians. There is an overview of parliamentary institutions, followed by entries on individual countries. The final section has topical essays looking at various aspects of parliamentary institutions. Provincial and state legislatures are not covered. *Class No:* 328(031)

Great Britain

Bibliographies

[1673]

MENHENNET, D. *and* WAINWRIGHT, J. 'POLIS' in Parliament: computer-based information retrieval in the House of Commons Library'. In *Journal of documentation.* v.38(2), June 1982, p.72-93.

Describes the organization of the House of Common Library and history of POLIS (the Parliamentary on-line information system) operational from 1980. Includes 8 references and the House of Commons thesaurus. (POLIS database is now managed by Meridian Systems Management Ltd. who charge 'a very high monthly rental to external users'. (*Refer,* v.5(4), Autumn 1989, p.22). *Class No:* 328(410)(01)

[1674]

PATTERSON, S.C. 'Understanding the British Parliament'. In *Political studies,* v.37(3), September 1989, p.449-462.

A review article with 64 footnotes, including titles. Text is in 5 sections: MP-constituency linkages - MPs political orientation - MPs voting behaviour - Committee-centre studies - Conclusion. *Class No:* 328(410)(01)

[1675]

RUSH, M. Parliament and government: an annotated bibliography of government publications for the 1986-87 Parliamentary session'. In *Parliamentary affairs,* v.41(4), October 1988, p.556-565.

Covers Parliamentary procedure, Parliamentary privilege, services and facilities, broadcasting of Parliamentary proceedings, the Ombudsman, Parliament and the EEC, Parliamentary control of the executive, the Civil Service, elections and electoral reform, official information and rights, the register of members' interests. Similar bibliographies were published for the 1978-1979 and 1982-83 sessions. *Class No:* 328(410)(01)

Handbooks & Manuals

[1676]

GRIFFITH, J.A.G. *and* RYLE, M. Parliament: functions, practice and procedures. London, Sweet & Maxwell, 1989. xxvii,538p. £21. ISBN: 042143970x.

Notes on references, table of Statutes, table of Standing Orders, and detailed contents list precede the 13 chapters in 5 parts: 1. Functions, powers and membership - 2. The framework of Parliament - 3. The use of opportunities - 4. The Lords - 5. Evaluations. Footnotes. Bibliography, p.525-7. Analytical index, p.529-38. *Class No:* 328(410)(035)

[1677]

The Guide to the House of Lords, 1997. Carlton, I., *ed.* London, Carlton, 1997. 346p. ISBN: 0952482355. ISSN: 13625241.

Published annually.

Data and contact information on Members of House of Lords. How the committees of the House of Lords are structured. Seperate lists of hereditary and life peers. *Class No:* 328(410)(035)

[1678]

SHELL, D. The House of Lords. 2nd ed. Hemel Hempstead, Herts, Harvester Wheatsheaf, 1992. xi,276p. illus. £40; $68. ISBN: 0745012019.

lst published 1988 by Barnes & Noble.

Describes and discusses the House of Lords and constitutional development, membership, the role of political parties, procedure and organization, legislative work, treatment of government legislation, (1979-1990), deliberative work, select committees and secondary legislation. *Class No:* 328(410)(035)

Periodicals & Progress Reports

[1679]

GREAT BRITAIN. House of Commons. Public Information Office. Weekly information bulletin. London, HMSO, £88.80pa; £2.30 each issue. ISSN: 02619229.

Information on the work of the House for the period of the bulletin and on forthcoming business for the following week. A users' guide is available from the Office also (Factsheet no.29). *Class No:* 328(410)(05)

[1680]

—GREAT BRITAIN. House of Commons. Public Information Office. Sessional information digest. 1991-92. London, HMSO, 1992. [3],47p. £6. ISSN: 02668343.

First published for 1983/84.

An index and companion publication to the above, as well as providing additional information. Issued about 10-12 weeks after the end of the Session. *Class No:* 328(410)(05)

Commonwealth

Histories

[1681]

GREY, I. The Parliamentarians: the history of the Commonwealth Parliamentary Association, 1911-1985. Aldershot, Hants. Gower Publishing Group Ltd., 1986. 336p. £29.45. ISBN: 0566051990.

Founded by leading Commonwealth statesmen and MPs, the original aim was to forge closer bonds between the parliamentary democracies of the world, and the book records the development and expanding activities of the Association. Chapters are arranged chronologically, and are followed by appendices and an index. *Class No:* 328(41-44)(091)

Canada

Yearbooks & Directories

[1682]

Canadian parliamentary guide Canada, Gale, 1996 1193p. £38.60 ISBN: 1896413013, CA.

Contains bibliographic information on Canada's parliamentarians *Class No:* 328(71)(058)

Mexico

Biographies

[1683]

CAMP, R.A. Mexican political biographies 1935-1993. 3rd ed.(rev. and expanded) Austin, Texas, University of Texas Press, 1995. xxxiv,985p. (*ILAS special publication.*) ISBN: 0292711743, US.

Includes bibliographic references.

Covers politicans of the last half century, and gives an exhaustive list of 1,950 of those active in poltical life since 1935. Entries have 12 catagories of information from birth to death. *Class No:* 328(72)(092)

USA

[1684]

SHERRILL, R. **Why they call it politics: a guide to America's government** 6th edition. Harcourt College Publishers, 2000. 678p. £14.95. ISBN: 0155072749.

Covers the fundamentals of US government. It is critical, and entertaining, and succeeds in explaining why power (and wealth) is in the hands of the few. This latest edition includes coverage of the 1998 election. *Class No: 328(73)*

Bibliographies

[1685]

The Speakers of the US House of Representatives: a bibliography, 1789-1984. Baltimore, MD., Johns Hopkins University 1986. xxx,323p. $37.50. ISBN: 0801827868.

Sponsored by the US Capitol Historical Society.

4280 partly-annotated books, journal articles, dissertations and also manuscript collections. An overview of the Office of Speaker precedes the bibliography, which is arranged in 4 chronological sections, each containing a general bibliography, followed by bibliographies of the 46 individual Speakers. Author index. Detailed subject index, and also detailed table of contents. *Class No: 328(73)(01)*

Encyclopaedias

[1686]

Congress A to Z: CQ's ready reference encyclopedia. 2nd ed. Washington, DC., Congressional Quarterly, 1993. 650p. $110. ISBN: 0871878267.

First published 1988.

Aims to be a comprehensive encyclopedia concerning the structure and operations of Congress. Includes explanations (several pages for each) of 30 basic processes (*e.g.* legislation, impeachment, lobbying, reapportionment). Also 250 definitions of terms; committee profiles; biographies of selected members; and historical facts. A 75-page appendix has historical lists of members of Congress; historical statistics on re-elections; party affiliations; vetoes; etc. Index of names and topics. '... indispensible source book ...' (*Choice*, v.26(7), March 1989, p.1120) of the 1st ed. *Class No: 328(73)(031)*

Tables & Data Books

[1687]

STANLEY, H. *and* NIEMI, R. **Vital statistics on American politics.** 5th ed. Washington, Congressional Quarterly, 1995. xviii,440p. ISBN: 0871877937.

13 topical chapters, each concluding with study questions, presenting statistical data on such subjects as state governors' terms and limits on succession, public opinion on the death penalty and abortion, apportioning among the states of seats in the House of Representatives, etc. Annotated bibliography arranged by topical sections. Index. ' ... although designed as a textbook ... has uses as a reference book' (*Wilson library bulletin*, October, 1988, p.105, on which this entry is based). *Class No: 328(73)(083)*

Biographies

[1688]

Biographical directory of the United States Congress, 1774-1989. 15th ed. Washington, D.C., Government Printing Office, 1989. 2104p. $82.

First published 1859 under the title 'Dictionary of Congress'.

In 2 sections, Preliminary and Biographical. The Preliminary section includes a complete list of members of each Presidential cabinet, membership and leadership of the Congresses, etc. The Biographical section (¾ of the book) is arranged A-Z by individual's surname and includes biographies of senators, representatives, delegates, resident commissioners, and vice-presidents. Data includes office held, State or territory represented, place and date of birth, education, profession, jobs held, party affiliation, election history. Entries average a paragraph in length. No photographs or portraits. *Class No: 328(73)(092)*

Libraries

Great Britain

[1689]

MENHENNET, D. **The House of Commons Library: a history.** London, HMSO, 1991. xi,162p. illus. £25. ((*House of Commons Library document no.21*).) ISBN: 010850641x.

A history of the library from earliest beginnings - appointment of the first librarian (1818) - developing from when it served mainly as a gentleman's club library to the research library it is now. *Class No: 328:061:026/027(410)*

Lobbying

Europe—Western

[1690]

PHILIP, A.B., *ed*. **Directory of pressure groups in the E.U.** 2nd ed. London, Cartermill, 1996 xliv,569 ISBN: 1860670733.

Previously published under the title *Directory of pressure groups in the European Community*, Harlow, Longman, 1992

Profiles of over 800 pressure groups operating at EC level. Organized by country, each entry includes details of the constitutional structure, election summary, data on political parties and major pressure groups (contact details, structure, funding, activities, achievements, and assessment of group's influence). *Class No: 328LOB(400)*

Great Britain

[1691]

DUBS, A. **Lobbying - an insider's guide to the Parliamentary process.** London, Pluto Press, 1988. ix, 221p. tables, figures. £30. ISBN: 0745301371.

A handbook to provide ordinary people with the knowledge they need to exert pressure on those in power in order to get results. 14 chapters (*e.g.* 4. Raising an issue in the House - 5. Legislation - 6. How an MP can help in other ways - 8. How to use election campaigns - 9. Influencing political parties - 10. House of Lords - 11. The European Parliament and other international bodies - 12. Councillors - 14. Commercial lobbying). 5 appendices (1. Commons glossary - 2. Lords glossary - 3. European glossary - 4. Political lobbying companies; specialist public affairs companies ; public relations companies offering lobbying services; Monitoring services - 5. Useful addresses and phone numbers). Bibliography. p.224-225. Index. p. 226-228. *Class No: 328LOB(410)*

[1692]

JORDAN, G. **'Insider lobbying':** the British version. In *Political studies,* v.37(1), 1989, p.107-113.

Includes 8 references and footnotes. *Class No: 328LOB(410)*

[1693]

MILLER, C. **Lobbying:** understanding and influencing the corridors of power. 2nd ed. Oxford, Blackwell, 1990. xv,250p. £40. ISBN: 0631172122.

1st published in 1987 as *Lobbying government*.

A manual of the techniques of access to and influence over power. In 3 chapters: 1. Government - the components of power; 2. Decision-makers - how do they work? 3. Dealing with government. 5 appendices. Index, p.245-250. *Class No: 328LOB(410)*

Lobbyists

USA

[1694]

The American lobbyists directory. Wilson, R., *ed*. Detroit, Mich., Gale Research Company, 1989. 1588p. $194.93. ISBN: 0810348144.

A guide to American registered lobbyists and their concerns. Includes a list of Federal lobbyists, arranged A-Z, *c.*9000 organizations represented by 6000 active lobbyists; a list of State lobbyists, arranged State-by-State, subdivided by the organizations and the *c.*35,000 lobbyists that represent them; and an appendix listing State and Federal government offices regulating lobbying activities. Indexes by name of lobbyist, by organization represented, and by subject areas of interest. *Class No: 328LOB(73)*

[1695]

—Beacham's guide to key lobbyists: an analysis of their issues and impact. Beacham, W., *and others, eds*. Washington, D.C., Beacham Publishing, 1989. 632p. illus. $195. ISBN: 093383313x.

A directory of lobbyists considered to be the most effective and influential on Capital Hill. Each profile has a black-and-white photograph, address, issue specialities, clients, party affiliation, history of lobbying activities, etc. '... more anecdotal than analytical ... more useful than the bare-bones biographies in many directories ... (*Choice*, November 1989, v.27(3), p.455). *Class No: 328LOB(73)*

[1696]

Washington's representatives ... who does what for whom in the nation's capital. Close, A.C., *and others, eds*. 17th ed. Annual. Washington, Columbia Books,1993. 723p. $70. ISBN: 1880873036.

A directory of lobbyists, listing over 12000 individuals and 11000 companies, interest groups and public relations firms. A-Z list of companies and organizations (names and addresses) - Index of companies and organizations grouped by subject or industry group - Country-by-country listing of foreign governments and representatives in Washington. 6-page introduction gives an overview of lobbying in the capital. *Class No: 328LOB(73)*

Parties & Movements

Dictionaries

[1697]

DOCHERTY, J.C. **Historical dictionary of socialism.** Lanham, Scarecrow, 1997. 376p. £45.60. $48. (*Religions, philosophies, and movements series, no. 16..*) ISBN: 0810833581.

Covers the evolution of socialism from the early 19th century to the present. *Class No: 329(038)*

[1698]

PAPADAKIS, E. **Historical dictionary of the Green movement.** Lanham, Scarecrow, 1998. 256p. $62. (*Religions, philosophies, and movements series, no. 20..*) ISBN: 0810835029. *Class No: 329(038)*

Worldwide

[1699]

DAY, A.J., *and others.* **Political parties of the world.** 4th ed. London, Cartermill; New York, Stockton, 1996. ix, 683p. ISBN: 1860670296, UK; 1561591440, US.

First published 1980.

A guide to over 2000 political parties (Bangladesh has 127) worldwide, arranged A-Z (Afghanistan ... Zimbabwe), with brief introduction on each country. Little data given for some parties but the aim is to give information on historical development; structure; leadership; membership; policy; publications; international affiliations when available. Appendices on international party organizations. Index of people, organizations & countries. *Class No: 329(100)*

[1700]

DELURY, G.E., *ed.* **The World encyclopedia of political systems and parties.** 2nd ed. New York, Facts on File; Harlow, Essex, Longman Group, 1987. 2v.(1410p.;697p.). £120; $175. ISBN: 0816015392.

First published 1983.

Covers 170 states and 8 dependent territories in articles of varying lengths. Arrangement is A-Z by country (v.1. Afghanistan ... Mozambique; v.2 Nepal ... Zimbabwe and smaller countries and microstates). Includes data on the history of the party system, organization, membership and/or constituency, leadership, and prospect. *Class No: 329(100)*

Histories

[1701]

BRAUNTHAL, J. **History of the International.** Clark, J., *translator.* London, Nelson, 1967. 2v. illus.

V.1 covers 1864-1914; v.2, 1914-1943. 'Will become as essential for students of the European Labour movement as the late G.D.H. Cole's classic *History of socialist thought'* (*TLS* no.3440, 1 February 1968, p.105).

V.3, *History of the International: world socialism, 1943-1968* (London, Gollancz; Westview Press, 1980. 656p. $61. ISBN 0891583696) concludes the work. One section deals with the expansion of Socialism and Communism in Asia since 1945. *Class No: 329(100)(091)*

Communism

[1702]

FURTAK, R.K. **The Political systems of the Socialist States: an introduction to Marxist-Leninist regimes.** Brighton, Sussex, Harvester/Wheatsheaf, 1986. xi,308p. tables. £40; $70.80. ISBN: 0745000487.

A brief introductory survey of the characteristics and common features of Socialist States precedes in-depth studies of 15 individual countries (Albania, Bulgaria, Republic of China, Cuba, Czechoslovakia, German Democratic Republic, Hungary, Korea, Laos, Mongolia, Poland, Rumania, USSR, Vietnam, Yugoslavia). Notes for further reading are given at the end of each chapter. Name index, p.300-301; subject index, p.302-308. *Class No: 329(100)COM*

[1703]

HOBDAY, C. **Communist and Marxist parties of the world.** Bell, D. *and* East, R. 2nd ed. rev. and updated. Chicago, St. James Press, 1990. xii,596p. £85. ISBN: 1558620737, US; 0582860389, UK.

"First edition compiled and written by Charles Hobday. This edition revised and updated under the general editorship of Roger East, by David Bell ..."

Section 1: Historical and international perspectives, includes a historical essay on the rise and evolution of Communist and Marxist parties. Section 2: Communist and Marxist parties, (the bulk of the book), is a descriptive list of international Communist organizations arranged in 8 geographical areas subdivided by country, A-Z, and again subdivided by name of organization, A-Z. Section 3: Appendices, has a lengthy list of documents, with extracts, and a select bibliography grouped as in Section 2, subdivided A-Z by author. Index of names. 'Easy to use, clearly written' (*Library journal*, v.111 (18), 1

....(contd.)

November 1986, p.87). '... Communist and Marxist parties in the broadest sense ...' (*International affairs*, v.62(4), Autumn 1986, p.719). *Class No: 329(100)COM*

[1704]

Marxist governments: a world survey. Szajkowski, B., *ed.* London, Macmillan Press; New York, St. Martin's, 1981. 3v. (1761p.), maps. £20 each vol.; $27.50 each vol. ISBN: 0312518579, v.1; 0312518587, v.2; 0312518587, v.3.

V.1 Albania - The Congo; v.2. Cuba - Mongolia; v.3. Mozambique - Yugoslavia. 25 regimes, self-described. Each includes a history of the country's transition from colonialism or capitalism to Marxist; a description of the country's party and government structure; biographies of leading officials; and military, economic and demographic data. China and USSR are only given 119p. but coverage is adequate for lesser-known regimes. Limited bibliographies. 'Indispensable for anyone interested in comparative Communism or individual Marxist governments' (*British book news,* December 1981, p.727). '... a good reference tool for students' (*Library journal,* 1 November 1981, p.2128). *Class No: 329(100)COM*

[1705]

WHITE, S., *and others.* **Communist and post-Communist political systems:** an introduction. 3rd rev. ed. London, Macmillan Press, 1990. xi,357p. figs., tables. £40. ISBN: 0333535472.

First published 1982.

A comparative study of 16 states. 8 chapters: 1. The comparative study of Communist and post-Communist states - 2. Histories, societies and political cultures - 3. Structure of government - 4. The party system - 5. The leaderships - 6. The policy process 7. Democracy and citizen politics - 8. Communist and post-Communist states in comparative perspective. Bibliography, p.337-352. Index, p.353-357. *Class No: 329(100)COM*

[1706]

Yearbook on international Communist affairs: parties and political movements, 1991. Staar, F., *ed.* 25th ed. Stanford, CA., Hoover Institution Press, 1991. 675p. $59.95. ISBN: 0817991611.

First published 1968 (covering 1966).

Describes the activities of 107 organizations during the previous year. The party profiles are arranged geographically by region subdivided by country, some including directory type information and there are 12 biographies. Includes the Warsaw Treaty Organization, the C.M.U.A., and 12 International Communist Front organizations. Select bibliography. Index of names of persons. 'The volume should prove very valuable in any reference library specialising in political affairs' (*International affairs*, v.54(3), July 1978, p.549, of an earlier edition). *Class No: 329(100)COM*

Radical Right

[1707]

Ó'MAOLÁIN, C., *comp.* **The radical right:** a world directory. Harlow, Essex, Longman Group Ltd., 1987 (distributed in US by ABC-Clio). 500p. £73.95. (*Keesing's reference publications.*) ISBN: 0582902703.

The radical right is here viewed as comprising ultra-conservatism, anti-communism, and right-wing extremism. About 3,000 organizations are listed in all. Profiles of about 1,500 parties, movements and groups in over 100 countries known to have far-right organizations, including anti-semitic and racist groups, right-wing guerrilla groups, right-wing conservative fringe groups and extreme nationalist groups, are arranged A-Z by country or territory. Each country section begins with a brief survey of recent political history and the evolution of the far right. Information for each organization includes name in the vernacular and in English, address, history, structure, membership, ideology, activities, finances, publications, and national and international affiliations. There are also brief notes on defunct organizations, lesser-known groups, and unaffiliated individuals. 'There is no comparable work' (*Choice*, v.26(1), September 1988, p.86). '... The most comprehensive listing...' (*Reference books bulletin,* 1 September 1988). *Class No: 329(100)RAD*

Europe

[1708]

McHALE, V.E. *and* SHOWRORSKI, S., *eds.* **Political parties of Europe.** Westport, CT., Greenwood Press, 1983. 2v. (1400p.). illus. $125 the set. (*Historical encyclopedia of the world's political parties series, v.2.*) ISBN: 0313244050.

V.1: Albania ... Norway; v.2: Poland ... Yugoslavia. Aims to provide a comprehensive reference guide to all significant parties in Europe through brief biographical sketches of the parties, covering such information as date and circumstances of foundation, evolution of ideology and programme, evolution of organization (including splits, mergers, associations and alliances), and impact of government and society. 39 distinct party systems are included. Country sections by contributing scholars have introductory essay and bibliography

....(contd.)
preceding the A-Z listing of the country's parties, which includes cross-references for varient and successive party names, initials and translations. *Library journal* (15 March 1983, p.577) considers the information given to be 'essentially factually correct and generally adequate for quick reference' but the bibliographies inadequate.
Class No: 329(4)

Europe—Western
[1709]
DAALDER, H., *ed*. **Party systems in Denmark, Austria, Switzerland, the Netherlands and Belgium.** London, Frances Pinter Publishers, 1987. xiii,372p. tables. £25. (*European party systems series*.) ISBN: 0861873696.
Studies of continuity and change in the party systems of five smaller European democracies from the aftermath of World War II to the present. Notes and references are given after each chapter. There are five chapters, one for each of the countries studied. Index, p.365-372.
Class No: 329(400)

[1710]
JACOBS, F., *ed. & comp*. **Western European political parties: a comprehensive guide.** Harlow, Essex, Longman Group, 1989. 730p illus., tables, maps. £95. ISBN: 0582001137.
Aim is to provide up-to-date information on all the major and minor political parties currently active in Western Europe. Two main sections cover the countries of the European Community and the other democracies, a third section outlining the continent's various multi-party political groupings. Arrangement is A-Z by country; for each country a map showing its political divisions, a historical and current overview of its political institutions and activities (with statistical tables), and a detailed examination of its political parties. '... a superb achievement ... (*Library Association record*, v.92(4), April 1990, p.345). *Class No:* 329(400)

Europe—Eastern
Encyclopaedias
[1711]
Political and economic encyclopedia of the Soviet Union and Eastern Europe. White, S., *ed*. Harlow, Essex, Longman; Chicago, St. James Press, 1990. xii,328p. illus. Maps. £65. $85. ISBN: 0582060362, UK; 1558620702, US.
A description of the political and economic histories and systems, from 1945 to 1990, of Albania, Bulgaria, Czechoslovakia, East Germany, Hungary, Poland, Romania, and the Soviet Union. Clear and detailed entries for each country and on leading personalities. Cross-references. Chronological table precedes the encyclopedia. Index of entries, p.325-8. '... a very useful reference work ... against a background of recent fundamental change' (*International affairs*, v.67(3), July 1991, p.608). *Class No:* 329(401)(031)

Biographies
[1712]
Who's who in the Socialist countries of Europe: a biographical encyclopedia of more than 12,600 leading personalities in Albania, Bulgaria, Czechoslovakia, German Democratic Republic, Hungary, Poland, Romania, Yugoslavia. Stroynowski, J., *ed*. New York, Munich, K.G. Saur, 1989. 3v. (lx,1367p.). $375. ISBN: 359810636x.
First published in 1978, covering 16 Socialist countries, including the USSR, Vietnam, China, etc.
Includes biographies of eminent people from spheres of party, government, military, diplomacy, economics, science, literature, religion, art and the press. V.1 includes a list of abbreviations, a name index arranged by country, and biographies, A-H; v.2 has biographies, I-O; and v.3 P-Z. Entries vary in length from 3 or 4 lines to ¾ column. *Class No:* 329(401)(092)

Great Britain
[1713]
BEER, S.H. **Modern British politics:** parties and pressure groups in the collectivist age. 3rd ed. London, Faber & Faber, 1982. xiv, 434, xivp. £4.95. ISBN: 0571180647.
First published 1965. First and second editions were sub-titled *'a study of parties and pressure groups'*.
Mainly concerned with the rise of collectivism from the late 19th century to the early 20th century. 13 chapters in 3 parts (1. Five types of politics - 2. The Labour party - 3. The Conservative party) are followed by a Conclusion, an Epilogue, and a detailed index (p.i-xiv).
Class No: 329(410)

[1714]
The Blackwell biographical dictionary of British political life in the twentieth century. Robbins, K., *ed*. Oxford, Blackwell Reference, 1990. 449p. illus. £30. ISBN: 0631157689.
Main focus is on politicians, but also includes information on the careers of church leaders, writers, the Royal Family, scientists, soldiers and businessmen, including some pre-1900 and Irish figures. Gives guidance on further reading. Has fewer facts than in *Dod's Parliamentary companion* or the *Civil Service yearbook,* but has much more qualitative comment. Full index. *Class No:* 329(410)

[1715]
REES, P. **Biographical dictionary of the extreme right since 1890:** an international biographical dictionary. Hemel Hempstead, Herts, Harvester Wheatsheaf, 1990. xx,418p. ISBN: 0710810199.
Profiles of 500 major figures on the radical right, extreme right and revolutionary right from 1890 to the present, arranged A-Z by surname. Entries include short bibliographies. *Class No:* 329(410)

Dictionaries
[1716]
DAY, A. **Political and economic dictionary of Eastern Europe.** London, Europa Publications, 2000. 500p. £65. ISBN: 1857430638.
Over 800 entries covering the politics and economics of Eastern Europe. Useful guide to the countries, regions, ethnic groups, political parties, leading politicians, geography and religions.
Class No: 329(410)(038)

Yearbooks & Directories
[1717]
MERCER, P. **Directory of British political organizations.** London, Longman Current Affairs, 1994 448p. ISBN: 0582237297.
An accessible guide to political organizations based in Britain or associated with British politcal parties. Wide coverage of charities and semi-official bodies which are not obviously political but related to the political process. Some foreign organizations are included if closely associated with British politics or affiliated with British political organizations. Information on each group covers purpose, beliefs, those in charge, publications, size, location, date of foundation, and source of funding. *Class No:* 329(410)(058)

Histories
[1718]
HILL, B.W. **The Growth of British parliamentary parties, 1689-1742.** London, George Allen & Unwin Ltd., 1976. 265p. £30. ISBN: 0049421492.
Traces the development of the early parties in the new situation brought about by the Revolution of 1688. 12 chapters in 3 parts: 1. The shaping of the parties - 2. The heydey of the parties - 3. The parties in the age of Walpole. A conclusion is followed by Notes (p.232-247) arranged by chapter; a select bibliography (p.248-254) divided into MS collections, printed sources, and secondary works; and an index (p.255-265). *Class No:* 329(410)(091)

[1719]
—HILL, B.W. **British parliamentary parties, 1742-1832, from the fall of Walpole to the first Reform Act.** London, Allen & Unwin, 1985. x,272p. £18. ISBN: 0049421875.
A sequel to his previous book, *The growth of British parliamentary parties, 1689-1742.*
13 chapters in 4 parts: 1. Introductory - 2. The early parties in decline - 3. Party tradition versus Court tradition - 4. The revival of the Tory party. An appendix, 'Later allegiance of 113 Tories elected in the 1761 General Election' is followed by Notes (p.239-254) arranged by chapters; Select bibliography (p.255-260); and analytical index (p.261-272). *Class No:* 329(410)(091)

Conservative Party
[1720]
A History of the Conservative Party. London, Longman Group, 1978-. v.1-. £24.50 each. ISBN: 058250712x, v.1; 0582507138, v.2; 0582507146, v.3; 0582096081, v.4; 0582504635, v.5; 0582275709, v.6.
V.1: *The foundation of the Conservative Party, 1830-1867*, by R. Stewart (xviii, 427p.); v.2: *The age of Disraeli, 1868-1881 : the rise of democracy.* v.3: *The age of Balfour and Baldwin, 1902-1940*, by J. Ramsden (xii, 413p.); v.4: *The age of Salisbury, 1881-1902 : unionism and empire*, by R. Shannon (vii,569p.); v.5: *The age of Churchill and Eden, 1940-1957* (ix,350p.); v.6: *The winds of change : Macmillan to Heath, 1957-1975* by J. Ramsden (x,485p.). V.1 deals not only with the leading figures but also minor characters, as well as party organization. Bibliography p.393-406. V.3 'will be regarded as a standard work for a long time' (*History*, v.65, 1980, p.149). *Class No:* 329(410)CON

[1721]

—LINDSAY, T.F. *and* HARRINGTON, M. The Conservative Party, 1918-1979. 2nd ed. London, Macmillan, 1979. 295p.

First published 1974 (New York, St. Martin's Press).

Provides chronological treatment in 19 chapters. Bibliographies, p.287-9. Non-analytical index. *Class No:* 329(410)CON

Labour Party

[1722]

HINTON, J. **Labour and Socialism:** a history of the British labour movement 1967 - 1974. Brighton, Sussex, Wheatsheaf Books Ltd., 1983. ix, 212p. £19.95. ISBN: 071080184x.

Traces the changing relationship between the Labour movement and the broader working-class constituency. 11 chapters (working-class organization in mid-Victorian Britain; Society, politics and the Labour movement, 1875-1914; Socialism and the new unionism, 1884-95; The Labour Alliance, 1895-1914; The labour unrest, 1910-1914; The impact of war, 1914-1921; Working-class organization between the wars; Labour governnment and general strike 1924-31; The thirties; Labour and the nation, 1939-51; The Labour movement in crisis, 1951-74. Further reading, p.201-206. Index. p.207-212. *Class No:* 329(410)LAB

[1723]

MORGAN, K.O. **Labour people:** leaders and lieutenants: Hardie to Kinnock. 2nd ed. Oxford, Oxford University Press, 1992. x,372p. illus. £8.99. ISBN: 0192852701.

First published 1987.

Examines *c*.30 key personalities in the history of the British labour movement between 1900 and 1987. 28 sections, each devoted to one or more personalities are grouped in 4 chapters: 1. The founding fathers, 1900-1931 - 2. Towards Jerusalem, 1931-1945 - 3. The years of power, 1945-1970 - 4. Retreat and renewal - 1970-1987. Select bibliography, p.346-360, Index. p.361-372. *Class No:* 329(410)LAB

[1724]

PELLING, H. **A Short history of the Labour Party.** 10th ed. London, Macmillan, 1993. 225p. illus., plates. £35. ISBN: 0333594754.

A brief introductory account of the Labour Party from its foundation to the present. 11 of the 12 chapters chronlogically arranged (from 1906 to 1992, the 12th chapter being conclusions. 4 appendices: A. Party membership; B. General election results; C. Chairmen and leaders of the Parliamentary party; D. Party secretaries. Index. *Class No:* 329(410)LAB

Liberal Party

[1725]

COOK, C. **A Short history of the Liberal Party, 1900-88.** 3rd ed. (A 4th ed. covering 1900-1992 was isued in 1993. 250p. illus. £40. ISBN 0333558219). London, Macmillan Press, 1989. 192p. £33. ISBN: 0333448839.

Covers the electoral fortunes of the party, personalities and the policies that have constituted an integral part of the party since 1900. 3 appendices: I. Major holders of party office, 1900-1988; II. The Liberal vote, 1918-1988; III. Liberal by-election victories since 1945. Bibliographical note. Index. *Class No:* 329(410)LIB

[1726]

DOUGLAS, R. **The History of the Liberal Party, 1895-1970.** London, Sidgwick & Jackson, 1971. xx, 330p. illus.

15 chapters, well footnoted, followed by biographical notes (p.303-13). Short bibliography, p.315-8 (1. Private papers - 2. Periodicals, etc. - 3. Books). Non-analytical index, p.319-30. *Class No:* 329(410)LIB

Scotland

[1727]

KELLAS, J.G. **The Scottish political system.** 4th ed. Cambridge, Cambridge University Press, 1989. xii, 286p. diagr., 28 tables,map. £12.50. ISBN: 0521363195.

First published 1973. 3rd ed., 1984, was completely revised.

14 sections: 1. Scotland as a political system - 2. The constitutional inheritance ... 5. Parliament - 6. Political parties and electoral behaviour - 7. Nationalism - 8. Devolution ... 12. The policy-making process - 13. The Highland periphery - 14. Conclusion. Notes, p.273-286, are arranged by chapter and include references. Bibliography, p.287-289, is A-Z. Index, p.291-296. *Class No:* 329(411)

Biographies

[1728]

Scottish labour leaders, 1918-1939: a biographical dictionary. Knox, W., *ed.* Edinburgh and Washington, Mainstream Publishing Co., (Edinburgh) Ltd., 1984. 304p. tables. £10. $39.95. ISBN: 0906391407.

Introduction, p.1-57 with 235 notes, is followed by the biographical entries. Entries, mostly 3-4 pages long, all end with lists of writings and sources. Entries marked with an asterisk denote information taken from the *Dictionary of labour biography* (qv). *Class No:* 329(411)(092)

France

[1729]

FREAR, J.R. **Political parties and elections in the French Fifth Republic.** London, C. Hurst; New York, St. Martin's Press, 1977. 292p. tables. $25. ISBN: 0312623313.

17 chapters, each with notes, on the period 1945-77: 1. French politics and the role of parties ... 4/5. Parties of the Majorité ... 12. Presidential elections in the Fifth Republic ... 15. Referenda - 16. Aspects of electoral behaviour - 17. Conclusion. 8 appendices (8. Glossary: elections, assemblies, etc.). Bibliographies, p.279-86. Analytical index. *Class No:* 329(44)

Italy

[1730]

Italian politics: a review, 1986-. Annual. V.8 (1993. 256p. £39.50. ISBN 185367159x) London, Pinter Publishing Ltd., 1987-. ISSN: 09523243.

Analyses the events and changes in contemporary Italian politics, economics and social events of the previous year in a historical and theoretical context. *Class No:* 329(450)

Russia

Encyclopaedias & Dictionaries

[1731]

ZEMTSOV, I. **Encyclopedia of Soviet life.** New Brunswick, NJ, Transaction, 1991. 376p. $59.95.

c.250 fairly lengthy entries which include Russian terms, colloquialisms, euphemisms and idioms. Russian and English subject indexes. An updated version of the author's *Lexicon of Soviet political terms* (1984). Complements the above entry. *Class No:* 329(47)(03)

Official Records

[1732]

GILL, G., *ed.* **The Rules of the Communist party of the Soviet Union.** London, Macmillan, 1988. xi, 264p. £29.50. ISBN: 0333387910.

Includes the texts of all the rules that have been adopted by the Soviet Communist party between its foundation 1898 and the XXVII Congress of 1986, plus amendments adopted at various stages of the party's history. All rules have been freshly translated for this volume with indications of amendments made. A substantial introduction traces the evolution of party rules. Glossary. 'This is the fullest treatment of the subject now available in English ...' (*Political studies*, v.37(1), March 1989, p.147). *Class No:* 329(47)(093.2)

Asia

[1733]

Political parties of Asia and the Pacific. Fukui, H., *ed.* Westport, Conn., and London, Greenwood Press, 1985. 2v. (xviii, 678p. and viii, 679p.) tables. $145; £165.50 the set. ISBN: 031321350x.

Arranged by country, A-Z (v.1: Afghanistan-Korea; v.2: Laos-Western Samoa), covering 82 countries. 72 academic specialist contributors. For each country; concise overview, selective bibliography, and detailed party histories. Cross-references. Coverage up to late 1983 in most cases. Clear and consistant style. 3 appendices; Chronology of events; Genealogy of parties; Typology of parties. Index of people, organizations, ideologies and events (p.1269-1346). "In depth and scope this ... is the most comprehensive available" (*Choice*, v.23(10), June 1986, p.1824). *Class No:* 329(5)

China

Communism

[1734]

HSÜEH, C.-T. **The Chinese Communist movement, 1937-1949.** Stanford, Calif., Hoover Institution on War, Revolution and Peace, Stanford University, 1962. x, 311p. $8.95. ISBN: 0817921125.

23 sections in 3 parts, all entries being annotated: 1. General works - 2. The war period, 1937-1945 - 3. The post-war period. In each part a

....(contd.)
general section precedes sections on specific aspects of the subject. Appendices list personal, geographic and corporate names appearing in the annotations, and a list of publishers.

An earlier volume covers the years 1921-1937 (1960, vii, 131p. $6.95. ISBN 081792082x) and follows the same pattern.
Class No: 329(510)COM

Africa
[1735]
Political leaders of contemporary Africa south of the Sahara: a biographical dictionary. Glickman, H., *ed.* Westport. CT, Greenwood Press, 1992. xxii,362p. $65. ISBN: 0313267812.

Biographies of 54 'contemporary' political leaders (*e.g.* since the mid-1950s), with bibliographies after each entry. Daniel Arap Moi (6p.) ; Jomo Kenyatta (over 5p.) ; Desmond Tutu (5p.) (Nelson Mandela is not included). Chronology. Bibliographical references, p.[337]-339. Index. *Class No:* 329(6)

America
[1736]
ALEXANDER, R.J. Political parties of the Americas: Canada, Latin America, and the West Indies. Westport, CT., Greenwood Press, 1982. 2v. (864p.. $65 the set,. (*Greenwood historical encyclopedia of the world's political parties.*) ISBN: 0313214743.

Arranged A-Z by country (v.1 Anguilla ... Grenada; v.2. Guadeloupe ... Virgin Islands of the United States). For each country there is an introduction with information on history, race, politics, labour, etc., followed by a select bibliography and a list of political parties by their English-language designations, with information on origin, development and leaders. Comprehensive index. 'Includes precise party histories, especially useful regarding Latin American politics' (*Wilson library bulletin,* May, 1983, p.789). '... highly recommended ...' (*Choice,* v.20(10), June 1983, p.1436).
Class No: 329(7)

[1737]
—Political parties of the Americas, 1980s to 1990s, Canada, Latin America and the West Indies. Ameringer, C.D., *ed.* Westport, CT, Greenwood Press, 1992. 697p. $99.50. ISBN: 0313274185.

Intended to complement the above. Contains updated country essays and bibliographies, and an inventory of active political parties, with a description of each. Each chapter written by an expert. Arrangement is by country, each entry including a narrative followed by a bibliography and a list of parties. Extensive cross-references. Appendix has a chronology. 'Highly commended for all reference collections' (*Library journal,* 15 March 1993, p.72,74).
Class No: 329

Canada
[1738]
HEGGIE, G.F. Canadian political parties, 1867-1968: a historical bibliography. Toronto, Macmillan, 1977. 603p.

8850 annotated entries; chronological/topical arrangement. Detailed subject index. 'Very thorough coverage ... Essential for every university-level library and every Canadian library of any pretensions whatsoever' (*Choice,* v.15(3), May 1978, p.374). *Class No:* 329(71)

Latin America
Bibliographies
[1739]
Latin American politics: a historical bibliography. Santa Barbara, CA., ABC-Clio, 1984. 290p. $75. (*Clio bibliography series, 16.*) ISBN: 0874363772.

Lists *c.*3000 journal articles on Latin American and Caribbean politics and political history published between 1973 and 1982. Some entries have short abstracts. Arranged geographically, subdivided chronologically. Items taken from the ABC-Clio database. Author index, cross-referenced subject index, and list of journal titles covered. *Class No:* 329(729.99)(01)

Handbooks & Manuals
[1740]
Ó MAOLÁIN, C. Latin American political movements. Harlow, Essex, Longman Group, 1986. 296p. £15.95. ISBN: 0582902754.

Data on *c.*700 legal and illegal political parties, left-wing and right-wing guerrilla movements, human rights pressure groups, politically active trade unions, and externally based groups (*e.g.* the Cubans in the US) active in continental and insular Latin America. Detailed information on each party is given, and also an account of the political background of each country. Index of names.
Class No: 329(729.99)(035)

Biographies
[1741]
ALEXANDER, R.J., *ed.* Biographical dictionary of Latin American and Caribbean leaders. New York, Greenwood Press, 1988. x, 509p. $75. ISBN: 0313243530.

Intended as a partial companion to the 1982 *Political parties of the Americas*.

'Over 450 biographical sketches of the most important political figures in the 19th and 20th centuries in Latin America and the Caribbean' (Preface). Emphasis is on leaders (presidents, dictators, prime ministers) but often more minor figures are often mentioned in the signed essays. Entries include bibliographies. No cross-references. Appendix A: Chronology of political events; appendix B: Biographies by countries. Index of people and places, p.481-506. List of contributors, p.507-509. '... useful for thumbnail sketches of specific political figures'. (*College & research libraries,* v.50(1), January 1989, p.85). *Class No:* 329(729.99)(092)

USA
Encyclopaedias
[1742]
Encyclopedia of the American Left. Buble, M.J., *and others, eds.* New York, Garland, 1990. 928p. illus. $95. (*Garland reference library of the social sciences, 502.*) ISBN: 0824047818.

'American Left' defined as 'that segment of society which has sought fundamental changes in the economic, political and cultural systems'. *c.*600 articles by *c.*300 contributors. Includes people, organizations and events associated with movements of radical social change and leftist positions on general topics (*e.g.* Abortion ... Utopianism). Majority of articles about a page in length and include 3 to 5 references. Glossary of terms and acronyms. Name and subject indexes. '... offers a fine introduction to many subjects otherwise difficult to find in reference works...the organization of the work is less praiseworthy than its content, however, and may cause difficulties for readers unfamiliar with radical history and vocabulary ... nonetheless strongly recommended ...'(*Choice,* v.28(2), October 1990, p.281). *Class No:* 329(73)(031)

Maps & Atlases
[1743]
MARTIS, K.C. The Historical atlas of political parties in the United States Congress, 1787-1988. New York, Collier Macmillan, 1989. 368p. illus., charts, maps. $160; £128. ISBN: 0029201705.

Continues Martis's *Historical atlas of the United States Congressional districts, 1789-1983,* published in 1983, which delineates district boundaries for the first 97 Congresses and names representatives from each district.

A complete history of political representation in America, claiming to be the first accurate, documented source of information about political party membership in the history of the US congress to the 100th (1989). Multicolour maps for each Congress show party representation by district; smaller maps on the same pages show party representation in the Senate. Pages facing the maps list the senators and representatives from each State and district with their party designations. The remainder of the work is explanatory text and a 700-item bibliography. 'This rich, beautifully presented compilation is a wellspring for research' (*Choice,* v.27(1), September 1989, p.84-88). *Class No:* 329(73)(084.3)

Biographies
[1744]
JOHNPOLL, B. *and* KLEHR, H., *eds.* Biographical dictionary of the American Left. Westport, CT., Greenwood Press, 1986. xiv,493p. $65. ISBN: 0313242003.

A collection of esssays on 275 individuals, mostly born between 1870 and 1920 and prominent in the major left wing organizations of the first half of the 20th century, and the history of the parties to which they belong(ed.). Entries normally 1-2 pages in length, some 4 pages. 6 appendices (A. Chronology of key events - B. Major radical party affiliation and year of entry - C. Place of birth - D. Birthdate (with date of death) - E. Those who abandoned the radical movement - F. Ethnic origin). Index, p.465-489. List of contributors. 'Objective, scholarly tone...' (*Wilson library bulletin,* January 1987, p.76). *Class No:* 329(73)(092)

[1745]

Who's who in American politics, 1993-94. 14th ed. New York, R.R. Bowker, 1993. 2v. $225. ISBN: 0835237859.

First published 1967. Issued biennially.

About 25000 biographical sketches of US office-holders, persons active in party politics, campaigners, etc. Information gathered primarily from answers to questionnaires includes party affiliations; birth date and place; names of parents; spouse; children; education; political, governmental and business positions held; memberships; voting residence; address; etc. *Class No:* 329(73)(092)

[1746]

—MORRIS, D. *and* MORRIS, I. Who was who in American politics: a biographical dictionary of over 4,000 men and women who contributed to the United States political scene, from colonial days up to and including the immediate past. New York, Hawthorn Books, 1974. 637p.

Complementary to the above. *Class No:* 329(73)(092)

Australia

[1747]

JAENSCH, D. *and* TEICHMANN, M. **Macmillan dictionary of Australian politics.** 4th ed. Crow's Nest, NSW, Macmillan of Australia, 1992. 256p. £35. ISBN: 0732914450.

Third ed. was published in 1988.

Guide for both student and lay person, providing a deeper understanding of the background to current events. *Class No:* 329(94)

Working class movements

Great Britain

Biographies

[1748]

BAYLEN, J.O. *and* GOSSMAN, N.J., *eds.* **Biographical dictionary of modern British radicals.** Hassocks, Sussex, Harvester Press (later Hemel Hempstead, Herts., Harvester Wheatsheaf), 1976-88. 3v. in 4. (2112p.). V.1&2: £85 each; v.3: £150. ISBN: 0855274042, v.1; 0855274948, v.2; 0710813198, v.3.

V.1: 1770-1830; v.2: 1830-1870; v.3 (in 2v.): 1870-1914. Biographies of *c.*900 British radicals active between 1770 and 1914, 'Radicals' covering middle as well as working class radicals in numerous radical, social, economic and religious groups and movements. Each entry details the subject's career and writings, and includes a bibliography of both primary and secondary sources. *Class No:* 329WOR(410)(092)

[1749]

GREAVES, R.L. *and* ZALLER, R., *eds.* **Biographical dictionary of British radicals in the seventeenth century.** Brighton, Sussex, Harvester Press, 1982-1985. 3v. ISBN: 0855271337, v.1; 071080430x, v.2; 0710804865, v.3.

An informative introduction on radicals of the 17th century precedes the lengthy biographies (*e.g.* Ashley, 1st Earl of Shaftesbury: over 7 columns; Henry Ireton (Cromwell's man): 8 cols.; Oliver Cromwell: over 7 cols.). V.3 has a supplementary bibliography, p.349-351, 3½ page corrigenda relating to v.1 and 2, and an index, A-Z by name of radicals included in the dictionary, p.356-371. *Class No:* 329WOR(410)(092)

33 Economics

[1763]
HARVARD UNIVERSITY. Graduate School of Business Administration. Baker Library. **The Kress Library of Business and Economics. Catalogue** covering material published through 1776, with data upon cognate items in other Harvard libraries. Boston, Mass., Baker Library, Harvard Graduate School of Business Administration, 1940. x,414p.

Supplement... 1776 (1956.vi,175p.); *Catalogue, 1777-1817 ...* (1957.[x],397p.); *Catalogue,1818-1848* (1964.viii,397p.); *Catalogue supplement, 1473-1848* (1967.[iv],453p.).

The 1940 volume has 7279 items, including 23 incunabula; 6 locations. Supplement: 2569 items, plus errata; 6 locations. 1957 vol.:7085 items; 10 locations., 1964v. 7642 items; 8 locations. Arranged chronologically by year, then A-Z by author. The 1957v. has a narrower interpretation of 'economics' than the previous volumes. The 1964v. omits government publications except those of chambers of commerce or boards of trade, but it includes books and pamphlets in the main Baker Library. *Class No:* 330(01)

[1764]
Index to economic articles in journals and collective volumes, 1886/1924-, v.1-. Homewood, Ill., Richard D. Irwin Inc., 1961-.

Prepared under the auspices of *The Journal of economic literature* of the American Economic Association. Prior to the 1966 ed., title was *Index of economic journals* and each ed. covered two or more years.

V.29, 1987 (published 1990) lists, by subject and author, *c.*40,000 articles published in 312 major economic journals and in collective volumes published in 1987, in English or with English summaries. Includes a list of journals and collective volumes indexes, the 4-digit classification scheme used and a topical guide to the classification schedules. Subject and author indexes. *Class No:* 330(01)

[1765]
International bibliography of economics. British Library of Political and Economic Science, *comp.* London and New York, Routledge, 1955-. v.1-. Annual. ISSN: 0085204x.

References to books, periodical articles, and documents, arranged in 15 sections, each subdivided: A. Preliminaries - B. Methods - C. General and basic works - D. History of economic thought - E. Economic history - F. Economic activity - G. Organization of production - H. Production (goods and services) - I. Prices and markets - J. Money and finance - K. Income and income distribution - L. Demand (use of income) - M. Social economics and policy - N. Public economy - O. International economics. Author and subject indexes. V.41: 1992 was published in 1993 (xxxii,450p. ISBN 0415692124). Supported by *Thematic list of descriptors: economics, 1989* (Routledge, 1989. 494p. ISBN 0415017777) and updated by *International current awareness service: economics and related disciplines* (November 1990-. Monthly. ISSN 0960152x). *Class No:* 330(01)

[1766]
LAVIN, M.R. Business information: how to find it, how to use it. Phoenix, AZ., Oryx Press, 1987. x, 299p. $49.50. ISBN: 0897741579.

16 chapters in 4 main sections: General introduction - Information about companies - Statistical information - Special topics (marketing information, business law, tax law, information for job hunters and consumers). 750 sources are described, 132 in detail (85% annotated). Each chapter ends with a list 'For further reading'. A detailed look at categories of information, mentioning a limited number of reference tools, rather than a comprehensive list of business information sources. Good subject and title indexes. 'Not a substitute for Daniells' *Business information sources (qv)*, the undisputed classic in the field of business information guides ... will serve as a teaching and ready reference tool'. (*Reference books bulletin*, 1986/87, p.108).

A 2nd ed. was issued in 1992 (512p. $49.95. ISBN 0897745566). *Class No:* 330(01)

[1767]
LONDON UNIVERSITY. Library. Catalogue of the Goldsmiths' Library of economic literature. Canney, M., *and others, comps.*

V.1 & 2, Cambridge, Cambridge University Press, for the University of London Library; v.3 & 4, University of London, Athlone Press. 4v.

V.1: *Printed books, to 1800* (1970, xxiii, 838p.); v.2: *Printed books, 1801-1850* (1975. vii, 772p.); v.3: *Periodicals which began before 1851, manuscripts, and additions* (1982. 223p.); v.4: *Index to entire catalogue* (1984. 459p.). One of the world's leading collections of early literature on the subject. *Class No:* 330(01)

[1768]
Management contents, 1975-. New York, Find-SVP (previously Skokie, Ill., Management Contents Ltd.), 1975-. Semi-monthly. $102 per hour.

Tables of contents of more than 320 business magazines and journals. Available only online (BRS, DIALOG, DataStar). *Class No:* 330(01)

[1769]
The Official index to the *Financial times.* Reading, Berks, Research Publications Ltd., 1981-. £610. ISSN: 02636891.

Prior to 1988 issue, title was *Annual index to the financial times*.

Compiled from the final London edition, plus references from the international (Frankfurt) edition. Cross-references. Date, page and column references are given. Also available on CD-ROM. *Class No:* 330(01)

[1770]
—Monthly index to the *Financial times.* London, Financial Times Business Information Ltd., 1981-. £297pa.

Electronically compiled index in 3 sections: corporate; general (including book reviews); personalities. Cross-referenced. Entries include brief descriptions of subjects covered, issue date, page number, and item identification. Published about 4 months after the month of the issues. Also available online (DIALOG, Information Services Inc.) *Class No:* 330(01)

[1771]
SCIMP: European index of management periodicals. Manchester, distributed by Manchester Business School Library for the European Business School Librarians Group, 1978-. 10pa. £75pa. FIM 650. ISSN: 01415077.

SCIMP (Selective Co-operative Index of Management Periodicals) is a co-operative effort of 18 European business school libraries. Indexes over 160 journals, the main ones exhaustively, covering the fields of management, finance and economics, industry and marketing, and associated subjects. Articles are listed in broad subject groups, with detailed permuted subject and author indexes (the subject index is cumulated 3 times a year). Articles in English from Scandinavian journals are included in particular issues 4 times a year. List of periodicals indexed in each issue. Also available for searching online on the database at Helsinki School of Economics, and on CD-ROM. *Class No:* 330(01)

[1772]
—CLEAVE, G.E., *ed.* SCIMP/SCANP thesaurus. 9th. ed. Warwick, European Business Schools Librarians Group, 1992. 268p. (*Occasional Publications/University of Warwick; no.21.*) ISBN: 0903220334.

Primarily an indexing tool for retrieving information on-line from the database at Helsinki. *Class No:* 330(01)

[1773]
STRAUSS, D.W. Handbook of business information: a guide for librarians, students and researchers. Littleton, Col., Libraries Unlimited, 1988. 537p. $37.50. ISBN: 0872876071.

Arranged in 18 chapters in 2 sections, the first section dealing with guides, bibliographies, periodicals, newspapers, loose-leaf services, and electronic forms of business information. The second section deals with special fields of business, including marketing, banking, real estate, etc. Sample pages are included for illustration. Good index. '... a very useful and detailed handbook that complements ... Daniells' *Business information sources*'. (*Choice,* v.26(10) June 1989, p.1668). *Class No:* 330(01)

[1774]
THWEATT, W.O. Classical political economy: a survey of recent literature. Boston, Mass., Kluwer-Academic Publishers, 1988. viii,275p. $50. ISBN: 0898382297.

Updates Schumpeter's *History of economic analysis*.

5 main chapters, each dealing with a leading classical political economist (Adam Smith, Malthus, Ricardo, J.S. Mill and Marx), plus a chapter devoted to six 'minor' figures. Each chapter surveying the literature is followed by a commentary. 'Its comprehensiveness, its lively style, the scholarship of its contributors, make it valuable to both novice and master in the history of economic thought, as well as an excellent reference' (Journal of economic history, v.69(1), March 1989, p.252-4). *Class No:* 330(01)

Indexes

[1775]
IntlEc CDROM the index to international economics, development and finance. Cambridge, Chadwyck-Healy, 1990

Published quarterly

Bibliographic index to international economic development and finance. Information provided by the International Monetary Fund/ World Bank Library from 1981. About a third of the records have searchable abstracts. Searches can be done by region, country, subject, keyword, title, author and language. It covers over 2,000 journal titles and 700 research titles. *Class No:* 330(014)

Encyclopaedias

[1776]

GREENWALD, D., *ed*. The McGraw-Hill encyclopedia of economics. 2nd ed. New York, London, McGraw-Hill Book Company, 1994. xi, 1093p. illus. $99.50; £80.95. ISBN: 0070244103.

First published 1982. Revised ed. of Encyclopedia of Economics

A detailed contents list precedes over 300 signed articles on wide-ranging topics by eminent contributors, with up-to-date authoritative discussions. References are appended to each article, which provides a definition and explanation of the subject, discusses its importance, its relationship to other concepts and opposing viewpoints. No biographies. 2 appendices: I: Classification of articles by economic fields; II: Time table of economic events. Name index. Subject index is analytical. US slanted. *Class No*: 330(031)

[1777]

O'HARA, P.A., *ed*. Encyclopedia of political economy. London, Routledge, 1999. 2v. (xxxiv,1302p.) £160. ISBN: 004151526x.

Around 450 entries by an international team of 120 scholars taking a "global or multinational view". Each article is signed, has subheadings, cross references, sources and selected reading. There is a comprehensive index. *Class No*: 330(031)

[1778]

PALGRAVE, R.H.I. The New Palgrave: a dictionary of economics. Eatwell, J., *and others, eds*. London, Macmillan Press; New York, Stockton Press, 1988. 4v. (3500p.). £395; $650. ISBN: 0333372352, UK; 0935859101, US.

First published 1894-96 as the *Dictionary of political economy*, reprinted 1984, 1896 & 1899; new ed. published 1923-26 as *Palgrave's Dictionary of political economy*.

The new edition 'like its predecessor, attempts to define the state of the discipline by presenting a comprehensive and critical account of economic thought' (Publisher's note, v.1, p.vii). About 900 scholars participated. *c*.2000 signed entries in the 4 volumes (1300 subject entries and 900 biographical entries). Length of articles varies (*e.g.* 'Econometrics', 11p.; 'Mathematical economics', 4p.) as do the bibliographies at the end of each article (less than 10 to over 200 items). The biographies, of economists born before 1st January 1916, list both selected works of the biographee and works about him/her. Extensive cross-references. Detailed analytical index, and appendix classifying entries by major subject area. '... succeeds in its attempt to be a modern treatise on economics. It will undoubtedly become the classic for this century that its predecessor was for the preceding one. However, its scholarly and mathematical approach to the material means its usefulness is limited to serious researchers in economics and related social sciences'. (*Reference books bulletin*, 1st April 1988, p.1320). *Class No*: 330(031)

[1779]

—The New Palgrave dictionary of money and finance. Newman, P., *and others, eds*. London, Macmillan; New York, Stockton Press, 1992. 3v.(2621p.). illus. £350; $595. ISBN: 156159041x, US; 0333527224, UK.

Companion to the above. Over 1000 essays by 800 contributors ('absolute priority rule'...'Zero coupon bonds'). Cross-references. Appendices include a list of entries, A-Z; subject classification; and a list of 104 subheadings. 'The especially fine write-up on Japan constitutes a minitreatise' (*Library journal*, January 1993, p.104,100). *Class No*: 330(031)

Handbooks & Manuals

[1780]

A Guide to modern economics. Greenaway, D. *and* Bleaney, M. *and* Stewart, I., *ed*. London, Routledge, 1996 xiii,604p. £19.99 ISBN: 0415144272.

Published in two volumes. Volume 2 will include Methodological Perspectives and Interfaces.

Reissue of "Companion to contemporary economic thought", published in 1991.

Divided into two parts: Economic Theory and Applied Economics. Includes a 'valuable review of the most important developments in economic theory and its implications over the last decade.' Containing 27 specially commissioned overviews, it is a 'student friendly guide to contemporary economics.' *Class No*: 330(035)

Dictionaries

[1781]

BANNOCK, G. *and* BAXTER, R.E. *and* DAVIS, E. The Penguin dictionary of economics. 5th. ed. Harmondsworth, Middlesex, Penguin Books, 1992 427p. £6.99 ISBN: 0140512551.

Previously published in 1972, 1978, 1984 and 1987.

This revised and updated edition contains over 150 new entries. Intended for students and the general reader. Gives a comprehensive coverage of the teminology used in both Britain and the United States. Extensive cross-references. *Class No*: 330(038)

[1782]

BEYNON, R., *ed*. The Routledge critical dictionary of global economics. London, Routledge, 1999. 374p. $22.99. £14.61. ISBN: 0415923522.

Detailed definitions by impressive list of contributors. Essays cover topics such as "The new economics", "The global context", "The world tomorrow" and have appended bibliographies. *Class No*: 330(038)

[1783]

The Macmillan dictionary of modern economics. Pearce, D.W., *ed*. 4th ed. London, Macmillan Press, 1992. 560p. £35. (*Macmillan dictionary series*.) ISBN: 0333576026.

First published 1981. Published in USA by MIT as *The MIT dictionary of modern economics*. (3rd ed. ISBN 0262161044 (USA).

Designed for the needs of students of economics, and useful to students of business and the social sciences. Over 2,800 entries and 14 contributors. Entries (A-Z) include biographies (*e.g.* 'J.M. Galbraith': over 1½ col., including brief summaries of major works. 'International Monetary Fund': 3½ cols.). No bibliographies. Review of the American edition states 'For currency and readability, this work supersedes Douglas Greenwald's 'McGraw-Hill dictionary of modern economics' (3rd ed., 1983) and Douglas A.L. Auld's 'American dictionary of economics' (1983) (*Choice*, v.24 (11/12), July/August 1987, p.1678). *Class No*: 330(038)

[1784]

PAENSON, I., *comp*. Systematic glossary, English-French-Spanish-Russian, of selected economic and social terms. Oxford, Pergamon Press, 1963. xxxv, 414p. diagrs., Loose leaf. £47. ISBN: 0080164358.

A co-operative effort involving NIESR, Institut National de Statistique et des Études Économiques, UNECLA and Institute of World Economy and International Relations, Moscow.

About 7,000 terms are defined and explained (sometimes at length) in all 4 languages. 8 chapters, with detailed subdivisions: 1. Demand - 2. Production - 3. Business economics - 4. Labour and social security questions - 5/6. Financial questions - 7. Economic theories - 8. International trade and other forms of international economic relations. A-Z index for each language. *Class No*: 330(038)

[1785]

RUTHERFORD, D. Routledge dictionary of economics. London, Routledge, 1995. viii, 539p. £50. ISBN: 0415122910.

First published in 1992 as Dictionary of economics

c.4300 A-Z entries for the key terms, issues, theories and concepts of mainstream economic theory and related disciplines. Includes biographies of eminent economists, profiles of organizations, acronyms and jargon. Concise and authoritative definitions, illustrated by graphs, models and diagrams as necessary. Cross-references. Classified index. '... a dictionary for economists rather than a dictionary of economics ...' (*Introduction*). *Class No*: 330(038)

Polyglot

[1786]

BERNARD, Y *and* COLLI, J.-C. Dictionnaire économique et financier: Français-anglais-allemande-espagnol. 5e éd. Paris, Editions du Seuil, 1989. 1438p. £57.

First published 1975.

A dictionary of economic, social and financial terms, each term fully defined and explained in French, with equivalents in the other 3 languages. *Class No*: 330(038)=00

[1787]

—BERNARD, Y *and* COLLI, J.-C. Vocabulaire économique et financier. 6th rev. ed. Paris, Editions du Seuil, 1989. 372p. £5.70.

Abbreviated version of the above. *Class No*: 330(038)=00

[1788]

—BERNARD, Y *and* COLLI, J.-C. Wörterbuch der Wirtschaft und Finanzen... Paris, Editions du Seuil,1989. 458p. £17.25.

An abbreviated version of the French original. Terms defined in German. Multilingual index. *Class No*: 330(038)=00

[1789]

DE JONG, F.J., *and others, eds*. Quadrilingual economics dictionary: English/American, French, German, Dutch. The Hague, Netherlands, Martinus Nijhoff; Deventer/Antwerp, Kluwer, 1980. ix, 686p. Dfl.95.; £48.50; $48. ISBN: 9024722438.

c.11,000 terms altogether (2400 Dutch, 2900 French) arranged in 4 sections: 1. English/American terms, A-Z, each term followed by equivalents in the other three languages; 2. French terms ...; 3. German terms ...; 4. Dutch terms ... Words included are current as of the mid-1970s. *Class No*: 330(038)=00

[1790]
Diccionario de derecho, economia y politica Inglés-español, Español-Inglés. [Dictionary of law, economics and politics English-Spanish, Spanish-English.] Lacasa, N. R. *and* Bustamante, I. D. de, *ed*. 4th ed. Madrid, Spain, Editorial Revista de Derecho Privado, Editoriales de Derecho Reunidas, 1991 763 p. (*Diccionarios y Enciclopedias*.) ISBN: 847130306x.
Previously published in 1980, 1986 and 1989.
Divided into two parts: white pages (English to Spanish section), and cream coloured pages (Spanish to English section). It gives basic definitions of terms and expressions, as well as synonyms. No cross reference available. *Class No:* 330(038)=00

[1791]
EUROPEAN PARLIAMENT. Translation Division. **Terminologie économique** (français/italien/anglais/allemand/néerlandais/danois). 3e.éd. Luxembourg, The Parliament, 1979. 287; 163p. £6.30.
First published 1968.
A-Z listing of French terms with definitions, corresponding terms and indexes in the other 5 languages. *Class No:* 330(038)=00

[1792]
HERBST, R. Dictionary of commercial, financial and legal terms 4th ed. rev. and enl. Thun (Switzerland), Translegal, 1982-1989. 3v. £93.50 each vol. ISBN: 3859420143, v.1; 385942016x, v.2; 3859420127, v.3.
First published 1955-1965 and 1979-1985.
V.1: English-French-German; v.2: German-English-French; v.3: French-German-English. About 30,000 head-words in each volume. Separate entries for different meanings of words. Differentiates between British and US English, Swiss and German German. Compounds are entered under both parts. *Class No:* 330(038)=00

[1793]
IMF glossary: English-French-Spanish. IMF Bureau of Language Services, *comp*. 4th rev. ed. Washington, DC., International Monetary Fund, 1992. vii, 341p. £11.25. ISBN: 1557752672.
First published 1979.
About 2000 words, phrases and institutional titles most commonly encountered in IMF documents in areas such as money and banking, public finance, balance of payments and economic growth, arranged A-Z by English name. French and Spanish indexes lead to numbered English entries. Appendixes include: III: Multilingual index of abbreviations and acronyms; IV: Currency units of various countries and areas. *Class No:* 330(038)=00

[1794]
ISAACS, A. Multilingual commercial dictionary. New York, Facts on File, 1980 (available from Books Demand UMI). 400p. $123.
c.3,000 commercial words and phrases in common commercial use with equivalent terms in other languages (English/American, French, German, Italian, Portuguese, Spanish). *Class No:* 330(038)=00

[1795]
KOHLS, S., *ed*. Dictionary of international economics: German, Russian, English, French, Spanish. Leiden, Netherlands, Sijthoff & Noordhoff International Publishers, 1976. 620p. Dfl.65; £26.50; $32.50. ISBN: 9028605053.
Main part has 6500 German entries, A-Z, with equivalents in the other languages (9700 in Russian, 9300 in English, 9500 in French, & 9400 in Spanish). Indexes in the other languages refer to the German entries. *Class No:* 330(038)=00

[1796]
MUNNIKSMA, F. International business dictionary in nine languages/... English/Esperanto/Deutsch/Español/Français/Italiano/Nederlands/Portuguese/ Svensk. London, Harrap, 1974. xvi,535p.
2812 English-base entries, with English and Esperanto explanations, equivalents in the other 7 languages, and indexes in 8 languages. *Class No:* 330(038)=00

[1797]
NASR, Z. The Dictionary of economics and commerce: English, French, Arabic. London, Macmillan, 1980. xii,212p. £12.95. ISBN: 0333231090.
Arranged A-Z by the English headword, giving French and Arabic translations. No indexes. *Class No:* 330(038)=00

English

[1798]
AMMER, C. *and* **AMMER, D.S.** Dictionary of business and economics. 2nd ed. New York & London, Collier Macmillan, 1984. 507p. $29.95; £26.50. ISBN: 0029007909.
First published 1977.
An encyclopedic dictionary of over 3,000 entries covering general theory of economics, history of economics and business, prices and income, banking and finance, accounting, law, investments, econometrics, labour, consumer economics, tax laws, microcomputers, etc. Includes biographies of important economists with emphasis on

....(contd.)
their ideas. Substantial descriptions but with a definite US slant (examples are all from US publications; includes terms peculiar to USA). *Class No:* 330(038)=20

[1799]
BROWNSTONE, D.M., *and others*. The VNR dictionary of business and finance. New York, Van Nostrand Reinhold, 1980. 293p. $35.
Defines keywords and phrases from all major business, financial and related subject fields, including industrial relations, marketing, real estate, insurance, statistics, etc. *Class No:* 330(038)=20

[1800]
DEANE, P. *and* **KUPER, J.,** *eds*. A Lexicon of economics. London, Routledge, 1988. xxviii,380p. £9.95. (*Social science lexicons*.) ISBN: 0415002346.
One of a series of social science lexicons based on the *Social science encyclopedia*.
A lengthy historical introduction to economics (p.xv-xxvii) is followed by articles on specific economics arranged by subject and including biographies. References for 'further reading' are given after the introduction and each entry. 81 contributors. There is a contents list of subjects. *Class No:* 330(038)=20

[1801]
GREENWALD, D., *ed*. The McGraw-Hill dictionary of modern economics: a handbook of terms and organizations. 3rd ed. New York, McGraw-Hill, 1983. xiii, 632p. illus. $57.50; £49.95. ISBN: 007024376x.
First published 1965.
Simple definitions of *c*.1400 frequently used modern economic terms, plus references to sources; followed by descriptions of *c*.200 private, public and non-profit associations and research organizations. Heavily US slanted. 'A welcome updating of a useful work' (*Wilson library bulletin*, v.48(1), September 1973, p.84, of the 2nd ed.). *Class No:* 330(038)=20

[1802]
—**GREENWALD, D.** The Concise McGraw-Hill dictionary of modern economics. New York, McGraw-Hill, 1984. 396p. $19.95; £16.50. ISBN: 0070243875.
Based on the 3rd ed. of *The McGraw-Hill dictionary of modern economics*, but has fewer descriptions of actual organizations and does not contain some 250 terms largely related to the accounting profession and insurance industry. *Class No:* 330(038)=20

[1803]
HANSON, J.L. A Dictionary of economics and commerce. 6th ed., rev. & updated. London, Macdonald and Evans, 1986. [4], 396p. illus. £7.50. (*M & E professional dictionaries*.) ISBN: 0712106499.
First published 1965.
Over 5,000 explanations and definitions of current economic and commercial terms and phrases. Covers economic theory, applied economics, economic history and commerce. Includes abbreviations and acronyms in current use, and also organizations (e.g., banks). Many cross-references. 'Balance of payments': 2 columns, 1 table. British slant. Useful to students. *Class No:* 330(038)=20

[1804]
MOFFAT, D. Economics dictionary. 2nd ed. Amsterdam, New York, Oxford, Elsevier, 1983. xiii,[1],331p. tables. £37.54; $38; Dfl.125. ISBN: 0444007989.
First published 1976.
Over 5000 concise entries, with extensive cross-references. Separate section for abbreviations. Mathematical appendix gives details relevant to analytical methods, plus weighted price indexes and weighted aggregative indexes. Entries vary in length (*e.g.* 'Balance of payments': 5 cols. & 2p. of tables; 'Collusion': 2 lines; 'Gross national product': nearly 1 col.; 'Sanctions': 12 lines). *Class No:* 330(038)=20

[1805]
NEMMER, E.E. Dictionary of economics and business. Enl.ed. Totowa, N.J., Littlefield, Adams, 1978. 523p. $12.50. ISBN: 0822600331.
First published 1959.
Over 5000 brief entries, with numerous cross-references. Enters organizations under known abbreviated form, cross-referring from the full form. Primarily for use in US colleges. *Class No:* 330(038)=20

[1806]
PASS, C., *and others*. Collins dictionary of economics. 2nd ed. Glasgow, HarperCollins, 1993. 576p. 190 illus. tables. £7.99. ISBN: 0004703723.
Previously published as Dictionary of Economics.
Over 2500 entries defined and explained, both for the general reader and for the student of economics, and many including explanatory diagrams. Longer entries summarize some of the major theoretical principles of economics. New terms are included (ie 'Big Bang', 'insider trading'). Cross-references. Appendix of mathematical symbols. *Class No:* 330(038)=20

[1807]

Reuter's glossary of international financial and economic terms. 3rd ed. London, Cartermill, 1996. vi, 138p. £12.95. ISBN: 186067108x.

First published 1982 by Heinemann.

Compiled and edited by the senior staff of Reuters Limited. Completely revised edition, contains nearly 3,000 specialized definitions of terms used in banking, shipping, brokerage, trading and business management, including derivatives. A-Z in each section. Cross-references. Abbreviations and acronyms. Double-column index. 'Designed for Reuter journalists, but also of great importance to business professionals, students and anyone interested in financial markets.' *Class No:* 330(038)=20

[1808]

SELDON, A. *and* PENNANCE, F.G. **Everyman's dictionary of economics.** 2nd ed. London, Dent, 1976 (Paperback edition published 1980). 416p. £6.95. ISBN: 0460030280.

First published 1965.

Sub-title 'an alphabetical exposition of economic concepts and their application'. About 500 entries, including biographies (*e.g.* 'Hayek'). 'Mercantilism': 2 columns: 'Journals, economic': 11/3 col.: 'Social ownership': 3 cols.: 'Stagflation': 1/3 col. 'Related subject index' (grouping entries under 14 heads), p.xi-xxiii, Reading lists, p.xxiii-xxiv. A handy reference tool for all types of library.

Class No: 330(038)=20

[1809]

The World Bank glossary.... 3rd rev. ed. Washington, D.C., The World Bank, 1986. 2v. (457 ++ 445. p.). v.1 £44.50; $.95. v.2. £33.95. $37.95. Reprinted 1991. ISBN: 0821317334, v.1; 0821317342, v.2.

Intended to assist the Bank's translators and interpreters, and other Bank staff. Includes terms used in economics and finance plus terminology common in such sections of Bank work as agriculture, education, energy, urban development, public health, transport, etc. Also lists acronyms frequently found in Bank texts and has a list of international, regional and national organizations.

Class No: 330(038)=20

French

[1810]

Dictionnaire économique de l'Anglais et du Français Rochard, M., *ed.* Paris, France, Economica, 1992 232p. 250 FF (*Collection Documentation et Information..*) ISBN: 2717822798, v.1; 2717823581, v.2.

Volume 1: Le système bancaire: Institutions, activités et dépôts, surveillance; Volume 2: Credit, taux d'interet

Published in two parts, the first (*Les concepts anglais*) covers financial institutions, banking and deposit, and banking supervision from an English perspective, and the second (*Les concepts français*) from a French perspective. Each term is defined and translated, and a context of use is also given. Synonyms in both French and English are also included for most entries. The second volume also includes an index to Volume 1 at the end of each section. Both volumes contain index and bibliography (p.220-232, v.1, and p. 166-179, v.2).

Class No: 330(038)=20=40

[1811]

KETTRIDGE, J.O. **French-English and English-French dictionary of commercial and financial terms, phrases and practice.** 3rd ed. London, Routledge, 1990. xii, 655p. £25. ISBN: 0415018676.

First published 1931.

About 12,000 main entries in each half, appendices of conventional signs, French syllabilification, abbreviations and conversion tables. Many phrases (*e.g.* 'actions': 3½ columns); also cautionary notes on usage in French and explanatory text in both languages.

Class No: 330(038)=20=40

German

[1812]

EICHBORN, R., *von.* **Cambridge-Eichborn German dictionary:** economics, law, administration, business, general. Cambridge, Cambridge University Press, 1983. 2v. (xii,1163p.viii,1399p.). £100 each vol. v.1: $130; v.2: $140. ISBN: 0521258456, v.1; 0521258464, v.2.

First published as *Wirtschaftswörterbuch* 1947; later editions titled *Der Grosse Eichborn* (Düsseldorf, Econ-Verlag GmbH.).

V.1: English-German; v.2: German-English. about 50,000 main entry words in each volume, the most comprehensive English-German/German-English dictionary of legal, economic, business and administrative terms and phrases available to date. A particular strength lies in the distinctions given between the British and American equivalents of German words and their different usages. Also includes a large number of common or specialized phrases and colloquialisms.

Class No: 330(038)=30

[1813]

—EICHBORN, R., *von.* Shorter Cambridge-Eichborn German dictionary: business and business law. economics, administration. Cambridge, Cambridge University Press, 1984. 2v. (xi,868; ix,977p.). £20 each vol. ISBN: 0521258138, v.1; 0521258146, v.2.

The condensed version of the above, with 140,000 entries per vol., based on a study of specialist works, newspapers, journals and official documents' (*Foreword*). *Class No:* 330(038)=30

[1814]

RENNER, R. *and* SACHS, R. **Wirtschaftssprache/Economic terminology** (German/English; English/German). 4. Aufl., 4th ed. München, Max Hueber Verlag, 1982. 543p. £20.60. ISBN: 3190062013.

First published in 1965.

About 7,000 items in 25 sections (with subsections), ranging from general economics, money and currencies, banking and bookkeeping, through bankruptcy, international trade, advertising and publishing, to transport, insurance and statistics, with an appendix on office equipment. Each section has English and German translation exercises, a key to the exercises being available separately.

Class No: 330(038)=30

Swedish

[1815]

GULLBERG, I.F. **Svensk-engelsk fackordbok för näringsliv, förvaltning, undervisning och forskning/A Swedish-English dictionary** of technical terms used in business, industry, administration, education and research. 2. revid uppl., med suppl. Stockholm, Norstedt, 1977. xix,[i],1722p.

First published 1964.

The 2nd ed. has an extensive supplement of *c.*40,000 new terms, giving a total of *c.*175,000 categorised terms. Rich in idioms. Includes many proper names ('Internationella': nearly 36 colums). British and US usages not differentiated. Includes abbreviations; list of important dictionaries in 50 languages. Well-produced and a fine example of its kind. *Class No:* 330(038)=397

Italian

[1816]

EDLER, F. **Glossary of mediaeval terms of business.** Italian series, 1200-1600. New York, Klaus Reprint Co., 1970. xx, 430p. $36. ISBN: 052701690x.

Glossary of c.2,000 terms, each with some six samples of usages, on OED lines. Classified list appended. List of primary and secondary sources precedes, p.1-17. *Class No:* 330(038)=50

[1817]

MOTTA, G. **Dizionario commerciale,** inglese-italiano, italiano-inglese: economica-legge-finanza. Milano, Signorelli, 1961 (Reprinted 1975). x,[i], 1051p. £18.95.

English-Italian, p.1-515; Italian-English, p.519-1051. About 15,000 main entries in each half. Many compounds and idioms (*e.g.* 'Account':2½ columns; 'Parts':1). English nouns are categorised; stress in Italian not shown. Intended for Italian rather than British users. English terms are sometimes suspect. *Class No:* 330(038)=50

[1818]

PICCHI, F. **Economics and business:** dizionario enciclopedico economico e commerciale; inglese-italiano, italiano-inglese. 2nd revised ed. Bologna, Nicola Zanichelli, S.p.A., 1990. 1594p. £53.

Entries, A-Z, in the English language with definitions in Italian, followed by Italian terms, A-Z, referring to English equivalents (straight translations, with no definitions). *Class No:* 330(038)=50

Spanish

[1819]

LOZANO IRUESTE, J.M. **Diccionario bilingüe de economía y empresa.** Madrid, Piramide, 1989. 799p. £38.80. ISBN: 8436804562.

Nearly 30,000 words and expressions in Spanish and English. Includes Spanish-American terms in use. *Class No:* 330(038)=60

Portuguese

[1820]

LEWIS, T., *and others, eds.* **Harrap's English-Brazilian Portuguese business dictionary.** London, Harrap's, 1982. [6], 283, [33]p. £35. ISBN: 0245538208.

A basic translating tool for everyday business language, including terms and expressions used in a wide range of commercial contexts such as banking, stock exchange, accountancy, insurance, commerce and law, drawing upon commercial correspondence, company reports, contracts, newspapers and magazines, etc. Translates only from English into Brazilian Portuguese. Cross-references.

Class No: 330(038)=690

Russian

[1821]

English-Russian dictionary of economics and finance : about 75,000 entries [Anglo-Russkii slovar po ekonomike i finansam : okolo 75,000 slov i vyrazhenii] Anikin, A.V., *ed.* Sankt Peterburg, Russia : Ekonomicheskaya Shkola, 1993 588 p. (*Biblioteka Ekonomicheskoi Shkoly*.) ISBN: 5900428052.

Published by the School of Economics Press

Gives Russian translations of English and American economic and related terms. Also gives practical examples of usage, variants, and translations. In alphabetical order, also includes an appendix of currency names translated into Russian, as well as their symbols and English equivalents *Class No:* 330(038)=82

Arabic

[1822]

HALEEM, M.A.A. *and* **KAY, E. English-Arabic business dictionary.** London, Graham & Trotman, 1984. xxxii, 263p. £22. ISBN: 0860104486.

About 5000 terms arranged by the English form, A-Z, with transliteration of the Arabic, and then in Arabic script. Some basic grammatical points, a few basic phrases for everyday use, and a listing of Arabic numerals precede the main dictionary. A section at the end lists countries and currencies of the major countries of the world with Arabic equivalents and transliterations. *Class No:* 330(038)=927

Chinese

[1823]

BROADBENT, K.A. A Chinese-English dictionary of China's rural economy. Farnham Royal, Hants, Commonwealth Agricultural Bureaux, 1978. xiii,406p.

Terms are listed in both Chinese characters and Roman letters. Includes a glossary of current terms and an English-Chinese index. *Class No:* 330(038)=951

Japanese

[1824]

Oriental economist's new Japanese-English dictionary of economic terms. Tokyo, Oriental Economist, 1977. 561,79p.

Earlier eds. published 1970 and 1974.

Both Roman and Japanese characters, with English translations of the terms. Reported to be of high quality. *Class No:* 330(038)=956

[1825]

—FUJITA, J. Kenkyusha's English-Japanese dictionary of trade and industry. New ed. Tokyo, Kenkyusha, 1970. xv,1181p.

This dictionary is also well thought of. *Class No:* 330(038)=956

Theses

Bibliographies

[1826]

The Comprehensive dissertation index (1861-1972). Vols. 25-26: Business and economics. High Wycombe, Bucks., University Microfilms, 1973. 2v. (734p.).

An index of 22,500 dissertations, copies of the majority of which are available from University Microfilms. Supplements are published annually by University Microfilms, Ann Arbor, Mich. (v.4, part 2 includes business and economics) and there are also five-& ten-year indexes (1973-82; 1983-87). *Class No:* 330(043)(01)

Reviews & Abstracts

[1827]

Econlit CDROM WinSpirs version 1.01 Bishop, B. *and* Goldie, J. *and* Lovy, D. *and* Harrison, A. *and* Roberts, N. *and* Robertson, I. *and* Sanders, P. London, SilverPlatter, 1991-

Published quarterly

'A comprehensive indexed bibliography with selected abstracts of the World's economic literature produced by the American Economic Association. Coverage of over 400 major journals, as well as articles in collective volumes (essays, proceedings etc.), books, book reviews, dissertations, and working papers licenced from the Cambridge University Press abstract of working papers in economics.' 99% of articles are in English or include English subtitles *Class No:* 330(048)

[1828]

The Economic journal: the quarterly journal of the Royal Economic Society. Oxford, Basil Blackwell Ltd. (previously Cambridge, the Society), 1891-. v.1, no.1-. £60.50pa; $112.50pa. ISSN: 00130133.

A valuable bibliographical tool, a substantial amount of each issue being devoted to reviews and lists of books and articles. The June 1989 issue (v.99, no.396) reviews 18 items (p.491-514), and has sections 'Book notes' (p.515-550) and 'Books received' (p.551-559). An annual index includes book reviews, A-Z by authors of books, and also an index of reviewers. *Class No:* 330(048)

[1829]

Economic titles/abstracts: semi-monthly review (with annual index) providing concise information of interest to business, trade, industry, economic libraries and research institutes. Dordrecht, Netherlands, Martinus Nijhoff, for the Netherlands Foreign Trade Agency EVD of the Ministry of Economic Affairs, V.1-18, 1974-1991. ISSN: 01665057.

A continuation of *Economic abstracts* 1953-1973) and *Economic titles* (1973).

Compiled by the staff of the Library of the Economic Information Service, the Netherlands Ministry of Economic Affairs. About 500 abstracts per issue, arranged by UDC, of items in more than 1800 of the world's leading economic journals, trade journals, bank letters, and professional journals of all sectors and branches of industry, as well as books, special studies, and reports in the same fields. Bibliographical data for entries is 1-4 keywords in English and an abstract in the original language of the publication. Analytical subject index in each issue and cumulative annual subject index. The printed version of the online Foreign Trade & Economic Abstracts database, *Economic abstracts international*. Vendors: Belindis, Data-Star, DIALOG. *Class No:* 330(048)

[1830]

—Economic abstracts international. The Hague, Netherlands, Ministry of Economic Affairs, 1974-.

The online database, updated semi-monthly. *Class No:* 330(048)

[1831]

—Key to economic science: semi-monthly review of abstracts in economics, finance, trade, industry, foreign aid, management, marketing, labour. Dordrecht, Netherlands, Martinus Nijhoff, 1953-87. ISSN: 01654748.

Offers a selection of the abstracts published in *Economic titles/abstracts*. Annual index. *Class No:* 330(048)

[1832]

Journal of economic literature. Nashville, Tenn., American Economic Association, 1963-. v.1, no.1-. Quarterly. $130pa., including *American economic review*. ISSN: 00220515.

Incorporating *The journal of economic abstracts*.

A guide for economists to ongoing research and publications. Focuses on research topics. Available online (DIALOG) and on CD-ROM. *Class No:* 330(048)

[1833]

—Economic literature index (ELI), 1969-. Nashville, Tenn., American Economic Association.

Online database for *Journal of economic literature*. Coverage is from 1969 to date, updated quarterly. A 'core' specialist database currently available on interactive public systems. *Class No:* 330(01)

[1834]

World agricultural economics and rural sociology abstracts (WAERSA). Wallingford, Oxon, CAB International, 1958-. Monthly. £320pa. $602pa. ISSN: 00438219.

About 7000 abstracts pa. 10 main sections: Agricultural economics - Agricultural policy - Supply, demand and prices - Marketing and distribution - International trade - Finance and credit policy - Farm economics - Cooperatives and collectives - Education, extension and resource - Rural sociology. Author and subject indexes per issue and annually. Annual geographical index. Online through CAB ABSTRACTS database, and also available on floppy disk.. *Class No:* 330(048)

Periodicals

[1835]

Economic journals and serials: an analytical guide. Sichel, B. *and* Sichel, W., *comps.* Westport, Conn., Greenwood Press, 1986. 285p. $45.00; £45.00. (*Annotated bibliographies of serials, 5.*) ISBN: 0313238103.

An alphabetical listing of 450 economic journals and serials published more than once a year. Each entry is in 3 parts (concise bibliographical information; narrative covering scope of content, editorial objectives, authority of contributors, technical level, and where applicable, comparison to related publications; format, number of articles, special features). Titles mainly from commercial publishing houses and university presses, but important US government and international organization's publications and some newsletters are also

....(contd.)
included. '... excellent notations that are both descriptive and evaluative' (*Library journal*, v.111(12), July 1986, p.73). *Class No:* 330(051)

[1836]
The Economist on CD-ROM. Cambridge, Chadwick-Healey, 1994-
Updated and published quarterly.
Provides full access to the text of the Economist from January 1991 onwards. Searches can be made using keywords and journalist names. The headlines alone or the text as a whole can be searched. The date can be set to a specific day or time period. Other types of search are also possible. Records can be printed out or downloaded to disc. *Class No:* 330(051)

Teaching Materials
[1837]
HEATHFIELD, D. *and* RUSSELL, M. **Modern economics.** 2nd ed. Hemel Hempstead, Harvester Wheatsheaf, 1992 xiii,461p. £14.99 ISBN: 0745011802.
First published 1987
Directed to needs of A Level students, with exercises and multiple choice questions. Suitable for BTEC or degree level course. In five parts 1. Introduction : Economics, an overview 2. Microeconomics 3. Macroeconomics 4. The open economy 5. Current Issues. Contains a glossary of terms and an index *Class No:* 330(072)

Quotations
[1838]
JACKMAN, M., *ed.* **The Macmillan book of business and economic quotations.** New York, Macmillan, 1984. 302p. $19.95. ISBN: 0025582208.
*c.*5000 quotations arranged under 62 A-Z subject categories, and taken from about 1000 sources. Chronological arrangement within each category. Citations include the quotation, the speaker/writer, and the year, but not the source. Period covered is from 400 B.C. to A.D. 1984. Keyword and name indexes. *Class No:* 330(082.2)

[1839]
JAMES, S., *ed.* **A Dictionary of economic quotations.** 2nd ed. London, Croom Helm; Totowa, N.J., Barnes & Noble, 1984. xi,240p. £25. ISBN: 0709914296, UK; 0389202304, US.
First published 1981.
A collection of *c.*2000 quotations arranged by topic in 133 subject sections, A-Z (Advertising ... Work). As well as economics, covers related areas of economic history, law, mathematics, politics and statistics. Keyword index, p.201-232. Author and source index, p.233-240. *Class No:* 330(082.2)

Histories
[1840]
CAMERON, R. **A Concise economic history of the world:** from Paleolithic times to the present. 2nd ed. Oxford, Oxford University Press, 1993. xxi,464p. illus., maps. £35. ISBN: 0195074459.
First published 1989.
Intended for the student and the general reader, the work is in two parts. The first part surveys world history, with emphasis on Europe, from ancient times to the end of the 18th century. The second half investigates, in greater detail, the related processes of industrialization and urbanization in the 19th and 20th centuries. *Class No:* 330(091)

[1841]
CARUS-WILSON, E.M. **Essays in economic history:** reprints edited for the Economic History Society. London, Arnold. 1954-62. (Reprinted 1969, New York, St. Martin's Press). 3v. V.1&3: $10.95 each; v.2: $14.95. ISBN: 0312260059, v.1; 0312260407, v.2; 0687011884, v.3.
V.1 contains reprints selected from the first twenty years of *Economic history*, 1926-41, and *Economic history review*, 1927-, articles substantially incorporated in later published work have not been included. 'The aim of the present collection therefore is to make easily accessible in one volume a selection of those articles which have proved most in demand from students'. Articles in v.2-3 'range widely over a century of writing about economic history in a dozen different periodicals and one symposium'. *Class No:* 330(091)

[1842]
HOWEY, R.S., *ed.* **A Bibliography of general histories of economics, 1692-1975.** Regents Press of Kansas, 1982. xii,244p. $29.95. ISBN: 0700602194.
Citations for 998 book-length histories are detailed and include information on later editions, translations, comments, and location of copies. 3 appendices, including citations for 215 essay-length histories taken from general treatises on economics. *Class No:* 330(091)

[1843]
SCHLEIFFER, H. *and* CRANDALL, R. **Index to economic history essays in Festschriften, 1900-1950.** Cambridge, Mass., Harvard University Press, 1953. 68p.
Arranged by broad subject headings; index of authors and proper names. *Class No:* 330(091)

Reviews & Abstracts
[1844]
The Journal of economic history. Cambridge, Cambridge University Press, for the Economic History Association, 1941-. Quarterly. £42;$75pa. ISSN: 00220507.
V.53(4), December 1993 contains 7 articles; Notes and discussion (3 items); 1 review article and 40 signed reviews of books, arranged by geographical region. *Class No:* 330(091)(048)

Biographies
[1845]
BLAUG, M. **Great economists since Keynes:** an introduction to the lives and works of one hundred modern economists. Cambridge, Cambridge University Press, 1988. [6],267p. illus. £50.$88.50. ISBN: 0521367425.
Alphabetical list of entries precedes the sketches of careers and professional contributions of living or recently deceased (post-1970) economists, including representatives of the major contrasting 'schools', as well as practitioners of distinctive methodological approaches. Lightly written but seriously conceived vignettes and, as the author intended, a reference work useful to students in early stages of their studies in economics. Secondary literature is listed after each biography. Index of names; index of subjects. *Class No:* 330(092)

[1846]
—BLAUG, M. **Great economists before Keynes:** an introduction to the lives and works of 100 great economists of the past. Cheltenham, Elgar, 1997. xi,286p. £50; $39.95. ISBN: 1858985714.
A companion volume to *Great economists since Keynes (qv)* in the same format. *Class No:* 330(092)

[1847]
—BLAUG, M., *ed.* **Who's who in economics:** a biographical dictionary of major economists, 1700-1987. 2nd ed. Cambridge, Mass., M.I.T. Press; Hemel Hempstead, Herts., Wheatsheaf Books Ltd., 1986. xxiii, 936p. $115; £95. ISBN: 0262022567, US; 0745002307, UK.
First published 1983, covering 1700-1981.
More than 1400 economists ('one who publishes more or less regularly in one of the hundreds of learned journals of economics'), including 1000 living economists who supplied the data in this volume themselves. Information for each biography includes name, year and place of birth, current and previous positions, education, prizes, principal fields of interest, list of publications, brief statements about their principal contributions to the science. Economists included from 25 countries, but half of them from US. Appendices: Index of principal fields of interest; Index of country of residence if not US; Index of country of birth if not US; Names without entry. Editor is the Professor of Economics of Education at London University. *Class No:* 330(092)

[1848]
MAI, L.H. **Men and ideas in economics:** a dictionary of world economists past and present. Totowa, N.J., Littlefield Co., 1975 (Reprinted by Littlefield/Quality Paperbacks). xiii, 270p. $9.95. ISBN: 0822602849.
Preceded by an introduction on the growth of economic thought, the biographical profiles of men and women in economics and selected influential personalities in related fields are arranged A-Z by name. Appendices are a brief state of the art essay on the present generation of economists, a historical outline of the schools of economic thought, and a short bibliography (less than 2 pages). '... a handy reference tool for the undergraduate student ... and for the lay reader ...' (*Library journal*, 15 January 1976, p.327-8). *Class No:* 330(092)

Developing Countries
[1849]
Dictionary of development: Third World economy, environment, society. Welsh, B.W.W. *and* Butorin, P., *eds.* New York, Garland, 1990. 2v. (lxv,1194p.). $130. ISBN: 0824014472.
V.1: A-I; v.2: I-Index. Introduction and 'Developing countries indicators' (by countries, A-Z, providing economic and statistical data concerning Third World societies and economies) precede the dictionary, which contains short definitions of terms, with origins, plus articles. Profuse cross-references. List of periodicals devoted to development topics, with publishers' addresses, completes the volume. *Class No:* 330(4/9-77)

Handbooks & Manuals

[1850]

Third World economic handbook. Sinclair, S. 2nd ed. London, Euromonitor Publications, 1989. 250p. tables. £45; $80. ISBN: 0863381634.

First published 1986.

Covers major economic developments and opportunities in third world countries and highlights short and long term economic opportunities. Regional analysis over 4 groups (Latin America, West Asia, South Asia, East Asia) is followed by detailed overviews for each country. Includes *c.*150 statistical tables. *Class No:* 330(4/9-77)(035)

Europe

Histories

[1851]

ALDCROFT, D.H. *and* RODGER, R., *comps.* **Bibliography of European economic and social history.** 2nd ed. Manchester, Manchester University Press, 1993. 192p. £45. ISBN: 0719034922.

First published 1984.

10,000 entries for English-language books, articles and conference proceedings published in 30 European countries arranged geographically (Europe - Western Europe - East, Central and South - Eastern Europe - Southern Europe - Scandinavia - The Baltic States). Each geographical section subdivided by subject (General economic and social history - agriculture and rural society - industry and external trade ... money, banking and finance ... population and migration ...urban history ... economic aspects of war ... historiography and bibliography - statistical series). Period covered is 1700-1939. No annotations. *Class No:* 330(4)(091)

[1852]

HACKEN, R.D., *comp.* **Central European economic history from Waterloo to OPEC, 1815-1975:** a bibliography. Westport, Conn., Greenwood Press, 1987. xviii, 270p. (Bibliographies & indexes in economics and economic history, 6). $45. ISBN: 0313254605.

5,373 unannotated, numbered entries arranged in five broad subject areas: Economic conditions - Agriculture - Industry - Business and commerce - Finance. Each area subdividied geographically and chronologically. Author index, p.237-270. Purports to cover all Central Europe but focuses on the German-speaking countries and Germany in particular. Mainly German language material. *Class No:* 330(4)(091)

Europe—Western

[1853]

Western European economic organizations: a comprehensive guide. Fraser, R., *ed.* Harlow, Longman Current Affairs, 1992. ix,448p. £85. ISBN: 0582068452.

A statistical overview by country with data on area, population, exchange rate, GNP, trade balance, precedes the main directory. The main directory is in 2 parts: 1. International organizations (Bank of International Settlements ... UNECE); 2. Country-by-country (Austria ... United Kingdom). For each country, an introduction reviews the political structure, pattern of government, economic development, and industrial organization. Then follows details of the central bank, government, stock exchange, political parties, industrial organizations, trade unions, etc., information including name; address; telephone, telex & fax numbers; history; principal officers; organization; structure; aims & objectives; methods and operations. Index of country and organization names, p.423-48. *Class No:* 330(400)

Histories

[1854]

TAYLOR, B., *comp.* **Society and economy in early modern Europe, 1450-1789:** a bibliography of post-war research. Manchester, Manchester University Press, 1989. 303p. ISBN: 0719019486.

About 4000 annotated entries representing the most important and useful books and journal articles written since 1945 on the subject. Arranged under 14 topical headings, subdivided by topic and countries. Includes works in French, Italian, Spanish and German as well as English. Annotations are brief but significant and the longer ones include references to review articles. Indexes of authors and place names. Complements the above. *Class No:* 330(400)(091)

Europe—Eastern

Histories

[1855]

KASER, M.C. *and* RADICE, E.A., *eds.* **The Economic history of Eastern Europe, 1919-1975.** Oxford, Clarendon Press, 1986-. To be in 5v. tables, maps. V.1 & 2: £45 each; v.3: £32.50. ISBN: 0198284446, v.1; 0198284454, v.2; 0198284462, v.3.

....(contd.)

V.1. *Economic structure and performance between the two wars* (1986. 636p.); v.2. *Interwar policy: the war and reconstruction* (1987. 680p.); v.3. *Institutional change within a planned economy* (1987. 328p.). Promises to be a monumental history of Eastern Europe (Albania, Bulgaria, Czechoslovakia, German Democratic Republic, Hungary, Poland, Romania and Yugoslavia) in the 20th century. Aims to be a definitive analysis. Less than favourable review essay in *Economic history review* (v.41(4), November 1988, p.592-602) which does, however, state that 'The erudition ... is not in question ... may overwhelm the inexperienced reader ... Very much for scholars in the best continental tradition'. *Class No:* 330(401)(091)

Great Britain

[1856]

Who's who in British economics: a directory of economists in higher education, business and government. Sturges, P. *and* Sturges, C., *eds.* Aldershot, Hants, Edward Elgar Publishing Ltd., 1990. ix,627p. £75. ISBN: 185278105x.

For each name included gives address, post, qualifications, offices, expertise, publications, the information provided by the people themselves. Nearly 1700 entries. Subject index, p.563-627. *Class No:* 330(410)

Periodicals

[1857]

Bank of England quarterly bulletin. London, Economics Department of the Bank, 1960-. £27. ISSN: 00055166.

First published 1960.

Invaluable on the British economy. Includes articles and an annex of statistics, some of which are not available elsewhere. *Class No:* 330(410)(051)

Histories

[1858]

British business history: a bibliography. Zarach, S., *ed.* 2nd ed. Basingstoke, Macmillan, 1994. ix, 333p. £50. ISBN: 0333592875.

Lists over 2500 business histories. *Class No:* 330(410)(091)

Italy

[1859]

BARUCCI, P. *and* CARPENTER, K., *comps.* **Italian economic literature in the Kress Library, 1475-1850.** Cambridge, Mass., Kress Library, Harvard University; Rome, Banco di Roma, 1985. 2v. (xxii, 490p.). $25.

1203 titles arranged chronologically by date of publication, then A-Z by author's name. Some entries are different editions of the same work. Cross-references. Several indexes. Includes a 13-page bibliography of Italian economic history. *Class No:* 330(450)

Scandinavia

Libraries

[1860]

RUOKONEN, K *and* RINNE, B. **Economic and business libraries in Scandinavia.** 3rd ed. Helsinki, Helsinki School of Economics Library, 1987. [3],123,[9], 8p. $25. (*Helsinki School of Economics, Reports and catalogues, F;49.*) ISBN: 9517003242.

First published 1976.

Data for 68 libraries arranged by country (Denmark, Finland, Iceland, Norway, Sweden) subdivided by name of library, A-Z. Entries include address, telephone number, date established, person in charge, hours, conditions of use, major library units, number of staff, size of collection, subjects, special collections, classification systems, services offered, library publications, automated operations in use, and co-operative projects. Excludes university libraries. Indexes of library names, English names of libraries, personal names and subjects. *Class No:* 330(48):061:026/027

Japan

[1861]

RUOKONEN, K. *and* MIYAKAWA, T. **Japan** Sources of economic and business information. Helsinki, Finland, School of Economic and Business Administration Library, 1991 100p. (*Reports and catalogues, E-70.*) ISBN: 9517009364. ISSN: 03579131.

A selection of mainly English language sources published both in Japan and other countries on Japanese business and economics. The information is divided into two main groups, reference sources and recent general publications. Also lists publishers, libraries and institutions, bookstores and other sources. Indexes cover author, organization and subject. *Class No:* 330(52)

USA

Handbooks & Manuals

[1862]

HOEL, A.A., *and others*. **Economic sourcebook of government statistics.** Lexington, Mass., Lexington Books, 1983. xv,272p. tables. £25. ISBN: 066906579x.

Explains how the many statistical series are compiled, their strengths and weaknesses, what they describe and do not describe (warnings of pitfalls). 6 sections 1. Measures of inflation - 2. Profits: indicators of general business conditions - 3. Interest rates and other financial indicators - 4. Measures of employment, unemployment and earnings - 5. Indicators of international finance and trade - 6. Indicators of government influence. 4 appendices (A. Selected sources of business and financial information; B. Financial statements; C. The Standard Industrial Classification; D. Value added and gross national product). Glossary. Index, p.264-71. Intended for the use of journalists.
Class No: 330(73)(035)

Writing & Lecturing

[1863]

The Economist style guide. New ed. London, Hamish Hamilton, in association with The Economist Books, 1996. 140p. £12.99. ISBN: 0241135567.

Based on *The Economist's* own house-style manual. Includes a new 'fast-checking section' with a glossary, covering everything from the stock markets to the laws of nature, science and economics.
Class No: 330:001.81

Information Management

[1864]

INTERNATIONAL ECONOMIC ASSOCIATION. **The Organisation and retrieval of economic knowledge:** proceedings of a conference held ... at Kiel, West Germany. Perlman, M., *ed.* London, Macmillan, 1977. xiii, 520p. £50. ISBN: 0333217071.

26 papers presented to the conference in 1975 by economist and librarians, arranged in four parts: 1. The technology of the library industry and its use for economic research - 2. The economics of the economics library industry and its implications - 3. The information needs of researchers and their implications for the organization of economic knowledge. Index. *Class No:* 330:025.4

Classification Systems

[1865]

BAKEWELL, K.G.B. *and* COTTON, D.A., *eds.* **The London classification of business studies** a classification and thesaurus for business libraries. 2nd ed. rev. London, Aslib, 1979. 253p. £21. ISBN: 0851421245.

First published 1970, ed. by K.G.B. Bakewell & V. Lang.

A thesaurus of indexing terms in the areas of business and management, as well as a classification scheme, with *c.*4000 terms.
Class No: 330:025.44

Institutions & Associations

[1866]

MEERHAEGHE, M.S.G., van. **International economic institutions.** 5th rev. ed. Dordrecht, Netherlands, Martinus Nijhoff, 1987 (distributed by Kluwer Academic Publishers). xxviii,368p. tables. £70. ISBN: 9024735130.

First published in German in 1964; in English 1966.

Introduction on the United Nations and its special agencies, the Bank for International Settlements, regional integration, etc. Part 1 with world organizations (KNF, World Bank, International Development Association, IFC. GATT, commodity agreements). Part 2 with European organizations (Benelux, OECD, CMEA, European Communities and EFTA). Origins, objectives, functions, operations, are given for each organization; bibliographies for most of them. Author and subject indexes. *Class No:* 330:061:061.2

Poverty

[1867]

World poverty: an economic survey of the 20th century. Pollard, G.S., *ed.* London, Harrap, 1990. 256p. illus., charts, tables. £18.95 ISBN: 024560023x.

Arranged in 6 periods: 1900-14. 1014-29, 1929-45, 1945-60, 1960-73 (The consumer boom), 1973-89 (The worldwide network). Biographies, p.230-47. Glossary. Further reading, p.250. Editor is Emeritus Professor of Economics at Bielefeld, West Germany.
Class No: 330.16

Reviews & Abstracts

[1868]

Human resources abstracts. Newbury Park, CA., Sage Publications Inc., 1975-. Quarterly. 37.00/00 (institutions); $85pa (individuals). ISSN: 00992453.

Continues *Poverty and human resources abstracts.* v.1-9, 1966-74. Published with the co-operation of the Institute of Labor and Industrial Relations, University of Michigan and Wayne State University.

About 200 journals, mainly US, are scanned and each issue contains *c.*250 abstracts of journal articles, books and reports on employment and related topics such as economic structure and planning, labour markets and participation, labour and industrial relations, earnings and benefits, human resources and society, immigration and migration. Broadly classified arrangement in *c.*15 categories. Author and subject indexes in each issue and cumulated annually. 'A reference tool of high quality' (*Reference services review,* v.7(4), 1979, p.70).
Class No: 330.16(048)

Development & Growth

Yearbooks & Directories

[1869]

State economic agencies of the world: an international directory of government organisations concerned with economic development and planning. ed. by A.J. Day. Harlow, Essex, Longman, 1985. (distributed in USA and Canada by Gale Research Co., Detroit). x, 546p. (Keesings reference series). £48; $78. ISBN: 0582902533, UK; 0810321041, US.

Published in the USA as 'Government economic agencies of the world'.

Lists *c.*2000 state agencies and organizations in 170 countries active in economic spheres (*e.g.* national, regional and sectoral planning, industrial development, agrarian reform, export promotion, etc.). Arranged A-Z by country. For each country basic economic data and a brief résumé of the prevailing political and economic conditons precede the listing of the economic agencies, which include chambers of commerce, tourist organizations, development banks, central banks, central statistical offices, customs, and various government departments and their agencies. *Class No:* 330.34(058)

Europe

[1870]

Economic growth in Europe since 1945. Crafts, N. *and* Toniolo, G., *ed.* Cambridge, Cambridge University Press, 1996 600p. £80.00 ISBN: 0521496276.

Contains bibliography and index.

Collection of papers on economic growth, combining applied economics with economics history. Case studies for several countries help to give a clear and informative view of postwar economic growth.
Class No: 330.34(4)

Economic Theories

[1871]

Companion to contemporary economic thought. Greenaway, D., *and others, eds.* London & New York, Routledge, 1991. 858p. £85. ISBN: 0415026121.

Articles are structured to survey today's economic concerns. Thematically arranged, the 41 essays cover a wide range of issues within the field and associated disciplines. Detailed notes, extensive bibliographies, and suggestions for further reading. *Class No:* 330.8

[1872]

A **Modern guide to economic thought:** an introduction to comparative schools of thought in economics. Mair, D. *and* Miller, A., *eds.* Aldershot, Hants, Edward Elgar, 1991. xi,281p. figures. £45. $39.95. ISBN: 1852783230.

Describes the main schools of contemporary economic thinking, stated in their own terms, their aims on issues, and the reasoning behind those aims. 9 chapters: 1. Introduction; 2. The philosophy and methodology of economics; 3. The Austrian school; 4. The Neoclassical school; 5. The macroeconomics of the Chicago school; 6. The orthodox Keynesian school; 7. The post-Keynesian school; 8. The Institutionalist (evolutionary) school; 9. Marxism and radical economics. 11 contributors. Bibliography, p.263-74. Index, p.275-81.
Class No: 330.8

[1873]

ROSTOW, W.W. **Theorists of economic growth** from David Hume to the present: with a perspective on the next century. Oxford, Oxford University Press, 1990. xx,712p. tables. £35. ISBN: 0195058372.

21 chapters in 4 parts: 1. Six classical economists: David Hume to Karl Marx; 2. Growth theory moves to the periphery, 1870-1939; 3. Growth analysis post-1945: a three-ring circus; 4. Problems and prospects. Appendix: Models of economic growth. Notes, p.571-682. Author index, p.682-688, subject index, p.689-712. *Class No:* 330.8

Bibliographies

[1874]

BATSON, H.E., *comp*. **A Select bibliography of modern economic theory, 1870-1929.** London, Routledge, 1930 (Reprinted 1968 by Kelley). 224p. $27.50. ISBN: 0678065098.

About 2000 entries. Pt.1: Subject bibliography (annotated); pt.2: Author bibliography (English authors; German authors; French authors), including periodical articles and reviews, items not in the British Library of Political and Economic Science are asterisked. Index of authors. A standard guide to the literature of the period. *Class No:* 330.8(01)

Histories

[1875]

GIDE, C. *and* RIST, C. **A History of economic doctrines,** from the time of the Physiocrats to the present day. Authorised translation by R. Richards. 2nd English ed., with additional matter from the latest French edition, translated by E.F. Row. London, Harrap, 1948. 800p. O.P.

First published 1915. The original, *Histoire des doctrines économiques,* was first published in 1909.

The 2nd English edition includes matter from the 7th French edition. Footnote references; analytical index. The standard history. *Class No:* 330.8(091)

[1876]

ROLL, E. **A History of economic thought.** 5th ed. London, Faber, 1992. xiv,592p. £20. $29.95. ISBN: 0571165532.

First published 1938.

13 chapters: 1. The beginnings - 2. Commercial capitalism and its theory ... 8. Modern economics - 9. The beginning of American economics ... 11. Macroeconomics and economic management - 12. The age of doubt and the new counter-revolution - 13. A new certainty? Conclusion. Index, p.580-92. For this edition, Lord Roll has revised the early chapters and added new material; later sections have been expended and updated. Essential reading. *Class No:* 330.8(091)

Bibliographies

[1877]

FUNDABURK, E.L., *ed*. **The History of economic thought and analysis:** a selective international bibliography. v.1: *The development of economic thought and analysis.* Metuchen, N.J., Scarecrow Press, 1974. 931p. $30. ISBN: 0810805804.

6 volumes were projected but only one published.

Over 10,000 references (including major periodical articles). Sections: General works - Specific works - Periods and schools. Author-subject index; short title index. 'The work is designated as selective but no criteria for the inclusion of different items are given' (*RQ,* v.13(4), Summer 1974, p.355). *Class No:* 330.8(091)(01)

[1878]

HUTCHINSON, W.K. **History of economic analysis:** a guide to information sources. Detroit, Mich., Gale, 1976. xii, 243p. Economics information guide series, vol. 3). $68. ISBN: 0810312956.

Covers the period from 1600 to 1940, citing more than 1,000 sources in the English language. 6 chapters are devoted to the forerunners of classical economics, Keynesian economics, and 20th century British economic thought. Appendices list major organizations concerned with the subject, and journals that print articles pertaining to the field. Author, title and subject indexes. *Choice*(v.14,no.1, March 1977,p.44) recommends it as 'a handy sourcebook for undergraduate and graduate students and professors', but the review in *The Economic Journal* (v.87, no.2, 1977, p.407) mentions numerous gaps in coverage, judgements that do not inspire confidence in the compiler's ability to act as a guide, and the mixture of 'extracts, textbooks and ephemeral articles [that] jostle side by side with classic contributions ...'. *Class No:* 330.8(091)(01)

Official Records

[1879]

STURGES, R.P. **Economists' papers, 1750-1950:** a guide to archive and other manuscript sources for the history of British and Irish economic thought. London, Macmillan, 1975. xxiv, 140p. ISBN: 0333149998.

Compiled for the Committee of the Guide to Archive Sources in the History of Economic Thought, Royal Economic Society.

A finding list of personal papers and correspondence of the most distinguished British economists (*e.g.* Sir James Stewart (1712-80), R.H. Tawney (1882-1962)), indicating the nature and location of the archival material and the principal published collections. 'A well-designed search-guide' (*The Economic Journal,* v.85, 1975, p.974). *Class No:* 330.8(093.2)

Labour & Employment

Bibliographies

[1880]

AZEVEDO, R.E. **Labor economics:** a guide to information services. Detroit, Mich., Gale Research Co., 1978. xii, 261p. (Economics information guide series, v.8). $62. ISBN: 0810312972.

51 specialized subject sections (*e.g.*Automation; Collective Bargaining;) are preceded by a section on textbooks and general works, and one on general journals, government publications, and information services. In each section an introduction precedes an annotated list of books and journals. US slant. Author, title and subject indexes. *Class No:* 331(01)

[1881]

INTERNATIONAL LABOUR OFFICE. **Bibliography of published research of the World Employment Programme.** 9th edition. Geneva, ILO., 1991. ix, 130p. SFr.17.50; £7.70; ⹂ 505.00/00 Presents information on research published up to March 1991 in the form of studies, monographs, articles and World Employment Programme research working papers. ISBN: 9221077462. ISSN: 10108206. *Class No:* 331(01)

[1882]

—INTERNATIONAL LABOUR OFFICE. **Annotated bibliography on clandestine employment.** Geneva, I.L.O., 1987. iii,132p. SFr.17.50; £7.70; $12.25. (*International labour bibliography, no.2.*) ISBN: 9221057267.

Provides a wide range of references to publications on the subject of clandestine employment and related issues, including monographs, journal articles, reports and conference proceedings. *Class No:* 331(01)

[1883]

—INTERNATIONAL LABOUR OFFICE. **Catalogue of publications in print,** 1994-95. Geneva, ILO Publications, 1994. 246p. *Gratis.* ISBN: 922106090x. ISSN: 10110569.

Lists ILO publications and documents available in English and offered for sale. Includes monographs, international comparative studies, manuals, codes of practice and reports of conferences and meetings, etc. Updated by the quarterly *ILO publications*. *Class No:* 331(01)

[1884]

International labour review. Geneva, International Labour Office, 1921-. Bi-monthly. SFr.17.50pa;$60pa. ISSN: 00207780.

Includes articles and notices of new books. V.132(5-6), 1993, 5 has news briefs and news features, 7 articles, and a bibliography (new ILO publications, with descriptions. *Class No:* 331(01)

[1885]

UNITED STATES. Department of Labor. **Catalog ...** Boston, Mass., G.K. Hall, 1975. 38v. (27, 638p.).

829,000 photographically reproduced catalogue cards, covering books, periodicals, reports, microfilm, microfiche and cassettes. The Library 'is the largest, most complete, and probably the oldest special library in its field' (G.K. Hall & Co. *Catalog of publications, 1979-1980,* p.58). *Class No:* 331(01)

Handbooks & Manuals

[1886]

WALSH, K. *and* PEARSON, R. **UK labour market guide.** 2nd ed. Aldershot, Hants., Gower Publishing Co., 1984. xi, 268p. £18.50. ISBN: 0566007185.

First published 1980.

Aim was to structure the guide so that the user can quickly and easily identify the range of labour market information available to meet the specific need, and then to select the most appropriate published sources or points of further contact. Part 1: Introduction; pt.2: Sources of labour market information (25 sections: How to use this section; Population and related statistics; Economic activity; Employment ... Training ... Labour mobility ... Earnings ... Industrial disputes); pt.3: Reference section (Labour market institutions; Other organizations providing information; index to key publications. List of abbreviations. Glossary (p.255-258). Index to numbered items (p.259-268). *Class No:* 331(035)

[1887]

WARREN, C. **Personnel administration manual.** London, Kogan Page, 1991. 400p. £35. ISBN: 0749401354.

Sections: Recruitment - Training, development and career progression - Maintaining standards of performance and conduct - Severance of the employment relationship - Money matters and the employee - Safety and security - Standard letters - Miscellaneous policies and procedures. *Class No:* 331(035)

Dictionaries

Polyglot

[1888]
EUROPEAN COMMUNITIES. Commission. **Glossary of labour and the trade union movement.** Luxembourg, Office for Official Publications of the European Communities, 1983. 216p. £11.50. ISBN: 9282533204.

Terms in English, French, German, Italian, Dutch, Greek, Danish, Swedish, Norwegian and Spanish. *Class No:* 331(038)=00

[1889]
KUNHARDT, U. von *and* LLISTOSELLA-MATZKY, I., *comps.* **Elsevier's dictionary of the labour market: in English, German, Swedish, Spanish and French.** Amsterdam, Elsevier Science Publishers, 1988. xii, 366p. Dfl.400; $210.50. ISBN: 0444428844.

Aimed at those working in the field of labour relations, and based on terminology that has largely been collected in the course of the authors' practical work. Includes multiword expressions, conference terminology, and names of institutions, government agencies and international organizations. A bibliography of dictionaries (p.xi-xii) precedes the 'Basic table' listing entries A-Z in English, each numbered, followed by equivalents in the other four languages. 4 indexes in those languages refer to the numbered English section. *Class No:* 331(038)=00

Reviews & Abstracts

[1890]
International labour documentation (New series). Geneva, International Labour Office, Central Library and Documentation Branch, 1949-. Monthly. SFr.90; £39.60; $72pa. ISSN: 00207756.

Frequency has varied.

An abstracting bulletin based on current acquisitions in the I.L.O. Central Library, covering the fields of industrial relations, labour law, employment, working conditions, management, vocational training, labour-related aspects of economics, social development, rural development, technological change, etc. Quarterly indexes. *Labordoc* (1965-, monthly update) is the machine-readable version, available for interactive and retrospective online searching. *Class No:* 331(048)

Periodicals

[1891]
HARRISON, R., *and others, comps.* **The Warwick guide to British labour periodicals, 1790-1970:** a check list ... Hassocks, Sussex, Harvester Press; Atlantic Highlands, N.J., Humanities Press, 1977. xxiii, 685p.

Lists 4,125 labour periodicals arranged A-Z by title, with dates and place of publication, editors and publishers, some indication of content if title not explicit, price, and library holdings information for 138 British repositories. 'Labour periodicals' are defined by the editors as those produced 'by an organised body ... of wage-earners or collectively dependent employees', papers produced 'in the avowed interest of the working class ...', and those 'produced for wage-earners by members of other social classes who sought to improve them, instruct them, or entertain them'. Chronological and thematic indexes. A review in *Social history* v.3. 1978. p.413-4) generally welcomes the guide but points out a number of omissions and criticizes the alphabetical arrangement. *Class No:* 331(051)

[1892]
INTERNATIONAL LABOUR OFFICE. **Register of periodicals in the ILO library.** Geneva, ILO., 1987. 420 frames. SFr.35. ISBN: 922106171x.

On COM microfiche.

Over 10,000 titles, listed by title and country. Journals scanned for input to *International labour documentation* are flagged. *Class No:* 331(051)

[1893]
—INTERNATIONAL LABOUR ORGANISATION. **Bibliography of periodicals on the quality of life.** Geneva, ILO, 1983. x,88p. SFr.15; £5; $8.55. ISBN: 9221034755.

Selective bibliography, with international coverage. Subjects include labour law, personnel management, ergonomics, industrial psychology and sociology, in addition to government documents and employer and worker organization publications. *Class No:* 331(051)

Yearbooks & Directories

[1894]
Conditions of work and quality of working life: a directory of institutions, edited by Linda Stoddart, assisted by Kristine Falciola. 2nd ed. Geneva, ILO, 1986. xxi, 306p. £14.55; SFr.40. ISBN: 9221053288.

First published 1981.

Lists 288 institutions in 56 countries, including government agencies, employers' organizations, trade unions, research institutions,

....(contd.)
university departments, etc. Each entry has details on staff, funding, information services, training programmes, research projects, meetings and publications. Arranged by area or country, A-Z, subdivided by organizations, A-Z. *Class No:* 331(058)

Histories

USA

[1895]
NEUFELD, M.E. *and* LEAB, D.J. **American working class history:** a representative bibliography. New York, Bowker, 1983. 356p. $39.95. ISBN: 0835217523.

First published in 1964 as *A representative bibliography of American labor history.*

A revised and greatly expanded edition. Lists nearly 7,300 items published through January 1983, including books, periodicals, certain government publications and films. Arranged in classified order, with a detailed table of contents and an author index. *Class No:* 331(091)(73)

Archives

[1896]
INTERNATIONAL LABOUR OFFICE. **International labour conventions and recommendations, 1919-1991, with supplements 1992-1993.** Geneva, ILO, 1992. 2v. (xlv, 762; xxi, 718) SFr.95; £41.80; $76. ISBN: 922107756x.

First published in 1966, covering the first 50 sessions, since when 30 conventions and 38 recommendations have been adopted. *Class No:* 331(093.20)

Worldwide

Encyclopaedias

[1897]
Encyclopedia of global industries. Sawinski, D.M. *and* Mason, W.H., *eds.* Gale, 1996 1,034p. $395.00 ISBN: 0810397676.

Contains bibliography, charts and index. *Class No:* 331(100)(031)

Tables & Data Books

[1898]
BEAN, R., *ed.* **International labour statistics:** a handbook,. guide, and recent trends. London, Routledge, 1989. xi,306p. £75. ISBN: 0415021790.

Part 1 is a guide to the use of labour statistics in 9 chapters by subject, pt.2 has 2 chapters on labour statistics from individual countries. Sources and examples are given. An appendix lists membership of the international trade secretariats. Index, p.294-306. *Class No:* 331(100)(083)

[1899]
HOBBS, S. *and* McKECHNIE, J. *and* LAVALETTE, M. **Child labor:** a world history companion. Oxford, ABC-Clio, 1999. 292p. $65. £41.30. (*World history companion series.*) ISBN: 0874369568.

Includes information on children's rights and child labour organizations. Appendix has bibliography, index, lists of acronyms and web sites. *Class No:* 331(100)(083)

[1900]
INTERNATIONAL LABOUR OFFICE. **Bulletin of labour statistics.** Geneva, ILO., 1965-. Quarterly, with 4 supplements a year. SwF.100pa. ISSN: 00074950; 03785505, supplements.

Contains articles and notes relevant to the production and analysis of labour statistics, as well as the most recent time series on employment, unemployment, hours of work, consumer prices. Methodological descriptions are included. Data is for several quarters and years to the latest available. The supplements provide interim release of the most recent information available on the basic statistical series. *Class No:* 331(100)(083)

[1901]
—INTERNATIONAL LABOUR OFFICE. **Yearbook of labour statistics,** 1993. 52nd issue. Geneva, ILO., 1993. xix,1225p. SwF.195. ISBN: 9220073420. ISSN: 00843857.

First published 1936 (for 1935/36).

31 tables, with explanatory notes, in 9 chapters (1. Total and economically active population - 2. Employment - 3. Unemployment - 4. Hours of work - 5. Wages - 6. Labour cost - 7. Consumer prices - 8. Occupational injuries - 9. Strikes and lockouts). Statistics cover 1983-1992. Covers *c.*180 countries. Appendix includes International standard industrial classification of all economic activities (ISIC) and International classification of occupations (ISCO. References and sources, p.1187-1208. Index of countries, territories and areas.

Complemented by data presented each quarter in the *Bulletin of labour statistics.* (ISSN 00074950). *Class No:* 331(100)(083)

[1902]

WALSH, K. *and* KING, A. **Handbook of international manpower market comparisons.** New York, New York University (distributed by Columbia), 1987. 318p. $90. ISBN: 0814792170.

Annual statistics for the last decade on population, labour force, unemployment, educational supply, industrial relations, labour costs, and consumer prices, grouped by country for the European Community, Norway, Sweden, Japan, and United States. An appendix gives selected indicators for each category. Another appendix lists sources, which are not included at the foot of each table. *Class No:* 331(100)(083)

Great Britain

Bibliographies

[1903]

BURNETT, J., *and others, eds.* **The Autobiography of the working class: an annotated critical bibliography.** New York, New York University Press (distributed by Columbia); Brighton, Sussex, Harvester Press, 1984-89. 3v. (1203p.). $125 each vol. £80 each vol. ISBN: 0710806809, UK; 0811471079, US; 0710806970, UK; 0814710948, US; 0710811675, UK.

V.1 covers 1750-1900; v.2 1900-1945; v.3 is a supplement, covering 1750-1945. Over 2000 autobiographies of members of the British working class are included in v.1 and 2, including unpublished diaries, typescripts, newspaper and magazine serializations, as well as published accounts. All critically analysed and annotated. Entries are numbered and information includes full bibliographical data, family life, occupations, activities and comments. 7 appendices (A. Miscellaneous - B. Oral - C. Politics - D. Military - E. Work - F. Collections - G. Diaries). 6 indexes (general - places - occupations - education - dates - appendix authors). 'An extremely valuable tool...' (*Choice*, v.25(3), November 1987, p.452). *Class No:* 331(410)(01)

[1904]

GREAT BRITAIN. HM Stationery Office. **Government publications. Sectional list 21: Employment, health and safety..** Revised May 1990. London, HMSO, 1990. 40p. Gratis.

Main sections: Employment - Health and safety.

Class No: 331(410)(01)

Tables & Data Books

[1905]

Employment gazette. Department of Employment. London, Harrington Kilbride plc.(previously HMSO) 1971-. tables. Monthly. £52.50pa; $4.95 single issue. ISSN: 02647052.

Succeeds *Ministry of Labour gazette* (1893-1968), thereafter as *Employment and productivity gazette* (1968-1970) and *Department of Employment gazette* (1971-1979).

V.102(1), January 1994, includes News; Special features (3 items); Questions in Parliament; Labour market statistics (on tinted paper) with information on employment, unemployment, vacancies, industrial disputes, earnings, retail prices, labour force survey; tourism; training and enterprise programmes; Reviews (5 short items); LFS (Labour force survey) help-line (on tinted paper). Index.

Class No: 331(410)(083)

[1906]

LEE, C.H. **British regional employment statistics, 1841-1971.** Cambridge, Cambridge University Press, 1980. 428p. ISBN: 052122666x.

Reclassifies data from the censuses of population into two series of employment tables, one from 1841 to 1911 and the other from 1901 to 1971, devised to give the longest possible time span without losing internal consistance. Data is broken down by the counties and regions of GB and into 27 industrial areas based on the current government industrial classifications. 'This is a thorough and scholarly work' (*Journal of the Royal Statistical Society*, Series A, v.143(3), 1980, p.370). 'Dr. Lee has made the census of occupations and employment much more accessible for testing hypotheses about the development of the economy' (*Economic history review*, v.33(3), 1980, p.430). *Class No:* 331(410)(083)

Histories

[1907]

HUNT, E.H. **British labour history, 1815-1914.** London, Weidenfeld & Nicolson, 1981. xiv,428p. £18.50. ISBN: 0297777858.

The first part of the book discussed the character and condition of labour in 5 chapters (1. Work and the workers - 2. Population: births and deaths - 3. Wages and living standards - 4. Poverty - 5. Migrants, emigrants and immigrants). The second part is concerned with the organized responses of labour to the changing conditions in 4 chronologically arranged chapters. Notes, p.343-398, are by chapter. 'Further reading', p.399-406, also by chapter. Index, p.407-428. 'It is

....(contd.)

a strength of this book that it seeks to see labour as it was ...' (*Economic history review*, November 1981, p.657).

Class No: 331(410)(091)

[1908]

LUNN, K. **A Social history of British labour, 1870-1970.** London, E. Arnold, 1992. 224p. £7.99. ISBN: 0713164786.

Considers union and party policy vis-01a-vis leisure, the family, health, welfare and economic change in the context of the aspirations and life-styles of its members. Work on the history of the subject is reflected in the analysis. *Class No:* 331(410)(091)

Biographies

[1909]

BELLAMY, J.M. *and* SAVILLE, J. **Dictionary of labour biography.** London, Macmillan Press, 1972-93. 9v. V.1-7; £30 each; v.8: £35; v.9: £55: 9-volume set: £445. ISBN: 0333131800, v.1; 0333140389, v.2; 0333144155, v.3; 0333197046, v.4; 0333220153, v.5; 0333240952, v.6; 0333331818, v.7; 0333387821, v.8; 033338783x, v.9.

Covers not only the national personalities of the British Labour movement, but also the activists at regional and local level. Based on data collected by G.D.H. Cole. Time span: *c.*1790 to the present day. Each volume is self-contained, although volumes after v.1 have a 'Consolidated list of names'. The first seven volumes covered a wide range of entries from most periods of labour history, with v.6 specializing on the radical movements of the early 19th century, and vol.7 mainly concerned with personalities of the 20th Century. V.8 spans two centuries of radicals, trade unionists and socialists. v.9 is especially concerned with 20th century activists and intellectuals. Each volume has its own index. *Class No:* 331(410)(092)

Official Records

[1910]

GREAT BRITAIN. Public Record Office. **Records of interest to social scientists, 1919-1939: Employment and unemployment.** Swann, B. *and* Turnbull, M. London, HMSO, 1978. v. 590p. (*Public Record Office handbooks, no.18.*)

7 chapters: 1. Introduction - 2. General policy - 3. Spheres of government activity (p.86-173) - 4. Cabinet and Departmental records: Code R (p.174-382) - 5. Cabinet annd Departmental records: Code C (p.383-532) - 6. Legislation: Code L (annotated) - 7. Parliamentary Papers: Code P. Appendices: 1. Abbreviations; 2. Unemployment figures; 3. Unemployment Act, 1934. *Class No:* 331(410)(093.2)

Laws

[1911]

WALTON, F., *comp. & ed.* **The Encyclopedia of employment law and practice.** 2nd ed. London, Professional Publishing, 1985. loose-leaf. ISBN: 094655921x.

A guide to aspects of employment legislation in the UK, kept up-to-date by a quarterly amendment service. Main index (31p.) and table of cases (21p.) are followed by the encyclopedia, A-Z (Advisory, Conciliation and Arbitration Service (ACAS) ... Youth training scheme). As an example, the entry for 'Lock-out' is in 6 sections: 1. Definition - 2. Lock-outs as breaches of contracts of employment - 3. Dismissal of lock-out employees - 4. Meaning of 'directly interested' in a dispute - 5. Status of the contract of employment during lock-outs - 6. Action by an employer contemplating a lock-out.

Class No: 331(410)(094.1)

Dictionaries

[1912]

CHANDLER, P. **An A-Z of employment law: a complete reference source for managers.** London, Kogan Page, 1995. xvii, 608p., facsims., tables. £16.95. ISBN: 0749412208.

Previously published in 1981 as *An A-Z of employment and safety law*

3 parts: 1. A-Z of employment and safety law (Abrasive wheels ... Young persons, employment of), including abstracts of regulations and summaries of Acts. - 2. Key codes of practice (e.g., Code of industrial relations practice; Picketing) - 3. Addresses and sources of further information. Appendix: Computing a period of continuous employment. Analytical index. Compact; well produced.

Class No: 331(410)(094.1)(038)

[1913]

SELWYN, N. **Dictionary of employment law.** London, Butterworths, 1985. [4], 165p. £15. ISBN: 0406207909.

Aims to provide a quick reference to key words and phrases used in modern employment law, with special emphasis on how the courts and tribunals interpret the various statutory provisions. Entries range in length from two or three lines to a page or more. Cross-references. Entries often refer to cases. *Class No:* 331(410)(094.1)(038)

Scotland

[1914]

MacDOUGALL, I. A Catalogue of some labour records in Scotland and some Scots records outside Scotland. Edinburgh, Scottish Labour History Society, 1978. xvi, 598p. £11.50. ISBN: 0950693308.

A comprehensive catalogue of primary and secondary sources relating to labour history of Scotland. In 7 sections: Records and publications of 1800 friendly societies - History of Co-operative Society records - 500 labour political organisations' records - Trade union organizations - Miscellaneous organizations and activities - Newspapers annd periodicals published in England, Ireland and Scotland: holdings in Scottish libraries - [People] in working class movements. Favourably reviewed in the Society for the Study of Labour History's *Bulletin*. no. 38. p.49. *Class No:* 331(411)

Latin America

[1915]

GREENFIELD, G.M. *and* MARAM, S.L., *eds*. Latin American labor organizations. Westport, Conn., Greenwood, 1987. 929p. $125. ISBN: 0313228345.

Short histories of all Latin American republics and Puerto Rico, Cuba, French Guiana, Guyana, Haiti, Jamaica, Suriname and Belize, focusing on labour relations and including information on the various unions, co-operatives, sindicatos and mutual aid societies. Detail given varies from country to country. There are appendices on international labor organizations, a country-by-country chronology of major events, and a country-by-country glossary of terms, people and events, plus a 98-page index. '... indispensable work for any collection on Latin America ... cannot be too highly recommended ...' (*Choice*, v.25(11/12), July/August 1988, p.1675). *Class No:* 331(729.99)

USA

Bibliographies

[1916]

Labor in America: a historical bibliography. Santa Barbara, CA., ABC-Clio, 1985. viii, 307p. $69; £66.70. (*Clio bibliography series, no 18*.) ISBN: 0874363977.

Information taken from the ABC-Clio database.

2865 abstracts of articles published between 1973 and 1983. In 5 chronological chapters (1. Labor in America: multiperiod - 2. Early American labor, to 1865 - 3. Labor in post-bellum America, to 1900 - 4. Labor in the new century, 1900 to 1945 - 5. Modern labor, 1945 to 1982). Each chapter is subdivided topically (*e.g.* General: the worker - The labor movement, government programs, policies and politics - Racial, ethnic and sex discrimination - Economic statistics of labor). Analytical subject index, p.201-294; author index, p.295-301; List of periodicals, p.303-305. *Class No:* 331(73)(01)

Yearbooks & Directories

[1917]

Training and development organizations directory. McLean, J., *ed*. 5th ed. Detroit, Mich., Gale Research Co., 1991. 684p. $310. ISBN: 0810343495.

Lists over 2300 training firms offering seminars and workshops, videos, and other training programmes that can enhance skills and personal development. Data for each firm includes name, address, telephone number, names of principals, staff size, areas of course emphasis, typical clients/target audience, course titles and fees. Arrangement is A-Z by company or organization name. Geographical, subject, and principal officers' names indexes. Available online. *Class No:* 331(73)(058)

Thesauri

[1918]

INTERNATIONAL LABOUR OFFICE. ILO Thesaurus: labour, employment and training terminology. 4th ed. Geneva,ILO,1992. xxxix, 557p. SFr.90. £39.60. $72. ISBN: 9220064294.

First published in 1976.

A thesaurus of English/French/Spanish descriptors used in the ILO library for information processing. An alphabetical index of terms (separate sequences for the three languages) refers to a systematic display using ILO's faceted classification scheme. *Class No:* 331:025.43

Institutions & Associations

[1919]

Employers' organizations of the world. Upham, M., *ed*. Harlow, Longman; New York, St. James Press, 1993. xiv,237p. £75. (*International reference*).) ISBN: 0582060370, UK; 1558620680, US.

Arranged by country, A-Z (Afghanistan ... Zimbabwe), with background information, followed by organizations with addresses, telephone numbers, leadership, total membership, affiliations, government bodies in which represented, aims and objectives, services provided to members, publications, date of foundation. International organizations. Select list of acronyms. Index of major employers' associations, p.234-7.

A new edition was issued in 1993 (loose-leaf, *c.*608p. £245. ISBN 0582100380). *Class No:* 331:061:061.2

Manpower

Worldwide

[1920]

ORGANISATION FOR ECONOMIC CO-OPERATION AND DEVELOPMENT. Labour force statistics, 1970-1990. Paris, OECD, 1992. 510p. tables, graphs. £24; $43; F.395. ISBN: 9264036857.

First published 1968. Annual. Superseded *Manpower statistics,* published from 1961 to 1965.

Definitions, symbols employed, sources precede the 3 main sections: I. General tables and graphs - II. Country tables - III. Participation rates and unemployment rates. Data is given for each of the member countries and includes population, labour force, unemployment and employment.

Updated by *Quarterly labour force statistics* (1975-. £24.pa. $43pa. F.195pa ISSN 02553627). *Class No:* 331.024(100)

Great Britain

[1921]

YOUNG, J.D. Socialism and the English working class: a history of English labour, 1883-1939. Hemel Hempstead,Herts., Harvester Wheatsheaf, 1989. x,273 p. £28.50 $50.45. ISBN: 0710812051.

Explores the connection between the social history of the English working class and the history of the Labour Movement. 8 chapters (Labour historiography and the English working class; English working class attitudes to State intervention and the labour unrest, 1906-1914 ... Militancy, English Socialism and The Ragged Trousered Philanthropists ... English workers, mass unemployment and the Left, 1924-1939. 600 notes, all referring to publications, p.234-264. Index, p.265-273. *Class No:* 331.024(410)

Industrial Relations

[1922]

GREAT BRITAIN. Department of Employment. Directory of employers; associations, trade unions, joint organisations, etc. London, HMSO. Semi-annual. £11.25 (September 1992 issue). ISSN: 09659633.

'Provides comprehensive lists of United Kingdom organizations whose objects include the negotiation of, or making of recommendations on wages and working conditions, or which provide representatives of organizations which are so concerned (*Introduction*). Organizations are grouped according to industries in which they function (SIC 1980 revision). Main sections: Employers' Associations - Trade union federations, trade union and other employees associations - Joint organizations, wages, councils, and arbitration boards, etc. Index. *Class No:* 331.1

Bibliographies

[1923]

BAIN, G.S. *and* WOOLVEN, G.B. A Bibliography of British industrial relations. Cambridge, Cambridge University Press, 1979. xxiii, 665p. ISBN: 0521215471.

Aims 'to bring together all the secondary source material, except that of an ephemeral or strictly propagandist nature, published in English between 1880 and 1970 on British industrial relations. It includes books, pamphlets, articles in learned and professional journals, theses and government reports' *(Preface)*. 15,056 numbered items; 7 parts, closely subdivided (1. General (bibliographies, guides and archival sources) - 2. Employees: industrial attitudes and behaviour - 3. Employee organisation - 4. Employers and their organisation - 5. Labour-management relations - 6. The labour force, labour markets and conditions of employment (p.205-413) - 7. The State and its agencies. Index of authors, subjects, periodical titles (*c.*500). etc. 'A large and most impressive book' (*British book news*, October 1979, p.812).

A welcome supplement has now been issued (A bibliography of British industrial relations, 1971-1979, by G.S. Bain and J.D. Bennett.

....(contd.)

Cambridge University Press, 1985. xix, 258p. £42. ISBN 0521266998). Since 1980 this is updated by annual articles in the *British journal of industrial relations. Class No:* 331.1(01)

[1924]

BENNETT, J. *and* **FAWCETT, J.,** comps. **Industrial relations:** an international and comparative bibliography. London, Mansell Publishing Ltd., 1985. xi,172p. £18.50. ISBN: 0720117879.

Compiled for the British Universities Industrial Relations Association.

Entries for major works are arranged A-Z by country, subdivided by chronological arrangement and then A-Z by author. Includes material on collective bargaining, industrial conflict, the institutions of industrial relations, labour economy, labour history, labour law, and the management of labour. Books, journal articles, essays in books of readings, and a few theses are included, mainly in English-language, but some French, German and Spanish. Author index, p.143-163. Subject index, p.164-172. *Class No:* 331.1(01)

[1925]

PETTMAN, B.O. **Industrial democracy:** a selected bibliography. Bradford, Yorks, MCB Publications, 1979. vii, 95p. £29.95. ISBN: 0905440617.

A selective listing of over 3000 items (articles, books, theses and reports) published between 1950 and 1978, divided into general, comparative, and country studies. Author index. *Class No:* 331.1(01)

[1926]

WALSH, R.M. *and* **BIRKIN, S.J.** **Job satisfaction and motivation:** an annotated bibliography. Westport, Conn., & London, Greenwood Press, 1979. viii, 643p. $50.95; £40.50. ISBN: 031320635x.

946 items relating to research and field studies published between 1970 and 1979. Some books, dissertations, documents, etc. are included but emphasis is on journal articles in disciplines such as psychology, management and public administration. Arranged in 3 parts: author index, subject (keyword in context) index, and abstracts for each of the items. *Class No:* 331.1(01)

Handbooks & Manuals

[1927]

A Handbook of industrial relations practice: practice and law in the employer relationship. Towers, B., *ed.* 3rd ed. London, Kogan Page, 1992. xvii, 431p. £18.95. ISBN: 0749407158.

First published 1979, edited by K. Hawkins.

17 chapters in 3 parts, pt.1 relates to the background of the subject; pt.2 The practice of industrial relations; pt.3 The law in industrial relations. List of cases cited. Useful addresses. Analytical index. *Class No:* 331.1(035)

[1928]

International handbook of industrial relations: contemporary developments and research. Blum, A.A., *ed.* Westport, CT., Greenwood Press; London, Aldwych Press, 1981. xiv, 690p. illus., tables. $67.95; £34.50. ISBN: 0313213038, US; 0861720105, UK.

27 essays, arranged A-Z by country, attempt 'to describe how workers and managers around the world deal with their problems at the workplace' (*Preface*). Includes both Western European countries and developing countries. 29 contributors. Select bibliography on comparative industrial relations. Index, p.679-696. *Class No:* 331.1(035)

[1929]

TORRINGTON, D.P., *ed.* **Handbook of industrial relations.** Epping, Essex, Gower Press, 1972. xix,328p. illus. ISBN: 0716101203.

'An attempt to help managers in their handling of industrial relations within the organization they run' (*Preface*). In 4 parts, with 14 contributors, on the national and company framework, the union viewpoint, and the social framework. Bibliography, p.313-8. Non-analytical index. D.P. Torrington's *Who's who in personnel administration and industrial relations* (1973. 518p.) has over 2500 biographies of leading individuals in the field. *Class No:* 331.1(035)

Dictionaries

English

[1930]

KELLY, M.A. **Labor and industrial relations:** terms, laws, court decisions, and arbitration standards. Baltimore, Johns Hopkins University Press, 1987. 200p. $26.50. ISBN: 0801833108.

A basic glossary of labour-related terms and a compendia of labour relations law, protective labour legislation, and major court decisions and arbitration standards. US oriented. Good index. More selective than Shafritz's *Facts on file dictionary of personnel management and labor relations* (qv). 'Definitions of terms are precise ...' (*Choice,* October 1987, p.286). *Class No:* 331.1(038)=20

[1931]

MARSH, A. **Concise encyclopedia of industrial relations,** with bibliography. Aldershot, Hants, Gower Press, 1979. [vi], 423p. £26. ISBN: 0566020955.

Originally issued as *Dictionary of industrial relations* in 1973.

About 3,000 entries. 'Donovan Commission': over 2 columns, with 2/3 col. of references. 'Transport and General Workers' Union: 3 cols. (amalgamations, in chronological order). Profuse references to Acts, Command Papers, Reports etc. Cross-references. Bibliography, p.355-423, listing all books and periodical articles cited in the text. British slant, but includes Ireland. 'An essential work of reference for librarians and teachers concerned with British industrial relations' (*British book news,* August 1979, p.650). *Class No:* 331.1(038)=20

[1932]

ROBERTS, H.S. **Robert's dictionary of industrial relations.** Industrial Relations Center. University of Hawaii at Manoa, *ed.* 3rd ed. Washington, DC, BNA Books, 1986. xxi, 811p. $65. ISBN: 0871794888.

First published 1966; rev. ed. 1971.

More than 4400 entries, including significant court cases and legislation, international unions, and government agencies, as well as terms and phrases used in labour-management relations. No biographical entries. '... a helpful, up-to-date source of information on terms, cases and organizations involved in industrial relations'. (*Reference books bulletin,* 1986/87, p.72). *Class No:* 331.1(038)=20

French

[1933]

DION, G. **Dictionnaire canadien des relations du travail.** 2e. rev. Quebec, Les Presses de l'Université Laval, 1987. 993p. £63.

First published 1976.

Has French definitions and an English-French index. Appendices include abbreviations in English and French of numerous North American and international employer, employee and government organizations; chronologies of Canadian and Quebec legislation and of important industrial relations events, etc. Bibliography of relevant dictionaries. *Class No:* 331.1(038)=40

Reviews & Abstracts

[1934]

Employee relations bibliography and abstracts. Marsh, A., *ed. and comp.* Oxford, Employee Relations Bibliography and Abstracts, 1985, plus 3 supplements, 1986-1987. xxxi,667p. Supplements 679, 260&280p. With supplement 1. £93.75; supplements 2 & 3. £37.50 each. ISBN: 094787500x, inc. suppl.1; 0947875026, suppl.2; 0947875034, suppl.3.

Classification and keyword index precede the bibliography, which is in 8 sections (General - Union-management relations - Relations at the place of work - Remuneration - Labour force - Trade unions - Industry - Psychology and sociology - Countries). 17103 entries. Author index. *Class No:* 331.1(048)

[1935]

—**Employee relations bibliography and abstracts.** 1989-. v.1-. Quarterly. Marsh, A., *ed. & comp.* Oxford, Employee Relations Bibliography and Abstracts, 1989-. ISSN: 09549064.

Continues the above.

c.2000 items each issue. Arrangement is as above except that there is a 9th section for United Kingdom regions. *Class No:* 331.1(048)

[1936]

Work related abstracts Detroit, Mich., Information Coordinators Inc., 1950-. Monthly. $455pa including subject heading list). ISSN: 02733234.

Formerly *Employment related abstracts*

A guide to current materials in labour relations and personnel management. About 6000 informative and indicative abstracts pa from over 275 labour, government and business journals, arranged by broad topic. Subject index to each issue, cumulating annually. *Work related abstracts subject heading list* (1972-. $15.) is issued biennially. *Class No:* 331.1(048)

Periodicals

[1937]

British journal of industrial relations. London School of Economics. London, London School of Economics (previously Oxford, Basil Blackwell, 1963-. quarterly (previously 3pa.). £72; $130pa. ISSN: 00071080.

V.31(4), December 1993 has 7 articles, 10 book reviews and a listing of books received (p.641-42). Indexed annually. *Class No:* 331.1(051)

Great Britain

Bibliographies

[1938]

GOTTSCHALK, A.W., *and others*. **British industrial relations:** an annotated bibliography. Nottingham, University of Nottingham, Department of Adult education, [1969?]. 72p. £0.75. ISBN: 0902031031.

About 750 entries, briefly annotated, in 5 sections: 1. Industrial relations at the place of work - 2. Industry wide bargaining - 3. The parties to collective bargaining - 4. Industrial relations: wider aspects - 5. Case studies and sources of information.
Employment relations in the United Kingdom, compiled by M. MacCafferty (London, Aslib, 1976. vi, 48p. £5.00. 0851420834) has 455 references to books, periodical and press articles covering January 1974-December 1975. Author index. *Class No:* 331.1(410)(01)

Histories

[1939]

WRIGLEY, C., *ed*. **A History of British industrial relations.** Brighton, Sussex, Harvester Wheatsheaf, 1982-87. v. 1&2 (xv, 269p.; vii, 328p.) tables, graphs. £42.50 each vol; $75.20 each vol. Cheltenham, Edward Elgar, 1996 v.3 (viii, 239p.) ISBN: 0710803168, v.1; 0710809336, v.2; 1852788925, v.3.

V.1: 1875-1914; v.2: 1914-1939; v.3 1939-1979. V.1 has 12 essays (1. Some aspects of the labour market in Britain ... 2. The rise of the mass labour movement ... - 3. Rank-and-file dissent - 4. Strikes, 1870-1914 - 5. Employers and managers ... - 6. Trade unions and the law - 7. The government and industrial relations - 8. Government administration - 9-12 are industrial relations case studies on 4 industries. Index, p.266-269. V.2 has 6 essays on the impact of State intervention on industrial relations during World War I; the interwar trade union development; rank-and-file movements and unions; the growth of white-collar trade unionism; employers' organizations and management strategy; the role of governments and the importance of social welfare. Also 3 industrial relations case studies. V.2 is considered disappointing, not maintaining the standard of v.1, but 'Taken together, the chapters represent a useful addition to the literature of interwar industrial relations ...' (*Economic history review,* November 1987, p.666). V.3: Industrial relations in a declining economy. *Class No:* 331.1(410)(091)

Germany

Bibliographies

[1940]

CHAMBERLIN, W. **Industrial relations in Germany, 1914-1939:** annotated bibliography of materials in the Hoover Library on War, Revolution and Peace and the Stanford University Library. Stanford, Calif., Stanford University Press, 1942 (Reprinted New York, AMS Press, 1974). xv, 403p. $35.00. ISBN: 0404564003.

A note on German labour law precedes the bibliography, which is divided into 7 chapters of documents, society publications, newspapers and periodical publications; and then monographs, studies and articles generally for 1914-1918, and 1933-1940. Index.
Class No: 331.1(430)(01)

Tribunals

[1941]

GOODMAN, M.J. **Industrial tribunals: practice and procedure.** 4th ed. London, Sweet and Maxwell, 1987. xxv, 120p. £15. ISBN: 0421391200.

First published 1976 as *Industrial tribunal's procedure.*

Aimed at helping the non-legal practitioner through the intricacies of industrial tribunal rules, regulations and procedure, providing an overall view of the tribunal's principal jurisdictions and detailed analyses of practice and procedure. Updated to include changes in the law since 1985, particularly the Wages Act 1986. Author is part-time chairman of the industrial tribunals and Social Security Commissioner. *Class No:* 331.15

Salaries & Wages

Great Britain

[1942]

Incomes data report. London, Incomes Data Services Ltd., 1966-. Semi-monthly. £125. pa. ISSN: 00193461.

An intelligence service on wages and incomes in Britain, including reviews of current activities in industries and of firms, settlements, intelligence reports on various subjects, and statistical tables of economic forecasts, labour turnover, and a data check (time series). *Class No:* 331.2(410)

[1943]

New earnings survey. Department of Employment. London, HMSO, 1968-. Annual. 6 parts each year. £12.50 each part; £69 the set. ISSN: 02620553.

Contents: A: Streamlined and summary analyses. Description of the survey; B: Analysis by agreement; C: Analyses of industry; D: Analyses by occupation; E: Analyses by region. Analyses by age group; F: Distribution of hours. Joint distributions of earnings and hours. Analysis of earnings and hours for part-time women employees. *Class No:* 331.2(410)

Occupations & Careers

[1944]

DIBDEN, K. *and* TOMLINSON, J., *eds*. **Information sources in education and work.** Sevenoaks, Kent, Butterworth, 1981. xiii, 166p. £22.50. (*Butterworths Guides to information sources.*) ISBN: 0408709235.

Directed at those responsible for advising young people and young people themselves on career choices. 11 chapters in 6 sections: 1 Setting the scene - 2 & 3. The right answer at the right time (before and in 6th form, beyond school, at university) - 4. Vocational and professional training - 5. Choosing and finding a job - 6. Information sources for the careers adviser. Bibliography relates to each chapter (pp. 150-166). No index. *Class No:* 331.5

[1945]

INTERNATIONAL LABOUR OFFICE. **International standard classification of occupations.** Rev, ed, Geneva, I.L.O., 1990. vii,457p. illus. SFr.65. $52. £28.60. ISBN: 9221064387.

Structured on the basis of type of work performed. *Class No:* 331.5

[1946]

Occupations, 93. Davies, K. Sheffield, Careers and Occupational Information Centre (COIC), 1992. 640p. £21.50. ISBN: 0861106342.

Entries for *c.*600 jobs and careers, with information on the work involved, the work environment, pay and conditions, vacancies, prospects for promotion, entry requirements, training courses, and address for further information. Subject index. *Class No:* 331.5

Handbooks & Manuals

[1947]

DONALD, V. **How to choose a career.** 4th. ed. London, Kogan Page, 1996. 128p. £6.99. (*(Kogan Page careers series).*) ISBN: 0749419342.

lst published 1986.

Advice not only on traditional career paths, but also on new growth areas likely to provide a career. 10 sections in 4 parts: 1. Good prospects - 2. What do you want from a career? - 3. Training - 4. Where to go for further career advice. 'Further reading' (11 items published by Kogan Page). Index. *Class No:* 331.5(035)

[1948]

GOLZEN, G. The *Daily Telegraph* guide to working abroad. 19th ed. London, Kogan Page, 1996. 336p. £9.99. ISBN: 0749419709.

Contains practical advice and detailed information on the overseas job market, including salary level comparisons, pensions, national insurance contributions, financial and tax planning, moving house, educating children, etc. *Class No:* 331.5(035)

[1949]

Working holidays: the complete international guide to seasonal job opportunities, 1993. London, Central Bureau, 1992. Annual. 320p. £7.95; $18.95. ISBN: 0900087891.

Published each December and valid only for the following year.

Practical information (*e.g.* Visas/work permits, travel insurance, advertising for a job); Jobs index, arranged geographically (Africa, Asia, Australia ... Yugoslavia, Worldwide) each subdivided and giving useful addresses, information, regulations, etc., for each.
Class No: 331.5(035)

Yearbooks & Directories

[1950]

The Directory of jobs and careers abroad. de Vries, A. 8th ed. with additional research by G. Adams London, Vacation work, 1993. 408p. £15.95. ISBN: 1854580256. ISSN: 01433482.

First published 1971.

In 3 parts: The general approach (Discovering your employment potential - Getting the job - Rules and regulations - Learning the language - Preparation and follow-up - Home letting) - Specific careers (17 sections, all subdivided) - Worldwide employment (by regions, subdivided by country; contacts; etc.). 5 appendices, including a Bibliography; Application procedure; Worldwide taxation; Worldwide living standards; Key to company classifications. Index to organizations. *Class No:* 331.5(058)

[1951]

Summer jobs abroad. Woodworth, D., *ed*. Annual. Oxford, Vacation Work, 1989-. 214p. £7.95. ISBN: 1854580051. ISSN: 03087123.

Earlier title was *Directory of summer jobs abroad.*

Aims to help students and other young people find jobs outside Britain during their long summer vacations. Valid for the 1989 summer season only. Lists 30,000 varied vacancies in over 40 different countries, excluding US, stating salaries, hours and periods of work, under countries A-Z: 'au pair, paying guests, and exchange visits'; 'visa, residence and working regulations, useful publications, travel and holidays'.

Also published by this publisher are *Summer employment directory of the US; Emploi d'été en France; Kibbutz volunteer; International directory of voluntary work* (see 362(100)(058)).
Class No: 331.5(058)

Great Britain

[1952]

ROUTH, G. **Occupations of the people of Great Britain, 1801-1981:** with a compendium of a paper 'Occupations of the people of the United Kingdom, 1801-81' by Charles Booth. London, Macmillan, 1987. xiv, 98p. figs., tables. £29.50. ISBN: 0333434978.

Extends Charles Booth's analysis to 1981, and presents a retrospect of the transformation that has occurred in 180 years. 6 chapters: 1. Charles Booth's paper - 2. 1881-1911 - 3. 1911-1951 - 4. 1951-1981 - 5. Retrospect - 6. Britain in its world setting. Appendix: Allocation of 1981 occupational units to occupational classes. Bibliography, A-Z by author, p.95-96. Index, p.97-98. Author is a former Reader in Economics at University of Sussex. *Class No:* 331.5(410)

Handbooks & Manuals

[1953]

BURSTON, D., *ed*. **An A-Z of careers and jobs.** 7th ed. London, Kogan Page, 1995. 432p. £9.99. ISBN: 0749417609.

First published 1984.

'... aimed primarily at young people still at school ...' (*Introduction*). Covers a range of careers and jobs, 350 different occupations from accountant to zoologist. Information given is description of job, qualifications and training, personal qualities, starting salary, further information (organizations and addresses), and publications. Cross-references. 2 appendices: 1. Youth Training Scheme - 2. Useful addresses. Index. *Class No:* 331.5(410)(035)

[1954]

Which subject? Which career? Jamieson, A., *ed*. 6th ed. London, Consumers' Association, in association with Hobsons Publishing, 1996. 594p. ISBN: 0852025890.

1st published 1987.

21 sections in 2 parts: 1. School courses; 2. Further and higher education. A Part 3, the bulk of the book, is an A-Z of careers (Accountancy ... Zookeeping). *Class No:* 331.5(410)(035)

Yearbooks & Directories

[1955]

Cassell career encyclopedia. Lea, K., *ed*. 14th ed. London, Cassell, 1997. xi, 754p. £35. $70. ISBN: 0304337404.

First published 1952.

Designed to be read to provide a broad general survey of the state of careers and employment, and the related areas of education and training. 11 sections (each subdivided, with appended 'Further reading',and 'Further information'): Academic and vocational qualifications - Academic and vocational studies and where they can lead - The world of work. The information society - Commerce, administration and finance - Creative, cultural and entertainment work - Land- and environment-related work - Central and local government and the armed forces - Manufacturing and production - Professional, scientific and social services - The service industries - Working overseas. 2 appendices: I: Organizations providing further information; II: Higher and further education institutions. Index to advertisers. Index. *Class No:* 331.5(410)(058)

[1956]

Jobfile: the comprehensive careers handbook. Miller, I.M., *and others, comps*. London, Hodder & Stoughton, 1988-. 571p. £22.99. ISBN: 0340587652.

Annual. First published 1988.

Annually revised career guide designed to give careers staff, teachers, students and others the chance to identify a realistic range of job opportunities. A-Z index of types of work, Careers areas index, Jobfile sections index precede profiles of 642 jobs, with description of job, qualifications, skills, notes, references, adult notes for each. *Class No:* 331.5(410)(058)

[1957]

Prospects directory: jobs and postgraduate study. Manchester, Central Services Unit, 1994-. 224p. £8.45. ISSN: 13609084.

continues *The career services' guide to graduate opportunities*

An index of institutions precedes the main directory, which is arranged A-Z under the names of the colleges, universities and polytechnics to which the careers services are attached. Information given includes name of service, address, personnel, term dates, directions, graduating force. There follows a section relating to disabled graduates. Index of personnel; index of term dates. *Class No:* 331.5(410)(058)

USA

Bibliographies

[1958]

Professional careers sourcebook. Dorgan, C.A., *and others, eds*. 3rd rev. ed. Detroit, Mich., Gale Research International Ltd. 1993. 1049p. $80.44 £47.50 ISBN: 0810375737.

First published 1990.

Presents over 100 professional career profiles, including information on general career guides, career information and services provided by professional associations, standards and certification agencies, directories of educational programmes and institutions, basic reference guides and handbooks related to the profession, professional and trade periodicals, etc. A master index lists all publications, organizations and information sources. *Class No:* 331.5(73)(01)

Yearbooks & Directories

[1959]

Career discovering encyclopedia. Primm, E.R., *ed*. Chicago, Ill., Ferguson, 1990. 6v. illus. $99.95. ISBN: 0894341065.

Supersedes Hopke, W.E., *ed*. *The Encyclopedia of careers and vocational guidance*. 7th ed. 1988.

Describes 504 careers, A-Z. Each career has a 2-page spread and includes information on type of work, education and training required, salary, future prospects, sources of further information, other related occupations. Index and glossary for all volumes at end of each volume. V.6 also indexes careers by cluster. '... clearly written, attractive, and well organized.' (*Booklist*, 15 May 1990, p.1836). *Class No:* 331.5(73)(058)

[1960]

VGM's careers encyclopedia. Norback, C.T. 3rd ed. Lincolnwood, Ill., National Textbook Co./VGM Careers Books, 1991. 464p. $39.95. ISBN: 0844261327.

Details of nearly 200 Careers, A-Z, including general descriptions, places of employment, qualifications, working conditions, education and training, advancement, income, etc. Index. *Class No:* 331.5(73)(058)

Unemployment

Bibliographies

[1961]

FARMER, P., *comp. & ed*. **The Social and economic impact of unemployment, 1979-85:** a select bibliography. Letchworth, Herts, Technical Communications, 1985. xix, 176p. ISBN: 0946655057.

Over 1,100 entries. Entries on UK press comment are followed by sections on Social impact - Physical and psychological effects - Economic and technological impact - Alternatives to unemployment - Employer and trade union attitudes to unemployment - Future projections on unemployment. For each entry there is title, author, publisher and price, and pagination, or journal or report details, and annotation. Corporate organizations index and author index. *Class No:* 331.56(01)

Great Britain

Official Records

[1962]

GREAT BRITAIN. Public Record Office. **Records of interest to social scientists: unemployment insurance 1911-1939.** London, HMSO., 1975. 268p. £4.50. (*Public Record Office handbooks, no.16*.) ISBN: 0114400636.

8 chapters, documenting the policy changes of successive governments (Liberal government, 1908/1914 ... National government, 1931/1939). Royal Commission on Unemployment Insurance, 1930-32. Committees dealing with unemployment insurance. 9 appendices (*e.g.* 6. Statistics; 9. Précis of Acts of Parliament dealing with unemployment insurance). *Class No:* 331.56(410)(093.2)

Technical Training

Dictionaries

Polyglot

[1963]
Vocational training: glossarium: a comparison of concepts from 12 member states of the European Union in nine languages: elaborated within the framework of a GIIT-CEDEFOP Project. Linshoft-Stiller, B., *project coordinator*. Luxembourg, Office for Official Publications of the European Communities, 1996 545p. ISBN: 928278326x.

Includes terms selected on the basis of need for precise definitions of modern vocational training terms. *Class No:* 331.86(038)=00

English

[1964]
MANPOWER SERVICES COMMISSION. Training Services. Glossary of training terms. 3rd ed. London, HMSO, for the Commission, 1981. [9],93p. £4.50. ISBN: 0118885111.

First published 1967,. 1st and 2nd eds. produced by the Department of Employment.

Defines over 300 terms, including names of organizations. 3 appendices: A. Abbreviations and acronyms - B. Industrial Training Boards and other training organizations - C. Names and addresses of organizations. *Class No:* 331.86(038)=20

Reviews & Abstracts

[1965]
Technical education abstracts from British sources. Leicester University. Library, *comp.* Abingdon, Oxon. Carfax (previously London, National Federation for Educational Research in England and Wales, and later Liverpool, Information for Education Ltd.), 1961-. v.1, no.1-. Quarterly. £112pa. ISSN: 00400920.

*c.*500 indicative and informative abstracts pa, drawn from *c.*50 major journals, monographs, reports and conference proceedings. Arranged in 24 subject divisions: Administration - Adult education - Business studies ... Teacher education ... Special education - Tourism. Author and subject indexes, cumulating annually. Intended for those working in science, technical and further education, including education and training for industry and commerce.
Class No: 331.86(048)

Great Britain

[1966]
The Training directory 2nd ed. London, Kogan Page, in association with BACIE, 1993. 296. £25. ISBN: 0749409568.

First published 1989.

Details government initiatives and proposals for vocational training in the United Kingdom; operations of TECs and LECs, government funding for employee training and industrial training groups; lists of suppliers of training materials and equipment. *Class No:* 331.86(410)

Trade Unions

[1967]
Trade unions of the world. Upham, M., *ed.* 4th ed. London, Cartermill, 1996. 447p. ISBN: 1860671306, UK.

First published 1987.

An international guide to trade unions and their activities. Arrangement is by country and territory, and for each there is background information, a discussion of trade unionism there, and full details of the central trade unions and other unions active there. For each trade union the information given includes the original and English translation of title; address; leadership; telephone, fax., telex, cable numbers; history and character; structure; publications; and international affiliations. A separate section gives information on international organizations. There is also a select index of acronyms, and an index of trade union organizations. 'A handy compendium of basic information on the worldwide status of the labor movement' (*Choice*, v.25(7), March 1988, p.1072, review of the first edition).
Class No: 331.881

Dictionaries

Polyglot

[1968]
EUROPEAN COMMUNITIES. Commission. Glossary of labour and the trade union movement. Luxembourg, Office for Official Publications of the European Communities, 1983. 216p. £11.50. ECU 17.41. ISBN: 0444428844.

400 terms in 10 languages on labour terminology and the vocabulary

....(contd.)
used in the trade union movement. Short definitions. Names and abbreviations of the most important trade union organizations are also listed. *Class No:* 331.881(038)=00

Periodicals

[1969]
TRADE UNION CONGRESS. Library. List of current trade union periodicals. London, the Library, 1991. 15p. Gratis.

Mimeographed.

A-Z list of unions publishing periodicals, with the titles of the periodicals they publish, with frequencies. Title index.
Class No: 331.881(051)

Europe—Western

Biographies

[1970]
ANDREUCCI, F. *and* DETTI, T. Il movimento operaio italiano: dizionario biografico, 1853-1943. Roma, Editori Riuniti, 1975-1978. 5v.

A biographical dictionary of the Italian labour movement, arranged A-Z by biographee throughout the 5v. *Class No:* 331.881(400)(092)

Great Britain

[1971]
JONES, J. *and* MORRIS, M. A-Z of trade unionism and industrial relations. New ed. London, Sphere Books Ltd., 1986. 368p. £5.95. ISBN: 0722151756.

First published 1983 by Heinemann.

'Aims to fill the absence of a *single* source of basic information on what may be broadly described as the world of labour (*Preface*). Detailed contents list precedes the main A-Z listing (Ability to pay ... Zero rating). 2 appendices: a list of trade unions in England and Scotland, A-Z under each country; and a list of names and addresses of institutions. 'Compact source book of basic definitions and background information covering *c.*500 terms used in discussions of trade unionism and industrial relations'. (*British book news,* March 1983, p.160, of the 1st edition). *Class No:* 331.881(410)

Bibliographies

[1972]
SMITH, H., *ed.* The British labour movement to 1970: a bibliography. London, Mansell, 1981. 268p. £30. ISBN: 0720109248.

3,838 numbered entries for books, pamphlets and periodical articles in English, published 1945-70. 140 periodicals are indexed. Arranged in sections: General (including biographical sources (making extensive use of Boase and *DNB*) and sources for research, study and teaching) - Socialism: history and theory - Early radicalism (*e.g.* Chartism) - Labour Party and Labour governments - Labour movement - Other organizations (*e.g.* Fabian Society; Communist Party) - Trade Unionism - Co-operation (*e.g.* Co-operative Society histories). Bibliographies, p.xv-xviii. Detailed index, p.221-50.

The same compiler's article. 'From Chartism to Callaghan; historiography and bibliography' (*Library review*, v.29, Winter 1980. p.271-4) surveys writings on the history of the British labour movement, with special mention of the *Dictionary of labour biography, Warwick guide to British labour periodicals. 1790-1970,* and the Scottish Labour Historical Society's *A catalogue of some Labour records in Scotland and some Scots records outside Scotland,* compiled and edited by Ian McDougall. *Class No:* 331.881(410)(01)

Yearbooks & Directories

[1973]
MARSH, A. *and* RYAN, V. Historical directory of trade unions. Aldershot, Hants., Gower Publishing Co Ltd., 1980-88. 4v. £45.00 each vol. ISBN: 0566021609, v.1; 0566021617, v.2; 0566021625, v.3; 0566021635, v.4.

Lists over 5,000 British trade unions, past and present. Entries in each volume A-Z by name of union, with information on foundation date, name changes, amalgamations, cessations, characteristics of policy, membership characteristics and numbers, sources of information (books, articles, minutes, etc.) and location of documentation. Cross-references. Index at end of vol.4. Contents: v.1: Non-manual unions; v.2: Trade unions in engineering. Coal-mining and iron and steel, agriculture, chemicals; v.3: Trade unions in building and allied trades, leather workers, enginemen and tobacco workers; v.4: Trade unions in textiles, printing, retail distribution, government and general unions, miscellaneous industries.
Class No: 331.881(410)(058)

[1974]

MARSH, A. **Trade union handbook:** a guide and directory to the structure, membership, policy and personnel of the British Trade unions. 5th ed. Aldershot, Hants, Gower Press, 1991. 350p. tables. £38. ISBN: 0566029758.

First published 1979.

4 parts: 1. The trade union movement in the United Kingdom - 2. Trade union organizations - 3. Directory of 402 trade unions - 4. Addresses of other industrial relations institutions. This edition updated to the beginning of 1987. A bibliography, included in earlier editions, has been omitted because such information is available from the author's *Employment relations bibliography and abstracts* (published 6-monthly). Author is Fellow in Industrial Relations at St. Edmund Hall, Oxford. *Class No:* 331.881(410)(058)

Histories

[1975]

CLEGG, H.A., *and others.* **A History of British trade unions since 1889.** Oxford, Clarendon Press, 1964-1994. v.1-. v.1: ix, [1], 514p. tables. v.2: xiii, 619p. v.3 viii, 458p. v.1: £45; v.2: £40. ISBN: 019828229x, v.1; 0198283075, v.2; 019820406x, v.3.

V.2 and v.3 appeared 20 and 30 years after v.1 and were written by H.A. Clegg alone.

V.1: *1889-1910;* v.2: *1911-1933.* v.3 *1934-1951* The only previous history of note is Sidney and Beatrice Webb's *History of trade unionism* (1894), the later editions of which (*e.g.* 1920) add little of value. This scholarly continuation, in 3v., is a detailed survey with profuse footnote references and notes, and bibliography. Partly analytical indexes. *Class No:* 331.881(410)(091)

[1976]

PELLING, H. **A History of British trade unionism.** 5th ed. London, Macmillan Press Ltd., 1992. 360p. illus. £40. ISBN: 0333577663.

First published 1963.

A standard work, revised and updated to take account of recent research and to explain the course of events up to the early 1990's. In 3 main parts: 1. The emergence of trade unions; 2. The consolidation of labour; 3. Problems of national integration. A statistical table covering the years 1893-1985 has numbers of trade unions, members, affiliations to the TUC, stoppages, and working days lost. Further reading is in 3 sections: 1. General; 2. Histories of individual unions; 3. Additional sources for particular topics (by chapters). There is a detailed index. *Class No:* 331.881(410)(091)

[1977]

PROCHASKA, A. **History of the General Federation of Trade Unions, 1899-1980.** London, George Allen & Unwin, 1982. xiv,274p. £15. ISBN: 0043310877.

7 chapters: 1. The beginnings to the General Federation of Trade Unions, 1890-1900 - 2. Growth: internal affairs, 1900-10 - 3. The General Federation in a wider world, 1900-10 - 4. The turbulent decade. The challenges of syndicalism and war, 1910-20 - 5. International affairs and the exclusion of the General Federation from British representation, 1913-22 - 6. Between the wars - 7. From the 1940s to the 1970s. Appendix: membership of the General Federation of Trade Unions, 1899-1980. Sources and select bibliography, p.254-261. Index, p.262-274. *Class No:* 331.881(410)(091)

Official Records

[1978]

BENNETT, J. *and* STOREY, R. *and* TOUGH, A., *comp.* **Trade union and related records.** 6th. ed. Coventry, University of Warwick Library, 1991. 48p. illus. (*University of Warwick Library Occasional Publications, no.5.*)

Details the principal groups of trade unions' and related records outside the custody of the union headquarters. Arranged A-Z by trade unions, indicating locations. *Class No:* 331.881(410)(093.2)

England

[1979]

BROWN, D. **The English labour movement, 1700-1951.** Dublin, Gill & Macmillan, 1982. [3], 322p. £20. ISBN: 717108708.

Outlines the development of working class organization in England since the industrial revolution.

In 8 chapters: 1. Trade unionism to *c.*1840-2 - 2. The making of the working class? - 3. Chartism - 4. The years of adjustment, 1850-75 - 5. Trade unionism and socialism, *c.*1875-1900 - 6. The emergence of labour, 1900-21 - 7. Triumph and defeat, 1921-27 - 8. Depression and apathy, 1927-39 - Postscript: Cradle to grave? Labour, 1939-51. 658 notes (mainly bibliographical sources on which book is based). Index, p.317-22 double column. *Class No:* 331.881(420)

Bibliographies

[1980]

POTTS, A. *and* JONES, E.R., *comps.* **Northern labour history: a bibliography.** London, Library Association, Reference, Special and Information Section 1981. [3],ii.122p. £22.50. ISBN: 0853659559.

Covering Cleveland, Cumbria, Durham, Northumberland and Tyne and Wear, the bibliography is arranged in 12 subject sections: Friendly and benefit societies, Co-Operatives, Political movements, Trade unionism, Strikes and disputes, Unemployment, Education and recreation, 20th century working class publications, and Individuals. (biographies, autobiographies, private papers, etc.). Includes printing and secondary sources. *Class No:* 331.881(420)(01)

Germany

[1981]

BARTEL, H., *ed.* **Sachwörterbuch der Geschischte Deutschlands und der deutscher Arbeiterbewegung.** Berlin, Dietz, 1969 - 1970. 2v. (1055 p. 877 p.) illus., maps.

An encyclopedia of the history of Germany and of the German working-class movement. V.1: A-K; v.2: L-Z.
Class No: 331.881(430)

France

[1982]

MAITRON, J., *ed.* **Dictionnaire biographique du mouvement ouvrier français de 1789-1939.** Paris, Éditions Ouvrières, 1964-93. v.1-4. 4 parts (43 volumes). Prices vary (*e.g.* Tome 27 (1986), FrF.230; £25).

1: (v.1-3): 1789-1864. De la Révolution français à la fondation de la Première Internationale; 2: (v.4-9): 1864-1871. De la fondation de la Première Internationale à la Commune; 3: (v.10-15): 1871-1914. De la Commune à la Grande Guerre; 4: (16-43): 1914-1939. De la Première à la Seconde Guerre Mondiale. Pt.1 contains 12,000 biographies A-Z. 'Important source material for the writing of the biographies was provided by the 10,000 dossiers relating to the June 1848 Rising and the Paris Commune of 1871 kept in the archives of the War Ministry and never previously used for the purposes of historical research' (*Times literary supplement,* no.3367, 8 September 1966, p.819). Biographies are unsigned, but lists of works, bibliography and iconography, as appropriate, are appended. V.10 (1973) has *c.*2500 short biographies, A-BOU, preceded by lists of delegates to congresses. Part 4 is now published. *Class No:* 331.881(44)

USA

Handbooks & Manuals

[1983]

FINK, G.M., *ed.* **Labor unions.** Westport,Conn., Greenwood, 1977. 544p. $50.95. (*Greenwood encyclopedia of American institutions.*) ISBN: 0837189381.

A handbook of historical sketches of more than 200 national labour unions, selected for importance as part of the American labour movement. Entries, arranged A-Z by name of union, are several pages in length, some signed, and all including suggestions for further reading. 5 appendices on national affiliations, chronology, union genealogies, executive leadership (of selected unions), and membership (of selected unions). Glossary and detailed index. Companion volume to the editor's *Biographical dictionary of American labor leaders (qv).* ' ... an excellent first choice for a good overview or survey ... (RQ, v.17, no.4, Summer 1978, p.360-61)...Original, useful, and altogether commendable reference work.' (*Library journal,* v.102, no.1, January 1, 1977, p.90). *Class No:* 331.881(73)(035)

Histories

[1984]

AMERICAN FEDERATION OF LABOR. **American Federation of Labor:** history, encyclopedia, reference book. New ed. New York, Greenwood Press, 1977 (now issued by the Federation). 3v. in 5. illus. $197.75 the set. ISBN: 0837195683, the set.

Originally published by authority of the 1916 and 1917 conventions. A reprint of the edition published by the Federation in Washington in 1919 and reprinted in 1960. *Class No:* 331.881(73)(091)

[1985]

—McBREARTY, J.C., *eds.* American labor history and comparative labor movements. A selected bibliography. Tucson, AZ., University of Arizona Press, 1973. (Available from Books Demand UMI). x, 262p. $68. ISBN: 0317105531. *Class No:* 331.881(73)(091)

Biographies

[1986]

FINK, G.M., *ed*. Biographical dictionary of American labor. Rev. ed. updated and expanded. Westport, CT., Greenwood Press, 1984. xvii,767p. ilus. $56.95 £45. ISBN: 0313228655.

First published 1974 as *Biographical dictionary of American labor leaders*.

Career biographies of *c*.734 men and women who have had a significant impact on the American labour movement. A main section, A-Z, by name, is supplemented by several appendices. Index. 'Essential for most academic and research libraries' (*Library journal*, 1 October 1984, p.1840), but *Choice* (v.22(9),May 1985, p.1302) complains that it is not representative. *Class No:* 331.881(73)(092)

Land & Property

Bibliographies

[1987]

DENMAN, D. R., *and others*. Bibliography of rural land economy and land ownership, 1900-1957: a full list of works relating to the British Isles and selected works from the United States and Western Europe. Cambridge, Cambridge University Press, 1958. xii, 412p.

A list of *c*.6500 works, first in classified order (p.1.-259). 8 classes: A. History - B. General works - C. Rural economy - D. Land economy - E. Estate economy - F. Research and education - G. Reference works - H. Foreign works; then under authors. Subject index. *Class No:* 332(01)

[1988]

GREAT BRITAIN. HM Stationery Office. Government publications. Sectional list 43, revised February 1992. London, HMSO, 1992. vii,12p. tables. Gratis.

Land Registry forms are listed and described. Also includes list of revelant official publications. *Class No:* 332(01)

[1989]

NURCOMBE, V.J. International real estate valuation, investment and development: a select bibliography. London, E. & F. Spon, 1987. viii, 232p. £15. ISBN: 0419136908.

3768 unannotated entries. An introduction (with 9 references) is followed by subject sections (General - Techniques - Technical topics (subdivided by subjects) - Industrial land and building (subdivided by countries) - Commercial property (subdivided by countries) - Retail property (subdivided by countries) - Residential property - Rural leisure and other property (subdivided by subject) - Property market (subdivided by countries) - Real estate practice - Finance and investment). Appendices of dictionaries and encyclopedias and of journals. Author index, p.181-207; analytical subject index, p.208-232. *Class No:* 332(01)

Dictionaries

[1990]

ABBOTT, D. Encyclopedia of real estate terms. Aldershot, Hants, Gower Technical Press, 1987. xiii, 1102p. £120. ISBN: 0291397026.

Definitions and explanations of over 5,000 terms and phrases used in real estate. Primarily UK usage but also includes terms used in US and France. Many entries are supported by reference to legal decisions. Cross-references. Appendices include a bibliography (p.1061-1099) arranged in subject groupings, and tables of measurement. *Class No:* 332(038)

[1991]

The Multilingual dictionary of real estate a guide for the property professional in the single European market.. Brugel, L. van *and* Williams, R.H. *and* Wood, B., *eds*. London, E. & F. Span, 1993 xii,392p.

Includes bibiographical references (pp. 391-392) and index. *Class No:* 332(038)

English

[1992]

FRIEDMAN, J.P., *and others*. Dictionary of real estate terms. Woodbury, NY., Barron's, 1984. 320p. $5.95. ISBN: 0812025210.

Similar to *Barron's real estate handbook*, except that the handbook has an additional 251p. of tables.

Over 1400 concise definitions of real estate and related legal, financial and architectural terms, with examples and, in some cases, diagrams, sketches, and calculations used to explain terms. 10-page appendix includes mortgage tables, measurement tables, and mathematical formulae. *Choice* (v.22(9), May 1985, p.1304) recommends that libraries purchase the Handbook. *Class No:* 332(038)=20

[1993]

THOMSETT, M.C., *comp*. Real estate dictionary. Jefferson, NC., McFarland & Company Inc., 1988. 220p. illus., charts, diagrs. $29.95; £22.45. ISBN: 0899503217.

Over 1100 entries, including words and phrases, legal concepts and rules, agencies, associations and regulatory bodies involved in real estate. Concentrates on residential and commercial property, real estate investment, mortgage loans, and legal terms. Succinct definitions and helpful charts, tables and diagrams. Cross-references. Also includes a buyers' checklist, amortization tables, and remaining balance tables. A handy source for consumers. *Class No:* 332(038)=20

[1994]

Webster's new world illustrated encyclopedic dictionary of real estate. Gross, J.S., *ed*. 3rd ed. Englewood Cliffs, N.J., Prentice-Hall, 1987. 418p. illus. $12.95. ISBN: 0139473181.

Previous ed. was *Illustrated encyclopedic dictionary of real estate*.

Includes a 251-page dictionary and 165-page portfolio of real estate forms. Entries in the dictionary are for real estate jargon, construction terms, and legal terminology for the layman; they vary in length from a sentence to a third of a page, and many have simple line-drawings for illustration. US-slanted. *Class No:* 332(038)=20

Spanish

[1995]

GOLDSTONE, H.P. Real estate/Bienes raíces: a bilingual dictionary, Spanish-English and English-Spanish... Jefferson, N.C., McFarland & Co., 1986. 136p. $15.95; £11.95. ISBN: 0899501966.

Includes about 4000 entries in each section. *Class No:* 332(038)=60

England & Wales

Handbooks & Manuals

[1996]

Walmsley's rural estate management: compendium at the service of agricultural landowners, practising land agents, and students for the profession in England and Wales. Miles, C.W.N., *and others*. 6th ed. London, Estates Gazette, 1979. xxvi, 589p. £20. ISBN: 0728200414.

First published 1948.

A list of references for further reading is appended to each chapter. Analytical index. *Class No:* 332(42)(035)

Common Land

[1997]

HOSKINS, W.G. *and* STAMP, L.D. The Common lands of England and Wales. London, Collins, 1963. xvii, 366p. illus. maps. (*The new naturalist*.)

The authors were members of the Royal Commission on Common Land, 1955-58. 25 chapters (1-7, by W.G. Hoskins; 8-25 on detailed regions by L.D. Stamp). Appendix: The commons of England. County lists, p.243-350 (name; acreage, nature; rights ownership). Favourably reviewed in *Geographical review,* v.55, no.4, October 1965, p.583-4. *Class No:* 332.24.33

Property Market

Dictionaries

[1998]

AMERICAN INSTITUTE OF REAL ESTATE APPRAISERS. The Dictionary of real estate appraisal. 2nd ed. Chicago, Ill., the Institute, 1989. 366p. $28.50. ISBN: 0911780939.

First published 1984.

c.3000 words and phrases related to the valuation of all types of real property, including accounting, arbitration, banking, construction, finance, insurance, law, and urban planning, etc. Short, concise definitions. Cross-references. List of information sources. *Class No:* 332.72(038)

[1999]

WEST, B. W. *and* DICKINSON, R.L. Street talk in real estate. Alameda, CA., Unique Publishing Co., 1987. vi. 216 p. $9.95. ISBN: 0934189013.

c.1500 standard, technical and colloquial words and phrases, expressions, and acronyms commonly used in real estate transactions. U.S. usage. *Class No:* 332.72(038)

Yearbooks & Directories

[2000]

Barron's real estate handbook. Harris, J.C. *and* Friedman, J.P., *eds.* 2nd ed. (A 3rd ed. was issued in 1993. 700p. $2995.). New York, Barron's, 1988. 700 p. illus., tables. $ 19.95. ISBN: 0812057589.

Combines a glossary of real estate terms with guides for buyers, sellers, professionals, and potential professionals. Several text chapters precede the glossary of *c.*1500 terms, covering finance, law, architecture, construction, associations and organizations. Brief descriptions, often followed by examples. Over 200-pages of mortgage tables, measurement tables, sample forms and worksheets. Bibliography. 3-page index. A comprehensive reference source. *Class No:* 332.72(058)

[2001]

Kemp's property industry year book. London, Kemps, 1980-. ISBN: 086259104x.

First published 1974. From 1974 to 1979 as *Kemp's estate agents yearbook and directory.* Annual.

Directory of estate agents and specialist services in the UK; Development and investment companies; Pension funds; and Property services. Each section arranged in classified order. *Class No:* 332.72(058)

Great Britain

Bibliographies

[2002]

RAMSAY, A., *comp.* **Property development and management into the nineties:** a guide to sources of information. London, British Library, 1988. [4], 59p. £19.50. ISBN: 071230763x.

10 chapters, each with an introduction and bibliography (arranged by author, A-Z, and unannotated): 1. Agents involved in property - 2. Development planning - 3. Project appraisal - 4. Property promotion - 5. Property management - 6. Management of property in general - 7. Management of residential property - 8. Management of commercial and industrial property - 9. Management of property in communal use - 10. Land management. Appendix: Directory of relevant organizations. *Class No:* 332.72(410)(01)

[2003]

SCARRETT, D., *ed.* **Sources of property market information:** a bibliography of practice-based market research reports and indices. Aldershot, Hants, Gower Publishing Ltd., 1988. viii,64p. £25. ISBN: 0566056631.

First published by Leicester Polytechnic Press in 3 eds., 1984, 1986, 1987.

Itemises the sources of information and also points to useful reports issued by stockbrokers and others. Part I: Agents reports; pt. II: Stockbrokers' reports; pt. III: Technical specifications of property indices. Index, p.58-64. *Class No:* 332.72(410)(01)

Cooperative Movements

Dictionaries

[2004]

SCAFFER, J. Historical dictionary of the cooperative movement. Lanham, Scarecrow, 1999. 784p. $110. (*Religions, philosophies, and movements series, no. 26.*) ISBN: 0810836661.

A good source for information on the different kinds of cooperatives, significant figures, including philosophers, pioneers, officials and leaders in a large number of countries. With a list of acronyms, extensive chronology, appendices and a comprehensive bibliography. *Class No:* 334(038)

Great Britain

[2005]

SMETHURST, J.M., *ed.* **A Bibliography of co-operative societies' histories.** Manchester, Co-operative Union, 1973. vi, 122p. £3. ISBN: 0851950949.

Section 1: General books on co-operation with particular reference to those which relate to societies and the history of the movement; 2: Histories of consumer co-operation societies; 3: Agricultural, manufacturing, production and co-partnership co-operative societies. Section 1 includes a few annotated items. Author index to each section. *Class No:* 334(410)

Business Relationships & Organization

[2006]

Kelly's East Grinstead, W. Sussex, Reed Information Services Ltd, 1993-. xxxv,2186p. ISBN: 061000641x. ISSN: 02699265.

continues *Kelly's business directory* (1986-1993), previously *Kelly's manufacturers amd merchants directory*

About 82000 industrial product and service companies in the UK are listed. Arranged in 4 sections: Reader reply section (reply paid cards for product literature); Industrial products and services section (with details of manufacturers, merchants, wholesalers and firms offering an industrial service, arranged under classified trade and professional headings); Oil and gas industry section (arranged similarly); Company information section (companies listed A-Z, with trade description, address and telecommunications details). *Class No:* 334.7

[2007]

Kompass: the authority on British Industry: 1995/96 United Kingdom. East Grinstead, Reed Information Services, 1995. 6v. £924. ISBN: 0862683106.

First published 1962. Annual.

Lists manufacturers, suppliers, distributors, products and services. V.I has *c.*41,000 different products and services offered by British industrial companies; v.II. Corporate information on 43,500 leading companies in British industry; [v.III]. Financial data; [v.IV]. Parents and subsidiaries; [v.V]. Industrial trade names; [v.6]. Quality assessed companies. Also available on CD-ROM. *Class No:* 334.7

Abbreviations & Symbols

[2008]

TOWELL, J.E., *ed.* **Business acronyms:** a selection of approximately 25,000 acronyms, initialisms, abbreviations, contractions, alphabetic symbols, and similar condensed appellations. 1st ed. Detroit, Mich., Gale Research Co., 1988. 414p. $74.75. (*Acronyms, initialisms & abbreviations dictionary subject guide series,* 2.) ISBN: 0810325497.

Definitions are taken from *Acronyms, initialisms & abbreviations dictionary* (Gale, 2nd ed., 1987-88. 3v.) and include all aspects of business, including banking, finance, commerce, trade, economics and statistics, plus stock exchange symbols, etc. 2 listings - by acronym and by term or phrase. *Class No:* 334.7(003)

Databases

[2009]

NOBARI, N.S., *ed.* **Books and periodicals on line:** a guide to publication contents of business and legal data bases, V.1., Part 1-, 1987-. New York, Library Alliance Inc. 1987-. Annual. $249. ISSN: 0951838x.

Aims to help researchers to use online time efficiently by providing them with a directory of over 6800 periodicals and serials which are available on such databases. In 4 sections: Alphabetical listing of periodicals and serials (name of publication; country of origin if not US, and journal code; name of publisher; name of database; name of producer; scope of editorial coverage, including starting date (and ending date if applicable); name of vendors) - Publishers' names and addresses - Producers' and vendors' names and addresses - Books and periodicals by database (A-Z by database, subdivided by A-Z list of titles). Available online and on CD-ROM. *Class No:* 334.7(003.4)

[2010]

Online/CD-ROM business sourcebook. Foster, P. *and* Foster, A. East Grinstead, Headland Press, 1989-. 2pa. £175. ISSN: 09535055.

Emphasis on UK and European electronic databases. Information on 70 hosts, and 1962 electronic databases. The databases are arranged into 17 areas, including financial data, business opportunities, legislation and regulations, market data, business and management literature and trademarks. *Class No:* 334.7(003.4)

Bibliographies

[2011]

BALL, S. The Directory of international sources of business information. 2nd ed. London, Pitman, 1991. 864p. £125. ISBN: 0273032844.

First published 1989.

Arranged in 3 main sections: country data sources; industry data sources; online data bases; preceded by an introduction and a section on European business information brokers and Euro-Info centres. The section on country data sources covers 32 countries, mostly European, arranged A-Z, with each entry including stock exchange members, chambers of commerce, embassies, major government offices devoted to commerce, and sources of statistics. The industry data sources section is arranged in 11 broad industrial groups, listing major international associations dealing with each group, directories, market research services, and journals. 4 appendices (1. Publishers of market research reports - 2. Data base hosts and producers - 3. Data base

....*(contd.)*

country coverage - 4. International telephone codes, etc.). 'The descriptions are well-written and provide sufficient information for users to make basic evaluative decisions' (*Choice*, v.27(2), October 1989, p.278) of the 1st ed. *Class No:* 334.7(01)

[2012]

Business index. Menlo Park, CA., Information Access Corporation, Sept. 1980-. Monthly. $1860pa. ($3500 on CD-ROM). ISSN: 02733684.

Indexes, cover-to-cover, the contents of over 325 business periodical titles, in addition to the *Wall street journal, Barron's National business and financial weekly*, and the financial section of *The New York times*, plus selected articles containing business information from over 1100 general and legal periodical and business books and reports from the Library of Congress MARC database. End of film has abstracts from *Management contents* database. Computer output microfilm. Available online (DIALOG, BRS, Mead Data Centre). *Class No:* 334.7(01)

[2013]

Business information alert. January 1989-. v.1,no.1-. Chicago, Ill. Alert Publications Inc., 1989- 10pa. $115pa. ISSN: 10420746.

Designed to keep libraries and related information professionals informed of new literature and information services in the field of business. Newsletter format. In 4 sections: Lead article - New publications (descriptive and critical book reviews, which take up about half the issue) - Database news - FYI section (brief descriptions of other news and resources 'for your information'). *Class No:* 334.7(01)

[2014]

CAMPBELL, M.J., *ed.* **Manual of business library practice.** 2nd ed. London, Clive Bingley Ltd., 1985. x,238p. £14.75. ISBN: 0851573606.

First published 1975.

Covers both public and company libraries, and sources of business information. 13 chapters: 1. Information for business: the pattern of business information provision ... 5. Directories and company information sources - 6 & 7. Statistics and market research sources ... 9. Management literature ... References and further reading, p.201-211, entries relating to chapters. Appendix: List of 'hosts' with databases provided. Index, p.205-218. *Class No:* 334.7(01)

[2015]

OWEN, T. Mind your own local business: where to find and how to use local economic and business information. 2nd ed. Newbury, Berks, Eurofi, 1988. xiii,450p. charts. £37.50. ISBN: 0907304435.

First published 1986.

8 chapters: 1. The tools for the job (sources of information and document supply - 2. Getting to know your area (regional and local statistics) - 3. Who are the local businesses? (information on individual enterprises) - 4. Who is going to buy? (marketing and product information sources) - 5. Answering the impossible questions (online information services) - 6. Who will back it? (guide to sources of finance) - 7. Dealing with the EEC (sources of information on the EEC) - 8. Is it clean? (contract compliance and ethical investment). There follows a complete guide to all the information sources discussed. Subject index, p.421-450. Comprehensive and readable. *Class No:* 334.7(01)

[2016]

RYANS, C.C. International business reference sources: developing a corporate library. Lexington, Mass., Lexington Books, 1983. xvii,195p. ISBN: 0669066125.

'Presents a representative list of the more essential sources of information useful to companies involved in doing business overseas' (*Introduction*). 4 chapters: 1. Government publications - 2. Subscriptions and continuations (journals, annuals, loose-leaf services) - 3. International business data sources (directories, almanacs, handbooks) - 4. International business books (marketing, finance, economics). All arranged A-Z by title. Data includes publication date or starting date and frequency, price, publisher's name & address, and brief description. Appendix: Additional names and addresses of organizations where country and product data may be obtained (subdivided by type of organization). Index, p.185-195. *Class No:* 334.7(01)

[2017]

SCHLESSINGER, B.S., *and others, eds.* **The Basic business library:** core resources. 2nd ed. New York, Oryx Press, 1989. 278p. $32.50. ISBN: 0897744519.

3 parts: 1. Core list of business reference sources - 2. The literature of business reference and business libraries - 3. Business reference sources and services: essays (10 signed essays, and index). US slant. *Class No:* 334.7(01)

Handbooks & Manuals

[2018]

Company administration handbook. Beattie, D., *ed.* 7th ed. Aldershot, Hants., Gower Publishing Co. Ltd., 1990. c.900p. £65. ISBN: 0566026678.

First published 1970.

34 chapters covering all aspects of company administration, including constitution and conduct of companies, accounting and finance, commercial functions, office administration, the company and its employees, and management of physical assets, each by a recognised expert in the field. Index, p.729-864. *Class No:* 334.7(035)

[2019]

Secretarial administration. Birds, J., *and others, eds.* Bristol, Jordans, 1993. 1800p.(looseleaf). £95. Updating releases are published twice a year (*c*.£45 each). ISBN: 0853080747.

An authority on company procedure. For company secretaries on company law and procedure. 10 chapters, each subdivided: 1.The position of secretary - 2. Constitution and organisation of a limited company - 3. Procedures - 4. Officers of a company - 5. Company meetings - 6. Public companies and investment regulation - 7. Insolvency - 8. Employment law - 9. Corporate insurance - 10. EEC. 5 appendices. Index. *Class No:* 334.7(035)

Dictionaries

[2020]

PASS, C., *and others.* **Collins dictionary of business.** 2nd ed. Glasgow, HarperCollins, 1995. 706p. illus. £16.95. ISBN: 0004708032.

For students taking a business-studies course at school or in further education, or as a professional seeking further qualifications. *Class No:* 334.7(038)

Laws

[2021]

MARSH, S.B. *and* **BAILEY, J.B. Terminology of business and company law.** Rev. ed. London, Chartered Institute of Management Accountants, 1993 143p. ISBN: 1874784132.

Aimed at students of business law and company law. Definitions vary in length from 1 line to 12 lines. Some common abbreviations included. *Class No:* 334.7(038)(094.1)

Polyglot

[2022]

APPLEBY, B.L., *comp.* **Elsevier's dictionary of commercial terms and phrases in five languages:** English, German, Spanish, French and Swedish. Amsterdam, Elsevier Science Publishers, 1984. [4],1083p. Dfl.515; £154.65; $271. ISBN: 0444422706.

An 'attempt to bring together in one volume terms and expressions from the multitude of different fields, accounting, banking, computing, economics, etc., which are intimately involved with the world of modern business (*Preface*). 10,163 terms are included, the basic table being English, followed by translations in the other four languages. Indexes in all five languages refer to the numbered English entries in the basic listing. *Class No:* 334.7(038)=00

[2023]

Harrap's five-language business dictionary. Angerer, M., *and others.* London, Harrap, 1991. 448p. ISBN: 0245603476.

Arranged in one A-Z sequence, the dictionary has 20,000 key business words from English, French, German, Italian and Spanish. *Class No:* 334.7(038)=00

[2024]

Six language business dictionary. British Chamber of Commerce. Cambridge, Colt Books Ltd., with the Association of British Chambers of Commerce, 1978 (reprinted 1991). 637p. £25. ISBN: 0905899032.

First published by Pan Books in 1978 as *Multilingual commercial dictionary*.

English, French, German, Italian, Portuguese and Spanish terms in one A-Z listing, each term folowed by its equivalents in the five other languages. *Class No:* 334.7(038)=00

[2025]

West's Law and commercial dictionary in five languages: definitions of the legal and commercial terms and phrases of American, English and civil law jurisdictions. English, German, Spanish, French & Italian. Epstein, R., *ed.* St. Paul, MN, West Publishing Company, München, Beck, 1985. 2v. (xvi, 885p.; xvi; 899p.). ISBN: 0314805028.

One volume has a pronunciation guide followed by the dictionary, A-J; the other continues the dictionary, K-Z and includes a list of legal abbreviations. Entries are for the English terms and phrases, with definitions, with the German, Spanish, French and Italian equivalents listed below. Includes terms related to systems in the other four

....*(contd.)*

countries. '... most unusual, but most practical ...' (*International journal of legal information*, v.15(5 & 6), p.77).
Class No: 334.7(038)=00

English

[2026]

A Concise dictionary of business. Isaacs, A. and others, *ed and* Market House Books, *comp.*. Oxford, Oxford University Press, 1990. 401p. £17.50 (*Oxford Reference*.) ISBN: 0192852310.

Over 4000 entries covering all the traditional areas of business, as well as the new terminology that has grown up around the globalization of stock, commodity, and financial markets.
Class No: 334.7(038)=20

[2027]

LAMMING, R. *and* **BESSANT, J. Macmillan dictionary of business and management.** London, Macmillan Press, 1988. [3],225p. diagrs. £30. (*Macmillan reference books*.) ISBN: 0333390547.

Compiled to help both students and practitioners to understand more about the terminology and technology of modern international business and management. Basic terms found in general dictionaries are omitted. Short entries of 2-20 lines include abbreviations and use diagrams to clarify descriptions. 'See' and 'see also' references.
Class No: 334.7(038)=20

[2028]

STEER, M. Dictionary of business studies. 2nd ed. London, Pitman Publsihing, 1989. xvii, 286p. £5.95. ISBN: 0273030779.

First published 1985.

Intended for students but useful to the general reader. Aims to provide a comprehensive reference companion for students of business studies at intermediate and advanced levels. Clear, detailed explanations. Extensive cross-references. *Class No:* 334.7(038)=20

German

[2029]

Business German dictionary English-German, German-English. Collin, P.H., *et al* eds.. Teddington, Peter Collin, 1994 641p. ISBN: 0948549505. *Class No:* 334.7(038)=30

French

[2030]

COLLIN, P.H., *and others*. **Business French dictionary:** French/English, English/French Rev. ed. Teddington, Surrey, P. Collin, 1995. 637p. ISBN: 0948549831; 0948549645.

Previously published in 1990 as *Dictionary of business*. About 3500 main entries in each half ('Mail': 1 column). 'Supplement' (19p): La France. les régions ... United Kingdom - Weights and measures - Numbers - Business letters - Curriculum vitae. Examples and quotations showing usage. *Class No:* 334.7(038)=40

[2031]

LAURENDEAU-COLLIN, F., *and others, eds.* **Harrap's business French-English dictionary:** dictionnaire Anglais-Français. 3rd rev ed. London & Paris, Harrap, 1991. xvi, 604p. £19.95. ISBN: 0245542531.

Aims to provide a basic translating tool for everyday business language. Emphasis is on providing practical examples to show terms and phrases used in context. Gives only the strictly commercial meanings of the words. Also includes some useful supplementary material concerning international organizations, international currencies, typical American business expressions, comparisons between English and French balance sheets.
Class No: 334.7(038)=40

Arabic

[2032]

SABA & CO. The English-Arabic dictionary of professional business terms. London, Middle East Economic Digest (MEED), 1987. [3], 210p. ISBN: 0946510334.

Includes *c*.11,000 terms, phrases, names of major organizations, government bodies, and formal titles of qualifications and positions A-Z in English, followed by the Arabic equivalents. '... should be considered a supplement to a standard English-Arabic dictionary ... structured for maximum convenience ...' (*Introduction*).
Class No: 334.7(038)=927

Chinese

[2033]

Business Chinese dictionary English/Chinese. Collin, P.H., *et al* editors. Teddington, Peter Collin, 1995 522p. ISBN: 0948549637. *Class No:* 334.7(038)=951

Japanese

[2034]

MITSUBISHI CORPORATION, *comp*. **Japanese business language:** an essential dictionary. London, K.P.I. Ltd., 1987 (Distributed by Routledge & Kegan Paul). xiii, 221p. £9.95. ISBN: 0710301995.

Analyses over 500 key words and phrases that are essential for doing or understanding business in Japan. Clarifies many points of verbal and social misunderstanding, and provides insights into differences in Japanese and Western business practices.
Class No: 334.7(038)=956

[2035]

Tatemae and honne: distinguishing between good form and real intention in Japanese business culture. Mitsubishi Corporation. New York, Free Press, 1988. 182p. $19.95. ISBN: 0029215919.

A revision of *Japanese business glossary* (1983), which was based on the 'Business glossary' column in the *Tokyo newsletter*.

A glossary of *c*.500 words and idiomatic phrases used in the Japanese company world, which could be misunderstood or misinterpreted by non-Japanese. Includes a 'simplified pronunciation guide'. Cross-references. Index of English words with Japanese equivalents and page numbers. *Class No:* 334.7(038)=956

Reports Literature

Bibliographies

[2036]

Index to business reports. Hunter, N.R., *comp*. Harrogate, North Yorks., Quarry Press (previously Headland Press), 1978-. 2 pa. £16.95 pa. $32.95 pa. ISSN: 02660180.

Indexes reports in a wide range of newspapers and journals. About 400 reports indexed in each issue and each January-June issue is superseded by the following January-December issue. Arrangement is by subject term, A-Z, followed by the journal abbreviation, day, month, year, and page number of the issue. *Class No:* 334.7(047)(01)

Yearbooks & Directories

[2037]

Political risk yearbook. Coplin, W.D. *and* O'Leary, M.K., *eds*. Syracuse, NY, Political Risk Services, 1992 (distributed outside US by Bowker-Saur). 7v. £750. ISBN: 1852711949.

A country-by-country analysis of risk instability, turmoil, economic and trade restrictions, all based on standardized data. Also data on heads of government, government officials, legislature, elections, economy, trade and social indicators, etc. For each country there are 18-month and 5-yearly forecasts of changes of regime, turmoil, and risks to international business with supporting data of all kinds. The 7v are arranged by continents, then A-Z by country. Each entry is of standard length and amount of data. '... a magnificent example of value-added in information analysis making it a quite invaluable reference item.'(*Reference reviews*, v.6(5), 1992, review 321, p.11). *Class No:* 334.7(058)

Quotations

[2038]

HAY, P. Harrap's book of business anecdotes. London, Harrap; New York, Facts on File, 1988. viii, 296p. $22.95. ISBN: 0045847436, UK; 0816015228, US.

The title of the US edition is *The Book of business anecdotes*.

Anecdotes are arranged in 12 subject groups, all subdivided (1. About money - 2. Banks and bankers ... 11. Business and the Muses - 12. Rewards). Extensive bibliography, p.279-290. Index, p.291-296. *Class No:* 334.7(082.2)

[2039]

The Hutchinson dictionary of business quotations. Cresswell, J. *and* Leinster, A. Oxford, Helicon, 1996 viii, 184p. ISBN: 1859860443. *Class No:* 334.7(082.2)

[2040]

Collins dictionary of business quotations. James, S. *and* Parker, R., *comps*. Glasgow, HarperCollins, 1991. 192p. £17.99; $40. ISBN: 0004343794.

Previously published by Routledge as *A dictionary of business quotations*.

Over 2500 quotations from across the globe, for browsing and reference. Arranged by 215 topics, A-Z (Accounts ... Workers). Includes 'see-also' references under topic headings. Very wide coverage. Index of authors and sources. Index of keywords. *Class No:* 334.7(082.2)

[2041]

MANSER, M., *comp*. **Chambers book of business quotations.** London, Chambers, 1987. 220p. 20 illus. £12.95. ISBN: 0550204881.

'Sayings from the famous, unknown and unacknowledged'. *c.2000* quotations on business and related subjects, arranged under 900 topics in 9 main sections. Illus. are line-drawings. Index. *Class No:* 334.7(082.2)

Tables & Data Books

[2042]

Key note guides: official business statistics. 1st ed. Hampton, Middx., Key Note Publications Ltd., 1988. iii,125p. tables. ISBN: 1850566046.

10 chapters, most having key data available, key sources, contacts, the sources, the statistics (1. An overview - 2. Product and market statistics - 3. Industry statistics - 4. Import and export statistics - 5. Economic and financial statistics - 6. Labour market statistics - 7. Socio-economic statistics - 8. The reliability of official statistics - 9. Government contact points - 10. Trade association statistics). Appendices (Selective bibliography - Business monitors: the complete list - HMSO information and services). *Class No:* 334.7(083)

Biographies

[2043]

International businessmen's who's who. Kay, E., *ed*. 3rd ed. Cambridge, International Biographical Centre, 1986. [6],383p. £75. ISBN: 0900332387.

First published 1967. 1st & 2nd eds. published by Burke's Peerage Ltd.

Gives biographical data (business activities and appointments held, past positions, recreational and community activities) on *c.*3000 business executives in some 60 of the world's largest countries. About 10-30 lines each, longer entries than in previous editions. By no means definitive; slanted towards Britain, North America, Europe, Japan, Australia and New Zealand. *Class No:* 334.7(092)

Great Britain

[2044]

GREAT BRITAIN. Department of Trade and Industry. **DTI QA register: the United Kingdom register of quality assessed companies.** London, HMSO, [1993]. 3v.(2494p.). tables. £145 (incl. supplements for the year). ISBN: 0115153179.

Compendium of lists of manufacturers world wide whose quality management systems, and sometimes their products, have been assessed by a number of UK independent third party assessment bodies and significant purchasers. V.1. lists products; V.2 - 3 list companies, A-Z. *Class No:* 334.7(410)

[2045]

HARRISON, A., *ed*. **New sources of grants and aid for businessmen in the UK:** a practical guide to the financial support and advisory services available to UK companies from central government, local authorities and regional agencies. London, Weka Publishing, 1987. loose-leaf unpaged. maps, forms. £68. ISBN: 185303004x.

In 10 parts: 1. Guide to the reader - 2. Current information - 3. Capital investment - 4. Research and technology - 5. Marketing and business advisory services - 6. Employment - 7. Exporting - 8. Energy - 9. Local schemes - 10. Other schemes. General index and contents list to each part. Kept up-to-date by supplements. *Class No:* 334.7(410)

Databases

[2046]

BATER, P. *and* PARKINSON, H., *eds*. **Business and company databases, 1988.** 1st ed. London, Aslib, 1988. [6],86p. £18. ISBN: 0851422314.

Selective list of some of the best known databases available in the UK. International coverage. A-Z listing by name of database, with information on content, updating, producer, hosts, cost, user aids, and further information. Database, subject and host indexes. *Class No:* 334.7(410)(003.4)

Bibliographies

[2047]

BRITISH LIBRARY. Science Reference and Information Service. **Business information:** a brief guide to the reference sources of the British Library. 2nd ed. London, British Library, Science Reference and Information Service, 1988. [4],32p. *Gratis*. ISBN: 0712307567.

Information on the services and the stock of the library of use to businessmen. Index, p.30-31. *Class No:* 334.7(410)(01)

[2048]

BROOKS, M.J. **Sources of free business information.** 2nd ed. London, Kogan Page, 1988. 106p. £6.95. ISBN: 1850914923.

First published 1986.

Over 500 sources, arranged by topic: 1. Taxation - 2. Sources of business finance - 3. Official grants and incentives - 4. Exporting and doing business overseas - 5. General economic and business information - 6. Information and advice for smaller businesses - 7. Legal matters - 8. Computers - 9. Investment - 10. Miscellaneous - 11. Names and addresses of providers of information. Includes brief reviews of the publications, where they can be obtained, pages, frequency, and organizations to contact. Further reading. Subject index. Index of information providers. *Class No:* 334.7(410)(01)

Reports Literature

[2049]

GREAT BRITAIN. Department of Trade and Industry. **Companies in 1992-93;** report for the year ended 31 March 1993. London, HMSO, 1993. [4],62p. tables. £14.50. ISBN: 0115153403.

First published 1890- as *Companies: general annual report* of the Board of Trade. Annual.

Information on the administration of the Companies Act, plus statistics on registration of companies during the previous 10 years, by classes and amount of nominal capital. *Class No:* 334.7(410)(047)

Periodicals

[2050]

London gazette. London, HMSO., 1665-. 4 per week, excluding supplements annd indexes. £365pa., excluding supplements. ISSN: 03743721.

Apart from State intelligence and public notices, contains official notices relating to companies, bankruptcies, partnerships, dissolutions. Supplements are normally concerned with naval, military and civil awards (*e.g.* lists of New Year's honours, of Queen's Birthday honours, of Premium Bond winners). *Class No:* 334.7(410)(051)

Yearbooks & Directories

[2051]

Key British enterprises: Britain's top 50,000 companies. London, Dun & Bradstreet, 1991-. Annual. 6v. ISSN: 01425048.

continues *Dun & Bradstreet's guide to the key British enterprises*.

V.1, 2 & 3 have alphabetical listing of companies actively trading, with address, telephone/telex/fax numbers, named managing director and senior executives, line of business, sales turnover, export markets, capitalisation/ownership, number of employees, etc. V.4 has industrial and geographical cross-references; v.5 has trade names, export markets, director's names; and v.6 has business rankings. Updates are issued twice a year. *Class No:* 334.7(410)(058)

[2052]

TUDOR, J. **Macmillan directory of UK business information sources.** 3rd ed. London, Macmillan Publishers, 1992. xi,435p. £35. ISBN: 0333572718.

First published 1987.

A compendium of sources and resources: How to use this book; Finding business information; Directory of business information sources and centres; Foreign trade organizations of the UK (A-Z.); British trade press and their editorial offices (subject arrangement); Alphabetical index to NACE classification (SIC codes) and organization sources (both of these serve as indexes); and main directory, arranged by subject (SIC), subdivided by UK and European sources and information centres, with names, addresses, telephone numbers, contacts, and brief indication of activities in some entries. A-Z index to information centres. Classified list of NACE categories. *Class No:* 334.7(410)(058)

Histories

[2053]

ORBELL, J. **A Guide to tracing the history of a business.** Aldershot, Hants., Gower Publishing Co. Ltd., for the Business Archives Council, 1987. x,116p. £15. ISBN: 0566055910.

Arranged in 3 parts: 1. Locating the business and research strategy (Sources for locating the business - Research strategy - Approaching the business); 2. Locating records of the business (Records deposited in record offices - Registers of business records - Published guides to business records); 3. Information sources outside the records of the business (records of suppliers of goods and services, records of government departments, records of associations, printed sources, personal records, visual sources. Bibliography, p.90-100, is A-Z by author. Addresses of record offices, museums, libraries, societies, etc., quoted in the text, p.101-110. Double-column index, p.111-116. *Class No:* 334.7(410)(091)

Biographies

[2054]

JEREMY, D.J., *ed*. **Dictionary of business biography:** a biographical dictionary of business leaders active in Britain in the period 1860-1980. London, Butterworth, 1984-86. 5v. and Supplement. £150 each vol. ISBN: 0406273413, v.1; 0406273421, v.2; 040627343x, v.3; 0406273448, v.4; 0406273456, v.5; 0406273405, set.

Based on the work of the Business History Unit at London School of Economics, funded by the Economic and Social Research Council.

Aimed to cover the whole spectrum of business (mining, manufacturing, public utilities, construction, services, distribution) excluding academics, civil servants, trade unionists, etc. if involvement in the business world was incidental. Includes those who had a good impact for good or bad, from larger or small businesses (*e.g.* Thomas Beecham, Horatio Bottomley, Billy Butlin). Arranged A-Z by biographee: V.1: A-C; v.2: D-G; v.3: H-L; v.4: M-R; v.5: S-Z, and indexes, list of contributors, errata. A supplement to v.1-5 was published in 1986 (120p. ISBN 0406273405).
Class No: 334.7(410)(092)

Scotland

Bibliographies

[2055]

REID, C.D. 'Business information needs in Scotland'. In *Aslib proceedings,* v.38(2), February 1986, p.51-64.

Paper presented to joint conference organized by the Library Association, R.S. & I. Section (Scottish Group) and Aslib (Scottish Branch) on *Business information problems and prospects, 1985,* which includes a checklist of sources of business information (p.61-64).
Class No: 334.7(411)(01)

Italy

Bibliographies

[2056]

CUCCHI, L. 'How to find Italian business information'. In *Business information review,* v.4(2), April 1988, p.16-27.

Evaluates the major sources, including directories, statistics, market research organizations, and online databases.
Class No: 334.7(450)(01)

Russia

Bibliographies

[2057]

KONN, T. 'The Soviet Union': commercial and technical information sources. In *Business information review,* v.4(3), January 1988, p.1526.

Outlines the changes in the foreign trade structure, followed by an introduction to the main Russian and English language sources of commercial and technical information relating to the Soviet Union. Includes guides, national economic plans, newspapers, journals, updating services, trade statistics, reports, online databases and organizations. *Class No:* 334.7(47)(01)

Asia

Periodicals & Progress Reports

[2058]

JUNGE, A.R. 'Business information sources in Asia'. In *Special libraries,* v.70(2), December 1979, p.82-90.

A review article on periodicals published by banks, trade organizations, companies, etc., which supplement the standard business information sources. *Class No:* 334.7(5)(05)

Japan

Bibliographies

[2059]

EDWARDS, S. *and* THOMPSON, K. **Japanese business publications in English, 1987:** a select annotated list of recent publications held by the British Library. 2nd ed. London, British Library, 1987. [2],i,55p. £10. ISBN: 0712307435.

First published 1986.

232 entries arranged by form (Directories - Statistics, market information and industry surveys - Trade and business journals - Bibliographies and abstracting journals - Company reports), the first three sections subdivided by subject. These are followed by lists of suppliers of literature published in Japan, and alternative sources of information. Index of titles and organizations.
Class No: 334.7(52)(01)

Africa

Bibliographies

[2060]

African trade: a bibliography of information sources. 1st ed. Berkhamstead, Trade Research Publications, for The Association of African Trade Promotion Organisations, 1988. 219p. £35; $75. ISBN: 0904783251.

Aims to be a guide to reference books of use to the business community. More than 600 references arranged in 4 sections: A. AATPO publications - B. International publications - C. Publications relating to Africa as a whole and regions of Africa - D. Publications by country. Entries have full bibliographical description; description of publication; language; price; brief note of publication; last date published, frequency; SITC number. 15-page subject index.
Class No: 334.7(6)(01)

America—North

[2061]

Standard and Poor's register of corporations, directors and executives, 1994. 67th ed. New York, Standard and Poor, 1993. 3v. plus cumulative supplements and user's companion. ISSN: 03613623.

First published in 1928.

Lists *c.*55,000 corporations and 500,000 officers, directors, etc. Contents: V.1: Corporations; v.2: Key to abbreviations. Register of directors and executives; v.3: Executives. Also includes Standard and Poor's 500; US and Canadian securities exchanges and administration; Standard industrial classification index and codes; Geographic index; Corporate family indexes (cross-reference index; ultimate parent index); Obituary section; New individuals in this edition; New companies in this edition. *Class No:* 334.7(71+73)

USA

Bibliographies

[2062]

SMITH, G. 'How to find US business information'. In *Business information review,* v.4(1), July 1987, p.3-11.

Reviews major sources - directories, company information, statistics, market research sources, magazines and newspapers, indexes and abstracts, databases, online vendors, libraries and information services, and research guides. *Class No:* 334.7(73)(01)

Periodicals & Progress Reports

[2063]

GEAHIGAN, P.C. *and* ROSE, R.F. **Business serials of the US government.** 2nd ed. Chicago, Ill., American Library Association, 1988 (Distributed by Eurospan. 86p. $11.95; £8.50. ISBN: 0838933491.

First published 1979.

183 business serial publications of the US government are listed, with descriptive and evaluative annotations. Arrangement is in 14 broad subject categories, and information includes Superintendent of Documents class number, title changes, issuing authority, frequency, supplements (if any), but not prices. Detailed subject and title index includes alternative and previous titles. *Class No:* 334.7(73)(05)

Histories

[2064]

LARSON, H.M. **Guide to business history:** materials for the study of American business history and suggestions for their use. Cambridge, Mass., Harvard University Press, 1948 (Reprinted Boston, Mass., Canner, 1964). xxvi,1181p. $22.50. ISBN: 0910324042.

4904 numbered and annotated terms in 7 parts (87 sections): 1. General introduction - 2. Historical background and setting of American business - 3. Business administrators, biographical and autobiographical books, pamphlets and articles - 4. The history of individual business units - 5. History of industries - 6. General topics in business history - 7. Research and reference materials. Detailed, analytical index, p.1057-1181. An excellent compilation, with introductory notes in each section. *Class No:* 334.7(73)(091)

[2065]

—LOVETT, R.W., *ed*. American economic and business history information sources ... Detroit, Gale Research Co., 1971. 323p. $68. ISBN: 0810308231.

6 sections: economic, business, agricultural and labour history, history of science and technology, and general reference works.
Class No: 334.7(73)(091)

[2066]
PUSATERI, C.J. A History of American business. 2nd ed. Arlington Heights, Ill., Harlan Davidson Inc.; London, Eurospan, 1988. xiii,444p. 14 illus. ISBN: 0882958445.

First published 1984.

14 chapters arranged in 4 sections: I. Panorama - II. The age of the merchant - III. The age of transition - IV. The age of managerial capitalism. 'Some suggestions for further reading' (p.371-374) are followed by 3 appendices (A. A chronology of American business; B. The 25 largest industrial corporations; C. Roster of 50 major business leaders), notes, a glossary of American business terms (p.417-424), and an index (p.425-444). *Class No:* 334.7(73)(091)

Libraries

[2067]
HYDE, M. Library and information services to business and industry: study on levels of service, related costs and charging systems. London, British Library Research & Development Department, 1988. viii, 103p. £5. (*British Library research paper, 48.*) ISBN: 0712331743.

In 3 parts: 1. Background: aims and objectives of the project; the 'levels of service' approach; user response to 'levels of service', costs and charging; 2. Guidlines to 'levels of service'; 3. Financial management, conclusions and recommendations.
Class No: 334.7:061:026/027

[2068]
LIBRARY ASSOCIATION. Industrial Group. Industrial and commercial libraries: an introductory guide. the Group, 1986. viii,44p. £10. (*Library Association pamphlet 39.*) ISBN: 0853655774.

8 sections: The library in the industrial and commercial environment - Relationship with the parent organization - Staff - User education - Resources and services - Funding - Equipment and furniture - Accommodation and space requirements. 2 appendices: 1. Points of contact; 2. Further reading. Index. *Class No:* 334.7:061:026/027

Private Firms

Great Britain

[2069]
Macmillan's unquoted companies, 1994. ICC Business Publications Ltd., *comp.* London, Macmillan Press, 1994. Annual. 2v. (1800p.). £199 the set. ISBN: 0333599071. ISSN: 02674378.

V.1: A-J; v.2: K-Z. Alphabetical listing of the top 20,000 companies. Include only companies with individual turnovers in excess of £3m. pa., and data reflects a 3-year trading period with individual sector performance tables to enable comparisons between companies. Geographical and SIC index. *Class No:* 334.722(410)

USA

[2070]
Million dollar directory America's leading public and private companies. Previously published in 1993 and 1994. Bethlehem, Pa., Dun & Bradstreet, 1996. ISBN: 0872170705.

Over 9500 US companies, with nearly 4200 subsidiaries, with sales of $10 million or more. Detailed information given for parent companies is address, telephone/fax, type of business, major officers, principal owners, assets, liabilities, net worth, sales, date of fiscal year end, number of employees, state of incorporation, number of US and foreign offices or manufacturing facilities, computer system hardware, wholly-owned subsidiaries, and names of outside services used. Main directory is arranged A-Z by name of parent company. A-Z cross-referencing index; geographic and SIC indexes.
Class No: 334.722(73)

Multinationals

Bibliographies

[2071]
UNITED NATIONS. Centre for Transnational Corporations. UNCTC bibliography, 1974-1987. New York, United Nations, 1988. v,83p. illus. $12; £8. (*CT/CTC/88.*) ISBN: 9211042186.

Arranged by subject in 18 main sections (I. Trends in the activities of transnational corporations ... VII. Manufacturing and extractive sectors - VIII. Service sector and transborder data flows ... XV. Data and information systems and sources ... XVIII. The *CTC reporter* and other journals. *Class No:* 334.726(01)

Dictionaries

[2072]
HOOGVELT, A. *and* PUXTY, A. Multinational enterprise: an encyclopedic dictionary of concepts and terms. Consultant editor: John Stopford. London, Macmillan, 1987. 261p. £29.95; $52.50. (*Macmillan reference library.*) ISBN: 033337603x, UK; 0893972495, USA.

Attempts to provide definitions for the specialized and multidisciplinary vocabulary used in the world of international business and multinational enterprises. Brings together relevant concepts and terms from economics, international law, management theory, sociology, and politics. Also included are entries for international organizations, regulations, codes and treaties and major national legislation. Includes a full bibliography, index and resource file of libraries, databases and research organizations. 'The definitions are often gems of concise insight ... '(*Choice*, June 1987, p. 1538).
Class No: 334.726(038)

Yearbooks & Directories

[2073]
Directory of multinationals. Stopford, J., *ed.* 4th ed. London, Macmillan, 1992. 2v.(1600p). £295. ISBN: 0333577566.

First published 1980.

Information on 428 industrial enterprises with global turnover in excess of £1 billion. Company profiles include name, address, directors, structure, products, background and current situation, 5-year financial data. *Class No:* 334.726(058)

Small Businesses

[2074]
MANCUSO, J. Mancuso's small business resource guide. New York, Prentice-Hall, 1988. 557p. $39.95. ISBN: 0138130809.

An updated and expanded version of Mancuso's *Small business survival guide* (1981).

Arranged A-Z by topical chapters (*e.g.* Advertising ... Venture capital) the guide describes associations, books, journals, government agencies and private sources which will assist those running small businesses. 'An excellent source ... (*Choice*) v.26(5), January 1989, p.785). *Class No:* 334.746.4

Bibliographies

[2075]
KRYSZAK, W.D. The Small business index. Metuchen, N.J., Scarecrow Press, 1978-85. 2v. (228p.;320p.). ISBN: 0810811502; 0810818175.

Indexes American and Canadian books, pamphlets and periodicals which contain information on starting a small business. Subject index includes more than 250 kinds of business. *Class No:* 334.746.4(01)

[2076]
The London Business School small business bibliography. Edwards, H. *and* Hughes, D., *eds.* 1989 ed. London, London Business School Library, 1990. xii,153p. £25. ISBN: 0902583204.

First published 1980.

A listing of *c.*1500 items, adding to the 12,000 collected in the five previous volumes. Arranged in 3 main parts: Part 1. Literature review on employment and unemployment relations in the small enterprise. Part 2. Subject bibliography in 15 sections, mostly subdivided (1. Entrepreneurship - 2. Starting new businesses - 3. Managing the on-going small business - 4. Business policy and organizational development - 5. Education, training, information, advice and consultancy. 6. Financing the small business ... 11. Particular types of small business - 12. Employment and small business ... 14. The small firm and its environment in the UK - 15. The small firm and its environment in other countries). Part 3. Author bibliography. Appendices: List of journals from which articles have been included; List of institutions. *Class No:* 334.746.4(01)

[2077]
Small business sourcebook. Dorgan, C.A., *ed.* 3rd ed. Detroit, Mich., Gale Research Co., 1988. 2v. (1913p.). $180. ISBN: 0810326485.

First published 1983.

Covers 163 specific small businesses. Information sources: general; counselling; financial. Specific businesses (Accounting ... Word processing). Organizations (government; state; trade and professional organizations; educational institutions; etc.). Comprehensive index.

A 6th ed. by C.A.Schwarz was published in 1992 ($220. ISBN 0810380765). *Class No:* 334.746.4(01)

[2078]

—The Small business guide: sources of information for new and small businesses. Rev. ed. London, Oryx Press, 1984. 399p. ISBN: 0563211105.

First published 1982.

12 sections (*e.g.* 2. Sources of direct help and advice - 3. Business opportunities ... 6. Raising the money - 7. Business and the law - 8. Training for business ... 10. Starting up overseas - 11. Glossary of key business terms (p.347-52). Index of enterprise agency sponsors. General index. *Class No:* 334.746.4(01)

Handbooks & Manuals

[2079]

How to set up & run your own business. 11th ed. London, Kogan Page, 1995. 237p. facsims., diagrs., forms, tables. (*The Daily telegraph* business enterprise book.) ISBN: 0749413743.

First published 1983 by Telegraph Publications.

18 contributors. 10 sections 1. What types of capital are there? - 2. Presenting your case - 3. Finding the right premises - 4. Marketing and sales - 5. Control and finance management - 6. Bookkeeping and administration systems - 7. NIS, corporation tax and VAT - 8. Planning the tax and using the incentives? - 9. Recruitment and employment law - 10. Starting off in export. 4 appendices (1. The costs of different methods of raising finance ... 3. Select bibliography - 4. Useful addresses. Index. Index of advertisers.

Class No: 334.746.4(035)

[2080]

MOGANO, M. How to start and run your own business. 7th ed. London, Graham & Trotman, 1989. vii,158p. £8.75 (*Better business series*.) ISBN: 1853332887.

A practical handbook of essential advice and information. 11 chapters: 1. Making a start - 2. Investigating the market - 3. Finding start-up money and using it effectively - 4. Getting the business going - 5. Taking professional advice - 6. Sales and marketing - 7. Exporting - 8. Planning and financial control - 9. Obtaining further finance - 10. The importance of people - 11. Growing larger. Useful addresses. Appendix: Budget update. Index, p.155-158.

Class No: 334.746.4(035)

Europe—Western

[2081]

HASKINS, G., *and others*. A Guide to small firms assistance in Europe. Aldershot, Hants., Gower, 1986. vii,363p. £35. ISBN: 056605082x.

Edited and co-ordinated for the European Foundation for Management Development and the European Association for National Productivity Centres.

In 3 parts: I. Reviewing the services: comparative analysis and the scope for transfer of ideas - II. Country overviews - III. Assistance in key areas. Includes a directory of all major national and regional organizations providing small firm services in 17 European countries; special tables showing the support provided for exports, start-ups, technological innovation, and research and development, etc.

Class No: 334.746.4(400)

USA

[2082]

Directory of federal and state business assistance: a guide for new and growing companies. National Technical Information Services, *ed.* National Technical Information Service (NTIS), 1986. xii,159p. $19. ISBN: 0934213038.

First published in 1984 as *Guide to innovative resources and planning for small business*.

2 main sections: Federal assistance section - State assistance section. The Federal assistance section has 182 entries from 47 federal departments, arranged A-Z by department, and entries include a one-sentence description of services offered to business, together with name and address, telephone number, sometimes a contact name, and 6 possible terms to designate type of assistance. The State assistance section has 406 entries and is similarly organized. 7 appendices list federal offices, etc. Subject index. *Class No:* 334.746.4(73)

Monopolies

Dictionaries

[2083]

ORGANISATION FOR ECONOMIC CO-OPERATION AND DEVELOPMENT. Glossaire de termes relatifs aux pratiques communicales restrictives/Glossary of terms relating to restrictive business practices. Paris, OECD, 1965. 100p. £2.20; $5.

60 terms are defined, with commentary (*e.g.* 'Unfair competition': 25-word definition plus 1½p. of commentary including quotation from a Convention of 1883). Four chapters. A. Terms relating to economic

.... (contd.)

concentration - B. Terms relating to arrangements between enterprises - C. Actions by enterprises - D. Other terms. Index.

Class No: 334.75(038)

Mergers

[2084]

COOKE, T.E. International mergers and acquisitions. London, Blackwell, in association with Arthur Young International, 1988. [5],516p. tables. £70. ISBN: 0631147489.

Provides detailed information on mergers and acquisitions in 12 key geographical areas, including UK, USA, Europe and Japan. Details forms of business organizations, merger registrations and controls, taxation and accounting implications, foreign investment and exchange controls, etc. *Class No:* 334.751

[2085]

EATON, J. Source guide to mergers and acquisitions information. London, London Business School Information Service, 1991. 764p. £20. ISBN: 0951440144.

Details of 91 publications arranged by type (*e.g.* databases (online - CD-ROM - diskette), annual directories, official publications, and online hosts. Followed by a miscellaneous section and sections on books, reports and surveys, periodicals and reference works. Does not claim to be comprehensive. *Class No:* 334.751

[2086]

GEORGE, K.D., *ed.* Macmillan's mergers and acquisitions yearbook. London, Macmillan Press, 1988. xxxv,799p. tables. £150. ISBN: 0333458656.

Takes a chronological look at events in the field in 6 key articles, followed by a section on 'How to use the book and read the financial data' and a 'Company information section' in 4 parts: 1. Mergers - 2. Acquisitions - 3. Divestments - 4. Management buyouts. Each section is arranged A-Z by name of company and includes information on bidder, target, diary of announcement, terms, financial statistics, and financial advisers. SIC code index. General index by name of company, p.795-799. *Class No:* 334.751

Finance

[2087]

CROPLEY, J. Directory of financial information sources. London, Woodhead-Faulkner, 1991. xii,308p. £65. ISBN: 0859415643.

Each entry provides data on institutions, databases and publications. Arrangement is in 10 sections, mostly subdivided: 1. The financial scene - 2. Markets - 3. Financial institutions and credit operations - 4. Corporate institutions and operations - 5. Investment media - 6. Trade - 7. Law and regulations - 8. Economics - 9. People, systems and services - 10. Addresses. Author and title index, p.264-302. Subject index, p.303-308. *Class No:* 336

[2088]

International banking and financial centers. Park, Y.S. *and* Essayyad, M., *eds.* Dordrecht, Kluwer Academic Publishers, 1989. xiv,271p. tables. Dfl.135; £35.25. ISBN: 0792390164.

A study to reflect recent trends and to present an in-depth look into the various aspects of IFCs: definitions; organization; competition; innovations; and evaluation of their contributions to international financing and investment and to the economies of host countries. 16 chapters in 4 parts: 1. Recent developments in international financial centers - 2. Cost/benefit analysis of international financial centers - 3. New appraisal of international banking facilities - 4. Global perspective of international financial centers. References are included at the end of each chapter. Index, p.269-271. *Class No:* 336

Databases

[2089]

Business-line finance: the international directory of online financial information. EDI Ltd. (Publishing), *comp. & ed.* London, EDI:Euromonitor Publications Ltd., 1987. ISBN: 0863382339.

Database directory arranged by subject, A-Z (Accounting - Banking services and information - Commodities/futures - Economics - Financial and insurance services - General business news and information - Insurance - Investment - Money markets - Over the counter listings - Stock market and securities). Indexes of hosts, producers and addresses. *Class No:* 336(003.4)

[2090]

Online databases in the securities and financial markets. New York, Cuadra/Elsevier, 1987. xxii,322p. $39.95. ISBN: 0444012761.

Descriptions of the databases are arranged A-Z by name, with information on type, subject, producer, online service, conditions, content, language, coverage, time span, updating (*i.e.,* monthly). There follows addresses of online databases, and indexes (subject, subdivided by database titles; online service/gateway index; master index). *Class No:* 336(003.4)

Bibliographies of Bibliographies

[2091]

LESTER, R. **Information sources in finance and banking.** Bowker-Saur, 1996 820p. £75.00 ISBN: 1857390377. *Class No:* 336(009)

Bibliographies

[2092]

BREALEY, R.A *and* EDWARDS, H. **A Bibliography of finance.** Cambridge, Mass., M.I.T., 1991. 822p. $60. ISBN: 0262023199.

Over 12,000 entries (over half for articles published 1980-89) taken from *c.*120 periodicals in finance and related fields. Entries grouped in 40 chapters, further subdivided into 373 individual subjects. Contents list; author and keyword indexes. Both authors at the London Business School. '... a large and impressive work ...'(*Choice*, v.28(11/12), July/August 1991, p.1754). *Class No:* 336(01)

[2093]

COHEN, J. **Special bibliography in monetary economics and finance.** London, Gordon & Breach, 1976. xiii,200p. £61.90. ISBN: 067700690x.

Covers the years 1953-73. In 7 sections (1. Monetary and financial theory - 2. Banks - 3. Financial intermediaries - 4. Financial markets - 5. Monetary statistics - 6. General texts - 7. Bibliographies; reference works). *Class No:* 336(01)

[2094]

LESTER, R.G. *and* CROPLEY, I., *eds.* **Information sources in finance and banking.** Sevenoaks, Kent, Bowker-Saur, 1994. To be in 2v. £55. ISBN: 1857390377, v.1.

V.1: Data sources; v.2: Evaluating financial information. V.1 is arranged by subject, entries including brief notes on sources, frequency of publication, price and serial information. *Class No:* 336(01)

[2095]

ROCK, J.M. **Money, banking and macroeconomics: a guide to information sources.** Detroit, Mich., Gale, 1977. 304p. $68. (*Economics information guide series, v.11.*) ISBN: 0810313006.

A selective, annotated bibliography of books and journal articles on inflation, the relation between income and prices, fiscal policy, and the history of macro-monetary theory. A general chapter (overview; introduction; general; special and secondary sources) precedes the four main chapters relating to financial intermediaries, macro-monetary theory, central banking, and stabilisation policy. Author, title and subject indexes. *Class No:* 336(01)

Encyclopaedias

[2096]

Enzyklapädisches Lexikon für das Geld-, Bank- und Borsenwesen. Achterberg, E. *and* Lanz, K., *eds.* 3.Aufl.redigiert und ergänzt. Frankfurt am Main, Knapp, 1967-68. 2v. (xi,1894p.).tables.

First published 1957.

V.1: A-H; v.2: I-Z. Includes country entries (*e.g.* U.S.: 5 pts., 34 sections, p.1686-1723). Includes some biographies (*e.g.* 'Smith, Adam': ½col.; 'Keynes': 2 cols., plus bibliography of 17 lines). International panel of 200 contributors. *Class No:* 336(031)

[2097]

MUNN, G. G. **Encyclopedia of banking and finance.** Woefel, C.J., *ed.* 9th ed. New York & London, McGraw-Hill Book Company 1991. xxvi,1097p. tables, charts. £89; $95. ISBN: 0077073940.

First published 1924; 8th ed. 1983.

c. 4200 lengthy entries, in addition to thousands of basic banking, business and financial terms. 'The in-depth entries provide a wealth of valuable information, such as historical background, analysis of recent trends, illustrative examples, statistical data, and citations to applicable laws and regulations (*Publisher's foreword*). Cross-references, but no index to this edition. *Class No:* 336(031)

[2098]

—DAVIDS, L.E. **Dictionary of banking and finance.** Totowa, N.J., Rowman & Littlefield, 1979. 229p. $8.95. ISBN: 0822603365.

Concentrates on developments since the mid-1960s in banking, defining *c.* 5400 terms and phrases. Suggested (*Choice* April 1979, p.200,202) as a quick-reference tool and supplement to Munn. *Class No:* 336(031)

[2099]

—RACHLIN, H. **The Money encyclopedia.** New York, Harper & Row, 1984. 669p., tables. $26.50. ISBN: 0061817112.

Less comprehensive than Munn, but a clear, readable source of information on economic terms commonly encountered by the general public. Entries written by experts from the banking, securities and insurance fields. *Class No:* 336(031)

Handbooks & Manuals

[2100]

GARNER, P., *and others, eds.* **Financial management handbook.** 3rd ed. Brentford, Middx., Kluwer Publishing Ltd., 1988. Loose-leaf, with updates. ISBN: 0903393336.

First published in 1977, edited by G.M. Dickinson and J.E. Lewis.

Part 1: Corporate strategy and financial planning - 2: Evaluation of capital outlays - 3: Financing and dividend policy - 4: Sources of external funds - 5: The management of working capital - 6: Financial control systems and the measurement of performance - 7: Mergers and takeovers - 8: International financial management - 9: Financial management and its economic environment - 10: Using business computers. Each part contains several signed contributions, many by well-known contributors, which include bibliographies. The loose-leaf format is for regular updating. 30-page index. *Class No:* 336(035)

[2101]

MASON, S. **The McGraw-Hill handbook of British finance and trade.** Maidenhead, Berks, McGraw-Hill Book Company (UK) Ltd., 1983. [8] 467p. £29.95p. ISBN: 0070845905.

Preface claims that it includes practically all basic information for businesses. 16 chapters:- 1. Money and interest rates - 2. The national economy - 3. Financial incentives, governnment and institutional aid - 4. International trade - 5. Taxation - 6. Investment - 7. Company structure/company demise - 8. Management analysis and techniques - 9. The mechanics of finance - 10. Sources and methods of finance - 11. The City of London: its institutions and markets - 12. Banks and banking institutions - 13. Commercial and financial institutions - 14. Developments in finance - 15. Miscellaneous financial organizations and activities - 16. Contact points. *Class No:* 336(035)

[2102]

ROWLEY, E.E. **The Financial system today:** understanding financial information. Manchester, Manchester University Press, 1987. ix,228p. tables. £22.50. ISBN: 0719014875.

A practical guide in 9 sections: 1. British government securities - 2. Measuring share price changes - 3. The retail price index - 4. The European currency unit - 5. Evaluation of a company - 6. London traded share options market - 7. Investment trusts and unit trusts - 8. The markets for foreign currencies - 9. The Eurocurrencies market. Index, p.223-228. Notes follow each chapter and include references. *Class No:* 336(035)

Dictionaries

[2103]

The New Penguin dictionary of money and finance. Newman, P. *and* Milgate, M. *and* Eatwell, J., *ed.* London, Macmillan, 1992 ISBN: 0333527224.

Contains indexes.

Over 1,000 entries by more than 800 contributors, on institutional and descriptive monetary history, and problems of financial regulation. It covers the monetary and financial systems of about 30 countries. There are many cross-references; Vol. 3 contains a subject classification listing the entries under 12 groups, and subdivided under 104 subheadings. Each volume includes a list of entries in that volume, with cross-references. Articles are signed and have bibliographies. It is the companion work to *The new Palgrave : a dictionary of economics*, published in 4 vols in 1987. *Class No:* 336(038)

[2104]

A World Bank glossary: a glossary of finance and debt. Washington, World Bank, 1991. vii,213p. $18.95; £17.95. ISBN: 0821316443.

Supersedes *Borrowing and lending terminology*(1984).

Main section (in English) defines terms used in major world financial markets, and also provides equivalent words or phrases in French and Spanish. Also includes a list of relevant acronyms in English, French and Spanish, and glossaries (with no definitions) translating French and Spanish terms into English. *Class No:* 336(038)

Polyglot

[2105]

DE MUNTER, M. *and* BAUDUIN, C. **Elsevier's fiscal and customs dictionary in five languages:** English/American, French, Dutch, and German. Amsterdam, Elsevier Science Publishers, 1988. xxxii,718p. Dfl.500; $285.50 ISBN: 0444428917.

Aimed at theoreticians and practitioners of fiscal law (including customs law), officials of tax administration, etc. 4845 numbered terms (words and phrases) in the English language, followed by French,

....(contd.)

Dutch and German equivalents. A bibliography (p.xv-xxxi) precedes, with dictionary item numbers in brackets for connection with legal, etc., documents. Includes certain legal and economic as well as purely fiscal terms. Indexes in all 4 languages. *Class No:* 336(038)=00

[2106]

EUROPEAN PARLIAMENT. Glossary of fiscal terminology: French/ Italian/English/German/Dutch. Luxembourg, European Parliament, 1975. 253p. £6.50.

Arranged under French terms, with keyword indexes in the other languages referring to the main sequence. A supplement, 'List of taxes and duties levied in the member states' includes the Danish language. *Class No:* 336(038)=00

[2107]

GOLDSMITH, DEVOLVÉ ET ASSOCIÉS, *and others*. Multilingual glossary of tax, financial and commercial terms. London, Oyez, Longman Group, 1983. 164p. £8.50. ISBN: 0851207618.

Arrangement is A-Z under the English-language terms, followed by French, German and Spanish equivalents in neighbouring columns. No indexes. *Class No:* 336(038)=00

[2108]

The IFR financial glossary. 3rd ed. London, IFR Publishing Ltd., 1992. 354p. £33. ISBN: 1873446012.

Covers terms used in short-term money, equity and bond markets; loans; financial instruments; Japanese, American, German and French terminology now internationally used; institutions and associations and their acronyms, differentiating between those words that have different meanings in different markets. Length of entries varies from 2 or 3 lines to over 20 lines. Extensive cross-references. *Class No:* 336(038)=00

[2109]

THOMSON, F.J. Elsevier's dictionary of financial terms in English, German, Spanish, French, Italian and Dutch. Amsterdam, Elsevier Scientific Publishing Ltd., 1979. [6], 496p. Dfl.290. $152.75. ISBN: 0444417753.

2379 numbered entries in English, followed by translations into the other five languages. Indexes in the other five languages followed by the entry numbers. No descriptions, but alternative terms are given. *Class No:* 336(038)=00

English

[2110]

AVEYNON, E.A., *ed*. Dictionary of finance. New York, Collier-Macmillan, 1988. 486p. illus., tables, charts. $50. ISBN: 0029164206.

Definitions for over 6000 terms in the area of finance and topics relating to finance (*e.g.* banking, law, marketing, economics). Entries include multiple meanings for many terms. Cross-references. *Class No:* 336(038)=20

[2111]

BANNOCK, G. *and* MANSER, W. International dictionary of finance. London, Hutchinson, in association with Economist Books, 1989. 220p. £19.95. ISBN: 0091743443.

Concerned not only with international finance but with domestic financial matters in major countries, particularly UK and US. Main subjects covered are money markets, commodity markets, securities markets, banking and insurance, and terms and phrases are limited to the specialized terminology of finance. Entries vary in length from 2 lines to ½-page. Cross-references. List of abbreviations precedes the dictionary. 'Comprehensive and concise reference guide for those wanting to be well-informed about the international world of finance' (*British book news*, January 1990, p.38). *Class No:* 336(038)=20

[2112]

BROSTER, E.J. Glossary of applied management and financial statistics. London, Gower Press, 1974. [v], 243p. illus., tables. £22.50. ISBN: 0716101742.

Defines a few hundred terms, some at length (*e.g.* Index numbers, 5 pages). Cross-references, examples and formulae. Annotated bibliography of 16 general works and 30 special works in 11 subject sections. *Class No:* 336(038)=20

[2113]

PERRY, F.E., *ed*. A Selected vocabulary of financial terms. London, Waterlow Publishers Ltd., 1981. [3],125p. £4.50. ISBN: 0900791705.

An A-Z listing (Acceptance credit ... Zero budgeting) of terms, with cross-references. Descriptions vary in length from a line to 1½ pages. Includes organizations. UK orientated. *Class No:* 336(038)=20

[2114]

ROSENBERG, J.M., *ed*. Dictionary of banking and financial services. 3rd ed. New York, Wiley, 1993. 369p. illus. $39.95. ISBN: 047157435x.

First published in 1982 with the title *Dictionary of banking and finance*.

Includes *c.*7500 words, phrases and abbreviations in an A-Z sequence. Entries vary in length from 3 or 4 words to about 150 words, and include definitions and alternative words. Excellent clear and concise definitions. 'Terms added, but - unfortunately - others dropped.'(*Wilson library bulletin*, v.67(8), April 1993, p.118). *Class No:* 336(038)=20

[2115]

WALMESLEY, J. Dictionary of international finance. 2nd ed. London, Macmillan, 1985. [5], 222p. £27.50. (*Macmillan dictionary series*.) ISBN: 0333370708.

First published 1979.

Several hundred entries for terms in trade finance, foreign exchange and economics. Al ... Zero coupon. 'Special drawing rights': ¾p., with 4 references; 'Eurodollar': 2/3p., with 6 references. Includes abbreviations and organizations (*e.g.* Carribean Community and Common Market; Association of South-East Asian Nations). The author is a vice-president of Barclays Bank. "The jargon of international trade, insurance, economics and securities trading is clearly, completely, yet succinctly defined" (*RQ,*v.19, no. 4, Summer 1980, p.390 on first ed.). *Class No:* 336(038)=20

German

[2116]

GUNSTON, C.A. *and* CORNER, C.M. German-English glossary of financial and economic terms. 8th ed. Frankfurt am Main, Knapp, 1983. xviii,918p. £54.

First published 1953.

About 20,000 main entries, including abbreviations and names of German associations and organizations. Swiss, US, etc. terminology is differentiated. Some explanation of scope of terms. Well spoken of by translators. New ed. in preparation. *Class No:* 336(038)=30

French

[2117]

LAMBERT, D.-C. Dictionnaire français-anglais de l'économie monétaire. 2e.éd. Paris, Éditions Économie et Humanisme, 1975. 261p. £9.90.

First published 1970.

About 500 entries, including biographies and abbreviations. The text of the entry comprises an explanation of the word, and a brief outline of the practice in various countries. Definitions are in French. French and English indexes. *Class No:* 336(038)=40

Spanish

[2118]

DONAGHY, P.J. *and* LAIDLER, J., *comps*. Dictionary of the language of financial reports: Spanish-English, English-Spanish. Bilbao, Ediciones Deusto, 1983 (distributed by Christopher Percival, Durham City). 222p. £11.50. ISBN: 8423405435.

Also available under the Spanish title *Diccionario de terminos usados en informes financieros...*

Translations of *c.*8000 specialized terms found in annual reports of companies, annual financial statements, etc. *Class No:* 336(038)=60

Arabic

[2119]

ABDEEN, A. English-Arabic dictionary of accounting and finance, with an Arabic-English glossary. Beirut, Librairie du Liban; Chichester, Sussex, John Wiley & Sons, 1981. xi,226,[41]p. ISBN: 0471276731.

Gives explanations of terms in English and Arabic, supported by examples and illustrations. Terms arranged A-Z in English. Appendices: 1. Financial ratios; 2. Currencies in the Arab world; 3. Metric conversion tables; 4. Illustrations. Finally, an Arabic-English glossary. *Class No:* 336(038)=927

Japanese

[2120]

WILLIAMS, D. A Dictionary of Japanese financial terms. Japan Library: Paul Norbury, 1992. 200p. £35. ISBN: 1873410115.

Each entry in phonetic English, kanji and English, plus brief supporting text. *Class No:* 336(038)=956

Periodicals & Progress Reports

[2121]

FISHER, W.H. Financial journals and serials: an analytical guide to accounting, banking, finance, insurance & investment periodicals. Westport, CT. Greenwood Press, 1986. 201p. $65.00. (*Annotated bibliography series, no.6.*) ISBN: 0313241953.

Over 500 English-language journals, briefly annotated. Arranged in 6 chapters, A-Z by title within each: Accounting, auditing and taxation - Banking - Finance - Insurance - Investments - Indexes and abstracts. Geographical, title, publisher and subject indexes. 'The depth of analysis, frequently several paragraphs in addition to the usual bibliographical data, is the basis for acquiring this work' (*Choice,* December 1986, p.606) but the review also mentions that there are some glaring omissions. *Class No: 336(05)*

Tables & Data Books

[2122]

International financial statistics. New York, International Monetary Fund, 1948-. v.1,no.1-. graphs, tables. Monthly. $218pa for 12 issues and yearbook; $50 for yearbook. ISBN: 1557752974, 1993 yearbook. ISSN: 02507463.

Preliminary pages have data on the IMF, exchange rates; fund accounts; international liquidity; international banking; money and banking; interest rates; prices, wages, production and employment; international transactions, government finance; national accounts and population; world tables. 'Country pages' covers *c.*100 countries (excluding Sino-Soviet bloc), Afghanistan ... Zimbabwe, followed by notes on tables. The February 1994 issue (v.47(2) gives time series 1988-92 yearly; 1992 & 1993 quarterly; latest 5 or 6 months, monthly. *Class No: 336(083)*

[2123]

ORGANISATION FOR ECONOMIC CO-OPERATION AND DEVELOPMENT. Published official sources of financial statistics. Paris, OECD, 1980. 132p. £4.90; $11. ISBN: 9264020950.

Information on the offical institutions in 17 countries publishing financial statistics, including their publications. Also information on the financial statistical publications of four international organizations, including OECD. *Class No: 336(083)*

Bibliographies

[2124]

BALACHANDRAN, M. A Guide to statistical sources in money, banking and finance. Phoenix, Ariz., Oryx, 1988. 119p. $45. ISBN: 0897742656.

A selected and annotated bibliography of 480 serial publications dealing with banking and monetary statistics. Arranged in 6 chapters: State services - Regional sources - National sources - Foreign country sources - International sources - Databases (63 entries). Annotations vary from one sentence to half a page. Omits USSR in foreign country section. Title and subject index. Directory of publishers. '... excellent source' (*RQ*, v.27(3), Spring 1988, p.429). 'A useful bibliography for business collections' (*Choice*, v.25(10), June 1988, p.1529). *Class No: 336(083)(01)*

Laws

Great Britain

[2125]

MILLER, J. Dictionary of financial regulations, 1988/89. London, London & International Publishers, under licence to The International Stock Exchange of the United Kingdom and the Republic of Ireland Ltd., 1988. xxvi,238p. £29.95. ISBN: 0948209291.

A guide to the vocabulary adopted in the regulation of financial services under the Financial Services Act, 1986. An overview, describing the way in which the headwords of the main text relate to the regulating system and to one another, is followed by the dictionary of over 900 entries, with extensive cross-references. Index of headwords, p.231,233-238. *Class No: 336(094.1)(410)*

Europe

Histories

[2126]

KINDLEBERGER, C.P. A Financial history of Western Europe. 2nd ed. New York, Oxford University Press, 1993. xviii,524p. illus (cartoons), tables, maps. £35. $29.95. ISBN: 0195077377.

First published 1984.

Introduction, p.1-14, includes chronologies (1. Wars - 2. Monetary events - 3. Banking landmarks - 4. Financial events), is followed by 24 chapters in 5 parts: 1. Money - 2. Banking - 3. Finance - 4. The interwar period - 5. After World War II. Each part has an introduction

....(contd.)
and each chapter ends with 'Suggested supplementary reading'. Glossary, p.465-473. Bibliography, p.477-511, A-Z by author. Index, p.513-525. *Class No: 336(4)(091)*

Great Britain

Tables & Data Books

[2127]

Financial statistics. Central Statistical Office. London, HMSO, 1962- no.1-. tables. Monthly. £120pa including explanatory handbook. £10 each issue. ISSN: 0015203x.

Prepared in collaboration with the Statistics Divisions of government departments and the Bank of England.

Brings together key financial and monetary statistics of the United Kingdom. 14 sections: 1. Financial accounts ... 3. Central government ... 6. Banks and building societies - 7. Other financial institutions - 8. Companies - 9. Personal sector - 10. Overseas sector ... 13. Exchange rates, interest rates and security prices - 14. Sectoral balance sheet. Supplementary tables. data and information (for figures in CSO databank). Index. *Financial statistics: explanatory handbook* is published annually. *Class No: 336(410)(083)*

Histories

[2128]

COLLINS, M. Money and banking in the U.K.: a history. London, Croom Helm, 1988. [12], 640p. tables, figs. £49.50. ISBN: 0709907605.

16 chapters in three parts covering the period 1826-1985: 1. 1826-1913;2. 1914-1939; 3. 1939-1986. Deals for each period with the general economic and legislative context determining the growth of monetary and financial assets; the developing form of banking business; the domestic monetary policy, and international monetary factors affecting the UK. Notes and further reading follow each chapter. Bibliography (p.593-626) of books, official publications and reports, articles, essays and papers. General index (p.627-638) and index of names (p.639-640). *Class No: 336(410)(091)*

London

Yearbooks & Directories

[2129]

The City directory, 1992. Cambridge, Woodhead-Faulkner, 1992. 328p. £98. ISBN: 0859417735.

First published 1976 by the *Investor's chronicle* and Woodhead-Faulkner, and later editions by Woodhead-Faulkner.

A comprehensive guide to the banks, financial organizations and other companies and services which make up the City of London. *Class No: 336(421)(058)*

France

Histories

[2130]

SAINT MARC, M. Histoire monetaire de la France, 1800-1980. Paris, Presses Universitaire de France, 1983. 441p. tables.

A thorough study of monetary history in France in 3 parts: Part 1 has the data (series of annual monetary statistics mainly from primary sources); pt.2 is historical; pt.3 is theoretical and empirical. Each chapter has a bibliography and the work is illustrated with graphs and tables. No index. '... presents a useful account of the historical evolution of money'. ... a valuable addition to the literature' (*Economic history review*, v.37 (1984), p.455). *Class No: 336(44)(091)*

Japan

Histories

[2131]

SUZUKI, Y, ed. The Japanese financial system. Oxford, Clarendon Press, 1987. £35. xi,358p. tables. ISBN: 0198285965.

Prepared by the staff of the Monetary and Economic Studies, Bank of Japan.

Part I outlines the features and changes in the Japanese financial system and economy after World War II; pt. II gives detailed descriptions of various assets, rates, financial institutions and monetary policy. Bibliography (62 items). Subject index, p.349-358. *Class No: 336(52)*

Asia—Near East

Bibliographies

[2132]

NICHOLAS, D. **The Middle East: its oil, economics and investment policies:** a guide to sources of financial information. London, Mansell, 1981. xxiv,199p. £45. ISBN: 0720109078. *Class No:* 336(56)(01)

Yearbooks & Directories

[2133]

The **MEED/TAIC Middle East financial directory, 1986.** London, Middle East Economic Digest, in association with The Arab Investment Company SAA, 1985. xi,453p. £60. ISBN: 0946510164. ISSN: 02662094.

First published 1975 as *Middle East financial directory;* from 9th ed., 1985 under the current title. Annual.

For 24 Middle East countries, arranged A-Z, general information, and information on central banks, commercial banks, specialized banks, and other financial institutions. Data includes addresses and telephone numbers, activities, management, head office, directors, finance, branches, and subsidiaries. Also a section on banks and other financial institutions in other countries (p.221-322). Indexes of institutions and persons. Glossary of acronyms and abbreviations. *Class No:* 336(56)(058)

Islamic World

Yearbooks & Directories

[2134]

PRESLEY, J.R., *ed*. **A Directory of Islamic financial institutions.** Croom Helm, 1988. 304p. $120; £50. ISBN: 0709913478.

In 4 sections: Part 1 has 7 articles on the theoretical bases and practical operations of Islamic banking; pt.2 is a directory of Islamic financial institutions, arranged by country, and listing for each institution address; telephone/telex/cable numbers for head and branch offices; names of directors and senior management; financial statistics; number of employees; and areas of operation, objectives, types of investment accounts and banking operations, and future developments. Pt.3 has case studies in Islamic banking and banking laws for certain Islamic countries translated into English; and pt.4 is on ownership, control and management of Islamic banks. Recommended by *Choice* (v.26(7), March 1989, p.1120) for comprehensive collections. *Class No:* 336(5.297)(058)

USA

Yearbooks & Directories

[2135]

The **Financial 1000:** a directory of who runs the leading 1000 US financial organizations. Marsh, J.E., *ed*. New York, Monitor Publishing Co., 1988. 553p. $100. ISSN: 08947627.

An A-Z list of companies, with names of officers, management, boards of directors, major subsidiaries and divisions, and telephone numbers. Covers banks, thrift institutions, insurance companies, and Wall Street firms. 3 indexes: geographical; individual names; by financial services rendered. *Class No:* 336(73)(058)

Public Finance

Bibliographies

[2136]

Financial sourcebooks' sources: the directory of financial research, marketing surveys, and services. Napierville, Jl., Financial Sourcebooks, 1987. 454p. $165.00. ISBN: 0942061004. ISSN: 08927812.

Directory of more than 500 reports, published by over 100 organizations, that range from free government and association publications to surveys from private research firms (priced at $30,000 upwards). Reports grouped in 8 chapters: The consumer - Consumer segments - Consumer financial products - Business and institutional services - Institutions - US geographical area information - International sources - Marketing, advertising and media. Each chapter is subdivided, subject-wise. Entries contain description of report, publishers address, frequency or date of publication, and in most cases length of report and price. Covers 1984- plus census data from the 1980 census. Appendices include a list of reports by publisher, a publisher's directory, and a directory of contacts at the US Census Bureau for demographic and economic information. US oriented. *Class No:* 336.1(01)

Tables & Data Books

[2137]

Government finance statistics yearbook, 1992. v.16. Washington, DC., International Monetary Fund, 1992. 710p. tables. $48. ISBN: 1557753008. ISSN: 02507374.

First published 1977. Annual.

Data for *c.*120 countries for 1977 to 1990, with 1991 estimates. 'United Kingdom': Table A: Revenues and grants; B. Expenditure by function; C. Expenditure and lending; D. Financing, by type of debt holder; E. Financing, by type of debt instrument; F. Outstanding debt by type of debt holder; G. Outstanding debt by type of debt instrument. Data is based on *A Manual on government financial statistics* (Rev. ed., 1986. $10). Also available on CD-ROM. *Class No:* 336.1(083)

[2138]

INTERNATIONAL MONETARY FUND. **A Manual on government finance statistics.** Washington, DC., the IMF, 1986. vii,[1],373p. illus., tables. %c $93.80. ISBN: 0939934442.

Compiled to assist those who are called upon to organize statistics of government finance for various purposes. In 6 chapters: I. Coverage (has sections A-K) - II. Selection and preparation of data - III. Analytical framework - IV.Classification - V. Relationships with other data systems - VI. Nonfinancial public enterprises and the nonfinancial public sector. List of tables; bridge tables; list of working tables; list of charts. *Class No:* 336.1(083)

Europe—Western

[2139]

EUROPEAN COMMUNITIES. Commission. **The European monetary system:** origins, operation, and outlook. Ypersele, J. van *and* Koeune, J.-C. Luxembourg, Office for Official Publications of the European Communities; Cambridge, Woodhead-Faulkner, 1985. 139,[4]p. tables. ECU.25. ISBN: 9282534685, EC; 0859413136, UK.

5 chapters: I. International motives for the EEC initiative - II. The ebb and flow of European monetary integration - III. The EMS and the conditions for its proper operation - IV. Five years with the EMS - V. The future of the EMS. 4 annexes (Timetable of events - Act of foundation of the European Monetary System - Versailles summit - European Parliament resolution of 16 February 1984). *Class No:* 336.1(400)

USA

Bibliographies

[2140]

MARSHALL, M.B. **Public finance;** an information sourcebook. Phoenix, AZ., Oryx Press, 1987. xviii,287p. $39.50. (*Oryx sourcebook series in business and management, 6.*) ISBN: 0897742761.

A briefly annotated bibliography of 1205 entries, focusing on policy issues and theory of public finance. Subject arrangement. Detailed table of contents and excellent indexes (Author index, p.253-260; title index, p.261-278; analytical subject index, p.279-287). 'A helpful feature is a core collection of important sources... ' (*Choice,* v.25(9), May 1988, p.1384). *Class No:* 336.1(73)(01)

Budgets

[2141]

BRITTAIN, H. **The British budgetary system.** London, Allen & Unwin, 1959. 320p.

A standard work. The composition of the budget is closely discussed item by item and is followed by a chapter on the national debt. Finally, the control of government expenditure by Parliament and the Treasury is explained in detail. Detailed index: no bibliography. *Class No:* 336.12

[2142]

PREST, A.R. *and* BARR, N.A. **Public finance in theory and practice.** 7th rev. ed. by N.A. Barr. London, Weidenfeld & Nicolson, 1985. 576p. £20. ISBN: 0297787527.

First published 1960.

More general in scope than Brittain (q.v.) as a text book, and includes chapters on US and Canada. *Class No:* 336.12

Accounts

Worldwide

Tables & Data Books

[2143]

ORGANISATION FOR ECONOMIC CO-OPERATION AND DEVELOPMENT. **National accounts of OECD countries, 1955/64-.** Paris, OECD, 1966-. tables. Annual. ISSN: 02567571.

Two volumes each year: v.1. *Main aggregates, 1960-1991.* (1993.

....(contd.)
160p. F.150. £25. $38.00.); v.2 *Detailed tables, 1979-1991* (1993. 588p. F.530. £87. $125.). V.1 shows for each member country the main aggregates calculated according to either the present or the former system of national accounts. V.2 shows each country's detailed statistics. Annex 1 is a glossary of the technical terms used in the system of national accounts; annex 2 gives a full set of English and French translations of the item descriptions in the detailed country tables. Updated by *Quarterly national accounts* (1976-. F.320. £40. $68pa.). *Class No:* 336.126(100)(083)

[2144]
UNITED NATIONS. Department of International Economic and Social Affairs. Statistical Office. **Yearbook of national accounts statistics, 1990:** main aggregates and detailed tables. New York, United Nations, 1992. 2v. ISBN: 9211613515.
First published 1957. Annual.
International coverage of statistical data on national accounts estimates for 170 countries and areas, giving specific data on gross domestic product, national income and capital transactions, government and consumer expenditures, social security and household funds. One volume devoted to main aggregates; the other to detailed tables. Issued separately is *National accounts statistics: analysis of main aggregates,* presenting in the form of statistical tables, a summary of main national aggregates. *Class No:* 336.126(100)(083)

Great Britain

Tables & Data Books

[2145]
GREAT BRITAIN. Central Statistical Office. **United Kingdom national accounts, 1993.** London, HMSO, 1993. vii,168p. tables. £15.50. ISBN: 0116205889. ISSN: 02678691.
First published for 1938/40. Prior to 1984 title was *National income and expenditure.* Known as *The Blue book.* Annual.
17 chapters in 5 sections: 1. The national accounts - 2. The main analyses - 3. The sector accounts - 4. Capital formation and capital stocks - 5. Other analyses and derived statistics. A 6th section has supplementary information (Glossary of terms; methodological notes; revisions; and index). Data is for several years to 1992.
Class No: 336.126(410)(083)

[2146]
—COPEMAN, H. The National accounts: a short guide. London, HMSO., 1981. various pagings. £5.50. (*Studies in official statistics, no.36.*) ISBN: 0116200006.
Provides a broad description of the accounts and a detailed commentary on their structure. *Class No:* 336.126(410)(083)

Taxation

[2147]
PLATT, C.J. Tax systems of Africa, Asia and Middle East: a guide for business and the professions. Aldershot, Hants, Gower Publishing Company, 1982. xxii, 240p. £27. ISBN: 0566023350.
Summarizes tax arrangements in 35 countries of Africa, Asia, and the Near and Middle East. A companion volume to the one on Western Europe. Similar arrangement to companion volume by Platt at 336.2(4). *Class No:* 336.2

[2148]
PLATT, C.J. Tax systems of Western Europe: a guide for business and the professions. 3rd ed. Aldershot, Hants, Gower, 1985. xxii, 171p. £15; $30.50. ISBN: 0566025345.
First published 1980.
Summarizes tax arrangements in 23 European countries, arranged A-Z. Each entry begins with a brief 'tax profile' followed by a summary of taxes in force (income tax, corporation tax, capital tax), notes on legislation, detail of income tax (basis of assessment, computation of taxable income, current allowances, etc.), details of corporation tax, notes on double taxation agreements and rates of tax. *Class No:* 336.2

Laws

[2149]
DIAMOND, W.H. *and* DIAMOND, D.B., *eds.* **International tax treaties of all nations.** Dobbs Ferry, N.Y., Oceana,1975-83. 34v. (Series A, 14v.; series B, 25v.). Series A plus loose-leaf index $710; Series B $1290. ISBN: 0379007258.
950 bilateral treaties, originally published by the United Nations, in sequence of their dates of issue by the League of Nations and the United Nations, together with individual editorial commentary, current effective status, etc. Supplement and cumulative index was published in 1983 (loose-leaf. $50. ISBN 0379007452). *Class No:* 336.2(094.1)

Europe

[2150]
Supplementary service to European taxation. Amsterdam, International Bureau of Fiscal Documentation, 1963-. Loose-leaf in 14 binders. Dfl.2400 for basic volume, binders & monthly updates for the year; Renewal: Dfl.860. ISSN: 00395927.
Includes tax tables (corporation and individual) for each European country; English-language texts of tax treaties; texts (in English) of official reports, including E.C. directives on taxation; and worldwide bibliography of new tax documents and publications. The Bureau also issues a series of loose-leaf guides to European taxation: v.1, *Taxation of patent royalties, dividends, interest in Europe;* v.2, *The taxation of companies in Europe;* v.3, *The taxation of private investment income;* v.4, *Value added tax in Europe;* and v.5, *Taxation in European Socialist countries.* *Class No:* 336.2(4)

Great Britain

Bibliographies

[2151]
GREAT BRITAIN. HM Stationery Office. **Government publications. Sectional list 29, revised January 1992. Inland Revenue.** London, HMSO., 1992. vi,14p. *Gratis.*
Includes references to the Tax Acts, tax cases and leaflets, tax reports, etc. *Class No:* 336.2(410)(01)

Encyclopaedias

[2152]
British tax encyclopaedia. Lawton, P., *ed.* London, Sweet & Maxwell, 1970-. 6v. (looseleaf). Annual service. £625. (including service).
First published 1921.
V.1 is a narrative treatise on the definition of income for tax purposes. V.2-5 contain the relevant statutory material, fully annotated. V.6 has a comprehensive index to the whole work, full tables, current up-dating releases, etc. Plentiful and detailed cross-references. *Class No:* 336.2(410)(031)

Handbooks & Manuals

[2153]
BROOKE-TAYLOR, D. **Guide to stamp duties.** Bicester, Oxfordshire, CCH Editions Ltd., 1988. xiii,378p. £19.50. ISBN: 0863251153.
Claims to be a straighforward and all-round guide to stamp duties. In 4 parts: 1: General principles; 2. Individual duties - conveyancing; 3: Individual duties - companies; 4: Individual duties - miscellaneous. Appendices: I: Table of duties; II: Companies Act forms; III: Relevant legislation. Case table. Legislation finding list. Double-column subject index, p.359-378, relating to paragraph numbers.
Class No: 336.2(410)(035)

[2154]
Butterworth's yellow tax handbook, 1993-94: Taxes Acts relating to income tax, corporation tax and capital gains tax... Sadikali, M., *ed.* 33rd ed. London, Butterworths, 1993. £20. (*A Butterworth taxbook annual.*) ISBN: 0406015937.
First published 1962. Annual.
'Provides plain text of the Taxes Acts relating to income tax, corporation tax and capital gains tax. *Moore & Rowlands yellow tax guide* (1989-90 ed. 1988. 1301p. £27.95. ISBN 0406366039. ISSN 09518231) explains the practical effects of all the legislation contained in the above. *Class No:* 336.2(410)(035)

[2155]
—Butterworth's orange tax handbook, 1993-94... inheritance tax, National Insurance contributions, stamp duties, value added tax. London, Butterworth, 1993. £20 ISBN: 0406015945.
First published 1976.
Companion volume to *Butterworths yellow tax handbook, Moores & Rowland orange tax guide* (1989-90. 1988. 1293p. £27.95. ISBN 0406365032. ISSN 09518223) explains the practical effects of all the legislation contained in the above. *Class No:* 336.2(410)(035)

[2156]
The Touche Ross tax guide for the self-employed. Packer, B. *and* Sandy, C. 4th ed. London, Macmillan Press, 1988. xiv,213p. £4.95. ISBN: 0333468368.
First published 1985.
Written by two tax specialists at Touche Ross, the guide aims to include every inmportant tax aspect of self-employment and running a small business, including setting up the business, salaries versus profits, national insurance, VAT registration and payment, tax records, capital expenditure, employees, raising finance, and pension plans, plus a series of tax-planning guidelines and hints.
Class No: 336.2(410)(035)

[2157]
WEBB, H.B. *and* COLLIER, R. **Butterworth's stamp duties guide.** London, Butterworths, 1988. xiv,163p. £21.95. ISBN: 0406260303.

An introduction to stamp duty, capital duty, and stamp duty reserve tax, written for the non-specialist. 8 chapters (1. The three duties in outline - 2. Stamp duty ... 7. Procedure, appeals and enforcement - 8. The new approach and future developments). Table of Statutes. 5 appendices (I. Outline of main heads of change for stamp duty; II. Specimen forms; V. Stamp offices - addresses and phone numbers). Index, p.147-163. *Class No:* 336.2(410)(035)

Dictionaries

[2158]
HART, G. **Dictionary of taxation.** London, Butterworth, 1981. v, 236p. £16.50. (*Butterworth's professional dictionaries series*.) ISBN: 040652159x.

Defines about 900 words and phrases, including definitions from the Finance Act, 1981. Entries vary from 2 lines to 2 pages in length, and sources (*e.g.* Acts, etc.) are given. Cross-referenced. *Class No:* 336.2(410)(038)

Yearbooks & Directories

[2159]
Butterworth's UK tax guide, 1993-94. Tiley, J., *ed.* 10th ed. London, Butterworths, 1993. 1680p. £17.95. ISBN: 0406015929.

Now issued annually, soon after each year's Finance Act.

'Developed from Tiley's *Revenue law,* it is designed to be both a comprehensive tax textbook and a pointer, by means of extensive cross-referencing, to the more detailed narrative in Butterworths loose-leaf tax encyclopedia' (Preface). In 11 parts I: Introduction; II: Income tax; III: Capital gains tax; IV: Corporate tax; V: Savings; VI: Anti-avoidance; VII: The international dimension; VIII: Inheritance tax; IX: National insurance contributions; X: Stamp duty and stamp duty reserve tax; XI: Value added tax. Tables of Statutes and tables of cases are followed by a 139p. index. *Class No:* 336.2(410)(058)

Laws

[2160]
HARRISON, E.R. **A Digest and index of tax cases ...** being a judicial dictionary of the law. Garland, C.E., *ed.* 6th ed. London, HMSO, 1949-. 2v. (loose-leaf) with cumulative supplements.

Cases indexed are those reported in the official *Reports of tax cases,* 1875-, although other reports are included. V.2 is a supplementary volume, updating v.1 and cumulated by periodical addition and replacement by new sheets. Each volume has 3 sections: tables of tax cases, names of parties and subject matter. This last is arranged A-Z by subject and gives a brief account of each relevant case, plus judicial finding. *Class No:* 336.2(410)(094.1)

China

[2161]
MOSER, M.J. *and* ZEE, W.K. **China tax guide.** 2nd ed. Hong Kong, Oxford University Press, 1993. xii,316p. £35. ISBN: 0195857240.

lst published 1988.

An introduction to a complex tax system. Chapter 2 is on forms of doing business in China; Ch.3 on individual income tax; the following chapters are on various business taxes. Includes specimens of tax forms; and a listing of 'selected legislation'. *Class No:* 336.2(510)

Customs & Excise

[2162]
GREAT BRITAIN. HM Customs and Excise. **Integrated tariff of the United Kingdom.** 1993 ed. London, HMSO., 1993. 3v.(1200 leaves). £120pa including amendments. ISBN: 0117292052. ISSN: 02620421.

Earlier title was *Tariff and overseas trade classification in the United Kingdom.* Annual.

V.1 General information; v.2. Schedules of duty and trade statistical descriptions, codes and rates; v.3. Customs freight procedures. *Class No:* 336.4

Commercial Finance

Bibliographies

[2163]
LISTER, J. *and* LISTER, R.E. **Annotated bibliography of corporate finance.** London, Macmillan Press, 1979. v, 240p.

1270 annotated entries for English language works of lasting interest and directly relevant to the theory and practice of corporate financing decisions. The bibliography is preceded by a list of the 117 periodicals consulted and the classification scheme employed for arrangement. Author and subject indexes. *Class No:* 336.6(01)

[2164]
London Business School bibliography of financial markets, 1987/88. Edwards, H., *ed.* London, London Business School Library, 1989. 365p. £35. ISBN: 0902583115.

First published for 1985/86. Annual.

*c.*5000 references to books, journal articles, working papers, reports and reference works published in English. In 3 main parts: Part 1. Subject bibliography (1. Financial markets - 2. Financial intermediation - 3. Market efficiency - 4. Common stocks - 5. Portfolio investment ... 10. Corporate finance ... 13. Information technology in financial markets - 14. Reference works). All sections are subdivded. Part 2. Country bibliography (by contents, subdivided by countries, A-Z). Part 3. Author bibliography. No annotations. Appendices list journals covered and there is also a list of institutions. *Class No:* 336.6(01)

Handbooks & Manuals

[2165]
DIBBEN, M. **The Guardian money guide.** 3rd ed. London, William Collins & Sons Ltd., 1988. 256p. £5.95. ISBN: 0004104498.

First published 1984.

18 chapters: 1. Budgeting - 2. Banking - 3. Savings - 4. Borrowing - 5. Buying your home - 6. How to sell a house ... 13. Wills ... 17. Holidays - 18. The law. Useful addresses, p.248-250. Index, p.251-256. '... offers straightforward advice on all the usual financial activities ...' (*Banking world,* October 1988, p.44). *Class No:* 336.6(035)

[2166]
DOWNES, J. *and* GOODMAN, J.E. **Barron's finance and investment handbook.** Woodbury, NY., Barron's, 1986. xiv, 994p. charts, tables. $18.95. ISBN: 0812057295.

In 5 major parts: Part 1 explains 30 types of personal investment; part 2 is on how to read an annual report; part 3 is on how to read more important daily financial pages and ticker tape; part 4 has definitions of more than 2500 financial and investment terms, and includes examples and illustrations taken from financial sources; and part 5 is a directory listing some 4700 companies, A-Z. '... the best introductory handbook for public and academic libraries'. (*Reference books bulletin,* 1986/87, p.75). *Class No:* 336.6(035)

[2167]
GEISST, C.R. **A Guide to financial institutions.** London, Macmillan, 1987. 144p. tables. £27.50. ISBN: 033338623x.

Provides a description of the major types of financial institution in both the United States and the United Kingdom, showing the inter-relationship between the major types of institution beginning with international financial institutions, and continuing with commercial banking, investment banking, building associations, life insurance companies and pension funds, and American federal agencies. There is also an 11-page index. *Class No:* 336.6(035)

Yearbooks & Directories

[2168]
Macmillan directory of global financial markets. Graham, J, *and others.* London, Macmillan Press, 1989. 464p. £95. ISBN: 0333483234.

In 3 parts: 1. Introduction to global financial markets - 2. Directory guide to market participation (introduction - UK organizations - US organizations - Japanese organizations) - 3. Dictionary of terminology and techniques (UK, US and Japanese). Aim is to provide a fully integrated guide to the structural and operational dynamics of the emerging global financial markets, the participant financial organizations, the techniques of financial engineering in complex global markets, and information systems technology. Includes a bibliography and index. *Class No:* 336.6(058)

Laws

[2169]
LOMNICKA, E. *and* POWELL, J.L. **Encyclopedia of financial services law.** London, Sweet & Maxwell, 1987-. 2v. (loose-leaf). £220 (inc. service to end of 1988). ISBN: 0421368802.

V.1 contains an introductory section; full text of the Financial Services Act 1986, with annotations; Statutes related to the Act; Orders and Regulations made under the Act; full text of the SIB's rule book, including explanatory notes and a list of definitions; relevant EEC directives and selected abstracts from the SIB's annual reports. V.2 has the rules of the recognised self regulating organizations, the recognised investment exchanges, and the recognised professional bodies. Both volumes are to be updated with specialist commentary. *Class No:* 336.6(094.1)

Worldwide

[2170]

SMOLKA-DAY, M.I. **Bibliographic guide to the legal aspects of international finance.** In *International journal of legal information*, v.18(3), Winter 1990, p.205-214.

A selection of some important or representative general materials in English, the emphasis being on recent publications. General material - International monetary system - International investments - Financing international trade - Eurobonds and Eurocurrency markets.
Class No: 336.6(100)

Europe—Western

Yearbooks & Directories

[2171]

European directory of financial information sources. London, Euromonitor, 1990 (distributed in US by Omnigraphics Inc.). xiv,386p. £160. $335. ISBN: 0863383696.

In 6 sections: 1. Financial services in Europe: a new era - 2. Company information sources (Pan-Europe, then by country, A-Z) - 3. Major banking and financial information - 4. Major banking and financial trade journals - 5. Major banking and finance associations - 6. Major financial operations, by country subdivided by type of business. *Class No:* 336.6(400)(058)

[2172]

Major financial institutions of Europe, 1994. Whiteside, R.M., *ed.* 3rd ed. London, Graham & Trotman, 1993. 336p. £195. ISBN: 1853339660.

Covers 17 Western European countries. Arranged A-Z by country, subdivided A-Z by name of institution. Entries give name and address of institution; telephone, cable, telex numbers; management; principal activities; financial information; principal shareholders; trade names; and number of employees. Index. *Class No:* 336.6(400)(058)

Great Britain

Yearbooks & Directories

[2173]

Sunday telegraph **business finance directory, 1987:** the guide to sources of corporate finance in Britain. 3rd ed. London, Graham & Trotman, 1987. [5],319p. £90; $158. ISSN: 02682249.

First published 1985. Annual.

Lists sources of finance, including banks, venture capital companies, stockbrokers,licensed dealers, finance houses, leasing companies, investment trusts, etc. Indexes of institutions, A-Z, institutions by category, and a classified index. *Class No:* 336.6(410)(058)

Biographies

[2174]

Who's who in the City, 1993. Williams, L., *ed.* London, Macmillan, under licence from the International Stock Exchange of the United Kingdom and the Republic of Ireland, 1993. 800p. £95. ISBN: 0333564057.

First edition 1988.

Brief biographical profiles of over 10,000 people, mainly directors or partners, in the financial community, A-Z by name. Two indexes list companies, A-Z, with address, telephone number, telex and fax numbers, and names of senior personnel; and list companies grouped by sector. *Class No:* 336.6(410)(092)

Scotland

[2175]

DRAPER, P., *and others.* **The Scottish financial sector.** Edinburgh, Edinburgh University Press, 1988. xiv, 347p. tables. £45. (*Scottish industrial policy, series 4*.) ISBN: 0852245505.

Outlines the past, present and future development of capital markets and financial intermediation in Scotland in 12 chapters: 1. Historical and economic perspective; 2. Financial flows and employment in the financial sectors in Scotland; 3. Scottish financial markets; 4. The Scottish clearing banks; 5. Retail deposit institutions; 6. Other banking and deposit institutions; 7. Insurance funds and insurance broking; 8. Investment management; 9. Public venture capital; 10. Innovation in financial markets and institutions; 11. Summary; 12. Conclusions. Bibliography (p.337-41, 105 items, A-Z by author); Double column index (p.342-7). *Class No:* 336.6(411)

London

[2176]

McCULLOGH, V. **Pocket guide to the new City.** Oxford, Basil Blackwell and The Economist Publications, 1988. [4],121p. illus. £15. ISBN: 0631162836.

An A-Z guide to the types of people, activities, institutions and instruments which populate the 'Square Mile' [the City of London], post the Big Bang. Cross-references. Entries vary from 2 lines to half a page, and are entertaining as well as informative.
Class No: 336.6(421)

USA

Biographies

[2177]

Who's who in finance and industry, 1992-1993. 27th ed. Chicago, Ill., Marquis Who's Who, 1991. 942p. $220. ISBN: 0837903270.

First published 1936 as *Who's who in commerce and industry,* later as *World who's who in finance and industry.*

An extension of *Who's who in America.* Biographical sketches of American leading men and women in finance and industry. Profiles the top executives of America's largest corporations as well as leaders of small and medium-size firms. *Class No:* 336.6(73)(092)

Capital & Investment

Bibliographies

[2178]

WALLACE, C.D., *ed.* **Foreign direct investment and the multinational enterprise: a bibliography.** Dordrecht, Martinus Nijhoff, 1988. xi,355p. Dfl.195 $100. £59. ISBN: 9024736579.

c.3500 unannotated entries arranged in 23 subject and geographical categories, A-Z by author. Includes monographs, journal articles, some government and international agency documents, and a few newspaper articles, mainly in English. ' ... excellent bibliographic survey ... ' (*International journal of legal information,*v.17 (1), Spring 1989, p.70-71). *Class No:* 336.60(01)

Handbooks & Manuals

[2179]

CROSSAN, R. *and* JOHNSON, M. **The Guide to international capital markets, 1991.** London, Euromoney Publications plc, 1991. [6],270p. 75. ISBN: 1855640708.

An earlier ed. was issued in 1988, edited by B. de Caires.

26 chapters: 1. Introduction - 2-22, each on a country's currency (Australian dollar...US dollar), with data on growth and development of the market, market size; breakdown of investors by type; regulations affecting investment; listing, payment and delivery; secondary market activity - 23. Swaps - 24. Commercial paper - 25. Medium term notes - 26. Corporate bond defaults and default rate. *Class No:* 336.60(035)

Dictionaries

[2180]

ROSENBERG, J.M. **Dictionary of investing.** New York, John Wiley & Sons, 1993. 368p. $39.95. ISBN: 0471574333.

First published 1986 as *The Investor's dictionary*

c.8000 terms used by the securities exchange system, the commodity and futures exchange system, and the more recent development in US financial markets, are defined. Also includes commonly-used symbols, acronyms and abbreviations. Cross-references. Many words given multiple definitions based on their utilization in various fields of activity. Short definitions (c.2 to c.15 lines). '... both current and comprehensive'. (*RQ,* v.26(4), p.517) of the earlier edition. *Class No:* 336.60(038)

Great Britain

[2181]

1992 guide to grants for business. Martin, M., *comp.* Swindon, Associated Management Services, 1992. 119p. £39.50

UK government grants; grants from the EC; assistance from local government in the UK. Each type of grant treated according to a standard format - title, objective, benefits, eligibility, amount available, your costs, whom to contact: Compiler is a consultant for the DTI Enterprise Initiative (Marketing). Favourably reviewed in *Reference review,* v.6(3), 1992. *Class No:* 336.60(410)

[2182]

Government funding for United Kingdom business: a complete guide to sources, grants and application procedures. Walker, R., *and others, eds.* 8th ed. London, Kogan Page, 1993. 668p. £50. ISBN: 0749409614.

Previously published by the Centre for the Study of Public Policy, University of Strathclyde, as *Governement support for British business*

Aims to provide detailed information on the many financial assistance schemes available for business development from government departments and other public sector agencies. 8 main sections: General investment/business development - Employment and training - R & D - Exporting - Tourism and recreation - Community and social projects - Transport and freight - Agriculture, forestry and fisheries support. Information for each scheme is in 14 sections. Cross-references. Text is taken directly from the AIMS online grants information service of the European Policies Research Centre. *Class No:* 336.60(410)

Handbooks & Manuals

[2183]

Handbook of market leaders. London, Extel Financial Ltd., 1976- 2pa. *c.*750p each issue. £185pa.

A comprehensive reference book detailing 650 British companies listed in the *Financial times actuaries all share index.* Arranged A-Z by firm, with a page allocated to each. Information includes chairman, registered office, profit and loss record, ordinary share record, net asset value, cash flow, dividend, etc. *Class No:* 336.60(410)(035)

Monetary System

Dictionaries

[2184]

HUMPHREYS, N.K. Historical dictionary of the International Monetary Fund 2nd ed. Lanham, Scarecrow, 1999. 368p.,illus. $60. (*International organisations series, no. 17.*) ISBN: 0810836599.

Entries describe the economic and financial concepts used by the IMF, its operational activities, departmental structure and staffing, and its decision-making authority, including the system of weighted voting by member countries. *Class No:* 336.7(038)

Histories

[2185]

ALLEN, L. The ABC-CLIO world history companion to capitalism. ABC-Clio, 1998. 404p. 14.99. ISBN: 0874369444.

Entries cover the development of capitalism from 1450 to the present day, with emphasis on the movements and ideas that shaped capitalism rather than individuals. Entries include "see also" references and bibliographies. *Class No:* 336.7(091)

Worldwide

[2186]

FRASER, R., *comp.* **The World financial system, 1944-86;** a comprehensive reference guide. Harlow, Essex, Longman Group, Phoenix, Ariz., Oryx, 1987. xiv, 582p. £50; $95. (*A Keesing's reference publication.*) ISBN: 0582902789, UK; 089774473x, US.

A guide to the evolution of the international monetary system, including extracts from key documents and decisions of the period. Part 1 is a comprehensive historical analysis of international monetary relations from the Second World War to 1986 in 23 chapters; part 2 has information on over 50 major international or regional organizations in the monetary or financial sphere grouped into general economic organizations, monetary and development organizations, and trade associations; part 3 outlines the International Development Strategy for the Third UN Development Decade (1981-90) and the New International Economic Order together with the programme of action. Appendices include data on membership growth of the UN and IMF, and patterns of currency fluctuation, 1970-86. Select bibliography, p.565. Detailed general index, p.567-82. '... well-produced ... a concise and very comprehensive guide to the increasingly complex world monetary system' (*Reference reviews,* v.2(1), March 1988, p.9).

A 2nd ed., which claims to be fully updated, was issued in 1992 by Longman Group and by Gale International Research Co.in 1992 (600p. £95;$165. ISBNs 0582209064 (UK) & 0882096529 (US)). *Class No:* 336.7(100)

Biographies

[2187]

Who's who in international banking. 6th ed. London, Bowker-Saur, 1993. xvii,625p. £125. $225. ISBN: 1857390407.

Concise biographical information on *c.*4000 leading bankers worldwide, plus a banking directory spanning 130 territories. The biographies cover the main aspects of the entrant's personal and professional life, with special emphasis on professional career and interests. The directory includes full contact details and an index of senior executives of the banks. *Class No:* 336.7(100)(092)

Europe—Western

[2188]

Banking in the EC: structure and sources of finance. London, Financial Times Business Information, 1991. xvi,363p. tables. ISBN: 1853341428.

Arranged by country, A-Z. For each country an introduction is followed by sections on banking control and supervision; banking institutions; banking associations; organizations which mobilise and guarantee credit; financial intermediaries; the markets; financing of firms by banks; export finance; business organization; banks [in the country]. *Class No:* 336.7(400)

Great Britain

Handbooks & Manuals

[2189]

TEMPERTON, P. A Guide to UK monetary policy. London, Macmillan Press, 1986. xxiv,165p. tables, diagrs., figs. £35. ISBN: 0333392084.

Aims to be the definitive guide to the current analysis and operation of monetary policy in the UK. A glossary of terms precedes the 9 chapters (Background to the introduction of monetary targets in the UK - Monetary targets in the UK - Analysing broad money - Analysing narrow money - Setting short term interest rates: the policy process - Setting short term interest rates in the money market - Funding the PSBR and monetary growth - The gilt edged market - Conclusion). Two appendices: 1. Official interest rates, 1932 to 1985; 2. Monetary policy measures, 1970 to 1985. Index, p.159-165. *Class No:* 336.7(410)(035)

Histories

[2190]

CAPIE, F. *and* **WEBBER, A. A Monetary history of the United Kingdom, 1870-1982.** Vol.1: Data, sources, methods. London, Allen & Unwin, 1985. xxiv,596p. tables. £40. ISBN: 004332097x.

Research project undertaken by the Centre for Banking and International Finance, City University, for The Economic and Social Research Council. Vol.2 will provide analyses.

In 3 parts: 1. Monetary aggregates and proximate determinants - 2. Components of the monetary aggregates and monetary measures - 3. Money and banking data series. 4 appendices. Bibliography, p.580-588. Index, p.589-596. '... provides all the sources of the primary data and outlines in painstaking detail the methodology and the transformations employed' (*Economic history review,* August 1986, p.475-6. *Class No:* 336.7(410)(091)

Banking

Bibliographies

[2191]

BURGESS, N. How to find out about banking and investment. Oxford, Pergamon Press, 1969. xii, 300p. facsims. £7.00. ISBN: 0080130453.

27 chapters; 1. Careers - 2. Dictionaries and encyclopedias - 3. Libraries and guides to libraries - 4. Bibliographies and literature guides - 5. Periodical literature - 6/27 (subject chapters, using the Dewey classification). Appendices: 1. Proceedings of the International Banking Summer School - 2. Societies and institutions. The detailed index (p.287-300) includes author/title entries. British slanted. *Class No:* 336.71(01)

[2192]

WELCH, J.M. Free bank letters as sources of economic and financial information. In *Journal of business and finance librarianship,* v.1(2), 1990. p,5-17.

Includes an appendix 'List of bank letters by country'. U.S., then by country, A-Z, with name of bank and title of newsletter only. *Class No:* 336.71(01)

[2193]

WILSON, C.R. **The World Bank Group:** a guide to information sources. New York, Garland, 1991. xviii,322p. $45. ISBN: 0824044290.

A bibliography citing books, articles, pamphlets, reports and dissertations by and about the International Bank for Reconstruction and Development, the International Development Association, and the International Finance Corporation of the World Bank Group. Over 1000 entries for items published or translated into English (mainly US sources) from 1944 through 1988 or later. Annotated. Cross-references. Indexes of names, divisions/affiliates, subjects and titles. *Class No:* 336.71(01)

Dictionaries

[2194]

Banking · terminology. 3rd ed. Washington, American Bankers Association, 1989. 409p. $34. ISBN: 0899823602.

Concise definitions (1-5 sentences in length) of terms and concepts used in banking. Cross-references. 5 appemdices includes a list of acronyms and abbreviations, bank performance ratios, and a glossary of economic indicators. '... does a good job defining some of the more popular terms and concepts used in banking ...' (*Booklist*, v.86(15), 1 April 1990, p.1573). *Class No:* 336.71(038)

[2195]

COLLIN, P.H. **Dictionary of banking and finance.** London, Peter Collin Publishing, 1991. [v],260,[17]p. £6.95 ISBN: 0948549122.

Vocabulary of *c.*4000 words and expressions covering a range of topics relating to personal and corporate finance. Quotes for examples are given in boxes. British and American usage. *Class No:* 336.71(038)

Polyglot

[2196]

RICCI, J. **Elsevier's banking dictionary:** English/American, French, Italian, Spanish, Portuguese, Dutch and German. 3rd rev & enl. ed. Amsterdam, Elsevier, 1990. x, 360p. £85. ISBN: 0444886674.

2765 numbered entries in English/American, with equivalents and indexes in the other 6 languages. Includes phrases such as 'Mutilated cheque' and 'Token payment'. *Class No:* 336.71(038)=00

[2197]

SCHARF, T. *and* SHETTY, M.C. **Dictionary of development banking:** a compilation of terms in English, French and German, with definitions in English. Amsterdam, Elsevier, 1972. vii, 214p. £66.18. ISBN: 0444410287.

First published in 1969.

Over 1,200 terms arranged in 3 broad sections: the environmental framework - development banking - development banks. Each section subdivided. Indexes in each of the 3 languages. *Class No:* 336.71(038)=00

English

[2198]

HANSON, D.G. **Dictionary of banking and finance:** a commentary on banking, financial services and corporate and personal finance. London, Pitman Publishing, 1985. x,691p. £39.95. ISBN: 0273018590.

Successor to *Thomson's dictionary of banking* (12th ed. 1974), first published in 1912.

Provides comprehensive coverage of the whole range of financial activities, both corporate and personal. Many cross-references. *Class No:* 336.71(038)=20

[2199]

PERRY, F.E. **Dictionary of banking.** 4th ed. revised by G. Klein. London, Pitman Publishing, in association with The Chartered Institute of Bankers, 1992. 368p. £14.95. ISBN: 0273037889.

First published 1977, by Macdonald & Evans.

A comprehensive dictionary of *c.*7000 words and expressions, including jargon, a wide selection of French and German terms, and many cross-references. Fully updated, and directed towards bankers in any position, with particular emphasis on British bankers serving abroad in one or other countries of the European Community. *Class No:* 336.71(038)=20

German

[2200]

FELDBAUSCH, F.K. **Bankwörterbuch/Banking dictionary.** Deutsch-Englisch, Englisch-Deutsch. 3rd ed. München, Verlag Modern Industrie, 1984. 400p. £27.90. $85. ISBN: 3478512409.

First published 1972.

About 10,000 terms in each part, German-English and English-

....(contd.)

German. Terms are those used in the US, Britain, Germany, Austria and German-speaking Switzerland. Country origin of terms is shown. *Class No:* 336.71(038)=30

[2201]

ZAHN, H.L. **Wörterbuch für das Bank- und Börsenwesen. Deutsch-Englisch, Englisch-Deutsch. Dictionary of banking and stock trading.** 3rd ed. Frankfurt am Main, F. Knapp; London. Pitman, 1984. viii,440p. New ed. in preparation, 1994. ISBN: 3781920224, German; 071215471x, UK.

First published 1982.

Contains *c.*11,000 terms in current use and practice. Primary sources were documentation used by banks, financial dailies and reports of international lending activities. A specialist dictionary, economic terms outside the field of banking and stock trading being omitted. Short explanations of terms given as necessary. Designed to meet the needs of bankers and translators. *Class No:* 336.71(038)=30

[2202]

—KLAUS, H., *ed.* Banking dictionary: English-German. 7th rev. ed. Bern, P. Haupt: London, Macdonald & Evans, 1990. 220p. £16.95. *Class No:* 336.71(038)=30

French

[2203]

KLAUS, H., *ed.* Banking dictionary: English-French/French-English. Association Suisse du Employés de Banque. Bern, P. Haupt, 1987. 264p. £20.50. ISBN: 3258033404. *Class No:* 336.71(038)=40

Reviews & Abstracts

[2204]

World banking abstracts, 1984-. Oxford, Blackwell, for the Institute of European Finance, 1984-. 6 pa. £250 pa. ISSN: 02659484.

over 400 current banking finance magazines and journals, plus research reports and studies, are reviewed for each issue. Sections, each subdivided, are: Institutions - Instruments and markets - Operations and services - Management, accounting and technology - Policy, law and regulations- International and national economics - Principles and methods. There is a list of periodicals and an index. *Class No:* 336.71(048)

Yearbooks & Directories

[2205]

The Bankers' almanac and year book ... 1993. 148th year. East Grinstead, London, Reed Information Services, 1993. Annual. 3v. ISBN: 0611008149.

V.1 & 2 is a directory of some 4000 major international banks and their 165,000 branches worldwide arranged A-Z (name, address, telephone/telex/fax numbers, history, ownership, president, managing director, head of international division, correspondents, consolidated balance sheet, meetings (dates), wholly-owned subsidiaries), etc. V.3 has a geographical listing of those banks and their branches. Also an index of banks in the Almanac for the first time and those which have merged or changed name since the last edition. *Class No:* 336.71(058)

[2206]

Directory of European banking and financial associations. Molyneux, P., *comp.* Cambridge, Woodhead-Faulkner; Chicago, St. James Press, 1990. xxi,217p. $65. ISBN: 0859416534, UK; 155862077x, US.

Details of the financial infrastructure of 20 European countries. Introduction: Trends and developments in European banking. Part 1: Europe - general; pt.2: Europe by country (Austria ... West Germany). Each section subdivided - banking; capital markets; insurance; other associations and organizations. Appendix of late entries. Index of offices, p.203-6. Index of organizations, p.207-14. Index of publications, p.215-7. *Class No:* 336.71(058)

[2207]

Who owns what in world banking. Power, E., *ed.* 3rd ed. London, Financial times business information, 1993. x,180p. ISBN: 1853342017.

First published in 1983.

A directory of the world's major banks, their subsidiaries and affiliates and, in the case of consortia, their shareholder banks. Information on each includes name, address, description, financial summary, subsidiaries and associate companies, etc., and foreign offices. No introduction. Index of banks, p.143-180. *Class No:* 336.71(058)

Almanacs

[2208]

Banker's almanac 3000 world ranking, 1994. 11th ed. East Grinstead, Sussex, Reed Information Services, 1993. £121. ISBN: 0611008076.

First published 1985. Annual.

A list of main exchange rates used precedes the 3 main sections, each section on a different coloured paper. On yellow paper is an A-Z index of 3400 banks. On white paper, the country rankings of 160 individual countries, A-Z by country, with information on current and previous rank, name of bank, location of registered office, total assets in US dollars, indication where figures consolidated, growth in assets from previous year, capital in US dollars, date of balance sheet. On green paper, world rankings, rankings by assets of *c*.3100 international banks with similar information to the above. *Class No:* 336.71(059)

Histories

Bibliographies

[2209]

VAN DILLEN, J.G. History of the principal public banks. London. Frank Cass, 1934 (reprinted 1964). xii, 480 p. £28. ISBN: 0714612553.

Includes extensive bibliographies of the history of banking and credit in 11 European countries (p.355-480). Also 'Modern bibliography of banking and currency (British Empire) from the XVth century to 1815', compiled under the direction of J. H. Clapham (p.449-56). *Class No:* 336.71(091)(01)

Laws

[2210]

Paget's law of banking. Megrah, M. *and* Ryder, F.R., *eds.* 9th rev. ed. London, Butterworths, 1982. lxxv,678p. £60. ISBN: 0406333521.

26 sections arranged in 4 parts: I: Banker & customer; II: Cheques and other orders for payment; III: Security for advances; IV: Commercial credits: international banking. Appendices : Uniform customs and practice for documentary credits; The Cheque Act, 1957. Detailed subject index, p.607-678. *Class No:* 336.71(094.1)

Great Britain

Histories

[2211]

GRADY, J. *and* WEALE, M. British banking, 1960-85. London, Macmillan, 1986. vii, 232p. tables. £29.50. ISBN: 0333375084.

Describes the evolution of the banking system since 1960 in 9 chapters: 1. An overview of the economy - 2. Risk and financial institutions - 3. Bank of England control and supervision - 4. The traditional banking system - 5. The accepting houses - 6. The new money markets - 7. The other British non-clearing banks - 8. International problems - 9. Conclusions. Notes and references to the chapters, p.207-211. Glossary, p.213-5. Bibliography of 162 items and 21 statistical sources. Index. *Class No:* 336.71(410)(091)

Archives

[2212]

PRESSNELL, L.S. *and* ORBELL, J., *and others*. A Guide to the historical records of British banking. Aldershot, Hants., Gower Publishing Ltd., 1985. xxv,1300p. £25. ISBN: 0566035421.

Describes the surviving records of over 600 operating or defunct banks in England, Scotland and Wales. A section on the use of the guide (Archive resources of the British banking community - Functions and structure of British banking - Use of historical records of banks) precedes the A-Z list of records, which gives the name of the bank, location, history, records and records location. Information relates to 639 banks. Select bibliography, p.118-122, arranged A-Z by author. Index to lists of records, p.123-130.
Class No: 336.71(410)(091)(093.20)

Germany

[2213]

MARSH, D. The Bundesbank: the bank that rules Europe. London, Heinemann, 1992. 359p. £18.99. ISBN: 0434451169.

A detailed account of the nature and role of the organization, together with an examination of the political and economic changes, including German unification. *Class No:* 336.71(430)

Bank of England

Histories

[2214]

CLAPHAM, J. The Bank of England: a history. Cambridge, Cambridge University Press, 1944 (reprinted 1958). 2v. (x, 305p.; [4], 460p.).

V.1, 1694-1797; v.2, 1797-1914, with an *Epilogue: The Bank as it is*, which takes the history to immediately before the Second World War. Written at the invitation of the authorities, treatment is chronological, tracing in detail the growth of bank practices (the use of bills and discounts, the insurance of currency, establishment of the reserve rates, use of cheques) and also records the role of the Bank in relation to contemporary political and economic happenings. Numerous footnotes. V.1 has 8 chapters and 6 appendices (F: The books of the Bank, to end of eighteenth century). V.2 also has 8 chapters and 6 appendices, mainly financial tables. Also an analytical index to both volumes, p.443-460. *Class No:* 336.711(091)

[2215]

—**ACRES, W.M. The Bank of England from within, 1694-1900.** London, printed for the Governor and Company of the Bank of England by Oxford University Press, 1931. 2v.

Deals more with internal and staff matters than does Clapham. V.2 includes a list of directors of the Bank, and of principal officials, 1694-1900, plus a 'List of the principal banks, pamphlets, etc. referred to in the text' (p.633-40). General, analytical index also in v.2. Numerous footnote references are listed in v.1, p.xv-xvi. *Class No:* 336.711(091)

[2216]

SAYERS, R.S. The Bank of England, 1891-1944. Cambridge, Cambridge University Press, 1976. 3v. (409, 313, 411p.). New ed. in 1v. (1986. 680p. £30. ISBN 0521310229). ISBN: 0521214750.

A history of the Bank. V.1 and 2 have 22 chapters arranged chronologically, followed by a list of publications cited in the text (p.655-659) and an analytical index. V.3 contains 42 appendices relating to the text of v.1 and 2, the final ones being a list of governors and other officers of the bank, a chronological list of events with chapter references, a list of committees, and references to unpublished sources. '... this most stimulating and enjoyable contribution to monetary (and economic) history by the doyen of monetary historians' (*The Economic journal*, v.,87, March 1977, p.145). *Class No:* 336.711(091)

Savings Banks

[2217]

HORNE, H.O. A History of savings banks. London, Oxford University Press, 1947. xv, 407p. ports., maps. *Class No:* 336.72

Building Societies

[2218]

Building societies year book: official handbook of the Building Societies Association, with Council of Mortgage Lenders yearbook. 1993-94 ed. London, Franey & Co Ltd., 1927-. Annual. 848p. £58. ISBN: 0900382694. ISSN: 00683566.

Data on each building society include names of directors and abridged balance sheet. Geographical list of building society offices. List of members of the Building Societies Association and Building Societies Institute. Geographical directory of surveyors, valuers, auctioneers, estate agents. *Class No:* 336.732

[2219]

NORKETT, P. The Building societies facts file. Harlow, Essex, Longman Group Ltd., in conjunction with Tekron Publications Ltd., 1987. [4], 232p. £100. ISBN: 0582022363.

Designed to give a complete overview of the financial performance of all building societies in the United Kingdom. Arranged in three categories: large (total assets over £250m), medium (£25m-£250m), and small (under £25m). The societies are ranked according to total assets, and there is a financial data sheet for each, giving annual results for 5 years to 1986 in a standard format for easy comparison, and percentage analyses of income, expenditure and balance sheet items. An appendix lists all societies, A-Z. *Class No:* 336.732

Money (Currency)

[2220]

DUNKLING, L. *and* ROOM, A. The Guinness book of money. New York, Facts on File, 1990. 191p. 24 illus. $19.95. ISBN: 0816025207.

Aimed at those only averagely versed in business and finance, a compilation of facts and literary quotations about money. Mini-

....(contd.)

glossaries define monetary slang throughout the ages. 2 indexes: quotations and references - subjects. 'A good addition to a reference collection' (*RQ*, v.31(1), Fall 1991). *Class No:* 336.74

[2221]
WESTON, R. Gold: a world survey. Beckenham, Kent, Croom Helm, 1983. ix,406p. charts, tables. £40. ISBN: 0709902026, UK; 0312331584, Australia.

6 parts: 1. The role of gold in the international monetary system, 1960-1980 - 2. The demand for gold, its forms and uses - 3/4. The supply of gold - 5. Spot and future market for gold - 6. How the price of gold is determined. Index. 'This book will be of great benefit to the specialist student of international economics. At the same time it is highly recommended for professional and financial analysts and advisers' (*British book news*, March 1984, p.169). *Class No:* 336.74

Bibliographies

[2222]
The International Monetary Fund. Salda, A.C.M., *comp.* Oxford, Clio Press, 1992. xxxviii,295p. £41. (*(International organizations,4)*.) ISBN: 1851091491.

A bibliography of books and articles, mostly in English. Indexes of authors, titles and subjects. *Class No:* 336.74(01)

[2223]
—JOHNSON, M.E. The International Monetary Fund, 1944-1992: a research guide. New York, Garland, 1993. 486p. $73. (*(Research and information guides in business, industry and economic institutions, 9)*.) ISBN: 0815302304.

An annotated bibliography of English-language monographs and articles. *Class No:* 336.74(01)

Handbooks & Manuals

[2224]
EDWARDS, A.D.P. The Exporter's and importer's handbook on foreign currencies. London, Macmillan, 1990. 192p. £40. ISBN: 0333534190.

22 chapters, including: A background to foreign exchange - The Eurocurrency market ... Selling and buying currencies ... What is a forward rate? ... Currency options - Financial futures ... The Treasury function ... Buying from UK importing agents - Conclusion. Glossary. *Class No:* 336.74(035)

[2225]
SUTTON, W. The Currency options handbook. Cambridge, Woodhead-Faulkner, 1988. [5], 208p. £45. ISBN: 0859413233.

Describes how options are traded and discusses their uses. Part 1. Inside currency options; part 2. Hedging foreign exchange risk using currency options; part 3. Currency option trading strategies; part 4. Conclusion. Glossary of terms. Bibliography (21 items). Index (p.207-8). Author is in charge of foreign currency options trading in London for Merrill Lynch.

A 2nd ed. was issued in 1990 (224p. £65. ISBN 0859416658). *Class No:* 336.74(035)

Dictionaries

[2226]
EATWELL, J., *and others, eds.* Money. London, Macmillan Press, 1989. 352p. £17.50. ISBN: 0333495268.

A series of reprints from *The New Palgrave: a dictionary of economics* (qv), gathering together 42 essay-length contributions on the subject of money. *Class No:* 336.74(038)

Yearbooks & Directories

[2227]
COWITT, P.P., *ed.* World currency yearbook. 24th ed. Brooklyn, NY., International Currency Analysis Inc., 1985. 974p. illus., tables. $225. ISBN: 0917645015.

Continues *Pick's currency yearbook,* published from 1955 to the 22nd ed. 1977-1978 (1979).

Descriptions of 145 major currencies, under countries, A-Z, preceded by a monetary glossary (p.10-13), 9 essays on currencies and a supplementary currency list. Also includes an essay on the Eurocurrency Market, and a central bank directory. Index (p.967-74) is of countries and currencies.

A 26th ed. for 1988/1989 was issued in 1991 (900p. $250. ISBN 0917645030). *Class No:* 336.74(058)

[2228]
—PICK, F. *and* SÉDILLOT, R. All the monies of the world: a chronicle of currency values. New York, Pick Publishing Corporation, 1971. xviii,, 613p.

Original ed. as *Toutes les monnaies du monde. Dictionnaire des changes,* by R. Sédillot (Paris, Sirey, 1955. 555p.). Translated by Carol J. Golden.

About 1500 concise entries, arranged A-Z under countries and currencies, with definitions and historical accounts of monetary systems. Cross-references. Bibliography, p.612-3. *Class No:* 336.74(058)

Histories

[2229]
A New history of the Royal Mint. Challis, C.E., *ed.* Cambridge, Cambridge University Press, 1992. 816p. illus. 92 tables. 79 maps. £95. ISBN: 0521240263.

The development of English minting from its origins in the 7th century down to the highly mechanised factory production of today. 5 chapters on the location of minting, the chronology and size of output, mint personnel and organization, and the main technology employed. 2 appendices: Output from 1200 to 1985; Mint contracts for 1279-1817. Select bibliography. *Class No:* 336.74(091)

[2230]
VILAR, P. A History of gold and money, 1450-1920. London, Verso Editions, 1984. 360p. 5 maps. £6.95. ISBN: 0860917983.

First English ed. 1976. Translated from the Spanish by J. White.

36 chapters, chronologically arranged, giving a comprehensive account of the role of bullion and currency since the beginning of the early modern epoch. A survey of the role of gold in its various forms of currency used in the ancient world and middle ages precedes an analysis of the gold and silver drive behind the voyages of discovery to Africa, America and Asia. Then traces banking and financial institutions. *Class No:* 336.74(091)

Bank Notes (Paper Money)

Great Britain

[2231]
MACKENZIE, A.D. The Bank of England note: a history of its printing. London, Cambridge University Press, 1953. x,163p. illus.

Covers the history of English banknote production up to the Second World War. More recently, *The search for the inimitable note,* by Clive Goodacre (*Penrose,* v.74, 1982, p.8-82) is an article on the subject profusely illustrated in colour. Whilst the classic work on the history of English coinage and paper money is A.E. Feavearyear's *The pound sterling: a history of English money* (2nd ed. rev. by E.V. Morgan. London, Oxford University Press, 1963, 458p.). *Class No:* 336.747(410)

Exchange Rates

[2232]
FLIGHT, H. *and* LEE-SWAN, B. All you need to know about exchange rates. London, Sidgewick & Jackson, 1988. 208p. £14.95. ISBN: 0283996269.

Aims to set out, for the layman, the intricacies of how the international monetary system functions. 17 chapters (Dispelling exchange rate myths - Setting the scene - Appraising currency movement - The balance of payments - The role of the Euromarkets ... Currency hedging instruments - Exchange rates and equity investment ... Man-made currencies ... Exchange-rate systems - The future outlook). Glossary, p.195-203. Analytical index, p.205-208. *Class No:* 336.748

Stock Markets & Exchanges

[2233]
The Money book: sources of finance and business information for businesses - from start-up to conglomerates. London, Mercury, 1993. 192p. £25. ISBN: 1852521120.

Aimed at professionals and lay people involved in raising money for new, emergent and established businesses. *Class No:* 336.76

ECONOMICS

Abbreviations & Symbols

[2234]
ROSENBERG, J.M. McGraw-Hill dictionary of Wall Street acronyms, initials, and abbreviations. New York, McGraw-Hill, 1992. 235p. $24.95. ISBN: 0070539340.

Over 10,000 entries for terms relevant to the stock and commodity markets. Overlaps with the *McGraw-Hill dictionary of business acronyms, initials, and abbreviations* (q.v.). *Class No:* 336.76(003)

Encyclopaedias

[2235]
SHEIMO, S., *et al., eds.* International encyclopedia of the stock market. Chicago, Fitzroy Dearborn, 1999. 2v. (1320p.),illus. $275. ISBN: 1884964354.

Includes index, appendicies, bibliography.

Defines over 2,000 terms relating to regional and world stock market practice. Describes economics of countries, and has entries also on individuals and institutions. There are historical entires which cover, for example, banking in ancient Egypt and Greece. Many entries have valuable directory information - including trading hours, contact names and addresses. *Class No:* 336.76(031)

Handbooks & Manuals

[2236]
GEISST, C.R. A Guide to the financial markets. 2nd ed. London, Macmillan Press, 1989. vi,164p. tables. £29.50. ISBN: 033348990x.

First published 1982.

Written from the investor's point of view, the guide discusses the 6 major financial markets - stock markets - money markets - bond markets - commodity future markets - options markets - new financial markets. Each chapter commences with basic definitions and ends with current problems. Notes follow each chapter. Index.
Class No: 336.76(035)

[2237]
The Handbook of world stock and commodity exchanges. Oxford, Blackwell, 1993. Annual. [18],585p. 250. ISBN: 0631188886.

In 2 parts: Part 1 has 27 short essays. Pt.2 has market indices - International security market - then by country A-Z (Argentina ... Yugoslavia), with data on exchanges, including address, principal officers, brief history, structure, official trading hours, number of securities listed, securities traded, trading system, selling and clearing, commission rates and other client costs, taxation and regulations affecting foreign investors. Abbreviations and acronyms. Glossary. Indexes of personnel, contracts, exchanges, trading systems, and information vendors. *Class No:* 336.76(035)

Dictionaries

Polyglot

[2238]
THOLE, B.L.L.M., *comp.* Elsevier's lexicon of stock-market terms. English/American-French-German-Dutch. Amsterdam, Elsevier, 1965. [viii], 131p.

c. 1000 numbered English/American specialised terms relating to investment, bonds, shares and other securities, payments, coupons, dividends and conversions, etc., with equivalents and indexes in French, German and Dutch. Includes phrases *e.g.* 'Raise a dividend', 'General meeting of shareholders'), and states genders. Critically reviewed in *Lebende Sprachen* (v.14(2), March/April 1969,p.59) for omissions and mistranslations *Class No:* 336.76(038)=00

[2239]
VALENTINE, S. International dictionary of the securities industry. 2nd ed. London, Macmillan Press, 1989. 300p. £45; $49.95. ISBN: 0333449738.

First published 1985.

Defines c.2000 terms and phrases used on the stock exchanges in North America, Great Britain, Netherlands, Japan, Italy, France, Germany and the Spanish-speaking world. Cross-references. Some single-item bibliographies. Revised and expanded principally because of the restructuring of the London stock market following the deregulation of The Stock Exchange, but the coverage of terms used in the other countries has also been revised and expanded. The author is Economic Adviser to The Stock Exchange.
Class No: 336.76(038)=00

Yearbooks & Directories

[2240]
BATTLEY, N. McGraw-Hill world futures and options directory, 1991-92. Maidenhead, Berks, McGraw-Hill, 1991. 663p. £65. $95. ISBN: 0077073436.

8 sections: A. Exchanges - B. Agricultural contracts - C. Financial contracts - D. Metal contracts - E. Petroleum/gas-engineering contracts - F. Stock index and equity contracts - G. Miscellaneous contracts - H. Membership listings. Each section starts with a listing of contracts. '... well-produced ... providing clearly laid out information in a standardized format.'(*Reference reviews*, v.5(2), 1991, p.14).
Class No: 336.76(058)

[2241]
Directory of world stock exchanges. Bootle, R., *ed.* Baltimore, MD., Johns Hopkins University Press; Cambridge, Woodhead-Faulkner Ltd., for The Economist, 1988. [6],469p. $89.50. ISBN: 0801837170, US; 085058275x, UK.

Data collected by questionnaire from 45 countries, is geared to professionals engaged in international trading. Entries include addresses of the stock exchanges; telephone/telex/cable/fax numbers; information on trading hours; the organization; type of securities traded; regulatory and tax regimes; lists of publications; historical background; and statistics of trading volume. *Class No:* 336.76(058)

[2242]
FITZGERALD, M.D. Directory of financial futures exchanges. London, Macmillan, 1987; New York, Stockton Press, 1988. xxv, 251p. £90; $180. ISBN: 0333390806 UK;; 0935859039 USA.

Intended to be a comprehensive directory of financial futures and options exchanges worldwide. Three introductory chapters explain the basic features of the financial futures market, followed by a directory section divided into exchanges, listing the types of contracts traded, and giving details of the members. There is a short bibliography of important books and articles, and a glossary of terms.
Class No: 336.76(058)

[2243]
Handbook of world commodity and stock exchanges. Oxford, Blackwell, 1991. 482p. £225; $245. ISBN: 0631179313.

Part 1 has 31 brief essays dealing with the history and present concerns of various exchanges. Pt.2 is the directory of stock, equity, commodities, futures and option exchanges in 50 countries. Each is arranged by country, then name. Entries include address, telephone number, principal officers, brief history, structure, official hours, etc. A glossary defines unfamiliar terms. Commodity index.
Class No: 336.76(058)

[2244]
The International Stock Exchange official yearbook, 1934-. 1993-1994 ed. London, Macmillan; New York, Stockton Press, 1993. lxiii, 958p. ISBN: 0333586980, UK; 156159105x, US. ISSN: 09536329.

Published by Skinner, 1934-1980; Macmillan, under licence from the International Stock Exchange of the United Kingdom and the Republic of Ireland 1981-. Annual. Title was *The Stock Exchange official yearbook* until 1987.

Contains details of all officially listed securities, fully indexed. Main sections are: The securities market in the UK; Overseas stock exchanges; Companies and public corporations in alphabetical order; List of companies in administration; List of companies in receivership; List of companies in liquidation; Register of defunct and other companies. Index (p.943-958). *Class No:* 336.76(058)

[2245]
—Register of defunct companies. London, Macmillan Press, in association with the London International Stock Exchange, 1990. 320p. £65. ISBN: 0333515293.

Lists companies removed from the London International Stock Exchange yearbook and its predecessors. *Class No:* 336.76(058)

[2246]
The Spicer and Oppenheim guide to securities markets around the world. Oliver, P.J. *and* Press, J., *eds.* New York, Wiley, 1988. vii,248p. $19.95. £17.50. ISBN: 0471612898.

First published 1986.

Focuses on 26 of the most important securities markets in the world, arranged A-Z (Australia ... United States of America), each with sections on stock exchanges - overview of bond and equity markets - futures and options trading - regulations affecting new entrants to the markets - outline of tax considerations - prospective developments. Also an actuaries world index; pound sterling index; securities markets around the world - a quick comparison; and international securities industry contact partners (names; addresses; telephone, telex and fax data). *Class No:* 336.76(058)

172

EIGHTH EDITION

Worldwide

Handbooks & Manuals

[2247]

World stock exchange fact book historical securities data for the international investor. Morris Plains, New Jersey, Electronic Commerce Inc., 1996 509p. +3.5" diskette (IBM-PC) $390.00 ISBN: 0964893002.

Arranged by country with statistics from 47 stock exchanges. Latest data for late 1995. Annual statistics generally include trading volume, investment capitalization, price/earnings ratio, total yield, and economic indicators for the particular country. There is an accompanying floppy disk containing the data, and annual updates are planned. *Class No:* 336.76(100)(035)

Yearbooks & Directories

[2248]

World directory of stock exchanges Volume 1$bWorld review of stock exchanges 1992/93. Garneau, M., *comp.* 3rd ed. Montreal, Canada, W.I.S.E.R Research, 1992 565p. Canadian $195.00 ISBN: 0969492839, CA. ISSN: 11818573, CA.

Contains subject index on pp. 387-390.

Offers basic fundemental and technical details of the securities industry around the world. Contains - 1. An alphabetical list of stock exchanges arranged by country - 2. Share trading values - 3. Market value of equity shares - 4. Debt securities - 5. Investment ratios - 6. Major stock indexes - 7. International stock index analysis - 8. Other stock exchanges. *Class No:* 336.76(100)(058)

Europe

Handbooks & Manuals

[2249]

STONHAM, P. Major stock markets of Europe. Aldershot, Hants, Gower Publishing Company, 1982. xv, 244p. diagr., tables. £40.50. ISBN: 0566003791.

Aims to assess the scale, importance and efficiency of six major European stock markets - Belgium, France, Germany, Italy, Netherlands and the United Kingdom. Presents information for each country on company financing; central government and local authority financing; structure and practice of stock exchange; performance and efficiency of stock market; new legislation and stock market reform; other prescriptions for stock market reform; and fiscal, company and savings/investment incentives. A summary is followed by notes and references. *Class No:* 336.76(4)(035)

Great Britain

[2250]

Studies in capital formation in the United Kingdom, 1750-1920. Feinstein, C. *and* Pollard, S., *ed.* Cambridge, Clarendon Press: C.U.P., 1988. £48. ISBN: 019828408x.

A comprehensive and highly specialized collection of essays. This study 'supplies the first comprehensive set of national estimates of capital formation and capital stocks from the Industrial Revolution to the First World War.'(*British book news*, March 1991, p.154). *Class No:* 336.76(410)

Tables & Data Books

[2251]

The Stock Exchange daily official list. London, Extel Financial Ltd., on behalf of the Council of the London Stock Exchange, 1843-. Daily.

Cites the quotations for securities, plus data on business actually transacted. Government, then commercial and industrial companies arranged in broad groups under various subject headings. The *List* is a complete and official record of price movements from day to day. Important not only in investment activities but also as the accepted basis for estate duty, probate valuations and investment holding-values in balance sheets. *Class No:* 336.76(410)(083)

[2252]

—Weekly official intelligence. London, Extel Financial Ltd. on behalf of the Council of the London Stock Exchange, 1882-. £186 per half-year.

Until recently titled 'Stock Exchange weekly official intelligence'.

Contains the official notices of the Council and various data, including dividends, meetings, new issues, etc. *Class No:* 336.76(410)(083)

Eire

[2253]

THOMAS, W.A. The Stock exchanges of Ireland. Liverpool, Francis Cairns, 1986. [8],273p. 9 illus. plus 8 black & white plates. £30. (*Studies in financial and economic history, v.1.*) ISBN: 0905205340.

The history of the Irish stock exchanges in 12 chapters, beginning in the late 18th century and reaching, in chapter 11, the unificiation of British and Irish exchanges in 1973 and the 'Big Bang' in 1986. Chapter 12 is on the Belfast Stock Exchange. Appendices have information about public loans raised in Ireland, limited company registrations, turnover on the exchanges, etc. Sources used include offical reports, business archives, the *Journal of the House of Commons,* etc. *Class No:* 336.76(417)

Investment

[2254]

CHAPMAN, K. Investment statistics locator. Phoenix, Ariz., Oryx Press, 1988. 182p. $45.00. ISBN: 0897743679.

An annotated list of 22 basic sources of statistics about stocks, bonds, and other investment vehicles, describing their characteristics and offering hints for efficient use. Detailed A-Z index lists topics and identifies sources that publish statistics on those topics. There is also a list of title abbreviations used in the index. US slanted. A welcome update of James Woy's *Investment information: a detailed guide to selected sources* (Gale, 1970). '... important for effective retrieval of financial statistics'. (*Wilson library bulletin,* May, 1988, p.111). *Class No:* 336.767

[2255]

MASEY, A. Financial times guide: investment trusts. London, Financial Times Business Information, 1988. [6],195p. £8.95. ISBN: 1853340189.

21 chapters (1. Introduction to investment trusts - 2. What is an investment trust? ... 4. How investment trusts work - 5. Investment trusts versus unit trusts ... 13. How to choose investment trusts ... 16. Reading the charts and ratios - 17. How to read the reports and accounts ... 21. The future. 5 appendices, mainly statistical plus a directory of management companies. Glossary, p.178-185. Index, p.187-195. *Class No:* 336.767

[2256]

STOPP, C. Financial times guides: unit trusts. London, Financial Times Business Information, 1988. [7],176p. £8.95. ISBN: 1853340170.

10 chapters (Why should you buy unit trusts? - What are you buying - Looking at performance - How to choose a unit trust - Unit trusts for income - How to deal in units - Getting advice - Getting technical: pricing, distribution, and tax - Unit trusts or insurance bonds - The future for unit trusts). Appendices: 1. Guide to the groups; 2. Guide to the stock markets. Glossary, p.159-167. Index, p.169-176. *Class No:* 336.767

[2257]

WILLIAMSON, G.K. The Longman investment companion: a comparative guide to market performance. Harlow, Essex, Longman, 1990. vi,162p. 71 illus. £20.50. ISBN: 0884628329.

7 topical chapters on bonds, currencies, interest rates, market indicators, mutual funds, stocks, and tangibles. Each entry describes the investment vehicle (over 70 in all), plus 20-year and year-by-year performance tables. *Class No:* 336.767

Dictionaries

[2258]

HILDRETH, S.S. The A to Z of Wall Street: 2500 terms for the street smart investor. Harlow, Essex, Longman Group Ltd., 1988. 299p. tables, charts. $13.95; £9.95. ISBN: 088462711x.

2500 investment terms defined in non-technical language. Overlaps considerably with *Words of Wall Street* and *More words of Wall Street.* 'Main problem involves the precision and fullness of its definitions' (*Reference books bulletin,* 1 March 1988, p.1101). *Class No:* 336.767(038)

[2259]

SCOTT, D.L. Wall Street words. Houghton Mifflin, 1988. xi,404p. $18.95. ISBN: 0395437474.

Defines 3600 investment terms encountered in US financial journals and newsletters. Definitions are in non-technical language. Includes a brief annotated bibliography of outstanding books on the investment field. *Library journal* (15 February 1988, p.160) prefers *Barron's finance & investment handbook (q.v.). Class No:* 336.767(038)

[2260]

—PESSIN, A.H. *and* ROSS, J.A. More words of Wall Street: 2000 investment terms defined. New York, Dow-Jones-Irwin, 1986. v,269p. $35. ISBN: 087094701x.

Companion volume to *Words of Wall Street,* defining terms in lay language. Includes abbreviations, acronyms, slang, basic investment words and phrases. Entries often amplified with examples. Cross-references. *Class No:* 336.767(038)

[2261]

—PESSIN, A.H. *and* ROSS, J. A. Still more words of Wall Street. New York, Business One Irwin , 1990. 292p. $18. ISBN: 1556233299.

A sequel to the above. *Class No:* 336.767(038)

[2262]

THOMSETT, M.C., *comp.* **Investment and securities dictionary.** Jefferson, NJ, McFarland, 1986. vii, 328p. charts, tables. $29.95. ISBN: 0899502253.

Definitions of more than 2000 technical words and phrases used by US investment professionals and financial planners. Definitions are clear and concise, often with tables, charts and graphs. Cross-references. The dictionary proper is followed by an alphabetical list of more than 170 abbreviations used in the securities industry; a section describing for lay persons what is contained in prospectuses or offering documents; and a bond classification list showing various classes of debt securities and distinctions between them. *Class No:* 336.767(038)

Yearbooks & Directories

[2263]

Allied Dunbar investment and savings guide, 1993. Robinson, C.P., *ed.* London, Longman Group Ltd., 1993. 468p. £19.99. ISBN: 0752000209.

First published for 1980/81. Annual.

Contains a wide range of investment know-how. 8 main sections, all subdivided: 1. The investor and his investment policy - 2. Real property - 3. Securities - 4. Business ventures (without pariticpation in management) - 5. Collective investment media - 6. Life assurance - 7. Commodities - 8. Alternative investments. Most sections end with lists of sources of further information. Useful addresses, p.300. Index, p.301-317. *Class No:* 336.767(058)

[2264]

Macmillan directory of international asset managers. Scott-Roberts, F. London, Macmillan Press, 1989. 300p. £95. ISBN: 0333494156.

Directory of the leading investment fund managers, A-Z by name. Data includes address; telephone/telex/fax numbers; company history; profiles of investment managers; size of funds under management; list of major clients; management fees; expenses; management policy and objectives; global asset allocation; statistical performance and performance ranking. *Class No:* 336.767(058)

Great Britain

Yearbooks & Directories

[2265]

Unit trust year book, 1993. London, Financial Times Business Information, 1993. Annual. 587p. £95. ISBN: 1853340707.

The year book is published in April each year and there is an *Autumn update* published in September.

The official year book of the Unit Trust Association, it covers 160 management groups and 1215 authorised unit trusts funds. In 3 sections: 1: Unit trusts:commentary and reference; 2: Statistics; 3: Management groups and unit trust details. Section 3 includes a directory of management groups (giving details of address, telephone number, telex, fax; funds managed; history) and details of the unit trusts (group, trustee, date formed, type of fund, investment, number of securities, unit accounts, portfolio distribution, trust record, etc.). *Class No:* 336.767(410)(058)

Russia

[2266]

SLAVENS, T.P. **Sources of information for investors in the Commonwealth of Independent States (formerly: The Soviet Union).** In *The Reference Librarian,* no.40, 1993, p.107-119.

Sections: Periodicals - Statistics - Economic theory - Economic conditions - Commerce - Dictionaries - Bibliographies. Short descriptions. *Class No:* 336.767(47)

USA

Venture capital

[2267]

SILVER, D.A. **Who's who in venture capital.** 3rd ed. New York, John Wiley & Sons, 1986. 468p. $29.95. £28.95. ISBN: 047101172x.

First published 1984.

In two sections: the first has four chapters on opinion, fact, concepts, ideas, etc.; the second, of 350 pages, has details of more than 600 funds and more than 1100 venture capitalists throughout the United States. 'As a reference book for both entrepreneurs, fund managers, and private investors looking for funds in the United States, it is extremely useful'. (*International small business journal,* v.6(2), January-March 1988, p.85-86). *Class No:* 336.767(73)VEN

Economic Surveys

[2268]

WORLD BANK. **World development report, 1993.** 16th. New York, Oxford University Press, for the World Bank, 1993. xii,329p. tables. ISBN: 0195208900. ISSN: 01635085.

First published 1978 (1979).

Designed to provide a comprehensive, continuing assessment of global development issues. The 1993 report examines the role of financial systems in development, preceded by a chapter reviewing recent trends. Bibliographical note. Statistical appendix. *Class No:* 338

Handbooks & Manuals

[2269]

Chisholm's handbook of commercial geography. Entirely rewritten by Sir Dudley Stamp. Blake, G.N. *and* Clark, A.N., *eds.* 20th ed. London & New York, 1980. xxxii,984p. tables, maps.

First published 1889.

4 main sections: 1. General factors affecting the production and distribution of commodities - 2. Circumstances connected with the exchange of commodities (transport, etc.) - 3. Commodities - 4. Regional geography (Europe ... Australia, New Zealand and the Pacific Islands, p.319-905). 6 appendices (1. Distribution maps (13); 3. International trade (statistics); 6. Conversion tables. Analytical index, p.933-84. 106 tables in main text. Standard text-book. *Class No:* 338(035)

[2270]

THE ECONOMIST. **The Economist guide to global economic indicators.** London, The Economist Books, 1992 viii,216p. $17.95 ISBN: 0471305537.

Previously published as the *The Economist guide to economic indicators: making sense of economics.* Contains subject index (pp. 210-216)

Practical guide for people with little knowledge of economics and finance, helps to insert economic facts in various areas of the field. Gives concise explanations of economic terms, divided by subject chapters. *Class No:* 338(035)

Reports Literature

[2271]

CITY UNIVERSITY. Business School. **Working paper series, 1977-.** London, City University, 1977-. 4pa.

A series of working papers on the subject of research in business and management studies, some of which are bibliographies (*e.g. The recruitment and retention of hospital auxiliary staff: a review of the literature and bibliography,* by A.P.O. Williams and others (1977), *The marketing of financial services: a bibliography.* by F.A. Johne and J. Montgomery-Smith (1978), and *Product policy and development in manufacturing firms: an annotated bibliography,* by F.A. Johne and Patricia A. Snelson (1987). *Class No:* 338(047)

Maps & Atlases

[2272]

Oxford economic atlas of the world. Jones, D.B., *ed.* 4th ed. London, Oxford University Press, 1972. viii, 239p. tables, maps. £20. ISBN: 0198941064.

Prepared by the Cartographic Department of the Clarendon Press, and first published 1954.

91p. of maps in colour. 13 sections: Environment - Crops - Livestock - Forestry and fishing - Fibres and textiles - Energy - Minerals and metals - Transport industries - Manufacturing industries - Demography - Disease - Society and politics - Surface and air communications. Index-gazetteer of *c.*4000 names of places and specific sites (*e.g.* mines, dams). Statistical supplement, p.117-239): countries, A-Z; statistics largely for 1963-65, with 1953-9

...(contd.)

comparisons. Page size, 37.5 x 28.5 cm. Oxford regional economic atlases: *Western Europe* (1971. 162p.);*U.S.S.R. and Eastern Europe* (New ed., 1971. 140p.); *India and Ceylon* (1953. 141p.); *Pakistan* (1955. 142p.); *Middle East and North Africa* (1960. 143p.); *Africa* (1971. 230p.); *United States and Canada* (2nd ed. 1975. 176p.
Class No: 338(084.3)

Histories

[2273]

The Cambridge economic history of Europe. Cambridge, Cambridge University Press, 1941-89. 8v. in 9v. illus., tables, maps. £45-£75. ISBN: 0521045053, v.1; 0521087090, v.2; 0521045061, v.3; 052104507x, v.4; 0521087104, v.5; 0521045088, v.6; 0521215900 & 0521215919, v.7-2 vols; 0521225043, v.8.

1: The agrarian life of the Middle Ages (2nd ed. 1966) 2: Trade and industry in the Middle Ages (2nd ed. 1987) 3: Economic organization and policies in the Middle Ages 1963) 4: The economy of expanding Europe in the sixteenth and seventeenth centuries (1967) 5: The economic organization of early modern Europe (1977) 6: The industrial revolutions and after: incomes, population and technical change (1965) 7: The industrial economies: capital, labour and enterprise. 1. Britain, France, Germany and Scandinavia (1978) 2. The United States, Japan, and Russia (1978) 8: The industrial economies: the development of economic and social policies (1989). Originally planned by Sir John Clapham and Eileen Power, aiming to provide an authoritative survey of an aspect omitted from the Cambridge medieval and modern histories. Terminal date is mid-20th century.
Class No: 338(091)

[2274]

HEICHELHEIM, F.M. **An Ancient economic history,** from the Palaeolithic Age to the migrations of the Germanic, Slavic and Arab nations. Rev. and complete English ed. Leiden, 1958-70. 3v.

Original as *Wirtschaftgeschichte des Altertums* (1938, 2v; bibliography, p.863-1277). Translated by Mrs Joyce Stevens.
Class No: 338(091)

Periodicals & Progress Reports

[2275]

The Economic history review, v.1, no.1-. 1927-. Oxford, Basil Blackwell Ltd., for the Economic History Society (previously by several other publishers). £54;$95 pa. ISSN: 00130117.

2nd series, v.47(1), February 1994 contains 5 articles (*e.g.* 'The industrial revolution and British imperialism, 1750-1850';'The Australian role in Britain's return to the gold standard'); one article in a series 'Surveys and speculations'. A book review section contains 24 book reviews; and there is a review of periodical literature, 1992. The 4th issue each year includes 'List of publications on the economic and social history of Great Britain and Ireland published in the previous year'. Keys to earlier volumes: *Economic history review: an index to the first series, v.1-18, 1927-48* (Utrecht, Oosthoek, 1965. 59p. £4.50); *Economic history review: index to second series, v.1-23, 1948-70* (Welwyn Garden City, Broadwater Press Ltd., 1972. £7.95).
Class No: 338(091)(05)

Worldwide

Bibliographies

[2276]

ORGANISATION FOR ECONOMIC CO-OPERATION AND DEVELOPMENT. **Catalogue of publication.** Paris, OECD. Annual (previously biennial), with quarterly supplements. *c.*100p. Gratis.

A sales list of OECD publications. 12 sections in the 1989 edition (published early 1989 and including publications on sale as at 1st January 1989): General economic analysis and forecasting - Energy - Development and aid - Labour market and social problems - Industry: science and technology - Financial and fiscal affairs - Accounting standards, competitions and consumer policy - Education - Environment - Regional development, public management - Food, agriculture, fisheries - Transport, tourism. A-Z of series, titles and authors. *Class No:* 338(100)(01)

[2277]

Predicasts F & S index Europe. Cleveland, Ohio, Predicasts Inc., 1978-. Monthly. Quarterly and annual cumulations. ISSN: 02704536.

A companion volume to *Predicasts F & S index international.*

Indexes articles and news items relative to the European Communities countries, other Western European countries, and Eastern Europe. Database 1970-. *Class No:* 338(100)(01)

[2278]

—Predicasts F & S index United States. Cleveland, Ohio, Predicasts Inc., 1960-. Quarterly. Annual cumulations. $850pa. ISSN: 02704544.

Title was *F & S index of corporations and industries* from 1960 to 1978.

Indexes articles and news items on US corporations and industries. Database, 1970-. *Class No:* 338(100)(01)

[2279]

Predicasts F & S index international. Cleveland, Ohio, Predicasts Inc., 1967-. Quarterly. Annual cumulation. $800pa. ISSN: 02704528.

Formerly F & S international.

Indexes articles and news items, being complementary to *Predicasts F & S index United States.* In 3 sections: 1. Industry and product (arranged by industry group, preceded by list of groups and subdivisions); 2. Countries, by region; 3. Companies, A-Z. Now limited to Canada, Latin America, Africa, Middle East, and Oceania. Also available online.=2 F & S index plus text=* (1991-) is the CD-ROM version. *Class No:* 338(100)(01)

[2280]

World development. Oxford, Pergamon Press, 1972-. Monthly. £462pa. ISSN: 0305750x.

A multidisciplinary journal on the social, economic and political consequences of development, focusing on reforms and co-operative efforts to eliminate disease, poverty and illiteracy. Includes a section of 'Book notes'. *Class No:* 338(100)(01)

Handbooks & Manuals

[2281]

GREAT BRITAIN. Department of Trade and Industry. **Hints to exporters visiting...** London, the Department. £6 each.

Continues *Hints to businessmen.*

About 100 country reports, revised bienially. Topics include preparation for the trip, travel and currency information, economic factors, import and exchange control regulations, methods of doing business and general information. Maps. *Class No:* 338(100)(035)

Reviews & Abstracts

[2282]

ECONOMIST INTELLIGENCE UNIT. **Country reports.** London, the Unit, 1952-. diagrs., charts, tables. £160. $315 pa for 4 quarterly issues per country.

Early title was *Quarterly economic review series.*

There are reviews for 180 countries, each containing an executive summary; an outlook section on political and economic prospects for the next 12-18 months; a 10-20p. review section analysing political developments, government policies, trends in production and demand, monetary and fiscal conditions, etc.; statistical appendices. Valuable, if expensive, economic digests. *Class No:* 338(100)(048)

Yearbooks & Directories

[2283]

ORGANISATION FOR ECONOMIC CO-OPERATION AND DEVELOPMENT. **OECD economic surveys.** Paris, OECD, 1953-. illus., tables. Annual. £110; $195 pa. ISSN: 03766438.

Previously as *Economic conditions in member and associated countries* and originally part of the O.E.C.D. annual report, 1949-52.

Country surveys, mostly north and western European, but including Japan, US, Canada, Yugoslavia, Turkey, Australia and New Zealand in a full year, although some countries are surveyed every other year (*e.g.* 17 countries were surveyed in 1989/90). Such published reports are agreed documents, and analyse recent developments and immediate prospects (demand; output; wages and prices; money and capital markets; balance of payments; government policies and the problems facing them. *Class No:* 338(100)(058)

[2284]

—ORGANISATION FOR ECONOMIC CO-OPERATION AND DEVELOPMENT. **OECD economic outlook.** Paris, OECD, 1960-. 2pa. £29.00; $25; Ff.150. ISSN: 04745574.

Published in June & December each year.

Surveys the latest economic developments in the OECD area and assesses future prospects. Includes up-to-date statistical information on the growth of real GNP and GDP, development of domestic demand, employment, output, foreign trade, productivity, etc.
Class No: 338(100)(058)

[2285]

—ORGANISATION FOR ECONOMIC CO-OPERATION AND DEVELOPMENT. OECD economic outlook - historical statistics, 1960-1989. 3rd ed. Paris, OECD, 1991. 170p. £14; $26; Ffl10 ISBN: 9264033483.

First published 1987, covering 1960-1985.

Shows how OECD countries' economies have evolved since 1960, expressed in terms of rates of change or percentage shares. The statistics provide the historical background to the *O.E.C.D. economic outlook's* current analysis and forecasts. *Class No:* 338(100)(058)

[2286]

UNITED NATIONS. Department of International Economic and Social Affairs. **World economic survey, 1993: current trends and policies in the world economy.** New York, United Nations, 1993. 273p. tables, graphs. $55. £42. ISBN: 9211091268. ISSN: 00841714.

First published 1949-. Annual. Initially *World economic report,* a continuation of the League of Nations *World economic survey* (1927-44. 11v.).

7 chapters: 1. The state of the world economy - 2. Trends in global output and policies - 3. International trade - 4. Saving, investment and the international transfer of resources - 5. Energy - 6. Conversion and the peace dividend - 7. Entrepreneurship. Annex: 39 tables. Explanatory notes precede, and sources are given in footnotes. *Class No:* 338(100)(058)

Tables & Data Books

[2287]

LIESNER, T. **One hundred years of economic statistics.** New ed. of *Economic statistics, 1900-1983,* revised and expanded to 1987. London, Economist Publications,1990. viii,344p. charts, tables. ISBN: 0850582792.

Presents time series, mainly from the 1950s, for UK, USA, Australia, Canada, France, Germany, Italy, Japan and Sweden. Includes trends and cycles in the total economy; growth of output by sector and commodity; capital formation; income and expenditure; prices; earnings and productivity ; employment and unemployment; population; education; trade and balance of payments; finance; transport; and energy. Data taken predominantly from official sources. Detailed notes explain how the series were constructed from diverse sources and normalized. Final section shows cross-national comparisons for 16 variables. *Class No:* 338(100)(083)

[2288]

MOORE, G.H. *and* MOORE, M.H. **International economic indicators:** a sourcebook. Westport, CT. Greenwood Press, 1985. ix,373p. $45; £42.50. ISBN: 0313219893.

An in-depth study of the economic indicators of the world's major industrialized nations, undertaken as part of the long-term project of The Center for International Business Cycle Research (CIBCR). '... a most useful body of data to apply to a variety of historical analyses' (*Journal of economic history,* June 1986, v.46(2), p.580). *Class No:* 338(100)(083)

[2289]

ORGANISATION FOR ECONOMIC CO-OPERATION AND DEVELOPMENT. **Main economic indicators, 1965-. Monthly.** Paris, OECD. £144pa; $195pa; F.950pa. ISSN: 04745523.

Contains *c.*1500 economic indicators appearing in major statistical bulletins published by OECD member countries. 1. Indicators by subject - 2. Indicators by country - 3. Appendix: Gross domestic product; purchasing power parities; comparative price levels; exchange rates; population. A historical volume is published from time to time: *Main economic indicators: historical statistics,* 1962-1991 (1993, 368p. $58. F.240. ISBN 9264038736). *Class No:* 338(100)(083)

[2290]

—Indicators of industrial activity. Paris, Organisation for Economic Co-operation and Development, 1979-. Quarterly. £26.30; F.225; $50pa. ISSN: 02504278.

Continues *Industrial production: quarterly supplement to 'Main economic indicators'.*

Provides an overall view of short-term economic developments in different industries for all OECD member countries, including indices of output, orders, prices and employment. *Class No:* 338(100)(083)

Bibliographies

[2291]

VERWEY, G. *and* RENOOIJ, D.C. **The Economist's handbook:** a manual of statistical sources. Amsterdam, Economist's handbook, 1934. Supplement, 1937. (Reprinted in 1.v. Detroit, Mich., Gale Research Co., 1971). viii,1460p.; iii, 79p. $65. ISBN: 0810337282.

The main section consists (p.39-200) of subjects, arranged A-Z with country sub-division. Column form is used to facilitate reference, sources of information being given in the right-hand column. An equally extensive section follows (p.203-415) listing the sources quoted (general; then by countries A-Z; then by frequency of publication - annual, quarterly, monthly, etc.) with notes on their scope. Finally, an

....(contd.)

A-Z index of sources. Countries drawn upon are: Belgium, France, Germany, Netherlands, Switzerland, the UK and USA. The Supplement lists additional source material and gives corrigenda. Now largely of historical value only. *Class No:* 338(100)(083)(01)

Developing Countries

Yearbooks & Directories

[2292]

Third World directory. Stubbs, L., *ed.* 2nd ed. London, Directory of Social Change, 1993. *c.*130p. £9.95. ISBN: 187386003x.

1st published in 1990.

A guide to over 200 development organizations, covering their history, geography, major projects, and future plans. Also volunteering opportunities and research into trusts. Index. *Class No:* 338(4/9-77)(058)

Europe

Bibliographies

[2293]

Sources of European economic and business information. University of Warwick. Business Information Service. 5th ed. Aldershot, Gower Publishing Group, 1989. 288p. £75. ISBN: 0566026589.

First published 1974.

*c.*6000 entries, covering 32 countries of Western and Eastern Europe. Part 1 lists source publications (International, then A-Z by country, subdivided by title. For each numbered entry - publisher, country coverage, frequency, language, and brief description). Pt.2 lists the publishing bodies. Indexes list the sources alphabetically, by subject, and by country. *Class No:* 338(4)(01)

Yearbooks & Directories

[2294]

UNITED NATIONS. Economic Commission for Europe. **Economic survey of Europe, 1992-1993.** New York, United Nations, 1993. ix,291p. tables, map. £42. ISBN: 9211165555. ISSN: 00708712.

First published for 1946/47. Annual.

5 chapters: 1. The transition economies in 1992-1993: an overview - 2. Macro-economic developments and outlook - 3. International economic relations - 4. The hard road to market economy: problems and policies - 5. Explaining unemployment in the market economies: theories and evidence. 6. Statistical appendices (A. Western Europe and North America; B. Eastern Europe with the Soviet Union; C. International trade and payments). Tables and charts throughout. Data for 1992-93. Kept up-to-date by the *Economic Bulletin for Europe* (1948-. Quarterly). *Class No:* 338(4)(058)

Histories

[2295]

The Fontana economic history of Europe. Cipolla, C.M., *ed.* London, Collins/Fontana Books, 1973-76. 6v. graphs, tables, maps.

V.1 *The Middle Ages* - 2. *The sixteenth and seventeenth centuries* - 3. *The Industrial Revolution* - 4. *The emergence of industrial societies* - 5. *The twentieth century* (in 2 parts) - 6. *Contemporary economies* (in 2 parts). Designed to fill a gap, by covering Europe both as a whole and in terms of individual countries, 'concise enough for convenient use and yet full enough to include the results of individual and detailed scholarship' (Series note). *Class No:* 338(4)(091)

Bibliographies

[2296]

WILSON, C. *and* PARKER, G., *eds.* **An Introduction to the sources of European economic history, 1500-1800. V.1: Western Europe.** London, Weidenfeld & Nicolson, 1977; Cornell University Press, 1978. xxx, 256p. diagrs., tables. $32.50. (*World economic history series.*) ISBN: 0801411092.

Was to be in two volumes, the second volume dealing with Northern, Central and Eastern Europe.

7 chapters on Italy, Spain the Low Countries, the British Isles, France and Germany, each divided by subjects, including population, industry, currency and finance, wealth and social structure, etc. 90 tables and 104 diagrams; notes and references (p.224-245). 13 contributors. *Class No:* 338(4)(091)(01)

Europe—Western

Handbooks & Manuals

[2297]

West European economic handbook. London, Euromonitor Publications Ltd., 1987. xii, 184p. tables, charts. £45. ISBN: 0863381421.

Examines the political, economic and social structure of the European Communities and the other principal countries of Western Europe. 9 chapters: 1. West Europe: an international perspective - 2. The European Communities: its economic role in Europe today - 3. Political and defence issues - 4. Pan-European economic trends - 5. Finance and banking in Europe - 6. Industrial development in Europe - 7. External trade flows and patterns - 8. The European market - 9. Future outlook. *Class No:* 338(400)(035)

Europe—Eastern

Bibliographies

[2298]

ABSEES (Abstracts: Soviet and East European series): a journal of Soviet and East European economic affairs. London, British Association for Slavonic and East European Studies (previously Oxford, Pergamon Press and Glasgow University Institute of Soviet and East European studies), 1970-. v.1, no.1-. 3 pa (previously quarterly). $695 pa. ISSN: 00445622.

Primarily a microfiche journal; each issue has printed summaries.

Subject coverage: Agriculture - COMECON - Economic planning - Economic policy and theory - Finance - Foreign trade and payments - Industry and construction - Labour and wages - Management - Science and technology - Social questions - Tourism - Trade and services - Transport and communications. Subject index only.

Class No: 338(401)(01)

[2299]

O'RELLEY, Z.E. Soviet-type economic systems: a guide to information sources. Detroit, Mich., Gale Research Co., 1978. 228p., $68. ISBN: 0810313065.

Lists and annotates books and journal articles in English relating to the economies of Bulgaria, Czechoslovakia, German Democratic Republic, Hungary, Poland, Rumania and the Soviet Union. Arrangement is under broad subject headings (*e.g.* prices and inflation, labour force, foreign trade, efficiency and productivity).

Class No: 338(401)(01)

Handbooks & Manuals

[2300]

East European economic handbook. Smith, A.H. London, Euromonitor Publications Ltd., 1985. vi, 325p. tables, 8 maps. £45; $70. ISBN: 0863380298.

A regional overview precedes separate chapters on the economies of 7 nations: Bulgaria, Czechoslovakia, German Democratic Republic, Hungary, Poland, Romania and Yugoslavia. Consideration is given to political factors affecting economic performance, the country and its people,. government and political organization, economic growth, economic planning, etc. A 'Fact file' has 20 statistical tables comparing the countries along various economic variables.

Class No: 338(401)(035)

Great Britain

[2301]

ALDCROFT, H. The British economy. v.1.$aThe years of turmoil, 1920-1951. Hemel Hempstead, Herts., Wheatsheaf Books Ltd., 1986. vii, 264p. £28.50. ISBN: 0710801149.

The first volume of what is intended to be an extended study of the British economy from 1920 to the present day.

8 chapters (Chequered decade: the 1920s - Depression and recovery, 1929-1939: an overview - Economic policy and recovery: external policy - Macroeconomic policy in the 1930s - Regional and industrial policies - Natural forces of recovery - The war economy and its consequences - Facing the future with Labour, 1945-1951), with 102 notes. Select reading, p.253. Political glossary - chief economic Ministers, p.254-258, chronological arrangement. Index, p.259-164.

Class No: 338(410)

Bibliographies

[2302]

GREAT BRITAIN. HM Stationery Office. Government publications. Sectional list 3, revised June 1988: Energy, trade and industry. London, HMSO, 1988. iv, 36p. *Gratis.*

Lists, with prices, publications of the Departments of Energy and of Trade and Industry. Sections: Serial publications and annual reports - Energy - Trade and industry (including Business Monitor). Index.

Class No: 338(410)(01)

[2303]

—GREAT BRITAIN. Department of Trade and Industry. Libraries. Publications London, Department of Trade and Industry Headquarters Library and Information Centre. Annual. *Gratis.*

An annual list of publications issued by the Department of Trade and Industry, Department of Energy (now merged with the Department of Trade and Industry), Monopolies and Mergers Commission, Office of Electricity Regulation, Office of Fair Trading, Office of Gas Supply, and Office of Telecommunications, issued by the Departments and through HMSO. *Class No:* 338(410)(01)

Handbooks & Manuals

[2304]

MORT, D., *comp.* **The Counties and regions of the United Kingdom:** a statistical and economic review. Warwick Statistics Service. Rev. ed. Aldershot, Hants., Gower Publishing Company Ltd., 1988. 224p. £27.50. ISBN: 0566027550.

First published 1983.

A study of the main demographic, economic and employment trends in the 54 counties of England and Wales, the 12 regional and island areas of Scotland and Northern Ireland and its districts. Provides key statistics on population trends and characteristics, district sizes, unemployment, earnings, housing, industrial structure, and local authority expenditure. Bibliography. List of selected libraries/information services. *Class No:* 338(410)(035)

Tables & Data Books

[2305]

CAPIE, F. *and* **COLLINS, M. The Inter-war British economy:** a statistical abstract. Manchester, Manchester University Press, 1983. [5], 118p. tables. £32.50. ISBN: 0719009014.

Mainly tables (142) and arranged in 8 sections: 1. Production - 2. Prices and retail sales - 3. Level of business activity - 4. Labour - 5. Overseas trade and shipping - 6. Money and banking - 7. Interest rates - 8. Capital. Index, p.117-118. *Class No:* 338(410)(083)

[2306]

Economic trends. Central Statistical Office. London, HMSO,., 1953-. no.1-. diagrs., charts, tables. Monthly. £155pa; £12.75 each issue. ISSN: 00130400.

Brings together all the main economic indicators, time series and graphs over the last five years or so. Preceded by several pages of current information, and followed by an analysis of indications in relation to the business cycle over the last 20 years. Other articles comment on and analyse economic statistics. *Class No:* 338(410)(083)

[2307]

First releases. London, Central Statistical Office: Press Office; Newport, Gwent, Business Statistics Office Library. *c.*100pa. Prices vary.

Continues *Business bulletins* from 1st January 1994.

Provides the statistical data previously published in *British business,* covering both sectoral and cross-sectoral data, as well as information of more general interest to business and commerce.

Class No: 338(410)(083)

[2308]

—Business briefing. London, Association of British Chambers of Commerce. Weekly. .

Aims to provide business-related news items drawn from government and private sector sources, together with some statistical information. An attempt to replace in part the defunct *British business*.

Class No: 338(410)(05)

Maps & Atlases

[2309]

Atlas of industrializing Britain, 1780-1914. Langton, J. *and* Morris, R.J., *eds.* London, Methuen, 1986. 272p. illus., tables, maps. £25. ISBN: 0416302904.

Aimed at teachers, the atlas is arranged in 31 chapters (Physical environment - Population - Regional structure and change - Agriculture - Rural settlement - Wages - Wind and water power - Coal and steam power - Transport - Sea trade - Textiles - Chemicals - Brewing and distillary - Leather footwear - Iron and steel - Shipbuilding - Engineering - Services - Banking and finance - Wealth and the wealthy - Poor law and pauperism - Urbanization - Retail patterns - Labour protest, 1780-1859 - Unionization - Popular institutions - Sport - Languages and dialects - Education - Religion - The electoral system). Sources of maps listed on p.228-235. Bibliography, p.236-246, A-Z by author. *Class No:* 338(410)(084.3)

Histories

[2310]

FLOUD, R. *and* McGLOSKEY, D., *eds*. **The Economic history of Britain since 1700**. 2nd ed. Cambridge, Cambridge University Press, 1984. 3v. (432; 536; 400p.). tables. ISBN: 0521459613.

First published 1981 in 2v.

V.1. 1700-1860; v.,2 1860 to the 1970s; v.3 1939-1992. V.1 has 13 chapters in 5 overlapping chronological divisions, each division, except the last, beginning with a general survey followed by a number of chapters which consider the main problems which have arisen in the historical interpretation of that period. Each division, except first and last, conclude with chapters dealing with the social history of the period in relation to economic change. V.2 and v.3 follow the same pattern. Each volume has bibliographies, indexes and glossaries. *Class No:* 338(410)(091)

Bibliographies

[2311]

CHALONER, W.H. *and* RICHARDSON, R.C., *comps*. **Bibliography of British economic and social history**. New ed. Manchester, Manchester University Press, 1984. xiv, 208p. £36. ISBN: 0719008883.

First published in 1976 as *British economic and social history: a bibliography*.

5780 numbered entries for books and periodical articles. Sections: General works - England, 1066-1300 - England, 1300-1500 - England, 1500-1700 (General works; Population; Agriculture and rural society; Industry; Towns; Alien migrants; Commerce and colonization; The concept of mercantilism; Communications and internal trade; Prices, public finance, banking and financial dealings; Government policy and administration, law and order; Classes and social groups; Poor relief; Charity and the Poor Law; Labour; Standards of living; Civil War; Interregnum, Restoration and Revolution, 1640-89; Religion; Education and learning) - England, 1700-1970 (p.83-155) - Wales before 1700 - Wales after 1700 - Scotland before 1700 - Scotland after 1700 - Ireland before 1700 - Ireland after 1700. Index of authors and editors, p.186-208. A bibliography easy to consult. *Class No:* 338(410)(091)(01)

Middle Ages

[2312]

BOLTON, J.L. **The Medieval English economy, 1150-1500**. London, Dent, 1980 (Reprinted 1985, Everyman Univ. Pubs.). 416p. £7.95. ISBN: 0460152742.

A general survey of 10 chapters: 1. Introduction: settlement and society - 2. Patterns of demand - 3. Overcrowded island - 4. The growth of the market - 5. Supplying the market - 6. Towards a crisis - 7. Crisis and change in agrarian reform - 8. Freedom versus restriction: town and countryside in the later Middle Ages - 9. English trade in the late Middle Ages: the triumph of the English - 10. Economics and ideas. Followed by conclusion, notes, a bibliography (p.357-378); and an index. 'An exemplary guide; (*TLS*, 26 September 1980, p.1069). *Class No:* 338(410)"01/14"

19th Century

[2313]

PORTER, G.R. **The Progress of the nation in its various social and economic relations from the beginning of the nineteenth century**. 3rd ed. 1851 (Reprinted New York, Kelley, 1970). xvi, 735p. $5032. ISBN: 0678005389.

First published 1836; 2nd ed. 1846.

A statistical and descriptive study of the social, economic, commercial and fiscal changes which took place in the United Kingdom during the first half of the 19th century. *Class No:* 338(410)"18"

Scotland

Periodicals & Progress Reports

[2314]

Scottish economic bulletin. Scottish Office. Edinburgh, HMSO, 1971-. no.1-. 2pa. £11.50 each issue.

No.48, Winter 1993/94 (ISBN 0114952353) includes an Economic review; Consumer prices in the Highlands and Islands; Scottish results of the 1991 census of employment: a statistical note; Charts and statistics: Main quarterly economic series; Main annual economic series; Articles published in recent issues of *Scottish economic bulletin*. *Class No:* 338(411)(05)

Histories

[2315]

MARWICK, W.H. 'A Bibliography of Scottish economic history during the last decade: 1963-1970'. In *Economic history review*, 2nd series, v.24(3), 1971, p.469-479.

An evaluative running commentary. Sections: General - Medieval - The seventeenth century - The eighteenth century - The nineteenth and twentieth centuries. Preceded by the author's contributions to *Economic history review*, 2nd series, v.16(1), 1963, p.147-54; v.4(3), 1952, p.377-82; and v.3(1), 1931, p.117-37. *Class No:* 338(411)(091)

Ireland

Tables & Data Books

[2316]

KIRWAN, F. *and* McGILVRAY, J. **Irish economic statistics**. Dublin, Institute of Public Administration, 1983. 225p. illus., tables, map. £7.95. ISBN: 0906980143.

First ed., by J. McGilvray, published in 1968.

Designed as a guide to the sources, of collection, presentation and analysis of the major branches of economic statistics in Ireland. Bibliography, p.213-221. Index. *Class No:* 338(415)(083)

Northern Ireland

Histories

[2317]

KENNEDY, L. *and* OLLERENSHAW, P., *eds*. **An Economic history of Ulster, 1820-1940**. Manchester, Manchester University Press, 1985. [6],248p. tables, maps. £25. ISBN: 0719017505.

Arranged in 7 chapters (1. The rural economy, 1820-1914 - 2. Industry, 1820-1914 - 3. Transport, 1820-1914 - 4. Population change and urbanisation, 1821-1911 - 5. Industrial labour and the labour movement, 1920-1914 - 6. The Northern Ireland economy, 1914-1939 - 7. The economic history of Ulster: a perspective. Many notes, including references, at the end of each chapter. Select bibliography, p.241-242, by chapter. Index of places, p.243-245; index of subjects, p.246-248. *Class No:* 338(416)(091)

Eire

Bibliographies

[2318]

PAGE, R. **Sources of economic information: Ireland**. Dublin, Institute of Public Administration, 1985. [5],112p. $19.95. ISBN: 0906980410.

Arranged in 21 subject sections A-Z: 1. Agriculture and fisheries 2. Balance of payments ... 19. Transport - 20. Data banks - 21. Journals, newspapers. Each section divided into official publications; other publications: Irish; other publications: British; publications of international organizations. Subject, title and author indexes. *Class No:* 338(417)(01)

Yearbooks & Directories

[2319]

EIRE. Department of Finance. **Economic review and outlook**. Dublin, Stationery Office, 1988. 56p. £2.60.

Published annually each summer.

Contains a detailed report on economic trends and includes an appendix of economic statistics. *Economic background to the budget*, published each January, is a companion volume summarizing economic development over the past year and assessing pre-budgetary prospects for the following year. *Class No:* 338(417)(058)

England

Histories

[2320]

CLAPP, B.W., *ed*. **Documents in English economic history: England from 1000 to 1760**. London, Bell, 1977 (Paperback ed. Bell & Hyman, 1984). 576p. £7.95. ISBN: 0713524693. *Class No:* 338(420)(091)

[2321]

—CLAPP, B.W., *ed*. Documents in English economic history: England since 1760. London, Bell, 1976. 544p.

For each volume the documents, and some comment, are arranged in 10 chapters: 1. General view - 2. Agriculture - 3. Evolution of industry - 4. Transport and internal trade - 5. Finance - 6. Foreign trade - 7. The workers - 8. Poor law and public health - 9. The consumer - 10. Economic policy and taxation. 'A valuable reference work' (*New history*, no.7, p.7). *Class No:* 338(420)(091)

Bibliographies

[2322]

WILLIAMS, J.B. A Guide to the printed materials for English social and economic history. 1750-1850. New York, Columbia University Press, 1926, (Reprinted Dublin, Irish University Press, 1968). 2.v.

About 7,500 selected entries - Pt.1., 'Works of general reference' (including bibliographies and catalogues; encyclopedias; local histories; biographies; in 11 sections) - pt.2, Special subjects (economic theory; economic conditions and questions; industry; social and economic conditions and movements; social political theory and movements; sections 12-16). All items are briefly annotated. V.2. includes author (plus brief title) and non-analytical subject indexes. *Class No:* 338(420)(091)(01)

Middle Ages

[2323]

HALL, H., *ed.* A Select bibliography for the study, sources and literature of English mediaeval economic history. London, King, 1914 (reprinted New York, B. Franklin, 1960). xiii, 350p. $23.50. (*Studies in economics and political science. Series of bibliographies, 41.*) ISBN: 0833715488.

Compiled by a seminar of the London School of Economics under the supervision of Hubert Hall.

A classified bibliography of 3200 items, with author and title index. Appended list of learned social journals and of periodicals. Still of considerable value on manuscript sources. *Class No:* 338(420)"01/14"

Wales

Yearbooks & Directories

[2324]

Welsh economic trends/Tueddiadau'r economi, 1992. Welsh Office. No.13. Cardiff, the Office, 1993. £10. ISBN: 0750402016.

First published for 1974. Annual.

Over 100 tables in 9 sections: Population - Regional income and expenditure - Earnings and hours - Personal incomes - Household income and expenditure - Industrial activity - Aids to industry - Capital expenditure - Public expenditure. Sources of further information are included in an appendix. *Class No:* 338(429)(058)

Germany

Periodicals

[2325]

Wirtschaft und Statistik. Stuttgart, Verlag Metzler-Poeschel, for Statistisches Bundesamt, 1921-. Monthly. DM.184pa. ISSN: 00436143.

About 50 pages of survey articles (economic survey; graphs on economic developments; economic indicators; price index) and 80-odd pages of statistical tables, with figures for previous months and years and cumulative statistical contents for the year. *Class No:* 338(430)(051)

German Democratic Republic

[2326]

The East German economy. Jeffries, E., *and others*. Beckenham, Kent, Croom Helm, 1987. [8],328p. figs., tables. £35. ISBN: 0709914695.

Surveys the current state of the East German Economy in 14 chapters: 1. The GDR in historical and international perspective - 2. Command planning and the production unit ... 4. The economic strategy of the 1980s and the limits to possible reforms ... 8. Product and process renewal in GDR economic strategy ... 10. The GDR financial system ... 13. The role of the GDR in Comecon: some economic aspects - 14. Economic reform of the GDR: causes and effects. 12 contributors. Glossary, p.306-313. References, p.314-322. Index, p.323-328. *Class No:* 338(430.2)

[2327]

GERMAN INSTITUTE FOR ECONOMIC RESEARCH. Handbook of the economy of the German Democratic Republic. Pohl, R., *ed.* Farnborough, Hants., Saxon House, 1979. xxiv, 366p. tables. £27.50. ISBN: 0566002566.

First published in German in 1977.

Aims to give a comprehensive view of East German achievements and problems. In 7 chapters: 1. Economic development and basic factors - 2. Economic organizations and planning system - 3. National accounts - 4. Production in the individual economic sectors - 5. Use and distribution of product and incomes - 6. Foreign economic relations - 7. The GDR and the CMEA. Appendix of tables. Index. *Class No:* 338(430.2)

Hungary

Bibliographies

[2328]

HORCHLER, G.F. Hungarian economic reforms: a selective, partially annotated bibliography. New Brunswick, The Hungarian Research Center, 1977. 190p. $8.95. (*Hungarian reference shelf, no.3.*) ISBN: 0686234057.

1620 entries, arranged by topics, are preceded by an initial section of references. bibliographical and serial publications. Covers books and articles, including those in a number of Western and Eastern European languages. Author index. *Class No:* 338(439)(01)

[2329]

—HANÁK, P. 'Short survey of recent literature on Hungarian economic history'. (in *Economic history review,* 2nd series, v.24(4), 1971, p.677-81).

An evaluative essay and select bibliography of 122 items in various languages. 3 sections: 1. Historical demography and historical statistics - 2. Economic history - 3. Social history. *Class No:* 338(439)(01)

France

Histories

[2330]

CARON, F. An Economic history of modern France. Translated from the French by Barbara Bray. London, Methuen, 1979 (Reprinted 1983). [xi],384p. illus., tables. £8.95. ISBN: 0416364705.

Part 1: The nineteenth century (1815-1914) (8 chapters, *e.g.* 5. The development of trade; 6. Agriculture) - Part 2. The twentieth century (Chapters 9-14; 14. State policy and business management, 1950-1973). Conclusions. Analytical index, p.371-84. Chapter bibliographies (mostly books and articles cited or directly used). Many tables. *Class No:* 338(44)(091)

Spain

[2331]

LIEBERMAN, S. The Contemporary Spanish economy: a historical perspective. London, Allen & Unwin, 1982. xiii,378p. tables, figs. £20. ISBN: 0043390269.

An introduction, 'Institutions and economic development: the Spanish case', is followed by 7 chapters: 1. Contemporary Spanish agriculture in historical perspective - 2. Agricultural policy since 1939 - 3. The long road to Spain's industrial revolution - 4. The Spanish industrial revolution of the 1960s - 5. The economic crisis of the 1970s - 6. The restoration of free trade unions - 7. Quo Vadis, Hispania? Notes and references follow each chapter. Bibliography, p.360-365, A-Z by author. Index, p.366-378. *Class No:* 338(460)

Bibliographies

[2332]

MACKAY, J. 'Recent literature on Spanish economic history'. In *Economic history review,* 2nd series, v.31(1), 1978, p.129-45.

Evaluative commentary, followed by a select bibliography of 204 titles in Spanish, arranged A-Z by author and indicating relevant pages as necessary. *Class No:* 338(460)(01)

[2333]

—HARRISON, J. 'Spanish economic history from the restoration to the Franco regime (essays in bibliography and criticism)'. In *Economic history review,* 2nd series, v.33(2), May 1980, p.259-75.

Follows up the earlier contribution by Mackay (*qv*) and includes 194 entries in the select bibliography. *Class No:* 338(460)(01)

Histories

[2334]

HARRISON, J. An Economic history of modern Spain. Manchester, Manchester University; New York, Holmes & Meier, 1978. xi,187p. £26.50; $32.50. ISBN: 0719007046, UK; 0841904111, US.

7 chapters take the history chronologically from the middle of the 18th century to early 1978, while an 8th chapter is devoted to the rise of organized labour from the beginning of the 1930s. Good bibliography of English-language works, mainly American. *Class No:* 338(460)(091)

[2335]

—VIVES, J.V., *ed.* An Economic history of Spain. 3rd ed. Princeton, N.J., Princeton University Press, 1969. xii,825p.

Translated from the Spanish by F.M. López-Morillas, and first published in 1955. Includes an extensive bibliography. *Class No:* 338(460)(091)

Russia

Yearbooks & Directories

[2336]

USSR economic handbook. Scrivener, R.S., *ed*. London, Euromonitor Publications Ltd., 1986. viii,246p. tables. £45; $80. ISBN: 0863381561.

Examines the economy of the USSR from 1917 to the present day. 10 chapters: Soviet economic history and growth - The Soviet Union in a world context - Resources and planning - Industrial growth and production - Transport and communications - Agriculture, forestry and fisheries - Foreign trade and tourism - Finance and banking - The USSR a market for consumer goods - Outlook. Index and list of tables. *Class No:* 338(47)(058)

Tables & Data Books

[2337]

CLARKE, R.A. *and* **MATKO, D.J.I. Soviet economic facts, 1917-80.** 2nd ed. London, Macmillan Press, 1983. 244p. £33. ISBN: 0333333624.

First ed. by Clarke, covered 1917-1970, published in 1972.

A statistical compilation containing the most important economic statistics of the Soviet Union since the Revolution, and providing a set of recalculated figures by Western scholars for comparison. Compiled exclusively from Soviet original sources. *Class No:* 338(47)(083)

[2338]

—**TREML, V.G.** *and* **HARDT, J.P.,** *eds*. Soviet economic statistics. Durham, N.C., Duke University Press, 1972. xii,457p. $37.50. ISBN: 0822502519.

A collection of 18 papers in 6 topic sections concerned with the evaluation of availability, credibility and reliability of Soviet statistical data, and with the intepretation of methodological and classification problems. *Class No:* 338(47)(083)

Maps & Atlases

[2339]

KISH, G. Economic atlas of the Soviet Union. 2nd ed. rev. Ann Arbor, University of Michigan Press; London, Cresset Press, 1971. 90p.

First published, 1960.

4 general maps of the Soviet Union. (vegetation, administrative divisions; air lines; population distribution), plus maps of 15 regions, 4 per region: A. Agriculture and land use - B. Mining and minerals - C. Industry - D. Transportation and cities. 3-colour clear maps; regional map scales vary from 1:6,000,000 to 1:12,000,000. Brief text on each region. Appended bibliography (mainly Russian sources) and index-gazetteer to regional maps. Page size, 26 x 26 cm. *Class No:* 338(47)(084.3)

Histories

Bibliographies

[2340]

KAZMER, D.R. *and* **KAZMER, Y. Russian economic history:** a guide to information sources. Detroit, Mich., Gale Research Company, 1977. x,520p. $68. (*Economic information guide series, v.4.*) ISBN: 0810313049.

Annotated, selective bibliography; 36 subject chapters on Russian economic history during the pre-revolutionary and Soviet periods. English-language sources published 1900-1974 (but omitting JPRS *Translations on USSR economic affairs*). *Class No:* 338(47)(091)(01)

20th Century

[2341]

HILL, R.J. The Soviet Union: politics, economics and society, from Lenin to Gorbachov. London, Frances Pinter, 1985. xix,232p. illus., tables, map. (*Marxist regime series.*) ISBN: 0861874463.

Basic data (p.xv-xvii) and glossary and list of abbreviations (p.xix) precede the 5 chapters: 1. History and political tradition - 2. Social structures - 3. The political system - 4. The economic system - 5. The regime's policies. Bibliography, p.211-223,. Index, p.224-232. *Class No:* 338(47)"19"

Finland

Yearbooks & Directories

[2342]

FINLAND. Ministry of Finance. Economics Department. **Economic survey.** Helsinki, Valtion Painatuskeskus, 1949-. Annual. Fmk 100.

Supplement to the annual budget proposal. The 1992 issue surveys

....(contd.)

the economy for recent years and forecasts it for 1993. 40 tables. Full Finnish and Swedish editions, abridged in English. *Class No:* 338(480)(058)

Sweden

[2343]

The Swedish economy. Stockholm, Konjunkturinstitut, 1960- 2pa. not priced. ISSN: 00397296.

Articles and statistical tables on the general economy. Many tables and graphs, sources and notes. English and Swedish editions. *Class No:* 338(485)

Asia

Bibliographies

[2344]

BLAUVELT, E. *and* **DURLACHER, J. Sources of Asian/Pacific economic information.** Farnborough, Hants, Gower Publishing Co. Ltd., 1980. 2v.(408 p.; 384 p.). £35. ISBN: 0566022958.

A bibliography of sources (over 5000 descriptive entries). Areas covered include Japan, China, Australia, New Zealand, South Korea, Taiwan, Hong Kong, Thailand, the Philippines, Malaysia, Singapore, Indonesia, India, Pakistan, Sri Lanka, Bangladesh, Papua New Guinea annd the Pacific Islands. Title and subject (subdivided by country) indexes. *Class No:* 338(5)(01)

[2345]

CHEN, V. The Economic conditions of East and Southeast Asia: a bibliography of English-language materials, 1965-1977. Westport, CT., Greenwood Press, 1978. lii,788 p. $125. ISBN: 0313205655.

Entries, mainly for journal articles, are arranged in a section for general works, and then in sections for the countries to which they refer, A-Z (Burma, Hong Kong, India, Japan, Malaysia, Philippines, Singapore, South Korea, Taiwan and Thailand), the entries in each section being preceded by an introduction mentioning important titles and including bibliographies. In each section entries are arranged by detailed subject headings, A-Z. Lists of journals and a list of subject headings are included. *Class No:* 338(5)(01)

[2346]

LEE, M.K.S.C., *ed*. **East Asian economics:** a guide to information sources. Detroit, Mich., Gale Research Company, 1979. x,326p. $68. ISBN: 0810314274.

An annotated bibliography of 1,700 selected English-language materials relating to the economies of China, Japan, South Korea and Taiwan, from 1900 to the present. In 7 chapters: 1-5 for Asia and the individual countries, each subdivided into general and 6 subject sections (Agriculture - Commerce and industry - Economic growth - International economics and trade - Labour - Finance); chapters 6 and 7, for journals and serials, and bibliographies, each subdivided geographically. Author, title and analytical subject indexes. *Class No:* 338(5)(01)

Handbooks & Manuals

[2347]

Asian economic handbook. Wong, J. London, Euromonitor Publications Ltd., 1987. [6],272p. tables, charts. £45; $80. ISBN 0863381413.

A regional overview precedes economic profiles for 18 nations of the continent's four major regions: East Asia (Taiwan, Hong Kong, North Korea, South Korea, Macao), ASEAN countries (Malaysia, Indonesia, Singapore, the Philippines, Thailand), Indochina (Vietnam, Laos, Burma, Kampuchea), and the Indian sub-continent (India, Pakistan, Bangladesh, Sri Lanka). A statistical 'Factfile', with comparative statistics, supplements other statistical data included in the handbook. Index. *Class No:* 338(5)(035)

[2348]

The Pacific Basin: economic handbook. Sinclair, S. London, Euromonitor Publications Ltd., 1987. x,204p. tables, map. £45. ISBN 0863381391.

10 chapters: 1. The Pacific Basin: the region and its importance to the world - 2. Political and economic issues - 3. Commodities and commodity trade - 4. Energy - 5. Banking and capital markets - 6 Social issues - 7. Manufacturing - 8. Trade - 9. The future of the Pacific Basin: problems and opportunities - 10. Statistical datafile (4 charts, 74 tables). List of tables. Index, p.195-204. *Class No:* 338(5)(035)

China

Bibliographies

[2349]

SCHMIDT, M. **Economic reforms in the People's Republic of China since 1979:** a bibliography of articles and publications in English-language magazines and newspapers. West Cornwall, CT., Locust Hill Press, 1987. xvi, 177p. $25. ISBN: 0933951108.

1898 unannotated items from more than 280 journals and newspapers in a classified arrangement (General economics - Economic growth, development, planning, fluctuation - Quantitative economic methods and data - Domestic monetary and fiscal theory and institutions - International economics - Administration, business finance, marketing, accounting - Industrial organization, technical change, industry studies - Agriculture: natural resources - Manpower, labour, population - Welfare programs, consumer economics, urban and regional economics). No sub-divisions. Author index. 'Heavy emphasis on well-known sources, but others included' (*Choice*, October 1987, p.290). *Class No:* 338(510)(01)

Handbooks & Manuals

[2350]

China economic handbook. Grummit, K.P. London, Euromonitor Ltd., 1986. 246p. tables, charts. £45. ISBN: 0863381553.

Includes 9 chapters covering the various aspects of China's economy: The historical background: Socialist economic development - The four modernizations - Human resources - Agriculture and rural developments - Industry and energy - Transport and communications - Foreign trade and tourism - Finance and banking - The new consumer markets. Also includes a bibliography (p.135-138); a directory of useful names and addresses; and statistical data from 1949 to about 1984. Index. *Class No:* 338(510)(035)

Japan

Yearbooks & Directories

[2351]

JAPAN. Economic Planning Agency. **Economic survey of Japan.** Tokyo, Japan Times Ltd., 1969-. Annual. 3900 yen; $23. ISSN: 00214833.

Superseded *Japanese economic statistics*.

The English-language edition of the Economic Planning Agency's annual economic white paper. *Class No:* 338(52)(058)

[2352]

-BANK OF JAPAN. **Economic statistics annual.** Tokyo, the Bank, 1966-. ISSN: 09106006.

Contains annual statistics on money and banking, securities and public finance, balance of payments, and foreign exchange. Supported by the Bank's *Economic statistics monthly* (1946-).
Class No: 338(52)(058)

Asia—Middle & Near East

Bibliographies

[2353]

BLAUVELT, E. *and* DURLACHER, J., *eds*. **Sources of African and Middle Eastern economic information.** Aldershot, Hants., Gower Publishing Co. Ltd., 1982. 288p. ISBN: 0866022788.

Arranged in 2 parts: pt.1: Source publications; pt.2: The publishing bodies. Part 1 lists the sources by Middle Eastern country: part 2 has 2 indexes: 1. Sources listed alphabeticaly - 2. Sources by subject and country. *Class No:* 338(53+56)(01)

Handbooks & Manuals

[2354]

Middle East economic handbook. Sinclair, S. London, Euromonitor Publications Ltd., 1986. [6],487p. tables, charts, maps. £45; $70. ISBN: 086338126x.

A regional overview precedes 19 chapters on individual Middle Eastern countries (Algeria ... United Arab Emirates), with discussions on the country's economy, political system, etc. A 'Factfile' of statistical data compares various economic aspects of the countries. *Class No:* 338(53+56)(035)

Reports Literature

[2355]

The Middle East review: economic and business report, 1989. 15th ed. Saffron Walden, Essex, World of Information, 1989. 191 p. tables, maps. £25. ISSN: 03053210.

First published 1974. Annual.

A general chapter precedes chapters on individual countries, arranged

....(contd.)
A-Z (Afghanistan ... Yemen,PDR). For each chapter an introductory article is followed by key facts, key indicators, country profile, and business guide. *Class No:* 338(53+56)(047)

Gulf States

Tables & Data Books

[2356]

KUBURSI, A. **The Economics of the Arabian Gulf:** a statistical sourcebook. Beckenham, Kent. Croom Helm, 1984. xi,206p. £45. ISBN: 0709915438.

A list of the 154 tables and an introduction precede the 10 subject sections of tables: 1. General statistics - 2. National statistics - 3. Oil and gas - 4. Trade and international transactions - 5. Population and employment - 6. Public finance - 7. Agriculture - 8. Industry - 9. Money and credit - 10. Education. Each section has a brief introduction and sources are indicated. *Class No:* 338(536)(083)

India

Yearbooks & Directories

[2357]

INDIA. Ministry of Finance (Economic Division). **Economic survey ...** 1993-94 New Delhi, Government of India Press, 1993. 162p.+ 115p. of statistics. Rs.10; £2; $4.

Annual.

9 chapters on the economic situation are followed by an appendix of statistical tables, arranged in 9 subject sections, all subdivided. Data is for 1992/93. *Class No:* 338(540)(058)

Histories

[2358]

The Cambridge economic history of India. Cambridge, Cambridge University Press, 1982-83. 2v. diagrs, tables, maps. v.1 £60; v.2. £80. ISBN: 0521226929, v.1; 0521228026, v.2.

V.1: *c.*1200-1750; edited by T. Raychaudhuri and L. Habib; v.2: *c.* 1757-*c.*1970; edited by D. Kumar and M. Desai.

Brings together the work of economists, historians, sociologists, social anthropologists and demographers, to summarize existing knowledge and undertake new research. *Class No:* 338(540)(091)

[2359]

ROTHERMUND, D. **An Economic history of India.** London, Routledge & Kegan Paul, 1988. iv, 224p. £40. ISBN: 0709942281.

A summary of the structure and dynamics of the Indian economy from pre-colonial times to 1986. 12 chapters: 1. The structure of the traditional economy - 2. The development of maritime trade and the beginnings of colonial rule - 3. The agrarian State and the Company ... 10. India's dilemma; dynamic industrialization and static agriculture - 11. The 'Green Revolution' and the industrial recession -12. Population growth and economic development. Index. 'Focuses on 20th rather than 19th century and on issues of India's aborted growth and restricted development' (*The Economic history review*, second series, v.42(2), May, 1989. *Class No:* 338(540)(091)

Bibliographies

[2360]

Annotated bibliography on the economic history of India (1500 AD to 1947 AD). Gokhale Institute of Politics and Economics *and* Indian Council of Social Science Research. Colombia, Mo, South Asia Books, 1978. 4v.

V.1:(1) Selections from the records; (2) Survey and settlement reports; (3) Gazetteers; (4) Acts and regulations. V.2: (5) British parliamentary papers; (6) Reports of committees and commissions. V.3: (7) Census reports; (8) Serials. V.4: (9) Books; (10) Articles; (11) Theses. V. 1-3 are in the form of source materials, v.4 mostly research work. Statistical content annotated exhaustively. Subject, region and author indexes at the end of each part.
Class No: 338(540)(091)(01)

Thailand

Yearbooks & Directories

[2361]

BANK OF THAILAND. **Annual economic report, 1991.** Bangkok, the Bank, 1992. [4], 135p. *Gratis*.

First published 1943. Annual.

Contains a summary report on developments in 1991 and outlook for 1992. Also a report on the activities of the Bank in 1991. A statistical section has data to 1991. Information is updated by the Bank's *Quarterly Bulletin* (previously *Monthly bulletin*). 1961 -. ISSN 0125605x). *Class No:* 338(593)(058)

Malaysia

Periodicals

[2362]
BANK NEGARA MALAYSIA. Quarterly bulletin, 1968-. Kuala Lumpur, the Bank. not priced. ISSN: 01278428.
Early title was *Quarterly economic bulletin*.
A review of economic conditions in Malaysia precedes a statistical section of 63 tables relating to money and banking, foreign trade and payments, production and prices, etc., with data for more than 10 years to the present. *Class No:* 338(595)(051)

Islamic World

Bibliographies

[2363]
SIDDIQI, M. N. Contemporary literature on Islamic economics: a selected classified bibliography of works in English, Arabic and Urdu up to 1975. Jeddah. International Centre for Research on Islamic Economics; Leicester, Islamic Foundation 1978. [2], 69p. (*Research report.1.*)
700 entries arranged in 7 sections: Economic philosophy of Islam - Economic system of Islam - Islamic critique of contemporary economics - Economic analyses in Islamic framework - History of economic thought in Islam - Miscellaneous - Bibliographies. English translations of Arabic and Urdu titles are given in brackets. Author index. *Class No:* 338(5.297)(01)

Africa

Bibliographies

[2364]
BLAUVELT, E. *and* DURLACHER, J., *eds.* Sources of African and Middle Eastern economic information. Aldershot, Hants., Gower Publishing Co. Ltd., 1982. 320p. ISBN: 0566022796.
Arranged in 2 parts: pt.1: Source publications; pt.2: The publishing bodies. Part 1 lists the sources by African country; part 2 has 2 indexes: 1. Sources listed alphabetically - 2 Sources by subject and country. *Class No:* 338(6)(01)

Handbooks & Manuals

[2365]
African economic handbook. Hodd, M. London, Euromonitor Publications Ltd., 1986. [6],335p. tables, charts. £45; $70. ISBN: 0863380883.
A regional overview is followed by sections on East, West, Central and Southern Africa, covering Kenya, Sudan, Tanzania, Ghana, Ivory Coast, Nigeria, Cameroon, Congo, Zaire, South Africa, Zambia and Zimbabwe. For each country economic profiles with in-depth statistical data. No index. *Class No:* 338(6)(035)

Histories

[2366]
KONCZACKI, Z.A. *and* KONCZACKI, J., *eds.* An Economic history of tropical Africa. London, Cass, 1977. 2v. (xx,310 & xv,260p.) illus., maps. £22.50 each vol. ISBN: 0714629197, v.1; 0714629154, v.2.
V.1: The pre-colonial period; v.2: The colonial period. Each volume reprints selected articles; v.1 having 28 articles in 7 subject groups, and v.2 having 22 articles in 5 subject groups. Index to each v. *Class No:* 338(6)(091)

Egypt

Periodicals

[2367]
Economic review. Cairo, Central Bank of Egypt, 1961-. Quarterly. ISSN: 00089249.
Each issue contains 1 or 2 articles, and sections on national developments, international developments, and statistics. The statistical section is mainly concerned with financial statistics, but also includes economic data. *Class No:* 338(620)(051)

Africa—East & Equatorial

Bibliographies

[2368]
KILLICK, A. The Economies of East Africa: a bibliography, 1963-1975. Boston, Mass., G.K. Hall, 1976. xxiv, 150p.
Nearly 1000 entries for English-language printed publications, plus mimeographed items and government documents, on the economies of

....(contd.)
Kenya. Tanzania and Uganda. Arranged by subject areas. Two indexes - to subjects and places, and to authors, editors and chairmen. *Class No:* 338(67)(01)

[2369]
—KILLICK, A., *and others*. The Economies of East Africa: a bibliography, 1974-1980. Boston, Mass., G.K. Hall, 1984. $55. ISBN: 0816185832.
Nearly 2000 entries published between 1974-1980, focusing broadly on the economies of Kenya, Tanzania and Uganda. Brief introductory essays compare 1872 entries in this work with 968 entries in the previous one. 8 broad subject categories, each subdivded. Useful indexes and appendices include a list of abbreviations, about 30 frequently cited serials, author index and subject index. *Class No:* 338(67)(01)

South Africa

[2370]
JONES, S. *and* MUELLER, A. The South African economy, 1910-1990. London, Macmillan, 1992. 380p. 47.50. Maps. ISBN: 0333515307.
27 chapters in 3 parts: A: Laying the foundations of a modern economy; B: The open economy; C: The modern economy takes shape since 1961. Index. *Class No:* 338(680)

Handbooks & Manuals

[2371]
HOUGHTON, D.H. The South African economy. 4th ed. Cape Town, Oxford, Oxford University Press, 1976. xiii, 310p. illus., graphs, tables, map. £12.50. ISBN: 0195700805.
First published 1964.
12 chapters relate the economic story of South Africa from the beginnings to 1975, the final chapter being on conditions for sustained progress. A statistical appendix of 25 tables, a select reading list (p.294-304) arranged according to chapters, and an analytical index Intended primarily for South African readers. *Class No:* 338(680)(035)

America—North & Central

Handbooks & Manuals

[2372]
Central American economic handbook. London, Euromonitor Publications Ltd., 1987. x,172p. tables, charts. £45. ISBN: 0863382185.
Examines the socio-economic trends and developments in several central American countries. 11 chapters: 1. Central America in a world context - 2. Regional interdependence - 3. Mexico - 4. Costa Rica - 5 El Salvador - 6. Guatemala - 7. Honduras - 8. Nicaragua - 9. Panama - 10. Future outlook - 11. Factfile (statistics). Index, p.165-172 (double-column, with tables indicated in bold). *Class No:* 338(71/73)(035)

Canada

Bibliographies

[2373]
BROWN, B.E., *ed.* Canadian business and economics: a guide to sources of information. Rev. ed. Ottawa, Canadian Library Association, 1984. 469p. Can$90. ISBN: 0888021615.
First published 1976.
Over 6500 entries for government publications, monographs, reference works, serials and theses, plus business databases and services. Omits periodical articles, newspapers, and most government statistical series, and highly specialized reports. 22 subject areas. Many cross-references. Dictionary index in English and French, listing subjects, titles, authors and publishers. '... a valuable, comprehensive and unique reference tool' (*RQ*, Fall, 1984, p.102). *Class No:* 338(71)(01)

Histories

Bibliographies

[2374]
DICK, T.J.O. Economic history of Canada: a guide to information sources. Detroit, Mich., Gale Research Co., 1978. vii,174p. $68. ISBN: 0810312921.
Nearly 1000 items listed in 5 chapters: 1. Interpretive and bibliographic sources - 2. From colonial times to the present - 3. The colonial period to 1867 - 4. Confederation (1867) to 1920 - 5. From 1920 to the present. Each chapter and section has a short introduction and is subdivided into general works, statistical records, theses o

..(contd.)

economic growth, sectors and industries, economic organization, technology and productivity change, and welfare resources. Author, title and subject indexes. *Class No:* 338(71)(091)(01)

Caribbean

Handbooks & Manuals

[2375]

Caribbean economic handbook. Fraser, P.D. London, Euromonitor Publications Ltd., 1985. vi,241p. tables. £45; $70. ISBN: 0863380891.

Aims to covert all aspects of the economies of the major islands of the region, including the Bahamas, Bermuda, Barbados, Cuba, the Dominican Republic, Haiti, Jamaica, Puerta Rico, and Trinidad and Tobago. 3 chapters: The Caribbean in a world context - Regional overview - Outlook. A 'Factfile' has comparative statistical data in 28 tables on population, distribution, retail sales, imports, health care, etc. *Class No:* 338(729)(035)

Latin America

Handbooks & Manuals

[2376]

UNITED NATIONS. Economic Commission for Latin America and the Caribbean. **Economic survey of Latin America and the Caribbean, 1985.** New York United Nations, 1987. 660p. $65. ISBN: 9211211352.

First published 1948. Annual.

Reviews trends in the Latin American and Caribbean economic situation, including inflation, trade, output, external finance, and foreign trade. Data for the whole region and individual countries. *Class No:* 338(729.99)(035)

Histories

[2377]

CORTÉS CONDE, R. *and* STEIN, S.J., *eds*. **Latin America: a guide to economic history, 1830-1930.** Berkely, CA., University of California Press, 1977. xviii, 685p. $75. ISBN: 0520029569.

Commissioned by the Joint Committee on Latin American Studies of the ACLS, the SSRC and the Consejo Latinamericano de Ciencia Sociales.

4450 mostly annotated items, in 8 sections; each written by a Latin American or US scholar: a historiographical introduction (in Spanish and English) - General bibliography (English) - Argentina (Spanish) - Brazil (Portuguese) - Chile (Spanish) - Colombia (English) - Mexico (Spanish) - Peru (Spanish). Each section begins with an introductory essay, followed by a section on reference works and major archival sources, and 8 topical sections. Author and journal indexes. '... an indispensible research tool for the student ...' (*Journal of social history*, Summer 1980, p.664-6). *Class No:* 338(729.99)(091)

[2378]

GRIFFIN, C.C., *ed*. **Latin American: a guide to historical literature.** Austin, Texas, University of Texas Press, 1972 (Reprinted 1979 by University of Wisconsin Press). xxx,700p. $35. ISBN: 0299082202.

Published for the Conference on Latin American History and issued as Publication no.4 of the Conference ...

Contains 7087 annotated entries in 7 chronological sections. Includes references to items on education, government and parties, foreign relations, law, society and labour. *Class No:* 338(729.99)(091)

USA

[2379]

PORTER, G., *ed*. **Encyclopedia of American economic history.** New York, Scribner's, 1980. 3v. (xii,1286p.). $225. ISBN: 0684162717.

In 5 sections: 1. The historiography of American economic history - 2. The chronology of American economic history - 3. The framework of American economic growth - 4. The institutional framework - 5. The social framework. Includes 72 interpretative and signed articles (e.g., on slavery, prices and wages, the automobile, immigration, women). Glossary. Comprehensive index. 'A superb addition to the reference literature on American economic history' (*RQ*, v.20(1), Fall 1980, p.93). *Class No:* 338(73)

Handbooks & Manuals

[2380]

O'HARA, F.M. *and* SICIGNANO, R. **Handbook of United States economic and financial indicators.** Westport, CT., Greenwood Press, 1985. vi,224p. $42.95; £35. ISBN: 0313239541.

Brings together reference data on more than 200 major standard measures of economic activity in the US, arranged in dictionary format (Accession rate, manufacturing ... Workweek, average

....(contd.)

manufacturing). Entries include description, derivation, publisher, announced in, cumulations (tables), projections, more information. 3 appendices: Nonquantitative indicators - Abbreviation list & guide to sources - List of compilers of indicators. Index, p.215-224. *Class No:* 338(73)(035)

Tables & Data Books

[2381]

Economic indicators. US Congress for the Joint Economic Committee, *prepared by the Council of Economic Advisors*. Washington, DC., Government Printing Office, 1948-. tables, graphs, Monthly. $28pa.

Data on prices, wages, production, business activity, purchasing power, credit money and Federal finance. Available online (DIALOG). *Class No:* 338(73)(083)

[2382]

Survey of current business. US Department of Commerce. Bureau of Economic Analysis. Washington, DC., the Department, 1921-. Monthly. $29pa. ISSN: 00396222.

Consists of a general survey and articles, with invaluable centre pages on blue-tinted paper - 'Current business statistics'. Each issue carries a detailed subject index to sections and individual series of statistics. Available online (DIALOG) *Class No:* 338(73)(083)

Histories

[2383]

OLSON, J.S. **Dictionary of United States economic history.** Westport, CT, Greenwood Press, 1992. 667p. $85. ISBN: 0313265321.

Over 1300 concise entries, averaging 250-500 words each and including brief bibliographies. Wide subject coverage, including biographies of prominent people. Selected bibliography. Brief chronology. Name and subject index. '... useful tool ...' (*Choice*, v.20(7), March 1993,, p.1118). *Class No:* 338(73)(091)

[2384]

POULSON, B.W. **Economic history of the United States.** New York, Macmillan Publishing Co. Ltd., 1981. x,672p. tables. ISBN: 0023962208.

A textbook of 23 chapters arranged chronologically in 3 sections: 1. Economic growth in the colonial and early national period: to 1790- 2. The transition to modern economic growth: 1790-1890 - 3. A mature economy: 1890 to the present. Footnotes, and suggested readings after each chapter. Index, p.661-672. *Class No:* 338(73)(091)

Bibliographies

[2385]

HUTCHINSON, W.K., *ed*. **American economic history:** a guide to information sources. Detroit, Mich., Gale Research Co., 1980. xii, 296p. $68. ISBN: 0810312875.

Covers American economic history from the colonial period to about 1960. Arranged in 10 chapters (e.g., Population and labor force - Land and agricultural development - Industrial growth and structure - Monetary and financial developments) within which annotated entries are complemented by unannotated listings of works for further study. Appendices list the major organizations concerned with American economic history and the major journals in the field. *Class No:* 338(73)(091)(01)

[2386]

ORSAGH, T., *and others, eds*. **The Economic history of the United States prior to 1860:** an annotated bibliography. Santa Barbara, CA., Clio Press, 1975. xiii, 100p.

799 entries for monographs and journal articles, arranged in 16 subject groupings, preceded by a general section. Most of the entries are annotated, if only briefly. Author and subject indexes. *Class No:* 338(73)(091)(01)

America—South

Handbooks & Manuals

[2387]

South American economic handbook. Blakemore, H. London, Euromonitor Publications Ltd., 1986. [5],274p. tables, charts. £45; $80. ISBN: 0863381251.

A regional overview precedes economic profiles for the 13 nations of South America (Argentina, Bolivia, Brazil, Chile, Colombia, Ecuador, the Guianas, Paraguay, Peru, Uruguay, Venezuela). *Class No:* 338(8)(035)

Uruguay

[2388]

FINCH, M.H.J. **A Political economy of Uruguay since 1870.** London, Macmillan Press; New York, St. Martin's Press, 1981. xiii,339p. tables, figs., map. £35; $29.95. ISBN: 0333278526, UK; 0312622449, US.

Published in association with the Center for Latin American Studies. 9 chapters: 1. The ideology of Batllismo, 1870-1970 - 2. Population and society - 3. Agrarian structure and performance - 4. Taxation and agricultural stagnation - 5. Exports and the meat industry - 6. Imports and industrialisation - 7. Public utilities and public corporations - 8. The economic crisis - 9. The military regime since 1973. Appendix: Foreign trade data. Notes (p.279-309) by chapter. Select bibliography (p.310-328), A-Z by author. Index (p.329-339). *Class No:* 338(899)

Australia

Periodicals

[2389]

The Australian economic review. Parkville, Institute of Applied Economic and Social Research, University of Melbourne, 1963-. Quarterly. A$145pa. ISSN: 00049018.

Each issue contains a summary of the economic situation and several chapters on specific economic and social issues. Lists special articles, monographs by members of the Institute's staff, and technical papers. Modelled on the *National Institute economic review.*
Class No: 338(94)(051)

Institutions & Associations

[2390]

FRASER, R. **Western European economic organizations.** Harlow, Essex, Longman, 1992. 448p. $145; £85. ISBN: 0582068452.

Data on international organizations precedes information on economic policy making in 19 Western European countries. Includes central banks, government agencies, regulatory bodies, stock exchanges and other organizations with input into economic policy making. Data includes postal address, telephone & fax numbers, principal officers, structure, funding, aims and objectives, history, affiliations, publications. Index of country and organization names. *Class No:* 338:061:061.2

Economic Policies & Controls

China

[2391]

HOWE, C. *and* WALKER, K.R. **The Foundations of the Chinese planned economy: a documentary survey, 1953-65.** London, Macmillan Press, 1989. 384p. £45. ISBN: 033346186X.

Traces the important changes in China in that period, through the medium of Chinese economic documents, most of which have not previously been translated. In 4 parts: 1. Strategy and planning - 2. Industrial development and organization - 3. Agricultural development - 4. Population and labour and urbanization. Index. *Class No:* 338.1/.5(510)

Economic Development

[2392]

Development index. East Kilbride, Glasgow (previously London), Overseas Development Administration, Library Services. 1967-. Monthly.

A list of periodical articles indexed by the Library of the Overseas Development Administration for current awareness. About 150 briefly annotated entries per issue, arranged under topics (*e.g.* Agricultural credit ... Women workers), on Third World countries. The country index is no longer provided. *Class No:* 338.1

[2393]

—Development contents. Glasgow, Overseas Development Administration Library. Monthly.

Contents pages of 'core' journals in the field of economic development. Reference numbers are given for articles listed in the above. *Class No:* 338.1(01)

Bibliographies

[2394]

GORMAN, G.E. *and* MAHONEY, M., *comps. & eds*. **Index to development studies literature.** Wokingham, Van Nostrand Reinhold (UK) Co Ltd., 1985. xxix,266p. £33. ISBN: 0442306342.

4452 items, arranged in subject groups, each sub-divided (International co-operation/international relations - economic policy/social policy/planning - economic conditions/economic research/economic system - institutional framework - culture/society - education/training - agriculture - industry - trade - transport - public finance/banking/international monetary relations - management/productivity - labour - demography/population - biology/food/health - environment/natural resources - earth science/space sciences - science/research/methodology - information/documentation). Author index, p.205-238. Keyword index, p.239-266. *Class No:* 338.1(01)

[2395]

GREAT BRITAIN. Department of Trade and Industry. **Index to development plans.** London, the Department, [1989]. [10]p. *Gratis.*

New eds. published at intervals.

A comprehensive list of current development plans available in the Export Market Information Centre of the Department.
Class No: 338.1(01)

[2396]

International development abstracts. Norwich, Geo Abstracts, 1982-. 6pa. £250pa (including annual index). ISSN: 02620855.

Compiled by members of the staff at the Centre for Development Studies, University College of Swansea.

Arranged in 22 subject sections, including urbanization, regional and spacial planning; education and training; international relations, conflict, cooperation and aid; and trade. Worldwide coverage. The annual *International development index* has author, subject and regional indexes. Available online (DIALOG) *Class No:* 338.1(01)

Handbooks & Manuals

[2397]

METRA CONSULTING. **Handbook of national development plans.** Gorle, P., *ed.* 2nd ed. London, Graham & Trotman, 1987. 2v.(400p.). loose-leaf., + supplements. £70. ISBN: 0860108376; 0860108384 Supp.1; 0860108392 Supp.2.

First published 1963, with updating supplements.

Summaries of national development plans for over 70 countries arranged A-Z by country. For each country a fact sheet with background data, comments on previous plans, summary of present plan (main assumptions - plan's strategy - priorities), allocation of funds by sectors, expected effect of plan on GDP, recent performance of plan. Half-yearly supplements. *Class No:* 338.1(035)

Dictionaries

[2398]

FRY, G.W. *and* MARTIN, G.R. **The International development dictionary** Santa Barbara, CA, ABC-Clio, 1991. 445p. $49. ISBN 0874365457.

458 terms, arranged A-Z under four major subject categories (Development thinkers/theorists, leaders and practitioners - Basic development concepts - Analytical concepts - Development movements, projects and organizations). Entries vary in length from one half to 3 pages. Numerous cross-references, a detailed index, and an A-Z list of entries facilitate access. Substantial bibliography of c350 books and articles. *Class No:* 338.1(038)

Polyglot

[2399]

SCHARF, T. *and* BALIN, M., *comps*. **Dictionary of development economics: economic terminology in three languages: English, French, German.** Amsterdam, Elsevier, 1969. xiii,268p.

3122 entries, in 12 chapters (1. Developing - 2. Planning - 3. Agriculture ... 12. Development statistics). English, French and German indexes. 'Slightly padded with matter extraneous to the subject, and in some cases carelessly edited, this is a useful little book which fills a definite need' (*Finance and development,* 1970, no.1 p.53-54). *Class No:* 338.1(038)=00

[2400]

—Dictionary of development banking. Amsterdam, Elsevier, 1972. vii,214p. Dfl.150; $79. ISBN: 0444410287.

1257 terms with English definitions, and French and German indexes. *Class No:* 338.1(038)=00

French

[2401]
UNITED NATIONS. Industrial Development Organization (UNIDO), Vienna. **Thesaurus of individual development terms** (English-French). Viet, J., *comp*. Vienna, the Organization, 1976. xi. 152p.
Also a French-English version. *Class No:* 338.1(038)=40

Developing Countries

Bibliographies

[2402]
Industrial development abstracts. United Nations. Industrial Development Organization (UNIDO), Vienna. New York, United Nations, 1971-. 2-4pa. price varies. (*UNIDO industrial information system INDIS*.) ISSN: 03782654.
About 200 indicative abstracts per issue of 'printed publications, such as major studies and reports, publications in series, and selected articles; from the reports and proceedings of expert working groups, workshops and seminars; internal studies; public information series; and reports related to technical assistance'. (*Introduction*). Arranged by computer access number. Subject and personal author indexes precede. *Class No:* 338.1(4/9-77)(01)

Great Britain

Bibliographies

[2403]
STONEY, P.J.M. *and* PATERSON, A.T. **A Bibliography of studies in regional industrial development**. Liverpool, University of Liverpool, Department of Business Studies, 1978. Supplement 1979. x,145p. £5. Supplement £1.50. ISBN: 0950631701; 095063171x, supplement.
Emanated from an empirical study of the Merseyside regions, but includes shorter sections of entries for other British regions and for the rest of the world. For Merseyside and the North West, the bibliography is a listing of titles arranged A-Z by author under subjects subdivided by form: Trade and industry - Regional science - Structure planning and development strategy - Urban studies. Author index. *Class No:* 338.1(410)(01)

Forecasting

Bibliographies

[2404]
FILDES, R., *ed*. **World index of economic forecasts**. 3rd ed. Aldershot, Hants, Gower Press, 1988. 400p. £75. ISBN: 056602702x.
First published in 1978, the first and second eds. edited by G.R. Cyriax.
A guide to econometric-based forecasting work of interest to businessmen and professional economists. Includes details of 470 forecasting groups in over 170 countries, together with their coverage, method and published output. *Class No:* 338.246(01)

Production

Worldwide

Tables & Data Books

[2405]
UNITED NATIONS. Department of International Economic and Social Affairs. **Industrial statistics yearbook, 1988**. 22nd ed. New York, United Nations, 1990. 2v. $50 each vol. ISBN: 9211613205 v.1; 9210611373 v.2; 9211613213 set.
First published for 1938/62. Early title was *Growth of world industry* then *Yearbook of industrial statistics*.
V.1. *General industrial statistics*; v.2. *Commodity production statistics, 1979-1988*. V.1. contains general industrial statistics providing the basic country data as well as a selection of indicators showing global and regional trends in industrial activity. V.2. deals specifically with annual statistics of production of individual commodities. *Class No:* 338.3/.4(100)(083)

Great Britain

Tables & Data Books

[2406]
GREAT BRITAIN. Department of Industry. Business Statistics Office. **Historical record of the census of production, 1907-1970**. London, HMSO, 1979. 402, lxvp. tables.
Contains 11 tables (*e.g.* 6. Analysis of employment, wages and salaries within industry, 1907 to 1970). 3 appendices (1: S.I.C., revised 1968). Bibliographies: A. Bibliography of census of production reports: B. Bibliography of associated publications. *Class No:* 338.3/.4(410)(083)

[2407]
—GREAT BRITAIN. Department of Industry. Business Statistics Office. **Annual census of production reports** ... 1970 -. London HMSO, 1971 -.
Continues *Report on the census of production* ... (1907-1968), which was normally five-yearly, covering mining and quarrying, manufacturing, construction, gas, electricity and water.
Annual census, 1971-; results for each industry published separately in the 'Business monitor: production series'(PA).
Others in the 'Business monitor: production series' give more up-to-date quarterly or annual production statistics for particular industries. *Class No:* 338.3/.4(410)(083)

[2408]
—Guides to official sources. No.6: Census of production reports. Interdepartmental Committee on Social and Economic Research. London, HMSO, 1961. x,86p.
Covers 'statistics prepared by the Board of Trade and published in the reports of the Census of Production and the Import Duties Act Inquiries for years from 1907 to 1958 (*Introduction*). *Class No:* 338.3/.4(410)(083)

Tourism

[2409]
ORGANISATION FOR ECONOMIC CO-OPERATION AND DEVELOPMENT. **Tourism policy and international tourism in OECD member countries, 1990-1991**. Paris, OECD, 1993. 202p. tables. F.180; £30; $42. ISBN: 9264138293.
Published annually since the 1970 ed.
Information on government policies in the field of tourism, accompanied by a statistical annex on recent trends (tourist flow, accommodation, payments, motives, transport, employment and prices). *Class No:* 338.48

[2410]
Travel trade gazette directory. 37th ed. London, Morgan-Grampion plc., in association with *Travel trade gazette*, 1993. £55. ISBN: 0862132193. ISSN: 09664297.
Sections, each starting with A-Z index: Travel agents - Car travel - Coach travel - Sea travel - Air travel - Travel trade information (National tourist and information offices; visa and passport offices; U.K. resort and regional information offices; associations, organizations and societies; national travel association) - Travel trade services - Tour operators - Special interest holidays - Hotels. Index to advertisers. *Class No:* 338.48

Bibliographies

[2411]
OVERTON, D. **Tourism: a guide to sources of information**. 2nd ed. London, Capital Planning Information, 1988. vi,82p. £16.50. (*CPI Information Reviews; no.4*.) ISBN: 0906011493.
1. Introduction (scope and purpose; general books; tourism textbooks) - 2. Sources of data - 3. Administration of tourism - 4. Tourist management, development and planning - 5. Environment - 6. Tourism for the disadvantaged - 7. Recreational and educational tourism - 8. Conference and business tourism - 9. Training - 10. Jobs - 11. Accommodation. Very sound literature guide. *Class No:* 338.48(01)

Handbooks & Manuals

[2412]
BAR-ON, R. **Travel and tourism data: a comprehensive research handbook on the world travel directory**. London Euromonitor, 1989. ix,366p. ISBN: 0863381316.
8 sections: 1. Travel and tourism: an overview - 2. International and domestic tourism: their scope and definition - 3. The principal sources of tourism data - 4. Methods of collecting tourism data - 5. The presentation, analysis and forecasting of time series - 6. Classification of travel and tourism data - 7. World tourism statistics, 1982-1986 - 8. Public sources of tourism data. Bibliography, p.339-351. Index to countries and subjects, p.359-366. *Class No:* 338.48(035)

Tables & Data Books

[2413]
ORGANISATION FOR ECONOMIC CO-OPERATION AND DEVELOPMENT. **National and international tourism statistics, 1974-1985**. 1st ed. Paris, OECD, 1989. 727p. £45; $80; F.380. ISBN: 9264032215.
Tables and graphs showing the trend of national and international demand over nearly two decades. In 2 parts: National tourism, by country of OECD plus US, Canada and Japan, A-Z; International tourism, similarly arranged. Data includes arrivals, nights spent, receipts, expenditures, etc. *Class No:* 338.48(083)

[2414]

WORLD TOURISM ORGANIZATION. Compendium of tourism statistics, 1987-1991. 13th ed. Madrid, Organizacion Mundial del Turismo, 1993. x,216p. tables. $50;£38. ISBN: 9284400049. ISSN: 10141744.

First published for 1976.

Provides in a condensed form the basic statistical series on national and international tourism supply and demand in the various countries and regions of the world. Following the main statistical section are: World and regional totals (on tinted paper); Technical notes; and Main sources of information, p.214. Both the above are updated by the quarterly *Travel and tourism indicators*. *Class No:* 338.48(083)

Prices & Costs

Worldwide

[2415]

UNION BANK OF SWITZERLAND. Prices and earnings around the globe: a comparison of purchasing power in 52 cities. Zurich, the Bank, 1988. 44p. tables, illus. *Gratis. (UBS publications on business, banking and monetary topics, no.108.)* ISBN: x21091010x.

International price comparison (of 14 items); wages and salaries around the world (5 sections); appendix of 27 tables (p.29-44). *Class No:* 338.5(100)

Trade & Commerce

Bibliographies

[2416]

NICHOLAS, D. Commodities futures trading: a guide to information sources and computerized services. London, Mansell, 1985. x,144p. £18. ISBN: 0720117038.

Arranged in 6 sections (Market trading and price distribution services - newspapers - newsletters - journals and magazines - yearbooks, directories and reference works - books). There are introductions to each section and subsection, and arrangement within sections is A-Z by service or title. An appendix gives addresses of online database hosts. Index, p.139-144. Mainly relates to computerized services, mainly in UK and US, some Netherlands. *Class No:* 339(01)

Protectionism

[2417]

LUTZ, J.M. Protectionism: an annotated bibliography with analytical introductions. Ann Arbor, Mich., Peiron Press, 1989. 207p. $40. (*Resources on contemporary issues.*) ISBN: 0876502494.

Each chapter has in introduction and ends with an annotated bibliography of *c.*20-200 items. Topics covered include the rise of protectionism, tariffs, non-tariff barriers to trade, hegemony, the General Agreement on Tariffs and Trade (GATT), customs unions, free trade areas, trading blocs, etc. As well as the US, other industrialized countries and developing countries are covered. Chronology since World War II. Glossary. Author and title indexes. '... a thorough treatment of protectionism as an economic tool since World War II in an easy-to-read format' (*Choice*, v.26(10), July 1989, p.1664). *Class No:* 339(01)PRO

Dictionaries

[2418]

BRANCH, A.E., *ed*. Dictionary of commercial terms and abbreviations. London, Witherby & Co., 1984. xiii,458p. £9.50. ISBN: 0900886900.

Aimed at students and includes terms found in accountancy, advertising, commerce, computers, economics, insurance, international trade, law, marketing, personnel management, real estate, selling, statistics, tourism and transport. Definitions are brief. 5 appendices (A. Further recommended textbook reading - B. Addresses and roles of professional institutions/associations - C. World currencies - D. Conversion weights and measures and conversion factors - E. List of chambers of commerce in the UK.). *Class No:* 339(038)

Polyglot

[2419]

Multilingual dictionary of commercial international trade and shipping terms: English-French-Spanish-German. Branch, A.E., *and others*. London, Witherby, 1990. 255p. £19.95 ISBN: 0948691905.

Lists some 2200 English terms used in the daily conduct of international trade and commerce with, under each term, the French, Spanish and German equivalents. *Class No:* 339(038)=00

Spanish

[2420]

RODRIGUES, L.J. *and* BERNET SOLER, J. Harrap's glossary of English and Spanish commercial and industrial terms. London, Harrap, 1990. 288p. £14.99. ISBN: 0245600183.

Class No: 339(038)=60

Arabic

[2421]

BRANCH, A.E. *and* HAKMEH, J.A. Dictionary of English-Arabic commercial, international trade and shipping terms. London, Witherby & Co., Ltd. 1988. 257p. £21. ISBN: 0948691611.

Wide coverage of the business sector, including commerce, customs, documentation, economics, exports, tourism, etc. *Class No:* 339(038)=927

Reviews & Abstracts

[2422]

Wilson business abstracts. New York, Wilson, 1982-.

Claims to provide cover-to-cover indexing and abstracts for the 350 most-demanded business periodicals. Indexing coverage from July 1982; abstracting coverage from June 1990. Available only online, on CD-ROM and on magnetic tape. *Class No:* 339(048)

Periodicals

Bibliographies

[2423]

European directory of trade and business journals. London, Euromonitor Publications Ltd., 1990. [6],339p. £135. ISBN: 0813383394.

Arranged geographically (a Pan-European and International section, followed by 17 West European countries), then subdivided by journal title, A-Z. Data include name of publisher, address, circulation, scope of readership, periodicity and editorial content. Included are the 'main journals which can be accessed for companies, organizations and individuals interested in finding information on Western European markets and industries, particularly in member countries of the forthcoming Single European Market' (*Foreword*). General index, p.289-308; subject index, p.309-339. *Class No:* 339(051)(01)

Europe

Handbooks & Manuals

[2424]

The European marketplace Hogan, J., *ed*. London, Macmillan, 1990. 650p. 50. ISBN: 0333518586.

Step-by-step business information path through the European market as a whole and 12 individual member states. 7 parts: 1. The European marketplace - 2. The economics of Europe - 3. Financing European business - 4. European Community law - 5. Training and education - 6. Official information sources - 7. Published information sources. Bibliography. Index. *Class No:* 339(4)(035)

Great Britain

Yearbooks & Directories

[2425]

MILLARD, P., *ed*. Trade associations and professional bodies of the United Kingdom. 12th rev. ed. Andover, Hants., Gale Research International, 1993. 800p. £75. ISBN: 187347721x.

First published 1962. First 9 editions by Pergamon Press.

An alphabetical and subject classified guide, arranged in 3 parts: Alphabetical list of trade associations and professional bodies; Chambers of commerce, trade, industry and shipping; Overseas chambers of commerce with offices in the UK. Subject index (p.557-606); Geographic index by town (p.607-648). The Part 1 listing is arranged by name, with address and telephone/telex/fax numbers. *Class No:* 339(410)(058)

Tables & Data Books

[2426]

GREAT BRITAIN. Central Statistical Office. Overseas trade statistics of the United Kingdom. London, HMSO, 1970-. Monthly. £385pa.

First published 1848. Previously (1965-69) as Board of Trade's *Overseas trade accounts of the United Kingdom*. Now issued in the Business Statistics Office's *Business monitor* series, MM20.

Detailed statistics of exports and imports compiled from declarations made to HM Customs and Excise by importers and exporters and their agents. Tables: General summary - Summary of imports and exports by area and country - Imports summary by commodities and countries

....*(contd.)*

- Imports by commodities and countries - Imports by detailed commodities - Exports summary by commodities and countries - Exports by commodities and countries - Exports by detailed commodities. Index of commodities. Monthly issues give cumulative totals, the December issue having annual figures.
Class No: 339(410)(083)

[2427]

—Guide to the classification for overseas trade statistics. Central Statistical Office. London, HMSO, 1992. 375p. £34. (*Business monitor, MA21*.) ISBN: 0115351787.

Arranged by Standard International Trade Classification number (SITC), followed by Commodity code number, and trade description. Subject index. *Class No:* 339(410)(083)

Russia

Handbooks & Manuals

[2428]

KNIGHT, M.G. **How to do business with Russians:** a handbook and guide for Western world business people. New York, Quorum Books, 1987. xxiv,311p. £40.50; $45. ISBN: 0899302114.

24 chapters arranged in 2 parts: 1. Trading with the Soviet Union: the way it operates - 2. The structure of Soviet foreign trade operations and orders of a business transaction. *Class No:* 339(47)(035)

Libraries

[2429]

European directory of business information libraries. Euromonitor, 1990. xi,193p. £160. ISBN: 086338367x.

A Pan-European and international section is followed by country sections. A-Z, (Austria ... United Kingdom - West Germany), subdivided by name of organizations.Data includes address; telephone, fax & telex numbers; contact; availability; stock; and services. General and subject indexes. *Class No:* 339:061:026/027

Institutions & Associations

[2430]

EUROPEAN COMMUNITIES. Commission. **Directory of European Communities trade and professional associations.** 5th ed. Luxembourg. Office for Official Publications of the European Community, 1992. 516p. ISBN: 9282641627. ISSN: 07717865.

In French, English and German. 11 sections, some subdivided: Chambers of commerce and industry; Industry; Crafts; Small & medium-sized enterprises; Trade; Transport; Professional; Other activities; Unions; Consumer and other organizations; Miscellaneous. Entries give addresses, telephone and fax numbers, date started, chairman, secretary general. Index of acronyms and abbreviations. Analytical index, p.494-508. Name index, p.509-16.
Class No: 339:061:061.2

Balance of Payments

[2431]

INTERNATIONAL MONETARY FUND. **Balance of payments yearbook, 1938, 1946, 1947-.** Washington, D.C., I.M.F., 1949-. tables. $56pa for the 1993 2-part yearbook). ISSN: 02523035.

Continues the series of figures issued by the League of Nations, covering 1926 (1910 in a few cases) to 1938, and the United Nations, covering 1939 to 1945.

Covers *c.*140 countries, A-Z. Part 1 has aggregated and detailed tables,standard presentation for each country giving data under headings in 8 subdivided sections (A. Current account - B. Direct investment and other long-term capital - C. Other short-term capital - D. Net errors and omissions - E. Counterpart items - F. Exceptional financing - G. Liabilities constituting foreign authorities' reserves - H. Total change in reserves.). Notes on tables. Part 2 has 55 tables of area and world totals of balance of payments components and aggregates.Information on countries is based partly on requirements laid down in the *Balance of payments manual* (4th ed., 1977).
Class No: 339.053

Great Britain

[2432]

GREAT BRITAIN. Central Statistical Office. **United Kingdom balance of payments, 1993.** London, HMSO., 1993. Annual. 89p. £13.25. ISBN: 0116205970. ISSN: 09507558.

10 sections: 1. General description of accounts - 2. Visible trade - 3. Invisibles: services ... 6. Invisibles: earnings on UK external assets and liabilities. 7 Transactions in UK external assets and liabilities ... 10. Exchange rates. Glossary. Index. Known as the 'Pink book'.
Class No: 339.053(410)

Businesses

[2433]

Who owns whom, 1993: United Kingdom and Republic of Ireland. High Wycombe, Bucks, Dun & Bradstreet International, 1993. 2v. ISBN: 0901491314. ISSN: 01404040.

First published 1958. Annual, with quarterly supplements.

Designed to help anyone needing to know about company connections. V.3 lists subsidiaries and associates of parent companies registered in the UK and in the Republic of Ireland; foreign parent companies and their subsidiaries and associates in the UK and Ireland. V.2 is an A-Z index of subsidiary and associated companies, showing their parents. Parent companies are also listed and marked 'Parent entry'. Who owns whom online is also available via the publisher.

Similar volumes are published for Continental Europe (now issued as V.1 & 2 of the volumes for Continental Europe, V.3 & 4 being those listed above), North America, and Australia and the Far East.
Class No: 339.1

Databases

[2434]

BASCH, R. **Finding foreign firms:** a survey of international company directories. In *Database*, v.12(2), April 1989, p.13-25.

On the capabilities - and quirks - of company directory databases. Compares 25 databases (numbers of companies included, information given, price, reliability, etc.). Appendix A lists additional international business directory-type databases. *Class No:* 339.1(003.4)

[2435]

The **Instant guide to company information online:** Europe. Spencer, N., *ed.* 2nd ed. London, The British Library, *Science Reference and Information Library*, 1993. [iii],64p. tables. £35. ISBN: 0712308032.

First published 1991.

Tabulates *c.*100 databases containing company data for each of 16 Western European countries (EC members, Austria, Switzerland, Norway and Sweden), indicating industry, product, codes, number of employees, profit and loss, etc. Separate A-Z listing of databases gives contact details, coverage, language and special features.
Class No: 339.1(003.4)

[2436]

RYAN, F.J. **Company information online:** buyer's guide to British directory databases. In *Business information review*, v.1(2), October 1984, p.26-43.

Discusses 4 databases in detail (ICC British company directory; ICC British company financial datasheets; JLS - Jordan line services; File KBE - Key British enterprises) and adds information on a fifth (EKOL - European Kompass online). *Class No:* 339.1(003.4)

Bibliographies

[2437]

Legal industrial espionage: a sourcebook and guide to finding company information. Newbury, Berks, Eurofi plc., 1988. [3],195p. £42.50. ISBN: 0907304427.

8 chapters: 1. Covert intelligence - 2. Statutory information - 3. Published sources (directories and yearbooks, periodicals, card index services, trade literature) - 4. Online access to information - 5. Patents, trade marks and industrial design - 6. Specialized information services - 7. Market research reports and services - 8. Libraries. Aims to show how anyone can set about obtaining detailed and in-depth company information by legal means. Index, p.189-195. *Class No:* 339.1(01)

[2438]

Research index: the fortnightly library service which indexes the news, views and comments on industries and companies. Dorset, Broadmayne, Business Surveys Ltd., 1965- Fortnightly, with half-yearly cumulation. £250pa. ISSN: 00345296.

Indexes *c.*100,000 articles and news items pa in *c.*130 British business, economic and trade periodicals, and the national press. Section 1 (pink pages) covers industrial and commercial news and reports not dealing specifically with a particular company. A-Z headings, *c.*180, Accountancy ... Yugoslavia. Section 2: Company, A-Z. A current awareness service. *Class No:* 339.1(01)

Dictionaries

Polyglot

[2439]

EUROPEAN PARLIAMENT. **Terminologie le la société anonyme européenne/Terminology of the European company.** 3rd ed. Luxembourg. the Parliament, 1981. . 319p. £8.50.

First published, 1968.

A six - language list of words and expressions. (English/French/German/Italian/Dutch/Danish). First listing in English with equivalents in the other languages. Indexes in the other languages referring to the English list. *Class No:* 339.1(038)=00

Histories

[2440]

DERDAK, T., *ed*. International directory of company histories. Chicago, Ill., St. James Press, 1987-. To be in 5v., plus supplementary vols. £85. $130 each vol. ISBN: 0912289104, v.1; 1558620125, v.2; 1558620591, v.3; 1558620605, v.4; 1558621768, v.5; 1558620346, set.

Compiled with the assistance of the Faculty of History, University of Chicago.

Basic information and short company histories for *c*.1250 leading companies in the United States, Canada, Great Britain, Europe and Japan, arranged A-Z by business category (Advertising ... Utilities). Each entry is about 1500-3000 words in length and includes basic information (Headquarters, capitalization, subsidiaries, etc.) and a company history written by a trained historian. A v.6 (ISBN 1558621768) is the first of the supplementary volumes, to be published twice a year, containing additional company entries and revised entries. *Class No:* 339.1(091)

[2441]

GRANT, D. Business histories and biographies an introduction. In *Business information review*, v.4(2), October 1987, p.29-32.

Evaluates the use of business histories and biographies as source materials, and provides a bibliography of 20 up-to-date sources. *Class No:* 339.1(091)

[2442]

ROOM, A. Corporate eponymy: a biographical dictionary of persons behind the names of major American, British, European and Asian businesses. Jefferson, NC, & London, McFarland, 1992. xx,280p. $35. £29.75. ISBN: 0899506798.

Arranged A-Z by name of business (*e.g.* Cadbury; Jack Daniels; Steinway; Ritz; Barclay). Short entries with basic information on who, where, when and how businesses were named, with concise description of products. Mainly the English-speaking world. Short selected bibliography. Complements Room's *Dictionary of trade name origins* (1982) which is broader in scope. '... worthwhile addition to any business collection and will intrigue many who happen to pick it up.'(*Booklist*, v.89(7), 1 December 1992, p.687). *Class No:* 339.1(091)

Official Records

[2443]

ARMSTRONG, J. *and* JONES, S. Business documents their origins, sources and uses in historical research. London, Mansell Publishing Ltd., 1987. xvi,251p. illus. £30. ISBN: 0720118468.

An introduction for the archivist and researcher to business documents and their value for historical research. 15 sections, preceded by an introduction on document creation: 1. Prospectuses - 2. Articles of association - 3. Board minute books - 4. Letter books - 5. Chairman's statement - 6. Registers of directors - 7. Registers of members - 8. Diaries - 9. Book-keeping records: journals and ledgers - 10. Balance sheets and profit and loss accounts - 11. Staff records - 12. Patents - 13. Licences - 14. Premises records - 15. Dealers and agency agreements. Bibliography, p.231-235. List of useful addresses. Analytical index, p.239-251. Authors are with the Business Archives Council. '... clear, readable guide to the subject of company records ...' (*Business history*, v.30(2), April 1988). *Class No:* 339.1(093.2)

Worldwide

Yearbooks & Directories

[2444]

DUNNING, J.H. *and* PEARCE, R.D. The World's largest industrial enterprises, 1962-83. 2nd. rev. ed. Aldershot, Hants., Gower Publishing Co, 1985. v.186p.tables. £57.50. ISBN: 0566006405.

First published 1981.

Details of the world's largest industrial enterprises in 1983, and for the years 1962, 1967, 1972, and 1982, classified into 20 industrial sectors. Sections: Introduction; The data for 1983; Changes in the sample composition, 1962-1982; Employment of the world's largest enterprises; Concentration, size and diversification; Profitability and growth, 1962-82; International operations; Research and development expenditures of the world's largest enterprises. Appendices: tables. *Class No:* 339.1(100)(058)

[2445]

The International corporate 1000. 3rd ed. London, Graham & Trotman Limited, 1990. 627p. £145; $280. ISBN: 1853333093.

First published 1988. Annual.

Lists the 1000 leading companies outside the US. Arranged by region (Europe, Far East and Australasia, Middle East and Africa, Latin America, and Canada). Data include names and titles of executives of the corporations; names of board members; address, telephone - telex - fax numbers; description of business and subsidiaries. *Class No:* 339.1(100)(058)

[2446]

The Times 1000 ... 1994: the indispensable annual review of the world's leading industrial and financial companies. London, Times Books, 1994. Annual. 128p. £29.50. ISBN: 0723005133. ISSN: 00824429.

First published for 1979-1980.

Listings of 1. World's top 50 industrial companies...7. The UK's top 1000 - 8. Europe's top 1000 - 9. USA's top 1000 - 10. Japan's top 1000...18. UK's top 25 banks - 19. Europe's top 25 banks - 20. UK's top 30 insurance companies - 21. UK's top 25 property companies - 22. UK's top 25 building societies - 23. UK's top 50 investment trusts. Index. *Class No:* 339.1(100)(058)

[2447]

World business directory. O'Meara, M. *and* Patterson, K., *eds*. 1st ed. Detroit, Mich, & Andover, Hants, Gale, 1992. 4v.(5314p). £250. ISBN: 0810377152.

Over 105,000 businesses involved in international trade (company name and variations; address; telephone, fax and telex numbers; WTC affiliation; key officers; revenue data; number of employees; type of business; year established; products; parent company). Industry, company name and product indexes. 3v. arranged by country; v.4 has indexes. *Class No:* 339.1(100)(058)

Europe

[2448]

European business rankings: lists of companies, products, services and activities compiled from a variety of published sources. Newman, O. *and* Foster, A., *comps*. Detroit & Andover, Hants, Gale Research International Ltd., 1992. 437p. $140. £95. ISBN: 1873477007.

Includes 2260 lists from more than 800 periodicals, newspapers, financial services, directories, statistical annuals, etc., held by Manchester Business School Library. Contents list (subject headings) serves as a finding list. Sources of lists cited and bibliography of sources included. *Class No:* 339.1(4)

Yearbooks & Directories

[2449]

Directory of European business. Cambridge Market Intelligence, *comp.* New York, Bowker-Saur, 1992. xxv,366p. tables. $195. ISBN: 0862916178.

User's guide, currency table, and list of abbreviations precedes. *c*.4000 leading business firms - service companies, organizations, government agencies and top manufacturing companies in 35 countries of East and West Europe, arranged A-Z by country (Albania ... Commonwealth of Independent States ... United Kingdom ... Yugoslavia}. Introduction to each country section on business environment (political system, economic policy, accounting rules, standards, tax system), followed by list of business services (subdivided by subject: Accounts ... Public relations companies); business organizations (Chambers of Commerce, professional bodies, trade associations); leading companies; government (foreign representation, ministeries, regulatory agencies); business information (statistical sources, national newspapers, business periodicals). *Class No:* 339.1(4)(058)

[2450]

European business services directory. Huellmantel, M.B., *ed*. Detroit, Gale, 1993. 1374p. $275. ISBN: 0810379163.

Lists business service providers that service other companies in 30 European countries, including former Soviet republics. In 3 sections: Service listing, profiles more than 20,000 comlanies arranged by topic according to their major service (*eg*, advertising, construction, finance); Geographic listing, with entry numbers referring to profiles; and A-Z list of companies, also with entry numbers referring to profiles. Preceding are an introduction and user's guide in English, French and German; a list of symbols and abbreviations; a table of currency abbreviations; and a list of SIC codes. Also available on magnetic tape and floppy disk. *Class No:* 339.1(4)(058)

Biographies

[2451]

Who's who in European business . East Grinstead, West Sussex, Bowker-Saur, 1993. 432p. £99. ISBN: 0862917956.

Biographies of the 5000 business leaders in 37 countries of Eastern and Western Europe. Entries arranged A-Z and tailored for the business user, with emphasis on professional career details. *Class No:* 339.1(4)(092)

Europe—Western

Handbooks & Manuals

[2452]
Guide to European company information: EEC countries. London Business School Information Service. 3rd ed. London, London Business School, 1989. [3],124p. map. £45. ISBN: 0951440101.

First and second editions were produced as handouts for seminars.
In 3 sections. 1st section has 12 country chapters (one for each of the 12 EEC countries) giving brief outlines of the main legal forms of companies, the disclosure requirements, and how to access these public filings. Followed in each chapter, apart from UK. by detailed descriptions of the directories, and online databases which are the main source of company information for each country. A pan-European chapter describes sources for more than one country. The 2nd section is on UK library resources, giving details of over 50 publicly available collections of these directories, together with summaries of the services they offer. The 3rd section has data on agencies that will obtain company accounts information, and describes the services offered by the major business and credit reporting agencies in terms of what they can provide, how long it takes, and cost. *Class No:* 339.1(400)(035)

[2453]
The Tavistock handbook and directory: business centres and managed workspace, 1993. Goodwin, G., *ed.* London, Kogan Page, 1993. 236p. maps. £14.95. ISBN: 0749409304.

Key to the areas covered precedes the introduction (Advantages of short-term accommodation over conventional office space; How to find the right accommodation for your business). Entries are arranged by region, subdivided by towns, and includes name of organization, address, telephone & fax numbers, type of accommodation offered. Index, p.221-36. *Class No:* 339.1(400)(035)

Yearbooks & Directories

[2454]
Major companies of Europe, 1993/94. 13th ed. London, Graham & Trotman, 1993. 3v. (1552p.). £599 the set; v.1 £320; v.2 & 3 £160 each. (*Major companies of the world series ..*) ISBN: 1853338893, set; 1853335969, v.1; 1853335977, v.2; 1853335985, v.3. ISSN: 0266934x, v.1; 02684667, v.2; 02684675, v.3.

First published 1980.
A directory of 9000 of Europe's largest companies. V.1: Continental European Community; v.2: United Kingdom; v.3: Western Europe outside the European Community. Data includes addresses; telephone/cable/telex/fax numbers; board of directors; senior executives; principal activities; trade names; subsidiary companies; principal bankers; financial information; and number of employees.
Class No: 339.1(400)(058)

[2455]
—**Medium companies of Europe, 1993-94.** London, Graham & Trotman, 1993. 3v. £599. ISBN: 1853338932. ISSN: 09601449.

1st published 1990. Annual.
c.7000 entries for medium-sized companies, following a similar format to the above. *Class No:* 339.1(400)(058)

Europe—Eastern

Yearbooks & Directories

[2456]
East European business directory. Didik, F.X., *ed.* Andover, Hants & Detroit, Gale Research International Ltd., 1991. lx,962p. £185. ISBN: 0810384019.

A guide to *c.*5000 of the largest business, commercial enterprises and special interest associations in Bulgaria, Czechoslovakia, Hungary, Poland, Romania, the western USSR, and the former East Germany. Classification is by products and services, and entries include full address of the organization; telephone, telex & fax numbers; contact name; details of product or service in which the business specializes. Production service section, A-Z by products. Geographical section, A-Z by country, subdivided by city or region. Alphabetical listing by company name. *Class No:* 339.1(401)(058)

Great Britain

Yearbooks & Directories

[2457]
Britain's privately owned companies. Bristol, Avon, Jordan, 1989. 3v. £125 each volume.

Formerly titled *Britain's top 2000 private companies*.
V.1 and 2 cover the larger companies, including 2000 companies in each vol. V.3 also has 2000 smaller companies. For each company financial data is given, including fixed assets, current assets, current liabilities, stock/work in progress, cash, numbers employed, total wage bill, average remuneration per employee. *Class No:* 339.1(410)(058)

[2458]
Extel Financial UK listed companies. London, Extel Financial Ltd., 1927-. Daily. £3970pa.

Details of *c.*2500 British quoted companies listed on the Stock Exchange. For each company there is an annual card showing the company's activities, balance sheets, board members, capital (with history), chairman's statement, dividend record, profit and loss account, yield earnings, etc. Cumulative new cards are issued for each company as and when dividends are announced or other news justifies. Extel also offers other services, including 'Extel European company service' and 8 overseas company services. *Class No:* 339.1(410)(058)

[2459]
GREAT BRITAIN. Central Statistical Office. United Kingdom directory of manufacturing businesses, 1993. London, HMSO, 1993. 759,xlviiip. £160. (*(Business monitor PO 1007A).*) ISBN: 0115363084.

First published 1989. Annual.
*c.*19800 entries, compiled from the CSO's register of businesses. Arranged by subject (SIC), subdivided by name of firm, A-Z. Name and address only. Includes key to the SIC (1980 Standard Industrial Classification). *Class No:* 339.1(410)(058)

Histories

[2460]
Debrett's bibliography of business history. Zarach, S., *ed.* London, Macmillan Press in association with Debrett's Business History Research Ltd., 1987. xv,278p. £35. ISBN: 0333424042.

Over 2000 titles are listed, arranged A-Z by subject (Accountancy ... Wines and spirits). Under each subject, general titles are followed by company histories arranged A-Z by name of company. Information given is author, title, publisher, date of publication, no. of pages. No annotations. Confined to histories published or printed in this century and '... no attempt to pass judgement on their value' (*Preface*). A list of 'Books of general use to the business historian' (p.251-253) is A-Z by author. Index of companies, p.254-278. *Class No:* 339.1(410)(091)

[2461]
FANNING, D. 'Business history and biography'. In *British book news,* February 1986, p.78-82.

A book survey followed by a bibliography of 89 books, arranged A-Z by author. The survey is in 5 sections: Outstanding contributions; Collected biography; Individual biographies; Individual corporate history; and Business and industrial history.
Class No: 339.1(410)(091)

[2462]
GOODALL, F. A Bibliography of British business histories. Aldershot, Hants., Gower, 1987. v,638p. £45. (*Business history series, v.3.*) ISBN: 0566053071.

A preface and user's guide precedes the 'Author index', which is the bibliography of works published during the last 150 years. Entries include title, publisher, name(s) of firm(s), description of content, SIC, and source library. Extensive cross-references. Company index, p.455-533. Industry classification index. p. 535-638.
Class No: 339.1(410)(091)

[2463]
HEALD, T. By appointment: 150 years of the Royal Warrant and its holders. London, Macdonald: Queen Anne Press. 1990. £40. ISBN: 0356170993.

The Royal Warrant holders number over 850 companies who are allowed to display the Royal Arms with the words 'By Appointment'. Includes descriptions of these 'Best of Britain' companies.
Class No: 339.1(410)(091)

Biographies

[2464]
The Directory of directors ... a list of the directors of the principal public and private companies in the United Kingdom, with the names of the concerns with which they are associated, 1993. 114th ed. East Grinstead, West Sussex,Reed Information Services Ltd., 1992. 2v. ISBN: 0611008157.

First published 1880.
V.1 lists *c.*58,000 directors, A-Z, the name being followed by companies of which the person is a director. V.2 lists *c.*16,000 companies and *c.*85,000 board members. Company information includes name, subject, address, telephone number, telex number, parent company, directors, date of accounts, financial data showing up to 3 years of accounts. *Class No:* 339.1(410)(092)

Archives

[2465]

RICHMOND, L. *and* STOCKFORD, B. **Company archives:** the survey of the records of 1000 of the first registered companies in England and Wales. Aldershot, Hants., Gower Publishing Co. Ltd., 1986. xxi,593p. £48. ISBN: 0566035472.

The survey was undertaken by the Business Archives Council with support from the Economic and Social Research Council.

The survey traced 1000 of the oldest surviving limited companies in England and Wales, embracing all kinds of business activity. An introduction and a user's guide precede the list of records, and are followed by name, place and subject indexes. '... a wonderful book for business historians'. (*Business history,* October 1986, p.126).
Class No: 339.1(410)(093.20)

Eire

Yearbooks & Directories

[2466]

EIRE. Department of Industry and Commerce. **Directory of Irish company names, 1988.** Dublin, Stationery Office, 1988. 2v.([8],1808p.). IR£100.

V.1: A-J; v.2:K-Z. Listing gives the company's registered number, its name (A-Z) and address. Indications are given if a company is in liquidation, receivership or dissolved. *Class No:* 339.1(417)(058)

England

Histories

[2467]

BELLAMY, J.M., *ed*. **Yorkshire business histories:** a bibliography. Bradford, Bradford University Press, in association with Crosby Lockwood, London, 1970. xxii,480p.

Edited for the Yorkshire Group, Reference, Special and Information Section of the Library Association.

Nearly 4000 firms, A-Z (p.1-386); 42 library locations. Industrial analysis, p.395-446 (24 classes). Data: name of firm; type of business; town; reference. Appendices: 1. General business histories, theses, etc. - 2. Periodical locations - 3. List of periodicals indexed.
Class No: 339.1(420)(091)

[2468]

GUILDHALL LIBRARY. London. **London business house histories:** a handlist. London, Corporation of City of London, [1965]. [56]p.

Four sections: 1. Index of firms - 2. 715 items, under trades, A-Z - 3. Collective histories (items 716-33) - 4. Archives (items 734-801). Addenda (7 items). Many of the items were issued privately and not to be found in standard bibliographies. (The Guildhall Library has an interleaved and updated reference copy). *Class No:* 339.1(420)(091)

[2469]

HORROCKS, S., *comp*. **Lancashire business histories.** Manchester, Joint Committee on the Lancashire Bibliography, 1971. xii,116p. (*A contribution towards Lancashire bibliography, 3*.)

General histories, p.1-16 (260 items); business histories, p.16-99 (979 entries). Includes many periodical articles; numerous cross-references. Indexes: name (personalia; organizations and firms); industrial; topographical (general; industrial localities). Locations in 58 libraries. *Class No:* 339.1(420)(091)

[2470]

ROWE, D.J., *ed*. **Northern business histories:** a bibliography. London, Library Association, Reference, Special and Information Section, 1979. [1],[1],7,191p. £27.50. ISBN: 0853659001.

3092 numbered entries (with locations in 38 libraries), under authors, companies, etc., A-Z. Appendix 1: Record Office holdings of business archives - 2. Law reports - 3. General histories (6 sections, including 6: Journals). 'Industrial analysis (*i.e.,* detailed subject index), also grouped under 23 heads (*e.g.* 20: Distributive trades: 7 columns, further subdivided). *Class No:* 339.1(420)(091)

Germany

[2471]

COVILL, L. **Germany's top 300:** a guide to Germany's largest corporations. London, Kogan Page, 1992. [424]p. £60. ISBN: 0749406577.

First published in 1991 by *Frankfurter Algemeine Zeitung.*

A *c*.50-page introduction to modern German commerce is followed by descriptions of 300 companies in detail, with date of establishment, address, contact numbers, business activities, SIC codes, locations, management personnel, employees, subsidiaries and participations, capital, major shareholders, turnover and pre-tax profits. Company, industry and location indexes. *Class No:* 339.1(430)

Russia

[2472]

SIBD, 92-93: the business directory for the Soviet region. North River, FYI Information Sources/Cooperative Reserve, 1992. 2v.(894p). $240. ISBN: 0963226304.

Update of the *Soviet independent business directory*: SIBD 1991 ed.

Purpose is to allow business people to 'identify, contact, evaluate, and communicate with potential business associates [in the Soviet Union]'(*Preface*). Lists over 2000 companies, A-Z, with indexes by products, geographical location, leaders (company officers), and business activities. An appendix lists the 500 largest enterprises.
Class No: 339.1(47)

Asia—Far East

[2473]

Major companies of the Far East and Australasia, 1993-94. 10th ed. London, Graham & Trotman, 1993. 3v. 370 or $1030 the set. (*Major companies of the world series*.) ISBN: 1853338982.

First published 1984.

V.1 South East Asia (Brunei, Indonesia, Malaysia, The Philippines, Singapore, Thailand); v.2. East Asia (People's Republic of China, Hong Kong, Japan, Republic of Korea, Taiwan); v.3. Australasia. *c*.5000 companies selected on a basis of business activity or business importance within the country. Each entry lists company name; address; telephone number; and principal activities. When available, also offices, establishment date, telex, cable and fax numbers; branches; principal agencies; shareholders; bankers; number of employees; and associate, parent or subsidiary company. Financial data is included in many entries. Indexes to each volume of company names, company names listed by country, and business activities.
Class No: 339.1(51/52+57)

Japan

Yearbooks & Directories

[2474]

Japan company handbook. Tokyo, Toyo Keizai Inc., 1974-. 2v. issued quarterly (previously 2pa). Yen18400; $204pa.

First section covers Blue Chip companies; nthe second section covers younger growth companies. One page for each company, grouped by industries, services, banks, etc. For each company there is general information, financial information, business results, etc. Company index, A-Z by name. *Class No:* 339.1(52)(058)

Islamic World

[2475]

Major companies of the Arab world, 1993/94. 17th year. London, Graham & Trotman, 1993. 1152p. £360; $560. (*Major companies of the world series*.) ISBN: 185333894x.

First published for 1976/77.

Lists *c*.6700 top Arab companies. Arrangement is by countries, A-Z, subdivided alphabetically by name of company. Data given include address, principal activities, financial information, branches, date of foundation, number of employees, etc. Indexes by name of company, by country, and by business activity. *Class No:* 339.1(5.297)

Canada

[2476]

The Globe and Mail report on business: Canada company handbook, 1992. 4th ed. Austin, Texas, Reference Press, 1992. 590p. charts, tables. $39.95. ISBN: 0921925212.

Basic business information on more than 1300 of Canada's largest companies. Full-page profiles are included for more than 400 of them, with summary stock market information, statistical information, business description, current news synopsis, and general information for investors. Arrangement is by industry, subdivided A-Z by company. Tinted pages have company address, type, industry, description of business, and total revenue from latest annual report.
Class No: 339.1(71)

Latin America

[2477]

Dun & Bradstreet's key business directory of Latin America, 1993/94. Bethlehem, PA, Dun & Bradstreet, 1993. 2v.(xxiv,6021p).

Previously *Dun's Latin America's top 25,000 companies*.

V.1: Businesses geographically (A-Z); businesses alphabetically; v.2: Businesses by industry classification (on tinted paper); Top 1000 businesses ranked by employee size. Data includes name and address; telephone and telex numbers; employee total; sales; SIC number; director/president, etc. *Class No:* 339.1(729.99)

USA

Bibliographies

[2478]

Corporate America: a historical bibliography. Santa Barbara, CA., ABC-Clio Information Services, 1984. xii,341p. $34; £26.35. (*ABC-Clio research guides, no.5*.) ISBN: 0874363624.

An annotated bibliography of 1358 short abstracts of articles on American business, published between 1973 and 1982, taken from *c*.2000 periodicals issued in 90 countries. 10 sections (1. Multinationals, conglomerates, and big business - 2. Banking, investments and service industries - 3. Transportation - 4. Communications - 5. Energy - 6. Food and fiber - 7. Mining - 8. Manufacturing and merchandising - 9. Social effects and environmental impacts - 10. Government regulation and intervention). Items drawn from the ABC-Clio Information Services database. Detailed subject index, p.255-334; author index, p.335-341. *Class No:* 339.1(73)(01)

[2479]

KLEIN, B., *ed*. Guide to American directories: a guide to the major directories of the United States, covering all industrial, professional, and mercantile categories. 13th ed. West Nyack, N.Y., Todd Publications, 1993. 600p. $95. ISBN: 091534422x.

10th ed. was published in 1979.

Describes over 6000 industrial, mercantile, and professional directories. Each concise entry includes publisher's name and address, date of publication, number and type of name listed, and price. Subject and title indexes. *Class No:* 339.1(73)(01)

Yearbooks & Directories

[2480]

Business organizations, agencies, and publications directory. Ehr, C.M. *and* Estell, K., *eds*. 7th ed. Detroit, Mich., Gale Research International Ltd., 1993. 1423p. £225. $330. ISBN: 0810383551.

First published, 1980.

26,000 entries covering 39 types of business information source in the US, arranged in 5 broad categories: US and international organizations - Government agencies and programmes - Facilities and services - Research and education facilities - Publications and information services. Master name and keyword indexes. *Class No:* 339.1(73)(058)

[2481]

Major companies of the USA, 1989/90. 3rd ed. London, Graham & Trotman, 1989. 1100p. £350; $665. (*Major companies of the world series*.)

First published 1987.

Covers 5200 major companies, arranged A-Z by company names. Data includes address; telephone/cable/telex/fax numbers; board of directors; senior executives; principal activities; trade names; subsidiaries; principal bankers; financial information and number of employees. *Class No:* 339.1(73)(058)

[2482]

Ward's business directory of US private and public companies, 1994. Detroit, Mich., Gale Research Company, 1994. Annual. 5v. V.1-4 $1045; v,5 $710. ISSN: 10488707.

Data on over 85,000 US businesses. V.1-3 have alphabetical and geographical listings in a single A-Z sequence, regardless of company size. V.4 has special features and geographical listing. V/5 has companies ranked by sales. Also available on magnetic tape and floppy disk. *Class No:* 339.1(73)(058)

Biographies

[2483]

Business master biography index. McNeil, B. *and* Unterberger, A., *eds*. Detroit, Mich., Gale Research Company, 1987. 630p. $180. (*Gale biographical index series, no.10*.) ISBN: 0810314991.

A spin-off from Gale's *Biography and genealogy master index* and its supplements. Refers to 26,000 biographical sketches. *Class No:* 339.1(73)(092)

[2484]

INGHAM, J.W., *ed*. Biographical dictionary of American business leaders. 2nd ed. Westport, CT. Greenwood Press, 1983. 4v. (xvii,2026p.). $225; £187.95 the set. ISBN: 0313213623.

835 biographical entries provide information on 1159 historically significant individuals, ranging from colonial to contemporary times. Includes colonial merchants, early national fur-traders, late 19th century iron and steel barons, early 20th century financiers, aircraft manufacturers, etc. 8 appendices list the entrepreneurs in a variety of ways. Lengthy index. Favourable review in *Business history* (July 1986, p.153-4) from which this annotation is taken. *Class No:* 339.1(73)(092)

Australia

Biographies

[2485]

The Business who's who of Australia, 1983. 17th ed. Crown's Nest, NSW., Riddell Publishing Pty Ltd., 1983. 848p. A$305. $245. ISSN: 00684503.

First published 1964.

Data on *c*.9000 companies, including addresses, activities, directors, capital, etc., listed A-Z by names of companies. In a separate section a 'directory of directors' lists, in a single alphabet, the names of all directors and the name(s) of the firm(s) with which they are associated. There is also a listing by the names of subsidiary companies, indicating the parent companies. Additional material includes information about Australian government offices and departments, diplomatic representatives,etc. *Class No:* 339.1(94)(092)

Market Structure

Licences and Permits

[2486]

BAILLIE, I.C. Licensing: a practical guide for the businessman. Harlow, Essex, Longman Group Ltd., 1987. xi,120p. £75. ISBN: 0851211321.

In 15 sections, written from the businessman's point of view: 1. Licensing and its alternatives - 2. What to license - 3. Government regulations - 4. Exclusion agreements - 5. Establishing and negotiating licenses - 6. Confidentiality - 7. The nature of a licensing agreement - 8. Style of agreement - 9. Structure of an agreement - 10. Considerations (payout) - 11. Managing a license - 12. Disputes - 13. Termination of the agreement - 14. Revision of the agreement - 15. Special types of licensing. Author is a member of the New York Bar and a Chartered Patent Agent. *Class No:* 339.13.025

Foreign Trade

Handbooks & Manuals

[2487]

BROOKE, M.Z. *and* BUCKLEY, P.J., *eds*. Handbook of international trade. London, Macmillan Press, 1988. xiv,460p. £125. ISBN: 0333453336. ISSN: 09536248.

First published 1982.

A survey of sources of information arranged in 9 sections: 1. Strategic issues - 2. Export and import - 3. Licensing, franchising, and other contractual arrangements - 4. Foreign investment - 5. Key markets - 6. Special industrial sectors - 7. Influence of treaty organizations - 8. Sources of information - 9. Indexes (subjects; abbreviations; countries and regions; treaties; companies and other relevant organizations; publications). *Class No:* 339.5(035)

[2488]

World trade resources guide: a guide to resources on importing from and exporting to the major trading nations of the world. Estell, K., *ed*. Detroit, Gale International Research Company, 1992. 891p. $169. ISBN: 0810384043.

A directory of more than 1000 foreign trade contacts and information sources in 80 of the largest and most significant trading nations of the world. The first section is arranged A-Z by country. Each country section begins with a map and brief profile, including population, GDP, foreign trade balance, etc., followed by entries for government agencies, chambers of commerce, banks, research services, trade associations, free trade zones, port authorities, airports, shipping lines, freight forwarders, publications, statistical sources, databases, libraries, comsultants, etc.Keyword and name index. *Class No:* 339.5(035)

Dictionaries

Polyglot

[2489]

INTERNATIONAL CHAMBERS OF COMMERCE. Key words in international trade. 3rd ed. Paris, ICC Publishing SA., 1989. 416p. £25.

First published 1981.

A glossary of *c*.1500 technical English words and phrases dealing with international commerce, arranged A-Z, with equivalents in German, Spanish, French and Italian. Indexes in German, Spanish, French and Italian. The 2nd ed. is also available with Arabic instead of Italian (£21). *Class No:* 339.5(038)=00

Tables & Data Books

[2490]

SLATER, C.M. *and* RICE, J.B., *eds*. **Foreign trade of the United States:** including state and metro area export data, 1999. 2nd ed. Lanham, MD, Bernan, 1999. 444p. $65. ISBN: 0890591601.

Includes statistics on imports and exports for each US state by country and industry. Detailed subject index and tables.
Class No: 339.5(083)

[2491]

UNITED NATIONS. Statistical Office. **International trade statistics yearbook, 1990.** New York, United Nations, 1993. 2v. $125. ISBN: 9210611446.

First published for 1950. Annual.

V.1, Trade by country; v.2. Trade by commodity matrix tables. International coverage of foreign trade statistics through summary tables showing overall trade by regions and countries; world exports by origin and area of destination as well as by product.
Class No: 339.5(083)

Europe—Eastern

Yearbooks & Directories

[2492]

Directory of foreign trade organizations in Eastern Europe: Bulgaria, Czechoslovakia, East Germany, Hungary, Poland, Romania and the USSR. San Francisco, CA., International Trade Press, 1989. 293p. $85. ISBN: 0926476009.

Lists chambers of commerce, banks, trade ministries, state committees and agencies that trade and deal in manufactured goods; joint ventures, agencies providing consumer goods. Information is limited to addresses and telephone numbers.
Class No: 339.5(401)(058)

China

Yearbooks & Directories

[2493]

Trade contacts in China: a directory of import and export corporations. London, Kogan Page, in association with Prospect Publishing House, China, 1987. 374p. £60; $110. ISBN: 1850913404.

An enlarged version of United States International Trade Administration's *Doing business with China* (1983).

Introductory chapter on traders in trading corporations, special Economic Zones, import duties and regulations, business laws and regulations, etc,; followed by a guide to over 600 trading corporations in Mainland China interested in developing international trade. Information includes name; address; telephone, telex and cable numbers; key personnel; business activities; subsidiary and branch offices. Indexes by industry, name and province.
Class No: 339.5(510)(058)

Trade Fairs

[2494]

International tradeshow directory, 1993/94. Frankfurt am Main, M & A Publishers for Fairs, Exhibitions and Conventions Ltd., 1993. 2 pa. £130 each issue; £180 pa.

First published 1919- in German.

Advertisers index and introduction (on how to use the directory) precede the main contents, which are divided into 'registers': 1. Trade fairs by country, subdivided A-Z by city or town, then chronologically. Contact addresses are given but other information varies - 2. Chronological listing of trade fairs and exhibitions to November 1995 - 3. A-Z index of 150 topics - 4. A-Z list of official names and abbreviations of events. Parts 2-4 refer back to part 1, which has entry numbers. Also available on electronic book and floppy disk. *Class No:* 339.52

Imports

Great Britain

Yearbooks & Directories

[2495]

The Directory of British importers. Mcleod, S., *ed*. 8th ed. Berkhamsted, Herts., Trade Research Publications, 1993. 2v.(800p.). £120. ISBN: 0904783324.

Sponsored by The British Importers Confederation.

V.1: Editorial and indexes; v.2: Register of importing firms. Indexes are by products imported/importing firms; countries imported from/importing firms; associates abroad/importing firms; brand and trade names/importing firms. The register of importing firms is arranged by

....(contd.)

name of firm, A-Z, address, telephone-telex-fax number, type of goods imported, import turnover (an indication), and countries imported from. *Class No:* 339.562(410)(058)

Exports

[2496]

MATTHEWS, R. **Finding export markets:** a guide to methods and information sources in the UK and worldwide. Berkhampstead, Herts, Trade Research Publications, 1986. various pagings. ISBN: 0904783197.

Includes list of countries covered, information sources for each country, and list of publishers. *Class No:* 339.564

Dictionaries

[2497]

DORSCHEID, P. **Elsevier's dictionary of export financing** and credit insurance, in English, German and French. London, Elsevier, 1989. viii,314p. £85.90; Dfl.263; $150.50. ISBN: 0444874968.

*c.*2100 terms of export credit insurance. *Class No:* 339.564(038)

Great Britain

Yearbooks & Directories

[2498]

British exports, 1994. 26th ed. East Grinstead, West Sussex, Kompass-Reed Information Services, 1993. xxxii,3221p. ISBN: 0862682827. ISSN: 13506986.

Prior to the 24th edition, title was *Kelly's United Kingdom exports*.

Lists more than 10,000 major UK exporters under 16,500 product and service classifications. V.1. Products and services (Indices to products. Product and service section). V.2. Company information (Product information pages. Trade names section. Company information section, with their overseas agents, branches and subsidiaries). *Class No:* 339.564(410)(058)

[2499]

The Directory of export buyers in the UK. 6th ed. Berkhamsted, Herts., Trade Research Publications, 1988. 360p. £65. ISBN: 0904783316.

First published 1978.

The register is arranged A-Z by name of firm, with address, telephone,-telex-fax number, products bought, and countries bought for. 3 indexes: Countries/export buyers; Foreign firms bought for/export buyers; and services provided by export buyers. Also international freight services for exporters.
Class No: 339.564(410)(058)

[2500]

The Export handbook, 1992. London, Kogan Page: London Chamber of Commerce, 1992. 450p. £30. ISBN: 0749406356.

Directory of export services for over 150 subject areas, offering information on embassies and government agencies, and including practical articles on all aspects of exporting.
Class No: 339.564(410)(058)

Laws

[2501]

SCHMITTHOFF, C.M. **The Export trade:** the law and practice of international trade. 9th ed. London, Stevens & Sons, 1986. £53. ISBN: 042048180x.

First published 1948.

A well-known text, aimed at both lawyers and laymen. 5 chapters: 1. International sale of goods - 2. Representations abroad - 3. Matters incidental to exporting - 4. Long-term contracts - 5. Customs law. Appendices on insurance of exports, carriage of exports by sea and air, exchange control, and freight forwarders. Analytical index.
Class No: 339.564(410)(094.1)

65 Business & Management

Yearbooks & Directories

[2502]

ENGHOLM, C. *and* GRIMES, S. **The Prentice-Hall directory of online business information** 1997. Prentice-Hall, 1996. 524p. $34.95. ISBN: 0132552825.

Contains illustrations, index and CDROM.

Useful guide to online services and selected web sites for business professionals. The first four chapters have general information on the Internet, how to get connected, and use of navigational tools. The rest of the book is divided into various chapters dealing with "Career Advancements", personal finance, business services, and resources by industry. The authors rate each site for content, ease of use, speed, and value. *Class No:* 65(058)

Worldwide

Bibliographies of Bibliographies

[2503]

DEANS, C. *and* DAKIN, S. **The Thunderbird guide to international business resources on the World Wide Web.** Wiley, 1997. 142p. $21.95. ISBN: 0471160164.

The work has 6 introductory essays covering Asia, Africa and the Middle East, Western and Eastern Europe, and America both North and South. The essays look at political and economic developement likely to affect trade. URLs are provided for Web pages relating to each region. Entries include country, category (information on the country, business topics, government resources, information providers), title, URL and brief description. The contents can be upgraded on Thunderbird's web site (http://www.t-bird.edu). *Choice* January 1997 v.34,5. *Class No:* 65(100)(009)

Business Methods & Organization

[2504]

ALLEN, M. *and* HODGKINSON, R. **Buying a business:** a guide to the decisions. 2nd ed. London, Graham & Trotman, 1989. xvi,209p. 39.50. $75. ISBN: 1853332771.

1st published 1986.

29 chapters each subdivided: 1. Synopsis - 2. Strategic ground rules ... 8. Valuation - 9. Financing ... 13. Legal protection ... 19. Acquiring abroad - 20. The aftermath. 3 appendices: I: Issues management guide; II: Areas to investigate before buying; III: Outline warranties and indemnities. Index. *Class No:* 650.011

[2505]

LOOSE, P., *and others*. **The Company director:** powers and duties. 7th ed. Bristol, Jordans, 1992. 583p. £34.95. ISBN: 085308162x.

Includes the Companies Act of 1989 and other recent developments. *Class No:* 650.011

Abbreviations & Symbols

[2506]

Business acronyms. Towell, J.E., *ed.* Detroit, Mich., Gale, 1988. xxiv, 414p. $60. ISBN: 0810325497.

25,000 acronyms and abbreviations, drawn from the 450,000-entry *Acronyms, initialisms and abbreviations dictionary*, plus additions. Two sequences, one arranged by acronyms, the other by definitions. *Class No:* 650.011(003)

[2507]

ROSENBERG, J.M. **McGraw-Hill dictionary of business acronyms,** initials, and abbreviations. New York, McGraw-Hill, 1992. 352p. $29.95. ISBN: 0070537348.

More than 15,000 entries from the area of general business, including science, technology and the latest government acronyms and abbreviations. *Class No:* 650.011(003)

Databases

[2508]

ARMSTRONG, C.J. *and* FENTON, R.R. **World databases in company information.** Bowker-Saur, 1996. 1147p. £195.00; $325.00. ISBN: 1857391950.

Contains indexes.

This work is an annotated list of electronically published databases from around the world. Each producer is described and their main products noted. Where there are variations between the coverage of the print and electronic resources, these are listed. *Class No:* 650.011(003.4)

[2509]

FOSTER, A. *and* SMITH, G. **Online business sourcebook.** Hartlepool, Headland, 1985. Looseleaf. ISBN: 090688912x.

Delineates 8 types of business database: A. Company information; B. Business news; C. Prices; D. Product and market data; E. Economics and finance; F. Trade; G. Media and consumer data; H. Business management. Data include cost of online connect time. *Class No:* 650.011(003.4)

[2510]

NEWHAM, G., *and others*. **'Choosing a business database: the expert approach.'** In *Business information review* v.5(1), July 1988, p.27-41.

Outlines the results of a pilot research project carried out at Loughborough University. First choice, basic bases: PTS Promt. 13 references; 8 tables, 1 chart. *Class No:* 650.011(003.4)

Bibliographies

[2511]

BAKEWELL, K.G.B. **How to organize information:** a manager's guide to techniques and sources, with a checklist for secretaries and assistants. Aldershot, Hants., Gower, 1984. 225p. £17.50. ISBN: 0566023970.

4 parts. 1. The information overload - 2. Using outside sources (libraries; abstracts, indexes and contents lists; fee-based information services; on-line services; videotext systems; other sources of information) p.11-73 - 3. The information file - 4. Directory of sources (Abstracting and indexing services ... Word processing). Loose insert; 'checklist for secretaries and assistants'. A concise, practical guide. *Class No:* 650.011(01)

[2512]

Bibliographic guide to business and economics, 1975-. Boston, Mass., G.K. Hall, 1976-. Annual. $550. ISSN: 03602702.

Each annual bibliography comprises an A-Z sequence of authors, titles, series and subjects of relevant publications catalogued by the New York Public Library, plus additions from Library of Congress MARC tapes. Coverage includes transportation and communication, commerce, business administration and finance, as well as serial titles. No language bar. *Class No:* 650.011(01)

[2513]

BRITISH LIBRARY. Science Reference and Information Service. **Business information:** a brief guide to the reference resources of the British Library. London, British Library, Business Information Service, 1987. 32p. illus., plan, chart. *Gratis*. ISBN: 0712307443.

Business stock location marks (directories, business books and market research reports, journals, abstracts) - Company information - Product information - Market information - Journals, house journals and newspapers - Statistics - Stockbrokers' reports - Abstracting and indexing services - Online database search service - Selected publicly available sources of business information in the UK - Guides to the business literature held at SRIS. Detailed index. An excellent example of a guide to a library's business resources. *Class No:* 650.011(01)

[2514]

—BROOKS, M. Sources of free business information. 2nd ed. London, Kogan Page, 1988. 91p. £5.95. ISBN: 1850914923.

First published 1986.

Has 11 sections, *e.g.* 5. General economic and business information; 6. Information and advice for smaller businesses; 8. Computers; 11. Names and addresses of providers of information. Details of more than 500 booklets 'Further reading from Kogan Page'. Subject index. Index of information providers. *Class No:* 650.011(01)

[2515]

Business and economics books, 1876-1983. New York, Bowker, 1983. 4v. (5256p.). $199. ISBN: 0835216144.

1-3. *Subject index.* 4. *Title index.*

Lists virtually every title on business and economics published or distributed in the US, 1876-1983, - more than 150,000 entries. V.1-3 adopt 50,000 Library of Congress subject headings.

Class No: 650.011(01)

[2516]

—Business and economics books and serials in print, 1981. New York, Bowker, [1981]. 1836p. ISBN: 0835218060.

First published 1973.

Provides author, title and subject access to *c*.50,000 in-print and forthcoming books. A separate section lists over 7,500 periodicals under 250 subject headings. Online through DIALOG.

Class No: 650.011(01)

[2517]

DANIELLS, L.M. Business information sources. 2nd rev. ed. Berkeley, Calif., Univ. of California Press, 1985. xv, 673p. $40. ISBN: 0520053354.

First published 1976.

21 chapters (1. Methods of locating facts ... 3. US business and economic trends ... 5. Foreign statistics and economic trends ... 10. Management ... 16. International management ... 20. Production and operations management - 21. A basic bookshelf, p.549-54 (briefly annotated)). Detailed analytical index. Confined to English-language sources. A standard work, US-slanted.

A 3rd ed. was published in 1993 (xix,725p. $35. ISBN 0520081803). *Class No:* 650.011(01)

[2518]

HARVARD UNIVERSITY. Graduate School of Business Administration. Baker Library. **Core collection: an author and subject guide, 1970/71-.** Boston, Mass., Baker Library, 1971-. Annual.

Bibliography of 4,000 titles, based on reading lists used on business courses at Harvard. Annual revision, with monthly updating in *Recent additions to Baker Library. Class No:* 650.011(01)

[2519]

HOGAN, J. Macmillan directory of EC business information sources. London, Macmillan, 1992. xxi,294p. £75. ISBN: 0333372726.

Guidance to both published and organized sources, stressing practicality throughout. Sections: 1. Directory of EC industry contacts (arranged by NACE product classification system)- 2. EC on-line databases - 3. EC-funded research and development programmes - 4. Business co-operation network (BC-NET) - 5. European business network (BICs) - 6. Economic and social committee members - 7. Glossary of abbreviations, acronyms, commercial, scientific and technical terms (over 700 terms in European languages). Index.

Class No: 650.011(01)

[2520]

LAVIN, M.R. Business information: how to find it, how to use it. 2nd ed. Phoenix, AZ, Oryx, 1992. 499p. tables. $49.95. ISBN: 0897745566.

First published 1987.

Designed to provide in-depth descriptions of major business publications, including electronic products and especially CD-ROM. Title and subject indexes. *Class No:* 650.011(01)

[2521]

SCHLESSINGER, B.S., *and others, eds.* **The Basic business library:** core resources. 3rd ed. New York, Oryx, 1994. 256p. $39.50 ISBN: 0897747399.

3 sections: 1. Core list of printed business reference sources; 2. The literature of business reference and business libraries. Part 3 contains 10 state-of-the-art essays concerning business reference sources and services. Useful for its annotated bibliography on business reference and business librarianship and the essays on business reference sources and services. *Class No:* 650.011(01)

[2522]

TUDOR, J. Macmillan directory of business information sources. 3rd ed. London, Macmillan Publishers Ltd., 1992. 500p. £75. ISBN: 0333579718.

Sections: Finding business information (primary sources; secondary sources; computer-based information services; libraries; business related databases: selected list covering UK industries) - Directory of business information sources and centres (based on Standard Industrial Classification) - Foreign trade organisations in the UK - British trade publications and their editorial offices. Alphabetical index to Standard Industrial Classifications - Alphabetical index to organisation sources. Aims 'to provide guidance on both the published and organisational sources relevant to the needs of the non-professional business researcher' (*Preface*). *Class No:* 650.011(01)

Encyclopaedias

[2523]

Encyclopedia of business. Maurer, J.G., *et al. eds.* Gale, 1996. 1584p. $395.00. ISBN: 0810391872.

Published in two volumes. Contains bibliography, charts and index.

Lists 700 topics in business, finance, human resources, and marketing. Entries are signed and vary in length from less than a column to over 10 pages. Written in non-technical language by business writers, academics and business persons. The general index has references to important or unusual terms, company names, US government agencies and legislation. *Class No:* 650.011(031)

Dictionaries

[2524]

ADAM, J.H. Longman dictionary of business English. 2nd rev. ed. Harlow, Essex, Longman, 1989. xvi, 564p. £15.99. ISBN: 0582050294.

Defines *c*.2,000 words and phrases used in current business and commerce. Includes abbreviations, organizations and brief biographical notices. Full cross-references. Appended 'Useful information' (15 tables of measures, weights, etc.). Clear and simple definitions, showing terms in context. Specially suitable for students of English.

Class No: 650.011(038)

[2525]

GREENER, M. The Penguin business dictionary. New ed. Harmondsworth, Middx., Penguin Books; Viking, 1987. [xv], 316p. £5.99. ISBN: 0670814245.

About 3,000 entries. Includes international bodies, organizations, economic and commercial phrases (*e.g.* 'Kennedy Round'). Ample cross-references. Lengthy list of abbreviations precedes.

Class No: 650.011(038)

[2526]

Macmillan dictionary of business and management. Lamming, R. *and* Bessant, E. London, Macmillan, 1987. 320p. diagrs., graphs, maps. £30. ISBN: 0333390547.

About 4,000 concise entries and cross-references, omitting some of the more basic terms. Includes entries for abbreviations, organizations, Acts and some biographies. 'European Community': 6½ columns; 'Line management': ½ column. 'It is intended as a handy general reference tool for all occasions' (*Preface*). *Class No:* 650.011(038)

Polyglot

[2527]

FERBER, G. Cassell English-Japanese business dictionary. London, Cassell, 1993. xiii,632p. ISBN: 030432552x.

Contains index.

Over 15,000 terms are defined, with additional notes on etymology, usage, etiquette, and psychology in Japanese business. The work is divided into five chapters covering - 1. Economics; Trade and Industry - 2. Finance - 3. Insurance - 4. Business; Company Law - 5. Employment; Personnel. The Japanese words are given in transliterated form, and there is a separate (romanized) Japanese-English index at the back of the work. *Class No:* 650.011(038)=00

[2528]

MAY, R. French dictionary of business, commerce, and finance; Dictionaire anglais des affaires, du commerce et de la finance. London, Routledge, 1996. xxiii,1123p. ISBN: 0415093945.

A major bilingual dictionary. Terms entered in alphabetical order. Useful appendices with abbreviations in the subject area covered, examples of French/English business letters, job titles in commerce, etc. *Class No:* 650.011(038)=00

German

[2529]

Collins business German: a dictionary of 12,000 essential words and phrases. London, HarperCollins, 1992. xvi,271p. £7.90. ISBN: 0004336240.

Word lists in over 20 fields, under topic (*eg*, accounting, advertising, computing, EEC finance, import/export, insurance, manufacturing, marketing, sales). German-English glossary, p.221-271. *Class No:* 650.011(038)=30

[2530]

NEUHAUS, K. *and* **HALTERN, M. Euro-business: German.** Bochum, ILT-Verlag, 1991. £7.95; DM17.80. (Euro-business - Sprachführer). ISBN: 3927899011.

Guide to the language of commerce, industry and services for the businessman (exhibitions, sales, marketing, advertising, promotion, meetings, data processing, joint ventures, personnel, import and export). Also useful general phrases for conversation, background information on Germany and its customs, over 150 essential addresses for travellers, etc. *Class No:* 650.011(038)=30

French

[2531]

Harrap's business French-English dictionary. Laurendeau-Collin, J.P., *and others, eds.* 3rd ed. London, Harrap, 1991. xvi, 604p. map. £19.95. ISBN: 024560149x.

Early ed. as *Harrap's French and English business dictionary* (1981).

English-French, French-English dictionary, with *c.*3,000 entries in each part. Includes terms used in banking, stock exchange dealings, accountancy, insurance, commerce, law, etc. Appended abbreviations, conversion tables. *Class No:* 650.011(038)=40

Italian

[2532]

RAGAZZINI, G. *and* GAGLIARDELLI, G. Harrap's business Italian dictionary. Italian-English. Concise ed. London, Harrap; Milan, Mursia, 1990. xiv, 672p. £15.95. ISBN: 0245601341.

Previously published in 1984 as *Dizionario commerciale Inglese-Italiano, Italiano-Inglese* *Class No:* 650.011(038)=50

Reviews & Abstracts

[2533]

Business periodicals index. New York, H.W. Wilson, 1958-. 11pa.; cumulated 4pa. and annually. ISSN: 00076961.

Its parent is *Industrial arts index*, 1913-57, from which both *Business periodicals index* and *Applied science and technology index* have stemmed.

Subject index to articles in over 250 English-language periodicals of which *c.*12 are British. Full cross-references. Appended 'Book reviews'. Available online through WILSONLINE and also available on CD-ROM. *Class No:* 650.011(048)

[2534]

Business publications index and abstracts. Detroit, Mich., Gale, 1983-. Monthly, with quarterly & annual cumulations.

Continues *Management contents* (1975-82).

1985: *c.*24,000 abstracts, covering periodical articles and book chapters. The 1985 cumulation occupies 4v.: *Abstracts* (2v.); *Subject/author citations* (2v.). Covers over 700 periodicals, - more extensive than either its predecessor (*c.*375 titles) or H.W. Wilson's *Business periodicals index* (*c.*275 titles). Forms the printed version of the *Management contents* database. *Class No:* 650.011(048)

Periodicals

[2535]

Business information review. Headland, Cleveland, Headland Press, 1984-. 4pa. $99pa.

Includes articles written by field exports about business information sources - print and electronic. Analyses information sources in specific industry sectors and countries, and the use of business information. *Class No:* 650.011(051)

Quotations

[2536]

The Chambers book of business quotations. Manser, M.H., *comp.* Edinburgh, W. & E. Chambers, 1987. vii, 211p. illus. £12.95. ISBN: 0550204881.

About 2,000 quotations on business and related subjects. 9 major sections, each with short introduction and subdivision: Success and wealth - Business activities - Finance and institutions - Economics and background sciences - Human resources - Time - Business facts of life - Business operations. Ambrose Bierce, Churchill, Emerson, Dr. Johnson, Adam Smith, Shakespeare, Shaw and Oscar Wilde. One of the most frequently cited sources. The sources are insufficiently detailed (*e.g* title only, for books; no pagination). *Class No:* 650.011(082.2)

Histories

[2537]

Business history of the world: a chronology. Robinson, R., *comp.* Westport, CT, Greenwood Press, 1993. 562p. $75. ISBN: 031326094x.

Aim was to include representative trend-setting occurrences, and most of those included are European. Formal chronology runs from 10,000 BC to AD 1988 in general. Early entries are, perforce, brief, but later ones can be several pages long. From 1600 material is divided into 'General events' and 'Business events'. Index of names, places and subjects. *Class No:* 650.011(091)

Biographies

[2538]

Dictionary of business biography: a biographical dictionary of business leaders active in Britain in the period 1860-1980. Jeremy, D.J., *ed.* London, Butterworth, 1984-86. 5v. & Supplement. facsims, ports. £72ea. ISBN: 0406273413, v.1; 0406273421, v.2; 040627343x, v.3; 0406273448, v.4; 0406273456, v.5; 0406273405, 5v, with supplement.

5v.: A-C, D-G, H-L, Mc-R, S-Z. Supplement: Indexes, contributors, errata. About 1,000 signed biographies in all, with emphasis on business careers. V.1, p.547-54 is devoted to George Cadbury, with appendix on writings and sources (unpublished and published). Living businessmen are included only if they have now retired from full-time office. Serves to supplement entries in *The Times* obituary columns and the *Dictionary of national biography*, which tend to pass over businessmen. The editor: Research Fellow, Business History Unit, London School of Economics and Political Science. *Class No:* 650.011(092)

[2539]

Dictionary of Scottish business biography, 1860-1960. Slaven, A *and* Checkland, S., *eds.* Aberdeen, Aberdeen University Press, 1986 - 1989. 2v. illus. v.1. £44; v.2. £48. ISBN: 0080303986 v.1; 0080303994 v.2.

V.1.:*The staple industries* is arranged in 9 sections, by industry (Extractive industries - Metals ... Shipbuilding ... Clothing ... Leather and footwear), each section having an essay, followed by a bibliography, A-Z by biographee. Personal name and subject indexes. V.2. *Processing, distributing, services* is arranged in 10 chapters (Food, drink and tobacco ... Construction ... Distributive trades - Banking, insurance and finance). *Class No:* 650.011(092)

USA

Tables & Data Books

[2540]

Business statistics of the United States. Slater, C.M., *ed.* 1995 ed. Bernan, 1996. 391p. $49.00. ISBN: 0890590400.

Contains index.

This work is in two sections, the US economy and industry profiles. Annual statistics for 1966-94 are listed, with monthly updates for 1991-94. Industry profiles follow the structure of the Standard Industrial Classification (SIC) for details on contruction and housing; mining, oil and gas; manufacturing; transportation; communications and utilities; retail and wholesale trade; services and government. *Class No:* 650.011(73)(083)

Information Management

[2541]

Manual of business library practice. Campbell, M.J., *ed.* 2nd rev. ed. London, Bingley, 1985. x, 238p. £30. ISBN: 0851573606.

First published 1973.

9 contributors. 13 chapters (2. Organization and administration: objectives, planning and staffing; 5. Directories and company information sources; 9. Management literature; 12. The use of external sources of information - 13. The impact of information technology). References and further reading, p.201-11. Appendix: Databases, p.212-14. Detailed, analytical index, p.215-38. *Class No:* 650.011:025.4

[2542]

—VERNON, K.D.C. *and* LANG, V. The London classification of business studies: a classification and thesaurus for business libraries. 2nd ed., revised by K.G.B. Bakewell and D.R. Cotton. London, Aslib, 1979. 253p. ISBN: 0851421245.

First published by the London Graduate School of Business Studies. *Class No:* 650.011:025.4

Institutions & Associations

[2543]

Business organizations, agencies and publications directory. Ehr, C.M. *and* Estell, K., *eds.* 7th ed. Detroit, Mich., Gale, 1993. 1423p. £225. $330. ISBN: 0810383551. ISSN: 08881413.

First published 1980.

26,000 entries covering 39 types of business in the United States, arranged in 5 broad categories: US and international organizations (subdivided by type) - Government agencies and programmes - Facilities and services - Research and education facilities - Publications and information services. Master name and keyword index. *Class No:* 650.011:061:061.2

[2544]
The International directory of business information sources and services. 2nd ed. London, Europa, 1996. xi, 550p. £115.00. ISBN: 1857430077.

A directory of business organizations in over 20 countries, and international organizations. Subdivisions covering: Chambers of commerce; International trade; Government organizations; Sources of statistical information; Business libraries. Detailed index. *Class No:* 650.011:061:061.2

[2545]
TUDOR, J. Macmillan directory of business information sources. 3rd ed. Basingstoke, Macmillan Publishers, 1992. 500p. £75. ISBN: 0333579718.

First published 1987.

Directory of business information sources (journals, etc.) and centres, is followed by foreign trade organizations in the UK and British trade publications and their editorial offices. A-Z index to Standard Industrial Classification (SIC Code), A-Z index to organization sources. *Class No:* 650.011:061:061.2

Mechanization

[2546]
Key abstracts, business automation, 1989-. Stevenage, Herts, INSPEC, IEE, 1989-. Monthly. £90. $165 pa. ISSN: 09549153.

48 subject sections in the fields of communications, computers and office systems in business and commerce, including banking, financial markets and retailing. *c.*50 abstracts in each issue. Subject index. Also available online (BRS,CEDOCAR, CISTI, Data-Star, Dialog, etc.). *Class No:* 650.011.54

Operational Research

[2547]
A Guide to operational research. Duckworth, W.E., *and others.* 3rd ed. London, Chapman & Hall, 1977. ix, 205p. ISBN: 0412135000.

First published 1962.

12 chapters: 1. What operational research is and does - 2. Measuring uncertainty - 3. Queuing problem - 4. Business forecasting (12 references; bibliography of 9 items) - 5. Simulation and Monte Carlo methods - 6. Stock and production control models - 7. Resource allocation - 8. Planning projects - 9. Analysing decisions - 10. Operational gaming - 11. Other research techniques - 12. Conclusions. Name index; general index. Favourably reviewed in *Aslib book list*, April 1978, entry 216. *Class No:* 650.012.122

Psychology

[2548]
McCORMICK, E.J. *and* ILGEN, D.R. Industrial and organizational psychology. 8th ed. London, Allen & Unwin, 1987. xii, 468p. diagrs., tables, graphs. £63.15. ISBN: 0044450028.

First published 1952.

6 sections: 1. Introduction - 2. Job-related behavior and its measurement - 3. Personnel selection - 4. Personnel training and development - 5. The organizational and social context of human work - 6. The job and work environment. 4 appendices: A. Elementary descriptive statistics ... D. Representative personnel tests. Bibliographies appended to each chapter. *Class No:* 650.013

Work Study

[2549]
BRITISH STANDARDS INSTITUTION. Glossary of terms used in work study and organizational methods (O & M). London, the Institution, 1979. 36p. diagr. £25.60. (*BS 3138:1979.*)

Defines terms for operator and machine-controlled work, with sections on organization study, method study, work management and work performance control. Examples of construction of standard time. BS 3375: parts 1-4: 1984-86 is also relevant. It deals with organization and method study, work measurement, and work performance control. *Class No:* 650.015

Office Practice

[2550]
GARTSIDE, L. Modern business correspondence: a comprehensive business guide to business writing and related office services. 4th ed. London, Pitman, 1986. x, 529p. illus. ISBN: 0273025759.

3rd ed., 1976.

2 parts (23 chapters): 1. The English background (principles of good business writing: style; presentation; spelling) - 2. Business correspondence (including filing and indexing systems; office machine

....(contd.)
systems; typing; letter styles). 4 appendices (C. Glossary of business terms, p.429-97; D. Abbreviations used in business). Detailed, analytical index. 48 illus. *Class No:* 651

[2551]
MILLS, G., *and others.* Modern office management. 7th ed. London, Pitman, 1986. xii,496p.

First published 1953; title for first 6 eds. was *Office organization and method.*.

8 parts (30 chapters): 1. Administration and organization - 2. Communications - 3. Other office services - 4. Data processing - 5. Financial and accounting services - 6. Environment - 7. Personnel - 8. Planning and control. Glossary of terms, p.478-87. Bibliography, p.385-7. Analytical index, p.488-96. Aims to provide a compact work for reference for company secretaries, accountants, cost accountants and administrative managers generally, and a textbook for students. *Class No:* 651

[2552]
TITMAN, L. The Effective office: a handbook of modern office management. London, Cassell, 1991. 544p. £45. $90. ISBN: 0304316768.

A guide to modern office techniques, including traditional techniques, electronic and technological aspects of office management. Chapters: The basics - Technology enlacement - Managerial tools - Method - Design - Work quantification - Support techniques - Final notes - Index. *Class No:* 651

Dictionaries

Polyglot

[2553]
CENTRE DE TERMINOLOGIE DE BRUXELLES. Elsevier's dictionary of office automation in four languages. Amsterdam, Elsevier, 1991. xxi,462p. ISBN: 0444880658.

In English, German, French and Dutch. Numbered descriptions are given in English followed by translations of the terms in the three other languages. Term lists in those languages refer to the numbered entries in English. Cross-references. Bibliography precedes (p.xi-xxi). *Class No:* 651(038)=00

Equipment

[2554]
BARCOMB, D. Office automation: a survey of tools and technology. 2nd ed. Bedford, Mass., Digital Press, 1989. viii, 339p. illus., diagrs.

2 parts: 1. Overview of office automation - 2. The tools of office automation (5. Text management and graphics ... 7. Electronic mail systems ... 9. Micrographics) - 3. Putting it all together (10. Integrated office automation systems ... 12. Coming soon to an office near you). Short bibliographies for each chapter. Glossary, p.311-26. *Class No:* 651.2

[2555]
Business equipment digest. Wallington, Surrey, BED Business Books, 1961-87. Monthly.

Covers all aspects of office business equipment, supplies and services. Addressed to senior executives who are responsible for puchasing office equipment, supplies and services. *Class No:* 651.2

Secretarial Work

[2556]
HUTCHINSON, L. Standard handbook for secretaries. 8th ed. New York, etc., McGraw-Hill, 1969. x, 638p. $16.95.

A mine of information on a variety of topics: letter and letter writing; dictation; typewritten work; copy for the press; filing; legal papers; patents and trademarks; copyright; government information; business and banking papers; securities; foreign exchange; financial statements; petty cash; insurance. Abbreviations; various tables; reference books. Detailed, analytical index. A basic title on the more conventional aspects of secretarial work. *Class No:* 651.44

[2557]
Webster's secretarial handbook. Springfield, Mass., Merriam-Webster, 1984. 550p. diagrs. $10.95. ISBN: 0877791368.

15 chapters cover communications, career-path development, meetings and conference arrangements, dictation, automated equipment, business correspondence, business English, management of business records, secretarial accounting, telecommunications. Cross-references. Bibliography. Index. *Class No:* 651.44

Correspondence

[2558]
FORMAN, J. *and* KELLY, K.A. **The Random House guide to business writing.** New York, McGraw-Hill, 1990. xxiii,856p. £20.95. (*McGraw-Hill English language series*).) ISBN: 0075572214.

15 chapters: 1. Introduction ... 4. The basics of business letters: writing to readers outside the organization ... 6. Letters that persuade - 7. Goodwill letters - 8. Memos - 9. The basics of report writing ... 12. Speaking - 13. Visual aids ... 15. The business writer and the computer. 2 appemdices: 1. Writing responses to cases; 2. A brief guide to grammar and punctuation. Notes, p.833-7. Index, p.839-56. *Class No: 651.7*

[2559]
HARVARD, J. **Bilingual guides to business and professional correspondence.** Oxford, etc., Pergamon Press, 1965-72 (and reprints).

English-German, by J. Harvard. 1965. x, 140p. *German-English*, by J. Harvard. 1965. [ix], 140p. *English-French*, by J. Harvard, and F. Rose. 1969. 236p. *French-English*, by J. Harvard, and F. Rose. 1965. ix, 140p. *English-Italian*, by J. Harvard, and M.M. Miletto. 1972. 232p. *Italian-English* by J. Harvard, and M.M. Miletto. *English-Spanish*, by J. Harvard, and I.F. Ariza. 1970. 236p. *Spanish-English*, by J. Harvard, and I.F. Ariza. 1970. 236p.

The *French-English* guide has 9 sections: 1. The layout of a French business letter - 2. The contents of a French business letter - 3. Business organisations - 4. Business transactions ... 8. Inquiry and information - 9. Applications and references. English page on left, French facing. English and French abbreviations. Differences between British and American vocabulary and spelling included. *Class No: 651.7*

[2560]
HORTEN, H.E. **Export-import correspondence in four languages.** London, Gower Press, 1970. xi, 2-316p. £25. ISBN: 0716100274.

The first part consists of a four-way parallel text, (English, French, German and Spanish) on topics such as orders, dispatch notice, acknowledgement of payment (p.2-87) which aims to help the business man to compose his own letters. English, French, German and Spanish indexes. Part 2 consists of 4 parallel dictionaries, each with *c*.1,000 entry-words. *Class No: 651.7*

[2561]
WHITEHEAD, G. *and* WHITEHEAD, D.H. **Pitman business correspondence.** London, Pitman Business Ltd., 1982. xii, 372p. £5.95. ISBN: 0273017977.

23 sections (2. The layout of a business letter; 5. Orders; 8. Complaints and their adjustment; 14/15. Export trade; 21. Organising a business correspondence department. Glossary of terms, p.363-8. Detailed, analytical index, p.369-72. Furnishes numerous examples (1 per page) of business letters and in-house memos serving the whole range of business activity.

A later ed. was issued in 1988. *Class No: 651.7*

Bibliographies

[2562]
Better said and clearly written: an annotated guide to business communication sources, skills and samples. Belanger, S.E., *comp*. Westport, CT, Greenwood Press, 1989. xiv,196p. $37.95. (*Bibliographies and indexes in mass media and communications,3*.) ISBN: 0313266417.

Over 1000 sources listed, including books, periodicals, databases and programmed-instructive workbooks. In 2 parts: 1. Research guides, resources, information; 2. Communication skills. Aimed primarily at business and engineering students, faculty, librarians and other working professionals. *Class No: 651.7(01)*

Dictionaries

Polyglot

[2563]
DUTTWEILER, C. *and* DUTTWEILER, G. **The 20,000 sentences and expressions of business and personal correspondence.** OTT Verlag, Switzerland, 1989. 3v.(493+459+422p). £33.90 each vol.; £99 the set.

Volumes are for German-French-English; French-German-English; English-German-French. Each volume has examples of usage in the first language of the volume. *Class No: 651.7(038)=00*

[2564]
The Multilingual business handbook: a guide to international correspondence. Ferney, D., *and others*. 2nd rev. ed. London, Macmillan, 1990. 352p. illus. £27.50; £9.99. ISBN: 0333512480, HB; 0333512499, pbk.

First published in 1983 by Pan Books, edited by P. Hartley and others.

A glossary of commercial expressions used in business correspondence in English, French, German, Spanish and Italian. Covers sales and distribution, agencies, customers, property, sales, rentals, hotel and travel reservations, and vocabulary relating to banking, post office, telephone, etc. *Class No: 651.7(038)=00*

Spanish

[2565]
GIRAUD, A.F.-S. **Diccionario comercial español-inglés, inglés-español. El secretario.** 3rd ed. Barcelona, Editoria Juventud, 1977. 158;137p.

First published 1940.

Intended for commercial correspondence. Includes about 4000 headwords in each half. Particular attention is given to terms and phrases used in commercial correspondence. *Class No: 651.7(038)=60*

Italian

[2566]
DAVIES, S. *and* ARDUINI, A.M. **Manuale bilingue di corrispondinza e comunicazione commerciale. Italiane-Inglese.** Hemel Hempstead, Herts, Prentice-Hall, 1989. viii,210p. £6.50.

First part is Italian-English, the second part English-Italian. Each in 3 sections: A. Commercial correspondence - B. Business communication - C. Business and cultural briefing on Italy. Cross-references. List of abbreviations. *Class No: 651.7=50*

Typing

[2567]
BENNETT, P. **The Typewriting dictionary.** Maidenhead, Berks, McGraw-Hill Book Company (UK) Ltd., 1987. 99p. £3.50. ISBN: 0070849927.

Complete dictionary of typewriting terms, rules and standard practice. Abbreviations - Accents - Accuracy speed tests ... Guide keys - Half-space correcting ... Paper sizes ... Words or figures. *Class No: 651.923*

Shorthand

[2568]
The Pitman 2000 dictionary of English and shorthand. London, Pitman, 1982. 848p. £19.99. ISBN: 0273016180.

Based on the original work by Sir Isaac Pitman, *Stenographic soundhand* (1837).

Total number of shorthand outlines is now over 75,000. '*Pitman 2000* shorthand is a modified form of Pitman's shorthand as it has been known and practised in its New Era form over the past fifty-nine years' (*Preface*). *Class No: 651.93*

[2569]
—Gregg shorthand dictionary. Gregg, J.R. 2nd ed. New York, etc., McGraw-Hill, 1974. 408p. (*Diamond Jubilee series*.)

Has outlines for 35,000 words, and *c*.4,000 names and geographical expressions. Now includes syllabication. *Class No: 651.93*

Accountancy

Bibliographies

[2570]
Current accounting literature, 1971-74: a catalogue of books and pamphlets in the Members' Reference Library of the Institute of Chartered Accountants in England and Wales... London, Mansell, 1972-82. 4v. £10 each.

8,188 author entries for material, mostly post-1960. Subject index. Annual supplements are union catalogues of recent accessions of the libraries of the Association of Certified Accountants, Institute of Chartered Accountants in Ireland, Institute of Chartered Accountants of Scotland, Institute of Cost and Management Accountants, and Liverpool Society of Chartered Accountants.

Earlier items are covered in the ICA's *Historical accounting literature* (Mansell, 1975. 360p.), listing *c*.3,000 entries for 2,500 works on accounting published since the late 15th century. Author index. *Class No: 652.7(01)*

[2571]
MOWAT, M. 'Information sources on accountancy and finance'. In *Business library review*, v.3(2), October 1986, p.3-9.

A helpful survey of relevant journals, directories, annuals and abstracting services (ANBAR; *ICMA abstracts*; *Research index*). Also mentions government publications, publications from professional bodies and accounting firms, specialist publishers and information services, business libraries and online information services. 1 reference. *Class No: 652.7(01)*

[2572]
PRYCE-JONES, J.E. Accounting in Scotland: a historical bibliography. Edinburgh, The Institute of Chartered Accountants of Scotland/Scottish Committee on Accounting History, 1974. 96p. illus.

323 entries, most of them annotated. 3 parts: 1. Books printed in Scotland, 1683-1320 - 2. Printed transcripts of accounts (books printed) - 3. History of Scottish accounting. Indexes of authors and titles. *Class No: 652.7(01)*

Encyclopaedias

[2573]
CHATFIELD, M. *and* VANDERMEERSCH, R. The History of accounting: an international encyclopedia. Garland, 1996 649p. $95.00. ISBN: 0815308094.

Contains bibliographies and index.

Entries on over 400 topics, covering accounting and economic concepts, and accounting practices in different countries. Articles are signed and include bibliographies and a list of cross-references. The book has a thorough index. Amongst the entries are biographical articles on economists and accountants. *Class No: 652.7(031)*

Handbooks & Manuals

[2574]
Handbook of modern accounting. Davidson, S. *and* Weil, R.L., *eds*. 3rd ed. New York, etc., McGraw-Hill, 1983. 1408p. illus. ISBN: 0070154929.

First published 1970.

42 briefly documented chapters by specialists (Accounting concepts and principles, and auditing standards and opinions ... Accounting for nonprofit organizations). Index. A comprehensive handbook.

From the British angle,-. *Class No: 652.7(035)*

Dictionaries

[2575]
BROCKINGTON, R. A Concise dictionary of accounting and finance. London, Pitman, 1986. vii, 127, [8]p. (*M & E Professional dictionaries*.) ISBN: 0712106847.

About 1,200 terms defined. American terminology is differentiated. 7 appendices (5. The contents of a company's annual report and accounts). Intended as a work of reference for those studying the literature of accounting and finance, and for the reader of the financial press. *Class No: 652.7(038)*

[2576]
FRENCH, D. Dictionary of accounting terms. New ed. Kingston upon Thames, Surrey, Croner Publications, 1991. xii,296p. £14.95. ISBN: 1855240459.

First published by Financial Training Publications in 1985.

Defines more than 3,500 words and expressions used with a special meaning in accountancy. Includes abbreviations, synonyms. 'Profit and loss account': nearly ½p.; 'Holding company': 2/3p. *Class No: 652.7(038)*

[2577]
Kohler's dictionary for accountants. 6th ed., edited by W.W. Cooper and Y. Ijiri. Englewood Cliffs, N.J., Prentice-Hall, 1983. xi, 574p. ISBN: 0135166586.

First published 1952; 5th ed. 1975.

20 contributors. 4,538 terms defined (5th ed.: *c*.3,000 entries). The entries - well over half, new material - range in length from 75 to 100 words. Examples of usage. The standard dictionary of accountancy. *Class No: 652.7(038)*

[2578]
Management accounting: offical terminology. 3rd ed. Chartered Institute of Management Accountants, 1996. ISBN: 1874784493.

This is a useful guide to terms used in management accountancy. *Class No: 652.7(038)*

[2579]
PARKER, R.H. Macmillan dictionary of accounting. 2nd ed. London, Macmillan Press, 1992. xvii,307p. £40. ISBN: 0333455487.

First published in 1984.

Has *c*.1,000 entries ('Depreciation': 2 columns; 'Merger accountancy': 1½ columns. Abbreviations and acronyms, p.vii-xi. For students, teachers and practitioners of accountancy. *Class No: 652.7(038)*

Polyglot

[2580]
UNION EUROPÉENNE DES EXPERTS COMPTABLES ÉCONOMIQUE ET FINANCIERS. Lexique UEC. 2.éd. Düsseldorf, Institut der Wirtschaftsprüfer-Verlag, 1974. 879p. ISBN: 3802100735.

First published 1961.

A dictionary of *c*.1,300 accountancy terms in French, German, English/American, Dutch, Danish, Italian, Spanish and Portuguese. Main A-Z sequence of terms, with definitions and indexes in each language. *Class No: 652.7(038)=00*

Arabic

[2581]
ABU-GHAZALEH, T. The Abu-Ghazaleh English-Arabic dictionary of accountancy. London, Macmillan, 1978. 210p. ISBN: 0333214684.

Arabic translation of the English entry-word appears in both Latin and Arabic characters. *Class No: 652.7(038)=927*

Reviews & Abstracts

[2582]
Accounting and finance abstracts. Bradford, Yorks., ANBAR Management Publications, in association with the Institute of Chartered Accountants in England and Wales, 1971-. monthly, previously 8pa. $1549.95 including cumulative index and *Compleat Anbar*. ISSN: 00014796.

Supersedes *Accounting + data processing abstracts*, previously *Anbar management services abstracts*.

Abstracts of articles from more than 300 international management journals. Covers financial accounts, software, internal and external auditing, computer management, capital investment, and data transmission. *Class No: 652.7(048)*

[2583]
Accounting and tax index: a bibliography of accounting literature. New York, American Institute of Certified Public Accountants, 1921-. Quarterly, with annual cumulation.

About 10,000 references pa. to periodical articles, books, government publications, etc. Author and subject sequence. Comprehensive coverage of accountancy, auditing, data processing, finance, investments, law, management and taxation. Restricted to English-language material. Also available online (Orbit Search, Service (ACCT) and CD-ROM. *Class No: 652.7(048)*

Periodicals

[2584]
SPICELAND, J.D. *and* AGRAWAL, S.P. International guide to accounting journals. New York, Markus Wiener Publishing, 1988. 291p. ISBN: 0910129630.

A 2nd ed. was issued in 1993 (320p. $49.95. ISBN 1558760679).

Covers journals in 33 countries and is concerned mainly with journals for research. 2 sections: information listed alphabetically by journal and journals by country. The first section includes information on primary readership, language, circulation, publisher, style, length, sponsor and percentage of articles on accounting topics. *Class No: 652.7(051)*

Yearbooks & Directories

[2585]
ACCA directory of members 1994/1995. London, Chartered Association of Certified Accountants, 1994. £20. ISBN: 1859080901.

Published in two volumes.

Alphabetical listing of ACCA members and information on ACCA in the first volume. The second volume lists members in practise, and contains a topographical list of firms both in the UK and overseas. *Class No: 652.7(058)*

[2586]
European accountancy yearbook, 1992. 1st ed. London, Graham & Trotman, 1991. 400p. £125. $240.

Lists *c*.2000 offices of major accountancy firms in Europe, with addresses; telephone, fax & telex numbers; names of partners and functions; nature of firm's European coverage; fee income by sector and total; main services; major public company clients; history; etc. *Class No: 652.7(058)*

Biographies

[2587]

Who's who in accountancy. [London], Chapter 3 Publications, in association with Longman, 1987. xiv, [1], 394p. £27.00. ISBN: 0851210627.

3 parts: 1. Index of individual entries in alphabetical order - 2. Indices of a more specialised nature (*e.g.* 4. Accountants who are members of Parliament; 7. Editors of accountancy journals) - 3. Index of accountants according to the Industrial Classification (Accountancy services ... Transport). *Class No:* 652.7(092)

Great Britain

Yearbooks & Directories

[2588]

INSTITUTE OF CHARTERED ACCOUNTANTS OF ENGLAND AND WALES. Directory of firms. Macmillan Press, 1994. 950p. £63. ISBN: 0333585178.

Detailed information on the specialization of chartered accountancy firms, arranged A-Z by towns, plus an overseas section. *Class No:* 652.7(410)(058)

Book-keeping

[2589]

Spicer and Pegler's book-keeping and accounts. Spicer, E.E. *and* Pegler, E.C. 22nd ed. London, Butterworth, 1993. 608p. £17.95. ISBN: 0406022364.

26 chapters (1. Incomplete records ... 26. Special reports including Stock Exchange situations). Detailed contents. Detailed, analytical index, p.557-66. 'Prepared with the examination needs of the student primarily in mind' (*Preface*). *Class No:* 652.71

Costing

Dictionaries

[2590]

INSTITUTE OF COST AND MANAGEMENT ACCOUNTANTS. Terminology of management and financial accountancy. London, Institute of Cost and Management Accountants, 1974. x, 95p.

· Third major revision of *Costing terminology*, first published in the Institute's *Journal.* Defines *c.*400 terms; includes basic and full contextual classifications. Detailed analytical index, p.77-95. *Class No:* 652.747(038)

Reviews & Abstracts

[2591]

Management and accounting research. London, Academic Press, for the Chartered Institute of Management Accountants, 1983-. Quarterly. ISSN: 10445005.

Title previously *ICMA abstracts bulletin.*

Aims to encourage scholarship and empirical research in management accounting by providing a vehicle for publishing original research in the field.*c.*100 abstracts per issue on cost and financial accountancy; finance and financial management; industry, services and computer applications. Author and subject indexes per issue and annually. *Class No:* 652.747(048)

Auditing

[2592]

ATTWOOD, F.A. *and* **STEIN, N.D. De Paula's auditing.** 17th ed. London, Pitman, 1986. xiv, 682p. ISBN: 0273025015.

First published 1970.

24 chapters (1. How to study auditing ... 24. Investigations). Appendix: Auditing standards and guidelines, and other professional announcements. Detailed, analytical index, p.675-82. Student orientated. *Class No:* 652.76

[2593]

Cashin's handbook for auditors. Cashin, J.A., *and others.* 2nd ed. by P.D. Neuwirth and J.F. Levy. New York, etc., McGraw-Hill, 1985. 1376p. illus. £85. ISBN: 0070102643.

First published 1971 (1344p.).

7 parts (with documented chapters by specialists): 1. Principles, standards and responsibilities - 2. Principal types of auditing - 3. Planning, evaluation and administration - 4. Audit program objectives and procedures - 5. Analytical methods - 6. Conclusion, review and reporting - 7. Professional developments. Index. *Class No:* 652.76

[2594]

CHARTERED INSTITUTE OF PUBLIC FINANCE & ACCOUNTANCY. Glossary of audit terms. London, Chartered Institute of Public Finance & Accountancy, 1988. [v], 40p. £14.25. ISBN: 0852993684.

Defines *c.*300 terms (Access control ... Working files). *Class No:* 652.76

[2595]

SPICER, C.C. *and* **PEGLER, E.C. Spicer and Pegler's practical auditing.** 17th ed. London, Butterworths, 1985. xi, 365p. diagrs., charts, tables. £13.50. ISBN: 0406678014.

2 parts (28 chapters): 1. The firm's audit account - 2. Approach to specific areas (*e.g.* 14. Expenditure; 19. Tangible and intangible fixed assets; 23. Taxation; 24. Group accounts). Glossary of terms, p.351-7. Detailed, analytical index, p.359-65. Includes quotations and abstracts from the Institute of Chartered Accountants in England and Wales' auditing standards and guidelines, etc. Standard textbook; well laid out. *Class No:* 652.76

Management

Databases

[2596]

HOWITT, DORAN AND WEINBERGER, MARVIN, Inc. Databasics: your guide to online business information. New York, etc., Garland, 1984. xx, 614p.

5 parts, of which part 2 (chapters 13-23) is 'A guide to selected business databases', p.93-286. The major hosts are DIALOG, DATA-STAR, DATASOLVE, PERGAMON INFOLINE and FINSBURY DATA SERVICES. *Class No:* 652.8(003.4)

Bibliographies

[2597]

ASHRIDGE MANAGEMENT COLLEGE. Management for the future: a bibliography, undertaken on behalf of, and sponsored by, the Federation for Management Education. Ashridge, Bucks., Ashridge Management College, 1986. v.p.

About 800 entries, each with descriptors and abstracts. 6 sections: A. The future - general issues & trends - B. Management: general - C. Strategic management, corporate planning & operational/functional implications - D. Other organizational issues - E. People management & human resources issues - F. Individual companies, (divided by type of industry, *e.g.* Food and drink; Construction). Author and company indexes. *Class No:* 652.8(01)

Encyclopaedias

[2598]

The Encyclopedia of management. Heyel, C., *ed.* 3rd ed. New York, Van Nostrand Reinhold, 1982. xxx, [1], 1371p. diagrs., graphs, tables, maps. ISBN: 0442251653.

Over 200 contributors. More than 350 documented articles, A-Z, ranging in length from half a page to 30p. 'Quality control and quality assurance': p.998-1009, carrying 7 exhibits, 35 references and 5 cross-references. 3 appendices: A. Universities and colleges (all US); B. Sources of information (organizations, A-Z); C. Sources of information (journals cited). Detailed analytical index, p.1361-71. 'A much-needed compendium of management information' (*Reference books bulletin*, 1983-1984, p.84). *Class No:* 652.8(031)

[2599]

The International encyclopedia of business & management. Warner, M., *ed.* London, Routledge, 1996. $999.95. ISBN: 0415073995.

Published in six volumes. Contains bibliography, index and tables.

Volumes 1-5 have entries covering biography, country-specific management topics, as well as topics in general business and management. All entries include an annotated bibliography, and there are adequate cross-references. Length of biographical articles range from 4 to 8 pages, and some thematic topics have up to 20 pages. Many entries include tables, charts and graphs. Volume 6 is a detailed keyword index to the work. 'Excellent comprehensive coverage of business and management around the world for students, businesspersons and scholars' *Booklist* (ALA) v. 96,6 Nov. 15 1996. *Class No:* 652.8(031)

Handbooks & Manuals

[2600]

Company administration handbook. Beattie, D., *ed.* 7th ed. Aldershot, Hants., Gower, 1990. xxiii,1005p. illus., plans, tables. £65. ISBN: 0566028557.

First published 1970.

28 contributors. 6 parts (34 documented chapters): 1. The constitution and conduct of companies - 2. Accounting and finance - 3. Commercial functions - 4. Office administration - 5. The company and its employees - 6. The management of physical assets. Detailed analytical index. A comprehensive textbook for company secretaries, managers and personnel executives. *Class No:* 652.8(035)

[2601]

The Complete guide to managing your business. Cheltenham, Stottard & Co., 1988-. v.p. Loose-leaf; updating service.

22 contributors. 20 chapters (*e.g.* 2. Financial planning and management; 4. Buying and selling a business; 17. Selling your product or service; 18. Marketing and advertising; 19. Exporting overseas). Includes forms, useful addresses and some publications. 39-p. index. *Class No:* 652.8(035)

[2602]

Croner's executive companion. New Malden, Surrey, Croner, 1988. Loose-leaf. ISBN: 0900319615.

12 sections. 1. Sources of law in the UK. Consumer protection; 2. Legal aspects, finance, taxes; 3. Taxation; 4. Communications; 5. Exporting & importing; 6. Property; 7. Government departments & industry; 9. Social security; 10. Manpower; 11. Economic review; 12. General information. 16-p. index. For managers, company secretaries, supervisors and administrators. *Class No:* 652.8(035)

[2603]

Handbook of human factors. Salvendy, G., *ed.* New York, Wiley, 1987. 1874p. illus. $150. ISBN: 0471880159.

Gives 'information about the effective design and use of systems requiring the interaction among human, machine (computer) and environment' (*Preface*). 68 documented chapters by specialists. Index. *Class No:* 652.8(035)

[2604]

Handbook of management. Lock, D., *ed.* 3rd ed. Aldershot, Hants, Gower, 1992. xli,1002p. 271 illus. £60. ISBN: 056602974x.

First published 1983.

73 chapters in 10 parts: 1. Principles, policy & organization; 2. Financial management; 3. Marketing; 4. Research, engineering & design; 5. Purchasing & inventory management; 6. Manufacturing management; 7. Logistics management; 8. Administration; 9. Human resource management; 10. The skills of management. 68 contributors. 'Further reading' after each chapter. Analytical index (double-column), p.989-1002. *Class No:* 652.8(035)

[2605]

Handbook of management skills. Stewart, D.M., *ed.* 2nd ed. Aldershot, Hants, Gower, 1992. xxvi,537p. 161 illus (figures & charts) £42.50. ISBN: 0566029693.

First published 1987.

33 chapters in 4 parts: 1. Managing yourself - 2. Managing other people - 3. Managing a specialist department - 4. Managing the business. 33 contributors. Analytical index, p.529-37 (double-column). '... this book is the one to keep in your desk drawer ... [until] you need the information' (the editor). *Class No:* 652.8(035)

[2606]

The New manager's handbook: a reference guide. Armstrong, M., *ed.* London, Kogan Page, 1990. 438p. tables, charts. £19.95. ISBN: 0749402563.

Designed for quick reference, with chapters on the European Community, human resources management, sales and marketing, production and operations management, financial planning, and strategic management. Includes case studies. Appendices contain useful addresses, details of foreign currencies, time zones, travel information, etc. *Class No:* 652.8(035)

[2607]

SIEGAL, J.G., and others. The McGraw-Hill pocket guide to business finance: 201 decision-making tools for managers. New York, McGraw-Hill, 1992. 354p. $29.95. ISBN: 0070575770.

'a handy reference' for financial professionals. 'Tools' are some of the most commonly used financial computations ranging from basic ratios to complex multiple regression tests. For each tool there is a brief definition, statement of computational method, examples of practical use, and identification of professions most likely to use it. Clear, well-organized entries. Well indexed. 'A good supplement to more in-depth financial handbooks'(*Choice*, v.30(3), November 1992, p.450). *Class No:* 652.8(035)

Dictionaries

[2608]

BLAKE, J. and LAWRENCE, P. The ABC of management: a handbook of management terms and concepts. London, Cassell, 1989. [3],133p. £6.95. $12.95. ISBN: 0304322288.

International in scope, with more detailed explanations than a simple dictionary. As well as defining terms, it provides details on key figures in business and management. Cross-references. Aimed at managers at all levels. *Class No:* 652.8(038)

[2609]

JOHANNSEN, H. and PAGE, G.T. International dictionary of management. 4th ed. London, Kogan Page, 1990. 388p. illus. £20. ISBN: 0749400153.

First published 1975.

Has over 6000 brief entries for terms, organizations, abbreviations and acronyms. 'It has both omissions and errors' (*Choice*, v.19(6), February 1982, p.744), of the 3rd ed. Use to supplement other business dictionaries. *Class No:* 652.8(038)

[2610]

ROSENBERG, J.M. Dictionary of business and management. New revision. New York, Wiley, 1993. x,374p. tables. $39.45. ISBN: 0471578126.

First published 1978; 2nd ed. 1983.

Defines over 7,500 terms for such areas of business as accounting, banking and finance, data processing, labour relations, management, marketing, real estate and transportation. Appendices A-M of tables of measures, interest, etc. Provides more terms than other such dictionaries, although some definitions are gratuitous. *Class No:* 652.8(038)

[2611]

STATT, D. A. Concise dictionary of business management 2nd edition London, Routledge, 1999 x, 187p. £55.00 ISBN: 0415188660.

This book was originally published as the "Concise dictionary of management" in 1991. The new edition adds many terms and buzz-words and also covers people who have contributed to the theory of management. The entries are quite short. *Class No:* 652.8(038)

German

[2612]

COVENEY, J., and others. Harrap's glossary of business management terms. German-English, English-German. London, Harrap, 1991. 256p. £4.50. ISBN: 0245603573.

Includes terms not usually found in existing general dictionaries. Covers the main areas of management interest. *Class No:* 652.8(038)=30

[2613]

SOMMER, W. and SCHÖNFELD, H.-M. Management dictionary: dictionary of accountancy, economic and tax law, and data processing. 4th-5th rev. ed. New York, de Gruyter, 1978-79. ISBN: 3110077086, v.1.

1. *English-German.* 5th rev. and enld. ed. 1979. 620p. 2. *Deutsch-Englisch.* 4th rev. and enld. ed. 1978. 542p. *Class No:* 652.8(038)=30

French

[2614]

QUEBEC OFFICE DE LA LANGUE FRANÇAISE. Terminologie de la gestion: vocabulaire des imprimés administratifs lexique, français et anglais. Quebec, Office de la langue française, 1974. 311p.

French-English, English-French dictionary of management terms. *Class No:* 652.8(038)=40

Theses

[2615]

Selected list of UK theses and dissertations in management studies. Sheffield City Polytechnic Library, for the British Business Schools' Libraries Group, 1975-. Annual. ISSN: 01407414.

12th annual listing, 1987, ([7], 472p.) lists *c.*1,500 theses and dissertations, with locations. 3 parts: 1. Subject grouping; 2. Author index; 3. Subject index. 19 Library locations. *Class No:* 652.8(043)

Reviews & Abstracts

[2616]

Business publications index and abstracts. Prepared by Management Contents. Detroit, Mich., Gale, 1983-198? Monthly, with annual cumulation. ISSN: 0739618x.

Subject-author citations. 1985 cumulation. 2v. (1127p.). 1986. *Abstracts.* 1985 cumulation in 2v. (1375p.).

The 1985 volumes index *c.*24,000 articles, with 50-200-word abstracts in the second two-volume set. Sources comprise over 700

....(contd.)

periodicals proceedings and transactions. The set constitutes the printed version of Management Contents database (qv). Retrospective volumes are planned. *Class No:* 652.8(048)

[2617]

Compleat ANBAR. Bradford, Yorks, ANBAR Management Publications, 1972-. Annual.

Reproduces all the abstracts appearing throughout the year in 5 ANBAR abstracting services, - *Accounting and finance abstracts, Marketing and distribution abstracts, Personnel and training abstracts, Top management abstracts, Operations + production abstracts.* Cumulated abstracts are grouped: 1. Users; 2. Techniques; 3. Applications; 4. Equipment, premises, suppliers. Indexes: subjects; authors (books). Bibliography (list of monographs, etc.).

Class No: 652.8(048)

[2618]

Management and marketing abstracts. Leatherhead, Surrey, PIRA [Paper Industry Research Association], in association with British Institute of Management, 1976-. Monthly. $846. ISSN: 03082172.

Formerly *Marketing abstracts.*

Over 3600 abstracts a year in 26 sections, including management techniques, personnel, education and training, marketing, etc. Author and subjects pa. Stresses practical aspects. Online: PERGAMON INFOLINE, DIALOG, ORBIT (1973-). *Class No:* 652.8(048)

[2619]

Management bibliographies and reviews. Bradford, Yorks., ANBAR Management Publications, 1987-. 8 pa (previously quarterly). £999.95. $2629.95 pa. ISSN: 09535713.

Continues *Anbar management publications* and *The ANBAR management bibliography.*

Provides up-to-date information on new developments and thinking in management practice and serves as a resource for research workers and practicing managers. *Class No:* 652.8(048)

[2620]

SCIMP [Selective cooperative index of management periodicals]: European index of management periodicals. European Business School Librarians Group. Helsinki, Helsinki School of Economics Library, previously Manchester, Manchester Business School Library, 1978-. 10pa. £75;FIM650pa. ISSN: 07822979.

Over 5,000 references pa.; *c.*150 journals scanned. Subject classes (100 General management; 200 Finance and economics; 300 Industry and marketing; 400 Associated subjects (*e.g.* Psychology; Communications). Author, company, and permitted subject indexes per issue, cumulated 3 times a year. A truly international effort: indexing is shared amongst 7 different countries; the database functions at Helsinki, editing at Delft, printing at Manchester, and the *SCIMP/SCAMP thesaurus* at the London Business School Library. Also available on CD-ROM. *Class No:* 652.8(048)

[2621]

Top management abstracts. Bradford, Yorks.,ANBAR Management Publications, in association with the British Institute of Management, 1971-. monthly (previously 8 pa). £689.95 pa. ISSN: 00494100.

Supersedes in part *ANBAR management services abstracts.*

About 120 short abstracts per issue, with critical comments italicized (*e.g.* "A bit of plugging for the author's organization here"). Brief subject index ('At a glance'). Cross-references. Asterisked items are mentioned in an introductory 'Highlights'. Some 250 journals are monitored. Annual index. Intended for directors, senior managers and senior staff officers. *Class No:* 652.8(048)

[2622]

Women in management review and abstracts. Equal Opportunities Commission. Bradford, Yorks., ANBAR Publications, Ltd., 1985-. 7 pa (previously quarterly). ISSN: 09558357.

Includes articles, news items, and book reviews, as well as *c.*50 abstracts per issue of articles in other management journals. Leavitt, J.A. *Women in management: an annotated bibiliography and sourcelist* (Phoenix, Ariz., Oryx Press, 1982. 197p.) covers items published/ written 1970-81, in 20 sections, with author index.

Class No: 652.8(048)

Progress Reports

[2623]

Current research in management. Hammond, V., *ed.* London & Dover, N.H., Frances Pinter (Publishers), for the Association of Teachers of Management, 1985. xv, 265p. £30. ISBN: 086187546x.

24 contributors. 5 parts (16 well-documented chapters): 1. Understanding organisations and culture - 2. Understanding managers and their needs - 3. Developments in personnel and industrial relations - 4. New directives in business - 5. Research into practice. Complete list of papers presented at Current Research in Management Conference, p.261-5. *Class No:* 652.8(055)

Audio-Visual Materials

[2624]

Films and videograms for managers: British National Film & Video catalogue. Brown, M., *ed.* London, British Film Institute, 1984. vi, 181p. (*British national film and video catalogue subject listing no.2.*) ISBN: 0851701698.

'A subject listing of recent films and videograms on management and selected topics drawn from the published records of the British National Film and Video catalogue for the year 1980 to 1983 inclusive'. *Class No:* 652.8(086)

[2625]

Management media directory: an annotated guide of commercially available audiovisual programs for business and management schools, in-house training and development programs, management consultants and human resource managers. Proven, J. *and* Glogowski, M.P., *eds.* Detroit, Gale Research Co., 1982. vi, 506p. $200. ISBN: 0810301709.

Data on over 3,500 programmes used by American business and management schools. Media include films, sound filmstrips, audiocassettes and videos. More than 230 distributors. Title and subject indexes. *Class No:* 652.8(086)

Information Services

[2626]

LONG, L. **Management information systems.** Englewood Cliffs, N.J., Prentice-Hall, 1989. $42.67. ISBN: 0135515988.

In 5 parts: Information - Computing institutions - MIS (Management Information Systems) concepts - Planning and implementation - Managing information and computing resources. Geared to undergraduate and graduate students. *Class No:* 652.8:061:025.5

Personnel Management

[2627]

ARMSTRONG, M. **A Handbook of personnel management.** 3rd ed. London, Kogan Page, 1988. xix, 712p. tables. ISBN: 1850913366.

7 sections: 1. Personnel management - an overview - 2. Organizational behaviour - 3. Organizational planning and development - 4. Employee resourcing - 5. Employment and personnel administration - 6. Reward management - 7. Employee relations. Appendicies A-L (A. Personnel policies ... H. Disciplinary procedure ... L. Assessment centres). Bibliographies throughout.

Class No: 652.83

[2628]

—An International dictionary of personnel terms. 2nd ed. London, European Association of Personnel Management, 1980. 157p.

Provides equivalents of terms in 10 languages, - French, Norwegian, English, Spanish, Finnish, German, Portuguese, Dutch. Swedish and Danish - in a grouped sequence. The index covers all 10 languages. A separate Italian section completes coverage of Western and Northern Europe. *Class No:* 652.83

[2629]

The Human resources management yearbook, 1993. London, A.P.Information Services, 1993. Annual. £22.50 ISBN: 0814581607. ISSN: 03066673.

First published 1969 by Kogan Page.

In 6 parts: Part 1 has articles by leading experts; pt 2 is a survey of major areas of employment, trade union and health and safety legislation; pts 3,4,5 are directories of course providers, consultancy and service providers, officials and public bodies of HRD; and pt 6 is a bibliography of recent books and journals on human resource management, grouped under 18 headings. *Class No:* 652.83

[2630]

Personnel + training abstracts. Bradford, Yorks, Anbar Publications Ltd., in association with The Institute of Personnel Managament, 1971-. monthly (previously 8 pa). $1549.95 including cumulative index and *Compleat Anbar* ISSN: 0305067x.

Supersedes in part *Anbar management services abstracts.*

Abstracts of articles selected from over 300 international management journals. Covers such topics as health and safety, management development, industrial relations. *Class No:* 652.83

[2631]

TORRINGTON, D. *and* EARNSHAW, J. **Pocket employer.** Oxford, Basil Blackwell and the Economist Publications, 1988. [ii], 252p. ISBN: 0631153896.

Contains *c.*300 terms related to the management of employment. Definitions and explanations of terms from employment law, academic research, and personnel management methods. Cross references and suggestions for further reading contained in text. *Class No:* 652.83

Dictionaries

[2632]

BENNETT, R. **Dictionary of personnel and human resources management.** London, Pitman Publishing, 1992. [ii],231p. £12.99. ISBN: 027303877x.

Over 3500 definitions covering the practical and utilitarian aspects of the personnel function (laws and regulations, methods, systems, procedures and techniques, plus broader topics concerned with organizational behaviour, human resources, planning, strategy and control. Intended for both student and practitioner. Fully cross-referenced. Includes acronyms. *Class No:* 652.83(038)

[2633]

TRACEY, W.R. **The Human resources glossary:** a complete desk reference for HR professionals. New York, AMACOM, 1991. 416p. $49.95. ISBN: 0814450113.

Over 3000 terms relating to human resources specializations, plus key terms from selected business and management disciplines, with explanation of context, use and managerial implications. Index of key terms. 'There are few glossaries one would wish to read cover to cover. This is one of them. It reads well, is thoughtfully organized ...' (*Choice*, v.29(2). October 1991, p.267). *Class No:* 652.83(038)

Yearbooks & Directories

[2634]

The Personnel manager's yearbook 1999/2000. Irwin, H., *ed.* London, AP Information Services, 1999. 1250p. £89.50. ISBN: 1902202120.

Contains indexes.

9,000 companies are listed with their addresses, telephone and fax numbers, names of senior staff, and number of employees. The second part of the book lists personnel advisors and suppliers of services for personnel managers. There is also an annotated bibliography for "Human Resource Development". *Class No:* 652.83(058)

Ergonomics

[2635]

Ergonomics abstracts. Basingstoke, Hants, Taylor & Francis, for the Ergonomics Information Analysis Centre, School of Manufacturing and Mechanical Engineering, University of Birmingham, 1969-. 6pa. £393:$677pa. ISSN: 00462446.

*c.*750 abstracts per issue on working efficiency of human beings. Irregular author and subject indexes. Available on microform from MIM. *Class No:* 652.83.04

Production Management

[2636]

BRITISH STANDARDS INSTITUTION. **Glossary of production planning and control terms.** London, The Institution, 1975. 40p. (*BS 5191: 1975*.)

Lists and defines general terms used in quality assurance, with an appendix defining related common words. *Class No:* 652.85

[2637]

—BURBRIDGE, J.L. IFIP glossary of terms used in production control. Amsterdam, North-Holland, 1987. ix, 113p. diagrs. ISBN: 0444702873.

3 parts: 1. Introduction - 2. Classified glossary (A. - J.: A. Management ... D. Purchasing ... J. Secretarial) - 3. Alphabetical glossary. Index. *Class No:* 652.85

[2638]

Industrial engineering handbook. Maynard, H.B., *ed.* 3rd ed. New York, etc., McGraw-Hill, 1971. [xvii, 1891]p. illus., diagrs., tables. $132. ISBN: 0070410844.

First published 1956.

About 75 contributors. 13 sections: 1. The industrial engineering function - 2. Methods - 3. Work measurement techniques ... 6. Wage and salary administration ... 8. Planning and control procedures ... 12. Industrial engineering tools - 13. Industrial engineering applications. Based on US practice. *Class No:* 652.85

[2639]

Operations + production abstracts. Bradford, Yorks, Anbar Publications, Ltd., in conjunction with the Institute of Management Services, 1973-. monthly (loose-leaf). $1549.95 including the *Compleat Anbar* ISSN: 09524614.

Formerly *Work study + O and M abstracts.* Supersedes in part *Anbar management services abstracts*, and later *Management services ++ production abstracts.*

Abstracts selected from over 300 international management journals, covering productivity, industrial engineering, work measurement, operational research, safety, and production methods. *Class No:* 652.85

[2640]

—Work Research Unit Information Service news and abstracts. London, the Service, 1978-. 6pa. *Gratis*.

Provides 30 items per issue on aspects of working conditions, including automation and robotics. *Class No:* 652.85

Quality Control

[2641]

EUROPEAN ORGANISATION FOR QUALITY CONTROL. Glossary Committee. **Glossary of terms used in the management of quality control,** with their equivalents in Arabic, Chinese, Czech, Danish, Dutch, Finnish, French, German, Greek, Hungarian, Italian, Japanese, Norwegian, Polish, Portuguese, Russian, Spanish, Swedish. 6th ed. Bern, the Organisation, 1989. 777p. £49.95.

First published in 1965.

457 English-based terms, with definitions (p.9-82), and equivalents and indexes in the other 18 languages. *Class No:* 652.856

[2642]

Juran's quality control handbook. Juran, J.M., *ed.-in-chief.* 4th ed. New York, etc., McGraw-Hill, 1988. [1774]p. illus. £93.50. ISBN: 0070331766.

3rd ed. 1974. [1600]p.

Revised and updated 4th ed. includes chapters on companywide planning for quality; quality improvement; quality costs; computers and quality; managing human performance; training for quality; quality programmes in service industries; marketing; upper management and quality. Index. *Class No:* 652.856

[2643]

LOCK, D., *ed.* **Gower handbook of quality management.** Aldershot, Hants, Gower, 1990. xxi,649p. £50 ISBN: 0366027704.

Contributions by professionals on a broad range of issues. 'It provides a full and instructive discussion of quality programmes and their implementation. Comprehensive'. (*British book news,* September 1990, p.575). *Class No:* 652.856

[2644]

Quality control and applied statistics: international literature digest service. Davenport, Iowa, Executive Sciences Institute, 1956-. Monthly. $148pa. ISSN: 00335207.

Formerly *Quality control and applied statistics, including Operations research, yearbook,* 1960-62.

50 abstracts per issue. 5 sections: Statistical process control - Mathematical statistics and possibility theory - Experimentation and correlation - Managerial applications - Reliability of complex assemblies. Appended list of publications abstracted. Author, subject and classification code indexes. *Class No:* 652.856

Purchasing

[2645]

Purchasing and materials management. Dobler, D.W., *and others.* 4th ed. New York, etc., McGraw-Hill, 1984. 736p. $33.95. ISBN: 0070370427.

6 parts: 1. The functions of purchasing and materials management - 2. Fundamentals - 3. Related materials functions - 4. Management - 5. Institutional and government purchasing - 6. Cases for study and analysis. Appendices. Indexes. *Instructor's manual* is also available. *Class No:* 652.87

Marketing & Sales

[2646]

Macmillan dictionary of marketing and advertising. Baker, M.J., *ed.* 2nd ed. London, Macmillan Press, 1990. [vi],271p. £20. ISBN: 0333516044.

First published in 1984.

About 2000 initialled entries, by 26 contributors, of terms commonly used in marketing and advertising, including thumb-nail sketches of key concepts and ideas. Fully cross-referenced. Intended readership: practitioners, managers, students and lay persons. *Class No:* 652.88

Bibliographies

[2647]

The European directory of marketing information sources, 1991. 2nd ed. London, Euromonitor, 1991. xix, 674p. charts, tables. ISBN: 0863384005.

First published 1987.

Over 2,000 entries, arranged in 10 main sections, all subdivided by country: 1. Official sources and publications; 2. Libraries and information services; 3. Leading market research companies; 4. Leading consumer research publishers; 5. Information databases and databanks; 6. Abstracts and indexes; 7. Major business and marketing journals; 8. Major business and marketing associations; 9. European business contacts; 10. Socio-economic profiles. Coverage: 17 Western European countries. Subject and A-Z indexes. *Class No:* 652.88(01)

[2648]

HEROLD, J. Marketing and sales management an information sourcebook. Phoenix, Ariz., Oryx, 1988. $39.50. (*Oryx sourcebook series in business and management.*) ISBN: 0897744063.

Contains 1,000 entries on reference works, indexes, abstracting journals, periodicals, serials, statistical sources, databases and vendors, CD-ROMS, and associations. Covers English-language material only from 1980 to the present. Numbered entries with annotations. Final chapter, 'Core Library Collection'. *Class No:* 652.88(01)

[2649]

International directory of marketing information sources 1988. London, Euromonitor, 1988. xxi, 362p. ISBN: 0863381618.

8 broad sections: 1. Official sources and publications - 2. Major reference libraries - 3. Leading market research companies - 4. Information databases - 5. Abstracts and indices - 6. Major business and marketing journals - 7. Leading general business and marketing associations - 8. International business contacts. General index, p.335-62. *Class No:* 652.88(01)

Encyclopaedias

[2650]

Companion encyclopedia of marketing. Baker, M.J., *ed.* London, Routledge, 1995. xxxiii,1061p. ISBN: 0415093953.

Contains indexes.

Contains 56 long articles grouped into 6 sections: Nature and Scope of Marketing; Theoretical Foundations; Marketing Management; The Marketing Mix; Marketing in Practice; Special Topics. Each article has a bibliography and a list for further reading. The index is comprehensive. *Class No:* 652.88(031)

Handbooks & Manuals

[2651]

BUELL, V.P. Handbook of modern marketing. 2nd ed. New York, McGraw-Hill, 1986. [1312]p. illus. $84.95. ISBN: 0070088543.

First published 1970.

107 essays on a wide range of marketing topics, by practitioners and academics. 19 subject areas. 'Of limited value to faculty and graduate level researchers, but useful treatment for students and practitioners' (*Choice*, v.24(3), November 1986, p.521). *Class No:* 652.88(035)

[2652]

PALEY, N. The Manager's guide to competitive marketing strategies 2nd edition St Lucie, 1999 427p. $49.95 ISBN: 1574442341.

Aimed at helping managers to understand market research, pricing policy, promotion and distribution in the context of both national and global markets. Good on the historical context for marketing. Can be used as a work-book for training marketing personnel, but the case studies provided make it also a useful academic text. *Class No:* 652.88(035)

Dictionaries

[2653]

HART, N.A. *and* STAPLETON, J. The Marketing dictionary. 4th ed. London, Butterworth-Heinemann, in association with the Chartered Institute of Marketing,1992. 240p. £12.95. ISBN: 0750602082.

First published 1977. The first 3 eds. were titled *Glossary of marketing terms.*

Contains *c.*3,000 terms used in present-day marketing and associated terminology, including research management, export, packaging, advertising, raw materials, selling, public relations, law, etc. Aimed at students taking diploma and degree examinations in the marketing field. *Class No:* 652.88(038)

[2654]

IVANOVIC, A. Dictionary of marketing. Teddington, Peter Collin Publishing, 1989. 207p. ISBN: 0948549084.

Contains *c.*3,500 terms and phrases used in marketing services and goods, *e.g.* market research, presentation and packaging, publicity and television advertising. Extensive use of bold type throughout text when giving examples. Supplement includes: British socio-economic groups ... Technical information for a periodical. *Class No:* 652.88(038)

[2655]

IVANOVIC, A., *and others.* English-German dictionary of marketing. Teddington, Mddx, Peter Collin, 1991. 350p. £25. ISBN: 094854922x.

Transation of the *Pons Fachwörterbuch Marketing.* Terms are defined in English. *Class No:* 652.88(038)

[2656]

OSTROW, R. *and* SMITH, S.R. The Dictionary of marketing. New York, Fairchild Publications, 1988. 258p. illus. $25.00. ISBN: 0870055739.

Has *c.*1,900 definitions of words and phrases. Some graphs and charts plus numerous cross-references. Also contains profiles of principal marketing trade associations. *Class No:* 652.88(038)

Glossaries

[2657]

CLEMENTS, M.N. The Marketing glossary: key items, concepts and applications in marketing management, advertising, sales promotion, public relations, direct marketing, market research, sales. New York, AMACOM, 1992. 392p. illus. charts, diagrs. $34.95. ISBN: 081445030x.

Over 1400 definitions for terms in marketing, aranged A-Z by key term. Cross-references. Appendices includes addresses and telephone numbers of marketing and advertising trade publications. Bibliography. *Class No:* 652.88(038.1)

Reviews & Abstracts

[2658]

Marketing + distribution abstracts. Bradford, Yorks., ANBAR Publications Ltd, 1971-. monthly (previously 8pa). £689.95 pa. ISSN: 03050661.

About 100 abstracts per issue. Some items are asterisked, for mention in the 'Highlights' introduction. Others may be given critical comment, italicized (*e.g.* "Rather involved"; "A well presented article in an area of increasing importance"). Subject index precedes, cumulated annually. Items are drawn from a core list of *c.*250 journals, listed in April and October issues. *Class No:* 652.88(048)

Worldwide

[2659]

International marketing data and statistics. London, Euromonitor Publications, Ltd., 1975-. Annual. tables. £145. ISSN: 03082938.

17th annual ed., 1993 (viii, 652p.) covers all major and selected minor countries, except European countries (in another volume). 25 data sections in the fields of population, employment, production, trade, economy, standard of living, consumption, housing, health, education, communications, transport, tourism, etc. Footnoted sources. Statistics are the latest available at time of publication. 'An essential source for international studies and marketing collections'(*Choice*,v.30(10), June 1993, p.1604). *Class No:* 652.88(100)

[2660]

International marketing handbook. 3rd ed., edited by F.E. Bair. Detroit, Mich., Gale, 1988. 3v. (4036p.). charts, tables, maps. $235.

Detailed marketing profiles for 141 countries. Trade and economic data on each country include foreign trade outlook; industry trends; transportation and utilities; distribution and sales channels; advertising and research; credit; trade regulations; investment; guidance for business visitors; sources of economic and commercial information.

A 4th ed. is planned for late 1995 (3v. $235. ISBN 0810373122). *Class No:* 652.88(100)

Europe

[2661]

European marketing data and statistics, 1998. 34th ed. London, Euromonitor Publications, 1998. Annual. 483p., tables, maps. £185. ISBN: 0863388213. ISSN: 00712930.

First published 1964.

Covers the 33 countries of Eastern and Western Europe. Profiles of the countries are followed by some 24 subject areas containing statistics on marketing geography, demographic trends and forecasts, economic indicators, finance and banking, external trade, labour force indicators, industrial resources and output, energy resources and output, defence, environmental data, consumer expenditure patterns, retailing, advertising, consumer markets, housing, health, education, agriculture, telecommunications, transport, tourism and culture. Subject index. *Class No:* 652.88(4)

Europe—Western

[2662]

Guide to European market information: EC countries. London, London Business School Information Service, 1991. £50. $100. ISBN: 0951440136.

11 chapters aranged by country (excluding UK) provide details of published market research studies, marketing and advertising journals, statistical series on trade and industry, online sources of market data, subscription services, trade and official bodies. The most important industries are listed for each country, with leading media and marketing organizations. Also, a Pan-European chapter covering international sources. Subject, title and type of source indexes. *Class No:* 652.88(400)

Bibliographies

[2663]

FOSTER, P. **How to find information 1992:** the European Single Market. In *Business information review*, v.5(4), April 1989, p.3-19.

Reviews the major sources of information on the European Single Market, covering books, pamphlets, directories, journals, newsletters, looseleaf services, current awareness services, EC official publications, market reports, information packs, seminars, information services, consultancy and seminars, care services, videos and online databases (*Author abstract*). *Class No:* 652.88(400)(01)

Great Britain

[2664]

Compendium of marketing information sources. London, Euromonitor Publications, 1989. xi,258p. ISBN: 0863382495. ISSN: 09572376.

'... a comprehensive one-stop guide to assessing the UK marketplace with classified entries identifying primary sources of market information available from official and unofficial sources on UK markets' (*Foreword*. In 7 sections, all subdivided and with brief annotations or descriptions: 1. Libraries and information services - 2. Abstracts and indexes - 3. Online databases and databanks - 4. Official sources - 5. Non official sources - 6. Market research agencies - 7. Company information. Products and services index; General index. *Class No:* 652.88(410)

Yearbooks & Directories

[2665]

The Marketing manager's yearbook 1996. Linch, K., *ed*. London, AP Information Services, 1996. ISBN: 0906247640.

Contains indexes.

Comprehensive source of information on buyers and sellers of marketing services, with 9,000 UK companies listed. Gives details of marketing departments, lists of advertising agencies, PR agencies, design companies, direct marketing companies, marketing consultants, etc. *Class No:* 652.88(410)(058)

Japan

[2666]

Japan marketing handbook. London, Euromonitor, 1988. 160p. $160. ISBN: 0863382134.

6 sections: Market overview - Economic and government policies - Japanese industry, technology and markets - Business and management - The Japanese consumer market - Conclusions. Appendices: Fact file - A to Z of Japanese markets - Some useful addresses. *Class No:* 652.88(52)

USA

Encyclopaedias

[2667]

Encyclopedia of consumer brands. Jorgensen, J., *ed*. Detroit, St. James Press, 1994. ISBN: 1558623361.

Published in three volumes. Contains illustrations and indexes.

Provides "substantive information on products that have been leaders in their respective brand categories, and have had decided impact in American business and popular culture." Covers around 600 of the most popular American brands. Entries are alphabetical, and give a history of the brand, in terms of its advertising history and marketing context. Each entry includes a bibliography. There are indexes of brand names, companies and persons, advertising agencies, and brand categories. *Class No:* 652.88(73)(031)

Market Research

[2668]

ASSOCIATION OF BRITISH MARKET RESEARCH COMPANIES. ABMRC handbook and guide to commissioning market research surveys 1991. London, Carrick James Market Research. 207p.

Main section: Industrial companies. Other sections include index by type of research, index by services offered, cfd index, personnel index, companies working overseas, index of publications, index of software packages. Chief aim of the Association is to assist clients in the selection of a research agency to meet their needs. *Class No:* 652.880

[2669]

BRITISH LIBRARY. Science Reference and Information Service. **Market research: a guide to British Library holdings.** Leydon, M., *ed*. 7th ed. London, SRIS, 1991. ix, 194p. (*Key to British Library holdings series*.) ISBN: 0712307745.

Sub-title varies.

List over 2000 current reports, arranged by subject. Subject index precedes (p.v-ix) the list of research reports, industry surveys and county profiles (p.1-168). Publishers' directory, p.169-194. British Library reference and loan copies (from the British Library Documents Supply Centre) are indicated. *Class No:* 652.880

[2670]

DICKINSON, J.R. The Bibliography of marketing research methods. Lexington, Mass., D.C.Heath, for Marketing Science Institute, 1986. xxxi,[1],758,[1]p.

Over 9200 entries, classified under *c*.800 headings and subheadings. Arranged in 3 broad categories: Market research function; data collection methods; data analysis techniques. Despite 'methods' in title, 'applications' subheadings are used, by way of illustration. *Class No:* 652.880

[2671]

International directory of market research organizations. Fuller, J.R., *ed*. 11th ed. London, Market Research Society, 1993. xx,[776]p. ISBN: 0906117143. ISSN: 09606718.

10th ed. was published in 1990.

Nearly 2000 companies in over 80 countries are listed. Arranged A-Z by country (Argentine ... Zimbabwe) subdivided by names of organizations. Data includes company address, telephone & fax numbers, contact, parent or subsidiary, membership [of organizations], research facilities, data services, product group expertise, international experience, staff, turnover, company description. 8 appendices including A. Principal market research associations; C1. Index of research facilities by country; C2. Index of data collection and processing services by country; D1.Publications by company; D2. Publications by title. *Class No:* 652.880

[2672]

Market research abstracts. London, Market Research Society, 1963-. 2pa. 60pa. ISSN: 00253596.

About 400 abstracts pa., covering market surveys, statistics, advertising and media research, psychology, etc. Subject and author indexes per issue. Online DEMOTAB. Available on microfilm from UMI. *Class No:* 652.880

[2673]

Market research: international directory of published market research. 16th ed. London, Arlington Management Publications Ltd., 1992. Annual. 751p. tables. £69.75.

First published 1976.

Lists *c*.700 major consulting and market research firms worldwide, A-Z; *c*.19,000 professional market reports covering over 100 countries; Organizations, firms and other producers of reports, A-Z. Products and services index. Price includes supplementary publication each September and a telephone enquiry service for new reports. *Class No:* 652.880

[2674]

—**Marketsearch: international directory of published market research.** 17th ed. London, Arlington Management Publications Ltd., 1993. Annual. 640p. £69.75. ISBN: 090661614x.

c.17,000 research studies of which many are completely new works. Worldwide coverage of over 150 countries. Semi-annual supplement published in the second half of the year updates. *Class No:* 652.880

Wholesale Selling

[2675]

American wholesalers and distributors directory: a comprehensive guide offering industry details on more than 18,000 wholesalers and distributors in the United States. Burek, D.M., *ed*. Gale, 1992. 1745p. $150. £95. ISBN: 0810382482.

Main arrangement is A-Z by name of firm, with access to entries by SIC code or geographically. Each entry includes all contact details, SIC code, major product lines, number of employees, estimated sales, and principal executives. A statistical section ranks the top 50 companies in each SIC section by sales. '... no other single comparable directory of this type.'(*Choice*,November 1992). *Class No:* 652.886

[2676]

European wholesalers and distributors directory. Irwin, L., *and others, eds*. Detroit, Gale, 1992. 677p. $175. ISBN: 0810383543.

Profiles more than 5000 major wholesalers and distributors in *c*.40 European countries. Arranged in four sections: by SIC subdivided by country; by specific product line; by countries in which company distributes products, subdivided by SIC; and A-Z by company name. Each main entry includes address; telephone, fax and telex numbers; executives; primary and additional SICs; number of employees; products and territories of distribution. *Class No:* 652.886

Retail Selling

[2677]

Macmillan dictionary of retailing. Baron, S. *and* Jones, P., *eds.* London, Macmillan, 1991. 312p. £35. ISBN: 0333537580.

Defines terms emanating from the Department of Retail Marketing at Manchester Polytechnic and top companies in retailing.
Class No: 652.887

[2678]

Retail trade international. London, Euromonitor Publications Ltd., 1992. 3v. tables. £650. $1300 the set. ISBN: 0863384072, v.1 & 2; 0863384471, v.3. ISSN: 09510737, v.1 & 2; 09510745, v.3.

Data on trends in retailing; consumer spending; retail sales by commodity, outlets, organizations (including mail order). V.1 & 2 cover Western European countries, A-Z, followed by Eastern European countries; v.3 has international data. *Class No:* 652.887

[2679]

Retailing in the European single market, 1993. Luxembourg, Office for Official Publications of the European Community, 1993. xii,213p. tables, diagrams. £34. $52. ECU 40. ISBN: 9282654583.

In 3 parts: I. Retail trade in Europe: structure, strategies, prospects (5 sections, all subdivided) - II. Retail trade in the single market: country reports (for each country key statistics, employment, activity, etc.) - III. Glossary. Data sources, p.211-2. Symbols and abbreviations. *Class No:* 652.887

Handbooks & Manuals

[2680]

BAILLIEU, D. Streetwise franchising: everything you need to know about taking up and running a successful franchise. London, Hutchinson Business, 1988. xvi,187p. £16.95. ISBN: 0091736803.

Aims to provide a guide to the issues and problems. 12 chapters: 1. Franchising as a legal concept ... 3. Raising finance - 4. Organizations to consult ... 11. Other sources of information - 12. The future of franchising; growth and new developments. 8 appendices include: Summary of franchise listing; sources of finance; Franchising trade associations. Index. *Class No:* 652.887(035)

[2681]

BARROW, C. and GOLZEN, G. Taking up a franchise: the *Daily telegraph* guide. 6th ed. London, Kogan Page, 1989. 283p. £6.99. ISBN: 1850919925.

Explanation of the meaning of franchising. 12 sections: 1. What franchising means - 2. Advantages and disadvantages of taking up a franchise ... 6. Financing a franchise ... 8. Current franchising opportunities: a guide ... 11. The British Franchise Association - 12. Useful organizations and publications. Index, p.267-275. '... somewhat journalistic format' (*International small business journal*, v.7(3), April/June, 1989, p.88). *Class No:* 652.887(035)

[2682]

MENDELSOHN, M. The Guide to franchising. 5th ed. London, Cassell, 1992. 368p. £45;$80. ISBN: 0805019766.

16 sections: The concept of franchising - History and development - Why franchise your business? ... How to become a franchiser ... Legal aspects ... Franchising internationally ... The British Franchise Association - Franchise consultants and their profession. Appendix. *Class No:* 652.887(035)

Yearbooks & Directories

[2683]

Markets yearbook. 33rd ed. Oldham, The 'World's Fair' Ltd., 1993. 264p. £8.

A list of markets in England, Wales and Scotland, with market days, owners and superintendents, etc. Directory (one alphabetical sequence), Aberdare ... Ystradgynlais, p.17-191. Wholesalers directory, p.192-246. Market operators, p.247-252. List of market venues, p.253-257. Index to advertisers. *Class No:* 652.887(058)

[2684]

Worldwide franchise directory: a guide offering details for comparing franchises and franchise investment opportunities around the world. Martin, S.B., *ed.* Detroit, Gale, 1991. 620p. $129.50. ISBN: 0810378051. ISSN: 1056456x.

Lists of 1600 franchising companies in 15 countries (c.1000 in US); lists of c.80 franchise consulting firms and c.40 franchising associations, are followed by the main entries for franchising firms, arranged A-Z by types of business (Accounting/tax services ... Weight control). Information for each includes name, address, telephone number, year franchise began, number of outlets, initial franchise fee, general description, background of franchising company, and franchise agreement information. Master name and keyword index, p.535-68. Geographical index. Personal name index, p.607-20. *Class No:* 652.887(058)

Great Britain

Yearbooks & Directories

[2685]

Retail directory of the UK 1997. Redman, C., *ed.* ISBN: 0707969816.
Previously published in 1990.

Aims to present all the significant companies involved in retailing in the UK and Ireland. It gives addresses, telephone numbers, names of buyers and managers. There is also useful information and plans of the important shopping areas in over 450 towns.
Class No: 652.887(410)(058)

USA

[2686]

FOSTER, D.L. The Encyclopedia of franchises and franchising. New York, Facts on File, 1989. 465p. $65. ISBN: 0816020817.

A-Z arrangement includes franchise histories, biographical sketches of business leaders, industry capsules (*eg* fast food), summaries of franchise regulations, and legal explanations and forms. Appendices include investment data, a ranking of 583 franchises by number of outlets, a list of franchises by type of business, and an index. A sequel to the author's *Rating guide to franchises* (1988).
Class No: 652.887(73)

Mail Order Selling

[2687]

The Royal Mail direct mail handbook. Andrews, L., *ed.* 2nd ed. Watford, Herts., Exley, 1988. 284p. illus. (incl. col.), ports., forms. £19.95. ISBN: 1850150729.

8 chapters. 1. The why and wherefore of mailing lists - 2. Direct mail production ... 7. Direct mail, the law, and advertising standards - 8. A guide to Royal Mail services. Bibliography, p.251-5. Glossary. Index. *Class No:* 652.887.2

Publicity

Advertising

[2688]

Advertiser's annual, 1994. East Grinstead, Reed Information Services Ltd. 1993. 3v. £162 the set; £99 each volume. ISBN: 0611008262. ISSN: 00653578.
First published 1915. (Business Pubns., Ltd.).

Data on over 2,500 advertising agencies, sales promotion consultants, sponsorship consultants, recruitment advertising agents, and public relations companies. V.1: Agencies and advertisers - v.2: Media (newspapers and periodicals; TV and radio; outdoor advertising) - v.3: Overseas media. Index to classified headings. Services and supplies. New sections in this ed.: advertising agencies; new agency contact companies. Nearly 3,500 major national advertisers are now listed. *Class No:* 652.91

Encyclopaedias & Dictionaries

[2689]

GRAHAM, I. Encyclopedia of advertising: an encyclopedia containing more than 1,100 entries relating to advertising, marketing, publishing, law, research, public relations, publicity and the graphic arts ... for everyday use by advertisers, agencies, advertising practitioners, businessmen and students. New York, Fairchild, 1969. xiii, 494p. illus. $132.60. ISBN: 0317581651.
First published 1952.

3 sections: 1. Advertising terminology, A-Z - 2. Terms grouped according to subject matter - 3. Directory of associations. No index. 'A useful source of information about graphic arts, commercial TV, copywriting and other aspects of advertising' (*Library journal*, 1 March 1970, p.864). *Class No:* 652.91(03)

[2690]

GRUBER, C.M. Wörterbuch der Werbung und des Marketing, Englisch-Deutsch, Deutsch-Englisch. [Dictionary of advertising and marketing.] Munich, Hueber, 1977. 312p., tables.

About 4,500 entry-words in each half. Arrangement is A-Z by keywords, with other terms arranged hierarchically under the keywords. Includes tables of paper sizes, etc., and lists of type sizes, etc. *Class No:* 652.91(03)

[2691]
JEFKINS, F. **Dictionary of advertising, direct response marketing and sales promotion.** London, Pitman, 1990. 236p. ISBN: 0273031368.

Contains c.1,500 definitions. Includes abbreviations, *e.g.* CAVIAR, EPOS. Cross references in upper case throughout text. Also includes entries for the more important advertising publications and legislation. *Class No:* 652.91(03)

[2692]
PAETZEL, H.W. **Complete multilingual dictionary of advertising, marketing and communications: English, French, German.** Lincolnwood, Ill., Passport Books, 1984. 606p. $39.95. ISBN: 0844291110.

First published 1972 (Essen, Stamm-Verlag, GmbH).

About 8,.000 terms; in three sequences, English, French and German, each with equivalents in the other two languages. *Class No:* 652.91(03)

[2693]
URDANG, L. **Dictionary of advertising terms.** Chicago, Ill., Tatham-Laird & Kudner, 1977. 209p. illus.

About 4,000 entries, with brief definitions, for terms and abbreviations in advertising and marketing. 'Especially valuable is the inclusion of special meanings of ordinary words, words unique in a single speciality and extensive cross-references for abbreviations, acronyms and synonyms' (*Library journal*, v.102(15), September 1977, p.1748). *Class No:* 652.91(03)

Yearbooks & Directories

[2694]
European advertising, marketing and media yearbook...a directory and source book. 2nd ed. London, Euromonitor, 1992 (distributed in US by Gale). Annual. xxxvi,771p. £195. $390. ISBN: 0863384129.

First published 1989.

Advertising profiles of 16 West European countries and limited data on 8 East European markets, including the former USSR and East Germany. Part 1 has historical and some forecasted data on demographic information, trends in gross domestic product and retail sales, consumer spending, advertising expenditures, and media by specific country. Part 2 is a directory, by country, of advertising agencies, top advertisers, publishers, broadcasters, and market research firms. Part 3 has brief overviews of advertising regulations in West European countries. No index, but detailed table of contents. *Class No:* 652.91(058)

[2695]
Graphis design: international annual of design and illustration. Zurich, Graphis Press Corp. illus., (incl. col.). SFr.123. $69.

Early title was *Graphis annual*. *Class No:* 652.91(058)

[2696]
Standard directory of international advertisers & agencies, 1993. Stokie, Ill., National Register Pubg. Co., 1964-. Annual.. 1560p. $325. ISBN: 0872171442. ISSN: 00814229.

International in scope, with data on c.17,000 companies (*e.g.* kind of media used; products; trademarks). *Class No:* 652.91(058)

[2697]
World advertising review. Kleinman, P., *ed.* London, Cassell; Holt, Rinehart & Winston, 1924-91. Annual. v.p. illus. (mostly col.). ISBN: 0304318205.

Previously as *Modern publicity*, first published as *Posters and their designers* (1924).

21 sections - (Alcoholic drinks - Automotive - Clothing and footwear ... Toiletries and cosmetics - Travel and tourism). List of credits. Index of agencies and studios. Index of advertisers. 425 well-captioned illus. International in scope. *Class No:* 652.91(058)

Great Britain

[2698]
NEVETT, T.R. **Advertising in Britain: a history.** London, Heinemann, on behalf of The History of Advertising Trust, 1982. xii, 213p. illus. (incl. ports.). facsims., ports., and tables. ISBN: 0434496421.

11 chapters (4. Advertising takes shape, 1800-1855; 6. Criticism and control in the nineteenth century; 8. The inter-war period. 3 appendices (A. Organisations whose represenatives constitute the Code of Advertising Committee; C. Table of legal cases). References (by chapters, p.215-7). Grouped bibliography, p.213-5. Non-analytical index. *Class No:* 652.91(410)

Media Advertising

[2699]
BRAD/British rate and data: media facts at your fingertips. London, Maclean Hunter, for British Rate and Data, 1954-. Monthly. £230. ISSN: 02633515.

The November 1991 issue has 4 main sections: Newspapers - Consumer and special interest publications - Business and professional publications, subjects, A-Z) - Other media (*e.g.* cinema advertising; radio stations; television data; video tape publications). Data include advertising rates per page, part of page, etc. Primarily for advertising, but also valuable for near-current facts on several thousand British newspapers and periodicals. Standard Rate and Data Service (Skorkie, Ill.) provides a more extensive US rate-and-advertising data, now in 13 sections, varying in frequency. The original *Standard rate and data service* ran between 1919 and 1950. *Class No:* 652.913/.916

[2700]
British television advertising: the first thirty years. Henry, B., *ed.* London, Century Benham, 1986. 527p. illus. (mostly col.), port., diagrs., graphs, tables, maps. ISBN: 0091658004.

14 contributors. The history (1955-), p.2-237; The television commercial; an essay, p.251-85; The agency viewpoint (3 contributors), p.419-53. Glossary of abbreviations, p.454-70. 12 appendices, A-M (Acts; Committees; Finance; M: 'Top twenty television advertising spenders by brand'). Detailed index, p.522-7. Well organized. *Class No:* 652.913/.916

Dictionaries

[2701]
DUVILLIER, F. *and* GRÜBER, U. **Dictionnaire bilingue de la publicité et de la communication.** London, Grant & Cutler, 1990. 464p. £49.25.

French and English, with terms defined in French. *Class No:* 652.913/.916(038)

Visual

Inn Signs

[2702]
LARWOOD, J., pseud. (*i.e* H.D.J. van Schevichaven) *and* HOTTEN, J.C. **English inn signs.** being a revised and modernized version of 'History of signboards', with a chapter on the modern inn sign, by G. Millar. Exeter, Blaketon Hall, 1985. xv, 336p. illus. ISBN: 0907854982.

Reprint of 1965 ed.

This edition is confined to inn signs, although earlier editions (1866-1907) included tradesmen's signs, - now covered partly by Heal, Sir A. *Signboards of old London shops* (1947). Larwood includes a brief bibliography, p.316. *Class No:* 652.9133

[2703]
LILLYWHITE, B. **London signs:** a reference book of London signs from earliest times to about the mid-nineteenth century. London, Allen & Unwin, 1972. xviii, 696p. illus. ISBN: 0049421018.

A-Z index to over 17,000 signs in the 19 manuscript volumes bequeathed by the compiler for use at the Guildhall Library. Data include location, approximate dates when in use and, often, notes on meaning or rarity of a sign. 'These must be of inestimable value to students of London topography, history and social life' (*TLS*, no.3678, 25 August 1972). *Class No:* 652.9133

Management Consultancy Services

[2704]
BRITISH CONSULTANTS BUREAU. **Directory,** 1993-94. London, the Bureau, 1993. 516p. £49.50. ISBN: 0950562130.

List of 275 BCB members in 8 sections, by type of activity: Engineers - Architects, planners - Management and economic consultants - Surveyors - Mining, minerals, geotechnical and geological consultants - Agricultural and fisheries consultants - Specialist categories - Nationalised industries' overseas group. Appendix: list (blue pages) of all members irrespective of their fields of activity. *Class No:* 652.92

[2705]
Consultants and consulting organizations directory a reference guide to more than 20,000 concerns and individuals engaged in consultation for business, industry and government. 14th ed. Detroit, Mich., Gale, 1993. 2v. (3026p.). $460. ISBN: 0810380455.

First published 1966.

Entries for 20,311 North American organizations and individuals, in more than 120 special fields. Geographical, subject and personnel indexes. *New consultants* provides interim supplements (2pa.) between editions. *Class No:* 652.92

[2706]

Directory of management consultants in the UK, 1993. Lambert, H., *comp. & ed.* 9th ed. London, TFPL Publishing, 1992. Annual. 497p. £75. ISBN: 1870889126.

First published 1983 (1983/84 ed.).

1500 management consulting firms, A-Z, with details of company activities. Index of specializations; Industry area index; Geographical index; Index of directors, partners, principals. *Class No:* 652.92

[2707]

European consultants directory, 1991. Koek, K.E., *ed.* Andover, Hants & Detroit, Mich., Gale Research International, 1992. 1038p. £150. $225. ISBN: 0810383136.

Companion volume to *Consultants and consulting organizations directory* covering the US and Canada.

Lists *c.*7500 consultancies operating in 34 European countries. Arranged in country order, subdivided by 15 headings (Agriculture, forestry and landscaping to the Environment and Politics). Details for each consultancy includes full contact information, date of formation of company, number of employees, names of senior consulting staff, annual turnover, indication of areas of specialization and geographical areas covered, branches, and variant names. Four indexes: Named consultants; Thesaurus of terms; Consulting activities; A-Z index of all consulting firms. *Class No:* 652.92

[2708]

European technical consultancies. Tomlinson, D.M., *ed.* Harlow, Essex, Longman Group, 1988. 352p. £75. ISBN: 0582031877.

Directory of more than 700 technical consultancies, in country order. Data (with effective use of symbols) on each consultancy include names of senior staff, roles and industrial categories. 4 indexes: company names, senior executives, consultancy services, industries served. *Class No:* 652.92

Public Relations

[2709]

BLACK, S. *and* SHARPE, M.L. Practical public relations: common-sense guidelines for business and professional people. 5th ed. London; Englewood Cliffs, Prentice-Hall, 1983. ix,214p. ISBN: 0136935311.

First published 1962.

4 parts (21 chapters): 1. Defining the subject: theory and practice - 2. Methods of public relations - 3. Public relations in action (including case histories) - 4. Educational, organisational, historical. Appendices: 1. Examinations in public relations; 2. Codes of professional conduct and ethics; 3. Public relations organizations. Bibliography, (p.223-4; 9 sections). Analytical index. *Class No:* 652.94

[2710]

Hollis UK press & public relations annual, 1993-94. 25th ed. Sunbury-on-Thames, Mddx., Hollis Directories Ltd., 1993. xciii,1010p. £65. ISBN: 0900967005. ISSN: 00733059.

First published 1967 as 'Contact'.

Arranged in 12 sections, each on a different tinted paper: 1. Media sources - 2. Media and corporate sources - 3. Reference and research - 4. Official and public information sources - 5. Consultancy specializations - 6. Public relations consultancies (UK and Ireland) - 7. Public relations: UK regional guide - 8. Public relations: overseas - 9. Sponsorship consultants - 10. Government relations and Parliamentary consultants - 11. Services - 12. Master index. Advertisers' index. *Class No:* 652.94

[2711]

Public relations consultancy...Public relations year book, 1992. Financial Times Business Information, for Public Relations Consultants Association, 1992. 311p. £40. ISBN: 1853340324.

Members of PRCA, A-Z with data on number of employees and range of services offered. Index of clients; index of directors and partners; index of holders of public office. Biographies of 650 PR partners and directors. *Class No:* 652.94

[2712]

Public relations handbook. 3rd ed. Englewood Cliffs, N.J., Prentice-Hall, 1983. 718p. illus.

First published 1950.

7 sections of chapters: 1. What public relations is and does - 2. What public relations includes - 3. How an organization utilizes public relations - 4. Analysis and preparation - 5. The techniques of communication - 6. The practice of public relations - 7. Emergency principles and trends. Bibliography. Glossary. Codes of ethics. List of associations. Index. *Class No:* 652.94

[2713]

WRAGG, D.W. The Public relations handbook. Oxford, Blackwell, 1992. xiii,354p. £55. ISBN: 0631184589.

51 chapters in 11 sections: 1: An introduction to public relations; 2. Media relations; 3. Financial and corporate relations; 4. Employee communications; 5. Political and community relations; 6. Sponsorship; 7. Events; 8. The application of public relations; 9. Developing public relations skills and activities; 10. Ancillary services; 11. Public relations today and tomorrow. Appendix: The IPR's code of professional conduct: PRCA professional charter. Index, p.352-4. *Class No:* 652.94

Dictionaries

[2714]

Glossary of public relations terms in seven languages (English-French-German-Spanish-Dutch-Finnish-Italian). Nally, M., *ed.* 2nd ed. Paris, CERP: European Public Relations Confederation, 1990. 83p. £23.50. *Class No:* 652.94(038)

34 Law

Law

Abbreviations & Symbols

[2715]
FONG, C. *and* EDWARDS, A.J. **Australian and New Zealand legal abbreviations.** 2nd ed. Sydney, Australian Law Librarians Group, New South Wales Branch, 1995. ISBN: 0959135987.

Aims to include abbreviations for Australian and New Zealand published law reports and journals and also for journals, from other countries regularly publishing articles of Australian and New Zealand interest. Cross-references. *Class No:* 340(003)

[2716]
SPRUDZS, A., *comp.* **Italian abbreviations and symbols:** law and related subjects. Dobbs Ferry, N.Y., Oceana, 1969. [iii],124p. $20. ISBN: 0379004518.

Aims to provide a simple key to the multitude of Italian abbreviations and symbols as they are found in contemporary Italian writings on law and related subjects. About 2600 abbreviations; no English translation of full Italian terms. 4 categories: (1) Legal, commercial and related terms; (2) Law reviews; (3) Names of Italian trade unions, political parties, etc.; (4) Italian names of European and international organizations concerned with law and related matters. Other volumes by A. Sprudzs: *Benelux abbreviations and symbols: law and related subjects* (1971. iii.129p. $20. ISBN 0379001209); *Foreign law abbreviations: French* (1967. ii.103p.). *Class No:* 340(003)

Databases

[2717]
NOBARI, N.S., *ed.* **Books and periodicals on line:** a guide to publication contents of business and legal data bases, V.1., Part 1-, 1987-. New York, Library Alliance Inc. 1987 -. Annual. $249. ISSN: 0951838x.

Aims to help researchers to use online time efficiently by providing them with a directory of over 6800 periodicals and serials which are available on such databases. In 4 sections: Alphabetical listing of periodicals and serials (name of publication; country of origin if not US, and journal code; name of publisher; name of database; name of producer; scope of editorial coverage, including starting date (and ending date if applicable); name of vendors) - Publishers' names and addresses - Producers' and vendors' names and addresses - Books and periodicals by database (A-Z by database, subdivided by A-Z list of titles). Available online and on CD-ROM. *Class No:* 340(003.4)

[2718]
RAPER, D., *ed.* **Law databases, 1988.** London, Aslib, 1988. [3],70p. £15. (*An Aslib online guide.*) ISBN: 0851422284.

First published 1983.

Details of 35 databases 'from the material supplied, in the main, by database producers' (*Introduction*). Information includes name, content, period of coverage, updating, producer, host, cost. There is a list of countries covered by the databases, and a list of host/producer addresses. A bibliography of 23 items completes the book. *Class No:* 340(003.4)

Bibliographies of Bibliographies

[2719]
FRIEND, W.L. **Anglo-American legal bibliographies:** an annotated guide. Washington, DC., Government Printing Office, 1944. (Reprinted by Rothman) ($15. 0837721288) and AMS Press ($15. 0404025994).

Lists nearly 300 legal bibliographies and bibliographical writings in books and journals. *Class No:* 340(009)

[2720]
LANSKY, R. **Bibliographische Handbuch der Rechts- und Verwaltungswissenschaften:** erläuteinde Bibliographie nationaler und internationaler Bibliographien/Bibliographical handbook on law and public administration: annotated bibliography of national and international bibliographies and other reference guides and information sources. Frankfurt am Main, Vittorio Klostermann, 1987-. To be in 3v. V.1: DM.156-.

V.1 was published in 1987; v.2 will be published 'in a few years'; v.3 will contain supplement and general index.

V.1: *General part and Europe* has 1269 annotated entries for

....(contd.)
bibliographies of bibliographies issued as books, bibliographical articles, library catalogues, and on-going listings in journals. Also includes basic reference aids such as encyclopedias and dictionaries, handbooks, biographical indexes, institutional directories, etc. Arranged by geographical region, subdivided A-Z by country, then by form or subject category. Entries are numbered, have full bibliographical description, concise annotation, and one location indication. Annotations are informative rather than critical. 'Not only a bibliography of bibliographies but a veritable vade mecum through the maze of legal reference materials in the areas of foreign, comparative and international law' (*International journal of legal information,* v.16(1), Spring 1988, p.24-27). *Class No:* 340(009)

Bibliographies

[2721]
ANDREWS, J.A. *and* HINES, W.D. **'Recent periodicals and source materials in law'.** In *British book news,* September 1988, p.644-647, 649.

Reviews the more significant serial publications that have appeared in the last 10 years. 45 titles listed in the bibliography. Written with the interest of overseas readers in mind. *Class No:* 340(01)

[2722]
Bibliographic guide to law. 1975- Annual. Library of Congress Staff. Boston, Mass., G.K. Hall (*Biblioguides*), 1991. 2v.(1053p) $340 ISBN: 0816170746.

Formerly *Law book guide.* First published 1975. Annual.

Lists all material catalogued during the year by the Library of Congress, covering all aspects of law, including that of the United States, international law, international organizations, criminology and forensic medicine. One A-Z sequence. *Class No:* 340(01)

[2723]
CAMBRIDGE UNIVERSITY. Squire Law Library. **The Squire Law Library: law catalogue.** Lekner, M.A., *comp.* Dobbs Ferry, N.Y. Oceana Publications, 1974. 15v.

V.1. Classification scheme - List of periodicals - Collections of legislation - Collections of law reports - Collections of treaties - United Kingdom: Parliamentary papers. V.2-7: Authors (c. 30,000 entries). V. 8-14: Subjects. V.15: Classification scheme: a list of subject headings for the Squire Law Library. *Class No:* 340(01)

[2724]
COLEMAN, K. **Legal reference work in non-law libraries:** a review of the literature. In *Special libraries,* v.71(1), January 1981, p.51-58.

Reviews library literature pertaining to the development and use of legal materials in non-law libraries in the US and Canada. Includes descriptions of model programmes and staff training workshops; recommendations for effective library service with law books; and bibliographical essays describing legal material appropriate for laymen. 22 citations. *Class No:* 340(01)

[2725]
COPE, C. *and* THOMAS, P.A. **How to use a law library** an introduction to legal skills. 3rd ed. London, Sweet & Maxwell, 1996. 292p. £13.50. ISBN: 0421460903.

First published 1979.

Includes sections on using a library; law reports; legislation; periodicals; government publications; European Union law. Author index. Detailed, analytical subject index. 'An essential reference book for new law students and new law library staff ... But it must be regarded as an elementary manual' (*The Law librarian,* v.10(3),. December 1979, p.56, of the 1st ed). *Class No:* 340(01)

[2726]
Current law index: multiple access to legal periodicals in print. Belmont, CA., Information Access Company, with the American Association of Law Libraries, 1980-.v.1-. Monthly. $395pa. ISSN: 01961780.

Covers *c.*700 law journals published in the US, Canada, UK, Ireland, Australia and New Zealand, and includes allied disciplines such as criminology and accounting. March, June and September issues are quarterly cumulations and the December issue is the annual 2-volume cumulation. Part A: Subject index, has bibliographical details, brief descriptions, and cross-references. Part B: Author/title index, table of contents, table of statutes. Also available online (BRS, DIALOG, etc.). *Class No:* 340(01)

[2727]

Index to legal books, 1989. New York, Bowker, 1989. Annual. 6v. $600 the set. ISBN: 0835226522.

Arranged in major legal subject categories, cites entries for leading law books, national in scope and importance. Cross-references.
Class No: 340(01)

[2728]

Index to legal periodicals, 1908-. New York, H.W. Wilson Company, in co-operation with the American Association of Law Libraries, 1909-. Monthly (except September), cumulating quarterly, annually and 3-yearly. $180pa. ISSN: 00194077.

Subject and author index to more than 400 legal periodicals from common-law countries (US and Commonwealth). Separate indexing of legal cases commented on (under plaintiff's name A-Z) and of book reviews. Pronounced US slant. Also available online, WESTLAW, Wilsonline and CD-ROM. *Class No:* 340(01)

[2729]

—**Index to foreign legal periodicals.** London, Institute of Advanced Legal Studies, in co-operation with the American Association of Law Libraries, 1960-,v.1,no.1-. Quarterly, cumulating annually & 3-yearly. $450pa. ISSN: 0019400x.

Complementary to *Index to legal periodicals,* in that it covers public and private international law, comparative law and municipal law of countries other than the US and Commonwealth. Covers *c.*300 leading legal periodicals. Comprises subject, geographical, book-review and author indexes. *Class No:* 340(01)

[2730]

Index to legal periodicals: thesaurus. New York, H.W. Wilson Company, 1988. 80p. $65. ISBN: 0824207629.

A ready-reference guide to the subject terms used in *Index to legal periodicals.* Includes broad, narrow and related terms in one list. *Class No:* 340(01)

[2731]

Index to periodical articles related to law: selected from journals not included in the 'Index to legal periodicals'. Dobbs Ferry, N.Y., Glanville Publications Inc., 1958-. Quarterly. $45pa. ISSN: 00194093.

A subject index to substantial articles published throughout the world that in the opinion of the editors are of research value, and are not in *Current law index, Index of foreign legal periodicals, Index to legal periodicals, Legal resource index,* or *Legaltrac.* The final issue each year is cumulative, and a 30-year index (1958-1988. v.1-30) has been published (4v. $450. ISBN 0878020632) which replaces the 10 and 5-year indexes. *Class No:* 340(01)

[2732]

Law books and serials in print: a multimedia sourcebook. New York, Bowker, 1992. 3v.(2345p.). $575.

Attempts to list all legal titles available within the US and, to a lesser extent, those published internationally. Over 53,000 publications listed, emphasis being on English-language publications. Indexed in 3 ways (v.1. by subject (Library of Congress subject headings); v.2. Author and title indexes; v.3. Separate subject and title indexes for serials, non-print media, microforms. List of publishers, distributors and producers. *Class No:* 340(01)

[2733]

Law books in review: a quarterly journal of reviews of current publications in law and related fields. Dobbs Ferry, NY., Glanville, 1974-. Quarterly. $55pa. ISSN: 08860408.

*c.*150 reviews pa. Arranged by subject, A-Z, and including sections on Legal law; Legal reference; International law; Reviews in brief. Author/title index and addresses of publishers. *Class No:* 340(01)

[2734]

Legal contents: the bi-weekly compilation of tables of contents from law: reviews, journals and symposia. New York, Find/SVP, 1972-. Monthly. ISSN: 02795787.

Previously as *Contents of current legal periodicals,* incorporating *Survey of law reviews.* and *CCLP: Contents of current legal periodicals.* Also available online.

Covers more than 320 business magazines and journals. *Class No:* 340(01)

[2735]

Legaltrac, 1980-. Foster City, CA., Information Access Company, with American Association of Law Libraries, 1980-. Monthly. $3500pa.

Issued on microfilm, and also available online.

Early title was *Legal resource index.*

Comprehensive guide to law journals, legal newspapers and articles selected from the general press. US-slanted. *Class No:* 340(01)

[2736]

LONDON UNIVERSITY. Institute of Advanced Legal Studies. **Catalogue of the Library** of the Institute of Advanced Legal Studies. Boston, Mass., G.K. Hall, 1978. 6v. (5085p.). $595. (*Hall library.*) ISBN: 0816100993.

106,700 photolithographed catalogue cards. The Library has extensive collections of public international law, English and Commonwealth law (including South African) and law of the European Communities, Western European countries and North America. 130,000v. of serials and monographs. *Class No:* 340(01)

[2737]

NEMES, I. *and* **COSS, G.** **Effective legal research.** Sydney, Butterworths, 1998. xi,379p. ISBN: 0409311588. *Class No:* 340(01)

[2738]

RAISTRICK, D. **Lawyers' law books:** a practical index to legal literature. 3rd ed. London, Butterworths, 1994. 732p. £28. (*Professional Books law reference library, vol.1.*) ISBN: 1857390873. First published 1977.

Contains a list of subject headings and cross-references. About 8,000 unannotated entries (author, title, edition and date, but not publisher). Lengthier topics have sub-headings. Regnal years of English sovereigns; Law reports of the United Kingdom and Ireland; and an author and short-title index. 'It is an extremely useful reference work that should fill a widely felt need' (Review of 1st ed. in *International journal of law libraries,* v.6(1), 1978, p.113). *Class No:* 340(01)

[2739]

SMITH, N. **Legal research techniques.** Hebden Bridge, Yorks., Legal Information Resources Ltd., 1987. ii,40p. £4.50. ISBN: 1870369017.

Includes sections on Preliminary search; Finding textbooks and articles on a subject; Finding cases; Finding Statutes; Finding Statutory Instruments; Words and phrases; EEC law. Appendix: Law report series. A must for public libraries and the lay person. *Class No:* 340(01)

[2740]

SZLADITS, C., *comp.* **A Bibliography of foreign and comparative law:** books and articles in English, 1953-1980. Dobbs Ferry, N.Y., Oceana, for the Parker School of Foreign and Comparative Law, Columbia University, 1955-82. 5v.+7 supplements. Supplements; $32.50-$35 each.

Chiefly concerned with foreign (*i.e.,* other than that of the common-law jurisdictions) and private international law. Each volume has *c.*13,000 entries. *Class No:* 340(01)

[2741]

TREVIÑO, A.J. **The Sociology of law:** a bibliography of theoretical literature. 2nd ed. E. Mellen, 1998. 188p. $79.95. ISBN: 0773483187.

"This bibliography should be of immense value to scholars, and to students who want to quickly locate major writings on major topics in the field." - *Choice* March 1999, p.1248. *Class No:* 340(01)

[2742]

WINTERTON, J. *and* **MOYS, E.M.,** *eds.* **Information sources in law.** 2nd ed. London, Bowker-Saur, 1997. xxii, 673p. £69. (*Guides to information sources.*) ISBN: 1857390415.

A bibliographical survey of the whole range of general and specialist literature which is available to those engaged in legal study and research. *Class No:* 340(01)

Encyclopaedias

[2743]

WALKER, D.M. **The Oxford companion to law.** Oxford, Clarendon Press, 1980. ix,[1],1366p. £25. ISBN: 019866110x.

Concise information 'about some of the principal legal institutions, courts, judges and jurists, systems of law, branches of law, legal ideas and concepts, important doctrines and principles of law, and other legal matters ...' (*Preface*). Coverage extends to English-speaking and Western European countries. 'South African law' (sectionalised): p.1159-62; 9 references. Brief biographies (*e.g.* Montesquieu: ½ column; 1 reference). Appendix 1: 'List of the holders of various offices since 1660' (UK, p.1316-62); 2: 'Bibliographical notes' (p.1363-66—: 1. Bibliographies - 2. Indexes to periodical literature - 3. Legal biography and profession - 4. Legal history - 5. Jurisprudence - 6. Comparative legal studies - 7. International law and institutions - 8. European Communities law - 9. Commonwealth law - 10. Particular countries (Australia ... USA). Not a concise legal encyclopaedia of the law of any country; 'still less ... a layman's Home Lawyer' (*Preface*). Note occasional double entries, *e.g.* both 'Tender, legal' and 'Legal tender' - by different contributors. *Class No:* 340(031)

Handbooks & Manuals

[2744]
MOYS, E.M., *ed*. **Manual of law librarianship:** the use and organization of legal literature. 2nd ed. Aldershot, Gower, in association with the British and Irish Association of Law Librarians, 1987. xxxv,915p. £47.50. ISBN: 056603512x.

First published 1976.

20 contributors and 3 consultants. 4 parts (18 chapters): 1. Introduction (2 chapters: Law libraries and their users; Legal systems and legal literature) - 2. Legal literature of the British Isles and other common law systems (Primary sources: legislation; Primary sources: law reports; Secondary sources: Government publications; Historical sources; Commonwealth and the US; Reference sources: common law systems) - 3. Legal literature of other legal systems - 4. Law library practice. Bibliographies for further reading are appended to each chapter. Glossary. Extensive index of works cited, p.801-891 (*c*.5000 entries); substantial subject index, p.892-915. Main coverage is still the British Isles, but now includes chapters on the European Community and the Commonwealth. A standard guide to the intricacies of legal literature. '... the only comprehensive general treatise in this area of librarianship ...' (*Library Association record*, January 1988, p.49). '... most highly recommended to anyone who wishes to know about law librarianship' (*The law librarian*, v.18(3), December 1987, p.105). *Class No:* 340(035)

Dictionaries

[2745]
MARTIN, E.A., *ed*. **A Dictionary of law.** 4th ed. Oxford, Oxford University Press, 1997. 522p. £8.99. (*Oxford reference.*) ISBN: 0192800663.

Intended not for lawyers, but for those who need some legal knowledge in their work. *c*.1700 terms, concepts, processes and organizations of the law are defined and explained, a typical entry containing a succinct definition followed by further explanation. Includes foreign terms (italicised). 'Based on the expertise of a team of academic and practising British lawyers, this work amasses an array of substantive articles ...' (*Choice*, v.22(2), October 1984, p.246), of the first edition. *Class No:* 340(038)

[2746]
STROUD, F. **Stroud's judicial dictionary of words and phrases.** James, J.S., *ed*. 5th ed. London, Sweet & Maxwell, 1986. 6v. £380 (1993 supplement: £28.50). ISBN: 0421366303; 0421371307, supplement.

First published 1890; 4th ed. 1971-75, with supplements.

A dictionary of words and phrases that have been interpreted by the judges, giving their interpretations. Statutory definitions not judicially interpreted are referred to. Cross-references. V.1: A-C; v.2: D-H; v.3: I-O; v.4: P-R; v.5: S-Z; v.6: Tables of cases and statutes. The first supplement is now issued annually. Rearrangement of the articles has improved access to the contents. 'This dictionary enjoys a well-merited reputation and the frequently heard question 'have you checked Stroud?' is a tiny indication of this. It has the authority of reliability and comprehensiveness achieved over nearly one hundred years and through five editions ...' (*Law librarian*, v.18(2), August 1987, p.68-69). *Class No:* 340(038)

Polyglot

[2747]
BUTLER, W.E. *and* NATHANSON, A.T., *eds*. **Mongolian-English-Russian dictionary of legal terms and concepts.** The Hague, Nijhoff, 1982. 745p. £103.50. ISBN: 9024726778.

Terminology also touches upon most branches of the social sciences, military affairs, medicine and some areas of the natural sciences. *Class No:* 340(038)=00

[2748]
DOUCET, M. **Dictionnaire juridique et économique. Wörterbuch der Rechts ...** Fleck, K.W., *ed*. 4 éd. rev. et remaniée. München, C.H. Beck'she Verlagsbuchhandlung, 1988. 2v. (xix,634p.; xvi, 656p.). ISBN: 3406314104, v.1; 3406098614, v.2.

2nd ed. published 1967-80.

French-German and German-French dictionaries of law and economics. *Class No:* 340(038)=00

[2749]
EGBERT, L.D. *and* MORALES-MACEDO, L. **Multilingual law dictionary,** English-français-español-Deutsch. Alphen aan den Rÿn, Sÿthoff; Dobbs Ferry, N.Y. Oceana, 1978. xxii,551p. £34.95.

6300 English-base terms, with French, Spanish and German equivalents and indexes. Where equivalents are lacking in the other languages (*e.g.* for 'Writ of scire facias'), explanations may be given. 4 appendices (1. Select list of definitions; 2. Law dictionaries, p.511-4; 3. Select references to law litérature, p.515-6. Aimed at practising lawyers, legal scholars and language specialists. 'Certainly achieves a great deal' (*International journal of law libraries*, v.6(3), November 1978, p.312). *Class No:* 340(038)=00

[2750]
EUROPEAN PARLIAMENT. **Legal terminology of the European Communities.** Luxembourg, Office for Official Publications of the European Community, 1976. 2v. (873 p.). £6.

Terms in French-Italian-English-German-Dutch-Danish, arranged under 632 classified French keywords, followed by equivalents in the other languages. V.2. is the index. *Class No:* 340(038)=00

[2751]
GARCÍA, I.R. **Diccionario de términos juridicos.** 2nd ed. rev. London, Butterworths, 1985. xi,704p. £39.50. (*Butterworths legal publications*.) ISBN: 0880635002.

English-Spanish; Latin-Spanish; French-Spanish. Terms are explained in Spanish, and there is a 237-page section of words and phrases defined by the Supreme Tribunal of Puerto Rico. *Class No:* 340(038)=00

[2752]
LE DOCTE, E. **Dictionnaire de termes juridiques en quatre langues ... Legal dictionary in four languages.** 2e (bewerkte en vermeerderde) druk. Brussels, Bruylant, 1995. 854p. ISBN 9062150500.

First published 1978.

c.12,000 words & phrases: French-base, with Spanish, English and German equivalents across a double-page. Very brief definitions, but includes alternative terms. Indexes in Spanish, English and German refer to page numbers. *Class No:* 340(038)=00

English

[2753]
COLLIN, P.H. **Dictionary of law.** Teddington, Mddx., Peter Collin Publishers, 1993. 400p. £9.95. ISBN: 1901659437.

Originally published in 1986 as *English law dictionary*.

Some 6000 words and phrases, the basic vocabulary in British and American law, are explained, using a limited vocabulary of 500 words. Examples are given as necessary. Cross-references. *Class No:* 340(038)=20

[2754]
GARNER, B.A. **A Dictionary of modern legal usage.** Oxford, Oxford University Press, 1991. xxvi,953p. £42.50. ISBN: 0195077695.

A dictionary of American and British usage. Classification guide, pronunciation guide, and list of abbreviations precede the dictionary. Entries vary in length from one line to over a column ('Metaphors': 4 columns), point out distinctions among variant forms and include brief essays on special topics. Cross-references. Select bibliography. 'Its strengths are depth in explanations, careful distinctions, and engaging style' (*Library journal*, on 1st ed., 15 September 1987, p.74). *Class No:* 340(038)=20

[2755]
SAUNDERS, J.B., *ed*. **Words and phrases legally defined.** 3rd ed. Butterworth and Co., (Publishers) Ltd., 1988-89. 4v. £220 the set. ISBN: 0406080402, Set; 0406080410, v.1; 0406080429, v.2; 0406080437, v.3; 0406080445, v.4.

First published about 1950.

An A-Z listing over the four volumes (e.g., v.1: A-C) aiming at accurate definitions of legal terms. Scope of the 3rd ed. broadened by the addition of selections of statutory definitions and extracts from textbooks (*e.g. Halsbury's laws of England*). Cross-references. Indications given when a term relates to a particular country such as Canada or Australia. A useful companion to *Halsbury's laws* .... *Class No:* 340(038)=20

[2756]
—BURTON, W.C., *ed*. **Burton's legal thesaurus.** 2nd ed. New York, Macmillan, 1998. 1120p. £75.95. ISBN: 0028649869.

First published 1982. *Class No:* 340(038)=20

[2757]
—CURZON, L.B. **A Dictionary of law.** 4th ed. London, Pitman Publishing, 1993. 480p. £13.99. ISBN: 0273601016.

First published 1979; 1st and 2nd eds. published by Macdonald & Evans.

A classic concise dictionary, compiled primarily for students, both in the UK and overseas, as a guide to the specialised vocabulary of the principles, practices and procedures of English law. Full references are given to cases and Statutes. *Class No:* 340(038)=20

[2758]
—Mozley & Whiteley's law dictionary. Ivamy, E.R.H., *ed*. 11th ed. London, Butterworth & Co., (Publishers) Ltd., 1993. vii,511p. £8.95. ISBN: 0406014205.

First published 1876.

A concise legal dictionary with over 3000 entries and cross-references. Its purpose is to give an exposition of legal terms and phrases of past and present use. 10th ed. adds definitions of terms used in the commercial and business world. *Class No:* 340(038)

[2759]

—OSBORN, P.G. *and* RUTHERFORD, L. *and* BONE, S. Osborne's concise law dictionary. 8th ed. London, Sweet & Maxwell, 1993. vii,392p. £8.95. ISBN: 0421389001.

Considered one of the best concise law dictionaries. Includes definitions of legal words and phrases, Roman law terms and maxims, and a list of law reports together with their abbreviations. *Class No:* 340(038)=20

German

[2760]

BESELER, D. von *and* JACOBS-WÜSTEFELD, B. Englisch-deutsches und deutsch-englisches Wörterbuch der Rechts und Geschäftssprache. Law dictionary: technical dictionary of the Anglo-American legal terminology, including commercial and statistical terms. 4th rev. ed.0 Berlin, de Gruyter, 1986-91. 2v. (xxii,1932p.). Eng.-Ger. 4th rev. ed. 1986. £176.95. Ger.-Eng. 4th ed., 1991. £264.95.

A technical dictionary of the Anglo-American legal terminology, including commercial and statistical terms. *Class No:* 340(038)=30

Scandinavian

[2761]

ANDERSON, R.J.B. Anglo-Scandinavian law dictionary of legal terms used in professional and commercial practice. Oslo, Universitetsforlaget, 1977. 137p. £12.95. ISBN: 8200023656.

Prepared under the auspices of the Royal Norwegian Ministry of Justice.

English base-term definitions, with equivalents in Swedish, Norwegian and Danish, followed by Norwegian - English - Swedish - Danish; Swedish - Norwegian - Danish - English; and Danish - English - Norwegian - Swedish sequences. *Class No:* 340(038)=395

French

[2762]

BAKER, J.H. Manual of law French. 2nd ed. Aldershot, Hants., Scolar Press, 1989. ix,219p. £52. ISBN: 0859677451.

Claims to be the first law French glossary to be produced since 1779, and is intended for students and practitioners concerned with English legal history. An introduction to law French (history, study, grammar, common abbreviations and contractions) is followed by a 'Bibliography of aids to interpretation' (1. Law French and Anglo-Norman glossaries - 2. Dictionaries of old French and French etymologies - 3. English dictionaries - 4. Latin dictionaries - 5. Translations and parallel texts - 6. Guides to grammar and morphology). Glossary, A-Z French and English translations. Index of persons. *Class No:* 340(038)=40

[2763]

QUEMNER, Th.A. Dictionnaire juridique, nouveau dictionnaire ... français/anglais, English/French: administration, assurances, bourse, commerce, douanes, droit ... Baleyte, J., ed. 6.ré éd. Paris, Editions de Navarre, 1977. 311, 415p. £30.20.

First published 1953-55.

Wide-ranging, covering legal, financial, commercial, fiscal and allied terms. Appendix of Latin and English/French legal terms. Pays particular attention to differences between Anglo-American concepts and those prevailing in France. *Class No:* 340(038)=40

Italian

[2764]

FRANCHIS, F. de. Dizionario giuridico. Law dictionary. Milano, Giuffrè Editore, 1984-1996. 2v. (xi, 1545p.; 1467p.) ISBN: 8814003165, v.1; 8814050015, v.2.

V.1 has over 10,000 entries of English/American law terms, with descriptions in Italian, covering constitutional law, administrative law, civil and criminal procedures, commercial law and the newest contractual techniques, international law, etc. Descriptions are often small essays (*e.g.* 'Bankruptcy': 10 cols; 'Company': 15 cols.). Bibliographies are attached to many entries. V.2 Italian-English dictionary. *Class No:* 340(038)=50

Spanish

[2765]

ROBB, L.A., *and others*. Diccionario de términos legales. Spanish-English and English-Spanish dictionary of legal terms. New York, Wiley, 1955. xii,228p. £34.85.

Includes terms used in Latin American countries (indicating name of country), and economic terminology. Well set out. Very favourably reviewed in *The Incorporated linguist*. v.18(1), Winter 1979, p.27). *Class No:* 340(038)=60

Latin

[2766]

Latin for lawyers. 3rd ed. London. Sweet & Maxwell, 1960. viii,287p. First published 1915.

Includes vocabulary of over 1000 Latin maxims, etc., with English translation. *Class No:* 340(038)=71

Russian

[2767]

PRISCHEPENKO, N.P. Russian-English law dictionary. New York University School of Law, ed. New York, Praeger, 1969. vii,146p. 9700 entries for Russian technical legal terms. Russian-English only. *Class No:* 340(038)=82

Polish

[2768]

POLISH ACADEMY OF SCIENCES. Institute of State and Law. Polish/English dictionary of legal terms. Warsaw, Ossolineum, 1986. [6],211p. £11.95. ISBN: 8304018977.

The first of four versions planned of the *Foreign-language dictionary of legal terms*. The others will be Polish/Russian, Polish/German, and Polish/French.

A-Z listing of *c.*11,000 headwords in Polish with English translations or equivalents. English-Polish index. *Class No:* 340(038)=84

[2769]

RYDLEWSKA-SZEWCZYKOWA, D. *and* ZACZKIEWICZOWA, J. Slownik prawniczy polsko-angielski/Polish-English dictionary of legal terms. Wroclaw, Zaklad Narodowy im Ossolinskich, 1986. 211p.

Published under the auspices of the Polish Academy of Sciences Institute of State and Law. The first of a series of foreign language dictionaries of legal terms planned to be published in Poland.

*c.*11,000 main entries arranged A-Z by the Polish term, with English equivalents. Supplemented by an index of the main English/Polish noun headwords. *Class No:* 340(038)=84

Welsh

[2770]

LEWIS, R. Termau cyfraith/Welsh terms ... gyda rhagair gan Arglwydd Morris o Borth-Y-Gest. Llandysul, Gwasg Gower, 1972. xxxiii,226p. ISBN: 0850881404.

Parallel Welsh and English text. Bibliography, p.219-216. *Class No:* 340(038)=916.6

Arabic

[2771]

FARUQI, H.S. Faruqi's law dictionary, English-Arabic: meanings and definitions of terms of English and American jurisprudence (ancient and modern). 3rd rev. ed. Beirut, Librairie du Liban, 1980. 758,[10]p.

Wide-ranging coverage, including terms in forensic medicine, commerce, banking, insurance, civil aviation, diplomacy and petroluem. *Class No:* 340(038)=927

[2772]

—FARUQI, H.S. Faruqi's law dictionary, Arabic-English: containing terms of jurisprudence (ancient and modern), forensic medicine, commerce, banking, insurance, civil aviation, diplomacy and petroleum. 3rd rev. ed. Beirut, Librairie du Liban, 1997.

Listed by the Arabic terms, with English equivalents. *Class No:* 340(038)=927

Reviews & Abstracts

[2773]

Legal reference services quarterly. New York, Hawarth Press Inc., 1981-. v.1(1)- $105pa. ISSN: 0270319x.

As well as articles, it contains book reviews and an annotated bibliography on a specific subject in each issue. *Class No:* 340(048)

Periodicals & Progress Reports

[2774]

International journal of legal information: the official journal of the International Association of Law Librarians. 1973-. 3pa. Washington, DC., The Institute for International Legal Information. $80pa. ISSN: 07311265.

Early title was *International journal of law libraries*, published by the International Association of Law Libraries.

Includes articles on legal perspectives and law librarianship, bibliographies, notes and comments, periodical reviews, international documentation, book reviews, books received and noted. *Class No:* 340(05)

[2775]

The Law librarian: journal of the British and Irish Association of Law Librarians. London, Sweet & Maxwell, for the Association, 1970-. 4pa. £35pa. ISSN: 00239275.

Early sub-title was *bulletin*....

V.24(1), March 1993 (52p.) is devoted to the use of information technology in law libraries; 15 case studies by law librariansry'); a 'Current awareness' section (Bibliographical guides ... Dictionaries ... Legal research and method...Periodicals (new)...Statistics. Lengthy signed book reviews, p.44-52. *Class No:* 340(05)

Periodicals

[2776]

WYPYSKI, E.M. **Legal periodicals in English.** Dobbs Ferry, N.Y., Glanville Press, 1976. 5 binders. $525 the set. ISBN: 0878020543.

Succeeds L.W. Marse's *Checklist of Anglo-American legal periodicals* (1962).

A page is allocated to each title, with data on frequency, previous title(s) (if any), subject, and where indexed, reprinted, microfilmed or cited. Cumulative indexes. *Class No:* 340(051)

[2777]

—MERSKY, R.M., *and others, eds.* Author's guide to journals in law, criminal justice and criminology. New York, Haworth Press, 1979. 243p. $32.95. ISBN: 0917724062.

Includes 'only those journals that accept manuscripts from outside sources' (*American book review annual*, 1980, item 519). 4 sections, covering general and specialized law-school reviews, association publications and commercial journals. *Class No:* 340(051)(01)

Bibliographies

[2778]

Legal journals index. Hebden Bridge, Legal Information Resources, 1986-. Monthly, with quarterly and annual cumulations. Annual issue is bound vol. £560pa. ISSN: 09504206.

Indexes over 155 British legal journals, including all items, case reports, comments and legislation, nearly 4000 items in each issue. A list of journals indexed precedes the subject index, with items arranged A-Z by subject, full citations and cross-references. This is followed by an author index, case index, legislation index, and book review index. *Class No:* 340(051)(01)

Quotations

[2779]

JAMES, S. *and* STEBBINGS, C., *comps. & eds.* **A Dictionary of legal quotations.** London, Croom Helm, 1987. xiv,209p. £12.95. ISBN: 0709913032.

Arranged A-Z by 160 subject terms (Accomplice ... Witnesses). Quotations under each subject are numbered and give source of quotation. 'Comprehensibility' has 16 quotations; 'Law' has 210, and 'see' references to Civil law, Common law, International law, Jurisprudence and Legislation. Index of authors and sources, p.178-184. Index of key words, p.185-209. *Class No:* 340(082.2)

[2780]

Oxford dictionary of American legal quotations. Shapero, F.R., *ed.* New York, Oxford University Press, 1993. xv,582p. $49.95. £35. ISBN: 0195058593.

3500 quotations, arranged by broad topic. Appendix: The Constitution. Author and rotated keyword indexes. 'Essential for law libraries that want a traditional and timely resource (*Choice*, v.31(2), October 93, p.273). *Class No:* 340(082.2)

Festschriften

Bibliographies

[2781]

DAU, H., *comp.* **Bibliographie juristischer Festschriften und Festschriftenbeträge:** Deutschland, Schweiz, Österreich/Bibliography of legal Festschriften: titles and contents, Germany, Switzerland, Austria. Berlin, Berlin Verlag Arno Spitz, 1962-87. 6v. V.5: DM.150-.

Now covers 120 years: Band O: *1864-1944* (1984); 1: *1945-1961* (1962); 2: *1962-1966* (1967); 3. *1967-1974* (1977); 4. *1975-1979* (1981); 5. *1980-1984* (c.1987). V.5 is in 4 main sections: A. Bibliography of Festschriften, arranged under 44 subject headings in A-Z order; B. Analytical bibliography of Festschriften; C. Indexes (author, name, geographical, subject); D. Supplement of Festschriften published in 1985/86. The very detailed subject index (p.526-617) is in German, but there is a useful listing of major subject areas in English, with German equivalents. *Class No:* 340(082.20)(01)

Histories

Bibliographies

[2782]

GILISSEN, J., *ed.* **Introduction bibliographique à l'histoire du dro**ﬞ **et à l'ethnologie juridique/Bibliographical introduction to leg**ﬞ **history and ethnology.** Bruxelles, Éditions de l'Institut de Sociologi￼ 1965-1988. 9v. (Loose-leaf binders). (*Études d'histoire et d'ethnolog*￼ *juridiques.*)

Some chapters not published. The majority of the sections are ﬞ English or French. *Class No:* 340(091)(01)

Developing Countries

Bibliographies

[2783

LANSKY, R. **Handbuch der Bibliographien zum Recht de** **Entwicklungsländer/Handbook of bibliographies on the laws** ﬞ **developing countries.** Hamburg, Übersee - Dokumentation i￼ Verband der Stiftung Deutsches Übersee - Institut, 1981. xxxiii, 633ﬞ ISBN: 3465014464.

Preliminary edition published 1977.

Annotated entries for 1494 bibliographies and reference tools ﬞ various languages. Arranged in geographical order (A. Multipﬞ regions - B. Middle East (Islamic legal systems) in general - C. Afri￼ - D. Asia - E. Oceana - F. Latin America). Items starred with oﬞ asterisk - important, items with two - very important. Titles in origiﬞ languages, descriptions in German. Summary, p.515-532; Indeﬞ p.533-615, in English & German in one sequence; Supplement, p.61￼ 633. *Class No:* 340(4/9-77)(01)

Europe

Yearbooks & Directories

[2784

Yearbook of European law, 1981-. Oxford, Clarendon Press, 1982-.

V.11, 1991/92, (1992. xvii,682p. £90. ISBN 0198257791) contaiﬞ 14 essays (*e.g.* 'The future of the Court of Justice of the Europeaﬞ Communities'; 'The Europe of universities') and 6 annual surveﬞ (Legal developments in the European Parliament - Competition law European political co-operation, 1989-91 - The Brussels Convention Council of Europe legal co-operation in 1991 - The Europeaﬞ Convention on Human Rights). 18 book reviews - Books received Table of cases - Commission decisions on competitions. Index. *Class No:* 340(4)(058)

Middle Ages

[2785

ULLMANN, W. **Law and politics in the Middle Ages:** an introductioﬞ to the sources of medieval political ideas. Cambridge, Cambridgﬞ University Press (first published by The Sources of History Ltd). 197￼ 320p. £17. (*Sources of history series.*) ISBN: 0521214599.

8 chapters: 2. The Roman law - 3. The scholarship of Roman law 4. Canon law - 5. The scholarship of Canon law - 6. Non-Romﬞ secular law - 7. Governmental doctrines in literary sources - 8. Thﬞ new science of politics. Footnotes. Select bibliography. p.307-10 (bﬞ chapters). Non-analytical index. 'One of the first attempts to preseﬞ the principal sources of medieval political ideas in an integrated anﬞ coherent manner' (*Preface*). *Class No:* 340(4)"01/14"

Europe—Western

Bibliographies

[2786

GRAULICH, D. *and* GRAULICH, C. **Guide to foreign leg**ﬞ **materials: Belgium, Luxembourg, Netherlands.** Dobbs Ferry, N.Yﬞ Oceana, 1968, for the Parker School of Foreign and Comparativﬞ Law, Columbia University. 258p. $17.50. (*Parker School studies* ﬞ *foreign and comparative law, v.3.*) ISBN: 0379117533. *Class No:* 340(400)(01)

[2787

SZLADITS, C. **Guide to foreign legal materials, French, Germa**ﬞ **Swiss.** New York, Oceana Publications, for Parker School of Foreiﬞ and Comparative Law, Columbia University, 1959. xv,599p. $30.00.

A 2nd ed. is being compiled in several parts. See 340(44)(01) for thﬞ guide to French materials, and 340(43)(01) for German materials.

French law, p.3-116; German law, p.118-330; Swiss law, p.33ﬞ 507. In the case of Swiss law, subdivision is: pt.1, Sources of laﬞ pt.2, Repositories of the law (bibliographies; legislative materials anﬞ commentaries; case law; encyclopedias and dictionaries; doctrinﬞ writings; list of legal abbreviations). Many footnote references. Indﬞ

..(contd.)

of authors and titles; index to subjects. A guide for the common-law lawyer to the use of foreign legal materials - laws, reports, books. *Class No:* 340(400)(01)

Great Britain

[2788]

Current law London, Sweet & Maxwell and Stevens, 1946-. Monthly. £190pa (with yearbook and citators: £265pa; with Statutes, yearbook and citators: £335pa). ISSN: 0011362x.

Cumulated annually. The yearbook is an annual consolidation of the monthly citation indexes to all developments since 1947, covering case law, Statute law, and Statutory instruments.

A survey by subject, believed to be complete, of all legal developments, legislation, decisions and literature. Full references to law reports, periodicals, etc., are given, and full indexes are provided, including case and Statute citators (*i.e.,* tables of earlier cases and Statutes affected by current development, legislative, judicial or literary). The making of orders, etc., under powers conferred by a Statute is shown in the citator. *Current law statutes annotated* (1948-. Annual) contains the Statutes and Church Assembly Measures passed during the calendar year. *Class No:* 340(410)

[2789]

GREAT BRITAIN. Statutory Instruments. 1890-. London, HMSO, 1890-.

Initially (and until 1947) as *Statutory Rules and Orders* ('S.R. & O.'). Cumulation, to December 31, 1948 (HMSO, 1949-52. 25v.), as *S.R. & O. and S.I. revised*.

Statutory Instruments ('S.I.'),. each issued separately and cumulated annually (less local S.I.s and revocations), consist of subordinate legislation, - Orders in Council and Orders, rules, regulations, etc. made by Ministers and others. A biennial subject index is provided in *Index to Governmental Orders in force* ... The annual *Table of Government Orders* is in numerical order. *Class No:* 340(410)

[2790]

GREAT BRITAIN. Statutory Publications Office. The Public General Acts and General Synod Measures. London, HMSO, [1831]-. Annual (formerly sessional).

Early title was *The Public General Acts and Church Assembly Measures. Class No:* 340(410)

[2791]

Halsbury's Statutes of England and Wales. 4th ed. London, Butterworths, 1985-92. 50v. ISBN: 0406214093.

First published 1930. Companion to *Halsbury's Laws of England* (*qv*).

Aim is to provide the user with an up-to-date version of the amended text of every Public General Act or Ecclesiastical Measure in force in England and Wales, with detailed annotations to each section and schedule. Arrangement is A-Z by subject and there is an index to each volume. V.50 includes Treaties of the European Communities. *Cumulative supplement*, 1989 (1989. ISBN 0406043442). *Tables of Statutes and general index, 1989-90* (1989. ISBN 0406214727) refers to v.1-39 & 41-50. 'Particularly useful for tracing Acts on a particular subject' (Dane, J., and Thomas, P.A. *How to use a law library* (1979),p.51) of the 3rd ed. *Class No:* 340(410)

Bibliographies

[2792]

CHLOROS, A.G., *ed.* Bibliographical guide to the law of the United Kingdom, the Channel Islands and the Isle of Man. 2nd ed. London, University of London, Institute of Advanced Legal Studies, 1973. xvii,301p. £7.50. ISBN: 0901190144.

First published 1956. Published in co-operation with the United Kingdom National Committee of Comparative Law, and under the auspices of Unesco and the International Association of Legal Science.

Contributions by more than 30 lawyers. 21 chapters, sectionalised, with introductions and select bibliographies (1. Bibliographies and general accounts - 2. The sources of English law ... 7. Civil law (entries for books written primarily for students are single-asterisked; those for students coming to the subject for the first time are double-asterisked) ... 12. International law - 13. Northern Ireland - 14. Scots law ... 17. The Commonwealth ... 21. Common Market). Index of authors and editors; subject index. 'Prepared mainly in order to introduce English law to foreign lawyers and especially to "Civilians" (*Foreword*). *Class No:* 340(410)(01)

Reports Literature

[2793]

All England law reports. London, Butterworths, 1936-. Weekly.

A series of reports of decisions of all the courts; in suitable cases editorial notes are given, explaining the legal significance. Cases are speedily reported. Annual cumulative index and 'noter-up'. This also contains a table of cases, a table of statutes judicially considered, and a table of cases judicially noticed in later editions.

All England law reports reprint, 1558-1935 (London, Butterworths, 1966-68. 36v. and index. ISBN 040600000x) is a selection in the same styles as the *All England law reports*.

LEXIS, a computer-based legal research service, launched by Butterworths in 1980, contains the full text of all English cases reported in the main series of law reports since 1945. *Class No:* 340(410)(047)

[2794]

DICKMAN, P. *and* MISKIN, C., *eds*. Daily law reports index. Hebden Bridge, West Yorks., Legal Information Resources Ltd., July, 1988-. Weekly. £285 including bound annual volume.

A quick access index to law reports appearing in UK daily newspapers (*e.g., The Times, Financial times, Independent, Guardian* and *Daily telegraph*). Each issue appears in the week following the last week of the fortnight covered. Indexed by case, keywords and legislation judicially considered. Individual issues are filed behind numbered tags in a loose-leaf binder; bound cumulations also contain a checklist of cases, and a Case report index, detailing cases subsequently reported fully in the major series (*e.g., Law reports, Criminal appeal reports, Local government reports, Tax cases,* etc.). 'The editors ... have filled a very important gap in aids available to legal research' (*The Law librarian,* v.20(2). August 1989, p.70). *Class No:* 340(410)(047)

Yearbooks & Directories

[2795]

Butterworth's legal services directory, 1999. 10th ed. Bowker-Saur, 1999. £25. ISBN: 1857392124.

First published 1988.

Covers investigators, expert witnesses, company registration agents, process servers, bailiffs, etc. *Class No:* 340(410)(058)

[2796]

The legal 500: the definitive guide to law firms and barristers chambers in Britain. Pritchard, J., *ed*. London, Legalease, 1999. 548p. £99. ISBN: 1870854381.

First published 1988. Annual.

Also available on CD-Rom.

Aims to be an introductory guide to leading law firms, the factual information being supplied by the firms. A regional survey, by area, precedes the listing of 500 firms, A-Z, by name, followed by address, recruitment, agency work, types of work undertaken. Then a list of foreign law firms in London, a list of recruitment agencies, etc. *Class No:* 340(410)(058)

Histories

[2797]

BLAND, D.S., *comp*. A Bibliography of the Inns of Court and Chancery. London, Seldon Society, 1965. xi,75p. £10. ISBN: 0854231161.

Comprises 862 numbered items, with many cross-references. 15 sections, including A. Manuscript sources- B. Histories, descriptions and general works - J. Drama - K. Literature, general - L. Libraries - M. Education - N. 19th century reform - O. The legal profession. Indexes of authors, subjects and persons. *Class No:* 340(410)(091)

[2798]

YALE, D.E.C. *and* BAKER, J.H., *eds*. A Centenary guide to the publications of the Seldon Society. London, Seldon Society, 1987. xxiv,242p. £30.

Supersedes the *General guide to the Society's publications,* by Kiralfy & Jones (1960).

A detailed index and summary of the contents of the Introductions to volumes 1-102 of the main series of the Society's publications, and also the supplementary series and the occasional publications. V.1 was published in 1887. Thorough indexes of names and subjects. The Seldon Society aims to study the history of law, prints, and ancient records, and the editors are literary directors of the Society. An informative review of the Society and the guide by Peter Luther is published in *The Law library,* v.20(1), April 1989, p.90-91. *Class No:* 340(410)(091)

Bibliographies

[2799]
HINES, W., *comp*. 'Bibliography on British and Irish legal history (works published after 1985)'. In *Cambrian law review*, v.18, 1988, p.80-90.

An unannotated bibliography of 195 items, mainly journal articles but some books. In 7 sections (General and miscellaneous works - Medieval (before 1500) - Early modern (1500-1800) - Modern (from *c*.1800) - Ireland - Scotland - Wales). Arrangement within sections is A-Z by author. No introduction. Works published before 1985 were listed in earlier issues of *Cambrian law review*.
Class No: 340(410)(091)(01)

Laws

[2800]
GREAT BRITAIN. Chronological table of the Statutes, covering the legislation from 1235 to the end of 1990. London, HMSO, 1990. 2v. (ix,874; 875-1946p.). £170. ISBN: 0118403222.

Issued annually.

Part 1: 1235-1950; pt.2: 1951 to end of 1990. Does not include local or personal Acts. *Class No:* 340(410)(094.1)

[2801]
GREAT BRITAIN. Statutory Publications Office. Statutes in force. London, HMSO, 1972-. Loose-leaf, with 64 binders.

Replaces *The Statutes revised*.

A series of booklets, in subject groups, A-Z.
Class No: 340(410)(094.1)

[2802]
Is it in force? 1993: a guide to the commencement of the Statutes of England and Wales and of Scotland passed since 1 January 1965. Butterworth's Editorial staff. London, Butterworths, 1993. Annual. viii,615p. £21. ISBN: 0406015880.

Arranged chronologically, 1965-, subdivided by the Acts, arranged A-Z by short title, with chapter number, date of Royal Assent, list of provisions, etc. *Class No:* 340(410)(094.1)

Scotland

Handbooks & Manuals

[2803]
WALKER, D.M. The Scottish legal system: an introduction to the study of Scots law. 6th ed. Edinburgh, W. Green, 1992. 552p.8 illus. £35. ISBN: 0414010124.

First published 1959.

Written primarily as a textbook for the introductory course in the legal curriculum of Glasgow University. 15 chapters, each with 'further readings' (3. The branches of legal science - 4. The development of Scots law ... 7. The modern judicial system ... 10. The sources of Scots law - 11. The repositories of Scots law ... 14. The administration of criminal justice - 15. The making of new law. Many footnotes referring to books, articles, case law, and Statutes.
Class No: 340(411)(035)

Dictionaries

[2804]
GIBB, A.D. Students glossary of Scottish legal terms.
Duncan, A.G.M., *ed.* 2nd ed. Edinburgh, W. Green & Son Ltd., 1982. 100p. £6. ISBN: 0414006968.

First published 1946.

A list of books of reference precedes the glossary, which has short, clear definitions of about 15 words for *c*.1000 words. (Concerned almost exclusively with legal expressions which are truly and exclusively lawyers' expressions' (*Introduction* to 1st ed.). Adequate cross-references. *Class No:* 340(411)(038)

Yearbooks & Directories

[2805]
Scottish current law year book ... 1948-. Edinburgh, W. Green & Sons, 1949-. Annual. £320. ISSN: 02656159.

Annual cumulation of the monthly *Current law* (Scottish ed.). Sold only with *Scottish current law citator*.

The 1984 *year book* has tables of cases, statutory instruments and abbreviations, followed by subjects (Administrative law ... Workmen's compensation). Appended: 'Books and articles' (78p. under subjects, A-Z). Analytical index. *Class No:* 340(411)(058)

[2806]
—Encyclopaedia of the laws of Scotland. Viscount Dunedin, *and others*, *eds.* Edinburgh, W. Green & Sons, 1926-35. v.1-16; supplementary volume, pts.1-2, and Appendix, 1949-52. 3v.

No further volumes published. Should be supplemented by *Scottish current law year book. Class No:* 340(411)(058)

Histories

[2807]
WALKER, D.M. A Legal history of Scotland. v.1. The beginnings to AD 1286. Edinburgh, W. Green, 1988. xxi,435p. £64. ISBN 0414008162.

An account of the historical development of legal institutions and the system of concepts, doctrines and principles in Scottish law, both public and private. A chronological approach, with 2 chapters on the early period and 15 chapters on the feudal period. Bibliography (p.409-420) is divided into reference books, general histories, record publications, sources, and literary sources, each subdivided A-Z by author. Analytical subject index (p.421-435). *Class No:* 340(411)(091)

Manuscripts & Incunabula

[2808]
STAIR SOCIETY. An Introductory survey of the sources and literature of Scots Law. Edinburgh, Stair Society, 1936. 486p.

The inaugural volume of the Stair Society, presenting the first comprehensive survey of the sources of Scots law which has ever been essayed. A complete guide, well documented and equipped with bibliographies. 38 contributions by specialists in 4 sections: Native sources - Non-native sources - Indirect sources - Special subjects. *Index*, compiled by J.C. Brown (Edinburgh, Stair Society, 1939, 66p.), in two parts: index of cases cited; index of subjects.
Class No: 340(411)(093)

Laws

[2809]
SCOTLAND. Parliament. The Acts of the Parliaments of Scotland, 1424-1707. 2nd rev. ed. Edinburgh, HMSO, 1966. lix,191p. tables.

First published 1908.

The 1908 ed. contains a chronological table of all the Acts, the text of Acts of a public nature and still in force, and a digested index of those still in force. Omits local and personal Acts (Minto, J. *Reference books* (1929), p.72). Insert: *Index of short titles of the current Acts of the Parliament of Scotland*, 1424-1707 (1967.4p.).
Class No: 340(411)(094.1)

Northern Ireland

Manuscripts & Incunabula

[2810]
NORTHERN IRELAND. The Statutes revised, Northern Ireland, AD1226-1950 inclusive (as amended up to the end of 1954). Belfast, HMSO, 1956. 16v.

V.1: Legislation pre-1800 - 2-8. UK enactments, 1801-1920; 9-12: UK enactments, 1921-1950; 13-16: Northern Ireland enactments, 1921-1950. These volumes contain all the enactments affecting Northern Ireland. *Chronological table of the Statutes* (covering 1226 onwards) and *Index to the Statutes in force* are issued at 3-yearly intervals.

Subordinate legislation is published singly and bound annually as *Statutory rules and orders of Northern Ireland. Index to the Statutory rules and orders of Northern Ireland in force on 31 December 1992* (1993. £150. ISBN 0337902925). *Class No:* 340(416)(093)

Eire

Bibliographies

[2811]
PAWLOSKI, B.M. 'Gaelic law in early and medieval Ireland; a bibliography' In *Law library journal*. v.79(2), Spring 1987, p. 305-31.

A bibliography of 365 books and articles on all aspects of early Irish law (pre-history to the Elizabethan era), arranged in 15 sections: 1. The Brehon law system; II. The King; III. Courts; IV. Irish parliament; V. Local law and administration; VI. Law of the family; VII. Honour and status; VIII. Land law; IX.. Charters and deeds; X. Agriculture; XI. Sick-maintenance; XII. Distraint; XIII. The Church; XIV. Influence of English Law; XV. Other influences. Double column author index, p. 332-3. *Class No:* 340(417)(01)

Handbooks & Manuals

[2812]
DOOLAN, B. Principles of Irish Law. 5th ed. Dublin, Gill & Macmillan, 1999. £19.99. ISBN: 0707128393.

First published 1981.

Claims to be the standard introduction to Irish law, each major area of law being comprehensively treated with a jargon-free explanation. Index. *Class No:* 340(417)(035)

Dictionaries

[2813]

MURDOCH, H. **A Dictionary of Irish law.** Dun Loaghaire, Co. Dublin, Topaz Publications, 1988. xiii,569p. IR£38. ISBN: 0951403206.

Provides in one volume definitions of the principal words and phrases which are encountered in Irish law giving, in most instances, the legal sources of the definitions, whether statutory or judicial, and a brief introduction to the relevant law. '... designed primarily for busy practising lawyers, whether barrister or solicitor, who want an *aide memoire* or an introduction to an area of law with which they are not immediately familiar ...' Endeavours to cover all areas of law. Extensive cross-references. 3 appendices: 1. Books on Irish law referred to in the dictionary (A-Z by author); books on UK law, of relevance to Irish law, referred to in the dictionary; 2. Law reports; 3. Law Reform Commission's reports/working papers. *Class No:* 340(417)(038)

Laws

[2814]

EIRE. **Actanna an Oireachtais/The Acts of the Oireachtais passed in the year ... consisting of the Public General Acts and the Private Acts, with tables and index.** Dublin, Stationery Office, 1922-. Annual.

Irish and English on opposite pages.

Index to the legislation passed by the Oireachtais ... 1922 to 1975 (Dublin, Stationery office, 1977) is updated at intervals. Subordinate legislation is issued singly and bound annually as *Statutory Rules, Orders and Regulations for Eire,* with cumulative indexes. *Class No:* 340(417)(094.1)

Commonwealth

[2815]

Law reform in the Commonwealth: law reform proposals and their implementation, 1987. London, Commonwealth Secretariat, 1988. v,191p. £7.50.

First published 1981. Annual.

A register of Commonwealth law reform agency proposals in law reform, and monitors the progress made in the implementation of such proposals. Also lists government departments concerned with legal research. *Class No:* 340(41-44)

Bibliographies

[2816]

NEWTON, V. **Commonwealth Caribbean legal literature:** a bibliography of primary sources to date and secondary sources for 1971-85. 2nd ed. Cave Hill, Barbados, Faculty of Law Library, University of the West Indies, 1987. xxiv, 492p. $50; Barbados$70.

First published as *Legal literature and conditions affecting legal publishing in the Commonwealth Caribbean: a bibliography* (1979).

3439 numbered entries, arranged by different types of sources (*e.g.* Constitutions; Law reports; Bibliographies; Theses). Most materials cited held in the University's libraries, but also includes materials held in other Caribbean law libraries. '... well suited to supporting research comparing the law of different Caribbean countries in particular fields and for checking collections by topic' (*International journal of legal information,* v.16(1), Spring 1988, p.38-39). *Class No:* 340(41-44)(01)

Reviews & Abstracts

[2817]

English and Empire digest, with complete and exhaustive annotations. Stickland, P., *ed.* Rev. ed. London, Butterworth, 1971. 66v. £2350. ISBN: 0406025002, the set.

Cumulative annual supplements, continuation and replacement volumes.

Digests every English case reported in a law report or series of reports, from early times onwards and (in smaller type) of many cases decoded in Commonwealth countries. A note of the decision is always given, with references to all published reports of the case, plus reference to later cases in which it has been judicially noticed. Cases are arranged systematically under broad subject headings (*e.g.* 'Contract'; 'Evidence'; 'Companies'; 'Negligence'; 'Criminal law and procedure'), *Class No:* 340(41-44)(048)

Yearbooks & Directories

[2818]

Annual survey of Commonwealth law, 1965-1977, v.1-13. Oxford, Clarendon Press, 1966-1978. 13v.

Various contributors to each issue. Covers all types of law, providing commentary on judicial decisions from most of the jurisidications of the Commonwealth and collections of legislative material. Heavily footnoted. Analytical subject and territorial indexes to each vol. *Class No:* 340(41-44)(058)

[2819]

Commonwealth law bulletin. London, Commonwealth Secretariat, 1975-. v.1,no.1-. Quarterly. £20pa. ISSN: 03050718.

Contains details of legislation, judicial decisions, international agreements, law reform. A 'Miscellaneous' section includes review of books, a list of recent periodical articles. The editorial note that precedes highlights developments. *Class No:* 340(41-44)(058)

England & Wales

Reports Literature

[2820]

Weekly law reports. London, Incorporated Council of Law Reporting for England and Wales, 1953-. Weekly. £175pa. ISSN: 00193518.

The series contains decisions of all courts, the most important of them being reported more fully in the *Law reports,* later. Here cases are reported speedily.

The annual cumulative index covering this series and *Law reports* also contains tables of cases and statutes judicially considered. Also available online.

The history of *Law reports* and other law series is described in section 5. 'The reports, abridgements, digests, collections of cases and statutes, and dictionaries', in v.15 (1965) of Sir W. Holdsworth's *A history of English law.* Also available online. *Class No:* 340(42)(047)

Laws

[2821]

Halsbury's Statutory Instruments; being a companion work to *Halsbury's Statutes of England.* Butterworth's Legal Editorial staff. 4th re-issue. London, Butterworth, 1979-. 23v. £400. ISBN: 0406045003.

Annotated edition of all Statutory Rules and Orders and Statutory Instruments in force, arranged under topics. Not all Instruments in force are reprinted in full. Updated by loose-leaf supplementary service. *Class No:* 340(42)(094.1)

England

Bibliographies

[2822]

WILLIAMS, G. **Learning the law.** 11th ed. London, Stevenson & Sons, 1982. viii,241p. £4.25. ISBN: 0420462902.

First published 1945; 10th ed. 1978.

Handbook for the law student, to prepare him/her for reading legal textbooks. 14 chapters (1. The divisions of the law ... 5. Technical terms ... 7. The interpretation of the statutes ... 12. Legal research ... 14. General reading (p.226-237, in 10 subject sections)). Index, p.239-241. *Class No:* 340(420)(01)

Encyclopaedias

[2823]

Halsbury's Laws of England. Lord Hailsham, *ed.* 4th ed. London, Butterworths, 1973-. 56v. *Annual abridgement* (v.1, 1974-); *Cumulative supplement* (2 parts, 1989); Current service *Monthly review. Monthly review* £35pa. ISSN: 03084388, Annual abridgement; 03079821, Monthly review.

First published 1907-17; 3rd ed. 1952-64 (43v.).

An encyclopaedia of English law, consisting of separate treatises on individual subjects, A-Z. The article 'Juries' (v.26, p.313-39, paras 601-654/700) is subdivided: 1. Constitution and duties of juries - 2. Qualification, exemption and excusability of juries - 3. Summoning of jurors - 4. Proceedings before juries - 5. Payment of jurors - 6. Common law offences. V.23 (1978) is devoted entirely to 'Income taxation' (1298p.), with a detailed index (p.1225-89) and a 'Words and phrases' index. Definitions; footnoted Acts and case law. V.53 (2v.) is a consolidated table of Statutes; v.54 (2v.) a consolidated table of cases; v.55-56 a consolidated index. *Class No:* 340(420)(031)

[2824]

—**Halsbury's Laws of England: a user's guide.** London, Butterworths, 1983. 30p.

Contents: Introduction - Component parts of Halsbury's Laws - keeping Halsbury's Laws up to date - Halsbury's annual abridgement - How to use Halsbury's Laws - Tables of titles (to the 4th ed.). Index key. *Class No:* 340(410)

[2825]
JOWITT W.A., 1st Earl Jowitt *and* WALSH, C. The Dictionary of English law. Burke, J., *ed.* 2nd ed. London, Sweet & Maxwell, 1977. 2v. (1952p.). £144 for 2v. & 1985 supplement. Supplement only, £23. ISBN: 0421230908, the set; 0421293705, supplement only. First published 1959.

Substantial definitions and explanations of English legal terms, A-K, L-Z, plus references to the relevant statutes, cases and standard text books. Many cross-references. 'Witness': 2 columns. Some biographies are included, with emphasis on legal careers or writings (*e.g.* Bracton). Bibliography (A-Z, authors), p.1923-35. 'It is thoroughly recommended to law librarians and to professional and business offices throughout the common law world ...' (*British book news,* June 1977, p.452). *Class No:* 340(420)(031)

Dictionaries

[2826]
McFARLANE, G. The Layman's dictionary of English law. London, Waterlow Publishers Ltd., 1984. vi,[2],319p. £12.95. ISBN: 0080391613.

Designed to give speedy explanations of legal words and phrases used in newspapers and broadcasting, etc., and in legal offices and documents. Very brief definitions. Includes Latin and French terms. *Class No:* 340(420)(038)

Quotations

[2827]
NORTON-KYSHE, J.W. The Dictionary of legal quotations: or, Selected dicta of English Chancellors and judges, from the earliest periods to the present time. With explanatory notes and references. Reprint of 1904 edition published by W.S. Hein, Buffalo, N.Y., 1984. xxi,344p. $40. ISBN: 0899413757. *Class No:* 340(420)(082.2)

Histories

[2828]
HOLDSWORTH, W.S. A History of English law. Rev. ed. London, Methuen; etc., 1956-72. 17v. £39. each vol. ISBN: 0421051604, v.1; 0421050209, v.2; 0421050306, v.3; 0421050403, v.4; 0421050500, v.5; 0421050608, v.6; 0421050705, v.7; 0421050802, v.8; 042105090x, v.9; 0421051000, v.10; 0421051108, v.11; 0421051205, v.12; 0421041900, v.14; 0421042001, v.15; 042105140x, v.16; 0421175605, v.17.

V.1: *The judicial system.* 7th ed.; revised by S.B. Chrimes and others. 1956. Index to v.1-9, by E. Potten; v.13 was published posthumously in 1953; v.16 (1966) is the final volume. V.17: *General index* (Sweet & Maxwell, 1972. 551p.). The great history of English law; indispensable for detailed information. *Class No:* 340(420)(091)

[2829]
MANCHESTER, A.H. Sources of English legal history: law, history and society in England and Wales, 1750-1950. New ed. London, Butterworths, 1984. xiv,443p. tables. £36. ISBN: 0406516596.

First published in 1980 as *A modern legal history of England and Wales, 1750-1950.*

Systematically covers the sources of the law, the legal profession, courts, criminal law, civil liability, the law of property and family law. The 15 chapters are preceded by a table of Statutes and list of cases. Each chapter commences with references to Statutes, cases, etc. Analytical index, p.435-443. *Class No:* 340(420)(091)

[2830]
SAINTY, J., *comp.* A List of English law officers, King's Counsel and holders of patents of procedure. London, Seldon Society, 1987. xviii,330p. £32. (*Seldon Society supplementary series, v.7.*)

Compiled for the Seldon Society.

'Lists are arranged in chronological order of appointment: Lists of holders of the offices of King's Serjeants at law (1278-1866); King's Prime or Ancient Serjeant (1623-1866); Attorney General (1315-1984); Solicitor General (1461-1984); Advocate General (1604-1872); King's Counsel (1604-1984); and holders of patents of precedence (1687-1897). Includes a few samples of letters patent, and a full list of names from each section. Each list preceded by a brief introduction giving details of the method of appointment, tenure and renumeration, and including reference to sources where history of each office can be found' (*The Law Librarian,* v.19(3), December 1988, p.114). *Class No:* 340(420)(091)

Official Records

[2831]
WINFIELD, P.H. The Chief sources of English legal history. Cambridge, Mass., Harvard University Press, 1925 (Reprinted in 1972 by B. Franklin and in 1983 by W.S. Hein). xviii, 374p. $40. (*Historical reprints in jurisprudence and legal literature series.*) ISBN: 0899412556.

Based on a course of lectures delivered in the Harvard Law School in 1923, this essential guide discusses problems involved in the study of English legal history and the equipment needed to face them; to each chapter is appended a critical list of printed sources and secondary works. Subjects: Existing bibliographical guides, Anglo-Saxon law, influence of Roman law on English law, statutes, public records, case law, abridgements, textbooks and books of practice. *Class No:* 340(420)(093.2)

[2832]
—COWLEY, J.D. A Bibliography of abridgements, digests, dictionaries and indexes of English law to the year 1800. London, Quarich, 1932 (now available from the Seldon Society). xcv,[1],196p. illus. £22. ISBN: 0854231080. *Class No:* 340(420)(093.2)

[2833]
—LOGAN, R.G. 'Bibliographical guide to early British law books'. In *Law librarian,* v.4(1), April/July 1973, p.9-12. *Class No:* 340(420)(093.2)

Laws

[2834]
GREAT BRITAIN. Index to local and personal Acts; consisting of classified lists of the local and personal and private Acts and special Orders and special procedure Orders 1801-1947. London, HMSO, 1949. viii,1140p.

Repeals and amendments are shown, but the information about repeals, etc. prior to 1901 is not complete. An earlier ed., covering 1801-1890, contains Irish entries omitted from the 1801-1947 ed. The local and personal Acts themselves are published individually, with annual tables and index. *Supplementary index to the local and personal Acts, 1948-1966: classified list of the local and personal Acts (together with alphabetical and chronological lists) for the years 1948-1966 inclusive* (Prepared in the Statutory Publications Office under the authority of the Statutory Law Committee. London, HMSO, 1967.228p.). The Statutory Publications Office's *Chronological list of the local and personal Acts, 1887-1947* also appeared in 1967 (200p.). According to J.L. Hobbs (*Local history and the library* (1962), p.39), the best guides to earlier private Acts are Vardon's *Index to local and personal and private Acts (1798-1840)* and Bramwell's *Analytical table of private Statutes* (1813. 2v.). *Class No:* 340(420)(094.1)

Germany

Bibliographies

[2835]
KEARLEY, T. *and* FISCHER, W. Charles Szladits' guide to foreign legal materials: German. 2nd rev. ed. Dobb's Ferry, NY, Oceana Publications Inc., 1990. xxiii,318p. $75.

Follows the format of the original (see 340(400)(01)) but also adds a description of legal education and the legal profession in West Germany, covering private and commercial law, procedural and penal law, public and administrative law, legal history, legal philosophy, statutes, customary law, judicial decisions, legal writings, and general principles of law in 12 chapters. List of abbreviations. List of English-language titles cited. Author-title and subject indexes. *Class No:* 340(430)(01)

Handbooks & Manuals

[2836]
COHN, E.J., *and others.* Manual of German law. Rev. ed. Dobbs Ferry, N.Y., Oceana, 1968-71. 2v. (350p.;311p.). V.1: $34; v.2: $23; set: $58. ISBN: 0379002965, v.1; 0379002973, v.2; 0686968204, set.

V.1 describes the structure and history of the German legal system and deals with civil law. V.2 covers commercial law, conflicts, civil procedure, bankruptcy, German law of nationality and East German law, plus indexes, glossary of German terms, and table of cases. *Class No:* 340(430)(035)

[2837]
—The German civil code, as amended to January 1, 1975. Amsterdam, North-Holland Publishing Co., 1975. xxxvii,434p.

Translated from the German. *Class No:* 340(430)(035)

LAW

Austria

Bibliographies

[2838]
FOX, J.R. 'A Guide to Austrian legal research'. In *Law library journal,* v.80(1), Winter 1988, p.99-113.

An overview of the Austrian legal system, including a bibliography of primary and secondary source materials in Austrian law (constitutional law, federal and provincial statutes and administrative law, courts and procedure, the civil code, health and safety law, business and tax law, and criminal law). Also lists Austrian law reviews and publishers. *Class No:* 340(436)(01)

Hungary

[2839]
Bibliography of Hungarian legal literature, 1945-1980. Nagy, L., *ed.*

Budapest, Akadémiai Kiadó, under the auspices of the International Association of Legal Science and the International Committee for Social Science Information and Documentation, for the Institute for Legal and Administrative Sciences of the Hungarian Academy of Sciencss, 1988. 429p.

Previous edition, covering 1945-65, was issued in 1966.

A learned and informative introduction precedes 19 subject chapters with a wide selection of books, articles and papers in Hungarian and other languages on the various fields of law. Each subject chapter has a concise introduction written by a well-known Hungarian specialist. 3316 entries have full bibliographical information and English translations of titles. List of abbreviations. Author index and broad subject index according to the language of the works listed. '... this very impressive bibliography ...'(*International journal of legal information,* v.17(2), Summer 1989, p.164-5). *Class No:* 340(439)

France

Bibliographies

[2840]
DUNES, A. **Documentation juridique.** Paris, Dalloz, 1977. viii,158p. (*Méthodes du droit.*)

Part 1 considers the functions of documentation, with particular reference to law. Part 2 deals with types of material (compendia; codes; reviews; monographs). Appended contents list and subject index. Recommended as a 'refresher' for French law-librarians and documentalists (*Bulletin des bibliothèques de France,* v.23(8), August 1978, item 1657). *Class No:* 340(44)(01)

[2841]
—COMBE, D.A. 'French legal bibliographies'. In *International journal of law libraries,* v6(2), July 1978, p.183-204. *Class No:* 340(44)(01)

[2842]
SZLADITS, C. *and* GERMAIN, C.M. **Guide to foreign legal materials: French.** 2nd rev. ed. Dobbs Ferry, N.Y., Oceana, 1985. xi, 205p. $35. ISBN: 0379117541.

First published 1959.

A guide for common law lawyers to the use of French legal materials. 10 chapters in 2 parts. Part 1 describes sources, their character and position in the French legal system (I. Legislation - II. Custom - III. Case law - IV. Legal science - V. General principles and equity). Part 2. (2/3rds of the work) is bibliographical (VI. Bibliographies (current bibliographies, retrospective bibliographies, guides to legal research, guides to libraries) - VII. Legislative materials - VIII. Case law (jurisprudence) - IX. Encyclopedias and legal dictionaries - X. Doctrinal writings). All chapters are subdivided. Conclusions, are followed by a list of legal abbreviations (p.171-182), a subject index (p.183-191), and an author/title index (p.193-205). *Class No:* 340(44)(01)

Handbooks & Manuals

[2843]
KAHN-FREUND, O., *and others*. **A Source-book on French law:** public law: constitutional and administrative law, private law: structure, contract. 3rd rev. ed. Oxford, Clarendon Press, 1991. xxix,523p. £19.99. ISBN: 0198762488.

First published 1973.

Bibliography, index. *Class No:* 340(44)(035)

Italy

[2844]
CERTOMA, G.L. **The Italian legal system.** London, Butterworth, 1985. xxiii,520p. £29.50. (*Butterworth's legal systems of the world.*) ISBN: 040639993x.

Aims 'to present the first comprehensive study of the Italian legal system. A table of the principal legislation Acts is followed by 12 chapters in 5 parts: 1. The historical development of the ... system - 2.

....(contd.)
Public law - 3. Private law - 4. Hybrid categories of law - 5. The research of Italian law. Legal research and bibliographical notes, p.491-500. Analytical index, p.501-520. *Class No:* 340(450)

Bibliographies

[2845]
GRISOLI, A. **Guide to foreign legal materials: Italian.** Dobbs Ferry, N.Y., Oceana, 1965, for the Parker School of Foreign and Comparative Law, Columbia University. xv,272p. $17.50. (*Parker School studies in foreign and comparative law, v.2.*) ISBN: 0379117525.

Primarily for the common-law lawyer. Part 1, Sources of Italian law (chapters 1-6); part 2, Repositories of the law (1. Bibliographies - 2. Legislative materials - 3. Case law - 4. Encyclopedias, form books and legal dictionaries - 5. Doctrinal). Appendices: Current legal abbreviations, abbreviations of periodicals. Index to subjects. Index to authors and titles. *Class No:* 340(450)(01)

Handbooks & Manuals

[2846]
GIANNANTONIO, E. **Italian legal information network: a handbook** ... Milano, Dott. A. Giuffrè Editore, 1984. xii,181p. ISBN: 881400143x.

A handbook on how to use databases in the system. In 4 parts: 1. Introduction to Italian law - 2. The information retrieval system - 3. Databases - 4. Retrieval aids. Appendix: Terminals connected via Euronet or via the public telephone network: initial procedure. Index, p.179-181. *Class No:* 340(450)(035)

Russia

[2847]
BUTLER, W.E. **Russian law.** [3rd ed.] Oxford, Oxford University Press, 1999. xlii,692p. £95. ISBN: 0198260326.

First published 1953. Previous ed. (1988) entitled: Soviet law.

Emphasis on post-Soviet law reform, with chapters on entrepreneurial law, securities regulation, banking and investment law. *Class No:* 340(47)

Encyclopaedias & Dictionaries

[2848]
Encyclopaedia of Soviet law. Feldbrugge, F.J.M., *ed.* 2nd ed. Leiden, Nijhoff, 1985. 964p. £124.75.

First published 1973.

Entries arranged A-Z by subject heading, most have subdivisions, all are signed, and end with 'see also' references to other headings. A select list of statutory materials is also included. *Class No:* 340(47)(03)

Greece

Bibliographies

[2849]
SPIROU, C.D.C. **English, French, German, and Italian language materials relating to Greek law:** a selected annotated bibliography. In *International journal of legal information,* v.17(1), Spring, 1989, p.10-31.

305 entries relating to books and articles, most material dating from 1980. Arranged A-Z by main entry. Subject-keyword index to numbered entries. *Class No:* 340(495)(01)

China

[2850]
TANNER, M.S. **The politics of law making in China: institutions, processes and democratic prospects** Oxford, Clarendon Press, 1999 286p. £45.00 ISBN: 0198293399.

Working often from original documents not meant for Western eyes, and from interviews with officials and others, Tanner produces an immpressive account of the changes in law-making procedures in China since the death of Mao, and the gradual (and probably unintended) democratization. The book is strong on the historical context of law-making institutions, and has detailed case studies of two particular laws. *Class No:* 340(510)

LAW

Bibliographies

[2851]
LANGEVOORT, J.J. **Chinese law in English: a selected bibliography.** In *International journal of legal information,* v.14(3-4), June-August 1986, p.111-154.

An unannotated list of 498 citations, arranged A-Z in each section, of books and articles on the law of Mainland china published in English from 1980. Part I. Primary source material; II. Other books and articles. Subject and keyword index, p.150-154.
Class No: 340(510)(01)

Chinese

[2852]
BILANCIA, P.R. **Dictionary of Chinese law and government: Chinese-English.** Stanford, CA., Stanford University Press, 1981. xv,822p. $75. ISBN: 0804708649.

Claims to have entries for 25,000 terms, with 15,000 examples of usage and 30,000 cross-references (*The Bookseller,* 8 August 1981. p.648). *Class No:* 340(510)=951

India

Bibliographies

[2853]
JAIN, H.C. **Indian legal materials: a bibliographical guide.** Bombay, N.M. Tripathe; Dobbs Ferry, N.Y., Oceana, 1970. xxiii,123p. $8.50. ISBN: 0379004666. *Class No:* 340(540)(01)

Israel

[2854]
SNYDER, E. M. **'Guide to Israel legal bibliography: primary sources'** In *Law library journal* v.70(1), February 1977, p.14-29.

Covers statutes, regulations and decisions published officially and by private publishers - 'pre-State materials since 1917, and publications after the establishment of the State in 1948, including brief discussions of the Knesset, the national legislature and the court structure. A separate section briefly touches upon Jewish law' (*Abstract*) Index. *Class No:* 340(569.4)

Islamic World

Bibliographies

[2855]
MAKDISI, J. **'Islamic law bibliography'.** In *Law library journal,* v.78(1), Winter 1986, p.103-189.

A survey of the publications of primary sources of islamic law (in Arabic) and secondary sources (in English and French). Introduction discusses the basic sources of the law and schools of legal doctrine, and provides a brief treatment of the development of Islamic law. 865 references. Author index. *Class No:* 340(5.297)(01)

Africa

Bibliographies

[2856]
MWALIMU, C. **'A Bibliographic essay of selected secondary sources on the common law and customary law of English speaking Sub-Saharan Africa'.** In *Law library journal,* v.80(2), Spring 1988, p.241-289.

In 5 parts: I. Introduction - II. The reception, influence, and impact of common law on African traditional legal systems, 1954-85 - III. African customary law in its interaction with common law, the results of interaction, and judicial approaches to the resolution of conflicts, 1954-85 - IV. Integration, unification, harmonization, and codification of laws of English-speaking Sub-Saharan Africa, 1897-1972 - V. Key provisions of legislation on the application of common law and customary law in English-speaking Sub-Saharan Africa (subdivided by country). 189 footnotes, many indicating sources. 2 appendices of sources (A. The legal profession and legal education in English-speaking Sub-Saharan Africa, 1967-81; B. General African law materials relevant to common law and customary law in the legal systems of English-speaking Sub-Saharan Africa, 1962-85.
Class No: 340(6)(01)

Canada

Bibliographies

[2857]
MacELLVEN, D.T. **Legal research handbook.** 4th ed. Toronto, Butterworths, 1998. xxiii,427p. Can$49.95. ISBN: 0433409444.

19 chapters, all subdivided: 1. Legal research concepts - 2. Law reports - 3. Digests and indexes for law reports - 4. Statutes - 5. Subordinate legislation - 6. Statutes and case citations - 7. Legal encyclopedias - 8. Legal periodicals and legal periodical indexes - 9. Other secondary literature research sources - 10. Computerized legal research ... 18. Social science and government publications research - 19. Improving legal writing. 3 appendices (B. Selected sources for further study; C. Glossary of legal research terms and concepts). Index. *Class No:* 340(71)(01)

Yearbooks & Directories

[2858]
Canadian legal directory, 1987. Hintauer, S., *ed.* 77th ed. Richard de Boo Publishers (distributed in US by Gale Research Co.), 1987. xii,1138p. $70. ISBN: 0888202407.

First published 1911. Annual.

The standard reference book for information about Canada's attorneys and law firms, relevant government offices, departments and judicial systems. Also includes details of law firms based outside Canada that are licenced to practice law in Canada.
Class No: 340(71)(058)

Latin America

Laws

Bibliographies

[2859]
UNITED STATES. Library of Congress. Law Library. **Index to Latin American legislation,** 1950 through 1960. Boston, Mass., G.K. Hall, 1961. 2v. Supplements 1-3 (1970-78). $195.00; $120 each supplement. ISBN: 0816105944.

30,900 catalogue cards photolithographically reproduced. Covers the principal laws, decrees, regulations and administrative rulings of twenty Latin American republics. Arranged by country, then by subject and chronologically thereafter. The 3 supplements add *c.*70,000 cards.

Earlier material is covered by *Bibliografia juridica de América latina (1810-1965);* compiled by Alberto Villalón (Santiago, Editorial Juridica de Chile, [1970]. 5v.). *Class No:* 340(729.99)(094.1)(01)

USA

Bibliographies

[2860]
Encyclopedia of legal information sources. Baker, B.L. *and* Petit, P.J., *eds.* 2nd ed. Detroit, Mich., Gale Research Co., 1993. xxv,1083p. $165. ISBN: 0810374390.

First published 1988.

*c.*29,000 citations on 480 law-related subjects, arranged A-Z by subject (Actions and defenses ... Zoning and planning). Intended to meet the needs of both professionals and laypersons. Includes laws, loose-leaf services, reference works, indexes, newsletters, statistics and audiovisual material, mainly published since 1980. Emphasis is on federal law and national organizations, but sections listing sources for each State are included. Detailed outline of contents, but no title or organization indexes. Cross-references. Supplements are planned to update the work. *Class No:* 340(73)(01)

[2861]
REAMS, B.D., *and others*. **American legal literature: a guide to** selected legal resources. Littleton, Col., Libraries Unlimited, 1985. 239p. $27.50. ISBN: 0872875148.

Intended for the layman. 3 sections (List of primary materials such as statutes, case reports and finding aids useful for finding such - List of legal reference materials such as law dictionaries, directories of lawyers, bibliographies, and research guides - List of monographs on the law accessible to a reader with no legal training). Short appendices include one on major American law book publishers. Unannotated.
Class No: 340(73)(01)

Encyclopaedias

[2862]

The Guide to American law: everyone's legal encyclopedia. St. Paul, MN., West Publishing Co., 1983-85. 12v. (6446p.). illus. $660 the set. ISBN: 0314732241.

Intended for students and the general reader rather than the professional. Articles range in length from long signed essays to short unsigned contributions. Definitions are in small open boxes. Includes historical and biographical entries and famous trials. Numerous case citations. Each volume has an index and a cumulated index is included in V.12. V.11 relates to classical legal documents.
Class No: 340(73)(031)

[2863]

—The Guide to American law yearbook, 1987: everyone's legal encyclopedia. St. Paul, MN, West Publishing Co., 1987. xvi, 580p. illus. $95. ISSN: 08950989.

Supplements the above by both updating some entries and adding new ones, its aim being 'to examine the major legal documents of recent years'. Mainly covers 1984 to early 1987.
Class No: 340(73)(031)

Handbooks & Manuals

[2864]

Encyclopedia of the American judicial system: studies of the principal institutions and processes of law. Janosik, R.J., *ed.* New York, Charles Scribner and Sons, 1987. 3v. (1420p.). $225. (*American civilization.*) ISBN: 0684178079.

Intended to meet the need for easier access to the subject matter of the American legal system. 88 lengthy essays analysing a wide array of aspects of American law are arranged in 6 subject sections (legal history - substantive law - institutions and personnel - process and behaviour - constitutional law and issues - methodology). Each article lists relevant court cases, a select bibliography, and cross-references to related articles, and averages 15 pages in length. Index at end of 3rd vol. *Class No:* 340(73)(035)

Yearbooks & Directories

[2865]

National directory of legal services. Davidson, R.L., *ed.* Englewood Cliffs, N.J., Prentice Hall Press, 1989. 589p. $79.95. ISBN: 0136093973.

Lists over 700 businesses serving the legal profession, providing attorneys and law officers with listings of individuals and organizations that can serve important needs of a law practice (*e.g.* expert witnesses; investigators; detectives; model makers; photographers, In 4 sections: Glossary of abbreviations and acronyms used - 'Discovery key indexing' (641 subject headings, each divided into general services and computer services) - General services listing - Computer services listing. Under the last 2 sections, organizations are arranged A-Z by name. *Class No:* 340(73)(058)

[2866]

WASSERMAN, S. *and* **O'BRIEN, J.W.,** *eds.* **Law and legal information directory.** 5th ed. Detroit, Mich., Gale Research Co., 1988. 1120p. $280. ISBN: 0810326477. ISSN: 0740090x.

First published 1981.

13,500 entries grouped in 21 chapters (9 of the 21 consist mainly of entries from other Gale publications): National and international organizations - Bar associations ... Federal Court system ... Law schools ... Special libraries - Information systems and services - Research centers - Legal periodicals - Book and media publishers ... Small Claims Court - Corporation departments of State. Chapters individually indexed.

A 7th ed. was published in 1992 in 2v. *Class No:* 340(73)(058)

Laws

Bibliographies

[2867]

LONDON UNIVERSITY. Institute of Advanced Legal Studies. **Union list of United States legal literature:** holdings of legislation, law reports and digests in libraries in Oxford, Cambridge and London. 2nd ed. London, the Institute, 1967. xii,82p.

Covers federal and state Statutes, the code of federal regulations, law reports and digests of cases. Treatises and periodicals are excluded, but reports of decisions of administrative tribunals and agencies are shown. Details of the years held are given.
Class No: 340(73)(094.1)(01)

New Zealand

Bibliographies

[2868]

PALMER, K.A., *ed.* **Index to New Zealand legal writing and cases.** 2nd ed. Auckland, N.Z. Legal Research Foundation Inc., 1982-87. 2v. V.1. NZ$24.20; v.2. NZ$66.

First published 1977.

V.1: 1954-1981; V.2. 1982-1985. Detailed coverage of writings on New Zealand law, including material published outside New Zealand. Entries arranged by subject, mostly subdivided. Cross-references. Each volume is in 2 parts; the first part indexes books, theses, dissertations, journal articles, law reform publications, and selected government publications; the second part indexes case notes, with reference to published reports, etc. *Class No:* 340(931)(01)

18th Century

Bibliographies

[2869]

ADAMS, J. *and* **AVERLEY, G. A Bibliography of eighteenth century legal literature:** a subject and author catalogue of law treatises and all law related literature held in the main legal collections in England. Newcastle-upon-Tyne, Avero Publications Ltd., 1982. 924p. with six microfiche. £220. ISBN: 0907977014.

Arranged by a special detailed classification scheme created for the work. 14 libraries were searched (locations given) as well as publishers' catalogues, etc. Entries are in 3 parts: Authors name - title, class no. - imprint information for every edition held in the source libraries (in chronological order). Separate author catalogue in fiche form in pocket. Somewhat difficult to use. *Class No:* 340"17"(01)

Research Methods

[2870]

JACOBSTEIN, J.M. *and* **MERSKY, R.M. Fundamentals of legal research.** 3rd ed. New York, Foundation Press, 1985. 705p. $22.95. (*University textbook series.*) ISBN: 0882772457.

First published 1977 as a successor to E.H. Pollack's *Fundamentals of legal research* (4th ed. 1973).

Designed as an aid to students learning to do legal research, especially in Anglo-American law. Includes information on computers and microforms, etc. Also helpful for research work.
Class No: 340:001.891

Information Services

[2871]

MISKIN, C. Library and information services for the legal profession. London, British Library Research and Development Department, 1981. iv,68p. £8. (*B.L.R & D Report, no.5633.*) ISBN: 0905984730.

In 9 sections: Introduction and methodology - The legal database - Law publishers - The legal profession - Library services and information units - Law librarians - Online systems (subdivided by country) - User studies - Conclusions and recommendations - References, p.52-55 (79 items). *Class No:* 340:061:025.5

[2872]

—LOGAN, R.G. 'Law libraries in Oxford'. In *The Law librarian,* v.20(2), August 1989, p.49-54. *Class No:* 340:061:025.5

Libraries

[2873]

MISKIN, C., *ed.* **Directory of law libraries in the British Isles.** 3rd ed. Hebden Bridge, West Yorks, Legal Information Resources Ltd., 1988, for the British and Irish Association of Law Libraries. ix,120p. £15. ISBN: 1870369025.

First published 1976 by the Association and edited by B. Mangles.

Entries for 317 libraries, based on replies to a postal questionnaire, with supplementary information. Arranged by place (England; Ireland; Scotland; Wales; Channel Islands and other islands). Data: name and address; telephone-telex-fax numbers; opening hours; terms of admission; loans; facilities and services; stock; subject coverage; affiliation, etc. 4 indexes - by name of organization, type of organization, contact name, special collection name. 'Presentation and layout is excellent; (*The Law librarian,* v.20(2), May 1989, p.71).
Class No: 340:061:026/027

Research Projects

[2874]

Legal research in the United Kingdom, 1905-1984: classified list of legal theses and dissertations successfully completed for postgraduate degrees awarded by universities and polytechnics in the United Kingdom from 1905 to 1984. University of London. Institute of Advanced Legal Studies. London, the Institute, 1986. various pagings. £12.50. ISBN: 0901190292.

Supersedes all earlier eds.

Nearly 2700 numbered entries listed in A-Z order of subject, subdivided chronologically. Each entry includes name of scholar, degree granting institution, degree, year awarded, and full title of thesis. Includes both an A-Z and a classified list of subject headings. Author and geographical indexes. *Class No:* 340:061:061.62.005

Bibliographies

[2875]

CORBIN, J. **Find the law in the library:** a guide to legal research. Chicago, Ill., American Library Association, 1989. 327p. $58. ISBN: 0838905021.

'... responds to students' needs to locate primary legal sources (*e.g.* statutes and court decisions) and to use secondary legal sources (*e.g.* encyclopedias and treatises) in dealing with legal research problems and writing library research reports ... excellent guide ...' (*Choice,* v.27(5), January 1990, p.766). *Class No:* 340:061:061.62.005(01)

Law Schools

[2876]

TSENG, H.P. **The Law schools of the world.** Buffalo,N.Y., W.S. Hein, 1977. ix, 419p. $47.50. ISBN: 0930342097.

'A current and fairly accurate international directory of law schools' (*International journal of law libraries,* v.6(3), November 1978, p.329). *Class No:* 340:061:378.4

Legal Aid

[2877]

Legal aid handbook. Legal Aid Board. 1998/99 ed. London, Sweet & Maxwell, 1998. xviii,779p. £13.50. ISBN: 0421641002.

First published 1950 by HMSO. From 1990 ed. by Sweet & Maxwell.

Sets out the 1988 Legal Aid Act and the references, together with eligibility tables, list of legal aid forms, and an updated version of the Law Society's *Notes for guidance*. Index. *Class No:* 340.028

Jurisprudence

[2878]

DIAS, R.W.M. **A Bibliography of jurisprudence.** 3rd ed. London, Butterworth, 1979. ix,453p. £22.95. ISBN: 0406574286.

A companion to his *Jurisprudence* (4th ed. 1976).

About 3500 briefly annotated entries in 22 sections: 1. General - 2. Advantages and disadvantages - 3. Justice perspectives of power and liberty ... 6. Precedent - 7. Statutory interpretation - 8. Custom - 9. Values - 10. Duty - 11. Conduct - 12. Persons - 13. Possessions - 14. Ownership - 15. Legal change - 16. Positivism. British theories - 17. The pure theory - 18. Historical and anthropological approaches - 19. Economic approach - 20. Sociological approaches - 21. Modern realism - 22. National law. Bibliographical index (authors, A-Z); case index; general index. *Class No:* 340.143

Bibliographies

[2879]

DREWRY, G. **'Judiciary and government'.** In Englefield, D *and* Drewry, G's *Information sources in politics and political science: a survey worldwide* (Butterworth, 1986, p.209-225).

In 6 parts: Partial revival of a lost tradition? - The judicial process - Judicial institutions and the machinery of justice - Administrative law - Present trends in law and politics - Law reports and lawyers' journals. *Class No:* 340.143(01)

Scotland

Biographies

[2880]

WALKER, D.M. **The Scottish jurists.** Edinburgh, W. Green & Sons Ltd., 1985. xv,492p. illus. £39. ISBN: 0414007573.

29 chapters on the major jurists of the 15th to 20th centuries, arranged chronologically (1. The concept of a Scottish jurist - 2. The early jurists - 3-27. on individual jurists, one per chapter - 28. The minor jurists of the 20th century - 29. The contribution of the Scottish jurists to the science of law in Scotland. Textual and bibliographical footnotes. An appendix reports on decisions of the Court of Session,

....(contd.)

etc. A bibliography (p.451-466) is extensive and includes works of reference, historical papers, Parliamentary papers, and writings of Scottish jurists. Excellent index (p.467-492). No bibliography of the works of the jurists but these are accessible through the index. '... a welcome addition to the literature of Scottish legal history ...' (*International journal of legal information,* v.15(1-2), February-March, 1987, p.72-3). *Class No:* 340.143(411)(092)

Comparative Law

Encyclopaedias

[2881]

INTERNATIONAL ASSOCIATION OF LEGAL SCIENCE. **International encyclopedia of comparative law.** New York, Kluwer Academic (early issues by Sijthoff & Noordhoff); Tübingen, J.C.B. Mohr; The Hague, Martinus Nijhoff Publishers, 1972-1989. 17v. $100-$138.50 each vol.

Contents: 1. National reports on the legal system of the world's states - 2. The legal systems of the world/their comparison and unification - 3. Private international law - 4. Persons and family - 5. Succession ... 11. Torts ... 13. Business and private organizations ... 15. Labour law - 16. Civil procedure - 17. State and economy. Heavily footnoted; bibliographies. *Class No:* 340.5(031)

Handbooks & Manuals

[2882]

DAVID, R. *and* BRIERLEY, J.E.C. **Major legal systems of the world today:** an introduction to the comparative study of law. 3rd ed. London, Stevens & Sons, 1985. xvi,624p. £28. ISBN: 0420473408.

First published 1978. Translation of *Les Grands systèmes de droit contemporains.*

4 parts: 1. The Romano-Germanic family - 2. Socialist laws - 3. The common law (English law; law of the US) - 4. Other conceptions of law and the social order (Muslim law; Law of India; Laws of the Far East; Laws of Africa and Malagasy). Appendix 1: 'Bibliographical information' (brief notes); 9 sections: Bibliographical tools ... Unification and harmonisation of law), p.577-609. Appendix 2: 'Useful information and references' (Centres of comparative law; Comparative law studies; Comparative law libraries). Bibliography, p.577-613. Index, p.615-624. *Class No:* 340.5(035)

Medical Jurisprudence

[2883]

WILSON, C. **Written in blood:** a history of forensic medicine. London, Grafton Books, 1991. 533p. 16 illus. £14.95. ISBN: 1853360554.

Analytical table of contents, followed by 10 chapters: 1. The science of detection; 2. The power of poison; 3. The discovery of fingerprints; 4. Whose body? 5. If blood could speak; 6. Every bullet has a fingerprint; 7. The microscope as detective; 8. The sexual criminal; 9. The craft of the manhunter; 10. The soul of the criminal. Select bibliography, p.505-10. Index, p.511-23. *Class No:* 340.6

Encyclopaedias

[2884]

LANE, E. **The Encyclopedia of forensic science.** London, Headline Book Publishing, 1992. [9],415p. illus. £17.99. ISBN: 0747205892.

123 entries A-Z (Acid ... Voiceprints), each subdivided and many including case studies. Introduction includes a chronology to 'some of the landmarks in the history of forensic science' (p.9). Index, p.407-15. *Class No:* 340.6(031)

Dictionaries

[2885]

BANDER, E.J. *and* WALLACH, J. **Medical legal dictionary.** Dobbs Ferry, N.Y., Oceana, 1970. vii,114p. $17.50. ISBN: 0379141019.

'This dictionary defines medical terms for the lawyer and legal terms for the physician. It contains many references to legal resources to enable the practitioner to obtain further information' (*Bibliography, documentation, terminology,* v.20(2), March 1970, p.83). *Class No:* 340.6(038)

International Law

Bibliographies

[2886]
BEVERLY, E. **Public international law:** a guide to information sources. London, Mansell, 1991. 334p. £60; $90. ISBN: 0720120829.

Part 1: Sources of information: a documentary typology of public international law; pt.2: Sources of information & selected subject bibliography: topical approach. 'Scholarly treatment' (*Library association record*, v.91(11), November 1991, p.760).
Class No: 341(01)

[2887]
CAMBRIDGE UNIVERSITY. Squire Law Library. **Catalogue of international law.** Lekner, M.A., *comp.* Dobbs Ferry, N.Y., Oceana, 1972. 4v. $200 the set. ISBN: 0379200309.

About 12,000 entries; v.1-2: Author catalogue; v.3-4: Subject catalogue. V.4 includes a list of periodicals, collections of legislation, law reports, treaties, UK Parliamentary papers and UN documents. Primarily late 19th-century and early 20th-century materials in the Western world, with sparing cross-references in the author catalogue, according to *Choice*, v.9(9), November 1972, p.1115-6. Type (computer print-out) could be more legible. *Class No:* 341(01)

[2888]
MERRILL, J.G. **A Current bibliography of international law.** London, Butterworth, 1978. xx,277p. £30. ISBN: 0406623767.

Confined to English-language monographs (including translations) and especially periodical articles published since 1960, thus excluding some important foreign literature. Author index; no subject index, but a detailed list of contents. *Class No:* 341(01)

[2889]
—DELUPIS, I. Bibliography of international law. New York, Bowker, 1976. 670p.

Lists over 5000 books and periodical articles in major European languages, published 1920-1974. 14 sections, each with introduction highlighting important works, states *Library journal*, v.101(13), July 1976, p.1512). *Class No:* 341(01)

[2890]
Public international law: a current bibliography of articles. New York and Berlin., Springer-Verlag, for Max-Planck Institute for Comparative Public Law and International Law, 1975 -. 2pa. DM120. $88.50 pa. ISSN: 03407349.

Lists foreign and English books and articles on public international law. *Class No:* 341(01)

Canada

[2891]
WIKTOR, C.L. **Canadian bibliography of international law.** Toronto, University of Toronto Press, 1984. 767p. $95. ISBN: 0802056156.

A major bibliography reflecting Canada's international legal practice from its beginnings through the early 1980s. Over 9000 entries arranged under topical headings, following the outline of many international law textbooks. Many subjects reflect particular Canadian emphasis. Citations include books, articles, documents and official papers, chapters and proceedings. Includes both English- and French-language literature. No annotations. Introduction provides a statistical analysis of citations by subject and period. 'A valuable guide ...' (*Choice*, v.22(5), January 1985, p.668). *Class No:* 341(01)(71)

Encyclopaedias

[2892]
Encyclopedia of public international law. Bernhardt, R. Amsterdam, North-Holland Publishing Company, 1981-1992. 5v. $2,486.

Published under the auspices of the Max-Planck-Institute for Comparative Public Law and International Law.

First issued in subject instalments: 1. Settlement of disputes - 2. Decisions of international courts ... - 3. & 4. Use of force ... - 5. International organizations in general ... - 6. Regional co-operation ... - 7. History of international law ... - 8. Human rights and the individual in international law. International economic relations - 9. International relations ... - 10. States. Responsibility of States ... - 11. Law of the sea - 12. Geographical issues. Instalment 8 (1985. xv,551p.) has 129 entries by 87 authors. 'Lists of articles' in each instalment is a subject list relating to the complete work. Articles are signed and include bibliographies. Cross-references.
Class No: 341(031)

Dictionaries

Polyglot

[2893]
LINDBERG, G. **International law dictionary** English/French/German. Blackstone Press, 1992. vii,439p. £18. ISBN: 1854311190.

Gives brief translations of all the major legal terms. Includes basic legal terminology, plus the most frequently used law-related terms from banking, finance, insurance, industry, and taxation. Also includes supplements of Latin and EC abbreviations. *Class No:* 341(038)=00

[2894]
PAENSON, I. **Manual of the terminology of public international law (peace) and international organization: English-French-Spanish-Russian.** Bruxelles, Bruylant, for Institut Universitaire de Hautes Études Internationales, Geneve; Derventer, Kluwer Academic, 1983. xlviii, 846 p. £163 $295. ISBN: 2802702831 belgium; 9065440526 netherlands.

Terms are listed in English-French-Spanish-Russian across the pages, and are arranged in 8 subject chapters, all subdivided. Terms are fully defined in all 4 languages. For each language there is a general index, an index of bi- or multilateral international transactions, an index of declarations and of resolutions of international organizations, an index of international conferences, and an index of cases submitted to international tribunals. Footnotes.
Class No: 341(038)=00

English

[2895]
LINDBERGH, E. **International law dictionary.** London, Blackstone, 1992. viii,439p. £35. ISBN: 1854311190. *Class No:* 341(038)=20

[2896]
PARRY, C., *and others, eds.* **Encyclopedic dictionary of international law.** Dobbs Ferry, N.Y., Oceana, 1986. xix,564p. $60. ISBN: 0379208288.

Designed for the contemporary student. Short, concise articles giving thorough information on the subjects covered. Includes not only the concepts of international law, but also important cases, treaties, and select biographies of major literary figures, but omits all topics of international law on war and the law of international organizations. Extensive cross-references. A documents section has the Charter of the United Nations and other contemporary international instruments.
Class No: 341(038)=20

German

[2897]
GILBERTSON, G. **Harrap's German and English glossary of terms in international law.** London, George G. Harrap & Co. Ltd., 1980. xi,355p. £25. ISBN: 0245535241.

Over 9000 headwords, phrases and contextual examples used in theoretical international law and international law as codified in treaties and agreements. 3 main parts: I. German-English section - headword entries arranged in strict alphabetical order; subheadings indented; II. 21 annexes (*e.g.* a selection of extended extracts from a variety of international instruments); III. English register, referring to Part I. 12,500 precise references for all English terms in parts I & II. Cross-references. *Class No:* 341(038)=30

Yearbooks & Directories

[2898]
The British year book of international law, 1998. Brownlie, I. *and* Crawford, J., *eds.* 69th ed. Oxford, Oxford University Press, 1999. 658p. £110. ISBN: 0198269005.

First published 1920. Annual.

Contains articles, book reviews, summaries of decisions in English and European Courts. Analytical index. *Class No:* 341(058)

Law of International Organizations

Bibliographies

[2899]
BAER, G.W., *comp. & ed.* **International organisations, 1918-1945:** a guide to research and research materials. Rev. ed. Wilmington, DE., Scholarly Press Inc., 1991. xii,212p. (*Guides to European diplomatic history research and research materials.*.)

Over 1600 entries, many with annotations. Chapter 1 commences with an overview, followed by a list of 117 selected works on international affairs, organizations, law, and diplomacy; ch.2 has details of the archives of international organizations; ch.3 & 4 describe archival and other related resources in the US, UK, France and other European countries, including resources of libraries and international affairs institutions. 13 other chapters deal with aspects of the League of

....(contd.)

Nations, etc., and the final chapter is on World War II conference diplomacy and the founding of the United Nations. *Class No:* 341.1/.8(01)

[2900]
HAMERTON, D.N. 'Exploiting the publications of international organisations'. In *Use of social science literature,* edited by N. Roberts (1977) p.303-322.

A valuable concise running commentary. Contents: Introduction - International organisations - League of Nations - International Labour Organization - World Court - United Nations - International Court of Justice - Documentation - Intergovernmental regional organisations - European Community - O.E.C.D. - Council of Europe - Organization of American States - Organization of African Unity - Defence organisations - Conferences - Periodicals - Conclusions. *Class No:* 341.1/.8(01)

[2901]
International bibliography: publications of intergovernmental organizations. White Plains, N.Y., Kraus International Publications; Oxford, Marsten Book Services Ltd. 1973-. Quarterly. $100pa. ISSN: 02561042.

Until 1983 title was *International bibliogaphy, information, documentation: publications of international organizations,* published by Bowker.

'Bibliographic record': *c.*500 annotated entries in each issue under broad subject headings (Agriculture and related subjects ... Youth). 'Periodicals record': contents-listing of over 100 periodicals. Subject index. Organizations index. Title index. Indexes cumulate annually. *Class No:* 341.1/.8(01)

[2902]
World bibliography of international documentation. Dimitrov, T.D., *comp. and ed.* Pleasantville, N.Y., UNIFO, 1981. 2v (826p.). $95. ISBN: 0891110100.

V.1: *International organizations* is in 2 parts: pt.1. 'International organizations. Activities, structure, policies, document control' has 4 chapters (1. Nature, structure and activities of international governmental organizations - 2. Basic documents ... - 3. Secretaries-General - 4. Policies and research on international documentation); pt.2. 'Bibliographic control of international documents'. V.2. *Politics and world affairs* is in 3 parts: I. Multinational diplomacy and international relations - II. International periodicals - III. Annexes (1. Major intergovernmental conferences.). Author index, p.323-340. Index of organizations, p.341-348. Subject index, p.349-352. " ... a work of considerable value ... ' (*International affairs* v.58(4), Autumn 1982, p.737). *Class No:* 341.1/.8(01)

Official Records

[2903]
PEASLEE, A.J., *ed.* International governmental organizations: constitutional documents. Xydis, D.P., *ed.* 3rd ed. The Hague, Martinus Nijhoff, 1974-1979. 5v.

First published 1956; 2nd ed. 1961.

Contents: 1. *General and regional, political economic, social, legal defense* (1974. 2v. (xiii,xv,1479p.) - 2. *Agriculture, commodities, fisheries, food, plants* (1975. xii,633p.) - 3. *Education, culture, copyright* (1979) - 4. *Science, health* (1979) - 5. *Communications, transport, travel* (1976. xi,686p.). Texts of the basic constitutional documents of leading international organizations, plus background data and select bibliographies. 'An invaluable source' (D.N. Hamerton, in *Use of social sciences literature,* edited by N. Roberts (1977), p.304). *Class No:* 341.1/.8(093.2)

Archives

[2904]
Guide to the archives of international organizations. V.1: the United Nations system. Unesco. Paris, Unesco, 1984. 279p. £14.25 F.95. (*Documents, libraries and archives: bibliographies and reference works, 8.*) ISBN: 9231020900.

A preliminary version was published in 1979.

Data on the archives of 34 United Nations agencies and their subordinate institutions, and other bodies. Information includes address, opening hours, working languages, administrative history, structure, select bibliography, and description of the archives. *Class No:* 341.1/.8(093.20)

League of Nations

Bibliographies

[2905]
BIRCHFIELD, M.E. Consolidated catalog of League of Nations publications offered for sale. Dobbs Ferry, N.Y., Oceana, 1976. ix,477p. $55. ISBN: 0379003287.

A guide to both series and monographs, arranged by the 17 League

....(contd.)

of Nations publications categories (Assembly; Council; Library; Information and general questions; Periodicals; and subject divisions of the Secretariat). 3 indexes: official number, sales number and subject. 'A comprehensive checklist and index' (*RQ,* v.16(3), Spring 1977, p.253). *Class No:* 341.121(01)

[2906]
—GHÉBALI, V.Y. *and* GHÉBALI, C., *comps. & eds.* A Repertoire of League of Nations serial documents, 1919-1947. Dobbs Ferry, N.Y., Oceana, 1973. 2v. (773p.). $85. ISBN: 0379003716.

Complements the above. Limited to serial documents but does include publications not for sale, unnumbered series and commission, conference and Secretariat documents. *Class No:* 341.121(01)

Histories

[2907]
WALTERS, F.P. A History of the League of Nations. London, Oxford University Press, under the auspices of the Royal Institute of International Affairs, 1952 (Reprinted in one vol. in 1986 by Greenwood Press). xvi,833p. ISBN: 0313250561.

First published 1952 in 2v.

The standard work on the League of Nations. An objective account by a member of the Secretariat, 1919-40. 67 chapters, taking the narrative up to 1946. No bibliography, but a rather general appendix note on sources. Supported by a very good analytical index. *Class No:* 341.121(091)

United Nations

Encyclopaedias

[2908]
OSMÁNCZYK, E.J. The Encyclopedia of the United Nations and international relations. 3rd ed. Philadelphia; London, Taylor and Francis, 1998. xvii,1220p. £199. ISBN: 1560324120. *Class No:* 341.123(031)

Handbooks & Manuals

[2909]
The Encyclopaedia of the United Nations and international agreements. Osmánczyk, E.J. 2nd ed. London & Philadelphia, Taylor & Francis, 1985. xv, 1059p. £170. $295. ISBN: 0850668336.

First published 1974 in Polish (Warsaw); 2nd ed. in Spanish, 1976.

A compendium of political, economic and social information, including data on the structure of the United Nations; its specialised agencies, and the many intergovernmental and non-governmental organizations that co-operate with the UN. Over 7000 entries, more than half of them having short explanations of words or names; other entries comprise descriptions of all the States in the world, and vary in length from a third to a full page. Sources are given for most entries. Also includes 'World population statistics, 1985-2025'; a list of acronyms and abbreviations; a selective index (p.975-1046); and an index to agreements, conventions and treaties (p.1047-1059). '...continues to be a convenient one-stop source...' (*Booklist,* v.87(12), 15/2/91, p.1248). *Class No:* 341.123(035)

[2910]
RIGGS, R. *and* PLANO, J. *and* ZIRINA, L. The United Nations: international organization and world politics. 2nd edition. Harcourt College Publishers, 1999. 560p. £19.95. ISBN: 0155078658.

Covers the history as well and the structure and procedures of the UN. This edition reflects the changes consequent upon the end of the cold war. It is objective in its approach, listing the UN's strengths and weaknesses - there is particularly good treatment of arms' control. The book also discusses the nature of international organisations as such. There are many charts and tables in the text, which make the book much easier to understand. *Class No:* 341.123(035)

[2911]
UNITED NATIONS. Department of Public Information. Basic facts about the United Nations. New ed. New York, United Nations, 1998. 348p. £7.50. $10. ISBN: 9211007933.

8 chapters: 1. Origins of the United Nations; 2. Organization of the United Nations; 3. International peace and security; 4. Economic and social development; 5. Human rights and humanitarian assistance; 6. Decolonization; 7. International law; 8. Intergovernmental agencies related to the United Nations. Appendices include 'For further reading' and index. *Class No:* 341.123(035)

Histories

[2912]
A Chronology and fact book of the United Nations, 1941-1991.
Hovet, T. *and* Trover, E.L. 8th ed. by Kumiko Matsuura and others.
Dobbs Ferry, N.Y.. Oceana, 1992. 598p. $75.00. (*Annual review of United Nations affairs series*.) ISBN: 0379212005.
4th ed. published 1976, covering 1941-1976.
A chronology with subject index list of members of UN organs and agencies, and texts of the Charter and of the General Assembly's rules of procedure. 'An indispensable starting point for research on UN activities and organization' (*International affairs*, April 1977, p.335, of the 4th ed). *Class No:* 341.123(091)

[2913]
Everyone's United Nations a handbook on the work of the United Nations. 10th ed. New York, United Nations Department of Public Information, 1986. [6],484p. $14.95. ISBN: 9211002737.
First published in 1948 as *Everyman's United Nations*.
Exposition of the work of the U.N. and its associated 18 intergovernmental agencies in 9 chapters: 1. The organization - 2. Peacemaking - 3. Peace-keeping - 4. Disarmament - 5. Economic and social development - 6. Human rights - 7. Decolonization - 8. International law - 9. Intergovernmental organizations. U.N. Charter p.429-50. Statutes of the International Court of Justice p.451-461. Universal Declaration of Human Rights p.462-6. Index, p.467-484.
Class No: 341.123(091)

[2914]
LUARD, E. A History of the United Nations. London, Macmillan Press, 1982-. v.1:£35; v.2: £45. ISBN: 0333243897, v.1; 0333244249, v.2.
V.1. *The years of Western domination, 1945-1955* (1982. 416p.); v.2. *The age of decolonization, 1955-1965* (1989. 592p.). V.1 is a critical account of the planning and setting up of the UN and of its responses to the various problems with which it found itself confronted during the first 10 years. V.2 deals with the period when the UN was involved with major crises throughout the world, and includes four of its peace-keeping operations. *Class No:* 341.123(091)

Official Records

Bibliographies

[2915]
UNDOC: current index. United Nations documents index. New York, and Geneva, United Nations Publications, 1979-. v.1, no.1/2-. Quarterly, with annual cumulations on microfiche. $150 for complete service. ISSN: 02505584.
Comprehensive coverage of UN documentation, including full bibliographical descriptions. Subject, author and title indexes. Also a check-list of new UN documents received at headquarters.
Class No: 341.123(093.2)(01)

Unesco

Bibliographies

[2916]
UNESCO. Bibliography of publications issued by Unesco or under its auspices (1946-1971). Paris, Unesco, 1973. xviii,385p. F.30. ISBN: 9230010375.
Over 5000 entries for books and journals, grouped by subjects. Coverage: 1946 to the end of 1971. *Class No:* 341.16(01)

[2917]
—**UNESCO. Unesco publishing catalogue, 1993.** Paris, Unesco, 1993. 162p. illus. *Gratis.*
Published annually.
Sections: Books - Periodicals - Electronic publishing - Publications of Unesco's regional offices. Alphabetical index and price list of titles in English, French and Spanish (p.129-143). *Class No:* 341.16(01)

[2918]
—**Unesco lists of documents and publications, 1972/76-.** Paris, Unesco, 1979-.
Published every three years. 1987/89 volume was published in 1993 (ISBN 9230028401).
Each is issued in 2 volumes: 1. Annotated list of documents and publications; 2. subject index; personal name index; conference index.
Class No: 341.16(01)

European Community

[2919]
CENTRE FOR EUROPEAN POLICY STUDIES. Annual review of European Community affairs, 1992. First issued for 1990. Annual. London, Brassey's (UK) Ltd., 1992. 475p. £40. ISSN: 09623868.
Aims to provide EC specialists, students and general readers with a comprehensive and authoritative account of EC developments.
Class No: 341.174

[2920]
The European Communities encyclopedia and directory, 1992. London, Europa, 1991. (distributed in US and Canada by Gale Research Ltd.). xix,390p. tables. £155; $325. ISBN: 0946653658.
In 4 parts: 1 has information on the European Communities, arranged A-Z, covering personalities, politics, programmes, reports and committees, acronyms, catch terms and phrases, etc. Pt.2 is a collection of essays by British academics on the political, legal, and social activities of the EC. Pt.3 is a detailed statistical survey. Pt.4 is a directory of EC institutions, including MEPs. Appendices summarize 3 original treaties, list measures involved in the implementation of the internal market, and give information on EC databases.
Class No: 341.174

[2921]
The European Community 1992: annual review of activities. Nugent, N., *ed*. Annual. In *Journal of Common Market studies*, v.31, 1993, p.1-163.
Includes a bibliography. *Class No:* 341.174

Abbreviations & Symbols

[2922]
RAMSAY, A. Eurojargon a dictionary of European Union acronyms, abbreviations and soubriquets. 5th ed. Stamford, Capital Planning Information, 1997. x,227p. 24.50. ISBN: 1898869308.
Arrangement is A-Z by acronyms, etc., with 'see' references. Bibliography. *Class No:* 341.174(003)

Databases

[2923]
HANSON, T. Directory of European Community and related databases. European Information Association, 1991 (available from Barbara Vickery, University of Nottingham Library, NG72RD). 78p. ISBN: 0948272244.
Introduction is followed by database records (p.3-69); index by database category; and index by host of distributor. Bibliography, p.77-8 *Class No:* 341.174(003.4)

Bibliographies

[2924]
JEFFRIES, J. A Guide to the official publications of the European Communities. 2nd ed. London, Mansell, 1981. xiv,i, 318p. £21; $36. ISBN: 0720115960.
First published 1978.
10 sections: 1, Introduction - 2. Publications of the European Communities - 3. Commission: general publications (*e.g.* Official journal; Treaties) - 4. Commission; non-statistical publications - 5. Eurostat - 6. Council of Ministers - 7. European Parliament - 8. Court of Justice of the European Communities - 9. Other bodies - 10. Bibliographic aids (*e.g., Euro abstracts; European bibliography*). 3 appendices (2. European documentation centre and depository libraries; 3 Further reading on the European Communities, p284-7. Detailed, analytical index. Includes titles up to the end of 1979. Attractively produced. A historical volume is *Reports of the European Communities, 1952-1977:* an index to authors and chairmen; compiled by June Neilson (London, Mansell, 1981. 576p. £35. ISBN 0720115922). (qv). *Class No:* 341.174(01)

[2925]
RAMSAY, A. European Union information. 2nd ed., fully revised and expanded. Halifax, Association of Assistant Librarians, 1997. 69p. £13. ISBN: 1901353052. *Class No:* 341.174(01)

[2926]
THOMSON, I. The Documentation of the European Communities: a guide. London, Mansell Publishing, 1989. 396p. £35; $60. ISBN: 0720120225.
Describes the many publicly available printed documents, many in series, that emanate from the Community. Also information on the structure of all its institutions. Appendices cover such topics as EEC online databases, EC information centres, and depository libraries.
Class No: 341.174(01)

Encyclopaedias

[2927]
DINAN, D., *ed*. Encyclopedia of the European Union. L. Rienner, 1998. 565p. $110. ISBN: 155587634x.
The entries cover "concepts, issues, developments, institutions, policies, events, negotiations, treaties, national interests, and personalities related to European integration." There are about 700 entries; larger entries are signed, some with bibliographies. Extensive cross references and a comprehensive index. *Class No:* 341.174(031)

[2928]
Encyclopedia of European Community law. Simmonds, K.R., *ed.*
London, Sweet & Maxwell, 1973-. 3v.(loose-leaf). V.A: £335; V.B:
£480; V.C: £990. ISBN: 0421193506, v.A; 0421193603, v.B;
0421207604, v.C.

Vol. A: United Kingdom sources (2 loose-leaf binders); v.B:
European Community treaties (3 loose-leaf binders); v.C: Community
Secondary legislation (7 loose-leaf binders). Text, with commentary in
smaller type; definitions. Brief bibliographies. Kept up-to-date with
amendments.

Secondary legislation (regulations, directories, decisions,
recommendations and opinions made by the Council of the European
Communities) is published in *Official journal of the European
Communities). Class No:* 341.174(031)

[2929]
Oxford encyclopaedia of European Community law. Oxford,
Clarendon Press, 1990-. To be in 3v. V.1:xcviii,550p. £75. ISBN:
0198255896.

V.1, *Institutional law*, has over 300 concise and lucid entries, A-Z,
each explaining a particular concept or point of law, fully documented
with case and treaty references. Also suggestions for further reading.
Class No: 341.174(031)

Handbooks & Manuals

[2930]
COE, A. *and* FURLONG, P. A Modern companion to the European
Community: a guide to key facts, institutions and terms. Aldershot,
Hants, Edward Elgar, 1992. 327p. £35. ISBN: 1852785160.

Includes a brief historical overview of the development of the EC
and a description of the major Directorates and policy making
functions. Also included are basic statistics on population, GNP, trade
performance, and the economic potential of each member country; and
explanations of over 1000 commonly used acronyms and
abbreviations. *Class No:* 341.174(035)

[2931]
LEONARD, D. Pocket guide to the European Community. Oxford,
Basil Blackwell Ltd; London, Economist Publications, 1988. xiii,210p.
tables, graphs. £15; $29.95. ISBN: 0631162844.

An introduction to the history, institutions and functions of the
European Community. 4 sections: The background - The institutions -
The competances - Special problems. Cross-references. 8 appendices
(1. Basic statistics of member states; 2. Presidents of the High
Authority and the Community; 5. Elections to the European
Parliament; 7. The single European Act; 9. Eurojargon). Suggestions
for further reading, p.201-202. Index, p.203-210.
Class No: 341.174(035)

[2932]
MATHIJSEN, P.S.R.F. A Guide to European Union law. 7th ed.
London, Sweet & Maxwell, 1999. 588 p. £26. ISBN: 0421635002.
Includes bibliographies. *Class No:* 341.174(035)

Dictionaries

[2933]
DINAN, D. Historical dictionary of the European Community.
Metuchen, NJ, Scarecrow Press, 1993. 319p. charts, maps. $37.50.
(*(International organizations)*.) ISBN: 0810826666.

160 brief descriptive and analytical entries on politicians, statesmen,
events and organizations in the history of the European Community.
Includes short pieces on each member state, but 25% of the entries are
biographical, with emphasis on how individuals influenced the EC's
development. Each entry has 250-300 or more words. Cross-
references. Lengthy introduction precedes. Classified bibliography lists
monographs and official documents. Detailed chronology; 20p. of
tables and graphs; and 5 political maps complete the dictionary.
Class No: 341.174(038)

[2934]
PARKER, G. *and* PARKER, B. A Dictionary of the European
Communities. London, Butterworth, 1981. [4], 84p. ISBN:
0408107332.

Concise definitions of terms relating to the European Communities,
covering institutions, policies and people, as well as including many
miscellaneous terms in common use. Cross-references. Reading list of
13 items. *Class No:* 341.174(038)

[2935]
PAXTON, J., *ed.* A Dictionary of the European Communities. 2nd
ed. London, Macmillan Press, 1982. 240p. £25. ISBN: 0333334388.

First published in 1977 as *A dictionary of the European Economic
Community*.

Entries A.A.S.M. ... Zollverein. Lengthier articles (*e.g.* 'Rome,
Treaty of' p.219-221) are sectionalised. That on 'Referendum, United
Kingdom', p.222-226, has detailed breakdown by counties of voting.
Includes brief biographies, and abbreviations. Cross-references, *e.g.*
from French terms to English. Select bibliography (grouped), p.279-
282. A handy quick-reference tool. *Class No:* 341.174(038)

Polyglot

[2936]
EUROPEAN COMMUNITIES. Council. Multilingual glossary of
abbreviations. 2nd ed. Luxembourg, Office for Official Publications
of the European Communities, 1982. xxxii,589p. £10.30. ECU 18.62.
First published 1980.

A glossary in 6 languages (French/German/English/Italian/Dutch/
Danish) containing *c.*8000 multilingual entries, plus their
abbreviations, on the internal and external activities of the European
Community. Includes technical terms, concepts, international bodies
and Community institutions. *Class No:* 341.174(038)=00

Reports Literature

[2937]
NEILSON, J., *comp.* Reports of the European Communities, 1952-
1977: an index to authors and chairmen. London, Mansell
Publishing, 1981. xiv, 561p. £27.50. ISBN: 0720115922.

Author index with over 2200 entries, A-Z, with full bibliographical
details. English and/or French translations of titles. Coverage is to the
end of 1977. Detailed subject index, p.503-561, refers to numbered
entries in the author (and chairmen) index. *Class No:* 341.174(047)

Periodicals & Progress Reports

[2938]
European access, February 1989-. Cambridge, Chadwick-Healey; in
association with the United Kingdom Offices of the European
Commission, 1989-. Bi-monthly. £110pa. ISSN: 02647362.

A current awareness guide to the development, activities and policies
of the European Communities. 1989(2), April issue has 119p. and
contains: Chronology of events in the European Community - The
European Parliament in election year - Commentary - Education and R
& D funding news - European Community information developments -
Documentation of the European Communities - Bibliographic review -
Recent references (brief entries) - Alphabetical list of subject headings
- List of useful addresses. *Class No:* 341.174(05)

Yearbooks & Directories

[2939]
The Europe 1992 directory: a research and information guide. London,
HMSO, for the Information Technology Consultancy Unit, Coventry
Polytechnic, 1992. 97p. £10.95.
First published 1989.

Sections: Glossary - Organizations - Principal Community
documents - Books, monographs, pamphlets - Journals (including list
of major articles on 1992), periodicals, magazines - Speeches (on
1992) - Research and training programmes - Databases for 1992 -
Audio-visual material - Management consultancies - Legal
consultancies - European documentation centres in the UK - Who's
who in the European Commission. Index. *Class No:* 341.174(058)

[2940]
EUROPEAN COMMUNITIES. Commission. Directory of the
Commission of the European Communities (September 1988).
Luxembourg, Office for Official Publications of the European
Community, 1988. 132p. ECU 3.50 £2.50.

A directory of the services and key personnel of the Commission.
Class No: 341.174(058)

[2941]
MARTENS, H. EC direct: a comprehensive directory of EC contacts.
Oxford, Blackwell, 1992. xiv,230p. $34.95. ISBN: 0631187960.

A handbook for companies interested in the European Community
and in the EC Commission. 12 chapters, all subdivided: 1.
Introduction: the single market - 2. The EC Commission: institutions
and persons - 3. Other EC institutions to contact ... 5. Private
organizations ... 8. Financial support and grants - 9. Databases - 10.
Economic data for EC countries ... 12. Glossary of terms and
abbreviations. Further reading, p.204. Index, p.205-19. Name index,
p.220-30. *Class No:* 341.174(058)

Tables & Data Books

Bibliographies

[2942]
EUROPEAN COMMUNITIES. Statistical Office. **Eurostat catalogue: publications and electronic services.** Luxembourg, the Office. Annual. *Gratis.*

Lists each title with bibliographical details and a brief description of contents. *Class No:* 341.174(083)(01)

Maps & Atlases

[2943]
HUDSON, R., *and others*. **An Atlas of EEC affairs.** London, Methuen, 1984. xiv,158p. illus., maps, tables.

Account in 6 chapters of the Community's history, organizational structure, population, labour market, economic performance and resources, social conditions, and prospects for the year 2000 A.D. 'A most welcome contribution to a field in which little has been published' (*International affairs*, v.61,no.1, Winter 1984-85, p.189-190). *Class No:* 341.174(084.3)

Laws

[2944]
EUROPEAN COMMUNITIES. Commission. **Directory of Community legislation in force** and other Acts of the Community institutions (recompiled and updated every six months) - all institutions. 19th ed. Luxembourg, Office for Offical Publications of the European Communities, 1992. 2v. (1064p.). ECU 90. £64 for 2v.

V.1 Analytical register; v.2. Chronological index. Alphabetical index. Enables the user to find the current instruments of Community legislation. *Class No:* 341.174(094.1)

Asian Regional Organizations

Official Records

[2945]
HAAS, M., *ed.* **Basic documents of Asian regional organizations.** Dobbs Ferry, N.Y. Oceana, 1974-85. 9v. v.1-8: $47.50 each; v.9: $50. Set: $430. ISBN: 0379001772.

V.1-7 are concerned with documentary history of international organizations with headquarters in Asia. V.8 has analytical treatment of the history, structure and functioning of the various Asian intergovernmental organizations. V.9 puts the data available from the preceding 8v. into a format to facilitate comparisons. *Class No:* 341.175(093.2)

African Regional Organizations

Official Records

[2946]
SOHN, L.B., *ed.* **Basic documents of African regional organizations.** Dobbs Ferry, N.Y., Oceana, for the Inter-American Institute of International Legal Studies, 1971-73. 4v. $190 the set. ISBN: 0379003619.

Texts of constitutions and other relevant documents, backed by bibliographies of books, periodical articles and documents. Main subdivisions: Organization of African Unity - African Development Bank - Regional groups in French-speaking Africa - Regional co-operation in West Africa - Maghreb Permanent Consultative Committee - East African organizations - Association of African States with the European Community. *Class No:* 341.176(093.2)

Frontiers

[2947]
DAY, A.J. **Border and territorial disputes.** 3rd ed. Harlow, Essex, Longman Group, 1992. (distributed in US and Canada by Gale Research Co.). x, 562p. 67 maps. £135 $245. (*Keesing's reference publication*.) ISBN: 0582209315, UK.

First published 1982.

Details of some 84 contemporary border and territorial disputes throughout the world. Coverage is limited to land-based disputes which are of territorial and/or political significance and involve contentious territorial claims by one nation against another. In five sections: Europe; Africa; Middle East; Asia and Far East; The Americas and Antarctica. Comprehensive index and a select bibliography. Noteworthy for "its lengthy in-depth explanations of each dispute's history, significant efforts and resolution, legal bases, etc. (*Wilson library bulletin*, V.67(8), April 1993, p.118). *Class No:* 341.222

[2948]
DOWNING, D. **An Atlas of territorial and border disputes.** London, New English Library, 1980. 121p. £7.95. ISBN: 0450048047.

30 maps arranged by region (Asia, the Middle East, Africa, the Americas, Europe). Examines, in textual and cartographic form the border disputes most likely to disturb the local or the international peace in the 1980s. Bibliography, p.116. Index, p.119-120. *Class No:* 341.222

[2949]
PRESCOTT, J.R.V. **The Maritime political boundaries of the world.** London, Methuen, 1985. xv,[1],377p. tables, diagrs. £35. ISBN: 0416417507.

14 chapters, each with conclusions and references: 1. Political geography of the oceans - 2. The physical nature of oceans and coasts - 3. National maritime claims - 4. International maritime boundaries - 5. International maritime zones - 6-14. on individual oceans and seas. Suggested reading list p.355-360, by chapter subject. Glossary, p.361-366. Name index, p.367-368; analytical subject index, p.369-377. *Class No:* 341.222

Africa

[2950]
BROWNLIE, L. *and* BURNS, I.R. **African boundaries:** a legal and diplomatic encyclopaedia. London, C. Hurst; Berkeley & Los Angeles, University of California Press, for the Royal Institute of International Affairs, 1979. xxvi, 1355p. 8 maps. £70. ISBN: 0903983877.

5 parts: 1. States of the Mediterranean littoral (15 boundaries) - 2. States of West Africa and the Western Sahara (28) - 3. The succession States of French Equatorial Africa, with Cameroun, Equatorial Guinea and Zaire (24) - 4. Sudan, Ethiopia, Somalia and East Africa (18) - 5. Southern Africa, including Angola, Zambia, Malawi and Mozambique (20). Rhodesia (Zimbabwe) - Zambia: p.1304-12 (General provenance; Alignment; Evidence, including Schedule; Current issues; Bibliography of 19 items). At least one sketch map accompanies each separate alignment; plus 8 other maps. Introduction concludes with a 'Select general bibliography', p.22-24. *Class No:* 341.222(6)

Law of the Sea

[2951]
Maritime affairs: a world handbook. Gold, E., *ed.* 2nd ed. Harlow, Essex, Longman, 1991. xxv,479p. £95. ISBN: 0582086930.

First published 1985, edited by H.W.Degenhardt.

A reference guide for modern ocean policy and management. 14 chapters: 1. Maritime affairs: the setting; 2. The modern law of the sea; 3. Maritime organizations and institutions...10. The coastal zone; 11. The Polar areas...13. The resolution of maritime disputes; 14. Maritime education and training. Appendices: A. United Nations Convention on the Law of the Sea; C. Selected maritime periodicals listing; D. Selected maritime reference bibliography. Index, p.471-9. *Class No:* 341.225

[2952]
WANG, J.C. **Handbook on ocean politics and law.** Westport, CT. & London, Greenwood Press, 1992. 592p. tables, charts, maps. $95. £85. ISBN: 0313264341.

A comprehensive work, with chapters surveying physical aspects of the oceans, international conferences on the law of the sea, living and non-living resources (with their economic and political management, environmental protection and pollution, military uses, navigation and transport, and marine scientific research. The author expresses his own opinion and summarizes those of others. Each chapter has bibliographical references and there is also a select bibliography. 7 appendices. Index. *Class No:* 341.225

Bibliographies

[2953]
The Law of the Sea: a selected bibliography, 1991. Annual. United Nations. Office for Ocean Affairs and the Law of the Sea. New York, United Nations, 1993. 61p. £15. ISBN: 9211334519.

Divided into 22 subject categories based mainly on the major topics in the United Nations Convention on the Law of the Sea. Author index. *Class No:* 341.225(01)

[2954]
—UNITED NATIONS. Office for Ocean Affairs and the Law of the Sea. **The Law of the Sea:** a bibliography on the law of the sea, 1968-1988: two decades of lawmaking, state practice and doctrine. New York, United Nations, 1991. 472p. $25. ISBN: 9210330684. *Class No:* 341.225(01)

[2955]

PAPPADAKIS, N. *and* GLASSNER, M., *eds*. **International law of the sea and marine affairs:** a bibliography. The Hague, Martinus Nijhoff, 1984. xxvi,579p. £88.95. ISBN: 9024728150.

Arranged in 9 sections: I. Introduction - the marine environment and the Law of the Sea - II. Maritime zones and maritime jurisdiction - III. The legal regime of the sea bed ... - IV. Main resources - V. Protection and preservation of the marine environment - VI. Marine scientific research - VII. Military uses and arms control - VIII. Ocean policy making - IX. Settlement of disputes. 2 appendices (1. Bibliographies, reference works, indexes, directories, dictionaries and guides to documents on the Law of the Sea and marine affairs, p.491-499 (343 items); 2. List of journals and periodical publications consulted). Author index. Index to documents, etc.
Class No: 341.225(01)

Dictionaries

Russian

[2956]

ZHELTOV, L.M. *and* KNIAZEV, V.S. **Anglo-russkii i russko-angliiskii slovar po morskomu pravu/English-Russian and Russian-English law of the sea dictionary.** Moskva, Voen, 1988. 207p. Rub.1.80. *Class No:* 341.225(038)=82

Independence of Nations

Official Records

[2957]

BLAUSTEIN, A.P., *and others, comps*. **Independence documents of the world.** Dobbs Ferry, N.Y., Oceana, 1977. 2v. $85. ISBN: 0379007940, v.1; 0379007959, v.2.

Texts, mostly in full and all translated into English, of documents covering 150 of some 160 nations of the world; introductory brief political histories. 'An excellent compilation' (*Choice*, v.14(12), February 1978, p.1624). *Class No:* 341.231(093.2)

Alliances & Treaties

[2958]

BOWMAN, M.J. *and* HARRIS, D.J., *eds*. **Multilateral treaties:** index and current status. London, Butterworth, 1984. 516p. £60.

An index to more than 800 of the most important multilateral treaties, relating to both public and private international law, that were concluded between 1856 and June 1983. Listing is in chronological order. Information in each entry includes entry into force, duration, signatories, parties, territorial scope, reservations, amendments, authentic texts, and sources of publication. Cross-references. Subject and word indexes. *Class No:* 341.232/.24

[2959]

MILLER, T.B., *ed*. **Current international treaties.** London, Croom Helm, 1984. [9],558p. £35. ISBN: 0709917589.

'... attempt to bring together in a single volume the texts of the main bilateral and multilateral treaties which form the legal skeleton of so much of current international relations ...' (*Preface*). Entries broadly grouped by subject (The convention of international diplomacy - Global political institutions - Economic treaties - Regional agreements - The control of nuclear weapons - Security treaties - Human rights), each group subdivided. Preambles and less essential clauses usually omitted and commentary kept to a minimum. 2 appendices: A. Signatories to multilateral instruments in this volume; B. Bilateral treaties in this volume. Index, p.553-558. 'Chief deficiency is omission of date and place of signatures' (*International affairs*, v.61(1), Winter 1984/85). *Class No:* 341.232/.24

[2960]

UNITED NATIONS. **Treaty series: treaties and international agreements registered or filed and recorded with the Secretariat of the United Nations ... 1946/47-.** New York, United Nations, 1947-.v.1-. ISSN: 03798267.

Texts are in the original languages, with English and French translations. Cumulative indexes are produced from time to time (v.1-100, 101-200...) comprising chronological and subject indexes. *Class No:* 341.232/.24

[2961]

—Multinational treaties deposited with the Secretary-General as at 31 December 1985. New York, United Nations, 1986. xxiv. 871p. $60 £60. (*ST/LEG/SER.E/4*.) ISBN: 9211332931.

Lists 833 treaties in chronological order, concluded from 1856.
Class No: 341.232/.24

Handbooks & Manuals

[2962]

REUTER, P. **Introduction to the law of treaties.** London, Kegan Paul, 1995. xviii,296p. £75. ISBN: 0710305028.

Originally a publication of the Graduate Institute of International Studies, Geneva. 1st French ed. published by Armond Colin, 1972. Translated by José Mico and Peter Haggenmacher.

In-depth treatment of the subject in 4 chapters, all subdivided: 1. Treaties (1. Historical aspects - 2. Fundamental legal aspects - 3. Definition and classification of international treaties - 4. Work on international treaties); 2. Conclusion, entry into foreign participation; 3. The effects of treaties; 4. Non-application of treaties.
Class No: 341.232/.24(035)

Dictionaries

Polyglot

[2963]

EUROPEAN COMMUNITIES. Commission. **European treaty vocabulary.** 2nd ed. Brussels, the Commission, 1983. 414p. £13.50.

French - German - English - Italian - Dutch - Danish. Indexes in each language. *Class No:* 341.232/.24(038)=00

Histories

[2964]

HARVARD UNIVERSITY. Law School. Library. **Index to multilateral treaties:** a chronological list of multi-party international agreements, from the sixteenth century through 1963, with citations to the text. Mostecky, V. Dobbs Ferry, N.Y., Oceana, 1965. x,301p. $40.00. ISBN: 0379003848.

3859 numbered items, 1596-1963. Entries state number, date, subject and sources. 'Subject and regional guide' (p.253-301), listing each treaty under one or more of the following: topic, area (if regional), country or city, place of signature and date (if popularly known), name of person(s) instrumental in drafting, and name of international organization (in English), if the treaty is a charter, etc., of that organization. 'While the list is comprehensive for the period preceding 1960, it is necessarily incomplete for the most recent years because the texts of some treaties were not available in printed form at press time' (*Preface*). *Class No:* 341.232/.24(091)

[2965]

TOSCANO, M. **The History of treaties and international politics.** Baltimore, MD., Johns Hopkins Press, 1966. (Available from Books Demand UMI). xv,[1],685p. $160. ISBN: 0317423592.

English translations of *Storia dei trattati e politica internazione. I, Parte generale* (Turin, Giappichelli, 1963), expanded edition of *Lezioni di storia dei trattati e politica internazionale. I, Parte generale* (Turin, Giappichelli, 1958).

An indispensable, evaluative guide to the source material of 20th-century international history. Particularly valuable, states *International affairs* (v.43(3), July 1967, p.537) on documents on the literature of World Wars I and II and memoir sources for the two wars. 'The Italian side understandably receives great emphasis'. *Class No:* 341.232/.24(091)

Official Records

[2966]

The Consolidated treaty series, 1648-1918: annotated. Parry, C., *ed*. Dobbs Ferry, N.Y., Oceana Publications, 1970-77. 243v. in 12v. indexed set. $11,000 the set. ISBN: 0379130009.

Extends from the Peace of Westphalia (1648) to the beginning of the League of Nations. Texts of treaties in original languages, plus English or French translations/summaries. Some annotations. Arranged chronologically. *Class No:* 341.232/.24(093.2)

Great Britain

[2967]

GREAT BRITAIN. Foreign and Commonwealth Office. **British and foreign state papers,** with which is incorporated [in v.116-157] Hertslet's Commercial treaties. London, Ridgway (then HMSO), 1841-1976. 170v.

v.1.(1841) covered 1812-14; v.169 (1976) covered 1967-68 v.170: index to v.166-169. This completes the series.

Items are arranged chronologically and consist of texts of agreements, treaties to which Great Britain was a partner. Orders in Council, appropriate Acts of Parliament (*e.g.* European Payments Union (Financial provisions), letters patent, etc.). Chronological index precedes. Subject and country indexes per volume and interim-cumulative (*e.g.* v.65 is index to v.139-164). An important source. *Class No:* 341.232/.24(410)

[2968]
GREAT BRITAIN. Foreign Office. **Treaty series, 1892-.** London, HMSO, 1892-. Annual.

Treaties to which the United Kingdom is a party and which have come into force are published as Command Papers in a special series. They have their Command number and their Treaty series number (beginning with no.1. each year). They are published individually as presented to Parliament. Many treaties are published as Command Papers outside the Treaty series when concluded but before they have come into force; when they have come into force, they are again published in the Treaty series with a different Command number. *Class No: 341.232/.24(410)*

[2969]
PARRY, C. *and* HOPKINS, C., *comps*. **An Index of British Treaties, 1101-1968.** Harris, D.J. *and* Shepherd, J.A. London, HMSO, 1970-1992. 4v. ISBN: 0115916814.

Compiled and annotated under the auspices of the International Law Fund and the British Institute of International and Comparative Law. V.1. contains the index of multilateral treaties by subjects; index of bilateral treaties by country, etc,; and index of bilateral treaties by subjects. V.2. Chronological list of treaties, 1101 - 1925. V.3. Chronological list of treaties, 1926 - 1968. V.4. Consolidated index to treaty series of the UK and other treaty series. Dates of entry into force and Command Paper number are given in V. 2-3. *Class No: 341.232/.24(410)*

[2970]
—GREAT BRITAIN. Foreign and Commonwealth Office. **Index to treaty series.** London, HMSO.

Continues the series of treaty indexes listed in HMSO's *Sectional list No.7: Treaty series, 1910-1962* The Index for 1992 (1993) was issued as Cm.2352 (£4.50. ISBN 0101235224). *Class No: 341.232/.24(410)*

USA

[2971]
KAVASS, I.I. *and* SPRUDZS, A. **A Guide to the United States treaties in force.** Buffalo, N.Y., W.S. Hein, 1992. 2v. $142.50. ISBN: 0685573419, v.1; 089941768x, v.2.

V.1. Numerical list of bilateral and multilateral treaties and agreements of the United States in force; v.2 Multilateral treaties and other agreements. 'May stand alone as handy reference but will be most useful as a complement to *Treaties in force* (1983), the standard Department of State list of agreements still in effect' (*Choice*, v.22(3), November 1984, p.402-3) of an earlier edition. *Class No: 341.232/.24(73)*

19th Century

[2972]
HURST, M., *ed*. **Key treaties for the Great Powers, 1814-1914.** Newton Abbot, Devon, David & Charles, 1972. 2v. (948p.).

Provides the text of 194 documents. Analytical index, p.918-948. *Class No: 341.232/.24"18"*

20th Century

[2973]
GRENVILLE, J.A.S. **The Major international treaties, 1914-1945** a history and guide with texts. London, Methuen, 1987. xviii,268p. 4 maps. £40. ISBN: 0416080928.

Supersedes, in part, Grenville's *The major international treaties, 1914-1973* ... (1974).

An introduction is followed by 10 chapters: 1. Secret agreements and treaties of the first world war - 2. The peace settlements and the League of Nations - 3. France, Britain, Italy and Germany, 1921-33 - 4. France and the eastern allies, 1921-39 - 5. The Soviet Union and her neighbours, 1919-37 - 6. The collapse of the territorial settlements of Versailles, 1931-8 - 7. From peace to world war in Europe and Asia, 1937-41 - 8. The Grand Alliance: Britain and the United States and the Soviet Union, 1941-45 - 9. The Allied conferences and the political settlement of Europe, 1943-5 - 10. The alliance and alignments of the United States from the League of Nations to the United Nations. Source references for the principal treaties, p.256-261. Analytical index, p.263-268. *Class No: 341.232/.24"19"*

[2974]
—GRENVILLE, J.A.S. *and* WASSERSTEIN, B. **The Major international treaties since 1945:** a history and guide with texts. London, Methuen, 1987. xiv,528p. £50; $85. ISBN: 0416380808.

Supersedes, in part, J.A.S. Grenville's *The major international treaties, 1914-1973* ... (1974).

An introduction on international treaties is followed by 10 chapters: 1. The foundations of post-war diplomacy - 2. The United States treaty system - 3. The Soviet treaty system - 4. The German question - 5. West European integration - 6. South and East Asia and the Pacific - 7. Africa - 8. The Middle East and East Mediterranean - 9. Latin America and the South Atlantic - 10. Détente and arms control.

....(contd.)
Appendix: Multilateral treaties on human rights and the environment. Sources for treaty texts, p.500-506. Analytical index, p.507-528. *Class No: 341.232/.24"19"*

[2975]
LEAGUE OF NATIONS. **Treaty series:** publications of treaties and international engagements registered with the Secretariat of the League. Geneva, League of Nations; London, Harrison, 1920-46. (Reprinted Dobbs Ferry, NY., Oceana, 1970). 9v. *Class No: 341.232/.24"19"*

[2976]
ROHN, P.H. **World treaty index.** 2nd ed. Santa Barbara, CA., ABC-Clio, 1984. 5v.(4271p.). $999 the set. ISBN: 0874361419.

First published 1975 in 6v.

V.1 Reference volume - 2. Main entry section, 1900-1959 - 3. Main entry section, 1960-1980 - 4. Keyword index - 5. Party index. Information includes: Type of agreement; date signed; registered; articles; language; head note; topic; concepts; parties (countries). *Class No: 341.232/.24"19"*

Aid & Development

Abbreviations & Symbols

[2977]
CARROLL, M., *comp*. **Acronyms relating to international development/Liste de sigles en développement international/Sigles relacionadas con desarrollo internacional.** Ottawa, International Development Research Centre, 1980. (Available from Unipub). 162p. $9.50. ISBN: 0839362084.

About 1500 entries (AAACU ... ZPG) giving abbreviations, full name, place and country. *Class No: 341.232(003)*

Dictionaries

[2978]
GREAT BRITAIN. Overseas Development Administration. **ABC of aid and development:** some terms and institutions. 4th rev. ed. London, ODA, 1986. 100p. Gratis.

First published 1971.

About 320 terms are defined, with background information, (*e.g.* 'Inter American Development Bank (IDB)': 2/3p.). 'Aims to explain as simply as possible phrases, terms and organizations commonly referred to by those who are involved in overseas aid and development' (*Preface*). Cross-references. Abbreviations, p.5-13). *Class No: 341.232(038)*

Yearbooks & Directories

[2979]
Development aid: a guide to national and international agencies. Sevenoaks, Kent, Butterworths; Newbury, Berks, Eurofi, 1988. [22],583p. 55. ISBN: 0408009918.

Listings of agencies providing aid for development. In two sections: 1. International agencies - 2. National agencies, arranged by continent, subdivided by countries, A-Z. For each entry: executive summary, followed by precise details of the nature and scope of the funding available. Includes addresses, telephone and telex numbers. *Class No: 341.232(058)*

Great Britain

Yearbooks & Directories

[2980]
Development guide: a directory of non-commercial organisations in Britain entirely concerned in overseas development and training. 3rd ed. London, Overseas Development Institute; Hemel Hempstead, Herts, Allen & Unwin, 1978. ix,216p. £10. ISBN: 0043600476.

First published 1962.

200 organizations (Action in Distress (AID) ... Young Women's Christian Association (YWCA) of Great Britain), p.3-202 - 1 per page. Data: name and address; aims; number of members; research; education; training; information and advice; publications; when founded; how financed; name of president. 'Overseas sources of information; (countries, A-Z), p.205-8. Index (partly analytical). *Class No: 341.232(410)(058)*

Atlantic Alliance

[2981]

The North Atlantic Treaty Organisation: facts and figures. llth ed., fully rev. & re-set with new graphics & an extended alphabetical index. Brussels, NATO Information Service, 1989. xii,575p. ISBN: 9284500419.

First published 1955 under title *NATO: the first five years*; 10th ed., 1981.

Includes an index and bibliographical references.
Class No: 341.232.1

Bibliographies

[2982]

GORDON, C. The Atlantic Alliance: a bibliography. London, Frances Pinter, 1978. 216p. £20. ISBN: 0903804328.

About 3000 references, drawn from British, Canadian, US, Scandinavian and Soviet sources. General bibliographical introduction (background material, p.11-15). 4 sections: 1. The genesis of the Alliance, 1945-1955; 2. The years of strain and stress, 1955-1962; 3. The search for a *modus vivendi*, 1962-1970; 4. The onset of *Détente*, 1970-1977 (books; economic and social aspects; legal aspects; industrial aspects; national and regional aspects; politico-military aspects; military-strategic aspects; reports, papers and pamphlets are similarly divided). Each of the 4 sections has an introduction.
Class No: 341.232.1(01)

[2983]

NORTON, A.R., *and others*. NATO: a bibliography and resource guide. New York, Garland, 1985. xiii,252p. $50. ISBN: 0824093313.

A general section, with entries arranged chronologically in 5-year periods to 1979, then 1980-81, is followed by entries for member states (A-Z), 'Issues in NATO'. 'Doctrines, strategies and military issues', 'Alliance politics', and 'Warsaw Pact'. No annotations. Index, p.227-252. *Class No:* 341.232.1(01)

Handbooks & Manuals

[2984]

Jane's NATO handbook, 1991/92. George, B., *ed*. Coulsdon, Surrey, Jane's Information Group, 1991. 450p. £125. ISBN: 0710609760.

Includes a chronology, directory of personalities, and documentation section. '...constitutes an all-embracing NATO scrapbook' (*The RUSI journal*, Spring 1990, p.84). *Class No:* 341.232.1(035)

International Court of Justice

Bibliographies

[2985]

INTERNATIONAL COURT OF JUSTICE. Library. Bibliographie de la Cour ... Bibliography of the International Court of Justice. The Hague, International Court of Justice, 1947-. No.1-.

A continuation of the lists published in chapter 9 of the *Yearbook* and *Annuaire* of the Court from 1946/47 to 1963/64, using the same grouping (sections A-L) and continuing numbering. Each annual issue has *c*.250 entries and profuse cross-references. Name and analytical subject indexes. (No.40, 1986, p.149-180, xxviip. £2.75. ISBN 0119097435). *Class No:* 341.646(01)

Yearbooks & Directories

[2986]

INTERNATIONAL COURT OF JUSTICE. Year book, 1987-88. No. 42. The Hague, the Court, 1989. xii,193p.

First published 1947. Annual.

Contains general information in 8 chapters on the organization, jurisdiction, activities and administration of the Court.
Class No: 341.646(058)

Disarmament

[2987]

MENOS, D., *comp*. Arms control fact book. Jefferson, N.C., McFarland, 1985. 140p. $15.95. ISBN: 0899501583.

According to the *Preface*, the aim is to help the general reader to understand the basic issues underlying arms control, its accomplishments to date, and the challenges for the future. The first half is a dictionary of frequently used terms in the arms control literature, each entry about half-page in length. There follows a directory, arranged A-Z, of selected national and international organizations active in arms control and disarmament. There is also a chronology of key arms control events. *RQ* (v.25(3), p.387) reports inconsistancies and incomplete indexing, but says there is no comparable work so it fills a definite need. *Class No:* 341.67

[2988]

—GAY, W. *and* PEARSON, M. The Nuclear arms race. Chicago, Ill., American Library Association, 1988. 270p. $29.95. (*Last quarter century, no.1*.) ISBN: 083890467x.

An overview of major issues (nuclear policies, nuclear war, arms control, deterrence, strategic theory, etc.). An annotated bibliography of books, articles, reports, etc., and a list of sources are included in each chapter. 'A comprehensive, well-conceived and well-organized sourcebook' (*Library journal*, v.113(7), April 1988, p.32-33).
Class No: 341.67

[2989]

The Nuclear almanac: confronting the atom in war and peace, edited by J. Dennis, Massachusetts Institute of Technology. Reading, Mass., Addison - Wesley, 1984. 546p. photos. tables. $35. ISBN: 0201053314.

A factual account of the discovery, development and use of nuclear energy, and a critical evaluation of possible issues raised by nuclear armaments and nuclear power. Signed essays are grouped under major headings: The history of nuclear weapons - The effects of nuclear weapons - Atomic warfare, its technologies and its consequences - International issues, including arms control negotiations - The non-military uses and abuses of nuclear energy - Public response - Scientific background. Each essay includes photographs, chronologies, tables, documentary excerpts, etc., as well as short 'Suggested readings' lists. Detailed index. *Class No:* 341.67

Bibliographies of Bibliographies

[2990]

CARROLL, B.A., *and others*. Peace and war: a guide to bibliographies. Santa Barbara, CA., ABC-Clio, 1983. xxi,580p. $42.50; £32.75. (*War and peace bibliography series, 16*.) ISBN: 0874363225.

Produced in co-operation with California State University Center for the Study of Armament and Disarmament.

Includes 1398 bibliographies published separately or as parts of books and articles, etc. from 1785 to 1980. Arranged under 34 subject groups (*e.g.* Women, peace and war; Peace education; Economic aspects of war). Gives detailed bibliographical information, number of items included, main language, proportion of items annotated, kinds of material included, and descriptive rather than evaluative annotations of *c*.30 words. Author index. *Class No:* 341.67(009)

Bibliographies

[2991]

ATKINS, S.E. Arms control and disarmament, defense and military, international security and peace: an annotated guide to sources, 1980-1987. Santa Barbara, CA., ABC-Clio 1988. 411p. $65. ISBN: 0874364884.

Nearly 1600 important works are annotated, mostly in English, and published between 1980 and 1987. Includes microform sets and textbooks, as well as printed sources. '... very welcome and surprisingly unique in its capture of all four major subtopics' (*Choice* v.26 (11/12), July-August, 1989. p. 1805-6). *Class No:* 341.67(01)

[2992]

BURNS, R.D., *comp*. Arms control and disarmament: a bibliography. Santa Barbara, CA, ABC-Clio, 1977. xv. 430p. (*The War/peace bibliography series, no.6*.)

8847 numbered references (many to periodical articles) arranged in 13 chapters in 2 parts. Each chapter is prefaced by an essay. Part 1. Views, overviews and theory (1. Research resources, and arms control and disarmament organizations ... 3. Historical surveys and contemporary views - 4. League of Nations and United Nations - 5. Special issues: inspection, verification, and supervision ...); Part 2. Accords, proposals and treaties (... 12. Controlling proliferation of nuclear weapons - 13. Rules of war and stabilizing the international environment). Subject and author indexes. *Class No:* 341.67(01)

[2993]

Card catalog of the Peace Palace Library, The Hague. Microfiche edition. Bethesda, MD., C I S Academic Editions, 1988. 1090 fiche and 724 fiche. $3545 and $2030. $4350 for both.

Comprises a universal bibliographical catalogue (a file containing *c*.350,000 entries for books, pamphlets and other materials, including correspondence) and a periodicals reference guide (an index to the contents of more than 2300 journals currently received, plus those no longer published). *Class No:* 341.67(01)

[2994]

FERMANN, G. Bibliography on international peacekeeping. Dordrecht, The Netherlands, & London, M.Nijhoff, 1992. xiii,291p. £59. ISBN: 0792320115.

1148 numbered items covering academic literature from banks, reports and journals, etc. Arranged in 14 chapters of which 1 to 10 are general, theoretical and conceptual, including case studies and brief reviews of operations. Chapter 11. Biographies and memoirs; 12. Book reviews; 13. Documentary collections; 14. Bibliographies. Data is from 1946/47 onwards. Subject index, p.256-71. General index, p.272-87. Journals & yearbooks, p.288. *Class No:* 341.67(01)

[2995]

McHUGH, D. Peace information sources: a guide to 31 British collections with comprehensive subject index. London, Infoshare Project, 1987. [4],83p. £2.50.

Listings of 23 national peace organizations, A-Z by name, and 9 peace centres (A-Z by town). For each entry: name and address, telephone number, access, aims, activities, publications, overview (main types of material, archives, human expertise), detailed analysis (subjects/important materials, organization/accessibility) of the various resources. Detailed subject index, p.67-83. *Class No:* 341.67(01)

[2996]

PASKINS, B. 'Peace studies and disarmament.' In *British book news*, July 1985, p. 387-91.

A literature survey with sections on The new peace movement, The effects of nuclear war, Ideas of deterrence, History and power politics, Philosophers and theologians, Psychologists and economists, Civil nuclear power, and finally, General guides and bibliographies. A bibliography lists the 98 book titles and two periodical titles referred to in the text. *Class No:* 341.67(01)

[2997]

RIDINGER, R.B.M. The Peace Corps: an annotated bibliography. Boston, Mass., G.K. Hall & Co., 1989. 384p. $35. ISBN: 0816189129.

A guide to the history of the United States Peace Corps from its inception in 1961 to 1986. Lists over 1400 selected sources, including books, newspaper and periodical articles, videotapes, memoirs, dissertations, research monographs and government documents, all annotated. 3 sections: 1. History of the Peace Corps; 2. Country programs; 3. Returned volunteers. 2 appendices: List of the Directors of the Peace Corps, 1961-1986; Periodicals of the Peace Corps. Name and subject index. *Class No:* 341.67(01)

[2998]

WOITO, R.S., *ed.* To end war a new approach to international conflict. 6th ed. New York, Pilgrim Press, 1982. 755p. $25. ISBN: 0829804641.

First published 1967.

21 chapters, each with an introductory essay of c.10p., preceding a bibliography on a particular subject (military, political, economic, ethical, religious, etc., connected with peace studies). Also includes a 200p. section of practical guidance, listings of organizations and resources. 'Not only the best bibliography by far on peace studies but also a superb guide to many issues ...' (*Choice*, v.20(8), April 1983, p.1114). *Class No:* 341.67(01)

Encyclopaedias

[2999]

Encyclopedia of arms control and disarmament. Burns, R.D., *ed.* New York, Scribner, 1993. 3v. $280. ISBN: 0684192810.

Includes 76 original articles and 150 excerpts of treaties. V.1 has signed articles in 2 parts: 1. has detailed histories of military activity and peace movements; 2. on a variety of themes and institutions, V.2 surveys historical dementions to 1945 and covers covert arms control activities since 1945. V.3 has a chronology of treaties and excerpts from treaties; a list of the 83 contributors; a list of acronyms; and a detailed index. Annotated bibliographies are included at the end of each article. *Class No:* 341.67(031)

[3000]

World encyclopedia of peace. Laszlo, E. *and* Yoo, J.Y., *eds.* Oxford, Pergamon Press, 1986. 4v. (1930p.). illus. £295; $530. ISBN: 0080326854.

Over 3000 literary references by over 200 experts from more than 30 countries, predominantly Western European and American. V.1-2 has a 36p. essay of introduction and history of peace encyclopedias, followed by a series of c.500 articles arranged A-Z by subject. V.3 has reprints of texts of peace treaties and conventions since 1919, a chronology of the peace movement, and Nobel Peace Prize laureates. V.4 lists peace organizations and institutions, A-Z by country; a bibliography arranged thematically (p.69-135); a list of journals arranged thematically (p.136-155) and devoted to peace research, peace activism, and international relations; and a list of contributors. Also a name index (p.173-230) and an analytical subject index (p.231-294) to the whole work. 'As the introductory essay ... suggests, this is a unique endeavor in many ways: it is also a fair achievement and

.... (contd.)

deserves a place in all but the smallest reference collections' (*College & research libraries*, v.48(4), July 1987, p.358). '... includes some noteworthy flaws' (*Choice*, October 1987, p.292). *Class No:* 341.67(031)

Handbooks & Manuals

[3001]

Peace resource book: a comprehensive guide to issues, groups and literature, 1986, edited by E. Bernstein and others for The Institute for Defense and Disarmament Studies. Cambridge, Mass., Ballinger Publishing Company 1986. 414p. $14.95. ISBN: 0887300383.

Supersedes *American peace directory*, 1984.

Issued as a working tool for those who are active in efforts for arms control, disarmament, and world peace. Arranged in 3 parts: 1. Peace issues and strategies (a useful 27-page introduction to the world military system, to government arms control negotiations, and to peace movement alternatives); 2. Directory of US peace organizations, listing about 400 national peace groups and 100 peace-oriented educational programmes. Also 5,700 national and local groups, arranged by A-Z and by Zipcode; 3. A briefly annotated bibliography of some 800 books, pamphlets and documents published between 1980 and 1985, arranged by topic. An author index and a list of publishers and distributors. Favourable review in *Choice*, v.23(7), March 1986, p.1042. *Class No:* 341.67(035)

Dictionaries

Polyglot

[3002]

Disarmament terminology. Foreign Office of the Federal Republic of Germany. Berlin, de Gruyter, 1982. xii,645p. £34.60. (*Terminological series, v.1.*)

2459 numbered terms and phrases related to disarmament, as well as designations of relevant organizations, authorities, conferences, bilateral and multilateral agreements. Listed A-Z in English, each entry followed by equivalents in German, French, Spanish and Russian. Indexes in all 5 languages. (A Chinese index is also available, £21.95). *Class No:* 341.67(038)=00

English

[3003]

ELLIOT, J.M. *and* ELLIOT, R.R. The Arms control, disarmament and military security dictionary. Santa Barbara, CA, ABC-Clio, 1989. 349p. $44.50. ISBN: 0874364302.

268 numbered entries, designed to complement by definition and organization those terms noted in standard texts on the topics. Arrangement is A-Z within subject-matter chapters. Extensive cross-references. US slant. Includes 24p. of notes. *Class No:* 341.67(038)=20

Russian

[3004]

DMITRICHEV, T.F. English-Russian dictionary on disarmament: about 12,000 terms ... Anglo-Russkii terminologicheskii slovar po voprasam razoruzhaniia. Moskva, Russky Yazuk Publishers, 1987. 377p.

Terms and sub-terms arranged A-Z by the English language terms, followed by the Russian equivalents. 5 annexes: I. Multilateral and bilateral agreements and other documents concerning arms limitation and disarmament. II. Peace initiatives of the Soviet Union and other Socialist countries in the field of arms limitation - III. Conferences, meetings and other international forums for peace and disarmament - IV. International and national bodies - V. International and national non-governmental organizations, research institutes, etc. A Russian-English volume was published in 1990 (560p. £7.965). *Class No:* 341.67(038)=82

Reviews & Abstracts

[3005]

Peace research abstracts journal. Newbury Park, CA., Sage Publications (Dundas,. Ontario, Peace Research Institute until 1994 issues), 1964-. v.1, no.1-. Bi-monthly. $193pa. ISSN: 00313599.

About 5000 abstracts pa of papers, articles and books dealing with questions of war and peace. Arranged in 10 subject sections, subdivided geographically as necessary. Author and subject indexes. *Class No:* 341.67(048)

Yearbooks & Directories

[3006]

MEYER, R.S. **Peace organizations, past and present:** a survey and directory. Jefferson, N.C., McFarland, 1988. 266p. $24.95. ISBN: 0899503403.

Profiles of 92 selected peace organizations, mainly US-based or international with US branches. Information included varies in length and content, but usually covers history, and political, philosophical or religious thrust, with examples of efforts and accomplishments. Final chapter has author's observations on the organizations and his throughts on search for peace. 'Main value is in profiles of lesser-known groups' (*Choice*, v.26(7), March 1989,. p.1128).
Class No: 341.67(058)

[3007]

—TRZYNA, T.C., *ed.* International peace directory. Californian Institute of Public Affairs, in co-operation with the University of Peace, Ciudad Colon, Costa Rica., 1984. 63p. $19.95. (*Who's doing what series, no. 10. University of Peace information guides, 1.*) ISBN: 0912102721.

A directory of leading organizations working for peace. *c.*100 entries, A-Z by name. Entries vary in length from a column to a page. Highly selective. *Class No:* 341.67(058)

[3008]

Peace movements of the world: an international directory. Day, A.J., *ed.* Harlow, Essex, Longman Group; Phoenix, Ariz., 1987. viii,398p. £48; $74.50. ISBN: 0582902681, UK; 0897744381, US.

Provides factual and objective data on over 1000 peace and anti-nuclear movements throughout the world. Arranged A-Z by country within broad geographical areas. Includes details of the origin, precise aims and activities of each movement, placed within the context of a description of prevailing issues in the particular country or continent. Index of movements, p.373-392; index of publications, p.392-398. '... useful directory of groups working for peace and disarmament' (*Choice*, v.25(8), April 1988, p.1224). '... by far this is the best source of information on peace organizations' (*Wilson library bulletin*, v.62(6), February 1988, p.102). *Class No:* 341.67(058)

[3009]

SIPRI: **yearbook:** world armaments and disarmament, 1993. Stockholm International Peace Research Institute. 24th ed. Oxford, Oxford University Press, for SIPRI, 1993. 600p. tables. £40; $75.00. ISBN: 0198291663. ISSN: 09530282.

1st issue (1970) covered 1968/69.

Up-to-date information on war, strategic and peace studies, and international relations. In 4 parts: 1. Weapons and technology - 2. Military expenditure, the arms trade and armed conflicts - 3. Developments in arms control - 4. Special features. Annexes: A. Major multilateral arms control agreements; B. Chronology. Abstracts. Index. *Class No:* 341.67(058)

[3010]

—SIPRI yearbooks: world armaments and disarmament, 1968-1979: cumulative index. London, Taylor & Francis Ltd., 1980. vii,90p. £25. ISBN: 0850661897. *Class No:* 341.67(058)

[3011]

The United Nations disarmament yearbook, 1992. V.17. New York, United Nations, 1992. 393p. $50. ISBN: 9211421934. ISSN: 02525607.

First published 1976. Annual.

Covers the deliberations, negotiations and actions related to documents occurring during the year concerned in the UN or under the auspices of the UNO and in committees on disarmament.
Class No: 341.67(058)

[3012]

WOODHOUSE, T., *ed.* **The International peace directory.** Plymouth, Northgate House Publishers Ltd., 1988. 189p. £19.95; $52.50. ISBN: 0746303793.

Covers *c.*600 peace organizations. Arranged in 4 parts: Part 1.: Introduction; pt.2: The organizations (A-Z by country, subdivided A-Z by name of organization, giving name and address, telephone number; membership and affiliations; meetings, publications, library; objectives; functions; placements; grants; issues); pt.3: Peace literature (comprising directories and guides; bibliographies; guide to current periodicals); pt.4: Statistical and reference analyses of returns (organizations identified by issues covered, by membership type; organizations making awards, prizes, scholarships and fellowships; organizations accepting voluntary work, placements, internships). Index to organizations. *Class No:* 341.67(058)

[3013]

—KINCADE, W.H. *and* HAYNER, P.B., *eds.* The Access resource guide: an international directory of information on war, peace and security. Cambridge, Mass., Ballinger Publishing Company, 1988. xxxvii,238p. $14.95; £23.50. ISBN: 0887302602.

*c.*600 organizations are listed, giving address, telephone number, membership, publications, meetings, internships, objectives and issues of concern. *Class No:* 341.67(058)

Biographies

[3014]

JOSEPHSON, H., *ed.* **Biographical dictionary of modern peace leaders.** Westport, Conn., Greenwood Press, 1985. 1133p. $145. ISBN: 0313225656.

Surveys the field of peace activism from 1800 to 1980. 750 biographical essays by over 250 authors from 15 nations, focusing on individuals who viewed the issues of war and peace from various approaches. Each essay contains an introductory paragraph including information about birth, death, education and career, followed by a study of the subject's work, thought and activity as a peace leader, and concludes with a bibliography. Wide definition of peace leadership (includes Czar Nicholas II, Kwame Nkrumah, and Haile Sellassie), but ' ... provides a useful source for quick, general reference ...' (*RUSI journal*, v.133(1), Spring 1988, p.91). *Class No:* 341.67(092)

USA

Yearbooks & Directories

[3015]

FINE, M. *and* STEVEN, P.M., *eds.* **American peace directory.** Institute for Defense & Disarmament Studies. 1st ed. Cambridge, Mass., Ballinger Publishing Company, 1984. ix,225p. ISBN: 0884109968.

In 2 parts, preceded by a 'Users'; guide'. Part 1 has alphabetical lists of peace groups in 5 sections; pt.2, 'Reference sections', has a list of groups by State and Zip-code, and US house of Representatives for 1984. Indexes (Peace forces - Structure - Constituency - Alphabetical). *Class No:* 341.67(73)(058)

Research Establishments

[3016]

UNESCO. Social and Human Sciences Documentation Centre and International Federation of Documentation's Social Science Information and Documentation Committee (FID/SD). **World directory of peace research and training institutions, 1991.** 7th ed. Paris, Unesco, 1991. xiii,[2],351p. ISBN: 9230027529.

First published 1973 as *International repertory of institutions for peace and conflict research.* Title changes slightly with each ed.

Includes institutions wholly or partly engaged in peace and conflict research and also institutions that support or promote such research in 66 countries. 7 sections: 1. Index of names and acronyms of institutions - 2. List of entries. International/regional institutions. National institutions - 3. Index of research subjects with indication of host country of the institution - 4. Geographical index - 5. Index by senior staff involved in peace activities - 6. Index of courses and subjects taught with indication of host country - 7. Index of institutions providing scholarships. *Class No:* 341.67:061:061.62

Constitutional Law

Dictionaries

[3017]

CHANDLER, R., *and others.* **Constitutional law dictionary.** Santa Barbara, ABC-Clio, 1985-87. 2v. (1244p.). v.1: $47.50; £35.25. v.2: $50; £41.50. (*Clio dictionaries in political science, 8 & 13.*) ISBN: 0874360315, v.1; 087436440x, v.2.

V.1 *Individual rights;* v.2. *Governmental powers.* V.1 focuses on concepts of constitutionalism, words and phrases common to American constitutional law, and leading case decisions by the United States Supreme Court. V.2 summarizes important cases in US legal history. Cross-references. Index. *Class No:* 342(038)

Worldwide

[3018]

MADDEX, Robert L. **Constitutions of the world.** London, Routledge, 1997 xxi,338p. ISBN: 0415164362.

Contains bibliography and index.

Each constitution is described by paragraphs on general information. Constitutional History: The constitution is divided into fundamental rights, division of powers, the Executive, the Legislature, the Judiciary and Amending the Constitution. Tables are given which show at a glance which type of government a country has, what the nature of its state is, its most recent constitution, what types of legislature, form of constitutional review, and complaints proceedure (Ombudsman) are available. The book explains important constitutions of the world in terms of their history, organization, and operation, and their stated goals for efficient and humane goverment. *Class No:* 342(100)

Government State Papers

[3019]

BLAUSTEIN, A.P. *and* FLANZ, G.H. **Constitutions of the countries of the world.** Dobbs Ferry, N.Y., Oceana, 1971-. 20 binders. Loose-leaf. $1500 for 20v. + supplement binder. ISBN: 0379004674.

Each binder has full text (translated, as necessary) of *c*.10 constitutions. Each text is accompanied by a concise chronology of events leading up to its adoption and a brief annotated bibliography for further reference. *Class No:* 342(100)(093.200)

[3020]

—BLAUSTEIN, A.P. *and* BLAUSTEIN, E.B. Constitutions of dependencies and special sovereignties. Dobbs Ferry, N.Y., Oceana, 1975-76. 7 binders, and yearly supplements. $625. ISBN: 0379002787.

Covers British, French and American dependencies.
Class No: 342(100)(093.200)

Europe—Western

[3021]

WEATHERILL, S. *and* BEAUMONT, P. **EC law:** the essential guide to the legal working of the European Community. London, Penguin Books, 1993. 846p. £20. ISBN: 0140145070.

An in-depth analysis of the constitutional law of the law and legislation of EC countries. *Class No:* 342(400)

USA

Bibliographies

[3022]

KURLAND, P. B. *and* LERNER, R., *eds*. **The Founders' constitution.** Chicago, University of Chicago Press, 1988. 5v.(3250p.). $300. ISBN: 0226463877.

Contains documents, letters, broadsides, etc., bearing on the creation of the United States Constitution, and its first 12 amendments from the 17th-century to the first third of the 19th-century. V.1. deals with philosophical and theoretical principles; v.2 - 4 proceed from the Preamble through the Articles; v.5. deals with Amendments I-XII. *Class No:* 342(73)(01)

[3023]

McCARRICK, E.M., *ed*. **US constitution:** a guide to information sources. Detroit, Mich., Gale Research Co., 1980. x,390p. $65; £14.50. (*American government and history information guide series, 4.*) ISBN: 0810302134, US; 0874362040, UK.

Annotated bibliography in chapter form. Chapters 1-5 cover general sources; background; framing, etc,; general interpretative works; basic principles. Chapters 6-12 deal with specific articles of and amendments to the US constitution. *Class No:* 342(73)(01)

[3024]

—MEYERS, A. 'Reference sources on the US Constitution.' In *Reference books bulletin*, 1986/1987, p.18-19.

Includes 20 annotated entries for encyclopedias and dictionaries, bibliographies, sources, Supreme Court decisions, etc.
Class No: 342(73)(01)

Encyclopaedias

[3025]

LEVY, L.W., *and others*. **Encyclopedia of the American Constitution.** New York, Macmillan Publishing Company; London, Collier-Macmillan, 1987. 4v.(1500p.). $400. the set. Supplement 1 (1992. 616p. $90). ISBN: 0029186102.

Over 2200 articles by nearly 300 scholarly contributors (historians, lawyers and political scientists) on all aspects of the American Constitution. Entries vary in length from a paragraph to several pages (*e.g.* 'Constitutional interpretation': 14¼ cols., 15 references; 'Watergate and the Constitution': 2 cols., 3 references; 'Humphrey, Hubert H. (1911-1978)': 1 col., 1 reference; 'Johnson, Lyndon B. (1908-1973)': over 60 cols., 4 references). Fully cross-referenced. Bibliographies appended to many articles. V.1 has a preface, a list of articles and a list of contributors preceding the encyclopedia entries. The final volume has a glossary and 3 indexes (general, names, and cases). 'This is certainly one of the most innovative, ambitious, and useful of the scholarly publications celebrating the bicentennial of the US Constitution' (*Library journal*, v.111(20), December 1986, p.96). *Class No:* 342(73)(031)

[3026]

PLANO, J.C. *and* GREENBERG, M. **The American political dictionary.** 8th ed. Fort Worth, Holt, Rinehart Winston Inc., 1989. x,608p. ISBN: 0030028442.

First published 1962.

Entries A-Z within 14 chapters: 1. Political ideas - 2. United States constitution and the federal union - 3. Parties, politics, pressure groups, and elections - 4. The legislative process: Congress and the state legislatures - 5. The Executive Office and powers - 6. Public administration: organization and personnel - 7. The judicial process: courts and law enforcement - 8. Civil liberties, civil rights, immigration and citizenship - 9. Finance and taxation - 10. Business and labor - 11. Agriculture, energy and environment - 12. Health, education and welfare - 13. Foreign policy and national defense - 14. State and local government. About 1000 entries in all (definition; significance to overall operations, theories and problems of American government; cross-references). The Constitution of the United States. Index, p.577-608. A standard encyclopedic dictionary. *Class No:* 342(73)(031)

[3027]

—SMITH, E.C. *and* ZURCHER, A.J. Dictionary of American politics. 2nd ed. New York, Baines & Noble, 1968. vii, [1]. 434p. illus., maps. $26.50. ISBN: 0064808033.

First published 1888.

*c.*4500 entries, giving definitions, categories, usage, plus etymology (where relevant). Appendices include text of American constitution, statistical data on the 50 states (with their nicknames), and a list of presidents. *Class No:* 342(73)(031)

Handbooks & Manuals

[3028]

LEES, J.D. **The Political system of the United States.** 3rd. London, Faber & Faber, 1983. 406p. £6.95. ISBN: 057118068x.

First published 1969.

12 chapters (*e.g.* 3. The nature of American federalism; 8. The Congress: legislative representation and action; 12. The political system and social change). Appendices: A. The Consititution; B. Presidents of the United States; C. Election results, 1944-80; D. Notes on further reading (by chapters, with general introduction, p.386-392). Analytical index, p.393-406. 'An attempt to provide an introduction to American politics which is as useful to students of the United States as to students of politics' (*Acknowledgements* in the 2nd ed.). *Class No:* 342(73)(035)

Parliaments

Handbooks & Manuals

[3029]

Parliaments of the world: a comparative reference compendium, prepared by the Inter-Parliamentary Union. 2nd ed. Aldershot, Hants, Gower Publishing Company Ltd; New York, Facts on File, 1986. 2v. (1440p). tables. £135. ISBN: 0566053810, (UK); 0810611869, (US).

First published in 1976 by Macmillan Press.

A comparative study of the structure and operation of parliaments throughout the world. An introduction is followed by chapters on The parliaments of the world - Parliament and its membership - Parliamentary procedure - Proceedings and debates - Parliamentary groupings - Parliamentary committees - Parliament and its means of information - Parliament and the media - Legislation - The budget - Parliament and the Government - Parliament and emergency - Constitutionality of laws - Dissolution of Parliament - Judicial and other functions of Parliament. Index. ' ... a potpourri of useful and otherwise difficult-to-locate information about this branch of government in 83 countries ...' (*Reference books bulletin*, 1986/7, p.68). *Class No:* 342.53(035)

[3030]

PAXTON, J., *ed*. **World legislatures.** London, Macmillan, 1974. xiii,169p. £10. ISBN: 0333148495.

Concise data on the formal procedures and constitutions of the world. A-Z (legislative authority; frequency of election; initiation of bills; referenda; etc.). Covers states (*e.g.* USA, Australia), provinces (*e.g.* Canada), Länder (*e.g.* West Germany) and republics (*e.g.* USSR). Selected bibliography, p.159-64; glossary, p.165-9. *Class No:* 342.53(035)

Europe—Western

[3031]

COCKS, B. **The European Parliament:** structure, procedure & practice. London, HMSO, 1973. [xi],336p.

Parts : 1. Structure of the European Parliament - 2. The external relations of the Communities - 3. Procedure of the European Parliament (chapters 9-19). Appendices A-D (A. Treaty establishing the E.E.C. (80p.)) ... C. Principal debates, reports and resolutions of the Parliament, 1958-1972 - D. Presidents of the Parliament). Index,

.... *(contd.)*

p.321-36. 'Designed to help Members of the United Parliament' (*Preface*). The author is Clerk of the House of Commons. 'An indispensable guide' (*International affairs,* v.49,no.3, July 1973, p.528). *Class No:* 342.53(400)

[3032]

European handbook of organisations. London, Whurr Publications, 1992. £29.95. ISBN: 1870332296.

Each entry starts with mention of a treaty or convention that established the organization, followed by clear sections on purpose, members countries, structure and activities. Brief chronology, up to the Maastricht Treaty. Country-by-country tabulation of who belongs to what. List of acronyms. Similar to Vachers (*qv*) but Whurr has better descriptions of what bodies do, according to *Refer,* v.9(2), Spring 1993, p.27. *Class No:* 342.53(400)

[3033]

Vacher's European companion: a diplomatic, political and commercial reference book. Berkhampstead, Herts., Vacher's Publications, 1972-. no.1-. Quarterly. £35.50pa. ISSN: 09580336.

A directory. Contents: The European Communities (The Commission, the European Parliament, the Court of Justice, Directorates General); other international organizations; National sections; European Documentation Centres and Deposit Libraries. Glossary of abbreviations. No index. *Class No:* 342.53(400)

Great Britain

[3034]

GREAT BRITAIN. House of Commons. **The Parliamentary debates. Fifth series. House of Commons: official report 1909-.** London, HMSO, 1909-.

Originally published as a private venture. (Cobbett's *Parliamentary History of England from ... 1066 to 12th August 1803.* London, Hansard, 1806-20. 36v., and its continuations). It became an official report in 1909: substantially verbatim.

Issued daily during the session; cumulated in bound volumes, with general detailed index (speakers and topics) to each session. A.J.P.Taylor (*English History, 1914-1945,* p.606) notes two limitations to Hansard. 'The reporters do not include casual cries, unless these contributed to the progress of the debate; hence, for instance, they omitted Amery's famous call to Greenwood on 2 September 1939. Nor was any record kept of the secret sessions, held in both World Wars - unlike the French Chamber, which kept a secret record, published later.' Also available on CD-ROM. *Class No:* 342.53(410)

[3035]

GREAT BRITAIN. House of Lords. **The Parliamentary debates. Fifth series. House of Lords: official report, 1909-.** London HMSO. 1909-.

Issued daily during the session; cumulated and indexed similarly to the House of Commons *Debates.* Also available on CD-ROM. *Class No:* 342.53(410)

[3036]

—**GREAT BRITAIN.** House of Lords. **Journals, 1509-.** London, HMSO.

The *Journals* of the House of Lords, issued sessionally, are a record of what was done in the House of Lords, not what was said. *Class No:* 342.53(410)

[3037]

Manual of procedure in the public business: laid on the table by Mr. Speaker for the use of Members. House of Commons. 13th ed. London, HMSO, 1984. xix, 287 p. £14.95. ISBN: 0108360156.

Contents of chapters: 1. Meetings of Parliament - 2. Election and admission of Members - 3. The Speaker and Chairmen of Committees - 4. Officers and Departments of the House - 5. Sittings of the House and arrangement of business - 6. Matters taken ... - 7. General rules of procedure - 8. Public bills - 9. Committees - 10. Financial business - 11. Relations between the two Houses - 12. Communications between the Crown and the House - 13. Witnesses ... - 14. Accounts and papers - 15. Records of the House - 16. Miscellaneous - 17. Private bills - 18. Special procedure orders - 19. Procedure under the Parliament Acts of 1911 and 1949 - 20. European legislation and international assemblies. *Class No:* 342.53(410)

[3038]

RADICE, L., *and others.* **Member of Parliament:** the job of the backbencher. London, Macmillan, 1990. 208p. £40. ISBN: 0333491211.

Chapters: The role of the Honourable Member - Getting in - The job in Parliament - A Parliamentary day - Pay and conditions - The job outside the House - Backbench views of the job - A month in the life of four backbenchers - Changes. Bibliography. Index. *Class No:* 342.53(410)

Bibliographies

[3039]

FORD, P. *and* **FORD, G. A Guide to Parliamentary Papers:** What they are, how to find them, how to use them. 3rd ed. Shannon, Irish University Press, 1972. 87p. £12.50. (*Southampton University Studies in Parliamentary Papers.*) ISBN: 0716514184.

First published 1955.

'Our main aim is to familiarise the researcher with the different kinds of papers, to explain the apparatus for finding them and to indicate the most profitable way of extracting information from them' (*Preface to the third edition*). Bibliographical aids, p.71-80; index, p.81-85. A valuable introduction to a complex subject. *Class No:* 342.53(410)(01)

[3040]

GOEHLERT, R.U. *and* **FENTON, S.M. The Parliament of Great Britain:** a bibliography. Lexington, Mass., Lexington Books, 1983. 240p. $30. (*Lexington Books special series on libraries and librarianship.*) ISBN: 0669057002.

Includes works dealing with the history, development and legislative processes of the Parliament, coverage being limited to works in English published in the last 100 years, monographs, essays in collections, journal articles, and dissertations and theses. Not evaluative, but introduction suggests basic introductory works. Author and subject indexes. *Choice* (v.20(9), May 1983, p.1264) suggests it could be used in conjunction with Wilding & Laundy's *An encyclopaedia of Parliament* (*q.v.*). *Class No:* 342.53(410)(01)

[3041]

GREAT BRITAIN. House of Commons. **A Bibliography of Parliamentary debates of Great Britain.** London, HMSO, 1956. 62p. (*House of Commons Library document no.2.*)

A bibliography of debates of both Houses of Parliament, including not only the standard sets of debates, both official and unofficial, but also information from diaries, etc. 94 numbered items. Helpful evaluative notes; a chronological chart of debates, diaries and proceedings, 1066-1953, assists quick reference. Debates in the Irish House of Commons are covered in an appendix. *Class No:* 342.53(410)(01)

[3042]

JONES, D.L. Debates and proceedings of the British Parliaments: a guide to printed sources. London, HMSO., 1986. vi,152p. £9.10. (*House of Commons library document, no.16.*) ISBN: 0108506150.

Lists, with suitable annotations, the printed sources of the proceedings (the record of what is done) and for the debates (the record of what is said) of the Parliaments held in the United Kingdom. The work is divided into sections based on the different Parliaments: the Parliaments at Westminster, the Irish Parliament, Parliamentary institutions in Northern Ireland, and the Scottish Parliament. Entries are arranged chronologically within each section by the earliest date of the work. Index referring to the principal elements of the text, p.145-152. *Class No:* 342.53(410)(01)

[3043]

Subject catalogue of the House of Commons Parliamentary papers, 1801-1900. Cockton, P., *comp.* Cambridge; Alexandria, VA., Chadwyck-Healey, 1988. 5v.(4500p.). $1500; £900. ISBN: 0859641333.

The papers are divided into 19 subject areas (*e.g.* Central government and administration; National finance and financial institutions; Population and demography;; Statistics; Agriculture and rural society; Industry and industrial society), each subject area being subdivided (Central government and administration has 4 sections). Then arranged according to traditional classification of Bills, Reports of select committees, Reports of commissions, Accounts and papers, arranged A-Z by descriptors, an index of descriptors is at the end of v.5. '... careful and scholarly approaches ... essential tool for study of 19c. Britain' (*Parliamentary affairs,* v.42(1), January 1989, p.134). *Class No:* 342.53(410)(01)

Handbooks & Manuals

[3044]

Erskine May's Treatise on the law, privileges, proceedings and usage of Parliament. Boulton, C., *ed.* 21st ed. London, Butterworths, 1989. xliv,1079p. ISBN: 0406114714.

First published 1844; 18th ed. 1971.

Parts: 1. Constitution, powers and privileges of Parliament (chapters 1-11) - 2. Proceedings in Parliament: public business (12-34) - 3. Proceedings in Parliament: private business. Table of abbreviations (references to sources), p.xxxix-xliv. Detailed table of contents. Appendix: House of Commons Standing Orders relative to public business. Detailed, analytical index, p.1025-1079. 'Erskine May' is not official; next to the *Journals* of both Houses, it is accepted as the great secondary authority. For the parliamentary and constitutional specialist; whereas *Abraham and Hawtrey's Parliamentary dictionary* (3rd ed., by S.C. Hawtry and H.M. Barclay. London, Butterworth, 1970. viii,248p.) is for the general political audience (*T.L.S.* no.3625, 20 August 1971, p.985).

...(contd.)

For the historical development of parliamentary procedure: Campion, G.F.M., 1st baron Campion. *An introduction to the procedure of the House of Commons* (2nd ed. London, Macmillan, 1950. 348p.); and, complementary, from the historical viewpoint, to Erskine May, - Redlich, J. *The procedure of the House of Commons: a study of its history and present form* (London, Constable, 1908. 3v.). *Class No:* 342.53(410)(035)

[3045]
MENHENNET, D. **The Journal of the House of Commons: a bibliographical and historical guide.** London, HMSO, 1971. viii,96p. facsims. (*House of Commons Library document no.7.*)

1. Introduction - 2. The official Record of Proceedings - 3. Origins: the Commons manuscript *Journal,* 1547 to 1800 - 4. The printing of the *Journal* - 5. The indexing of the *Journal* - 6. Contents and historical value of the Commons *Journal.* 3 appendices (1. Availability of the present Commons *Journal* volumes and of the general indexes, p.52-7; 25 locations). Analytical index. Bibliography, p.92-94. The House of Commons *Journals,* published each session, are a record of what was done in the House of Commons, not what was said. They also record all papers laid before the House. The *Journals* constitute the authentic record of the proceedings of the House and primary authority on parliamentary procedure. House of Commons' *Standing Committee debates* is issued daily when Committees meet; - a verbatim report of proceedings in Standing Committee published by HMSO since 1919. *Class No:* 342.53(410)(035)

Dictionaries

[3046]
HAWTREY, S.C. *and* BARCLAY, H.M. **Abraham and Hawtrey's parliamentary dictionary.** 3rd ed. London, Butterworth, 1970. viii, 248p.

First published 1956 as *A Parliamentary dictionary,* by L. A. Abraham and S. C. Hawtrey.

An A-Z guide to expressions in common usage in the Houses of Parliament with explanation and comment. Understood to refer to House of Commons unless the context obviously requires otherwise. Some footnotes. Cross-references. Detailed, analytical index, p.241-8. *Class No:* 342.53(410)(038)

Periodicals

[3047]
The House magazine. London, Parliamentary Communications, Ltd., 1976-. v.1,no.1-. Weekly. £115pa.

The weekly journal of the House of Commons, with sections on the Commons diary; The week; The week in Washington; 'Committee corridors', features (*e.g.* the issue for 11 June 1990 includes several items on prisons). 'Parliamentary and European business' is printed on blue-tinted paper. *Class No:* 342.53(410)(051)

Published Series

20th Century

[3048]
RODGER, F. **Serial publications in the British Parliamentary Papers, 1900-1968.** London, Library Association, 1971. xix, 146p. £7.50. ISBN: 0838900860.

1273 entries in all, aiming 'to list by issuing agency all serials which have appeared in the House of Commons Sessional Papers at any time during the present century and to indicate briefly their publishing history: earliest and latest dates of issue, relationship to other publications and details of non-parliamentary publications when this occurs' (*Introduction*). Great Britain, excluding Ireland: p.1-119 (1207 items); Ireland: p.113-8. Detailed analytical index of subjects , bodies, areas/countries. 'A guide of inestimable value to the annual reports, accounts, statistics and other serial publications of government departments which are embodied in this century's sessional papers of the House of Commons' (*Library Association record,* v.74(3), March 1972, p.62). *Class No:* 342.53(410)(082.1)"19"

Tables & Data Books

[3049]
CREWE, I. *and* FOX, A. **British Parliamentary constituencies: a statistical compendium.** London, Faber and Faber, 1984. 397p. tables, maps. £25. ISBN: 0571132367.

Up-to-date electoral, political and socio-economic information on each of the 650 constituencies, in the 1983 election results. *Class No:* 342.53(410)(083)

Histories

[3050]
BUTT, R. **A History of Parliament. V.1: The Middle ages.** London, Constable, 1989. xxiii,662p. 22 illus (1 col). £30. ISBN: 0094706301.

'... describes growth of medieval Parliament by placing it in a continuous narrative of political history ...' (*Preface,* p.xv). Footnotes. Select bibliography, p.635-8. Analytical index, p.639-62. *Class No:* 342.53(410)(091)

[3051]
HISTORY OF PARLIAMENT TRUST. **The History of Parliament.** London, HMSO, 1964-. Secker & Warburg, 1983-. (Alan Sutton Publishing from 1991).

It is planned to cover the Westminster Parliament from 1264 to the present day. The introductory surveys (each with its index) and especially the biographies are particularly valuable. The latter are signed, have quotations, and give sources. Published so far:- The House of Commons, 1715-1754, by Romney Sedgwick (2v. 1970. £50); The House of Commons, 1754-1970, by Sir Lewis Namier and John Brook (3v. 1964. £80); The House of Commons, 1660-90, by B.D. Henning (1983, 3v. £120. ISBN 0436192748); The House of Commons, 1509-1558, by S.T. Bindoff (1983. 3v. ISBN 0436042827); The House of Commons, 1558-1603, by P.W. Hasler (1982. 3v. £95. ISBN 0118875019); The House of Commons, 1790-1820, by R.G. Thorne (1986. 5v. £225): The House of Commons, 1386-1421, by J.S. Roskill and others(1993. 4v. 276p. ISBN 086299943x). *Class No:* 342.53(410)(091)

[3052]
WEDGEWOOD, J.C. **History of Parliament, 1439-1509.** London, HMSO, 1936-38. 2v.

V.1: Biographies of members of the Commons House, 1439-1509; v.2: Register of the ministers and of the members of both Houses, 1439-1509. *Class No:* 342.53(410)(091)

Biographies

[3053]
STENTON, M., *ed.* **Who's who of British Members of Parliament: a biographical dictionary of the House of Commons, based on annual volumes of *Dod's parliamentary companion,* and other sources.** Brighton, Sussex, Harvester Press, 1976-1981. 4v. (1724p.). £80 each vol. ISBN: 0855273151, v.2; 0855273259, v.3; 0855273356, v.4.

Contents: V.1: 1832-1885; v.2: 1886-1918; v.3: 1919-1945; v.4: 1945-1979. *Dod's parliamentary companion* (*q.v.*) began publication in 1832. This biographical dictionary adds more career data, including date of death. Since earlier volumes of *Dod's* are not readily available, this work has its place. 'However, Stenton's efforts at revision and updating are disappointingly sparse' (*Library journal,* 1 May 1977, p.1005). *Class No:* 342.53(410)(092)

[3054]
—Dod's Parliamentary companion, 1999. 167th year. Hurst Green, East Sussex, Dod's Parliamentary Companion, 1999. 1400p. illus. £105. ISBN: 0905702271. ISSN: 00707007.

First published 1832.

Sections: The Royal Family - Biographies of Peers - composition of the House of Lords - Biographies of Peers of Ireland who are not Peers of Parliament - Precedence - Addressing letters - Biographies of Members of the House of Commons - Constituencies and polling, etc. - The Ministerial responsibilities - Government and public offices. Index. *Class No:* 342.53(410)(035)

[3055]
—Vacher's parliamentary companion: a reference book for Parliament, national organisations and public offices. Berkhamstead, Herts., Vacher's Publications, 1831-. Quarterly. £23. ISSN: 09580328.

Provides more concise information more frequently than the above. A-Z list of members of both Houses, with members' town addresses, constituencies, etc. Also available on microform from UMI. *Class No:* 342.53(410)(092)

[3056]
—ZETTER, L. Vachers biographical guide, 1990. London, A.S.Kerswill, 1990. 370p. £25.

Includes sections on members of both Houses of Parliament and British members of the European Parliament. Each entry lists name, political allegiance, date of birth, marital status, education, previous occupation(s), political career, and political and personal interests. *Class No:* 342.53(410)(092)

Official Records

[3057]
BOND, M.F. **Guide to the records of Parliament.** London, HMSO, 1971. x,352p. illus.

'This guide describes the complete range of records preserved within the Palace of Westminster: the records of both Houses of Parliament; all documents which have been presented to the two Houses or purchased by them; - and the papers which have accumulated in the

....(contd.)

various Parliamentary and non-Parliamentary offices of the Palace' (*Preface*). 6 parts; 1. Records of the House of Lords (p.13-194) - 2. Records of the House of Commons of Westminster. Appendices: 1. List of Clerks of the Parliaments; 2. List of Clerks of the House of Commons. Table of Acts cited. Detailed, analytical index, p.313-52. A comprehensive guide; well produced. *Class No:* 342.53(410)(093.2)

[3058]

POLDEN, P. Guide to the records of the Lord Chancellor's Department. Brunel: the University of West London. London, HMSO, 1988. xxx,376p. £35. ISBN: 0113800150.

21 chapters arranged in 4 main sections: 1. The Lord Chancellor and his office - 2. The administration of justice - 3. Reforms in the law - 4. Church and State. Introductions to each section; short prefaces to chapters and notes after them. 4 appendices: 1. The Lord Chancellors and their staff, 1872-1951 - 2. Reports of committees - 3. Statutes and bills - 4. Decided cases. Bibliographies of books, p.371-374, and articles and lectures, p.374-376. No index. A comprehensive and accessible guide to the records. *Class No:* 342.53(410)(093.2)

17th Century

[3059]

HAYTON, D. and JONES, C. and DITCHFIELD, G.M., eds. British parliamentary lists, 1660-1800: a register. London, Hambledon Press, 1995. xxi,151p. illus., plan. £28. ISBN: 1852851317.

Revised and expanded version of: A register of parliamentary lists, 1660-1761, but omitting the previously included lists for the Parliament of Ireland. *Class No:* 342.53(410)"16"

[3060]

KEELER, M.F. The Long Parliament, 1640-1641: a bibliographical study of its members. Philadelphia, Pa., American Philosophical Society, 1956. ix,410p.

In three parts: 1. Portrait of a Parliament - 2. Elections and returns - 3. Biographical directory of the Parliament Men (p.81-404; *c.*650 entries, A-Z). Profuse footnotes (*c.*20 per page). Index to part 1. *Class No:* 342.53(410)"16"

18th Century

[3061]

Hansard's catalogue and breviate of Parliamentary Papers, 1696-1834. Ford, P. and Ford, G. Oxford, Blackwell, 1953. 220p.

Reprinted in facsimile.

A classified list, together with a breviate of the Papers arranged under subject headings. This reprint includes a select list of House of Lords Papers not in Hansard's *Breviate*. There is a very full index to the papers, and a helpful introduction. *Class No:* 342.53(410)"17"

[3062]

JUDD, G.P. Members of Parliament, 1734-1832. New Haven, CT, Yale University Press; London, Oxford University Press, 1955. Reprinted 1972 by Shoestring. vii,389p. $43.50 ISBN: 0208012303.

Attempts to show the relationship between the British ruling class 'a cohesive group ... toughly knit' and the House of Commons, 1734-1832 by a detailed statistical analysis of 5034 Members. 10 chapters (*e.g.* 4. The age of members - 5. Length of service - 6. Social status and family background, etc.), followed by 'Check list of members (p.95-385). This list consists of 5034 numbered entries (full name; dates of birth and death; position(s) held; parliamentary career (seat(s) and date(s)); sources (*e.g.* D.N.B., G.E.C. [Cokayne], *Alumni Oxon.*), with many cross-references. analytical index to chapters 1-10. *Class No:* 342.53(410)"17"

[3063]

LAMBERT, S., ed. Sessional Papers of the eighteenth century: George I and II. Wilmington, Del., Scholarly Resources Inc., 1975. 20v. diagrs., graphs, charts, maps.

Claims to provide a complete collection of the Parliamentary Papers of the period, covering trade, taxation, colonies, crime, religion and politics under the early Hanoverians. 'Indispensable' (*Choice*, v.13(12), February 1977, p.1570). *Class No:* 342.53(410)"17"

[3064]

—LAMBERT, S., ed. Sessional Papers of the eighteenth century: George III. Wilmington, Del. Scholarly Resources Inc. 1975. 127v. *Class No:* 342.53(410)"17"

19th Century

[3065]

FORD, P. and FORD, G. Select list of British Parliamentary Papers, 1833-1899. Rev. ed. Shannon, Irish University Press, 1970. xxii,166p. £17.50. ISBN: 0716505746.

First published 1953.

A classified list of reports and other material 'issued by commissions or similar bodies of investigation into economic, social and constitutional questions, and matters of law and administration'.

....(contd.)

Valuable subject index, over 4500 papers listed; references are to the House of Commons' volume arrangement. *Class No:* 342.53(410)"18"

20th Century

[3066]

FORD, P. and FORD, G. A Breviate of Parliamentary Papers, 1900-1916: the foundation of the Welfare State. Oxford, Blackwell, 1957 (Reprinted Shannon, Irish University Press, 1969). xlix,470p. £27.50. ISBN: 0716505754. *Class No:* 342.53(410)"19"

[3067]

—FORD, P. and FORD, G. A Breviate of Parliamentary Papers, 1917-1939. Oxford, Blackwell, 1951 (Reprinted Shannon, Irish University Press, 1969). [1],xlviii,571p. £27.50. ISBN: 0716505762. *Class No:* 342.53(410)"19"

[3068]

—FORD, P. and FORD, G. A Breviate of Parliamentary Papers, 1940-1954: War and reconstruction. Oxford, Blackwell, 1961. [1],515p.

Each volume consists of summaries of selected Parliamentary Papers, - 'the reports of committees, royal commissions and similar bodies in matters which have been, or might have been, the subject of legislation or have dealt with public policy' (*Introduction*, 1917-1939 vol.). The 1940-1954 vol. is arranged in 16 sections (17 in the 1900-1916 vol., which includes 'Irish Papers'): 1. Machinery of government - 2. National finance - 3. Monetary and economic policy, financial institutions- 4. Agriculture and food supply - 5. Trade and industry - 6. Coal, fuel, power, water - 7. Transport - 8A. Post Office, telegraphy - 8B. Broadcasting, the press - 9. Inventions, patents, copyright - 10. Labour - 11. Social security - 12. Health - 13A. Housing - 13B. Town and country planning - 14. Education - 15A. Population - 15B. Social problems - 16. Legal administration, police, law. *Class No:* 342.53(410)"19"

[3069]

Ford list of British Parliamentary papers, 1974-1983, together with specialist commentaries. Marshallsay, D. Cambridge, Chadwick-Healey, 1989. xlviii,694p. £70. ((*Southampton University studies in Parliamentary papers*).)

Includes reports and published evidence of all types of committee, commission, working party and other enquiry bodies, plus White and Green Papers. Selected reports of the Foreign Affairs Committee are listed for the first time. Commentaries, editor's note, abbreviations, and subject classification of papers precedes. Appendices: 1. Select list of annual reports; 2. Select list of research series. Alphabetical subject/title index, p.655-83. Chairmen and author index, p.684-94. *Class No:* 342.53(410)"19"

Scotland

[3070]

YOUNG, M.D., ed. The Parliaments of Scotland. Edinburgh, Scottish Academic Press, 1992-93. 2v. illus. £35 each vol. ISBN: 0707307058.

Biographies of the burgh and shire commissioners of Scotland, 1357-1707 (the Treaty of Union). V.1:A-K; v.2:L-Z. *Class No:* 342.53(411)

Ireland

[3071]

ENGLEFIELD, D. Printed records of the Parliament of Ireland, 1613-1800: a survey and bibliographical guide. London, Lemon Tree Press, 1978. 52p. *Class No:* 342.53(415)

Northern Ireland

[3072]

MALTBY, A. The Government of Northern Ireland, 1922-72: a catalogue and breviate of Parliamentary Papers. Dublin, Irish University Press, 1974. xxii,235p. £19.50; $35. ISBN: 0716521512.

16 classes: 1. Machinery of government - 2. National finance ... 16. Legal administration, police, the law. Appendix 1: Westminster reports concerning Northern Ireland. 2: Select list of annual and other recurring reports. Index of chairmen and authors; title index. *Class No:* 342.53(416)

Eire

[3073]

EIRE. Dail Eireann. Diosbóireachtai pairliminte/Parliamentary debates: tuairsig oifigiúil/official report, 9th September 1922-. Dublin, Stationery Office, 1922-. v.1-.

Daily parts, followed by bound volumes. Each volume is indexed. *Class No:* 342.53(417)

19th Century

[3074]

MALTBY, A. *and* MALTBY, J. Ireland in the nineteenth-century: a breviate of offical publications. Oxford, Pergamon Press, 1979. 269p. £37. ISBN: 008023688x.

Lists and digests over 600 nineteenth-century reports relating to Ireland, under broad subject headings. 'Combines scholarship and liveliness' (*Library review,* v.29, Winter 1980, p.51).
Class No: 342.53(417)"18"

20th Century

[3075]

FORD, P. *and* FORD, G. A Select list of reports of enquiries of the Irish Dáil and Senate, 1922-1972. Dublin, Irish University Press, 1974. 64p. v £12.50. (*Southampton University studies in Parliamentary Papers.*) ISBN: 0716522365.

In 17 classes (1. Machinery of government - 2. National finance ... 17. Legal administration, police, law). Analytical subject index. Aims 'to help students to follow the development of thought in Eire's main lines of domestic policy since the foundation of the State' (*Scope and arrangement*). *Class No:* 342.53(417)"19"

Commonwealth

Encyclopaedias

[3076]

WILDING, N. *and* LAUNDY, P. An Encyclopaedia of Parliament. Completely rev. 4th ed. London, Cassell, 1971. ix,931p.

First published 1958.

'Abjuration Act' ... 'Zinoviev letter'. Covers British and Commonwealth Parliaments, giving definitions of terms (*e.g.* 'Closure'), background history (*e.g.* 'Elizabeth I (1533-1603) and Parliament'), and notes on procedure, privileges and customs of Parliament. Lengthier articles have brief bibliographies, for further reading. 34 appendices (2. Salaries of Ministers, Speakers and Members ... 34. Bibliography, p.892-931 with subdivisions). Well produced. Both authors were members of the Federal and Southern Rhodesian Parliaments. The standard work. *Class No:* 342.53(41-44)(031)

France

[3077]

PICKLES, D. The Government and politics of France. London, Methuen, 1972-73. 2v.(xii,453p.;xii,500p.).

V.1: *Institutions and parties;* 2: *Politics.* V.1 has 11 chapters on institutions, and parties and interest groups. Appendix 2: The French Constitution of 4 October 1958. Notes, p.321-410. Bibliography of French and English items. Analytical index, p.417-53. V.2 has 3 parts: 1. Internal politics; 2. Foreign policy; 3. Reflections by way of conclusion. Notes, p.356-476. Bibliography (grouped), p.477-83. Analytical index. Covers events up to 1973. A standard work. *Class No:* 342.53(44)

[3078]

WRIGHT, V. The Government and politics of France. 3rd ed. London, Unwin-Hyman; New York, Holmes & Meier, 1989. xii,402p. £9.95; $44.50. ISBN: 0091731437, UK; 0841912394, US.

First published 1978.

A leading text on the government and politics of France, taking account of events up to and including the presidential elections of 1988. *Class No:* 342.53(44)

USA

Bibliographies

[3079]

HALL, K.L. A Comprehensive bibliography of American constitutional and legal history, 1896-1979. Millwood, NY, Kraus International Publications, 1984. 5v.(3443p.). $650 for 5v. Supplement 1980-1987 (1991. $155. 021.00/00 0527374083

68063 numbered entries for books, journal articles, and doctoral dissertations published in English in the United States, journal articles accounting for a high percentage of citations. Items grouped in topical subdivisions within 7 chapters: 1. General surveys and texts - 2. Institutions - 3. Constitutional doctrine - 4. Legal doctrine - 5. Biographical - 6. Chronological - 7. Geographical. Some duplication of entries. Supplements promised. *Class No:* 342.53(73)(01)

[3080]

REAMS, B.D. *and* YOAK, S.D. The Constitution of the United States a guide and bibliography to current scholarly research. Dobbs Ferry, N.Y., Oceana Publications Inc., 1987. xvii,[4],545p. $65. ISBN: 0379208881.

Produced to mark the celebrations of the Bicentenary of the signing of the US Constitution in 1787.

An unannotated bibliography arranged according to sections and amendments of the Constitution, listed in reverse chronological order. Covers essays, articles and books in one sequence, and government documents in another, published between 1970 and 1986. Also includes selected general texts, other bibliographies, and a selection of government documents. Author, title and subject indexes.
Class No: 342.53(73)(01)

[3081]

—REAMS, B.D. *and* YOAK, S.D. The Constitutions of the States: a state by state guide and bibliography to current scholarly research. Dobbs Ferry, N.Y., Oceana Publications Inc., 1988. 554p. $60. ISBN: 0379209705.

A companion volume to the above.

Each chapter devoted to the Constitution of a State. Coverage almost entirely a survey of periodical literature. Indexes by title, author and case name. *Class No:* 342.53(73)(01)

[3082]

ZWIRN, J., *comp.* Accessing U.S. government information: subject guide to jurisdiction of the executive and legislative branches. Revised and expanded edition. Westport, CT, Greenwood Press, 1996. xvii,178p. £46.95. (*Bibliographies and indexes in law and political science, no.24.*) ISBN: 0313297657. ISSN: 07426909.

Includes general and specific subjects which form the jurisdiction of the US government, this volume details legal authorities, principal offices, financial resources and their patterns of interaction in order to illustrate the most appropriate methods/authors accessing federal data. *Class No:* 342.53(73)(01)

[3083]

ZWIRN, J. Congressional publications: a research guide to legislation, budgets and treaties. Littleton, Col., Libraries Unlimited, 1983. 195p. $22.50. ISBN: 0872873587.

An explanation of how political, social and economic forces shape national public policy, followed by chapters on the relationship of congressional strategy to its information gathering and producing role. The main part of the book deals with the legislative process (policy research, hearings, reports, debates, voting, bills and resolutions). Basic sources are included at the end of most chapters. Document and subject indexes. '... marred by poor proofreading and the author's convoluted sentence structure' (*Choice,* v.20(10), June 1983, p.1440). *Class No:* 342.53(73)(01)

Handbooks & Manuals

[3084]

Congressional quarterly's guide to the Congress of the United States. 3rd ed. Washington, Congressional Quarterly Inc., 1982,. xx, [1],1185p. illus. $90. ISBN: 0871872390.

First published 1971.

Carefully defines and explains, with full footnotes, the complex procedures and issues of the US House of Representatives and Senate. 7 chapters: 1. The origins and development of Congress - 2. Powers of Congress - 3. Congressional procedures - 4. Housing and support of Congress - 5. Congress and the electorate - 6. Pressures on Congress - 7. Qualifications and conduct. Several appendices (Biographical index of members, 1789-1982; Constitution; Documents of the pre-Constitutional period; Congressional statistics; Congressional rules; Glossary of Congressional terms; Lobbying; etc.). Detailed index. 'An essential reference work' (*Choice,* May 1977, p.344, of the 2nd ed.). *Class No:* 342.53(73)(035)

Reviews & Abstracts

[3085]

CIS/Index. Congressional Information Service/Index to publications of the United States Congress. Washington, D.C., Congressional Information Service, 1970 - . Monthly; quarterly and annual cumulations. Service basis. ISSN: 00078514.

Abstracts and indexes US Congressional hearings, reports, committee prints, and other Congressional papers issued during the previous month. Very detailed indexing. 'In every respect the master index to the total prolific output of the US Congress' (*RQ,* v.11(1), Fall, 1972, p.32). Available on CD-ROM (Congressional Masterfile). *Class No:* 342.53(73)(048)

Yearbooks & Directories

[3086]

The Almanac of American politics, 1990: the Senators, the Representatives, the Governors - their records, States and districts. New York, National Journal (previously Dutton), 1989. 1500p. $56.95. ISBN: 0892340436.

First published 1972. Biennial.

Data under States (Alabama ... Wyoming) and Congressional districts. Senate and House of Representatives committees. Name index. *Class No:* 342.53(73)(058)

Maps & Atlases

[3087]

MARTIN, K.C. The Historical atlas of the United States Congressional Districts, 1789-1983. New York, Macmillan/Free Press, 1982. 302p. $150.

Includes an index to members of the House of Representatives, identifying the Congress(es) each served in. *Class No:* 342.53(73)(084.3)

Libraries

[3088]

World directory of national parliamentary libraries. Dietz, W., *ed.* IFLA, Section of Parliamentary Libraries, 1985. x,379p.

Entries arranged by countries, A-Z, by the English names (Albania ...Zimbabwe), with 'see references' from earlier names. Information given includes library address, telephone number, person in charge; parliamentary papers (*e.g.* Hansard, Votes and proceedings, Standing orders, Bills, Committee papers, journals, etc.); publications concerning the library; and publications by the library. Descriptions are brief. *Class No:* 342.53:061:026/027

Human Rights

[3089]

DEVINE, C., *et al.* Human rights: the essential reference Poole, H., *ed.* London, Oryx, 1999 311p. £51.95. ISBN: 157356205x.

Apart from the texts of declarations of human rights of one type or another, the volume provides a history of human rights before 1945, and account of the Universal Declaration of Human Rights, accounts of contemporary human rights movements - including the biographies of c. 40 activists - and a discussion of current issues including HIV. *Class No:* 342.7

Bibliographies

[3090]

ANDREWS, J.A. *and* HINES, W.D. Keyguide to information sources on the international protection of human rights. London, Mansell; New York, Facts on File, 1987. 169p. £28; $40. ISBN: 0720118735, UK; 0816018227, US.

An introduction to the international and regional protection of human rights, and to its literature. Part 1. General background, has overviews of the history of human rights, international treaties and conventions, and individual rights; pt.2 is an annotated bibliography arranged by general topics (*e.g.* treaties, constitutional protection) and by format (*e.g.* by law reports, bibliographies); and p.3 has brief descriptions of a wide range of organizations. Index to authors, titles, subjects and organizations. 'An essential and timely research tool' (*International affairs*, v.63(4), Autumn 1987, p.725). 'Highly recommended' (*Choice*, v.25(6), February 1988, p.881). *Class No:* 342.7(01)

[3091]

ANDREWS, J.A. *and* HINES, W.D. 'The Literature of human rights'. In *British book news*, July 1984, p.390-3.

Sections on sources of material, periodicals, theoretical and general works, textbooks on international protection, human rights in Europe, and human rights in UK law. Lists 44 books and 10 reports and journals. *Class No:* 342.7(01)

[3092]

COLUMBIA UNIVERSITY. Center for the Study of Human Rights. Human rights: a topical bibliography. Boulder, Col., Westview, 1983. xii,299p. $29.95. ISBN: 086531571x.

2500 entries arranged in over 150 categories. Main sections, each subdivided, are: 1. General and introductory works - 2. Philosophical and theoretical works - 3. National and international perspectives - 4. Specific rights (47 subdivisions) - 5. Related topics - 6. Teaching human rights - 7. Reference materials (collected documents, bibliographies, directories, selected journals, organizations providing regular human rights reports). Index of authors, p.271-296; brief subject index, p.297-299. *Class No:* 342.7(01)

[3093]

FRIEDMAN, J.R. *and* SHERMAN, M.I., *eds. & comps.* Human rights: an international and comparative law bibliography. Westport, CT., Greenwood Press, 1985. xxvi,868p. $76.95; £64.50. (*Bibliographies and indexes in law and political science, no.4.*) ISBN: 0313247676.

Authorised by the Division of Human Rights and Peace of Unesco.

In 3 parts: 1. Rights - 2. Institutions - 3. Source guide. Part 1 is arranged A-Z by subjects (Aliens - Associations - Asylum ... Children - Civil and political rights - Conscience - Cultural rights - Detention ... Privacy - Peace ... Women) subdivided A-Z by authors. 4306 citations, in over 20 languages with English translation in brackets for all other languages except French. Part 2 covers organizations, procedures, doctrines, and practices, etc. Author index, p.809-854; secondary subject index, p.855-868 is not sufficiently detailed. *Class No:* 342.7(01)

[3094]

Human rights bibliography. Geneva,United Nations Centre for Human Rights, 1992. 5v.(2086p.). $95 (CD-ROM, 1980-93. $190). ISBN: 9211003776.

Bibliography of UN documents and publications on human rights, racial discrimination, apartheid, etc., published from 1980-1990. Over 9000 entries grouped according to the human rights classification, subdivided A-Z by title. Each entry includes title, publication place and date, pagination, notes on document content, and other relevant information.. Author and subject indexes. *Class No:* 342.7(01)

[3095]

VERSTAPPEN, B., . *comp. and ed.* Human rights reports: ar annotated bibliography of fact-finding missions. New York, K.G. Saur Inc., 1987. xiii,393p. $75. DM198. ISBN: 0905450353, US; 3598107456, Germany.

Prepared under the auspices of the Netherlands Institute of Human Rights.

An annotated bibliography reporting on fact-finding missions sponsored by both governmental and non-governmental organizations. Covers a wide range of subjects, including arrest and detention, prison conditions, religious freedom and the position of the churches, refugees and displaced persons, trade unions and freedom of association. *c.*550 reports conducted between 1970 and 1986, classified by country or region. Subject and organization indexes. *Class No:* 342.7(01)

[3096]

WHALEN, L. Human rights: a reference handbook. Santa Barbara, CA, ABC-Clio, 1989. 218p. $37. ISBN: 0874360935.

Primary purpose is to bring together those materials on human rights that would be useful to researchers, teachers, students, activists and others interested in the subject. An annotated bibliography of print and non-print materials on the subject produced betwen 1982 and 1988, including indexes and abstracts, directories, anthologies, monographs, periodicals, films, videos, filmstrips, audiotapes, and databases. The bibliography is preceded by a chronology from 1941 to 1988, a 14 page biographical section on 15 people, and an annotated directory of human rights organizations. Also included are texts of important human rights documents. Index of authors, subjects and organizations. *Class No:* 342.7(01)

Encyclopaedias

[3097]

Encyclopedia of human rights. Lawson, E.H. *and* Ayala-Lasso, J. and Wiseberg, L.S., *eds.* London, Taylor & Francis, 1996. xli,1715p. £275. ISBN: 1560323620.

A major compendium, arranged A-Z. Includes over 300 original texts of international and regional treaties; reports on general and specialized subjects (*eg* health care, the environment, women's and children's rights, rights of minorities and indigenous peoples), specialized conventions and declarations on apartheid, terrorism, etc. guarantees of fundamental rights around the world and an overview of the human rights situation in more than 150 countries; plus information on over 130 non-governmental and intergovernmental organization (*e.g.* UN, OAS). Fully cross-referenced. 100-page bibliography. 16 appendices. 'No other work approaches the massive scope of this encyclopedia'(*Booklist*, v.99(6), 15 November 1991, p.642). *Class No:* 342.7(031)

Handbooks & Manuals

[3098]

BROWNLIE, I. Basic documents on human rights. 3rd ed. Oxford, Clarendon Press, 1992. x,631p. £20. ISBN: 0198256833.

First published in 1971; 2nd ed. 1981.

Designed to provide a collection of sources on human rights issues in the form of a handbook. Covers recent UN declarations and conventions, European institutions, the contribution of the ILO, and developments in the Third World. *Class No:* 342.7(035)

[3099]
World human rights guide. Humana, C., *comp.* 2nd ed. New York, Facts on File; London, Hodder & Stoughton, 1986. xviii,344p. tables, charts, maps. $35; £19.95. ISBN: 0816014043, US; 0850580757, UK.

First published 1983.

Assesses information about human rights in 120 major countries, from data compiled from a 40-item questionnaire based on 3 UN documents (Universal Declaration of Human Rights. International Covenant on Economic, Social and Cultural Rights. International Convenant on Civil and Political Rights). Arranged A-Z by country and including human rights rating; life expectancy; infant mortality; form of government; UN covenants ratified; income per head; percentage of gross national product on military; state of health; education; factors affecting human rights; summary. The amount of information depending on what could be collected by questionnaire and extensive literature search. *Class No:* 342.7(035)

Dictionaries

[3100]
CONDÉ, H.V. A Handbook of international human rights terminology. University of Nebraska Press, 1999. 256p. $35. £33.25. ISBN: 0803215010.

Thorough definitions of about 800 terms and acronyms commonly found in contemporary human rights literature. Includes bibliography. *Class No:* 342.7(038)

[3101]
EUROPEAN PARLIAMENT. Terminology of human rights: English/French/German/Italian/Dutch/Danish/Greek. 3rd ed. Luxembourg, European Parliament, 1982. 342p. £11.

Rev. ed. published 1977.

English-based terms with equivalents and reverse indexes in the other languages. 'This valuable glossary' (*The Incorporated Linguist*,Autumn 1976, p.106, of the revised 1977 ed.). *Class No:* 342.7(038)

[3102]
Human rights organizations and periodicals directory, 1993. Ginger, A.F., *and others, eds.* Irregular in the past, now biennial. Berkeley, CA, Meiklejohn Civil Liberties Institute.

Over 1000 entries arranged A-Z, describing US-based organizations, periodicals, publishers and library collections that focus on human rights, civil rights, and civil liberties, etc. Directory information and brief descriptions are based on replies to a questionnaire and on the Federal agencies guide. Indexes by subject and type of activity, by periodical title, and by geographical area. *Class No:* 342.7(038)

[3103]
MARIE J.-B. Glossaire des droits de l'homme: termes fondamentaux dans les instruments universels et régionaux: Français-Anglais. Glossary of human rights: basic terms in universal and regional instruments: English-French. Paris, Editions de la Maison des Sciences de l'Homme, under the auspices of Institut International des Droits de l'Homme, 1981. 339p. £13.35. *Class No:* 342.7(038)

Yearbooks & Directories

[3104]
Human rights directory: Latin America, Africa, Asia. Wiseberg, L.S. and Scoble, H.M., *eds and* Human Rights Internet staff, *comp.*. 2nd ed. Garrett Park, Washington, Human Rights Internet, 1987. 243p. $30. ISBN: 0939338009.

First published 1981.

c.400 organizations, including 32 PEN affiliates and 20 Amnesty International affiliates, from c.70 countries. Emphasis is on Latin America, The Caribbean, Africa, the Middle East, Asia and the Pacific, but there is also a listing of 70 organizations based in Europe and North America. Amount of information varies from simple name and address to entries including origin, purposes, programmes, publications, presidents, etc. Initial arrangement is by countries. Indexes of English-name, non-English name, acronyms and subjects. *Class No:* 342.7(058)

[3105]
—WISEBERG, L.S., *and others, eds.* Human rights directory: Latin America and the Caribbean. Cambridge, MA, Human Rights Internet (USA), Harvard Law School, 1990. 528p. $50. (*(Human rights internal reporter, 13, no.2-3)*.)

First published 1981. Early editions also covered Africa, Asia, etc. (see above).

34 chapters (area, individual countries, international organizations). More than 800 organizations, primarily non-governmental, operating inside or outside Latin America, whose primary concern is human rights in that region. Civil, political and economic prerogatives of the individual, *and* also rights specific to women, children, indigenous peoples, refugees, etc. Omits 'universal' organizations (included in the 1987 volume). Bilingual text. Cross-references. Index. *Class No:* 342.7(058)

[3106]
Yearbook on human rights. First published 1946. Annual. New York, United Nations.

Extracted texts and summaries of significant national constitutional, legislative and judicial developments on personal, civil, political,economic, social and cultural rights. Covers national developments in 30 countries, the activities of the supervisory bodies on racial discrimination, and international developments in the United Nations and Specialized Agencies. *Class No:* 342.7(058)

Worldwide

Encyclopaedias

[3107]
LANGLEY, W.E. Encyclopedia of human rights issues since 1945. London, Fitzroy Dearborn, 1999. 422p. $65. £45. ISBN: 1579581668.

than 400 entries on incidents, violations, countries and human rights activists. Each topic includes brief bibliography. *Class No:* 342.7(100)(031)

Africa

Encyclopaedias & Dictionaries

[3108]
SAHA, S. Dictionary of human rights advocacy organizations in Africa Westport CT, London, Greenwood, 1999 290p. £47.95 ISBN: 0313309450.

Nearly 400 organizations, mostly in Africa itself but some outside, are listed alphabetically, with descriptions of them, their history and their specific area of concern - often, of course a specific country. There are two appendixes, the first of which lists the countries of Africa which have human rights provisions written into their constitutions, the second has a number of declarationf of human rights - beginning with Magna Carta. *Class No:* 342.7(6)(03)

USA

Yearbooks & Directories

[3109]
O'CONNOR, K. *and* **EPSTEIN, L. Public interest law groups:** institutional profiles. Westport, CT., Greenwood Press, 1989. 261p. $45. ISBN: 0313247870.

Detailed profiles for c.170 US public interest groups concerned with the protection of civil rights, legal aid, conservation, consumer interest, abortion, and capital punishment. Information includes a brief history of the organization, sometimes with discussion of legal cases with which it has been concerned. Entries average 1-page, and usually include references. Appendix A has brief descriptions of c.50 more groups. Index of cases cited. *Class No:* 342.7(73)(058)

Thesauri

[3110]
STORMORKEN, B. *and* **ZWAAK, L. Human rights terminology in international law:** a thesaurus. Dordrecht, Martinus Nijhoff, 1988. 234p. Dfl.100; £30.95.

Based on actual texts of 8 most important human rights conventions. 4 sections: Master listing (the thesaurus) - A-Z listing of all terms - KWOC listing - Articles listing by convention in abbreviated form. Stormorken is Head of the Human Rights Documentation Centre of the Council of Europe in Strasbourg. *Class No:* 342.7:025.43

Education Institutions

[3111]
World directory of human rights teaching and research institutions. Social and Human Sciences Documentation Centre and the Division of Human Rights and Peace. Paris, Unesco/Berg, 1988. xxiv,216p. F.125; $49.95. ISBN: 923102504x, Unesco; 0854962298, Berg.

An inventory of all human rights higher education programmes which contain the academic, technical and financial information required by potential candidates. Field codes and an index of countries precedes the directory, which is in 5 sections: I. Index of names and acronyms of institutions - II. List of entries (divided into 2 groups: International and regional institutions - National institutions; and include name, address, date created, staff, type of organization, human rights education programme) - III. Index by research subject, with indication of host country of the institute - IV. Index of courses and subjects taught, with indication of the host country of the institution - V. Index of institutions providing scholarships.

A 2nd ed. was published in 1992. *Class No:* 342.7:061:37

Citizens Rights

Great Britain

[3112]

NATIONAL COUNCIL FOR CIVIL LIBERTIES. **Civil liberty:** the NCCL guide to your rights. Grant, L., *and others*. 3rd ed. Harmondsworth, Mddx, Penguin Books, 1978. 618p. illus. £1.95.

First published 1972.

29 sections: 1. The powers of the police - 2. Your rights in the criminal courts ... 5. Motorists - 6. Drugs - 7. Sex - 8. The worker and the law - 9. Consumer rights - 10. Race discrimination - 11. Your rights in the civil courts ... 13. Censorship and secrecy - 14. Industrial privacy ... 22. Housing - 23. Medical rights - 24. Death ... 26. Complaints against government, public authorities and the professions ... 29. European Commission on Human Rights. 3 appendices (*e.g.* Organizations which give help and advice; Index of Acts of Parliament). Analytical index, p.605-18. *Class No:* 342.71(410)

[3113]

Reader's Digest you and your rights: an A to Z guide to the law. Williams, D.W., *ed.* 9th ed. London, Reader's Digest Association Ltd., 1986. 752p. illus. £16.95.

A to Z entries (Abandoned vehicle ... Zebra crossing). Written in simple language and well sectionalised, it makes good use of two-colour illustrations, facsimiles, and cross-references. Quotes cases and decisions. 'How to make a complaint', p.736-752. Index. A 10th ed. was published in 1991 (ISBN 0276420055). *Class No:* 342.71(410)

Bibliographies

[3114]

MORBY, G. **Know how to find out about your rights.** 2nd ed. London, Pluto Press & Library Association Publishing Ltd., 1982. 188p. £3.95. ISBN: 0861043596.

First published as *Know how guide to information training and campaigning materials for information and advice workers*.

A critical guide to the literature. Sections: General reference and information services - Immigration, nationality and race - Sex and sexual discrimination - Battered women and refuges - Family law - Housing - Money, tax and debt - Consumer rights - Health, mental health and drugs - Retirement, death, and coping with bereavement - The police and the criminal law - The legal system and general principles of law - Children, young people's rights and education - Employment and unemployment - Group work, campaigning and fund raising - Training materials - Publishers and their addresses. Index, p.174-188. *Class No:* 342.71(410)(01)

Criminal Justice

[3115]

Vandalism: a state of the art review and guide to sources of information. Farmer, P. 2nd ed. Stamford, Lincs., Capital Planning Information, 1987. 61p. £7.75. (*CPI Topicguide, no.5.*) ISBN: 0906011434.

First published 1982. *Class No:* 343.1

Bibliographies

[3116]

BEST,, R.A. *and* PICQUET, D.C. **Computer crime, abuse, liability and security:** a comprehensive bibliography, 1970-1984. Jefferson, N.C., McFarland & Co, 1985. iv,155p. $33. £24.75. ISBN: 0899501486.

1704 unannotated entries for journal articles and 293 books, for the subjects in the title plus privacy, patents, copyright, antitrust and trade regulation. Books arranged A-Z by author, articles by title. No subdivisions. English-language material only. Co-author and detailed subject indexes. *Class No:* 343.1(01)

[3117]

Criminal justice periodical index. Ann Arbor, Mich., University Microfilms International, Serials Index, 1975-. 3pa. (Base vol. & semi-annual update.). $260pa. ISSN: 01465818.

Lists *c.*30,000 references a year under subjects, A-Z, from *c.*100 titles (mostly US) covering criminal law, criminology, drug abuse, family law, juvenile justice, police studies, prison administration, rehabilitation, security systems, etc. Includes book reviews. Extensive cross-references. Author index each issue. 3rd issue each year is cumulation for the year. Also available online. *Class No:* 343.1(01)

[3118]

DEIGHTON, S., *ed.* **The New criminals:** a bibliography of computer related crime. 2nd ed. London, Institution of Electrical Engineers, 1979. [44p.]. £10. ISBN: 0852964560.

112 annotated entries arranged in two main sections, each subdivided: 1. Computer abuse (1. Books - 2. General - 3. The crime - 4. The criminals); 2. Protection and security (1. Books - 2. General - 3. Security systems - 4. Auditing - 5. Legal aspects - 6. Insurance). References were taken from INSPEC and the *Quarterly bibliography of computers and data processing,* and include all relevant material in the joint library of the IEE and the British Computer Society. *Class No:* 343.1(01)

Encyclopaedias

[3119]

Encyclopaedia of world crime, criminal justice, criminology and law enforcement. Nash, J.R. Wilmette, Il., Crime Books Inc. (distributed by Marhsall Cavendish), 1990. 6v (5500p.) illus. $600 the set. ISBN: 0923582002.

V.1-4 have over 50,000 articles, with 4000 illustrations, including stories of criminals, prosecutors, executioners, legal theorists, assassination victims, notorious prisons, organized crime syndicates, crime fighters, and fictional works based on real crime. Length of articles varies from a few sentences to several pages. V.5 is a dictionary of 20000 terms from law enforcement, the underworld, current slang, etc., and also includes summaries of court decisions and legislation. V.6 has an index of proper names; a subject index, and a bibliography of over 25000 books. 'An important work ...' (*RQ* v.30(3), Spring 1991, p.416). *Class No:* 343.1(031)

[3120]

KADISH, S.H., *ed.* **Encyclopedia of crime and justice.** New York, Collier Macmillan, 1983. 4v.(1790p.). $300. ISBN: 0029181100.

286 articles organized topically, which present all sides of the cogent arguments. Reading lists are given after each article. Several multi-articles on the biggest problem areas (*e.g.* sentencing (10 articles); police (9 articles); prisons (6 articles)) All are well-written. Cross references. Glossary of terms, and excellent index. 'An invaluable interdisciplinary study of the field of criminal justice.' (*Library journal*, v.109(1) January 1984, p.74). *Class No:* 343.1(031)

Reviews & Abstracts

[3121]

Criminal justice abstracts. Monsey, N.Y., Willow Tree Press Inc. (previously the National Council on Crime and Delinquency), 1968-. Quarterly. $140pa. ISSN: 01469177.

Continues *Crime and delinquency literature.* previously as *Selected highlights of crime and delinquency literature* and *Information review on crime and delinquency.*

About 400 informative abstracts in each issue. Claims to cover all criminal justice literature from all disciplines. Subject and geographical index. Author index. Indexes cumulate annually. Cumulated author and subject index, 1968-1985, was published in 1988 (ISBN 0960696059). US slanted. *Class No:* 343.1(048)

[3122]

Criminology, penology & police science abstracts. Criminologica Foundation, the University of Leiden, and Joint Bureaus for Dutch Child Welfare (WIJN), Utrecht, *eds.* Amstelveen, Netherlands, Kugler Publications b.v., for the Criminologica Foundation, London, 1961-. v.1-. 6pa. Dfl.630 pa. $450pa.

Formed by a merger of *Police science abstracts* and *Criminology and penology abstracts*. The former was previously *Abstracts on police science*; the latter *Excerpta criminologica* (v.1-8. 1961-68) and *Abstracts on criminology and penology...* (v.9-19. 1969-79).

Covers the etiology of crime and juvenile delinquency, the control and treatment of offenders, criminal procedure, the administration of justice, and forensic and police science, including forensic medicine. indexes. *Class No:* 343.1(048)

Worldwide

Yearbooks & Directories

[3123]

International directory of private investigators, private detectives, process servers, security guards, security equipment suppliers, security services, debt collecting agencies, covering also certificated bailiffs, status enquiry agents and trade protection societies, 1986-87. 20th ed. Folkestone, Kent, Regency International Publications, 1986. 480p. £19.50. ISBN: 0900618728.

First published 1967. Annual. *Class No:* 343.1(100)(058)

[3124]

A World directory of criminological institutes. Santoro, C.M., *ed.* 5th ed. Rome, United Nations Interregional Crime and Justice Research Institute, 1990. xxxiii,661p. $54. ISBN: 9290780096.

First published 1974; 4th ed. 1986.

Lists *c.*400 criminological organizations and institutes, many international in scope, located in 55 countries. International bodies are followed by countries, A-Z (Argentine ... Zaire - CERDAS - Kinshasa), subdivided by names of organisations, A-Z. Entries have full name and address, history, method of governance, type of activities, staff, finances and publications. *Class No:* 343.1(100)(058)

England & Wales

Tables & Data Books

[3125]

GREAT BRITAIN. Home Office. Criminal statistics, England and Wales, 1992. London, HMSO, 1993. Annual. 230p. tables. £22.70. (*Cm.2410.*) ISBN: 010124102x.

8 sections: 1. Introduction and summary - 2. Notifiable offences recorded by the police - 3. Notifiable offences in which firearms were reported to have been used or stolen - 4. Homicide - 5. Offences cautioned or found guilty - 6. Court proceedings - 7. Sentencing - 8. Use of police bail and court remand. 7 appendices (*e.g.* 5. Standard list offences - 6. Glossary of terms - 7. Statistics on the criminal justice system. *Class No:* 343.1(42)(083)

USA

[3126]

WALSH, J. Crime and criminal justice reference sources. In *Booklist,* v.88(10), January 15, 1992, p.363-4,966.

Lists guides to the literature, bibliographies, dictionaries and encyclopedias, directories, statistical sources, and electronic reference sources. *Class No:* 343.1(73)

Handbooks & Manuals

[3127]

BAILEY, W.G., *ed.* **The Encyclopedia of police science.** New York, Garland, 1989. 718p. illus. $77. (*Garland reference library of social science, 413.*) ISBN: 0824066278.

143 entries on American law enforcement topics, covering technology, administration, history, values and future trends. Intended to be an introduction to the subject, the entries are general in scope and 2 to 14 pages in length. Bibliographies are appended to each entry and two other bibliographies are included: 'Bibliography of police history', including books, dissertations and articles, and 'Bibliography of bibliographies' listing 71 works in chronological order by publication date. 2 Sections of black-and-white photographs. Complementary to J.J. Fay's *Police dictionary and encyclopedia* (1988). *Class No:* 343.1(73)(035)

Criminal Law

Bibliographies

[3128]

DE SCHUTTER, B. *and* **ELIAERTS, C. Bibliography on international criminal law.** Leiden, Sijthoff, 1972. li,423p.

5201 numbered items (books, periodical articles, typescripts) in 11 sections (1. General studies - 2. Extraterritorial jurisdiction - 3. Extradition - 4. Transmission of prosecutions ... 7. War crimes - 8. Other international crimes - 9. Humanitarian law - 10. International Criminal Court - 11. United Nations concern with international criminal law). Index of persons; subject index. *Class No:* 343.5(01)

[3129]

WERNER, J. 'Recent literature on organized crime'. In *International journal of legal information,* v.14(3-4), June-August 1986, p.155-169.

A 2-page essay precedes the bibliography, which is arranged in 3 parts: Books & TV material; Articles; Bibliographies. *c.*250 entries, unannotated, arranged A-Z within the 3 sections. *Class No:* 343.5(01)

Periodicals & Progress Reports

Bibliographies

[3130]

RANK, R. 'Criminal law and criminology': a bibliography of periodicals. In *Law library journal,* v.60(3), August 1967, p.249-71.

Part 1: 320 titles, A-Z, with details of start and frequency; includes

....(contd.)

ceased journals. Part 2 is a list of titles, under 41 countries. 'Especially useful for "dead" periodicals' (*Use of social sciences literature,* ed. by N. Roberts (1977), p.225). *Class No:* 343.5(05)(01)

England

Histories

[3131]

RADZINOWICZ, L. A History of English criminal law and its administration from 1750. London, Stevens & Sons, 1948-86, under the auspices of the Pilgrim Trust. 5v. £100 each vol. ISBN: 0420374604, v.1; 0420374470, v.2; 0420374809, v.3; 0420415904, v.4; 0420462805, v.5; 0420475206, set.

Volumes are: 1. The movement for reform - 2. The clash between private initiative and public interest in the enforcement of law - 3. Cross-currents in the movement for the reform of the police - 4. Grappling for control - 5. The emergence of penal policy. *Class No:* 343.5(420)(091)

Industrial Espionage

[3132]

CORNWALL, H. The Industrial espionage handbook. London, Ebury, 1992. 131p. £9.99

First published 1990.

A handbook on the collection and compilation of commercial intelligence - how to spy, how others could be spying on you, and the resources, disciplines, techniques and technologies available in the service of the industrial espionage operative. 6 appendices, including a list of terms, online services, costs, and useful addresses. Bibliography, p.125-6. Index, p.127-31. *Class No:* 343.534

Murder

Bibliographies

[3133]

ABEL, E., *comp.* **Homicide** a bibliography. Westport, CT., Greenwood Press, 1987. xiii,169p. $29.95. (*Bibliographies and indexes in sociology, no.11.*) ISBN: 0131259011.

1919 unannotated entries relating to articles, monographs and documents on homicide from the scientific literature, arranged A-Z by author. Most citations are from the late 1970s or early 1980s, plus a few classics. Subject index, p.157-169, has broad headings. *Class No:* 343.611(01)

[3134]

CHARNY, I.W., *ed.* **Genocide:** a critical bibliographic review. London, Mansell Publishing Ltd., 1988. xiv,273p. £36.50. ISBN: 072011876x.

A publication of the Institute of the International Conference on the Holocaust and Genocide.

'Each chapter ... is intended to present an authoritative, encyclopedia-like statement of the knowledge base in a given field or area of study of genocide, and an annotated critical bibliography' (*Introduction*). 13 chapters: 1. The study of genocide - 2. Intervention and prevention of genocide - 3. The history and sociology of genocidal killings - 4. The Holocaust ... 5. The Armenian genocide - 6. Genocide in the USSR ... 11-13. are on literature, art and film. Bibliographies follow each chapter. Index, p.257-273. *Class No:* 343.611(01)

[3135]

NEWTON, M. Mass murder: an annotated bibliography. New York, Garland, 1988. 378 p. $45. (*Garland reference library of social science, 427.*) ISBN: 0824066197.

A bibliography and biographical dictionary of men and women who have perpetrated murders and killings. Over 600 annotated entries, avoiding sensational works ' ... a welcome research guide' (*Choice,* v.25(10), June 1988, p. 1538). *Class No:* 343.611(01)

Encyclopaedias

[3136]

WILSON, C. *and* **PITMAN, P. Encyclopaedia of murder.** Rev. ed. London, Pan Books, 1984. 672p. illus. £4.95. ISBN: 0330283006.

First published 1961 by Arthur Barker Ltd.

A detailed contents list is followed by 2 essays ('The study of murder' by Colin Wilson and 'Why an encyclopaedia of murder?' by Patricia Pitman). The main part of the book consists of biographies of murderers, arranged A-Z by name followed by a select bibliography and a classified index. *Class No:* 343.611(031)

[3137]

—WILSON, C. *and* SEAMAN, D. Encyclopaedia of modern murder, 1962-82. London, Arthur Barker Ltd., 1983. xx,267p. illus. £10.95. ISBN: 0213168766.

'The age of murder', an introductory essay by Colin Wilson, is followed by the main section of the work, 'A-Z of murderers, terrorist organizations and victims' which has 102 names, mainly UK and US. A select bibliography, p.255-256; a classified index, p.257-258; and a name index, p.259-267 complete the book, which is a sequel to *Encyclopaedia of murder (qv)*. *Class No:* 343.611(031)

Biographies

[3138]

GAUTE, J.H.H. *and* ODELL, R. **New Murderer's who's who.** New ed. London, Headline, 1989. 512p. illus. £7.99. ISBN: 0747232709.

Biographical sketches of 360 murderers (mostly British; 85 are American). Limited to crimes on which books have appeared. Bibliography of 746 items fails to state publishers and dates of publication. Arrangement and faulty subject index are criticised in *Library review* (v.29. Autumn 1980, p.217). 'Still, an essential reference book' (*Library journal* 1 May 1979, p.1042).

Class No: 343.611(092)

Suicide

Bibliographies

[3139]

LESTER, D., *and others*. **Suicide:** a guide to information sources. Detroit, Mich., Gale Research Company, 1980. xiv. 294p. $68. (*Social issues and social problems information guide sources,v.3.*) ISBN: 0810314150.

The first and main part covers the various sources on the subject in general (*e.g.* bibliographies; basic reference sources; dissertations and theses; statistics; the news media). The 4 remaining parts concern Theories of suicide; Social and environmental correlates of suicide; Psychological correlates and analyses of suicide; and Suicide prevention. Included: a checklist of doctoral dissertations, of authors who committed suicide, and of suicide in literature and mythology. Author, title and subject indexes. *Class No:* 343.614(01)

[3140]

—McINTOSH, J.L., *comp*. Research on suicide: a bibliography. Westport, CT., Greenwood Press, 1985. xiii,323p. $35. (*Bibliographies and indexes in psychology, no.2.*) ISBN: 0313239924.

Updates and expands Lester's work. Over 2300 entries, mainly 1970-, arranged in 10 chapters, all subdivided: 1. Overview works - 2. Definitions and the variety of self-destructive behaviour - 3. Historical background - 4. Theories of suicide - 5. Demography and epidemiology of suicide: statistics and risk factors - 6. Prevention, intervention, treatment, assessment and prediction of suicidal behaviour - 7. The need for education about suicide - 8. Ethics of suicide: moral, philosophical, religious and legal aspects - 9. After suicide: prevention - 10. Suicide literature directed to specific gatekeepers and suicide and art. Noteworthy items and uninformative titles only are annotated. Selected sources have asterisks. Author index, p. 288-314. Subject index, p.315-323. *Class No:* 343.614(01)

[3141]

—PRENTICE, A.E. Suicide: a selective bibliography of over 2,200 items. Metuchen, N.J., Scarecrow Press, 1974. 227p. $19. ISBN: 0810807734.

Covers English-language material, mostly published 1960-73, and is narrower in scope as well as being less current than the above. *Class No:* 343.614(01)

[3142]

Suicide and the elderly: an annotated bibliography and review. Osgood, N.J. *and* McIntosh, J.L. Westport, CT., Greenwood Press, 1986. xiii,193 p. $59.95. (*Bibliographies and indexes in gerontology . 3.*) ISBN: 0313247862.

A 36-page literature review is followed by an annotated list of bibliographical sources, with fairly lengthy descriptions, and a list of non-English works, some annotated. An appendix gives sources of demographic data. Author and subject indexes ' ... an excellent source ... ' (*Choice* v.24(7), March 1987 p.1034). *Class No:* 343.614(01)

Encyclopaedias

[3143]

EVANS, G. *and* FARBEROW, N.L. **The Encyclopedia of suicide.** New York. Facts on File, 1988. 434p.tables,charts. $40. ISBN: 0816013977.

Intended as a companion volume to the publisher's encyclopedias on alcohol and drug abuse.

An introduction giving an overview of suicide as a social, cultural and historical phenomenon, precedes the encyclopedia of over 500 entries treating the various aspects of the subject. Entries range in

....(contd.)

length from a few sentences to long essays, averaging about 700 words. Includes biographies of famous suicides, noted authors and researchers, as well as historical events involving suicide. Extensive bibliography as well as publications mentioned in the text. Subject index. ' ... comprehensive work on a socially prevalent and disturbing problem' (*Reference books bulletin*, 15 November 1988, p 552).

Class No: 343.614(031)

Prisons

Russia

[3144]

ROSSI, J. **The Gulag handbook:** a historical dictionary of Soviet penitentiary institutions and terms related to the forced labour camps. London, Overseas Publications Exchange Ltd., 1987. 546p. ISBN: 0903868970.

Published in USSR in 1987, and in New York in 1988 as *The Gulag handbook: an encyclopedic dictionary of Soviet penal institutions ...*, translated by William Burhans (Paragon House. 608p. $55. ISBN 1557780242).

A linguistic, encyclopedic guide, cross-referencing thousands of terms invented by, for and about the Gulag. *Class No:* 343.81(47)

Libraries

Bibliographies

[3145]

HARTZ, F.R., *and others*. **Prison librarianship:** a selective, annotated, classified bibliography, 1945-1985. Jefferson, N. Carolina, McFarland & Company, 1987. ix,115p. £19.95. ISBN: 089950258x.

185 lengthy entries arranged in 19 sections and including Administration and planning of correctional libraries; Background reading; Bibliographies; Censorship issues; Libraries and educational rehabilitation; Law libraries; and Library services. Author and subject indexes. US slant. *Class No:* 343.81:061:026/027(01)

Criminology

[3146]

RADZINOWICZ, L. **The Cambridge Institute of Criminology:** its background and scope. London, HMSO, 1988. 96p. £11.50. ISBN: 0113408846.

Outlines the early problems of the Institute, established 1959, examines the scope and content of courses offered, and looks at how the work has evolved over the years. *Class No:* 343.9

Bibliographies of Bibliographies

[3147]

DAVIES, B.L. Criminological bibliographies: uniform citations to bibliographies, indexes and review articles of the literature of crime study in the United States. Westport, CT., Greenwood Press, 1978. xxvi,182p. $36.95. ISBN: 0313205450.

Over 1400 references, in 7 subject sections. Indexed by subject, compiler and issuing body. *Class No:* 343.9(009)

Bibliographies

[3148]

Criminology and forensic sciences: an international bibliography, 1950-1980. Vomende, R., *comp.* Munich, K. G. Saur, 1981-82. 3v. (xv, 2389p.). £110. DM420. $300. ISBN: 3598103743.

An extended survey of 30 years' publication in criminology and related sciences, law and humanities in *c.* 50 countries. Includes *c.* 400,000 published items arranged A-Z by author, with citations in the original language of publication. Books, journal articles, collective works, conference papers, etc., are included. No subject or classified listing. *Class No:* 343.9(01)

[3149]

HOWARD LEAGUE FOR PENAL REFORM. John Howard Library of Criminology and Penology. **Catalogue, 1963.** London, the League, 1963,. 82p.

A list of nearly 3000 items in 8 main sections: 1. Social problems and social services - 2. Crime and criminals - 3. Child welfare and juvenile delinquency - 4. Law and penal procedure - 5. Treatment of offenders and penal institutions - 6. Capital punishment - 7. Biography and memoirs - 8. Miscellaneous: philosophy; psychology. Offical journals and statistics received. Author index. The John Howard Library no longer exists. *Class No:* 343.9(01)

[3150]
PERRY, R. 'Criminology and its literature' In *Use of social sciences literature* ., edited by N. Roberts (1977), p.219-39.

Sections: Introduction - Guide to the literature, bibliographies and library catalogues - Abstracting and indexing services - Periodicals - Official publications - Statistics - Legislation - Conference and Congress proceedings - Books of readings, Festshriften and other collections - Encyclopedias, dictionaries and other reference works - Information and current awareness services - Research in progress. 5 references. Helpful running commentary. *Class No: 343.9(01)*

[3151]
RADZINOWICZ, L. *and* HOOD, R.G. Criminology and the administration of criminal justice: a bibliography. London, Mansell; Westport, CT., Greenwood Press, 1976. 414p. ISBN: 0837190681.

Main sequence of *c.*4500 entries, primarily covering literature published within the last 20 years. 19 subject headings, with chronological sub-arrangement. A supplement (1500 entries) updates to 1976. Concerns the sociology of crime, criminal justice and penology. Author index. 'Much more concerned with issues of policy and research on criminals than with day-to-day practical matters' (*British book news*, April 1977, p.274-5). 'Highly commended' (*Library journal*, v.102, no.12, 1 September 1977, p.1747). Winner of the 1977 Joseph L. Andrews Bibliographic Award of the American Association of Law Libraries. *Class No: 343.9(01)*

[3152]
WRIGHT, M., *ed*. Use of criminology literature. London, Butterworth, 1974. [xii], 242p. (*Information sources for research and development*.)

16 contributors. 13 sections (1. Conducting a search for information on criminology - 2. Sociological aspects of criminology - 3. Psychiatric aspects of crime - 4. Criminological aspects of psychology - 5. Alcoholism and crime: an introductory bibliography - 6. Introduction to the literature of drug dependence - 7. The treatment of offenders - 8. Criminal law and administration of criminal justice - 9. Police literature - 10. Criminal and related statistics - 11. The history of prisons and penal practice - 12. Illustrations in criminological and penal literature - 13. Official publications. Running commentary; well sectionalised chapters. Subject and name index only. 'A useful guide to literature and information in the whole field of criminology, concentrating on British publications, but also referring to some foreign material' (*Brtish book news*, November 1978, p.871). Author was Director of the Howard League for Criminal Reform. *Class No: 343.9(01)*

Handbooks & Manuals

[3153]
International handbook of contemporary developments in criminology. Johnson, E.H., *ed*. Westport, CT., Greenwood Press, 1983. 2v. illus. $125 the set. V.1. $65; V.2.$85. ISBN: 0313210594 v.1; 0313238030 v.2.

V.1. *General issues and the Americas*; v.2. *Europe, Africa, the Middle East and Asia*. Essays on criminology as it is carried out in the differing political-legal contexts of the US and 39 other countries. Collectively, the two volumes are an inventory of variations in the conceptions and work of criminologists around the world. Most articles are followed by bibliographies and many bibliographical entries are annnotated. 'This handbook is unique in its intellectual richness and transnational criminological perspective. (*Choice*, March 1984, p.954). *Class No: 343.9(035)*

Dictionaries

[3154]
DE SOLA, R. Crime dictionary. 2nd ed., rev. & expanded. New York, Facts on File, 1988. xiii,222p. $24.95; £18.50. ISBN: 0816018723.

First published 1981.

Over 10,000 terms, including 1500 new entries, used by criminals and law enforcement professionals, including legal, medical and psychiatric terms; abbreviations; weapons; nicknames of prisons; criminal gangs and terrorist groups; government crime-fighting agencies; criminal and drug-culture slang; criminal and white-collar crime; etc. 3 appendices (Foreign terms - Place-name nicknames - Selected sources. US oriented. *Class No: 343.9(038)*

Polyglot

[3155]
ADLER, J.A., *ed*. Elsevier's dictionary of criminal science in eight languages: English/American - French - Italian - Spanish - Portuguese - Dutch - Swedish - German. Amsterdam, London, etc., Elsevier, 1960. xv,1460p.

10,930 numbered English/American terms, with one-word equivalents in the other 7 languages across the double page, and keys to those languages. Coverage: 'the prevention, detection and suppression of crime, including the physical state, physical conditions and special circumstances of law-breakers, witnesses, and victims'

....(contd.)
(*Preface*). Terms are categorised. The review in *Babel* (v.9(1-2), p.110-1) notes mistranslations and omissions. *Class No: 343.9(038)=00*

English

[3156]
WALSH, D. *and* POOLE, A., *eds*. A Dictionary of criminology. London, Routledge & Kegan Paul, 1983. xi,242p. £14.95. ISBN: 071009549x.

Intended for students, this guide to concepts and terminology frequently used in criminology, includes terms selected from the fields of psychology, psychiatry, penology, sociology, social work, and the law of England and Wales. Cross-references. British slant. 34 contributors. 'Too many entries are merely legal definitions' (*Times educational supplement*, 18 May 1984, p.31). *Class No: 343.9(038)=20*

USA

Bibliographies

[3157]
Crime and punishment in America: a historical bibliography. Santa Barbara, CA., ABC-Clio, 1984. 346p. $38.50. ISBN: 0874363632.

Information taken from the ABC-Clio database.

1396 abstracts of periodical articles published between 1973 and 1982 on crime, criminals, and criminal justice in America from Colonial times to the present day. Topics arranged in 8 chapters and within each chapter arranged by author, A-Z. Subject index with terms rotated. Author index. '... a good basic starting point for research in particular topics in the field ...; (*Choice*, v.21(10), June '1984, p.1440). *Class No: 343.9(73)(01)*

Mafia

[3158]
CAMBRIDGE UNIVERSITY. Institute of Criminology. Mafia: a selected annotated bibliography. Trott, L. *and* Smith, D.C., *comps*. Cambridge, the Institute, 1977. [viii], 141p. Mimeographed.

*c.*1000 annotated entries. Classes A - I (A: Mafia as a criminal organization that operates internationally ... C: Mafia's share in US crime ... F: Mafia seen as a Sicilian sub-culture - G: Mafia as a state of mind rather than an organization - H: Mafia represented in art - I: Unannotated and unclassified references. Author and short title index, p. 114-41. *Class No: 343.91*

Commercial Law

Dictionaries

English

[3159]
FOSTER, S. Business law terms. Edinburgh, W. & R. Chambers Ltd. 1988,. [4],115p. £2.50. ISBN: 0550180656.

A compact guide to the key business law words and phrases used in the commercial world. Short, clear explanations are given. *Class No: 347.7(038)=20*

[3160]
HUDSON, A.H. Dictionary of commercial law. London, Butterworth & Co (Publishers) Ltd., 1983. [4],289p. £9.95. (*Butterworth's professional dictionary series*.) ISBN: 0406681600.

Intended to provide ready access to basic information relating to the terminology of most of the principal topics of both commercial law and intellectual property, describing rather than merely defining words and phrases. Cross-references. 'Copyright' itself: 2 pages, but with Copyright exemptions, in sound recording, literary, dramatic, etc.: 6 pages. 'Form of contract': 2 pages. 'Guarantee': 2 pages. *Class No: 347.7(038)=20*

[3161]
IVAMY, E.R.H. Dictionary of company law. 2nd ed. London, Butterworth, 1985. 264p. £14. (*Butterworths professional dictionary series*.) ISBN: 0406681635.

First published 1983.

Words and phrases used in company law, each entry containing a concise statement of the relevant provisions of the Companies Acts and of significant case law. Entries vary in length (*e.g.* Debenture, 6½ pages; Deed of settlement, 3½ lines; Fraudulent trading, *c.* 600 words). Cross-references. This second edition brings the dictionary up-

....(contd.)
to-date with the Companies Act, 1985, Companies Securities (Insider Dealing) Act, 1985, and the Business Names Act, 1985. *Class No:* 347.7(038)=20

German

[3162]
CREIFELDS, C. **Rechtswörterbuch**. Kauffmann, H., *ed.* 13., neuarbeitete Aufl. München, C.H. Beck, 1996. xvi,1568p. ISBN: 3406401309.
German law dictionary. *Class No:* 347.7(038)=30

[3163]
ROMAIN, A., *and others*. **Dictionary of legal and commercial terms.** v.1: 4th rev. ed.; v.2: 2nd. rev. ed. London, Butterworths; München, C. H. Beck'sche Verlagsbuchhandlung, 1985-1989. 2v .(viii,854; viii,883). £45 each vol. ISBN: 0406038112 v.1.(UK); 0406038120 v.2.(UK); 0406038103 set.
First published 1975. German title is *Wörterbuch der rechts- und wirtschaftssprache*.
v.1. English-German; v.2. German-English. A very detailed dictionary. *Class No:* 347.7(038)=30

Persian (Farsi)

[3164]
FAHIM, K., *and others*. **English-Persian dictionary of legal and commercial terms.** Leiden, E.J. Brill, 1989. xviii,81p. Gld.150; $75. ISBN: 9004084150.
Compiled primarily for the use of the Iran-United States Claims Tribunal at the Hague.
Lists *c.*5000 key legal and commercial English terms and their equivalents in Persian. A companion Persian-English volume is in preparation. *Class No:* 347.7(038)=915.5

Worldwide

[3165]
Digest of commercial laws of the world. Kohlick, G., *ed.* Dobbs Ferry, N.Y., Oceana, for National Association of Credit Management, 1966-72. 11 loose-leaf binders, including forms of commercial agreements and state variations. $850 + supplementary service. ISBN: 0379010003.
Each volume covers a set of countries; each digest deals with such matters as contracts, agency and representation, forms of business organizations, bills of exchange, and recognition of foreign judgement. *Class No:* 347.7(100)

Europe—Western

Handbooks & Manuals

[3166]
THOMAS, R., *general editor*. **Company law in Europe.** London, Butterworths, 1992. 1v. (loose-leaf). £150. ISBN: 0406168016.
Survey of the law relating to companies within individual countries of Europe, the information given extending from general data to detailed notes on specific subjects. *Class No:* 347.7(400)(035)

Great Britain

Bibliographies

[3167]
CLINCH, P. **Business law: an introduction to information sources.** In *Business information review*, v.5(1), July 1989, p.3-17.
The sources of business law, including statutes, statutory instruments, case law and extra-legal sources, are described and evaluated with, in addition, practical advice on their use in enquiry work. (Author's abstract). *Class No:* 347.7(410)(01)

Handbooks & Manuals

[3168]
Butterworths company law handbook, 1993. Walmsley, K., *ed.* 9th ed. London, Butterworths, 1993. xvii,2066p. ISBN: 0406020078.
'The aim is to make available in a convenient and up-to-date form the full text of the most important company law statutes, statutory instruments and European legislation'(Introduction). In 6 parts: 1. Company legislation; 2. Other legislation; 3. Statutory instruments; 4. Selected stamp duties provision; 5. Securities and Investment Board rules and regulations; 6. European Community legislation. Index (to paragraph numbers), p.2027-63. Glossary, p.2065-6. *Class No:* 347.7(410)(035)

[3169]
MEINHARDT, P. *and* DAVIS, N. **Company law in Great Britain.** Aldershot, Hants., Gower Publishing Co. Ltd., 1982. 300p. £22.50. ISBN: 056602389x.
Sets out the main features of company law in Britain in 26 sections: 1. Basic law - 2. Formation of a limited company ... 8. Capital ... 10. Allotment and transfer of shares ... 13. Minority rights and investigation - 13A. Insider dealing ... 20. Audit ... 24. Private companies ... 26. Reform. Select bibliography (2p.). Index (18p.). *Class No:* 347.7(410)(035)

[3170]
Palmer's company law. Schmitthoff, C.M., *and others, eds.* 25th ed. London, Sweet & Maxwell, 1992-. 5v. (looseleaf). £295, updating service: £180 pa. ISBN: 0420446605.
V.1 & 2 have narrative texts (16 parts); v.3 & 4 are on the Companies Acts and other measures (pts A-K); v.5 has tables and index. *Class No:* 347.7(410)(035)

Canada

Handbooks & Manuals

[3171]
FRASER, W. **Fraser's handbook of Canadian company law.** 7th ed. Toronto, Carswell Co. Ltd., 1985. 733p.
6th ed., 1975.
Presented in logical sequence in 23 chapters. Covers the law of several provinces as well as Federal law. Table of fees. List of Statutes applicable in the Dominion. Table of contents. Index. 'Each subject thoroughly explained and discussed and the wealth of information so accumulated is presented in a clear and readable form' (*International journal of legal information*, v.14(1-2), February-April 1986, p.73). *Class No:* 347.7(71)(035)

Consumer Protection

Bibliographies

[3172]
FOREMAN, S. **Consumer monitor: an annotated bibliography of British government and other official publications relating to consumer issues.** Aldershot, Hants., Gower Publishing, 1987. 460p. £35. ISBN: 0566054019.
Prepared on behalf of the National Consumer Council.
*c.*2000 annotated entries in broad subject arrangement, aiming to be comprehensive for the period 1980 to 1 April 1986, and also including some older material. Detailed subject index. 'A little extra background text and explanation would not have gone amiss.' (*Library Association record*, v.89(7), July 1987, p.338). *Class No:* 347.731(01)

[3173]
—GOUKER, D. 'Consumer information sources'. In *Reference books bulletin*, July 1988, p.1791-2, 1794, 1796, 1798, 1800, 1802, 1806-7.
Over 80 titles arranged by general sources (indexes and abstracts, directories, periodicals, and loose-leaf services), followed by individual product groups. *Class No:* 347.731(01)

Handbooks & Manuals

[3174]
HARRIES, J.N. **Consumers: know your rights.** 3rd ed. London, Oyez Longman, 1983. xii, 235p. £5.95. ISBN: 0851207804.
Chapters: 1. The consumer bargain - 2. Buying goods - 3. Consumer safety - 4. Credit - 5. Contractors, repairers and other services - 6. Business practices - 7. Manufacturers' liability for defective products - 8. Who can help? - 9. The European Economic Community. Analytical index, p.227-235. Sectionalised chapters; good use of bold type. *Class No:* 347.731(035)

Ownership & Property

Handbooks & Manuals

[3175]
WILLIAMS, J.F. **A Manager's guide to patents, trade marks & copyright.** London, Kogan Page, 1986. 168p. £12.95. ISBN 1850912033.
16 chapters written in clear, non-legal language: 1. What is 'intellectual property'? ... 3. Advisers ... 7. Trade marks - 8. Copyright - 9. Registered designs - 10. Industrial design copyright 11. Ownership of rights ... 16. The future. 14 appendices (8. Summary of copyright rules; 13. Further reading; 14. Useful names and addresses). Index, p.165-168. *Class No:* 347.77(035)

Dictionaries

Polyglot

[3176]

HIATELLO, A. Glossario trilingue della proprietà industriale ... Trilingual glossary on industrial property. Torino, Albert Meynier, 1985. 93p. L.60,000; SwF.80.

Includes over 500 terms and phrases relative to industrial property. In 3 sections: French-Italian - English-Italian - Italian-French-English. *Class No:* 347.77(038)=00

Copyright

[3177]

GOLDSTEIN, P.M. Copyright: principles, law and practice. Boston, Mass., Little, Brown, & Co., 1989. Supplement: 1991. 3v. and cumulative supplement (xi,486p). ISBN: 0316319651, v.1; 0316319643, v.2; 0316319651, v.3; 0316319694, supplement.

First published in 1949.

16 chapters in v.1 & 2 dealing with rights, infringements, defences, remedies, procedures, other sources of protection, etc. V.3 has Appendices: A: Statutes, legislation, reports & regulations; B: Copyright conventions; C: Forms. Table of cases. Table of statutes. Index, p.949-91.The supplement updates and is superseded from time to time. *Class No:* 347.78

[3178]

TONE, P. Copyright law in the United Kingdom and the European Community. London, Athlone Press, 1990. x,233p. *((European Community law series).)*

'... seeks both to expound the new British law of copyright under the 1988 Act ... and to examine ... the relevant existing rules of Community law ...' *(Preface)*. 8 chapters: 1. Introduction - 2. Subsistence - 3. Infringement - 4. Remedies - 5. Licences - 6. Moral right - 7. Performers' rights - 8. Industrial design. Notes, p.172-223. Bibliography, p.224. Table of cases, p.225-231. Index, p.232-3. *Class No:* 347.78

Handbooks & Manuals

[3179]

Copinger and Skone James on copyright, including international copyright. Garnett, K., *and others, eds.* 14th ed. London, Sweet & Maxwell, 1998. 2v. £250. ISBN: 0421589108.

First published 1870.

11 parts (32 chapters: 1. Introductory and historical - 2. Copyright in literary, dramatic, musical and artistic works and published editions - 3. Related forms of protection - 4. Copyright in cinematographic films, sound recordings and broadcasts - 5. Copyright in special circumstances (*e.g.* public lending right) - 6. European Economic Community - 7. Transitional provisions - 8. Arrangements between authors and publishers, etc. 9. International copyright and the protection of works originating outside the United Kingdom - 10. Copyright law of America and other foreign countries - 11. Forms and precedents. Appendices A-F (A. U.K. Statutes; B. U.K. Orders; C. Copyright conventions and agreements; F. Treaty of Rome). Analytical subject index. The basic manual on the subject. *Class No:* 347.78(035)

[3180]

LINT, M.F. A User's guide to copyright. 4th ed. London, Butterworth, 1997. xxv,451p. illus., 1 form. £42.50. ISBN: 0406046085.

First published 1979.

Explains the law and scope of copyright and provides answers to problems that arise in practice. The text considers the significant developments principally from the EU taking place in this area of law in the context of rental and lending rights and copyright in cable and satellite TV. *Class No:* 347.78(035)

[3181]

THORN, E.A. Understanding copyright: a practical guide. Tunbridge Wells, Jay Books, 1989. 128p. illus. £4.95. ISBN: 1870404033.

Arranged in 8 sections: 1. Defines ownership of copyright, including significance of the copyright symbol - 2. Photocopying and duplication - 3. Copyright of books, film and video rights, etc. Public Lending Right - 4. Sound recordings - 5. Television and video - 6. Problems with copyright for computer programs and software piracy - 7. Artistic works (including photographic work) - 8. Live performances. 7 appendices (Examples of copyright notices - useful organizations - recorded music libraries - signatories to the Berne Convention - further reading (10 items)). Index, p.127-128. Written in non-legal language. Biassed towards the view of the publisher or other owner of the copyright. *Class No:* 347.78(035)

Dictionaries

Polyglot

[3182]

WORLD INTELLECTUAL PROPERTY ORGANIZATION (WIPO). WIPO glossary of terms of the law of copyright and neighbouring rights. Geneva, WIPO, 1980. 281p. £19.50.

In English/ French/Spanish. Also available in English/French/Arabic and English/French/Russian. *Class No:* 347.78(038)=00

Laws

[3183]

Copyright laws and treaties of the world. Unesco *and* World Intellectual Property Organization (WIPO), *and others.* Paris, Unesco; Washington, Bureau of National Affairs Inc., 1956-. Annual Supplements. 3v. (loose-leaf). $ 655 for 3 loose-leaf vols. updated to 1987, including supplements.

'A compilation of the laws, orders, rules, regulations, conventions and treaties which establish, in and between the different countries of the world, the legal provisions for the protection of copyright' *(Explanatory notes).* Arranged by countries. A-Z. *Class No:* 347.78(094.1)

Air Law

Bibliographies

[3184]

HEERE, W.P. International bibliography of air law, 1900-1971. Leiden, Sijthoff; Dobbs Ferry, N.Y., Oceana, 1972. xxvi,569p. $40. ISBN: 0379000105.

Supplements 1972-1976 (1976. xxii, 169p. $22); 1977-1980 (1981. 394p. $69.50. ISBN 90224725550); 1981-1984 (Deventer, Kluwer and Taxation Publishers, 1985. xxxiv, 250p.).

About 10,000 entries in the main work. 16 chapters: 1. General subjects - 2. Organizations in the field of civil international aviation - 3. The administration of national and international aviation - 4. The aviation industry - 5. Aircraft - 6. Aviation personnel - 7. Airports and air navigation facilities - 8. Air transport - 9. Damage to third parties - 10. Accidents, towage and salvage - 11. Insurance - 12. Criminal law - 13. Acts on board aircraft - 14. Military aviation - 15. The laws of war and neutrality - 16. Miscellaneous. Index of names; analytical subject index. The supplements are similarly arranged. *Class No:* 347.8(01)

[3185]

LONDON UNIVERSITY. Institute of Advanced Legal Studies. Union list of air and space law literature in the libraries of Oxford, Cambridge and London. 2nd ed. London, the Institute, 1975. xii,301p. *(Union catalogue no.4, 2nd ed.)*

First published 1956.

About 2000 items with locations in 22 libraries. Part 1: Background works and source materials (dictionaries, bibliographies, etc.) - 2: Works on air and space law in general and on specific topics (*e.g.* legal aspects of military aviation and astronautics). Index of authors and editors, corporate author index; subject index. *Class No:* 347.8(01)

Legal Procedures & Personnel

[3186]

Stone's justice's manual, 1993. Richman, J. *and* Draycott, A.T., *eds.* 125th ed. London, Butterworth & Co (Publishers) Ltd.; Shaw & Sons Ltd., 1993. 3v. ISBN: 040601602x.

First published 1842.

Detailed authoritative information. 10 parts in 3v. V.1. Part 1. Magistrate's Courts, procedure - II. Evidence - III. Sentencing - IV. Family law - V. Youth Courts - VI. Licensing. V.2. Part VII. Offences, matters of complaint, etc. V.3. Part VIII. Transport - IX. Precedents and forms - X. Miscellaneous legislation. Table of Statutes and treaties. A-Z table of Statutory Instruments and EEC regulations. Chronological list of S.I.'s. Table of cases. Index, p.401-731. *Class No:* 347.9

Encyclopaedias

[3187]
REDDEN, K.R. Modern legal systems cyclopedia. Buffalo, N.Y., William S. Hein & Co., 1984. 10v. (loose-leaf, various pagings). $1375 the set; $175 each vol. ISBN: 0899413005, the set.

Designed as a standard reference source for practising attorneys and academic institutions. Each volume covers a particular geographic region:- 1. North America - 2. Pacific Basin - 3. Western Europe (EEC countries) - 4. Western Europe (non-EEC countries) - 5. Middle East - 6. Africa - 7. Central America and Caribbean - 8. Eastern Europe - 9. Asia - 10. South America. Annotated bibliography follows each chapter. Value is enhanced by periodic supplementation and regional coverage, according to *International journal of legal information,* v.14(5-6), October-December, 1986, p.236).
Class No: 347.9(031)

Ireland

Bibliographies

[3188]
O'HIGGINS, P. Bibliography of Irish trials and other legal proceedings. Abingdon, Oxon, Professional Books, 1986. 300p. £42.50. ISBN: 0862050804.

Nearly 2000 entries in 12 sections: 1. Digests - 2. Law reports - 3. Reports of single trials by named reporters - 4. Anonymous reports of trials - 5. Election cases - 6. Fishery cases - 7. Judge's charges to Grand Juries - 8. Books containing reports of trials - 9. Speeches by Counsel - 10. Speeches from the dock - 11. Counsel's opinion - 12. Miscellaneous. Indexes of cases, persons, and subjects.
Class No: 347.9(415)(01)

Costume & Dress

[3189]
HARGREAVES-MAWDSLEY, W.N. A History of legal dress in Europe until the end of the eighteenth century. Oxford, Clarendon Press, 1963. xii,151p. illus.

Chapters: 1. Italy, Spain and Portugal - 2. France - 3. Great Britain and Ireland - 4. German-speaking countries, the Low Countries, Switzerland, Scandinavia, Hungary and Poland. Short glossary of terms, with line-drawings. Most of the illustrations are half-tones, not particularly clear or numerous, but backed by handy descriptions (*e.g.* of the dress of the Chief of Police in France). The 'Critical bibliography' (p.121-9) covers manuscripts and books but it is not annotated. Analytical index. *Class No:* 347.90:391

Civil Proceedings

[3190]
The Encyclopedia of forms and precedents other than court forms. Walton R., Sir. 5th ed. London, Butterworths, 1985-93. ISBN: 0406023603, the set.

3rd ed. 1945-50. 20v.; 4th ed. 1964-73, 24v.

Aim is 'to provide a form for at least every ordinary transaction which occurs in practice and for all those except such as are purely academic. To present these forms in a simple and straightforward manner so that the nature and effect can be understood at a glance. To collect and arrange them so that they can be found with the utmost facility' (*Publishers' note*). Arranged under topics, A-Z. *A consolidated index, 1988/89, to published volumes* was issued in 1989. Also two loose-leaf 'service' volumes. *Class No:* 347.91/.98

[3191]
—Atkin's encyclopaedia of court forms in civil proceedings. Jacob J.I.H., Sir, *and others, eds.* 2nd ed. London, Butterworth, 1961-. 41v. loose-leaf supplementary service. £966. ISBN: 040601020x.

First published 1937 in 16v.

Arranged under topic, A-Z. *Class No:* 347.91/.98

Arbitration

Bibliographies

[3192]
ZAGORIN, J.S. Bibliography of books and articles on international commercial arbitration. In *International journal of legal information,* v.17(3), Winter 1989, p.233-54.

Based on the library collection of Baker & McKenzie, New York. 9 sections: General - Arbitrability - Coice of law - Procedure - Awards - Enforcement - Treaties - Local and regional arbitration. Includes a list of serials which regularly publish articles on arbitration, and a list of national arbitration associations and their publications.
Class No: 347.918(01)

Dictionaries

[3193]
LEE, E.H. Dictionary of arbitration law and practice. London, Mansfield Law Publishers, 1986. [5],185p.

Claims to be the first of its kind to be devoted to the subject. Table of contents, by subject A-Z, precedes the dictionary, which includes terms and phrases familiar and less familiar relating to the subject. Also terms connected with arbitration law and practice. Entries may be definitions or judicial interpretations. Cross-references. Table of cases and table of Statutes and Rules of the Supreme Court.
Class No: 347.918(038)

[3194]
SEIDE, K., *ed.* A Dictionary of arbitration and its terms. Dobbs Ferry, N.Y., Oceana, for the American Arbitration Association, 1970. 334p. $21. ISBN: 0379003864.

Defines *c.*700 arbitration terms, with source and case citations. Cross-references. Appendices on rules of arbitration procedures, arbitration statutes and uniform laws, international conventions, plus extensive bibliographies of commercial arbitration, international public arbitration and labour arbitration. *Class No:* 347.918(038)

Lawyers, Solicitors & Legal Officials

Worldwide

Yearbooks & Directories

[3195]
Kime's international law directory, 2000 107th ed. London, Sweet and Maxwell, 1999. £80. ISBN: 0421674903.

First published 1892.

Practitioners' names are arranged under continents, countries, states and towns. Separate sequences for foreign lawyers resident in London, New York and Paris; international commissioners, etc.
Class No: 347.96(100)(058)

Great Britain

Yearbooks & Directories

[3196]
Butterworths law directory, 1993: a directory of solicitors and barristers in private practice, commerce, local government and public authorities in England, Scotland and Wales. 9th ed. London, Martindale-Hubbell, in association with the Butterworth Group, 1993. xi,1767p. £45. ISBN: 1857390717.

A-Z indexes, with contact details, of solicitors in private practice, in commerce, and firms in private practice. Agency commissions. A-Z indexes of barristers in private practice, in commerce. Geographical list of chambers. List of organizations employing solicitors and barristers. Scottish section. International section. Members of the Institute of Legal Executives. *Class No:* 347.96(410)(058)

[3197]
Directory of solicitors and barristers, 1992. London, The Law Society, 1992. 1313p. £48. ISBN: 1853280631.

Succeeds *The Law list* (1641-1976), *The Bar list* (1977-1989), and *The Solicitor's and barrister's directory.*

Contents include: Solicitors (solicitors firms in London, in England & Wales, overseas; Employed solicitors; firms index; solicitors index; notaries index); Barristers (chambers; individual barristers); Legal executives (A-Z listing). *Class No:* 347.96(410)(058)

[3198]
Hazell's guide to the judiciary and the courts with the Holborn Law Society's Bar list by chambers with index, 1987. Editorial Staff of R. Hazell & Co., *eds.* 3rd ed. Henley-on-Thames, Oxon, R. Hazell & Co., 1988. xi[1],335p. £17. ISBN: 0901718416. ISSN: 02663597.

First published 1985.

In 9 sections: The judiciary - The courts in England and Wales (Circuits, Crown courts, Country courts, Magistrates' courts, Crown prosecution service) - Bar list by chambers - Northern Ireland - Scotland - Isle of Man - Jersey - Guernsey and Alderney - Police forces in England and Wales, Scotland, Northern Ireland, Isle of Man and the Channel Islands. A handy source of information.
Class No: 347.96(410)(058)

Scotland

Yearbooks & Directories

[3199]
The Scottish law directory, 2000. Edinburgh, T & T Clark, 2000. £34. ISBN: 0567005518. ISSN: 00808083.

First published 1895.

Covers certificated solicitors practising in Scotland by authority of the Law Society of Scotland. *Class No:* 347.96(411)(058)

Courts

[3200]

ivil court practice. Thompson, P.K.J., *ed*. London, Butterworth, 1999. Annual. £100. ISBN: 0406927634.

Supersedes *County court practice*. *Class No:* 347.97/.99

[3201]

Reference guide to the United States Supreme Court. Elliott, S.P., *ed*. New York, Facts on File, 1986. 476p. illus. $50. ISBN: 0816010188.

6 major sections: The role of the Supreme Court - The constitutional powers of the branches of federal government - Division of power - Individual rights - Landmark cases - Biographies of the Justices (a concise biography, A-Z, of every Justice who has served on the Supreme Court). Several appendices of chronological listings. The bibliography includes books on the Court itself as well as on individual Justices. Index to cases, individuals and subjects. Supplements Congressional Quarterly's *Guide to the United States Supreme Court*(1979). *Class No:* 347.97/.99

[3202]

KYRME, T. History of the Justices of the Peace. Chichester, West Sussex, Barry Rose, 1991. 3v. £75 each volume. ISBN: 1872328458, v.1; 1872328504, v.2; 1872328555, v.3.

History of JPs and magistrates from medieval England to date, including chapters on development in the United Kingdom and in Commonwealth countries. V.1. England to 1689 - v.2. England, 1689-1989 - v.3. Territories beyond England. Includes bibliographies and indexes. *Class No:* 347.97/.99

England & Wales

[3203]

he Supreme Court practice 1999. Jacob, I.H. *and* Scott, R., *eds*. Sweet & Maxwell, 1999. 3v. £430 [book]; £600 [CD-Rom]. ISBN: 0421653906; 042164110x, cd-rom. ISSN: 00395978.

First published 1967. New eds. were issued at 3-yearly, but now two-yearly intervals, kept up-to-date by biannual cumulative supplements.

"The white book" provides an authoritative guide to civil court practice and procedure in England and Wales. Includes forms, practice directions, procedural tables and relevant statutory materials. *Class No:* 347.97/.99(42)

Handbooks & Manuals

[3204]

KE, G.C. Oke's Magisterial formulist ... Pearson, J.E., *ed*. 20th ed. London, Butterworth, 1985. 700p. in 2 loose-leaf binders. £125. ISBN: 040632400x.

First published 1850; 19th ed. 1979.

A companion volume to *Stone's Justice's manual*. Part 1. deals with forms for use before Magistrate's Courts; part 2. deals with precedents for offences, matters of complaint, search warrents, etc., divided A-R. Table of penalties. Tables of Statutes, Statutory Instruments. Detailed index, p.101-184, to divisions and paragraph numbers. Kept up to date. *Class No:* 347.97/.99(42)(035)

Yearbooks & Directories

[3205]

REAT BRITAIN. Lord Chancellor's Department. County Courts Branch. County Court districts (England and Wales): index of place names. 14th ed. London, HMSO, 1992. [iv],181p. £15.95. ISBN: 0113800525.

Over 30,000 place-names, A-Z, with county and place of County Court. *Class No:* 347.97/.99(42)(058)

[3206]

haw's directory of courts in the United Kingdom. 1999. London, Shaw & Sons, 1999. 464p. £37.50. ISBN: 0721914063.

First published 1973. Annual.

Details all changes in staff, sittings of courts, addresses, court code number and telephone numbers each year. Covers prisons, crown courts, county courts, magistrates' courts, other courts of summary jurisdiction and the Crown Prosecution Service. *Class No:* 347.97/.99(42)(058)

USA

[3207]

LANDFORD, L.A. *and* EVANS, P.R., *eds*. Supreme Court of the United States, 1789 - 1982: an index of opinions. Millwood, N.Y., Kraus International, 1983. 2v. (1182 p.). $85. ISBN: 0527279528.

Arranged chronologically by the term of each justice. Opinions are classified in 7 categories (majority opinions - concurring opinions - dissenting opinions - opinions announcing judgement (plurality opinions) - separate opinions (views of individual justices) - statements (reasons for decisions based on precedents - opinions as circuit justices

....(contd.)
(opinions written during justice's service in such courts). 'Meticulous work' (*College and research libraries*, v.45 (1), January 1984, p.54 - 55).

First supplement, 1981-1991 (1993. ISBN 0527279552).
Class No: 347.97/.99(73)

[3208]

Guide to the US Supreme Court. 2nd ed. Washington, Congressional Quarterly, 1989. 1060p. $179.95 ISBN: 0685335585.

First published 1979.

Guide to the origins, development, operation and decisions and impact of the Supreme Court. 'Members of the Court' provides brief biographies of the 101 Supreme Court justices. 'Major decisions of the Court, 1790-1979' summarises Supreme Court rulings. 'Case index' - Appended documents, glossary and detailed subject index. (Based on entry in *College & research libraries* July 1980, p.345-6). *Class No:* 347.97/.99(73)

[3209]

The Oxford companion to the Supreme Court of the United States. Hall, K.L., *ed*. New York, Oxford University Press, 1992. 1028p. illus. $49.95. ISBN: 0195058356.

A political, economic, cultural and legal history of the Court. Over 1000 entries by *c*.300 contributors, including biographies, court decisions, terms, etc. Cross-references. Case-name and topical indexes and extensive appendices. *Class No:* 347.97/.99(73)

Canon Law

[3210]

Canon law abstracts: a half-yearly review of periodical literature in canon law. By members of the Canon Law Society of Great Britain and Ireland. Melrose, the Society, 1959-. no.1-. 2pa. £10pa. ISSN: 00085650.

The 1988, no.2 issue (no.60) covers articles on the canon law of the Roman Catholic Church in journals appearing in July-December, 1987. Sections: General subjects - Oriental law - Historical subjects - Book 1: General works ... Book 7: Processes. *Class No:* 348

[3211]

The Code of canon law. Canon Law Society of Great Britain and Ireland. New revised English translation. London, HarperCollins, 1997. xvi,508p. £12.99. ISBN: 000599375x.

Includes index. *Class No:* 348

[3212]

CORIDEN, J., *and others, eds*. The Code of canon law: a text and commentary. New ed. London, Cassell, 1990. 1184p. £35. ISBN: 0809128373.

First published by G. Chapman, 1985. 505.00/00$aA commentary on the revised code of canon law, written and edited by members of the Canon Law Society of America. Each section is followed by a bibliography. Complete analytical index. *Class No:* 348

35 Public Administration

.... (contd.)

textbooks. Appendices include a copy of the US Constitution. '*A* masterly codification by an eminent authority in public administration' (*Choice*, July/August 1986). *Class No:* 350(038)

Public Administration

Bibliographies

[3213]
BUTCHER, T. 'Public administration and policy studies'. In *Information sources in politics and political science* ... (ed. by Englefield & Drewry. Butterworth, 1986.) p.189-208.

An introduction precedes 10 sections: Approaches to the study of public administration - Traditional approaches - Public administration as the study of organizations - Policy studies - British public administration - Central administration - The Civil Service - Control of the administration - Policy studies in Britain - Other literature and information sources. *Class No:* 350(01)

[3214]
CALIFORNIA UNIVERSITY. Institute of Governmental Studies Library. **Subject catalog...** Boston, Mass., G.K. Hall, 1970. 26v. (21,981p.). First supplement. 1978. 5v. (4051p.). $2830 the set. ISBN: 0816109079.

813,000 photolithographed catalogue cards. 'A collection of pamphlets, government documents, and periodicals covering a wide range of subjects of public interest, both past and present'. (G.K. Hall & Co. *Catalog,* 1979-1980, p.34). *Class No:* 350(01)

[3215]
GREAT BRITAIN. Overseas Development Administration. Library Services. **Public administration:** a select bibliography. 7th ed. London, the Library, 1987. [26p.]. *Gratis.*

First published 1967.

152 numbered items in 26 sections: Administrative law ... Government and public administration - Legislatures ... Management ... Population planning ... Rural development ... Urban and regional planning. Does not now include official publications which are included in *Technical co-operation.* Bibliographies; author and geographical indexes. *Class No:* 350(01)

[3216]
WRIGHT, M. 'The Literature and sources of public administration'. In *Use of social sciences literature* (ed. N. Roberts. London, Butterworth, 1977), p.192-218.

Running commentary. Sections: Public administration as a discipline - Approaches to the study of public administration [central and local government] - Information for research (Official documents; Unpublished material; Research; Government publications; Statistics; Secondary sources (journals). *Class No:* 350(01)

Encyclopaedias

[3217]
SHAFRITZ, J.M., *ed.* **The international encyclopedia of public policy and administration.** Boulder, Westview Press, 1997. 2750p. £379.50 $550. ISBN: 0813399777. *Class No:* 350(031)

Dictionaries

[3218]
COLLIN, P.H. **Dictionary of government and politics.** 2nd ed. London, P. Collin Publishing, 1997. 302p. £9.95. ISBN: 1579580726.

*c.*5000 main words and phrases covering national legislatures, elections, local government, parliamentary and council procedure, international affairs and political parties and theories. Aims to cover both British and American terminology. A supplement gives information about the political and legislative systems in both Britain and the United States, together with the reproduction of relevant documents. Examples given. *Class No:* 350(038)

[3219]
SHAFRITZ, J.M. **The Facts on File dictionary of public administration.** New York, Facts on File, 1986. [9], 610p. $29.95. ISBN: 0816012660.

Short entries covering a great many terms and concepts in the traditional A-Z arrangement. Many entries include references to books and journals for further study. Includes short biographies of prominent persons in the field; court decisions, statutes, regulations, organisations and journals. Many cross-references. Also information on indexes, abstracts, databases, etc. relevant to public administration; a list of significant journals in the field; and a historical list of significant

Reviews & Abstracts

[3220]
FRANCIS. 528. **Bulletin signalétique.** 528. Bibliographie internationale de science administrative. International bibliography of administrative science. Paris, Institut de l'Information Scientifique et Technique. Science Humaines et Sociales. Centre National de la Recherche Scientifique, 1971-.v.1-. Quarterly. F.560pa. ISSN: 01508695.

Previously *Bulletin signalétique. 528. Science administrative,* 1947-1970, then *Bulletin signalétique. 528. Bibliographie interational de science administrative.*

V.42(4) (1988): Items 3335-4232 of indicative abstracts and references. Sections: 01. Administrative science - 02. History - 03. Methods of administrative science - 04. Administrative structures - 05. Civil Service - 06. Means of action of administration - 07. Control of public order - 08. Public enterprise. List of journals scanned, index of concepts, index of authors per issue and annually. Contents list in English and French, but abstracts only in French. Available online (Telesystems, Questel) and on CD-ROM. Class No: 350(048)

[3221]
International review of administrative sciences. Brussels, International Institute of Administrative Sciences, 1928-. v.1, no.1-. Quarterly. £60pa.; $99pa. ISSN: 00208523.

An English-language edition has been published by Sage Publications since 1957. There is also a Spanish edition.

Includes a selective bibliography of between 60 and 100 books each issue, arranged by subject. *Class No:* 350(048)

[3222]
Sage public administration abstracts. Newbury Park, CA., Sage Publications, 1974-. Quarterly. $235pa. ISSN: 00946958.

Each issue has *c.*250 abstracts of books, pamphlets, government publications, significant speeches, legislative research studies and periodical articles from *c.*200 English-language periodicals in a wide range of subject fields relating to public administration. Many author abstracts. Arranged in 13 subject groups. Author and subject indexes (cumulated in the 4th issue each year) plus 'related citations' (lists of articles and books not abstracted). Journals and subject matter predominantly North American. *Class No:* 350(048)

Scotland

Yearbooks & Directories

[3223]
The Scottish government yearbook, 1992. Paterson, L. *and* McCrone, D., *eds.* Edinburgh, University of Edinburgh, Unit for the Study of Government in Scotland, 1992. 282p. £8.95. ISBN: 0951805304.

First published 1979.

20 sections. The editors' introduction is followed by 2. The political year in Westminster, 3-8 are articles on constitutional issues, 9-11 on education, 12-15 on general matters, 16-19 on reference (opinion polls, Scottish legislation, structure of the Scottish Office, Parliamentary by-elections. 20 is on recent publications (452 items on Scottish government and administration.

From 1993 the title changed to *Scottish affairs.* issued quarterly. *Class No:* 350(411)(058)

USA

Bibliographies

[3224]
CAIDEN, E.G., *and others.* **American public administration:** a bibliographical guide to the literature. New York, Garland, 1983. xvii,201p. $30. (*Public affairs and administration series, v.3. Garland reference library of social science, v.169.*)

1220 items with descriptive annotations, arranged in 4 sections: 1. The scope of American public administration - 2. Abstracts, indexes and continuing bibliographies in public affairs and administration - 3. Professional journals in public affairs and administration - 4. A select bibliography of books. Index of abstracts, indexes and continuing

...*(contd.)*
bibliographies; index of journals; and author index. Intended for students of American public administration. One of *Choice's* outstanding academic books, 1984-85. *Class No:* 350(73)(01)

Handbooks & Manuals

[3225]
SHAFRITZ, J.M. **The Dorsey dictionary of American government and politics.** Chicago, Dorsey Press, 1989. xxxii,661p. illus., tables. $34.95. ISBN: 0256056390.
Over 4000 entries on Federal, State and local government and politics. Entries include important US Supreme Court decisions, political slang, and biographies, and most have bibliographical references. 5 appendices (including one treating online databases). Key concept list organizes all entries under wide headings. 'The work's careful scholarship, ease of use, comprehensiveness, and depth recommend it highly...' (*Choice,* October 1988, p.296).
Class No: 350(73)(035)

[3226]
SHAFRITZ, J.M. The HarperCollins dictionary of American government and politics. New York, HarperCollins, 1992. 656p. illus. tables, charts. $50. ISBN: 0062700316.
About half of the material has been taken from the Dorsey dictionary (see above), but *c.*1000 new terms are included, including current slang. Over 5000 entries, from a sentence to 250 words in length, noting the term's origins. Cross-references. Boxed features with many entries with lists, statistical summaries, quotes, and primary source material. 'Anything but dry, it is both erudite and readable.' (*Booklist,*v.88(17), 1 May 1992, p.1623). *Class No:* 350(73)(035)

Biographies

[3227]
American leaders,1789-1991: a biographical summary. Washington, D.C., Congressional Quarterly, 1991. 450p. $27.95. ISBN: 0871875942.
Summary biographies of from two to six lines each, containing facts about American leaders at Federal and State levels (only governors at State level). 'A general potpourri ... useful at general reference desk' (*Choice,* v.25(4),December 1987, p595) of the first edition.
Class No: 350(73)(092)

Libraries

[3228]
IMMLER, O., ed. World directory of administrative libraries: a guide to libraries serving national, state, provincial and Länder libraries. Munich, K.G. Saur (previously Verlag Dokumentation), 1976. 475p. DM60. ISBN: 3794044274.
A directory, under countries A-Z; entries 1 per page for major libraries. Data stress specialisation, stock, service. Index of libraries; index under countries; index of official and English names. Includes entries for all European Community libraries.
Class No: 350:061:026/027

Government Bodies

Worldwide

[3229]
State economic agencies of the world: an international directory of governmental organizations concerned with economics development and planning. Day, A.J., ed. Harlow, Essex, Longman, 1985. (Dist. in US & Canada by Gale Research Co.). x, 546p. £48; $78. (*Keesing's reference services.*) ISBN: 0582902533, UK; 0810321041, US.
Issued in the US as 'Governmental economic agencies of the world ...'.
*c.*2,000 state and parastatal agencies and organizations throughout the world active in economic spheres (*e.g.* national, regional and sectoral planning, industrial development, agrarian reform, export promotion etc.). Covers 170 countries, arranged A-Z, with, for each one, basic economic data and a brief résumé of the prevailing political and economic conditions preceding the listing of the economic agencies (*e.g.* trade agencies, central banks, nationalized banks, trading organizations, chambers of commerce, central statistical offices). *Class No:* 350.07(100)

Great Britain

[3230]
GREAT BRITAIN. Cabinet Office. **Public bodies, 1993.** London, HMSO, 1993. xii,81p. tables. £12. ISBN: 0114300933.
First published 1988.
Lists nationalized industries, public corporations, non-departmental public bodies, and National Health Service authorities, and gives some basic facts about them, including information about annual reports published, addresses of sponsor departments, number of members appointed and their remuneration, other financial information, etc. Index. *Class No:* 350.07(410)

[3231]
The Guide to the executive agencies. Carlton, I., *ed.* London, Carlton, 2000. £75.00 ISBN: 1901581179. ISSN: 13606689.
Published annually.
Covers the agencies created by the former government to deal with areas such as Employment Services, Child Support, Prisons, NHS and Social Security Contributions. Contains "data on all agencies now operating, contact details for key personnel, addresses of head and regional offices, functions and spending power of each agency and a list of proposals for agency status". *Class No:* 350.07(410)

Yearbooks & Directories

[3232]
Councils, committees & boards: a handbook of advisory, consultative, executive & similar bodies in British public life. Glanville, M.P., *ed.* 9th ed. Beckenham, Kent, CBD Research, 1999. 530p. £142.50. ISBN: 0900246847.
First published 1970.
About 1270 entries (Aberdeen and District Milk Marketing Board ... Youth Committee for Northern Ireland). Includes Crown Agents, BBC and National Health Service. Data on each body: name; abbreviation; validity indication; address; telephone & telex number; establishment and membership; terms of reference, objects or duties; activities and supplementary information; publications; notes re imminent or proposed changes which will affect status/functions. Cross-references. Abbreviations index; index of chairmen, presidents and chief executives; subject index. 'An essential reference tool' (*Trade and industry,* 25 November 1977, p.386, on the 3rd ed.).
Class No: 350.07(410)(058)

Russia

Biographies

[3233]
LAZITCH, B.M. *and* DRACHKOVITCH, M.M. **Biographical dictionary of the Comintern.** New, rev. & expanded ed. Stanford, CA., Hoover Institution Press, 1986. lv,532p. $44.95. ISBN: 0817984011.
First published 1973.
A new introduction is followed by 753 biographical sketches ranging in length from several lines to several pages, of which some 230 have been updated and corrected. There follows a guide to abbreviations, a list of biographees, and a list of 435 pseudonyms. Does not indicate sources or include suggestions for further reading. 'The work should prove invaluable to those looking for information about persons who played little publicized roles in the Communist International' (*College & research libraries,* v.36(1), January 1975, p.63-4, of the 1st ed.).
Class No: 350.07(47)(092)

USA

Handbooks & Manuals

[3234]
United States government manual, 1999-2000. Office of the Federal Register, National Archives and Records Service. Washington, The Federal Register, 1999. vii,859p. tables, map. £32. ISBN: 0160501172.
First published 1935. Annual.
The official handbook of the Federal government. Describes the purposes and programmes of most government agencies and lists top personnel. *Class No:* 350.07(73)(035)

Meetings

[3235]
Shackleton on the law and practice of meetings. Shearman, I., *ed.* 9th ed. London, Sweet & Maxwell, 1997. 381p. £79. ISBN: 0421539100.
First published 1934.
5 parts: 1. Public meetings - 2. Meetings for the transaction of business: general rules 3. Meetings relating to companies - 4. Meetings of local authorities - 5. Defamatory statements. Analytical index, p.321-330. *Class No:* 350.077.5

[3236]

WARD, S. A-Z of meetings: how they work and how to run them. London, Pluto Press, 1985. ix,241p. illus., forms. £3.95. (*Pluto handbook*.) ISBN: 0745301037.

In 10 chapters: 1. Constitutions and rules - 2. Standing orders - 3. Alternative standing orders - 4. Meetings in practice - 5. Alternative practice for meetings - 6. Annual General Meetings - 7. Large conferences - 8. Running your own conference - 9. Discussion conferences - 10. The Law. Appendices: 1. Meetingspeak; 2. A guide to etiquette; 3. Sample trust deed. Index, p.211-214. *Class No:* 350.077.5

China

[3237]

LIEBERTHAL, K.G. *and* DICKSON, B.J. Research guide to central party and government meetings in China, 1949-1986. Rev. & expanded ed. Armonk, N.Y., M.E. Sharpe Inc., 1989. 339p. $50. ISBN: 0873324927.

First published 1976 covering 1949-75.

Covers over 500 meetings that could be documented. Information given includes dates, type of meetings (*e.g.* Party Congress, Politburo, Report meetings, etc.), place, attendance, major items on the agenda, speeches and reports, documents passed, other decisions or actions, and additional comments. Chronological arrangement. Index of people, places, organizations and issues. '... a unique and invaluable resource for China students and scholars' (*Choice*, v.27(4), December 1989, p.613p.). *Class No:* 350.077.5(510)

Civil Service

Great Britain

[3238]

DREWRY, G. *and* BUTCHER, T. The Civil Service today. Oxford, Basil Blackwell, 1988. x,259p. tables. £29.95. ISBN: 0631154280.

A prologue: some crises of the 1980s, precedes 11 chapters (1. Charting the territory - 2. How things came to be - 3. Some facts and figures - 4. The universal department - 5. Recruitment and training - 6. Conditions of service - 7. The working context - 8. Ministers and civil servants - 9. The public face of private government - 10. Slimmer and fitter: the quest for efficiency and effectiveness - 11. Conclusion: the Civil Service at the crossroads?. 422 notes, by chapter headings, p.222-244. Select bibliography, by subject sections with no annotations, p.245-252. Index, p.253-259. (A 2nd ed. was issued in 1991. x,281p. £12.99. ISBN 0631181725). *Class No:* 350.08(410)

[3239]

GREAT BRITAIN. Committee on the Civil Service, 1966-68. Chairman: Lord Fulton. [Report on the Civil Service]. London, HMSO, 1968-9. 5v. in 7.

1: Report of the Committee. 1968. (Cmnd.3638); 2: Report of a Management Consultancy Group. (1968); 3: (2 pts): Surveys and investigations; 4: Factual, statistical and explanatory paper (1968); 5: (2 pts): Proposals and opinions (1968). *Class No:* 350.08(410)

Bibliographies

[3240]

GREAT BRITAIN. HM Stationery Office. Government publications. Sectional list 44, revised January 1991: Treasury and Civil Service. London, HMSO, 1991. viii,139p. Gratis.

Includes sections on the Civil Service College - Civil Service Department - Committee of enquiry into Civil Service Pay - Equal Opportunities Division - Treasury and Civil Service Committee. *Class No:* 350.08(410)(01)

Yearbooks & Directories

[3241]

The Civil Service year book, 1993. Cabinet Office. London, HMSO., 1993. viii.885,ix-lxxxip. £19.50. ISBN: 0114300755.

Issued annually.

6 chapters: 1. The Royal Household - 2. Parliamentary Offices - 3. Ministers, Departments and Executive Agencies - 4. Libraries, museums and galleries. Research councils. Other organizations - 5. Departments and other organizations (Northern Ireland; Scotland; Wales) - 6. Salary tables. Entries briefly state scope of office and give telephone numbers for contacting. Index to individual officers. Index to departments and sub-departments precedes. Subject index, p.xliii-lxxvi. Essential to any reference library. *Class No:* 350.08(410)(058)

Police

Bibliographies

[3242]

LOS ANGELES PUBLIC LIBRARY. Catalog of the Police Library. Boston, Mass., G.K. Hall, 1972. 2v. (1546p.). $200. ISBN: 0816109648.

35,000 photolithographic reproductions of a card dictionary catalogue, covering books, pamphlets and periodical articles, The collection is strong in criminology, scientific investigation, crime and criminals, riots, violence and police history. First supplement published 1980 ($255. ISBN 0816103281 *Class No:* 351.74(01)

[3243]

Police science abstracts: an international abstracting service covering police science, the forensic sciences and forensic medicine. Amstelveen, Netherlands, Kugler Publications, for Criminologica Foundation, (early issues published by Kluwer D.V.), 1973-?. v.1-?. 6pa. ISSN: 01666282.

Continues *Abstracts on police science* (1973-1979). Prepared by Criminologica Foundation in co-operation with the University of Leiden and the Netherlands Institute for Advanced Training of Senior Police Officers, Warnsveld. Now superseded by *Criminology, penology and police science abstracts*.

About 1500 indicative and informative abstracts and references pa. 14 sections: 1. General - 2. Police organization - 3. Police personnel - 4. Police equipment - 5. Finances, budget - 6. Police power - 7. Police operations - 8. Traffic and traffic control - 9. Crime prevention - 10. Crime control, criminal investigation - 11. Police work in relation to special kinds of persons - 12. Police work in relation to special types of offences - 13. Forensic science - 14. Forensic medicine. Cross-references. Cumulative author and subject indexes. List of journals received for abstracting. *Class No:* 351.74(01)

[3244]

—WHITEHOUSE, J.E. A Police bibliography. New York, AMS Press, 1980. 2v.(525p.). $95. (*Studies in criminal justice, no.3*.) ISBN: 0404160409.

17,400 entries. Useful for retrospective coverage, with emphasis on the 1960-1970 period. *Class No:* 351.74(01)

Encyclopaedias

[3245]

KURIAN, G.T. World encyclopedia of police forces and penal systems. New York, Facts on File, 1989. 582p. tables, charts. $95. ISBN: 0816010196.

Data on law enforcement systems and correction systems in 183 countries. Countries are listed A-Z within 3 categories - major, smaller, micro. Entries for each country include a basic fact sheet with information on area, population, type of government, population per police officer, and police expenditure per 1000 inhabitants. Length of entries varies (UK:15p.; US:52p.) and for smaller countries, merely the basic fact sheet, plus short descriptions. For larger countries there are 4 headings (History and background - Structure and organization - Recruitment, education and training - The penal system). 4 appendices: Interpol (12p.); Directory of addresses of police HQs in 141 countries; Bibliography (34 titles, unannotated); Table of comparative statistics on police protection covering 125 countries. 'Although the information it contains is largely undocumented ... [the] encyclopedia ... brings together in one source much useful material' *Reference books bulletin*, v.86(2), 15 September 1989, p.211). *Class No:* 351.74(031)

[3246]

—FAY, J. Police dictionary and encyclopedia. Springfield, Ill., C.C. Thomas, 1988. 378p. $29.75. ISBN: 0398054940.

4500 brief entries, including more than 6300 terms. International in coverage. ' ... a dictionary in format and contents ... '(*Library journal*, 15 April 1989, p.68). *Class No:* 351.74(031)

Dictionaries

[3247]

INGLETON, R. Elsevier's dictionary of police and criminal law: English-French and French-English. New York, Elsevier Science, 1999. 1 CD-ROM. $185.50. ISBN: 0444501320.

Originally published 1992.

12,500 terms relating to the organization and functions of the police, the criminal law, and rules of evidence, traffic control, drugs, terrorism, accidents and disasters. Includes many slang and jargon terms. *Class No:* 351.74(038)

Yearbooks & Directories

[3248]

ANDRADE, J. **World police and paramilitary forces.** London, Macmillan Press,; New York, Stockton Press, 1985. xiii,245p. illus. £55.; $90. ISBN: 0333386299, UK; 0943818141, US.

Directory of police forces in almost every country of the world. 177 entries covering the history, organization and strength of each force and its role in maintaining internal security, criminal statistics, and operations and equipment. Part 1: Introduction; 2: Country-by-country survey, A-Z, plus Interpol; 3: Directory of internal security equipment. Select bibliography, p.xiii. 'Expensive, but worth the money' (*Reference books bulletin*, 1986/87). *Class No: 351.74(058)*

Great Britain

[3249]

PARKER, C.G.A. **Police and constabulary almanac.** London, Police Review, 1998. £25. ISBN: 0901718777. ISSN: 04772008.

First published 1861.

A directory of Home Office officials, police organiozations; police forces; chief police officers; defence services, transport and local police; prisons, etc.; motor licence authorities and index; police and professional societies, associations, etc.; gazetteer; civil defence, emergency planning; fire brigade; ambulance services; charitable societies, associations, etc.; advertisements. Index. Courts on yellow paper. *Class No: 351.74(410)*

Bibliographies

[3250]

BRETT, D.T., *comp*. **The Police of England and Wales:** a bibliography. 3rd ed. Bramshill, Hartley Wintney, Hants., Police Staff College, 1979. [i],[1],129p. £0.30. ISBN: 0903727927.

First published *c*.1964.

About 1000 unannotated entries under 7 heads (*e.g.* General information sources; Office of constable; General history and description; Committee reports; Police forces and areas). Little or no reference to special branches or departments such as the CID or women police. *Class No: 351.74(410)(01)*

Security

Dictionaries

[3251]

FAY, J.J., *ed*. **Butterworth's security dictionary:** terms and concepts. Stoneham, MA., Butterworths publishers, 1987. [5], 277p. illus. (16 line drawings). $24.95. £35. ISBN: 0409900338.

Intended for security personnel who need to know the language used in all areas. Arranged in 3 sections: Procedural concepts - Legal concepts - Organizational concepts. Includes disciplines of law, investigations, risk management, personnel administration, safety, and electronics technology. Explains and describes terms and phrases rather than merely defining them, and includes examples where needed. Bibliography of *c*.120 items. Appendices include a list of terrorist groups; electronic security symbols, conversion tables, properties of flammable liquids and gases, etc. *Class No: 351.75(038)*

[3252]

KIDD, S. **Dictionary of industrial security.** London, Routledge, 1987. 141p. £16.95; $39.95. ISBN: 0710207948.

c.1000 entries for terms, phrases, acronyms, abbreviations, and names of associations and institutions related to the industrial security industry. Clearly written. Intended for managers of security firms, crime prevention agencies and the like. Includes a select bibliography and an appendix on UK and US security standards. Author is a British security manager. *Class No: 351.75(038)*

Yearbooks & Directories

[3253]

International security directory, 1987-88. 20th ed. Henley-on-Thames, Oxon., R. Hazell & Co. (Court & Judicial Publishing) 1987. [4],108p. £19.50. ISBN: 0901718424. ISSN: 00747890.

Annual since 1963.

Sections on international organizations (UN, NATO, Commonwealth Secretariat, ICPO Interpol) and national days (for all countries) precede the main section, Countries of the world (United Kingdom - Afghanistan ... Zimbabwe), with information for each country on population, alliance, defence, police and fire HQs, associations, and companies. Index of products, services and suppliers. *Class No: 351.75(058)*

Russia

Bibliographies

[3254]

ROCCA, R.G. *and* DZIAK, J.J. **Bibliography on Soviet intelligence and security services.** Boulder, Col., Westview Press, 1985. xi, 203p. $16.25. (*A Westview special study*.) ISBN: 0813370485.

The authors were assisted by the staff of the Consortium for the Study of Intelligence. Copyright is with the National Strategy Information Center, New York.

An annotated list of 518 books, articles, chapters of books, and documents on the KGB and other Soviet intelligence agencies, arranged A-Z by authors in each section: 1. Select bibliographies and other reference works - 2. Russian/Soviet accounts - 3. Defector/firsthand accounts - 4. Secondary accounts - 5. Congressional and other government documents. Appendices: Glossary of abbreviations and terms; KGB leadership; GRU leadership; Chart: Development of Soviet intelligence and security services. Author/source index, p.174-186; title index, p.187-203. '... of particular interest are chapters on Russian sources and writings by defectors and other eyewitnesses.' (*College & research libraries news*, v.46(9), October 1985, p.508-511). *Class No: 351.75(47)(01)*

USA

[3255]

HAINES, G.K. *and* LANGBART, D.A. **Unlocking the files of the FBI:** a guide to its records and classification system. Wilmington, Del, Scholarly resources, 1993. xviii,348p. $60. ISBN: 0842023380.

Designed for researchers who require access to the extensive records and papers of the Federal Bureau of Investigation. Provides number, title, description, extent of records, date span, location, disposition, and procedures required to gain access. There are 278 classifications in the system. Includes bibliographical references and index. 'A welcome finding aid ...'(*Choice*, v.30(11), July/August 1993, p.1749). *Class No: 351.75(73)*

Housing

[3256]

Housing. Great Britain. Department of the Environment, Transport and the Regions. Rev. ed. London, Stationery Office, 2000. (*Planning policy guidance, PPG3..*) *Class No: 351.778.5*

Dictionaries

[3257]

SAYEGH, K.S. **Housing** a multidisciplinary dictionary. Ottawa, ABCD-Academy Book, 1987. 626p. $31. ISBN: 0921139012.

c. 28,000 terms giving clear, concise and useful definitions from a wide variety of disciplines. *Class No: 351.778.5(038)*

Europe

Tables & Data Books

[3258]

UNITED NATIONS. Economic Commission for Europe. **Annual bulletin of housing and building statistics for Europe.** 1998 ed. New York, United Nations, 1998. 89p. £19. ISBN: 9210163346.

First published 1957. Annual.

Statistical data on dwelling construction, materials used, employment in the construction industry, and wholesale price indices of building materials in Europe, Canada and the United States. *Class No: 351.778.5(4)(083)*

Great Britain

Bibliographies

[3259]

A Housing bibliography. Newson, T., *ed*. 5th ed. Birmingham, University of Birmingham, School of Public Policy, 1988. 214p. £12.

First and second eds. (1976 & 1978) published by Lancaster University; 3rd & 4th eds. by Birmingham University, Centre for Urban and Regional Studies. Early editions compiled by J.M. Stewart.

A comprehensive listing of literature published on British housing policy over the last five years. Subject and author indexes. *Class No: 351.778.5(410)(01)*

Yearbooks & Directories

[3260]

Housing year book, 1996. Harlow, Essex, Longman Group (UK) Ltd., 1996. Annual. £75. ISBN: 0273616838. ISSN: 02645181.

First published 1983.

A guide to local and central government departments, institutions, and people concerned with housing issues and problems in the UK. Preliminaries, including a gazetteer, are followed by 21 sections relating to local authorities, housing, rent and rates, etc., and including 20: Sources of information. Index. Advertisers' index.

Class No: 351.778.5(410)(058)

Tables & Data Books

[3261]

GREAT BRITAIN. Department of the Environment. Scottish Development Department and Welsh Office. **Housing and construction statistics, 1982-1992, Great Britain.** 14th ed. London, HMSO., 1993. vii[2],226p. illus. tables. £24. ISBN: 0117528862.

First published for 1969-1979.

Designed to provide a broad perspective on developments over the past decade. Includes data on orders, output, labour, structure, materials and investment on construction; housebuilding, renovations, slum clearance, stock of dwellings, finance, rents, etc. relating to housing.

A 2-part quarterly, also titled *Housing and construction statistics* (1972-. £30pa. ISBN 03089819) has monthly and quarterly statistical data for the main series published in the annual.

Class No: 351.778.5(410)(083)

England

Histories

[3262]

BURNETT, J. A Social history of housing, 1815-1985. Rev. ed. London, Methuen, 1986. 387p. £35. $39.95. ISBN: 0416367704.

First published by David & Charles in 1978, covering the years 1815-1970.

11 chapters, in 3 main periods: 1. 1815-1850 (1. People and houses; 2. The cottage homes of England; 3. The housing of the urban working classes; 4. Middle class housing) - 2. 1850-1914 - 3. 1918-1985. Chapter 11: Retrospect and prospect. Chapter notes and references, p.346-373. Index (small type), p.374-387.

Class No: 351.778.5(420)(091)

Economic Legislation

Dictionaries

[3263]

DRAZIL, J.V. Quantities and units of measurement: a dictionary and handbook. London, Mansell Publishing, 1983. [V],313p. £15. ISBN: 0720116651.

Supersedes the author's *Dictionary of quantities and units* (1971).

In 3 parts: 1. A dictionary of units of measurements, their symbols and abbreviations - 2. A dictionary of quantities and selected constants - 3. Symbols denoting qualities and constants. 4 appendices (2. UK and US units; 4. Bibliography (p 287-294). French and German indexes with references to corresponding English terms in pt.2.

Class No: 351.82(038)

Weights & Measures

[3264]

The Economist desk companion. London, Century Business/Economist Books, 1992. 272p. £20. ISBN: 0712698167.

Adapted from *The World measurement guide*. Mostly conversion tables. In 4 parts: pt.1 is an introduction describing the three major world measurement systems; pt.2 has definitions, special measurements, formulae and calculations for 24 subject areas; pt.3 has 175 pages of conversion tables; and pt.4 has appendices. 'This is 'top desk publishing', but probably not a book for the layman' (*Library association record*, v.94(10), October 1992, p.668).

Class No: 351.821

[3265]

NAFT, S *and* **SOLA, R.de.** International conversion tables. Rev. and enl. ed. by P.H.Bigg. London, Cassell, 1965. liii,351 p.

First published 1961. Originally S. Naft's *Conversion equivalents in international trade* (1931).

6 sections: 1. Conversion factors - 2. Conversion tables - 3. Compound conversion factors - 4. Special measures used in various industries, commerce and engineering (Automobiles ... Water. Typographical point system. Clothing and shoe sizes: English, US and continental/metric) - 5. Geography of weights and measures (84 countries) - 6. Other useful data (alphabets; chemical elements; electrical units; international standards; signs and symbols). Detailed contents list; no index. Key passages are in French, German, Italian and Spanish, as well as English. *Class No:* 351.821

[3266]

The World measurement guide. 4th ed. London, The Economist Newspaper, 1980. 240p. illus. £30.; $55. ISBN: 085058040455.

First published as *The Economist' guide to weights and measures* in 1954. 3rd ed. (1975) was titled *'The Economist measurement guide and reckoner'*.

A guide to conversions between measuring systems; explains, defines, comments on and illustrates national and international measures and statistics. Quick reference - Systems of measurement (metric, UK, US, other countries) - Conversion tables - Special measurements (space and time; agriculture, fishing and forestry; industry) - Useful definitions and formulae - General tables (annual percentage rates, interest rates, growth rates, etc.) - Glossary (p.224-229) - Index (p.234-240). *Class No:* 351.821

Dictionaries

Polyglot

[3267]

CLASON, W.E., *comp.* Elsevier's lexicon of international and national units; English/American - German - Spanish - French - Italian - Japanese - Dutch - Portuguese - Polish - Swedish - Russian. Amsterdam, Elsevier, 1964. 75 p. (*Elsevier lexica.*)

299 English/American terms, with definitions, plus equivalents (but not indicating genders or plural forms) in 10 other languages. A second section lists units (300-368) used in different parts of the world, A-Z by 69 countries.' Index of international and national units' (p.61-72), covering 10 of the 11 languages in one A-Z sequence; 'Russian index ... ', p.73-74. Appended is a bibliography of dictionaries, glossaries and vocabularies, and of textbooks.

Class No: 351.821(038)=00

French

[3268]

DOURSTHER, H. Dictionnaire universel des poids et mesures anciens et modernes, contenant des tables des monnaies de tous les pays. Bruxelles, Hayez, 1840. (reprinted Amsterdam, Meridian Publishing Co., 1965). iv,604p.

Extremely full A-Z list of units, with French, English and decimal equivalents; for monetary units gives French and English weights, content and value. About 10-20,000 different units in all. Invaluable on Asiastic, historical and obscure currencies of weights and measures (*e.g.* Paolo; Ghersch; Platt; Batman; Line; Mud; Muck; Mun).

Class No: 351.821(038)=40

Great Britain

Yearbooks & Directories

[3269]

BRITISH STANDARDS INSTITUTION. British standards catalogue, **1993.** London, BSI., 1993. xxi,798p. £36; loose-leaf ed. £52. Supplement (usually monthly): £108 pa. ISBN: 0580219704. ISSN: 09530339.

First published 1937. Title varies. Originally *Handbook of information*.

A numerical, briefly annotated list of current British Standards: General series (p.1-452), followed by BS CECC publications - BS QC publications - Codes of practice (p.453-472) - Automobile series - Marine series - Aerospace series - Handbooks - Published documents - Drafts for development - Education publications - British Standards Society publications - European standards - ETSI publications - Information service publications - BSI QA publications - Miscellaneous items - Corresponding international/British standards index. 'Complete sets of British Standards maintained for reference in the United Kingdom' (p.xiii). Subject index, p.621-798.

Class No: 351.821(410)(058)

Histories

[3270]

CONNOR, R.D. The Weights and measures of England. London, HMSO, 1987. xxvi,422p; illus. £30. ISBN: 0112904351.

14 chapters (1. From early beginnings to Roman times - 2. The natural and drusian foot - 3. The Saxon gyrd, the rod, and the acre ... 7. The early currency - 8. The origins of the units of commercial weight ... 13. The onset of metrication: The nineteenth century - 14. Britain goes metric: the twentieth century). 4 appendices (*e.g.* D. Tables of pre-metric British measures). Glossary of unit terms. Bibliography, p.373-387, A-Z by author. Analytical index, p.388-422. *Class No:* 351.821(410)(091)

[3271]

ZUPKO, R.E. British weights and measures: a history from antiquity to the seventeenth century. Madison, University of Wisconsin Press, 1977. xvi,248p. tables. ISBN: 0299073408.

Arranged in four chapters, all subdivided: 1. Roman, Anglo-Saxon, and Norman legacies - 2. Medieval times: refinement and proliferation - 3. The Tudor era - 4. Epilogue. 4 appendices include: B. British pre-Imperial units; C. British Imperial Units; D. Pre-metric weights and measures in Western and Eastern Europe. Bibliography (p.193-234) is arranged in four sections (MS., Monographs, Articles, Documents, Reference works, other works). Analytical index, p.235-248. *Class No:* 351.821(410)(091)

[3272]

ZUPKO, R.E. A Dictionary of English weights and measures, from Anglo-Saxon times to the nineteenth century. Madison, University of Wisconsin Press, 1968 (Available from Books Demand UMI). xvi,224p. $60. ISBN: 031708979x.

Dictionary, p.3-184 ('Acre' ... 'Yoke of land'). 'Pennyweight': 1½p. (etymology; definition; quotations). Ample cross-references; references. *Library journal* (v.93(16), 15 September 1968) notes that much material is drawn from *Oxford English dictionary* but there is new material as well. Valuable annotated bibliography, p.195-224. Appendix 2: Fundamental English laws on weights and measures. *Class No:* 351.821(410)(091)

Metric System

Dictionaries

[3273]

BRITISH STANDARDS INSTITUTION. Vocabulary of legal metrology: fundamental terms. London, BSI, 1971. 184p.

French ed. 1969, by Organisation Internationale de Metrologie Légale (93p.).

Defines *c.*280 terms on metrology, organizations and services, activities, documentation and markings for the service of legal metrology, quantities and units of measurement ... A-Z index in English and French. *Class No:* 351.821.1(038)

[3274]

—BRITISH STANDARDS INSTITUTION. Glossary of terms used in metrology. Rev. ed. London, BSI, 1986. 28p. (*BS 5233:1986.*)

First published 1975.

Defines fundamental terms, basic to all aspects of measurement. *Class No:* 351.821.1(038)

Local Government

[3275]

YOUNGS, F.A. Guide to the local administrative units of England. London, Royal Historical Society, 1980-1991. 2v. (xx,830p.;xx,919p.). ISBN: 0901050679, v.1; 0861932781, v.2.

Vol I. Southern England; vol II. Northern England. Each volume in 4 parts: 1. The parishes of England (V.I p.1-554; v.II. p.1-635) - 2. Local government units - 3. Parliamentary constituencies - 4. The dioceses of England. Parts 2-4 summarise the information in pts. 1 of each volume. Dividing line between volumes is roughly from the Severn to the Wash. Detailed lists of sources. *Class No:* 352

Bibliographies

[3276]

HILL, D.M. 'Local government'. In *Information sources in politics and political science* ... (Englefield & Drewry, eds., 1986), p.226-241.

An introduction is followed by sections on: Theories and definitions - Historical works and texts - Area studies, including London - Comparative studies - Representation and participation - Functions - Finance - Management - Central-local relations - Reform - Official material and bibliography. *Class No:* 352(01)

[3277]

INTERNATIONAL UNION OF LOCAL AUTHORITIES. Bibliographia: new publications in the library. The Hague, the Union, 1963-. no.1-. 6pa.

About 100 items (usually annotated) per issue. Annotations are in the language of the original. Sections, A-Z, by subject. No index. *Class No:* 352(01)

Handbooks & Manuals

[3278]

ROWAT, D.C. International handbook on local government reorganization: contemporary issues. Westport, CT., Greenwood Press, 1980. xv, 626p. illus. tables. $76.95. ISBN: 0313212694.

A comparative study, worldwide. 5 parts: 1. The government of metropolitan areas - 2. Regional or county government - 3. The basic units in developed countries - 4. The basic units in developing countries - 5. Conclusion, trends and problems. Appended list of comparative materials. *Class No:* 352(035)

Europe—Western

[3279]

European municipal directory = Annuaire des communes et regions d'Europe = Das europaische Kommunal- und Regionalregister. London, Newmedia Publishing, 2000. £298. ISBN: 1902812018.

Each country listing is introduced by an explanation of how local government works in that country; what spending and other powers are available, and how budgets are raised. In English and 8 other European languages. *Class No:* 352(400)

Great Britain

Bibliographies

[3280]

GREAT BRITAIN. HM Stationery Office. Government publications. Sectional list 5, revised August 1991: Environment. London, HMSO, 1991. viii,68. *Gratis.*

Covers publications issued principally by the Department of the Environment (including those of its predecessor, the Ministry of Housing and Local Government, which are still available.

Covers in-print publications on the environment (local government, housing, conservation, polution control, etc.) available from HMSO, and also includes relevant publications from other organizations. *Class No:* 352(410)(01)

[3281]

LOGA: local government annotations service. Romford, Essex, Havering Public Libraries, 1966-. Bi-monthly (previously monthly). £10pa. ISSN: 00236349.

Issued on behalf of the Association of London Chief Librarians in co-operation with other London public libraries.

Entries arranged A-Z by subject sections (General - Accidents ... Youth, youth employment and youth services). V.21, 1988/89 has 1142 indicative abstracts, covering journal articles, monographs and reports. 78 periodical titles are scanned (listed on back cover). Index to subjects. *Class No:* 352(410)(01)

[3282]

—WATSON, J., *comp.* Bibliography of ephemeral community information materials. Leeds, Leeds Polytechnic School of Librarianship, Public Libraries Management Research Institute, 1979. 2v. (*British Library Research and Development report, 5521.*)

Part 1: A sources guide; part 2: An assessment of BNB coverage of housing and education titles from January 1977 to April 1979. *Class No:* 352(410)(01)

Handbooks & Manuals

[3283]

HARRISON, T. Access to information in local government. London, Sweet & Maxwell, 1988. xv,107p. £12.50. ISBN: 0421384107.

'Designed as a concise and practical guide to the law governing access to information held by local authorities and access to meetings generally'. Contents: 1. Access by the public (I. The Local Government (Access to Information) Act, 1985; II. Access to outside the 1985 Act) - 2. Access by local authority members - 3. Personal information - access and confidentiality - 4. The Data Protection Act, 1984 - 5. The Access to Personal Files Act, 1987. App.1: Text of the 1985 Act; App.2: List of enactments conferring rights to attend meetings or inspect documents. *Class No:* 352(410)(035)

Yearbooks & Directories

[3284]

Longman directory of local authorities, 1993. London, Longman Law, Tax and Finance, 1993. 224p. £19.50. ISBN: 0851219675.

First published 1961.

Part 1. *Local authorities in England and Wales,* and part 2: *Local authorities in Scotland* both list county councils and district authorities, followed by a section giving names and alphabetical list of parishes, villages and other smaller places. Part 3. *General information and addresses* aims to help the user in the course of conveyancing work. *Class No:* 352(410)(058)

[3285]

Shaw's local government directory, 2000/2001. Callow, P., *ed.* Crayford, Shaw, 2000. 432 p. £35. ISBN: 0721915043.

Class No: 352(410)(058)

Tables & Data Books

Bibliographies

[3286]

MORT, D. 'How to find UK local statistics'. In *Business information review,* v.5(1), July 1988, p.3-14.

Outlines the range of sources produced by local authorities, CIPFA, Chambers of Commerce, TV companies, market research companies and specialist consultants, etc. *Class No:* 352(410)(083)(01)

Histories

[3287]

KEITH-LUCAS, B *and* RICHARDS, P. G. A History of local government in the twentieth century. London, Allen & Unwin, 1978. 268p. *(New local government series, 17.)*

11 chapters, on constitution, functions, popularisms, councillors and permanent staff, party politics, central control, local government associations, 20th-century reorganizations, Local Government Act, 1972 and the changed system it created. ' ... The standard work on the subject' *(British book news,* November 1978, p.904).

Class No: 352(410)(091)

Scotland

[3288]

Scotland's regions, incorporating *County & municipal year book for Scotland,* 1994. 62nd ed. Coupar Angus, Perthshire, Wm Culross & Son Ltd., 1993. xi,390p. ISBN: 1873891148.

The ... *County & municipal year book for Scotland* was first published in 1934.

4 parts: 1. Offices and staff of government departments - 2. Scotland's regions: Regional, District Council and Development Corporation officials - 3. Scottish Health Service (p.125-217). National and local authority associations (p.218-382) - 4. Advertisers (by names and trades). *Class No:* 352(411)

England & Wales

Handbooks & Manuals

[3289]

GREAT BRITAIN. Department of the Environment *and* Welsh Office. **Local government in England and Wales:** a guide to the new system. London, HMSO, 1974. iv,275p. tables, maps. £4. ISBN: 0117508470.

The re-organization came into full operation on 1 April 1974. 10 sections: 1. General outlines of the new system - 2. Local authority functions in England and Wales - 3. Areas of the new local authorities - 4. Parishes, communities, etc. - 5. Electoral arrangements - 6. Chief executives and addresses of principal authorities - 7. National Health Service reorganization - 8. Water reorganization - 9. Names and addresses of bodies at national level - 10. Selection of publications (p.272-5). 3 folding maps: administrative, health and water areas. *Class No:* 352(42)(035)

[3290]

LABOUR PARTY. Local government handbook, England and Wales. 6th ed. London, Labour Party, 1977. xiv,381p. tables. (loose-leaf). £2.50.

First published 1920.

18 sections: 1. Structure of local government in England and Wales - 2. How local authorities work - 3. Councillors' rights and responsibilities ... 5. Local government finance - 6. Education - 7. Housing - 8. Social services - 9. Planning - 10. Transport ... 13. Environmental health - 14. Consumer protection - 15. Information services ... 17. Regional administration - 18. The Labour Group. Periodicals. *Class No:* 352(42)(035)

England

Histories

[3291]

REDLICH, J. *and* HIRST, F.W. The History of local government in England. 2nd ed. London, Macmillan, 1970. (Facsimile ed., by Kelley, 1980). xv,261p. £18. ISBN: 0678070059.

A re-issue of Book 1 of 'Local government in England' (1903), edited with an introduction and epilogue by B. Keith-Lucas.

The best account of the development of local government in the 19th century. Excellent evaluative footnote references to the literature; bibliography, p.253-6.

The massive *English local government, from the Revolution to the Municipal Corporation Act,* by Beatrice and Sidney Webb (London, Longmans, 1909-29, 11v.) was reprinted in 1963 (London, Cass), V.1, *The parish and the county* (xxxiv,664p.) has footnote references, an index of subjects of authors and other persons, and index of places. *Class No:* 352(420)(091)

USA

Bibliographies

[3292]

SHEARER, B.S. *and* SHEARER, B.F. Periodical literature on United States cities: a bibliography and subject guide. Westport, CT., Greenwood Press, 1983. xi,574p. $56.95. ISBN: 0313235112.

4919 periodical articles on the 170 US cities having a population of 100,000 or more, arranged by name of city, A-Z. Includes articles published between 1970 and 1981, selected by value of information and availability. 8 categories (not all used for each city): General - Architecture and the arts - Education and the media - Environment - Government and politics - Housing and urban development - Social and economic conditions - Transportation. List of cities by States, with entry numbers. Author and subject indexes. 'A most useful selection' *(College & research libraries,* v.45(1), January 1984, p.52-53).

Class No: 352(73)(01)

Information Services

Great Britain

[3293]

GRAYSON, L. Library and information services for local government in Great Britain. London, Library Association, 1978. 242p. £11.50; $15. ISBN: 0853658102.

9 chapters, each with 'References and notes': 1. Developments promoting information flow in local government ... 4. The development of documentary information services ... 7. Co-operation between information services ... 9. The future. Appendix: 'Local government and other organisations involved in the provision of documentary information services', p.170-4. Bibliography of 283 annotated items, p.175-228. Analytical index, p.229-42. Useful to local councillors as well as librarians. *Class No:* 352:061:025.5(410)

Urban Areas (Towns & Cities)

[3294]

MARLIN, J.T., *and others.* Book of world city rankings. New York, Free Press, 1986. 604p. 82 tables. $29.95. ISBN: 0029202302.

Supersedes *The book of city rankings* (1984).

Information on the quality of life and work in over 100 metropolitan areas around the world, using vital statistics, demographics, economy, health, crime, and many other important social criteria to ascertain rankings. In 2 parts: 1. Cities subdivided by geographical regions - 2. Comparative data on land and environment, demography, economy, transport, health, housing, education and crime. Useful table of contents but no general index. Bibliographical references follow each section. *Class No:* 352.075.1

Reviews & Abstracts

[3295]

Sage urban studies abstracts. Newbury Park, CA., Sage Publications, 1973-. v.1-. Quarterly. $232pa. ISSN: 00905747.

*c.*250 indicative and informative abstracts in each issue. Sections: Trends in urbanization and urban society - Urban history - Architecture and urban design - Housing - Urban development and redevelopment - Urban planning and land use - Environment and resource conservation - Transportation and communication - Crime, criminal justice, and law enforcement - Urban economics - Social and public services - Government, administration and politics - Urban fiscal and budgeting policy - Social issues and trends - Urban theory and research. Author and subject indexes. List of periodicals abstracted and cumulative index published in the 4th issue each year. *Class No:* 352.075.1(048)

Yearbooks & Directories

[3296]

Urban history yearbook, 1991. Reeder, D.A., *ed*. Leicester, Leicester University Press, 1991. 300p. £39.50. ISBN: 0718560914.

First published 1974. Annual.

A research tool and forum of discussion for urban historians.
Class No: 352.075.1(058)

Histories

[3297]

CHANDLER, T. Four thousand years of urban growth: an historical census. Rev. ed. Lewiston, N.Y., St. David's University Press, 1987. 656p. tables. $129.95. ISBN: 0889462070.

First published 1974 as *3000 years of urban growth,* by Chandler and Fox.

Covers the period from 2250 BC. to AD. 1975. Time series population data is given for the years available for individual cities. Sources are cited and indications given to which figures are estimated. Other tables rank cities by population. An introductory chapter on methodology precedes the main part of the work, which is arranged in broad geographic areas, subdivided by country or region. Historical names are used. Index of city, country and regional names, but no cross-references to current names. *Class No:* 352.075.1(091)

Europe

Histories

[3298]

BARLEY, M.W., *ed*. European towns: their archaeology and early history. London, New York, Academic Press, for the Council for British Archaeology, 1977. xxvii,521p. illus. (incl. pl.). £74. ISBN: 0120788500.

30 contributors. 3 parts: 1. Country surveys (1-18; *e.g.* 2. Urban archaeology in Scotland, p.19-35. 30 references. Résumés in French and German) - 2. Origins of towns (16-23; *e.g.* 22. Novgorod, p.391-403; bibliographical note of ½p.) - 3. The town as a political centre (*e.g.* 27. Northern Italy, p.475-85. 12 notes). Index (non-analytical), p.511-21. *Class No:* 352.075.1(4)(091)

Europe—Western

Histories

[3299]

GUTKIND, E.A., *and others*. International history of city development. London, Collier-Macmillan, 1964-72. 8v. illus., facsims., plans, maps. £40. each vol. ISBN: 0029132509, v.1; 0029132606, v.2; 0029132703, v.3; 0029132800, v.4; 0029133009, v.5; 0029133106, v.6; (no information on v.7); 0029133300, v.8.

Contents: v.1. Urban development in Central Europe (1964); v.2 Urban development in the Alpine and Scandinavian countries (1965); v.3. Urban development in Southern Europe: Spain and Portugal (1967); v.4. Urban development in Southern Europe: Italy and Greece (1969); v.5. Urban development in Western Europe: France and Belgium (1970); v.6. Urban development in Western Europe: the Netherlands and Great Britain (1971); v.7 Urban development in East-Central Europe: Poland, Czechoslovakia and Hungary (1972); v.8 Urban development in East Europe: Bulgaria, Romania and the U.S.S.R. (1972). V.6 (xv,512p.) devotes p.127-473 to Great Britain (chapters: 5. Origin and spread of settlement; 6. The Roman interlude; 7. Invasion and settlements; 8. The Middle Ages; 9 Utopia. Reality. Subtopia; 10. City survey (24 cities); bibliography, p.492-504). V.6 has 294 captioned illus. in all. *Class No:* 352.075.1(400)(091)

Great Britain

Reviews & Abstracts

[3300]

Urban abstracts. London Research Centre. Research Library, *comp*. London, Research Centre (previously London, Greater London Council Research Library, and later Letchworth, Herts., Technical Communications), 1974-. v.1-. Monthly. £98pa. ISSN: 0305103x.

Previously compiled by the Greater London Council's Research Library.

About 3000 indicative abstracts pa., arranged under 16 subject headings: Government and politics - Local government - Education - Emergency services and planning - Health - Housing - Industry and employment - Leisure and recreation - Personnel and training - Social issues and policy - Social services - Urban and regional planning - Transportation - Building, construction and architecture - Engineering and electronics - Environment and pollution. Also available on ACOMPLINE and URBALINE databases, and on CD-ROM..
Class No: 352.075.1(410)(048)

Yearbooks & Directories

[3301]

The Municipal year book and public services directory. 1999 ed. London, Municipal Journal Ltd., 1999. 2v. maps. Annual. £173 for 2v. ISBN: 0707970083. ISSN: 03055906.

First published 1898.

46 sections of general information on public services. V.1. Functions and officers (35 sections: 1. Administrative and legal services ... 31. Water - 32. National associations of local authorities - 33. Organizations - 34. Maps - 35. Late information). V.2 Authorities and members (sections 36 to 46: 36. County councils of England ... 46. Central government of England).General index; index to local authorities; index to advertisers. *Class No:* 352.075.1(410)(058)

Histories

[3302]

GROSS, C. A Bibliography of British municipal history. 2nd ed. Leicester, Leicester University Press, 1966 (Reprinted New York, B. Franklin). vi,xvi,vii,xxxiv,461p. $32.50. ISBN: 8833714651.

First published 1897 by Harvard University Press.

3092 numbered items (with interpolations) - books, pamphlets, articles - on the constitutional history of British boroughs. Introductory 'Survey of principal public and local records for municipal history and town chronicles'. Part 1: General works (including bibliographies, sources, secondary works) on municipal history (including countries), arranged by period and by subject. Part 2: Works on individual towns, A-Z (p.150-430). Particularly important items (*e.g.* Anderson) are asterisked. Index, p.433-461. A basic critical bibliography. The 2nd ed. is a reprint, with an essay on Gross and his contributions to urban studies, by G.H. Martin. *Class No:* 352.075.1(410)(091)

[3303]

—MARTIN, G.H. *and* McINTYRE, S. A Bibliography of British and Irish municipal history. v.1: General works. Leicester, Leicester University Press, 1972. lviii,806p. £30. ISBN: 0718510933.

Excludes titles cited in Gross, which it supplements. 6006 entries cover the period from earliest times to 1966. Main sections (closely subdivided): Bibliographies and guides - General printed records: texts and calendars - General history - The urban community - Municipal administration (p.295-544) - Wales, Scotland, Ireland (p.545-703). Valuable general introduction; numerous sectional prefaces. Author and subject index, p. 717-806. *Class No:* 352.075.1(410)(091)

England

[3304]

BERESFORD, M.W. *and* FINBERG, H.P.R. English medieval boroughs: a hand-list. Newton Abbot, Devon, David & Charles, 1973. 200p. tables.

Introduction (p.21-57; 10 sections, *e.g.* 10: Nature of sources for first evidence) - Handlist of English medieval boroughs, arranged by counties, p.65-193. 'A gazetteer of places which in their day were reckoned to be boroughs' (*Introduction*). Entries consist of date, brief description, source. Call numbers are given for classes of documents cited from the Public Record Office. *Class No:* 352.075.1(420)

[3305]

—REYNOLDS, S. An Introduction to the history of English medieval towns. Oxford, Clarendon Press, 1977. xiv,234p. illus. (pl.), maps. £17.50. ISBN: 0198224559.

Concerns towns, not boroughs. Refers to European parallels. Bibliography, p.202-23. Index. 'For the undergraduate and the interested layman' (*British book news,* January 1978, p.74). *Class No:* 352.075.1(420)

[3306]

PATTEN, J. English towns, 1500-1700. Folkestone, Dawson, 1978. 360p. 15 tables, 25 figs., maps. £14; $30. ISBN: 0712907939, UK; 0208617216, US.

Concentrates on themes of population, occupation and town-and-country relationships during the period, following examination of medieval town patterns and anticedents. The concluding chapter focuses on a comparative study of towns in Norfolk and Suffolk. *Class No:* 352.075.1(420)

Africa

Bibliographies

[3307]

O'CONNOR, A.M. Urbanization in tropical Africa an annotated bibliography. Boston, Mass., G.K. Hall, 1981. xxx,380p. maps (on end papers). $46. (*Bibliographies and guides in African studies.*) ISBN: 0816182620.

Annotated entries for scholarly literature written in English or French and published between 1960 and 1979 in the disciplines of sociology, demography, geography and urban planning. Geographical

....(contd.)

arrangement subdivided by countries, then cities. Cross-references. Includes a list of periodicals, and indexes by place names and authors. *Class No:* 352.075.1(6)(01)

USA

Bibliographies

[3308]

BUENKER, J.D., *and others*. **Urban history:** a guide to information sources. Detroit, Mich., Gale Research Co., 1981. 448p. $68. (*American government and history information guide series, 9.*) ISBN: 0810314797.

*c.*1900 entries, divided into topical chapters: General studies - The urbanization process - The city in American thought - Regional studies - Studies of colonial cities and towns - Urban institutions - Planning, architecture and urban renewal - Class, ethnicity and race - Urban politics and government - Bosses, machines and urban reform. Author, title and subject indexes. *Class No:* 352.075.1(73)(01)

[3309]

Index to current urban documents. Westport, CT., Greenwood Press, 1973-. Quarterly, with annual cumulations. $350pa. ISSN: 00468908.

Documents are listed geographically by US state and city or county, subdivided by government agency. Short annotations appended as necessary to convey content. Subject index. Also available online. *Class No:* 352.075.1(73)(01)

[3310]

—HECKART, R.J. 'A Fresh look at the *Index to current urban documents* and the *Urban documents microfiche collection*'. In *RSR*, v.17(3), Fall, 1989, p.79-82.

'Despite the fact that these two resources constitute the only ongoing, fully indexed national resource for local government documents, many libraries fail to use them' (the author). The article explains how they can be used, and includes 6 references. *Class No:* 352.075.1(73)(01)

[3311]

UNITED STATES. Department of Housing and Urban Development. Library and Information Division. **Dictionary catalog of the United States Department of Housing and Urban Development Library and Information Division.** Boston, Mass., G.K. Hall, 1972-75. 19v. (14,936p.); 2 supplements (2v. each). $1880 for 19v.; $220 for supplements. ISBN: 0816110077, the set of 19v; 0816111359, the set of supplements.

About 350,000 photolithographically reproduced catalogue cards. Includes over 12,000 Comprehensive Planning Reports and Model Cities Reports. The HUD Library is the national information resource for urban regional planning literature, covering housing, urban renewal, race relations, community development environment, law and legislation. *Class No:* 352.075.1(73)(01)

Reviews & Abstracts

[3312]

Urban affairs abstracts. Washington, National League of Cities, 1971-. Weekly, with semi-annual and annual cumulations. $275pa. ISSN: 03006859.

Draws upon 400 journals on urban affairs. Mainly US. Subject arrangement. *Class No:* 352.075.1(73)(048)

Yearbooks & Directories

[3313]

The Municipal year book, 2000. V.67. Washington, DC., ICMA, 2000. charts, tables. $84.95. ISBN: 0873269756. ISSN: 00772186.

First published 1934.

The basic reference annual on United States local government. In 6 sections: 1. Five substantial articles on selected current issues - 2. Four surveys of intergovernmental developments - 3. Salary surveys - 4. Profiles of individual cities and counties in tabular form - 5. Ten directory listings of local government associations, top municipal officials, etc., and descriptions of 73 organizations providing professional services. Also includes a bibliography with references under 17 headings (reference - statistical sources - 15 functional areas); an annotated list of books and reports, followed by periodicals and descriptions of online services; a list of publishers' addresses. *Class No:* 352.075.1(73)(058)

Counties

England & Wales

Histories

[3314]

STEPHENS, E., *comp*. **The Clerks of the Counties, 1360-1960.** London, Society of Clerks of the Peace of Counties and of Clerks of County Councils, 1961. xiv,[1],274p. illus.

Lists *c.*2800 names, arranged A-Z according to counties, of those known to have held office of Clerk of the Peace in the counties of England and Wales, 1360-1960, and the office of the Clerk of the County Council from 1889 to 1960 (p.51-193). 7 columns, stating period of office, name, dates of birth and death, and biographical notes. 5 appendices. Index of names of Clerks of the Counties. *Class No:* 353(42)(091)

USA

Dictionaries

[3315]

ELLIOTT, J.M. *and* ALI, S.R. **The State and local government political dictionary.** Santa Barbara, CA., ABC-Clio, 1988. 325p. $37.50. (*Clio dictionary in politics*.) ISBN: 0874364175.

The author describes the work as a 'dictionary, reference guide, study guide, supplement to a textbook, source of review material and/or a social science aid. '... a useful and well-organized tool that defines and describes the significance of major concepts and terms used to study American state and local government' (*Choice*, v.26(5), January, 1989, p.780). *Class No:* 353(73)(038)

Yearbooks & Directories

[3316]

The Book of the States, 1998-99. Lexington, KY, Council of State Governments, 1999. $99.00. ISSN: 00680125.

First published 1935. Biennial. Available on microfiche from W.S. Hein and from Kraus Microform.

A general survey of the constitution, organization, financing and functioning of State governments is followed by data on individual States (*e.g.* nickname, motto, flower, bird, tree, song). Separately paged supplements accompany most issues. *Class No:* 353(73)(058)

Biographies

[3317]

SOBEL, R. *and* RAIMO, J., *eds*. **Biographical directory of the governors of the United States, 1789-1978.** Westport, CT., Meckler Books, 1978. 4v.

117 contributors. Entries are in chronological order under States, A-Z. Biographical data include names and occupations of parents; family; religion; political affiliation; election results; political and private careers; accomplishments in office; bibliography (including location of governor's papers). 'This excellent set' (*Choice*, December 1978, p.1344). *Class No:* 353(73)(092)

[3318]

—RAIMO, J.W., *ed*. Biographical directory of the governors of the United States, 1978-1983. Westport, CT., Meckler Books, 1985. 352p. $45.

Continues the above. *Class No:* 353(73)(092)

Central Government

[3319]

'The Economist' dictionary of political biography. London, Economist Books Ltd., 1990. 335p. ISBN: 009174847x.

Over 2000 entries, including brief biographies (*e.g.* 'Mitterand': 1¾ columns. A glossary and list of abbreviations follow. The index arranges entries under countries, Afghanistan ... Zimbabwe. Very readable text. *Class No:* 354

Worldwide

[3320]

BLONDEL, J. **The Organization of governments:** a comparative analysis of governmental structures. Beverley Hills, CA., Sage Publications, 1980. [6],242p. illus. $28. (*Political executives in comparative perspective: a cross-national empirical study, v.2.*) ISBN: 0803997760.

Arranged in 8 chapters, followed by a select bibliography (p.235-6). Index, p.237-242. *Class No:* 354(100)

Yearbooks & Directories

[3321]

BLONDEL, J. **Government ministers in the contemporary world.** London, Beverley Hills., CA., Sage, 1985. viii,291p. 1 illus., tables, charts. £25. (*Political executives in comparative perspective: a cross-national empirical study, v.3.*) ISBN: 0803997507.

Devoted to an anatomy of ministerial careers throughout the governments of the world since 1945. In 3 parts: I. Background (the social background of ministers; the routes to ministerial office) - II. The duration of ministers in office - III. Ministers in government (including amateurs and specialists, long-lasting ministers, one-post ministers). Appendix I. The sources of this study; II. Country characteristics of ministers, 1945-1982. Bibliography, p.282-283. Index, p.284-290. *Class No:* 354(100)(058)

[3322]

Countries of the world and their leaders, 1994. Detroit, Mich., Gale Research Company, 1993. Annual. 2v.(1990p.). illus., 70 maps and other illus. ISBN: 081038227x. ISSN: 01962809.

Basic social, political and economic data for 170 countries of the world, provided by the US State Department and other government sources. Also other information of use to American businessmen and other travellers, including the CIA's list of 'Chiefs of State and Cabinet members of foreign governments' and reports on OAU, NATO, OECD, UN, ASEAN and the EC. *Class No:* 354(100)(058)

[3323]

DA GRAÇA, J. **Heads of state and government:** a comprehensive international historical directory. New York, New York University Press; London, Macmillan, 1985. [7], 265p. $65; £33. ISBN: 0814717780, US; 0333392817, UK.

Updates *Rulers and governors of the world*, ed. by B. Spuler (New York, Bowker, 1977-78), which was a translation of *Regenten und Regierungen der Welt* (Würzburg, Ploetz, first published 1953).

Arranged in two main sections: A. Major international organizations (Arab League - ASEAN- Caribbean Community - Commonwealth of Nations - CMEA - Council of Europe - European Community - NATO - UAU - OAS - Organization of the Islamic Conference - South Pacific Commission - UN); B. Countries and regions, A-Z, (Afghanistan ... Zimbabwe). Under each organization, country or region is a chronological list of names and dates of office of all the leaders, each entry being preceded by a concise historical note and some general facts about the country, etc. Covers over 500 countries, regions and territories, and contains the names of nearly 10,000 leaders. Index, cross-referenced. *Class No:* 354(100)(058)

Europe

[3324]

Who's who in European politics. 2nd ed. London, Bowker-Saur, 1993. xxiii,1016p. £149. $215. ISBN: 1857390210.

Section 1 has 8170 short biographies of active politicians (heads of state, members of government, national legislatures, political parties, trade unions, and prominent regional leaders) arranged A-Z in one sequence. Section 2 is a country by country political directory and index, listing heads of State, all members of national governments, leading political party members, etc. *Class No:* 354(4)

Great Britain

[3325]

BRAZIER, R. **Ministers of the Crown.** Oxford, Clarendon, 1997. xxxv, 379 p. £45. ISBN: 0198259883.

Includes bibliographical references and index. *Class No:* 354(410)

[3326]

HARRISON, E. **Officials of royal commission of enquiry, 1870-1939.** London, University of London, Institute of Historical Research, 1995. xxvii, 124 p. (*Officer-holders in modern Britain ; 10.*) ISBN: 1871348293.

Includes index. *Class No:* 354(410)

[3327]

The New Whitehall series. London, Allen & Unwin, for the Royal Institute of Public Administration, 1954-79. No. 16 is available from the Institute, £10.

1. *The Home Office,* by Sir F.A. Newsam, 1954; 2nd ed. 1955. 2. *The Foreign Office,* by First Baron Strong, and others. 1955. 3. *The Colonial Office,* by Sir C. Jeffries. 1956. 4. *The Ministry of Works,* by Sir H. Emmerson. 1956. 5. *The Scottish Office, and other Scottish government departments,* by Sir D. Milne. 1957. 6. *The Ministry of Pensions and National Insurance. 1958. 7. The Ministry of Transport and Civil Aviation,* by Sir G. Jenkins. 1959. 8. *The Ministry of Labour and National Service,* by Sir G. Ince. 1960. 9. *The Department of Scientific and Industrial Research,* by Sir H. Melville. 1962. 10. *Her Majesty's Custom & Excise,* by Sir J. Crombie. 1962. 11. *The Ministry of Agriculture, Fisheries and Food,* by Sir J. Winnifrith. 1962. 12. *The Treasury,* by Lord Bridges, 1966; 2nd ed. 1967. 13. *The Inland Revenue,* by Sir A. Johnston, 1965. 14. *The Ministry of Housing and Local Government,* by Lady E. Sharp. 1969. 15. *The Central Office of*

....*(contd.)*

Information, by Sir F. Clark. 1970. 16. *The Department of Education and Science,* by Sir W.D. Pile. 1979. Authoritative description of the work of major central government depts., past and present; each with list of ministers, etc., footnote references and an analytical index. Nos. 12 and 14 are praised (in *Use of social sciences literature* (1977. p.205), as rising above the level of being 'dull, pedestrian and uninformative'. All titles except the last in the series are op. *Class No:* 354(410)

[3328]

SAINTY, J.C. **Office-holders in modern Britain.** London, Athlone Press, for the University of London, Institute of Historical Research, 1972-79. 8v. £4-£7 each vol. ISBN: 0485171414, v.1; 0485171422, v.2; 0485171430, v.3; 0485171449, v.4; 0485171457, v.5; 0901179353, v.6; 0901179531, v.7; 0901179558, v.8.

1: *Treasury officials, 1660-1780* (1972. xiv,161p.). 2: *Officials of the Secretaries of State, 1660-1780* (1973. xii,119p.). 3: *Officials of the Board of Trade, 1660-1870.* (1974. xiv,124p.). 4: *Admiralty officials, 1660-1870,* (1975. xiv,159p.). 5: *Home Office officials, 1782-1870.* (1975. xv,62p.). 6: *Colonial Office officials: Officials of the Secretary of State for War and Colonies, 1801-1854, and of the Secretary of State for Colonies, 1854-1879.* (1976. x,52p.). 7: *Navy Board officials, 1660-1832,* by J.M. Collinge. (1979. 165p.). 8: *Foreign Office officials, 1782-1870,* by J.M. Collinge. (1979. 93p.). Each volume contains chronological and A-Z lists of officials, with notes and a scholarly introduction. *Class No:* 354(410)

[3329]

—COLLINGE, J.M. Officials of Royal Commissions of Inquiry, 1815-70. University of London, Institute of Historical Research, 1984. vii,108p. £8. ISBN: 0901179809. *Class No:* 354(410)

[3330]

SAINTY, J.C., *and others.* **Officials of the royal household 1660-1837** : Department of the Lord Chamberlain and associated offices. London, Institute of Historical Research, 1997. 2 v. £41 (*Office-holders in modern Britain ; 11.*) ISBN: 1871348404.

Includes bibliographical references and index.

Pt.1 Department of the Lord Chamberlain and associated offices. - Pt.2 Departments of the Lord Steward and the Master of the Horse. *Class No:* 354(410)

Bibliographies

[3331]

GREAT BRITAIN. HM Stationery Office. **Government publications. Sectional list 26, (revised September 1987): Home Office.** London, HMSO, 1987. 16p. *Gratis.*

Sections: Animals - Betting, gaming and lotteries - Broadcasting - Charities - Children - Civil defence - Community relations - Criminal matters - Drugs - Elections - Fire - Firearms - Immigration and nationality - Northern Ireland - Police - Prisons, probation and after-care, parole - Research and Planning Unit publications - Safety - Shops - Miscellaneous. The Home Office Information and Library Services issues a list, annually, of publications of the Office not handled by H.M. Stationery Office. *Class No:* 354(410)(01)

Yearbooks & Directories

[3332]

The London diplomatic list (incorporating *Directory of international organizations*). Foreign and Commonwealth Office. London, HMSO., 1964-. 2pa (previously quarterly). £3.95 each issue. ISSN: 09506918.

Alphabetical list of all the representatives of foreign States and Commonwealth countries in London, with names and descriptions of the persons returned as composing their diplomatic staff. Includes addresses and telephone numbers of each department, and list of representatives in order of their precedence. *Class No:* 354(410)(058)

Histories

[3333]

GREAT BRITAIN. Public Record Office. **The Cabinet Office, to 1945.** Wilson, S.S. London, HMSO, 1975. vii,252p. £6. (*Public Record Office handbook, no. 17.*) ISBN: 0114400342.

10 sections: 1. Introduction - 2. The general procedures of the Cabinet Office, 1917-1945 - 3. The Cabinet and Committee of Imperial Defence before 1917 - 4. The War Cabinet, 1916-1919, and the Lloyd George administration to October 1922 ... 8. Imperial and International Conferences, 1915-1939 - 9. The War Cabinet, 1939-1945 - 10. The Historical Section. Annexes 1-12 (11: List of committees). Index, p.244-52. *Class No:* 354(410)(091)

[3334]

JENNINGS, J. **Cabinet government.** 3rd ed. Cambridge, Cambridge University Press, 1959. x,587p.

First published 1936.

A description of the central administration and its historical development during the last hundred years, in 15 chapters. Appendix 1: Governments since 1835. Appendix 4: Biographical and bibliographical notes (p.546-70). Covers material available up to the middle of 1957. *Class No:* 354(410)(091)

Eire

[3335]

O'DONNELL, J.D. **How Ireland is governed.** 6th ed. Dublin, Institute of Public Administration, 1979. vii,152p.

First published 1965.

16 chapters (*e.g.* 4. The House of the Oireachtas; 9. Local government; 11. The judiciary; 14. The Government of Northern Ireland). Appendices A-E (A: The Departments and major offices). Partly analytical index. *Class No:* 354(417)

England

[3336]

BELL, G.M. **A Handlist of British diplomatic representation, 1509-1688.** London, Royal Historical Society, 1990. viii,306p. £25;$52. ISBN: 0861931238.

Continues *Lists of British diplomatic representatives (1689-1789),* edited by D.M.Horn (London, 1932) and *Lists of British diplomatic representatives (1789-1852),* edited by S.T.Bindoff (London, 1934).

Names of England's 602 diplomats and their 1320 missions. Each entry gives brief career details, with dates, plus sources (instructions, correspondence). List of abbreviations and symbols for sources. Index of persons, p.295-306. *Class No:* 354(420)

Russia

[3337]

Current Soviet leaders ... a cumulative guide to officials and notables in the USSR. Oakville, Ontario, Mosaic Press, 1974-1982. 2pa. ISSN: 03182037.

Based on official Soviet sources and compiled by the Borys Lewytzkyj Research Bureau.

Sections: 1. Communist Party of the Soviet Union (USSR; Union Republics) - 2. Soviet government (USSR; Union Republics) - 3. Public organizations (*e.g.* Komsomol; Trade Unions) - 4. Foreign trade agencies and organizations - 5. Soviet delegations abroad - 6. Activities of L.I. Brezhnev and A.N.Kosygin - 7. Honours - 8. Deaths - 9. Index. Changes in position and of occupants are noted. *Class No:* 354(47)

Denmark

[3338]

Kongelig dansk Hof- og Statskalender. Statshåndbog for kongeriget Danmark... København, Schultz, 1734-. Annual. ISSN: 00852589.

Detailed directory of Danish government departments and officials, plus organizations, universities, etc. Name index and subject index. *Class No:* 354(489)

Belgium

[3339]

Annuaire administratif et judiciaire de Belgique et de la capitale du royaume. Brussels, Bruylant. Annual. BFr.57100. ISSN: 00662461.

Detailed directory of Belgian central and local government departments and officials. Includes a list of Brussels streets, communes, and faubourgs. Index of departments and subjects. *Class No:* 354(493)

China

[3340]

LAMB, M. **Directory of officials and organisations in China :** a quarter-century guide. Armonk, N.Y., & London, M.E. Sharpe, 1994. xxxiii,1355p. £215; $341.75. (*Contemporary China papers no. 22..*) ISBN: 1563244276.

Intended for analysts of political and organizational developments in China since the Cultural Revolution. In 5 sections: A. The Communist Party of China (subdivided by committees, commissions, departments, institutes, etc.); B. The State structure; C. Ministers and commissions of the State Council; D. Abolished ministers and commissions; E. Bureau and specialized agencies subordinate to the State Council. *Class No:* 354(510)

[3341]

SAICH, T. **China: politics and government.** London, Macmillan Press, 1981. xiii,265p. tables, map. £8.50. ISBN: 0333287436.

11 chapters: 1. From revolution to liberation: the emergence and triumph of the Chinese Communist Party - 2. The first seventeen years ... 3. The Cultural Revolution and its aftermath - 4. Marxism-Leninism-Mao Zedong thought - 5. The Chinese Communist Party - 6. The State structure - 7. The People's Liberation Army - 8. Social and political control - 9. Urban China - 10. Rural China - 11. Epilogue. References to chapters and footnotes, p.229-253. Selected further reading (by chapter), p.254-261. Analytical index, p.262-265. '... authoritative ...' (*British book news,* April, 1982, p.221). *Class No:* 354(510)

India

[3342]

RANA, M.S., *ed.* **Indian government and politics:** a bibliographical study. v.1: 1885-1980. New Delhi, Wiley Eastern Ltd., 1981. xxviii,648p. £30. ISBN: 0852267630.

To be in 2 v.

c.11,000 items arranged in 8 subject sections: I. Ancient political thought and institutions - II. Medieval political thought and institutions - III. Modern political developments - IV. Political thinkers and leaders - V. Collected biographies - VI. Nationalism - VII. Democracy. Political ideologies. Political movements. Politico-social issues. Muslim politics - issues and ideas - VIII. A classified list of PhD theses. Author index, p.595-648. *Class No:* 354(540)

Asia—Near East

[3343]

Political leaders of the contemporary Middle East and North Africa: a biographical dictionary. Reich, B., *ed.* Westport, CT., Greenwood Press, 1990. 557p. £69.95. $85. ISBN: 0313262136.

Profiles 70 men and women who have had a significant impact on the political development of the Arabic-speaking countries of the area since World War II. Each entry (7-10p.) is signed and concludes with a list of additional sources as well as noting the political leader's own writings. A chronology of the region, up to 1989, precedes a bibliography of general sources and a detailed index. 'Strongly recommended'. (*Choice,* v.27(11/12), July-August 1990, p.1810). *Class No:* 354(56)

Africa

[3344]

BIDWELL, R.L. **Guide to African ministers.** London, Rex Collings, 1978. [iv], 79p. tables. £10. ISBN: 0860360644.

6 tabular sections: Heads of State (including, where appropriate, Colonial governors) - Prime Ministers - Ministers of Foreign Affairs - Ministers of War or Defence - Ministers of the Interior or of Local Government - Ministers of Finance. Each section is subdivided into 8 groups, 'representing countries grouped together for geographical or historical reasons' (*e.g.* groups D & E: Francophone Equatorial and West Africa). Period: 1950-1976. Exact dates are given. 60 notes. No index. *Class No:* 354(6)

USA

Bibliographies

[3345]

VOSE, C.E. **A Guide to library resources in political science:** American government. Washington, DC., American Political Science Association, 1975. viii,135p. illus. $6.50. (*Instructional resource monographs, no.1.*) ISBN: 0915654032.

Essays on how political scientists might garner knowledge from libraries. In 3 parts: 1. American national government (Government publications - the Constitution - Congress - The Executive Branch - Federal Courts); 2. General reference books (Almanacs - biographies - political dictionaries - encyclopedias); 3. Library basics (files, archives and manuscripts). Bibliographies attached to each essay. 'A selection tool rather than a reference work' (*R.Q.,* v.15(2), Winter 1975, p.180). *Class No:* 354(73)(01)

Yearbooks & Directories

[3346]

CONGRESSIONAL QUARTERLY INC. **Washington information directory, 1993-94.** Washington, D.C., Congressional Quarterly, 1993. Annual. 1100p. $89.95. ISBN: 0871877720.

First published 1976.

Names, telephone numbers, addresses and responsibilities of more than 5000 key personnel and agencies located in Washington, arranged in subject chapters, each followed by a bibliography. Subject index;

....(contd.)

agency and organization index. 'An invaluable guide to the working of official and unofficial Washington' (*American reference book annual*, 1980, entry 49C). *Class No:* 354(73)(058)

[3347]

—Encyclopedia of governmental advisory organizations. Batten, D. *and* Dresser, P., *eds*. 9th ed. Detroit, Mich., Gale Research Company, 1989. $505. ISBN: 0810374609.

First edition 1973-75.

Reports on the advisory organizations at work in the US today. Nearly 6000 entries describing the activities and personnel of the committees advising the President and various departments and bureaus of the Federal government (organization name and address; telephone number; executive secretary's name, history and authority; programme; membership; staff; etc.). Also includes information on White House conferences and other conferences sponsored by the Federal government, groups under contract doing studies for the Federal government, and Congressional committees doing studies of current topical interest. 5 indexes; alphabetical and keyword, personnel, publications and reports, organizations by Federal department or agency, organizations by Presidential administration. *Class No:* 354(73)(058)

[3348]

LARSON, D.R. Guide to US government directories. Phoenix, AZ., Oryx Press, 1981-1985. 2v. (436p.). $60.50; £45 each vol. ISBN: 0912700637, v.1; 0897741625, v.2.

V.1: 1970-1980; v.2: 1980-1984. Includes all types of publications (serials, appendices, articles, as well as individual volumes (with some 'location identification or contact codes' for the names of people, groups or places. Extensive analytical subject index to each volume. *Class No:* 354(73)(058)

Biographies

[3349]

SOBEL, R., *ed*. Biographical directory of the United States executive branch, 1774-1989. 2nd rev. ed. Westport, CT., Greenwood Press, 1990. 600p. $95. ISBN: 0313265933.

First published 1971.

Contains biographical data on *c.*500 persons. *Class No:* 354(73)(092)

Diplomatic Service

Worldwide

Handbooks & Manuals

[3350]

FELTHAM, R.G. Diplomatic handbook. 7th ed. London, Longman., 1998. 216p. £20.99. ISBN: 0582317169.

First published 1970.

10 sections: 1. Diplomatic relations (*e.g.* the establishment of diplomatic missions and of permanent diplomatic missions) - 2. The Ministry of Foreign Affairs - 3. The diplomatic mission - 4. Protocol and procedure - 5. Diplomatic privileges and immunities - 6. Consular offices and consular posts - 7. The United Nations - 8. International organizations and agreements outside the UN - 9. International law and practice - 10. Conferences. Appendices A-E (E: Glossary of diplomatic, consular, legal and economic terms). Analytical index. Author is former Director of the Foreign Service Programme at the University of Oxford. 'An exceptionally handy little book' (*International affairs*, v.56(4), Autumn 1980, p.682) of the 3rd ed. *Class No:* 354DIP(100)(035)

[3351]

—Satow's guide to diplomatic practice. Gore-Booth, Lord . 5th ed. London, Longman, 1979. xix,544p. £29.95. ISBN: 0582501091.

First published 1917.

5 books (44 chapters): 1. Diplomacy in general - 2. Diplomatic agents in general - 3. Consular matters - 4. International transactions - 5. International organizations. 6 appendices (*e.g.* 1. Definitions and terms; 4. Specialized agencies). Chapter notes, p.489-521; bibliography, p.522-31; index, p.532-44. A more detailed, legalistic approach than Feltham's *Diplomatic handbook*. *Class No:* 354(100)(035)

Great Britain

Yearbooks & Directories

[3352]

The Diplomatic Service list: 1999. Foreign and Commonwealth Office. 28th ed. London, Stationery Office Books, 1999. £27.50. ISBN: 0115917659. ISSN: 04191714.

Succeeds *The Foreign Office list* (1806-1965). Annual.

In 4 parts: 1. Home departments - 2. British representatives overseas

....(contd.)

- 3. Chronological lists, from 1972, of Secretaries of State, Ministers of State, Permanent Under-Secretaries, Ambassadors, High Commissioners and permanent representatives to international organizations - 4. Biographical notes, and lists of staff (of Senior Grade to Grade 10 of the Diplomatic Service, officers of Grades S1-S3 of the Secretarial Branch and officers of the Security Officer Branch). *Class No:* 354DIP(410)(058)

Armed Forces

[3353]

WISE, T. A Guide to military museums. 5th rev. ed. Doncaster, S. Yorks., Athena Books, 1988. [80]p.

First published 1969.

211 main entries, arranged under regiments (descriptive notes; hours, curator, approaches; marginal badges of regiments). Index of special museums (*e.g.* German occupation: Channel Islands). 72 entries on 'other places of interest'. *Class No:* 355

[3354]

World defence forces, 1989: a compendium of current military information of all countries of the world. Pope, B.H., *ed*. Santa Barbara, CA, ABC-Clio Press, 1989. 137p. $28.95;£17.15. ISBN: 0874362733. *Class No:* 355

Abbreviations & Symbols

[3355]

Defence terminology: an A-Z of military abbreviations, acronyms and special-purpose words. Lee, R.G., *ed*. London, Brasseys (UK) Ltd., 1991. vi,225p. £15.95. ISBN: 008041320x.

A compilation of current terms (including combat terms, mnemonics and special-purpose words), abbreviations and acronyms. Over 4200 definitions from '"A" weighting' to 'Zoom systems'. Includes army, navy and air force terms from both sides of the Atlantic. *Class No:* 355(003)

[3356]

PRETZ, B., *ed*. Dictionary of military technological abbreviations and acronyms. London, Routledge & Kegan Paul, 1983. [2],496p. £37.50. ISBN: 0710092741.

*c.*50,000 abbreviations and acronyms used by the British, American, German and Soviet military. Covers all the services and their technology. A-Z throughout. *Class No:* 355(003)

[3357]

SCOTT, B.K.C. Dictionary of military abbreviations. Hastings, Tamarisk Books, 1982. [4], 117p. £7. ISBN: 0907221017.

Over 5000 abbreviations and acronyms used by and about the military forces of the UK, Europe and Commonwealth, past and present, that may be found in official documents, on items of equipment, in military histories or contemporary accounts. *Class No:* 355(003)

Bibliographies

[3358]

Air University Library index to military periodicals. Alabama, Maxwell Air Force Base, Air University Library, 1949-, v.1, no.1-. Quarterly. ISSN: 00022586.

As *Air University periodical index*, 1949-62.

'A subject index to significant articles, news items and editorials appearing in 76 English-language military and aeronautical periodicals' (*Preface*). Arranged A-Z authors and subjects in one sequence, with further subdivision as necessary, and finally A-Z by title. *Class No:* 355(01)

[3359]

COCKLE, M.J.D. A Bibliography of English military books up to 1642. New ed. London, Holland Press, 1982. xl,269p. illus. £25. ISBN: 0900470704.

First published 1900.

Entries nos.1-166 consist of books in English, arranged chronologically; nos. 500-950 cover foreign books, arranged according to subjects A-Z, with final chronological order. Nos. 167-499 are not used. Index (p.251-68) includes names of English printers. *Class No:* 355(01)

[3360]

Current military and political literature. Oxford, The Military Press Ltd., 1983-. 6pa. £60pa. ISSN: 09543589.

Early title was *Current military literature*.

Comment, abstracts and citations of important articles from journals and monographs about international strategic and defence studies, military science, political science and international affairs. Arranged in subject sections. Author, source journals and geographical indexes. *Class No:* 355(01)

[3361]

SCRIVENER, D. *and* SHEEHAN, M. **Bibliography of arms control verification.** Aldershot, Hants, Dartmouth Publishing Company, 1990. [6],176p. £30. ISBN: 1855210444.

Bibliography of recent research on arms control verification, both Western sources and Soviet writings. Also includes two essays on the problems of verification and the difference between Western and Soviet attitudes . Bibliographical data includes books and articles, unannotated. *Class No:* 355(01)

Encyclopaedias

[3362]

International military and defense encyclopedia. Dupuy, T.N., *and others, eds*. Washington, Brassey's (US), 1993. 6v.(3132p). £1000. $1250. ISBN: 0028810112.

785 articles (including 129 for regions or countries complete with historical data) each of 100-10,000 words in length, by over 400 authors. Articles are arranged in 17 major subject areas (*e.g.* Aerospace forces; Logistics; Combat). Emphasis is on current events, theories, etc., but there are numerous historical and biographical articles also. Each article carries a bibliography. V.1 lists all authors and articles. Lists of acronyms and abbreviations are in each volume. Meticulous, easy-to-use index of more than 25,000 index terms. 'This work is essential for military, government, and academic collections and is highly recommended for large public libraries'. (*Library journal*, 15 March 1993, p.70). *Class No:* 355(031)

[3363]

MACKSEY, K. *and* WOODHOUSE, W. **The Penguin encyclopedia of modern warfare,** 1850 to the present. Harmondsworth, Mddx., Viking, 1991. x,373p. diagrs, maps. £18.99. ISBN: 0670826987.

More than 30 maps and a useful chronology covering the last 150 years. Bibliography, p.361-2. Index, p.363-73. 'A useful desk-reference book, supporting Dupuy's *The Encyclopedia of military history*'(1986). (*Library journal*, 1 November 1991, p.90.). *Class No:* 355(031)

Histories

[3364]

WARRY, J. **Warfare in the classical world:** an illustrated encyclopedia of weapons, warriors and warfare in the ancient civilisations of Greece and Rome. New York, St. Martin's Press; 1981. 224p. illus, diagrs., maps. $24.95. ISBN: 0312856148.

First published in London in 1980 by Salamander Books Ltd.

15 chapters on the soldiers of Greece and Rome from the rise of Mycenae to the decline of the Roman Empire, 1600 BC - AD 800: The pronunciation of ancient languages - Homeric and Mycenaean warfare - The Persian wars ... Alexander the Great ... Pompey and his epoch - Julius Caesar ... The coming of the Barbarians. Glossary, p.218-219. Detailed analytical index, p.220-224. Includes over 125 photographs, the majority in colour, 50 battle plans, and tactical diagrams. 'A magnificent colour encyclopedia ...' (*Library journal,* August 1981, p.1528). *Class No:* 355(031)(091)

Russian

[3365]

Sovetskaya voennaya entisiklopediya. Moscow, Voennoe Izdat. Ministerstva Oborony SSSR, 1976-80. 4v.illus. (some.col.), tables, maps.

'Soviet military encyclopedia'. Entries A-Z (*e.g.* 'Samokhodnaya artilleriiskaya' [artillery self-propelled gun]: 3p., 9 illus., 1 table). Campaign maps (*e.g.* World War II) are a feature. Cross-references. Coloured illustrations of flags, etc. Each volume has *c*.650p. *Class No:* 355(031)=82

[3366]

—ROMER, J.-C. Le Dictionnaire encyclopédique militaire soviétique: d'une édition à l'autre. In Strategique, no.35, 1987, p.5-23.

Discusses changes in the new 1986 edition of the Soviet military encyclopedia. *Class No:* 355(031)=82

Handbooks & Manuals

[3367]

Defense and foreign affairs handbook, 1999. Copley, G.R., *ed.* New York, International Strategic Studies Association, 1999. $242 CD-ROM $429. ISBN: 1892998033; 1892998025, CDROM.

Political, economic and defence data on *c*.200 countries. *Class No:* 355(035)

[3368]

ROBERTSON, D. **Guide to modern defense and strategy:** a complete description of the terms, tactics, organizations and accords of today's defense. Detroit, Mich., Gale Research International Ltd., 1988. xii. 324p. $65. ISBN: 0810350432.

A handbook of defence terms and concepts, emphasising 'modern' and 'strategy'. Long definitions and discussions of broad military and naval terms and concepts, half a page to a page or more in length. Cross-references. List of *c*.150 acronyms. No index and no bibliography. British slant, but US topics and concepts included. *Class No:* 355(035)

Dictionaries

Polyglot

[3369]

Brassey's multilingual military dictionary. Oxford, Pergamon & Brassey's Defence Publications, 1987. Reprinted 1989. xvii,815p. £48. ISBN: 0080270328.

c.7000 key military words and phrases in the English language, with definitions in English, numbered, and followed by equivalents in French, Spanish, German, Russian and Arabic. 6 indexes, one in each of the languages, including English, refer to the numbered items. Index of definitions and equivalents in British English and US usage, p.447-457. Appendices (*e.g.* A. Ranks; B. Units/formations). *Class No:* 355(038)=00

English

[3370]

AMMER, C. **Fighting words:** from war, rebellion, and other combative capers. New York, Paragon House, 1989. 256p. illus. $19.95. ISBN: 1557780560.

Definitions of originally military terms in short informative essays. *Class No:* 355(038)=20

[3371]

Department of Defense dictionary of military and associated terms: incorporating the NATO (English and French). United States. Joint Chiefs of Staff. Washington, G.P.O., 1990-.

First published 1972, 1979 & 1988 by the Hemisphere Publishing Corporation. Now to be updated by supplements.

c. 6000 entries for military and 'Pentagonese' terms arranged in subject groups. Many cross-references. An appendix is a directory of departments, agencies and facilities of the Department of Defense and the Coast Guard. 'may be useful in the interpretation of military documents' (*Choice*, v.25 (10), June 1988, p.1532). *Class No:* 355(038)=20

[3372]

Dictionary of military terms. US Joint Chiefs of Staff. New rev. & exp. ed. London, Greenhill Books, 1999. 493p. £25. ISBN: 1853673862.

At head of title-page - US Department of Defense. First published by the Joint Chiefs of Staff as JCS Pub.1.

More than 6000 concise entries for current military and associated terms. Symbols indicate the origin of the terms. *Class No:* 355(038)=20

[3373]

Jane's dictionary of military terms. Hayward, P.H.C., *comp*. London, Macdonald & Jane, 1975. [iv],201p.

c.2500 concise entries, some terms having a number of meanings (*e.g.* 'Cluster' has 5). Cross-references. Appendix 1: Abbreviations, p.179-98; 3: The order of precedence of corps and regiments of the Regular Army. British slant. *Class No:* 355(038)=20

[3374]

SHAFRITZ, J.M., *and others*. **The Facts on File dictionary of military science.** New York, Facts on File, 1989. 498p. $40. ISBN: 0816018235.

Over 5000 entries, primarily those associated with strategy, logistics, military law, weapons, technology, administration and weapons procurement from the age of Napoleon to the 1980s. Systematic sequence: (1) Headword (2) Definition number when more than one meaning (3) Definition. Many 'see also' references and full bibliographical references. '... a useful reference work ...'(*Reference books bulletin*, 1 November 1989, p.606). *Class No:* 355(038)=20

German

[3375]
EITZEN, K.H. German-English, English-German military dictionary, with detailed lists of abbreviations, American and British tables of measurements, coins and weights, ranks, calibres, conversion tables, NATO-ABC, etc. 4th ed. London, Atlantic Press, 1957. 549p. Reprinted 1988 as *The military Eitzen*. £22.90.

Each half has *c*.10,000 entries, including many compounds. Particularly strong on colloquialisms (especially US). Some 2,000 abbreviations are explained on p.467-530, with references to the main text. *Class No: 355(038)=30*

Norwegian

[3376]
MARM, L.   Engelsk-Amerikansk-Norsk,   Norsk-Engelsk-Amerikansk... militaeir ordbok. Oslo, Fabritius, 1977. x,276p.

English/American - Norwegian, Norwegian - English/American military dictionary. More recent is: *Class No: 355(038)=396*

[3377]
—ARK, O.I. English-Norwegian military dictionary. New York; French and European Publications, 1985. 459p. $95; £29.50. ISBN: 0828819076.

English into Norwegian. *Class No: 355(038)=396*

French

[3378]
NATO glossary of terms and definitions (English and French), listing terms of military significance and their definitions for use in NATO, together with an index of NATO agreed documents containing specialist terms and definitions. [Brussels], NATO, 1988. (*Allied administrative publications/North Atlantic Treaty Organization, 6*.)
Class No: 355(038)=40

Russian

[3379]
Russian-English military dictionary. Joint Technical Language Service of the War Office. London, HMSO, 1983. 688p. £25. ISBN: 0112300189.

Produced for military translators and interpreters, this revised ed. is the first to be made available to the public. *Class No: 355(038)=82*

Arabic

[3380]
Arabic military dictionary: English-Arabic, Arabic-English. Multi-lingual International Publishers Ltd., *comp and* Kay, E., *ed..* London, Routledge & Kegan Paul, 1986. [7],171,[133]p. £30. ISBN: 0710204582.

Compiled for use by military personnel and by anyone who is directly or indirectly involved in military technology. Includes the terms and phrases in everyday use in the field or in headquarters. No definitions. Includes abbreviations. The first section has the terms, A-Z in English, with transliterated Arabic and Arabic script; the second section has terms in Arabic script, with English translations.
Class No: 355(038)=927

[3381]
KAYYALI, M.S. Modern military dictionary: English-Arabic, Arabic-English. London, Third World Centre for Research and Publishing; Beirut, Arab Institute for Research and Publishing, 1986. 118,[135]p. £22. ISBN: 0861990218. *Class No: 355(038)=927*

Chinese

[3382]
LOWE, J. D-H. A Dictionary of military terms and military intelligence phrases: Chinese-English, English-Chinese. Boulder, Col., Westview Press, 1992. 725p. maps. $95
Class No: 355(038)=951

Reviews & Abstracts

[3383]
Abstracts of military biography. Ramirez Mitchell, R.A., *ed.* Buenos Aires, Ruben A. Ramirez Mitchell, 1967-. v.1, no.1-. Quarterly. $70pa.

Former titles were *Resumenes analyticos sobre defensa y seguridad nacional* and *Resúmes analiticos de bibliografia militar,* published by Instituto de Publicaciones Navales.

World coverage of literature (books, periodicals, government reports) on warfare, national defence and international relations. A-Z subject order. Abstracts are in Spanish and English.
Class No: 355(048)

Periodicals

Bibliographies

[3384]
IMPERIAL WAR MUSEUM. Department of Printed Books. List of current journals,1991. London, the Museum, 1991. 83p. £14.

Includes *c*.500 titles, A-Z, followed by a 26-page subject index.
Class No: 355(051)(01)

Yearbooks & Directories

[3385]
R.U.S.I. and Brassey's defence yearbook, 1991. Royal United Services Institute for Defence Studies, *ed.* 101st ed. London, Brassey's U.K. Ltd., 1991. viii,336p. illus. ISBN: 0080407102.

First published jointly 1974 (1974/56 ed.). 1886-1949 as *Brassey's naval and shipping manual*.

Up-to-date surveys and analyses of the defence world. This ed. has 18 articles by well-known experts, arranged in 5 subject sections: European security - Security policies and military concepts - Defence industries and the market place - The place of the military in regional stability - Signposts (3 items including a directory of educational establishments teaching strategic studies, and statistics of NATO defence expenditure, 1985-1989. Notes including bibliographical references, follow each article. One of the most authoritative sources on the defence field. *Class No: 355(058)*

Quotations

[3386]
A Dictionary of military quotations. Royle, T., *comp.* London, Routledge; New York, Simon and Schuster, 1990. [xii],210p. $40. ISBN: 0415041384, UK; 0132101130, US.

Nearly 3500 quotations arranged in 5 major categories: 1. Captains and kings - 2. Battles and wars - 3. Armies and soldiers - 4. War and peace - 5. Last post. Author index, p.191-198. Subject index, p.199-210. *Class No: 355(082.2)*

[3387]
HEINL, R.D. Dictionary of military and naval quotations. Annapolis, MD., U.S. Naval Institute Press, 1966. xl,[i],367p. ports. $21.95. ISBN: 0870211498.

About 6000 quotations from more than 1400 individuals under 800 subjects, A-Z; range extends chronologically from Homer to Liddell Hart. Gives sources and date of quotation, where known and applicable. Index of authors of quotations. *Class No: 355(082.2)*

[3388]
SHAFRITZ, J.M. War on words: including quotations from ancient times to the present. Englewood Cliffs, NJ, Prentice-Hall, 1990. 559p. $29.35. ISBN: 013209875x.

Far more helpful to students than M. Hastings (1985) or J. Wintle (1987), and more of a follow-up to the classic *Dictionary of military and naval quotations*, by R.D.Heinl, (*q.v.*) according to *Choice*, December 1990, p.616. *Class No: 355(082.2)*

[3389]
TSOURIS, P.G. Warriers' words: a quotation book: from Sesostris III to Schwarzkopf, 1871 BC to AD 1991. London, Arms & Armour Press, 1992. 534p. £15.99. $29.95. ISBN: 1854090887.

Quotations from more than 250 military personalities who have 'exercised the profession of arms', arranged in *c*.350 subject areas ('War' has 12 subheadings). Entries list author, title, date of source, translator, complete bibliographical details being given at the end of the book. Biographical index of sources provides brief summaries of military career. *Class No: 355(082.2)*

Histories

[3390]
DUPUY, R.E. *and* DUPUY, T.N. The Encyclopedia of military history, from 3500 B.C. to the present. 4th rev. ed. New York & London, Harper-Collins, 1993. 1654p. illus. maps. $65;£30. ISBN: 0062700561, US; 0004701437, UK.

First published 1970. Title in USA is The Harper encyclopedia of military history...

21 chapters (1. The dawn of military history ... 21. Superpowers in the nuclear age, 1945-1991). Each begins with an essay assessing military trends, leaders, weapons, etc., followed by data chronologically arranged. Thus, ch. 14, 'The beginning of modern warfare, 1600-1700', deals with military trends, then major wars (*e.g.* Thirty Years' War, 1618-48, with events chronologically tabulated), and finally with areas and countries (Western Europe ... Spanish America, Portuguese America). Bibliography by chapters. 150 illus., 75 campaign and other maps. General index (*c*.15,000 entries); index of battles and sieges; index of wars. A valuable contribution.
Class No: 355(091)

[3391]
JESSUP, J.E. *and* COAKLEY, R.W. A Guide to the study and use of **military history.** Center of Military History, United States Army. Washington, D.C., Government Printing Office, reprinted 1982. xv,507p. $250.00.

23 chapters in 4 parts: 1. Military history, its nature and use - 2. Bibliographical guide - 3. Army programs, activities, and uses - 4. History outside the US Army. 2 appendices: A: Reference works: a select list; B: Historical journals and societies. Index, p.457-507. Footnotes, and lengthy bibliographies after each chapter. '... designed to foster appreciation of the value of military history and explain its uses and the resources available for study' (*Preface*).
Class No: 355(091)

Maps & Atlases
[3392]
HARTMAN, T *and* MITCHELL, J. A World atlas of military **history, 1945-1984.** London, Leo Cooper/Secker & Warburg, 1984. xi, 108p. tables. 93 maps. £16. $24.95. ISBN: 0436191474.

Covers the major and minor wars fought since 1945 in Europe, the Middle East, the Gulf, Africa, India, China and Korea, South East Asia, Central and South America. Includes text, statistical tables and maps. Name index, p. 93-96. Gazetteer, p.97-108.
Class No: 355(091)(084.3)

Biographies
[3393]
DUPUY, T.N., *and others*. The Harper encyclopedia of military **biography** Edison, NJ, Castle, 1995. 834 p. £25. ISBN: 0785804374.
Class No: 355(092)

[3394]
KEEGAN, J. *and* WHEATCROFT, A. Who's who in military **history,** from 1453 to the present day. New ed. London, Hutchinson, 1987. 376p. illus. £25. ISBN: 0091705207.

First published, 1976. by Weidenfeld and Nicolson.

'We have dealt with the Great Captains at length, as they deserve; but beyond them we have written as the interest or curiosity of the topic demanded' (*Introduction*). For popular consumption.
Class No: 355(092)

Worldwide

Encyclopaedias
[3395]
The International military encyclopaedia. Tobias, N., *ed.* Gulf Breeze, Ill., Academic International Press, 1992-. To be in *c.*50v. v.1: $37. ISBN: 0875691595, v.1.

Primarily a work of military history and affairs, with emphasis on the post- World War II period. V.1 has 197 entries (A...). *Wilson library bulletin* (February 1993, p.105) considers the *Encyclopedia of military history* will suffice for most libraries.
Class No: 355(100)(031)

Handbooks & Manuals
[3396]
The Military balance, 1993-94. Oxford, Brassey's for the International Institute for Strategic Studies, 1993. Annual. 268p. illus., tables. £36. ISBN: 1857530381. ISSN: 04597222.

First published 1959 as *The Soviet Union and the NATO powers: the military balance*.

In 2 parts: 1. Countries and principal facts - 2. Tables and analysis. Provides an authoritative assessment of the military strength and defence spending of every country possessing armed forces. Country entries detail military organization and list equipment holdings, manpower and relevant economic data. *Class No:* 355(100)(035)

[3397]
Strategic survey, 1992-93. International Institute for Strategic Studies. First published 1967. Annual. London, Brassey's (UK), 1992. 248p. £21; $29. ISBN: 1857530039.

The Institute's annual analytical review of international security-related events, and likely future international developments.
Class No: 355(100)(035)

[3398]
International defence directory. Thompson, S., *ed.* 11th ed. Coulsdon, Surrey, Jane's, 1993. xci.1223p. £250. $395. ISSN: 02567822.

Lists *c.*15000 defence companies and *c.*350000 key personnel in 172 countries. Entries include company name, key personnel, product and service description. Quick reference section (on tinted paper) precedes. Product/service index. Product supplier link. Also available on CD-ROM. *Class No:* 355(100)(058)

[3399]
KEEGAN, J., *ed.* World armies. 2nd ed. London, Macmillan; Detroit, Mich., Gale Research Co., 1983. xlvi, 688p. £45; $80. ISBN: 0333340795, UK; 0810315157, US.

First published 1979.

18 contributions. Data on the armies of 150 countries, Afghanistan ... Zimbabwe (*e.g.* Finland, p.183-6. History and introduction - Strength and budget - Command and constitutional status - Role commitment, deployment and recent operations - Organization - Recruitment, training and reserves - Equipment and arms industry - Rank, dress and distinctions - Current developments). Appendices: 1. The armies of Africa; 2. The armies of India, Pakistan, Burma, Sri Lanka and Bangladesh. Adds flesh to the bare bones provided by *The Military balance* (International Institute for Strategic Studies) (*qv*), but the latter has the decided advantage of being annual.
Class No: 355(100)(058)

Tables & Data Books
[3400]
World military and social expenditure, 1996. Sivard, R.L. Washington, World Priorities, 1996. 56p., col.illus., maps. $9.00. ISSN: 03634795.

First published 1974. Annual.

A report on the use of world resources for two kinds of priorities: military power and human needs. Includes factual background data for *c.*150 countries, with comparative figures not readily available elsewhere. *Class No:* 355(100)(083)

Great Britain
[3401]
GORDON, L.L. British battles and medals: a description of every campaign medal and bar awarded since the Armada, with the historical reasons for their awards, and the names of all the ships, regiments and squadrons of the Royal Air Force whose personnel are entitled to them. Joslin, E.C., *ed.* 6th ed. London, Spink & Son, 1988. viii,299p. illus. (some col.). £38. ISBN: 0907605257.

First published 1947.

10 sections: Campaign medals from 1588 to 1982 listed in chronological order - Polar medals - United Nations medals - Indian Army ranks and British equivalents - List of regiments and corps as at 1987 - Precedence of corps and infantry regiments - Cavalry and infantry regiments - Bibliography - Index of medals - Index of bars. Profusely illustrated in black-and-white, and 4 pages of bars in colour. A standard reference work for medal collectors. *Class No:* 355(410)

Handbooks & Manuals
[3402]
CHANT, C. Handbook of British regiments. London, Routledge, 1988. xi,313p. illus. £20. ISBN: 0415002419.

Information on *c.*85 regiments and corps which form the current British Army 'from the Household Cavalry to the Royal Dental Corps, from the SAS to Queen Alexandra's Nursing Corps and the Royal Army Chaplain's Department' (book jacket). Each has a separate entry giving factual details in a standardized layout for easy comparison, including current title, colonel-in-chief, battle honours, uniform, history, nicknames, mottoes and marches, and illustration of cap badge. Index to corps and regiments, p.310-313.
Class No: 355(410)(035)

[3403]
FREDERICK, J.B.M., *comp*. Lineage book of British land forces, **1660-1978:** biographical outlines of cavalry, yeomanry, armour, artillery, infantry, marines and air force land troops of the regular and reserve forces. 2nd ed. Pontefract, W. Yorks., Lofthouse Publications, 1987. 2v. (532p.,534p.). £25 each vol. ISBN: 1851170073, v.1; 1851170081, v.2; 185117009x, set.

First published 1969 by Hopefarm Press, Cornwallville, N.Y.

Skeleton histories of well-known and also little-known regiments of the British Army, including those formed for short periods of war service. Under each regiment - regular units, militia, special reserve, territorials and volunteers, as well as new armies and war-formed units. Also a section on disbanded regiments and corps.
Class No: 355(410)(035)

Yearbooks & Directories

[3404]

Brassey's armed services careers yearbook, 1987/88. London; Brassey's Defence Publishers, 1988. xxii,345p. 12 illus. £35; $52.50. ISBN: 0080335985.

Arranged in 3 parts: 1. The Royal Navy and Royal Marine - 2. The Army - 3. The Royal Air Force. In each part there is information on organization and role, opportunities, selection and training, career development for commissioned and non-commissioned officers. Appendices have more specific details. *Class No:* 355(410)(058)

[3405]

British defence directory. Lycett—Gregson D.C., *ed.* London, Brasseys (UK) Ltd., 1982-. Quarterly. £228 pa. ISSN: 02724782.

Quarterly computerized directory of senior service and civilian personnel in the Ministry of Defence, Royal Navy, Army, *eg*Royal Air Force, NATO and Diplomatic service. Includes hierarchical charts. Comprehensive address code index. Name index.
Class No: 355(410)(058)

Official Records

[3406]

HIGHAM, R., *ed.* **A Guide to the sources of British military history.** London, Routledge; Berkeley, CA., University of California Press, 1971. xxi,630p. (*Conference in British studies, no.1.*) ISBN: 0710072511, UK; 0520016742, US.

25 chapters, by various hands (1. Introduction - 2. Military developments from prehistoric times to 1485 - 3. Military developments of the Renaissance - 4. The Navy, to 1714... 11. Colonial warfare, 1815-1970... 16. The development of the Royal Air Force, 1909-1945... 24. The evolution of naval medicine - 25. The history of military and martial law. Includes information on access to special collections and private archives. Appended bibliography of 362 items. No index. 'Nearly all 25 chapters are very good and some are outstanding' (*Journal of modern history,* v.45(1), March 1973, p.92-93. *British military history: a supplement to Robin Higham's guide...* (New York, Garland, $67. xii,586. ISBN 0824084500) was published in 1988. *Class No:* 355(410)(093.2)

Germany

[3407]

SEATON, A. The German army; 1933-45. London, Weidenfeld & Nicolson, 1982. xxiv. 310p. 7 maps. £16.50. ISBN: 0297780328.

A full length analytical study in 12 chapters, arranged chronologically (1. The Legacy - 2. In the grip of fear ... 7. New commitments, 1941 - 8. Barbarossa ... 12. The collapse). 3 appendices (1. Army groups in the West and South; 2. Army groups in the East; Notes on the main German arms). Notes and sources, p.270-282, by chapter; Bibliography, p.283-292; Name and general indexes, p.293-310. *Class No:* 355(430)

Histories

[3408]

MEIER-WELCKER, H. Handbuch zur deutschen Militärgeschichte, 1648-1939. Militärgeschichtlichen Forschungsant durch Friedrich Forstmeier ... [et al]. München, Bernard & Graefe, 1979-1981. 6v.

A handbook of German military history. *Class No:* 355(430)(091)

[3409]

SHOWALTER, D.E. German military history, 1648-1982: a critical bibliography. New York, Garland Publishing Inc., 1984. xxxiii,331p. $45. (*Military history bibliographies, 3. Garland reference library of social science, 113.*) ISBN: 0824092686.

A historical preface is followed by 4055 numbered entries, arranged in 10 chapters, each chapter having an introduction: 1. General works - 2. The age of absolutism: 1648-1789 - 3. Revolution and reform: 1789-1815 - 4. Confederation and unification: 1815-1871 - 5. The Second Empire: 1871-1914 - 6. The Great War: 1914-1918 - 7. The Weimar Republic: 1918-1933 - 8. The Nazi years: 1933-1945 - 9. The Wehrmacht, institutions and operations: 1933-1945 - 10. The two Germanies, 1945-1980. Author index, p.309-331.
Class No: 355(430)(091)

France

Histories

[3410]

HEGGOY, A.A. *and* **HAAR, J.M. The Military in imperial history:** the French connection. New York, Garland, 1984. x,302p. $50. (*Military history bibliographies, 4. Garland reference library of social science, 192.*) ISBN: 0824090608.

Claims to be the first English-language guide devoted exclusively to literature on French overseas military affairs from the Crusades to the present. Arranged in 20 chapters by topic and geographic location: I. French military organization and theory - II. French colonization and

....(contd.)

imperialism - III. French foreign legion... - IV-XVIII deal with overseas territories. - XIX Comparative and general works on imperialism - XX. Bibliographies, serials. Each section has an introduction. 'Some conclusions' are followed by a chronology of selected events in French imperialist history; a short bibliography (p.269-272); and an index (p.273-302). *Class No:* 355(44)(091)

[3411]

ROSS,, S.T. French military history, 1661-1799: a guide to the literature. New York, Garland Publishing, 1984. 305p. $54. (*Military history bibliographies, 6. Garland reference library of social science, 190.*) ISBN: 0824090624.

In 3 parts, general works, the old regime, and the French revolution. Each part is divided into 4 sections, each treating a different theme. Informative essays begin every part and section and conclude with bibliographical listings. Author, but no subject, index. 'This approach is very helpful in outlining and providing expert commentary on historiographic developments in a maze of sources, many of which are in French' (*Choice* v.22(6) February 1985, p.798, on which this entry is based). *Class No:* 355(44)(091)

Russia

[3412]

SCOTT, H.F. *and* **SCOTT, W.F. Armed forces of the USSR.** 2nd ed. rev. & updated. London, Arms and Armour Press, with the Royal United Services Institute for Defence Studies, 1981. xxiv.447p. illus. tables. £14.95. ISBN: 0853682879.

First published, 1979.

12 chapters, arranged in 3 parts: 1. Fundamentals of Soviet military doctrine and strategy - 2. Military force for the nuclear age -3. A nation in arms. Many footnotes, including bibliographical references. Selected bibliography, p.401-412. Name index, p.423 -430. Subject index. p.431-447. *Class No:* 355(47)

[3413]

The Soviet military encyclopedia. Green, W.C. *and* Reeves, W.R., *eds.* Westview Press, 1993. 4v.(404,403, 407,222p). $375. ISBN: 0813314321.

Abridged English-language edition of an 8v. Russian-language encyclopedia published by the Soviet Ministry of Defence between 1976 and 1980. V.1-3 have signed entries arranged A-Z by English terms (with Russian in parenthesis), many entries including lengthy lists of references. V.4 is the index in two sections - English terms and Russian terms used in the original edition. No cross-references. '... a treasure trove of insights into Soviet military organization, doctrine and tactics ...'(*Choice,* v.31(5), January 1994, p.762). *Class No:* 355(47)

Yearbooks & Directories

[3414]

Soviet armed forces review annual. Jones, D.R., *ed.* Gulf Breeze FL., Academic International Press, 1988. 375p. $71. ISBN: 0875691005.

First published 1977. Annual. The responsibility of Russia Research Center at Dalhousie University in Nova Scotia.

A survey of Soviet military developments for the past decade, with data to 1987. Detailed charts on people, weapons and policies. (... the SAFRA series remains unique and handy ... ' (*International affairs,* v.65(3) Summer 1989 p.607). *Class No:* 355(47)(058)

[3415]

—The Military-naval encyclopedia of Russia and the Soviet Union. Jones, D.R., *ed.* Gulf Breeze, FL., Academic International Press, 1978-. V.1-. ISBN: 0875690289 set.

Projected in *c.*50v., each with *c.*250p. and *c.*200 documented articles (lengthier articles being signed. Aim was to complete at the rate of 2-3v. pa., but editor 'badly need(s) co-operation of scholars and specialists ... '.

So far published: v.1. "A" (Gliders) - Administration, Military (1978); v.2. Administration, Military, Science of - Admiral Makarov (ship); v.3. Admiral Murgescu (ship) - Adp. Adp-tail 1981; v.4. Adrian I Nataliia (ship) - Adzhariia (1984) [deals largely with Russian tactical formations]. 'This is an excellent, though specialized, reference work of great utility to university libraries' (*Choice* v.16 (11), January 1980, p. 1422). *Class No:* 355(47)(058)

Balkan States

[3416]

JESSUP, J.E. Balkan military history: a bibliography. New York, Garland, 1986. xii,478p. $66. (*Military history bibliography, 8. Garland reference library of social sciences, 234.*) ISBN: 0824089634.

Lists unannotated citations of literature on Balkan military history from the 14th century to 1983. Includes what is now Albania, Bulgaria, Greece, Hungary, Romania, Yugoslavia, European Turkey, Serbia, Macedonia and Montenegro. A section on sources for the region as a whole is followed by 8 chronological chapters. Each chapter has an informative essay on sources and then a bibliographic

....(contd.)
listing of books, monographs, journal articles, essays, documents, dissertations, etc. in Balkan and Western European languages. Author and subject indexes. *Class No:* 355(497)

Japan
[3417]

KONDO, S. **Japanese military history:** a guide to the literature. New York, Garland, 1984. xii,88p. $35. (*Military history bibliography series, 5.*) ISBN: 0824090578.
6 sections: 1. Survey histories of the modern period - 2. From the ancient era to the restoration of 1868 - 3. From the creation of a modern army to the China Incident - 4. The Pacific War (1): survey histories - 5. The Pacific War (2): campaign and combat histories - 6. The history of the conclusion of the war, memoirs and biographies. Bibliography of 443 items, A-Z (p.51-81). Index (p.83-88). *Class No:* 355(52)

Israel
[3418]

WALLACH, J.L. **Israeli military history:** a guide to the sources. New York, Garland, 1984. xii,291p. $39. (*Military history bibliographies 1. Garland reference library of social science, 191.*) ISBN: 0824090616.
1715 entries arranged in 11 chronological chapters from *c.*1300 B.C. to 1974 and after. Each chapter begins with an informative essay on the sources and concludes with a bibliographical listing of books, monographs, journal articles, dissertations and documents published in Western languages. Appendix: Archives, libraries, museums, periodicals. Author index, p.273-291, but no subject index. *Class No:* 355(569.4)

Latin America
[3419]

ENGLISH, A.J. **Armed forces in Latin America:** their histories, development, present strength and military potential. London, Jane's, 1984. 490p. illus. £30. ISBN: 0710603215.
Covers the countries of Central and South America, and also Haiti, Jamaica, Cuba, and Trinidad and Tobago. Data for each country includes vital statistics, historical outline, politico-strategic position, general structure of armed forces (army, navy, air force), paramilitary forces, sources of supply, defence production, summary and prospects. Glossary in English, Spanish and Portuguese. Select bibliography, p.481-486, arranged by chapter. Index, p.487-490. *Class No:* 355(729.99)

USA
[3420]

EVINGER, W.R., *ed.* **Directory of US military bases worldwide.** 3rd ed. Phoenix, AZ, Oryx Press, 1998. 424p. £93.50. $147.75. ISBN: 1573560499. *Class No:* 355(73)

[3421]

TOMAJCZYK, S.F. **Dictionary of the modern American military :** over 15000 weapons, agencies, acronyms, slang, installations, medical terms, and other lexical units of warfare. Jefferson, NC, McFarland, 1996. xiii,785p., illus.,charts,tables. £112.50. ISBN: 0786401273. *Class No:* 355(73)

Yearbooks & Directories
[3422]

American military defense annual, 1987. Kruzel, J., *ed.* Lexington, Lexington Books, 1987. 228p. illus.,charts,tables. $35.£27. ISBN: 0669150916.
First published for 1985-1986. Annual.
Claims to be a definitive, up-to-the-minute guide by recognised experts with a wide range of views on the latest topics in defence. 11 chapters: 1. Perspectives - 2. US Defense strategy: a debate - 3. The defense budget - 4. Strategic forces - 5. Theater forces: US defense policy in NATO - 6. Seapower and projections forces - 7. Manpower - 8. Organization and management - 9. Arms control - 10. Special supplement: the Strategic Defense Initiative - 11. Special supplement: low intensity conflict. Defense bibliography, 1984, p.241-250. Notes. Index. *Class No:* 355(73)(058)

Histories
[3423]

Reference guide to United States military history. Shrader, C.R., *ed.* New York, Facts on File, 1993-2000. 5v. illus. maps. £36 $75 each volume. ISBN: 0816018375, v.2; 0816018383, v.3; 0816018391, v.4; 0816018405, v.5.
V.1 deals with the period 1607-1815; v.2 with 1815-1865; v.3 with 1865-1919; v.4 with 1919-1945; and v.5 with 1945-1993. First half of each volume is an overview of major trends and developments in the US military for that period, followed by six chronological narrative chapters, and then by brief biographical and 'battles and events' sections. Each volume has a short bibliography and an index. '... concise introductions ... but do not supersede existing standard and specialised reference sources.'(*Choice,*v.31(3), November 1993, p.438). *Class No:* 355(73)(091)

Bibliographies
[3424]

LANE, J.C., *ed.* **America's military past:** a guide to information sources. Detroit, Mich., Gale Research Co., 1980. xi,280p. $68. (*American government and history information guide series, 7.*) ISBN: 0810312050.
1743 items, with short annotations, arranged A-Z in each of 8 chapters: 1. Foundations of the American military experience - 2. Origins of the American military experience - 3. The military in the new republic (1783-1815) - 4. The military in the era of nationalism and westward expansion (1815-1877) - 5. The military and America's rise to world power - 6. The military in the age of total war (1914-45) - 7. The military in the nuclear age (since 1945) - 8. The military and the limited wars. Author index, p.253-267; subject index, p.269-280. *Class No:* 355(73)(091)(01)

Reviews & Abstracts
[3425]

KINNELL, S.K., *ed.* **Military history of the United States:** an annotated bibliography. Santa Barbara, CA., ABC-Clio, 1986. x,333p. $88.95. (*Clio bibliography series, 23.*) ISBN: 0874364744.
A collection of 3825 abstracts of scholarly journal articles originally published in *America: history and life* between 1974 and 1985. Subject arrangement, with subject and author indexes. Complements *A Guide to the sources of United States military history*, ed. by R. Higham (*qv*). *Class No:* 355(73)(091)(048)

Biographies
[3426]

SPILLER, R.J. *and* DAWSON, J.G., *eds.* **Dictionary of American military biography.** Westport. CT., Greenwood Press, 1984. 3v. (xv,1368p.). $175 £136.50. ISBN: 0313214336.
*c.*400 biographical essays, written by *c.*200 scholarly contributors, of pertinent individuals from the French and Indian Wars to the Vietnam war. Includes both native Americans and non-Americans, and all branches of the military are represented. Arrangement is A-Z by name of biographee. Essays average *c.*1500 words, include factual information (birth, death dates, etc.,) and brief bibliographies. Cross-references. Appendices. Subject index. 'A well-constructed scholarly publication that will appeal to the casual reader of American military history' (*Choice* v.22(9) May 1985., p 1303.). 'A good starting place for research on a person or period ... ' (*Library journal* December 1984, p.2264). *Class No:* 355(73)(092)

[3427]

Webster's American military biographies. McHenry, R., *ed.* Springfield, Mass., Meriam 1978 (reprinted 1984 by Dover). xi 548p. $11.95. ISBN: 0486247589.
1033 capsule biographies. MacArthur: 22/3 columns; Ulysses S. Grant: 3½ cols. Addenda (p.498-548): 1. Secretaries of War ... Commanders of NATO forces, 1960-; 2/4. Army, Navy, Marine Corps (Chief Officers. Chronology and Commanders), Air Force (Chief Officers, Commanders); Career categories (A/Z, p.544-8). *Class No:* 355(73)(092)

20th Century
[3428]

CARVER, **Field Marshall, Lord. Twentieth century warriors:** the development of the armed forces of the major military nations in the twentieth century. London, Weidenfeld & Nicolson, 1987. [4], 468p. 6 maps. £16.95. ISBN: 0297791605.
Aims to trace the development of the armed forces of the major military nations of the century, with a chapter for each country (Britain - France - Germany - Russia - the Soviet Union - USA - Japan - China) and a ninth chapter of conclusions. Select bibliography, p.447-450, by chapter; notes, p.451-452; analytical index, p.453-468. *Class No:* 355"19"

Decorations

Worldwide

[3429]
CLARKE, J.D. Gallantry medals and awards of the world. Sparkford, Stephens, 1993. 248p. illus. (some col.) ISBN: 1852603038.
Class No: 355.134(100)

Great Britain

[3430]
ABBOTT, P.E. and TAMPLIN, J.M.A. British gallantry awards: the standard reference work on awards for gallantry or distinguished service, 1855-1979. Hayward, J.B., *ed.* 2nd ed. London, Nimrod Dix Co., 1981. xx,316p. illus. £25. ISBN: 0902633740.
First published 1971 by Guiness Superlatives Ltd.
44 selected awards, A-Z (Air Force Cross ... Victoria Cross). Information given for each includes origin and development; description; verifications and citations; numbers awarded; illustrative award (showing reason for award in a particular instance); illustrations (some in colour). Includes information on 'copies' and 'fakes'. Bibliography, p.xvii-xviii. *Class No:* 355.134(410)

[3431]
LESLIE, N.B. The Battle honours of the British and Indian armies, 1695-1914. London, Leo Cooper, 1970. xiii,145p.
Regiments of the British army - Regiments of the Indian army - Battle honours: (a) Europe; (b) Asia; (c) Africa; (d) America; (e) West Indies; (f) Antipodes. Careful detail (name and date of battle; abbreviated title of regiment; title; date of award - Army Ordnance and date). 'An extremely valuable ... reference book' (*TLS*, 2 April 1971).
Two older works are still of value: J.H. Mayo's *Medals and decorations of the British army and navy* (London, Constable, 1897, 2v. illus. (incl. col. pl.)), detailing all British and Indian medals and decorations issued up to date of publication, and reprinting official warrants and orders in full; and C.B. Norman's *Battle honours of the British army*, from Tangier, 1662 to the commencement of the reign of King Edward VII (London, Murray, 1911. xxviii,500p. illus. maps), with notes on the battles for which honours were awarded to British regiments, recording numbers taking part, casualties, etc.
Class No: 355.134(410)

[3432]
PILLINGER, D. and STAUNTON, A. Victoria Cross locator. 2nd ed., revised & updated. Maidenhead, D. Pillinger, 1997. iii,58p. ISBN: 064605225x. *Class No:* 355.134(410)

[3433]
CREAGH, O'M. and HUMPHRIS, E.M., *eds.* Distinguished Service Order, 1886-1923: a complete record of the recipients of the Distinguished Service Order, 1886-1923, with citations, services and other biographical and related details. New ed. of 1924 ed. Colchester, J.B. Hayward & Son, 1978. 777p. 1020 illus. £50. ISBN: 0903754126.
Companion volume to the above. *Class No:* 355.134(410)

Uniforms & Insignia

Worldwide

[3434]
CAMPBELL, B.L. and REYNOLDS, R. Marine badges and insignia of the world, including marines, commandos and naval infantrymen. Poole, Dorset, Blandford, 1983. 191p. illus. £8.95; $16.95. ISBN: 0713711388.
Arranged in 19 sections, by country (US; UK; European countries; other). Text concentrates on describing the badges and insignia and includes a certain amount of background history. There are 48 colour plates of over 1000 badges and insignia on centre pages, as well as black and white illustrations in the text. Index, p.189-191, has references to illustrations in italics. *Class No:* 355.14(100)

[3435]
ROSIGNOLI, G. Air Force badges and insignia of World War 2. Poole, Dorset, Blandford Press, 1976. 200p. illus (col.).
Covers 19 countries (Great Britain, p.11-16, plates 1-6; USSR, p.118-20, pl.15-20; US, p.135-47, pl.29-39). Brief historical background is provided. Index (under countries).
Class No: 355.14(100)

[3436]
ROSIGNOLI, G. Army badges and insignia of World War 2: Great Britain, Poland, Belgium, Italy, USSR, US, Germany. 2nd ed. London, Blandford Press, 1974. 288p. illus. £8.95. ISBN: 071370697x.
First published 1972.
88 plates, many in colour. Index of countries, subdivided by type of badge, etc. *Class No:* 355.14(100)

[3437]
ROSIGNOLI, G. Army badges and insignia of World War 2, Book 2:$bBritish Commonwealth, Canada, South Africa, British African territories, India, British overseas territories, Finland, France, Japan, Netherlands, Yugoslavia, China, Denmark, Czechoslovakia. London, Blandford Press, 1975. 198p. illus. ISBN: 071370747x.
80 colour plates, illustrating over 2000 badges. Index, by country.
Class No: 355.14(100)

[3438]
THOMPSON, L. Badges and insignia of the elite forces. London, Cassell, 1999. 144p. illus. £14.99. ISBN: 1854095110.
Arranged by region (Africa - The Americas - Asia - Middle East - Europe), each subdivided by country. Brief descriptions and history of badges and insignia, with colour plates. *Class No:* 355.14(100)

Handbooks & Manuals

[3439]
KNÖTEL, R. Uniforms of the world: a compendium of army, navy and air force uniforms, 1700-1937. Knötel, H. *and* Sieg, H., *eds.* Rev. & enl. ed. New York, Scribner; London, Arms and Armour Press, 1980 (reissued by Arms and Armour Press in 1988). 483p. illus. $30; £5.99. ISBN: 0684103047, US; 1850791090, UK.
Originally published 1896. Translated from the 1956 ed. by R.G. Bell.
Broad chronological and geographical coverage. 1600 illus. 'Leans rather heavily on the uniforms of the preunified states of Germany ... Recommended for all libraries' (*Choice*, v.18(4), December 1980, p.507-8). *Class No:* 355.14(100)(035)

[3440]
KANNIK, P. Military uniforms in colour. English ed., edited by W.Y. Carman. London, Blandford Press, 1968. 278p. illus.
Translated from the Danish, *Alverdens uniformer i farver* (1967).
International in scope, with pride of place to the Napoleonic Wars. Comparatively meagre on British colonial and Indian units. Military terminology, p.257-70. Analytical index, under countries. 512 small coloured illus. (4 per page), chronologically from the Papal Swiss Guard of 1506 to 1960 units (including UN troops, 1950). Editor was Assistant Director, Imperial War Museum.
Class No: 355.14(100)(035)

[3441]
MOLLO, A. *and* SMITH, D. World army uniforms since 1939. London, Blandford Press, 1981. 359p. 122p. of col. illus., with 260 illus in all. *Class No:* 355.14(100)(035)

Europe—Eastern

[3442]
WIENER, F, *comp.* Army, navy and air force uniforms of the Warsaw Pact. London, Arms and Armour Press, 1978. 64p. illus. (inc. col. pl.).
Translated from the German original *Die Armeen der Warscheven-Pakt-Staaten* (M. Lehmanns, 1975).
Brief text supported by 654 illus. (including 16p. of col. plates). Covers current uniforms, badges and insignia. Warsaw Pact countries: USSR, Bulgaria, East Germany, Poland, Czechoslovakia, Hungary, Romania and Yugoslavia. *Class No:* 355.14(401)

[3443]
Soviet army uniforms and insignia (1945-75). London, Arms and Armour Press, 1981. 149p. illus.
Originally produced under the direction of Chief of Imperial General Staff, War Office, London. Has 9 p. of plates and nearly 300 drawings. *Class No:* 355.14(47)

Great Britain

[3444]
CHICHESTER, H.M. *and* BURGES-SHORT, G. The Records and badges of every regiment and corps in the British Army. 2nd ed. London, Greenhill Books, 1986. 984p. 24 col. illus. £30. ISBN: 0947898220.
First published in 1900 by Gale & Polden, Aldershot.
An authoritative account of British regiments and corps, and their predecessors, up to 1900, with data on badges, lists of unit histories, and information on uniforms, colours and standards.
Class No: 355.14(410)

[3445]
DAVIS, B.L. British army cloth insignia: 1940 to the present: an illustrated reference guide for collectors. London, Arms & Armour Press, 1985. 72p. 600 illus. £7.95. ISBN: 0853687099.
A price guide, mainly illustrations. Bibliography, p.17-18.
Class No: 355.14(410)

[3446]

EDWARDS, T.T. **Regimental badges.** 6th ed. London, Charles Knight, 1974. xiv,361p. illus.

First published 1951.

An illustrated record of cap badges of regiments and corps of the British Army, with notes on origin. Sections: 1. Regular Army - 2. Territorial and Army Volunteer Reserve - 3. Departments and Corps - 4. Miscellaneous - 5. Officers Training Corps - 6. Some discontinued badges. 5 appendices (The Garter ... The bugle). Brief index. *Class No:* 355.14(410)

[3447]

—KIPLING, A.L. *and* KING, H.L. Head-dress badges of the British Army. London, F. Muller, 1973-79. 2v. illus. V.1: £50; v.2: £35. ISBN: 0584109474, v.1; 0584109490, v.2.

The two volumes have 3100 black and white illustrations. V.1 has 36 sections (1. Early badges ... 36. The marching regiments of foot, 1914). V.2 has 22 sections, from the end of the Great War to the present day. Each volume has an index. *Class No:* 355.14(410)(035)

[3448]

JARRETT, D. **British naval dress.** London, Dent, 1960. 148p. illus.

Four sections: 1. Before 1748; 2. 1748 to 1829; 3. 1830 to 1900; 4. After 1900 . Profusely illustrated (86 plates and 19 line-drawings), many of the originals being in the National Maritime Museum. Illustrations also include badges. Detailed index. 'A most interesting book for the general reader as well as a handbook for film and theatrical producers and for historical illustrations; (*The Naval review,* v.49(1), January 1961, p.88). *Class No:* 355.14(410)

[3449]

—MOLL, J. Uniforms of the Royal Navy during the Napoleonic Wars. London, Evelyn, 1965. [7],43p. illus.

Contains 20 coloured plates in the form of modern silhouettes and includes a bibliography. *Class No:* 355.14(410)

[3450]

WILKINSON, F. **Badges of the British Army,** 1820 to the present, an illustrated reference guide for collectors. 10th ed. London, Cassell, 1997. 95p. illus. £14.99. ISBN: 1854094262.

First published 1969.

A guide for the collector, with photographs and a price guide. Also information on badge collections, how to purchase, sell, store, renovate and record them. *Class No:* 355.14(410)

Handbooks & Manuals

[3451]

DAVIS, B.L. **British army uniforms and insignia of World War II.** Rev. ed. London, Arms and Armour Press, 1992. 276p. £16.95. ISBN: 085409159x.

First published 1983.

Arranged in 6 parts: 1. Ranks and appointments - 2. Badges and insignia - 3. Uniforms and clothing - 4. Specialist and protective clothing - 5. Equipment - 6. Local Defence Volunteers and the Home Guard. 3 appendices (1. Glossary; 2. The Army Council; 3. Army numbers). Profusely illustrated. No index. *Class No:* 355.14(410)(035)

Illustrations

[3452]

ARMY MUSEUMS OGILBY TRUST. **Index to British military costume prints, 1500-1914.** London, the Trust, 1972. 493p. illus.

2584 numbered items; an index to published prints, recording more than 15,000. Two parts: 1. Sets; 2. Single prints. Index to artists, authors, engravers, lithographers, printers and publishers; index to regiments, corps and subjects; index to persons and plates. Good reproductions (51 plates). 'An exceptionally full and thorough checklist' (*British book news,* September 1972, p.784). *Class No:* 355.14(410)(084.1)

[3453]

—CARMAN, W.Y. British military uniforms from contemporary pictures: Henry VII to the present day. London, Spring Books: Hamlyn, 1968 (a reprint of the 1957 volume published by Leonard Hill). xiv,168p. illus.

Has 109 monochrome and colour plates; sources stated. Detailed lists (*e.g.* 'Dress of infantry', p.160-2: regiment/uniform/piping). Index. *Class No:* 355.14(410)(084.1)

Histories

[3454]

LAWSON, C.C.P. **A History of the uniforms of the British army,** from its beginnings to 1760. London, Norman Military Publications, 1940-67. 5v. illus. (incl. col. pl.), tables.

An authoritative record, based on official records and warrants. V.3 (1961) has a chapter on the Amerian colonies and a bibliography. V.4 (1966), covering c.1797-1815, introduces the foreign regiments in

....(contd.)

British Service. Profusely illustrated (*e.g.* v.4 has 4 colour-plates and 150 black-and-white drawings). Effective use of tables (*e.g.* p.115-7: 'Scottish fencibles'; tabulated data: regiment; date; facings; dress; lace; details; reference). *Class No:* 355.14(410)(091)

Scotland

[3455]

COCHRANE, P. **Scottish military dress.** London, Blandford Press, 1987. 128p. 92 illus. (90 in col.). £12.95. ISBN: 0713717386.

Arranged chronologically in 6 chapters (Late Middle Ages - 17th century - 18th century - The French wars, 1793-1815 - 19th century - 20th century. An appendix lists regimental titles and numbers. Bibliography of sources consulted (p.116-117). Index (p.122-128). *Class No:* 355.14(411)

Germany

[3456]

ELLIS, C. **A Collector's guide to the history and uniform of Das Heer:** the German Army, 1933-45. Addlestone, Surrey, Ian Allan, 1993. 160p. 170 illus. £10.99. ISBN: 0711021937.

A historical account of the German Army through the years of Nazi domination. *Class No:* 355.14(430)

[3457]

STEIN, H.-P *and* OTTMER, H.-M. **Symbole und Zeremoniell in deutschen Striekräften vom 18. bis zum. 20. Jahrhundert.** Herford, Mittler, 1984. 320p. illus (inc. 18 col. pl.). (*Entwicklung deutscher militärischer Tradition, Band 3.*) ISBN: 3813201619.

Arranged in 3 main sections, each subdivided. A general section of military symbols and ceremonial (4 parts) is followed by a section on symbols (10 parts) and a section on ceremonial (4 parts). Bibliography, p.310-314. Index. p.315-318. *Class No:* 355.14(430)

USA

[3458]

DAVIS, B.L. **United States army cloth insignia:** 1941 to the present day. London, Arms & Armour Press, 1987. 68p. 370 illus. £6.95. ISBN: 0853688508.

A price guide, mainly illustrations. *Class No:* 355.14(73)

[3459]

EMERSON, W.K. **Chevrons:** illustrated history and catalogue of U.S. Army insignia. Washington, DC., Smithsonian Institute Press, 1983. 298p. illus. tables. $49.50. ISBN: 0874744121.

Designed for use by military personnel, historians, museum curators, and uniform buffs. 8 chapters: 1. The story of chevrons, uniforms and service stripes - 2. Evolution of early chevrons, pre-1872 - 3. History, 1872-1902 - 4. Catalog of 1872-1902 - 5. History, 1902-1920 - 6. Catalog, 1902-1920 - 7. History, post 1920 - 8. History and catalog of special chevrons, awards and insignia. Includes illustrations of 637 chevrons, inc. 50 in colour. 3 appendices (Summary of manufacturing code letters; Alphabetical listing of rank titles with corresponding catalog numbers). Notes after each chapter. *Class No:* 355.14(73)

Standards & Colours

Commonwealth

[3460]

EDWARDS, T.J. **Standards, guidons and colours of the Commonwealth forces.** Aldershot, Gale & Polden, 1953. xvi,239p illus (15 col. pl.).

Provides a historical commentary on the official warrants, regulations and orders relating to regimental colours. Well documented, with excellent illus. *Class No:* 355.15(41-44)

Battles & Battlefields

Dictionaries

[3461]

EGGENBERGER, D. **Encyclopedia of British battles,** 1479 to the present. New ed. London, Dover Publications, 1986. 546p. 50 illus. maps. £13.45. ISBN: 0486249131.

First published 1967 as *A dictionary of battles*.

Recreates the scenes and actions of nearly 1600 military engagements in the period covered. 'Suggestions for further reading' Detailed index of all persons and places mentioned. *Class No:* 355.422(038)

[3462]

AFFIN, J. **Brassey's battles:** 3,500 years of conflict, campaigns and wars from A to Z. Revised ed. London, Brassey's, 1995. 514p., illus., maps. ISBN: 0185753160.

A dictionary of over 7000 entries for battles, campaigns and wars. Contents: Chronicle from Greek-Persian wars to W.W.II; Major wars and 'incidents' since 1945. List of battles, campaigns and wars A-Z by name of battle. 'Textual entries are clear, concise and informative and quality of design and production is first class' (*British book news,* May 1986, p.293). *Class No:* 355.422(038)

[3463]

SWEETMAN, J. **A Dictionary of European land battles:** from the earliest times to 1945. London, Hale, 1984; New York, Macmillan, 1985. 309p. £10.50; $19.95. ISBN: 0029317002, UK.

Ready reference to *c.*2400 European land battles. In 4 parts, the main 266-page section listing the battles with concise descriptions and details of strategy, weapons, casualities, the political background and the ramifications of the outcome. There follows a list of wars and battles fought within them; a select bibliography (1½p.); and index of persons involved in the battles described, including biographical data. *Class No:* 355.422(038)

Histories

[3464]

CHANDLER, D.G. **Battles and battlescenes of World War Two.** New York, Macmillan, 1989. 160p. illus., maps. $19.95. ISBN: 0028971752.

Information on 52 selected engagements, arranged A-Z by title of battle or battlefield. Entries include essential facts such as date, location, object, opposing sides, forces engaged, casualties, and result. Also a list of suggested readings and a 2-3 page narrative about the engagement. Small black-and-white maps and photographs accompany each entry. Chronological table. Index. *Class No:* 355.422(091)

[3465]

CONNOLLY, P. **Greece and Rome at war.** New and revised edition. London, Greenhill Books, 1998. 350p. illus (col). £25. ISBN: 185367303x.

The author has recast his 3 earlier books to make this general sketch of the historical background from early Greek times to the fall of the Roman Empire. The text has been expanded in places to recount the course of some individual battles and campaigns in detail. In 4 parts: Greece and Macedonia - Italy and the Western Mediterranean - The Roman Empire - The later Empire, AD200-450. Profusely illustrated. Bibliography. *Class No:* 355.422(091)

[3466]

CORDESMAN, A.H. *and* WAGNER, A.R. **The Lessons of modern war.** Boulder, Col., Westview Press; London, Mansell Publishing Ltd., 1989-98. 4v. $88. £35 each volume. ISBN: 0813309549, v.1 (US); 0720120454, v.1 (UK); 0813309557, v.2 (US); 0720120446, v.2 (UK); 0813309565, v.3 (US); 0720120438, v.3 (UK); 0813386020, v.4 (US).

Focuses on military events and lessons, the politics, strategy and tactics of five recent major conflicts. V.1: The Arab-Israeli conflicts, 1973-1989; v.2: The Iran-Iraq war; v.3: The Afghan and Falklands conflicts; v.4: The Gulf war. *Class No:* 355.422(091)

[3467]

SEYMOUR, W. **Great sieges of history.** London, Brassey's (UK), 1991. xviii,338p. illus, maps. ISBN: 0080376967.

List of maps and illustrations, and glossary precedes. An introduction is followed by 17 chapters, except for ch.1 each on a siege: 1. The mechanics of a siege - 2. Acre 1189-91 ... 7. Londonderry 1689 ... 11. Ladysmith 1899-1900 ... 14. The Alcásar of Toledo, July-September 1936 ... 16. Leningrad September 1941-January 1944 - 17. Dien Bien Phu ... Appendix: Notes for visitors to the sites of the sieges. Bibliography (by chapter), p.324-9. Index, 330-338. *Class No:* 355.422(091)

[3468]

WEIGLEY, R.F. **The Age of battles:** the quest for decisive warfare from Breitenfeld to Waterloo. London, Vintage Ebury/Pimlico, 1993. £14. ISBN: 0712658564.

Originally published Indiana University Press, 1991.

A narrative history that considers all aspects of the topic, the historical circumstances and political conditions of the adversaries, strategic thinking, personalities of the commanders,tactical maneuvers on the field, the role of armaments and technology, etc. 20 chapters in 3 parts: 1. The profession of officership and the birth of modern war; 2. The eighteenth century: classical epoch of modern war; 3. Thunderstrokes of battle: the French revolutionary and Napoleonic wars. *Class No:* 355.422(091)

Great Britain

[3469]

SEYMOUR, W. **Battles in Britain,** and their political background. London, Sidgwick & Jackson, 1975. 2v. (232p.; 231p.). illus, plans, charts.

V.1: 1066-1547; V.2. 1642-1746. V.1. has chapter bibliographies, plus a list of books studied in connection with armour, weapons, and uniforms. V.2. has 11 chapters. 'Marston Moor', p.83-107, with 2 illus. 1 plan. 4p. shows types of weapons used in the Civil War. Bibliography, p.225-7. Each volume has a non-analytical index. *Class No:* 355.422(410)

[3470]

—GREEN, H. Guide to the battlefields of Great Britain and Ireland. Rev. ed. London, Constable, 1983. 288p. 32 illus., 49 maps. £6.50. ISBN: 0094645205.

First published 1973.

A brief account and sketch map of 52 battles, often with photographs showing how the ground looks today. *Class No:* 355.422(410)

[3471]

SMURTHWAITE, D., *ed.* **The Ordnance Survey complete guide to the battlefields of Britain.** London, Penguin, 1993. 224p. 140 illus. (50 col.), 133 maps (col.). £13.99. ISBN: 0718136551.

Chronological arrangement (The Romans in Britain, 55 BC-AD 409 - Early England, 410-1060 - The Middle Ages, 1066-1450 - The age of the Wars of the Roses, 1450-1550 - The English Civil War, 1642-51 - Warfare in the age of reason, 1660-1746 - The Battle of Britain: the Royal Air Force, 1918-40). Tables of regiments. Gazetteer. Glossary. Further reading (p.221). Analytical index, p.222-224. *Class No:* 355.422(410)

France

Dictionaries

[3472]

CHANDLER, D.G. **Dictionary of the Napoleonic wars.** London, Greenhill Books, 1993. 608p. ports., maps. £29.95.

Entries for 1200 battles and campaigns, A-Z. Also biographies. Appendix: Napoleon's military movements, 1796-1815. Bibliography (authors, A-Z). Chronological tables. 85 maps. No index. *Class No:* 355.422(44)(038)

[3473]

—HAYTHORNTHWAITE, P.J. The Napoleonic source book. London, Arms & Armour, 1995. 416p.,ill.,maps. ISBN: 1854092871.

Very selective (*e.g.* only 14 of the 26 Napoleonic marshals are included). Gives brief sketches of the 60 'nations' involved. The above title is more useful for persons and places. *Class No:* 355.422(44)(038)

[3474]

POPE, S. *and* ROBBINS, K., *eds*. **The Cassell dictionary of the Napoleonic wars.** London, Cassell, 1999. 572p., illus.,maps. £35. ISBN: 0304352292. *Class No:* 355.422(44)(038)

USA

[3475]

MACDONALD, J. **Great battles of the American Civil War.** London, Michael Joseph, 1988. 200p. illus. ISBN: 0718131029.

Introduction on the nation divided, followed by 18 chapters on individual battles (including Fredericksburg, Gettysburg, Chattanooga, etc.), and final chapter on the nation reunited. Gazetteer, p.192-4. Bibliography, p.195. Index, p.196-99. *Class No:* 355.422(73)

Strategy

[3476]

HOUSE, J.M. **Military intelligence, 1870-1991:** a research guide. Westport, CT, Greenwood Press, 1993. xv,165p. $59.95. (*(Research guides in military studies, 6).*) ISBN: 0313274037.

English-language books and articles arranged in 5 chapters (General and strategic intelligence - Institutional studies - Tactical intelligence - Human intelligence - Counter intelligence) subdivided by author, A-Z. Most entries have short, but frequently critical annotations. Introduction discusses the nature and history of military intelligence. Author and subject indexes. '... a very useful source.'(*Choice,*v.31(3), November 1993, p.434). *Class No:* 355.43

[3477]

Jane's C31 systems. Rackham, P., *ed.* Coulsdon, Surrey, Jane's, 1993. 380p. £145. ISBN: 0710610734.

A guide to command, control, communication and major subsystems. Also on CD-ROM. *Class No:* 355.43

Bibliographies

[3478]

Current world affairs: a quarterly bibliography. Alexandria, VA., John C. Damon (previously Boston, VA, American Security Council Education Foundation of the Center for International Security Studies), 1977-. no.1-. $140pa. ISSN: 10504850.

Prior to 1989 title was *Quarterly strategic bibliography*, which superseded *Current bibliographic survey of national defense*.

*c.*800 references per issue, arranged under Periodicals (titles, A-Z): Congressional documents; Books; Other documents, Appended list of periodicals consulted. Glossary. Subject index. *Class No:* 355.43(01)

[3479]

LAWRENCE, R.M. Strategic defense initiative: bibliography and research guide. Boulder, Col., Westview Press, in co-operation with the Center for Space Law and Policy, University of Colorado at Boulder; London, Mansell, 1987. xiii,352p. $29.50; £27.50. ISBN: 0813372291, US; 0720118689, UK.

*c.*1000 citations that reflect the full spectrum of thought on the issue. In 3 sections: Technical background of the debate - Arguments in favour of SDI - Arguments against SDI. Each section includes an essay integrating and amplifying the information presented in the abstracted materials. No annotations. No indexes. *Class No:* 355.43(01)

[3480]

—TUTTLE, A.C. 'The Strategic defense initiative'. In *Choice*, v.27(1), September 1989, p.61-63, 66-73.

A bibliographic essay citing 63 items. Sections on historical context, early proponents, SDI technology, SDI and the USSR, SDI and the American economy, ethics of SDI, SDI and the future; SDI and the strategic policy debate. *Class No:* 355.43(01)

Dictionaries

[3481]

ROBERTSON, D. A Dictionary of modern defense and strategy. London, Europa Publications, 1987. xii,324p. £12.95. ISBN: 0946653674, UK.

Distributed in US & Canada by Gale Research Co., under the title *Guide to modern defense and strategy*.

Over 400 entries describing the terms, tactics, organizations, and accords governing today's defence. Entries arranged A-Z and each defined by an essay of *c.*350 words. Extensive cross-references. Uses non-technical language. British bias. A new ed. was published in 1990 (ISBN 0946653674). *Class No:* 355.43(038)

[3482]

WALDMAN, H. The Dictionary of SDI. Wilmington, Del., Scholarly Resources, 1988. 182 p. $35. ISBN: 0842022813.

c. 800 concise definitions of words and phrases relating to the 'strategic defense initiative' (SDI), including some personal and organizational names. Includes text and agreed statements of the 1972 Antiballistic Missile Treaty and a list of members of the Defensive Technologies Study Team. *Class No:* 355.43(038)

Polyglot

[3483]

SCHWARZ, U. *and* HADIK, L. Strategic terminology: a trilingual glossary. New York, Praeger, 1966. 157p. $12.50. ISBN: 0686572173.

Published under the auspices of the Graduate School of International Studies, Geneva.

About 4000 English, French and German terms are defined in those languages, with supporting quotations from 29 authorities (*e.g.* Clausewitz; *Dictionary of United States military terms* ... (1964). The English term and definition plus quotation(s) are followed by the French and German entries (normally supported by citations from authorities in those languages). French and German indexes (including equivalents); bibliography of authorities cited, p.155-7. *Class No:* 355.43(038)=00

Maps & Atlases

[3484]

CHALIAND, G. *and* RAGEAU, J-P. A Strategic atlas: comparative geopolitics of the world powers. Translated by Tony Berrett; maps by Catherine Petit. 3rd rev. and updated ed. New York, Harper & Row, 1993. 224p. maps. $40:00. ISBN: 0062715542.

First published in France in 1983 as *Atlas stratique*.

Shows the economic, political, cultural and military relationships of the world in a special and geographical context, emphasizing the geopolitical position in which individual nations and groups of nations see themselves in today's world. Extensive maps and charts, circular polar projection maps introduced to avoid distortion. A readable text accompanies the maps. *Class No:* 355.43(084.3)

[3485]

FREEDMAN, L. Atlas of global strategy. London, Macmillan Press; New York, Facts on File, 1985. 192p. 90 illus., tables, 120 maps. £18.95; $22.95. ISBN: 0333384164, UK; 0816010587, US.

Examines the role of war in the modern world. An extensive introduction (p.9-24) is followed by 6 sections (The changing international order - The changing pattern of warfare - The nuclear arms race - Conventional war - Warfare since 1945 - What's to be done?). Chronology, 1945-1985. Bibliography, p.185-187. Index, p.189-192. 'An atlas for quick reference on strategic concerns', the author 'overcomes the picture-book format ... by combining an unbiased narrative of the superpower relationship with innovative cartography' (*Library journal*, v.111(3), 15 February 1986, p.173). *Class No:* 355.43(084.3)

USA

[3486]

DANIELS, G., *ed.* A Guide to the reports of the United States strategic bombing survey ... London, Boydell & Brewer, for the Royal Historical Society, 1981. xxvi, 115p. £12; $22. (*Guides and handbooks. Supplementary series* 2.) ISBN: 0901050717.

1. European survey (p.3-66) - 2. Pacific survey (p.69-115). A closely classified inventory, providing contents of each report, its documentary exhibits and appendices. Valuable historical introduction No indexes, but a detailed contents list. *Class No:* 355.43(73)

[3487]

—COULTER, E. 'Evolution of nuclear strategy in the United States'. In *Choice*, v.25(10), June 1988, p.1519-1527.

A bibliographical essay, with sections on the generalists, foreign generalists, the hardliners, the skeptics, the philosophers. 93 cited works listed A-Z by author. *Class No:* 355.43(73)

Army

[3488]

The Army list. 1814-. London, HMSO, 1914-. Frequency varies. 2v (xii,534p.;780p.). Part 1 £18; part 2 £24. ISBN: 0117726575, Part 1 (1993 ed.); 0117720585, Part 2 (1993 ed.).

Part 1 is in 4 sections: 1. Queen and Royal Family; 2. Defence councils, Army commands, Establishments; 3. Regular Army; 4 Territorial Army. Index of names (p.411-533). Subject index (p.534) Part 2 lists officers in receipt of retired pay. *Class No:* 356

[3489]

The World's armies: an illustrated review of the armies of the world Westhorp, C., *ed.* London, Salamander Books Ltd., 1991. 143p. illus (col). maps. £18.95. ISBN: 0861015878.

Chapters by area (North America - Central & South America - Asia & the Far East - Oceania - Europe - North Africa & Middle East - Sub-Saharan Africa), subdivided by country. Deals with the composition and capabilities of each army. Text is accompanied by equipment tables of principal items in service, colour flags and maps, diagrams and colour photographs. *Class No:* 356

Encyclopaedias

[3490]

HOGG, I.V. The Illustrated encyclopaedia of artillery. London, Stanley Paul & Co. Ltd., 1987. 256p. illus. (photos, some in col.). diagrs. £16.95. ISBN: 0091726549.

In two sections: a short history of artillery from 1325, and (c.200p.) an A-Z encyclopedia covering weapons, technical terminology, gunnery shorthand, and notable personalities involved in the development of artillery weapons. Covers all nations, some sketchily (*e.g.* USSR) Clear and concise layout. Presumably aimed at the layman, but equally of interest to the professional or military historian. *Class No:* 356(031)

Handbooks & Manuals

[3491]

Jane's world armies. Coulsdon, Jane's Information Group, 1996. 605p (ringbinder) CD-ROM £506.38. Ringbinder £565. ISBN: 0710614748, CDROM; 071061389x, ringbinder. *Class No:* 356(035)

[3492]

WEEKS, J., *comp.* Jane's pocket-book: armies of the world. London, Jane's, 1981. 224p. illus. £5.95. (*Jane's pocket book.*) ISBN: 0710601492.

Sections arranged A-Z by country (Afghanistan ... Zimbabwe), with details of strength of the army, military service, background, structure and equipment. *Class No:* 356(035)

Maps & Atlases

[3493]

BANKS, A. **A World atlas of military history to 1500.** New ed. London, Secker & Warburg, 1984. 12.95. ISBN: 0436032295.

154 clear, easily understood, black-and-white maps, some with double-page spread. Adequate legends. Some battles are shown in phases (*e.g.* Cannae: 3 phases, p.56). Includes general as well as war maps. Index of battles, sieges, wars, campaigns, etc.; index of individuals; index of races, tribes and all named groups of people. Page size, 22 x 17 cm. *Class No:* 356(084.3)

[3494]

—BANKS, A. **A World atlas of military history, 1861 - 1945.** London, Seeley Service, 1978. [ix],160,[22]p. ISBN: 0854221409.

145 maps, covering the American Civil War, the European, colonial and Far Eastern wars, 1860 - 1914, and World Wars I and II. ' ... an easily accessible and handy guide to the strategic and tactical geography of the wars of the 19th and 20th centuries' (*British book news*, June 1978, p468). Page size, 22 x 17 cm. *Class No:* 356(084.3)

[3495]

—CHANDLER, D.G. **Atlas of military strategy: the art, theory and practice of war.** London, Cassell Military, 1996. 208p. illus., maps. £25.

Reprint of 1980 edition. 200 two-colour maps, including campaign and battle plans. Bibliography. Over 120 illus. *Class No:* 356(084.3)

Histories

[3496]

BARTHORP, M. **The Armies of Britain, 1485-1980.** London, National Army Museum; Guernsey, Seagull S.A., [1981]. 296p. illus., maps. £4.50. ISBN: 0901721069.

A popular account in 22 chapters. Appendices: 1. Regiments and corps of the British army in 1979 and their chief forbears; 2. Command of the army, 1485-1980. Chapter references, p.290-8. Index to text and illus.

For detailed period histories of army organization and administration, best sources are: Cruickshank, C.G. *Elizabeth's army* (1946); Fifth, Sir C.H. *Cromwell's army* (3rd ed., 1932); Walton, C. *History of the British standing army, 1660-1700* (1894); Curtis, E.E. *The organization of the British army in the American revolution* (1926); Oman, Sir C. *Wellington's army* (1912); and Dunlop, J.K. *The development of the British army, 1899-1914* (1938).

Class No: 356(091)

Great Britain

[3497]

LEWIS, J.E. **The Handbook of the SAS and elite forces: how the professionals fight and win.** London, Constable Robinson, 1997. 504p.,illus. £6.99. ISBN: 1854877046.

One-volume encyclopedia covering special forces (including the SAS) and their tactics worldwide, with a collection of accounts of their operations since 1945. *Class No:* 356(410)

Bibliographies

[3498]

BRUCE, A.P.C. **A Bibliography of the British Army, 1660-1914.** 2nd ed. London, Munich, New York, K.G. Saur, 1985. xii,422p. £35; DM.120; $45. ISBN: 0862912873, UK; 0862912873, US; 3598105746, German.

First published 1975 as *An annotated bibliography of the British Army, 1660-1914* (New York, Garland).

5656 entries, some annotated, arranged in 24 chapters in 4 parts: 1. Bibliographies, indexes and general works - 2. Organization, management and personnel - 3. Military theory, tactics, drill and equipment - 4. Military operations and overseas garrisons (arranged geographically, then by subject). No introductions to either chapters or parts. Author index, p.351-390. Subject index, p.391-422. 'In all, it gives fine coverage of a somewhat narrow topic' (*Library journal*, v.101(13), July 1976, p.1512, of the 1st ed.). *Class No:* 356(410)(01)

[3499]

—BRUCE, A. **A Bibliography of British military history, from the Roman invasion to the Restoration, 1660.** Munich, K. G. Saur, 1981. x, 350p. Dm.56-. $31. £18.50. ISBN: 359810359x.

3280 annotated entries arranged in 17 chapters in 4 parts: 1. Guides, indexes and sources - 2. General military works - 3. Organizations, campaigns and military leaders - 4. Fortifications, castles, weapons and uniforms. Each part and chapter begins with a brief introductory paragraph followed by an A-Z list by author. Strong emphasis on books and periodical articles, including the popular. Very short annotations. Follows the same selection criteria as the above. *Class No:* 356(410)(091)

[3500]

STRACHAN, H. 'The British Army, 1815-1856: recent writing reviewed'. In *Journal of the Society for Army Historical Research*, Summer 1985, p.68-79.

Includes references to *c.*84 books, articles and theses. *Class No:* 356(410)(01)

[3501]

—SPIERS, E.M. 'The British Army, 1856-1914: recent writing reviewed'. In *Journal of the Society for Army Historical Research*, Winter 1985, p.194-207.

Includes references to over 150 items. *Class No:* 356(410)(01)

Encyclopaedias

[3502]

GRIFFIN, D. **Encyclopaedia of modern British army regiments.** Wellingborough, Northants. P. Stephens, 1985. 236p. illus. £16.50. ISBN: 0850597080.

Deals, in order of seniority, with each of the regiments left in the modern army. Includes information on insignia, honours, anniversaries, customs, mascots, dress distinctions, marches, etc., plus a 'family tree' for each regiment showing its lineage. Many photographs and other illustrations. *Class No:* 356(410)(031)

[3503]

PEEDLE, R. **Encyclopaedia of the modern territorial army.** Wellingborough, Patrick Stephens, 1990. 232p. illus. diagrs, maps. £22.50. ISBN: 0850599385.

Explains the role of the Territorial Army, its history and structure. Chapters: A brief history - The Territorial Army today - The Yeomanry - The Artillery - The Corps of Royal Engineers - The Infantry - Airborne units - The corps and services. 5 appendices: 1. Chronological table of significant dates; 2. Sandhurst; 3. Council of TAVRAs; 4. Some Victoria Crosses of the Territorial Army; 5. Territorial Army order of precedence; 6. Regimental quick marches. Index, p.229-232. *Class No:* 356(410)(031)

Handbooks & Manuals

[3504]

ASCOLI, D. **A Companion to the British Army, 1660-1983.** London, Harrap Ltd., 1983. 319p. illus. £14.50. ISBN: 0245539603.

A *vade-mecum* to the Army's origins and development from the first standing regiments of Charles II to the present day. A lengthy introduction (p.13-57) and an A-Z listing of regiments, titled *The Spinal column*, precedes the 6 main sections: A. Orders of precedence - B. Information on regiments - C. The anatomy of the Army - D. Battle honours - E. Headdress badges - F. Chronology of political and military control. Select bibliography, p.313-314. Analytical index, p.315-319. *Class No:* 356(410)(035)

[3505]

BRERETON, J.M. **A Guide to the regiments and corps of the British Army** on the regular establishment. London, The Bodley Head, 1985. 288p. illus. £10.95. ISBN: 0370305787.

'... unravels at a glance the complex amalgamations underlying the present day units. All regiments and corps ever raised are listed if they subsist in the units of today's British regular army. The Royal Marines are also included'. (Dust jacket). A select bibliography of 19 items, explanatory notes, and a list of precedence of regiments and corps, precedes the main part of the guide. This includes information in respect of each unit, whether existing or previously merged: date of raising, successive titles, battle honours, motto, uniform, regimental marches, journal, headquarters, museum, nicknames, and cap badge. Index to regiments and corps, p.183-288. *Class No:* 356(410)(035)

[3506]

HALLOWS, I.S. **Regiments and corps of the British Army.** London, Arms & Armour Press, 1991. 320p. illus. £19.95.

A useful general reference work tracing the history and traditions of every regiment and corps in the Army's 1991 Order of Battle. Covers dress, regimental marches, battle honours and anniversaries. Includes addresses of museums and associations, and a bibliography of each regiment and corps. *Class No:* 356(410)(035)

Dictionaries

[3507]

GANDER, T. **Encyclopedia of the modern British army.** 3rd ed. Wellingborough, Northants, P. Stephens, 1986. 312p. 650 illus., diagrs. £19.95. ISBN: 085059684x.

First published 1980.

In 4 sections: The British army since 1945 (p.6-18) - Organization (p.19-99) giving information and hierarchy diagrams of each of the regiments - Weapons and equipment (p.100-287) - Uniforms and insignia (p.288-306). 4-columned index (p.307-312) is combined with a glossary of abbreviations. Cross-referenced. *Class No:* 356(410)(038)

Histories

[3508]

DIETZ, P. **The Last of the regiments:** their rise and fall. London, Brassey's (UK), 1990. viii,271p. 10 illus. £31.50. ISBN: 0080347614.

A study of the creation of the British military tradition and of the regimental system in particular. 10 chapters: 1. The origins of the British Army ... 3. The golden age of the regiments ... 5. The regiments in India ... 8. Action, reaction and intervention - 9. The long armistice and the second world war - 10. The end of the family. 4 appendices. Notes and references. Bibliography, p.255-8. Index, p.259-71. *Class No:* 356(410)(091)

[3509]

FORTESCUE, J.W. **A History of the British Army.** London, Macmillan, 1899-1930. (Reprinted by AMS Press). 13v. with 6v. of maps. ISBN: 0404025501, the set.

Usually accepted as the standard work on British Army history. It suffers, however, from a lack of proportion: the majority of the volumes are devoted to the period between 1763 and 1810. Furthermore, it contains little or no information on the development of army organizations and administration. *Class No:* 356(410)(091)

[3510]

WHITE, A.S., *comp.* **A Bibliography of regimental histories of the British Army.** Rev. ed. London, London Stamp Exchange, 1988. viii,317p. £16.95. ISBN: 094813061x.

First published in 1965 by the Society for Army Historical Research, with The Army Museums Ogilby Trust.

*c.*2500 briefly annotated entries. Sections: 1. General - 2. Regular army - 3. Departments, Corps - 4. Auxiliary forces - 5. Miscellaneous (*e.g.* Women's corps; Disbanded regiments). Appendix shows present day titles of regiments. Index, p.309-317.

An addendum was issued in 1992 (viii,331p. £24.95). *Class No:* 356(410)(091)

Scotland

Histories

[3511]

BARNES, R.M., *and others.* **The Uniforms and history of the Scottish regiments:** Britain - Canada - Australia - New Zealand - South Africa, 1625 to the present day. London, Seeley Service, [1956]. 351p. illus. (12 col. pl.), tables.

16 chapters, 12 of which cover the history, 1625-1954, by periods. Chapter 13: Early Scottish weapons; 14: The pipes; 15-16: Uniforms of the Scottish regiments. Appendices consist of abbreviated regimental histories (Scottish regiments of Britain, of Canada, of Australia, etc.) noting H.Q. or depot, brief chronology, uniforms, battle honours, number of battalions in 1914-18, regimental march and motto, and affiliated or allied regiments. No bibliography. Index, giving names of regiments in capitals. 83 uniforms illustrated in colour on 12 plates; 26 line-drawings. *Class No:* 356(411)(091)

British Colonies

Histories

[3512]

Regiments of the Empire: a bibliography of their published histories. Perkins, R., *comp.* Newton Abbott (privately published), 1989. 382p. illus. £24.50. ISBN: 0950642916.

A glossary of acronyms and abbreviations precedes the bibliography of over 800 items arranged in 8 geographical groups: 1.Colonies, protectorates and other territories; 2. Africa; 3. India; 4. Canada; 5. New Zealand and Australian forces in Korea; 6. New Zealand and Australian forces in South Vietnam; 7. New Zealand; 8. Australia. Index is by chapter. *Class No:* 356(41-5)(091)

France

Histories

[3513]

HORWARD, D.D., *ed.* **Napoleonic military history:** a bibliography. London, Greenhill Books, Lionel Leventhal Ltd.; New York, Garland, 1986. xiii,689p. £30.00. (*Garland reference library of social science, 194. Military history bibliographies, 9.*) ISBN: 0947898441.

7740 entries arranged in 24 chapters, each chapter having an introduction: I. Introduction to Napoleonic research - II. Armies of the Napoleonic period ... V. The Egyptian campaign (1798-1801) ... VII. England at war (1798-1815) ... XVI. St. Helena and the Napoleonic legend... XXIV. The Ottoman Empire. *Class No:* 356(44)(091)

Russia

[3514]

HERSPRING, D.R. **The Soviet High Command, 1967-1989:** personalities and politics. Lawrenceville, NJ, Princeton University Press, 1990. 296p. $45 ISBN: 0691078440.

A study, based on primary written source materials, of the evolutions of civil-military relations in the Soviet Union from 1967, including the ideas and personalities of the 8 key military leaders. *Class No:* 356(47)

Bibliographies

[3515]

SMITH, M.J. **The Soviet army, 1939-1980:** a guide to sources in English, with a historical introduction by John Erickson. Santa Barbara, CA., ABC-Clio, 1982. lviii,551p. $26.25. ISBN 0874363071.

Brief historical introduction precedes the unannotated bibliography of 5743 items arranged in 5 sections: 1. Reference works (subdivided A-Z; Bibliographies - Abstracts ... Biographies) - 2. The era of World War II, 1939-1945 -3. The Soviet economy and defense establishments - 4. The Soviet ground forces, 1946 to the present - 5. The Soviet army and military assistance around the globe, 1945 to the present. Each section has a short introduction. 2 appendices (I. List of journals consulted; II. Selected Soviet military lives: a bibliographical directory (p.475-522). Author index, p.523-551. 'An excellent general reference tool for non-specialized research on the Soviet military ... ' (*Choice* v.20(9), May 1983 p.1270). *Class No:* 356(47)(01)

Canada

Bibliographies

[3516]

COOKE, O.A., *ed.* **The Canadian military experience, 1867-1983:** a bibliography. Department of National Defence of Canada. 2nd ed. Ottawa, Canadian Government Publishing Centre, 1984. xix,329p. Can.$11.95. (*Department of National Defence, Directorate of History, monograph series, no.2.*) ISBN: 0660526492.

First published 1979. The 2nd ed. has an added section covering the period since the amalgamation of the Canadian services in 1968.

Now in 6 sections: Bibliography - Defence policy and general works - and sections on each of the three services (subdivided chronologically) and one on the combined forces since 1968. No annotations. Subject index, p.270-293; persons index, 294-295 Services, branches, formations, units, p.296-329. 'Overall ... this is a valuable update of a valuable handbook ...' (*RUSI journal,* v.130(1) March 1985, p.82). *Class No:* 356(71)(01)

USA

[3517]

ANCELL, R.M. *and* MILLER, C.M. **The biographical dictionary of World War II generals and flag officers.** Westport, CT, Greenwood Press, 1996. 720p. £82.50. ISBN: 0313295468.

Covers officers of the United States Army on active duty between 1941 to 1945. *Class No:* 356(73)

Bibliographies

[3518]

FLETCHER, M. **The Peacetime army, 1900-1941:** a research guide. Westport, CT. Greenwood Press, 1988. 177p. $37.95. (*Research guides in military studies, 1.*) ISBN: 0313259879.

Over 900 annotated entries, chronologically subdivided into 1900-1917 and 1919-1941. A substantial introduction precedes the bibliography of English-language books, scholarly and popular journal articles, and dissertations. Omits first-hand narratives, naval studies and accounts of the rise of air power. Includes a chronology. Author subject index. 'A high-quality work ...' (*Choice,* v.26(10), June 1989 p.1660). *Class No:* 356(73)(01)

Histories

[3519]

HIGHAM, R., *ed.* **A Guide to sources of US military history.** Hamden, CT., Archon: Shoestring Press, 1981. xiii,559p. ISBN 0208014993.

19 chapters - bibliographical essays on major sources by specialists 1. Introduction - 2. European background of American military affairs - 3. Colonial forces, 1607-1776 - 4. The American revolution ... 6. The Navy in the nineteenth century, 1789-1889 ... 10. Science and technology in the twentieth century ... 12. Military and naval medicine ... 17. The Army, 1945-1973 - 18. The Navy, 1941-1973 - 19 Museums as historical resources. Lengthy bibliographies after each essay (*e.g.* 17. The Army: 390 references, A-Z). Introductory essay ends with suggestions for further research, then a bibliography. 643 bibliographical references in all.

...(contd.)

2 supplements have been published - 1. by Shoestring Press (1981. xiv,332p. ISBN 020801750x); 2-3. by Archon Books (1993. 531p. ISBN 0208022147). *Class No:* 356(73)(091)

Air Force

[3520]

LINTHAM, V. **Air wars and aircraft:** a detailed record of air combat, 1945 to the present. New York, Facts on File, 1990. 415p. illus. tables. maps. $50. ISBN: 0816023565.

Aims to identify aircraft used in major and minor wars worldwide since 1945. Conflicts are arranged chronologically within 12 geographical regions. Entries describe political and social problems causing armed conflict and detail how military aircraft were used. Includes *c.*100 tables, 221 black & white photographs, and 100 maps. Glossary of abbreviations. Bibliography. *Class No:* 358.4

Worldwide

[3521]

Jane's world air forces. Coulsdon, Jane's Information Group, 1996. CD-ROM; ringbinder 400p. £595 (CD-ROM); £540 (ringbinder). ISBN: 0710614888. *Class No:* 358.4(100)

Encyclopaedias

[3522]

TAYLOR, M.J.H. **Encyclopedia of the world's air forces.** New York. Facts on file; Wellingborough, Northants. Patrick Stephens Ltd., 1988. 216p. $35 £21.50. ISBN: 0816020043 US; 1852601353 UK.

Largely updates M. Hewish's *Air forces of the world* (1979).

'Details of the world's aircraft from single aircraft operated by the Comores Air Force to the many thousands operated by the super powers' (*Stephen's catalogue*). Arranged A-Z by country, each country entry includes a map showing geographical location and a brief history of its air force, followed by information on current strength, air bases, commitments, budgets, and air policies, etc., Comparative specifications for aircraft types are in data tables at the end of the book. The author is a noted British aviation authority. *Class No:* 358.4(100)(031)

20th Century

[3523]

NOFFSINGER, J.P. **World Ward I aviation :** a bibliography of books in English, French, German and Italian :$bwith a price list supplement. Rev. ed. Scarecrow Press, 1996. 576p. $98. ISBN: 081083085x. *Class No:* 358.4(100)"19"

Great Britain

[3524]

NESBIT, R.C. **An Illustrated history of the R.A.F.** London, Hutchinson, 1990. illus. £25. ISBN: 0091746566.

Published to commemorate the 50th anniversary of the Battle of Britain. Includes over 600 black and white and full-colour photographs and illustrations, with detailed captions. *Class No:* 358.4(410)

[3525]

NESBIT, R.C. **RAF:** a complete history 1918-1998. Sutton Publishing/ RAF Museum, Hendon, 1978. 279p. illus. (some col.) £25. ISBN: 0750919493. *Class No:* 358.4(410)

[3526]

—LEWIS, P. **Squadron histories: R.F.C., R.N.A.S. and R.A.F.,** 1912-59. London, Putnam, 1959. 208p. illus. (incl. col. pl.).

Provides very brief squadron histories (nos.1-695), p.11-124. 13 appendices, including: 1. Aircraft used as equipment or for service trials by squadrons (keyed to squadrons 1-695) - 2. Aircraft specifications - 3. Titles of squadron ... 7. Squadron and unit code lettering. Illus. of flight-squadron markings. *Class No:* 358.4(410)(091)

Handbooks & Manuals

[3527]

GANDER, T. **Encyclopaedia of the modern Royal Air Force.** 2nd ed. Wellingborough, Northants, Patrick Stephens, 1987. 256p. illus. £19.95. ISBN: 0850598591.

First published 1984.

A guide to the organization, structure, role and equipment of the RAF today, including aircraft, bombs, guns, missiles, and uniforms. Profusely illustrated with black-and-white photographs and diagrams. *Class No:* 358.4(410)(035)

Yearbooks & Directories

[3528]

The Air Force List, 1999. London, Stationery Office Agencies, 1999. 464p. £22. ISBN: 011772887x. ISSN: 02668610.

First published 1949. Annual. Previously *The Monthly Air Force list* February, 1919-1939.

Arranged by Commands/Branches, etc.; R.A.F. Voluntary Reserve. Index of names. *Class No:* 358.4(410)(058)

France

Bibliographies

[3529]

CHRISTIENNE, C., *and others.* **French military aviation:** a bibliographical guide. New York, Garland, 1989. 255p. $35. (*Military history bibliographies, 11. Garland reference library in the humanities, 381.*) ISBN: 0824085183.

Intended as a guide for researchers in the field of French military aeronautics. In 2 parts; the first part containing an 84-page treatise by General Christienne on the development of French military aviation and the research challenges and opportunities offered. The second part is a bibliography of *c.*2000 books, articles, documents, and dissertations, almost all in French. *Class No:* 358.4(44)(01)

Russia

Bibliographies

[3530]

SMITH, M.J. **The Soviet air and strategic rocket forces, 1939-1980:** a guide to sources in English. Oxford, Clio Press, 1981. xliv, 321p. £22.85 $45. (*War/peace bibliography series 10.*) ISBN: 0874363063.

3350 unannotated entries arranged in 7 sections, each section having a brief introduction and subdivisions: 1. Reference works - 2. The era of World War II, 1939-45 - 3. The Soviet economy and defense establishments - 4. Soviet aerospace forces, 1946 to the present - 5. Soviet aerospace weapons systems - 6. Arms competition, arms control, and the balance of power. - 7. Soviet aerospace arms and assistance around the globe. Includes books., journal articles, documents, papers and reports. 4 appendices (Late entries; List of journals consulted; Selected Soviet aerospace biographies; Charts). Author index, p.305-321. Well researched and detailed bibliography. *Class No:* 358.4(47)(01)

USA

[3531]

TERRY, M.R. **Historical dictionary of the United States Air Force.** Lanham, MD, Scarecrow Press, 2000. 624p., illus.,maps,charts. £80.55. (*Historical dictionaries of war, revolution and civil unrest, no. 11..*) ISBN: 0810836319.

Entries give information on aircraft, weapons, air operations and wars, as well as USAF's organizational forms and behind-the-scenes politics. *Class No:* 358.4(73)

Navy

[3532]

OBIN, A. **Bibliography of nautical books, 2000.** Warsash, Southampton, Warsash Publishing, 2000. £90. ISBN: 0948646152.

First ed. published 1985.

11 sections: 1. Books, main listing by title - 2. Books, main listing by author - 3. Books, main listing by subject - 4. Hydrographic Department (Admiralty) - 5. International Maritime Organization - 6. Statutory instruments - 7. M notices (Department of Transport) - 8. British standards - 9. Journals and periodicals - 10. Video cassettes - 11. Publishers and suppliers (addresses and telephone numbers). Coverage of shipping, naval, maritime, yachting, and marine engineering items in print, forthcoming, and out of print. *Class No:* 359

[3533]

PEMSEL, H. **Atlas of naval warfare:** an atlas and chronology of conflict at sea, from the earliest times to the present day. London, Arms and Armour Press, 1977. 176p. illus., tables, maps.

First German ed. 1975.

4 sections: The age of galleys - The age of sail - The iron and steel - The nuclear age. Traces events up to 1973 (the Arab-Israeli 'Yom Kippur' war). 'The war in the Pacific', 1941-42: p.125-8; 8 maps; 8 illus. of ships. 9 appendices (*e.g.* 'The world's naval powers', by number of ships, 1859-1977). Select bibliography, p.165-6. Index. 'An excellent work, well researched and attractively put together' (*American reference books annual,* 1979, v.10, item 1604). *Class No:* 359

[3534]

—LLOYD, C. Atlas of maritime history. London, Hamlyn, 1975. 144p. illus. (some col.), maps.

Divided into chronological periods (from Phoenicians and Greeks to the nuclear submarine); 2p. per period, consisting of map, text and illus. 6-colour maps. Some British slant. 'Recommended enthusiastically for the undergraduate and graduate library; (*Choice*, April 1976, p.204,206 - on which the foregoing is based). *Class No:* 359(084.3)

Abbreviations & Symbols

[3535]

BAHJAT, A.H. *and* WEDERTZ, B. Dictionary of naval abbreviations. 4th ed. Annapolis, Md., Naval Institute Press, 2000. 320p. $29.95. ISBN: 1557501661.

First published 1969.

Contains over 45,000 abbreviations, including a complete listing of US Marine Corps and Coast Guard abbreviations, terms which may have been of army origin but now navy. *Class No:* 359(003)

Bibliographies

[3536]

GREAT BRITAIN. Ministry of Defence. Author and subject catalogues of the Royal Navy Library, Ministry of Defence, London. Boston, Mass., G.K. Hall, 1967. 5v. $495. ISBN: 0816107556.

Claimed to be the world's largest collection of naval and maritime books, mainly devoted to naval and general history, voyages, hydrographic surveys and the like. 78,000 entries, photolithographically reproduced from cards. Entries include charts and maps. *Class No:* 359(01)

20th Century

[3537]

LAW, D.G. The Royal Navy in World War Two: an annotated bibliography. London, Greenhill Books; Lionel Leventhal United, 1988. 305p. £27.50. ISBN: 1853670022.

Claims to be an annotated bibliography of all primary and secondary published monographs describing the role of British, Dominion and minor allied forces in the naval war against the Axis. Also covers other groups such as Coastal Command, the Merchant Navy and Combined Operations. 30 chapters in 4 sections: 1. Campaign histories - 2. Allied unit histories - 3. The Axis forces - 4. Technical studies and miscellanea. Altogether 1883 numbered entries. Only includes books in the English language, and published before the end of 1987. Cross-references to related material. Indexes of authors, titles, and ships. *Class No:* 359(01)"19"

Handbooks & Manuals

[3538]

MILLER, D. The World's navies. London, Salamander Books, 1992. 160p. 250 illus. £13.95. ((*Armed forces, v.3*).) ISBN: 0861016424.

Details by region, with brief notes on equipment, size and organization of such services. Highlights major warships, submarines and weapons. *Class No:* 359(035)

Dictionaries

[3539]

GRANVILLE, W. A Dictionary of sailors' slang. London. Andre Deutsch, 1962 (reprinted 1972). 136p.

'... slang and colloquial speech of the Royal and Merchant Navies, the fishing fleets, yachtsmen, lightshipmen and the crews of the barges and 'narrow boats' ... also records of speech habits of dock workers, harbourmen, and those who labour on the fringes of maritime endeavour' (*Preface*). Omits Cockney rhyming slang. Explanations, as well as definitions, are given when necessary. *Class No:* 359(038)

[3540]

HARD, J. Royal Navy language. Lewis, Sussex, The Book Guild Ltd., 1991. 310p. £12.50. ISBN: 0863325580.

Over 3000 terms and expressions are explained briefly, each entry being from a line to 5 or 6 lines in length. Arranged in 23 chapters: 1. The Royal Navy, Naval Reserve & assorted services - 2. Ships and aircraft ... 5. Ranks, rates and jobs - 6. Dress...12. Parts of a ship and equipment ... 17. Boats ... 21. Traditional tallies (nicknames) - 22. Royal Navy slang - 23. The language of the sea ashore. Cross-references. *Class No:* 359(038)

[3541]

PALMER, J., *comp*. Jane's dictionary of naval terms. London, Macdonald & Jane's. 1975. [iv],342p. ISBN: 035608258x.

Over 6000 entries for maritime military terms, terms of general seamanship and some purely mercantile terms ('Davit': ¾ col. 'Shackle': 1 column). Different meanings are numbered. Many cross-references. Sources (p.2) include Royal Navy, US Navy and NATO manuals. *Class No:* 359(038)

[3542]

—NOEL, J.V. Naval terms dictionary. 5th ed. Annapolis, Md., Naval Institute Press, 1988. 336p. 80 illus. £21.95. ISBN: 087021571x.

First published 1952.

c.6000 entry-words, - US Navy colloquialisms, slang and technical terminology, including abbreviations. 5 appendices (*e.g.* ship, aircraft and missile designation systems; electronic nomenclature. *Class No:* 359(038)

Yearbooks & Directories

[3543]

JONES, J.M. Historic warships: a directory of 140 museums and memorials worldwide. Jefferson, NJ, McFarland, 1993. 245p. illus. $45. ISBN: 0899507794.

Describes 144 warships built between the 16th and 20th centuries, which are now in parks or museums in 25 countries. Entries, arranged by country where located (about half in the US), include battle record, technical information, black and white photographs, and information on the museums, etc. where situated, with address and telephone number. *Class No:* 359(058)

[3544]

SILVERSTONE, P.H. Directory of the world's capital ships. London, Ian Allan, 1984. 496p. illus. £35. ISBN: 0711012229.

Aim was to produce an illustrated work of reference, covering the capital ships of 21 of the world's most important navies, from the mid-nineteenth century to the late twentieth century. Includes 1000 ships in some 500 classes. Definition of capital ships is broad and includes battleships, battle cruisers, monitors, coastal defence ships, aircraft carriers, etc. A preliminary section, 'How to use this book', includes lists of operations of the US Civil War, W.W.1 and W.W.2, A-Z by name of operation, and a list of shipbuilders, A-Z by name plus town and country. The main part of the directory is arranged A-Z by country (Argentine ... USA) with, for each country, brief background information; class details (displacement, dimensions, armour, complement, etc.); individual ships (A-Z by name, with data on history of its career, type, class, nomenclature (meaning of name), details of construction, war service, ultimate fate). Index, p.491-496. *Class No:* 359(058)

Histories

[3545]

BRUCE, A.P.C. *and* COGAR, W.B. An Encyclopedia of naval history. Chicago, Facts On File; London, Fitzroy Dearborn, 1998. vii,448p., illus.,ports. $50. $35. ISBN: 0816026971, US; 1579581099, UK.

International in scope but with a focus on Great Britain and the United States. *Class No:* 359(091)

[3546]

COLETTA, P.E. American naval history: a guide. 3rd ed. Lanham, MD, Scarecrow Press, 2000. 936p.,illus.,maps. £112.50. (*Historical dictionaries of ancient civilizastions and historical eras.*.) ISBN: 0810833026. *Class No:* 359(091)

[3547]

MARCUS, G.J. A Naval history of England. London, Allen & Unwin, 1961-71. 2v. (xii,494p.; 523p.). maps.

V.1: *The formative years [to 1973]*; v.2: *The age of Nelson*. V.2. is well formulated and has chapter bibliographies. p.505-20. Non-analytical index, but ships are listed in detail. Very readable narrative. Aims to be a compromise between the short and the full-scale history. '... a must for all secondary schools and libraries' (*British book news*, June 1971, p. 498). *Class No:* 359(091)

[3548]

—NATIONAL MARITIME MUSEUM. The Commissioned sea officers of the Royal Navy, 1660-1815. London, the Museum, 1954. 3v.

Provides a complete list of naval officers for the period. *Class No:* 359(410)(091)

[3549]
SWEETMAN, J., *ed.* **American naval history:** an illustrated chronology of the U.S. Navy and Marine Corps, 1775 - present. 2nd ed. Annapolis, Md., Naval Institute Press, 1991. 376p. illus., maps. $36.95. ISBN: 1557507856.

First published 1984.

Year-by-year summary of major events in the history of the US Navy and Marine Corps from the American Revolution to the late 1980s. Covers battles, warships, personnel, exploration, etc. *c.*200 illustrations and several specially drawn maps. Bibliography. Calendar, vessel and general indexes. *Class No:* 359(091)

Bibliographies

[3550]
ALBION, R.G. **Naval and maritime history:** an annotated bibliography. 4th ed. rev. & expanded. Mystic, CT., Munson Institute of American Maritime History, the Marine Historical Association, Inc., 1972. ix,370p. $10. ISBN: 0913372056.

First published 1951.

Lists *c.*5000 books in English, plus PhD. theses. In 7 main sections: 1. Reference works (A-G, including F: Lists of ships; G: Lists of men) - 2. Merchantmen and warships - 3. Captains and crews - 4. Maritime science, exploration and expansion - 5. Commerce and shipping - 6. Navies (naval history, by periods, p.229-302) - 7. Special topics (*e.g.* Auxiliary services; Main American maritime museums). Books asterisked represent 'the select minority of the more substantial and useful'. Author and subject indexes. 'An indispensable companion to any writer on maritime subjects' (E.G.R. Taylor, on the 3rd ed., in *Journal of the Institute of Navigation,* v.17(2), April 1964, p.211). US-slanted. *Class No:* 359(091)(01)

Europe

[3551]
LEWIS, A.R. *and* RUNYAN, T.J. **European naval and maritime history, 300-1500.** Bloomington, Ind.,Indiana University Press, 1985. 208p. $22.95. ISBN: 0253320828.

Focuses on Western Europe, including the Baltic, North Sea and Atlantic traditions, and on the Mediterranean, particularly Byzantine and Moslem naval history. Scholarly. *Class No:* 359(4)

Great Britain

[3552]
RASOR, E.L. **British naval history since 1815:** a guide to the literature. New York, Garland, 1990. xxi,841p. $90. (*(Military history bibliographies, v.13).*) ISBN: 0824077350.

Part 1: Historiographical narrative (1. Introduction & sources - 2. Naval writers and historians - 3. Strategy, sea power, and international relations - 4. Intelligence - 5. Admiralty, logistics, warships & naval aviation - 6. Human resources, war and society - 7. The Merchant Marine and the fishing fleet - 8. Imperialism and reconnaisance - 9. Chronology - 10. Genre). Part 2: Bibliographical listing (3125 entries by name). *Class No:* 359(410)

[3553]
WEIGHTMAN, A.E. **Heraldry in the Royal Navy:** crests and badges of H.M. ships. Aldershot, Gale & Polden, 1957. xviii,514p. illus.

Arrangement is by name of ships, A-Z. Diagrams of badges are accompanied by heraldic descriptions, origin and notes on historical background and battle honours. *Class No:* 359(410)

Encyclopaedias

[3554]
BEAVER, P., *ed.* **Encyclopaedia of the modern Royal Navy:** including the Fleet Air Arm and Royal Marines. 3rd ed. Wellingborough, Northants, Patrick Stephens, 1987. 329p. illus., maps, tables. £19.95. ISBN: 0850598605.

First published 1982.

'Aims to illustrate the many facets of the modern Royal Navy ... remains the only comprehensive guide to all these elements' (*Introduction*). The introduction is followed by essays on the Royal Navy since 1945, organization and role, Royal Navy warships, the Fleet Air Arm, the Royal Marines, auxiliary services, other services, naval equipment weapons and services, uniforms and insignia. Also a glossary and an index. *Class No:* 359(410)(031)

Handbooks & Manuals

[3555]
THOMAS, D.A. **A Companion to the Royal Navy.** London, Harrap Ltd., 1988. xvi,443p. illus., maps. £19.95. ISBN: 0245545727.

The story of the Royal Navy in 5 sections: 1. The Admiralty - 2. Ship's names and badges (A-Z by name of ship) - 3. Naval battles (chronological, then A-Z by name) - 4. Battle honours (name of battle & date; list of ships) - 5. Naval chronology, 1660-1987. No index. *Class No:* 359(410)(035)

Yearbooks & Directories

[3556]
GREAT BRITAIN. Ministry of Defence. Navy Department. **The Navy list:** containing lists of ships, establishments and officers of the Fleet, 1998. London, Stationery Office Books, 1998. 300p. £21.50. ISBN: 0117728926. ISSN: 01416081.

First published April 1814. Annual. Not published for sale between September 1939 and May 1949. July and January supplements cover selective promotions, Queen's Birthday and New Year honours, and changes.

Contents include: 2. Alphabetical list of officers - 3. Seniority lists of officers on active list - 4. Key Royal Navy personnel - 5. Ships and units of the fleet and establishments - 6. Key addresses - 7. Reserves - 8. Obituary ... Also *The Navy list of retired officers ....* *Class No:* 359(410)(058)

Histories

[3557]
BEAVER, P. **Britain's modern Royal Navy.** Sparkford, Haynes/Patrick Stephens, 1996. 192p., illus. £19.99. ISBN: 1852604425.

Includes comprehensive details of all ships currently in naval service, including support vessels. Describes naval weapons and sensors, with specifications of naval aircraft and their weapons. Also descriptions of naval bases, dockyards and key establishments. *Class No:* 359(410)(091)

[3558]
CLOWES, W.L. **The Royal Navy:** a history from the earliest times to the present. London, Sampson Low, 1897-1903. (Reprinted by AMS Press). 7v. illus., maps. $290 the set; $41.50 each vol. ISBN: 0404016405, the set.

V.7 has a sub-title '... to the death of Queen Victoria', and goes up to 1900. A most detailed work. And the standard history; full index, and many appendices of flag officers and of ships lost, etc. *Class No:* 359(410)(091)

[3559]
COLLEDGE, J.J. **Ships of the Royal Navy:** complete record of all fighting ships of the Royal Navy from the 15th century to the present. Rev. ed. London, Greenhill Books, 1987. 388p. £30. ISBN: 0947898751.

Rev. ed. of *Ships of the Royal Navy: an historical index* (David & Charles, 1969-70) V.1: major ships (excluding trawlers, drifters, tugs, etc.).

Preliminaries describing the scope of the book are followed by a listing, A-Z by type or name of ship ('A' class submarines ... Zulu). Includes over 13,000 names. *Class No:* 359(410)(091)

[3560]
—COLLEDGE, J.J. Ships of the Royal Navy: an historical index. V.2: Navy-built trawlers, drifters, tugs and requisitioned ships. Newton Abbot, Devon, David & Charles, 1970. 400p.

*c.*11,000 names are listed, stating tonnage, dimensions, armament, dates, shipyard, etc. *Class No:* 359(410)(091)

[3561]
—MANNING, T.D. *and* WALKER, C.F. British warship names. London, Putnam, 1959. 498p.

*c.*20,000 entries, A-Z, giving name, meaning/derivation and a 1-2 line history. Ships of the same name are numbered under each name entry. When gaps occur in the enumerated sequence, the ships 'do not qualify for inclusion'. A history of names rather than of warships as such. *Class No:* 359(410)(091)

[3562]
—YOUNG, J. A Dictionary of ships of the Royal Navy of the Second World War. Cambridge, Stephens, 1975. . 192p. illus.

Records over 2000 vessels, 27 photographs. *Class No:* 359(410)(091)

[3563]
KEMP, P. **The Admiralty regrets:** British warship losses of the 20th century. Stroud, Sutton, 1999. xii,275p., illus.,1port. £25. ISBN: 0750915676.

The warship losses are presented chronologically. Includes a bibliography. *Class No:* 359(410)(091)

[3564]

LENTON, H.T. **British and Empire warships of the Second World War.** London, Greenhill, 1998. 752p., illus. $135. ISBN: 1853672777. *Class No:* 359(410)(091)

[3565]

LYON, D.J. **The Sailing Navy list:** all the ships of the Royal Navy (built, purchased and captured), 1688-1855. Conway, Maritime, 1993. 352p. 300 illus. £60. ISBN: 0851776175.

Arranged by types and classes, with notes on design and designer. D.J.Lyon is Curator, National Maritime Museum.
Class No: 359(410)(091)

[3566]

The Royal Navy day by day. Sainsbury, A.B., *ed.* Shepperton, Surrey, Ian Allan Publishing, in association with the National Maritime Museum, 1992. vi,424p. illus. £29.95 ISBN: 0711021236.

A history, in diary form, of daily events (not just great battles) in the Navy's 700-year tradition. Bibliography, p.365-77. General index, p.378-424. *Class No:* 359(410)(091)

[3567]

SMITH, P.C. *and* OAKLEY, D. **The Royal Marines - a pictorial history, 1664-1988.** Tunbridge Wells, Kent, Spellmount, 1988. 256p. 366 illus. (16 in col.). £25. ISBN: 0946771324.

11 chapters chronologically arranged, 50/50 text and illustrations. Includes a short bibliography (p.247) and index (p.248-256). *Class No:* 359(410)(091)

[3568]

THOMAS, D.A. **Battles and honours of the Royal Navy.** Barnsley, Pen & Sword Books/Leo Cooper, 1998. 362p. illus. £25. ISBN: 085052623x. *Class No:* 359(410)(091)

[3569]

WARNER, O. **Battle honours of the Royal Navy.** London, Philip, 1956. 199p. illus.

A tabulated list of naval actions from 1588 to 1953, and details of single ship actions, listed alphabetically. Lists, with battle honours, follow of ships of the Royal and Commonwealth Navies now in commission, of Fleet Air Arm squadrons which have been in action, and of regiments with naval battle honours. A final section gives illustrations of ships' badges. *Class No:* 359(410)(091)

Biographies

[3570]

Naval who's who, 1917. Polstead, Suffolk, J.B. Hayward & Son, 1981 (Distributed by London Stamp Exchange Ltd, London). 344p. £19.

A facsimile of the 1st ed., originally titled *The Royal Navy list of Who's Who in the Navy.*

Uninteresting data and advertising material deleted and text of Admiral Jellicoe's Despatch for the Battle of Jutland added, together with a casualty roll of all ranks. Includes a list of abbreviations, etc.; a chronological list of notable naval events, 1213-1914; Services, honours and special qualifications of officers, active and retired; and *War supplement,* giving service details and acts of gallantry which, although they may have culminated in an award, did not always appear in the *London gazette. Class No:* 359(410)(092)

Germany

[3571]

BIRD, K.W. **German naval history:** a guide to the literature. New York, Garland, 1985. xx,1121p. $154. (*Military history bibliographies, 7. Garland reference library of social science, 215.*) ISBN: 0824090241.

Includes 4871 citations devoted to literature on the German navies from before Bismarck to 1983. 9 chapters discuss the craft and sources of German naval history, each beginning by examining current research themes and proceeding to a bibliographic essay keyed to the bibliography proper, and ending with suggestions for further research. The bibliography is arranged by author, A-Z, and there is no subject index. '... one of the finest naval bibliographies available on any foreign fleet' (*Choice*, v.22(8), April 1985, p.1136, on which this annotation is based). *Class No:* 359(430)

France

[3572]

POLAK, J. **Bibliographie maritime française depuis les temps les plus reculés jusquà 1914.** Grenoble, Éditions de Quatre Seigneurs, 1976. 367,[1]p. facsims.

9627 numbered entries arranged under authors, A-Z. Bibliographical and source notes. Ships index; subject index (non-analytical). List of sources precedes. *Class No:* 359(44)

[3573]

—JENKINS, E.H. **History of the French Navy,** from its beginnnings to the present. London, Macdonald and Jane's, 1973. 364p. illus. (inc. 17p. of pl.)., ports., maps, plans.

Bibliography, p.349-51. *Class No:* 359(44)

Russia

[3574]

POLMAR, N. **Guide to the Soviet Navy.** 5th ed. Annapolic, MD, US Naval Institute Press, 1991. 608p. illus., charts, tables. £32.95. ISBN: 0870212419.

First published 1977. *Class No:* 359(47)

Bibliographies

[3575]

SMITH, M.J. **The Soviet navy, 1941-1978:** a guide to sources in English. Santa Barbara, CA., ABC-Clio Press, 1980. xiv,211p; illus (incl.pl.). $26.25. (*War/peace bibliography series, 9.*) ISBN: 0874362652.

About 1750 entries for monographs, periodical articles and theses, indexed by authors. 'A valuable and extensive bibliography for both general and specific research needs at all academic levels' (*Choice,* December 1980, p.512). *Class No:* 359(47)(01)

Handbooks & Manuals

[3576]

JORDAN, J. **An Illustrated guide to the modern Soviet navy.** London, Salamander Books Ltd., 1982. 159p. illus. £4.95. ISBN: 0861011465.

A popular work, with more than 150 photographs (70 in colour) and 30 dawings. Sections on the organization of the Soviet surface navy, and on ocean-going ships, are followed by chapters by class of ship, and then weapons and sensors, ship-borne aircraft, and weapons by type. *Class No:* 359(47)(035)

Latin America

Histories

[3577]

SCHEINA, R.L. **Latin America: a naval history, 1810-1985.** Annapolis, MD., Naval Institute Press, 1987. xv,442p. $34.95; £25.25. ISBN: 0870212958. *Class No:* 359(729.99)(091)

USA

[3578]

JORDAN, J. **An Illustrated guide to the modern US Navy:** the world's most advanced naval power. London, Salamander Books Ltd., 1982. 159p. illus. £4.95. ISBN: 0861011511.

Chapters arranged by classes of vessels - aircraft carriers, cruisers, destroyers, frigates, patrol combatants, amphibious warfare vessels, support ships, replenishment ships, weapons and sensors. Popular rather than scholarly. *Class No:* 359(73)

Bibliographies

[3579]

SMITH, M.J., *comp.* **The United States Navy and Coast Guard, 1946-1983:** a bibliography of English-language works and 16mm films. Jefferson, N.C., McFarland & Company, 1984. xx,539p. $65; £48.75. ISBN: 0899501222.

10,057 entries arranged topically. No annotations. A historical note and list of periodicals consulted are followed by the bibliography in 8 sections: 1. Reference works - 2. The American Defense Establishment - 3. The US Navy and US Coast Guard - 4. The balance of power and arms control - 5. The US Navy and Coast Guard operations - 6. Warships, warplanes and hardware. 16mm film guide, Author index, p.473-519; subject index p.520-539. *Class No:* 359(73)(01)

Histories

[3580]

BAUER, K.J. *and* ROBERTS, S.S. **Register of ships of the U.S. Navy, 1775-1990: major combatants.** New York & London, Greenwood Press, 1991. xxiii,350p. illus. $85. £79.95. ISBN: 0313262020.

1: The sail navy, 1775-1853; 2: The old steam navy, 1814-1876; 3: The new navy, 1883-1990. Bibliography, p.299-302. Hull number index. Index, p.309-350. The first of 3v. designed to update Bauer's *Ships of the Navy, 1775-1969* (Rensselaer Polytechnic Institute, 1969). *Class No:* 359(73)(091)

[3581]

NORRIS, J.M. **History of the US Navy.** Feltham, Middx., Hamlyn, 1984. (Distributors for Bison Books Ltd.). 224p. illus., plans, ports. (some col.). £9.95. ISBN: 0600385914.

Introduction (p.6-13) is a brief history, and is followed by 10 chapters in 3 parts (I. A reluctant naval power - II. A naval power born to glory - III. New naval missions). Profusely illustrated. Index, p.222-224. *Class No:* 359(73)(091)

Bibliographies

[3582]

A **Bibliography of American naval history.** Coletta, P.E., *ed.* Annapolis, Naval Institute Press, 1981. 453p. $15.95; £9. ISBN: 0870211056.

Includes diplomatic, political, economic and social history, as well as the history of US Navy, Marine Corps and Coast Guard (when part of the Navy Department). 4822 entries for English-language works (journal articles, essays, books, theses, government publications, oral history reviews). Arrangement is chronological, subdivided by type of publication, preceded by an international section of bibliographical aids and reference works. Subject index. Complements Myron Smith's books. *Class No:* 359(73)(091)(01)

[3583]

—A Selected and annotated bibliography of American naval history. Coletta, P.E., *ed.* Lanham, MD; London, University Press of America, 1988. xi,523p. $34.50. ISBN: 0819171115.

Updates the above by providing new titles in military literature that have appeared since the end of 1979. Entries arranged in 23 special topics (*eg* Amphibious operations ... Women in the Navy) as well as titles in chapters that proceed in chronological order. *Class No:* 359(73)(091)(01)

[3584]

UNITED STATES. Department of the Navy. US Naval History Divison. **US naval history sources in the United States.** Allard, D.C., *and others, eds.* Washington, DC., United States Government Printing Office, 1979. viii,235p. illus.

'... seeks to aid students of naval history by identifying manuscripts, archival and other special collections deposited in more than 200 American archives and libraries'. Arrangement is by US state, A-Z (Alabama ... Wyoming), subdivided by the name of the library of other organization. Lists of papers are given by name, date and volume. Index, p.207-235, of names and places. *Class No:* 359(73)(091)(01)

Dictionaries

[3585]

MORRIS, J.M. *and* KEARNS, P.M. **Historical dictionary of the United States Navy.** Lanham, MD, Scarecrow Press, 1998. 488p.,illus. £80.75. (*Historical dictionaries of war, revolution, and civil unrest..*) ISBN: 0810834065.

Entries arranged alphabetically. Cross referenced selections include acronyms and abbreviations, ship type designations, major ship types by class, every type of naval aeroplane and airship in the Navy's inventory, major weapons used from the beginning to the present day, and a useful section on naval and vessel terminology. *Class No:* 359(73)(091)(038)

36 Social Services & Welfare

Charities & Foundations

Bibliographies

[3586]

HARRIS, M. *and* BILLIS, D. **Organizing voluntary agencies:** a guide through the literature. London, Bedford Square Press, 1986. [4],125p. £7.95. ISBN: 0719911478.

An introduction precedes the bibliographic section, arranged A-Z by author. Entries are annotated, varying in length from 2 lines to a page, covering the relevant literature published during the ten years to 1984 generally. Cross-references. Also includes a user's guide to topics and issues; a list of journals cited; and a list of useful addresses. *Class No:* 36.075(01)

[3587]

LAYTON, D.N. **Philanthropy and voluntarism:** an annotated bibliography. New York, Foundation Center, 1987. 308p. $18.50. ISBN: 0879541989.

Entries for 1614 items, 244 annotated, on the philanthropic tradition. The author is mainly concerned with the history, philosophy and theory of philanthropy in the US, the UK and other countries. Includes 1614 items, of which about a sixth are annotated, on the philanthropic tradition, drawn from writings in history, economics, sociology, journalism and statistics. *Class No:* 36.075(01)

Handbooks & Manuals

[3588]

The Complete fundraising handbook. Clarke, S. *and* Norton, M., *eds.* 3rd ed. London, Directory of Social Change, 1997. 432p. £14.95. ISBN: 1900360098.

First published in 1992.

Bibliography - Index. *Class No:* 36.075(035)

[3589]

EAGLESHAM, N. **Researching local charities:** a practical guide to making better use of charitable resources. London, Directory of Social Change, 1988. v,73p. £3.95. ISBN: 0907164382.

4 sections: Local charities [a description of what they are, etc.]; Sources of information [index of charities and other sources]; Building a charity profile; Producing a finished profile, 6 appendices include the Charities Acts 1960 & 1985. *Class No:* 36.075(035)

Yearbooks & Directories

[3590]

Directory of grant-making trusts. 1999-2000 ed. West Malling, Kent, Charities Aid Foundation, 1999. £89.95. ISBN: 1859340784.

First published 1968 by National Council of Social Service, Charities Aid Fund.

4 parts: 1. Classification of charitable purposes - 2. Trusts listed under classifications. Alphabetical list of trusts empowered to give to general charitable trusts - 3. Register of grant-making charitable trusts. Trusts deleted from Part III - 4. Geographical index of trusts. Alphabetical index of subjects. Some entries include titles of publications. *Class No:* 36.075(058)

[3591]

The FIAC directory of independent advice centres. Newton, D. *and* Kirkwood, J. *and* Lunn, S., *ed.* Liverpool, Federation of Independant Advice Centres, 1990 416 p.

Major organizations are listed on a nationwide basis, but most are listed according to region and area. Each entry lists the address, a brief description of the organization and those for whom its service is intended, and the types of service provided. Information on additional languages spoken, contact details, and opening hours is also furnished. *Class No:* 36.075(058)

[3592]

The International foundation directory. Pilling, S. *and* Kirby, D., *eds.* 9th ed. London, Europa Publications, 2000. 820p. £120. ISBN: 1857430883.

First published 1974.

A directory of institutions in 50 countries, A-Z, covering foundations, trusts and similar non-profit institutions in many fields. Data on each: name and address; founding data; brief history; activities; finance; names of officers; publications (if any). Bibliography: index. Coverage is wide-ranging, including science,

.... (contd.)

medicine, education, social welfare, the arts and humanities, aid t‹ less-developed countries, and international relations. *Class No:* 36.075(058)

[3593]

Voluntary agencies directory 1997. National Council for Voluntar‹ Organizations. 16th ed. NCVO Publications, 1997 407p. £18.95 ISBN: 071991485x.

Published annually

Covers those agencies which are non profit making, have n‹ political slant and receive their funding from public donation or gran aid. Symbols are used to show if an agency is a designated charity, o‹ has sub-branches, paid staff, or information services. Entry i alphabetic, with telephone and address details given, as well as the dat‹ of formation, its objectives and activities. *Class No:* 36.075(058)

Great Britain

Handbooks & Manuals

[3594]

Charities and broadcasting: a guide to radio and television appeals an‹ grants. Parker, N., *ed.* London, Directory of Social Change, 1988 vi, 250p. £5.95. ISBN: 090716434x.

Provides practical information about every television company, radi‹ station and cable operator in the United Kingdom, with details of thei policy towards charities and voluntary groups. Part 1: Th‹ background; part 2: Regional and local classification (for eac‹ company, showing information on total raised for charity, donation‹ appeals, social action broadcasts, etc.). 3 appendices (1. Rules an‹ guidelines; 2. Further information (Broadcasters - further names an‹ addresses; Useful contacts; Suggested further reading). Index o‹ television companies, radio stations, and cable operators precedes. *Class No:* 36.075(410)(035)

[3595]

NORTON, M. **A Guide to the benefits of charitable status.** 2nd ed‹ London, Directory of Social Change, 1988. [5], 230p. £5.95. ISBN‹ 0907164269.

First published 1983.

Provides information on all the important tax reliefs and othe‹ benefits available to charities. 9 sections: 1. Value added tax; 2. Rates‹ 3. Investment of charity funds; 4. Individual giving; 5. Gifts of capital‹ 6. Grants and donations; 7. Lotteries, gaming and competitions; 8‹ Charity trading; 9. Salaries. 8 appendices (Appendix 8; Resources‹ useful publications and organizations (p.225-230). No index, bu‹ detailed table of contents. *Class No:* 36.075(410)(035)

Yearbooks & Directories

[3596]

BAWTREE, D. *and* KIRKLAND, K. **Tolley's charities administratio‹ handbook.** 2nd ed. London, Tolley Publishing, 1999. £41.95. ISBN‹ 0754502686.

Provides useful information for effective charity management, an‹ offers practical advice and assistance for likely problems. Als‹ includes the requirements of the Charities Act. *Class No:* 36.075(410)(058)

[3597]

Charities digest, 1991. Chapman, M.D., *ed.* London, Waterlo‹ Professional Publishing, 2000. Annual. £22.95. ISBN: 1857839315.

First published 1882 as *The annual charities register and digest.* Title varies.

A detailed directory of charitable trusts and associations for specia‹ and general classes. *Class No:* 36.075(410)(058)

Laws

[3598]

LLOYD, S. *and* MIDDLETON, F. **The Charities Acts handbook.** 2n‹ ed. Bristol, Jordans/Directory of Social Change, 1996. 280p. £24.95‹ ISBN: 0853082928.

Revised edition of *Charities: the new law.* *Class No:* 36.075(410)(094.1)

England & Wales

Histories

[3599]
CROWTHER, M.A. The Workhouse system, 1834-1929: a history of an English social institution. London, Methuen & Co. Ltd., 1983. 316p. £11.99. ISBN: 0416360904.

First published 1981 by Batsford Academic and Educational Ltd.

10 chapters in 2 parts: I: Administrators (ch.1-7); II: Inmates (ch.8-10); followed by Conclusions. Notes (p.273-291) include references. Select bibliography (p.292-295). Index (p.296-316).
Class No: 36.075(42)(091)

USA

Yearbooks & Directories

[3600]
Corporate 500: the directory of corporate philanthropy. 12th ed. San Francisco, CA., Public Management Institute, 1994. 1400p. $365. ISBN: 0916664570. ISSN: 0197937x.

First published 1982.

Factual information on the funding programmes of the 580 American corporations with the most active programmes. Includes profiles of 70 corporations responsible for gifts of $95m. to non-profit organizations. *Class No:* 36.075(73)(058)

[3601]
Foundations. Keele, H.M. *and* Kiger, J.C., *eds.* Westport, CT., Greenwood Press, 1984. 516p. illus. $56.95. (*Greenwood encyclopedia of American institutions, 8.*) ISBN: 0313225567.

Lists 230 foundations, selected from the core group of *c*.3400 large foundations described in the 9th ed. of the Foundation Center's *Foundation directory*. Descriptions, up to 3p. long, are on the history and current giving interests. 227 of the foundations selected have assets of over $30 million; 199 are private, independent foundations; 31 are company-sponsored or community foundations. Entries vary widely in quality. Arrangement is A-Z by the first word of the foundation's name. *Class No:* 36.075(73)(058)

Social Services

[3602]
BUNCH, A. Community information. In *Printed reference material* (3rd ed., 1990, edited by P.W. Lea and A. Day), p.324-359.

General sources - Government publications - Subject areas (careers ... women). 6 references. An important and timely contribution.
Class No: 362

[3603]
BUNCH, A.J. Community information services: their origin, scope and development. London, Clive Bingley Ltd., 1982. viii, 168p. £20. ISBN: 0851573185.

7 chapters: 1. Community information - meaning and origins; 2. The United States - the information and referral model; 3. Community information services in Britain - non-public library; 4. Public library community information services in Britain; 5. Community information services to rural areas; 6. Developments in community information services in other countries; 7. Community information and new technology. References are appended to each chapter. Index, p.164-168. *Class No:* 362

[3604]
Social services year book, 2000. London, Financial Times Prentice Hall, 2000. Annual. £125. ISBN: 027364503x. ISSN: 0307093x.

First published 1972 (for 1972/73).

Covers local government, England and Wales (including social services and allied departments), health authorities, advice and counselling, voluntary service, elderly people's welfare organizations, social services and allied organizations. Index. Bibliography arranged by subject. *Class No:* 362

Abbreviations & Symbols

[3605]
CENTRAL COUNCIL FOR EDUCATION AND TRAINING IN SOCIAL WORK. Glossary of abbreviations. 2nd ed. the Council, 1986. [1],21p. (spiral binding). £1. ISBN: 0904488063.

First published 1985.

Arranged A-Z (AA Alcoholics Anonymous ... YWCA), giving only full title (no address). Titles in brackets no longer exist or have been changed or incorporated into those of other organizations. Also includes CCETSW's awards and programmes, and former awards.
Class No: 362(003)

Databases

[3606]
Online information sources on social and community issues. Harman, J., *comp.* New ed. Berkhamsted, Volnet UK, 1993. 43p. illus. Spiral binding. £7.50. ISBN: 1897708459.

First issued in 1992 as an online pack.

Sources of online information (hosts and databases) in the field are listed and and described. Alphabetical and subject index to databases.
Class No: 362(003.4)

Bibliographies

[3607]
CONRAD, J.H. Reference sources in social work: an annotated bibliography. Metuchen, NJ., Scarecrow Press, 1982. vi,201p. $17.50; £13.85. ISBN: 0810815036.

656 entries, with very short annotations, arranged in 6 groups: 1. General - 2. History of social work - 3. Allied fields (A. Psychiatry and psychology; B. Sociology and anthropology; C. Economics; D. Political science; E. Urban affairs) - 4. Fields of service (Adoption ... Women) - 5. Service methods - 6. Social work profession. Appendices list social work journals, social service organizations, and social work libraries. Author, title and subject indexes. US slant.
Class No: 362(01)

[3608]
CROWN, A.D., *comp.* A Bibliography of the Samaritans. 2nd ed. Metuchen, N.J., Scarecrow Press, and The American Theological Library Assocation, 1992 338p. $39.50. (*ATLA bibliography series, no.10.*) ISBN: 0810826461.

An expansion of Leo A. Meyer's *Bibliography of the Samaritans,* edited by D. Broadribb (1964).

Nearly 6000 annotated items, with class numbers after the entries giving a clue to the subject. Subject index with class numbers and subject terms. *Class No:* 362(01)

[3609]
MENDELSOHN, H.N. A Guide to information sources for social work and the human services. Phoenix, Ariz., Oryx, 1987. viii,136p. $28.50. ISBN: 0897743385.

Aims to systematically present pertinent sources that social work practitioners, educators and students can use to locate information in libraries. 11 bibliographic essays, some on types of material, some on techniques, some on topics. Each chapter ends with a bibliography. Title, organization and subject index. '... an excellent introductory source for social work students' (*Wilson library bulletin,* December 1987, p.92). 'This well-conceived bibliographic guide fills a gap ...' (*Reference books bulletin,* 1 March 1988, p.1120). *Class No:* 362(01)

Dictionaries

[3610]
BARKER, R.L. The Social work dictionary. 4th ed. Washington, NASW Press, 1999. $34.95. £26.99. ISBN: 0871012987.

1st published 1987.

Defines nearly 5000 terms used in social work administration, research, policy development and planning, health, etc.
Class No: 362(038)

[3611]
CLEGG, J. Dictionary of social services: policy and practice. 3rd ed. London, Bedford Square Press for the National Council for Voluntary Organisations, 1980. x, 148p. £5.95. ISBN: 0719910390.

First published 1971.

Defines c.500 words, phrases and names of government departments commonly used in social services, 'Ability ... Zoning'. Outlines reorganization of local government and the National Health Service in 1974. *Class No:* 362(038)

Reviews & Abstracts

[3612]
Social service abstracts: monthly summaries of selected documents. Department of Health and Social Security. Library Services. London, HMSO (previously the Library), 1972-. Monthly. £98. ISSN: 03094693.

Includes over 2000 abstracts a year. Sections: Social policy - Social services - Social work - Services for the elderly and the handicapped - Services for children and young people - Services for other special needs - DHSS circulars - Bibliographies. Author and analytical subject index per issue; cumulated annually. Covers the whole range of the personal social services, with particular emphasis on literature originating in Britain. *Class No:* 362(048)

[3613]
Social work research and abstracts. Washington, NASW Press (previously New York, National Association of Social Workers, 1965-. Quarterly. $100pa. ISSN: 01480847.

Early title was *Abstracts for social workers*.

Nearly 2000 abstracts pa from about 200 journals. Arranged in 4 main subject sections, each subdivided; Social work profession - Theory and practice - Area of service - Social issues/social problems. 2 essays and a list of journals scanned precedes. Author and subject indexes. Available online (BRS) and also on microform from UMI. *Class No:* 362(048)

Yearbooks & Directories

[3614]
International directory of voluntary work. Pybus, V. 7th ed. Oxford, Vacation Work, 2000. 304p. £15.95. ISBN: 1854582380. ISSN: 01433474.

First published 1979.

Details of over 700 organizations offering residential work, long and short term, subdivided geographically (United Kingdom, by type of activity; Europe, subdivided by country; North America, Israel and the Middle East; Africa; Asia and Australia.

Non-residential work, by type of activity. Further reading. Index of organizations. *Class No:* 362(058)

Great Britain

Bibliographies

[3615]
BUNCH, A.J. Sources of community information. St. Albans, Branch and Mobile Libraries Group of the Library Association, [1986]. [3],64p. £3. (*Basic library guides, 8*.) ISBN: 0946461066.

Arranged in 4 sections: Introduction - General sources - Official sources - Non-official sources. Each section includes information on organizations and agencies, annotated entries for reference books and periodicals, and information on databases. No index. *Class No:* 362(410)(01)

[3616]
STEWART, G., *comp.* **Personal social services bibliography.** 2nd ed. London, Library Association, 1980. xiii, 129p. £12.50. ISBN: 0853655138.

First published 1978.

3,435 references, covering the literature from 1977 to May 1980. Subject area: 'Domicillary fieldwork and residential local services ...' (*Introduction*). 43 sections, with extensive subdivision , and cross-references (*e.g.* 1. General - 2. Advice centres - 3. Alcoholism ... 6. Children ... 16. Elderly ... 27. Offenders ... 30. Racial minorities ... 41. Youth). Many periodical articles. About 75% of the references are British; 25%, North America. Appended: Abbreviations. Compiler is Lecturer in Social Policy, Univ. of Lancaster. *Class No:* 362(410)(01)

Handbooks & Manuals

[3617]
The FIAC directory of independent advice centres. Thackeray, A. *and* Jones, M. London, Federation of Independent Advice Centres, 1988. £8.95. ISBN: 1871181003.

Lists the 450 independent advice agencies and organisations who are members of FIAC, a coordinating, resource and service agency. Geographical arrangement, subivided as necessary. Each entry has name and address, telephone number, services offered, subjects on which advice can be given, representation, languages, translators, and users. Several indexes. *Class No:* 362(410)(035)

[3618]
Guide to the social services, 2000/2001. Chapman, M.B. London, Waterlow Professional Publishing, 2000. x, 354p. £19.95. ISBN: 1857838548.

First published 1882, as part of *Charities digest*.

Details resources offered by statutory and voluntary organizations involved with administration of public social services. The aim is to provide signposts to further help, and detailed advice. Covers mainly England and Wales, divided by the services provided. *Class No:* 362(410)(035)

Theses

[3619]
TAYLOR, M. *and* **PRESLEY, F. Community work in the UK, 1982-1986:** a review and digest of abstracts. London, Library Association Publishing Ltd., in association with C.P.F. (Community Projects Foundation) and Calouste Gulbenkian Foundation, 1987. [4], 148p. £20. ISBN: 0853659974.

An introductory review (p.1-24) is followed by the digest (p.25-122), with 16 subject sections of abstracts (A,. Directories ... C. Community work theory - D. Community work practice ... H. Race

....(contd.)
and sex equality ... P. Funding and legal). Author and selected subject indexes. Lists of organizations and abbreviations. Selected journals list. *Class No:* 362(410)(043)

Yearbooks & Directories

[3620]
The Self-help guide: a directory of self-help organizations in the United Kingdom. Knight, S. *and* Gann, R. London, Chapman & Hall, 1988. [6],125p. £6.95. ISBN: 0412293706.

Lists over 500 organizations arranged in 5 sections: 1. Introduction (with 16 references) - 2. Organizing and using self-help information - 3. Self-help literature (A-Z, numbered items. Name, address, telephone number and contact, publications, aims) - 4. Where to go for more information - 5. Directory of self-help groups. 2-page subject index. Directory index (refers to numbered items). *Class No:* 362(410)(058)

[3621]
The Social work and social welfare yearbook, 1991. Carter, P., *and others, eds.* Milton Keynes, Open University Press, 1991. viii,216p. £19.99. ISBN: 0335097960.

First published 1989. Annual.

Provides a range of critical commissioned articles on current concerns in social work and social welfare. 16 essays *e.g.* 2: Social work, justice and common good - 5. Family centres - 9. Drug problems in social work - 12. How social fund officers make decisions. *Class No:* 362(410)(058)

Laws

[3622]
CANS (Citizens Advice Notes): a service of information ... compiled from authoritative sources. Cumulative ed. to 1993. London, NCVO (National Council for Voluntary Organisations), CANS Department, 1991. 3v. plus supplements. 1st year's subscription: £95; annual renewal: £62. Loose-leaf.

First published as *Notes on new emergency regulations, 1939*.

Continuously updated digest of social legislation. 16 sections: 1. Administration of justice ... 3. British nationality and migration - 4. Business and industry - 5. Consumer protection ... 7. Education - 8. Employment ... 11. Housing, general - 12. Housing: Rent Acts - 13. Local government and public health - 14. Married persons and children ... 17. Personal health and welfare services ... 21. Town and country planning - 22. Transport (Roads). Index precedes, p.1-109. *Class No:* 362(410)(094.1)

Scotland

[3623]
Directory of national voluntary organisations in Scotland. Saunders, M. *and* Scott, M. Edinburgh, Scottish Council for Voluntary Organisations, 1987. 135p. illus. £5.50. ISBN: 0903589974.

Lists over 400 organizations, A-Z. Each entry includes name of organization, address, telephone number, contact name, and brief description of the organization's work, aims, and activities. Title index and classified index. *Class No:* 362(411)

[3624]
ENGLISH, J., *ed.* **Social services in Scotland.** 4th ed. Edinburgh, Mercat Press, 1998. 180p. diagrs., tables. £14.95. ISBN: 1873644779.

First published 1979.

Provides an introduction to all the main social services in Scotland. Contains chapters on central and local government, social security, health services, mental health services, housing, personal social services, children's hearings, education, employment services, services for the elderly and for the physically handicapped, urban social policy. References and 'further reading' follow each chapter. Index. *Class No:* 362(411)

USA

Bibliographies

[3625]
TRATTNER, W.L. *and* **ACHENBAUM, W.A.,** *eds.* **Social welfare in America:** an annotated bibliography. Westport, CT., Greenwood Press, 1983. xxxiii,324p. $36.95. ISBN: 0313230021.

Over 1400 annotated entries relating to major works written since 1956 on the subject of public welfare in America. Arranged in topical subject groups, subdivided chronologically. Subject and author indexes. '... remarkably thorough collection of sources ...' (*Choice*, v.21(8), April 1984, p.1117-8). *Class No:* 362(73)(01)

Encyclopaedias

[3626]

Encyclopedia of social work. Edwards, R.L. *and* Hopps, J.G., *eds*. 19th ed. Silver Springs, Md., National Association of Social Workers, 1995. 3v. $129 (including supplement). ISBN: 0871012553; 0871012774, supplement. ISSN: 00710237.

16th ed., 1971-. Continues *Social work year book* (Russell Sage Foundation, 1929-.).

Topical articles on social work and social welfare activities in the US, written by specialists in the field. Arranged in sections covering fields of practice, populations, social issues and problems, social work practice, social institutions, human development, research, professions, etc. Cross-references. Includes biographies. Detailed index. A statistical supplement, 1997 is a separate volume for frequent updating. 'There are no similar sources to which this invaluable collection of information can be compared' (*Choice*, v.14(11), January 1978, p.1478, of the 17th ed.). *Class No:* 362(73)(031)

[3627]

The Social work reference library: Encyclopedia of social work, 19th ed., the Social work dictionary, 3rd ed., Social work almanac, 2nd ed. Edwards, R.L., *ed.* Silver Springs, Md., National Association of Social Workers, 1997. 1 CD-ROM. $279. ISBN: 0871012898.

Class No: 362(73)(031)

Yearbooks & Directories

[3628]

Volunteerism: the directory of organizations, training, programs and publications. Kipps, H.C., *ed.* 3rd ed. New York. Bowker, 1991. 1164p. $104.95. ISBN: 0835227391.

Previously published in 1980 as *411: community resource tie line* and *Community green sheets*, and in 1984 as *Community resources directory* (Gale Research Co.).

In 3 sections: 1. Resource groups and publications (listed generally by types of assistance such as Health, Employment and Consumer Services) - 2. Training programs (arranged by States) - 3. Program profiles (emphasizing those organizations that administer volunteer groups). Indexes of organizations and program emphasis. Identifies more than 5000 organizations. Index access by type of organization, organization name, and geographical location. *Class No:* 362(73)(058)

Histories

[3629]

BLAIR, K.J. The History of American women's voluntary organizations, 1810-1960: a guide to sources. Boston, Mass., G.K. Hall, 1988. 363p. $45. ISBN: 0816186480.

678 annotated entries for books and journal articles, arranged A-Z by author and coded to show whether a work concentrates on a charitable organization or one dedicated to peace, patriotism, religion, suffrage, temperence, etc. List of sources consulted. Subject and name index. No geographical index. Publisher claims this to be the first annotated bibliography on the subject ... 'from 1810, when women first began to gain influence in the public sphere through the formation of clubs, to 1960, when the contemporary women's movement emerged'. *Class No:* 362(73)(091)

Biographies

[3630]

TRATTNER, W.I., *ed.* **Biographical dictionary of social welfare in America.** Westport, CT., Greenwood Press, 1986. 897p. $76.95; £75. ISBN: 0313230013.

Biographical sketches of some 300 prominent Americans who were active in social work or other related endeavours. Women and minorities well-represented. Excludes theorists, philanthropists and persons still living. Most entries concisely and clearly written, containing relevant remarks about a person's importance in the history of social reform and social welfare. Includes a list of current sources for further information. (Information based on a review in *Choice* (v.24(2), October 1986). *Class No:* 362(73)(092)

Health & Welfare

[3631]

National health systems of the world. Oxford, Oxford University Press, 1991-93. 2v. (663,356p.). V.1.£75; v.2.£45. ISBN: 0195053206, v.1; 0195078454, v.2.

V.1: The countries; v.2: The issues. Examines health systems in 68 countries. Introduction explains benefits from a comparison of the systems, followed by sections on individual countries grouped in three major categories (industrialized - transitional - very poor). Length of

....(contd.)

entries varies from short ones for Eastern European countries to 23p. for the US. '... indispensable ...'(*Choice*, v.29(2), October 1991, p.263) on V.1. *Class No:* 362.1

Bibliographies

[3632]

BLADES, C.A., and others. The International bibliography of health economics: a comprehensive annotated guide to English language sources since 1914. New York, Macmillan; Brighton, Sussex, Wheatsheaf, 1986. 2v. (xviii,1092p.). $180; £90. ISBN: 0028959906, US; 074500086x, v.1 UK; 0745001599, v.2 UK.

First published in 1977 as *An annotated bibliography of health economics*.

5180 numbered entries for books, chapters of books, government publications, and articles from *c.*440 journals, on health economics published between 1914 and 1982. Part 1: General works - Demand/need for health care - Supply of health services - Estimating the contribution of health services. Part 2: Finance and organization of health services - Planning whole systems - Bibliographies - Supplementary entries. Entries are annotated with 50-100 word descriptions. Author and very detailed subject indexes. *Class No:* 362.1(01)

[3633]

ELLING, R.H., ed. Cross-national study of health systems - countries, world regions, and special problems: a guide to information sources. Detroit, Mich., Gale Research Co., 1980. xviii,687p. $68. (*Health affairs information guide series, v.3.*) ISBN: 0810314533.

Complementary to *Cross-national study of health systems - concepts, methods and data sources.* (Transaction Books, 1980).

Identifies 17 types of special problems in health systems. Specific countries (including Canada, Cuba, People's Republic of China, Sweden, UK and USSR - but not USA, dealt with elsewhere in the Health affairs series), and other world regions are then covered. The annotated bibliography records research monographs, periodical articles, official reports and unpublished dissertations. *Class No:* 362.1(01)

[3634]

Encyclopedia of health information sources. Wasserman, P., *ed.* 2nd ed. Detroit, Mich., Gale Research Company, 1993. *c.*500p. $165.00. ISBN: 0810369095.

First published 1987.

13,000 citations for *c.*450 health-related topics, listed A-Z. Under each topic heading are listed the citations for up to 14 types of sources, including abstract services, annuals, associations, bibliographies, biographical sources, dictionaries, directories, encyclopedias, institutes, online data bases, periodicals, professional societies, statistical sources, textbooks. Cross-references. List of subjects. A 3rd ed. is planned for 1996. *Class No:* 362.1(01)

[3635]

HASSELBAUER, K.J. A Research guide to the health sciences: medical, nutritional, and environmental. New York, Greenwood Press, 1987. 657p. $49.95. (*Reference sources for the social sciences and humanities, 4.*) ISBN: 0313235309.

Over 2000 citations in 4 parts: General works - Basic sciences - Social aspects of the health sciences - Medical specialties. The first part includes research guides, bibliographies, indexes, bibliographical sources, directories, encyclopedias. The other three parts also include textbooks. *Class No:* 362.1(01)

[3636]

REES, A.N. The Consumer health information source book. 6th ed. Oryx Press, 2000. 232p. $70.25. ISBN: 1573561231.

First published 1981.

Includes annotated entries for books, booklets and pamphlets. Cross-references. Directory of publishers. Title and subject indexes. *Class No:* 362.1(01)

[3637]

ROPER, F.W. *and* **BOORKMAN, J.A., eds. Introduction to reference sources in the health sciences.** 3rd ed. Chicago, Ill., Medical Library Association, 1994. 312p. $37. ISBN: 0810828898.

First published 1980.

Bibliographic sources. Information sources. Index. '... does an excellent job of discussing various types of reference and information sources and their use in reference work in the health sciences' (*Journal of academic librarianship*, v.11(4), September 1985, p.255). *Class No:* 362.1(01)

Dictionaries

[3638]

DEARLING, A. **The Social welfare word book.** Harlow, Longman, 1993. xxiii,203p. £15.99. ISBN: 0582219760.

A 13-page list of acronyms and abbreviations precedes. The main dictionary entries are about a paragraph in length, with description, background and context. Many have examples, and all end with references to related headings. *Class No:* 362.1(038)

[3639]

TIMMS, N. *and* TIMMS, R., *eds.* **Dictionary of social welfare.** London, Routledge & Kegan Paul, 1982. vi, 217p. £40. ISBN: 0710090846.

c.300 entries, arranged A-Z. Each entry indicates the meaning or range of meanings of the word, and then outlines its application in welfare, and use by practitioners. Most entries conclude with references to works which deal with the subject. Cross-referenced. *Class No:* 362.1(038)

Reviews & Abstracts

[3640]

Health service abstracts. London, Department of Health and Social Security Library, 1974-. no.1-. Monthly. £29pa. ISSN: 02680459.

Succeeds *Current literature on personal social services* and, later, *Current literature on health services.* As from May 1985 incorporates *Hospital abstracts* and *Current literature on general medical practice* also.

About 150 brief summaries of journal articles, reports, books, and references per issue. Headings: Services for special groups (Maternity - Children - Elderly - Terminally ill - Physically handicapped - Psychiatric services - Mentally handicapped - Ethnic minorities - Prison medical services); Services for special diseases; NHS reports; DHSS publications; Circulars and other guidance material. Cross-references. Author and subject indexes. Database is DATASTAR. *Class No:* 362.1(048)

[3641]

Quality assurance abstracts. DHSS Library and King's Fund Centre. Quality Insurance Project. London, Department of Health and Social Security Library *and* King Edward's Hospital Fund for London, 1986-92. 6pa. ISSN: 0269297x.

Over 800 abstracts pa. Arranged in 28 broad subject divisions: General items and comment ... Quality assurance in the United Kingdom ... Hospitals (various subdivisions) ... Primary health care ... Nursing ... Bibliography and reference materials. Subject and author indexes. Produced for DHSS-DATA, the DHSS Library database. *Class No:* 362.1(048)

Yearbooks & Directories

[3642]

Directory of organisations in allied and complementary health care. Madge, D., *ed.* London, British Library Publishing, 2000. 150p. £37. ISBN: 0712308547.

Each chapter covers a specific area, such as acupuncture, herbalism, reflexology. There are brief descriptions of the therapy and a list of associations and societies. Covers UK and Europe. *Class No:* 362.1(058)

[3643]

The Health and safety at work directory, 1998/99. Kingston upon Thames, Croner Publications, 1998. vi,193p. ISBN: 1855245053.

Aims to be a comprehensive collection of names and addresses of organizations and people interested in, or involved with, health and safety. Formerly: The health and safety directory. *Class No:* 362.1(058)

Tables & Data Books

[3644]

World health statistics annual. Geneva, World Health Organization. tables. ISSN: 02503794.

Initially as *Annual epidemiological and vital statistics.* Until recently issued in 3v. First published for 1939/46, then annually.

In 4 main sections: A. Global overview - B. Special topic (in this issue 'Implementation of the global strategy for health for all by the year 2000: regional perspectives of achievement') - C. Vital statistics and life tables - D. Causes of death (subdivided by region and country). 2 Annexes (II. List of member states of WHO, by region).

Supplemented by *World health statistics quarterly* (1978-. SFr.100pa.). *Class No:* 362.1(083)

Laws

[3645]

The Journal of social welfare law and family law. London, Sweet & Maxwell, Stevens Journal, 1978-. 6pa. £72 pa. ISSN: 01418033.

Each issue usually includes 3-4 articles; Recent legislation and reports; Recent Social Security Commissioners' decisions; and one or two lengthy book reviews. *Class No:* 362.1(094.1)

Great Britain

[3646]

The Hospitals and health services yearbook ... an annual record of the hospitals and health services of Great Britain and Northern Ireland, incorporating *Burdett's Hospitals and charities,* founded 1889. London, Institute of Health Services Management. Various pagings.

23 sections, including directories of health authorities in England, in Wales and in Scotland; Statutory instruments and circulars; Summaries of reports; Health Service literature; a short bibliography; and Directory of hospital suppliers. Indexes (on green paper); Health authorities, hospitals; general index; advertisers. *Class No:* 362.1(410)

[3647]

LAING, W. **Laing's review of private health care ... and directory of independent hospitals,** residential and nursing homes and related services 1992. 4th ed. London, Laing & Buisson Publications, 1992. 1220p., tables, map. £95. ISBN: 185440024x. ISSN: 09539050.

Lists *c*12,000+ private and voluntary homes for the elderly, plus independent hospitals, screening clinics, and homes and hospitals for the mentally ill. *Class No:* 362.1(410)

[3648]

Wellard's NHS handbook, 2000/2001. Merry, P., *ed.* 15th ed. Tunbridge Wells, JMH Publishing, 2000. xv,312p. £45. ISBN: 0953368424.

First ed. published 1980.

Formerly *NHS handbook.*

Aims to make NHS easily understood by those without prior knowledge of its structure and to provide an up-to-date reference for those already working in the NHS and related fields. Also a quick reference section and an index. *Class No:* 362.1(410)

Bibliographies

[3649]

GREAT BRITAIN. HM Stationery Office. **Government publications. Sectional list 11, revised December 1988: Department of Health and Social Security.** London, HMSO., 1989. 35p. *Gratis.*

Two lists of items currently in print: 'Health and social services' (sections include: Children and child abuse; Drugs and pharmaceuticals; Health equipment notes; Hospitals, administration and organization; Medical practitioners; National Health Service; Social services; Statistical and research reports) - 'Social security' (*e.g.* National insurance (industrial injuries); Pensions; Occupational pensions). *Class No:* 362.1(410)(01)

[3650]

Health education index and guide to voluntary and other support organisations and self-help groups concerned with health care. Edsall, B., *comp. & ed.* 9th ed. London, B. Edsall & Co., 1988. 414p. £40. ISBN: 0902623508. ISSN: 01403273.

First published 1970.

Lists over 13,000 references to health education material (p.18-359) arranged in 170 subject areas, A-Z. Includes booklets and pamphlets, books, films, film strips and slides, flannelgraphs, lecture notes, loops, transparencies, tapes and tape cassettes, posters, video cassettes, wallcharts, etc. Sources of supply index, p.7-15. Also lists professional organizations (p.361-362) and 'People who help, index of voluntary and other support organizations ...' (p.363-413). *Class No:* 362.1(410)(01)

[3651]

HUSTWIT, J. *and* WEBLEY, M. **Information in social welfare:** a survey of resources. London, National Institute for Social Work, 1977. 95p. £2.50. (*NISW no. 6.*) ISBN: 0902789090.

Based on a report on information resources in social welfare prepared for the British Library Research and Development Dept.

Pt. 1: Development in social welfare information resources in the 1970's - Pt. 2: Social welfare information resource - a guide (142 references). Appendix A: Current awareness sources - B. A short bibliography of social welfare and related information research (1968-), by date. *Class No:* 362.1(410)(01)

Handbooks & Manuals

[3652]

Registered Nursing Home Association: reference book, 1990/91: registered nursing homes, clinics and hospitals in the UK. 15th ed. Birmingham, the Association, 1990. 210p. maps.

Contents: Summary of National Health Service beds - List of N.H.S. in region/district order - Regional health authorities/boards - Alphabetical list of members of the R.N.H. Association - Town/district locations of members of the R.N.H. Association.
Class No: 362.1(410)(035)

Yearbooks & Directories

[3653]

Croner's care homes guide. New Maldon, Croner Publications, 1987. 2v. £28.50 each vol. ISBN: 0900319518, South; 0900319526, North & Midlands. ISSN: 09525157.

One volume covers the South of England, the other the North and Midlands. Each volume is arranged by counties and then alphabetically by town in postal address. Together they list over 10,000 homes. Each entry includes full name of home, date established, full postal address, telephone number, name of proprietor, ownership status, special services offered, visiting arrangements, fees, number of residents, conditions of acceptance, licensing authority, details of accommodation available, arrangements for meals, lifts, TV, telephone, heating, etc. A-Z index by names of homes. *Class No:* 362.1(410)(058)

[3654]

Directory of independent hospitals and health services, 1997. London, FT Pharmaceuticals, 1997. 896p. £110. ISBN: 0443057702. ISSN: 09510561.

First published 1980. The first 5 eds. published by Medical Marketing Information Ltd. Former title was *Directory of private hospital and health services.*

Includes chapters on independent hospitals, screening clinics, private bed accommodation in NHS hospitals, private nursing homes, voluntary homes, dual registered homes. Arrangement is A-Z by organization, with address, telephone, matron's name, etc. Followed by guides to English health regions, health authorities, and English counties; a buyers' guide, general index, and index of advertisers.
Class No: 362.1(410)(058)

Scotland

Bibliographies

[3655]

GREAT BRITAIN. HM Stationery Office. Government publications. Sectional list 71: revised 1 June 1989. Scotland. London, HMSO, 1989. 45p. *Gratis.*

Includes a section on the Scottish Home and Health Department (p.24-29). Sections: Home affairs (Criminal matters - Fire - Licensing ... Police - Prisons); Health (Alcohol - Child health ... Food, hygiene, nutrition - Health buildings and equipment ... Mental health and welfare ...). *Class No:* 362.1(411)(01)

England & Wales

Tables & Data Books

[3656]

Health and personal social service statistics for England, 1997. Department of Health and Social Security. London, Stationery Office Agencies, 1998. 84p. maps. £16.50. ISBN: 0113221088.

First published 1969. Annual.

13 sections: 1. Population and vital statistics - 2. Finance - 3. Manpower - 4. N.H.S. hospital administrative service - 5. Family Practitioner Committee services - 6. Community health service - 7. Personal health services - 8. Maternity and child health and social services - 9. Psychiatric services - 10. Preventive medicine - 11. Morbidity - 12. Abortions notified under the Abortion Act, 1967 - 13. Miscellaneous health statistics. Appendices: 1. General notes; 2. List of publications; 3. Regional health authority areas.
Class No: 362.1(42)(083)

[3657]

—**Health and personal social services statistics for Wales, 1991.** Welsh Office. no.18. Cardiff, E & S. S Division, Welsh Office, 1991. £5. ISBN: 0750401982.

First published 1969. Annual.

Similar content to the above, with 12 sections and 2 appendices.
Class No: 362.1(42)(083)

USA

Yearbooks & Directories

[3658]

Medical and health information directory. 11th ed. Detroit, Mich., Gale, 2000. 3v. $336.50 set. ISBN: 0787634808, v.1; 0787634832, v.2; 0787634867, v.3. ISSN: 07499973.

First published 1977.

V.1: Organizations, agencies and institutions - v.2: Publications, libraries and other information resources - v.3: Health services. Intended for US medical and health professionals, government officials, librarians, consumers, and others. Each volume is self contained. *Class No:* 362.1(73)(058)

Libraries

[3659]

Directory of medical and health care libraries in the United Kingdom, 2000-2001. Forrester, W.H., *ed.* 11th ed. London, Library Association Publishing, 2000. 288p. £35. ISBN: 1856043789.

First published 1957, the 1st-4th editions entitled *Directory of medical libraries in the British Isles.*

Lists specialist libraries, with details of address, telephone and fax numbers, email addresses, URLs, librarian, readers, stock policy, opening hours, publications, branches, holdings, etc. 2 appendices, including 1. List of members of NHS Regional Libraries Group. List of libraries arranged A-Z by town. Indexes of personal names, establishments, counties, and named collections. Subject index to special collections. Selected subject index to libraries.
Class No: 362.1:061:026/027

National Health Service

[3660]

A Patient's guide to the National Health Services. Hessayon, A., *comp.* London, Consumers' Association and Hodder & Stoughton, 1983. 223p. £3.95. ISBN: 0340335467.

Topics covered include: How to choose your GP, dentist, optician; Maternity and child health services; All aspects of going into hospital; Mental health services; The care of the elderly; The roles of different health workers; Questions of medical records and confidentiality, and consent and medical research. Further chapter considers the pros and cons of private treatment. Finally, there is a chapter on the structure of the NHS; a list of useful addresses (p.215-8); and an index (p.219-223). *Class No:* 362.1:061:061.1

Hospitals

Reviews & Abstracts

[3661]

Hospital literature index. Chicago, Ill., American Hospital Association, 1945-. Quarterly (from 1945 to 1961, 2pa.) 4th quarter is annual hardbound issue. 5-year cumulations. $290pa. ISSN: 00185736.

From 1978 compiled with the co-operation of the National Library of Medicine.

About 10,000 references pa from *c.*500 English-language journals. An A-Z author-subject index of literature about hospital administration, planning and financing, and administrative aspects of medical, paramedical, etc., fields. Includes references to significant books as well as periodical articles. Also available online; Vendors: DIMDI; National Library of Medicine. *Class No:* 362.11(048)

Great Britain

[3662]

Directory of hospitals. 5th ed. Edinburgh, Churchill Livingstone Medical Journals, 1992. 490p. £34. ISBN: 058209626x.

Lists all hospitals in the United Kingdom and Eire (NHS and independent) plus names of consultants for each hospital by specialities. Features RHS/DHA/FHSA addresses, NHS Trusts. Index of consultants by medical specialty. *Class No:* 362.11(410)

Libraries

[3663]

Directory of domiciliary and hospital patients' library services in the United Kingdom. Collison, J., *and others, eds.* Manchester, Library Association, Medical, Health and Welfare Libraries Group *and* Department of Library and Information Studies, Manchester Polytechnic, 1984. viii,854p. £12. ISBN: 0950989703.

Geographical arrangement: Domiciliary library services (Public library services in the UK - Other public libraries in the British Isles); Hospital public library services (England: Regional health authorities, by authority - Northern Ireland: Health and personal social services, by authority - Northern Ireland: Health and personal social services, by authority - Scotland: Health boards, by authority - Wales: Regional health authority - Isle of Man and Channel Islands - London post-

....(contd.)
graduate teaching hospitals - Special hospitals). Index of hospitals, district health authorities and place names.
Class No: 362.11(410):061:026/027

England

Middle Ages

[3664]
CLAY, R.M. **The Mediaeval hospitals of England.** London, Methuen, 1909 (Reprinted by Cass, 1966). xxii,357p. illus. £25. ISBN: 0714612928.
The most valuable part of this history lies in appendix B, which is a list of nearly 800 houses for wayfarers, sick, aged, infirm, insane, and lepers founded before 1547, arranged by counties. Appended list of sources. Well produced. 'It should be available in every historical and good general library' (*British medical journal,* no.5503, 25 June 1966, p.1590. *Class No:* 362.11(420)"01/14"

Family Planning

[3665]
LOUDON, N. *and* GLASSIER, A. *and* GEBBIE, A., *eds.* **Handbook of family planning and reproductive healthcare.** 3rd ed. Edinburgh, Churchill Livingstone, 1995. 462p. illus. £43.95. ISBN: 0443051577. *Class No:* 362.178

Reviews & Abstracts

[3666]
Latest literature in family planning. London, Family Planning Information Service, 1974-90. 6pa. ISSN: 03088774.
Formerly *Current literature in family planning.*
About 100 abstracts pa, drawn from English-language books, pamphlets, periodicals, monographs and reports. Subject fields: Family planning - medical and non-medical. *Class No:* 362.178(048)

Developing Countries

[3667]
ROSS, J. A., *and others.* **Family planning and child survival:** 100 developing countries. New York, Center for Population and Family Health, Columbia University, 1988. 247p. Gratis (later eds. $5 each). ISBN: 0962095206.
Intended to be issued biennially. Successor to *Population and family planning programs,* Population Council fact book series issued 1969-1985.
Statistical data compiled from returned questionnaires and standard secondary sources. (*e.g.* UN's Demographic yearbook). No index. Useful table of contents. *Class No:* 362.178(4/9-77)

Disabled & Handicapped

Bibliographies

[3668]
LANE, E. *and* LANE, J. **'Reference materials for the disabled'.** In *RSR* v.10(3), Fall, 1982, p.73-76.
Includes 23 annotated citations and also organizations, etc., that help, arranged in 6 sections (Guides - Aids for independent living - Service agencies - Library resources - Specialized formats - Utilizing technology. US oriented. *Class No:* 362.4(01)

[3669]
LANE, P. **'Books on disability'.** In *British book news,* April 1984, p.199-204.
A literature review, with sections on Children; Toys; Education; Employment; The sociology of disability; The Snowball effect of Snowdon; Social work and community care; Careers with disabled people; Attitudes; Self-help; Leisure; Access and design; Aids costs, Women; Preventable disability; Third world; Libraries. Also a bibliography of the 129 books referred to in the text.
Class No: 362.4(01)

[3670]
NATIONAL LIBRARY FOR THE HANDICAPPED CHILD. **Catalogue of library holdings.** London, the Library, 1986. 800p. £7.50. ISBN: 0948664002.
A list of books, computer software, sound tapes, slides, film strips, 16mm film, videos, jigsaws, pictures and multi-media packs. Includes details of books on the care and education of handicapped children. Listed by author, by title, and by handicap. *Class No:* 362.4(01)

Dictionaries

[3671]
INTERNATIONAL LABOUR OFFICE. **Vocational rehabilitation and the employment of the disabled:** a glossary. Geneva, ILO., 1981. 182p. Sw.F.15. £6.60. ISBN: 922002571x. *Class No:* 362.4(038)

[3672]
LINDSEY, M.P. **Dictionary of mental handicap.** London, Routledge, 1989. vi,345p. £42.50. ISBN: 0415028108.
Bringing together terms and concepts from a wide variety of fields, this is '... an attempt to demystify the terms so that they can be more readily understood by lay people, unqualified staff, and staff from the same and other disciplines.' (*Preface*). Short descriptions vary in length from a few lines to a page. Cross-references. References for further reading are added to many entries. *Class No:* 362.4(038)

Yearbooks & Directories

[3673]
Directory for disabled people. Darnborough, A. *and* Kinrade, D., *comps.* 8th ed. New Jersey, Prentice Hall, 1998. 536p. £17.95. ISBN: 013736489x.
First published 1977.
16 sections ... 2. Financial benefits and allowances - 3. Aids: their provision and availability ... 7. Employment - 8. Mobility and motoring ... 11. Sport and leisure ... 16. Helpful organizations. 2 appendices: A. Selected further information, including bibliographies; B. Addresses of publishers and stockists mentioned. Index.
Class No: 362.4(058)

[3674]
HALE, G., *ed.* **The New source book for the disabled:** an illustrated guide to easier and more independent living for physically disabled people, their families and friends. 2nd ed. London, Heinemann, 1983. 288p, illus. £9.95. ISBN: 0434311596.
First published in 1979 by Paddington Press.
A quarto which includes sections on resources (*e.g.* organizations; general reference books; periodicals; leisure activities). Index.
Class No: 362.4(058)

[3675]
NORCROSS, J.C., *et al.* **Authoritative guide to self-help resources in mental health.** New York, Guilford Press, 2000. 432p. £24.95. $35. ISBN: 1572305061. *Class No:* 362.4(058)

[3676]
SANDHU, J., *and others. eds.* **Directory of non-medical research relating to handicapped people, 1987.** 4th ed. Newcastle-upon-Tyne, Handicapped Persons Research Unit, Newcastle Polytechnic, 1987. [6], 479p. £15. ISBN: 0906721296.
First published 1932.
Sections on education, communication, family, post school, recreation, social and personal, services, community care, institutional care, health care, rehabilitation, functional/clinical assessment, elderly, mobility, miscellaneous. Information given for each project is project title, aims and methods, institution/organization (name, address, telephone no.), investigator's name, funded by, starting date, publications/progress report. Indexes of workers, institutions, and subjects.
A new ed. was issued in 1993 as *Directory of non-medical research on disability, 1989-93,* edited by E.Humphries & O.Paget (University of Northumbria at Newcastle, 210p. £9. ISBN 0906721555).
Class No: 362.4(058)

The Blind

Bibliographies

[3677]
AMERICAN FOUNDATION FOR THE BLIND. New York City. M.C. Migel Memorial Library. **Dictionary catalog of the M.C. Migel Memorial Library ...** Boston, Mass., G.K. Hall, 1970. 2v. $156 the set. ISBN: 081610705x.
A catalogue of 23,000 photolithographically reproduced cards, on every phase of blindness. Typical subject headings include Preschool child, Reading, Public school classes, Space perception, Personality development, Counseling, Vocational guidance and placement, the Deaf-blind, and the War-blinded. *Class No:* 362.41(01)

[3678]
—ROYAL NATIONAL INSTITUTE FOR THE BLIND. Reference Library. **Works on blindness and associated subjects.** London, the Institute, 1962, with supplements in 1964, 1969, 1971.
Since 1974 the Library has produced select accessions lists.
Class No: 362.41(01)

The Deaf

Dictionaries

[3679]

Gallaudet encyclopedia of deaf people and deafness. Van Cleve, J.V., *ed*. New York, McGraw-Hill, 1987. 3v. (xiii,1322p.). illus. $300 the set. ISBN: 0070792291.

Sponsored by Gallaudet University.

273 entries discussing the sociology, audiology, law, education, psychology, history and rehabilitation of deaf people. Articles are signed, vary in length between half a page to 30 pages, with subsections and bibliographies. 10 associate editors and 400 distinguished contributors in all. Includes biographical entries. International in scope. 'Excellently done' (*Library journal*, v.111(17), 15 October 1986, p.86). '... an encyclopedia on and for the deaf that is likely to become the standard work in its field' (*Choice*, April 1987, p.1198). '... a unique set with no competition ... written in a clear and generally accessible manner ...' (*Reference books bulletin*, 1986/87, p.84). *Class No: 362.42(038)*

Poor & Destitute

Bibliographies

[3680]

HENSLIN, J.M. Homelessness: an annotated bibliography. New York, Garland, 1993. 2v.(1092p). $125. ISBN: 0824041151.

V.1 has 3300 annotated entries arranged by author, A-Z, each entry being from a sentence to a paragraph in length. V.2 lists the same citations in 41 subject sections (Advocacy ... Homeless women), with full citations but no annotations. Author index. '... brings together a wide array of sources on a critical global social issue'(*Booklist*, v.90(1), 1 September 1993, p.88). *Class No: 362.5(01)*

[3681]

KUTAIS, B.G. *and* SHOHOV, T., *eds*. **Homelessness:** a guide to the literature. 2nd ed. Nova Science Pub., 1999. 259p. £50.99. $69. ISBN: 1560727012. *Class No: 362.5(01)*

Child Welfare

[3682]

UNICEF. State of the world's children, 2000. New York, United Bations, 2000. 100p. tables, charts. £7.95. ISBN: 9280635328. ISSN: 0265718x.

Annual, first published 1980.

In 2 parts: A report submitting 10 specific propositions for ending the poverty of one quarter of mankind, and a section of statistical tables; footnotes. *Class No: 362.7*

Bibliographies

[3683]

HAAG, E.E. Research guide for studies in infancy and childhood. Westport, CT., Greenwood Press, 1988. 430p. $55. (*Reference sources for the social sciences and humanities, 8.*) ISBN: 0313247633.

Section 1 has chapters on search strategy, databases, and general reference works, by type. Section 2 has specialised subject bibliographies on families; child care; communication; cognition; behaviour, social/cultural, physical and atypical development; and creativity. Each section is subdivided. Annotations are descriptive. Subject, title and author indexes. Complements Woodbury's *Childhood information sources* (1985). *Class No: 362.7(01)*

[3684]

PARDECK, J.T., *and others, comps*. **Child welfare training and practice:** an annotated bibliography. Westport, CT., Greenwood Press, 1982. 143p. £45. $49.95. ISBN: 0313233837.

In 7 sections: Abuse and neglect - Law and court - Substitute care - In-home services and parent education - Institutions and special-needs children - Minority clients - Training and interviewing methods. Annotated entries. Non-print media included. Cross-references. Author, institutional, audiovisual and subject indexes. *Class No: 362.7(01)*

[3685]

SCHEIMAN, D.L. *and* SLONIM, M. **Resources for middle childhood;** a source book. New York, Garland, 1988. 138p. $27. (*Garland reference library of social sciences, 433.*) ISBN: 0824077776.

Concerned with children who are 6 to 12 years old. Arranged in 8 broad groupings (Physical development - psychosocial development - cognitive development - family interaction - play - peer relationships - schooling - societal impact). Each section has an essay, followed by an annotated bibliography. Author and title indexes, but no subject index. *Class No: 362.7(01)*

[3686]

WOODBURY, M. Childhood information resources. New York, Information Resources, 1985. 593p. $45. ISBN: 087815051x.

789 annotated entries for information published by all kinds of child study agencies, in all disciplines regarding children. Each chapter has a 3-5 page introduction describing coverage, subject category, research methodology, etc. Covers 150 periodicals, 173 organizations, and 40 databases. Lengthy author/title/subject index. ' ... a useful sourcebook ... ' (*Choice* v.23(2) October 1985 p.278). *Class No: 362.7(01)*

USA

Yearbooks & Directories

[3687]

POSNER, J.L. CWLA's guide to adoption agencies: a national directory of adoption agencies and adoption resources. New York, Child Welfare League of America, 1989. 668p. tables. $15.95. ISBN: 0878683453.

Lists both public and private adoption agencies in the US. Arranged by State, subdivided by name of agency. Data includes address of agency, director's name, adoption procedures, programme summary, accreditation, children placed (age, ethnicity, etc.), requirements for adoptive parents (age, religion, marital status, etc.), and average cost and waiting time. *Class No: 362.7(73)(058)*

Youth Welfare

[3688]

Directory of youth services and child care in the UK. 2nd ed. Harlow, Essex, Longman, 1992. xvii,346p. £40. (*Longman community information guide.*) ISBN: 0582087864.

First published 1990.

A comprehensive, detailed listing of local authority, independent and voluntary organizations. In 2 parts: 1. Public and statutory services, central and local government, England, Wales, Scotland and Northern Ireland - 2. Voluntary, private and non-statutory services. Index, p.340-345. *Class No: 362.8*

[3689]

Youth movements of the world. Angel, W.D. Harlow, Essex, Longman, 1991. 700p. illus. £99. (*Longman current affairs.*) ISBN: 0582062713.

Lists over 1000 youth organizations and government and non-government agencies under countries A-Z. Introduction on each country gives statistics (demography, education, employment and health) and information on government youth ministries and youth policies. On each organization: contact; office holders; membership; history; aims; activities; affiliations. *Class No: 362.8*

Bibliographies

[3690]

DERRICK, D., *comp*. **Selected and annotated bibliography of youth, youth work and provision for youth.** Leicester, National Youth Bureau, 1976. ix,411p. £3.50. ISBN: 0902095269.

Over 2000 entries, with concise, expository annotations. Classes A-S (with further subdivision): A. Social studies - B. Psychology and human behaviour - C. Social services - D. Community development - E. Education - F. Adolescence - G. Transition from school to work - H. Leisure - I. Handicapped - J. Delinquency - K. Young volunteers - L. Drugs - M. Counselling - N. Sex - O. Detailed youth work - P. The youth service - Q. Training for youth and community work - R. Training - S. Management. Key to publishers. Indexes of authors and subjects. *Class No: 362.8(01)*

[3691]

Young people now. Leicester, National Youth Agency, 1973- First 6pa, then monthly. £22.80pa. ISSN: 09562842.

As *Youth service information centre digest*, 1969-73. Incorporated *Youth social work bulletin*, then *Youth in society* umtil 1988. Current title from 1990. Focuses on issues that affect young people and those who work for them. *Class No: 362.8(01)*

Counselling

[3692]

FELTHAM, C. *and* DRYDEN, W. **Dictionary of counselling.** London, Whurr Publishers Ltd., 1993. xii,216p. £22.50. ISBN: 1870332083.

A list of 8 consultants, conventions used, and a list of abbreviations precede the dictionary. Entries are from 2 or 3 lines to over a column in length ('Counselling skills': nearly a column). References [a bibliography], p.212-6. *Class No: 364.44*

Insurance

Bibliographies

[3693]

CHARTERED INSURANCE INSTITUTE. Library. **Insurance reading list**: a selection of useful books and periodicals on insurance and related subjects. 7th ed. London, the Library, 1986. 23p. £2.

First published 1972 as *Select list of useful books*....

About 300 unannotated entries (but stating prices, or if op). 17 sections (with subdivisions): General ... Marine ... Fire ... Life ... Pensions ... Accident ... Liability ... Aviation ... Periodicals.

The *Journal* of the Institute (6pa each £2.) regularly carries a feature 'In print', - a checklist for books and periodical articles. Prices are given for photocopying articles. The Institute also issues *gratis* select subject bibliographies (*e.g. Householders' insurance; Life insurance*). *Class No:* 368(01)

[3694]

CUNNEW, R. **The Insurance sourcebook.** Harlow, Essex, Longman, 1991. x,246p. £40 ISBN: 058208556x.

Comprehensive guide to sources of information on and for insurance, in the UK and internationally. *Class No:* 368(01)

Dictionaries

Polyglot

[3695]

DE LUCCA, J.L. **Elsevier's dictionary of insurance and risk prevention in English, French, Spanish, German and Portuguese.** Amsterdam, Elsevier, 1997. 1 CD-ROM. ISBN: 0444826963, CDROM.

Gives definitions of 3962 terms. *Class No:* 368(038)=00

[3696]

DRUDE, G. *and* SACHS, W, *eds*. **Lebensversicherungs-technisches Wörterbuch,** Deutsch-Englisch-Französisch-Italienisch-Spanisch. Dictionary of actuarial and life insurance terms. 3.Aufl. Karlsruhe, Verlag Versicherungswirtschaft, 1983. 611p. £45.50.

2nd ed. published 1964 with supplement, 1972.

A dictionary of actuarial and life insurance terms, with equivalents. Five sequences: German-English-French-Italian-Spanish; English-French-Italian-Spanish-German; French-Italian-Spanish-German-English; Italian-Spanish-German-English-French; and Spanish-German-English-French-Italian. *Class No:* 368(038)=00

[3697]

MÜLLER-LUTZ, H.L., *ed*. **Four-language insurance dictionaries.** Rev. eds. Karlsruhe, Verlag Versicherungswirtschaft e.V., 1971-90. £16.50 each.

A series of polyglot insurance dictionaries; English, French and German equivalents figure in each dictionary, the other languages being, respectively: Bulgarian, Chinese, Czech, Danish, Dutch, Greek, Hungarian, Japanese, Norwegian, Polish, Portuguese, Romanian, Russian, Swedish, Turkish. Each dictionary has *c.* 270 p. *Class No:* 368(038)=00

[3698]

—MÜLLER-LUTZ, H.L. *and* CHIDIAC, J.S. Insurance dictionary: English-French-Arabic, French-English-Arabic, Arabic-English-French. Karlsruhe, Verlag Versicherungswirtschaft e.V., 1971. 134, 64p. *Class No:* 368(038)=00

English

[3699]

BROWN, R.H. **Dictionary of marine insurance terms and clauses.** 5th ed. London, Witherby & Co. Ltd., 1989. 656p. £25. ISBN: 0948691433.

First published 1962.

About 4000 entries for terms, abbreviations and clauses. Concise definitions, and references to Acts. Cross-references. This edition includes summaries of the new sets of clauses which have been published by the Institute of London Underwriters, and comments on most of the individual clauses. *Class No:* 368(038)=20

[3700]

CLARK, J. **Dictionary of insurance and finance terms.** London, CIB Publishing, 1998. 341p. £19.95. ISBN: 0852974949. *Class No:* 368(038)=20

[3701]

COCKERELL, H. **Witherby's dictionary of insurance.** 3rd ed. London, Witherby & Co. Ltd., 1997. 378p. £22.85. ISBN: 1856090833.

First published 1980.

About 2000 terms, with brief (*c*.20-word) definitions. List of abbreviations precedes. Appendix. 'Institutions of insurance. 'Intended to help people who practice insurance or who need to read about it, to understand the terms and abbreviations they may encounter. It is not encyclopedic' (*Preface*). *Class No:* 368(038)=20

[3702]

International dictionary of insurance and finance. Clarke, J., *ed*. London, Fitzroy Dearborn, 1999. 350p. £38. ISBN: 1579581617.

Covers all aspects of international insurance - health, property, casualty, marine, disability, copyright and trademark protection. Entries arranged alphabetically, and provide definitions, explanations and illustrations of each term. *Class No:* 368(038)=20

[3703]

RUBIN, H.W. **Dictionary of insurance terms.** 4th ed. York, Barrons Educational, 2000. 512p. $12.95. (*Barrons business dictionaries*..) ISBN: 0764112627. *Class No:* 368(038)=20

[3704]

THOMSETT, M.C., *comp*. **Insurance dictionary illustrated.** Jefferson, N.C., McFarland, 1989. 243p. $29.95. ISBN: 0899503918.

Includes over 1000 words and phrases used in the insurance industry. Definitions are clear even though complex. Covers all types of insurance but the emphasis is on those most likely to be needed by consumers. Includes examples and cross-references. Includes a directory of addresses. Fewer terms than L.E. David's *Dictionary of insurance* (6th ed., 1984) and H. Rubin's *Dictionary of insurance terms* (1987). *Class No:* 368(038)=20

German

[3705]

STOCKS, K.-H. **Wörterbuch für alle Sparten der Versicherung.** Düsseldorf, Buchverlag Annaliese Rettinghausen, 1988. 2v. (634p.). ISBN: 3980155404, v.1; 3980155412, v.2.

Bande I: Deutsch-Englisch; Bande II: Englisch-Deutsch. Includes *c*.7500 terms, including *c*.200 technical words. Keywords (headwords) are followed by indented connections. *Class No:* 368(038)=30

French

[3706]

DINSDALE, W. A. *and* PEARCE, E A. **French for insurance officials,** with French-English and English-French glossaries. Jory, G. A., *ed*. 3rd ed. London, Chartered Insurance Institue, 1968. xii, 13-313p. £4.

Chapters 1-7: Introduction - Accident insurance - Fire insurance - Life insurance - Marine insurance - Aviation insurance - Reinsurance. Letters, policy forms, etc., in French. French-English technical terms (*c*. 1000) p.232-72, plus common abbreviations; English-French technical terms, p 277-313. Appendices: 1. Miscellaneous forms, p. 177-224. 2. Bibliography p.225-7. *Class No:* 368(038)=40

[3707]

LESOBRE, J. *and* SOMMER, H. **Lexique: risque, assurance, réassurance: français - anglais/américain, anglais/américain - français. Lexicon: risk, insurance, reinsurance.** 2nd é. Paris, Berger-Levrault, 1981. 396p. ISBN: 2701304059.

Includes 5300 terms and expressions, 1600 abbreviations, and 98 pages of technical tables. Part 1. English/American - French; French - English/American; part 2. Abbreviations and initials: (1. English and American; 2. French); part 3. Tables; part 4. Bibliography, p.387-394. *Class No:* 368(038)=40

Spanish

[3708]

BROWN, A.C.S. *and* DINSDALE, W.A. **Spanish for insurance officials.** with Spanish-English and English-Spanish glossaries. London, Chartered Insurance Institute, 1957. vii,9-189 p. £4.

Chapters 1-5: Introduction - Accident insurance - Fire insurance - Life insurance - Marine insurance (p.9-135). Letter forms, policy forms etc., in Spanish. Appendix; bibliography, p.136-8. Glossaries: Spanish-English technical terms (*c*. 1500 words), p.142-65; English-Spanish, p.166-88. Very brief index of subjects. *Class No:* 368(038)=60

Arabic

[3709]
TREKY, T.H., *ed*. Dictionary of insurance terms. In English and Arabic. London, Witherby & Co. Ltd., 1985. 395p. £30. ISBN: 090088696x.

Gives the Arabic equivalent of various insurance terms, explaining them in simple clear language. Various usages are given.
Class No: 368(038)=927

Biographies

[3710]
Who's who in world insurance Harlow, Essex, Longman; Chicago, St. James Press, 1991. xiii,280p. £135. (*Longman business information*.) ISBN: 0582085209, UK; 1558621687, US.

Details principal corporate insurance personnel, to provide insurance professionals with key contacts within the industry. Preceded by lists of abbreviations and company designations, is an A-Z listing of 3421 personnel, with name, current appointment, current employer, business address, telephone, telex, cable and fax numbers. Company index, p.229-60. Geographical index (countries A-Z. subdivided by personnel, A-Z), p.263-80. *Class No:* 368(092)

Worldwide

Yearbooks & Directories

[3711]
Financial times world insurance year book, 1993. Harlow, Essex, Longman Group (UK) Ltd.; Detroit, Gale, 1993. xxi,580p. £125. ISBN: 0582217369.

Entries for 1143 companies and 50 associations in 84 countries, arranged geographically (Argentina ... Zimbabwe). Each country section is prefaced by selected statistics and details of leading national insurance associations and institutes. Information for each insurance firm is foundation, head office, directors, management, classes written, activities, capital, ownership, financial results (data for the last three years available). Preliminary sections are: Currency conversion rates and abbreviations - Company designations - Financial terms defined - Lloyds of London. Indexes of classes written (p.479-508), companies (p.509-576), international professional services, and advertisers (p.580). *Class No:* 368(100)(058)

[3712]
Lloyd's nautical year book, 1999. Hughes, D. Colchester, Essex, LLP Professional Publishing, 1998. 350p. illus., maps. £48. ISBN: 1859788408. ISSN: 09525394.

Published from 1892 - annually. Early title was *Lloyd's nautical year book and calendar.*

Contains current information relating to offshore and onshore ship management. Sections: The shipping industry (includes an annual review of developments and trends in all aspects of ship management) - Lloyd's and insurance (including marine insurance) - Legal/ international regulations - General information (including shipping, insurance and legal terms) - A-Z index. *Class No:* 368(100)(058)

Great Britain

Yearbooks & Directories

[3713]
The Insurance directory and year book (*Post magazine green book*). London, Bouverie Data Services, on behalf of Buckley Press Ltd., 1992. Annual. 3v. (xxx,1958p.). £235 for 3v.; v.1 & 2 £65 each; v.3 £145. ISBN: 090023637x, v.1; 0900236388, v.2; 0900236450, v.3; 0900236469, set. ISSN: 00740691.

First published 1842.

V.1: Insurance companies, Lloyd's syndicates, unit trusts; v.2: Brokers and intermediaries; v.3: Statistics. *Class No:* 368(410)(058)

[3714]
REW, J. *and* STURGE, C. Macmillan directory of Lloyds of London. London, Macmillan Press, 1989. 310p. tables. £70. ISBN: 0333491815.

Claims to be a directory explaining the working of Lloyds without technical jargon. Editorial review of the year, with tables and statistics, is followed by a directory of agencies, Lloyd's brokers, Lloyd's departments, Lloyd's associations, back-up services, and professional bodies. Index. *Class No:* 368(410)(058)

Tables & Data Books

[3715]
ASSOCIATION OF BRITISH INSURERS. Insurance statistics, 1988-1992. London, the Association, 1993. 28p. tables. ISSN: 09503668.

First published for 1981-1985. Annual.

Long-term business (premiums and benefit - individual life insurance - individual pensions - individual annuities - health insurance - occupational pensions and life insurance schemes); General business (worldwide premium income - UK motor insurance - UK non-motor insurance - overseas insurance - marine, aviation and transport insurance - worldwide reinsurance - overall trading results - invisible earnings investments - family spending). Sources of further statistics. *Class No:* 368(410)(083)

Archives

[3716]
COCKERELL, H.A.L. *and* GREEN, E. The British insurance business, 1547-1970: an introduction and guide to historical records in the United Kingdom. London, Heinemann Educational Books, 1976. xiii,142p. illus. (pl.), tables.

The historical scope of business (chapters 1-5) - pt.2 A guide to insurance archives in the United Kingdom, p.76-132. 4 sections: 1. The archives of British assurance companies (brief inventory; business; linkages; records; locations); 2. Marine insurance underwriters: a guide to risk books; 3. Local insurance agents: a guide to research in the UK; 4. Insurance institutions: a guide. Further reading, p.133-4. Analytical index. *Class No:* 368(410)(093.20)

Laws

[3717]
IVAMY, E.R.H. Dictionary of insurance law. London, Butterworth, 1981. [3],166p. £9.95. (*Butterworth's professional dictionary series*.) ISBN: 0406603006.

Includes terms in general use in marine and non-marine insurance which have been legally defined, either in Statute or case law. Excludes general legal terms. When possible includes detailed extracts from relevant legal decisions to support the meaning given. Copiously cross-referenced. *Class No:* 368(410)(094.1)

Social Security

Bibliographies

[3718]
Bibliographie universelle de securité sociale/World bibliography of social security. Genève, Association Internationale de la Sécurité Sociale/International Social Security Association, 1963-. no.1-. 2pa (previously quarterly). SFr.50pa. ISSN: 00061476.

c.3000 references pa. Arranged A-Z by country, subdivided by subjects, followed by international and regional sections, also subdivided by subjects. French, English, Spanish and German indexes refer to the numbered items. *Class No:* 368.4(01)

Dictionaries

Polyglot

[3719]
EUROPEAN PARLIAMENT. Terminologie de la sécurité sociale ... Luxembourg, the Parliament, 1974. [234]p. £2.50.

Replaces the 1967 ed., adding English and Danish terminology.

237 French-base terms, A-Z, with equivalents and indexes in Italian, English, German, Dutch and Danish. *Class No:* 368.4(038)=00

Great Britain

Tables & Data Books

[3720]
Social security statistics. Department of Social Security. 24th ed. London, Stationery Office Books, 1996. 331p. illus. charts. tables. £33. ISBN: 0117624330.

First published for 1972. Annual. Replaces tables previously included in the annual report of what was then the Department of Health and Social Security.

In 8 sections: A. Income related benefits - B. Elderly - C. Unemployment - D. Incapable of work because of sickness - E. Disabled and carers - F. War pensions and industrial injuries - G. Mothers, widows and families - H. Other statistics. Appendices (*e.g.* 3. Useful publications - 4. Description of standard regions). *Class No:* 368.4(410)(083)

Laws

[3721]

O'HIGGINS, P. *and* PARTINGTON, M. **Social security law in Britain and Ireland:** a bibliography. London, Mansell Publishing Ltd., 1986. xxiv, 417p. £65. ISBN: 0720117941.

Includes more than 5500 items, arranged in broad subject categories, drawing together books, pamphlets and periodical articles published up to and including 1983. 4 main sections, all subdivided: 1. History of social security to 1946; 2. Social security since 1946; 3. Social security: International and European influences; 4. Miscellaneous works. Author index. 'The main fault ... lies in its format, and the resulting difficulty in being able to access information quickly'. (*Library review*, Spring, 1987, p.70). *Class No:* 368.4(410)(094.1)

Unemployment Insurance

Great Britain

Official Records

[3722]

GREAT BRITAIN. Public Record Office. **Records of interest to social scientists: unemployment insurance 1911-1939.** London, HMSO, 1975. 268p. £4.50. (*Public Record Office handbooks, no. 16.*) ISBN: 0114400636.

8 chapters, documenting the policy changes of successive governments (Liberal government, 1908/1914 ... National government, 1931/1939). Royal Commission on Unemployment Insurance, 1930-32. Committees dealing with unemployment insurance. 9 appendices (*e.g.* 6. Statistics; 9. Précis of Acts of Parliament dealing with unemployment insurance).

Class No: 368.44(410)(093.2)

37 Education

Education

[3723]
The International encyclopedia of education: research and studies. Huson, T. *and* Postlethwaite, T.N., *eds*. 2nd ed. Oxford, Pergamon Press, 1994. 12v. illus. $3902. ISBN: 0080410464.

Entries cover major areas of education (adult education, counselling, curriculum, economics, administration, policy, educational technology, evaluation, higher education, national systems, pre-school education, education research, special education, teaching, vocational education, and industrial education). Strong US emphasis. Lengthy entries. Last volume contains a classified list of entries, a list of contributors, author and subject indexes, and a list of major educational journals. *Class No:* 370

[3724]
—Encyclopedia of comparative education and national systems of education. Postlethwaite, T.N., *ed*. Oxford, Pergamon Press, 1988. 806p. 200 illus. £85. (*Advances in education.*) ISBN: 0080308538.

1200 entries, thematically organized. Detailed descriptions of the educational systems in 159 countries, and articles outlining major aspects of comparative education. Also based on the above. *Class No:* 370(031)

[3725]
—International encyclopedia of educational technology. Plomp, T. *and* Ely, D.P. 2nd ed. Oxford, Pergamon Press, 1996. 700p. $219.75. ISBN: 0080423078.

Provides state-of-the-art reports covering the whole field of educational technology from a largely international perspective. Contributors, name and subject indexes. *Class No:* 370(031)

Bibliographies of Bibliographies

[3726]
HOUNSELL, D., *and others*. Bibliographic services in education: a survey and analysis of secondary services in the United Kingdom. Lancaster, University of Lancaster, Centre for Educational Research and Development, 1978. vi,66p. diagrs., charts, tables. (*BL R & D report no. 5447.*)

Report to the British Library Research and Develpment Department on Project SI/CT/011.

Pt.1: Survey of recurrent secondary services in education; pt.2: Analysis of selected secondary services in education (detailed examination of *British education index, Research into higher education abstracts, Sociology of education abstracts,* and *Technical education abstracts*. Appendix 1: 'An annotated list of British secondary services covering the literature of education', p.57-62 (33 indexing and abstracting services). *Class No:* 370(009)

[3727]
—BESTERMAN, T. Education - a bibliography of bibliographies. Totowa, N.J., Rowman & Littlefield, 1971. 306p.

Extracted from the author's *A world bibliography of bibliographies* (1965-66. 4v. and index). *Class No:* 370(009)

[3728]
—HOUNSELL, D., *and others*. Bibliographic and information services in education: final report to the British Library R & D Department on Project SI/CT/011. Lancaster, University of Lancaster, Centre for Educational Research and Development, 1980. [6],110.[51]p. (*BL R&D report no. 5610.*)

7 sections: Personnel in education and training - ERIC feasibility study - An inventory of information services - Bibliographic services in education - the *Current index to journals in education* - The experimental information service - Concluding comments. References (2p.). 16 appendices. *Class No:* 370(009)

[3729]
SHANKS, D. Guide to bibliographies on education. Winnipeg, University of Manitoba, Department of Educational Administration and Foundations, Faculty of Education, 1982. 144p. Can$6. (*Monographs in education, 7.*)

947 entries arranged by the L Schedule of the Library of Congress classification scheme. An explicit introduction precedes the entries, which are for publications issued between 1964 and 1980 (continuing T. Besterman's *Education: a bibliography of bibliographies* (1971) which covered to 1964. Author, title and subject indexes. 'Though

....(contd.)
modest in size, this bibliography is a welcome addition to the field, both for its coverage and for its ease of use' (*Choice*, v.20(7), March 1983, p.960). *Class No:* 370(009)

Bibliographies

[3730]
ALTBACH, P.G., *and others*. International bibliography of comparative education. New York, Praeger, 1981. xvii,300p. $52.95; £26. (*Praeger special studies series in comparative education.*)

Includes an extensive essay on comparative education, followed by two bibliographies, a general one on the definition and development of the discipline and topics of major interest within the field, and one on education in various countries of the world, excluding the US. Over 3000 unannotated bibliographical citations of books and journal articles, arranged under broad categories or geographical areas. Cross-referenced subject index. *Class No:* 370(01)

[3731]
ALTBACH, P.G., *and others*. Research on foreign students and international study: an overview and bibliography. New York, Praeger, 1985. 403p. $35.95. (*The Praeger special studies series in comparative education.*) ISBN: 0030719224.

Published in co-operation with the Comparative Education Center at Suny, Buffalo.

Over 2800 entries arranged in 37 topical categories (*e.g.* economic aspects, academic performance, cross-cultural issues), subdivided by form (books, articles, dissertations, theses, government documents, reports). Most entries are annotated and the majority in English, published over the last 20 years. No. index. *Class No:* 370(01)

[3732]
AMBERT, A.N. *and* MELENDEZ, S.E. Bilingual education: a sourcebook. New York, Garland, 1985. 355p. $45. (*Garland reference library of social science, v.197.*) ISBN: 0824009551.

11 chapters: Bilingual education program models - Legal issues - English as a second language - Assessment - Reading - Bilingual special education - Bilingual vocational education - Program evaluation - Parental involvement and participation - Teachers and teacher training - Antibilingualism. Clearly written and readable. US slant. *Class No:* 370(01)

[3733]
BAATZ, C.A. The Philosophy of education: a guide to information sources. Detroit, Mich., Gale Research Co., 1980. 344p. $68. (*Education information guide series, v.6.*) ISBN: 0810314525.

Partly annotated bibliography of recent works from the mid-1960s to the mid-1970s, following a concise and well-written introduction. *Choice*, (v.18(5), January 1981, p.631) reports that annotations are not complete, nor are they uniform, but 'It is a real help to faculty and students alike...' *Class No:* 370(01)

[3734]
BERRY, D.M. A Bibliographic guide to educational research. 2nd ed. Metuchen, N.J., Scarecrow Press, 1980. 215p. £18.75. ISBN: 081081742x.

First published 1976.

772 annotated entries for books, periodicals, research studies, government publications, textbooks, tests, audiovisual materials, etc., arranged by type of publication (*e.g.* Instructional materials), subdivided by subject categories. Designed for students on education courses. Excellent subject index, and also author and title indexes.

A 3rd ed. was issued in 1990 (508p. $49.50. ISBN 0810823438). *Class No:* 370(01)

[3735]
Bibliographical aids and reference tools for the literature of education: a guide to works relating to education held by Southampton University Library. Balakrishnan, M. *and* Chadwick, C., *eds*. 6th ed. Southamptonn, University of Southampton Library, 1986. [4],54,[3]p. £5. ISBN: 0854322736.

The 4th ed. was published in 1978.

340 briefly annotated entries. 12 sections: Guides to the literature of education - Guides to British governmental and official publications - Directories and yearbooks, with a section on entry requirements and courses in adult and higher education - Dictionaries, encyclopaedias and surveys - Indexing and abstracting periodicals - Guides to the research literature (research registers; surveys of research) - Research methods - Statistical methods - Statistics of education: guides and

....(contd.)

sources - Preparing research papers and publications, with a note on copyright - The law of education - Bibliographies - Tests: bibliographies. Name index. A basic user's guide. *Class No:* 370(01)

[3736]

BLAUG, M. **Economics of education:** a selected annotated bibliography. 3rd ed. Oxford, Pergamon Press, 1978. vi, 421p. £33. ISBN: 0080206273.

First published 1966.

2002 briefly annotated entries in 4 main sections: A. Developed countries (1. General surveys ... 4. Educational planning ... 8. The economics of health) - B. Developing countries - C. Bibliographies (items 1880-1937) - D. Items (65) received too late for classification. Includes French and German items. Brief evaluative section introductions. *Class No:* 370(01)

[3737]

British education index. 1954-.v.1-. Leeds, University of Leeds (previously London, Library Association, then British Library Bibliographic Division), 1954-58; 1968-. 3 quarterly issues and annual cumulation. £92pa. ISSN: 00070637.

An index of articles of permanent educational interest, published in a wide range of English-language periodicals. Arranged by author, with full bibliographical citations, then by subject. List of indexed journals. Also available online. Vendors: DIALOG. *Class No:* 370(01)

[3738]

Bulletin of the International Bureau of Education. Geneva, Unesco for the International Bureau of Education, 1926-. no.1-. Quarterly. SFr.65pa. ISSN: 10141715.

Formerly *International Bureau of Education bulletin*, later *Education documentation and information: bulletin of the International Bureau of Education*. Now incorporates the bulletin, and *Awareness list* and *Cooperative education abstracting service*.

Each issue is devoted to a particular theme. Thus, no.250, 63rd year, 1st quarter 1989: 'Computers in education: the shape of things to come; (p.7-88) including an annotated bibliography of 302 items in 5 sections (General reference - National policies - Training teachers and the development of human resources - Informatics as a subject for education and culture - Computerized ways and means for education). Index of authors and editors. *Class No:* 370(01)

[3739]

CLARKE, P.B. **Finding out in education:** a guide to sources of information. 2nd rev. ed. Harlow, Essex, Longman, 1993. ix,217p. £95. ISBN: 0582217970.

Annotated entries, arranged in form rather than subject sections. 29 sections in all: 1. Introduction ... 3. Guides to libraries ... 7-17 General reference sources - 18-20. Bibliographies - 21-24. Periodicals - 25-26. Educational research - 27. Conclusion - 28. Title index (p.194-211) - 29. Subject index (p.212-217). No author index. Author was formerly librarian at Jordanhill College of Education, Glasgow. *Class No:* 370(01)

[3740]

Contents pages in education. Abingdon, Oxon, Carfax, 1986-. Monthly. £276. $569 pa. ISSN: 02659220.

Covers over 700 international journals; *c.* 2000 contents pages in each annual volume. *Class No:* 370(01)

[3741]

Core list of books & journals in education. O'Brien, P. *and* Fabiano, E., *eds.* Phoenix, Ariz., Oryx, 1990. 125p. $39.95. ISBN: 0597745590.

Mainly limited to English-language imprint material. Entries have detailed annotations. 3 indexes: author/title; title; subject. *Class No:* 370(01)

[3742]

Education index. New York, H.W. Wilson, 1932-. v.1-. Monthly (except July and August), cumulates quarterly and annually (July-June). Service basis. ISSN: 00131385.

An index to *c.*350 selected educational journals, proceedings and yearbooks. A-Z order of subjects and authors, list of book reviews appended. Journals covered are predominantly US. Also available online. (Vendors: Wilsonline (EDI)) and on CD-ROM. *Class No:* 370(01)

[3743]

—Education literature, 1907-1932. Facsimile ed. New York, Garland, 1979. 12v. $40. ISBN: 0824037111.

Usefully precedes *Education index*. Over 44,000 references; separate volume of cumulated proper name and subject index. *Class No:* 370(01)

[3744]

FOSKETT, D.J. 'The Literature and sources of education'. In *Use of social sciences literature,* ed. by N. Roberts (1977), p.149-75.

Succinctly covers many aspects of educational literature and organizations. *Class No:* 370(01)

[3745]

HUMBY, M. **A Guide to the literature of education.** London, University of London, Institute of Education Library, 1975. vi, 142p. £1. (*Education libraries bulletin, Supplement 1. 3rd ed.*) ISBN: 0900008202.

Based on *A guide to the literature of education*, by S K. Kimmance (2nd ed., 1961), first published 1958.

Aims 'not to provide a comprehensive bibliography, but to give selected examples of the various types of printed material to be found in an education library'(*Introduction*). 572 concisely and well-annotated entries, arranged in 15 sections: 2. Guides to the literature of education - 3. Bibliographies of education - 4. Educational research - 5. Encyclopedias of education - 6. Dictionaries of education - 7. Educational directories and yearbooks - 8. Educational organizations - 9. Educational periodicals (including indexing and abstracting services) - 10. Biographies in education - 11. Official publications concerning education - 12. Education statistics - 13. School textbooks and other teaching aids - 14. Classification schemes for education - 15. Education libraries and information services. Index of authors and titles. *Class No:* 370(01)

[3746]

MONROE, W.S. **Bibliography of education.** New York, Appleton, 1897. (Reprinted Detroit, Mich., Gale, 1968). 228p. $35. ISBN: 0810333376.

A bibliography of 3200 books and pamphlets; restricted to books in English. According to the 1968 introduction by Dr. Cordasco, it 'continues to serve as a major initial source in education bibliography. *Class No:* 370(01)

[3747]

RAMSAY, P.G., *and others.* **Multicultural education:** a source book. New York, Garland, 1989. 177p. .$25. ISBN: 0824085582.

Theoretical, research and practical information related to the implementation of a multicultural education programme in pre-school and elementary school classrooms. Omits bilingual education. Each chapter reviews major issues, historical changes, and related research in its subject area and includes an annotated list of 30-50 titles. Includes literature published since 1976. US slant. ' ... a fine sourcebook ... '(*Choice* v.26(11/12), July-August 1989, p.1818). *Class No:* 370(01)

[3748]

WOODBURY, M. **A Guide to sources of educational information.** 2nd ed., completely rev. Arlington, VA., Information Resources Press, 1982. xii,430p. facsims. £36.80. ISBN: 0878150412.

First published 1976.

636 annotated entries. 5 main parts (19 chapters): 1. Effective research - 2. Printed research tools (dictionaries, encyclopedias, thesauri; directories; yearbooks; monograph series, periodicals, news letters; bibliographies and review sources; statistical sources; abstracting, indexing and current awareness services) - 3. Special subjects (*e.g.* special education; tests and assessment instruments) - 4. Non-print sources (*e.g.* directory and institutional information sources; computerized retrieval sources) - 5. Follow-through (guides to routers). Well annotated. Analytical index. US-slant. 'The best guide to education's reference literature' (*Wilson library bulletin*, February, 1986, p.60). *Class No:* 370(01)

[3749]

—O'BRIEN, N.P. **Education:** a guide to reference and information sources. 2nd ed. Englewood, Col., Libraries Unlimited, 2000. $40. (*Reference sources in the social sciences, series 2.*.)

Describes *c.*750 major sources of educational information from the elementary level to higher education. Arranged in 20 broad subject-orientated chapters, subdivided by type of material. Includes online databases, educational research centres and other organizations, and periodical titles, as well as printed sources. Annotations are evaluative and descriptive. Emphasis is on US works published since 1980. *Class No:* 370(01)

Encyclopaedias

[3750]

BAKER, C. *and* JONES, S.P., *eds.* **Encyclopedia of bilingualism and bilingual education.** Clevedon, Multilingual Matters, 1999. 766p., illus.,graphs,maps,diagrams. £99. $169.95. ISBN: 1853593621.

Divided into 3 sections: Individual bilingualism, Bilingualism in society, Bilingual education. Includes a bibliography and glossary. *Class No:* 370(031)

[3751]
BLISHEN, E., *ed*. Blond's encyclopedia of education. London, Blond Educational, 1969. xi,882p.
'A-level' ... 'Zoning'; *c*.2150 entries, with numerous cross-references; *c*.150 contributors. Some articles carry short bibliographies (*e.g.* 'South Africa, Education in': 7 items). 6½ columns on 'School leaving age'. Includes biographies. Deals primarily with British educational practice, plus brief notes on other countries. 15 appendices (14. Educational journals - 15. Selected museums and art galleries). *Class No:* 370(031)

[3752]
CHAMBLISS, J.J., *ed*. Philosophy of education: an encyclopedia. New York; London, Garland, 1996. xvi,720p. $130. ISBN: 081531177x. *Class No:* 370(031)

[3753]
DEJNOZKA, E.L. *and* KAPEL, D.E. American educators' encyclopedia. Revised ed. Westport, CT., Greenwood Press, 1991. xvii,597p. illus. $95. ISBN: 0313252696.
First published 1982.
Over 2000 articles arranged A-Z by subject. Covers all aspects of education and includes names as well as topics and terms most frequently used in elementary, secondary and higher education. Suggestions for further study follow most entries. Cross-references. Topical index. 27 appendices provide variety of tabular information. *Class No:* 370(031)

[3754]
The Encyclopedia of education. Deighton, L.C., *ed*. New York, Macmillan and the Free Press, 1971. 10v. (*c*.6000p.). $199 the set. ISBN: 0028953002.
About 1000 contributors. In more than 1000 articles it offers a view of institutions and people, of the processes and products, found in educational practice. 'The articles deal with the history, theory, research, and philosophy, as well as the structure and fabric of education' (*Preface*). Well documented ('Test reliability': v.9, p.143-53, with nearly a column of bibliography). The article on education bibliographies gives an 'excellent brief overview of bibliographies, indexes, abstracts, encyclopedias, directories, government publications' (*Wilson library bulletin*, v.46(4), December 1971, p.365-6). V.10 includes 'Guide to articles', p.117-228, and an index with *c*.50,000 entries. Strongly US-slanted. *Class No:* 370(031)

German

[3755]
Lexikon der Pädagogik. Willmann-Institut, München-Wein. Leitung der Herausgabe: Heinrich Rombach. Neue Ausg. Freiburg in Briesgau, Herder, [1970] -1971. 4v. (*c.* 2000 p.).
First published 1930-32; 2nd ed. 1960-64.
More international in scope than previous editions, although the viewpoint is Roman Catholic. Most articles carry bibliographies (*e.g.* 'Kuba': 21/3 columns; 11½ lines of bibliography). 'It is not an exhaustive dictionary of pedagogics, but contains selected entries in which foreign educational thinking figures as prominently as German. It has a triple reference system: cross-references to key terms selected as headings; cross-references between words in the entry texts and their headings; and cross-references at the end of the entries to headings dealing with a related subject' (*Bibliography, documentation, terminology*, v.13, No.1. January 1973, p. 39). General index of persons and subjects appended to v.4. A standard work. *Class No:* 370(031)=30

Handbooks & Manuals

[3756]
A Parents' guide to education. London, Fontana/Collins, 1986. 352p. £3.95. ISBN: 0006368069.
First published by Hodder & Stoughton in 1983.
In 6 chapters: 1. The educational system - 2. The pre-school child - 3. The primary child - 4. The secondary pupil - 5. Beyond sixteen - 6. Children with problems. Address and book list, p.335-340. Index, p.341-352. *Class No:* 370(035)

Dictionaries

English

[3757]
BARROW, R. *and* MILBURN, G. A Critical dictionary of educational concepts: an appraisal of selected ideas and issues in educational theory and practice. 2nd ed. New York, St. Martin's Press; Hemel Hempstead, Herts, Harvester Wheatsheaf Publications, 1990. 350p. $43.95. £50. ISBN: 0807730580, US; 0745009190, UK.
Essay length entries analysing such major subjects as assessment, culture, emotional development, teacher effectiveness, development

....(contd.)
theory, knowledge, learning, curriculum, etc. References are attached to the longer entries. Cross references. Bibliography, A-Z by author. *Class No:* 370(038)=20

[3758]
COLLINS, K.T., *and others*. Key words in education. London, Longmans, 1973. [iii],240p.
Arranged A-Z (Abacus-Aberdare Report (1881) ... Youth service (references to 2 reports). Includes brief biographies. Cross-references. Appendix 1: The educational system in Great Britain - 2: Important Education Acts in England and Wales - 3: Important Education Reports since 1926 - 4: Education journals. *Class No:* 370(038)=20

[3759]
DEJNOZKA, E.L. Educational administration glossary. Westport, CT., Greenwood Press, 1983. xii,247p. $50.95. ISBN: 0313233012.
c.1400 terms in educational administration are defined. The glossary is supplemented by 15 appendices, including the American Association of School Administrators' code of ethics; a list of major school administration journals; the names of institutional members of the University Council for Educational Administration; and a listing of all nationally accredited school administration programs. *Class No:* 370(038)=20

[3760]
GORDON, P. *and* LAWTON, D. A Guide to English educational terms. London, Batsford Academic and Educational Ltd., 1984. xvii, 220p. £14.95. ISBN: 0713443758.
Aim is to provide concise definitions of those terms most likely to be encountered in current discussion on educational matters. Many entries have short well-chosen bibliographies for further reading. 'An outline of the educational system in England and Wales: 2½p,;' 'Landmarks in the development of English education since 1800': 6p.; 'Education acronyms': 5½p.; 'Ministers of education': 1¾p. '... this really is a good job, sensible and helpfully done' (*The Times educational supplement*, 18 May 1984, p.32). *Class No:* 370(038)=20

[3761]
HILLS, P.J., *ed*. A Dictionary of education. London, Routledge & Kegan Paul,1982. 5,284p. £15. (*Routledge education books*.) ISBN: 0710008716.
A 'conceptual dictionary' for students, teachers, administrators and the general reader. 2 parts: Part 1: Areas of education (brief articles on topics such as 'educational research', 'curriculum development', with references for further reading. Part 2 is the dictionary proper, with terms fully explained. *Class No:* 370(038)=20

[3762]
LAWTON, D. *and* GORDON, P. Dictionary of education. 2nd ed. London, Hodder & Stoughton, 1996. 256p. £15.99. ISBN: 0340648155.
A guide to the language of education. In 3 sections: 1. Discussion of some key concepts - 2. The dictionary: an alphabetical list of definitions - 3. Acronyms and abbreviations. The dictionary incorporates recent changes, has short definitions from one or two lines to half a page (nearly a page for 'Local government acts'), and has cross-references. *Class No:* 370(038)=20

[3763]
PAGE, G.T. *and* THOMAS, J.B. International dictionary of education. London, Kogan Page, 1977. 381p. diagrs. £14.95. ISBN: 0850383013.
Over 10,000 entries, ranging from the fine points of curriculum development and educational research to the colloquialisms of the classroom and lecture theatre (*Introduction*). Brief definitions (maximum: *c*.150 words); numbered meanings. Very concise bibliographies; entries for international organizations and major national institutions and associations. Appendix of abbreviations, and of American honor societies, professional fraternities and sororities. British and US emphasis. *Class No:* 370(038)=20

[3764]
ROWNTREE, D. A Dictionary of education. London, Harper & Row; Totowa, N.J., Barnes & Noble, 1981. viii, 354p. £15.95 $22.50. ISBN: 0063181576 UK; 0389202630 US.
Over 3000 entries providing a guide to the intricacies of educational jargon in the US and UK. Includes brief entries on educationalists and descriptions of educational reports. Definitions are short, *c*.1-10 lines, and indicate US or UK usage. Cross-references. *Class No:* 370(038)=20

Theses

Bibliographies

[3765]

British education theses index (BETI), 1950-1980. Johnston, J.B.V. *and* Marder, J.V., *eds*. Leicester, Librarians of Institutes and Schools of Education, 1980. Microfiche 48X, with a full-size hard-copy introduction. £33. A thesaurus was published in 1986 (150p. £13.50. ISBN 090192217x). *Class No:* 370(043)(01)

[3766]

—British education theses index. Thesaurus. Johnston, J.B.V. *and* Marder, J.V., *eds*. Leicester, Librarians of Institutes and Schools of Education, 1986. 150p. £13.50. ISBN: 090192217x.

Developed from the ERIC thesaurus for use with *British education theses index. Class No:* 370(043)(01)

Reviews & Abstracts

[3767]

Current index to journals in education. Phoenix, AZ., Oryx Press (previously New York, CCM Information Sciences Inc.), 1969-. v.1,no,.1-. Monthly. $235pa.; semi-annual indexes, $198. ISSN: 00113565.

Published in co-operation with the Educational Resources Information Center (ERIC) of the US Office of Education.

Covers *c.*740 major education and education-related journals. About 2000 articles are indexed monthly. 4 sections: main entry section (using ERIC descriptors), with 3 indexes - subject, author and journal content. Has references to textbooks in each issue. More comprehensive, by far, than *British education index* and *Education index. Current index to journals in education: cumulated author index, 1969-1984* was published by Oryx Press in 1985 (2218p. $100. ISBN 0897742354). The on-line database ERIC (Washington, Educational Resources Information Center, 1966-), covering both periodical articles and reports, is updated monthly. *Class No:* 370(048)

[3768]

Educational administration abstracts. Beverley Hills, CA., Sage Publications, in cooperation with the University Council for Educational Administration, 1966-. Quarterly. $175; £134pa. ISSN: 00131601.

Previously *Educational abstracts*.

*c.*250 abstracts each issue of articles from more than 140 professional journals. Broad topical arrangement (*e.g.* personnel, curriculum, school-community relations, supervision, minority group relations, professional education, etc.). Cross-references. Author index. *Class No:* 370(048)

[3769]

FRANCIS. 520. Bulletin signalétique. 520. Sciences de l'éducation. Paris, Centre National de la Recherche Scientifique: Centre de Documentation Sciences Humaines, 1947-. v.1-.no.1-. Quarterly. F.520pa. ISSN: 0223341x.

Previously *Bulletin analytique. Philosophie* (v.1-9, 1947-55, *Bulletin signalétique. 19: Philosophie, Sciences humaines* (1956-60), and *Bulletin signalétique. 20: Psychologie. Pédagogie* (in 19-24: *Sciences humaines. Philosophie* (1961-)), later as *Bulletin signalétique. 520. Sciences de l'éducation.*

*c.*4000 indicative abstracts and references a year. Classes: 01. History and philosophy of education - 02. Educational policy - 03. Planning and economics of education - 04. Educational organization - 05. Life-long education and employment - 06. Educational research - 07. Teaching methods - 08. Teaching aids - 09. Educational personnel - 10. School life - 11. School work, docimology, guidance - 12. Maladjustment - 13. Education and psychology - 14. Sociology of education. Cumulative list of journals searched. Indexes of concepts and authors. Available online (Telesystem, Questel) and CD-ROM. e *Class No:* 370(048)

[3770]

Multicultural education abstracts. Abingdon, Oxon, Carfax Publishing, 1982-. v.1,no.1-. Quarterly. ISSN: 02609770.

A current awareness service drawing on a wide range of international sources. Non-evaluative abstracts. *c.*400 abstracts pa, mainly of journal articles but includes some books. *c.*750 journal titles are scanned. Author and subject indexes to each issue, cumulated annually. *Class No:* 370(048)

[3771]

Sociology of education abstracts. Abingdon, Oxon, Carfax Publishing Co., (previously Liverpool, Information for Education Ltd.), 1965-. v.1,no.1-. Quarterly. ISSN: 00380415.

*c.*600 indicative and informative abstracts pa, arranged under authors, A-Z. Includes abstracts of books and journal articles, *c.*400 journal titles being scanned. Author and subject indexes, cumulating annually. *Class No:* 370(048)

Periodicals & Progress Reports

Bibliographies

[3772]

COLLINS, M.E., *comp*. **Education journals and serials:** an analytical guide. Westport, CT., Greenwood Press, 1988. 355p. $49.95. (*Annotated bibliography serials: a subject approach series, no.12.*) ISBN: 0313245142.

An aid to selection of serials for library collections. Includes serials published abroad in English, and interdisciplinary journals with substantial coverage of education. Entries are numbered and grouped under broad headings. Annotations are in 2 parts: general topical areas covered and description of contents; they include starting date, frequency, price, publishers' address, circulation, and former titles. Features noted included index, book reviews, adverts, major indexes and databases that index the journal, and target audience. 'Well-organized, thoroughly indexed, and easy to read...' (*Choice*, v.26(1), September 1988, p.76). *Class No:* 370(05)(01)

Yearbooks & Directories

[3773]

Directory of educational documentation and information services. Unesco. International Bureau of Education, *ed*. 5th ed. Paris, Unesco, 1988. x,114p. F.35. ISBN: 9230025186.

A reference book for those engaged in the field. Arranged in 5 sections: National services - Regional services - International services - Other member institutions - Inventory of international databases on education. *Class No:* 370(058)

[3774]

World year book of education, 2000. London, Kogan Page, 1999. 288p. £45. ISBN: 0749425040.

First published 1932. From 1965 to 1974 issued by Evans Bros. Ltd.

Each issue is devoted to a special theme (1987 'Vocational education'; 1988 'Education for the new technologies'; 1989 'Health education'; 1994 'The gender gap in higher education') and reviews the nature and practice of health education in over 15 countries. *Class No:* 370(058)

Histories

Bibliographies

[3775]

HIGSON, C.W.J., *ed*. **Sources for the history of education:** a list of material (including school books) contained in libraries of the Institutes and Schools of Education, together with works from the libraries of the Universities of Nottingham and Reading. London, Library Association, 1967. x,196p. Supplement. (for 1965-74). 1976. x,221p.

Sections A-D cover books, textbooks and children's books published up to 1870, by periods; E: Government publications up to and including 1918. About 5500, British-slanted items in all. Detailed, analytical subject index; author index to government publications. The *Supplement* lists *c.*4000 items, with 22 locations, for sections F-J (covering the same periods as in the parent work). Subject index; author index to government publications. *Class No:* 370(091)(01)

[3776]

McCARTHY, J.M. An International list of articles on the history of education published in non-educational serials, 1965-1974. New York, Garland, 1977. xxv,228p. $33. ISBN: 0824099095.

2817 references in 8 sections: 1. Ancient world and general - 2. Europe (p.5-93: General; countries, A-Z) - 3. Mid-East (General. Israel, Lebanon. Syria. Turkey) - 4. Africa (General; countries, A-Z) - 5. Asia - 6. Oceania - 7. South America - 8. North America (US: p. 149-201). Cross references. Author index. Complementary to Higson, in covering only periodical articles. *Class No:* 370(091)(01)

Worldwide

Encyclopaedias

[3777]

World education encyclopedia. Kurian, G.T., *ed*. New York, Facts on File, 1988. 3v. (1720p). illus., tables, charts, maps. $175. ISBN: 0871967480.

181 countries are divided into major, middle or minor according to the amount of information available, and arranged A-Z in each category. V.1. Major countries. Algeria - Hungary; V.2. Major countries; Iceland - Sri Lanka; V.3. Major countries; Sudan - Zambia. Middle countries. Minor countries. So far as information is available, the essays for each country include recent history, background, legal foundations, an overview, pre-primary and primary schooling, secondary education, higher education, non-formal education, the teaching profession, a glossary, and a brief bibliography. The aim is to compare and analyse the various education systems, but not to evaluate, criticize or judge them. 67 contributors. Appendices (I.

....(contd.)

Global education rankings; II. Global and regional bibliography). Index, p. 1685-1720. 'The strength of the encyclopedia lies in the consistency with which it presents its data'(*Reference books bulletin*, 1 November 1989, p. 722-3). *Class No:* 370(100)(031)

Handbooks & Manuals

[3778]

FINDLAY, B. **International education handbook.** London, Kogan Page, 1997. 352p. £18.95. ISBN: 0749419555.
Class No: 370(100)(035)

[3779]

International handbook of educational systems. Chichester, Wiley, 1983-84. 3v. (738+906+854p.). illus. v.1: £35.95. v.2: £38. v.3. £38.90. ISBN: 0471900788, v.1; 0471900796, v.2; 0471902144, v.3.
V.1: *Europe and Canada,* ed. by B. Homes; v.2: *Africa and the Middle East,* by J. Cameron and P. Hirst; v.3: *Asia; Australia and Latin America,* by Robert Cowen and Martin McClean. Contain a wealth of valuable information concerning the education systems of 60 countries, including historical developments, social structure, economics. Systematically arranged so that comparisons between countries can be made. Statistical data and information on relevant legislation is included when available. *Class No:* 370(100)(035)

Developing Countries

Bibliographies

[3780]

CLAYTON, D. *and* JAMESON, E., *comps.* **Bibliography of policy related education documents in selected countries in Africa, Asia, the Caribbean and the Pacific.** 2nd ed. London, Overseas Development Administration, 1988. 2v.
V.1 Africa and the Caribbean; v.2. Asia and the Pacific. Arranged by countries, A-Z, under each region. Publications, mainly of the countries themselves, are arranged in 5 sections for each country: 1 Development plans - 2. Statistics, annual reports, yearbooks and directories - 3. Legislation and policy statements - 4. Reports of committees and commissions - 5. General education documents. Where applicable, a further section covering curriculum and syllabuses is added. A-Z by author in each section. List of locations at end of each volume. No index. *Class No:* 370(4/9-77)(01)

Europe

Histories

[3781]

BOWEN, J. **A History of Western education.** London, Methuen, 1972-81. 3v. (416p.;xxii,504p.;630p.). illus., maps. v.1. £35; v.2. £27.50; v.3. £32.50. ISBN: 0416161103, v.1; 0416161200, v.2; 0416161308, v.3.
V.1: *The ancient world: Orient and Mediterranean, 2000B.C.-A.D.1054* (1972); v.2: *Civilization of Europe, sixth to sixteenth century* (1975); v.3: *The modern West: Europe and the New World* (1981). A comprehensive account of theories, educational institutions and practices. Include bibliographies and analytical indexes in each volume. Scholarly, with many quotations from primary sources.
Class No: 370(4)(091)

Great Britain

Bibliographies

[3782]

GREAT BRITAIN. HM Stationery Office. **Government publications. Sectional list 2. Revised May 1988: Education and science.** London, HMSO, 1988. 28p. *Gratis.*
Part 1: General, adult and further education ... curriculum and examinations - health and physical education - higher education - middle schools - primary education - safety - school meals ... secondary education - special education - statistics - teachers - youth - series lists - Assessment of Performance Unit. Pt.2: University Grants Committee. Pt.3: Legislation. Title index (excluding legislation). *Class No:* 370(410)(01)

Yearbooks & Directories

[3783]

The Education authorities directory and annual, 1991. 90th year of publication. Merstham, Redhill, School Government Publishing Ltd., 1993. lxxx,1290p. £58. ISBN: 0900640316. ISSN: 00709131.
First published 1909.
Various sections: Government departments, public offices, examination organizations - Local education authorities - Secondary and middle schools (p.156-559) - Teachers' centres - Further education

....(contd.)

- Polytechnics and Scottish central institutions - Institutes/colleges of higher education (teacher training) - Universities - Special schools and homes for the handicapped - Special community homes - Directors of social services - Educational psychological service - Careers centres - Public library authorities - Organizations concerned with education (p.1198-1249) - Education publishers and equipment suppliers - Commonwealth education departments and universities (p.1264-1280). Preliminary pages include: Index to local education authorities and secondary schools; General index (p.xi-xxvi); Index to place names; Index to advertisers; Buyer's guide; 'Coming events in education, 1991'. *Class No:* 370(410)(058)

[3784]

The Education factbook: an A-Z guide to education and training in Britain. Pates, A., *and others.* London, Macmillan Press, 1983 (Reprinted 1986). ix, 268p. £14.95. (*Macmillan reference books.*) ISBN: 0333274695.
Main body of the work is a list of terms, arranged A-Z, and including names, initials, phrases, etc., each briefly described and explained. Length of entries varies from 2-3 lines to 2 columns. Address list, p.240-264. Book list, A-Z by author, p.266-268.
Class No: 370(410)(058)

[3785]

Education year book. Harlow, Essex, Longman Group.
First published 1939. Previously *Education committees year book.*
A detailed compendium in 29 sections, including: 3. County Council Education departments - 4. London district education departments - 8. Independent secondary schools - 11. Higher, further and vocational education - 17. Employment and careers - 18. Teachers' and other educational organizations - 24. Overseas education - 26. Broadcasting, audio-visual education and computers in education - 29. Buyers' guide. Index and index to advertisers. *Class No:* 370(410)(058)

Government Publications

[3786]

ARGLES, M. *and* VAUGHAN, J.E. **British government publications concerning education during the 20th century.** 4th ed. Lancaster, History of Education Society, 1982. iii,60p. £4.50. (*Guides to sources in the history of education, no.7.*) ISBN: 0905090144.
First published 1963.
Running commentary and literature in closely divided sections. A. Short bibliography and book list of helpful works - B. Introduction - C. The central authorities: a historical note - D. United Kingdom Departments of State, etc., which issue or have issued documents relating to education - E. Official literature of education - F. Two special periods, 1900-1946; 1969-1980 - G. Reports: a list of popular (chairmen's) names and official titles - H. Short selective index of bodies and topics mentioned in the text and not listed under 'contents'. *Class No:* 370(410)(061.1)

[3787]

—ARGLES, M. British government publications in education during the 19th century. Lancaster, History of Education Society, 1971. 20p. £0.25. ISBN: 0950106437. *Class No:* 370(410)(061.1)

Tables & Data Books

[3788]

Education and training statistics for the United Kingdom. 1997 ed. London, Stationery Office Books, 1998. 112p. chiefly tables. £12. ISBN: 0112710220. *Class No:* 370(410)(083)

[3789]

Education statistics for the United Kingdom. Department of Education and Science. Welsh Office, Scottish Education Department, Department of Education for Northern Ireland, University Grants Committee. London, Stationery Office Books. tables.
First published 1967. Annual.
Contents: Population - Number of institutions - Finance - Teaching staff - Schools - Curriculum - Post-compulsory participation rates - Further and higher education - Qualifications and destinations.
Class No: 370(410)(083)

Scotland

Bibliographies

[3790]

CRAIGIE, J., *ed.* **A Bibliography of Scottish education before 1872.** New ed. Scottish Council for Research in Education, 1984. 251p. £7.50. (*Publications of the Scottish Council for Research in Education, 60.*) ISBN: 0901116599.
First publisheed 1970, by University of London Press.
Draws on 24 library collections. 4 parts: 1. Works of general reference. General histories of Scottish education - 2. Acts of the

....*(contd.)*
Parliament of Scotland ... 3. Administration. Biographies. Curriculum ... Historical studies. Local history ... 4. The Scottish universities. Indexes of writers, subject, places. *Class No:* 370(411)(01)

[3791]
—CRAIGIE, J., *ed.* A Bibliography of Scottish education, 1872-1972. New ed. Scottish Council for Research in Education, 1984. 279p. £7.50. ISBN: 0901116629.
First published in 1974 by University of London Press.
Continues the above. *Class No:* 370(411)(01)

England & Wales

Histories

[3792]
ARMYTAGE, W.H.G. Four hundred years of English education. Cambridge, Cambridge University Press,1964. viii,353p.
Covers the period 1563-1963 in 12 chapters. Chapter notes, p.270-324; references to general sources used, p.vii-viii. Analytical index. Author was Professor of Education, University of Sheffield. *Class No:* 370(42)(091)

[3793]
LOWNDES, G.A.N. The Silent social revolution: an account of the expansion of public education in England and Wales, 1895-1935. London, Oxford University Press, 1937. xii,274p.
A standard work, dealing mainly with the development of elementary and secondary education during the period covered, but with a chapter on technical and further education. Extensive chapter bibliographies. *Class No:* 370(42)(091)

[3794]
—BIRCHENOUGH, C. History of elementary education in England and Wales, from 1800 to the present day. 3rd ed. London, University Tutorial Press, 1938. xxi,572p.
The most comprehensive history of elementary education for that period. *Class No:* 370(42)(091)

[3795]
—CUNNINGHAM, P. Local history of education in England and Wales: a bibliography. Leeds, University of Leeds, Museum of the History of Education, 1971 (Reprinted in paperback, 1976). 190p. £2.50. ISBN: 0904427056.
*c.*3000 entries, with very occasional explanatory notes), arranged by counties and towns. Appended sections on the Isle of Man and the Channel Islands. *Class No:* 370(42)(091)

[3796]
MACLURE, J.S. Educational documents in England and Wales, 1816 to the present day. 5th ed. London, Methuen, 1986. x,445p. £9.95. ISBN: 0416394701.
First published 1965.
Aim is to bring together selected extracts from the leading official documents which plot the development of a public system of education in England and Wales since 1816. A lengthy introduction precedes 65 excerpts arranged chronologically, with bibliographical details. Index of members of committees, assessors, etc. Short general index, p.437-439. '... an essential companion for those who wish to learn from primary sources of the most crucial developments in public education ... since the early years of the nineteenth century'. (*British journal of educational studies,* February 1987, p.89). *Class No:* 370(42)(091)

Biographies

[3797]
CHRISTOPHERS, A. An Index to nineteenth-century British educational biography. London, University of London, Institute of Education, 1965. xii,88p. £1.05. (*Education libraries bulletin. Supplement 10.*) ISBN: 0900008067.
Sections: 1. Collected biography (19 items) - 2. Individual biography (450 numbered items, under biographees, A-Z). Subject index. Dates and very brief notes on careers of biographees are given in section 2. Includes many analyticals (*e.g.* references to entries in DNB). No annotations. *Class No:* 370(42)(092)

Germany

[3798]
RUST, V.D. Education in East and West Germany: a bibliography. New York, Garland, 1984. 227p. $35. (*Reference library of social science, 202.*) ISBN: 0824090500.
Long introductory essay on the history of German education precedes a bibliography of over 1100 English-language books and periodical articles on all phases of German education, mainly regarding the period since 1945. Arrangement is in 11 general subject categories, and most items have annotations. Journal, name and subject indexes. '... a valuable annotated bibliography ...' (*Choice,* v.22(8), April 1985, p.1147). *Class No:* 370(430)

China

[3799]
FRASER, S.E. *and* HSU, K.-L. Chinese education and society: a bibliographic guide: the cultural revolution and its aftermath. White Plains, N.Y., International Arts and Sciences, 1972. (available Books Demand Unlimited). 204p. $53.50. ISBN: 0317102338.
14 sections, sections 4-14 concerned specifically with education. Entries usually annotated. Many of the items listed were originally written in Chinese; full references to translations. Favourably reviewed. *Class No:* 370(510)

Japan

[3800]
BEAUCHAMP, E.R. *and* RUBINGER, R. Education in Japan: a source book. New York, Garland, 1989. 300p. $42. (*Reference books in international education, 5. Garland reference liibrary of social science, 329.*) ISBN: 082408635x.
A successor to Herbert Passin's *Japanese education: a bibliography of materials in the English language.* (1971).
About 2000 entries arranged in 14 chapters, each preceded by an essay on the major themes and developments. Many entries are annotated. Historical emphasis is from the Tokugaswa period (1603-1867) forward, and a third are pre-1970. The main Western and Japanese scholars are cited. Subject index. 'Essential for graduate collection in international education' (*Choice,* v.27(1), September 1989, p.76). *Class No:* 370(52)

[3801]
TEICHLER, U. *and* VOSS, F. Bibliography of Japanese education/ Bibliographie zum japanischen Erziehungswesen: postwar publications in Western languages. Munich, K.G. Saur, 1974. 294p.
Over 2000 entries, under 25 subject heads. Items are mostly in English, followed by German and French. *Class No:* 370(52)

India

[3802]
GREAVES, M.A. Education in British India, 1698-1947: a bibliography and guide to the sources of information in London. London, University of London, Institute of Education, 1967. xx,182p. maps. £1.50. (*Education libraries bulletin. Supplement 13.*)
1379 unannotated items. Books, pamphlets, reports and theses are listed under authors, A-Z; index to those items with specific subjects; select list of journals; manuscripts and records. A select list of reference works used in compiling the bibliography precedes. Continued in part by S.R. Mittal's *Bibliography of Indian education, 1947-1966,* a thesis accepted for the LA diploma. *Class No:* 370(540)

Islamic World

Bibliographies

[3803]
PANTELIDIS, V.S. Arab education, 1956-78: a bibliography. London, Mansell Publishing Co., 1982. xviii,552p. £45; $96. ISBN: 0720115884.
Lists over 5600 sources of information on education in the 21 countries of the Arab world. Arrangement is by country, then subject (Accountability - Administration and supervision - Adult education ... Bibliographies ... Women's education - Writing), not in A-Z order. Items are numbered and cover books, journal articles, dissertations, conference and working papers, government and non-government reports, information and other pamphlets, photographs and maps in books and articles. English-language materials only. Generous cross references. Items are *very* briefly annotated. Author, title and subject index (p.481-552) related to item numbers. 'It will become a standard in its field' (*Choice,* v.20(3), November 1982, p.409). *Class No:* 370(5.297)(01)

Africa

Bibliographies

[3804]
COUCH, M., *comp.* Education in Africa: a select bibliography. London, University of London, Institute of Education, 1962-65. 2v. (121p. xii, 116p.). v.1. £0.65; v.2. £1.05. (*Education libraries bulletin, supplement 5,9.*) ISBN: 0900008008 v.1; 0800008016 v.2.
1. *British and former British territories in Africa.*1962. x, 121p. 2. *French-speaking territories (former French and Belgian colonies); Portuguese and Spanish territories; Ethiopia and Eritrea; Liberia; and general African references, 1962-64.* 1965, xii, 116p. Pt 1 (*c.* 1,300 entries) excludes the Republic of South Africa. It is selected from the catalogue of the Library of the Department of Education in Tropical Areas of the Univ. of London, Institute of Education, and contains material listed to the end of 1961. General; then countries A-Z, with subdivisions (*eg.* Nyasaland: General - Primary - Secondary - Higher -

....*(contd.)*
Adult - Women and girls) and final chronological order. Pt.2. is similarly arranged; items starred were not available for checking by the compiler. Each pt. has a list of more than 200 periodicals cited.
Class No: 370(6)(01)

Latin America

Bibliographies

[3805]
LAUERHASS, L. *and* HAUGSE, V.L. Education in Latin America: a bibliography. Boston, Mass., G.K. Hall; Los Angeles, CA., UCLA Latin American Centre Publications, University of California, 1981. xviii,431p. $63.50. (*UCLA Latin American Center Publications, Reference series, v.9.*) ISBN: 0816185166.
Designed as an introductory reference volume for research on education in Latin America in all its formal and nonformal aspects from its beginning in pre-Columbian times to the mid-1970s. 4 main sections: Latin America: general - Middle America and the Caribbean (subdivided by countries) - Spanish South America (subdivided by countries) - Brazil. 9866 numbered, unannotated entries with, for each division, sections on serials and reference sources; education in general; in-school education; out-of-school education and special programmes; educational planning and administration. Index, p.369-431. *Class No:* 370(729.99)(01)

USA

Bibliographies

[3806]
American education: a guide to information sources. Durnin, R.G., *ed.* Detroit, Mich., Gale Research Co., 1982. xvi,247p. $68. (*American studies information guide series, v.14.*) ISBN: 0810312654.
107 topical chapters (Art ... Utilization of teachers) each listing up to 40 books, mostly annotated, and in some cases relevant bibliographies. Includes a bibliographic essay with a list of the most influential books on education published in the last 200 years. 'On balance, the editor has done a good job of choosing the important books on most topics, although significant omissions are almost inevitable in a work of this scope' (*Library journal,* 14 January 1983, p.121). *Class No:* 370(73)(01)

Reviews & Abstracts

[3807]
Resources in education (RIE), 1975-. v.10, no.1-. ERIC, *comp.* Washington, Superintendent of Documents, Government Publishing Office. Monthly. $94pa. ISSN: 00980897.
Previously as *Research in education* (Washington, Education Resources Information Center (ERIC), US Office of Education, 1966-74.
About 15,000 digests pa of documents (largely US) in education, giving ERIC clearinghouse numbers/ED number cross-references, plus descriptors and identifiers. Subject arrangement in broad groups. Semi-annual indexes (subject, author, institution, type of publication).
The online database ERIC (Washington, Education Resources Information, 1966-), covers both reports and periodical articles, and is up-dated monthly. *Class No:* 370(73)(048)

Yearbooks & Directories

[3808]
KLEIN, B.T., *ed.* Guide to American educational directories. 8th ed. New York, Todd Publications, 1998. $75. ISBN: 0915344696.
First published 1963. A 'spin-off' of the publisher's *Guide to American directories.*
Lists *c.*3000 US and Canadian directories, under *c.*100 subjects A-Z. Broad subject arrangement. Each entry of 30-50 words has title, brief description of contents, pagination, publisher's address and telephone number, and price. Title index. *Class No:* 370(73)(058)

Biographies

[3809]
GORDON, P. *and* ALDRICH, R. Biographical dictionary of North American and European educationists. Woburn Press, 1997. $67.50. (*Woburn education series.*) ISBN: 0713002050.
Class No: 370(73)(092)

[3810]
OHLES, J.F. Biographical dictionary of American educators. Westport, CT. Greenwood Press, 1978. 3v. (1666p.). $65 each vol.; $150 for 3v. ISBN: 0837198941, v.1; 083719899x, v.2; 0837198968, v.3; 0837198933, set.
470 contributors. Biographical sketches of 1665 leaders in American education from the 1700s to the present day. Entries contain references to other sources (*e.g.* general biographical dictionaries; obituaries). Appendices group names by birth-places and dates, States and specializations. Usefully assembles data scattered elsewhere. *Class No:* 370(73)(092)

Research Methods

Handbooks & Manuals

[3811]
Educational research, methodology, and measurement: an international handbook. Keeves, J.P., *ed.* 2nd ed. Oxford, Pergamon Press, 1997. 964p. $219.75. ISBN: 0080427103.
Arranged in 4 sections (1. The methods of educational enquiry - 2. The creation, diffusion, and utilization of knowledge - 3. Measurement of educational research - 4. Research techniques and statistical analysis. Each section has an introductory essay. *Class No:* 370:001.891(035)

Thesauri

[3812]
British education thesaurus. Marder, J.V., *ed.* Leeds, Leeds University Press, 1988. xii, [2],426p. £40. ISBN: 0853161445.
Alphabetical descriptor display, p.1-254, is followed by Rotated descriptor display, p.255-426. Preliminary items include 'Indexing and retrieval in the British education databases', 'Thesaurus construction and format' and 'How to search effectively using the British Education Thesaurus'. *Class No:* 370:025.43

[3813]
EUDISED; multilingual thesaurus for information processing in the field of education. English version. Viet, J. *and* Slype, G.van. New ed. Berlin, Mouton Publishers, 1984. xix[307]p. ISBN: 3110098474.
Previous ed. published 1982. Also available in French, German, Spanish and Dutch.
Designed by the European Documentation and Information System for Education (EUDISED), using documentary language specially conceived for the processing of information in member states. An introduction precedes the structured alphabetical thesaurus, terminographs, list of terminographs, and rotated alphabetical thesaurus. *Class No:* 370:025.43

[3814]
EUROPEAN CENTRE FOR THE DEVELOPMENT OF VOCATIONAL TRAINING (CEDEFO). Thesaurus of vocational training. Viet, J., *and others.* 2nd ed. Luxembourg, Office for Official Publications of the European Communities, 1988. xiii,234p. ECU12. ISBN: 9282580482.
First published 1986. Also available in 7 other languages.
An introduction precedes the structured alphabetical thesaurus, a list of 'top terms', a permuted index, and a list of 'candidate descriptors'. *Class No:* 370:025.43

[3815]
Unesco: IBE education thesaurus: a list of terms for indexing and retrieving documents and data in the field of education, with French and Spanish equivalents. International Bureau of Education. 4th rev. ed. Paris, Unesco, 1984. xvi,345 p. £9. (*Ibedata series.*) ISBN: 9231020617.
First published 1973.
Covers the field of 'education and training' for use in the computerized indexing and retrieval of educational information at an international level. *Class No:* 370:025.43

[3816]
—EDUCATIONAL RESOURCES INFORMATION CENTRE (ERIC). Thesaurus of ERIC descriptors. Houston, J.E., *ed.* 13th ed. Phoenix, AZ., Oryx Press, 1995. 656p. £51.95. ISBN: 0897747887.
A-Z list of descriptors - rotated descriptor display - hierarchical term display - descriptor group display. *Class No:* 370:025.43

[3817]
—FOSKETT, D.J. *and* FOSKETT, J. The London education classification: a thesaurus/classification of British educational terms. 2nd ed. London, University of London, Institute of Education Library, 1974. [i], 165 p. (*Education Library bulletin. Supplement 6.*) *Class No:* 370:025.43

Information Services

[3818]

Directory of educational documentation and information services. Unesco. International Bureau of Education. 5th ed. Paris, Unesco, 1988. x,114p. ISBN: 9230025186.

In 4 sections: 1. National services - 2. Regional services - 3. International services - 4. Other member institutions. Data for each service include name (official and translated); address; country; year of creation; parent organization; present head; size of staff, type of activities; people served; services given; fields covered, size of collection; methods of data processing; classification systems; audio-visual material; reprographic services; periodical publications. Within the 4 sections, the organizations are arranged A-Z by country. Entries in English, French or Spanish; title page and preliminaries in all 3 languages. *Class No:* 370:061:025.5

Research Projects

[3819]

Review of educational research. Washington, American Educational Research Association, 1931-. Quarterly (previously 5pa). $46pa (institutions); $37pa (individuals). ISSN: 00346543.

Each issue consists of lengthy, well-documented contributions on topical themes (until June 1970 articles on 15 major themes were updated triennially). *Class No:* 370:061:061.62.005

[3820]

SACHS, M. **EUDISED R & D bulletin, no.1,1976-.** Quarterly. Munich, K.G. Saur, for EUDISED, Council of Europe. £55pa. ISSN: 03787192.

Each issue contains *c.*250 reports on current or recently completed projects in the field of educational research and development. Also available online. *Class No:* 370:061:061.62.005

Encyclopaedias

[3821]

ALKIN, M.C., *ed.* **Encyclopedia of educational research.** 6th ed. London, Macmillan Library Reference, 1992. 4v. (1664p.) illus. $450. ISBN: 0029004314.

First published in 1941. Sponsored by the American Educational Research Association.

Presents a critical synthesis and interpretation of reported research in the field. 256 lengthy articles by 300 specialists, with extensive bibliographies (*e.g.* 'Bilingual education': 18 cols., with 'see also' references and 39 bibliographical references; 'Computer-based education': 29 cols. in 15 sections, with 'see also' references and including 7½ columns of bibliographical references. Cross references. ' ... an essential purchase for libraries serving students and professionals in education' (*Library journal*, 1 January, 1983, p.42). *Class No:* 370:061:061.62.005(031)

[3822]

—**Handbook of research on social studies teaching and learning.** Shaver, J., *ed.* New York, Macmillan, 1991. 603p. $63. ISBN: 0028957903.

A project of the National Council for the Social Studies modelled on the aging *Encyclopedia of educational research* (*qv*). 53 topical chapters. Appended bibliographies. *Class No:* 370:061:061.62.005(031)

Women

Developing Countries

Bibliographies

[3823]

KELLY, D.H. **Women's education in the Third World** - an annotated bibliography. New York, Garland, 1989. 478p. $52. (*Reference books in international education, 5. Garland reference library of social science, 544.*) ISBN: 0824086341.

1200 annotated entries, mainly from 1970 onwards, including journal articles, monographs, chapters of books, arranged in 15 topic groups, subdivided geographically. Cross-references. Excellent introduction and introductory essays to each topic. Items mainly in English, but do include some Spanish, French, Portuguese and German publications. Author and geographic indexes. *Class No:* 370-0055.2(4/9-77)(01)

Education Theory

[3824]

DUFOUR, B., *ed.* **New movements in the social sciences and humanities.** London, M.T. Smith, 1982. xii,287p. £13.50. ISBN: 0851171931.

Surveys new developments in the study and teaching of the whole range of the subjects and also interdisciplinary areas. 19 chapters in 2 parts: Part 1. The social sciences in higher education: academic developments in the subjects; pt.2. The social sciences and humanities in secondary education: the subjects in the schools. References, p.237-260. arranged by chapter. Further reading and useful addresses, p.261-284. Notes on the contributors, p.285-287. *Class No:* 370.01

[3825]

HILGARD, E.R. *and* BOWER, G.H. **Theories of learning.** 5th ed. Englewood Cliffs, N.J. Prentice-Hall, 1981. 640p. illus. $41; £43.85. ISBN: 0139144323.

First published 1948.

A scholarly introduction to the major current theories of learning. Extensive bibliography. *Class No:* 370.01

[3826]

—CURTIS, S.J. *and* BOULTWOOD, M.E.A. A Short history of educational ideas. 5th ed. London, University Tutorial Press, 1978. x,685p.

4th ed. published 1965.

21 chapters, each with 'suggestions for further reading'. Chapter 17: 'John Dewey (1859-1952). Footnote references. Index of names and titles mentioned in the text. *Class No:* 370.01

Religious Education

Bibliographies

[3827]

HUNT, T.C. *and* CARPER, J.C. **Religious colleges and universities in America:** a selected bibliography. New York, Garland, 1988. 374p. $54. (*Garland reference library of social science, 422.*) ISBN: 0824066480.

Arranged in 24 chapters, the first one having *c.*400 annotated entries on religion and higher education, as well as government aid to, and regulation of church-affiliated institutions. The following 23 chapters are organized by denomination, with *c.*1900 partially annotated entries. 35 contributors. Index to topics and individual institutions. 'No other book approaches this in coverage of the subject'. (*Choice,* v.26(6), February 1989, p.920). A companion work is *Religious schools in America: a select bibliography,* by T.C. Hunt and others (1986. 416p. $47. 0824085833). *Class No:* 370.014.52(01)

Dictionaries

[3828]

SUTCLIFFE, J.M., *ed.* **A Dictionary of religious education.** London, SCM Press, in association with The Christian Education Movement, 1984. xvi,[1],376. £14.95. ISBN: 0334019680.

A guide to religious education around the world, concentrating 'on methods of teaching rather than the content of what is taught' (*Preface*). Lengthy signed entries of ¼ to 3 pages, each having a short bibliography. Select bibliography, p.373-374. Name index, p.375-376. *Class No:* 370.014.52(038)

Educational Psychology

Bibliographies

[3829]

BAATZ, O.K. *and* BAATZ, C.A., *eds.* **The Psychological foundations of education:** a guide to information sources. Detroit, Mich., Gale Research Co., 1981. 481p. $68. (*Educational information guide series, v.10.*) ISBN: 0810314673.

Topical arrangement in 9 chapters; within each chapter the authors include objective; curriculum design; the role of learners, parents, teachers and schools; process, structure and methods of teaching and learning; theory, research sources, and teacher education and preparation. Many entries have descriptive and evaluative annotations. Author, title and subject indexes. *Class No:* 370.015.3(01)

Dictionaries

[3830]

HARRÉ, R. *and* LAMB, R., *eds.* **The Dictionary of developmental and educational psychology.** Oxford, Basil Blackwell Ltd., 1986. xi,271p. £25. ISBN: 0631146032.

Based on material from *The encyclopedic dictionary of psychology* (1983), material being selected and up-dated, bibliographies revised and new entries added, and including more biographies. 97 contributors. Short bibliographies follow most entries. Cross-

...(contd.)

references. 'Absence from school and truency': 6 cols., 16 references in bibliography; 'Freud, Sigmond': 6½ cols., 15 references; 'Ontogenetic sequence': ¼ col. *Class No:* 370.015.3(038)

Teachers & Teaching

Bibliographies
[3831]

HAYWOOD, P.G., *comp.* **A Bibliography of adult teaching, psychology and research:** a sourcebook. Nottingham, University of Nottingham, Department of Adult Education, 1981. [2],48p. £1.50. ISBN: 0902031678.

Unannotated bibliography on student motivation and learning application in 4 sections: 1. a. General works; b. Mature students - 2. Teaching methods and evaluation (subdivided, A-E) - 3. University and adult education - 4. Education in retirement. *Class No:* 371(01)

Encyclopaedias
[3832]

The International encyclopedia of teaching and teacher education. Dunkin, M.J., *ed.* Oxford, Pergamon Press, 1987. 900p. £65. (*Advances in education.*) ISBN: 008030852x.

Based on *The International encyclopedia of education: research and studies,* ed. by T. Huson and T.N. Postlethwaite (1985) (*qv*).

2000 literary references, thematically organized in 124 articles on all aspects of the subject. *Class No:* 371(031)

Great Britain
[3833]

Treasure chest for teachers: services available to teachers and schools. 12th ed. Kettering, Northants., The Teachers Publishing Co. Ltd., [1988]. [4],204p. £3.50. ISBN: 0900642351.

First published 1960.

5 parts: 1. Societies and associations providing services and materials for teachers and schools (p.2-56; data; name & address; secretary; subscription; activities; aims) - 2. Materials and services relating to individual countries from embassies, legations and bodies for the promotion of travel and good relations - 3. Commercial, industrial and nationalized concerns providing services and materials for teachers and schools - 4. Places to visit (A-Z under country headings) - 5. Educational equipment manufacturers and suppliers. Classified index to parts 1-3 (p.186-194). General index, mainly of organizations, p.196-204. *Class No:* 371(410)

Education & Training
[3834]

University courses in education open to students from overseas, 1990-91. London, University Council for the Education of Teachers, 1989. 156p. £3.75. ISBN: 0903509121.

Lists advanced courses available in United Kingdom universities, and short courses for teachers, identifying those unikversities that offer tailor-made courses. *Class No:* 371:377.8

Teaching Materials

[3835]

Audiovisual and microcomputer handbook: the SCET guide to educational and training equipment. Henderson, J. *and* Humphreys, F., *eds.* 4th ed. London, Kogan Page, 1983. 160p. £12.95. ISBN: 0850387817.

First published 1980.

A products directory for equipment, software, services, etc., giving names, addresses and telephone numbers. Also listings of training and information organizations, professional organizations, film libraries, professional and trade journals, a selective bibliography (p.118-129), and a microcomputer supplement. *Class No:* 371.64/.69

Bibliographies
[3836]

El-Hi textbooks and serials in print: including related teaching materials, 2000. New York, Bowker, 2000. 2750p. $206.75. ISBN: 0835242706. ISSN: 00000825.

First published 1969. Annual.

Bibliographic information on texts, text series, reference and professional books, arranged by subject. Indexed by author, title and series. *Class No:* 371.64/.69(01)

Yearbooks & Directories
[3837]

Educational media and technology yearbook, 2000. v.25. Englewood Cliffs, Col., Libraries Unlimited, 2000. 300p. £63.50. ISBN: 1563088401. ISSN: 87552094.

First published 1973. Annual.

Provides an up-to-date overview of the subjects, including information on professional associations, graduate programmes, foundations and funding sources. *Class No:* 371.64/.69(058)

Audio-Visual Aids
[3838]

COPPEN, H.E., *comp.* **Survey of British research in audio-visual aids, 1945-71.** 3rd ed. London, National Committee for Audio-Visual Aids in Education, Educational Foundation for Visual Aids, 1972. iii,271p. £1.50. Supplements 1-5: £0.70-£1.50.

First published 1965.

Bibliography is in 10 sections: 1. Films - 2. Still projected media ... 8. Television - 9. Programmed learning and teaching machines - 10. Unclassified. Abstracts are similarly grouped. *Class No:* 371.67

Bibliographies
[3839]

WICKS, P. **'Audio-visual aids in education'.** In *British book news,* May 1988, p.340-343.

A book survey on the subject, including a list of 18 book titles, some free booklets, and 5 periodical serial titles. *Class No:* 371.67(01)

Education Technology
[3840]

International yearbook of educational and training technology, 1991. Osbourne, C., *ed.* 9th ed. London, Kogan Page, in association with the Association for Educational and Training Technology, 1991. Annual. 508p. ISBN: 0749403780. ISSN: 03709732.

First published in 1976. Previously as *APLET yearbook of educational and instructional technology, 1972/73* (1972).

Arranged in 4 parts: 1. International and regional centres of activity - 2. Centres of activity in the United Kingdom - 3. Centres of activity in the United States (by State, A-Z) - 4. Centres of activity worldwide (by country, A-Z). Each section lists organizations actively involved in the development of educational and training technology and includes addresses, telephone and telex numbers, contact names, area of interest, details of current and future research and development projects, main services offered, keywords summarizing the organization's activities, and recent publications by staff or personnel. Index of institutions. *Class No:* 371.68/69

Dictionaries

English
[3841]

ELLINGTON, H. *and* HARRIS, D. **Dictionary of instructional technology.** London, Kogan Page; New York, Nichols Publishing Company, 1986. 189p. illus. £15.95; $34.50. (*AETT occasional publication, no.6.*) ISBN: 1850910723, UK; 0893972436, US.

Aims to be a comprehensive glossary of the most important terms that educational and training technologists are liable to come across in their daily work. Includes both British and US terms, as well as terms used in other English-speaking countries. Over 2800 terms from instructional technology, educational psychology, statistics, film & TV production, photography, reprography, computing and information technology. Many cross-references. *Class No:* 371.68/69(038)=20

French

[3842]

Glossary of educational technology terms. Unesco, for the International Bureau of Education, Methods, Materials and Techniques of Education Section. 2nd. ed. rev. & enl. Paris, Unesco, 1988. 263 p. F60 £9. ISBN: 9230025178.

First published 1984.

Groups in one volume the terms related to educational technology. English-French edition, with each term defined in both languages. (English-Spanish and English-Russian editions are also available). *Class No:* 371.68/69(038)=40

Reviews & Abstracts

[3843]

Educational technology abstracts. Abingdon, Oxon, Carfax Publishing Company, 1985-. 6pa. £45; $120pa. ISSN: 02663368.

Provides *c.*900 indicative abstracts pa from a wide range of international journals and books. About 3400 journals scanned. Arrangement is by broad subject groups: Design and planning - Teaching methods - Instructional media - Instructional resources - Learning - Assessment and evaluation. List of journals covered. Author and subject indexes. *Class No:* 371.68/69(048)

Games & Simulators

[3844]

BELCH, J., *ed.* **Contemporary games:** a directory and bibliography covering games and play situations or simulations used for construction and training by schools, colleges and universities, government, business and management. Detroit, Mich, Gale Research Co., 1973-74. 2v. (560p.; 408p.). v.1: $110; v.2: $98. ISBN: 0810309688, v.1; 0810309696, v.2.

v.1: Directory; v.2: Bibliography. V.1 lists and describes *c.*900 games, under titles A-Z, with references. V.2 has 2375 entries in 3 main subject groups. *Class No:* 371.69

[3845]

GIBBS, G.I. Dictionary of gaming, modelling & simulation. Beverly Hills, CA., Sage Publications, 1979 (Available from Books Demand UMI). 159p. illus. $43.50. ISBN: 0317110195.

Provides illustrations to bring out the meanings of some terms, plus mathematical formulae for the many statistical tests included. 'A small, attractive work' (*Choice,* v.17(1), March 1980, p.48). *Class No:* 371.69

Schools

Bibliographies

[3846]

BURGESS, R.G. 'Studying schooling'. In *British book news,* April 1988, p.254-7,259.

A book survey in 4 sections: Basic texts - Social and political context - Studies of schools and classrooms - Studies of curriculum and assessment. Includes a bibliography of 75 books. *Class No:* 373(01)

[3847]

The School administrator's resource guide. Clay, K., *ed.* Phoenix, AZ., Oryx Press, 1988. viii,104p. $22. ISBN: 0897744462.

An annotated bibliography of 548 entries, arranged in 9 overlapping chapters. Document format (journal articles, microfiche documents, books, dissertations) relating mainly to 1982-1987. Author, subject and title indexes. '... the best and most current thinking in the field of school administration' (*Reference books bulletin,* 1 May, 1988). *Class No:* 373(01)

Dictionaries

[3848]

GORTON, R.A., *and others, eds.* **Encyclopedia of school administration & supervision.** Phoenix, AZ., Oryx Press, 1988. 352p. $74.50. ISBN: 089774232x.

Intended for administrators in elementary and secondary schools. 300 practical or theoretical topics arranged A-Z by subject. Entries are signed, average length is one page, include cross-references and bibliographies of up to 3 books or journal articles. 200 contributors. 'A guide to related topics' groups titles of individual articles under broader headings. *Class No:* 373(038)

Reviews & Abstracts

[3849]

School organization and management abstracts. Abingdon, Oxon, Carfax, 1982-. V.1(1)-. Quarterly. £112. ISSN: 02612755.

In 3 sections: Abstracts of journal articles: Abstracts of books, Abstracts of theses and dissertations. Aims to focus particularly on the organization and management of the school as a complex institution. Journals covered (*c.* 200) are listed in each issue. Author and subject indexes, which are cumulated and bound in the final issue of each volume. *Class No:* 373(048)

Great Britain

Yearbooks & Directories

[3850]

The Gabbitas, Truman & Thring guide to boarding schools and colleges, 1988/89. Henderson, M., *ed.* Plymouth, Northcote House, 1988. 374p. £8.95. ISBN: 1869863070. ISSN: 0951872x.

First published 1987/88.

Includes over 900 independent and state boarding schools, arranged in 5 sections: Pre-prep and preparatory schools - Senior independent schools - State maintained boarding schools - Boarding at 16 and over - International schools in the UK and overseas. A guide for parents, which also contains a number of articles contributed by experts.

A 7th ed. was published by John Catt in 1993 for 1994, edited by D. Bingham. (370p. 130 illus. 17 maps. £9.95. ISBN 1869863453). *Class No:* 373(410)(058)

[3851]

Independent schools yearbook, 1999-2000. Rev. ed.. London, A. & C Black, 1999. Annual. 1170p. £27. ISBN: 0713651687.

Prior to 1992-93 edition, separate volumes for girls' schools and for boys' schools, co-educational schools and preparatory schools.

Full details of all the schools in the Headmasters Conference, Girls Schools Association schools. *Class No:* 373(410)(058)

USA

Yearbooks & Directories

[3852]

Private schools of the United States. Council for American Private Education (CAPE) Schools. Shelton, CT., Market Data Retrieval 1988. 2v. $75. ISBN: 0897705025, v.1; 0897705033, v.2.

Information on 15,000 elementary and secondary private schools, members of 13 diverse national private school associations. The first vol. lists the schools A-Z by State, subdivided A-Z by school name. All entries have school name, address, telephone no., grades, principal's name and enrollment; some entries include more specific information. The second vol. has indexes to schools by association membership and by grade level, and a complete A-Z listing of schools. *Class No:* 373(73)(058)

Libraries

[3853]

HERRING, J.E. School librarianship. 2nd ed. London, Clive Bingley Ltd., 1988. xii,81p. £11.95. ISBN: 0851574238.

A general survey of the place of school librarianship within education, management, organization and the provision of information. Bibliography, p.78-80, A-Z by author. Index, p.81. *Class No:* 373:061:026/027

Catholic Schools

Handbooks & Manuals

[3854]

Catholic education: a handbook. 12th ed. London, Catholic Education Council for England and Wales, 1984. £4. ISBN: 0950156248.

Basically a 'General list of schools by diocese and local education authorities' (p.25-149), preceded by an index. Appended, lists of Catholic boarding schools, special schools for handicapped pupils, and community homes (providing educational and training facilities). *Class No:* 373:283(035)

Primary Schools

England & Wales

[3855]

The Routledge compendium of primary education. Campbell, R.J., *ed* London, Routledge & Kegan Paul, 1988. x,250p. £6.95. ISBN 0415002206.

Designed as a guide and reference source to the theory, practice and policy in primary education. Part 1 consists of 14 extended analyses and discussions of the main ideas in the field, such as classroom

...(contd.)

processes, home-school relationships, and children's development and learning. Part 2 is a glossary, including definitions of complex or controversial ideas; a list of 'Further reading', and outlines of important reports, surveys, Education Acts, and leading figures in primary education. *Class No:* 373.3(42)

Secondary & Sixth Form Schools

Great Britain

[3856]
The Parents' guide to independent schools. Tyrrell, C., *ed.* 12th ed. Maidenhead, Berks., SFIA Educational Trust, 1993. 2v. in 1 (902p.). £31.95. ISBN: 090669518x.

First published 1981.

V.1 consists mainly of nearly 1300 school profiles; arranged by countries and counties. Data on each school: type (*e.g.* girls - board; day); name of head; entry; curriculum; reports and consultation; leavers; sports; activities; religious service; comment. 44 coloured maps. Preliminary 14 sections deal with the independent school system, choice of school, schools for children with special needs, abilities, and disabilities; glossary. V.2, largely tables, reviews and details schemes designed for the financing of school fees. Tables of comparative school details, supporting the school profile in v.1. Index of school types; index of schools, by categories; index of schools, by religious denominations. *Class No:* 373.5(410)

Eire

[3857]
EIRE. Department of Education. Liosta a iarbhunscoileanna (List of post-primary schools). 1987-88. Dublin. Stationery Office, 1988. . £2.25. *Class No:* 373.5(417)

Adult Education

Bibliographies

[3858]
FRENCH, J. Adult literacy: a source book and guide. New York. Garland, 1987. 435p. $58. (*Garland reference library of social science, 346. Sourcebooks on education, 14.*) ISBN: 0824085744.

A literature review precedes 591 numbered and annotated entries for books, journal articles, documents, federal and state monographs published in the last five years. Arrangement is by topic, subdivided A-Z by author. Author and subject indexes. US bias. 'Informative, easy to use, and more comprehensive than other literary bibliographies ... ' (*Choice* v.25(6),February 1988, p.886). *Class No:* 374.7(01)

[3859]
HAYWOOD, P., *comp.* Bibliography of comparative adult education: a source book. 2nd ed. Nottingham, University of Nottingham, Department of Adult Education, 1983. xi,203p.(spiral binding). £12.50 ISBN: 0902031686.

First published 1981.

A subject index (p I-XI) precedes the main text, which is arranged geographically (General and international - Africa - Americas - Asia - Australasia - Europe). 2467 unannotated entries in all, mainly related to 1960-. Includes 5 supplements. *Class No:* 374.7(01)

Encyclopaedias

[3860]
JARVIS, P. The International dictionary of adult education. London, Kogan Page, 1999. 288p. £35. ISBN: 0749426713.

Provides a detailed reference to the concepts, organizations and figures in adult education. *Class No:* 374.7(031)

Handbooks & Manuals

[3861]
BRODGE, S. Adult education. Newcastle-under-Lyme, AAL Publishing, 1988. [2],53p. £6. ISBN: 0900092696.

Sections: Information about adult classes - Providing resources for adult classes - Adult basic education - Provision for independent learners - Supporting open learning packages - Education guidance services - Twenty-five practical ways to work with adult learners - References and further reading (p.52-3). *Class No:* 374.7(035)

[3862]
STEPHENS, M.D., *ed.* International organizations in education. New York, Routledge, 1989. 165p. $42.50. ISBN: 0415021839.

A collection of 10 authoritative essays dealing with various aspects of organizations involved in adult education on an international scale, including 2 overviews, 3 articles on broadly international organizations, and 5 essays on regional organizations. Essays are analytical and evaluative. *Class No:* 374.7(035)

Histories

Great Britain

[3863]
KELLY, T. A History of adult education in Great Britain. 3rd ed. Liverpool, Liverpool University Press, 1991. liv,425p. £20. ISBN: 0853234078.

First published 1962.

A revised 38-page prologue is followed by 26 chapters, with footnotes, and a bibliography to 1990 (p.397-9). Detailed, analytical index (p.401-425). *Class No:* 374.7(091)(410)

Biographies

[3864]
International biography of adult education. Thomas, J.E. *and* Elsey, B., *eds.* Nottingham, University of Nottingham, Department of Adult Education, 1985. xxii,709p. £27. (*Nottingham studies in the theory and practice of the education of adults.*) ISBN: 1850410011.

A world wide collection of biographies of people who have played a significant part in the development of adult education. Arranged A-Z by name (Abdullah, Hagia Dadasore (b.1917) ... Zilsel, Edgar (1891 - 1944), the entries are signed and vary in length from one to 8 pages, usually ending with one or two references. Thematic index, p. 686 - 705; subject index, p. 706 - 709. *Class No:* 374.7(092)

Europe

Bibliographies

[3865]
KULICH, J. Adult education in continental Europe: an annotated bibliography of English-language materials, 1983-1985. Vancouver, University of British Columbia, Centre for Continuing Education, 1987. [5].ii,145 p. Can$ 18. (*Monographs on comparative and area studies in adult education, 12.*) ISBN: 088843135x.

First ed. was for 1945-1969 (1971); followed by eds. for 1971-1974 (1975), 1975-1979 (1982), 1980-1982 (1984).

661 unannotated entries, arranged by country, subdivided by subject. Index. ' ... most useful volume' (*Adult education*, v.60 (4)). *Class No:* 374.7(4)(01)

Great Britain

Bibliographies

[3866]
DALE, S. *and* CARTY, J. Finding out about continuing education: Sources of information and their uses. Milton Keynes, Open University Press, 1985. vi[1] 101p. £7.95. ISBN: 0335150241.

In 7 sections (1. Introduction - 2. Libraries - 3. Literature search procedure - 4. Bibliographical tools - 5. Audio-visual materials - 6. Organizations and associations - 7. Conclusions. Finally,'A corollary: libraries in continuing education. No index. *Class No:* 374.7(410)(01)

[3867]
A Select bibliography of adult continuing education in Great Britain, including works published to the end of the year 1981. Thomas, J.E. *and* Davies, J.H., *eds.* Leicester, National Institute of Adult Continuing Education, 1984. xvi,158p. ISBN: 0900559470.

First published 1952; 3rd ed. 1974, edited by T. Kelly.

1156 numbered entries, some annotated and referring to other items. 4 main parts: 1. General - 2. The social and educational background - 3. History and organization of adult education (p.12-91) - 4. Theory and method. Includes periodical articles. Cross-references. Author and subject indexes. *Class No:* 374.7(410)(01)

Great Britain

Yearbooks & Directories

[3868]
SLADE, A.L. *and* KASCUS, M. Library services for open and distance learning. 3rd ed. Libraries Unlimited, 2000. $75. ISBN: 1563087456. *Class No:* 374.7OPE(410)(058)

England & Wales

Yearbooks & Directories

[3869]

Returning to work: a directory of education and training for women. Network. London, P. Chapman, 1996. $24.95. ISBN: 1853963372. ISSN: 09574808.

A glossary of acronyms precedes the directory of courses and county contacts, arranged by county. Followed by 'sources of information: national schemes and organizations' and 'Useful publications'. Subject, college and advertisers' indexes. *Class No:* 374.7(42)(058)

Information Services

[3870]

UNESCO. Directory of adult education documentation and information services. 3rd ed. Paris, Unesco, 1984. x,76p. F.20. ISBN: 9230021881.

2nd ed. published 1980.

Data on *c.*160 documentation services world wide, including national, regional and international services. An annex lists adult-education abstracting services. *Class No:* 374.7:061:025.5

Open Learning

Yearbooks & Directories

[3871]

Open learning directory, 1997. Oxford, Butterworth-Heinemann, 1997. xv,736p. ISBN: 0750633387.

Details of open learning training courses. Indexes. *Class No:* 374.7OPE(058)

Great Britain

Yearbooks & Directories

[3872]

ADAMS, M., *ed*. **Libraries and open learning:** a directory of college libraries involvement with open learning. Library Association, Colleges of Further and Higher Education Group, 1988. [3], 51p. £5. ISBN: 186997705x.

114 entries, giving name of college, address, telephone number, name of contact, position, provision, library involvement, and comment. Further surveys are promised. *Class No:* 374.7OPE(410)(058)

Special Education

Bibliographies

[3873]

DAVIS, W.E. Resource guide to special education: terms, laws, assessment procedures, organizations. 2nd ed. Newton, Mass., Allyn & Bacon, 1986. 329p. $37.95. ISBN: 0205085466.

First ed. was titled *Educators' resource guide to special education.* 5 sections: 1. Terms employed in special education and related areas - 2. A list of commonly used acronyms and abbreviations - 3. A listing and description of educational and psychological tests and inventories - 4. Concise summaries of key pieces of legislation and litigation affecting the handicapped - 5. A list of organizations and agencies concerned with exceptional persons. US emphasis. *Class No:* 377(01)

[3874]

GREENLAW, M.J. and McINTOSH, M.E. Educating the gifted: a sourcebook. Chicago, Ill., American Library Association, 1988. viii,469p. $45; £35.25. ISBN: 0838904831.

'... purpose is to serve as a concise, clear reference tool for persons interested in the gifted individual. (*Preface*). 8 chapters: 1. A historical look at gifted education - 2. Who are the gifted? - 3. Indentification of the gifted - 4. Counseling the gifted and those around them - 5. Programming for the gifted - 6. Academic curriculum for the gifted - 7. Education for teachers of the gifted - 8. Parenting gifted children. Selected bibliographies follow each chapter. US-slant. Index, p.459-469. *Class No:* 377(01)

[3875]

Special education: a source book. Sternlicht,, M., *comp*. New York, Garland, 1987. 431p. $50. (*Garland reference library of social science, 375.*) ISBN: 0824085248.

Annotated bibliography on special education for teachers of exceptional students and others interested in the field. Arranged in 10 chapters (Mental retardation - Giftedness - Visual impairments - Hearing impairments - Learning disabilities - Brain damage - Speech and language inpairments - Orthopedic and other physical impairments

....(contd.)

- Emotional and behavioural impairments - and mainstreaming. Each chapter prefaced by an information survey article. Most citations are to periodical articles. Author and subject indexes. '... fills a gap in special education scholarship ...' (*Choice*,v.25(3), November 1987, p.458). *Class No:* 377(01)

Encyclopaedias

[3876]

REYNOLDS, C.R. and FLETCHER-JANZEN, E., *eds*. **Encyclopedia of special education.** 2nd ed. New York, Wiley, 1987. 1980p. $375. ISBN: 047125309x.

Designed to present a comprehensive view of what special education is about in a readable, understandable, usable and summative form. Worldwide coverage but with US bias. Topics covered include clinical disorders and syndromes, testing, intervention techniques, education methods and legal considerations. Biographies of prominent practitioners and theorists. Articles are followed by bibliographical references. Name index. Subject index. 'An invaluable resource' (*Library journal* v.113(7), 15 April 1988, p.32). *Class No:* 377(031)

[3877]

—**REYNOLDS, C.R.** *and* **FLETCHER-JANZEN, E. Concise encyclopedia of special education.** New York, Wiley, 1990. 1215p. $89.95. ISBN: 0471515272.

An abridged version, based on the above. Articles are unsigned and most, according to the editors, have been 'condensed and streamlined to give basic facts and reference ideas'. *Class No:* 377(031)

Handbooks & Manuals

[3878]

FARRELL, M. The Special education handbook. London, David Fulton Publishers, 1997. v,217p. ISBN: 1853464678. *Class No:* 377(035)

[3879]

Handbook of special education. Kauffman, J.W. *and* Hallahan, D.P., *eds*. Englewood Cliffs, N.J., Prentice-Hall, 1981. xv,807p. illus. ISBN: 0133817563.

Aimed at students, professionals and practitioners involved in the education of exceptional children. Chapters are arranged in 5 sections: Introduction (covers history, trends and European practice) - Conceptual foundations (disabilities and special characteristics) - Delivery systems - Curriculum and methods - Environmental management. Includes bibliographies. Index. *Class No:* 377(035)

[3880]

Handbook of special education: research and practice. Wang, M.C., *and others, eds*. Oxford, Pergamon Press, 1987-1991. 4v. (xi,387p.;xi,392 p.;ix,376 p.;340p.). £50 each vol.; £140 the set (*Advances in education..*) ISBN: 0080333834, vol.1; 0080333842, vol.2; 0080333850, vol.3; 0080408176, vol.4.

V.1. Learner characteristics and adaptive education; v.2. Mildly handicapped conditions; v.3. Low incidence conditions. The 3 vols contain 45 chapters in 9 sections, each summarizing the well confirmed knowledge in a particular area, giving attention to the research literature, tested experience and practice of leading professionals. Each vol. has a bibliography, author and subject index. Synthesis of findings published 1990 (236p. ISBN 0080402380, 0080402372).

2nd ed. published 1995 under title: *Handbook of special and remedial education: research and practice.* xii,468p. ISBN 0080425666. *Class No:* 377(035)

Dictionaries

[3881]

WILLIAMS, P., *ed*. **A Glossary of special education (children with special needs).** Milton Keynes, Open University Press, 1987. 192p. £20. ISBN: 0335159966.

Brief explanations of the terminology of education, psychology, medicine and social work used in special education. *Class No:* 377(038)

Polyglot

[3882]

BRUNET, L., *and others*. **Terminology of special education.** Rev. ed. Paris, Unesco: International Bureau of Education, 1983. 368p. F.30; £11.50. (*Ibedata series.*) ISBN: 923002127x.

First published 1977.

English, Spanish, French and Russian terms in 4 separate glossaries following a preliminary section, 'Group clusters'. English glossary has over 500 terms: English definitions with Spanish, French and Russian equivalents. Spanish, French and Russian glossaries are on the same pattern. *Class No:* 377(038)=00

English

[3883]

IOORE, B.C., *and others.* **A Dictionary of special education terms.** Springfield, Ill., C.C.Thomas, 1980. 128p. (spiral binding). $17.00. ISBN: 0398040095.

Includes mental retardation, emotional handicap, hearing, vision and learning disability, speech handicap, physical handicaps, and giftedness. *Class No:* 377(038)=20

Reviews & Abstracts

[3884]

xceptional child education resources. Reston, VA., Council for Exceptional Children, 1968-. Quarterly. $90pa. ISSN: 01604309.

As *Exceptional child education abstracts* until May 1977.

Abstracts periodical articles from over 250 journals, as well as books, reports, surveys, doctoral dissertations, and nonprint professional media. Covers education of both handicapped and gifted children. Numerical order, with author, subject and title index, per issue and annually. The Council acts as a clearinghouse for ERIC programmes in this field. On-line database available, 1966- (updated quarterly). *Class No:* 377(048)

Yearbooks & Directories

[3885]

irectory of special education. International Bureau of Education. Paris, Unesco, 1986. 104p. $5; F.25; £3.75. ISBN: 9230024139.

First published in 1969 as *Special education.*

'Special education' is designed as 'covering all general or vocational education given to children who are physically handicapped, mentally handicapped, socially maladjusted or are in other special categories' (1969 ed.). Lists governmental and non-governmental agencies responsible for the provision of special education in 136 countries and territories. Arranged A-Z by English names. *Class No:* 377(058)

Executive Education

[3886]

cNULTY, N.G., *ed.* **International directory of executive education.** Oxford, Pergamon Press, 1985. 528p. £84; $125. ISBN: 0080309887.

In-depth descriptions of 4 aspects of executive education and training services in 92 countries (Programmes in general management; Programmes in functional management; In-company training; Master's degree programmes for executives). Management consultancy services. Description of schools. Index of acronyms of schools; Index to acronyms and terms used in text; Matrix index of programmes by country. *Class No:* 377.3

Further & Higher Education

Bibliographies

[3887]

LTBACH, P.G. Comparative higher education abroad: bibliography and analysis. New York, Praeger, with the International Council for Educational Development, 1976. xii,274p. $5.50. ISBN: 0891922229.

More than 1700 unannotated references to books, periodical articles and dissertations on countries in Africa, Asia, Canada, Europe, Latin America, the Middle East, and Oceania. Includes two bibliographical essays and an annotated list of relevant books published in 1974. *Class No:* 378(01)

[3888]

ALTBACH, P.G. Comparative higher education: research trends and bibliography. London, Mansell, 1979. xi,[1],206p. ISBN: 072010825x.

The essay on recent trends (p.3-113) indicates directions for future research and is well footnoted. Bibliography of 1116 numbered entries with interpolations. Topic cross-reference index; country and region index; author index. *Class No:* 378(01)

[3889]

LTBACH, P.G. *and* **KELLY, D.H. Higher education in international perspective:** a survey and bibliography. London, Mansell Publishing Ltd., 1985. xviii,583p. £40. ISBN: 0720117070.

The two reports of the survey, *Perspectives on comparative higher education, a survey of research and literature* and *Research on higher education in European socialist countries* includes 82 and 210 references respectively. The bibliography of 6901 items, has 22 subject sections, each subdivided by geographical regions, then by books and articles, and finally A-Z by author, followed by bibliographies, again by region. *Class No:* 378(01)

[3890]

MENGE, R.S. *and* **MATHIS, B.C. Key resources on teaching, learning, curriculum and faculty development:** a guide to the higher education literature. San Francisco, CA., Jossey-Bass Publishers, 1988. xix,406p. $35; £32. (*Higher education series.*) ISBN: 1555421180.

686 annotated items, books and periodical articles, on teaching, learning, curriculum and faculty development in colleges and universities. Arranged in subject chapters, each with an introduction, references, and bibliography, subdivided by general and then subject and A-Z by author. Cross-references. Includes information on periodicals and databases. Author index, p.373-384; analytical subject index, p.385-406. *Class No:* 378(01)

[3891]

—REID, B.J. 'Higher education', 1980-85. In *British book news,* August 1985, p.450-58.

A review of recent books covering a wide subject area (General - Learning and teaching - Entry to higher education - Students study courses in particular disciplines - Higher education staff, research, finance and management - Distance education - Industry and employment - Books and libraries - Overseas students and higher education overseas - Adult education). Includes 206 books, 2 serials, 3 abstracting and indexing journals, and 4 directories. *Class No:* 378(01)

Encyclopaedias

[3892]

The International encyclopedia of higher education. Knowles, A.S., *ed.* Washington, Jossey-Bass Publishers, 1977. 10v. (5208p.). $700 the set. ISBN: 0875893236.

V.1. *Contents. Contributors, Acronyms. Glossary.* v.2-9. A-Z entries. v.10. *Index.* About 500 named contributors. Appended to each substantial article are lists of (a) major international and national organizations; (b) principal information sources. 'Adult education': v.2. p.120-73: 7 sections, plus two appendices (p.168-73). Country entries are a feature. V.9 concludes with 'International directory' (p.4477-4588). V.10: *Index* comprises a name index and a subject index (p.4633-5208). Somewhat elaborate layout. For the very large reference library. 'A unique source for state-of-the-art surveys, and particularly for comparative studies ... (*Library journal,* 15th April 1979, p.886). *Class No:* 378(031)

[3893]

—ALTBACH, P.G. International higher education: an encyclopedia. New York, Garland, 1991. 2v.(1165p.) $150. £110. ISBN: 0824048474, US; 1558621520, UK.

52 country and regional profiles (mainly underdeveloped areas) arranged by countries, blend description and analysis into short overviews of 10 to 20 pages, covering historical developments, current trends, structure and governance, higher education's relationship with political systems and labour markets, etc. Also included are 15 cross-cultural topics, including foreign education, graduate education, private higher education, and academic freedom. Updates, in part, the above, aging encyclopedia. *Class No:* 378(031)

Reviews & Abstracts

[3894]

Research into higher education abstracts. Abingdon, Oxon, Carfax Publishing Co., for the Society for Research into Higher Education, 1967-. v.1,no.1-. 3pa (previously quarterly). £112. ISSN: 00345326.

About 200 abstracts per issue. Sections: A. General - B. Systems and institutions - C. Teaching and learning - D. Students - E. Staff - F. Student assessment and course evaluation - G. Continuing education - H. Information technology and networks. Over 500 journals scanned. Author and subject indexes each issue, cumulating in the 3rd issue each year. *Class No:* 378(048)

Yearbooks & Directories

[3895]

Directory of technical and further education, 1993. 27th ed. Harlow, Longman, 1993. xi,509p. illus. £65. ISBN: 0582096049.

Includes both public and private education in the United Kingdom, with courses and careers from 16 to restart, and from adult education to polytechnics. 11 chapters: 1. Central government; 2. Regional framework for further education; 3. Local government education departments; 4. Further education colleges; 5. Tertiary colleges; 6. Sixth form colleges; 7. Correspondence colleges; 8. Examining bodies; 9. Employment and careers; 10. CBI; TUC; 11. Allied organizations. Subject, geographical and general indexes. *Class No:* 378(058)

[3896]

Vacation study abroad, 2000/2001: the complete guide to Summer and short term study. Steen, S.J. Institute of International Education, 2000. ISBN: 0872062503.

First published 1951. Annual.

Designed to assist students planning summer study abroad, with relevant information on more than 850 study abroad programmes.

Class No: 378(058)

Developing Countries

Bibliographies

[3897]

ALTBACH, P.G. **Higher education in developing nations:** a select bibliography, 1969-1974. New York, Praeger, with the International Council for Educational Development, 1975. iv,229,[1]. $6. ISBN: 0891922210.

Continues the author's *Higher education in developing countries* (Cambridge, Mass., Harvard University, Center for International Affairs, 1970).

Bibliography of 2438 references (general perspectives; developing countries; regions and countries; Africa (Botswana ... Zambia); Asia; Latin America; Middle East and North Africa) - largely for periodical articles. Appended list of bibliographies and journals. Cross-reference index. Appendix: International and regional agencies concerned with research and education in higher education. *Class No:* 378(4/9-77)(01)

Europe

Handbooks & Manuals

[3898]

RASHDALL, H. **The Universities of Europe in the Middle Ages.** Powicke, F. M. *and* Emden, A.B., *eds.* new ed. London, Oxford University Press, 1936,(reprinted 1987). 3.v.(1587p.)illus. v.1. £55; v.2.£35; v.3. £50. ISBN: 019822981x v.1; 0198229828 v.2; 0198229836 v.3.

First published 1895.

A scholarly account, heavily footnoted. Bibliographies precede accounts of individual universities (*e.g.* Vienna, in v.2:one page of bibliography). Appendices of documents and notes. General index in v.3. p.497-558. Folding map. *Class No:* 378(4)(035)

Europe—Western

Handbooks & Manuals

[3899]

Higher education in the European Community: student handbook. 7th ed. Phoenix, AZ, Oryx Press, 2000. $32.50. ISBN: 0897747852.

First published 1977.

A directory of courses and institutions in the European Union. Arranged by country, under organizations of higher education (type, student statistics, organization and validity of courses); admission and registration; knowledge of the language of instruction, language courses, and other courses; financial assistance and scholarships; entry and residence regulations; social aspects (social security and health insurance, advisory services, student employment, cost of living, accommodation, etc.). Appendix to each entry lists organizations and institutions from which further information and application forms may be obtained, a bibliography of national information material and, in most cases, a table of subjects taught at each institution. Also includes information on the European University Institute, Florence; College of Europe; Bruges; and information on the Erasmus programme, ECTS, Comett, Lingua and Naric. *Class No:* 378(400)(035)

Great Britain

[3900]

UNIVERSITY CENTRAL ADMISSION SERVICE (UCAS). **A parents' guide to higher education.** Richmond, Trotman, 1997. 88p. £7.99. ISBN: 0856603600.

Handbook for parents to help them through their children's applications yo higher education, with suggestions on how parents can help children through the selection process and into university or college. Advice on choosing a course, applying through UCAS, money matters and student life. *Class No:* 378(410)

Handbooks & Manuals

[3901]

College administration a handbook. Locke, M., *and others*. 2nd ed Longman Group UK Ltd., in association with NATFHE, 1988. xii [1], 498p. £19.95. ISBN: 0582901170.

First published 1980.

Describes in detail the administration of public sector post-schoo education in England and Wales. 4 basic sections: 1. Th administrative framework - 2. The institutions and the staff - 3 Curriculum and students - 4. Buildings. Cross-references. References A-Z by author, p.477-485, with further reading lists attached to man subsections. Triple-column detailed index, p.490-498.

Class No: 378(410)(035)

[3902]

NATFHE handbook of initial teacher training, 1996. Central Registe and Clearing Houses Ltd., *comp.* London, National Association o Teachers in Further and Higher Education, 1996. Annual. £12. ISBN 0901390445.

First published 1954.

Detailed guide to courses of training for teaching, and a wide rang of other courses. For each institution; general information; course offered; method of application. Lists courses within the CRCH scheme, A-Z by name, followed by entries for colleges of dance music, drama, etc. Index of subjects and courses. Index of institutions.

Class No: 378(410)(035)

Reports Literature

[3903]

GREAT BRITAIN. Committee on Higher Education. **Report of th Committee appointed ... under the chairmanship of Lord Robbins 1961-1963.** London, HMSO, 1963. 7v. (*Cmnd 2154.*)

The Report is accompanied by 5 Appendices: 1. The demand fo places in higher education (2 pts.) - 3 Teachers in higher education - 4. Administrative, financial an economic aspects - 5. Higher education in other countries (1(countries; 'Principal written sources', p.300-6).

Class No: 378(410)(047)

Yearbooks & Directories

[3904]

The Gabbitas-Thring guide to independent further education 1989/1990. 3rd ed. London, John Catt Ltd., 1989. £7.95. ISSN 0269588x.

First published 1986.

Lists a wide variety of schools and colleges, including tutoria colleges and professional/vocational training establishments.

Class No: 378(410)(058)

USA

Bibliographies

[3905]

BEACH, M., *comp.* **A Subject bibliography of the history o American higher education.** Westport, CT., Greenwood Press, 1984 vii,165p. $36.95. ISBN: 0313232768.

A bibliography of major books, journal articles and dissertations o the subject, arranged A-Z by subject (Academic costume ... Zoology) Unannotated. Author and subject indexes. A companion volume to th author's *Bibliographic guide to American colleges and universitie* (1976). *Class No:* 378(73)(01)

[3906]

PARKER, F. *and* PARKER, B.J. **US higher education:** a guide t information sources. Detroit, Mich., Gale Research Co., 1980 xii,675p. $68. (*Gale information library: Education information guid series, v.9.*) ISBN: 0810314762.

Annotated bibliography of books and reports on the history philosophy, administration, finance, governance, curriculum, studen life, library and audiovisual services, and custodian concerns of th field. Author arrangement, with detailed subject index.

Class No: 378(73)(01)

Research Establishments

[3907]

International directory of research institutions on higher education European Centre for Higher Education (CEPES). 2nd rev. ed. Paris Unesco, 1988. xv,134p. F.30; £6. (*IBEDATA series.*) ISBN 923002576x.

First published 1981 as *International directory of higher educatio research institutions*.

Particular emphasis on the research and publication functions o institutions, listing extensively the books, periodicals, documents an papers which they have published since 1983.

Class No: 378:061:061.62

Education Institutions

Worldwide

[3908]
:ademic year abroad, 2000/2001. Steen, S.J. New York, Institute of
International Education, 2000. $46.95. ISBN: 087206249x.
First published 1964. Annual.
Geographical arrangement of each part by region, subdivided by
country, city, and sponsoring institution. Information includes dates,
subjects offered, credit eligibility, language of instruction, highlights,
costs, housing, contact person, etc. Indexes by sponsoring body and
by field of study. '... the most comprehensive source ...' (*Reference
books bulletin*, 1 November 1989, p.598),.
Class No: 378:061:37(100)

Academic Dress

[3909]
RANKLYN, C.A.H. Academical dress, from the Middle Ages to the
present day, including Lambeth degrees. Hassocks, Sussex, the
Author, 1970. vii,254p. illus.
15 chapters, devoted to the academical dress of graduates (1. The
origin of academical dress ... 8. The University of Oxford - 9. The
University of Cambridge - 10. The University of London - 11. Other
universities ... 15. Bibliography (58 items). Small black-and-white
illustrations. *Class No:* 378:391

[3910]
AYCRAFT, F.W., *comp.* Degrees and hoods of the world's
universities and colleges. 5th ed., rev. and enl. by F.R.S.Rogers and
others. Hassocks, Sussex, C.A.H.Franklyn, 1972. xvii,162p.illus.
First published 1923.
Short historical introduction. Main section gives, under each
country, its universities and under each university its degrees and
details of the shape and colours of its degree hoods. Separate sections
for theological colleges and learned societies. Illus. include hoods in
full colour and a section showing hood shapes. A comprehensive index
is provided. *Class No:* 378:391

[3911]
MITH, H. *and* SHEARD, W. Academic dress and insignia of the
world: gowns, hats, chains of office, hoods, rings, medals and other
degree insignia of universities and other institutions of learning. Cape
Town, Balkema, 1970. 3v. (1843p.). illus.
V.1: *General introduction. British Commonwealth, Irish Republic
(Eire) & Republic of South Africa;* v.2: *Europe, Africa, Asia, United
States of America, Central and South America;* v.3: *Glossary and
definitions.* Hood identification tables (p.1646-1771; by colours). US
Inter Collegiate Code. Abbreviations, Index (p.1825-41). Detailed full-
page black-and-white illus. 442 plates, with notes usually facing.
Class No: 378:391

Europe

[3912]
ARGREAVES-MAWDSLEY, W.N. A History of academical dress
in Europe until the end of the eighteenth century. Oxford, Clarendon
Press, 1963. (Reprinted Greenwood Press, 1978). xiii,235p. illus (21
pl.). £22.50. ISBN: 0313202508.
Chapters: 1. Italy, Spain, Portugal and Malta - 2. France - 3-4.
Great Britain and Ireland - 5. German-speaking countries, the Low
Countries, Switzerland, Scandinavia, Hungary and Poland. A scholarly
survey, with profuse footnotes. Glossary of terms (p.190-5); critical
bibliography (p.196-210: A. Manuscripts - B. Printed books).
Analytical index. Not very fully illustrated (colour frontispiece and 21
black-and-white half-tones, 17 drawings), but descriptions are detailed.
Class No: 378:391(4)

Great Britain

[3913]
IAW, G.W. Academical dress of British and Irish universities.
Phillimore, 1995. 264p. illus. £20.
Originally published 1966 as *Academical dress of British
universities.*
Descriptions and diagrams of gowns, hoods, robes and caps worn by
graduates and undergraduates. Index of universities and degrees;
useful list of abbreviations of degrees. *Class No:* 378:391(410)

Degrees & Qualifications

Worldwide

Handbooks & Manuals

[3914]
International guide to qualifications in education. National Academic
Recognition Information Centre, British Council. 4th ed. London,
Mansell Publishing, in association with the British Council, 1995.
896p. £112.55. ISBN: 0720122171.
First published 1984.
Chapters on each of *c.*150 countries, arranged A-Z, from which
students come to Britain for further study, training or employment. For
each country there is a brief introduction to education, evaluation of
recognition normally accorded to key qualifications, description of
marking systems used at secondary and tertiary levels, and a survey of
the structure of education in the country. Appendices on examination
bodies and international organizations. *Class No:* 378.2(100)(035)

Great Britain

[3915]
British qualifications: a complete guide to educational, technical,
professional and academic qualifications in Britain. 30th ed.
London, Kogan Page, 2000. Annual. xliv,751p. $85. ISBN:
0749431652. ISSN: 01415972.
First published 1966.
A comprehensive guide to educational, technical, professional and
academic qualifications in Britain. 7 parts: 1. Teaching establishments
- 2. Secondary school examinations - 3. Further education
examinations - 4. Awards made by universities and designated
institutions - 5. Qualifications, listed by trades & professions (*c.*200
career fields and professions (Accountancy ... Youth and community
service) - 6. Bodies crediting independent institutions - 7. Study
associations and the 'learned societies'. Detailed index preceded by
index of advertisers. *Class No:* 378.2(410)

[3916]
Which degree? 1999. Cambridge, Hobsons, 1998. Annual. 4v. (*CRAC
student guides..*) ISBN: 1860170498, v.1; 1860172563, v.2;
1860172571, v.3; 186017051x, v.4.
Successor to *Which university?.*
A subject listing of over 12,000 degree courses in the UK, stating
content and entrance requirements followed by sections on universities,
polytechnics and colleges, stating amenities, etc. Volumes are arranged
by subject: 1: Arts, humanities, languages - 2. Engineering,
technology, geography - 3. Sciences, medicine, mathematics - 4.
Social sciences, business, education, law. Essential reading. Indexes to
all 4 vols. *Class No:* 378.2(410)

USA

[3917]
Peterson's guide to certificate programs at American colleges and
universities. Lopos, G.J., *and others, eds.* Princeton, N.J.,
Peterson's Guides, 1988. 343p. $35.95. ISBN: 0878667415.
Developed in co-operation with the National University Continuing
Education Association.
Information on over 1400 programmes, representing nearly 300 US
four-year colleges & universities, arranged A-Z by state, subdivided
by programme classification. Each entry has programme content,
format, evaluation criteria, enrollment requirements, cost, student
services, contact person. Geared towards adult part-time learners and
heavily career-oriented. Indexes to institutions and programmes.
Class No: 378.2(73)

Scholarships & Postgraduate Awards

[3918]
The Awards almanac: an international guide to careers, research and
education funds. Schmidt, G.W. *and* Singson, K.P., *eds.* Detroit &
London, St. James Press, 1993. xi,749p. £61. $90. ISBN:
155862144x.
Aimed at individuals (not organizations) requiring funds to continue
education or to carry out activities related to their career. Arranged A-
Z under the name of the grant-awarding body, each entry has contact
names and addresses, brief description of purpose of award, areas of
study it encompasses, details of requirement of award, method of
application, deadlines, amounts awarded, ratio of applicants and
awards offered. Indexes of awards by name and by subject covered,
granting organizations, and keywords. *Class No:* 378.3

[3919]

BRITISH COUNCIL. **Scholarships abroad:** scholarships offered to British students by overseas governments and universities, 1991/92. London, for British Council, 1990. Annual. 58p. £4.95. ISBN: 0117015008.

Lists over 300 foreign government awards available to British postgraduate students, with details of how to apply. Arranged by country, A-Z. Followed by information on the Commonwealth Scholarship and Fellowship Plan, Council of Europe, and NATO. *Class No:* 378.3

[3920]

The Grants register, 2001. 19th ed. London, Macmillan Reference, 2000. 1024p. £99. ISBN: 0333773330. ISSN: 00725471.

First published 1969 (for 1969-70). Editor of early issues was C.A.Lerner.

Details of awards and grants worldwide. Subject index, index of awards and awarding bodies. Complementary to Unesco's annual *Study abroad (qv). Class No:* 378.3

[3921]

Study abroad, 1998-1999. 30th ed. Paris, Unesco, 1997. £21.28 (CD-ROM).

First published 1948.

A directory of nearly 3000 opportunities for further study and training in all academic and professional fields, offered by international organizations, governments, private and public foundations, universities and other institutions in more than 124 countries.

Class No: 378.3

Great Britain

Yearbooks & Directories

[3922]

The Educational grants directory, 1998/99: voluntary and charitable help for children and students in need. Harland, S. 5th ed. London, The Directory of Social Change, 1998. 256p. £18.95. ISBN: 1900360314.

Details over 200 national and general sources of help, A-Z by name; 900 local and parochial educational charities; and nearly 100 companies sponsoring degree courses. Details are given of eligibility, policy/practice, grants, correspondent, and address. Other sections: musical education (choir schools, music scholarships); assisted places scheme; education authorities; and sources of further information and advice. Index. *Class No:* 378.3(410)(058)

USA

Yearbooks & Directories

[3923]

Directory of research grants 2000. Phoenix, AZ., Oryx Press, 2000. 1264p. $159.50. ISBN: 1573561894.

First published for 1983. Annual.

Arrangement is by subject areas. A tool for scholars, grants administrators, faculty members and any person or organization looking for a way to get support for research projects.

Class No: 378.3(73)(058)

Universities, Polytechnics & Colleges

[3924]

The Encyclopedia of higher education. Clarke, B.R. *and* Neave, G.R., *eds.* Oxford, Elsevier Science/Pergamon Press, 1994. 4v.(2530p). £857.15. ISBN: 0080372511.

V.1 analyses more than 135 national systems of higher education; v.2 & 3 have papers on an extensive range of issues and problems in the fields; and v.4 offers a unique and comprehensive review of the development of core academic disciplines. In all, over 300 essays. Indexes of contributors, names and subjects. '... a monumental achievement ...' (*Choice*, v.30(6), February 1993, p.938).

Class No: 378.4/.6

[3925]

History of universities. Brockliss, L., *ed.* Oxford, Oxford University Press, 1981-. Annual. c.£50 each volume. ISSN: 01445138.

V.12, published in 1994 (502p. illus. £50. ISBN 0198204604) includes studies of English collegiate statutes in the later Middle Ages, teaching of natural philosophy in 17th century Paris, women academics in England, 1870-1930, an item of research in progress, conference reports, an essay review, book reviews. Index. *Class No:* 378.4/.6

[392

International handbook of universities. International Association Universities. 16th ed. London, Macmillan Reference, 2000. 2000 £149. ISBN: 0333945131.

First published 1959.

Includes universities in 115 countries, arranged A-Z by countr with brief descriptions of faculties and departments, names of dea and principals, admission requirements, degrees and diplom awarded, publications, number of academic staff, student enrollme library (stock and publications). Index. *Class No:* 378.4/.6

Yearbooks & Directories

[392

European education yearbook: the annual guide to study abroad, 199 Swanley, Kent, Nexus Business Connections Ltd., 364p. a supplement, 'Course and program selector'. ISSN: 0968168x.

Details of over 700 universities, colleges and institutions worldwid Index of institutions and courses guide precede. Main section 'Studying in Europe' (A-Z by country, with an introduction to country followed by a list of universities, etc.); 'Higher educati overseas'(profiles of institutions); and 'Learning English oversea Many advertisements of educational institutions. *Class No:* 378.4/ .6(058)

[392

The World list of universities/Liste mondiale des universit International Association of Universities, *comp.* 22nd ed. Londc Macmillan Reference, 1999. 1600p. £99. ISBN: 0333671511.

Directory of universities and other institutions of higher education over 150 countries and a guide to the principal national a international organizations concerned with higher education. Part Institutions and national organizations - Part 2: International a regional organizations. University vacations. Appendix: T International Association of Universities (officers; membe publications). Index. In English and French. *Class No:* 378.4/.6(058

[392

The World of learning, 1999. 50th ed. London, Europa Publicatio 1999. Annual. 2085p. £280. ISBN: 1857430646. ISSN: 00842117.

A directory of universities, colleges, libraries, learned societi museums, art galleries and research institutes in more than 1 countries, arranged A-Z (International - Afghanistan ... Zimbabw Includes over 26,000 institutional names, addresses, etc., and li more than 150,000 individuals. The international section has details more than 400 international educational, scientific and cultu organizations. Includes 'open' and 'free' universities. Index institutions. *Class No:* 378.4/.6(058)

Histories

[393

The Illustrated history of Oxford University. Prest, J., *ed.* Oxfo Oxford University Press, 1993. 500p. 224 illus. 5 maps. £25. ISBI 0198201583.

Contains separate chapters on Oxford's contribution to religic classical studies, the arts, and the life and physical science Chronology. Guide to further reading. Index. *Class No:* 378.4/.6(09

Europe

[393

BOSWICK, S. **Guide to the universities of Europe.** New York, Fac on File, 1991. 296p. $35. ISBN: 081602359x.

A directory of 275 universities in 26 European countries, arrang A-Z by country. Information for prospective applicants includ admission requirement, application procedures and deadlines, degr requirements, visas, costs, scholarships available, etc. Aimed at Nor American applicants. Both public and private universities are include Universities of Eastern Europe are treated separately.

Class No: 378.4/.6(4)

Europe—Western

[393

Directory of higher education institutions in the Europe Community. London, Kogan Page; Luxembourg, Office for offic Publications of the European Community, 1992. 544p. illus. map £25. ISBN: 0749404892, UK; 9282627500, EC.

Over 4000 entries, giving address, number of students, and subj areas covered. In English and French. *Class No:* 378.4/.6(400)

Great Britain

Handbooks & Manuals

[3933]

ASSOCIATION OF COMMONWEALTH UNIVERSITIES. **Higher education in the United Kingdom, 1992-93.** Harlow, Essex, Longman Group UK Ltd., 1992. Biennial. 312p. illus. £14.95. ISBN: 0582081955. ISSN: 03061744.

First published 1936.

A guide for overseas students wishing to study in Britain and their advisers. Lists 150 subjects, A-Z, with, under each subject heading, a list of courses available and where offered. A list of useful addresses. A list for further reading. *Class No: 378.4/.6(410)(035)*

[3934]

Graduate studies: the complete guide to over 6000 post-graduate courses in the UK. CRAC (Careers Research and Advisory Centre). Cambridge, Hobson Publishing Plc.

First published 1972. Annual.

Summaries of research facilities and courses and basic information about the institutions in which postgraduate study is available. In 4 parts: 111 subject sections, A-Z (Accounting and finance...Zoology), each entry naming the institutions concerned, with title of course of study area. qualifications, period of study, any specific entrance requirements, and a brief synopsis - Institutions address list - Research establishments - Research institutes... Index of course titles. Index of subject headings and applied sciences. Each entry gives the name of the institution, title of course or study area, qualification, period of study, any specific entrance requirements, and a brief synopsis. Cross-references. Institutions address list; Index of course titles; Index of subject headings; and index of advertisers. *Class No: 378.4/.6(410)(035)*

[3935]

The NatWest student book 2001 entry. Boehm, K. *and* Lees-Spalding, J. Richmond, Trotman, 2000. Annual. 650p. illus., maps. £12.99. ISBN: 085660531x.

First published 1979.

A book for those applying for a degree course in UK colleges, polytechnics and universities. Content: How to go about it - Where to study - Maps - Subject/place index - What to study. Index. *Class No: 378.4/.6(410)(035)*

[3936]

Where to study in the UK. London, Kogan Page, 1999. £7.99.

First published 1986.

Contains information relating to the qualifications of professional associations and examining bodies, with details of the colleges and schools in the independent and public sectors which prepare students for the professional associations' examinations. In 5 parts: 1. The professional associations; 2. Business, commercial, secretarial and technical examining bodies; 3. Colleges offering professional courses; 4. Post-experience and postgraduate courses; 5. English language colleges. A list of useful addresses is followed by indexes of professional assocations and advertisers. *Class No: 378.4/.6(410)(035)*

Yearbooks & Directories

[3937]

The Times' good universities guide: the definitive guide to Britain's universities. O'Leary, J. *and* Cannon, T. London, Bartholomew & Times, 1993. 216p. £8.99.

A complete list of all 96 UK universities, each with facts, figures, and a short profile. Also rankings (league tables of performance according to clear criteria), and listing 'top' universities by subject. (Entry taken from *The good book guide*, v.63, July/August 1993, p.15). *Class No: 378.4/.6(410)(058)*

Histories

[3938]

GABRIEL, A.L. **Summary bibliography of the history of the universities of Great Britain and Ireland up to 1800,** covering publications between 1900 and 1968. Notre Dame, Indiana, Medieval Institute, University of Notre Dame, 1974. 154p. (*Texts and studies in the history of medieval education, no.14.*)

1514 entries, in 6 sections, on the history of education in Europe and England up to 1800, and on English, Scottish, Welsh and Irish universities. Author and subject indexes. *Class No: 378.4/.6(410)(091)*

[3939]

The History of British Universities, 1800-1969: a bibliography, excluding Oxford and Cambridge. London, Society for Research into Higher Education, 1970. xv,264p.

7 general sections, followed by entries on the universities, A-Z (p.59-250). 'University of York' (p.248-50: 40 entries). Data on each, as appropriate: (a) books and pamphlets; (b) theses and dissertations; (c) reports; (d) periodical articles; (e) bibliographies. Author index. *Class No: 378.4/.6(410)(091)*

[3940]

The History of the University of Oxford. Oxford, Oxford University Press, 1984-. To be in 8v.

A completely new and full-scale history, from its obscure origins in the 12th century to the late 20th century. 8 chronologically arranged volumes are planned: two on the Middle Ages; three spanning the early modern period to 1800; two on the 19th century; one on the 20th century. Published so far: v.1: *The early Oxford Schools,* ed. by J.I. Catto (1984. 670p. £55); v.II: *Late medieval Oxford* ed. by J.I. Catto & T.A.R. Evans (1992. 823p. illus. £90); v.III: *The collegiate university,* ed. by James McConica (1986. 800p. £65); v.V: *The eighteenth century,* ed. by L.S. Sutherland and L.G. Mitchell (1986. 968p. illus.£75). *Class No: 378.4/.6(410)(091)*

[3941]

LEADER, D.R. **A History of the University of Cambridge. V.1: The University to 1546.** Cambridge, Cambridge University Press, 1988. xxi,399p. illus. (18 half-tones), 2 maps. £35. ISBN: 0521328829.

To be in 4v. V.1: *The University to 1546,* by D.R. Leader; v.2: *1546-1750,* by V. Morgan; v.3: *1750-1870,* by P. Searby; v.4: *1870-1990,* by C. Brooke.

V.1. has 13 sections: 1. Origins - 2. Hostels, convents and colleges - 3. Teaching - 4. The trivium - 5. The Quadrivium - 6. The philosophers - 7. Theology - 8. Law - 9. Medicine - 10. Interlude and expansion - 11. Internal reform - 12. John Fisher and Lady Margaret - 13. The Henrician reformation. Bibliography, p.352-379. Index, mainly of people, p.381-399. *Class No: 378.4/.6(410)(091)*

Scotland

Biographies

[3942]

WATT, D.E.R. **A Biographical dictionary of Scottish graduates,** to AD 1410. Oxford, Clarendon Press, 1977. 607p.

Biographical data on *c.*1100 graduates who attended universities in England and the continent before the foundation in 1411 of St. Andrews, the oldest of the Scottish universities. 'Will take its place naturally on the reference shelves of all libraries with any pretence to holdings in medieval history' (*Library review,* v.27, Winter 1978, p.264). *Class No: 378.4/.6(411)(092)*

Commonwealth

Yearbooks & Directories

[3943]

Commonwealth universities yearbook, 1999: a directory to the universities of the Commonwealth and the handbook of their Association. 74th ed. London, Association of Commonwealth Universities, 1999. 2v.(1,220p.). £155. ISBN: 085143164x. ISSN: 00697745.

First published 1914.

V.1: Australia to Nigeria. v.2: Pakistan to Zimbabwe. The UK has 500 pages in v.2. Entries give information on address, numbers of staff and students, types of courses, income, etc. Abbreviations. Indexes. *Class No: 378.4/.6(41-44)(058)*

Japan

[3944]

Japanese colleges and universities, 1989: a guide to institutions of higher education in Japan. Association of International Education, Japan, *comp. & ed.* Tokyo, Marazon Co. Ltd., 1989. xviii,781p. diagrs. maps. ISBN: 4621033573.

3 sections: 1. National colleges and universities (A-Z by name); 2. Local public colleges and universities; 3. Private colleges and universities. Other sections include: School fees; Scholarships; Programs. Japanese-English names list of the colleges and universities. Index. *Class No: 378.4/.6(52)*

Africa

Yearbooks & Directories

[3945]

Directory of African universities. Association of African Universities. 5th ed. Accra North, A.A.U. Documentation Centre, 1988. [4],viii,495p.

3rd ed. published 1983.

Arrangement is A-Z by country, subdivided A-Z by name of university. Information includes address, telephone number, academic year, foundation date, language of instruction, senior staff, council, statistics of personnel (administrative and teaching), number of students, faculties, conditions of admission, libraries, publications. Entries are in the European language of the country. *Class No: 378.4/.6(6)(058)*

America—North & Central

Yearbooks & Directories

[3946]

The Faculty directory of higher education. 1st ed. Detroit, Mich., Gale Research Co., 1988. 12v.(6635p.). $785 the set. (individual subject vols. available separately). ISBN: 0810327503. ISSN: 08949476.

Classified directory of names, addresses and titles of courses taught by some 623,000 faculty members in more than 31000 US and 220 Canadian colleges and universities. 11 discipline-oriented volumes cover business, economics and law; communications; computer science and data processing; education; engineering; fine and applied arts; humanities; language and literature; medicine and nursing; science and mathematics; and social sciences. Each volume has a short guide to subject coverage and a key to abbreviations. V.12 is the master A-Z index of faculty members, and also has a list of institutions. Competes with *The National faculty directory*. 'Primary value will be as a marketing aid' (*Choice,* v.25)7), March 1988, p.1062).
Class No: 378.4/.6(71/73)(058)

Caribbean

Bibliographies

[3947]

Universities in the Caribbean region - struggles to democratize: an annotated bibliography. Waggoner, B.A. *and* Waggoner, G.R., *comps.* Boston, Mass., G.K. Hall, 1986. 368p. $55. ISBN: 0816181594.

Over 1600 annotated entries on the rapid growth of higher education in the Caribbean after World War II. *Class No:* 378.4/.6(729)(01)

USA

Yearbooks & Directories

[3948]

American universities and colleges. 14th ed. New York, deGruyter, 1992. 2200p. $149.95. ISBN: 0899258611. ISSN: 00660922.

First published 1928.

Describes over 1900 institutions in detail. Profiles are arranged by state and include information on history, admission requirements, programmes offered, degrees conferred, enrollment, fees and financial aid, faculty size, administration, buildings and grounds, etc. Institution and general indexes. *Class No:* 378.4/.6(73)(058)

[3949]

Faculty white pages, 1991. CMG Information Services, *comp.* Detroit, Mich., Gale Research Co., 1991. 1837p. Annual. $135. ISBN: 0810371782.

Lists names, addresses and telephone numbers of more than 510,000 teaching faculty at over 3,000 US colleges, universities and other institutions of higher learning. Arranged in 41 subject sections, and A-Z by name within each section. A guide to subject coverage lists over 300 specific disciplines that are covered in the general subject sections. 'Roster of colleges and universities' provides name, city, State, and zipcode for each of the institutions covered. *Class No:* 378.4/.6(73)(058)

[3950]

The National faculty directory. 31st ed. Detroit, Mich., Gale Research, 1999. 3v. $770. ISBN: 0787633712. ISSN: 00774472.

First published 1970.

Covers about 3200 junior colleges, colleges and universities in the US and 120 selected Canadian institutions. Single A-Z sequence of entries, which give individual's name, department, institution, address, city, state, and zip code. Geographic listing of the institutions covered. Six-monthly supplement updates the main edition. *Class No:* 378.4/.6(73)(058)

[3951]

Yearbook of American universities and colleges, 1986-1987. Kurian, G.T., *ed.* New York, Garland, 1988. *c*1637p. charts, tables. $95. ISBN: 0824079426. ISSN: 08961034.

First published for 1986-1987. To be annual.

A review of major developments in US higher education in 15 sections: 2. Principal sectors of higher education - 3. Issues - 4. Statistics - 5. People ... 10. Selected state reports on higher education... 15. Bibliography (p.615-632). Index, p.633-653.
Class No: 378.4/.6(73)(058)

39 Customs & Traditions

Costume

[3952]
ULLOLPH, A. **The Fashion book.** London, Phaidon Press, 1998.
512p. illus. (some col.) $39.95. ISBN: 071483808x. *Class No:* 391

Bibliographies

[3953]
NTHONY, P. *and* ARNOLD, J. **Costume: a general bibliography.**
London, Costume Society, c/o Department of Textiles, 1974. vi,42p.
£1. ISBN: 090340706x.
First published 1966.
A selection of *c.*500 periodical articles, books and journals, mainly
published after 1900, dealing primarily with the history of Western
European costume. (*Introduction*). 35 sections of briefly annotated
entries (sections by form and by subject). No index.
Class No: 391(01)

[3954]
ostume index: a subject index to plates and illustrated text. Monro, I.S.
and Cook, D.E. New York, H.W. Wilson Co., 1937. Supplement,
1957. x,338p. Supplement. x,210p.
Indexes illustrations of costume in 615 books; entries are under
countries, types of people wearing costume, and specific articles.
Locations in 33 libraries. The supplement adds 347 titles.
Class No: 391(01)

[3955]
ILER, H. *and* HILER, M., *comps.* **Bibliography of costume:** a
dictionary catalog of about eight thousand books and periodicals.
Cushing, H.G., *ed.* New York, Wilson, 1939 (Reprinted New York,
Arno Press, 1976). xl,911p.
Author, title, subject, editor, illustrator, engraver and other entries
in one alphabet; *c.*8400 items. The fullest information, including non-
evaluative annotation, is given in the author entry. 'The items listed
include books, periodicals and portfolios of plates dealing with dress,
jewelry, and decoration of the body, in general and for special
occasions, of all countries, times, and peoples ... In addition to books
on costume many books of travel, history and antiquities are listed
since they include text or illustrations of costume value' (*Preface*).
Class No: 391(01)

Encyclopaedias

[3956]
RELAND, P.J. **Encyclopedia of fashion details.** London, Batsford,
1989. 264p. 512 illus. £17.99. ISBN: 071346433x.
Fashion details (*e.g.* pleats, tucks, piping, pockets, collars).
Arrangement is A-Z and illustrates some of the ways in which style
and decorative effects may feature in the design of a garment.
Class No: 391(031)

[3957]
LANCHÉ, J.R. **A Cyclopaedia of costume;** or, Dictionary of dress,
including notices of contemporaneous fashions on the continent; and a
general chronological history of the costumes of the principal countries
of Europe, from the commencement of the Christian era to the
accession of George the Third. London, Chatto & Windus, 1876-79
(Reprinted Gale Research Co., Detroit, 1969). 2v. illus (some col.).
V.1 contains the dictionary and covers a wide variety of costumes,
material, armour, etc., from lace, hood, sleeves, pin and wimple to
crozier, helmet, gauntlet and sword; many quotations; some footnote
references. V.2 is a history from 53B.C. to A.D.1760. Despite its age,
it is still valuable for details of costume of the medieval and
renaissance periods. *Class No:* 391(031)

[3958]
ACINET, A. **The Historical encyclopedia of costumes.** New York,
Checkmark Books, 1995. 320p. illus. (some col.). $45. ISBN:
0816019762.
Originally published in 20 instalments, *c.*1876-86, in *Le costume
historique*. In 1888 a 2000-page work in 6 vols. was fashioned from
the earlier periodical instalments.
The 1888 work was the basis for the English ed., condensed to one
vol., edited in chronological order, and redesigned into a more
accessible form. In 4 parts: *The ancient world - Nineteenth century
antique civilizations - Europe from Byzantium to the 1800s -*

....(contd.)
Traditional costumes of the 1800s. Each part is subdivided
geographically. Index by country. 'The scope of the work is
impressive' (*RQ*, v.28(4), Summer 1989, p.565). *Class No:* 391(031)

[3959]
—BOUCHER, F. **20,000 years of fashion:** the history of costume &
personal adornment. New ed. Abrams, 1987. 356p. illus. $45. ISBN:
0810916932.
Devoted only to Western fashion, but covers more chronological
ground than the above, having been updated to include the 1970s and
1980s. *Class No:* 391(031)

Handbooks & Manuals

[3960]
ARNOLD, J. **A Handbook of costume.** London, Macmillan Press, 1973
(Reprinted 1978). 336p. illus., facsims., ports. ISBN: 0333244893.
1. Primary sources (1. Paintings - 2. Sculpture... 6. Monumental
brasses... 9. Dolls - 10. Tapestries, embroidery, printed and woven
textiles - 11. Archival material, literary sources, periodicals and
newspapers) - 2. Dating costumes from construction techniques - 3.
Costume conservation, storage and display - 4. Costume for children
and students (use of library and museums; collection of reproductions
showing primary source material) - 5. Custume for the stage - 6.
Costume bibliography (p.217-32; 18 sections; *c.*500 items) - 7.
Collections of costume and costume accessories in England, Scotland
and Wales (over 80 collections under places, A-Z, p.233-336). Each
part of section 1 has list and notes of books with 'useful' illustrations
or a list of primary source books. Over 240 illus. (photography; line
drawings) in all. No index. A valuable guide to sources.
Class No: 391(035)

[3961]
ARNOLD, J. **Patterns of fashion.** London, Macmillan Press, 1972-85.
3v. (72p., 88p., 128p.). £12.95 each vol. ISBN: 0333136063, v.1;
0333136071, v.2; 0333382846, v.3.
V.1 is sub-titled 'Englishwomen's dresses and their construction,
*c.*1660-1860'; v.2 '... *c.*1860-1940' v.3 'the cut and construction of
clothes for men and women, *c.*1560-1620. *Class No:* 391(035)

[3962]
HOUCK, C. **The Fashion encyclopedia:** an essential guide to
everything you need to know about clothes. New York, St., Martin's
Press, 1982. 236p. illus. $22.50. ISBN: 0312284004.
A highly readable survey of the field of fashion, covering style,
personalities, production, care, and purchasing of material, clothing
and accessories. Arranged A-Z by topic. Many black-and-white
illustrations. *Class No:* 391(035)

[3963]
McKELVEY, K. **Fashion source book.** Oxford, Blackwell Scientific,
1996. 271p. illus. £15.99. $34.95. ISBN: 0632039930.
Comprehensive in scope, and designed to meet the need of fashion
students. Every item is illustrated, and there are 1600 copyright-free
illustrations which readers may use and adapt. *Class No:* 391(035)

[3964]
YARWOOD, D. **Costume in the Western world:** pictorial guide and
glossary. New York, St. Martin's Press; London, Lutterworth Press;
1981. 192p. illus. $17.50; £7.95. ISBN: 0312170130, US;
0718824784, UK.
Supplements 'The encyclopedia of world costume' (1979). Focuses
on fashion and costume in the Western world and North America from
the early Middle Ages to the present, emphasising in particular the
sixteenth to nineteenth centuries. *Class No:* 391(035)

[3965]
—YARWOOD, D. **The Encyclopedia of world costume.** London,
Batsford, 1978. (Reprinted 1986). 472p. illus. £14.95. ISBN:
0713413409.
This work, in A-Z order, has 2164 careful line-drawings and 8p. of
coloured illustrations. 'Sleeves' (p.377-84): 39 illus.; 'Lace' (p.264-
72) includes specific laces and lace terms. Bibliography (grouped),
p.454-9. Detailed index. 'This book should be in every school and
public library' (*New history*, no.11., 1979, p.8). *Class No:* 391

Dictionaries

[3966]

PICKEN, M.B. A Dictionary of costume and fashion: historic and modern: with over 950 illustrations. New York, Dover, 1999. 446p. $14.95. ISBN: 0486402940. *Class No:* 391(038)

[3967]

PICKEN, M.B. The Fashion dictionary: fabric, sewing and apparel in the language of fashion. Rev. & enl. ed. New York, Funk & Wagnall, 1973. xii,[1],434p. illus.

First published 1939 as *The Language of fashion*. Rev. ed. 1957.

More than 10,000 words briefly defined, with pronunciation. 109 group terms (*e.g.* Linens, Heels). Includes obsolete terms. 'Sleeves': 5½ columns in the 1959 ed., describing *c.*50 types of sleeve, with 11 small line-drawings. 202 half-tones, plus *c.*2 line-drawings per page. Analytical index of illustrations. Adequate cross-references. A standard work in its field. *Class No:* 391(038)

[3968]

WILCOX, R.T. The Dictionary of costume. London, Batsford, 1992. 416p. illus. £19.99.

Over 3200 entries and over 2000 line drawings. Covers all periods worldwide. All aspects of costume from 'aal' (source of red dye) to 'zukin' (Japanese scarf); accessories, underwear, hairstyles, cosmetics, clothing materials, embroideries, lace, etc. *Haute couture*, folk costume, military and ecclesiastical dress, tailoring and dressmaking tools. *Class No:* 391(038)

Reviews & Abstracts

[3969]

Costume: the journal of the Costume Society. London, the Society, 1967-. Annual. £15. ISSN: 05908876.

The history of clothing. Includes numerous short articles, *c.*30 book reviews, lists of new books (including museum publications) and periodical articles. *Class No:* 391(048)

Yearbooks & Directories

[3970]

LAMBERT, E. World of fashion: people, places, resources. New York, R.R. Bowker, 1976. 361p. $18.95. ISBN: 0835206270.

Arrangement is geographical, entries for each country including a brief history and economic survey of the industry. This is followed by a biographical directory of leading designers and firms, a section of 'Fashion influentials' (editors and writers, fashion historians, photographers, illustrators, merchandisers), trade associations, awards, schools and colleges, costume museums, and fashion periodicals. Bibliography. Index. *Class No:* 391(058)

Histories

[3971]

BOEHN, M. von. Modes and manners from the Middle Ages to the end of the eighteenth century. London, Harrap, 1932-5 (reprinted by Blom Publications, 4v. in 2). 4v. illus. $50. ISBN: 0405082800.

Translation of the original German, *Die Möde, Menschen und Modern* (München, Bruckmann, 1923-28. 8v. in 5).

1: *From the decline of the ancient world to the Renaissance;* 2: *The sixteenth century;* 3. *The seventeenth century;* 4. *The eighteenth century.* *Class No:* 391(091)

[3972]

—BOEHN, M. von *and* FISCHEL, O. Modes and manners of the nineteenth century. Rev. ed. London, Dent, 1927 (Reprinted by Blom Publications, 4v. in 2). 4v. illus. $50. ISBN: 0405082835.

Covers 1790-1914, by periods; illustrated from contemporary sources. 'Especially valuable for its illustrations from works of art often unfamiliar to English students' (*Art libraries journal*, v.1(3), Summer 1976, p.6). *Class No:* 391(091)

[3973]

BOUCHER, F. A History of costume in the West. Rev. ed. London, Thames & Hudson, 1987. 464p. 1300 illus. (365 in col.). £32. ISBN: 0500014167.

Translation of *Histoire du costume en occident, de l'antiquité à nos jours* (Paris, Flammarion, 1965), by John Ross.

A particularly well-illustrated history, arranged chronologically by periods from prehistory to 1964, 12 chapters, each with short bibliography appended. General bibliography in 4 form sections. Index. *Class No:* 391(091)

[3974]

BRUHN, W. *and* TILKE, M.A. A Pictorial history of costume: a survey of costume of all periods and peoples from antiquity to modern times, including national costume in Europe and non-European countries. Tübingen, Wasmuth; London, Zwemmer, 1955. 277p. 200 illus. (120 col.). £32.50. ISBN: 0302002693.

Based on the German edition, *Das Kostümwerk* (1941). The colour plates illustrate about 4000 costumes up to the end of the 19th century. *Class No:* 391(091)

[3975]

—TILKE, M. Costume patterns and designs a survey of costume patterns and designs of all periods and nations, from antiquity to modern times. London, Magna Books, 1990. 128p. 112 illus. £19.99. ISBN 1854221965.

Planned as a supplement to Bruhn and Tilke. Many of the plates are in colour, explanatory text preceding. The drawings are mostly to scale 1:10. *Class No:* 391(091)

[3976]

CUNNINGTON, C.W. *and* CUNNINGTON, P. The History of underclothes. Mansfield, A.D. *and* Mansfield, V., *eds.* New rev. ed. New York, Dover, 1995. 185p. illus. £9.95. ISBN: 0486271242.

First published 1951.

Chronological treatment in 14 chapters (1. Medieval period; 2-13 periods 1585-1939; 14. 1940-1950). 157 black-and-white illus. Appendix on clothes rationing. Glossary of materials. Bibliography of primarily and secondary sources (2p.). Sources of illus. Detailed index, p.183-185. *Class No:* 391(091)

[3977]

EWING, E. History of twentieth-century fashion. Mackrell, A., *ed.* 3rd ed. London, Batsford, 1992. xii,300p. 307 illus (some col.). £25. ISBN: 0713468181.

Written by E.Ewing, this edition revised and updated by A Mackrell. Looks behind the scenes for an understanding of the social, economic and technical changes which have made fashion available to all. Bibliography precedes, p.iv-v. Index, p.299-300. *Class No:* 391(091)

[3978]

GORSLINE, D. A History of fashion. London, Fitzhouse Books (an imprint of B.T. Batsford), 1991. xiii,266p. illus. ISBN: 0713465921.

First published in 1953; first published in Great Britian by Batsford in 1955.

A historical and visual study of dress from the ancient world to the middle of the 20th century. In 3 parts, all subdivided: I. Costume of the ancient world; II. European costume; III. American costume. Detailed contents list precedes. *c.*1800 illustrations. Bibliography p.249-256. Sources, p.257-266. Essentially pictorial with a minimum amount of explanatory material. 'A reference for professionals and students alike' (*British book news,* January 1991, p.64). *Class No:* 391(091)

[3979]

HANSEN, H.H. Costume cavalcade: 689 examples of historic costume in colour. 2nd rev. ed. London, Methuen, 1972. 160p. illus. (mostly col.). £6.50. ISBN: 0413288005.

First published 1956, a translation of *Klaededratsen kavalcade* (Copenhagen, Politikens Forlag).

Text in chronological periods (Egypt. *c.*3000-500 B.C. ... Twentieth century, 1900-1970. 689 six-colour photolithographed illus. (re-drawn from original dress), plus small line-drawings. 'Some books on costume', p.[6]. 'Sources used for the illustrations', p.[7] Bibliography, p.156. Index. *Class No:* 391(091)

[3980]

PEACOCK, J. Costume, 1066-1966. Rev. ed. London, Thames & Hudson, 1994. 135p. illus. $16.95. ISBN: 0500277915.

A sketchbook of dress arranged under the reigns of English kings and queens. Each page has 8 sketches; no text, apart from an introduction, the aim being to make each costume self-explanatory, but there are brief notes around each sketch. Sources of sketches are not indicated. List of books for further reading. *Class No:* 391(091)

[3981]

SMITH, G. Inspiration and information: sources for the fashion designer and historian. In *Art librarian's journal,* 1989, 14/4, p.11-16

Text of a paper presented to the IFLA Sectionn of Art Libraries, at Paris, August 1989. 50 references to sources other than books on costume history. *Class No:* 391(091)

[3982]

A Visual history of costume. London, Batsford, 1984-86. 6v. illus £12.95 each vol. Volumes for the 19th & 20th centuries were reprinted (revised and reprinted) in 1992 (£15.99 each vol.). ISBN 0713440937; 0713440953; 0713448571; 0713448598; 0713440996 0713440910.

Devised for those who need reliable, easy-to-use reference material on the history of dress. The central part of each volume is a series of illustrations taken from the time of the dress itself. Clothes described and significance explained. Arranged chronologically. Glossaries

..(contd.)
designed to also act as indexes. Volume titles: *14th & 15th centuries*, M. Scott. (1986. 152p. 150 illus); *16th century*, by J. Ashelford. (1983. 144p. 156 illus (8 col.)); *17th century* (1983. 144p. 158 illus (8 col.)); *18th century*,by A. Ribeiro (1983. 144p. 156 illus (8 col.)); *19th century* (1984. 144p. 158 illus (8 col.)); *20th century, by* P. Byrde (1986. 152p. 162 illus.). *Class No:* 391(091)

Biographies
[3983]
TEGEMEYER, A., *comp*. **Who's who in fashion.** 3rd ed. New York, Fairchild, 1995. 300p. illus. $49. ISBN: 1563670402.

First published 1980.

The people chosen for inclusion are '... designers with an international track record ...'. Entries, which vary in length from a paragraph or two to 2 or 3 pages, include date and place of birth (and death), fashion awards, background, education, philosophy, career, etc. A-Z arrangement by name. Bibliography. Index.
Class No: 391(092)

[3984]
Who's who in fashion: a biographical encyclopedia of the International Red Series containing some 6000 biographies. Strute, K. *and* Dolken, T., *eds*. 2nd ed. New York, Bowker; Zurich, Who's who in the International Red Series, 1983. 3v. (1000p.).

First published 1982.

A directory of important personalities and institutions related to fashion in Western European countries. V.1 covers fashion, v.2-3 cover beauty and jewelry. *Class No:* 391(092)

Europe
Bibliographies
[3985]
NOWDON, J. **European folk dress:** a guide to 555 books and other sources of illustrations and information. London, The Costume Society, 1973. 60p. £2.50. (*Bibliography, no.2.*) ISBN: 0903407043.

Entries for bibliographies, periodicals, and general works are followed by entries grouped in European areas, subdivided by countries. For each entry, author, title, place of publication and publisher, year of publication. Many entries also have brief descriptions or comments. No indexes. *Class No:* 391(4)(01)

Handbooks & Manuals
[3986]
NOWDON, J. **The Folk dress of Europe.** London, Mills & Boon Ltd., 1979. 160p. illus. £8.95. ISBN: 0263063976.

Arranged by country, A-Z (The Austrian-Hungarian Empire - Czechoslovakia ... Spain - Portugal). Includes 145 black-and-white illustrations in the text and 24 colour plates. Bibliography, p.153-160. *Class No:* 391(4)(035)

Histories
[3987]
EACOCK, J. **The Chronicle of Western fashion.** New York, Abrams, 1991. 224p. illus. $29.95. ISBN: 0810939533.

c.1000 full-colour, detailed drawings in chronological order (ancient civilisation grouped by nationalities, later nationalities mingle). 8-10 figures a page, with descriptions of each figure accompanied by small outline replicas). Bibliography. Illustrated glossary.
Class No: 391(4)(091)

England
Dictionaries
[3988]
UNNINGTON, C.W., *and others*. **A Dictionary of English costume.** 900-1900. London, Black, 1960. (Reprinted 1982). 292p. illus. £7.50.

Concise descriptions of all items of English costume from contemporary sources, plus approximate date of their coming into fashion and in many cases a quotation to illustrate their nature and function. Extensive glossary of materials and over 300 illustrations. *Class No:* 391(420)(038)

Histories
[3989]
ROOKE, I. **English costume...** London, Black, 1929-50. 7v. £4.50 each volume.

English costume of the early Middle Ages: the 10th to the 13th centuries ... the later Middle Ages: the 14th and 15th centuries ... in the age of Elizabeth; the 16th century ... the seventeenth century ... the eighteenth century ... the nineteenth century ... English children's

....(contd.)
costume since 1775. A popular series that aims to be a useful guide and not a serious text-book. Uniform pattern. Thus, *English costume of the seventeenth century* has 89 pages, plus 40 pages of illus. (8 in colour), with descriptive text facing; treatment is chronological, by 10-year periods. No Index. *Class No:* 391(420)(091)

Middle Ages
[3990]
OWEN-CROCKER, G.R. **Dress in Anglo-Saxon England.** Manchester, Manchester University Press, 1986. xi,241p. illus. £35. ISBN: 0719018188.

Arranged chronologically and profusely illustrated: 1. Introduction - 2. Germanic tradition - 3-8. are devoted to women's and men's costumes in the 5th & 6th, 7th to 9th, 10th & 11th centuries - 9. Textile production - 10. Conclusions. Appendix, p.203-208, old English garment names. Notes, p.211-225, by chapter. Bibliography, p.227-234, A-Z. Index, p.235-241. *Class No:* 391(420)"01/14"

19th Century
[3991]
CUNNINGTON, C.W. **English women's clothing in the nineteenth century:** a comprehensive guide with 1,117 illustrations. New York, Dover, 1990. $24.95. ISBN: 0486263231. *Class No:* 391(420)"18"

Africa
[3992]
POKORNOWSKI, I.M. *and* EICHER, J.B. *and* HARRIS, M.F. **African dress II:** a select and annotated bibliography. East Lansing, Michigan State University, 1985. $11.25. ISBN: 9996653544.

Lists over 100 sources in English. *Class No:* 391(6)

USA
[3993]
WARWICK, E., *and others*. **Early American dress;** the Colonial and Revolutionary periods. New York, Blom, 1965 (Reprinted by Alexander Wyckoff and other. 428p. illus., maps. $45. (*History of American dress, v.2.*) ISBN: 0943276101.

Based on *Early American costume* (1929), By E. Warwick and H.C. Pitz.

A chronological survey in 9 chapters, from the founding of the colonies to the US of 1790. Costume of men and women are given separate treatment in chapters 2-7; 8: 'Children in North America, 1785-1790'; 9: 'Frontier life'. Well produced, careful drawings from original sources. Major items in the bibliography, p.389-98. Evaluative annotations. Analytical index, p.399-425,. *Class No:* 391(73)

19th Century
[3994]
BYRDE, P. **Nineteenth century fashion.** London, Batsford, 1992. 192p. 138 illus (8 col). £30. ISBN: 0713455462.

Traces the evolution of men's, women's and children's clothes throughout the age. Illustrations, in black & white and in colour, include contemporary portraits, cartoons, fashion plates, advertisements, etc. *Class No:* 391"18"

20th Century
[3995]
The Guinness guide to 20th-century fashion. Bond, D. 2nd ed. Enfield, Middx., Guinness Publishing Ltd., 1985 (Reprinted 1988). 240p. illus (some col.). £32.95. ISBN: 0851123562.

First published 1981.

Chapters for each of the decades from the 1900s to the 1980s, the text describing the decade and fashions, supported by the many illustrations. Index, p.237-240. *Class No:* 391"19"

[3996]
PEACOCK, J. **20th century fashion:** the complete sourcebook. London. Thames & Hudson, 1993. 240p. illus. £18.95. ISBN: 0500015643.

Detailed history and sourcebook, with 1100 coloured illustrations, charts the development of women's fashion in all its aspects (couture wear, day wear, underwear, leisure wear, evening wear, bridal wear, and accessories). Designers and designs. *Class No:* 391"19"

Stage Costume

[3997]

KESLER, J. **Theatre costume:** a guide to information sources. Detroit, Mich., Gale Research Co., 1979. 308p. (*Performing arts information guide series, v.6.*)

Over 1700 titles, concisely and accurately annotated.
Class No: 391:792

[3998]

Stage costume source book. London, Cassell/Ward Lock, 1998. 128p. illus.(some col.) £18.99. ISBN: 0304350680.

Offers stage costumes including period, animal and children's costumes. Covers period drama, opera, pantomime, musicals, ballet, fantasy and review. Some backcloth designs are included.
Class No: 391:792

[3999]

—BROOKE, I. **Western European costume ... and its relation to the theatre.** London, Harrap, 1939-40. 2v. illus (incl. pl.).

V.1 covers 13th-16th century; v.2, 17th-19th century. 32 colour plates, 176 black-and-white illustrations in all. Aims 'to give some of the more usual styles and fashions worn since the theatre commenced to be a leading interest in Western Europe' (*Introduction*). No bibliographies; index in v.2. *Class No:* 391:792

[4000]

—TRUMAN, N. **Historic costuming.** London, Pitman, 1936. 2v. illus.

A chronological survey, 550 B.C. - A.D. 1910. Numerous keyed black-and-white illustrations and 1 colour plate. Of value to theatrical producers and designers, covering civil, ecclesiastical and military dress. *Class No:* 391:792

Yearbooks & Directories

[4001]

Directory of theatre resources. A guide to research collections and information services. Howard, D., *comp.* 2nd ed. London, Library Association Information Services Group and The Society for Theatre Research, 1986. 144p. £10.50. ISBN: 0946347085.

A survey was carried out in 1985/86 to provide information for the Working Party on Library Provision for Theatre Research.

In 2 parts: part 1 is a directory of public and private collections open to the public, 256 entries arranged A-Z by place; part 2 has entries for those societies and associations serving the theatre which provide information services. 46 entries arranged by name of organization. Information was collected by questionnaire and is uneven, but entries name a contact, give opening hours and note conditions of admission; some give details of catalogues, indexes and publications. Index to collections, p.134-137; subject index, p.139-142.
Class No: 391:792(058)

[4002]

FRANCHI, F. *and* HUDSON, C., *comps.* **Directory of performing arts resources.** 3rd ed. London, Society for Theatre Research and the Theatre Museum, 1998. ISBN: 0854300635. *Class No:* 391:792(058)

Men's Fashions

[4003]

Esquire's encyclopedia of 20th century men's fashions. Schoeffler, O.E. *and* Gale, W. New York, McGraw-Hill, 1973. xi,709p. illus. (incl. col.). xi,709p. illus. (incl. col.).

51 sections on all items of men's clothing (Suits ... Designers), illustrated from *Esquire,* etc. Captions give dates. 'Footwear': p.292-320, subdivided into decades, to show fashion changes; 38 illus. plus 1 col.plate. Later sections cover materials and manufacture of fabrics. Glossary, well illustrated, p.644-89. Analytical index, p.690-709.
Class No: 391.1

[4004]

WAUGH, N. **The Cut of men's clothes, 1600-1900.** London, Faber & Faber, 1964. 160p. illus., diagrs. £35. ISBN: 0571057144.

Originally published 1964.

A chronological survey, in three main periods: 1600-1680, 1680-1800, 1800-1900. Includes quotations from contemporary sources. Bibliography (c.35 books; 4 journals); list of museums with costume collections (p.157). List of artists, engravers and illustrators. Index (accessories and detail, *e.g.* buttons; cravet; ruffles). 29 plates and frontice-piece; 42 cutting diagrmas; 27 tailors' patterns.
Class No: 391.1

Women's Fashions

[4005]

BRADFIELD, N. **Costume in detail: women's dress, 1730-1930.** New ed. London, Harrap, 1981. ix,391p. illus. £15.95. ISBN: 0245536086.

First published 1968.

Chronological treatment, in 5 chapters. 'The Charles Wade Collection at Snowhill Manor, now a property of the National Trust,

....(contd.)
proved a valuable starting point for local research, and from there tl circle widened' (*Introduction*). 370 full-page drawings (colour plate were included in the 1st ed.) and highly detailed studies, together wi scholarly and informative text. Detailed, non-analytical index, p.38 91. 'Books consulted', p.384-5. 'Most valuable for anyone studyii fashion and design, and for those concerned with the datin conversation and repair of historic costume' (*British book nev* January 1969, p.23) of the 1st ed. *Class No:* 391.2

[400?]

COLEMAN, E.A. **The Opulent era: fashions of Worth, Doucet ar Pingat.** London, Thames & Hudson, [1989]. 208p. 192 illus (52 col.). £24. ISBN: 0500014760.

A survey of *fin de siècle* couture, including many reproductions the most sumptuous gowns. Designs, fabrics and clients are discusse and compared, setting their work in a larger social and cultur context. Author is an American museum curator. *Class No:* 391.2

[400?]

WAUGH, N. **The Cut of women's clothes, 1600-1930.** London Fab & Faber, 1968. 336p. illus., diagrs. £20. ISBN: 0571085946.

A chronological survey in 4 parts (17th-20th centuries). 75 cuttii diagrams; 54 tailors' patterns; 71 plates. 'The diagrams have bee chosen as far as possible from existing patterns in order to show sequence of cut' (*Introduction*) Hair-styles and accessories a included. Bibliography, p.320-1, with a separate list of technical bool and a selection of journals. Partly analytical index, p.323-36.
Class No: 391.2

Encyclopaedias

[400?]

O'HARA, G. **The Encyclopedia of fashion from 1840 to the 1980** New York, Abrams, 1986. 272p. illus. $27.50. ISBN: 0810908824.

Covers the multifarious subject from 1840, when sewing machin came into use, and concentrates on the five major fashion capitals the 19th and 20th centuries, Paris, London, New York, Rome, ai latterly, Milan. More than 1000 entries, A-Z, including individuals the fashion industry or influencing it, styles, trends, fabrics, fur retailers etc. Numerous cross-references. 365 illustrations, 27 colour. Length of entries varies from 2 lines to half a pag Bibliography, p.269-272 (General, dictionaries & encyclopedia books about fashion and costume design, books by fashion ar costume designers, magazines, etc.). *Class No:* 391.2(031)

Dictionaries

[400?]

CALLAN, G.O. **Dictionary of fashion and fashion designers.** Rev. ar expanded ed. London, Thames & Hudson, 1998. 272p. illus. (son col.) $16.05. ISBN: 050020313x. *Class No:* 391.2(038)

[401?]

Fairchild's dictionary of fashion. Calasibetta, C.M. 2nd ed. Ne York, Fairchild, 1988. 749p. illus. $50. ISBN: 0870056352.

First published 1976.

A significantly revised and updated edition of 10,000 entries, A-? for organizations, persons, slang terms, trademarks, clothing, ha styles, jewelry and fabrics. Numerous cross-references. Black-an white drawings illustrate the terms, and there are 16 full-colour pag with 50 illustrations of costume from Ancient Egypt to 1988 Americ An appendix of 171 brief biographical entries for fashion designers followed by black-and-white portraits of some 64 of then 'Authoritative, well-designed ...' (*Reference books bulletin,* 1 December 1988, p.690). *Class No:* 391.2(038)

Children's Fashions

England

[401?]

CUNNINGTON, P. *and* BUCK, A. **Children's costume in Englan 1300-1900.** London, Black, 1965. 236p. 15 illus. £9.50. ISBN 0713603712.

One chapter per century; many contemporary quotations. Deals wi children from infancy to the age of *c.16*. Particularly rich in illu Bibliography, p.226-9 (manuscript sources; printed manuscripts ar books; dress and domestic economy; journals; secondary sources Non-analytical index. *Class No:* 391.31(420)

Hairstyles

Histories

[4012]

CORSON, R. **Fashions in hair:** the first five thousand years. London, Peter Owen, 2000. 719p. illus. (incl. pl.). £60. ISBN: 0720610931.

First published 1965.

A well-illustrated historical survey, with plates and black-and-white illus. Plates are on rectos, with descriptive notes facing. Chapters: 1. The wheel of fashion - 2. Ancient civilizations ... 6. The fifteenth century ... 14. The twentieth century: women. Index covers plates. *Class No:* 391.5(091)

Regalia

England

[4013]

HOLMES, M. *and* SITWELL, H.D.W. **The English regalia:** their history, custody & display. London, HMSO., 1972. ix,83p. illus. (pl.).

The history of the regalia - The history of the Crown jewels and their custody. References, p.82-83. Lists: 'Keepers of the Crown jewels before the Civil War'; 'Musters and Treasurers of the jewels and plate of the Jewel House, 1660-1782'; 'Keepers of the Jewel House at the Tower of London': etc. 42 well-coloured plates. Attractive production. *Class No:* 391.7(420)

Customs

[4014]

KIGHTLY, C. **The Customs and ceremonies of Britain:** an encyclopaedia of living traditions. London, Thames & Hudson, 1986. 248p. illus., map. £12.50; $24.95. ISBN: 0500250960.

Over 200 entries describing English, Scottish and Welsh customs and ceremonies (*e.g.* 'Pig-face Sunday', 'Cheese rolling', 'Whuppity Stourie') arranged A-Z by name of custom or ceremony (or under a group title whenever a custom does not warrant a separate entry). Entries include dates, times and locations of the ceremonies when appropriate. Over 200 illus. (12 in col.). Cross-references. Includes a calendar of customs; a select (brief) bibliography (1p.); a regional map; and a regional gazeteer (England divided into 12 regions; Scotland and Wales separate) listing customs and places where they occur. '... fascinating ...' (*Choice*, v.24(2), October 1986, p.280). *Class No:* 392

Festivals

[4015]

COOPER, J.C. **The Aquarian dictionary of festivals.** Wellingborough, Northants, 1990. 224p. illus. £7.99. $12.75. ISBN: 0850308488.

A detailed history of all festivals celebrated by humankind from tribal communities to urban societies. Reflects the origins of ancient beliefs and customs. Cross-references. Bibliography, p.221-4. *Class No:* 394.2

[4016]

GRIFFIN, R. *and* SHURGIN, A.H., *eds.* **The Folklore of world holidays.** 2nd ed. Detroit, Gale, 1998. 841p. $105. ISBN: 0810389010.

Entries for each day of the year; country/countries plus references. Over 340 holidays and festivals for over 150 countries, being particularly strong on non-European countries. Detailed index. A useful companion to *Holidays and anniversaries of the world*' (2nd ed., Gale, 1990). *Class No:* 394.2

[4017]

SPICER, D.G. **The Book of festivals.** Detroit, Mich., Gale Research Co., 1969 (Reprinted by Omnigraphics Inc., 1990). xiv,429p. $52. ISBN: 1558888411.

Part 1: The festivals of different peoples (p.3-347; A-Z; 'Festivals of Albania' ... 'Festivals of Yugoslavia'). Pt.2: The story of the calendars (Armenian, Chinese, Gregorian, Hindu, Jewish, Julian, Mohammedan). Appendix: 'Glossary of familiar religious and festival terms'. Selected bibliography on festivals, p.389-420 (by countries). Index of festivals. *Class No:* 394.2

[4018]

MERIN, J. *and* BURDICK, E.B. **International directory of theatre, dance and folk festivals.** Westport, CT., Greenwood Press, 1978. 480p. $35. ISBN: 0313209936.

Sponsored by the International Theatre Institute of the United States. Records over 850 festivals in 56 countries, with brief description of programmes and attractions offered. *Class No:* 394.2

Handbooks & Manuals

[4019]

Festivals in world religions, edited by Alan Brown on behalf of the Shap Working Party on World Religions in Education, compiled by A. Brown. New ed. London & New York, Longmans, 1993. x, 290p. illus. £9.99. ISBN: 0582361974.

First published 1986.

Explains in detail how many religions and many countries celebrate their major festivals. Chapter 1: Introduction (Feasts and festivals, Natural cycles and festivals. Sacred history. Sacred times. Sacred places. The Gregorian calendar) is followed by chapters on Baha'i, Buddhist, Chinese, Christian, Hindu, Jaina, Japanese, Jewish, Muslim, Sikh, Zoroastrian (Parsi), National and secular festivals, and Observing festivals in schools. 16 specialist contributors. Bibliography of 11 items plus 6 on Shap Working Party. Double column index, p.283-89. *Class No:* 394.2(035)

Scotland

[4020]

McNEILL, F.M. **The Silver bough:** a four-volume study of the national and local festivals of Scotland. Glasgow. Maclellen, 1957-90. 4v. V.1. & v.4: £7.50 each. ISBN: 0853351619, v.1; 0948474041, v.3; 0853350027, v.4.

V.1: *Scottish folk-lore and folk-belief* (1957); 2: *A calendar of Scottish national festivals, Candlemas to Harvest Home* (1959); 3: *A calendar of Scottish national festivals. Halloe'en to Yule* (1990); 4. *The local festivals of Scotland* (1970). V.2-4 deal with festivals in calendar order. V.1 carries a brief bibliography; that in v.2 is a little fuller (but authors and titles only). V.2 is well illustrated and carries many quotations. 'A valuable compendium of information' (*Scottish studies*, v.4, 1960, p.219-22). *Class No:* 394.2(411)

England

[4021]

WHISTLER, L. **The English festivals.** London, Heinemann, 1947. 241p. illus.

The calendar festivals described in some detail, with helpful bibliographical footnotes. An appendix indexes carols in several collected volumes. *Class No:* 394.2(420)

Yearbooks & Directories

[4022]

SPICER, D.G. **Yearbook of English festivals.** New York, Wilson, 1954 (Reprinted Omnigraphics, 1993). xxv,298p. map. $38. ISBN: 0780800028.

Part 1: Chronological survey; part 2: The Easter cycle. In calendar order; gives very readable, rather popularised accounts of current festivals, thus supplementing Chambers; *Book of days*. Glossary; bibliography; indexes of customs, counties and regions. *Class No:* 394.2(420)(058)

USA

[4023]

COHEN, H. *and* COFFIN, T.P., *eds.* **The Folklore of American holidays:** a compilation of more than 600 beliefs, legends, superstitions ... 3rd ed. Detroit, Mich., Gale Research, 1998. 608p. $138.75. ISBN: 0810388642.

Concentrates on the lore and legend associated with *c.*125 American calendar holidays and festivals. Describes the way they are celebrated, historical origin, general characteristics, etc., followed by 'Sources and comments' (Bibliographical information for published sources, informant information for oral sources), and comments from editors. Entries vary from one to 5 pages in length. 5 indexes (Subject - Ethnic and geographic - Collectors, informants and translators - Song titles and first lines - Motifs and tale types). *Class No:* 394.2(73)

[4024]

Festivals sourcebook: reference guide to fairs, festivals and celebrations in agriculture; antiques; the arts, theatre and drama, arts and crafts; community; dance; ethnic events; film; folk; food and drink; history; Indians; marine; music; seasons and wildlife. Wasserman, P., *ed.* 2nd ed. Detroit, Mich., Gale Research Co., 1984. 736p. $135. ISBN: 081030323x.

Lists more than 4000 festivals. *Class No:* 394.2(73)

[4025]

—HILL, K.T. **Festivals USA.** New York, Wiley, 1988. 242p. $12.95. ISBN: 0471626368.

Lists the nation's best 1000 festivals, as identified by the author. Arranged geographically by region, subdivided by State and then by month. Includes date and location of festival, description of the event, foods served, and (because designed as a travel guide) information on accommodation, restaurants, etc. Glossary of local terminology and jargon. Subject index. *Class No:* 394.2(73)

[4026]

SHEMANSKI, F. **A Guide to fairs and festivals in the United States.** Westport, CT., Greenwood Press, 1984. viii,339p. $42.95. ISBN: 0313214379.

Identifies several hundred of the main United States events, arranged by State, then city or town. Appendix by type of event and a calender of events by State and month. *Class No:* 394.2(73)

Special Days

[4027]

GROSS, E. **This day in religion.** New York, Neal-Schuman, 1990. 294p. $39.95. ISBN: 1555700454.

A chronological 'book of days' for religion. Covers every day of the year, the time period being *c*.300 CE to 1989. Describes in 1-2 sentences religious events that happened on each day. Non-Christian religions included. Index of names and subjects. Brief glossary. Bibliography. '... offering more current and diverse information on religion than any similar work available'(p.6). *Class No:* 394.268

[4028]

Holidays and anniversaries of the world. Mossman, J., *ed.* 2nd ed. Detroit, Mich., Gale Research Co., 1990. 1080p. ISBN: 0810348705.

First published 1985.

Lists 23000 regional, national and international holidays and anniversaries for each of the 366 days of the Gregorian year. Includes birthdates of famous people of all ages; days of the Saints, Holy Days and other days of religious significance; historical events; etc. Glossary of time words. Index. *Class No:* 394.268

Dictionaries

[4029]

DUNKLING, L. **A Dictionary of days.** London, Routledge & Kegan Paul; New York, Facts on File, 1988. xiii,156p. £14.95; $21.95. ISBN: 0415002397, UK; 0816019169, US.

A compendium of over 850 named days celebrated in literature and in real life in the English-speaking world. 27 categories. Entries generally brief, usually less than 300 words. Includes occasional quotations, and references are cited. List of specifically dated days in calendar order. 'Eminently readable source' (*Library review*, v.37(2), 1988, p.62). *Class No:* 394.268(038)

USA

[4030]

GREGORY, R.W. **Anniversaries and holidays.** 4th ed. Chicago, Ill., American Library Association, 1983. xiii,262p. $25; £18.50. ISBN: 0838903894.

First published 1928.

'The purpose... is to provide a quick identification of notable anniversaries, holy days, holidays and special event days, and to link outstanding days to books for further information or background' (*Preface*). Arranged in 3 parts: 1. Calendar of fixed days - 2. Calendar of movable days - 3. Books related to anniversaries and holidays (p.184-244. 875 briefly annotated entries, A-Z). Index, p.245-262. *Class No:* 394.268(73)

[4031]

HATCH, J.M. **The American book of days.** 3rd ed. New York, Wilson, 1978. 1214p. $75. ISBN: 0824205936.

2nd ed. 1948, by G.W. Douglas.

Over 700 articles, each of 300-8000 words. Covers holidays, anniversaries, religious and secular festivals, celebrations, birthdays of prominent Americans, etc. 'Recommended as an essential purchase for all academic libraries' (*Choice*, v.16(5/6), July/August, 1979, p.648). *Class No:* 394.268(73)

Official Ceremonies

[4032]

GARNER, J.F. **Civic ceremonial: a handbook of practice and procedure.** Waldram, G.N., *ed.* 3rd ed. London, Shaw & Sons, 1979 (reprinted 1984). xiv,204p. £10. ISBN: 072190162x.

First published 1953.

9 chapters: 1. Historical background - 2. The office of mayor or chairman - 3. The ceremonial position of mayor or chairman - 4. The expenses of office - 5. Royal and State visits - 6. Civic ceremonies and functions - 7. Town twinning - 8. Civic insignia - 9. Ceremonial officers. 2 appendices: A. Specimen orders of procedure; B. Attendance of mayor/chairman at non-civic functions - specimen forms. Index of towns. Alphabetical index. No illustrations. *Class No:* 394.4

England

Histories

[4033]

MILTON, R. **The English ceremonial book: a history of robes, insignia and ceremonies still in use in England.** Newton Abbot, Devon, David & Charles, 1972. 216p. illus.

6 chapters: The heralds and the college of Arms - 2. The coronation: the royal robes and regalia - 3. Robes and coronets of the peers - 4. Robes of judges, serjeants and barristers - 5. Knighthood: insignia and robes of orders of chivalry - 6. Civic robes and insignia. Chapter notes and short bibliography, p.208. Authorities personally consulted, p.209. Detailed index. 61 illustrations (8 in colour). *Class No:* 394.4(420)(091)

Chivalry

[4034]

BARBER, R. *and* BARKER, J. **Tournaments, jousts, chivalry and pageants in the Middle Ages.** Woodbury, Suffolk, Boydell Press, 1989. 240p. illus. £19.95. ISBN: 0851154700.

Aims to present a coherent picture of the tournament from its beginnings in the 12th century until the close of the medieval period. Includes 40 coloured and 80 black-and-white illus. *Class No:* 394.7

Dictionaries

[4035]

BROUGHTON, B.B., *comp.* **Dictionary of medieval knighthood and chivalry:** concepts and terms. New York, Greenwood Press, 1986. 614p. illus. $67.95; £65. ISBN: 0313245525.

Intended as a resource for medievalists at all levels and areas of interest. Topical arrangement of entries, which have quick definitions and in-depth discussions of chivalry and knighthood as practised in England and France. Extensive cross-referencing. Most entries include one or more bibliographical references and there is also a lengthy bibliography. Calendar of feast days and saint's days. Index. *Class No:* 394.7(038)

[4036]

BROUGHTON, B.B., *comp.* **Dictionary of medieval knighthood and chivalry:** people, places and events. New York, Greenwood Press, 1988. 774p. charts. $55. ISBN: 0313253471.

Companion volume to *Dictionary of medieval knighthood and chivalry: concepts and terms* (1986) above.

Over 700 entries with wide coverage of Britain and France. Extensive cross-reference to items in both this and the previous volume. Entries are fairly short and include bibliographical references. Separate bibliography of 249 items of mainly secondary sources. Appendices include genealogical charts of reigning families. 70-page double-column index. *Class No:* 394.7(038)

[4037]

UDEN, G. **A Dictionary of chivalry.** London, Kestrel Books, 1977 vii,352p. illus., ports.

Originally published 1968.

Over 1000 entries, 'Abatement of honour' ... 'Zutphen, Honour of'. Lavishly and well illustrated in margins; 96 illus. in colour. Articles concern arms and armour, battles and warfare, tournaments and pennons, sports and pastimes, biographies of knights (*e.g.* Sir Philip Sidney: 1 column). Few references to sources; no bibliography. For the young. *Class No:* 394.7(038)

Etiquette

[4038]

COLLETT, P. **Foreign bodies:** a guide to European mannerisms. London, Simon & Schuster, 1992. 368p. £14.99. ISBN: 067171063x.

Explores the way Europeans behave towards each other - revealing much about the British national character. *Class No:* 395

[4039]

DE COURCY, A. **A Guide to modern manners.** London, Thames & Hudson, 1985. 160p. 25 illus. £5.95. ISBN: 050001373x.

'In this book I have tried to define some major social groupings together with pitfalls unknown to earlier manuals of correct behaviour in short, to write a guide to truly modern manners'; (*Introduction*). 2 chapters, amusing and lightly written. *Class No:* 395

Handbooks & Manuals

[4040]

Debrett's new guide to etiquette and modern manners. Morgan, J. London, Headline, 1999. 382p. illus. £12.99. ISBN: 074727715x.

First published 1981.

Gives precise guidance: Births and the ceremonies of childhood; Weddings; Table manners; Parties; Invitations, letters and talk; Visitors and houseguests; Public occasions and events; Courtship;

...(contd.)

Household staff - 15. Sports and games; Dress. Appendix: Initials and abbreviations of rank, honours and degrees: Precedence in England and Wales; Scotland. Analytical index. *Class No:* 395(035)

[4041]

POST, E.P. **Emily Post's etiquette.** 16th ed. New York, HarperCollins, 1997. 845p. $35. ISBN: 0062700782.

First published 1922.

The standard US handbook, legislating for every conceivable social occasion. Includes a section on unmarried couples living together and expanded section on divorce. *Class No:* 395(035)

[4042]

—The **Amy Vanderbilt complete book of etiquette:** a guide to contemporary living. Tuckerman, N. *and* Dunnan, N. *and* Aher, J. Rev. & updated ed. New York, Doubleday, 2000. 800p. illus. $32. ISBN: 0385413424.

'The emphasis, where appropriate, is on handling the sometimes difficult and awkward situations that arise as a result of changing attitudes towards marriage, divorce, living together, sex and feminism' (*American reference book annual*, 1980, item 1100). *Class No:* 395(035)

[4043]

—EDWARDS, A. *and* BEYFUS, D. **Lady behave:** a guide to modern manners. London, Cassell, 1969. 380p.

4th ed. published 1957.

A British equivalent to Emily Post. Modern, practical and reasonably comprehensive, amusing as well as informative. Examples of invitation cards, etc. Appendix: 'How to address titled people' (p.307-19). Analytical index. *Class No:* 395(035)

Dictionaries

[4044]

BÄUML, B.J. *and* BÄUML, F.H. **A Dictionary of gestures.** Metuchen, N.J., Scarecrow Press, 1975. 284p. illus. $22.50; £15.75. ISBN: 0810808653.

'Culturally transmitted (semiotic) gestures' (*Introduction*), as cited in works of literature and art. 53p. of finger gestures. Bibliography of 512 sources. Indexed by significance of gesture and body part (*e.g.* Neck). Negligible illus. 'An impressive compendium of erudite research' (*Choice*, v.14(1), March 1977, p.40, on which this annotation is based). *Class No:* 395(038)

[4045]

BÄUML, B.J. *and* BÄUML, F.H. **A Dictionary of worldwide gestures.** 2nd ed. Metuchen, NJ, Scarecrow Press, 1997. 604p. $79.50. ISBN: 0810831899. *Class No:* 395(038)

Forms of Address

[4046]

Debrett's correct form: standard modes of address for everyone from peers to presidents. Noel, C., *ed.* Rev. ed. London, Headline, 1999. 381p. £20. ISBN: 0747223300.

First published 1970.

7 parts: 1. The Royal Family - 2. The Peerage - 3. Other titles and styles - 4. Styles by office (*e.g.* Legal) - 5. Official and social occasions - 6. American usage - 7. Usages in other foreign countries. Appendices: Rules for hoisting flags ... Pronunciation of titles and surnames. Detailed, analytical index. *Class No:* 395.6

Great Britain

[4047]

Titles and forms of address: a guide to their correct use. 19th rev. ed. London, A & C Black, 1990. xxxviii,185p. £7.99. ISBN: 0713631325.

First published 1918.

Sections: Royalty - The peerage - Dukes and duchesses - Marquesses and marchionesses - Earls and countesses - Viscounts and viscountesses ... Chiefs of Scottish clans ... Ecclesiastical - The Royal Navy - The Army - The Royal Air Force ... Law, diplomatic and government - Honours, qualifications and appointments - The universities. Some pronunciations of proper names. Analytical index, p.179-185. Confined to English titles, including those of the church and civic dignitaries. *Class No:* 395.6(410)

Women & Society

[4048]

CARTER, S. *and* RITCHIE, M. **Women's studies:** a guide to information sources. London, Mansell; Jefferson, NC., McFarland, 1990. 288p. £42.75. ISBN: 0720120586, UK; 0899505341, US.

Over 1000 English-language works published mainly between 1978 and 1988. Arranged in 3 main sections: General material (*e.g.* reference sources, biographies, women's studies) - Women in the world (subdivided geographically) - Special subjects (13 topics). Annotations vary in length from two lines to two paragraphs. Indexed by author, title and subject. Updates S.E. Searing's *Introduction to library research in women's studies* (1985) and K. Loeb's *Women's studies: a recommended core bibliography* (1987). *Class No:* 396

[4049]

HUMM, M. **The Dictionary of feminist theory.** 2nd ed. Harlow, Prentice Hall/Harvester Wheatsheaf, 1995. 320p. £14.95. ISBN: 0133553892.

'A broad, cross-cultural and international account of contemporary feminist thought' (*Preface*). Includes entries relating to family, work, sexuality, gender, race. Bibliography. *Class No:* 396

Databases

[4050]

Women online: research in women's studies using online databases. Atkinson, S.D. *and* Hudson, J., *eds.* New York, Haworth Press, 1990. 420p. £35.50. (*Haworth series in library and information, v.3..*) ISBN: 1560240377.

Chapters on online searching, by specialists, are followed by a directory of the online services mentioned. Database Matrix (not exhaustive). (Neither *Women's studies abstracts* nor *Women's abstracts* is online). *Class No:* 396(003.4)

Bibliographies of Bibliographies

[4051]

BALLOU, P.K. **Women:** a bibliography of bibliographies. 2nd ed. Boston, Mass., G.K. Hall, 1986. 288p. $30. ISBN: 0816187290.

First published 1980.

A mainly annotated list of 906 books, parts of books, pamphlets, journal articles, microforms and documents published between 1970 and June 1985. Items selected for scope, availability, organization and commentary. A wide range of topics, with 200 subject headings. Cross-references. Subject, title and author indexes. 'An excellent starting point, the volume will be useful to both beginning and advanced women's studies researchers' (*Choice*, March 1987, p.1025). *Class No:* 396(009)

[4052]

RICHIE, M., *comp.* **Women's studies:** a checklist of bibliographies. London, Mansell, 1980. xv, 107p. £15. ISBN: 0720109183.

489 unannotated entries. Sections: General (including special issues of periodicals; library-holdings) - Anthropology - Area studies - Arts - Criminology - Economics -, Education - Geography - Health and medicine - History - Language - Law and women's rights - Literature - Politics - Psychology and psychiatry - Religion - Science - Sex roles - Sociology. Appendix. Author and keyword indexes. *Class No:* 396(009)

Bibliographies

[4053]

AMICO, E., *ed.* **Reader's guide to women's studies.** London, Fitzroy Dearborn, 1998. 1000p. £95. ISBN: 188496477x.

Entries on 600 topics in women's studies and women's history. Most entries are essays of 800 to 1000 words, with bibliographies. *Class No:* 396(01)

[4054]

BARROW, M. **Women, 1870-1928:** a select guide to printed sources in the United Kingdom. London, Mansell; New York, Garland, 1981. 249p. £25; $73. ISBN: 072010923x, UK; 0824094506, US.

Originally as a thesis accepted for Fellowship of the Library Association, 1977, with its 4 major sections: 1. Archives (Collections; Education; Emigration ...) - 2. Printed works (Collections; Bibliographies; Biographies; Diaries ...) - 3. Non-book material (*e.g.* artefacts; films; oral history) - 4. Index. *Class No:* 396(01)

[4055]

—OAKES, E.H. *and* SHELDON, K.E. **A Guide to social science resources in women's studies.** Santa Barbara, CA, Clio Books, 1978. xi,162p.

Items arranged by academic discipline, with subdivisions as warranted. Includes books, bibliographies, and other resources. Author and subject indexes. *Class No:* 396(01)

[4056]

Bibliofem: a joint library catalogue and continuing bibliography on women. London, City & London Polytechnic, Fawcett Library, 1978-1986. Monthly. (Microfiche). ISSN: 01416456.

Co-sponsored by the Equal Opportunities Commission.
Class No: 396(01)

[4057]

A Bibliographic guide to studies on the status of women: development and population trends. Paris, Unesco; New York, UNIPUB; Epping, Essex, R.R. Bowker, 1983. xii,292p. F.175; $41; £14.95. ISBN: 9231021222, France; 0859350673, UK; 0890590281, US.

597 annotated items arranged in regional sections (including Western and Eastern Europe, North America, Latin America, Africa, Asia and the Arab States), subdivided into thematic sub-sections. The sub-sections each provide an overview and list the main existing bibliographies, followed by items on women's work and labour force participations, family and household concerns, education and demography. Includes theses and unpublished documents as well as books and other sources of information. Country, subject and author indexes. *Class No:* 396(01)

[4058]

GILBERT, V.F. *and* TATLA, D.S. Women's studies: a bibliography of dissertations, 1870-1982. Oxford, Blackwell Reference, 1985. xiv,496p. £57.50. ISBN: 0631137149.

Over 12,000 unpublished dissertations relevant to women's studies, retrieved from the archives of American British and Irish universities. Subject guide, a very detailed contents list, is followed by the bibliography, arranged in 23 subject sections (Arts - Criminology - Demography - Education ... Feminism - Health ... Philosophy - Physiology - Politics ... Religion - Reproduction - Sexuality - Sociology ... Women in the Third World. Each section subdivided and subdivided again by authors, A-Z. No annotations. 'See also' references at beginning of each subsection. Checklist of bibliographical and reference sources, p.461-466. Index, p.467-496.
Class No: 396(01)

[4059]

HUMM, M. An Annotated critical bibliography of feminist criticism. Boston, Mass., G.K. Hall, 1987. 240p. $35. ISBN: 0816189374.

An annotated list of 907 English-language books and articles published in the United States and Great Britain between 1950 and 1985. Entries chronologically arranged within 8 subject areas (Theory and sexual politics; literary criticism; sociology; psychology; history; anthropology and myth; education; and women's studies). Indexes to subjects (topics and authors) and contributors. Includes works not in Stineman and Loeb, but has fewer entries. 'Recommended as a supplement to Stineman and Loeb', (*Choice*, v.25 (7), March 1988, p.1066). *Class No:* 396(01)

[4060]

LOEB, K., *and others*. Women's studies: a recommended core bibliography, 1980-1985. Littleton, Col., Libraries Unlimited, 1987. xvi, 538p. $85; £55. ISBN: 0872874729.

An abridged edition was also published in 1987 (*c*.250p. £23.50; $28. 0872875989).

Annotated entries for 1154 English-language books and 57 periodicals relating to women. Arranged in 18 broad categories, the entries are both descriptive and evaluative. Author, title and subject indexes, the latter rich in multiple levels of access. '... offers an excellent review of current scholarship ...' (*Choice*, June 1987, p.1536).

A predecessor, E. Stineman's 'Women's studies: a recommended core bibliography' was published in 1979 and included 1,763 annotated entries. *Class No:* 396(01)

[4061]

ROSENBERG, M.B. *and* BERGSTROM, L.V., *comps. & eds*. Women and society: a critical review of the literature, with a selected annotated bibliography. Beverley Hills, CA., Sage Publications, 1975 (Available from Books Demand UMI). [vi], 354p. $90. ISBN: 0317106198.

3612 briefly annotated entries in 12 sections: 1. Sociology - 2. Political science (entries 878-1542) - 3. History - 4. Women in philosophy and religion - 5. Women in medicine and health - 6. Women in biography, autobiography and memoirs - 7. Women in literature and the arts - 8. Women in psychology - 9. Women in anthropology - 10. Women in economics - 11. General reference works on women (A. Bibliographies; E. Women's collections and libraries) - 12. Addendum. Indexes: author organization; journal issues entirely devoted to women; persons not cited as authors; indexes of places, subjects and topics. *Class No:* 396(01)

[4062]

RYAN, B. The Women's movement: references and resources. G.K. Hall, 1996. $45. (*Reference publications on American social movements*..) ISBN: 0816172544. *Class No:* 396(01)

[4063]

STAFFORD, B. 'Best reference works for the study of minority and third world women'. In *Special collections,* v.3(3/4), Spring/Summer 1986, p.173-189.

Aims to provide an overview or guide to the best women's studie reference sources published within roughly the past five years Sections: Afro-American women in North America - Native America women - Latins in the United States - Asian-American women - Jewish women - Muslim women - Women in international development Subsaharan Africa - The Arab world - South Asia - China - Korea and Japan - South-east Asia - Latin America - General. *Class No:* 396(01)

[4064]

WARREN, M.A. The Nature of women: an encyclopedia & guide to the literature. Point Reyes, CA., Edgepress, 1980. 708p. $20. ISBN 0918528070.

Describes and analyses the scholarly works that shaped the western tradition with regard to thought about women. 'Authors and topics' (A-Z, monographs). 'Anthologies and sourcebooks; (broad categories) followed by a directory of periodicals, a bibliography, glossary and comprehensive index. 'While her impressive work lacks bibliographic precision, it is, for extensive analysis of individual works, an achievement unequaled in the women's studies area (*Library journal* v.107(6), 15 March 1980, p.712-3). *Class No:* 396(01)

Encyclopaedias

[4065]

TUTTLE, L., *ed*. Encyclopedia of feminism. Harlow, Essex, Longman Group UK Ltd.; New York, Facts on File, 1986. 399p. £9.95 $24.95. ISBN: 0582893461, UK; 0816014248, US.

Aims to provide, in one volume, ready access to major events people, ideas, organizations and publications in the contemporary and past women's movements. Emphasis on America and Western Europe Arrangement is A-Z, length of entries varying from *c*.30 words to 2½ columns (*e.g.*, 'Holloway brooch':1 col; 'Housework': 2½ cols. 'Liberal feminism': 2½ cols.). Many entries are about people. Good cross-reference structure. Extensive bibliography, p.375-399, by authors, A-Z. 'An excellent reference guide to a vast body of information;' (*Choice*, v.24(8), April 1987, p.1204). *Class No:* 396(031)

[4066]

Women studies encyclopedia. Tierney, H., *ed*. Revised & expanded ed. London, Aldwych Press, 1999. 3v. £234.50. ISBN: 086172111x.

V.1 Views from the sciences; v.2. Literature, art and learning; v.3 History, philosophy and religion. Focuses on recent feminist research in the natural, behavioural and social sciences, health and medicine economics, linguistics, political sciences, and the law. Articles provide a definitive historical overview and current research findings. Most articles include selected references. *Class No:* 396(031)

Dictionaries

[4067]

A Women's thesaurus: an index of language used to describe and locate information by and about women, edited by M.E.S. Capek. New York, Harper & Row, 1987. 1052p. $37.50. ISBN: 0060157755.

A joint project of the National Council for Research on Women and the Business and Professional Women's Foundation, with assistance from the American Library Association and others.

c.5000 terms that can be used as a controlled vocabulary to index and research for information for materials in 11 broad subject areas Attempts to bring together all related terms and to suggest alternatives An introduction explains thesaurus construction and applications. 'No other work so comprehensive' (*Choice*, v.25 (6), February 1988 p.888). *Class No:* 396(038)

Reviews & Abstracts

[4068]

Studies on women abstracts. Abingdon, Oxon, Carfax Publishing Co. 1983-. v.1, no.1-. 6pa. £136. ISSN: 02625644.

c.800 indicative and informative abstracts pa. Covers books and journal articles in all main areas of women's studies (education employment, women in the family and community, medicine and health, female sex and gender role socialization, social policy, social psychology of women, female culture, media treatment of women biography, literary criticism, and historical studies. List of book received for inclusion. List of journals covered (396). Author and subject indexes, cumulated annually. *Class No:* 396(048)

[4069]

Women studies abstracts. Rush, N.Y., Rush Publishing Co., 1972-.no.1-. Quarterly. $56pa. ISSN: 00497835.

About 200 indicative and informative abstracts per issue, arranged in 22 subject sections: Education, localization - Sex roles, characteristics, differences and similarities - Employment - Sexuality - Family ... History - Literature and art ... Women's Liberation Movement. Appended is an extensive listing of book reviews. Author and subject indexes, cumulating in the 4th issue each year. 'Recommended for the basic women's studies collection in college libraries (*Choice*, v.12(12), February 1976, p.1544). Also available on microform from UMI. *Class No:* 396(048)

[4070]

—Women's studies index. 1989-. Boston, Mass., G.K. Hall, 1991-. Annual. $165. ISSN: 10586369.

Covers over 100 journal titles, ranging from popular to scholarly. Whereas *Women's studies abstracts* offers depth, this index offers breadth. Author and subject access. *Class No:* 396(048)

[4071]

Women's studies index 1997. Farmington Hills, MI, G.K. Hall, 1998. 750p. £196.99. ISBN: 0783800770.

Covers articles appearing in over 80 journals dealing with a range of topics and issues of concern to women. *Class No:* 396(048)

Periodicals & Progress Reports

[4072]

DOUGHAN, D. *and* SANCHEZ, D., *comps*. **Feminist periodicals, 1855-1984:** an annotated, critical bibliography of British, Irish, Commonwealth and international titles, compiled by David Doughan and Denise Sanchez. Brighton, Harvester Press, 1986; New York, New York University Press (Dist. by Columbia), 1987. 316p. £60; $75. ISBN: 0710809921, UK; 0814717985, US.

920 titles, 229 antedating 1960, arranged chronologically, of journals, broadsheets and other periodicals relating to women. Include brief annotations and locations in major London libraries. Includes an essay on women's periodicals, a short bibliography and indexes of persons, titles, subjects and dates. A good source guide for working on 19th and 20th century social and feminist histories. David Doughan is librarian of the Fawcett Library. *Class No:* 396(05)

Yearbooks & Directories

[4073]

COWLEY, R. **What about women? Information sources for women's studies.** Manchester, Fanfare Press, 1984. [4],103p. £2.85. ISBN: 0947813004.

Includes nearly 140 addresses of British and foreign organizations of importance to women, plus details of their resource centre holdings and their services. Arranged in 3 sections: I. Directory of organizations (England, Scotland, Wales, international, some overseas governmental organizations) - II. Developing a resource collection, 1: Basic resource list for women's studies - III. Developing a resource collection, 2: Organization of materials. The directory in section I includes for each organization, name, address, telephone number, aims, publications, stock and policy, services offered. *Class No:* 396(058)

Quotations

[4074]

PARTNOW, E. **The New quotable woman.** New York, Facts on File, 1992. 714p. $40. ISBN: 0816021341.

Combines, revises and updates two previous volumes, *The Quotable woman from Eve to 1979*(1986) and *The Quotable woman...1800-1981*(1983).

Organized chronologically by birthdates, subdivided by speakers. Sources given. Biographical index indicates subject, career and occupation, ethnicity and nationality. *Class No:* 396(082.2)

Tables & Data Books

[4075]

Statistical record of women worldwide Schmittroth, L., *comp. & ed.* 2nd ed. Detroit, Gale, 1995. $105. ISBN: 0810388723.

Emphasis on US. Source notes are given for each table. Subject and geographic index. *Class No:* 396(083)

Maps & Atlases

[4076]

SEAGER, J. *and* OLSON, A. **Women in the world** an international atlas. Touchstone, Simon & Schuster; London, Pan Books, 1986. 128p. illus., tables, maps. $19.95; £7.95. ISBN: 0671602977, US; 0330291939, UK.

Global information on the lives of women arranged in 40 chapters within 10 central topics (The second sex - marriage - motherhood - work - resources - welfare - authority - body politics - change - statistical politics). Maps and short tables, supported by text, showing the differences and similarities among women throughout the world. Country table. Notes on maps. Bibliography, p.121-126. Index, p.127-128. 'A major tool' (*Library journal*, v.111(19), 15 November 1986, p.87). *Class No:* 396(084.3)

Histories

[4077]

KANNER, B., *ed.* **The Women of England,** from Anglo-Saxon times to the present: interpretative bibliographical essays. Hamden, CT., Archon; Shoestring, 1979; London, Mansell, 1980. 429p. $37.50; £30. ISBN: 0208016392, US; 0720115647, UK.

13 contributors. 12 bibliographical essays (*e.g.* 'Women in Norman and Plantagenet times', p.83-123; 55 notes; bibliography, p.113-23. 'A survey of primary sources and archives for the history of early twentieth-century English women', p.388-409; 21 notes; bibliography (*i.e.*, library and society sources), p.410-8). Index. 'This belongs in any library used by students of literature, history, or the social sciences. (*Library journal*, v.104(14), August 1979, p.1552). *Class No:* 396(091)

[4078]

O'DAY, R. **'The History of women and the family'.** In *British book news*, July 1986, p.383-386.

A literature survey of 55 books, arranged in 4 sections: Demographic history; The 'sentiments' school; The 'household economics' approach; Other works on women. *Class No:* 396(091)

Bibliographies

[4079]

FREY, L., *and others, comps*. **Women in Western European history:** a select chronological, geographical and topical bibliography from antiquity to the French Revolution. Westport, CT., Greenwood Press, 1982. lv,760p. $49.95.

A historical outline and topical guide to citations, p.xv-l, (serves as a detailed contents list) is followed by a Guide to quotations (names A-Z & pages on which quoted). The bibliography is arranged in 6 sections: 1. Historical surveys - 2. Antiquity - 3. Middle Ages - 4. Renaissance/ Reformation - 5. Seventeenth century - 6. Eighteenth century. Entries are numbered and arranged by subject in each section, subdivided by authors, A-Z. No annotations. Subject index, p.633-639; name index, p.641-660; author index, p.661-760. *Class No:* 396(091)(01)

[4080]

—FREY, L., *and others, eds. & comps*. Women in Western European history: a select chronological, geographical and topical bibliography, the nineteenth and twentieth centuries. Westport, CT., Greenwood Press, 1984. liv,1025p. $115. 021.00/00 0313228590

Similar arrangement to the above, with 4 sections: 1. Nineteenth and twentieth centuries - 2. Nineteenth century (*c.*1789-1914) - 3. Early twentieth century, 1914-1945 - 4. Twentieth century since 1945. A first supplement (1986. 699p. 0313251098) supplements the two earlier volumes, with more recently discovered or published material. *Class No:* 396(091)(01)

Biographies

[4081]

The International who's who of women 2000. 63rd book & CD ed. London, Europa, 1999. $680. ISBN: 1857430735.

Contains *c.*5000 biographies, with a 17-category occupations index. *Class No:* 396(092)

[4082]

UGLOW, J.S., *ed.* **The Macmillan dictionary of women's biography.** Rev. ed. London, Macmillan, 1998. 642p. illus. £25. £12. ISBN: 0333674421, hbk; 0333725735, pbk.

First published 1982.

Aims to be the first comprehensive biographical dictionary of women, including entries on women of outstanding achievement and influence from all parts of the world and all eras of history. Emphasis is on The British Isles, North America, the Commonwealth and Europe. Prefaced by additional reference sources chosen from all periods and cultures, the main part of the dictionary has 1500 entries, A-Z, and where possible entries include reference to an autobiography or serious biographical study, following a resumé of basic facts (name, dates, nationality, reason for inclusion, and brief biography). Length of entries varies from 1/3 col. to 1col. Cross-references to alternative

....*(contd.)*

names or spellings. Subject index in 4 parts (Public life - Cultural life - Physical achievements - Colourful characters), each subdivided. Names are listed A-Z with dates and nationalities. *Class No:* 396(092)

Laws

[4083]

CHARLES, N. *and* JAMES, J. **The Rights of women:** the essential question and answer guide to women's legal problems. London, Arrow Books, 1990. 224p. ISBN: 0099662302.

Gives answers to queries about women's legal problems, from sexual harassment at work to compensation claims. *Class No:* 396(094.1)

Developing Countries

Bibliographies

[4084]

BYRNE, P.R. *and* ONTIVEROS, S.R., *eds*. **Women in the Third World:** a historical bibliography. Santa Barbara, CA., ABC-Clio, 1986. 152p. $28. ISBN: 0874364590.

600 annotated entries for journal articles, selected from *c.*2000 journal titles and published between 1970 and 1985. Arranged by geographical area (Africa - Asia - Middle East - Pacific region - Latin America - West Indies). Subject and author indexes. *Class No:* 396(4/9-77)(01)

[4085]

FENTON, T.P. *and* HEFFRON, M.J., *comps. & eds*. **Women in the Third World:** a directory of resources. Maryknell, N.Y., Orbis Books, 1987. 160p. $9.95. ISBN: 0883445301.

In 5 sections, annotated entries for books, periodicals, pamphlets and articles, audiovisual materials, and organizations, with unannotated supplementary lists in each section. Material mainly published between 1971 and 1986. 'An excellent complement to Byrne & Ontivero's *Women in the Third World: a historical bibliography* (1986)' (*Choice*, v.25(1), September 1987, p.86). *Class No:* 396(4/9-77)(01)

[4086]

TOWNSEND, J. **Women in developing countries;** a select annotated bibliography for development organisations. Brighton, Sussex, Institute of Development Studies, 1988. v,190p. £7.50 + £1.50 p & p. (*Development bibliography series, 1.*) ISBN: 0903354802.

Assembled with the help of IDS, War on Want, and Oxfam.

Items arranged by country, with a general section for each continent, and also a final general section. All items annotated and relative importance is indicated. *Class No:* 396(4/9-77)(01)

Europe

Almanacs

[4087]

SNYDER, P. **The European women's almanac.** New York, Columbia, 1992. 399p. $35. ISBN: 0231080646.

A 'snapshot' of women's status and conditions in 26 countries. Chapters are arranged A-Z by country, each beginning with a map and description of political and cultural status, followed by statistics for 1987-91 of vital issues (equal rights, health care, parental leave, lesbian rights, employment, education). Comparative tables give information on women's life expectancy, no. of TV sets in homes, women's suffrage, etc. *Class No:* 396(4)(059)

Great Britain

[4088]

SMITH, H.L. **British feminism in the twentieth century.** Aldershot, Hants, Edward Elgar, 1990. x,214p. £57.50. ISBN: 1852780967.

11 specially commissioned essays arranged in 3 parts, with extensive notes after each chapter: 1. Feminism in the early 20th century; 2: Feminism in the interwar years; 3: Feminism from the second world war to the present. Select bibliography (books and articles), p.205-7. Index, p.209-14. *Class No:* 396(410)

[4089]

SMITH, H.L. **British women in the 20th century.** In *Choice*, v.31(6), February 1994, p.900-08.

116 citations arranged A-Z by author in the following sections: The suffrage movement - WWI and the interwar years - WW2 and the postwar years - Contemporary feminism - Social and policy issues - Work, family and the law - Women in Scotland, Wales and Ireland. *Class No:* 396(410)

Biographies

[4090]

BANKS, O. **The Biographical dictionary of British feminists:** v.1. 1800-1930. Brighton, Harvester Wheatsheaf, 1985. 256p. £70. $133. ISBN: 0710801327.

Entries arranged under 32 broad headings/categories. *Class No:* 396(410)(092)

[4091]

—BANKS, O. **The Biographical dictionary of British feminists. V.2:** A supplement, 1900-1945. Hemel Hempstead, Herts, Harvester Wheatsheaf, 1990. 243p. £80.95. $114. ISBN: 0745001122.

Adds new material on Fabian women and feminist writers. Subject index covers more than 300 specific topics. *Class No:* 396(410)(092)

Scotland

Bibliographies

[4092]

MARSHALL, R.K. **Virgins and virago:** a bibliography of women in Scotland from 1080 to 1980. London, Collins, 1983. 365p. 8 illus. (ports). ISBN: 0002160390.

Reprinted: Chicago, IL, Academy of Chicago Publications. ISBN 0897330757 £9.50.

An attempt to examine the activities of women in Scotland. 14 chapters in 4 parts: 1. To 1560: the passive woman? - 2. 1560-1709: wives and mothers - 3. 1707-1830: women in society - 4. 1830-1980: the active woman. Notes, p.317-340, by chapters, include refeences Index, p.341-365. *Class No:* 396(411)(01)

Ireland

Bibliographies

[4093]

BRADY, A., *comp*. **Women in Ireland:** an annotated bibliography. Westport, CT., Greenwood Press, 1988. xxxiii,478p. $45. (*Bibliographies and indexes in women's studies, 6.*) ISBN: 0313244863.

2312 briefly annotated entries for books, book chapters, periodical articles, theses and dissertations and treat all aspects of Irish women's lives. Arranged A-Z by author under subject categories (Biography and Autobiography - Literature, folklore and mythology (entries 824-1003) - Education - Religion and witchcraft - Community studies - Marriage and the family - Human sexuality, reproduction and health - Psychology - Law - Employment and economic life - History - Politics - Revolutionary movements - Perspectives on women's literature - General - Doctoral dissertations - Masters' theses). Each category begins with a scope note on contents. Annotations are descriptive and most items included are in English. Author index, p.421-438; subject index, p.439-478, is analytical. *Class No:* 396(415)(01)

England

Bibliographies

[4094]

KANNER, B. **Women in English social history, 1800-1914:** a guide to research. New York, Garland, 1990. 3v. ISBN: 0824092015, v.1 0824092058, v.2.

*c.*20,000 primary and secondary sources from the onset of the 19th century to World War I. Entries are mainly annotated and evaluative,and include journal articles. V.3 has autobiographical writings. Index to each volume. *Class No:* 396(420)(01)

China

Bibliographies

[4095]

WEI, K.T. **Women in China:** a selected and annotated bibliography. Westport, CT., Greenwood Press, 1984. 250p. $65. (*Bibliographies and indexes in women's studies, 1.*) ISBN: 0313242348.

Expanded version of the author's bibliographical essay published in *Choice*, November 1982.

Over 1100 annotated entries of books, periodical articles, theses, dissertations and reports. Arranged in broad subject chapters (*e.g.*education, legal status). Cross-references listed at end of each chapter. Most items in English, some in European languages; Chinese publications are transliterated into English. Emphasis is on 19th and 20th century publications. Lacks a specific subject index. 'One of th more important reference tools on the subject ...' (*Choice*, v.22(6) February 1985, p.801). *Class No:* 396(510)(01)

Japan

[4096]
HUBER, K.R. **Women in Japanese society:** an annotated bibliography of selected English language materials. Westport, CT, Greenwood Press, 1992. xviii,485p. $75. ((*Bibliographies and indexes in women's studies*).) ISBN: 0313252963.

19 sections of journal articles, book chapters and books published through 1990 arranged in 5 groups: Women's place - Women in the private sphere - Women in the public sphere - Women as artists, performers and writers - Other. Concise informative annotations. Chronology of historical periods. Indexes by author, title, translator, interviewee; by title phrase, series, proceedings; and by subject. *Class No:* 396(52)

Asia—South & South East

[4097]
SAKALA, C. **Women in South Asia: A guide to resources.** New York, Kraus International, 1980. 517p. $40. ISBN: 0527785741.

Sponsored by The Association for Asian Studies.

'This book organizes an unprecedented and perhaps unanticipated wealth of materials related to South Asian women. The materials cover both historical and contemporary South Asia, which includes India, Pakistan, Bangladesh, Sri Lanka and Nepal' (*the author*). In 2 sections: *Published resources* is a bibliography of *c*.4600 Western language entries for books, films, recordings, etc., most of which were examined and are annotated; and *Libraries, archives and other local sources. Class No:* 396(54+59)

USA

[4098]
BASS, D.C. *and* BOYD, S.H. **Women in American religious history:** an annotated bibliography and guide to sources. Boston, Mass., G.K. Hall, 1986. xiv,155p. $30. (*Reference publications in women's studies*.) ISBN: 0816181519.

Claims to be the first to list and extensively annotate writings about women in religion from colonial times through 1985, exploring the connection between the history of American women and religion in America. 568 items, including books, parts of books, reference works, and periodicals. Cross-references. Index to proper names, authors, editors and historical figures. 'A scholarly addition ...' (*Reference books bulletin*, 1986/87, p.55). *Class No:* 396(73)

[4099]
HILDENBRAND, S., *ed.* **Women's collections:** libraries, archives and consciousness. New York, Howarth Press, 1986. 194p. $32.95. ISBN: 0866562737.

Describes the major library holdings of women's collections in the United States, as well as excellent private collections. Also examines the history of women's collections through the years. *Class No:* 396(73)

Bibliographies

[4100]
COYLE, J.M., *comp.* **Women and aging:** a selected, annotated bibliography. Westport, CT., Greenwood Press, 1989. 135p. $35.95. (*Bibliographies and indexes in gerontology,9*.) ISBN: 0313260214.

622 annotated items arranged in 13 sections (Roles and relationships - Economics - Employment - Retirement - Health - Sexuality - Religion - Housing - Racial and ethnic groups - Policy issues - International concerns - Middle age - General), subdivided A-Z by author in format categories in each section (books - articles - films - government documents - dissertations). Primary focus is on the older American woman, but includes the middle-aged. Author and subject indexes. ' ... although the subject index does not always include items under all relevant listings' (*Choice*, v.27(1), September 1989, p78). *Class No:* 396(73)(01)

[4101]
Women's history sources: a guide to archives and manuscript collections in the United States. Hinding, A., *ed. in association with the University of Minnesota.* New York, R.R. Bowker, 1979. 2v. $189.95. ISBN: 0835211037.

Devotes V.1 (Collections) to descriptions of over 18,000 collections held by 2000 depositories, arranged under States, then towns, A-Z. V.2 forms the index. *Class No:* 396(73)(01)

Reviews & Abstracts

[4102]
HARRISON, C.L. **Women in American history:** a bibliography. Byrne, P.R. Santa Barbara, CA., ABC-Clio, 1975-85.

2v.(374p.383p.). v.1 $15; v.2 $75. (*Clio bibliography series, nos. 5 & 20*.) ISBN: 0874362601, v.1; 0874364507, v.2.

V.1 covers the period 1964-77; v.2 1978-84. Abstracts and annotations pertaining to American and Canadian women, chosen from *c*.600 international serials and anthologies, are arranged topically in 11

....(contd.)

headings (*e.g.* Women and ethnicity; Women and religion), each subdivided. Subject indexes are cross-referenced. Author index. List of periodicals. *Choice*, (v.23(8), April 1986, p.1196) says it will not replace *Women's studies abstracts* but it is easy to use. *Class No:* 396(73)(048)

Yearbooks & Directories

[4103]
DOSS, M., *ed.* **Women's organizations:** a national directory. 2nd ed. Garrett Park, MD., Garrett Park Press, 1986. 302p. $25. ISBN: 0912048425.

An expanded version of *The directory of special opportunities for women* (1981).

Some 2,000 organizations and their branches, including professional and trade associations, networking groups, government commissions, community and college-based women's centres, and resource and research centres specialising in women's issues and concerns. Arranged A-Z, with address, telephone number, code letter for category, and brief (4-5 sentence) explanation of purpose if one is known. Index by state and by broad subject category. Comprehensive in scope. '... some indexing eccentricities' (*Wilson library bulletin*, February 1987, p.68). *Class No:* 396(73)(058)

Histories

[4104]
TINLING, M. **Women remembered:** a guide to landmarks of women's history in the United States. Westport, CT., Greenwood Press, 1986. 810p. $89.50. ISBN: 0313239843.

Entries are from 1 to 4 paragraphs long and concentrate on the accomplishments of the women. Arrangement is geographical, eventually subdivided by personal name, A-Z. At the end of each State listing are bibliographical notes. Finally, a general bibliographical essay on women's studies. 'A major ready reference source... ' (*Library journal*, 1 October 1986, p.88). *Class No:* 396(73)(091)

Negro-African

Bibliographies

[4105]
SIMS, J.L., *comp.* **The Progress of Afro-American women:** a selected bibliography and resource guide. Westport, CT., Greenwood Press, 1980. 387p. $49.95. ISBN: 0313220832.

The first major bibliography in the field since L.G. Davis's *The black woman in American society* (1976).

c.4000 unannotated items, including books, magazine and newspaper articles, dissertations, theses and government documents, arranged in 34 subject sections, each subdivided. Coverage is from slavery to participation in the women and rights movement. *Class No:* 396(73)=96(01)

Jews

Bibliographies

[4106]
RUUD, I.M. **Women and Judaism:** a select annotated bibliography. New York, Garland, 1988. 232p. $45. (*Garland reference library of social science, 316*.) ISBN: 0824086899.

Over 800 informatively, but uncritically annotated entries for monographs, journal articles, essays and dissertations, mainly published in the twentieth century. English, French and Scandinavian language material, but no Hebrew. Arrangement is A-Z by author, and items are numbered. Topographical, author and subject indexes. 'A significant contribution to a growing field ...' (*Choice*, v.25(11/12), July/August 1988, p.1677). *Class No:* 396(=924)(01)

Islamic Peoples

Bibliographies

[4107]
MEGHDESSIAN, S.R., *comp.* **The Status of the Arab woman:** a select bibliography. Westport, CT., Greenwood Press, 1980. 176p. $49.95. ISBN: 0313225486.

Compiled under the auspices of the Institute for Women's Studies in the Arab World, Beirut University College, Lebanon.

1616 entries mainly in English or French, for journal articles, books, dissertations, reports, etc., published since 1950. General items are grouped (Cultural and social background of the Middle East - Conferences and seminars on the Arab woman - Women in Islam and the law - Women in the Arab Middle East - Women in North Africa), followed by items on specific Arab countries (by country, A-Z)).

....(contd.)
Author index, p.159-171, and a poor subject index, p.173-176, with long lists of item numbers under each term.
Class No: 396(=95.297)(01)

Thesauri
[4108]
CAPEK, M.E.S., *ed*. **A Women's thesaurus:** an index of language used to describe and locate information by and about women. The National Council for Research on Women. New Yorker, Harper and Row, 1987. xxxv,1052p. $37.50. ISBN: 0060157755.
A section on thesaurus construction and use precedes the displays (alphabetical, rotated, hierarchical, subject groups, use/do not display, delimiters display). *Class No:* 396:025.43

Libraries
[4109]
SEARING, S.E. *and* GOETSCH, L. **Introduction to library research in women's studies.** 2nd ed. Boulder, Col., Westview Press, 1999. $69. (*Westview guides to library research.*) ISBN: 0813320151.
In 2 parts: Part 1: *Using the library* is in 5 sections, with notes. Part 2: *The tools of research* is a selective, annotated bibliography describing the major tools (guides, bibliographies and indexes, catalogues, biographical sources, directories, microforms, online sources, periodicals, handbooks). 3 appendices, including C. Review essays in Signs. Author, title and subject indexes.
Class No: 396:061:026/027

Institutions & Associations
[4110]
Encyclopedia of women's associations worldwide: a guide to over 3400 national and multinational nonprofit women's and women-related organizations Greenfield, L.R., *ed*. Farmington Hills, MI, Gale, 1993. 471p. £65. $80. ISBN: 1873477252.
Lists 6000 established and emerging women's associations intended to be used to promote communication and networking. Geographical arrangement, with some countries having only one entry. Activities index. *Class No:* 396:061:061.2

Research Projects
[4111]
FRANSELLA, F. *and* FROST, K. **On being a woman:** a review of research on how women see themselves. London, Tavistock Publications, 1977. 237p. £9.95. (*Tavistock women's studies.*) ISBN: 0422760706.
Chapters cover such topics as the development of self-esteem, research on pregnancy and childbirth, and female mental health. In each chapter research findings are summarised, plus a useful commentary. 'All in all, it is a very valuable volume, packed with information and references, and offering succinct summaries of countless different topics' (*British book news,* November 1977, p.847). *Class No:* 396:061:061.62.005

Gypsies
[4112]
FRASER, A. **The Gypsies.** Revised paperback ed. Oxford, Blackwell,1995. 376p., illus., maps. £16.99. (*The Peoples of Europe.*) ISBN: 0631196056.
Sections: 1: Bibliographical works; 2: Periodicals; 3: General studies; 4. Asian backround; 5: Particular European countries; 6: Pre-1800 European history; 7: 19th & 20th centuries; 8: North America; 9: Physical anthropology; 10: Language; 11: Music; 12: Folktales; 13: Pollution code; 14: Religion; 15: Other travellers; 16: Gypsies in art and literature. Bibliography. Index. *Class No:* 397

Bibliographies
[4113]
BINNS, D. **A Gypsy bibliography:** a bibliography of recent books, pamphlets, articles, broadsheets, theses and dissertations pertaining to gypsies and other travellers that the author is aware of at the time of printing. Manchester, Dennis Binns Publications, 1982. [108]p. ISBN: 0950829005.
1306 items (1289 arranged A-Z by author; the rest are of records currently available). Includes materials from 1500 to the present day, but pre-1914 titles are omitted if unattainable or obscure or in a foreign language. *Class No:* 397(01)

[4114]
BLACK, G.F. **A Gypsy bibliography.** London, Quaritch, for the Gypsy Lore Society, 1914. vii,226p. (*Gypsy Lore Society monographs, no.1.*) Preliminary ed., 1909 (139p.).
4577 items in author order, with subject index. *Class No:* 397(01)

[4115]
—LIVERPOOL UNIVERSITY. Library. **A Catalogue of the gypsy books** collected by the late Robert Andrew Scott Macfie. Liverpool, the University, 1936. 178p.
Brief author catalogue only; appendix of songs and music. *Class No:* 397(01)

[4116]
KENNINGTON, D. **Gypsies and travelling people:** a select guide to documentary and organisational sources of information. 5th ed., revised by D. Barton & edited by M Ashcroft. Stamford, Lincs., Capital Planning Information, 1992. iii,73p. £15. (*CPI topic guide, no. 1.*) ISBN: 0906011833. ISSN: 01421859.
3rd ed., 1986.
In 10 sections: Historical background - The travelling population - Official publications and legislation (subdivided by area, etc.) - Social characteristics, history and traditions - Planning, legal and environmental issues - Education of travellers - Bibliographies - Organizations - Local authority liaison officers/advisers - Libraries and information sources. Entries include brief annotations. Name index. *Class No:* 397(01)

[4117]
LEEDS UNIVERSITY. Brotherton Library. **Catalogue of the Romany Collection** formed by D.U. McGrigor Phillips and presented to the University of Leeds. Edinburgh, Nelson, for the Brotherton Collection, 1962. xii,[1],227p.
20 sections, including drawings and paintings, photographs, gramophone records, letters, playbills and press cuttings. International coverage. Section 1. Bibliographies and other general works; 2. Official documents. 1234 numbered items, each with brief bibliographical descriptions. Index. *Class No:* 397(01)

Handbooks & Manuals
[4118]
OKELY, J. **The Traveller-gypsies.** Cambridge, Cambridge University Press, 1983. xii,254p. 16 illus., 9 diagrs., 15 tables. £16.95. (*Changing cultures.*) ISBN: 0521288703, pbk.
12 chapters examine the historical origins of the gypsies, their economy, travelling patterns, self ascription, kinship and political groupings, and their marriage choices, upbringing and gender divisions. References, p.241-247, by author, A-Z. Glossary (including Romany terms), p.249-250. Analytical index, p.251-254. *Class No:* 397(035)

Dictionaries
[4119]
WEDECK, H.E. **Dictionary of gypsy life and lore.** London, Peter Owen, 1973. vi, 518p. illus. £4.50. ISBN: 0720601630.
Includes material from the collection of *The Journal* of the Gypsy Lore Society.
Spans the history of gypsies in each continent where they exist, chronicling their origins, beliefs, customs, folklore and related subjects. A-Z arrangement. Entries mainly short from 2 to 3 lines to a page. *Class No:* 397(038)

Folklore & Folktales

Bibliographies
[4120]
ASHLIMAN, D.L. **A Guide to folktales in the English language:** based on the Aarne-Thompson classification system. New York, Greenwood, [1987]. 368p. $79.50 (*Bibliographies and indexes in world literature, no. 11*). ISBN: 0313259615.
Aims to help readers find reliable texts of any given folktale, not only in its best-known version, but also in less familiar variants (*Introduction*). Short plot summaries for the stories are followed by lists of several collections in which versions of the stories are included. There is a separate list of titles of Grimm's tales; a list of folk-tale collections; and an index of titles of better-known stories and keywords from typical plots. 'More selective than N.O. Ireland's 'Index of fairy tales ...' but plot summaries and arrangement make identifying stories easier' (*College and research libraries,* v.49(4), July 1988, p.345). *Class No:* 398(01)

[4121]
AZZOLINO, D.S. Tale type- and motif-indexes: an annotated bibliography. New York, Garland, 1987. 105p. $33. (*Garland folklore bibliographies, v.11. Garland reference library of the humanities, v.565.*) ISBN: 0824087887.

186 entries, arranged A-Z by author, of type and motif indexes with which folklorists can arrange tales and elements in tales in numeric sequences, which make comparisons easier (Best known is the Aarne-Thompson classification system). Subject and geographical indexes. *Class No:* 398(01)

[4122]
BONSER, W. A Bibliography of folklore, as contained in the first eighty years of the publications of the Folklore Society. London, W. Glaisher, for the Folklore Society, 1961. Supplement, 1969. xv, 126p. Supplement, 54p. £4.50. Supplement, £6. ISBN: 0903515024; 0903515032, Supplement.

Preceded by N.W. Thomas's *Bibliography of anthropology and folklore* (London, Nutt, for the Folklore Society, 1906-7. 2v.).

2626 entries in the main volume; a classified index to *Folk-lore record, Folk-lore journal, Folk-lore* and the Society's extra publications, 1878-1957. Classes A-P: A. General topics - B. Folklore of the British Isles - C. Folklore of other countries and races - D. Mankind - E. Human activities - F. Natural history - G. Natural phenomena - K. Calendar customs - L. Religious folklore & the supernatural - M. Miscellaneous aspects of folklore - N. Narrative folklore - P. Folklore in literature and art. Brief notes explain or expand titles of articles. Indexes: authors, topography of the British Isles; foreign countries, races and tribes; subjects. The supplement covers 1958-1967; the original volume, 1878-1957.
Class No: 398(01)

[4123]
CARNES, P. Fable scholarship: an annotated bibliography. New York, Garland, 1985. 382p. $65. (*Garland folklore bibliographies, v.8. Garland reference library of the humanities, v.367.*) ISBN: 0824092295.

Fables defined as literary tales 'generally assumed to comfortably fit under the rubric "Aesopic"' (*Introduction*). 1452 items of scholarly works appearing in books, dissertations and journal articles published between 1880 and 1982. Extensively annotated. Many cross-references. Arranged A-Z by author, with separate indexes for names and subjects, listing of fables by Perry number, and motif index. 'Complexity of indexes and most criticism cited not in English indicates limited to scholars' (*College & research libraries*, January 1987, p.68). 'This work's greatest strength ... lies in the number and variety of the entries - embracing monographs, articles, and both domestic and foreign dissertations' (*Choice*, v.23(5), January 1986, p.724). *Class No:* 398(01)

[4124]
CLEVELAND PUBLIC LIBRARY. John G. White Department. Catalog of folklore, folklife and folk songs. 2nd ed. Boston, Mass., G.K. Hall, 1978. 3v. (2456p.). $255. ISBN: 081610249x.

First published 1965.

51,500 photolithographed catalogue cards for over 36,000v. of monographs and serials. Most entries are for subjects (over 1100 subject headings), including analytical entries. International in scope, embracing 'Märchen, jests, legends, exempla, fables, and heroic fairy and etiological tales, ballads, folk songs, children's songs, folk dances, proverbs, riddles, wit and humour, and the folklore of physical objects ...' (G.K. Hall & Co., *Catalog of publications, 1979-80*, p.27). *Class No:* 398(01)

[4125]
—ZIEGLER, E.B. Folklore: an annotated bibliography and index to single editions. Boston, Mass., Fazon, 1973. 203p. $12. ISBN: 087305100x.

Confined to singly published editions of folklore, as opposed to stories in collections. Arranged by titles. Separate indexes for subject, motif, country, type of folklore and illustrator. *Class No:* 398(01)

[4126]
Internationale volkskundliche Bibliographie/International folklore and folklife bibliography/... 1939/41-. Bonn, (previously Basle), Rudolf Habelt Verlag GmbH, for Société Internationale d'Ethnologie et de Folklore, 1949-.Biennial. ISSN: 00749737.

Under the auspices of the Conseil International de la Philosophie et des Sciences Humaines, with Unesco support. Continues *Volkskundliche Bibliographie* (Berlin, de Gruyter, for Verband Deutsche Vereine für Volkskunde, 1919-41. v.1-13: 1917-36, which itself continues *Catalogus* van Volklorein de Koninklijke Bibliotheek (The Hague, Drukkerij 'Humanitas', 1919-22. 3v. in 2).

The 1985-1986 volume, published 1991, has *c*.11,600 items in 21 classes (1. Folklore and folklife in general - 2. Settlement - 3. Buildings - 4. Objects - 5. Signs - 6. Technology, arts and crafts, industries - 7. Characteristics and types of people - 8. Costume, - 9. Food - 10. Manners and customs, festivals, pastimes - 11. Social groups, common law - 12. Popular beliefs - 13. Folk medicine - 14. Popular science - 15. Folk literature - 16. Popular poetry - 17. Music

....(contd.)
and dance - 18. Folk-tales, myths, legends ... 21. Popular speech. List of periodicals precedes. Author and subject indexes.
Class No: 398(01)

[4127]
SHANNON, G.W.B., *comp.* 'Folk literature and children': an annotated bibliography of secondary materials. Westport, CT., Greenwood Press, 1981. 124p. $36.95. ISBN: 0313228086.

465 annotated entries for essays, monographs, articles, portions of books, dissertations, theses, etc., that deal with folk literature and its effect on children. Introduction summarises arguments both for and against folk tales, followed by the bibliography in 3 main sections (Literature - Education - Psychology) covering the period 1693-1979. Author, title and subject indexes. 'A valuable reference tool ...' (*Choice*, v.19(9), May 1982, p.1220). *Class No:* 398(01)

[4128]
STEINFIRST, S. Folklore and folklife: a guide to English-language reference sources. New York, Garland, 1992. 2v.(1208p). $120. (*Folklore bibliographies, v.16.*) ISBN: 0815300689.

A general bibliographical survey aimed at the beginner in research. Entries include descriptive annotations. Sections have bibliographical essays. One chapter discusses folklore associations and periodicals. Author, title and subject indexes. *Class No:* 398(01)

[4129]
The Storyteller's sourcebook: a subject, title and motif index to folklore collections for children. MacDonald, M.R., *ed.* 2nd ed. Detroit, Mich., Gale Research, 1995. $138.54. ISBN: 0810304716.

An index to children's folktales in 556 collections and 389 picture books published during the last 20 years. 4 main parts: Motif index, following the folktale indexing system designed by Stith Thompson - Tale title index - Subject index - Ethnic and geographic index, arranged by geographical area, subdivided and followed by an ethnic group index. *Class No:* 398(01)

[4130]
—The Storyteller's sourcebook, vol. 2. MacDonald, M.R. *and* Sturm, B. Gale Group, 2000. $105. ISBN: 0810354853. *Class No:* 398(01)

[4131]
THOMPSON, S., *ed.* Motif-index of folk-literature: a classification of narrative elements in folk tales, ballads, myths, fables, medieval romances, exempla, fabliaux, jest books, and local legends. Rev. ed. Bloomington, Indiana State University Press, 1989-90. 6v. $400 the set. ISBN: 0253338875.

First published Bloomington, 1932-36. 6v.

A systematic thematic index, covering a vast collection of folk-literature; references and some source material are cited. A-Z index and list of sources. The scope of the revised ed. is extended to include Icelandic sagas, early Irish literature, and oral tales of India. V.6, as before, provides a detailed A-Z index of motifs. An indispensable study of the subject. *Class No:* 398(01)

Encyclopaedias

[4132]
Enzyklopädie des Märchens. Handwörterbuch zur historischen und vergleichenden Erzählforschung. Hrsg.von Kurt Ranke [u.a.]. Berlin, de Gruyter, 1977-.v.1-. prices vary.

To be in 12v. (v.5 issues were published in 1985/86).

Articles on specific figures (*e.g.* Faust), tales, customs, supernatural, etc. Biographies of folklorists are a special feature. Most contributors are from German-speaking countries. 'The set is indispensable for any folklore collection;' (*American notes & queries*, v.23(16), January - February 1985, p.89). *Class No:* 398(031)

Reviews & Abstracts

[4133]
Abstracts of folklore studies. Austin, Texas, University of Texas Press, for the American Folklore Society, 1963-1975, v.1-13. Quarterly.

About 1000 indicative and informative abstracts were arranged pa under periodical titles, A-Z (*Alabama review ... Zeitschrift für Volkskunde*). 49 journals featured in the Winter 1975 issue. Final section listed book reviews. Annual author and subject indexes.
Class No: 398(048)

[4134]
Folklore. London, Folklore Society, 1959-. 2pa. £24pa. ISSN: 0015587x.

The journal of the society, with scholarly articles on all aspects of traditional culture in Britain, Europe and related cultures, plus a review section. *Class No:* 398(048)

Yearbooks & Directories

[4135]

Folk directory, 1965-. 1994-95 ed. London, English Folk Dance and Song Society. 176p £5.95 ISBN: 0946247005.

Includes a calendar of traditional customs; and lists of conferences and lectures; Folk festivals; district secretaries of the society; performers; films; archives, libraries and museums; and folk organizations (national, regional, international). *Class No:* 398(058)

Great Britain

[4136]

ALEXANDER, M. British folklore, myths and legends. London, Weidenfeld & Nicolson, 1982. 224p. 90 illus. (24 in colour). ISBN: 0297781510.

Examines the survival of different legends and customs and charts the evolution of folk belief. 9 sections: The magical island - Stones, graves and chalk images - 'There were giants in the earth' - The fabulous bestiary - The secret commonwealth - The Devil's congregation - The ghostlore of Britain - Rebels and champions - The Pagan inheritance. Picture sources. Index. *Class No:* 398(410)

[4137]

BARBER, R., *ed*. Myths and legends of the British Isles. Boydell & Brewer, 2000. 640p. $55. ISBN: 0851157483. *Class No:* 398(410)

[4138]

Folklore, myths and legends of Britain. 2nd ed. London, Reader's Digest Association, 1977. 552p. illus. (some in colour). ISBN: 0340163979.

First published 1973.

In 3 parts: 1. Lore of Britain - 2. Romance of Britain - 3. People of myth. 28 contributors. Detailed index, p.542-550. Lavishly illustrated. *Class No:* 398(410)

[4139]

The Folklore of the British Isles. Newell, V.J., *ed*. London, Batsford, 1973-1977. 18v. illus., examples, maps.

Cornwall, by T. Deane and T. Shaw. 1975. *The Cotswolds*, by K. Briggs. 1974. *Devon*, by R.Whitlock. 1977. *East Anglia*, by E. Porter. 1974. *Hampshire and the Isle of Wight*, by W. Boase. 1976. *Hertfordshire*, by D. Jones-Baker. 1977. *Ireland*, by S. O'Sullivan. 1974. £6.95. (David & Charles). *The Isle of Man*, by M. Killip. 1975. *The Lake District*, by M. Rowling. 1976. *Orkney and Shetlands*, by E.W. Marwick. 1975. £6.95. *The Scottish Highlands*, by A. Ross. 1976. *Somerset*, by K. Palmer. 1976. *Staffordshire*, by J. Raven. 1978. *Sussex*, by J. Simpson. 1973. *Warwickshire*, by R. Palmer. 1976. *The Welsh Border*, by J. Simpson. 1976. *Wiltshire*, by R. Whitlock. 1976. *Legends from Ireland*, by S. O'Sullivan. 1974. The volume *The folklore of Staffordshire*, by J. Raven (1978. 223p.) has 9 chapters (1. Ghosts and graves ... 6. The turning year ... 9. Sports and pastimes), with chapter notes, p.183-209. Quotes rhymes, charters, church records, etc. Bibliography, p.210-11. Index of tale types. Motif index (following Stith Thompson's *Index* (1966) and E. Baughman's *Type and motif index of the folktales of England and North America* (1966). General index, p.217-23. *Class No:* 398(410)

[4140]

FOLKLORE SOCIETY. British calendar customs. London, Glaisher, 1936-46. 7v.

Content: *England*, ed.by A.R.Wright & T.E.Jones. 3v. 1936-40. (v.1. Movable festivals; 2-3. Fixed festivals). Index in v.3. *Orkneys and Shetlands*, ed.by M.M.Banks, 1946. *Scotland*, ed by M.M.Banks. 3v. 1937-41. (v.1. Movable festivals; v.2-3. Fixed festivals). Index in v.3. Arranged in calendar order; lists of authorities. *Class No:* 398(410)

[4141]

GOMME, A.B. The Traditional games of England, Scotland and Ireland, collected and annotated by Alice Bertha Gomme. New York, Dover, 1964 (Reprinted London, Thames & Hudson, 1984, in one vol.). 1016p. illus. $18.95.

Unabridged reprint of *Dictionary of British folk-lore* (London, Nutt, 1984-8. 2v.).

More than 800 games are listed (A-Z), described and analysed. Rhymes are given in full, with local versions. 'Memoir on the study of children's games', p.458-531. The standard authority. *Class No:* 398(410)

[4142]

McINTYRE, F. What was that dance? Aylesbury, Bucks, the Author, 1993. £9.65.

Based on an earlier book with the same title produced by Bob Howe in 1968.

An index to 3000 folk dances, indicating for each the dance type, the music, a published source, and availability on record or cassette.(Information taken from *Refer*, v.9(1), Winter 1993). *Class No:* 398(410)

Bibliographies

[4143]

BAER, F.E. Folklore and literature of the British Isles: an annotated bibliography. New York, Garland, 1986. 355p. $43. (*Folklore bibliographies, no.11*.) ISBN: 082408660.

Entries for 1039 books, journals articles and dissertations published between 1890 and 1980 on the relation of folklore to English literature. Includes scholarly and popular items, arranged A-Z and numbered. 84-page general index. Annotations are descriptive and range in length from a phrase to *c.*200 words. 'An excellent and welcome addition ... (*Choice*, v.24(8), April 1987, p.1193). *Class No:* 398(410)(01)

Encyclopaedias

[4144]

BRAND, J. Brand's popular antiquities of Great Britain. Faiths and folk-lore: a dictionary of national beliefs, superstitions and popular customs, past and current, with their classical and foreign analogues, described and illustrated. London, Reeves & Turner, 1905 (Reprinted New York, Blom; London, Blond, 1967. 2v. illus.

Forming a new edition of *The popular antiquities of Great Britain*, by Brand and Ellis, largely extended, corrected and brought down to the present time and now first alphabetically arranged by W.C. Hazlitt. Brand's original work: *Observations on popular antiquities* (1777), had a new edition by Sir Henry Ellis in 1813.

In the Hazlitt edition, the editor makes his own comments and retains many illustrative passages from the obscurer Elizabethan and Jacobean writers. Entries A-Z (Abbot of Bon Accord ... Yule log), and far easier to use than Brand's *Observations*. *Class No:* 398(410)(031)

Dictionaries

[4145]

BRIGGS, K.M. A Dictionary of British folk-tales in the English language, incorporating the F.J. Norton Collection. New ed. London, Routledge & Kegan Paul, 1991. 2v.(1472p.) £45 each vol. £70 the set. A paperback edition in 2 vols. was published in 1991 (Pt.A: Folk narratives (1168p. £35. ISBN 0415066948); Pt.B: Folk legends (1472p. £35. ISBN 0415066956). ISBN: 0415066964, set.

A: Folk narratives (1168p.) B: Folk legends (1472p.). . Folk-tales are narrated in full and embrace verse tales (*e.g.* Child's *English and Scottish ballads*), giving source, type and motifs and comment, if considered necessary. 'Recommended for public and academic libraries' (*Library journal*, 1 December 1976, p.2470). *Class No:* 398(410)(038)

[4146]

HOLE, C. A Dictionary of British folk customs. Oxford, Helicon, 1995. 352p., tables, maps. £10.99. (*Helicon Reference Classics.*.) ISBN: 1859861296.

Published originally as *British folk customs* (1976).

Customs: All Fool's Day ... Yule Candle (over 4p.). Select calandar. Select bibliography (A-Z authors). Index. Succinct; very readable. *Class No:* 398(410)(038)

Ireland

[4147]

O SÚILLEABHÁIN, S. A Handbook of Irish folklore. Dublin, Educational Co. of Ireland, Ltd., for the Folklore of Ireland Society, 1942 (Reprinted Detroit, Mich., Singing Tree: Gale Research Co., 1971). xxxi,699p. $58. ISBN: 6810335611.

14 chapters (1. Settlement and dwelling ... 13. Popular oral literature - 14. Sports and pastimes). No index, but a detailed contents list (p.xix-xxxi); no sources. 'The main purpose ... is to serve as a guidance for collectors of Irish oral tradition' (*Introduction to collectors*). A mine of information and also, because of the many questions listed, a guide for further research. *Class No:* 398(415)

[4148]

—Ó DANACHAIR, C., *comp*. A Bibliography of Irish ethnology and folk tradition. Dublin & Cork, The Mercier Press, 1978. 95p. £13. ISBN: 085342490x.

In 2 parts: pt.1. Subjects (Settlement and dwelling - Livlihood and household support - Communications and trade - The community - Human life - Nature - Medicine - Time - Principles and rules of popular belief and practice - Mythological tradition - Historical tradition - Religious tradition - Folk narrative and the verbal wit - Folk poetry - Sports and pastimes - Miscellanies - Study and reesearch. Pt.2 is an alphabetical list of authors. Entries are arranged according to the O Súilleabháin handbook. *Class No:* 398(415)(01)

[4149]

O'HOGAIN, D. **Myth, legend and romance:** an encyclopaedia of the Irish folk tradition. London, Harrap: Ryan Publishing, 1990. 500p. illus. £19.95. ISBN: 1870805119.

Covers all of the stories in the narrative history of the Irish tradition. 284 entries, A-Z, incorporate the mythological cycle, the Ulster cycle, the Fianna cycle, the King's cycle, as well as the hagiography, folktales and customs of Ireland. List of sources in abbreviated form follow each entry, referring to the complete bibliography forming a separate part of the volume. There are several indexes, a short introduction to Gaelic, and a pronunciation guide. *Class No:* 398(415)

England

[4150]

CHANDLER, K. **Morris dancing** in the English South Midlands, 1660-1900: a chronological gazetteer. Enfield Lock, Mddx, Hisarlik Press, 1993. 208p. £10.95. (Publications of the Folklore Society: Tradition 2) ISBN: 1874312079.

A county-by-county listing of the 147 confirmed performance locations of morris dancing in the region during the period. Each entry includes, where available, chronology of performance, with details of context and activity, participants, musicians, etc. *Class No:* 398(420)

[4151]

CHANDLER, K. **"Ribbons, bells and squeaking fiddles":** the social history of morris dancing in the English South Midlands. 1660-1900. Enfield Lock, Mddx, Hisarlik Press, 1993. 208p. £12.95. (Publications of the Folklore Society: Tradition 1) ISBN: 1874312060.

Examines the historical development and performance aspects of the dance. *Class No:* 398(420)

Wales

[4152]

RHYS, J. **Celtic folklore: Welsh and Manx.** New ed. London, Wildwood House, 1980. 2v.(400p.;318p.). v.1 £5.50; v.2. £4.95. ISBN: 0704504057, v.1; 0704504103, v.2.

First published 1901, by Clarendon Press, Oxford.

A pioneer treatment of Welsh folklore, with a useful list of bibliographical references appended. *Class No:* 398(429)

Handbooks & Manuals

[4153]

OWEN, T.M. **Welsh folk customs.** 5th ed. Llandysul, Dyfed, Gomer Press, 1987. 197p. 16p. of plates (black & white). £4.95. ISBN: 0863833470.

First published 1959, 1st to 4th eds. published by the National Museum of Wales, Cardiff.

Chapters: 1. The Christmas season - 2. Candlemas and the movable festivals - 3. May and midsummer - 4. Harvest and winter's eve - 5. Birth, marriage and death. Select bibliography (p.187-189) A-Z by author. Index (p.190-197). 'The text provides an integrated study of the subject based on the literature, on replies to questionnaires and on information collected in the field' (*Foreword* to an earlier edition). Well documented. *Class No:* 398(429)(035)

China

Bibliographies

[4154]

TING, N.-T. *and* TING, L.-H. **Chinese folk narratives:** a bibliographical guide. San Francisco, CA., Chinese Materials Center, Inc., 1975. 68p. (*Bibliographical aids series, no.4.*)

A selective annotated bibliography of primary sources, confined to publications in major American and West European libraries, and in the authors' private collection. 3 parts: bibliographies; classical literary versions (title entry); modern oral versions (author entry; under title if authorship is corporate). Titles appear in romanised form, plus Chinese script form and often with English translations. *Class No:* 398(510)(01)

[4155]

YIN-LIEN C. CHIN, *and others.* **Traditional Chinese folktales.** Armonk, New York, M.E. Sharpe, 1996. 192p. illus. $15.95. ISBN: 156324800x.

Originally published 1989. *Class No:* 398(510)(01)

Japan

Bibliographies

[4156]

ALGARIN, J.P. **Japanese folk literature:** a core collection and reference guide. New York, R.R. Bowker, 1982. 226p. $29.95. ISBN: 0835215164.

Annotated bibliography of mainly English-language sources of Japanese folk literature. An introduction tracing its developments precedes the bibliography, which is in 3 parts: Works on Japanese folklore (63 titles) - Japanese folktale anthologies (48 titles) - Classic folktales of Japan (27 titles), which summarises the best-known tales. Indexes include a folktale index. 'The work fills a gap in the bibliographies of Japanese studies' (*Choice*, v.20(6), February 1983, p.805). *Class No:* 398(52)(01)

America

Bibliographies

[4157]

FLANAGAN, C.C. *and* FLANAGAN, J.T. **American folklore:** a bibliography, 1950-1974. Metuchen, N.J., Scarecrow Press, 1977. vi,406p. $27.50; £20.60. ISBN: 0810810735.

3639 numbered entries, with very brief annotations for some 16 sections: 1. List of magazines and abbreviations - 2. Festschriften, symposia, collections - 3. Bibliography, dictionaries, archives - 4. Folklore: study and teaching - 5. General folklore - 6. Ballads and songs - 7. Tales and narrative material - 8. Legends (theory; history; collections) - 9. Myth and mythology - 10. Beliefs, customs, superstitions, cures - 11. Folk heroes - 12. Folklore in literature - 13. Proverbs, riddles, Wellerisms, limericks - 14. Speech, names, cries, etc. - 15. Minor genres (*e.g.* rhymes; graffiti) - 16. Obituaries (of prominent folklorists). Includes some Canadian, Mexican and Caribbean material. *Class No:* 398(7)(01)

Canada

Bibliographies

[4158]

BLANCHETTE, J.-F., *and others.* 'Une Bibliographie de la culture materielle traditionelle au Canada, 1965-1982/A Bibliography of folk material culture in Canada, 1965-1982'. In *Canadian folklore Canadien*, v.4(1-2), 1984, p.107-146.

Lists works on the material culture of 'People who came to Canada after the fifteenth century'. *Class No:* 398(71)(01)

Latin America

Bibliographies

[4159]

BOGGS, R.S. **Bibliography of Latin American folklore.** New York, Wilson, 1940 (Reprinted Detroit, Mich., Ethridge, 1975). x,109p.

643 numbered, briefly annotated entries in 15 sections: Bibliography - Periodicals, serial publications and organizations - General and miscellaneous works (Argentina ... Venezuela) - Mythology, legends and traditions - Folktales - Poetry, music, dancing and games - Festivals and games - Drama - Arts and crafts, including dress and ornament - Food and drink - Belief, witchcraft, medicine and magic - Folk speech - Proverbs - Riddles. Subdivision by countries throughout. Detailed index. Supplemented by entries in 'Folklore bibliography' (*Southern folklore quarterly*, 1941-. ISSN 00384127). *Class No:* 398(729.99)(01)

USA

Bibliographies

[4160]

KIBBEE, J. **American folklore** a guide to reference sources. In *R.S.R.*, v.17(3), Fall, 1989, p.37-44.

39 references which it is suggested could serve as a core collection of reference materials on American folklore for both scholars and the general public, reflecting the scope of folk studies as it has evolved during the past 100 years. *Class No:* 398(73)(01)

Encyclopaedias

[4161]

BRUNVAND, J.H., *ed.* **American folklore:** an encyclopedia. New York, London, Garland, 1996. xviii,794p.,illus. $125 (hardback). $34.95 (paper). (*Garland Reference Library of the Humanities, vol. 155.*) ISBN: 0815307519, hbk; 0815333501, pbk.
Class No: 398(73)(031)

Handbooks & Manuals

[4162]

DORSON, R.M., *ed*. **Handbook of American folklore.** Bloomington, Indiana University Press, 1996. xix,584p. illus. $18.95. ISBN: 0253203732.

Originally published 1983.

About 70 essays present the state of the art, with evaluations of the scholarly literature and other pertinent work. Bibliographical notes are appended to each chapter, and there is a 23-page general bibliography. General index. 'A basic work' (*American notes and queries*, v.23(16), January/February 1985, p.90). *Class No:* 398(73)(035)

[4163]

PUCKETT, N.N., *comp*. **Popular beliefs and superstitions: a** compendium of American folklore. Hand, W.D., *and others*. Boston, Mass., G.K. Hall, 1981. 3v. (1903p.). $125. ISBN: 0816185859.

36,209 entries, interpreting nearly every imaginable human experience. Aimed at serious students of American culture, anthropology and folklore. *Class No:* 398(73)(035)

Theses

[4164]

DUNDES, A. **Folklore theses and dissertations in the United States.** Austin, Texas, University of Texas Press, for the American Folklore Society, 1976. 610p. $27.50. ISBN: 0292724136.

Chronological listing of over 7000 dissertations and masters' essays accepted by US universities before 1969. Indexes of authors and institutions. 'All in all this is a very useful, well-executed bibliography' (*College & research libraries*, v.38, July 1977, p.328). *Class No:* 398(73)(043)

Films

[4165]

American folklore films and video tapes: a catalog. Center for Southern Folklore Staff. New York, R.R. Bowker, 1982. 424p. $39.95; £34.75. ISBN: 0835215369.

An earlier catalogue was published by the Center with the title *American folklore films and video tapes: an index* (1976. $15. ISBN 0892670002).

Lists over 2000 films, etc., available for rental or sale, with details of title, length, format, date, producer, distributor, and brief synopsis. Detailed subject index. *Class No:* 398(73)(084.122)

Australia

[4166]

The Oxford companion to Australian folklore. Davey, G.B. *and* Seal, G., *eds*. Oxford, Oxford University Press (Australia), 1993. xvii,381p. illus. A$49.95; £30. ISBN: 0195530578.

Attempts 'to draw together the various threads of what is known' (*Preface*). Covers the major genres and ethnic groups, longer articles being signed and many including bibliographies. Also includes biographical entries, descriptions of institutions, and publications. *Class No:* 398(94)

Jews

[4167]

YASSIF, E. **Jewish folklore: an** annotated bibliography. New York, Garland, 1986. 341p. $65. (*Garland folklore bibliographies, 10. Garland reference library of the humanities, 450*.) ISBN: 082409039x.

Choice (v.24(2), October 1986, p.289) considers that '*A bibliography of Jewish folkloristics* would be a more appropriate title for this critical annotated study, which focuses on the scholarly contributions about folklore of all Jewish groups rather than actual texts'. More than 1300 informative and evaluative annotations for books and articles published over the last 100 years are arranged A-Z by author, with an appendix of late additions. Bibliographic information omits publishers. Few cross-references. Subject (keywords from titles) and name index. 'A major contribution to the study of Jewish folklore' (*Choice*, v.24(2), October 1986, p.290). *Class No:* 398(=924)

Children

[4168]

OPIE, L. *and* OPIE, P. **The Lore and language of school-children.** Oxford, Clarendon Press, 1959 (Paperback issued 1987). 438p. £4.95. ISBN: 0192820591.

'The present study is based on the contributions of some 5000 children attending seventy schools, primary, secondary modern and grammar, in different parts of England, Scotland, and Wales, and one school in Dublin' (*Preface*). Riddles, topical rhymes, nicknames, pranks, street names, superstitions, first-line and general indexes. 11 distribution maps. Fully illustrated by examples. *Class No:* 398-0053

Metrical Romances

Bibliographies

[4169]

Arthurian legend and literature: an international bibliography. Reiss, E., *and others*. New York, Garland, 1984-. 2v. V.1: $48; V.2: $34. (*Garland reference library in the humanities, v.415*.)

V.1: *The Middle ages*, has *c*.400 entries arranged by broad subject headings. Author and title index. V.2 covers post-medieval treatment of Arthurian legend. Updates and complements Loumis's *Arthurian literature in Middle Ages* (1959). *Class No:* 398.22(01)

[4170]

Bulletin bibliographique des études arthuriennes. Paris, Société International Arthurienne; Seattle, W.A., University of Washington, International Arthurian Society, 1949- Annual. $20. ISSN: 00267929.

Includes lists of books, articles and theses published in *c*.15 countries. Indexes of authors and subjects; list of members. *Class No:* 398.22(01)

[4171]

Clwyd Library Service catalogue of the collection of Arthurian literature. Davies, G., *ed*. [ii]. 2,83, 591p.

Cover title: 'Casgliat Arthuraidd'.

Two sequences: 1. Authors and titles, A-Z (*c*.2500 entries) - 2. Classified. *Class No:* 398.22(01)

[4172]

FLETCHER, R.H. **The Arthurian material in the Chronicles,** especially those of Great Britain and France. 2nd ed. New York, B. Franklin, 1966 (Reprinted 1973). ix,335p. $75. ISBN: 0833711539.

First published 1906. The 2nd ed. was expanded by a bibliography and critical essay for the period 1905-1965, by L.S. Loomis.

Aims to show what Arthurian material is contained in the European Chronicles, especially those of Great Britain and France. Treats more than 200 Chronicles, ranging from mid-6th to end of 16th century. 12 chapters (*e.g.* 3. Geoffrey of Monmouth, p.43-115). Numerous footnote references to the literature. Supplementary bibliography, 1905-65, p.333-5. *Class No:* 398.22(01)

[4173]

PICKFORD, C.B. *and* LAST, R. **The Arthurian bibliography.** Woodbridge, Suffolk, Boydell & Brewer, 1981-1998. 3v. (820p., 352p.,694p.) £120. ISBN: 0859910695, v.1; 0859910997, v.2; 0859913996, v.3.

V.3 edited by C. Palmer.

Claims to be a complete listing of all critical writing on King Arthur and the Arthurian romance down to 1975. Computer-compiled. V.1: Author listing; v.2: subject index; v.3: Author listing: subject order. *Class No:* 398.22(01)

Encyclopaedias

[4174]

LACY, N.C., *and others*, *eds*. **The New Arthurian encyclopedia.** Updated ed. New York, Garland, 1996. xxxviii,577p., illus. £34.95. $27.96. (*Garland reference library of the humanities, v.585*.) ISBN: 0815323034.

First ed. published in 1986.

Over 1200 essay entries and a large number of brief and informative entries, by 130 contributing scholars. Treats major authors and texts as well as broad subjects, covering the Arthur legend from the earliest tales to the present day in literature, history, art, music, films, etc. Each essay has a short bibliography of 1-4 items appended. Cross-references. Subject list of entries by category. Index, including all authors, artists, and important themes and motifs. Recommended as 'an important beginning in Arthurian studies' (*Library journal*, 1 Sept., 1991, p.182). *Class No:* 398.22(031)

Handbooks & Manuals

[4175]

LACY, N.J. *and* ASHE, G. *and* MANCOFF, D.N. **The Arthurian handbook.** 2nd ed. New York, Garland Publishing, 1997. 400p. $23.95. (*Garland Reference Library of the Humanities, v.1920.*) ISBN: 0815320817.

Aims to provide both an introduction for the general reader and a useful summation for the specialist. A chronology precedes 5 chapters: 1. Origins - 2. Early Arthurian literature - 3. Modern Arthurian literature - 4. Arthur in the arts - 5. An Arthurian glossary. Index. *Class No:* 398.22(035)

Dictionaries

[4176]

MINARY, R. *and* MOORMAN, C. **An Arthurian dictionary.** Rev. ed. Chicago, IL, Academy Chicago Publishers, 2000. xxvi,117p. illus. $12.95. ISBN: 0897333489.

Entries for 'mythological and literary characters, historic personages, authors, works and place names in terms of their connection with the historic and literary Arthur'. (*Choice*, v.16(2), April 1979, p.206). Short bibliography. *Class No:* 398.22(038)

Histories

[4177]

LOOMIS, R.S., *ed*. **Arthurian literature in the Middle Ages: a** collaborative history. Oxford, Clarendon Press, 1959. xvi,574p. illus.

41 chapters (1. The Arthur of history ... 5. The Welsh Triads ... 12. The origin and growth of the Tristan legend ... 15. Chrétien de Troyes ... 21. The origin of the Grail legend ... 29. The troubadours ... 34. The Dutch romance ... 37. The English rimed and prose romances ... 40. St. Thomas Malory - 41. Arthurian influence on sport and spectacle. Epilogue. Detailed, non-analytical index. Gives quotations. Pays tribute to James Douglas Bruce's *Evolution of Arthurian Romance from the beginnings down to the year 1300* (1923). *Class No:* 398.22(091)

Superstitions

Encyclopaedias

[4178]

Zolar's encyclopaedia of omens, signs and superstitions. Englewood Cliffs, N.J. Prentice Hall Press, 1989. 400p. $11.95; £6.95. ISBN: 0671653172.

Explains the origin, hidden meaning, and significance of more than 650 omens, signs and superstitions. *Class No:* 398.3(031)

Dictionaries

[4179]

OPIE, I. *and* TATEM, M., *eds.* **A Dictionary of superstitions.** Oxford, Oxford University Press, 1989. xiii,[1],494p. £17.50. ISBN: 0192115979.

1600 entries, arranged A-Z by subject, that treat superstitions of the British Isles that have survived to the nineteenth and twentieth centuries. Each superstition is illustrated by one or more quotations in chronological order to show the history and development of the superstition, the quotations being from a wide range of published and unpublished sources. Geographical locations and other clarifying information is given in brackets. Extensive cross-references. Entries vary in length from 2 or 3 lines to over a column. Select bibliography of 16th to 20th-century books and periodicals, p.455-462. Analytical index, p.463-494. *Class No:* 398.3(038)

[4180]

PICKERING, D. **Cassell dictionary of superstitions.** London, Cassell/ Ward Lock, 1995. vi,294p. £16.99. ISBN: 0304345350.

Covers superstitions from around the world, including those dealing with ailments, weather, and childbirth. Arranged alphabetically by subject. *Class No:* 398.3(038)

Fallacies

[4181]

ACKERMANN, A.S.E. **Popular fallacies:** a book of common errors explained and corrected, with copious references to authorities. 4th ed. London, Old Westminster Press, 1950 (reprinted Detroit, Mich., Gale,1970). xv,843p. $74. ISBN: 0810332957.

A hotchpotch of curious information, not always authoritative but frequently useful. *Class No:* 398.3FAL

[4182]

WARD, P. **A Dictionary of common fallacies.** 2nd ed. Cambridge, Oleander Press, 1980 (reprinted New York, Prometheus, 1989 in 1v.). 2v.(viii,303;xii,313). Reprint:636p. £10 each vol. $49.95 for reprint. ISBN: 0900891653, set; 0900891637, v.1; 0900891645, v,2; 0879755113, Reprint.

First published 1978 in 1v.

Each volume has entries, A-Z, covering commonly-held beliefs and sayings (*e.g.* that Aethelred was 'unready', 'The earth is flat' and 'History repeats itself'), as well as phenomena (*e.g.* Ectoplasm). Keywords are used for entry, which may be the name of a person. Each volume has a bibliography of authorities and an index. *Class No:* 398.3FAL

Fairies & Goblins

Bibliographies

[4183]

EASTMAN, M.H. **Index to fairy tales, myths and legends.** 2nd ed. Boston, Faxon, 1926. Supplement, 1937; 2nd supplement, 1952. ix,610p. (1st supplement, ix,566p.; 2nd supplement, 370p.). $14. ISBN: 0873050282.

About 30,000 references in an alphabetical analytical index, with list of books analysed; geographical list; bibliography of books on the art of story telling. Includes some modern stories. Continued by: *Class No:* 398.43(01)

[4184]

—IRELAND, N.O. **Index to fairy tales, 1949-1972 including folklore, legends and myths in collections.** Westwood, Mass., Faxon, 1973. (Available Metuchen, N.J. Scarecrow). 741p. Supplements, 1973-77 (1979. 259p.), 1978-1986 (1989, 575p.) and 1987-1991 (1994, 602p.), published by Scarecrow. $62.50. Supplement: $62.50. ISBN: 0810820110; 0810818558; 081082194x; 0810827506.

Main work indexes 406 books. Innovations are the comprehensive subject index of stories and the single A-Z sequence. *Class No:* 398.43(01)

Dictionaries

[4185]

BARBER, R. *and* RICHES, A. **A Dictionary of fabulous beasts.** New ed. Woodbridge, Boydell Press, 1996. 168p., illus. £15.99. ISBN: 0851156851.

First published 1971 by Macmillan Press.

Fabulous beasts, A-Z, from the Asbaia to the Zû. Bibliography of over 200 items, with references from the text, is arranged chronologically. The black-and-white illus. are few and far between, and *RQ* (v.12(1), Fall, 1972, p.86) recommends, for illus., *A fantastic bestiary*. by Ernest Lehner, with over 300 illus. *Class No:* 398.43(038)

[4186]

BRIGGS, K.M. **A Dictionary of fairies,** hobgoblins, brownies, bogies and other supernatural creatures. New ed. London, Penguin, 1993. 512p.illus. £9.99. ISBN: 0140176586.

First published by Allen Lane in 1976.

Entries A-Z include such unlikely headwords as 'Faults condemned by fairies'. Also entries for W.B. Yeates and Milton, but not Shakespeare, for his Ariel. 'Wizards': over 2p., with appended motif numbers. 'Tom Tit Tot' has an entry, with the tale reproduced in full. Book-list (A-Z authors), p.455-62. 'A note on the pronunciation of Celtic names'. Index of types and motifs, using the Antti-Aarne + Stith Thompson standard method of cataloguing folk-tales. *Class No:* 398.43(038)

Singing Games

[4187]

OPIE, I. *and* OPIE, P. **Children's games in street and playground;** chasing, catching, seeking, hunting, racing, duelling, exerting, daring, guessing, acting, pretending. London, Oxford University Press, 1969 (paperback ed., 1984). xvi,371p. illus, maps. £8.99. ISBN: 0192814893.

Concerned solely with games that children (aged about 6-12) play of their own accord when out of doors, and usually out of sight. About 2500 names of games and game-rhymes appear in the index (p.345-71); over 10,000 children were interviewed. Notes on histories of individual games. *Class No:* 398.8

[4188]

OPIE, I. *and* OPIE, P. **The Singing game.** Oxford, Oxford University Press, 1988. 544p. 28 illus. £9.99. ISBN: 0192840193.

'Presents the singing games and clapping games that used to be, or still are, played by children in Great Britain, with as much of their histories as could be discovered. Information chiefly drawn from the nationwide surveys undertaken in the 1950s and 1960s' (*Preface*). Chapter 1. The singing game - 2. Chains and captives - 3. Match-making - 4. Mating - 5. Wedding rings - 6. Cushion dances ... 12. Mimicry ... 16. Static circles - 17. Eccentric circles ... 20. Clapping. Music and verses are included in the text. List of illustrations; list of abbreviations; select bibliography; general index; A-Z index of songs, games and dances. *Class No:* 398.8

[4189]
The Oxford dictionary of nursery rhymes. Opie, I. *and* Opie, P., *eds.* 2nd ed. Oxford, Oxford University Press, 1997. xxix,559p. illus. (incl. pl.). £25. ISBN: 0198600887.

Entries on more than 500 rhymes and songs traditionally handed on by young children. Entry is usually under the most prominent word or subject; data on history of each rhyme, parallels and first appearance, source and variations. The illustrations are taken from drawings or old ballad sheets. Index of notable figures; index of first lines. *Class No:* 398.8

[4190]
—NORTHAL, G.F. English folk-rhymes: a collection of traditional verses relating to places and persons, customs, superstitions, etc. London, Kegan Paul, Trench, Trübner, 1892. xii,565p.

17 subject sections (*e.g.* 11. Games - 12. The almanac - 13. Weather), plus 18. Additions and corrections. Many quotations; references to sources. Sources, p.ix-xii. *Class No:* 398.8

Proverbs

[4191]
The Concise Oxford dictionary of proverbs. Simpson, J.A., *ed and* Speake, J. 3rd ed. Oxford, Oxford University Press, 1998. 333p. £6.99. ISBN: 0192800841.

First published 1982.

Nominally an abridgement of the standard work, *The Oxford dictionary of English proverbs* (3rd ed. 1970). Includes over 1000 proverbs from around the world, giving full documentary information from the point when each proverb entered the English language. Many illustrative quotations. 2½-page bibliography of major proverb collections and works cited from modern editions, A-Z by author. Thematic index. '...abundant cross-references, and the attractive layout make the book more enjoyable to browse than many older, standard sources.'(*Choice*, v.30(7) March 1993, p.1122). *Class No:* 398.9

[4192]
CORDY, H.V. The Multicultural dictionary of proverbs: over 20,000 adages from more than 120 languages, nationalities and ethnic groups. Jefferson, NC, McFarland, 1997. x,406p. $47.50. £42.75. ISBN: 0786402512.

Includes bibliography and index. *Class No:* 398.9

[4193]
FERGUSON, R. The Penguin dictionary of proverbs. London, Allen Lane: Penguin Books Ltd., New York, Facts on File, 1983. xii, 331p. £8.95; £3.95; $24.95. ISBN: 0713915404, UK; 0871962985, US.

Published in the US as *The facts on file dictionary of proverbs*.

A collection of over 6000 proverbs, numbered, from all over the world, arranged in 188 categories, A-Z (Absence ... Corruption ... Love ... Royalty ... Writing), each category subdivided into various aspects of the main theme. Identification of the origins of the proverbs and explanations of the meanings are given as necessary. Index, p.271-331, indexes each proverb under its first keyword, followed by the complete phrase or opening phrase, with category and item number. 'The proverbs, displaying their folkloric foundings, range from the mundane to the witty' (*Wilson library bulletin*, November 1983, p.225). *Class No:* 398.9

[4194]
FLEXNER, S. *and* FLEXNER, D. Wise words and wives tales: the origins, meanings and time-honored wisdom of proverbs and folk sayings, olde and new. New York, Avon, 1993. 218p. $9. ISBN: 0380762382.

Entries note the earliest recorded appearance of each saying, followed by variations in form and meaning as they evolved. Limited to the English-speaking world. Cross-references. *Booklist* (v.90(1), 9/1/93, p.92) comments that a thematic index would have been a useful addition. *Class No:* 398.9

[4195]
GLUSKI, J., *comp. & ed.* Proverbs / Proverbes / Sprichwörter / Proverbi / Proverbios / Poslovity: a comparative book of English, French, German, Italian, Spanish and Russian proverbs, with a Latin appendix. Amsterdam, Elsevier, 1971 (paperback ed. 1989). xxxviii,448p. £48.75; Dfl.95. ISBN: 0444409041; 0444873503.

More than 1100 proverbs and proverbial phrases, more or less current, in each of the 6 languages, under 48 topic-sections (1. Words and deeds - 2. Truth:lie ... 47. Ethics: practical philosophy - 48. Miscellaneous). 6 language indexes (indexed by catchwords). Entries asterisked in the main sequence have equivalents in the Latin appendix (p.433-46). *Class No:* 398.9

[4196]
PACZOLAY, G. European proverbs: in 55 languages, with equivalents in Arabic, Persian, Sanskrit, Chinese and Japanese = Europai kosmondasok 55 nyelven, arab, perzsa, szanszkrit, kinai es Japan megfelelokkel. Veszprem [Hungary], Veszpremi Nyomda, 1997. 527p. ISBN: 9638096012.

English and Hungarian. *Class No:* 398.9

[4197]
PICKERING, D. The Cassell dictionary of proverbs. London, Cassell/ Ward Lock, 1997. vi,297p. £14.99. $24.95. ISBN: 0304349119.

Entries explain the meanings and origins of each proverb. The proverbs are from the English-speaking world with parallels from other cultures. *Class No:* 398.9

[4198]
STEVENSON, B.E. Stevenson's book of proverbs, maxims and familiar phrases. New York, Macmillan, 1948; London, Routledge, 1949 (Reprinted 1965). viii,2957p.

Contains more than 73,000 proverbs, maxims and phrases. Subject arrangement, with dates; full index of keywords. Overlaps considerably with Stevenson's *Book of quotations*. Gives precise citations; international in scope. Proverbs in foreign languages are first translated, then given in the original. The 1965 reprint has the title *Macmillan book of proverbs, maxims and familiar phrases.* *Class No:* 398.9

England

[4199]
The Oxford dictionary of English proverbs. Wilson, F.P., *ed.* 3rd ed. rev. Oxford, Clarendon Press, 1970. xv,[1], 930p. £19.50; $45. ISBN: 0198691181.

First published 1935.

About 14,000 entries, A-Z, under first significant word. Cites variants (*e.g.* 'House is his castle. A man's (Englishman's)'). Cross-references from other key words, but not necessarily from first word of proverb. Cites sources and users, chronologically, with dates. Sources, p.xi-xv. Smallish print; entries not sufficiently conspicuous. Many new entries, thanks to permitted unrestricted use of M.P. Tilley's *A dictionary of the proverbs in England in the* sixteenth and seventeenth centuries (1950). No index.

Two older storehouses of proverbs, English and foreign, are: *Lean's Collectanea*, by V.S. Lean (1902-04), classified in various ways by country, calendar, subject-matter, etc.; and H.G. Bohn's *Handbook of proverbs* (1889), based on the collections of John Ray (1670) and David Ferguson (1641). *Class No:* 398.9(420)

[4200]
TILLEY, M.P. A Dictionary of the proverbs in England in the sixteenth and seventeenth centuries: a collection of the proverbs found in English literature and the dictionaries of the period. Ann Arbor, Mich., University of Michigan Press; London, Oxford University Press, 1950. (Reprinted AMS Press). xiii,854p. $115. ISBN: 0404188990.

Subject entry, items A-Z thereunder, citing sources; bibliography of works quoted, p.769-802. Indexes of significant words in proverbs (p.809-54; and a Shakespeare index (p.803-08), giving exact references. About 11,780 proverbs are listed. *The Oxford dictionary of English proverbs* (3rd ed., 1970, p.x) refers to Tilley's work as 'exemplary for clarity, for references, particularly to Shakespeare, and for paucity of errors'. *Class No:* 398.9(420)

[4201]
WHITING, B.J. *and* WHITING, H.W. Proverbs, sentences and proverbial phrases, from English writings mainly before 1500. Cambridge, Mass., Belknap Press of Harvard University Press; London, Oxford University Press, 1968. li,733p. $51. ISBN: 0674719506.

About 10,000 entries, A-Z by keyword, and then chronologically, with exact citation to source. Where appropriate, references to other standard collections are cited. Indexes: important words; proper nouns. 'It will not be superseded' (*Library journal*, v.93(21), 1 December 1968, p.4543). *Class No:* 398.9(420)

[4202]
—WHITING, B.J. Modern proverbs and proverbial sayings. Cambridge, Mass., Harvard University Press, 1989. 709p. $39.95. ISBN: 0674580532.

5567 entries of material published between c.1930 to the early 1980s, arranged by keyword, with bibliographical sources indicated. A very wide variety of sources were scanned throughout the years for this compilation. Unfortunately, only one keyword, usually the first noun, is used for each proverb; no definitions are given, even for abstract or metaphorical proverbs; and no oral proverbs are included. However, 'No other compilation of proverbs covers the twentieth century with such comprehensiveness ... Whiting's crowning work will become a standard reference source for proverbs and should delight both the scholar and the casual browser' (*Reference books bulletin*, November 15, 1989, p.696). *Class No:* 398.9(420)

Wales

[4203]

VAUGHAN, H.H., *ed*. **Welsh proverbs with English translations.**
Facsim. ed. Felinfach, Llanerch Publishers, 1995. vi,378p. £9.95.
ISBN: 1897853246.
  A collection of 2259 Welsh proverbs in metrical English, with Welsh
originals. *Class No:* 398.9(429)

[4204]

—**EVANS, J.J. Welsh proverbs, in English and Welsh.** Llandyssul,
Cardiganshire, Gomerian Press (J.D. Lewis & Sons Ltd.), 1965.
147,59p.
  About 1400 selected entries, under first words, A-Z of the proverbs
in Welsh. Parallel Welsh and English text. *Class No:* 398.8(429)

China

[4205]

SCARBOROUGH, W. A Collection of Chinese proverbs. 2nd ed.
Shanghai, Presbyterian Misson Press, 1926 (Reprinted New York,
Paragon Book Reprint Corp., 1964). vi,381,xivp.
  Grouped under broad headings, with a topical index. Proverbs in
Chinese script, with transliteration and translation.
Class No: 398.9(510)

USA

[4206]

TAYLOR, A. *and* **WHITING, B.J. A Dictionary of American
proverbs and proverbial phrases, 1820-1880.** Cambridge, Mass.,
Belknap Press of Harvard University Press, 1958. xxii,[1],418p.
  Arranged A-Z by keyword, with full references to book and page.
Includes proverbs used by American authors of the period, even if the
proverbs are not American in origin. 10-page bibliography of texts and
reference works (p.xiii-xxii). *Class No:* 398.9(73)

[4207]

—**WHITING, B.J. Early American proverbs and proverbial phrases.**
Cambridge, Mass., Harvard University Press, 1977. 576p. $42.50.
ISBN: 0674219813.
  Covers 1620-1820. Arranged under keywords, A-Z, p.1-506, with
cross-references to similar sayings and to entries in standard collections
of English proverbs. Bibliography of sources, p.xxiii-lxiv. Index of
keywords. The period was one in which 'proverbs were used seriously
to instruct, warn, cajole or just grumble about life in general' (*TLS*,
no.3969, 28 April, p.483). *Class No:* 398.9(73)

90 Archaeology

[4208]

RENFREW, C. *and* BAHN, P. **Archaeology** theories, methods, and practice. London, Thames and Hudson, 1991. 544p. illus., diagrs., maps, bibliog., index. pbk. £18.95. ISBN: 0500276056.

Comprehensive introduction to what archaeology is and to what archaeologists do. 3 main parts: 1. Framework of archaeology - 2. Discovering the variety of human experience - 3. The World of archaeology. 87 special features on key topics *e.g.* underwater archaeology, radiocarbon dating, origins of farming, collapse of civilizations, and summaries of 25 significant excavations. 'Serves as an important showcase for modern archaeological science' (*Antiquity*, v.66, no.250, March 1992, p.272-3). *Class No: 902*

Bibliographies

[4209]

Archäologische Bibliographie. Berlin, Walter de Gruyter, 1913-. Annual. ISSN: 03418308.

Succeeded bibliographies printed in *Jahrbuch Deutschen Archäologischen Instituts* (1886-88) and *Archäologischer Anzeiger* (1889-1912).

1992v. (1993. lii,484p.) 13146 references in 24 subject sections (*e.g.* Praxis und Institutionen; Topographie; Urgeschichte). Systematic subject index. A comprehensive and authoritative bibliography of mammouth proportions. *Class No: 902(01)*

[4210]

CHAMPION, S. 'Archaeology on the World Wide Web: a user's field-guide' Special Review Section: Electronic Archaeology, *Antiquity*, v.71, no.774, December 1997, p.1027-38.

'Outlines some of the categories of information about archaeology on the World Wide Web, illustrated by good examples; it introduces the "official" places which catalogue information and provide easy navigation; and offers ... some tips for frustration free searching to those looking for specific items of interest'. Includes virtual libraries; books, journals; communication; institutions, organizations and societies; sites and monuments; and using search engines. *Class No: 902(01)*

[4211]

WOODHEAD, P. **Keyguide to information sources in archaeology.** London, Mansell, 1985. xiv,219p. diagr. £25. ISBN: 0720117453.

Part 1. Overview of archaeology and its literature in 7 chapters: 1. History and scope - 2. Archaeological information - 3. Who, what, where? - 4. Keeping up to date with current publications, developments and events - 5. Finding out about the literature - 6. The literature of archaeology - 7. Other sources of information. Pt. 2 Bibliographical listing (an annotated bibliography of reference sources). Pt. 3 List of selected organizations. 'A work of great interest and quite widespread usefulness' (*Library Review*, v.35, no.2, Summer 1986, p.136-7). *Class No: 902(01)*

Encyclopaedias

[4212]

The Cambridge encyclopedia of archaeology. Sherratt, A., *ed.* Cambridge, Cambridge Univ. Press, 1980. 495p. illus., charts, maps, plans.

55 contributors. 3 parts (10 sections; 62 chapters): 1/1. The development of modern archaeology ... 2/2. Man the hunter; 2/3. The postglacial revolution; 2/4.The early empires of the western Old World; 2/5. Empires in the eastern Old World; 2/6. Old empires and new forces; 2/7. On the edge of the Old World; 2/8. The New World (*e.g.* chapter 59: Andean South America); 2/9. Pattern and process ... 3/10. Framework; dating and distribution. Chronological atlas, p.437-52 (36 col. maps). Bibliography (by chapters), p.453-65. Further reading (by parts and sections), p.416-7. Analytical index, p.468-95. 500 illus. (150 col.), with descriptive captions. Omits industrial archaeology.'The selection of topics is excellent and as comprehensive as positive' (*Choice*, v.18, no.2, October 1980, p.220). 'A volume with wide appeal' (*Nature*, v.288, 6 November 1980, p.42). 'More likely to be used for browsing than for quick reference' (*College & Research Libraries*, January 1981, p.49). *Class No: 902(031)*

[4213]

Encyclopedia of archaeology. Santa Barbara, Calif., and Oxford, ABC-Clio, 5v., 1999-2000. £270.

Pt.1: The Great archaeologists (2v.). 1999. 960p. illus., bibliogs., index. $150. £95. ISBN 1576071995. 58 A-Z cross-referenced essays, arranged chronologically, on prominent archaeologists of the past contributed by leading archaeologists of today, consisting a history of archaeology from the Renaissance to the present. Each essay begins with the life and career of the biographee and concludes with bibliographies of original source material and later assessments. Also included is a glossary and a subject index.

Pt.2: Histories and discoveries (3v.) 2000. 1,500p. illus., maps, bibliog., index. $275. £175. 1576071987. A-Z entries, ranging from brief definitions and identifications to discursive essays, spotlight archaeological pioneers, discoveries and debates, concepts and techniques, periods and regions etc. A timeline, a general bibliography, and a full index complement the text. 'This new one-of-a-kind collective biography is quite scholarly and belongs in all serious archaeology/anthropology collections', (*Booklist*, v.96, nos. 9+10, 1+15, January 2000, p.974). *Class No: 902(031)*

[4214]

The Oxford companion to archaeology. Fagan, B.M., *ed.* New York, Oxford Univ. Press USA, 1996. xx,844p. maps, charts, bibliogs., index. $55. ISBN: 0195076184.

c370 contributors. 700 A-Z cross-referenced entries on virtually every aspect of archaeology *e.g.* Egyptian hieroglyphics, luminescence dating, the Mayan calendar, Olduvai Gorge, the history of archaeology, excavation methods, leading archaeologists, and human culture. 29 full page maps. 14 chronological tables. Analytical index p.820-44. *Class No: 902(031)*

[4215]

TATTERSALL, I., *and others, eds.* **Encyclopedia of human evolution and prehistory.** New York Garland Publishing, 1988. xxxvi, 603p. illus., diagrs., maps. $87.50. ISBN: 0824093755.

40 academic contributors. 1200 A-Z topic heading entries about half being cross-references to associated articles. Entries are initialled and all but the shortest carry bibliographical references. Main subject areas covered include Fossil and archaeological localities; Archaeology (general terms and concepts); and Archaeological sites. Subject list by topics (summary of major subject areas) p.xiii-xxiv. 'A comprehensive and authoritative source, filling a unique niche, that will be essential to academic libraries' (*Booklist*, v.85, no.11, 1 February 1989, p.922+924). *Class No: 902(031)*

Handbooks & Manuals

[4216]

Handbuch der Vorgeschichte. Müller-Karpe, H. München, C.H. Beck, 1966-. V.1-.

1. *Altsteinzeit* 1966; 2nd ed. 1977. xi, 359p.+274p. plates and drawings. 2. *Jungsteinzeit Text.* 1968. xiii, 612p. *Tafeln* 1968. vi, 327p. 3. *Kupferzeit Text* 1974. xiii, 770p. 3406054218. *Regesten* 1974. 771-1124p. 3406054226. *Tafeln* 1974. 746p. 3406054234. 4. *Bronzezeit Text.* 1980. vii, 496p. 340679415. *Text und Register.* 1980. 497-866p. 3406079423. *Tafeln.* 1980. 602p. 340607943 3v. DM548. To be completed with an Iron Age volume. This monumental series provides an account of world prehistory, continent by continent, country by country, with a distinct European bias. Each chapter begins with a historical survey of archaeological work. 'Almost unreadable as a book, because of the vast array of cross-references and footnotes, nonetheless there is buried here an immense learning' (*Antiquity*, v. LVI, no.218, November 1982, p.233-234). *Class No: 902(035)*

Dictionaries

[4217]

BAHN, P., *ed.* **Collins dictionary of archaeology.** Glasgow, Harper Collins, 1992. iv,654p. maps, bibliog. £15.99. ISBN: 0004341570.

3,000 entries including definitions of archaeological terms, worldwide sites and artefacts, explanations of archaeological theory and methods, biographical sketches of important archaeologists. Map section p.556-641. Bibliography p.642-50. *Class No: 902(038)*

[4218]
SHAW, I. *and* JAMESON, R. A Dictionary of archaeology. Oxford, Blackwell, 1999. xv,624p. illus., tables, bibliogs. ISBN: 0631174230.
41 contributors. 'The principal aim of this dictionary is to provide readers with a reference tool for the terms, techniques and major sites in archaeology' (*Preface*). To that end definitions of varying length, key words in contemporary archaeology, including industrial and marine archaeology are combined with major essays on continents, countries and regions. Excludes Greek and Roman history and sites in favour of a more comprehensive coverage of the archaeology of China, Japan, and Oceania. Reading lists follow virtually every entry. *Class No: 902(038)*

[4219]
WHITEHOUSE, R.D., *ed*. The Macmillan dictionary of archaeology. London, Macmillan Press, 1983. xi,597p. bibliog., index. £25.00. ISBN: 0333271904.
Over 3500 entries covering the themes, concepts, and discoveries in archaeology. Bibliography p.592-97. Subject index. *Class No: 902(038)*

Glossaries

[4220]
SEEBERG, E.S. Dictionary of archaeology: English, German, Norwegian. 3rd ed. Oslo Univ. Museum of Cultural Heritage, 1999. 323p. pbk. ISBN: 8271811541.
Terms and definitions in English A-Z plus separate indexes for German and Norwegian equivalents. *Class No: 902(038.1)*

Periodicals

[4221]
MUSTY, J. The Origins of the archaeological periodical *Current Archaeology*. v.9, no.5. June 1986, p.142-143.
Notes on UK journals 1665-1979. *Class No: 902(051)*

Maps & Atlases

[4222]
ASTON, M. *and* TAYLOR, T. The Atlas of archaeology. London, Dorling Kindersley, 1998. 208p. col.illus., col.maps, bibliog., index. £20. ISBN: 0751303208.
Popular style but academically respectable overview of the world's most celebrated archaeological sites and finds in 9 chronological chapters. Gazetteer of 1200+ sites indicated on 14 full-colour regional maps (p.136-57) supplemented by Gazetteer Listings, profiles of date, location, type of site, and site details (p.158-97). Glossary p.198-200. Bibliography p.201. Analytical index. *Class No: 902(084.3)*

[4223]
The Times of archaeology of the world. Scarre, C., *ed*. London, Times Books, 1999. 320p. col. illus., col. maps, tables, bibliog, index. £35. ISBN: 0723010323.
First published 1989 as *Past worlds. The Times atlas of archaeology*. 90 academic contributors (31 from Cambridge University). 122 double page pictorial and cartographic features arranged in 7 main sections: 1. Understanding the past - 2. Human origins 16 million-10,000BC. - 3. The agricultural revolution 10,000-4,000BC. - 4. The first cities and states 4000-1000BC. - 5. Empires of the Old World 1000BC-AD650 - 6. The New World 10,000BC-AD1600 - 7. Towards the modern world AD650-1800. Chronology in 5 colour code for geographical regions p.11-21. Glossary p.281-4. Bibliography p.285-8. 750 col. illus.
'Without question, this is now the standard archaeological atlas' (*Wilson Library Bulletin*), v.63, no.5, January 1989, p.127). *Class No: 902(084.3)*

[4224]
The World atlas of archaeology. Flon, C., *ed*. London, Mitchell Beazeley International Ltd., Boston, G.K. Hall, 1985. 423p. col.illus., col. maps, bibliog., index. £29.95; $83.00. ISBN: 0855335538, UK; 0816187479, US.
English language edition of *Le grand atlas de l'archéologie* (Encyclopaedia Universalis, 1985).
Over 90 contributors present a superb visual survey closely integrated with authoritative text arranged in chronological, thematic and regional chapters: Prehistoric Europe - The Classical World - The early Middle Ages - Middle Ages - Byzantine World - Islam - Near East - Egypt and Sudan - Scythia and the Steppes - Central Asia - The Indian World - Southeast Asia - China - Vietnam - Korea and Japan - Africa - The Americas - Oceania - Modern period (Archaeological background ... Archaeology and East-West exchange ... Industrial archaeology). Glossary p.405-418. Bibliography p.394-403. More than 100 maps. Over 1000 photographs. Emphasis is on social aspects i.e., food and drink, clothing, everyday life, commercial interchange etc. 'A most useful and necessary work for the professional scholar' (*Antiquity*, v.60, no.229, July 1986, p.154). *Class No: 902(084.3)*

Chronologies

[4225]
GRASLUND, B. The Birth of prehistoric chronology dating methods and dating systems in nineteenth century Scandinavia. Cambridge, Cambridge University Press, 1987. iv, 132p., illus., bibliog., index. £25.00. $39.50. (*New studies in antiquity*.) ISBN: 0521322499.
15 Well documented chapters analysing the basic elements of archaeological dating systems and tracing the origins and development of those sytems. *Class No: 902(090)*

Histories

[4226]
TRIGGER, B.G. A History of archaeological thought. Cambridge, Cambridge Univ. Press, 1989. xv,500p. illus., bibliog., index. ISBN: 0521328780.
'A history of archaeology from medieval times to the present in world-wide perspective'. 1. Relevance of archaeological history - 2. Classical archaeology and antiquarianism - 3. Beginnings of scientific archaeology - 4. The imperial synthesis - 5. Culture-historical archaeology - 6. Soviet archaeology - 7. Functionalism in Western archaeology - 8. Neo-evolutionism and the New Archaeology - 9. The explanations of diversity - 10. Archaeology and its social context. Bibliographical essay p.412-28. References p.429-76. Analytical index. 'The best intellectual history of the discipline to date' (review article, *Journal of Field Archaeology*, v.18, no.1, Spring 1991, p.106-11). *Class No: 902(091)*

Worldwide

Bibliographies

Internet

[4227]
ArchNet: WWW virtual library - archeology. URL:http:/ archnet.uconn.edu/
Coverage: academic departments and programmes worldwide, museums and research facilities, electronic journals, and archaeology-related newsgroups and listservers. Specific subject areas include archaeology historic preservation, geoarchaeology, historic archeology, hypertext site reports. Also Regional Views (list of archaeological resources on specific areas). 'Should be a standard bookmark for every library and institution where graduate or undergraduate courses ... are regularly offered' (*Choice*, Supplement to v.36, August 1999, p.36-37). *Class No: 902(100)(01)(003.41)*

Pacific Ocean

[4228]
IRWIN, G. The Prehistoric exploration and colonisation of the Pacific. Cambridge, Cambridge Univ. Press, 1992. viii,240p. maps, tables, bibliog., index. £30. ISBN: 0521403715.
'Concerned with two distinct episodes of voyaging and colonisation. The first began some 50,000 years ago in the tropical region of Island Southeast Asia, the continent of Australia and its Pleistocene outliers ... The second episode began after 3,500 years ago and was a burst of sophisticated maritime and neolithic settlement in the remote Pacific' (*Introduction*). Bibliography p.223-31. Analytical index. *Class No: 902(265)*

Asia—South East

[4229]
BELLWOOD, P. Man's conquest of the Pacific the prehistory of Southeast Asia and Oceania. Auckland, Collins, 1978. 462p. illus., maps, bibliog., index. £20.00. ISBN: 0002169118.
13 chapters: 1. Introduction; 2. Human populations - past and present; 3. Cultural foundations; 4. The cultures of Southeast Asia and Oceania; 5. The linguistic history of the Pacific area; 6. Subsistence pattern and the prehistoric implications; 7. Neolithic and Early Metal Age cultures on the Southeast Asian mainland; 8. Neolithic and Early Metal Age Inland Southeast Asia; 9. The prehistory of Melanesia; 10. Prehistory of Micronesia; 11-12. Prehistory of Polynesia; 13. Prehistory of New Zealand. Glossary p.424. Important bibliography p.425-451. *Class No: 902(265)(59)*

Ancient Egypt

Bibliographies

[4230]
Annual Egyptological bibliography/Bibliographie Egyptologique annuelle/Jährbuch Agyptologische bibliographie. Zonhoven, L.M.J., *ed*. Leiden, International Association of Egyptologists in cooperation with the Nederlands Instituut voor het Nabije Oosten, 1948-. Annual.
The 1984v. (1987. xi, 251p. 9072147030) has 1331 numbered

....(contd.)

abstracts sytematically classified in 10 sections: 1. General (History of Egyptology, Obituaries, Present day Egyptology, Reports, Methodology, Research tools) - 2. Scripts and language - 3. Texts and philology - 4. History - 5. Art and archaeology - 6. Religion - 7. Society and culture - 8. Science and technology - 9. The country and neighbouring areas - 10. Nubian studies. Author and title indexes. Published on the recommendation of the International Council for Philosophy and Humanistic Studies, with the financial assistance of UNESCO and the Nederlandse organistie voor zuiver-wetenschappenijk onderzoek ZWO.

Janssen, J.M.A. *Annual Egyptological Bibliography indexes 1947-1956.* Leiden, E.J. Brill, 1960. xviii, 475p. *Class No:* 902(32)(01)

Encyclopaedias

[4231]

Lexikon der Ägyptologie. Helck, W. *and* Westendorf, W., eds. Wiesbaden, Otto Harrassowitz, 7v., 1975-1992

V.6: *Stele-Zyppresse* (1986.1455p. ISBN 3447026634). V.7: *Nachträge, Korrecturen und Indices.* 1992. xli,841p.+ 16 folded maps. 3447033320. International cooperative encyclopedia of immense scholarly distinction. Initialled articles end with lists of reference. *Class No:* 902(32)(031)

Biographies

[4232]

DAWSON, W. R. *and* UPHILL, E. P. *and* BIERBRIER, M. L. Who was who in Egyptology. 3rd ed. London, Egypt Exploration Society, 1995. 455p. port. ISBN: 0856981257.

First published 1952. 2nd ed. 1972.

About 1,000 entries. Howard Carter 54 lines; Geroge Edward Stanhope Molyneux, 5th Earl of Carnarvon 24 lines *Class No:* 902(32)(092)

Holy Land (Ancient World)

[4233]

AMIHAI MAZAR. Archaeology of the land of the Bible 10,000-586 B.C.E. New York, Doubleday, 1990. Published for Center for Judaic-Christian Studies, Dayton, OH. xxx,572p. illus., maps, bibliog., indexes. $30. (*The Anchor Bible Reference Library*.) ISBN: 038523970x.

Comprehensive chronological overview of the archaeological research of Old Testament Palestine from the earliest settlements to the Babylonian destruction of the first temple. Bibliographical note and abbreviations p.xix-xxiii. Glossary of geographic terms (Hebrew, Arabic, English) p.xxx. 11 maps. 'Of special value ... is Mazar's superb 34-page introduction to the technical realia of Palestinian archaeology; nothing better is currently in print; (*Choice*, v.28, no.4, December 1990, p.688). *Class No:* 902(33)

[4234]

AMNON BEN-TOR, *ed.* The Archaeology of ancient Israel. New Haven, Yale Univ. Press, 1992. xxi,398p. +41p. col. pl. maps, tables, bibliog., index. £30. ISBN: 0300047681.

Translation by R. Greenberg of the original Hebrew edition published by The Open University of Israel.

7 Academic contributors. Survey of a century of research into the history of ancient Israel from the Neolithic era to the fall of Jerusalem and the destruction of the Temple in 586 BC. Introduction reviews the past 40 years of archaeological activity in Israel. Bibliography p.377-84. Supersedes W.F. Albright's *The archaeology of Palestine* (3rd ed. 1956), K. Kenyon's *Archaeology in the Holy Land* (1965), and Y. Aharoni's *The archaeology of the land of Israel* (1982). *Class No:* 902(33)

[4235]

The New encyclopedia of archaeological excavations in the Holy Land. Stern, E., *ed.* Jerusalem, Israel Exploration Society and Carta; New York, Simon & Schuster, 4v., 1993. xxii,1552p. col.illus., maps, plans, bibliogs., indexes. $355; £199. ISBN: 9652202096, (Is); 0132762889, US, set.

Updated and enlarged edition of *Encyclopedia of archaeological excavations in the Holy Land* edited by M. Avi-Yonash (Prentice Hall, 1976-8).

365 signed articles from 200+ archaeologists each providing a detailed excavation report and a bibliography. Chronological tables p.1529-34. Glossary p.1535-40. Name, place and Biblical references index. 'Scholars and researchers will find this reference set indispensable' (*Library Journal*, v.118, no.14, 1 September 1993, p.173-4). *Class No:* 902(33)

Mesopotamia

Maps & Atlases

[4236]

LLOYD, S. The Archaeology of Mesopotamia from the Old Stone Age to the Persian conquest. London, Thames & Hudson, 1978. 252p. illus., ports., maps, plans, index. (*The World of Archaeology*.)

10 chapters (1. The land and its rivers - 2. The twilight of Neolithic man ... 9. The late Assyrian period - 10. Babylon: the last Mesopotamian monarchy). Notes on the text, p.232-7. Bibliography p.238-43 (under authors). 'Analyses systematically the wealth of material produced by major and minor excavations since 1900 ... an invaluable reference work' (A.J. Abdulrahman. *Iraq*, 1984 Entry 144). *Class No:* 902(35)(084.3)

Persia, Ancient

Bibliographies

[4237]

PEARSON, J.D., *ed.* A Bibliography of pre-Islamic Persia. London, Mansell, 1975. 288p.

Compiled under the auspices of the Royal Institute of Translation and Publication of Iran.

Over 7,000 entries, in 4 main parts (1: Languages and literatures - 2. History, including numismatics, chronology, historical geography, law - 3. Religions, including folklore and Iranian epic - 4. Art & archaeology (general; archaeological travels; exhibition catalogues; history of art; artifacts). Attempts to list 'all the printed literature in Western European languages' (*Introduction*) - books and periodical articles - on the pre-Islamic period locatable in relevant libraries, museums and periodicals. *Class No:* 902(355)(01)

Ancient Greece & Rome

[4238]

GRANT, M. The Visible past Greek and Roman history from archaeology 1960-1990. London, Weidenfeld and Nicolson, 1990. xvii,258p. illus., maps, bibliog., index. £17. ISBN: 0297820397.

9 chapters arranged chronologically in 2 parts (1. The Greeks - 2. Italy and the Roman Empire) describe and assess 50 archaeological sites or projects, including underwater archaeology and the findings of air photography, that have transformed our knowledge of classical history. Chapter references p.186-92. Notes p.193-216. Bibliography p.220-40. 9 maps. *Class No:* 902(37/38)

[4239]

STILLWELL, R., *and others eds.* The Princeton encyclopaedia of classical sites. Princeton, New Jersey, Princeton Univ. Press, 1976. xxi, 1019p. $215. ISBN: 0691035423.

Data on over 2,800 archaeological sites. Aardenburg ... Zoster. About 400 contributors. Period: 750BC-AD565. All entries, however, short, have references, ('Corinth'; 6 columns; 2/3 col. of bibiliography; 'Carthage': 1¼ cols., 5 references; 'Katana' (Catania, Sicily); 21/3 cols. of bibliography). Map references to 24p. of 3-colour maps; map indexes, p.1011-19. Glossary of technical terms. Scholarly, readable text. A handsome volume. 'This first-class reference book' (*Library Journal*, v.101, 1 October 1976, p.2050). *Class No:* 902(37/38)

Maps & Atlases

[4240]

FINLEY, M.I. Atlas of classical archaeology. London, Chatto & Windus, 1977. 256p. illus., plans, maps.

Period covered is mainly 1000B.C.-500A.D. Sections: Introduction - Roman Britain - The Roman Rhine - Danube frontier - Provence - The Iberian Peninsula - North Africa - Sicily - Italy - Illyricum, Moesia and Dacia - Greece (p.141-83) - Cyprus - Black Sea - Asia Minor - Syria - Palestine - East of Palmyra. Each section has reference appended. Appended: Chronological table; Roman emperors; Glossary; Greek vase types; The Greek architectural orders. Excellent photographs and ground plans; small diagrams and maps. *Class No:* 902(37/38)(084.3)

Ancient Greece

Bibliographies

Internet

[4241]

The Prehistoric archaeology of the Aegean. Rutter, J. URL:http://devlab.cs.dartmouth.adu/history/bronze age/

'It is immediately apparent that this site has the potential to be the most comprehensive Web site on prehistoric Greece down to the collapse of Mycenaean civilization. Sites available until now have included excellent collections of images of Bronze Age Greece ... but none, to this reviewer's knowledge, has combined the authority of

....(contd.)

Rutter's text and bibliography with a huge collection of images and sophisticated Web design and navigation tools' (*Choice*, Supplement to v.36, p.162). *Class No:* 902(37)(01)(003.41)

Europe

[4242]
CHAMPION, T., *and others*. **Prehistoric Europe.** London, Academic Press, 1984. x, 359p. illus., maps, bibliog., index. £37.00.

Comprehensive synthesis of new interpretations (based on recent archaeological data) in 9 chronological chapters each equipped with numerous maps and drawings. References p.327-35. 'It will at once take its place as a new standard work, for it is quite simply the best introduction to European prehistory which is currently available' (*Nature*, v.314, no.6006, 7 March 1985, p.28-29). *Class No:* 902(4)

[4243]
COLLIS, J. **The European Iron Age.** London, B.T. Batsford, 1984. 192p. illus., map, bibliog. £19,95. ISBN: 0713434511.

General introduction demonstrating the links between the classical Mediterranean world and the more shadowy regions of Central Europe. Notes and bibliography p.181-188. Index p.189-192. 'A magnificent survey of a whole continent' (*Current Archaeology*, v. ix, no.2, July 1985, p.46). *Class No:* 902(4)

[4244]
GAMBLE, C. **The Palaeolithic settlement of Europe.** Cambridge, Cambridge Univ Press, 1986. xix, 471p. illus., tables, bibliog. £45.00. ISBN: 0521245141.

Surveys the hunter-gatherer societies of Europe in 9 chapters (1. European paleolithic studies: history and approaches; 9. The palaeolithic settlement in Europe). Extensive bibliography p.411-459. Site index p.460-462. General index p.463-471. *Class No:* 902(4)

[4245]
SCHUTZ, H. **The Prehistory of Germanic Europe.** New Haven, Yale Univ Press, 1983. viii, 421p. illus., (some col.), maps, tables, index. $60.00. £45.00. ISBN: 0300028636.

Systematic survey of Central European cultural history in 7 chapters: 1. The Palaeolithic; 2. The Ceramic Age; 3. The Bronze Age; 4. Hallstatt; 5. The La Tene culture; 6. Northern genesis; 7. Conclusion. Chapter notes p.355-399. Bibliography p.400-407. Aim is to make accessible a summary of modern research to students and scholars. *Class No:* 902(4)

[4246]
SKLENAR, K. **Archaeology in Central Europe** the first 500 years. Leicester, Leicester Univ. Press; New York, St. Martin's Press, 1983. viii, 182p. illus., maps. ISBN: 0718512049, UK; 0312047215, US.

The development of prehistoric and protohistoric archaeology in Central Europe and in each of the countries concerned. Bibliography p.170-174. Index p.176-182. *Class No:* 902(4)

[4247]
WHITE, A.W.R. **Neolithic Europe** a survey. Cambridge, Cambridge Univ. Press, 1985. xiv,363p. illus., maps, bibliog. £27.50. (*Cambridge World Archaeology*.) ISBN: 0521247993.

Wide ranging survey of the archaeological evidence 8000-2000BC. Each chapter reviews nature of the evidence, the environment, chronology and cultural sequences, settlements, and social context of production. Bibliography p.342-355. Index p.356-363. 'A balanced and well-referenced summary of the subject' (*Choice*, v.23, no.7, March 1986, p.1126). *Class No:* 902(4)

Bibliographies

Internet

[4248]
Archeological resource guide for Europe WWW virtual library for European archaeology. URL:http://odur.let.rug.nl/arge/

Indexed collection of almost 1,100 hypertext links from 38 countries indicating current archaeological communications and information resources across Europe. 13 categories in home page navigation bar include geographical, thematic, and chronological indexes. 'A superb site, useful to the general public and professionals' (*Choice*, Supplement to v.36, August 1999, p.169). *Class No:* 902(4)(01)(003.41)

Encyclopaedias

[4249]
FILIP, J. **Enzyklopädisches Handbuch zur Ur-und Frühgeschichte Europas.** Stuttgart, Kohlhammer, 2v., 1966-69. xv, 1756p. illus. (incl. pl.), tables, maps, bibliogs.

1: A-K; v.2: L-Z und Nachträge.

About 250 contributors. Many short articles on the prehistory, and early history of Europe, some of them signed; references appended. Helpful entries under 'Inventaria archeologia', 'Izvestija'. 'Bretagne':

....(contd.)

5 cols; 'Kroatien': 6 cols. listing publications produced locally; 'England': nearly 4 cols., with ½col. of bibliography. Includes biographies (*e.g.* Müller-Karpe, H.: ½col.). Numerous small, good line-drawings; 92 plates appended. *Class No:* 902(4)(031)

Great Britain

[4250]
Archaeology in Britain. London, Council for British Archaeology, 1977-. Annual. ISSN: 03088456.

Before 1977 published with C.B.A.'s *Annual Report*.

1991 volume edited by Morris, R. and Heyworth, M. (1992, vi,143p. illus., index. ISBN 1872414362) includes directory information and annual reports of official bodies (*e.g.* Cadw. Welsh Historic Monuments; Department of the Environment for Northern Ireland; English Heritage; Historic Scotland, *etc.*); Nautical bodies (*e.g.* C.B.A. Nautical Archaeology Society); Research Projects; and city, county, district and regional organizations. *Class No:* 902(410)

[4251]
The Archaeology resource book 1992. Halkon, P., *and others*, *eds.* London, English Heritage and Council for British Archaeology, 1992. iii,146p. softcover. £6. ISBN: 1872414230.

Expands and replaces M.J. Corbishley's *Archaeological resources handbook for teachers* (London, CBA., 2nd ed., 1983).

1. Archaeology in education (including National Curriculum, Examinations, Careers) - 2. Archaeology in Action (National agencies, Professional units and trusts, National, regional and local archaeological societies, Museums) - 3. Research (reading archaeology, Audio-visual materials, computer software). *Class No:* 902(410)

[4252]
CUNLIFFE, B. **Iron Age communities in Britain** an account of England, Scotland and Wales from the seventh century BC until the Roman Conquest. 3rd ed. London, Routledge, 1991. xii,685p. illus., maps, drawings, bibliog., index. ISBN: 0415054168.

1st ed. 1974; 2nd ed. 1979.

Comprehensive account of the British Iron Age. 21 chapters in 4 parts: 1. Introduction (development of Iron Age studies) - 2. Space & time (from a chronological and regional standpoint) - 3. Themes (pattern of settlement, development of hill-forts etc.) - 4. Systems (Iron Age society and social change). Appendix A. Pottery - B. Selected radiocarbon dates - C. List of principal sites (p.609-23). Chapter notes p.624-6. Bibliography p.631-73. This edition is substantially revised. *Class No:* 902(410)

[4253]
HUNTER, J. *and* RALSTON, I., *eds.* **The Archaeology of Britain** an introduction from the Upper Palaeolithic to the Industrial Revolution. London, Routledge, 1999. xiv,327p. illus., tables, bibliog. £60. ISBN: 0415135877.

16 contributors. 17 overview chapters (*e.g.* 1. British archaeology since the end of the Second World War ... 9. Roman Britain: civil and rural society ... 16. The Workshop of the World: The Industrial Revolution). 'Where it is unusual as a textbook is that it really is accessible and readable. No specialist knowledge is required to understand it, yet the chapters do not trivialise their subjects ... What it obviously cannot be, however, is comprehensive ... and is not, in general, the text one would turn to for detailed information about a specific site' (*Reference Reviews*, v.14, no.2, 2000, p.45). *Class No:* 902(410)

[4254]
Medieval archaeology Journal of the Society for Medieval Archaeology. London, Society for Medieval Archaeology, 1957-. Annual. ISSN: 00766097.

Regular feature 'Medieval Britain and Ireland' includes Specialist Group reports and Excavation Reports (A-Z by site) for England, Northern Ireland, Republic of Ireland, Scotland, and Wales. V.41. 1997. has B.S. Nenk and others, 'Medieval Britain and Ireland in 1991' (p.241-328).

Index volumes: V.1-5, *1957-1961* (1965); V.6-10, *1962-1966* (1968); V.11-15, *1967-1971* (1973); V.16-20, *1972-1976* (1978); V.21-25, *1977-1981* (1982); V.26-30, *1982-1986* (1988); V.31-35, *1987-1991* (1993); and V.36-40, *1992-1996* compiled by A. Hudson, 1999. 78p. *Class No:* 902(410)

[4255]
MEGAW, J.V.S. *and* SIMPSON, D.D.A. **Introduction to British prehistory** from the arrival of *Homo Sapiens* to the Claudian invasion. Leicester, Leicester Univ. Press, 1979. xv, 560p. illus., plans, tables, maps, pbk. £12.95. ISBN: 0718511727.

7 contributors. 7 chapters: 1. The environmental background to British prehistory - 2. Exploitation and adaptation in pre-agricultural communities - 3. The first agricultural communities (*c.*3,500-2,500BC) - 4. The Later Neolithic (*c.*2,500-1,700BC) - 5. The Early Bronze Age (*c.*2,000-1,300BC) - 6. The Later Bronze Age (1400-500BC) - The Iron Age (*c.*BC-AD200) (p.344-501). Some chapter notes.

....*(contd.)*

Abbreviations (sources. Bibliography (A/Z authors), p.503-44. Analytical subject index; index of places. Well produced; finely drawn illus. *Class No:* 902(410)

[4256]

Post-Medieval Archaeology. London, The Journal of The Society For Post-Medieval Archaeology, 1968-. Annual. ISSN: 00794326.

Regularly includes 2 features: 'Post-medieval Britain and Ireland' consisting of excavation reports (ecclesiastical buildings; military and naval earthworks and structures; wrecks; towns and corporate buildings; manors, country houses *etc;* farms and small domestic buildings; industry; communications;) and 'Post-medieval Britain in periodic literarure' A-Z periodical title.

V.31 *1997* (1998). Index volumes: V.1-5, *1967-1971* (1973) and V.6-11, *1972-1976* (1978); Index to volumes 11-20, 1977-1986 is incorporated in V.22 *1988. Class No:* 902(410)

[4257]

SELKIRK, A. The Riches of British archaeology. Cambridge, Cambridge Univ. Press, 1988. 208p. illus., maps, index. ISBN: 0521321328.

50 significant sites excavated in Britain over the last 20 years, on double-paged spreads, arranged in 5 chronological sections: Earlier prehistory - Later prehistory - Roman Britain - The Dark Ages - Saxon and Medieval Britain. With a glossary and list of sites and museums to visit. *Class No:* 902(410)

Bibliographies

[4258]

BONSER, W. A Prehistoric bibliography. Troy, Jane, *added to and extended by.* Oxford, Blackwell, 1976. xvi, 425p. ISBN: 0631170901.

Companion to Bonser's *Romano-British bibliography* (1964) and *Anglo-Saxon and Celtic bibliography* (1957).

9,020 entries for books and periodical articles, many drawn from British local history, archaeological and antiquarian society publications. Topical arrangement under 5 main heads: A. Men and methods in archaeology - B. Field archaeology - C. Specific sites - D. Material funds - E. Culture. (B.C. and D. are further divided into 6 geographical zones of the British Isles). Index of authors and subjects. Long list of *corrigenda* issued. *Class No:* 902(410)(01)

[4259]

British and Irish archaeological bibliography. York, Council for British Archaeology, 1997-. Two issues per year. Institutions £99. £1.105. $200. ISSN: 13674765.

Formerly *British archaeological bibliography* (1992-1996). Continues series of *British archaeological abstracts* (1968-1991).

Contains hundreds of references and abstracts from a wide variety of books and journals. It includes monographs, conference proceedings, postgraduate theses, articles of relevance to British and Irish archaeology which appear in the literature of other disciplines, *Ancient Monuments Laboratory Reports,* fieldwork reports, Society newsletters, and postgraduate theses. References are classified according to period and subject, and are indexed annually. Each issue has an author index, full details of all journals cited, a directory of relevant book publishers and references to British, Irish and European parliamentary activity relating to archaeology. V.3, no.2, October 1999 contains abstracts 99/1001-99/2100. The perceived role, aims and objectives of *BAB* is spelled out in v.1, no.1, April 1992, p.14-15. *Class No:* 902(410)(01)

[4260]

—British and Irish archaeological bibliography online database. http://ads.ahds.ac.uk./catalogue/biab.html via Archaeology Data Service.

100,000 references to material published 1695-1991 in G.L. Gomme's *Index of archaeological papers 1665-1890; Archaeological Bulletin for Great Britain and Ireland* (CBA. 1940-1950); *British archaeological abstractgs* (CBA. 1968-1991) and *British Archaeological Bulletin* (1992).made available in the first instance in free-text search only format. Further work is underway to connect references into a standard searchable database (see CBA's *Briefing,* March 1999, p.16 issued with *British Archaeology,* no.42). *Class No:* 902(410)(01)

[4261]

—British and Irish archaeological bibliography World Wide Web. http://www.britarch.ac.uk/biab.

Also includes information on the scope, aim, background and history of the BIAB project together with details or archaeological serial publications and contact details of publishers and/or editors. *Class No:* 902(410)(01)

[4262]

British and Irish archaeology a bibliographical guide. King, A C., *comp.* Manchester Univ. Press, 1994. xii,324p. index. (*History And Related Disciplines Select Bibliographies.*) ISBN: 0719018757.

7,777 mainly English-language items published 1960-90 entered under heavily sub-divided period divisions generally used by British and Irish archaeologists. Many entries are briefly annotated. Index of authors, editors and organisations p.301-24. *Class No:* 902(410)(01)

[4263]

LAVELL, C. The Handbook for British and Irish archaeology sources and resources. Edinburgh Univ. Press, 1997. xii,421p. index. pbk £29.95. ISBN: 0748607641.

1. Bibliographies and Libraries - 2. Unpublished sources and record offices - 3. Periodicals - 4. Organisations, institutions and societies - 5. Photographic resources - 6. Select Archaeological Bibliography (27 sub-sections providing references to every aspect of British archaeology). Awarded the Library Association Besterman Medal 1998 for an outstanding bibliography. Lavell was compiler of *British Archaeological Abstracts 1968-1991. Class No:* 902(410)(01)

Handbooks & Manuals

[4264]

ADKINS, L. *and* **ADKINS, R.A. The Handbook of British archaeology.** 3rd ed. London, Constable, 1998. 319p. illus. bibliog. pbk. £14.99. ISBN: 0094783306.

First published by David & Charles and in the US by Barnes & Noble in 1982 under the title of *A thesaurus of British archaeology.*

8 chronological chapters from the palaeolithic to the medieval period are followed by 2 others, 'Archaeological Techniques' and a miscellaneous chapter. Text entries end with sources for further reading and there is an extensive bibliography (p.285-296). Index p.292-319. More than 500 line drawings. 'Excellent detailed work explaining the technical terms and jargon found in British archaeology' (Woodhead: *Keyguide to information sources in archaeology,* 1985). *Class No:* 902(410)(035)

Reviews & Abstracts

[4265]

British archaeological abstracts. London, Council for British Archaeology, 1967-1991. no.1-. 2 *pa.* ISSN: 00070270.

1989: 1892 abstracts on the archaeology of Great Britain and Ireland. Arranged by periods: 1. General, multi-period undated - 2. Palaeolithic and Mesolithic - 3. Neolithic - 4. Bronze Age - 5. Iron Age - 6. Roman Britain - 7. Migration/Early medieval - 8. Medieval - 9. Post-medieval/Industrial. Recent, then by subjects. Annual author and subject indexes. When CBA's *Archaeological bibliography for Great Britain and Ireland* folded with the 1980 issue coverage of abstracts ceased to be selective and comprehensivity is now attempted from *c.*165 British and 130 foreign journals. There is a microfiche edition. *Archaeological site index to radiocarbon dates for Great Britain and Ireland,* 1971-1982 is a supplement to *British archaeological abstracts.* Lavell, C. *British archaeological thesaurus for use with British archaeological abstracts and other publications in British archaeology* (CBA, 1989). 69p. refs., pbk. £4.95. ISBN 0906780772 is 'a standard list of words in current use in British archaeology' (*British archaeological abstracts* Entry 89/893). *Class No:* 902(410)(048)

Yearbooks & Directories

[4266]

The 1997 directory of British archaeology. London, Current Archaeology, 1997. 32p. (*Issued gratis with Current Archaeology.*)

729 entries (359 societies, 118 professional organisations, 37 universities, 52 county archaeologists) arranged A-Z in 16 sections: National organisations, Scotland, Wales, 12 English regions, Northern Ireland and the Isle of Man. *Class No:* 902(410)(058)

[4267]

British archaeological yearbook 1995-1996. York, Council for British Archeology, 1995. £24. ISBN: 1872414516. ISSN: 13550462.

Contents of this compendium include information on archaeology in education; detailed listings of archaeological organisations in Britain and Europe; a guide to archaeological resources on the Internet; events and conferences; and grants and funds available to British archaeologists. *Class No:* 902(410)(058)

Maps & Atlases

[4268]

ELLYER, R. 'The Archaeological and historical maps of the Ordnance Survey', *The Cartographical Journal*, v.26, no.2, December 1989, p.111-133. figs, plans, tables.

Important research article. 'Discusses the making of these maps and cites the known cartographical, bibliographical and manuscript sources relevant both to the published maps and to those which failed to reach publication' (*Abstract*). Bibliography p.131-3. Table 1: Period maps prepared by the O.S. *Class No:* 902(410)(084.3)

[4269]

ANLEY, J. Atlas of prehistoric Britain. Oxford, Phaidon, 1989. 160p. illus., (some col.), maps, bibliog., index. £22.50. ISBN: 0714825697.

A chronological approach, 'no more than a rough guide' (Preface) to 'the principal concentrations of major prehistoric monuments in Britain and Ireland'. Date charts p.152-53. Sites to visit p.154-57. Bibliography p.157. 139 illus. (41 in colour).
Class No: 902(410)(084.3)

Middle Ages

[4270]

UIR, R. The Lost villages of Britain. London, Michael Joseph, 1982. 285p.+16p. col. plates. illus., diagrs., bibliogs., index. £11.95. ISBN: 0718120361.

12 thematic chapters *e.g.* 2. Meeting the medieval village ... 7. The Highlands made desert ... 9. The price of a park. Appendix 1. Reading on p.271-2 - 2. Main sites, A-Z by county p.273-8. For the non-specialist reader. 'Fills a notable gap on the archaeologist's bookshelf' (*Current Archaeology*, v.8, no.4, June 1983, p.123-4).
Class No: 902(410)"01/14"

Modern Times

[4271]

ROSSLEY, D. Post-medieval archaeology in Britain. Leicester, Leicester Univ. Press, 1990. ix,328p. illus., plans bibliog., index. £52.50; $49. ISBN: 0718512855.

Overview in 12 chapters: 1. Post-medieval rural landscape - 2. Post-medieval town - 3. Church archaeology - 4. Fortifications - 5. Shipwrecks - 6. Sources of power before the invention of the steam engine - 7/8. Metals - 9. Mining and quarrying - 10. Other industries - 11. Glass - 12. Ceramics. Bibliography p.291-308. 'To have written a book which encapsulates current research in post-medieval archaeology so clearly is a considerable achievement, but to direct the reader so firmly to the tasks for the next generation of scholars is of even greater benefit. It ensures that its value as a work of reference is greatly enhanced' (*Post-Medieval Archaeology*, no.25, 1991, p.189-91).
Class No: 902(410)"15/19"

Scotland

[4272]

iscovery & Exploration In Scotland an annual survey of Scottish archaeological discoveries, excavation and fieldwork. Edinburgh, Scottish Regional Group Council for British Archaeology, later The Council For Scottish Archaeology, 1955-. ISSN: 0419411x.

1990 volume edited by Proudfoot, E.V.W. and Proudfoot, B.E. (1992. 64p.) illus., map, charts, indexes, sd. ISBN 090135211x) includes brief reports of excavations A-Z by locality within regions/districts; report of Royal Commission On the Ancient and Historical Monuments of Scotland (Archeology and Buildings programmes and accessions to the National Monument Record of Scotland).
Class No: 902(411)

[4273]

ANSON, W.S. *and* **SLATER, E.A.,** *eds.* **Scottish archaeology** new perceptions. Aberdeen Univ. Press, 1991. xi,228p. illus., maps, tables, bibliogs., index. limp cover. £14.95. ISBN: 0080412122.

13 papers by different hands, each ending with a bibliography, provide authoritative overviews on the current state of knowledge of all periods of Scottish archaeology *e.g.* 2. Skara Brae: revisiting a Neolithic village in Orkney ... 4. Future of Roman Scotland ... 7. Surveying for the future: RCAHMS archaeological survey ... 13. Managing output rather than input? The implications of computerising the National Museum of Scotland's archaeological information.
Class No: 902(411)

[4274]

HUNTER, J.R. Fair Isle the archaeology of an island community. Edinburgh, HMSO for the National Trust for Scotland, 1996. viii,280p. illus., maps, plans, bibliog., index. £19.95. ISBN: 0114957509.

Resulting from a systematic survey of 750 sites, and exploratory excavations, 1984-1989, this account in 15 chapters is arranged on a broad chronological basis. Inventory of sites p.217-63. Bibliography p.265-72. Analytical index. 'A near comprehensive story of an island's archaeology from earliest times until the present, addressing a broad sweep of sites, finds and landscapes' (*Journal of the British Archaeological Association*, v.151, 1998, p.242-3).
Class No: 902(411)

[4275]

RITCHIE, A. Prehistoric Orkney. London, Batsford for Historic Scotland, 1995. 128p. illus. (some col.), pbk. £14.99. ISBN: 0713475935.

'An excellent summary of the modern campaign of excavation ... and of what one might call the consensus reconstruction of Orkney's neolithic society' (*Antiquaries Journal*, v.76,1996, p.280-81).
Class No: 902(411)

[4276]

RITCHIE, G. *and* **RITCHIE, A. Scotland: archaeology and early history.** London, Thames & Hudson, 1981. 192p. illus., map, bibliog. (*Ancient peoples and places.*) ISBN: 0500021007.

8 chapters: 1. Hunters and fishers; 2. Early farming communities; 3. Henge monuments and stone circles; 4. The first metalworkers; 5. Warrior Celts; 6. Roman Scotland; 7. Britons, Angles and Scots; 8. The Pictish kingdom. Extensive bibliography p.183-186. Index p.159-192. 'Scholars will consult it many times' (*Choice*, v.19,no.2, October 1981, p.292). *Class No:* 902(411)

Ireland

[4277]

EDWARDS, N. The Archaeology of early medieval Ireland. London, B.T. Batsford, 1990. 256p. illus. bibliog., index. £35.00. ISBN: 0713453672.

1. The Roman impact on Ireland - 2. Settlement: ring forts - 3. Other settlement types - 4. Food and farming - 5. Craft - 6. The Church - 7. Art - 8. The Vikings. New critical introduction to the archaeological evidence. *Class No:* 902(415)

[4278]

O'KELLY, M.J. Early Ireland: an introduction to Irish prehistory. Cambridge, Cambridge Univ. Press, 1989. xiii, 375p. illus., maps, plans, bibliog., index. £35.00. ISBN: 0521334896.

12 chronological and thematic chapters: 1. The Ice Age ... 10. The Iron Age - 11. Later prehistoric settlement - 12. Iron Age burial. 4 Appendices: Radio-carbon dating; Dendochronology; Pollen analysis; and Calibration of radio-carbon dating. Bibliography p.353-70.
Class No: 902(415)

[4279]

WADDELL, J. The Prehistoric archaeology of Ireland. Galway Univ. Press, 1998. xii,433p. maps, illus., tables, bibliog., pbk. 25. ISBN: 1901421104.

'Overall this book provides a sound, detailed and up-to-date account...it is essentially a textbook and sourcebook rolled into one' (*Antiquity*, v.73, no.279, March 1999, p.232-33). *Class No:* 902(415)

Dictionaries

[4280]

FLANAGAN, L. A Dictionary of Irish archaeology. Dublin, Gill and Macmillan, 1992, 222p. illus., bibliog. ISBN: 0717118355.

Entries for major excavated sites and major finds, religious sites, standing stones, earthworks etc. from the Mesolithic to end of the medieval period. Bibliography p.221. Flanaghan was formerly Keeper of Antiquities in the Ulster Museum. *Class No:* 902(415)(038)

Yearbooks & Directories

[4281]

The Irish heritage and environment directory 1999. Bray, Co. Wicklow, Archaeology Ireland, 1998.$b400p.$c£19.99. ISBN: 0953442608.

Up-to-date information on a number of key areas of interest to people involved in heritage and the environment in the Republic of Ireland and Northern Ireland, including current legislation; organisations and interest groups; professional consultants; museums, interpretative centres and heritage gardens open to the public; education opportunities at all levels in heritage areas; resources, including specialist libraries and genealogy centres; and a 1999 planner. Also essays on built heritage and natural heritage legislation, rights of way and REP Schemes by leading experts in each field. The

....(contd.)
listings provide contact information and descriptions of a wide variety of heritage and environment organisations at national, regional and local levels. *Class No:* 902(415)(058)

Northern Ireland
[4282]
GREAT BRITAIN. Department of Environment for Northern Ireland. **Pieces of the past** archaeological excavations by the Department of the Environment for Northern Ireland 1970-1986. Hamlin, A. *and* Lynn, C. Belfast, HMSO, 1988. xxi, 109p. col. illus., col. maps, diagrs., bibliog., index. £6.90. ISBN: 0337082162.
Describes 35 excavations. Appendix 1. Archaeological excavations organized by the Department 1970-1986. Glossary p.99-102. Bibliography p.102. For the general reader. *Class No:* 902(416)

[4283]
GREAT BRITAIN. Department Of The Environment (Northern Ireland). **Finding and minding** a series of reports on archaeological work in Northern Ireland. Belfast, HMSO, 1990, 16p. col. illus., pbk. £2.90. ISBN: 0337082456.
How Northern Ireland's heritage is identified, excavated, recorded, and protected. *Class No:* 902(416)

[4284]
MALLORY, J.P. *and* McNEILL, T.E. **The Archaeology of Ulster** from colonization to plantation. Belfast, The Institute of Irish Studies, The Queen's Univ. of Belfast, 1991. 367p. illus., maps, diagrs., bibliog. index. £15. ISBN: 0853893527.
Chronological narrative and interpretation of archaeology in Ulster c.7000 BC - 1800 AD. Important bibliography p.338-56. Mainly confined to the 9 counties of modern Ulster although some details of archaeological sites in Donegal, Cavan, and Monaghan. 'A very valuable up-to-date discussion on the archaeology of Ireland in general, and not just Ulster alone' (*Antiquity,* v.66, no.251, June 1992, p.559). *Class No:* 902(416)

England
[4285]
WILSON, D.M., *ed*. **The Archaeology of Anglo-Saxon England.** London, Methuen, 1976. xvl,532p. illus., facsims., tables, plans, index.
11 contributors. 10 sections: 1. Agricultural and rural settlement - 2. Buildings and rural settlement - 3. Towns - 4. Ecclesiastical architecture - 5. Monastic sites - 6. Crafts and industry - 7. The pottery - 8. The coins - 9. The animal resources - 10. The Scandinavians. Appendices (A-C (A: Gazetteer of Anglo-Saxon settlement sites (tabulated under 9 heads; p.405-52). List of sources, p.463-511. *Class No:* 902(420)

Middle Ages
[4286]
CLARKE, H. **The Archaeology of medieval England.** London, British Museum Publications, 1984. 224p. illus., maps, bibliog. £12.95. ISBN: 0714180386.
Reviews knowledge of medieval England derived from archaeological sources. Chapter notes p.195-201 and valuable bibliography p.204-218. Index p.221-224.
Class No: 902(420)"01/14"

Channel Islands
[4287]
The Channel Islands an archaeological guide. Chichester, Sussex, Phillimore, 1981. xv.144p.illus.(inc.16p.plates), maps, diagrs. bibliog. index. £14.95. ISBN: 0850333954.
Part 1 is a summary account of the state of archaeological knowledge in 9 sections *e.g.* Palaeolithic man ... The Roman period ... Antiquities and scholars. Part 2 Sites and Monuments, is a complete gazetteer of sites. Bibliography p,.137-140. 40 plates. 71 figures. 'Essential for all visitors with any interest in the Islands' past' (*British Book News,* December 1981,p.766). *Class No:* 902(423.4)

Wales
[4288]
STANFORD, S.C. **The Archaeology of the Welsh Marches.** 2nd ed. Ludlow, Salop, S.C. Stanford, 1991. ii,190p. illus., maps, bibliog., index. £7.95. ISBN: 0950327158.
First published London, Collins, 1980.
'An essay on the problems of community survival within the geographical and political limitations of the Welsh Marches' (*Preface*). 2. Palaeolithic hunters and their descendants - 3. Neolithic settlers and

....(contd.)
traders ... 9. Castles in the Marches ... 11. Archaeology of rural industries. Places to visit p.171. Bibliography p.172-8.
Class No: 902(429)

Glossaries
[4289]
WILLIAMS, J. Ll., *ed*. **Geiriadur termau archaeolog/** A dictionary of archeological terms in English and Welsh. Cardiff, University of Wales Press, 1999. 228p. £7.99. ISBN: 0708316069.
Covers the complete time-span of archaeology from earliest times to the present day. 'It is not a book I would use as a reliable term list for archaeology in English ... but it does appear to represent the wide range of current archaeological usage' (*Reference Reviews,* v.14, no.2, 2000, p.44-45). *Class No:* 902(429)(038.1)

Germany

Encyclopaedias
[4290]
Reallexikon der germanischen Altertumskunde, von Johannes Hoops. 2nd revised ed. Berlin & New York, W. de Gruyter, 1968-. Lieferung 1-. illus., (incl. pl.), plans, tables, maps.
First published 1911-19 (4v.).
v.1-13. (1973-1999). Aachen-Hardaknut. An encylopaedia of German archaeology. Longer articles are sub-divided into sections, each with a bibliography. Originally intended to be completed in 8v., this scholarly work now stretches into the distant future.
Class No: 902(430)(031)

Czechoslovakia
[4291]
SKLENAR, K. **The History of archaeology in Czechoslovakia,** chap. 14, *Towards a history of archaeology* edited by Glyn Daniel (Thames & Hudson, 1981). *Class No:* 902(437)

Poland
[4292]
'A Panorama of Polish archaeology', *Antiquity,* v.65, no. 248, September 1991, p.583-721. illus., diagrs., maps, bibliogs.
11 papers by separate hands surveying recent discoveries and excavations methods introduced by the title paper which includes sections on historical and ethnic geography, the origins of growth or archaeology in Poland. *Class No:* 902(438)

France
[4293]
Archéologie de la France 30 ans de découvertes. Paris, Éditions de la Réunion des musées nationaux, 1989. 495p. illus. (many col.), drawings, maps, bibliog., indexes. A4 soft cover. 390F. ISBN 2711822516.
39 chapters organized in 8 main sections: 1. Paléolithique inférieur et moyen - 2. Paléolithique supérieur - 3. Le Néolithique - 4. L'Âge du Bronze - 5. L'Âge du Fer - 6. La Gaulle Romaine - 7. Antiquité tardive et début de Moyen Âge: L'évêque et le Compte - 8. Moyen Âge et temps modernes: La construction de la France. 8 Annexes: 1 Organisation et réglementales de la recherche archéologique en France (p.462-3) - 2. Les Musées d'archéologie en France (p.264) - 3 Archéologie et archéometrie - 4. Glossaire (p.466) - 5. Tableau chronologie (p.467-74) ... 8. Bibliographie (p.479). Produced as a catalogue of an exhibition organized by La Réunion des Musées Nationaux, La Direction due Patrimoine, and La Direction des Musées de France in 1989. *Class No:* 902(44)

[4294]
BENDER, B. **The Archaeology of Brittany, Normandy and the Channel Islands** an introduction and guide. London, Faber, 1986 246p. illus., maps, bibliog. £14.95. ISBN: 0571099572.
A detailed up-to-date account of the archaeological background precedes a systematic guide: Brittany (p.65-162); Normandy (p.163-217); Channel Is. (p.218-243). Glossary p.245. Bibliography p.246-247. Index p.249-254. *Class No:* 902(44)

[4295]
La France explore son passé depuis 30 ans l'archéologie territorial dernier bilans et dernières recherches, Dijon, Les Dossier D'Archéologie, no. 250. Fevrier 2000. Ff70.
Survey of French archaeology and research 1970-2000 in 32 mainly regional articles: Régions Nord. Parisienne, Centre et Oeust, Sud. *Class No:* 902(44)

[4296]

CARRE, C., *ed*. Ancient France 6,000-2,000 BC Neolithic societies
and their landscape. Edinburgh, Edinburgh Univ. Press, 1984. viii,
390p. illus., maps, bibliog. £25.00. ISBN: 085224441x.

8 regional chapters relate the story of France's early farming
societies. Each chapter includes a brief geographical account and a
short history of previous research. Important bibliography p.344-380.
Index p.383-390. 'An excellently factual and stimulating reference
work' (*Antiquity*, LXVIII, no.223, July 1984, p.146).
Class No: 902(44)

Bibliographies

[4297]

Gallia informations: préhistoire et histoire. Paris, Éditions du Centre
National de la Recherche Scientifique, 1990-. 2pa. ISSN: 09948899.

Derives from features in *Gallia* v.1-15 (1943-1957) and *Gallia
Préhistoire* v.1-32 (1958-1990).

Descriptive excavation reports and bibliographies region by region
in progressive volumes. 1990. 1++2 (1990. 319p. illus., maps,
drawings. F270. ISBN 2222046165) covers Bretagne and Provence-
Alpes - Côte d'Azur. *Class No: 902(44)(01)*

Italy

[4298]

PIVEY, N. *and* STODDART, S. Etruscan Italy an archaeological
account. London, Batsford, 1990. 168p. illus., bibliog., index.
£29.95. ISBN: 0713465212.

1. Physical environment and prehistoric background - 2. Settlement
and territory - 3. Subsistence technology and production - 4. Trade and
exchange - 5. Myth, language and literacy - 6. Ritual - 7. Warfare - 8.
Social organization. Traveller's gazetteer p.153-7. Glossary p.158-9.
Bibliography p.160-3. *Class No: 902(450)*

Scandinavia

[4299]

LINDT-JENSEN, O. A History of Scandinavian archaeology.
London, Thames & Hudson, 1975. 144p. illus., facsims, ports, plans,
maps, index. (*The World Of Archaeology*.)

A survey of the past 400 years with biographical sketches of key
figures. Bibliography p.139-41. 129 illus. *Class No: 902(48)*

Denmark

[4300]

VASS, S. *and* STORGAARD, B. Digging into the past 25 years of
archaeology in Denmark. Copenhagen, The Royal Society of Northern
Antiquities; H. Kojbjerg, Jutland Archaeological Society, 1993. 312p.
illus. (many col.), maps, plans, tables, bibliog. ISBN: 8772885688.

76 contributors. Record of Danish archaeology 1968-1993. 83
articles in 7 sections: 1. Man and the environment - 2/6 Late
Palaeolithic to The Middle Ages and more recent times - 7.
Archaeological institutions. Extensive bibliography (imnportant for
Scandinavian languages material) p.288-312. *Class No: 902(489)*

[4301]

ENSEN, J. The Prehistory of Denmark. London, Methuen, 1983.
xviii, 330p. illus., maps, bibliog. ISBN: 041634190x.

19 interdisciplinary chapters examine the whole of Denmark's
cultural prehistory from Stone Age hunters *c*.11,000 BC to the end of
the Iron Age 800 AD. An extensive bibliography (p.287-321) enhances
an 'outstanding and important book' (*Antiquity* v.57, no.221,
November 1983, p.230). Index p.322-330. *Class No: 902(489)*

[4302]

OESDAHL, E. Viking age Denmark. London, British Museum
Publications, 1982. 172p. illus., map, bibliog., index. ISBN:
0714150270.

Covers the period *c*.800-1050 in 12 thematic chapters *e.g.* 4.
Settlement and survival ... 8. Arms and fortifications ... 9. Pagans and
Christians. Appendix: Finds list. Viking Age settlements in present day
Denmark traced archaeologically p.249-50. Extremely useful
bibliography p.255-268. 51 plates. Analytical index.
Class No: 902(489)

Albania

[4303]

NDREA, Zh. 'Archaeology in Albania', *Archaeological Reports For
1991-1992*, p.71-88. illus., maps.

'Archaeology in Albania 1973-83' was published in *Archaeological
Reports 1983-84.* p.102-19.

Descriptive reports of excavations by district and by site.
Class No: 902(496.5)

China

[4304]

CHANG, Kwang-Chih. The Archaeology of ancient China. 4th ed.
New Haven, Yale Univ. Press 1987. xxv, 450p. illus., maps, tables,
bibliog. $52.00. £50.00. ISBN: 0300037821.

First published 1963. 'This edition ... bears very little resemblance
to its previous incarnations ... I no longer intend to cover the whole
field and cite every available reference ... now ends with the rise of
civilization and no longer includes the very rich and complex period of
ancient history after about 1000 BC.'

Introduction (geographical review, traditional historiography and
antiquarianism, modern and contemporary archaeology) - 1.
Palaeolithic foundations - 2. The early farms - 3-4. Neolithic
developments - 5. The Chinese interaction sphere and the foundations
of civilization - 6-7. The first Chous. Glossary of Chinese characters
p.423-438. Bibliography p.443-450. *Class No: 902(510)*

[4305]

JIA LANPO *and* HUANG WEIWEN. The Story of Peking Man from
archaeology to mystery. Beijing, Foreign Language Press; Hong
Kong, Oxford Univ. Press, 1990. vii,270p. illus., map, index. £19.50;
$29.95. ISBN: 0195851889.

An illustrated account of the excavation of the fossilized remains of
Peking Man at Zhoukoudian in 1929. Jia Lianpo was one of the
excavation team. *Class No: 902(510)*

[4306]

KEIGHTLEY, D.N. The Origins of Chinese civilization. Berkeley,
Univ. of California Press, 1983. xxix, 617p. illus. maps, tables. index.
$50. ISBN: 0520042298.

17 academic contributors giving a multidisciplinary approach to the
early cultural development of China. Arranged in 4 parts: environment
and agriculture; culture and peoples; language and writers; tribe and
state. Extensive English and Chinese language references to each
chapter. Finding list of Carbon - 14 dates cited p.583-585. Index and
glossary p.587-617. *Class No: 902(510)*

[4307]

NELSON, S.M., *ed*. The Archeology of Northeast China beyond the
Great Wall. London, Routledge, 1995. 288p. illus., maps. £40. ISBN:
0415117550.

Collective synthesis by 8 Chinese archaeologists on the prehistory
and archaeology of Dongbei (i.e. Manchuria) based on recent
discoveries. *Class No: 902(510)*

Korea

[4308]

NELSON, S.M. The Archaeology of Korea. Cambridge Univ. Press,
1993. xvi,307p. illus., maps, bibliog., index. £35. (*Cambridge World
Archaeology*.) ISBN: 0521404436.

Survey of Korean prehistory from earliest palaeolithic settlers to
AD668 in 8 chronological and thematic chapters (*e.g.* 1. Introduction
(including Data sources and Korean archaeological sequences) - 2.
Environment ... 5. Megaliths, rice and bronze 2000 to 550BC ... 8.
Ethnicity in retrospect. Bibliography p.268-301 includes items in
Chinese and Korean languages. *Class No: 902(519)*

Japan

[4309]

AIKENS, C.M. *and* TAKAYASU HIGUCHI. Prehistory of Japan.
New York, Academic Press, 1982. xv, 354p. illus., maps, bibliog.,
index. $39.50. £26.50. ISBN: 0120452804.

6 chapters describe the archaeological evidence of human activity in
the Japanese islands from Palaeolithic times to the emergence of the
historic Yamato states *c*. AD 700. Bibliography A-Z by author, p.339-
347. 'Welcomed as a general textbook and for reference use'
(*Antiquity*, v.56, no. 218, December 1982, p.238). *Class No: 902(52)*

[4310]

PEARSON, R.J., *and others, eds*. Windows on the Japanese past:
studies in archaeology and prehistory. Ann Arbor, Michigan, Center
for Japanese Studies, Univ. of Michigan, 1986. 629p. maps, bibliog.
$48.95. ISBN: 0939512238.

32 Japanese and American academic contributors. 'The volume's
110-page glossary of place-names, personal names, site names, type
names, and technical terms constitutes an important reference aid for
the field of Japanese archaeology' (Shulman, F.J. *Japan*. 1989. Entry
109). *Class No: 902(52)*

[4311]

Recent archaeological discoveries in Japan. Tsuboi Kiyotari, *ed*. Paris, UNESCO; Tokyo, Centre for East Asian Cultural Studies, 1987. Available in UK from HMSO. xiii,108p.+ 20p. col. pl. illus., maps, bibliog. pbk. ISBN: 9231024515, UNESCO; 4896564030, CEACS.

A summary of the results of surveys in different regions of Japan by government agencies and various institutes in 6 chapters by different hands: 1. Palaeolithic age - 2. Jomon culture - 3. Protection of archaeological sites in Japan. Chronology p.101-2. Bibliography p.103-6. *Class No: 902(52)*

Asia—Middle & Near East

Encyclopaedias

[4312]

The Oxford encyclopedia of archaeology in the Near East. New York, Oxford Univ. Press, USA, 5v., 1997. v.1. xxii,492p. 2/5. vi,449p. 489p. 536p. 553p. bibliogs., maps. $335. ISBN: 0195065123, (set).

Published under the auspices of the American Schools of Oriental Research.

560 contributors. 1125 cross-referenced A-Z entries (inc. 450 archaeological sites) relating to archaeological methods, organisations and institutions, major excavations, scientific techniques, biographies of prominent archaeologists now deceased *etc.* and special topics (*e.g.* Museums and Archaeology, Tourism and Archaeology). Although Syria and Palestine sites are the core, the Encyclopedia ranges from Anatolia in the North, Morocco in the West, to Ethiopia and the Peninsula in the South and to Iran in the East. 415 halftones. 220 line drawings. 30 maps. Each entry ends with a scholarly bibliography. Appendix 1. Egyptian Aramaic Texts (v.5, p.393-410) - 2. Chronologies (p.411-16) - 3. Maps (p.417-30). Directory of contributors (p.431-50). Synoptic outline of contents (p.451-59). Analytical index (p.461-553). 'The contents of these volumes are remarkable for their accuracy and high level of scholarship' (*Bulletin of the American School of Oriental Research*, no.314, May 1999, p.71-75).

Meyer, E.M. 'The Making of the Oxford Encyclopedia of Archaeology in the Near East', *Biblical Archaeologist*, v.59, no.4, December 1996, p.194-97. *Class No: 902(53+56)(031)*

[4313]

Reallexikon der Assyriologie und vorderasiatischen Archäologie. Edzard, D.O., *ed*. Berlin & New York, Walter de Gruyter, 1928-. Lieferung 1-. illus., charts.

Published first in fascicules and consolidated in bound volumes at 4-yearly intervals. V.1-7: A-Medizin (1931-1990). A scholarly archaeological encyclopaedia of Assyriology and archaeology of the Near East. Articles are signed and end with lists of references. Bd.7 Libanukšabaš-Medizin. 1990. xxvii,631p. ISBN 3110104377. *Class No: 902(53+56)(031)*

India

[4314]

ALLCHIN, B. *and* **ALLCHIN, R. The Rise of civilization in India and Pakistan.** Cambridge, Cambridge Univ. Press, 1982. xiv,379p. illus., maps, tables, bibliog., index. £25.00. (*Cambridge World Archaeology*.) ISBN: 0521242444.

Lineal descendant of *The Birth of Indian civilization* (1968).

Introductory chapter 'Archaeology in South Asia', then 13 chapters (grouped in 3 sections: 1. Constituent elements - 2. Indus urbanism - 3. The legacy of the Indus civilization) tracing the origins and development of culture in India and Pakistan from its earliest roots in Palaeolithic times, through the rise and disintegration of the great Indus civilization, to the emergence of regional cultures and the arrival and spread of Indo-Aryan speaking peoples'. Bibliography (by chapter) p.362-371. *Class No: 902(540)*

[4315]

THAPER, B.K. Recent archaeological discoveries in India. Paris, Unesco, and Tokyo, The Centre for East Asian Cultural Studies, 1985. Available in UK from HMSO. xiii,159p. +12p. col. pl. illus (some col.), bibliog., pbk. £16.50. ISBN: 9231023853, Unesco; 4896564022, CEACS.

A state of the art review of Indian excavation and publication highlighting recent advances in knowledge of the cultural history of each period: Palaeolithic, Mesolithic, Neolithic, the Indus civilization, Megalithic, and the historical period. Bibliography p.149-59. *Class No: 902(540)*

Encyclopaedias

[4316]

An Encyclopedia of Indian archaeology. Ghosh, A., *ed*. New Delhi Munshiram Manoharlal, 1989; Leiden and New York, E.J. Brill, 2v. 1990. xvi,413p. +470p. illus., bibliogs., index. $228.57. ISBN 8121500877, India; 9004092641, Holland & US.

V.1: Subjects; v.2: A Gazetteer of explored and excavated sites. Over 100 Indian anthropologists, archaeologists and historians examine the findings of 150 years of excavation in 20 subject based sub-divided chapters (e.g. dating, rock art, cultures, technology, coins and seals settlements, pottery, writing). Sections within chapters end with bibliographies. V.2 is a gazetteer of sites in v.1 with expansive treatment of the larger and more important sites. 'This work should take its place as the classic statement of Indian archaeology for many years' (*Library Journal*, v.116, no.7, 15 April 1991, p.82). *Class No: 902(540)(031)*

Bangladesh

[4317]

CHAKRABARTI, D.K. Ancient Bangladesh a study of the archaeological sources. Delhi, Oxford Univ. Press India, 1992 xii,200p.+ 8p. plates. £17.50. ISBN: 0195628799.

1. Introduction (Geographical background, Ancient Historical Geographical units) - 2. Prehistory (inc. inventory of sites and artifacts) - 3. Early history - 4. Excavated data - 5. Miscellaneous data on ancient settlements - 6. Summary. Bibliography p.186-7. Systematic review of the pre-Islamic archaeological data. *Class No: 902(549.3)*

Turkey

[4318]

GATES, M-H. 'Archaeology in Turkey'. American Journal of Archaeology, v.100,no.2, April 1996, p.277-335. illus., bibliog.

Overview of recent excavation arranged by archaeological period and location. Bibliography (conferences, journals and general publications, festschrifts and memorials) p.280. *Class No: 902(560)*

Iraq

Maps & Atlases

[4319]

BEEK, M.A. Atlas of Mesopotamia a survey of the history and civilization of Mesopotamia from the Stone Age to the fall of Babylon London, Nelson, 1962. 164p. illus., maps.

Text on the civilizations of Sumeria, Assyria and Babylonia in 10 sections 'The accompanying maps provide comprehensive information concerning ancient empires, the chief excavation sites and the major discoveries' (A.J. Abdulrahman. *Iraq*, 1984, Entry 92). 290 photogravure illus. and 22 maps. *Class No: 902(567)(084.3)*

Asia—South East

[4320]

HIGHAM, C. The Archaeology of mainland Southeast Asia from 10,000 BC to the fall of Angkor. Cambridge, Cambridge Univ. Press 1989. xvi,387p. illus., maps, plans, bibliog., index. £35. (*Cambridge World Archaeology*.) ISBN: 0521255236.

Scholarly prehistory of the area covered by the valleys of the Red Mekong and Chao Phraya rivers and the intervening terrain, *i.e* Thailand, Vietnam, Kampuchea, Laos and adjacent areas Chronological table p.xv-xvi. References p.363-77. *Class No: 902(59)*

Africa

[4321]

The Archaeology of Africa food, metals and towns. Shaw, T., *and others, eds*. London, Routledge, 1993. xxxvii,857p. illus., maps diagrs., tables, bibliog., index. £75. (*One Wolrd Archaeology*.) ISBN 041508444x.

61 contributors. Academic archaeological and palaeoenvironmental survey of change in Africa, principally over the last 10 millenia, in 44 chapters. Important bibliography p.750-833. Analytical index. *Class No: 902(6)*

[4322]

PHILLIPSON, D.W. African archaeology. 2nd rev. ed. Cambridge Cambridge Univ. Press, 1993. 300p. illus., maps, bibliog., index £40. ISBN: 052144103x.

Up to date survey in 8 chapters (2. The emergence of man in Afric ... 5. Beginnings of permanent settlement ... 8. The second millenium AD in sub-Saharan Africa). Bibliography p.212-27. *Class No: 902(6)*

[4323]

ROBERTSHAW, P., *ed*. **A History of African archaeology.** London, James Currey, 1990. viii,378p. illus., maps, bibliog., index. £35. ISBN: 0852550200.

Primarly a regional survey but also includes the personal memoirs of Desmond Clark, Peter Shinnie and Thurstan Shaw and essays on early prehistory, rock art, and African archaeology in a world perspective. Bibliography p.310-71. Criticised for its exiguous coverage of some regions in *Antiquity*, v.65, no.246, March 1991, p.174-5. *Class No: 902(6)*

Encyclopaedias

[4324]

Encyclopedia of precolonial Africa archaeology, history, languages, cultures and environments. Vogel, Joseph O. *and* Vogel, Jean. Walnut Creek, CA, Alta Mira Press, 1997. 605p. bibliogs., index. $125. £95. ISBN: 0761989021.

90+ articles, each with bibliography, dealing mostly with Sub-Saharan black Africa before colonial expansion in early 1800s following 5 main themes: 1. Environment (geography, geology, climate) - 2. Research (archaeology, history) - 3. Technology - 4. People and culture - 5. Prehistory. *Class No: 902(6)(031)*

Maps & Atlases

[4325]

CLARK, J.D., *comp*. **Atlas of African prehistory.** Chicago, Univ. of Chicago Press, 1967. 62p. maps.

12 base-maps (1. Topography; 2. Geology; 3. Soils; 4. Mean annual rainfall; 5. Main vegetation types; 6/7. Hypothetical rainfall; 8/11. Hypothetical vegetation zones; 12. Simplified vegetation), 11 of them 1:20 million. 38 transparent overlays (*e.g.* 9/11. Fossil man in Africa; 24 Neolithic industries of sub-Saharan Africa; 25/26. Prehistoric art; 27. Distribution of white rhinoceros). Page size, 42.5 x 50cm. A 62p. booklet includes a gazetteer, listing sites by countries, subdivided by industries or culture, with geographical co-ordinates. *Class No: 902(6)(084.3)*

Africa—North

Bibliographies

CD-ROM

[4326]

WENDORF, F. *and* APPLEGATE, A., *comps*. **Bibliography of North African prehistory.** New York, Plenum Publishing Corporation, 1997. CD—ROM Macintosh Computer with 68020 or greater processor. Apple System Software version 7.0 or greater. Windows 386 or 486 based computer. Microsoft Windows 3.1 or greater. 4 MB of RAM. CD—ROM drive. $150. ISBN: 0306454203.

6,000 entries in 10 languages indexed by 100+ categories. Covers all aspects of prehistory in North Africa from Mediterranean Sea to the Sahel in the south and from Atlantic in the West to the Red Sea in the East but excludes Dynastic Egypt. *Class No: 902(61/65)(01)(003.40)*

America

[4327]

FAGAN, B.M. **The Great journey the peopling of ancient America.** London, Thames and Hudson, 1987. 228p. illus., bibliog., index. £14.95. $19.95. ISBN: 0500050457.

'A quest for early artifacts and human fossils, for indisputable proof of the antiquity of humankind in the Americas.' Further reading p.263-276. 'A conservative and very carefully reasoned overview' (*Choice*, v.25, no.8, April 1988, p.1282). *Class No: 902(7)*

[4328]

FIEDEL,, S.J. **Prehistory of the Americas.** 2nd ed. Cambridge, Cambridge Univ. Press, 1992. xix,400p, illus., maps, table, bibliog., index. £40. ISBN: 0521415322.

1st ed. 1987.

1. The development of American archaeology - 2. From Africa to Siberia: early human migration in the old world - 3. The Paleo-Indians - 4. The Archaic:post Pleictocene foragers - 5. The origins of agriculture and village life - 6. Chiefdoms and states - 7. Parallel worlds. References p.358-378. Author and subject indexes. Chronology p.xv-xix. Bibliography p.367-91. *Class No: 902(7)*

Maps & Atlases

[4329]

COE, M., *and others*. **Atlas of ancient America.** New York and Oxford, Facts on File, 1986. 284p. illus., maps, bibliog., index. $40.00. £18.95. ISBN: 0816011990.

20 thematic and 25 site features arranged in 6 sections: The new world - The first Americans - North America - Mesoamerica - South America - The living heritage. Bibliography p.226-7. Gazetteer p.228-236. 200 colour illus. 60 maps. 'Instructive to refer to and a delight to dip into' (*Bulletin Society of University Cartographers*, v.22, no.1, 1988, p.40-41). *Class No: 902(7)(084.3)*

Chronologies

[4330]

TAYLOR, R.E. *and* MEIGHAN, C.W., *eds*. **Chronologies in New World archaeology.** New York and London, Academic Press. xiii,587p. maps, tables, bibliogs., index. chronological charts on endpapers. $49.50. (*Studies in Archaeology*.) ISBN: 0126857504.

Chapter 1. 'Dating methods in New World archaeology followed by 15 chronological chapters, each by a different hand, and each furnished with its own bibliography. General bibliography p.558-563. 'General chronology for the whole of the New World with a view toward providing a general reference work that can allow more reading, understanding and comparison of chronological information for New World archaeology'. *Class No: 902(7)(090)*

America—North

[4331]

FAGAN, B.M. **Ancient North America: the archaeology of a continent.** 2nd ed. London, Thames and Hudson, 1995. 525p. illus., maps, diagrs., bibliog., index. £16.95. ISBN: 0500278172.

1st ed. 1991.

22 chapters narrative account of the diverse prehistoric societies of North America, from first settlement c.12,000 BC to the period of European contact, arranged in 7 parts: 1. Background (inc. Discovery and Culture history and North American archaeology) - 2. Palao-Indians - 3. Great Plains - 4. Far North - 5. The West - 6. Eastern woodlands - 7. After Columbus. Each chapter ends with list of further reading. 'This is a definitive introduction to the archaeology of the native people of North America by an expert who has written extensively on the subject' (*Reference Reviews*, v.10,no.3, 1996, p.47). *Class No: 902(71+73)*

Encyclopaedias

[4332]

GIBBON, G., *ed*. **Archaeology of prehistoric Native America an encyclopedia.** New York, Garland, 1998. 941p. illus., maps, tables, bibliog., index. $165. ISBN: 081530275x.

Compiled by academics, state and federal government personnel, and representatives of museums and historical societies etc., this scholarly encyclopedia contains introductory essays identifying the major culture areas (*e.g.*Arctic/subarctic; North West Coast; pre-Clovis/Paleoindian) and covers the whole of North America. 750 signed A-Z entries relate to sites, cultures, artifacts etc., and end with brief bibliographies. *Class No: 902(71+73)(031)*

Dictionaries

[4333]

JELKS, E.B., *ed*. **Historical dictionary of North American archaeology.** Westport, Connecticut, Greenwood Press,1988. xvii, 760p. Bibliog., index. $95.00. £77.95. ISBN: 0313243077.

151 contributors. Over 1800 signed entries of varying length relating to significant sites, artifacts, and major prehistoric cultures, each concluding with a list of selected sources. Dictionary p.1-546. Appendix: Sites listed geographically p.547-553. Sources A-Z by author p.569-705. Analytical index. 'Indispensable in reference work and collection development' (*Booklist*, v.85, no.2, 15 September 1988, p.136+138). *Class No: 902(71+73)(038)*

Mexico

[4334]

BERNAL, J. **A History of Mexican archaeology the vanished civilizations of Middle America.** London & New York, Thames and Hudson, 1980. 208p. illus., maps, bibliog., index. £12.50. (*The World of Archaeology*.) ISBN: 0500780080.

8 chapters *e.g.* 1. American-Indian origins ... 3. Research in the archives ... 5. Historians and travellers (1825-1880) - 6. Museums and the protection of antiquities. Bibliography p.190-203. *Class No: 902(72)*

Bahamas

Bibliographies

[4335]
GRANBERRY, J.A. **Bibliography of Bahaman prehistory.** 2nd ed. Nassau, Bahamas Archaeological Team, 1988.
1st ed. 1982.
103 unannotated items. New editions are planned on a quinquennial basis. *Class No: 902(729.6)(01)*

Brazil

[4336]
KIPNIS, R., *and others*. **'Issues in Brazilian archaeology'** *Antiquity*, v.72, no.277, September 1998, p.571-675. illus., maps, refs.
9 well-documented papers by separate hands including C. Barreto's 'Brazilian archaeology from a Brazilian perspective' (p.573-91) and E.G. Neves' 'Twenty years of Amazonian archaeology in Brazil 1977-1997' (p.625-32). *Class No: 902(81)*

[4337]
PROUS, A. **Arquelogia Brasileira.** Brasília, Editora Universidade de Brasíla, 1991. 605p. illus., bibliog., indexes. ISBN: 8523003169.
15 chapters (*e.g.* 1. História du pesquisa e da bibliografia arquéologia no Brasil - 2. Sítios e vestígios pré-históricos no Brasil ... 12. A pré-história amazônica ... 15. Arquelogia histórica. Bibliography p.577-88. *Class No: 902(81)*

Peru

[4338]
KEATINGE, R.W., *ed*. **Peruvian prehistory** an overview of pre-Inca and Inca society. Cambridge, Cambridge Univ. Press, 1988. xvii, 364p. illus., figs., tables, maps, bibliog., index. £35.00. $49.50. ISBN: 0521255600.
Supersedes *A reappraisal of Peruvian archaeology* edited by W. Bennett (Society for American archaeology, 1948) as the standard work.
11 papers from different hands either review a specific period of Peruvian history or examine recent research results *e.g.* 8. Progress and prospect in the archaeology of the Inca -9. From event to process: the recovery of late Andean organizational structure by means of Spanish colonial written records ... 11. A summary view of Peruvian prehistory. Bibliography p.319-355. *Class No: 902(85)*

Australasia & Oceania

[4339]
WHITE, J.P. *and* O'CONNELL, J.F. **A Prehistory of Australia, New Guinea and Sahul.** Sydney, Academic Press, 1982. xii,286p. atlas, maps, tables, bibliog., index. ISBN: 0127467505.
1. Perspectus - 2. Land, people and research - 3. Sahul early prehistory ... 5. Australia the last 10,000 years - 6. New Guinea - 7. Sahul - 8. Update. Bibliography p.237. References p.239-66. *Class No: 902(9)*

Indonesia

[4340]
BELLWOOD, P. **Prehistory of the Indo-Malaysian archipelago.** Sydney, Academic Press, 1985. x, 370p. illus., maps, bibliog., index. A$34.50. £45.00. ISBN: 0120853701.
10 chronological chapters relating the human prehistory of the islands of Indonesia from the initial hominid settlement to the eve of the historical Hindu and Buddhist civilizations. 'A balanced, thorough and reasonable presentation on the state of Indo-Malaysian prehistoric research' (*Antiquity*, v.61, no.232, July 1987, p.325-326). *Class No: 902(910)*

New Zealand

[4341]
ANDERSON, A. **'The Chronology of colonization in New Zealand',** *Antiquity*, v.65, no.249, December 1991, p.767-95, map, tables, refs.
Assesses the likely period of the prehistoric colonization of New Zealand according to radio carbon dates. References p.793-5. *Class No: 902(931)*

[4342]
DAVIDSON, J. **The Prehistory of New Zealand.** 2nd ed. Auckland, Longman Paul, 1987. iv, 270p. illus., maps. ISBN: 9582718120.
1st ed. 1984.
10 extensively documented chapters *e.g.* 2. Maori origins ... 5. Material culture ... 6. Subsistence economics ... 10. From East Polynesian to Maori: conclusion and prospect. Bibliography p.227-41. Glossary of Maori and other Polynesian words p.243. List of sites and places of archaeological interest p.247-59. Authoritative state of the art review. *Class No: 902(931)*

[4343]
PRICKETT, N., *ed*. **The First thousand years** regional perspectives in New Zealand archeology. Palmerston North, The Dunmore Press, 1982. 204p. maps, illus., bibliog. $27.95. ISBN: 090856483x.
10 regional chapters by 8 contributors record progress in New Zealand archaeology since 1957. Bibliography p. 179-199. Index of sites p.201-202. 'A useful summary of the present state of New Zealand archaeology' (*Antiquity* v.58, no.224, November 1984, p.234-235). *Class No: 902(931)*

Australia

[4344]
CONNAH, G. **Of the hut I builded:** the archaeology of Australia's history. Cambridge, Cambridge Univ. Press, 1988. xvi, 176p. illus. diagrs., bibliog., index. Aust$35.00; £19.50. ISBN: 0521345677.
10 chapters *e.g.* 1. The material heritage of Australian history - 2 The historical archaeology of precolonial contact ... 9. Information from industrial relics - 10. Potential of Australian historica archaeology. Bibliography p.164-168. Author is Professor o Archaeology and Palaeoanthropology, Univ. of New England in Armisdale. *Class No: 902(94)*

[4345]
FLOOD, J. **Archaeology of the dreamtime.** Sydney, Collins, 1983 288p., illus., (some col.), bibliog. ISBN: 0002164442.
18 chapters in five sections (Introduction; Human origins; Ice Age beginnings; The rising of the seas; The last two thousand years examine what is known of Australian prehistory. Incorporates the results of much recent archaeological work. Chapter notes p.254-256 Glossary p.267-274. Further reading p.275-277. Index p.278-288. 'A generally clear, well-informed and well-balanced account of Australian prehistory' (*Antiquity*, v.58, no.224, November 1984, p.232-233). *Class No: 902(94)*

Nautical Archaeology

[4346]
GREENHILL, D. *and* MORRISON, J. **The Archaeology of boats and ships** an introduction. London, Conway Maritime Press, 1995. 288p., illus., maps, bibliog., index. £30. ISBN: 0851776523.
Updated version of Greenhill's *The Archaeology of the boa* (London, A & C. Black, 1976).
Authoritative survey of the development of boatbuilding in 20 chapters arranged in 3 parts: 1. General theory - 2. Roots o boatbuilding - 3. Aspects of the evolution of boats and vessels in Europe, North America and Asia. Glossary p.283-84. Bibliography p.274-82. *Class No: 902.034*

[4347]
KUPPURAM, G. *and* KUMUDAMANI, G., *eds*. **Marine archaeology** the global perspectives. Delhi, Sundeep Prakashan, 2v., 1996 xiv,643p.+52pl. (some col.), tables, bibliogs. Rs1850. ISBN 8185067910.
34 contributors. 50 articles within 8 sections: 1. Submarine archaeological investigations - 2. Shipwrecks and ancient shipping - 3 Water crafts, maritime trade and cultural interaction - 4. Ancient ports and harbours - 5. Marine archaeology - 6. Conservation of sunken cultural property - 7. Protection of underwater cultural heritage - 8. Miscellaneous. Chapter bibliographies. *Class No: 902.034*

[4348]
PEARSON, C., *ed*. **Conservation of maritime archaeological objects.** London, Butterworth, 1987. iv,297p. illus. £55.
Compendium of 12 essays from 8 contributors on the marine environment; the deterioration of materials and the corrosion of metals; on-site and off-site conservation treatments; and environmental and storage factors. *Class No: 902.034*

Bibliographies

[4349]
ILLSLEY, J.S., *comp*. **An Indexed bibliography of underwater archaeology** and related topics. Oswestry, Anthony Nelson, 1996. 360p. indexes. (*International Maritime Archaeology Series, no.3.*) ISBN: 0904614573. ISSN: 1356983x.
12,093 unannotated entries under 7 subdivided sections: 1. General guides - 2. Shipbuilding and naval architecture - 3. Underwater archaeology - 4. Artefacts - 5. Conservation - 6. Archaeological sites - 7. Miscellaneous topics. Author and keyword indexes. *Class No: 902.034(01)*

Encyclopaedias

[4350]

ncyclopaedia of underwater and maritime archaeology.
Delgado, J.P., *ed*. London, British Museum Press, 1997. 493p. illus.
(some col.), index. £29.95. ISBN: 0714121290.

172 contributors. 500 cross-referenced topic entries A-Z, mostly
ending with references to additional reading. Topics include sites
(shipwrecks, groups of wrecks, submerged cities and harbours),
research themes, legislation, practical techniques, organisations,
institutions and agencies, prehistoric settlements, and overview articles
examining underwater archaeology in its broader regional, national,
and scientific contexts. Subject list by topics p.13-15. Glossary of
nautical terms p.479-81. *Class No: 902.034(031)*

Handbooks & Manuals

[4351]

EAN, M., *and others, eds*. **Archaeology underwater** the NAS guide
to principles and practice. Denbigh, Clwyd, Nautical Archaeological
Society and Archetype Publications, 1992. ix,336p. illus., diagrs.,
bibliog., index. ISBN: 1873132255.

19 contributors. Comprehensive guide and textbook. Topics include
project planning, recording, position fixing, search methods,
surveying, investigative techniques, post-fieldwork recording, analysis,
and publication. Chapter reading lists. Bibliography p.282-98.
Class No: 902.034(035)

[4352]

REEN, J. Maritime archaeology: a technical handbook. London &
San Diego, Academic Press, 1990. xx,282p. illus., diagrs., bibliog.,
index. $27. ISBN: 012298630x.

With the emphasis on technical matters this handbook covers 5
broad areas: searching for sites; recording sites; excavation;
management of collections; and study, research and publication.
Bibliography p.267-78. Analytical index. 'There is a heavy bias
towards shipwrecks, and relatively modern ones at that' (*Preface*).
Class No: 902.034(035)

Maps & Atlases

[4353]

1UCKLEROY, K., *ed*. **Archaeology under water** an atlas of the
world's submerged sites. New York and London, McGraw-Hill, 1980.
192p. illus. (some col.), maps, bibliog. index. ISBN: 0070439561.

1. Techniques and approaches - 2. Mediterranean wreck sites and
classical seafaring - 3. European shipwrecks over 3000 years - 4.
Shipwrecks in the wake of Columbus - 5. Structures under water - 6.
Preservation. Bibliography p.188-189. Analytical index. 'A broad
picture of how and where underwater archaeology has advanced'
(Prologue). A good state of the art report. *Class No: 902.034(084.3)*

Indian Ocean

[4354]

RAO, S.R., *ed*. **Marine archaeology of Indian Ocean countries:**
proceedings of the First International Conference on Marine
Archaeology of Indian Ocean countries, October 1987. Goa, National
Institute of Oceanography, 1988. xlvi,164p. illus. (some col.). Rs500.
ISBN: 819007408.

60 papers by geologists, geophysicists, oceanographers and
archaeologists in 2 sections: 1. Organization of the Conference,
general problems, and the future of marine archaeology - 2. Research
areas (problems of marine archaeology; ancient shipping and
shipwrecks; exploitation of submerged ports; underwater survey
techniques; sea-level fluctuations; marine art; ancient ports in India;
conservation; the underwater cultural heritage of Indian Ocean
countries; and marine technology in archaeology).
Class No: 902.034(267)

Ancient Greece & Rome

[4355]

**ARKER, A.J. Ancient shipwrecks of the Mediterranean & the
Roman Provinces.** Oxford, Tempvs Reparatvm, 1992. 569p. illus.,
maps, bibliog., index. (*British Archeological Reports International
Series, no.580*.) ISBN: 0860547361.

5 descriptive historical chapters (*e.g.* 2. Shipwrecks in Ancient
History ... 3. Shipwrecks and Commerce) then Catalogue of 1,259
wrecks arranged A-Z by location p.39-460. Data: name, reference to
map, nationality, latitude and longitude, cargo category and date.
Glossary of technical terms p.36-38. List of references p.461-513. 15
maps. '*A catalogue raisonné* of shipwrecks of the Mediterranean
region which date before AD1500 together with Roman ships and
boats from outside the region ... concerned essentially with sea-going
ships of the Graeco-Roman world. *Class No: 902.034(37/38)*

Great Britain

[4356]

FENWICK, V. *and* **GALE, A. Historic shipwrecks** discovered,
protected and investigated. Stroud, Glos., Tempus, 1998. 160p. illus.
(inc. 16 col. plates), map, bibliog., index. £18.99. $29.99. ISBN:
075241416x.

Informative account in 9 chapters (*e.g.* 1. Untold voyages - 2. The
King's ships ... 4. Discoveries, dates & doubts ... 6. Outward bound
for the Indies) of the 47 sites designated under the Protection of
Wrecks Act 1973. Historic Wreck location map p.7. A-Z list of wrecks
p.15. Glossary p.152. Bibliography p.153. Analytical index. 'Marred
by out-of-date and inaccurate information (*British Archaeology*, no.43,
April 1999, p.16). *Class No: 902.034(410)*

[4357]

MARSDEN, P. English Heritage book of ships and shipwrecks
London, B.T. Batsford/English Heritage, 1997. 128p. illus. (some
col.pl.) maps, bibliog., index. ISBN: 0713475358.

1. Maritime archaeology in Britain - 2. Earlier boats - 3. Late Iron
Age and Roman ships ... 5. Medieval seafarers ... 7. Global seafaring:
seventeenth to early nineteenth century - 8. From sail to steam.
Glossary p.117. Places to visit p.118-20. Bibliography (by chapter)
p.121-23. Analytical index. Detailed summary of maritime discoveries
in Britain. *Class No: 902.034(410)*

Scotland

[4358]

MACDONALD, R. Dive Scotland's greatest wrecks. Edinburgh,
Mainstream Publishing, 1993. 176p. illus. (some col.), maps, bibliog.,
index. £12.99. ISBN: 185158532x.

'Detailed description of Scotland's most famous wrecks. Data
includes location, tidal conditions, maximum depth, visibility, nearest
coastguard and police stations. Bibliography p.170-172.
Class No: 902.034(411)

[4359]

MARTIN, C. Scotland's historic shipwrecks London, B.T. Batsford/
Historic Scotland, 1998. 128p. illus. (some col.), bibliog., index.
£15.99. ISBN: 071348327x.

Survey of the most famous wrecks in Scottish waters. Scotland's
sunken treasures p.109-119. Glossary p.121. Bibliography p.122-23.
Data includes list of events in which the ship wrecked played a part
and the circumstances of its loss. Author is Reader in Maritime Studies
in the University of St. Andrews. *Class No: 902.034(411)*

London

[4360]

MARSDEN, P. Ships of the Port of London first to eleventh centuries
AD. London, English Heritage, 1994. 237p. illus., maps, plans,
tables, bibliog., index. (*Archaeological Report, no.3*.) ISBN:
185704470x.

3 specialist chapters on Blackfriars Ship 1962, New Guy's boat
1958, and County Hall Ship 1910 among 6 general chapters on the
Port of London during the early medieval period. Appendix 9 Glossary
of nautical terms p.215-16. Bibliography p.221-25.
Class No: 902.034(421)

Scandinavia

[4361]

Aspects of maritime Scandinavia. Proceedings of the Nordic Seminar
on Maritime Aspects of Archaeology, Roskilde, 13th-15th March,
1989. Crumlin-Pedersen, O., *ed*. Roskilde, Denmark, The Viking
Ship Museum, 1991. 291p. illus., tables, maps, bibliogs., index.
ISBN: 8785180173.

23 papers by independent hands, each with its own bibliography,
arranged in 7 thematic sections: 1. Archaeological background - 2.
Aspects of maritime archaeology - 3. Routes, portages and havens - 4.
Non-urban ports and trading stations - 5. Other non-urban sites - 6.
Ports - 7. Tracing maritime sites. Chronological Table p.185. Index of
finds, sites and sea-routes p.287-89. *Class No: 902.034(48)*

America

[4362]

BASS, G.F. Ships and shipwrecks of the Americas a history based on
underwater archaeology. 2nd ed. London, Thames and Hudson, 1996.
272p. illus. (many col.), maps, bibliog., index. pbk. £16.95 ISBN:
050027892x.

1st ed. 1988..

12 essays by different hands record the triumphs of marine
archaeology in the New World in chronological order: Viking
longboats to the Titanic. Glossary p.260-61. Brief guide to museums
and research institutes p.261-62. Bibliography p.263-67. 376 illus. (80
col.). 'Its only disappointing feature is that the paperback edition is

....(contd.)

updated merely by a few paragraphs dovetailed into the Introduction and Epilogue' (*Reference Reviews*, vol.11,no.1, 1997, p.42).
Class No: 902.034(7)

Australia

[4363]

HENDERSON, G. **Maritime archaeology in Australia.** Nedlands, Univ. of Western Australian Press, 1986. ix, 201p. illus., tables, bibliog., index. £12.00. ISBN: 0855642416.

Complete account of the archaeological resource and an overview of the progress of the discipline in Australia, with some pointers to future directions in 10 chapters e.g., 3. Ships in Australian waters before European settlement - 4. After European settlement - 5. Finders and the law - 6-9. Maritime archaeology in the various States - 10. Reflective overview and prospects. Appendix: Shipwrecks declared under legislation p.173-8. Bibliography p.179-85.
Class No: 902.034(94)

Fieldwork Techniques

[4364]

Archaeological site manual. 3rd ed. London, Museum of London Archaeology Service, 1994. variously paginated in loose-leaf binder. ISBN: 0904818403.

1st ed. 1980; 2nd ed. 1990.

Designed for on-site use, this guide to the compilation of archaeological site records assists in recording methods, excavation techniques, finds on site, and order of operations. *Class No:* 902.2

Great Britain

[4365]

BINKS, G., *and others eds*. **Visitors welcome** a manual on the presentation and interpretation of archaeological excavations. London, HMSO, 1988. 162p. illus. (some col.), bibliog., index. pbk. £25.00. ISBN: 0117012106.

Part 1. Section 1. Why invite visitors to your dig? The benefits of presentation and interpretation - 2. What is it realistic to provide for the visitor? Planning the interpretative programme - 3. Who is really likely to visit ... and what will they be interested in? - 4. How are you going to get your interpretation across to visitors? - 5. Encouraging school visits - 6. Opportunities for generating income - 7. Who can help? Grant aid and sponsorship - 8. Public relations. Part 2. Technical Appendix (*e.g.* funding ... useful addresses ... setting up a trading company ... guided tours ... publication design ... audio systems). Bibliography p.156-9. *Class No:* 902.2(410)

[4366]

WOOD, E.S. **Collins field guide to archaeology in Britain.** 5th ed. London, Collins, 1979. 389p. illus. (inc.pl.), maps, indexes. ISBN: 0002192357.

1st ed. 1963.

4 parts: 1. General background - 2. Types of field antiquities; fixtures (p.88-246; Caves and rock shelters ... Deceptive natural features) - 3. Types of field antiquities: surface findings (*e.g.* flint; pottery) - 4. Books to read (sectionalised; running commentary; p.350-66). A key to over 200 varieties of earthworks. Neat production.
Class No: 902.2(410)

America—North

[4367]

McMILLON, B. **The Archaeology handbook** a field manual and resource guide. New York, John Wiley, 1991. iv,259p. illus., bibliog., index. $24.95; £10.95. ISBN: 0471530514.

Excavation guide for North American amateur archaeologists and archaeological volunteers. Resource section (travel agencies; museums; sites; excavations; field schools; state archaeologists and state historical reservation officers; archaeological organizations) p.142-248. Bibliography p.249-53. 'A good practical guide to archaeological techniques' (*Reference Reviews*, v.6, no.2, 1992, p.44).
Class No: 902.2(71+73)

Antiquities

[4368]

CLEERE, H.F., *ed*. **Archaeological heritage management in the modern world.** London, Unwin, Hyman, 1989. xxiv, 318p. maps, tables, diagrs., bibliogs., index. £35.00. (*One World Archaeology series, no.9*.) ISBN: 0044450281.

....(contd.)

33 contributors from 18 countries. Compendium of papers arranged in 4 sections: 1. Approaches to heritage management - 2. Regional and country studies - 3. Case studies - 4. Training and qualification of archaeologists for heritage management. Most papers have lists of references appended. *Class No:* 904

[4369]

JOUSSAUME, R. **Dolmens for the dead** : megalith building throughout the world. Translated by A. and C. Chippindale. London, B.T Batsford Ltd., 1988. 320p. illus., maps, bibliog., index. £19.95 ISBN: 0713453699.

First published in Paris by Hachette as *Les dolmens pour les mort* 1985.

13 geographical chapters with marked European emphasis but with worldwide coverage nevertheless: 8. Africa, the Arabian peninsula and Madagascar - 9. Syria, Lebanon and Israel - 10. The Caucasus 11. India - 12. China, Korea and Japan - 13. South America Introduction (p16-24) attempts a definition of dolmen whilst Translator's preface (p.11-15) distinguishes between British and continental usage. Bibliography p.299-315. 26 plates and 65 drawings.
Class No: 904

[4370]

MOHEN, J-P. **The World of megaliths.** London, Cassell, 1989; New York, Facts On File, 1990. 318p. illus. (some col.), maps, bibliog. index. $35. ISBN: 0304318795, UK; 0816022518, US.

Originally published as *Le Monde des mégalithes* (Tournai Casterman, 1989).

Worldwide survey of menhirs, dolmens and cromlechs together with a discussion of current views of megalithic societies. 9 chapters in 4 sections: Sites and legends - Three thousand years of building - Secre of the builders - Sacred world of megaliths. Chronological table p.284 Table of contemporaneous megalithic cultures p.285. Glossary p.290 8. Bibliography (with French and German language titles p.286-9) Geographic index p.299-318. *Class No:* 904

Worldwide

[4371]

The Collections of the British Museum. Wilson, D.M., *ed*. London British Museum Publications, 1989. 304p. illus. (many col.), bibliog. index. ISBN: 0714116823.

Descriptive handbook to British Museum antiquities arranged by Departments: 1. Classical collections - 2. Coins and medals - 3 Egyptian antiquities - 4. Ethnographic collection - 5. Medieval and modern collection - 6. Oriental collections - 7. Prehistoric and Roman Britain - 8. Prints and drawings - 9. Western Asiatic antiquities - 10 Conservation and scientific research. Bibliography p.289-90. Galleries of the BM. p.291-4. *Class No:* 904(100)

Holy Land (Ancient World)

[4372]

MURPHY-O'CONNOR, J. **The Holy Land: an Oxford archaeological guide** from earliest times to 1700. 4th ed. Oxford Univ. Press, 1998 xxiv,459p. illus., maps, bibliog., index. £12.99. (*Oxford Archaeological Guides*.) ISBN: 0192880136.

Introduction (historical outline, scope, use) - 2. Pt.1: City of Jerusalem - 2. A-Z guide to the remainder of the Holy Land. Covers 150 archaeological sites and includes information on museums and advice on visiting desert areas. Bibliography p.xix-xxii.
Class No: 904(33)

Ancient Rome

[4373]

CLARIDGE, A. **Rome.** rev. ed. Oxford Univ. Press, 1999. 480p. illus. maps, plans, index, pbk. £18.95. (*Oxford Archaeological Guides*.) ISBN: 0192880039.

'Illustrated guide to all the major sites in twelve areas in central Rome and four in Greater Rome, including the Capitoline Hill, Roman Forum, Colosseum, Mausoleums of Augustus and Hadrian, the Circus Maximus, Catacombs, Ostia, and Tivoli. The introduction offers an assessment of Roman achievement and its status as the capital of the Roman Empire, explaining how Rome has survived to become the largest and most complex archaeological site in the world' (*publisher's announcement*). *Class No:* 904(38)

Europe

[4374]

BALFOUR, M. **Megalithic mysteries** an illustrated guide to Europe's ancient sites. Limpsfield, Sy. Dragon's World, 1992. 192p. col. illus. maps, diagrs., bibliog., index. £19.95. ISBN: 1850281637.

Selective A-Z gazetteer by area and country which includes road directions and map references. 'Europe' includes parts of North

...(contd.)
Africa; British sites are well represented. 'All the well-known monuments in Europe are here and plenty which are scarcely known at all' (*Reference Reviews*, v.7, no.3, 1993, p.42). *Class No:* 904(4)

[4375]
SERVICE, A. *and* BRADBERY, J. **The Standing stones of Europe** a guide to the great megalithic monuments. Rev. ed. London, Dent, 1993. 287p. illus., maps, bibliog., index. ISBN: 0460861158.
First published by Weidenfeld & Nicolson 1979.
Descriptive gazetteer and guidebook to Northern and Southern Europe. Megalithic sites to visit in British Isles p.254-64. Glossary p.270-2. References and bibliography p.273-9. Map sources for locating megalithic sites (by country) p.280-1. *Class No:* 904(4)

Great Britain

[4376]
AUBREY, J. **Monumenta Britannica.** Fowles, J., *ed.* Sherborne, Dorset, Dorset Publishing Co., 2 vols., 1982. 1143p. facsims. maps, indexes. £95.; $250. each vol. ISBN: 0902129406, v.1; 0902129503, v.2.
Monumenta Britannica: a miscellanie of British antiquities remained in manuscript form from 1693 to its first printing in this limited edition of 595 copies.
A survey of British field antiquities from the prehistoric to the medieval period commissioned by Charles II. Aubrey's manuscript is here reproduced in facsimile with a facing modern English printed text. *Class No:* 904(410)

[4377]
BURL, A. **A Guide to the stone circles of Britain, Ireland and Brittany.** New Haven, Yale Univ. Press, 1995. 276p. illus., plans, bibliog., index, pbk. ISBN: 0300063318.
390 numbered sites A-Z x county in UK and Republic of Ireland, A-Z x department in France. Data: location, description, best approach, known archaeology, rating in terms of condition, bibliographical references. Glossary p.263-4. Bibliography p.266-8. An eminently practical and informative guide. *Class No:* 904(410)

[4378]
BURL, A. **The Stone circles of the British Isles.** New Haven, Yale Univ. Press, 1976. xxii,410p. illus., maps, diagrs., tables, bibliog., index. £40.00. ISBN: 0300019726.
9 chapters *e.g.* 1. The earlier work on stone circles - 2. Origins - and regional chapters 4-9. Appendix 1. A county gazetteer of the stone circles of the British Isles p.335-71. Bibliography p.376-95. *Class No:* 904(410)

[4379]
–BURL, A. **Great stone circles fables fictions facts.** New Haven, Yale University Press, 1999. 199p. illus. (some col.), maps, bibliog., index. ISBN: 0300076894.
Selects a dozen attractive and ecovative stone rings (e.g. Rollright Stones, Stonehenge) for close examination and to answer standard questions: their purpose, construction, age, distribution, design, art, legend, and relation to astronomy. Chapter notes (mostly reference citations) p.187-93. Bibliography p.194-96. *Class No:* 904(410)

[4380]
CANBY, C. **A Guide to the archaeological sites of the British Isles.** New York and Oxford, Facts on File, 1988. 358p. illus. index. $24.95. £13.95. (*Guide to the archeological sites of Europe & the Mediterranean no.1.*) ISBN: 0816015708.
750 cross-referenced entries relating to monuments, churches, castles, towns and cities, Palaeolithic period to 12th century, A-Z in 3 sections: England and Wales, Scotland and Ireland. Sites are located by distance from the nearest major town. No bibliography. Intended as a travel book and as an archaeological reference work but 'while it has some reference value, public libraries serving travellers will not find it a worthwhile addition as a guidebook' (*Booklist*, v.85, no.14, 15 March 1989, p.1265-6). *Class No:* 904(410)

[4381]
CASTLEDEN, R. **Neolithic Britain** New Stone Age sites of England, Scotland and Wales. London, Routledge, 1992. xiv,432p. illus., plans, bibliog., index. £40. ISBN: 0415058457.
1,100 domestic, ceremonial, and burial sites, some of them recently discovered, belonging to the period 4700-2000 BC, are described A-Z within the 'new counties'. Appendix: radiocarbon dates p.403-4. Bibliography p.405-9. *Class No:* 904(410)

[4382]
CLAYTON, P. **Guide to the archaeological sites of Britain.** 2nd ed. London, B.T. Batsford, 1985. 239p. illus., bibliog., index. £14.95. ISBN: 0713448431.
First published as *Archaeological sites of Britain* Weidenfeld & Nicolson, 1976.
250 of the more notable sites described in 7 regional sections (1. The South East ... 7. The North). Some museums to visit p.232-5. Glossary p.230-1. Bibliography p.229. 180 illustrations. *Class No:* 904(410)

[4383]
COPE, J. **The Modern antiquarian** a pre-millenial odyssey through Megalithic Britain including a guide to over 300 pehistoric sites. London, Thorsons, 1998. x,438p. col.illus., col.maps, bibliog., index. £29.99. ISBN: 0722535996.
Lavishly illustrated popular encyclopedic work in 2 parts: 1. Series of 7 essays (*e.g.* In search of Megalithic Britain ... The Landscape temples) - 2. Gazetteer arranged regionally, a highly personal interpretation of 300+ 'Of the very best sites' selected from hundreds visited over an 8 year period. Bibliography p.430-31. 'It will probably sell more than all the combined archaeological books published in [the] last decade put together; more people will read it than have ever studied an excavation report' (*Antiquity*, v.73, no.279, March 1999, p.236-38). *Class No:* 904(410)

[4384]
ELLIS, P.B. **A Guide to early Celtic remains in Britain.** London, Constable, 1991. 272p. illus., bibliog., index. £11.95. ISBN: 0094692009.
Divided into 9 regions this guide contains descriptions of the visible remains of the Early Celtic period from the 8th century BC to the arrival of the Romans in the 1st centry AD. All the most scenic and the most significant sites - hillforts, cliff castles, hillside carvings, burial mounds *etc.* - are included. Glossary p.255-9. Bibliography p.260-4. *Class No:* 904(410)

[4385]
HAYES, A. **Archaeology of the British Isles** with a gazetteer of sites in England, Wales, Scotland and Ireland. London, Batsford, 1993. 206p. illus., maps, bibliog., index. £25. ISBN: 0713472278.
Popular account of Britain's archaeological heritage from 250,000 BC to AD 1500. Gazetteer of 450 sites p.159-200. Bibliography p.201-2. *Class No:* 904(410)

[4386]
HOGG, A.H.A. **Hill-forts of Britain** London, Hart-Davis, Macgibbon, 1975. xvi. 17p + 304 p. illus. (inc. pl.), ground plans, maps, index.
12 chapters. 1. Names - 2. Modern research ... 5. Distribution and regional types ... 7. Building the hill-fort ... 10. The interior - 11. The Romans and after - 12. Four important hill-forts. Bibliography. 103-11. Gazetteer. A-Z, p.112-299 (with ground plans, grid references, bibliographical references). Illus. include aerial views, location maps. *Class No:* 904(410)

Bibliographies

[4387]
'**Books: a review of ten years of books and articles on Hadrian's Wall**', *Current Archaeology*, v.14, no.8 (No.164), August 1999, p.303-305.
Bibliographical essay on select items from the 190+ books and articles published in the 1990s. *Class No:* 904(410)(01)

Maps & Atlases

[4388]
GREAT BRITAIN. Ordnance Survey. **Ancient Britain (map).** Southampton, Ordnance Survey. folded map, col.illus. £6.25. ISBN: 031929028x.
Illustrates (with text) highlighted buildings and monuments, with historical information portrayed against a modern background, showing the geographical distribution of some of the most visible ancient monuments of Great Britain. *Class No:* 904(410)(084.3)

Roman Times

[4389]
COLLINGWOOD, R.G. *and* WRIGHT, R.P. **The Roman inscriptions of Britain: 1. Inscriptions on stone.** Oxford, Clarendon Press, 1965. 824p. illus. (incl.pl.).
A finely produced work, with details of 2,400 inscriptions; entries arranged under regions and counties, then towns. In each case, a reproduction of the original plus transcription and translation. 'Milestones' are covered in items 2219-2400. Short glossary and translation of military terms; index of sites. Bibliography (p.xix-xxxiii): A. Abbreviations of periodicals and serial works - B. Manuscript sources - C. Separate works - D. Museum catalogues.
Goodburn, R. and Waugh, H. *Inscriptions on stone. Epigraphic indexes.* Gloucester, Alan Sutton. 1990. 128p. £18. 0862990262. Key

....*(contd.)*

to analysis of inscriptions' contents: 64 separate indexes in 16 major reference groups.

A facsimile edition is published by Alan Sutton which includes a new section of *Addenda and Corrigenda*. 852p. £90. ISBN 075090917x. *Class No:* 904(410)"0055-0449"

[4390]

—FRERE, S.S. *and* TOMLIN, R.S.O., *eds*. The Roman inscriptions of Britain: 2. Instrumentum Domesticum. Gloucester, Alan Sutton, 1990.

1. *The military diplomata; metal ingots, tesserae, dies; labels; and lead sealings*. 1990. xiv,126p.++ 8p. pl. £35. ISBN 0862997755. Bibliography p.xiii-xiv. - 2. *Weights, gold vessels, silver vessels, bronze vessels, lead vessels, pewter vessels, shale vessels, glass vessels, spoons*. 1991. xiii,146p.++ 8p. plates (twice). £35. 0862998204. Bibliography p.xiii. - 3. *Brooches, rings, gems, bracelets, helmets, shields, weapons, iron tools, baldric fittings, votives in gold, silver and bronze, lead pipes, roundels, sheets and other lead objects, stone roundels, pottery and bone roundels, other objects of bone*. 1991. xiii,176p.++ 16p. pl. £35. 0862999359. Bibliography p.xiii. - 4. *Wooden barrels, stilus tablets, leather stamps, oculists stamps, wall plaster, mosaics, handmills, stone tablets, balls, pebbles, etc*. 1992. 244p. £35. 0750900865.- 5. *Tiles and tile stamps*. 176p. £35. 0750903198 - 6. *Dipinti and graffiti on amphorae, mortaria and course pottery*. 224p. £34. 0750905360 - 7. *Graffiti on Samian ware*. 168p. £35. 0750907436 - 8. *Graffiti on course pottery. Addenda and Corrigenda Fasc. 1-7*.

Frere. S.S. *Epigraphic indexes*. 1999. £20. 0750909188. As indispensable companion comprising 78 separate indexes plus a concordance with published sources. *Class No:* 904(410)"0055-0449"

[4391]

—TOMLIN, R.S.O. Britannia Romana a history of Roman Britiain from inscriptions. Stroud, Gloucs., Alan Sutton, 1999. 256p. illus. £20. ISBN: 0862997976.

Narrative history which includes the inscription, a full translation, and a linking commentary. *Class No:* 904(410)'0055-0449'

[4392]

DE LA BÉDOYÈRE, G. The Finds of Roman Britain. London, B.T. Batsford, 1989. 242p. illus. (inc. some col. pl.), tables, bibliog., index. £19.95. ISBN: 0713460822.

Emphasis on artefacts sharing a common function: 1. The Roman army in Britain - 2. Crafts, trade and industries - 3. Household life - 4. The individual - 5. Public and social life - 6. Religion and superstition - 7. Death and burial - 8. Christianity - 9. Coinage. Appendix: Museums p.209-22 (list of most important holding Romano-British collections). Table of events p.212-13. Bibliography p.227-37. Over 500 illustrations. *Class No:* 904(410)"0055-0449"

[4393]

WILSON, R.J.A. A Guide to the Roman remains in Britain. 3rd ed. London, Constable, 1988. xvi, 453p. illus., maps, bibliog., indexes. £8.95. ISBN: 0094686507.

1st ed. 1978.

Survey of all visible antiquities in 10 regional chapters. Sites are grouped according to their nature and not to their proximity. Introduction (p.1-30) includes sections on Roman army in Britain; Military remains (by type); Historical outline; and Glossary (p.26-30). Appendix 1. Gazetteer of visible remains not mentioned in text p.408-19 - 2. Some museums displaying Romano-British material (p.420-1) - 3. Bibliography p.422-444. Index of sites and types of monument. Designed primarily for the ordinary individual who has an interest in the Roman past but no prior specialized knowledge. *Class No:* 904(410)"0055-0449"

Maps & Atlases

[4394]

GREAT BRITAIN. Ordnance Survey. **Roman Britain map.** Southampton, Ordnance Survey, 2000. folded map, col.illus. £6.25.

Scale, 1:625,000. (1 inch to 10 miles). Shows known Roman military sites, roads and place names against a background of modern Britain. *Class No:* 904(410)"0055-0449"(084.3)

Scotland

[4395]

ALLEN, J.R. *and* ANDERSON, J. **The Early Christian monuments of Scotland.** Balgravies, Angus, The Pinkfoot Press, 2v., 1993. 1200p. illus. £49. ISBN: 1874012059.

First published by The Society of Antiquaries of Scotland in 3v. (1903).

V.1: Artistic and historical appraisal of monuments and illustrated analysis of symbols. V.2-3: Classified and descriptive catalogue. *Class No:* 904(411)

[4396]

ARMIT, I. Scotland's hidden history. Stroud. Glos., Tempus, 1998. 160p., col.illus. £18.99. $29.99. ISBN: 0752414062.

8 chronological chapters, sub-divided by site type, provide descriptions of 100 sites that may be visited in Scotland and the Northern Isles. Good direction and access notes. Period covered is from Neolithic times to the Vikings. *Class No:* 904(411)

[4397]

BREEZE, D. Historic Scotland: 5000 years of Scotland's heritage. London, Batsford, 1998. 128p. col.illus., bibliog., index. £14.99. ISBN: 0713483946.

Tells the story of Scotland and its people through descriptions and illustrations of sites and buildings in the care of Historic Scotland. The text is by the Chief Inspector of Ancient Monuments. *Class No:* 904(411)

[4398]

Exploring Scotland's heritage. Edinburgh, HMSO for Royal Commission on the Ancient and Historical Monuments of Scotland, 1985-. col.illus., maps, bibliog., index, pbk. £10.95. each.

Popular but authoritative handbooks introducing Scotland's most interesting and best preserved monuments which are grouped according to character and date. The use of O.S. 1:50,000 Landranger maps is recommended. Ritchie, G. and Harman, M. *Argyll and the Western Isles*. 2nd ed. 1996. ISBN 0114952876. Baldwin, J. *Edinburgh, Lothian and the Borders*. 2nd ed. 1996. ISBN 0114952922. Snell, G. *Dumfries and Galloway*. 2nd ed. 1996. ISBN 0114952949. Shepherd, I.A.G. *Grampian*. 1986. ISBN 0114924538. Close-Brooks, J. *The Highlands*. 2nd ed. 1995. ISBN 0114952930. Walker, B. and Ritchie, G. *Fife, Perthshire and Angus*. 2nd ed. 1996. ISBN 0114952868. Shepherd, I. *Aberdeen and North-East Scotland*, 2nd ed. 1996. 0114952906. Ritchie, A. *Orkney*. 1996. 0114952884. Ritchie, A. *Shetland*. 1996. 0114952892. Stevenson, J.B. *Glasgow, Clydeside and Stirling*. 2nd ed. 1995. 0114952914. 'Essential to complete the libraries of tourist guides, antiquarians and historians, and intelligent visitors to Scotland' (*Local Historian*, v.17, no.3, August 1986, p.184). *Class No:* 904(411)

[4399]

FOJUT, N. *and* PRINGLE, D. The Ancient monuments of Shetland. London, HMSO, 1993. 64p. col. illus. col.map, bibliog., pbk. £3.95. ISBN: 0114942005.

Illustrated gazetteer to the antiquities of Shetland from Neolithic settlements to 18th century coastal defences. Bibliography p.64. *Class No:* 904(411)

[4400]

FOJUT, N., *and others*. The Ancient Monuments of the Western Isles. Edinburgh, HMSO for Historic Scotland and Western Islands Tourist Board and Western Islands Enterprise, 1994. 72p. col.illus. pbk. £3.95. ISBN: 0114952019.

Descriptive gazetteer of island's monuments. *Class No:* 904(411)

[4401]

FOJUT, N. A Guide to Prehistoric and Viking Shetland. 3rd ed. Lerwick, Shetland Times, 1994. iv,128p. col.illus., maps, pbk. £12. ISBN: 0900662913.

Contents include descriptions of culture periods and their remains together with a gazetteer of the most significant sites and a number of suggested tour itineraries. 'An excellent guide to its subject' (*Reference Reviews*, v.11,no.8, 1997, p.40). *Class No:* 904(411)

[4402]

GRAHAM-CAMPBELL, J. *and* BATEY, C.E. Vikings in Scotland: an archeological survey. Edinburgh University Press, 1998. xix,296p. illus., maps, bibliog., index. £14.95. ISBN: 074860863x.

13 thematic chapters (*e.g.* 1. Scotland before the Vikings - 2. Norwegian background - 3. Sources - 4/6. Regional surveys). Further reading p.265-80. Analytical index. Comprehensive overview based on recent fieldwork and excavation. 'Makes a wealth of material available to the general public, and certainly deserves to become a standard text for students with an interest in Norse Scotland' (*Medieval Archaeology*, v.43, 1999, p.317-19). *Class No:* 904(411)

[4403]

GREAT BRITAIN. Historic Buildings And Monuments Scotland. A List of ancient monuments in Scotland 1990. Edinburgh, Scottish Development Department, 1990. 51p. ISBN: 0748003274.

A-Z regional guide arranged according to local authority areas. Data: 1:50,000 O.S. sheet and National Grid number within broad categories: prehistoric ritual and funerary; domestic and defensive; Roman; Crosses and canal stones; Ecclesiastical; secular; industrial. List of addresses of national organizations and regional archaeologists inside end cover. *Class No:* 904(411)

[4404]
Historic Scotland the sites to see. Edinburgh, Historic Scotland. 48p.
col. illus., maps. £1.95.
Contains descriptions of 300+ sites in the care of Historic Scotland
grouped into geographical areas and listed A-Z. *Historic Scotland map*
(24cmx15cm folded). £3.95. ISBN 0860846741 shows their location
and is indexed. *Class No:* 904(411)

[4405]
—Welcome to Historic Scotland over 60 historic attractions to visit.
Edinburgh, Historic Scotland, 2000. 24p. 10cmx21cm col. illus., col.
maps. gratis.
Brief description of 68 abbeys, castles, towers, gardens, distilleries,
prehistoric monuments etc. arranged in 13 regions (*e.g.* Kingdom of
Fife, Borders, Western Isles). Data: location, telephone, access, tour
facilities, restaurant and bookshop (if available). *Class No:* 904(411)

[4406]
HUNTER, J.R. Fair Isle. The archaeology of an island community.
Edinburgh, HMSO for The National Trust for Scotland, 1996.
viii,279p. illus., maps, bibliog., index. £19.95. ISBN: 0114957509.
13 chapters (*e.g.* 4. Earthworks and field systems ... 8. Viking and
Norse settlement - 12. Watermilling on Fair Isle). Appendix: Inventory
of 750 sites p.217-63. Bibliography p.265-73. *Class No:* 904(411)

[4407]
JENNER, M. Scotland through the ages. London, Mermaid, 1989.
256p. illus. (many col.), maps, bibliog., index. £10.95. ISBN:
0718132807.
First published by Penguin 1987.
Historical background with maps and gazetteers to over 400 major
archaeological and historic sites. *Class No:* 904(411)

[4408]
MACK, A. Field guide to the Pictish symbol stones. Balgravies,
Angus, The Pinkfoot Press, 1997. xiv,191p. maps, illus. ISBN:
1874012067.
1. The symbols - 2/14. Museums by region (stones in the collection,
findspot, present location, and description) ... 17. References given in
text p.146-50 - 18. Maps and map notes p.151-64.
Class No: 904(411)

[4409]
MacSWEEN, A. and SHARP, M. Prehistoric Scotland. London,
Batsford, 1989. 208p. illus., maps, bibliog., index. £15.95. ISBN:
071346173x.
A lavishly illustrated guide to over 100 outstanding prehistoric sites
to stand as exemplars of the various types: settlement, defence, tombs
and burial; ritual, and stones & henges. An introductory chapter
summarizes the periods of Scottish prehistory. Glossary p.195-8.
Gazetteer p.199-203. Bibliography p.204. *Class No:* 904(411)

[4410]
Reports and inventories. Great Britain. Royal Commission on the
Ancient and Historical Monuments of Scotland. Edinburgh,
HMSO,1909-.
1.*Berwick*, 1909. 2. *Sutherland*. 1911. 3. *Caithness*. 1911. 4/5.
Galloway. 1912-14. 2v. 6. *Berwick*. Rev. issue. 1915. 7.
Dumfriesshire. 1920. 8. *East Lothian*. 1924. 9. *Outer Hebrides, Skye
and the Small Isles*. 1928. 10. *Midlothian and West Lothian*. 1929. 11.
Fife, Kinross and Clackmannan. 1933. 12. *Orkney and Shetland*.
1946. 3v. 13. *City of Edinburgh*. 1951. 14. *Roxburghshire*. 1956. 2v.
15. *Selkirkshire*. 1957. 16. *Stirlingshire*. 1963. v.1-2. £15. 17.
Peebleshire. 1967. 2v. £10; £17.50; $20.00. 18. *Argyle*. v.1: *Kintyre*.
1972; v.2: *Lorn*. 1975; v.3: *Mull, Tiree, Coll & N. Argyle*; v.4: *Iona*.
1982; v.5: *Islay, Jura, Colonsay & Oronsay*. 1984. £45. 0114917280;
v.6: *Mid-Argyll & Cowal*. 1988. v.7: *Mid Argyll & Cowal: medieval
and later monuments*. 1992. £120. 0114940940; 19/20. *Lanarkshire*.
1978. (v.20. £20). *North-east Perth: an archaeological landscape*.
1990. £35. 0114934460 is the first in a series of RCAHMS
archaeological surveys. Occasional publications designed to give fuller
treatment to subjects which cannot be embraced within the normal
course of the Commission's publication programme include: *Late
medieval monumental sculpture in the West Highlands*. 1977.
230p.+45p., plates. £14.50. *Monuments of industry: an illustrated
historical record*. 1986. xiii, 248p. £28.00. 0114924570.
In the numbered series descriptions are arranged by parish. Until
1938 monuments erected up to 1707 were included; in 1938 The
Commissioners were empowered to cover up to 1815; after 1948 the
terminal date has been left to their discretion. S.P. Halliday and J.B.
Stevenson's 'Surveying for the future: RCAHMS Archaeological
Survey 1908-1990', *Scottish Archaeology: new perceptions*. 1991.
p.129-39. bibliog. relates its development and progress. See also: 'The
Royal Commission on the Ancient and Historical Monuments of
Scotland: the first eighty years', *Transactions Ancient Monuments
Society*, v.36, 1992, p.13-77. *Class No:* 904(411)

[4411]
—GREAT BRITAIN. Royal Commission on the Ancient and Historical
Monuments of Scotland. National Monuments Record of Scotland
Jubilee a guide to the collections, 1941-1991. Edinburgh, HMSO,
1991. xvii,77p. illus., index. £14.95. ISBN: 0114941254.
A-Z cumulative descriptive list of NMRS's historical collections.
Does not include NMRS Library or material emanating from
RCAHMS' field investigations. *Class No:* 904(411)

[4412]
RITCHIE, A. and RITCHIE, G. The Ancient monuments of Orkney.
3rd ed. Edinburgh, HMSO for Historic Scotland and Orkney Islands
Council, 1995. 76p. col.illus., col.maps, bibliog. £4.95. ISBN:
0114957347.
1st ed. 1978; 2nd ed. 1986.
Illustrated guide and gazetteer to the monuments of Orkney from the
prehistoric settlement of Skara Brae to the Second World War.
Bibliography p.76. *Class No:* 904(411)

[4413]
RITCHIE, A. and BREEZE, D.J. Invaders of Scotland an introduction
to the archaeology of the Romans, Scots, Angles and Vikings,
highlighting the monuments in the care of the Secretary of State for
Scotland. Edinburgh, HMSO for Historic Buildings and Monuments,
1991. vi,58p. col. illus., map on endpaper, bibliog., indexes,
flexicover. £4.95. ISBN: 011494136x.
Colourfully illustrated descriptive guide to Scotland's most
interesting and important archeological sites. Bibliography p.56.
Class No: 904(411)

[4414]
RITCHIE, A. Iona. London, B.T. Batsford/Edinburgh, Historic
Scotland, 1997. 128p. illus. (inc. 12 col.pl.), map, bibliog., index.
£15.99. ISBN: 0713478551.
Archaeological description and historical overview in 9 chapters
(*e.g.* 1. Island of Iona - 2. Prehistory - Columba and Iona ... 9. Iona in
medieval times). Places to visit p.117-18. Bibliography p.119-20.
Glossary p.121-22. Authoritative and well illustrated.
Class No: 904(411)

[4415]
RITCHIE, A. Picts an introduction to the life of the Picts and to the
carved stones in the care of the Secretary of State for Scotland.
Edinburgh, HMSO, for Historic Buildings and Monuments, 1989. 64p.
col. illus. pbk. £3.95. ISBN: 0114934916.
Illustrated introduction to Pictish Scotland 400-800 AD. and a guide
to the surviving antiquities. *Class No:* 904(411)

[4416]
RITCHIE, A. Scotland BC historical buildings and monuments.
Edinburgh, H.M. Stationery Office, 1988. Published for Scottish
Development Department (Historic Buildings and Monuments). 80p.
illus. (some col.), pbk. £3.95. ISBN: 0114934274.
Description of stone circles, tombs, rock carvings, Celtic forts *etc.*,
(many in state care and open to the public) on mainland Scotland and
on the Northern and Western Isles. *Class No:* 904(411)

[4417]
ROBERTSON, A.S. The Antonine Wall: a handbook to the surviving
remains. Keppie, L. 4th ed. Glasgow Archaeological Society, 1990.
v,113p. illus., maps, bibliog., index. ISBN: 0904254127.
1st ed. 1960.
Authoritative and detailed guide. Bibliography p.102-9. Museums
holding Antonine Wall material p.109-110. *Class No:* 904(411)

[4418]
Scheduled ancient monuments a guide for owners, occupiers and land
managers. Edinburgh, Historic Scotland, 1996. 24p. col.illus. gratis.
A guide to scheduling under the Ancient Monuments and
Archaeological Areas Act 1979 and the Ancient Monuments (Class
Consents) (Scotland) 1996. In question and answer form.
Class No: 904(411)

[4419]
—Grants for ancient monuments a guide to grants available for the
preservation, maintenance and management of ancient monuments.
Edinburgh, Historic Scotland, 1997. 24p. col. illus. sd. gratis.
Explains the procedure for applying for and claiming an Ancient
Monuments Grant. *Class No:* 904(411)

[4420]
TURNER, V. Ancient Shetland. London, Batsford:Edinburgh, Historic
Scotland, 1998. 128p. illus. (few col.), index. £15.99. ISBN:
0713480009.
11 thematic chapters (*e.g.* 3. The first farmers ... Gateways to the
Sea). Places to visit *i.e.* a descriptive gazetteer) p.119-22. Bibliography
p.123. 'Can be thoroughly recommended to libraries interested in
Scottish antiquities' (*Reference Reviews*,v.13, no.1, 1999, p.45-46).
Class No: 904(411)

Bibliographies

[4421]

CROSS, M. **Bibliography of monuments in the care of the Secretary of State for Scotland.** Department of Archaeology, University of Glasgow and Historic Scotland, 1994. xxxiv,602p. ISBN: 0852614586.

15,000+ annotated entries relating to 328 sites of outstanding historic or archaeological interest arranged by location A-Z. Archives and libraries consulted p.xv. Guardianship sites for which guidebooks have been published p.xv-xvi. List of bibliographies consulted p.xvi-xvii. List of publications consulted p.xviii-xxxiv. *Class No:* 904(411)(01)

Gazetteers

[4422]

PIGGOTT, S. *and* RITCHIE, G. **Scotland before history with a gazetteer of ancient monuments.** 2nd ed. Edinburgh, Edinburgh Univ. Press, 1982. 196p. illus., map, pbk. £13.50. ISBN: 0852244703.

Non-technical account of human settlement and development from the earliest times to the Roman occupation accompanied by a gazetteer of 255 sites of the best preserved, most dramatic, and most typical field monuments, arranged A-Z by region and district. Index of sites. Favourable reception in *Antiquity*, v.57, no.221, November 1983, p.230-231. *Class No:* 904(411)(083.86)

Roman Times

[4423]

KEPPIE, L. **Scotland's Roman remains:** an introduction and handbook. Edinburgh, John Donald, 1986. ix, 188p., illus., maps, plans, diagrs., bibliog., index, pbk. £7.50. ISBN: 0859761576.

Part 1: Romans in Scotland has 9 chapters *e.g.* 1. Scotland on the eve of the Roman invasion - 2. Romans in Scotland: an historical outline ... 9. Impact of Romans. Part 2. Visiting Scotland's Roman remains (p.72-170) is in 3 geographical regional chapters. Bibliography p.173-84. *Class No:* 904(411)"0055-0449"

Ireland

[4424]

Archaeological survey of Ireland. Dublin, The Stationery Office, 1986-. illus., maps, indexes.

Buckley V.M. *Archaeological inventory of County Louth.* 1986. 135p. £16.50. ISBN 070700286; Moore, M.J. *County Meath.* 1987. £18.50. 0707600316. Brindley, A. and Kilfeather, A. *County Carlow.* 1993. 128p. £11. 0707603242. Moore, M.J. *County Wexford.* 1996. x,262p. illus. (many col.), indexes. £22. 070762326x is arranged under 27 types sites (*e.g.* megalithic structures, hillforts, moated sites, churches and monastic remains ... industrial sites. Glossary p.198-200. Bibliography p.201-203. Townland and subject indexes p.204-230. 28 location maps p.231-62.

Ongoing series of county inventories prepared and published by the Archaeological Survey of the Office of Public Works. Data: county reference, number, name, locational information, height above sea level, 10 figure Irish National Grid number. *Class No:* 904(415)

[4425]

HARBISON, P. **Guide to national and historic monuments of Ireland:** including a selection of other monuments not in state care. 3rd ed. Dublin, Gill and Macmillan, 1992. xiv,378p.+ 8p. maps, bibliog., index.

1st ed. 1970 as *Guide to the national momuments of Ireland.* 2nd ed. 1975.

Introduction (p.1-32) is an overview of Irish geology and of Irish monuments from the Stone Age to the medieval period. Main gazetteer is arranged A-Z by country. Data: history and description of monument; bibliographical reference, map coordinates. Glossary p.349-52. Sources p.353-55. 8 site location maps. This redesigned edition includes the 6 northern counties. *Class No:* 904(415)

[4426]

McNALLY, K. **Standing stones.** Belfast, Appletree Press, 1991. 128p. illus. IR£6.99. ISBN: 0862812011.

Guide to Irish field monuments illustrated by over 70 photographs. *Class No:* 904(415)

[4427]

WEIR, A. **Early Ireland** a field guide. Belfast, Blackstaff Press, 1980. vii, 245p. illus., index. £7.95. ISBN: 0856402125.

In 2 distinct sections: a chronological survey incorporating the dating of prehistoric monuments and the archaeological background; and a gazetteer (p.93-233) arranged A-Z by counties. Only those monuments offering the visitor/general reader some visual reward find a place. Glossary p.235-239. Place-name index p.241-245. *Class No:* 904(415)

Northern Ireland

[4428]

HAMLIN, A. **Historic monuments of Northern Ireland.** 6th ed Belfast, HMSO for Department of the Environment (Northern Ireland) 1988. xii,168p. illus. (some col.), map, bibliog., index. pbk. £6.90 ISBN: 0337082162.

1st ed. 1926.

Traces the province's prehistoric and historic background and cover: 154 sites in state care A-Z by county and lists over 250 othe: monuments. Bibliography p.157-60. *Class No:* 904(416)

England & Wales

[4429]

The Penguin guide to prehistoric England and Wales. Dyer, J. Harmondsworth, Allen Lane, 1981. 384p. illus., maps.

Published in Penguin Books 1982.

Descriptive guide to prehistoric monuments, 3-4 entries to the page grouped under 'new' county sections. Each entry is provided with a national grid reference number and the use of Ordnance Survey 1:50,000 maps is recommended. Map section p.18-27. Reference: p.363-366. Glossary p.369-372. Index of sites p.374-384. 'Extensive, detailed, informative and in general acurate and reliable' (*Antiquity*, v.56, no.216, March 1982, p.74-75). *Class No:* 904(42)

Laws

[4430]

The Treasure Act 1996 Code of practice (England and Wales). London, Department of National Heritage, 1997. 78p. bibliog., index.

A Welsh-language version is also published.

The Treasure Act 1996 replaced the common law of treasure trove, 24 September 1997. This guide, in 13 sections, covers the definition of treasure, inquests, acquisition and valuation, and rewards etc. Appendix 1. The Act in full - 2. Pilot schemes for voluntary recording of all archaeological finds - 3. Sources of further advice: A. Coroners' addresses A-Z by county - B. Sites and monuments records, and local government archivists (p.42-64). *Class No:* 904(42)(094.1)

England

[4431]

BIDWELL, P., *ed.* **Hadrian's Wall 1989-1999** A summary of recent excavations and research prepared for The Twelfth Pilgrimage of Hadrian's Wall 14-21 August 1999. Carlisle, Cumberland and Westmorland Antiquarian and Archaeological Society and the Society of Antiquaries of Newcastle-upon-Tyne, 1999. vii,224p. illlus., bibliog. £10. ISBN: 1873124295.

Includes specialist chapters on Vindolanda writing tablets and the management of the wall, and an extensive bibliography (p.203-224). *Class No:* 904(420)

[4432]

COLVIN, H.M., *ed.* **The History of the King's Works.** London, H.M. Stationery Office, 6v., 1973-1982.

1-2. *The Middle Ages.* 1976. £52.00 (these volumes are not sold separately). 0116704497. 2. *1485-1660* Pt.1. 1975. 011670568x. 4. *1485-1660* Pt.2. 1982. £55.00. 0116708328. 5. *1670-1782.* 1976. £32.00. 011670571x. 6. *1782-1851.* 1973. £40.00. 0116702869. Portfolio plans V-VII complementing v.4-5 sold separately from volumes of text. £11.00. 0116711167. Surveys royal building in England from the era of Offa's Dyke to the establishment of the Victorian Office of Works in 1851. *Class No:* 904(420)

[4433]

DARVILL, T. **Ancient monuments in the countryside:** an archaeological management review. London, Historic Buildings & Monuments Commission for England, 1987. viii,188p. illus., maps, plans, tables, bibliog., index. Softcover. £12.50. (*Archeological Report, no.5.*) ISBN: 1850741670.

A detailed framework for the enjoyment, preservation, and conservation of ancient monuments in rural areas ranging from prehistoric sites to 19th century industrial remains. 1. Archaeology and management (archaeological evidence; development of the countryside; resource management; legislative background) - 2/3. Semi-natural and man-made landscapes - 4. Looking forward. Appendix A: Names and addresses of archaeological organizations in England - B. Ancient Monuments and related legislation - C. Code of practice for mineral operators. Notes p.174-8. Glossary P.179-80. Bibliography p.181-8. *Class No:* 904(420)

[4434]

GREAT BRITAIN. Royal Commission on the Ancient and Historical Monuments of England. **Inventories.** London, HMSO, 1910-. illus., maps, plans.

Buckinghamshire, 2v., 1912-13. *City of Cambridge,* 2v., 1959. reprinted 1988. 500p. pbk. £35. ISBN 0113000235. *County of Cambridge,* 2v., 1968-72. *Dorset,* 5v., 1952-75. *Essex,* 4v., 1916-23. *Herefordshire,* 3v., 1931-34. *Hertfordshire,* 1911. *Huntingdonshire,* 1926. *London,* 5v., 1924-30 including v.3 *Roman London,* 1928. *Middlesex,* 1937. *Lincolnshire: Town of Stamford,* 1977. 0117007129. *County of Northamptonshire,* 6v., 1975-84. *City of Oxford,* 1939. *City of Salisbury,* v.1. 1980. 0117008494. *Gloucestershire. 1. Iron Age and Romano-British monuments in the Gloucestershire Cotswolds.* 1977. 282p. 0117007137. *Shielings and Bastles,* 1970. *Westmorland,* 1936. *City of York,* 5v., 1962-81. *County of Cambridgeshire,* v.1: *West Cambridgeshire* (1968. lxix,256p.) covers 37 civil parishes, each with village plan, description, parish church, etc. Sectional preface (natural background, building materials, ecclesiastical buildings, earthworks, etc.). Armorial index; glossary; analytical index. 120 maps, plates, ground plans. V.2: *North East Cambridgeshire.* 1972. lxvi,163p.

The Royal Commissions on Historical Monuments of England, Scotland and Wales were set up to make an inventory of the ancient and historical monuments and constructions connected with or illustrative of the contemporary culture, civilization and living conditions of ordinary people. *Class No:* 904(420)

Glossaries

[4435]

Thesaurus of archaeological site types. London, Royal Commission on the Historical Monuments of England and English Heritage, 1992. xxvi,213p. bibliog. £10. ISBN: 1873592078.

Descends from RCHME's *Thesaurus of archaeological terms* (1986).

'This thesaurus is concerned with aiding the indexing and retrieval of archaeological site type terms by establishing the relationships of the source terms and then developing these into a classification of classes' (*Introduction*). Scope: archaeological site types in England. Includes 3,000+ terms. A-Z list p.1-147. Class list p.148-213. Glossary p.xvii-xviii. Class definitions p.xx-xxi. Bibliography p.xix. *Class No:* 904(420)(038.1)

Isle of Man

[4436]

MANX MUSEUM AND NATIONAL TRUST. The Ancient and historic monuments of the Isle of Man: a general guide including a select list with notes. 4th ed. Douglas (I.of M.), Manx Museum and National Trust. 49p. illus., map, index. pbk. £0.50p. ISBN: 0901106135.

1st ed. 1958; 3rd ed. 1967.

Contents: The early history of the Isle of Man - Suggestions for further reading (p.17) - The ancient monuments - Administration in the Isle of Man - Illustrations (p.19-30) - Map of sites - The Ancient and historical monuments of the Isle of Man: a selected list with notes (p.31-47). Alphabetical index to sites. *Class No:* 904(428.9)

Wales

[4437]

GREAT BRITAIN. Cadw: Welsh Historic Monuments. A Guide to ancient and historic Wales. London, HMSO for Cadw, 1991-. illus., maps, bibliogs., index.

1. Rees, S. *Dyfed.* 1992. x,241p. illus., pbk. £11.95. ISBN 0117012203. 2. Whittle, E. *Glamorgan and Gwent.* 1992. 244p. illus. pbk. £11.95. ISBN 0117012211. 3. Lynch, F. *Gwynedd.* 1995. x,220p. pbk. £11.95. 917015741. 4. Burnham, H. *Clwyd and Powys.* 1995. x,220p. pbk. £11.95. 011701575x. Descriptive A-Z county gazetteers of sites and buildings in the care of CADW. *Dyfed* has 8 chapters: 1. Earliest prehistoric periods ... 5. Roman period ... 8. Medieval churches. Summary of dates p.218-20. Glossary p.221-4. Bibliography p.225-9. 3 maps. *Class No:* 904(429)

[4438]

GREAT BRITAIN. Royal Commission on the Ancient And Historical Monuments In Wales. **Inventories.** Cardiff, H.M. Stationery Office, 1911-.

1. *Montgomery* 1911. 2. *Flint* 1912. 3. *Radnor* 1913. 4. *Denbigh* 1914. 5. *Carmarthen* 1917 6. *Merioneth* 1921. 7. *Pembroke* 1925. 8. *Anglesey* 1937. 9. *Caenarvon* 3v., 1956-64. *Glamorgan* v.1: *Pre-Norman.* Pt.1. *The Stone and Bronze Ages.* 1976 xxx,144p. ISBN 0117005886. *Pt.2 The Iron Age and the Roman occupation.* 1976. xxx,135p.16p.pl. 0117005894. *Pt.3 The early Christian period.* 1976. xxx,80p.15p.pl. 0117005908. V.3: *Medieval secular monuments.* *Pt.1A: The early castles from the Norman Conquest to 1217.* 1991. xv,391p. 0113000359. *Pt.2.* *Non-defensive.* 1982. xxxviii,397p.44p.pl. 011701141x. V.4: *Domestic architecture from the*

....(contd.)

Reformation to the Industrial Revolution. Pt.1. The Greater houses. 1981. xl,379p. 0117007544. *Pt.2. Farmhouses and cottages.* 1988. xviii,661p. 0113000200.

11. *Brecknock. V.1: The prehistoric and Roman monuments. Part 2. Hill forts and Roman remains.* 1987. xxxii,196p. 18p.pl. £45.00. 0113000030. All volumes arranged by parishes with glossaries, numerous illustrations and maps. *Class No:* 904(429)

[4439]

GREGORY, D. Wales before 1066: a guide. Llanrwst, Gwynedd, Gwasg Carreg Gwalch, 1989. 144p. illus., maps, bibliog., index. pbk. £30. ISBN: 0863811175.

4 chronological parts, each comprising a general historical survey followed by a descriptive guide to surviving ruins and monuments: 1. Prehistoric times - 2. Roman interlude - 3. Celtic church - 4. External threats. Short bibliography p.139. 4 maps. *Class No:* 904(429)

[4440]

ROBINSON, D. Heritage in Wales : a guide to the ancient and historic sites in the care of Cadw: Welsh Historic Monuments. London, Macdonald Queen Anne Press, 1989. 208p. illus. (many col.), index. £14.95. ISBN: 0356172783.

Introduction: The work of Cadw (p.8-9) is followed by A-Z county descriptive gazetteer. Biographical notes: key historical figures p.181-7. Glossary p. 188-93. Gazetteer: the location of properties and details of access p.194-200. Bibliography (200-201) includes list of Cadw's official guidebooks. *Class No:* 904(429)

Maps & Atlases

[4441]

GREAT BRITAIN. Cadw: Welsh Historic Monuments. Map of Wales a map and gazetteer to the ancient & historic sites in the care of Cadw: Welsh Historic Monuments. Cardiff, Cadw: Welsh Historic Monuments, 1990. single sheet folded, col. illus. £1.25. ISBN: 0948329513.

A comprehensive guide to over 120 properties of major importance in the direct care of the Secretary of State for Wales. The gazetteer gives brief historic notes, details of rail and road access, and an indication of those sites with exhibitions or other displays. *Class No:* 904(429)(084.3)

Germany

Roman Times

[4442]

VON ELBE, J. *and* VON ELBE, D. Roman Germany a guide to sites and museums. Mainz, Verlag Philipp von Zabern, 1975. 523p. folding map in pocket, bibliog.

141 locations. 'More than a mere guidebook ... also a companion to the study of Roman Germany, with well-written authoritative descriptions and explanations of archaeological sites, museum holdings, and their historical significance' (D.S. and J.E. Detweiler. *West Germany,* 1987. Entry 37). *Class No:* 904(430)"0055-0449"

[4443]

—VON ELBE, J. The Romans in Cologne and Lower Germany a guide to Roman sites and monuments Düsseldorf, Ursula Preis, 1995. 204p. illus., index. ISBN: 3980441806.

A partly enlarged reissue of the chapters on Cologne in *Roman Germany* (2ed., 1977).

Aims 'to guide the non-specialised friend of Roman antiquities to selected Roman sites and monuments which because of the quality of visible remains or Roman artifacts are considered worth a visit'. List of monuments p.203-204. *Class No:* 904(430)"0055-0449"

Hungary

[4444]

Pannonia Hungarica Antiqua. Hajnóczi, G., *and others.* Budapest, Archaelingua Foundation, 1998. 121p. illus. (many col.), col. maps, plans. £14.95. ISBN: 9638046112.

3 intineraries: 1. Relics along the Road - 2. The Danube limes - 3. Internal Pannonia. Each includes topography, history, descriptions of each site and monument accessible to visitors, information of excavation or monument reconstruction, and a bibliography. Glossary p.108-121. *Class No:* 904(439)

Italy

[4445]

CARPICECI, A.C. Pompeii 2000 years ago and today. 3rd ed. Firenze, Bonechi Edizione Il Turismo, 1997. 127p. col.illus., map. index. Lire 16,000. ISBN: 8872043069.

1st ed. 1997: 2nd ed. 1991.

Introduction (*e.g.* Origins and History, Pompeii's destruction. Plan

....*(contd.)*

of typical *Domus Pompeiana* etc.) p.4-9. 100 sites described, illustrated and linked to loose map enclosed. Index of sites p.127. *Class No:* 904(450)

[4446]
COARELLI, F. Roma. 3rd ed. Milano, Mondadori, 1997. 383p. col.illus., maps, bibliog., index. (*Guide Archeologiche Mondadori.*) ISBN: 8804429461.

1st ed. 1974.

1. Le grandi opera pubbliche - 2. Il centro monumentale. 3. Le regioni augustee. Appendice: La technica edilizia e i materiali da costruzione. Imperatori romania p.369. Bibliografia p.370-77. First class guide to the antiquities of the eternal city. *Class No:* 904(450)

Bibliographies

[4447]
McILWAINE, I.C. Herculaneum: a guide to printed sources. Napoli, Bibliopolis, 2v., 1988. 1029p. maps, plans, index. L200,000. ISBN: 8870882099.

Monumental work with 3 chaps: 1. Excavation of Herculaneum - 2. Papyri - 3. Impact of the discovery - and 14 sections: 1. Source materials - 2. Campania, Naples and Vesuvius - 3. Herculaneum: history and excavation - 4. The town and its buildings - 5. People - 6. Neapolitan Academies - 7. National Museum - 8. Art in general - 9. Paintings and mosaics - 10. Sculpture - 11. Other fine and applied arts and technologies - 12. Epigraphy and wax tablets - 13. Papyri - 14. Biographical sources. 12 Appendices. Chronology p.27-29. Name and subject indexes p.917-1028. A scholarly work of high distinction. *Class No:* 904(450)(01)

Spain

[4448]
COLLINS, R. Spain. Oxford Univ. Pres, 1998. 344p. illus., maps, plans, pbk. £11.99. (*An Oxford Archaeological Guide.*) ISBN: 0192853007.

'Practical guide to over 100 of the best archeological sites in Spain, ranging from the Roman remains of Cordoba to the Islamic palace and minarets of Seville, and including on-site information about forums, temples, theatres, villas, mosques, and medieval churches. The introduction gives a brief historical and archaeological outline from the Neolithic to the medieval period. Appendices gives sites arranged by province and sites' (*publisher's announcement*). *Class No:* 904(460)

Portugal

[4449]
Subterranean Lisbon. Lisboa, Electa, 1994. 278p. illus. (many col.), maps, bibliogs.

21 contributors. 23 papers (*e.g.* The first inhabitants of the Lisbon region ... Roman and Visigothic Lisbon ... Moslem Lisbon ... Estuary of the River Tagus). Bibliography p.133-40. Plus descriptive and illustrated catalogue of 395 exhibits of the Lisbon European Capital of Culture 1994 Exhibition at the Museu Nacional de Arqueologia. Bibliography p.275-79. *Class No:* 904(469)

Asia—Near East

[4450]
CANBY, C. A Guide to the archaeological sites of Israel, Egypt and North Africa. New York and Oxford, Facts On File, 1990. vi,272p. illus., maps, plans, index. £13.95. $29.95. ISBN: 0816010544.

Description of 300+ sites in Israel, Egypt, Libya, Tunisia, Algeria and Morocco. Data: location; history and excavations; important finds; museums. Introductory essays provide a chronological framework. 'Suffers from a lack of chronological and geographic coherence and sufficient detail for the serious traveller' (*Booklist,* v.86,n o.19, 1 June 1990, p.1923-4). *Class No:* 904(56)

Maps & Atlases

[4451]
ROAF, M. Cultural atlas of Mesopotamia and the Ancient Near East. New York and Oxford, Facts On File, 1990. 238p. col. illus., col. maps, bibliog., index. £19.50. ISBN: 0816022186.

Pictorial atlas covers the geography, history, archaeology of the Near East from prehistory to 330 BC, combining text, maps and photographs in 3 parts: 1. Villages - 2. Cities - 3. Empires. Also 24 special features (*e.g.* Archaeology in the Near East ... Origins of writing ... Discovery of Mesopotamia); 20 site features (*e.g.* Jericho ... Nineveh ... Persepolis); 16 King Lists; and 46 maps. Chronological table p.8-9. Bibliography p.224. Glossary p.225. Gazetteer p.230-2. The author was Director of the British School of Archaeology in Iraq 1981-85. *Class No:* 904(56)(084.3)

Syria

[4452]
BURNS, R. Monuments of Syria a historical guide. London, I.B Tauris, 1993. 350p. illus., maps, plans. £49.50. ISBN: 1850434964.

Gazetteer and encyclopedic architectural and historical survey of al main and secondary sites and monuments. Comprehensive chronologies and glossaries. *Class No:* 904(569.1)

Bibliographies

[4453
BYBEE, H.C. *and* L'HEUREUX, C. Bibliography of Syria archaelogical sites to 1980. Lewiston, NJ., E. Mellen, 1995. 248p bibliog., indexes. $89.95. ISBN: 077349040x.

1800 entries for articles and books ordered in 3 parts: A-Z by site; topical sections; sources used in compilation. *Class No:* 904(569.1)(01)

Jordan

[4454
MAQSOOD, R. Petra: a traveller's guide. Rev. ed. Reading, Garnet 1996. x,189p. col.illus., maps, bibliog., index. £9.95. ISBN 1859640729.

1st ed. 1994.

A complete tour of the monuments, tombs and ancient religious site with 18 detailed maps of walks round the city, practical advice o accommodation, and a full account of Petra's Nabatean, Biblical an Roman history. Bibliography p.177. *Class No:* 904(569.5)

Egypt

[4455
REEVES, N. The Complete Tutankhamun: the king, the tomb, th royal treasure. 260 London, Thames & Hudson, 1990. 224p. illus (many col.), maps, bibliog., index. £15.95. ISBN: 0500050589.

1. Tutankhamun and his time - 2. Search and discovery - 3 Archaeology of the tomb - 4. Pharaoh's burial - 5. Treasures of th tomb. Chronology and family relationships p.8-9. The story of th tomb (dates of burial, discovery, and location of objects discovered p.210-1. Bibliography p.214-7. Lavishly illustrated handbook. *Class No:* 904(620)

[4456
REEVES, N. *and* WILKINSON, R.H. The Complete Valley of th Kings: tombs and treasures of Egypt's greatest pharaohs. London Thames and Hudson, 1996. 224p. illus. (some col.), maps. £19.95 ISBN: 0500050805.

Introductory sections on the geology of the Valley, planning an cutting of the tombs, archaeological discovery, followed by a guide t individual tombs. *Class No:* 904(620)

America—North

[4457
THOMAS, D.H. Exploring ancient North America an archaeologica guide. London, Routledge, 1999. 336p. pbk. £11.99. ISBN 041592359x.

Combining the latest field research with accounts of tribal life, th guide covers 400+ accessible prehistoric sites. *Class No:* 904(71+73

Mexico

[4458
COE, A. Archaeological Mexico: a traveler's guide to ancient cities an sacred sites. Chicago, Calif., Moon Publications, 1998. xvi,391p illus., maps, bibliog. $19.95. £13.99. ISBN: 1566911052.

Historical overview and step-by-step tours of 52 significant site Also hints on close-by accommodation. Suggested reading in essa form p.361-65. *Class No:* 904(72)

Latin America

Bibliographies

Internet

[445
Ancient Mesoamerican civilizations. URL:http://222.angelfire.com/c humanorigens.

Explores sites and sounds of Mesoamerica, including Aztec, May Mixtec and Zapotec cultures (archaeology, history, writing system with bibliographical references and links to other Internet sites. 'A excellent resource for various academic disciplines and a real treat f the general audience of all ages' (*Choice,* Supplement to v.36, Augu 1999, p.142). *Class No:* 904(729.99)(01)(003.41)

Australia

[4460]

LOOD, J. **The Riches of ancient Australia:** a journey into prehistory. St. Lucia, Univ. of Queensland Press, 1990. xxii,373p. illus., maps, table, index. pbk. Aust$34.95. ISBN: 0702222593.

Guide to the prehistoric sites of Australia in 20 chapters region by region. 'Each chapter summarizes the prehistory of an area and then tells where the sites are and how to reach them, well informed and well illustrated (*Antiquity*, v.65, no.248, September 1992, p.726).
Class No: 904(94)

Hawaii

[4461]

IRCH, P.V. **Legacy of the landscape** an illustrated guide to Hawaiian archaeological sites. University of Hawaii Press, 1996. 132p. illus. (5 col.), maps. $45. ISBN: 0824818164.

Authoritative handbook to 50 habitation sites, dryland agriculture complexes, petroglyphs, heiau, etc. Site locations depicted on individual island maps. *Class No:* 904(969)

Industrial Antiquities

[4462]

LFREY, J. *and* PUTNAM, T. **The Industrial heritage** managing resources and uses. London, Routledge, 1992. xii,327p. illus., bibliog., index. £40. ISBN: 041504068x.

The assessment, conservation, interpretation, financing and management of the heritage of industrial cultures. Bibliography p.310-20. *Class No:* 904:6

[4463]

ALMER, M. *and* NEAVERSON, P. **Industrial archaeology principles and practice.** London, Routledge, 1998. 180p. illus. £65. ISBN: 0415166268.

Part 1 discusses industrial archaeology's theoretical basis; defines and describes the variety of industrial landscapes, buildings, structures and machinery; and considers the social and environmental factors. Part 2 is concerned with cultural resource management: sites, documents, museums, heritage centres, and archival policies.
Class No: 904:6

Encyclopaedias

[4464]

he **Blackwell encyclopedia of industrial archaeology.** Trinder, B., *ed.* Oxford, Blackwell, 1992. xxii,964p. illus., maps, bibliogs., index. £100. ISBN: 0631142169.

59 contributors. Signed articles of varying length and ending with a list of locations and a bibliography provide a guide to the monuments, settlements, landscapes, and museums holding industrial artefacts. National articles for 31 countries: Albania, Australia, Austria, Belgium, Bulgaria, Canada, Czechoslovakia, Denmark, England, Finland, Germany, Greece, Hungary, Iceland, Ireland, Italy, Netherlands, New Zealand, Norway, Poland, Portugal, Romania, Scotland, Spain, Sweden, Switzerland, Turkey, USSR, USA, Wales, and Yugoslavia. Also biographical entries for significant industrial pioneers 1650-1950 and articles on technology in 18 subject groups (*e.g.* transport, chemicals, public utilities). Appendix: guide to contents by subject p.861-72. Bibliography p.873-930. Analytical index. Editor is Lecturer and Historical Adviser, Institute of Industrial Archaeology, Ironbridge. *Class No:* 904:6(031)

[4465]

INES, C. **Companion to the Industrial Revolution.** New York and Oxford, Facts On File, 1990. x,262p. illus., maps, tables, bibliog. ISBN: 0816021570.

Over 1000 A-Z entries (200-1000 words in length) relating to people, places, events and technological achievements of historical significance. Many entries identify places to visit or end with suggestions for further reading. Chronology (1702-1867) p.246-56.
Class No: 904:6(031)

Dictionaries

[4466]

ONES, W. **Dictionary of industrial archaeology.** Stroud, Sutton Publishing, 1996. xvii,461p. illus., diagrs., bibliogs., indexes. £40. ISBN: 0750910216.

2,600 cross-referenced entries provide clear definitions of the terms and words commonly used in industrial archaeology with full descriptions of function and design. Period covered is mainly 1750 to 1850 although, where relevant, the earlier or later history of particular industries is included. Major entries end with short bibliographies. Indexes to 31 selected industries p.441-57. General bibliography p.458-61. *Class No:* 904:6(038)

Great Britain

[4467]

COSSON, B.P. **The BP book of industrial archaeology.** 2nd ed. Newton Abbot, Devon, David & Charles, 1987. 384p. illus. bibliog. £16. ISBN: 0715389319.

First published 1975.

17 chapters: 1. Nature of industrial archaeology; 2. The industrialization of Britain; 3. Wind and water power; 4. Steam and internal combustion engines; 5. Coal; 6. Iron and steel; 7. Engineering 8. Non-ferrous metals; 9. Stone, clay and glass; 10. Textiles; 11. The chemical industries; 12. Public utilities; 13. Roads and bridges; 14. Rivers and canals; 15. Railways; 16. Ports and shipping; 17. Conclusion.

4 Appendices: 1. Gazetteer of sites p.323-350; 2. Museums of industry p.351-360; 3. Useful addresses p.361-364; 4. Bibliography p.365-376. Index p.377-384. 246 illus. 'A vast amount of information both verbal and visual, both for the casual reader and for the dedicated student' (*Industrial Archaeology Review*, v.10, no.1, Autumn 1987, p.100-101. *Class No:* 904:6(410)

[4468]

MINCHINTON, W. **Guide to industrial archaeology sites in Britain.** London, Granada, 1984. 192p. illus., maps, bibliog., index. £10.95. ISBN: 0246117818.

Almost 100 sites of major importance arranged in 7 regional sections (sub-divided by county). Lists of other sites worth visiting for each county. Bibliography p.181-3. 'Easy to follow, eminently readable and within the limited choice of sites, quite informative' (*Industrial Archaeology Review*, v.8, no.2, Spring 1986, p.217).
Class No: 904:6(410)

Gazetteers

[4469]

The National Trust guide to our industrial past. Burton, A. London, George Philip in association with The National Trust and The National Trust for Scotland, 1983. 240p. illus. (some col.), maps, bibliog. £12.50. ISBN: 0540010723.

9 chapters. Gazetteers of sites and monuments open to the public in United Kingdom arranged by modern counties p.187-226. Bibliography p.227-228; maps, p.230-234; index p.235-240. 'Everything is superficial, and nothing is treated in depth' (*Industrial Archaeology Review*, v.6, no.3, Autumn 1982, p.249-250).
Class No: 904:6(410)(083.86)

Scotland

[4470]

GREAT BRITAIN. Royal Commission on the Ancient and Historical Monuments of Scotland. **Catalogue of records, Scottish Industrial Archaeology Survey 1977-85.** Edinburgh, Royal Commission on the Ancient and Historical Monuments of Scotland, 1989. 106p. £2. ISBN: 0748003053.

1500 industrial sites arranged in 3 sections: Topographical; Industrial classification; Thematic surveys. Data: site name, industrial classification, type of site, National Grid reference, and parish or burgh. 'Whilst the book is not a comprehensive gazetteer it presents a useful record of demolished or threatened sites on mainland Scotland ... and as such will be a valuable source of reference' (*Industrial Archaeology Review*, v.12,no.2, Spring 1990, p.223-4).
Class No: 904:6(411)

[4471]

HUME, J.R. **Scotland's industrial past** an introduction to Scotland's industrial history with a catalogue of preserved material. Edinburgh, National Museums of Scotland in association with the Scottish Museums Council, 1990. vii,72p. illus., indexes. £11.95. ISBN: 094863622x.

Narrative overview of industrial collections of Scotland, Scotland's industrial history, and the Industrial Heritage - Scotland Project. Catalogue of 378 items grouped under 9 thematic sub-headings (*e.g.* textiles, engineering and shipbuilding, public utilities). Name and location indexes. *Class No:* 904:6(411)

[4472]

McDONALD, M.R., *ed*. **A Guide to Scottish industrial heritage.** Glasgow, Scottish Industrial Heritage Society, 1996. 40p. illus., maps, index. £2.95. ISBN: 095285550x.

137 sites or groups of sites (200+ in all). Also lists 37 museums with industrial exhibits. Thematic index. 'It will prove a valuable pocket guide for industrial archaeologists and represents excellent value' (*Industrial Archaeology Review*, v.19, 1997, p.109).
Class No: 904:6(411)

Northern Ireland

[4473]

McCUTCHEON, W.A. The Industrial archaeology of Northern Ireland. Belfast, HMSO; 1980. Fairleigh Dickinson, 1984. xlv, 395p. illus., tables, bibliog., indexes. £55. $75. ISBN: 0337081549, UK; 0838631258, US.

A major conspectus of the industrial history and landscape of Northern Ireland in 7 chapters each furnished with extensive notes and bibliographical references: 1. Roads and bridges - 2. Canals and internal navigations - 3. Railways - 4. Animal, wind and water power - 5. Flax and linen - 6. Tyrone coalfield - 7. Conservation and preservation. Appendix of 35 plates covers topics and themes which for lack of space could not be the subject of separate chapters. 177 figures. 156 plates. 35 tables. Author is Director of the Ulster Museum. 'This book is a major contribution ... it sets a standard of coverage and research that is very much higher than we have seen. It could prove to be a pivotal book - the trend of publishing and even of industrial archaeology itself may well come to move along new lines' (*Industrial Archaeology*, v.16, no.1, Spring 1981, p.84-89).
Class No: 904:6(416)

England

[4474]

INSTITUTION OF CIVIL ENGINEERS. The Civil Engineering Heritage Series. London, Thomas Telford Services, 4v., 1996.
1. Northern England. 2nd ed. 1996. £12.50. ISBN 027725181; 2. Southern England. 199? £12.50. 0727719718; 3. Eastern & Central England. 199? £12.50. 072771970x; 4. Wales & Western England. 2nd ed. 1997. £8.75. 072770236x. Expert guidebooks for exploring the principal landmarks of British engineering history.
Class No: 904:6(420)

Bibliographies

[4475]

GREENWOOD, J. Industrial archaeology and industrial history series. Cranfield, Kewdale Press, 1985-.
1. *Industrial archeology and industrial history of Northern England: a bibliography.* 1985. 300p. index. ISBN 0951038907. 3050 entries in 7 regional chapters. 2. *-of the English Midlands: a bibliography.* 1987. 410p. index. 0951038915. 3. *-of London: a bibliography.* 1988. 259p. index. 0951038923. 4. *-of South-eastern England: a bibliography.* 1990. 450p. indexes. 0951038931. 5151 numbered entries (books and articles from 420 periodicals). *Class No: 904:6(420)(01)*

Gazetteers

[4476]

ALDERTON, D. *and* BOOKER, J. The Batsford guide to the industrial archaeology of East Anglia: Cambridgeshire. Essex. Norfolk. Suffolk. London, B.H. Batsford, 1980. 192p. illus., maps, bibliog., index. (*The Batsford Guide to the Industrial Archaeology of the British Isles.*) ISBN: 0713422335.
Introductory chapter p.13-34 relates the region's basic changes in industries, communications and economic structure. Descriptive gazetteer A-Z by county. Bibliography p.181-183. Glossary p.183. Index of sites by industry p.184-192. 65 photographs, 5 maps.
Class No: 904:6(420)(083.86)

[4477]

ASHMORE, O. The Industrial archaeology of North-west England. Manchester, Manchester Univ. Press, 1982. 241p. illus., maps., bibliog., index. £9.95. ISBN: 0719008204.
Descriptive gazetteer of industrial archaeological sites in 4 A-Z sequences: Cheshire, Greater Manchester, Merseyside, and Lancashire selected to illustrate their range and type, geographical distribution, and historical development. Bibliography (by industrial type) p.230-235. Subject index. 'The publisher can fairly claim that this is an essential reference gazetteer for enthusiasts, students, teachers, planners and environmentalists' (*British Book News*, January 1883, p.35). *Class No: 904:6(420)(083.86)*

[4478]

A Brief guide to the industrial heritage of West Yorkshire. Thompson, W.J., *ed.* Telford, Salop, Association for Industrial Archaeology, 1989. 52p. illus., maps, bibliog. sd. ISBN: 0950844837.
5 contributors. Essays and descriptive gazetteer of sites for Calderdale, Kirklees, Bradford, Leeds, and Wakefield. Bibliography inside back cover. Published on the occasion of the Association's annual conference in Huddersfield in 1989.
Class No: 904:6(420)(083.86)

[4479]

BROOK, F. The Industrial archaeology of the British Isles 1. The West Midlands: Hereford-Worcester. Shropshire. Staffordshire. Warwickshire. West Midlands. London, B.T. Batsford, 1977. 223p. illus., maps, diagrs., bibliog., index. (*The Industrial Archaeology of the British Isles.*) ISBN: 071340924x.
Introduction (p.15-39) surveys the region's major industries. A-Z gazetteer of 1200 sites in 5 county sequences. Bibliography p.211-213. *Class No: 904:6(420)(083.86)*

[4480]

DAY, J. A Guide to the industrial heritage of Avon and its borders. Telford, Shropshire, Association for Industrial Archaeology, 1987. 51p. (inc. covers). illus., maps, bibliog., index. sd.
Descriptive gazetteer of 268 sites grouped in 10 area sections vi Bath; Bristol; Bristol Port; Kingsdown; Northavon; Wansdyke; Woodspring; Gloucester; Wiltshire and Somerset borders. Bibliography p.50. Subject index. Published on the occasion of the Association for Industrial Archaeology's annual conference, University of Bath, September 1987. *Class No: 904:6(420)(083.86)*

[4481]

HASELFOOT, A.J. The Batsford guide to the industrial archaeology of South-East England: Kent Surrey East Sussex West Sussex. London B.T. Batsford, 1978. 152p. illus., maps, bibliog., index. (*The Batsford Guide to the Industrial Arcaeology of the British Isles.*) ISBN 0713415614.
Introduction surveys extractive industries, power supplies and services, transport, and miscellaneous industries. Gazetteer A-Z by county. Bibliography p.147-148. Glossary p.149. 65 photographs. maps. Unfavourable review in *Industrial Archaeology Review* v.3, no.3, Summer 1979, p.276 which concludes 'nevertheless it is worth buying .. because it does draw attention to a number of interesting sites'. *Class No: 904:6(420)(083.86)*

[4482]

WRIGHT, N.R. A Guide to the industrial archaeology of Lincolnshire including South Humberside. Telford, Shropshire, Association for Industrial Archaeology and The Society for Lincolnshire History and Archaeology, 1983. 40p. (inc. covers). illus., maps, bibliog. sd. 95p ISBN: 0903582007.
A-Z gazetteer of sites and museums at 97 locations. Bibliography p.3-4. Published on the occasion of the Association for Industrial Archaeology's annual conference, Lincoln, September 1983.
Class No: 904:6(420)(083.86)

Wales

[4483]

KEEN, R. 'The Archaeology of industrial Wales', *Industrial Archaeology Review*, vol.17, no.1, Autumn 1995, p.63-82. illus. bibliog.
Overview of Welsh industrial archaeology covering iron, steel and tinplate; coal; slate; metal mining; transport; and the landed estate. Bibliog. p.82-83. *Class No: 904:6(429)*

Gazetteers

[4484]

HUGHES, S. *and* REYNOLDS, P. Industrial archaeology of the Swansea region. Telford, Shropshire, Association for Industrial Archaeology, in association with the Royal Commission of Ancient and Historical Monuments in Wales and the South West Wales Industrial Archaeology Society, 1988. 55p. (inc. covers) illus. maps bibliog. sd. £1.95. ISBN: 0950844829.
Gazetteer of 173 sites arranged in industrial groups. Site plan p.28-29. Bibliography, museums and conservation societys, p.55. Published for the Association for Industrial Archaeology's Annual Conference Swansea, 1988. *Class No: 904:6(429)(083.86)*

Netherlands

[4485]

NIJHOF, P. 'Industrial archaeology in the Netherlands' *Industrial Archaeology Review*, v.13, no.2, Spring 1991 p.103-13.
Early days - Involvement of local institutions - Surveys and documentation ... Museums - Company archives. Appendix: Classification of industrial and technological monuments.
Class No: 904:6(492)

Belgium

[4486]

BAETENS, R. Industrielle archeologie in Vlaanderen :theorie en praktijk. Antwerpen, Standard Uitgeverij, 1988. 271p. illus. Fr.198? ISBN: 9002152787.
Contents: definitions, methodology and progress of industrial archaeology since 1965 - documentary and other sources - list of

....(contd.)

monuments classified by industry - provincial case studies. Favourably reviewed in *Industrial Archaeology Review*, v.12, no.1, Autumn 1988, p.101-102. *Class No:* 904:6(493)

South Africa

[4487]

HARRIS, D.E. 'Some notes on the industrial archaeology of South Africa', *Industrial Archaeology*, 1980, p.359-365.
Class No: 904:6(680)

New Zealand

[4488]

THORNTON, G. 'Industrial archaeology in New Zealand' *Industrial Archaeology Review*, v.10, no.1, Autumn 1987, p.23-39. 26 plates, map, refs.
Review of the industrial archaeology of 18 industries plus a final section on the present position of industrial archaeological studies.
Class No: 904:6(931)

Australia

[4489]

DONNACHIE, I. 'Industrial archaeology in Australia'. *Industrial Archaeology Review*, v.5, no.2, Spring 1981, p.96-113. illus. refs.
'Examines something of the development and progress of industrial archaeology in Australia, the recording of its industrial heritage, the range of survivals, the achievements in excavation and conservation, the work of museums and universities, and the growing volume of literature.' 38 refs. *Class No:* 904:6(94)

[4490]

DONNACHIE, J. 'The industrial heritage of Australia and New Zealand': an essay in bibliography and criticism, *Industrial Archaeology Review*, v.7, no.2, Spring 1985, p.200-209. illus. refs.
Review article of recent works of note. *Class No:* 904:6(94)

Institutions & Associations

[4491]

'Industrial Archaeology institutions and societies' *Industrial Archaeology* Index to v.1-15. (1964-1980).1984.
Directory and activity information of 17 of the most influential institutions, associations and societies. *Class No:* 904:6:061:061.2

908 Area Studies

Worldwide

[4492]

CENTRAL INTELLIGENCE AGENCY. **The World factbook 1998.**
Washington, Central Intelligence Agency, 1998. xx,639. maps, tables.
£98. ISBN: 002881052x.

Sourcebook of important CIA unclassified data on 266 nations,
dependent areas, and other geographical and geopolitical entities
arranged A-Z providing basic information on each country's area,
climate, recent international disputes, natural resources, environment,
population, inflation rate, GDP, agriculture, industry, defence
expenditure, national holidays, literacy rate, legal system, and labour
force. Appendixes: A. United Nations system ... C. International
Organizations and Groups ... H. Cross-reference list of geographical
names.

Also available on CD-ROM as part of the *National Trade Data
Bank*. *Class No:* 908(100)

[4493]

—World factbook. URL:http://www.odci.gov/cia/publications/factbook/
index.html

Minor flaws (noted in *Choice,* Supplement to v.36, August 1999,
p.68) include the frame may cut off words in the introductory matter;
the home page is not well worded; and clicking on the large World
Factbook graphic can inadvertently hit the CIA home page.
Class No: 908(100)

[4494]

Guinness world fact book. Carpenter, C., *ed.* Enfield, Mdx., Guinness,
1994. 448p. tables, index. £14.99. ISBN: 0851127983.

Review of state of the world in mid-1990s arranged A-Z by country
within 12 regional sections (*e.g.* Africa south of the Sahara ...
Commonwealth of Independent States ... Southern and Antarctic
Territories) and World political figures (biographies of Heads of State
and others). Factual data on government, geography, economy and
recent history plus special short essays on topics of world importance
(*e.g.*Trading blocks, Population trends). *Class No:* 908(100)

[4495]

NOLAN, C.J. **The Longman guide to world affairs.** New York,
Longman Publishers USA, 1998. vi+24p. maps, 450p. softcover.
£13.99.

4,600 cross-referenced A-Z entries cover historical and
contemporary affairs, law, organisations, wars and world crises, and
political geography, and profiles of leading political figures.
Class No: 908(100)

[4496]

SEGAL, G. **The World affairs companion** the essential one-volume
guide to global issues. 3rd ed. London, Simon & Schuster, 1991.
xxiv,310p. maps, tables, bibliogs., index. pbk. £8.99; $24.95.

Overview of world affairs since 1945 concentrating on current issues
in a series of c.1000 word essays arranged in 9 subdivided thematic
and regional sections: 1. Power of politics - 2. Shaping the new agenda
- 3. Modern warfare - 4. The new Europe ... 8. The Middle East - 9.
Africa. Section bibliographies. *Class No:* 908(100)

[4497]

The World today a nation-by-nation guide. Spence, J.E., *ed.* London,
Cassell, 1994. 256p. illus. (many col.), col.maps, bibliog., index.
£18.99. ISBN: 0304344842.

26 contributors. Analyses of the political, economic, social and
cultural trends of each of the world's 100 largest countries arranged in
5 regional sections. A data panel for each country includes map, flag,
chronology of events from 1900, national statistics, and outline of
constitution. Smaller countries included in regional gazetteers.
Glossary of international organisations p.248-49. Bibliography p.250.
Editor is Director of Studies at the Royal Institute of International
Affairs. *Class No:* 908(100)

Internet

[4498]

NativeWeb. URL:http://www.nativeweb.org/

Orignally focussed on North America when launched in 1994 but
now extended to indigenous peoples worldwide. 3 links from Home
Page: 1. Resource Center (searchable by geographic region, keywords,
genealogy etc.) - 2. Communication Center (news, events calendar) -
3. General information (history and description of NativeWeb). 'One
of the more stable and frequently updated sites on the Web that deal
with indigenous peoples' (*Choice,* Supplement to v.36, August 1999,
p.168). *Class No:* 908(100)(003.41)

Encyclopaedias

[4499]

KURIAN, G.T., *ed.* **The Encyclopedia of the First World.** New York
and Oxford, Facts On File, 2v., 1990. 1436p. maps, tables, bibliogs.
£145. ISBN: 0816012334.

Detailed country by country coverage of the world's 26 most
economically advanced countries. Each country is profiled in terms of
its geographical features, climate and weather, population, ethnic
composition, languages, religion, historical background, constitution
and government, political parties, manufacturing, mining, energy,
foreign commerce, defense, legal system and law enforcement,
freedom and human rights, *etc.* *Class No:* 908(100)(031)

[4500]

NESS, I. **Encyclopedia of world cities.** Chicago and London, Fitzroy
Dearborn, 1999. xvii,739p. maps, tables, bibliog., index. £95. ISBN:
1579581315.

132 city profiles comprising a full-page map, a text divided into 10
key areas (*e.g.*location, history, government and politics), and a
statistical factbox, for each city. Bibliography p.695-97. Analytical
index. 'Shrieks out for shelf space in large public and academic
libraries' (*Reference Reviews,* v.13, no.8, 1999, p.37).
Class No: 908(100)(031)

[4501]

Worldmark encyclopedia of the nations: a practical guide to the
geographic, historical, political, social & economic status of all
nations, their international relationships, and the United Nations
system. Gall, T.L., *ed.* 9th ed. Detroit, Gale Reference, 5v., 1998.
2573p. illus., maps (some col.), bibliogs., index. £265. ISBN:
0787600741.

First published in 1v., 1960.

V.1: United Nations; v.2 Africa; v.3 Americas; v.4 Asia & Oceania;
v.5 Europe. Comprehensive geographic, historical, political, and
economic data on 202 nations and 80 dependencies arranged under 50
numbered headings e.g., 1. Location - 2. Topography ... 12. History
... 47. Tourism - 48. Famous persons ... 50. Bibliography. 200 maps.
A master index is provided at the end of each volume.
Class No: 908(100)(031)

Databases

[4502]

Countries of the world encyclopedia. Bureau of Electronic Publishing
Inc. IBM Compatible PC, XT, AT, PS/2, VGA Card, Apple
Macintosh Classic, SE, II, MS-DOS 3.1 or higher. Apple 640K
(DOS); 1Mb (Mac), networkable. $395.

Over 60,000 pages detailing world history, culture and economy.
Includes in depth country analyses written by US State Department.
Class No: 908(100)(031)(003.4)

Handbooks & Manuals

[4503]

Cities of the world: a compilation of current information on cultural,
geographical, and political conditions in the countries and cities of six
continents. 5th ed. Detroit, Gale Research Co., 4v., 1998. 4016p.
illus., maps. index. £245. ISBN: 0810376911, set.

1st published in 1982. Based on official briefings issued as *Post
reports* by the US Department of State.

1. *Africa.* 081037692x. 2. *Western Hemisphere (excluding US,*
0810376938. 3. *Europe and the Mediterranean Middle East.*
0810376946. 4. *Asia, the Pacific, and the Asiatic Middle East.*
0810376954. 177 background country articles cover social, political
and economic conditions, population, history, commerce and industry
etc. With reports on 507 major + 2900 smaller cities. Cumulative
index in v.4. *Class No:* 908(100)(035)

[4504]

UNITED STATES. Department of The Army. **Country studies**
Washington, Federal Research Division, Library of Congress 1957-
(*Area Handbook Series/American Univ. Foreign Area Studies*).

109 volumes on individual countries, some now in revised editions.
The series aims 'to provide a compact and objective composition and
analysis of the dominant social, political and economic characteristic
... Topics covered include: government, population, topography,
language, religion, health, climate, justice, economics, trade,
communications, transportation, international affairs, and armed
forces'. Volumes include *Afghanistan; Albania; Algeria; Angola;
Argentina; Australia; Austria; Bangladesh; Belgium; Bolivia; Brazil*

....(contd.)

Bulgaria; Burma; Burundi; Cambodia; Cameroon; Chad; Chile; China; Republic of China; Colombia; Congo; Costa Rica; Cuba; Cyprus; Czechoslovakia; Dominican Republic; Ecuador; Egypt; El Salvador; Ethiopa; Finland; East Germany; Federal Republic of Germany; Ghana; Greece; Guatemala; Guinea; Guyana; Haiti; Honduras; Hungary; India; Indian Ocean; Indonesia; Iran; Iraq; Israel; Italy; Ivory Coast; Jamaica; Japan; Jordan; Kenya; North Korea; South Korea; Laos; Lebanon; Libya; Malawi; Malaysia; Mauritania; Mexico; Mongolia; Mozambique; Morocco; Nepal; Bhutan; Sikkim; Nicaragua; Nigeria; Oceania; Pakistan; Panama; Paraguay; Persian Gulf States; Peru; Philippines; Poland; Portugal; Romania; Rwanda; Saudi Arabia; Senegal; Sierra Leone; Singapore; Somalia; South Africa; Soviet Union; Spain; Sri Lanka; Sudan; Syria; Tanzania; Thailand; Trinidad & Tobago; Tunisia; Turkey; Uganda; Uruguay; Venezuela; North Vietnam; South Vietnam; The Yemens; Yugoslavia; Zaire; Zambia. *Class No:* 908(100)(035)

[4505]
—The Library of Congress: country studies. URL:http://lcweb2.loc.gov/frd/cs/cshome.html.

85 country studies. 'Overall, this site is visually appealing, quite easy, and compact, yet it offers a number of links to other locations ... This superb literary resource should be bookmarked widely' (*Choice*, Supplement to v.36, August 1999, p.158). *Class No:* 908(100)(035)

Yearbooks & Directories

[4506]
The Europa world year book, 2000. 41st ed. London, Europa Publications, 2v., 2000. 4100p. maps, tables, index. £450. ISBN: 1857430751, (set). ISSN: 09562273.

First published 1926. Under various titles, latterly *Europa yearbook: a world survey*. From 1960 as an annual publication in 2v.

V.1: includes 1,650 International Organisations *e.g.* The United Nations ... The Commonwealth ... European Communities (data: history, publications, and directory type information) and Countries Afghanistan-Jordan. V.2: Countries Kazakstan-Zimbabwe. Country surveys follow a set pattern: 1. Introductory survey covering recent history and economic affairs, social welfare and brief geographical details - 2. Statistical survey - 3. Directory information on the constitution, government legislature, political organizations, diplomatic representation, judicial system, religion, press, radio and television, finance, trade and industry, transport, tourism, atomic energy. 'A consistently reliable and comprehensive reference work, essential to both general and special libraries *International Affairs*, v.61, no.4, Autumn 1985, p.737). *Class No:* 908(100)(058)

[4507]
LEVY, C.J. *and* **SCHULTZ, J.D. Global links** a guide to key people and institutions worldwide. London, Fitzroy Dearborn, 1998. ix,177p. indexes.

Published in US by The Oryx Press. $59.95. ISBN 1573562246.

Entries A-Z by country. Data: executives (president, prime minister, first deputy prime minister), minister/ministries (from agriculture to youth), legislative leaders, judicial leaders, selected diplomats (ambassador to US, ambassador to UN, US embassies), major political parties, central bank, media and communication, contact information (name, address, telephone and fax numbers, Web site address, e-mail addresses). 2 indexes: 1. Web sites- 2. Heads of State. *Class No:* 908(100)(058)

[4508]
The Statesman's year-book the politics, cultures and economies of the world 2000. Turner, B. 136th ed. London, Macmillan Reference Books, 1999. xxxii,2024p. tables, diagrs., col. graphs, maps. ISBN: 0333733355.

Published annually since 1864.

Pt.1. International organizations (p.3-115). Pt.2. 192 Countries of the world A-Z. New and improved features reported in this edition include Thoroughly revised content, Specially commissioned essays from major political and academic figures, New statistics revealing internet usage, number of PC's and mobile phones, Considerably increased coverage of social statistics and trends, and Extended bibliography for each entry. Chronology p.xv-xxvi *Class No:* 908(100)(058)

[4509]
—Statesman's year book centenary collection. London, Macmillan, 2000. Boxed set of 2v. £125. ISBN: 0333801814.

A copy of the 2000 edition together with a facsimile of the 1900 edition. *Class No:* 908(100)(058)

[4510]
—Statesman's yearbook factbooks. London, Macmillan, 1999-. £14.99.

Single-volume profiles of individual countries and regions complementing and augmenting information available in *The Statesman's Yearbook*. 1999 titles: *China profiled* 0333780582; *France profiled* 0333780566; *Germany profiled* 0333780558; *Italy profiled* 033780574. Further titles planned for this series include Eastern Europe, Southern Africa, Latin America, Scandinavia, Russia, Japan, Benelux, and USA. *Class No:* 908(100)(058)

[4511]
—The World Today essential facts in an ever changing world 2000. London, Macmillan, 2000. 1097p. £14.99. ISBN: 0333792254.

Derived from the database of Stateman's yearbook. 'Makes no acknowledgement of its illustrious origins; it offers no preliminaries nor index; it would benefit greatly from a simple map for each country; it contains few statistics; and it manages to ignore international organisations completely. Perhaps most disappointingly of all, it fails to give suggestions for further reading' (*Library Association Record* v.102, no.5, May 2000, p.283). But, 'there is likely to be little doubt about the quality and authoritativeness of the contents'. *Class No:* 908(100)(058)

[4512]
Worldmark yearbook 2000. Chicago, Gale Group, 2v., 2000. c.3000p. $275. £173.25. ISBN: 0787649317.

Approximately 230 countries and territories with comprehensive features including statistical surveys; detailed directories of political, social and economic entities; and a bibliography. Flags and colour emblems, regional maps and black-and-white country maps in regional context are included. Volume 1 begins with an introductory essay that summarizes the major international events of the past year. Country A-Z entries follow. Volume 2 provides a comprehensive directory of international organizations with brief descriptions and extensive contact information, including 3-mail and internet home pages as available. *Class No:* 908(100)(058)

Nomenclatures

[4513]
WILCOCKS, J. Countries and islands of the world a guide to nomenclature. 2nd ed. London, Clive Bingley, 1985. vii, 124p. bibliog. £11.50. ISBN: 0851573835.

First published 1981.

'A reference guide to the many changes in name and government in states all over the world in modern historical times'. *Class No:* 908(100)(083.72)

Maps & Atlases

[4514]
BOYD, A. An Atlas of world affairs. 10th ed. London, Routledge, 1998. 252p. maps, index. £35. ISBN: 0415106710.

1st ed. 1957 published by Methuen; 9th ed. by Routledge in 1991.

Arranged in 10 thematic sections (*e.g.* oil, nuclear geography) and 63 geo-political sections (*e.g.* Russia's territorial gains, Northern Seas, Suez and Indian Ocean). Long-serving general guide to international affairs since 1945. New issues covered in this edition include the break-up of the Soviet Union, Czechoslovakia, the expansion of the European Union, and the new order in South Africa. *Class No:* 908(100)(084.3)

Biographies

[4515]
HAMILTON, N.A. Founders of modern nations. Santa Barbara, Calif., ABC-Clio, 1995. xviii,505p. illus., maps, bibliog., index. £24.95. ISBN: 0874367506.

A-Z biographical entries for the dominant military, political and intellectual figures largely responsible for the founding of modern nation states (p.3-423). Country profiles p.424-62. Chronology p.463-64. Bibliography p.473-82. 6 maps. *Class No:* 908(100)(092)

Asian Races

Encyclopaedias

[4516]
The Encyclopedia of the Chinese overseas. Pan, L., *ed.* Singapore, Archipelago Press and Landmark Books, 1998. 399p. illus. (many col.), tables, maps, bibliog., index. ISBN: 9183018925.

Published under the aegis of the Chinese Heritage Centre in Singapore, founded by the Singapore Federation of Chinese Clan Associations in 1995. Published in UK by Curzon, 1999. 0700711228.

53 contributors from East and West. Profiles of 37 Chinese communities in Southeast Asia, The Americas, Australasia - Oceania, Europe, Africa, and the Indian Ocean area, their relations with China, plus introductory chapters on their origins, migration patterns,

....(contd.)

institutions, and inter-ethnic relations. Timelines (an illustrated chronology) p.364-67. Bibliography p.375-87.
Class No: 908(100)(=95)(031)

Atlantic Ocean

Bibliographies

[4517]

KING, H.G.R. **Atlantic Ocean.** Santa Barbara, California and Oxford, Clio Press, 1985. xix, 250p.+2p. map, index. £36.50. $41.50. (*World Bibliographical Series; no. 61*.) ISBN: 1851090045.

913 annotated entries. 16 sections: The Atlantic region in general - History - The Atlantic as a strategic military area and contemporary foreign relations ... Tourism ... Research institutions, libraries, art galleries, museums and archives ... Atlantic islands in general - North Atlantic Islands - South Atlantic islands. Author, title and subject index. *Class No:* 908(261)(01)

Pacific Ocean

Bibliographies

[4518]

MAURICIO, R., *comps.* **Pacific Basin and Oceania.** Fry, G.W. Santa Barbara, California and Oxford, Clio Press, 1987. xxxvi, 468p. + 2p. maps, index. £64.95; $55.00. (*World Bibliographical Series, no.70.*) ISBN: 1851090150.

1178 annotated entries. 38 sections: The Pacific region in general - History - Law of the sea ... Tourism and travel accounts - Small boat voyages - Periodicals - Research institutions, libraries and archives - The Pacific Islands in general - Prehistory and archaeology - Geography - History ... Libraries, archives, and museums - Periodicals - Bibliographies - Contemporary foreign relations - Melanesia - The islands of Melanesia - Micronesia - The islands of Micronesia - Polynesia - The islands of Polynesia - Other Pacific Islands. Single author, title, subject index. *Class No:* 908(265)(01)

Indian Ocean

Bibliographies

[4519]

GOTTHOLD, J.J., *comp.* **Indian Ocean.** Santa Barbara, California and Oxford, Clio Press, 1988. xxix, 329p.+2p., map, index. £47.95. $55.00. (*World Bibliographical Series; no.85.*) ISBN: 1851090347.

804 annotated entries. 12 sections: The Indian Ocean in general - History (8 subdivisions) ... Atlases, maps and charts ... Encyclopaedias, yearbooks, indexes and gazetteers ... Bibliographies - Indian Ocean island groups. *Class No:* 908(267)(01)

Ancient Greece & Rome

[4520]

METZ, D. **Famous firsts in the ancient Greek and Roman World.** Jefferson, NC., McFarland, 2000. 154p. bibliog., indexes. £26.25. ISBN: 0786405996.

Covering the period from the earliest times to the 2nd Century A.D., this volume ranges over all recorded aspects of the Classical World, and is arranged in 6 thematic sections: 1. Mythological firsts - 2. Politics, law, oratory, government - 3. Military and foreign affairs - 4. Art, architecture, literature, science - 5. Miscellaneous (*e.g.*sport, the stage, clothing) - 6. Innovations and inventions of noted individuals. Bibliography p.137-140. *Class No:* 908(37/38)

Developing Countries

Encyclopaedias

[4521]

Encyclopedia of the Third World. Kurian, G.T. 4th ed. New York, Facts on File, 3v., 1992. lv,2363p. illus., diagrs., tables, maps, bibliog., index. £125. ISBN: 0816022615.

First published in 2v. 1979; revised edition 3v. 1981.

Europa year-book type data and discursive text describing the dominant political, economic and social systems of 126 countries A-Z. Bibliography p.2241-56. *Class No:* 908(4/9-77)(031)

Handbooks & Manuals

[4522]

ARNOLD, G. **Third World Handbook.** London, Cassell, New York, St. James Press 1994. 221p. illus., maps. index. £35. ISBN: 0304328375, UK.

9 chapters: 1. End of empires - 2. The United Nations - 3. The Third World and non-alignment - 4. The (six) regional groupings (p.56-136) - 5. Aid and its agencies - 6. OPEC and oil power - 7. A new international economic order - 8. The population factor - 9. Resources and exploitation. Country gazetteers (statistical informtion) p.189-205. *Class No:* 908(4/9-77)(035)

[4523]

The World guide 1999/1000 a view from the South. Bissio, R., *ed.* Millennium ed. Montevideo, Instituto del Tercer Mundo;Oxford, New Internationalist Publications, 1999. 631p. maps, diagrs., tables, bibliog., index. £24.95. ISBN: 1869847687.

First published published in Mexico as *Guia de tercer mundo* (1979). First English language edition as *Third World guide* (1986). Previous ed. 1997.

Global issues. An overview of the Twentieth Century (81 topics gathered under 5 subject headings: 1. The earth and its people - 2. Society - 3. Science and Technology - 4. Economics - 5. International Relations) followed by 217 country profiles consisting of map, graphic charts of public expenditure, workers, land use etc., with accompanying text on its environment, society and the state, and with statistics on demography, health, education, communications, economy and energy (p.85-601). Bibliography p.602-604. Review of the major environmental, social and technological and economic trends of the century. 'Can be characterized as a *Europa Yearbook* written from a Third World perspective. Clearly, it does not provide an objective treatment, but libraries seeking an alternative perspective may find this volume useful.' (*Booklist*, v.86, no.12, 15 February 1990, p.119). *Class No:* 908(4/9-77)(035)

Dictionaries

[4524]

HADJOR, K.B. **Dictionary of Third World terms.** London, I.B. Tauris, 1992. 303p. £24.95. ISBN: 1850433461.

Additional entries in *Penguin dictionary of Third World Terms.* 1993. £6.99. 0140512934.

Entries include short factual items, biographical data on key Third World figures, information on economic and social realities, and discursive and critical summaries of controversial words and concepts. *Class No:* 908(4/9-77)(038)

[4525]

KURIAN, G.T. **Glossary of the Third World:** words for understanding Third World peoples and cultures. New York and Oxford, Facts On File,1989. 300p. $45.00. ISBN: 0816018421.

This A-Z list of mostly non-English terms is intended 'to survey, explore, and illustrate the rich variety of Third World cultures' and to complement the author's *Encyclopedia of the Third World*. Its organization, conceptual basis, and contents are described as limited in *Choice* (v.27, no.3, November 1988, p.466). *Class No:* 908(4/9-77)(038)

Maps & Atlases

[4526]

Atlas of the Third World. Kurian, G. 2nd ed. New York and Oxford, Facts on File, 1989. 400p. maps, tables, bibliog., index. $175.00. ISBN: 0816019304.

1st ed. 1983. Companion to *Encyclopaedia of the Third World*.

Comprehensive selection of maps and statistical information in graphic form. 1. Introduction provides a review and interpretation of the data presented - 2. Thematic profiles: 14 topics identified as critical issues in Third World development - 3. 80 Country profiles A-Z concentrating on natural resources, population, and social and economic performance. Over 600 maps and 2000 charts and graphs. 'Because of the mamy revisions and the new countries that were not in existence in 1982, the *Encyclopedia* is a worthwhile purchase even for libraries that own the earlier edition. The dynamic conditions in much of the Third World merit the publication and purchase of a new edition every five years'. (*Reference Books Bulletin 1987-1988*, p.140). *Class No:* 908(4/9-77)(084.3)

Europe

[4527]

DROST, H. **What's what and who's who in Europe** the pre-eminent factbook on people, places, organizations, events and terms across Europe. London, Cassell, 1995. x,646p. £40. ISBN: 0304341177.

4,500+ entries on people, places, organizations, movements etc. including country profiles (geography, population, economy, trade, political structure, armed forces, alliances and history), technical terms and concepts. Excludes countries formerly part of the Soviet Union. *Class No:* 908(4)

[4528]
The Guinness European data book. Enfield, Mdx., Guinness Publishing, 1994. 192p. col.illus., (flags), col.maps. £11.99. ISBN: 0851125239.

Compendium of essential information, facts, and analyses of all 45 European countries (official data; government, cabinet, geography, economics, recent history etc.) plus general sections of continental importance (*e.g.*European Community, Treaty of Maastricht, Social Policy, urbanization, health care, labour force, regional policy etc.).
Class No: 908(4)

Europe—Western

Yearbooks & Directories
[4529]
Western Europe 2000. 3rd ed. London, Europa, 1999. 660p. maps, tables, bibliogs. £255. (*Regional Surveys of the World.*) ISBN: 1857430662. ISSN: 09536906.

1st ed. 1989.

Section 1. Background to the region (essays presenting an overview of important and topical issues relating to the region as a whole). Section 2. Country surveys of 32 countries and territories detailing the country's geographical, political and economic background. An at-a-glance historical chronology for each country is new to this edition. 'In an otherwise increasingly crowded market the Europa titles continue to stand out ... the sheer breadth, depth and quality of their coverage'. *Reference Reviews*, v.14, no.3,2000, p.47-48).
Class No: 908(400)(058)

Europe—Eastern

Bibliographies
[4530]
The American bibliography of Slavic and East European studies. New York, M.E. Sharpe, 1972 - Annual, $100. ISBN: 156324750x. ISSN: 00943770.

Succeeds *American bibliography of Russian and East European studies*, 1955-66 (Bloomington, Indiana Univ., 1957-67, 11v.).

1993 (1996). 632p. Citation source for North American scholarship on Eastern and Central Europe, the Balkans, the Baltic states, and the former Soviet Union. Bibliographies are arranged by discipline subdivided by geographical regions. Citations are to books, journal articles, government and research reports, dissertations, and book reviews. *Class No:* 908(401)(01)

[4531]
Bibliographic guide to Slavic, Baltic, and Eurasian studies 1978-1994. New York, G.K. Hall, 1978-. Annual.

Previously published as *Bibliographic guide to Soviet and East European studies*.

1994 (3v. 1995). 1800p. $666 ISBN 073821964 lists all publications on or from the former Soviet Union and Eastern Europe catalogued during the past year by the Research Libraries of New York Public Library with additional entries from LC MARC tapes. It is, in effect, an annual supplement to the New York Public Library's *Dictionary catalog of the Slavonic Collection* (2nd ed. G.K. Hall, 1974, 44v).
Class No: 908(401)(01)

[4532]
MAGOCSI, P.R. Carpatho-Rusyn studies: an annotated bibliography. New York, Garland, 1988-. viii, 143p. maps, index. (*Garland Reference Library of The Humanities; no. 824.*) ISBN: 0824058364.

V.1 *1975-1984* (1988). V.2 planned for publication 1995. 649 extensively annotated entries arranged on an annalistic basis. 4 Appendices: Transliteration tables; Language, subject and places of publication. The Carpatho-Rusyn area is defined as far western Ukraine, the Lemko region of Poland, the Prešov region of north-east Czechoslovakia, and the Vojvodinian villages of Yugoslavia. The present intention is for future volumes to appear at 10 year intervals.
Class No: 908(401)(01)

[4533]
Slavic studies a guide to bibliographies, encyclopedias, and handbooks. Croucher, M., *comps.* Wilmington, Delaware, Scholarly Resources, 2v., 1993. xiv,986p. ISBN: 0842023747.

5210 items relating to Slavic studies in English, German, French and Slavic languages. Vol.1: Area studies, Eastern Europe and the Balkans, Bulgaria, Czechoslovakia, Poland. Vol.2: Soviet Union, Former Yugoslavia, General references. Author and title indexes. 'It contains only reference works that, arranged by subject, allow researchers to find materials in their areas of interest without having to know the author or title of any specific work' (*Introduction*).
Class No: 908(401)(01)

Encyclopaedias
[4534]
Encyclopedia of the Second World. Kurian, G. *and* Karch, J., *eds.* New York and Oxford, Facts On File, 1991. 614p. maps,. charts, tables, bibliog., index. $95. £85. ISBN: 0816012326.

National profiles (at Janaury 1990) of Albania, Bulgaria, China, Czechoslovakia, East Germany, Hungary, Mongolia, Poland, Rumania, Soviet Union, and Yugoslavia, provide information on over 30 subject fields (*e.g.* geographical features, historical background, human rights, defence, foreign policy). By virtue of unfortunate timing now largely outdated by events although it remains 'a valuable source of historical information on the rise and reign of communism in these eleven countries' (*Wilson Library Bulletin*, v.65,no.10, June 1991, p.134). *Class No:* 908(401)(031)

Yearbooks & Directories
[4535]
Eastern Europe and the Commonwealth of Independent States 1999. 4th ed. London, Europa, 1998. xiv,1004p. maps, tables, bibliogs. £255. (*Regional Surveys of the World.*) ISBN: 1857430581.

1st ed. 1991.

48 specialist contributors. Part 1. Background to the region *i.e.* introductory essays. Part 2: Individual country chapters A-Z on Albania, Armenia, Azerbaijan, Beralrus, Bosnia and Herzegovina, Bulgaria, Croatia, Czech Republic, Estonia, Georgia, Hungary, Kazakstan, Kyrgyzstan, Latvia, Lithuania, Macedonia, Moldova, Poland, Romania, Russian Federation, Slovakia, Slovenia, Tajikstan, Turkmenistan, Ukraine, Uzbekistan and Yugoslavia. These include a geographical profile, chronology, essays on recent history and the economy, statistical survey and directory material on the constitution, government, defence and military, foreign embassies, judicial system, news media, finance, trade, tourism, industry, *etc.* and a bibliography. Part 3: Political profiles of the region. 2nd ed (1995) was named Directory of the Year by the Directory Publishers Association.
Class No: 908(401)(058)

Great Britain
[4536]
OAKLAND, J. British civilization: an introduction. 3rd ed. London, Routledge, 1995. 368p. illus., bibliog., index. pbk. £10.99. ISBN: 0415122589.

Comprehensive introduction to a wide range of aspects of contemporary Britain: 1. The country - 2. People - 3. Political institutions - 4. Local government - 5. International relations - 6. Legal system - 7. Economic and industrial institutions - 8. Social security - 9. Education - 10. The media - 11. Religion - 12. Leisure, sports and the arts.

Oakland's *Dictionary of British institutions: a student's guide* (London, Routledge, 1993. 176p. index. pbk. £9.99. 0415071100) is a guide to institutional terminology widely employed in contemporary life. *Class No:* 908(410)

CD-ROM
[4537]
Facts about Britain 1945 to 1995 on CD-ROM. London, HMSO, 1995. Windows TM 3.1 or higher, and requires an IBM 386/486 PC or 100% compatible with 4Mb extended RAM, hard disk drive, CD-ROM drive, and VGA monitor (SVGA recommended)., illus., maps, diagrs., tables. £49. ISBN: 0115264620.

A wealth of factual data on Britain's resources, infrastructure, machinery of government and more, selected by COI and HMSO from the 46 editions of the *Britain Handbook* and from the *Aspects of Britain* series.

The *Aspects of Britain* series was launched in 1991 to give more detailed information on individual topics than the Handbook could supply; the series now runs to over 50 titles, 16 of which can be found on this CD-ROM. *Class No:* 908(410)(003.40)

Internet
[4538]
KnowUK. Cambridge, Chadwyck-Healey, 1999. WWW.Netscape Navigator 1.2 and above. Microsoft Internet Explorer 3.0 and above. PC. Macintosh or Unix computer sufficient to run browsers. £3.495. Special terms for those wishing to offer multiple service points.

At the heart of *KnowUK* is *KnowUK:Central,* which brings together the key reference sources of British people, government and places as well as information sources for libraries, archives, associations, charities and quangos. It is not a collection of links to information elsewhere on the Internet. It delivers reliable and constantly updated information gathered and prepared by experienced editorial teams from the finest British reference directories:- *e.g.*Who's Who, Debrett's People of today. The service has been designed so that it can be used by library customers with little or no help from librarians.
Class No: 908(410)(003.41)

Bibliographies

[4539]

JACKSON, P. **British sources of information: a subject guide and bibliography.** London and New York, Routledge & Kegan Paul, 1987. xvii, 526p. £35.00. ISBN: 0710206968.

4 Parts: 1. The select bibliography (40 chaps.) e.g., Commonwealth and Europe ... Geography ... History ... Northern Ireland ... Scotland ... Travel and tourism in Britain ... Wales - 2. Periodicals, journals, magazines (24 chaps.) - 3. Sources of Information (33 chaps.) - 4. Teaching resources. 'This subject guide to books and sources aims to provide assistance above all to the general reader but also to the student and teacher in locating texts, information and teaching resources on major aspects of British life, society and culture' (*Preface*). *Class No:* 908(410)(01)

Encyclopaedias

[4540]

GASCOIGNE, B. **Encyclopaedia of Britain.** London, Macmillan, 1993. 720p. illus. (many col.), tables, bibliog. £29.95. ISBN: 0333547640.

6000 A-Z cross-referenced entries covering every aspect of British life and history with specific fact-box items. 'A highly successful attempt to distil virtually a reference library into a single book' (*Reference Reviews*, v.8, no.1, 1994, p.43. *Class No:* 908(410)(031)

[4541]

The Hutchinson encyclopedia of Britain 1999. Oxford, Helicon, 1999. 1015p. illus. (30 col.), maps. £35. ISBN: 1859862756.

Some content lifted from the *Hutchinson illustrated encyclopedia of British history* (q.v.). Distributed in US by Gale. $ 75. ISBN 1859862756

14 contributors. 6,000 cross-referenced entries, mostly 2 paragraphs in length plus 45 featured articles (1-2 pages) on famous people, events, movements, metropolitan areas, tourist attractions, national features and monuments. Also World Heritage sites, organisations and institutions, art, leisure, customs and traditions. Many chronologies and sidebars, list of 684 useful Web sites p.995-1007. Chronology of British History p.1008-15. 27 maps. Focuses on Britain's cultural, historical and geographic heritage. *Class No:* 908(410)(031)

[4542]

Twentieth-century Britain an encyclopedia. Leventhal, F.M., *ed.* 902p. bibliogs., index. $95. ISBN: 0824072057.

Over 200 contributors 600+ signed cross-referenced entries 500 to 3000 words long relating to events, leading figures, social issues, institutions etc. Chronology p.xxii-xxxv. Guide To Further Research (bibliogs., guides to sources, reference works, biographies, dissertations) p.869-70. Analytical index. 'Brief bibliographies concluding each signed article provide pointers for readers who need more than ready-reference information' (*Booklist*, v.92, no.11, 1 February 1996, p.958). *Class No:* 908(410)(031)

Dictionaries

[4543]

JACOBS, A. *and* MONK, J., *eds.* **The Cambridge illustrated dictionary of British heritage.** Cambridge, Cambridge Univ. Press, 1987. viii,484p. illus., maps, bibliog., index. £14.95; $24.95. ISBN: 0521302145.

'Encapsulates the essence of Britain and British life in 1500 entries, 200-300 words in length. Fields covered include arts; buildings; ceremonies; cuisine; customs; education; finance; geography; government; history; languages; law; monarchy; monuments; organizations; religion; societies; and sports. Bibliography (by topic) p.480-3. *Class No:* 908(410)(038)

[4544]

JOSEPH, T. *and* SAGAR, D.J., *eds.* **Cassell dictionary of modern Britain.** London, Cassell, 1995. xiii,306p. map, tables, index. £18.99. ISBN: 0304345881.

9 contributors. 1500+ A-Z entries relating to events and major public figures who shaped the contemporary social and political scene from 1945 onwards. Appendix 1. Decolonization - 2. General elections - 3. Senior Government members - 4. Demography - 5. Economic data - 7. Social data. *Class No:* 908(410)(038)

Yearbooks & Directories

[4545]

GREAT BRITAIN. Office for National Statistics. **Britain 2000** the official handbook of the United Kingdom. Pearce, N., *ed.* 51st ed. London, The Stationery Office, 1999. xii,564p. illus. (many col.), maps, diagrs., tables, index. £37.50. ISBN: 0116210982.

1st ed. 1946.

All the latest facts, figures, and developments about British life in 30 sections arranged in 5 parts: 1. Britain and its people - 2. Government and foreign affairs - 3. Social and Cultural affairs - 4. The Environment and Transport. 5. Economic Affairs. Genealogical table

....(contd.)

shows Royal Family from the reign of Queen Victoria to July 1999. Colour maps on endpapers include Physical Features; Major conservation and recreation areas; Passenger rail network; and Motorway and major trunk roads. Further reading and websites at end of each section. 'A telling snapshot of modern life' (*The Times*, no.66670, 12 November 1999, p.14).

Britain 1999 (50th ed.) included a special essay, 'Fifty not out', written by the editor. Although personal in tone it nevertheless effectively summarized the social changes that dominated the years 1946-1999 in Britain. *Class No:* 908(410)(058)

Scotland

Bibliographies

[4546]

SMITH, D., *comp.* **Scotland.** 2nd ed. Santa Barbara, California and Oxford, Clio Press. 1998. 476p.+1p., map, index. £80. (*World Bibliographical Series; no.34.*) ISBN: 1851092803.

1st ed., compiled by E.G. Grant, published in 1982.

1287 annotated entries. 34 sections: The country and its people - Geography and geology - Tourism - Travel, topography and local history ... Prehistory and archaeology - History - Genealogy, clans and military history ... Libraries, museums and art galleries ... Bibliographies. Author, title and subject index. *Class No:* 908(411)(01)

Encyclopaedias

[4547]

FISHER, J. **The Glasgow encyclopedia.** Edinburgh, Mainstream Publishing, 1994. 415p. illus. bibliog., index. £20. ISBN: 1851582126.

Popular guide encompassing 126 A-Z subject categories *e.g.* Archaeology - Archives ... Coats of Arms ... Historians ... Topography and Geology. Bibliography p.401-03. *Class No:* 908(411)(031)

[4548]

MULLAY, A.J. **The Edinburgh encyclopedia.** Edinburgh, Mainstream Publishing, 1997. 384p. illus., bibliog., index. £20. ISBN: 1851587624.

104 cross-referenced entries of varying length for Edinburgh's institutions, buildings, history, society, pastimes, people and events, in a single A-Z sequence. Bibliography p.373-75. *Class No:* 908(411)(031)

Ireland

[4549]

Facts about Ireland. 16th ed. Dublin, Department of Foreign Affairs, Government of Ireland, 1995. 225p. col.illus., col.maps, tables, bibliog., index. £10.95. ISBN: 0906404215.

1st ed. 1963.

General overview of Irish life in 7 main sections: Land and people - The Irish State - Northern Ireland - Ireland in the world - Economy - Services - Culture. *Class No:* 908(415)

[4550]

Irish almanack and yearbook of facts 1999. McArt, P. Inishowen, Co. Donegal, 1999. vii,490p., col.illus., col. maps, index, softcover £8.95. ISBN: 0952959631.

Quotes of the year., Chronology (1998) p.9-25. History, geography, population, counties of Ireland. Who Is Who. Who Was Who etc. 'A busy-looking little reference book jamb-packed with facts, figures and useful information'. (*Books Ireland*, no.200, December 1996, p.377). *Class No:* 908(415)

Bibliographies of Bibliographies

[4551]

EAGER, A.R. **A Guide to Irish bibliographical material** a bibliography of Irish bibliographies and sources of information. 2nd ed. London, Library Association, Westport, Connecticut, Greenwood Press, 1980. xv, 502p. £55. ISBN: 0853659311, UK; 0313223432, US.

1st ed. 1964.

9,517 unannotated entries (5,700 more than 1st ed).

Sections: General works (bibliography; librarianship; periodicals; newspapers; directories and almanacs; museums; manuscripts; incunabula; binding; censorship) - Philosophy - Religion - Sociology - Philology - Science - Useful arts - Fine arts - Literature - Geography, travel - Biography - History (by period; Ulster, Connaught; Leinster; Munster; The Irish abroad).

Object: 'to provide a bibliographic index covering Irish enumerative bibliography and aims to serve as a quick reference guide to all who are interested in Irish studies and research studies' (*Introduction*).

....(contd.)
Includes unpublished material and work in progress. 'This excellent guide ... can be recommended enthusiastically' (*Choice*, v.18 no.9 May 1981, p.1234). *Class No:* 908(415)(009)

Bibliographies
[4552]
SHANNON, M.O. **Modern Ireland:** a bibliography on politics, planning, research, and development. Westport, Connecticut, Greenwood Press; London. The Library Association. 1981. xxvi, 733p. indexes. £55.00; $67.95. ISBN: 0853659141, UK; 0313229031, US.
5425 entries (some briefly annotated), with particular emphasis on items relating to the 20th century, grouped in 29 sections e.g., 1. General (reference works and bibliographies) - 2. History ... 7. Islands ... 23. Major regions of the Republic - 24. Dublin ... 26. Belfast - 27. Selected counties and towns of Northern Ireland. Name, subject and geographical indexes. *Class No:* 908(415)(01)

Encyclopaedias
[4553]
The Hutchinson encyclopedia of Ireland. Oxford, Helcon, 2000. 384p. £25. ISBN: 1859863205.
1300 A-Z cross-referenced entries covering Irish men and women in all fields of human activity; Irish history, politics, business, and government; towns and places in Ireland, including key tourist attractions; Ireland's cultural heritage; literature, music, sport, humour; the Irish around the world, particularly Irish Americans; and quotations on Ireland and the Irish way of life. A chronology of Irish history provides a quick reference guide to key issues.
Class No: 908(415)(031)

Northern Ireland
[4554]
Northern Ireland. 2nd ed. London, HMSO, 1995. iv,131p. £5.95, tables bibliog., index. (*Aspects of Britain*.) ISBN: 0117020095.
1st ed. 1992.
Prepared by the Central Office of Information, this booklet outlines the background to the conflict in Northern Ireland and provincial affairs. History - Progress towards a political settlement - Government and administration - Human rights - Justice and the law - Social affairs - Economy - Media - Cultural and social life. Appendix 1. 1985 Anglo-Irish Agreement - 2. Downing Street Declaration - 3. Frameworks for the future. Bibliography p.127. *Class No:* 908(416)

Bibliographies
[4555]
SHANNON, M.O., *comp.* **Northern Ireland.** Santa Barbara, Calif., and Oxford, 1991. xxxviii,603p. +1p. map. indexes. £79. (*World Bibliographical Series, no. 129.*) ISBN: 1851090320.
1962 annotated entries in 52 sections: Province and its people - Geography - Tourism and travel guides - City and regional guides ... Prehistory - Archaeology - History - Biography ... Military, police and security forces ... Encyclopaedias and directories - Bibliographies. Glossary p. xxxi-xxxviii. *Class No:* 908(416)(01)

Eire

Bibliographies
[4556]
SHANNON, M.O., *comp.* **Irish Republic.** Santa Barbara, California and Oxford, Clio Press, 1986. xxiv, 404p.+1p. map, index. £59.95. $55.00. (*World Bibliographical Series; no.69.*) ISBN: 1851090142.
1459 annotated entries. 48 sections: The country and its people - Geography - Travellers' accounts - Tourism and travel guides - City and regional studies ... Prehistory - Archaeology - History ... Genealogy ... Libraries ... Encyclopaedias and directories - Bibliographies. Glossary p.xxiii-xxiv. Author, title and subject index. *Class No:* 908(417)(01)

Yearbooks & Directories
[4557]
Ireland: a directory 2000. O'Donnell, J., *ed.* 30th ed. Dublin, Institute of Public Administration. An Foras Riaracháin, 1999. 487p. maps, ports., tables, index. ISBN: 1902448243. ISSN: 07901070.
'A complete directory of Irish life, covering the private as well as the public sector': Legislature, executive and judiciary - Diplomatic representation - Civil service - Defence forces - Garda Síochána - Local administration - Public voluntary hospitals - State-sponsored bodies - Financial institutions - Major companies and corporations - Communications - Higher education - Religious denominations - Trade

....(contd.)
& professional organizations - Social, cultural and political organizations - Northern Ireland - European Community - International organizations - Institute of Public Administration - Statistics - General information (basic facts, mileage chart, postal charges etc.). 'I can safely say that were my reference collection to be limited to half a dozen books, this directory would be one of them' (Librarian, Northern Ireland Assembly Library. Stormont, (*Reference Reviews*, v.8,no.7, 1994, p.43-44), *Class No:* 908(417)(058)

Commonwealth
[4558]
LARBY, P.M. *and* HANHAM, H. **The Commonwealth.** Oxford, Clio Press, 1993. xxxvii,254p.+ 3p. maps, index. (*International Organizations Series, no.5.*) ISBN: 1851091866.
970 annotated entries under 36 headings: Countries of the Commonwealth ... History ... Constitutional development ... Archives and manuscripts - Bibliographies ... Reference works - Research. Author, title and subject index. Both authors are senior librarians well versed in Commonwealth studies. *Class No:* 908(41-44)

Bibliographies
[4559]
The Catalogues of the Library of the Institute of Commonwealth Studies, University of London. Cambridge, Chadwyck-Healey, 1979. 1. £180.00. 2. £250.00. 3. £10.00. 4. £100.00. Complete set £475.00.
Author catalogue: 55,000 catalogue cards on 136 microfiche - Subject catalogue: 81,000 cards on 195 fiche - Periodicals catalogue: 1,500 cards on 5 fiche - Bibliography of bibliographies: 9,000 pages on 30 fiche. Individual catalogues are available separately. Subject coverage includes the history of the Commonwealth and its member states since 1850; relations between them; and political, economic and social problems. Since the 1960s the Library has specialised in acquisitions from the Commonwealth Caribbean. *Class No:* 908(41-44)(01)

[4560]
ROYAL COMMONWEALTH SOCIETY. **Subject catalogue of the Library of the Royal Empire Society,** formerly the Royal Colonial Institute. Lewin, E., *comp.* London, The Society, 4v., 1930-37. Reprinted Dawsons Pall Mall Press 1967.
1: *British Empire generally, and Africa.*
2: *Australia, New Zealand, South Africa. General voyages and travels, Arctic and Antarctic.*
3: *Canada, Newfoundland, West Indies, Colonial America.*
4: *Mediterranean dependencies, Middle East, India, Burmah, Ceylon, Malaya, East Indies, Far East.*
The Royal Commonwealth Society Library contains an estimated 400,000 items. Geographical areas are divided by subjects; final chronological order. Although the Society's library was damaged in World War II, and the catalogue no longer strictly applies to it, the listing remains an indispensable bibliography. 'Perhaps the finest private library on imperial history in the world' (Flint, J.E. *Books on the British Empire and Commonwealth* (1968), Foreword).
Supplemented by: *Biography catalogue of the Library of the Royal Commonwealth Society,* edited by Donald H. Simpson (1961, xxiii, 511p. and *Manuscript catalogue of the Library of the Royal Commonwealth Society,* also edited by Donald H. Simpson (London, Mansell, 1975).
The *Subject catalogue* and *Biography catalogue* are updated in *Subject catalogue of the Royal Commonwealth Society* (Boston, Mass., G.K. Hall, 1971, 7v.; *First supplement.* 1977. 2v.) reproducing a total of 157,000 catalogue cards. *Class No:* 908(41-44)(01)

Yearbooks & Directories
[4561]
The Commonwealth yearbook 1999. Green, R., *ed.* 9th ed. London, Hanson Cooke for the Commonwealth Secretariat. xv,472p. col.illus., col.map, tables. £68.75. ISBN: 1902221184.
Formerly *A yearbook of the Commonwealth* (1969-1986) itself a successor to the *Commonwealth Office yearbook.*
Pt.1: The Commonwealth in 1999 (50th anniversary, history etc.). - 2. The Commonwealth In Action (biennial summits, calendar of meetings. Commonwealth Games) - 3. Commonwealth Beliefs (Declaration of Principles, The Lusaka Declaration, summit statements on position and action) - 4. Member Countries A-Z (geography, society, communications, transport, economy, travellers' information, history, constitution etc.) - 5. Organizations (Secretariat, Foundation) - 6. Statements and communiqués - 7. Acronyms and abbreviations. *Class No:* 908(41-44)(058)

[4562]
—The Commonwealth online. URL:http://www.tcol.co.uk/index.htm.
An electronic version of *The Commonwealth yearbook.*
Class No: 908(41-44)(058)

Manuscripts & Incunabula

[4563]

ROYAL COMMONWEALTH SOCIETY. The Manuscript catalogue of the library ... Simpson, D.H., *ed*. London, Mansell, 1975.

'The word *"manuscript"* has been somewhat liberally interpreted' (*Introduction*) and embraces minute books, letter books, correspondence, autographs and portraits. Sections: Collections (library talks; Walter Frewen Lord Prize essays) - General material (*e.g.* Voyages and travel) - Europe - Asia - Africa (p.77-129) - The Americas - Australasia. Cross-references. Notes on character and provenance of each item. Index of names; index of subjects and organizations. The fourth supplement, 'Manuscripts newly catalogued 1983-1989', is printed in Royal Commonwealth Society *Library Notes*, no. 293 (new series), October 1989, p.1-5. Previous supplements appeared in issues nos. 217, 225 and 253. 'Certainly no research library in a Commonwealth or ex-Commonwealth country can afford to be without it' (British Book News, September 1975, p.622).
Class No: 908(41-44)(093)

England

Bibliographies

[4564]

DAY, A., *comp*. England. Santa Barbara, Calif., and Oxford, Clio Press, 1998. xvii,591p. +1p. map, index. £87.50. (*World Bibliographical Series, no.160*.) ISBN: 1851090401.

2,364 annotated entries arranged in 44 sections: Country and its people - Travellers' accounts - Geography and geology ... Tourism and travel guides - Prehistory and archaeology - History ... Monarchy ... Armed forces and defence ... Directories - Bibliography. Author, title and subject index. 'A well rounded portrait of England from historical and contemporary perspective ... This bibliography is an essential purchase for the reference library' (*Reference Reviews*, v.8,no.7, 1994, p.42-43). *Choice* Outstanding Academic Reference Book 1995. *Class No:* 908(420)(01)

London

Bibliographies

[4565]

CREATON, H., *comp*. London. Oxford and Santa Barbara, Calif., 1996. xxxi,165p. + 1p. map. index. £32. (*World Bibliographical Series, no.189*.) ISBN: 185109248x.

600 annotated entries grouped in 25 sections: London and its people - Geography - Guide books ... Biographies, diaries and letters - History ... Open spaces - Libraries, museums, archives, and learned societies - Bibliographies. Heather Creaton is Deputy Directory of the Centre for Metropolitan History at the Institute of Historical Research in the Univ. of London. *Class No:* 908(421)(01)

Channel Islands

Bibliographies

[4566]

GARDINER, V., *comp*. The Channel Islands. Oxford and Santa Barbara, Calif., Clio Press, 1998. xxvi,179p.+2p. maps, indexes. £35. (*World Bibliographical Series, no.209*.) ISBN: 1851093028.

650 entries in 34 sections: Islands and their people - Place names - Geography - Maps and charts ... Travel guides and tourism - Travellers' accounts ... Archaeology - History - German occupation during Second World War - Biography and autobiography ... Bibliographies. Chronology p.xxv-xxvi. Author, title and subject indexes. *Class No:* 908(423.4)(01)

Wales

[4567]

Reference Wales. May, J., *comp*. Cardiff, University of Wales Press, 1994. xi,356p. bibliog., pbk. £9.95. ISBN: 0708312349.

Factual information presented under 17 subject headings: 1. Physical characteristics - 2. Population - 3. Government and Politics - 4. Welsh language, National and Urdd Eisteddfodau - 5. Religion - 6. Education - 7. Health Services - 8. Media - 9. Transport - 10. Economy - 11. Armed Forces and Wales - 12. Arts - 13. Sport - 14. Disasters, Battles, Deaths and Disturbances - 15. Wales and the Welsh in Europe and the Rest of the World - 16. Wales and the Welsh in Britain - 17. Wales and the Welsh. 'John May's labour of love has a vast store of facts one would sweat blood to find elsewhere' (*Reference Reviews*, v.9,no.4, 1995, p.44). *Class No:* 908(429)

Bibliographies

[4568]

HUWS, G. *and* ROBERTS, D.H.E., *comp*. Wales. Santa Barbara, Calif., and Oxford, Clio Press, 1991. xv,247p.+1p. map, indexes. (*World Bibliographical Series, no.122*.) ISBN: 1851091181.

876 annotated entries arranged in 33 sections: Country and its people - Geography and geology - Tourism and travel ... Prehistory and archaeology - History and genealogy ... Welsh overseas - Libraries, art galleries, museums and archives - Books ... Directories - Bibliographies. Author, subject and title indexes.
Class No: 908(429)(01)

Germany

Bibliographies

[4569]

WALLACE, W., *comp*. Berlin. Santa Barbara, Calif., Oxford, Clio Press, 1993. xx,160p. + 1p. map, indexes. £29. (*World Bibliographical Series, no.155*.) ISBN: 1851091424.

429 annotated entries in 19 sections: Berlin and its people - Geography - Guide Books ... Biographies, autobiographies, memoirs and diaries - History ... Bibliographies. Author, title and subject indexes.. *Class No:* 908(430)(01)

Federal Republic of Germany

Bibliographies

[4570]

DETWEILER, D.S. *and* DETWEILER, J.E., *comps*. West Germany The Federal Republic of Germany. Santa Barbara, California and Oxford, Clio Press, 1987. xv, 353p.+1p. map, index. £49.95. $55.00. (*World Bibliographical Series; no.72*.) ISBN: 1851090177.

534 annotated entries. 35 sections: The country and its people: Reference and general works - Geography ... Prehistory and archaeology - History ... West Berlin and it special status ... Archives, libraries and museums - Directories and encyclopaedias - Bibliographies. Author, title and subject index. 'An essential bibliographical guide' (*Choice*, v.26, no.11-12, July-August 1989, p.1809). *Class No:* 908(430.1)(01)

German Democratic Republic

Bibliographies

[4571]

WALLACE, J. East Germany. Santa Barbara, California and Oxford, Clio Press, 1987. xviii, 293p.+1p., map, index. £40.95. $51.50. (*World Bibliographical Series, no.77*.) ISBN: 1851090231.

739 annotated entries. 36 sections: The country and its people - Geography - Tourism and travel guides - Travellers' accounts and descriptions of East Germany by GDR citizens, émigrés from GDR and Westerners ... History ... Berlin (East), the Wall and escapes ... Reference works - Bibliographies - Documentary collections. Author, title and subject index. *Class No:* 908(430.2)(01)

Luxembourg

Bibliographies

[4572]

CHRISTOFORY, C. *and* THOMAS, E., *comps*. Luxembourg. rev. ed. Santa Barbara, California and Oxford, Clio Press, 1997. xxxiv,327p.+1p. map, index. (*World Bibliographical Series; no.23*.) ISBN: 1851092498.

1st ed. 1981.

1058 annotated entries (487 in previous ed.). 37 sections: The country and its people - Geography ... Tourism and Travel ... Prehistory + Archaeology - History ... Biographies ... Bibliographies. Author, title and subject indexes. *Class No:* 908(435.9)(01)

Austria

Bibliographies

[4573]

PENISTON-BIRD, C.M., *comp*. Vienna. Oxford and Santa Barbara, Calif., Clio Press, 1997. xxxv,159p.+1p. map, index. £34. (*World Bibliographical Series, no.201*.) ISBN: 1851092757.

494 annotated entries in 27 sections: Vienna and its people - Geography ... Tourism and guide books - Travellers' accounts - History - Biographies, autobiographies, memoirs, diaries and letters ... International agencies ... Reference texts and bibliographies. Introduction (history, economy, politics) p.xv-xxxiv. Glossary of German terms p.xxxv. Author, title and subject indexes.
Class No: 908(436)(01)

[4574]

SALT, D. *and* RADLEY, A.F., *comps*. **Austria**. Santa Barbara, California and Oxford, Clio Press, 1986. xxxviii, 318p. + 1p. map, index. £46.95; ℒ52.25. (*World Bibliographical Series, no. 66.*) ISBN: 1851090096.

847 unannotated entries. 34 sections: The country and its people - Geography- Traveller's accounts ... Prehistory and archaeology - History... Encyclopaedias, directories and reference works - Museums, libraries, art galleries and archives ... Bibliographies. Glossary p.xxxi-xxxiv. Austrian rulers p.xxxv-xxxviii. Author, title and subject index. *Class No:* 908(436)(01)

Czechoslovakia

Bibliographies

[4575]

SHORT, D., *comp*. **Czechoslovakia**. Santa Barbara, California and Oxford, Clio Press, 1986. xxv, 409p.+1p. map, index. £57.50. $55.00. (*World Bibliographical Series, no.68.*) ISBN: 1851090118.

1,000 annotated entries. 41 sections: The country and its people - Geography - Travellers' accounts - Tourism and travel guides ... Prehistory and archaeology - History - Nationalities and minorities ... Encyclopaedias and directories - Archives and libraries - Bibliographies - Document collections. A note on the language of Czechoslovakia p.xxiii-xxv. Author, title and subject index. *Class No:* 908(437)(01)

Czech

Bibliographies

[4576]

LUNT, S., *comp*. **Prague**. Oxford and Santa Barbara, Calif., Clio Press, 1997. xviii,182p. +1p. map. indexes. £35. (*World Bibliographical Series, no. 195.*) ISBN: 1851092528.

533 annotated entries arranged in 29 sections: City and its people - Geography - Guide Books - Travellers' Accounts - Prehistory and archaeology - Life in Prague - History ... Bibliographies - Publishers. *Class No:* 908(437.1)(01)

Slovakia

Encyclopaedias

[4577]

Slovakia and the Slovaks a concise encyclopedia. Bratislava, Encyclopedical Institute of the Slovak Academy of Sciences/Goldpress Publishers, 1994. xv,727p. col.illus., col. map on front endpaper ISBN: 8085584115.

c.200 contributors. Published to mark the foundation of Slovakia as an independent nation, this wide-ranging encyclopedia identifies its most significant personalities and events, its cultural, political and economic developments, and its characteristic features. *Class No:* 908(437.6)(031)

Poland

Bibliographies

[4578]

SANFORD, G. *and* GOZDECKA-SANFORD, A., *comps*. **Poland**. 2nd ed. Santa Barbara, California and Oxford, Clio Press, 1993. xxiii,250p.++ 1p. map, index. £40.50. (*World Bibliographical Series; no. 32.*) ISBN: 1851091807.

1st ed. 1984.

914 annotated entries: 35 sections: The country and its people - Geography - Tourism and travel ... Prehistory and archaeology - History - Poles abroad ... Encyclopaedias and directories - Bibliographies ... Libraries, archives and museums. *Class No:* 908(438)(01)

Encyclopaedias

[4579]

Encuyklopedia Warszawy. Warszawa, Wydawnictwo Naukowe PWN, 1994. 1072p. illus. (many col.), maps, tables, bibliog. ISBN: 8301088362.

7,000 entries relating to all aspects of history and contemporary life in the Polish capital city. Chronology p.1039-51. Bibliography p.1052-63. *Class No:* 908(438)(031)

Hungary

[4580]

MOLNÁR, E., *ed*. **Hungary. Essential facts and figures**. Budapest. MTI Media Data Bank, 1995. 320p. col.illus., col.maps, index.

75 sections grouped under 11 thematic headings (*e.g.* 1. Country and its people - 2. History - 3. Structure of the State ... 9. Tourism). Appendix with map of Budapest (*i.e.* official information: Passport & visa regulations... Currency exchange... Important addresses) p.283-314. *Class No:* 908(439)

Bibliographies

[4581]

KABDEBO, T., *comp*. **Hungary**. Santa Barbara, California and Oxford, Clio Press, 1980. lvi, 280p.+1p. map, index. £38.95. $34.75. (*World Bibliographical Series; no.15.*) ISBN: 0903450283.

1094 annotated entries. 37 sections: The country and its people - Geography - Prehistory, archaeology - History ... Libraries, art galleries, museums and archives ... Encyclopaedias, directories - Bibliographies. Glossary p.liv-lvi. Author, title and subject index. *Class No:* 908(439)(01)

[4582]

SÁRKŽI, M., *comp*. **Budapest** Oxford and Santa Barbara, Calif., ABC-Clio, 1997. xx,109p., map, indexes. £20. (*World Bibliographical Series, no 198.*) ISBN: 1851092617.

341 annotated entries in 21 sections: Budapest and its people - Geography ... Memoirs and travellers' accounts - History ... Reference works - Bibliographies. Introduction (origins and history) p.xi-xx. Author, title and subject indexes. *Class No:* 908(439)(01)

France

[4583]

CORDELLIER, S. *and* POISSON, E., *eds*. **L'état de France** un panorama unique complet de la France 1999-2000. Paris, La Découverte, 1999. 640p. maps, tables, bibliogs., index. pbk. Ffr. 149. £18.25. ISBN: 2707130494.

150 specialist contributors. In 6 sections: 1. Enjeux et débats - 2. Modes et conditions de vie - 3. Culture, éducation, médias - 4. Régions et territoires (Métropole et Outre-Mer) - 5. Radioscopie de l'économie - 6. État et politique. Chronologie (Avril 1998-Mars 1999) p.17-22. Chronologie retrospective (1992-1998) p.595-613. An enormous amount of information packed into a compact paperback format. *Class No:* 908(44)

[4584]

NORTHCUTT, W. **The Regions of France** a reference guide to history and culture. Westport, CT., Greenwood Press, 1997. xii,310p. illus., maps, bibliogs., index. $55. ISBN: 031329223x.

Concise information on 22 French regions. Data: map, regional geography, history, recent politics, population, economy, culture (including cuisine), architecture, noteworthy sites and bibliography. Chronology p.261-65. General bibliography (A-Z by author) p.271-76. 23 maps. Analytical index. *Class No:* 908(44)

Bibliographies

[4585]

CHAMBERS, F., *comp*. **France**. 2nd ed. Santa Barbara, California and Oxford, Clio Press, 1990. xv,290p.++ 1p. map, indexes. £52.00; $31.50. (*World Bibliographical Series; no.13.*) ISBN: 1851090827.

1st ed. 1980.

942 entries in 49 sections: Country and its people - Paris - Maps, atlases and gazetteers - Travel guides ... Prehistory and archaeology - Historiography - History ... Nationalities and minorities ... Fashion - Food and Drink ... Reference works - Bibliographies. Author, title and subject indexes. *Class No:* 908(44)(01)

[4586]

CHAMBERS, F., *comp*. **Paris**. Oxford and Santa Barbara (Calif.), Clio Press, 1998. xviii,138p.+2p. map, indexes. £30. (*World Bibliographical Series, no.206.*) ISBN: 1851092714.

430 annotated entries in 22 sections: Paris and its people - Geography - Guidebooks ... History - Biographies, autobiographies, memoirs and diaries ... Encyclopedias, directories and reference works. Author, title and subject indexes. *Class No:* 908(44)(01)

Dictionaries

[4587]

FIERRO, A. **Histoire et dictionnaire de Paris**. Paris, Laffont, 1996. 1580p. maps, bibliog. indexes. Fr.189. ISBN: 2221078624.

In 5 sections: 1. Narrative history to 1995 - 2. Paris of today - 3. Chronology - 4. Dictionary of Parisian topics - 5. Bibliography. 'Ce dictionnaire thématique couvre tous les aspects de la vie parisienne: les institutions, la réligion, l'économie, les transports, la santé, l'approvisionement, l'alimentation, la vie quotidienne, les moeurs, les fêtes, l'urbanisme et l'architecture, la topographie générale, le soi et le

....*(contd.)*

sous-soi, la vie animale et végétale'. (*Livres Hebdo*, no.205, 17 Mai 1996, p.72). Author is Conservateur de la Bibliothéque de la Ville de Paris. *Class No:* 908(44)(038)

Corsica

Bibliographies

[4588]

HUDSON, G.L., *comp.* **Corsica.** Oxford and Santa Barbara, Calif., Clio Press, 1997 xxxvii,200p.+1p. maps, indexes. £43. (*World Bibliographical Series, no.202.*) ISBN: 1851092633.

433 annotated entries in 39 sections: The Island and its people - Geography ... Tourism and travel guides - Travellers' accounts ... Prehistory and archaeology - History - Biographies, autobiographies and memoirs ... Nationalities and minorities ... Bibliographies. Introduction (general account) p.xvii-xxxii. Chronology p.xxxiii-xxxvi. Useful addresses p.xxxvii. Author, title and subject indexes. *Class No:* 908(449.45)(01)

Monaco

Bibliographies

[4589]

HUDSON, G.L., *comp.* **Monaco.** Santa Barbara, Calif. and Oxford, Clio Press, 1991. xxxiii,193p. +1p. map. index. £30; $70. (*World Bibliographical Series, no.120.*) ISBN: 1851091173.

511 annotated entries arranged in 30 sections: The Principality and its people - Geography and tourism - Travellers' accounts ... Archaeology and prehistory - Genealogy and heraldry ... Casino ... Archives, libraries and museums ... Bibliographies. Reigns of the Lords and Princes of Monaco, House of Grimaldi p.xxix-xxxi. Author, subject and title index. *Class No:* 908(449.49)(01)

Italy

Bibliographies

[4590]

BULL, M.J. **Contemporary Italy** a research guide. Westport, Conn., Greenwood Press, 1996. xvii,141p. bibliog., indexes. (*Bibliographies and Indexes in World History, no.43.*) ISBN: 0313291373. ISSN: 07426852.

Introduction: Evolution of research on contemporary Italy. Pt.1: Survey and analysis: 1. History - 2. Politics - 3. Government - 4. Economy - 5. Society. Pt.2: Annotated bibliography (in same 5 sections) p.61-127. Author, and subject indexes. Both English and Italian language items are entered. *Class No:* 908(450)(01)

[4591]

SPONZA, L. *and* ZANCANI, D., *comps.* **Italy.** Oxford and Santa Barbara, Calif., Clio Press, 1995. xxxi,412p.+2p. maps. indexes. £67.50. (*World Bibliographical Series, no. 30.*) ISBN: 0903450445.

1076 annotated entries divided into 43 sections: Country and its people - Geography - Tourism and travel guides - Travellers' accounts and companions ... History - Biography and memoirs... The Arts ... Reference works - Bibliographies. Chronology p.xix-xxxi. Author, title and subject indexes. *Class No:* 908(450)(01)

Sicily

Bibliographies

[4592]

OLIVASTRI, V., *comp.* **Sicily.** Oxford and Santa Barbara, Calif., Clio Press, 1998. xxix,188p.+1p. map. indexes. £37. (*World Bibliographical Series, no.213.*) ISBN: 1851092919.

456 annotated entries in 36 sections: Island and its people - Geography - Travel and tourism - Travellers' accounts and companions ... History - Biography and memoirs ... Law and order ... Archaeology ... Reference works - Bibliographies. Introduction (historical overview) p.xv-xix. Chronology p.xxi-xxix. Author, title and subject indexes. *Class No:* 908(450.82)(01)

San Marino

Bibliographies

[4593]

EDWARDS, E. *and* MICHAELIDES, C., *comps.* **San Marino.** Oxford and Santa Barbara, Calif., Clio Press, 1996. xxxvi,100p.+1p. map. indexes. £30. (*World Bibliographical Series, no. 188.*) ISBN: 1851092420.

246 annotated entries arranged under 32 headings : Country and its people - Geography - Travel ... Prehistory, archaeology and palaeontology - History - Stamps and coins ... Bibliographies.

....*(contd.)*

Chronology p.xxi-xxx. Captains Regent of San Marino p.xxxi-xxxvi. Author, title and subject indexes. 'A pioneering work of bibliographic skill and scholarship' (*Reference Reviews*, v.10,no.7, 1996, p.48). *Class No:* 908(454.4)(01)

Vatican City

Bibliographies

[4594]

WALSH, M.J. **Vatican City State.** Santa Barbara, California and Oxford, Clio Press, 1983. xxxv, 105p.+2p. plan, index. £18.95. $22.00. (*World Bibliographical Series; no.41.*) ISBN: 0903450720.

368 annotated entries. 18 sections: The city and its citizens - Guides for visitors - Archaeology - History ... Papal Office and Court ... Diplomacy ... Services to culture and scholarship ... Reference works. Introduction (p.xv-xxxv) includes The states of the church; The Popes and their capital; The Roman question; Constitution; Legal status; Administrative organization; College of Cardinals *etc.* Author, title and subject index. *Class No:* 908(456.31)(01)

Malta

Bibliographies

[4595]

BOSWELL, D. *and* BEELEY, B., *comps.* **Malta.** 2nd ed. Santa Barabara, California and Oxford, Clio Press, 1998. xxvii,274p.+1p. map, index. £52. (*World Bibliographical Series; no. 64.*) ISBN: 1851092692.

1st edition, compiled by J.R. Thackrah, published in 1985.

980 annotated entries. 30 sections: The country and its people - Geography and geology - Travellers' accounts - Travel guides and tourism ... Prehistory, archaeology and ethnography - History - Knights of St. John - Genealogy and heraldry... Bibliographies. Author, title and subject indexes. Few entries printed in the 1st ed. survive in this later compilation. *Class No:* 908(458.2)(01)

Yearbooks & Directories

[4596]

Malta year book 1999. Clews, J.A. 47th ed. Sliema, Malta, De la Salle Brothers Publications, 1999. 505p. col.illus., tables, bibliog. ISBN. 9990953066.

27 sections (*e.g.* The Maltese Islands - Philately and books ... The Maltese nobility ... Orders of chivalry ... Gozo supplement. 8 special articles including The Nation of Gozo. Not an official handbook but authoritative and reliable. *Class No:* 908(458.2)(058)

Spain

[4597]

KERN, R.W. **The Regions of Spain** a reference guide to history and culture. Westport CT., Greenwood Press, 1995. xii,411p. illus., maps, bibliog., index. £56.50. ISBN: 0313292248.

Concise information on all Spain's 18 regions and 50 provinces A-Z by region. Standard entry: map and regional characteristics and ther each province's vital statistics, economy, history, literature, art, music, customs, historic sites and cuisines. Glossary p.355-57. Chronology p.359-66. Bibliography p.367-73. 19 maps. Analytical index. One-stop, easy to use guide. *Class No:* 908(460)

[4598]

VINCENT, M. *and* STRADLING, R.A. **Cultural atlas of Spain and Portugal.** Amsterdam, Time-Life Books, 1994. 240p. col.illus., col maps, bibliog., index. ISBN: 070540871x.

13 chapters arranged in 3 parts: 1. Physical background - 2. History of the Peninsula - 3. Geographical regions. 29 Special Features (*e.g.* Art of the Iberians, Portuguese navigators, Posters of the Spanish Civil War). Chronology p.8-9. Ruling Houses of Spain and Portugal (531AD to date) p.224. Glossary p.225-27. Bibliography p.228. Gazetteer p.231-34. Sumptuous production aimed at showing how identity of both countries was shaped by their physical background and by the events of history. *Class No:* 908(460)

Bibliographies

[4599]

SHIELDS, G., *comp.* **Madrid.** Oxford and Santa Barbara, Calif., Clio Press, 1996. xxxv,250p.+3p. maps, indexes. (*World Bibliographical Series, no.193.*) ISBN: 1851092501.

538 annotated entries ordered into 33 sections: Madrid and its people - Geography - Atlases and maps - Tourism - Guidebooks Travellers' accounts - Archaeology and prehistory - History ... Bibliographies. Chronology p.xxv-xxviii. Useful addresses p.xxix xxxv. Author, title and subject indexes. *Class No:* 908(460)(01)

[4600]

SHIELDS, G.J. **Spain.** 2nd ed. Santa Barbara, California and Oxford, Clio Press, 1994. xxxii,448p.+2p. map, index. £68. (*World Bibliographical Series; no.60.*) ISBN: 185109220x.

1st ed. 1985.

1135 annotated entries. 43 sections: The country and its people - Travellers' accounts - Geography - Atlases and maps - Tourism - Travel guides ... Archaeology and prehistory - History - Empire - Bibliographies. Chronology p.xxv-xxvii. Rulers of Spain p.xxix-xxx. Author, title and subject indexes. *Class No:* 908(460)(01)

Dictionaries

[4601]

TRUSCOTT, S. *and* GARCÍA, M. **A Dictionary of contemporary Spain.** London, Hodder & Stoughton, 1998 301p. pbk. £32. ISBN: 0340655178.

Cross-referenced A-Z entries on abbreviations, cultural phenomena, the media, literary and political personalities, events in recent history, political and legal institutions, and national and local government. 'This would have been better produced as an encyclopedia with fuller entries, plenty of illustrations and with cross-references and mention of historical sources (*Reference Reviews*, v.13, no.7, 1992:42). *Class No:* 908(460)(038)

Andorra

Bibliographies

[4602]

TAYLOR, B., *comp.* **Andorra.** Santa Barbara, Calif., Oxford, Clio Press, 1993. xxxv,97p. + 1p. map, indexes £22. (*World Bibliographical Series, no.167.*) ISBN: 1851092110.

268 annotated entries arranged in 35 sections: Country and its people - Travellers' accounts - Geography - Travel guides ... Prehistory and archaeology - History ... Languages and dialects ... Encyclopedias and directories - Bibliographies. Chronology p.xvii-xxvi. Rulers p.xxvii-xxxi. Author, title and subject indexes. *Class No:* 908(467.2)(01)

[4603]

WEST, G., *comp.* **The Basque Region.** Oxford and Santa Barbara, Calif., Clio Press, 1998. xxvi,148p.+1p. map, indexes. £34. (*World Bibliographical Series, no.212.*) ISBN: 1851092587.

410 annotated entries divided into 32 sections: Regions and its people - Geography - Tourist guides ... Origins and prehistory - History ... Language ... Encyclopaedias and directories - Bibliographies. Chronology p.xxiii-xxvi. Author, title and subject indexes. *Class No:* 908(467.2)(01)

Gibraltar

Bibliographies

[4604]

SHIELDS, G.J., *comp.* **Gibraltar.** Santa Barbara, California and Oxford, Clio Press, 1987. xxxiii, 100p.+2p. map, index. £18.50. (*World Bibliographical Series, no.87.*) ISBN: 1851090452.

260 annotated entries. 28 sections: The Rock and its people - Geography and geology - Travellers' accounts - Guidebooks and maps ... Archaeology and prehistory - History ... Anglo Spanish dispute ... Libraries and museums ... Yearbooks and directories - Bibliographies - Theses and Dissertations. Chronology p.xxxi-xxxiii. Author, title and subject index. *Class No:* 908(468.2)(01)

Portugal

Bibliographies

[4605]

LAIDLAR, J., *comp.* **Lisbon.** Oxford and Santa Barbara, Calif., Clio Press, 1997. l.252p.+1p. map, indexes. £52. (*World Bibliographical Series, no.199.*) ISBN: 1851092684.

692 entries in 38 main sections: Lisbon and its people - Geography ... tourist and travel guide books - Travellers' accounts ... Prehistory and archaeology - History - Biographies and autobiographies ... Bibliographies and catalogues. Introduction (site, climate, origins, history, Lisbon today) p.xxi-xlvii. Administration of Lisbon (with list of Freguesias, *i.e.* parishes) p.xlix-l. Appendix: Portuguese works on Lisbon (21 unannotated entries) p.209-11. Author, title and subject indexes. *Class No:* 908(469)(01)

[4606]

UNWIN, P.T.H. **Portugal.** Santa Barbara, California and Oxford, Clio Press, 1987. xxxlx, 269p.+1p. map, index. £40.95. $50.50. (*World Bibliographical Series; no.71.*) ISBN: 1851090169.

787 annotated entries. 29 sections: The country and its people - Geography and geology ... Travellers' accounts - Tourism - Prehistory and archaeology - History - Overseas territories ... Bibliographies and catalogues. Author, title and subject index. *Class No:* 908(469)(01)

Russia

[4607]

The Territories of the Russian Federation. London, Europa, 1999. xi.,286p. maps, indexes. £55. ISBN: 1857430700.

Part 1. Background to the Federation including a Chronology of Russia (p.15-21) - Pt.2: Territorial surveys of chapter length on all 89 members of the Russian Federation, including a map, geographical description, its location and population, a short historical introduction, an account of the current political situation, an economic survey, and a directory of leading political officials. Largely recycled from *Eastern Europe And The Commonwealth Of Independent States 1999 (q.v.).* *Class No:* 908(47)

Bibliographies

[4608]

BOILARD, S.D. **Reinterpreting Russia:** an annotated bibliography of books on Russia, the Soviet Union, and the Russian Federation, 1991-1996. Lanham, Md., Scarecrow Press and Pasadena/Englewood Cliffs, Calif., 1997. xxii,283p. bibliog., indexes. £39.50. ISBN: 0810832984.

617 English-language titles primarily concerned with Russian/Soviet politics, government, history, and society arranged in 5 parts: 1. Reference works - 2. Medieval Russia - 3. Imperial Russia - 4. U.S.S.R.- 5. Russian Federation. *Class No:* 908(47)(01)

[4609]

PITMAN, L., *comp.* **Russia/USSR** 2nd ed. Oxford and Santa Barbara, Calif., Clio Press, 1994. xxiv,.384p.+2p. map. indexes. £58. (*World Bibliographical Series, no.6.*) ISBN: 1851092118.

Replaces A. Thompson's *Russia/USSR* (1979).

1274 annotated entries in 35 sections: Country and its people - Geography - Travel guides - Travellers' accounts - History ... Circus ... Bibliographies. Author, title and subject indexes. *Class No:* 908(47)(01)

[4610]

Soviet studies guide. Konn, T., *ed.* London, Bowker Saur, 1992. xvi,237p. maps, bibliogs., index. £39. (*Area Study Guide Series, no.1.*) ISBN: 0862917905.

10 thematic bibliographical essays by different hands: 1. Land, environment, people - 2. History - 3. Society and culture - 4. Government and politics - 5. International relations - 6. Armed Forces - 7. Economy - 8. Business - 9. Science and technology - 10. General reference. Each essay ends with consolidated annotated bibliography. Although collapse of USSR overtook publication this guide retains considerable reference value. *Class No:* 908(47)(01)

Encyclopaedias

[4611]

The Cambridge encyclopedia of Russia and the former Soviet Union. Brown, A., *and others, eds.* 2nd ed. Cambridge University Press, 1994. xii,604p. illus. (some col.), col. maps, tables, bibliog., index. ISBN: 0521355931.

Previously as *The Cambridge encyclopediua of Russia and the Soviet Union* (1982).

132 academic contributors. Well presented encyclopedia in 13 main sections: 1. The physical environment - 2. Peoples - 3. Religion - 4. History - 5. Art and architecture - 6. Language and literature - 7. Cultural life - 8. Sciences - 9. Politics - 10. Economy - 11. Society - 12. Military power - 13. International Relations . Glossary p.568-69. Bibliography (by chapter) p.570-80. 52 col.maps and charts. *Class No:* 908(47)(031)

Baltic States

Bibliographies

[4612]

SMITH, I.A. *and* GRUNTS, M.V., *comps.* **Baltic States.** Santa Barbara, Calif., Oxford, Clio Press, 1993. lxxvii,169p. map, index. £39.50. (*World Bibliographical Series, no.161.*) ISBN: 1851091963.

554 annotated entries grouped in 32 sections: Countries and their peoples - Geography and the environment - Tourism and Travel guides - Travellers' and personal accounts ... Prehistory and archaeology - History ... Encyclopedias, directories and reference works - Bibliographies. *Class No:* 908(474)(01)

Lithuania

Bibliographies

[4613]

KANTAUTAS, A. *and* KANTAUTAS, F. A Lithuanian bibliography: a checklist of books and articles held by the major libraries in Canada and the United States. Edmonton, Univ. of Alberta Press, 1975. xxxix, 725p. £16.55. ISBN: 0888640684.

10168 entries, classified in 13 categories e.g., 4. Bibliographic aids, general reference works, serials, locating copies. Author and subject indexes.

Supplement to a Lithuanian bibliography: a further checklist... 1979. xxviii, 316p. 0888640684. £5.50. *Class No:* 908(474.5)(01)

Encyclopaedias

[4614]

Encyclopedia Lituanica. Sužiedélis, S. *and* Vesaitis, A., *eds.* Boston, Encyclopedia Lituanica, 6v., 1970-1978.

Based on the same publishers *Lithuanian encyclopaedia* (1953-1969) - the first complete general encyclopedia ever published in Lithuania.

V.6 *V-Z* and *Supplement A-Z*. 1978. 540p. illus., map, index. 38 contributors. Includes list of contributors to entire work. Essential reference source to Lithuania from the earliest times.

Class No: 908(474.5)(031)

[4615]

Lithuania: an encyclopaedic survey. Demskis, E., *ed.* Vilnius, Encyclopedia Publishers, 1986. 431p. illus. (many col.), col. maps, tables, index.

Over 50 contributors. Illustrated sections on General information - Natural Features - Population and settlements - Constitution and government - History - Communist Party of Lithuania - Economy - Public Health - Sports and tourism - Education - Science - Publishing - TV and radio - Literature and art - Religion - Honorary titles and prizes. *Class No:* 908(474.5)(031)

Ukraine

Bibliographies

[4616]

MAGOCSI, P.R., *comp.* Ucrainica at the University of Toronto Library a catalogue of holdings. Toronto, University of Toronto Press, 2v., 1985. xviii, 1845p. ISBN: 0802034306.

Library catalogue entries arranged in 31 chapters *e.g.* 1. Reference aids and general works - 2. Serials ... 6. Guidebooks ... 8. Maps and atlases ... 15. Numismatics, genealogy and sphragistics - 16 Archaeology - 17. History ... 31 Ucrainica abroad.

Class No: 908(477)(01)

[4617]

WYNAR, B.S. Ukraine a bibliographic guide to English-language publications. Englewood, Colo., Ukranian Academic Press, 1990. xiii, ,406p. index. $85. ISBN: 0872877612.

1084 critically annotated entries, plus thousands of subsumed entries, covering the period early 1950s to mid-1989, arranged in 13 categories (e.g. 1. General reference sources ... 5. Ethnic studies ... 7. Geography and travel - 8. History and political science). Entries include unpublished doctoral dissertations, books, symposia, pamphlets, selected articles in scholarly journals, and, in some instances, review citations. An important reference source.

Class No: 908(477)(01)

Encyclopaedias

[4618]

Encyclopedia of Ukraine. Kubijovyč, V., *ed.* Toronto, Univ. of Toronto Press, for the Canadian Institute of Ukrainian Studies, the Shevchenko Scientific Society, and the Canadian Foundation for Ukrainian Studies. 5v., 1984-1993. illus. maps. ports. bibliogs. $700.

Revision of *Entsklopediia Ukrainoznavstva*. Preface discusses earlier Soviet and non-Soviet Ukrainian encyclopedias.

v.1 *A-F.* 1984. xv,952p. 0802033628. v.2 *G-K* 1988. 737p. 0802034446 100 scholars are engaged worldwide on a comprehensive guide to the life and culture of the Ukraine. Most of the longer entries include a bibliography. Each volume contains approximately 3,000 entries, two to three pages of four-colour illustrations, 800 black-and-white half-tones, 36 black-and-white maps, and two four-colour maps. A comprehensive name index will be prepared and published in a separate volume, within the next two years. 'Sets a standard which other such projects will find it difficult to equal' (*Canadian American Slavic Studies*, v.25, nos.1-4, 1991. p.381). *Class No:* 908(477)(031)

[4619]

—KUBIJOVYČ, V. *and* SHUKOVSKY, A. Encyclopedia of Ukraine. Map and gazetteer (scale 1:2,000,000). Toronto, Univ. of Toronto Press for the Canadian Institute of Ukrainian Studies, 1984. 30p. folded col. maps tipped in inside back cover. ISBN: 0802033628.

Gazetteer p.10-30. *Class No:* 908(477)(031)

[4620]

—KUBIJOVYČ, V., *ed.* Ukraine a concise encyclopedia. Toronto, Univ. of Toronto Press, 2v. 1963-71.

Based on *Entsyklopediya Ukrainoznavsta* (München & New York, 3v. 1949-52).

Arranged by topics. V.1: physical geography, natural history, population, ethnography, history, culture and literature: v.2 (xiiii, 1394p.): law and government ... social sciences, culture ... concluding with the Ukranian diaspora. V.2 has 87 contributors.

Class No: 908(477)(031)

Armenia

Bibliographies

[4621]

NERCESSIAN, V.N., *comp.* Armenia. Oxford and Santa Barbara, Calif., Clio Press, 1993. xxiii,304p.+1p. map, indexes. £49.50. (*World Bibliographical Series, no.163.*) ISBN: 1851091440.

879 annotated entries in 25 sections: Country and its people - Geography and geology - Travellers' accounts - Travel guides ... Prehistory and archeology - History - Biographies and memoirs ... Cuisine ... Bibliographies. Author, title and subject indexes.

Class No: 908(479.25)(01)

Finland

[4622]

Facts about Finland. Helsinki, Otava Publishing Co., 1999. 165p. col.illus., col.maps, index. ISBN: 9511155148.

1. Finland in Europe - 2. A Land of many faces - 3. Finland through the centuries - 4. A Society of Nordic values - 5. Economy - 6. Scientific facts - 7. The Modern welfare state - 8. Culture - 9. Finland in the 21st century. *Class No:* 908(480)

Bibliographies

[4623]

SCREEN, J.E.O., *comp.* Finland. 2nd ed. Santa Barbara, California and Oxford, Clio Press, 1997. xxi, 246p.+1p. map, index. £42. (*World Bibliographical Series; no.31.*) ISBN: 185109265x.

1st ed. 1981.

802 annotated entries. 29 sections: Introductory works - Geography - Travel and Tourism - Prehistory, archaeology, ethnography and genealogy - History ... Encyclopaedias, yearbooks and biographical dictionaries - Bibliographies. Author, title and subject index.

Class No: 908(480)(01)

Norway

Bibliographies

[4624]

SATHER, L.B., *comp.* Norway. Santa Barbara, California and Oxford, Clio Press, 1986. xxiv, 293p.+1p. map, index. £42.50. $46.95. (*World Bibliographical Series; no.67.*) ISBN: 185109010x.

942 annotated entries. 41 sections: The country and its people - Travellers' accounts - Geography - Tourism and travel guides ... Prehistory and archaeology - History - Modern explorers ... Reference books, directories and biographical dicitionaries. Author, title and subject index. *Class No:* 908(481)(01)

Yearbooks & Directories

[4625]

Hvem, Hva, hvor. [Who, what, when.] Oslo, Chr. Schibsteds, 1934- Annual.

Almanac including summaries of the past years' national events. 'A frequently used reference guide' (L.B. Sother. *Norway*, 1986. Entry 904). *Class No:* 908(481)(058)

Sweden

Bibliographies

[4626]

SATHER, L.B. *and* SWANSON, A., *comps.* Sweden. Santa Barbara California and Oxford, Clio Press, 1987. xxiv, 370p.+1p. map, index. £49.95. $55.00. (*World Bibliographical Series; no.80.*) ISBN 1851090355.

1015 annotated entries. 44 sections: The country and its people -

....(contd.)
Travellers' accounts - Geography - Tourism and travel guides ...
Prehistory and archaeology - History ... The social welfare state ...
Nobel prizes ... Libraries, archives and museums ... Reference works
and directories ... Bibliographies. *Class No:* 908(485)(01)

Denmark

Bibliographies

[4627]
MILLER, K.E., *comp*. **Denmark**. Santa Barbara, California and
Oxford, Clio Press, 1987. xix, 216p.+1p., map, index. £31.95.
$50.50. (*World Bibliographical Series; no.83*.) ISBN: 1851090428.
730 annotated entries. 33 sections: The country and its people -
Geography - Tourism and travel ... Prehistory and archaeology -
History ... Libraries and museums ... Encyclopaedias and directories -
Bibliographies -The Faroe Islands - Greenland. Author, title and
subject index. *Class No:* 908(489)(01)

Iceland

Bibliographies

[4628]
McBRIDE, F., *comp*. **Iceland**. 2nd ed. Santa Barbara, California and
Oxford, Clio Press, 1996. xxvii,345p.+2p., map, indexes. £60.
(*World Bibliographical Series; no.37*.) ISBN: 1851092374.
Replaces J.J. Horton's *Iceland* (1983).
970 annotated entries. 40 sections: The country and its people -
Geography ... Tourism and Travel guides - Travellers' accounts ...
Archaeology - History - Genealogy - Catalogues and bibliographies.
Author, title and subject indexes. More than 700 new entries.
Class No: 908(491.1)(01)

Netherlands

Bibliographies

[4629]
KING, P. *and* WINTLE, M., *comps*. **The Netherlands**. Santa Barbara,
California and Oxford, Clio Press. 1988. xix, 308p.+1p., map, index.
£43.95. $52.50. (*World Bibliographical Series; no.88*.) ISBN:
185109041x.
1025 annotated entries. 35 sections: The country and its people -
Geography ... Prehistory and archaeology - History - Voyages of
discovery and colonies ... Archives, libraries, galleries and museums
... Directories - Bibliographies. Glossary p.xix. Author, title and
subject index. *Class No:* 908(492)(01)

[4630]
OS, A. van, *comp*. **Amsterdam**. Oxford and Santa Barbara, Calif., Clio
Press, 1997. xxiv,104p.+1p. map, index. £30. (*World
Bibliographical Series, no.203*.) ISBN: 1851092773.
326 annotated entries in 22 sections: Amsterdam and its people -
Geography - Tourism and travel guides ... History (inc. archaeology)
... Bibliography. Useful addresses p.xxiii-xxiv.
Class No: 908(492)(01)

Belgium

Bibliographies

[4631]
RILEY, R.C., *comp*. **Belgium**. Santa Barbara, California and Oxford,
Clio Press, 1989. xxxviii, 269p.+1p. map, indexes. £38.00. (*World
Bibliographical Series; No.104*.) ISBN: 1851090991.
819 annotated entries. 37 Sections: The country and its people -
Geography and geology ... Archaeology and prehistory - History ...
The EEC ... Libraries, art galleries and museums ... Encyclopaedias,
directories and reference works - Bibliographies. Theses and
dissertations on Belgium p.xxix-xxxviii. Author, subject and title
indexes. *Class No:* 908(493)(01)

Switzerland

Bibliographies

[4632]
MEIER, H.K. *and* MEIER, R.A., *comps*. **Switzerland**. Santa Barbara,
California and Oxford, Clio Press, 1990. xviii,409 +1p. map.
indexes. £55.95; $65. (*World Bibliographical Series, no. 114*.) ISBN:
1851091076.
974 annotated entries in 42 chapters: The Country and its people -
Travel - Geography ... Archaeology and prehistory - History -
Genealogy ... Emigration: The Swiss abroad - Languages and dialects
... Tourism ... Museums, libraries and archives - Books and

....(contd.)
bookmaking ... Reference books - Bibliographies. Author, title and
subject index. 'There is nothing comparable available' (*Choice*, v.28,
no.9, May 1991, p.1462). *Class No:* 908(494)(01)

Liechtenstein

Bibliographies

[4633]
MEIER, R.A., *comp*. **Liechtenstein**. Santa Barbara, Calif., Oxford,
Clio Press, 1993. xx,123p+1p. map, index. £30. (*World
Bibliographical Series, no.159*.) ISBN: 1851092013.
267 annotated entries in 34 sections: Country and people - Travel -
Geography ... House of Liechtenstein - History and archaeology ...
Tourism ... Philately ... Reference Books *Class No:* 908(494.9)(01)

Greece

Bibliographies

[4634]
CONSTANTINIDES, S. **Greece in modern times** an annotated
bibliography of works published in English in 22 academic disciplines
during the twentieth century. Lanham, MD., Scarecrow Press, 1999.
656p. $115. ISBN: 0810836580.
Indexes nearly 4,000 books and articles concerned with the
development of modern Greece from the beginning of the 19th to the
end of the 20th century. Disciplinary categories are sub-divided into
small thematic subsections. Entries are cross-referenced, and when
appropriate they point to other texts. *Class No:* 908(495)(01)

[4635]
VEREMIS, T. *and* DRAGOUMIS, M. **Greece**. 2nd ed. Santa Barbara,
California and Oxford, Clio Press, 1998. 434p.+1p. map, index. £73.
(*World Bibliographical Series; no.17*.) ISBN: 1851092862.
Replaces 1st ed. (1980).
998 annotated entries. 33 sections: The country and its people -
Geography - Prehistory and archaeology - History ... Greeks overseas
... Encyclopaedias - Bibliographies. Author, title and subject index.
Class No: 908(495)(01)

Albania

Bibliographies

[4636]
YOUNG, A., *comp*. **Albania**. Rev. ed. Santa Barbara, California and
Oxford, Clio Press. 1997. xlviii,294p. + 1p. map, indexes. (*World
Bibliographical Series: no.94*.) ISBN: 1851092609.
1st ed. 1988 (893 entries).
911 annotated entries. 41 sections: The country and its people -
Geography - Travel and travellers' accounts ... Archaeology and
prehistory - History ... Nationalities and minorities - Bibliographies.
Introduction (name, history, language, religion, publishing, press)
p.xvii-xxv. Chronology p.xxvii-xxxvi. Individuals of note in Albania's
history p.xli-xlvi. Author, title and subject indexes.
Class No: 908(496.5)(01)

Yugoslavia

Bibliographies

[4637]
HORTON, J.J. **Yugoslavia**. Rev. and expanded ed. Santa Barbara,
California and Oxford, Clio Press, 1990. xxi, 279p. + 1p. map,
index. (*World Bibliographical Series, No. 1*.) ISBN: 185109105x.
First published 1977.
921 annotated entries in 41 sections: The country and its people -
Travel and description - Geography . . . Archaeology - History ...
Nationalities . . . Tourism . . . Directories - Museums and libraries - -
Bibliographies. A note on the languages of Yugoslavia p.xxi. Author,
subject and title index. *Class No:* 908(497.1)(01)

Slovenia

Bibliographies

[4638]
CARMICHAEL, C., *comp*. **Slovenia**. Oxford and Santa Barbara,
Calif., Clio Press, 1996. xv,176p.+1p. map. indexes. £31. (*World
Bibliographical Series, no. 186*.) ISBN: 1851092390.
601 annotated entries in 36 categories: The country and its people -
Geography - Tourism and travel guides - Travellers' accounts ...
Prehistory and Archaeology - History ... Overseas populations ...
Bibliographies. Author, title and subject indexes. 'Carmichael's
annotations reflect a scholar's knowledge of current events (*Choice*,
v.34,no.5, January 1997, p.766). *Class No:* 908(497.12)(01)

Croatia

Bibliographies

[4639]

CARMICHAEL, C., *comp.* **Croatia.** Oxford and Santa Barbara, Calif., ABC-Clio, 1999. xxv,194p.+1p. map, indexes. £38. (*World Bibliographical Series, no.216.*) ISBN: 1851092854.

775 annotated entries arranged in 34 sections: Country and its people - Geography ... Tourism and travel guides - Travellers' accounts, memoirs and correspondence - History - The National Question ... Croatian War of Independence (1990-1995) ... Encyclopedias and reference books - Bibliographies. Author, title and subject indexes. *Class No:* 908(497.13)(01)

[4640]

FRANOLIĆ, B., *comp.* **Books on Croatia and Croatians** recorded in the British Library General Catalogue. Zagreb and London, Croation Information Centre, 2v., 1996 and 1999.

V.1. 1996. 246p. ISBN 9536525038. c.1650 unannotated entries listed in order of date of publication under 3 main sub-divided headings: 1. General reference and descriptive works (A. Bibliographies - B. Biography, genealogy, heraldry - C. Travel accounts and guide books - D. Ethnology, geography, topography - E. Croats abroad - Burgenland Croats) - 2. History (13 form, thematic and chronological sub-divisions) - 3. Cities and Towns (13 A-Z). V.2. 1999. 216p. ISBN 9536058278. A further 1400 items mainly dealing with Croatian culture arranged within 32 form and thematic sections. Data: author, title, imprint, collation, and British Library shelfmark. Intended as a research guide. *Class No:* 908(497.13)(01)

Bulgaria

Bibliographies

[4641]

CRAMPTON, R.J. **Bulgaria.** Santa Barbara, California and Oxford, Clio Press, 1989. xxxiii,232p., map, indexes. £39. (*World Bibliographical Series; no.107.*) ISBN: 1851091041.

794 annotated entries. 38 sections: The country and its people - Geography - Tourist guides - Travel accounts - Bulgaria before the Bulgarians - History ... Libraries, museums and archives ... Directories - Bibliographies. Author, title and subject indexes. *Class No:* 908(497.2)(01)

Romania

Bibliographies

[4642]

SIANI-DAVIES, P. *and* SIANI-DAVIES, M., *comps.* **Romania.** 2nd ed. Santa Barbara, California and Oxford, Clio Press, 1998. 386p.+1p. map, index. £66. (*World Bibliographical Series; no.59.*) ISBN: 1851092447.

1st ed. compiled by A. Deletant and D. Deletant 1985.

977 annotated entries. 31 sections: The country and its people - Geography - Prehistory, archaeology and ethnography - History ... Nationalities and minorities ... Encyclopaedias and directories - Libraries and collections - Bibliographies. Author, title and subject index. 'An excellent guide to relevant material ... one of the best so far in the series' (*Choice*, v.24, no.3, November 1986, p.452). *Class No:* 908(498)(01)

Crete

Bibliographies

[4643]

EDWARDS, A., *comp.* **Crete.** Oxford and Santa Barbara, Calif., Clio Press, 1998. xlvii,134p.+1p. map. indexes. £32. (*World Bibliographical Series, no.215.*) ISBN: 1851091734.

386 annotated entries group in 27 sections: Island and its people - Geography .... Tourism and travel guides - Travellers' accounts ... Archaeology - Prehistory and ancient history - Medieval and modern history - Biographies, autobiographies and memoirs - Internet sites and databases. Introduction (history of Crete) p.xv-xxvii. Chronology p.xxix-xxxv. Rulers of Crete p.xxxviii-xxxix. Author, title and subject indexes. *Class No:* 908(499.8)(01)

Asia

Bibliographies

[4644]

Bibliography of Asian studies. Surdam, W., *ed.* Ann Arbor, Association for Asian Studies, Univ. of Michigan, 1956-. Annual. ISSN: 00677159.

Previously published as *Bulletin of Far Eastern bibliography* 1936-40; and as 'Far Eastern bibliography' in *Far Eastern Quarterly*, 1941-

....(contd.)
46.

1990 volume (1996. lii,710p.) has 34,119 unannotated entries for monographs, periodical articles, articles included in festschriften and commemorative volumes arranged in 35 geographical divisions, subdivided under 15 subject classifications (including Geography, History, Library and Information Sciences) further subdivided under *c.*150 subject headings. Also in 4 superclasses (Bibliography, References, Sources, Study and Teaching). *Class No:* 908(5)(01)

Yearbooks & Directories

[4645]

FENTON, T.P. *and* HEFFRON, M.J., *comps.* **Asia and Pacific: a directory of resources.** Maryknoll, New York, Orbis Books; London, Zed Books, 1986. xx, 137p., bibliogs., indexes, pbk. £18.95; $9.95. ISBN: 088344528x, US; 0862326354, UK.

Updates and expands the Asia and Pacific chapter of *The Third World resource directory* (Orbis Books, 1984).

6 Chapters: 1. Organizations - 2. Books - 3. Periodicals - 4. Pamphlets and articles - 5. Audiovisuals - 6. Other resources. Clearly intended for US use: 'We have probably overlooked significant organizations and resources in Europe, Asia, the Pacific, and elsewhere' (*Introduction*, p.xix). *Class No:* 908(5)(058)

Central Asia

[4646]

CAPISANI, G.R. **The Handbook of Central Asia** a comprehensive survey of the new republics. London, I.B. Taurus, 2000. xxii,264p. maps, bibliogs., index. £45. ISBN: 1860644295.

An examination of the present political, social and cultural structure of Kazakstan, Usbekistan, Turkmenistan, Tajikistan and Krgyzstan, together with an analaysis of geo-political issues, their compalex ethnic, religious and linguistic composition, and a skilful overview of the region's history. *Class No:* 908(50)

Asia—Far East

Bibliographies

[4647]

Bibliographic guide to East Asian studies. New York, G.K. Hall, 1990-. Annual.

1994 (1995). $200. ISBN 07382176x. Covers Japan, China, North and South Korea, Hong Kong, and Taiwan, with approximately 3500 listings from LC MARC tapes and the Oriental Division of the New York Public Library. It includes publications about East Asia; materials published in any of the relevant countries; and publications in the Chinese, Japanese and Korean languages. *Class No:* 908(51/52+57)(01)

Yearbooks & Directories

[4648]

The Far East and Australasia 2000. 31st ed. London, Europa, 1999. xxiv,1407p. maps, tables, bibliogs. Annual. £220. (*Regional Surveys of the World.*) ISBN: 185743062x. ISSN: 00713791.

First published 1969.

77 contributors provide a compendium guide and systematic political and economic guide to all the countries and territories of East Asia, Southeast Asia, the Asiatic countries of the former USSR, Australia, New Zealand, and the Pacific Islands. Pt.1 General survey comprises a series of introductory essays (*e.g.* Population in Asia and the South Pacific; Asian-Pacific community in the Pacific century) - 2. Country surveys including Physical and social geography, History, Economy, Statistical survey, Directory (*i.e.* constitution, government, political organizations, diplomatic representation, judiciary, religion, the media, finance, tourism, *etc.* with a bibliography) - 3. Regional organizations (*i.e.* comprehensive information on the major organizations active within the region). Select bibliography Books (p.1396-1400), Periodicals (p.1401-1407). 'Tho continued existence of this work of reference is a blessing for all reference libraries sensible enough to stock it' (*Reference Reviews*, v.12,no.4, 1998, p.53). *Class No:* 908(51/52+57)(058)

China

[4649]

Chinese studies papers presented at a colloquium at the School of Oriental and African Studies, University of London 24-26 August 1987. Sponsored jointly by the British Library, the School of Oriental and African Studies, University of London and the China Library Group. Wood, F., *ed.* London, The British Library, 1988. 232p. illus. £23.50. (*British Library Occasional Papers, No.10.*) ISBN: 0712301569.

....*(contd.)*

25 papers presenting an overview of resources for Chinese studies in UK libraries; paper and book in China; and automation and cooperation. *Class No:* 908(510)

Bibliographies

[4650]
HAYFORD, C.W., *comp*. China. 2nd ed. Santa Barbara, California and Oxford, Clio Press, 1997. xx, 632p.+1p. map, index. £75. (*World Bibliographical Series; no. 35.*) ISBN: 1851092358.

Replaces P. Cheng's *China* (1983).

1500+ annotated entries. Primarily relating to recent English language books covering all aspects of China: The country and its people - Geography - Tourism and travellers' accounts ... Prehistory and archaeology - History - Biographical works ... Overseas Chinese - Bibliographies and directories. Author and subject index.
Class No: 908(510)(01)

[4651]
WANG, R.T. Area bibliography of China. Lanham, MD., Scarecrow Press, 1997. Distributed in UK by Shelwing Ltd., 4 Pleydell Gdns, Folkestone, CT20 2DN. xiii,334p. index. £56.05. (*Area Bibliographies, no.13.*) ISBN: 0810833506.

4,150 unannotated cross-referenced entries arranged A-Z under Library of Congress subject headings. Entries consist mainly of recently published English language titles. Author index p.295-334.
Class No: 908(510)(01)

Encyclopaedias

[4652]
The Cambridge encyclopedia of China. Hook, B. *and* Twitchett, D., *eds*. 2nd ed. Cambridge Univ. Press, 1991. 512p. illus. (some col.), maps, bibliog., index. £35. $49.50. ISBN: 052135594x.

1st ed. 1982.

79 contributors. Covers all aspects of China: history, geography, economics, politics, the arts, wildlife, customs, food and drink, social organization, law, education, literature etc. Arranged thematically, this edition charts the political unrest of 1989. 60 maps.
Class No: 908(510)(031)

[4653]
COULING, S. The Encyclopaedia Sinica. Hong Kong, Oxford Univ. Press, 1983. xiv, 633p. bibliog. £18.00. ISBN: 0195815955.

Facsimile edition of a work originally published by Kelly and Walsh, Shanghai, 1917.

A scholarly work still of considerable value. Articles A-Z. with short addenda and corrigenda. A mine of information (*e.g.* on 'Names'); 'Han Dynasty' includes list of rulers with names in Chinese characters as well as in romanised form. Biographies; many cross-references. Author was one-time Honorary Secretary and Editor, North-China Branch, Royal Asiatic Society. *Class No:* 908(510)(031)

[4654]
Encyclopedia of China: the essential reference to China, its history and culture. Perkins, D., *ed*. Chicago & London, Fitzroy Dearborn, 1999. ix,662p. illus., bibliog., index. £65. ISBN: 1579581102.

1000+ cross-referenced A-Z entries explore all aspects of the history and culture of China. Major cities and provinces; historical eras and figures; government and politics; economics; religion; language and the writing system; food and customs; sports and martial arts; crafts and architecture; important Chinese figures outside of mainland China. Bibliography p.633-35. 'Well worth a place on the reference shelves as a first port of call and makes a fascinating introduction to this remarkable country' (*Reference Reviews*, v.13, no.5, 1999. p.50).
Class No: 908(510)(031)

[4655]
Encyclopedia of New China. Luo Liang, *ed*. Beijing, Foreign Languages Press, 1987. 990p. illus. (mostly col.), col. maps, tables, index. £49.00. ISBN: 0835119696, UK; 711900086-1/217.

38 contributors. 5 main sections: 1. The land and the people - 2. History - 3. Politics - 4. Economy - 5. Culture. Appendix 1. The constitution and other important laws - 2. Brief guide to China's leading officials (p.831-908) - 3. A chronology of the People's Republic of China 1949-1985 (p.911-970) - 4. Miscellaneous tables including Brief chronological table of Chinese history p.973.
Class No: 908(510)(031)

Handbooks & Manuals

[4656]
MACKERRAS, C. *and* YORKE, A. The Cambridge handbook of contemporary China. Cambridge, Cambridge Univ. Press, 1991. x,266p. maps, tables, bibliog., index. £35; $37.50. ISBN: 0521383420.

1. Chronology 1900-April 1990 (p.1-58) - 2. Politics - 3. Eminent contemporary figures (p.73-119) - 4. Classified and annotated bibliography (p.120-45) - 5. Foreign relations - 6. China's economy - 7. Population - 8. Gazetteer (p.183-204) - 9. China's minority nationalities - 10. Education - 11. Culture and Society. Chapter notes p.240-2. *Class No:* 908(510)(035)

Yearbooks & Directories

[4657]
China directory 1996. 24th ed. Tokyo, Radiopress Inc., 1995. 523+88p. maps on end papers, index. Annual. ISBN: 4947638966.

Lists leaders and members of party and government, constitutional, and other official bodies such as 13th Central Committee, National Peoples Congress and the State Council and Commissions. Name index in Pinyin. *Class No:* 908(510)(058)

Maps & Atlases

[4658]
BLUNDEN, C. *and* ELVIN, M. Cultural atlas of China. Oxford, Phaidon; New York, Facts on File, 1983. 237p. illus. (mostly col.), col. maps, tables, bibliog., index. £18.50; $40.00. ISBN: 0714823090, UK; 0871961326, US.

1. Space (geographic and demographic context) - 2. Time (survey of Chinese culture from Beijing Man to the present) - 3. Symbols and society (thematic coverage). Bibliography p.225-27. Gazetteer p.229-34. 58 maps. 204 col.illus. *Class No:* 908(510)(084.3)

Hong Kong

Bibliographies

[4659]
SCOTT, I., *comp*. Hong Kong. Santa Barbara, California, and Oxford, Clio Press, 1990. xxiii,248p.++ 1p. map, indexes. £35.95; $64.00. (*World Bibliographical Series, no.115.*) ISBN: 1851090894.

838 annotated entries in 30 sections: Territory and its people - Geography ... Archaeology and prehistory - History ... Urban society and problems ... Bibliographies. Author, title and subject indexes.
Class No: 908(512.317)(01)

Yearbooks & Directories

[4660]
Hong Kong, 1996. Howlett, R., *ed*. Hong Kong, Government Information Services Department, 1996. 494p. col. illus., tables, maps, index. HK$80. ISBN: 9620202201.

26 sections *e.g.* 19. Travel and tourism ... 26. History.
Class No: 908(512.317)(058)

Macao

Bibliographies

[4661]
EDMONDS, R.L., *comp*. Macau. Santa Barbara, California and Oxford, Clio Press, 1989. 1v, 110p.+1p. map, index. £21.00. (*World Bibliographical Series, no.105.*) ISBN: 1851090908.

381 annotated entries. 22 sections: The territory and its people - Geography and geology ... Travellers' accounts - History ... Libraries, art galleries, museums and archives ... Directories ... Bibliographies. Glossary of place names p.lv. Author, title and subject index.
Class No: 908(512.318)(01)

Tibet

Bibliographies

[4662]
PINFOLD, J., *comp*. Tibet. Santa Barbara, Calif., and Oxford, Clio Press, 1991. xxvi,157p. +1p. map. indexes. £26.95. (*World Bibliographical Series, no. 128.*) ISBN: 1851091580.

559 annotated entries in 25 sections The country and its people - Geography - Travel and exploration ... History ... Language - Religion ... Human rights ... Bibliographies. Author, title and subject indexes. 'An ideal source for further study ... it will prove a valuable resource for academic, geographical and many general reference collections' (*Reference Reviews*, v,5, 1991, p.36). *Class No:* 908(515)(01)

Mongolia

Bibliographies

[4663]

NORDBY, J., *comp*. **Mongolia**. Santa Barbara, California and Oxford, Clio Press, 1993. xxix,192p.++ 1p. map, index. £44.00; $75.00. (*World Bibliographical Series, no.156*.) ISBN: 1851091297.

489 annotated entries in 36 sections: Country and its people - Travellers' accounts - Tourism and travel guides - Geography ... Archaeology - History ... Mongolian nationalism ... Bibliographies. Author, title, and subject index. *Class No:* 908(517)(01)

Encyclopaedias

[4664]

Information Mongolia the comprehensive reference source of the People's Republic of Mongolia (MPR). The Academy of Sciences MPR, *comp*. Oxford, New York, and Beijing, Pergamon Press, 1990. xxxviii,505p. illus. (some col.), col. maps, tables, bibliogs., index. £120; $200. (*Countries Of The World Information Series*.) ISBN: 0080361935.

79 contributors. Part 1. Land and people - 2. History of Mongolia - 3. Political system of the Mongolian People's Republic - 4. The Armed Forces - 5. National economy. Each part is sustained by a substantial bibliography. 19 maps. 67 tables. Analytical subject index p.483-505. Encyclopedic coverage of all aspects of Mongolian life 'within a detailed historical framework'. 'With information largely through 1989, the book is already dated by the political and social changes in Mongolia, but ... this is still a very useful work' (*Choice*, v.28, no.4, December 1990, p.608). *Class No:* 908(517)(031)

Korea

Bibliographies

[4665]

HOARE, J.E., *comp*. **Korea**. Oxford and Santa Barbara, Calif., Clio Press, 1997. xxxii,334p.+1p. map, indexes. £63. (*World Bibliographical Series, no.204*.) ISBN: 1851092463.

1,101 annotated entries in 3 parts in 67 sections: Part 1. General works on Korea (geography ... travellers' and residents' accounts - Tourism and travel guides ... Prehistory and archaeology - History - Korean War ... Bibliographies. Part 2. The Democratic People's Republic of Korea (North Korea) and Part 3. The Republic of Korea (South Korea) with similar sections and others as appropriate. Author, title and subject indexes. *Class No:* 908(519)(01)

Handbooks & Manuals

[4666]

A Handbook of Korea. 8th ed. Seoul, Korean Overseas Information Service, 1990. 571p. col.illus., col.maps, bibliog., index.

First published 1978.

Sections: Land - People and language - History - Belief, philosophy and religions - Culture and arts - Customs and tradition - Constitution and government - Foreign relations - Unification policy - National defense - Finance - Economy - Industry - Agriculture, forestry and fisheries - Transporation and telecommunications - Science and technology - Education - Mass communications - Social development - Quality of life - Sports - Tourism. Bibliography p.549-61. *Class No:* 908(519)(035)

Yearbooks & Directories

[4667]

Korea Annual 1996. 33rd ed. Seoul, Yonhap News Agency, 1996. 820p. illus. col.maps, index. ISBN: 8974330369. ISSN: 12250147.

Chronology 1995 p.5-14. Chronology of South Korea in 20th century p.15-45. Review of all aspects of Korean life e.g., government; economic and social affairs; North Korea today and general information. Who's who p.465-788. Who's Who in North Korea p.789-813 *Class No:* 908(519)(058)

Japan

[4668]

Japan. Eyes on the country views of the 47 prefectures. Tokyo, Foreign Press Center, 1997. 415p. col.illus., col.maps, tables. Y.2,000.

Published to mark the 20th anniversary of the founding of the Foreign Press Center.

Compact yet detailed compilation of the features and policies of each of the 47 prefectures within 8 regions: Hokkaido/Tohoku, Kanto, Hokuriku, Clenbu, Kiski, Chungoku, Shikoku, and Kynshu/Okinawa. Contents: directory information and a brief history, prefecture philosophy (projects and goals, focus on internationalization, notable features, towards the 21st century, and a map). Reference section (*i.e.*

....(contd.)

glossary, periods of Japanese history, and local government administration) p.2-4. Appendix: A. Statistical look at Japan's 47 prefectures, p.406-09. *Class No:* 908(52)

[4669]

Japanese studies: papers presented at a colloquium at the School of Oriental and African Studies, University of London 14-16 September 1988. Brown, Y-Y., *ed*. London, The British Library, 1990. xvi,398p. illus., facsims. (*British Library Occasional Papers, no.11*.) ISBN: 071230178x.

Sessions at the colloquium were devoted to 3 areas: 1. Overview of resources for Japanese studies (*e.g.* Japanese studies in Britain 1945-88. Map and map collections in Japan) - 2. Printing, publishing and the art of the Japanese book - 3. Automation and cooperation. *Class No:* 908(52)

Bibliographies

[4670]

BRUIJN, R.K. de-. **Area bibliography of Japan**. Lanham, Md., Scarecrow Press, 1998. 320p. £45.60. (*Scarecrow Area Bibliographies, no.14*.) ISBN: 0810833743.

'Provides a general overview of literature relating to Japan and covers a broad range of subject matter: from art, feminism and linguistics, to corporate culture, history and medicine. It includes books published since 1980 that are related to the geographical area of Japan and to Japanese culture within that area, placing emphasis on current literature and topics and providing information about the enormous changes that have occurred in Japan in recent years. Entries are arranged alphabetically by subject' (publishers advt.). *Class No:* 908(52)(01)

[4671]

EADES, J.S., *comp*. **Tokyo**. Oxford and Santa Barbara, Calif., Clio Press, 1999. xxxvi,288p.+2p. maps, tables, indexes. £55. (*World Bibliographical Series, no.214*.) ISBN: 1851092927.

806 annotated entries entered under 27 subject headings. Tokyo and its people - Geography - Guidebooks - Biographies, Autobiographies, memoirs and diaries - History ... Information resources. Introduction (Tokyo's history) p.xvii-xxxvi. Author, title and subject indexes. *Class No:* 908(52)(01)

[4672]

MAKINO, Y. *and* MIKI, M. **Japan and the Japanese** a bibliographic guide to reference sources. Westport, CT., Greenwood Press, 1996. x,157p. indexes. (*Bibliographies and Indexes in Asia Studies, no.1*.) ISBN: 0313263116.

532 annotated entries arranged in 2 main sub-divided parts: 1. General reference works - 2. Subject bibliographies and reference works in 31 thematic sections (including geography, history, and World War II and the Allied occupation). Author, title and subject indexes. *Class No:* 908(52)(01)

[4673]

PERREN, R. **Japanese studies** from prehistory to 1990: a bibliographical guide. Manchester Univ. Press, 1992. x,172p. index. £45. (*History and Related Disciplines Select Bibliographies*.) ISBN: 0719024587.

4069 Western language items (many annotated) in 6 uniformly sub-divided sections under 20 thematic headings (*e.g.* population and demography ... foreign trade and culture ... imperialism ... art and culture). *Class No:* 908(52)(01)

[4674]

SHULMAN, F.J. **Japan**. Santa Barbara, California, and Oxford, Clio Press, 1989. xix, 873p. and 2p. maps, index. (*World Bibliographical Series, no.103*.) ISBN: 1851090746.

1615 annotated entries in 46 sections: The country and its people - Geography and geology ... Travellers' accounts - Tourism and travel guides - Prehistory and Archaeology - History - Biographical and autobiographical accounts ... Minorities: the Ainu, Burakumin, and Koreans - Overseas Japanese ... Libraries and Museums - Encyclopaedias, directories and subject dictionaries - Bibliographies and research guides. Chronology p.xxi. Author, subject and title index. *Class No:* 908(52)(01)

Encyclopaedias

[4675]

The Cambridge encyclopedia of Japan. Bowring, R. *and* Kornicki, P., *eds*. Cambridge, Cambridge Univ. Press, 1993. 408p. col. illus., col. maps, tables, diagrs., bibliogs., index. £29.95. (*Cambridge World Encyclopedias*.) ISBN: 0521403529.

54 contributors. *Contents*: Geography - History - Language and literature - Thought and religion - Arts and crafts - Society - Politics - Economy in thematically arranged text with boxed features highlighting important topics. *Class No:* 908(52)(031)

[4676]

Kodansha encyclopedia of Japan. London, Kodansha Europe Ltd., 9v. 1983. Distributed in UK by International Book Distributors and in US by Harper & Row. V.1-8. 352p. each; v.9. 288p. £720.00 (set including *Supplement*). ISBN: 0870116207, UK; 4061445316, Japan.

680 Japanese and 524 international contributors. Over 10,000 articles cover all aspects of Japanese life: technology, economics law and business with the greatest emphasis on history, geography, fine arts, and literature. V.9 is a analytical index: list of contributors p.ix-xxii. 'The long pieces on the major aspects of Japan are of the highest quality, all of them written by top-notch scholars' (Encyclopaedia of Japan, *Choice*, v.21, no. 11-12, July-August 1984, p.1576).

Supplement/1987. 64p. illus. index. $20.00. 'Overviews and in-depth analyses of the newest developments in Japanese society'.
Class No: 908(52)(031)

[4677]

—CD-ROM Encyclopedia of Japan. London, Kodansha Europe, 1999. Single 12cm disc for Windows. Minimum System Requirements: processor; Pentium 90MHz and above Memory; 32MB Hard Disc; 120MB free space CD-ROM Drive; 4x Operating System; Windows 95/98/NT4.0(SP3) and above either English or Japanese version; English Windows will operate all Japanese text. ISBN: 4062099373.

Published to mark Kodansha's 90th anniversary.

Utilises the resources of the 9v. *Kodansha encyclopedia of Japan* and the 2v. *Japan: an illustrated encyclopedia (qqv.)* 12,000 entries (3,000 fully revised; 160 new entries). Search via English or romanised Japanese keywords corresponding to the alpha-sequence entry headwords. The whole resource can be accessed by entering a keyword, browsing through the index, or selecting a subject field or topic through the *Special Tours* feature. Related articles can also be found using the linked photograph *Gallery,* and the detailed *Timeline* places the Encyclopedia in a chronological context and facilitates access via any point in Japanese history. Click on the links proivded to access related English language web sites on the Internet.
Class No: 908(52)(031)

[4678]

—Japan an illustrated encyclopedia. London, Kodansha Europe Ltd., 2v., 1993. 1964p. col.illus., maps, bibliog., index. £175. ISBN: 4069310983.

Based on *Kodansha encyclopedia of Japan* (Tokyo, Kodansha, 9v. 1983).

700 Japanese and 700 international contributors. 12,168 revised, updated, cross-referenced entries, plus 2,000 new to this title to strengthen coverage of current affairs and business and technology developments, and nearly 100 feature articles and pictorial essays, covering all aspects of modern Japanese life. 14p. bibliography of major works in English, 24p. chronology, 4,000 illustrations, 24p. maps. English-Roman and Japanese orthography index.

Japan. profile of a nation (Kodansha, 1994. 520p. illus., col. map, index, pbk. £30. ISBN 4770023847) is 'a generous selection of entries' from *Japan: an illustrated encyclopedia.*
Class No: 908(52)(031)

[4679]

—The Kodansha bilingual encyclopedia of Japan a unique, fully bilingual guide to the people and culture of Japan London, Kodansha Europe, 1999. 944p. illus. index. £75. ISBN: 4770021305.

Up-to-date political and economic developments explained in detail to give an accurate picture of modern Japan. With sections covering diverse aspects of Japan from government and economy to traditional culture, lifestyle and sports. Appendices present bilingual versions of important documents such as the Constitution of Japan, U.S.-Japan Security Treaty, and so on. *Class No:* 908(52)(031)

Dictionaries

[4680]

)E MENTE, B.L. **Japan encyclopedia.** Lincolnwood, Illinois, Passport Books, 1995. 558p. illus., maps. £18.95. ISBN: 0844284351.

Wideranging introduction to all aspects of Japanese events, culture, and people. English language sources of further information p.543-556. *Class No:* 908(52)(038)

[4681]

'ERKINS, D. **Encyclopedia of Japan:** Japanese history and culture, from Abacus to Zori. New York and Oxford, Facts on File, 1991. 410p. illus., maps, charts. £21.95. ISBN: 0816019347.

1,000+ A-Z cross-referenced entries relating to Japanese history, culture, business, government, arts and crafts, language and literature, food, and religion. List of Emperors p.79. Prime Ministers since 1945 p.269. Bibliography p.394-401. 'Well balanced and accurate survey for the general reader' (*Reference Reviews,* v.6, no.5, 1992, p.47).
Class No: 908(52)(038)

Taiwan

[4682]

COPPER, J.F. **Taiwan** nation-state or province? Boulder, Colo., Westview Press, 1990. xi,148p. illus., map, bibliog., index. $32.50; £21. (*Westview Profiles Nations of Contemporary Asia.*) ISBN: 081330444x.

1. Land and the people - 2. History - 3. Society and culture - 4. Political system - 5. Economy - 6. Foreign and military policies - 7. Future. Chapter notes p.129-36. Bibliography p.137-41.
Class No: 908(529)

Bibliographies

[4683]

WEI-CHIN LEE, *comp.* **Taiwan.** Santa Barbara, California and Oxford, Clio Press, 1990. xxxiv,247p.++ 1p. map, indexes. £38.00; $68.00. (*World Bibliographical Series, no.113.*) ISBN: 1851090916.

825 entries in 37 sections: Country and its people - Tourism and traveller's accounts - Geography ... Prehistory and archaeology - History - Religion ... Indigenous minority peoples ... Military affairs ... Bibliographies and directories. Romanization of Chinese names and terms p.xxix. Author, title and subject indexes. Concentrates on post-1980 English language publications. *Class No:* 908(529)(01)

Yearbooks & Directories

[4684]

CHANG YING, *ed.* **The Republic of China yearbook 1996.** Taipei, Government Information Office, 1996. xvii,790p. col. illus., col. maps, col. tables, index. $45. ISBN: 9570066598. ISSN: 10130942.

Previously published as *Republic of China reference book.*

National symbols (Anthem, Flag etc.) p.x-xvii. 25 sections (*e.g.* 1. Geography - 2. People ... 3. History ... 8. National Defense - 9. Foreign Affairs ... 22. Tourism). Who's who in the Republic of China p.429-639. Appendix 1. Chronology January 1911 to June 1995 - 2. Constitution p.666-81 - 3. Government directory p.682-90. One of the most informative of all official yearbooks. *Class No:* 908(529)(058)

Asia—Middle & Near East

Bibliographies

[4685]

AUCHTERLONIE, P. **Introductory guide to Middle Eastern and Islamic bibliography.** Oxford, Middle East Libraries Committee, 1990. v,84p. index, A4 soft cover. £7.50. (*MELC Research Guides, no.5.*) ISBN: 0948889407.

Basic bibliography (in form sections) providing a concise and straightforward guidance to the range of reference materials available for Middle Eastern studies. *Class No:* 908(53+56)(01)

[4686]

Bibliographic guide to Middle Eastern studies. New York, G.K. Hall, 1991-. Annual.

1994 (1995). 500p. $205. ISBN 0783821921. Lists all materials cataloged during the past year by the Library of Congress, the Middle East section of the NYPL's renowned Oriental Division, and the modern Hebrew language books in the NYPL's Jewish Division. The Guide covers books published in the modern Arabic, Persian and Turkish languages in Egypt, Israel, Iran, Iraq, Jordan, Saudi Arabia, Libya and other Middle Eastern and North African countries. It also includes books published on the Middle East in Western languages and in Western countries. *Class No:* 908(53+56)(01)

[4687]

FENTON, T.P. *and* HEFFRON, M.J., *comps.* **Middle East: a directory of resources.** Maryknoll, New York, Orbis Books, 1988. 144p. indexes, pbk. $9.95. ISBN: 0883445336.

Updates and expands the Middle East chapter in *Third World resource directory* (Orbis, 1984).

1. Organizations - 2. Books - 3. Periodicals - 4. Pamphlets and articles - 5. Audiovisuals. *Class No:* 908(53+56)(01)

Encyclopaedias

[4688]

The Cambridge encyclopedia of the Middle East and North Africa. Mostyn, T. *and* Hourani, A., *eds.* Cambridge, Cambridge Univ. Press, 1988. 504p. illus., (some col.), col. maps., bibliogs., index. £30.00; $49.50. ISBN: 0521321905.

Over 80 contributors. Authoritative essays grouped in 6 parts sub-divided into headed sections: 1. Lands and peoples - 2. History (Ancient history of the Near East to The Middle East and North Africa 1800-1939 in 8 sections) - 3. Societies and economies - 4. Culture - 5. The countries (28) and peoples without countries (Armenians, Kurds, Palestinians) - 6. Inter-state relations. Section bibliogs. 36 maps. 50 colour and 100 black and white illus. 'An authoritative source of

....*(contd.)*

information on the history, culture and political situation of the Middle East' (*Reference Reviews,* v.3, no.2, June 1989, p.93).
Class No: 908(53+56)(031)

[4689]

Encyclopedia of the modern Middle East. Simon, R.S., *and others, eds.* New York, Macmillan, 4v., 1996. 2182p. illus., maps, geneal. tables, bibliog., index. $350. ISBN: 0028960114.
300 academic contributors. c.4,000 cross-referenced entries (1500 biographies), relating mainly to events, leading figures, locations, and prominent companies, in 24 Middle Eastern countries, from Morocco to Afghanistan, over the last 200 years, ranging in length from short definitions to 8-page essays with bibliographies.
Class No: 908(53+56)(031)

Yearbooks & Directories

[4690]

The Middle East and North Africa 2000. 46th ed. London, Europa, 1999. Annual. xvii,1228p. maps, tables, bibliogs. £235. $435. (*Regional Surveys of the world.*) ISBN: 1857430611. ISSN: 00768502.
Part 1. General survey, authoritative essays on issues of contemporary interest - 2. Regional organizations: comprehensive information on the United Nations and the other major organizations active in the region - 3. Country surveys Algeria to Yemen: Geography; History; Economy; Statistical survey; Directory (the constitution, government, legislature, political organizations, diplomatic representation, judicial system, religion, press, publishers, radio and TV, finance, trade and industry, transport, tourism, atomic energy, defence, education). Calendar of political events October 1998-September 1999 p.xiv-xvi. 'This series has no serious rival for its comprehensive coverage, international scope and regular updating' (*Reference Reviews,* v.11, no.2, 1997, p.52-53).
Class No: 908(53+56)(058)

[4691]

The Middle East annual issues and events. Partington, D.H., *ed.* Boston, G.K. Hall, 1981-. Annual (v.3. 1983). xiii, 269p. maps on endpapers. index.
1983 edition has 6 articles: Islamic fundamentalism - PLO since Beirut - Soviet Union, Syria, and the crisis in Lebanon - Chad - Middle East in the US Media - The year's publications in Middle Eastern studies. Essays included in v.1-2 listed p.269. 'Offers convenient access to authoritative analyses of important issues' (*Wilson Library Bulletin,* v.57, no.8, April 1983, p.708).
Class No: 908(53+56)(058)

Saudi Arabia

[4692]

FOUAD AL-FARSY. Modernity and tradition the Saudi equation. London, Kegan Paul International, 1990. xxiii,337p. illus., maps, tables, bibliog., index. ISBN: 0710303955.
Supersedes the author's *Saudi Arabia: a case study in development.*
1. The geography of the Kingdom - 2. Historical and cultural background - 3. Islam ... 5. Political system - 6. Kingdom's ministries - 7. Government agencies - 8. Petroleum - 9. Economy - 10. Planning - 11. Industrial development - 12. Agricultural development ... 18. Foreign relations ... 20. How others see us. Bibliography p.322. 4 maps. 'Primary objective of this work is to deal as comprehensively as possible with the development of Saudi Arabia as a political, economic and social system' (*Introduction*). *Class No:* 908(532)

Bibliographies

[4693]

CLEMENTS, F.A., *comp.* **Saudi Arabia.** 2nd ed. Santa Barbara, California and Oxford, Clio Press, 1988. xxix, 354p.+1p. map, index. £44.95. $55.00. (*World Bibliographical Series; no.5.*) ISBN: 1851090673.
1361 annotated entries (789 in 1st ed.). 34 sections: The country and its people - Exploration and travel - Geography ... History ... Libraries - Bibliographies. Theses and dissertations on Saudi Arabia p.xviii-xxix. Author, title and subject index. *Class No:* 908(532)(01)

Yemen

Bibliographies

[4694]

AUCHTERLONIE, P., *comp.* **Yemen.** Rev. ed. Santa Barbara, California and Oxford, Clio Press, 1998. 372p.+1p. map, index. £63. (*World Bibliographical Series; no.50.*) ISBN: 1851092552.
First published as *The Yemens: the Yemen Arab Republic and the people's Democratic Republic of Yemen* edited by G. R. Smith in 1984.
938 annotated entries. 34 sections: The country and its people - Geography - Tourism - Travellers' accounts ... Prehistory and

....*(contd.)*

archaeology - History ... Museums and archives ... Directories - Bibliographies. Author, title and subject index. This edition contains more than twice as many entries as the first edition. 'A work of considerable scholarship' (*Reference Reviews,* v.12,no.4, 1998, p.52). 'A highly commendable work for both the initiate and the seasoned Saudi Arabian scholar' (*Bulletin School of Oriental and African Studies,* v.61, no.3, 1998, p.546). *Class No:* 908(533)(01)

Oman

[4695]

Oman '97. Oman, Ministry of Information, nd. 246p. col.illus., col.maps.
33 sections (*e.g.*H.M. The Sultan, Basic statute of the state, history, geography, foreign affairs, defence, regional municipalities and environment). *Class No:* 908(535)

Bibliographies

[4696]

CLEMENTS, F.A., *comp.* **Oman.** 2nd ed. Santa Barbara, California and Oxford, Clio Press, 1994. xxii,346p.+1p., map, indexes. £52. (*World Bibliographical Series, no.29.*) ISBN: 1851091971.
1st ed. 1981.
1175 annotated entries. 36 sections: The country and its people - Oman in general works on the Middle East - Exploration and travel - Geography ... Prehistory and archaeology - History ... Oil ... Bibliographies. Author, title and subject indexes.
Class No: 908(535)(01)

Gulf States

[4697]

The United Arab Emirates 1996. London, Trident Press, 1996. 280p. illus. (many col.), tables. ISBN: 1900724014.
A comprehensive review of significant events in the UAE in 1996 set in the context of the previous 25 years. 6 sections: 1. Government - 2. Economy - 3. General Infrastructure - 4. Social development - 5. Information and culture - 6. Heritage. Appendix: UAE at a glance (general information and statistical tables) p.268-71.
Class No: 908(536)

Bibliographies

[4698]

CLEMENTS, F.A., *comp.* **United Arab Emirates.** 2nd ed. Santa Barbara, California and Oxford, Clio Press, 1998. 274p.+1p. map, index. £47. (*World Bibliographical Series, no.43.*) ISBN: 1851092749.
1st edition 1983.
690 annotated entries. 30 sections: The country and its people - UAE in general works on the Middle East - Exploration and travel - Geography ... Prehistory and archaeology - History ... Bibliographies. Author, title and subject index. *Class No:* 908(536)(01)

[4699]

UNWIN, P.T.H., *comp.* **Qatar.** Santa Barbara, California and Oxford, Clio Press, 1982. xxv, 162p+1p. map, index. £24.95. $30.00. (*World Bibliographical Series, no.36.*) ISBN: 0903450666.
574 annotated entries. 29 sections: The country and its people - Geography and geology - Travel and exploration ... Prehistory and archaeology - History ... Bibliographies. Author, title and subject index. *Class No:* 908(536)(01)

Bahrain

[4700]

LAWSON, F.H. Bahrain the modernization of autocracy. Boulder, Colo., Westview Press, 1989. xiv,146p. illus., map, bibliog., index. (*Profiles Nations Of The Middle East.*) ISBN: 0813301238.
1. Geographical and social structure - 2. Establishment of British Imperial order - 3. Nationalist movements of 1950s - 4. Contemporary politics - 5. Contemporary economic affairs - 6. Foreign relations Bibliography p.137-42. *Class No:* 908(536.5)

Bibliographies

[4701]

UNWIN, P.T.H., *comp.* **Bahrain.** Santa Barbara, California and Oxford, Clio Press, 1984. xxxii, 265p.+1p. map, index. £39.50. $43.50. (*World Bibliographical Series no.49.*) ISBN: 0903450860.
911 annotated entries. 31 sections: The country and its people - Geography and geology - Travel and exploration ... Prehistory and archaeology - History ... Oil industry ... Bibliographies. Author, subject and title index. *Class No:* 908(536.5)(01)

Kuwait

[4702]

RYSTAL, J. **Kuwait** the transformation of an oil state. Boulder, Colo., Westview Press, 1992. xii,194p. illus., map, tables, bibliog., index. (*Nations Of The Contemporary Middle East.*) ISBN: 0813308887.

1. Introduction - 2. History - 3. Oil economy - 4. Kuwaiti society - 5. Political institutions and processes - 6. Foreign policy - 7. Aftermath of the invasion. Chronology (1756-1991) p.179-80. Bibliographic essay, p.181-5. *Class No: 908(536.8)*

Bibliographies

[4703]

LEMENTS, F.A., *comp.* **Kuwait**. 2nd ed. Santa Barbara, California and Oxford, Clio Press, 1996. xxiii,340p.+1p. map, indexes. £64. (*World Bibliographical Series, no.56.*) ISBN: 0903450992.

1st ed. 1985.

1,116 annotated entries (799 in 1st ed). 33 sections: The country and its people - Kuwait in general works on the Middle East - Exploration and travel - Geography ... History ... Gulf War ... Libraries - Bibliographies. Author, title and subject indexes. *Class No: 908(536.8)(01)*

Asia—South & South East

Bibliographies

[4704]

ELSON, D.N. **Bibliography of South Asia.** Metuchen, NJ., Scarecrow Press, 1994. xv,466p. index. £52.50. (*Scarecrow Area Bibliographies, no.4.*) ISBN: 0810828545.

3115 unannotated mostly English-language entries limited to monographs published 1982 - relating to Afghanistan, Bangladesh, Bhutan, India, Maldives, Nepal, Pakistan and Sri Lanka, arranged under subject headings. The introduction (p.i-xv) includes a survey of other bibliographical and reference works. Author index. 'Will be of inestimable value to many academic and other large reference collections' (*Reference Reviews*, v.9,no.4, 1995, p.47). *Class No: 908(54+59)(01)*

[4705]

EARSON, J.D., *ed.* **South Asian bibliography** a handbook and guide. Hassocks, Sussex, Harvester Press; Atlantic Highlands, New Jersey, Humanities Press, 1979. xiii, 381p. ISBN: 0855278919, UK; 0391008196, US.

26 contributors. Sections: Manuscripts. Archives. Theses - Printed books (1. Special forms: Periodicals and newspapers; Official publications, to 1947: Government publications, since 1947; Maps. 2. Subjects: Religions; Anthropology and sociology: Art and archaeology; Music and the dance; Language and literature; Historical writing, Law; Economics; Traditional science and technology; Modern science and technology - 3. Regions and countries (India, Pakistan, Bangladesh, Afghanistan, Ceylon (Sri Lanka), Maldives, Burma, the Himalayas and Tibet). Running commentary in subsections (India: bibliographies; reference books: India in general; the states). Index of authors, p.361-81 - *c*.1,600 entries. An important and scholarly bibliography: awarded the LA's Besterman Medal for 1979. *Class No: 908(54+59)(01)*

Encyclopaedias

[4706]

he **Cambridge encyclopedia of India, Pakistan, Bangladesh, Sri Lanka, Nepal, Bhutan and the Maldives.** Robinson, F., *ed.* Cambridge, Cambridge Univ. Press, 1989. 520p. illus., (many col.), maps, tables, index. £30.0; $49.50. ISBN: 0521334519.

69 contributors. 85 authoritative essays grouped in 9 sections: 1. Land - 2. Peoples - 3. History to independence - 4. Politics - 5. Foreign policy - 6. Economics - 7. Religions - 8. Societies - 9. Culture. Section bibliographies. Glossary p.505-7. 75 maps. 69 tables. Analytical index. 'The best available single-volume treatment of South Asia' (*Library Journal*, v.114, no.9, 15 May 1989, p.65). *Class No: 908(54+59)(031)*

Maps & Atlases

[4707]

lly annotated atlas of South Asia. Dutt, A.K. *and* Geib, M.M. Boulder, Colorado, Westview Press, 1987. xxiii,231p. illus., maps, bibliog. $29.50. ISBN: 0813300444.

Introduction to South Asia followed by 6 national sections on India, Bangladesh, Pakistan, Sri Lanka, Nepal and Bhutan. Bibliography p.225-231. 'More appropriate to have published this text as an introductory textbook on South Asia, rather than an atlas' (*Cartographica* v.25,no.4, 1988, p.92-93). *Class No: 908(54+59)(084.3)*

Libraries

[4708]

GAUR, A., *ed.* **South Asian studies** papers presented at a colloquium on 24-26 April 1986. London, The British Library, 1986. xvii, 327p. £19.50. (*British Library Occasional Papers, No. 7.*) ISBN: 0712300953.

Devoted to 3 main topics: 1. Resources in the United Kingdom (with special reference to the British Library's collections - 2. Bibliographical research, and facilities - 3. Resources in the libraries of South Asia and other countries, and the prospects for international cooperation. 'This is bound to emerge as a standard work in its field' (*Library Association Record*, v.89, no.6, June 1987, p.293). *Class No: 908(54+59):061:026/027*

India

Bibliographies

[4709]

BRAY, J. *and* NAWANG TSERING SHAKSPO. **A Bibliography of Ladakh.** Warminster, Wiltshire, Aris & Phillips, 1988. 153p. index. £17.50. ISBN: 085668435x.

Close to 1000 annotated entries listing books, articles, sound discs, tapes and academic theses which appeared before mid-1987 in India, Europe, North America and Japan. The emphasis is on academic studies on Ladakhi history and culture. *Class No: 908(540)(01)*

[4710]

DARSHAN SINGH TATLA *and* TALBOT, I., *comps.* **Punjab.** Oxford and Santa Barbara, Calif., Clio Press, 1995. xlix,323p.+2p. maps. indexes. £56.75. (*World Bibliographical Series, no. 180.*) ISBN: 1851092323.

1051 annotated entries registered in 31 sections: The Punjab and its people - Geography - Tourism and travel guides ... Travellers' accounts - Archaeology and ancient history - History - Biographies and memoirs ... Encyclopedias and directories. Chronology p.xxxix-xlii. Glossary p.xliii-xlvi. Author, title and subject indexes. *Class No: 908(540)(01)*

[4711]

DEVONSHIRE, I.D., *comp.* **India.** 2nd ed. Santa Barbara, California and Oxford, Clio Press, 1995. 356p.+2p., map, indexes. £58.50. (*World Bibliographical Series; no.26.*) ISBN: 1851092005.

1st ed. compiled by B.K. Gupta and D.S. Kharbas 1984.

1039 annotated entries. 35 sections: The country and its people - Geography and Travel ... Archaeology and prehistory - History ... Minorities and tribal communities - Indians abroad ... Bibliographies, abstracts and indexes. Chronology p.xxvii-xxx. Author, title and subject indexes. *Class No: 908(540)(01)*

[4712]

GREAT BRITAIN. India Office Library and Records. **Catalogue of European printed books, India Office Library.** Boston, Mass., G.K. Hall, 10v., 1964. 7225p. $835.00 (Export $1010.00). ISBN: 0816106711.

110,000 photolithographed catalogue cards. Scope is every aspect of the history and culture of the peoples of the Indian subcontinent and contiguous territories of related culture. Particularly strong in art and archaeology, history, philosophy and religion, linguistics, anthropology, and economics and politics, the collection includes many official British and Indian publications. *Class No: 908(540)(01)*

[4713]

RAMESH CHANDER DOGRA. **Jammu and Kashmir:** a select and annotated bibliography of manuscripts books and articles together with a survey of its history, languages and literature. Delhi, Ajanta Publications, 1986. viii, 417p. indexes. Rs300. $60.00.

11 introductory essays precede a classified bibliography. 'A most useful cumulation of knowledge' (*Bulletin of School of Oriental and African Studies*, v.51, no.1, 1988, p.193-194). *Class No: 908(540)(01)*

Dictionaries

[4714]

ROY, A.K. *and* GIDWANI, N.N. **A Dictionary of Indology.** New Delhi, Oxford & IBH Publishing; Atlantic Highlands, N.J., Humanities Press, 4v., 1983-1986. iii,327p, 349p, 287p, 337p.

Encyclopedic dictionary of terms and topics relating to, amongst other subjects, ancient geography, archaeology, epigraphy, history, and palaeography. *Class No: 908(540)(038)*

Yearbooks & Directories

[4715]

Hindustan yearbook and who's who 1999. Sarkar, S., *ed.* 4th ed. Calcutta, M.C. Sarkar, 1999. 275p. Rs7,500. £5. $10. ISSN: 09701168.

Pt.1 43 thematic sections including chronology, geographical information, world gazetteer, and tourism - 2. 32 sections including all Indian states and territories, Who's who, national honours and awards, Indian events 1998, Pakistan 1998. *Class No:* 908(540)(058)

[4716]

India 1999 a reference annual. 43rd ed. New Delhi, Publications Division, Ministry of Information and Broadcasting, 1999. 775p. maps, tables, index. Rs.250. ISBN: 8123007124. ISSN: 00736090.

1st ed. 1953.

31 sections (*e.g.*Land and people - 2. National symbols ... 28. India and the world - 29. States and Union Territories - 30. Diary of national events 1997-1998 - 31. General Information (Presidents, Chief Justices, Nobel Laureates etc.) 7 Appendixes (1. Government of India - 2. Members of Parliament etc. Compiled from official sources. *Class No:* 908(540)(058)

Gazetteers

[4717]

The Gazetteer of India. Chopra, P.N., *ed.* New Delhi, Gazetteer Unit, Ministry of Education and Social Welfare, 4v., 1965-78. maps.

V.1 (xii, 657p.) has 10 chapters, with section specialists: 1. Physiography - 2. Weather and climate - 3. Geology - 4. Flora - 5. Fauna - 6. The people - 7. Languages - 8. Religions - 9. Social structure - 10. Social life (20p. only). Index. 'For all its faults, the *Country and people* volume probably contains a wider range of useful information than any work of comparable length' (*Journal of Asian Studies*, v.26. no.2. February 1967, p.318).
Class No: 908(540)(083.86)

Bhutan

Bibliographies

[4718]

DOGRA, R.C., *comp.* **Bhutan.** Santa Barbara, California and Oxford, Clio Press. 1990. xxxiii,124p.++ 1p. map, index. £21. (*World Bibliographical Series, no.116.*) ISBN: 1851091289.

403 annotated entries in 21 sections: Country and its people - Geography and geology ... History ... Foreign relations ... Yearbooks, encyclopedias and directories - Bibliographies. Chronology p.xxi-xxiv. Rulers and dignitaries of Bhutan (1616 to date) p.xxv-xxvi. Glossary p.xxvii=xxxiii. Author, title and subject index.
Class No: 908(541.31)(01)

Nepal

[4719]

MAN MOHAN SHARMA. An Introduction to the mountain kingdom of Nepal. Pokhara (Nepal) and Noida (India), Dattatreya Prakashan, 1995. 358p. illus. (inc. 23p. pl.), maps, indexes. ISBN: 8185384185.

Pt.1 Introduction (location and legendary origins; Entry to Nepal; People; Festivals; Languages) - 2. Lore and legends - 3. Trekking (Travel Agencies p.320-35; Rafting Agencies p.336-7) - 4. Appendices (Bibliography p.339-42; Glossary p.343-8; Indexes).
Class No: 908(541.35)

Bibliographies

[4720]

WHELPTON, J. Nepal. Santa Barbara, California and Oxford, 1990. xxv,295p.+1p. map, index. £44.95; $75.00. (*World Bibliographical Series, no.38.*) ISBN: 0903450682.

917 annotated entries in 33 sections: Country and its people - Travellers' accounts - Geography and geology - Tourist guides ... Archaeology and prehistory - History ... Brigade of Gurkhas ... Reference works - Bibliographies. Author, title and subject index.

Sri Lanka

Bibliographies

[4721]

SAMARAWEERA, V., *comp.* **Sri Lanka.** Santa Barbara, California and Oxford, Clio Press, 1987. xliii, 194p.+1p. map, index. £32.50. $40.50. (*World Bibliographical Series; no.20.*) ISBN: 090345033x.

631 annotated entries. 34 sections: The country and its people - Geography - Travel guides - Travellers' accounts ... Prehistory - Archaeology and epigraphy - History ... Politics ... Libraries,

....(contd.)

museums and archives ... Bibliographies and indexes. Chronolog p.xxxix-xliii. Author, title and subject index.
Class No: 908(548.7)(01)

Pakistan

[4722]

KENNEDY, C.H. *and* **RAIS, R.B. Pakistan, 1995.** Boulder, Colo. Westview Press, 1995. 229p. £31.95. ISBN: 0813387280.

An analysis of social, political, religious and economic change sinc the early 1990s. *Class No:* 908(549)

Bibliographies

[4723]

TAYLOR, D., *comp.* **Pakistan.** Santa Barbara, California and Oxford Clio Press, 1990. xxxi,259p.+1p. map, indexes. (*Worl Bibliographical Series, no.10.*) ISBN: 1851090819.

797 annotated entries in 37 sections: The country and its people Geography ... Travellers' accounts - Tourism- Archaeology an prehistory - History - Biographies and autobiographies ... Arme forces ... Reference works - Bibliographies. Chronology p.xxix-xxx Heads of State and Prime Ministers p.xxxi. Author, title and subjec indexes. *Class No:* 908(549)(01)

Yearbooks & Directories

[4724]

Pakistan: an official handbook. Islamabad, Government of Pakista Directorate of Films and Publications. Ministry of Information an Broadcasting. Annual.

Originally as *West Pakistan yearbook.*

1995 volume (v,289p. col.illus. col. port., fold-in-map, index). 1 Pakistan (history) - 2. Foreign relations - 3. Justice - 4. Parliamentar affairs - 5. Federal government - 6. National Economy ... 8. Industr ... 29. Punjab - 30. Sindh - 31. Northwest Frontier Province - 32 Baluchistan - 26. States and frontier regions - 33. Azad Kashmir. ' review of government progress and achievements mainly economic .. the tone is inevitably bland but a considerable amount of informatio can be derived from it'. *Class No:* 908(549)(058)

[4725]

RAFIQUE AKHTAR. Pakistan year book 1993-94. 21st ed. Karach and Lahore, East and West Publishing Co., 1993. 592p. illus., ports. tables, index. ISBN: 9698017003.

1st ed. 1973.

38 sections deployed under 4 headings 1. The land and people - 2 The cultural heritage (History ... Archaeology ... Tourism) - 3. Th Government and its services - 4. The Economy. Analytical index.
Class No: 908(549)(058)

Bangladesh

[4726]

BAXTER, C. Bangladesh a new nation in an old setting. Boulder Colorado, Westview Press, 1984. xii, 130p. illus. map, bibliog. index $30.00. (*Nations of Contemporary Asia.*) ISBN: 0865316309.

9 chapters: 1. A delta and its people - 2. Hindu, Buddhists, an Muslims - 3. Bengal under the British - 4. A province of Pakistan - 5 A new nation-state - 6. Administration: civil and military - 7 Economic and social development - 8. Bangladesh in the world system - 9. Prospects: hope or despair? Annotated bibliography p.117-120.
Class No: 908(549.3)

Iran

Bibliographies

[4727]

FARHAD DIBA. A Bibliography of Iran. Tauris, 2v., 1989. 1200p index. £100.00. ISBN: 1850431213.

More than 14,000 items in several languages cover Iranian culture history, politics and economics *etc.. Class No:* 908(55)(01)

[4728]

NAVABPOUR, R., *comp.* **Iran.** Santa Barabara, California and Oxford Clio Press, 1988. xviii, 308p.+1p., map, index. £43.50. $52.00 (*World Bibliographical Series; no.81.*) ISBN: 1851090363.

787 annotated entries. 39 sections: The country and its people Geography and Geology - Travellers' accounts - Tourism and trave guides ... Prehistory and archaeology - History ... Ayatollah Khomei and the Iranian Revolution ... Iranian collections in foreign librarie museums and galleries ... Bibliographies. Author, title and subjec index. *Class No:* 908(55)(01)

Encyclopaedias

[4729]

ncyclopaedia Iranica. Yarshater, E., *ed.* New York, Columbia University Press; London, Routledge and Kegan Paul, 8v. 1985-. illus., maps, bibliog., index.

V.4 BAYJU-CARPETS. 896p.p. (2 cols.). ISBN 0710091311. $300.00; £200.00. In process of publication in fascicules (6pa.) each of 112 pages with 8 fascicules comprising one volume with the exception of v.1 which has 9. When complete the *Encyclopaedia* will consist of 18v., an index volume, and a single-volume supplement. Research tool covering archaeological, geographical, ethnographic, historical, artistic, literary, religious, linguistic, philosophical, scientific, and folklore studies. Coverage extends to surrounding areas and their cultural relations with Iran. 'As it is an unprecendented enterprise, many of the articles are the first comprehensive and systematic treatment of the topics they cover ... the most important and ambitious scholarly publication ever attempted in the field of Iranian studies' (*Middle Eastern Studies*, v.24, no.3, July 1988, p.391-392.

V.7 is on the Internet: www.iranica.com. *Class No:* 908(55)(031)

Turkey

Bibliographies

[4730]

ALIM-HARDING, C., *comp.* Turkey. 2nd ed. Santa Barbara, California and Oxford, Clio Press, 1999. xliii,407p.+2p. map, indexes. (*World Bibliographical Series; no.27.*) ISBN: 1851092951.

Replaces M. Güllcküü's *Turkey* (1981).

1434 annotated entries in 36 sections: The country and its people - Travel and tourism - Geology and Geography ... Archaeology and prehistory - History ... Overseas populations ... Encyclopaedias and reference works - Bibliographies. Author, title and subject indexes. The majority of the works cited have been published since 1980. Unlike other volumes in the series, this particular volume is a cooperative work, no fewer than 32 contributors were involved. *Class No:* 908(560)(01)

Cyprus

Bibliographies

[4731]

ITROMILIDES, P.M. *and* EVRIVIADES, M.L., *comps.* Cyprus. 2nd ed. Santa Barbara, California and Oxford, 1995. xli,264p.+2p. map, indexes. £46.50. (*World Bibliographical Series; no.28.*) ISBN: 1851092137.

1st ed. 1982.

931 annotated entries (689 in 1st ed.) in 33 subject divisions. The country and its people - Travel and tourism - Geology and geography - Cartography, maps and gazetteers ... Prehistory and archaeology - History - Foreign relations - Bibliographies. Chronology p.xxxii-xl. Author, title and subject indexes. *Class No:* 908(564.3)(01)

Handbooks & Manuals

[4732]

he Almanac of Cyprus 1999. Nicosia, Press and Information Office, 1999. 395p. illus. (many col.), tables, map. ISBN: 9963381952.

Compendium of local political, economic and cultural developments in 9 chapters: 1. Island of Cyprus - 2.History - 3. The Cyprus problems - 4. Political system - 5. Cyprus in the world - 6. Economy - 7. Society - Social Policy - 8. Education and culture - 9. Useful information. *Class No:* 908(564.3)(035)

Iraq

Bibliographies

[4733]

LEANEY, C.H., *comp.* Iraq. 2nd ed. Santa Barbara, California and Oxford, Clio Press, 1995. xxiii,362p. + 1p. map, index. £39.95. (*World Bibliographical Series; no.42.*) ISBN: 1851092293.

1st ed. compiled by A.J. Abdulrahman 1984.

827 annotated entries. 34 sections: The country and its people - Geography and geology - Travel ... Prehistory, archaeology and numismatics - History - Foreign Relations - Armed Forces and National Security ... Bibliographies. Author, title and subject index. *Class No:* 908(567)(01)

[4734]

McLACHLAN, K.S. *and* SCHOFIELD, R.N. A Bibliography of the Iran-Irak borderland. Wisbech, Cambridgeshire, Middle East & Northern African Studies Press, 1987. xii, 383p. index. £30. ISBN: 0906559219.

Almost 3,400 entries arranged in 5 chapters: 1. Geography; 2. Geology and geomorphology; 3. Maps; 4. Modern history and international relations; 5. Treaties, reports and bibliographies. Notes on library resources in London p.viii-xi. 'Attempts to review the literature germane to disputes over the boundary including matters affecting the entire frontier zone.' For recent newspaper and current affairs journal articles readers are referred to A. Mahrad's *Der Iran-Irak Konflikt*. *Class No:* 908(567)(01)

Syria

Bibliographies

[4735]

SECCOMBE, I.J., *comp.* Syria. Santa Barbara, California and Oxford, Clio Press, 1987. xxxii, 341p.+2p. map, index. £49.50. $55.00. (*World Bibliographical Series; no. 73.*) ISBN: 1851090185.

903 annotated entries. 32 sections - The country and its people - Travel guides and travelogues - Explorers' and travellers' accounts - Geography ... Prehistory and archaeology - History ... Minorities ... Libraries and archives ... Bibliographies. Author, title and subject index. *Class No:* 908(569.1)(01)

Lebanon

Bibliographies

[4736]

BLEANEY, C.H., *comp.* Lebanon. 2nd ed. Santa Barbara, California and Oxford, Clio Press, 1991. xxxi,230p.++ 1p. map, index. £39.; $84. (*World Bibliographical Series; no.2.*) ISBN: 1851091505.

1st ed. 1979 compiled by Shereen Khairallah

724 annotated entries in 34 sections: Country and its people - Geography - Travellers' accounts ... Prehistory and archaeology ... History ... Foreign relations ... Bibliographies. Author, title and subject index. Majority of the new entries in this edition relate to the civil war which broke out in 1975. *Class No:* 908(569.3)(01)

Israel

[4737]

HIRSCH, E., *ed.* Facts about Israel 1998. Jerusalem, Israeli Information Centre, 1998. 287p. col.illus.

History (Biblical times, Foreign domination, State of Israel) - The State - Land and people - Society - Health and Social Services - Education - Science and Technology - Economy - Culture - Israel among the nations. *Class No:* 908(569.4)

Bibliographies

[4738]

BLEANEY, C.H., *comp.* Israel. Santa Barbara, California and Oxford, Clio Press, 1994. xix,367. +1p. map, indexes. £56. (*World Bibliographical Series; no.58.*) ISBN: 1851091769.

Replaces E.M. Snyder and E. Kreiner's *Israel* (1985).

1010 annotated entries. 41 sections: The country and its people - Geography and geology - Travellers' accounts and photographs ... Archaeology and numismatics - History - PLO and the Palestinians in exile ... Jerusalem ... Biographies and Autobiographies ... Bibliographies. Glossary p.xvii-xix. Author, title and subject indexes. This edition concentrates on material published 1984-92. *Class No:* 908(569.4)(01)

Yearbooks & Directories

[4739]

The Israel year book and almanac 1999. Schramm, L., *ed.* 53rd ed. Jerusalem, IBRT Translation/Documentation, 1999. x,310p. illus., map tables, index. ISBN: 9659015623. ISSN: 00751413.

Incorporating *The Palestine yearbook and Israel annual*, formerly published in US for the Zionist Organization of America, and the *Anglo-Palestine year book* formerly published in UK.

1. General information (Physical data and human resources - Agriculture - Archaeology - Arts - Defense - Economy - Education - Environment - Foreign Affairs - Government - Health - Immigration and adoption - Judea, Samaria and Gaza - Justice - Media - National Institutions - Religion - Science and technology - Sports - Women - Awards and prices - Obituaries) 2. There is also a lexicon of Israeli 'English' (*e.g.* an academic is any person with a university education!). *Class No:* 908(569.4)(058)

Jordan

Bibliographies

[4740]
SECCOMBE, I.J., *comp*. **Jordan**. Santa Barbara, California and Oxford, Clio Press, 1984. xliii, 278p.+1p. map, index. £42.95. $45.00. (*World Bibliographical Series; no.55*.) ISBN: 0903450925.

834 annotated entries. 34 sections: The country and its people - Travel guides, travelogues and tourism - Explorers and travellers' accounts - Geography ... Prehistory and archaeology - History ... The West Bank since 1967 ... Libraries ... Bibliographies. Author, title and subject index. *Class No:* 908(569.5)(01)

Russia in Asia

[4741]
BATALDEN, S.K. *and* BATALDEN, S.L. **The Newly independent states of Eurasia** handbook of former Soviet Republics. 2nd ed. Phoenix, Oryx, 1997. 248p. maps, tables. $34.95. ISBN: 0897749405.

1st ed. 1993.

Up-to-date statistical profiles of each new republic, covering demography, government, education, economics, and communications, based on the most reliable sources available. Each profile is followed by an analytical discussion of the current political, cultural, and economic issues facing that country. A succinct summary of each republic's geography and history is also included. The countries profiled are Armenia, Azerbaijan, Belarus, Georgia, Kazakhstan, Kyrgyzstan, Moldova, the Russian Federation, Tajikistan, Turkmenistan, Ukraine, and Uzbekistan. A map of each republic and general maps of various regions are also provided. *Class No:* 908(57)

Siberia

[4742]
COLLINS, D.O., *comp*. **Siberia and the Soviet Far East**. Santa Barbara, Calif. and Oxford, Clio Press, 1991. xx,217p.+ 4p. maps, indexes. £35. (*World Bibliographical Series, no. 127*.) ISBN: 1851091572.

735 annotated entries in 27 sections: General works - Travellers' accounts - Travel guides - Geography ... Prehistory and archaeology - History - Ethnography ... Bibliographies - Encyclopaedias and reference works - Periodicals. Ethonyms p.xv-xvii. Author, title and subject indexes. *Class No:* 908(571)

Afghanistan

Bibliographies

[4743]
JONES, S., *comp*. **Afghanistan**. Santa Barbara, Calif., and Oxford, Clio Press, 1992. xxv,279p. +1p. map. indexes. £43.95. (*World Bibliographical Series, no.135*.) ISBN: 1851091405.

1014 annotated entries in 37 sections: Country and its people - Geography and geology - Tourism and guide books - Travel and exploration ... Archaeology - History - Soviet invasion and occupation ... Libraries, galleries, museums and archives ... Reference works - Bibliographies. Author, title and subject indexes.
Class No: 908(581)(01)

Asia—South East

[4744]
Southeast Asian affairs 1993. 20th ed. Singapore, Institute of Southeast Asian Studies, 1974-. Annual. xvii,372p. maps on endpapers. ISSN: 03775437.

Comprehensive coverage on Southeast Asian politics, economics, and social trends and developments in the form of analyses and writings primarily from contributors in the region. Part 1: Regional and ASEAN overviews; 2: Internal developments in each of 10 ASEAN countries. Bibliographical notes appended to each essay.
Class No: 908(59)

Maps & Atlases

[4745]
ULACK, R. *and* PAUER, G. **Atlas of Southeast Asia**. New York Macmillan Publishing Co.; London, Collier Macmillan Publishers, 1989. xvii, 171p. col. illus., col. maps, tables, bibliog., index. $95.00. £45.00. ISBN: 0029332001.

Part 1. Regional overview: 1. Physical environment and resources - 2. Historical and political background - 3. Cultural characteristics - 4. Regional population and urban characteristics. Part 2: 10 chapters on the nation - states of the region. Integrated text, maps and illustrations. Bibliography p.153-157. 70 maps. 'Fills a gap that has existed in the literature for many years' (*Booklist*, v. 85, no.16, 15 April 1989, p.1442-3). *Class No:* 908(59)(084.3)

Libraries

[4746]
Directory of South-East Asian library collections in the United Kingdom and Western Europe. Karni, R.S., *ed*. 3rd ed. Oxford Hans Zell on behalf of the South East Asia Library Group, 198? 240p. £35.00. ISBN: 0905450604.

150 libraries and documentation centres with sizeable holdings of printed materials on Southeast Asia. Data: full name and address plus collections, services and facilities information.
Class No: 908(59):061:026/027

Myanmar

Bibliographies

[4747]
HERBERT, P.M., *comp*. **Burma**. Santa Barbara, Calif., and Oxford Clio Press, 1991. xxiv,327p. +1p. map. indexes. £49. (*World Bibliographical Series, no.132*.) ISBN: 1851090886.

850 annotated entries in 30 sections: Country and its people - Travellers' accounts and guide books - Geography and geology . Prehistory and archaeology - History ... Religion ... Yearbook directories and statistics - Bibliographies and research guides. Author title and subject indexes. *Class No:* 908(591)(01)

Thailand

[4748]
KEYES, C.F. **Thailand:** Buddhist kingdom and modern nation-state Boulder, Colo., Westview Press, 1987; Bangkok, Editions Duang Kamos, 1989. xviii,252p. illus., maps, tables, bibliog., index.

6 chronological and thematic chapters. 'An accessible introduction to modern Thailand which, remarkably, also offers the specialist insight and information on virtually every page' (*Journal of Southeast Asia Studies*, v.22, no.2, September 1991, p.455-6). *Class No:* 908(593)

Bibliographies

[4749]
SMYTH, D. **Thailand**. 2nd ed. Santa Barbara, California and Oxford Clio Press, 1998. xxiv,226p.+1p. map, indexes. £56. (*World Bibliographical Series; no.65*.) ISBN: 1851092544.

1st ed. compiled by M. Watts 1986. (818 entries).

724 annotated entries. 32 sections: The country and its people Travel - Geography ... Prehistory and archaeology - History .. Yearbooks ... Bibliographies. Glossary p.xxiii-xxiv. Chronolog p.xix-xxii. Author, title and subject indexes. *Class No:* 908(593)(01)

Malaysia

[4750]
Malaysian studies archaeology, historiography, geography, and bibliography. Lent, J.A. *and* Mulliner, K., *eds*. Dekalb, Illinois Northern Illinois University Center for Southeast Asian Studies, 1986 Distribution by Cellar Book Shop. xi, 240p. bibliog. $14.00 (*Occasional Papers SEA Studies, no. 11*.) ISBN: 0318200708.

7 contributors. 5 essays each with a bibliography: 1. Archaeology in Malaysia, Brunei and Singapore - 2. Historiography of Peninsula Malaysia - 3. Survey and evaluation of the literature on modern Sarawak and Sabah history - 4. Geographical studies of Malaysia - 5 Recent bibliographical activities in Malaysia and Sarawak 'Recommended for graduate and upper-division collections .. particularly as a guide to essential Malay sources' (*Choice*, v.24, no.9 May 1987, p.1382). *Class No:* 908(595)

Bibliographies

[4751]
BROWN, I. *and* AMPALAVANAR, R., *comps*. **Malaysia**. Santa Barbara, California and Oxford, Clio Press, 1986. xxxv, 308p.+2p maps, index. £43.95. $53.50. (*World Bibliographical Series; no.12*.) ISBN: 0903450232.

754 annotated entries, 34 sections: The country and its people Geography ... Prehistory and archaeology - History ... Indigenous minority peoples ... Libraries ... Directories - General bibliographies Glossary p. xxxiii-xxxv. Author, title and subject index.
Class No: 908(595)(01)

[4764]

—Index Islamicus, 1665-1905: a bibliography on Islamic subjects in peridoicals and other collective publications. Behn, W.A., *comp*. Millersville, Pennsylvania, Adiyok Publications, 1989. 869p. map on front end papers, indexes. $125.00.

Extends coverage to Pearson's *Index Islamicus* back to the mid-17th century with 21,000 items in Western languages. The compiler was also joint compiler with Pearson on the *Fifth supplement* to the main work (1983). 'A required purchase for all libraries with research-level collections in Middle East studies' (*Choice*, v.27,no.2, October 1989, p.278). *Class No:* 908(5.297)(01)

[4765]

—Index Islamicus on CD-ROM. Roper, G.J. *and* Bleaney, C.H., *eds*. 3rd ed. East Grinstead, Sussex, Bowker Saur, 2000. Annual update. Windows 3.1. £1995. ISBN: 1857392507.

First published 1998. Excludes *Index Islamicus 1665-1905*.

224,000 entries. Coverage extends over the whole Muslim world, 1906-1998, including all aspects of Muslim life past and present. Publications are clearly recorded in two different categories and the index includes references from over 24,000 monographs and over 172,000 articles. As well as the books by individual authors, there are conference papers, celebration, presentation, memorial volumes and collections of essays.

Easy to use search screen combined with linked browse function, allows simple search routines to be conducted, ideal for both experienced and first time users. Hypertext searching across the database to enable users to refine or extend search results. Search criteria includes subject, author, title, title keyword, key word, publication date, record type and source. *Class No:* 908(5.297)(01)

[4766]

—ROPER, G. The Bibliography of the Arab Middle East with particular reference to Index Islamicus, p.11-37, *Arabic resources acquisition and management in British Libraries* (Mansell, 1986).
Class No: 908(5.297)(01)

Encyclopaedias

[4767]

The Oxford encyclopedia of the modern Islamic world. Exposito, J.L., *ed.* New York, Oxford Univ. Press, USA, 4 vols., 1995. 1902p. maps, bibliog., index. £295. ISBN: 0195066138.

750 A-Z cross-referenced entries 'dedicated to the institutions, religion, politics, and culture in Muslim societies throughout the world, with particular emphasis on the nineteenth and twentieth centuries'. Length of entries varies between brief articles to major analytical essays. Includes regional overviews and information on specific countries and c.100 biographical entries on political, religious, and literary figures. The inclusion of contributors from many parts of the world has helped to avoid what the editor calls the "pitfalls of Orientalism" ... an important purchase for academic and public libraries' (*Booklist*, v.91, no.17, 1 May, 1995, p.1588).
Class No: 908(5.297)(031)

Maps & Atlases

[4768]

Atlas of the Islamic world since 1500. Robinson, F. Oxford, Phaidon; New York, Facts On File, 1982. 238p. illus. (mostly col.), maps (mostly col.), bibliog., index. £18.50; $40.00. ISBN: 0714822000, UK; 0871966298, US.

Pt 1. Revelation and Muslim history - 2. To be a Muslim (religious life, Arts of Islam) and 10 specified features *e.g.* 'The Mughal World' and 'Ottoman World'. Chronological table p.8-9. Islamic rulers p.10-11. Glossary p.224-5. Bibliography p.229-31. Gazetteer p.232-4. 50 Maps. 'A mine of information on Islam and the Islamic world since A.D. 1500' (*Choice*, v.20, no.8, April 1983, p.114).
Class No: 908(5.297)(084.3)

Africa

[4769]

Africa today. 3rd ed. London, Africa Books Ltd., 1996. 1500p.+ 24p. col. maps. tables. £195. $295. (*Know Africa.*) ISBN: 0903274221. ISSN: 02611562.

1st ed. 1981. Companion volume to *Africa today* and *Makers of modern Africa (q.q.v.).*

Compendious reference work on 54 African countries presenting a detailed record of modern African history and the political, economic and social development, from an African viewpoint, arranged in 6 pts: 1. General (geography, languages, religion) - 2. Organizations (political and economic) - 3. A-Z Country surveys - 4. sports - 5. Quick reference - 6. Atlas. *Class No:* 908(6)

[4770]

BAKER, P., *comp*. International directory to African studies research. 3rd ed. London, Hans Zell, 1995. xxii,319p. indexes. £95. ISBN: 1873836368.

First published 1975 as *International guide to African studies research*.

Over 1800 entries (as compared to 1137 in the 2nd ed.) listing relevant research institution A-Z by country and by name of organization. Data: directory information, library holdings, publications, and summary of main areas of research. 5 indexes: serials, personnel, ethonyms and language names, international organizations, and a thematic index. *Class No:* 908(6)

[4771]

BUTE, E.L. *and* HARMER, H.J.P. The Black handbook the people, history and politics of Africa and the African diaspora. London, Cassell, 1997. vii,392p. index. ISBN: 0304335428.

4 introductory essays (People, Places and events, Terms, movements and ideas, and Colonialism, liberation, and war) precede country profiles A-Z (basic facts, geography, language, religions, population, defence, education, communications etc.) p.205-232. Political parties and leaders p.233-77. Intergovernmental organizations and treaties p.278-98. Rebellion, emancipation and civil rights in the U.S. p.299-321. Chronology of Africa and the African diaspora (1494-) p.325-85. First-class single-volume compendium of key events, facts and figures of historical and contemporary Africa. *Class No:* 908(6)

[4772]

YAKAN, M.Z. Almanac of African peoples and nations. New Brunswick, US., and London, Transaction Publishers, 1999. vii,847p. bibliog., index. ISBN: 1560004339.

8 parts: 1. Introduction - 2. African language families - 3. Languages by country - 4. African peoples and nations A-Z (p.27-134) - 5. African peoples and nations (p.137-713) - 6. Endnotes (459 references) p.717-33. Bibliography p.737-55. Index p.759-847. Comprehensive survey of ethnic groups, highlighting their contribution to the overall African scene, and the basic features of their respective cultures. *Class No:* 908(6)

[4773]

ZELL, H.M. *and* LOMER, C., *eds*. The African studies companion a resource guide and directory. 2nd ed. London, Hans Zell, 1997. xvi,276p. £40. ISBN: 1873836414.

1st ed. 1989.

Annotated guide to 935 major information sources arranged in 11 sections: 1. General reference sources - 2. Current bibliographies - 3. Journals and magazines - 4. Major libraries and documentation centres - 5. Publishers - 6. Dealers and distributors of African Studies materials - 7. Organizations - 8. Associations and Societies - 9. Foundations - 10. Awards and prizes. *Class No:* 908(6)

Bibliographies of Bibliographies

[4774]

SCHEVEN, Y. Bibliographies for African studies 1987-1993 Oxford, Hans Zell Publishers, 1994. xxi,176p. index. £42. ISBN: 1873836511.

Preceded by *Bibliographies for African studies 1970-1986*.

Brief annotations (inc. number of entries) on 800 separately published bibliographies on Sub-Sahara Africa arranged in 2 sections: 1. Topical (under 36 subject headings) - 2. Geographical (by 9 regions and 48 countries) 'Thorough, meticulously compiled, and totally essential' (*African Research and Documentation*, no.48, 1988, p.40-42). 'This volume will undoubtedly be used as a starting point for researchers on a very regular basis' (*Library Association Record*, v.97,no.8, August 1995, p.445). *Class No:* 908(6)(009)

Bibliographies

[4775]

Africa bibliography. Blackhurst, H., *in association with International African Institute, comp*. Manchester, Manchester Univ. Press, 1984 -. 1 - Annual. Distributed in North American by St. Martin's Press.

Records publications principally in the humanities, social sciences, and arts under 33 subject headings. Data sources are the book and periodical acquisitions of the John Rylands University Library of Manchester and material received by the International African Institute in London. 1987 volume includes 4031 entries from works published in 1986 and 1987 and indexes almost 400 journals. Review in *Journal of African History*, v.28, no.1, 1987, p. 175-6 compares its coverage with *International African Bibliography*. *Class No:* 908(6)(01)

Yearbooks & Directories

[4752]
Information Malaysia 1994 Yearbook. 14th ed. Kuala Lumpur, Berita Publishing, 1994. viii,633p. maps, tables. ISSN: 01266195.
43 sections: 1. Historical background ... 4. National symbols... 21. Constitution - 22. Monarchy... 30. Johor Darul Takzim - 31. Kedah - 32. Kelantan... 39. Sabah - 40. Sarawak - 41. Selangor - 42. Terengganu - 43. Federal territory. Exhaustive and authoritative yearbook. *Class No:* 908(595)(058)

Singapore

[4753]
Singapore facts and pictures 1997. Singapore, Ministry of Information and the Arts, 1997. 205p. col. illus., col. map, tables, index, pbk. ISSN: 02177773.
Illustrated compendium of popular appeal in 30 sections (Land and people - History - Government ... Tourism - General information for tourists - Places of interest - Islands). *Class No:* 908(595.13)

Bibliographies

[4754]
QUAH, S.R. *and* **QUAH, J.S.T.,** *comps.* **Singapore.** Santa Barbara, California and Oxford, Clio Press, 1988. xv, 258p.+2p. maps, indexes. £39.50. $55.00. (*World Bibliographical Series; no.95.*) ISBN: 1851090711.
764 annotated entries. 33 sections: The country and its people - Geography and Tourism ... History ... Finance and banking ... Libraries and museums - Directories ... Bibliographies. Author, title, and subject indexes. *Class No:* 908(595.13)(01)

Yearbooks & Directories

[4755]
Singapore 1998. Singapore, Publicity Division, Ministry of Information and the Arts, 1998. 386p. col. illus., tables, maps on endpapers. S$23.10. ISSN: 0129766x.
23 sections: Singapore in 1997 - Awards, events and milestones - History - Land - People ... International relations ... Tourism etc. *Class No:* 908(595.13)(058)

Kampuchea (Cambodia)

Bibliographies

[4756]
JARVIS, H., *comp.* **Cambodia.** Santa Barbara, Calif., and Oxford, Clio Press, 1997. lxiv,412p.+1p. map, indexes. £79. (*World Bibliographical Series, no.200.*) ISBN: 1851091777.
933 annotated entries in 38 sections: Country and its people - Geography, maps and atlases - Tourism and travel guides - Travellers' accounts and exploration ... Archaeology - History - Personal accounts, biographies and autobiographies... Bibliographies ... Internet sites and databases. Introduction (*i.e.* outline history) p.xix-xxxii. Chronology p.xxxv-lxii. Author, title and subject indexes. *Class No:* 908(596)(01)

Vietnam

[4757]
SARDESAI, D.R. Vietnam the struggle for national unity. 2nd ed. Boulder, Colo., Westview Press, 1992. xi,192p. maps, bibliog., index. ISBN: 0813381967.
1st ed. 1988 published by Promilla.
1. Ethnicity, geography, and early history - 2. Millenium of freedom - 3. French conquest - 4. Nationalist movement - 5. Roots of second Indochina war - 6. Indochina imbroglio - 7. New Vietnam - 8. International relations - 9. Cambodia question and US-Vietnamese relations. Chronology p.153-7. Chapter notes p.159-64. Bibliography p.165-77. 3 maps. *Class No:* 908(597)

Bibliographies

[4758]
MARR, D.G., *comp.* **Vietnam.** Santa Barbara, Calif., and Oxford, Clio Press, 1992. lxxviii,393p. +1p. map. indexes. £65. (*World Bibliographical Series, no.147.*) ISBN: 1851090924.
1038 annotated entries in 32 sections: Country and its people - Traveller's accounts - Geography ... Archaeology and prehistory - History - Biography and autobiography ... Minorities and nationalities ... Foreign relations ... Bibliographies. Chronology p.xlvii-lxxvi. Glossary p. lxxvii-lxxviii. Author, title, and subject indexes. *Class No:* 908(597)(01)

Laos

Bibliographies

[4759]
CORDELL, H., *comp.* **Laos.** Santa Barbara, Calif. and Oxford, Cl Press, 1991. xxxvi, 215p. +1p. map. indexes. £36. (*Worl Bibliographical Series, no.133.*) ISBN: 1851090754.
548 annotated entries in 34 sections: Country and its people Travellers' accounts and travel guides - Geography and geology . Prehistory and archaeology - History ... Ethnic groups ... Annuals a directories - Manuscripts and archives - Bibliographies. Author, tit and subject indexes. *Class No:* 908(598)(01)

Islamic World

[4760]
ULPH, S. Handbook to the Islamic Middle East. London, Cassel 1994. 480p. illus., maps, tables, index. £35. $70. ISBN: 0304324809
Concise, quick-reference guide to the religion, history, literature ar culture of the Islamic Middle East, divided into broad subject section each of which includes introductory essays, feature article chronologies, who's whos, glossaries, indexes, tables and maps. *Class No:* 908(5.297)

Bibliographies

[4761]
Bibliography of Islamic Central Asia. Bregel, Y., *comp.* Bloomingto IN., Research Institute for Inner Asian Studies, Univ. of Indian 1995. lixx,2276p. (*$299.* (*Indiana Univ. Uralic and Altaic Studie no.160.*).)
30,000+ entries relating to the Inner Asian heartland from th introduction of Islam in the 8th century A-D, to the introduction Communism, arranged in 19 sub-divided sections (*e.g.* archaeolog history, description and travel). Entries cited in all major language except Chinese and Japanese. 'A real spur to further endeavours in th field of Central Asian studies' *Bulletin of the School of Oriental ar African Studies,* v.61,no.3, 1998, p.581-82). *Class No:* 908(5.297)(01)

[4762]
Index Islamicus 1906-1955 a catalogue of articles on Islamic subjects i periodicals and other collective publications. Pearson, J.D. an Ashton, J.F., *comps.* Cambridge, Heffer, 1958 (reprinted Mansel 1961, with minor corrections). xxxvi,895p. £65.00. ISBN 0702103800. ISSN: 03069524.
Supplement 1956-1960 (1962) xxviii,316p. £48.00. 0720103819 *Second supplement 1961-1965* (1967) xxx,342p. £48.00. 0720103827 *Third supplement 1966-1970* London, Mansell, 1972. xxxvi,384p £48.00. ISBN 0720102820. *Fourth Supplement 1971-1975* (1977 xlii,429p. £48.00. 0720106397. ISSN 03069524. *Fifth supplemer 1976-1980* (2v., 1983). *part 1. Articles,* xliii,539p. Part 2 *Monographs,* xii,348p. £110.00. 0720116503 set. *Index Islamicu 1981-1985:current books, articles and papers on Islamic subject* compiled by G.J. Roper, 2v., 1990. 1216p. £100.00. $200.00 0720120098 set. Some 30,000 items some of which do not appear i the *Quarterly. Index Islamicus: a bibliography of books and articles o the Muslim World* compiled by G.J. Roper. Bowker-Saur, 2v. 1991 1347p. 6th quinquennial supplement 1981-1985. 34,382 entries. Th main volume has more than 26,000 entries drawn from 51 periodicals, plus Festschriften, other collective works and congres proceedings. Aims to cover the whole field of Islamic studies, pur science and technology alone being excluded. Not confined to Islami countries but includes items of Islamic interest from elsewhere Restricted to material in Western languages, including Russian Classified arrangement with main divisions: General works an bibliography - Religion and theology - Law - Philosophy and science Art - Geography - Ethnology and history - Language - Literature Education. Author index. Unquestionably the basic bibliographical too in its field. *The Quarterly Index Islamicus* (1986-1992) £95.p (institutions) £24. (individuals) ISSN 03087395 draws on over 1,10 sources in all European languages. *Class No:* 908(5.297)(01)

[4763]
—Index Islamicus New books, articles and reviews on Islam and th Muslim world. Roper, G.J. *and* Bleaney, C.H., *comps.* Eas Grinstead, Bowker Saur, 1994-. 3 issues per annum. ISSN: 13600982.
Replaces *Quarterly index Islamicus* (1986-1993).
Arranged in 95 form, thematic and country sections (*e.g.* 1. Islami studies history and organization, institutions and scholars; genera reference works 15. Geography and Ecology, Travel and exploratio ... 18. Archaeology ... 21/22. History ... 31/92. Muslims in regior and separate countries across Africa, Asia, and Europe. *Class No:* 908(5.297)(01)

[4776]

frica since 1914. Santa Barbara, California and Oxford, ABC-Clio Information Services, 1985. ix, 402p. indexes. £60.50. $75.00. (*Clio Bibliography Series.*) ISBN: 0874363950.

4329 abstracts of journal articles printed 1973-1982 extracted from the ABC - Clio databank and arranged in 11 chapters: 1. General - 2. Pan African integration and cooperation - 3. African politics - 4. International relations and trade - 5. Africa in the world wars - 6. Society and culture - plus five regional chapters. 'A worthwhile acquisition for specialist libraries'. (*Journal of African History*, v.28, no.3, 1987, p.469). *Class No:* 908(6)(01)

[4777]

ENTON, T. and HEFFRON, M.J., *comps.* Africa a directory of resources. New York, Orbis Books, 1987. 144p. pbk. $9.94. ISBN: 0883445328.

Organizations, reference books, pamphlets, articles, and audiovisual materials. 'A useful work that deserves frequent updating' (*Choice*, v.25,no.11-12, July-August 1988, p.1674). *Class No:* 908(6)(01)

[4778]

ARRIS, G. Central and Equatorial Africa area bibliography. Lanham, MD., Scarecrow Press, 1999. xli,209p. index. £55.10. (*Scarecrow Area Bibliographies, no.18.*) ISBN: 0810836068.

1,763 unannotated entries, including some for French, German and Spanish publications, relating to Chad, Central African Republic, São Thomé Principe, Equatorial Guinea, Gabon, People's Republic of Congo (Congo Brazzaville), Democratic Republic of Congo (Congo-Kinshasa and Zaire), Rwanda, Burundi, Zambia, and Malawi. Introduction (p.ix-xli) consists of a long bibliographical essay which highlights items listed in the text. Arranged by country A-Z and by subject. *Class No:* 908(6)(01)

[4779]

nternational African bibliography current books, articles and papers in African studies. Hall, D., *ed.* London, Mansell, 1971-. Quarterly. ISSN: 00205877.

Appeared as a supplement to the International African Institute's journal, *Africana*, until 1970. A fuller history of the project up to 1972 appears in R. Jones' introduction to the Institute's *Cumulative bibliography of African studies* (2v., 1973) (*q.v.*).

This quarterly bibliography lists serious and authoritative work in African studies, covering the whole of the African continent (and adjacent islands), except for Egypt. The main focus is on the arts and humanities, but there is some coverage of scientific publications, especially relating to geography, natural resources and environmental issues. Arrangement is primarily geographical, but to aid a subject approach, one or more subject tracings are included at the end of each entry so that the user may rapidly scan the page to pick out a particular subject. The first section, covering Africa in general, is subdivided into broad subject groupings.

International African bibliography 1973-1978: books, articles and papers in African studies edited by J.D. Pearson (Mansell, 1982. xxx,343p. ISBN 0720115655) covers v.3-8 plus 3000 items not recorded in the quarterly issues. *Class No:* 908(6)(01)

[4780]

KAGAN, A. and SCHEVEN, Y. Reference guide to Africa a bibliography of sources. Lanham, MD., Scarecrow Press, 1999. vii,262p. $49.50. ISBN: 0810835851.

944 entries relating to continental Africa arranged in 2 main parts: 1. General sources (inc. bibliographies, indexes, guides, handbooks, encyclopedias, biographical works, and government publications) - 2. Subject sources (17 disciplines). Author, title and subject indexes. 'An excellent reference source' (*Choice*, v.36, no.10, June 1999, p.1754). *Choice* Outstanding Academic Title 1999. *Class No:* 908(6)(01)

[4781]

McILVAINE, J. Africa: a guide to reference material. Oxford, Hans Zell, 1992. xxv,507p. indexes. £75. (*Regional Reference Guides, no. 1.*) ISBN: 0905450434.

Annotated guide to 1766, factual reference works relating to Africa south of the Sahara including encyclopaedias, dictionaries, directories, handbooks, gazetteers, almanacs, yearbooks, topographic reference sources, biographical sources, statistical sources and other categories. Appendix includes Annual Reports on British possessions in Africa from 1846 until date of independence. 'Will be an essential companion to African studies for many years' (*Library Association Record*, v.95, no.10, October 1993, p.574). *Class No:* 908(6)(01)

Encyclopaedias

[4782]

Africana the encyclopedia of the African and African American experience. Appiah, K.A. and Gates, H.L., *eds.* New York, Basic Civitas Books, 1999. xxxvii,2095p. col.illus., col.maps, tables, bibliog. $100. ISBN: 0465000711.

3,500+ cross-referenced A-Z entries from 225 contributors relating to every facet of Africa and the African diaspora although primarily focused on political, social and cultural history. The aim is 'to give a

....(contd.)

sense of the wide diversity of peoples, cultures, and traditions that we know about Africa in historical times, a feel for the environment in which that history was lived, and a broad outline of the contributions of people of African descent, especially in the Americas, but, more generally around the world' (*Introduction*). 12 featured articles up to 15 pages each; shorter entries from 1/2 column to 5 pages. Bibliography p.2065-95. 'The strength of Africana's unique linkage of the African and African American worlds becomes evident in comparison to other reference works treating one or the other half of that whole' (*Booklist*, v.96, no.12, 15 February 2000, p.1132+1134). 'Avoids extreme idealogical stands' (*Library Journal*, v.124, no.19, 15 November 1999, p.58). *Class No:* 908(6)(031)

[4783]

Encyclopedia of Africa South of the Sahara. Middleton, J., *and others, eds.* New York, Charles Scribers' Sons, 4v., 1997. xli,555p.+586p.+614p.+711p. illus., maps, col.maps on endpapers, bibliogs., index. ISBN: 0684804670, v.1; 0684804689, v.2; 0864804697, v.3; 0684804700, v.4; 0684804662, set.

c.700 contributors. A-Z cross-referenced, signed articles, each with a short list of references, encompassing African history, geography, religion, economy, medicine, nationalism, ideologies, historical and cultural interpretation etc. The aim is to present 'What is today generally known and accepted about human endeavour and achievement in Africa' (*editor's preface*). Appendix A. African studies outside Africa v.4, p.435-59. B. Chronology (comparative timelines) p.461-76. C. Ethnic groups (A-Z by country tables: alternative name, location, linguistic affiliation, population, notes) p.477-563. Analytical index p.585-711. *Class No:* 908(6)(031)

[4784]

OLIVER, R. and CROWDER, M. The Cambridge encyclopedia of Africa. Cambridge, Cambridge Univ. Press, 1981. 492p. illus. (some col.), maps (some col.), tables, diagrs. £27.50 $35.00. ISBN: 0521230969.

99 contributors. 4 sections: 1. The African continent - 2. The African past before European colonisation - 3. Contemporary Africa - 4. Africa and the World. Bibliography (by chapter) p.485-491. 'There is really no other work on the market at present that is so comprehensive and useful as this handsome publication' (*Choice*, v.19, no.10, June 1982, p.1374). *Class No:* 908(6)(031)

Yearbooks & Directories

[4785]

Africa South of the Sahara 2000. 29th ed. London, Europa, 1999. Annual. xix,1210p. maps, tables, bibliogs. £240.$445. (*Regional Surveys of the World.*) ISBN: 1857430603. ISSN: 00653896.

First published 1971.

51 contributors. Part 1. Background to the continent: 3 featured essays (European colonial rule in Africa, Date of Independence of African countries) - 2. Regional Organizations, all major organizations working in the region: their aims activities, publications etc. Pt.3. Country surveys A-Z: Physical and social geography; Recent history; The Economy; Statistical survey; Directory (i.e. constitution; government; political organizations; diplomatic representation; religion; news media; finance; trade/industry; transport; tourism; atomic energy; power; defence; and Bibliography. Calendar of political events 1998-1999 p.xvi-xviii. 'This is a reference book which is unsurpassed and I would think unsurpassable' 'An excellent reference tool for detailed information about the countries included' (*Reference Reviews*, v.14, no.3, 2000, p.54-55). *Class No:* 908(6)(058)

[4786]

New African yearbook 1997-1998 Rake, A., *ed.* 11th ed. London, I.C. Publications, 1997. 540p. maps, tables. ISBN: 0905268628. ISSN: 01401378.

African organizations (directory) p.9-18. 63 A-Z by country summary articles on each country's political history, banking, communications, economy, current events, politics, and statistics, p.20-540. *Class No:* 908(6)(058)

Libraries

[4787]

STANDING CONFERENCE ON LIBRARY MATERIALS ON AFRICA. SCOLMA directory of Libraries and special collections on Africa in the UK and in Europe. French, T. 5th ed. Oxford, Hans Zell, 1993. 355p. index. £58. ISBN: 0905450892.

First published in 1963.

Over 300 collections identified and described. Arranged geographically by country. Data includes name of librarian; hours of opening; subject coverage; special services; publications; CD-ROM and online databases *etc*. Detailed index of subjects, territories, authors and organizations. *Class No:* 908(6)(058):061:026/027

Maps & Atlases

[4788]
GRIFFITHS, I.Ll. **An Atlas of African affairs.** 2nd ed. London, Routledge, 1994. x,233p., maps, tables, bibliog., index. £37.50. ISBN: 0415054885.

65 enviromental, historical, political, economic and southern Africa sections each containing a map or group of maps with 2-4 pages of text. Chronology of African independence (States, capitals, changes of government, and political leaders of post-colonial Africa). Redrawn maps are of high quality - 'Considering the limitations of working without colour, the maps in general achieve wonders of compression and exposition' (*The Year In Reference* 1994, p.32-33).
Class No: 908(6)(084.3)

[4789]
MURRAY, J., *ed.* **Cultural atlas of Africa.** Oxford, Phaidon; New York, Facts on File, 1981. 240p. illus. (mostly col.). col. maps. bibliog., index. £17.95. $29.95. ISBN: 0714820458.

1. Physical background (natural geographical phenomena) - 2. Cultural - 3. Nations of Africa, a country by country survey grouped regionally. Also 16 special features (*e.g.* Great Zimbabwe; Source of the Nile debate; Mapping of Africa; Flags-symbols of nationhood). Bibliography p.227-229. Gazetteer p.230-235. 84 maps. 'A great deal of information in an extraordinarily attractive book' (*Choice*, v.19, no.1, September 1981, p.52). *Class No:* 908(6)(084.3)

Black Races

Handbooks & Manuals

[4790]
MORRISON, D.G., *and others.* **Black Africa** a comparative handbook. 2nd ed. New York, Paragon House; London, Collier Macmillan, 1989. 720p. maps, charts, tables. $169.50. £99. ISBN: 0887020429, US; 0333498631, UK.

1st ed. 1972.

Systematic data on 41 nations (32 in 1st ed.). Pt1. Comparative profiles with notes on the uses and limitations of cross-national data; measures, models and meaning in aggregate data; ethnic unit classification and analysis, *etc.* Pt2. Country profiles A-Z. Sources are given; select bibliography for each territory. 'An essential reference work for students, scholars and organizations requiring quantitive comparative information relevant to problems of development in Africa' (*Choice*, v.10, no.3, May 1973, p.429-30).
Class No: 908(6)(=96)(035)

Africa—North

Bibliographies

[4791]
BLACKHURST, H. **East and Northeast Africa bibliography** Lanham, Md., Scarecrow Press, 1996. xiv,299p. index. (*Scarecrow Area Bibliographies, no.7.*) ISBN: 0810830906.

3838 unannotated entries, arranged under A-Z subject headings, relating to post-1960 books or booklets of at least 40 pages. Covers the countries of Djibuti, Eritrea, Ethiopia, Kenya, Somalia, Sudan, Tanzania and Uganda. Author index p.165-99.
Class No: 908(61/65)(01)

Maghreb

Bibliographies

[4792]
PAZZANITA, A.G., *comp.* **The Maghreb.** Oxford and Santa Barbara, Calif., Clio Press, 1998. xxxiv,328p.+1p. map. indexes. £57. (*World Bibliographical Series, no.208.*) ISBN: 1851093109.

531 annotated entries in 21 sections: Region and its people - Geography and the environment - Explorers and early travellers' accounts - Travel memoirs and travel guides - Prehistory and archaeology - History ... Dictionaries and bibliographies. Introduction (history, colonialism, overview of the Arab Maghreb Union and its French-language publications) p.xvii-xxxii. Glossary p.xxxiii-xxxiv. Author, title and subject indexes. *Class No:* 908(61/66)(01)

Tunisia

Bibliographies

[4793]
LAWLESS, R.I., *and others, comp.* **Tunisia.** Santa Barbara, California and Oxford, Clio Press, 1982. xxviii, 251p. map, index. £35.95. $36.00. (*World Bibliographical Series; no.33.*) ISBN: 0903450631.

895 annotated entries. 35 sections: The country and its people - Travel and travel guides - Tourism - Geography and geology ...

....(contd.)
Prehistory and archaeology ... Libraries and archives .. Bibliographies. Author, title and subject index.
Class No: 908(611)(01)

Libya

Bibliographies

[4794]
BESCHORNER, N., *comp.* **Bibliography of Libya 1970-1990** London, Centre of Near and Middle Eastern Studies, SOAS, Univ. o London, and Society for Libyan Studies. vi,110p. softcover. ISBN 0728601729.

528 unannotated entries for books and pamphlets mainly in Wester languages but a few in Arabic script arranged under 9 headings bibliography, economics, Islam, law, natural resources/environment politics, sociology, transport, and urbanization. Locations (with shelfmarks) are given for 8 London and 1 Libyan libraries.
Class No: 908(612)(01)

[4795]
LAWLESS, R.I., *comp.* **Libya.** Santa Barbara, California and Oxford Clio Press, 1987. xxi, 243p.+1p. map, index. £35.95. $47.75. (*World Bibliographical Series; no.79.*) ISBN: 1851090339.

626 annotated entries. 31 sections: The country and its people Travellers' accounts and travel guides - Geography and geology Prehistory and archaeology - History ... Foreign relations ... Librarie and archives ... Bibliographies. Author, title and subject index.
Class No: 908(612)(01)

Egypt

Bibliographies

[4796]
MAKER, R.N., *comp.* **Egypt.** Santa Barbara, California and Oxford Clio Press, 1988. xxxi, 306p.+1p. map, indexes. £46.95. $55.00 (*World Bibliographical Series; no.86.*) ISBN: 1851090398.

1022 annotated entries. 31 sections: The country and its people Geography, maps and geology - Tourism and travel guides Travellers' accounts - History ... Libraries and museums Bibliographies. Chronology p. xxi-xxv. Glossary p. xxvii-xxxi Author, title and subject indexes. *Class No:* 908(620)(01)

Sudan

Bibliographies

[4797]
DALY, M.W., *comp.* **Sudan.** Rev. and expanded ed. Santa Barbara California and Oxford, Clio Press, 1992. 194p.++ 1p., indexes £24.95. (*World Bibliographical Series; no.40.*) ISBN: 1851091874.

First published 1983.

708 annotated entries. 29 sections: Land and people - Geography and Geology - Exploration and travel ... History - Biography and autobiography ... Libraries and archives - Bibliographies. Author, title and subject indexes. *Class No:* 908(624)(01)

[4798]
HILL, R.L. **A Bibliography of the Anglo-Egyptian Sudan** from the earliest times to 1937. London, Oxford Univ. Press, 1939. 213p., indexes.

About 5,000 items, on all aspects of knowledge. History, p.113-52 includes biography and genealogy, and is arranged under periods Indexes of persons and subjects. *Class No:* 908(624)(01)

[4799]
—EL NASRI, A.R., *comp.* **A Bibliography of the Sudan 1938-1958.** London, Oxford Univ. Press for Univ. of Khartoum, 1962. x, 171p.

Continues R.H. Hill's *A bibliography of the Anglo-Egyptian Sudan* (1939) (*qv*). 2,763 items, the largest section being on government and politics. Agriculture, anthropology, economics, history, language and literature, medicine also figure. The compiler was librarian of the Univ. of Khartoum.

Supplemented by 'Sudan bibliography, 1959-1963' and 'A bibliography of the Sudan, 1964-1966,' by Ibrahim and A.R. El Nasri, in *Sudan notes and records*, v.46, 1965, p. 130-66, and v.49, 1968. 162-91: 1,893 unannotated items in all, under sections.
Class No: 908(624)(01)

Ethiopia

Bibliographies

[4800]

ILKIAS, P. **Ethiopia:** a comprehensive bibliography. Boston, Massachusetts, G.K. Hall, 1989. 650p. index. $75.00. Export $85.00. ISBN: 0816190666.

Over 16,000 items listed covering all aspects of Ethiopian history, culture and society arranged thematically. Includes much material previously unrecorded outside Ethiopia. *Class No:* 908(63)(01)

[4801]

IUNRO-HAY, S. *and* PANKHURST, R., *comps*. **Ethiopia.** Oxford and Santa Barbara, Calif., Clio Press, 1995. xxxiii,225p.+1p. map. index. £39.95. (*World Bibliographical Series, no. 179.*) ISBN: 1851091114.

610 annotated entries in 30 sections: Country and its people - Travellers' accounts and travel guides - Geography and geology ... Prehistory and archaeology - History - Eritrean conflict ... Drought, famine and international aid ... Bibliographies and reference works. Chronology and list of rulers p.xxiii-xxvii. Theses and dissertations p.xxix-xxxiii. Author, title and subject indexes. *Class No:* 908(63)(01)

Eritrea

Bibliographies

[4802]

EGLEY, R., *comp*. **Eritrea.** Oxford and Santa Barbara, Calif., Clio Press, 1995. lix,125p.+1p. map, index. £28.50. (*World Bibliographical Series, no.181.*) ISBN: 1851092455.

341 annotated entries arranged in 31 sections: Country and its people - Travel guides - Explorers' and Travellers' accounts - Geography ... Prehistory and archaeology - History ... Biographies ... Reference works and scholarly journals - Bibliographies. Author, title and subject index. A long introduction contains useful information on Eritrean history. *Class No:* 908(635)(01)

Morocco

Bibliographies

[4803]

INDLAY, A.M., *and others, comps.* **Morocco.** 2nd ed. Santa Barbara, California and Oxford, Clio Press, 1995. xxxii,178p.+1p. map, indexes. £32.50. (*World Bibliographical Series; no.47.*) ISBN: 1851092161.

1st ed. 1984.

622 annotated entries. 38 sections: The country and its people - Geography - Travel guides, and tourism - Travellers' accounts - Prehistory and archaeology - History ... Western Sahara ... Bibliographies. Author, title and subject indexes. This revised volume retains key works from the first edition whilst focusing primarily on literature published in the last ten years, which has tended to concentrate on political, economic and environmental issues. *Class No:* 908(64)(01)

Western Sahara

Bibliographies

[4804]

*AZZANITA, A.G., *comp*. **Western Sahara.** Oxford and Santa Barbara. Calif., Clio Press, 1996. xl,259p.+1p. map, indexes. £49. (*World Bibliographical Series, no.190.*) ISBN: 1851092560.

620 annotated entries grouped in 13 sections: Territory and its people - Geography - Travel memoirs - History ... Politicans and foreign relations ... Bibliographies. Glossary p.xxxix-xl. Chronology p.xxxv-xxxvii. Author, title and subject indexes. *Class No:* 908(648)(01)

Azores

Bibliographies

[4805]

MONIZ, M., *comp*. **Azores.** Oxford and Santa Barbara, Calif., ABC-Clio, 1999. lv,312p.+1p. map, indexes. £42. (*World Bibliographical Series, no 221.*) ISBN: 1851092838.

777 annotated entries arranged in 34 sections: Region and its people - Navigation, pilot guides and the coast - Geography, geology, and volcanology ... Tourism and travel guides ... Travellers' accounts - History ... Biographies, autobiographies, memoirs and correspondence ... Bibliographies and catalogues. Introduction (geography, political history and development etc.) p.xxiii-l. Author, title and subject indexes. *Class No:* 908(649.9)(01)

Algeria

Bibliographies

[4806]

LAWLESS, R.I., *comp*. **Algeria.** 2nd ed. Santa Barbara, California and Oxford, Clio Press, 1995. lxxv,309p.+1p. map, indexes. £58.00. (*World Bibliographical Series; no.19.*) ISBN: 1851091300.

1st ed. 1980.

886 annotated entries. 36 sections: The country and its people - Tourism and travel - Geography and Geology ... Prehistory and archaeology - History ... Maghreb unity ... Nomadism ... Bibliographies. Theses and dissertations in English on Algeria p.lvii-lxxv.Author, title and subject indexes. *Class No:* 908(65)(01)

Mauritania

Bibliographies

[4807]

CALDERINI, S., *and others, comps*. **Mauretania.** Santa Barbara, Calif., and Oxford, Clio Press, 1992. xvii,165p +1p. map. indexes. £27.95. (*World Bibliographical Series, no.141.*) ISBN: 1851091521.

405 annotated entries in 29 sections: Country and its people - Travel memoirs and travel guides - Explorers and early travellers' accounts - Geography ... Prehistory and archaeology - History ... Slavery ... Foreign aid ... Bibliographies. Author, title, and subject indexes. *Class No:* 908(661.2)(01)

Mali

[4808]

IMPERATO, P.J. **Mali** a search for direction. Boulder, Colo., Westview Press; London, Dartmouth, 1989. xiv,170p. illus., maps, bibliog., index. $29. (*Profiles. Nations Of Contemporary Africa.*) ISBN: 0813303419.

1. Introduction - 2. Early history - 3. Conquest, colonial rule, and independence. 4. Malian politics since independence - 5. Culture and society - 6. Economy - 7. International relations. Chapter notes p.149-58. Bibliography p.159-62. *Class No:* 908(662.1)

Bibliographies

[4809]

STAMM, A.L., *and others, comps*. **Mali** Oxford and Santa Barbara, Calif., Clio Press, 1998. xxxv,327p.+1p. map, indexes. (*World Bibliographical Series, no. 207.*) ISBN: 1851091661.

910 English - and French-language annotated items in 35 sections: Country and its people - Explorers and Travellers' accounts - Recent travel and guidebooks - Geography ... Prehistory and archaeology - History ... Bibliographies. Introduction (peoples, early and modern history) p.xvii-xxxv. Author, title and subject indexes. *Class No:* 908(662.1)(01)

Burkina Faso

[4810]

ENGLEBERT, P. **Burkina Faso:** unsteady statehood in West Africa. Boulder, Colo., Westview Press, 1996. 224p. illus., maps, bibliog., index. £63.00. £46.95. (*Nations of the Modern World: Africa.*) ISBN: 0813382491.

Burkina Faso's precolonial and colonial history; its political instability, economy, poverty, society, culture and foreign relations. *Class No:* 908(662.5)

Bibliographies

[4811]

DECALO, S., *comp*. **Burkina Faso.** Oxford and Santa Barbara, Calif., Clio Press, 1994. 132p.+1p. map, indexes. 24.50 $48.50. (*World Bibliographical Series, (no.169).*) ISBN: 1851092145.

412 annotated entries in 25 sections: The country and its people, Geography and geology ... Prehistory and archaeology - History - The peoples ... Conservation, Drought and Ecology ... Travel and tourism - Reference works, bibliographies and research guides. Author, title and subject indexes. *Class No:* 908(662.5)(01)

Niger

[4812]

CHARLICK, R.B. **Niger** personal rule and survival in the Sahel. Boulder, Colo., Westview Press; London, Dartmouth, 1991. xv,189p. illus., tables, maps, bibliog., index. £20. (*Profiles Nations of Contemporary Africa.*) ISBN: 0891589686, US; 1855212226, UK.

1. The Sahel and its people - 2. Historical background to contemporary Niger - 3. Nigerien political system - 4. Economy - 5. Niger in the world. Bibliography p.171-5. *Class No:* 908(662.6)

Bibliographies

[4813]

ZAMPONI, L.F., *comp*. **Niger.** Santa Barbara, Calif., and Oxford, Clio Press, 1994. xl,233p. + 1p. map, indexes. £39.95. (*World Bibliographical Series, no.164.*) ISBN: 1851092048.

431 annotated entries in 32 sections: Country and its people - Geography - Travel guides - Explorers' and travellers' accounts ... Prehistory and archaeology - History ... Drought and famine ... Bibliographies. Author, title and subject indexes.
Class No: 908(662.6)(01)

Senegal

Bibliographies

[4814]

EADES, J. *and* DILLEY, R.M., *comps*. **Senegal.** Santa Barbara, Calif., and Oxford, Clio Press, 1994. xlii,284p. + 1p. map, indexes. £48. (*World Bibliographical Series, no.166.*) ISBN: 1851091564.

860 annotated entries in 33 sections: Country and its people - Geography ... Maps and atlases - Travel guides - Explorers' and travellers' accounts ... History ... Tourism - Research resources. Author, title and subject indexes. *Class No:* 908(663)(01)

Sierra Leone

Bibliographies

[4815]

BINNS, M. *and* BINNS, T., *comps*. **Sierra Leone.** Santa Barbara, Calif., and Oxford, Clio Press, 1992. xliv,235p. +2p. maps, indexes. £24.50. (*World Bibliographical Series no.148.*) ISBN: 1851091017.

627 annotated entries in 37 sections: Country and its people - Geography ... Environment and conservation - Archaeology - Travellers' accounts - History ... Customs and rituals ... Bibliographies. Author, title, and subject indexes.
Class No: 908(664)(01)

Gambia

Bibliographies

[4816]

GAMBLE, D.P., *comp*. **The Gambia.** Santa Barbara, California and Oxford, Clio Press, 1988. xxxiv, 135p.+2p. maps, index. £22.95. $32.50. (*World Bibliographical Series, no.91.*) ISBN: 1851090681.

334 annotated entries. 32 sections: Place names and orthography - The country and its people - Travel guides, travelogues and tourism - Explorers and travellers' accounts - Geography ... Prehistory and archaeology - History ... Libraries ... Bibliographies. Author, title and subject index. 'This is an excellent bibliography' (*Choice*, v.26, no.11-12, July-August 1989, p. 1812). *Class No:* 908(665.1)(01)

Guinea

[4817]

SUNDIATA, I.K. **Equatorial Guinea** colonialism, state terror, and the search for stability. Boulder, Colo., Westview Press, 1990. x,179p. illus., maps, tables, bibliog., index. $29. (*Westview Profiles. Nations Of Contemporary Africa.*) ISBN: 0813304296.

1. Land and people - 2. History - 3. Politics - 4. Society and culture. Bibliography p.155-61. *Class No:* 908(665.2)

Bibliographies

[4818]

BINNS, M., *comp*. **Guinea.** Oxford and Santa Barbara, Calif., Clio Press, 1996. 89p. + 1p. map, index. £30. (*World Bibliographical Seires, no. 191.*) ISBN: 1851091483.

225 annotated entries arranged in 33 sections: Country and its people - Geography ... Travel guides - Travellers' accounts ... History - Biography and autobiography... Bibliographies. Author, title and subject index. *Class No:* 908(665.2)(01)

[4819]

FEGLEY, R., *comp*. **Equatorial Guinea.** Santa Barbara, Calif., and Oxford, Clio Press, 1991. lvii,118p.+ 1p. map, index. £26. (*World Bibliographical Series, no.136.*) ISBN: 185109167x.

339 annotated entries arranged in 35 sections: Names and orthography - The country and its people - Travel guides - Explorers' and travellers' accounts - Geography ... Migrations, exiles and refugees ... Biographies - Reference works - Bibliographies. Author, subject and title index. *Class No:* 908(665.2)(01)

Guinea-Bissau

[4820

FOREST, J.B. **Guinea-Bissau:** power, conflict and renewal in a Wes African nation. Boulder, Colo., Westview Press, 1992. x,165p. illus. maps, tables, bibliog., index. ISBN: 0865316813, t/p; 0813316813 rear cover.

1. Historical context - 2. Politics - 3. Economy - 4. Society - 5 Future. Bibliography p.153-4. *Class No:* 908(665.7)

Bibliographies

[4821

GALLI, R.E., *comp*. **Guinea-Bissau.** Santa Barbara, Calif., Oxford Clio Press, 1990. xxiv,180p.+ 1p. map. indexes. $57; £27. (*Worl Bibliographical Series, no.121.*) ISBN: 1851091084.

584 annotated entries in 21 sections: The country and its people Geography and geology ... History ... Bibliographies - Reference books. Theses and dissertations on Guinea-Bissau p.xiii-xxiv. Author title and subject indexes. Very useful for its record of Portugues language material. *Class No:* 908(665.7)(01)

Cape Verde Islands

Bibliographies

[4822

SHAW, C.S., *comp*. **Cape Verde.** Santa Barbara, Calif., and Oxford Clio Press, 1991. 190p.+ 1p. map, index. £29. (*Worl Bibliographical Series, no.123.*) ISBN: 185109119x.

484 annotated entries arranged in 28 sections: The country and it people - Geography ... Tourism and travel guides - Travellers accounts - History ... Libraries, archives and research ... Genera reference sources - Bibliographies. Author, title and subject index. *Class No:* 908(665.8)(01)

Liberia

Bibliographies

[4823

DUNN, D.E., *comp*. **Liberia.** Oxford and Santa Barbara, Calif., Clic Press, 1995. lxii,207p.+1p. map. indexes. £45.50. (*Worl Bibliographical Series, no. 157.*) ISBN: 1851091785.

656 annotated entries arranged in 28 sections: country and its peopl - Geography and geology ... Tourism and travel guides - Travellers accounts and memoirs - History - Historical biographies ... Majo population groups ... Human rights ... Encyclopedias and reference works - Bibliographies. List of theses and dissertations p.xxix-lxii Author, title and subject indexes. *Class No:* 908(666.2)(01)

Ivory Coast

Bibliographies

[4824

DANIELS, M., *comp*. **Côte D'Ivoire.** Oxford and Santa Barbara, Calif. Clio Press, 1996. xxviii,231p.+1p. map. indexes. (*Worl Bibliographical Series, no. 131.*) ISBN: 1851091203.

786 annotated entries in 31 sections: The country and its people Geography and geology - Travel guides - Travellers' accounts .. Prehistory and archaeology - History ... Ethnic groups .. Bibliographies. Author, title and subject indexes.
Class No: 908(666.8)(01)

Ghana

Bibliographies

[4825

MYERS, R.A., *comp*. **Ghana.** Santa Barbara, Calif., and Oxford, Clic Press, 1991. xxvii,436p. +1p. map. index. £65.95. (*Worla Bibliographical Series, no. 124.*) ISBN: 1851091351.

781 annotated entries in 35 categories: The country and its people Geography and geology ... Prehistory and archaeology - Explorers', travellers' and missionaries' accounts - History ... Ethnic groups .. Archives, libraries and museums ... Encyclopaedias and directories Bibliographies. Author, title, and subject index.
Class No: 908(667)(01)

Togo

Bibliographies

[4826]

ECALO, S., *comp*. Togo. Santa Barbara, Calif., Oxford, Clio Press, 1995. xxviii,168p.+1p. map, indexes. £36. (*World Bibliographical Series. no.178*.) ISBN: 1851091602.
c.565 annotated entries in 28 sections: Country and people - Travel and tourism ... History ... Bibliographies and reference works. Introduction (history, economy, politics) p.xi-xxi. Theses and dissertations on Togo p.xxiii-xxviii. Author, title and subject indexes.
Class No: 908(668)(01)

Benin

Bibliographies

[4827]

ADES, J.S. *and* ALLEN, C., *comps*. Benin Oxford and Santa Barbara, Clio Press, 1996. xliii,261p.+1p. map. indexes. (*World Bibliographical Series, no.192*.) ISBN: 1851091459.
759 annotated entries in 38 sections: Country and its peoples - Geography ... Travel guides ... Travellers' accounts - Prehistory and archaeology - History ... International relations ... Bibliographies etc. Author, title and subject indexes. *Class No:* 908(668.2)(01)

Nigeria

[4828]

igeria: giant in the tropics a compendium. Lagos, Gabumo Publishing Co., 2v., 1993. ISBN: 9780101446, set.
1. Edited by Adalemo, I.A. and Baba, J.M. 496p. illus. (some col.) tables, maps. ISBN 978010156x. Chapters on Natural resources - Making of a nation - Economic development since 1960 - Political economy 1965-93 - Foreign relations since 1960 - National defence and internal security - Education, science and technology - Social development - Changing status and roles of women - Mass media, culture, arts - Sports - Tourism - Areas of Nigeria. 2. *State Surveys*, edited by Udo, R.K. and Mamman, A.B. 598p. illus. (some col.) ISBN 9780101683. Survey of Abia, Andamawa, Akwa Ibom, Anambra, Bauchi, Benue, Borno, Cross River, Delta, Edo, Enugu, Imo, Jigawa, Kaduna, Kano, Katsina, Kebbi, Kogi, Kawara, Lagos, Niger, Ogun, Ondo, Osan, Oyo, Plateau Rivers, Sokoto, Taraba, and Yobe states. Nigeria: a chronology p.479-93. Atlas of Nigerian states p.501-98. *Class No:* 908(669)

Bibliographies

[4829]

1YERS, R.A., *comp*. Nigeria. Santa Barbara, California and Oxford, Clio Press, 1989. xxxii, 462p.+1p. map, index. £57.50. $55.00. (*World Bibliographical Series; no.100*.) ISBN: 1851090835.
1150 annotated entries. 39 sections: The country and its people - Geography and geology - Explorers', travellers' and missionaries' accounts ... Prehistory and archaeology - History ... Ethnic groups ... Museums ... Libraries and archives ... Encyclopaedias and directories - Bibliographies. Author, title and subject index.
Class No: 908(669)(01)

Maps & Atlases

[4830]

ARBOUR, K.M., *and others*. Nigeria in maps. London, Hodder and Stoughton, New York, Holmes and Meier, 1982. vii,148p. maps, diagrs., tables, bibliog. ISBN: 0340184256, UK; 0841907633, US.
60 maps with accompanying text divided into general, physical geography, prehistory and historical and political evolution, social conditions, agriculture and fishers, rural and urban life, manufacturing and power, commerce, and communications, transport and planning. Glossary p.142. Bibliography p.143-148. 21 contributors mostly drawn from Univ. of Ibadan. 'An extremely well thought-out range of topics included ... one would need an encyclopaedic knowledge of Nigeria to detect errors of substance' (*Geographical Journal*, v.149, no.3, November 1983, p.390-301). *Class No:* 908(669)(084.3)

Sao Tome & Principe

Bibliographies

[4831]

HAW, C.S., *comp*. São Tomé and Príncipe. Oxford, Clio Press, 1994. xxvi,183p.+2p. maps, index. £29.95. (*World Bibliographical Series, no.172*.) ISBN: 1851091815.
417 annotated entries in 25 sections. The country and its people - Geography ... Tourism, transport and communications - Travellers' accounts - History ... Angolars ... General reference works - Bibliographies. Author, title and subject indexes.
Class No: 908(669.95)(01)

Cameroon

[4832]

DELANCEY, M.W. Cameroon dependence and independence. Boulder, Colo., Westview Press; London, Dartmouth, 1989. ix,193p. illus., tables, maps, index. (*Profiles. Nations Of Contemporary Africa*.) ISBN: 1855210533.
1. Introduction - 2. Precolonial and colonial heritage - 3. Political system - 4. Society and culture - 5. Economy - 6. Foreign policy - 7. Cameroon looks to the future. Bibliography p.177-83. 'The chapters on politics and economics are excellent ... A most sensible, well-done book' (*Choice*, v.27, no.9, May 1990, p.1556). *Class No:* 908(671.1)

Bibliographies

[4833]

DELANCEY, M.W. *and* DELANCEY, M.D., *comps*. Cameroon. Rev. ed. Santa Barbara, California and Oxford, Clio Press, 1999. xxvi, 207p.+1p. map, indexes. £40. (*World Bibliographical Series; no.63*.) ISBN: 185109301x.
1st ed. 1986. (502 entries).
654 annotated entries. 26 sections: The country and its people - Geography - Travel and tourism ...Archaeology and prehistory - History ... Museums, archives and libraries - Bibliographies. Author, title and subject indexes. 'There is no comparable work' (*Choice*, v.37, no.5, January 2000, p.908). *Class No:* 908(671.1)(01)

Gabon

[4834]

AICARDI DE SAINT-PAUL, M. Gabon: the development of a nation. London, Routledge, 1989. x,145p. maps, tables, index. ISBN: 0415039053.
First published by Albatros (Paris, 1987) as *Le Gabon: du roi Denis à Omar Bongo*.
1. The country and its people - 2. From discovery to independence - 3. Institutional, administrative and political framework - 4. Analysis of Gabonese economy - 5. Infrastructures - 6. Social policies - 7. Gabon and the world. Chapter notes p.98-107. Bibliography p.129-38.
Class No: 908(672.1)

Bibliographies

[4835]

GARDINIER, D.E., *comp*. Gabon. Santa Barbara, Calif., and Oxford, Clio Press, 1992. xxxvii,178p. +1p. map. indexes. £32. (*World Bibliographical Series, no.149*.) ISBN: 1851091742.
549 annotated entries in 32 sections: The country and its people - Geography ... Archaelogy and prehistory - History ... Religions and missions ... Bibliographies. Author, title and subject indexes.
Class No: 908(672.1)(01)

Congo

[4836]

FEGLEY, R., *comp*. The Congo. Santa Barbara, Calif., and Oxford, Clio Press, 1993. 1,168p.+ 1p. map, index. (*World Bibliographical Series, no. 162*.) ISBN: 1851091998.
536 annotated entries in 34 sections: Country and its people - Travel guides - Explorers' and travellers; accounts - Geography ... Prehistory and archaeology - History ... Ethnic groups ... Reference works and scholarly journals - Bibliographies. Author, title and subject index.
Class No: 908(672.4)

Angola

Bibliographies

[4837]

BLACK, R., *comp*. Angola. Santa Barbara, Calif, and Oxford, Clio Press, 1992. xxvii,176p. +1p. map indexes. £29.50. (*World Bibliographical Series no.151*.) ISBN: 1851091432.
565 annotated entries arranged in 31 sections: The country and its people - Geography and geology ... Prehistory and archaeology - History ... Foreign relations and foreign intervention ... Directories and Current reference sources. Glossary p.xxv. Theses and dissertations on Angola p.xxvii. Author, subject, and title indexes.
Class No: 908(673)(01)

Central African Republic

[4838]

O'TOOLE, T. The Central African Republic: the continent's hidden heart. Boulder, Colorado, Westview Press; London, Gower, 1986. xiv,174p. illus., maps, bibliog., index. $34.00; £19.50. (*Profiles/ Nations of Contemporary Africa*.) ISBN: 086531647, US; 0566007738, UK.
1. The physical setting - 2. Historical context - 3. The Central

....*(contd.)*

African policy - 4. Society and change - 5. Economic and political dependence - 6. The Central African Republic and the world. Bibliography (by chapter) p.152-6. *Class No:* 908(674.1)

Bibliographies

[4839]

KALCK, P., *comp*. **Central African Republic**. Santa Barbara, Calif., and Oxford, Clio Press, 1993. liv,153p.+ 1pl. map, indexes. £36. (*World Bibliographical Series, no.152*.) ISBN: 1851091726.

538 annotated entries (mostly French language) in 22 sections: Country and its people - Geography and geology - Maps - Tourist guides - Expeditions and exploration ... Peoples - Prehistory and History ... Bibliographies - Biographies. Chronology p.xliv-liv. Author, title and subject indexes. *Class No:* 908(674.1)(01)

Chad

Bibliographies

[4840]

JOFFÉ, G. *and* DEY-VIAUD, V., *comps*. **Chad**. Oxford and Santa Barbara, Calif., Clio Press, 1995. xxviii,268p.+1p. map. indexes. £33. (*World Bibliographical Series, no. 177*.) ISBN: 1851092315.

650 annotated entries in 21 sections: Country and its people - Travellers' accounts - Geography ... Prehistory and archeology - History ... Ethnic groups ... Bibliographies. Author, title and subject indexes. *Class No:* 908(674.3)(01)

Zaire

Bibliographies

[4841]

WILLIAMS, D.B., *and others, comps*. **Zaire**. Oxford and Santa Barbara, Calif., Clio Press, 1995. xxxii,268p.+1p. map. indexes. £45.95. (*World Bibliographical Series, no. 176*.) ISBN: 1851092188.

829 annotated entries in 38 sections: Country and its people - Explorers' accounts - Travel guides and tourism - Geography ... Prehistory and archaeology - History ... Ethnic groups ... Bibliographies. Chronology p.xxiii-xxx. Guide to current and former names p.xxxi-xxxii. Author, title and subject indexes. *Class No:* 908(675)(01)

Burundi

[4842]

DANIELS, M., *comp*. **Burundi**. Santa Barbara, Calif., and Oxford, Clio Press, 1992. xxv,135pp.+ 1p. map. indexes. £24.50. (*World Bibliographical Series, no.145*.) ISBN: 1851091947.

463 annotated entries in 25 sections: The country and its people - Geography ... Prehistory and archaeology - History ... Ethnic groups ... Bibliographies. Chronology p.xix,xxv. Author, title and subject indexes. *Class No:* 908(675.97)

Rwanda

[4843]

FEGLEY, R., *comp*. **Rwanda**. Santa Barbara, Calif., and Oxford, Clio Press, 1993. xxxvi,161p.+ 1p. map, index. (*World Bibliographical Series, no.154*.) ISBN: 1851092021.

521 annotated entries in 34 sections: Country and its people - Travel guides - Explorers' and Travellers' accounts - Geography ... Prehistory and archaeology - History ... Reference works and scholarly journals - Bibliographies. Author, title and subject index. *Class No:* 908(675.978)

Uganda

Bibliographies

[4844]

NYEKO, B., *comp*. **Uganda**. 2nd ed. Santa Barbara, California and Oxford, Clio Press, 1996. xlvii,364p.+1p. map, indexes. £56. (*World Bibliographical Series; no.11*.) ISBN: 1851092439.

Replaces R.L. Collison's *Uganda* (1981).

798 annotated entries. 34 sections: The country and its people - Geography - Travel and tourism ... Prehistory and archaeology - History - Autobiographies, biographies and memoirs ... Water resources ... - Bibliographies. Chronology p.xxxv-xlvii. Author, title and subject indexes. *Class No:* 908(676.1)(01)

Kenya

Bibliographies

[4845]

COGER, D., *comp*. **Kenya**. 2nd ed. Santa Barbara, California and Oxford, Clio Press, 1996. xxxvi,276p. map, indexes. £50. (*World Bibliographical Series; no.25*.) ISBN: 0903450348.

1st ed. by R.L. Collinson 1982.

840 annotated entries. 32 sections: The country and its peoples Geography ... Tourism and travel guides ... Prehistory and archaeology - History ... Nationalities, minority and ethnic groups ... Bibliographies. Chronology p.xxi-xxxvi. Author, title and subject index. *Class No:* 908(676.2)(01)

Somalia

[4846]

LAITIN, D.D. *and* SAMATAR, S.S. **Somalia** nation in search of state. Boulder, Colo., Westview Press; London, Gower, 1987 xvii,198p. illus., map, bibliog., index. (*Profiles: Nations C Contemporary Africa*.) ISBN: 0865315558, US; 0566054590, UK.

1. Peopling of the Somali peninsula - 2. Society and culture - 3 Colonialism and the struggle for national independence - 4 Government and politics - 5. Economy - 6. Foreign relations - 7. Int the 1990s. Chapter notes p.171-81. Bibliography p.182-3. *Class No:* 908(677)

Bibliographies

[4847]

DE LANCEY, M.W., *and others, comps*. **Somalia**. Santa Barbara California and Oxford, Clio Press, 1988. xxviii, 191p.+1p. map indexes. £32.95. $43.50. (*World Bibliographical Series; no.92* ISBN: 185109038x.

584 annotated entries. 26 sections: The country and its people Geography - Travellers' accounts ... History ... Libraries, museum and archives ... Bibliographies. Author, title and subject indexes 'Recommended for all research collections' (*Choice*, v.27, no.2 October 1989, p.293-4). *Class No:* 908(677)(01)

Djibouti

Bibliographies

[4848]

SCHRAEDER, P.J., *comp*. **Djibouti**. Santa Barbara, Calif., an Oxford, Clio Press, 1991. xxxix,239p.+ 1p. map, index. £38. (*World Bibliographical Series, no.118*.) ISBN: 1851090843.

409 annotated entries arranged under 22 subject headings: Th country and its people - Tourist guides - Geography and earth science - Travellers' accounts ... History ... Migration and refugees - Ethnicit and population ... Bibliographies. Author, title and subject index. *Class No:* 908(677.1)(01)

Tanzania

Bibliographies

[4849]

DARCH, C., *comp*. **Tanzania**. 2nd ed. Santa Barbara, California an Oxford, Clio Press, 1996. xxxii,379p.+1p. map, indexes. £66. (*World Bibliographical Series; no.54*.) ISBN: 1851092196.

1st ed. 1985.

808 annotated entries. 32 sections: The country and its people Geography - European travel and exploration - Travel guides ... Archaeology and pre-colonial history - History ... Bibliographies Author, title and subject indexes. 600 entries are new to this edition. *Class No:* 908(678)(01)

Mozambique

Bibliographies

[4850]

DARCH, C., *comp*. **Mozambique**. Santa Barbara, California an Oxford, Clio Press, 1987. xxvi, 360p.+1p. map, index. £49.95 $55.00. (*World Bibliographical Series; no.78*.) ISBN: 1851090258.

735 annotated entries. 32 sections: The country and its people Travellers' accounts and exploration - Geography ... Prehistory an archaeology - History ... Foreign and economic relations ... Museum and archives ... Directories and current reference sources Bibliographies. Author, title and subject index. *Class No:* 908(679)(01)

Africa—Southern

Bibliographies

[4851]

MUSIKER, R. *and* MUSIKER, N. **Southern African bibliography.** Lanham, MD., Scarecrow Press, 1996. 264p. $52. (*Scarecrow Area Bibliographies, no.11.*) ISBN: 0810831759.

Lists the significant books and monographs on Angola, Botswana, Lesotho, Malawi, Namibia, Mozambique, South Africa, Swaziland, Zambia, and Zibabwe published since 1945 covering art, culture, economy, history, politics, religion, society, and important persons, places, events and movements. The work is arranged by subject and contains detailed author, title and subject indexes.
Class No: 908(68)(01)

Yearbooks & Directories

[4852]

Southern African annual review. Pycroft, C *and* Munslow, B. Oxford, Hans Zell, 1989-.

1. 1987/88. v.1: Country reviews. 404p. £48. $85. ISBN 0905450035. v.2: Regional reviews. 470p. £48. $85. 0905450043. Set 2v. 1989. £96. $170. 0905450027.

2. 1989. v.1: Country reviews. 320p. £35. $65. 0905450747. v.2 Regional reviews. 320p. £35. $65. 0905450795. Set 2v. 1990. £70. $130. 0905450698.

Volume 1 provides extensive coverage of press sources on the region, whilst Volume 2 deals with the important issues of the period, revealing the motivating forces for regional integration, confrontation, and negotiation. Based on the Southern Africa Computerized Data/ Text (SACDT) System developed by the Centre of African Studies in the University of Liverpool. 'Uneven, disjointed, patchy in quality, highly selective and difficult to use' (*Reference Reviews*, v.4,no.3, 1990, p.31-2). *Class No:* 908(68)(058)

South Africa

[4853]

South Africa yearbook 1995. 2nd ed. Pretoria, South African Communication Service, 1995. 446p. col.illus., col.maps, tables, index. ISBN: 0797031928. ISSN: 10229515.

1st. 1994. Replaces *South Africa ... official yearbook of the Republic of South Africa* (1974-1993).

1. A rainbow country - 2. History - 3. Dawn of a new era (*i.e.* post-1994 election result) - 4. Wildlife and tourism ... 9. Foreign relations ... 11. Safety and order ... 22. Science and technology.
Class No: 908(680)

Bibliographies

[4854]

DAVIS, G.V., *comp*. **South Africa.** 2nd ed. Santa Barbara, California and Oxford, Clio Press, 1994. xxvii,463p.+1p. map, index. £69.50. (*World Bibliographical Series; no.7.*) ISBN: 185109203x.

1st ed. compiled by R. Musiker 1979.

1252 annotated entries. 52 sections: The country and its people - Geography - Travellers' accounts ... Prehistory - Historiography - History ... Minorities ... Autobiography - Biography ... Bibliographies - Africana. Author, title and subject indexes. *Class No:* 908(680)(01)

Botswana

Bibliographies

[4855]

WISEMAN, J.A., *comp*. **Botswana.** Santa Barbara, Calif., and Oxford, Clio Press, 1992. xxvii,187p. +1p. map. indexes. £32. (*World Bibliographical Series, no. 150.*) ISBN: 1851091718.

723 annotated entries in 30 sections: Country and its people - Geography and geology - Travellers' and Explorers' accounts ... Prehistory and archaeology - History ... Peoples of Botswana - Bibliographies and libraries. Author, title and subject indexes.
Class No: 908(681)(01)

Swaziland

[4856]

DAVIES, R.H. **The Kingdom of Swaziland** a profile. London, Zed Books, 1985. Distributed in US by Biblio Distribution Center, Totowa (New Jersey). x, 82p. tables. £13.95. (*Third World Books.*) ISBN: 0862324491.

Swaziland under colonialism - 2. Process of decolonization - 3 Structure of the Swaziland economy - 4. Outline of the class structure - 5. Political struggles since independence - 6. Swaziland in the regional struggle. Notes p.76-81. *Class No:* 908(683.4)

Bibliographies

[4857]

NYEKO, B., *comp*. **Swaziland.** 2nd ed. Santa Barbara, Calif., and Oxford, Clio Press, 1994. xxx,241p. +1p. map. indexes. £39. (*World Bibliographical Series, no. 24.*) ISBN: 1851092269.

1st ed. 1982.

705 annotated entries in 28 sections: Country and its people - Geography and geology - Tourism and travel guides ... Prehistory and archaeology - History ... Foreign relations ... Bibliographies. Theses and dissertations p.xxi-xxx. Author, title and subject index.
Class No: 908(683.4)(01)

Lesotho

Bibliographies

[4858]

JOHNSTON, D., *comp*. **Lesotho.** 2nd ed. Santa Barbara, California and Oxford, Clio Press. 1996-. xxxvi,197p.+2p. map, indexes. (*World Bibliographical Series; no.3.*) ISBN: 1851092471.

Replaces S.M. Willett and D.P. Ambrose's *Lesotho: a comprehensive bibliography* (1980).

563 annotated entries. 38 sections: Country and its people - Geography ... Tourism and travel guides ... Prehistory and archaeology - History - Biographies, autobiographies and memoirs ... Bibliographies. Glossary p.xxxiii. Author, title and subject index.
Class No: 908(686.1)(01)

Namibia

Bibliographies

[4859]

SCHOEMAN, S. *and* SCHOEMAN, E., *comps*. **Namibia.** 2nd ed. Santa Barbara, California and Oxford, Clio Press, 1997. xxxviii,294p. +1p. map. index. £57. (*World Bibliographical Series, no. 53.*) ISBN: 1851092781.

1st ed. 1984.

843 annotated entries. 33 sections: The country and its people - Geography ... Archaeology and rock art - History - Biographies ... Politics and the international status issue ... Libraries and archives ... Bibliographies. Author, title and subject index.
Class No: 908(688)(01)

[4860]

TRUSCHEL, L.W. **German South West Africa:** a centennial bibliographic essay, *African Journal*, v.14, no.4, 1983, p.277-291.

Literature review with consolidated bibliography p.289-91.
Class No: 908(688)(01)

Zimbabwe

[4861]

SYLVESTER, C. **Zimbabwe** the terrain of contradictory development. Boulder, Colo., Westview Press; London, Dartmouth, 1991. xii,212p. illus., maps, bibliog., index. (*Profiles: Nations Of Contemporary Africa.*) ISBN: 0813306906, US; 1855212560, UK.

1. Historical kaleidoscope - 2. Contradictions of Rhodesia (1923-1979) - 3. State and politics in contemporary Zimbabwe - 4. Political economy of 'growth and equity' - 5. Civil society and state-society relations - 6. Z.'s international profile - 7. Less contradictory future? Bibliography p.191-7. *Class No:* 908(689.1)

Bibliographies

[4862]

POTTS, D., *comp*. **Zimbabwe.** 2nd ed. Oxford, Clio Press; Santa Barbara, Calif., ABC-Clio, 1993. 368p.+1p. map. £56.50. (*World Bibliographical Series, no.4.*) ISBN: 1851091955.

Replaces Pollak, OB. and Pollak, K. comps. *Rhodesia/Zimbabwe.* Oxford, Clio Press, 1979.

879 annotated entries arranged in 37 sections: The country and its people - Geography ... Prehistory and Archaeology - History ... Languages ... Military and police ... Encyclopaedias and directories - Bibliographies. Author, title and subject indexes.
Class No: 908(689.1)(01)

Encyclopaedias

[4863]

A Concise encyclopedia of Zimbabwe. Berens, D., *ed*. Gweru, Mambo Press, 1988. 444p. illus. (some col.), col.maps, tables, softcover. £6.95. ISBN: 0869224417.

Compact general knowledge book encompassing flora and fauna, history and geography, religion and culture, politics, economics, and social life. *Class No:* 908(689.1)(031)

[4864]

Tabex encyclopedia Zimbabwe. 2nd ed. Stanton, Arlington Business Corporation, 1989. xv,448p., illus., col. maps, index. $42.70. ISBN: 0951450506, UK; 0908306040, Zim.

First published in 1987 by Quest Publishing of Harare.

All aspects of present-day Zimbabwe presented in a single A-Z sequence with the emphasis on sport and the natural sciences. Some entries end with lists of further reading. Zimbabwean chronology p.xiii-xv. 'An excellent single-volume reference work appropriate for a wide range of audiences' (*Choice*, v.27, no.11-12, July/August 1990, p.1810). *Class No:* 908(689.1)(031)

Zambia

Bibliographies

[4865]

BLISS, A.M. *and* **RIGG, J.A.,** *comps.* **Zambia.** Santa Barbara, California and Oxford, Clio Press, 1984. xviii, 233p.+1p. map, index. £33.95. $38.00. (*World Bibliographical Series, no.51.*) ISBN: 0903450887.

829 annotated entries. 34 setions: The country and its people - Geography and geology ... Prehistory and archaeology - History ... Peoples of Zambia ... Libraries, museums and archives ... Bibliographies. Place names in Zambia (old and new) p. xviii. Author, title and subject index. *Class No:* 908(689.4)(01)

Malawi

Bibliographies

[4866]

DECALO, S., *comp.* **Malawi.** 2nd ed. Santa Barbara, California and Oxford, Clio Press, 1995. xxii, 188p. map, indexes. £33.50. $28.50. (*World Bibliographical Series; no.8.*) ISBN: 1851092382.

Replaces R.B. Boeder's *Malawi* (1979).

508 annotated entries. 35 sections: The country and its people - Travel and tourism - Geography and geology ... Archaeology - History ... Reference works and bibliographies. Author, title and subject indexes. *Class No:* 908(689.7)(01)

Madagascar

Bibliographies

[4867]

BRADT, H., *comp.* **Madagascar.** Santa Barbara, Calif., and Oxford, Clio Press, 1993. xviii,118p. + 1p. maps, indexes. £24. (*World Bibliographical Series, no.165.*) ISBN: 1851091793.

341 Annotated entries in 27 sections: Country and its people - Geography - Travellers' accounts - Travel guides ... History ... Philately and numismatics ... Bibliographies. Author, title and subject indexes. *Class No:* 908(691)(01)

Seychelles

Bibliographies

[4868]

BENNETT, G. *and* **BENNETT, P.R.,** *comps.* **Seychelles.** Santa Barbara, Calif; Oxford, Clio Press, 1993. xxix,113p. + 2p. maps, indexes. £24.50. (*World Bibliographical Series, no.153.*) ISBN: 1851091823.

339 annotated entries in 27 sections: Country and its people - Geography - Travellers' accounts ... History ... Aldabra ... Bibliographies. Chronology p.xxiii-xxvi. Glossary p.xxviii - Author, title and subject indexes. *Class No:* 908(696)(01)

Mauritius

[4869]

BOWMAN, L.W. Mauritius democracy and development in the Indian Ocean. Boulder, Colo., Westview Press; London, Dartmouth, 1991. xv,208p. illus., maps, tables, bibliog., index. (*Profiles. Nations of Contemporary Africa.*) ISBN: 081330508x, US; 185521248x, UK.

1. Geographic and physical setting - 2. Historical background - 3. Society and culture - 4. Politics of independent Mauritius - 5. Economy - 6. International relations - 7. Mauritius and the future. Chapter notes p.169-88. Bibliography p.189-95. 2 maps. 'This most informative, well-written book provides a wealth of up-to-date facts ... a valuable addition to the literature on off-shore Africa' (*Journal of Modern African Studies*, v.29, no.4, December 1991, p.715-6). *Class No:* 908(698.2)

Bibliographies

[4870]

BENNETT, P.R. *and* **BENNETT, G.J.,** *comps.* **Mauritius.** Santa Barbara, Calif., and Oxford, Clio Press, 1992. xxv,151p. +2p. maps index. £26.95. (*World Bibliographical Series, no. 140.*) ISBN 185109153x.

537 annotated entries in 27 sections: Country and its people Geography - Travellers' accounts ... History ... Cuisine ... Directorie - Bibliographies. Glossary p. xxiii-xiv. Author, subject and title index. *Class No:* 908(698.2)(01)

St. Helena

Bibliographies

[4871]

DAY, A., *comp.* **St. Helena, Ascension and Tristan da Cunha.** Oxfor and Santa Barbara, Calif., Clio Press, 1997. xxi,260p. + 2p. maps index. £44. (*World Bibliographical Series, no.197.*) ISBN 1851092722.

754 annotated entries grouped in 35 sections: Islands and Thei People - Discovery and early voyages - Visitors' Accounts Geography ... Tourism and Travel Guides - Maritime History - History - Napoleon Bonaparte ... Bibliographies. Author, title and subjec index. 'The annotations everywhere are lucid, scholarly in approach and exceptionally informative' (*Reference Reviews*,v.11, no.6, 1997 p.58). *Class No:* 908(699.25)(01)

[4872]

HELYER, P. *and* **SWALES, W. Bibliography of Tristan da Cunha** Oswestry, Anthony Nelson, 1998. 175p. illus., maps, index. £25 ISBN: 090461462x.

Arranged under 22 A-Z subject headings (*e.g.* Archival sources an audio-visual ...Bibliographies and biographies ... Expeditions .. Geography, geology and cartography ... History ... Naval, maritim and hydrography ... Voyages. Citations give author, date, title pagination. *Class No:* 908(699.25)(01)

America—North

Yearbooks & Directories

[4873]

The USA and Canada 1998. 3rd ed. London, Europa Publications 1997. 600p. maps, tables, bibliogs. £235. (*Regional Surveys of th World.*) ISBN: 1857430441. ISSN: 09560904.

Revised every 2 years.

Separate sections for each country provide introductory historical geographical and demographic data. There follow essays (plu bibliographies) on the political and administrative system, th economy, social issues, and international relations. Extensive statistica and directory type information is listed under Public affairs; Th economy; Society; Transport and utilities; and Tourism. A group o essays examine topics currently affecting US and Canada equally. 'It i difficult to see how any other single volume of comparable size coul possibly improve its coverage' (*Reference Reviews*, v.4, no.4, 1990 p.36). *Class No:* 908(71+73)(058)

Canada

[4874]

Canada: a portrait. The official handbook of present conditions an recent progress. 56th ed. Ottawa, Statistics Canada, 2000. biennial 204p.+ 2p. map, col. illus., tables. ISBN: 0660177803. ISSN 08406022.

First published 1931. Recently known as *Canada handbook*.

Succinct and popular account published 'to survey the Canadia situation as a whole within a reasonable space, in a popular an attractive format, and at a cost which makes possible a wid distribution' 1. The Land - 2. The People - 3. The Society - 4. Art and Leisure - 5. The Economy - 6. Canada in the world. *Class No:* 908(71)

[4875]

WEIHS, J. Facts about Canada its provinces and territories. New York, H.W. Wilson, 1995. 262p. illus. $35 US and Can. $40 overseas. ISBN: 0824208641.

Concise guide to sources of information and thousands of facts fo each province and territory in 31 categories including premiers an Lieutenant Governors, geography and climate, time zones, importan historical dates, flag description, coat of arms, motto and emblems date of entry into Confederation, national and provincial parks, historistes. *Class No:* 908(71)

Bibliographies

[4876]

NGLES, E., *comp*. **Canada**. Santa Barbara, Calif., Oxford, Clio Press, 1990. xxx,393 +1p. map. indexes. £55.95. (*World Bibliographical Series, no.62*.) ISBN: 1851090053.

1316 annotated entries arranged in 37 sections: The country and its people - Geography ... Prehistory - History ... Nationalities and minorities - Aboriginal peoples ... Languages ... National identity ... Libraries, museums and archives - Book industries and trade ... General reference works. Author, title and subject indexes. *Class No:* 908(71)(01)

Encyclopaedias

[4877]

The Canadian encyclopaedia. Marsh, J.H., *ed*. Year 2000 ed. Toronto, McClelland & Stewart, 1999. 2640p. illus (many col.), col. maps, bibliog., index. Can $64. ISBN: 0771020996.

*c.*10,000 signed entries, with short reading lists 'to provide coverage of all aspects of life in Canada, of all regions, over a vast time scale from the geological formation of the ancient rocks ... to the most recent political events'. Analytical index. A CD-ROM edition is available. CD-ROM Find It TM software and instruction manual. 1990. 0888303424. *Class No:* 908(71)(031)

[4878]

COLOMBO, J.R. **Colombo's Canadian references**. Toronto, Oxford Univ. Press, 1976. viii, 576p. ISBN: 0195402537.

Over 6,000 brief entries, A-Z Encyclopaedic in scope containing biographies (*e.g.* Jacques Cartier: ½ col., 3 cross-references), historical and geographical data, literary terms, abbreviations, *etc.*, as well as notes on current topics. Handy lists (*e.g.* Canada's prime ministers; winners of the Stanley Cup; Canada's 100 largest companies). Good use of cross-references. 'This excellent mini-encyclopaedia' (*RQ*, Fall 1977, p.72), No illus., maps or bibliographies. *Class No:* 908(71)(031)

[4879]

LANDRY, L. **Encyclopédie du Québec** un panorama de la vie québécoise. Montréal et Bruxelles, Les Éditions de l'Homme, 2v., 1973. xliii, 1010p. illus., tables, maps. ISBN: 0775903671, v.1; 0775903795, v.2.

A compendium with many statistical data and listings. Unusually arranged in Dewey Classification order (010 Bibliographie. Générale ... 929. Armoiries). Sections include directory material, 1-2 line biographies, bibliographies and statistics. Subject index to each volume (v.1: 0-6; v.2: 7-9). Aimed at student and laymen. *Class No:* 908(71)(031)

Yearbooks & Directories

[4880]

Canadian almanac and directory 2000. 153rd year of publication. Toronto, Micromedia, 1999 (variously paginated), maps, tables. £75. ISBN: 189502157x. ISSN: 00688193.

47,000+ facts and figures about Canada in 10 sections: 1. Almanac and miscellany (Canadian flags, British and Commonwealth Honours etc.) - 2. Organizations - 3. Government directory - 4. Municipal - 5. Communications and information management - 6. Arts and culture - 7. Business and finance - 8. Health - 9. Education - 10. Legal.

A CD-ROM version is produced. *Class No:* 908(71)(058)

Quebec

Bibliographies

[4881]

GAGNON, A-G., *comp*. **Québec**. Oxford and Santa Barbara, Calif., Clio Press, 1999. xxvi,350p.+1p. map. indexes. £63. (*World Bibliographical Series, no.211*.) ISBN: 1851092900.

1,050 annotated entries arranged in 40 thematic sections: Québec and its people - Geography ... History - Biography ... Aboriginal inhabitants ... General reference works. Introduction (p.xiii-xxiii) concerns the city's history and landmarks. Glossary p.xxv-xxvi. *Class No:* 908(714)(01)

Newfoundland

Bibliographies

[4882]

O'DEA, A.C., *comp*. **Bibliography of Newfoundland**. Toronto, Univ. of Toronto Press in association with Memorial Univ. of Newfoundland, 2v., 1986. xx,1450p. index. $175.00; £122.50. ISBN: 0802024025.

v.1 5911 entries. Collections and sources p.xvi-xx. v.2 378 annuals. Author, title and subject indexes p.885-1450. Major work 'to record, chronologically, the printed works relating to Newfoundland from the early voyages of discovery to 1975 ... intended to inform or interest

....(contd.)

the scholar, the intelligent reader, and the collector' (*Preface*). 'Meets an undoubted need, and meets it in a way that can be described as definitive' (*Canadian Historical Review* v.69, no.3, September 1988, p.418-420). *Class No:* 908(718)(01)

Encyclopaedias

[4883]

Encyclopedia of Newfoundland and Labrador. Smallwood, J.R. *and* Pitt, R.D.W. St. Johns, Newfoundland Book Publishers, 1981-.

1. A-E. 914p. illus., maps. 1981. $39.00. ISBN 0920508146. Covers all aspects of life past and present with long articles (with list of references) for major topics. 18p. of maps. 'Much useful information that would be difficult to find elsewhere' (*Choice*, v.19,no.10, June 1982, p.1376). *Class No:* 908(718)(031)

Mexico

Bibliographies

[4884]

PHILIP, G.D.E., *comp*. **Mexico**. 2nd ed. Santa Barbara, California and Oxford, Clio Press, 1993. xviii,194p.+1p. maps indexes. £29.95. (*World Bibliographical Series, no.48*.) ISBN: 185109198x.

1st ed. compiled by N.C. Robbins 1984

750 annotated entries. 29 sections: The country and its people - Tourism and travel guides - Geography ... Archaeology and prehistory - History ... Bibliographies and Reference works. Author, title, and subject index. *Class No:* 908(72)(01)

Guatemala

Bibliographies

[4885]

WOODWARD, R.L., *comp*. **Guatemala**. Revised and enlarged ed. Santa Barbara, California and Oxford, Clio Press, 1992. xxix,269p.++ 1p. map, indexes. £42.50. (*World Bibliographical Series; no.9*.) ISBN: 1851091882.

First published with W.B. Franklin as compiler in 1984.

843 annotated entries in 34 sections: Country and its people - Geography - Travellers' accounts ... Prehistory and archaeology - History ... Human rights.Bibliographies. Author, title and subject index. *Class No:* 908(728.1)(01)

Belize

Bibliographies

[4886]

WRIGHT, P. *and* COUTTS, B.E. **Belize**. 2nd ed. Santa Barbara, California and Oxford, Clio Press, 1993. xxiv, 307p.+1p. map, indexes. £49.95. (*World Bibliographical Series, no.21*.) ISBN: 1851091327.

1st ed. compiled by R.L. Woodward, 1980.

964 annotated entries. 42 sections: The country and its people - Geography - Tourism and travel guides - Traveller's accounts ... Prehistory and archaeology - History ... Bibliographies. Author, title, and subject indexes. *Class No:* 908(728.2)(01)

Honduras

Bibliographies

[4887]

HOWARD-REGUINDID, P.F., *comp*. **Honduras**. Santa Barbara, Calif., and Oxford, Clio Press, 1992. xx,258p. +1p. map. indexes. £39.95. (*World Bibliographical Series, no.139*.) ISBN: 1851091378.

788 annotated entries in 38 sections: Country and its people - Geography - Tourism - Travellers' accounts ... Prehistory and archaeology - History ... Ethnic groups and refugees ... Libraries and archives ... Encyclopedias and directories - Bibliographies. *Class No:* 908(728.3)(01)

El Salvador

Bibliographies

[4888]

WOODWARD, R.L., *ed*. **El Salvador**. Santa Barbara, California and Oxford, Clio Press, 1988. xxix, 213p.+1p. map, index. £32.95; $39.00. (*World Bibliographical Series, no.98*.) ISBN: 0851090738.

659 annotated entries. 40 sections: The country and its people - Geography - Travellers' accounts ... Prehistory and archaeology -

....(contd.)

History ... Human rights ... Libraries, museums and archives ... Encyclopaedias and directories - Bibliographies. Author, title, and subject index. *Class No:* 908(728.4)(01)

Nicaragua
[4889]

WALKER, T.W. **Nicaragua** the land of Sandino. 3rd ed. Boulder, Colo., Westview Press, 1991. xvi,202p. illus., map, bibliog., index. £26.95. (*Westview Profiles: Nations Of Contemporary Latin America.*) ISBN: 0813310903.

1st ed. 1981; 2nd ed. 1986.

1. Introduction - 2. Early history: pre-Columbian period to the mid-1930s - 3. Recent history - 4. Economic dimension - 5. Culture and society - 6. Government and politics - 7. International dimension. Bibliography p.173-84. *Class No:* 908(728.5)

Bibliographies
[4890]

WOODWARD, R.L., *comp.* **Nicaragua.** 2nd ed. Santa Barbara, California, and Oxford, Clio Press, 1994. xxv, 294p.+1p. map, index. £44. (*World Bibliographical Series, no.44.*) ISBN: 1851091890.

1st ed. 1983.

918 annotated entries. 33 sections: The country and its people - Geography - Travellers' accounts ... Prehistory and archaeology - History ... Human rights - Bibliographies. Author, title, and subject index. 'Should be at the top of the must-buy list for nearly every library because it provides such comprehensive coverage' (*Choice,* v.21, no.9, May 1984, p.1284). *Class No:* 908(728.5)(01)

Costa Rica

Bibliographies
[4891]

STANSIFER, C.L., *comp.* **Costa Rica.** Santa Barbara, Calif., and Oxford, Clio Press, 1991. xxiii,292p. +1p. map. indexes. £44.95. (*World Bibliographical Series, no. 126.*) ISBN: 1851090274.

706 annotated entries in 39 sections: The Country and its people - Geography and geology - Travellers' accounts ... Prehistory and archaeology - History ... Human rights ... Libraries, archives and museums ... Biographies - Directories - Bibliographies. Dissertations on Costa Rica p.xix-xxiii. Author, title and subject indexes. *Class No:* 908(728.6)(01)

Panama

Bibliographies
[4892]

LANGSTAFF, E.D., *comp.* **Panama.** Santa Barbara, California and Oxford, Clio Press, 1982. vii, 184p. + 1p. map, index. £25.95; $28.00. (*World Bibliographical Series, no.14.*) ISBN: 0903450267.

641 annotated entries. 34 sections: The country and its people - Geography ... Travel - Prehistory and archaeology - History - Peoples ... Periodicals - Reference Books - Libraries, museums and archives - Bibliography and bibliographies. Author, title, and subject index. *Class No:* 908(728.7)(01)

Caribbean
[4893]

DYDE, B. **Caribbean companion** the A to Z reference. London, Macmillan, 1995. 192p. £4.95. ISBN: 0333546571.

Facts and figures on people and places; artists and writers; politics and politicians; sport; music; folklore and culture; flora and fauna; historical and recent events; and geography and marine environment. *Class No:* 908(729)

Bibliographies of Bibliographies
[4894]

JORDAN, A. *and* COMISSIONG, B., *comps.* **The English-speaking Caribbean** a bibliography of Bibliographies. Boston, G.K. Hall, 1984. xxiv, 411p. indexes. $61.00. ISBN: 0816186073.

1406 annotated entries divided into 5 bibliographical and 59 (country sub-divided) subject listings *e.g.* Archaeology (entries 517-520); History (766-808); and Geography (732-742). Name and subject indexes. Based on collections of St. Augustine campus library of University of West Indies where the compilers are University Librarian and Deputy Librarian. *Class No:* 908(729)(009)

Bibliographies
[4895]

GOSLINGA, M. **A Bibliography of the Caribbean.** Metuchen, N.J., Scarecrow Press, 1996. 343p. indexes. £75.05. (*Area Bibliography Series.*) ISBN: 0810830973.

3600 entries (all monographs of at least 50 pages), relating to literature on the Caribbean islands, and also to mainland Belize, French Guiana, Guyana, and Suriname, organised into several sub-divided sections. Geographical, author and title indexes. *Class No:* 908(729)(01)

Encyclopaedias
[4896]

The Cambridge encyclopedia of Latin America and the Caribbean. Collier, S., *and others, eds.* 2nd rev. ed. Cambridge, Cambridge Univ. Press, 1992. 480p. illus. (some col.), maps, tables. £35. ISBN: 0521413222.

1st ed. 1985.

68 contributors. 6 sections: 1. Physical environment - 2. Economy - 3. Peoples - 4. History - 5. Politics and society - 6. Culture. Glossary p.8-9. Detailed analytical index. Articles append further reading lists. 70 maps. 'Destined to become the standard single-volume work on Latin America' (*Choice,* v.23, no.7, March 1986, p.1036-37). *Class No:* 908(729)(031)

Handbooks & Manuals
[4897]

The Caribbean handbook 1995/96. Tortola, BVI, FT Caribbean 1995. 268p. illus. (some col.), maps, tables, bibliog. Softcovers. ISBN: 9768033119.

Section A. Caribbean profile: regional survey, business review - B. Caribbean countries A-Z: Key facts, business/tourist information, location and physical features, travel, official public holidays, the economy, utilities *etc.* Bibliography p.261-65. *Class No:* 908(729)(035)

Yearbooks & Directories
[4898]

MACDONALD, R. *and* TRAVIS, C. **Libraries and special collections on Latin America and the Caribbean:** a directory of European resources. London, Athlone Press for the Institute of Latin American Studies, Univ. of London, 1988. 339p. index. £32. ISBN: 0485177145.

2nd ed. of B. Taylor's *Directory of Libraries and special collections on Latin America and the West Indies* (1975). Completely revised and extended to cover holdings in Europe.

195 UK and 272 European collections recorded (3 times the number in the earlier work) for material relating to regions south of the Rio Grande and reasonably adjacent islands. Main emphasis is on printed material. Full directory information. 'A useful guide to the existence and availability of special research materials' (Reference Reviews, v.2, no.3, September 1988, p.110). *Class No:* 908(729)(058)

Cuba

Bibliographies
[4899]

PEREZ, L.A. **Cuba** an annotated bibliography. New York, Garland Press, 1988. xiii, 301p. index. $45.00 £36.95. (*Bibliographies and Indexes in World History; no.10.*) ISBN: 0313261628. ISSN: 07426852.

1120 items identifying the major written works on Cuba arranged in 45 categories (*e.g.* 2. Geography ... 5. Prehistory and archaeology - 6. History (7 subdivisions) - 7. Genealogy ... 45. Bibliographies. Preference given to works in English. 'Only titles that are generally available to readers are included' (*Introduction*). Compiler is Graduate Research Professor in the Department of History, Univ. of South Florida. *Class No:* 908(729.1)(01)

[4900]

STUBBS, J., *and others, comps.* **Cuba.** Oxford and Santa Barbara, Calif., Clio Press, 1996. xxx,337p.+1p. map, indexes. £59.50 (*World Bibliographical Series, no.75.*) ISBN: 1851090215.

1172 annotated entries in 38 sections: The Country and its people - Geography - Tourism and travel guides - Travellers' accounts ... Prehistory and archaeology - History - Revolution - Biographies ... Bibliographies. Author, title and subject indexes. Introductory overview on Cuba's history, economy, constitution, political system, society and culture p.xv-xxx. *Class No:* 908(729.1)(01)

Jamaica

Bibliographies

[4901]

INGRAM, K.E. Jamaica. 2nd ed. Santa Barbara, California and Oxford, Clio Press, 1997. xxviii,366p. + 1p. map, index. £67. (*World Bibliographical Series, no.45.*) ISBN: 1851092676.

1st ed. 1984.

1182 annotated entries. 36 sections: The country and its people - Geography ... Prehistory and archaeology - History and collective biography ... Labour movement and Trade Unions ... Libraries, archives and information systems ... General directories and handbooks - Bibliographies. Author, title, and subject index. *Class No:* 908(729.2)(01)

Cayman Islands

Bibliographies

[4902]

BOULTBEE, P.G., *comp*. Cayman Islands Oxford & St. Barbara, Calif., Clio Press, 1996. xviii,129p.+1p. map. index (*World Bibliographical Series, no. 187.*) ISBN: 1851092404.

447 annotated entries in 30 sections: Country and its people - Geography ... Oceanography - Travel guides - Travellers' accounts ... Prehistory and archaeology - History ... Bibliographies. Author, title and subject index. *Class No:* 908(729.29)(01)

Yearbooks & Directories

[4903]

Cayman Islands yearbook and business directory 1990. Winker, C. *and* Martins, D., *eds*. Grand Cayman, Cayman Free News, 1985-. Annual. 480p. illus. (some col.), tables index.

1. Cayman Islands and its people (History, geography, culture, the year in review *etc*.) - 2. Government - 3. Finance and investment - 4. Business and commerce - 5. Living and working - 6. Reference (Tourist information A-Z). *Class No:* 908(729.29)(058)

Dominican Republic

Bibliographies

[4904]

SCHOENHALS, K., *comp*. Dominican Republic. Santa Barbara, California, and Oxford, Clio Press, 1990. xxx, 210p. map. index. (*World Bibliographical Series, no.111.*) ISBN: 1851091106.

913 annotated entries in 40 sections: The country and its people - Geography ... Travellers' accounts ... Prehistory and Archaeology: pre-Columbian inhabitants - History ... Voodoo ... Encyclopaedias and directories - Bibliographies. Author, subject and title index. *Class No:* 908(729.3)(01)

Haiti

[4905]

BELLEGARDE-SMITH, P. Haiti the breached citadel. Boulder, Colo., Westview Press, 1990. xxi,217p. illus., maps, bibliog., index. $34. (*Westview Profiles. Nations of Contemporary Latin America.*) ISBN: 0813371724.

1. The nature of Haiti: Land and society - 2. Context of Haitian development and underdevelopment - 3. Modernization and dependence - 4. Haitian economy and the National Security state - 5. Politics and government. Appendix 1. Significant dates in Haitian history p.181-7. Chapter notes p.191-7. Bibliographical essay p.199-207. 'A useful summary of Haiti's history' (*Choice*, v.27, no.10, June 1990, p.1736). *Class No:* 908(729.4)

Bibliographies

[4906]

CHAMBERS, F., *comp*. Haiti. 2nd ed. Santa Barbara, California and Oxford, Clio Press, 1994. xxvi, 270p.+1p. map, indexes. £42. (*World Bibliographical Series; no.39.*) ISBN: 1851092153.

1st ed. 1983

913 annotated entries. 42 sections: - The country and its people - Geography - Maps, atlases and gazetteers ... Travel guides - Travellers' accounts ... Prehistory and archaeology - History ... Voodoo ... - Bibliographies. Chronology p.xix-xxiv. Author, title and subject index. *Class No:* 908(729.4)(01)

[4907]

LAGUERRE, M.S. The Complete Haitiana a bibliographic guide to the scholarly literature 1900-1980. Millwood, New York, Kraus International Publications, 2v., 1982. lxxiii, xix, 1562p. maps on endpapers, index. ISBN: 0527540404, set.

A companion work to L. Comitas' *The complete Caribbeana* (*qv*).

65 chapters divided into 11 general thematic sections: 1. Introduction to Haiti - 2. Ecological setting - 3. History of Haiti - 4. Population - 5. Culture - 6. Structure of Haitian society - 7. Health and medicine - 8. Educational system - 9. Political and legal processes - 10. Socio-economic system - 11. Rural and urban developments. Includes books, articles, government documents and essays that form part of a book, in several languages including Haitian creole. Most references include a library code indicating location. *Class No:* 908(729.4)(01)

[4908]

PRATT, F., *ed*. Haiti guide to the periodical literature in English, 1800-1990. Westport, Conn., Greenwood Press, 1991. xiv,310p. indexes. £33.95. ISBN: 0313278555.

Over 5,000 citations arranged chronologically within 9 sections: 1. Physical setting - 2. Human element - 3. Cultural environment ... 5. Geopolitical influence - 6. Historical background ... 8. Bibliographies. Computerized index. *Class No:* 908(729.4)(01)

Puerto Rico

Bibliographies

[4909]

CEVALLOS, E.E., *comp*. Puerto Rico. Santa Barbara, California and Oxford, Clio Press, 1985. xiii, 193p. + 1p. map, index. £28.50. (*World Bibliographical Series, no. 52.*) ISBN: 0903450895.

605 annotated entries. 34 sections: The country and its people - Geography ... Archaeology and prehistory - History - Folklore ... Migration ... Encyclopaedias - Museums, archives and libraries - Bibliographies. Author, title and subject index. *Class No:* 908(729.5)(01)

Encyclopaedias

[4910]

FERNANDEZ, R., *and others eds*. Puerto Rico past and present an encyclopedia. Westport, Conn., Greenwood Press, 1998. 375p. bibliog., index. $59.95. ISBN: 031329822x.

Contents include history and legacy of Taino Indians and all aspects of Puerto Rican history and society including biographical entries. All entries carry select bibliographies. *Class No:* 908(729.5)(031)

[4911]

La Gran encicyclopedia de Puerto Rico. Baez, V., *ed*. Madrid, Ediciones R., 14v., 1976. illus., bibliogs., indexes.

Thematic volumes: 1. Historia - 2. Politica ... 14. Diccionario histórico - biográfico. 'Without question, this is a comprehensive encyclopaedia of Puerto Rican cultural, political, and social history' (F.E. Cevallos. *Puerto Rico*. 1985. Entry 574). *Class No:* 908(729.5)(031)

Bahamas

Bibliographies

[4912]

BOULTBEE, P.G., *comp*. The Bahamas. Santa Barbara, California and Oxford, Clio Press, 1989. xx, 195p.+1p. map, index. £37.00. (*World Bibliographical Series; no.108.*) ISBN: 1851091025.

703 annotated entries. 36 sections: The country and its people - Geography ... Travel guides - Travellers' accounts - Tourism ... Prehistory and archaeology - History ... Obeah ... Libraries and archives ... Directories - Bibliographies. Author, title and subject index. *Class No:* 908(729.6)(01)

Handbooks & Manuals

[4913]

Bahamas handbook and businessman's annual 1997. Nassau, Etienne Dupuch, 1996. 559p. illus. (some col.), maps, tables, index. Soft cover. ISBN: 0914755633. ISSN: 00672912.

8 glossy sections: 1. Features including Treasure Seekers (i.e. Marine archaeology) - 2. Leisure and vacations - 3. The family islands - 4. Business and finance - 5. Bahamas information - 8. Government. *Class No:* 908(729.6)(035)

Turks & Caicos Islands

Bibliographies

[4914]

BOULTBEE, P.F., *comp*. **Turks and Caicos Islands.** Santa Barbara, Calif., and Oxford, Clio Press, 1991. xvii,97p.+ 1p. map. index. £19. (*World Bibliographical Series, no.137.*) ISBN: 1851091629.

305 annotated entries in 25 sections: The country and its people - Geography ... Travel guides - Traveller's accounts - Tourism ... Prehistory and archaeology - History ... Philately and numismatics ... Libraries Directories - Bibliographies. *Class No:* 908(729.68)(01)

Leeward & Windward Islands

Bibliographies

[4915]

BERLEANT-SCHILLER, R.   *and*   LOWES, S.   *and* BENJAMIN, M., *comps*. **Antigua and Barbuda.** Oxford and Santa Barbara, Calif., Clio Press, 1995. xxxviii,210p.+2p. maps, indexes. (*World Bibliographical Series, no. 182.*) ISBN: 1851092285.

633 annotated entries divided into 24 sections: Country and its people - Travel guides and travellers' accounts - Geography ... Prehistory and archaeology - History ... Sport ... Reference sources. Author, title and subject indexes. *Class No:* 908(729.7)(01)

[4916]

CRANE, J., *comp*. **Martinique.** Oxford and Santa Barbara, Calif., Clio Press, 1995. xxxi,140p.+1p. map. indexes. £26. (*World Bibliographical Series, no. 175.*) ISBN: 1851091513.

380 annotated entries in 21 sections: Department and its people - Geography - Travellers' accounts ... Travel guides and tourism - Prehistory and archaeology - History ... Reference sources. Author, title and subject indexes. *Class No:* 908(729.7)(01)

[4917]

MOLL, V.P., *comp*. **St. Kitts-Nevis.** Oxford and Santa Barbara, Calif., Clio Press, 1995. xxiii,185p.+1p. map. indexes. £32. (*World Bibliographical Series, no. 174.*) ISBN: 1851092226.

565 annotated entries in 42 sections: Country and its people - Geography - Travellers' accounts - Tourism ... Prehistory and archaeology - History ... Abstracts and bibliographies. Author, title and subject indexes. *Class No:* 908(729.7)(01)

[4918]

MOMSEN, J.H., *comp*. **St. Lucia.** Oxford, Clio Press, 1996. xxxi,179p.+1p. map. indexes. £34.50. (*World Bibliographical Series, no. 185.*) ISBN: 185109136x.

531 annotated entries grouped in 33 sections: Country and its people - Geography ... Tourism and travel guides- Prehistory and archaeology - History ... Banana industry ... Directories, yearbooks and handbooks - Bibliographies. Author, title and subject indexes. Attempts to identify everything published in England about the island. *Class No:* 908(729.7)(01)

Virgin Islands

Bibliographies

[4919]

MOLL, V.P., *comp*. **Virgin Islands.** Santa Barbara, Calif., and Oxford, Clio Press, 1991. xxv,210p.+ 2p. maps, indexes. £34. (*World Bibliographical Series, no.138.*) ISBN: 1851091653.

614 annotated entries in 40 sections: Islands and their peoples - Geography - Travellers' accounts - Tourism ... Prehistory and archaeology - History ... Environment ... Books and publishing ... Bibliographies and abstracts. Author, title, and subject indexes. *Class No:* 908(729.72)(01)

Montserrat

Bibliographies

[4920]

BERLEANT-SCHILLER, R., *comp*. **Montserrat.** Santa Barbara, Calif., and Oxford Clio Press, 1991. xxviii,102p.+ 1p. map, indexes. £22. (*World Bibliographical Series, no.134.*) ISBN: 1851091548.

341 annotated entries arranged under 20 headings: 1. Country and its people - Geography - Tourism and travel ... Natural hazards ... Archaeology - History ... Reference sources. Author, title and subject indexes. *Class No:* 908(729.727)(01)

Dominica

[4921]

MYERS, R.A., *comp*. **Dominica.** Santa Barbara, California and Oxford, Clio Press, 1987. xxv, 190p.+1p. map. index. £31.95' $40.50. (*World Bibliographical Series, v.82.*) ISBN: 1851090312.

493 annotated entries. 28 sections: The country and its people - Geography - Travel guides and tourism ... Amerindians - History ... Libraries and archives ... Encyclopaedias and directories - bibliographies. Author, title and subject index. *Class No:* 908(729.821)

[4922]

MYERS, R.A., *comp*. **A Resource guide to Dominica 1493-1986.** New Haven, Connecticut, Human Relations Area Files, 1987. 649 leaves. maps.

Includes an outline history of Dominica and 25 sections arranged by topic. Also location guide to documents in UK, Europe, US, and West Indian archives. Name and subject index p.580-649. *Class No:* 908(729.821)

St. Vincent & the Grenadines

Bibliographies

[4923]

POTTER, R.B., *comp*. **St. Vincent and the Grenadines.** Santa Barbara, Calif., and Oxford, Clio Press, 1992. xxviii,212p.+ 1p. map, indexes. £34.50. (*World Bibliographical Series, no.143.*) ISBN: 1851091831.

631 annotated entries in 33 sections: Country and its people - Geography ... Tourism - Travellers' accounts ... Prehistory - History ... Language and dialect ... Bibliographies. Glossary p.xxvii-xxviii. Author, title, and subject indexes. *Class No:* 908(729.824)(01)

Grenada

Bibliographies

[4924]

SCHOENHALS, K., *comp*. **Grenada.** Santa Barbara, Calif., Oxford, Clio Press, 1990. xxxviii,179p.+ 1p. map, index. £33. (*World Bibliographical Series, no.119.*) ISBN: 1851091262.

793 annotated entries in 37 sections: The country and its people - Geography ... Travellers' accounts ... Prehistory and archaeology - History ... Nationalities and minorities ... Encyclopaedias and directories - Bibliographies. Author, title and subject index. Events leading to the US invasion are well summarized in the introduction. *Class No:* 908(729.828)(01)

Barbados

Bibliographies

[4925]

POTTER, R.B. *and* DANN, G.M.S. **Barbados.** Santa Barbara, California and Oxford, Clio Press, 1987. xxxix, 356p.+1p. map, index. £49.95. $55.00. (*World Bibliographical Series; no.76.*) ISBN: 1851090223.

958 annotated entries. 39 sections: The country and its people - Geography ... Travellers' accounts - Tourism ... Prehistory and archaeology - History ...Constitution and the legal system ... Libraries ... Directories, yearbooks and handbooks - Bibliographies. Glossary p. xxxv-xxxix. Author, subject and title index. *Class No:* 908(729.86)(01)

Trinidad & Tobago

Bibliographies

[4926]

CHAMBERS, F., *comp*. **Trinidad and Tobago.** Santa Barbara, California and Oxford, Clio Press, 1986. xv, 213p. + 1p. map, index. £30.50; $ 35.00. (*World Bibliographical Series, no.74.*) ISBN: 1851090207.

641 unannotated entries. 43 sections: The country and its people - Geography ... Travel guides - Travellers' accounts ... Prehistory and archaeology ... Historiography - History ... Calypso - Festivals - Carnival ... Libraries and archives ... Reference works - Bibliographies. Author, title and subject index. *Class No:* 908(729.87)(01)

Netherlands Antilles

Bibliographies

[4927]
CHOENHALS, K. **Netherlands Antilles and Aruba.** Oxford and Santa Barbara, Calif., Clio Press, 1993. xxii,160p.+2p. maps, index. £27.50. (*World Bibliographical Series, no.168*.) ISBN: 1851092102.

565 annotated entries in 40 sections: Islands and their people - Geography ... Travellers' accounts ... Prehistory and archaeology - History ... Nationalities and minorities ... Bibliographies. Introduction (historical overview) p.xvii-xxii. Author, title and subject indexes. *Class No:* 908(729.88)(01)

Bermuda

Bibliographies

[4928]
OULTBEE, P.G. *and* RAINE, D.F., *comps*. **Bermuda.** Oxford and Santa Barbara, Calif., Clio Press, 1998. xviii,165p.+1p. map, index. £32. (*World Bibliographical Series, no.205*.) ISBN: 185109170x.

545 annotated entries in 37 sections: Country and its people - Geography ... Travel guides - Travellers' accounts - Tourism ... Archaeology - History - Genealogy - Slavery ... Bibliographies. Author, title and subject indexes. *Class No:* 908(729.9)(01)

Latin America

Bibliographies

[4929]
Bibliographic guide to Latin American studies. New York, G.K. Hall, 1978-. Annual.

1994 (2v. 1995). 1722p. $580. ISBN 0783821859. Includes acquisitions cataloged during the past year by two of the world's most comprehensive collections - the Nettie Lee Benson Latin American Collection at the Univesity of Texas Library, Austin, and the Library of Congress. Entries cover library materials written by Latin American authors, materials published anywhere in the world pertaining to Latin America and materials written in any language. A supplement to the *Catalogue of the Latin American Collection of the University of Texas Library* (G.K. Hall, 1969). *Class No:* 908(729.99)(01)

[4930]
British bulletin of publications on Latin America the Caribbean Portugal and Spain. London, The Hispanic and Luso-Brazilian Council, 1950-. v.1-. 2 *pa*. £10.00. *pa*. ISSN: 02682400.

Annotates 200-250 English-language books and lists a large number of periodical articles per issue. Nos.1-45 are available on a 35mm. microfilm (£20.00). *Class No:* 908(729.99)(01)

[4931]
ENTON, T.P. *and* HEFFRON, M.J., *comps*. **Latin America and Caribbean: a directory of resources.** New York, Orbis Books; London, Zed Books, 1986. xvi,142p. indexes. $9.95; £18.95. ISBN: 0862326370, UK; 0883445298, US.

An expansion of the Latin American and Caribbean chapter in the compilers' *Third World resource directory* (Orbis, 1984).

1. Organizations - 2. Books - 3. Periodicals - 4. Pamphlets and articles - 5. Audiovisuals - 6. Other resources. Emphasis on 'alternative' sources; some standard works are omitted. *Class No:* 908(729.99)(01)

[4932]
HALLEWELL, L. 'Latin American area librarianship a guide for collection development' (*Choice*, v.33,no.10, June 1996, p.1593-1605).

Surveys the origin and development of Latin American Studies collections. Other topics include Latin American book trade, bibliographic control problems, serials and other sources of information, and North American collections of Latin Americana. Bibliography of 169 books, serials and journal articles p.1599-1605. Lawrence Hallewell is Latin American Studies Librarian, Colombia University Libraries. *Class No:* 908(729.99)(01)

[4933]
Latin American studies a basic guide to sources. McNeil, R.A., *ed.* 2nd ed. Metuchen, N.J., Scarecrow Press, 1990. xi,458p. indexes. $42.50. £40.40. ISBN: 0810822369.

A rev. ed. of *Latin American bibliography: a guide* edited by L. Hallewell (1978).

36 contributors. A form-based introductory guide to research on Latin America in the humanities and social sciences divided in 6 main parts: 1. Libraries and their use (leading Latin American collections in UK, US and Europe) - 2. Bibliographies - 3. Other printed sources (encyclopedias, handbooks, guides, directories, maps and atlases etc.) - 4. Non print sources - 5. Specialised information - 6. Research and career development. Subject and reference source indexes. Prepared under the auspices of the Standing Committee of National and University Libraries' Advisory Committee on Latin American

....(contd.)
Materials. 'Essential for any library with a serious interest in Latin America' (*Choice*, v.28,no.1, September 1990, p.78).
Class No: 908(729.99)(01)

Handbooks & Manuals

[4934]
Handbook of Latin American studies. Martin, D.M., *ed.* Austin, Univ. of Texas, 1936-. v.1-. Annual. ISSN: 00729833.

V. 1-3 published by Harvard Univ. Press, then by Univ. of Florida Press. Latterly prepared 'by a number of scholars for the Hispanic Division of the Library of Congress'.

As from v.26 (1964) coverage has been split, 'Humanities' and 'Social sciences' volumes being published in alternative years. Thus v.51 *Social sciences* (1992. xx,901p. 0292751494) has 5109 concisely annotated entries for Bibliography and general works, Anthropology (including Archaeology) - Economics - Education - Geography - Government and politics - International relations - Sociology. 55 contributing editors. V.52 *Humanities* (1993. xxiii,934p. 0292751567) has 5444 entries for Bibliography and general works - Art - Film - History (in 7 main divisions) - Language - Literature - Music - Philosophy. 68 contributing editors.

Handbook of Latin American Studies CD-ROM. Edited by Hispanic Division Library of Congress. Fundacion MAPFRE America. 1995. V.1-53 (1936-1994). 1. Disc. Windows 3.1 or higher. 0848952306. $150. Easy to use CD providing access to 250,000+ entries. *Class No:* 908(729.99)(035)

[4935]
—Library of Congress HLAS online handbook of Latin American studies. URL:http://lcweb2.loc.gov/hlas/

Includes entries v.56-60. Help screens currently in English only but Spanish and Portuguese translations are planned. 'Reflects how the World Wide Web can best promote scholarship and learning' (*Choice*, Supplement to v.36, August 1999, p.164).
Class No: 908(729.99)(035)

Dictionaries

[4936]
NUÑEZ, B., *with the assistance of the African Bibliographical Center*. **Dictionary of Afro-Latin American civilization.** Westport, Connecticut, Greenwood Press, 1980. xxxv, 525p. illus., maps, indexes. $56.95. ISBN: 0313211388.

Historical and descriptive dictionary of more than 4500 entries relating to terms and places, and including biographies of Afro-Latin American political leaders, writers *etc.* involved in Afro-Latin American civilization. From English, French, Portuguese and Spanish sources. 'Provides a unique documentation and illustration of the impact of African civilization and peoples upon - and contributions to - the New World' (*Foreword*). *Class No:* 908(729.99)(038)

Yearbooks & Directories

[4937]
South America, Central America and the Caribbean 2000. 8th ed. London, Europa, 2000. 810p. maps, tables, bibliogs. £235. (*Regional Surveys of the World*.) ISBN: 1857430670.

Over 20 specialist contributors. Part 1. Background to the region consists of signed introductory essays (*e.g.* Economic background, Democratization) - 2. Country surveys: 49 A-Z chapters on all countries and territories containing concise historical, geographical and economic information, using the latest official statistics on finance, industry, agriculture, trade, population, education, transport, tourism, and the news media. Also a government, political and constitutional directory and a bibliography for each of the major countries - 3. Regional organizations *i.e.* all principal organizations working in the region with the emphasis on United Nations activities. 'Has deservedly won generous plaudits for its comprehensive coverage of three quite distinct geopolitical areas' (*Reference Reviews*, v.5,no.2, 1991, p.39-40). *Class No:* 908(729.99)(058)

USA

[4938]
CARPENTER, A. *and* PROVORSE, C. **Facts about the cities.** 2nd ed. New York, H.W. Wilson, 1996. $55.US and Can.5760, elsewhere.

Latest available data on 371 cities (41 more than 1st ed.) covering inter alia history, climate, population, conventions and tourism. *Class No:* 908(73)

[4939]

DUCHAK, A. **A-Z of modern America.** London, Routledge, 1999. xv,405p. indexes. £45. ISBN: 0415187559.

Cultural dictionary containing 3,000+ cross-referenced entries relating to key people; American life and customs; legal, religious and government practices; and multiculturalism, minorities and civil rights. The aim is to define contemporary America through its history and culture. *Class No:* 908(73)

[4940]

KANE, J.N., *and others, comps.* **Facts about the States.** 2nd ed. New York, H.W. Wilson, 1994. 632p. bibliogs., tables. US and Canada $60. $75 other countries. ISBN: 0824208498.

1st ed. 1989.

Part one contains a chapter for each state that includes in-depth information on: state names, mottos, songs, seals, flags, and other official symbols; geography, climate, and land use; demography; major cities; state governors; culture, sports, education, and state holidays; economy; national sites; landmark dates in state history; the environment; government and politics; state finances; unusual state facts; plus three bibliographic sections: The State in Literature; A Guide to Resources; and Selected Nonfiction Sources.

Part 2: comparative tables that rank states by area and population density, order of settlement and statehood, average temperature and rainfall, highest and lowest levels of literacy, personal wealth, presidential voting patterns, geographic characteristics. *Class No:* 908(73)

[4941]

World Almanac of the USA. Carpenter, A. *and* Provorse, C., *eds.* New York, World Almanac, 1993. 400p. col. maps, tables, flags. $18.95. ISBN: 0886877245.

Detailed portrait of each State in the Union: its history, geography, notable sons and daughters, laws, climate, environment, statistics, sport, transport, and religion. *Class No:* 908(73)

Bibliographies

[4942]

The American West in the twentieth century a bibliography. Etulain, R. W., *ed.* Norman, Univ. of Oklahoma, 1994. vii,456p. index. $60. ISBN: 0806126582.

Published in cooperation with The Center for the American West, Univ. of New Mexico.

8187 unannotated items arranged in 12 subdivided sections: 1. Bibliographies and reference works - 2. General works - 3. Regional and State history - 4/8. Social, Political, Economic, Environmental and Constitutional History - 9. Science, Medicine and Technology - 10. Sports, Recreation and Leisure - 11. Public policy - 12. Cultural and intellectual history. Overall the books, essays and dissertations entered focus on the post-1900 West. *Class No:* 908(73)(01)

[4943]

HERSTEIN, S.R. *and* ROBBINS, N.C., *comps.* **United States of America.** Santa Barbara, California and Oxford, Clio Press, 1982. xii. 307p.+1p. map, index. £42.50. $45.00. (*World Bibliographical Series; no. 16.*) ISBN: 1851090444.

1126 annotated entries. 36 sections: The country and its people - Geography - Archaeology and prehistory - History - Nationalities and minorities ... Reference works.. *Class No:* 908(73)(01)

[4944]

LOPEZ, M.D. **New York:** a guide to information and reference sources 1979-1986. Metuchen, N.J., Scarecrow Press, 1987. xi,372p. indexes. £26.25. ISBN: 0810820188.

1065 fully annotated entries arranged in 2 parts (New York State and New York City) and divided under 30 and 36 headings respectively: *e.g.* Biography and Autobiography ... Bibliographies and indexes ... Description and travel ... Geography ... History. Follows the author's *New York: a guide to information and reference sources.* Scarecrow Press, 1980. x,307p. *Class No:* 908(73)(01)

[4945]

MARTEN, J., *comp.* **Texas.** Santa Barbara, Calif., and Oxford, Clio Press, 1992. xxiii,229p.+ 1p. map, index. £36. (*World Bibliographical Series, no.144.*) ISBN: 185109184x.

708 annotated entries in 20 sections: State of Texas and its people - Geography and natural history - History - Military affairs ... Ethnic groups ... Reference works and bibliographies. Author, title and subject index. *Class No:* 908(73)(01)

[4946]

SALZMAN, J., *ed.* **American studies** an annotated bibliography. Cambridge University Press, 3v., 1986. xii,2058p. ISBN: 0521266866; 0521266874, v.1; 0521266883, v.2; 0521325552, set.

Replaces An annotated bibliography of works on the civilizations of the United States (US Information Agency, 1982).

V.1 Anthropology and folklore; Art and Architecture; History (p.237-707). V.2 Literature; Music; Political science; Popular culture; Psychology; Religion; Science, technology and medicine. V.3 Author, title and subject indexes. Prefaces to each section introduce the basic

....(contd.)

bibliographic resources for research in that discipline. 'A valuable set because of the huge number of books it lists, the meaningful way in which they are arranged, and the prefaces that precede each section' (*Reference Books Bulletin,* 1986-1987, p.156). *Class No:* 908(73)(01)

[4947]

—SALZMAN, J., *ed.* American studies an annotated bibliography, 1984-1988. Cambridge University Press, 1990. xi,1085p. indexes. £75. $95. ISBN: 0521365597.

Interim supplements are printed in *Prospects: an annual of American Cultural Studies.*

Over 200 contributors. This supplement to the original bibliography contains 3,872 annotated items published in US. Similar supplements, a volume for material published outside US, and a volume devoted to journal articles, are planned. Author and title indexes. 'A thoroughly commendable compilation' (*Choice,* v.28,no.4, December 1990, p.614). *Class No:* 908(73)(01)

Encyclopaedias

[4948]

The American regional encyclopedia series. New York and Oxford, Facts On File, 1985-. illus. (some col), maps, tables, bibliogs., indexes. £40.00 each.

1. *The Encyclopedia of New England* edited by R. O'Brien and R.D. Brown. 1985. ix,613p. ISBN 0871967596. Connecticut, Maine, Massachusetts, New Hampshire, Rhode Island, Vermont. 2. *The Encyclopedia of the South* edited by R. O'Brien and H.H. Martin. 1986. viii,583p. 0871967286. Alabama, Arkansas, Florida, Georgia, Kentucky, Louisiana, Maryland, Mississippi, Missouri, North and South Carolina, Tennessee, Texas, Virginia and West Virginia. 3. *The Encyclopedia of the Midwest* edited by A. Carpenter. 1989. 544p. 0816016607. Illinois, Indiana, Iowa, Michigan, Minnesota, Missouri, Ohio and Wisconsin. 4. *The encyclopedia of the Central West* edited by A. Carpenter. 1990. 544p. 0816016615. Colorado, Kansas, Montana, Nebraska, New Mexico, North and South Dakota, Oklahoma, Texas and Wyoming. 5. *The Encyclopedia of the Far West* edited by A. Carpenter. 1991. 0816016623. Alaska, Arizona, California, Hawaii, Idaho, Nevada, Oregon, Washington, Utah, Samoa, Guan, U.S. Trust Territories *Class No:* 908(73)(031)

[4949]

Encyclopedia of Southern culture. Center for the Study of Southern Culture, Univ. of Mississippi *and* Wilson, C.R. *and* Ferris, W., *eds.* Chapel Hill, Univ. of North Carolina Press, 1989. 1,634p. illus. (incl. pl.), maps, tables, charts, bibliogs., index.

Over 800 contributors. 1300 signed, well-documented, cross-referenced entries deployed in 24 major thematic sections *e.g.* Agriculture; Art and architecture; Black life; Environment; Ethnic life; Folklore; History and manners; Industry; Language; Law; Media; Music; Politics; Recreation; Religion; Violence; Women's life *etc.* Scope covers the 11 Confederate States of the Civil War and also midwestern and Middle Atlantic states. Includes biographies. 'This compendium has no contemporary rival' (*Booklist,* v.86, no.1, 1 September 1989, p.97-98). *Class No:* 908(73)(031)

[4950]

GLAZIER, M., *ed.* **The Encyclopedia of the Irish in America.** Chicago, Univ. of Notre Dame Press, 1999. 1012p. illus. $89.95. £58. ISBN: 0268027552.

250 academic contributors. c.800 entries relate to notable personalities, historical events, places, institutions, publications, with major essays on key topics. 'A very valuable reference and browser' (*Books Ireland,* no.229, March 2000, p.78). *Class No:* 908(73)(031)

[4951]

KUTLER, S.I., *and others, eds.* **Encyclopedia of the United States in the twentieth century.** New York, Scribner, Simon & Schuster, Prentice Hall International, 4v. + index v. 1941p.+89p. $385. ISBN: 0132105357.

80 academic contributors. 74 independent essays in 6 broad sections: The American people - Politics - Global America - Science, technology and medicine - Economy - Culture. 'A masterly edited publication that captures the essence of many political, social, cultural, and technological developments that have occurred in the United States this century' (*Choice,* v.33,no.8, April 1996, p.1284).

Encyclopedia of the United States Index. 1996. xxxvii,89p. 064804816. Chronology (American people; Politics; Global America; Science, technology and medicine; Economy; Culture) p.xviii-xxxvii. Analytical index p.1-89. *Class No:* 908(73)(031)

[4952]
Worldmark encyclopedia of the States a practical guide to the geographic, demographic, historical, political, economic and social development of the United States. Gall, T.L., *ed*. 4th ed. Detroit, Gale Research, 1998. 800p. maps, tables, bibliogs. £110. ISBN: 0787600806.

1st ed. 1981.

A detailed portrait of each state, the District of Columbia, Puerto Rico, US Virgin Islands, American Samoa, Guam, and the US Pacific and Caribbean territories and dependencies organized under 50 numbered headings *e.g.* 1. Location ... 11. History ... 47. Tourism ... 49. Famous persons - 50. Bibliography. Each entry begins with a "ready-reference" guide to information that is frequently requested, such as state song, bird and flag. The volume also provides state maps, a bibliographic list of additional sources of information, a chart of U.S. presidents and a glossary of terms. 'A convenient package of statistical data with general review information. However it is presently revised too infrequently and contains too little unique material to be recommended for purchase by most libraries' (*Reference Books Bulletin 1986-87*, p.155). *Class No:* 908(73)(031)

Handbooks & Manuals

[4953]
Cities of the United States a compilation of current information on economic, cultural, geographic and social conditions. Straub, D.A., *ed*. 3rd ed. Detroit, Gale Research, 4v., 1998. 2212p. illus., maps, index. £285. ISBN: 0810364352, set.

1. *The South* 0810364360. 2. *The West* 0810383934. 3. *The Midwest* 0810364397. 4. *The Northwest* 0810364395.

Historical and present-day information on over 100 key cities of historical, political, or commercial significance organized in 12 data sections - 1. The city in brief - 2. Geography and climate - 3. History - 4. Population - 5. Municipal government - 6. Economy - 7. Education and research - 8. Health care - 9. Recreation - 10. Convention facilities - 11. Transport - 12. Communications. 'Useful to business researchers, marketing specialists, tourists, history students, and students of urban affairs. Although ... most of the information ... can be derived from other sources, it is always useful to be able to find it in one place' (*Choice*, v.26, no.7, March 1989, p.1118). *Class No:* 908(73)(035)

Government Publications

Bibliographies

[4954]
PARISH, D.W. Bibliography of State bibliographies 1970-82. Littleton, Colorado, Libraries Unlimited, 1985. xiii, 267p. indexes. ISBN: 0872874664.

1031 annotated entries relating to material published by US State governments arranged A-Z by State and alphabetically within States under broad subject headings *e.g.* Archaeology - Area Studies - Drug use and abuse ... Geography ... History ... Libraries ... Native people ... Politics and government ... Space exploration. Appendix: Acquisition guide and agency addresses p.217-39. Title and subject indexes. *Class No:* 908(73)(061.1)(01)

Maps & Atlases

[4955]
Macmillan color atlas of the states. Old Tappan, NJ., Macmillan Reference, Prentice Hall International, 1996. 377p. col. illus., col. maps. $100. ISBN: 0028646592.

A-Z 4 colour guide tour of all 50 states with notes on State Seals, legal holidays, state flags, facts, sources of information etc. enhanced with generous provision graphs and charts. *Class No:* 908(73)(084.3)

Hispanic Peoples

[4956]
KANELLOS, N. The Hispanic American almanac. 2nd ed. Detroit, Gale Research, 1996. 884p. illus., maps, bibliogs., index. £84.50 ISBN: 0810385953.

Major aspects of the culture and civilization of Hispanic Americans living in the United States, including Spanish explorers and colonizers, Significant documents, Historic landmarks, Labor and employment, Women, Religion, Prominent Hispanics, Military, Business, and Race. A bibliography has been included at the end of each chapter to facilitate further research. Features of the *Almanac* include a glossary and a keyword index. *Class No:* 908(73)(=60)

Yearbooks & Directories

[4957]
Hispanic American information directory. Detroit, Gale Research Co., 1990. 395p. indexes. $69.50. ISBN: 0810374447.

Selected material in 8 out of 16 chapters was taken from other Gale titles and re-edited for this publication.

4700 resources available to Hispanic Americans organized in 16 sections including national associations, library collections, industrial service companies, government programmes, publications *etc*. Name and keyword indexes. *Class No:* 908(73)(=60)(058)

Jews

[4958]
American Jewish desk reference the ultimate one-volume reference to the Jewish experience in America. New York, Random, 1999. 642p. illus., bibliog., index. $39.95. ISBN: 0375402438.

900 A-Z cross-referenced entries, 85% of which are biographical, of varying length (500-3,000 words) arranged in 14 broad thematic chapters. *Class No:* 908(73)(=924)

Bibliographies

[4959]
KARKHANIS, S. Jewish heritage in America an annotated bibliography. New York, Garland Press, 1988. xx,434p. indexes. $59. ISBN: 0824075382.

1100 annotated items arranged in 7 sections: 1. Reference and research - 2. Historical perspectives - 3. Antisemitism - 4. Religious traditions - 5. Intellectual and literary traditions - 6. Sociological impact - 7. Political activism. Author, title and subject indexes. *Class No:* 908(73)(=924)(01)

Asian Races

[4960]
The Asian American almanac. Detroit, Gale Research, 1995. 834p. illus., maps, tables, bibliog., index. £73. ISBN: 0810391937.

40+ chapters on all major aspects of Asian American life and culture 1830s to date. Subject index. *Class No:* 908(73)(=95)

Encyclopaedias

[4961]
MARSHALL, F.N., *ed*. The Asian-American encyclopedia. New York, Marshall Cavendish, 6v., 1994. 1818p. illus., maps, tables, diagrs., bibliogs., indexes. $449.95. ISBN: 1854336771.

2,000+ cross-referenced entries, ranging from brief 2-3 lines to essays several pages in length, on historical events, laws and court cases, leading personalities, places, religion, and publications. V.6 contains a chronology, a directory of Asian-American organisations, museums, libraries etc. and a 40p. bibliography. Ethnic and subject indexes. *Class No:* 908(73)(=95)(031)

Black Races

[4962]
The African American almanac. Carney, J., *and others, eds*. 8th ed. Detroit, Gale Research, 1999. 1270p. tables, bibliog., index. $170. ISBN: 0787617504.

Historical and current information in 29 subject areas *e.g.* African American history, society and culture including the African diaspora, organizations, population, inventors and scientists, entertainers, religious traditions, black nationalism, civil rights, and African-American firsts from 1600. *Class No:* 908(73)(=96)

[4963]
Encyclopedia of African-American culture and history. Salzman, J., *and others, eds*. New York, Macmillan, 5v., 1996. 3200p. illus., tables, bibliogs., index. $425. ISBN: 0028973453.

Over 600 contributors. 2,200 signed cross-referenced articles relating to key individuals, historical events, important legal decisions, institutions and organisations, publications, and social, cultural and political concepts. 'In recent years, numerous important reference sources on black Americans have appeared but none is more authoritative, comprehensive, and impressive as this new work' (*Library Journal*, v.121, no.12, July 1996, p.100,102). Selected as one of *Choice's* Outstanding Academic Books of 1996. *Class No:* 908(73)(=96)

[4964]
SCHONBERG CENTER FOR RESEARCH IN BLACK CULTURE. The New York Public Library African American desk reference. New York, Wiley, 1999. 608p. tables. $34.95. ISBN: 0471239240.

5,000+ information capsules on statistics, culture, customs, history, and contemporary issues. 500 biographical profiles. 120 sidebars on topics of particular significance. 20 timelines. *Class No:* 908(73)(=96)

Bibliographies

[4965]

The Kaiser index to black resources 1948-1986. Kaiser, E.D., *comp.* New York, Carlson Publishing, 5v., 1992. 2600p. $995. ISBN: 0926019600.

Index of 174,000 items relating to articles in newspapers and over 170 periodicals held in the Schomburg Center for Research in Black Culture of The New York Public Library arranged under 15,000 subdivided Library of Congress subject headings. Much of the material is not indexed elsewhere. *Class No:* 908(73)(=96)(01)

Amerindians, North

[4966]

CHAMPAGNE, D., *ed.* **The Native North American almanac.** Detroit, Gale Research, 1994. 1275p. maps, tables, bibliog., indexes. £57.50. ISBN: 0810388650.

Comprehensive coverage of all major aspects of the civilization and culture of the indigenous peoples of the US and Canada. 17 sections include signed essays, annotated directory information, documentary excerpts and biographies. Each chapter includes a subject-specific bibliography and photographs, maps and charts and a detailed table of contents, alphabetical and geographical lists of tribes, multimedia bibliography, glossary, appendix of tables and charts and occupational and keyword indexes. *Class No:* 908(73)(=97)

[4967]

HIRSCHFELDER, A. *and* MONTANO, M.K. de. **The Native American almanack** a portrait of native America today. New York, Prentice Hall, 1993, x,341p. illus., maps, tables, bibliog., index. $25. ISBN: 0671850121.

14 sections portraying all aspects of Native American life: 1. Historical review of relations between Native Americans in the United States - 2. Native Americans today (population, tribes, reservations) ... 4. Treaties - 5. Bureau of Indian Affairs and Indian Health Service ... 14. Military service. Appendix 1. Tribes by State - 2. Reservations, rancherias, colonies and historic Indian areas - 3. Chronology of Indian treaties 1778-1868 - 4. Native landmarks - 5. Chronology (1492-1992) p.301-33. Bibliography (by chapter) p.315-327. *Class No:* 908(73)(=97)

Bibliographies

[4968]

Native American Bibliography Series. Marken, J.W. Metuchen, N.J., Scarecrow Press, 1980-.

1. Marken, J.W. and Hoover, H.T. *Bibliography of the Sioux.* 1980. 338p. $27.50. ISBN 0810813564.

4. *Anderson, W.L. and Lewis, J.A. A guide to Cherokee documents in foreign archives.* 1983. 768p. $40. 081081630x.

6. Wilson, T.P. *Bibliography of the Osage.* 1985. 172p. $20. 0810818051.

7. Kutsche, P. *A guide to Cherokee documents in the Northeastern United States.* 1986. 541p. $79. 0810818272.

9. *Tate, M.L. The Indians of Texas: an annotated research bibliography.* 1986. 514p. $52. 0810818523.

10 Blumer, T.J. *Bibliography of the Catawba.* 1987. 575p. $59.50. 0810819864.

11. Hoyt, A.K. *Bibliography of the Chickasaw.* 1987. 230p. $25. 0810819953.

12. Edmunds, R.D. *Kinsmen through time: an annotated bibliography of Potawatomi history.* 1987. 237p. $27.50. 081082020x.

13. Dempsey, H.A. and Moir, L. *Bibliography of the Blackfoot.* 1989. 255p. $27.50. 0810822113.

14. Tate, M.L. *The Upstream people: an annotated research bibliography of the Omaha tribe* 1991. 522p. maps. $27.50. 0810823721.

The series of bibliographies on Native American tribes also includes bibliographies of general topics concerning Native Americans. The compilers aim to be comprehensive, annotate the more important items, and produced bibliographies ranging from 2000 to 5000 entries. *Class No:* 908(73)(=97)(01)

[4969]

WHITE, P.M. **American Indian studies** a bibliographic guide. Boulder, Colo., Libraries Unlimited, 1995. 163p. indexes. $29. ISBN: 1563082438.

Guide to sources 1970-1993 arranged by form: guides, directories, encyclopedias, bibliographies, biographical sources, theses, government publications, microforms, databases, newspapers and periodicals. *Class No:* 908(73)(=97)(01)

Encyclopaedias

[4970]

MALINOWSKI, S. *and* SHEETS, A., *eds.* **The Gale encyclopedia of Native American tribes.** Detroit, Gale, 4v., 1998. illus., maps bibliogs. index. $349. ISBN: 0787610852.

Signed articles, arranged geographically, in 4 volumes: 1. Northeast and southeast - 2. Arctic and subarctic - 3. Plateaux and Great Plains 4. Pacific northwest and California. Regional essays introduce each section. History, culture, current issues, biographies, and tribal legends are the main themes. *Class No:* 908(73)(=97)(031)

[4971]

The Reference encyclopedia of the American Indian. Klein, B.T., *ed.* 8th ed. Nyack, NY, Todd Publications, 1998. ii,727p. bibliog. $125.

1. Source listings (reservations, communities and tribal councils, government agencies, museums, events etc.) - 2. Canadian listings - 3. Bibliography (4500 in print books) - 4. 2500 biographical sketches. *Class No:* 908(73)(=97)(031)

Amerindian

Bibliographies

[4972]

HELMER, D. 'Native American reference sources', *Booklist,* v.96, no.9/10, 1+ 15 January 2000, p.956, 958, 960, 962.

Annotated list of recently published materials (*i.e.* 1990s). arranged in 3 sections: 1. General resources (first choices for high school, public and undergraduate libraries) - 2. Additional resources (more specialized titles) - 3. School library resources. *Class No:* 908(73)=97(01)

Alaska

Bibliographies

[4973]

FELK, M.W., *Comp.* **Alaska.** Oxford and Santa Barbara, Calif., Clio Press, 1995. xxxi,219p.+2p. maps, indexes. £38.50. (*World Bibliographical Series, no.183.*) ISBN: 1851091416.

793 annotated entries arranged in 25 sections: The State and its people - Geography - Travel guides - Travel narratives ... Prehistory and archaeology - History ... Recreation ... Bibliographies. Author, title and subject indexes. 'This professionally researched, carefully shaped, and carefully integrated bibliography reveals an awful lot of information, either long buried in obscure and perhaps forgotten publications or in hard to track down works still in print' (*Reference Reviews,* vol.10,no.4, 1996, p.48). *Class No:* 908(798)(01)

Handbooks & Manuals

[4974]

WOERNER, R.K. **The Alaska handbook.** Jefferson, North Carolina, and London, McFarland & Co., 1986. ix, 220p. illus., ports., maps, tables, index. $19.95. ISBN: 0899502199.

10 chapters: 1. Alaska: an overview - 2. Land regions - 3. Transport - 4. Land ownership and disposal - 5. National Parklands - 6. Cities - 7. Flying to Alaska - 8. Camping - 9. Floating Alaska's rivers - 10. Wildlife, fishing and hunting. Appendix F. Other information sources. *Class No:* 908(798)(035)

Brazil

Bibliographies

[4975]

DICKENSON, J., *comp.* **Brazil.** 2nd ed. Santa Barbara, California and Oxford, Clio Press, 1997. xxviii,246p + 1p. map. index. £47. (*World Bibliographical Series, no. 57.*) ISBN: 1851092595.

Replaces S.V. Bryant's *Brazil* (1985).

903 annotated entries. 36 sections: The country and its people - Geography ... Archaeology and prehistory - History ... Nationalities, minorities and immigrants - Museums and libraries ... General bibliographies. Author, title and subject index. *Class No:* 908(81)(01)

[4976]

HARTNESS, A. **Brasil obras de referência 1965-1998** Uma bibliografia commentada. Brasilia, Briquet De Lemos/Livros, 1999. x,435p. indexes. ISBN: 8585637145.

2913 (mostly annotated) entries arranged in 28 sections (*e.g.* 1. Bibliografias ... Bibliotecas, arquives, museus ... Biografia ... Geografia ... História). *Class No:* 908(81)(01)

Argentina

Bibliographies

[4977]

IGGINS, A., *comp*. **Argentina**. Santa Barbara, Calif., and Oxford, Clio Press, 1991. xxvi,460p. +1p. map indexes. £65. (*World Bibliographical Series, no.130*.) ISBN: 1851091092.

1350 annotated entries in 42 sections: Country and its people - Geography - Travellers' accounts ... Archaeology and prehistory - History ... The Gaucho ... Falklands Islands dispute ... Encyclopaedias, directories and biographical dictionaries - Bibliographies. Author, title and subject index. *Class No:* 908(82)(01)

[4978]

NIVERSITY OF BUENOS AIRES. **Argentine bibliography:** a union catalogue of Argentinian holdings in the libraries of the University of Buenos Aires. Boston, Mass., G.K. Hall, 7v., 1980. 5000p. $689.00 (Export $830.00). ISBN: 0816103178.

The *Argentine Bibliography* reproduces in book form more than 105,000 cards in the card catalogs of the 53 libraries of the University of Buenos Aires. The Bibliography lists all works written by Argentine authors and works about Argentina published anywhere in the world through 1977. *Class No:* 908(82)(01)

Falkland Islands

[4979]

HEADLAND, R. **The Island of South Georgia**. Cambridge, Cambridge Univ. Press, 1984. xvi, 293p. illus., maps, tables, bibliog. £22.50. ISBN: 0521252741.

9 chapters: 1. Geography, administration and population - 2. Discovery - 3. Early history and the first epoch of sealing - 4. Expeditions, visits and other events - 5. Whaling, second sealing epoch - 6. Travel and communications - 7. Physical sciences, the land, ocean and atmosphere - 8. Natural history - 9. Military action, events on South Georgia in 1982 and the island's future. Bibliography p.270-5. 'A truly splendid book by a knowledgeable scholar, catholic in interest and qualified by extensive personal experience of the island' (*Geographical Journal*, v.151, no.2, July 1985, p.261). *Class No:* 908(829.1)

Bibliographies

[4980]

DAY, A., *comp*. **The Falkland Islands**, South Georgia and The South Sandwich Islands. Oxford and Santa Barbara, Calif., Clio Press, 1996. xvii,231p.+2p. maps, index. £40.50. (*World Bibliographical Series, no.184*.) ISBN: 1851092366.

693 annotated entries in 31 sections: The Islands and their people - Discovery and early voyages - Travellers' accounts - Geography and geology ... Tourism and travel guides - Prehistory and archaeology - Maritime archaeology - History - Sovereignty - War in the South Atlantic 1982 ... Bibliographies - South Georgia - South Sandwich Islands. Author, title and subject indexes. 'An excellent starting point for anyone interested in researching a particular topic and has many intriguing ... entries leaving one wishing for immediate access to a huge library' (*Warrah*, v.9, May 1996,. p.12). *Class No:* 908(829.1)(01)

[4981]

HEADLAND, R. **South Georgia** a bibliography. Cambridge, British Antarctic Survey, 1982. 180p. £3.00. ISBN: 0856650951.

'A definitive work in this field, computer-set and likely to be updated periodically' (H.G.R. King. *The Atlantic Ocean*, 1985. Entry 886). *Class No:* 908(829.1)(01)

Chile

Bibliographies

[4982]

BLAKEMORE, H., *comp*. **Chile**. Santa Barbara, California and Oxford, Clio Press, 1988. xiv, 197p. + 2p. maps, indexes. £28.50; $42.50. (*World Bibliographical Series, no. 97*.) ISBN: 1851090266.

642 annotated entries. 29 sections: The country and its people - Geography - Exploration and travel ... Archaeology ... History ... Government and politics ... Museums and libraries ... Bibliographies. Author, title and subject indexes. *Class No:* 908(83)(01)

Bolivia

Bibliographies

[4983]

YEAGER, G.M., *comp*. **Bolivia**. Santa Barbara, California and Oxford, Clio Press, 1988. xv, 228p.+1p. map. index. £32.95; $41.00. (*World Bibliographical Series, no.89*.) ISBN: 0851090665.

816 annotated entries. 36 sections: The country and people - Geography - Tourism and travel guides - Travellers' accounts ...

....(*contd.*)

Prehistory and archaeology - History ... Social conditions ... Bibliographies - Reference Works and encyclopaedias - Dictionaries. Author, title and subject index. *Class No:* 908(84)(01)

Peru

Bibliographies

[4984]

FISHER, R., *comp*. **Peru**. Santa Barbara, California and Oxford, Clio Press, 1989. xvii, 193p.+1p. map, indexes. £34.00. (*World Bibliographical Series; no.109*.) ISBN: 1851091009.

705 annotated entries. 31 sections: The country and its people - Geography - Tourism and travel guides - Exploration and travellers' accounts ... Archaeology and prehistory - History ... Libraries and archives ... Reference works ... Bibliographies. Author, title and subject indexes. *Class No:* 908(85)(01)

Colombia

Bibliographies

[4985]

DAVIS, R.H., *comp*. **Columbia**. Santa Barbara, California and Oxford, Clio Press, 1990. xxi,204 +1p. map. indexes. £29.95. (*World Bibliographical Series, no.112*.) ISBN: 1851090932.

662 annotated entries in 29 sections: Country and its people - Geography and the environment ... Exploration and travellers' accounts - Archaeology and prehistory - History ... La Violencia ... Archives ... Reference works - Bibliographies. Author, title and subject index. *Class No:* 908(86)(01)

Ecuador

Bibliographies

[4986]

Ecuador. Corkill, D., *comp*. Santa Barbara, California and Oxford, Clio Press, 1989. xxi, 155p. + 1p. map. indexes. £32.00; $45.00. (*World Bibliographical Series, no. 101*.) ISBN: 085109069x.

557 annotated entries. 28 sections. The country and its people - Geography - Exploration and travellers' accounts - Tourism and travel guides ... Archaeology and prehistory - History ... Directories and current reference books - Bibliographies - Professional periodicals. Author, title, and subject indexes. *Class No:* 908(866)(01)

Venezuela

Bibliographies

[4987]

WADDELL, D.A.G., *comp*. **Venezuela**. Santa Barbara, California and Oxford, Clio Press, 1990. xviii,206p. map, index. £29.95; $29.95. (*World Bibliographical Series, no.110*.) ISBN: 1851091068.

815 annotated entries in 29 sections. Country and its people - Geography - Description and travel ... Prehistory and archaeology - Native peoples - History ... Bibliographies. Author, subject and title index. *Class No:* 908(87)(01)

Guyana

Bibliographies

[4988]

CHAMBERS, F. **Guyana**. Santa Barbara, California and Oxford, Clio Press, 1989. xv, 206p. + 1p. map. indexes. £31.95; $45.00. (*World Bibliographical Series, no. 96*.) ISBN: 1851090703.

606 annotated entries. 36 sections: The country and people - Geography - Maps, atlases and gazetteers ... Travel guides - Travellers' and explorers' accounts ... Prehistory and archaeology - Historiography - History ... Libraries, archives and museums ... Reference works - Bibliographies. Separate author, title and subject indexes. *Class No:* 908(88)(01)

French Guiana

Bibliographies

[4989]

CRANE, J., *comp*. **French Guiana**. Oxford and Santa Barbara, Calif., Clio Press, 1999. xxxiii,160p.+1p. map, indexes. £34. (*World Bibliographical Series, no.210*.) ISBN: 1851092412.

405 annotated entries arranged under 22 headings: The Department and its people - Geography - Travellers' accounts ... Travel guides and tourism - Prehistory and archaeology - History ... Reference sources.

....*(contd.)*
Introduction (geophysical environment - climate - history - contemporary Guyane) p.xv-xxxiii. Author, title and subject indexes.
Class No: 908(882)(01)

Suriname

Bibliographies
[4990]
HOEFTE, R., *comp*. **Suriname**. Santa Barbara, Calif., Oxford, Clio Press, 1990. xxx,227p.+ 1p. map, index. £34. (*World Bibliographical Series, no.117.*) ISBN: 1851091033.
731 annotated entries in 30 sections: The country and its people - Geography and geology - Travellers' accounts ... Prehistory and archaeology - History ... Languages ... Libraries and archives ... Reference Books - Bibliographies. Author, title and subject index.
Class No: 908(883)(01)

Paraguay
[4991]
ROETT, R. *and* SACKS, R.S. **Paraguay** the personalist legacy. Boulder, Colo., Westview Press, 1991. xviii,188p. illus., tables, map, bibliog., index. £21.95. (*Profiles. Nations Of Contemporary America.*) ISBN: 0865312729.
1. Introduction - 2. History 1524-1904 - 3. Modern history - 4. Economy - 5. Culture and society - 6. Politics and government - 7. International relations. Bibliography p.171-7. *Class No:* 908(892)

Bibliographies
[4992]
Paraguay. Nickson, R.A. Rev. ed. Santa Barbara, California and Oxford, Clio Press, 1999. xxiv, 249p.+1p. map. index. £34. ISBN: 1851093206.
1st ed. 1987.
724 annotated entries. 45 sections: The country and its people - Geography ... Tourism and travel guides - Travellers' accounts Archaeology - History ... Biographies, autobiographies and memoirs - Bibliographies. Author, title, and subject indexes.
Class No: 908(892)(01)

Uruguay

Bibliographies
[4993]
FINCH, M.H.J. **Uruguay**. Santa Barbara, California and Oxford, Clio Press, 1989. xxix, 232p. + 1p. map, indexes. £34.95. (*World Bibliographical Series, no.102.*) ISBN: 0851090983.
667 annotated entries. 34 sections: The country and its people - Tourism and travel guides - Geography ... Prehistory and archaeology - History ... Politics ... Museums and archives - Directories - Bibliographies. Theses and dissertations on Uruguay p.xxvii-xxix.
Class No: 908(899)(01)

Australasia & Oceania

Bibliographies of Bibliographies
[4994]
THOMPSON, A.G. **The Southwest Pacific:** an annotated guide to bibliographies, indexes and collections in Australian libraries. Canberra, Research School of Pacific Studies, The Australian National University in association with The Academy of Social Sciences in Australia, 1986. x, 127p. indexes, softcover. ISBN: 0867848327.
479 annotated items listed under 6 geographical headings subdivided into broad subject categories. Author and subject indexes.
Class No: 908(9)(009)

Bibliographies
[4995]
TAYLOR, C.R.H., *comp*. **A Pacific bibliography** printed matter relating to the native peoples of Polynesia, Melanesia, and Micronesia. 2nd ed. London, Oxford Univ. Press, 1965. xx, 692p.
First published 1951 (xxix, 492p.).
More than 16,000 references (to periodical articles as well as books), classified by island groups and by subjects. Covers every island group of Polynesia, Melanesia and Micronesia, and includes New Zealand. According to Ad Orientem *Catalogue nine*, 1967, (p.147). over 13% of the entries concern the Maori, over 5%, Hawaii and 4%, the Fiji Islands. 'One of the major bibliographies on the Pacific' (G.W. Fry and R. Mauricio. *Pacific Basin and Oceania*, 1987. Entry 488). *Class No:* 908(9)(01)

[4996]
THAWLEY, J. **Australasia and South Pacific Islands bibliography** Lanham, Md., Scarecrow Press, 1997. xvii,588p. £70.30. ISBN 0810832402.
5,918 items mainly English language books published in the last 5 years, but including 26 computer databases and 38 major journals arranged by country and island groups: South Pacific, Australia, Papu New Guinea, New Zealand, and 23 small island states in Melanesia Micrtonesia and Polynesia. 'An intelligent, competent, and remarkabl wide-ranging compilation which students ... will find of real servic and value as a first guide to a dauntingly extensive and widel scattered specialist literature' (*Reference Reviews*, vol.11,no.7, 1997 p.48-49). *Class No:* 908(9)(01)

Yearbooks & Directories
[4997]
Pacific Islands Yearbook. 17th ed. Suva, Fiji, Fiji Times, 1994 vii,767p. map in end-pocket. ISBN: 9822010028.
Preceded by *Stewart's Handbook of the Pacific Islands: a reliabl guide to all the inhabited islands of the Pacific for tourists, traders settlers* (Sydney, McCarren, Stewart, 1908-1929 annual). Unde present title since 1932.
Descriptive gazetteer A-Z by island or island group *e.g.* Tokela (Government - Justice - Defence - Education - Labour - Health Housing - Economy - Manufacturing -Local Commerce - Tourism Overseas trade - Finance - Transport - Communications - Utilities Major office holders - Visitors information (p.618-630). Pacifi chronology p.7-10. Index of islands, atolls and inlets p.759-67. Cover. 34 island groups and territories. *Class No:* 908(9)(058)

Indonesia

Bibliographies
[4998]
BUTLER, A. **A New Guinea bibliography**. Waigani, Univ. of New Guinea Press, 5v, 1984-1990. xxvii, 2604p. index, reproduced from typescript..
'An attempt to list in subject order all the monographs, pamphlets, theses, reports, government documents, seminar papers, journals, *etc* which are published either in New Guinea or which deal with Papua New Guinea or Irian Jayan topics' (*Preface*). V.5: *Indexes* (1990) includes contents tables for v.1-4; author and name index; and subject index. The *Bibliography* is part of the Papua New Guinea Information Network project. *Class No:* 908(910)(01)

[4999]
KRAUSSE, G.H. *and* KRAUSSE, S.C.E., *comps*. **Indonesia**. Santa Barbara, California and Oxford, Clio Press, 1994. xlv,407p.++ 1p. map, indexes. £64.50. (*World Bibliographical Series, no.170.*) ISBN: 1851091270.
1083 entries in 36 sections: Country and its People - Travellers Accounts - Tourism and Travel Guides - Geography ... Prehistory and archaeology - History - Biography and Memoirs ... Cuisine ... Bibliography. Author, title and subject indexes. Introduction (p.xix-xlv) gives useful introduction to the history of Indonesia.
Class No: 908(910)(01)

[5000]
VAN BOAL, J., *and others*. **West Irian:** a bibliography. Dordrecht, Foris Publications Holland; Cinnaminson, New Jersey, Foris Publications USA, 1984. xiv, 307p. index. (*Koninklijk Institute Voor Taal-Land-En Volkenkunde Bibliographical Series; no.15.*) ISBN: 9067650595.
Approximately 3,000 entries arranged in 9 subdivided chapters: 1. General - 2. Climate, geology - 3. Zoology and botany - 4. Physical anthropology and demography - 5. Linguistics - 6. History (p.41-76) - 7. Cultural anthropology - 8. Ethnology, regional studies - 9. Economics and socio-cultural development after 1950. Each chapter contains an introduction to and a description of relevant literature followed by a list of titles A-Z by author. Intended as a concise guide, not 'a voluminous work referring to a confusing mass of literature of often uncertain value'. Author index and index of geographical and tribal names.
Appendix: P. Nienhuis' 'Inventaris van het rapportenarchief van het kantooos voor bevolkingszaken (Nederlands-Nieuw Guinea) 1951-1962' *i.e.* an inventory of reports of the Bureau of the Adviser on Native affairs, p.206-307. *Class No:* 908(910)(01)

Brunei
[5001]
Brunei Darussalem in profile. London, Shandwick, 1988. Published on behalf of The Government of Brunei Darussalam. 164p. col.illus. col.map. tables, index. ISBN: 095138550x.
Contents: Introduction (Location, size, race, religion; Short history; Key dates; Future) - The Constitution - Structure of government -

..(contd.)
Heraldry - The Sultans of Brunei - Economic profile - Commercial
information - Practical information. 8p. street maps.
Class No: 908(911.13)

Bibliographies

[5002]
RAUSSE, S.C. *and* KRAUSSE, G.H. **Brunei.** Santa Barbara,
California and Oxford, Clio Press, 1988. xliii, 249p. + 2p. maps,
geneal. tables. index. £39.50. (*World Bibliographical Series, no. 93.*)
ISBN: 1851090290.

660 annotated entries. 31 sections: The country and its people -
Brunei in general works on Southeast Asia - Geography ...
Archaeology and prehistory - History - The Sultans - Politics and
government ... Tourism and recreation ... Libraries and Museums ...
Bibliographies and indexes. Sultans of Brunei: a genealogy p.xlii-xliii.
Author, subject and title index. *Class No:* 908(911.13)(01)

Philippines

Bibliographies

[5003]
RICHARDSON, J. **Philippines.** Santa Barbara, California and Oxford,
Clio Press, 1989. xx, 372p.+1p. map. index. £37.00. (*World
Bibliographical Series, no.106.*) ISBN: 0851090770.

955 annotated entries. 39 sections: The country and its people -
Tourism and travel guides ... Archaeology and pre-Spanish history -
History - Politics since independence - Libraries and Museums ...
Encyclopaedias, directories and yearbooks - Bibliographies. Author,
title, subject index. *Class No:* 908(914)(01)

Timor

Bibliographies

[5004]
ROWLAND, I., *comp*. **Timor.** Santa Barbara, Calif., and Oxford, Clio
Press, 1992. xli,117p.+ 2p. maps, index. £32. (*World Bibliographical
Series, no.142.*) ISBN: 1851091599.

348 annotated entries in 22 sections: Island and its people - Travel
guides - Travellers' accounts - Geography ... Archaeology and
prehistory - History - Timorese peoples... Indonesian invasion and
foreign relations ... Bibliographies - Periodicals. Chronology p.xxxix-
xli. Author, title and subject index. *Class No:* 908(923.52)(01)

New Zealand

[5005]
Facts New Zealand. Pullar, V., *comp.* 2nd ed. Wellington, Statistics
New Zealand, 1995. 210p. maps, tables, index. pbk. ISSN: 11715057.
1st ed. 1992.

Concise digest on all aspects of contemporary New Zealand in 9
sections: 1. Land and people - 2. Social organization - 3. Work and
leisure - 4. Maori - 5. Primary production - 6. Industry and business -
7. Economics - 8. International comparisons. History (chronological
table c.1300-1995) p.35-45. *Class No:* 908(931)

Bibliographies

[5006]
MARTIN, M.S. **'New Zealand at 150',** a sesquicentennial booklist,
Choice, v.27, no.9, May 1990, p.1460-4.

Running commentary with consolidated list of books mentioned on
political, historical and social issues (including race and the
environment). *Class No:* 908(931)(01)

[5007]
NESBITT, M., *comp*. **New Zealand** a basic annotated bibliography for
students, librarians and general readers. London, Commonwealth
Institute Staff & Research Library, 1988. vi. 62p. sd. ISBN:
094614043x. ISSN: 03061124.

Unnumbered entries in 17 sections *e.g.* General background
(includes Bibliographies, Indexes, Reference Books and Travel Guides)
... History ... Society and people. Other sources p.61-62.
Class No: 908(931)(01)

[5008]
PATTERSON, B. *and* PATTERSON, K., *comps.* **New Zealand.** 2nd
ed. Santa Barbara, California and Oxford, Clio Press, 1998. 416p. +
2p. maps, index. £69. (*World Bibliographical Series, No.18.*) ISBN:
185109279x.

1st ed., compiled by R.F. Grover, published in 1982.
972 annotated entries. 40 sections: The country and people -
Geography ... History of the Pacific - Prehistory and archaeology -
History of New Zealand ... Maori people ... Politics ... Libraries, art
galleries, museums and archives ... Encyclopedias and directories -
Bibliographies. *Class No:* 908(931)(01)

Encyclopaedias

[5009]
The Concise encyclopedia of Australia and New Zealand.
Stewart, P., *ed*. Rev. ed. Sydney, Horwitz Graham, 1991, 2v. 1068p.
col.illus., col.maps. $A100. ISBN: 0725522364.

Revised edition of *New National Australian encyclopedia* which was
first published in 1964 as *The Modern encyclopedia of Australia and
New Zealand*. Frequently reprinted.

V.1: Australian maps. Chronology p.17-38. Constitution p.39-54.
Facts and Figures (geographical, political, industrial, agricultural,
sport) p.55-136. Australia A-L. V.2: Australia M-Z. NZ maps.
Chronology p.892-904. Facts and Figures p.905-13. NZ. A-Z. Good
home, office, school reference source. *Class No:* 908(931)(031)

[5010]
The Illustrated encyclopedia of New Zealand. McLauchlan, G., *ed*.
Auckland, David Bateman, 1990. Distributed in North America by
G.K. Hall. 1448p. $75. ISBN: 0869530071, US.

Expanded version of *The Bateman New Zealand encyclopedia* (2nd
ed. 1988).

*c.*2500 articles cover all aspects of New Zealand life. Chronology of
New Zealand history to the end of 1988. Entirely redesigned with
pages divided into 3 columns. 2,200 colour and 800 black and white
illustrations. Good index serves cross-reference role. 'Articles are well
developed, readable, and much more extensive than in *Bateman*'
(*Booklist*, v.87, no.6, 15 November 1990. p.682).
Class No: 908(931)(031)

[5011]
McLINTOCK, A.H., *ed*. **An Encyclopaedia of New Zealand.**
Wellington, Owen, Government Printer, 3v., 1966. illus., tables,
maps.

Signed articles by *c.*350 countributors, usually with references (*e.g.*
'Otago province': 6½p. 4 maps, 6 references; 'Welfare services'; 4p.
5 references). Some 700 biographies, including 'Expatriates -
Biographies' (v.1, p.575-604). The 500 maps are a feature. 96 plates
in all, with 3, 4 or 6 illus. per page; also numerous small text
illustrations. Analytical index. v.3, p.713-843. Well produced.
Class No: 908(931)(031)

Yearbooks & Directories

[5012]
New Zealand official yearbook 1996 Te pukapuka Houanga Whaimana
o Aotearoa. 99th ed. Wellington, Statistics New Zealand, 1996.
viii,592p. illus., col. maps, tables, diagrs., bibliogs., index. $49.50.
ISSN: 00780170.
1st ed. 1893.

Compendium of facts and figures on all aspects of New Zealand's
social, economic and cultural life presented in 28 sections: 1.
Geography - History - 3. Government ... 11. Leisure and tourism ...
14. Land and environment, each with its own bibliography. Analytical
index. *Class No:* 908(931)(058)

Libraries

[5013]
Australian and New Zealand studies papers presented at a colloquium at
the British Library 7-9 February 1984. McLaren-Turner, P., *ed*.
London, The British Library, 1985. [x] 213p. £13.95. (*British Library
Occasional Papers.*) ISBN: 0712300481.

31 papers mainly devoted to the resources of the British Library and
other UK research libraries. *Class No:* 908(931):061:026/027

Melanesia

Bibliographies

[5014]
EDRIDGE, S. **Solomon Islands bibliography up to 1980.** Suva Institute
of Pacific Studies, University of the South Pacific; Wellington,
Alexander Turnbull Library; Honiara, Sol. Is., National Library,
1985. xvi, 476p. maps on endpapers, index. ISBN: 0908702035.

Books, pamphlets and periodical articles published within Solomon

....(contd.)

Islands, or relating to them, arranged as a classifed catalogue. All works published by Solomon Islanders are included regardless of subject. *Class No:* 908(932)(01)

[5015]

O'REILLY, P. **Bibliographie méthodique, analytique et critique de la Nouvelle - Calédonie.** Paris, Musée de l'Homme: 1955. 361p. index. *(Publications de la Société des Océanistes; no.4.)*

4181 items published 1774-1954 covering all aspects of New Caledonia's life and history - geography, geology, zoology, botany, ethnology, economy, literature *etc*. 'Still a valuable comprehensive annotated bibliography' (G.W. Fry and R. Mauricio *Pacific Basin and Oceania,* 1987. Entry 566). *Class No:* 908(932)(01)

[5016]

—PISIER, G. **Bibliographie méthodique, analytique et critique de la Nouvelle - Calédonie 1955-1982.** Nouméa, Publications de la Société Études Historiques de la Nouvelle - Calédonie; 1983. 350p. illus., indexes.

Modelled on P. O'Reilly's *Bibliographie ... de la Nouvelle - Calédonie* (1955) which it updates.

3338 references. 20 Sections: 1. Bibliography and general reference works - 2. Geography ... 11. History ... 18. Periodical publications .. *etc*. Author, place and subject indexes. *Class No:* 908(932)(01)

[5017]

O'REILLY, P. **Bibliographie méthodique, analytique et critique des îles Wallis et Futuna.** Paris, Musée de l'Homme, 1964. 68p. *(Publications de la Société des Océanistes, no.13.)*

491 items in subject divisions *e.g*. Geography and climate; Ethnology; History *etc.,* 'This carefully annotated and comprehensive bibliography; (G.W. Fry and R. Mauricio *Pacific Basin and Oceania.* 1987. Entry 1157). *Class No:* 908(932)(01)

[5018]

O'REILLY, P. **Bibliographie méthodique, analytique et critique des Nouvelles - Hébrides.** Paris, Musée de l'Homme, 1958. 305p. *(Publications de la Société des Océanistes; no.8.)*

Mostly annotated entries relating to all aspects of the islands. 'A comprehensive bibliography' (G.W. Fry and R. Mauricio. *Pacific Basin and Oceania,* 1987, Entry 631). *Class No:* 908(932)(01)

Australia

[5019]

Reader's Digest country Australia the land and the people. Sydney, Reader's Digest, 1989. col. illus., diagrs., col. maps. $45.00. ISBN: 0864380526.

Over 800 A-Z entries relating to Australian history, wildlife, lore and legends illustrated with 1300 photographs *etc*. *Class No:* 908(94)

CD-ROM

[5020]

Aboriginal and Torres Strait Islander CD-ROM. Melbourne, RMIT Publishing. Semi-Annual. Available from Silverplatter Information Ltd., Merlin House, 20 Belmont Terrace, Chiswick, London, W4 5UG. CD-ROM. Single Disc.

ATSIROM is a collection of significant Australian databases containing 70,000+ bibliographic records from 11 leading sources on Aboriginal and Torres Strait Islander people. It contains references to published and unpublished material, including journal articles, newspaper and newsletter articles, conference proceedings, royal commissions, and government department reports across a broad range of topics. *Class No:* 908(94)(003.40)

Bibliographies

[5021]

CLINCH, M.A. **Guide to Northern Territory research resources in Northern Territory collections.** Darwin, North Australia Research Unit of the Australian National Univ., 1981. ix, 374p. maps, bibliog.

5 major parts: 1. Directory of collections - 2. Finding list (8200 A-Z by author entries with locations) - 3. Union list of Northern Territory newspapers - 4. Appendices (including B. Brief chronology of the Northern Territory p. 359-62). Maps p.369-74. Bibliography p.374. 'Starting point for anyone ... who wants to find out something about the Territory' *(Foreword).* *Class No:* 908(94)(01)

[5022]

CUMPSTON, J. **Macquarie Islands** a bibliography. Gemorne, New South Wales, The Stone Copying Co., 1958. ii, 32p. map. sd. *Class No:* 908(94)(01)

[5023]

KEPARS, I. **Australia.** 2nd ed. Santa Barbara, California and Oxford, Clio Press, 1994. 260p. + 2p. map, index. £42. *(World Bibliographical Series, no. 46.)* ISBN: 185109122x.

1st ed. 1985.

1004 annotated entries. 42 sections: The country and people - Geography ... History ... Defence and military history ... Australian Aborigines ... Reference works. Author, title and subject indexes. *Class No:* 908(94)(01)

[5024]

KEPARS, I., *comp*. **Tasmania.** Oxford and Santa Barbara, Calif., Clio Press, 1997. xx,164p.+1p. map, indexes. £32. *(World Bibliographical Series, no.194.)* ISBN: 1851092730.

537 annotated entries in 30 chapters: Island and its people - Geography - Discovery and exploration - Tourst and travel guides .. History - Biographies and autobiographies - Convicts - Aborigines ... Reference works. Author, title and subject indexes. *Class No:* 908(94)(01)

[5025]

MILLS, C.M. **A Bibliography of the Northern Territory.** Canberra, College of Advanced Education Library, 1977-. ISBN: 0858990607, set.

1. *Monographs. Pt.1. Sciences, primary industry and recreation.* 1977. xiv, 168p. index. 0858990615. 1236 entries in 12 sections including C. Geography and L. Maps and atlases.

2. *General, Travels, History, Humanities and religion.* 1978. xvi, 465p. index. 0858990828. Over 2000 entries in 15 sections *e.g*. M. General, travels - N. Bibliographies and catalogues - O. History - P. Biographies - Q. Journals, diaries, logs, letters - R. Exploration and survey.

3. *The Social Sciences (excluding material relating to the Aborigines)* 1981, xxii, 174p. 0858990913. 848 entries in 9 sections. Summary of Northern Territory historical events p.xi-xvii.

4. *The Aborigines; plus supplementary entries to Pts. 1-3, to 1981 and consolidated index to the complete bibliography,* 2v., 1983. xii, 751p. 08589902324. 2623 entries in 21 sections including AG. Prehistory and archaeology ... AL. Bibliography - AM. Tribes. Index p.609-751. *Class No:* 908(94)(01)

Encyclopaedias

[5026]

The Angus & Robertson concise Australian encyclopedia. rev. ed. North Ryde, New South Wales, Angus and Robertson, 1986. 505p. col. illus., tables, col. maps, index. ISBN: 0207153051.

First published 1983.

Almost 1000 cross referenced entries illuminating the most significant geographical, historical, cultural, social, political and commercial events that have shaped modern Australia. Suitable for home and school use. *Class No:* 908(94)(031)

[5027]

The Australian encyclopaedia. 4th ed. Sydney, Grolier Society of Australia, 12v., 1983. illus. (many col.), maps, diagrs. ISBN: 0959660429.

First published 1925/26. 3rd. ed. 1977.

A comprehensive picture of Australia and its people both past and present. V.12 *Index and Appendix* (p.1-86) includes lists of awards, sporting achievements, and statistical data. 100 new topics in this edition not counting biographical entries. *Class No:* 908(94)(031)

[5028]

The Australian people: an encyclopedia of the nation, its people and their origins. Jupp, J., *gen. ed*. North Ryde, New South Wales, Angus & Robertson, 1988. xvi, 1040p. illus. (some col.), bibliog., tables, index. Aust$80.00; £47.75. ISBN: 0207154279.

250 Contributors. 290 articles deployed in 4 main sections: 1. Aspects of the peopling of Australia (The Aboriginals and the convict period; Imperial settlement; Immigration since the Second World War) - 2. Australian Aborigines (Society; Culture; Economy; Politics *etc.,*) - 3. The Settlers (Afghans to Yugoslavs) - 4. Immigrants and immigration. Appendix 1. 1986 Census data - 2. Chronology (p.973-978). Bibliography p.979-1022. Supported by Australian Bicentennial Authority to lend a multicultural dimension to the Bicentennial publications. For general and academic use. *Class No:* 908(94)(031)

[5029]

The Bateman concise encyclopaedia of Australia. Shaw, J., *ed*. 2nd ed. Bunderim, Queensland, David Bateman. Distributed in North America by G.K. Hall. xxvi, 848p. illus (some col.), col. maps. Aust $39.93; US$54.95. ISBN: 0949135232.

1st ed. 1984 as *Collins Australian encyclopedia.*

Popular, family reference work containing over 1000 cross-referenced articles. Few changes from 1984 edition. *Class No:* 908(94)(031)

[5030]
The Cambridge encyclopedia of Australia. Bambrick, S., *ed.*
Cambridge, Cambridge Univ. Press, 1994. 400p. illus., col. maps,
tables. £35. (*Cambridge World Encyclopedias Series.*) ISBN:
0521365112.
70 contributors. 8 major sections examine all the key aspects of the
continent, past and present: the physical environment, traditional
aboriginal society, history since European contact, economy, society,
government, culture and the arts, and scientific research. Individual
states receive individual attention, but the emphasis throughout is on
Australia-wide trends and the way these interact with developments in
the world outside, in North America and Europe quite as much as in the
Pacific. *Class No:* 908(94)(031)

Yearbooks & Directories

[5031]
The Book of Australia. Sydney, Waterworth Press, 1997. 602p. tables,
index. softcover.
Almanac in 16 sections: climate, geography, flora and fauna,
environment, population, history, government, law, economy,
transport, defence, health, education, employment and training, the
media, arts, and sport. Unofficial but a well-designed guide to
Australia and contemorary Australian scene. *Class No:* 908(94)(058)

Aborigines

[5032]
The Encyclopaedia of Aboriginal Australia. Aboriginal and Torres
Strait Islander history, society and culture. Horton, D., *ed.*
Canberra, Aboriginal Studies Press for the Australian Institute of
Aboriginal and Torres Strait Islander Studies, 2v., 1994. xxxiii,1340p.
illus. (mostly col.), col.maps, bibliog., index. ISBN: 0855752491,
v.1; 0855752505, v.2; 0855752343, set.
Over 200 contributors. 18 key entries introduce initialled cross-
referenced entries, each with further reading details, covering art,
economics, education, food, health, history, land ownership, language,
law, literature, medicine, music, politics, prehistory, religion, social
organization, sport, and technology. Includes much biographical
information. Bibliography p.1246-72. Time line (p.1326-29) included
in Entry Guide p.1307-40. A major and definitive reference work.
Class No: 908(94)(=995)

Bibliographies

[5033]
THAWLEY, J. *and* GAUCI, S. Bibliographies on the Australian
aborigines an annotated listing. 2nd ed. Bundoora, Victoria, The
Borchardt Library, La Trobe Univ., 1987. v, 44p. index. softcover.
ISBN: 0858166623.
1st ed. 1979.
163 entries A-Z by author with subject and geographical index.
Class No: 908(94)(=995)(01)

Papua—New Guinea

[5034]
RANNELLS, J. PNG: a factbook on modern Papua New Guinea. 2nd
ed. Oxford Univ. Press, 1995. 212p. maps, bibliog., index. pbk.
ISBN: 0195536797.
A-Z entries relating to PNG's government, economy, natural
resources geography, biology, and society. Much statistical
information. *Class No:* 908(954)

Bibliographies

[5035]
McCONNELL, F. Papua New Guinea. Santa Barbara, California and
Oxford, Clio Press, 1988. xxviii, 379p. map, index. £49.95; $55.00.
(*World Bibliographical Series, no. 90.*) ISBN: 1851090304.
865 well-annotated entries. 33 sections: The country and its people -
Geography ... Prehistory and archaeology - History - Biographies ...
Libraries, museums and archives ... Encyclopaedias, directories and
reference works - Bibliographies. Publishers and research institutions
p.xxvii-xxviii. *Class No:* 908(954)(01)

Encyclopaedias

[5036]
The Encyclopedia of Papua and New Guinea. Ryan, P., *ed.*
Melbourne Univ. Press in association with the Univ. of Papua and
New Guinea, 2v. and index. 1231p.+83p. illus., maps and index.
ISBN: 0522840256.
About 200 contributors; signed articles. 'Art' (v.1, p.20-50): over 1
column of references; cross-references, 'Port Moresby'; 3½ cols. of
bibliographies. V.3 has detailed index, p.33-83; gazetteer of place-
names; 10 colour lift out maps. *Choice* (v.9, no.12, February 1973,

....(contd.)
p.1572) commends the biographical articles as being more evaluative
than in most encyclopaedias. Well written and well produced. At
various times the prospect of updating the encyclopedia has been
discussed but to no avail. *Class No:* 908(954)(031)

Polynesia

Bibliographies

[5037]
DE RIETZ, R. Bibliotheca Polynesia: a catalogue of some of the books
in the Polynesiana collection formed by the late Bjarne Kroepelian and
now in the University Library Oslo. Stockholm, Almquist & Wiksell,
1969. 455p.
'Meticulous analysis of over 1300 items (*TLS*, no.3,564, 18 June
1970, p.669). *Class No:* 908(96)(01)

[5038]
HANSON, F.A. *and* O'REILLY, P., *eds.* Bibliographie de Rapa,
Polynésie Française. Paris, Musée de l'Homme, 1973. (*Publications
de la Société des Océanistes; no.32.*)
259 entries, many annotated. *Class No:* 908(96)(01)

[5039]
O'REILLY, P. *and* REITMAN, R. Bibliographie de la Tahiti et de la
Polynésie française. Paris, Musée de l'Homme, 1967. 1046p. index.
(*Publications de la Société des Océanistes; no.14.*)
10,501 annotated items organized under by subject *e.g.*
Bibliographies; Voyages; Geography; Ethnology; History.
Class No: 908(96)(01)

Encyclopaedias

[5040]
L'Encyclopédie de la Polynésie. Salvat, B, *and others, eds.* Papeete,
Christian Gleizal-Multipress, 9v., 1986-1988.
100 contributors. Covers 118 islands but concentrates largely on
French possessions. V.1-3 are concernned with the physical
environment, climate etc.; v.4-5 consider Polynesian civilization
before the arrival of European expeditions; v.6-7 deal with the
colonization of Polynesia; whilst v.8-9 focus on the period 1960-1987,
especially upon political affairs, new institutions such as L'Université
du Pacifique, and the establishment of an economy based on tourism.
4000 col. illus. 'Cette Encyclopédie ... réunit une documentation
considérable présentée de façon très agréable, avec notamment une
iconographie très abondante, très variée et de grande qualité' (*Cahiers
D'Outre-Mer*, no.170, Avril-Juin 1990, p.208).
Class No: 908(96)(031)

Fiji

Bibliographies

[5041]
GORMAN, G.E. *and* MILLS, J.J., *comps.* Fiji. Oxford, Clio Press,
1994. xxvii,207p.+1p. map, £35. (*World Bibliographical Series,
no.173.*) ISBN: 1851090789.
673 annotated entries in 28 sections: The country and its people -
Travel guides ... Archaeology and prehistory - History ... Land tenure
... General bibliographies. Chronology p.xxv-xxvii. Author, subject
and title indexes. *Class No:* 908(961.1)(01)

[5042]
N'YEURT, A. De R., *and others.* A Bibliography of Rotuma. Suva,
Pacific Information Centre and Marine Studies Programme, Univ. of
the South Pacific, 1996. xiii,131p. index. F$20. ISBN: 9820102928.
900+ entries comprising books, journals, newspaper articles,
microfilms, and audiovisual records, theses and dissertations arranged
by broad subject headings. 'This painstaking bibliography at last puts
Rotuma studies on to a sound academic basis, and should be acquired
by any reference librarian with Pacific Islands and Polynesian
specializations' (*Reference Reviews*, v.11,no.4, 1997, p.42).
Class No: 908(961.1)(01)

[5043]
SNOW, P.A. A Bibliography of Fiji, Tonga and Rotuma. Canberra,
Australian National Univ. Press, 1969. xliii,418p. maps.
Over 10,000 entries. Fiji (p.80-295) has 63 sections (1. Bibliography
- 2. Biography - 3. Research - 4. Origins and migrations ... 62.
Philately). Alphabetical index of names, p.357-418. List of journals
and bibliography precede. 'So comprehensive that it should be
classified as a national bibliography' (*Library Journal*, v.94,no.21, 1
December 1969, p.4420-1). *Class No:* 908(961.1)(01)

Tonga

Bibliographies

[5044]

DALY, M., *comp*. Tonga. Oxford and Santa Barbara, Calif., ABC-Clio, 1999. xxxvi,185p.+1p. map, indexes. £37. (*World Bibliographical Series, no.217*.) ISBN: 1851092935.

452 annotated entries deployed in 28 sections: Country and its people - Geography and environment - Tourism and travel guides - Travellers' accounts ... Prehistory and archaeology - History ... Encyclopedias and reference works - General bibliographies. Introduction (geography, history, political system, foreign relations, essence of Tonga etc.) p.xi-xxix. Chronology p.xxxi-xxxii. Author, title and subject indexes. *Class No: 908(961.2)(01)*

Samoa

Bibliographies

[5045]

HUGHES, H.G.A., *comp*. Samoa (American Samoa and Western Samoa, Samoans abroad). Oxford and Santa Barbara, Calif., Clio Press, 1997. lxxxix,342p.+2p. maps, indexes. £75. (*World Bibliographical Series, no.196*.) ISBN: 1851092536.

950 annotated entries in 42 sections: Samoa and the Samoans - Geography - Travellers' accounts and reminiscences - Tourism ... Prehistory and archeology - History ... Robert Louis Stevenson ... Bibliographies and catalogues - Audio-Video media. Introduction (land, climate, vegetation and fauna, social organization, language, history) p.xix-xxxv. Theses p.xxxvii-liv. Chronology p.lv-lxxi. Administrators 1900-97, p.lxxiii-lxxvi. Glossary p.lxxvii-lxxxii. Author, title and subject indexes. *Class No: 908(961.3)(01)*

Micronesia

Bibliographies

[5046]

POLLOCK, N.J., *comp*. Nauru bibliography. Univ. of Wellington, 1994. ii,33p. $NZ20.

Replaces Krauss, N.L.H. *Bibliography of Nauru, Western Pacific* (Honolulu, 1970, 14p. sd.).

c.500 unannotated A-Z by author entries with location in Australian and New Zealand libraries. 'This represents a real quantitative advance in Nauruan bibliography' (*Reference Reviews*, v.10,no.5, 1996, p.47). *Class No: 908(965)(01)*

[5047]

STORIE, M.C. *and* WUERCH, W.L., *comps*. Micronesia. Oxford and Santa Barbara, Calif., Clio Press, 1999. lxviii, 215p.+5p. maps, indexes. £42. (*World Bibliographical Series, no.220*.) ISBN: 1851092897.

739 annotated entries relating to Guam, Gilbert Islands, Phoenix Islands, Line Islands, Marianna Islands, Marshall Islands and Nauru, arranged in 23 sections: Islands and their people - Prehistory - The Second World War: The Pacific War ... Geography ... Tourism and travel guides ... Navigation and seafaring ... Bibliographies. Chronology p.xix-xxxv. Government leaders of Micronesia p.xxvii-xxxiii. Author, title and subject indexes. *Class No: 908(965)(01)*

Hawaii

[5048]

OLIVER, A.M. Hawaii fact and reference book recent and historical facts and events in the fiftieth state. Honolulu, Mutual Publishing, 1995. xiii,274p. index. $12.95. ISBN: 1566470617.

Arranged in 11 sub-divided sections: Facts about the State and the counties of Hawaii - People and health - Education - Government and public affairs - Environment - Culture - Sports - Business, labor and the economy - Transportation - Rankings - Chronology. *Class No: 908(969)*

Bibliographies

[5049]

MORRIS, N.J. *and* DEAN, L., *comps*. Hawai'i. Santa Barbara, Calif., and Oxford, Clio Press, 1992. xxxv,324p. +2p. map. indexes. £49. (*World Bibliographical Series, no. 146*.) ISBN: 1851091750.

812 annotated entries in 36 sections: The islands and the people - Geography ... Prehistory and archaeology - History - Voyaging - Maritime history - Specific islands ... Bibliographies. Chronology p. xxi-xxxv. Author, title and subject indexes. *Class No: 908(969)(01)*

Polar Regions

Bibliographies

[5050]

MILLS, W. *and* SPEAK, P. Keyguide to information sources on the Polar and Cold Regions. London, Mansell, 1998. xiv,330p. maps, bibliogs., index. £70. ISBN: 0720121760.

1781 entries arranged in 3 sections: 1. Survey of the Polar and Cold regions and information sources relating to them (p.1-95) including list of relevant libraries, archives and museums worldwide - 2. Bibliography (45 form and subject sections *e.g.* bibliographic databases, internet resources, archaeology, history, travel and expeditions, tourism, maps and atlases) - 3. Directory of selected organizations (*e.g.* national and international research organizations, publishers, and special suppliers of polar and cold regions books). Scholarly, authoritative and comprehensive study of major importance. *Class No: 908(98/99)(01)*

Reviews & Abstracts

[5051]

Polar and glaciological abstracts. Cambridge, Cambridge University Press, 1990-. Quarterly. £24.00 (Individuals. £32.00 (Institutions). ISSN: 09575073.

Abstracting service offering comprehensive coverage of the world's polar regions scanning over 900 serials plus relevant books, reports and theses. Each issue contains author, subject and geographic indexes cumulated annually. Archaeology, history and expeditions and exploration are 3 specialized areas included. *Class No: 908(98/99)(048)*

Arctic

Bibliographies

[5052]

KING, H.G.R. The Arctic. Santa Barbara, California and Oxford, Clio Press, 1989. xvi, 272p. + 3p. map, indexes. £39.50; $55.00. (*World Bibliographical Series, no. 99*.) ISBN: 185109072x.

935 annotated entries. 37 sections: The Arctic Region in General - Geography ... Prehistory and archaeology - History - Biographies of Arctic explorers ... Arctic peoples ... Expedition planning and survival ... Libraries, museums, archives and academic institutions - Bibliographies - Svalbard - Jan Mayen - Greenland - Arctic Canada - Alaska - Soviet Asia/Siberia - Scandinavian Arctic and Lapland - The Arctic Ocean. Author, subject and title indexes. *Class No: 908(98)(01)*

Greenland

[5053]

This is Greenland '99 the official directory, country, products and services. Danker, P., *ed*. Copenhagen, Government of Greenald in cooperation with the Royal Danish Ministry of Foreign Affairs, 1999-. Annual. 336p. col.illus., col.map, tables. ISBN: 8789685105.

1. A guide to Greenland (Official Greenland. Politics. Public administration. Church and religion. Economy. Trade And Industry. Establishing a business. Infrastructure. Technical Administration. Conditions of life. Culture. Geography/The Environment. History. Practical information) p.13-167. List of goods and services (by professional categories) p.169-210. List of firms and institutions (A-Z with contact details) p.213-265. Comprehensive index of goods and services p.271-332. Lavishly illustrated reference and guide book destined to be the most frequently updated and most reliable international source. *Class No: 908(988)*

Bibliographies

[5054]

HØYER, B., *ed*. Groenlandica. Catalogue of Groenlandica collection in the National Library of Greenland. Nuuk, Nunatta Atnagaateqarfia, 1986. 585p. indexes.

Annotated. Books in Greenlandic - Books on Greenland and the Arctic. Alphabetical and subject indexes. *Class No: 908(988)(01)*

[5055]

MILLER, K.E., *comp*. Greenland. Santa Barbara, Calif., and Oxford, Clio Press, 1991. xix,111p. +1p. map. index. £18.95. (*World Bibliographical Series, no. 125*.) ISBN: 1851091394.

375 annotated entries in 18 sections: Greenland and its people - Explorations - Geography and geology ... Prehistory and archaeology - History ... Foreign relations ... Libraries and museums ... Bibliographies. Author, title and subject index. *Class No: 908(988)(01)*

Antarctic

[5056]

TRIGGS, G.D., *ed*. **The Antarctic Treaty regime:** law, environment and resources. Cambridge Univ. Press, 1987. xxii,239p. diagrs., tables, map, bibliog. £30. (*Studies in Polar Research*.) ISBN: 0521327660.

24 papers from the Proceedings of a conference organized by the British Institute of International and Comparative Law, April 1985, examine the legal structure established by the Treaty and discuss the legal, political and environmental issues involved. Bibliography (by topic) p.234-5.

A similar work is *The Antarctic legal regime,* edited by C.C. Joyner and S.K. Chopra, Dordrecht, Martinus Nijhoff, 1985, xi,288p. map, index. This includes 11 papers by different hands in 2 sections: Law and politics and Resource regimes and environmental protection.
Class No: 908(99)

Bibliographies

[5057]

Australian Antarctic bibliography. Hobart, Institute of Antarctic and Southern Ocean Studies, Univ. of Tasmania, 1987. v, 463p. in spiral binding. ISBN: 0859013707.

8 sections: 1. General (expeditions, voyages, travel) - 2. Atmospheric physics - 3. Bases and logistics - 4. Biological sciences - 5. Terrestial sciences - 6. Oceanography - 7. Medical sciences - 8. Socio-economic sciences. No annotation. Relates to Australian Antarctic Territory and the Heard, Macquarie, and McDonald Islands.
Class No: 908(99)(01)

[5058]

MEADOWS, J., *and others, comps*. **The Antarctic.** Oxford, Clio Press, 1994. xxvi,383p.+2p. map index. £57.95. (*World Bibliographical Series, no. 171*.) ISBN: 1851091211.

1195 annotated entries arranged in 41 sub-divided sections: Antarctic region in general - Geography ... Southern Ocean - Development of Antarctic science - History - International relations and geopolitics ... Sub-Antarctic and other islands. Author, subject and title index. 'It really does unlock an enormous amount of information that might otherwise be hard to come by' (*Reference Reviews,* v.9,no.1, 1995, p.48). *Class No:* 908(99)(01)

91 Geography, Exploration, Travel

Geography & Travel

Bibliographies

[5059]

A **Bibliography of geographic thought.** Brown, C.L. *and* Wheeler, J.O., *comps*. Westport, Conn., Greenwood Press, 1989. x,521p. indexes. $55. (*Bibliographies and Indexes in Geography, no.1*.) ISBN: 0313268991. ISSN: 10448349.

A revised and expanded edition of Wheeler's *Bibliography on geographic thought* (1983).

6,196 citations (over 5,500 articles and 453 books listed separately) divided into 9 subsections: 1. Biography - 2. Geography - 3. Geography in other countries - 4. Techniques and models - 5. Philosophy - 6. The profession - 7. Subdisciplines - 8. Applied geography - 9. Educational. Author, subject and biographical indexes. 'Represents an impressive benchmark that documents a lengthy and proud record of geographical scholarship' (*Bulletin, Special Libraries Association Geographical and Map Division*, no.162, December 1990, p.43-4). *Class No:* 91.0(01)

[5060]

GREAT BRITAIN. National Maritime Museum. **Catalogue of the library.** London. H.M. Stationery Office, 1968-. illus., ports., facsims., maps.

1.*Voyages & travel.* 1968. xi,403p. 2. *Biography.* 2v., 1969. 501p.475p. ISBN 0112900046. 3. *Atlases & cartography.* 2v., 1971. vi,lx, 1166p. 0112900585. 4. *Piracy & privateering.* 1972. ix,175p. 0112901190. 5. *Naval history. pt.1: The Middle Ages to 1815.* 1977. 218p. 0118807609. V.1 has 1,240 numbered entries, usually with annotations or bibliographical notes. Sections (each preceded by a chronological table): Collective voyages - Circumnavigations (items 17-125, chronologically) Africa - America - East Indies - Europe and Mediterranean - Far East - Pacific - Polar: Arctic - Polar: Antarctic - General voyages. Detailed index; index of ships. Well produced. *Class No:* 91.0(01)

Encyclopaedias

[5061]

DOUGLAS, I., *and others, eds*. **Companion encyclopedia of geography** the environment and humankind. London, Routledge, 1996. xxviii,1021p. diagrs. ISBN: 0415074177.

47 contributors. 45 thematic chapters, examining both physical and human geography, divided into 6 parts: 1. A differentiated world - 2. A world transformed by the growth of a global economy - 3. The global scale of habitat modification - 4. A world of questions - 5. Changing worlds, changing geographies - 6. Geographical futures. 'An indispensable item for any library that wishes to strengthen its reference section and for the professional geographer who wants to keep abreast of developments' (*Choice*, v.34, no.6, February 1997, p.940). *Class No:* 91.0(031)

Exploration & Travel

[5062]

Guinness book of explorers and exploration. Gavet-Imbert, M., *ed.* Enfield, Mdx., Guinness Publishing, 1991. 285p. col. illus., col. maps, index. £19.95. ISBN: 0851129730.

12 contributors. Recounts travels, discoveries and explorations in 11 historical and continental sections: 1. Antiquity - 2. Medieval adventures - 3. Islamic travellers - 4/8. by continent - 9. The Poles - 10. Mountains and oceans, caves and volcanoes - 11. Space. *Class No:* 910

Bibliographies

[5063]

COX, E.G. A Reference guide to the literature of travel including voyages, geographical descriptions, adventures, shipwrecks and expeditions. Seattle, Univ. of Washington, 3v., 1935-49. Reprinted Westport, Connecticut, Greenwood Press, 1970. $125.00. ISBN: 0837125065, v.1; 0837121620, v.2.

1. *The Old World.* 1935. 2. *The New World.* 1938. 3. *Great Britain.*

....(contd.)
1949. Source material is covered up to 1800. Entries, usually annotated are arranged chronologically under sea or subject. V.3 includes chapters on maps and charts, general reference books, and bibliographies. Indexes of personal names in v.2 (covering v.1-2) and v.3. *Class No:* 910(01)

[5064]

SMITH, H.F. American travellers abroad a bibliography of accounts published before 1900. Lanham, MD., Scarecrow Press, 1999. ix,383p. bibliog., indexes. £57. ISBN: 0810835541.

c.1360 annotated entries A-Z by author within letter groups relating to books narrating the travels of American citizens outside the 48 continental United States. Bibliography p.353-56. Indexes of places and authors' occupations. *Class No:* 910(01)

Encyclopaedias

[5065]

DELPAR, H., *ed*. The Discoverers an encyclopedia of explorers and exploration. New York, McGraw-Hill, 1980. viii,471p. illus., ports., facsims, maps. £45.00. ISBN: 0070162646.

28 contributors (5 British). 250 signed articles, with brief bibliographies appended, on world exploration since the 15th century, 'Aerial exploration' ... 'Zagoskin'. 'Maritime exploration': p.225-38; 18 references; 6 cross-references. 'Literature and exploration': p.209-17; quotations; 13 references. 'Women in travel and exploration' has 5 ports. and 18 references. Includes entries under continents and countries. Emphasis on Western European discoverers. 'The volume is beautifully illustrated with photographs, engravings, maps and other reproductions' (*Current Geographical Publications*, v.43, no.5, May 1980, p.396). *Class No:* 910(031)

Handbooks & Manuals

[5066]

DAY, A.E. Discovery and exploration: a reference handbook. The Old World. London and New York, K.G. Saur - Clive Bingley, 1980. 295p. £22.50. ISBN: 0851572561, UK; 0896641791, US.

Covers the continents of Europe, Asia and Africa, 455 entries, A-Z, over half of them biographical (Livingstone: nearly 4p.: Marco Polo: 2p.). Also entries for associations, institutions (*e.g.* Hakluyt Society and its publications: 13p.), book and periodical titles. Regional index of discovery and exploration, including names of explorers, books, etc: index of titles. Aimed at sixth form and undergraduate students specialising. 'It will guide young students directly to the more available and useful English printed sources' (*British Book News*, September 1980, p.569). *Class No:* 910(035)

Maps & Atlases

[5067]

Atlas of Columbus and the great discoveries. Nebenzahl, K. Chicago, Rand McNally, 1990. 168p. illus (some col.), maps (some col.), bibliog. $75. col. maps, bibliog. ISBN: 052883407x.

50 late 15th century and early 16th century maps depicting contemporary geographical knowledge and speculation of the world's oceans and new lands. Each map is accompanied by a short documented essay. *Class No:* 910(084.3)

[5068]

NEWBY, E. The Mitchell Beazley world atlas of exploration. London, Mitchell Beazley, 1975. 288p. illus., facsims., ports., plans, maps.

Some full-page, 3-colour maps, but the maps are an adjunct to text and illus. 'South America: a land of scientists', p.180-9 (11 illus., 3 ports., 3 maps). Concludes with 'The last frontier' (outer space), p.266-7; and 'Men of the world' (listing over 600 explorers, subdivided by continents, 6 illus., 9 maps). Bibliography (by continents), p.274-5. Index, p.176-88. Over 600 illus. Page size:29x23cm. 'If it is not strictly speaking an "atlas", it is still a highly desirable book' (*Bulletin of the Society of University Cartographers*, v.13,no.1, 1979, p.63). *Class No:* 910(084.3)

[5069]

Philip's atlas of exploration. London, Philips, 1996. 248p. illus. (mostly col.), col.maps, index. £19.99. ISBN: 0540061913.

91 map/illustration/text features in 10 sections: 1. Early exploration - 2. Asia - 3. Africa - 4. Central and South America - 5. North America - 6. Pacific, Australia and New Zealand - 7. Arctic - 8. Antarctic - 9. Oceanography - 10. Exploration today. Biographies (200) p.224-34. Time chart of exploration (8 cols. across double page) p.235-41. Comprehensive guide attractively presented. *Class No:* 910(084.3)

[5070]

Thomas Cook world atlas of travel. Taylor, M., *ed.* London, Thomas Cook and Columbus Press, 1998. viii,216p. col.maps, col. tables, index. £24.99. ISBN: 1900341557.

Contents: general maps (1-46). Specialist maps. *i.e.* climate, time, health, tourism, sport, driving, IATA areas, flight times, heritage sites etc. (p.47-127). Relief maps (p.128-36). Transport maps (p.137-68). Appendices (geographical definitions, U.S. states, Canadian provinces and territories, Australian states and territories, French départements, world's major urban areas, highest and lowest, conversions. International glossary) p.169-72. 50 tables. *Class No:* 910(084.3)

[5071]

The Times atlas of world exploration. Fernández-Armesto, F., *ed.* London, Times Books, 1991. 286p. col. illus., col. maps, facsims, index. £35. ISBN: 0723003440.

18 contributors. 46 chapters arranged in 12 mainly continent and ocean sections. Chronology in continent time bands p.10-15. Glossary of technical terms p.243-4. Biographical glossary (*c.*400 explorers) p.245-72. Index of place-names (over 12,000 entries) p.273-86. Facsimiles of over 180 period maps and 130 specially commissioned topographical maps showing discovery and exploration routes. Excellent atlas covering over 3,000 years of exploration. Generally superior to *Royal Geographical Society history of world exploration* (*qv*) but with inexplicable omission of any sort of bibliographical apparatus apart from list of antique maps reproduced in the *Atlas* with their sources. *Class No:* 910(084.3)

Biographies

[5072]

BAKER, D.B., *ed.* **Explorers and discoverers of the world.** Detroit, Gale Research, 1993. xli,637p. illus., maps, bibliogs., index. ISBN: 0810354217.

Biographies of 320 world explorers in single A-Z sequence. Entries (1-4p. in length) examine historical significance and consequences of discoveries and explorations. Political, economic, and religious contexts assessed. Select bibliography for each entry. Chronology of exploration p.xvii-xxiii (by area). *Class No:* 910(092)

[5073]

Dictionary of British and Irish travellers in Italy 1701-1800. Ingamells, J., *comp.* New Haven, Yale Univ. Press for The Paul Mellon Centre For Studies in British Art, 1997. lii,1070p. ISBN: 0300071655.

Identifies 6,000 travellers. Data: biographical profile (education, appointments); itinerary and experiences in Italy; journals; and publications. *Class No:* 910(092)

[5074]

WALDMAN, C. *and* **WEXLER, A. Who was who in world exploration.** New York and Oxford, Facts On File, 1992. viii,712p. ports., maps, bibliog. $65. ISBN: 0816021724.

800 profiles of explorers and discoverers A-Z. Data: birth and death dates; nationality; occupation; capsule chronology expedition or voyage; biography; description of expedition. Appendix 1. Explorers by region of exploration (p.671-82) - 2. Maps (p.684-98). Bibliography (by region) p.699-712. *Class No:* 910(092)

[5075]

World explorers and discoverers. Bohlander, R.E., *ed.* New York, Macmillan, 1992. xi,532p. illus., maps, bibliog., index. $80. ISBN: 002897445x.

313 profiles of 'the most significant men and women in the history of world exploration ranging in length from 450 to 4000 words. Glossary p.467-76. Explorers (by nationality) p.477-81. Explorers (by area of exploration) p.483-88. Bibliography p.489-511. *Class No:* 910(092)

Pacific Ocean

[5076]

BADGER, G. The Explorers of the Pacific. Kenthurst, Kangaroo Press, 1988. 248p. illus. (some col.), maps, bibliog., index. ISBN: 0864172117.

Historical narrative in 21 chapters with 8 appendices. Notes p.230-5. Bibliography p.236-42. *Class No:* 910(265)

[5077]

MARTIN, M.S. 'The Other ocean: the discovery and exploration of the Pacific', *Choice*, v.30, no.8, April 1993, p.1277-86.

Bibliographic essay covering non-European and European voyages, navigation, the people, exploration and science, culture contact, and literary responses. Works cited p.1284-6. *Class No:* 910(265)

Biographies

[5078]

DUNMORE, J. Who's who in Pacific navigation. Honolulu, Univ. of Hawaii Press, 1991. xvi,312p. bibliog., indexes. $34. ISBN: 0824813502.

Life and achievements of 256 British, Spanish, French and Dutch voyagers and researchers. Bibliography p.273-300. 'This thoroughly researched and well-prepared work will be an excellent source of information for historians, subject specialists, and others who are interested in the Pacific areas' (*ARBA Guide to Biographical Resources 1986-1997.* 1998, p.91). *Class No:* 910(265)(092)

Tibet

[5079]

WALKER, D. The Pundits: British exploration of Tibet and Central Asia. Lexington, Univ. Press of Kentucky, 1990. viii,327p. maps, bibliog., index. $30. ISBN: 081311666x.

Narrative account of the explorations and surveys of Nepal, Sikkim, Bhutan and Tibet, 1866-1885, undertaken by the 'Pundits', the trained native Indian personnel emploped by the Great Trigonometrical Survey of India. 7 maps. 'A major contribution to the history of exploration beyond the Indian frontiers' (*Geographical Journal*, v.157, no.1, March 1991, p.79). Accounts of the more important surveys were first published in the Survey's *General Reports* and subsequently collected in v.8 of the *Records of the Survey of India* (Dehra Dun, 1915). *Class No:* 910(515)

Africa

[5080]

CASADA, J.A. An Annotated bibliography of exploration in Africa. Oxford, Hans Zell, 1990. 400p. indexes. £48.00; $85.00. ISBN: 0905450272.

Covers African exploration from the earliest period to modern times and includes major articles as well as books. The emphasis is on English language material but significant works in other languages find a place. A substantial introduction investigates the present state of reference sources on African exploration. *Class No:* 910(6)

America—North

[5081]

North American exploration. Allen, J.L., *ed.* Lincoln, Univ. of Nebraska Press, 3v., 1997.

V.1: *A New World disclosed.* xvii,538p. illus., maps, bibliog., index. ISBN 09803210159. Chapter notes p.453-510. Bibliography p.511-14. 14 maps.

V.2: *A Continent defined.* ix,472p. illus., maps, bibliog., index. 080321023x. Chapter notes p.397-436. Bibliography p.437-44. 16 maps.

V.3: *A Continent comprehended.* x,656p. illus., maps, bibliog., index. 0803210434. Chapter notes p.547-604. Bibliography p.605-18. 12 maps.

24 contributors. First-class, well-documented narrative history. 'The focus is, firstly, on the relationship between pre-existing and preconceived geographical lore and the evolution of the goals of exploration; secondly, upon the links between that lore, the new material obtained during explorations and the decisions explorers made; and finally, on the connections between these processes and the resulting geographical pictures of newly discovered lands'. *Geographical Journal*, v.164,no.2, July 1998, p.215-16). See also Barry Gough's 'Terra Cognita', *Pacific Historical Review*, v.63,no.3, August 1999, p.451-56 (a review essay). *Class No:* 910(71+73)

Maps & Atlases

[5082]

GOETZMANN, W. H. *and* **WILLIAMS, G. The Atlas of North American exploration** from the Norse voyages to the race to the Pole. New York, Prentice Hall, 1992. 224p. illus., col.maps, bibliog., index. $40. ISBN: 0132971283.

Double-page spreads (analysis of the exploration, historical and modern maps, illustrations, and extract from the explorer's own record) arranged in 5 historical and geographical sections: 1. American continent: on the edge of the world - 2. Opening of the continent - 3. Expanding frontiers - 4. Ocean to ocean - 5. Far North. Bibliography p.204-209. *Class No:* 910(71+73)(084.3)

Arctic

[5083]

HOLLAND, C., *ed*. **Furthest North:** a history of North Polar exploration. London, Robinson Publishing, 1994. 305p. maps. £16.99. ISBN: 1854872826.

History of all known attempts to reach the North Pole (1527-) through the explorer's own accounts and records. *Class No:* 910(98)

Antarctic

[5084]

FOGG, G.E. *and* SMITH, D. **The Exploration of Antarctica** the last unspoilt continent. London, Cassell, 1990. 224p. illus. (mostly col.), bibliog., index. £16.95; $24.95. ISBN: 0304318132.

Combines a history of Antarctic exploration with a description of the continent's geography, geology, and its continuing scientific and ecological significance. Bibliography p.218-21. Superbly illustrated. 7 maps. *Class No:* 910(99)

Women

[5085]

TINLING, M. **Women into the unknown** a sourcebook on women explorers and travellers. Westport, Conn., Greenwood Press, 1989. xxvi,356p. maps, bibliogs., index. $55. ISBN: 0313253285.

42 short biographical and travel essays each with a respectable bibliography. Appendix: Books of exploration and travel (written by women) in the English language p.314-42. Bibliography p.343-4. 9 maps. *Class No:* 910-0055.2

Planning & Field Work

[5086]

WINSER, S. *and* McWILLIAM, N. **Expedition planners' handbook and directory 1993-94.** London, Expedition Advisory Centre, Royal Geographical Society, 1992. 319p. illus., bibliogs. £12.95.

1. Expedition planning - 2. Organization - 3. Choosing expedition projects - 4. Scientific fieldwork - 5. Environmental logistics - 6. Expedition techniques - 7. Post-expedition responsibilities - 8. Appendices (Expedition Advisory Centre; Young Explorers Trust) - 9. Expedition Directories (reference sources; grant-giving organizations; equipment and services directory). *Class No:* 910.2

Expeditions, Voyages, Travel

[5087]

GREAT BRITAIN. Department of Health. **Health advice for travellers.** London, Department of Health, 1999. 52p. tables, bibliog. sd. 10cmx21cm. gratis. available from Post Offices.

3 colour-coded sections: 1. Health risks around the world ... and how to avoid them (eat and drink safely, be safe out of doors, major diseases, immunisation summary, worldwide country-by-country disease and immunisation checklist). - 2. Planning ahead (health insurance, emergency health checklist etc.) - 3. Getting treatment around the world). Sources of further information (publications, advice centres) p.52. *Class No:* 910.4

[5088]

HARRINGTON, R. **Trouble-free travel:** an insider's guide. 2nd ed. London, WEXAS Ltd., 1987. 96p. illus., pbk. £2.75. ISBN: 0905802039.

1st ed. 1982.

14 chapters *e.g.* 2. Maps: the good and the bad ... 4. Money matters - 5. Travel tip-offs - 6. Visas: a bureaucratic jungle. Practical tips not for total beginners. 'It assumes you are already a 'traveller' - someone who avoids conventional package holidays like the plague and probably has some experience of independent travel in the Third World' (*Introduction*). *Class No:* 910.4

[5089]

KEAY, W. **Expedition guide.** London, The Duke of Edinburgh's Award, 1987. 208p. col.illus., diagrs., bibliog. £7.95. ISBN: 0905425014.

17 chapters (1. Equipment ... 5. Planning ... 7. First aid) providing guidance for trainers, supervisors and assessors, and instructions in expedition skills. Also contains the syllabus, conditions, Course Directors' and Tutors' notes for the Basic Expedition Training Award of the Central Council of Physical Recreation. Bibliography p.205. *Class No:* 910.4

[5090]

TULLY, C. **The A-Z guide for lightweight travellers.** Mulbarton, Norfolk, Writer's Block, 1988. 160p. cartoons, pocket-size, pbk. £4.00. ISBN: 0951341006.

Chatty but informative notes. Airports p.118-9. Conversion charts (length, temperature, volume, weight) p.122-4. National Tourist Offices p.125-6. Also visa and vaccination regulations for 180 countries, time zones, short wave radio frequencies *etc*. *Class No:* 910.4

Bibliographies

[5091]

PROVOST, F. **Columbus, an annotated guide to the scholarship on his life and writings 1750-1988.** Detroit, Omnigraphics, 1991. xxxii,225p. indexes. $48.

Continues Columbus references in *European America: a chronological guide to works printed in Europe relating to the Americas 1493-1750* (6v., 1980-).

780 items in 7 sections: 1. Collections of sources, texts and studies - 2/3. Primary documents - 4. Life - 5. Columbiana - 6. Bibliographies - 7. Columbus scholarship. 'Gives easy access to nearly every aspect of Columbus and his enterprise in a usable format with every entry annotated' (*William and Mary Quarterly*, 3rd ser, v.49, no.2, April 1992, p.254).

Supplementing this Guide, Provost's *Columbus dictionary* (Omnigraphics, 1991. 142p. bibliog refs. $75. ISBN 1558881581) includes entries for persons, places, and events associated with Columbus' voyages. *Class No:* 910.4(01)

[5092]

SORENSON, J.L. *and* RAISH, M.L. **Pre-Columbian contact with the Americas across the oceans** an annotated bibliography. Provo, Utah, Research Pr., 2v., 1990. 1350p. index. $89. ISBN: 0934893144.

5613 items relating to the theme: 'to what degree were the pre-Columbia American peoples and their cultures dependent on or independent of those in the Old World'. *Class No:* 910.4(01)

[5093]

UNIVERSITY OF WASHINGTON. Fisheries-Oceanography Library. **Selected references to literature on marine expeditions, 1700-1960.** Boston, Massachusetts, G.K. Hall, 1972. iv,517p.

9,000 references, arranged A/Z by ship or name of expedition. No subject or author index; infrequent cross-references. Poor-quality print for some catalogue cards, but accuracy of citation is high (*RQ*, v.13,no.4, Summer 1974, p.354-5). *Class No:* 910.4(01)

Encyclopaedias

[5094]

FRITZE, R.H. **Travel legend and lore** an encyclopedia. Santa Barbara, Calif., and Oxford, ABC-Clio, 1998. xiv,443p. illus., bibliogs., index £44.95. ISBN: 087436759x.

284 A-Z cross-referenced entries, mostly furnished with a short reading list, focusing on journeys for the purposes of trade, diplomacy, missionary work, pleasure, and surveying, historical figures, animals, events, places, and institutions, dating from antiquity to the dawn of the 19th century. Bibliography p.403-23. *Class No:* 910.4(031)

Handbooks & Manuals

[5095]

LORIE, J. *and* SOHANPAUL, A. **The Traveller's handbook.** 8th ed London, WEXAS, 2000. 950p. maps, index, soft-cover. £14.99.

7th ed. 1998.

13 celebrity contributors. Pt.1: How to travel. 1. Where and when (information on each country including visa requirements) - 2. Finding out more (books, maps etc.) - 3. Specialist travel? - 4/6. Getting there - 7. Great journeys overland - 8. Paperwork and money - 9. A place to stay - 10. Health guide - 11. Equipping for a trip - 12 Communications - 13. When things go wrong - 14. Travel writing films and photography - 15. And finally (customs, ticket out, coming home).

Pt.2: Directory to each of above sections. 'A mass of information much of which is just impossible to locate easily elsewhere. An indispensable guide for the independent traveller' (*Reference Reviews* v.3,no.1, March 1989, p.40-41). *Class No:* 910.4(035)

Quotations

[5096]

YAPP, P., *ed*. **The Travellers' dictionary of quotations:** who said what, about where? London, Routledge and Kegan Paul, 1983. xvi 1022p.

More than 10,000 quotations, drawn principally from English language sources, arranged A-Z by existing countries, subdivided by regions and smaller units. 'A wealth of material on a very wide range of places' (*Geographical Journal*, v.150, no.1, March 1984, p.113). *Class No:* 910.4(082.2)

Histories

[5097]

BRIDGES, R.C. *and* HAIR, P.E.H., *eds*. **Compassing the vaste globe of the Earth** studies in the history of the Hakluyt Society 1846-1996 With a complete list of the Society's publications. London, Hakluyt Society, 1996. xi,336p. illus., maps, bibliog., indexes. £30. ISBN 0904180441. ISSN: 00729396.

8 contributors. Published to celebrate 150th anniversary of Hakluyt Society. Contents: 1. Prolegomena (HS. from past to future) - 2. 19th

.(contd.)
Century: Victorian figures (W.D. Cooley. R.H. Major. Henry Yule. Clements Markham) - 3. 20th century: Recollected figures (William Foster. R.A. Skelton. Edmond S. de Beer) - 4. Epilogue (HS. and World history). Appendices (Publications 1847-1995. List of officers 1846-1996). *Class No:* 910.4(091)

[5098]
RANCK, I.M. *and* BROWNSTONE, D.M. **To the ends of the earth** the great travel and trade routes of human history. New York and Oxford, Facts on File, 1984. xiv, 427p. illus. (some col.), maps, bibliogs., index. $35.00. ISBN: 0911818251.
31 chapters trace 45 of the principal routes following their history in contemporary accounts *e.g.* The Northeast Passage (p.282-92) has map, 4 illus. and 7 citations. In contrast The Northwest Passage has no entry and only 5 slight references. All chapters are equipped with bibliographies of varying length. *Class No:* 910.4(091)

[5099]
QUINN, D.B., *ed.* **The Hakluyt handbook.** London, the Hakluyt Society, 2v., 1974. xxvi,332p.; xiii,333-707p. facsims, maps. (*Hakluyt Society, 2nd series, nos.144,145.*) ISBN: 0521086949, v.1; 0521202116, v.2; 0521202124, set.
29 essays and bibliographical studies by various hands, arranged in 5 parts, provide 'a reference guide to the publications of Richard Hakluyt (1552-1616) and a critical evaluation of his work in the field of travel literature' (*Geographical Journal*, v.142,no.1, March 1976, p.163-4). Part 1: A Hakluyt perspective (7. Hakluyt's maps - 8. From Hakluyt to Purchase - 9. Tudor travel literature). Part 2: Hakluyt's use of the materials available to him. Part 3: From 1552 to 1616 (A Hakluyt chronology). Part 4: Contents and sources of the three major works. Part 5. Hakluyt's books and sources (27. The primary Hakluyt bibliography - 28. Secondary works on Hakluyt and his circle - 29. Works published by the Hakluyt Society 1846-1973). D.B. Quinn's 'Richard Hakluyt and his followers' in the Society's *Annual Report 1972* is an account of the *Handbook's* conception and birth. Hakluyt Society publications subsequent to the *Handbook* and volumes in preparation are recorded in the Society's *Publications in print and preparation 1999-2000* (1999). 16p. *Class No:* 910.4(091)

[5100]
The **Royal Geographical Society history of world exploration.** Keay, J., *ed.* London, Hamlyn, 1991. 320p. illus. (some col.), col. maps, bibliog., index. £20.
10 sections by different hands: 1. Early exploration - 2. Asia - 3. Africa - 4. North America - 5. Central and South America - 6. Pacific, Australia and New Zealand - 7. Arctic - 8. Antarctic - 9. Oceanography - 10. Exploration today. Each consists of historical narrative with boxed features on chief explorers, their key routes, and their equipment etc., and a discovery map. A running chronological frieze adorns every page. Bibliography p.314. *Class No:* 910.4(091)

Manuscripts & Incunabula

[5101]
GREAT BRITAIN. National Maritime Museum. **Guide to the manuscripts in the National Maritime Museum.** London, Mansell, 2v., 1977-80. facsims., maps, indexes.
1. *The Personal collections.* edited by R.J.B. Knight. 1977. xxiv,234p. £28.00,. ISBN 0720107148. 2. *Public records, business records and artificial collections.* 1980. 251p. £28.00. 0720115914. V.1 has 300 annotated entries, briefly outlining careers of individuals concerned, plus description of each description. Arranged A-Z under names of persons. Detailed general index; ship index. *Class No:* 910.4(093)

Tropics

[5102]
ÉBERT, J. **Travelling in tropical countries** a guide for Africa, the South Seas, Latin America, Asia and the West Indies. Edmonton, Hurtig Publishers, 1986. 250p. illus. Can $14.95. ISBN: 0888303033.
Translation of *Voyager en pays tropical* (Montreal, Les Éditions du Boréal Express, 1984).
14 chapters. 1. The tourist - 2. The young traveller - 3. Other kinds of travellers - 4. Passport - 5. Visas, immigration and customs - 6. Baggage - 7. Money, mail - 8. Rules of hygiene - 9. Air travel - 10. Automobile trips - 11. The World's great itineraries - 12. Other kinds of transportation - 13. Respect for other cultures - 14. Appendices. (12 of Canadian interest only). *Class No:* 910.4(213)

Treasure Trove

[5103]
HAYDOCK, T. **Treasure trove** where to find the great lost treasures of the world. London, Fourth Estate, 1986. 160p. illus., maps, tables, index. £9.95. ISBN: 0947795308.
15 sites 'where the exact location of the treasure has been recorded with a promising degree of precision'. *Class No:* 910.4:351.759.5

Maps & Atlases

[5104]
WILSON, D. **The World atlas of treasure.** London, Collins, 1981. 256p. illus. maps. ISBN: 0002168774.
Popular account of the world's buried and sunken treasure. Of limited reference value. *Class No:* 910.4:351.759.5(084.3)

Disasters

[5105]
DAVIS, L. **Encyclopedia of natural disasters.** London, Headline, 1993. xii,433p. illus., index. pbk. bibliog. £6.99. ISBN: 0747243433.
1. Avalanches and landslides - 2. Earthquakes - 3. Famines and droughts - 3. Floods ... 5. Plagues and epidemics - 6. Cyclones - 7. Hurricanes - 8. Icestorms and snowstorms - 9. Tornadoes - 10. Typhoons - 11. Storms - 12. Volcanic eruptions and natural explosions. Chapter chronologies. Bibliography p.411-6. Nearly 400 entries. *Class No:* 910.4:502.5

[5106]
NEWSON, L. **The Atlas of the world's worst natural disasters.** London, Dorling Kindersley, 1998. 139p. col. illus., col. maps, index. £17.99. ISBN: 0751306061.
Earthquakes, hurricanes, typhoons, volcanoes, cyclones, and floods, are included in this gazetteer of over 500 natural disasters. Detailed maps locate the main danger zones. *Class No:* 910.4:502.5

[5107]
SMITH, R. **Catastrophes and disasters.** Edinburgh, Chambers, 1992. x,246p. illus., tables, index. pbk. £6.99. ISBN: 0550170154.
Accounts of air disasters; avalanches, rockfalls, mudslides; earthquakes; environmental disasters; famine; fire; floods; industrial disasters; pandemics; road and rail; disasters at sea; space; sporting disasters; Tsunamis; volcanoes; and windstorms. Chronological list of events p.viii-x. *Class No:* 910.4:502.5

Shipwrecks

[5108]
CAHILL, R.A. **Disasters at sea** Titanic to Exxon Valdez. London, Century, 1990. xv,272p. illus., bibliog., index. £16.99. ISBN: 0712638148.
Narrative of maritime diasters by unsafe design, foundering, fire, explosion, collision, and stranding. Chapter notes p.249-59. Bibliography p.259-62. *Class No:* 910.4:656.6

[5109]
HOCKING, C. **Dictionary of disasters at sea** during the age of steam including sailing ships and ships of war lost in action 1824-1962. London, London Stamp Exchange, 1989. 779p. £35. ISBN: 0948130725.
First published in 2v. by Lloyd's Register of Shipping in 1969.
Shipping losses on the high seas and in inland waters arranged A-Z by name of ship. Data: owners, launch date, builders, displacement, engine power, maximum speed, and circumstances of loss. *Class No:* 910.4:656.6

[5110]
HOOKE, N. **Modern shipping disasters 1963-1987.** London, Lloyd's of London Press, 1989. ix,539p. £35. ISBN: 1850442118.
A-Z entries by name of ship on all merchant and naval vessels over 500 tons gross reported to have been totally lost or to have been declared constructive total losses due to all causes including war. Data: nationality, ship's name, shipping company, date of construction, shipbuilder, tonnage, and descriptive report and circumstances of loss. *Class No:* 910.4:656.6

[5111]
WATSON, M.H. **Disasters at sea** every ocean-going passenger ship catastrophe since 1900. 2nd ed. updated and expanded by Miller, W.H. Yeovil, Patrick Stephens, 1995. 216p. illus., tables, index, bibliog. £17.99. ISBN: 1852605057.
1st ed. 1987.
10 chronological chapters (by decades) arranged by date of disaster. Data: ship's name; owners; previous names; builders; particulars (tonnage and dimensions); machinery; passenger accommodation; date of disaster; and circumstances. Glossary p.211. Bibliography p.212-13. Index to vessels p.214-16. *Class No:* 910.4:656.6

Dictionaries

[5112]
RITCHIE, D. **Shipwrecks** an encyclopedia of the world's worst disasters at sea. New York, Facts On File, 1996. 320p. illus., bibliog., index. $40. ISBN: 0816031630.
Several hundred wrecks listed A-Z by name of ship, most belonging to the period from the 1800s to the 1940s but excluding wartime losses. Data: when, where, how ship went to the bottom. *Class No:* 910.4:656.6(038)

Maps & Atlases

[5113]

PICKFORD, N. The Atlas of ship wreck & treasure the history, location and treasures of ships lost at sea. London, Dorling Kindersley, 1994. 200p. col.illus., col. maps, bibliog., index. £20. ISBN: 1564585999.

Pt.1: Shipwrecks (40 most significant) in 14 chronological sections (Bronze Age to Byzantium ... 2nd World War). Pt.2: Gazetteer (*i.e.* 20 Maps p.124-59 and 1400+ shipwreck listing p.160-93). Data: type of ship, route, cargo, if an when salvaged, plotted on preceding maps. Glossary p.194. Bibliography p.195. *Class No:* 910.4:656.6(084.3)

Great Britain

[5114]

Shipwreck index of the British Isles. Larn, R. *and* Larn, B. London, Lloyd's Register of Shipping, 10v., 1995-.

Vol.1 Isles of Scilly, Cornwall, Devon, Dorset, unnumbered pagination after the preliminaries. illus., maps, bibliogs., index. £49. ISBN 09000528885. Introduction (p.vi-xii) has sections on the development of the ship; shipwrecks and their causes; Select Committee on Shipwrecks; Lloyd's Register of Shipping; and the Merchant Shipping Act. Main text records 7,100 losses in chronological within 6 geographical areas each with location map. Data: name of vessel; date lost; ship type; cargo; crew; passengers; total lost, port of registration; flag; owner; construction; propulsion; horse-power; boilers; tonnages; dimensions; armament; voyage from/ to; location; latitude and longitude; loss category; circumstances of loss; and bibliography.

Vol.2. Hampshire, Isle of Wight, Sussex, Kent (Mainland), Kent (The Downs) Goodwin Sands, Thames. 1995. £49. 0900528990. *Vol.3 The East coast of England.* In 7 sections: Essex, Suffolk, Norfolk, Lincolnshire, Yorkshire, Co. Durham, Northumberland. Primary Research Locations, p.xxiv-xxxi. *Index to Volumes 1-3.* 1997. This is a full ship name index, detailing its owner, construction, area code and date of loss. *Class No:* 910.4:656.6(410)

Expeditions, Voyages, Travel

Women

[5115]

MOSS, M. *and* **MOSS, G. Handbook for women travellers.** 2nd ed. London, Piatkus, 1995. xvi.288p. illus., bibliog., index. £8.99. ISBN: 0749914394.

1st ed. 1987.

1. Thinking ahead - 2. What to carry - 3. What to wear - 4. Getting ready to go - 5. On the move - 6. Staying healthy - 7. Women only - 8. Travelling Green - 9. Disorientation - 10. Making contact - 11. Personal safety - 12. Coming back. Appendix A. The traveller's code - Recommended reading p.273-75. *Class No:* 910.4-0055.2

Geography

[5116]

National Geographic desk reference a geographical reference with hundreds of photographs, maps, charts, and graphs. Washington, National Geographic, 1999. 704p. col.illus., maps. $40. £25. ISBN: 0792270827.

Single-source reference to the places, people, and dynamics that shape our world. 4 sections: 1. What is geography - 2. Physical geography (planet Earth, climate and weather) - 3. Human geography (population, migration, cultural, economic, urban and political geography) - 4. Places (including A-Z listing of the world's nations). World maps p.676-85. Glossary p.686-691. 'Should become a classic on many reference shelves ... there is no other reference work exactly like this' (*Library Journal*, v.125, no.4, 1 March 2000 p.70). *Class No:* 911

Bibliographies

[5117]

AMERICAN GEOGRAPHICAL SOCIETY. Research catalogue. Boston, Mass., G.K. Hall, 15v. and map suppt., 1962. 1043p.

V.1 & 2: General - 3. Regional North America - 4-5. United States - 6-7. Mexico, Central America, Bermuda, West Indies, South America - 8-10. Europe - 11. Africa - 12-13. Asia - 14. Australasia - 15. Polar regions, Oceania, Tropics. Map supplement is merely a map key to the classification used.

First Supplement: Regional catalogue 2v., 1972. 1414p. $260.00 (Export $315.00). ISBN 0816109990. *Topical catalogue,* 2v. 1974. 1483p. is available on microfilm by request. $265.00 ($320.00). *Second Supplement* 2v., 1978. 1300p. $260.00 ($315.00). ISBN 0816100810.

More than 200,000 photolithographed catalogue cards. Particularly

....(contd.)

strong in periodical-article entries. Includes maps. The Library is the largest of its kind in the Western hemisphere. Updated in *Current geographical publications: additions to the Research catalogue of the American Geographical Society (qv).* *Class No:* 911(01)

[5118]

HARRIS, C.D. Bibliography of Geography. Chicago, Department of Geography, Univ. of Chicago, 1976-. ISBN: 0890650861.

Pt.1: *Introduction to general aids.* 1976. ix, 276p.

585 main entries, some (*e.g.* the 6 major comprehensive current bibliographies of geography, p.25-26) with extensive analysis of contents and all annotated. 16 sections: 1. Bibliographies of bibliographies - 2. Comprehensive current bibliographies - 3. Comprehensive retrospective bibliographies - 4. Specialized bibliographies - 5. Books - 6. Serials - 7. Government documents - 8. Dissertations - 9. Photographs - 10. Maps and atlases - 11. Gazetteers - 12. Place-name dictionaries - 13. Dictionaries - 14. Encyclopedias - 15. Statistics - 16. Methodology. Appendices: 1. Gazetteers of the US Board on Geographic Names; 2. A small geographical reference collection (items 530-85). Detailed index of authors and titles Prepared primarily for use by geographers.

Pt.2: *Regional v.1 The United States of America.* 1984. viii, 178p index. $12.00. 0890651124.

Almost 1000 briefly annotated entries in 5 sections: Preliminary (worldwide bibliographies and guides, maps and atlases etc.) - 1 General aids - 2. Physical geography, related earth services, the environment, and resources - 3. Human geography and related social sciences - 4. Regions of the United States. Limited to separately published bibliographies, commercial, university presses, government sources or associations with the emphasis on works printed in the previous 15 years.

Pt.2: *Regional* will eventually comprise 5 sequences, the others to be USSR; The Americas excluding United States; Europe excluding Soviet Union; and Africa, Asia, Australia and the Pacific.

A worthy successor to J.K. Wright and E.T. Platt's *Aids to geographical research* (1947). *Class No:* 911(01)

[5119]

LOCK, C.B.M. Geography and cartography: a reference handbook. London, Clive Bingley, 1976. 762p.

An integration of *Geography: a reference handbook* (1968; 2nd ed 1972.529p.) and *Modern maps and atlases* (1969).

1,400 entries, A-Z (titles of works, forms of literature, biographies, topics), with a strong bibliographical and cartobibliographical slant Extended entries on Cartography (p.159-95); Audio visual aids; Bibliographies, national; Classification; Education in geography and cartography; Globes; Map librarianship (p.427-51); Maps (historical); Abstracts. Extensive index, p.635-762. The work does not fully integrate *Modern maps and atlases*, which should be retained for its coverage of national, regional and thematic maps and atlases (*RQ*, v.16,no.3, Spring 1977, p.258-9). A-Z order of entry has value for quick reference, but it is apt to scatter related material and choice of entry-words can be capricious (*e.g.* 'Man and wildlife'). Sample maps would have been an asset. A bulky but highly rewarding volume; 'for all geographical libraries' (*Library Review,* v.26,1977/8,p.144). *Class No:* 911(01)

Encyclopaedias

[5120]

BIGER, E., *ed.* **The Encyclopedia of international boundaries.** New York, Facts On File, 1995. 543p. illus., maps, bibliog. $125. ISBN 0816032335.

International land boundaries for all continental states 'formed on the basis of international agreements'. For each state: background summary and pairing sections with each neighbouring state Geographical setting; Historical background; Present situation. *Class No:* 911(031)

[5121]

DUNBAR, G.S., *ed.* **Modern geography: an encyclopedic survey.** New York, Garland; London, St. James Press, 1991. xx,219p. index. $45 £40. ISBN: 0824053435, US; 1558621229, UK.

95 contributors. 'An overview of developments in the field of geography from about 1890 to the present, with emphasis on personalities, institutions, major concepts, subfields, and the evolution of the discipline in various countries' (*Introduction*). Entries are A-Z with some cross-referencing, many have bibliographies (maximum of 6 items). 300 biographies (birth and death dates, highest academic qualification, institutional affiliation, major publications). 'Highest recommendation for all academic libraries' (*Choice,* v.28,no.8, April 1991, p.1292). *Class No:* 911(031)

[5122]

The Encyclopedia of world geography. Bateman, G. *and* Egan, V., *eds*. Oxford, Roundhouse Reference Books, 1993. 512p. col.illus., col.maps, tables, bibliog., index. £29.95. ISBN: 1857100158.

Detailed country profiles, grouped in regions, of 188 nations of the world, of varying length, and in 3 sections: geography, society, and economy. Fact panels give current population, economic statistics, physical characteristics, and nature of government. Bibliography p.502. Over 200 maps and 500 full colour illustrations. Analytical index. *Class No:* 911(031)

[5123]

World geographical encyclopedia. Bonapace, V. *and* Laureti, L., *eds*. New York, McGraw-Hill, 5v., 1994. col.illus., col.maps, col.tables, bibliog., index. ISBN: 0079114962.

Originally published *Enciclopedia geografica universale* (Milan, Federico Motta Editore, 1994).

1. *Africa.* 350p. 2. *The Americas.* 352p. 3. *Asia.* 352p. 4. *Europe.* 350p. 5. *Oceania; Index.* 357p. Each vol. includes a continental overview (physical geography, geology, climate, economy, history, culture); summary table of political and statistical data for each country; detailed regional analyses; geographical summaries of individual countries; historical and cultural itineries. V.5: includes World statistics (p.241-98); Lexicon (p.299-304); Great routes of discovery (p.305-315). Bibliography (p.317-24) contains many Italian-language titles. Index (p.325-57). 'This photographic panorama of the world deserves a place in any academic library' (*Choice*, v.35,no.5, January 1996, p.771). Selected as one of *Choice's* Outstanding Academic Books of 1996. *Class No:* 911(031)

Dictionaries

[5124]

MAYHEW, S. A Dictionary of geography. 2nd ed. Oxford, Oxford Univ. Press, 1997. 460p. pbk. £6.99. ISBN: 0192800345.

First published as *The Concise Oxford dictionary of geography* (1992).

Definitions of over 6,000 terms used in all aspects of human and physical geography including cartography, surveying, ecology, population, agriculture, and transport. *Class No:* 911(038)

[5125]

Philip's geography dictionary. 2nd ed. London, George Philip, 2000. 240p. illus., maps, tables. £6.99. ISBN: 0540078247.

1st ed. 1995.

1500+ A-Z cross-referenced entries defining the major terms used in physical, human and environmental geography. Areas covered include the atmosphere, weather and climate, coastal formation, geomorphology, settlement, and economic development. *Class No:* 911(038)

[5126]

SKINNER, M., *and others, eds*. Dictionary of Geography. Chicago & London, Fitzroy Dearborn, 1999. 311p. illus. $40. ISBN: 1579581544.

Cross-referenced definitions for words in physical, economic, and historical geography. 'Each entry is defined with a complete sentence, and the concept is then elaborated in one or more sentences, many accompanied by examples and illustrations ... a valuable resource for readers of elementary to advanced textbooks and journal articles'. (*Choice*, v.37, no.6, February 2000, p.1084). *Class No:* 911(038)

Reviews & Abstracts

[5127]

Geo abstracts. Norwich, Elsevier/Geo Abstracts, 1972-.

Preceded by *Geomorphological abstracts* (1960-65) and *Geographical abstracts* (1966-71).

1972-1988 in 7 separate sections: A. Landforms and the Quaternary - B. Biogeography and climatology - C. Economic geography - D. Social and historical geography - E. Sedimentology - F. Regional and community planning - G. Remote sensing and cartography. Annual index in 2v. Index to A.B.E. and F. and C.D. and F.

Physical geography See *Walford's Guide to Reference Material Vol.1* (7th ed., 1996) items 1675 and 1891.

Human geography (1989-. £165 UK; £180 or $333.00 overseas. ISSN 09539611). 6pa. 15 sections: Methodology and theory; Techniques; Environment; Environmental resources; Historical; Population; People and regions; Rural studies; Urban studies; Regional and community planning; Trade; Agriculture; Industry; Transport and communications; Recreational geography (inc. Tourism). Regional index in each issue. Annual thematic and geographical index and list of journals scanned.

GEOBASE (DIALOG file 292) is the online database of *Geo abstracts.* Over 58% of its records cover physical and human geography 1980-. E.H. Ferrell's 'GEOBASE: the online bibliographical database of Geo Abstracts', *SLA G&M Bulletin,* no.153, Sep. 1988, p.11-13 discusses its search capabilities, finding

....(contd.)

strategies *etc.* Also available on SilverPlatter CD-ROM, updated quarterly with coverage options 1980-Present; 1980-1989; 1990-Present. *Class No:* 911(048)

Periodicals

Bibliographies

[5128]

National Geographic index 1888-1988. Washington, National Geographic Society, 1989. 1216p. col. illus., col. maps. $24.95. ISBN: 0870447645.

Supersedes 3 previous indexes.

Indexes by subject, title, author, and photographer some 7000 articles published in 1148 issues of *National Geographic Magazine* (subsequently *National Geographic*) . *Class No:* 911(051)(01)

Yearbooks & Directories

[5129]

EHLERS, E., *ed. In cooperation with the International Geographical Union.* Orbis geographicus 1992-1993/World directory of geography ... 7th ed. Wiesbaden, Franz Steiner Verlag, 1992. xviii,546p. maps, index. DM108.00. ISBN: 3515043268.

First issued in 1952 on the occasion of the International Geographical Congress, Washington.

Departments of geography - Geographical societies and associations - Geographical institutions and their members A-Z by country. 'Highly useful international directory' (C.D. Harris. *Annotated world list of selected current geographical serials.* 4th ed., 1980, p.55). *Class No:* 911(058)

Tables & Data Books

[5130]

Philip's geographical digest 1998-1999 Rayner, C., *and others, eds*. London, Heinemann. 1998. 128p. maps, tables. £18.50 ISBN: 0435350226.

World statistical coverage A-Z by country: Summaries (area and population; production; manufactures; trade) - Population - Agriculture - Energy - World trade - Gross National Product - Money exchange rates - Production statistics - 2. Key world developments - 3. World tourist statistics. An authoritative reference work giving facts and figures on geographical topics. *Class No:* 911(083)

Histories

[5131]

KIMBLE, G.H.T. Geography in the Middle Ages. London, Methuen, 1938. xi,272p. illus., bibliog.

A survey in 10 chapters, with 20 illustrations. Numerous footnote references. The select bibliography (p.245-57) contains valuable lists of texts and of secondary materials, including periodical articles. *Class No:* 911(091)

[5132]

THOMSON, J.O. History of ancient geography. Cambridge, Cambridge Univ. Press, 1948. xi,427p. illus., maps.

12 chapters, ending with the 5th century A.D. A scholarly survey of the beliefs and theories about the cosmos, heavens and earth, by the one-time Professor of Latin in the University of Birmingham. Profuse footnote references, but with citations drastically curtailed. Notes on books, etc., p.392-4, 66 illus. in the text and maps. Detailed index. Very readable: 'the definitive work on the legacy of classicial geographers' (Parry, J.H. *The age of reconnaissance* (1963), p.347). *Class No:* 911(091)

Bibliographies

[5133]

DUNBAR, G.S. The History of modern geography: an annotated bibliography of selected works. New York, Garland, 1985. xvi,386p. index. $53.50. (*Bibliographies of the history of science and technology, no.9.*) ISBN: 0824090667.

1717 entries assembled in 3 Pts. (22 chapters): General and topical; Geography in various countries; Biographical works. Author and subject indexes. 'A guide to the literature in the history of geography from the mid-eighteenth century' (*Introduction*). *Class No:* 911(091)(01)

20th Century

[5134]

JOHNSTON, R.A. *and* CLAVAL, P. Geography since the Second World War: an international survey. London, Croom Helm; Totowa, New Jersey, Barnes & Noble, 1984. 290p. £30.00. ISBN: 0709914113, UK; 0389204811, US.

1. Introduction: the international study of the history of geography - followed by individual studies on France, Italy, South-east Europe, Soviet Union, United Kingdom, Poland, the German-speaking countries, North America, the Netherlands, Japan, the Iberian Peninsula and Latin America. Extensive chapter references.
Class No: 911(091)"19"

Biographies

[5135]

LARKIN, R.P. *and* PETERS, G.L. Biographical dictionary of geography. Westport, Conn., Greenwood Press, 1993. xii,361p. bibliogs., index. ISBN: 0313276626.

Career profiles and biographical sketches, chronologies, and selected bibliographies of 77 geographers and cartographers of all periods.
Class No: 911(092)

[5136]

MARTIN, G.J., *ed and* ARMSTRONG, P.H., *ed..* Geographers: bibliographical studies. London and New York, Mansell, 1976-. v.1-. Annual. ISSN: 03086992.

Studies of geographers, cartographers, mariners, surveyors, etc. 'who have made major contributions to the development of geographical thought and of geography as a scientific subject and academic discipline'. Includes names whose significance has hitherto been neglected. Thus v.18. (1998. ix,147p. 0720123399) includes T.F. Armstrong, C.F. Brooks, S.P. Chatterjee, F.E. Clements, R. Dion, F. Magellan, K.J. Mason, J.L. Stokes, D. Thompson, and C.W. Thornthwaite.

Each study describes the education, life and work of its subject, scientific ideas and geographical thought, and the influence and spread of those ideas. In addition, for each individual, there is a bibliography, list of sources, summary chronology of his/her life, and a portrait. An index completes each volume. Almost 250 individuals have been profiled since the annual studies started in 1976. *Class No:* 911(092)

Developing Countries

[5137]

DICKENSON, J., *and others*. A Geography of the Third World. 2nd ed. London, Routledge, 1996. xiii,344p. illus., maps, tables, bibliogs., index. ISBN: 0415106729.

Comprehensive standard text which outlines major Third World themes and issues in 11 well-documented chapters (*e.g.* Historical perspective ... 9. National economic management - 10. External relationships. Glossary p.312-14. Further reading (by chapter) p.326-30. References p.331-33. *Class No:* 911(4/9-77)

Europe

[5138]

HOFFMAN, G.W., *ed.* Europe in the 1990s a geographic analysis. 6th ed. New York, Wiley, 1989. xxiv,759 +28 index pages. illus., tables, maps, bibliogs. ISBN: 047162280x.

1st ed. 1953; 5th ed. 1983. Formerly titled *A Geography of Europe: Problems and prospects.*

7 contributors. A geographical analysis of Europe's major regions in 12 chapters: 1. Historical geography - 2. Physical environment - 3. Social and economic change - 4. Regional and environmental problems, policies, and institutions - 5. The British Isles - 6/10. Western, Northern, Central, Southern, and Eastern Europe - 11. Soviet Union - 12. Europe in the 1990s. Glossary p.752-4. Chapter bibliographies. 'This edition takes particular note of the dramatic changes that have taken place since the mid-1980s, and it focusses on expected changes in the 1990s. (*Preface*). *Class No:* 911(4)

Great Britain

[5139]

CHAMPION, A.G. *and* TOWNSEND, A.R. Contemporary Britain: a geographical passport. London, Edward Arnold, 1990. x,310p. bibliog., index. £12.95. ISBN: 0713165804.

12 documented chapters arranged in 4 parts: 1. Faces of change - 2. Geographical impact - 3. Local outcomes and government responses - 4. The next decade. Bibliography p.277-300. *Class No:* 911(410)

Histories

[5140]

FREEMAN, T.W. A History of modern British geography. London, Longman, 1980. ix,258p. illus., maps, bibliolg., index. ISBN 0582300304.

10 chronological chapters trace the development of academi geography, discuss seminal books, individuals and groups, and rela the growth of the discipline to intellectual, social and economi circumstances. Geographical biographies (over 60 leading Britis geographers) p.205-239. Bibliography p.240-250. Publicatio coincided with the 150th anniversary of the Royal Geographica Society. *Class No:* 911(410)(091)

[5141]

STEEL, R.W., *ed.* British geography 1918-1945. Cambridge Cambridge Univ. Press. 1987. xi,189p. index. £27.50. ISBN 052124790x.

12 chapters, each by a different hand, trace the foundations o modern British geography *e.g.* Darby, H.C. 'On the writing o Historical Geography 1918-1945'. *Class No:* 911(410)(091)

Ireland

[5142]

GRAHAM, B.J. *and* PROUDFOOT, L.J. Historical geography o Ireland. London, Academic Press, 1993. 454p. £24.95. ISBN 0122948815.

11 Contributors. Period 500-early 1920s covered in 9 themati chapters (Irish emigration to Britain, US and Australia, urbanizatio industrialization). 'Has some revealing insights on the separat development of historical geography in Ireland and in Britain (*Geographical Journal*, v.159. no.3. November 1993, p.346-7). *Class No:* 911(415)

London

Bibliographies

[5143]

DOPHIN, P., *and others*. The London Region an annotate geographical bibliography. London, Mansell, 1981. xvi,379p. maps indexes. ISBN: 0720115981.

1909 annotated entries in 9 sections: 1. General bibliographies statistical sources and atlas - 2. General works - 3. Physica environment - 4. Historical patterns of growth and development - 5 Economic structure and patterns - 6. Transport - 7. Social patterns an processes - 8. Planning the metropolis and beyond - 9. Environmenta problems: conservation, pollution and control. Appendix: Libraries i London containing collections on the London region (p.322-5). Nam and subject indexes. 'This work may possibly be one of the mor important reference tools on London' (*Choice*, v.20 no.2 Octobe 1982, p.242). *Class No:* 911(421)(01)

Federal Republic of Germany

[5144]

Geographie Deutschlands Bundesrepublik Deutschland. Staat-Natu Wirtschaft. Tietze, W., *and others, eds.* Berlin & Stuttgart, Gebrüde Borntraeger, 1990. xii,687p. illus., maps, tables, bibliog., index.

11 contributors. A. Politisch-geographische Grundlagen - B Landesnatur - C. Grundlagen und strukturräumliche Entwicklungen de Wirtschaft in der Bundesrepublik Deutschland - D. Kartographisch Quellenlage - E. Die Verwendung vond Zahlen der amtlichen Statisti in der geographischen Landeskunde. A monumental work o scholarship. Bibliographies are appended to each section.
Class No: 911(430.1)

France

[5145]

Atlas et géographie de la France moderne. Papy, L., *ed.* Paris Flammarion, 16v., 1976-83.

Brétagne by A. Meynier. 1976. *La Region Lyonnaise* by R. Lebeau 1976. *Alsace et Lorraine* by E. Juillard. 1977. *Normandie* by A Fremont. 1977. *Paris* by J. Beaujeu-Garnier 2v. 1977. *Haut Bourgogne et Franche-Compté* by P. Claval. 1978. *Midi Touloussai* by F. Taillefer. 1978. *Pays de la Loire* by P. Fenelon. 1978 *Provence, Côte d'Azur et Corse* by R. Livet. 1978. *Alpes Française* by Paul G. Veyret. 1979. *Languedoc et Roussillon* by R. Ferras an others. 1979. *Nord et Picardie* by P. Flatres. 1980. *Champagne Pay de Meuse et Basse Bourgogne* by R. Brunet. 1981. *Massif Central b* A. Fel and G. Bouet. 1981. 348p. illus., maps. In 3 sections: L Massif Central, L'Auvergne, Le Limousin. 32p. maps between p.30 and 306. Statistical tables p.306-317. Place name index p.320-324 Bibliography p.325-338. *Midi atlantique* by L. Papy. 1982. Thes attractive volumes are intended for a wide readership; and present 'un image vivante de la France au début du dernier quart du xxième siècle (*Preface*). *Class No:* 911(44)

[5146]

INCHEMEL, P. **France** a geographical, social and economic survey. Elkins, D. *and* Elkins, T.H., *translators*. Cambridge, Cambridge Univ. Press; Paris, Editions De La Maison Des Sciences De l'Homme, 1986. xxvi,660p. illus., maps, tables, bibliog., index. £40.00. ISBN: 0521249872, UK; 2735101754, Fr.

Originally as *La France* (Paris, Armand Colin, 1980).

39 chapters deployed in 8 main parts: 12. The natural environment - 2. People - 3. Actors and policies in the spatial structures of France - 4. Resources, economic activity and economic enterprises - 5. The infrastructure of spatial interaction - 6. Landscape and environment in rural France - 7. The urban environment - 8. Conclusion. Bibliography p.605-49. Analytical index. *Class No:* 911(44)

Belgium

[5147]

éographie de la Belgique. Denis, J., *ed*. Bruxelles, Crédit Communal, 1992. 624p. illus. (some col), maps, diagrs. (some col.), bibliogs.

14 sections by a team of 33 contributors: La structure géologique - Le Climat - Les Formes du relief - L'Hydrologie - Les Sols - Les Ecotypes - La Population - L'Agriculture - L'Industrie - Le Secteur Tertiaire - Les Villes - Les Campagnes - L'Espace économique et l'aménagement du territoire - Une vocation internationale - L'Atlas de Belgique. All sections end with long lists of references.

Class No: 911(493)

Hawaii

[5148]

ORGAN, J.R. **Hawaii** a geography. Boulder, Colorado, Westview Press, 1983. xxiv,293p. illus., maps, bibliogs., index. (*Geographies of the United States*.) ISBN: 0891589422.

6 contributors. 24 well-documented chapters lined up in 5 parts: 1. Introduction - 2. Physical environments - 3. Human activities and economic geography (including Tourism) - 4. The Islands (Oahu, Hawaii, Maui, Kauai and Niihau, Mokolai and Lanai, The problem or Kahoolawe) - 5. Conclusions. Hawaiian place-names p.267-74.

Class No: 911(969)

Institutions & Associations

[5149]

RYAN, C.D.B. **The National Geographic Society** 100 years of adventure and discovery. Washington, National Geographic Society; Oxford, Phaidon, 1987. 484p. illus. (mostly col.), bibliog., index. £35. ISBN: 0714824852, UK.

Lavishly illustrated history of the Society: 10 chronological chapters interspersed with 10 thematic chapters *e.g.* polar exploration, archaeology, natural disasters, space exploration. Bibliography p.476. See also G.M. Grosvenor's 'A hundred years of the National Geographic Society', *Geographical Journal*, v.154, no.1, March 1988, p.87-92. *Class No:* 911:061:061.2

Conferences

[5150]

ISH, G., *ed*. **Bibliography of international geography congresses 1871-1976**. Boston, G.K. Hall, 1979. viii,540p.

6969 papers presented at 23 congresses from Antwerp 1871 to Moscow 1976 listed in chronological order with author and subject indexes. 'Of permanent value to students of the history of geography' (*Geographical Journal*, v.147,no.2, July 1981, p.251). *Class No:* 911:061:061.3

Historical Geography

Encyclopaedias

[5151]

ENN, J.R. **Encyclopedia of geographical features in world history** Europe and the Americas. Santa Barbara, Calif., and Oxford, ABC-Clio, 1998. 344p. illus., maps, bibliog., index. £29.95. $55. ISBN: 0874367603.

Explores the historical and cultural significance of mountains, plateaus, basins, land gateways, rivers, straits, and seas of Europe and the Americas, including c.150 alphabetically arranged entries, each with geological, geographic, and historical information and cross-references. A-to-Z entries for North America, Mexico, Central America, the Caribbean, South America, Europe, and Russia as far as the Ural Mountains. *Class No:* 911.0(031)

Europe

[5152]

POUNDS, N.J.G. **An Historical geography of Europe**. Cambridge University Press, 1990. xiii,484p. maps, diagrs., tables, bibliogs., index. £30. $17.95. ISBN: 0521322170.

12 alternating chapters on the changing pattern of human history during the last 2,500 years of Europe's history. One set of 7 captures Europe at particular celebrated points, the other 5 chapters trace the changes in the intervening periods. Chapter bibliographies. Based on 3v. work of the same title (1973-85). 'A superb summary of Europe's historical geography in one succinct volume' (*Choice*, v.28,no.7, March 1991, p.1205). *Class No:* 911.0(4)

Europe—Eastern

[5153]

TURNOCK, D. **Eastern Europe** an historical geography 1815-1945. London and New York, Routledge, 1989. ix,357p. maps, tables, bibliogs., index. £35.00. ISBN: 0415012694.

8 broad thematic chapters arranged in 2 pts. Pt.1. The century of peace 1815-1914: 1. Political geography - 2. Economic development: Germany and the Hapsburg lands - 4. The Russian and Ottoman Empires - 5. Settlement geography. Pt.2. The Era of World War 1914-1945. 6. Political geography - 7. Economic geography - 8. Transport power and settlement. Extensive chapter bibliographies plus (general) Bibliography p.330-9. *Class No:* 911.0(401)

Great Britain

[5154]

SHAW, G. **British directories** as sources in historical geography. London, Geo Books, 1982. 60p. illus., tables. sd. £5.00. (*Historical Geography Research Series*.) ISBN: 0860941094. ISSN: 0143683x.

An introductory survey in 6 chapters: 1. Introduction - 2. Evolution and development - 3. Contents - 4. Spatial and temporal coverage - 5. Reliability - 6. Use of directory material in urban historical geography. Notes p.54-60. *Class No:* 911.0(410)

Scotland

Bibliographies

[5155]

WHYTE, J.D. *and* WHYTE, K.H. **Sources for Scottish historical geography** an introductory guide. Norwich, Geo Abstracts, 1981. ii,46p. bibliog., sd. £5.00. (*History of Research Series no.6.*) ISBN: 0860940667. ISSN: 0143683x.

1. Introduction (location of source material) - 2. General research aids - 3. Sources (18 categories *e.g.* 12 maps ... 16. Statistical accounts). Bibliography p.38-46. *Class No:* 911.0(411)(01)

England & Wales

[5156]

DODGSHON, R.A. *and* BUTLIN, R.A., *eds*. **An Historical geography of England and Wales**. 2nd ed. New York, Academic Press, 1990. xxi,589p. diagrs., tables, maps, bibliog., index. £39. ISBN: 0122192532.

14 contributors (British academics, etc.). Extends from prehistory to date. Well-documented overview of all aspects of human geography, population changes, agriculture, transport and communications, landscape, towns and industries, and overseas trade. Detailed subject index. 'A most methodical analysis of recent researches into the various themes discussed' (*British Book News*, February 1979, p.171). *Class No:* 911.0(42)

France

[5157]

PLANHOL, X. de. **An Historical geography of France**. Cambridge Univ. Press, 1994. xxiii,563p. maps, figs., bibliog., index. ISBN: 0521322081.

First published as *Géographie historique de la France* (Paris, Fayard, 1988).

11 chapters organized in 3 parts: 1. Genesis of France - 2. Traditional organization of the territory of France - 3. Centralization and diversification of the French space. Chapter notes p.469-503. Guide to further reading p.504-505. Bibliography p.507-532. 'A major work of historical geography which will doubtless have much to offer geographers, but which is also important for historians'. (*French History*, v.8,no.4, December 1994, p.470-72). *Class No:* 911.0(44)

Scandinavia

[5158]

MEAD, W.R. An Historical geography of Scandinavia. London and New York, Academic Press, 1981. xviii,313p. maps, tables, diagrs., bibliogs., index. £41.00; $74.00. ISBN: 0124874207.

12 chapters *e.g.* 2. The concept of Scandinavia ... 4. From Middle Ages to Baroque Empire ... 11. Fin de siècle *c.*1900 - 12. The process and problems of fulfilment. Ch. bibliographies. *Class No:* 911.0(48)

Caribbean

[5159]

WATTS, D. The West Indies patterns of development, culture and environmental change since 1492. Cambridge, Cambridge Univ. Press, 1987. xxii,609p. illus., maps, tables, bibliog., index. £50.00. (*Cambridge Studies in Historical Geography no.8.*) ISBN: 0521245559.

3 main themes (total removal of a large aboriginal population; development of plantation agriculture; and resulting environment changes) unravelled in 11 chapters: 1. The environment - 2. Aboriginal settlement and culture - 3. Spanish intrusion and colonization - 4. Early northwest European plantations - 5. Northwest European sugar estates 1645-1665 - 6-9. Extension of the West Indian sugar estate economy 1665-1833 - 10. Post 1833 adjustments - 11. Twentieth-century trends. Notes p.540-52. Bibliography p.553-85. Analytical index. *Class No:* 911.0(729)

USA

[5160]

MEINIG, D.W. The Shaping of America: a geographical perspective on 500 years of history. New Haven and London, Yale Univ. Press, 3v., 1986-.

1: *Atlantic America 1492-1800.* 1986. xxii,500p. illus., maps, tables, bibliog., index. 2: *Continental America 1800-1867.* 1993. xix,636p. 0300056583. 3. *Transcontinental America 1850-1915.* 0300075928. 40 maps. 4. *Global America 1915-1992.* (to be published). The author is Maxwell Professor of Geography at Syracuse University.

See Meinig's 'The Shaping of America 1850-1915' *Journal of Historical Geography,* v.25, no.1, January 1999, p.1-8 Cole Harris' 'Comments on The Shaping of America', *ibid,* p.9-11; and Carville Earle's 'Continuity or discontinuity, that is the question! The Shaping of America in the gilded age and progressive era', *ibid,* p.12-16. *Class No:* 911.0(73)

Bibliographies

[5161]

CONZEN, M.P., *and others.* A Scholar's guide to geographical writing on the American and Canadian past. University of Chicago Press, 1993. indexes. £29.95.

10,000+ entries presenting a comprehensive review of geographical writings about the American past concentrating on complete research before 1990. Arranged in general and regional sections sub-divided by provinces, states and subjects. Author and subject indexes. 'An essential reference volume for researchers of the historical geography of North America' (*Geographical Journal,* v.160, no.3, November 1994, p.348). *Class No:* 911.0(73)(01)

[5162]

GRIM, R.E. Historical geography of the United States: a guide to information sources. Detroit, Gale Research Co., 1982. xix,291p. indexes. (*Geography and Travel Information Guide Series.*) ISBN: 0810314711.

686 annotated entries 'limited almost exclusively to the United States from the beginning of the sixteenth century until the early twentieth century' arranged in 21 chapters divided into 3 parts: Cartographic sources; Archival and other historical sources; Selected literature in historical geography. Author, title and subject indexes. Because of its emphasis on 'recent and current literature, *i.e.,* published or reprinted 1965-1980, it complements rather than duplicates D.R. McManis' *Historical geography of the United States* (1965). 'Recommended for all academic libraries (*Choice,* v.20,no.8, April 1983, p.1110). *Class No:* 911.0(73)(01)

New Zealand

[5163]

GREY, A. Aotearoa and New Zealand: a historical geography. Christchurch, Canterbury Univ. Press, 1994. maps, index. NZ$29.95. ISBN: 0908812345.

'A masterly work of reference covering the history and geography of the two islands from their origins to the year 1935, with an Afterword summarizing subsequent developments' (*Geographical Journal,* v.162, no.1, March 1996, p.117). *Class No:* 911.0(931)

Australia

[5164]

POWELL, J.M. An Historical geography of modern Australia. The restive fringe. Cambridge, Cambridge Univ. Press, 1988. xx,400p. illus., maps, tables, bibliog., index. £30.00. (*Cambridge Studies in Historical Geography no.11.*) ISBN: 0521256194.

'A broad interpretative thesis' in 10 chapters *e.g.* 3. Imperialism, protectionism, democratic nationalism ... 5. Science and the frontier .. 9. Agriculture and the modern federation. Notes p.342-76 Bibliography p.377-86. Analytical index. 'A fine achievement, good for historical geography, and good as well for Australia (*Geographical Journal,* v.158, no.2, July 1992. p.231). *Class No:* 911.0(94)

Research Methods

[5165]

BAKER, A.R.H. *and* BILLINGE, M. Period and place. Research methods in historical geography. Cambridge, Cambridge Univ. Press, 1982. x,377p. illus., maps, bibliog., index. £25.00. (*Cambridge Studies in Historical Geography no.1.*) ISBN: 052124272x.

31 papers presented at a workshop organized by the International Geographical Union's Working Group on Historical changes in Spational Organization in Cambridge, July 1979, arranged under headings: 1. Developments in Historical Geography - 2 Reconstructing past geographies - 3. Identification and interpretation of geographical change - 4. Behavioural approaches - 5. Theoretical approaches - 6. Historical sources and techniques. Notes p.313-61 Bibliography p.363-72. *Class No:* 911.0:001.891

Human Geography

Dictionaries

[5166]

BRAND, D. *and* DUROUSSET, M. Dictionnaire thématique histori géographie. 4th ed. Paris, Sirey, 1995. 560p. Fr.156. ISBN 2247019285.

6,000 terms which include a few from other disciplines like demography, economics, political science, and geology. *Class No:* 911.3(038)

[5167]

GOODALL, B. The Facts on File dictionary of human geography New York, and Oxford, Facts on File, 1987. 507p. diagrs., graphs $29.95; £15.00. ISBN: 0816017387.

Over 3000 definitions (1 line to 1 page in length) including some obsolete terms students may still encounter, and in foreign languages in common international use. 'Inevitably, this volume will be compared - to its detriment - to the *Dictionary of Human Geography* edited by R.L. Johnston' (*Choice,* v.24, no.11/12, July/August 1987 p.1676). *Class No:* 911.3(038)

[5168]

JOHNSTON, R.J., *ed.* The Dictionary of human geography. 3rd ed Oxford, Blackwell Reference, 1994. xx,724p. diagrs., graphs, index pbk. £14. ISBN: 0631181415.

Concerned with English-language words and terms in common usage in contemporary human geography. Many entries end with references suggested readings, or both. Abbreviations in Human Geography. For this editions the signed, cross-referenced articles are greatly expanded. *Class No:* 911.3(038)

Glossaries

[5169]

McDOWELL, L. *and* SHARPE, J.P. A Feminist glossary of human geography. London, Arnold, 1999. x,372p. bibliog. £50. ISBN 0340706597.

42 contributors, 400+ cross-referenced definitions of term employed in feminist debates that students of geography need to know Bibliography p.301-72. *Class No:* 911.3(038.1)

912 Maps & Atlases

Map Collections

[5170]
ARSGAARD, M.L. **Map librarianship.** 3rd ed. Littleton, Colorado, Libraries Unlimited Inc., 1987. 475p. illus., maps, index. £68.50. ISBN: 1563084740.

7 chapters: 1. Selection and acquisition - 2. Classification - 3. Cataloguing and computer applications - 4. Storage, care and repair - 5. Reference services - 6. Public relations - 7. Education. 'The focus is on theory, techniques, and practices, and on the practical short-term, and long-term aspects of working with cartographic material; thus the volume may be used as a classroom text, a working manual, and a reference source' (*Introduction*). *Class No:* 912:026

Bibliographies

[5171]
NEW YORK PUBLIC LIBRARY. Research Libraries. Map Division. **Dictionary catalog of the Map Division.** Boston, Mass., G.K. Hall, 10v., 1971. 8898p. $990.00 (Export $1198.00). ISBN: 0816107831.

187,000 photolithographed catalogue cards. Represented are the 280,000 sheet maps of the Map Division. Included are nearly 11,000v. other than atlases on the techniques of map making; analytical cards for periodical articles and bibliographies.

Supplemented by *Bibliographic guide to maps and atlases*. 1979-. *Class No:* 912:026(01)

Maps & Atlases

Bibliographies

[5172]
Bibliographic guide to maps and atlases. Boston, Mass., G.K. Hall, 1979-. Annual. ISBN: 078381335x.

Supplements *Dictionary catalog of the map division* Research Libraries, New York Public Library (1971).

1995. (1996) has v,804p. Lists materials catalogued during the past year by the New York Public Library Map Division, and the Geography and Map Division of Library of Congress. Includes in dictionary format maps, atlases, charts, plans and globes, as well as books about maps and cartography, plus periodicals and periodical articles. 'Not a work of scholarship but merely the commercial exploitation of automated records' (*Geographical Journal*, v.147, no.3, November 1981, p.381). *Class No:* 912.0(01)

[5173]
BRITISH LIBRARY. **Catalogue of printed maps, charts and plans.** Photolithographed ed. London, Trustees of the British Museum, 15v., 1967. Corrections and additions. 1967. 7822p. + 55p. £400.00. ISBN: 0714103241.

First published as *Catalogue of the printed maps, plans and charts in the British Museum* compiled by R.K. Douglas (London, 1885. 2v.); supplemented by the annual *Catalogue of printed maps in the British Museum: accessions* (1884-).

The 15v. ed. records British Museum holdings up to 1964 and is in the same format as the *General catalogue of printed books*. Entries have brief bibliographical notes (*e.g.* scale, map size). Arrangement is by localities. A-Z, with subdivision (*e.g.* London, v.9, p.13-202) as relevant.

The British Library catalogue of printed maps charts and plans Ten-year supplement 1965-1974. 1978. 690p. £45.00. ISBN 0714103667.

Catalogue of cartographic materials in the British Library 1975-1988, London, Bowker-Saur, 3v., 1989. 1201p. £36.00. 0862917654. 48,000 entries relating to atlases, single sheet maps, map series, maritime charts, plans, globes, and other relevant material acquired by the British Library Map Library. Also details of 260 digital cartographic and remote sensing databases in the UK located as a result of a British Library sponsored research project. 3 sequences: 1. Geographic names A-Z using BL Map Library headings - 2. Names/ titles - 3. Subjects *i.e.* reference works, books and serials relating to all aspects of cartography. Also available on 48 x reduction microfiche.

British Library Catalogue of Cartographic Materials: Accessions

....(*contd.*)
1975-1988. 15 x 1.48 microfiche on Datox sheets filed in a ring-bound folder accompanied by an explanatory introduction. *Class No:* 912.0(01)

[5174]
The British Library map catalogue on CD-ROM. Reading, Primary Source Media, 1996. CD-ROM. MS-Windows. £1495.

Providing access to the map catalogue's 300,000 records, this new CD-ROM brings together all 19 published volumes of the British Library's catalogues of these maps, as well as the automated file of post-1974 accessions. Entries can now be retrieved by searching on a combination of different fields, including geographical area, period, theme, cartographer or publisher, title, country or place of publication, physical form, on a range of scales. Includes a printed users guide to searching the British Library map catalogue on CD-ROM and a user manual for more technical queries. *Class No:* 912.0(01)

[5175]
Encyclopedias, atlases, and dictionaries. Sader, M., *ed and* Lewis, A., *ed.*. New York and London, R.B. Bowker & Co., 1995. 495p. illus., bibliog., maps, index, tables. $85. ISBN: 0835236692.

Originally published as *General reference books for adults* (1988).

4 major sections: 1. Introduction (on how to choose for home and library purchase with comparative charts) - 2. Reviews (facts, format, authority, currency, accuracy, clarity, objectivity, legibility) - 3. Electronic versions - 4. Large print reference works. 'Users will find the well-written summaries, which often compare the merits of the work in question with those of similar titles, very convenient' (*Booklist*, v.92, no.11, 1 February 1996, p.954-55). *Class No:* 912.0(01)

[5176]
GeoKatalog. Stuttgart, Geo Center Internationales Landkartenhause, 2v., 1975-1983. Loose-leaf.

A detailed trade catalogue of national and international maps and atlases, thematic maps and atlases, plans, guides and globes.

GeoKartenbrief (*c.3pa*). no.317, June 1990 notes new maps, atlases and books comprising all topics in the field of regional geography and, at the same time, acts as a Supplement to *GeoKatalog*. *Class No:* 912.0(01)

[5177]
GREAT BRITAIN. National Maritime Museum. **Catalogue of the Library. Volume 3: Atlases and cartography.** London, HMSO, 2v., 1971. xi, lx, 1166p. illus. facsims.

765 numbered items. V.1: Ptolemy - Italian atlases - Dutch and Flemish atlases - French atlases - British atlases (p.343-524) - German, Russian, Spanish & American atlases - Cartography & historiography. V.2: Index (lx p., p.655-1166), - detailed and analytical. V.1 states contents of *Imago mundi* (annual) and of atlases. (Noting every map and chart). Well produced. *Class No:* 912.0(01)

[5178]
PODELL, D.K. **Thematic atlases for public, academic, and High School libraries.** Metuchen, NJ., Scarecrow Press, 1994. xxxii,175p. bibliog., indexes. £27.50. ISBN: 0810828669.

Evaluates 100 thematic atlases in wide variety of subject areas. Data: Full imprint, features, price, ISBN; Topics and coverage; Contents; and Noteworthy qualities. Glossary p.147-49. Bibliography p.151-52. Index to publishers p.153-58. Name/Title and Subject Indexes. 'An excellent guide for the non-specialist, and not only provides reviews of a number of thematic atlases but also gives some pertinent advice on how to evaluate atlases for yourself' (*Reference Reviews*, v.9,no.4, 1995, p.42). *Class No:* 912.0(01)

[5179]
UNITED STATES. Library of Congress. **A List of geographical atlases in the Library of Congress** with bibliographical notes. Washington, Library of Congress, 8v., 1909-74.

V.1-4 (1909-20), compiled by P.L. Phillips; v.5-6 (1958-63), compiled by C. E. LeGear.

V.6. covering titles 7624-10254, covers nearly 2,500 items received 1956-60, including *800* Oriental publications. Arranged by continent and country. Author lists and topographical indexes in v.2-6, with cumulated index to v.1-4 in v.4 Entries sometimes have biobibliographical notes, often extensive. V.5 deals with world atlases, special and general. While v.6 records atlases of Europe, Asia, Africa, Oceania, the Polar regions and Oceania, v.7 (1973) lists titles 10255-18435, dealing with the Western hemisphere and individual countries of North and South America. V.8 (1974) is an integrated author list and index. *Class No:* 912.0(01)

Worldwide

[5180]

Lonely Planet Travel Atlases. Hawthorn, Victoria, Lonely Planet Publications, 1996-. col.maps, indexes.

Australia. 2000. ISBN 1864500654. 128p.; *Chile and Easter Island.* 1996. 0864425171. 96p.' *Egypt.* 1996. 72p. 0864423764; *India and Bangladesh.* 1996. 164p. 0864422709; *Israel & the Palestinian Territories.* 1996. 64p. 086442440x; *Jordan, Syria & Lebanon.* 1996. 96p. 0864424418; *Kenya.* 1997. 80p. 0864424426; *Portugal.* 1997. 88p. 0864424809; *Southern Africa.* 2000. 128p. 1864501014; *Thailand, Vietnam, Laos & Cambodia.* 2000. 112p. 1864501022; and *Turkey.* 1997. 128p. 0864422725. The comprehensive information in the atlases has been fully cross-referenced with Lonely Planet guidebooks. Other features of the series include distance and climate charts, plus a complete index of all map features.
Class No: 912.0(100)

Pacific Ocean

[5181]

Atlas of the South Pacific. 2nd ed. Wellington, External Intelligence Bureau of New Zealand, 1986. 48p. col. maps. $NZ59.95.

First published 1978.

Maps (1:40,000 to 1:7.500,000) and descriptive text on facing pages cover Micronesia, Melanesia, Polynesia, and New Zealand. 20 plates. Gazetteer p.40-48. *Class No:* 912.0(265)

[5182]

BIER, J. A. Reference map of Oceania: the Pacific islands of Micronesia, Polynesia, Melanesia. Honolulu, Univ. of Hawai'i Press, 1995. Double sided 36cmx23cm (6cmx9cm folded). $7.95. ISBN: 0824816870.

Double sided colour map including 52 inset maps depicting capitals, principal cities towns and villages, airports, active volcanoes, corral reefs *etc.* Index of 3,300+ place-names and their geographic location. Scale: 1:17,460,000. *Class No:* 912.0(265)

[5183]

KENNEDY, T.F.A. A Descriptive atlas of the Pacific Islands: New Zealand, Australia, Polynesia, Melanesia, Micronesia, Philippines. 3rd ed. Wellington, A.H. Reed, 1975. 79p. 67p.

1st ed. 1966.

Grey, black-and-white maps only, illustrating each of the principal island groups. Concise supporting text. Written on a very elementary level; designed for use in school and general libraries (*Library Journal,* v.93, no.22, 15 December 1968, p.4641). Page size: 23 x 17.5cm. *Class No:* 912.0(265)

Developing Countries

[5184]

CROW, B. *and* **THOMAS, A. Third World atlas.** New ed. Milton Keynes, Buckinghamshire, and Philadelphia, Open Univ. Press, 1994. 80p. col.tables, col.maps, diagrs. ISBN: 0335190774.

37 features (maps, text, diagrams) arranged in 3 sections: 1. Definitions of 'Third World' and 'development' - 2. The making of the Third World - 3. Issue challenges in contemporary development. Data tables p.74-78. Notes p.79. Sources p.80 Sources p.72.
Class No: 912.0(4/9-77)

Europe

[5185]

AA road atlas Europe. Basingstoke, Hants., Automobile Association Publishing, 2000. 224p. col.maps. £9.99. ISBN: 0749523638.

44 European countries. 58 city environs plans. Through-route maps for easy journey planning. Local place names to assist navigation.
Class No: 912.0(4)

[5186]

Baedeker/European maps. Basingstoke, Hampshire, The Automobile Association. Double-sided map. Scales ranging from 4 to 8 miles to 1 inch with smaller scales for the multi-country/large area titles. £4.99 each.

Alps ISBN 0861454464 - *Austria* 0749515376 - *Belgium/ Luxembourg* 0749517735 - *Czech Republic* 0749510609 - *Europe* 0749517727 - *France* 0749515384 - *Germany* 0749515392 - *Great Britain and Ireland* 0749515406 - *Italy* 074951541 - *Netherlands* 0749515422 - *Switzerland* 0749515430 - *Western Turkey* 0749515449. Designed to complement guidebook series, road, rail and tourist information. *Class No:* 912.0(4)

[5187]

Europe: a thematic atlas. London, Century Business in association with The Economist Books, 1992. 288p. col. illus., col. maps, tables, index. £39.95. ISBN: 071265383x.

Map features assembled in 9 main sections: History, Communications, Business, Finance, Politics, International relations, War and defence, Environment, and People and culture. Country analyses give basic reference information (area, climate, population, government, *etc.*). Chronology p.274-83. Sources p.288. 'This splendid reference work ... gives a thorough overview of Europe as a whole' (*Reference Reviews,* v.7, no.2, 1993, p.43).
Class No: 912.0(4)

[5188]

GREAT BRITAIN. Public Record Office. Maps and plans in the Public Record Office 4. Europe and Turkey. London, The Stationery Office, 1998. xv,1080p. £150. ISBN: 0114402752.

Contains more that 2,500 entries describing over 7,200 maps and plans transferred to the PRO from the Colonial Office, the Foreign Office, the War Office and other government departments. Within each topographical section the arrangement is chronological. Full PRO document references are given for each map. *Class No:* 912.0(4)

[5189]

The New Europe an encyclopedic atlas. Blombach-Schäfer, U., *and others eds.* London, Mitchell Beazley, 1992. 288p. col. illus., col maps, index. £19.99. ISBN: 0855339225.

Published in conjunction with Bertelsmann Lexikon Verlag of Gütersloh/München.

30 contributors. 3 general sections: Europe land and people, European Community origins and the Community today. Relief map and factbox of each nation whilst text summarises its history, environment, culture, tradition, economics, and political system. Profusely illustrated. *Class No:* 912.0(4)

Bibliographies

[5190]

BEECH, G., *ed.* **Maps and plans in the Public Record Office. 4 Europe and Turkey.** London, The Stationery Office, 1998. xiii,1064p. bibliog., index. ISBN: 0114402752.

5,168 annotated entries A-Z Europe (by 5 regions); A-Z by country, Seas. Data: area, date, full-title, number of sheets, imprint, and PRO requisition number. Many of the maps are of non-British origin. Bibliography p.947. British Admiralty charts p.948-52. Numbered War Office maps p.953-61. Indexes to official mapmaking bodies, persons and organisations, and places. *Class No:* 912.0(4)(01)

Europe—Eastern

[5191]

Atlas der Donauländer. [Atlas of Danubian lands.] Breu, J., *ed.* Wien, Franz Deutike Verlagsgesellschaft for Österreichisches Ost-und Südosteuropa Institut, 10 lieferung in loose-leaf binder, 1970-1989. $7,200. ISBN: 3700590180.

A massive and monumental thematic atlas, the work of 35 cartographers over two decades, with 48 fold-out plates (95cm x 68cm) each accompanied by a page of text. The area covered extends from the northern boundary of Czechoslovakia to the southern boundary of Albania; from just west of Regensburg in Bavaria to Odessa in the east, thus excluding the Danube headwaters. There are 43 physical, 3 population, and 67 economic and communication maps, whose texts end with bibliographical references. Standard scale is 1:2,000,000. Contents table and introduction printed in German, Russian, French and English. 'A first-rate, innovative, most attractive atlas unfortunately affordable only [by] the world's leading libraries' (*Cartographica,* v.27, no.1, Spring 1990, p.93-5).
Class No: 912.0(401)

[5192]

—Atlas der Donauländer. Register. Wien, Österreichisches Ost-und Südosteuropa-Institut, 1989. xxv,139p. ISBN: 370050019x.

Comprehensive multilingual gazetteer of the geographical names in the *Atlas. Class No:* 912.0(401)

[5193]

Atlas Ost-und Südosteuropa /Atlas of Eastern and Southeastern Europe. Jordan, P. *and* Kelnhofer, F., *eds.* Wien, Österreiches Ost-und Südosteuropa- Institut, 1989-. 4 sheets per year. DM28.(DM21. for subscribers to the complete atlas).

Map 5.1 G1. *Administrative subdivision of Eastern and South eastern Europe.* 1989. DM28.

Map 5.1 H1. *The expansion of tourism from Western countries to Hungary in the eighties.* 1989. DM28.

Atlas in progress: loose-leaf collection of standard size sheets (74 x 59cm), each sheet with one or more maps on a particular theme. Each map sheet is accompanied by a booklet with background text to the map's theme and with methodological notes on its compilation and design. Aims to provide up-to-date information on the nine former socialist countries of Eastern Europe in 5 broad thematic sections.

..(contd.)
ecology, population, economy, transport, and planning. Titles, legends and text in German and English. 'Likely to become a valuable reference work' (*Cartographica*, v.28,no.1, Spring 1991, p.118-9 from where this information is derived). *Class No:* 912.0(401)

Great Britain

[5194]
A Great Britain road atlas 2000. Basingstoke, Hampshire, Automobile Association, 1999. xviii, 318p. col.maps, indexes. £20. ISBN: 0749521783.

1st ed. 1986.

Preliminaries including 5 double-page route planning maps and mileage chart. Road maps (3m to 1 inch). Ports and airports. London's orbital motorway. London districts, Central London Street map with index. Fully indexed map of Ireland, 5 district maps, 86 fully-indexed town plans. New to this edition is a M60 Manchester orbital roadway map. Bestselling road atlas with 'new digitised mapping'.
Class No: 912.0(410)

[5195]
A Great Britain town plans. Basingstoke, Hampshire, Automobile Association, 1999. 96p. col. maps. £7.99. ISBN: 0749519819.

85 full colour maps of 85 towns plus central London with district maps of London, Birmingham, Manchester, Glasgow, and Tyne & Wear, 11 Airport maps, 9 port maps and Channel Tunnel terminal plans. *Class No:* 912.0(410)

[5196]
A motoring atlas Britain 2000. 22nd ed. Basingstoke, AA Publishing, 1999. xvi,192p. col.maps, index. £14.99. ISBN: 0749522062.

First published in 1979 as *The Complete atlas of Britain*.

Preliminaries (p.i-xvi) includes 3. routeplanner maps; road signs; motorway junctions; and mileage chart. Maps (4 miles to one inch) p.2-105. 46 Town plans p.106-27. City district maps (including London). Central London street index p.150-56. Index to 23,000+ place names p.157-192. Highly recommended. Available in many 'remainder' book shops at a much reduced price (c.£3.99) very close to publication date. *Class No:* 912.0(410)

[5197]
The Atlas of Britain and Northern Ireland. Planned and directed by D.P. Bickmore and M.A. Shaw. Oxford, Clarendon Press, 1963. xli,200p. of maps, 22p. of gazetteer.

Standard scale, 1:2M, enlarged by 1:1M and 1:½M for regions, and reduced to 1:8M for small distribution-maps. The 1:2M and 1:1M maps are used for physical geography, agriculture, fisheries, industry, demography, housing, administrative boundaries, communications and trade. Many fascinating and unusual maps, although some aspects are ignored, *e.g.* education, health, culture, history, scenery. Gazetteer has c.15,000 entries, with grid references. Separate transparent overlay at 1:2M. Dudley Stamp calls the atlas 'a landmark in the history of British cartography, with originality and freshness of approach as the most striking feature (*Geographical Journal*, v.129, pt.4, December 1963, p.506-7). *Class No:* 912.0(410)

[5198]
Collins postcode atlas of Great Britain and Northern Ireland. London, Harper Collins, 1999. 216p. maps, indexes. £49.99. ISBN: 0004488369.

All postcode boundaries clearly depicted on detailed background maps. Scale: 4.15 miles to 1 inch; Central London 1m to 3.17 inches. *Class No:* 912.0(410)

[5199]
GREAT BRITAIN. Ordnance Survey. Explorer maps. Southampton, Ordnance Survey. flat or folded. £5.50.

The new larger format Explorer maps will cover the parts of Great Britain not already covered by Outdoor Leisure maps. The geographically-based sheetlines will cater for regional tourism as well as for local walkers and cyclists. Rights of way information is included. National Trail and Recreational Path routes are shown. Scale: 1:25,000 (21/2 inches to 1 mile).

17 maps track the Greenwich Meridien through town and villages and across the countryside: Sheet 122. *South Downs Way - Steyning to Newhaven* to sheet 292. *Withernsea & Spurn Head*.
Class No: 912.0(410)

[5200]
GREAT BRITAIN. Ordnance Survey. Outdoor Leisure maps. Southampton, Ordnance Survey. flat or folded. £6.50.

45 Outdoor Leisure maps cover Britain's most popular holiday destinations like National Parks and selected Areas of Outstanding Natural Beauty. Packed with detail they are invaluable to the tourist and holidaymaker as well as walkers and climbers. Sample titles: 20. *South Devon-Brixham to Newton Ferrers*; 38. *Ben Nevis & Glen Coe*. Scale 1:25,000 (21/2 inches to the mile). *Class No:* 912.0(410)

[5201]
GREAT BRITAIN. Ordnance Survey. Pathfinder maps. Southampton, Ordnance Survey. Sheet size: folded 5 x 9 inches; flat 39 x 18 inches. £4.50.

Replace renowned 1:25,000 First Series maps. Coverage of the country completed in 1989.

Particularly useful for walking and rambling showing rights of way, thus revealing the country's footpath network. Scale: 2½ inches to 1 mile (1:25,000). The Pathway series will complete the coverage of Great Britain at 1:25,000 scale until the Explorer upgrading programme is finalised. Pathfinder maps completely covered by Outdoor Leisure Maps, or Explorer Maps (*qqv*) have been withdrawn and are no longer available. Some 500 are still in print.
Class No: 912.0(410)

[5202]
Reader's Digest book of the road. London, Reader's Digest, 1996. 527p. col.illus., col.maps, index. £24.95. ISBN: 0276421906.

Replaces *Reader's Digest atlas of the British Isles* (1st ed. 1988) which itself succeeded the *Reader's Digest book of the road* and *New book of the road*.

'The complete driver's atlas and touring guide to Britain and Ireland'. 159 col.maps (mostly at 3 miles to 1 inch), 26p. of route planning maps, 14p. maps of routes round large cities. 158p. of motorists information (emergency and legal information, motorway guides, town plants *e.g.*). Guide to places of interest behind the relevant maps. Favourably reviewed in *Bulletin Of The Society of Cartographers*, v.29, no.2, 1995, p.34-35. *Class No:* 912.0(410)

CD-ROM

[5203]
AND Route '99 UK & Ireland. Oxford, AND, 1998. PC Intel 486. 8Mb.Ram, 4 Mb of hard drive space. CD-ROM drive. £39.99.

1:750.000 mapping covers all 5 continents, the first PC title to detail the world's road networks. 'Routes are planned by entering departure and arrival points from pull-down menus and, in seconds, displayed on atlas-style topographic maps. The optimum and, where applicable, alternative routes are also detailed with concise text directions. An interactive map provides the low-down on any route, letting the user zoom in on defined sections with a simple mouse click.' (*The Times, Interface*, 3rd February 1999, p.5). *Class No:* 912.0(410)(003.40)

[5204]
Ordnance Survey interactive atlas of Great Britain CD-ROM. 4th ed. Southampton, Ordnance Survey/Attica Interactive, 2000. Windows 95, 98, NT4 or 2000, Pentium 90 processor or higher, 5Mb hard drive space, 5Mb RAM, 256 colour, 800x600 monitor, CDD-ROM drive with 4x or faster speed, 16 bit sound card or 100% compatible (recommended), Internet access (recommended), printer (recommended). ISBN: 1873472579, single user.

1st ed. 1996.

A definitive and fully interactive reference atlas of Great Britain combining Ordnance Survey mapping at a variety of scales, together with video, pictures and sound. The product also incorporates statistics and text resources which address geographical issues at national and European levels.

Extensive range of Ordnance Survey mapping from 1:600,000 to 1:10.000 scale; selected mapping arranged in recognisable layers (water, roads, vegetation etc.) which can be turned on or off and progressively built-up on top of each other; rapid and seamless zoom and pan between and across map scales; colourful small scale maps of the counties, regions and countries that comprise Great Britain and the European Union; cursor tracking displays its position by six-figure National Grid and Latitutde and Longitude references as well as county name; fast and comprehensive Gazetteer search function; distance measurement between two or more locations in Britain; export map images to graphics application for annotation and overlay; detailed nationwide and European database. *Class No:* 912.0(410)(003.40)

Bibliographies

[5205]
GREAT BRITAIN. Ordnance Survey. Maps, atlases and guides. Catalogue 1999. Southampton, Ordnance Survey, 1998. An annual publication. 56p. col. illus. sd. *gratis.*

Previously published as *Ordnance Survey map catalogue: maps, atlases, guides and services.*

Contents include descriptive lists of all OS map series intended for business, educational and leisure use *e.g.* Landranger, Pathfinder, Travelmaster, and Explorer maps, touring and holiday maps, historical maps and guides, atlases and administrative and geological maps, and street atlases, books, and CD-ROM. A 12-page price list is inserted. *Class No:* 912.0(410)(01)

[5206]

PERKINS, C.R. *and* **PARRY, R.B. Mapping the UK.** London, Bowker-Saur, 1996. xiv,397p. illus. (14p. col.pl.), maps, tables, bibliogs., indexes. £125. ISBN: 185739030x.

Overview and definitive guide to contemporary British-produced mapping of the United Kingdom in traditional and innovative formats arranged thematically in 22 chapters (*e.g.*Ordnance Survey history, policy and function - 3/6. Topographic mapping ... 13. Nautical charts ... 15. Boundaries and gazetteers ... 22. Future of the UK map). Appendix A. Specialist map retailers and data sources in the UK - B. Map libraries. Bibliographies at end of each chapter. 'An essential reference tool for all those dealing with mapping, whether they be involved in educational or commercial sectors as map makers or map users' (*Geographical Journal*, v.164, no.3, November 1998, p.351). *Class No:* 912.0(410)(01)

Indexes

[5207]

GREAT BRITAIN. Ordnance Survey. **Mapping index.** Southampton, Ordnance Survey, 2000. flat or folded. gratis. ISBN: 0319009556, flat; 0319009548, folded.

This index, based on the 1:625,000 scale Travelmaster 1, shows the relationship between Landranger, Outdoor Leisure, Explorer and Pathfinder maps and also features an area diagram on the Travelmaster series. The index is now updated every six months to reflect the continual change to the Outdoor Leisure, Explorer and Pathfinder series during the upgrading progamme. *Class No:* 912.0(410)(014)

[5208]

HELLYER, R. Ordnance Survey small-scale maps. Indexes 1801-1998. Newtown, Montgomeryshire, David Archer, 1999. xxiv,264p. facsims., bibliog., index. ISBN: 0951757954.

Indexes all OS maps on scale of 1:50,000 or smaller scales. Data: no. map sheet, area covered and colourings. *Class No:* 912.0(410)(014)

Scotland

[5209]

Collin's Scotland atlas and gazetteer. London, HarperCollins, 1999. xii,244p. col.maps. £10.99. ISBN: 0004488431.

Road maps on scale 3.2 inches to 1 mile, p.2-85. Types of feature shown p.86. Administrative areas p.87-90. Gazetteer (17,500 entries) including settlements, physical features, locations, places of interest, population) p.91-244. Curiously, also included is a feature on the new Scottish Parliament p.vii-x. *Class No:* 912.0(411)

[5210]

GREAT BRITAIN. Ordnance Survey. **Touring map Scotland.** Southampton, Ordnance Survey, 2000. flat or folded. £3.95. ISBN: 0319250288, folded map only.

Tourist information, Picnic areas and viewpoints, Camping and caravan sites, and Selected Recreational Paths. Scale: 1:500,000 (1 inch to 21/2 miles). *Class No:* 912.0(411)

Ireland

[5211]

ANDREWS, J.H. History in the Ordnance Map: an introduction for Irish readers. 2nd ed. Newtown, Montgomeryshire, David Archer, 1993. 63p. illus., bibliog. ISBN: 095175792x.

First published by Director at the Ordnance Survey Office, Dublin (1974).

Describes the principal maps of the whole or parts of Ireland produced by the Ordnance Survey of the UK 1824-1922. References p.62. Bibliography p.63. *Class No:* 912.0(415)

[5212]

Atlas of Ireland. Irish National Committee for Geography. Dublin, Royal Irish Academy, 1979. 104p. illus., table, maps.

Sections: General reference - Geology and geophysics - Geomorphology and hydrology - Soils - Climate - Flora and fauna - Settlement (*e.g.* Prehistoric sites) - Population - Primary production - Manufacturing - Tertiary activities - Social and culture. Includes 5 town plans. Notes to maps. Table of English and Irish place-names. Air photographs: 'The Irish landscape'. Index (*c.*800 place-names). Page size: 33x41.5cm. 'This is an important reference volume on Ireland' (M.O. Shannon. *Irish Republic*, 1986. Entry 57). *Class No:* 912.0(415)

[5213]

Bartholomew All Ireland road atlas. London, Bartholomew, 1996. 56p. col.illus., col.maps, index. ISBN: 0702832693.

Places of interest p.3-7. Maps p.10-37. Tourist Information Centres p.38-39. Town plans of Belfast, Cork, Dublin and Limerick. Index to place names p.46-56. *Class No:* 912.0(415)

[521]

Collins road atlas Ireland. London, HarperCollins, 1999. 56 col.maps, index. set. £4.50. ISBN: 0004489691.

Cheap and colourfully cheerful atlas on a scale of 5 miles to t inch. Maps p.10-37. Tourist Information Centres p.38-39. Town pla p.42-45. Index of placenames p.46-56. *Class No:* 912.0(415)

Commonwealth

[521]

Atlas of British overseas expansion. Porter, A.N., *ed.* Londo Routledge, 1991. x,279p. maps, plans, bibliog., index. £50. ISBN 0415019184.

92 chronological map/text features chart and chronicle Britain growth as a maritime commercial power from the late 15th century the postwar withdrawal from Empire (*e.g.* Bristol and the Atlan 1480 to 1509 ... Exports from the West Indies ... The Commonweal 1931 to 1989). Also 20 shorter features on 20 towns and cities imperial significance. Bibliography p.238-50. 137 black/white map More academic in tone and content than C. Bayly's *Atlas of the Britis Empire. Class No:* 912.0(41-44)

England & Wales

[521]

GREAT BRITAIN. Ordnance Survey. **Landranger map** Southampton, Ordnance Survey. Sheet size: flat 39 x 35 inches; folde 5½ x 9 inches. £5.25.

204 maps cover England and Wales (listed in *Maps, atlases ar guides catalogue 1997*). Each map encompasses an area 25 x 25 mil and shows tourist information such as camping and caravan site viewpoint, selected places of interest, rights of way information, cyc routes, and footpaths and bridleways. Scale 1¼ inches to 1 mi (1:50,000). *Class No:* 912.0(42)

London

[521]

Collin's Greater London street atlas comprehensive edition. Londo HarperCollins, 1998. 433p. col. maps, indexes. £16.99. ISBN 0004488075.

First published by Geographia in 1977.

Route planning maps (inc. M25 London Orbital Motorway) p.1-1 Urban area maps (1:50,000) p.17-25. London Street maps (1.20,00 p.26-279; Information pages p.280-433. Indexes to places of interes place-names, street names, British Rail stations. London Undergroun map *etc.* Information includes hospitals, police stations, sportir venues, museums, galleries, and underground stations. 80,000 full indexed streets. *Class No:* 912.0(421)

Wales

[521]

Atlas cenedlaethol Cymru/National atlas of Wales. Carter, H., *ed* Aberystwyth, University of Wales Press for the Social Scienc Committee, Board of Celtic Studies, Univ. of Wales, 1981-198 illus., maps, bibliogs. £250.00. ISBN: 0708307752.

Over 200 thematic map sheets compiled by 20 specialists fro universities and other higher education institutions in and beyor Wales. Sheets are grouped and numbered in 9 sections and housed in stout box folder: 1. Physical environment - 2. Political development 3. Culture - 4. Economic history - 5. Land use and agriculture - Industry - 7. Services and communications - 8. Population an settlement - 9. Regional policy and planning. Maps are drawn b Geoprojects (UK) Ltd. and the Department of Geography, Universi College of Wales, Aberystwyth, on a general scale of 8 miles to 1 inc (1:500,000). Transparent reference overlays incorporate National Gr to facilitate precise location of the mapped information. The maps a fully bilingual and are accompanied by a commentary text wi bibliographies. H.M. Griffiths' 'The National Atlas of Wales (*Cartographical Journal*, v.26, no.1, June 1989, p.7-14) traces i origins and the factors influencing its development and outlines aspec of its design, compilation and production. *Class No:* 912.0(429)

[521]

Welsh Office atlas/Atlas y Swyddfa Cymreig. Cardiff, HM Statione Office, 1972-75. maps.

An atlas of planning maps, 1:425,000, based on Ordnance Surve maps. 23 maps: 1. General reference map - 2. Administrative areas 3. Parliamentary constituencies - 4. Home population - 7. Forestry 8.8a. Traffic volumes, 1965, 1972 - 9. Rate support grant, 1971-72 10. Local office areas and assisted areas - 11. Water resources - 1 Energy facilities, production and distribution - 13. Derelict land, 197 72 - 14. Agricultural land - 15. Conservation of the countryside - 1 Population distribution, 1971 - 17. Health facilities - 18. Populatic density, 1971 - 19. Communications - 20. Annual average rainfa 1941-1970 - 20a. Climate. Map size, 35.5 x 22cm. *Class No:* 912.0(429)

Germany

[5220]

A big road atlas Germany. Basingstoke, Hants., Automobile Association, 1999. 224p. col. maps, index. £14.99. ISBN: 0749520213.

Produced in conjunction with ADAC (German Automobile Club) this large scale atlas has maps on the scale of 2.4 miles to 1 inch. 90,000 place names are indexed, the motorway network is clearly numbered, scenic routes and views are highlighted, and detailed tourist information is included. *Class No:* 912.0(430)

[5221]

CHÄFERS, B. The State of Germany atlas. London, Routledge, 1998. 128p. col.maps, col.tables, index. £9.99. ISBN: 0415188261.

First published in a German language edition (Bonn, Verlag J.H.W. Dietz Nachfolger, 1997).

35 double-page spreads illustrating how Germany is changing and the continuing differences between *Länder* in East and West Germany. 5 parts: 1. People - 2. Society - 3. Work and welfare - 4. Economy - 5. The State and politics. Major sources p.8. Commentary p.92-126. Almost every map compares Germany with its 15 European partners. *Class No:* 912.0(430)

[5222]

opographischer atlas Berlin Entwicklung und Struktur der Stadt Berlin in 55 Karten und 20 Luftbildern mit erläuternden Texten. Pape, C. *and* Freitag, V., *eds.* Berlin, Dietrich Reimer Verlag, 1987. 189p. illus. (some col.), maps (some col.), bibliog., index. ISBN: 3496008970.

74 explanatory text and maps in double-page features organized in 8 sections: 1. Die geographische Lage Berlins - 2. Das Stadtgebiet im Naturraum - 3. Die Entwicklung des Stadtgebietes - 4. Zentren städtischen Lebens - 5. Typen städtischer Wohngebiete - 6. Raumtypen städtischer Wirtschaft und Verwaltung - 7. Kultur-und Freizeitstätten - 8. Die amtlichen Karten Berlins. Auswahl aus dem neueren Schriftums p.184-89. Published to mark Berlin's 750th anniversary. *Class No:* 912.0(430)

Luxembourg

[5223]

tlas du Luxembourg. Department of Geography, Univ. of Nottingham (prepared in collaboration with a group of Luxembourg geographers). Luxembourg, Board of National Education, 1971-76. 3pts. loose-leaf.

The completed atlas consists of some 70 sheets. The 42 sheets forming pts. 1-2 are in 6 sections - historical, physical, administrative, demographic, economic and social. The relief and geological sheets are on a scale 1:200,000. Favourably reviewed in *Geography* (v.58, pt.1, no. 258, January 1973, p.100). Sheet size, 37.5x50cm. *Class No:* 912.0(435.9)

Austria

[5224]

tlas der Republik Österreich. Hrsg. von der Kommission für Raumforschung der (Österreichischen Akademie der Wissenschaften unter der Gesamtleitung ihres Obmannes Hans Bobek. Wien, Kartographische Anstalt Freytag-Berndt und Artaria, 1961-.

85 major maps, 1:1M. 12 sections - general, topographical, climate, hydrology, soil, flora and fauna, economy, population, agriculture and forestry, industry, power, mining, trade, transport and communications, culture. *Class No:* 912.0(436)

Czechoslovakia

[5225]

tlas Ceskoslovenské Socialistické Republiky. Praha, Ustrední Správa Geodézie a Kartografie, 1966. 16p. 58pl. of maps.

58 maps covering geology, geomorphology, climate, biogeography, population, mining, industries (chemicals; textiles), agriculture, transport, trade, housing, health, social security, education and culture of Czechoslovakia. Headings and explanatory notes on maps in Czech, English and Russian. Index-gazetteer of *c.*5,500 names. Very favourably reviewed in *The Geographical Journal,* (v.136, pt.3, September 1970, p.487). Page size, 49x43.5cm. *Class No:* 912.0(437)

[5226]

tlas SSR. [Atlas of the Slovak Socialist Republic.] Mazúr, E., *and others, eds.* Bratislava, Slovensá Kartografia, 1980. 1,136p. maps.

161 contributors. General key to the atlas, map titles and texts in the appendix given in English and Russian as well as Slovak. 'This is the first complete Slovak atlas and covers ever aspect of the country's geography' (D. Short. *Czechoslovakia*, 1986. Entry 46). *Class No:* 912.0(437)

Hungary

[5227]

Magyarorsz ag nemzeti atlasza. National atlas of Hungary. Budapest, Cartographica on behalf of the Hungarian Academy of Sciences and the Ministry of Agriculture and Food, 1989. 395p. col.maps, tables. ISBN: 9633515084, CM.

Previous ed. 1967.

180 contributors. Bilingual Hungarian-English thematic atlas in 19 sections: 2. Surveying and mapping (details of maps 1528-1885) ... 5. Climate ... 15. Transport, post and telecommunications ... 17. Tourism. Explanatory notes p.293-395. Objectives are to present a complete picture of Hungary in early 1980s and to survey changes of previous two decades. *Class No:* 912.0(439)

[5228]

Magyarország autóatlasza. [Road atlas of Hungary.] Budapest, Cartographia, 1993. 204p. col.maps, index. ISBN: 9633525012.

Tables of distances p.4-5. Budapest p.12-13. Maps p.14-59. Accommodation p.61-83. Sketch maps (localities) p.84-197. Scale 1:360,000. Preliminaries in English, German, French, and Russia. *Class No:* 912.0(439)

France

[5229]

AA road atlas France 2000. Basingstoke, Hants, AA Publishing, 2000. 144p. col.maps, index. £9.99. ISBN: 0749522852.

IGN mapping 4 miles to the inch. 60 town plans, 36,000 places indexed. Includes street and environs maps of Paris. *Class No:* 912.0(44)

[5230]

Atlas de France. Comité National de Géographie. 2nd ed. Paris Éditions Géographiques de France, 1951-59. 80pl. of maps.

First published 1933-45.

The 2nd ed. has its 80 sheets divided as follows: Géographie physique (26) - Biogéographie (8) - Géographie économique (29) - Géographie humaine et géographique politique (17). Where information was unchanged, plates were repeated from the 1st ed. Each sheet may contain various maps. Thus, sheet no.80, Santé publique, comprises 14 maps, showing incidence of major diseases, etc. in France. Distributions are mainly shown by départements, in flat tints. More important maps are in 4 sheets at 1:1M. No index gazetteer. Page size, 50x38.5cm. *Class No:* 912.0(44)

[5231]

Atlas de France. Montpellier and Paris, RECLUS. La Documentation Française, 14v., 1995. col.maps. Fr.220 each volume.

1. *La France dans le Monde.* - 2. *Population* - 3. *Emplois et entreprises* - 4. *Formation et recherche* - 5. *Société et culture* - 6. *Milieux et ressources* - 7. *Tourisme et loisirs* - 8. *L'Espace rural* - 9. *Industries* - 10. *Services et commerces* - 11. *Transports et communications* - 12. *L'Espace des villes* - 13. *La France d'outre-mer* - 14. *Territoire et aménagement.* *Class No:* 912.0(44)

[5232]

Atlas de la France et de ses régions un atlas cartographique au 1:250.000. Paris, Sélection du Readers Digest, 1993. 278p. maps. 420F. ISBN: 2709804670. *Class No:* 912.0(44)

[5233]

Atlas des départments français d'Outre-mer. Bordeaux-Talence, Centre d'Études de Géographie Tropicale du CRNS, 1975-.

1. *La Réunion.* 1976. 192p. 250F. ISBN 2222019117. 37 maps (1:150,000). 'The range of subject matter covers virtually every aspect of Réunion's geography and the written material both complements and supplements the cartography' (*Geographical Journal, v.144,no.2, July 1978, p.376-7*). 2. *La Martinique.* 1977. 120p. 430F. 2222021642. 3. *La Guadeloupe.* 1982. 430F. 2222031052. 4. *La Guyane.* 1979. 222202501x. 36 col. map features: 1. Situation - 2. La Région des Guyanes ... 17. Archéologie - 18. Cartes anciennes - 19. Histoire Coloniale. *Class No:* 912.0(44)

[5234]

Atlas Paris par arrondissements. Clermont-Ferrand, Services de Tourisme Michelin, 1988. 70p. col.maps. Softcover. ISBN: 206000151x.

Les rues de Paris p.6-20. Plan de Paris p.21-51 with other maps Boulogne-Billancourt; Clichy, Levallois-Perret, Neuilly-sur-Seine; Saint Ouen p.54-8. Also Métro, Résau Express Régional, Autobus, Lignes Urbaines, and Aéroports p.60-65. Les Bois de Paris p.68-9. *Class No:* 912.0(44)

[5235]

Michelin regional maps - France. Watford, Michelin Tyre PLC., Travel Publications Department. £4.

Bretagne - Normandie - Pays de Loire - Poitou-Charentes - Aquitaine - Midi-Pyrénées - Nord de la France - Ile-de-France - Centre - Auvergne Limousin - Languedoc Roussillon - Champagne Ardennes - Alsace et Lorraine - Bourgogne Franche-Comte - Rhône Alpes - Provence côte d'Azur - Vallée du Rhône (enlargement of Lyon and Marseille to 1:100,000) - and Fort Noire - Alsace. Scale 1:200,000 (1 cm = 2 km). *Class No:* 912.0(44)

[5236]

Philip's France, Belgium, Luxembourg road atlas 2000. London, Philip, 2000. 304p. maps, index. Spiral bound. £9.99. ISBN: 0540078646.

Detaled 1:250,000 mapping, showing many minor roads and including motorway-junction layouts, names, and tolls. The extensive tourist information features highlighted sites and places of interest and numerous scenic routes. 12 detailed town plans each covering a full page (Paris two pages), give particularly comprehensive coverage as well as a map of the Paris region approaches. A distances table and a comprehensive index containing over 36,000 place names complete this useful atlas. *Class No:* 912.0(44)

CD-ROM

[5237]

CD-Atlas de France. Paris, Chadwyck-Healey France. IBM Compatible PC; Apple Macintosh, MS-DOS 3.1 or higher; Apple Macintosh, 640k, networkable. £995. Ffr.25,000.

Administrative maps. Data: information on population, economy, agriculture, trade and industry, transport and communications, tourism, and history. Arranged by regions, départements, cantons and communes.

Developed by GIP Reclus, Argo-Infographie, and the publishers. *Class No:* 912.0(44)(003.40)

Italy

[5238]

AA road atlas Italy. Basingstoke, Hants, Automobile Association Publications, 1999. 128p. col.maps, £13.99. ISBN: 0749523336.

4 miles to 1 inch scale 30 town plans. Includes Sardinia and Sicily. Motorway maps, through routes, places of interest, and a distance chart. *Class No:* 912.0(450)

[5239]

Atlante stradale d'Italia. Milano, Touring Club Italiano, 3v. L81,000 set. L28,500 single volumes.

3v. road atlas: *Nord*; *Centro*; *Sud*. Scale 1:200,000. A fully annotated review of the more important tourist localities is placed at the beginning of each volume. *Class No:* 912.0(450)

[5240]

Atlante tematico d'Italia. Milano, Touring Club Italiano and Consiglio Nazionale delle Ricerche, 4 boxed sets, 1990-. 800p. col. maps, tables, bibliogs. ISBN: 8836504299.

This new social, economic, environmental and cultural profile of Italy has 126 numbered fascicules arranged in 4 thematic boxed sets: 1. Referimenti generali ed elementi fisico-ambientali - 2. Popolazione e insediamenti - 3. Risorse e attivitá economiche - 4. Patrimonio culturale e ambiente. Each fascicule consists of text, map(s), and sources and bibliography. At the time of compilation 32 fascicules had been issued *e.g.* 3. Italy in the Mediterranean area ... 52. Urban system ... 72. Energy ... 96-7. Folklore (All fascicules have Italian and English titles). Maps: 8 colours. Scale varies 1:1 million - 1:12 million. 'The team effort of some 220 scientific coordinators, designers and cartographers ... has created in this comprehensive, authoritative and up-to-date portrayal of the physical, economic, social and cultural geography of Italy an atlas that will rank with the best of national atlases' (*Geographical Journal,* v.161, no.2, July 1995, p.216-17). *Class No:* 912.0(450)

Spain

[5241]

Atlas grafico de España Aguilar. 2nd ed. Madrid, Aguilar, 1982. 507p. col.illus., col.maps, index. ISBN: 8403421087.

Sumptuous pictorial atlas with 124 physical and thematic map features. Place name index p.439-507. Most maps on scale 1:250,000. *Class No:* 912.0(460)

[5242]

Gran atlas de Carreteras España Portugal. Barcelona, Plaza & Janes, 1992. ix,320p. col. maps, index. ISBN: 3575188696.

Available from Geo-Center International with cover title of *Euro-road Atlas Spain and Portugal.* £9.99. 357511381

Maps on scale of 1:300,000 and A-Z of places p.10-278. 60 towns plans and index p.279-320. Preliminaries and guide to index in 5 Iberian and 3 Western European languages. *Class No:* 912.0(460)

[524.

INSTITUTO GEOGRÁFICO NACIONAL. Atlas nacional de Españ Madrid, Ministerio de Obras Públicas, Transportes y Medio Ambient 1990-. col.maps, col.illus., indexes. ISBN: 8478190295.

Supersedes *Atlas nacionale de España* (Madrid, Instituto Geofráfi y Catastral, 1965-68).

Published in laminated covered facsicules: Sección 1. Grupo *Referencias Generales.* 2nd ed. 1993. 23p. - 3a & 3b *Referenci cartográficas. Tablas de datos geográphicas.* 1994. 34+12p. - 3 *Imagen y paisaje.* 1992. 36p. - 7. *Edafología.* 1992. 10p. - *Geofísica.* 1992. 20p. - 9. *Climatología.* 1992. 24p. - 10. *Hidrologí* 1993. 32p. - 11.+12. *Bigeografía, flora, fauna y espacios natural protegidos.* 1992. 17+6p.

3.13 *El medio marino.* 24p. - 4.14 *Información demográfica.* 199 46p. - 4.14b *Potenciales demográficos.* 1992. 23p. - 4.18 *Energi* 1991. 20p. - 5.16 *Minerica.* 1994. 20p. - 5.17 *Agricultura, ganaderí y pesca.* 1992. 40p. - 7.25 *Transporte maritimo.* 1994. 20p.

8.31 *Finanzas y hacienda.* 1992. 18p. - 9.33 *Turismo.* 1994. 34p. 36b. *Deportes.* 1994. 54p. - 37. *Trapajo, securidad social y servici sociales.* 1994. 24p. - 10.39. *Prolemas medioambientales.* 16p. 11.41. *El conocimiento del territorios: otros organismos officiale* 1992. 26p. - 12.42. *Sociología familiar.* 1994. 22p.

Class No: 912.0(460)

Portugal

[524

Atlas de Portugal. Lisboa, Cartas do Instituto Geográphico e Cadastra 1988. (Selecções do Reader's Digest). 159p. illus., col.maps, table index.

1. Portugal no mundo - 2. Mapas de Portugal (p.10-40) - 3. Portug hogie e ortem (geology; parks; vegetation; rivers; temperature ar climate; fishing; tourism; agriculture; industry; architectur Portuguese overseas discoveries p.41-88). 4. Almanaque (geographic tables p.89-104) - 5. Portugal em imagens (pictorial feature p.10 120). *Class No:* 912.0(469)

[524!

Atlas turístico de Portugal. Lisboa, Lucidus, 1986. 392p. col.illus col.maps, tables, index.

Less an atlas, more a sumptuously illustrated guidebook whic includes Azores, Madeira and Macao. General tourist and geographic data and information p.343-387. Index of places p.389-90. Mostly Portuguese but occasional short passages in English. *Class No:* 912.0(469)

Russia

[524

Atlas of Russia and the post-Soviet republics. Hastings, East Susse Arguments and Facts Media, in conjunction with ATKAR-PK Kartografija Moscow, 1994. 64p. col.maps, index. ISBN 1873976046.

27 maps reflecting the geopolitical interests of the former USS Individual maps show the Baltic states, the Transcaucasian regio Ukraine, and Moldova. Central Asian states are presented as a whol Index of geographic names p.41-64. *Class No:* 912.0(47)

[524

BREWER, M. Atlas of Russia and the independent republics. Ne York, Simon & Schuster, 1995. 144p. illus., maps, bibliog., inde $75. ISBN: 0130519960.

Introductory section on former Soviet Union followed by separa chapters on each Republic - Armenia, Azerbaijan, Belarus, Estoni Georgia, Kazakhstan, Kyrgyzstan, Latvia, Lithuania, Moldova, Russi Tajikstan, Turkmenistan, Ukraine, Uzbekistan - covering politic boundaries, agricultural output, and industrial production, with 3+ tw colour maps and a capital city map. *Class No:* 912.0(47)

[524

BRUNET, R., *and others.* **Atlas de la Russie** et des pays proches. Par RECLUS-La Documentation Française, 1995. 208p. col. maps, inde F220. ISBN: 2110034289.

160 map features in 6 main sections: 1. Territoires - 2. Production et ressources - 3. Environnement - 4. Espaces de view - 5. La Russi transformations et tensions - 6. Nouveaux horizons. Well produce atlas of all aspects of contemporary Russia. *Class No:* 912.0(47)

[524

HARRIS, G. *and* **DIAKONOV, S.A. Mapping Russia and i neighbours:** the new atlas of the changed geographical face of th former Soviet Union. Los Angeles, The Americas Group, 199 1p.+6p. transparent overlays+12p. $29.95. ISBN: 093504714x.

Scale 1:34,000,000 (i.e. 900 miles: 45mm). *Class No:* 912.0(47)

Poland

[5250]

Iarodowy atlas Polski. Warszawa, Polska Akademia Nauk, Instytut Geografii, 1973-78. xlp. 127 pl. of maps.

127 folding coloured maps - general, analytical, socioeconomic and sociocultural at scale 1:200,000 and smaller. English language version as *National atlas of Poland* (186p). *Class No:* 912.0(475)

Scandinavia

[5251]

Cappelens bilatlas Norden. [Cappelen's car atlas of the Nordic states.] Oslo, J.W. Cappelens Forlag. 1981. In cooperation with Norges Automobil-Forbund. 287p. maps.

Detailed maps of Norway, Denmark, Sweden and Finland (Scale 1:6,000,000). Text in English, French, German, Dutch as well as Scandinavian languages. *Class No:* 912.0(48)

Finland

[5252]

Pennia suuri Suomi-Kartasto/Kartverk över Finland/Finland in maps/ Finnischer atlas 1:250,000. Helsinki, Maanmittanshallitus (*i.e.,* National Board of Survey) ja Weilin and Göös, 1979. 224p. col.mnaps, index. ISBN: 0513519554.

GT road maps on scale (1:250,000) larger than in any previous atlas of Finland. 102 town plans (1:40,000). Distances tables p.165. Gazetteer of 9000 place names. *Class No:* 912.0(480)

[5253]

Suomen Kartasto/Atlas of Finland/Atlas över Finland. Helsinki, Kustannososakeyhti ö Otava, 1960. viii, 39 pl. of maps.

Originally Atlas de Finlande (Helsinki, Société de Géographie de Finlande, 2v. 1899). Under present title 2v., 1925-29.

39 double plates of special maps of excellent quality; scales, 1:1M., 1:6M., etc. 455 maps, covering altitudes and depths, geodesy and mapping, geology, climate (34 maps), hydrology, fauna, flora, vegetation zones, forests and peatlands, population (37 maps), arable area, agriculture (64 maps), forestry, industry, foreign trade and harbours, traffic, inland trade, co-operative movement, finance, education, health and medical care, history, elections, geographic regions, communications. There are even maps showing distribution of dentists, blue-and-grey-eyed people. Norwegian lemmings, and sausage factories. Largest scale, 1:1M. (population maps); usually each double-plate has several small maps. No subject index, although there is a detailed contents list in Finnish, English and Swedish. Legends are also trilingual. Page size 45 x 36cm.

Separate [*Explanatory notes*] in Finnish (1962. 122p.) describes and supplements the maps. An English edition of this has been promised.

5th edition 1977-1992 published by National Board of Survey and Suomen Maantietaellinen Seura in 62 folios (various pagination) *e.g.* 111 *Introduction* (1993) *Mapping of Finland* (1984), 312 *Publication administration* (1977). Maps and figures in Finnish, Swedish and English. Accompanying articles in Finnish with Swedish and English in enclosures. *Class No:* 912.0(480)

Norway

[5254]

Det store Norges-Atlas Henriksen, P., *ed.* Oslo, Hjemmets Bokforlag, 1992. 224p. col.illus., col.maps, index. ISBN: 8259008742.

Includes the coats of arms of Norwegian municipalities and local districts (p.148-155) and a place-name index comprising 40,000 entries. *Class No:* 912.0(481)

Sweden

[5255]

National atlas of Sweden. Wastenson, L., *ed.* Stockholm, SNA Publishing, 17v., 1990-96. col.illus., col.maps. ISBN: 9187760045, (set).

English edition published under the auspices of the Royal Swedish Academy of Sciences by the National Committee of Geography.

1. *Maps and mapping.* - 2. *The Forests.* - 3. *Population.* - 4. *The Environment* - 5. *Agriculture* - 6. *Infrastructure* - 7. *Sea and coast* - 8. *Cultural life, recreation and tourism* - 9. *Sweden in the world* - 10. *Work and leisure* - 11. *Cultural heritage and preservation* - 12. *Genealogy* - 13. *Landscape and settlements* - 14. *Climate, lakes and rivers* - 15. *Manufacturing services* - 16. *Geography of plants and animals* - 17. *The Geography of Sweden.* *Class No:* 912.0(485)

Denmark

[5256]

Atlas over Danmark. København, Det Konelige Danske Geografiske Selskab, 1976-. illus., maps, bibliog.

1st series.

1. *Landskabsformerne* (The landscapes). 1949. 32p.; explanatory booklet. 129p.

2. *Befolkningen* (The population). 1961. 2p.; explanatory booklet. 124p.

V.1 has many sectional maps, with text and indexes to types of landscape, in Danish and English. V.2 consists of population maps, 1:200,000, each dot respresenting 25 persons. The booklets include illustrations and bibliographies. Page size, 55 x 37.5cm.

2nd series.

1. *Opgivne og tilplantede landburgsarealer:Jylland* (Abandoned and afforested agricultural lands in Central Jutland). 1976. 46p. 10p. pl.

2. *Topografisk atlas Danmark* 1976. 192p. Includes 79 main maps and encompasses Greenland. English summaries of commentary. Bibliography p.178-79. No gazetteer/index. *Class No:* 912.0(489)

[5257]

Danmark 1:100 000 topografisk atlas. 3rd ed. København, Kort-og Matrikelstyrelsen, 1989. 161p. maps, tables, index. ISBN: 8774500686.

60 x double page dated maps supported by 22,000 gazetteer entries. Most detailed map of Denmark. *Class No:* 912.0(489)

Netherlands

[5258]

Atlas van Nederland/Atlas of the Netherlands. Compiled for the Federation for the Scientific Atlas of the Netherlands. 's- Gravenhage, Staatsdrukkerij- en Uitgeverijbedrift, 1963-77. Supplements 1978-1981. diagrs., tables, maps. Looseleaf.

98 map plates (double-page spreads), backed by commentary or other maps. 17 sections (1. Topography and cartography - 2. Geology, geophysics, mineral resources - 3. Geomorphology - 4. Soils (9 plates, 1:200,000) - 5. Climate - 6. Vegetation and biogeography - 7. Water management - 8. Historical geography - 9. Settlements - 10. Dialect and regional - 11. Population - 12. Public utilities - 13. Agriculture - 14. Fisheries - 15. Manufacturing industries - 16. Commerce and transportation - 17. Physical training). No gazetteer. *Class No:* 912.0(492)

[5259]

—**Atlas van Nederland.** 's-Gravenhage, Staatsdrukkerij/uitgeverij, 21v. 20 parts each of 24p. col.illus., col.maps, col.graphs, tables, bibliogs, sd. ISBN: 901205006, set.

Under the auspices of the Stichting Wetenschappelijke *Atlas van Nederland* (1977).

1. *Bevolking* - 2. *Bewoningsgeschiedenis* - 3. *Steden* - 4. *Dorpen* - 5. *Wonen* - 6. *Voorzieningen* - 7. *Recreatie* - 8. *Werken* - 9. *Bedrijven* - 10. *Landbouw* - 11. *Poort van Europa* - 12. *Infrastructuur* - 13. *Geologie* - 14. *Bodem* - 15. *Water* - 16. *Landschap* - 17. *Milieu* - 18. *Ruimtelijke ordening* - 19. *Stadsinrichting* - 20. *Landinrichting* - 21. *Registers en indexen.* All volumes are equipped with a glossary and a bibliography. *Class No:* 912.0(492)

[5260]

TAMSMA, R. The Netherlands in 50 maps. Amsterdam, Koninklijk Nederlands Aardrijkskundig Genootschap, 1988. 126p. DFL24.90. ISBN: 9068090623.

Continuation of *The Netherlands in 100 maps* (1977).

Brings together maps first printed in issues of *Tijdschrift voor Economische en Sociale Geografie* with original commentaries. 'An essential compendium of information about the current geography of the Netherlands and is highly recommended because the commentaries ... enhance considerably the value of the original journal maps' (*Bulletin of Society of University of Cartographers*, v.22, no.1, 1988, p.46). *Class No:* 912.0(492)

Belgium

[5261]

Atlas de Belgique/ Atlas van Belgie. De Smet, R.E., *and others.* Bruxelles, Royaume de Belgique Comité National de Géographie, 1950-1972. 266p. bibliogs.

65 maps (50x60cm) grouped under 13 headings: 1. Belgium in Europe - 2. Cartography and geophysics - 3. Soils and sub-soils - 4. Climatology - 5. Hydrology - 6. The North Sea coast - 7. Biogeography - 8. Human geography - 9. Forestry and agriculture - 10. Industry - 11. Transport and commerce - 12. Regional geography - 13. Administrative areas. Each map accompanied by text and bibliography. *Class No:* 912.0(493)

[5262]
Atlas of Belgium. Bruxelles, Belgian Information and Documentation Institute, 1987. 30p. maps.

10 topical maps accompanied by text: 1. Belgium in Europe - 2. Political structure - 3. Population - 4. Agriculture - 5. Metallurgy - 6. Chemicals and textiles - 7. Energy - 8. Roads - 9. Railways - 10. Inland waterways. 'A useful, if general, up-to-date picture of the state of the nation' (R.C. Riley *Belgium,* 1989, Entry 59).
Class No: 912.0(493)

Switzerland
[5263]
Atlas der Schweiz. Imhof, E. Berne, Verlag der Eidgenössischen Landestopographie, 1965-78. illus., tables, maps. Looseleaf.

General scale (double-spread): 1:½M., with large-scale topographical maps at 1:50,000 of Aletsch Glacier and other selected areas. More than 404 coloured maps. Topographical relief plates from the *Schweizerischer Mittelschulatlas.* Thematic maps on 9 topics, from topography to traffic. Explanatory notes and statistical tables accompany each map. Good choice of colours for contours, rocks, snowfields and glaciers. Page size, 50 x 37.5cm.

'It is no doubt the finest national atlas ever produced' (*The Geographical Magazine,* August 1978, p.772). *Class No:* 912.0(494)

Slovenia
[5264]
Atlas Slovenije: 109 preglednih kart v merilu 1:50,000 in Slovenija v sliki in besedi. [Atlas of Slovenia. 109 maps on the scale 1:50,000 and Slovenia in pictures and words.] Ljubljana, Mladinska knjiga za Geodelski zavod Slovenije, 1986. 365p. illus., maps.

'A beautifully produced, large-format atlas ... with text describing special features' (Carmichael, C. *Slovenia,* item no.51).
Class No: 912.0(497.12)

Croatia
[5265]
A Concise atlas of the Republic of Croatia and of the Republic of Bosnia and Hercegovina. Zagreb, Miroslav Krle za Lexicographical Institute, 1993. 159p. col.illus., col.maps, index.

Based partly on *Zemljopisni atlas Republike Hrvatske* (1992).

Contents: State symbols (flag, coat of arms, national anthem. flag of the President, parliament) p.1-7; Topographic maps (internal maps scale 1:500,000) p.9-41; Thematic maps (with text) p.43-81; History and historic maps (with text), p.83-100; Constitutional systems p.102-3; and Statistics p.106-26. *Class No:* 912.0(497.13)

Romania
[5266]
Atlasul Republicii Socialiste România. Bucharest, Editura Academiei Republicii Socialiste România, 1974-79. 5 fascicules.

'This definitive atlas of Romania is divided into thirteen sections containing seventy-six maps which present aspects of the physical, economic and social geography of the country' (A. and D. Deletant. *Romania,* 1985. Entry 29). *Class No:* 912.0(498)

[5267]
România: atlas rutier. Dragomir, V., *and others.* Bucharest, Editura Sport-Tourism, 1982. 204p. maps, index.

73 maps at a scale of 1:350,000. 40p. of town plans. Glossary of road signs. Place-name index 'The most detailed road atlas of Rumania published since the last war' (A. and D. Deletant. *Romania,* 1985. Entry 32). *Class No:* 912.0(498)

China
[5268]
Atlas of China. Chicago, Rand McNally, 1990. 48p. illus., maps, index. pbk. $8.95. ISBN: 0528833855.

Two-page maps of The World, Asia, China, and 4 regional maps of China (1:3,000,000) including Tibet followed by single page maps of areas surrounding major cities (1:1,000,000). Updated from *The international atlas* (1969) showing political capitals and boundaries with cultural, transport, hydrographic and topographic features. Detailed index of 11,000 entries. For home and school use.
Class No: 912.0(510)

[5269]
Atlas of the People's Republic of China. Yang Dan, *ed.* Beijing Foreign Languages Press China Cartographic Publishing House, 1989. Distributed by China International Book Trading Corporation, Beijing variously paginated but 58 mostly double page maps +112p. index col. maps. $49.95. ISBN: 0835123197; 711900560x.

Based on Chinese pinyin edition 1983.

32 administrative maps of provinces, autonomous regions and Beijing municipality mostly on scale 1:2,000,000 (table of facts of short articles on back of each map covering population, area, climate major products, and administrative set up December 1987). 1 topographical maps on various scales. Finely produced atlas.
Class No: 912.0(510)

[5270]
HSIEH CHIAO-MIN *and* **HSIEH, J. K. China: a provincial atlas.** New York, Macmillan/Prentice Hall, 1995. 303p. maps, bibliog., index. $125. ISBN: 0028971841.

Maps arranged in 2 sections: 1. 15 thematic maps (political boundaries, population, geography, natural resources, agriculture industry etc.). 2. Topographical maps of 23 provinces, 5 autonomous regions, and 3 municipalities. Glossary of physical, geographical and administrative terms in English translation. Locator index of 4,35 place-names. 'The text that accompanies the maps is well written and easily read: it is not too dense, and is well-balanced' (*Western Association of Map Librarians Information Bulletin,* v.27, no.3, July 1996, p.141-42). *Class No:* 912.0(510)

[5271]
Times atlas of China. Geelan, P.J.M. *and* Twitchett, D.C. London Times Books, 1974. xl, 144p.+27p. maps.

First published (in part) by Kyobunkaku Ltd., Tokyo, 1973.

Sections: History - Modern China (population: agriculture .. China's frontiers) - Physical maps (by Bartholomew) - Provincial map and notes - 31 city plans (main sheets named). Glossary, p.144. Index gazetteer of *c.* 25,000 place-names. 'Destined to become the standard in its field' (*Library Journal,* v.101, no.8, 15 April 1976, p.968) 'Hardly a monumental work' (*Geographical Journal,* v.142, pt.2 1976, p.359). Page size, 36 x 26cm. *Class No:* 912.0(510)

[5272]
Tourist atlas of China. Zhao Xilin, *ed.* Shanghai, Cartographi Publishing House China, 1985. 99p.+12p. col. plates. col. illus., col maps. softcover. £6.95.

Principal details and coloured maps of 56 main cities and areas open to foreign tourists. Chronology of Chinese historical periods p.3 Information for tourists p.96-99 includes official travel agency trave service details, important anniversaries and holidays in China, climatic data *etc.* Tall pocket size. *Class No:* 912.0(510)

Hong Kong
[5273]
Hong Kong atlas. Hong Kong, Hai Feng Publishing, 1991. 66p.++ 1 unnumbered pages. col. maps, tables, index. £14.25. ISBN 9622381820.

Includes general, thematic, and street maps. Bilingual introduction other preliminaries, and street index. *Class No:* 912.0(512.317)

Mongolia
[5274]
Bügd Nairamdakh Mongol Ard Uls ündesnii atlas. [Mongolian People Republic national atlas.] Ulaanbaatar, Academy of Sciences, 1990 144p.

Physical geography, history, demography, political geography *etc* thematic maps. Gazetteer. List of contents only in English.
Class No: 912.0(517)

Japan
[5275]
COLLCUT, M., *and others.* **Cultural atlas of Japan.** Oxford, Phaidon New York, Facts On File, 1988. 240p. col. illus., col. maps, bibliog. index. $40. ISBN: 0714825263, UK; 0816019274, US.

9 chapters (*i.e.* map, illustrations and text) in 3 divisions: 1. Origins - 2. Historical period - 3. Modern Japan with 19 special features (*e.g* Ainu of Hokkaido, Samurai society in the medieval age, Japan and the West) and 12 site features. The rulers of Japan p.228-9. Chronolog p.8-9. Glossary p.230-1. Gazetteer p.233-6. Bibliography p.225-7. 40 maps. *Class No:* 912.0(52)

[5276]
Japan: a bilingual atlas. London, Kodansha Europe, 1999(?). 128p maps, index, pbk. £12.99. ISBN: 4770015364.

51 colour and b/w maps include detailed maps of major cities tourist attractions, national parks, and transport networks.
Class No: 912.0(52)

[5277]

he National atlas of Japan. Compiled by Geographical Survey Institute, Ministry of Information. Tokyo, Japan Map Center, 1977. x,367, illus., maps.

216 maps (50 at 1:2,500,000; 166 at 1:4,000,000), with explanatory notes and small supporting maps. Nearly half the maps are thematic, covering agriculture, industry, communications and trade. Several maps concern environmental problems. Gazetteer: List of administrative areas; Index to place names (p.359-65; c.5,000 entries). 'A superb example of the high standards which characterize Japanese cartography' (*Geographical Journal*, v.144, 1978, p.369). *Class No:* 912.0(52)

Asia—Middle & Near East

[5278]

tlas of the Middle East. Brawer, M., *ed.* New York, Macmillan; London, Collier Macmillan, 1988. 140p. maps, tables, diagrs., bibliog., index. ISBN: 0029052718.

Covers 19 countries from Libya in the West to Iran in the east and Turkey to the north. A regional overview is followed by country surveys *e.g.* Iran p.86-93 has sections on topography, climate, population, agriculture, history, government and politics, and 3 maps. *Class No:* 912.0(53+56)

[5279]

LAKE, G., *and others.* The Cambridge atlas of the Middle East and North Africa. Cambridge, Cambridge Univ. Press, 1987. vii,124p. col.maps, bibliog. £45.00; $75.00. ISBN: 0521242436.

Maps and accompanying text in 7 sections: 1. Introductory - 2. Physical environment - 3. Cultural - 4. Demographic - 5. Economic - 6. Communications - 7. Special topics. Gazetteer (*i.e.,* country profiles) p.120-1. Bibliography p.122-4. 'A well-executed, scholarly work of enduring value' (*Reference Books Bulletin 1987-1988*, p.146-8). There is a map by map appraisal in *Middle Eastern Studies*, v.27, no.1, January 1991, p.172-9. *Class No:* 912.0(53+56)

Gulf States

[5280]

ational atlas of The United Arab Emirates. Al Ain, United Arab Emirates in association with Reading, GEOprojects, 1993. 189p. illus., maps, diagrs. ISBN: 0863511007.

Available in Arabic and English-language editions.

1. Maps of U.A.E. (history of cartographic knowledge; topography; topographical map coverage *etc.*) - 2. U.A.E. from space - 3. International, regional and local - 4. Heritage and history - 5. Geology and geomorphology - 6. Climate - 7. Water resources - 8. Biogeography - 9. Population - 10. Land use - 11. Economic - 12. Transport and communication - 13. Education and Health - 14. Cultural. 154 plates in all. Index of geographic names p.155-64. Large format. *Class No:* 912.0(536)

India

[5281]

n Atlas of India. Muthiah, S., *ed.* Delhi, Oxford Univ. Press, 1990. vi,185p. col. maps, tables, index. £30; $79.95. ISBN: 0195625536.

18 general maps for India then physical geography, administration, population, transport and tourism, agriculture, industry, minerals, economic development, and mass communication maps for each of India's 32 states and union territories, 212 maps in all on various scales. 'The administrative maps that show the district and smaller Taluk boundaries within each state and their principal cities are particularly noteworthy' (*Choice*, v.30, no.2. October 1992, p.267). 'Provides a wealth of data ... the definitive atlas for the world's second most-populous nation' (*Booklist*, v.88, no.22, Aug 1992, p.203+4). *Class No:* 912.0(540)

[5282]

ational atlas of India. Calcutta, National Atlas and Thematic Mapping Organization, Department of Science and Technology, Government of India, 1984.

Massive work, 25 years in the making, in 8 large loose-leaf volumes: 1. General and political maps - 2. Physical and geomorphological - 3. Climatic and biogeographical - 4. Population and transport - 5. Land use and industrial - 6. Agricultural and economic - 7. Social and regional - 8. Historical and cultural. In all 300 variously dated maps on basic scale 1:6,000,000. Format allows for extracting single or more maps for detailed scrutiny or for class use.

Despite the maps' old-fashioned and cluttered appearance, the atlas remains a colossal achievement, fully justifying the sense of pride evident in S.P. Dasgupta's preface to v.1. *Class No:* 912.0(540)

Bibliographies

[5283]

GOLE, S. India within the Ganges. New Delhi, Jayaprints, 1983. 239p. facsims., bibliog., index.

1. Indigenous maps - 2. Early European contacts - 3. Portuguese foothold - 4. Finding the way - 5. European rivalry -6. British conquest - 7. Survey maps. Bibliography p.102. 8. Printed maps in India 1447-1800 p.103-228. Division into 2 parts reflects the book's purpose: as a text on how the maps come to be drawn and, secondly, to serve as a reference guide. *Class No:* 912.0(540)(01)

Nepal

[5284]

SILL, M. *and* KIRKBY, J. The Atlas of Nepal in the modern world. London, Earthscan Publications in association with the ETC Foundation. 1991. 159p. illus., maps, tables, bibliog., index. ISBN: 1853830321.

Part 1. Nepal today. Part 2: Natural resources and hazards; water and its uses; tourism and the environment; people and language; towns and industry; land management; land and food; energy; transport; education. Bibliography p.153-6. 'An attempt to provide analytical information that can be used in detailed discussions of environmental and developmental issues' (*Foreword*). *Class No:* 912.0(541.35)

Sri Lanka

[5285]

The National atlas of Sri Lanka. Colombo, Survey Department (Ministry of Lands and Land Development) Sri Lanka, 1988. x,142p. col. illus., maps (some col.), diagrs., tables, index. ISBN: 9559059009.

59 mostly double-paged maps, with authoritative accompanying texts, arranged in 9 categories: 1. Location maps - 2. Maps of Sri Lanka (Ancient and modern maps Geodetic control) - 3. Physical - 4. Archaeology and history - 5. People - 6. Agriculture - 7. Industry, power and transport - Commerce - 9. Government, administration and justice. 'Designed to suit users with a good secondary education. It is not meant for specialists in their own fields'. *Class No:* 912.0(548.7)

Iran

[5286]

HOURCADE, B., *and others*. Atlas d'Iran. Paris, RECLUS-La Documentation Française, 1998. 192p. col.maps, bibliog., index. F320. ISSN: 09990089.

1. The land of Iran - 2. Population - 3. Cultures - 4. Villages - 5. Cities and development - 6. Unequal development - 7. Models of Iranian space. Bibliography p.180-81. 250 maps. Contents page in French and English. *Class No:* 912.0(55)

Turkey

[5287]

Türkiye atlasi/Atlas of Turkey. Istanbul, Milli Egitim Basimevi, 1961. 23 double pl.

Publication of the Faculty of Letters, University of Istanbul. The first national atlas of Turkey. No explanatory text. 87 maps and diagrams, mostly based on original research, but some are compilations or are taken from other sources. Thus, the 44 small maps on climate are based on data of the General Directorate of Meteorology. *Class No:* 912.0(560)

Israel

[5288]

BAHAT, D. *and* RUBENSTEIN, C.T. The Illustrated atlas of Jerusalem. New York, Simon & Schuster, 1990. 152p. illus. col. maps and plans, bibliog., index. $95. ISBN: 0134516427.

First published in Hebrew (Jerusalem, Carta, 1989).

An introductory chapter on topography, and 14 others on the city's history, cover the period from 1,000 BC to the present day. Based on archaeological findings and written sources from each period including *The Bible*. Lavishly illustrated. For this English language edition there is a new section on Jerusalem at the time of Christ and a bibliography (p.148). *Class No:* 912.0(569.4)

[5289]

BENVENISTI, M. *and* KHAYAT, S. The West Bank and Gaza atlas. Jersualem (?), West Bank Data Bank Project, 1990. (Distributed in North America by Westview Press). 140p. maps, tables, pbk. ISBN: 9653560026.

60 thematic maps covering topography, Israeli and Arab population growth and distribution, administrative boundaries, roads, transportation, health, land use *etc*. *Class No:* 912.0(569.4)

[5290]

SURVEY OF ISRAEL. Atlas of Israel cartography physical and human geography. 3rd ed. London, Collier Macmillan, New York, Macmillan, 1985. 232p. $175.00. ISBN: 002905050x.

1st Hebrew ed. published in Tel-Aviv by The Survey of Israel 1956-64. 2nd English ed. 1970. contained 550 colour maps including some not to be found in the 3rd ed.

55 contributors (leading Israeli geographers, cartographers *etc.*). This bilingual Hebrew-English edition contains 400 col. maps on 40 sheets (each sheet consisting of a double-page) 2/3 of which are devoted to settlement patterns and economic geography. Following the map sheets is an English language narrative section which includes statistical data and bibliographies. 'The currency of the third edition both in terms of data and boundaries, and the new thematic maps ... will require that academic and large public libraries purchase it. The second edition should not be discarded, since the volumes complement each other' (*Reference Books Bulletin 1986-1987* p.149).
Class No: 912.0(569.4)

Afghanistan

[5291]

National atlas of the Democratic Republic of Afghanistan. Warsaw, Geokart Poland, 1985(?). xiv,36p. col. maps, bibliog., index. ISBN: 8300023275.

Published in cooperation with the Afghan Geodesy and Cartography Head Office in Kabul.

63 maps depict Afghanistan's physical and socio-economic geography. Bibliography p.xiii-xiv. Published in two versions: in English and in Dari. *Class No:* 912.0(581)

Vietnam

[5292]

LAP, V.T. *and* TAILLARD, C. Atlas du Viêtnam an atlas of Vietnam. Paris, Reclus-La Documentation Française, 1993. 422p. maps. FF298. ISBN: 2110030976.

Thematic maps, mostly dating from 1987, endeavour to present an integrated geographical approach to North and South Vietnam. 'A front runner in a narrow field and an excellent production, this book is highly recommended' (*Geographical Journal*, v.162,no.1, March 1996, p.89). *Class No:* 912.0(597)

Laos

[5293]

Atlas of the Lao P.D.R. Vientiane, National Geographical Department, 1995. 24p. col.illus., col,maps.

17 col.maps compiled from 1990-93 data implemented with the cooperation of the Cartographic Institute for Land Administration. Scale: 1:24,000. *Class No:* 912.0(598)

Islamic World

[5294]

BOUSTANI, R. *and* FARGUES, F. The Atlas of the Arab World geopolitics and society. New York, Facts on File, 1991. 144p. col. illus., col. maps, col. diagrs., tables, index. ISBN: 0816023468.

First published: Paris, Bordas, *Atlas du monde arabe* (1990).

11 thematic map sections including narrative analysis of issues indicated in sub-title: 1. Borders - 2. Ethnic groups - 3. Population ... 8. Oil and industry - 9. Regional unity - 10. The state - 11. Palestine. References p.142. Maps and their sources p.143-4.
Class No: 912.0(5.297)

Africa

Bibliographies

[5295]

McILWAINE, J. Maps and mapping of Africa a resource guide. London, Hans Zell, 1997. xxviii,391p., indexes £60. ISBN: 1873836767.

c.3131 bibliographical references to writings about maps, mapping and toponymy of Africa - both historical and contemporary - including bibliographies and catalogues, mapping and survey material, together with a directory of overseas libraries and archives with African map collections, arranged in 3 parts: 1. Africa in general (map collections; atlases and gazetteers, toponymy, maps & survey) - 2. Africa as mapped by colonial and overseas agencies - 3. By region and country. Name and subject indexes p.353-91. *Class No:* 912.0(6)(01)

[529_]

Maps and plans in the Public Record Office 3. Afric Penfold, P.A., *ed.* London, HMSO, 1982. xii, 426p. index. £36.0 ISBN: 0114401098.

3647 items described with PRO order reference number arranged / Z by country. Illustrate especially the European expansion in th nineteenth and early twentieth centuries, boundary disputes, territori claims, and settlements. Former colonies with their present nam p.vii. Key to record references p.397-399. *Class No:* 912.0(6)(01)

[529_]

NORWICH, O.I. Maps of Africa: an illustrated and annotated cart bibliography. Bibliographical descriptions by Pam Kolb Johannesburg and Cape Town, A.D. Donker, 1983. 444p. illus. (son col.) facsims (some col.) maps on endpapers, index. Rand 95. £65.0 $120.00. ISBN: 0868520284.

345 maps, each with its own cartobibliography, in 8 sections: Continent of Africa - 2. Southern Africa - 3. Cape of Good Hope - Sea charts - 5. North Africa - 6. East Africa - 7. West Africa - { Islands, towns, ports, etc. Historical survey of maps of Africa p.13-3 'Chiefly of interest to collectors and scholars concerned with th authentication of maps' (*Geographical Journal*, v.150, no.2, Ju 1984, p.289-290). *Class No:* 912.0(6)(01)

Tunisia

[529_]

Atlas de Tunisie. Fakhfakh, M., *ed.* Paris, Jeune Afrique, 1979. 72 maps, bibliog.

44 thematic maps and accompanying text. 'A very valuab geographical source book' (A.M. Findlay and others. *Tunisia*, 198 Entry 97). *Class No:* 912.0(611)

Ethiopia

[529_]

National atlas of Ethiopia. Addis Abeba, Ethiopian Mapping Authority 1988. vii,81p. col. maps., illus., diagrs.

76 map features (facing pages of maps and text): Ethiopia in Afric ... Administrative divisions - Topography ... Tourism - Addis Abeb city ... Ancient Ethiopia c.2800 BC to 1270 AD ... Imperi Abassi Geographica ... Ethiopia and the post-colonial neighbouring state 1910-1987 - Wars and invasions. Gazetteer p.153-7.
Class No: 912.0(63)

Morocco

[530_]

Atlas du Maroc. Comité de Géographie du Maroc. Rabat, Institu Scientifique Chérifien, 1956-. maps.

A series of loose maps with explanatory handbooks (30-40p.) Som 200 maps covering 54 topics. *Class No:* 912.0(64)

Mauritania

[530_]

Atlas de la République Islamique de Mauritanie. Paris, editions j.a. 1977. 64p. col.maps, tables, bibliog., index. (*les atlas jeune afrique*. ISBN: 2852580845.

19 thematic maps with text. Documentation et bibliographie p.64.
Class No: 912.0(661.2)

Mali

[530_]

Atlas du Mali. Paris, éditions jeune Afrique, 1980. 64p. col. maps bibliog., index.

20 thematic map features including La Bouche du Niger ... Le Delt Intérieur ... Bamako et sa région. Lexique p.62.
Class No: 912.0(662.1)

Burkina Faso

[530_]

Atlas de la Haute-Volta. Paris. éditions ja., 1975. 47p. col.maps. index ISBN: 2852580144.

15 thematic maps including Histoire ... Tourisme.
Class No: 912.0(662.5)

Niger

[530_]

Atlas du Niger. Paris, éditions j.a., 1980. 64p. col.maps, tables bibliog., index. (*les atlas jeune afrique*.) ISBN: 2852581515. ISSN 03370658.

19 thematic maps with text. Lexique p.62. Documentation e Bibliographie p.64. *Class No:* 912.0(662.6)

Senegal

[5305]

Atlas du Senegal. Pélissier, P., *comp.* 2nd ed. Paris, les éditions jeune afrique, 1983. 72p. col.maps, tables, bibliog., index. (*les atlas jeune afrique.*) ISBN: 2852582880. ISSN: 03370658.

First published 1980.

19 thematic maps with text. Documentation et bibliographie p.72. *Class No:* 912.0(663)

Sierra Leone

[5306]

CLARKE, J.L. Sierra Leone in maps. 2nd ed. London, Univ. of London Press, 1969. 120p.

51 black-and-white maps (usually 1:30M), with explanatory text facing each map. 13 contributors. Bibliography, p.115-20, including many periodical articles. *Class No:* 912.0(664)

Liberia

[5307]

GNIELINSKI, S. van, *ed.* Liberia in maps. London, Univ. of London Press, 1972. 111p. maps, plans.

Black-and-white maps in 50 sections (1. Liberia in Africa - 2. Liberia and her neighbours - 3. Historical background - 4. Geology ... 12. Wildlife ... 22/23. Urban land use - 32. Economic history - 43. Electric power and water supply ... 49. Ports - 50. External trade). 14. contributors - past and present members of the Department of Geography, Univ. of Liberia. Text on left-hand page, facing map. Bibliography, p.109-11. *Class No:* 912.0(666.2)

Ivory Coast

[5308]

Atlas de la Côte d'Ivoire. Vennetier, P., *comp.* 2nd ed. Paris, les éditions jeune afrique, 1983. 72p. col.maps, tables, bibliog., index. (*les atlas jeune afrique.*) ISBN: 2852582872.

First published 1978.

20 thematic maps with text. Bibliographie et documentation p.72. *Class No:* 912.0(666.8)

Cameroon

[5309]

Atlas of the United Republic of Cameroon. Laclavère, G., *ed.* Paris, Éditions Jeune Afrique, 1980. 72p.

33 thematic maps 'A superb document ... very concise, detailed while at the same time being highly informative' (M.W. Delaney and P.J. Schraeder. *Cameroon,* 1986. Entry 13). *Class No:* 912.0(671.1)

Gabon

[5310]

Géographie et cartographie du Gabon: atlas illustré. Barret, J., *ed.* Paris, EDICEP. 1983. 135p. maps. *Class No:* 912.0(672.1)

Congo

[5311]

Atlas de la République Populaire du Congo. Paris, éditions j.a., 1977. 64p. col.maps, bibliog., index. ISBN: 2852580438.

18 thematic map features (inc. Divisions administratives ... Région du Pool ... Région du Niari ... Congo Septentrional). Bibliography p.64. *Class No:* 912.0(672.4)

Central African Republic

[5312]

Atlas de la République Centrafricaine. Vennetier, P., *comp.* Paris, les éditions jeune afrique, 1984. 64p. col. maps, tables, index. (*les atlas jeune afrique.*) ISBN: 2852583127. ISSN: 03370658.

19 thematic map features (inc. Préhistoire et histoire ... Tourisme). Lexique p.60-61. Bibliographie p.64. *Class No:* 912.0(674.1)

Uganda

[5313]

Atlas of Uganda. Uganda Lands and Surveys' Department. 2nd ed. Kampala, Government Printer Uganda, 1967. 81p. maps, illus.

First published 1962.

40 pages of coloured maps (mostly 1:1,500,000), sometimes 12 to a page, each accompanied by explanatory text. Ranges from external communications, physical geography, climate, flora and fauna, human geography, rural economy, industry and trade, to history. Town plans of Kampala and Jinja. Brief gazetteer. 48 x 51cm. *Class No:* 912.0(676.1)

Kenya

[5314]

KENYA. Survey of Kenya. National Atlas of Kenya. 3rd ed. Nairobi, the Survey, 1970. 103p. illus., maps.

43 plates of maps, mostly at 1:3M, with descriptive text facing, and a comprehensive gazetteer. 'Better, more attractive and more informative than its 1959 precedessor' (*The Geographical Journal,* v.137, pt.4, December 1971, p.590-1). *Class No:* 912.0(676.2)

Africa—Southern

[5315]

Reader's Digest atlas of Southern Africa. Cape Town, Reader's Digest Association of South Africa, 1984. Produced in conjunction with the Directorate of Surveys and Mapping, Department of Community Development. 256p. illus., maps, bibliog. £45.00. ISBN: 09477008020.

213 pictorial map features in 3 sections: 1. Anatomy of South Africa (a compendium of facts and figures) - 2. Africa south of the Sahara (a broader view of the African continent with detailed thematic maps and concise notes on the history, economy, population and government of 42 independent states) - 3. Our land in close up. Gazetteer and index (30,000 names) p.214-54. Extensive bibliography (in very small print) p.255-56. Map scales vary but 1:500,000 most common. *Class No:* 912.0(68)

Bibliographies

[5316]

Braby's maps of Southern Africa/Brabyse kaarte van Suidelike Afrika. Durban, A.C. Brady, nd. 24p. sd.

Descriptive catalogue and price list of maps of Transvaal, Orange Free State, Natal, Cape Province and other areas (inc. South African homelands). *Class No:* 912.0(68)(01)

South Africa

[5317]

TALBOT, A.M. *and* TALBOT, W.J. Atlas of the Union of South Africa. Pretoria, Government Printer, 1960. lxiv,177p. maps, tables.

Prepared in collaboration with the Trigonometrical Survey Office and under the aegis of the National Council for Social Research. English and Afrikaans text. All the maps (about 700), except for a few relief, geological and vegetation maps, are black and white, Sections: 1. Relief, geology, mining, soils, vegetation and fisheries - 2. Climate and water resources - 3. Population - 4. Agriculture - 5. Industries and occupations - 6. Transportation - 7. External trade. A scale of 1:8M is used for most maps. Page size. 41 x 56cm. *Class No:* 912.0(680)

Namibia

[5318]

National atlas of South West Africa (Namibia)/ Nasionale atlas van Suidwes-Afrika (Namibie). Van der Merwe, J.H., *ed.* Cape Town. Prepared by the Institute for Cartographic Analysis, University of Stellenbosch for Directorate Development Coordination SWA, 1983. 184 unnumbered pages, tables, diagrs., bibliog. ISBN: 0797200207.

92 full-page maps (each accompanied by a page of text containing a summary of data sources and computational procedures) arranged in 7 sections: 1. Orientation - 2. Natural environment - 3. Settlement structure - 4. Population - 5. Economic structure - 6. Infrastructure - 7. Urban structure. Designed as an official source of spatial information for national and international publication. A short list of reference works is presented 'to gain a perspective of the country as a whole for more background information about specific themes'. *Class No:* 912.0(688)

Zambia

[5319]

DAVIES, D.H., *ed.* Zambia in maps. London, Univ. of London Press, 1971. 128p. maps.

55 black-and-white maps, with text facing (1. Political geography ... 10/11. Early man ... 21. Administrative divisions ... 39. Lusaka ... 55. Regional inequalities and the First National Devlopment Plan). 21 contributors. References p.123. *Class No:* 912.0(689.4)

Malawi

[5320]

The National atlas of Malawi. Lilongwe, Malawi Department of Surveys, 1983. 70p. col.maps.

Maps and explanatory text in loose-leaf binder to allow for new or replacement maps. *Class No:* 912.0(689.7)

Madagascar

[5321]

ASSOCIATION DES GÉOGRAPHES DE MADAGASCAR Tananarive. **Atlas de Madagascar.** Le Bourdiec, F., *sous la direction de*. Tananarive, Bureau pour le Développement de la Production Agricole, Agence de Madagascar, avec la collaboration du Centre de l'Institut Géographique National à Madagascar. 1969-71.

62 maps, 1:4M; 106p. of commentary. 7 sections; Physical, human and rural geography; resources and industries; vie de relations; équipment divers; synethèse regional. Favourably reviewed in *Africa* (v.42, no.3, July 1972, p.261). Page size 40 x 31 cm. *Class No:* 912.0(691)

Mauritius

[5322]

DEVI VENKATASAMY, *and others*. **Philip's atlas of Mauritius.** London, George Philip, 1991. 47p.

'Comprehensive and elaborate in its presentation of the geographical, economic and social features of the islands ... the cartography is of high quality' (Bennett, P.R. and Bennett G.J. *Mauritius*, 1992. Entry no 77). *Class No:* 912.0(698.2)

America—North

[5323]

Basic map library. New York, H.W. Wilson. $59.95. (*Map Library.*)

Basic map library contains 30 maps, including 25 road maps that cover all 50 states, regional maps of the Eastern and Western US, a detailed street map of Washington D.C. and wall maps of the US and the world. Interstate highway system, details of roads in major cities and areas of special interest, and toll road & bridges information, are all featured. *Class No:* 912.0(71+73)

[5324]

—Canadian supplement. New York, H.W. Wilson. $29.95. (*Map Library.*)

12 maps and index dividers designed as a supplement either to *Map Library* or *City map library*. Extends coverage to major metropolitan areas and provinces of Canada. *Class No:* 912.0(71+73)

[5325]

—City map library. New York, H.W. Wilson. $69.96. (*Map Library.*)

37 maps, case and index dividers. Street maps of major US cities with street indexes. *Class No:* 912.0(71+73)

America—North & Central

[5326]

AA big road atlas USA, Canada and Mexico. Basingstoke, Hants, Automobile Association Publications, 2000. 144p. col.maps. £10.99. ISBN: 0749522615.

Published by arrangement with the American Automobile Association.

270 city, national park and recreational maps, 58,400 towns and cities indexed. Border crossing regulations, traffic rules and driving times map. *Class No:* 912.0(71/73)

[5327]

Rand McNally road atlas United States, Canada. Mexico 1999. Chicago, Rand McNally, 1998. 160p. Pbk. £8.99 ISBN: 0528840177. 75th anniversary ed.

407 state, province and country maps, incorporating 320+ city map references. Travel planning information and directories. New to this edition are an 8-page expansion, 24 city maps and 5 larger state maps reflecting population drifts and today's recent tourist destinations. *Class No:* 912.0(71/73)

Canada

[5328]

Atlas of Canada. Reader's Digest Association (Canada) in conjunction with the Canadian Automobile Association, 1981. 220p. col.illus., col.maps, tables, graphs, index. £17.95. ISBN: 0888500963.

1. Thematic features (p.6-59) on geography, geology, history, society, population - 2. Facts about Canada: a compendium of basic knowledge (p.60-76) - 3. Maps of Canada (p.77-177) on various scales drawn with cooperation of Surveys and Mapping Branch. Energy, Mines and Resources Canada - 4. Gazetteer index (p.178-219). *Class No:* 912.0(71)

[5329]

FARLEY, A.L. **Atlas of British Columbia** people, environment and resource use. Vancouver, Univ. of British Columbia Press, 1979. 144p. illus. (some col.), graphs, diagrs, maps.

61 maps sheets (people (11 maps); environment (15); resource use (35). Text, facing map sheets, include references. The reviewer in *Geography* (v.65, pt.3, no.288, July 1980, p.263) considers that the *Atlas* needs more tabulated data and fewer unnecessarily large colour photographs. Page size, 35.5 x 28.5cm. *Class No:* 912.0(71)

[5330]

MATTHEWS, G.J. *and* MORROW, R. **Canada and the world** an atlas resource. Scarborough, Ontario, Prentice Hall Canada. 1985. vii, 201p. illus., maps, graphs, tables, bibliog. ISBN: 0131138464.

1. Canada and the world. 2. Canada: 59 mostly double page regional and thematic maps *e.g.* Exploration; the Provinces today; Native peoples; Far North; Great Lakes. 3. World thematic maps. 4. World regional maps. 5. Canadian statistics. 6. World statistics. Glossary p.185-92. Gazetteer p.193-200. Sources p.201. *Class No:* 912.0(71)

[5331]

National Atlas of Canada. 5th ed. Ottawa, Energy Mines and Resources Canada, 1986-. Box $30.00. Each map $5.50.

First published as *Atlas of Canada* by the Department of the Interior in 1906. 4th ed. under the present title issued in 1974 by the Macmillan Company of Canada.

'The 5th edition is planned as a continuing serial publication of separate but related maps, collectively dealing with all aspects of Canada. When comprehensive coverage of about two hundred map subjects is eventually reached, revision of the original maps will also be underway. The production of revised versions of each map will, in general, depend on the national importance of the subject, the state of scientific and scholarly knowledge in the field, and the public demand for such information' (*The fifth edition The National Atlas of Canada. An Information System*, a brochure issued *gratis* by Energy, Mines and Resources Canada, Canada Map Office, 615 Booth Street, Ottawa, Ontario, KIA OE9). A French version, *L'Atlas National du Canada* is available.

'Eventually all National Atlas data will be stored in digital form to allow rapid updating and information transfer as new research material is received into the National Atlas Information System' (*ibid.*). *Class No:* 912.0(71)

[5332]

North of 50°: an atlas of Far Northern Ontario. Toronto, Univ. of Toronto Press for Royal Commission on the Northern Environment on behalf of the Government of Ontario. xviii, 54 plates, 112-119p. col. maps. ISBN: 0802033873.

54 maps in atlas designed to aid decision-making in the development of Northern Ontario. *Class No:* 912.0(71)

[5333]

RICHARDS, J.H. *and* FUNG, K.I. **Atlas of Saskatchewan.** Saskatoon, Univ. of Saskatchewan, 1969. viii, 236p.

51 Canadian academic contributors. Maps grouped in 12 sections each of which deals with 'a specific but not necessarily separate theme' *e.g.* 2. Historical geography ... 4. Physical geography ... 6-10. Economic geography. Chapter references p.199-201. Gazetteer p.202-236. *Class No:* 912.0(71)

Bibliographies

[5334]

NICHOLSON, N.L. *and* SEBERT, L.M. **The Maps of Canada** a guide to official Canadian maps, charts, atlases and gazetteers. Folkestone, William Dawson and Sons Ltd; Hamden (Conn), Archon Books, The Shoe String Press Inc., 1981. x, 251p., illus., maps, tables. £20.00. ISBN: 0712909117, UK; 0208017828, US.

Comprehensive survey in 17 chapters and 8 appendices. Appendix 1. Some significant dates in the evolution of Canadian mapping. 4. Map coverage of the provinces and territories of Canada. 8. Availability of official Canadian maps, charts, atlases and gazetteers. Notes and references (by chapter) p.240-245; glossary of mapping terms p.246-247; index p.248-251. 'Highly recommended' (*Library Journal*, 1 May 1982, p.878). *Class No:* 912.0(71)(01)

Newfoundland

[5335]

McMANUS, G.E. *and* WOOD, C.H. **Atlas of Newfoundland and Labrador.** St. Johns, Breakwater, 1991. vii,77p. illus., diagrs., bibliog. $49.95. ISBN: 1550810006.

23 thematic map features (including text, graphs, diagrams, illus.) covering environment, culture, demography, communications, tourism, fishing, forestry, energy, *etc.* Gazetteer p.55-65. References and credits p.67-77. *Class No:* 912.0(718)

Mexico

[5336]

tlas of Mexico. Bonine, M.E., *and others*. Rev. ed. Austin, Univ. of Texas, Bureau of Business Research, 1975. 138p. diagrs., tables, maps, pbk. $20.00. ISBN: 0877551871.

1st ed. 1970.

5 major sections of black-and-white maps: Physical setting - Population - Agriculture - Transportation, services and commerce - Industry. Sources stated. Appended statistical tables and diagrams. Appended 2p. of 'General publications'. Uniform scale of maps; 3.5cm: 100 miles. Page size 28 x 37cm. *Class No:* 912.0(72)

[5337]

tlas of Mexico. Pick, J.B., *and others*. Boulder, Colo., Westview Press, 1989. xxi,367p. maps, tables, bibliog., index. $55. ISBN: 0813376955.

135 black and white maps computer plotted from data derived from 1980 census and subsequent annual statistical reports. All but 13 maps focus on political and administrative units. 93 tables.
Class No: 912.0(72)

America—Central

[5338]

RBINGAST, S.A., *and others*. Atlas of Central America. Austin, Univ. of Texas, Bureau of Business Research, 1979. 62p. maps, pbk. $18. ISBN: 0877552622.

38 maps covering terrain, administration, population, economic activity, transportation and geology. Colouring is criticised for lack of clarity. Nevertheless, 'a welcome addition to printed sources dealing with Central America' (*Choice* v.17, no.4, June 1980, p.515).
Class No: 912.0(728)

Costa Rica

[5339]

ALENCIANO, E.C. Atlas cantonal de Costa Rica. San José, Instituto de Fomento y Asesoría Municipal, 1987. 395p. col. maps, bibliog.

Detailed maps of Costa Rica's 7 provinces and of its 81 cantons (counties) each accompanied by a narrative text with information on population statistics, geology, land use, history etc. 'The atlas is a monumental contribution to basic knowledge about Costa Rica and will be of use to researchers and casual students as well as to tourists and investors' (Stansifer, C.L. *Costa Rica*, 1991, entry no.49).
Class No: 912.0(728.6)

Panama

[5340]

tlas nacional de la Republica de Panama. 3rd ed. Panama, Instituto Geographico Nacional, 1988. x,222p. maps. $80.

15 sections combining maps, text, graphs and diagrams: 1. General maps - 2. Physical geography - 3. Natural resources - 4. Population - 5. Silviculture and fishing - 6. Agriculture - 7. Industry - 8. Transport and communication - 9. Commerce - 10. Education and culture - 11. Health and social welfare - 12. Elections - 13. Regional and urban maps - 14. Administrative areas - 15. Index. Scale ranges from 1:500,000 - 1:125,000,000 although mostly 1:1 million. 304 maps *in toto*. 'The atlas is better than similar atlases in Latin America and the Third World. The quality of information the manner of presentation, the volume and thoroughness of the data are first rate' (*Cartographica*, v.28, no.2, Summer 1991, p.115-6). *Class No:* 912.0(728.7)

Caribbean

[5341]

he Atlas of Central America and the Caribbean. New York, Macmillan; London, Collier Macmillan, 1985. 144p. illus. (some col.); col.maps, col.plans, coats of arms, bibliog., index. $40.00; £50.00. ISBN: 0029080207.

Part 1. Regional profile consisting of 7 brief thematic essays - 2. Central America (12 country essays) - 3. The Caribbean (22 essays). Bibliography p.138-41. 'Plagued by so many problems of both a technical and intellectual nature that it is not possible to recommend the purchase of the atlas for either personal or library use' (*The American Cartographer*, v.14,no.2, April 1987, p.183-4). *Class No:* 912.0(729)

Cuba

[5342]

tlas de Cuba XX aniversari del triunfo de la Revolución Cubana. La Habana, Instituto Cubano de Geodesia y Cartografia, 1978. 168p. col. maps, index.

71 maps arranged in 6 sections: 1. Introducción (Cuba y los países vecinos; División político - administrativa 1975, 1979) - 2. Mapas de la naturaleza y recursos - 3. De la economía - 4. De la población y cultura - 5. De la historia - 6. Mapa geográfico general.
Class No: 912.0(729.1)

[5343]

Atlas nacional de Cuba/Natsional'nyi atlas Kuby. Moskva, Glanoe Upravlenie Geodezii i Kartografii MVD SSSR, 1970. 144p. maps.

A co-operative effort of the Cuban and Soviet Institutes of Geography of the Academy of Sciences and the Academia de Ciencias de Cuba.

105 maps. on scales 1:75,000 to 1:1M. General, physical, agricultural, industrial, cultural, historical and population maps, with explanatory text for each group. 23p. of text; 7p. index-gazetteer. (Based on review in *Library of Congress information bulletin*, v.30, no.27, 8 July 1971, p.407). 'An excellent recent atlas' (*Latin American bibliography*. edited by L. Hallewell (1978), p.123. *National atlas of Cuba; complete translation of the Russian-language atlas* (Springfield, Va., 1971, 309p.) (US Joint Publications Research Service. Translations on Latin America, 525) is a translation of the text only. *Class No:* 912.0(729.1)

Jamaica

[5344]

CLARKE, C.G. Jamaica in maps. London, Univ. of London Press, 1974. 104p., diagrs., maps.

42 maps, with text facing (*e.g.* 4. Geology and drainage; 8. Distribution of population; 19. Rural settlement; 22. Selected small towns; 23/25. Kingston (land use; population; housing); 30/32. Export crops; 39. Electricity; 42. External trade. Bibliography p.98-104. Page size 22.5 x 30cm. *Class No:* 912.0(729.2)

[5345]

National atlas of Jamaica. Kingston, Town Planning Department, Ministry of Finance & Planning, 1971. 79p. col. illus., tables, maps.

Maps (on rectos, with descriptive text facing): Location and size - Geology ... Water resources ... Soils and land capability ... Sugar ... Coffee ... Manufacturing - Transportation ... Education ... Monument, historic and archaeological sites - Bathing beaches. 41 tables. Statistical sources. Page size, 30 x 55cm. *Class No:* 912.0(729.2)

Bahamas

[5346]

Atlas of the Commonwealth of the Bahamas. Kingston Publishers. Rev. ed. Nassau, Ministry of Education, 1985. 48p. maps, plans.

38 thematic maps and 45 plans of cities, towns and settlements.
Class No: 912.0(729.6)

Trinidad & Tobago

[5347]

AKAI, A. *and* MATADEEN, J. Atlas for Guyana and Trinidad and Tobago. Rev. ed. London, Macmillan, 1982. 32p. maps.

For school use. *Class No:* 912.0(729.87)

USA

[5348]

The National atlas of the United States. Gerlach, A.C., *ed*. Washington, U.S. Geological Survey, 1970. xiii,417p. maps, diagrs.

765 maps, mostly in colour and many with a two-page spread. General reference maps, followed by thematic maps: physical, climatic and water (74p.); historical (24p.); economic (89p., *i.e.*, 187 maps, including sets); sociocultural (30p.; administrative (24p.); mapping and charting (34p.); political (7p.). One drawback: The tight binding prevents two-page spread maps from being visible at the inner edges. 'Ranks amoung the finest national atlases yet produced' (*Geographical Review*, v.62, no.1, January 1972, p.97). 'The general layout and design is quite superb' (*Cartographic Journal*, v.9, no.1, June 1972, p.65-66). Page size: 47 x 34.5cm. *Class No:* 912.0(73)

[5349]

Rand McNally Quick reference United States atlas. Chicago, Rand McNally, 1998. 64p. col.maps, pbk. £4.99. ISBN: 0528837710.

Individual maps of all 50 states and a 2,500-entry index. Terrain shading shows each state's topography in detail. *Class No:* 912.0(73)

[5350]

Rand McNally state map collection. Chicago, Rand McNally. 1998. $49.95. complete in laminated case. ISBN: 0528811916.

41 individual road maps covering all 50 US states plus US Interstate Highway map. *Class No:* 912.0(73)

[5351]

Rand McNally zip code finder 1999. Stokie, Il., Rand McNally, 1998. 432p. pbk. £6.99. ISBN: 0528839918.

Updated annually.

Over 120,000 ZIP Codes for cities, towns and places. Postal and private carrier rate information. 3-digit ZIP Code maps of all 50 states and Washington, D.C. Detailed ZIP Code maps of 17 major cities
Class No: 912.0(73)

[5352]

USA State maps on file. New York and Oxford, Facts On File, 7v. £250.00 the set or £40.00 each volume. Replacement pages 75p. each.

1200 loose leaf, copyright free outline maps in 7 ring binder volumes: *Mid-Atlantic; Southwest; Mountain and Prairie; West; Midwest; New England;* and *Southeast.* Topics include politics, environment, demographics, physical geography, climate, and history. For school use. *Class No:* 912.0(73)

[5353]

WURMAN, R.S. US atlas. New York, Access Press, 1990. Distributed by Prentice Hall. 144p. col.maps, index. pbk. $12.95. ISBN: 0130017604.

Divides US into 70 maps each 250 miles by 250 miles at a uniform scale of 1:15,480.000. Also 34 metropolitan maps (50 miles by 50 miles) and 8 downtown cente maps (5 miles by 5 miles). Tourist information includes food and accommodation, museums and amusement parks, architecture, weather extremes, and a calendar of events. Index of *c.*10,000 place names. 'US Atlas is a good road atlas. It would be a useful addition to any reference collection' (*Booklist,* v.86,no.12, 15 February 1990, p.1191-2). *Class No:* 912.0(73)

CD-ROM

[5354]

Rand McNally StreetFinder 1999. Chicago, Rand McNally, 1998. CD-ROM Windows. £39.99.

StreetFinder software is the fundamental US street-mapping tool, with new features such as an easier-to-use interface and address-to-address directions via the Internet. *Class No:* 912.0(73)(003.40)

[5355]

Street atlas USA. Freeport, ME, Delorme Mapping, 1994. Distributed by Gale Research Co. CD-ROM. £65. ISBN: 0899339530.

Complete street map of US on a single CD-ROM. Records 12 million street segments and 1 million lakes, ponds, rivers, parks, and railways. Search by phone number, ZIP code or name of city, town, or street. Maps provide data on thousands of streets and developments that didn't exist a few years ago. *Class No:* 912.0(73)(003.40)

[5356]

US atlas. Software Toolworks/Mindscape International. Apple Macintosh, LC or higher, 256 colour monitor, Apple, System 7 or higher, 4Mb, IBM Compatible PC. $59.95.

130 high resolution reference and relief maps, including state maps, regional city maps, county names and boundaries. *Class No:* 912.0(73)(003.40)

Micromaterials

[5357]

PC USA Version 2.0. Mildenhall, Suffolk, Global Network. £59.95.

Electronic atlas which provides current and historical information for all 50 states and Puerto Rico. Included is a self-updating time zone map, detailed state and city data, colorful state flags. System requires IBM PC/XT/AT/PS2 or compatibles with min. 640K RAM floppy drive or hard disk DOS 2.0+. *Class No:* 912.0(73)(003.5)

Bibliographies

[5358]

MAKOWER, J., *ed.* The Map catalog: every kind of map and chart on earth and even some above it. 2nd ed. New York, Vintage Books, 1990. 364p. illus., maps, facsims. $27.50. ISBN: 0394383264.

1st ed. 1986.

Directory of the map resources of the United States in 10 main sections: 1. Travel - 2. Specific areas - 3. Boundaries - 4. Scientific - 5. History - 6. Utility/Services - 7. Water - 8. Sky - 9. Images - 10. Atlases/Globes (in 41 map themes). This edition is significantly restructured. 'Possibly the very best starting point for anyone who wants to obtain a map or information about maps, especially for uncommon types or remote areas ... every map librarian should have a copy' (*Cartographica,* v.28, no.2, Summer 1991, p.107-8). *Class No:* 912.0(73)(01)

[5359]

MILLER, E.W. 'State atlases': major sources of spatial information;, *Journal of Geography,* v.81,no.1, January/February 1982, p.34-6.

Brief reviews of 7 state atlases and a list of 44 others A-Z by state. *Class No:* 912.0(73)(01)

[5360]

SCHWARTZKOPF, R.B. 'State atlases from the eighties', Special Libraries Association. Geography and Map Division *Bulletin* No.155, March 1989, p.21-25.

Bibliography of current State atlases *i.e.* 1980 onwards arranged A-Z by State. 7 references. *Class No:* 912.0(73)(01)

Amerindians, North

[5361]

PRUCHA, F.P. Atlas of American Indian affairs. Lincoln, Univ. of Nebraska Press, 1990. x,191p. maps, bibliog., tables, index. $47.50. ISBN: 0803236891.

109 black and white maps and statistical information covering 'Native Americans' in United States, but not Canada, arranged by topic *e.g.* population by counties and rural areas, land cessions, reservations, sites of Indian uprisings and military operations, using census data up to 1980. 'Lacks focus, balance or consistency as well as an interpretative framework that would enable to reader to make sense of the author's selection of information' (*Journal of the Early Republic,* v.11, no.3, Fall 1991, p.400-1). *Class No:* 912.0(73)(=97)

Alaska

[5362]

Alaska atlas and gazetteer. Freeport, Maine, DeLorme Mapping, 1992. 156p. col.maps, tables, index, softcover. $19.95. £14.95. ISBN: 0899332013.

135 maps reproduced from United States Geological Survey topographical maps on scales of 1:300,000 for densely populated areas and of 1:1,400,000 for remote areas. Gazetteer (visitors information centers, parklands, freshwater fishing, natural features, wildlife refuges, main highway system etc.) p.6-15. Index of place-names and physical features p.146-56. *Class No:* 912.0(798)

Bibliographies

[5363]

FALK, M.W. Alaskan maps: a cartobibliography of Alaska to 1900. New York, Garland, 1983. xxiii,245p. $68.00. ISBN: 0824091329.

1. History of Alaskan cartography (1300-1900) p.xi-xv. 2. Alaskan maps listed chronologically p.3-192. Bibliography p.193-201. *Class No:* 912.0(798)(01)

America—South

[5364]

Atlas of South America. Brawer, M., *ed.* New York, Simon & Schuster, London, Macmillan, 1991. 144p. col. illus., diagrs., col. maps, indexes. $65; £35. ISBN: 0130506427, US; 0333559010, UK.

Pt.1: Overview of region. Pt.2: Physical environment, climate, economy, agriculture, industry and minerals, history, government and politics of South American countries and territories. Sources p.131. Annotated bibliography compiled by Linda Vertrees p.132-8. Glossary p.139. Indexes of place-names and persons. *Class No:* 912.0(8)

Brazil

[5365]

Atlas nacional do Brasil. new ed. Rio de Janeiro, Instituto Brasileiro de Geografia e Estatistica, Conselho Nacional de Geografia, 1966.

50 map-plates (chiefly thematic maps), with statistical data and explanatory text. 5 sections; 1. Political and administrative - 2. Physical - 3. Demographic - 4. Economic - 5. Socio-cultural. Map size 57.48cm. *Class No:* 912.0(81)

Argentina

[5366]

Atlas de la República Argentina. 6th ed. Buenos Ayres, Instituto Geográfico Militar, 1989. 81p. col. maps, tables.

1st ed. 1965.

36 col. maps of provinces and major cities supplemented with physical and socioeconomic information. *Class No:* 912.0(82)

[5367]

RANDLE, P.H. Atlas del Desarrollo Territorial de La Argentina. Buenos Aires, Oikos, 3v., 1981. ISBN: 8449948525 (complete set).

Atlas. xvii, 312 plates, 1p. 8449948523. Maps grouped in 4 sections. 1. El territorio se configura (Cartografia antigua; Etnografia; Expediciones exploraciones y viages; Fronteras internas; Jurisdicciones politicas; J. eclesiasticas; J. de la Justicia Federal; Universidades; Limites internacionales) - 2. La produccion y la poblacion - 3. El equipamiente territorial - 4. El proceso de urbanizacion. Massive 53 cm x 35½ cm format. *Memoria.* 146p. 8449948521. Commentary on maps in atlas. *Serie de estidisticas historicas.* ix, 283p. 844994852x. Statistical table to accompany Pt.2. of Atlas: La produccion y la poblacion. *Class No:* 912.0(82)

Chile

[5368]

tlas de la Republica de Chile. 2nd ed. Valparaiso (?) Instuto Geografico Militar, 1983. 352p. maps.

1st ed. 1982.

196 maps deployed in 4 parts: 1. Antecedentes generales - 2. Mapa Físico de Chile - 3. Mapas temáticos nacionales - 4. Mapas temáticos régionales (Tarapacá; Antofagasta; Atacama; Coquimbo; Valparaíso; Santiago; Libertador General Bernardo O'Higgins; Maule; Bío-Bío; La Araucania; Los Lagos; General Carlos Ibáñez del Campo; Magallanes y de la Antártica Chilena) - 5. Índice de nombres geográficos. *Class No:* 912.0(83)

Bolivia

[5369]

tlas de Bolivia. Barcelona, Ediciones Geomundo, 1985. xii,227p. col. illus., col. maps. ISBN: 8459957012.

121 maps supported by text and illustrations divided in 5 parts: 1. La Tierra y el Espacio - 2. Bolivia y su desarrollo histórico - 3. Bolivia y su divisón politica - 4. Mappas temáticos de Boliva - 5. Población y recursos humanos. *Class No:* 912.0(84) .

Peru

[5370]

EÑAHERRERA DEL AGUILA, C. Atlas del Peru. Lima, Instituto Geografico Nacional, 1989. 399p. illus., maps, tables.

Updates and replaces Aguilla's *Atlas histórico geográfico y de paisajes Peruanos* (1963-70).

Contents include maps and text on locational maps, astronomy, the earth and projection; historical maps, topographical sheets, political and urban maps; physical landscapes; economic and population maps; and Regional and Departmental maps. 'A significant contribution to an understanding of Peru' (*Cartographia*, vol.31,no.3, Autumn 1994, p.66-67). *Class No:* 912.0(85)

[5371]

AVINES, R. Atlas geografico e historico del Peru. Lima, Editorial Bresa, 1996. 259p. col.illus., col.maps, tables. ISBN: 8483891735.

Maps of Peru's 23 Departments A-Z (*e.g.*Amazon, Arequipa, Huancavelica, Lima, San Martin). *Class No:* 912.0(85)

Colombia

[5372]

tlas de Colombia planeó y dirigió la obra. 3rd ed. Bogotá, Instituto Geográfico Agustín Codazzi, 1977. 283p.

190 maps, most of them in colour. 70p. of maps: *c.*300 illus. on 50 plates. 'Of major interest to geographers is the thematic part of the work' (*The Geographical review*, v.59, no.2, April 1969, p.301-2). For the general public rather than the specialist. Page size, 44 x 31cm. *Class No:* 912.0(86)

Venezuela

[5373]

tlas de Venezuela. 2nd ed. Caracas, Direccion de Cartografia Nacional, Ministerio del Ambiente y de los Recursos Naturales Renovables, 1979. viii,331p. col. illus., col. maps.

First published 1969.

Major atlas of 300 maps and text in 8 sections: 1. Referencias Generales - 2. Venezuela historica - 3. Caracas historica - 4. Cartografia basica - 5. Mapas de las Entidades Federales - 6. Mapas regionales - 7. Cartografia tematica - 8. Miscelaneas. *Class No:* 912.0(87)

Australasia & Oceania

[5374]

NTHEUME, B. *and* **BONNEMAISON, J. Atlas des îles et états du Pacifique Sud.** Montpellier, GIP Reclus; Paris, Publisud, 1988. 126p. col.maps, tables, bibliog. ISBN: 286600417135; 2869120213.

In 2 main sections: 1. Le Pacifique, les Pacifiques? 14 thematic chapters *e.g.* origins of peoples; discovery; population intensity; migration; trade, commerce, tourism *etc.* 2. Le Pacifique Sud d' île en île: each island described with map, statistical tables, and references. Bibliography p.124-6. 'Cet atlas est un instrument de travail moderne, attrayant, indispensable pour tous ceux qui veulent s'initier aux réalités de Pacifique d'aujourd'hui' (*Les Cahiers D'Outre-Mer*, no.170, Avril-Juin 1990, p.205-60). *Class No:* 912.0(9)

Indonesia

[5375]

SCARLETT, C. Road atlas of Indonesia. London, New Holland, 1996. 72p. col.illus., col.maps, tables, index. pbk. £6.99. (*Globetrotter Travel Atlas*.) ISBN: 1853684465.

Featuring locator maps, climatic charts, representational road maps and distances, large scale maps, and travel information panels. *Class No:* 912.0(910)

Philippines

[5376]

The Philippine atlas. Manila, Fund for Assistance to Private Education, 2v., 1975. illus., diagrs., tables, maps & overlays.

1. *A historical, economic and educational profile of the Philippines.* 304p. 2. *Directory of schools, assistance groupings and index.* 125p. V.1 has good coloured maps, with text facing. V.2 includes distribution maps of universities and institutions (governmental and non-governmental), a glossary and place-name index (*c.*2,500 entries), as well as a general index. Page size, 31 x 38cm. *Class No:* 912.0(914)

New Zealand

[5377]

AA illustrated road atlas of New Zealand. Auckland (?), Landsdowne Press (?), 1997. 112p. col.illus., col.maps, index. ISBN: 1869582195.

A combination of a New Zealand road atlas and a colourful travel guide 30 pages of mapping and a 16 page place name index. The 60 page Travel and Recreation Guide includes detailed information of what to see and do. *Class No:* 912.0(931)

[5378]

GREAT BRITAIN. Ordnance Survey. New Zealand touring atlas. Southampton, Ordnance Survey, 1998. softback. £11.99. ISBN: 1875992901.

Ordnance Survey also publish maps of *New Zealand* (1875992111); *Auckland* (1875992146); *North Island* (18759212x); and *South Island* (1875992138). *Class No:* 912.0(931)

[5379]

KELLY, J. *and* **MARSHALL, B. Atlas of New Zealand boundaries.** University of Auckland Press, 1996. 325p. ISBN: 1869401492. ISSN: 01121545.

Maps on scale 1:600,000 depicting administrative and statistical boundaries arranged in 13 sections. V.1 includes 1. Territorial and statistical - 2. Environment - 3. Land - 4. Agriculture and fisheries - 5. Forest, power and mineral resources. V.2. 6. Trade and industry - 7. Planning and development - 8. Transport and communications - 9. Judicial - 10. Finance and insurance - 11. Services, welfare and defence - 12. Government and politics - 13. Religion, culture and sport. Ring binder format allows for convenient insertion of updated material. *Class No:* 912.0(931)

[5380]

MacKENZIE, D.W., *ed.* **Heinemann New Zealand atlas.** Auckland, Heinemann in association with the Department of Survey and Land Information, 1987. 31p. of text+117 pages of maps +46 unnumbered pages of gazetteer. $NZ75.00.

117 sectional maps on scale 1:250,000 based on the Department's New Zealand Map Series. Text gives information on plate tectonics, climate, vegetation, forestry, urbanization *etc.* Gazetteer of 20,000 entries. *Class No:* 912.0(931)

Australia

[5381]

Atlas of Australia. 2nd ed. Sydney, Reader's Digest (Australia), 1994. 304p. col.illus., col.maps, index. ISBN: 0864386958.

Profiles of Australia (*e.g.* Land we live in ... Coast of the island continent ... Aboriginal lands and claims) p.8-57; Capital cities p.58-73; Australian maps (scale 1:1 million) p.74-223. Gazetteer p.225-304. *Class No:* 912.0(94)

[5382]

Atlas of South Australia. Griffin, T. *and* McCaskill, M., *eds.* Adelaide, South Australian Government Printing Division, 1986. xiv,134p. maps, bibliog., index. A$55.00. ISBN: 0724346880.

55 thematic map features in 5 main sections: 1. Course of settlement - 2. Environment and resources - 3. Production - 4. South Australians - 5. Regional maps. Gazetteer of 2000 place-names (p.121-8). Chronology p.129-30. Map sources p.130-1. Bibliography p.131. 'Should become a milestone of its type in cartography' (*Bulletin. Society of University Cartographers*, v.21, no.2, 1988, p.117). *Class No:* 912.0(94)

[5383]

Atlas of Victoria. Duncan, J.S., *ed*. Melbourne, Victoria Government Printing Office, 1982. xv,239p. col.illus., col.maps, tables, diagrs. A$39.95. ISBN: 0724182551.

40 thematic sections *e.g.* 14. Prehistory ... 15. History ...38. Topography forming an inventory of resources and a portrayal of the State in the late 1970s. Section 39 Gazetteer (names on topographic maps) p.217-225. Section 40 Index. 170 maps and diagrams, 209 illus. 'A handsome work, at once technically impressive and aesthetically pleasing' (*Geographical Journal*,v.149, no.3, November 1983, p.392-4.). *Class No:* 912.0(94)

[5384]

Australia road atlas. Southampton, Ordnance Survey, 1997. 12.99. ISBN: 0319008991.

Includes 4WD section, full National Park listings, quick find distance chart, and place name gazetteer. *Class No:* 912.0(94)

[5385]

Philip's illustrated atlas of Australia. Rev. ed. 1981. South Yarra, Victoria, George Philip, 1981. 178p. col. illus., col. maps, col. diagrs. ISBN: 0855507128.

First published 1977 as *The pictorial atlas of Australia*.

The physical, economic and social aspects of each state presented on a scale appropriate to its size. Includes sections on New Zealand, Islands of the West Pacific, and Papua New Guinea. Gazetteer (over 7000 entries) p.150-178. Over 100 maps. For home and school use. *Class No:* 912.0(94)

Bibliographies

[5386]

Australian maps. Canberra, National Library of Australia, 1968-. Quarterly with annual compilations (1968-1981); annual 1982-. ISSN: 00450677.

1987v. (1988. viii, 171p.+6p. maps.) Aims to provide a comprehensive list of published maps representing areas within Australia and its territories and other maps with Australian associations. Based on acquisitions at the National Library of Australia and arranged according to the classification set out in Boggs. S.W. and Lewis, D.C.*The classification and cataloguing of maps and atlases* (New York, SLA, 1945) with the Australasia area developed by the Mitchell Library of the State Library of New South Wales. Directory of Australian map publishers and retailers p.129-171. *Class No:* 912.0(94)(01)

Papua—New Guinea

[5387]

Papua New Guinea atlas. King, D. *and* Ranck, S., *eds*. Robert Brown (Australia) in conjunction with Univ. of Papua New Guinea, 1980. 109p. col. illus., maps (some col.), bibliogs.

Over 40 contributors. Arranged in 3 parts: 1. The changing face of the nation (archaeology and early man) - 2. The physical environment - 3. Information resources. Well-documented. *Class No:* 912.0(954)

Polynesia

[5388]

Atlas de la nouvelle - Calédonie et Dépendences. Combroux, J. Paris, Éditions de l'Office de la Recherche Scientifique et Technique Outre-mer, 1981. ISBN: 2709906015.

53 map features in 6 sections: 1. L'Environement géographique et océanique - La Nature dans l'Archipel Nouvelle - Calédonien - 3. Les populations, leur origine et leur implantation - 4. L' Espace rural: son occupation et son utilisation - 5. L'Économie Calédonienne - 6. L'Encadrement, les équipements sociaux, l'urbanisation. *Class No:* 912.0(96)

Micronesia

[5389]

KAROLLE, B.G. Atlas of Micronesia. 2nd ed. Honolulu, Bess Press, 1993. 122p. maps, tables, bibliog, index. ISBN: 1880188503.

3 sections: 1. Introduction to Micronesia (physical setting, flora, prehistory, contact with Europeans, colonial rule). 2. Micronesia as a whole (population, canoes and navigation, economic development, tourism, education, and gazetteer. 3. Focus on Guam, Saipan, Palau, Yap, Chuuk, Pohnpei, Kosrue, Majuro Atoll, and Kwajalein. Bibliography p.113-16. *Class No:* 912.0(965)

Hawaii

[5390]

Atlas of Hawaii. 2nd ed. Honolulu, Univ. of Hawaii Press, 1983. 238p col.illus. col.maps, tables, bibliog., index. ISBN: 0824808371.

First published 1973.

Nearly 300 reference, environment, cultural, and social map followed by an extensive Bibliography (46 sections) p.223-230 an Gazetteer p.231-238. 'Characterized by careful scholarship completeness and vivacity of presentation' (*American Reference Boo Annual*, 1974, item 476). *Class No:* 912.0(969)

Polar Regions

[5391]

UNITED STATES. Central Intelligence Agency. **Polar regions atlas** Washington, Superintendent of Documents, CIA, 1978. 65p. illus. diagrs., maps.

The two Polar regions are dealt with separately but similarly. Each part consists of double-page maps (35 x 45cm.) on 15 'issues' o themes (*e.g.* Arctic, p.6-33: Arctic issues - Discovery - Climate - Physical features - Sea ice - Climatic change - Permafrost - Northern development - Aboriginal people - Fisheries - Mining - Oil and gas - Transportation - Environmental protection - Science programs - Sovereignty problems). Arctic gazetteer/index, p.58-63 (*c.*1,20 entries); Antarctic gazetteer, p.64-65 (*c.*400 entries), - including name of national research stations. Folding map of each region 1:17,250,000. Well-drawn maps. 'An invaluable summary of the geography of both polar regions' (H.G.R. King *The Arctic*, entry 21). *Class No:* 912.0(98/99)

Antarctic

[5392]

Antarctica great stories from the frozen continent. Sydney, Reader's Digest, 1985. 320p. illus. (many col.), col. maps. £17.95. ISBN 0949819646.

39 major contributors. 1. Continent and its wildlife (21 species and geographical double-page spreads - 2. The explorers in chronological order - 3. Atlas (p.286-91) and chronology (p.292-91). Good quality pictorial and encyclopedic atlas. *Class No:* 912.0(99)

World Atlases

[5393]

Atlante Enciclopedico Touring. Milano, Touring Club Italiano, 3v-. 1986-.

V.1. *Italia* 1986. xviii, 160p. 8836502989. Explanatory sections as how maps are made *i.e.*, impact of scale, use of satellite imagery, and Glossary. 4 Major sections: 1. Thematic maps on various scales *e.g.* geomorphology, land use, vegetation, settlement, urban development - 2. Regional analysis: satellite, physical, political, environmental and industrial maps of each of Italy's 6 major regions - 3. National synthesis: general physical, population, migration, industrial employment, energy and regional data for Italy's 20 administrative regions - 4. International comparative maps setting Italy in its E.E.C. and world contexts. Glossary p.131-143. Bibliography p.144-45. V.2 *Europa* 180p. 8836502997. 3 major sections: 1. General and thematic maps with essential geographical, economic and political features, mostly at 1:20,000,000 - 2. Principal European regions *e.g.* Scandinavia, Iberia, Italy and the Balkans, Soviet Union at 1:5,000,000 - 3. Physical-political maps at 1:2,500,000 mostly duplicating previous information. Glossary p.135-45. Bibliography p.146-47. V.3: *Paesi Extraeuropei*. 1988. 189p. 8836503004. 5 main sections (Asia, Africa, The Americas, Australia including Pacific and Polar regions). Each set: standard set of maps, physical environment, politics and administration, economy, geography. Final section of thematic maps. 'As in the first two volumes, the quality of cartography and printing is by and large excellent' (*Bulletin of The Society o University Cartographers*), v.23, no.2, December 1991, p.53). *Class No:* 912.01

[5394]

Bartholomew world atlas. 13th ed. Edinburgh, John Bartholomew, 1985. xvi,100,79p. col.illus., col.maps, index. ISBN: 0702806196.

First published as *The Edinburgh world atlas*, 1st-8th eds. (1954-73) and subsequently under its present title, 9th-12th eds. (1974-82).

1. Introductory features (geographical terms; projections; world climate; communication, exploration *etc.*) - 2. Maps are mainly physical but also with a heavy thematic coverage. 17 different layer colours. Gazetteer of 30,000 place names. An excellent general-purpose world atlas. *Class No:* 912.01

[5395]

he Book of the World. Rev. ed. New York, Macmillan, 1999. 533p. col.illus., col.maps, index. $465. ISBN: 0028649664.

1st published 1996.

World regional maps on scale of 1:4,000,000; North America maps 1:2,000,000. Includes 64p. section of maps of major cities and 85p. section on natural landscapes extending over 29 climatic zones. 'A magnificent example of bookmaking as well as digitised mapmaking that also utilizes color photography, effective and attractive page and symbol design, and descriptive text to convey a real sense of the planet's beauty and grandeur' (Booklist, v.92, no.21, July 1996, p.1845-46). 'Any library without the first edition should certainly consider purchase of this fantastic atlas' (Booklist, v.95, no.19/20, 1+15 June 1999, p.1872).

The Macmillan World Atlas. 1996. 415p. col.maps, index, $59.95. 0028608127. 100 double page maps of world at 1:4,500,000 and 31 maps North America at 1:2,250,000. Separate section of physical maps of continents and oceans at 1:40,000,000. *Class No:* 912.01

[5396]

he Cartographic satellite atlas of the world. London, Map Marketing Ltd., 1998. 144p. index.

Based on a true (not simulated) view of earth from 800 kms into space, the images have been created by processing signals gathered by circling satellites. Glossary and index of 11,000 names. *Class No:* 912.01

[5397]

:ollins atlas of the world. 4th ed. London, Harper Collins, 1999, xl,224p. col.illus., col.maps, index. £30. ISBN: 0004485629.

1. Geographical encyclopaedia: 15 double-page spreads *e.g.* Earth structure, Oceans, History of maps, Key to maps, Use of maps. 2. World atlas of 128p. of maps on different large (1:1,000,000 or 1:2,500,000), medium (1:7,500,000), or small scales according to shape, size, and density of detail. 3. Geographical data (world physical and political data, and Nations of the World. Glossary p.136-8. Place-name index (40,000 names) p.141-224. *Collins concise atlas of the world.* 200p. ISBN 000447824x is based on the full atlas and has 96p. of full colour maps. *Class No:* 912.01

[5398]

he Dorling Kindersley world reference atlas. 2nd ed. London, Dorling Kindersley, 1996. 757p. col.illus., col.maps, index. £35. $49.95. ISBN: 0751303925.

1st ed. 1994.

4 sections: The World Today (historical and physical maps p.14-49) - 2. Nations of the World (for each nation a summary overview, maps, and information on climate, communications, tourism, politics, defence, economy, resources, ecology etc. plus historical chronology and flag p.52-651) - 3. Global issues (population, hunger and disease, world economy, communications etc.) - 4. Index - Gazetteer. (International Organisations, geographical place-names, glossary of geographical terms, A-Z index/gazetteer of 20,000 places) p.654-755. More than 6,000 maps in all. A satisfying world atlas and geographical compendium.

World reference atlas CD-ROM. Windows version 0751315095; Mac version 075131346. *Class No:* 912.01

[5399]

:oode's world atlas. Espenshade, E.B., *ed.* 20th ed. Chicago, Rand McNally, 1999. 384p. col. illus., col. maps, tables, indexes. £24.99. ISBN: 0528839985.

Emphasis on newly updated physical-political maps and especially on US thematic maps 'addressing current societal concerns: education, wealth, poverty, hazardous waste sites, and health care'. Also world thematic maps (military and economic alliances, nuclear and solar energy, agriculture, minerals) and large-scale maps (1:300,000) of 62 metropolitan areas. 'An excellent supplement to larger atlases ... few atlases of this size are in *Goode's* class' (*General Reference Books for Adults*, 1988, p.208). *Class No:* 912.01

[5400]

The Hammond atlas of the world with CD-ROM. Maplewood, NJ., Hammond, 1997. 303p. col.maps, index. $79.95. ISBN: 0843711752.

Created from a digitized database, incorporating data from orbiting satellites, satellite imagery, and unique software, and drawn on the Optimal Conformal projection, the maps in this atlas are claimed to have only a 2% distortion. *Contents:* Interpreting maps (evolution of cartography, map projections) - Quick/ref guide (A-Z listing of all the world's political entities, their size and population) - Global relationships (environmental concerns, energy and resources, climate, vegetation) - Physical world (13 'Terrascape' TM physical maps) - Maps of the World (in 6 continental regions, with 70 inset maps for metropolitan and special areas) (p.50-208) - Statistical tables and 115,000 entry index. 'Overall, this superb atlas is clear, accurate, attractive and a great pleasure to use' (*Reference Reviews*, v.8,no.6 (1994), p.39-40).

'CD-ROM offers a number of attractive features including a tool bar with icons that enable functions such as measuring distance and determining population and current time; an advanced search function; and an almanac that is hyperlinked with the maps. Other features

....(contd.)

include the ability to display thematic maps and to convert the information in the thematic maps to pie charts and graphs' (*Booklist*, v.94, no.2, 15 September 1997, p.264). *Class No:* 912.01

[5401]

'National Geographic' Atlas of the world. 7th ed. Washington, National Geographic Society, 1999. 280p.+136 index p., col.illus., col.maps, col.graphs. $125. ISBN: 0792275284.

First published 1963. Fully revised since 1992 edition.

Fully revised up to date (*e.g.* Hong Kong and Macao reverted to China, new Canadian province of Nunavut). 300 maps, 13 satellite images. Each continent is introduced by satellite, political and physical maps and a country summary section; Political maps follow for countries and regions. Detail maps of 231 cities and urban areas. Thematic maps on climate, world population, the biosphere etc. Glossary of foreign terms. Index of 150,000+ place names. A very attractive large atlas. 'Should not be absent from the shelves of any respectable library' (*Geographical Journal*, v.158, no.1, March 1992, p.95).

Continually updated on *National Geographic's* web resource: nationalgeographic.com/mapmachine. *Class No:* 912.01

[5402]

The New international atlas. 25th anniversary edition. Chicago, Rand McNally, 1999 (updated). 560p. col.maps, tables, index. £99. ISBN: 0528838083.

25th anniversary edition first published 1992.

Rand McNally's flagship atlas. 255 map pages include world, ocean, continental maps; 50 x 16 miles to the inch (1:1,000,000) maps of key regional areas of exceptional economic importance, high density of population, or confronting complex transport needs; and 60 urban maps at scale of 5 miles to the inch (1:300,000) for major world metropolitan areas. Textual matter is in 5 languages: English, French, German, Portuguese and Spanish, with place-names in the local language (country names in English and in local official form). An unusual feature is three-dimensional shadings for mountains and valleys. 160,000 world names (including 35,800 US) are indexed. 'If a collection lacks the twenty-fifth anniversary edition of the New International, it is sadly and inexplicably deficient' (*Wilson Library Bulletin*, v.69, no.7, March 1995, p.83. *Class No:* 912.01

[5403]

Peters atlas of the world. Harlow, Longman, 1989. 226p. illus., col. maps. bibliog. £29.95. ISBN: 0582035015.

1. The world in 43 double page maps each representing 1/60 of the earth's surface. 2. Nature, man and society *i.e.*, 246 thematic maps (each showing global data by colour, not symbols). 3. Index p.189-226. Principal sources of information on thematic maps p.96. The distinctive feature of this atlas is the use of Arno Peter's own projection, designed to show the Earth in its true proportion, which lends the continental outlines an unfamiliar aspect. 'The very demerits of the Peters world projection could well be commercially helpful for sales of the atlas in developing countries but only the cartographically naive will be deceived and fail to be exasperated by the pretentious and misleading claims made for the atlas by the authors and publishers' (*Geographical Journal*, v.155,no.2, July 1989, p.295-7). *Class No:* 912.01

[5404]

Philip's atlas of the World. Comprehensive edition. 10th ed. London, George Philips in association with the Royal Geographical Society, 2000. 416p. col.maps, col. tables, index. £50. ISBN: 054007893x.

As well as 176 pages of the latest digital world mapping and 6 pages of detailed world statistics, it contains the highly informative 48-page *Introduction to World Geography* which combines text, maps, charts and diagrams to explain key world themes. An added feature for this edition is a new City Maps section, featuring large-scale and fully indexed city centre plans along with brand new approach maps to 67 of the world's most important cities. The 128-page, 75,000-entry index includes geographical features as well as place names. Attractively produced to a high standard. *Class No:* 912.01

[5405]

Philip's encyclopedic world atlas. London, Philip in association with the Royal Geographical Society, 2000. 288p. £25. ISBN: 0540077704.

The atlas opens with a 18-page section, which includes country, city and physical statistics, and is followed by a 32-page introduction to the continents of the world. The main body of the atlas is arranged alphabetically, country-by-country, each country profiled with a concise text describing the main features of landscape, climate, history, politics and economy, and accompanied by a full-colour map. Cities, towns and major communication routes are marked and a 25,000-name index provides rapid reference to the maps. *Class No:* 912.01

[5406]

Rand McNally Cosmopolitan world atlas. Chicago, Rand McNally, 1999. 336p. col.maps, index. £49. ISBN: 0528838091.

Part of the Rand McNally atlas list for more than 40 years. The *Cosmopolitan* includes maps of each U.S. state and Canadian province - a special Rand McNally feature. Highlights include: 221 maps featuring topographical relief and colorful "ribbons" delineating today's political boundaries. More than 69,000 indexed place names, "Real World" section offering encyclopedic information on economic activity, terrain, languages and, population tables and U.S. ZIP Code information.

Rand McNally Today's World. 1999. 200p. col.maps, index. £19.99. features a collection of maps excerpted from the Cosmopolitan World Atlas. 59,000 indexed place names. *Class No:* 912.01

[5407]

Rand McNally travelers' world atlas and guide. Chicago, Rand McNally, 1998. 256p. col. maps, index. £11.50 ISBN: 0528837192.

This guide includes a full 62-page world atlas plus detailed maps of more than 60 major cities. Other features include an extensive country-by-country section highlighting important travel information such as clothing needs, climate, telephone dialing codes, holidays around the world and international travel tips. *Class No:* 912.01

[5408]

Rand McNally world atlas of nations. Chicago, Rand McNally, 1995. 256p. col. illus., col. maps. $39.95. ISBN: 0528836188.

Maps of 216 nations, dependencies, protectorates *etc.* presented A-Z and not geographically. 'The arrangement, as text, statistical data, and color photographs are more prominent than the maps' making it 'an effective ready-reference source for basic information and a quick overview' (*Booklist,* v.85, no.10. 15 January 1989, p.853). *Class No:* 912.01

[5409]

Reader's Digest illustrated world atlas. Rev. ed. London, The Reader's Digest Association, 1997. 288p. col. maps. £29.95. ISBN: 0276422899.

Previously published as *Reader's Digest atlas of the world.*

Totally redesigned, this edition is presented in 4 main sections: 1. The story of the earth - 2. The World in maps (supplied by Rand McNally— 3. Nations of the World (brief guide to 192 nations) - 4. World gazetteer (42,000 names). 'This atlas is a mixed bag ... if you require a reasonable level of detail in maps combined with a basic introduction to the geographical concepts and not too high a price, then [this atlas] may well fill the bill' (*The Bulletin of The Society of Cartographers,* v.31,no.1, 1997, p.38-39). *Class No:* 912.01

[5410]

SMITH, D. **The State of the world atlas.** 6th ed. London, Penguin Reference, 1999. 144p. col. maps, tables, index, pbk. £11. ISBN: 0140514465.

5th ed. 1995.

50 extensively revised double-page maps in 6 pts: 1. Intimations of mortality - 2. People - 3. Work and business - 4. The State - 5. Holds on the mind - 6. Numbers game. Notes to maps p.133-54. Sources p.155-57. *Class No:* 912.01

[5411]

The Times atlas of the world. Comprehensive ed. 10th ed. London, Times Books, 1999. 544p. col.illus., col. maps,. diagrs., index. £125. ISBN: 0723007926.

2000 Millenium edition is the 'first completely revised and redesigned edition' since the 1st ed. (1967). Published in the U.S. by Random House. $250. ISBN 081295265x.

124 plates of maps (nearly all double page spread). Various scales: most European countries at scales ranging from 1:500,000 to 1:250,000; most cities and islands inset maps are at 1:250,000. 15 different styles of Times Roman lettering ensures high standards of legibility. Spelling of place names corresponds to the principles and practices of the British Permanent Committee on Geographical names. English conventional names of important places added where space permits. Chinese names in Pinyin style. Preliminaries include 'The Earth Today; Stars and planets; The World in 2000; Mapping the world; and Geographical information are produced by digital technology and are arranged by continent: Oceania (Pacific Islands, Australasia and Southwest Pacific, New Zealand and Australia) - Asia - Europe - North America - South America - Antarctica. Following the maps are a Glossary (p.1-5) and an Index-Gazetteer of 200,000+ place names (p.6-223).

'This new edition of a classic reference source is a beautiful, comprehensive, and well-done depiction of the world at the beginning of a new millennium. Its closest competitor is the second edition of *The Book of the World,* which is larger and flashier but has an index half the size. Priced at about half the cost of *The Book of the World, The Times Atlas of the World* should be considered for purchase by all libraries'. (*Booklist,* v.96, nos. 9/10, 1+15 January 2000). *Class No:* 912.01

[5412]

—**The Times atlas of the world. Concise ed.** Barraclough, G., *ed.* 7th.ed. London, Times Books, 1997. 84p.+179p. maps + 110p. index. col.illus., col.maps, col.diagrs. ISBN: 0723007187, UK.

178 pages of entirely new world reference mapping based for the first time on Bartholonew's digitised databases. Maps were selected with historical, cultural, political and economic links in mind as well as physical geography. Scales: continental maps 1:15.5 million and 1.30m; regional maps 1.7.5m to 1:12.6m; local maps: 1.3m and 1:6.6m. Map sequence starts at International Date Line in the Pacific and works westwards. Guide to the states and territories p.10-33. Physical earth p.34-47. Geological comparisons p.48-49. Climate p.54-55. Vegetation p.56-57. Earthquakes and volcanoes p.58-59. City plans p.65-80. *Class No:* 912.01

[5413]

—**The Times atlas of the world. Family edition.** 3rd ed. London, Times Books; 1996. 68+156p. maps, tables, index. £17. ISBN: 0723008094, UK.

Introductory section includes states and territories of the world (col. flag, area, population, capital, currency *etc.*), physical maps, solar system, earthquakes and volcanoes, annual rainfall, population and geographic dictionary (p.94-9). Plans of 50 cities. Index of 30,000 entries. For home, school and office use. 'Excellent value, although obviously less comprehensive than the main edition' (*Good Book Guide,* no.44, September/October 1989, p.18). *Class No:* 912.01

[5414]

Today's world a world atlas from the cartographers of Rand McNally. Stokie, Il., Rand McNally, 1992. 200p. col. maps, index. $29.95. ISBN: 0528835009.

New, accurate, large-format political and topographical atlas. National boundaries clearly shown with special markings for disputed, undefined, or indefinite frontiers. Alternative and historical names of cities indicated. Up-to-date information on united Germany, divided Soviet Union, and confused Yugoslavia. Large-scale regional maps of US and Canada. Place-name index of over 45000 entries. 'Does an admirable job of portraying the countries of the world with current boundaries' (*Booklist,* v.89, no.11, 1 Feb 1993, p.1005). *Class No:* 912.01

Databases

[5415]

The Times world map and database. Glasgow, Harper Collins, 1994. £45. ISBN: 0723006962.

Mapping includes *5,000 places and geographical features; 50 statistical categories; 6 map scales from 1:96 million to 1:4 million; 9 colour palettes; Over 1,000 map views; Over 400,000 different map combinations; World time zones with animated clock face; and rapid zoom and pan facilities.* Search and locate facilities include full index search; point and click to name a feature; and rapid pinpointing. This product requires a PC with hard disk and 3.5" floppy disk plus a mouse or other pointing device, running Windows 3.1 or above. *Class No:* 912.01(003.4)

CD-ROM

[5416]

3D atlas 98 CD-ROM. Langley, Berks., Creative Wonders, Electronic Arts Ltd., 1998. PC and Apple Mac.

Updates original *3D Atlas* (1996).

Maps reflect changes in world boundaries and demographic information. Statistics on world's cities and 200 city maps. Profiles of 250 countries. 2000 photographs. Web access. *Class No:* 912.01(003.40)

[5417]

Global Explorer CD-ROM. Freeport, ME, Delorme Mapping, 1994. Distributed by Gale Research Co. CD-ROM DOS stand-alone. £57. ISBN: 0899339522.

Provides detailed maps of the globe with planning, zooming and other features to help users locate specific places. Users can point and click on any worldwide destination to obtain detailed maps and pinpoint national and provincial boundaries, bodies of water, urban highways and major highways. Also presents elevation data and coverage patterns indicating wet-lands, glaciers, oil fields and other features. Brief text descriptions for 20,000 points of interest, spanning categories from archeological sites to volcanoes. Detailed street maps for 100 international cities. Text, statistics and charts present general information about the geography, government, economy and population of countries and dependencies around the globe. *Class No:* 912.01(003.40)

[5418]
ational Geographic maps on CD-ROM. PC Windows 95/98. £59.99.
'A powerful search engine lets you explore the entire catalogue of maps through a number of options - continent, country, geographical regions such as the Mediterranean, even titles like "exploration and discovery" - or the publication date of the magazine and the former country names ... Although this is well presented and the maps are of an excellent quality, it is difficult not to feel that *National Geographic* has simply scanned a pile of maps from the past 109 years of its history and simply put them on to CD-Roms.' (*Times Interface,* 28 April 1999, p.7). *Class No:* 912.01(003.40)

Micromaterials
[5419]
C Globe version 4.0. Mildenhall, Suffolk, Global Network. £59.95.
An electronic desk-top atlas, which provides instant profiles of 190 countries and dependencies in one source. Annually updated, the profiles include maps, graphics, facts and figures, a picture of the national flag and even a rendition of the national anthem. With world, continent and country maps, the atlas can also display major city locations, landscape elevations, lakes, rivers, mountains. System requires IBM PC/XT/AT/PS2 or compatibles with min. 640K RAM floppy drive or hard disk DOS 2.0+. *Class No:* 912.01(003.5)

Regional Atlases

Marine World
[5420]
he Times atlas and encyclopaedia of the sea. Couper, A., *ed.* 2nd ed. London, Times Books, 1989. 272p. col. illus., col. maps, bibliog., index. £27.50. ISBN: 0723003181.
Previously published as *The Times atlas of the oceans* (1983).
26 contributors. *Contents:* 1. The ocean environment - 2. Resources of the ocean - 3. Ocean trade - 4. The world ocean. 11 appendices: 2. Geography of oceans and seas ... 7. Shipping routes - 8. The strategic use of the oceans (world naval operations and gunboat diplomacy 1950-88) - 9. Study of the sea (Maritime Museums A-Z by country; Programmes conducted within the International Decade of Ocean Exploration 1971-80) ... 11. Law of the sea (p.241-7). Glossary p.248-54. Sources p.255-6. Bibliography p.256-7. *Class No:* 912.6

914/919 Gazetteers & Guide Books

Gazetteers & Guide Books

[5421]
Baedeker guides. Basingstoke, Hampshire, The Automobile Association. Average 335p. col. illus., maps, plans, pbk. Prices vary from £8.99 to £14.99.

Titles: Algarve, Amsterdam, Australia, Austria, Bali, Barcelona, Belgium, Berlin, Brazil, California, Canada, Caribbean, China, Copenhagen, Crete, Cyprus, Czech & Slovak Republics, Florence, Florida, France, Germany, Great Britain, Greece, Greek Islands, Hawaii, Hong Kong, Hungary, Ireland, Israel, Italy, Lisbon, London, Madeira, Madrid, Majorca, Mexico, Moscow, Nepal, Netherlands, New York, New Zealand, Paris, Prague, Portugal, Provence & Cote D'Azur, Rome, San Francisco, Scandinavia, Scotland, Seychelles, South Africa, Spain, Switzerland, Tenerife, Thailand, Turkey, USA, Venice and Vienna. Art, culture, history, climate, places of interest and scenic beauty spots. Each guide now includes a separate folded map. *Class No: 914/919.9*

[5422]
Blue guides. London, Ernest Benn (later A & C. Black), 1918-. maps, plans.

'Blue guides', *Geographical Journal* v.144, no.3, November 1978, p.533 gives the series' background history.

200 titles: *Amsterdam.* 2nd ed.; *Austria.* 4th ed.; *Barcelona.* 2nd ed.; *Belgium.* 9th ed.; *Crete.* 7th ed.' *Madrid.* 2nd ed.; *Istanbul. Romania.* (new); *Turkey.* 3rd ed.; *Umbria.* 3rd.; and *Washington.* (new).

1999 titles: *Athens.* 4th ed. £12.99. ISBN 0173648430; *Australia.* £16.00, 017363846; *Czech and Slovak Republics.* 2nd ed. £14.99. 017364429x; *Java, Bali and Lombok.* £15.00. 0173639156; *Oxford and Cambridge.* 5th ed. £12.99. 0173648848; *Poland.* £15.99. 0173638990; *Prague.* £10.99. 0173644281; *Provence and the Côte d'Azur.* £12.99. 0173639814; *Sicily.* 5th ed. £13.99. 0173649089; *Southern Italy.* 9th ed. £14.99. 0173650028; *Tuscany.* 3rd ed. £14.99. 0173649720.

Earlier titles in print: *Albania.* 2nd ed. £12.99. 0173642572; *Berlin and Eastern Germany.* £13.99. 0173638710; *Boston & Cambridge.* 2nd ed. £14.99. 0173631708; *Budapest.* £10.99. 0173640774; *Bulgaria.* £13.99. 0173641010; *Channel Islands.* 3rd ed. £10.99. 0173638524; *China.* £16.99. 0173630272; *Corsica.* 2nd ed. £9.99. 0173635894; *Country Houses of England.* £15.99. 0173637803. *Cyprus.* 4th ed. £12.99. 0173639865; *Denmark.* 2nd ed. £13.99. 017363474x.

Egypt. 3rd ed. £19.99. 0173635908; *England.* 11th ed. £15.99. 0173638745; *Florence.* 7th ed. £11.99. 0173649070; *France.* 4th ed. £16.99. 0173643315; *Greece.* 6th ed. £17.99. 017363250x; *Hungary.* 2nd ed. £14.99. 0173645598; *Ireland.* 8th ed. £14.99. 0173645504; *Jordan.* £12.99. 0173646462; *Loire Valley.* £10.99. 0173635729; *London.* 5th ed. £14.99. 0173646780; *Malaysia & Singapore.* £13.99. 0173641576; *Mexico.* £19.99. 017362776x; *Mid-Pyrénées.* £10.99. 0173638532; *Morocco.* 3rd ed. £12.99. 0173646772; *Museums and Galleries of New York.* £17.99. 0173639385.

Netherlands. 6th ed. £13.99. 0173645784; *New York.* 2nd ed. £17.99. 0173631694; *Normandy.* £9.99. 0173637307; *Northern Italy.* 10th ed. £14.99. 0173632763; *Paris & Versailles.* 9th ed. £12.99. 0173644478; *Portugal.* 4th ed. £12.99. 0173642347; *Rhodes & The Dodecanese.* £10.99. 0173640936; *Rome.* 6th ed. £13.99. 0173646691; *Southern India.* £16.99. 0173641584; *South-west France.* £9.99. 0173639105; *Switzerland.* 5th ed. £11.99. 0173635592; *Thailand.* £14.99. 0173639059. *Tunisia.* £11.99. 01783641053; *Venice.* 6th ed. £11.99. 0173647982; *Vienna.* £10.99. 0173639369; *Wales.* 8th ed. £12.99. 017364074x.

Renowned for detailed coverage of architecture, art history *etc.*, with practical information on accommodation, eating out, and local events and festivals. 'The best guides to have appeared since the nineteenth century Baedeckers' (*Reference Reviews*, v.5, no.1, 1991. p.43). *Class No: 914/919.9*

[5423]
Chambers World gazetteer: an A-Z of geographical information. Munro, D., *ed.* 5th ed. Edinburgh and Cambridge, Chambers/ Cambridge, 1988. xviii, 733p.+112p. World Atlas. £30.00. $34.50. ISBN: 1852962003.

First published 1895. Last edition (1965) published as *Chamber's World gazetteer and geographical dictionary.* This edition is the most comprehensive revision since the *Gazetteer's* first publication.

Standard international directory of 20,000 world place names: cities, regions, countries, places of touristic interest, notable archaeological and religious sites *etc.* 150 line maps illustrate political divisions and administrative areas. United States countries listed under State headings. Entries include information on location, pronunciation, topography, history, economic activity and key calendar dates. 120p. colour atlas. 'Generally, more and smaller, place name locations appear in Webster, but the Chambers entries are more informative' (*Choice*, v.26, no.7, March 1989, p.1118). *Class No: 914/919.9*

[5424]
The Columbia gazetteer of the world. Cohen, S. B., *ed.* New York, Columbia Univ. Press, 3v., 1998. xxiv,3578p. tables. $750. £500. ISBN: 0231110405.

Completely revised edition of *Columbia-Lippincott Gazetteer of the World* (1952).

175,000 entries (30,000 new to this edition). Data: pronunciation guide; latitude, longitude and altitude readings; population; description and type of location; with economic, cultural, political and historical information. 'Remains the essential world gazetteer. No other work gets anywhere near it for the scale of its coverage' (*Refer*, v.15,no.1, Winter 1999, p.13). *Choice* Outstanding Academic Book 1998.

The Columbia gazetteer of the world online ed. by S. Cohen, 2000. ISBN 0231119060. *Class No: 914/919.9*

[5425]
FISHER, M. Provinces and provincial capitals of the world. 2nd ed. Metuchen, New Jersey, Scarecrow Press, 1985. ix, 248p. index. £19.50; $21.00. ISBN: 0810817586.

224 countries A-Z. Data: commonly used name of country; official name in its accepted English form; Romanized native form; general location; capital; number and type of major administrative units or provinces; name of these units and their capitals. *Class No: 914/919.9*

[5426]
FITZPATRICK, G.L. and MODLIN, M.J. Direct-line distances. (1) International and (2) United States editions. Metuchen, New Jersey, Scarecrow, 1986. xliii,275p. maps. £42.50 each or £72.50 for both. ISBN: 0810818728, Int. ed; 081081871x, US ed.

Tables of distances, measured in kilometres, between 1001 cities, towns, islands, and other strategically located places assembled in 50 sections of 20 columns each. Leeds and Manchester (UK) not included although there is an entry for Manchester (New Hampshire). The United States edition includes 312 places in the US not found in the International edition and gives distances in statute miles. 'Will fill a void in reference libraries and collections' (*Geographical Journal*, v.154, no.1, March 1988, p.141). *Class No: 914/919.9*

[5427]
HARDING, L. Dead countries of the nineteenth and twentieth centuries Aden to Zululand. Lanham, Md., Scarecrow Press, 1998. xi,393p. maps, illus., bibliog., index. £42.75. ISBN: 0810834456.

Identifies 'all the countries, colonies, protectorates, princely states etc ... that have existed since 1800 but now do not' and provides 'some basic statistics and a short almanac-type entry for each, explaining how it came into existence, what happened to it while it did exist and why it does not exist now' (*Preface*). Arranged in 15 regional chapters. Bibliography p.365-75.3 maps. *Class No: 914/919.9*

[5428]
HART, M., ed. World travel guide 1996/97. 15th ed. London, Columbus Press, 1996. 1152p. col. illus., maps (some col.), tables. ISBN: 0946393621. ISSN: 02678738.

Preliminaries (Calendar of events, How to use this book, International Organizations, World and regional maps) p.A1-A64. A-Z country by country guide, US state by state, p.1-1091. Data: Map showing location within its general region, population, language, religion, time, communications, passports and visas, money, health, travel and social and business profiles. Appendices: education, international trade travel media, health, disabled, World of Islam, Christianity. Buddhism. Weather etc. *Class No: 914/919.9*

[5429]

The Hutchinson guide to the world. 4th ed. Oxford, Helicon, 1998. vi,666p. maps, tables. £30.

First published as *The Hutchinson paperback guide to the world* (1990).

Countries of the world A-Z (Data: thumbnail map, government, economy and resources, population and society, transport, chronology, practical information for the visitor and traveller, historical overview) p.1-290. Gazetteer (6000 towns and regions, natural features, major landmarks) p.293-628. 47 appendices (administrative divisions, world geography, countries and population) p.631-66. Up-to-date quick reference work incorporating expanded information on European and North American towns and regions in this edition. *Class No:* 914/919.9

[5430]

International dictionary of historic places. Ring, T., *ed.* Chicago, Fitzroy Dearborn, 5v., 1995. illus., maps on endpapers, index. £95. per volume; £375. (set) ISBN: 1884964052, set.

1. *The Americas.* xv,804p. illus., maps on endpapers, index. 1884964001. 2. *Northern Europe* 188496401x. 3. *Southern Europe.* 818p. 1884964028. 4. *Africa and Middle East.* 1884964036. 5. *Asia and Oceania.* xvii,955p. 1884964044. V.1 has 3-4000 word essays on 160 sites in the US and Canada, Mexico, the Caribbean, Central America and South America, each ending with a list of further readings. All sites have witnessed important events in human history and have been preserved for the benefit of future generations. Entries conclude with an annotated *Bibliography* of books/articles pertaining to the site. Entries are illustrated with a current or historic photograph, a plan, or an artist's rendering of the site. Each volume concludes with an Index; volume 5 has an index to the entire series. *Class No:* 914/919.9

[5431]

KURIAN, G. The World gazetteer of boundaries. Santa Barbara, California, ABC-Clio, 1988. 900p. maps, tables, bibliog. £77.45. ISBN: 087436504x.

Definitive inventory of world land and maritime boundary changes since 1917 arranged by continent or region. Also includes descriptions of current and dormant boundary disputes and summaries of boundary treaties. *Class No:* 914/919.9

[5432]

KURIAN, G.T. Geo-data the world almanac gazetteer. Detroit, Gale Research Co., 1982. 624p. $60.00. ISBN: 0810316056.

In 4 major parts: 1. United States (detailed information on 50 states, 3142 counties, and 2492 towns and cities of over 10,000 population) - 2. World countries, cities and administrative divisions - 3. Geographical gazetteer of the world (data on continents, oceans, seas, rivers, islands mountains *etc.*) - 4. Rankings (comparative areas, heights, depths *etc.*). *Choice,* v.20,no.11-12, July-August 1983, p.1576-7 would have preferred a single A-Z sequence and concludes 'most libraries would be better served by the standard Webster's New Geographical Dictionary'. *Class No:* 914/919.9

[5433]

LAW, G. Administrative subdivisions of countries. Jefferson, NC., McFarland, 2000. 457p. ISBN: 0786407298.

Each country's entry gives the ISO 3166 country code, basic facts on language(s), its time zone relative to Greenwich Mean Time, its capital, a brief history showing changes in status and territory since 1900, ISO and FIPS codes, population, area, and its postal code system. 'An amazing exercise of scholarship ... a mine of factual information, and anyone involved in political history, international trade and travel will find much that is of use' (*Reference Reviews*, v.14, no.4, 2000, p.35). *Class No:* 914/919.9

[5434]

Lonely Planet catalogue. Hawthorn, Victoria, Australia, Lonely Planet 2000-. 112p. col.illus., index. gratis.

Titles and publication details of all Lonely Planet's renowned and immensely successful guidebooks, wildlife and walking guides, phrasebooks, travel literature, and travel atlases *(q.v.)* etc. *Class No:* 914/919.9

[5435]

Lonely Planet online.

Lonley Planet's Web site has information on hundreds of destinations ranging from Amsterdam to Zimbabwe, complete with interactive maps and colour photographs of almost every spot on the globe, including places far off the beaten track. In all, Lonely Planet covers up to 500 destinations online, each including descriptive content on things to see and do; insight into being there; background information; planning help; and links to Lonely Planet's bulletin board, reports from travellers on the road and links to other Web resources. Updating. Our digital information is updated constantly as news breaks, elections are won, and floods and accidents necessitate changes to travel information. Lonely Planet has scores of researchers on the road as well as a network of locally based reliable sources positioned throughout the world. *Class No:* 914/919.9

[5436]

Merriam-Webster's geographical dictionary. Hopkins, D.J., *ed.* 3rd ed. Springfield, Massachusetts, Merriam-Webster, 1997. 26A,1361p. tables, maps. $29.95. ISBN: 0877795460.

First published 1949 as *Webster's geographical dictionary*.

A gazetteer, not a dictionary of geographical terms. Over 48,000 place-names entries, including all US places with 2,500+ inhabitants, plus over 15,000 cross-references. Geographical terms (over 450 in c.12 languages),. Entries state pronunciation, word division and basic data (location; features; history) on countries, regions, cities and natural features. 252 black-and-white maps. 'Libraries ... will want to update and supplement their geographical reference collection with this new edition' (*Booklist,* v.93, no.22, August 1997, p.1928). *Class No:* 914/919.9

[5437]

PAXTON, J. The Penguin encyclopedia of places. 3rd ed. London, Penguin, 1999. 1030p. £11.99. ISBN: 0140512756.

1st ed. 1971.

Geographical and historical notes on 12,000 places ranging from detailed accounts of individual countries to brief descriptions of geographical features. *Class No:* 914/919.9

[5438]

Philip's world handbook country by country. Widdows, R., *comp.* London, George Philip, 1993. vi,298p. col. maps, tables. ISBN: 0540057290.

1. World maps (different scales) p.1 to 37 - 2. World gazetteer (220++ countries) describing each nation's geography, history, economy, culture, and politics (p.38-232) - 3. World statistics (physical dimensions, demography, cities, energy, gross national product *etc.*). *Class No:* 914/919.9

[5439]

Reader's Digest guide to places of the world. London, The Reader's Digest Association Limited, 1987. 735p. col. illus., col. maps. £26.95. $29.95. ISBN: 0276398262.

Contents: 1. A-Z guide to the nations of the world, places of interest and geographical terms in common use, p.10-730; 2. Flags of the world p.731-733; 3. International organizations and alliances p.734-735.

158 full-colour maps, 250 colour illustrations and 7000 features and articles. 'Heartily recommended as a reference work or as study material for any cartographic office as well as being the ideal home geographical encyclopedia' (*Bulletin of Society of University Cartographers,* v.21, no.2, 1988, p.115-6). *Class No:* 914/919.9

[5440]

ROOM, A. Place-name changes since 1900: a world gazetteer. Metuchen, New Jersey, Scarecrow Press, 1979; London, Routledge & Kegan Paul, 1980. xxii, 202p. £20.00. ISBN: 0710007027.

Gazetteer of c.7500 entries and cross-references. 3 appendices (1. Official names of countries, 1 November 1978). Bibliography p.189-202. *Class No:* 914/919.9

[5441]

The Rough Guides London, Rough Guides, 1982-. col. illus., maps.

Currently there are 140 travel guides inprint, including over 50 published new titles or new editions published in 2000. A full list is to be found in *2000 The Rough Guides* (80p.) which may be obtained from Rough Guides, 62-70 Shorts Gardens, London, WC2H 9AB. This also contains an interview conducted by Jeremy Atiyah, travel editor of *The Independent on Sunday,* with Mark Ellingham, co-founder and publisher of the guides. *Class No:* 914/919.9

[5442]

—The Rough guide to travel online. http://travel.roughguides.com.

Access to 10,000 destinations world-wide, including points of interest, historical sites, and museums. Each week a travel essay spotlights focusing on a particular destination. Contents menu: basics, best of, eating, accommodation, entertainment, sights, districts, and vicinity. *Class No:* 914/919.9

[5443]

SHOWERS, V. World facts and figures: a unique authoritative collection of comparative facts on the cities, countries, and geographic features of the world. 3rd ed. New York, Wiley, 1989. 721p. illus., bibliog., index. $74.95. ISBN: 0471857750.

First published as *The world in figures* (1973).

Comparative tables on largest, longest, highest *etc.* geographical features plus city, country and continent gazetteer information. Bibliography p.679-88. *Class No:* 914/919.9

[5444]

UNITED STATES. Board on Geographic Names. **Gazetteers.** Washington, Defense Mapping Agency Combat Support Center, 1955-. tables.

A world series of country gazetteers, Afghanistan-Zambia, of standard names approved by the Board on Geographic Names and unapproved variants. The single line entries include coordinates, evaluation of the quality of the names, designations (*i.e.*, cities, mountains, rivers *etc.*), and political administrative unit. Includes undersea features. By far the most comprehensive and detailed of their kind.

Foreign names decisions of the US Board on Geographic Names contains information about recent decisions. They are not cumulative. *Names of political entities of the world* is published approximately every 15 months. *Class No: 914/919.9*

[5445]

—Foreign gazetteers of the US Board on Geographic Names, Microfiche Collection. Washington, D.C., Congressional Information Service, 1987. 1505 microfiche (negative polarity) 24:1 reduction ratio. 15p. printed bibliography. $3,000.00.

Only the most current gazetteer for each country is reproduced in this collection.

'Not all these gazetteers were distributed through the Government Printing Office's depository program ... Tragically, several gazetteers from the 1980s have been witheld from depository libraries due to bureaucratic definitions of proprietary information ... The printed bibliography is excellent and can stand on its own as a superb reference tool. It alphabetically lists the countries included in the collection, with cross references to previous names of a country (if any) and countries grouped together in one gazetteer' (*Information Bulletin* Western Association of Map Librarians, v.19,no.2, March 1988, p.114-5). *Class No: 914/919.9*

[5446]

World Boundaries series. London, Routledge, 5v., 1994.

1. Schofield, C.H., ed. *Global boundaries.* 144p. illus. 6 maps, £40. ISBN 0415088380. 2. Schofield, C.H. and Schofield, R., eds. *The Middle East and North Africa.* 244p. illus., 18 maps. £40. 0415088399. 3. Grundy-Warr, C., ed. *Eurasia.* 256p. £40. 0415088348. 4. Girrot, P., ed. *The Americas.* 224p. illus., 21 maps. £40. 0415088364. 5. Blake, G., ed. *Maritime boundaries.* 192p. illus. 40 maps. £40. 0415088356. Covers the theory and practice of boundary delimitation, management, disputes, conflict resolution, and territorial change. *Class No: 914/919.9*

Bibliographies

[5447]

ANDERSON, S. **Anderson's travel companion.** Aldershot, Hants., Scolar Press, 1996. £39.50. ISBN: 1859280137.

Lists recommended guides and travel literature, inc. fiction, for each country of the world. Sarah Anderson is the founder of the Travel Bookshop, London. 'If you find that even with all the titles you already keep on your shelves you still haven't got the subject covered, I suggest you refer to her remarkable directory' (*Bookseller*, no.4699, 12 January 1996, p.54). *Class No: 914/919.9(01)*

Encyclopaedias

[5448]

CANBY, C. **The Encyclopaedia of historic places.** New York, Facts On File; London, Mansell Publishing Ltd., 2 vols, 1984. v,1051p. illus. £85. $160. ISBN: 0720116902, the set; 0720116937, vol.1; 0720116945, vol.2.

Geographic locations of historic significance (towns, cities, countries, provinces and regions, empires, deserts, forts and battle sites, lakes and rivers, mountains, shrines and archaeological sites 'including many places not found in standard reference books') pinpointed in A-Z entries by most common English name. 'Should become librarians' first choice as a source of short histories' (*Wilson Library Bulletin*, v.58, no.10, June 1984, p.753).
Class No: 914/919.9(031)

Dictionaries

[5449]

The Oxford dictionary of the world. Munro, D. Oxford Univ. Press, 1995. xi,686p.+16p. col.maps, tables. £17.99. ISBN: 0198661843.

15,000 A-Z entries of varying length on countries, regions, cities and important towns, peoples, languages, religions, natural features, and historic sites and buildings. Long series of appendices containing data on mountains, rivers, lakes, deserts, population etc. 250 location and country maps. Descriptive gazetteer/topographical index. Core text of 3,000 entries drawn from *Oxford English Reference Dictionary*. 'A must for the reference shelves and a joy for the armchair browser' (*Reference Reviews*, v.10,no.7, 1996, p.40). Selected as one of *Choice's* Outstanding Academic Books of 1996.
Class No: 914/919.9(038)

Europe

[5450]

TOURING CLUB ITALIANO. **Guida d'Europa.** Milano, Touring Club Italiano, 16v. illus., maps, plans.

Periodically updated, each volume begins with a comprehensive geographic, artistic and economic overview. This is followed by motoring itineraries and an A-Z gazetteer of places to visit. Also general information on hotels, restaurants, camp sites etc., with plentiful maps, town plans and drawings. *Titles: Spagna e Portogallo*, 502p. L49.000; *Francia*, 444p. L44,000; *Parigi e dintori*, 296p. L39,000; *Gran Bretagna e Irlanda*, 367p. L40,000; *Londra e dintori*, 272p. L39,000; *Germania-Repubblica Federale*, 496p. L49,000; *Belgio, Olanda, Lussemburgo*, 272p. L38,000; *Svizzera*, 280p. L39,000; *Austria*, 290p. L39,000; *Iugoslavia*, 256p. L39,000; *Grecia*, 190p. L40,000; *Bulgaria e Romania*, 240p. L30,000; *Ungheria*, 144p. L28,000; *Cecoslovacchia*, 232p. L30,000; *Mosca e Leningrado*, 192p. L30,000; *Danimarca e Islanda*, L33,000; *Svezia, Norvegia, Finlandia*, L40,000. *Class No: 914*

Great Britain

[5451]

AA **book of British towns.** London, Drive Publications for The Automobile Association, 1982. 432p. illus. (mostly col.), col.maps. £12.95.

First published 1979.

Complete guide to 691 towns and cities (more than 20,000 population) with guided tours of 11 largest. Exploring London p.224-71. Glossary of architectural and historical terms p.430.1. 212 maps in colour. 616 colour and 248 b/w. illustrations. *Class No: 914.10*

[5452]

AA **book of British villages** a guide to 700 of the most interesting and attractive villages in Britain. Reprinted with amendments. London, Drive Publications for The Automobile Association, 1985. 448p. col.illus., maps, indexes. £16.95. ISBN: 0903356287.

First published 1980.

A-Z gazetteer p.8-416 plus 13 special features e.g., 'Discovering village history' (R. Parker); 'How villages got their names' (M. Gelling); 'Lost villages' (W.S. Hoskins). 13 Regional maps. Gazetteer of village craft centres p.444-47. *Class No: 914.10*

[5453]

AA **days out in Britain and Ireland 1997.** Basingstoke, Hants., Automobile Association, 1997. 256p. col.maps. ISBN: 0749513853.

Over 2,250 historic houses, castles, museums and galleries, ancient monuments, wildlife parks, nature reserves etc. to visit with prices, opening times, and disabled facilities. 12 page colour road atlas.

AA Days out in Britain and Ireland CD-ROM 1997. ISBN 0749515368. 'The easy-to-use search facility will instantly identify the day out closest to your requirements from over 2,000 heritage and leisure attractions in Britain and Ireland. Nearby attractions are listed as well' (*advt*). *Class No: 914.10*

[5454]

AA **guide to National Trust properties in Britain.** Powell, R., *ed.* Basingstoke, Hampshire, The Automobile Association, 1986. 192p. col.illus., col.maps, index. £9.95. ISBN: 0861451988.

A-Z by location within 7 regional sections. Glossary p.188. Sumptuously illustrated. *Class No: 914.10*

[5455]

AA **illustrated guide to Britain.** Basingstoke, AA Publishing, 1999. 256p. col. illus., col. maps. £12.99. ISBN: 0749517719.

500 places of interest described in words and pictures with 3 miles to one inch scale AA map extracts and practical information on major personalities, myths and legends, local delicacies, customs and festivals. *Class No: 914.10*

[5456]

AA **illustrated guide to Britain's coast.** Reprinted with amendments 1987. London, Drive Publications for The Automobile Association, 1984. 383p. col.illus., col.maps, index. £16.95. ISBN: 0903356333.

A richly illustrated mile by mile survey (p.8-349) starting at the Severn estuary near Bristol and continuing anti-clockwise round the entire coastline and the main offshore islands, dividing the coast into 145 sections each covering a strip of coast (typically) of 35 miles. Each section embodies a descriptive text accompanied by a map and boxed local information and places to see inland. 13 special double-pages features, *e.g.* 'Bristol, seafaring city' and 'Coastal lands lost and won'. Also 'Exploring the living world of our seashore' (p.350-369). Key to *Guide* on endpapers. *Class No: 914.10*

[5457]

AA illustrated guide to country towns and villages of Britain. London, Drive Publications for The Automobile Associations, 1985. 448p. col.illus., col.maps, index.

21 major contributors. Descriptive gazetteer of over 500 country towns and villages chosen for their outstanding beauty and interest A-Z in 36 areas. Detailed maps of each area indicate locations of places to visit. Aspects of life (6 special features) p.415-439. Index of towns and villages and general index. *Class No:* 914.10

[5458]

AA/Ordnance Survey leisure guides. Basingstoke, Hampshire, Automobile Association; Southampton, Ordnance Survey, 1985-. 128p. col.illus., col.maps, index. £7.99/£8.99.

Cornwall & the Isles of Scilly 0749520523; *Cotswolds* 0749520531; *Devon & Exmoor* 074952054x; *Hampshire & Isle of Wight* 074951194x; *Lake District* 0749520558; *Northumbria* 0749520594; *North York Moors* 0749520566 *Peak District* 0749520582; *Scottish Highlands and Islands* 0749520590; *Yorkshire Dales* 0749520604.

Now organised by area with 10 scenic walks and 2 car tours within each section . Tourist areas explored and explained. In-depth descriptions of all the major attractions. All walks illustrated with OS mapping, plus an AA road atlas of the region A-Z gazetteer of interesting towns and villages. Check list for each region - essential information and fact files: customs, traditions, history, local legends and places of special interest to children. *Class No:* 914.10

[5459]

AA roadbook of Britain A-Z gazetteer. The reference guide to places in Britain. Cavendish, R., *ed.* Basingstoke, Hants, A.A. Publications, 1995. 656p. illus., index. £20. ISBN: 0749511400.

Preliminaries include Counties in Britain; Population and Profiles of counties and regions. Main gazetteer of 9000+ entries with descriptive annotations p.39-630. Vehicle index marks p.630-32. Picnic sites p.633-35. National Parks and National Scenic Areas p.636-38. Kings and Queens p.639-41. Parish Church (inc. cutaway diagram) p.642-43. Architectural glossary p.644-48. Index to famous people p.649-51. Where to find well-known places of interest p.652-56. *Class No:* 914.10

[5460]

AA the Britain guide 2000. Basingstoke, Hampshire, 1999. 464p. col.illus., col. maps, softback. £9.99. ISBN: 0749522445.

1000+ heritage sites to visit, stately homes, castles, gardens, galleries, museums in Britain and Ireland, each described with up-to-date details and prices. *Class No:* 914.10

[5461]

AA touring Britain and Ireland. Basingstoke, Hants., Automobile Association Publications, 1996. 288p. col.illus., col.maps. ISBN: 0749507853.

Two books in one - an illustrated tour guide and a complete atlas. 4 miles to 1 inch mapping, 47 circular scenic tours highlighted on double page atlas spreads. Special feature on Britain's top 20 attractions. *Class No:* 914.10

[5462]

AA walkers' Britain. Basingstoke, Hampshire, Automobile Association, 1999. 256p. col.illus., col.maps. £12.99. ISBN: 0749520914.

Describes 30 outstanding long-distance paths, each divided into sections for an average day's walk, with detailed route directions and essential practical information. *Class No:* 914.10

[5463]

—**AA book of Britain's walks.** Basingstoke, Hampshire, Automobile Association, 1999. 288p. col.illus., col.maps. £30. ISBN: 0749522429.

120 themed circular walks. 8 main themes: ancient tracks, spectacular landscapes, wartime Britain, wilderness, flora and fauna, mystery, famous people, urban and industrial heritage. Plus *AA Pocket book of Britain's walks.* (128p. 2000. £6.99. 0749522437) with detailed route instructions and maps for use on the ground. *Class No:* 914.10

[5464]

Britain map. London, British Tourist Authority. Single sheet 59cmx84cm folded to 10cmx21cm. £1.30.

Road map (its legend in 4 languages) on one side; a list of Tourist Information Centres (telephone & fax numbers), a mileage chart, and traffic signs etc. on the other. *Class No:* 914.10

[5465]

Collins British atlas and gazetteer. London, HarperCollins, 1999. 512p. maps. £39. ISBN: 0004487907.

Road maps on scale 4.15 miles: 1 inch (p.2-109). Gazetteer (55,000 entries) give succinct information on settlements, physical features, points of interest, and National Grid references (p.137-512). *Class No:* 914.10

[5466]

GAUNT, P. The Cromwellian gazetteer an illustrated guide to Britain in the Civil War and Commonwealth. Gloucester, Alan Sutton and The Cromwell Association, 1987. xiv,241p. illus., maps, geneal tables, index. £14.95. ISBN: 0862992915.

A guide to sites in Britain and Ireland associated with the parliamentary cause 1642-1660 with emphasis on Cromwell himself. Arranged A-Z by country. Appendix: A Cromwell itinerary p.224-228. 9p. of maps. *Class No:* 914.10

[5467]

GOODMAN, A. *and* **CYPRIEN, M. A Traveller's guide to early medieval Britain.** London, Routledge and Kegan Paul; Harrisburg, Pennsylvania, Historical Times Inc., 1986. 128p. illus., map, bibliog. £12.95. ISBN: 0710209428, UK; 0918678161, US.

Gazetteer p.8-122 incl. 11 special essays *e.g.* Magna Carta and the beginnings of parliament, Holidays and Holy-days. List of Kings p. 123-4. Glossary p.125-6. Further reading p.127. *Class No:* 914.10

[5468]

GREAT BRITAIN. Ordnance Survey. **The Ordnance Survey gazetteer of Great Britain.** 4th ed. Southampton, Ordnance Survey; London, Macmillan Reference Books, 1999. xviii,791p. £99. ISBN: 0333770293.

1st ed. 1987. 3rd ed. 1996.

Lists 256,000 named features on O.S. Landranger Map Series (1:50,000 *i.e.* 1½ inches to the mile) covering England, Scotland and Wales on 204 sheets. Data: Name; County; National Grid Reference; Latitude and Longitude; Feature code (antiquity, forest, hill *etc.*); and Sheet number. The O.S. Landranger Map on which the feature appears is also noticed. This edition is completely revised and includes latest county and unitary boundaries. 'The sheer scale of the work makes it an invaluable tool' (*Refer*, v.4, no.1, Spring 1986, p.16). *Class No:* 914.10

[5469]

HAMMOND, C. Ricardian Britain a guide to places connected with Richard III. 5th ed. London, Richard III Society, 1988. 48p. map, index. sd. £2.50. ISBN: 0904893138.

1st ed. by V. Giles and C. Hicks (now Hammond) 1968.

88 entries A-Z by historic counties. Data: Description; Hours; Directions. Appendix: Portraits of Richard III. *Class No:* 914.10

[5470]

HUDSON, K. *and* **NICHOLLS, A. The Cambridge guide to the historic places of Britain and Ireland.** Cambridge, Cambridge Univ. Press, 1989. viii, [16]p., maps, 326p. illus. (28 col.), indexes. £14.95. ISBN: 0521360773.

Descriptive gazetteer of the amenities and opening hours of 1567 monuments and buildings including all major National Trust and English Heritage sites, industrial monuments, gardens, battlefields, literary shrines, spas, shops, theatres *etc.*, 8 regional double-page location maps. Place and subject indexes. *Class No:* 914.10

[5471]

The Hutchinson guide to Britain. Oxford, Helicon, 2000. 512p. pbk. £12.99. ISBN: 1859863361.

A-Z guide to places, history and culture. 2000+ cross-referenced entries relating to British men and women in all fields of human activity; UK history, politics, government and business; towns and places in the UK, including key tourist attractions; and Britain's cultural heritage: writers, visual arts, architecture, music, TV, film, sport, and more. Britain's modern-day institutions, its customs, and tourist attractions are comprehensively covered. Major UK themes (such as Northern Ireland, the UK contribution, The Scottish and Welsh assemblies) and the quirkier side of British life are given special feature coverage. *Class No:* 914.10

[5472]

JACKSON, R. Dark Age Britain: what to see and where. Cambridge, Patrick Stephens, 1984. 208p. illus., maps, index. £10.95. ISBN: 085059622x.

Historical text for the general reader interspersed with descriptions and illustrations of visible Dark Age remains. Arranged in 3 Parts (15 chapters): 1. The British resistance 410-642AD - 2. The Anglo-Saxon kingdoms 642-800AD - 3. 'From the fury of the Northmen, O Lord, deliver us'. List of sites which may be visited p.6-7. 160 photographs. 6 maps. *Class No:* 914.10

[5473]

KERR, N. *and* **KERR, M. A Guide to medieval sites in Britain.** London, Grafton Books, 1988. 270p. maps, illus., index. £14.95. ISBN: 0246124709.

160 entries relating to over 200 sites belonging to the period 1200-1485 grouped in 8 geographical regions. Each contains an architectural and historical description and clear map directions. 'As an aid to planning outings rather than as a comprehensive reference work it is an attractive and useful book' (*Reference Reviews*, v.2, no.3, September 1988, p.161). *Class No:* 914.10

[5474]

KERR, N. *and* **KERR, M. A Guide to Norman sites in Britain.** London, Granada, 1984. 192p. illus. maps, bibliog. £10.95. ISBN: 0246119764.

156 sites grouped geographically (Southern England p.12-53; East Anglia p.54-79; Central England p.80-107; Wales and the Marches p.108-137; Northern England p.138-159; Scotland and the Borders p.160-185) of the visible physical remains of the period 1066-1200. Each site is located in detail and is furnished with a six-figure Ordnance Survey grid reference. Glossary p.186-188. Index p.189-192. *Class No:* 914.10

[5475]

MUIR, R. *and* **WELFARE, H. The National Trust guide to prehistoric and Roman Britain.** London, George Philip in association with The National Trust and the National Trust for Scotland. 272p. illus. (a few col.), maps, bibliog., index. £12.50. ISBN: 0540010766.

10 chronological and thematic chapters each ending with an extensive list of places to visit with O.S. grid references and location maps. Bibliography p.261. *Class No:* 914.10

[5476]

The National Trust guide to Dark Age and Medieval Britain 400-1350. Muir, R. London, George Philip/The National Trust/The National Trust for Scotland, 1985. 256p. maps, illus. (some col), bibliog. £14.95. ISBN: 0540010901.

10 thematic, generously illustrated chapters supported by a gazetteer (p.235-241) introduce surviving monuments and attempt to explain their significance. Maps p.242-250. Bibliography p.251. Index 252-256. *Class No:* 914.10

[5477]

OTTAWAY, P. *and* **CYPRIEN, M. A Traveller's guide to Roman Britain.** London, Routledge & Kegan Paul; Harrisburg, Pennsylvania, Historical Times Inc., 1987. 128p. illus., map, bibliog. ISBN: 0710209438, UK; 0918678196, US.

Gazetteer of sites p.10-124 incl. 11 special articles *e.g.* Emperors in Britain, Towns. List of prominent individuals p.125-6. Glossary of terms p.126-7. Further reading p.128. *Class No:* 914.10

[5478]

Philip's navigator Britain. London, Philip, 2000. 368p. col.maps, index. ISBN: 0540078174.

Shows the smallest roads and lanes - including those that are often missed off less detailed mapping. For main roads and motorways every roundabout, junction and slip-road is shown in detail. In country areas thousands of individual houses and farms are marked and named, along with footpaths and tracks. Also includes tourist information - showing marinas, ferries, county showgrounds, tourist and leisure attractions and 50 detailed town and city plans, route-planning maps, a distances table and a 41,000 name index. Scale 1.5 miles to 1 inch. *Class No:* 914.10

[5479]

PLATT, C. The National Trust guide to late medieval and renaissance Britain: from the Black Death to the Civil War. London, George Philip in association with the National Trust and the National Trust for Scotland, 1986. 239p. illus. (some col.), map, bibliog., index. ISBN: 0540011088.

7 thematic chapters (e.g. High chivalry ... Spoil of the abbeys ... The War of the Three Kingdoms) are supported by a descriptive gazetteer (p.207-25) of some notable buildings of the period with some indications of access. Glossary p.228-31. Bibliography p.230-1. As a guide this beautifully illustrated volume falls down because of its exiguous direction details. *Class No:* 914.10

[5480]

Portrait of Britain. Leapman, M., *main contributor*. London, Dorling Kindersley, 1999. 721p. col.illus., col. maps, index. £29.99. ISBN: 0751308080.

Adapted and extended from the Eyewitness Travel Guides.

Introducing Great Britain (maps, contemporary and historical Britain, Great Britain through the year, including regional climate tables) p.1-73. Tourist guide and descriptive gazetteer in 7 regional sections (historic towns and cities, castles, cathedrals, stately homes, landscapes, in fact all the heritage bits with gorgeous illustrations) p.76-701. Projects for the Millennium p.721. Suitable for all public library service points. *Class No:* 914.10

[5481]

The Readers' Digest good beach guide 1996. The Marine Conservation Society, *comp.* Newton Abbot, David & Charles, 1996. 255p. col.illus., col.maps, tables. ISBN: 0715304968.

Previously published as *The Heinz good beach guide.*

Introduction (How to use guide; European Community Bathing Water Directive; Mandatory standards etc.). 8 regional chapters cover British Isles. Data for each beach: Water quality; bathing safety; access; public transport; toilets; food; seaside activities; wet weather alternatives; wildlife and walks. *Class No:* 914.10

[5482]

Reader's Digest illustrated encyclopedia of Britain. London, Reader's Digest Association, 1999. 512p. col.illus., col.maps, col.tables.

Sumptuous and colourful A-Z presentation in 200 entries of Britain's heritage, its countryside and towns, its pastimes, arts, sports and culture, its politics and institutions. It might almost be described as 'the people's encyclopedia'. But, truely, it is better than that. Maps p.492-500. *Class No:* 914.10

[5483]

Reader's Digest town tours in Britain: a walker's guide. London, Reader's Digest Association, 1990. [6p. + 104 folded double p. + 24p.] looseleaf in ring-binder. col. illus., col. maps. £25.95. ISBN: 0276420098.

Pictorial birds-eye view maps outline half-day circular walking tours of 155 towns, all beginning and ending in a central car park (underground station in Central London). Places of interest are clearly marked and are supplemented by detailed notes and colour photographs. Generally each double page is devoted to a single town although, occasionally, two smaller towns are accommodated. There are 45 quick tours of other towns. 'A very useful compendium of attractively presented, concise, and up-to-date local information ... of value and interest to a wider audience than the tourist' (*Reference Reviews*, v.4, no.2, 1990, p.37). *Class No:* 914.10

[5484]

ROSS, A. *and* **CYPRIEN, M. A Traveller's guide to Celtic Britain.** London, Routledge & Kegan Paul, 1985. 128p. illus., map, bibliog. £9.95. ISBN: 0710206321.

1. Celtic sites in Britain (map) - 2. Celtic Britain, a descriptive gazetteer of 124 significant sites A-Z by location. Glossary of characters p.124-6. Glossary of terms p.127-8. Bibliography p.128. *Class No:* 914.10

[5485]

WALTON, J. The National Trust guide to Late Georgian and Victorian Britain: from the Industrial Revolution to World War I. London, George Philip in association with The National Trust, 1989. 269 illus. (some col.), maps, bibliog., index. ISBN: 0540011851.

Pictorial guide to Britain 1750-1914 with chapters on Prestige and property; country houses; factories and industries; transport, travel and trade; towns and cities; urban working class; church, chapel and people; leisure and enjoyment; countryside and people. Emphasis on National Trust properties. Bibliography p.258-61. 3 maps. *Class No:* 914.10

[5486]

WHEATLEY, K. National Maritime Museum guide to maritime Britain. Exeter, Webb & Bower, 1990. 206p. illus. (some col.), maps on endpapers, index. £15.95. ISBN: 0863502687.

A region by region account of Britain's maritime history with special emphasis on heritage docks, ship preservation, underwater archaeology, museums, maritime research, the coastline, and leisure. Each regional chapter includes a gazetteer giving local information. *Class No:* 914.10

CD-ROM

[5487]

AA MileMaster Britain and Ireland. Basingstoke, Hants., AA Multimedia, 1997. CD-ROM for Windows. ISBN: 0749515090.

Just enter your starting point and destination and your exact route is overlaid on the AA's superb 3 mile to 1 inch mapping. Magnify it to get more detail,. Print it out. Get about in town using the AA's town plans. (*advt.*). *Class No:* 914.10(003.40)

[5488]

Interactive Britain & Ireland. Farnborough, AA Multimedia. CD-ROM. £29.99.

5 rooms: 1. What (miscellaneous) - 2. Where (information on 10,000 of Britain's most interesting places - 3. When (timeline of British history with text, videos & sounds for the main events) - 4. Who (2,800 biographies) - 5. Index. 'The main problem ... is that it tries to cram in too many different subjects on to one CD, which results in a lack of detail' (*Library Technology*, v.3,no.2, April 1998, p.32). *Class No:* 914.10(003.40)

Standards

[5489]

British standard specification for codes for the representation of names of counties and similar areas. Milton Keynes, Bucks, BSI 6879-1987. 26p. £19.10.

Replaces Colin Chapman's *Chapman County codes* (Federation of Family History Societies, 1979).

Codes refer to names in use and include all the main names used for UK subdivisions over the years. *Class No:* 914.10(083.74)

Islands

[5490]

NEWTON, N. The Shell guide to the islands of Britain. Newton Abbot, David & Charles, 1992. 224p. illus. (some col.), index, maps. £16.99. ISBN: 0715398830.

Part 1: Early settlements and archeology; islands and Christianity; folklore; commerce and tourism; dispersal and emigration. Part 2: Individual islands, their characteristics, tourist information, and travel directions. *Class No:* 914.10(210.7)

Women

[5491]

LEGGET, J. Local heroines a women's historical gazetteer of England, Scotland and Wales. London, Pandora, 1988. xxxiii, 382p. illus., maps, index. £15.95. ISBN: 0863580378.

1. 5 maps p.xxiv-xxxiii. 2. Gazetteer, A-Z by city, town or village, or nearest sizeable community or local landmark. Data: names or events associated with place mentioned, where traced, location, location and brief description of relevant buildings, monuments, gravemarkers, plaques *etc.*, and some information about the women concerned and the nature of the association. 3. Biographical index p.295-367. 4. How to find out more (books, courses, women's historical groups, museums and art galleries, Record Offices and archives, holidays) p.368-375. *Class No:* 914.10-0055.2

Scotland

[5492]

Chambers Scottish guides. Woolnough, K., *ed.* Edinburgh, Chambers, 1992. maps, plans, pbk. £7.99 each.

Smith, R. *Highlands and islands.* xiii,226p. ISBN 0550221026. Woolnough, K. *South-east Scotland* 055022100x; Bathgate, S. *South-west Scotland.* 0550221018.

In 3 sections: 1. National Fact File (activities, food and drink, money, accommodation *etc.*) - 2. Regional Fact File (local features, cinemas, galleries, sport) - 3. Regional Gazetteer (A-Z list of places to visit and things to do with special interest panels and maps). *Class No:* 914.11

[5493]

CROWL, P.A. The Intelligent traveller's guide to historic Scotland. London, Sidgwick and Jackson, 1986. xix, 625p. illus., maps, geneal. tables, bibliog., index. £12.95. ISBN: 0283993820.

Pt.1. Narrative history (p.4-371) in 9 sections comprises a chronological account of Scotland's past with an emphasis on its visible and visitable remains. Pt.2. Gazetteer (p.373-571) arranges sites mentioned in Pt.1 in 7 geographical regions sub-divided by historical counties. Bibliography p.579-87. Analytical index. *Class No:* 914.11

[5494]

HASWELL-SMITH, H. The Scottish islands a comprehensive guide to every Scottish Island. Edinburgh, Canongate Books, 1996. 423p. illus., maps, tables, bibliog., index. £25. ISBN: 0862415799.

165 islands (at least 40 hectares in area) arranged within 12 geographical districts. Data for each island: Gaelic pronunciation, map reference, area and height, ownership, population (current and historic), geology, history, wildlife, access, anchorages, map. 'Without doubt the most comprehensive guide available to Scottish islands' (*Reference Reviews*, v.11, no.1, 1997, p.54). *Class No:* 914.11

[5495]

JOHNSTON, W. and JOHNSTON, A.K. Gazetteer of Scotland including a glossary of the most common Gaelic names. 3rd ed. revised by R.W. Munro. Edinburgh and London, Johnston & Bacon, 1973. x,353p. maps.

Identifies all named places. Most entries give locational information only. *Class No:* 914.11

[5496]

Scottish historical guides. Edinburgh, Birlinn, 1996-. illus., maps, index. £6.99-£8.99.

Oram, R. *Angus & The Mearns - A Historical Guide.* 1996. 256p. ISBN 1874744475; Collard, M. *Lothian.* 1998. 126p. 1874744459; Oram, R. *Moray & Badenhoch.* 1996. 182p. 1874744467; Wickham-Jones, C. *Orkney.* 1998. 156p, 1874744718; Gourlay, R. *Sutherland.* 112p. 1874744440.

Each paperback title comprises a guidebook, a history, and a gazetteer. *Class No:* 914.11

[5497]

TRANTER, N. and CYPRIEN, M. A Traveller's guide to the Scotland of Robert the Bruce. London, Routledge and Kegan Paul, 1985. 128p. illus., bibliog. ISBN: 0710206887.

Illustrated gazetteer to sites including 8 background articles p.8-123. Rivals for the throne and Pride of Bruces (family trees) p.124-7. Bibliography p.128. *Class No:* 914.11

[5498]

The Which? guide to Scotland. Leslie, A., *ed.* Rev. ed. London, Consumers' Association, 1994. 520p. map, index. pbk. £12. ISBN: 0852025173.

Introduction (history, religion, birdwatching, golf, travel to Scotland, food and drink) and 123 regional guides each of which includes a gazetteer on places to see and advice on where to stay and where to eat. 'The perfect all-in-one companion to the traveller in Scotland'. *Class No:* 914.11

[5499]

WHYTE, J.D. and WHYTE, K. Exploring Scotland's historic landscapes. Edinburgh, John Donald Publishers, 1987. v, 314p. illus., maps, bibliog., index, pbk. £10.00. ISBN: 0859761665.

18 trails 'which include a range of landscape features ... important for understanding how the Scottish landscape has developed. A map accompanies each trail. Bibliography p.306-7. *Class No:* 914.11

[5500]

WRIGHT, G., ed. A Guide to the Orkney Islands. 2nd ed. Edinburgh, Gordon Wright Publishing, 1989. 64p. illus. £2.50. ISBN: 0903065673.

17 sections by various Orcadian hands. 'For anyone planning to visit the Orkneys this will prove an invaluable introduction to what to expect and what to look for - it is equally useful to those non-visitors who simply want to know more about the islands and their culture' (*Library Review*, v.39, no.2., 1990, p.71-72). *Class No:* 914.11

Ireland

[5501]

AA all-in-one guide Ireland. Basingstoke, AA Publishing, 1998. 256p. col.illus., col.maps, index. £8.99. ISBN: 0749517646.

In 6 colour-coded sections: Dublin and the Eastern Counties, the Southern, Western, Northwestern Counties, Lakeland, Belfast and Northern Ireland. Information on events and festivals, where to go and what to do, where to stay and where to eat, places to visit (museums, galleries, historic and ancient sites) and essential practical information. *Class No:* 914.15

[5502]

AA Reader's Digest illustrated guide to Ireland. London, Reader's Digest Association, 1991. 352p. col. illus., col. maps, index. £45. ISBN: 0276420330.

Place by place guide with information on touring centres, local customs, regular events, places of special and historical interest, fishing, golfing, natural history *etc.* 10 route maps. 35 regional maps. 'A good and comprehensive touring companion' (*Traveller*, v.22, no.2, Spring 1992, p.15). *Class No:* 914.15

[5503]

Ireland the complete guide and road atlas. Belfast, Appletree Press, 1995. 176p. col. illus., col. maps, index. Flexible cover. £9.99. ISBN: 0862815074.

1. Introduction (outline history, geography, genealogy, accommodation, further reading) - 2. Touring in Ireland (10 tours) - 3. 4 regional descriptive gazetteers viz. Dublin and the East, South, West, and Northern Ireland (p.30-108) - 4. Road atlas p.143-65. Scale 3 inches to 25 miles (1:443,520). *Class No:* 914.15

[5504]

LEWIS, S. A Topographical dictionary of Ireland comprising the several counties, boroughs, corporate market, and post towns, parishes and villages with historical and statistical descriptions... 2nd ed. Port Washington, New York, Kennikat Press, 2v., and atlas, 1971.

First published London, S. Lewis, 1837. 2nd ed. 1849.

Despite its date, this pre-famine gazetteer is indispensable for research of any nature involving topographical detail. An atlas volume was also issued but it is now only of historical interest.

A 2v. facsimile edition was published by Kenny's Bookshop (Galway) in 1995. £145. ISBN 0906312415. *Class No:* 914.15

[5505]

SHEEHAN, S. and LEVY, P. Ireland handbook. Bath, Footprint Handbooks, 2000. 713p.+7p. col.maps, col.illus. £11.99. ISBN: 1900949555.

1 Footsteps in the door - 2. Essentials - 3. Republic of Ireland: Dublin - Central North - Counties of Wicklow and Wexford - Waterford, Tipperary and Limerick - Co. Cork - Kerry - Clare - Galway and Roscommon - Mayo, Sligo and Leitrim - Donegal - Northern Ireland: Derry and Antrim - Belfast - Down and Ardagh - Tyrone and Fermanagh - Background - Footnotes. Special features include ecological tours, walks, and shopping. *Class No:* 914.15

[5506]

Shell guide to Ireland. Killanin, Lord *and* Duignan, M.V., *Updated by Peter Harbison.* Rev. ed. London, Macmillan, 1989. 340p. illus. (some col.), col. maps, bibliog., index. £16.95. ISBN: 0333469577.

1st ed. 1962.

This edition is substantially revised. Bibliography p.340. 'One of the very few reliable and comprehensive guides to the monuments, museums, and culture of the island' (*The Times*, no.63489, p.31). *Class No:* 914.15

Eire

[5507]

Heritage: a visitors guide Brennan, E., *ed.* Dublin, Office of Public Works, 1992. 208p. col. illus. I£9.95. ISBN: 0707601029.

Annually issued illustrated guide to national monuments, national parks and gardens, nature reserves, and 600 kilometres of inland waterways, in the care of The Office of Public Works. *Class No:* 914.17

[5508]

Ireland guide. Dublin, Gill & Macmillan, 1993. 512p.++ 24p. col. illus., maps, pbk. £8.99. ISBN: 0717119769.

Gazetteer emphasising history, archaeology, and architecture, arranged by province, county and place. Includes Ulster. 3 maps. 'Lies somewhere between the gorgeous *AA/Reader's Digest illustrated guide to Ireland* (over three times the price but six times the value) and the compact *Michelin Green Guide* ... either of which makes this one look a bit old-fashioned and dull' (*Books Ireland*, no.167, April 1993, p.88). *Class No:* 914.17

[5509]

LALOR, B. Ultimate Dublin guide: an A-Z of everything. Dublin, O'Brien Press, 1991. 309p. illus., maps, pbk. IR£6.95. ISBN: 0862782201.

2500 descriptive annotated entries giving basic information on art galleries, churches, cinemas, hostels, hotels, libraries, monuments, museums, music, parks, plaques, pubs, restuarants, sport, theatres, and walks. 7 maps. 'A rather appealing mini-encyclopedia of Dublin and environs' (*Books Ireland*, no.150, May 1991, p.99). *Class No:* 914.17

England & Wales

[5510]

GREAT BRITAIN. Office of Population Census and Surveys Census of 1981. England and Wales. **Index of place names.** London, HMSO., 2v., 1985. vii,849p. ISBN: 0116910658.

First produced in the series of Census publications in 1831. This ed. 13th in series.

About 62000 entries in all (A-K, L-Z) including *c*.30,000 villages, hamlets and localities, without legally defined boundaries. Data (tabular): description, county, district, registered district number, national grid reference, and population 1981. Appendix A Topographical arrangement of Registration Districts and Sub-districts. Based on the 1981 Census records updated to include changes to statutory boundaries and/or names up to 1 January 1985. *Class No:* 914.2

England

[5511]

AA touring England. Hicks, P., *ed.* Rev. ed. Basingstoke, Automobile Association, 1996. 608p. col. illus., col. maps, index.

First published 1987.

Map, text and illustrated motor tours of West Country, South and Southeast England, Central England and East Anglia, and North Country p.34-324. Town plans p.328-443. Atlas p.446-601. Fully up to AA's high standard and lavishly illustrated guidebooks. *Class No:* 914.20

[5512]

The English Heritage visitor's handbook 1996-97. London, English Heritage, 1996. 224p. col.illus., col.maps, index. pbk. £4.50. ISBN: 1850746249.

The Historic Buildings & Monuments Commission for England (English Heritage) was set up by the Government under the National Heritage Act 1983. This descriptive handbook and gazetteer is arranged in six regional sections with further sections on other historic sites in England, Historic Scotland; Cadw; Welsh Historic Monuments; and Manx National Heritage. 7 location maps.

English Heritage Visitor's Map 1996-97 (£1.95) is a single sheet 58cmx83cm featuring locations of 400+ English Heritage properties. Scale: 22 miles to one inch. *Class No:* 914.20

[5513]

GREENWOOD, D. Who's buried where in England. 3rd ed. London, Constable, 1999. 368p. illus., map, index. £12.99. ISBN: 0094793107.

1st ed. 1982. 2nd ed. 1990.

The burial places of over 500 men and women listed in 8 categories: Sovereigns - Royal consorts and nobles - Statesmen, politicians and warriors - Churchmen, philosophers, lawyers and scholars - Scientists, doctors, business men, engineers and industrialists - Authors, playwrights and poets - Actors, artists and musicians - Explorers, sportsmen, reformers, outlaws, heroines, criminals and miscellaneous. Persons cremated at Golders Green, p.21-22. Geographical checklist A-Z county p.349-58. *Class No:* 914.20

[5514]

The Holiday Which? guide to the Lake District. Locke, T., *ed.* London, Consumers' Association and Hodder & Stoughton, 1991. 280p. maps, index. pbk. £8.95. ISBN: 0340544112.

Previous ed. 1989.

A practical and informative guide divided into 4 regions. Touring routes are designed to cover major places of interest. Walks p.211-59. Information (Tourist Information Centres; accommodation; entertainment; maps; transport; outdoor activities) p.260-72. Calendar of events p.273-5. Introduced by The Natural Setting p.11-15 and Man's Lakeland History p.16-35. *Class No:* 914.20

[5515]

KERR, N. *and* KERR, M. A Guide to Anglo-Saxon sites. London, Granada, 1982. 207p. illus. maps. ISBN: 0246117753.

101 sites selected either as a good example of a particular type of monument, or for its historical associations, or because it enjoys a fine setting, arranged under the major Anglo-Saxon kingdoms: Northumbria p.16-60; Mercia p.62-107; East Anglia p.110-147; Wessex p.150-197. Glossary p.199-203. Museums with important Anglo-Saxon collections p.204. Index 205-207. *Class No:* 914.20

[5516]

The King's England. Mee, A., *ed.* Barnsley, Yorkshire, The King's England Press, 41v., 1989-90. £650. Also priced individually.

First published 1936-53 by Hodder & Stoughton. Text for this facsimile edition is usually that of each volume's first printing.

Complete historical and geographical account of England immediately before the Second World War in 41v. Introductory volume *Enchanted land* and one volume per historical county (combined v. for Bedfordshire and Huntingdonshire; Hampshire and Isle of Wight; the Lake Counties; Leicestershire and Rutland; and 3v. for the Yorkshire Ridings). In each volume the places described are arranged A-Z, historical, architectural and biographical notes being included. Richard Dalby's 'Arthur Mee's King's England series', *Book and Magazine Collector*, no.36, March 1987, p.20-25 describes the background to this well-loved series. *Class No:* 914.20

[5517]

PLATT, C. Travellers' guide to medieval England. London, Secker & Warburg, 1985. xix,249p. illus., map, index. £12.95. ISBN: 0436375591.

8 regional weekend/short break tours each with map, background historical text and gazetteer entries. Glossary p.xiii-xix. *Class No:* 914.20

[5518]

SHIPLEY, D. *and* PEPLOW, M. England's undiscovered heritage: a guide to 100 unusual sites and monuments. London, Weidenfeld & Nicolson, 1988. 160p. illus. (some col.), maps, geneal tables. £10.95. ISBN: 0297792687.

A-Z descriptive gazetteer of 100 of the least well known monuments in the care of English Heritage. Tour planner county maps p.134-45. Royal houses of England p.146-57. Glossary p.158-60. *Class No:* 914.20

[5519]

WAINWRIGHT, M. *and* LOCKE, T. The Which? guide to Yorkshire and the Peak District. London, Consumers' Association and Hodder & Stoughton, 1992. 288p. illus., maps, index. £10.99. ISBN: 034055035x.

8 topographical chapters: 1. West Yorkshire ... 4. North Yorkshire Moors ... 8. Peak District and 9. Walking. Final practical information section includes notes on accommodation, markets, entertainment, and travel *etc*. *Class No:* 914.20

[5520]

The Which? guide to the West Country. London, Consumer's Association and Hodder & Stoughton, 1991. 337p. maps, index. pbk. £9.95. ISBN: 0340514434.

Points the way to the best West Country attractions. Arranged in 12 topographical sections (11 regional + Walking). Each section ends with 2-tier system highlighting first and second division attractions. Information (p.322-32) includes Tourist Information Centres, public travel details, cinemas, market days *etc*. Covers Somerset, Devon, Cornwall, Isle of Scilly. *Class No:* 914.20

Bibliographies

[5521]

English places. London, British Library, 1998. 12p. bibliogs., sd. *gratis.* (Humanities Readers Guide no.3)

Short guide to printed sources of information in the Humanities collections of the British Library: General works and bibliographies; Victoria County History; Directories; Gazetteers and books of travel; Domesday Book; Towns; London; Buildings; Place names; Illustrations; Maps and atlases; Newspapers and general periodicals; and other resources. *Class No:* 914.20(01)

London

[5522]

AA complete book of London. Basingstoke, Hants., Automobile Publishing, 1996. 192p. col.illus., col.maps. ISBN: 0749503955.

31 tourist attractions and areas explored Central street atlas and theatreland maps. Illustrated with colour photographs. Details on shopping, pubs, entertainment and eating out. 'On the Perimeter' guide to the outer limits of the city. 6-page river map. *Class No:* 914.21

[5523]

Guide to London docklands. Monahan, P., *ed.* London, William Curtis, 1989. 144p. col.illus. £2.50. ISBN: 1871967066.

Docklands past and present - Residential property - Getting about - Eating out - Good pub guide - Sport - Things to do - Green spaces - Shopping - Consumer services - A place to do business. *Class No:* 914.21

[5524]

London city and docklands atlas. Reading, GEO Projects, 1998. 38p. maps. £4.50. ISBN: 0863510051.

Brings together the City of London map at 1:4,500 and the London Docklands at 1:10,000 in paginated form showing detailed streets, community facilities, land use categories, important buildings and places of interest. Featuring City traffic restrictions. British Rail, Docklands Light Railway and Underground stations shown. Places to visit guides and street name indexes for both areas. London Underground map. *Class No:* 914.21

[5525]

PHILLIPS, T. A London Docklands guide: a gazetteer of historical and architectural interest in St. Katherine's, Wapping, Shadwell, Ratcliff, Limehouse, Poplar, Blackwall, Isle of Dogs, Silvertown, North Woolwich, Beckton, Bermondsey, and Rotherhithe, with maps and photographs. High Wycombe, Buckinghamshire, Peter Marcan Publications, 1986. vi,58p. illus., maps, bibliog. £5.95. ISBN: 0951028952.

A useful guidebook in 8 chapters encompassing the London dockland Boroughs of Southwark, Tower Hamlets, and Newham. Short histories of each region are followed by imaginatively illustrated accounts of their surviving landmarks. Bibliography p.58. 13 individually drawn street maps. *Class No:* 914.21

CD-ROM

[5526]

StreetMaster London Your street-level journey planner and electronic atlas. Basingstoke, Hants., AA Multimedia, 1997. CD-ROM for Windows. ISBN: 0749515104.

AA StreetMaster London is based on the sophisticated mapping and route-planning capabilities developed for in-car navigational systems ... Simply select your location and destination and AA StreetMaster London will calculate your quickest or shortest route (*advt.*), but 'wherever you are bound within the M25, you will get there much faster with an old fashioned printed street map' (*The Times. Interface*) section 3 March 1999, p.11). *Class No:* 914.21(003.40)

Channel Islands

[5527]

STEVENS, J. and JEE, N. The New Shell guide to the Channel Islands. London, Michael Joseph, 1987. 192p. illus. (many col.), maps, bibliog., index. £12.95. (*New Shell Guides.*) ISBN: 0718127609.

Descriptive gazetteer of 1. The Bailiwick of Jersey (including boxed essays on such topics as the Jersey militia, Museum of La Société Jersiaise) - 2. Guernsey (including Sark, Alderney and the smaller islands). Glossary p.174. Bibliography p.175. 8 maps. *Class No:* 914.234

Wales

[5528]

BREVERTON, T. An A to Z of Wales and the Welsh. Swansea, Christopher Davies, 2000. 296p. £14.99. ISBN: 0175407341.

'A dip-in dip-out A-Z supplement for conventional tourist books/ histories' (*Introduction*). *Class No:* 914.29

[5529]

GREAT BRITAIN. Cadw: Welsh Historic Monuments. **A Nation under siege** The Civil War in Wales 1642-48. London, HMSO, 1991. 80p. col. illus. pbk. £6.95. ISBN: 011701222x.

Pictorial guide to over 30 castles and a number of walled towns, great houses, and churches associated with the Civil War. *Class No:* 914.29

[5530]

TOMES, J. Blue Guide Wales. 8th ed. London, A & C Black, 1995. 326p. illus., maps, index. £12.95.

Formerly published as *Blue Guide Wales and the Marches.*

1A. Background information (Countries of Wales, Eisteddfod, The Flag (Red Dragon), Industrial archaeology, History p.25-42, Biographical notes p.42-53 etc.) - 1B. Practical information (Organizations like Wales Tourist Board. CADW, Welsh Development Agency) - 2. Detailed descriptions of 46 routes criss-crossing the Principality, illustrated and with maps and plans. An indispensable guide 'excellent on detailed historic and geographical background' (*Observer*, no.10,399, 3 February 1991, p.59). *Class No:* 914.29

Maps & Atlases

[5531]

Wales Tourist Board map. Norwich, Jarrolds, 1999(?). Single sheet folded to tall pocket size. £1.95. ISBN: 1850130825.

14 car tours. Details of National Parks, beaches, forests etc. List of Tourist Information Centres. Scale 5m:1inch. *Class No:* 914.29(084.3)

Germany

[5532]

ARDAGH, J. The Shell guide to Germany. London, Simon & Schuster, 1991. 332p. col. illus., maps, bibliog., index. pbk. £10.99. ISBN: 0671710214.

A guide to Germany in 8 chapters: 1. Introduction (Germany today, historical dates, travelling and accommodation etc. including a Glossary of German words p.25-7) - 2. North Rhine/Westphalia - 3. Rhineland/Palatinate - 4. Baden/Württemburg - 5. Bavaria - 6. Hessen - 7. Lower Saxony - 8 Hamburg - 9. Bremen - 10. Schleswig Holstein - 11. Berlin. Bibliography p.328. *Class No:* 914.30

France

[5533]

AA illustrated guide to France. Basingstoke, Automobile Association, 1992. 256p. col. illus., col. maps, index. £25. ISBN: 0749405001.

Comprehensive guide to all the French regions highlighting where to go and what to see. A special section is devoted to Paris. Michelin mapping. *Class No:* 914.4

[5534]

AA walks and tours in France. Basingstoke, Automobile Association, 1993. 256p. col.illus., col. maps. £19.99. ISBN: 0749505540.

11 contributors. 61 tours and 114 walks covering whole of France arranged by region. The Institut Géographique National de France p.5-6. Walk maps extracted from IGN 1:25,000 Série Bleue; Tour maps IGN 1:250,000 Série Rouge. Data: Route directions, route map and illustrations. Points of interest. *Class No:* 914.4

[5535]

The Holiday Which? guide to France. Ruck, A., *comp.* 4th ed. London, Consumers' Association and Hodder & Stoughton, 1991. 662p. illus., maps, index, pbk. £10.95. ISBN: 0340550287.

1st ed. 1982.

14 regional profiles (*e.g.* Paris - Isle de France ... Loire Valley - Britanny - Normandy) followed by sections on French history and architecture, eating and drinking in France, and general travel and accommodation information. 'An informative, practical and readable general purpose guide' (*Reference Reviews*, v.5, no.4, 1991, p.32). *Class No:* 914.4

[5536]

Index atlas de la France: liste des localités, nomenclature des communes, cartes départementales et plans de villes. New ed. Rennes, Oberthur, 1991. 989p. maps, tables, index. ISBN: 2901454022.

In 4 parts: 1. General (Tableau de la France administrative; tableaux des distances kiométriques entre 50 grandes villes; cartes de la France routières) - 2. Index des communes et localités p.32-112. 3. Cartes départementales p.113-304. 4. Nomenclature départementale des communes et localités p.305-432. 5. Plans de villes p.433-992. *Class No:* 914.4

[5537]

Michelin Green tourist guides - France. Guides verts touristiques. Watford, Michelin Tyre PLC, Travel Publications Department. £8.49 to £8.99.

2000 French language titles : *Alpes Du Nord - Alpes du Sud - Alsace et Lorraine - Auvergne - Bourbonnais - Berry-Limousin - Bourgogne - Bretagne - Champagne-Ardenne - Châteaux de la Loire - Corse - Côte D'Azur - Flandres, Artois, Picardie - Ile de France - Jura - Languedoc, Gorges du Tarn, Cévennes-Normandie Cotentin - Normandie - Vallée de la - Seine - Paris - Pays Rhenans-Périgord Quercy - Poitou Vendée Charentes - Provence - Pyrénées-Acquitaine - Pyrénées-Rousillon - Vallée du Rhoine.*

2000 English language titles: *Alsace Lorraine Champagne - Atlantic Coast-Auvergne/Rhone Valley-Brittany - Burgundy Jura - Châteaux of the Loire - Dordogne-Berry Limousin - French Alps - French Riviera - Languedoc, Roussillon and Tarn Gorges - Normandy - Northern France and the Paris region - Paris-Provence.*

Detailed descriptions of places of interest including town plans. Intended for use with 1:200,000 Michelin regional maps of France (*qv*). 'Are in a class of their own for sightseeing and route planning (*Sunday Times,* 8732, 29 Dec. 1991: p.3:9). *Class No: 914.4*

[5538]

OIZON, R. Dictionnaire géographique de la France: communes, départements, régions, population, économie, tourisme. Paris, Larousse, 1979. 915p. maps.

Records 36,394 communities, noting postal code, population and local features (*e.g.* industry). Unlike comparable gazetteers, has entries for natural regions (*e.g.* Vosges), historical sites (*e.g.* Touraine), tourist attractions (Loire Châteaux), rivers, peaks, national/regional parks, spas and winter sports centres. Overseas départements are included. 'It would be difficult to identify a more useful gazetteer for any country' (*American Notes & Queries,* October 1979, p.27). *Class No:* 914.4

[5539]

Regions of France. London, A. & C. Black. 1989- col. illus., maps, pbk. £11.99.

Auvergne and the Massif Central. 0747012202; *Brittany.* 0747039938; *Dordogne & Lot.* 3rd ed. 0713641193; *Languedoc and Roussillon.* 3rd ed. 0713645245; *The Loire Valley.* 0747039911; *Normandy, Picardy and Pas de Calais* 2nd ed. 0747042998; *Paris.* 0713680482; *Provence and the Côte d'Azur.* 0747039946; *Rhone Valley and Savoy.* 0747080326; *South-West France.* 074703992x. *Alsace: the complete guide.* 0747038281; *Champagne-Ardennes and Burgundy.* 0747041770.

Each book includes a lively account of the region's history, a section on food and drink, and a detailed narrative tour of all the region's notable features - cities, villages, chateaux, churches and monuments and areas of outstanding natural beauty. *Class No:* 914.4

[5540]

The Which? guide to Brittany and Normandy. The all-in-one guide to touring, walking, camping and beach holidays in North-West France. London, Consumers' Association and Hodder & Stoughton, 1993. 298p. maps, index. pbk. £11.99. ISBN: 0340564806.

Descriptive gazetteer in 7 regional chapters with final Practical Information section (travel, package holidays, accommodation, weather, *etc.*). *Class No:* 914.4

Italy

[5541]

The Holiday Which? guide to Italy. Morgan, I. rev. ed. London, The Consumers' Association and Hodder & Stoughton, 1992. 560p. illus., maps, index. £10.95. ISBN: 034053897x.

3 introductory essays on History; Art and Architecture; and Food and Wine precede 12 topographical chapters: 1. Lakes and mountains - 2. Venice - 3. Northern cities - 4. Liguria - 5. Florence - 6. Tuscany and Umbria - 7. Rome - 8. Central Italy - 9. Naples and Campania - 10. The South - 11. Sicily - 12. Sardinia. Each chapter contains an introduction 'to give a flavour of what the region or city or island is like'; descriptions of resorts, monuments, places of scenic interest, excursions, *etc.*; and recommended hotel information. A final general information section surveys travel arrangements, recommended books (p.512-5), maps, festivals, and the weather. 'Our aim has been to produce a guide that you won't need to supplement except with road maps and city plans' (*About this guide*). *Class No:* 914.50

[5542]

NORWICH, J.J., *ed.* **Regions of Italy.** London, A. & C. Black, 1995-. col.illus., maps, plans, pbk. £11.99 each volume.

Florence and Tuscany 0713638214; *Naples and Campania* 0713638230; *Umbria, The Marches & San Marino* 0713638222; *Venice and North East Italy* 0713643757.

Comprehensive guides to the towns, villages and countryside illustrated with specially commissioned full colour photographs and with historical and gastronomic background. Routes and walks with recommended sights and recommended hotels and restaurants. *Class No:* 914.50

[5543]

TOURING CLUB ITALIANO. Guida d'Italia. Milano, Touring Club Italiano. maps, plans, bibliogs.

First published 1914-29.

23 Regional volumes regularly updated. Ideal for detailed exploration of a particular region with very detailed information supported by maps, town plans and a bibliography. Titles: *Piemonte* 728p. L45.000; *Torino e Valle d'Aosta,* 408p. L47,000; *Lombardia* 1100p. L65,000; *Milano,* 671p. L54,000; *Veneto,* 740p. L47,000 *Venezia,* 794p. L56,000; *Trento-Alto Adige,* 576p. L47.000; *Friuli Venezia Giulia,* 573p. L47,000; *Liguria,* 778p. L55,000; *Emilia Romagna,* 787p. L54,000; *Toscana,* 816p. L.55,000; *Firenze e ditorni,* 496p. L47,000; *Marche,* 708p. L52,000; *Umbria,* 552p L47,000; *Lazio* 830p. L55,000; *Roma e dintori,* 830p. L54,000 *Abruzzo e Molise,* 534p. L47,000; *Campania,* 716p. L54,000; *Napoli e dintori,* 640p. L47,000; *Puglia,* 486p. L47,000; *Basilicata e Calabria,* 714p. L54,000; *Sardegna,* 704p. L54,000; *Sicilia,* L65,000 *Rome and Latium,* L15,000 160p. is available in an English language edition. *Class No:* 914.50

[5544]

—TOURING CLUB ITALIANO. Guide illustrata d'Italia. Milano Touring Club Italiano, 1984. 416p. illus, maps, plans. L42,000.

566 A-Z principal places of interest. 41 maps and plans of tours, archaeological sites, 34p. road maps, and short description of Italy's 20 administrative divisons. 777 col. photographs. Also *Guida ai centri minori-Italia Settentrionale,* 368p. L50,000; *Italia Centrale,* 400p L50,000; *Italia Meridionale,* 400p. L50,000. *Class No:* 914.50

[5545]

Touring Club of Italy guides. Basingstoke, Hampshire, Automobile Association. col.illus., maps. From £11.99 to £17.99.

Florence 0749520124; *Italy* 0749520132; *Marche: a complete guide to the region, its national parks and over a hundred towns, including Urbino.* 2000. 0749523441; *Milan* 0749520140; *Naples* 0749520159; *Rome* 0749520167; *Sicily* 0749520175; *Umbria* 2000. 0749523174; and *Venice* 0759420183. All complete with regional and town maps, hotels, restaurants, shops, cultural and historical detail, and walks and car tours with detailed route maps. *Class No:* 914.50

Spain

[5546]

Diccionário geográfico de España. Madrid, Ediciones de Movimiento, 17v., 1956-61.

'The fullest information about Spain yet collected in a single work' (*Times Literary Supplement,* no.3,176, 11 January 1963, p.28). In gazetteer form, entries A-Z, often containing very detailed information. v.17 (xxi,[1], 747p.) includes: 1. 'Plazas de soberania y provincias africanas': 2. 'Poblados nuevos': 3. 'Addenda'. Questionnaires were sent out to all the towns and villages of Spain, to be answered by the local authorities. *Class No:* 914.60

[5547]

MEAD, R. Andalucía handbook. 2nd ed. Bath, Footprint Handbooks; Lincolnwood, Ill., Passport Books, 1999. 354p.+6p. col. maps, col. illus., plans. £9.99; $17.95. (*Footprint Handbooks.*) ISBN: 190094927x, UK; 0844221252, US.

1st ed. 1997.

Fact-packed handbook in mainly regional sections 1. Footstep in the door 2. Essentials (land, wildlife, history, modern Andalucía) - 3. Andalucía (Málaga, Almería, Cádiz, Córdoba, Granada, Huelva, Jaén, and Sevilla Provinces , and Gibraltar) - 4. Background information for travellers (travel, accommodation, food and drink, entertainment, holidays and festivals etc.) - 5. Footnotes (useful addresses, words and phases, maps). Comprehensive, readable, and bang up to date. *Class No:* 914.60

[5548]

Regions of Spain London, A. & C. Black, 1995-. illus., maps, plans, pbk.

Barcelona & Catalonia 0747080296; *North-West Spain* 074708016x. Comprehensive guides to the towns, villages and countryside; routes and walks with recommended sights; background history, recommended hotels and restaurants. *Class No:* 914.60

[5549]

The Which? guide to Spain: a panorama of mainland Spain, plus Mallorca, Menorca, Ibiza and the Canary Islands, all in one volume. Belford, R., *and others.* London: Consumers' Association and Hodder & Stoughton, 1991. 631p. maps, bibliog., index. pbk. £12.95. ISBN: 0340521937.

Introduction (history, art and people, environment and wildlife, bullfighting ... eating in Spain, accommodation), 13 regional guides and gazetteers (Andalucia ... Valencia), and Balearic and Canary Islands. Glossary of art, architectural and gastronomic terms p.618-20. Bibliography p.617-8. *Class No:* 914.60

Gibraltar

[5550]

BENADY, T., *ed*. Gibraltar guidebook. 2nd ed. Grendon, Gibraltar Books, 1989. 47p. col. illus., maps, bibliog. £1.95. ISBN: 0948466138.

1st ed. 1982. Previous edition titled *Guide-book to Gibraltar* (1985). Gibraltar's historical background and places of interest. *Class No:* 914.682

Russia

[5551]

NOBLE, J., *and others*. Russia, Ukraine & Belarus. Hawthorne, Vict., Lonely Planet, 1996 (1999 reprint). 1187p. col.illus., maps, index.

Russia (Moscow and Around Moscow; St. Petersburg and Around St. Petersburg; West and North European Russia; Volga; Caucasus; Trans-Siberian Railway; Siberia and the Far East; Western Siberia) - Ukraine (Kiev; Central, Western and Southern Ukraine; the Crimea) - Belarus (Minsk; Elsewhere in Belarus). Glossary p.1164-1167. *Class No:* 914.7

Baltic States

[5552]

MUNRO, D., *comp*. The Scotia reference gazetteer of the Baltic States. Kinnesswood, Kinross, D. Munro, 1996. 144p. maps. ISBN: 0952861607.

Descriptive topographical guide to 800 places in 3 county sections (Estonia, Latvia, and Lithuania) each printing a glossary (English: other language), a Fact file (official name, language, religion, constitution), and a gazetteer. *Class No:* 914.74

Iceland

[5553]

HÁLFDÁNARSON, O., *ed*. Iceland road guide. 3rd ed. Reykjavik, Iceland Travel Books, 1981. 440p. maps, pbk.

Based on original Icelandic editions 1973 and 1974.

Single or double-page road sketches cover the whole national network with brief descriptions of all interesting places *en route*. Based on the road numbering system. 2 general and 9 area maps. *Class No:* 914.911

[5554]

SCHEI, L.K. and MOBERG, G. The Faroe Islands. London, John Murray, 1991. viii,248p. illus. (some col.), map, bibliog., index. £10.95. ISBN: 0719550092.

1. Nature - 2. Early times ... 4. Later history ... 6. People ... 9. Place-names ... 16. The Grind (whales) - 17/28. Island chapters. Glossary p.238-9. Bibliography p.240-1. *Class No:* 914.911

[5555]

SWANEY, D. Iceland, Greenland and the Faroe Islands. 3rd ed. Hawthorne, Vict., Lonely Planet, 1997. 627p. col.illus. maps, index. £12.99 $19.95.

Facts about the region - Facts for the visitor - Getting there and away - Iceland (Reykjavik; Rekjanes Peninsula; West and South Central Iceland; The Westfjords; North Central Iceland; Akureyri; North East, East, South West and Central Iceland) - Greenland (South, Southwestern Greenland; Disko Bay) - The Faroe Islands (Tórshavn; Streymoy and Eysturo, Outer Islands). *Class No:* 914.911

Greece

[5556]

The Holiday Which? guide to Greece and the Greek Islands. Morgan, I., *ed*. London, Consumers Association and Hodder & Stoughton, 1989. 710p. bibliog., maps, index, pbk. £10.95. ISBN: 0340504331.

3 parts: 1. Background information on history and architecture, mythology, wild flowers, eating and drinking - 2. The Mainland (Athens and Attica; The Peloponnese; Central Greece: Macedonia and Thrace) - 3. The Islands (Corfu and the Ionian Islands; The Peloponnese Islands: Evia and the Sporades; The Cyclades; Rhodes and the Dodecanese; The North-East Aegean Islands). Recommended books p.677-78. *Class No:* 914.95

China

[5557]

Collins China guides and Collins illustrated guides. London, Collins, 1985-. col. illus., col. maps, pbk. £8.95.

Collins illustrated guide to all China. 1988. ISBN 0002152398. Other titles: Fuijan; Guilin, Canton and Guangdong; Hangzhou and Zhejiand Province; Jiangsu; The Silk Road: Xian; Yangzi; Yangzi River; Yunnan. *A guide to Beijing.* 1987. 144p. 0002179458 has sections Life in Beijing; Getting to B.; General information for travellers; Climate and clothing; Hotels; Getting around;

....(contd.)

Recommended restaurants; Entertainment; Shopping; History of Beijing. Other titles: *Canton; Fujian; Jiangsu; Shanghai; etc.* *Class No:* 915.10

[5558]

—SCHWARTZ, B. China off the beaten track. London, Collins Harvill, 1985. viii,247+16p. maps, tables, bibliog., index, pbk. £8.95. (*China Guides Series.*) ISBN: 0002721147.

Background historical, political and cultural information and notes on travel arrangements and visas *etc.* precede descriptions of 37 areas and cities grouped in 6 regions: North China, Yellow River, Yangtse Basin, South China, Southwest, and Beyond the Wall (The Silk Road, Inner Mongolia, The Northeast, and Tibet). An appendix includes a phrasebook, main train timetables, a brief glimpse of Hong Kong and Macau, and a Bibliography (p.240-242). List of open cities p.iv. 24 city-centre maps. *Class No:* 915.10

Hong Kong

[5559]

MORAN, K. Hong Kong handbook including Macau and Guangzhou. Chico, California, Moon Publications, 1995. 347p. illus., maps, bibliog., index. $15.95. £10.95. ISBN: 1566910560. ISSN: 10790675.

Introduction (land, climate, history, government etc.) - Hong Kong basics (sport and recreation, accommodation, food and restaurants etc.) - Hong Kong island - Kowloon - New Territories - Outlying islands (Lantau, Cheung Chan. Lamma) - Macau - Guangzhou. Glossary p.327-30. Bibliography p.331-38. *Class No:* 915.123.17

Tibet

[5560]

CHAN, V. Tibet handbook: a pilgrimage guide. Chico, Calif., Moon Publications, 1994. 1100p. illus., maps, bibliog., index. £19.95. ISBN: 0918373905.

1. Introduction (history, art) - 2. Lhasa - 3. Pilgrimage and historical sites - 4. Works of art - 5. Pilgrimage and trekking routes - 6. Practical information. Glossary p.1044-52. Bibliography p.1062-64. 'A rich mine of information, complete with over 200 plans and trekking maps and an excellent introductory guide to spoken Tibetan. Monumentally definitive; an absolute must' (*Traveller*, v.26, no.4, Autumn 1996, p.52-53). *Class No:* 915.15

[5561]

DORJE, G. Tibet handbook. 2nd ed. Bath, Trade & Travel; Lincolnwood, Ill., Passport Books, 1999. 968p. illus., (some col.) maps (some col.), indexes. £12.99. $21.95. ISBN: 1900949334, (UK); 0844221902, (US).

1st ed. 1996.

Authoritative details of the entire country, including the far west, north and east not previously covered in any other guidebook. It gives a remarkable insight into Tibet and the mountain kingdom of Bhutan, with the access points for travellers from Kathmandu and China. An iconographic guide of Tibetan Buddhism p.883-916. Glossary p.919-30. *Class No:* 915.15

Korea

[5562]

NILSEN, R. South Korea handbook. Chico, California, Moon Publications, 1988. 600p. col. illus., maps, charts, bibliog., index, pbk. $14.95. ISBN: 0918373204.

Definitive travel guide. Korean glossary and language notes. Subject and place-name index. *Class No:* 915.19

Japan

[5563]

BISIGNANI, J.D. Japan handbook. Chico, California, Moon Publications, 1983. 504p. col.illus., maps, charts, bibliog., index, pbk. $12.95. ISBN: 0960332227.

Cultural and anthropological encyclopaedic guide to every aspect of Japanese life for the tourist and traveller. Appendix on Japanese life and glossary. 112 maps and plans. Subject and place-name index. *Class No:* 915.2

[5564]

PALEVSKY, N. *and* KINESHITA, J. Gateway to Japan. 3rd ed. London, Kodansha Europe. 808p. illus., maps, index. pbk. £15.99. ISBN: 477002018x.

The premier guide to Japan, offering a comprehensive survey of every region of the country, complete with historical and cultural notes. *Class No:* 915.2

[5565]
Tokyo city atlas a bilingual guide. London, Kodansha Europe, 1998(?). 124p. (84in. col.), maps, index, pbk. £13.99. ISBN: 4770017812.

A comprehensive guide to Metropolitan Tokyo, featuring 21 area maps with both *chome* and *banchi* numbers, subway station exit guides, 18 detailed maps, details of surrounding major urban centres, and an index of 3600 place names and landmarks. *Class No: 915.2*

Gulf States

[5566]
LORIMER, J.G. Gazetteer of the Persian Gulf, Oman and Central Arabia. Reading, Garnett for The Sultan Qaboos Univ., Oman, 19v., 1998. 2000p. maps, geneal tables, bibliog. £3,000 (set). Volumes also sold separately. ISBN: 185964127x.

A geographical and statistical volume was published in 1908, to be followed by a two-part historical 'volume' in 1915. A separate portfolio of genealogical charts of the ruling families of the region was also published.

Bilingual English and Arabic edition. The 2000-page, alphabetically ordered survey which comprises the geographical volume, and the large-scale fold-out map which accompanied it, is being published in seven volumes. The original historical volume, which includes the regions' general history from the Abbasid Caliphate of 1258 to the early twentieth century plus individual histories of the eleven political entities within the region, is published as a further ten volumes. In addition, there are two boxed volumes of maps and genealogical tables, bringing the total number of volumes in this set to nineteen. *Class No: 915.36*

[5567]
ROBISON, G. Arab Gulf States. 2nd ed. Melbourne, Lonely Planet Publications, 1999. 513p. col.illus., col.maps, index. £12.99. ISBN: 086442390x.

Facts about the region - Facts for the visitor - Getting there and around - Bahrein - Kuwait - Oman - Qatar - Saudi Arabia - United Arab Emirates. *Class No: 915.36*

India

[5568]
BHATT, S.C., *ed*. The Encyclopedic district gazetteers of India. New Delhi, Gyan Publishing House, 11v. and Supplement v., 1998. ISBN: 8121205255, set.

1. *Southern Zone*: Andaman and Nicobar Islands, Andhra Pradesh, Karnataka - 2. Kerala, Lackshadweep, Pondicherry, Tamil Nadu - 3. *Northern Zone*: Chandigargh, Delhi, Haryana, Himachal Pradesh, Jammu and Kashmir - 4. *Central Zone*: Madhya Pradesh - 6. Uttar Pradesh - 7. *Western Zone*: Dodra and Nagar Havell, Daman and Diu, Goa, Gujerat, Maharashtra - 8. *Eastern Zone*: Bihar - 9. Orissa, West Bengal - 10. *North-eastern Zone*: Arunchal Pradesh, Assam - 11. Manipur, Meghalaya, Mizoram, Nagaland, Sikkim, Tripura - *Supplement*: Karnataka, Haryana, Uttar Pradesh, Gujerat.

Data given in these substantial volumes: location and area, history, population, languages, religion, geographical and physical features, rivers and canals, waterways, towns villages, communications, agriculture and irrigation, animal husbandry, industry, trade commerce and exports, tourism, fairs and festivals, education, medicine, administration, and a map for each district. *Class No: 915.40*

[5569]
BRADNOCK, R. India 2001. 10th ed. Bath, Footprint Handbooks, 2000. 1408p.+24 col. maps, tables, index. £15.99. ISBN: 1900949644, UK.

1st ed. 1996.

1. A foot in the door - 2. Essentials - 3. Northern India (Uttar Pradesh, Madhya Pradesh, Rajasthan, Haryanna and Punjab, Himachal Pradesh, Jammu and Kashmir) - 4. Eastern India (Kolkata and West Bengal, Sikkim, Northeastern Hill States, Orissa, Bihar, Andaman and Nicobar Islands) - 5. Southern India (Tamil Nadu, Kerala, Kamatidia, Andhra Pradesh) - 6. Western India (Maharashtra and Mumbai) - 7. Background (history, culture, modern India) - 8. Footnotes (glossary, maps, index). *Class No: 915.40*

[5570]
BRADNOCK, Robert *and* BRADNOCK, Roma. Goa handbook. 3rd ed. Bath, Footprint Handbooks, 2000. 320p. illus., maps, bibliog., index. £9.99. ISBN: 1900949458, UK.

1. Introduction - 2. Horizons (land, culture, religion, history etc.) - 3. Around Goa (Panaji and Central Goa, special sites, Talukas, excursions outside Goa) - 4. Information for travellers - 5. Rounding up (further reading, useful addresses, index, maps). *Class No: 915.40*

[5571]
BRADNOCK, Robert *and* BRADNOCK, Roma. Indian Himalaya handbook. Bath, Footprint Handbooks, 2000. 320p. col.illus., col.maps, index. £10.99. ISBN: 1900949792.

When to go, with comprehensive information on climate and seasons - Guidance on where to trek and how to organise a trip - Listings on accommodation, eating and all practicalities - and Background information on culture, history, geography, religion and the people. Encompasses Garhwal and Kumaon Himalaya in Utter Pradesh, the Himalaya in Himachal Pradesh, Ladakh and Zanskar in the Western Himalaya and Darjeeling area, Sikkim in the Eastern region. *Class No: 915.40*

[5572]
BRADNOCK, Robert *and* BRADNOCK, Roma. South India handbook. Bath, Footprint Handbooks, 2000. 480p. col.illus., col.maps, index. £11.99. ISBN: 1900949814.

Guide to the highly diverse area of South India covering the popular destination of the state of Kerala plus the states of Tamil Nadu and Karnataka. *Class No: 915.40*

Bibliographies

[5573]
SCHOLBERG, H. The District Gazetteers of British India a bibliography. Zug, Switzerland, Inter Documentation, 1970. xii, 131p. map, index. (*Bibliotheca Asiatica, no.3*.)

'A complete and orderly list of the district and state gazetteers of British India'. 16 chapters: 1. History - 2. Bengal - 3. Bihar and Orissa - 4. Assam - 5. Madras - 6. Bombay - 7. North-West Provinces and United Provinces - 8. Central Provinces - 9. Central India - 10. Rajputana - 12. North-West Frontier Province - 13. Sind - 14. Baluchistan - 15. Burma - 16. Miscellaneous gazetteers. Series list p.54-94. Author list p.95-109. Place-name index p.110-131.

'A district gazetteer is a comprehensive description of a district or state of British India, published privately, in series, or under the auspices of a governmental body, and including historical, archaeological, political, economic, sociological, commercial and statistical data' (*Introduction*). *Class No: 915.40(01)*

Dictionaries

[5574]
SHARMA, J.S. The National geographical dictionary of India. New Delhi, Sterling Publishers, 1972. viii, 223p.

About 2,000 entries, A-Z, with some cross-references and index. Delhi: 2/3p.; Madras ½p. also 2-3 line entries. Unspecified references to classical Indian works; vague locations; no map references. *Class No: 915.40(038)*

Bhutan

[5575]
DORGE, P., *comp*. Tibet handbook. 2nd ed. Bath, Footprint Handbooks; Lincolnwood, Ill., Passport Books, 1999. 968p. illus. (some col.), maps (some col.), indexes. £12.99 $21.95. ISBN: 1900949334, UK; 0844221902, US.

Section 13 (p.823-82) Bhutan is divided into 6 sections: 1. Essentials (planning, travelling, accommodation, holidays and festivals etc.) - 2. Thimphu - 3/5. West, Central and East Bhutan - 6. Background (history, land and environment, culture, religion, modern Bhutan) 'What more can be said about these universally admired Footprint Handbooks that has not been repeated over and over? Well, in this instance, simply that if reference libraries stock just one book on Tibet, this must be it' (*Reference Reviews*, v.13, no.8, 1999, p.45). *Class No: 915.413.1*

Nepal

[5576]
WOODHATCH, T. Nepal handbook. 2nd ed. Bath, Footprint Handbooks; Lincolnwood, Passport Books, 1999. 565p.+6p. col. maps, illus., bibliog. £11.99. $17.95. ISBN: 190094944x, UK; 0658000160, US.

1st ed. 1997.

1. A Foot in the door - 2. Essentials (where to go, before you travel, money, getting there, further readings etc.) - 3. Trekking, mountaineering and rafting (Western Himalaya, Annapurna Himal, Langtang, Eastern Highlands) - 4/9. Kathmandu Valley, Beyond the three cities, Kathmandu to Pokhara, The Terai, Dolpa and Western Nepal, Road to Tibet - 10. Background (history, land, religion, culture, Modern Nepal) - 11. Footnotes (glossary, index, money etc.) Information for travellers - 5. Rounding up. 'This new edition at once becomes the new standard guide to one of the worlds most remote and fascinating countries' (*Reference Reviews*, v.14, no.4, 2000, p.43-44). *Class No: 915.413.5*

Sri Lanka
[5577]

BRADNOCK, R. and BRADNOCK, R. Sri Lanka handbook. 3rd ed. Bath, Footprint Handbooks, 2000. 416p. illus., col.maps, index. £11.95. ISBN: 1900949709, UK.

1st ed. 1996.

A Foot in the door (Travel FAQS, planning etc.) - 2. Horizons (land and environment, architecture and art, history, modern Sri Lanka) - 3. Around Sri Lanka (Columbo, Western and Northwestern, Southwestern and Central regions, Kandy and the Hill Country, Cultural Triangle, Eastern region, Jaffna and the Northern province) - 4. Information for Travellers - 5. Footnotes (further reading, useful addresses, words and phrases etc.). *Class No:* 915.487

Pakistan
[5578]

WINTER, D. and MANNHEIM, I. Pakistan handbook. 2nd ed. Bath, Footprint Handbooks; Lincolnwood, Ill., Passport Books, 1999. 676p.+10p. col. maps, illus., index. £12.95. $19.95. ISBN: 1900949377, UK; 0844221449, US.

1. A Foot in the door (rich history) - 2. Essentials - 3. Sind - 4. Baluchistan - 5. Punjab - 6. Azad Jammu - 7. North West Frontier Province - 8. Karakoram Highway and the northern areas - 9. Background (history, climate etc.) - 10. Footnotes (Urdu words, maps, index). 'An excellent addition to the travel reference shelves (*Reference Reviews*, v.14, no.4, 2000, p.42-43). *Class No:* 915.49

Turkey
[5579]

CARSON, D. Turkey. London, Collins, 1988. 251p. illus., maps, bibliog., index. £5.95. (*Collins Independent Travellers Guide*.) ISBN: 0004109716.

Background information (History, Turkey today, Weather, Travelling, Where to stay, Eating and drinking, Sport, Shopping, General Basics) p.13-69. 7 x A-Z regional gazetteers. Concise, reliable, informative. *Class No:* 915.60

Syria
[5580]

MANNHEIM, I. and WINTER, D. Jordan, Syria and Lebanon handbook. Bath, Footprint Handbooks; Lincolnwood, Ill., Passport Books, 1998. 686p. illus., maps, index. £12.99. $21.95. ISBN: 1900949148, UK; 0844248694, US.

1. International and regional travel - 2. Horizons (land, people, history etc.) - 3. Jordan - 4. Syria - 5. Lebanon - 6. Rounding up (further reading, index, maps). 'Scarcely can a page be turned without the eye alighting on some interesting historical or biblical fact' (*Reference Reviews*, v.13, no.4, 1999, p.54-55). *Class No:* 915.691

Israel
[5581]

WINTER, D. Israel handbook with the Palestinian Authority areas. 2nd ed. Bath, Footprint Handbooks, Lincolnwood, Ill., Passport Books, 1999. 841p.+8p. col. maps, indexes. £12.99. $19.95. ISBN: 1900949423, UK; 0658003682, US.

1st ed. 1998.

1. A Foot in the door - 2. Essentials - 3. Jerusalem - 4. The West Bank - 5. Dead Sea region - 6. Negev - 7. Gaza - 8. Tel Aviv/Jaffa - 9. Mediterranean coastal strip - 10. Haifa and the North coast - 11. Galilee and the Golan - 12. Background (history, land, modern Israel) - 13. Footnotes (maps, glossary of archaeology and architecture terms). *Class No:* 915.694

Jordan
[5582]

MANNHEIM, I. Jordan handbook. Bath, Footprint Handbooks, 2000. 416p. col.illus., col.maps, index. £11.99. ISBN: 1900949695.

Plans and details of all the major sites plus the less frequently visited sites - Coverage of the overland route from Europe - Background information on history, culture, religion, landscape and archaeology, and details of camal safaris, diving, snorkelling, rock climbing and archaeological digs. *Class No:* 915.695

Afghanistan
[5583]

Historical and political gazetteer of Afghanistan. Adamec, L.W., ed. Graz, Akademische Druck-und Verlagsanstalt, 6v., 1972-1985. 3388p.

Gazetteer of Afghanistan first prepared by General Staff of British India in 1871 as a secret reference source. Subsequent editions in 1882, 1894, 1907 and 1914. This edition consolidates new material up to 1970.

....*(contd.)*

1. *Badakhshan and Northeastern Afghanistan.* 1972. xiii,255p. Glossary p.198-218. 2. *Farah and Southwestern Afghanistan.* 1973. xv,385p. Glossary p.325-45. ISBN 3201008575. 3. *Herat and Northwestern Afghanistan.* 1975. xvi,519p. Glossary. 3201009423. 4. *Mazar-i-Sharif and North-Central Afghanistan.* 1979. xviii,693p. Glossary p.607-27. 320101898. 5. *Kandahar and South-Central Afghanistan.* 1980. xx,667p. Glossary p.579-601. 3201011258. 6. *Kabul and Southeastern Afghanistan.* 1985. xx,847p. Glossary p.825-47. 3201012726. All volumes have substantial unnumbered map sections. The gazetteer combines the most important geographical data with historical, political, and cultural information. *Class No:* 915.81

Myanmar
[5584]

ELIOT, J. Myanmar (Burma) handbook. Bath, Footprint Handbooks; Lincolnwood, Ill., Passport Books, 1997. 416p. illus., maps. £9.99; $16.95. ISBN: 0900751878, (UK); 084424919x, (US).

Originally published as part of *Thailand, Indochina & Burma handbook,* 1992 (4th ed. as *Thailand & Burma* handbook, 1996).

1. Introduction and hints (whether to go, where and how to go etc.) - 2. Horizons (land, history, modern Burma etc.) - 3. Burma (Yangon, Lower Myanmar, Central Myanmar, Eastern and Northern Hills. West Coast, The South) - 4. Bangkok and Chiang Mai - 5. Information for travellers - 6. Rounding Up (reading and listening, the internet, maps, glossary etc.) *Class No:* 915.91

Thailand
[5585]

ELIOT, J. and BICKERSTETH, J. Bangkok and the Beaches handbook. Bath, Footprint Handbooks, 2000. 448p. col.illus., col.maps, index. £10.99. ISBN: 1900949784.

Practical information on how to get about and where to stay and eat, with coverage of the popular destinations of Phuket and Koh Samui, Phi Phi, and beyond to the lesser knwon areas and islands. *Class No:* 915.93

[5586]

ELIOT, J. and BICKERSTETH, J. Thailand handbook. 2nd ed. Bath, Footprint Handbooks; Lincolnwood, Ill., Passport Books, 1999. 833p. illus., col. maps. £12.99. $19.95. ISBN: 1900949326, (UK); 0844222389, (US).

1st ed. 1997.

1. A foot in the door (how and when to go etc.) - 2. Essentials - 3. Bangkok - 4. Central Plains - 5/8. Northern, Northeastern, Eastern and Western Regions - 9. Southern Thailand) - 10. Background (history, politics, land and environment, modern Thailand) - 11. Footnotes (food glossary, maps, index etc.). *Class No:* 915.93

Malaysia
[5587]

Malaysia & Singapore handbook. Eliot, J. and Bickersteth, J., eds. 3rd ed. Bath, Footprint Handbooks, 2000. 820p. col.illus., col.maps, col.maps on endpapers, bibliogs., index. £12.99. ISBN: 1900949520.

First published in 1992 as part of *Indonesia, Malaysia & Singapore Handbook* (4th ed. 1995).

Contents: 1. A Foot in the door (where and how to go, cost etc.) - 2. Malaysia (7 geographical sections) - 3. Brunei - 4. Singapore - 5. Footnotes (health, words and phrases, eating out etc.). Glossary p.680-83. Comprehensive guide. 'This is a fascinating part of the world and one could not have a better guidebook than this one' (*Reference Reviews*,v.12,no.4, 1998, p.49-50). *Class No:* 915.95

Singapore
[5588]

ELIOT, J. and BICKERSTETH, J. Singapore handbook. Bath, Footprint Handbooks; Lincolnwood, Passport Books, 1999. 235p. illus. (some col.), maps (some col.), index. £9.99. $16.95. ISBN: 1900949199, UK.

1. A Foot in the Door (culture) - 2. Essentials - 3. Singapore Island - 4. Background (history, land and environment, modern Singapore) - 5. Footnotes (food glossary, maps, index). *Class No:* 915.951.3

Kampuchea (Cambodia)
[5589]

COLET, J. Cambodia handbook. 2nd ed. Bath, Footprint Handbooks; Lincolnwood, Ill., Passport Books, 2000. 214p.+6p. col. maps, col. illus. £9.99; $15.95. ISBN: 1900949474, UK; 0658000675, US.

1st ed. 1997.

Informative, practical guide in 7 chapters: 1. Foot in the door (where and how to go) - 2. Essentials (history, art and architecture) - 3. Phnom Penh, 4. Northeast Cambodia - 5. Northwest and the Tonlé

....*(contd.)*

Sap - 6. The South - Background (accommodation, food and drink, entertainment) - 7. Footnotes (reading and listening, health, glossary, maps, index). *Class No:* 915.96

Vietnam

[5590]

COLET, J. *and* ELIOT, J. **Vietnam handbook.** 2nd ed. 1999. Bath, Footprint Handbooks; Lincolnwood, Ill., Passport Books, 1999. 421p.+7p. col. maps, illus., index. £10.99. $16.95. ISBN: 1900949369, (UK); 0844221937, (US).

1st ed. 1997.

1. A Foot in the door (historical sites)- 2. Essentials - 3. Hanoi - 4. The North - 5. Central Region - 6. Saigon - 7. Mekong Delta - 8. Background (after the war, modern Vietnam etc.) - 9. Footnotes (glossary, index). 'These new-style Handbooks will prove at least as successful as the old ones' (*Reference Reviews*, v.13, no.7, 1999, p.42-43). *Class No:* 915.97

Laos

[5591]

ELIOT, J., *and others*. **Laos handbook.** Bath, Footprint Handbooks; Lincolnwood, Ill., Passport Books, 1999. 305p.+6p. col.maps, col. illus. £9.99. $15.95. ISBN: 1900949466, UK; 0658000144, US.

1st ed. 1992.

1. Foot in the door (how and where to go etc.) - 2. Essentials (land, history, art and architecture, modern Laos) - 3. Vientiane - 4. The North - 5. Central Province - 6. The South - 7. Background (travel, food, accommodation etc.) - 8. Footnotes (reading and listening, glossary etc.). *Class No:* 915.98

Africa

[5592]

KIRCHHERR, E.C. **Place names of Africa 1935-1986** a political gazetteer. Metuchen, New Jersey, Scarecrow Press, 1987. viii,136p. bibliolg., maps, tables. £13.15. ISBN: 0810820617.

A completely revised, enlarged and updated edition of the author's earlier *Abyssinia to Zimbabwe: a guide to the political units of Africa in the period 1947-1978* (Athens, Ohio, Ohio Univ. Center of International Studies, 3rd ed., 1979).

Pt.1 General introduction (need for a political gazetteer, notes on the maps *etc.*) - 2. Place names of the principal African states and adjacent islands A-Z (p.7-89) - 3. Supplementary notes and maps - 4. Bibliography p.125-36. 23 maps. 'The layout, the cross-referencing, the maps, the crisp, uncluttered explanations ... bring many disparate facts together' (*Geographical Journal*, v.155, no.2, July 1989, p.253). *Class No:* 916

Bibliographies

[5593]

TAUSSIG, L. **Resource guide to travel in Sub-Saharan Africa.** London, Hans Zell, 2v., 1994-1997. £135. set ISBN: 1873836554, set.

1. *East and West Africa.* 1994. 383p. £75. ISBN 1873836457. 2. *Central and Southern Africa (and Indian Ocean Islands).* 1996. xxx,468p. index. £75. 1873836503. 1,500+ entries provide annotated listings of guide books and maps, details of tourist offices, national parks, historical sites and monuments, plus language guides and courses. It also includes extensive directory-type listing of the book shops, libraries, and tourism centres, with a special section devoted to conservation and natural history organizations. 'Without doubt these two volumes constitute a major addition to the bibliography of African tourism and travel' (*Reference Reviews*, v.12, no.3, 1998, p.54-55). *Class No:* 916(01)

Tunisia

[5594]

McGUINNESS, J. **Tunisia handbook with Western Libya.** 2nd ed. Bath, Footprint Handbooks; Lincolnwood, Ill., Passport Books, 1999. 557p.+12p. col. maps., illus. (some col.). £10.99. $19.95. ISBN: 0900949342, (UK); 0844221929, (US).

1st ed. 1997.

1. A Foot in the door (highlights, the deep South, excursions in Western Libya) - 2. Essentials (planning, travel, where to stay, food and drink, shopping, further reading etc.) - 3. Tunis and around (history and background, Carthage) - 4. Cap Bon peninsula - 5/8. Northern, Central, Southwestern, Southeastern Tunisia - 9. Djerbo - 10. Background (history, land and environment, arts and architecture, culture, modern Tunisia). Undoubtedly the most practical and comprehensive guide to Tunisia currently on the market'. (*Reference Reviews*, v.14, no.4, 2000, p.44). *Class No:* 916.11

Libya

[5595]

McGUINNESS, J. **Libya handbook.** Bath, Footprint Handbooks, 2000. 352p. col.illus., col.maps, index. £12.99. ISBN: 1900949776.

Comprehensive information on how to plan a trip to Libya from getting the documents to when to go: Practical information on how to get about and where to stay: Background information written by an expert on culture, history, religion and art and architecture; and with details of excursions to Southeastern Tunisia and across the Egyptian frontier to Alexandria. *Class No:* 916.12

Egypt

[5596]

McLACHLAN, A. *and* McLACHLAN, K. **Egypt handbook.** 2nd ed Bath, Footprint Handbooks, 2000. 600p. col.illus., col.maps, bibliog. index. £12.99. ISBN: 090075172x; 1900949687, UK.

1st ed. 1996.

1. A Foot in the door (travelling in Islamic countries, history, travel and survival in the desert) - 2. Horizons (land, culture, history modern Egypt) - 3. Around Egypt (Cairo and environs, the Pyramids and El-Fayoun, The Nile Valley, Alexandria and the Mediterranean coast, Suez Canal zone, Sinai, Red Sea coast) - 4. Information for travellers - 5. Libya - 6. Footnotes (further reading, useful addresses index, maps). 'Librarians can stock this guide with confidence, and intending tourists ... should certainly invest in a copy' (*Reference Reviews*, v.13,no.2, 1999, p.49-50). *Class No:* 916.20

Morocco

[5597]

McGUINNESS, J. **Morocco handbook.** 2nd ed. Bath, Footprint Handbooks; Lincoln, Ill., Passport Books, 1999. 560p.+8p. col maps, illus., index. £11.99. ISBN: 1900949350, (UK); 0844221325 (US).

1st ed. 1997.

A Foot on the door (imperial cities, modern Morocco) - 2. Essential - 3. Tangier and the Northwest - 4. Rabat - 5. Casablanca and the Central Atlantic coast - 6. Imperial cities and the Middle Atlas - 7 Eastern Morocco - 8. Marrakech and the High Atlas - 9. Southern Morocco - 10. The deep South - 11. Background (history archaeology, arrival of Islam) - 12. Footnotes (language, maps glossary). *Class No:* 916.4

Africa—East & Equatorial

[5598]

HODD, M. **East Africa handbook 2001.** 7th ed. Bath, Footprint Handbooks, 2000. 864p.+9p. col. maps. £14.99. ISBN: 1900949652 (UK).

1. Foot in the door - 2. Essentials etc. - 3. Kenya - 4. Tanzania and Zanzibar - 5. Uganda - 6. Ethiopia - 7. Eritrea - 8. Djibouti - 9 Footnotes (books, index, maps). *Class No:* 916.7

South Africa

[5599]

BALLARD, S. **South Africa handbook 2001 with Lesotho and Swaziland.** 2nd ed. Bath, Footprint Handbooks, 2000. 1024p.+10p col. maps, index. £14.99. ISBN: 1900949660, (UK).

1st ed. 1999.

1. A Foot in the door - 2. Essentials - 3. Cape Town - 4. Western Cape - 5. Eastern Cape - 6. KwaZulu Natal - 7. Gauteng - 8. North West Province - 9. Mpumalanga - 10. Northern Province - 11. Free State - 12. Northern Cape - 13. Background (history, land and environment, modern South Africa) - 14. Lesotho - 15. Swaziland 16. Footnotes (travel, maps, index). *Class No:* 916.80

Namibia

[5600]

BALLARD, S. *and* SANTCROSS, N. **Namibia handbook.** 2nd ed Bath, Footprint Handbooks; Lincolnwood, Ill., Passport Books, 1999 320p. maps, illus., bibliog., index. £10.99. $21.95 ISBN 190094930x, UK; 0844221333, US.

1. A Foot in the Door (people and way of life, adventures in the desert) - 2. Essentials (shopping, holidays and festivals etc.) - 3. Windhoek - 4/7. The North - 8. The Coast - 9. Namib-Naukluft - 10 The South - 11. Background (history, land and environment, modern Namibia) - 12. Footnotes. *Class No:* 916.88

Zimbabwe

[5601]

BALLARD, S. *and* LINTON, R. **Zimbabwe and Malawi handbook** Bath, Footprint Handbooks; Lincolnwood, Ill. Passport Books, 1997. 576p. illus., maps. £11.99. ISBN: 0900751932, UK.
Class No: 916.891

Canada

[5602]

CANADA. Department of Mines And Technical Surveys. Geographical Branch. **Gazetteers of Canada.** Ottawa, Canadian Government Publishing Centre, 1952-. pbk or mircrofiche.

First published by the Canadian Permanent Committee on Geographical Names (1952-62).

List of place-names with brief description or identification, location and coordinates. *Alberta* C$19.50. ISBN 0660539842 - *British Columbia*, 3rd ed. 1985. C$22.50. 0660527731 - *Manitoba*, 3rd ed. 1981. C$8.00. 0660508486 - *New Brunswick* (Microfiche only) C$3.00 - *Newfoundland*, 2nd ed. 1983. C$12.00. 0660521911 - *Northwest Territories*, 1980. C$7.00. 0660504669 - *Nova Scotia*, 2nd ed. 1977. C$10.00. 0660016745 - *Ontario*, 3rd ed. 1988. C$ 19.95. 0660518644 - *Prince Edward Island*, 2nd ed. 1973. C$1.50 - *Saskatchewan*, 3rd ed. 1985. C$8.00. 0660530481 - *Yukon Territory*, 4th ed. 1981. (Microfiche only) C$2.00. Bilingual. *Class No:* 917.1

[5603]

HEMPSTEAD, A. **Alberta and the Northwest Territories handbook** including Banff, Jasper, and the Canadian Rockies. 3rd ed. Chico, Calif., Moon Publications, 1999. 491p. illus., col.maps, bibliog., index. $18.95. £12.99. ISBN: 1566911443. ISSN: 10799338.

Introduction (land, flora, fauna, history, geography and geology, people) - On the road (recreation, accommodation and food, transportation, other practicalities) - Calgary - Dinosaur Valley - Southern Alberta - West of Calgary - Banff National Park - Jasper National Park - Central Alberta - Edmonton - Northern Alberta - Northwest and Nunavut. Booklist p.400-403. *Class No:* 917.1

[5604]

LIGHTBODY, M., *and others*. **Canada.** 7th ed. Melbourne, Lonely Planet Publications, 1999. 992p. col.illus., col. maps, index. £14.99. ISBN: 0864427522.

Facts about Canada (history, geography etc.) - Facts for the visitor (tourism, post and communications etc.) - Getting there and away. Province by province tour and travel guide (Ontario, Quebec, Newfoundland and Labrador, Nova Scotia, Prince Edward Island, New Brunswick, Manitoba, Saskatchewan, Alberta, Yukon, North West Territories, Nunavut). Glossary p.967-69. *Class No:* 917.1

[5605]

The **Nunavut handbook.** Iqaluit, Nortext Multimedia, 1999. 454p. (20p. col.pl.). Cdn$29.95. US$21.50.

1st ed. 1997.

On 1 April 1999 Canada's latest province, Nunuvut, came into existence. This commemorative edition of what seems set fair to becoming an annual publication contains 100 chapters (accommodation, transport, the Government, national and territorial parks, and a chapter on every community. Available on the Internet at www.arctic-travel.com.

Lisa Sykes' 'Returned to the natives', (*Sunday Times*, 13 September 1998, Travel p.4-5) includes details of planning a trip, getting there, accommodation etc. Adrian Mourby's 'Living at the tip of the iceberg', (*The Times*, 27 March 1999, Travel p.28) includes a useful boxed factfile. See also Stuart Wavell's 'This land is our land' (*Sunday Times Magazine*, 28 March 1999, p.40-43, 45-47). *Class No:* 917.1

America—Central

[5606]

HUTCHISON, P. **Central America & Mexico handbook 2001.** Bath, Footprint Handbooks, 2000. 1376p. col.illus., col.maps, index. £15.99. ISBN: 1900949636.

Special feature on Central America 'at a glance' - where to go and how to get about - Comprehensive coverage of the whole region from the deserts of Northern Nexico to the lush rainforests of Cental America - Feature on the Maya World of Mexico, Honduras, Guatemala, El Salvador and Belize - Examines the Pacific and Caribbean beaches and the surfing scene (including Baja California) - Background information on ancient civilizations, and archaeological sites. Ranges across: Mexico, Guatemala, Costa Rica, Belize, Nicaragua, El Salvador, Honduras, Panama. *Class No:* 917.28

Belize

[5607]

MALLAN, C. **Belize handbook.** 2nd ed. Chico, Calif., Moon Publications, 1993. 263p. illus., maps, bibliog., index. $13.95. £8.95.

Introduction (land, sea, flora, fauna, history, economy, people, accommodation, transport etc.) - Mundo Maya (*i.e.* Maya archaeological sites) - Belize - The Cayes - Corozal - Orange Walk - Cayo - Stann Creek, and Toledo Districts. Bibliography p.255-56. *Class No:* 917.282

Costa Rica

[5608]

BAKER, C.P. **Costa Rica handbook.** 3rd ed. Chico, Calif., Moon Publications, 1999. 785p. illus., maps, index. $19.95. £12.99. ISBN: 1566911249.

Introduction (land, ecosystem, fauna, history, people) - On the road - San Jose - Central Highlands - Caribbean coast - Northern Lowlands - Guanacaste and the Northwest - Nicoya Peninsula - Central Pacific - Golfo Dulce - Peninusla de Osa - South Central Costa Rica. *Class No:* 917.286

Caribbean

[5609]

CAMERON, S. **Caribbean Islands handbook 2001.** 12th ed. Bath, Footprint Handbooks; Lincolnwood, Ill., Passport Books, 2000. 1168p.+12p. col. maps, index. £14.99; $22.95. ISBN: 1900949628, UK.

1st ed. 1989.

1. Beginners guide to the Caribbean - 2. Essentials - 3. The Bahamas - 4. Cuba - 5. Cayman Islands - 6. Jamaica - 7. Turks & Caicos Is. - 8. Haiti - 9. Dominican Republican - 10. Puerto Rico - 11/12. US + British Virgin Islands - 13. Leeward Islands - 14. Netherlands and French Antilles - 15. Windward Islands - 16. Barbados - 17. Trinidad & Tobago - 18. The Venezuelan Is. - 19. Netherlands Antilles and Aruba - 20. Footnotes (index, maps etc.). Winner of the Thomas Cook Award. *Class No:* 917.29

Bibliographies

[5610]

POYNTING, J. **Resource guide to travel in the Caribbean.** London, Hans Zell, 1996. 250p. £48.00. ISBN: 0905450620.

800 + entries including annotated listings of over 300 mainstream travel guide books, and general-purpose and thematic maps; reviews of specialist guides to historical sites, diving and snorkelling, and the region's birdlife cuisine and local languages; a broad selection of modern travel writing on the Caribbean; reviews of travel and special interest videos; extensive directory-type listings of travel bookshops, map specialists and major library collections in Europe, North America, and the Caribbean itself; sections on the services offered by government tourist organizations and both international and Caribbean-based conservation agencies. *Class No:* 917.29(01)

Cuba

[5611]

CAMERON, S. **Cuba handbook.** 2nd ed. Bath, Footprint Handbooks; Lincolnwood, Ill. 1999. 380p. illus., maps, index. £10.99. $19.95. ISBN: 1900949547, UK; 0844249483, US.

1. Cuba Introduction - 2. Horizons (pre-Columbian civilisations, history, culture, responsible tourism) - 3. Around Cuba (Havana, Pinar del Rio, Matanzas, Cienfuego, Villa Clara, Sancti Spiritus, Ciego de Avila, Les Tunas, Holguin, Santiago de Cuba, Granima, Guentanamo) - 4. Information for Travellers - 5. Rounding Up (index, events, food vocabulary. *Class No:* 917.291

Jamaica

[5612]

LUNTTA, K. **Jamaica handbook 2000.** 4th ed. Chico, Calif., Moon Publications, 1999. 375p. illus. (few col.), maps, bibliog., index. $15.95. £10.95. ISBN: 1566911613. ISSN: 10880941.

Introduction (land, history, government, economy, people etc.) - On the Road (events, arts, shopping, accommodation, food and drink, transport etc.) - Montego Bay - Negril - Southwest coast and inland - Kingston - Blue Mts. - Port Antonio - Ocho Rios - Runaway Bay and the North Coast . Bibliography p.288-97. Glossary p.298-307. *Class No:* 917.292

Dominican Republic

[5613]
CAMERON, S. **Dominican Republic handbook.** Bath, Footprint Handbooks, 2000. 384p. col.illus., col.maps, index. £10.99. ISBN: 1900949601.

Special feature on the history and culture of the Republic - Explores inland as well as the coast - Full coverage of 'adventure' tourism (river rafting, climbing Pico Duarte, horse riding, walking) - Extensive listings of hotels, restaurants, care hire facilities. Comprehensive coverage of National Parks. *Class No: 917.293*

USA

[5614]
American places dictionary a guide to 45,000 populated places natural features and other places in the United States covering counties, cities, towns, townships, villages and boroughs, as well as Indian Reservations, military bases, and major geographical features, the entries providing descriptions, precise locations and name origin information and supported by maps and indexes. Abate, F.R., *ed.* Detroit, Omnigraphics, 5v., 1992. 3500p. tables. $350; $85 each vol. ISBN: 1558887474, set.

1. *Northeast.* 1558881468. 2. *South/Southeast.* 1558881476. 3. *Central.* 1558881484. 4. *West.* 1558881492. 5. *National index.* 1558881247. Information on every state, all 3,141 US countries, nearly 40,000 cities, towns, townships, boroughs. Indian reservations, and 170 major military installations (*i.e.* every place with a functioning government), includes legal status, ZIP and area code, latitude and longitude, and 1980 and 1990 census population. For larger towns and cities descriptive location, economic, and historical background is given. All main entries are listed in the index volume along with names of individuals, institutions and other text references. *Class No: 917.3*

[5615]
The Cambridge gazetteer of the United States and Canada a dictionary of places. Hobson, A., *ed.* Cambridge Univ. Press, 1995, xiv,743p. maps. £40. $49.94. ISBN: 0521415799.

12,000 entries, based on latest census details relating to all states, provinces and territories, and their capital cities, and all municipalities of 10,000 population (UK) and 8,000 (Can). Also industrial sites, national parks. Based on 2 questions: What is the essence of this place? Why is this place of enough interest to merit inclusion? Glossary entries (geological, physical, historical, governmental) listed p.xii-xiii. *Class No: 917.3*

[5616]
CANTOR, G. **Historic landmarks of Black America.** Detroit, Gale Research Co., 1991. 372p. illus., maps, bibliog., index. $29.95; £20. ISBN: 0810378094.

Over 300 significant sites, memorials, historical houses, museums, libraries, colleges, battlefields arranged A-Z by state and city in 6 regions. Idaho, Nevada, Wyoming, and North Dakota are not represented although southern Ontario is covered. Data: historical significance, location, directions, access. Chronology 1539-1919.
Historical black landmarks: a traveler's guide. Visible Ink (Gale), $17.95. ISBN 0810394081 is a paperback edition. *Class No: 917.3*

[5617]
CASTLEMAN, D. **Navada handbook.** 5th ed. Chico, Calif., Moon Publications, 1998. 530p. illus., maps, bibliog., index. $18.95. £12.99. ISBN: 1566911168. ISSN: 10785426.

Introduction - On the road (travel, accommodation etc.) - Reno and Western Nevada - Northwest, Northeast, and Central Nevada - Las Vegas and the Southern Corner. Booklist p.513-16. *Class No: 917.3*

[5618]
City profiles USA 1997: a traveler's guide to major U.S. cities. Kniskern, N.V., *ed.* 2nd ed. Detroit, Omnigraphics, 1997. xxvi,609p. $85. ISBN: 0780800931. ISSN: 10829938.

1st ed. 1996.

Provides important contact information for about 30,000 travel-related services, facilities, attractions, and events in more than 200 cities located throughout the United States. Included are the largest US cities by population, the capital city of each state, and other important US travel destinations ... balanced coverage of all states, with each state represented by at least two cities. The work focuses on individual cities rather than metropolitan areas. Data: brief description of the city, followed by listings of its population, land and water areas, latitude and longitude, county, time zone, and principal area code(s). *Class No: 917.3*

[5619]
The Complete guide to America's National Parks 1995-96 edition. Washington, National Park Foundation, 1994. 540p. maps. $14.95; £12.99. ISBN: 0679026762.

'The official and only comprehensive visitors' guide to the 367 National Parks'. National Park sites A-Z by State p.26-442. National Trains System p.443-58. National Rivers and National Wild and Science Rivers, p.451-70. Special Interest Parks p.471-74. Data: address, directions, visitor activities, permits, fees and limitations, accessibility, camping and lodging, food and supplies, first aid/hospitals, general information. *Class No: 917.3*

[5620]
Counties USA 1997. Detroit, Omnigraphics, 1997. 580p. maps, index. $65. ISBN: 078080094x.

Descriptive and contact information for each of the 3,100-plus counties in the United States: the county seat, with a complete mailing address for the county office, a general telephone and fax number, and Internet address when available; population statistics (1990 census and 1995 estimate); population density; land and water areas; elevation; and name origin. Arranged by state, with all counties listed alphabetically within these state chapters. County Index provides an alphabetical list of every county in the United States, together with the name of the state in which the county is located. *Class No: 917.3*

[5621]
EASTMAN, J. **Who lived where in the USA** a biographical guide to homes and museums. New York, Facts on File, 1983. xxii,513p. illus., indexes. £20.00. ISBN: 0871965623.

Aims 'to catalog and present data on the American residences of more than 600 persons whose lives had major effects on national society and history; and to enable travelers ... to find and view for themselves the homes or sites associated with these famous persons' (*Introduction*). Data: Year of construction, destruction, dates of occupance, 1982 status of home or site including street address and access information. Sites listed in 6 regions. *Class No: 917.3*

[5622]
A Historical guide to the United States. New York, W.W. Norton, 1986. 601p. illus., index. $25. £19.95. ISBN: 0393023834.

Short essays providing a practical guide (representative rather than exhaustive) to places of historical interest in every State of the Union. Well indexed (p.579-601). 'The strength of this book is that it presents a national overview of the major state and local museums and scenic and historical sites in one volume' (*Choice*, v.24, no.9, May 1987, p.1380). *Class No: 917.3*

[5623]
KANE, J.N. **The American counties:** origins of county names, dates of creation and organization, area, population including 1980 census figures, historical data, and published sources. 4th ed. Metuchen, New Jersey, Scarecrow Press, 1983. xi,546p. bibliogs. £47.40. ISBN: 0810815583.

1st ed. 1960.

3067 counties listed A-Z: data includes 'capsule bibliographies'. Other sections list counties by State, their date of creation, county seats, and those counties whose names have changed. Also persons for whom counties have been named, independent cities, and Alaska boroughs. *Class No: 917.3*

[5624]
McRAE, W. *and* JEWELL, J. **Montana handbook** including Glacier National Park. 4th ed. Chico, Calif., Moon Publications, 1999. 457p. illus., maps, bibliog., index. $17.95. £11.99. ISBN: 1566911427. ISSN: 10822654.

Introduction (land, geology, climate, flora and fauna, history, government and economy, arts and culture) - On the road (sightseeing highlights, recreation, accommodation and food, transportation, other practicalities) - Southern, Northeastern, North Central Montana - The Judith Base and Central Montana - South-Central and the Missouri headwaters, Southwestern and Northwestern Montana - Glacier National Park. Booklist p.427-32. *Class No: 917.3*

[5625]
National Geographic guide to America's hidden corners. New York, Random House, 1999. 384p. col.maps, col.illus. $25. ISBN: 0792272110.

Guide for 'hard-to-please travellers who prefer the lesser known, still unspoiled spots' to 75 off-the-beaten track US destinations. Contents include essays by regional travel writers and current visitor information. 76 full-colour maps. *Class No: 917.3*

[5626]
National Geographic's guide to State Parks of the United States 2nd ed. Washington, National Geographic Society 1998. 384p. col. illus., col.maps. £24. ISBN: 0792273648.

Covers 50 states. Data: location and size, telephone nos. driving routes, facilities, what to see and do, best times to visit. 32 col. maps 250 col. photographs. *Class No: 917.3*

[5627]

mni gazetteer of the United States of America. Abate, F.R., *ed*. Detroit, Omnigraphics, 11v., 1991. 9400p. $2,000 (set); $200 (individual volumes). ISBN: 1558883363, set.

1. *New England* - 2. *Northeastern States* - 3. *Southeast* (including Puerto Rico, Virgin Islands, other Caribbean islands) - 4. *South Central States* - 5. *Southwestern States* - 6. *Great Lake States* - 7. *Plains States* - 8. *Mountain States* - 9. *Pacific* - 10. *National Index* - 11. *US Data sourcebook*. Approximately 1.5 million single-line entries for all places of 5,000 population upwards. Data: name, place or feature, state, county, zip code or 1990 Census population, latitude and longitude United States Geological Survey map name. V.10 has detailed A-Z list of every entry in the 9 regional volumes. V.11 is a supplementary collection of 7 specialized lists of vital national data amd other places not noted in the regional volumes. 'The largest compilation of US place names ever published ... essential for large reference collections ... smaller libraries can acquire individual volumes as needed. A landmark reference work' (*Library Journal*, v.166, no.13, August 1991, p.86+88). 'Will be of inestimable value to historians, genealogists, goegraphers, cartographers, and anyone working with demographics' (*ibid*, v.117, no.7, 15 April 1992, p.45). Included in *Library Journal's* Best Reference Books 1991.

Omni Gazetteer of the United States CD-ROM Version. Edited by Frank R. Abate. Software produced by SilverPlatter. Published by Omnigraphics, Inc., 1992. $2000. ISBN 1558884181.

Class No: 917.3

[5628]

-Omni gazetteer state series. Abate, F.R., *ed*. Detroit, Omnigraphics, 50v., 1992-. $3750 (Set); $125. (individual volumes).

Extracted from *Omni gazetteer of the United States of America* (*q.v.*).

First volume published: *Omni gazetteer of New York State: a guide to more than 40,000 place names*. 1992. $125. ISBN 1558887709. Each volume will cover all populated places, structures, facilities, locales, historic places, and named geographic features.

Class No: 917.3

[5629]

arks directory of the United States a guide to 3,700 national and state parks, recreation areas, historic sites, battlefields, monuments, forests, preserves, memorials, seashores, and other designated recreation areas in the United States administered by national and state park agencies. Smith, D.L., *ed*. 2nd ed. Detroit, Omnigraphics, 1994. 813p. maps, indexes. $145. ISBN: 0780800184.

1st ed. 1992.

4,700+ detailed entries provide comprehensive coverage of every national and state park, including battlefields, historic sites, memorials, monuments, parks, preserves, recreation areas, seashores, wild and scenic rivers and riverways, and other units. New areas of coverage include national forests, national wildlife refuges, national scenic and historic trails, and more than 150 major urban parks. Data: acreage, facilities, recreational activities, and special features. Entries also include basic reference information, directions and address and telephone number. Special Features Index lists geographic and historical references, such as battles, forts, and historical figures, mentioned in the text of the entries. The Master Index provides an alphabetical listing of all parks covered in the Directory.

Class No: 917.3

[5630]

ERK, J. Massachusetts handbook. Chico, Calif., Moon Publications, 1998. 461p. illus., maps, bibliog., index. $18.95. £12.99. ISBN: 1566910838. ISSN: 10968535.

Introduction (land, history, government and economy) - On the road (sightseeing highlights, accommodation and food, transportation, information) - Greater Boston - North of Boston Metrowest - Southern Massachusetts - Cape Cod - The Islands: Martha's Vineyard and Nantucket - Central Massachusetts - Pioneer Valley - The Berkshires. Booklist p.432-43. *Class No:* 917.3

[5631]

eader's Digest travel guide USA. Pines, P., *ed*. Pleasantville, NY., Reader's Digest Association, 1994. 432p. col.illus., col.maps, index. $29.97. ISBN: 0895775646.

Part road atlas, part travel guide in series of two-page spreads. Features lighthouses, village greens, covered bridges, boating lakes, fishing streams, waterfalls, islands, forests, mountains, forts, parks, zoos, battlefields, Indian museums city centres, and major tourist areas. 198 maps. 'Simplifies and improves trip planning through its very convenient layout placing site descriptions and maps side by side' (*Wilson Library Bullet*, v.69,no,1, September 1994, September 1994, p.86-87). *Class No:* 917.3

[5632]

SMITH, D.L. *and* KNISKERN, N.V. The Traveler's sourcebook. Detroit, Omnigraphics, 1996. 306p. $48. ISBN: 0780801742.

85 A-Z subject chapters cover every type of travel interest to US internal travellers along with visa, customs, bureaux de change, embassies and foreign tourism offices for the international traveller. Every conceivable sport or recreation is included, popular destinations, and all types of accommodation. 'This practical consumer-oriented reference work is sure to be a winner with both librarians and the public' (*Booklist*, vol.93, no.4, 15 October 1996, p.453).

Class No: 917.3

[5633]

SMITH, J. Virginia handbook including Chesapeake Bay, Shenandoah Valley. Chico, Calif., Moon Publications, 1999. 378p. illus., maps, ports, bibliog., index. $15.95. £10.99. ISBN: 1566911419. ISSN: 10998853.

Introduction (land, history, economy and government, people) - On the road (recreation, tours, shopping, accommodation, information and sources) - The Piedmont - The Coast - Southwest Virginia - The Shenandoah - Northern Virginia - Sidetrip to Washington. Booklist p.349-51. *Class No:* 917.3

[5634]

WEIR, K. Los Angeles handbook. Chico, Calif., Moon Publications, 1999. 350p. illus., maps, bibliog., indexes. $16.95. £10.99. ISBN: 1566911559.

Introduction (Greater Los Angeles, Los Angeles as an idea, place, story, direction) - Pasadena and vicinity - Downtown and around - Hollywood - The West Side - Beverley Hills - Los Angeles coast - Diversions beyond Los Angeles. Booklist p.305-21. *Class No:* 917.3

CD-ROM

[5635]

NATIONAL GEOGRAPHIC. Trip planner platinum. Washington, National Geographic, 1999. CD-ROM.

Detailed guide to 300+ parks in US and Canada in addition to 21 video tours of key attractions. 'The redesigned trip wizard enables users to customize and print out information on everything from driving instructions to local contacts to hotel costs.' (*advt.*).

Class No: 917.3(003.40)

Micromaterials

[5636]

The National register of historic places 1984. Alexandria, Virginia and Cambridge, Chadwyck-Healey, 1984. 300 6497 98-frame silver positive microfiche. £63.50. Individual State registers are available and priced separately.

Supersedes *The National Register of Historic Places 1976*.

150,000 photographs and 130,000 pages of text comprise a record of 27,000 sites and structures of importance in American history, archaeology, architecture and engineering, arranged by State. Information includes name, location, narrative, descriptions, significance, period, geographical data, and major bibliographical references. Includes all properties, registered up to December 1982. The National Register is the official list of historic properties recognised by the Federal Government. *Class No:* 917.3(003.5)

[5637]

—National register of historic places index. Wayzata Technology Inc. Annual. IBM compatible PC; Apple Macintosh, MS-DOS (Microsoft Extensions required); Apple. $295.

52,000 place names of historic importance from the records of the Department of the Interior and National Park Service. Data: place name, state, county, street address, city, type of place, certification date, criterial indicators, and reference numbers.

Class No: 917.3(003.5)

Amerindians, North

[5638]

CONFEDERATION OF AMERICAN INDIANS, *comp*. Indian reservations: a State and Federal handbook. Jefferson, N.C., McFarland, 1986. 329p. $45. ISBN: 0899502008.

Page-long descriptions of 277 reservations in 31 states. Data: address, tribal land holdings, history, culture, government, population profile, tribal economy, climate, and recreation. 'A unique source' (*Reference Services Review*, v.17,no.4, Winter 1989, p.66-7).

Class No: 917.3(=97)

Alaska

[5639]

DALBY, R. **The Alaska guide.** 2nd ed. Golden, Colo., Fulcrum Publishing, 1996. ix,226p. illus., maps. $16.95. ISBN: 1555913067.

10 regional sections (*e.g.* Southeastern Alaska - Anchorage ... Prince William Sound ... Arctic) divided by tourist destinations and locations each with information on travel, events, outdoor activities, indoor attractions, and guide to food and accommodation. *Class No:* 917.98

[5640]

STANLEY, D. *and* CASTLEMAN, D. **Alaska-Yukon handbook** including the Canadian Rockies. 2nd ed. Chico, California, Moon Publications, 1991. 415p. col. illus., maps, bibliog., index, pbk. $10.95. ISBN: 0918373786.

Superbly illustrated comprehensive travel guide. 94 maps. Subject and place-name index. *Class No:* 917.98

America—South

[5641]

South American handbook, 2001. Cox, B., *ed.* 76th ed. Bath, Footprint Handbooks; Lincolnwood, Ill., Passport Books, 2000. 1680p.+17p. col. maps, tables, indexes. £21.99 ISBN: 190094961x, UK.

1st ed. 1924 published by South American Publications.

1. A foot in the door (travel information) - 2. Essentials - 3. Argentina - 4. Bolivia - 5. Brazil - 6. Chile. - 7. Colombia - 8. Ecuador - 9. Paraguay - 10. Peru - 11. Uruguay - 12. Venezuela - 13. The Guianas - 14. Falkland Islands - 4. Footnotes, index, map symbols). *Class No:* 918

Bibliographies

[5642]

WAGENHAUSER, B. **Resource guide to travel in South America.** London, Hans Zell, 1996. 350p. £75. ISBN: 1873836252.

1000+ entries comprising annotated listings of over 500 mainstream travel guide books and maps; specialist coverage of the region's flora and fauna, national parks, historical sites, mountains and hiking trails, railways and languages; directory-type listings of travel bookshops, map specialists and major library collections in Europe, North America and in South America itself; separate sections devoted to travel and special interest magazines, and travel publishers and distributors; in-depth profiles of international and South American-based conservation, natural history and ecotourist organizations. *Class No:* 918(01)

Brazil

[5643]

BOX, B. **Brazil handbook.** 2nd ed. Bath, Footprint Handbooks, 2000. 799p.+12p. col.maps, col.illus. £13.99. ISBN: 1900949504.

1. Footsteps in the door - 2. Essentials - 3. Rio de Janeiro - 4. São Paulo - 5. Minais Gerais and Espirito Santo - 5. Iguacu Falls and the South - 6. Bachia - 7. Recife and the Northeast Coast - 8. Fortaleza and the Northern Coast - 9. The Amazon - 10. Brasilia and the Pontanal - 11. Background - 12. Footnotes (further reading etc.). 'A quality guide to an increasingly popular tourist destination' (*Reference Reviews*, v.12, no.8, 1998, p.49-50). *Class No:* 918.1

[5644]

DAY, M. *and* BOX, B. **Rio & around handbook.** Bath, Footprint Handbooks, 2000. 288p. col.illus., col.maps, index. £9.99. ISBN: 1900949806.

What to see and do in Rio de Janeiro and in Rio state. *Class No:* 918.1

Argentina

[5645]

NURSE, C. **Argentina handbook.** 2nd ed. Bath, Footprint Handbooks; Lincolnwood, Illinois, 2000. 608p. col.maps, col.illus., bibliog., index. £12.99. ISBN: 1900949679, UK.

1st ed. 1998.

1. A Foot in the door (where and how to go) - 2. Horizons (history, people, culture, economy) - 3. Argentina (Buenos Aires, the Pampas, Central Sierras, The West, Northwest, Northeast, Lake District, Patagonia, Tierra del Fuego) - 4. Information for travellers - 5. Footnotes. 'If there's anything out, it completely eludes your reviewer' (*Reference Reviews*, v.12, no.7, 1998, p.54-55). *Class No:* 918.2

Falkland Islands

[5646]

GREAT BRITAIN. Foreign and Commonwealth Office. **Gazetteer o** **the Falkland Islands Dependencies** (South Georgia and the Sout Sandwich Islands). London HMSO, 1977. 9p. sd.

763 place names A-Z accepted for official use. Supplement 1979. *Class No:* 918.291

Chile

[5647]

NURSE, C. **Chile handbook.** 2nd ed. Bath, Footprint Handbooks Lincolnwood, Ill., Passport Books, 1999. 544p.+7p. col. maps index. $19.95. £11.99. ISBN: 1900949288, (UK); 0844221279, (US). 1st ed. 1997.

1. A Foot in the door (how and when to go) - 2. Essentials - 3 Santiago - 4. Valparaiso and Viña del Mar - 5. From Santiago to L Serena - 6. North of La Serena - 7. Antofagasta Calama and San Pedr - 8. Iquique-Arica and the Far North - 9. Through the Central Valley 10. The Lake District - 11. Chiloé - 12. The Camino Austral - 13. Th Far South - 14. Tierra del Fuego - 15. Chilean Pacific Islands - 16 Background (history, land and environmentals etc.) - 18. Footnote (further reading, websites). 'One can only marvel at this splendi achievement, surely the finest guide to Chile available at such a modes price (*Reference Reviews*, v.14, no.4, 2000, p.45-46). *Class No:* 918.3

Bolivia

[5648]

MURPHY, A. **Bolivia handbook.** Bath, Footprint Handbooks Lincolnwood, Ill., Passport Books, 1997. 368p. illus., maps, bibliog £11.99. $21.95. ISBN: 1900949091, UK; 0844249238, US.

1. Introduction and hints - 3. Horizons (history, climate etc.) - 3 Bolivia (La Paz, Lake Titicaca, North of La Paz, Las Yungas, Potos and Sucre, Southern Highlands, Cochabamba, Eastern Lowlands Amazonia Basin) - 4. Information for Travellers - 5. Rounding u (maps, index etc.). 'Another high quality addition to the Footprin series' (*Reference Reviews*, v.12, no.3, May 1998, p.55-56). *Class No:* 918.4

Peru

[5649]

MURPHY, A. **Peru handbook.** 2nd ed. Bath, Footprint Handbooks Lincolnwood, Ill., Passport Books, 1999. 560p.+12 col. maps, illus £11.99. $17.95. ISBN: 1900949318, (UK); 0844221872, (US). 1st ed. 1997.

1. A Foot in the door (how and when to go) - 2. Essential (shopping, holidays etc.) - 3. Lima - 4. Cusco and the Sacred Valley 5. Lake Titicaca - 6. Arequipa - 7. South Coast - 8. Cordillera Bianca 9. North Coast - 10. Northern Highlands - 11. Central Highlands - 12 Amazon Basin - 13. Background (history, politics, modern Peru) 14 Footnotes (maps, basic Spanish for travellers etc.). *Class No:* 918.5

Columbia

[5650]

POLLARD, P. **Colombia handbook.** 2nd ed. Bath, Footprin Handbooks, 2000 480p. maps, illus., bibliog., index. £10.99. ISBN 1900949717, UK.

1st ed. 1998.

1. A Foot in the door - 2. History - 3. Colombia (Bogota, Bogota t Cúcula, The North Coast and Islands, Up the Rio Magdalena Antioquia and Chocó, La Zona Cafetera and the Cauca Valley Popayán, Tierradentro and San Agustin, The Llanos and Amazonia) 4. Information for travellers - 5. Rounding Up. 'One of the best an most thorough guides to Colombia in existence' (*Reference Reviews* v.12, no.8, 1998, p.50). *Class No:* 918.6

Ecuador

[5651]

MURPHY, A. **Ecuador & Galápagos handbook.** 2nd ed. Bath Footprint Handbooks; Lincolnwood, Ill., Passport Books, 1999 448p.+13 col. maps, illus. £11.99. $19.95. ISBN: 1900949296 (UK); 0844221295, (US).

1st ed. 1997.

A Foot in the door - 2. Essentials - 3. Quito - 4. Northern Ecuador 5/6. Central and Southern Highlands - 7. Guayaquil and south to Per - 8. Pacific Islands - 9. The Oriente - 10. Galápagos Is. - 11 Background (history, politics, government, modern Ecuador) - 12 Footnotes (basic Spanish, maps, index etc.). *Class No:* 918.66

Venezuela

[5652]
MURPHY, A. Venezuela handbook. 2nd ed. Bath, Footprint Handbooks; Lincolnwood, Ill., Passport Books, 2000. 384p. illus., maps, bibliog., index. £11.99. ISBN: 190094958x.

A footstep in the Door. 1. Introduction and hints - 2. Horizons (history, economy, government etc.) - 3. Caracas, the Northwest Lara and Yaracuy, The Lowlands of Maracaibo, The Andes, The Llanos, Guyana and Orinoco - 4. Information for travellers - 5. Footnotes (further reading, index, maps). *Class No:* 918.7

Australasia & Oceania

Nomenclatures

[5653]
MOTTELER, L.S. Pacific island names a map and name guide to the New Pacific. 3rd ed. Honolulu, Bishop Museum Press, 1986. 91p. maps, index. (*Bishop Museum Miscellaneous Publications, no.34.*) ISBN: 0930897196. ISSN: 08886776.

First published 1960 as *Guide to Pacific Islands* compiled by E.H. Bryan. 2nd ed. 1972 *Guide to islands in the Tropical Pacific.* This edition greatly expanded and in a new format.

Lists 6,000 island names (4500 variants) in 2 sections: 1. Political guide to names - 2. Index. Primary area of coverage: Oceania between Tropics of Cancer and Capricorn with Northwestern Hawaiian islands, Austral Islands (French Polynesia), Pitcairn Island, and the Chilean islands in Southeast Pacific. Sectional maps p.6-12.
Class No: 919(083.72)

Indonesia

[5654]
DALTON, B. Indonesia handbook. 6th ed. Chico, Calif., Moon Publications, 1995. 1351p. illus., (few col.), maps, bibliog., index. $25. £15.95. ISBN: 1566910625. ISSN: 10785442.

1st ed. 1977.

Introduction (land, history, government, economy, people etc.) - On The Road (holidays/festivals/events, accommodation, food, transport etc.) - Java - Bali - Sumatra - Nusateng Kalimantan - Sulawesi - Maluku - Irian Java - Bahasa Indonesia. Glossary p.1308-18. Bibliography p.1319-30. *Class No:* 919.10

[5655]
ELIOT, J. Bali and the Eastern Isles handbook. Bath, Footprint Handbooks, 2000. 416p. col.illus., col.maps, index. £9.99. ISBN: 1900949733.

Covers the holiday island of Bali and its popular neighbour Lombok plus the less well known but easily accessible islands of Flores, Sumba and others in Eastern Nusa Tengarra. How to get about from island to island and how to plan an itinerary - background information on culture, history, religion and art and architecture with special features on beaches, diving and trekking. *Class No:* 919.10

[5656]
ELIOT, J. Indonesia handbook. Bath, Footprint Handbooks; Lincolnwood, Ill., Passport Books, 1998. 1,152p. illus., maps. £14.99. $24.95. ISBN: 1900949156, (UK); 0844249572, (US).

Originally published as part of *Indonesia, Malaysia & Singapore handbook,* 1992. (4th ed. 1996).

1. Introduction - 2. Horizons (land, history, modern Indonesia etc.) - 3. Indonesia (Java, Bali, Sumatra, Kalimantan, Sulawesi, Lombok and Sumbawa, East Nusa Tenggara and East Timor, Maluku, Irian Jaya) - 4. Information for Travellers - 5. Rounding Up (further reading, internet and radio, fares and timetables etc.). *Class No:* 919.10

Philippines

[5657]
HARPER, P. and FULLERTON, L. Philippines handbook. 2nd ed. Chico, Calif., Moon Publications, 1994. 638p. illus., maps, bibliog., index. $25. £15.95. ISBN: 1566910048.

1st ed. 1991.

Introduction (land, history, government, economy, people etc.) - Practicalities (shopping, entertainment, events, food, transport, accommodation etc.) - Luzon - Islands in the Stream (Mindoro, Palawan) - Visayas (Panay, Negros, Leyte, Samas) - Mindanao. *Class No:* 919.14

New Zealand

[5658]
KING, J. New Zealand handbook. 5th ed. Chico, California, Moon Publications, 1999. 512p. col.illus., maps, bibliog., index. $18.95; £12.99. ISBN: 1566911656. ISSN: 10852662.

1. Introduction (land, history, people, economy etc.) - 2. On The Road (food and drink, travel, accommodation etc.) - 3. North Island - 4. South Island - 5. Stewart Island. Glossary p.499-500. Booklist 502. *Class No:* 919.31

[5659]
The Past today historic places in New Zealand. Wilson, J., *ed.* Auckland, Pacific Publications for the New Zealand Historic Places Trust, 1987. vi, 183p., illus. (many col.), bibliogs., index. ISBN: 0864790015.

17 contributors. 19 chapters regional chapters on places of significance to Maoris and Europeans. Glossary of Maori terms p.173. Chapter bibliographies. For popular use. *Class No:* 919.31

[5660]
SHADBOLT, M. Reader's Digest guide to New Zealand. Sydney, Reader's Digest, 1988. 352p. col. illus., col. maps, index. $39.95. ISBN: 0864380372.

20 A-Z regional guides in gazetteer form with useful basic travel data. Special box features highlight wildlife, personalities and historical places. Well produced with 20 maps and over 500 photographs. *Class No:* 919.31

[5661]
Wises New Zealand guide a gazetteer of New Zealand. 8th ed. Auckland, Wises Publications, 1987. xxvi, 481p. col. illus., col. maps. ISBN: 0908794002.

Published as *Wises New Zealand index: every place in New Zealand 1899-1948.* First edition under current title 1952.

Descriptive guide (now incorporating historical detail) to towns, cities, localities, geographical and geological features, Maori folklore, and place-name meanings. General information (p.iv-xxvi) includes Maoris and European discovery, population, climate, main and suburban Post Offices. 23p. of maps. 63 col. plates. *Class No:* 919.31

Bibliographies

[5662]
AZZELINA, D.S. 'Trekking Australia and New Zealand' *Library Journal,* v.125, no.4, 1 March 2000, p.59-62.

Short bibliographical essay divided under the headings: Australia, general interest, New Zealand, language and literature, and web sites. Slightly flawed in that the writer of the essay labours under the illusion that New Zealanders are nicknamed Kiwis after the national fruit! *Class No:* 919.31(01)

Australia

[5663]
Australia's national parks. Sydney, Random House, 2000. 352p. col.illus., col.maps. $45. ISBN: 009183855x.

Over 125 parks are covered comprehensively, while additional text on another 160 parks and a detailed grid for every state gives information about access, facilities and activities for over 700 parks and reserves. *Class No:* 919.4

[5664]
The Cambridge dictionary of Australian places. Appleton, R. *and* Appleton, A., *comps.* Cambridge, Cambridge Univ. Press, 1992. xii,356p. maps. £40; $65. ISBN: 0521395062.

National gazetteer listing 'virtually every population centre in the country with pronunciation guide and etymological, geographical, and historical and economic information. 26 maps. *Class No:* 919.4

[5665]
Explore Australia 2000 the complete touring companion. 15th ed. London, Viking, 1999. vii,636p. col.illus., col.maps. index. £30. ISBN: 0670883611.

First published by George Philip and O'Neil 1980.

Introductory material for the motorist then A-Z touring guide, 750 towns and including places of historic interest, state by state with detailed maps for every State and Territory. Gazetteer of 9,000 place names. 15 inter-city route maps and complete road atlas of Australia. New to this edition: the best tours in each state, wildlife, national parks, and events listings. 'Easily the most comprehensive source around' (*Library Journal,* v.125, no.4, 1 March 2000. *Class No:* 919.4

[5666]
The Heritage of Australia the illustrated register of the national estate. Melbourne, Macmillan Company of Australia in association with Australian Heritage Commission, 1981. various pagination. illus., (some col.), maps, bibliogs., index. £40. ISBN: 0333337506.

6,600 places of historical interest (buildings and structures, national parks, Aboriginal sites, etc.) expertly described. Arranged State by State in 40 regional sections. Glossary p.86-89. Analytical index. Over 7,500 photographs. Monumental work. *Class No:* 919.4

[5667]
JOHNSON, M., *and others*. **Australia handbook**. Chico, Calif., Moon Publications, 1997. 913p. illus. (few col.), maps, bibliog., index. $21.95. £14.99. ISBN: 1566910722. ISSN: 10886427.

Introduction (land, history, government, people etc.) - On The Road (sport and recreation, accommodation, food and drink, travel, visas and officialdom, maps, tourist information etc.) - New South Wales - Northern Territories - Queensland, South Australia - Tasmania - Victoria - Western Australia. Glossary p.867-69. Bibliography p.870-74. *Class No:* 919.4

[5668]
JOHNSON, M. **Outback Australia handbook**. Chico, Calif., Moon Publications, 1996. 421p. illus., maps, bibliog. index. ISBN: 1566910471. ISSN: 10852670.

Introduction (land, history, government, languages etc.) - On The Road (sports, events/entertainment, accommodation, visas and officialdom etc.) - South Australia - Outback New South Wales and Queensland - Northern Territories - Western Australia. Glossary p.389-91. Bibliography p.392-96. *Class No:* 919.4

[5669]
MOON, R. *and* MOON, V., *eds*. **Discover Australia: national parks**. Sydney, Random House, 1999. 416p. col.illus., col.maps. $39.95. (*Discover Australia*.) ISBN: 0091837723.

Illustrated reference to over 1000 of Australia's national parks, reserves and state forests. The guide includes all new maps and information needed to explore. Arranged by state, the guide lists facilities available and walking and cycling tracks (with information on the length and the degree of difficulty) and camping restrictions. *Class No:* 919.4

[5670]
MOON, R. *and* MOON, V., *eds*. **Discover Australia: road guide**. Sydney, Random House, 1998. 416p. col.illus., col.maps. $39.95. (*Discover Australia*.) ISBN: 009183774x.

This guide gives detailed information on each town and its surrounding area; the main features of the town, the festivals, gatherings, sporting competitions and other attractions; and also suggestions on where to stay. *Class No:* 919.4

[5671]
Reader's Digest illustrated guide to Australian places. Sydney, Reader's Digest (Australia), 1993. 704p. col.illus., col.maps, index. ISBN: 0864383991.

178 maps describing 2,500 cities, towns, hamlets, national parks, monuments, and landmarks, including Aboriginal special places, state by state. Also traces course of European expansion. *Class No:* 919.4

Papua—New Guinea

[5672]
Papua New Guinea handbook : Business and travel guide. 11th ed. Sydney, Pacific Publications, 1985. 280p. illus., maps, plans.

First published as *The Handbook of Papua and New Guinea* in 1954. Revised at intervals.

Geography - History - The People - Land use - Finance - Commerce - Industry - Transport and communications - Social services - Religion. Pt.2: Provincial directory. *Class No:* 919.54

Polynesia

[5673]
STANLEY, D. **South Pacific handbook 2000**. 7th ed. Chico, California, Moon Publications, 2000. 976p. illus., maps, charts, bibliog., index. $23.95. £14.95. ISBN: 1566911729. ISSN: 10852700.

Comprehensive guide to the history, geography, climate, cultures and customs of the islands of Polynesia and Melanesia. Introduction (land, history, government, peoples etc.) - On The Road (accommodation, food, services and information, health, travel etc.) - Polynesia (Tahiti-Polynesia, Pitcairn Islands, Easter Island, Cook Islands, Niue, Tonga, Samoa, Tokelau, Wallis and Futuna Islands, Tuvalu) - Melanesia (Fiji, New Caledonia, Vanuatu, Solomon Islands). Resources (including a bibliography) p.929-56. Glossary p.957-61. 'Of particular value are the maps and information on how to get to remote outer islands of the various Pacific nations; (G.W. Fry and R. Mauricio. *The Pacific Basin and Oceania*, 1987. Entry 166). *Class No:* 919.6

[5674]
STANLEY, D. **Tahiti - Polynesia handbook**. 3rd ed. Chico, Calif., Moon Publications, 1996. 243p. illus. (some col.), maps, bibliog., index. $13.95. £8.95. ISBN: 1566910374. ISSN: 10824855.

Introduction (land, history, government, economy, people) - On The Road (entertainment, accommodation, sources of information, transport etc.) - Society Islands - Outer, Austral, Tuamotu, and Gambier Islands - Marquesas - Guidebooks - Reference Books - Map publishers. Glossary p.230-36. *Class No:* 919.6

[5675]
STANLEY, D. **Tonga - Samoa handbook**. Chico, Calif., Moon Publications, 1999. 321p. illus., maps, bibliog., index. $15.95. £9.99 ISBN: 1566911745.

Introduction (land, history, people etc.) - On the road. Samoa (Savai'i Opolu) - American Samoa (Tuila, Mann'a Group) - Tonga (Tongatapu, Ena Island, The Ha'apai Group. The Vava'u Group. The Ninas) - Niue. Bibliography p.289-301. Glossary p.303-04. *Class No:* 919.6

Fiji

[5676]
Fiji handbook business and travel guide. Douglas, N. *and* Douglas, N. Sydney and New York, Pacific Publications, 1987. 264p. illus. (some col.), maps, tables, bibliog., index, softcover. ISBN: 085807060x.

Previously published as *Fiji handbook and travel guide*.

1. The place, the past and the people - 2. Parliament, the public sector and productivity - 3. The traveller in Fiji. Chronology of Fiji p.21-24. Bibliography p.258-9. 9 maps and 16p. of coloured plates. *Class No:* 919.611

[5677]
STANLEY, D. **Finding Fiji**. Chico, California, Moon Publications, 1992. 127p. col. illus., maps, charts, bibliog., index, pbk. $6.95 ISBN: 0918373921.

Practical travel guide with Fijiian vocabulary. 26 maps. Subject and place-name index. Extracted from the author's *South Pacific handbook* (q.v.). *Class No:* 919.611

Micronesia

[5678]
LEVY, N.M. **Micronesia handbook** guide to the Caroline, Gilbert Mariana and Marshall Islands. 5th ed. Chico, California, Moon Publications, 2000. 308p., col. illus., maps, charts, bibliog., index pbk. $16.95. £10.99. ISBN: 1566911621. ISSN: 10880954.

Introduction (land, history, people) - On The Road (food, accommodation, travel, Information Services etc.) - Republic of the Marshall Islands - Federated States of Micronesia, Republic of Palau, Territory of Guam - Commonwealth of the Northern Marianas, Republic of Nauru - Republic of Kiribati - American possessions, Bibliography p.284-89. Glossary p.295-97. *Class No:* 919.65

Hawaii

[5679]
BISIGNANI, J.D. **Hawaii handbook. All Islands**. 5th ed. Chico, California, Moon Publications, 1999. 1100p. col.illus., maps, bibliog. index, pbk. $19.95. £13.95. ISBN: 1566911605. ISSN: 10785299.

Introduction (land, history, government) - Out and About (arts, sports, travel, accommodation) - Big Island - Maui - Kahoolawe, Lauai - Molokai - Nihau - Kauai. Glossary p.1062-66. Booklist p.1055-1061. *Class No:* 919.69

[5680]
NILSEN, R. **Honolulu-Waikiki handbook. The island of Oahu**. 3rd ed. Chico, Calif., Moon Publications, 1999. 328p. illus., maps, bibliog. indexes. $14.95. £10.99. ISBN: 1566911281. ISSN: 10772882.

Original text by J.D. Bisignani.

Introduction (overview) - On the road (food and drink, getting there information and services) - Honolulu-Waikiki (sights, shopping etc.) Central Oahu - Pearl City and vicinity) - Southeast Oahu - Windward Oahu - The North Shore - The Leeward Coast. Booklist p.302-308 Glossary p.309-313. *Class No:* 919.69

Greenland

[5681]
YDEGAARD, T. **Greenland**. Leicester, Cordee, 1990. 184p. £9.95 ISBN: 1871890004.

Complete trekking and travel guide. *Class No:* 919.88

Antarctic

[5682]
RUBIN, J. **Antarctica** a lonely planet survival kit. Hawthorne, Vict. Lonely Planet Publications, 1996. 362p. col.illus., maps, index £11.99. ISBN: 0864424159.

1. Facts about Antarctica - 2. Facts for the visitor - 3. Getting there and away - 4. Wildlife - 5. Environment - 6. Antarctic Science - 7 Private expeditions - 8. Antarctic gateways - 9. Southern Ocean and subantarctic islands - 10. Antarctic Peninsula & Weddell Sea - 11 Ross Sea - 12. East Antarctica - 13. South Pole. Appendix: The Antarctic Treaty. Glossary p.254-57. *Class No:* 919.9

Arctic

[5683]

WANEY, D. **The Arctic.** Melbourne, Lonely Planet, 1999. 456p. illus. (some col.), maps, index. $27.95. £12.99. ISBN: 0864426658.

Facts about the Arctic (history, geography, climate, environment and ecology). For the visitor (planning, tourist information, visas, books etc.). Travel, History. Indigenous peoples. Arctic Research. Literature. Guide to Arctic Alaska, Canada, Greenland, Iceland, Norway, Sweden, Finland, and Russia. 54 maps. *Class No:* 919.98

92 Biography

Biography

Worldwide

[5684]
Almanac of famous people a comprehensive reference guide to more than 25,000 famous and infamous newsmakers from Biblical times to the present. Stetler, S.L., *ed.* 4th ed. Detroit, Gale Research Co., 3v., 1989. 3083p. $103.50. ISBN: 0810327848. ISSN: 1040127x.

First published as *Biography almanac* (1981); 3rd ed. 1987.

V.1-2 Over 25000 Biographies including subject's name, nicknames, dates of birth and death (where appropriate), nationality, occupation or best-known activity, with citations to biographical sketches or articles appearing in over 300 readily available sources. V.3. Chronological, geographical and occupational indexes. 'It is basically a biographical dictionary ... contemporary popular singers, television stars, stage personalities, and cinema actors are covered more completely than in other biographical dictionaries' (*Choice,* v,.24,no.10, June 1987, p.1528). *Class No:* 929(100)

[5685]
The Cambridge biographical encyclopedia. Crystal, D., *ed.* 2nd ed. Cambridge University Press, 1998. xi,1179p. illus., maps, diagrs. £29.95. ISBN: 0521630991.

1st ed. 1994.

1. 16,000 short biographies A-Z with emphasis on 20th century. Ready Reference: tables and lists of 10,000+ political leaders and rulers A-Z by country; Saints (patronages and fast days); religious leaders; Justices of the US Supreme Court; Nobel Prize winners; Poets Laureate etc. Useful biographical compendium for home, school, and pub-quiz use but inappropriate for serious biographical research. 700 new A-Z entries in this edition.

Chrystal, D. ed. *The Cambridge biographical dictionary* (1996. 736p. pbk. £10.95. ISBN 0521567807) is a biographical compendium with essential concise information on 14,000 men and women. *Class No:* 929(100)

[5686]
Chambers biographical dictionary. Parry, M., *ed.* 6th ed. Centenary ed. Edinburgh, Chambers Harrap, 1997. 2008p. ports, £40. ISBN: 0550160604.

1st ed. 1897.

17,500 cross-referenced biographical entries (3,500 new to this edition). Data: nationality, occupation, and career achievements. 250 panels focus on particularly important people (*e.g.*Mark Anthony, J.M. Keynes). Extended coverage of science, music, art, political, television and film personnel. 'For the general reader looking for a clear authoritative assessment of the personalities who, for better or worse, have shaped our world' (*Preface*).

Chambers biographies on CD-ROM. £49.99. ISBN 0550107509. 24,000 lives. *Class No:* 929(100)

[5687]
Current biography. New York, H.W. Wilson, 1940-. Monthly except December. ports. $58.00 US and Canada; $68.00 elsewhere. ISSN: 00113344.

Each monthly issue now contains 15 profiles, some 2500-4500 words in length, of people 'who make today's headlines and tomorrow's history. Biographies are rewritten and updated when necessary. In December the monthly biographies are revised and cumulated into a single A-Z sequence in the *Current biography yearbook.* *Class No:* 929(100)

[5688]
—Current biography yearbook. New York, H.W. Wilson, 1940-. Annual. 1940- $69 US and Canada, $79 in other countries. 1986-1989 $58.00 US and Canada, $68.00 in other countries. ISSN: 00849499.

A cumulation, published in December, of all biographies printed in the previous 11 months issues of *Current biography* to which are added a list of sources consulted, a classification of the subjects profiled by their professions, and a cumulative index to the articles from all previous *Yearbooks* of the decade. 1996 vol. has 700p. ISBN 0824208781.

CD-ROM version. Single disc. All the profiles and obituaries that have appeared in *Current Biography Yearbook* since 1940 are now available electronically. More than 14,000 biographies and 8,900 obituaries, covering 15,000 individuals. Provides in-depth biographies of key individuals. Each entry contains 3,000 word profiles, along with up-to-date bibliographic information, and is fully searchable.

....(contd.)
From politics, the arts, and sports to science, the world of media, user get the facts on outstanding achievers, past and present. Each entr provides detailed bibliographic information, including profession gender, birthplace, date of birth, education, race/ethnicity, and more. *Class No:* 929(100)

[5689]
Current biography cumulated index 1940-1995. New York, H.W Wilson, 1996. 144p. $27 US. and Canada; $31. elsewhere. ISBN 0824208927.

Provides access to 14,000+ biographies. Lists subjects of all th articles and revisions and obituaries in *Current biography.* Entrie include changes in title and cross-references to variants an pseudonyms. *Class No:* 929(100)

[5690]
A Dictionary of twentieth-century world biography. Briggs, A., *ed.* Oxford, Oxford Univ. Press, 1992. 615p. £19.95. ISBN: 0192116797

Originally published as *Longman dictionary of 20th centur biography* (1985).

1750 A-Z biographies of those who have made their mark on th 20th century. Data: family background, education, achievements and or misdemeanours, and the events they influenced. *Class No:* 929(100)

[5691]
Dictionary of world biography. Aves, A., *and others, eds.* Chicag and London, Fitzroy Dearborn, 10v., 1998-1999. ports bibliogs. indexes. £750. (set). £95. for single volumes. ISBN: 1579580505, set.

A 'revision and reordering of Salem Press' 'Great Lives of History series originally published in 30v.

V.1 *The Ancient World.* 1998. xv,997p. £95. ISBN 1579580408 V.2. *The Middle Ages.* 1998. xvii,1049p. 1579580416. V.3. *Th Renaissance.* 1998. xv,813p. 1579580424. V.4. *The 17th and 18t Centuries.* 1999. xviii,1515p. 1579580432. V.5+6. *The 19th Century* 1999, xv,2455p. 157980440 and 1579580459. V.7-9. *The 20t Century.* 1999. 1579580467, 1579580475 and 1579580483. V.10 *Index.* 1999. 14579580491.

Each biographical 2-3,000 word essay (v.4 has 337 reprinted from the original 'Great lives of History' series plus 40 new essays) contain a core text divided in 3 parts: an early life section investigating th individual's upbringing and background, a life's work career an achievements outline, and an overview summary of the entrant's plac in history. An annotated evaluative bibliography completes the essay Area of achievement, geographical location, and name indexes. 'Th contributors present and interpret the known facts and weave them int a cogent and well-polished narrative' (*Reference Reviews,* v.13, no.7 1999, p.38-39). *Class No:* 929(100)

[5692]
Encyclopedia of world biography. Byers, P.K. 2nd ed. Detroit, Gale 17v., 1998. c10,000p. refs. indexes. $975. £750. ISBN: 0787622214.

1st ed. as *McGraw Hill encyclopedia of world biography* (17v. 1973).

Entirely revised and updated - the first complete revision in 25 year which includes: approximately 500 new entries, with more women multicultural and international coverage, bringing the total to approximately 7,000 biographies on notables from every part of th world and from all time periods; consolidated index that makes it easy for researchers to quickly locate needed data; Updated entries tha highlight newly discovered facts and interpretations of historica figures; and sources for further study. V.17 is an index volume. *Class No:* 929(100)

[5693]
—Abridged encyclopedia of world biography. Detroit, Gale, 6v., 1999 4000p. ports., bibliog., indexes. $495. ISBN: 0787639044.

Each volume devoted to a broad subject: American history - Worl history - Literature - Science and mathematics - Arts and entertainmen - Social sciences. A combination of 2000 entries in essay format with bibliography and 5000 basic fact entries of 2-3 lines. *Class No:* 929(100)

[5694]
Encyclopedia of world biography on CD-ROM Version 1.0. Detroit, Gale, 1999. Systems requirements. Windows 3.1 or higher. 8MB RAM. 5MB available hard disk space. $975. ISBN: 0787629391.

Contains 7,200 entries and 5,700 portraits. Searches available: name, subject, place of birth or death, works, or keywords. Timeline enables searching by year. Some additions to printed version of the Encyclopedia. 'Page design is clean and uncluttered. Text is on the right, and an enlargeable portrait and search results window are displayed on the left. Entries are hyperlinked, making it easy to move from one to another. Documentation, which consists of a user's manual and a Help card, is detailed and clear' (*Booklist*, v.95, no.18, 15 May 1999, p.1728). *Class No:* 929(100)

[5695]
istoric world leaders. Commire, A., *ed.* Detroit, Gale research Co., 5v., 1993. 1500p. illus., ports., maps. £176. (set). ISBN: 0810384086, set.

1. *Africa, Middle East, Australia and Asia.* £42. 0810384094; 2/3. *Europe* £80.50, 0810384108; 4/5. *North and South America.* £80.50. 0810384124. Profiles of and descriptive essays on social, political, and religious leaders from the earliest times. Each volume is arranged geographically and then A-Z by name. All entries end with a list of sources for further study. *Class No:* 929(100)

[5696]
he Hutchinson dictionary of biography. 2nd ed. Oxford, Helicon, 1993. 760p. index, ports. £20. ISBN: 0091776392.

Originally published as *The Hutchinson paperback dictionary of biography* (Arrow Books, 1990).

8000 entries (500 new to this ed.) on the 'most important topical or noteworthy people of our own times and previous eras'. *Reference Reviews*, 7(5), 1993: 40-41 goes overboard. 'This work approaches close to being the perfect reference book. Its subject matter is of high topicality and enduring interest'. *Class No:* 929(100)

[5697]
he International who's who 2001. 64th ed. London, Europa Publications, 2000. 1743p. £210. ISBN: 1857430816. ISSN: 00749613.

1st ed. 1935.

20,000 biographies (1000 new to this edition). Data: date and place of birth, nationality, education, career, honours, publications, and leisure interests. Includes a section on reigning royal families. 'Each new edition of this authoritative work of reference is the result of a thorough revision of its predecessor' (*International Affairs*, v.61, no.4, August 1985, p.736-7).

The International Who's who 2001 CD-ROM. £280. ISBN 1857430832. Key features include surname and combined searches; print output, design, note recording facility, and Help on-screen guidance. Required hardware: 486 SX25 or higher IBM compatible PC, CD-ROM drive, MS-DOS 5.0 or later, Windows 3.1, 95, 98, NT, 4MB RAM (8MB recommended), 10MB hard disk space (Windows), *A detailed "User Guide" is included in the CD-ROM pack.* *Class No:* 929(100)

[5698]
-Europa's 100 a selection of biographies taken from *The International who's who* 1935-2000. London, Europa, 1999. 13p.

See Alan Hamilton's 'Britons make mark on century's A-list'. *The Times*, no. 66526, 29 May 1999 p.7 where there can also be found the 100 names chosen. *Class No:* 929(100)

[5699]
AW, N.S., *comp.* Dictionary of international biography a biographical record of contemporary achievement. 26th ed. Cambridge, International Biographical Centre, 1998. clv,587p. ports. ISBN: 0948875860.

1st ed. 1963.

c.5800 biographical and career profiles reflecting 'contemporary achievement in every profession and field of interest within as many countries as possible' from information supplied by the entrants themselves. *Class No:* 929(100)

[5700]
he Macmillan dictionary of biography. Jones, B. *and* Dixon, M.V. 3rd ed. London, Macmillan, 1989. 917p. pbk. £12.99. ISBN: 0333514262.

First published by Macmillan Press in 1981.

7500 brief biographies, 400 new to this edition, with some minor figures dropped. Longest entries, *e.g.* Jesus, Lenin, Mozart run to 500-1000 words. Most end with references to other sources. First edition published under a cloud - see letter from Barry Jones in *TLS*, no.4135, 2 February 1982, p.719. 'As one of the ostensible co-authors I wish to dissociate myself from the book in every way as I think it lacks the fundamental prerequisite of any reference book, viz, accuracy. In a careful re-reading of the published text I have picked up at least 3000 factual errors, quite apart from absurdities in the text and gross omissions'. *Class No:* 929(100)

[5701]
Merriam-Webster's biographical dictionary. Springfield, Massachusetts, Merriam-Webster, 1995. 1170p. $27. ISBN: 0877797439.

Rev. ed. of *Webster's New Biographical Dictionary* (1985).

30,000 biographies 'present in a single volume biographical information on important, celebrated, or notorious figures from the last five thousand years, beginning with Menes, King of Egypt, *c.*3100 B.C. 'Given the low price, the comprehensive inclusion criteria, and the quality of presentation, this work remains a core research tool that must be considered an essential part of every library collection' (*ARBA Guide to Biographical Resources 1986-1997.* 1998, p.16).
Class No: 929(100)

[5702]
Who's who in the world 2000 Millenium edition. Eckes, K.A., *ed.* 17th ed. New Providence, NJ. Marquis Who's Who, 1999. xv,2552p. ISBN: 0837911230.

First published 1970.

55,000 sketches of world statesmen, major businessmen; high ranking military officers; heads of education, religious, professional and scientific organizations from 215 countries determined on position of responsibility held or level of achievement obtained. Professional index in 18 subdivided categories p.2423-2552. Available on CD-ROM as part of the *Complete Marquis Who's Who on CD-ROM*.
Class No: 929(100)

Databases

[5703]
Biography database 1680-1830 Oxford, ABC-Clio, 5 discs, 1998-2001. Fully IBM compatible computer with a minimum 4Mb RAM (under Windows 3.1) or 8Mb RAM (under Windows 95), 5Mb of free hard disk space, 3.5" floppy disk drive, Windows 3.1 or Windows 95, MS DOS CD-ROM extensions, minimum VGA colour monitor (super VGA preferred). CD-ROM player meeting ISO 9660 standard, and device driver (supplied with player), mouse. £7,500 complete in advance or £1,500 on publication of each CD. ISSN: 13658751.

Contains all UK and US directories, trade directories, book subscription lists, journal records (*e.g. Gentlemans Magazine*), society membership lists. Individuals can be searched by 15 categories including gender, address, religion, and occupation. This data is supplemented by summaries of biographies from the *Annual Biography and Obituary* (1817-) and the *Annual Register* (1758-) 'Non-computer literate users may find some of the language used in the Installation and User Guide daunting but it is not necessary to understand the structure of the Database fully in order to use it effectively; it is enough to rely on the browse facility' (*Local Historian*, v.29,no.1, July 1999, p.57-58). *Class No:* 929(100)(003.4)

[5704]
Internationaler Biographischer Index/World biographical index. 5th ed. München, K.G. Saur, 1998. 1 Disk OptiSearch Retrieval System by M.P.W. Software. Interface Microsoft Windows. DM 1,980. No charge for network use. ISBN: 3598404158.

A complete guide to, and an index to 4 million articles in 16 Biographical Archives published by K.G. Saur *viz* American, British, German, Italian, Polish, Spanish, Portuguese and Latin American, Australasian, Scandinavian, and Benelux archives *(q.q.v.).* Also an independent reference source on 2.5 million plus individuals.

Available with SilverPlatter software. The SilverPlatter CD-ROM can be used with all conventional servers, including Windows/NT, Sun Solaris, SLO-UNIX, IBM AIX, and LINUX.

Users can log in to the Internet by Allegro-W3 V.2 5u/or via K.G. Saur's home page http://www.saur.de. *Class No:* 929(100)(003.4)

CD-ROM

[5705]
Current biography on CD-ROM New York, H.W. Wilson, 1997. DOS and Macintosh. $449. Annual renewal $149.

2,000 biographies + 1800 obituaries available to researchers by integrating the full text of every *Current Biography* annual since 1983-1994. In-depth information on politicians, business people, journalists, actors, sports figures, artists, scientists, and others from nearly six decades of headlines and history. For a renewal fee, the *1940-Present* database is also updated annually, delivering all of the articles and obituaries from *Current Biography Yearbook*, plus numerous updates and about 250 shorter articles that do not appear in the printed version.

Data: detailed account of the subject's life and career, including the subject's own views, attitudes, and opinions, observations of journalists, colleagues, and associates, plus factual information such as birthdate, education, awards, marital status and concise lists of select biographical references for further research.
Class No: 929(100)(003.40)

[5706]

Wilson biographies. New York, H.W. Wilson, 1998. CD-ROM disk. Windows 3.1 or later; Macintosh DOS 3.1 or later; Internet Service; or magnetic tape. $945. (US); $1,050 (outside North America) single user; annual renewal $245. ($285.).

'Contains more than 38,000 profiles cumulating the full-text entries from 100 Wilson printed reference works ... In addition to factual details and accounts of the subjects; careers, entries may include observations from journalists, reviewers or colleagues and autobiographical statements written by the subjects. Entries also have lists of books and articles by and about each figure. Approximately 1,000 biographies are added to the databases each year'. (*Reference Reviews*, announcement). Search routes: name, profession, title, place of origin, gender, race. *Class No:* 929(100)(003.40)

Internet

[5707]

Biography resource center. Detroit, Gale Group, 1999. Internet database $3,000 single site, single user.

The Biography Resource Center, the first product to result from The Gale Group merger, combines the most frequently consulted Gale biographical databases with full-text periodicals from the former Information Access Company (IAC). Contains c.240,000 biographies, covering 170,000 individuals. In addition, there are articles by and about the biographees from 232 periodicals, journals, and newspapers. 3 Search levels are offered: Name, Custom (name, occupation, nationality, ethnicity, date or place of birth/death, and gender), and Fulltext and Boolean searches. 'Because most of the sources in BRC were published within the past 20 years and a large number are from the last 10 years, the majority of the biographical sketches are reasonably up-to-date. Generally, the bibliographical header at the beginning of a biography alerts the user to the date the material was originally published' (*Booklist*, 1 November 1999, p.552-53). *Class No:* 929(100)(003.41)

[5708]

Wilson biographies plus. New York, H.W. Wilson. Internet database.

45,000 biographies. Expanding links to related full text articles, abstracts and index citations from 4,000+ sources. 1000 full length profiles are added each year. *Class No:* 929(100)(003.41)

[5709]

World biographies plus illustrated. New York, H.W. Wilson, 1999. WilsonWebSystem. Internet:www.hwwilson.com. $1,495 single site, single user.

The largest of all Wilson biographical databases when introduced in 1999 although the 2000 version, *Wilson Biographies Mega*, will probably exceed it.

Contains full-text entries of 46,000 biographies and obituaries from 61 Wilson dictionaries and c.26,000 photographs and images, many in colour. Boolean Searching is possible through Searchplus, the most sophisticated search level, the others being Browse and Search. There are also entries from other publishers' reference works. 'A serious drawback to the WBPI database is the prevalence of older sources, which means that many of the biographies and their accompanying bibliographical references do not reflect current scholarship. In fact, more than 22,000 of the biographies in this database originally appeared in sources published before 1970 ... Although the links to recent periodical articles are helpful they cannot fully compensate for biographical essays that are truly out-of-date'. (*Booklist*, 1 November 1999, p.553). *Class No:* 929(100)(003.41)

Bibliographies

[5710]

ARBA guide to biographical resources 1986-1997. Wick, R.L. *and* Mood, T.A.   Englewood, Colo., Libraries Unlimited, 1998. xxxiv,604p. indexes. £57.50. ISBN: 1563084538.

Continuation of *ARBA guide to biographical dictionaries* (1986).

437 contributors. 1,180 signed critical evaluations of biographical reference works, either previously reviewed in *American Reference Books Annual*, or selected for their importance and value. Arranged in 2 pts: 1. International and national biographies - 2. Biographies in 24 professional fields (*e.g.* 3. History - 4. Geography) Data: author, title, publisher, date, price, ISBN/ISSN, LC number, and evaluation. Author, title and subject indexes. *Class No:* 929(100)(01)

[5711]

Biographical dictionaries and related works an international bibliography of more than 16,000 collective biographies, bio-bibliographies, collections of epitaphs, selected genealogical works, dictionaries of acronyms and pseudonyms, historical and specialized dictionaries, biographical materials in government manuals, bibliographies of biography, biographical indexes, and selected portrait catalogues. Slocum, R.B., *ed.*   2nd ed. Detroit, Gale Research Co., 2v., 1986. 1319p. bibliog., indexes. $150.00. ISBN: 0810302348.

First published 1967. Supplements 1972 and 1978.

In 3 sections: universal biography; foreign and U.S. biography by

.... (contd.)

area; and foreign and U.S. biography by vocation. Some entries are annotated. Author, title and subject indexes. Bibliography p.17-23. 4000 items are new to this edition. *Class No:* 929(100)(01)

[5712]

Biography index: a cumulative index to biographical material in books and magazines. New York, H.W. Wilson, 1946-, v.1-. Quarterly paperbound issues and an annual cumulation. Annual subscription $120.00 US and Canada $130.00 elsewhere. ISSN: 00063053.

Based on more than 2600 periodicals regularly scanned in the Wilson indexes plus works of individual and collective (auto)biographies, and obituaries. The main section is A-Z by biographees (full name, dates, nationality, profession, and full bibliographic citation). The 2nd section is an index to professions and occupations. There are 17 biennial or triennial retrospective volumes 1946-August 1992 each $160.00 US and Canada, $190.00 elsewhere.

Wilson biography index. Quarterly. Single disc. Biographical information about prominent people in every field. It covers information indexed from 3,000 periodicals; current English-language books - including 1,900 works of individual and collective biographies annually; autobiographies; memoirs; journals; diaries; letters; interviews; bibliographies; obituaries; fiction; drama; pictorial work; poetry. Also provides coverage of incidental biographical material found in otherwise nonbiographical books. 2 Indexes, the Name Index and the Index to Professions and Occupations. *Class No:* 929(100)(01)

[5713]

Dictionary of biographical reference. containing over one hundred thousand names; together with a classed index to the biographical literature of Europe and America. Phillips, L.B. 3rd ed. Detroit, Gale Research Co., 1982. xiv, 1038p. bibliog. $90.00. ISBN: 081033996x.

1st ed. published in 1871. 2nd ed. 1881 as *Great index of biographical reference* 3rd ed. first published by Sampson, Low, Marston & Co. (1889). This edition incorporated Frank Weitenkampf's supplement covering prominent people 1871-1888. Reprinted by Akademische Druk-und Verlagsanstalt of Graz in 1964.

Indexes 42 general and specialized biographical dictionaries. Includes an additional bibliography of c.1600 principal works of collective biography in 3 divisions: general biographies, national biographies, and class (*i.e.*, professional) biographies. *Class No:* 929(100)(01)

[5714]

Dictionary of universal biography of all ages and all peoples. Hyamson, A.M., *ed.* 2nd ed. (reprint). Detroit, Omnigraphics, 1994. xii,680p. $65. ISBN: 0780500109.

1st ed. 1916. 2nd ed. London, Routledge; New York, E.P. Dutton, 1951. Reprint by Gale Research 1981.

A finding list of c.110,000 biographies contained in the 23 most comprehensive biographical dictionaries and encyclopaedias. Does not include living persons. Entries, usually single-line, include name, nationality, profession, dates (where known) and a coded reference to original dictionary. *Class No:* 929(100)(01)

[5715]

LOBIES, J.P.   Index   bio-bibliographicus   notorum   hominum. Osnabrück, Biblio Verlag, 1972-. ISBN: 3764807261, complete work.

A. *Allgemeine Einführung.* 1972. B. List of bibliographical works 1972-73. Supplementunm (opera 5146-6215) 1992 C. *Corpus alphabeticum.* 1976-. v.1-. A (general introduction) has 3 sections: 1. Universal biographies; 2. Biographical works arranged on geographical, historical and linguistic principles (2,000 items); 3. Biographical reference works by vocations (subjects and activities). B. enumerates 5145 bibliographies cited in Part A; author and subject indexes. C. has entries under biographies A-Z. V.82 to Michel Gazil. V.23 has supplements to B. (entries 5146-5500); v.24 (entries 5501-5750; v.25 (entries 5751-6000); v.40 (entries 6001-6148); v.47 (entries 6149-6215) 1990. V.45/47. Supplement III. *Sectio Sinica cum supplemento Coreano* (v.1 1976) includes a foreword on How to use Index bibliographies for Chinese names. V.2. *Ban yong - Bo Zong* (1979). *Sectio Ameniaca. V.1A-D* (1982); *E-M* (1985); *N-V and Supplement A-V* (1987). 'The aim of this work is a world wide brief biographical presentation of all personalities - including those of the second or third rank - who have been significant in one or the other way for the history of mankind' 3-5 million entries will be listed eventually in this massive and tortuous index. *Class No:* 929(100)(01)

[5716]

St. James guide to biography. Schellinger, P.E., *ed.*   Chicago and London, St. James Press, 1991. x,870p. bibliogs. £90. ISBN: 1558621466.

Not a biographical dictionary but a bibliographic guide with signed critical essays on the biographies of over 700 major figures in world history. 313 contributors. *Class No:* 929(100)(01)

[5717]
World biographical information system. München, K.G. Saur, 1999. 30p. illus. sd. gratis.

Principally an annotated list of K.G. Saur's series of national biographical archives on microfiches, their printed indexes, those in process of publication, and those still at the planning stage. Also included is 'Towards a World Biographical Archive', detailing its origins and structure, the sources used, a small selection of the social and professional groups included, and the extent of the archives. *NB*: All World Biographical Archive titles are listed individually at the appropriate place in this present volume. *Class No:* 929(100)(01)

[5718]
—**Bibliographie zu den Biographischen Archiven.** 2nd rev. & expanded ed. München, K.G. Saur, 1998. 258p. ISBN: 3598337531.

Documents the 6394 biographical reference works, source works, lexica, handbooks and who's who which have been, and continue to be included for the publisher's microfiche archive series.
Class No: 929(100)(01)

Awards & Prizes

[5719]
Nobel Prize winners: an H.W. Wilson biographical dictionary. Wesson, T., *ed.* New York, H.W. Wilson, 1987. xxxiv,1165p. illus., bibliogs. $90.00 US and Canada. $100 other countries. ISBN: 0824207564.

566 x 1500 word profiles of Nobel Prize winners 1901-1986 offering 'a narrative overview of a laureate's life and career, while focussing on the individual's prizewinning work and attempting to assess its significance'. List of winners p.vii-xii. Winners by prize category p.xiii-xix. Alfred Nobel p.xxiii-xxviii. The Nobel Prizes and Nobel Institutions p.xxix-xxxiii. Quinquennial supplements will be published beginning in 1992. 'The work has more depth than *Who's Who of Nobel Prize Winners* ed. by Bernard S. and June H. Schlessinger (1986)' (*Choice* v.25,no.8, April 1988, p.1224).
Nobel prize winners supplement 1987-1991 edited by P. Maguire. 1992. 144p. $35. (US and Canada); $40 (elsewhere). Biographical sketches of 49 Nobel Prize winners.
Nobel prize winners 1992-1996 supplement. 1997. 160p. bibliog. 5735. (US and Canada); $40. (elsewhere). ISBN 0824209060. Biographies of 55 Nobel prize-winning men, women and institutions 1992-1996. *Class No:* 929(100)(079.2)

[5720]
WALTER, C. Winners the blue ribbon encyclopedia of awards. New York, Facts on File, 1982. ix,916p. index. ISBN: 0871963868.

Awards tabulated in 25 categories *e.g.* General achievement, Librarianship and information science, with lists of recipients on an annalistic pattern. *Class No:* 929(100)(079.2)

[5721]
The Who's who of Nobel Prize winners 1901-1995. Schlessinger, B.S. *and* Schlessinger, J.H., *eds.* 3rd ed. Phoenix, Arizona, Oryx Press, 1996. 288p. bibliog., indexes. $49.50. ISBN: 0897748999.

1st ed. 1986.
181 contributors, arranged by prize category on an annalistic basis. Data: family and personal, selected publications by and about, sources, and a commentary which quotes from the prize citation. Name, education, nationality and religion indexes. 'The first tool that provides biographical information on Nobel Prize winners in all categories ... a useful quick reference source' (*Reference Books Bulletin 1986-7* p.25).
Class No: 929(100)(079.2)

[5722]
World of winners: a current and historical perspective on awards and their winners. Siegman, G., *ed.* 2nd ed. Detroit, Gale Research Co., 1991. 1200p. indexes. $60.00. ISBN: 0810369818. ISSN: 10413529.

First published 1989.
Complete historical record of 75,000 winners and over 1,800 awards arranged alphabetically within 12 subject sections: Arts and letters; Business management, and marketing; Design and architecture, Health and medicine; Humanities, education and library science; Lifestyle; Live performance; Mass media; Music; Public affairs; Science; engineering, and technology; Sports and hobbies. Organization, winner, and award names indexes. Companion volume to *Awards, honors and prizes.* *Class No:* 929(100)(079.2)

[5723]
—**SIEGMAN, G.,** *ed.* Awards, honors, and prizes an international directory of awards and their donors. 17th ed. Detroit, Gale Research Co., 2v., 2000. 2210p. $475. £344.14. ISBN: 078763400x.

First published 1969.
1. *United States and Canada.* $245. £177.50. ISBN 0787634018 A-Z directory of 5216 organizations sponsoring over 15,500 awards *etc.* in virtually every field of human endeavour. 2. *International and foreign.* $275. £199.24. 07878634026. More than 9300 awards and prizes given in 100 countries other than US and Canada arranged A-Z by sponsoring organization within country sections. Data: purpose of award and elegibility factors; character (monetary, medal, plaque);

....(contd.)
frequency (year established). Organization, award name, and subject indexes. This edition gives e-mail address and URLs. 'Recognized as the standard work in its field' (*Booklist,* v.84,no.22, August 1988, p.1896). *Class No:* 929(100)(079.2)

Internet

[5724]
The Nobel Foundation the official website of the Nobel Foundation. http://www.nobel.ki.se/

'Clearly organized and up-to-date ... an authoritative source for both historical and current information about Nobel prizes, Nobel laureates and contains useful encyclopedic information ... apart from a few typographical errors, this site is an excellent source' (*Choice,* v.35,no.9, May 1998, p.1510). *Class No:* 929(100)(079.2)(003.41)

Jews

[5725]
International biographical dictionary of Central European emigrés 1933-1945. Straus, H.A. *and* Roeder, W., *eds.* München, New York. London, Paris, K.G. Saur, 3v. in 4, 1980-1983. Distributed in the Western Hemisphere by Gale Research Co. £425.00 set. ISBN: 3598100876, set.

1. *Biographisches handbuch der deutschsprachigen emigration nach 1933. Band 1. Politik, Wirtschaft, Öffentliches Leben* 1980. lviii,875p. £149.00. 3598100876 (Ger). 0896641015 (US). 014044818 (UK). 2. *International biographical dictionary of Central European emigrés 1933-1945. Sciences, Arts, Literature. Pt.1. A-K; Pt.2. L-Z* 1983. xciv,1316p. $220.00. £219.00. 359810089. 3. *Gesamtregister/Index.* 1983. xx,277p. $95.00. £99.00. 359810096 Bilingual key to v.1+2. Approximately 8700 biographies mostly of Jews forced to leave Germany, Austria, and Czechoslovakia during the Nazi era. Key for use of Dictionary p.1291-98 (v.2). Glossary p.1299-1301 (v.2). Sponsored by Research Federation for Jewish Immigration (New York) and Institut für Zeitgeschichte (München).
Kurzbiographien zur Geschichte der Juden 1918-1945 (K.G. Saur, 1990. 2598104774) 'Diese Biographie mit nahezu 5000 ergänzt das *Biographisches Handbuch der deutschsprachigen Emigration nach 1993* (dustwrapper). *Class No:* 929(100)(=924)

[5726]
Who's who in world Jewry: a biographical dictionary of outstanding Jews. Rosenblatt, J.T., *ed.* 7th ed. New York, Who's who in World Jewry, 1987. xix,631p. illus. $129.00. ISBN: 0961827203.

First published 1955.
'The personalities included were selected on the basis of their influence, position, and accomplishments, and the data used was supplied by them' (*Introduction*) but 'the list of persons not included is long' (*Booklist,* v.84,no.15, 1 April 1988, p.1327-8).
Class No: 929(100)(=924)

Black Races

[5727]
Contemporary Black biography. Bigelow, B.C., *ed.* Detroit, Gale Research, 1991-. Biannual.

Volume 12 (1996): £40. 0787601004 'This concise yet comprehensive biannual source covers prominent black individuals from around the world. Illustrated entries provide not only biography, but list writings and sources for further reading. Each throughly indexed volume contains about 70 full length biographies, divided into the following sections: portrait, date and place of birth, family names, education, address, career data, memberships, awards received, and books written. Sources for further reading as well as a full biographical profile.' *Class No:* 929(100)(=96)

Middle Ages

Women

[5728]
ECHOLS, A. *and* **WILLIAMS, M. An Annotated index of medieval women.** New York, Markus Wiener; Oxford. Berg Publications, 1992. xxiv,635p. bibliog. £40. ISBN: 0920129274.

1500 entries presenting cross-section of women who flourished AD800-1500 arranged A-Z by first name in 32 country sections although most are French or English of the 13th and 14th Centuries. Contents: 1. Readers Guide - 2. Main Listings (p.1-424). Data: brief biography and various cross-references to main areas of activity and prominence - 3. Cross Reference Listings (p.425-596) by date, country, biographical category, and last name, title, region or city - 4. Complete Bibliography (p.597-635) divided into Sources with and without authors. A work of detailed and estimable scholarship.
Class No: 929(100)"01/14"-0055.2

Women

[5729]
Chambers biographical dictionary of women. Parry, M., *ed.*
Edinburgh, Chambers, 1996. x,741p. ports. £25. ISBN: 0550150064.
21 contributors. 3000 entries (1800 derived from Chambers extensive database; 1200 freshly researched) spanning 80 vocational and subject categories. A Women's Chronology: key events and achievements p.715-31. 'Aims to document many of the women who, in the face of general opposition and prejudice, have been successful in their own right, and whose lives have made a mark on history without reaching the history books' (*Introduction*). Although universal in its coverage, the weighting is inevitably on 19th and 20th century women of the Western World. *Class No:* 929(100)-0055.2

[5730]
GERBER, J.B. Distinguished women of the twentieth century international biographies. Santa Barbara, Calif., and Oxford, ABC-Clio, 2000. 400p. ports., index. £44.95. ISBN: 1576070972.
Profiles the most extraordinary women of the twentieth century. The biographees come from all areas including anthropology, archaeology, architecture, the arts, astronomy, aviation and space, business and finance, computer science and artificial intelligence, education, engineering, environment, exploration and adventure, health and medicine, history, human rights, law, mathematics, media and journalism, music, politics and government, sciences, social activism, social sciences, sports, and stage and screen. *Class No:* 929(100)-0055.2

[5731]
The International who's who of women 1997. 2nd ed. London, Europa, 1997. 600+p. index. £215. ISBN: 1857430271. ISSN: 09653775.
1st ed. 1992.
Over 5,500 concise profiles of the world's most eminent and distinguished women. Data: name and title; academic degrees and professional qualifications; date and place of birth; nationality; family details; education; career history; major publications, films, plays; honours, awards and prizes; leisure interests. Occupational index. *Class No:* 929(100)-0055.2

[5732]
OLSEN, K. Chronology of women's history. Westport, CT., Greenwood Press, 1994. 512p. bibliog., index. $39.95. ISBN: 0313288038.
Entries are arranged by year(s) in a format of 10 subject categories (*e.g.* General status and daily life ... Athletics and exploration ... Religion). Brief entries summarize the most important or characteristic events of each period, while explanatory essays illuminate broad trends and outstanding aspects of women's life in a variety of cultures. *Class No:* 929(100)-0055.2

[5733]
The Penguin biographical dictionary of women. London, Penguin Books, 1998. 737p. indexes. £12.99. ISBN: 0140514066.
'This brilliant reference tool ... a carefully researched collection of 1600 biographies of the world's women - from household names to long-forgotten little-knowns' (*The Times*, 30 May 1998. *Metro* p.18) Iris Murdoch 61 lines, Jacquetta Hawkes 45 lines. Index by occupation p.715-24. Index by nationality p.725-27. *Class No:* 929(100)-0055.2

[5734]
The World's who's who of women 1995/96.. 13th ed. Cambridge, International Biographical Centre, 1995, cxxvii,511p. ports. £105. ISBN: 0948875127.
1st ed. 1973.
c.6000 entries for the leading women of the world today. Data: vital statistics; Honours; education; career and appointments; publications. Previous editions carried many more entries and so should not necessarily be discarded. *Class No:* 929(100)-0055.2

Bibliographies

[5735]
ADAMSON, L.G. Notable women in world history a guide to recommended biographies and autobiographies. Westport, CT., Greenwood Press, 1998. xiv,402p. bibliogs., index. ISBN: 0313298181.
Content for entries includes subject's vital statistics, a biographical sketch encompassing general achievement, parental heritage, education, public recognition, and an annotated list of readings. 3 appendices: notable women by date of birth, by country, and by title, occupation, or main area of interest. *Class No:* 929(100)-0055.2(01)

Europe—Western

Micromaterials

[5736]
Biografisch archief van de Benelux/Archives biographiques des Pays du Benelux. Biographical archive of the Benelux countries. Biographisches archiv der Benelux-länder. Gorzny, W. *and* Van de Meer, W., *comps.* München, K.G. Saur, 1992-94. 762 fiches (24x) Silver or diazo. DM 22,800 (silver); DM 21,000 (diazo) ISBN: 3598326300, Silver; 3598326106, Diazo.
Biographical entries. 160,000 individuals in a single A-Z sequence cumulated from 122 biographical reference works (1598 - beginning of 20th century). Covers former Dutch colonies in Indonesia, the Antilles, and Surinam, and the Belgian Congo. Indexed in printed form in *Biographische index van de Benelux*.
Biografisch archief van der Benelux Deel II/Archives biographiques des Pays du Bénélux. Deuxième Série/Biographical archive of the Benelux countries. Series II/Biographisches archiv der Benelux-Länder Neue Folge. 1999. 300 fiches. DM 16,800 (silver); DM 15,600 (diazo). ISBN 359834631x; 3598346301 (diazo). From a further 65 reference works covering the period 1860-1998.
Class No: 929(400)(003.5)

[5737]
—Biografisch index van de Benelux/Index biographique des Pays du Bénélux/Biographical index of the Benelux countries/Biographische index den Benelux-Länder. Van der Meer, W., *comp.* München, K.G. Saur, 4v., 1997. xix,1604p. DM 1,980. (DM 1,780 for subscribes to *Biografische architiet van de Benelux*.) ISBN: 3598326459.
A-Z list of biographies included in *Biografisch archief van de Benelux (q.v.)* *Class No:* 929(400)(003.5)

Great Britain

[5738]
Asian & who's who international. Sachar, J.S., *comp.* 12th ed. Ilford, Essex, Asian Who's Who International. 1999. 288p., col. illus., ports., pbk. £17.95. ISBN: 0905372190. ISSN: 01401076.
First published 1975-76.
Who's who of over 1000 prominent Asians living in UK and also (now) outside UK. Data: birth, marriage, education, arrival date in Britain, position, recreation. Also directory information for organizations involved in race relations, ethnic minority press plus section on Asian history, background, religious groups, festivals, and food. *Class No:* 929(410)

[5739]
BELL, P., *comp.* Victorian biography a checklist of contemporary biographies of British men and women dying between 1851 and 1901. Edinburgh, Peter Bell, 1993. 193p. bibliog. ISBN: 1871538114.
Lists 2,500 titles including 400 biographies of women. 'Especially valuable for reference to the many obscure biographies of minor figures which will prove difficult, if not impossible, to find' (Powell, J. *Art, truth, and high politics*. Lanham, Md., Scarecrow Press, 1996, p.8). *Class No:* 929(410)

[5740]
A Dictionary of Edwardian biography. Edinburgh, Peter Bell, 36v., 1987-.
First published by the Brighton publishers W.T. Pike 1898-1912 in 33 county volumes each of which combined a guide book with an illustrated biographical dictionary. This present series omits the topographical material.
Cheshire 223p. £36.00 ISBN 0946687145; *Dorset* 65p. £20.00. ISBN 0946687005; *Durham* 197p. £25.00. ISBN 0946687061; *Edinburgh and The Lothians* 219p. £25.00. ISBN 0946687102; *Lancashire* 319p. £40.00. ISBN 094668703x; *Leicester & Rutland* 123p. £25.00. ISBN 0946687021; *Liverpool* 183p. £36.00 ISBN 0946687137; *Manchester & Salford* 208p. £36.00 ISBN 0946687129; *Northumberland* 183p. £25.00 ISBN 0946687043; *Sheffield* 139p. £25.00. ISBN 0946687013; *South Wales & Monmouthshire* 155p. £25.00 ISBN 0946687110; *West Riding of Yorkshire* 307p. £40.00 ISBN 0946687080; *Wiltshire* 120p. £25.00 ISBN 0946687056.
Each volume consists on average of about 500 detailed and illustrated biographical sketches of local figures. All are arranged according to such categories as parliamentary, medical, legal, clerical, engineering, landowning and magistracy, business, commerce and insurance, the armed forces, accountants, surveyors, architects, vets & dentists, as well as "art, literature and education". Each volume has been separately indexed.
Master index to whole series and to individual vs. of Pike's New Century Series, 192p. £36.00, ISBN 0946687099. *Class No:* 929(410)

[5741]

he **Dictionary of national biography.** Oxford, Oxford Univ. Press, 1885-.

1. *The Dictionary of national biography, from the earliest times to 1900*. Edited by Sir Lesley Stephen and Sir Sidney Lee. London, Smith, Elder, 63v., 1885-1900. *First Supplement* in 3v. 1901 for those lives accidentally ommited or who had died after their letter was in print. Using thinner paper the standard edition is now reduced to 22v. incorporating 30,000 lives in 30,500p. retaining the two alphabetical sequences. £795.00. ISBN 0198651015.

2. *The Twentieth Century DNB. The Dictionary of national biography 1901-1911*, edited by Sir Sidney Lee. 1912. 2,088p. £65.00. ISBN 0198652011.

The Dictionary of national biography 1912-1921, edited by H.W.C. Davis and J.R.H. Weaver, 1927. xxvi, 623p. £60.00. ISBN 019865202x.

The Dictionary of National Biography 1922-1930, edited by J.R.H. Weaver, 1937, xiv, 962p. £65.00. ISBN 0198652038.

The Dictionary of National Biography 1931-1940, edited by L.G. Wickham Legg, 1949, xvi, 968p. £65.00. ISBN 0198652046.

The Dictionary of National Biography 1941-1950, edited by L.G. Wickham Legg, and E.T. Williams, 1959. xxi, 1031p. £65.00. ISBN 0198652054.

The Dictionary of National Biography 1951-1960, edited by E.T. Williams and Helen M. Palmer, 1971. xxvi, 1150p. £65.00. ISBN 0198652062.

The Dictionary of National Biography 1961-1970, edited by E.T. Williams and C.S. Nicholls, 1981. 1170p. £65.00. ISBN 0198652070.

The Dictionary of national biography 1971-1980, edited by Lord Blake and C.S. Nicholls, 1986. xix, 1010p. £65.00. ISBN 0198652089. With a cumulative index 1901-1980. 'De mortuis nil nisi bunkum - here was a principle which served the twentieth-century *DNB* for many years. In the latest volume, however, the new chief editor conclusively demonstrates that it has been abandoned' (*English Historical Review*, v.103, no.406, January 1988, p.156-8).

The Dictionary of national biography 1981-1985: with an index covering the years 1901-1985 in one alphabetical series, edited by Lord Blake and C.S. Nicholls, 1990. 608p. £40.00. ISBN 0198652100.

The Dictionary of national biography 1986-1990 with an index covering the years 1901-1990 in one alphabetical series edited by C.S. Nichols. 1996. 576p. £50. ISBN 0198652127. This is the final volume of The Dictionary of national biography.

'For more than a century it has furnished us with a carefully-written profile of every man or woman who has left a thumb-print on the island story. No other nation can boast a reference work so magisterially exact and yet so hypnotically readable' (*Sunday Times*, 25 March 1990, p.C7). 'The *DNB* is a National Portrait Gallery in print. The compositions are admirable and the colours vivid' (*The Times*, 27 June 1996, p.34).

Further information: 1. J.L. Kirby's 'The Dictionary of National Biography', *Library Association Record*, v.60, no.6, June 1958, p. 181-91-. 2. A. Bell's Leslie Stephen and DNB', *Times Literary Supplement*, 16 December 1977, p.1478 - 3. R.H. Fritze's 'The Dictionary of National Biography and its early editors and publisher', *Reference Services Review*, v.16, no.4, 1988, p.21-29).

Class No: 929(410)

[5742]

-The Concise dictionary of national biography from earliest times to 1985. Oxford, Oxford Univ. Press, 3v., 1992. 3340p. £125. ISBN: 0198653050.

Details of more than 32,500 men and women who died before 1945 condensed from the 31 volume *DNB* 'Though no substitute for that most readable of all reference books, the Concise DNB is a triumph of compression' (*Times*, 26 Mar 1992, p.5). *Class No:* 929(410)

[5743]

-The Contributor's index to the Dictionary of National Biography 1885-1901. Fenwick, G. Cirencester, Gloucestershire, St. Paul's Bibliographies; Detroit, Omnigraphics, 1989. xli, 413p. index. £50.00. ISBN: 0906795737, UK; 1558888152, US.

Lists 694 contributors and their articles, giving names, dates, *DNB* volume numbers and page references. Unsigned articles are listed separately. *Class No:* 929(410)

[5744]

-Dictionary of national biography. Missing persons. Nichols, C.S., *ed.* Oxford, Oxford Univ. Press. 1993. 768p. £80. ISBN: 0198652119.

Biographies of 1086 persons who for a variety of reasons were omitted from previous volumes. Compiled from over 100,000 suggestions from the general public and scholars. 12% of entrants in this volume are women compared to 3% in the *DNB* to date. Occupational index. *Class No:* 929(410)

[5745]

-Dictionary of national biography. Corrections and additions. Boston, G.K. Hall, 1966. iv, 212p.

Cumulated from the *Bulletin of the Institute of Historical Research* covering the year 1923-1963.

1,300 entries, photographically reproduced by offset. A cumulation, A-Z of 'Corrections and additions' to *DNB* appearing in the *Bulletin*, v.1(1923)-36 (1963). A number of corrections and additions are signed; corrections by the staff of the *Bulletin* are in square brackets. The entry 'Sir Robert Howard (1626-1698)' runs to 2½ columns of corrections and additions. An essential supplement to the main work. *Class No:* 929(410)

[5746]

-Dictionary of national biography. Errata. London, Smith, Elder & Co., 1904. vi, 300p.

Full use was made of the long list of corrections contributed by W.C. Boulter to *Notes And Queries*.

Issued 'to correct the inevitable misprints and misstatements' found in the substantive work. *Class No:* 929(410)

[5747]

Dictionary of national biography on CD-ROM. Oxford Univ. Press., 1995. IBM PC or full compatible with 80386 processor or above, 4Mb free RAM, DOS 5.0 or higher, 3Mb free hard-disk space, VGA or Super VGA monitor, CD-ROM drive, MSCDEX 2.1. Windows 3.1 or higher, Microsoft mouse or compatible. ISBN: 0192683128.

DNB up to 1985. 'Instant access to precise biographical information and can perform wide-ranging searches in ways impossible with the printed volumes. You can find details of a particular individual, identified by name, title, gender, dates, or occupation (or a combination of these), or a group of individuals that share certain characteristics. The results of your searches will be displayed instantly, saving you time and effort in your research'. (advt.).
Class No: 929(410)

[5748]

FENWICK, G. Women in the DNB a guide to DNB volumes 1885-1985 and Missing Persons. Aldershot, Scolar Press, 1994. x,181p. index. ISBN: 0859679144.

Data: career, education, family, club membership, contact addresses. Victorian *DNB* was largely a male domain - proprietor, editors, staff, contributors and subjects. The first volume had 505 biographies, only 35 of them women, by 87 contributors, four of whom were women. In the early twentieth-century volumes, there were still few women subjects and even a fall in women writers.
Class No: 929(410)

[5749]

MATTHEW, C. 'New Dictionary of National Biography', *The Historian*, no.4 Winter 1993, p.13-14.

An account of current progress on providing a new *DNB* for the new century and millennium outlining the editorial structure. The net result 'will be a New Dictionary of National Biography to 2000, with about 50,000 entries in 45 million words. It will be published in two formats - first as a traditional book with the 10,000 illustrations and second electronically'.

In almost every case, articles have been commissioned to academic experts who are familiar with their subjects' papers. Accompanying each biography will be a section listing sources used for the article and information on chief deposits of archives; standard biographies, collections of printed papers, and diaries; sound and film archives; notable ports., statues', (J. Powell. *Art, truth & high politics*. Lanham, Md. Scarecrow Press, 1996, p.10). See also Joanna Pitman's 'Portrait of a nation', *The Times*, no.65,003, 11 July 1994, p.14.
Class No: 929(410)

[5750]

MULLAY, A.J. British birthplaces: A 'Who Was Born Where' listing of cities, towns and villages where the famous were born. Complete with personal name index. Edinburgh, Wherewithal Books 1997. 202p. maps, index. £30. ISBN: 0906606160.

1,500 places in UK, registered A-Z, with listings of their famous sons and daughters. Data: birth and death dates and profession or occupation (*e.g.* military commander, soprano, South African statesman). c.3,500 individuals are included. Personal name index p.153-202. *Class No:* 929(410)

[5751]

People of today. Coles, A., *and others, eds.* 13th ed. London, Debrett's Peerage, 2000 Millenium Edition. 126p.+2164p. £120. ISBN: 1870520548.

1st ed. 1988. Previous editions under title of *Debrett's distinguished people of today*. This was a successor to *Debrett's Handbook* the 3rd and last edition of which appeared in 1986.

32,000 biographical entries encompassing top people in business, medicine, publishing, sport, education and academia, art and antiques, politics. (Anthony Charles Lynton Blair 11 lines; William Jefferson Hague 10 lines; Charles Peter Kennedy 13 lines; Baron Cowdrey of Tonbridge 14 lines). Preliminary pages include valuable reference information on The Royal Family and Royal households, Her

....(contd.)

Majesty's Officers of Arms, general tables of precedence, position of letters after the name, forms of address of persons of title, and a series of introductory essays on topics of current interest including Brave New Millenium (D. Starkey) and A Tribute to the Queen Mother (D. Williamson). *Class No:* 929(410)

[5752]

TOASE, C.A. 'Lives of lesser-known people indexes and collections', *Refer*, v.15,no.3, Autumn 1999, p.4-8.

Primarily concerned with Chadwyck-Healey's *British & Irish biographies* and K.G. Saur's *World biographical information system* series (including titles presently in progress), this illuminating article also deals with obscure British collective biographies and indexes.

Class No: 929(410)

[5753]

Who's who an annual biographical dictionary 2000. 152nd ed. London, A & C Black, 1849-. Annual. 64p.++2278p. £115. ISBN: 071365158x.

Published originally by Bailey Bros, and later by Simpkin, Marshall, Kent, it was in its early days mainly lists of names under various headings, *e.g.* Royal Household, House of Commons, etc, without any individual biographical details. It continued in this style until it was bought by A. & C. Black in 1896. The following year it became *Who's who*, 49th year, 1897 (first year of new issue, edited by Douglas Sladen). Its aim now was 'to include all the most prominent people in the Kingdom, whether their prominence is inherited, or depending upon office, or the result of ability which singles them out from their fellows in occupations open to every educated man and women'. In 1899 the title became *Who's who, 1988, an annual biographical dictionary*. In 1901 it incorporated *Men and women of the time*, adjusted its title and has appeared in this style ever since.

Obituary list October 1998 - October 1999, p.11-15. Abbreviations p.17-60. Royal Family p.62-63. An authoritative dictionary of contemporary biography, the aim being 'to furnish in as compact a form as possible a series of biographical sketches of eminent living persons of both sexes, in all parts of the civilized world'. The criterion of selection is that of 'personal achievement or prominence, and of a man's or woman's interest to the public at large or to any important section of that public'. Compilation. Initially a questionnaire is sent to a person chosen for inclusion and thereafter a proof of the entry is submitted annually to the biographee for revision. This edition has 30,000 entries (1,000 new): Anthony Charles Lynton Blair 9 lines, William Jefferson Hague 10 lines, Charles Peter Kennedy 15 lines.

Who's who CD-ROM 1897-1999. Over 100,000 biographies.

Class No: 929(410)

[5754]

—Who was who ... a companion to Who's who containing the biographies of those who died in the decade... London, A.C. Black, 1929-.

1897-1915. 7th ed., 1987. £40. ISBN 0713626704. *1916-1928.* 5th ed., 1992. £40. 0723601698. *1929-1940.* 2nd ed., 1967. £40. 0713601701. *1941-1950.* 5th ed., 1981. £40. 0713621311. *1951-1960.* 4th ed., 1984. £40. 0713625988. *1961-1970.* 2nd ed., 1979. £40. 0713620080. *1971-1980.* 1981. £40. 0713621761. *1981-1990.* 1992. 845p. 0713633360. *1991-1995. A companion to Who's Who containing the biographies of those who died in the period 1991-1995.* 1996. 619p. £55. 0713644966.

Gives birth and death dates and acts as a key to the appropriate volume. 'The entries are for the most part as they last appeared in Who's who, with the dates of death added and in some cases further additional information to bring them up to date' (*Preface*).

Who was who. A cumulated index 1897-1990. 1991. 850p. £50. 071363457x. Lists the names and years of birth and death of all those whose entries appear in *Who Was Who 1897-1990*.

Class No: 929(410)

CD-ROM

[5755]

People of today 1996 (CD-ROM edition). User Manual + Folio Infobase software. £199 + VAT.

34,000 entries (*The Times*), 35,313 (*Reference Reviews*) available for search under such headings as Names, Education, Marriage, Career, Clubs, Schools and Universities, Recreations, Publications etc. 'The names of the 34,000 leading lights of our meritocracy are now available for scrutiny by the bug-eyed nerds who prefer their reference libraries interactive' ('No Darrens in the Athenaeum', *The Times*, 2 April, p.17). *Class No:* 929(410)(003.40)

[5756]

Who's who 1897-1998 one hundred years of biography. Oxford Univ. Press, London, A & C Black, 1996. CD-ROM. Windows Macintosh. £250. + VAT.

116,000 biographies. The entire text of *Who Was Who and Who's Who 1998* on a single CD-ROM. 'The program runs smoothly and the layout of the menus is clear and concise. You can pull up overview lists of search findings or tick your way through the individual biography files, which invariable run to two pages. These can also be printed' (*Times Interface*, 19 August 1998, p.7).

Who's who 1897-1996 one hundred years of biography. London, A.C. Black and Oxford Univ. Press, 1996. 60p. spiral binding. User manual. Contents: 1. Introduction - 2. Getting started - 3. The Workplace - 4. Finding entries - 5. Viewing - 6. Who's who options. Index. *Class No:* 929(410)(003.40)

Micromaterials

[5757]

British and Irish biographies 1840-1940. Jones, D.L., *ed.* Cambridge and Alexandria, Virginia, Chadwyck-Healey, 6 parts, 1985-1991. 1400 silver halide microfiche 105mmx148mm, 24xreduction with a cumulated index of names and titles on COM. £30,000 set. £5,500 approx. per part.

Claimed to be the largest British biographical reference work ever compiled, this collection makes available 272 general, professional, and regional biographical dictionaries, containing 6½ million entries on 4 million people largely unrepresented in *DNB* or *Who's who*. 1. 382v. on 2218 microfiche with computer output microfiche (COM) index includes 10 general dictionaries: *Burke's handbook to the Most Excellent Order of the British Empire* (1921); *Burke's landed gentry* (1833-1947); *Celebrities of the century* (1890); *Hutchinson women's who's who* (1934); *Ladies who's who 1919-27* (1930); *Men and women of the day (1889-1894); Men of mark 1876-1873* by T. Cooper; *Men of the time 1852-87* continued as *Men and women of the time 1891-1899*; *People of the period* by A.T. Camden Pratt (1897); and *Women of the day* by F. Hoyt (1885). Plus 14 professional and 31 regional biographical dictionaries. 2. 168v. on 2179 microfiche includes *The biographical quarterly, recording biographical data of noteworthy citizens of the English-speaking countries 1935-36* and *Debrett's Peerage 1900-40* plus 10 professional and 32 regional works. 3. 236v. on 2455 microfiche includes *Debrett's Peerage 1864-1899* and *The Knightage of Great Britain and Ireland 1841* plus 10 professional and 25 regional works. 4. 164v. on *c.*2400 microfiche including *The upper ten thousand: an alphabetical list of all members of noble families, bishops, privy councillors, judges ... 1875-77* continued as *Kelly's handbook to the titled, landed and official classes 1880-1937* continued as *Kelly's handbook of distinguished people 1938-40* plus 10 professional and 21 regional works. 5. Published June 1990. 6. Published June 1991. Many of the works reproduced were originally printed in small editions and access is difficult in any other form.

Class No: 929(410)(003.5)

[5758]

British biographical archive. Baillie, L. *and* Sieveking, P., *eds.* London, K.G. Saur, 1984-1989. 1236 fiches (x24) either in Diazo or Silver edition. Diazo DM 20,800; Silver DM 22,800. ISBN: 3598304676, Diazo; 359850479x, Silver.

A single A-Z cumulation of full-text entries from 324 English language biographical reference works originally published 1601-1929 covering every aspect of British biography. *DNB* and *Who was who* are not included. Entries for each individual are arranged together in chronological order. 'British' is interpreted to include inhabitants of colonies born up to a year before independence or home rule and foreign nationals closely associated with Britain. Particularly useful for libraries not holding older standard biographical works. C.A. Toase's 'Micro biography', *Refer*, v.4, no.3, Spring 1987, p.1-5 compares the coverage, arrangement and presentation, and access in the library of *British & Irish biographies 1840-1940* and *British biographical archive*: 'There is hardly any overlap in titles between the two works'. *Class No:* 929(410)(003.5)

[5759]

—The British biographical archive. Series II. Esposito, A., *ed.* London, K.G. Saur, 1991-94. 632 fiches (24x) Silver or Diazo. DM 22,500 (silver); DM 20,480 (diazo). ISBN: 3598336292, silver; 3598336284, diazo.

Continuation of *British Biographical Archive*.

154,600 entries, compiled from 268 biographical sources published 1601-1978, extend the range of occupational groups, increases the sources on women, and includes a greater number of photographic portraits. Indexed in *British biographical index (q.v.)*.

Class No: 929(410)(003.5)

[5760]

-The British biographical index. Humanities Reference Unit. University of Glasgow, *comp*. 2nd cumulated and enlarged edition. London, K.G. Saur, 7v., 1998. cxcvi,3179p. DM 2,968 (DM 2,436 for subscribers to *British Biographical Archive*). ISBN: 3598336306.

Printed index to the first and second series of *British biographical archive* and a biographical dictionary in its own right. Data: name of biographee; basic biographical information, and listing of biographical citations and fiche reference no. for each person in the *Archive*. *Class No:* 929(410)(003.5)

Bibliographies

[5761]

HANDLEY, C.S. An Annotated bibliography of diaries printed in English. Aldeburgh, Hanover Press, 4v., 1997. ISBN: 0952597330.

In 4 ringbinders: 1. International index and appendices (Bibliography of bibliographies of diaries, including anthologies, collections, and studies; Index of diarists; and lists of fictional diaries) ISBN 0952597349 - 1. Bibliography of diaries printed in English to 1800. 095257357 - 3. 1801-1860. 0952597365 - 4. From 1861. 0952597373. *Class No:* 929(410)(01)

[5762]

LANHAM, H.J. 'Some neglected sources of biographical information: county biographical dictionaries 1890-1937', *Bulletin of the Institute of Historical Research*, v.34, no.89. May 1961, p.55-66.

There are two types of county biographical dictionary, the illustrated volume of local worthies and the county 'Who's who'. Unfortunately the value of all types of such dictionaries is diminished at present by the fact that there is no complete set in existence. The Press-Gaskell series, Pike's New Century series, and county 'Who's who' are briefly described. Appended is a summary of libraries' holdings arranged under English counties A-Z, followed by Wales, Scotland and Ireland. Usually only one major library holding is given per title. *Class No:* 929(410)(01)

[5763]

MATTHEWS, W., *comp*. British autobiographies: an annotated bibliography of British autobiographies published or written before 1951. Berkeley, Univ. of California Press, 1955. xiv,376p.

Reprinted Hamden, Conn., Archon Books, 1968.

6,654 very briefly annotated entries for persons 'born in the British Isles' and 'naturalised British subjects'. Arranged A-Z, anonymous works under the first word of the title. Subject and locality index of biographees. *Class No:* 929(410)(01)

[5764]

-MATTHEWS, W., *comp*. British diaries: an annotated bibliography of British diaries written between 1442 and 1942. Cambridge, Cambridge Univ. Press, 1950. xxxiv,339p. index.

Diaries arranged chronologically by date of first entry. '... includes diaries written by Englishmen, Scotsmen, Welshmen and Irishmen in the British Isles, in Europe, and on the high seas, and also the diaries of American and other travellers in the British Isles, so far as they have been published in England and in English'. Diaries in manuscript form are recorded with locations. *Class No:* 929(410)(01)

Women

[5765]

BELL, P., *comp*. Victorian women: an index to biographies and memoirs. Edinburgh, P. Bell, 1989. [130p.] pbk. ISBN: 1871538017.

2nd of 3 indexes which together will attempt to list all published biographies of British women from the late 18th century to the end of the First World War.

Online A-Z entries (name, status or position, title of biography). Scope: memoirs, autobiographies, journals, diaries, obituaries in book or pamphlet form. *Class No:* 929(410)-0055.2

[5766]

CRAWFORD, A., *and others*, eds. The Europa biographical dictionary of British women: over 1000 notable women from Britain's past. London, Europa Publications, 1983. Available in North America from G.K. Hall. ix,436p. £27.50; $55.00. ISBN: 0905118774, UK; 0810317893, US.

80 contributors. 'Women whose place in history is recognized' and 'women whose work has had some sort of public impact' (*Introduction*). Data: birth and death dates, synopsis of life and career, publications, with additional bibliographical references. *Class No:* 929(410)-0055.2

Bibliographies

[5767]

OLDFIELD, S., *comp*. Collected biography of women in Britain 1550-1900 a select annotated bibliography. London, Mansell, 1999. xx,168p. ports, index. £60. ISBN: 0720123216.

364 entries comprise 'an excellently researched and competently compiled book' which will be 'much sought after for those elusive notables on the fringe of mainstream biography and, of course, for many facets of feminist studies' (*Reference Reviews*, vol.13, no.6, 1999, p.42-43). *Class No:* 929(410)-0055.2(01)

Scotland

[5768]

BELL, P., *comp*. Who was who in Edwardian Scotland. Edinburgh, Peter Bell, 1986. 52 unnumbered pages. sd. ISBN: 0946687080.

Combined index in one A-Z sequence to ten illustrated county biographies published 1896-1912. Single-line entries give names, dates of birth and death, occupation, and reference to original and other biographical volumes. Biographical dictionaries indexed and other reference works cited p.[2-3]. *Class No:* 929(411)

[5769]

A Biographical dictionary of eminent Scotsmen. originally edited by Robert Chambers, New ed. revised under the care of the publishers. With a supplement volume, continuing the biographies to the present time. Thomson, T., *ed*. Edinburgh, Blackie, 5v., 1855.

The original edition (4v.) covered the period up to 1834, but for this edition the stereotypes were revised and reprinted, bringing the information up to 1844. V.5 contains additional entries and is up to 1855. The work contains entries for living persons and dates from the earliest times. *Class No:* 929(411)

[5770]

Chambers Scottish biographical dictionary. Goring, R., *ed*. Edinburgh, Chambers, 1992. xl,468p. index. £25. ISBN: 0550160434.

2400 profiles of 'eminent names from every era and discipline, focussing not just on the well-known, but also on those whose achievement has previously been neglected' (*dustwrapper*). 'Disappointing in its lack of depth and factual information' (*Reference Reviews*, v.7, no.1, 1993, p.42). *Class No:* 929(411)

[5771]

Dictionary of Scottish biography. Irvine, Strathclyde, Carrick Media, 1999-.

Roy, K. ed. *V.1: 1971-75*. 1999. 175p. £28. ISBN 0946724415. 24 contributors. 250 profiles of the great and the good ranging from brief factual accounts to specially commissioned essays enhanced by anecdotes and extracts from books and journals. Each volume will cover 5 years of deceased persons. *Class No:* 929(411)

[5772]

Who's who in Scotland 1998. 9th ed. Irvine, Carrick Media, 1999. 511p. £30. ISBN: 0946724423.

1st ed. 1986.

c.8000 entries relating to 'people of achievement and influence from all sections of Scottish society' Data: name, occupation, dates of birth and death, family, education, career, publication, recreations, contact address. The Who's Who in Scotland Directory (of official, cultural, religious etc. bodies, A-Z under subject he. *Class No:* 929(411)

Ireland

[5773]

BOYLAN, H., *ed*. Dictionary of Irish biography. 3rd ed. Dublin, Gill & Macmillan; New York, St. Martin's Press, 1998. xviii,462p. illus. bibliog. ISBN: 0717125076, UK.

First published 1978.

About 1700 entries (1300 2nd ed.); summarising the lives and achievements of Ireland's most distinguished people from AD 400 to the present day. Excludes living persons. Bibliography p.458-61. 'Simply cannot be faulted, and it is hard to realise that the modest inch of shelfspace contains so much information on 1600+ people' (*Books Ireland*, no.214, Summer 1998, p.180). *Choice* Outstanding Academic Title 1999. *Class No:* 929(415)

[5774]

A Dictionary of Irish biography.

Aidan Duggan's 'A dictionary of Irish biography', *Scholarly Publishing*, v.20,no.1, October 1988,p.39-42 is an account of the 10 year planning towards the launching in 1986 of the Royal Irish Academy's project: 'The Dictionary will contain biographies and assessments of all men and women of note who died on or before 31 December 1989 and who fall into one or other of the following four categories. i Those who were born in Ireland and who in some manner achieved a reputation within their native land. ii Those who were born outside Ireland but who came to Ireland and there in some manner achieved an Irish reputation. iii Those who were born in Ireland but who left their native land and in some manner achieved a reputation

....*(contd.)*

overseas. iv Those who were neither born in Ireland nor resident in Ireland but who achieved reputations and who clearly liked to think of themselves as essentially Irish. It is hoped that this first volume will be ready for publication in 1992 and that five more volumes will appear at approximately intervals of two to three years'. *Class No:* 929(415)

[5775]

McREDMOND, L., *ed*. **Modern Irish lives** dictionary of 20th-century biography. Dublin, Gill & Macmillan, 1996 xix,328p. I£19.99. ISBN: 0717121984.

c.1400 concise biographies on Irish personalities active in this century. Glossary of terms, abbreviations, acronyms and contractions p.xiii-xix. *Class No:* 929(415)

[5776]

WEBB, A. **Compendium of Irish biography:** sketches of distinguished Irishmen and of eminent persons connected with Ireland by office or by their writings. Atlantic Highlands, New Jersey, Humanities Press, 1974. xix,598p.

First published Dublin, Gill, 1878.

Compact sketches of the lives of deceased Irishmen and Irish women. Includes 'those who, though not born in Ireland, took a prominent part in the affairs of the country, or wrote important works respecting it' (*Library of Congress Information bulletin*, v.30,no.37, 16 September 1971). List of 478 authorities consulted. 'Invaluable, never wholly superseded' (Eager, A.R. *A guide to Irish bibliographical material* (1964)). *Class No:* 929(415)

Women

[5777]

O'CÈIRÌN, K. *and* O'CÈIRÌN, C. **Women of Ireland** a biographic dictionary. Minneapolis, MN., Irish Books and Media, 1996. 248p. ports., bibliog., index, pbk. $19.95. ISBN: 0937702161.

Brief entries for prominent Irish women from the 5th century AD to 1994. *Class No:* 929(415)-0055.2

Northern Ireland

[5778]

NEWMAN, K., *compiler for the Ulster History Circle*. **Dictionary of Ulster biography.** Belfast, Institute of Irish Studies. The Queen's Univ. of Belfast, 1993. viii,278po. bibliog. ISBN: 0853894787.

'This dictionary includes people from the nine counties of Ulster who have distinguished themselves. They have either been born here, or have been educated here, or have worked here, or have represented here, or have died here, or have been buried here. What unites them all is that they are no longer alive' (*Introduction*). Bibliography p.275-78. *Class No:* 929(416)

England

[5779]

BOASE, F. **Modern English biography.** London, F. Cass, 6v., 1985. £285.00. ISBN: 0714621188.

Originally published Truro, Netherton & Worth, 1892-1921.

A most valuable work, supplementing the *DNB*, particularly for the lesser-known personalities of the 19th century. Each volume contains an analytical index to the entries. About 30,000 short biographical sketches of persons who died between 1851 and 1900. Notes sources of portraits (photographs), lists published works, theatre performances and other facts sometimes omitted in larger works of reference, states the *Times Literary Supplement* leader (no.3,330, 23 December 1965, p.1189-90). Draws on obituaries and notices in *The Times, Illustrated London News* and journals, as well as local newspapers, records, etc., and so has a greater coverage of national and local celebrities who died in the latter part of the 19th century than *DNB* (*qv*). The sub-title of the supplement varies, stating the scope as covering those 'who have died during the years 1851-1900'.

Index to biographies of women in Boase's Modern English Biography, (Edinburgh, Peter Bell, 1986. 30 unnumbered pages, sd. ISBN 0946687072) identifies 1130 women entries. Data: birth and death dates and occupation. A number of other subject indexes will be published. *Class No:* 929(420)

Channel Islands

[5780]

LAYZELL, A., *ed*. **Who's who in the Channel Islands 1987.** Jersey, Who's Who in The Channel Islands, 1987. 156p. ports., pbk. £9.95. ISBN: 0951247018.

Biographies listed under individual islands - Jersey; Guernsey; Alderney; Sark; Herm (1); Brecqhou (1); Lihou(1); the other islands (0). *Class No:* 929(423.4)

[5781]

MARR, L.J. **Guernsey people.** Chichester, Sussex, Phillimore, 1984 xix,245p. index. ISBN: 0850335299.

Sequel to author's *A history of the Bailiwick of Guernsey*.

200 short biographies. Pt.1: Biographical dictionary (p.1-174) with Appendix on Second world War (p.175-8) - 2. Anecdotal jotting (p.181-203) - 3. Family trees (p.206-14) - 4. Early Bailiwick name (p.219-35). *Class No:* 929(423.4)

Wales

[5782]

The Dictionary of Welsh biography down to 1940. London Honourable Society of Cymmrodorion, 1959. lx,1157p.

Based on the Welsh ed. of 1953.

3,500 signed articles, covering all periods and walks of life. For inclusion the biographee or at least one parent had to be born in Wales 'The intervening years have enabled the editors to make many corrections' (*Preface*). Appendix of additional biographies.

Class No: 929(429)

[5783]

EVANS, G. **Welsh nation builders.** Llandysul, Dyfed, Gomer Press 1988. 356p. ports. ISBN: 0863834175.

65 biographical essays on 'people who have contributed to building the Welsh nation' (*Preface*), arranged chronologically, from Caradog (fl.30-50 AD) to Saunders Lewis (1893-1985). *Class No:* 929(429)

Germany

[5784]

Dictionary of German national biography. Killy, W. *and* Vierhaus, R., *eds*. München, K.G. Saur, 10v., 2000-2002 c.6850p DM 4,200. ISBN: 359823290x, set.

Originally published as *Deutsche bibliographische enzyklopädie* (10v. 1995-1999 and 2 supplementary vols., 1999-2000.

'The Dictionary of German National Biography' will not only include detailed accounts of the 'great names' of the past. It will also make accessible the biographies of as many people as possible who had some significant influence on their own time and later developments, whether in public life and politics or in any other field of activity, and who are indispensable to a picture of their time. Finally, a very large number of people will be mentioned who were figures of some bearing in their time, and who deserve to be remembered in their particular sphere of activity, scholarly discipline or artistic genre. 'Each entry heading comprises the name (with all name variations), first name and mark of nobility, as appropriate. Pseudonyms, maiden name, and wrongly attributed names are also given. The occupation of the biographee is followed by dates and places of birth and death.

The articles contain the most relevant, factual biographical details, informing the reader of the life and work of the biographees, their place of origin, education, significant encounters, career developments, places of activity, characteristic work, achievements, friendships and relationships, group and association affiliation, reception and, in individual cases, prizes and honours'. (*Prospectus*). 60,000 entrants from the German-speaking world.

Deutsche biographische enzyklopädie. German-English glossary of frequently-used terms (München, K.G. Saur, 1996. 24p.

Class No: 929(430)

[5785]

Wer ist wer 1999-2000? Das Deutsche who's who/The German who's who/Le Who's who allemand. 38th ed. Lübeck, Schmidt Römhild, 1999. xvi,1676p. ports. DM410. ISBN: 3795020263.

1st ed. *Wer ist's?* 1908. 10th ed. *Degener's wer ist's?* 1938.

About 33,000 biographies, of varying length, of front runners and trendsetters. Directory of Federal Republic of Germany and the Federal States p.1-6. Biographies p.7-1602. Necrology since 37th ed. p.1604-05. Birthday list A-Z by day p.1608-1663. *Class No:* 929(430)

[5786]

Who's who in Germany: a biographical encyclopedia ... containing about 11,000 biographies of top-ranking decision makers, politicians and other leading personalities operating in the fields of business and finance, politics, science, the arts and entertainment. Dove, J.C., *ed*. 35th ed. Milano, Who's Who in Italy, 2v., 1996. xxviii,3196p. $260. ISBN: 8885246249.

First published 1955.

1996 ed. Appendix outlines various aspects of German life and up-to-date statistics of leading enterprises. *Class No:* 929(430)

Micromaterials

[5787]

eutsches biographisches archiv/German biographical archive.
Fabian, B., *ed.* München, K.G. Saur, 1982-1985. 1447 (x24)
negative microfiches either in Diazo or Silver. DM 22,200 (silver);
DM 19,980 (diazo). ISBN: 3598304102, Diazo; 3598304218, Silver.

A cumulation of 264 German language biographical dictionaries
published 1707-1913. Entries number 480,000 covering 280,000
individuals in a single A-Z sequence. A complete listing of the
reference works used to compile the *Archiv* is available on request.
Indexed in printed form in *Deutscher biographischer index (q.v.).*
Class No: 929(430)(003.5)

[5788]

-Deutscher Biographischer Index/German biographical index.
Gorzny, W., *ed.* 2nd cumulative and enlarged edition. München,
K.G. Saur Verlag, 8v. 1997. cxcii,4017p. DM 3,465 (DM 2,800 to
Free of charge to subscribers of *Deutsches bibliographisches archiv*).
ISBN: 3598304323, set.

Index to *Deutsches bibliographisches Archiv.* Entries give dates of
birth and death, occupation or profession, and location of articles in
the *Archiv.* Notes on use (in German and English) p.ix-xi. List of
sources (Ger. and Eng.) p.xiii-xxvi. 'The usefulness of the *Index* in
drawing together a wide range of information not readily available
elsewhere is counterbalanced by the difficulty of using it effectively
without the *Archiv*' (*Reference Reviews*, v.1, no.2, June 1987, p.77).

CD-ROM edition 1998. DM 980 (Special price at DM 398 for
purchasers of the book editition of *Deutscher Biographischer Index
2nd, cumulative and enlarged edition*, for purchasers of the microfiche
edition *Deutsches Biographisches Archiv* as well as for the purchasers
of the CD-ROM edition of World Biographical Index). ISBN
3598402848. *Class No:* 929(430)(003.5)

[5789]

-Deutsches biographisches archiv. neue folge bis zur mitte des 2.
Jahrhunderst/German ... biographical archive$ba sequel up to the mid-
20th century. Gorzny, W., *ed.* München, K.G. Saur, 1989-1993.
1300 fiches (24x) DM 22,400 (silver); DM 19,980 (diazo). ISBN:
3598328206, Silver; 3598328346, Diazo.

Entries for c.280,000 individuals from the late 19th century to the
first half of the 20th century collated from 260 biographical
dictionaries into one A-Z sequence. Indexed in printed form in
Deutscher biographischer index (q.v.) Class No: 929(430)(003.5)

[5790]

-Deutsches biographisches archiv 1960-1999/German biographical
archive 1960-1999. Mediavilla, V.H., *comp.* München, K.G. Saur,
1999-. c.900 fiches in 12 instalments. Silver and diazo. DM 24,600
(silver); DM 22,800 (diazo). ISBN: 3598341512, silver; 3598341504,
diazo.

220,000 biographical entries on 180,000 personalities compiled from
364 reference works. All these sources complement the information
contained in the previous archives and extend the period under review
to the present day. *Class No:* 929(430)(003.5)

Luxembourg

[5791]

MERSCH, J. **Biographie nationale du pays de Luxembourg** depuis ses
origines jusqu' à nos jours. Luxembourg, Imprimerie de la Cour
Victor Buck, 1947-. fasc. 1-. illus., ports., indexes.

fasc. 1-22 (v.1-11). 1947-75. Not arranged A-Z; a series of lengthy
and scholarly contributions on promiment persons, famous families,
etc. Thus, fasc. 9 (1958-60. 280p.) includes 'Les rois du Pays-Bas,
grand ducs de Luxembourg', by Jules Mersch (p.30-280). Footnote
references; quotations from primary sources. *Class No:* 929(435.9)

Austria

[5792]

Neue Österreichische biographie ab 1815. Grosse Österreicher. Wien,
Amalthea-Verlag, 1923-.

Title has varied: v.1-8 (1923-1935) *Neue Österreichische biographie
1815-1918*; v.9 (1956) *Neue Österreichische biographie ab 1815*; v.10
(1956-) *Neue Österreichische biographie ab 1815 Grosse
Österreichischer.* Reprint volumes 1923-1935 carry the latest version
of the title.

18-20 lengthy signed and documented articles (not A-Z) on 19th and
20th century Austrians. Volume indexes, v.8- Band 1. 1977.
3850020754. Band 20. 1979. 3850021068. Band 21. 1982.
3850021572. Band 22. 1987. 3850022536. 18 essays with portraits.
Index of biographees v.1-22 in single A-Z sequence p.167-175.
Class No: 929(436)

[5793]

Österreiches biographisches Lexikon 1815-1950. Hrsg von der
Österreichischen Akademie der Wissenschaften. Redigiert von Eva
Obermayer-Marnarch. Graz-Köln-Wien, Böhlaus (v.1-5), Wien,
Verlag Österreichischen Akademie der Wissenschaften (v.6-.).

V.1-9 (1957-1988) A-Savić Žarko. 1988. xxix,448p. 3700114834.
Bibliographischer abschnitt p.xix-xxix. Lieferung 46. *Savinšek-Schou.*
1990. 370011687x.

Each volume contains c.2000 biographies, giving fairly concise
biographical data, with bibliographies. Covers personalities of the
Austro-Hungarian Empire which was dissolved in 1918. The entry for
Count Julius Andrassy runs to 1½ columns, including bibliography
(works by 2½ lines; material on 10½ lines, including a reference to
Neue deutsche Biogaphie). Frequently cited works are listed p.xxi-
xxix.

To some extent continues C. von Wurzbach's *Biographisches
Lexikon des Kaiserthums Oesterreich* (Vienna, Zamarski, 60v. 1865-
91).) which goes forward from 1750. *Class No:* 929(436)

[5794]

Who is Who in Österreich mit Südtiroltel eine personenenzyklopädie.
Hübner, R., *ed.* 14th ed. Zug, Switzerland, Who Is Who Verlag für
Personenenzyklopädien, 4v., 1998. 2032p. ports. ISBN: 372900025x.

Government directory p.11-44. Career profiles of leading figures.
Preliminaries include the words and music of the national anthem.
Class No: 929(436)

Czechoslovakia

Micromaterials

[5795]

Česky biografický archiv a Slovenský biografický archiv/
Tschechisches und Slovakisches biographisches archiv/Czech and
Slovakian biographical archive. München, K.G. Saur, 1993-1999.
687 fiches (24x) Silver or Diazo. DM 21,600 (silver); DM 19,800
(diazo). ISBN: 3598334311, silver; 3598334303, diazzo.

A single A-Z sequence cumulation of 150,000 entries for 100,000
individuals who influenced the history and culture of the lands now
designated the Czech Republic and Slovakia taken from 213 German,
Hungarian, Czech, and Slovak language biographical reference works
published from 1559-1992. Indexed in *Český biografichý a Slovenský
biografichý.* *Class No:* 929(437)(003.5)

[5796]

—Český biografický index a Slovenský biografický/Czech and Slovakian
biographical index. Kramme, U. *and* Muena, Z.U. München, K.G.
Saur, 4v., 1999. DM 1,980 (DM 1,780 for subscribers to *Česky
biografický archiv.* ISBN: 3598334605.

Printed index to *Česky biografický archiv (q.v.).*
Class No: 929(437)(003.5)

Slovakia

[5797]

Slovenský biografickík (od roku 833 do roku 1990). [Slovak
biographical dictionary.] Zväzok, I., *ed.* Matica Slovesnká, Martin,
1986-.

a *A-D.* 1986. 538p. 2. *E-J.* 1987. 587p. 3. *K-L.* 1989. 445p. ISBN
8070900194. 4. *M-Q.* 1990. 562p. 8070900709. When complete will
include 15,000 biographical sketches of leading personalities from the
time of the Great Moravian Empire to the present. Data: date and place
of birth and death; biography (education, occupation, activities); list of
published works; books about; monuments. Introduction in Slovak,
Russian, English and German. *Class No:* 929(437.6)

Hungary

[5798]

FEKETE, M., *ed.* **Prominent Hungarians, home and abroad.** 5th ed.
Budapest, HVG Publishing House, 1991. 506p. pbk. ISBN:
9637525025.

Editor regrets that many new government appointments and office
holders are held over to the next edition. Information on entrants is
sparse. *Class No:* 929(439)

Micromaterials

[5799]

Ungarisches biographisches archiv/Magyar Életrajzi Archivum/
Hungarian biographical archive. Kramme, U. *and* Muena, Z.U.
München, K.G. Saur, 1994-1999. 450 silver of diazo fiches (24x).
DM 21,840 (silver); DM 19,800 (diazo). ISBN: 3598337809, silver;
3598337633, diazo.

115,000 biographical articles, on 90,000 individuals, collected from
141 reference works published in Latin, Hungarian, German and
English, 1559-1995. Includes non-Hungarians who lived and worked

....(contd.)

in Upper Hungary and parts of Croatia, Slovenia, and the Kraina, Indexed in printed from in *Hungarian biographical Index. (q.v.)*
Class No: 929(439)(003.5)

[5800]
—Hungarian biographical Index/Magyar Életrajzi index. München, K.G. Saur, 3v., 2000. DM 1320 (DM 1194 for subscribers to *Hungarian Biographical Archive*. ISBN: 3598337949.

Printed index to *Hungarian biographical archive (Ungarisches bibliographisches archiv)*.

France
[5801]
Dictionnaire de biographie française. Paris, Librarie Letouzey et Ané, 1929-. v.1-. ISBN: 2706301589, complete work.

V.1-19 (1929-1999); A-La Rochefoucauld. Lengthy, authoritative, signed articles with good bibliographies and/or sources used. Includes outstanding Frenchmen and women from Metropolitan France and dependent territories, from the earliest times; also foreigners who have played an important part in the life of France. Excludes living persons. *DNB* was one of the models on which the work is based.
Class No: 929(44)

[5802]
Who's who in France 1996-1997 Qui est qui en France Dictionnaire biographique de personalités françaises vivant en France, dans les territoires d'Outre-mer où à l'étranger et de personalités étrangères résident en France 1991-1992. 28th ed. Paris, Éditions Jacques Lafitte, 1996. 1787p. col. illus. ISBN: 2857840349. ISSN: 00839531.

First published 1953.

Pt.1 Les Grands Institutions. Souverains et chefs d'État depuis l'an 751. Présidents de la République ... Decorations officielles françaises . Régions, départements et villes de France - 2. Le Who's Who des Enterprises - 3. Notices biographiques (p.81-1728) - 4. Le Who's Who des Régions (p.1731-60) 5. Vie practique *i.e.* essays on such topics as Tourisme et voyages, Guide des vins, Guide des médias. 20,000 biographies (900 new to this edition). *Class No:* 929(44)

Micromaterials
[5803]
Archives biographiques Françaises/French biographical archive. Bradley, S., *ed.* München, K. G. Saur, 1989-1991 1065 fiches in Diazo or Silver. Silver DM 22,800; Diazo DM 20,800. ISBN: 3598325797, Silver; 3598325649, Diazo.

A compilation of 180 original biographical reference works, 18th to 20th century, edited into a single A-Z sequence and providing 143.000 individual lives from the earliest period of French history. Covers Francophone Canada, Switzerland, and French colonies. Indexed in printed form in *Index biographique Français*.
Class No: 929(44)(003.5)

[5804]
—Archives biographiques Françaises. Deuxième Série/French biographical archive Series II/Französisches biographisches archiv Neue Folge. Nappo, T., *comp.* München, K.G. Saur, 1993-1996. 664 fiches (24x) Silver or Diazo. DM 24,600 (Silver); DM 22,800 (Diazo). ISBN: 3598335687, Silver; 3598335555, Diazo.

Special attention is paid to the 19th and 20th centuries in this second part. Indexed in printed form in *Index biographique Français. (q.v.)*
Supplément. 2000. c.100 fiches. DM 4,920 (silver); DM 4,520 (diazo). ISBN 3598335040 (silver); 3598335032 (diazo). The biographical information in Série II and the Supplément is taken from 197 biographical dictionaries and covers 201,100 individuals.
Class No: 929(44)(003.5)

[5805]
—Archives biographiques Françaises jusqu'à 1999/French biographical archive to 1999. München, K.G. Saur, In preparation c.170,000 biographical entries. *Class No:* 929(44)(003.5)

[5806]
—Index biographiqe Français/French biographical index. Dwyer, H., *ed.* 2nd cumulative and enlarged edition. K.G. Saur, 7v., 1997. clxi,3310p. DM 2,968 (DM 2,436 to purchasers of *Archives biographiques Françaises*). ISBN: 3598335814.

Detailed index to *Archives biographiques Françaises*. Data: basic biographical information, listing of biographical citations, and fiche reference numbers. Also a comprehensive biographical dictionary in its own right. *Class No:* 929(44)(003.5)

Italy
[5807]
Dizionario biografico degli Italiani. Roma, Istituto della Enciclopedia Italiana fondata da Giovanni Treccani, 1960-.

V.1-53 (1960-1999). *A-Ghisalberti. Index v.1-10.* The Italian equivalent to *DNB* but includes living persons. V.32 has 200 contributors and contains long signed articles (*e.g.* Gabriele D'Annunzio has 58 columns of text with 1 col. of bibliography) 'Some exceptional long articles, packed with the results of first-hand research, on comparatively minor characters' (*Times Literary Supplement,* no.3077, 17 February 1961, p.102). *Class No:* 929(450)

Micromaterials
[5808]
Archivo biografico Italiano/Italian biographical archive. Nappo, T and Furlani, S., *eds.* München, K.G. Saur, 1987-1991. 1406 fiche (24x). Silver DM 22,000; Diazo DM 19,800. ISBN: 3598315201, silver; 3598315406, diazo.

Biographical information on 150,500 individuals cumulated from 321 Italian-language biographical reference works 1646-1931, in a single A-Z sequence, from early Roman times to the 20th century. Coverage extends to the former kingdoms and duchies of Italy, Dalmatia, and Malta. *Class No:* 929(450)(003.5)

[5809]
—Archivio biografico Italiano sino al 1996/Italian biographical archive to 1996/Italienisches biographisches archiv bis 1996. München, K.G. Saur, 1998. c.470 silver or diazo fiches (24x). DM 22,200 (silver); DM 20,400 (diazo). ISBN: 3598343019, silver; 3598343000, diazo.

150,000 entries, drawn from reference works published since the 1960s, add biographies for a further 120,000 men and women including all members of the Italian parliament 1965-mid 1990s and politicians of the individual federal governments within Italy.
Class No: 929(450)(003.5)

[5810]
—Archivo biografico Italiano, nuova serie/Italian biographical archive. Series II. Nappo, T. *and* Furlani, S., *eds.* München, K.G. Saur, 1992-94. 710 fiches (24x) Silver or Diazo. DM 24,600 (silver); DM 22,600 (diazo). ISBN: 3598331541, Silver; 3598331401, Diazo.

180,000 entries cumulated from 124 Italian language biographical dictionaries. Overlaps with original volume in respect of 19th century material but mainly consists of 20th century biographical source material. Indexed in printed form in *Indice biografico Italiano (q.v.)*.
Supplemento. 1997. 95 fiches. DM 4,920 (silver); DM 4,520 (diazo). ISBN 3598333315 (silver); 3598333307 (diazo).
Class No: 929(450)(003.5)

[5811]
—Indico biografico Italiano/Italienischer biographischer index/Italian biographical index. Nappo, T., *comp.* 2nd cumulated and enlarged ed. München, K.G. Saur, 7v., 1996. ccxxiv,2650p. DM 2,968 (DM 2,436 to subscribers of *Archivo biografico Italiano*). ISBN: 3598331681.

Detailed index to *Archivo biografico Italiano*. Data: basic biographical information, listing of biographical citations, and fiche reference numbers. A comprehensive biographical dictionary in its own right.
CD-ROM edition 1998. DM.980 (DM.398 to purchasers of the book edition). ISBN 3598403798. c.268.000 individuals and families from the beginnings of Roman history to the mid-20th century.
Class No: 929(450)(003.5)

Spain
[5812]
Who's who in Spain 1996. Zurich, Verlag A.G., 1996. xxxiii,1660p col. ports. ISBN: 8885246326.

5,000 personal profiles of top-ranking decision makers. Spanish Royal Family p.xxx-xxxiii. *Class No:* 929(460)

Micromaterials
[5813]
Archivo biográfico de España, Portugal e Iberoamérica/Spanish, Portuguese and Latin American biographical archive. Mediavilla, V.H. *and* Nayle, R.A., *eds.* München, K.G. Saur, 1986-1989. 1144 microfiches (24x) in Silver or Diazo fiche. DM 23,800 (silver); DM 21,800 (diazo). ISBN: 3598320450, Silver; 3598320302, Diazo.

Single A-Z cumulation of full text entries from 304 biographical reference works published between the 17th and 20th centuries covering the cultural, social, and political history of the Iberian Peninsula and Latin America. *Indice biográfico de España Portugal e Iberoamérica. (q.v.)* is a printed index. *Class No:* 929(460)(003.5)

[5814]
–Archivo biográfico de España, Portugal e Iberoamérica 1960-1995/ Spanish, Portuguese and Latin American biographical archive 1960-1995/Spanisches, Portugiesisches und Iberoamerikanisches archiv, 1960-1995. Mediavilla, V.H., *comp.* München, K.G. Saur, 1996-1998. DM 21,840 (Silver); DM 19,800 (diazo). ISBN: 3598340311, silver; 3598340303, diazo.

180,000 entries on 110,000 personalities, collated from 227 biographical reference works published since the 1960s. *Indice biográfico de Espana, Portugal e Iberoamérica (q.v.)* is the printed index. *Class No:* 929(460)(003.5)

[5815]
–Indice biográfico de España, Portugal e Iberoamérica/Spanish, Portuguese and Latin American biographical index. Mediavilla, V.H. and Nayle, R.A., *eds.* 3rd cumulated and enlarged ed. München, K.G. Saur, 10v., 1999. DM 2,980 (DM 2,400 to subscribers to the *Archivo biográfico*). ISBN: 359834600x.

Detailed index to *Archivo biográfico de España, Portugal e Iberoamérica.* Data: basic biographical information, listing of biographical citations, and fiche reference numbers. Also a comprehensive biographical dictionary in its own right. Explanatory notes are in Spanish, Portuguese, English and German.

CD-ROM edition 1997. DM 980 (DM 398 for purchasers of the 1995 7v. edition of the printed index. 3598402856.
Class No: 929(460)(003.5)

[5816]
–MEDIAVILLA, V.H., *comp.* Archivo biográfico de España, Portugal e Iberoamérica. Nueve serie/Spanish, Portuguese and Latin-American biographical archive. Series II. München, K.G. Saur, 12 instalments, 1991-93. 1018 fiches (24x). DM 23,800 (silver): DM 21,800 (diazo). ISBN: 3598329644, Silver; 3598329776, diazzo.

204,000 entries cumulated from 333 Spanish and Portuguese language reference works, partly supplementary on persons previously entered in the main work, but including thousands of new entries for personalities from the first half of the 20th century. *Indice biográfico de España, Portugal e Iberoamérica* is a printed index.
Class No: 929(460)(003.5)

Portugal

[5817]
O Grande livro dos Portugueses 4000 personalidades em texto e imagem. Nomes, datas, factos com 980 Ilustrações. Lisboa (?), Círculo de Leitores, 1991. 518p. illus. (some col.), ports. (some col.). ISBN: 9724201430.

Brief biographical profiles of celebrated Portuguese men and women from all periods of history. *Class No:* 929(469)

Russia

[5818]
McCAULEY, M. Who's who in Russia since 1900. London, Routledge, 1997. xxiv,268p. maps, bibliog. ISBN: 0415138973.

Profiles of individuals active in all territories under Russian control (inc. most of the republics in the former Soviet Union), in politics, science and engineering, religion, sport, armed forces, arts, and literature. (Boris Pasternak 30 lines. Boris Yeltsin 2 pages). Chronology p.xviii-xxiv. Glossary of Russian terms, concepts and institutions p.244-56. Bibliography p.267-68. 'A refreshing blend of alternative subjects and provides a spotlight on many familiar names and events' (*Booklist*, v.94, no.6, 15 November 1997, p.582).
Class No: 929(47)

[5819]
VRONSKAYA, J. *and* CHUGUEV, V. A Biographical dictionary of the former Soviet Union: *prominent people in all fields from 1917 to the present.* 2nd ed. London, K.G. Saur, 1992. 643p. ports, maps on endpapers, index. £149; $275. ISBN: 0862916216.

First published as *A Biographical dictionary of the Soviet Union* (1989).

Information on more than 7500 personalities (including 200 new to this ed.). Includes 'people who emigrated, defected or moved for any other reason, and even those who were born abroad of Russian parentage or their activity involved them closely in Russian life' (*Author's note*). Index by occupations (40 categories) p.495-525. Heavy cultural bias. 'Many kinds of library should find the dictionary well worth the money' (*Reference Reviews*, v.3,no.3, September 1989,p.141). *Class No:* 929(47)

[5820]
Who's who in Russia. Colombo, G., *ed.* Zurich, Who's Who The International Red Series Verlag. Distributed in the UK by The Eurospan Group (London) xvii,1368p. map, index.

Biographies p.1-922. General overview of Russia p.927-29. History p.931-61. Political life p.953-1099. Economy p.1103-1279. Culture p.1285-1348. Goes way beyond the usual scope of a biographical dictionary, thus assembling a mass of quick-reference information not always easily accessible elsewhere. *Class No:* 929(47)

[5821]
Who's who in Russia and the CIS Republics. Morozov, V., *ed.* New York, Henry Holt, 1995. xvi,328p. index. ISBN: 0805026916.

Designed as a handy desk reference for researchers, journalists, business people, diplomats and students to Russian Orthodox Church leaders, presidents of commercial banks, gymnastic champions, opera singers, journalists, physicists, and actors etc. Data: last and first name; birthplace and date; nationality; education; career; major works; family information; address and telephone no. *Class No:* 929(47)

[5822]
Who's who in Russia and the new states. Geron, L. *and* Pravda, A., *eds.* 2nd ed. London I.B. Tauris, 1993. 672p. £95. ISBN: 1850434875.

First published as *The Tauris Soviet Directory the elite of the USSR today* (1989).

Part 1 lists the States alphabetically, with the names of ministries and the addresses of the parliamentary buildings, the state committees and other national bodies, as well as the holders of the most important offices. Part 2 has 4000 career profiles of leading figures in all areas of public life. Data: career history, publications, honours and awards, and personal details.

Covers Armenia, Azerbaijan, Belarus, Estonia, Georgia, Kazakhstan, Kyrgyzstan, Latvia, Lithuania, Moldova, Russian Federation, Tajikistan, Turkmenistan, Ukraine, and Uzbekistan.
Class No: 929(47)

Micromaterials

[5823]
Biographical archive of the Soviet Union (1917-1991). München, K.G. Saur, 2000. c.500 silver or diazo fiches (20x) in 12 instalments. DM22,200 (silver); DM20,400 (diazo). ISBN: 3598346913, silver; 3598346905, diazo.

c.130,000 biographical entries. *Class No:* 929(47)(003.5)

[5824]
FREY, A., *comp.* Russian biographical archive/Russisches biographisches archiv. München, K.G. Saur. c.500 silver of diazo fiches (24x) in 12 instalments. DM 20400 (silver); DM 21600 (diazo). ISBN: 3598340613, silver; 3598340605, diazo.

125,000 articles on 80,000 individuals of the pre-1917 period, from 162 Russian, English, French and German sources, 1827-1995. See also *Biographical archive of the Soviet Union (1917-1991)*. All Russian states are covered. *Class No:* 929(47)(003.5)

Baltic States

[5825]
Who is who in the Baltic States. Riga, Publishing House of Valeri Belokon, 1998. 608p. ISBN: 9984913457.

Pre-eminent politicians, businessmen, scientists, and men of culture in Latvia (3,500), Lithuania (3,000), and Estonia (1000), in 3 sequences. Data: current position, education, languages spoken, publications, publications. *Class No:* 929(474)

Micromaterials

[5826]
Baltic biographical archive/Baltisches biographisches archiv. Frey, A., *comp.* München, K.G. Saur, 1995-1998. 436 fiches (x24) silver or diazo. DM 21,840 (silver); DM 19,800 (diazo). ISBN: 359833821x, silver; 3598338201, diazo.

Biographical entries on 105,000 individuals entered in 218 Western and Eastern European language reference works, concentrating on the earlier period on German-Baltic people, although more and more Estonians, Latvians, Lithuanians, and Baltic emigrants find a place as the 20th century progresses. Indexed in printed form in *Baltic biographical index. (q.v.) Class No:* 929(474)(003.5)

[5827]
—Baltic biographical index. München, K.G. Saur, 3v. 1999. lxix,1089p. DM 1,320 (DM 1,194 for subscribers to *Baltic biographical archive*). ISBN: 3598338481.

Printed index to *Baltic biographical archive (q.v.)*
Class No: 929(474)(003.5)

Lithuania

[5828]
Who is who in Lithuania 97/98. Kaunas, Kas yra Kas Lietuvoje, 1998. 688p. ports. ISBN: 9986709040.

1st ed. in Lithuanian 1995.

3,500 biographies 'of most distinguished individuals at the current time in Lithuania'. Data, date and place of birth, academic progress, professional and public positions and organizations, family, education, employment, recreation, and photograph. State government institutions p.471-86. Local authorities and public administration institutions p.497-633. *Class No:* 929(474.5)

Poland

[5829]
Kto jest kim w Polsce informator biograficzny. 3rd ed. Warszawa, Wydawnictwo Interpress, 1993. 875p. ISBN: 8822326440.

1st ed. 1991.

3825 short biographical career sketches of which 767 are new to this edition *Class No:* 929(475)

[5830]
Polski słownik biograficzny. Cracow, Polska Akademia Nauk, Instytut Historii, 1935-. v.1-. ISBN: 8304001489.

V.1-37 (1935-1999) A-Skaradkiewicz. The definitive dictionary of Polish biography. V.1-v.7 (A-Frankowski) were published 1935-48 and publication was resumed in 1958. Scholarly, signed articles covering Poles of all historical periods and foreigners who have played an important part in Polish affairs. Articles include references to source material. *Class No:* 929(475)

[5831]
Who's who in Poland a biographical directory comprising about 4000 entries on leading personalities in Poland and information on major state, political, diplomatic, scientific and artistic institutions and organizations. Interpress Publications Warsaw, *ed.* Zurich, Who's Who the International Red Series, 1982. xi,1107p. DM240. £55.00. ISBN: 3921220564.

Following the 4000 biographies is a directory section (p.1058-1107) on *c.*800 institutions. 'A useful if expensive volume' (*International Affairs* v.59,no.3, Summer 1983, p.558-9). *Kto jest kim w Polsce: informator biograficzny* (Warszawa, Wyndawnictwo Interpress, 1984, 1175p. 8322320736) is a translation. *Class No:* 929(475)

Micromaterials

[5832]
Polskie archiwum biograficzne/Polnisches biographisches archiv/ Polish biographical archive. München, K.G. Saur, 1992-95. 625 fiches (24x) Silver or Diazo. DM 19,800 (silver); DM 18,000 (diazo). ISBN: 3598327013, silver; 3598327005, diazo.

A single A-Z sequence cumulation of biographical entries for people who lived and worked within the borders of the Polish state at any time during its history taken from 180 Polish, Russian, German, French, English and Latin language biographical reference works published from the 17th century to 1945.

Supplement. 1997. 93 fiches. DM 3,960 (silver); DM 3,600 (diazo). ISBN 3598327358 (silver); 359832734x (diazo). Index in printed form *Polski indeks biograficzy (q.v.). Class No:* 929(475)(003.5)

[5833]
—Polski indeks biograficzny/Polnischer biographischer Index/Polish biographical index. Baumgartner, G., *comp.* München, K.G. Saur, 4v., 1998. xxi,1467p. DM1,980 (DM1,780 for subscribers to the *Polskie archiwum biograficzne*). ISBN: 3598327285.

A-Z list of the 85,000 biographies on the 718 microfiches of the *Polish Biographical Archive* and *Supplement.* Data: location in PAB, fiche and frame number of the microfiche. *Class No:* 929(475)(003.5)

[5834]
—Polskie archiwum biograficzne. Seria nova/Polnisches biographisches archiv. Neue folge/Polish biographical archive. Series II. Baumgartner, G. München, K.G. Saur, 1999-. c430 silver or diazo fiches in 12 instalments. DM 22,200 (silver); DM 20,400 (diazo). ISBN: 3598344813, silver; 3598344805, diazo.

Based on 134 major Polish, English, French and German language reference guides, published 1946-1998. Includes 110,000 articles on 65,000 individuals: some providing additional information on existing entrants; others cover previously unlisted persons from the latter half of the 20th century.

Scandinavia

[5835]
Who's who in Scandinavia: a biographical encyclopedia of the international red series containing some 13,000 biographies of living prominent personalities in Denmark, Finland, Iceland, Norway and Sweden. Strute, K. *and* Doelken, T., *eds.* Zurich, Who's who International Red Series, 2v., 1983. viii,614p.+615-1186p. £80.00. ISBN: 3921220262.

'An extensive appendix gives up-to-date information on political, artistic, intellectual, economic and social life and internationally renown (sic) enterprises' (*Title page*). *Class No:* 929(48)

Micromaterials

[5836]
Scandinavian biographical archive/Skandinavisches biographisches archiv. Metherell, D. *and* Guthrie, P., *comps.* München, K.G. Saur, 1989-91 . 828 fiches (24x) Silver or Diazo. DM 22,800 (Silver); DM 20,800 (diazo). ISBN: 359832670x, Silver; 3598326505, Diazo.

Part A. *Denmark. Norway. Iceland.* 383 fiches.
Part B., *Sweden. Finland.* 445 fiches.

200,000 entries on 155,000 persons, compiled from 424 biographical reference works, 1621-1986, related to people who lived from the 8th to the early 20th century. Also includes persons in colonial territories and emigrants worldwide. *Scandinavian biographical index (q.v.)* is an index in printed form. *Class No:* 929(48)(003.5)

[5837]
—Scandinavian biographical index/Skandinavischer biographischer index. London, K.G. Saur, 4v., 1994. 2580p. DM 1,548 (free to subscribers to *Scandinavian biographical archive*) ISBN: 0862918294.

Detailed index to *Scandinavian biographical archive*. Data: basic biographical information, listing of biographical citations, and fiche reference numbers. A comprehensive biographical dictionary in itw own right. *Class No:* 929(48)(003.5)

Finland

[5838]
Kuka kukin on Who's who in Finland. Henkilötietoja nykypolven suomalaisista 1994 16th ed. Helsinglssä, Kustannusosakeyhtiö Otava, 1994. 1119p.

First published 1909; previous edition 1990.

About 4240 entries (1150 new to this edition), more detailed than the normal Who's who. Obituary p.1112-1119. In Finnish only but 'English equivalents of some common signs, words and abbreviations used in this book' p.10-11. *Class No:* 929(480)

[5839]
—Kuka kukin oli/Who was who in Finland. Henkilötietoja 1900 - luvulla kuolleista julkisuuden suomalaista. Helsingissä, Kustannusosakeyhtiö Otava, 1961. 543p.

2614 biographies of prominent people who died 1900-1961. *Class No:* 929(480)

[5840]
Vem och vad? biografisk handbok 1996. Ekberg, H., *ed.* Esbo, Holger Schildts Förlag. 1996. 714p. ISBN: 951500800x.

First published 1920.

3120 career profiles in a Finnish Who's who in Swedish. Also includes an Obituary. *Class No:* 929(480)

Norway

[5841]
Hvem er hvem 1994. 14th ed. Oslo, Kunnskapsforlaget Aschehoug - Gyldenal, 1994. vii,662p. ISBN: 8257304867.

First published 1912; 12th ed. 1979. Now published intermittently every 4 or 5 years.

4900 biographies with Obituary p.643-662. *Class No:* 929(481)

[5842]
Norge biografisk leksikon. Oslo, H. Aschehoug, 19v., 1923-1983.

Biographical portraits of Norwegians - living and dead - from the earliest times with extensive bibliographical references. A useful feature is the provision of outline family trees when several members of a family have articles devoted to them. *Class No:* 929(481)

Sweden

[5843]
Svenskt biografiskt lexikon. Stockholm, Bonnier (v.1-15); Norstedt & Söner (v.16-19); Norstedt Tryckeri (v.20-.), 1918, v.1-.

v.1-25 (1918-1987): A- Munck; Fasc 136-137 to Rudbeck (1989-1999). Includes prominent Swedish men and women from the earliest times and also those associated with the country over a long period. V.1-10 included living persons but these were excluded from v.11 onwards. Signed, well documented articles, some written by the editorial staff, others by independent experts. The work is under the supervision of Personhistoriska Instituet. *Class No:* 929(485)

[5844]
Vem är det: Svensk biografisk handbok 1995. Mortensen, J.S., *ed.* Stockholm, Norstedt's Förlag, 1997. 1290p. ISSN: 03473341.

1st ed. 1912.

The Swedish 'Who's who' containing about 10,000 short factual biographies. Heavy abbreviated entries. Obituary of the previous year. *Class No:* 929(485)

Denmark

[5845]
Dansk biografisk leksikon. Engelstoft, P. *and* Dahl, S., *eds.* 3rd ed. København, Gyldensal, 16v., 1979-1984. ISBN: 8700055514.
1st ed. 19v. 1887-1905. 2nd ed. 26v. 1933-1934.
Lengthy signed articles with bibliographies. 'Hans Christian Andersen' v.1, p.173-81, including 2 columns of bibliography. Each volume has list of contributors and subject index of biographees. V.16 (1984) includes Supplement p.249-351. *Class No:* 929(489)

[5846]
Kraks blå bog 1996: 8149 biografier over nulevende danske, faerø og grønlandske maend og kvinder. København, Krak, 1996. 1347p. ISBN: 8772255633. ISSN: 09001476.
First published 1910.
Entries include a list of publications where appropriate. Obituaries since previous edition.
Kraks Blå Bog Register over 16433 personer der er biograferet; Kraks Blå Bog 1910-1993. 149p. is an index volume.
Class No: 929(489)

Iceland

[5847]
Islenzkir samtídarmenn. [Icelandic contemporaries.] Gudnason, J. *and* Haraldsson, P., *eds.* Reykjavík, Bókaútgáfan Samtídarmenn, 2v., 1965-7.
Who's who of 5000 contemporary Icelanders. *Class No:* 929(491.1)

[5848]
OLASON, P.E. Islenzkar aeviskrár: frá landnámistímum Arsloka 1940. Reykyavík, Birt A Kostnad Hins Islenzka Bókmenntafélags, 6v., 1948-76.
c.10,000 biographies of eminent Icelanders from the times of the earliest settlements. *Class No:* 929(491.1)

Belgium

[5849]
Biographie nationale. Académie Royale Des Sciences, Des Lettres et Des Beaux-Arts de Belgique. Bruxelles, Bruylant, 1866-. v.1-.
v.1-28 (1866-1944); v.29-44 (*i.e.*, Supplément 1-16) (1957-1985). The Belgian *DNB.* Long, signed obituaries by specialists (*e.g.* Cardinal Mercier by A. Simon: 21½ columns, including 1 col. of bibliography; Henri Pirenne by F.L. Ganshof: 522/3cols, with sub-headings and 1 col. of bibliography). Each of the supplementary volumes has a separate A-Z sequence and list of contributors. *Class No:* 929(493)

[5850]
Le Dictionnaire des belges. Bruxelles, Paul Legrain, 1981. 570p.
90,000 short biographies 1830 to 1980. *Class No:* 929(493)

[5851]
National biografisch woordenboek. Koninklijke Vlaamse Academiën Van Belgïe. Brussel, Paleis Der Academiën, 1964-.
V.11. 1985. vii,870p. ISBN 9065690115. V.12. 1987. vii,847p. ISBN 9065690123. Flemish biographical dictionary which includes many people omitted from French-language *Biographie nationale (qv).* Also includes biographies of prominent Dutch personalities. Successive volumes have own A-Z sequence with a cumulative index. Well-documented with each entry ending with bibliographical citations. 'There emerges an impressive picture of the number of biographies which have been brought up-to-date' (*Acta Historiae Neerlandica,* v.8,1975,p.160). *Class No:* 929(493)

[5852]
Qui est qui en Belgique francophone 1985-1989. Deccan, R., *ed.* 2nd ed. Bruxelles, Éditions BRD, 1985. 1099p. ISBN: 9065980180. ISSN: 07713792.
First edition 1980.
12584 biographies (10109 in 1980 ed.) of leading personalities in public life, social organizations, liberal professions, science, the arts, the mass media *etc.* Royal Family p.13-14. A third edition is announced for 1990. *Class No:* 929(493)

[5853]
Wie is wie in Vlaanderen 1985-1989. Deccan, R., *ed.* 2nd ed. Brussel, Uitgeverij BRD, 1985. 1455p. ISBN: 9065980172. ISSN: 07717822.
1st ed. 1980.
15219 biographies compared to 12014 in 1ast ed. 'Het Koninklijk Huis (Royal family) p.13-14. A 3rd ed. is expected in 1990. *Class No:* 929(493)

Switzerland

[5854]
Who's who in Switzerland including the Principality of Liechtenstein 1990-1991: a biographical dictionary containing about 3500 biographies of prominent people in and of Switzerland (including the Principality of Liechtenstein. 16th ed. Geneva, Nagel, 1990. 555p. ISBN: 2826308289.
First published 1952.
Significant input of 200 new biographies in this edition. Glossary p.11-13. *Class No:* 929(494)

Greece

Micromaterials

[5855]
Greek biographical archive/Griechisches biographisches archiv. München, K.G. Saur, 1998-. c.400 fiches (silver or diazo) in 12 instalments. DM 22,400 (silver; DM 20,400 (diazo). ISBN: 3598341814, silver; 3598341806, diazo.
120,000 biographical articles, collected from 98 source works on 90,000 individuals living in Greece, Asia Minor, the Aegean Islands, and lower Italy (in the Byzantine period) from the 4th century AD to the present, thus covering Byzantine imperial history, 350 years of Ottoman Turk rule, and the 19th and 20th centuries. *Class No:* 929(495)(003.5)

Balkan States

Micromaterials

[5856]
Südosteuropäisches biographisches archiv/South-East European biographical archive. Kramme, U. *and* Muena, Z.U., *comps.* München, K.G. Saur, 1998-. x.450 silver or diazo fiches (24x) in 12 instalments. DM 22,200 (silver); DM 20,400 (diazo). ISBN: 3598341210, silver; 3598341202, diazo.
120,000 biographical entries, extracted from 175 reference works published in English, French, German and Italian, and in relevant South-East European languages, 1711-1995. Countries covered: Albania, Bulgaria, Romania, Slovenia, Croatia, Bosnia-Herzegovina, Macedonia, Serbia, and Montenegro. *Class No:* 929(497)(003.5)

Croatia

[5857]
Tko je tko uhrvatskoj. Who is who in Croatia. Zagreb, Golden Marketing, 1993. xviii,956p. ISBN: 9536168006.
Facing Croat and English entries for 4,000+ Croatian scholars, scientists, artists, businessmen, politicians, lawyers, generals, bishops, athletes and journalists from the homeland and the diaspora. Directory of organizations, associations and institutions p.861-956. *Class No:* 929(497.13)

Romania

[5858]
IONESCU, S.N. Who was who in twentieth century Romania. Boulder, Colo., East European Monographs; New York, Columbia Univ. Press, 1994. 318p. bibliog. $39. ISBN: 0880332921.
c.3,000 entries. Data: birth and death dates and places, education, career, publications. Also includes lists of rulers, prime ministers, and presidents of the Romanian Academy. *Class No:* 929(498)

Asia—Far East

[5859]
Who's who in Asia and the Pacific nations. Kay, B. *and* Bootman, C., *eds.* 4th ed. Cambridge, International Biographical Centre, 1999. xx,523p. ISBN: 0948875631.
Formerly published under the title *Who's who in Australasia and the Pacific* (1st ed. 1989; 3rd ed. 1997).
c.8000 entrants from 70+ countries and territories in the Asian Pacific area. Data: birth date, education, career, publications, honours and awards. Appendix A. Organizations and Associations (A-Z by country) p.491-504. *Class No:* 929(51/52+57)

China

[5860]
BOORMAN, H.L. *and* HOWARD, A.C., *eds.* Biographical dictionary of Republican China. New York, Columbia Univ. Press, 5v., 1967-79. 1853p. $60.00 each volume. ISBN: 0231089554, v.1; 0231089562, v.2; 0231089570, v.3; 0231089589, v.4; 0231045581, v.5.
About 600 essay-biographies of persons, living or dead, who were prominent during the Republican period, 1911-49. 'Chang Kai-shek':

....(contd.)

v.1, p.319-38; 1p. of bibliography. V.1 has appended 'General bibliographical reference works' (p.481-2). The bulk of v.4 is a valuable bibliography (p.97-418) by Joseph K.H. Cheng, following text order (A-Z, biographies). Most of the personalities are drawn from political, military, economic and academic spheres. Chinese characters follow romanised form of entry name. V.5: *A personal name index* (1979,[xiii],75p.) has 16 contributors. Entries are in romanised form, plus Chinese characters. Names are in bold type if the subject of a biographical essay in the dictionary. Non-analytical index ('Yuan Shih-k'ai': 1 column). *Class No:* 929(510)

[5861]

KLEIN, D.W. *and* **CLARK, A.B. Biographic dictionary of Chinese Communism 1921-1965.** Cambridge, Mass., Harvard Univ. Press, 2v., 1971. xvi,641p. 642p. maps. $81.00. ISBN: 0674074106.

433 biographies, plus 96 appendices on key events and organizations in the party's history. Well documented (*e.g.* Chou En-lai: v.1, p.204-19, including 1½ columns of bibliographical references). Selected bibliography, p.1031-8. Glossary - name index (p.1170-94): Chinese characters for *c.*1,750 names. Like Boorman (*qv*) bears 'the stamp of extensive research and scholarly analysis from the limited sources of information currently available ... Both Klein and Boorman adopt Wade's standard form of Romanization, thereby greatly facilitating comparative study' (*Asian Affairs*, v.60, pt.2, June 1973, p.196). Boorman is more readable; Klein, more informative (*The China Quarterly*, October/December 1971, p.741-8). *Class No:* 929(510)

[5862]

Who's who in China 1918-1950. With an index compiled by Jerome Cavenaugh. Hong Kong, Chinese Materials Center, 3v., 1983.

Material in these 3 reprint volumes was collected originally from *The China Weekly Review*, previously *Millard's Review*, printed in Shanghai. 'Although the publishers never managed to live up to their initial plan to publish a yearly volume, this was the first important attempt to collect biographical information on Chinese leaders in English. The *Who's who* was a direct offshoot of the weekly's practice of introducing important Chinese in the news through biographical sketches' (*Preface*).

Reprint v.1: Index p.1-198. *Who's who in China 1918-1920 containing the pictures and biographies of some of China's political, financial, business and professional leaders.* Also 2nd ed. (1920). Reprint v.2: 3rd ed. (1925) including Directory of American Returned Students. 972+25p. Supplement to 3rd ed. (1928) 168p. Reprint v.3: 4th ed. (1931) 512p.; Supplement to 4th ed. (1933) 136p. 5th ed. (1936) 300p.; Supplement to 5th ed. (1940) 83p. and 6th ed. (1950) 253p. *Class No:* 929(510)

Internet

[5863]

Chinese biographical databases. URL:http://exodus.lcsc.edu/cbiouser/

'A dynamic, interactive database moderated by scholars' in 6 sections: 1. Introduction (database description, uses, and objectives) - 2. Searches (22 options) - 3. Reports (individual biographical entries) - 4. New biographies (contribution from users) - 6. Feedback. 'Useful for quick searches for notable Chinese individuals; the historical event search is especially valuable' (*Choice*, Supplement to v.36, August 1999, p.56). *Class No:* 929(510)(003.41)

Micromaterials

[5864]

Chinesisches biographisches archiv/Chinese biographical archive. Minden, S. von, *ed*. München, K.G. Saur, 1996-1999. 453 fiches (24x). DM 23,400 (silver); DM 21,600 (diazo). ISBN: 3598339119, silver; 3598339100, diazo.

115,000 biographical entries, from 88 reference sources, published 1898-1994, on 67,200 individuals 'within the cultural sphere of China', from the historical beginnings to the present day. 44,000 entries from standard Chinese reference works are provided with English-language abstracts. Indexed in *Chinese biographical index*. *Class No:* 929(510)(003.5)

[5865]

—MINDEN, S. von, *ed*. Chinese biographical index. München, K.G. Saur, 3v., 2000. DM 1,320 (DM 1,194 for subscribers to *Chinesisches biographisches archiv*). ISBN: 3598339372.

Printed index to *Chinesisches biographisches archiv (q.v.)*. *Class No:* 929(510)(003.5)

20th Century

[5866]

BARTKE, W. A Biographical dictionary and analysis of China's Party leadership 1922-1988. München, K.G. Saur, 1990. xi,482p. ports, tables. £127.50. ISBN: 3598108761.

In 3 parts: 1. Biographies of 1049 members of the Central Committee 2nd-13th Central Committees. Data: name in Roman and Chinese script; career profile; visits abroad, A-Z by Western form - 2. Analyses of Central Committee cadres including the Politburo and Central committees - 3. Tables *i.e.*, information on all 13 Central Committees 1922-1988. *Class No:* 929(510)"19"

[5867]

BARTKE, W. Who's who in the People's Republic of China. 3rd ed. London, K.G. Saur, 2v., 1990. 900p. ports., index. £145.00. ISBN: 3598107714.

First published in New York by M.E. Sharpe Inc. and in Brighton, Sussex, by Harvester Press 1981. 2nd ed. published by K.G. Saur in 1987.

'Entries cover a whole range of living Chinese personalities: politicians, soldiers, academics, scientists, diplomats, religious and cultural leaders. Each biography lists posts held, thus enabling the user to assess at a glance the present importance of a party cadre, and includes a photograph where available. Names are also translated into Pinyin, together with Chinese characters... Also contains an occupation index and an appendix on the organisation of the People's Republic of China, with charts and tables detailing the composition and structure of the active leadership of todays China' (*K.G. Saur catalogue*). *Class No:* 929(510)"19"

Women

[5868]

Biographical dictionary of Chinese women the Qing period 1644-1911. Wing-Chung Ho, C., *and others, eds*. New York, M.E. Sharpe, 1998. 387p. bibliog., index. $87.95. ISBN: 0765600439.

80+ contributors. c.200 profiles of varying length of women of achievement. Further reading lists appended to all entries. *Class No:* 929(510)-0055.2

Korea

Micromaterials

[5869]

Korean biographical archive. München, K.G. Saur, In preparation. *Class No:* 929(519)(003.5)

Japan

[5870]

Who's who in Japan 1991-92. 3rd ed. Hong Kong, International Culture Institute, 1992. Distributed in North America by Gale Research Co. and in UK by K.G. Saur. [iv],1281p. £225. ISBN: 3598075804.

First ed. 1984-85.

About 51,000 brief biographies on leading figures in contemporary Japanese society arranged A-Z by family name. Data: name, degree or license, position, education, birthdate, career, honours, membership, hobbies, address and telephone numbers. The Directory of Public and Private Institutions also provides the official names, addresses and telephone numbers of Diet organs, ministries and government agencies, local government offices, companies listed in the First and Second Sections of the Tokyo Stock Exchange, public and private universities, non-profit foundations and organizations, libraries and museums. Biennial revisions are promised. 'Those who can justify purchase will find it to be money well spent' (*Reference Reviews*, v.3,no.1, March 1989, p.42-3). *Class No:* 929(52)

Micromaterials

[5871]

Japanese biographical archive/Japanisches biographisches archiv. Wispelwey, B., *comp*. München, K.G. Saur, 1999-. c.400 silver or diazo fiches (24x). DM 22,200 (silver); DM 20,400 (diazo). ISBN: 359834001x, silver; 3598340001, diazo.

An accumulation of c.120 biographical reference works on Japan, published up to 1998, including 70,000 individuals who shaped Japanese politics, economy, science, religion and culture during the varied course of its history. It also covers non-Japanese individuals who lived and worked in Japan. The biographies are written in Japanese, English, German, French and other Western languages. In order to make the biographical material accessible to readers without knowledge of Asian languages, approximately 25,000 entries from Japanese standard works will be provided with specifically written English-language abstracts. *Class No:* 929(52)(003.5)

Asia—South & South East

Micromaterials

[5872]
South-East Asian biographical archive/Südostasiatisches biographisches archiv. Wispelwey, B., *comp*. München, K.G. Saur, 1997-. c.430 silver or diazo fiches (24x) in 12 instalments. DM 23,400 (silver); DM 21,600 (diazo). ISBN: 359834511x, silver; 3598342101, diazo.

Comprises approximately 85,000 biographies on 55,000 persons, collected from 271 reference volumes, 1880-1997. Region covered includes the modern states of Brunei, Cambodia, Malaysia, Philippines, Thailand, Indonesia, Laos, Myanmar, Singapore, and Vietnam. *Class No:* 929(54+59)(003.5)

India

[5873]
BUCKLAND, C.E. Dictionary of Indian biography. New York, Haskell House Publishers, 1968. xii, 494p. bibliog. $85.00; £76.50. ISBN: 0838302777.

First published London, Sonnenschein, 1906.

'The main facts of the lives of about 2,600 persons - English, Indian, foreign, men or women, living or dead - who have been conspicuous in the history of India, or distinguished in the administration of the country, in one or other of its branches, or have contributed to its welfare service and advancement by their studies and literary products, or have gained some special notoriety. The entries date from 1750 'when the English power in India was being established'. It is still useful for the period covered and is not entirely superseded by any other work. Bibliography is appended, together with a list of the reference works consulted by the compiler of the *Dictionary*. *Class No:* 929(540)

[5874]
Eminent Indians who was who 1900-1980 also Annual diary of events. New Delhi, published under the auspices of Durga Das Pvt. Ltd., 1985. Rs.250. *Class No:* 929(540)

[5875]
India who's who 1997-98. Inder Jit, *ed*. 25th ed. New Delhi, INFA Publications 1997. lxiv,236p. + 164A+182B index. Rs500. $90.

1st published 1969.

5,000 concise biographies (500 new to this edition) Arranged in 7 categories: Public Affairs, Business Humanities, Sciences, Sciences Applied, Social Sciences and Law, Miscellaneous. 'A storehouse of basic biographical information about India's leading personalities who by their achievements and status have come to be acclaimed in their respective fields'. *Class No:* 929(540)

Micromaterials

[5876]
BAILLIE, L., *comp*. Indian biographical archive/Indisches biographisches archiv. München, K.G. Saur, 1997. 500 silver or diazo fiches (24x). DM 22,200 (silver); DM 20,400 (diazo). ISBN: 3598340915, silver; 3598340907, diazo.

Single A-Z cumulation of biographical material on 148,000 individuals, including English, French and Portuguese, from all periods of Indian history, collected from 184 source works published since the mid-1800s. Geographical scope includes the modern states of Pakistan, Bangladesh, and Sri Lanka. On completion of the editorial and microfilm work a printed index will be published. *Class No:* 929(540)(003.5)

Sri Lanka

[5877]
Personalities Sri Lanka a biographical study (15th-20th century) [1490-1990AD]. Wimalaratne, K.D.G., *comp*. Columbo, Ceylon Business Appliances, 1994. xxxix,149p. ISBN: 9559287001.

A-Z career profiles of 834 personalities belonging to all ethnic groups who have contributed to the development of Sri Lanka. *Class No:* 929(548.7)

Pakistan

[5878]
Biographical encyclopedia of Pakistan 1996-97. Muhammad Umar Kirmani, *ed*. Lahore, Biographical Encyclopedia of Pakistan, 1997. 956p.+xvp. index. ports.

Life sketches arranged in 12 occupational sections: Public life, science and technology, Engineering, Consultant engineers and architects, Education, literature and journalism, Medicine and public health, Law and justice, Administration, Industry and commerce, Business executive, Notable families, Land and farming, Religion, and Public and social life. *Class No:* 929(549)

Indian Subcontinent States

[5879]
SCHOLBERG, H., *ed*. The Biographical dictionary of Greater India. New Delhi, Promilla, 1998. (Distributed by South Asia Books). 406p. bibliogs., index. $72. ISBN: 8185002231.

157 biographies of men and women who shaped the destiny of South Asia from the earliest period to the 20th century arranged in 16 chronological and thematic chapters. 'Scholberg (a well-known author and librarian) offers a masterpiece for the benefit of South Asian scholars and researchers' (*Choice*, v.36, no.7, March 1999, p.1231). *Choice* Outstanding Academic Title 1999. *Class No:* 929(54.)

Iran

[5880]
BEHROUZ, K. *and* OURMAZDI, M. Iran's who's who 1993. 4th ed. Tehran, Iran Who's Who, 1993. 473p.

About 1,000 very brief biographical outlines. Data: date and place of birth, current position, education, travel, foreign language. *Class No:* 929(55)

Turkey

[5881]
Günümüz Türkiyesinde kim kimdir/Who's who in Turkey 1997-1998. 5th ed. Istanbul, Profesyonel, 1997. xviii,19-670p.

1st ed. 1985; 4th ed. 1990.

About 13,000 brief biographical sketches, three columns to the page. Only title/page in English *Class No:* 929(560)

Micromaterials

[5882]
Türkisches biographisches archiv/Turkish biographical archive. München, K.G. Saur, 1999-. c.380 silver or diazo fiches (20x) in 12 instalments. DM 22,200 (silver); DM 20,400 (diazo). ISBN: 3598342713, silver; 3598342705, diazo.

The biographies, predominantly written in Turkish, but also in English, French, German, Italian and Latin, have been compiled from approximately 220 sources published between 1709 and 1994. The Archive lists approximately 80,000 individuals and consists of about 150,000 biographical entries. It covers the period from the 11th century AD, when the Ottoman Empire was established, up to the present day, the time of the modern Turkish Republic. *Class No:* 929(560)(003.5)

Lebanon

[5883]
Who's who in Lebanon 1999-2000. Bustros, G., *ed*. 15th ed. Beirut, Publitec, 1998. 482p. £178.00. ISBN: 2903188165.

First published 1977. Now published biennially.

Concise biographies of 2000+ prominent personalities including some foreign residents plus a geographic, economic, political, legal, and cultural survey of Lebanon. Lists National Assembly members, ministers, official Lebanese decorations, diplomatic and consular missions. *Class No:* 929(569.3)

Israel

[5884]
Who's who in Israel and Jewish personalities from all the world 1999. Itzhak Ben, *ed*. Special Jubilee issue. Tel-Aviv, Who's Who in Israel, 1999.

'The Presidency of Israel', 'Members of the 11th Knesset' and 'Members of the Government' precede Pt.1. Personalia, (c.3000 biographies). Pt.2. Public and private enterprises: Government, official and public institutions and corporations, public and private enterprises, municipalities, cultural and educational institutions, commerce, industry, tourism. *Class No:* 929(569.4)

Afghanistan

[5885]
ADAMEC, L.W. Historical and political who's who of Afghanistan. Graz, Akademische Druk-u. Verlagsanstalt, 1975. ix,385p.

Brief biographies of *c*.1500 persons in 2 sequences: 1945-1974 and 1747-1945. Also Afghan Government members for 20th century. 92 genealogical tables of prominent families. Glossary p.379.85. *First supplement to the Who's who of Afghanistan: Democratic Republic of Afghanistan*. 1979. 53p. Includes corrections to the base volume. *Class No:* 929(581)

[5886]

—ADAMEC, L.W. A Biographical dictionary of contemporary Afghanistan. Graz, Akademische Druck-u. Verlagsanstalt, 1987. vi,252p.+24p. of photographs. ISBN: 3201013390.

Biographies of 1600 high government officials, political leaders, military officers, religious leaders *etc.* since 1945. Who's who p.1-209. Government 1919-1978 and 1978-1986 p.213-231. Diplomatic list p.232-242. PDPA leadership p.243-245. Glossary p.246-252.

Class No: 929(581)

Malaysia

[5887]

New Malaysian who's who. Kuala Lumpur, Kasuya Publishing, 3v. in 2, 1989. $700.

Part 1. Sabah and Sarawak. cdlix,744p. illus., ports, map. ISBN 9839624008. Biographical information on King and Queen, Malay rulers, government ministers *etc.* p.i-xlii. Brief chapters on general business information, Malay business law, economy, taxation, political parties, honours and awards, and 13 Malay states. p.xliv-cdlix. Personalities from East Malaysia p.1-744.

Part 2. West Malaysia. 2v. cdlix,1,498p. 9839624016. On same pattern as Part 1. Personalities from West Malaysia p.1-1,498p.

Biodata on 7,000 people of distinction: education, professional qualifications, career, affiliations, honours and awards, and foreign visits. *Class No:* 929(595)

Islamic World

[5888]

Arabian personalities of the early twentieth century. Bidwell, R., *ed.* Cambridge, Oleander Press, 1986. viii,362p. map. index. £29.,75. (*Arabia past and present, v.19.*) ISBN: 0906672392.

First published in a strictly limited and confidential edition in 1917.

Primary sourcebook of British intelligence material containing 3700 biographical sketches arranged in 7 regional sections: Hejaz, Asir, Yemen, Aden and Hadramaut, Gulf Coast, Central Arabia, Syrian Desert and Sinai. *Class No:* 929(5.297)

[5889]

Who's who in the Arab World 1999-2000. Bustros, G.M., *ed.* 14th ed. München, K.G. Saur. 1998. 968p. bibliog, index. £310. ISBN: 3598076711. ISSN: 00839752.

1st ed. 1966. Now issued biennially.

Part 1. Biographical section of *c.*6000 sketches of prominent persons in the Arab World indexed by country and profession - 2. Survey of 19 Arab countries Algeria - Yemen - 3. Outline of Arab World: General survey including History, The League of Arab States; Mahgreb Committee; Arab petroleum; etc.). Bibliography p.975-76. Index of biographees by profession and by country p.917-74.

Class No: 929(5.297)

Micromaterials

[5890]

Arab-Islamic biographical archive/Arabisch-Islamisches biographisches archiv. München, K.G. Saur, 1995-1998. 450 fiches (24x). DM 22,200 (silver; DM 20,400 (diazo). ISBN: 3598338813, silver; 3598338805, diazo.

95,000 biographical entries selected from 239 reference works in English, French, German, Italian and Spanish. On 80,000 individuals from the Mediterranean region, the Arab peninsula, Central Asia, and India, from pre-Islamic times to the present day.

Class No: 929(5.297)(003.5)

Bibliographies

[5891]

AUCHTERLONIE, P. Arabic biographical dictionaries: a summary guide and bibliography. Durham, Middle East Libraries Committee, 1987. iv,60p. bibliog. pbk. £5.25. ISBN: 0948889012.

Research guide in 4 sections: 1. Brief account of historical development of Arabic biographical dictionaries - 2. List of classical dictionaries - 3. Modern biographical dictionaries in Arabic and Western languages - 4. Brief summary of Western scholarship regarding most complete and well known dictionaries.

Class No: 929(5.297)(01)

Africa

[5892]

Africa who's who. 3rd ed. London, Africa Books Ltd., 1996. xi,1507p. 195. $295. (*Know Africa.*) ISBN: 090327423x. ISSN: 01611570.

1st ed. 1981. Companion volume of *Africa today* and *Makers of modern Africa* (qqv).

Biographical data on over 14000 eminent personalities: nationality

.... *(contd.)*

and occupation, date and place of birth, education, career, current occupation, publications, national and international honours.

Class No: 929(6)

[5893]

BROCKMAN, N. C. An African biographical dictionary. Santa Barbara, Calif., ABC-Clio, 1994. viii,440p. bibliog., maps, index. $60. ISBN: 0874367484.

550 biographical outlines of leading figures in African history with emphasis on the post-colonial period. Mostly political but with a generous selection of cultural figures, scientists, and religious personalities. List of sub-Saharan states with colonial name p.385-6. Africa since independence: nations and leaders p.391-94. Bibliography p.419. 3 maps. 'An excellent source for information not easily found elsewhere' (*Choice*, v.32,no.9, May 1995, p.1426. *Class No:* 929(6)

[5894]

The Encyclopaedia Africana dictionary of African Biography. New York, Reference Publications, 20v., 1977-. ports, maps, bibliogs., indexes. ISBN: 091725600x, set.

Compiled under the direction of the Secretariat of the Encyclopaedia Africana project in Accra.

1. *Ethiopia-Ghana.* 1977. 367p. ISBN 09117256018. 70 contributors. Signed biographical profiles of 146 Ethiopians and 138 Ghanaians. 2. *Sierra Leone - Zaire.* 1979. 372p. 0917256069. 40 contributors. 234 profiles (Sierra Leone 132 and Zaire 102). 3. *South Africa - Botswana - Lesotho - Swaziland.* 1995. 304p. 0917256212. 228 profiles. Each title incorporates an historical introduction to the country involved and a guide to names and terms. All entries are signed. *Class No:* 929(6)

[5895]

RAKE, A. Who's who in Africa leaders for the 1990s. Metuchen, N.J., Scarecrow Press, 1992. 448p. index. $59.50. ISBN: 0810825570.

Career profiles of more than 300 political figures in the 47 countries South of the Sahara A-Z by country. Each country section begins with basic geographical, constitutional, and political information.

Class No: 929(6)

Micromaterials

[5896]

African biographical archive/Archives Biographiques Africaines/Afrikanisches Biographisches Archiv. Mediavilla, V.H., *ed.* München, K.G. Saur, 1994-1997. 457 fiches (24x) silver or diazzo. £7294 (silver); £6631 (diazzo). ISBN: 3598331002, silver; 3598331010, diazzo.

A single sequence A-Z cumulation of biographical entries from 233 biographical reference works relating to Africa. Published in English, French, German and Italian 1840-1993. Post 1950 publications constitute 90% of all sources consulted. Contains approximately 113,000 biographical entries relating to 75,000 individuals. Indexed in *African biographical index/Index biographique Africain (q.v.)*.

Class No: 929(6)(003.5)

[5897]

—African biographical index/Index biographique Africain. Mediavilla, V.H., *ed.* München, K.G. Saur, 3v. 1999. xviii,1134p. DM 1,320. ISBN: 3598331282.

Indexes in printed form the *African biographical archive (q.v.)*.

Class No: 929(6)(003.5)

Nigeria

[5898]

Who's who in Nigeria. Nyaknno Osso, *ed.* Lagos, Newswatch Communications, 1990. 803p. ISBN: 9782704121.

Brief entries on 2500 Nigerian men and women of outstanding accomplishments in all walks of life. Data: birthdate, education and qualifications, awards, national honours, foreign decorations, published works. *Class No:* 929(669)

Uganda

[5899]

Who's who in Uganda 1993-94. Isingoma, D., *ed.* 2nd ed. Kampala, Fountain Publishers, 1994. v,102p. ISBN: 9970020277.

1st ed. 1989.

Brief details of 'those who through their careers affect the political, economic, social and cultural life of the country'. Data: date of birth, present post, career, special interests and achievements.

Class No: 929(676.1)

Africa—Southern

[5900]

Who's who of Southern Africa 2000: an illustrated biographical record of prominent personalities in the Republic of South Africa, Botswana, Mauritius, Namibia, Swaziland, Zimbabwe, and neighbouring countries in South Africa. Hayes, S.V., *ed.* Millenium ed. Craighall, Who's Who of Southern Africa, 1999. Annual. 633p. ports. ISBN: 0958426511. ISSN: 00839876.

First published 1907. Title changed from *South African who's who,* in 1959.

Republic of South Africa Official directory. Biographies p.47-415. Data: name, current position, date of birth, education, recreations, address, corporate information. Representatives of South Africa abroad p.463-499. Sections on Namibia, Botswana, Swaziland, Mauritius, Lesotho, Malawi, and Zimbabwe consisting of official directories.

Class No: 929(68)

South Africa

[5901]

BEER, M. de. Who did what in South Africa. Rev. ed. Jeppestown, AD Donker, 1995. 154p. ports. ISBN: 086852204x.

1st ed. 1986.

Collection of short biographical sketches of people known for their achievement in a wide diversity of fields. *Class No: 929(680)*

[5902]

Dictionary of South African biography. Beyers, C.J., *ed.* Various publishers for Human Sciences Research Council (Pretoria), 1968-. (v.1-5. 1968-1987).

V.4 (Butterworth & Co.,1981). xx,803p.ISBN 0409091839. V.5 (Johannesburg, Chris van Rensburg Publications, 1987). 909p. ISBN 0796904200. Biographies of persons who died before 1982. Signed articles. Each volume has an A-Z sequence. Hendrik Frensch Verwoerd (v.4) p.730-40 with half column of references. The whole is to run to several volumes, each with biographies of persons who died up to 5 years before publication, and each with cumulative indexes. A most important, authoritative source for South African biography. Published in English and Afrikaans. *Class No: 929(680)*

[5903]

–New dictionary of South African biography. Verwey, E.J., *ed.* Pretoria, Human Sciences Research Council, 1995-.

Complements *Dictionary of South African biography (q.v.)*

Vol.1: 1995. viii,310p. pbk. ISBN 0796916489. 129 entries aim 'to fill gaps in our history, highlighting in particular the significant roles played by black leaders from all walks of life, and the many women who dared to challenge the *status quo*' Each entry is given, where possible, a portrait and a list of references. List of contributors (and their contributions) p.iii-iv. *Class No: 929(680)*

[5904]

TOFFOLI, H.P. and SILBER, G. Who's really who in South Africa. Johannesburg, Jonathan Ball, 1989. ii,229p. illus. ISBN: 0947464077.

240 irreverent profiles of 'the buzz people of South Africa' whose 'words, deeds, and personalities are in some way woven into the rich and colourful fabric of South African society'. *Class No: 929(680)*

Zimbabwe

[5905]

Who's who in Zimbabwe a book providing biographical data on prominent Zimbabweans in various spheres of life: politicians, industrialists, professionals, academics, executives *etc.* 1993-1994. Harare, Argosy Press, 1994. 88p. ports., sd. ISBN: 0908309309.

Over 500 entrants: basic profiles of leading personalities and their careers. *Class No: 929(689.1)*

Mauritius

[5906]

Dictionnaire de biographie Mauricienne/Dictionary of Mauritian biography. Port Louis, Société de l'Histoire de l' Ile Maurice, 1941-.

Issued in fascicules: no.1 February 1941; 17p. no.45. April 1990. 1362p.++ 8p. *Mutanda* and *Addenda*. Documented entries for 'all those who, identified with Mauritius, whether by birth, adoption or temporary connection, played a part worth recording in the history of Mauritius' are in English or French (depending on country of origin). No living persons. *Class No: 929(698.2)*

Canada

[5907]

Canadian who's who 1999. Lumley, E., *ed.* 34th ed. Toronto, Univ. of Toronto Press, 1999. Annual. 1380p. $170. ISBN: 0802049311. ISSN: 00689963.

First published in London by Times Publishing Co. 1910. 2nd ed. 1936, substantially longer, incorporated *Canadian men and women of the time*. Then issued triennially with 5 supplementary booklets

....(contd.)

(*Canadian biographical service*) until University of Toronto acquired the publishing rights 1978. *Canadian who's who 1979* (1976-9).First annual volume 1980.

Essential details of some 15,000 (5000 new to this edition) prominent Canadians in all walks of life. Standard reference source of Canadian biography. Data: name, occupation, education and qualifications, career, publications, recreations.

Canadian who's who index 1898-1984 (1986) compiled by E. McMann is a complete index of entire backlist of Canadian who's who and 1898 and 1912 editions of *Canadian men and women of the time*. xi, 528p. 0802046339. Lists 33,230 names. History of *Canadian who's who* 1910 onwards p.vii-viii.

Canadian who's who on microfiche 1898-1975. Canadian who's who CD-ROM. 1996. $195. ISBN 0802049338. PC:Windows 95/98, Windows 3.1/Windows NT. Mackintosh: System 6 or higher. *Class No: 929(71)*

[5908]

Debrett's illustrated guide to the Canadian establishment. Newman, P.C., *ed.* Agincourt, Ontario, Methuen, 1983; London, Debrett's Peerage Ltd., 1984. 407p. col.illus. £19.95. ISBN: 0458976904.

Part 1. The power network - 2. The Dynasties (p.167-219) 'being portraits of 21 families that for at least three generations have exemplified prestige and leadership of the Canadian establishment' - 3. The Honours list *i.e.* a listing of Canadians of exceptional achievement in all aspects of contemporary Canadian society. Appendix: The Family Foundations (25 largest charitable funds based on family or personal wealth). *Class No: 929(71)*

[5909]

Dictionary of Canadian biography. Toronto, Univ. of Toronto Press, 20v., 1966-. bibliogs., indexes.

French ed. *Dictionnaire biographique du Canada* (Québec, Les Presses de l'Université Laval).

14 entirely self-contained volumes, each covering a specific number of years. The volume in which a biography is included is determined by the date of death or, if this is unknown, the 'floreat' date. 'Biographers should endeavour to provide a readable and stimulating treatment of their subject. Factual information should come from primary sources if possible' (*DCB's Directive to contributors*). Volumes published to date: 1. *1000 to 1700*. 1966. xxiii, 755p. ISBN 0802031420. 2. *1701 to 1740*. 1969. xli,759p. 0802032400. 3. *1741 to 1770*. 1974. xlii, 782p. 0802033148. 4. *1771 to 1800*. 1979. lvii,913p. 0802033512. 5. *1801 to 1820*. 1983. xxv,1044p. 0802033989. 6. *1821 to 1835*. 1987. xxiv,960p. 0802034365. 7. *1836 to 1850*. 1988. xxix,1088p. 0802034527. 8. *1851 to 1860*. 1985. xxxvii,1129p. 0802034225. 9. *1861 to 1870*. 1976. xiii,967p. 0802033199. 10. *1871 to 1880*. 1972. xxix,823p. 0802032877. 11. *1881 to 1890* 1982. xx,1092p. 0802032679. 12. *1891 to 1900*. 1990. 1200p. Can $75. 0802034608. *Index Vs.1-12. 1000-1900*. 1991. 568p. $60. 0802034640 is in 2 parts: (1) list of subjects of biographies; (2) Cumulative Nominal Index, 'a vast web of references and cross-references which stretches across the volumes'. 13. *1901 to 1910*. 1994. xxi,1295p. $85. 0802039987. 14. 1911-1920. 1999. xxi,1247p. 0802034764.

V.14 has 459 contributors; 648 well-documented biographies ranging from 600 to 10,000 words in length. General bibliography (Archival and manuscript collections; newspapers, published sources and theses) p.1093-1112. Index of identifications (38 categories of occupations) p.xiii-xviii. Geographical index p.1154-1175. Nominal index p.1119-1247. 'Characterized by careful scholarship, good writing and remarkable breadth of coverage' (*Choice*, v.9, no.12, February 1973, p.1572). F.G. Halpenny's 'The Dictionary of Canadian Biography/Dictionnaire biographique du Canada', *Canadian Studies* (British Library, 1984), p.133-43, has more detail. M. Dowding's 'Dictionary side-swiped by funding cutbacks', *Quill & Quires* v.56, no.4, April 1990, p.6 reports that the future volumes are imperilled through a serious loss of funding. *Class No: 929(71)*

[5910]

RAWLINSON, H.G. and GRANATSTEIN, J.L. The Canadian 100 The 100 most influential Canadians of the 20th century. Toronto, Mcarthur, 1998. 382p. $14.95. ISBN: 1552780058.

Biographical sketches of those who have had most impact on Canadian society in all arenas of life. *Class No: 929(71)*

[5911]

Who's who in Canada 1999: an illustrated biographical record of leading Canadians from business, the professions, government and academia. 90th ed. Toronto, Global Press, 1996. 1,798p. ports, index. $130. ISBN: 0771576137. ISSN: 00839450.

Biographies p.1-698. Rising Stars, p.699-722. Cross-reference listing by company position, name p.725-755. To celebrate its 90th anniversary this edition includes News-worthy names (in previous editions) p.xxv-l. *Class No: 929(71)*

Micromaterials

[5912]

Canadian biographical archive. München, K.G. Saur. At the planning stage.

c.110,000 biographical entries. *Class No:* 929(71)(003.5)

Newfoundland

[5913]

Dictionary of Newfoundland and Labrador biography. St. John's, Harry Cuff Publications, 1990. vi,408p. bibliog., indexes. ISBN: 0921191510.

Basic reference information on approximately 1,500 individuals 'who have influenced the development of Newfoundland and Labrador as colony, country and province, since the European re-discovery of America in 1497' (*Foreword*). Bibliographic note p.374-9. Geographic index p.380-92. Index of identifications (*i.e.* occupation or profession) p.393-408. 'A laudable contribution to the historical and cultural information about Newfoundland and Labrador (*ARBA guide to biographical resources 1986-1997*. 1998. p.42). *Class No:* 929(718)

Mexico

[5914]

CAMP, R.A. Who's who in Mexico today. 2nd ed. Boulder, Colo., Westview Press, 1993. 187p. £65. (*Westview Studies on Latin America and the Caribbean.*) ISBN: 0813384524.

1st ed. 1988.

Almost 400 biographies of contemporary leaders in all areas of Mexican life including prominent women, opposition political leaders, and members of the Colegio Nacional. Data: date of birth and birthplace; education; party and elected press; government appointments; family information; military service; national awards; and bibliographical references. Complements the author's *Mexican political biographies 1935-1981* (*q.v.*). 'A concise, accurate, and up-to-date biographical dictionary' (*Choice*, v.26, no.2, October 1988, p.284 +6). *Class No:* 929(72)

[5915]

Diccionario biográfico de Mexico. Monterrey, Editorial Revesa, 2v., 1968-1970. vii,643p. + vii,580p.

V.1 covers colonial and early independent Mexico (A-Z) and v.2 completes coverage to 1970. Includes Who's who on information on 5,500 living Mexicans. *Class No:* 929(72)

Bibliographies

[5916]

WOODS, R.D., *comp.* **Mexican autobiography** an annotated bibliography. La autobiografia Mexicana: una bibliografia razonada. Westport, Connecticut, Greenwood Press, 1988. 264p. bibliogs., indexes. $39.95; £30.50. (*Bibliographies and Indexes in World History, no.13.*) ISBN: 0313259453. ISSN: 07426801.

325 essays comprehending autobiographies proper, memoirs, diaries, collections of letters *etc*. Data includes basic bibliographical information, author's dates, narrative dates, and translation or primary edition in English. Translations indexed by author, title and subject. Other indexes provide access by subject, profession or outstanding characteristics of the author and chronological period. Parallel English and Spanish text. *Class No:* 929(72)(01)

Puerto Rico

Bibliographies

[5917]

FOWLIE-FLORES, F. Index to Puerto Rican collective biography. New York, Greenwood Press, 1987. xxi,215p. $42.95; £30.50. (*Bibliographies and Indexes in American History, no.5.*) ISBN: 0313251932. ISSN: 07426828.

Includes collective biographies, collections of essays, histories, published before or during 1985. Key to sources p.xv-xxi. Sources indexed p.203-212. Bibliography of related materials p.273-4. Bibliographies consulted p.215. *Class No:* 929(729.5)(01)

Latin America

Bibliographies

[5918]

Index to Spanish American collective biography. Mundo Lo, S. de. Boston, G.K. Hall, 6v., 1981-.

1. *The Andean countries*. 1981. xxix,466p. $60. ISBN 0816181810. 2. *Mexico*. 1982. xxix,373p. 0816185298. 3. *Central America and the Caribbean*. 1984. xxxiii,360p. 0816186367. 4. *The River Plate countries*. 1985. xxxi,388p. $94. 0816186502. Future volumes: 5. *Brazil*. 6. *General Spanish American sources.*

Provides access to references concerning individuals associated with

....(contd.)

Spanish America, its culture and institutions, as recorded in a variety of sources. The brief annotation includes bibliographical information, note of general content, and symbols of US and Canadian libraries where copies are located. Author, title, biographee, and geographic indexes. There are plans to issue supplements.
Class No: 929(729.99)(01)

USA

[5919]

American national biography. Garraty, J.A. *and* Carnes, M.C., *eds.* New York, Oxford Univ. Press, 24v., 1999. 23000p. bibliogs., indexes. $2,500. £1500. ISBN: 0195206355.

Replaces *Dictionary of American biography*. (*qv*).

6,000 contributors. 17,500 signed original biographies, each with its own bibliography of articles, books and archival resources, of men and women who have died up to and including 1995. Covers 'precolonial figures as far back as the Vikings; foreigners and expatriates who have influenced the American experience; women, African Americans and other groups whose contributions have become increasingly valued over the last 50 years; unexpected but influential people including criminals, socialites, sports figures and celebrities. The work reflects the influences of social and cultural aspects of history and the diverse character of American development. It will be continually updated. The American National Biography is a partnership between the American Council of Learned Societies and Oxford University Press, who have established a Center for American Biography devoted to the future of the ANB and its electronic maintenance'. (*Reference Reviews*, v.12,no.7, 1998, p.60). *Choice* Outstanding Academic Title 1999.

'From its position at the apex of America's intelligensia, the ACLS was able to exploit the academic network of the United States. Under the direction of managing editor Paul Betz, some 200 senior and associate editors divided into 19 categorical task forces. These committees selected the subjects, commissioned the essays from 6,100 contributors and completed the final review. They were supported by ranks of copy editors and fact-checkers at the Oxford University Press in North Carolina. Money came from the ACLS's own fund-raising as well as grants from the Mellon and Rockefeller Foundations and the National Endowment for the Humanities ... *American National Biography* represents such a colossal effort that it probably never would have taken flight without the psychological imperative of the looming millennium. But its publication now is indeed something to celebrate'. (*The Times*, no.66982, 8 April 1999, p.38). See also Faust, T. and Courtney, A. 'Its a Big Country: American National Biography', *Choice*, v.37,no.1, September 1999, p.99-100.

Librarians contemplating purchase of this work can obtain a 6-page A4 brochure from Oxford University Press, Great Clarendon Street, Oxford, OX2 6DP. *Class No:* 929(73)

[5920]

BEST, H. Debrett's Texas peerage. New York, Coward-McCann, 1983. 385p.illus., index. ISBN: 0698112444.

Part 1. Today's patrician Texans (26 chapters). Part 2. The peerage in 7 chapters: 1. The first families of the Republic of Texas - 2. Signers of the Declaration of Independence - 3. Heroes of the Alamo - 4. Senior officers at the Battle of San Jacinto - 5. Other notables and heroes - 6. The carriage trade of the Republic - 7. The 'Old Three Hundred'. *Class No:* 929(73)

[5921]

The Cambridge dictionary of American biography. Bowman, J.S., *ed.* Cambridge Univ. Press, 1995. xxxviii,903p. indexes. £40. $44.95. ISBN: 0521402581.

34 contributors. Over 9,000 entrants. including living people, covering all fields of endeavour. 'This book is written for anyone interested in having a basic but eminently readable reference to one's living contemporaries and their achievements as well as to historically important figures' (*dustwrapper*). *Class No:* 929(73)

[5922]

Dictionary of American biography. Sponsored by the American Council of Learned Societies, New York. New York, Charles Scribner's Sons 20v. 1996. $1,800. ISBN: 0684805405.

The lives of 19,173 men and women from over 700 fields of endeavour who died through 1980. ... 'who have made some significant contribution to American life in all its manifold aspects' in 10 base volumes and 10 supplements. Article length is determined by relative importance of the person, amount of available authentic material, the nature of his career, and completeness of biographies already published; and this also applies to the appended bibliographies. 'The monumental *D.A.B.*' (*RQ*, v.14, no.2, Winter 1974, p.169). W.K. McCoy's 'Dictionary of American Biography', *Reference Services Review*, v.11, no.3, Fall 1983, p.17-20. refs. is a good history and evaluation.

Dictionary of American biography. Comphrehensive index. 1996 $140. This series of volumes is now at an end. Indexes 19,173 entries by name, birthplace, college, occupation, subject, and by the name of the contributor. *Class No:* 929(73)

[5923]
Concise dictionary of American biography. 5th ed. New York, Scribner, 2v., 1997. 1700p. index. $235.00. ISBN: 0684805499.

1st ed. 1964. 4th ed. 1990.

Abridged version of all 19,173 biographies included in the full *Dictionary of American biography*, 1063 biographies 1870-1980 added since the 4th ed. Birthplace and Occupations indexes. *Class No:* 929(73)

[5924]
Dictionary of America Biography on CD-ROM. New York, Charles Scribner's Sons. Windows* and Macintosh $595. Single User/LAN ISBN: 0684806118.

Containing all 19,173 biographical entries from the bound set, the powerful search engine quickly finds the biography by name, birthplace, occupation, birth/death dates, sex, or keywords. Cross-references to the printed volumes allow the CD-ROM to be used as an index to the bound set. *Class No:* 929(73)

[5925]
ncyclopedia of Frontier biography. Thrapp, D.L. Glendale, California, Arthur H. Clark, 3v., 1988. 1698p. bibliogs., index. $175.00. ISBN: 0870621912.

Approximately 4500 biographies of western pioneers and native Americans each accompanied by a short bibliography. 'A wealth of information about persons who lived on the frontier, whether that was the trans-Appalachian frontier, the wide Missouri frontier, the mining regions of the Rockies, or the gold-mining/ranching frontiers of California, Oregon, or Arizona'. A bibliography attached to each main entry.

Encyclopedia of Frontier biography Vol.4: Supplemental volume. Spokane (Washington), Arthur H. Clark, 1994, 610p. index. $65. ISBN 0870622226. A further 1000 entries. 'The supplement, bound to match the basic set, is a must buy for all who have the earlier work. It rounds the set out, fills in the gaps brings it up-to-date, and is in itself fascinating reading' (*ARBA guide to biographical resources 1986-1997. 1998, p.84-85*). *Class No:* 929(73)

[5926]
Iarquis who's who regional library. New Providence, N.J. Marquis Who's Who.

1. *Who's Who in the Midwest 1998-1999*. 26th ed. 1998. 700p. £220. 083797284. 2. *Who's Who in the South and Southwest 1999-2000*. 26th ed. 1998. 800p. £220. 0837908299. 3. *Who's Who in the East 1999-2000*. 27th ed. 1998. 1213p. £220. 083790630x. 4. *Who's Who in the West 2000-2001*. 27th ed. 1999. 778p. £220. 0837909309. 'The Who's Who Regional Library features directories of individuals with a distinctly regional interest - most of whom do not appear in *Who's Who in America*. Each volume reaches deep into the political, cultural, business, and academic framework of the cities and states represented'. (*Reed Reference Publishing 1996 Catalogue*). Available as part of *The Complete Marquis Who's Who Plus. Class No:* 929(73)

[5927]
IEIER, M.S. Mexican American biographies: a historical dictionary 1836-1987. New York and London, Greenwood Press, 1988. ix,270p. index. $45.00; £35.95. ISBN: 0313245215.

270 biographies of historical and contemporary *prominentes* in all fields of the Mexican/American experience. Two appendices list biographees by profession and by State. 'Valuable as a starting point for further research' (*Booklist* v.84,no.18, 15 May 1988, p.1585). *Class No:* 929(73)

[5928]
IULLAY, A.J. Birthplaces USA who was born where. Edinburgh, Wherewithal Books, 1999. Available from Thomas Lyster Ltd, Ormskirk Industrial Park, Burscough Road, Ormskirk, LY39 2YW. 256p. indexes. £40. $87.50.

Details the birthplace of famous Americans. 2,240 placenames A-Z by state and town. Subjects taken from 4 unnamed major biographical dictionaries. 'Mullay and his team of helpers are to be commended for [their] notable achievement. It is excellent value for money' (*Reference Reviews*, v.13, no.1, 1999, p.41-42). *Class No:* 929(73)

[5929]
he National cyclopaedia of American biography being the history of the United States as illustrated in the lives of the founders, builders and defenders of the Republic, and of men and women who are doing the work and moulding the thought of the present time. New York, J.T. White, 1892-1984.

Comprising almost 70,000 biographies the work has a complicated structure. Originally planned to rank with the great European biographical dictionaries in 12v. it now encompasses : 1. *Permanent series* (numbered volumes) v.1-63, 1892-1984. Lengthy entries with portraits and facsimile signatures (the series thereby serves as a national portrait gallery or as an historic picture file). Until 1924 each volume contained biographies of both deceased and living persons. Biographies 'are grouped by occupation or location ... in this way, there appears to be a narrative history running over several pages instead of vignettes of isolated persons and incidents'. Access therefore depends largely on the *Index*. No bibliographies. 2. *Current series*

....(contd.)
(lettered volumes) A-N, 1924-1978. Covers living persons only, the eminent and not so eminent. It is estimated that 75% of those included in the lettered volumes eventually found a place in the *Permanent series*. 3. *N-63* (1984) reverted to the practice of including entries relating to both living and dead persons in the same volume, seemingly to mark the *Cyclopaedia's* demise: 'it is likely to be the final volume ... issued under the auspices of the present publisher' (*Preface*). In fact, after 111 years, the publisher has gone out of business. 4. *Index* 576p. 1984. Replaces the 1971 and 1979 indexes and covers the entire set as described above. W.K. McCoy's 'The National Cyclopedia of American Biography', *Reference Service Review*, v.9,no.4, October/December 1981, p.5-9, from which much of this information is derived, includes 15 refs. and a bibliography. *Class No:* 929(73)

[5930]
Notable Americans: what they did, from 1620 to the present. Hubbard, L.S., *ed.* 4th ed. Detroit, Gale Research Co., 1988. x,733p. indexes. $178.25. ISBN: 0810325349.

1st ed. as *The conspectus of American biography* (1906). Part of *The National Cyclopaedia of American Biography (qv)*. 2nd ed. *White's conspectus of American biography* (1937). 3rd ed. *Notable names in American history: a tabulated register* (1973).

A compendium of 42,000 US officeholders and award winners in government, the military, business, labour, philanthropy, religion, and national associations, arranged in 19 chapters. No biographical information, simply chronological lists of names. 'Even researchers with access to the multitude of specialized sources ... will appreciate the convenience of this volume' (*Booklist*, v.84,no.18, 15 May 1988, p.1586-6). *Class No:* 929(73)

[5931]
The Scribner encyclopedia of American lives. New York, Charles Scribner's Sons, 1998-.

Biographical dictionary series to be published quinquennially. Regarded as a continuation of the *Dictionary of American biography* lately deceased (R.I.P.).

1.*Notable Americans who died between 1981 and 1985*. 1998. 930p. ports., index. $125. ISBN 0684804921. 332 contributors. 494 signed biographies of those who made significant contributions to American life and culture or who otherwise deserve to be remembered. Occupational index. 'A valuable successor of the highly respected scholarly tradition set by *DAB*' (*Library Journal*, v.124, no.3, 15 Feb 1999, p.143-44).

1986-1990. 1999. xi,967p. ports. index. 0684804913. 506 signed biographies. Occupation index v.1+2 p.937-56. Alphabetical lists of subjects v.1+2, p.957-67. *Class No:* 929(73)

[5932]
Who was who in America. New Providence, NJ., Marquis Who's who 13v., 1966-1993. $620 the set. ISBN: 0837902320, set.

Historical volume (1607-1896). $69.50. 0837902002. 13,450 biographies from America's early days including Leif Ericsson, Columbus and John Cabot. Colour biographical map, time-line history chart and 'Facts at your finger tips' that puts American history into perspective 950A.D. - 20th century. 1. *1897-1942.* $69.50. 0837902010. 2. *1943-1950.* $69.50. 0837902061. 3. *1951-1960.* $69.50. 0837902037. 4. *1961-1968.* $69.50. 0837902045. 5. *1969-1973.* $69.50. 0837902053. 6. *1974-1976.* $69.50. 083790207x. 7. *1977-1987.* $69.50. 083790210x. 8. *1982-1985.* $69.50. 0837902142. 9. *1985-1989.* 1989. 392p. £60. 0837902177. 10. *1989-1993.* 1993. 416p. £60. 0837902207. 11. *1993-1996* 400p. $90. 0837902258. V.13. *1998-2000.* 2000. 0837902355. *Index Volume 1607-2000 $45.* 0837902215. *Almost 130,000 notable figures in American history are included.* Except for the *Historical volume* all biographies are taken from *Who's who in America*. Available as part of *The Complete Marquis Who's Who on CD-ROM (q.v.). Class No:* 929(73)

[5933]
Who's who in America 2000. Tiger, H.L., *ed.* 54th ed. New Providence, NJ., Marquis Who's Who 3v., 1999. 6000p. bibliogs., index. Biennial. £420. ISBN: 0837901995.

First published 1899.

More than 115,000 biographies (70,000 updated, 30,000 new to this edition). Each biennial edition is thoroughly revised and features a retiree index, *i.e.* biographies deleted because of career retirement; obituaries; and regional and topical listings. 'A unique reference source with no close competitor' (A. Ricker's Who's Who in America', *Reference Service Review*, v.8,no.4, October/December 1980, p.7-13). Also available as part of *The Complete Marquis Who's Who on CD-ROM. Class No:* 929(73)

[5934]

—The Complete Marquis who's who plus on CD-ROM. New Providence, NJ., Marquis Who's Who. 2 disc set. Price on application.

This CD-ROM integrates the current *Who's Who in America*, along with the complete library of accompanying regional and professional *Marquis Who's Who* directories, and recent volumes of *Who Was Who in America*. Profiles of more than 768,000 notable individuals of the past and present, from every field of human endeavour. Users can identify and retrieve information on individuals using 35 searchable characteristics. Updated twice a year. *Class No:* 929(73)(003.40)

[5935]

—Index to Marquis who's who publications 1999. New Providence, NJ., Marquis Who's Who, 1999. 535p. £90. ISBN: 0837914361.

Successor to *Marquis who's who publications: index to all books* first published 1978; in 2v. 1984.

Referral tool to more than 300,000 individuals listed in the latest editions of Marquis' 15 different who's who publications. *Class No:* 929(73)

[5936]

WIERZBIANSKI, B., *and others, eds*. Who's who in Polish America. Bicentennial Publishing Corporation, 1996. Distributed by Hippocrene Books. 571p. $60. ISBN: 0781805201.

Complements *Who's who in Polish America* (1939).

Entrants drawn 'from people from all parts of the United States in as wide a range of professional and social groups as possible'. 'The book fills a gap ... justifying its claim that no attempt of this nature on such a scale has been made for almost half a century' (*Choice*, v.34, no.4, December 1996, p.596). *Class No:* 929(73)

CD-ROM

[5937]

American leaders on CD-ROM. Santa Barbara, Calif., and Oxford, ABC-Clio, 1997. PC: Windows 95 (also compatible with Windows 3.1 and higher). 486SX/33 MHz or faster processor, 8MB RAM, hard drive with at least 4MB free, SVGA monitor (640x480, 256 colors), Windows-compatible mouse or pointing device, 2X CD-ROM drive. MAC: System 7.0 or higher, 68030/33 MHz or faster processor, 8Mb RAM, hard drive with at least 4MB free, 14-in. monitor (640.480, 256 Colors), 2X CD-ROM drive. Standalone $129. Network $299 (unlimited use). Lab pack (10 discs) $279.

1200+ biographies of political, cultural and social leaders. Boolean searching, name and subject indexes, and an attribute search feature. Timelines present entrant's life span, impact and importance. Glossary of terms provides definitions, analysis and perspective. Emphasis is on the 1990s. *Class No:* 929(73)(003.40)

Micromaterials

[5938]

The American biographical archive. Worters, G., *comp*. New York, K.G. Saur Inc., 1986-1991. 1842 fiches (24x) in Silver or Diazo fiche. Silver DM 22,800. Diazo DM 20,800 ISBN: 3598309511, silver; 3598309503, diazo.

A-Z cumulation of 500,000+ full text entries from 367 biographical works of reference in 630v. covering 280,000 individuals from the earliest period of North American History to the early 20th century. All entries concerning a single individual appear in one location on the microfiche arranged in chronological order by date of publication. Indexed in printed form in *American biographical index (q.v.)* *Class No:* 929(73)(003.5)

[5939]

—American biographical archive. Series II. München, K.G. Saur, 1993-96. 734 fiches (24x) silver or diazo DM 24,600 (silver); DM 22,800 (diazo). ISBN: 3598335342, Silver; 3598335202, Diazo.

Single A-Z sequence cumulated from a further 135 biographical dictionaries published in 19th and 20th centuries to 1974. Contains 215,000 biographical entries on 172,000 individuals. In this second archive greater attention has been paid to women and those segments of society underrepresented in the original set. Indexed in printed form in *American biographical index (q.v.)*. *Class No:* 929(73)(003.5)

[5940]

—American biographical index/Amerikanischer biographischer index. 2nd cumulated and enlarged ed. London, K.G. Saur, 10v., 1999. ccxl,4200p. £498. DM 3,980 (DM 2,980 to subscribers to *American biographical archive*). ISBN: 3598335482.

Basic biographical detail to all entries in *American biographical archive* together with listings of source works and fiche number in that work. *Class No:* 929(73)

Bibliographies

[5941]

American autobiography 1945-1980: a bibliography. Briscoe, M.L., *and others, eds*. Madison, Univ. of Wisconsin Press, 1982-. xiv,365p. index. $35.00; £32.95. ISBN: 0299090906.

Intended as a supplement to L. Kaplan's *Bibliography of American autobiographies (qv)*.

5008 descriptive entries compiled mainly from *Biography Index*. 'Because of the book's extensive coverage, coupled with the fact that it is a major work in the area and a supplement to Kaplan, this reference tool is an essential purchase for academic and larger public libraries' (*Choice*, v.20,no.8, April 1983, p.1105). *Class No:* 929(73)(01)

[5942]

American diaries: an annotated bibliography of published American diaries and journals. Arksey, L., *and others, eds*. Detroit, Gale Research Co., 2v., 1983-1987. xviii,311p.+Øviii,501p. indexes. $103.00; £78.00 each. ISBN: 0810318008, v.1; 0810318016, v.2.

Supersedes W. Matthew's *American diaries: an annotated bibliography of American diaries written prior to the year 1861* (Berkeley. University of California Press, 1945).

Chronologically arranged bibliography of printed American diaries and journals written 1492-1844 (v.1) and 1845-1980 (v.2). Annotation includes diary's emphasis, historic events mentioned, and diarist's background. 'A good bibliography covering a category of writing that has been increasing in demand' (*Choice*, v.21,no.9, May 1984, p.1271). *Class No:* 929(73)(01)

[5943]

Biography and genealogy master index: a consolidated index to more than 10 million listings in over 350 current and retrospective biographical dictionaries. Herbert, M.C. and McNeil, B., *eds*. 2nd ed. Detroit, Gale Research Co., 8v., 1980-1981. 6000p. $975. £626. (*Gale Biographical Index Series*.) ISBN: 0810310945. ISSN: 07301316.

First edition published 1975-76 *Biographical dictionaries master index* edited by D. Labeau and G.C. Tarbert.

More than 3.2 million citations to biographical articles from more than 350 sources. 'Entries give the individual's name, birth and death dates when provided by the indexed source, and a coded citation locating the indexed material ... However, this is neither a "genealogical" index (*e.g.* passenger and cemetery lists are absent) nor a "master" index (coverage is too narrow and selective, and the emphasis is mainly on the US)' [nevertheless] 'when used with care and an understanding of its limitations, the index serves as an important and valuable aid' (*Choice*, v.19, no.1, September 1981, p.45). English language sources only.

McNeil, B. ed. *Biography and genealogy master index 1981-1985 cumulation*, 5v., 1985. 4177p. £568. 0810315068. A cumulation of the 5 annual supplements that updated the base set. An additional 2.3 million citations are recorded. *Biography and genealogy master index 1986-90 cumulation*, 3v., 1990. 3387p. £602. 0810348039. Adds 1,895,000 citations to biographical articles appearing in more than 500 editions and volumes of over 250 sources. Since 1980 over 4 million citations have been added to the base record.

1996-2000 Cumulation 4v. 2000. $995. £626. 0810316188.

2001 ed. Pt.1 2000. 0787629979. Pt.2. 2000. 0878629987. Provides 450,000 citations to biographical articles appearing in 179 editions and columes of 113 biographical dictionaries and who's whos. Sources cover both living and deceased persons from every field of activity and from *many* countries of the world. *Class No:* 929(73)(01)

[5944]

—Abridged biography and genealogy master index. McNeil, B. and Unterburger, A.L., *eds*. Detroit, Gale Research Co., 3v., 1995. 4511p. £331. ISBN: 0810368781.

2.2 million citations from 266 reference works. 'Libraries unable to afford the full Biograpy and Genealogy Master Index should consider purchasing the abridged version. Highly recommended' (*Choice*, v.25, no.11/12, July/August, 1988, p.1671). *Class No:* 929(73)(01)

[5945]

—Bio-Base 2000 Master Cumulation. McNeil, B., *ed*. Detroit, Gale Research Co., 1999. 500 microfiches. $1,030. £648.90. ISBN: 0810320734.

B. Bonta and F. Cable's 'The Gale biography series', *Reference Services Review*, v.10, no.1, Spring 1982, p.25-33 is a comparative review of the history, background, coverage and editorial practices of *Biography and genealogy master index, Bio-Base*, and *Biography master index*.

The 2000 Master Cumulation on microfiche of the *Biography and Genealogy Master Index* database furnishes 12 million citations to biographical entries appearing in over 900 biographical dictionaries. Each citation provides the subject's full name (as given in the source indexed), birth and/or death dates, and a code indicating the source of biographical data. Printed bibliography of sources indexed accompanies each set.

This edition supersedes *Bio-Base 1990 Master Cumulation, Bio-Base 1995*, and *Bio-Base 1996-1999*. *Class No:* 929(73)(01)

[5946]

—Biography and genealogy master index. url. http://nw.gale.com/gale/galenet/gnetwork.html

Contains 11 million records (450,000 added annually) drawn from multi-volume printed set and supplements. Offers 3 search modes: 1. Simple search by name - 2. Extended search (several fields at once, Boolean operators, birth and death dates) - 3. Expert search. 'The site is well organized, loads and displays quickly, and is easy to navigate, search, and print' (*Choice*, v.36,no.1, September 1998, p.81).
Class No: 929(73)(01)

Encyclopaedias

[5947]

GARRATY, J.A. *and* STERNSTEIN, J.L., eds. Encyclopedia of American biography. 2nd ed. New York, HarperCollins, 1996. 1263p. $50. ISBN: 0062700170.

1st ed. 1974.

1000 Americans (80 new to this edition). Entries comprise an outline career guide together with short essay by a named scholar providing an in-depth analysis of entrants place in American history. 'A nice bridge between the short, fact-based biographical dictionary and the longer monograph' (*Booklist*, v.93, no.9/10, 1 and 15 January 1997, p.892).
Class No: 929(73)(031)

Hispanic Peoples

[5948]

MEIER, M.S. Notable Latino Americans a biographical dictionary. Westport, Conn., Greenwood Press, 1997. xv,413p. ports. ISBN: 0313291055.

127 profiles of men and women who made a major contribution to U.S. life and culture. List of further reading ends each entry.
Class No: 929(73)(=60)

[5949]

Who's who among Hispanic Americans. Unterburger, J.L., ed. 3rd ed. Detroit, Gale Research Co., 1994. 475p. indexes. £176.50. ISBN: 0810385503.

First ed. 1990.

11,000 A-Z entries for notable contemporary Hispanic Americans across a broad spectrum of professions and occupations. Geographic location, occupation and country of descent indexes. Data: occupation, education, career information, organization affiliations, honours and achievements, military service, sources of further information. Geographic location, occupation, and country of origin indexes. 'A significant tool about an import ethnic group' (*Booklist*, v.87, no.14, 15 March 1991, p.1525). Available online through NEXIS, on diskette, and magnetic tape. Class No: 929(73)(=60)

Jews

[5950]

The Concise dictionary of American Jewish biography. Marcus, J.R., ed. New York, Carlson, 2v., 1994. 711p. bibliogs. $200. ISBN: 0926019740.

Approximately 24,000 brief, cross-referenced biographies of American Jews who died before 1986. Data: more familiar version of names, vital statistics, place of death, immigration date, education, occupation, and position in Jewish community. Bibliogaphical citations to further information sources. Class No: 929(73)(=924)

Asian Races

[5951]

UNTERBERGER, A., ed. Who's who among Asian Americans. Detroit, Gale, 1994. 780p. indexes. £57.50. ISBN: 0810394332. ISSN: 09757104.

Occupation, ethnic and cultural heritage, personal data, education, career information, affiliations, honours and awards details of 6000 US citizens or residents whose ethnic background is either Asia or the Pacific Islands. 'An important new specialized source' (*Booklist*, v.91,no.3, 1 October 1994, p.363-64). Class No: 929(73)(=95)

[5952]

-Notable Asian Americans. Zia, H. *and* Gall, S.B., eds. Detroit, Gale Research, 1995. 468p. illus., indexes. £57.50. ISBN: 0810396238.

Signed biographical sketches (one to three pages long) on 250 prominent past and present Asian Americans. Data: personal, career and educational information and discussion of significant achievements. Subject, occupation and ethnicity indexes.
Class No: 929(73)(=95)

Black Races

[5953]

LOGAN, R.W. *and* WINSTON, M.R., eds. Dictionary of American Negro biography. New York, W.W. Norton, 1982. xxi,680p. $50.00. ISBN: 0393015130.

270 contributors. 632 extensive signed biographies of Negroes who attained historical significance (Martin Luther King 443 lines) spanning 300 years of American history. No living persons. Classified list of entries (88 categories) p.ix-xxi. 'The work is quite useful but does not replace Who's who of the colored race (1915) or Colored America (1928-50). 'Recommended as an essential purchase for all academic and public libraries' (*Choice* v.20,no.10, June 1983, p.1433-4).
Class No: 929(73)(=96)

[5954]

Who's who among African Americans 1996-97. 9th ed. Detroit, Gale Research, 1996. 1855p. indexes. £107. ISBN: 0810357283.

Biographical and career details on more than 20,000 notable African American individuals, including leaders from sports, the arts, business, religion. Obituary section contains fully updated entries for entrants who have died since the previous edition. Geographic and occupational indexes. Class No: 929(73)(=96)

[5955]

Who's who among Black Americans 1991-92. Cloyd, I., ed. 7th ed. Detroit, Gale Research, 1992. 1500p. indexes. ISBN: 0810354047.

1st ed. 1976. Formerly published by Educational Communications of Lake Forest. Illinois.

Biographical and career details on 19000 notable individuals. An obituary section contains updated entries for those who have died since being listed in the 6th ed. Geographic and occupations indexes. Previous editions should not be discarded because of large number of biographees who are subsequently deleted. 'An important tool because relatively few African Americans are listed in Who's who in America' (*Booklist*, v.86, no.21, July 1990, p.2118). Class No: 929(73)(=96)

Micromaterials

[5956]

The African-American biographical database. Burkett, R.K., *and others*, eds. http://aabd.chadwyck.com:8085/. £695p.a. (single user); £995 (5-8 concurrent users).

Brings together 50,000 biographies with access to 20,000+ illus., and full-text online access to 350+ reference works including state and local directories, church and missionary histories and yearbooks and publications of social clubs and fraternal orders. Material may be located by name, occupation, religion, birthplace, or date of birth or death. Two means of searching: Profile Search (browse) and Full Text Search. 'Numerous searches of the database during the month of review revealed no difficulty in connecting to the resource, searching the database, displaying the search results, or displaying the digitized images' (*Choice*, v.35,no.10, June 1998, p.1677).
Class No: 929(73)(=96)(003.5)

Amerindians, North

[5957]

JOHANSEN, B.C. *and* GRINDE, D.E. The Encyclopedia of Native American biography: six hundred life stories of important people from Powhatan to Wilma Mankiller. New York, H. Holt, 1997. 512p. illus., bibliog. $50. ISBN: 0805032703.

Includes many leading present day figures. Class No: 929(73)(=97)

[5958]

MALINOWSKI, S. *and* ABRAMS, G.H.J. Notable native Americans. Detroit Gale, 1995. 4902p. bibliogs., indexes $65. £57.50. ISBN: 0810396386.

265 signed biographical essays on outstanding Native American men and women in all fields of endeavour. Subject, occupation and tribal indexes. Class No: 929(73)(=97)

Women

[5959]

American women 1935-1940 a composite biographical dictionary; a consolidation of all material appearing in the 1939-1940 edition of American women, with a supplement of unduplicated entries from the 1935-1936 and 1937-1938 editions. Howes, D., ed. Detroit, Gale Research Co., 2v., 1981. clxii,1208p. indexes. $160.00. ISBN: 0810304031.

About 12000 women from education, the arts, the professions, science, club work, business, and governments. Data includes occupation, membership, public offices, political party, books, and honours. Geographical and occupational indexes. 'Might have been a good who's who at the time of its original publication, but its purchase now is questionable when other sources meet reserchers' needs with more thoroughly' (*Choice*, v.19,no.8, April 1982, p.1043).
Class No: 929(73)-0055.2

[5960]

HERMAN, K. Women in particular an index to American women. Phoenix, Arizona, Oryx, 1985. 740p. indexes. $95.00; £72.75. ISBN: 0897740882.

Biographies of c.15,000 women who made a significant contribution to American life. Data: Birth and death dates, career information, ethnicity, religion, and list of sources for further information. Despite some reservations *Library Journal* 15 May 1985, p.57 concluded that it is 'a useful tool that can be recommended for most libraries'. *Class No:* 929(73)-0055.2

[5961]

Who's who of American women 2000-2001. 22nd ed. New Providence, NJ, Marquis Who's Who, 2000. 1170p. Biennial. £210. ISBN: 0837904269.

First published 1958.

Over 27,000 (13,000 new) biographies. Data: personal, present position, education, career path covering a wide range of professions and disciplines including government, business, the arts, and medicine. *Class No:* 929(73)-0055.2

Bibliographies

[5962]

ADAMSON, L.G. Notable women in American history a guide to recommended biographies and autobiographies. Westport, CT., Greenwood Press, 1999. 450p. bibliogs., index. $49.95. ISBN: 0313295840.

Lists 500 women either born in America, or naturalised citizens, who made a significant contribution to American life, and who have had a full-length biography or autobiography published since 1970. Each entry ends with an annotated bibliography. 3 Appendices: notable women by year of birth, title, occupation or main area of interest, and by ethnicity. *Class No:* 929(73)-0055.2(01)

[5963]

ADDIS, P.K. Through a women's I. an annotated bibliography of American women's autobiographical writings 1946-1976. Metuchen, New Jersey, Scarecrow Press, 1983. xiv,607p. indexes. $37.50. ISBN: 0810815885.

Supplements L. Kaplan's *Bibliography of American autobiographies* (Univ. of Wisconsin Press, 1961) and M.L. Brisco's *American autobiography 1945-1980 (qv)*.

2217 descriptive entries A-Z by author. Introduction includes list of sources p.ix-xiv. *Class No:* 929(73)-0055.2(01)

Argentina

[5964]

CUTOLO, V.O. Nuevo diccionario biográfico argentino (1750-1930). Buenos Ayres, Editorial Elche, 7v., 1968-1985. 5053p.

V.1 has about 1000 entries relating to wide range of significant figures both native and foreign born. Data: date and place of birth, education, career, and major publications. Some entries carry extensive bibliographies). Covers January 1982 onwards. *Class No:* 929(82)

[5965]

UDAONDO, E. Diccionario biográfico argentino. Buenos Ayres, Imprenta y Casa Editoria Coni, 1938. 1151p.

c.3300 biographies for personalities active in the period 1800-1920. *Class No:* 929(82)

[5966]

UDAONDO, E. Diccionario biográfico colonial argentino. Buenos Ayres, Huarpes, 1945. 980p. illus.

Biographical dictionary from earliest colonial days to 1810. *Class No:* 929(82)

[5967]

UDAONDO, E., and others. Grandes hombres de nuestria patria. Buenos Ayres, Editorial Pleamar, 3v., 1968. 1160p. illus., ports, facsims.

c.300 biographies of outstanding figures in Argentine history. *Class No:* 929(82)

[5968]

VITAVER, P.R., ed. Quién es quién en América del Sur diccionario biográfico Argentino 1982-1983. Buenos Ayres, Publicaciones Referenciales Latino Americanas, 1982. xv,799p.

6000 biographies. Publicaciones Referenciales en el Mundo (list of 112 Who's whos) p.14. *Class No:* 929(82)

Ecuador

[5969]

Diccionario biografico del Ecuador. Pimentel, R.P. Guayaquil, Mayo, 3v., 1987. 511p.++ 469p.++ 538p. pbk.

Biographies of those who contributed to the progress and civilization of Ecuador. Not arranged A-Z. *Class No:* 929(866)

Guyana

[5970]

SEYMOUR, A. and SEYMOUR, E. Dictionary of Guyanese biography. Georgetown, A.J. Seymour, 2v., 1985-1986. bibliog., pbk. Mimeographed.

2 separate compilations: 1. *1985.* 118p. - 2. *1986.* 97p. Introduction to v.2 looks forward to the possibility of combining them into one compilation. *Class No:* 929(88)

Paraguay

[5971]

Quien es quien en el Paraguay. Monte-Domecq, R., *comp.* 9th ed. Asuncion, Editoria MD & Asociados, 1991. 220p. illus., ports, maps, index.

Historical synthesis p.19-39; Constitution p.41-61; Political divisions of Paraguay p.63-70; List of Governors-General and Presidents p.71-90. Biographies p.91-174. *Class No:* 929(892)

Uruguay

[5972]

FERNÁNDEZ SALDANA, J.M. Diccionario uruguayo de biografías 1810-1940. Montevideo, Amerinda, 1945. 1366p.

About 800 fairly lengthy biographies of significant historical figures. No bibliographies. *Class No:* 929(899)

Australasia & Oceania

Micromaterials

[5973]

Australasian biographical archive/Australasiatisches biographisches archiv. Mediavilla, V.H., *ed.* München, K.G. Saur. 1990-94. 423 fiches (x24) silver or diazzo. DM 16,800 (silver); DM 14,800 (diazzo). ISBN: 359832930x, silver; 359832944x, diazzo.

Arranged A-Z by subject's name, this single sequence cumulation of approx. 100,000 entries from 140 biographical works (1866-1987) covers Australia, New Zealand, Papua New Guinea, and South Pacific Islands, from the period of discovery and settlement to the post-war era.

Supplement. 1995. 119 fiches. DM 5,400 (silver); DM 4,800 (diazo). ISBN 3598329253 (silver); 3598329245 (diazo). Extends coverage to 174,600 biographical entries on 95,100 individuals. A concentrated effort has been made to find material on women, native populations and other categories underrepresented in the original archive. Indexed in printed form in *Australasian biographical index. (q.v.). Class No:* 929(9)(003.5)

[5974]

—Australasian biographical index/Australasien biographischer index. Mediavilla, V.H., *comp.* München, K.G. Saur. 1998. xv,1326p. DM 1,320 (DM 1,194 for subscribers to *Australasian biographical archive.* ISBN: 359832958x.

Printed index to *Australasian biographical index* (1990-1994) and its *Supplement* (1995) *(q.v.). Class No:* 929(9)(003.5)

Sarawak

[5975]

Who's who Sarawak 1985-86. 2nd ed. Kuching, Sarawak Publishing House, 1985. 406p. ports. ISSN: 01274619.

'Biographies of prominent people who have won recognition for notable achievements in various fields of human endeavour' (*Introduction*). Also directory information on the Government, M.P.s, Departments and Statutory bodies. *Class No:* 929(911.14)

Philippines

[5976]

MANUEL, E.A. Dictionary of Philippine biography. Quezon City, Filipiniana Publications, 1955, 1970, 1986.

V.1 1955. 511p. illus., index. V.2. 1970. 502p. illus., index. V.3 1986. xv, 566p. illus., index. All 3v. so far published are separate A-Z sequences of biographical sketches some of which, especially in v.3 are becoming encyclopaedic in nature with extensive bibliographies by and about the persons included. V.3 includes a foreword or documentation, general information, bibliographic features and Towards an encyclopaedia goal: national conditions and needs shaping its form and substance. Future volumes are expected: at what interval is not vouchsafed. *Class No:* 929(914)

[5977]

VILLAREL, H.K., and others. Eminent Filipines. Manila, National Historical Commission, 1965. xxvi,294p. ports. (*National Historical Commission Publication no.1.*)

About 220 brief biographies including many not found in Manuel's *Dictionary of Philippine biography (qv). Class No:* 929(914)

New Zealand

[5978]

The Dictionary of New Zealand biography. Wellington, Allen & Unwin New Zealand and Department of Internal Affairs, 1990-.

V.1: 1769-1869. 1990. xviii,674p. indexes. ISBN 004641052x. 572 biographical essays (20% of women; 30% Maoris). 'As well as for eminence on a national scale, the people in this Dictionary have been chosen for their standing within less extensive milieux, for their representativeness and for the balance their presence will give to the volume as a whole' (Introduction). Glossary of Maori words p.xiv-xv. Categories index (i.e. professions and occupations) p.615-25. Tribal and Hapu index p.627-9. Name index p.631-74. V.2: 1870-1900. xix,664p. 0908912498 has 617 biographical essays. V.3 1901-1920, Auckland Univ. Press, 1996. xxi,649p. 1869402006 has 606 biographies (419 men, 187 women) and V4. 1921-1940 (1999?) presents the lives of 613 people. V.1 won the Goodman Fielder Wattie Book of the Year Award in 1991.

Ngā Tāngata Taumata Rau (q.v.) are companion volumes in the Maori language. Class No: 929(931)

[5979]

–Ngā Tāngata Taumata Rau. Auckland Univ. Press, 3v., 1990-1996.

V.1 1769-1869 (1990); V.2 1870-1900 (1994); V.3 1901-1920 (1996) contain the Maori biographies included in The Dictionary of New Zealand biography (qv) in the Maori language.

Class No: 929(931)

[5980]

SCHOLFIELD, G.H., ed. A Dictionary of New Zealand biography. Wellington, Department of Internal Affairs, 2v., 1940.

Sponsored by the National Historical Committee as an official centennial publication. Entries are for persons, not necessarily resident in New Zealand, 'who had significance in the history of the Dominion' from roughly 1840 onwards. 95% of contributions are the work of the editor; the others are signed by the authors. Documented entries. Short glossaries of Maori words. Bibliography, v.1, p.xviii-xix. Modelled on the DNB. Class No: 929(931)

[5981]

Who's who in New Zealand. 12th ed. Wellington, Reed, 1991. ISBN: 0790002248.

First published 1908.

The backgrounds and achievements of almost 3000 prominent NZ men and women in all fields of activity, including business, politics, education, medicine, law, science, the arts, and sport. Data: academic achievements, professional qualifications, positions held, published works, awards and honours, recreations, and family details.

Class No: 929(931)

Women

[5982]

The Book of New Zealand women Ko Kui ma te kaupapa. Macdonald, C., and others, eds. Wellington, Bridget Williams Books, 1992. xiv,772p. ports, indexes. ISBN: 0908912048.

Signed biographical essays of 300 NZ women (with sources). Indexes to names, subjects, and authors. Class No: 929(931)-0055.2

Melanesia

[5983]

O'REILLY, P. Calédonians: répertoire biobibliographique de la Nouvelle-Calédonie. 2nd ed. Paris, Musée de l'Homme, 1980. 416p. ports. (Publications de la Société des Océanistes, No.3.)

First published 1953 (x,308p.).

French language who's who information on about 1000 living and dead prominent figures. Class No: 929(932)

[5984]

O'REILLY, P. Hébridais: répertoire bio-bibliographique des Nouvelles-Hébrides. Paris, Musée de l'Homme, 1957. 290p. ports. (Publications de la Société des Océanistes, no.6.)

Biographies not only of notable residents but also of historical figures connected with the island. Class No: 929(932)

Australia

[5985]

ATKINSON, A. The Dictionary of famous Australians. 2nd ed. St. Leonards, NSW, Allen & Unwin, 1995. xviii,268p. ports. ISBN: 1863738819.

1st ed. 1992.

Brief biographies of 600+ notable and notorious Australians. Data: vital statistics, career outlines, listing of works and deeds for which known. Class No: 929(94)

[5986]

Austral-Asian who's who. Singh, J., ed. 2nd ed. Adelaide, Oriental Publications, 1991. xxxiv,643p., ports., index. ISBN: 0646031902.

1st ed. 1981.

Biographical details of almost 500 leaders of various Asian communities arranged in 12 professional categories. AustralAsian associations and societies p.xix-xxxi. Greatly expanded from 1st ed.

Class No: 929(94)

[5987]

Australian dictionary of biography. Melbourne Univ. Press, 1966-. Distributed in UK by Europa Publications.

Period 1. Convicts and settlers 1788-1850. 1966-67. V.1-2. 1116 entries. Period 2. Gold rush & after 1851-1890. V.3-6. 1969-76. 2053 entries. Period 3. Federation and after 1891-1939. V.7-12. 1979-90. Index: volumes 1-12 1788-1939. 1991. xv,236p. 0522844596. bibliog. p.xv. Names (p.1-86). Places of birth (p.87-165). Occupations (p.166-285). Consolidated corrigenda (p.287-326). V.13 1940-1980 A-DE. 1993. xxvi,626p. 0522845126. A production of high standard. 'It is the great merit of the Australian Dictionary of Biography (unlike the DNB) that if offers a genuine cross-section of society' (Times Literary Supplement, no. 3435, 28 December 1967, p.1263).

V.14 1940-1980 Di-Kel. edited by J. Ritchie. 1996. xxviii,616p. ISBN 052284717x. £42.50 is the 2nd of 4v. dealing with the period 1940-1980 and includes 666 lives written by 572 authors.

Class No: 929(94)

[5988]

–GIBBNEY, H.J. and SMITH, A.G., comps. A Biographical register 1788-1939. Notes from the name index of the Australian Dictionary of Biography. Canberra, Australian National University, Australian Dictionary of Biography, 2v., 1987. xviii,403p.+429p. bibliog., index. ISBN: 0731501047, set.

1. A-K. 07351500989. 2. L-Z. 0731501039.

8100 entries. Data: name; leading occupation; main place associated with; birth, marriage, death details; biographical outline; and bibliographical references. By-product of 1st 12v. of Australian dictionary of biography. Based on a card index maintained since late 1950s which 'as an aid to the publication of the Dictionary, now extends far beyond this basic function and encompasses material on many thousands more men and women than those deemed appropriate for a Dictionary entry' (Introduction). Bibliography of collective biographical material p.xiii-xvii. Occupational index. p.361-429.

Class No: 929(94)

[5989]

Contemporary Australians 1995/96, Port Melbourne, Reed Reference Australia, 1995. xii,500p. index. ISBN: 1875589686.

One-stop reference book/media guide containing biographical, career, and contact details of 4,500+ people currently shaping Australia. Classified index in 26 professional/occupational categories p.485-500. Class No: 929(94)

[5990]

Debrett's handbook of Australia. 3rd (Bicentennial) ed. Sydney, Collins, 1987. 272+1098p. col. frontis., col. illus. ISBN: 0002178044. ISSN: 08193665.

First published as Debrett's handbook of Australia and New Zealand 1982; 2nd ed. 1984.

7000 biographical entries for leading men and women (Kerry Packer 20 lines, Rupert Murdoch 24 lines). Introductory features include J.C. Vaughan's 'New flags for Australia' p.95-96. Class No: 929(94)

[5991]

GILLEN, M. The Founders of Australia a biographical dictionary of the First Fleet. Sydney, Library of Australian History, 1989. xlviii, 624p. illus. facsims. bibliog. Aust $56.00. ISBN: 0908120699.

Biographical entries of all 1377 people known to have landed in Sydney Cove, January 1788. A series of appendices provide entries for those who embarked in the First Fleet but who never reached Sydney; non-English First Fleeters; Officers, Passengers, Free Women and Children, and ships and crews. Explanatory notes (on tracing First Fleeters) p.xxxix-xliii. Appendix 10. Abstract of biographical data. Appendix 12. Chronology. Bibliography p.537-544. Published to commemorate the Australian Bicentenary. Class No: 929(94)

[5992]

–FIDLON, P.G., and others, eds. The First Fleeters a comprehensive listing of convicts, marines, seamen, officers, wives, children and ships. Sydney, Australian Documents Library, 1981. ix, 86p. pbk.

Data: name, status, ship. Does not purport to be a complete list.

Class No: 929(94)

[5993]

–RYAN, R.B., ed. The Second Fleet convicts a comprehensive listing of convicts who sailed in HMS Guardian, Lady Juliana, Neptune, Scarborough and Surprise. Sydney, Australian Documents Library, 1982. xv, 95p. pbk. ISBN: 0908219067.

Data: name/place, date, sentence, ship. Class No: 929(94)

[5994]

—RYAN, R.J., *ed*. The Third Fleet convicts: an alphabetical listing of names, giving place and date of conviction, length of sentence and ship of transportation. Cammeray, Horwitz Grahame, 1983. xiv, 126p. ISBN: 072551521x.

Data: name/place,. date, sentence, ship. *Class No:* 929(94)

[5995]

Monash biographical dictionary of 20th century Australia. Arnold, J. *and* Morris, D. Port Melbourne, Reed Reference Publishing. 1994. xx,.568p. bibliog. $A60. £45. ISBN: 1875589198.

Revised paperback edition announced for publication within 2 yrs.

2,200+ career profiles of Australians from all ethnic backgrounds who achieved prominence and/or made a contribution to their country in 20th century. References p.xix-xx. Introduction (p.xi-xv) contains brief account of Australian biographical dictionaries.

Class No: 929(94)

[5996]

Northern Territory dictionary of biography. Carment, D. *and* Maynard, R. *and* Powell, A., *eds*. Casuarina, NT., NTU Press, 2v., 1990-92.

V.1: *To 1945*. 1990. xvi,325p. ISBN 094907022x. V.2: xiii,238p. 0949070378. 100 contributors. Full signed biographies which broadly reflect life in the Territory rather than focussing on eminent figures, including migrants, women, and Aborigenes. *Class No:* 929(94)

[5997]

Who's who in Australia 2000: an Australian biographical dictionary and register of prominent people with which is incorporated John's Notable Australians. Herd, M., *ed*. 36th ed. Melbourne, Information Australia, 1999. iv,1815p. illus., Now published annually. ISSN: 08108226.

1st ed. *John's notable Australians* 1906. 3rd ed. *Fred John's annual* 1912. 6th ed. *Who's who in Australia* 1992.

12,400 Biographies. Preliminary features include words and music Advance Australia fair; Royal style and titles; Order of precedence of honours and awards; Australian decorations (*illus*.); Australian winners of Nobel prizes; Diplomatic Corps in Australia *etc*. Data: career profiles, honours and awards, publications, recreation.

Class No: 929(94)

Bibliographies

[5998]

BORCHARDT, D.H. *and* MARSHALL, J.G. 'Biography', chapter 20, *Australians: a guide to sources* (v.10 *Australians. A historical library,* 1988).

Introductory essay and annotated bibliography divided into General biographical dictionaries and regional sources for New South Wales, Queensland, Tasmania, Victoria and Western Australia.

Class No: 929(94)(01)

Women

[5999]

Contemporary Australian women. Port Melbourne, Reed Reference Australia, 1996. 306p. $US35. ISBN: 1875589929.

2000+ entries relating to women active in all fields of endeavour although some entries are sketchy and exiguous. *Class No:* 929(94)-0055.2

[6000]

LOFTHOUSE, A., *comp*. Who's who of Australian women. North Ryde, New South Wales, Methuen Australia, 1982. 504p. frontis, index. ISBN: 0454004370.

Celebrates the lives of 1430 Australian women spanning 3 generations. *Class No:* 929(94)-0055.2

Polynesia

[6001]

O'REILLY, P. Tahitiens: répertoire bio-bibliographique de la Polynésie française. 2nd ed. Paris, Musée de l'Homme, 1975. 670p. ports., index.

Replaces 1st ed. 1962 (xvi, 535p.). and *Supplément,* 1966 (iv,104p.).

1875 annotated entries and includes a list of governors and commandants. 'A valuable who's who of French Polynesia' (G.W. Fry and R. Mauricio. *Pacific Basin and Oceania,* 1987. Entry 922).

Class No: 929(96)

Fiji

[6002]

Who's who in Fiji Fiji's golden book of record. Berwick, S. Suva Berwicks Publishing House, 1990. 307p. ports, maps. pbk. ISBN 0091005493.

A second edition is planned for 1995. Until then a supplement will be published every December to update existing entries and for the inclusion of new biographies.

3 parts: 1. Introduction (customs and traditions; historical background; people; constitutional developments) - 2. Who's who (p.89-242) - 3. Who was who (p.248-307). *Class No:* 929(961.1)

Hispanic Peoples

[6003]

Dictionary of Hispanic biography. Tardiff, J.C. *and* Mabunda, L.M., *eds*. Detroit, Gale Research, 1996. 1011p. illus. indexes. $120. £92. ISBN: 0810339822.

80 academic contributors. 471 biographical essays (1-3p.) of leading Hispanic figures from Spain, Spanish America and the US, ranging from the voyages of discovery to the present time.

Class No: 929(=06)

Jews

[6004]

WIGODER, G. Dictionary of Jewish biography. New York, Simon & Schuster, 1991. 567p. ports. $55. ISBN: 013210105x.

Over 750 biographical sketches, of varying length, with bibliographic citations, of famous and infamous Jews of all nationalities from biblical to modern times. Excludes living persons 'This exceedingly useful work ... can answer a great many reference questions' (*Library Journal,* 1 June 1992, p.188).

Class No: 929(=924)

Bibliographies

[6005]

ZUBATSKY, D.S. Jewish autobiographies and biographies an international bibliography of books and dissertations in English. New York, Garland, 1989. x,370p. $47. ISBN: 0824056434.

1,800 entries, arranged A-Z by biographee. Mostly confined to 20th century. Major sources consulted p.viii-x. Topical index (*i.e.* by profession or occupation). *Class No:* 929(=924)(01)

929.5/.9 Genealogy & Heraldry

Poland

Bibliographies

[6006]

OSKINS, J.W. **Polish genealogy and heraldry** an introduction to research. Washington, European Division, Library of Congress, 1987. xii, 114p. illus., map, index, softcover.

Pt.1: 1. Armorials and studies in heraldry - 2. Genealogy - 3. English language publications for Americans seeking their Polish heritage - 4. Select periodicals - 5. Bibliography. Pt.2: 6. Encyclopedias - 7. Biographies - 8. Geographical dictionaries, gazetteers and maps - 9. Histories - 10. Archives and printed sources - 11. Miscellaneous reference works. Chronology p.98-104. List of rulers p.105. See also B. Kles-Pilewski's 'Some sources for Polish genealogy', *Genealogist's Magazine*, v.16, no.4, December 1969, p.150-9, a briefly annotated list of 90 items. *Class No:* 929.50/.9(438)(01)

France

Bibliographies

[6007]

AFFROY, G. **Bibliographie généalogique, héraldique et nobiliaire de la France, des origines à nos jours.** Imprimés et manuscrits. Paris, Saffroy, 5v., 1968-88. Published with aid of the Centre National de la Recherche Scientifique.

1. *Généralités.* 1974. 2. *Provinces et colonies françaises. orient latin, refugiés.* 3. *Recueils généalogiques généraux, monographies, familiales et études particulières.* 1974. 830p. 4. *Table générale, auteurs, titres anonymes, matières.* 570p. *Supplément 1969-1983.* 1988. xvi, 286p. ISBN 2901541054.

V.1 contains a subject index. Entries are subdivided in detail. Items 1506-1931: 'Bibliographies héraldiques et généalogiques' subdivided by country). Includes coloured plates. *Class No:* 929.50/.9(44)(01)

Netherlands

Bibliographies

[6008]

EENAERTS, R.J. **Algemeen genealogisch-heraldisch repertorium voor die Zuildelijke Nederlanden** / Répertoire général généalogique et héraldique des Pays-Bas/Méridionaux/General genealogical and heraldic index of the Southern Netherlands. Handszame, Belgium, Familia et Patra (now Torhout, Belgium, Flandria Nostra), 8v., 1969-1985.

38,824 items from books, periodicals and newspapers. *Class No:* 929.50/.9(492)(01)

USA

Bibliographies

[6009]

ILBY, P.W., *comp*. **American and British genealogy and heraldry:** a selected list of books. 3rd ed. Boston, New England Historic Genealogical Society, 1983. xix, 940p. $49.95. ISBN: 0880820047.

First two editions published by the American Library Association in 1970 and 1975.

Almost 10,000 entries citing books and definitive periodical articles on genealogy, heraldry, and North American local history with a genealogical slant. Scope enlarged to almost double that of the previous edition. Extensive index of 20,000 entries. Treatment of black and ethnic genealogy is greatly expanded and a completely new section appears listing works in English covering non-English speaking countries. Described as 'unmatched in the field' by Evelyn Haynes' 'Encore Filby!' *Reference Services Review*, v.12, no.3, Fall 1984, p.70-72 which reports that compiler and publisher are contemplating annual or biennial supplements. *Class No:* 929.50/.9(73)(01)

Databases

[6010]

ARENDS, M. **Genealogy software guide.** Baltimore, MD, Genealogical Publishing, 1998. 269p. index, pbk. $19.95. ISBN: 0806315814.

Reviews of currently available IBM-compatible software and outlines the features of 27 database programmes for the PC snd 40+ utilities. Data: publisher/writer, contact information, cost, hardware requirements. *Class No:* 929.50(003.4)

[6011]

TAYLOR, N., *ed*. **Computers in genealogy beginners hand book.** London, Society of Genealogists, 1994. 66p. £4.50.

Supersedes *Computers in genealogy beginners' pack* (Society of Genealogists, 1993).

Contents include updated versions of listings of family history commercial and shareware packages and their suppliers plus articles on the use of computers for family history, data transfer between computers, and choosing a program. *Class No:* 929.50(003.4)

Bibliographies

[6012]

KEMP, T.J. **The Genealogist's virtual library** full text books on the World Wide Web. Wilmington, DE., Scholarly Resources, 2000. 282p. $70. ISBN: 0842028641.

Facilitates the identification of full-text books on the Internet. *Class No:* 929.50(003.4)(01)

Internet

[6013]

HOWELLS, C. **Cyndi's list of genealogy sites on the Internet.** http://www.CyndisList.com.

'What began on Mar 4, 1996, as a small set of bookmarked genealogy Web sites selected for the author's personal use, then shared with the Tacoma-Pierce County Genealogical Society, has exploded into nothing short of an electronic phenomenon. Cyndi's List has become the premier gateway for genealogical research on the internet, providing access to more than 40,000 genealogy sites, each thoroughly researched and categorized' (*Booklist*, v.96, no.6, 15 November 1999, p.644). *Class No:* 929.50(003.41)

[6014]

—HOWELLS, C. **Cyndi's list:** a comprehensive list of 40,000 genealogy sites on the Internet. Baltimore, Genealogical Publishing, 1999. xviii,855p. $49.94. ISBN: 0806315563.

'The print version, identical to the online version in scope, arrangement, and content'. Canada and the US sections arranged by province and state respectively, Europe by country or groups of countries. All sites indicate its complete Web address plus a brief description of its content when applicable. 'Regardless of where one needs to begin, be it with census records, cemetry lists, oral histories, ethnic special interest groups, or ship passenger and immigration records, Cyndi's List will guide the way' (*Booklist*, v.96, no.6, 15 November 1999, p.644). *Class No:* 929.50(003.41)

[6015]

KEMP, T.J. **Virtual roots:** a guide to genealogy and local history on the World Wide Web. Wilmington, DE., Scholarly Resources, 1997. 279p. $65. ISBN: 0842027181.

Guide to 1000+ www sites. Data: e-mail/postal addresses, tel/fax numbers. 217 Family Association sites. 'A much-needed guide to the Web's rich resources for genealogists, local historians, public libraries, archivists, and librarians (*Choice*, v.35,no.6, February 1998, p.966). *Class No:* 929.50(003.41)

Dictionaries

[6016]

HARRIS, M. *and* HARRIS, G., *comps*. **Ancestry's concise genealogical dictionary.** Salt Lake City, Ancestry, 1989. 259p. bibliog. $10.95. ISBN: 091648906x.

3500 genealogical and historical terms partially defined. 'The reader would profit from more complete explanations or choices';

....(contd.)

nevertheless 'this is a convenient little guide which many a genealogist will find useful' (*Choice*, v.27, no.3, April 1990, p.1298).
Class No: 929.50(038)

Periodicals

CD-ROM
[6017]

Periodical Source Index (PERSI). Salt Lake City, Ancestry for Allen County Library, 1997. CD-ROM for Windows 3.1/95. $99.95.

'Periodical Source Index is the largest index of genealogical and local history materials, listing more than 1.1 million articles from over 6000 journals published since 1800. It should be in every library and will be in constant use' (*Library Journal*, 1 April 1999, p.58).
Class No: 929.50(051)(003.40)

Yearbooks & Directories
[6018]

The Genealogical services directory 2000. York, Genealogical Services Directory, 1999. 360p. £4.95. ISBN: 0953029735.

Revised, updated and extended to 5000 organizations including archive repositories, museums, and local history groups), 1500 never before listed in a single publication, together with E-mail and Internet addresses. Feature articles include Libraries and Genealogy: Welsh Estate Records; Land Registry Records; Scottish Archives; Irish Records; and Internet Genealogy. *Class No:* 929.50(058)

Archives
[6019]

BEVAN, A. Tracing your ancestors in the Public Record Office. 6th ed. London, PRO, 1999. xvi,394p. illus. bibliog. £12.99. ISBN: 1873162618.

First published by Cox, J. and Padfield, T. in 1981. Census records, military service papers, court documents, wills, taxation records plus many more unique personal records are all held by the PRO. This book gives clear guidance on using these records and demonstrates by using cases of individual examples.

Includes newly released First World War Army and Navy records, Merchant Marine records, and changes caused by the opening of the Family Records Centre. Invaluable practical guide for all researchers and indispensable to the inexperienced visitor to the PRO. Completely revised and expanded for this edition. 'A much enlarged and improved edition of the guide you really must have access to if you are to make the most of a visit to the PRO' (*Lincolnshire Past & Present*, no.38, Winter 1999/2000, p.18-19). *Class No:* 929.50(093.20)

Worldwide
[6020]

JOHNSON, K.A. and SAINTY, M.R., eds. Genealogical research directory 2000. North Sydney, Genealogical Research Directory, 1985-. Annual. Available in UK from Mrs. E. Simpson, 2 Stella Grove, Tollerton, Notts., NG12 4EY 1216p. maps. £18.

Originally published by Library of Australian History, 1981, as *Genealogical research directory (Australasian ed.)*.

A medium by which family historians may exchange research data with distant relatives and others. Includes: (1) Directory of surnames (dates; family names; time period; town, county, province or state); (2) Subjects; (3) One-name studies and organizations; (4) Directory of 1400 genealogical societies and research repositories A-Z by country; (5) Professional notices. *Class No:* 929.50(100)

[6021]

—Genealogical research directory on CD-ROM 1990-1999. Windows 3.1 95, 98 and NT4 (PC only). £23.90.

Contains all the surname, subject and one-name sections from GRD 1990-96. An easy to use search filter allows user to select either name, interest or geographical area, and then collate a list of researchers with similar interests. 500,000 entries from 22,000 contributors. This edition has a new search engine and a new loading programe. 'A must for any person wishing to contact people with a similar area of interest, either genealogical or geographical' (*Family Tree Magazine*, v.13,no.2, December 1996, p.8). *Class No:* 929.50(100)

Databases
[6022]

International genealogical index.

Over 30 million baptismal entries from parish and non-parochial registers from all parts of England compiled and computerized by the Genealogical Department of the Church of Latter Day Saints, Salt Lake City, Utah. See J.W. Gibson's *Where to find the international*

....(contd.)

Genealogical Index (1984),. A specimen page is on p.146 of T.V.H. Fitzhughes' *The dictionary of genealogy* (rev.ed. 1985).
Class No: 929.50(100)(003.4)

Bibliographies
[6023]

HOFFMAN, M. Genealogical and local history books in print. 5th ed. Baltimore, MD., Genealogical Publishing, 4v., 1996-97. $100 set.

First published as *Genealogical books in print* 1975.

V.1: *Family history*. 1996. 477p. ISBN 080631513x. V.2: *General reference and world resources*. 1997. 375p. 0806315385. V.3: *U.S. sources and resources: Alabama-New York*. 1997. 574p. 0806315369. V.4: *North Carolina-Wyoming*. 1997. 530p. 0806315377. 'This welcome update of the field's most indispensable bibliographical tool lists individual books as well as family histories and compiled genealogies and includes names and addresses of vendors' (*Library Journal*, 1 April 1999, p.58). *Class No:* 929.50(100)(01)

[6024]

KAMINKOW, M.J., ed. Genealogies in the Library of Congress : a bibliography. Jamestown, Virginia, Magna Carta Book Company, 2v., 1972. Supplement 1972-1976, 1977. Second Supplement 1976-1986, 1987. 1800p.+285p.+850p. $175. $89.50. (2nd Supplt). ISBN 0910946159, 2v; 0910946302, (2nd Supplt.).

'This bibliography brings up to date similar printed works published in 1910 and 1919 under the title *American and English genealogies in the Library of Congress*, as well as the microcard edition which appeared in 1954' (*Editor's note*).

19,208 items plus addenda (734). Bibliographical notes; Library of Congress locations; nearly 25,000 cross-references (including references from family names to authors). Includes all entries in the Library of Congress 'Family name index', and lists not only American and English works but also holdings of Canadian, Irish, Welsh, Scottish, Australian, Latin American, Polish, German, Dutch, Scandinavian, French, Spanish, Italian, Portuguese and Asian sources. 'The most comprehensive bibliography available of family histories of America and Great Britain' (*Library Journal*, v.98, no.8, 15 April 1973, p.1243). Kaminkow's *A complement to Genealogies in the Library of Congress* (Magna Carta Books, 1981. 118p. $83.50 0910946248) adds a further 20,000 items.

Genealogies catalogued by the Library of Congress since 1986: with a list of established forms of family names and a list of genealogies converted to microform since 1983. Washington, Library of Congress 1992. 1349p. $70. *Class No:* 929.50(100)(01)

Official Records
[6025]

KEMP, T.J. Vital records handbook. Baltimore, Genealogical Publishing Co., 1988. ix, 231p. facsims. $19.95. ISBN: 0806312203.

Complete collection of vital records application forms (for photocopying) with essential data such as name and address of record office, 'phone, fees, and explanation of payment methods, for all record offices in 1. United States - 2. U.S. Trust Territories - 3 Canada, Ireland and United Kingdom. Dates of files held, gaps and omissions, and alternative locations are also indicated.
Class No: 929.50(100)(093.2)

Jews

Bibliographies
[6026]

ZUBATSKY, D.S. and BERENT, I.M., comps. Sourcebook for Jewish genealogies and family histories. 2nd ed. Bergenfield, NJ. Avotaynu, 1996. 456p. bibliog. $69.50. ISBN: 1886223033.

Information on 12,000 family names A-Z plus the location of related resources. Draws on the contents of the compilers' *Jewish genealogy a sourcebook of family histories and genealogies* (New York, Garland 2v., 1984-89). 'The compilers have made every effort to create the most comprehensive bibliography of available resources to date' (*Booklist*, v.93, no.9/10, 1+15 January 1997, p.900-901).
Class No: 929.50(100)(=924)(01)

Europe

Handbooks & Manuals
[6027]

BAXTER, A. In search of your European roots: a complete guide to tracing your ancestors in every country in Europe. Baltimore Genealogical Publishing Co., 1985. xix, 289p. bibliog. index, pbk $12.95. ISBN: 0806311142.

A-Z guides of 30 European countries (excluding the United Kingdom) are designed to guide the reader through the complexities of genealogical research. Up-to-date information on church, state, and

..(contd.)
provincial archives. European Jewish records p.11-20. Bibliography p.279-83. Genealogical organizations p.284-6.
Class No: 929.50(4)(035)

Great Britain

[6028]
MERY, A. **A-Z of British genealogical research.** Northlands, South Africa, Mantis Consulting, 1995. £3.50. ISBN: 0620196033.

A concise guide to researching British ancestry. 'Practically everything the family historian may want to know about is included' (*Family Tree Magazine,* v.12,no7, May 1996, p.20).
Class No: 929.50(410)

[6029]
ERBER, M.D. **Ancestral trails** the complete guide to British genealogy and family history. Baltimore, MD, Genealogical Publishing, 1997; Stroud, Glos., Sutton Publishing in association with the Society of Genealogists, 1998. 674p. illus., bibliog., index. $34.95. £30. ISBN: 0806315415, US; 0750914181, UK.

Detailed account of types of record available. 1. An introduction to genealogical research ... 4. Genealogical problems ... 11. Archives, libraries and family history societies ... 26. Peerages, the gentry, famous people and heraldry ... 29. Scotland, Wales, Ireland, Isle of Man and the Channel Islands. 8 Appendices (*e.g.* County Record Offices ... Commencement date of the reigns of English and British monarchs). Bibliography (by chapter) p.630-653. Analytical index p.654-74. 'This complete, current, and beautiful guide ultimately helps the researcher focus on how the ancestral trail begins and how to form a coherent picture of past generations and their links to the present' (*Library Journal,* v.123,no.4, 1 March 1998, p.80). Awarded Library Association McColvin Medal for an outstanding reference work 1998.
Class No: 929.50(410)

[6030]
EO, G., *comp.* **The British overseas:** a guide to records of their births, baptisms, marriages, deaths and burials, available in the United Kingdom. 2nd ed. London, Guildhall Library, 1988. 72p. pbk. ISBN: 0900422262.

First published 1984.

Part 1. Introduction to the sources. 2. List of known registers for individual places overseas. 'A very useful guide' (*Refer,* v.4, no.1, Spring 1986, p.15). *Class No:* 929.50(410)

Internet

[6031]
CHAEFER, C.K. **Instant information on the Internet:** (a genealogist's no-frills guide to the British Isles). Baltimore, Genealogical Publishing, 1999. $9.95. ISBN: 0806316144.

750 British and Irish internet sites listed A-Z by county. Includes record offices, public archives, parish and non-conformist records, libraries and museums. 'Despite its tendency to go out of date quickly, will give endless hours of enjoyment and provide access to much hitherto undisclosed information' (*Family Tree Magazine,* v.15, no.12, October 1999, p.52). *Class No:* 929.50(410)(003.41)

Bibliographies

[6032]
KAMINKOW, M.J. **A New bibliography of British genealogy** with notes. Baltimore, Maryland, Magna Carta Book Co., 1965. xvii,170p.

1,783 numbered entries, the most important being annotated. 8 parts: 1. General works (bibliography; manuals and introductions; indexes to pedigrees; other indexes; guides, calendars, indexes, etc. to manuscript collections; guide to microfilm holdings; library directories) - 2. Periodicals, including newspapers - 3. Particular subjects ('Army' to 'Wills') - 4. English counties, A-Z - 5. Ireland - 6. Scotland - 7. Wales - 8. Islands (including West Indies). Addenda. Index (authors, series, etc.). 'The main aim has been to list books that have not been listed elsewhere, and to indicate where to look for a list of those that have' (*Introduction*). 'One of the most important genealogical bibliographies published during recent years' (*Genealogists' Magazine,* v.15,no.7, Setpember 1966, p.255-7). Largely replaces H.G. Harrison's *Select bibliography of English genealogy* (1937).
Class No: 929.50(410)(01)

[6033]
RAYMOND, S. **British genealogical periodicals** a bibliography of their contents. Birmingham, Federation of Family History Societies. ISBN: 1872094201; 1872094236.

Bibliography of the contents of 19th and early 20th century periodicals. V.1 covers *Collectanea topographica et genealogica* (1834-43); *Topographer and genealogist* (1846-58); and *The Ancestor* (1902-5). 1991. 83p. £5. ISBN 1872094201. 2. *The Genealogist. Pt.1. Sources.* 1991. 40p. £3. *Pt.2. Family histories, Pedigrees, Bibliographical notes and obituaries.* 1991. 44p. £3. 1872094317. 3. *Miscellanea Genealogica Et Heraldica. Pt.1. Sources.* 1993. £4.50.

....(contd.)
1872094511. *Pt.2. Family histories* etc. 1993. £4. 187209452x. Supplement 1. *British genealogy in miscellaneous journals.* 1994. 80p. £7. 0958814449. *Class No:* 929.50(410)(01)

[6034]
RAYMOND, S. A. **British genealogical books in print.** Bury, Lancs, Federation of Family History Societies, 1999. ISBN: 1860060951. ISSN: 10332065.

Lists all inprint titles published anywhere in the world relating to England, Scotland and Wales, likely to be of interest to British genealogists. Arranged in three sections: those printed by commercial and private publishers, by societies, and by libraries and record offices. Excludes local history titles and the publications of the Federation of Family History Societies. These latter are already listed in John Perkins' *Current publications from member societies*
Class No: 929.50(410)(01)

Handbooks & Manuals

[6035]
BAXTER, A. **In search of your British and Irish roots** a complete guide to tracing your English, Welsh, Scottish and Irish ancestors. 4th ed. Baltimore, Genealogical Publishing Co., 1999. xiv, 304p. bibliog., index. $18.95. ISBN: 080631611x.

1st ed. 1982.

'An excellent book for both overseas and home researchers (but mainly the former) who want a clearly written, no frills explanation of how to compile their family tree' (*Family Tree Magazine,* v.10,no.1, November 1999, p.66). *Class No:* 929.50(410)(035)

[6036]
RODGER, N.A.M. **Naval records for genealogists.** London, HMSO, 1988. iv, 220p. tables, bibliog., index. £4.95. (*Public Record Office Handbooks.*) ISBN: 0114402094.

1. Introduction, scope, arrangement. Records elsewhere. Navy list - 2. Ranks and ratings - 3. Types of service record - 4. Musters and pay books. Appendix 1. Analysis of service records (p.67-136) - 2. Service records in series (p.137-187) - 3. Naval reserve and auxiliary forces. Author index. *Class No:* 929.50(410)(035)

Dictionaries

[6037]
FITZHUGH, T.V.H. **The Dictionary of genealogy.** Lumas, S., *for the Society of Genealogists.* 5th ed. London, A & C Black, 1994. 320p. illus., facsims. £24.99. ISBN: 0713648597.

1st ed. 1985.

Part 1. Guide to ancestry research 'outlines the various choices open to the researcher and describes step by step, the main sources of information and the techniques to be used in tracing the family back through time'. (*Foreword*). Part 2. The Dictionary contains over 1,000 descriptions, definitions and locations of virtually all the historical records likely to be examined by genealogists. Scholarly, informative, practical. 'Clearly the result of many years of research' (*Reference Reviews,* v.3,no.3, September 1989, p.140-1).
Class No: 929.50(410)(038)

Yearbooks & Directories

[6038]
OWEN, D.B. **Guide to genealogical resources in the British Isles.** Metuchen, New Jersey, Scarecrow Press, 1989. 399p. indexes. $39.50. ISBN: 0810821532.

279 institutions A-Z by locality with their resources and services. 'A valuable, fairly reasonably priced record useful both to special genealogical and historical collections' (*Choice,* v.27, no.5, January 1990, p.774+6). *Class No:* 929.50(410)(058)

Databases

[6039]
Vital Records Index British Isles (1538-1888). Salt Lake City, Utah, Church of Jesus Christ of Latterday Saints, 5 discs, 1998 plus printed manual. Windows 95+.

Genealogical data comprising birth, Christening and marriage records gathered from parish records, civil registrations etc. presented in an easy to search and read format. Manual offers good advice on using source limitations, variant spellings, and referencing the original microfilm record. Until content is put on the web, 'these discs will be the access means of choice for public libraries and genealogical collections' (*Library Journal,* v.124, no.10, 1 June 1999, p.196).
Class No: 929.50(410)(058)(003.4)

Libraries

[6040]

HARVEY, R. **Genealogy for librarians.** 2nd ed. London, Clive Bingley, 1992. viii,194p. bibliog., index. £27.50. ISBN: 0851574084.
1st ed. 1982.
Well documented guide to primary and secondary sources of information mainly confined to England but with some mention of Welsh, Scottish and Irish genealogy and a cursory look into Europe. Chapter 1. The Librarian and the genealogist examines the problems faced by librarians when attempting to provide a service for genealogists. New material in this edition includes divorce and adoption sources. Bibliography p.156-83.
Class No: 929.50(410):061:026/027

Scotland

[6041]

SINCLAIR, C. **Tracing your Scottish ancestors** a guide to ancestry research in the Scottish Record Office. Rev. ed. Edinburgh,The Stationery Office, 1997. x,155p. illus., map, bibliog., indexes. limp cover. £9.99. ISBN: 0114958653.
1st published 1990.
Authoritative survey of the range of materials held in the SRO with 28 chapters on the various types of national and local records associated with different professions and occupations (*e.g.* Tenants and crafters ... litigants ... coal miners). Appendix A: Useful addresses p.142-46 - B. Useful books p.147-8. Chap.3 on the General Register Office for Scotland rewritten to take account of post-1990 developments. 'A model of its kind ... an excellent, down-to-earth, step-by-step introduction to the whole business of ancestry research in Scotland' (*Reference Reviews*, v.5, no.1, 1991, p.37-8).
Class No: 929.50(411)

Handbooks & Manuals

[6042]

CORY, K.B. **Tracing your Scottish ancestry.** Edinburgh, Polygon 1990. xii,195p. map, facsim, bibliog., index, limp cover. ISBN: 0748660542.
Comprehensive manual for would-be family historians. Part 1: A guide to genealogy in Scotland (Search records in New Register House and Scottish Record Office ... Names ... Heraldry ... Clans and tartans *etc.*). Part 2: Step by step guide in searching for family records p.163-86. Appendix 1: Glossary of occupations - 2. Useful addresses - 3. List of parishes, counties and commissariots p.108-52 - 4. Book list p.153-6. Neatly complements C. Sinclair's *Tracing your Scottish ancestors* (*q.v.*).
A second edition, containing an explanation of the computer index programme in operation in New Register House, Edinburgh, was published in 1995. £7.95. ISBN 0748662154.
Class No: 929.50(411)(035)

[6043]

STEEL, D.J. *and* STEEL, A.E.F. **Sources for Scottish genealogy and family history.** Chichester, Sussex, Phillimore for the Society of Genealogists, 1970. xiii, 320p. (*National Index of Parish Registers, no.12.*)
Sections: Historical background - Scottish nomenclature (surnames; Christian names, titles and descriptions) - Parish registers - Ancillary sources (*e.g.* Irregular marriages: Court Records) - Nonconformists, Footnote references. Bibliography (bibliographies; genealogy and archives; history; p.249-76). 'A detailed and scholarly guidebook' (E.G. Grant. *Scotland*, 1982. entry 457). *Class No:* 929.50(411)(035)

[6044]

Tracing ancestors in Shetland. Sandison, A. 3rd ed. London, A. Sandison, 1985. 48p. bibliog., pbk. £1.50. ISBN: 0950619124.
First published in Lerwick by T. and J. Manson in 1972.
8 chapters on first steps, Scottish traditions, and sources for Lerwick and county parishes. Appendices on surnames, Shetland family historians, local registraries, and searching New Register House, Edinburgh. Bibliography p.40-43. Distributed in Lerwick by the *Shetland Times. Class No:* 929.50(411)(035)

Ireland

[6045]

BETIT, K.J. *and* RUDFORD, D.A. **Ireland: a genealogical guide for North Americans.** Salt Lake City, Irish at Home and Abroad, 1995. 62p. $14.95.
Research guide with references to other sources.
Class No: 929.50(415)

[604(]

DAVIS, B. **An Introduction to Irish research** Irish ancestry: beginner's guide. 2nd ed. Birmingham, Federation of Family Histor Societies, 1994. v,100p. bibliog., index. ISBN: 1872094910.
1st ed. 1992.
Introductory guide in 7 chapters (*e.g.* 1. Basics of Irish research - 2 Postal research ... 5. Archives - 6. Irish records). Appendix A Heritage and research centres in Ireland. Bibliography p.91-95.
Class No: 929.50(415)

[604'

McCARTHY, T. **The Irish roots guide.** Rev. ed. Dublin, Lilliput Pres 1997. ix,116p. illus. facsims., tables, bibliog., pbk. IR£4.99. ISBN 0946640777.
1st ed. 1991.
Guide to 12 most useful sources of genealogical information (*e.g* census returns ... Catholic parish records ... tithe applotment books . records of the graveyard) followed by step-by-step instructions on the use. Chapter 7 Future of Irish genealogy. Bibliography p.113-6. 'A invaluable handbook to reconstructing male and female lines' (*Book Ireland*, no.152, September 1991, p.155). *Class No:* 929.50(415)

Handbooks & Manuals

[604£

BEGLEY, D.F., *ed.* **Handbook on Irish genealogy:** how to trace you ancestors and relations in Ireland. 6th ed. Dublin, Heraldic Artis Ltd., 1984 160p. illus. maps, tables, index, pbk. £4.95. ISBN 0950245593.
First published 1970.
6 chapters: 1. Tracing ancestors and relations in Ireland - 2. Record and record repositories - 3. County maps - 4. Parish registers - 5 Preliminary research in home countries - 6. Emmigrant passenger list to America. Record repositories and their contents p.129-144 Pedigrees in printed books p.145-149. Published family historie p.150-152. Useful addresses p.154. Reproductions of maps printed t accompany Samuel Lewis' *A Topgraphical dictionary of Ireland* p.41 73. *Class No:* 929.50(415)(035)

[604£

—BEGLEY, D.F., *ed.* **Irish genealogy** a record finder. Dublin, Heraldi Artists Ltd., 1981. 257p. illus. index. ISBN: 0950245577.
Sequel to *Handbook on Irish genealogy* (6th ed, 1984).
1. The peoples of Ireland - 2. Historical and administrative division of Ireland - 3. Irish census returns - 4. Guide to Irish directories - 5 Genealogical matter in the publications of the Irish Manuscrir Commission - 6. Newspapers as a genealogical source - 7. Th Registry of Deeds for genealogical purposes - 8. Wills an administrations; 9. Early genealogical sources for attornies an barristers. 10. R.E. Matheson's special report on surnames in Ireland Gravestone inscriptions recorded in printed sources (arranged b parish) p.233-240; Miscellaneous genealogical sources p.241-248; Lis of libraries, archives and record offices p.249-251.
Class No: 929.50(415)(035)

[605(

FALLEY, M.D. **Irish and Scotch-Irish ancestral research** : a guide t the genealogical records, methods and sources in Ireland. Baltimore Genealogical Publishing, 2v., 1984. $60. ISBN: 0806301964.
Reprint of 1962 ed.
1: *Repositories and records.*
2: *Bibliography and family index.*
Deals comprehensively with every phase of record searching in th US and in Ireland (where research is virtually impossible because o the destruction of records in 1922). Includes sources of Irish materia not in Ireland. 'Easily the best Irish genealogical work ever to hav been published' (*Library Journal*, v.88, no.114, August 1963 p.2884). *Class No:* 929.50(415)(035)

[605

GRENHAM, J. **Tracing your Irish ancestors** the complete guide. 2n ed. Dublin, Gill and Macmillan, 1999. 396p. maps, facsims. bibliogs., pbk. £12.99. ISBN: 0717127966.
1st ed. 1992.
Pt. 1: Major sources: 1. Civil records - 2. Census - 3. Church - 4 Land records. Pt. 2: Other sources: 5. Wills - 6. The Genealogica Office - 7. Emigration - 8. Registry of deeds - 9. Newspapers - 10 Directories. Pt. 3: Reference guide: 11. Occupations - 12. Count source lists - 13. Family histories - 14. Church of Ireland publi records in Dublin repositories - 15. Research services, societies an repositories. Well-documented authoritative guide. New to this editio is a complete list of all known copies of Catholic church records 'Considerable detail on what is where, and how to consult it' (*Book Ireland*, no.223, Summer 1999, p.194-95).
Class No: 929.50(415)(035)

[6052]

'LAUGHLIN, M.C. The Complete book for tracing your Irish ancestors. Kansas City, Irish Genealogical Foundation, 1982. 224p. bibliog.

Guide to types of records, terminology, repositories and societies in England, Ireland, United States and Canada.
Class No: 929.50(415)(035)

Maps & Atlases

[6053]

ITCHELL, B. A New genealogical atlas of Ireland. Baltimore, Genealogical Publishing Co., 1988. 123p. maps, softcover. $18.95. ISBN: 0806311525.

Identifies and precisely locates 6 major administrative divisions: counties, baronies, civil parishes, dioceses, poor law and probate districts. 'To be used in conjunction with *General alphabetical index to the townlands and towns, parishes and baronies of Ireland* (Dublin, 1861 reprinted by Genealogical Publishing Co. 1984). This has data on localities A-Z including OS sheet number, acreage, name of county, baronry and civil parish in which it is situated.
Class No: 929.50(415)(084.3)

Eire

Archives

[6054]

YAN, J.G. A Guide to tracing your Dublin ancestors. Glenageary, Co. Dublin, Flyleaf Press, 1988. 96p. illus., index, pbk. £5.95. ISBN: 0950846619.

Complete listing of all the major record sources in county and city of Dublin. *Class No:* 929.50(417)(093.20)

England & Wales

Handbooks & Manuals

[6055]

AMP, A.J. My ancestor was a migrant: (in England and Wales): how can I trace where he came from? London, Society of Genealogists, 1987. 44p. index. sd. £2. ISBN: 0901878944.

'Attempts to set out the major record sources which may be used prior to 1851 to trace a movement within England and Wales. It assumes that the resources of the General Register Office after 1st July 1837 have been exhausted'. *Class No:* 929.50(42)(035)

[6056]

ARDNER, D.E. *and* SMITH, F. Genealogical research in England and Wales. Salt Lake City, Utah, Bookcraft Publishers, 3v., 1956-65. illus., facsims., maps.

V.1 (1956). 1. Brief historic and economic background - 2. Family sources ... - 3. Cemeteries, burial grounds and churchyards - 4. Civil registration of births, marriages and deaths - 5. Examples of civil registration - 6. The census records of England and Wales - 7. How to trace place and family in the 1841-1851 census records - 8. Street and local addresses in the 1851 census returns - 9. The parish and its administration - 10. The parish registers - 11. Laws relating to the keeping of parish registers - 12. How to use parish registers - 13. Bishop's transcripts and their value - 14. Marriage licences and the intention to marry - 15. The Nonconformists, their history and records - 16. The Jews in Great Britain and the Commonwealth - 17. The Roman Catholics and their records - 18. Surnames. Given names. Dialect.

V.2 (1959). 1. Planning research and recording research results - 2. An introduction to probate records - 3. Wills, administrations and inventories - 4. Probate calendars or indexes and act books - 5. Miscellaneous probate records - 6. Examples of the value of probate records - 7. Naval and military records. Merchant shipping records. Churches on foreign soil - 8. Historical events related to genealogical research - 9. The counties of England and Wales.

V.3 (1965) includes a discussion of apprentice and freeman records; reading early English script; Chancery proceedings, schools and university registers; poll books; feet of fines; inquisitions, post-mortems, and manor court rolls.

Gathers together a mass of data, simply explained; many footnote references and facsimiles. Each volume has an analytical index. Chapter 9 of v.2, 'The counties of England' (p.195-307) is supported by numerous black-and-white maps, but the lettering on these is far from clear in many cases, and there is no gazetteer. 'Contains the most up-to-date guide to the whereabouts of the genealogist's main series of records that there is' (*Genealogist's Magazine*, v.13, no.11, September 1961, p.345). The same review states that on probate records it is 'undoubtedly the best that has ever appeared in print'.
Class No: 929.50(42)(035)

[6057]

ROGERS, C.D. The Family tree detective a manual for analysing and solving genealogical problems in England and Wales, 1538 to the present day. 2nd ed. Manchester, Manchester University Press, 1985. xii, 164p. illus. bibliog. £15. ISBN: 0719018455.

First published 1983.

How to proceed when genealogical sources on parents, marriage, and deaths appear to be exhausted. Select bibliography p.156-159. Index p.160-164. Regarded by the author as being in some ways complementary to Cox and Padfield's *Tracing your ancestors in the Public Record Office* (qv). *Class No:* 929.50(42)(035)

England

[6058]

WAGNER, Sir Anthony. English genealogy. 3rd ed. Chichester, Sussex, Phillimore, 1983. xiii, 475p. tables. £20. ISBN: 085033473x.

First published Oxford, Clarendon Press, 1960.

1. Purpose - 2. The roots - 3. English and Norman - 4. The social framework - 5. The rise and fall of families - 6. Strangers - 7. Settlers - 8. The records (p.324-350) - 9. The study and literature of genealogy (p.351-407) - 10. The practical approach. Index p.439-475. 'It already has an established place in the literature of its subject' (*Archives*, v.11, no.49, Spring 1973, p.61). *Class No:* 929.50(420)

Bibliographies

[6059]

HUMPHERY-SMITH, C.R. A Genealogist's bibliography. 2nd rev. ed. Chichester, Sussex, Phillimore, 1985. viii, 128p. pbk. £7.95. ISBN: 0850334225.

First published 1976, 2nd rev. ed. 1981. Based on H.G. Harrison's *Select bibliography of English genealogy* (1937).

Classified list of books and articles arranged A-Z by historical counties. Glossary p.95-113; Bibliography p.114-128.
Class No: 929.50(420)(01)

[6060]

RAYMOND, S. English genealogy an introductory bibliography. 3rd ed. Bury, Federation of Family History Societies, 1996. 40p. £5. ISBN: 1872094198.

First ed. published 1988. 2nd ed. 1991.

Introductory guide to the published sources of genealogy. First volume in a series intended to include every county not only in England but also Scotland and Wales.

Buckinghamshire 1993. 57p. £5.50. ISBN 1872094724; *Cheshire V.1: Genealogical sources.* £10. V.2: *Family histories and pedigrees.* £7.25; *Cornwall* 2e 1994. 84p. £8.60. 0958814457; *Cumberland and Westmorland.* 1993 67p. £5.50. 1872094278; *Devon V.1: Genealogical sources* 2e 1994. 83p. £7.75. V.2: *Family histories and pedigrees* 2e 1994. 64p. £7.50. 09588144732; *Dorset.* 1991. vii,113p. £6.60. 187209421x; *Gloucestershire and Bristol.* 1992. 88p. £6.60. 1872094341; *Hampshire.* 1996(?). £9. *Kent* 2v. 1998: V.1 *Genealogical sources.* 1998. 108p. indexes £7.50. 1860060714. V.2 *Reports, inscriptions and wills.* 1998. 68p. index. £6. 1860060706. *Lancashire V.2: Registers, inscriptions & wills.* 1996(?). £5.50. *V.3: Family history and pedigrees* 1996(?) £5.50. *Lincolnshire.* 1996(?). £8.10; *London and Middlesex.* V.1. *Genealogical sources.* 1860060587. V.2. *Family histories and pedigrees.* £5. 1860060595. 1994. 128p. £7.60. 1872094775; *Norfolk.* 1993. 91p. £6.60. 1872094597; *Oxfordshire.* 1993. 59p. £5.50. 1872094570. *Somerset.* 1991. 107p. 1872094228; *Suffolk.* 1992. 91p. £6. 1872094414. *Wiltshire.* 1996(?). £6.60. Forthcoming: *Kent* (3 or 4 v.); *Lancashire V.1: Genealogical sources.*

Annotated bibliographies divided into form and thematic sections: History of country; Bibliography and archives; Names and dialect; Biographical dictionaries; Genealogical directories; Parish Registers; Directories, encyclopedias and maps etc. Family name, Place-name and Author indexes. *Class No:* 929.50(420)(01)

Gazetteers

[6061]

SMITH, F. A Genealogical gazetteer of England: an alphabetical dictionary of places, with the location, ecclesiastical jurisdiction, population, and the date of the earliest entry in the registers of every ancient parish in England. Baltimore, Maryland, Genealogical Publishing Co., 1987. xv,590p. $30.00.

Reprint of 1968 ed.

'One of the most outstanding works of its kind in the last decade' (*Library Journal*, v.93,no.15, 1 September 1968, p.2996).
Class No: 929.50(420)(083.86)

Archives

[6062]

COLWELL, S. **Dictionary of genealogical sources in the Public Record Office.** London, Weidenfeld & Nicolson, 1992. xvii,206p. £20. ISBN: 0297831402.

Introduction (p.vii-xv) guides the reader round PRO, explains how documents are organized, and outlines access procedures. Dictionary entries under countries, personal names, and types of record. Glossary p.198-206. *Class No:* 929.50(420)(093.20)

[6063]

REID, J.P. **Genealogical research in England's Public Record Office.** A guide for North Americans. Baltimore, Genealogical Publishing, 1996. 148p. illus., bibliog., maps, indexes. $22.50. ISBN: 0806315040.

Preliminary information includes how to find Chancery Lane and Kew Gardens, admission procedures, document codes and list of printed guides. Main text is concerned with descriptions of the types of document to be found. An appendix lists addresses of county record offices. *Class No:* 929.50(420)(093.20)

London

Handbooks & Manuals

[6064]

HARVEY, R., *comp.* **A Guide to genealogical sources in the Guildhall Library.** 3rd ed. London, Guildhall Library, 1988. 56p. index, sd. £4.00. (*Research Guide, no.1*.) ISBN: 0900422254.

2nd ed. 1979.

18 chapters *e.g.* 3. Poll books and registers of electors ... 5. Census returns ... 7. Parish registers ... 13. Apprenticeship - 14. Guilds and livery companies. 'A good starting point for the inexperienced researcher' (*Library Association Record*, v.91, no.1, January 1989, p.54). *Class No:* 929.50(421)(035)

Isle of Man

Handbooks & Manuals

[6065]

NARASINHAM, J. **The Manx family tree** a beginner's guide to records in the Isle of Man. Isle of Man, the author, 1986. vi,48p. map,facsims., index. sd.

Vital records; wills; census, property, ecclesiastical court and other records and their whereabouts. Glossary p.43-5.
Class No: 929.50(428.9)(035)

Wales

[6066]

BARTRUM, P.C., *comp.* **Welsh genealogies AD300-1400.** Cardiff, Univ. of Wales Press, for the Board of Celtic Studies, 8v., 1974. 941p., geneal. tables.

2nd ed. published on microfiche 1981 which incorporated three lists of additions and corrections.

Compiled mainly from manuscripts in the National Library of Wales. Purpose is to reduce Welsh pedigrees into order and to make the results available in convenient form. V.1-4 lists pedigrees A-Z; v.5-8 comprise classified geographical, alphabetical place name, person, and surname indexes.

Welsh genealogies AD1400-1500. 18v., 1983. 1776p. V.1-10 lists pedigrees: v.11-18: indexes. *Class No:* 929.50(429)

Handbooks & Manuals

[6067]

HAMILTON-EDWARDS, G. **In search of Welsh ancestry.** Chichester, Sussex, Phillimore, 1986. xi, 95p. illus. facsims. bibliog, index. £8.95. ISBN: 0850335639.

15 chapters *e.g.* 2. Welsh Christian and surnames - 3. Civil registrations - 4. Census returns - 5. Parish registers - 6. Nonconformists - 7. Wills and administrations - 8. Professional men - 9. Army and Navy records - 10. Merchant service and East India Company - 11. National Library of Wales - 12. Manor Court Chancery and other records. Appendix C. Useful addresses - D. County Record Offices in Wales - E. Family history societies of Wales. Bibliography p.83-87. *Class No:* 929.50(429)(035)

Germany

[6068]

BRANDT, E.R. **Germanic genealogy** a guide to worldwide sources and migration patterns. 2nd ed. St. Paul, MN, Germanic Genealogy Society, 1997. 517p. maps, bibliog., index. $32. ISBN: 0964433737.

1st ed. 1995.

Handbook for the Family history researcher covering 60 countries. Data and information: guides to sources, addresses of archives and

....(contd.)

societies, German world list and language hints; places of origin church and civil records. 24 historical and modern maps.
Class No: 929.50(430)

Handbooks & Manuals

[6069]

BAXTER, A. **In search of your German roots** a complete guide to tracing your ancestors in the Germanic areas of Europe. United Germany ed. Baltimore, Genealogical Publishing Co., 1991. xii, 122p. bibliog., softcover. $9.95. ISBN: 0806313110.

1st ed. 1988.

Expansion of chapter printed in *In search of your European roots* (1985).

12 chaps. *e.g.* 4. The records of the Mormon church - 5. Jewish records - 6. Archives - 7. The Lutheran Church - 8. The Germans in the United States - 9. The Germans in Canada - 10. Records in Germany - 12. German genealogical associations in North America p.113-15. Bibliography p.117-9. *Class No:* 929.50(430)(035)

Dictionaries

[6070]

THODE, E. **German-English genealogical dictionary.** Baltimore, Md. Genealogical Publishing, 1996. 318p. $29.95. ISBN: 0806313420.

Thousands of German words and short phrases associated with genealogy compiled from church records, civil administration records family correspondence, ship passenger lists, and emigration records. *Class No:* 929.50(430)(038)

Yearbooks & Directories

[6071]

THODE, E. **Address book for Germanic genealogy.** 6th ed. Baltimore, Md., Genealogical Publishing, 1997. 195p. $24.95. ISBN 0806315261.

Almost 2,000 entries relating to genealogical and related societies state and municipal archives, religious archives and organisations booksellers, and professional genealogists in Europe and North America. *Class No:* 929.50(430)(058)

Czechoslovakia

Handbooks & Manuals

[6072]

MILLER, O.K. **Genealogical research for Czech and Slovak Americans.** Detroit, Gale Research Co., 1978. xiv, tables, index. $68 (*Genealogy and Local History series, no.2.*) ISBN: 0810314045.

11 chapters: 1. The genealogical library of the Church of Jesus Christ of Latter-Day Saints - 2. History - 3. Geography - 4. Czech and Slovak immigration to America - 5. Sources for genealogical research in Czechoslovakia - 6. Archives - 7. Names - 8. The Calendar - 9 Language - 10 Nobility and Heraldry - 11. Conclusions. Appendix 1 Branch genealogical libraries of the Church of Jesus Christ of Latter Day Saints p.165-179. Each chapter is followed by a comprehensive bibliography of sources. 3 maps. *Class No:* 929.50(437)(035)

France

Handbooks & Manuals

[6073]

CURRER-BRIGGS, N. *and* GAMBIER, R. **Huguenot ancestry** Chichester, Sussex, Phillimore, 1985. x,150p., illus., geneal. tables bibliog., index. £11.95. ISBN: 0850335647.

7 Sections: 1. Introduction - 2. Areas of Huguenot settlement in Britain - 3. Huguenots in North America and South Africa - 4 Planning and organising a research project - 5. British research sources p.82-107 - 6. Research in France, the Netherlands, Germany and Switzerland p.108-21 - 7. Recording the results. Chronology p.128-131; Bibliography p.133-136. 24p. plates. The only book on the subject. *Class No:* 929.50(44)(035)

Italy

[6074]

COLE, T.R. **Italian genealogical records:** how to use Italian, civil ecclesiastical and other records in family history research. Salt Lake City, Ancestry, 1995. 265p. illus. $34.95. ISBN: 0916489582.

'A professional researcher of Italian genealogy, Cole traces the history of Italian record-keeping and explains the different types of records, with advice on how to approach Italian repositories'. (*Library Journal*, 1 April 1999, p.60). *Class No:* 929.50(450)

Vatican City

[6075]

WILLIAMS, G.L. Papal genealogy the families and descendants of the Pope. Jefferson, N.C., McFarland, 1998. 272p. tables, geneal.tables, index. £47.25. $52.50. ISBN: 0786403152.

All papal families from the beginning are covered in this comprehensive work. Genealogical charts give all descendants of the popes, showing in many cases the interrelationships between the papal families and the leading families of Europe. Detailed histories examine the impact of the papacy on each pope's family and how each influenced the history of the church. With tables, an appendix and an index. (*publisher's announcement*). *Class No:* 929.50(456.31)

Portugal

[6076]

HUMPHERY-SMITH, C.R. 'Genealogy in Portugal', *Family Tree Magazine*, v.12,no.11, September 1996, p.59-60. map.

Discursive article but some hard facts on archives and record depositories and some useful addresses. *Class No:* 929.50(469)

Poland

[6077]

CHORZEMPA, R.A. In search of Polish roots. Baltimore, Genealogical Publishing, 1993. 262p. illus., maps, pbk. $17.95. ISBN: 0806313781.

Investigates resources in Poland and North America. Chorzempa is Director of the Polish Genealogical Society of America. 'Highly recommended for research' (*Library Journal*, v.118, no.10, 1 June 1993. p.102). *Class No:* 929.50(475)

Sweden

Handbooks & Manuals

[6078]

OLSSON, N.W. Tracing your Swedish ancestry. Stockholm, Almquist & Wiksell, 1985. 26p. map.

First published 1963.

'Brief summary of the most useful Swedish documents for genealogical research, difficulties often encountered, and the addresses of Swedish archives and American institutions of greatest assistance in family history' (L.B. Sather and A. Swanson. *Sweden*, 1987. Entry 315). *Class No:* 929.50(485)(035)

China

Bibliographies

[6079]

TELFORD, T.A., *and others, comps.* Chinese genealogies at the Genealogical Society of Utah: an annotated bibliography. Taipei, Ch'eng Wen Publishing Co., 1983. 50+370p. index.

Covers Chinese class and lineage genealogies and other general works. Items arranged in order of country, province and hsien/shih. Introduction (Chinese genealogies as research sources; the problem of reliability; Chinese genealogies at the Genealogical Society of Utah; surnames; localities; progenitors; chronological distribution; overseas Chinese genealogies; access to the microfilm collection; purpose and arrangement of bibliography) p.1-50. Text (p.1-297) and Locality index (p.297-370) in Chinese script. *Class No:* 929.50(510)(01)

America

Encyclopaedias

[6080]

SCHAEFER, C.K. Genealogical encyclopedia of the Colonial Americas a complete digest of the records of all the countries of the Western hemisphere. Baltimore, MD, Genealogical Publishing Co., 1998. 204p. maps, bibliog., index. $57. £49.95. ISBN: 0806315768.

Covers Spanish, English, French, Portuguese colonies in the Caribbean, the 13 original United States, other states formed before the Revolution, and Canada. Data for each section: map, short history, extant land, military, church, tax etc. records. Web sites for major record repositories are indicated. *Class No:* 929.50(7)(031)

Canada

[6081]

DOUGLAS, A. 'Genealogical research in Canada' *Genealogists' Magazine*, v.23, no.6, June 1990, p.217-21.

Useful introductory guide. Lists Provincial Archives addresses. *Class No:* 929.50(71)

[6082]

WHYTE, D. A Dictionary of Scottish emigrants to Canada before Confederation. Toronto, Ontario Genealogical Society, 1986. xvi, 443p. bibliog., softcover. ISBN: 0920036090.

12501 entries listing name, parentage, place of origin, dates of birth and death, destination, date and ship, occupation, wife/husband parentage, date of marriage, children, sources of information. Bibliography - Guide to the references p.439-43. With dependants not separately listed records over 30000 names. *Class No:* 929.50(71)

Bibliographies

[6083]

MENNIE DE VARENNES, K. Bibliographie annotée d'ouvrages généalogiques au Canada / Annotated bibliography of genealogical works in Canada. Markham, Ontario, Fitzhenry & Whiteside in association with the National Library of Canada and the Canadian Government Publishing Centre, Supply and Services Canada, 6v., 1986. xvi, 2080p.

V.1: 0889029113 has author/title index (p.1-327); index of parishes (p.331-49); subject index (p.443-66); list of periodicals (p.467-70); list of genealogical societies in Canada (p.471-3). Monumental work of inestimable value. *Class No:* 929.50(71)(01)

Handbooks & Manuals

[6084]

BAXTER, A. In search of your roots: a guide for Canadians seeking their ancestors. Toronto, The Macmillan Company of Canada, 1978. 203p. bibliog., index. ISBN: 0770518559.

19 chapters detail all possible sources of pertinent information for every province in Canada and around the world. Bibliography (by chapter) p.277-291. *Class No:* 929.50(71)(035)

Jamaica

[6085]

WRIGHT, P. 'Materials for family history in Jamaica', *Genealogist's Magazine*, v.15, no.7, September 1966, p.239-250.

Discursive essay on the surviving records and monument inscriptions. *Class No:* 929.50(729.2)

Barbados

[6086]

BRANDOW, J., *comp.* Genealogies of Barbados families. Baltimore, Maryland, Genealogical Publishing Co., 1983. 753p. $40. ISBN: 0806310049.

Much material derives from V.L. Oliver: *Caribbeana: being miscellaneous papers relating to the history, genealogy, topography and antiquities of the British West Indies* (London, Mitchell Hughes & Clarke, 6v., 1912) and early issues of the *Journal of the Barbados Museum and Historical Society*.

*c.*100 well known families included. See also C.J. Stanford's 'Genealogical sources in Barbados', *Genealogist's Magazine*, v.17, no.9, March 1974, p.493-8 and no.10, June 1974, p.563-4. *Class No:* 929.50(729.86)

USA

[6087]

The Handbook for genealogists. 9th ed. Logan, UT, Everton Publishers, 1999. 380p. col.maps $34.99. ISBN: 1890895092.

1st ed. 1947.

A popular and comprehensive research aid for locating major State and County records with up-to-date listings of archives, genealogical societies and libraries. State profiles cover history and list map and church records sources. A coloured map is provided for each state. *Class No:* 929.50(73)

[6088]

COLDHAM, P.W. The Complete book of emigrants. Baltimore, Genealogical Publishing, 4v., 1987-93.

1. *1607-1660* (1987). 600p. ISBN 0806311924. $34.95. 2. *1661-1699* (1990). 900p. 0806312823. $49.95. 3. *1700-1750* (1992). 752p. 080631334x. $44.95. 4. *1751-1776* (1993). 357p. 0806313765. $29.95. Definitive list of c.100,000 passengers to the New World throughout the colonial period based on English sources. Arranged by year and date of record. Data: name, age, occupation, residence, ship, destination, and precise source citation. Each volume includes indexes to persons and ships. *Class No:* 929.50(73)

[6089]

FILBY, P.W. *and* MAYER, M.K., *eds*. **Passenger and immigration lists index** a guide to published arrival records of about 500,000 passengers who came to the United States and Canada in the seventeenth, eighteenth, and nineteenth centuries. Detroit, Gale Research Company, 1980-. ISSN: 07368267.

Replaced H. Lancour's *A bibliography of ship passenger lists 1538-1828* (3rd ed., 1963).

2. *1st edition* in 3 vols: A-G; H-N; O-Z. 1981. xxxv, 2339p. £337. 0810310996. This 3 volume base set indexed 300 published sources encompassing over 480,000 people. Sources indexed p.xiii-xxxv. Key to title codes for locating sources on endpapers. 3. *First edition 1982-1985 Cumulated Supplements* in 4 vols: A-E; F-K; L-R; S-Z. 1985. lxviii, 858p.+lxviii, 859-1698p.+lxviii, 1699-2609p.+lxviii, 2610-3404p. £360. $475. 0810317958. Cumulated Supplements, 1991-1995. ISBN 0810383373. 1986-1990. ISBN 0810325799. 1982-85. ISBN 0810317958, Price £406/each cumulated supplement. Latest cumulation is *A Guide to published records of more than 3,430,000 immigrants who came to the New World between the sixteenth and mid-twentieth centuies. 1996-2000.* 3v. 1999. 2340p. $550. £346.50. 0787637211. 2001 Supplement Pt.1: 2000. 575p. $245. £154.35. 0787632805. Pt.2: 2000. 575p. $245. £154.35. 0787632813

Enables researchers to locate ancestors who emigrated to North America and the West Indies in 16th-mid 20th centuries. Main entries contain (1) Name and age of immigrant as given in the original source; (2) year and place of arrival; (3) code indicating the specific source containing the arrival record; (4) page number on which the name appears in original source; (5) names of all accompanying passengers, their age, and their relationship to the main passenger. An insight into the compiler's aims and intention can be gleaned from P.W. Filby 'Passenger and naturalization lists: the new sources', *Reference Quarterly*, v.23, no.2, Winter 1983, p.193-194. *Class No:* 929.50(73)

[6090]

—Passenger and immigration lists index 1538-1940. CD-ROM.

Information on almost 3 million individuals who immigrated to the US. *Class No:* 929.50(73)

[6091]

Genealogy Sourcebook Series. Detroit, Gale Research, 4v., 1995. £159. set. ISBN: 0810385414.

1. *African-American genealogical sourcebook.* 244p. 1995. 0810392267. 'The most professional and extensive genealogical research guide for African Americans published during the last two decades' (*Choice*, v.33,no.3, November 1995, p.429). 2. *Asian American.* 280p. 0810392283. 3. *Hispanic American.* 224p. 0810392275. 4. *Native American.* 218p. 0810392291.

Information in each title includes: Emigration or migration history; Possible problems in interpreting data; Basic genealogical records and their applicability to the ethnic group - family records, census records, church records, etc; Genealogical records specific to the ethnic group; and Directory of genealogical information - archives and libraries, organizations, print sources and other media. *Class No:* 929.50(73)

[6092]

SCHAEFER, C.K. **Guide to naturalization records of the United States.** Baltimore, Md., Genealogical Publishing, 1997. 394p. illus., bibliog. $25. ISBN: 0806315326.

Main section is arranged A-Z by state and includes location of naturalization records, courthouses, county records, types of records, available indexes, and use instruction. Introductory matter encompasses US naturalization laws and the data to be found in declarations of intention, depositions, and certificates of naturalization. 'Since naturalization records are scattered, this book will be essential for genealogists' (*Booklist*, v.93,no./21, July 1997, p.1834). *Class No:* 929.50(73)

[6093]

TEPPER, M., *ed*. **Passengers to America:** a consolidation of ship passenger lists from the New England Historical and Genealogical Register. Baltimore, Genealogical Publishing Co., Inc., 1980. xii, 554p. $20. ISBN: 0806307676. *Class No:* 929.50(73)

[6094]

—TEPPER, M., *ed*. Emigrants to Pennsylvania, 1641-1819: a consolidation of ship passenger lists from the Pennsylvania Magazine of History and Biography. Baltimore, Genealogical Publishing Co., Inc., 1975. x, 292p. $15. ISBN: 0808306823. *Class No:* 929.50(73)

[6095]

—TEPPER, M., *ed*. Immigrants to the middle colonies: a consolidation of ship passenger lists and associated data from the New York Genealogical and Biographical Record. Baltimore, Genealogical Publishing Co., Inc., 1979. xiii, 178p. $12. ISBN: 0808307927. *Class No:* 929.50(73)

[6096]

—TEPPER, M., *ed*. New World immigrants: a consolidation of ship passenger lists and associated data from periodical literature. Baltimore, Genealogical Publishing Co., Inc., 2v. 1980. xxii, 568p.+vii, 602p. index. $40. ISBN: 0806308540.

Index of names and ships. *Class No:* 929.50(73)

CD-ROM

[6097]

ARENDS, M. **Genealogy on CD-ROM.** Baltimore, Genealogical Publishing, 1999. 266p. illus., index. $29.95. ISBN: 0806316233.

Surveys in expert fashion all currently available CD-ROMs of interest to genealogists and local historians. Entry data: title, publisher price, system requirements, and brief description of contents. Arranged by topic (*e.g.* biographies, military records, state and international resources etc.). *Class No:* 929.50(73)(003.40)

[6098]

NICHOLS, E.L. **Genealogy in the computer age:** understanding family search. Salt Lake City, Utah, Family History Educators, 1994. 56p illus., index, pbk. $9.95. ISBN: 1880473070.

Guide to the Family Search CD-ROM indexes produced by the Mormon Church explaining routes through the Ancestral File, the International Genealogical Index, the Social Security death index *etc*. *Class No:* 929.50(73)(003.40)

Internet

[6099]

CROWE, E.P. **Genealogy online** researching your roots. Web edition New York, McGraw-Hill, 1998. xxii,293p. illus., index. $24.95 £18.99. ISBN: 0070147221.

Guide to relevant web-sites. Services covered include the Usene Newsgroups; World Wide Web; Genealogy One: The National Genealogy Society BBS; The church of Latter-day Saints; MSN: the Microsoft Networks Genealogy Forum. One-stop guide to genealogical data available on the Internet. *Class No:* 929.50(73)(003.41)

[6100]

Genealogical archives online city directories of the United States Detroit and Andover, Hants, Gale Research Group (Primary Source Media, 1999.) www.citydirectories.psmedia.com.

A database of 100 US city directories centering on the periods an regions most studied by genealogists and historians. The directorie provide listings of names, occupations, street addresses, churches schools, associations, businesses, and local government and community leaders.

Searchable by full text, first name, last name, and street address etc 'Highly recommended for individuals specific cities and time frame research needs and for libraries, societies and archives' (*Library Journal*, v.124, no.8, 1 May 1999, p.120). *Class No:* 929.50(73)(003.41)

[6101]

SCHAEFER, C.K. **Instant information on the Internet** a genealogist' no-frills guide to the 50 states and District of Columbia. Baltimore Genealogical Publishing, 1999. $9.95. ISBN: 080631608x.

Guide to the most important genealogy sites on the Internet (stat vital records, archives, historical societies, state, regional and loca libraries). 'This is an invaluable index for anyone wishing to explor their ancestry in the U.S. and the information provided on the site gives leads to many other sources' (*Family Tree Magazine*, v.15 no.12, October 1999, p.52). *Class No:* 929.50(73)(003.41)

Bibliographies

[6102]

ACKERMANN, K.T., *ed*. **Genealogical Periodical Annual Index:** ke to the genealogical literature. Bowie, Maryland, Heritage Books, 1963 , Annual.

v.25: *1986* (1987. 256p. $17.50 ISBN 1556130724). A surname locality, topical and book review index to genealogical and related periodical literature (over 260 titles in all). Preceded by D.L. Jacobus' *Index to genealogical periodicals* (Baltimore, Genealogical Publishing Co., 1978. 365p. $17.50). which covers the years up to 1952. *Class No:* 929.50(73)(01)

[6103]

Bibliography of genealogy and local history periodicals with union lis of major US collections. Clegg, M.B., *ed*. Fort Wayne, Ind., Allen County Library Foundation, PERSI Project, 1990. unpaged, index $75.

c.5,500 genealogy and local history periodicals held in 11 libraries are listed A-Z by title under place and family names. The genealogica collections of the Allen County Public Library, Fort Wayne, form th base list. Reproduced from a computer database. *Class No:* 929.50(73)(01)

[6104]

FILBY, P.W., *ed*. **Passenger and immigration lists bibliography. 1538-1900**: being a guide to published lists of arrivals in the United States and Canada. 2nd ed. Detroit, Gale Research Co., 1988. xli, 324p. index. £84. $110. ISBN: 0810327406.

First edition published in 1981. *First Supplement* published 1984. To be used in conjunction with *Passenger and immigration lists index* (*qv*).

Lists over 2500 published sources incorporating those published in *First Supplement*, and adds more than 750 new sources. Numbered and annotated entries are arranged A-Z by author or title. The index provides access to places of emigration, immigration, ship names, ports of departure and arrival, and places of settlement. 'An essential source for research in immigration history, ethnic studies, and genealogy' (*Booklist*, v.85, no.5, 1 November 1988, p.464).
Class No: 929.50(73)(01)

[6105]

HOROWITZ, L. **A Bibliography of military name lists** from pre-1675 to 1900: a guide to genealogical sources. Metuchen, N.J., Scarecrow Press, 1990. xxxvii,1080p. £94.95. ISBN: 0810821664.

6656 briefly annotated entries 'designed to help genealogists and researchers identify a person through his military service' (*Introduction*) arranged in 10 chronological periods corresponding to American wars. Data is from payrolls, muster lists, obituaries, pension and bounty land records *etc*. but not from county or city histories.
Class No: 929.50(73)(01)

[6106]

KEMP, T.J. **The 1995 genealogy annual** a bibliography of published sources. Wilmington, DE, Scholarly Resources, 1995-. Annual. 397p. $95. ISBN: 0842026614.

In 3 parts: 1. Family histories (2/3 of the Annual) - 2. Guides and handbooks (US and international) - 3. Genealogical sources A-Z by state). 'Will in time prove to be a most valuable genealogical resource for worldwide information' (*Booklist*, v.93,no.13, 1 March 1997, p.1195). *Class No: 929.50(73)(01)*

[6107]

KEMP, T.J. **'The Roots of genealogy collections'** *Library Journal*, v.124, no.6, 1 March 1999, p.57-60.

Updates J. Reid's 'Branching out into genealogy', *Library Journal*, 11 January 1992, p.51-55.

'Highlights some of the best books, periodicals, CD-ROMs, and web sites that librarians will find invaluable in assisting genealogical researchers'. *Class No: 929.50(73)(01)*

[6108]

MEYERINK, K.L., *ed*. **Printed sources** a guide to published genealogical records. Salt Lake City, Ancestry, 1998. 840p. bibliog., index. $49.95. ISBN: 0916489701.

4 Sections: 1. reference works - 2. finding aids - 3. printed original records - 4. compiled records (*e.g.* family history). Text explains the nature and origin of printed sources, their content, and how to locate them. 3 appendices: 1. CD-ROMs - 2. Major US genealogical libraries - 3. Genealogical publishers and booksellers. Companion guide to Szucs, L.D. and Luebking, S.H. *The Source : guidebook of American genealogy (q.v.)* *Class No: 929.50(73)(01)*

[6109]

SCHAEFER, C.K. **The Center: a guide to genealogical research in the National Capital Area.** Baltimore, Genealogical Publishing, 1996. 148p. illus., bibliog., indexes. $19.95. ISBN: 0806315156.

Extensive guide to the genealogical research collections in Washington DC and its environs including Federal Government records, the collections of societies and associations, ethnic, cultural and religious groups, military records, and specialist research library collections. Data: address, telephone/fax numbers, public transport details, car parking, access regulations, opening hours, copying facilities. 'A truly valuable resource; libraries with genealogy collections will find it an important addition' (*Booklist*, v.93,no.4, 15 October 1996, p.448-49). *Class No: 929.50(73)(01)*

[6110]

UEBRICK-PACHELI, W. **'Select bibliography of genealogical research aids published by the National Archives and Records Administration'**, *Reference Services Review*, v.15, no.1, Spring 1987, p.43-45.

Descriptive guide to major NARA publications.
Class No: 929.50(73)(01)

[6111]

YOUNG, T.M. **Afro-American genealogy sourcebook.** New York, Garland, 1987. ix,199p. illus. $39. ISBN: 0824086848.

Lists and describes the most often used resources in genealogy and family history research of African-Americans. Arranged in 4 parts: 1. Background reading and basic reference sources - 2. Private resources - 3. Public records - 4. Directory of resources.
Class No: 929.50(73)(01)

Handbooks & Manuals

[6112]

GREENWOOD, V.D. **The Researcher's guide to American genealogy.** 2nd ed. Baltimore, Genealogical Publishing Co., Inc., 1990. 623p. illus. facsims. tables, index. $24.95.

24 well-documented chapters *e.g.* 5. An introduction to research tools: reference materials ... 11. Using census returns ... 16. Local land records, identify and evaluate the various types of records. The final chapter is on Canadian research. 'The most comprehensive how-to book on American genealogical and local history research' (*Library Journal*, v.99, no.12, 15 June 1974, p.1692).
Class No: 929.50(73)(035)

[6113]

LAW, H.T. **How to trace your ancestors to Europe:** 117 stories of how ancestors were traced to their birthplaces in 20 European countries. Salt Lake City, Cottonwood Books, 1987. 422p. illus. map. indexes. $19. ISBN: 0935775013.

Pt.1. Case studies of 117 successful searches for the home towns of European ancestors. Pt.2. Research methods and outline of 46 United States resource centres *Class No: 929.50(73)(035)*

[6114]

SMITH, J.C. **Ethnic genealogy** a research guide. Westport, Conn., Greenwood Press, 1983. xxxix, 440p. $46.95. ISBN: 0313225931.

Part 1. General information on sources, procedures, and genealogical research. Part 2. Utilizing major repositories with chapters on The National Archives and Records Services p.123-173 and The Genealogical Society of Utah Library p.175-205. Part 3. comprises separate chapters on American-Indian, Asian-American, Black American, and Hispanic American records and research. Each chapter is fully documented and equipped with an extended bibliography. Index p.403-435. 'The work is particularly helpful in identifying the location of resources that should be used to support the research' (*Choice*, v.21, no.8, April 1984, p.1110).
Class No: 929.50(73)(035)

[6115]

SZUCS, L.D. *and* LUEBKING, S.H., *comps*. **The Source** a guidebook of American genealogy. rev. ed. Salt Lake City, Ancestry Publishing Co., 1997. 846p. illus., facsims., maps., tables, bibliogs. $49.95. ISBN: 0916489671.

1st ed. 1984.

Chapter essays identify major record sources; published general sources; and special records (immigrant, urban, Indian, Spanish, Negro, Asian, Jewish). Appendix A. Regional Federal archives and record centres - B. State historical archives and record depositories - C. Historical societies and agencies in the US - D. Genealogical Society of Utah and branches - E. Selected research libraries - F. Where to write for vital records - G. Genealogical societies of the US - H. Genealogy book publishers. Chapter bibliographies. 'Compact yet wide-ranging, this authoritative work must surely remain the definitive textbook on genealogy in the United States for much time to come' (*Genealogists Magazine*, v.21, no.7, September 1984, p.256). 'Librarians can use *The Source* as a way of navigating the information on the Web by identifying types of date, titles of resources, and appropriate agencies prior to an internet search' (*Booklist*, v.95, no.17, 1 May 1999, p.1820). *Class No: 929.50(73)(035)*

Glossaries

[6116]

BENTLEY, E.P. **The Genealogist's address book.** 4th ed. Baltimore, Md., Genealogical Publishing Co., 1998. 442p. index, pbk. $39.95. ISBN: 0806315806.

1st ed. 1991.

Lists over 25,000 national and state genealogical: organizations: 1. National (including National Archives and its regional centres, government departments and agencies) - 2. State listings of vital records offices, county and regional archives, libraries and societies - 3. Ethnic archives *etc*. - 4. Special resources (hereditary societies, adoption information, immigration research centres *etc*.) - 5. Periodicals and newsletters. New to this edition are E-mail addresses and websites. 'Essential for institutions or individuals seriously pursuing genealogical research' (*Library Journal*, v.116,no.1, January 1991, p.88). *Class No: 929.50(73)(038.1)*

Yearbooks & Directories

[6117]

EICHHOLZ, A., *ed*. **Ancestry's red book:** American, state, county and town sources. Rev. ed. Salt Lake City, Ancestry, 1992. 858p. maps, bibliog., index. $49.95. ISBN: 0916489477.

1st ed. 1989.

Comprehensive guide to genealogical research resources arranged A-Z by State. All types of record are within its ambit and it also acts as a location guide for newspapers and periodicals, and private manuscript collections, and as a directory of archives, libraries and genealogical and historical societies. Special attention is given to

....(contd.)

immigration, naturalization and various ethnic groups. 'It becomes the new standard, quick-reference handbook for American genealogy' (*Library Journal*, v.115, no.7, 15 April 1990, p.80). *Class No:* 929.50(73)(058)

[6118]

MacSORLEY, M.E. Genealogical sources in the United States of America. Basingstoke, Hants, M.E. MacSorley, 1995. 112p. £6.

Research guide for UK researchers. Concentrates on pre-1620 era, British colonization, settlement, and immigration. Details location of State archives and public libraries, the National Archives and its 12 regional offices. *Class No:* 929.50(73)(058)

Archives

[6119]

Guide to genealogical research in the National Archives. Washington, National Archives Trust Fund Board, 1983. xiii, 304p. illus. geneal. tables, maps. $35. ISBN: 0911333002.

Supersedes *Guide to genealogical records in the National Archives* compiled by M.B. Colket and F.E. Bridgers (1964).

20 chapters: 1. Census records ... 2. Passenger arrival lists ... 12 Records of Black Americans ... 20. Cartographical records grouped in 4 sections, population and immigration, military, particular groups, and miscellaneous. Introduction (p.1-38) includes notes on the value and limitations of Federal records, research methods and aims, and the National Archives' resources and research facilities. Selected as an outstanding reference source by the American Library Association. *Class No:* 929.50(73)(093.20)

Hispanic Peoples

[6120]

RYSKAMP, G.R. Finding your Hispanic roots. Baltimore, MD, Genealogical Publishing, 1997. 290p. pbk. $19.95. ISBN: 0806315172.

'The most comprehensive manual on Hispanic ancestry discusses the basic records available and research techniques' (*Library Journal*, 1 April 1999, p.60). *Class No:* 929.50(73)(=60)

Libraries

[6121]

Directory of American libraries with genealogy or local history collections. Filby, P.W., *comp.* Wilmington, Delaware, Scholarly Resources, 1988. 319p. index. $75. ISBN: 0842022864.

A-Z State by State, town by town directory of US and Canadian libraries and archives. 'Even though admittedly incomplete ... a must purchase for libraries serving genealogists' (*Wilson Library Bulletin*, v.63, no.1, September 1988, p.95). *Class No:* 929.50(73):061:026/027

[6122]

PARKER, J.C. Library service for genealogists. Detroit, Gale Research Company, 1981. xii, 362p. $68. ISBN: 0810314894.

24 Chapters: 2. Collection development ... 6. How-to-do-it books - 7. Vital records - 8. Finding family histories - 9. Genealogical name indexes - 10. Genealogical periodicals and periodical indexes ... 12. Census schedules - 13. Finding county and city histories ... 15. Sources listing ancestors as individuals. Index p.311-362. *Class No:* 929.50(73):061:026/027

America—South

Handbooks & Manuals

[6123]

DE PLATT, L. Genealogical historical guide to Latin America. Detroit, Gale Research Co., 1978. xvi, 273p. tables, index. $68. (*Genealogy and Local History Series, no.4*.) ISBN: 0810313898.

29 chapters: 1. Research standards - 2. Civil registration - 3. Ecclesiastical records - 4. Palaeography - 5. Abbreviations used during 15th, 16th, 17th centuries - 5. Research aids - 7. Colonial calendar - 8. Ecclesiastical divisions of Latin America 1492-1912 (bibliog.) - 9. Popular movements - 10. Political divisions - 11-29. Latin America A-Z by country. *Class No:* 929.50(8)(035)

Australia

Handbooks & Manuals

[6124]

HAWKINGS, D.T. Bound for Australia. Chichester, Sussex, Phillimore, 1987. xvi, 269p. illus., facsims., tables, bibliog., index. £12.85. ISBN: 0850336147.

Guide in 9 chapters 'to enable the descendent of a convict to trace his ancestor and to discover as much as possible about that individual's

....(contd.)

personal life and crime; his (or her) journey to New South Wales; and his (or her) life in the colony' (*Preface*). Favourably received in *Archives* v.18, no.79, April 1988, p.175-6. *Class No:* 929.50(94)(035)

[6125]

McCLAUGHLIN, T. From shamrock to wattle digging up your Irish ancestors. Sydney, Collins, 1985. 162p. illus., facsims., gen. tables bibliog., index. pbk. ISBN: 0002173301.

Directs Australian family historians to available source material in Australia and Ireland. Bibliography p.145-53. *Class No:* 929.50(94)(035)

[6126]

REAKES, J. How to trace your convict ancestors their lives, times & records. Sydney, Hale & Iremonger, 1987. 71p. illus. ISBN 086806274x.

17 chapters *e.g.*. 2. Trials ... 3. Hulks ... 4. The voyage... 5 Assignment ... 8. Musters ... 9. Pardons ... 16. Books ... 17 Addresses guide the researcher through the key events in a convict's life, discussing the records most useful to family historians. Glossary p.67-69. *Class No:* 929.50(94)(035)

Jews

Bibliographies

[6127]

The Encyclopedia of Jewish genealogy Vol.1. Sources in the United States and Canada. Kurzweil, A. *and* Weiner, M., *eds.* Northvale, N.J., Jason Aronson, 1991. xxii,226p. bibliogs., index. $30; £16.95. ISBN: 0876688350.

1st of 3v. V.2 will cover sources in Europe, Australia and South America; v.3 will be arranged by topic *e.g.* The Holocaust; Sephardic Jewry.

1. Immigration and naturalization - 2. Institution resources in US (A-Z x state and city) - 3. Canadian resources. Extensive appendices include directories of Jewish genealogical and historical societies worldwide; Federal archives and research centres; and French German, Hungarian, and Polish-Jewish records in the Salt Lake City Family History Library. *Class No:* 929.50(=924)(01)

20th Century

Bibliographies

[6128]

SCHAEFER, C.K. The Great War a guide to the service record of all the world's fighting men and women. Baltimore, Md, Genealogical Publishing, 1998. 189p. illus., map, bibliog., index. $22.50. ISBN: 0806315547.

3 parts: 1. Military organizations and types of record available - 2. Nations involved A-Z. Each entry includes brief description of country's war time role and its records - 3. War's aftermath including new political boundaries. 'Schaefer has done an excellent job in getting this information and presenting it clearly. Highly recommended for genealogical collections' (*Library Journal*, v.123,no.19, 15 Nov 1998, p.62). *Class No:* 929.50"19"(01)

Family Histories

[6129]

BARDSLEY, A., *comp.* First name variants. Birmingham, Federation of Family History Societies, 1998. £4.95. ISBN: 1860060242.

Based on census records, parish registers, and printed directories, this list includes 8,000 variants of 1,300 names. *Class No:* 929.52

Databases

[6130]

BRADLEY, A. Family history on your PC a book for beginners. Wilmslow, Cheshire, Sigma Press, 1996. vii,221p. pbk. £9.95. ISBN: 1850585024.

1. Introduction - 2. Basics of family history - 3. Family history with a computer - 4. Centralised bureaucracy ... 10. Writing up. Appendix 1. Useful addresses - 2. Further reading (p.210-13) - 3. Chapman County Code (for pre-1974 counties). Sound basic guide to processes and records for computer literate family historians. *Class No:* 929.52(003.4)

Internet

[6131]

HAWGOOD, D. **Families on the Internet.** D. Hawgood and Federation of Family History Societies, 1999. 16p. £1.50.

Describes the key features of the www.familysearch.org website of the Church of Jesus Christ of Latter-day Saints, Salt Lake City, offering practical advice, guidance and tips for making best use of the system. 'An invaluable guide for those wishing to fully exploit the facilities of FamilySearch' (*Family Tree Magazine,* v.16, no.1, November 1999, p.39). *Class No:* 929.52(003.41)

Handbooks & Manuals

[6132]

HEY, D. **The Oxford guide to family history.** Oxford, Oxford Univ. Press, 1993. x,246p. illus. (a few col.), facsims, bibliog., indexes. £19.95. ISBN: 0198691777.

1. Study of family history - 2. Family names - 3. Mobility and stability - 4. Family and society - 5. Guide to the records. Bibliography p.231-6. Both a social history and a practical introductory guide to relevant records and their location. *Class No:* 929.52(035)

[6133]

LYNSKEY, M. **Family trees** a manual for their design, layout and display. Chichester, Phillimore, 1996. v,102p. illus., coats of arms, geneal tables (some col.), bibliog., index. £13.95. ISBN: 0850339804.

Detailed guide to the various ways to lay out and draw up a genealogical chart. No aspect of pedigree preparation and presentation is overlooked. Bibliography p.100. *Class No:* 929.52(035)

Worldwide

Internet

[6134]

Family Search Internet Genealogy Service. Salt Lake City, Utah, Church of Jesus Christ of Latter-day Saints, 1999. www.familysearch.org.

Contains 400 million names drawn from databases, public records and libraries. A major source is the International Genealogical Index, 'a massive 320 million records of births, christenings and marriages for more than 600 million people who lived between the 1500s and the early 1900s'. (*The Times,* 66,577, 27 July 1999, p.38). *Class No:* 929.52(100)(003.41)

Handbooks & Manuals

[6135]

CURRER-BRIGGS, N. **Worldwide family history.** London, Routledge & Kegan Paul, 1982. ix, 230p. maps. ISBN: 0710009348.

Explains how English-speaking people of foreign descent can begin tracing their ancestors. Part 1. describes the history and archives of Europe, Islam, China, and Japan. Part 2. deals with colonial shipping in the seventeenth and eighteenth centuries, the settlement of the Americas, including chapters on Anglo-Saxon, Dutch, Scandinavian, German, Polish, French, Spanish, Italian, Greek and Slav emigrants, and a record of the early European settlement of South Africa, Australia, and New Zealand. Appendix 1. Heraldry and genealogical research; 2. Chief sources of information in the form of a combined bibliography and list of addresses for Europe and the United States. *Class No:* 929.52(100)(035)

Europe

[6136]

DE RANDECK, J.H. **Les plus anciennes familles du monde** Répertoire encyclopédique des 1,400 plus anciennes familles du monde, encore existantes, originaires d'Europe. Genève, Éditions Slatkine, 2v., 1984. 1636p. ISBN: 2051005575.

Family history in brief with 'significant' persons enumerated A-Z by family. Strongest criterion for inclusion is longevity and continuity (not, it is claimed, nobility, power, wealth). *Class No:* 929.52(4)

Great Britain

[6137]

PRICE, V.J. **Register offices of births, deaths and marriages in Great Britain and Northern Ireland.** 2nd ed. Southport, Brewin Books, 1996. 37p; index. £3.95. ISBN: 1858580218.

1st ed. 1991.

A-Z index by counties and towns plus an index to place-names in 5 separate sequences for England, Wales, Northern Ireland, Scotland, and the Isle of Man. Also information on procedures to follow. *Class No:* 929.52(410)

[6138]

Sources and methods for family and community historians a handbook. Drake, M. *and* Finnegan, R., *eds.* Cambridge Univ. Press in association with The Open Univ., 1994. xiv,322p. illus., tables, bibliog., index. (*Studying Family and Community History 19th and 20th Centuries, no.4.*) ISBN: 0521460042.

22 contributors. 'Offers guidance on sources, research strategies and techniques, the relevant libraries and archives, and how to present research findings' in 13 chapters divided into 5 sections: 1. Some basics (Questions and strategies for research - primary sources) - 2. Using sources - 3. Methods and techniques - 4. Presentation, dissemination and publication - 5. Locating sources and references (Guide to record offices, libraries *etc.* - Selected reference and bibliographical resources). Appendix: Some key dates p.307-314. *Class No:* 929.52(410)

[6139]

TARVER, A. **Church court records:** an introduction for family and local historians. Chichester, Phillimore, 1995. xvi,143p. facsims, map, bibliog., indexes. £12.95. ISBN: 0850339278.

Introduction (problems, finding record offices and documents, process of law, language and handwriting) - 1. Process of law - 2. Official business - 3. Probate and testamentary business - 4. Marriage - 5. Tithes and Easter offerings - 6. Defamation. Chapter notes p.125-29. Table of Affinity p.131. Bibliography p.132-33. Glossary of Latin words and phrases p.134-35. English legal and technical terms p.136-38. *Class No:* 929.52(410)

[6140]

TITFORD, J. **'Emigration from Britain** a selected list of printed, microform and CD-ROM sources', *Family Tree Magazine,* v.13,no.1, November 1996, p.9-10; no.3, January 1997, p.25-26.

Enumerates sources that feature and name emigrants from UK to North America, Australia and New Zealand, South Africa, and the West Indies. *Class No:* 929.52(410)

[6141]

WOOD, T. **Record Offices for family historians.** 2nd ed. Bury, Federation of Family History Societies, 1999. 16p. bibliog. (*Basic Facts About....*) ISBN: 1860061095.

1st ed. 1996.

Introduction (national collections, the Public Record Office, Diocesan and County record offices, Libraries, museums and heritage centres, Family History Centres, Family History Societies) - Preparation beforehand - Reserving a research place - Do's and don'ts - Rules and regulations - Using time effectively - Getting help - Making notes - Alternatives to County Record Offices - Useful addresses. Bibliography p.15-16. *Class No:* 929.52(410)

Bibliographies

[6142]

British Family history London, the British Library, 1998. 20p. sd. *gratis.* (*Humanities Reader Guide no. 5.*)

First issued 1981.

Purpose is 'to help readers to find published genealogical sources in the humanities collections of the British Library'. Material listed includes bibliographies, guides, family histories, parish registers, biographical records, poll books and electoral registers, wills, libraries and record offices, and societies. *Class No:* 929.52(410)(01)

[6143]

FEDERATION OF FAMILY HISTORY SOCIETIES. **Current publications by member societies.** 2nd ed. Doncaster, FFHS, 1984. 32p. £1.25.

List of publications issued by The Society of Genealogists, The Heraldry Society, Institute of Heraldic and Genealogical Studies, local societies, A-Z, and of FFHS. *Class No:* 929.52(410)(01)

[6144]

THOMSON, T.R., *comp.* **A Catalogue of British family histories.** 3rd ed. with addenda by G. Barrow. London, Research Publishing Co., in conjunction with the Society of Genealogists, 1980. 229p. £6. ISBN: 0705000974.

First published 1928.

Nearly 2000 entries Abbot-Yvery. Entries are asterisked if items are privately printed. 'Purports to be a complete list of British Family histories' (*Preface*). 3rd edition includes 'Addenda', Acland-Yeamans (p.185-229). *Class No:* 929.52(410)(01)

Handbooks & Manuals

[6145]

COLE, J.A. *and* TITFORD, J. **Tracing your family tree:** the complete guide to discovering your family history. 2nd ed. Newbury Countryside Books, 1997. 208p. illus., maps, tables, bibliog., index. pbk. £9.99. ISBN: 1853064483.

1st ed. published by Equation 1988.

1. Where and how to start - 2. Civil registration of births, marriages and deaths - 3. The Census returns - 4. Parish registers - 5. Non-

....*(contd.)*

conformists and their records - 6. Wills and administrations - 7. Parish records, civil records, poor law, Quarter Sessions records and records of the Clerk of the Peace - 8. County Record Offices - 9. The Church of Jesus Christ of Later Day Saints and the International Genealogical Index - 10. Manorial records - 11. Directories and newspapers - 12. Miscellaneous sources - 13. The Public Record Office - 14. Genealogical societies. Appendix: Some useful dates for the family historian; some miscellaneous terms, abbreviations and colloquialisms; regnal years; useful addresses etc. p.195-204. Bibliography p.175-190. Glossary p.191-194. 'A complete workbook for the would-be genealogist'. *Class No:* 929.52(410)(035)

[6146]

COLWELL, S. The Family history book a guide to tracing your ancestors. 2nd rev. ed. Oxford, Phaidon, 1989. 192p. illus. genealogical tables, maps, bibliog. £14.95. ISBN: 0714825948.

1. Genealogy in the past and its uses; 2. Tracing your ancestors; 3. Using your sources; 4. How our ancestors lived; 5. Emigration and travel; 6. The study of names; 7. Heraldry. Appendix 1. Calendar of dates; 2. Registration Districts 1837-1851 and 1852-1946; 3. Useful addresses. *Class No:* 929.52(410)(035)

[6147]

COX, J. and COLWELL, S. Never been here before? A genealogist's guide to the Family Records Centre. Richmond, Sy., Public Record Office, 1997. vi,113p. illus., facsims., geneal. tables, bibliog. £5.99 (*Readers Guide, no.17.*) ISBN: 1873162413.

'An admirable, user-friendly guide to the FRC, written with clarity throughout, complete with maps of the floors, tabular summaries of specific collections, procedures for gaining access to the documents, charges where they are levied, in addition to numerous illustrations of typical examples of the millions of records held on-site' (*Archives.* v.23,no.99, October 1998, p.183) Bibliography p.112-13. *Class No:* 929.52(410)(035)

[6148]

COX, J. New to Kew? a first time guide for family historians at the Public Record Office, Kew Richmond, Sy., Public Record Office, 1997. vi,128p. illus., facsims, map, bibliog. £5.99. (*Readers Guide, no.16.*)

1. Introduction (vital sources elsewhere, International Genealogical Index, Society of Genealogists, Federation of Family History Societies etc.) - 2. Using P.R.O. at Kew (the building, what to do first) - 3. Records A-Z (27 categories *e.g.* apprenticeship records, change of names). Bibliography p.125-6. Useful addresses p.128. *Class No:* 929.52(410)(035)

[6149]

Debrett's guide to tracing your family tree. Currer-Briggs, N. and Gambier, R. Rev. ed. London, Headline, 1999. 152p. illus. (some col.), geneal tables, bibliog., maps. ISBN: 0747223319.

First published by Webb & Bower 1982.

17 chapters (*e.g.*1. Family History yesterday and today ... 8. Dating - 9. Celtic ancestors ... 14. Emigration). 16 maps. 4 Appendices: 1. Useful dates - 2. Checklist of genealogical sources 3. Useful addresses - 4. Recommended reading. *Class No:* 929.52(410)(035)

[6150]

The Family historian's enquire within. 5th ed. Birmingham, Federation of Family History Societies, 1995. 287p. illus., maps, bibliog., index. ISBN: 187209483x.

1st ed. 1985. Hardback edition published as *Tracing your ancestors.*

Invaluable compendium of definitions, explanations, record sources, locations, societies, publications, bibliographies, dates, *etc.* Appendix 1. PRO Records at Kew and Chancery Lane - 2. PRO Information Series pamphlets in numerical order p.257-60. 3. Units of the British Army - 4. Chapman country codes illustrating county boundaries before/after 1974-75. 8 maps 'Both an encyclopaedia and an omnium gatherum of sources and extinct occupations, with many references to publications on specific topics' (*Refer,* v.4, no.1, Spring 1984, p.16). *Class No:* 929.52(410)(035)

[6151]

PELLING, G. Beginning your family history. 5th ed. Newbury, Berkshire, Countryside Books in association with The Federation of Family History Societies, 1990. 80p. illus., facsims, bibliogs, index. £3.50. ISBN: 1853060844.

First published by FFHS 1980.

The aim of the fifth edition remains to provide the beginner with preliminary information on family sources, instructions on how to construct a pedigree chart, and with notes on the various types of source materials, their location, access and usefulness, necessary to research back to the sixteenth century. Chapter bibliographies and a comprehensive list of FFHS publications. *Class No:* 929.52(410)(035)

Dictionaries

[6152]

HEY, D. The Oxford dictionary of local and family history. Oxford Univ. Press, 1997. 297p. bibliog. £5.99. ISBN: 0198600801.

Quick reference tool of 1,500 A-Z entries encompassing legal and specialist terms, types of documentation and sources of information, institutions and organizations, historical and political events, family history records etc. Lists regnal years, Saint's days, locations of all UK national and local record offices. Bibliography arranged under thematic headings (demography, landscape history, publishers' series, agrarian history, academic journals etc.) p.286-97. *Class No:* 929.52(410)(038)

Scotland

[6153]

FULTON, A. Scotland and her tartans the romantic heritage of the Scottish clans and families. London, Hodder & Stoughton, 1991. 224p. col. illus., index. £14.99. ISBN: 0340572086.

Main section 'Clans and family tartans' (p.46-209) provides descriptive and historical notes on clans A-Z with Branches, Tartans and Motto. Col. illus. of 265 authentic tartan sets. Also The clan tradition - Kinship of the clan - Highland dress - The '45 rebellion - Suppression and dispersal - Wearing the tartan - Tracing your Scottish ancestry. *Class No:* 929.52(411)

[6154]

JAMES, A. Scottish roots a step-by-step guide for ancestor hunters. Rev.ed. Edinburgh, The Saltire Society, 1995. 159p. facsims. £4.99. ISBN: 0854110666.

First published 1981 by MacDonald Publishers.

Practical guide for would-be family historians starting from scratch: At home - New Register House - Scottish Record Office - Libraries - On location - Museums of Scotland - Doing it from a distance - Getting it all down. *Class No:* 929.52(411)

[6155]

MacLEAN, C. The Clan Almanac: an account of the origins of the principal tribes of Scotland. Illustrated with examples of the tartans adopted by each. Moffat, Lochar Publishing, 1990. 142p. col. illus., bibliog. £5.95. ISBN: 094840339x.

Definitive A-Z list of the clans and names of Scotland giving origin of names; lands; principal branches; slogan and motto; heraldic badge; leading figures; and tartan. Appendix 1. Clans, septs and dependants - 2. The Chief of clans and names - 3. Clan societies. Bibliography p.144. Pocket book size. *Class No:* 929.52(411)

[6156]

URQUHART, B., ed. Identifying tartans: the new compact study and identifier. London, Apple Press, 1994. 80p. col.illus., bibliog. £4.99. ISBN: 1850764999.

Contents: Origins of clans tartans - Using the guide - Sources of the earliest tartans - Glossary (p.79) - References and further reading (p.79-80) - Collections to visit. 140 clan and family tartans. Data: earliest known date and recorded source; status; type; notes; col. illustrations. *Class No:* 929.52(411)

CD-ROM

[6157]

The Clans and tartans of Scotland CD-ROM. Irvine, Sgian Dhu Interactive, 1998. Windows 3.1 or later. 486/33 Mhz or greater. 4 MBytes. £29.95.

130 full clan histories covering 700 family names and 2,000p. of information. Main screen options: clans, clan septs, maps, history, story of tartans, the clan system. 'Altogether an entertaining program, intended as a genealogical guide to the subject, but the serious student of Scottish history would find it very limiting' (*Family Tree Magazine,* v.15,no.1, November 1998, p.30). *Class No:* 929.52(411)(003.40)

Bibliographies

[6158]

FERGUSON, J.P., comp. Scottish family histories. 2nd ed. Edinburgh, National Library of Scotland, 1986. xii, 254p. £14.95. ISBN: 0902220683.

Scottish family histories held in Scottish libraries first published Edinburgh, Scottish Central Library, 1960.

Lists some 3200 works. This edition incorporates periodical articles and the holdings of the National Library of Scotland. Cooperating libraries are included in Key to Library Codes (p.x-xii). *Class No:* 929.52(411)(01)

Encyclopaedias

[6159]

WAY, G. *and* SQUIRE, R. **Collins Scottish clan and family encyclopedia.** Glasgow, Harper Collins. 1994. 512p. col.illus., col.maps, bibliog., index. £25. ISBN: 0004705475.

6 contributors. 4 Introductory essays by different hands: Clanship a historical perspective; Law of the clan; Tartan and the Highland dress; and Heraldry. Member clans of the Standing Council of Scottish chiefs p.63-343 (Data: Arms, Crest, Motto, Supporters, Standard, Brief history). The Armigerious clans and family of Scotland p.345-475 (Data: Arms, Crest, Motto, Brief history). Appendix 1. Chronology 400-1886 - 2. Scottish monarchs to 1707 - 3. Glossary of heraldic terms p.482-92 - 4. A-Z List of Scottish names associated with clans and families - 5. Genealogy in Scotland - 6. Commission by the Lord Lyon King of Arms in favour of the creann-cach. List of sources p.11. 2 maps: Old Counties of Scotland; Traditional clan territories. The definitive single volume reference work on the Scottish clans. *Class No:* 929.52(411)(031)

Handbooks & Manuals

[6160]

DAM, F. **The Clans, septs and regiments of the Scottish Highlands.** 8th ed. revised by Sir Thomas Innes of Learney. Edinburgh & London, Johnston & Bacon, 1970. 692p. illus. (pl.), map. £17.50. ISBN: 0717945006.

First published 1908.

6 parts: 1. History of the clan system - 2. Structure of the clan system - 3. Celtic culture - 4. Highland forces - 5. Clan insignia and heraldry - 6. Clan lists and culture. 17 plates and 56p. of tartans (112). Clan map of Scotland. A standard, well-documented account. *Class No:* 929.52(411)(035)

[6161]

MOODY, D. **Scottish family history.** London, B.T. Batsford, 1988. 219p. bibliog. index. £14.95. ISBN: 0713477244.

7 chaps: 1. The humble and the mighty: sources of biography - 2. Working lives - 3. Living, dying, moving house: the study of demography - 4. Kin, clan and community - 5. Exploring local society - 6. Culture and beliefs - 7. Family, church and state. Chapter bibliographies p.179-205. References p.206-213. Analytical index. *Class No:* 929.52(411)(035)

[6162]

Scottish clans & tartans **History of each Clan and full list of Septs.** London, New Orchard, 1991. 55p.+ 96 double pages print and col. illus. map. ISBN: 0850791635.

First published c.1891.

Concise guide to Gaelic language, highland dress, clan ceremonial, armorial bearings, clan systems *etc.* introduces 96 double pages each giving short history and colour illustration of individual clan tartans. *Class No:* 929.52(411)(035)

Ireland

[6163]

Burke's Irish family records. Montgomery-Massingberd, H.J. London, Burke's Peerage, 1976. 1300p.

Previously as *Burke's Genealogical and heraldic history of landed gentry of Ireland*, first published 1899; 4th ed. 1958.

The genealogical histories of 514 Irish families, Acton ... Yeats (*c.*100 of Celtic origin), from their earliest recorded male ancestor down to the present day. Includes biographical entries for each member of the family (living and dead). Full cross-references. Addenda, p.1235-7. *Class No:* 929.52(415)

[6164]

DAVIS, B. **An Introduction to Irish research.** Irish ancestry: a beginner's guide. 2nd ed. Birmingham, Federation Of Family History Societies, 1992. viii,100p. map, facsims., bibliog., index. ISBN: 1872094910.

1st ed. 1992.

1. Basics of Irish research - 2. Postal research - 3. Irish exodus - 4. The search begins - 5. Archives - 6. Records - 7. Worldwide Irish research. Appendix A. Heritage and research centres in Ireland - B. Useful addresses - C. Records and their sources - D. Bibliography (p.92-95). *Class No:* 929.52(415)

[6165]

GREENHAM, J. **Clans and families of Ireland** heritage and heraldry. Dublin: Gill & Macmillan, 1993. 184p., col. illus. I£12.99. ISBN: 0717120325.

A-Z listing of 200 family names, with short notes on their derivations, origins, and history, complemented with chapters on immigration, emigration, and Irish heraldry. *Class No:* 929.52(415)

[6166]

MACLYSAGHT, E. **Irish families** their names, arms and origins. 4th ed. Dublin, Hodges Figgis, 1978. 368p.

The main sequence is A-Z by family name ignoring prefixes 'O' and 'Mac'; it deals with names and origins. Coloured plates illustrate almost 250 Irish family arms and crests, with descriptive captions. Bibliography (p.316-38), in 2 parts: 1. Irish family histories: 2. General (including 'Periodicals containing much material for family history'); County, diocesan and local histories. Detailed index. The author was formerly Chief Herald of Ireland. *Class No:* 929.52(415)

[6167]

—MACLYSAGHT, E. **More Irish families** a new revised and enlarged edition ... incoporating Supplement to Irish families, with an essay on Irish chieftainries. Dublin, Irish Academic Press, 1982. 254p. port., maps, bibliog.

More Irish families first published by Gorman in 1960; *Supplement* by Helicon Press in 1964.

Forms single companion volume to *Irish families*. A-Z sequence by family name extending coverage p.21-213. Appendix 1. Additional information for articles in the basic work; 3. The commonest English, Scottish and Welsh surnames in modern Ireland; 4. Explanation of technical terms used in text; and 5. Bibliography of works relating to the Irish abroad p.232-233. Maps and index to maps p.235-243; Index p.244-254. *Class No:* 929.52(415)

[6168]

RYAN, J.G. **Irish records:** sources for family and local history. 2nd ed. Oram, Utah, Ancestry Publishing, 1997. 666p. $49.95.

1st ed. 1989.

Listing of sources for all Irish counties (census records, church registers, local family histories, commercial and social directories, gravestone inscriptions etc.). Also gives information on the Irish Genealogical Research Project (IGP). 'Every country should be so fortunate as to have such a well-written, comprehensive, and easy to use guide, which covers Ireland and Northern Ireland and spells out the key genealogical sources' (*Library Journal,* 1 April 1999, p.60. *Class No:* 929.52(415)

[6169]

YURDAN, M. **Irish family history.** London, B.T. Batsford, 1990. xii,194p. maps, bibliog., index. £14.95. ISBN: 0713462752.

Guidance on where to find relevant archives and on how to interpret the records available in 8 chapters e.g. 2. The leaving of Ireland - 3. Making a start with research - 4. The ancestor abroad. Conclusion: the future of Irish Family History Research p.168-71. Key dates in Irish history p.ix-xi. Glossary p.172-5. Useful addresses p.176-86. Bibliography p.187-91. *Class No:* 929.52(415)

Bibliographies

[6170]

MACLYSAGHT, E. **Bibliography of Irish family history.** 2nd ed. Shannon, Irish Academic Press, 1982. 71p. pbk. £2. ISBN: 071650507x.

Previously published in the author's *The Surnames of Ireland* (4th edition, revised and corrected 1978) but omitted from the 5th edition (1980). It was first issued as a separate publication in 1981 and is reissued in a 2nd edition revised and expanded.

850 entries A-Z by family. 'The reader is also advised to consult the list of reports in the National Library on manuscript collections in private keeping given in *Analecta Hibernica* v.XXII, p.371-387: these are supplementary to those in print in other numbers of *Analecta Hibernica* which are included in this bibliography' (Foreword). *Class No:* 929.52(415)(01)

Northern Ireland

[6171]

MAXWELL, I. **Tracing your ancestors in Northern Ireland.** a guide to ancestry research in the Public Record Office of Northern Ireland. Edinburgh, The Stationery Office, 1997. xiii,121p. illus., bibliog., index. ISBN: 0114958238.

Comprehensive overview in 29 sections of the records held in the Public Record Office of Northern Ireland. Covering national and local government, churches, courts, businesses and families through birth records, marriage licenses and death certificates, census reports, school registries, deed registrations, hospital and emigration files, voter and military records, wills and maps, and Royal Irish Constabulary records. Bibliography p.98-99. 'Will be of enormous help to researchers to follow their ancestry through Ulster back to Scotland ... here at last we have a comprehensive guide' (*Journal of the Society of Archivists,* v.19,no.2, October 1998, p.247-8). *Class No:* 929.52(416)

[6172]

O'NEILL, R.K. **Ulster libraries, archives, museums and ancestral heritage centres.** Belfast, Ulster Historical Foundation, 1997. xiv,178p. index. softcover. £6.99. ISBN: 0901905798.

Hints to visitors p.xii-xiv. A-Z by location. Data: contact information, hours and access, resources, sources, references, special collections, publications. *Class No:* 929.52(416)

Archives

[6173]

NEILL, K. **How to trace family history in Northern Ireland.** Belfast, Irish Heritage Association and Lisburn, Co. Antrim, B.Q. Publications, 1986. 92p. spiral binding. £5. ISBN: 095081931x.

Comprehensive guide to repositories and types of records including an introductory guide to the Public Record Office of Northern Ireland and A-Z list of civil parishes and local registrar district offices. For amateur and overseas researchers. *Class No:* 929.52(416)(093.20)

Commonwealth

[6174]

TITFORD, J. **Settlers of the Old Empire** *Family Tree Magazine.*
'Tristan da Cunha', *Family Tree Magazine,* v.14, February 1998, p.11-12 and v.14, no.5, March 1998, p.25-26; 'Ascension', *FTM,* v.14, no.7, May 1998, p.25-26; 'The Falkland Islands', *FTM,* v.14, no.11, September 1998, p.9-11; 'West Indies manuscript sources', *FTM,* v.15, no.1, November 1998, p.18-19; 'West Indies printed sources', *FTM,* v.15, no.3, January 1999, p.10-11; 'West Indies: unsettled settlers, pirates and buccaneers', *FTM,* v.15, no.5, March 1999, p.54-55; 'West Indies. St. Kitts', *FTM,* v.15, no.7, May 1999, p.54-56 and v.15, no.9, July 1999, p.24-26; 'The West Indies: Nevis', *FTM,* v.15, no.11, September 1999, p.9-11, v.16, no.1, November 1999, p.59-61, and v.16, no.3, January 2000, p.54-60. Essays reporting on the types of record, their location, indexes available, together with lists of further reading. *Class No:* 929.52(41-44)

England & Wales

[6175]

HAWKINGS, D.T. **Criminal ancestors** a guide to historical criminal records in England and Wales. Stroud, Gloucs., Alan Sutton, 1992. xiv,458p. illus., bibliog. £35. ISBN: 0862998174.

21 sections on different types of records (*e.g.* 1. Prisons and prison life - 2. Criminal registers ... 4. Courts of Quarter Session - 5. Assize Courts - 6. Old Bailey and Central Criminal Court ... 9. Petty Sessions and Juvenile Offenders ... 12/13 Transportation to America 1615-1868 ... 19. Records of the Director of Public Prosecutions - 20. Bankrupts and debtors. 8 Appendices on using the records *etc.* Bibliography p.344-49. Glossary p.350-53. *Class No:* 929.52(42)

Maps & Atlases

[6176]

FOOT, W. **Maps for family history** a guide to the records of the tithe, valuation office, and national farm surveys of England and Wales 1836-1943. London, PRO Publications, 1994, viii,85p. facsims., bibliog., index. £8.95. (*Public Record Office Readers Guide no.9.*) ISBN: 1873162170.

1. Use of maps for family history - 2. Introduction to the surveys - 3/5. Tithe, Valuation office and National Farm surveys - 6. Records in Scotland - 7. Care of maps - 8. Further reading (p.69). Appendices 1. Valuation Office Regions and District Offices - 2/3. Valuation Office maps: index of counties and index of places. Explains historical background, why and how records were created, and what information they contain. *Class No:* 929.52(42)(084.3)

England

[6177]

RAYMOND, S. **South West family histories.** Bury, Federation of Family History Societies, 1998. 28p. £7.50. ISBN: 1860060730.

Amalgamation of family history section from his county bibliographies (Cornwall, Devon, Dorset, Gloucestershire, Somerset and Wiltshire). *Class No:* 929.52(420)

[6178]

ROGERS, C.D. *and* SMITH, J.H. **Local family history in England 1538-1914.** Manchester, Manchester Univ. Press, 1991. vi,217p. tables, bibliog., index. ISBN: 0719803200.

In 3 parts: 1. History of the family 1538-1914 (marriage, children, widowed and aged in early modern period and in the industrial age) - 2. Exploitation of source material - 3. Family History agenda (organization, what to investigate, making it public). Resource Research List (bibliography) p.201-11. Brings together genealogy, family history, local history and demography. *Class No:* 929.52(420)

Bibliographies

[6179]

GANDY, M. **'Tracing your Catholic ancestors in England** What books are available?', *Family Tree Magazine,* v.12,no.10, August 1996, p.8-10.

Authoritative guide to sources of information and finding aids including non-Catholic records, mission registers, monumental inscriptions, wills and estates, biography and family history, education, and journals and periodicals. See also Gandy's 'Catholic ancestors', *Family History News and Digest,* v.8,no.1, April 1991, p.21-29. *Class No:* 929.52(420)(01)

Archives

[6180]

COLWELL, S. **Family roots** discovering the past in the Public Record Office. London, Weidenfeld and Nicolson, 1991. 231p. illus., facsims, geneal., tables, diagrs., bibliog., index. £15.99. ISBN: 0297830260.

Part 1. 'Understanding the sources': 1. The legal system - 2. Holding and transfer of land - 3. Tax and other sources of revenue - 4. Strangers and settlers. Part 2. 'The Sources at work' consists of 9 case studies containing examples of the types of information to be derived from the records in the PRO. Chapter notes p.207-16. Bibliography p.217-22. *Class No:* 929.52(420)(093.20)

London

Archives

[6181]

BOURNE, S. **Ten London repositories:** a practical guide for the family historian. 2nd ed. Northfleet, Kent, S. Bourne, 1987. [20]p. ISBN: 0951067834.

First published 1985.

Provides basic information on facilities and services, outlines the main groups of records held, points out practical problems, and suggests useful advance reading. *Class No:* 929.52(421)(093.20)

Wales

[6182]

ISTANCE, J. *and* CANN, E.E. **Researching family history in Wales.** Birmingham, Federation of Family History Societies, 1996. 87p. bibliog., pbk. £5.50. ISBN: 1860060307.

A companion volume to Rowlands, J. and others. *Welsh family history: a guide to research (q.v.).*

County by county guide to the location of archives and libraries. Data: address, telephone and fax numbers, hours, facilities, holdings, charges. Bibliography p.73-80. *Class No:* 929.52(429)

[6183]

ROWLANDS, J. *and* ROWLANDS, S., *eds.* **Welsh family history** a guide to research. 2nd ed. Birmingham, Federation of Family History Societies and The Association of Family History Societies of Wales, 1998. xii,325p. illus., facsims, maps, tables, geneal tables, bibliog., index. pbk. £9.95. ISBN: 186006065x.

1st ed. 1993.

20 contributors. Handbook divided into 25 chapters (*e.g.* 2. Archive repositories in Wales - 3. Family history societies ... 7. Surnames - 8. Place names - 9. Basic Welsh for Family Historians). Bibliography (p.315-17). *Class No:* 929.52(429)

Germany

[6184]

RIEMER, S.J. **The German research companion.** Sacramento, Calif., Lorelei Press, 1997. xxii,638p. bibliog., index. ISBN: 0965676145.

Buried within the 32 chapters of this massive Companion are a chronology of events (p.1-8) and other basic information, the foundation dates of the German länder, a major gazetteer of Eastern Europe; studies of German emigration and immigration; guides to various types of records located in Germany and the United States (archives and respositories, genealogical reference works, U.S. and German military resources, religious records etc.); a chapter on tourism; another on Pennsylvania; even a chapter headed This & That just in case anything had been overlooked. Truly described as 'a heavy-duty German reference assistant', it is hard to see what more historians of German born families could possibly require. Cited sources and references p.623-38. *Class No:* 929.52(430)

South Africa

[6185]

HARRISON, E. **Family history: a South African beginners' guide.** Gauteng, South Africa, Elly Harrison, 1996. £5.50 bibliog. ISBN: 0620196262.

Guide to civil and church records. List of useful addresses. *Class No:* 929.52(680)

Canada

Handbooks & Manuals

[6186]
BISHOP, J. 'Newfoundland family records', *Genealogists' Magazine*, v.20, no.9, March 1982, p.293-295. *Class No:* 929.52(71)(035)

Caribbean

[6187]
GRANNUM, G. **Tracing your West Indian ancestors** Sources in the Public Record Office. London, PRO Publications, 1995. x,102p. illus., facsims, bibliog., index. £8.95. (*PRO Readers Guide, no.11.*) ISBN: 1873162200.

Manual in 11 chapters (*e.g.* 3. Records of the Colonial Office ... 5. Life cycle records - 6. Land and property - 7. Military records - 8. Slaves ... 10. Emigration to the UK). Appendix 1. Colonial Office Classes ... 4. Geographical bibliography p.93-95. 'No other book does the job that this one does - and does it in a very professional manner' (*Journal of the Society of Archivists,* v.17, no.2, October 1996, p.230). *Class No:* 929.52(729)

USA

[6188]
The **American Family Tree series.** Phoenix, Oryx Press, 12v., 1995-. $24.95 each.

Robl, G. *A students guide to German American genealogy.* 1995. 192p. ISBN 0897749839; Brockman, T.C. ... *to Italian American genealogy.* 1995. 192p. 0897749731; Yamaguchi, Y ... *to Japanese American genealogy.* 1995. 208p. 0897749790; Kavash, E.B. ... *to Native American genealogy.* 1996. 192p. 0897749758; Paddock, L.O. and Rollyson, C.S. ... *to Scandinavian American genealogy.* 1995. 192p. 0897749782. McKenna, E. ... *to Irish American genealogy.* 1996. 0897749766. Other volumes in the series include British, African, Jewish, Polish, Chinese and Mexican American genealogy. *Class No:* 929.52(73)

[6189]
Burke's American families with British ancestry. Baltimore, MD, Genealogical Publishing Co., 1996. $47.50. ISBN: 0806306629.

First appeared in 16th ed. of *Burke's Landed Gentry* (1939). *Class No:* 929.52(73)

[6190]
Mayflower families through five generations: descendants of the Pilgrims who landed in Plymouth, Massachusets, December 1620. Plymouth, MA, General Society of Mayflower Descendants, 18v., 1975-. $25-35 each.

'An invaluable source for documenting some of America's original European settlers' (*Library Journal,* 1 April 1999. p.59). *Class No:* 929.52(73)

[6191]
Migration from the Russian Empire lists of passengers arriving at the port of New York. Vol.1: January 1875 - September 1882. Vol.2: October 1882 - April 1886. Glazier, I.A., *ed.* Baltimore, Md., Genealogical Publishing, 25v. 1995-. 703p.+631p. indexes. $60 each. ISBN: 0806314745, v.1; 0806314753, v.2.

Data (from original ships' manifests in the Temple - Balch Center for Immigration Research collections): date of arrival, name, age, sex, occupation, province or country, village, ship's name, port of embarkation. When completed the 25 volume project will cover the period 1871-1910. *Class No:* 929.52(73)

[6192]
WALCH, T., *comp.* **Our family, our town:** essays on family and local history sources in the National Archives. Washington, National Archives, 1987. 223p. illus. $20. ISBN: 0911333509.

Practical advice and encouragement for the use of federal records in family and local history research. Military pension records, census schedules, ship passenger lists, and court documents are among the materials discussed. *Class No:* 929.52(73)

Micromaterials

[6193]
City directories of the United States. Reading, Primary Source Microfilm, Gale Group, 1999. Online and Microform. 6292 fiche. On request.

Provides listings of names, occupations, street addresses, churches, schools, association, businesses, and local government and community leaders. This allows genealogists to create family histories, Cities and time periods offered in this database are selected to coincide with key events in history, such as the Civil War and waves of immigration. The database is also designed to support genealogical tools such as passenger lists, the federal census years, vital records, and others. Accompanied by printed guides.

Genealogical archives online: City directories of the United States is a full text searchable archival collection making it possible to search

....(contd.)
city directories using any word or string of words. Speach search fields provide more targeted data retrieval options. Enter a first name, last name, address, occupation, cultural or business institution, or search on ads across the entire database or on a single directory! Digital facsimiles can be magnified for viewing convenience, downloaded and printed as required. Both IP address verification and password protection registration options are available. *Class No:* 929.52(73)(003.5)

Bibliographies

[6194]
ROSENBERG, J. 'American family history', *Choice,* v.20, no.5, January 1983. p.675-684.

Literature review of general works and works on The European background; The Colonial family; Nineteenth-century families; The Black family; The Twentieth-century. List of works cited p.682-684. *Class No:* 929.52(73)(01)

Encyclopaedias

[6195]
ROBB, H.A., *ed.* **Encyclopedia of American family names.** New York, Harper Collins, 1995, 710p. $40. ISBN: 0062700758.

Based on *Report of Distribution of Surnames in the Social Security Number File* (1984).

5,000 most common US names A-Z. Data: Ranking on SSA list; number with that name; derivation of name and country of origin; brief etymology; published genealogies (if any). *Class No:* 929.52(73)(031)

Reviews & Abstracts

[6196]
American family history a historical bibliography. Brown, J.S. *and* Kinnell, S.K. Santa Barbara, California and Oxford, ABC-Clio Information Services, 1984. xii,282p. indexes. £28.70. (*ABC-Clio Research Guides, no.12.*) ISBN: 0874363802.

1167 abstracts and citations of journal articles A-Z by author arranged in 4 chapters - 1. The family in historical perspective - 2. The family and other social institutions - 3. Familial roles and relationships - 4. Individual family histories. Author and subject indexes. Compiled from the ABC-Clio historical database 1973-1982. 'A very useful source' (*Choice,* v.22,no.7, March 1985, p.959). *Class No:* 929.52(73)(048)

Yearbooks & Directories

[6197]
BENTLEY, E.P., *ed.* **Directory of family associations.** 3rd ed. Baltimore, Md., Genealogical Publishing, 1996. 355p. pbk. $34.95. ISBN: 0806315237.

Offers access to c.6,500 US. Family Associations. Data: name, address, 'phone no., contact person, publications, dates of annual reunions. *Class No:* 929.52(73)(058)

New Zealand

[6198]
BROMELL, A. **Tracing family history in New Zealand.** Rev. ed. Petone, G.P. Publications, 1991. 196p. illus., facsims., bibliog.

First published 1988.

Deals with research in New Zealand. *Class No:* 929.52(931)

[6199]
BROMELL, A. **Tracing your family outside New Zealand.** Petone, G.P. Publications, 1991. 196p.

Emphasis is on copy-records deposited in New Zealand but there is also a basic introduction to records held in Scotland, Ireland, and Australia. *Class No:* 929.52(931)

Handbooks & Manuals

[6200]
BROMELL, A. **Tracing family history in New Zealand.** Wellington, Government Printing Office, 1988. 196p. illus., map, facsims, bibliog., index. ISBN: 0477013767.

Supplements *Family history research in New Zealand: a beginner's guide* (NZ Society of Genealogists, 1984).

Authoritative manual in 19 chapters *e.g.* 4. Maori genealogy or whakapapa ... 5. Arrival in New Zealand ... 7. National archives ... 18. Researching overseas. Bibliography p.184-189. Useful addresses p.189-191. *Class No:* 929.52(931)(035)

[6201]

Family history at National Archives. Wellington, Allen & Unwin and National Archives, 1990. xiv,162p. illus.

Guide to immigration, tax, military, educational, and court records held in New Zealands' National Archives. 'Will surely channel the enthusiasm of New Zealand genealogists in many profitable directions' (*Journal of the Society of Archivists*, v.13, no.2, Autumn 1992, p.156-7). *Class No:* 929.52(931)(093.20)

Australia

[6202]

The Bicentennial dictionary of Western Australians pre 1829-1888. Erikson, R., *comp.* Nedlands, Univ. of Western Australia Press, 4v., 1987. xxiv, 3419p. ISBN: 0855642785, set.

Supersedes *Dictionary of Western Australians:* 1. *Early Settlers 1829-1850* (1979) and *Supplement* (1981) - 2. *Bond 1858-1868* (1979) - 3. *Free 1850-1868* (1979) - 4. *The challenging years 1868-1888* (2v., 1984-85) now described as working copies designed to encourage public participation in the collection of family records.

V.5. Atkinson, A. *Asian immigrants to Western Australia 1829-1901* (1988. xvi, 464p. illus.,map,tables. ISBN 0855642874 covers Chinese, Japanese, Indian, Filipino, Afghan and Malay immigration. Of the original set of volumes, *The golden years 1889-1914* (1986. 1006p. 0855642505), retains its value. This work is an official project of the Australian Bicentennial Authority. *Class No:* 929.52(94)

[6203]

COFFEY, H.W. *and* **MORGAN, M.J. Irish families in Australia and New Zealand.** Melbourne, P.O. Box 135, 1978-.

Preliminary paperback edition: 1. *1788-1878* (Abbott-Dwyer-Gray). 1978. 140p. 0959595228. 2. *1788-1979* (Eades-Kate). 1979. 141-307p. 0959595236. 3. *1788-1980* (Laffy-Quirke). 1980. 308-505p. 0959595244. 4. *1788-1981* (Rafferty-Young). 1981. 506-639p. 0959595252. A total of 2710 brief biographies.

Revised edition: 1. *1788-1983* (Abbot-Dynan). 1983. 248p. 0959595260. 1353 persons included compared to 580 entries in preliminary edition. *Class No:* 929.52(94)

[6204]

PEAKE, A.G. National register of ship arrivals Australia and New Zealand. Bayswater, Western Australia, Australian Federation of Family History Organizations, 1999.

Lists and locates the primary source records in named archives. *Class No:* 929.52(94)

Bibliographies

CD-ROM

[6205]

Family history on disc information resources for genealogists. Melbourne, RMIT Publishing. Annual. Available from SilverPlatter Information Ltd., Merlin House, 20 Belmont Terrace, Chiswick, London, W4 5UG. CD-ROM (single disc).

Contains information resources for genealogists, family historians, and researchers. A compilation of Australia's leading family history resource database, it covers family histories, cemetery records, memorial records, historical records, military ancestry, Who's Whos, and other genealogical resources. *Class No:* 929.52(94)(01)(003.40)

Handbooks & Manuals

[6206]

HALL, N.V. Tracing your family history in Australia. 2nd ed. Albert Park, Scriptorium Family History Centre, 1994. 657p. bibliog., index. ISBN: 1864040718.

1st ed. 1985.

Guide to Australian sources for tracing the family history and genealogy of people living in Australia accessible by personal consultation or correspondence arranged by states and territories. Contextual bibliography of published and unpublished Australian genealogical material with strong emphasis on finding aids p.512-623. *Class No:* 929.52(94)(035)

[6207]

RAY, P. *and* **JOHNSTON, K.** 'Genealogy', chapter 19, *Australians: a guide to sources* (v.10 *Australians. A historical Library*, 1988).

Introductory essay plus an annotated bibliography in 4 sections: Tracing your ancestors; Genealogical societies and congresses; Public records and listings; Vital registers and graveyard inscriptions. *Class No:* 929.52(94)(035)

[6208]

Relations in records a guide to family history sources in the Australian archives. Canberra, Australian Government Publishing Service, 1988. xx, 161p. illus., facsims., softcover. ISBN: 0644068477.

Comprehensive guide to Commonwealth archives of genealogical interest stored in the regional offices arranged in 4 categories: immigration and shipping; defence; population; Commonwealth government employees. Using the guide and Australian Archives control systems and finding aids p.xi-xx. Indispensable reference tool for all Australian genealogists and family historians. *Class No:* 929.52(94)(093.20)

Parish Registers

Great Britain

[6209]

SOCIETY OF GENEALOGISTS. Parish register copies. Part One Society of Genealogists Collection. 11th ed. London, Society of Genealogists, 1995. vi,152p. sd. ISBN: 1859510043.

First published in 1937 as *A catalogue of parish register copies in the possession of the Society of Genealogists* (1937).

1. A-Z by English county - 2. Channel Islands - 3. Isle of Man - 4. Ireland - 5. Scotland - 6. Wales - 7. Overseas. Data: place, dates, brief description. *Class No:* 929.53(410)

[6210]

—SOCIETY OF GENEALOGISTS. Parish register copies. Part Two other than the Society of Genealogists collection. 2nd ed. 1974. London, Society of Genealogists, 1978. xi,50p. sd. ISBN: 0901878375.

First published 1971.

A-Z list of English and Welsh counties. Key to locations p.v-x. Regarded as a temporary guide until all regional volumes of *National index of parish registers* are printed. *Class No:* 929.53(410)

Scotland

[6211]

STEEL, D.J. Sources for Scottish genealogy and family history. Chichester, Sussex, Phillimore for The Society of Genealogists, 1980. xiii,32p. bibliog., index. (*National Index of Parish Registers, v.12.*)

Historical background; Catholic nomenclature; Parish registers; Ancillary sources (*e.g.*Court records, inscriptions); Nonconformists. Bibliography. *Class No:* 929.53(411)

England & Wales

[6212]

Original parish registers in Record Offices and libraries. Matlock, Derbyshire, Local Population Studies, in association with the Cambridge Group for the History of Population and Social Structure, 1974-.

First published 1974. 128p. £3. 1st Supplt. 1976. 60p. £2. 2nd Supplt. 1978. 64p. £2. 3rd. Supplt. 1980. 92p. £3.75. Fourth Supplt. 1982. 96p. £4.50.

Sections: England (by counties); Wales (by counties); Isle of Man. Includes original registers, rough books of register entries, duplicate books made simultaneously, early replacement copies. *Class No:* 929.53(42)

Maps & Atlases

[6213]

The Phillimore atlas and index of parish registers. Humphery-Smith, C.R., *ed.* Chichester, Sussex, Phillimore, 1984. v, 92p. maps, 91-281p. index. £30.00. ISBN: 0850333989.

'Phillimore & Co. Ltd., had the idea of publishing a consolidated guide to parish records at the same time as the Institute of Heraldic and Genealogical Studies was considering a new edition of its book of parish maps with improved new maps and an index to parishes and research sources. The two ideas have been brought together'.

Atlas contains 42 full page historical county genealogical maps of pre-1832 parishes each accompanied by a reproduction of a topographical map from J. Bell's *A new and comprehensive gazetteer of England and Wales* (1834). 'Each parish map shows the ancient parochial boundaries, the probate court jurisdiction affecting each area by colour coding, the situation of churches and chapels where relevant, and the dates of commencement of the original registers of the parish that have survived'. The index is A-Z by county and is linked to the county maps by grid references and indicates whether parishes are included in the *International Genealogical Index*. A glowing review in *Genealogists Magazine*, v.21,no.7, September 1984, p.255 describes this as 'a genealogist's dream index'. *Class No:* 929.53(42)(084.3)

England

[6214]

ational index of parish registers. Chichester, Sussex, Phillimore for The Society of Genealogists. bibliogs., indexes.

Steel, D.J. *Sources of births, marriages and deaths before 1837.* rev. ed. 1976. 2. *Sources for nonconformist genealogy and family history* 1973. 3. Steel, D.J. and Samuel, E.R. *Sources for Roman Catholic and Jewish genealogy and family history.* 1974. 4. Palgrave-Moore, P.T.R. *South East England* 1980 partly superseded by 4.(1) Webb, C. *Surrey* 1990. Steel, D.J. *South Midlands and Welsh Border counties* new ed. 1977. 6.(1) Bloor, P.D. *The North Midlands: Staffordshire* 2nd rev. ed. 1992. 6.(2) Stott, W.T. and Webb, C. *Nottinghamshire* 1995. 7. Palgrave-Moore, P.T.R. *East Anglia* 1983. 8.(1) Wilcox, A. *Berkshire* 1989. 8.(2) Webb, C. *Wiltshire* 1992. 9.(1) *Bedfordshire and Huntingdonshire* 1991. 9.(2) *Northamptonshire* 1991. 9.(3) *Buckinghamshire* 1992. 9.(4) Wilcox, A. *Essex* 1993. 11. Neat, C.P. *Durham and Northumberland* 2nd rev. ed. 1984.

Class No: 929.53(420)

London

[6215]

uide to parish registers deposited in the Greater London Record office. Harris, T.C., *comp.* 2nd ed. London, Greater London Record office, 1991. 90p. ISBN: 0951810901.

1st ed. 1990.

In 2 parts: 1. Alphabetical list of parishes by name - List of parishes by place. Appendix 1. Record offices which hold parish registers for adjoining counties. *Class No:* 929.53(421)

[6216]

UILDHALL LIBRARY. London. A Handlist of parish registers, register transcripts and related records at Guildhall Library. Part One: City of London. 6th rev. ed. London, Guildhall Library, 1990. 130p. pbk. (*Guildhall Library Research Guide, no.4.*) ISBN: 0900422300.

1st ed. 1963.

Arranged A-Z by Church. *Class No:* 929.53(421)

Wales

[6217]

VILLIAMS, C.J. and WATTS-WILLIAMS, J., *eds.* Cofrestri plwyf Cymru/Parish registers of Wales. Aberystwyth, National Library of Wales & Welsh County Archivists Group in association with the Society of Genealogists, 1986. xliv, 217p. maps, facsims., index. £6.95. (*National Index of Parish Registers, no.13.*) ISBN: 0907158145.

Parish lists of the 13 historical counties of Wales describing the registers of over 1000 parishes and chapelries in existence before 1812, and of 200 post-1812 for which records are held by a repository. List of repositories p.xxx. Bilingual introduction.

Class No: 929.53(429)

Canada

Bibliographies

[6218]

IRKETT, P. Checklist of parish registers. 4th ed. Ottawa, Canadian Government Publishing Centre, 1986. 205p. C$12.00. ISBN: 0660538636.

Cross-referenced listing of parish registers on microfilm or microfiche at the National Archives that contain records of birth, baptisms, marriages and deaths. A-Z by place name within each province or region. *Class No:* 929.53(71)(01)

Heraldry

Handbooks & Manuals

[6219]

OUTELL, C. Boutell's heraldry revised by J.P. Brooke-Little. Rev. ed. London, Warne, 1983. x,368p. illus. (inc.pl.). ISBN: 0723230935.

First published 1950. Based on Boutell's *The manual of heraldry* (1863) and *English heraldry* (1867).

27 chapters (1. The beginning and growth of heraldry - 2. Definitions, heraldic language and blazonry ... 8. Heraldic charges ... 22. Flags ... 26. Recent trends and developments - 27. Heraldic authorities and sources. 28 col.pl. Critical bibliography (p.302-313) 'designed to be read as part of the book rather than used simply as a catalogue for reference'. Glossary and index p.314-68. 'A must for all heraldry addicts' (*TLS*, no.3755, 22 February 1974, p.189 on the 1973 ed.). *Class No:* 929.6(035)

[6220]

FRANKLYN, J. Shield and crest: an account of the art and science of heraldry. 3rd ed. London, MacGibbon & Kee, 1967,. xviii,521p. illus. (inc.col.pl.).

First published 1960.

A notable grammar of heraldic practice, with splendid examples in colour of shields and crests current in the 20th century. The blazonry and charges are described in great detail and with particular regard to their original use and meaning. Descriptions of plates are unhelpfully relegated to end of text. A good index of proper names, but some of the charges are given only under general headings, *e.g.* fish, flower. The 3rd ed. has *c.*24 pages of extra information, chiefly enlargements of existing sections; some extra illustrations. Almost every page reset. 'One of the standard textbooks of heraldry in English in the 20th century' (*Times Literary Supplement,* no.3,413, 27 July 1967, p.693). *Class No:* 929.6(035)

[6221]

GAYRE OF GAYRE *and* NIGG, R. Heraldic standards and their ensigns. Edinburgh, Oliver & Boyd, 1959. xix,132p. 16 col.pl., index.

The aim is to clarify and illustrate the various types of heraldic ensigns. Claims to be the first book devoted to the heraldic flag. 1. The pennon - 2. The lance pennon - 3. The personal banner - 4. The guidon - 5. The heraldic standard - 6. The streamer - 7. The heraldic household badge - 8. The gonfallon or gonfallion - 9. Heraldic vanes - 10. Banderolles and helm-streamers - 11. The armorial or heraldic flag. Footnote references. *Class No:* 929.6(035)

[6222]

NEUBECKER, O. Heraldry: sources, symbols and meaning. London, Little Brown, 1997. 288p. illus. (mainly col.). £16.99. ISBN: 0316641413.

First published London, Macdonald & Jane's 1976.

Sections: The herald - Terminology (p.42-55) - The shield - The sign - The helmet - The crown - Heraldic accessories (*e.g.* Badges) - The right of arms - Armorial display. Early armorials (p.268-72). Bibliography, p.273-5 (grouped). Index. Profusely illustrated (1,500 col. illus.). International in scope. *Class No:* 929.6(035)

[6223]

WOODCOCK, T. *and* ROBINSON, J.M. The Oxford guide to heraldry. Oxford, Oxford Univ. Press, 1988. xli, 233p. illus. (some col). bibliog. £17.50. ISBN: 0192116584.

1. Origins of heraldry - 2. English heraldry - 3. Grantees of English arms - 4. The shield of arms - 5. Crests - 6. Supporters, badges and mottoes - 7. Marshalling of arms - 8. Heraldic authority in Great Britain - 9. American heraldry - 10. The use of heraldry as decoration. Appendix A. The Royal Arms of Great Britain - B. English and Scottish Kings of Arms. Glossary of heraldic terms in open use p.197-206. Bibliography p.207-210. Analytical index. 'Illustrated guide to the history and uses of heraldic symbols ... intended as a non-specialist introduction ... written with full authority, avoiding romantic myths and pseudo-heraldic terms' (d/w). Authors are Somerset Herald and Fitzalan Pursuivant Extraordinary respectively. *Class No:* 929.6(035)

[6224]

WOODWARD, J. *and* BURNETT, G. A Treatise on heraldry, British and foreign, with English and French glossaries. Newton Abbot, Devon, David and Charles, 1969.

First published 1892. 2nd ed. Edinburgh, Johnston, 2v., 1896.

The best English survey of continental heraldic practice. The illustrations are excellent. It covers the origin, history, and practical application of armory. V.2 contains an index of proper names and subjects. This treatise serves as an introduction to Rietstap's *Armorial général (qv)*. *Class No:* 929.6(035)

Dictionaries

[6225]

BROOKE-LITTLE, J.P. An Heraldic alphabet. 4th rev. ed. London, Robson Books, 1996. ix,234p. illus. (incl.col.pl.) bibliog., pbk. £8.95. ISBN: 1861050771.

First published Macdonald. 1973.

Prefatory essay, followed by the alphabet, *c.*1,700 terms; numerous cross-references. The author is Clarenceaux King of Arms. 'Aims to explain the jargon as it is today' (*TLS*, no.3757, 25 January 1974, p.72). 'If your old copy is still in good condition I am not sure it is worth buying this new edition, although it is cheap enough and unquestionably authoritative' (*Reference Reviews*, v.11, no.3, 1997, p.20-21). *Class No:* 929.6(038)

[6226]

FOSTER, J. **The Dictionary of heraldry** feudal coats of arms and pedigrees. London, Studio Editions, 1992. xvi, 234p. illus., col. coats of arms, geneal. tables. ISBN: 1851709304.

First published as *Some feudal coats of arms* (London, James Parker, 1902).

Feudal coats of arms p.1-214 (A-Z by family and individuals); Men of coat armour their bearings and badges with many chart pedigrees and royal descents p.215-240. *Class No: 929.6(038)*

[6227]

FRANKLYN, J. *and* TANNER, J. **An encyclopaedic dictionary of heraldry.** Oxford, Pergamon Books, 1970. xiv,307p. illus. (inc.pl.); facsims.

The glossary, p.1-355, has c.8,000 entries and cross-references, 474 illus.; 18p. of colour plates; text facing illus. Appendix 2: Analysis of blazon, p.350-67. 'Even if Gough & Parker's *A Glossary of terms used in heraldry* (1967) is held, this work's illustrations make it indispensable' (*Library Journal,* v.95,no.15, 1 September 1970, p.2788). *Class No: 929.6(038)*

[6228]

FRIAR, S., *ed.* **A New dictionary of heraldry.** Sherborne, Dorset, Alphabooks, 1987. 384p. illus. (some col). coats of arms, bibliog. £15.95. $30. ISBN: 0906670446, UK; 0517566656, US.

Published in the United States by Harmony under the title *A dictionary of heraldry.*

34 distinguished contributors define and expand upon more than 1000 terms in heraldry and armory. A list of general books is included under the entry 'Bibliography in the A-Z sequence. 16 col. plates. 'The attention to modern (or vernacular) heraldry ... makes this book unique' (*Booklist,* v.84, no.15, 1 April 1988, p.1321). The editor is Keeper of the Heraldry Society's Register of Armorial Bearings. *Class No: 929.6(038)*

[6229]

PARKER, J. **A Glossary of terms used in heraldry.** Newton Abbot, Devon, David & Charles, 1970. xxxii, 659p. illus., col. frontis., index. ISBN: 715347640.

First published 1894.

Contents: A synoptical table of the chief terms used in British heraldry p.xv-xxxii; Glossary p.1-634. Index to the names etc., whose coats of arms will be found blazoned in the course of this glossary p.635-639. *Class No: 929.6(038)*

Worldwide

[6230]

The International armorial register. A register of armorial bearings in current use with the names and addresses of the bearers and the authority for their use. Dingli-Attard-Inguanez, M., *ed.* Missouri, Universal Intelligence Data Bank of America, 1984. 380p. $27.50. ISBN: 0961074000. *Class No: 929.6(100)*

Europe

[6231]

RIETSTAP, J.B. **Armorial général:** précédé d'un dictionnaire des termes du blason. 2nd ed. Gouda, Van Goor, 2v. , 1884-87. Reprinted Paris, Dupont, 1904; Institut Héraldique, 1905-14; The Hague, Nijhoff, 1926-34; New York, Barnes & Noble, 1965. illus.

First published 1861.

The standard encyclopaedia of European arms with entries arranged A-Z by families.

Supplément par V. Rolland and H. Rolland (The Hague, Nijhoff, 7v. in 8, 1926-54; London, Heraldry Today, 1965). *Table du Supplément* par H. Rolland (Lyon, Société Sauvegarde Historique, 1951. 190p.).

Plates illustrating the arms in Riestap's original work were published under the title *Armories des familles contenues dans l'Armorial Général* (Paris, Institut Héraldique Universel, 6v., 1903-26; The Hague, Nijhoff, 1938). A 3rd. ed. of these plates edited by V. Rolland and H. Rolland (with text in English) was published under the title *General illustrated armorial* (Lyon, Sauvegarde Historique, 6v., 1953). This was reprinted as *Illustrations to the 'Armorial Général' of J.B. Rietstap* (London, Heraldry Today, 3v., 1967). *Class No: 929.6(4)*

[6232]

VOLBORTH, C.A. von. **The Art of heraldry.** Poole, Dorset, Blandford Press, 1987. 224p. coats of arms (mostly col.), bibliog. £40. ISBN: 0713713909.

Originally planned as a replacement to the author's *Heraldry customs, rules and styles* (1981).

1. Heraldic design - 2. Heraldic art and craft over the centuries - 3. An international exhibition of heraldic works by artists and artisans from the end of the nineteenth century. Design of new armorial bearings p.218. Index of names p.222-224; general index p.224. *Class No: 929.6(4)*

Dictionaries

[6233]

STALINS, G.F.L., *and others.* **Vocabulaire-atlas héraldique en six langues:** Français - English - Deutsch - Español - Italiano - Nederlandsch. Paris, Société du Grand Armorial de France, 1952.

At head of title-page: Académie Internationale d'Héraldique. Pt.1 tabulates principal terms in heraldry in six languages - 2. A-Z listing of terms for each of the languages - 3. Black and white plates. *Class No: 929.6(4)(038)*

Great Britain

[6234]

BURKE, Sir J.B. **The General armory of England, Scotland, Ireland and Wales;** comprising a registry of armorial bearings from the earliest to the present time with a Supplement. London, Harrison, 1884. lxxix,50,1185p.

First published 1842. This edition reprinted London, Burke's Peerage, 1961 and Baltimore, Md., Genealogical Publishing Co. 1969.

The 1884 ed. contains descriptions of about 60,000 coats-of-arms. The work is in dictionary form, the entries being under the name of the family or corporation. The illustrations are confined to the arms of the English and Welsh dynasties. An index of mottoes includes the names of the families concerned.

Morant, A. *General armory two: additions and corrections to Burke's 'General armory',* edited by C.R. Humphery-Smith (East Ardsley, Wakefield, West Yorkshire. Tabard Press: Heraldry Today, 1973. 240p.). *Class No: 929.6(410)*

[6235]

The Cambridge armorial. Humphery-Smith, C., *ed.* London, Orbis 1985. 141p. coats of arms (some col.). ISBN: 0856138711.

Descriptive text with profuse illustrations of armorial bearings of the Colleges (in order of foundation), approved foundations, and 2 schools. Notes on their origins, historical associations, and heraldic significance. Glossary p.142-4. *Class No: 929.6(410)*

Bibliographies

[6236]

MOULE, T. **Biblioteca heraldica Magnae Britanniae:** a bibliography of heraldry, genealogy, nobility, knighthood and ceremonies from 1469-1821. London, Heraldry Today, 1966. 692p. illus. £30. ISBN 0900455144.

First published 1822.

A classic bibliography of 810 items, arranged chronologically. Includes lists of visitations and the principal foreign books or genealogy and heraldry. The reprint is less unwieldy than the original 'The outstanding bibliography of British heraldry' (*Oxford guide to heraldry,* 1988). *Class No: 929.6(410)(01)*

Handbooks & Manuals

[6237]

BRIGGS, G., *comp.* **Civic and corporate heraldry:** a dictionary of impersonal arms of England, Wales & Northern Ireland. London, Heraldry Today, 1971. 432p. illus.

Armorial bearings A-Z, p.24-428, preceded by an illustrated glossary of 162 heraldic terms. Supplementary list of obsolete civic authorities. Nearly 1,000 clear drawings. 'Impersonal' covers towns, counties and other civic authorities, as well as schools, colleges, univs., insurance companies, banks, industrial corporations and ecclesiastical bodies. *Class No: 929.6(410)(035)*

[6238]

FOX-DAVIES, A.C. **A Complete guide to heraldry:** revised and annotated by J.P. Brooke-Little. London, Orbis Books, 1985. xii,528p. illus., bibliog., index. £20.00.

First published 1909. Rev. ed. 1949.

A comprehensive, authoritative guide to the rules, practice and art of heraldry, revised by the Richmond Herald of Arms. Arranged in 42 systematic, short chapters, lavishly illustrated (nearly 800 drawings; 26 new coloured pl.). Comprises the history of armory; a detailed description of the treatment of charges used, regalia, seals, badges, cadency, the law of armorial bearings, and the artistic employment of heraldry. Bibliography, updated, p.486-8. *Class No: 929.6(410)(035)*

Dictionaries

[6239]

Dictionary of British Arms. Chesshyre, D.H.B. *and* Woodcock, T., *eds.* London, Society of Antiquaries, 1992-. Distributed by *Heraldry Today.*

Replaces J.W. Papworth's *Ordinary of British Armorials.* A photoreproduction of his *An Alphabetical dictionary of Coats of Arms* (1874).

Vol.1 Medieval Ordinary. London, 1992. lxvi,530p. index. £48. ISBN 0854312587. 74 contributors. History of the project p.viii-xiv.

....(contd.)
Structure of the Ordinary p.xv-xix. Sources p.xxvi-xxxvii. Terminology p.xxxviii-xlv. Index of headings p.xlix-lxvi. Index of names p.399-530. First in a series of 4 Ordinaries covering the period before the beginning of the heraldic visitations in 1530. Arms are listed A-Z under the heraldic charges.
Vol.2 1996. xciv, 533-677p. £66.50. ISBN 0854312864.
Class No: 929.6(410)(038)

Yearbooks & Directories
[6240]
FOX-DAVIES, A.C. **Armorial families;** a directory of gentlemen of coat-armour. 7th ed. London, Hurst & Blackett, 2v., 1929. Reprinted Newton Abbot, Devon, David & Charles, 1970.
First published 1895.
Introductory chapter on the abuse of arms. The entries are in A-Z order, by families. Only those arms which are officially recorded are included. Full heraldic descriptions are given, with accounts of the recent bearers of the arms. Well illustrated. Index of quarterings.
Class No: 929.6(410)(058)

[6241]
FOX-DAVIES, A.C. **The Book of public arms:** a complete encyclopaedia of all royal territorial, municipal, corporate, official and impersonal arms. London, Jack, 1915. xx,877p.
First published 1894.
Arranged in A-Z order of entries, this work is still the current authority. Each entry gives a full description of the arms, crest, and motto borne, together with the date of the grant, where such exists.
Class No: 929.6(410)(058)

Scotland
[6242]
BURNETT, C. *and* DENNIS, M. **Scotland's heraldic heritage** The Lion rejoicing. Edinburgh, The Stationery Office, 1997. 96p. col.illus. ISBN: 0114957843.
An introduction to the art of heraldry showing its form in different applications within Scotland throughout the centuries and interpreting its many representations. Illustrates the arms of the Scottish monarchs, and how heraldry can show ownership and demonstrate lineage and alliances. *Class No:* 929.6(411)

Handbooks & Manuals
[6243]
INNES OF LEARNEY, Sir T. **Scots heraldry** a practical handbook of the historical principles and modern application of the art and science. 2nd ed. Edinburgh, Oliver & Boyd, 1934. Reprinted Johnston & Bacon, 1978. xi,131p. illus., bibliog., index. ISBN: 0717942247.
The standard work on the Scottish practice of armory. Guide to further study of Scottish heraldry (a bibliography) p.119-21. Author was Lord Lyon King of Arms 1945-1969. *Class No:* 929.6(411)(035)

[6244]
PAUL, J.B. **An Ordinary of arms contained in the Public Register of all arms and bearings in Scotland.** Baltimore, Maryland, Genealogical Publisdhing Co., 1969. xxiv,428p. index.
First published Edinburgh, Green, 1893.
The Scottish equivalent of Papworth's Dictionary, the entries (over 5,500) being under the heraldic charges. Index of family names.
Class No: 929.6(411)(035)

[6245]
URQUHART, R.M. **Scottish burgh and county heraldry.** London, Heraldry Today, 1973. xii, 274p. illus., map. £25. ISBN: 0900455241.
The arms of the burghs and county councils are arranged under counties, with c.2-3 black-and-white illus. per page. Appendix: 'Chronological table of matriculations of boroughs, counties and county councils'. Bibliography, p.254-6. Reference notes. Index.
Class No: 929.6(411)(035)

[6246]
URQUHART, R.M. **Scottish civic heraldry:** regional, islands, districts. London, Heraldry Today, 1979. 101p. illus., maps, index. £15. ISBN: 0900455268.
1: The new councils and their heraldry; 2: The arms of the Councils. Bibliography, p.93-4. Reference notes. Black-and-white maps only. *Class No:* 929.6(411)(035)

England
[6247]
FRIAR, S. **Heraldry for the local historian and genealogist.** Gloucester, Alan Sutton, 1992. xi,271p. illus. (inc. col. pl.), bibliog. £16.99. ISBN: 086299893x.
1. Heraldry: an historical perspective - 2. Armigers: nobility and gentry - 3. Documents, seals and manuscripts - 4. Architectural and decorative features - 5. Monuments, effigies, brasses and hatchments - 6. Heraldic artefacts - 7. Blazon: terminology of armory - 8. Marshalling, cadency and augmentations of honour - 9. Liveries, badges - 10. Royal heraldry. Bibliography p.247-52. Glossary p.256-71. Fully illustrated sourcebook for all researchers not just local historians or genealogists. *Class No:* 929.6(420)

[6248]
SUMMERS, P., *ed.* **Hatchments in Britain.** Chichester, Sussex, Phillimore, 10v., 1974-1994.
1. *Northamptonshire, Warwickshire and Worcestershire.* 1975. xi, 113p. illus. £13.95. 0850330858.
2. *Norfolk and Suffolk.* 1976. xiv, 157p. illus. £13.95. 0850332303.
3. *The Northern Counties. Cumberland, Westmorland, Durham, Northumberland, Lancashire and Yorkshire.* 1979. xiv, 186p. illus. £13.95. 0850333296.
4. *Oxfordshire, Berkshire, Wiltshire, Buckinghamshire, Bedfordshire.* 1982. xv, 167p. illus. £13.95. 0850334519.
5. *Kent, Surrey and Sussex.* 1985. xv, 174p. illus. £13.95. 0850335353.
6. *Essex, Middesex, Hertfordshire, Cambridgeshire, Huntingdonshire.* 1985. xv, 166p. illus. £13.95. 085335361.
7. *Cornwall, Devon, Dorset, Somerset, Gloucestershire, Hampshire, Isle of Wight,.* 1988. 208p. £13.95. 0850336511.
8. *Lincolnshire, Nottinghamshire, Cheshire, Staffordshire, Derbyshire, Leicestershire, Rutland.* 1988. 192p. £13.95. 085033652x.
9. *Herefordshire, Shropshire, Wales, Scotland. Monmouthshire, Ireland, and hatchments in former British Colonies.* 1994. 136p. £13.95. 085033912x.
10. *The development and use of hatchments and Addenda and Corrigenda to Vols. 1-8.* 1994. 160p. £13.95. 0850339138. Appendix 1. Documents illustrating the use of hatchments and other funeral heraldry 1560-1816 ... 5. Index locorum vols. 1-10 (p.137-52). Bibliography p.153. Index. *Class No:* 929.6(420)

[6249]
WAGNER, A. **Heralds of England:** a history of the office and College of Arms. London, Heraldry Today, 1985. 634p. illus. (of coats of arms), ports. £48. ISBN: 0900455411.
Originally published by H.M. Stationery ffice, 1967.
An authoritative account, sumptuously printed and illustrated. 44p of plates, 13 in colour. *Class No:* 929.6(420)

[6250]
—CHESSHYRE, H. *and* AILES, A. **Heralds of today:** a biographical list of officers of the College of Arms, London, 1963-86. Gerrards Cross, Buckinghamshire, Van Duren, 1986. 71p. photos. index. ISBN: 0905715314.
Primarily intended as a supplement to the London Survey Committee's *The College of Arms London* (1963).
Brief history of the history and jurisdiction of the 13 offices of the College of Arms and of the 8 Officers of Arms Extraordinary together with biographical accounts of the holders. *Class No:* 929.6(420)

Handbooks & Manuals
[6251]
PINCHES, J.H. *and* PINCHES, R.V. **The Royal heraldry of England.** London, Heraldry Today, 1974. xviii,334p. illus. (incl.col.pl.), tables, bibliog., index. £40.00. ISBN: 090045525x.
Sections: The English - The Normans - The Plantagenets - The Lancastrians - The Yorkists - The Tudors - House of Hanover - House of Saxe-Coburg - House of Windsor... House of Mountbatten - Windsor. 258 black-and-white illus. Bibliography, p.ix-xii. Authoritative. 'Highly recommended' (*RQ*, v.14,no.3, Spring 1975, p.266-7). *Class No:* 929.6(420)(035)

Wales
[6252]
SIDDONS, M.P. **The Development of Welsh heraldry.** Aberystwyth, National Library of Wales, 3v., 1991-1993. £150.; $300.
V.1: 1991. xxvi,433p. illus. (inc. 24 col. pl.), index. £50. $100. ISBN 090715851x. Examines the origins and development of heraldry in Wales to the early 17th century. 1. Origin - 2. Sources other than manuscripts - 3. Heraldic manuscripts - 4. Heraldry in Welsh poetry - 5. Development and characteristics - 6. Advance - 7. Heraldry of the Welsh princes - 8. Influence of the Heralds. 16 Appendices including C. Welsh heraldic vocabulary and P. Dates of appearance of arms in Wales.
Volume 2 contains in Welsh armorial listing coats of arms in

....(contd.)

alphabetical order of the names of the pesons to whom they were attributed or the families bearing them, with sources.

Volume 3 is an ordinary of Welsh arms according to blazon in order to permit the identification of a given coat of arms.
Class No: 929.6(429)

Russia

[6253]

MANDICH, D.R. *and* PLACEK, J.A. **Russian heraldry and nobility.** Bynton Beach, Florida, Dramio, 1992. iv,700p. coats of arms ISBN: 0963306391.

Introduction (History and structure of Russian heraldry) p.1-8. Blazons of family arms p.9-213. Genealogical notes p.214-405. Coats of arms p.409-668. *Class No:* 929.6(47)

Australia

[6254]

LOW, C., *ed.* **A roll of Australian arms** corporate and personal borne by lawful authority. Adelaide, Rigby, 1971. xxxii, 184p. coats of arms (some col.), bibliog., index.

Corporate arms (Commonwealth and pan-Australia and then State by State) p.3-62. Personal arms p.65-171. Bibliography p.173. Glossary p.174-7. *Class No:* 929.6(94)

Ecclesiastical

Vatican City

[6255]

MARTIN, J. **Heraldry in the Vatican / L'Araldica in Vaticano / Heraldik im Vatikan.** Gerrards Cross, Buckinghamshire, Van Duren, 1987. 228p. illus. (some col.), coats of arms (some col.), plans, index. £36. ISBN: 090571525x.

Developed from articles first printed in *L'Osservatore della Domenica* (1969).

20 Heraldic tours of the Vatican. Appendix A. Plan of St. Peter's Basilica - B. Plan of Vatican City State. Text in English, Italian and German. Author is Prefect of the Pontifical Household.
Class No: 929.6:28(456.31)

Crests & Mottoes

Handbooks & Manuals

[6256]

ELVIN, C.N. **A Hand-book of mottoes borne by the nobility, gentry, cities, public companies, etc.** ... With Supplement by R. Pinches. London, Heraldry Today, 1971. £14. ISBN: 0900455047.

First published 1859.

The 1971 ed. is a reprint, with an added index and a supplement. The much-needed index contains 5,000 names. The original (names, A-Z) had annotations, but no details of dates or authorities. Often gives the address as well as name of family associated with each motto. 'This is by far the best edition and is heartily recommended for most libraries' (*RQ*, v.11, no.2, Winter 1971, p.184).
Class No: 929.624(035)

Great Britain

[6257]

FAIRBAIRN, J. **Fairbairn's Book of crests** of the families of Great Britain and Ireland. 4th ed. rev. and enl. by A.C. Fox-Davies. London, Heraldry Today, 1983. £45. ISBN: 0900455387.

First published 1859.

Crests arranged by surnames. *Class No:* 929.624(410)

Badges & Emblems

[6258]

GORMAN, J. **Banners bright** an illustrated history of the banners of the British trade union movement. London, Allen Lane, 1973. viii,184p. illus. (some col.)., index. ISBN: 0713902906.

Study of the rise and decline of trade union banners, especially their history, style, and subject matter. Illustrations p.57-182.
Class No: 929.628

[6259]

NAOKI MUKODA. **Emblems.** Tokyo, Bijutsu Shuppan-sha, 1987. 127p. col.illus. ISBN: 4568500834.

490 blazer badges grouped in 8 sections: 1. British military emblems - 2. University - 3. Sports - 4. United States uniform patches - 5. Regional emblems - 6. Emblems arranged by motifs - 7. Brand emblems - 8. Emblem variations. The story of emblems (bilingual Japanese and English text) p.113-25. *Class No:* 929.628

[6260]

WILLIAMS, D. *and* MUIRHEAD, G. **Northumberland miners' banners.** Ashington, Mid Northumberland Arts Group, 1987. 36p. illus., bibliog., pbk. £1.95. ISBN: 0904790584.

Description, history and significance of some colliery banners. Bibliography p.36. *Class No:* 929.628

[6261]

WILLIAMSON, D. **Debrett's guide to heraldry and regalia.** London, Headline, 1992. 160p. illus. (mostly col.), bibliog., index. £17.99. ISBN: 0747206090.

Pt.1: Heraldry: 1. Origin and development - 2. Rules - 3. Heralds and the College of Arms - 4. Scottish heraldry - 5. Modern heraldry - 6. Continental heraldry. Pt.2: Regalia: 7. Origins - 8. English regalia and the Coronation ceremony - 9. Non-royal - 10. Royal regalia and Coronations of the World. Appendix 1. Glossary (p.118-34) - 2. Royal regalia England and Scotland - 3. Coronations of British Sovereigns - 4. Royal regalia worldwide. Bibliography p.155-7. *Class No:* 929.628

Nobility

Europe

Middle Ages

[6262]

BOULTON, D'A.J.D. **Knights of the Crown:** the monarchial orders of knighthood in later medieval Europe 1325-1520. Woodbridge, Suffolk, The Boydell Press, 1987. xxv, 540p. illus. £45. ISBN: 0851154174.

Examines the historical background, foundation, statutes, name and title, members, privileges and obligations, officers, corporate attitudes, insignia and formal costume of 13 orders which attached the presidential office to the crown of the princely founder or made it hereditary in his house. Bibliography p.503-524.
Class No: 929.7(4)"01/14"

Great Britain

[6263]

The Complete peerage of England, Scotland, Ireland, Great Britain and the United Kingdom extant, extinct or dormant. Cokayne, G.E. Gloucester, Alan Sutton, 6 vols. 1984. £75. ISBN: 0904387828.

First edition published 1887-1898 in 8v.; new edition revised and enlarged in 12v. 1910-59. V.13 *Peers created 1901-1938* (1940). This present edition is reprinted photographically in reduced format enabling the complete work to be published in a 6v. boxed set.

V14. *Addenda and corrigenda.* 1998. 880p. £95. ISBN 0750901543. 'An essential work of reference for its numerous corrections and additions to previous volumes quite apart from the 20th-century additions'. A full historical and genealogical account of all peerages created in England, Scotland and Ireland since the conquest, each volume is arranged alphabetically and includes details of every peer's birth, parents, honours, offices, marriage, death and burial. *Class No:* 929.7(410)

[6264]

LEESON, F.L. **A Directory of British peerages:** from the earliest times to the present day. 2nd ed. London, Society of Genealogists, 1984. xi, 174p. index. ISBN: 0901878642.

Replaces E. Solly's *An index of hereditary English, Scottish and Irish titles of honour* (1880).

A-Z by title and surname in one sequence giving title, rank, period covered by peerage, its destination, and family name. Introduction p.v-x includes notes on other sources. 'Not intended as a work of expertise but as a ready-reference compilation for those wishing to find out quickly whether or when a certain peerage existed, with its rank(s), nationality, ownership, approximate period and fate' (*Introduction*).
Class No: 929.7(410)

[6265]

Peerage creations 1689-1800 a chronological list of creations in the peerage of England and Great Britain. Sainty, J.C., *comp.* London, Parliamentary History Yearbook Trust, 1998. vii,97p. index. pbk. £7. (*Parliamentary History Occasional Series, no.1.*) ISBN: 0953234908.

'Enables us to date peerage creations more accurately and to determine the correct spelling of peerages from the patents' (*Archives*, v.24, no.100, April 1999, p.84). *Class No:* 929.7(410)

CD-ROM

[6266]
Notable British families 1600s-1990s. Broderbund in association with Genealogical Publishing Company, 1999. U.K. distributors: S & N Genealogy Suppliers, Salisbury. CD-ROM. £29.95.

Facsimilies of 11 Burke publications: *A Genealogical History of the Dormant, Abeyant, Forfeited and Extinct Peerages of the British Empire; A Genealogical and Heraldic History of England, Ireland and Scotland; Burke's Family Records; A Genealogical and Heraldic History of the Colonial Gentry; The General Armorial of England, Scotland, Ireland and Wales; A Genealogical and Heraldic History of the Commoners of Great Britain and Ireland; Index to Pedigrees in Burke's Commoners;* and *The Prominent Families of the United States.* *Class No:* 929.7(410)(003.40)

Bibliographies

[6267]
Burke's family index. Montgomery-Massingberd, H.J., *ed.* London, Burke's Peerage, 1976. xxxii, 171p. £9.50. ISBN: 085011022x.

Two main features: 'A bibliography of *Burke's,* 1826-1976 (p.xiii-xxx) - 'The family index' (p.1-171). The latter is a comprehensive A-Z listing of the 20,000 families that have appeared in Burke's publications, 1826-1976. *Class No:* 929.7(410)(01)

Handbooks & Manuals

[6268]
Burke's peerage and baronetage. Mosley, C., *ed.* 106th ed. Crans, Swit., Burke's Peerage (Genealolgical Books) Ltd., 2v., 1999. cxx,3347p. coats of arms, index. £295. $395. ISBN: 2940085021.

First published 1826 as *Burke's Genealogical heraldic history of the peerage and baronetage of the United Kingdom.* This edition published for libraries worldwide by Fitzroy Dearborn (London and Chicago, ISBN 1579580831).

First revised and updated edition since 1970. Editorial team has adhered to the established format in listing the details of 108,000 living people, while incorporating some important changes that will make the new edition easier to use. These include: a full index for all listed living persons, a larger typeface and easy to follow layout, preliminary essays on the histories of major families and titles, articles on the principal houses and family seats, a thorough revision of all coats of arms (computer enhanced for greater clarity), and details on the correct forms of address for all living individuals listed'. But the most striking innovation is the inclusion of illegitimate offspring for the first time. (See Harlow J. and Corbidge R., 'Upper classes wake up on wrong side of the blankets', *Sunday Times,* 16 May 1999, p.9). List of titles p.vi-xxviii. Precedence in UK p.xxxiv-xl. Readers' guide p.ii-li. Glossary p.lii-lvii. Heraldic glossary p.lviii-lxiv. Abbreviations p.lxv-xcvii. Summary of peerage families p.ic-civ. The Royal Family p.cv-cxx. Peerage & Baronetage p.1-3104. Index p.3105-3347. *Class No:* 929.7(410)(035)

[6269]
Debrett's peerage and baronetage 2000. Kidd, C. *and* Williamson, D., *eds.* London, Debretts Peerage and Macmillan; 1999. 105p.+1817p.+1160p. col.port., illus., coats of arms. £250. ISBN: 033354577x, UK.

Founded in 1769; renamed Debrett in 1802. 'Modern technology has come to Debrett at last and the complete text of the Peerage and Baronetage has now been computerized. This means we shall be able to produce amended family articles between editions, which we hope will appear every five years (Preface to 1985 ed.).

Comprises information concerning the Royal Family, the Peerage, Privy Councillors, Scottish Lords of Session, Baronets, Chiefs of clans in Scotland. Other information includes H.M. Officers of Arms; tables of general precedence; guide to the wearing of Orders; Foreign and Commonwealth Orders. Entries provide illustration of coat of arms and lists of living relatives, collateral branches and predecessors. *Class No:* 929.7(410)(035)

Yearbooks & Directories

[6270]
Burke's genealogical and heraldic history of the landed gentry. Townsend, P., *ed.* 18th ed. London, Burke's Peerage, 3v., 1965-72.

1st ed., *Burke's Genealogical ... history of commoners* (1833-38. 4v.); 2nd ed. *Landed gentry of Great Britain and Ireland,* with an index of about 100,000 names (1843-49, 3v.).

Contains biographical sketches of *c.*600 distinguished families of England, Scotland and Wales; 500 armorial illustrations; index of families. Gives brief biographical sketch of present head of family; name of wife and children (if any); lineage; arms (both illustration and description); seat. Perhaps one-half of the families are no longer landowning. American families with British ancestry are included in the 1939 ed., p.2539-3021, published separately in 1948 as *Burke's Distinguished families of America: the lineages of 1,600 families of British origin now resident in the United States of America.* Burke, Sir

....(contd.)
J.B. *A genealogical and heraldic history of colonial gentry* (London, Harrison, 1891-95. 2v. illus.), with excellent reproductions of 120 coats of arms, was reprinted by Genealogical Publishing Co., Baltimore, Md., in 1970. *Class No:* 929.7(410)(058)

[6271]
—SAYER, M.J. 'The Scope of Burke's Landed Gentry', *Genealogist's Magazine,* v.19,no.4, December 1977, p.120-124 and 'Pedigrees of County Families, *ibid,* v.19,no.10, June 1979, p.354-362; v.20,no.2, June 1980, p.56-59; v.20,no.4, December 1980, p.135; v.20, no.5, March 1981, p.157-160; v.6,no.8, December 1981, p.267-273; v.7,no.9, March 1982,p.304-308.

Lists of landed families not appearing in any edition of *Burke's Landed Gentry.* *Class No:* 929.7(410)(058)

Scotland

Handbooks & Manuals

[6272]
The Scots peerage founded on Wood's edition of Sir Robert Dougals's Peerage of Scotland; containing an historical and genealogical account of the nobility of that kingdom. Paul J.B., Sir, *ed.* Edinburgh, Douglas, 9v., 1901-14. illus. (coats of arms).

Contains biographies in narrative form not only of title-holders but of all offspring in the male line. A very comprehensive name index is contained in v.9. *Class No:* 929.7(411)(035)

Commonwealth

[6273]
BURKE, Sir J.B. **A Genealogical history of the dormant, abeyant, forfeited, and extinct peerages of the British Empire.** New ed. London, Harrison, 1883. xii,642p.

Reprinted Baltimore, Genealogical Publishing Co., 1996.
Useful for ancestry and descendants of peers; but personal details should be taken from Cokayne (*qv.*). Refers to 40,000 persons.

A genealogical and heraldic history of the extinct and dormant baronetcies of England, Ireland and Scotland, by J. and J.B. Burke (2nd ed. London, 1844) has been reprinted (London, Burke's Peerage, 1964. 652p. armorial illus.). *Class No:* 929.7(41-44)

[6274]
—PINE, L.G. **The New extinct peerage 1184-1971:** containing extinct, abeyant, dormant and suspended peerages with genealogies and arms. London, Heraldry Today, 1972. xxviii,313p. ISBN: 0900455233.

Serves as a supplement to Burke's *Genealogical history ...* Index to surnames and title. *Class No:* 929.7(41-44)

France

[6275]
DE LA CHENAYE-DESBOIS ET BODIER, A. **Dictionnaire de la Noblesse:** contenant les généalogies, l'histoire & la chronologie des familles nobles de la France, l'explication de leurs armes et l'état des grandes terres du Royaume, possédées à titre de Principautés, Duchés, Marquisats, Comptés, Vicomptés, Baronies etc. ... 3rd ed. Nendeln, Liechtenstein, Kraus Reprints, 19v., 1969.

Reprint of 3rd ed. (Paris, 1863-78).
'On a jouit à ce dictionnaire Le Tableau Généalogique et Historique des Maisons Souveraines de l'Europe et une notice des familles étrangères, les plus anciennes, les plus nobles et les plus illustrées'. *Class No:* 929.7(44)

Spain

[6276]
Elenco de grandezas y titulos nobiliarios Españoles 1985. 18th ed. Madrid, Hidalguia, 1985. 1026p. bibliogs., index. softcover. ISBN: 840005895x.

Royal Family (including chronology of the Spanish monarchy) p.9-17. Nobility A-Z by title p.13-811. Name index p.815-903. Bibliografia fundamental para consulta relativa a legislacion nobiliaria p.1011-3. List of significant archive offices p.1015-1018. *Class No:* 929.7(460)

Orders & Decorations

[6277]
MĚŘIČKA, V. **The Book of Orders and decorations.** London, Hamlyn, 1975. 248p. illus. (some col.), bibliog. ISBN: 0600367312.

An exhaustive analytical survey including general sections on Awards in the Ancient World - Orders and general awards - Collecting Orders and decorations. A Collectors' vade mecum includes General standard terminology for Orders and decorations (p.211-8); Survey of

....(contd.)

mottoes (p.219-23); List of Orders according to country or place of origin (p.224-38); and Bibliography (p.239-41). 41 col.pl.
Class No: 929.71

[6278]

PATTERSON, S. **Royal insignia** British and foreign Orders of chivalry from the Royal Collection. London, Merrell Holberton, 1996. 208p. col.illus. bibliog. £45. ISBN: 1858940257.

Orders from over 30 countries with full-size colour illustrations. Provenances p.198-204. Orders held by members of the Royal Family p.205-207. Bibliography p.208. *Class No:* 929.71

Worldwide

[6279]

CLARKE, J.D. **Gallantry medals & awards of the world.** Yeovil, Som., Patrick Stephens, 1993. 248p. illus. (some col.), bibliog., index. £18.50. ISBN: 1852603038.

Describes and illustrates 2,204 examples from 37 countries listed A-Z. Data: clear identification and dimensions; where worn; requirements for bestowal. Glossary p.242-3. Bibliography p.244. 'A selection to reflect nations and awards most likely to be encountered when studying military conflict or civilian bravery' (*Introduction*). *Class No:* 929.71(100)

[6280]

DORLING, H. Taprell. **Ribbons and medals.** Ed. and rev. by A.A. Purves. London, Osprey in association with Spink & Son Ltd., 1983. 320p.+20p. col. illus. ISBN: 0850455162.

First published as an 80-page booklet by George Philip and Son in 1916. Eight revised editions 1919-1974 with supplements between editions.

5 chapters: 1. British orders and decorations - 2. Commonwealth awards - 3. United Nations awards - 4. Order of Malta - 5. Foreign countries awards. *Class No:* 929.71(100)

Europe

[6281]

HIERONYMUSSEN, P. **Orders, medals and decorations of Britain and Europe in colour.** London, Blandford Press, 1967. 256p. illus. (inc. col. pl).

Originally as *Europaeiske ordner i farver* [European orders in colour] (Copenhagen, Politikens Forlag, 1966).

The 80 coloured plates (450 photographs) of orders medals and decorations of 28 European nations are preceded by an introductory essay and followed by an encyclopaedia of orders (date of institution; to whom it may be given; classes; whether or not returnable on death of holder). 'An excellent general guide in a comparatively small volume' (*Times Literary Supplement*, no.3,414, 3 August 1967, p.713). *Class No:* 929.71(4)

Great Britain

[6282]

GALLOWAY, P. **Royal service.** London, Central Chancery, St. James's Palace, 1996. £45.

'A history of the Royal Victorian Order and its associated medal containing the names of all recipients and their citations since the old Queen started to bestow the blue, red and white ribbon 100 years ago' (*Sunday Telegraph*, no.1850, 23 November 1996, p.8). *Class No:* 929.71(410)

[6283]

HENDERSON, D.V. **Dragons can be defeated** a complete record of the George Medal's progress 1940-1983. London, Spink, 1984. 120p. tables, bibliog. £12. ISBN: 0907605141.

The creation of the G.M. - 2. The first few years - 3. The period since the war - 4. Honorary awards. Table 1. A-Z list of award winners: Name, rank, position, organization, action, place, date, London Gazette citation. Table 2. Alphabetical list of honorary awards to foreign nations. Bibliography p.117-8. *Class No:* 929.71(410)

[6284]

VICKERS, H. **Royal orders.** London, Boxtree, 1994. 192p. illus. (some col.), ports., bibliog. £25. ISBN: 1852835109.

Examines the history of the royal orders in 17 chapters: 1. The present Royal Family - 2/16. Garter, Thistle, St. Patrick, O.M., Bath, St. Michael and St. George, Royal Victorian Order, Royal Victorian Chain, C.H., O.B.E., Imperial Service Order, Indian Orders, St. John of Jerusalem, Commonwealth orders and decorations. Sources p.190-192.

An earlier work of value is Sir. Ivan De la Bere's *The Queen's orders of chivalry* (London, William Kimber, 1961). *Class No:* 929.71(410)

Bibliographies

[6285]

LITHERLAND, A.R. *and* SIMPKIN, B.T. **Spinks standard catalogue of British and associated orders decorations & medals** with valuations. London, Spink, 1990. 222p. col. illus., bibliog. £25. ISBN: 090760532x.

Historical and numismatic descriptions and illustrations to 336 orders, decorations and medals. Guide to order of wearing p.11-12. Bibliography p.202-3. *Class No:* 929.71(410)(01)

Ireland

[6286]

DOHERTY, R. *and* TRUESDALE, D. **Irish winners of the Victoria Cross** Dublin, Four Square, 2000. 224p. £30. ISBN: 185182491x.

Details of 170 Irish V.C.s. *Class No:* 929.71(415)

[6287]

GALLOWAY, P. **The Most illustrious Order** the Order of St. Patrick and its knights. London, Unicorn Press, 1999. 320p. col.illus., bibliog., index. ISBN: 0906290236.

Examines the history of this now virtually defunct Order in its political, social, cultural, and ceremonial context. Appendix 4. The Officers of the Order. Appendix 5. Letters patent, statutes, warrants, ordinances and other documents. Bibliography p.295-97. Chapter references p.298-309. Analytical index. *Class No:* 929.71(415)

Commonwealth

[6288]

BATE, C.K. *and* SMITH, M.G. **For bravery in the field** recipients of the Military Medal 1919-1939: 1939-1945: 1945-1991. London, Bayonet Publications, 1991. vii,542p. illus., index. £55. ISBN: 1873996004.

A roll of Military Medal recipients marshalled in 3 distinct chronological sections. An introduction (p.1-16) covers all aspects of the award: naming, verification, citations, recommendations, posthumous awards, investitures, forfeitures and restorations, gratuities, precedence *etc. Class No:* 929.71(41-44)

[6289]

GALLOWAY, P. **The Order of the British Empire.** London, Central Chancery of the Orders of Knighthood, 1996. 188p. col.illus. bibliog., index. £25. ISBN: 0907605656.

Based on official documentation this history traces the story of the changing appearance of its insignia, the repeated attempts to establish a chapel and concludes with the stability and popularity enjoyed by the Order today. *Class No:* 929.71(41-44)

[6290]

HARVEY, D. **Monuments to courage** Victoria Cross headstones & memorials. Weybridge, P.M. da Costa, 2v., 1999 £75.

Accurate locations of all but a dozen of the 1,322 deceased recipients final resting places, including the seemingly impossible 'lost 300' who lie in un-marked paupers' graves in overgrown Victorian graveyards and cemeteries from London to the North Indian plains. Data: photograph (if available), details of birth, death and final resting place, together with a description of the action when the V.C. was earned, and its present location. Appendix: list arranged by Country, county, town, and resting place. A-Z name list. *Class No:* 929.71(41-44)

[6291]

Honours and awards in the British Empire and Commonwealth. Pamm, A.N., *comp.* Aldershot, Hants, Scolar Press, 2v., 1994. xvi,1657p. £195. + £165. Set £295. ISBN: 085967911x, set.

1. *The United Kingdom and Eire.* ISBN 0859679845. 2. *The British Empire and Commonwealth.* 085969853. An encyclopedic reference work covering the receipt and bestowal of honours and rewards at all levels in the British Empire and Commonwealth. The books record honours and awards in approximately 100 countries. This publication deals with the more important and recognised levels, that is the bestowal of public position and rank, official titular honours, admission into state orders and the bestowal of decorations and medals. Within the country divisions, each awarding authority is listed, together with the system of awards that it instituted and the recipient population who received the awards. *Class No:* 929.71(41-44)

[6292]

JOCELYN, A. **Awards of honour:** the orders, decorations, medals and awards of Great Britain and the Commonwealth, from Edward III to Elizabeth II. London, A & C Black, 1956. xx, 276p. illus. (20 col. pl). index.

17 chapters: Introduction and definitions; Orders; Ribands of orders; Decorations and campaign medals; Long service and good conduct medals; Dominion and colonial decorations and medals; Miscellaneous decorations and medals; etc. The 20 colour-plates consist of mounted reproductions of medals and ribbons. Detailed index, p.265-76. Page size 31 x 25cm. *Class No:* 929.71(41-44)

[6293]

LAFFIN, J. **British V.C.s of World War Two** a study in heroism. Stroud, Glos., Sutton Publishing, 1997. xxv,258p. illus. (mostly ports), bibliog., index. £25. ISBN: 0750910267.

106 British VCs were awarded in the Second World War analysed here in the context of the campaigns and actions for which they were awarded. 12 Chapters in 3 sections: Royal Navy, The Army, Royal Air Force. Appendix 1 V.C. winners from Australia, Canada, India, New Zealand, South Africa and Fiji - 2. Living holders of the Victoria Cross in 1997. Bibliography p.245-46. *Class No:* 929.71(41-44)

[6294]

The Register of the George Cross. 2nd ed. Cheltenham, This England Books, 1992. 151p. ports., bibliog. £14.95. ISBN: 0906324173.

A-Z by recipient. Data: name, vital statistics, and short narrative of award and deed. Short history of the George Cross p.6-7. Town and county connections p.147-9. Bibliography p.150. *Class No:* 929.71(41-44)

[6295]

The Register of the Victoria Cross. 3rd. ed. Cheltenham, This England Books, 1997. 308p. ports., bibliog. £25. ISBN: 0906324270.

1,351 of recipients A-Z. Data: rank, unit, other decorations, place and date of deed, place of date of birth and death, place of memorial, town or county connection, and portrait. Short history of the V.C. p.6-7. Dates on which awards were published in *The London Gazette* p.284-289. Bibliography p.322. *Class No:* 929.71(41-44)

Bibliographies

[6296]

MULHOLLAND, J. and JORDAN, A., *eds.* **Victoria Cross bibliography.** London, Spink, 1999. xvii,217p. £25. ISBN: 190204021x.

'Part 1 contains a list of key VC titles, each with a description and annotation. Part two lists non-fiction and fictional books written by VC recipients. The index lists, in alphabetical order, every VC recipient and gives the date of the *London Gazette* citation. It also names the books in which the recipients are mentioned significantly, enabling the researcher to quickly identify key works.' (*Library Association Record,* v.102, no.3, March 2000, p.163). *Class No:* 929.71(41-44)(01)

Germany

[6297]

TREADWELL, T.C. and WOOD, A.C. **German Knights of the Air 1914-1918** the holders of the Orden Pour le Mérite. London, Brassey's, 1997. 208p. illus., ports., bibliog., index. £17.50. ISBN: 1857532317.

Career profiles and details of engagements for which the Order was received. Bibliography p.198. *Class No:* 929.71(430)

USA

[6298]

FOSTER, F. and BORTS, L. **US military medals.** 3rd ed. Fountain Inn, S.C., Medals of America Press, 1995. 79p. col.illus., index. $24.95. ISBN: 1884552124.

Covers US military medals and ribbons from World War II to the Gulf War for all services. Includes personal decorations, special service medals, and meritorious awards. *Class No:* 929.71(73)

[6299]

LANG, G., *and others.* **Medal of Honor recipients 1863-1994. V.1: Civil War to second Nicaraguan campaign. V.2: World War II to Somalia.** New York, Facts On File, 2v., 1995. 894p. bibliog., index. $80. ISBN: 0816025599.

c.3,400 entries arranged chronologically and ordered by war or specific military action. Data: rank, date of birth, military unit, citation, date of death, where buried. *Class No:* 929.71(73)

[6300]

VETTERAU, B. **The Presidential Medal of Freedom.** Washington, Congressional Quarterley, 1996. 546p. illus., bibliog., index. $67. ISBN: 1568021283.

Data: 1-2 page biographies of all recipients of the US's highest civilian honour (quote from citations, date and place of the award ceremony, and overview of medalist's achievements. Introductory chapters outlines history of the medal and of other American medals. *Class No:* 929.71(73)

New Zealand

[6301]

CHAMBERLAIN, H., *comp.* **Service lives remembered** the Meritorious Service Medal in New Zealand and its recipients 1895-1994. Wellington, Howard Chamberlain, 1995. 574p. £60. ISBN: 0473030470.

Biographies of all 488 recipients of MSM. 'The great strength of the book is ... the quality and quantity of biographical detail recorded' (*Reference Reviews*, vol.10,no.4, 1996, p.16-17). *Class No:* 929.71(931)

Australia

[6302]

Order of Australia 1975-1995. Kirkland, F., *ed.* Cremorna, NSW., Plaza Historical Services, 1995. 873p. ports (1 col.).

1st ed. 1993.

Contents: Honours system in Australia, Constitution of the Order of Australia, Insignia Ordinance of 1977, and information on the recipients. *Class No:* 929.71(94)

Rank & Precedence

[6303]

CARLISLE, N. **A Concise account of the several foreign orders of knighthood** and other marks of honourable distinction especially of such as have been conferred upon British subjects together with the names and achievements of those gallant men who have been presented with honorary sword, or plate, by The Patriotic Fund Institution. London, John Hearne, 1839. Reprinted by London Stamp Exchange, 1988. xxix, 582p. index. £38. ISBN: 094813027x.

1. Descriptive history of Foreign orders with annotated lists of British recipients A-Z by country: The Empire of Austria to Wurtemburg p.1-485. 2. Patriotic Fund awards p.486-539. *Class No:* 929.73

England & Wales

[6304]

SQUIBB, G.D. **Precedence in England and Wales.** Oxford, Clarendon Press, 1981. xviii,139p. bibliog. £40. ISBN: 0198253893.

Examines the manner in which laws of precedence have developed and presents tables of precedence 'which differ in some respects from those set out in current works of reference'. Appendix 4: Modern tables of precedence p.119-125. Bibliography p.126-130; index p.131-139. *Class No:* 929.73(42)

Vatican City

[6305]

CARDINALE, H.E. **Orders of knighthood, awards and the Holy See:** a historical, juridical and practical compendium. 3rd ed. Gerrards Cross, Bucks, Van Duren, 1985. 336p. illus. (many col.), bibliog. £29.50. ISBN: 0905715268.

1st ed. 1983; 2nd ed. 1984.

'Contains all the historical, juridical and practical information about each pontifical Order and Award and other Catholic or originally Catholic Orders of Knighthood' (*Preface to 1st ed.*). Bibliography p.317-8. *Class No:* 929.73(456.31)

China

[6306]

GARRETT, V.M. **Mandarin squares** mandarins and their insignia. Hong Kong, Oxford Univ. Press, 1990. vii,66p. illus. (some col.), bibliog., index. £6.95. (*Images of Asia.*) ISBN: 0195852397.

Mandarin squares are the embroidered insignia sewn on to the robes of the ruling mandarin classes in China's Qing dynasty (1644-1911). This short book provides an account of the Chinese system of government and traces the origin, development and symbolism of mandarin squares. Glossary p.60. Bibliography p.62-3. *Class No:* 929.73(510)

Royalty

[6307]

Almanach de Gotha. Kennedy, J., *ed.* 184th edition. London, Almanach de Gotha, 2v. 2000. Distributed by Boydell & Brewer.

Published annually 1763-1944 (181st ed.). French-language listing of complete genealogies of all Royal Families of Europe and South America, mediatized German princes, both reigning and formerly reigning. Publication resumed in 1998.

English language version: Vol.1: Pt.1: reigning and formerly reigning Royal and Princely houses of Europe and South America. Pt.2: Mediatized and sovereign houses of the Holy Roman Empire. 1000p. col.illus. £60. $110. ISBN 0953214222. Vol.2: The Non-

....(contd.)

Reigning Princely and Ducal houses of Europe. 1000p. col.illus. £60. $110. 0953214230. This is the first new edition of this volume since 1944. The ultimate authority on such matters. *Class No:* 929.731

[6308]

Burke's royal families of the world. London, Burke's Peerage, 2v., 1977-80.

1: *Europe & Latin America,* 1977. xxv,594p. 2: *Africa & the Middle East.* 1980. xvi.320p. V.1 is arranged under 48 countries (Albania ... Yugoslavia). Includes princely and ducal houses. Introductory historical essays; biographies; pedigrees. Appendices: A. The mediatized sovereign states of the Holy Roman Empire - B. Principal order of knighthood - C. Ancestral tables - D. Select bibliography, p.569-70. Index of names in the pedigrees, p.571-88. Addendum. 'Comprehensive and definitive ... will become an indispensable reference book' (*The Times,* 4 July 1977, p.14). *Class No:* 929.731

CD-ROM

[6309]

Royal families. London (?), BCA, 1996. CD-ROM. IBM-compatible PCs running Windows 3.1 or higher. £44.65 including accompanying video.

'There are 26,000 people named here, all cross-referenced and indexed like an interactive museum of nobility. Family trees pop up at the touch of a button; maps explain the rise and fall of nations and there are more dates here than in the whole of North Africa. Even Cadwallon the Long Handed of Gwynedd gets an entry' (*Sunday Times,* 21 July 1996, p.3:12) *Class No:* 929.731(003.40)

Encyclopaedias

[6310]

GURNEY, G. Kingdoms of Asia the Middle East and Africa: an illustrated encyclopedia of ruling monarchs from ancient times to the present. New York, Crown Publishers, 1986. viii, 438p. illus., maps, tables, index. $24.95. ISBN: 0517552566.

Historical record of 4000 royal sovereigns. 845 photographs. *Class No:* 929.731(031)

[6311]

TAPSELL, R.F., *comp.* **Monarchs, rulers, dynasties and kingdoms of the world.** New York, Facts on File, 1981. London, Thames and Hudson, 1983. 511p. $35.00. ISBN: 0871961210, US; 0500258055, UK.

An encyclopaedic guide to more than 13,000 rulers and 1,000 dynasties from 3000B.C. to the twentieth century. Section 1 Alphabetical guide to dynasties and states (1200 entries); Section 2. Dynastic lists. 17 genealogical charts. Introduction (p.8-12) includes notes on dynastic names, royal titles, classifications and definitions, personal names, and monarchy today. 'The chief virtues of the book are its inclusion of minor states and its coverage of the non-Western world' (*Choice,* v.21,no.1, September 1983, p.69).
Class No: 929.731(031)

Chronologies

[6312]

CARPENTER, C. The Guinness book of kings, rulers & statesmen. Enfield, Middlesex, Guinness Superlatives, 1978. vii,312p. index. ISBN: 090042446x.

Chronological lists of Heads of State and Government A-Z by State 3000BC to present day. *Class No:* 929.731(090)

[6313]

MORBY, J.E. Dynasties of the world a chronological and genealogical handbook. Oxford, Oxford Univ. Press, 1989. xv, 254p. tables, bibliogs., index. £29.95. ISBN: 0192158724.

1. Ancient Near East - 2. Hellenistic World - 3. Roman and Byzantine worlds - 4. Barbarian West - 5. Europe - 6. Islamic dynasties - 7. India - 8. Far East - 9. Africa - 10. New World. Chronological tables giving years of rule, family relationships of major world dynasties. Notes contain supplementary information regarding chronological problems, calendars, dating systems and royal styles.
Class No: 929.731(090)

Europe

[6314]

ARNOLD, J. The Royal houses of Europe The Family of Her Majesty Queen Victoria. West Malling, Kent, Patrica Arnold, 1998. variously paginated, geneal. tables., index. ISBN: 095332211x.

Queen Victoria's descendants now number 1130 in 8 generations. This extended family tree traces them all. *Class No:* 929.731(4)

[6315]

LOUDA, J. *and* **MacLAGEN, M. Lines of succession** heraldry of the royal families of Europe. Rev. ed. London, Little Brown, 1999. 308p. illus., col. heraldic and genealogical tables, maps, index. £19.95. ISBN: 0856054691.

First published by Macdonald (1981).

Detailed treatment of all the present and former kingdoms of Europe and all German and Italian grand-duchies from the eleventh century onwards. Heraldry is presented as an indispensable adjunct to royal genealogy, coats of arms in full colour are employed to illustrate 'the various matrimonial alliances and territorial acquisitions or losses, or rises in rank.' 37 chapters (*e.g.*2. Medieval England - 3. Great Britain - 4. Scotland). 7 maps. *Class No:* 929.731(4)

[6316]

McNAUGHTON, A., *comp.* **The Book of Kings: a royal genealogy.** New York, Quadrangle, New York Times Book Co., 3v., 1974. 1480p. illus.

1. *The Royal Houses.* 2. *The families.* 3. *Plates, indexes.* 'This very comprehensive catalog of all the legitimate descendants of George I (*Choice,* v.12,no.9, November, 1144). V.3 has over 100 plates and an extensive index. 'A clearly arranged and important reference source on European royalty' (*Library Journal,* 1 May 1975, p.836).
Class No: 929.731(4)

[6317]

OPFELL, O.S. Queens, Empresses, Grand Duchesses and Regents women rulers of Europe, A.D.1328-1989. Jefferson, McFarland, 1989. xiii,282p., ports., bibliog., index. $25.95. ISBN: 0899503853.

39 biographical chapters including material on their subjects' impact upon history. Bibliography (by ruler) p.161-70. For the general reader. *Class No:* 929.731(4)

[6318]

RUVIGNY AND RAINEVAL, 9th Marquis of. The Titled Nobility of Europe an international peerage and who's who of the sovereigns, princes and nobles of Europe. London, Harrison, 1914. lxxi,1605p., coats of arms, index.

Facsimile edition published by Burke's Peerage in 1980. ISBN 0850110289.

Abbreviations in 5 languages: English, French, German, Italian and Spanish p.xxii-xxv. Index to surnames p.xxix-lxx. Pt.1 Royal and Princely Houses p.1-206. Pt.2 The Mediatized Princely and Noble Houses p.207-1593. An account of all the European sovereigns and coats of arms with text in English and in their national language. Originally intended to be an annual publication but after the Great War scythed through the European royal houses it probably seemed pointless, but it remains a valuable historical record and reference source. *Class No:* 929.731(4)

[6319]

WILLIAMSON, D. Debrett's Kings and Queens of Europe. Exeter, Webb & Bower, 1988. 208p. illus. (some col.), maps, geneal. tables, bibliog., index. £19.95. ISBN: 086350194x.

Concise factual information on every monarch who has reigned over parts of Europe over the last thousand years, supported by outline historical text on each royal house, arranged in 8 regional chapters: The Iberian Peninsula to the Balkans. Appendix: 29 Genealogical tables. Bibliography p.204-205. The Monarchs of Europe and some claimants *i.e.* dynastic tables on endpapers. Omits Holy Roman Emperors and the Imperial German, Austrian and Russian dynasties and minor sovereigns, Grand Dukes, Electors *etc.*
Class No: 929.731(4)

Encyclopaedias

[6320]

GURNEY, G. Kingdoms of Europe an illustrated encyclopaedia of ruling monarchs from ancient times to the present. New York, Crown Publishers Inc., 1982. x,627p., map, illus., index. $24.95. ISBN: 0517543958.

Records the reigns of monarchs from the Roman Empire to Queen Elizabeth II in 20 geographical chapters plus six appendices for other independent grand duchies and principalities. 1700 illustrations. *Class No:* 929.731(4)(031)

Great Britain

[6321]

ASHLEY, M. British monarchs: the complete genealogy, gazetteer, and biographical encyclopedia of the Kings and Queens of Britain. London, Robinson, 1998. xiv,824p. illus., maps, geneal. tables, bibliog., index. £25. ISBN: 1854875043.

History and biographies of c.1,000 monarchs of the UK and its antecedent kingdoms in 4 main sections: 1. Royal Book of Records - 2. The Kingdoms of Britain (p.41-61) - 3. The Kings and Queens of Britain (biographies in 3 chronological sections: The Dark Ages to AD 900, The Fight for Britain 900-1300, Uniting the Kingdom 1300-) p.65-709 - 4. The World About Them: Legendary and European rulers

....*(contd.)*

(semi-historical kings of Britain, associated kingdoms, High Kings of Ireland, Viking rulers of Dublin, Scandinavia, Hanover) p.711-748. 51 genealogical tables, 13 maps. *Class No:* 929.731(410)

[6322]
Burke's guide to the Royal Family. Montgomery-Massingberd, H.J., *ed.* London, Burke's Peerage, 1973. xvi,358p. illus., diagrs. £21.85.

The monarchy in Britain, p.3-115; the Royal family (biographies of members (p.118-84); the Royal lineage (narrative pedigrees, p.185-333). Appendices (A-F; F: The list of Royal Warrant holders, p.342-56). 27 plates; 15 coloured drawings of royal heraldry; 24 portraits; Abbreviations, p.xiii-xvi. *Class No:* 929.731(410)

[6323]
Chronicle of the Royal Family. Mercer, D., *ed.* London, Chronicle Communications, 1991. 624p. £29.95. ISBN: 0582090067, UK; 187203120x, Can.

Intended to complement *Chronicle of Britain and Ireland.* (*q.v.*).

15 contributors. *Contents:* 1. From tribes to kingdoms (the story to 850 AD) - Chronicle from 850 to 1991 p.12-587. Appendix: A-Z gazetteer of palaces and royal residences p.588-611. Over 1750 illustrations. Accompanied by 55cm x 75cm wallchart, *Kings and Queens of England and Scotland,* displaying main lines of succession of royal houses. Follows Chronicle pattern of reporting historical events as though they had just happened. Book of descriptive reportage rather critical analysis. *Class No:* 929.731(410)

[6324]
Debrett's Kings and Queens of Britain. Williamson, D. Exeter, Webb & Bower/Michael Joseph, 1986. 240p. illus. (some col.), geneal. tables, bibliog. ISBN: 086350101x.

12 Sections: 1. Kingship in ancient Britain - 2. Roman Britain and the English settlements - 3. The Kings of Wessex and All England - 4-12. Sucessive Royal houses. Appendix B. Genealogical tables p.212-234. Index p.237-240. *Class No:* 929.731(410)

[6325]
MONTAGUE-SMITH, P.W. The Royal line of succession The British monarchy from Cerdic AD534 to Queen Elizabeth II. Andover, Hants, Pitkin Guides, 1998. 32p. col.ports., geneal. tables. £2.50. ISBN: 0853724040.

First published 1953(?).

Contents: The continuity of kingship - House of Cerdic - Cerdic & Denmark - Normandy, Blois & Anjou - Anjou - Tudor - Stuart & Orange - Hanover - Saxe Coburg & Gotha - Windsor - Kings of Scotland - Sovereign Princes of Wales - Kings of Ireland. 14 detailed geneal. tables. Author was at one time editor of *Debrett's Peerage.* *Class No:* 929.731(410)

[6326]
PARKER, M.St.J. Britain's Kings & Queens. Andover, Hants, Pitkin, 1997. 32p. col.ports, geneal. tables. £2.50 ISBN: 0853724504.

Descended from Sir George Bellew's *The Kings and Queens of Britain* (1953?). This edition first published 1990.

Short histories of the reigns of all English monarchs from the early Kings of Wessex to Elizabeth II. *Class No:* 929.731(410)

[6327]
WEIR, A. Britain's Royal Families the complete genealogy. London, The Bodley Head, 1989. 4b iv,386p. bibliog., index. £15.00. ISBN: 0370313100.

9 chronological chapters (1. The Saxon and Danish Kings of England... 9. The House of Saxe-Coburg-Gotha becomes the House of Windsor). Brief biographical data on all monarchs and their parents, siblings, issue (legitimate and bastard). Bibliography p.334-44. *Class No:* 929.731(410)

[6328]
WILLIAMSON, D. Brewer's British royalty. London, Cassell, 1996. v,392p. geneal.tables. £18.99. ISBN: 0304344273.

1500 A-Z cross-referenced entries relating to royal dynasties, myth, folklore, historical events, ceremonies and traditions, castles and palaces, key battles, individual monarchs and consorts, decorations etc. from the very earliest times to the present day. 37 Appendices (*e.g.* Kings of the Catuvellanni, Kings of Kent, Houses of Bruce and Stewart, Royal line of Powys, Genealogical triumph of Llywelyn the Great, Elizabeth II's descent from Irish kings). *Class No:* 929.731(410)

Scotland

[6329]
Debrett's Royal Scotland. Goodman, J. *and* Moncreiffe, Sir Ian. Exeter, Webb & Bower in association with Debrett's Peerage Ltd., 1983. 224p. illus. (many col.), map. bibliog. index. £12.95. ISBN: 0905649591.

Pt.1. Royal castles, palaces and houses - 2. Pageantry and ceremony (*e.g.* The Honours of Scotland; Royal Company of Archers; Order of

....*(contd.)*

the Thistle) - 3. Royal visits to Scotland (George IV to Prince Charles). Bibliography p.218-220. Monarchs of Scotland since AD 1005 p.218. The Royal Family of Scotland on endpapers. *Class No:* 929.731(411)

[6330]
ORAM, R. Scotland's Kings and Queens. Edinburgh, The Stationery Office, 1997. 108p. illus. bibliog., index. £12.99. (*Discovering Historic Scotland series.*) ISBN: 0114957835.

Traces the history of the Scottish monarchy from the 9th century (Constantine, King of Picts) to 1567 when James VI ascended the throne at the tender age of 1 year old. Also inspects the monarchy's social aspect, Crown/Church relationships, and royal and government administration. Glossary. List of sites to visit. 'A great deal is packed into this well-illustrated little book and, as an introduction to the subject, as well as a quick reference source, it fills a useful niche' (*Reference Reviews*, v.12, no.5, 1998, p.48).

Note also Bold, A. *Scotland's Kings and Queens* (Andover, Hants, Pitkin, 1996, 20p. col.illus. geneal. tables. ISBN 085372608) for short biographies of monarchs of the royal houses of Alpin, Dunkeld, Canmore, Balliol, Bruce and Stewart, 843 AD to 1746. *Class No:* 929.731(411)

[6331]
ROSS, S. The Monarchs of Scotland. Moffat, Dumfries & Galloway, Lochar Publishing, 1990. 192p. illus. (some col.), col. maps, facsims., geneal. tables, bibliog. £14.95. ISBN: 0948403225.

Their vital records, personalities, achievements, and role in the creation and presentation of the Kingdom of Scotland from Kenneth MacAlpin to Queen Anne. Bibliography p.6-7. Chronology p.185-8. *Class No:* 929.731(411)

Ireland

[6332]
BERRESFORD, P. Erin's blood royal the Gaelic noble dynasties in Ireland. London, Constable, 1999. 3452p. illus., bibliog., index. £20. ISBN: 0094786003.

19 surviving families of the 60 kings, dukes, baronets who ruled Ireland in 1541. *Class No:* 929.731(415)

England

[6333]
DYER, R. Royal tombs of England. Leeds, Pocket Booklets, 1985. 24p. illus., pbk. £1. $1.50. (*Britain's Heritage Series.*) ISBN: 0950978760.

Chronological list burial/tomb sites. *Class No:* 929.731(420)

Russia

[6334]
WARNES, D. Chronicles of the Russian Tsars the reign by reign record of the rulers of Imperial Russia. London, Thames And Hudson, 1999. 224p. illus. (some col.). £19.95. ISBN: 0500050937.

Narrative history of the reign of each Tsar, from the late 15th to the 20th century, interwoven with biographical portraits, and the key issues in Russian history. Generously supplied with timelines, datafiles and quotations. 248 illustrations (100 in colour). *Class No:* 929.731(47)

Scandinavia

[6335]
VAN DER KISTE, J. Northern Crowns the Kings of modern Scandinavia. Stroud, Gloucs., Sutton Publishing, 1996. xi,164p. illus. geneal. tables, bibliog., index. £16.99. ISBN: 0750911387.

Covers the royal families of Norway, Sweden, Denmark and, to a lesser extent, Finland. Particular attention is paid to family ties with the British royal family. Bibliography p.156-58. *Class No:* 929.731(48)

Islamic World

[6336]
BOSWORTH, C.E. The New Islamic dynasties a chronological and genealogical manual. Edinburgh Univ. Press, 1996. xxvi,389p. index. £49.50. ISBN: 074860684x.

Previously published as *The Islamic dynasties* (1967).

Considerably expanded edition extending coverage to Africa, South East Asia and Indonesia. 'No-nonsense approach to the complexities of Muslim royal nomenclature and precise AD/AH equivalences' (*Bulletin of the School of Oriental and African Studies*, v.61, no.2, 1998, p.406-7). *Class No:* 929.731(5.297)

Women

[6337]

JACKSON, G.M. **Women rulers throughout the ages** an illustrated guide. Santa Barbara, Calif., and Oxford, ABC-Clio, 1999 325p. ports. £44.95. ISBN: 1576070913:

Revised, expanded and updated from the 1990 publication *Women Who Ruled*.

More than 500 (150 new to this edition) biographies of queens, empresses, prime ministers, presidents, regent rulers, de facto rulers, constitutional monarchs, and other women rulers since the beginning of recorded history. The entries are presented alphabetically with geographical divisions, and the volume includes a country-by-country geographical index, arranged chronologically by centuries. *Class No: 929.731-0055.2*

Flags & Banners

[6338]

Complete flags of the world. London, Dorling Kindersley, 1998. 240p. col.illus., maps on endpapers, index. £9.99. ISBN: 0751311693.

1st published as *The Ultimate Pocket Flags of the world* (1997).

Text and illustration of national, international, official and provincial flags, with information on their historic and symbolic significance and their development. Key flags of the world (including the Red Flag and the Red Duster) p.6-7. Type of flag, parts of the flag, and heraldic terms (a sort of illustrated glossary) p.8-9. World guide (in 6 regional/continental divisions) p.10-235. International flags p.236-37. Signal flags p.238. *Class No: 929.9*

[6339]

CRAMPTON, W. **The Complete guide to flags.** London, Kingfisher Books, 1989. 136p. col. illus., col. maps, index. £9.95. ISBN: 086272466x.

Flags of all nations and states (including US states and British colonies) unusually grouped according to their common features *e.g.* heraldic devices, coloured crosses, and those related by political ideologies. Each flag is illustrated in colour with an explanation of its history and main features. Glossary p.132. *Class No: 929.9*

[6340]

GREAT BRITAIN. Ministry of Defence. Clothing & Textiles Agency. **Flags of all nations.** 2nd ed. London, The Stationery Office, 1999 reprint. Variously paginated, col. illus., diagrs. £49. ISBN: 0117729043.

First published for The Admiralty in 1956.

Authoritative illustrated description of British and Commonwealth, Royal Standards, military and non-military distinguishing flags, and the national flags, ensigns, and merchant flags of other countries. Loose leaf in substantial ring-binder to allow the insertion of new and revised information. *Class No: 929.9*

[6341]

PREBBLE, G.H. **The Symbols, standards, flags and banners of ancient and modern nations.** Boston, Massachusetts, G.K. Hall, 1980. 156p. illus.

A reprint of *History of flags of US and other nations.* Boston, Osgood, 1893.

Traces in detail the meanings, symbolism and uses of bannerets, banderoles, guidons, pennons, ensigns, gonfalons, standards and flags. *Class No: 929.9*

[6342]

TALOCCI, M. **Guide to the flags of the world.** Revised and updated by Whitney Smith. London, Sidgwick & Jackson, 1989. 271p. col. illus., maps, bibliog., index, pbk. £7.99. ISBN: 0283988703.

First published as *Guida alle bandiere di tutto il mondo* (Milano, Arnoldo Mondadori Editore, 1977). English edition first published 1982.

Vividly illustrated flags and arms A-Z by country within continents with final section on International flags. Glossary p.260-3. Bibliography p.271. *Class No: 929.9*

Bibliographies

[6343]

SMITH, S., *comp. and ed.* **The Bibliography of flags of foreign nations.** Boston, Massachusetts, G.K. Hall, 1965. viii, 169p.

3,053 numbered entries (plus interpolations), with brief notes. Two parts: 1. Topical entries (*e.g.* heraldic flags; naval flags; religious flags; legal aspects of flags) - 2. Countries (Afghanistan ... Zanzibar, p.44-163; UK: nos.2844-3011K). Cross-references. 3 appendices (2. Chronological list of general flag items through 1960; 3. Items on flag etiquette and ceremony. *Class No: 929.9(01)*

Encyclopaedias

[6344]

The Orbis encyclopedia of flags and coats of arms. Mucha, L. London, Orbis, 1985. 220p. illus. (many col.), col. maps, bibliog., index. £4.95. ISBN: 085613645x.

Pocket sized handbook introducing the basic history and rules of vexillology, describing and illustrating in colour the flags and coats of arms of all independent nations. Arranged in 8 sections: Europe, Asia, Africa; North and Central America; South America; Australia and Oceania; Antarctic; United Nations. Glossary p.211-215. Over 400 colour illustrations. 6 maps. *Class No: 929.9(031)*

[6345]

ZNAPIEROWSKI, A. **The World encyclopedia of flags:** the definitive guide to international flags, banners, standards and ensigns. London, Lorenz, 1999. 256p. col.illus., col.maps, bibliog., index. £17.95. ISBN: 0754801675.

In 2 sumptuously illustrated sections: 1. Flags through the ages: Origins and development; All about flags (design, types, materials and techniques, usage); Emperors, Sovereigns, Presidents; Government flags; Military signs; Navy ensigns and flags; Flag families (Christian cross, Muslim crescent, Union Jack etc.) - 2. The World of Flags (Europe, Asia, Australia and Oceania, The Americas, Africa, International Organizations, Regional and local flags, House and private flags). 600+ flags illustrated with information on date of adoption and symbolic message. Bibliography p.252. *Class No: 929.9(031)*

Great Britain

[6346]

PERRIN, W.G. **British flags:** their early history and their development at sea; with an account of the origin of the flag as a national device. Cambridge, Cambridge Univ. Press, 1922. xii, 207p. illus.

Chapters: 1. The origin of the flag and its development up to the end of the 13th century - 2. Early English, Scottish and Irish flags - 3. The union flags and jacks - 4. Flags of command - 5. Colours of distinction - 6. Flag signals - 7. Ceremonial and other usages. 13 coloured illus.; analytical index. *Class No: 929.9(410)*

[6347]

SWINSCOE, A. **The British flag** how? when? why? Glasgow, Brown, Son, & Ferguson, 1978. 20p., col. illus., sd. £2. ISBN: 0851743277.

First published 1954.

The patron Saints - Growth of the Union flag - Heraldic notes - Flying the flag - Story of the ensigns - Notes on the Commonwealth period. *Class No: 929.9(410)*

Scotland

[6348]

HARRIS, P., *ed.* **Story of Scotland's flag.** Glasgow, Lang Syne Publishers, 1992. 48p. illus. £4.95. ISBN: 1852171731.

Condensed, partly rewritten edition of McMillan, W. and Stewart, A. *The Story of the Scottish Flag* (1925).

The history of the St. Andrew's Cross from the Middle Ages to the 20th century. *Class No: 929.9(411)*

Ireland

[6349]

HAYES-MCCOY, G.A. **A History of Irish flags from earliest times.** Dublin, Academy Press; Boston, G.K. Hall, 1979. 240p. col. illus.

Comprehensive illustrated survey. *Class No: 929.9(415)*

Germany

[6350]

DAVIS, B.L. **Flags of the Third Reich.** London, Osprey, 1994. 48p.+8p. col.pl. illus., ports, bibliog., index. (*Men At Arms no.270.*) ISBN: 1855323176.

Bibliography p.43-44. *Class No: 929.9(430)*

Canada

[6351]

'The Canadian flag/Le drapeau canadien', *The Archivist,* v.17,no.1, January-February 1990.

Complete issue devoted to the Canadian flag with articles on Birth of a flag, Choosing a national flag, The Royal Mark in New France, Conserving the Proclamation of the Canadian flag, The Governor-General's flag, and others. *Class No: 929.9(71)*

USA

[6352]

CANNON, D.D. The Flags of the Confederacy : an illustrated history. Wilmington, North Carolina, Broadfoot, Publishing, 1988. 128p. col. illus. $29.95. ISBN: 0918518628.
  72 col. illus. *Class No:* 929.9(73)

[6353]

GUENTER, S.M. The American flag cultural shifts from creation to codification. Cranbury, N.J., Associated Univ. Presses, 1990. 254p. illus., bibliog., index. $34.50. ISBN: 0838633846.
  A study of the 'evolving relationship between the symbol of the American flag and the development of the nation' (Preface). Chapter notes p.213-37. Bibliography p.238-47.
  A complete history of 'Old Glory' is available in C.M. Debarr's and J.A. Bonkowske's *Saga of the American flag: an illustrated history* (Harbinger House, 1990. 91p. col. illus., bibliog.).
  Class No: 929.9(73)

[6354]

LOEFFELBEIN, R.L. The United States flag factbook: everything about Old Glory. Jefferson, NC., McFarland, 1996. 224p. illus., bibliog., index. $35. ISBN: 0768401567. *Class No:* 929.9(73)

[6355]

RICHARDSON, E.W. Standards and colors of the American Revolution. Philadelphia, Univ. of Pennsylvania Press and the Pennsylvania Society of the Revolution and its Color Guard, 1982. xvii, 341p. col. illus. ISBN: 0812278399.
  Sumptuously illustrated (64 col. plates) encyclopaedic work on the design, emblems, and unit descriptions of revolutionary flags. 22. chapters: 1. Flag design and symbols - 2. Liberty flags - 3. Continental and Union colours - 4. Continental army - 5. Navy privateers - 6-18. State flags A-Z - 19. French forces - 20. British and Loyalist colours - 21. German colours - 22. Post-war colours. Appendix 1. Chronological summary of George Washington correspondence, orders and events and other documentation relating to Continental Army standards and colours - 2. Philadelphia flagmakers and flagpainters. Glossary p.275-83. References and notes p.285-323. Bibliography p.325-333. *Class No:* 929.9(73)

[6356]

SHEARER, B.F. *and* SHEARER, B.S. State names, seals, flags and symbols. 2nd ed. Westport, Connecticut, Greenwood Press, 1994. 448p. col. illus. bibliog., index. $49.95. ISBN: 0313288623.
  1st ed. 1987. Replaces G.E. Shankle's *State names, flags, seals, songs, birds, flowers, and other symbols* (1938).
  9 well-documented chapters: 1. State names and nicknames - 2. Mottoes - 3. Seals - 4. Flags - 5. Capitals - 6. Flowers - 7. Trees - 8. Birds - 9. Songs. - 10 Legal holidays - 11. Automobile licence plates - 12. Festivals and fairs - 13. US postage stamps issued in honour of states and territories. 'Should be part of the basic reference collection of every academic, public, or school library'. (*Choice*, v.25, no.9, May 1988, p.1386). *Class No:* 929.9(73)

Australia

[6357]

The Australian national flag. 2nd ed. Canberra, Australian Government Publishing Service, 1985. 28p. illus. (some col.), diagrs., sd. ISBN: 0644040467.
  1st ed. 1982.
  Includes international rules for flying flags. *Class No:* 929.9(94)

93/99 History

Encyclopaedias

[6358]

LANGER, W.L., *comp. and ed*. An Encyclopedia of world history ancient, medieval and modern chronologically arranged. London, Harrap/Galley Press, 1987. viii,1609p. geneal.tables. ISBN: 0861366476.

First published 1940. This edition is text of *The new illustrated encyclopedia of world history* (Boston, Houghton Mifflin, 5th ed. 1972) with a new section covering the period 1971-1986, p.1359-1403.

7 major periods covering Palaeolithic period to the present time, subdivided by countries and areas. Appendix (p.1405-1417) lists Roman and Byzantine emperors, Caliphs, Roman Popes, Holy Roman Emperors, Kings of England and France, US Presidents, European and New World universities formed prior to 1900. *Class No:* 93/99(031)

History

[6359]

BARNES, H.E. A History of historical writing. 2nd ed. New York, Dover Publications, 1962; London, Constable, 1963. xiii, 440p. pbk. $5.60. ISBN: 048620104x.

First published 1937.

A running commentary in 15 chapters, each with updated 'Selected references' appended. Detailed index of authors and titles p.407-40. The succeeding period is dealt with in *Historiography, method, history teaching: a bibliography of books and articles in English 1965-1973* by A.S. Birkos and L.A. Tambs (Hamden, Connecticut, Shoe String Press, 1975. xi, 130p. $19.50. ISBN 0208014209). *Class No:* 930.0

[6360]

BENTLEY, M., *ed*. Companion to historiography. London, Routledge, 1997. xvii,997p. bibliogs, index. £100. ISBN: 0415030846.

39 international academic contributors. 39 essays arranged in 5 parts: 1. Beginnings - East and West - 2. Medieval World - 3. Early Modern historiography - 4. Reflecting on the modern Age - 6. Contexts for the writing of history (Hinterlands and Approaches). Each essay is minutely annotated and ends with an extensive list of references. 'Vastly superior to any comparable work in its field' (*International History Review,* v.20,no.4, December 1998, p.835-37). *Class No:* 930.0

[6361]

BOIA, L., *ed*. Great historians from antiquity to 1800: an international dictionary. Westport, Connecticut, Greenwood Press, 1989. 432p. $65.00; £58.50. ISBN: 0313245177.

Sponsored by the Commission on the History of Historiography of the International Committee of the Historical Sciences.

Brief articles on the life and work of 600 historians. *Class No:* 930.0

[6362]

—Great historians of the modern age: an international dictionary. Boia, L., *and other, eds*. Westport, Conn., Greenwood Press, 1990. 841p. indexes. $95; £75.85. ISBN: 0313273286.

Essays on 900 19th and 20th century historians arranged in 38 country or region chapters. 'Far more comprehensive coverage than *The Blackwell Dictionary of Historians* ... an excellent biographical dictionary' (*Choice,* v.29, no.3, November 1991, p.416). *Class No:* 930.0

[6363]

BOND, B., *ed*. The First World War and British military history. Oxford, Clarendon Press, 1991. xiv,330p. bibliog., index. ISBN: 0198222998.

11 essays by separate hands in 4 sections: 1. Establishing the historical foundation (*i.e.* preoccupations and limitations of authors in the field) - 2. Battle of the memoirs (bitter controversies of reputations of political and military leader) - 3. Indirect approaches (Middle East campaigns) - 4, Great War rediscovered (history in the wake of 1960's media saturation). Chronology of publications on First World War military histories p.vii-x. Concentrates heavily on Western Front. *Class No:* 930.0

[6364]

BREISACH, E. Historiography ancient, medieval & modern. Chicago, Univ. of Chicago Press, 1983. xii, 487p., bibliog., index. $35. ISBN: 0226072746.

Detailed chronological text of the historiography of the western world from the early Greeks to the 20th century. Bibliography p.429-464. 2nd ed. published 1994. *Class No:* 930.0

[6365]

DE SOUZA, J.P. *and* KULKARNI, C.M. Historiography in Indian languages. Delhi, Oriental, 1972. 275p. bibliogs.

21 essays on Bengali, Gujarati, Kannada, Malayalam, Marathi, Punjabi, Tamil and Telugu writings. *Class No:* 930.0

[6366]

HAY, D. Annalists and historians: Western historiography from the eighth to the eighteenth century. London, Methuen, 1977. viii, 215p. pbk. £8.95. ISBN: 0416811906.

Due emphasis on the importance of the Bible and the Lives of the Saints in the earlier period and on the Enlightenment historians in the later period. References; index. 'Fills a long-felt gap in the literature ... Ideally suited to that undergraduate audience for whom it is clearly intended' (*British Book News*, January, 1978, p.17). *Class No:* 930.0

[6367]

Historiography: an annotated bibliography of journal articles, books and dissertations. Kinnell, S., *ed*. Santa Barbara, California, ABC-Clio, 2v., 1987. 376p,482p., indexes. $137.50. £110. set. (*ABC-Clio Bibliography Series*.) ISBN: 0874364906, v.1; 0874364914, v.2.

8000 entries published 1970 onwards extracted from *America History and Life* and *Historical Abstracts*. V.1 treats broad topics *e.g.* individual historians whilst v.2 is arranged on a geographical basis. Author and subject indexes. *Class No:* 930.0

[6368]

MILLAR, T.B. Recent Australian historiography. London, University of London, Institute of Commonwealth Studies, 1987. 18p. sd. £1.50. (*Working papers in Australian studies*.) ISBN: 0902499653.

1. What is history?; 2. Large histories; 3. Aborigines in Australian history; 4. Women; 5. The growing diversity; 6. Documents. *Class No:* 930.0

[6369]

Philip's world history people, dates & events. London, Philip (1999)?. 320p. col.illus. pbk. £9.99. ISBN: 0540077178.

Lists more than 10,000 events from the earliest human origins to the present day. It is divided into four major geographical and town thematic categories - Asia and Australasia, Africa, Europe, The Americas, Science and Technology, and the Arts and Humanities - each detailing significant historical events, and enabling the reader to compare what was happening contemporaneously at any time in history in each category. More than 300 colour illustrations and an extensive biographical section. *Class No:* 930.0

Databases

[6370]

GREENSTEIN, D.L. A Historian's guide to computing. Oxford Univ. Press, 1994. 288p. illus., pbk. £30. ISBN: 0198235216.

For historians and other scholars with no prior expertise in the use of computers who need to know what kinds of problems computers can solve. Offers advice on how to exploit the computer and avoid potential pitfalls in day-to-day tasks, from bibliographic management to the use of electronic mail, and on-line library catalogues. The three central chapters on research methods examine databases and information management, numbers and measurement (including statistics, and graphical and tabular display); and document preparation and textual analysis. The final chapter offers an eight-point guide to project management which will help the user to harness the computer in a cost-effective, efficient, and productive manner for projects of any size and complexity. *Class No:* 930.0(003.4)

[6371]

LEWIS, M.J. *and* LLOYD-JONES, R. Using computers in history a practical guide. London, Routledge, 1996. 264p. illus. £45. ISBN: 0415103118.

Designed around practical workshop exercises. *Section 1: Introduction* 1. How to Use this Book and Getting Started 2. Introduction to History and Computing *Section 2: Spreadsheets and Graphs* 3. Spreadsheets, Graphs, and the Historian Chapter - 4. Presenting Historical Data With a Spreadsheet - 5. Presentation of Historical Information: Graphs - 6. The Historian and Data: The

...*(contd.)*
Material Conditions of the Working Class in Britain 1850-1914 - 7. Spreadsheets and Graphs: The Historian and Data *Section 3: Databases* - 8. Databases and the Historian - 9. Getting Started with a Database - 10. Databases and Independent Study.
Class No: 930.0(003.4)

[6372]
MAUDSLEY, E. *and* MUNCK, T. **Computing for historians** an introductory guide. Manchester Univ. Press, 1993. xvi,231p. figs., tables, bibliog., index. £40. ISBN: 0719035473.
12 chapters in 3 sections: 1. Background (History and computing: the second revolution; computer systems; word processing for historians) - 2. Census: an introductory historical database - 3. Sources. Appendix 2 CD—ROM and online history bibliography p.196-98. Glossary p.199-221. Bibliography p.222-27. Comprehensive introduction for those with no prior experience in historical computing.
Class No: 930.0(003.4)

[6373]
SCHÜRER, K. *and* ANDERSON, S.J. **A Guide to historical datafiles held in machine-readable form.** London, Association for History and Computing, 1992. v,339p. indexes. ISBN: 0951535218.
Part 1: Introduction (nature and scope) - 2. Inventory of historical datafiles - 3. Datafiles overseas - 4. Index. Information on 650 files. Data: study, purpose, content, period, place, reference.
Class No: 930.0(003.4)

[6374]
TRINKLE, D.A., *and others*. **The History highway** a guide to internet resources. Armonk, NY., Sharpe Reference, 1996. $56.95. ISBN: 0765600102.
'A roadmap to the burgeoning number of history sites (over 1000) that have sprung up along the information superhighway' (*publisher's advt.*). *Class No:* 930.0(003.4)

CD-ROM

[6375]
The Hutchinson history reference suite. Oxford, Helicon, 1996. Single CD-ROM for Windows; requires multimedia PC with a 386SX or higher processor, 4Mb of system memory, 4Mb of free hard-disc space, Microsoft Windows version 3.1 or later. £29.99. ISBN: 1859861229.
Originally published as *The Hutchinson history library CD-ROM* (1995).
7 reference works on a single disc including *Hutchinson Chronology of world history* (compact edition), *Hutchinson dictionary of world history*, *Hutchinson dictionary of historic quotations*, and the *Hutchinson directory of history web sites*. 500 colour and b/w illustrations. 50 maps. 'Essentially a collection of the reference works above, this title packs an immense amount of information, including quotations, tables, chronologies and 600 illustrations. The earliest entry in the Chronology is 10,000BC, spanning all the way to 1995 ... The historical content is vast. The biography is packed full of obscure German Philosophers and Nigerian ex-presidents, for example. However, most of these obscurer entries are skeletal, which perhaps leads us to the conclusion that this title is a great fact finding tool: more a workhorse reference tool than a DK-style interactive experience'. *Library Technology*, v.4,no.3, June 1999, p.46).
Class No: 930.0(003.40)

Internet

[6376]
History On-line. London, Institute of Historical Research, 1999. URL:htp://www.ihrinfo.ac.uk/welcome html.
'The principal components of the database are: books in print and forthcoming from leading publishers in the field, many with descriptions and even pictures of cover sleeves, and links to the publisher's sites for ordering; journal articles with abstracts; a directory of teachers of history with their interests; completed and in progress research degrees; and Institute seminars and conferences. All but the journals can be searched through the Institute's own in-house classification scheme, which organises items by subject, period and place. There are currently around 30,000 items in the database, and searching is powered by Roads software' (*Library Technology*, v.4, no.2, April 1999, p.24). *Class No:* 930.0(003.41)

Bibliographies

[6377]
The American Historical Association's Guide to historical literature. Norton, M. B. *and* Gerhardi, P., *eds*. New York, Oxford University Press, 2v., 1995. xxv,2027p. indexes. £100. $150. ISBN: 0195099524, vol.1; 0195099532, vol.2; 0195057279, set.
1st ed. 1931; 2nd ed. 1961.
370 contributors. 26,926 annotated, cross-referenced citations ordered in 48 chronological, national and regional sections, each

....*(contd.)*
introduced with a brief historiographical essay. Data: citation number, author/editor, title, edition, pagination, publishing (place, publisher, date), series title, ISBN/ISSN, Annotation (average 30 words), and contributor's initial. List of journals p.1613-21. Author index p.1623-1741. Subject index p.1743-2027. Systematic and critical overview of contemporary historical scholarship.
'An indispensable work for scholars, students, librarians and general readers' (*Library Journal*, 1 November 1994, p.71-advt.). 'The new edition remains a splendid achievement and is sure to be heavily consulted for years to come' (*Booklist*, vol.91,no.16, 15 April 1995, p.1517-18). *Class No:* 930.0(01)

[6378]
Annual bulletin of historical literature 83 a critical review of new publications of 1997. Laybourn, K. *and* MacKenney, R., *eds*. Oxford, Blackwell for The Historical Association, 1999. ISSN: 00663832.
First published 1912 (for 1911) and thence annually except for war years.
Running commentary by 28 contributors on several hundred items. 12 sections: 1. Ancient History - 2. Late Antiquity and early Middle Ages - 3. Central and late Middle Ages - 5/9. 16th century to 20th century - 10. Africa - 11. The Americas - 12. Middle East, Asia, Australia, New Zealand and the Pacific islands. *Class No:* 930.0(01)

[6379]
Bibliographie internationale des sciences historiques/International bibliography of historical sciences. Paris, Colin (now München, K.G. Saur), 1930-. Annual. Edited for the International Committee of Historical Sciences, Lausanne, Published with Unesco aid and under the patronage of the International Council for Philosophy and Humanistic Sciences. Available in North America from G.K. Hall. ISSN: 00742015.
V.63 *1994*(1999),498p. ISBN 3598204183. Arranged in Classes A-U, subdivided by countries, subjects and periods (*e.g.* A. Auxiliary historical sciences; C. Prehistory and protohistory; D. Ancient East; I. Middle Ages; K. Modern times; general works; L. Modern religious history; N. Modern economic and social history; P. International relations; modern history). Index of authors and persons; geographical index. Tardy appearance, but valuable for coverage of Africa, Asia, Eastern and Southern Europe. *Class No:* 930.0(01)

[6380]
Bibliographies in history: an index to bibliographies in history journals and dissertations ... Kinnell, S., *ed*. Santa Barbara, California, ABC-Clio, 2v., 1988. $144.50. £130. set. ISBN: 087436521x, set.
1. *Covering the US and Canada*. 137p. index. $85. £51. ISBN 0874365228. About 5100 entries. 2. *Covering all countries in the world except the US and Canada*. 322p. index. $85. £51. ISBN 0874365236. About 3000 entries. Entries relate to articles or dissertations published 1971-1987 extracted from *America History and Life* and *Historical Abstracts* with author and subject indexes. 'Students will be able to avoid the tedium of extensive searching in the print indexes' (*Choice*, v.26, no.10, June 1989, p.1652).
Class No: 930.0(01)

[6381]
D'ANIELLO, C.A., *ed*. **Teaching bibliographic skills in history:** a sourcebook for historians and librarians. Westport, Conn., Greenwood Press, 1993. 392pp. bibliog. £58.50. ISBN: 0313252661.
10 contributors. Pt.1 The study of history (Historical methodologies and research; Interdisciplinary history) - 2. Bibliographic instruction in History (Finding and using historical materials) - 3. Special topics (Catalogues and indexes; using reference sources; Sources for interdisciplinary research; Electronic information sources; Finding aids to archives and manuscript collections) - 4. Bibliography (Teaching the bibliography of history; Select annotated bibliography.
Class No: 930.0(01)

[6382]
Recently published articles. Washington, American Historical Association, 1976-. 3 *pa*. $20.00. members. $28.00. non-members and institutions. ISSN: 01455311.
Formerly (1895-1975) a section of *The American Historical Review*.
Lists more than 15,000 references *pa*. in all fields of history. Draws on over 3,000 periodicals, a fair proportion being in foreign languages. Systematically arranged (20 sections) by periods, continents and countries. Claims to be 'the most current and comprehensive bibliography of periodical literature about history available'.
Class No: 930.0(01)

[6383]

RICHARDSON, R.C. The Study of history: a bibliographical guide. Manchester, Manchester Univ. Press, 1988. Distributed in North America by St. Martins Press. xiv,98p. index. £29.95; $55.00. (*History and Related Disciplines Selected Bibliographies*.) ISBN: 0719018811.

Approximately 2,100 entries arranged in 9 chronological and thematic divisions: 1. General works *i.e.*, bibliographies, philosophy of history, methods and purposes, quantification, historiographical surveys - 2-9. Ancient History to Twentieth Century. 'Although the emphasis is heavily toward British historiography this book should prove very useful to undergraduates, beginning graduate students, and their instructors' (*Choice*, v.26,no.2, October 1988, p.295-6).
Class No: 930.0(01)

[6384]

SLAVENS, T.P. Sources of information for historical research. New York, Neal-Schuman, 1994. 577p. indexes. pbk. $39.95. ISBN: 1555700934.

Annotated entries on major reference works covering archives, history, heraldry, genealogy, and biography arranged by Library of Congress subject headings. 'Useful for both novice and experienced researchers' (*Choice*, v.32,no.2, October 1994, p.265).
Class No: 930.0(01)

Encyclopaedias

[6385]

Encyclopedia of historians and historical writing. Boyd, K., *ed.* Chicago & London, Fitzroy Dearborn, 2v., 1999. l,1562p. bibliogs., indexes. £175. ISBN: 1884964338.

Almost 400 academic contributors. 852 A-Z essays, each with extensive bibliographies, of 3 types: 1. Individual historians (scholarly career and publication record) born no later than 1945 - 2. Nations or geographical regions - 3. Topical essays relating to historical sub-disciplines, methods shaping historical writing, and the most studied historical debates. Alphabetical list of entries p.xv-xxii. Thematic list p.xxiii-xxxiii. Chronological list of historians p.xxxv-xl. Further Reading Index (*i.e.* general bibliography A-Z by author) p.1411-1535. 'It all adds up to a scholarly, well-documented reference work' (*Reference Reviews*, v.13, no.6, 1999, p.43-44). *Choice* Outstanding Academic Title 1999. *Class No:* 930.0(031)

[6386]

Encyclopedia of world history. Market House Books, *comp.* Oxford Univ. Press, 1998. vii,775p. illus. (inc. ports.), maps, tables, £30. $30. ISBN: 0198602235.

Core of this publication derived from the 2v. devoted to history in the *Oxford Illustrated Encyclopedia*: Judge, H. *World history from earliest times to 1800* and Blake, R. *World history from 1800 to the present day* (1988).
4000+ cross-referenced A-Z entries relating to events, historical and social concepts and movements, and the leading military, political and inventive figures from prehistory to the present day. Also detailed analysis of every world nation's history in the context of its physical location and economic development. Chronology of world events (in 3 vertical columns to the page) p.749-75. 50 maps.
Class No: 930.0(031)

[6387]

Family encyclopedia of world history. London, Reader's Digest Association, 1996. 752p. illus. (many col.), maps. £26.95. ISBN: 0276422872.

25 contributors. 3,000 A-Z entries (instant, easy to read accounts of key makers of history, the countries whose destinies they determined, and great events). 140+ features explain in detail why revolutions and movements happened when they did. Timelines of History (overview of 1700 highlights in chronological order) p.722-41. At-A-Glance reference lists (*e.g.* Holy Roman Emperors, dynasties of Islam, India and China etc.) p.742-49. 50+ maps. *Class No:* 930.0(031)

[6388]

History of humanity. London, Routledge, Paris, UNESCO, 7v. 1994-.
V.1: de Laet S.J., ed. From the origins of humanity to the third millenium. 1994. 1440p. maps, bibliog., index. £85. ISBN 0415093058. 40+ contributors. In 2 main sections: 1. From anthropogenesis to the beginnings of food production - 2. Food production to the first states.
V.2: Dani, A.H. and Mohen, J.P., eds. *From the third millenium to the seventh century BC.* 1995. 700p. illus., maps, bibliog., index. £85. 0415093066. Over 60 contributors. In 2 main sections: 1. Thematic (*e.g.* Technical aspects ... Measurement of time ... Song, music and dance) - 2. Regional.
V.3: Herrman, J. and Zurcher, E., eds. *From the seventh century BC to the seventh century AD.* 1996. 736p. illus., maps, bibliog., index. £95. 0415093074. In 2 sections: 1. Thematic, covering trends and developments of the period - 2. Geographical, study the progress of peoples worldwide.
V.4: *From the seventh to the sixteenth century*, June 1997. 0415093082. £95. V.5: Burke, P. and Inalchik, H. eds. *From the*

....(contd.)
sixteenth century to the eighteenth century, 1999. xxvi,508p. + 60p. col.pl. £95. 0415093090. Forthcoming. V.6: *The nineteenth century*, 0415093104. £95. V.7: *The twentieth century*, 0415093112. £95.

Edited by a team of internationally recognised scholars, each volume includes a *general introduction*, several *thematic chapters* dealing with the features of the period from a global viewpoint, a series of *regional chapters* examining the issues in more detail, and *detailed bibliographies* and an *exhaustive index*. *Class No:* 930.0(031)

[6389]

Philip's world history encyclopedia. London, Philip, 2000. 528p. col.illus., col.maps, col.diagrs. £30. ISBN: 0540078778.

6,500 cross-referenced A-Z articles featuring a chronology of people, dates and events spanning over 12,000 years; and a Ready Reference section which provides tabular information on key historical topics. Some 30 important subject areas appear as special extended features on double-page spreads.
Phillip's illustrated world history encyclopedia. 2000. 528p. illus., maps. £12.99. ISBN 0540078786. Paperback edition.
Class No: 930.0(031)

[6390]

STEWART, R. The Illustrated encyclopedia of historical facts from the dawn of the Christian era to the new world order. London, Simon & Schuster, 1992. 320p. illus. (some col.), col. maps, index. £17.50. ISBN: 0671711105.

Concentrates on 480 major world events with 5 pictorial introductory essays on successive historical periods. Micropedia of people p.280-95; of places p.296-300. Historical charts p.301-13. For family and school use. *Class No:* 930.0(031)

[6391]

WOOLF, D.R., *ed.* A Global encyclopedia of historical writing. New York, Garland, 2v., 1998. xxxiv,1047p. bibliogs., index. £125. (*Garland Reference Library Of The Humanities, no.1809.*) ISBN: 0815315147.

318 contributors. Signed cross-referenced entries fall into 3 categories: 1. Biographical entries on individual historians or sometimes individual works and genres of historiography not associated with a particular author - 2. Surveys of regional or national historiographies - 3. Topical articles on certain concepts, approaches or themes. Time span: from antiquity to the present day. Index p.993-1,047. 'Without descending into hyperbole, the width and depth of coverage is truly impressive and leaves little room for valid criticism' (*Reference Reviews*, v.12,no.8, 1998, p.46-47). *Choice* Oustanding Academic Title 1999. *Class No:* 930.0(031)

Dictionaries

[6392]

The Blackwell dictionary of historians. Cannon, J., *and others* eds. Oxford, Blackwell Reference, 1988. xiv,480p. bibliogs., index. £50. $75. ISBN: 063114708x.

200 contributors. Over 450 biographical entries including 50 living historians, 60 French, 40 Germans and 20 Italians. In addition there are 25 national historiographical surveys and 40 thematic entries. 'No reference library of reasonable size that lays claim to having any worthwhile coverage of British or overseas history should be without it' (*Library Association Record*, v.91, no.5, May 1989, p.291).
Class No: 930.0(038)

[6393]

Chambers dictionary of world history. Boyd, K., *ed.* Edinburgh Chambers, 1993. viii,996p. maps. £30. ISBN: 0550150056.

35 contributors. 7500 cross-referenced entries relating to political, military, and diplomatic history from the earliest times to the 1990s. 'A single volume of substantial size ... which will be useful for most quick reference purposes for professional and educational users' (*Preface*). 36 maps. *Class No:* 930.0(038)

[6394]

COOK, C. Macmillan dictionary of historical terms. 3rd ed. London Macmillan Press, 1998. 384p. ISBN: 0333673476.
First published 1983.
Over 2,000 terms 'frequently encountered by both undergraduate and research students', covering 1500 years of history from the onset of the Middle Ages, and the rise of Islam, to the closing decade of the twentieth century. *Class No:* 930.0(038)

[6395]

The Guinness history fact book. Enfield, Mdx., Guinness Publishing 1994. 256p. maps. £9.99. ISBN: 0851127827.

A-Z factfinder of 3000 entries giving key information on major rulers, statesmen, revolutionaries and ideologies, chronologies of leading nation-status *etc.* Preliminaries include a brief history of the world (in 6 periods) p.8-44. Time charts p.46-73. 25 maps. 'Pure genius this captivating book isn't, but it is a perfectly respectable source of historical information that deserves to be taken seriously' (*Reference Reviews*, v.8,no.8, 1994, p.40-41). *Class No:* 930.0(038)

[6396]
HARBOTTLE, T.B. **Dictionary of historical allusions:** a guide to names and nicknames, sobriquets and similar appellations ... and terms commonly found in historical writings, but omitted from standard dictionaries and encyclopedias. Detroit, Gale Research Co., 1968. 306p.

First published London, Sonnenschein, 1904.

'A useful source for indentification of fugitive phrases' (*Wilson Library Bulletin*, v.43, no.10, June 1969. p.1022). 'Leans towards English history' (*Choice*, v.6, no.12, February 1970, p.1731). *Class No:* 930.0(038)

[6397]
The **Hutchinson dictionary of world history.** Oxford, Helicon, 1993. x,699p. maps, tables, geneal. tables. £20. ISBN: 0091771528.

Over 5000 entries including longer feature articles (*e.g.* Age of Discovery, Gandhi and Indian Nationalism) relating to key individuals, events, major movements, and histories of every modern country, from prehistory to post-Communism. 7 Appendices. World Chronology p.676-99 and 100 thematic chronologies. 70 maps. *Class No:* 930.0(038)

[6398]
MOURRE, M. **Dictionnaire encyclopédique d'histoire.** Paris, Bordas, 5v., 1996. 6,000p. illus. col.plates.

19,200 entries (1715 new to this edition). Natural emphasis on France and French history does not detract from its authority. First great universal historical dictionary to be published in France since C. Dezobry and T. Bachelet's *Dictionnaire général de biographie et d'histoire* (1857).

Le petit Mourre: dictionnaire de l'histoire. new ed. 1994. 1072p. Fr320. ISBN 2040270655. 6,000 entries arranged A-Z under subject headings. *Class No:* 930.0(038)

[6399]
The **Oxford minidictionary of twentieth-century world history.** Oxford, Oxford Univ. Press, 1990. 444p. limp cover. £2.25. ISBN: 0198661614.

Covers the important events, individuals, and historical movements in c.1,000 cross-referenced entries. Well suited for examination revision. *Class No:* 930.0(038)

[6400]
TRUHART, P. **Historical dictionary of states.** States and state-like communities from their origins to the present/Lexikon der historischer Staatennamen. Staaten und-staatssähnliche Gemeinwesen von der Ursprüngen bis zur Gegenwart. München, K.G. Saur,1996. xxxiv,872p. bibliog., index. ISBN: 3598112920.

This incredibly detailed general survey of all the 'states' in the world since c.3,000BC (estimated to number some 7,500) presents basic information on the development of all geopolitical entities in antiquity, medieval, and modern times. Bibliography p.775-90. Index p.791-782. All chronological sections are divided by region. *Class No:* 930.0(038)

[6401]
VETTERAU, B., *comp.* **World history:** a dictionary of important people, places, and events from ancient times to the present. New York, Henry Holt, 1994. 1200p. $45. ISBN: 080507350x.

Revision of *Macmillan's concise dictionary of world history* (1983).

10,000 brief entries and over 100 longer entries on such topics as 'Holy Roman Empire' and 'American Revolution'. *Class No:* 930.0(038)

Reviews & Abstracts

[6402]
Historical Abstracts bibliography of the world's historical literature. Santa Barbara, California, ABC-Clio; Oxford, Clio Press, 1955-. Priced on Service Rate Principle depending on library's annual book fund. ISSN: 03632717.

1. Boehm H. ed. *Historical abstracts 1775-1945: bibliography of the world's periodical literature* v.1-16. 1955-1970. Up to 1964 this offered universal coverage but from 1965 US and Canada were removed and included in *America history and life* (*qv*). 2. V.17-. 1971-. Published in 2 parts: *Part A. Modern history abstracts 1450-1914* and *Part B. Twentieth century abstracts*. Entries relating to the period 1914-1945 appeared in both parts in v.17-20. 3. From 1980 (v.31) coverage was extended to books and dissertations. 4. 5 retrospective volumes were published 1980-1984 to include references that were previously outside *Historical Abstract's* scope and also references not available when the original volumes appeared. These retrospective volumes (26-30) can only be purchased in conjunction with the relevant current volumes *i.e.* 26/31, 27/32, 28/33, 29/34 and 30/35.

Each volune provides abstracts of over 18,000 articles from 2,000+ historical journals published worldwide and also cites 3,000 new books reviewed in key English language review journals whilst dissertations are derived from *Dissertation Abstracts International*. *Modern history abstracts 1450-1914* and *Twentieth century abstracts* are both

....(contd.)

published quarterly: nos. 1-3 contain references arranged by subject (vs. 1-2 have indexes) and no.4 contains a cumulative annual index. *Modern History Abstracts* is divided into 3 sub-parts: 1. General (*i.e.* bibliography, methodology, historiography, archive, libraries, societies *etc.*) - 2. Topics (*e.g.* international relations, wars, political history, science and technology) - 3. Area and Country (8 geographical divisions). *Twentieth century abstracts* omits sub-part 1. *Vol.50* (1999) has 11,475 entries in *Modern History abstracts* and 10,003 in *Twentieth-century abstracts*. Bibliographic entries printed in *Historical abstracts* are available online from File 39, DIALOG Information Services covering 1973 to date and through CompuServe.

Five year indexes are issued: V. 1-5 (1955-59) £240; vs. 6-10 (1960-64) £240; V.11-15 (1965-69) £240; vs. 16-20 (1970-74) £420; vs. 21-25 (1975-79) £420; vs. 31-35 (1980-84) £420; vs. 36-40 (1985-89) £375. v.26-30 (retrospective) £310. *Class No:* 930.0(048)

[6403]
—Historical abstracts (Internet database). Davis, R.W. *and* Speck, V., *eds.* Oxford and Santa Barbara, Calif., ABC-Clio, 1999. $6,800/network of 2-6 users.

'From the attractive blue-and-white opening page, navigation is straightforward; the minimal graphics and left-hand menu bar keep the screen uncluttered and response time respectable. The Web version covers items published from 1967 to the present and, in contrast to the CD-ROM versions, is updated monthly. The Web version also features timely "in-process" English-language article entries, which are added before they have been fully abstracted or assigned complete subject terms ... One can specify any combination of keyword, subject term, author/editor, title, language, document type, journal name, publication date, or time period covered; a magnifying glass icon indicates fields that allow browsing of alphabetical lists of subject terms, journal names, or other criteria. Boolean "and", "or", "not" and truncation (*) are available; the time period search has recently been reworked to allow more speedy retrieval by country (*e.g.*1800h) or decade (1990d) (*Choice*, Supplement 36, p.134). *Choice* Outstanding Academic Title 1999. *Class No:* 930.0(048)

[6404]
—Historical abstracts on disc. Davis, R.W., *ed.* Santa Barbara, Calif., ABC-Clio. Hardware: IBM PC/XT/AT or 100% compatible, 512Kb memory (384K free), 20 Mb hard drive. CD-ROM drive with appropriate controller card and interface cable (Hitachi, Philips, Sony, or any other CD-ROM drive with ISO 9660 compatible device driver). Operating System: MS-DOS 3.0 or higher.

Packed with annotated references to historical writings covering the years 1450 to the present, this quick, easy-to-run expanded reference tool provides access to more than 500,000 journal articles, over 23,500 disserations, and over 49,000 book citations. In all, more than 465,000 entries (from more than 50 languages.)

Basic Subscription: Includes an initial CD-ROM disc with information from 1982 to present, plus two cumulative updates. Your renewal includes three cumulative updates.

Expanded Subscription: Includes an initial Expanded Edition CD-ROM disc with retrospective information from 1979 to present, plus two cumulative updates. Your renewal includes three cumulative updates. Updates will include additional order as well as current data. *Class No:* 930.0(048)

Periodicals

[6405]
HENIGE, D., *comp.* **Serial bibliographies and abstracts in history:** an annotated guide . Westport, Conn., Greenwood Press, 1986. ix,220p. index. $35. £27.95. (*Bibliographies and Indexes in World History, no.2.*) ISBN: 0313250707.

874 annotated items A-Z by title consisting of 'all bibliographies which address in whole or in part any aspect of the past. Data: history and frequency of publication, types of indexes, kinds of material included, languages represented and, in some instances, a word of commendation. Subject index. 'Smaller or less well known sources that are nonetheless of enormous value can be identified through this tool' (*Reference Services Review*, v.17, no.4, Winter 1989, p.69-70). *Class No:* 930.0(051)

[6406]
STIEG, M.F. **The Origin and development of scholarly historical periodicals.** Tuscaloosa, Univ. of Alabama Press, 1986. xi,261p. tables, bibliog. $31.95. ISBN: 0817302735.

Chronological study with emphasis on *Historische Zeitschrift; English Historical Reivew; Deutsche Zeitschrift für Geschichtswissenschaft; Mississippi Valley Historical Review; Zeitschrift für Sozial-und Wirtschaftsgeschichte; Catholic Historical Review* and *Journal of the History of Ideas.* Chap.8. Bibliographic control and use. Chapter notes p.199-266; Bibliography p.227-247. Index p.249-261. *Class No:* 930.0(051)

Bibliographies

[6407]

BOEHM, E.H., *and others*. **Historical periodicals directory**. Santa Barbara, California and Oxford, ABC-Clio, 5v., 1981-1986. £339.50. ISBN: 0874361672, set.

Updates Boehm and Adolphus' *Historical periodicals* (*qv.*).

1. *US and Canada*. 1981. xii,180p. $95. £62.25. 0874360188. 2. *Europe: West, North, Central and South*. 1983. xv,597p. $110. £70.50. 0874360196. 3. *Europe, East and Southeast*. 1984. xv,252p. $95. £66.50. 087436020. 4. *Latin America and the West Indies* 1955. xiv,157p. $95. £67.50. 0874360218. 5. *Australia and New Zealand*. 1986. xiii,227p. $95. £73.50. 0874360226. Includes cumulative title index and subject/geographic index. 63 contributors covers 8900 titles. Lesser known titles deliberately sought to include information not found elsewhere. Aims to be comprehensive, for current periodicals and those that have ceased publication since 1960. Data: title; dates and frequency; address; scope; language; where abstracted; former title (if any). 'While the effort put into this set must be admired, it is really needed only in research libraries' (*Choice*, v.24, no.9, May 1987, p.1380). *Class No:* 930.0(051)(01)

[6408]

CARON, P. *and* JARYC, M. **World list of historical periodicals and bibliographies**. Oxford, etc., International Committee of Historical Sciences, 1939. 391p. indexes.

The original list of 3,103 periodicals is supplemented by annual additions in the *International bibliography of historical sciences*, v.16-, 1947-. A useful selection, but far from exhaustive for British periodicals and publications of societies. *Class No:* 930.0(051)(01)

[6409]

FYFE, J. **History journals and serials**: an analytical guide. Westport, Connecticut, Greenwood Press, 1986. xxiii,351p. index. $46.95. (*Annotated bibliographies of serials: a subject approach No.8*.) ISBN: 0313239991. ISSN: 07485190.

689 entries in 35 geographical and topical sections (1. Universal history ... 7. Genealogy and family history ... 22-34. Geographical regions ... 35. Indexes and abstracts) forming a comprehensive and detailed annotated bibliography of major journals of international reputation in the English language. Aimed primarily at helping the librarian to select journals and the historian for personal reading and the submission of manuscripts. Table of abstacts, indexes and databases p.xvii-xx. Directory of microform and reprint publishers p.xxi-xxiii. 'The compiler has done a good job' (*Choice*, v.24, no.3, November 1986, p.454). *Class No:* 930.0(051)(01)

Quotations

[6410]

Chronological dictionary of quotations. Wright, E., *ed.* rev. ed. London, Bloomsbury, 1993. ix,445p. indexes. £17.99. ISBN: 0747514755.

First published as *Who said what when* (1988).

Over 7000 quotations largely selected for their historical interest (*i.e.* for the light they throw on an important event or figure). Arranged in 13 sections: 1. The Old Testament .... 13. The Post-War World. Keyword and name indexes. *Class No:* 930.0(082.2)

[6411]

PALMER, A. *and* PALMER, V. **A Dictionary of historical quotations**. 2nd ed. London, Granada Publishing, 1985. xi,404p. pbk. £3.95. ISBN: 0586085076.

First edition published by Harvester Press in 1976 under the title of *Quotations in history*.

Over 2000 quotations ranging in time from the crowning of Charlemagne (AD800) to present day. Arranged A-Z by speakers. Key word indexes. A note on the circumstances of each remark would have been helpful; also a chronological index. 'Decidedly Western in orientation' (*sic!*) 'but it serves a vital need' (*Library Journal*, 15 December 1976, p.2259). *Class No:* 930.0(082.2)

Maps & Atlases

[6412]

BLACK, J. **Maps and history** constructing images of the past. New Haven, Yale Univ. Press, 1997. ix,267p. facsims of maps, index. ISBN: 0300069766.

Comprehensive and wide-ranging account of the role, development, and nature of historical atlases and their impact on the presentation of the past in 11 chapters (*e.g.* 1. Development to 1800 ... 3. Nationalism and Eurocentrism in 19th century historical atlases ... 5. War, environment and ideology 1914-45). Chapter notes (mostly bibliographical references and citations) p.242-59.

Black, J. 'Historical atlas reconsidered?', *The Historian*, no.39, Autumn 1993, p.16-20 is a bibliographical essay very much on the same lines. *Class No:* 930.0(084.3)

[6413]

Dorling Kindersley atlas of world history. London, Dorling Kindersley 1999. 352p. col.illus., col.maps, bibliog., index. £29.99. ISBN 075130179x.

Pt.1: Eras of world history (26 world maps and analytical text) p.10 113. Pt.2: 8 regional histories (North and South America, Africa Europe, West Asia, South and Southeast Asia, North and East Asia Australasia and Oceania) p.114-287. Subject index and glossary p.289 319. Index-Gazetteer (20,000 names) p.319-51. 470+ col. maps, 42 timelines, 1000+ illustrations. The publisher's inimitable and attractive style has failed to deflect strong words of criticism: 'duff design however, makes the atlas slick but unserviceable ... text is compresse for the short attention span, into embarrassing fatuities or litera nonsense' (*The Times*, no.66693, 9 December 1999, p.45). *Class No:* 930.0(084.3)

[6414]

GROVE, N. **National Geographic atlas of world history**. Washington National Geographic, 1998. 400p. illus., maps. $45. ISBN 0792270487.

Tells the story of human development from the European cave painters of the Ice Age to the computer revolution. Each chapte features fact boxes, short biographies and detailed maps, with tim lines giving access to the chronology of events. *Class No:* 930.0(084.3)

[6415]

HAYWOOD, J., *and others*. **The Cassell atlas of world history** London, Cassell, 1997. c.350p. (no continuous pagination), col.illus. col.maps, index. £30. ISBN: 0304348457.

168 double-page spreads (maps, texts, timelines) depicting rise an fall of empires, military history, growth of settlements, spread o agriculture, the spread and influence of different cultures, illustratin how human history was shaped by geography and environment arranged under 6 chronological headings: 1. The Ancient Worl (4,000,000-500BC) - 2. Classical World (500 BC-AD600) - 3. Th Medieval World (AD 600-1492) - 4. From Columbus to America Independence (1492-1783) - 5. Nineteenth Century World (1783-1914 - 6. From World War 1. to the present (1914-1997). *Class No:* 930.0(084.3)

[6416]

—HAYWOOD, J., *and others, eds*. Cassell historical atlases. London Cassell, 5v., 1998. col. illus., col. maps, index. £14.99 each.

1. *The Cassell atlas of the Classical World 500BC-AD60C* 0304350443. 2. *Medieval World AD600-1492*. 0304350427. 3. *Earl modern world 1492-1783*. 030435096x. 4. *Nineteenth century worl 1783-1914*. 0304350456. 5. *1914 to present*. 0304350508. Preser. overview of main themes of world history. Maps are supported by A-2 entries of people, places and events. Analytical indexes. *Class No:* 930.0(084.3)

[6417]

OVERY, R., *ed*. **The Times history of the world**. New ed. London Times Books, 1999. 357p. col.illus., col.maps, bibliog., index. £50 ISBN: 0723008949.

First published as *The Times atlas of world history* in 1978. Revise and reprinted at frequent intervals.

27 contributors. c.100 double page map features in 7 major sections 1. Human origins - 2. First civilizations - 3. Classical civilizations o Eurasia - 4. World of divided regions - 5. The Emerging West - 6 Age of European dominance - 7. Age of global civilization. Glossar (individuals, peoples, events) p.311-46. Chronology (5 regiona timelines) p.16-27. Bibliography p.310. 520+ computer generated col maps.

'Who would have guessed it, 25 years ago', *The Times*,10 Apri 1999, p.4 compares this new edition with the first but fails to mentio why a change of title was deemed necessary. *Class No:* 930.0(084.3)

[6418]

Philip's atlas of world history. O'Brien, P.K., *ed*. Rev. ed. London Philip, 1998. 368p. illus., col. maps, bibliogs., index. £17.99. ISBN 0540075833.

First published 1987. Published in the U.S. as *Atlas of world histor* (Oxford Univ. Press, $85. ISBN 0195215672).

135 double-page spreads, each of which portrays key development in a world region over a specific period of time. Each spread feature informative colour maps, together with complementary text discussin and explaining the historical, political, geographical, social, cultura and religious themes behind each topic. Additional historica information includes a detailed 22-page time chart, a 20-page gazettee of historical places, concise biographies of significant figures and a extensive index. The Atlas presents the entire story of civilisation in it physical setting. Specially designed to help the reader visualise grea historical themes and decisive monuments, it combines over 40 specially drawn maps graphically depicting the scope of these events. *Class No:* 930.0(084.3)

The Times concise atlas of world history. Barraclough, G., ed. 6th ed. [6419]
London, Time Books, 1997. viii,184p. col.maps, bibliog. £19.99.
ISBN: 0723009066.

1st ed. 1982.

In 4 sections: 1. Early man and the civilizations of the ancient world; 2. Decline and recovery the emergence of a new world; 3. The rise of the West; 4. The modern world. Although modelled on *The Times atlas of world history* it is not simply a condensed version but stands on its own merits as a compact historical atlas. 'No fewer than 70 of the 320 maps ... are entirely new or radically changed' (*Introduction*). Bibliography p.152. Index gazetteer p.153-154. This edition is substantially revised principally because of recent advances in archaeological knowledge and because of the collapse of Communist regimes in Eastern Europe. 'A superb work, not least because of its determined avoidance of an Eurocentric perspective' (*Archives*, v.20, no.89, April 1993. p.122). *Class No:* 930.0(084.3)

Biographies

People in world history an index to biographies in history journals and [6420]
dissertations covering all countries of the world except Canada and the U.S. Kinnell, S., ed. Santa Barbara, California, and Oxford, ABC-Clio, 2v., 1988. 800p. £113.95 set. ISBN: 0874365503, set; 0874365511, v.1; 087436552x, v.2.

A-Z reference guide to biographical material extracted from the ABC-Clio database with an introductory chapter consisting of article abstracts on biographical writing. A detailed subject index in v.2 allows access by career, politics, religion, ethnic group, place of residence, country of origin, or by the source of the biographical material. *Class No:* 930.0(092)

Women

Women in world history Vols. 1-3. Commire, A. *and* Klezmer, D., eds. [6421]
Detroit, Gale, 15v., 1999-2000. 17,500p. illus., geneal. charts. $995. ISBN: 078763736x.

International in scope from antiquity to the 20th century. Cross-referenced A-Z entries varying in length from a brief paragraph to several pages. On completion (December 2000) the 15v. will contain 10,000 biographies (6,000 signed) from 300 contributors across 20 different countries. Indexes will be published by mid-2001. Supplementary volumes are planned. 'There is nothing comparable to this encyclopedia's coverage of women from all over the world in all eras and all walks of life' (*Booklist*, v.96, no.13, 1 March 2000, p.1285). *Class No:* 930.0(092)-0055.2

Ancient Greece & Rome

MOMIGLIANO, A. The Classical foundations of modern [6422]
historiography. Berkely, Univ. of California Press, 1990. xiv,162p. bibliog., index. ISBN: 0520068904.

6 university lectures: 1. Persian, Greek, Jewish historiography - 2. Herodotean and Thucididean traditions - 3. Rise of antiquarian research - 4. Fabius Pictor and the origins of national history - 5. Tacitus and the Tacitist tradition - 6. Origins of ecclesiastical historiography. Bibliographical note p.xiii-xiv.
Class No: 930.0(37/38)

Ancient Greece

Greek historiography. Hornblower, S., ed. Oxford, Clarendon Press, [6423]
1994. xii,286p. bibliogs., index. £35. ISBN: 019814931x.

8 contributors. Contents: Polybius and his predecessors - Herodotus and religion - Herodotus on Alexander I of Macedon - Narratology and narrative techniques in Thucydides - World of Theophrastus - The tradition about the First Sacred War - Conformity and creativity: Diodorus and his sources - Symbol of unity? The Persian War tradition in the Roman Empire. *Class No:* 930.0(37)

Europe

Bibliographies

A Selected bibliography of modern historiography. Attila, Pók, ed. [6424]
Westport, Conn., Greenwood Press, 1992. xv,284p. indexes. £52.79. (*Bibliographies and Indexes in World History, no.24.*) ISBN: 031327231x. ISSN: 07426941.

Expands L.D. Stephens' *Historiography: a bibliography* (Metuchen, N.J., Scarecrow Press, 1975).

Listing of 2454 mostly unannotated entries relating to books and journal articles arranged in 6 geographically sub-divided national

....(contd.)

chapters. Strong Central European presence. Prepared under the auspices of the Institute of History of the Hungarian Academy of Sciences. *Class No:* 930.0(4)(01)

Great Britain

ARNSTEIN, W.L., ed. Recent historians of Great Britain essays on [6425]
the post-1945 generation. Ames, Iowa State University Press, 1990. x,207p. bibliogs., index. ISBN: 0813805929.

Assessments of the published works and achievements of 8 modern British historians. *Class No:* 930.0(410)

Bibliographies

ELTON, G.R. Modern historians on British history 1485-1945: a [6426]
critical bibliography. London, Methuen, 1970. viii,239p.

Based on English version of 'Literaturbericht' (to May 1967), appearing in *Sonderheft 3* (1969) of *Historische Zeitschrift*. Essays, in 13 sections: 1. Introduction - 2. Works of reference - 3. Sources - 4. General - 5. The sixteenth century - 6. The seventeenth century - 7. The eighteenth century 8. The nineteenth century - 9. The twentieth century - 10. Social history - 11. History of ideas - 12. Scotland - 13. Ireland. Indexes: authors and editors; subjects. 'A valuable element of the work is the references to reviews in scholarly journals of many of the works cited' (*Library Journal*, v.97, no.18, 15 April 1973, p.1384). *Class No:* 930.0(410)(01)

Scotland

'Writing Scotland's history proceedings of the Edinburgh Conference, [6427]
Nov. 1996', *Scottish Historical Review*, special issue, no.201, April 1997, p.1-114.

8 papers including D. Broun's 'The birth of Scottish history' (p.4-22); C. Kidd's 'The strange death of Scottish history' (p.86-102); and J. Stevenson's 'Writing Scotland's history in the twentieth century' (p.103-114). *Class No:* 930.0(411)

Ireland

Irish historiography. [6428]

1. *Irish historiography 1936-70* edited by T.W. Moody. Dublin, Irish Committee of Historical Sciences, 1971. viii,155p. 'Not a bibliography but an assessment and interpretation' (*Introductory*). 7 papers, arranged chronologically (1. Ireland before the Norman invasion ... 7. Twentieth-century Ireland, 1914-70), with an additional chapter on 'Thirty-five years of Irish historiography'. Appendix: 'A new History of Ireland under the auspices of the Royal Irish Academy (Stage I) conspectus'.

2. *Irish historiography 1970-79* edited by J. Lee. Cork Univ. Press, 1981, viii,238p. pbk. ISBN 0902561200. 9 papers: 1. Gaelic Ireland to 1603 - 2. Medieval Ireland 1169-1534 - 3. Ireland 1534-1660 - 4. 1660-1800 - 5. 1800-1921 - 6. Ireland since 1921-7. Irish ecclesiastical history since 1500 - 8. Irish economic history since 1500 - 9. Index to Bulletin of the Irish Committee of Historical Sciences 1939-1974. *Class No:* 930.0(415)

England

GRANSDEN, A. Historical writing in England. London, Routledge & [6429]
Kegan Paul; Ithaca, New York, Cornell Univ. Press, 2v., 1974-82. illus., facsims., bibliog., indexes.

1. *c.550-c.1307.* 1974. xxiv,610p. 071007476x. 21 chapters: 1. Gildas and Nennius - 2. Bede... 5. Anglo-Saxon chroniclers - 6. History of Norman Conquest ... 21. The chronicle of London. Appendix B. Local history in the thirteenth century (p.519-21) - D. Chronological index of the principal literary sources for English history to *c.*1307 (p.524-9).

2. *c. 1307 to the early sixteenth century.* 1982. xxiv,644p. 071000480x. 14 chapters: 1. Chroniclers of the reign of Edward II ... 7. The biographies of Henry V... 9. Chronicles of the Wars of the Roses: English. Epilogue (p.454-79) assesses the historiographical achievments of medieval England. Appendix H. Chronological Indices (The principal literary sources for English history ... 1307-1485; Annals; Local histories; Antiquarian works of the 15th century) p.499-503. Bibliography p.504-15. Extremely well-documented survey of medieval chronicles, annals, local history *etc*. *Class No:* 930.0(420)

China

[6430]

DIRLIK, A. 'Reversals, ironies, hegemonies. Notes on the contemporary historiography of modern China' *Modern China*, v.22,no.3, July 1996, p.243-84. bibliog.

Considers post-revolutionary histories. Bibliography p.282-84.
Class No: 930.0(510)

Asia—Middle & Near East

[6431]

LEWIS, B. *and* HOLT, P.M., *eds*. Historians of the Middle East. London, Oxford Univ. Press, 1962. xi,519p. index.

41 contributions, - papers presented at conferences held at the School of Oriental and African Studies, London University, 1956-58. Parts: 1. Arabic, Persian and Turkish historiography to the 12th/19th century (1-22) - 2. European (including Russian) historical writing on the Near and Middle East, from the Middle Ages to the present day (23-32) - 3. Modern Middle Eastern historical writing (33-38) - 4. General theories (39-41). Footnote references.
Class No: 930.0(53+56)

Asia—South & South East

[6432]

PHILIPS, C.H., *ed*. Historians of India, Pakistan and Ceylon. London, Oxford Univ. Press, 1961. x, 504p. index. (*Historical Writing On The People of Asia, no.1*.)

Papers presented at conferences held at the school of Oriental and African Studies, London University, 1956-58. Pt.1 deals with historiography current in the early empires; Pt.2 covers historical writings in the periods of European dominance and nationalist movements. Footnote references (for chapter 26, 115 such references).
Class No: 930.0(54+59)

Asia—South East

[6433]

HALL, D.G.E., *ed*. Historians of South-East Asia. London, Oxford Univ. Press, 1961. viii,342p. index. (*Historical writing on the people of Asia*.)

25 chapters, by various contributors, - papers presented at conferences held at the School of Oriental and African Studies. London University 1956-58. Pt.1: Indigenous writings (9 chapters; p.13-104); pt.2: Western writings (chapters, 10-25; p.107-335) (*e.g.* 'Some aspects of Spanish historical writing on the Philippines', by C.R. Boxer, p.200-12). Covers Malaya, Burma, Indonesia, Vietnam. Numerous footnote references.

The same editor has written a brief general survey, 'On the study of Southeast Asian history', in *Pacific Affairs*, v.33,no.3, September 1960, p.268-81. *Class No:* 930.0(59)

Islamic World

[6434]

CHOUEIRI, Y.M. Arab history and the nation state a study in modern Arab historiography' 1820-1980. London, Routledge, 1989. xix, 238p. bibliog., index. £30. ISBN: 0415031133.

6 well-annotated chapters separated into 2 parts: 1. Pioneers and amateurs 1820-1920 (a general development of Arab historiography with emphasis on Egypt, Syria and North Africa) - 2. The professional historians: managers of legitimation (a critical analysis and assessment of 3 modern Arab historians). Glossary p.220-2. List of dynasties p.223. Bibliography p.224-31. *Class No:* 930.0(5.297)

Africa

[6435]

JEWSIEWICKI, B. *and* NEWBURY, D. African historiographies: what history for which Africa? Beverley Hills, and London, Sage Publications, 1986. 320p. bibliog., index. $29.95. (*Sage series on African modernization and development*.) ISBN: 0803924984.

23 essays grouped in 5 categories: 1. The epistemology of African studies - 2. The historiography of oral discourse - 3. Africa from the outside - 4. Africa from within - 5. Which way out? Trends in the developing historiography of Africa. Bibliography p.279-316. 'Bound to make a significant contribution to the study and general understanding of African history' (*Choice*, v.24, no.4, December 1986, p.671). *Class No:* 930.0(6)

Latin America

[6436]

THOMAS, J.R. Biographical dictionary of Latin American historian and historiography. Westport, Connecticut, Greenwood Press, 1984 xiv, 420p. bibliog., index. $50.95. £38.50. ISBN: 0313230048.

Introduction (p.3-77): 'The men who wrote history'; 'The meaning of history'; 'Historic truth and the way to find it'; 'Literary style an type of history produced'; 'Historiographic polemics.' 250 Bio bibliographical sketches p.81-361. Appendix 1. Listing by birth place 2. By year of birth. 3. Careers. 4. Subjects researched by majo historians. *Class No:* 930.0(729.99)

[6437]

WILGUS, A.C. The Historiography of Latin America: a guide to historical writing 1500-1800. Metuchen, New Jersey, Scarecrow Press 1976. xvi,33p. tables. $32.50; £27.50. ISBN: 0810808595.

Biobibliographical data on European and American born historica writers of the period, writing in eight languages. Each century i treated as a unit. Bibliography of *c*.450 references.
Class No: 930.0(729.99)

USA

[6438]

Twentieth-century American historians. Wilson, C.N., *ed*. Detroit Gale Research Co., 1983. xi,519p. ports. $76.00. (*Dictionary o Literary Biography v.17*.) ISBN: 0810311445.

54 contributors. Literary biographies of 59 historians whose mos important work, published during the 20th-century, concentrate chiefly on US history. Bibliography p.489-492. *Class No:* 930.0(73)

[6439]

—American historians 1866-1912. Wilson, C.N., *ed*. Detroit, Gal Research Co., 1986. xiv,428p. ports., bibliog., index. $88.00 (*Dictionary of Literary Biography, v.47*.) ISBN: 0810317257.

Bio-critical essays on 46 historians. Appendix 'Recording the Civi War'. *Class No:* 930.0(73)

[6440]

—American historians 1607-1865. Wilson, C.N., *ed*. Detroit, Gal Research Co., 1984. xv,382p. ports. $82.00. (*Dictionary of Literar Biography v.30*.) ISBN: 0810317087.

35 contributors. Literary biographies of 46 historians - chroniclers o the Colonial and Revolutionary periods; the literary historians of th early - 19th century; and other popular and specialized historians of th same period. Bibliography p.347-351. *Class No:* 930.0(73)

Middle Ages

Encyclopaedias

[6441]

GRABOIS, A. The Illustrated encyclopedia of medieval civilization Jerusalem, The Jerusalem Publishing House Ltd.; London, Octopus 1980. Distributed in North America by Mayflower. 751p., illus., (inc col. pl.), maps, bibliog., tables, index. $25. ISBN: 070640856x.

Intended for the general public this impressive book has 4,000 entries (with 1-3 references appended) covering all aspects o Christendom, Islam, and the oriental civilizations of India, China an Japan from the 4th to the 15th century. Many cross references. Selec bibliography p.9-11. Chronological table (AD395-1429) p.741-745 'Index of persons, terms and symbols which are not title of entries i the encyclopedia'. 'Highly and enthusiastically recommended for al libraries' (*Choice*, v.18, no.6, February 1983, p.776).
Class No: 930.0"01/14"(031)

Maps & Atlases

[6442]

PLATT, C. The Atlas of medieval man. London, Macmillan Londo Ltd., 1979. 256p. illus. (many col.), maps. ISBN: 0333270797.

Profusely illustrated century by century overview of medieva politics, religion, warfare, exploration, technology and cultur A.D.1000-1500 with the world divided into 8 major areas: Wester and Eastern Europe; Near and Far East; South East Asia; India Africa; and the Americas. Particularly valuable for this comparativ approach. *Class No:* 930.0"01/14"(084.3)

18th Century

Dictionaries

[6443]

BLACK, J. *and* PORTER, R. A Dictionary of eighteenth centur world history. Oxford, Blackwell, 1994. xvii,880p.+20p. maps geneal. tables, bibliog. ISBN: 0631180680.

c.120 contributors. Extending from the wars of the 1690s to th defeat of Napoleon in 1815, it combines a compendium of facts an information on the chief personalities, events and conflicts, an

....(contd.)

political, social and intellectual developments with longer interpretative articles. Also includes surveys of such important centres of power and civilization as China, Japan, India and Persia. Bibliography p.799-807. Chronology p.810-75. Dynastic charts p.876-80. 10 maps.

The Penguin dictionary of eighteenth-century history London, Penguin Books, 1996. pbk. £9.99. ISBN 0140512586.

Class No: 930.0"17"(038)

19th Century

Dictionaries

[6444]

A Dictionary of nineteenth-century world history. Belchem, J. *and* Price, R., *eds.* Oxford, Blackwell Reference, 1994. xviii,746p. maps, index.

97 contributrors. 800 entries relating to political, diplomatic, military, social and economic history. Many biographical entries. Cultural disciplines *e.g.* architecture, painting, music, covered by overview entries. Longer entries (over 300 words) end with 103 references. Chronology (4 timelines across the double-page) p.676-717. 9 maps.

The Penguin dictionary of nineteenth-century history. London, Penguin Books, 1996. ISBN 0140512691. *Class No:* 930.0"18"(038)

20th Century

[6445]

COOK, C. Twentieth-century world history a guide to places and events. London, UCL Press, 1996. 288p. illus. £29.95. ISBN: 1857285328.

A-Z cross-referenced entries cover the key locations in 20th century world history. *Class No:* 930.0"19"

[6446]

COOK, C. *and* BEWES, D. What happened where a guide to places and events in twentieth-century history. London, UCL Press, 1997. x,310p. maps. ISBN: 1857285328.

Desk-top companion and guide to places and events featuring in 20th century world history. Diplomatic crises, world conferences, assassinations, massacres, battles, and treaties also find entry. Appendix 1. Changing nations of the 10th century - 2. Major wars. *Class No:* 930.0"19"

[6447]

YOUNG, J.W. The Longman companion to America, Russia, and the Cold War 1941-1998. 2nd ed. London, Longman, 1999. xiv,309p. maps, tables, bibliog., index. pbk. £14.99. (*Longman Companions to History.*) ISBN: 0582369010.

1st ed. published as *The Longman Companion to Cold War and detente* (1993).

Surveys East-West relations from the Grand Alliance of the Second World War to the aftermath of the disintegration of the U.S.S.R. 10 Sections: 1. Chronology (p.3-79) - 2. Crises and conflicts - 3. Conferences and summits - 4. Major treaties and organisations - 5. Major office-holders - 6. Biographies - 7. Glossary (p.239-66) - 8. Strategic nuclear weapons: the nuclear balance 1956/79 - 9. Bibliography (in form of extended essay, p.273-81) - 10. Maps. *Class No:* 930.0"19"

Encyclopaedias

[6448]

The Facts On File encyclopedia of the 20th century. Drexel, J., *ed.* New York and Oxford, Facts On File, 1991. ix,1046p. illus., maps, index. $79.95; £39.95. ISBN: 0816024618.

26 contributors. Over 8,000 A-Z entries, 3 columns to the page, covering all fields of human endeavour: art, literature, entertainment, exploration, science, politics, and warfare, providing a guide to the most significant events, people, places, and movements in 20th century history (Mikhail Sergeyevich Gorbachev, 90 lines; Popeye, the sailor man, 20 lines; Boris Nikolayevich Yeltsin, 40 lines). Country entries have boxed chronologies. 750 illus. 150 maps.

Class No: 930.0"19"(031)

Handbooks & Manuals

[6449]

COOK, C. *and* STEVENSON, J. The Longman handbook of world history since 1914. London, Longman, 1991. ix,539p. maps, bibliog., index. £22. ISBN: 0582485886.

Essential facts and figures on major aspects of world twentieth-century history from the outbreak of the First World War organized in 6 sections: 1. Political history in 6 regions + lists of Heads of State and selected ministers/rulers A-Z by country (p.182-244) - 2. Wars and international affairs - 3. Economic and social - 4. Biographies

....(contd.)

(p.371-409) - 5. Glossary of terms (p.413-62) - 6. Bibliography (p.465-506). 10 maps. A key one-stop compendium.

Class No: 930.0"19"(035)

Dictionaries

[6450]

Larousse dictionary of twentieth century history. Min Lee, *ed.* Edinburgh, Larousse, 1994. 767p. £8.99. ISBN: 0752300032.

Based on entries relating to the twentieth century printed in *Chambers dictionary of world history* (Edinburgh, Chambers, 1993) plus a few updates and revisions.

'Libraries already holding the Dictionary of World History should think twice about buying this spin-off work, but it is useful in its own right, providing a concise overview and a convenient guide to the key people, places, and events of the twentieth century in a single sequence' (*Reference Reviews*, v.9,no.3, 1995, p.43).

Class No: 930.0"19"(038)

[6451]

PALMOWSKI, J. A Dictionary of twentieth-century world history. Oxford Univ. Press, 1997. viii,693p. maps, tables, pbk. £7.99. ISBN: 0192800167.

2,500 cross-referenced entries for events, leading civil and military leaders, treaties, religious and political movements, world organisations etc. Omits nothing of importance.

Class No: 930.0"19"(038)

[6452]

TEED, P. Dictionary of twentieth-century history (1914-1990). Oxford, Oxford University Press, 1992. 630p. £14.95. ISBN: 0192116762.

Dictionary of nearly 2000 entries relating to major countries, figures, movements, and events that have shaped the century from the First World War to the Iraqi invasion of Kuwait in 1990. Also covers social, cultural, and technological developments.

Class No: 930.0"19"(038)

Maps & Atlases

[6453]

DOCKRILL, M.L. The Collins atlas of twentieth century world history. Glasgow, Harper Collins, 1991. 160p. illus., col. maps, bibliog., index. £14.99; $29.95. ISBN: 0004350618, UK; 0060160098, US.

Published in US as *Atlas of twentieth century world history.*

53 double-page map and text spreads under 5 chronological period divisions 1900-1990, each ending with a chronology of political, social, scientific, and cultural events since 1945. Also 10 essays on periods of strong significance in world history. Glossary p.154-5. Bibliography p.155. *Class No:* 930.0"19"(084.3)

Chronologies

[6454]

OCHOA, G. *and* COREY, M., *eds.* Fitzroy Dearborn guide to events of the 20th Century. London, Fitzroy Dearborn, 2000. 650p. £50. ISBN: 157958165x.

Coverage of more than 300 topics, capsule biographies of 800+ noteworthy figures, profiles of the countries of the world, and a timeline. *Class No:* 930.0"19"(090)

Contemporary

[6455]

BRIVATI, B., *and others, eds.* The Contemporary history handbook. Manchester Univ. Press, 1996. xxiv,488p. index. £45. ISBN: 0719048354.

41 well-documented chapters, by independent hands, ordered in 7 parts: 1. Debates (*i.e.* issues occupying current attention) - 2. International perspectives - 3/7. Archival, printed, oral and audio, visual, and electronic sources. *Class No:* 930.0"312"

Philosophy of History

[6456]

BENTLEY, M. Companion to historiography. London, Routledge, 1997. xvii,997p. bibliogs., index. ISBN: 0415030846.

39 analytically descriptive chapters, examining the moods and trends in historical throughout all its phases of development, arranged in 5 parts: 1. Beginnings, East and West - 2. Medieval World - 3. Early modern history - 4. Reflections on the modern age - 5. Contexts for the writing of history. Pages of references follow each section. *Class No:* 930.1

Bibliographies

[6457]

FRITZE, R.H., *and others, eds*. **Reference sources in history** an introductory guide. Santa Barbara, Calif. and Oxford, ABC-Clio, 1990. 319p. index. $49.50. £45.95. ISBN: 0874361648.

685 cross-referenced entries for major reference works listed in 14 form chapters *e.g.* book review indexes, core journals, dissertations and theses, archives and manuscripts. Entries consist of full bibliographical citations and evaluative annotations. Author and title index. Coverage is for all historical periods and for all geographical areas although the emphasis is on English-language items relating to Anglo-American and European history. 'An accurate, current and reliable work that supersedes Helen J. Poulton's classic but dated *The Historian's Handbook*' (*Library Journal*, v.116,no.7, 15 April 1991, p.84).

A second edition is due to be published in November 2000.c65. ISBN 0874368839. *Class No:* 930.1(01)

Dictionaries

[6458]

RITTER, H. **Dictionary of concepts in history.** Westport, Connecticut, Greenwood Press, 1986. xix,490p. index. $55.00; £49.50. ISBN: 0313227004. ISSN: 07303335.

Attempts 'to identify and discuss some of the key concepts of contemporary historical analysis'. Entries consist of a concise definition of the idea in question, a discussion of the history of the idea, an annotated list of references cited, and suggestions for follow-up reading. 'A phenomenal volume that deserves a place in every reference library' (*Libraries and Culture*, v.24,no.3, Summer 1989. p.396-7). *Class No:* 930.1(038)

Study Methods

[6459]

MARIUS, R. **A Short guide to writing about history.** 3rd ed. New York, Longman, 1999. xiii,1921p. index. pbk. ISBN: 0321023870. 2nd ed. 1994.

Instruction manual on methods in historical study and methods in writing arranged in 8 chapters: 1. The Essay in History ... 3. Modes of Historical Writing ... 6. Documenting Your Sources. Appendix A. Book Reviews - B. Essay Examinations. Intended for US and Canadian students but applicable universally. *Class No:* 930.2

[6460]

TRINKLE, D.A. **Writing, teaching and researching history in the electronic age** historians and computers. New York, M.E. Sharpe, 1998. 256p. $58.95 ISBN: 0765601788.

Examines how computer technology is changing historical research and teaching. *Class No:* 930.2

Chronology

[6461]

BEAL, G. **The Independent book of anniversaries.** London, Headline, 1992. viii,503p. indexes. £20. ISBN: 0747206848.

A page for every day of the year includes a list of the notable people who were born or died on that day and the significant events in history which occurred on that day. Sources discussed p.vii-viii. Indexes of people and events. *Class No:* 930.24

[6462]

Book of days: an encyclopedia of information sources on historical figures and events, keyed to calendar dates. Ann Arbor, Michigan, Pierian Press. Annual 1987-.

1987. 730p. $98. 0876502249. 08910146. 1988. 776p. $98. ISBN 0876502486. ISSN 08910146. Each annual volume contains hundreds of 'resource guides' (or, pathfinders) covering a broad range of subjects that can be precisely dated. Dates selected commemorate anniversaries of important historical events and well-known people. The research guides consist of an introductory essay; reference sources; adult, young adult and children's works on the subject; recordings; feature films; other A/V resources; discussion and project suggestions; sources of further information; cross-reference dates; background information on the contributor; and other events on the day in question. Subject, chronological and contributor indexes. *Reference Books Bulletin 1986-1987*, p.153-4 notes a 'wide variation in the quality of the guides' and recommends 'a more consistent and rigorously applied editorial standard for the bibliographies'. *Class No:* 930.24

[6463]

Chronology of world history. Santa Barbara, Calif., and Oxford, ABC Clio, 4v., 1999. 3109p. indexes. $375. ISBN: 1576071553.

Incorporates H.E.L. Mellersh's *Chronology of the Ancient World* (1976); R.J. Storey's *Chronology of the Medieval World* (1973); N William's *Chronology of the Expanding World* (1969) and *Chronology of the Modern world* (1966); and subsequent revised and enlarged editions. 'Now so thoroughly overhauled that it is not being billed as revised edition' (*Library Journal*, v.124, no.10, 1 June 1999, p.100).

1. *Prehistory-AD 1491 The Ancient and Medieval World.* 2. *1492 1775 The Expanding world.* 3. *1776-1900 The changing World.* 4 *1901-1998 The Modern world.*

27 contributors. 70,000 events chronicled, grouped by subject within year-by-year arrangement, covering political, social, scientifi and artistic affairs. 125 boxed special features are dispersed throughou the text. Choice Outsanding Academic Title 1999. *Class No:* 930.24

[6464]

Collins dictionary of dates. Butler, A., *ed.* 8th ed. London HarperCollins, 1996 xxiv,677p.. ISBN: 0004708989.

First published as *Everyman's dictionary of dates* (1911); 7th ed 1986.

Basic purpose remains 'to make useful dates accessible to the general reader'. Calendars (Christian, Jewish, Roman, Orthodox Muslim etc.) p.ix-xxiv. 8000 entries (500 new to this edition) A-Z an of 3 types: classified (longest); narrative; and short entries and cove history, science, technology, literature, arts, and sports. Chronology of events 30,000BC to date p.595-677. No index but 'likely to be the most useful for answering miscellaneous reference questions' (*RQ* v.11, no.2, Winter 1971, p.164-165). *Class No:* 930.24

[6465]

The Fitzroy Dearborn calendar of world history. Paxton, J. and Knappman, E.W., *eds.* Chicago and London, Fitzroy Dearborn 1999. xiv,460p. illus., maps, index. £45. ISBN: 1575981536.

Descends from S.H. Steinberg's *Historical Tables* (1st ed. 1939 12th ed. 1991).

9 contributors. Covers 25,000+ distinct events worldwide structured in 6 columns across the double page, 4 columns defining geographic regions, the remaining 2 dedicated to science, inventio and technology, and religion, culture and arts, and ordered in 7 majc historical epochs: 1. Ancient World - 2. Roman Imperium - 3. Middl Ages - 4. Renaissance & Enlightenment - 5. Industrial Age - 6. Worl War II - 7. Contemporary World. Particular effort to include in-dept coverage of African, Asian and Latin American events'. Encompasse social, religious, cultural artistic, scientific and economic milestones Analytical index p.387-460. *Class No:* 930.24

[6466]

FREEMAN-GRENVILLE, G.S.P. **Chronology of world history:** calendar of principal events from 3000 BC to AD 1976. 2nd ed London, Rex Collings, 1978. 746p. tables. £15. ISBN: 0860361039.

First published 1975.

Columns have 6 headings: Western Europe - Central & Easter Europe - Egypt & Africa - The Near East & India - The Far East Religion & culture. Records chiefly political and military events whereas B. Grun's *The timetables of history* (*qv*) 'stresses cultural scientific and other nonpolitical events and trends' (*Library Journal* March 1979, p.618). Index (*c.*20,000 entries). The 2nd ed. updates th chronology by 3 years, as well as making additions to the original. *Class No:* 930.24

[6467]

FREEMAN-GRENVILLE, G.S.P. **The Islamic and Christia calendars** AD622-2222 (AH1-1650). Reading, Berks., Garne Publishing, 1995, 112p. £12.95. ISBN: 1859640664.

Conversion method for any date from the beginning of the Islami era to the early years of the Christian 23rd century. Also Islamic date and festivals. *Class No:* 930.24

[6468]

GRUN, B. **The Timetables of history:** a chronology of world event based on Werner Stein's *Kulturfahrplan*. Rev. ed. New York, Simo & Schuster, 1987. 688p. $17.95. ISBN: 0317634356.

Kulturfahrplan first compiled 1946. This ed. first published 1975.

Information presented in 7 columns across the double page: 1 History and politics - 2. Literature, theater - 3. Religion, philosophy learning - 4. Visual arts - 5. Music - 6. Science, technology, growth 7. Daily life. Timetables start at 5000BC; annual from AD501. *Class No:* 930.24

[6469]

HAYDN, J. **Dictionary of dates and universal information** relating t all ages and nations. By the late Benjamin Vincent, rev. and brough up to date ... continuing the history of the world to midsummer 1910 25th ed. New York, Dover, 1969. xii, 1614p.

First published 1841.

A dictionary of miscellaneous subjects, arranged A-Z. Each subjec is treated chronologically (*e.g.* 'Coroner', in which some statute relating to coroners are mentioned; 'Mexico', in which *c.*200 event

..(contd.)

from 1503 onwards are recorded; and 'Telephone', a list of events in the history of the telephone. 'Useful in large libraries for older topics' (*RQ*, v.12, no.2, Winter 1971, p.164). *Class No:* 930.24

[6470]

Holidays, festivals, and celebrations of the World dictionary. Henderson, H. *and* Thompson, S.E., *eds.* 2nd ed. Detroit, Omnigraphics, 1997. 882p. bibliog., indexes. $84. ISBN: 0780800745.

1st ed. 1991.

200 holiday observations (500 new to this edition from U.S. and 100 other countries). A-Z entries describe religious, cultural, ethnic, historical and sports related events and celebrations. 23-page annotated bibliography. 8 indexes. *Class No:* 930.24

[6471]

-GULEVICH, T., *ed.* World holiday, festival and calendar books. Detroit, Omnigraphics, 1998. 477p. indexes. $55. ISBN: 0780800737.

1057 annotated citations for English language books on religious festivals, regional holidays, and calendar systems. Essentially a bibliographical support to *Holidays, festivals, and celebrations of the World dictionary (q.v.).* *Class No:* 930.24

[6472]

The Hutchinson chronology of world history Compact edition. Revised and updated ed. London, Helicon, 1998. vii,520p. index. £14.99. ISBN: 1859862500.

Single-volume abridgement of H.E.L.Mellersh's *Chronology of the ancient World*, R.J. Storey's *Chronology of the Medieval World*, and N. Williams' *Chronology of the Expanding World 1492-1762* and *Chronology of the Modern World 1763-1992.* 1st ed. 1985. Pbk. ed. 1996.

In 8 chronological sections the last of which is now headed The Making of Global Civilization 1946-1997. This is divided into general events and under 9 thematic headings (*e.g.* Science, technology and discovery; music, literature). Analytical index p.437-520. *Class No:* 930.24

[6473]

JOHNSON, D.E. From day to day; a calendar of notable birthdays and events. Metuchen, N.J., Scarecrow Press, 1990. ix,850p. index. $72.50. ISBN: 0810823543.

15000 entries arranged in monthly chapters each beginning with its history and special days. An introductory chapter on the calendar (p.1-8) covers its evolution, the moon cycle, the change from the Julian to the Gregorian calendar etc. A comprehensive index of proper names p.736-850. *Class No:* 930.24

[6474]

The Oxford companion to the year an exploration of calendar customs and time-reckoning. Oxford University Press, 1999. index. £35. ISBN: 0192142313.

Section 1: a day-by-day survey of the calendar year, revealing the history, literature, legend, and lore associated with each season, month, and day. Section 2: a broader study of time-reckoning: historical and modern calendars, religious and civil, are explained, with handy tables for the conversion of dates between various systems. Special attention is given to the calculation of Easter. *Class No:* 930.24

[6475]

Ribbons of time world history year by year since 1492. London, Mitchell Beazeley, 1988. 128p. col. illus., maps. bibliog. index. £8.95. ISBN: 0855337206.

Divided into 6 colour coded categories of human achievement: 1. World events - 2. Literature, religion and philosophy - 3. Art and architecture - 4. Music and other performing arts - 5. Science and technology - 6. National events (British Is.). Bibliography p.122. 50 time panoramas. Over 600 four-colour images. Family reference work. *Class No:* 930.24

[6476]

RICHARDS, E.G. Mapping time the calendar and its history. Oxford Univ. Press, 1998. xxi,438p. illus., tables, bibliog., index. ISBN: 0198504136.

30 chapters arranged in 4 parts: 1. The Calendar in theory - 2. Calendars of the world - 3. Calendar conversions (*i.e.* the mathematics involved) - 4. Easter. Appendix 1. Astronomical constants - 2. Names of days of the week - 3. French Republican calendar. Glossary p.401-410. Bibliography p.411-428. This is not a book to be picked up lightly, the scholarship shows. *Class No:* 930.24

[6477]

TRAGER, J. The People's chronology a year-by-year record of human events from prehistory to the present. Rev. ed. New York, Harry Holt; London, Aurum Press, 1992. ix,1237p. illus., index. $45; £30. ISBN: 0805017860, US; 1854102346, UK.

First published 1979.

Single sequence of 35000+ descriptive entries covers 30 different fields of human activity (*e.g.* politics, exploration, technology, sport, environment). Analytical index p.1127-1237. *Class No:* 930.24

[6478]

TRUHART, P. Regents of nations a systematic chronology of states and their political representatives in past and present. A biographical reference book. 2nd revised and expanded ed. München, K.G. Saur, 5v. 1999-2001. DM1980. ISBN: 3598215428, set.

1st published in 4v. 1985-1988.

1. *Antiquity worldwide.* 1999, 1312p. DM428. 3598215436. 2. *America. Africa.* 2000. 1128p. DM428. 3598215444. 3. *Asia.* 2000. 952p. DM428. 359815452. 4. *Europe.* 2001. 1224p. DM428. 3598215460. 5. *Index.* 2001. 660p. DM248. 3598215479. Biographical information on *c.*30,000 heads of state and premiers along with information on territorial and provincial governors of nations back to the Middle Ages. Entries include period of reign or office, name, title, place and date of birth and death, relation to predecessor, and outstanding events. Also included are the historical developments of present day nation states and a review of political structures. *Class No:* 930.24

[6479]

WETTERAU, B., *comp.* The New York Public Library book of chronologies. New York, Prentice Hall, 1990. 634p. bibliog., index. $29.95. ISBN: 0136204511.

Timelines arranged in 14 topical chapters *e.g.* Technology, Arts, Sports, War and military history, Politics and law, Education. Bibliography p.622-4. *Class No:* 930.24

[6480]

Worldmark chronology of the nations. Dickey, S., *ed.* Detroit, Gale, 4v., 1999. 2100p. illus., maps, bibliogs., indexes. $249. £230. ISBN: 0787605212.

4 geographic volumes: Asia (63 nations); Africa (56 nations); Europe (45 nations); Americas (40 nations). 7200 entries profiling events, persons and places range from 50 to 250 words, while overview essays on regions and nations run one to two pages. The focus is on the 20th century, but events with far-reaching consequences from ancient history are also covered. Each volume includes a graphical timeline that integrates the historical highlights from all countries, glossary, bibliographies for each country and an appendix of excerpts from primary documents. A subject index for each volume points researchers to terms, theories, practices, people, organizations and publications mentioned in the text. *Class No:* 930.24

CD-ROM

[6481]

Chronology of world history CD-ROM. Oxford, Helicon, 1995. Single CD-ROM for Windows; requires multimedia PC with a 386SX or higher processor, 4Mb of system memory, 4Mb of free hard-disc space, Microsoft Windows version 3.1 or later. Rights: Helicon. £150. ISBN: 185986001x.

Compiled from N. Williams' *Chronology of the expanding world 1492-1762* and *Chronology of the modern world 1763-1992,* H.E.L. Mellerh's *Chronology of the Ancient World,* and R.L. Storey's *Chronology of the medieval world (q.q.v).*

This electronic edition has compressed more than three thousand pages of detailed information onto a single compact disc, enabling searching across the whole of human history. Events can be located by any word of the text, by subject category (including science, the arts, and births and deaths), or by date. *Class No:* 930.24(003.40)

20th Century

[6482]

WALLER, P. *and* **ROWETT, J.,** *eds.* Chronology of the 20th century. Oxford, Helicon, 1995. x,630p. tables, index. £25. ISBN: 1859860346.

Derived from relevant section of N. Williams' *Chronology of the modern world.*

12 contributors. Record of political and international events on left hand page and record of activities in 11 thematic sections (*e.g.* science, technology, discovery) on right hand page. Statistics (p.530-35). Index (p.536-630). 'As a calendar of events, and as a record of activities in the twentieth century, this chronology will fulfil most libraries' requirements' (*Reference Reviews*, v.9,no.6, 1995. p.45). *Class No:* 930.24"19"

Women

[6483]

Chronology of women worldwide people, places, and events that shaped women's history. Detroit, Gale Research, 1997. 605p. index. £34.50. ISBN: 0787601543.

Focuses on key international happenings throughout the ages, with particular emphasis on the recent events of the 19th and 20th centuries. Brief biographies of important individuals are also featured. *Class No:* 930.24-0055.2

Archives

Dictionaries

[6484]

Dictionary of archival terminology. Dictionnaire de terminologie archivistique English and French with equivalents in Dutch, German, Italian, Russian and Spanish. Walne, P., *ed.* 2nd ed. München, K.G. Saur, 1988. 212p. indexes. £35. (*ICA Handbook Series, no.7.*) ISBN: 3598202792.

First published 1984 when it superseded *Lexicon of archival terminology* (Elsevier, 1964).

Lists *c.*500 specialist terms of archival science in 7 languages arranged A-Z with definitions in English language order followed by French equivalents and definitions and then by equivalent terms only for the other languages. *Class No:* 930.25(038)

[6485]

WILLIAMS, A.E. **Termau archifau/Archive terms.** Caernarfon, Gwaanaeth Archifau Gwynedd, 1986. iv, 55p. pbk. £4. ISBN: 0901337366.

A vocabulary of archive terms with Welsh-English, English-Welsh sections. Based primarily on the type of material found in local record offices. 'Will be a most useful and valuable reference work in those record offices where documents are catalogued in Welsh and where a large number of scholars are Welsh speaking' (*Journal of the Society of Archivists*, v.8, no.3, April 1987, p.171). *Class No:* 930.25(038)

Worldwide

[6486]

INTERNATIONAL COUNCIL ON ARCHIVES, *ed.* **Guides to the sources for the history of the nations/Guides des sources de l'histoire des nations.** 3rd series North Africa, Asia and Oceania. München, K.G. Saur, 1972-.

1. *Guide des sources de l'histoire d'Afrique du Nord, d'Asie et d'Océanie conservées en Belgique* compiled by E. Vandevoude and A. Vanrie. 1972. 622p. Edited by Archives Générales du Royaume.

2. *Sources de l'histoire d'Asie et de l'Océanie dans les archives et bibliothèques françaises* 2v., 1981. *Pt.1 Archives*, xxiii, 539p. DM298. ISBN 3598214723. *Pt.2 Bibliothèque Nationale* xi, 315p. DM168. 3598214731. Autres bibliothèques 1992. 330p. DM298. 359821488x.

3. *Sources on the history of North Africa, Asia and Oceania in Scandinavia. Pt.1 Denmark* compiled by R.C. Hansen. 1980. 842p. DM298. 359821474x. *Pt. 2 Finland, Norway, Sweden*, compiled by B. Federly and others. 1981. 224p. DM128. 3598214758. Edited by the National Archives of Denmark, Finland, Norway and Sweden.

4. *Sources on the history of Asia and Oceania in the Netherlands Pt.1 Up to 1796* compiled by P.H. Roessingh, 1982. 337p. DM168. 3598214766. *Pt.2 Sources 1796-1949* compiled by F.P. Jacquet. 1983. 547p. DM268. 3598214774. Edited by the Netherlands State Archive Service.

5. *Sources de l'histoire du Proche-Orient et de l'Afrique dans les archives et bibliothèques françaises Pt.1 Archives Nationales* 1996. xxx,463p. DM840. 3598214782. *Pt.2 Bibliothèque Nationale*, 1984. ix, 480p. £85.00. 3598214790. Edited by the Commission Française du Guide des Sources de l'Histoire des Nations.

6. *Quellen zur Geschichte Nordafrikas, Asiens und Ozeaniens in der Bundesrepublik Deutschland bis 1945* compiled by E. Ritter, 1984. xlvi, 386p. DM168. 3598214804.

7. *Guia de fuentes para la historia de Asia en España*, compiled by L.S. Belda, 1987. 242p. DM228. 3598214820.

8. *Quellen zur Geschichte Afrikas, Asiens und Ozeaniens im Österreichischen Staatsarchiv* 1986. xii, 273p. DM198. 3598214847. Edited by the International Council on Archives.

9. *Sources on the history of Africa, Asia, Australia and Oceania in Hungary*, With a supplement *Latin America* 1991. xvii,451p. DM298. 359214855. Edited by the National Archives of Hungary.

10. *Sources on the history of Africa, Asia and Oceania in Yugoslavia* 1991. vii,164p. DM168. 3598214863. Edited by the Union of the Societies of Archivists in Yugoslavia.

Invaluable for historical research this series also serves as a guide to the organization of European national archives. *Class No:* 930.25(100)

Pacific Ocean

[6487]

MANDER-JONES, P., *ed.* **Manuscripts in the British Isles relating to Australia, New Zealand and the Pacific.** Canberra, Australian National Univ. Press, 1973. Distributed by Angus & Robertson. xxiii, 697p.

Sponsored by the National Library of Australia and the Australian National Univ. Library.

Inventory of source material in nearly 100 public and private collections, societies (London: p.3-376), firms - arranged geographically 'British Isles' includes Eire. Area covered extends as far as Galápagos. Juan Fernandez, the Marianas, Hawaiian Is.,

....(contd.)

Antarctica. Very detailed index of 90p. 'Sets an even higher standar than its predecessors in this field' (*Commonwealth*, v.17, no.3, Jun 1973, p.82). *Class No:* 930.25(265)

[6488

Pacific history a list of primary sources held in University of Queenslan libraries. St. Lucia, Univ. of Queensland Library, 1989. 42p. sd *gratis.*

Briefly annotated list of government reports, consular despatches Colonial Office correspondence relating to the Pacific as a whole an specifically to Fiji, Hawaii, Kiribati, Nauru, New Caledonia, Norfol Islands, Papua New Guinea, Samoa, Solomon Is., Tahiti, Tonga, an Vanuatu. *Class No:* 930.25(265)

Europe

[6489

COOK, C. *and* PUGH, G. **Sources in European political history** London, Macmillan Press, 3v., 1987-1990.

1. Cook C. and Pugh G. *The European Left* 1987. £35.00. x 237p. 0333239962. 2. Cook C. and others *Diplomacy an international affairs* 1989. £90.00. 033277759. 3. Cook C. and othe *War and resistance* 1990. £35.00. 0333423690.

The aim is to provide 'a readily available register of Europea archives. V.1. is an A-Z guide to the personal papers of over 100 individuals active on the European left 1848-1945. Bibliograph p.237. 'A very helpful listing of archival resources' (*English Historicc Review*, v.103, no.407, April 1988, p.557). *Class No:* 930.25(4)

Great Britain

[6490

Calendars of charters and rolls in the manuscript collections of th British Library. Cambridge, Chadwyck-Healey, 1989. 18 reels c positive silver halide 35mm microfilm. £950.

Entries for over 75,000 documents including 6000 Europea documents mostly from France. These include deeds, royal letter papal bulls, monastic charters, manorial documents, farm accounts wills, treaties, diplomatic papers, royal household accounts, maps chronicles, heraldic and illustrated material. 'The calendars of charte are the only fully descriptive catalogue of the contents of thes collections. They contain short summaries of the contents of charter acquired by the Department of Manuscripts up to 1911 ... For othe types of records such as manorial documents a detailed listing i provided' (*Publisher's brochure*). *Class No:* 930.25(410)

[6491

COLE, J. *and* CHURCH, R., *comps.* **In and around recor repositories in Great Britain and Ireland.** 4th ed. Huntingdor Family Tree Magazine, 1998. 102p. bibliog., index. limp cove £4.95.

First published as *In and around record offices in Great Britain an Ireland* by Wiltshire Family History Society in 1987.

Detailed guide to the procedures and facilities of 740 repositorie which hold archives and local history collections. A-Z by 'ne counties'. Data: Car parks, facilities for children and disable document ordering, postal research, publications, places of interes nearby, nearest Tourist Information Centre. *Class No:* 930.25(410)

[6492

COOK, C., *and others, comps.* **The Longman guide to sources i contemporary British history.** London, Longman, 2v., 1994.

Direct successor to *Sources in British political history* (Macmillan 6v., 1975-1985).

1. *Organisations and societies* ed. by C. Cook and D. Waller. 384 index. £55. ISBN 0582209714. Compact guide to the records 1000+ organisations (political parties, trade unions, employer organisations, and pressure groups) arranged A-Z. Data: history an aims of organisation concerned; survey of surviving records; notes o location and availability. 2. *Individuals* ed. by C. Cook , J. Leonarc P. Leese. xii,353p. index. £55. 0582209722. Guide to the papers 1200+ individuals involved in British political life 1945-. Concentrate on 'those papers known to have been deposited, or where custodians paper still in private hands have indicated their willingness to facilita the needs of researchers' (*Introduction*). 'Likely to be the starting-poi in the research of generations of students and scholars' (*Archive* vol.22,no.94, April 1996, p.62). *Class No:* 930.25(410)

[6493

COX, J. **The Nation's memory: a pictorial guide to the Public Recor Office.** London, HMSO, 1988. 64p. illus. (some col). location ma on endpapers. pbk. £3.50. ISBN: 0114402167.

4 contributors. A popular guide to the buildings and to the P.R.O services. Attempts to convey something of the range of record available for consultation. Of particular value is 'Division of recor groups between Chancery Lane and Kew' p.28-29. *Class No:* 930.25(410)

[6494]

CRAWFORD, A. 'The Public Record Office', *History Today*, v.50, no.3, March 2000, p.26-27.

Descriptive article on the U.K.'s national archive of official documents and how it meets the changing needs of its users. *Class No:* 930.25(410)

[6495]

FOSTER, J. *and* SHEPPARD, J. **British archives:** a guide to archive resources in the United Kingdom. 3rd ed. London, Macmillan, 1995. 750p. bibliog., indexes. £85. ISBN: 0333532554.

1st ed. 1982. 2nd ed. 1989.

Over 1300 entries relating to national and local record offices, libraries and museums, collections and institutions, societies and associations. Data: address; telephone; enquiries to (*i.e.* named officer), hours, access, historical background, acquisition policy, major collections, significant non-manuscript material, finding aids, facilities, and publications.4 indexes: subject, collection, repository and country. 'Aims to consolidate information for the historian and archivist and provide a starting point for the first-time user of archives' (*Introduction*). The authors' 'British Archives and archives in Britain', *Journal of the Society of Archivists*, v.11, no.4, October 1990, p.151-5 is an illuminating commentary. *Class No:* 930.25(410)

[6496]

FOWLER, S., *and others, eds.* **RAF records in the PRO.** London, PRO Publications, 1995. £8.95. (*PRO Reader's Guide, no.8.*) ISBN: 1873162146.

Guide, designed for beginners, to the unique collections of aviation records - from the origins of military flying in Britain to the 1960s - held by the Office. Subjects covered include the following: organisation of the air services; operational records; aircraft and airships; records of individuals; women in the Royal Air Force and Air Transport Auxilliary; honours and awards; crashes and casualties; and photographic reconnaissance.

See also N. Hurst's bibliographical essay, 'Royal Air Force 1918-1948' *Family Tree Magazine*, v.13,no.2, December 1996, p.3-5. *Class No:* 930.25(410)

[6497]

GREAT BRITAIN. Public Record Office. **Guide to the contents of the Public Record Office.** London, HMSO, 3v., 1963-69.

Supersedes M.S. Guiseppi's *Guide to the manuscripts preserved in the Public Record Office* (1923-24. 2v.), of which it is largely a revision.

The Records transferred to the PRO between 1923 and 1960 'have not only lengthened previously existing series but have added upwards of two thousand classes not known to Giuseppi's *Guide* (*Preface*). Arrangement is by administrative provenance. General classes (*e.g.* Records of the High Court of Admiralty) are allotted separate sections, with introductions. Each type of record (*e.g.* Prize Appeal Records) is briefly annotated. Each volume has a key to regnal numbers; chronological index to statutes cited in text; index of persons and places; index of subject. V.1 has a glossary. V.3 has corrigenda and addenda to v.102.

Update on microfiche every 2 years. *Class No:* 930.25(410)

[6498]

GREAT BRITAIN. Public Record Office. **Information for readers.** London, Public Record Office. 7p. sd. *gratis.*

Basic information: 1. Introduction - 2. How to get there (Chancery Lane and Kew) - 3. Readers' tickets - 4. Hours of opening - 5. The reading rooms - 6. The records and their means of reference - 7. Photocopying services - 8. Other facilites - 9. Copyright - 10. Official records not in the PRO - 11. General rules - 12. Division of records between the buildings. Indispensable for the first-time researcher. *Class No:* 930.25(410)

[6499]

GREAT BRITAIN. Royal Commission on Historical Manuscripts. **Accessions to repositories and records added to the National Register of Archives.** London, HMSO. Annual. ISSN: 03080986.

1958-1971 as *List of accessions to repositories.*

1991 ed. (1992) vi,99p. £13.50 ISBN 0114402299. With contributions from over 200 repositories, this publication sets out to provide historians with a concise report of the more important or unusual accessions in the British Isles during the past year. Accessions are listed within sections relating to national, special and local repositories in England, Wales, Scotland and the Isle of Man. Also listed are reports added to the National Register of Archives in 1991. Lists of accessions to archives were published in the *Bulletin of the Institute of Historical Research* from 1923 to 1953. From 1954 to 1956 this was covered by the *Bulletin* of the National Register of Archives (London, NRA. Limited circulation), and from 1957 they were published separately as 'List of accessions to repositories'. *Class No:* 930.25(410)

[6500]

GREAT BRITAIN. Royal Commission on Historical Manuscripts. **Record repositories in Great Britain.** 11th ed. London, Public Record Office, 1999. vii,80p. index. £4.99. $7.95. ISBN: 1873162766.

First published by HMSO in 1964.

A geographical directory of 319 repositories which systematically collect and preserve written records. Data: addresses etc.; telephone and fax, internet, access hours, requirements for access, fees, wheelchair access, research services, contact personnel. 'There are three essential tools for the historian choosing to search the vast collections held by local record offices in Great Britain. This is one of them' (*Journal of the Society of Archivists*, v.29, no.9, May 1992, p.90). *Class No:* 930.25(410)

[6501]

GREAT BRITAIN. Royal Commission on Historical Manuscripts. **Surveys of historical manuscripts in the United Kingdom** a select bibliography. 3rd ed. London, HMSO, 1997. 35p. indexes. sd. £1.50. ISBN: 0953023907.

1st ed. 1989.

Details of nationwide completed and in progress surveys of historical records in business, economic, ecclesiastical, genealogical, legal, literary and artistic scientific and medical fields. 'It is in fact a very select bibliography' (*Journal of the Society of Archivists*, v.19, no.1, April 1998, p.124). *Class No:* 930.25(410)

[6502]

Guide to the location of collections described in the Reports and Calendars series 1870-1980. Great Britain. Royal Commission on Historical Manuscripts. London, HMSO., 1982. [x], 80p. £3.95. (*Guides to sources for British history No.3.*) ISBN: 0114401446.

Locates major groups of papers and the more important single documents recorded in the 236 volumes of Records and Calendars published by RCHMss since it was established. Arranged A-Z by owner. 'Each volume or group of volumes in the Reports and Calendar series is separately indexed. But these indexes are also amalgamated in the *Guide to the reports of the Royal Commission on Historical Manuscripts Pt.1. Topographical Reports issued 1870-1911*(1914); *1911-1957* (1973). *Pt.2. Index of persons: reports issued 1870-1911* (2v, 1935-1938); *1911-1957* (3v, 1966)' (*Bibliographical note*). *Class No:* 930.25(410)

[6503]

Guides to sources for British history based on the National Register of Archives. London, HMSO, 1982-.

1. *Papers of British cabinet ministers 1782-1900.* 1982. xi, 75p. £3.95. ISBN 0114401217. 2. *The manuscript papers of British scientists 1600-1940.* 1982. vii, 109p. £3.95. ISBN 0114401225. 3. *Guide to the location of collections described in the Reports and Calendar Series 1870-1980.* 1982. viii, 71p. £3.95. ISBN 0114401446. 4. *Private papers of British diplomats 1782-1900.* 1986. v, 80p. index. £5.95. ISBN 014401888. 5. *Private papers of British colonial governors 1782-1900.* 1986. vii, 66p. ISBN 011440206x. 6. *Papers of British churchmen 1780-1940* 1987, x, 96p. £7.95. ISBN 0114402124. 7. *Papers of British politicians 1782-1900.* 1989. 100p. £8. ISBN 011440223x. 8. *Records of British business and industry 1760-1914.* 1990. 146p. 0114402264. Royal Commission on Historical Manuscripts series of digests of privately owned collections of papers in 'the areas of historical study for which the information itself is most comprehensive and most obviously in scholarly demand.' *Class No:* 930.25(410)

[6504]

MACFARLANE, A. **A Guide to English historical records.** Cambridge, Cambridge Univ. Press, 1983. ix, 134p. bibliog. ISBN: 0521252253.

Describes the nature of historical records of the period 1200-1800 in five chapters: 1. Rediscovering the English past - 2. Some problems and limitations - 3. Records of the State - 4. Records of estates - 5. Ecclesiastical jurisdiction. Not to be regarded as a systematic guide. Bibliography p.127-134. No index. 'Gives helpful direction on how and where searches might be conducted' (*Choice*, v.21, no.10, June 1984, p.1448). *Class No:* 930.25(410)

[6505]

The National inventory of documentary sources in the United Kingdom and Ireland. Cambridge and Alexandria, Virginia, Chadwyck-Healey, 1985-. Silver halide positive microfiche at 24 x reduction. Two subscription plans. Large order discount.

NIDS is an open-ended series published in units (each containing several hundred finding aids) at the rate of 8 *per annum*. Units 25 x 32 are published 1988/89.

Provides immediate access to over 12000 archives and manuscript collections in national and local government records offices, government academic and public libraries, museums, specialist research institutions, and private collections, by reproducing their finding aids on microfiche. The indexing apparatus offers 3 possible access routes; a list of finding aids; a names and subjects index; and also by titles. A free handbook, *How to use the National Inventory of Documentary Sources in the United Kingdom and Ireland in your*

....*(contd.)*

research, is available to prospective users and purchasers. G. Palmer's 'The National Inventory and local history', *Local History*, no.6, May 1985, p.10-11 stresses its usefulness in that area. *CD-ROM index to NIDS*. 1996. Access by titles of collections within a repository, names, and subjects. *Class No:* 930.25(410)

[6506]

OLNEY, R.J. **Manuscript sources for British history.** Their nature, location and use. London, Institute of Historical Research, Univ. of London, 1995. x,72p. bibliog., soft cover. £5. ISBN: 1871348285. ISSN: 13591126.

Pt.1: Creation and distribution of manuscript material - 2. Finding and using the sources - 3. Further reading (bibliographies, surveys and general reference works, general directories, guides to repositories, type or classes of record, subject areas. Republic of Ireland, other useful works) p.32-67. 'Written primarily with the postgraduate student in mind, and more specifically the student undertaking a thesis in British history' (*Introduction*). 'Students should seriously consider buying it if their future research lies in British history' (*Journal of the Society of Archivists*, v.17,no.1, April 1996, p.127-28). *Class No:* 930.25(410)

[6507]

The Public Record Office guide 1999. (to microfiche ed.). Richmond, Surrey, PRO Publications, 1999. 40p. (unpaginated). ISBN: 1873162626.

1. The Records in the PRO - 2. Access - 3. Arrangement and scope. How to use records. Appendix 1. Table of reigns - 2. Glossary. This is the last edition to be published before the guide is available on the Internet. *Class No:* 930.25(410)

[6508]

The Records of the nation The Public Record Office 1838-1988. The British Record Society 1888-1988. Martin, G.H. *and* Spufford, P., *eds.* Woodbridge, Suffolk, Boydell Press/The British Record Society, 1990. viii,312p. tables, index. £35. $73. ISBN: 0851155383.

21 chapters by different hands in 4 sections: 1. The history and development of the PRO- - 2. Calendars and indexes - 3. Contrasting consumers - 4. The probate records of the nation: new approaches to wills, inventories and accounts. Includes chapter 8. The thirty-year rule and freedom of access ... 11. National Register of Archives and other nationwide finding aids ... 14. A genealogist's view of the Public Records. Edited texts of papers given at the historical conference in London to mark the PRO's 150th anniversary and the British Record Society's centenary. *Class No:* 930.25(410)

[6509]

SARGENT, D. **The National Register of Archives: an international perspective.** Essays in celebration of the fiftieth anniversary of the NRA. Institute of Historical Research, University of London. Special Supplement to *Historical Research*, no.13, June 1995. 103p. ISSN: 09503471.

Chap.1: The National Register of Archives (p.1-35) has sections on Establishment and early history; Origin and structure; Public Search Room; Archive services in the UK; Processing and management of information; Description of NRA (activities and publications); NRA indexes and databases; and Public services. *Class No:* 930.25(410)

Internet

[6510]

Public Record Office finding aids. URL:http://www.pro.gov.uk/finding/default.htm.

A database of over 8 million documents. 'Browsing is possible using letter codes, titles and classes of records. Subject-specific searching allows as many as three key words. Given the size and complexity of the underlying system, the site interface is remarkably simple, well-organized, and easy to navigate ... Also provided are links to the Public Record Office home pages' (*Choice*, v.37, no.7, March 2000, p.1279). *Class No:* 930.25(410)(003.41)

Scotland

[6511]

BARNES, I. **'National Register of Archives (Scotland)',** p.72-75, *The National Register of Archives: an international perspective* edited by D. Sargent (*q.v.*).

A brief outline. *Class No:* 930.25(411)

[6512]

GREAT BRITAIN. Scottish Record Office. **Guide to the national archives of Scotland.** Edinburgh, The Stationery Office for the Scottish Record Office and the Stair Society, 1996. x,253p. bibliog. £50.

Replaces M. Livingstone's *A Guide to the Public Records of Scotland* (1905).

Descriptive calendar dealing with records of the pre-Union administration, records of the law of Scotland, and SRO archives from 16th century to date. Appendix 1. The Record Officials p.225-31. 2 Record legislation p.232-34. Glossary p.235-47. Bibliography and list of abbreviations p.248-53. 'Takes in turn each of the pre-Union departments of state, the administration of justice at both central and local level, the great series of registers of deeds and of sasines and the records of diligence, tracing the development of each, examining its function and describing the records each generates ... a pudding full o, rich plums' (*Journal of the Society of Archivists*, v.19, no.1, p.125-26). *Class No:* 930.25(411)

[6513]

STEVENSON, D. *and* STEVENSON, W.R. **Scottish texts and calendars** an analytical guide to serial publications. London, Royal Historical Society; Edinburgh, Scottish Historical Society, 1987. xli 233p. ISBN: 0861931114, RHS; 0906245087, SHS.

Designed as a companion volume to E.L.C. Mullins' *Text and calendars (qv.)* and is therefore limited to private society publications. Updates, and to a certain extent, replaces C.S. Terry's *A catalogue of the publications of Scottish historical and kindred clubs and societies, and of the volumes relevant to Scottish history issued by His Majesty's Stationery Office 1780-1908* (1909) and C. Matheson's *A catalogue of the publications of Scottish historical and kindred clubs and societies 1908-1927* (1928). Also includes appendix: Royal Commission On The Ancient and Historical Monuments of Scotland Inventories p.189-191. Index p.193-233. *Class No:* 930.25(411)

Ireland

[6514]

HELFERTY, S. *and* REFAUSSÉ, R., *eds.* **Directory of Irish archives.** 3rd ed. Dublin, Four Courts Press, 1999. 192p. indexes. £30. ISBN 1851824685.

First published in 1988.

250 organizations and repositories holding educational, religious and cultural archival material or records of historical significance. A-Z by name of institution. Appendix: Institutions and organizations believed to hold archives but which did not respond to the questionnaires. County and subject indexes. 'The most useful work of reference of its kind to have appeared in this country in recent years' (*Irish Genealogist*, v.7, no.3, 1988, p.482). *Class No:* 930.25(415)

Commonwealth

[6515]

COMMONWEALTH ARCHIVISTS ASSOCIATION. **Colonial related archive and manuscript collections in the UK** summary guide to the archive and manuscript collections relevant to the former British Colonial territories in the UK. Burdett, A., *comp.* London, Commonwealth Archivists Association, 1988. 97p.

Lists almost 200 collections A-Z by repository in London, rest of England, Scotland, Wales and Northern Ireland. Omits Public Record Office collections, business archives, and regimental museums. *Class No:* 930.25(41-44)

[6516]

COMMONWEALTH ARCHIVISTS ASSOCIATION. **Commonwealth sources in British official records. Colonial and Dominion Offices.** London, Commonwealth Archivists Association, 1985. 93p. typescript, sd.

A catalogue produced by the Public Record Office and the Institute for Commonwealth Studies listing A-Z by country and subject the main Colonial and Dominion Offices record classes relating to Commonwealth countries. Also indicates records now on microfilm. *Class No:* 930.25(41-44)

[6517]

GIPSON, L.H. **A Guide to manuscripts relating to the history of the British Empire 1748-1776.** New York, Knopf, 1970. xxii,490, xxviip. (*The British Empire before the American Revolution, v.15.*)

A detailed guide to depositories and manuscript sources, official and also belonging to private societies, business firms and church organizations. 11 parts: 1. London depositories of manuscripts (p.3-324) - 2. The English counties (A-Z) - 3. Wales - 4. Scotland - 5. Northern Ireland - 6. Republic of Ireland - 7. France - 8. Spain - 9. Canada - 10. Atlantic and West Indies islands - 11. The United States (p.437-90). Index. *Class No:* 930.25(41-44)

London

[6518]

•EADMAN, H. *and* SCUDDER, E., *eds*. **An Introductory guide to The Corporation of London Record Office.** London, Corporation of London, 1994. 82p. illus., index. £5. ISBN: 085203038x.

Descriptive guide arranged by type of record in 20 sections *e.g.* Custumals; Charters; Records of Courts of Law; Almshouses and hospitals; Military and armed bands). *Class No:* 930.25(421)

[6519]

•ondon local archives a directory of local authority record offices and libraries. 3rd ed. London, Greater London Archives Network, 1994. 44p.

Data: address, telephone and fax numbers, opening hours, facilities, published guides, access arrangements, staff names, and special collections. *Class No:* 930.25(421)

German Democratic Republic

[6520]

•uide des archives d'Allemagne de l'Est. Berlin, Centro Franco-Allemand de Recherches en Sciences Sociales, 1994 (?).

Guide to 60 depositories in Berlin and the 5 new Länder arranged by region. Data: current location; access conditions; photocopying facilities; size, nature and quality of holdings. *Class No:* 930.25(430.2)

Hungary

[6521]

•URUCZ, G. **Guide to documents and manuscripts in Great Britain relating to the Kingdom of Hungary** from the earliest times to 1800. London, Mansell, 1992. xiv,708p. index. £85; $170. ISBN: 0720121469.

Archives and manuscripts (inc. diaries, travelogues, personal and institution papers) relating to Hungary, Austria, Turkey, and Transylvania, in 36 UK repositories arranged A-Z by location. 'This guide is the result of a painstaking piece of research, and will be of enormous value to historians' (*Reference Reviews*, v.7, no.2, 1993, p.46). *Class No:* 930.25(439)

France

[6522]

•es Inventaires des Archives Nationales de Paris. Paris, Chadwyck-Healey France in association with La Direction des Archives de France, 1991. Fr.215,000. £20,475. ISBN: 2869760116.

740 finding aids (95% not previously published) to the most important collections, and a 132p. printed catalogue and index with a bibliography of research guides and an introduction to the history and use of the Archives. Available either as a complete set or in discrete sections: Complete edition: *Les inventaires des Archives Nationales de Paris*. Separate sections: 1. *Section Ancienne* (Middle Ages and Ancien Regime (up to 1789)). Fr.117,600. £11,200. 2869760124. 2. *Section Moderne et Contemporaine* (1789-1940 and 1940-). Fr.62,500. £5,950. 2869760132. 3. *Archives Privées* Fr.44,100. 2869760140. £4,200. 4. *Plans* Fr.14,700. £1,400. 2869760159. *Subject subsections:* 1. *La révolution Francaise* Fr.36,700. £3,500. 2869760175. 2. *Les Beaux-Arts* Fr.11,000. £1,050. 2869760153.

Guide de l'utilisateur des Archives Nationales. pbk. 2869760167 is an extremely useful guide even for experienced users.

Les Archives nationales. La Memoire de la France, a glossay A4 brochure, is available from Chadwyck-Healey France, 3 rue de Marivaux, 75002 Paris. *Class No:* 930.25(44)

[6523]

•Les Archives Nationales. Etat général des fonds. Paris, Archives Nationales, 5v. 1978-88.

1. *L'ancien régime* edited by E. Taillemite. 1978. 820p. 2860000208. 2. *1789-1940* edited by R. Mathieu. 1978. 656p. 2860000216. 3. *Marine et outre-mer* edited by J. Favier. 1980. 713p. 2860000259. 4. *Fonds divers et additions et corrections aux tomes I, II et III.*. edited by R. Marquant. 1986. 432p. 2860000267. 5. *1940-1958 Fondes conservés à Paris.* 1988. Fr220. 2680001425. 'On y trouvera, en revanche, en cinq volumes l'ensemble des ressources documentaires offertes par les Archives Nationales à la date du 1er juillet 1976'. This detailed inventory is arranged in broad categories each of which is given an introduction to guide users. 'L'État général des fonds ne dispense pas du recours aux inventaires, il y conduit'. L.L. Frader's 'A guide to the Archives Nationales', *French Historical Studies*, v.15, no.1, Spring 1987, p.170-2 is useful.

A detailed survey of the Archives Nationales collection. L.L. Frader's 'A guide to the Archives Nationales', *French Historical Studies*, v.15, no.1, Spring 1987, p.170-2 is a useful introduction.

The two series, L'état général des fonds and L'état des inventaires, follow the same organization: major chronological divisions and then "série". There is no general index to the set, but the table of standard classification system used in the French archives and detailed

....(contd.)

tables of contents in each volume provide access to the section containing relevant material' (*College & Research Libraries*, v.52, no.2, March 1991, p.188-9. *Class No:* 930.25(44)

[6524]

—LES ARCHIVES NATIONALES. L'état des inventaires. Paris, Archives Nationales, 6v., 1985-. Distributed by La Documentation Française.

1. *Ancien régime.* 1985. Fr150. ISBN 28600000674. 2. *1789-1940.* 3. *Marine et Outre-Mer.* 4. *Fonds divers.* 1986. Fr160. 28600001034.

Together with *L'état des inventaires archives départementales, communales et hospitalières* (Paris, Archives Nationales, 2v., 1984. Fr390. set) the completed set of 6v. describe all inventories for regional and national archives, and constitute a major revision of H. Courteault's *État des inventaires des archives nationales, départementales, communales et hospitalières au ier. Janvier 1937* (Paris, Didier, 1938) and its *Supplement 1937-1954* (1955). This information is derived from 'France-Archives', *College & Research Libraries*, v.52, no.2, March 1991, p.188-191). *Class No:* 930.25(44)

[6525]

La Révolution Française à travers les archives des états géneraux au 18 brumaire. Paris, Archives Nationales - La Documentation Française, 1988. 438p. facsims. ISBN: 2860001433, Archives Nationales; 2110019964, La Documentation Française.

251 manuscript and printed documents arranged in 15 chronological and thematic chapters with historical commentary. Un mot sur la provenance des documents et sur les textes de présentation p.437. 'Cet ouvrage n'est ni un manual d'histoire, ni une catalogue d'exposition: il tient un peu des deux (*Avant-propos*). *Class No:* 930.25(44)

Italy

[6526]

Guida generale degli archivi di stato Italiani. Roma, Ministero Per I Beni Culturali E Ambientali. Ufficio Centrale Per I Beni Archivistici, 5v., 1981-1990.

1. *A-E* 1981. xviii, 1040p. 2. *F-M* 1983. xvi, 1088p. 3. *N-R* 1986. xiv, 1301p. 4. *S-Z.* 1994. xv,1411p. 887125080x. 'Archivo centrale dello Stata' with index v.1, p.33-295 then arrangement is A-Z by state archive. Descriptive entries, many with bibliographical references. To be completed in 5v. including an index volume. 'This will make available in print a summary description of what are probably the most extensive archival records, in terms of both chronological range and type of material preserved in a single country' (*Archives*, v.18, no.79, April 1988, p.167-168). *Class No:* 930.25(450)

Vatican City

[6527]

BOYLE, L.E. **A Survey of the Vatican archives** and of its medieval holdings. Toronto, Pontifical Institute of Medieval Studies, 1972. 250p. bibliog., index. ISBN: 0888443501.

General introduction. Bibliography p.173-221.

Class No: 930.25(456.31)

Bibliographies

[6528]

BLOUIN, F.X., *ed*. **Vatican archives** an inventory and guide to historical documents of the Holy See. Oxford Univ. Press, 1997. 840p. bibliog., indexes. $150. ISBN: 0195095529.

Produced by archivists and historians of the University of Michigan Vatican Archives project. 500 entries that provide detailed histories of each administrative agency of the Vatican, its purpose and workings, followed by a listing of the different records it produced. A-Z index of agencies and series titles, plus geographical and chronological indexes. Most items cited in the 45-page bibliography are in languages other than English. *Class No:* 930.25(456.31)(01)

Spain

[6529]

Guia de les archivos estatales Españoles. 2nd ed. Madrid, Ministerio De Cultura Direccion General De Bellas Artes Y Archivos. Subdireccion General De Archivos Inspeccion Tecnica De Archivos, 1984. 244p. illus. map, tables, index, pbk. ISBN: 8450506522.

First published 1977.

Directory arranged in 4 sections: Archives historicos Generales; Regionales; De Distrito; Provinciales. *Class No:* 930.25(460)

[6530]

SIERRA, C. 'Censo-guía de Archivos Españoles', p.86-90, *The Register of National Archives: an international perspective* edited by D.Sargent *(q.v.)*. [Survey guide to Spanish archives.]

Contents: Legislation - Objective - Methodology - Dissemination - Other databases in preparation at CIDA. *Class No:* 930.25(460)

Russia

[6531]

Archives in Russia a directory and bibliographical guide to holdings in Moscow and St. Petersburg. New York, M.E. Sharpe, 2v., 1998. bibliogs., indexes. £180. ISBN: 0765600348.

Extensive guide furnished with author and title, subject, manuscripts, and acronyms indexes. *Class No:* 930.25(47)

[6532]

GRANT, S.A. *and* **BROWN, J.H. The Russian Empire and the Soviet Union** : a guide to manuscript and archival materials in the United States. Boston, Massachusetts, G.K. Hall for the Kennan Institute for Advanced Russian Studies, The Wilson Center, 1981. xi, 632p. indexes. ISBN: 0816113009.

Arrangement is A-Z by state, city and thereunder by repository, institution or individual. *Class No:* 930.25(47)

[6533]

GRIMSTED, P.K. Archives and manuscript repositories in the USSR. Princeton, Princeton Univ. Press, 3v., 1972-1988.

1. *Moscow and Leningrad.* 1972. xxx, 436p. $64.50. ISBN 0691051496. Parts A-G (A. General archival bibliography and research aids - B. Central State archives of the USSR - C. Archives and manuscript collections of the Academy of Sciences of the USSR - D. Special archives - E. Manuscript divisions of libraries and museums in Leningrad - G. Republic and local archives in Moscow and Leningrad.) Appendix 2: Reference aids for paleography and ancillary history disciplines. Glossary of archival terms. Author-title index; subject index (p.415-36). 'Provides firm guidelines for those working with regional sources in the USSR today' *Library journal,* v.98, no.13, July 1973, p.2056).

—Supplement 1: Bibliographical addenda. Zug, Inter Documentation Co. AG, 1976, 217p.

425 annotated entries (*e.g.* for *c.*150 selected catalogues, etc. of medieval Slavic manuscript collections).

2. *Estonia, Latvia, Lithuania, and Belorussia..* 1981. xliii, 929p. $81.50. ISBN 0691052794. Parts H-L (H. General archival bibliography and research aids - I. Estonia - J. Latvia - K. Lithuania - L. Belorussia). Appendix 1. Procedural information: archival organization, access and working conditions - 2. Geographic name tables - 3. Charts and maps of administrative territorial divisions - 4. Glossary of archival terms (p.689-715). Pt. M. A preliminary bibliography of descriptions of archival materials ... now in collections outside the USSR. p.717-830. Author/title and subject indexes.

3. *Ukraine and Moldavia. Book 1. General bibliography and institutional directory.* 1988. liii,1107p. $125.00. ISBN 069105391x. In 3 parts: 1. Bibliographical list of reference literature relevant to historians, archivists *etc.* - 2. Specific archival and manuscript repositories (short description of institution; published lists of collection's holdings) - Appendix: Procedural information for research in Soviet archives. Book 2 will recount the historical development of these institutions. *Class No:* 930.25(47)

[6534]

—**GRIMSTEAD, P.K. A Handbook for archival research in the USSR.** International Research and Exchanges Board, Kennan Institute for Advanced Russian Studies, 1989. Distributed by IREX of Princeton, New Jersey. 430p. index, pbk. $19.95.

Definitive and well-documented work on Soviet archive administration and its terminology. Access to archival material is explicated and the major bibliographies and reference works listed. 3 appendices focus on the more important repositories in Leningrad and Moscow; the state archives of the Russian Soviet Republic; and the state archives of the non-Russian republic. 'This impressive, thorough, and well-organized reference tool will prove indispensable to anyone contemplating archival research in the Soviet Union' (*Choice,* v.27, no.2, October 1989, p.288). *Class No:* 930.25(47)

[6535]

—**GRIMSTED, P.K.** 'Recent publications on archives and manuscript collections in the Soviet Union' : a selective survey. *Slavic Review,* v.41, no.3, Fall 1982, p.511-533. Also distributed as an offprint. *Class No:* 930.25(47))

[6536]

—**GRIMSTED, P.K.** Recent Soviet archival literature: a review and preliminary bibliography of selected reference aids. Washington, DC., Kennan Institute for Advanced Russian Studies, 1987. 122p. sd. (*Occasional paper No.7.*)

Some material previously appeared as 'A new Soviet Directory of Archives and Manuscript Repositories: a major contribution,' *Slavic Review,* v.45, no.3, Fall 1986, p.534-544.

In 3 parts: 1. General archival bibliographies and reference aids - 2. Literature relating to individual repositories or systems - 3. Bibliography of selected recent Soviet archival literature. 'The present study is in origin ... an overgrown review article of a major new Soviet archival reference publication. At the same time and in a broader context, it is a hasty update of my earlier coverage and review of recent general Soviet archival reference literature, with emphasis on repositories in Moscow and Leningrad' (*Preface*). *Class No:* 930.25(47)

[6537]

Guide to the collections in the Hoover Institution archives relating to Imperial Russia, the Russian revolutions and civil war, and the first emigration. Leadenham, C.A., *comp.* Stanford, Calif., Stanford Univ., Hoover Institution Press, 1986. xx,208p.index. £16.60, $18.95. (*Hoover Bibliographic Series, no.68.*) ISBN: 081792681x.

Descriptive list of 676 archival collections arranged under 13 broad chronological, geographical and subject headings. List of collection titles A-Z p.1-14. Index p.147-208. The Hooverian Institution holds the largest archive pertaining to 20th century Russian affairs outside the Soviet Union. *Class No:* 930.25(47)

[6538]

HARTLEY, J.M., *ed.* **The Study of Russian history from British archival sources.** London, Mansell Publishing Ltd., 1986. lx, 184p. £26.00. ISBN: 0720117844.

11 papers read at a conference organized by the London School of Slavonic and East European Studies in 1984 as part of a project to prepare a comprehensive guide to sources in the British Isles. P.H. Grimsted's 'Foreign collections and Soviet archives' comments on the need to be aware of the corresponding papers in the Soviet Union. 'The hope she expresses, that other western countries will follow the British example and draw up a guide along the lines promised here will be widely shared' (*Archives,* v.18, no.78, 1987, p.115-116). *Class No:* 930.25(47)

[6539]

—**HARTLEY, J.M. Guide to documents and manuscripts in the United Kingdom relating to Russia and the Soviet Union.** London, Mansell Publishing Ltd., 1987. xxiii, 526p. bibliog., index. £50.00 $110.00. ISBN: 0720118050.

The product of a three-year project undertaken at the School of Slavonic and East European Studies 'to record systematically for the first time the location of documentary material relating to Russia and the Soviet Union in the United Kingdom' 331 repositories and their collections are listed A-Z by town. Bibliography p.xxiii. Does not cover material in the Public Record Office, the House of Lords, or the India Office Library and Records, whose collections were judged to be generally known. Unfortunately questionnaires to almost 400 institutions reasonably expected to hold important material either failed to elicit a reply or else resulted in a nil return. But Appendix 1. Privately held papers described in the printed reports of The Royal Commission on Historical Manuscripts, or listed in the National Register of Archives and the National Register of Archives of Scotland p.409-418. Appendix 2. Unrecorded papers in private ownership p.418-421. 'Of crucial value to historians, particularly as so much material in Russia is inaccessible' (*Archives,* v.18, no.78, 1987, p.124-125). *Class No:* 930.25(47)

Poland

[6540]

MILEWSKI, W., *and others.* **Guide to the archives of the Polish Institute and Sikorski Museum.** London, Orbis Books, 1985. xxiv, 25-375p. index. ISBN: 0901149284.

323 entries relating to Records of the Civil Service; Private collections; and Subject collections. An outline history of the Archives, p.xi-xviii. The Institute's archives contain the largest collection of primary sources ouside Poland, with special emphasis on the Second World War period. 3 further volumes are planned, the next to appear is expected to be *The Polish armed forces 1939-1947.* *Class No:* 930.25(475)

Sweden

[6541]

BJERSBY, M. 'The Swedish National Register of Private Archives', p.91-98, *The National Register of Archives: an international perspective,* edited by D. Sargent (*q.v.*).

Contents: Private archives in Swedish archival institutions: a brief survey - The National Register: background and activities - Computerisation of the National Register - National archival data-base - Making information available for public use - Reference service of the National Register. *Class No:* 930.25(485)

Netherlands

[6542]

RUITENBERG, G.N.W. 'The Central Register of Private Archives (CRPA) and the policy in the Netherlands regarding private archives', p.65-71, *The National Register of Archives: an international perspective* edited by D. Sargent (*q.v.*).

Basic principles of Governmental policy in the Netherlands regarding private archives - The establishment of CRPA - Acquisition. *Class No:* 930.25(492)

Belgium

[6543]

Het Rijkarchief in de provinciën Overzicht van de fondsen en verzamelingen 1. De Vlaamse provinciën. Brussel, Algemeen Rijksarchief, 1975. 405p.

Survey of material in the archive depositories of the provinces of Antwerp, Beveren-Waas, Bruges, Ghent, Hasselt, Kortrijk and Ronse. Data includes history, contents, and survey of printed and manuscript inventories. *Class No:* 930.25(493)

Asia

[6544]

NUNN, G.R. Asia and Oceania a guide to archival and manuscript sources in the United States. London and New York, Mansell Publishing Ltd., 5v., 1985. 2550p. £280.00; $415.00. ISBN: 0720117135.

V.1 Alabama - District of Columbia. [xxvi], 495p. Sources p.xvi-xxvi. V.2 District of Columbia. 496-1036p. V.3. Florida - Minnesota. 1037-1489p. V.4. Mississippi-Wyoming. 1491-1904p. V.5. Index. 1905-2456p. Annotated descriptive entries encompassing all unpublished materials, notably archives and manuscripts in 100 major and 360 smaller repositories, but excluding doctoral dissertations. Geographical coverage is Afghanistan eastwards *i.e.*, excluding Israel, Arab Middle East, Soviet Asia and also Hawaii and Australia. 'An indispensable research tool with which academic libraries will need to equip themselves' (*British Book News,* October 1985, p.588). *Class No:* 930.25(5)

[6545]

NUNN, G.R. Canada and Asia: a guide to archives and manuscripts. London, Mansell, 1993. 800p. £120; $240. ISBN: 0720121108.

Definitive listing of archival holdings listed by province, city or town, and name of repository. Exhaustive subject index. Complementary volume to the author's *Asia and Oceania: a guide to archival and manuscript sources in the United States (q.v.).* *Class No:* 930.25(5)

Asia—Far East

[6546]

MATTHEWS, N and WAINWRIGHT, M.D., *comps*. A Guide to manuscripts and documents in the British Isles relating to the Far East. London, Oxford Univ. Press, 1977. xiv, 182p. ISBN: 0197135919.

'Far East' embraces China, Japan, Korea, Mongolia, Tibet and Soviet Asia. The inventory covers such repositories as the Public Records Office, county record offices, missionary society archives and material still in private custody. *Class No:* 930.25(51/52+57)

Tibet

[6547]

SINGH, A.K.J. A Guide to source materials in the India Office Library and Records for the history of Tibet, Sikkim and Bhutan 1765-1950. London, The British Library, 1988. viii, 187p. £30. ISBN: 071230634x.

'The main emphasis of the guide is upon the archives held in India Office Records both official and private, which uniquely document the development of British India's political relations with the Himalayan region'. Appendix: Brief notes on other archival sources in Britain, India, Sikkim, Bhutan and China p.171-2. *Class No:* 930.25(515)

Japan

[6548]

BORSA, I. 'Archives in Japan,' *Journal of the Society of Archivists,* v.7,no.5, April 1984, p.287-298.

A brief examination of the National Archives of Japan; Imperial Household, Agency, Archives and Mausoleum Division; National Defence College; Diplomatic Record Office; and Yomei Library, Kyoto. *Class No:* 930.25(52)

Asia—Middle & Near East

[6549]

GREAT BRITAIN. India Office Library and Records. Sources for Middle East studies. Tuson, P. 2nd ed. London, India Office Library And Records, 1984. 21p. bibliog. sd. *gratis.*

Originally as *A brief guide to sources for Middle East studies in India Office Records* (1982).

Introduction (Britain, India and the Middle East; India Office Records) p.1-4. Descriptive list of IOR sources, p.5-14. Index of Middle East countries covered by the Records, p.15-21. Bibliography, p.21. *Class No:* 930.25(53+56)

[6550]

MATTHEWS, N. *and* WAINWRIGHT, M.D. A Guide to manuscripts and documents in the British Isles relating to the Middle East and North Africa. Oxford, Oxford Univ. Press, 1980. 482p.

One of a series of 4v. (the others concern the Far East, Africa south of the Sahara, and South and south-east Asia) recognised by the International Council on Archives and Unesco as the UK contribution to the 'Sources of history of the nations: Asia and North Africa' series.

Coverage: the Arab countries of Middle East and North Africa, Israel, Cyprus, Turkey, Iran and certain regions of the Caucasus, Central Asia and the Crimea. Sections: England (London, p.1-221); Rest of England (locations A-Z), Wales, Scotland, Northern Ireland, Eire. 'Papers in private custody', p.387-419. Some detail in inventories. Inclusion of material does not necessarily mean that is is available for study. Detailed index, p.421-82. An essential reference source 'until at least the end of the century' (*British book news,* July 1980, p.401). *Class No:* 930.25(53+56)

Asia—South & South East

[6551]

WAINWRIGHT, M.D. *and* MATTHEWS, N., *comps*. A Guide to Western manuscripts and documents in the British Isles relating to South and South East Asia. London, Oxford Univ. Press, 1965. xix,532p.

Lists of 80 manuscript depositories in London (p.1-258); England (excluding London (p.259-357); Wales and Monmouthshire; Scotland; Northern Ireland; Eire; Papers in private ownership (not deposited); Addenda. Omits the India Office Library collections; 'to have included these would at least have doubled the size of the work' (*Preface*). Detailed index, p.475-532. Well produced. 'An indispensable source of reference' (*Times Literary Supplement,* no.3,297, 6 May 1965, p.357). *Class No:* 930.25(54+59)

[6552]

—PEARSON, J.D. A Guide to manuscripts and documents in the British Isles relating to South and South-East Asia. London, Mansell, 2v., 1989-1990. ISBN: 0720119618.

Supplement to *A guide to Western manuscripts and documents in the British Isles relating to South and South East Asia* (1965).

1. *London.* 1989. vii,319p. index. £60.00. ISBN 0720119618. 2. *British Isles.* 1990. xvi,384p. index. £70.00. ISBN 072012011x. J.D. Pearson writes on 'The supplement to Wainwright and Matthews', *South Asian Studies* (British Library, 1986), p.106-8. *Class No:* 930.25(54+59)

India

[6553]

INTERNATIONAL COUNCIL ON ARCHIVES. Guide to the sources of Asian history 3. India. New Delhi, National Archives of India, 6v., 1987-.

1. National Archives. 1987. xi,165p. Guide to 11 A-Z ministry archives of Government of India. Each chapter gives genesis of the current structure of the Ministry concerned, its organizational history, access regulations, and photographic services. 'A useful source of information on the rich collections of the National Archives' (*Bulletin of the School of Oriental and African Studies, Univ. of London,* v.54, no.1, 1991, p.241-2). Projected volumes. 2. National Archives - 3/5. State/Union/Territory archives - 6. Directory of custodial institutions in India. *Class No:* 930.25(540)

[6554]

MOIR, M. A General guide to the India Office Records. London, The British Library, 1988. xvl, 331p. frontis., bibliog., index. £35.00. ISBN: 0712306293.

Extends W. Foster's *A guide to the India Office Records 1600-1858* (Eyre & Spottiswoode for The India Office, 1919).

1. The administrative background (p.3-124) - 2. The India Office Records (Summary list of 50 lettered classes p.129-30; Descriptive inventory A-Z p.131-275). Appendix 2. Notes on archival sources ... for areas outside British India or on its frontiers. Bibliography p.292-300. Analytical index. Authoritative, comprehensive and well-documented account of IOR holdings. IOR is 'the most important accumulation of historical source material in Britain for the study of politics, administration and commerce in South Asia and related areas from the early seventeenth to the mid-twentieth century' (*Preface*). *Class No:* 930.25(540)

[6555]

SETON, R. The Indian Mutiny 1857-58 a guide to source material in the India Office Library and Records. London, The British Library, 1986. xvi, 99p.+8p.pl. illus., bibliog., index. £12.95. ISBN: 0712300414.

Indispensable guide to the wealth of archival material dispersed in the IOLR's vast collections. Grouped in 4 main sections: 1. Records of the East India Company, the Board of Control, and the India Office - 2. Proceedings of the Government of India and of the Presidencies and

....(contd.)

Provinces - 3. Records of Residents and Agents in the Princely States - 4. Private papers. Bibliography p.89-94. Intended 'to facilitate access to the more rewarding sources' (*Introduction*). *Class No:* 930.25(540)

[6556]
SUTTON, S.C. A Guide to the India Office Library with a note on the India Office records. 2nd ed. London, HMSO, 1967. Reprinted with correction 1971. xii, 122p. illus., facsims.

First published 1952.

The India Office Library is one of the largest Orientalist libraries in the world. Resources comprise printed books; MSS; drawings and prints; photographs. The account of India Office records, a new feature 'will be useful until the full guide to the Records, now being prepared, is completed ... Indispensable for all serious orientalists' (*Times literary supplement*, no.3,442, 15 February 1968, p.166). *Class No:* 930.25(540)

Sri Lanka

[6557]
WIMALARATNE, K.D.G. An Introduction to the national archives - Sri Lanka. Colombo, National Science Council of Sri Lanka, 1978. 32p. bibliog.

'A survey of the development, functions and organization of Sri Lanka's national archives (V. Samaraweera. *Sri Lanka*, 1987. Entry 551). *Class No:* 930.25(548.7)

Pakistan

[6558]
ATIQUE ZAFAR SHEIKH. 'The National Archives of Pakistan' p.210-215, *South Asian studies* (British Library, 1986).

Includes a list of important holdings. *Class No:* 930.25(549)

[6559]
A Handbook of archives and material on Pakistan's freedom struggle. 3rd ed. Karachi, Archives of Freedom Movement, University of Karachi, 1988. xxxii,417p. col. illus. Rs300; $30. ISBN: 9698069003.

Detailed guide to All-India Muslim League (1906-47) and the Pakistan Muslim League (1947-69) archives. *Class No:* 930.25(549)

Turkey

[6560]
GRISWOLD, W. 'The National archives in Turkey' *Muslim World*, 64, 1974, p.40-44.

Supplemented by Kemal H. Karpat's 'An update on Turkish archives', *Middle East Studies Association Bulletin*, 23, 1989, p.181-87. *Class No:* 930.25(560)

Israel

[6561]
ALSBERG, P.A., *ed*. Guide to the archives of Israel. Jerusalem, Israel Archives Association, 1973. 257p.

Original ed. published in Hebrew 1966.

Inventories archives, and major collections of documents, papers and monographs dealing with Zionist, Jewish or Israeli history, sciences, politics, etc. Comprehensive and informative. B. Wassersteins 'Libraries and archives 12: Israel', *Archives*, v.60, 1975, p.56-61 gives a brief history of the collections in the Jewish National Library, the Hebrew University Library, and other archives in Jerusalem. *Class No:* 930.25(569.4)

[6562]
SEGALL, A., *ed*. Guide to Jewish archives. Jerusalem. World Council on Jewish Archives, 1981. 90p.

Lists repositories in Israel and elsewhere with details of history and scope of their collections. *Class No:* 930.25(569.4)

Myanmar

[6563]
GREAT BRITAIN. India Office Library and Records. A Brief guide to the sources for the study of Burma in the India Office Records. Griffin, A.A. London, India Office Library and Records, 1979. 25p., map.

Introduction (*c*. 1600-1795; 1795-1897; 1897-1948) - Sources (1. Correspondence; 2. Proceedings; 3. Minutes; 4. Departmental records; 5. Non-archival collections and special groups; 6. Official publications; 7. Maps; 8. European manuscripts; 9. Biographical sources). Appendices: 1. Summary list of main classes and series of official archives; 2. List of European manuscript collections (17). *Class No:* 930.25(591)

Africa

[6564]
'Archival resources for African studies in the United Kingdom, p.190-213, *African studies* (The British Library, 1986).

In government departments; societies and other organizations; local record and archives offices; and in private archives. *Class No:* 930.25(6)

[6565]
COOK, C., *comp*. The Making of modern Africa a guide to archives. New York, Facts On File, 1995. v,218p. bibliog., indexes. £32. $35. ISBN: 081602071x.

Lists A-Z by name of holder over 1,000 archival collections of personal papers 'of value to the historian of modern Africa'. No attempt is made to describe government and official archives of the former colonial powers or of the newly independent nations of Africa. Data: Name of archive; dates covered; career profile of holder; and description of archive and in what language. Bibliography p.203. Archive index (location) p.204-211. Subject index p.212-18. *Class No:* 930.25(6)

[6566]
HANNAM, H. 'The Documentation of colonial rule in Africa', *African Research and Documentation*, no.27, 1981, p.8-14.

A description of the various classes of documents produced in connection with British colonies. Useful table of Publications of British African colonies deposited in the Public Record Office, A-Z by colony, p.13-14. *Class No:* 930.25(6)

[6567]
MWIYERIWA, S.S. 'Developments in African archives', p.246-257, *African studies* (The British Library, 1986).

'The nature of the archival landscape in Africa' with specific reference to Uganda; Ghana; Senegal; Sudan; Nigeria; Kenya; Zanzibar; Zimbabwe, Zambia, Malawi; and elsewhere. 11 refs. *Class No:* 930.25(6)

[6568]
PEARSON, J.D. Guide to documents and manuscripts in the British Isles relating to Africa. London, Mansell, 2v., 1993-94. ISBN: 0720121671, set.

Much extended and revised edition of N. Matthews and M.D. Wainwrights *A Guide to manuscripts and documents in the British Isles relating to Africa* (OUP, 1971).

V.1: *London*. 1993. vii,375p. £100. 0720120888. V.2: *British Isles outside London*. 1994. x,566p. £125. 0720212090x. Lists and describes the archival holdings of 65 institutions, societies, museums, libraries and record offices in London and of 200 similar organizations in England, Wales, Scotland and Ireland arranged A-Z by location and by the name of the institution. Data: date, location mark or box number, brief indicative title. Analytical indexes. 'This massive work will be of inestimable value to researchers in all areas of African studies' (*Reference Reviews*, vol.9,no.5, 1995. p.46). *Class No:* 930.25(6)

[6569]
SOUTH, A., *comp*. Guide to non-Federal archives and manuscripts in the United States relating to Africa. London, Hans Zell for the National Archives and Records Administration, Washington, D.C., 2v., 1989. ix,1250p. £140.00. ISBN: 0905450566, v.1; 0905450574, v.2; 0905450558, set.

V.1: Alabama - New Mexico. V.2: New York - Wisconsin. Index. Describes printed and audio-visual material located in US A-Z by state, city and by series or collection. Entries include name of series or collection title, dates, amount of material, subjects, and areas of Africa concerned. Bibliography p.1106-9. Alphabetical list of repositories p.1110-21. 'A monumental and essential work that will be consulted for decades to come' (*African Research and Documentation*, no.50, 1989, p.22-24). *Class No:* 930.25(6)

Bibliographies

[6570]
McILWAINE, J. Writings on African archives. London, Hans Zell for the Standing Conference on Library Materials on Africa (SCOLMA), 1996. xviii,278p. index. £45. ISBN: 187383666x.

2,355 briefly annotated entries relating to monographs, articles, reports, conference papers *etc*. about archives and manuscript collections. Pt.1: Archives in Africa (Africa in General: archives and records management and archival sources in general, then A-Z by country within regional sections). Pt.2: Archives relating to Africa located to overseas: Europe; UK; North America; South America; and Asia. Locations given 'for some of the more fugitive material. *Class No:* 930.25(6)(01)

Africa—West

[6571]
COMMONWEALTH ARCHIVISTS ASSOCIATION. West African sources in British Colonial Office records. London, Commonwealth Archivists Association, 1987. 26p. A4 size typescript. sd.
Records relating to The Gambia, Sierra Leone, Ghana, Nigeria and Fernando Po. *Class No:* 930.25(66)

[6572]
Guide to materials for West African history in European archives. London, Athlone Press, 5v., 1962-73.
1. *Materials for West African history in the archives of Belgium and Holland*, by P. Carson. 1962. 86p. 2: *Materials for West African history in Portuguese archives*, by A.F.C. Ryder. 1965. vi,92p. 3: *Materials for West African history in Italian archives*, by J.R. Gray and D.S. Chambers. 1965. viii,104p. 4: *Materials for West African history in French archives*, by P. Carson. 1968. viii,170p. 5: *Materials for West African history in the archives of the United Kingdom*, by N. Matthews. 1973. 225p. V.2 deals with the main sources, in Lisbon, Coimbra, Evora and Porto. Individual volumes and documents are singled out for special mention. Detailed abstract of manuscript catalogues, indexes, etc., with an indication of inadequacies. Index. Most of the items in v.3 are in Rome, notably the Vatican archives. V.5 includes not only major collections, *e.g.* British Library and Rhodes House, but papers held in, for example, the Municipal Library, Warrington or the Companies Registration Office, Edinburgh. *Class No:* 930.25(66)

Kenya

[6573]
THURSTON, A. Guide to archives and manuscripts relating to Kenya and East Africa in the United Kingdom. Oxford, Hans Zell, 2v., 1991. xvii,1196p. index. £120; $222. ISBN: 0905450477.
A guide to official and non-official records, the bulk of which date from 1945, concerning the pre-independence period in more than 250 British archival repositories including the Public Record Office and Rhodes House Library. Oxford.
V.1: *Official Records*. xvii,617p. 0905450477. In 2 pts: 1. Official records (Public Record Office; Crown Agents for overseas governments; Foreign & Commonwealth Office; India Office Library & Records *etc.*) - 2. Non-official archives and manuscripts. Administrative chronology of Kenya and East Africa p.xiii. List of principal office holders in Kenya Colony and its predecessors p.xii.
V.2: *Non-official Archives and Manuscripts*. 618-1196p. index 090545099x. Private papers of organizations and individuals held in university libraries, local repositories, museums etc. Regionally arranged guide to records mostly dating from 1945 concerning the pre-independence period held in more than 150 repositories. 'A work of amazing diligence, which collates and integrates a vast body of scattered information' (*Library Association Record*, v.83, no.8, August 1991, p.543). *Class No:* 930.25(676.2)

Africa—Southern

[6574]
Directory of manuscript collections in Southern Africa. Cape Town, South African Library, 1986. viii, 89p. pbk. £4. ISBN: 0869680587.
102 of the more significant repositories in Malawi, South Africa, Zambia and Zimbabwe listed A-Z by institution. Information includes history of their collections, acquisition policy, area of specialization, and publications. 'A useful basic guide' (*African Research and Documentation*, no.42, 1986, p.50-51). *Class No:* 930.25(68)

South Africa

Databases

[6575]
KIRKWOOD, C. 'Inter-institutional co-operation in the computer retrieval of information on private archives: the South African National Register of Manuscripts (NAREM)', p.76-85, *The National Register of Archives: an international perspective* edited by D. Sargent (q.v.)
Contents: Origin of NAREM; Processing of information for NAREM; On-line retrieval of NAREM data; Information available in NAREM; National integration of archives. *Class No:* 930.25(680)(003.4)

Zimbabwe

[6576]
JOHNSTONE, I.J. A Guide to Zimbabwe-related documentation in Britain. Harare, National Archives of Zimbabwe, 1985. 503p. index.
A thorough guide to archives in London (A-Z by institution) and outside London (A-Z by town or city). Poorly reproduced from typescript. *Class No:* 930.25(689.1)

[6577]
KAMBA, A.S. 'National archives of Zimbabwe' *African Research and Documentation*, no.28, 1982, p.10-12.
Outline description of its organization, functions, and publications. *Class No:* 930.25(689.1)

Canada

[6578]
CANADA. Public Archives of Canada. Catalogue of the Public Archives/Catalogue de la Bibliothèque des Archives Publiques. Boston, Mass., G.K. Hall, 12v., 1979. $1250. Export $1510.00. ISBN: 081610316x.
Main author-catalogue of *c.*40,000 publications; chronological catalogue of pamphlets published between 1495 and 1950; list of catalogued periodicals. Covers all aspects of Canadian history and culture. *Class No:* 930.25(71)

[6579]
Guide des sources de l'histoire du Canada conservées en France. Ottawa, Archives Publiques Canada, 1982. xix, 157p. ISBN: 0660908867.
9 contributors. The results of a survey undertaken in the Archives Nationales (Paris), the archival repositories of the Départements, in government ministries, and the Bibliothèque Nationale. Chronological limits: from the origins of French Canada to 1940. Preliminaries also in English translation. *Class No:* 930.25(71)

[6580]
Manuscripts and Government Records in the United Kingdom and Ireland relating to Canada/ Manuscrits et documents au Royaume-Uni et au Irlande concernant Le Canada. Wilson, B.G., *ed*. Ottawa, National Archives of Canada, 1992. xxi,705p. indexes. ISBN: 0660574241.
Lists textual documentation of significance to the political, economic, social, intellectual, cultural and scientific history of Canada held in archives and record offices in England (A-Z by new counties), Wales, Scotland, Channel Islands, Isle of Man, Northern Ireland, and the Republic of Ireland. Name, topography and subject indexes p.583-705. *Class No:* 930.25(71)

[6581]
MARCOUX, Y. 'A National Register of Archives in mosaic form: the Canadian example' p.55-64, *The National Register of Archives: an international perspective* edited by D. Sargent (q.v.).
Canadian archives and society - Canadian Archival System - National Register of Archives - The future information system on Canadian archives. *Class No:* 930.25(71)

Caribbean

[6582]
INGRAM, K.E. Manuscripts relating to Commonwealth Caribbean countries in United States and Canadian repositories. St. Lawrence, Barbados, Caribbean Univs. Press in association with Bowker, New York, 1975. xxix, 422p. ISBN: 0854740295.
1,038 numbered entries (with interpolations). 91 repositories (including map collections), those visited being indicated. Geographical order of repositories; entries arranged chronologically. Data include extended descriptions, provenance notes, bibliographical references, and details of the existence of reproductions. Supplement: Chronological short list of entries, 1498-1959. 'List of works to which reference has been made', p.xii-xx. Index, p.345-422. *Class No:* 930.25(729)

[6583]
TYSON, G.F. A Guide to manuscript sources in United States and West Indian depositories relating to the British West Indies during the era of the American Revolution. Wilmington, Delaware, Scholarly Resources,1979. xvii,96p. bibliog. index. $25.00. ISBN: 0842021310.
Focuses specifically on manuscript materials relating to Antigua, Bahamas, Barbados, Bermuda, British Virgin Islands, Dominica, Grenada, Jamaica, Montserrat, Nevis, St. Kitts, St. Lucia, St. Vincent, and Tobago for the period 1763-1783. U.S. Depositories A-Z by State; West Indian depositories A-Z by island. Bibliography p.90. *Class No:* 930.25(729)

Jamaica

[6584]
INGRAM, K.E. Sources of Jamaican history 1655-1838 : a bibliographical survey with particular reference to manuscript sources. Zug, Switzerland, Inter Documentation Co., 2v., 1976. xvii+Øiii, 1310p. ISBN: 3857500174.
Part 1 (1-8 *e.g.* 2. British and Irish repositories and sources 3. Jamaican repositories and sources; 7. Some printed sources; 8. Maps and pictorial records) - Part 2: Descriptive lists, A-K (A. Descriptive list of manuscripts in British, Irish and Jamaican repositories, p.189-947, C. Bibliographies, catalogues and guides ... H. Newspapers and

....*(contd.)*

periodicals ... J. Law of Jamaica; K. Parliamentary papers). Supplement, p.1123-1200. Detailed index, p.1200-1310. A descriptive inventory, by the Librarian, Univ. of West Indies. 'Will ... remain for many years to come the most valuable guide to documentary material on Jamaican history for the pre-1838 period' (*Archives*, v.14, no.62, Autumn 1979, p.114-15). *Class No: 930.25(729.2)*

[6585]

—INGRAM, K.E. Sources for West Indian studies a supplementary listing with particular reference to manuscript sources. Zug, Switzerland, Inter Documentation Co., 1983. 412p.

1169 entries describe historical and literary source materials in West Indian depositories. Supplements his *Sources of Jamaican history* (1976). *Class No: 930.25(729)*

Leeward & Windward Islands

[6586]

BAKER, E.C. A Guide to records in the Leeward Islands. Oxford, Blackwell for the Univ. of the West Indies, 1965. x, 102p. map, index.

Based on a survey made in 1962. An inventory of records in Antigua, Montserrat, Nevis, St. Christopher and the British Virgin Islands, with some descriptive notes. Includes newspapers; one of the appendices covers maps, plans and drawings. *Class No: 930.25(729.7)*

[6587]

BAKER, E.C. A Guide to records in the Windward Islands. Oxford, Blackwell for the Univ. of the West Indies, 1968. xii, 95p., map, index.

An inventory of records in Grenada, St. Vincent, St. Lucia, and Dominica. 'An invaluable source' (R.A. Myers *Dominica*, 1987. Entry 455). *Class No: 930.25(729.7)*

Barbados

[6588]

CHANDLER, M.J. A Guide to records in Barbados. Oxford, Blackwell for the Univ. of West Indies, 1965. xi, 204p. map, index.

Based on a survey made in 1960, and the first of a series of volumes that are to cover the records of all the territories in the West Indies. The full inventory (p.1-164) is followed by appendices on special types of material (*e.g.* acts and laws, newspapers, maps and plans). Detailed index. *Class No: 930.25(729.86)*

Bermuda

[6589]

ROWE, H. A Guide to the records of Bermuda. Hamilton, Bermuda, 1984. 132p. $12.00.

'The result of painstaking and accurate research, it contains among other merits valuable historical notes about every agency and activity on which records are held' (*Library Association Record*, v.86,no.4, April 1984, p.179). *Class No: 930.25(729.9)*

Latin America

[6590]

INTERNATIONAL COUNCIL ON ARCHIVES. Guides to the sources for the history of the nations: A. Latin America.

1. *A guide to manuscript sources for the history of Latin America and the Caribbean in the British Isles* by P. Walne. London, Oxford Univ. Press, 1973. 2. *Führer durch die Quellen zur Lateinamerikas in der Bundesrepublik Deutschlands* by R. Hauschild-Thiessen and E. Bachman. Bremen, Schüneman, 1973. 3. *Übersicht über die Quellen zur Geschichte Lateinamerikas in Archiven der Deutschen Demokratischen Republik*. Potsdam, Staatliche Archivverwaltung, 1971. 4. *Guide du chercheur dans les archives françaises: les sources de l'histoire de l'Amérique latine* by D. Ozanam. Paris, Institute des Hautes Études de l'Amérique latine, 1963. 5. *Guida delle fonti per la storia dell'America latina esistenti in Italia* by E. Lodolini. Rome, Direzione Generale degli Archivi di Stato, 1976. 6. *Guida della fonti per la storia dell'America latina negli archivi della Santa Sede e negli archivi ecclesiastici d'Italia* by L. Pásztor. Vatican City, Archivo Vaticano, 1970. 7. *Guia di fuentes para la historia de Ibero-América conservados en España* Madrid, Dirección General de Archivos y Bibliotecas, 2v., 1966-69. 8. *Fuentes para la historia de Ibero-América: Escandinavia* by M. Mörner. Stockholm, Riksarkivet, 1968. 9. *Guide to the sources in the Netherlands for the history of Latin America* by M.P.H. Roessingh. The Hague, Algemeen Rijkarchief, 1968. 10. *Guide des sources de l'histoire d'Amérique latine conservées en Belgique* by L. Liagre & J. Barten, Bruxelles, Archives Généraux, 1967. *Class No: 930.25(729.99)*

[6591]

NAUMAN, A.K. A Handbook of Latin American and Caribbean national archives/Guia de los archivos nacionales de America Latino y el Caribe. Detroit, Blaine Ethridge, 1983. ix, 127p. bibliog.

Introduction to resources for potential first-time users. Collections, services, access A-Z by country omitting Cuba, Haiti, Trinidad & Tobago. English and Spanish text. *Class No: 930.25(729.99)*

[6592]

ULIBARRI, G.S. *and* HARRISON, J.P. Guide to materials on Latin America in the National Archives of the United States. Washington, National Archives and Records Service, 1974. 489p. $25.00. ISBN: 0911333223.

Supersedes J.P. Harrison's *Guide to materials on Latin America in the National Archives* (1961).

A detailed inventory, with notes on representative documents. Index of issuing bodies, geographic names and selected subjects. Appendices provide lists of National Archives files and of US diplomatic and consular posts with archival records. 'Materials' includes maps, photographs and films. 'An indispensiable aid for the researcher' (*Library of Congress information bulletin*, 4 July 1975, p.280-1). *Class No: 930.25(729.99)*

[6593]

WALNE, P., *ed*. A Guide to manuscript sources for the history of Latin America and the Caribbean in the British Isles. London, Oxford Univ. Press in collaboration with the Institute of Latin American Studies, Univ. of London, 1973. xx,580p.

A detailed inventory of public repositories. Appendix: 'The British in South America - an archive report'. Addenda. Index, p.521-80 (Ship's names: over 4 columns). A first-rate research tool in its field. 'This is a basic reference work' (*Library Journal*, v.98, no.14, August 1973, p.2266). *Class No: 930.25(729.99)*

USA

[6594]

LARSEN, J.C., *ed*. Researcher's guide to archives and regional history sources. Hamden, Connecticut, Shoe String Press, 1988. xiv, 167p. $27.50. £19.95. ISBN: 0208012442.

14 contributors. Basic information on skills needed for researching and on location of specific sources. *Class No: 930.25(73)*

[6595]

NATIONAL HISTORICAL PUBLICATIONS AND RECORDS COMMISSION. Directory of archives and manuscript repositories in the United States. 2nd ed. Phoenix, Arizona, Oryx, 1988. 853p. index. $55.00. £36.70. ISBN: 0897744756.

1st ed. 1978. This was a revised ed. of P.M. Hanser's *A Guide to archives and manuscripts in the United States* (1961).

Data on 4560 repositories (an increase of 1400 on the 1978 ed.), museums, galleries, archives and libraries in all 50 states. Arranged A-Z by state/territory, subdivided by locality. Index of entries in alphabetical order. 'Historians, graduate students, and genealogists will find it indispensable in planning research trips' (*Choice*, v.26, no.2, October 1988, p.286). *Class No: 930.25(73)*

[6596]

The National inventory of documentary sources in the United States. Alexandria, Virginia, and Cambridge, Chadwyck-Healey Inc., 1983-. Silver Halide (archivally permanent) 24 x microfiche in envelopes. Part 1. *Federal records*. 1985. 1911 microfiche. £3,750. 0898870267. 428 current finding aids in the National Archives and Record Service and a single-indexed finding aids to 7 Presidential Libraries. Separate printed index. Part 2. *Manuscript Division, Library of Congress*. 1983. 889 microfiche. £1,950. 0898870283. Registers to almost 800 of the most important collections. Separate printed index. Part 3. *State Archives, Libraries and Historical Societies*. Academic Libraries and other repositories. Published in 10 units per annum accompanied by COM indexes, 1984-. £6,000 annual subscription. Alternative subscription plans per unit are available. There is an annual updating service to parts 1 and 2. It is anticipated that Part 3 will continue for at least five years before the backlog of existing finding aids is exhausted.

An awesome reference work providing an immediate access to thousands of finding aids to collections the length and breadth of the United States. Potential subscribers are advised to apply for *Handbook for the researcher* and a booklet *NUCMC RLIN and NIDS* advertized as being available *gratis* from the publishers at 1021 Prince Street, VA 22314 or Cambridge Place, Cambridge, CB2 1 NR. *Class No: 930.25(73)*

[6597]

SZUCS, L. *and* LUEBKING, S.H. The Archives: a guide to the National Archives Field Branches. Salt Lake City, Ancestry, 1985. 340p. $35.95. ISBN: 091648923x.

Guide to the holdings of the National Archives' 11 regional archives. *Class No: 930.25(73)*

[6598]
UNITED STATES. National Archives. **Guide to cartographic records in the National Archives.** Washington, National Archives, 1971. 444p. index. $25. ISBN: 0911333193.

The National Archives has among its holdings more than 1.6 million maps and approximately 9 million aerial photographs. This guide describes those materials that are maintained in the Cartographic and Architectural Branch, as well as other maps filed with closely related textual records held by other custodial units of the National Archives. Entries arranged under Government departments, agencies, *etc.*
Class No: 930.25(73)

[6599]
UNITED STATES. National Archives and Records Administration. **Guide to Federal records in the National Archives of the United States.** Washington, D.C., National Archives and Records Administration, 3v., 1996. 2428p. Vol.3 is an index volume. $95. ISBN: 0160483123.

Supersedes *Guide to the National Archives of the United States* (1974 and later reprints).

This comprehensive guide describes the holdings in the Washington DC. area and those of NARA regional repositories as at 1 October 1994. Data: a brief administrative history, a summary description of archival holdings, their quantity, and notes on subject terms and finding aids. Also available on NARA web site at gopher:// clio.nara.gov/u/inform/guide. Ordered by almost 500 record groups, 'this magisterial reference work provides an introduction to more than 1.7 million cubic feet of textual records, 300,000 rolls of microfilm, 2.3 million maps and charts, 9.2 million aerial photographs, 7.4 million still pictures, 178.000 sound records, 123,000 motion picture reels, and 7,000 computer data sets (*Choice*, v.34,no.7, March 1997, p.1144). *Class No:* 930.25(73)

CD-ROM

[6600]
ArchivesUSA. Cambridge, Chadwyck-Healey, 1996. CD-ROM Windows.

Brings together in electronic form records from three important information sources - *The National Union Catalog of Manuscript Collections (NUCMC), The National Inventory of Documentary Sources in the United States (NIDS US)*, with their indexes, and *The Directory of Manuscript Repositories in the US (DAMRUS)*.

NUCMC was established in 1959 as a cooperative programme in which public US repositories reported their holdings of manuscript collections to the Library of Congress. Catalogue entries prepared from these reports were published annually in book form through 1987 and thereafter as machine-readable records. *NIDS US* is a compilation of over 52,000 archival and manuscript finding aids on microfiche from hundreds of repositories throughout the country.

ArchivesUSA contains all *NUCMC* records to date and the list of collections from *NIDS US* together with an extensive names and subjects index. The fully-updated *DAMRUS* listings provide important practical information on all manuscript repositories in the US including locations, opening times, phone and fax numbers and e-mail addresses. *Class No:* 930.25(73)(003.40)

[6601]
CD-ROM Index to NIDS. Cambridge, Chadwyck-Healey, 1996. CD-ROM. MS-DOS.

CD-ROM Index to NIDS *The National Inventory of Documentary Sources in the United Kingdom and Ireland* (NIDS UK) and the *National Inventory of Documentary Sources in the United States (NIDS US)* are reference works for anyone who wants to find out what is in a particular archive or manuscript collection. They reproduce on microfiche the finding aids to thousands of collections in libraries and record offices, museums and private collections throughout the UK, Ireland and the United States, *NIDS US* also has separate parts covering Federal Records and the Manuscript Division, Library of Congress. Specially-created indexes provide access by titles of collections within a repository, and by names and subjects. They are the link between researchers and the primary resources in repositories for which they are searching. *Class No:* 930.25(73)(003.40)

Bibliographies

[6602]
DE WITT, D.L., *comp.* **Articles describing archives and manuscript collections in the United States** an annotated bibliography. Westport, Conn., Greenwood Press, 1997. xi,458p. index. £71.50. ISBN: 0313295980. ISSN: 07426879.

2273 entries arranged in 13 heavily sub-divided sections: 1. General collections - 2. Business - 3. Ethnic, minorities and women - 4. Federal archives - 5. Fine Arts - 6. Literary - 7. Military - 8. Political - 9. Professional groups and organisations - 10. Regional - 11. Religious groups - 12. Foreign repositories - 13. US repositories holding foreign records or manuscripts. Analytical index p.361-458.
Class No: 930.25(73)(01)

[6603]
Guides to archives and manuscript collections in the United States an annotated bibliography. De Witt, D.L., *comp.* Westport, Conn., Greenwood Press, 1994. xi,478p. index. £75. (*Bibliographies and Indexes in Library and Information Science, no.8.*) ISBN: 0313284997.

2062 entries listed in 13 thematic groups: 1. General collections (archives and manuscripts; maps, oral histories and photographs) ... 4. Federal archives ... 8. Political collections ... 10. Regional collections ... 12. Foreign repositories holding US-related records - 13. US repositories holding foreign records or manuscripts. 'The purpose of this bibliography is to bring together in one volume finding aids to unpublished materials' (*Introduction*). *Class No:* 930.25(73)(01)

Amerindians, North

[6604]
HILL, E., *ed.* **Guide to records in the National Archives relating to American Indians.** Washington, National Archives, 1984. 467p. illus. $25.00. ISBN: 0911333134.

First published 1981.

Includes concise information about records that trace the evolution of federal Indian policy, the effects of national policies on traditional Indian culture, Indian wars and their results, and the role of Native Americans in the development of U.S. society.
Class No: 930.25(73)(=97)

Australasia & Oceania

[6605]
Catalogue of manuscripts of Australasia and the Pacific in the Mitchell Library Sydney. Sydney. Trustees of the Public Library of New South Wales. 1967 and 1969.

1. *Series A.* 1967. 293p. Primary and secondary source material catalogues 1945-1963. Subject and author indexes. 2. *Series B.* 1969. 500p. Material added 1963-1967. *Class No:* 930.25(9)

Brunei

[6606]
CHUA SUI GIM. 'Guide to modern archives and manuscripts found in the UK relating to Brunei, Sabah and Sarawak,' *Brunei Museum Journal*, v.5, no.1, 1981, p.56-77.

Covers the pre-1963 period. *Class No:* 930.25(911.13)

New Zealand

[6607]
Archives New Zealand a directory of archives and manuscript repositories in New Zealand, the Cook Islands, Fiji, Niue, Tokelau, Tonga, and Western Samoa. Rogers, F., *comp.* Auckland, Archives Press, 1984. vii, 65p. maps, index.

Directory information (inc. hours, fees, acquisition policy, access restriction, published guides) to 155 repositories. Bibliography p.v. 2 maps. Complements *National Register of Archives and Manuscripts in New Zealand. Class No:* 930.25(931)

[6608]
Directory of archives and manuscript repositories in New Zealand, the Cook Islands, Fiji, Niue, Tokelau, Tonga, and Western Samoa. 2nd ed. Plimmerton, Archives Press, Archives New Zealand. vi,73p. NZ$30. ISBN: 0959777741.

194 entries arranged geographically then A-Z by institution. Data: Name and address, access, guides and other publications, charges *etc.*
Class No: 930.25(931)

Australia

[6609]
Directory of archives in Australia. Burnstein, S., *and others, comps.* Granville, NSW, Ambassador Press for the Australian Society of Archivists, 1992. x,527p. index. A$30. ISBN: 0947219064.

458 entries arranged by jurisdiction and geographical area, then A-Z by name of institution. Data: name and address; access details, published guides *etc. Class No:* 930.25(94)

[6610]
Guide to collections of manuscripts relating to Australia a selective union list. Canberra, National Library of Australia, 1986. 21 microfiche set. 42 x reduction. $Aust.20.00. ISSN: 07259107.

First published 1965.

Lists collections of private papers, business records, certain restricted collections and 'fugitive' official collections (*i.e.* hard to find official records held outside the national or State archives offices). Includes some entries relating to other geographic regions notably the Pacific Islands and areas neighbouring Australia. Arranged in 2 pts:

....(contd.)

entries in numerical order and a consolidated name index of collections and sub-groups within collections. An invaluable tool for all those engaged in historical prime source material. *Class No:* 930.25(94)

[6611]

NATHAN, E. 'Archives', chapter 2, *Australians: a guide to sources* (v.10. *Australians. A historical library*, 1988).

Public records - Archives legislation - Official publications - Access to government archives - Guides and finding aids - Non-government archives. *Class No:* 930.25(94)

[6612]

POWELL, G. 'The Exchange of archival information in Australia', p.44-54, *The National Register of Archives: an international perspective* edited by Dick Sargent *(q.v.).*

Contents include a guide to collections of manuscripts relating to Australia; National Register of Records; Australian bibliographic network; Australian Historical Records Register; and published guides. *Class No:* 930.25(94)

Palaeography & Epigraphy

[6613]

BISCHOFF, B. Latin palaeography Antiquity and the Middle Ages. Cambridge Univ. Press in association with The Medieval Academy of Ireland, 1990. xi,291p. facsims., bibliog., indexes. £12.95. ISBN: 0521364736.

First published as *Paläographie des romischen Altertums und des abendländischen Mittelalters,* Berlin, Erich Schmidt Verlag, 1979. 2nd ed. 1986.

Authoritative and comprehensive account of the history of the Latin script: A. Codicology - B. History of the Latin script - C. Manuscripts in cultural history. *Class No:* 930.27

[6614]

BROWN, M.P. A Guide to Western historical scripts: from antiquity to 1600. London, The British Library, 1990. Published in North America by Univ. of Toronto Press. 138p. Facsims., bibliogs. £17.95. ISBN: 0712301771.

1. Roman system of scripts - 2. National hands - 3. The insular system of scripts - 4. Anglo-Saxon - 5. Caroline minuscule - 6. Protogothic - 7. Gothic - 8. Italic - 9. Humanistic system of scripts. Appendix: Some common abbreviations p.136. Glossary p.8. Bibliography p.9-12. Index of scripts p.137. Index of manuscripts p.138. 55 plates. A survey of the evolution of scripts with examples in broad chronological sequence. The author is a Curator in the Department of Manuscripts, the British Library. *Class No:* 930.27

[6615]

DANBURY, E. Palaeography for historians. Chichester, West Sussex, Phillimore, 2000. 160p. illus. £15.99. ISBN: 186077072x.

A practical guide for researchers bewildered by Latin, English and French primary sources which are firmly placed in their administrative and legal framework. *Class No:* 930.27

[6616]

DENHOLM-YOUNG, N. Handwriting in England and Wales. Cardiff, Univ. of Wales Press, 1954. xi, 102p. [33p] illus., maps.

An introduction to the study of palaeography, with bibliography and annotated plates for students beginning their research on some aspect of English or Welsh history or literature. Emphasis is on the period from the coming of the Caroline miniscule to the 17th century. Sections on types of hands are supplemented by valuable guidance on particular problems and on the use of palaeography in the criticism of texts. *Class No:* 930.27

[6617]

HECTOR, L.C. The Handwriting of English documents. 2nd ed. Dorking, Surrey, Kohler & Coombes, 1980. 136p. illus. (pl.), bibliog., index. £15.00. ISBN: 0903967162.

First published 1958. 2nd ed. London, E. Arnold, 1966.

Six chapters: 1. The equipment of the writers - 2. The equipment of the reader - 3. Abbreviations - 4. Scribal conventions and expedients - 5. English handwriting from the Conquest to 1500-6. English handwriting since 1500. Transcripts of passages represented in plates; bibliography, p.132-3 (works asterisked contain transcribed facsimiles); index. *Class No:* 930.27

[6618]

JENKINSON, H. The Later court hands in England, from the 15th to the 17th century, illustrated from the Common Papers of the Scriveners' Company of London, the English Writing Masters and the Public Records. Cambridge, Cambridge Univ., 2v., 1927.

Pt.1: Text; pt.2: plates.

Standard work on English hands of the 15th, 16th and 17th centuries, containing (pt.1) valuable study on various aspects, bibliography, and transcripts and notes for the plates in pt.2. Alphabets in pt.2. *Class No:* 930.27

[6619]

JOHNSON, C. *and* JENKINSON, H. English court hands AD1066-1500 illustrated chiefly from the Public Records. Oxford, Clarendon Press, 2v., 1915.

Pt.1: Text; pt.2: Plates.

Standard work on English medieval chancery, exchequer and legal hands, containing (pt.1) valuable study on various aspects and bibliography of development of individual letters, abbreviations, and transcripts (where necessary), with detailed notes for the plates in pt.2. *Class No:* 930.27

[6620]

PARKES, M.B. English cursive book hands 1250-1500. 2nd ed. London, Scholar Press, 1979. xxxii, 24p. facsims., bibliog. £15. ISBN: 0859675351.

First published Oxford, Clarendon Press, 1969.

Basically, 24 pages of examples of book hands, with notes and transcriptions facing. Preliminaries include notes on Anglicana book hands, the handwriting of university scribes, the handwriting of individual scribes, etc.' also a valuable introduction (footnoted), 'a note on palaeographic terms' (p.xxvi) and a select bibliography. *Class No:* 930.27

[6621]

WRIGHT, C.E. English vernacular hands from the twelfth to the fifteenth centuries. Oxford, Clarendon Press, 1960. xx,25p. facsims. bibliog.

24 facsimiles and transcriptions. The introduction (p.1-xx) discusses The Vernacular Manuscript Tradition and Handwriting. *Class No:* 930.27

Bibliographies

[6622]

JONES, L.E. Medieval Latin palaeography: a bibliographical introduction. Toronto, Univ. of Toronto Press, 1984. xvi, 399p. index. $35. £26. ISBN: 0802056121.

2207 briefly annotated entries constitute an 'outstanding bibliography' which 'provides a clear, thorough, and reliable introduction to the rich and complicated literature of medieval Latin palaeography' *(Choice,* v.22, no.10, June 1985, p.1467). Index locorum, nominum, rerum p.334-391. Index codicum p.392-399. *Class No:* 930.27(01)

[6623]

LONDON UNIVERSITY. Library. The Palaeography Collection in the University of London Library: an author and subject catalogue. Boston, Mass., G.K. Hall, 2v., 1968.

A collection primarily concerned with material for the study of the manuscript book in Greek, Latin and Western European languages. The author catalogue comprises *c.*10,800 cards; the subject catalogue *c.*13,100 cards. *Class No:* 930.27(01)

[6624]

THORP, J. Books on palaeography: sixteenth to eighteenth century handwriting, *Local Historian,* v.16, no.6, May 1985, p.327-334. *Class No:* 930.27(01)

Ancient Greece

[6625]

SCHUBART, W. Griechische paläographie. München, Verlag C.H. Beck, 1966. vii,184p.illus. ISBN: 3406013376.

Abteilung 1:4, 1 of the *Handbuch der Altertumswissenschaft. Class No:* 930.27(37)

Ancient Rome

[6626]

GORDON, A.E. Illustrated introduction to Latin epigraphy. Berkeley, Univ. of California Press, 1983. xxv, 264p.+64p. plates. bibliog. index. $50. ISBN: 0520038983.

2 Parts: Introduction - Latin epigraphy defined; provenience of Latin inscriptions; sources and collections; technical details; subject matter; problems of inscriptions; contents of this selection; miscellaneous information; bibliography p.54-65. The Inscriptions p.69-185. Concordances p.237-242. *Class No:* 930.27(38)

[6627]

LOWE, E.A., *ed.* Codices Latini antiquiores: a palaeographical guide to Latin manuscripts prior to the ninth century. Oxford, Clarendon Press, 1934-. illus., (pl.), maps.

Country locations:

1: *Vatican City.*

2: *Great Britain, Ireland,* 2nd ed. 1972. 84p. £17.50. Suppt. 1971. £17.50. 3/4: *Italy.* 5: *Paris.* 6: *France.* 7: *Switzerland.* 8/9: *Germany* 10: *Austria, Belgium, Czechoslovakia, Denmark, Egypt and Holland.* 11: *Hungary, Luxembourg, Poland, Russia, Spain, Sweden, United States and Yugoslavia. Supplement.* 1972. £55. ISBN 019818218x. *Class No:* 930.27(38)

USA

[6628]

SPERRY, K. **Reading early American handwriting**. Baltimore, Md Genealogical Publishing Co., 1998. 289p. bibliog. $29.99.

For American researchers using early American documents, it explains the techniques involved, provides some alphabets, and defines terminology, abbreviations, and contractions. Indicates sources for the study of palaeography on the Internet. *Class No:* 930.27(73)

Ancient History & Ancient Peoples

[6629]

BOWERSOCK, G., *and others eds*. **Late antiquity** a guide to the post classical world. Cambridge, Mass., The Belknap Press of Harvard Univ. Press, 1999. xvi,780p. illus. (some col.), bibliogs., index. ISBN: 0674511735.

Treating the period 200-800 AD as a distinctive period of history, and taking as its scope the vast regions covered by the Roman and Sassanian Empires, 11 academics contribute 10 introductory essays (*e.g.*Building the past, Barbarians and ethnicity, Christian triumph and controversy, Islam) and c.225 initialled A-Z entries, each with a bibliography, p.273-757 relating to important individuals, places, institutions etc. A commendable initiative, concentrating on a period and region relatively neglected in historical reference works. *Class No:* 931

[6630]

The Cambridge ancient history. Cambridge, Cambridge Univ. Press.

Originally published in 12v. and 5v. of plates (1923-1929). This new edition is totally rethought and rewritten with new text and plates, illustrations and bibliographies.

Pt.1: *Prolegomena and prehistory*. 3rd ed., 1970. £75. ISBN 0521070511. Pt.2: *Early history of the Middle East*. 3rd ed., 1971. £90. 0521077915. 2. Pt.1: *History of the Middle East and the Aegean region c.1800-1380 BC*. New ed; 1973. £80. 0521082307. 2. Pt.2: *c.1380-1000 BC* 3rd ed., 1975. £90. 0521086914. *Plates to volumes 1 and 2*. 1977. £45. 0521205719. 3. Pt.1: *The prehistory of the Balkans, the Middle East and the Aegean world 10th to 8th centuries BC*. 2nd ed., 1982. £90. 0521224969 3. Pt.2 *Assyrian and Babylonian Empires and other states of the Near East from the eighth to the sixth centures*. 2nd ed. 1992. £85. 0521227178. Pt.3 *The expansion of the Greek world, 8th to 6th centuries BC*. 2nd ed., 1982. £65. 0521234476. *Plates to v.3*. 1984. £49.95. 0521242894. 4. *Persia, Greece and the Western Mediterranean c.525-479 BC*. 2nd ed. 1988. £85. 0521228042. *Plates to volume 4* 1988. £50. 0521305802. 5. *The Fifth Century* 1992. 618p. £70. 052123347x. 6. The Fourth Century BC. 1994. £90. 0521233488. *Plates to v.5 & 6*. 1995. 0521233496 7. Pt.1: *The Hellenistic World*. 2nd ed., 1984. £70. 052123445x.*Plates to v.7 pt.1*. 1984. £45. 0521243548. 7. Pt.2: *The rise of Rome to 220 BC*. 1990. £75. 0521234468. 8. *Rome and the Mediterranean to 133 BC*. 2nd ed. 1989. £70. 0521234484. 9. *The last age of The Roman Republic 133-44 BC*. £85. 0521256038. 10. *The Augustan Empire 44 BC-AD70*. 1996. £90. 0521264308. *Plates to v.9 and 10*. 1997. £45. 0521267757. 11. *The Imperial Peace AD 70-192*. 1936. 052120449936. 12. *Imperial crisis and recovery AD 193-324*. 1939. £80. 05212044944. *Plates to v.11 & 12*. 1997. £45. 0521309735. 13. *The Late Empire AD337-425*. 1997. £85. 0521300205. 14. 1996. £85. 0521325919.

'A genuinely classic work now brought up-to-date: it is a staple item for any academic or major collection covering this period of history' (*Reference Reviews*,v.10,no.7, 1996. p.42 of v.10). *Class No:* 931

[6631]

COTTERELL, A. **The Pimlico dictionary of classical civilizations**. London, Pimlico, 1998. xi,438p. maps. £12.50. ISBN: 0712674969.

A-Z cross-referenced entries relating to peoples, individual leaders, dynasties, schools of philosophy, institutions, military campaigns and battles unusually covering the classical world, 600BC-600AD, as a whole, Greece, Rome, Persia, India and China. Further reading(s) are appended to each entry. Chronology p.452-63. Maps p.467-76. Index of names and subjects not titles of entries. *Class No:* 931

[6632]

CRAWFORD, M. **Sources for ancient history**. Cambridge, Cambridge Univ. Press, 1983. xi, 238p. illus. bibliog., index. £30.00. (*Studies in the Uses of Historical Evidence*.) ISBN: 0521247829.

4 essays examining the historical use and interpretation of ancient literature, classical epigraphy and archaeology, and numismatic evidence from the ancient Mediterranean. 'Spankingly up-to-date in their concepts, examples and bibliographies' (*Antiquity*, v.58, no.223, July 1984, p.149). *Class No:* 931

[6633]

The Seventy wonders of the ancient world the great monuments and how they were built. Scarre, C., *ed*. London, Thames and Hudson, 1999. 304p. illus. (mostly col.), bibliog., index. £24.95. ISBN: 0500050961.

16 contributors. 70 monuments described and illustrated under 6 categories: Seven wonders, Tombs and cemetries, Temples and shrines, Palaces, baths and fortifications, Harbours, hydraulics and roads, and Colossal statues and monoliths, dating from the 6th millenium BC. to the 16th century pyramids of the Aztecs. Bibliography p.293-97. *Class No:* 931

Encyclopaedias

[6634]

BROWN, A., *ed*. **Encyclopedia of the Ancient World**. London, Fitzroy Dearborn, 2000. 425p. col.illus., bibliog., index. £95. ISBN: 1579582818.

Cross-referenced entries on particular civilizations, and series of civilizations explain the historical context of their rise and fall. Each entry is a self-contained clearly defined essay extended by factboxes highlighting specific aspects of the subject. A glossary and a time-line tighten this colourful overview. *Class No:* 931(031)

[6635]

The Penguin encyclopedia of Classical civilizations. Cotterell, A., *ed*. London, Viking, 1993. xiv,290p. illus. (few col.), maps, bibliog., index. £20. $29.95. ISBN: 0670826995.

6 chapters, by separate hands, each with its own chronology cover the period 550BC to 600AD: Hellenic civilization; The Hellenistic age; The World of Rome; The Empires of Persia; Imperial India; and The Unification of China. Bibliography (by chapter) p.283-84. *Class No:* 931(031)

Maps & Atlases

[6636]

Atlas of the Greek and Roman world in antiquity. Hammond, N.G.L., *ed*. Park Ridge, New Jersey, Noyes Press, 1981. viii, 56p. maps. £44.24; $48.00. ISBN: 081555060x.

35 contributors. 46 maps (various scales) divided into 3 sections: 1. Greek prehistory and history - 2. Topographical maps - 3. Roman history. 10,000 sites are located although many identifications are no more than probables. Appendix 1. Founding dates of Greek colonies - 2. Modern names for sites in Roman Britain - 3. In Gaul, Germany and the Alps. *Class No:* 931(084.3)

[6637]

OLIPHANT, M. **The Atlas of the Ancient World**. Charting the great civilizations of the past. London, Ebury Press, 1992. 220p. illus. (many col.), col. maps, bibliog., index. £19.99. ISBN: 0091770408.

Popular illustrated atlas in 9 sub-divided sections: 1. Mesopotamia and Near East - 2. Egypt - 3. Persia - 4. Prehistoric Europe - 5. Greece and the Aegean - 6. Roman world - 7. India - 8. China - 9. The Americas. Chronology of the Ancient World p.202-11. Bibliography p.212-13. Analytical index. *Class No:* 931(084.3)

[6638]

Peoples and places of the past The National Geographic illustrated cultural atlas of the ancient world. 5th ed. Washington, National Geographic Society, 1983. 424p. col. illus., col. maps. $69.95. £49.95. ISBN: 087044462x.

16 textual, pictorial and cartographic chapters with chronologies and bibliographies provide a sumptuous folio volume for the well-heeled general reader. *Class No:* 931(084.3)

CD-ROM

[6639]

Atlas of the ancient World CD-ROM. London, Maris Multimedia, 1997. £29.99.

Covers 5 million years of human history from the Stone Age to the end of the Roman era. 8 regional overviews, 52 documentaries. 2,000 col.illus. 274 maps. Internet access to the latest archaeological research. Information from *Online & CD-ROM Review*, v.21, no.5, October 1997, p.295). *Class No:* 931(084.3)(003.40)

Chronologies

[6640]

BICKERMAN, E.J. **Chronology of the Ancient World**. Rev. ed. London, Thames & Hudson, Ithaca, New York, Cornell Univ. Press, 1980. 223p. illus., tables, index. $32.50. (*Aspects of Greek and Roman life*.) ISBN: 0500400393, UK; 080141282x, US.

First published in English 1968. Adopted from *Chronologie* published in Leipzig (2nd ed., 1963).

Elucidates the basic problems of ancient chronology ... 1. The Calendar - 2. Chronography (the principles of antiquity in computing the years) - 3. Applied chronology (rules derived from these principles

....(contd.)

to relate ancient dates to modern time reckoning - 4. Notes (p.96-108) - 5. The tables (p.109-218) including astronomical canon, Olympian years, Roman consuls and emperors, and ending with chronological tables of Greek and Roman history 776 BC and AD 476. Analytical index.

Note James, P. and others: *Centuries of darkness: a challenge to the conventional chronology of Old World archaeology* (London, Cape, 1991) argues for a radical shift in the currently accepted chronology of the ancient Near East and Mediterranean world. *Class No:* 931(090)

[6641]

JAMES, P., *and others*. **Centuries of darkness** a challenge to the conventional chronology of Old World archaeology. London, Jonathan Cape, 1991. xxii,434p. illus., maps, bibliog., index. £15.95. ISBN: 022402647x.

Argues for a radical shift in the currently accepted chronology of the ancient Near East and Mediterranean world to repair 'a gigantic academic blunder, perpetuated by the convenience of a seemingly reliable time-scale as well as the sheer complexity of the issues involved' (*p.320*). Appendix 1. Dendochronology and radiocarbon dating - 2. Greek and Roman theories on ancient chronology. Chapter notes and references p.345-94. Bibliography p.395-426. *Class No:* 931(090)

Asia—Middle & Near East

Dictionaries

[6642]

BIENKOWSKI, P. *and* MILLARD, A., *eds*. **A Dictionary of the ancient Near East.** London, British Museum Press, 2000. x,342p. illus., map, index. £29.99. ISBN: 0714111414.

500 signed cross-referenced entries explaining and describing the concepts, sites, peoples, and periods of history, from 13 contributors. Chronological chart p.vii. King lists p.330-35. *Class No:* 931(53+56)(038)

Ancient China

[6643]

LOEWE, M. *and* SHAUGHNESSY, E. **The Cambridge history of ancient China** from the origins of civilization to 221BC. Cambridge Univ. Press, 1999. xxix,1148p. illus., maps, tables, bibliog., index. $130. ISBN: 0521470307.

14 academic contributors, specialists in history, archaeology, palaeography and art history write the eight core chapters treating the Shang, Western Zhou, Spring and Autumn and Warring States periods. Chapters on the pre-historic background and the growth of language provide the major context of China's achievements during the 1500 years under review. Two final chapters show how China's developments relate to the growth of independent cultures in Central Asia. The last chapter leads the reader forward to imperial times as described in the volumes of *The Cambridge History of China (q.v.)*. Literature and material sources p.7-11. Calendar and chronology of events p.19-24. Reign dates p.25-29. *Class No:* 931.5

[6644]

WALDRON, A. **The Great Wall of China** from history to myth. Cambridge, Cambridge Univ. Press, 1990. xvi,296p. illus., maps, bibliog., index. £30. (*Cambridge Studies in Chinese History, Literature and Institutions.*) ISBN: 052136518x.

Historical narrative in 11 chapters: 1. Introduction: what is the Great Wall of China? - 2. Early Chinese walls - 3. Strategic origins ... 5. Security without walls: early Ming strategy and its collapse ... 7. Politics and military policy at the turn of the 16th century ... 11. The Wall acquires new meanings. Chapter notes p.227-55. Bibliography (Chinese and Japanese and Western materials) p.256-78. Glossary p.279-85. See also the author's 'The problem of the Great Wall of China', *Harvard Journal of Asiatic Studies*, v.43, no.2, 1983. *Class No:* 931.5

Ancient Egypt

[6645]

DAVIES, W.V. **Egypt and Africa** Nubia from prehistory to Islam. London, British Museum Press in association with the Egypt Exploration Society, 1991. x,320p.++16p. pl. maps, plans, bibliogs. ISBN: 0714109622.

30 essays by different hands on various aspects of the archaeology and early history of Nubia including Jean Vercoutter's L'Archéologie Nubrienne et Soudanaise: passé présent et futur'. Celebrates the opening of The Raymond and Sackler Gallery of Egypt and Africa, British Museum, July 1991. *Class No:* 932

[6646]

DODSON, A.M. **Monarchs of the Nile.** London, Rubicon Press, 1995. xviii,238p. illus., maps, bibliog., index. £17.95. ISBN: 094869520x.

Concise account of the lives and times of over 600 important Egyptian Pharaohs from the unification of Egypt c.3000BC to the Ptolemaic dynasty in the second century BC. Chronology and the Kings of Dynastic Egypt (3050BC-1953) p.204-212. Royal cemeteries p.213-17. Bibliography p.224-29. 5 maps. *Class No:* 932

[6647]

HART, G. **Pharaohs and pyramids:** a guide through Old Kingdom. Egypt. London, The Herbert Press, 1991. 240p. col. illus., map, bibliog., index. £17.95. ISBN: 1871569362.

A chronological history and guide to the principal pyramids and other surviving monuments constructed after the unification of Upper and Lower Egypt. King list p.9. Time chart p.10-11. Bibliography p.235-6. *Class No:* 932

[6648]

LEHNER, M. **The Complete Pyramids.** London, Thames And Hudson, 1997. 256p. illus. (some col.), facsims, maps (some col.), bibliog., index. £24.95. ISBN: 0500050848.

Fully illustrated survey in 5 sections: 1. Tomb and temple (ritual and mythology surrounding the death and burial of Egypt's pharaohs) - 2. Explorers and scientists (travellers, looters and archaeologists) - 3. Whole Pyramid catalogue (survey and description of 3,000 years of pyramid building) - 4. The living pyramid (building techniques) - 5. Overview. Visiting the pyramids (Giza, Saqqara, Dahshur, Abusir, Meidu) p.264-65. Bibliography p.246-52. Over 550 illustrations (83 in colour). *Class No:* 932

[6649]

QUIRKE, S. **Who were the Pharaohs?** a history of their names with a list of cartouches. London, British Museum Publications, 1990. 80p. illus., bibliog., index. £4.95. ISBN: 071410955x.

Traces the evolution of royal names from the dawn of Egyptian writing, c.3000 BC., to the Roman period. Section 5: The principal names of the kings of Egypt gives their cartouches. Bibliography p.79. *Class No:* 932

[6650]

WEST, J.A. **The Traveller's key to ancient Egypt:** a guide to the sacred places of ancient Egypt. New York, Knopf, 1985. London, Harrap Columbus, 1987. xiv,480p. illus., pbk. $18.45; £8.95. ISBN: 074710011x, UK; 0394514416, US.

Detailed and practical guidebook in 23 thematic and topographical chapters *e.g.* 1. Historical overview ... 2. Development of Egyptology ... 4-6. Giza ... 12. Cairo Museum. Appendix 1. Dynasties and kings - 2. Further reading (p.448-9) - 3. Egyptological, architectural, technical glossary p.450-4 - 4. Travelling tips. *Class No:* 932

Bibliographies

[6651]

MASKELL, H. 'Electronic Egypt: *The shape of archaeological knowledge on the Net'.* Review Section: Electronic Archaeology, *Antiquity*, v.71, no.774, December 1997, p.1073-76.

A tour of Web sites relating to Ancient Egypt. *Class No:* 932(01)

Encyclopaedias

[6652]

BARD, K.A., *ed*. **Encyclopedia of the archeology of Ancient Egypt.** London, Routledge, 1999. xxx,938p. illus., maps, tables, bibliogs., index. £150. $250. ISBN: 0415185890.

190 international academic contributors. 14 overview essays (*e.g.*Neolithic and predynastic periods ... Old Kingdom ... late Ptolemaic period). 300 cross-referenced and signed A-Z articles relating to important sites, geographical features, prominent archaeologists, and ending with short reading lists. Chronology of Ancient Egypt p.xxvii-xxx. Glossary p.891-93. 'This outstanding work is prepared by scholars for serious students ... Egyptologists, philologists, historians, classicists, art historians, and anthropologically trained archaeologists helped to write it' (*Booklist*, v.96, no.1, 1 September 1999, p.178). 'An excellent choice for libraries of all types and individuals who can afford it' (*Choice*, v.37, no.7, March 2000, p.1277). *Class No:* 932(031)

[6653]

The Oxford encyclopedia of Ancient Egypt. Redford, D.B., *ed*. Oxford Univ. Press, 3v., 2000. illus., maps, bibliogs., index. $450. ISBN: 0195102347.

600 cross-referenced articles on all aspects of Ancient Egypt, extending over 5,000 years of history including detailed articles on Egyptian archaeology, art, architecture, religion, literature, language, and politics. *Class No:* 932(031)

Dictionaries

[6654]

BIERBRIER, M. L. Historical dictionary of ancient Egypt. Lanham, MD., Scarecrow Press, 1999. xix,301p. (Historical Dictionaries of Ancient Civilizations and Historical Eras, no.1.) ISBN: 0810836149.

Introduction (historical overview) p.1-12. Dictionary (monuments, sites, pharaohs, patriarchs, dynasties and dynastic periods, places, events, etc. of note during the period 200,000BC to 642AD, and modern archaeologists and egyptologists) p.13-172. Bibliography arranged in 23 form and thematic divisions (e.g. Nubia, archaeology, museum collections, classical sources) p.174-255. Appendix 1. Dynastic lists (p.257-60) - 2. Museums with Egyptian collections (A-Z by country) p.267-302. Chronology p.xv-xvii. Class No: 932(038)

[6655]

SHAW, I. and NICHOLSON, P.T. British Museum dictionary of Ancient Egypt. London, British Museum Press, 1995. 328p. illus. (some col.), maps, bibliogs., index. £27.50. ISBN: 0714109827.

550 cross-referenced definitions of key terms in Egyptology and for people, sites, objects, physical characteristics etc. Chronology (i.e. that preferred by Dept. of Egyptian Antiquities, British Museum) p.310-312. Appendix 1: List of Egyptologists mentioned in text - 2. A-Z list of owners of tombs in Western Thebes. Short bibliographies accompany most entries. 165 col.illus. 60 maps and site plans. 'Very up-to-date in its scholarly research and sources ... of such high quality that it sets a standard that all such works should emulate and strive to attain' (Journal of Near Eastern Studies, v.58,no.3, July 1999, p.207-208). Class No: 932(038)

Maps & Atlases

[6656]

BAINES, J. and MÁLEK, J. Atlas of ancient Egypt. Oxford, Phaidon, 1980. 240p. illus. (mostly col.), col. maps, bibliog., index. £22.50. ISBN: 0714819581.

'A systematic survey of the most important sites with ancient Egyptian monuments, an assessment of their historical and cultural importance and a brief description of their salient features' (Introduction). 3 parts: 1. The cultural setting - 2. A journey down the Nile - 3. Aspects of Egyptian society. Museums with Egyptian collections p.224-5. Glossary p.226-7. Bibliography p.231-2. Gazetteer p.233-5. Analytical index. 36 maps. 530 illustrations (380 in colour). Class No: 932(084.3)

[6657]

MANLEY, B. The Penguin historical atlas of Ancient Egypt. London, Penguin Books, 1996. 144p. col.maps, col.illus., bibliog., index. £9.99. ISBN: 0140513310.

Over 60 coloured chronological thematic maps, on various scales, supported by authoritative text, arranged within five historical periods. Timeline 5,000BC-305BC in 4 cols.: Egypt, Nubia, Lands of the Bible, Europe and the Middle East p.8-11. Egyptian Kings and Rulers 2900-323BC p.132-35. Bibliography p.136. Class No: 932(084.3)

Biographies

[6658]

DAVID, R. and DAVID, A.E. A Biographical dictionary of ancient Egypt. London, Seaby, 1992. xxxvi,179p. maps, bibliog., indexes. £18.50; $39.95. ISBN: 1852640324.

More than 200 entries cover important historical and cultural figures of ancient Egypt during the period 3100BC to AD600. Data: name, brief identification, cross-refs., bibliographical reference. Chronological tables p.173-77. Bibliography p.179. Class No: 932(092)

[6659]

RICE, M. Who's who in Ancient Egypt. London, Routledge, 1999. lxi,257p. illus., maps, bibliog. £19.99. ISBN: 0415154480.

Almost 1,000 biographies, not only of the great and the good, but also of more humble folk such as grave-robbers, gardeners, and hairdressers, whose names have chanced to survive. Class No: 932(092)

Jewish History

[6660]

DOTHAN, T. The Philistines and their material culture. New Haven, Connecticut, Yale University Press, 1983. xxii, 310p. illus., tables, maps, index. $55.00. £58.75. ISBN: 0300022581.

Revised and expanded edition of the author's book of the same title published in Hebrew (Jerusalem, Bialik Institute and Israel Exploration Society, 1967).

6 chapters (1. The historical sources ... 6. Absolute chronology and conclusions). Copiously illustrated and heavily annotated account of the archaeological evidence set against the background known from textual sources of the period between the late Bronze and Early Iron Ages. Class No: 933

[6661]

SOGGIN, J.A. A History of ancient Israel from the beginnings to the Bar Kochba revolt AD 135. London, SCM Press, 1984; New York, Westminster, 1985. 436p. illus., bibliogs., index. £10.50. $29.95. ISBN: 0334020433, UK; 0664212581, US.

Tanslated from Storia d'Israele, dalle origine alla rivolta di Bar-Kochba 135 d.C. (Brescia, Case Editrice Paideia, 1985).

14 chronological and thematic chapters in 4 parts: 1. Introductory problems - 2. Traditions about the Proto-history of the people - 3. A house divided - 4. Under the empires of East and West. Chapter 2 Methodology, bibliography and sources p.18-40 is useful as are the extensive bibliographies included in all chapters. Appendix 1. An introduction to the archaeology of Syria and Palestine p.357-367 - 2. Chronology of the First Temple Period: a presentation and evaluation of the sources. Class No: 933

[6662]

YORAM TSAFRIR, and others. Tabula Imperii Romani: Iudea. Palaestina Eretz Israel in the Hellenistic, Roman and Byzantine periods. Jerusalem, The Israel Academy of Sciences And Humanities, 1994. x,263p. 4 maps in text, 5 maps in separate pocket inside front covers, bibliogs. ISBN: 9652081078.

Gazetteer p.55-263. Data: brief description; Greek Roman, Hebrew, and Aramaic literary sources; modern bibliographical citations; archaeological information from excavation reports and surveys. List of abbreviations used in gazetteer p.25-52. Maps in front pocket: General (1:100,000); 2 detailed maps North and South (1:25,000); Ancient synagogues and Jewish Centres; and Ancient churches and episcopal sees (1:400,000). Class No: 933

Bibliographies

[6663]

EDELHEIT, A.J. and EDELHEIT, H. The Jewish world in modern times: a selected, annotated bibliography. Boulder, Colarado, Westview Press; London, Mansell Publishing Ltd., 1988. xix,569p. £37.50; $65.00. ISBN: 0813305721, US; 072011988x, UK.

2170 descriptive and critically annotated entries limited to books, articles and pamphlets available to the American Jewish reading public. Part 1. The Jewish World: 1. Surveys of Jewish history - 2. Social History - 3. Emancipation and transformation of European Jewry - 4. Religious trends - 5. Cultural trends - 6. Antisemitism - 7. Public affairs - 8. The Holocaust - 9. Zionism and Jewish nationalism. Part 2. The Jewish Community: 10. Central Europe and Scandinavia - 11. Eastern Europe and the Balkans - 12. U.S.S.R. - 13. Western Europe - 14. The Americas - 15. US and Canada - 16. The Middle East - 17. Land of Israel - 18. Africa, Asia and the Pacific - 19. Bibliographies and guides (p.458-459). Introduction: The outline of modern Jewish history p.1-8. Class No: 933(01)

[6664]

MOR, M and RAPPAPORT, U. Bibliography of works on Jewish history in the Hellenistic and Roman periods 1976-1980. Jerusalem, The Zalman Shazar Center, 1982. xvii, 95p. index. ISSN: 03335119.

Continues Rappaport's 'Bibliography of works on Jewish history in the Hellenistic and Roman periods 1946-1970', Studies in the history of the Jewish people and the land of Israel, no.2, 1972, p.247-321 and Rappaport and Mors' Bibliography of works on Jewish history in the Hellenistic and Roman periods 1971-1975 published by The Institute of Advanced Studies in Jerusalem in 1976.

770 items in Western languages arranged in 34 sections covering the period from the Second Temple to the Herods. Compiled with the aid of Haifa On-line Bibliographical Text System (HOBITS) which is being used to keep current bibliographical database. Class No: 933(01)

[6665]

PURVIS, J.D. Jerusalem, the Holy City: a bibliography. Metuchen, New Jersey, Scarecrow Press, 1988. xii, 499p. index. $42.50. (American Theological Library Association Bibliography No.20.) ISBN: 0810819996.

5827 unannotated entries in 40 chapters grouped in 8 Parts: 1. General studies - 2. The Biblical period to 587BC - 3. Second Temple period - 4. Roman Jerusalem - 5. Judaism - 6. Christian Jerusalem - 7. A Muslim city - 8. Jerusalem in modern times. Author and subject indexes p.432-499. Class No: 933(01)

Encyclopaedias

[6666]

Encyclopedia of Jewish history: events and eras of the Jewish people. Shamir, I. and Shavit, S., eds. Jerusalem, Massada Publishers; New York, Facts On File, 1986. 288p. col. illus., maps, diagrs., index. £17.95. ISBN: 0816012202.

30 contributors. Concise information on events and key figures in the annals of the Jewish people, from the beginnings to modern times, arranged in over 100 historical entries with 12 appendices on Jewish culture and ethnology. Each entry comprises a central article of c.800 words accompanied by maps, photographs and diagrams.

....(contd.)

'Connections', appearing on each pair of facing pages, direct the reader to related chapters. Major themes p.13-19. Chronological chart of Jewish and World history p.247-263. Glossary p.265-274.
Class No: 933(031)

Maps & Atlases

[6667]
BACON, J. **The Illustrated atlas of Jewish civilization.** London, Deutsch; New York, Macmillan, 1990. 224p. illus (some col.), col. maps, index. £19.95. $35. ISBN: 0233985697, UK; 0025434152, US.
Introduction: Mapping Jewish history (by Martin Gilbert) - 1. From Abraham to the destruction of the Second Temple - 2. Age of prayer and thought C.E. 70 to the Spanish Inquisition - 3. High Middle Ages to Moses Mendelssohn - 4. Jewish enlightenment to the eve of Holocaust - 5. The dark side: anti-Semitism - 6. The Holocaust - 7. Israel and world Jewry following World War 2. No bibliography. 'A successful blend of beautiful cartography, arresting illustrations, and informative text covering the entire range of the Jewish historical experience from patriarchal times to the present' (*Library Journal*, v.116,no.4, 1 March 1991, p.84). *Class No:* 933(084.3)

[6668]
BARNAVI, E., *ed.* **A Historical atlas of the Jewish people** from the time of the Patriarchs to the present. London, Hutchinson, 1992. xi,299p. illus. (mostly col.), col.maps, index. £30. ISBN: 0091775930.
49 contributors. Beautifully illustrated and attractively produced atlas suitable for both academic and general readers. Glossary p.281-83.
Class No: 933(084.3)

[6669]
COHN-SHERBOCK, D. **Atlas of Jewish history.** London, Routledge, 1993. 224p. illus. maps. £35. ISBN: 0415086841.
Atlas and guide in 15 sections: 1. Ancient Near East and the Israelites ... 3. Captivity and return ... 6. Judaism under Islam in the Middle Ages - 7. Jews in medieval Christian Europe - 13. Jewry in 19th and early 20th centuries - 14. The Holocaust - 15. Israel. 113 maps. *Class No:* 933(084.3)

[6670]
FRIESEL, E. **Atlas of modern Jewish history.** New York, Oxford Univ. Press, 1990. 159p. illus., col. maps, diagrs., tables, bibliog., index. $49.95; £25. ISBN: 0195053931.
Revised from the 1983 Hebrew edition published by Carta, The Israel Map and Publishing Co.
185 three colour maps and dozens of charts and line drawings arranged in 7 main sections: 1. Jewish demography - 2. European countries 17th century to World War I - 3. Major themes in Jewish history - 4. Muslim countries - 5. European Jewry in the interwar years - 6. European Jewry 1940 to 1980s - 7. New centers of Jewry. Bibliography p.145-7. Greatly surpasses M. Gilbert's *Jewish history atlas.* 'Offers a unique perspective on the development of the Jewish people' (*Booklist*, v,87, no.1, 1 September 1990, p.79-80).
Class No: 933(084.3)

[6671]
GILBERT, M. **The Routledge atlas of Jewish history.** 2nd ed. London, Routledge, 1993. 148p. illus., maps. £25. ISBN: 0460861816.
132 black and white maps trace the Jewish diasporas from ancient Mesopotamia to modern Israel. Themes covered: prejudices and violence, migrations and movements, society and status, trade and culture, politics, government, and war. *Class No:* 933(084.3)

Chronologies

[6672]
BLOCH, A.P. **Once a day an anthology of Jewish historical anniversaries for every day of the year.** Hoboken, New Jersey, Ktav Publishing House, 1987. xv,376p. index. ISBN: 0881251089.
Summaries of events or capsule biographies of prominent figures in Jewish history noted for each day of the year (arranged according to the Christian calendar). *Class No:* 933(090)

[6673]
GRIBETZ, J., *and others.* **The Timelines of Jewish history:** a chronology of the most important people and events in Jewish history. New York, Simon & Schuster, 1993. 752p. illus., maps. $35. ISBN: 067140070.
Although over half the contents relate to 20th century, the chronology ranges from prehistoric times. Entries are tabulated under 3 headings: General history, Jewish history, Jewish culture.
Class No: 933(090)

Biographies

[6674]
COMAY, J. **Who's who in Jewish history after the period of the Old Testament.** 2nd ed. London, Routledge, 1995. xxxvi,467p. illus. (some col.), facsims., maps, chron.table, indexes. £35. ISBN: 0415125839.
1st ed. 1974.
Over 1000 A-Z entries covering period from Hasmonean Dynasty to modern Israel. With limited exceptions restricted to dead persons who have contributed significantly to Jewish history and thought. Glossary p.viii-x. Chronology p.xi-xxxiii. Thematic index p.397-407. No bibliographies. *Class No:* 933(092)

Micromaterials

[6675]
SCHMUCK, H., *comp.* **Jüdisches biographisches archiv/Jewish biographical archive.** München, K.G. Saur, 1994-1996. 690 silver or diazo fiches (24x). DM 24,600 (silver); DM 22,800 (diazo). ISBN: 3598336039, silver; 3598335903, diazo.
111,000 entries for 75,000 persons collected from 133 sources published 1781-1958. No national or geographic limits. Presents comprehensive picture of role of Jews in religion, culture, economics and politics from the beginnings to 1948 when Israel was founded. Indexed in printed form by *Jewish biographical index (q.v.)*
Supplement. 1998. 127 fiches. DM 4,920 (silver); DM 4,520 (diazo). ISBN 3598335164 (silver); 359833513x (diazo).
Class No: 933(092)(003.5)

[6676]
—Jewish biographical archive. Series II. München, K.G. Saur, in preparation.
c.100,000 biographical entries. *Class No:* 933(092)(003.5)

[6677]
—Jewish biographical index. München, K.G. Saur, 4v., 1998. lii,1401p. DM 1,980 (DM 1,780 for subscribers to *Jewish biographical archive*). ISBN: 3598336160.
Printed index to *Jewish biographical archive (Jüdisches biographisches archiv)* and its *Supplement. CD-ROM edition.* 2000. DM 980 (DM 398 for purchasers of the printed index. ISBN 3598404131. *Class No:* 933(092)(003.5)

Ancient India & Ancient Indo-China

[6678]
BHATTACHARJEE, A. **A History of ancient India.** 2nd ed. Liverpool, Lucas Publications, 1988. 480p. maps, geneal tables, bibliog., index. £15.95. ISBN: 1851800255.
1st ed. 1979.
17 chapters including 2. Sources of ancient Indian history - 3. Prehistory ... 16. The Deccan - 17. The distant South. Bibliography p.469-72. 'Purports to present within a single ambit and a convenient compass a critical approach to the history of ancient India' (*Preface to 1st ed.*). *Class No:* 934

Medo-Persians

Biographies

[6679]
LEICK, G. **Who's who in the Ancient Near East.** London, Routledge, 1999. 229p. maps, tables. £19.99. ISBN: 0415132304.
700 entries cover primarily the kings and other ruler's of the peoples of Mesopotamia, and the surrounding areas, from the times of the earliest documents to the end of the Selucid period, 2500-145BC. A 17-page glossary 'may actually be useful independently of the main text' (*Reference Reviews*, v.14, no.1, 2000, p.47). 4 maps.
Class No: 935(092)

North, West & East European Peoples

[6680]
BRAUND, D. **Georgia in antiquity** a history of Colchis and Transcaucasian Iberia 550BC-AD562. Oxford, Clarendon Press, 1994. xviii,359p. illus., maps, bibliog., index. £40. ISBN: 0198144733.
Thematic and chronological history in 9 chapters: 1. Imagining Georgia in antiquity - 2. Geography and economy of Ancient Georgia ... 6. Colchis under the Principate ... 9. War in Lazica. The fifth and sixth centuries. Bibliography p.315-48 includes items in non-Western European languages. 8 maps. *Class No:* 936

[6681]
BURNS, T.S. **A History of the Ostrogoths.** Bloomington, Indiana Univ. Press, 1984. xvii, 299p., illus., tables, maps, bibliog. $29.95. ISBN: 0253328314.
Well documented study based on primary Roman sources and modern archaeological research. Chapter notes p.221-257. Bibliography p.259-289. Index p.291-299. *Class No:* 936

[6682]

KING, J. Kingdoms of the Celts a history and a guide. London, Blandford, 1998. 256p. illus., maps, bibliog., index. £19.99. ISBN: 071372692x.

12 chapters: 1. Who were the Celts ... 3. From Gaul to Galatia: the earliest kingdoms - 4. Celtic Britain - 5. Ireland ... 10. Welsh and Breton royal dynasties ... 12. The royal Celtic legacy. Bibliography (classical, vernacular and medieval texts and translations, language, general) p.250-53. *Class No: 936*

[6683]

The Peoples of Europe series. Oxford, Blackwell, 1986-. illus., maps, tables, indexes. £20.

Collins, R. *The Basques.* 1986. 272p. ISBN 0631174786; James, E. *The Franks.* 1988. 265p. 0631148728; Galliou, P. and James, M. *The Bretons.* 1991. 334p. 0631164065' Christie, N. *The Lombards.* 1994. 320p. 0631182381; Wilkes, J. *The Illyrians.* 351p. 1992. 063114617; Todd, M. *The Early Germans.* 1992. 285p. 0631163972; Elton, G.R. *The English.* 1992. 264p. 0631176810. Fraser, A. *The Gypsies.* 1992. 0631159673; Thompson, E.A. *The Huns.* 1995. 256p. 0631158995; Heather, P. *The Goths.* 1996. 384p. 0631165363. Milner-Gulland, R. *The Russians* 1997. 260p. 0631188053

European tribes and peoples from their origins in prehistory according to the archaeological and historical evidence. *Class No: 936*

[6684]

WOLFRAM, W. History of the Goths. New and completely revised from 2nd German ed. Berkeley and London, Univ. of California Press, 1988. xii,613p. and 7p. maps. bibliog., index. $39.95. ISBN: 0520052595.

First published as *Geschichte der Goten: von den Anfängen bis zur Mitte des sechsten Jahrhunderts.* (München, Verlag C.H. Beck, 2nd ed. 1980)

Authoritative and comprehensive academic treatise arranged in 5 sections: 1. The names - 2. Formation of the Gothic tribes before the invasion of the Huns - 3. Forty-year migration and the formation of the Visigoths 376/378 to 416/418 - 4. Kingdom of Toulouse 418 to 507 - 5. The 'new' Ostrogoths. 3 Appendices: 1. Roman Experors - 2. Survey of Gothic history p.367-71 - 3. Genealogical charts. Chapter notes p.377-534. Bibliography p.537-73. Formidable and extremely well-documented work. *Class No: 936*

Ancient Greece & Rome

[6685]

GREEN, P. Alexander to Actium: the historical evolution of the Hellenistic Age. Berkeley/Los Angeles, Univ. of California Press; London, Thames & Hudson, 1990. xxiii,970p. illus., maps, geneal., tables, bibliog., index. £36. ISBN: 0520056116, US.

An extremely well-documented historical survey in 37 chapters divided in 5 parts: 1. Alexander's funeral games 323-276 BC. - 2. The zenith century 276-222 BC. - Phalanx and legion 221-168 BC. - 4. The breaking of nations 167-116 BC. - 5. Rome triumphant 116-30 BC. Chronological table p.683-727. Genealogical tables (Macedonian and Thracian dynasties; Seleucids; Ptolemies; Attalids; Greek Indo-Bactrian kings) p.732-9. Chapter notes p.741-908. Bibliography p.909-28. 'Green's encyclopedic zest for the classics is spiced by wide knowledge of other fields, literary and political. His masterpiece is crammed with generous allusion' (*Sunday Times,* no.8655, 3 February 1991, Section 6, p.1-2). *Class No: 937/938*

[6686]

Oxford history of the classical world. Boardman, J., *and others.* Oxford, Oxford University Press, 1986. x, 882p., illus., maps, tables. £27.50. ISBN: 0198721129.

Subsequently published in 2v. - 1. *Greece and the Hellenistic World.* 1988. 448p. illus., maps, bibliog., index, pbk. £9.95. ISBN 0192821652 - 2. *Rome.* 1988. 448p. illus (some col.), maps, ports., bibliog., index. pbk. £9.95. ISBN 0192821660.

32 chapters divided into three sections: Greece (8th-4th century BC); Greece and Rome; and Rome. Within each section political and social history chapters are interspersed with others relating to literature, philosophy and the arts. Chapter bibiliographies. Tables of events p.830-860. Index p.873-882. 16 col. plates. *Class No: 937/938*

Bibliographies

[6687]

HOPWOOD, K., comp. Ancient Greece and Rome a bibliographical guide. Manchester Univ. Press, 1995. xiv,450p. index. £50. ISBN: 0719024013.

8,000 briefly annotated items arranged in 16 chronological (950BC-565AD) and 5 general sections (maps/atlases; social and economic; general handbooks and surveys; 199 festschriften). *Class No: 937/938(01)*

Encyclopaedias

[6688]

GRANT, M. *and* KITZINGER, R. Civilization of the Ancient Mediterranean. Greece and Rome. New York, Charles Scribner's Sons, 3v., 1988. xxvii, xiv, xiv, 1980p. $225.00. £160.00. ISBN: 0684188643, v.1; 0684188651, v.2; 068418866x, v.3; 0684175940, set.

88 contributors. Historical summary of Greece (p.3-44); of Rome (p.45-85). 97 essays under broad subject headings: Land and Sea - Population - Agriculture and food - Technology - Government and society - Economics - Religion - Private and social life - Women and family life - Literary and performing arts - Philosophy - Visual arts. Each essay concludes with a bibliography. Epilogue: progress of classical scholarship p.1819-32. Chronological table p.xvii-xxiv. 'A comprehensive overview of current thinking about the classical world ... this set really stands alone as a unique source' (*Booklist,* v.84, no.20, 15 June 1988, p.1716). *Class No: 937/938(031)*

[6689]

GRANT, M. A Guide to the Ancient World : a dictionary of classical place-names. New York, H.W. Wilson, 1986. 14p., maps+728p. $65.00. US $75.00. other countries. £54.00. ISBN: 0824207424.

900 historical, geographical, archaeological essays (150 to 1500 words in length) on significant place-names of historical importance, ranging from the Atlantic Ocean to Pakistan, and from the Sahara to southern Russia, from the first millenium BC to the late 5th century AD, encompassing references to contemporary writers, modern names, and precise geographical locations. Bibliography p.711-28. 'For information on towns and cities the dated Princeton encyclopedia of classical sites ... covers similar ground with greater accuracy and completeness' (*Choice,* v.24, no.5, January 1987, p.742). *Class No: 937/938(031)*

[6690]

GRUMMOND, N.T. de, *ed.* An Encyclopedia of the history of classical archaeology. Westport, Conn., Greenwood Press, 2v., 1996. 1330p. illus., bibliog., index. $225. ISBN: 0313220662.

171 contributors. 1,125 entries relating to the visual remains of ancient Greece and Rome, the Bronze Age Aegean, the Etruscans, and the remains of these cultures in other regions. Also includes biographies of travellers, archaeologists, and scholars who have contributed to the study of classical archaeology and a chronology from the sack of Athens in 480BC to 1989. 'The scholarly nature of this encyclopedia will make it especially valuable to students, researchers, and teachers of archaeology, classics, history, and art and architectural history, and to curators in museums; (*Booklist,* v.93, no.11, 1 February 1997, p.964-65). *Class No: 937/938(031)*

[6691]

The Oxford companion to classical civilization. Hornblower, S. *and* Spawforth, A., *eds.* Oxford Univ. Press, 1998. xxv,804p. col.illus., maps, bibliog. £30. $49.95. ISBN: 0198601654.

c.300 contributors. 700+ A-Z cross-referenced entries encompassing essay length articles and short quick references examining Greek and Roman prehistory, history and politics, individuals, social and family life, war studies, literature, philosophy, mythology and religion, science, technology, medicine, art and architecture etc. Chronology p.789-93. Bibliography p.794. 9p. of maps. An up-to-date and erudite resource. *Class No: 937/938(031)*

[6692]

PAULY, A.F. von *and* WISSOWA, G. Pauly's Real-Encyklopädie der classichen Altertumswissenschaft. Stuttgart, Metzler (later München, Druckenmüller, 1894-.1967. Supplement - Bänden 1-. 1903-. (Supplt. 15. 1978).

Published in 2 parallel series. 1. Reihe A-Q (24v. in 32 pts.) completed 1963; 2. Reihe R-Z (110v. in 19 pts.) completed 1967.

Comprehensive signed articles, with adequate bibliographies, cover every aspect of classical literature, history, geography, antiquities and civilization. An indispensable work of scholarship for any library. Gärtner H. and Wünsch A. *Pauly's Real-Encyklopädie der classicher Altertumswissenschaft Register der Nachträge Und Supplemente* (1980). xxii, 250p. *Der Kleine Pauly. Lexikon der Antike auf der Grundlage von Pauly's Real-Encyclopädie der classichen Altertumswissenschaft* ... bearb. und hrsg. von K. Ziegler und W. Sontheimer, 5v., 1964-75 is the work of 99 contributors, mostly German. *Index to the supplements and supplementary volumes of Pauly-Wissowa's Real-Encyklopädie* ... compiled by J.P. Murphy (Chicago, Ares Publishers, 1976. 138p. 0890051747). Well produced. 'Indispensable supplement to the original and much easier to use' (*Papers of the Bibliographical Society of America,* v.70, no.2, 1976, p.303). *Class No: 937/938(031)*

[6693]

—Der Neue Pauly: enzyklopädie der Antike. Cancik, H. *and* Schneider, H., *eds.* Stuttgart, J. B. Metzler, 1996-.

1. *A-Ari.* 1996. liii,1154p. maps, tables. ISBN 347014703. 360+ contributors. Transcription table p.x-xi. Bibliographical abbreviations p.xv-xxxiv. Ancient authors and titles p.xxxiv-xlvii. This new dictionary of Greek and Roman antiquity looks set fair to replace the original work. All entries are initialled and are complemented by source references. Now reached V.7. *Lef-Men, 1999. xii,127p. ISBN 3476014770. A separate sequence, Rezeptions-und-Wissenschaftsgeschichte,* has commenced with v.13. A-Fo to 1999. ov, 1162p. *Class No: 937/938(031)*

Dictionaries

[6694]

A Dictionary of ancient history. Speake, G., *ed.* Oxford, Blackwell, 1994. x,758p. maps, geneal tables, bibliog. £35. ISBN: 0631180699.

11 academic contributors. 2000 cross-referenced A-Z entries relating to major events, institutions, individuals, periods, places *etc.* in the Ancient World from 776BC to AD476 linked by references to bibliography (p.685-734). Appendix includes 3 genealogical tables and list of Roman Emperors. 10 maps. *Class No: 937/938(038)*

[6695]

The Oxford classical dictionary. Hornblower, S. *and* Spawforth, A., *eds.* 3rd ed. Oxford Univ. Press, 1996. liv,1640p. ISBN: 019866172x.

1st ed. 1949; 2nd ed. 1970.

6,250 (nearly 1000 new) initialled and cross-referenced A-Z entries, by an international team of 361 scholars, relating to all aspects of the Ancient World. This is a completely new and largely rewritten edition to reflect advances in knowledge since the 1940s (list of new entries p.xi-xiv in 4 columns). No other single volume reference work comes near to *OCD's* comprehensive coverage. *Class No: 937/938(038)*

Maps & Atlases

[6696]

GRANT, M. The Routledge atlas of Classical History. 5th ed. London, Routledge, 1994. 93p.+[8p.] index. maps. £20. ISBN: 0415119340.

First published as *The Dent Atlas of Classical History* (1971).

92 black and white outline maps (5 new to this ed.), with copious informative legends, cover political, economic, cultural and religious themes from the Near East c.1700BC to The Byzantine Empire of Justinian. Index of place-names p.95-102. *Class No: 937/938(084.3)*

[6697]

TALBERT, R.J.A. Atlas of Classical History. London, Croom Helm; New York, Macmillan, 1985. 217p. maps, bibliog., tables. £19.95. $50.00. ISBN: 0709924216, UK; 0029331102, US.

134 maps arranged chronologically: 'The Aegean in the Bronze Age' - 'Dioceses and provinces of the Roman Empire in AD 314. Bibliography p.179-189. Gazetteer p.190-217. Primarily intended for A level and undergraduate level students. Concern about the clarity of its small scale maps is expressed in *Choice*, v.23, no.5, January 1986, p.723. *Class No: 937/938(084.3)*

Internet

[6698]

Atlas of the Greek and Roman world. Talbot, R., *and others, comps.* URL:http://www.unc.edu/depts/cl atlas.

History and progress of 'what promises to be the ultimate hard-copy atlas and gazetteer', due to be published in 2000, in which are included detailed colour topographic maps with precisely labelled towns, roads, canals etc. 'Talbot and his team offers a superb gateway to Web resources on the ancient world' (*Choice*, Supplement to v.36, August 199, p.161). *Class No: 937/938(084.3)(003.41)*

Biographies

[6699]

RADICE, B. Who's who in the Ancient World a handbook to the survival of the Greek and Roman classics. rev. ed. Harmondsworth, Middlesex, Penguin Books, 1973. xlvi, 225p. illus., pbk. £5.95. ISBN: 0140510559.

First published London, Blond, 1971.

An encyclopaedia of *c.1,00 historical and mythical persons and places ('Helen': 2+T columns; 'Seneca': 11/3 cols.; 'Odysseus': 4 cols.). References to paintings, sculpture, music and literature. Select bibliography, p.xlvi. Table of main dates (Greece; Rome; Near East). Detailed index, p.165-225. 'An extremely useful reference work for the average reader'* (Choice, v.9, no.1, March 1972, p.46). *Class No: 937/938(092)*

Micromaterials

[6700]

Biographical archive of the Classical World/Biographisches archiv der Antike. Schmuck, H., *ed.* München, K.G. Saur, 1996-1999. 700 fiches in 12 instalments. Silver or diazo. DM 22,200. ISBN: 3598339712, silver; 3598339704, diazo.

170,000 biographical articles, culled from 90 reference sources and prosopographic compilations, on 120,000 personalities, who shaped and moulded, everyday life, culture and political development, from the 8th century BC to the 5th century AD throughout the entire Western world. Reflects modern research up to the 1990s. Indexed in printed form in *Biographical index of the Classical World (q.v.).* *Class No: 937/938(092)(003.5)*

[6701]

—Biographical index of the Classical World. Schmuck, H., *comp.* München, K.G. Saur, 4v., 2000. DM 1,900 (DM 1,780 for purchasers of the *Biographical archive of the Classical World.*

Index to the *Biographical archive of the Classical World (q.v.)* containing names and biographical dates, sources, and location in the *Archive.* *Class No: 937/938(092)(003.5)*

Women

[6702]

LIGHTMAN, M. *and* LIGHTMAN, B. Biographical dictionary of Ancient Greek and Roman women. New York and Oxford, Facts On File, 1999. 320p. illus., bibliog., index. $45. ISBN: 0816031126.

Focuses on women mentioned in classical Greek and Roman history and literature. Data: regional affiliation, time period, with a descriptive profile. Some puzzling inclusions and exclusions. *Class No: 937/938(092)-0055.2*

Ancient Greece

Bibliographies

[6703]

FEUER, B. Mycenaean civilization a research guide. New York, Garland, 1996. 412p., indexes. $75. (*Research Guides To Ancient Civilizations, no.5.*) ISBN: 0815306024.

Annotated bibliography covering Bronze Age and Aegean World consisting of mainly English language items but also including French, German, modern Greek, and Italian - language publications. Introduction contains a chronology and a short account of the origins, history and destruction of the Mycenaean civilization. *Class No: 937(01)*

Encyclopaedias

[6704]

SACKS, D. Encyclopedia of the Ancient Greek world. New York, Facts On File; London, Constable, 1996. xiii,306p. illus., maps, bibliog., index. $40. £24.95. ISBN: 0816023239, (US); 0094752702, (UK).

550+ A-Z entries (300-1000 words) encompass politics, geography, philosophy, and Greek culture over 2,000 years. Bibliography p.272-75. *Class No: 937(031)*

Handbooks & Manuals

[6705]

ADKINS, L. *and* ADKINS, R.A. Ancient Greece a handbook. Stroud, Gloucs., Sutton Publishing, 1998. viii,472p. illus., maps, plans, bibliog., index. £20. ISBN: 0750919736.

First published in US. as *Handbook to life in Ancient Greece* (New York, Facts On File, 1997).

Chapters cover civilizations, city-states and empires; rulers and leaders; military affairs; geography of the Greek world; economy, trade and transport; towns and countryside; written evidence; religion and mythology; art, science and philosophy; everyday life, each ending with readings lists. Time period: advent of Minoan civilization to Roman conquest of 30 BC. Bibliography p.427-39. Analytical index p.440-72. *Class No: 937(035)*

Maps & Atlases

[6706]

MORKOT, R. The Penguin historical atlas of Ancient Greece. London, Penguin Books, 1996. 144p. col.illus., col.maps, bibliog., index. £9.99. ISBN: 0140513353.

40 generously illustrated map features arranged in five chronological sections: Crete, Mycenae and the Heroic Age - 2. Dark Age to Athenian Ascendancy - 3. The Persian rival - 4. Perikles to Philip - 5. Alexander and after. Timeline 7000BC-30BC in 4 geographical and thematic strands p.8-11. Bibliography p.136. Over 60 full colour maps. *Class No: 937(084.3)*

Chronologies

[6707]

WARREN, P. *and* HANKEY, V. **Aegean Bronze Age chronology.** Bristol, Bristol Classical Press, 1989. x,230p. illus., tables. £24. ISBN: 090651567x.

3 main chapters: 1. Introduction (inc. evidence that has become available in recent years) - 2. Relative (pottery based) chronology - 3. Absolute chronology recorded by radiocarbon dating and ceramic synchronisms. *Class No:* 937(090)

Biographies

[6708]

BOWDER, D., *ed.* **Who was who in the Greek World 776BC-30BC.** Oxford, Phaidon; Ithaca, New York, Cornell Univ. Press, 1982. 239p. illus., maps, geneal tables, bibliog., index. £18.00; $35.00. ISBN: 0714822078, UK; 0801415381, US.

12 contributors. Over 750 entries 'to provide a scholarly and readable account of the lives, achievements, and works of all the more notable personages' (*Introduction*). Entries end with bibliographical source references. A brief essay on the Mycenean and Minoan periods, 'The Homeric heroes', carries entries for legendary leaders. Chronology p.6-9. Glossary p.217-23. Bibliography p.224-7. 'Its major virtue is to bring together in short compass the most recent biographical and historical information on a large number of ancient Greek (and a few non-Greek) personages' (*Choice,* v.20,no.8, April 1983, p.116). *Class No:* 937(092)

[6709]

DEVELIN, R. **Athenian officials 684-321 BC.** Cambridge, Cambridge Univ. Press, 1989. xix,556p. bibliog., indexes. £55. ISBN: 0521328802.

A year-by-year list of officials from archaic and classical Athens with a short notice of their activities and the evidence relating to an individual's office in a particular year. Also contains all state decrees datable to any year or which include relevant information. Chronology p.xi-xii. References and bibliography p.xiii-xix. Modelled on T.R.S. Broughton's *The Magistrates of the Roman Republic. Class No:* 937(092)

[6710]

HAZEL, J. **Who's who in the Greek world.** London, Routledge, 1999. 320p. maps. £29.99. ISBN: 0415124972.

A-Z profiles of Greek historians, philosophers, and literary men of significance selected on the basis of their impact on Greek society 750-1000BC. Entries range from a single paragraph to a few pages in length and are accompanied by a glossary. 3 maps. *Class No:* 937(092)

Archives

[6711]

SICKINGER, J.P. **Public records and archives in classical Athens.** Univ. of North Carolina Press, 1999. 274p. bibliog., index. $49.95. ISBN: 0807824690.

Examines the evidence for the existence of copious archives maintained by Athenian magistrates. 'Only readers thoroughly familiar with the details of Athenian history will be able to follow the argument. This is an important book, but for a very specialized audience' (*Choice,* v.37, no.2 October 1999, p.385). *Class No:* 937(093.20)

Ancient Rome

[6712]

AUFSTIEG UND NIEDERGANG DER RÖMISCHEN WELT. Geschichte und Kultur Roms im Spiegel der neueren Forschung. **Rise and decline of the Roman world.** Temporini, H. *and* Haase, W., eds. Berlin & New York, Walter de Gruyter, 1972-.

Teil 1: *Von den Aufängen Roms bis zum Ausgang der Republik,* 4v. in 1 and *Tafeln* (1972-73). Teil 2: *Principat. Politische Geschichte,* 11 in 15v, (1974-88) *Künste,* 1v. in 3 (1981-85); *Recht,* 3v. (1976-82); *Religion,* 28v. in 11 (1978-93); *Sprache und Literatur,* 6v. in 22 (1980-94); *Philosophie, Wissenschaften, Technik,* 2v. in 10 (1987-95). V.18.2 *Religion (Heidentum: Die Religiösen Verhältnisse In Den Provinzen)* edited by W. Haase. 1989. xi, 875-1655p. ISBN 3110103664 has 15 chapters by various hands in 3 languages. Most have bibliographies and/or lists of illustration sources. A truly remarkable and impressive work of scholarship.

Inhaltsverzeichnis mit Autorenregister (Stand. Ende 1996) edited by S. Schwerdtfeger and U. Ilchmann 1997. vii,155p.. ISBN 3110155745 reflects all entries in volumes published up to and including 1996. *Class No:* 938

[6713]

BRAUND, D. **Augustus to Nero** a sourcebook on Roman history 31BC-AD68. London, Croom Helm, 1985. xiii, 334p. bibliog., index. £17.95. $28.95. ISBN: 0709906595.

849 sources - inscriptions, coins, papyri, literary texts - arranged in 8 sections and translated: 1. Imperial family - 2. Imperial household - 3. Senators - 4. Equites - 5. Armed forces - 6. Imperial administration - 7. Kings, cities, and towns - 8. Society and economy. Bibliographical note p.v-xi. *Class No:* 938

[6714]

RICHARDSON, L. **A New topographical dictionary of Ancient Rome.** Baltimore, John Hopkins Univ. Press, 1992. 458p., illus., plans. £49. ISBN: 0810843006.

Updates S.B. Platner's *Topographical dictionary of Ancient Rome* (1929).

Description and concise history, geographical and topographical features, of the known buildings and monuments of ancient Rome, with measurements, dates and references to significant ancient and modern sources. Entries extend from a few lines to 2000 word essays. 'No book for beginners. A basic knowledge of Latin and Roman civilization is required' (*Choice,* v.30, no.8, April 1993, p.1299). *Class No:* 938

[6715]

SCARRE, C. **Chronicle of the Roman Emperors** the reign by reign record of the rulers of Imperial Rome. London, Thames and Hudson, 1995. 240p. illus. (many col.), maps, diagrs., tables, bibliog., index. £17.95. ISBN: 0500050775.

Chapter length studies of all Emperors 31BC to AD476 arranged in 4 chronological sections: The first Emperors (31BC-AD96); High point of Empire (AD96-AD235); Crisis and renewal (AD235-AD337); The last emperors (AD337-AD476). Factboxes summarise events. 'A very attractive and useful volume covering its subject concisely, consistently and clearly' (*Reference Reviews,* v.10,no.3, 1996. p.42-43). *Class No:* 938

Bibliographies

[6716]

ROLLINS, A. **Rome in the fourth century** an annotated bibliography with historical overview. Jefferson, N. Carolina, McFarland, 1991. xxxiii,324p. index. $48.50; £36. ISBN: 0899506240.

1432 entries restricted to 20th century material in the English language arranged in 12 thematic sections: 1. General works - 2. Politics and government - 3. Military matters - 4. Literature and education - 5. Monetary matters - 6. Economy, technology, science and medicine - 7. Society and art - 8. Foreign affairs and barbarians - 9. Religion and philosophy - 10. Christianity - 11. Church and state. The period covered is AD 284 - AD 395. *Class No:* 938(01)

[6717]

ROLLINS, A.M., *comp.* **The Fall of Rome** a reference guide. Jefferson, North Carolina, McFarland, 1983. xiv, 130p. index. $19.95. £14.35. ISBN: 089950034x.

260 items forming 'a select and selectively annotated guide to twentieth century literature in English on the fall of Rome' (*Introduction*). Chronology p. xiii-xiv. *Class No:* 938(01)

Encyclopaedias

[6718]

BUNSON, M. **Encyclopedia of the Roman Empire.** New York, Facts On File, 1994. xviii,494p. illus., maps, bibliog., index $45. £24.95. ISBN: 081602135x.

A-Z guide (1900 entries) to the peoples, places, events, and culture of the Roman Empire from the period of Julius Caesar and the Gallic Wars (59-51BC) to the fall of the Empire in the West (476AD). Chronology of major events p.xvi-xviii. Appendix 1. Emperors 27BC-476AD - 2. The Julio-Claudians. Glossary of governmental, military and social titles p.473. Bibliography p.475-6. 4 maps. 'The encyclopedia does not disappoint in its generally excellent coverage of the Roman Empire. There are several entries that the general reader may be hard pressed to find in other reference works' (*Booklist,* v.90,nos 19+20, 1st and 15 June 1994, p.1876). *Class No:* 938(031)

[6719]

WACHER, J., *ed.* **The Roman world.** London, Routledge & Kegan Paul, 2v., 1987. 1,478+Øiv,479-872p. maps, plans, diagrs., bibliog., index. £120.00. ISBN: 0710208944, v.1; 0710208952, v.2; 0710099754, set.

Encyclopaedic survey by 33 archaeologists and historians on all aspects of the Roman world organized in 11 parts each ending with an extensive bibliography: 1. Introduction - 2. The rise of the Empire - 3. The Army - 4. The Frontiers - 5. Cities, towns and villages - 6. Government and law - 7. Rural life - 8. Economy - 9. Society - 10. Religion and burial - 11. Postscript. General Bibliography p.xxv-xxx. Chronological table p.xxiv-xliii. Glossary p.xliv-l. *Class No:* 938(031)

Dictionaries

[6720]

STEINBY, E.M., *ed*. **Lexicon topographicum Urbis Romae.** Roma, Editioni Quasar, 1993-.

Replaces S.B. Platner's *Topographical dictionary of ancient Rome* (1929) and complements L. Richardson's *A new topographical dictionary of ancient Rome* (1992).

Vol.1: *A-C*. 1993. 479p. illus., bibliogs. L.240,000. ISBN 8870970191. Vol.2: *D-G*. 1995. 500p. 8871400739. Vol.3: *H-O*. 1996. 8871400968. International team of 73 contributors. Its distinctive feature is the inlcusion of early Christian monuments up to the 7th century. R.B. Ulrich's review article, 'Archaeological reference texts and the information age' *American Journal of Archaeology*, v.99,no.1, January 1995, p.147-50, considers the role of electronic publishing in archaeological scholarship and reference works of this nature. *Class No: 938(038)*

Portraits

[6721]

TOYNBEE, J.M.C. **Roman historical portraits.** London, Thames & Hudson, 1978. 409p. ports. £18.00. ISBN: 0500232776.

Covers the late Republic and Augustan period. A catalogue of portraits of identifiable notables of the age precedes entries on the individuals concerned, with commentary on the portraiture. Largely devoted, despite the title, 'to portraits of foreign (*i.e.*, non-Roman) rulers from the third century B.C. to the fifth century A.D. who were in one way or another involved in the history of Rome as allies, client princes or antagonists' (*Annual Bulletin of Historical Literature*, v.64, 1980, p.18). *Class No: 938(084.10)*

Maps & Atlases

[6722]

CORNELL, T. *and* MATTHEWS, J. **Atlas of the Roman world.** Oxford, Phaidon; New York, Facts on File, 1982. 240p. col. illus., col., maps, bibliog., index. £18.50. $40.00. ISBN: 0714821527, UK; 0871966522, US.

Pt.1. Early history and the Republic - 2. From Republic to Empire - 3. Provinces of the Empire - 4. The Empire in Decline. 21 special features *e.g.* Roman patriotism, The city of Constantine, The Roman legacy. Chronological table p.6-7. Bibliography p.228-230. Gazetteer p.231-236. Analytical index. 62 maps. 470 illustrations (257 in colour). 'Superior to most other introductory surveys of Rome' (*Choice*, v.20, no.3, November 1982, p.406). *Class No: 938(084.3)*

Chronologies

[6723]

BAGNALL, R.S., *and others*. **Consuls of the Later Roman Empire.** Atlanta, Georgia, Scholars Press for The American Philological Association, 1987. viii,759p. tables, bibliog., indexes. (*Philological Monographs no.36.*) ISBN: 155540099x.

1. History of the Consulate - 2. The Evidence (p.97-617) - 3. Critical appraisal - 4. Bibliography (p.700-8) - 5. Indices. 'This book is not so much concerned with these men as figures in the society of late antiquity as it is devoted to their utility for identifying years: consulates as a means of reckoning time' (*Preface*). *Class No: 938(090)*

[6724]

MATZ, D. **An Ancient Rome chronology** 264-27 BC. Jefferson, N.C., McFarland, 1997. 240p. bibliog., index. $34.50. £31.05. ISBN: 0786401613.

Chronology of the major events in later Roman republican history. Divided into 6 sections:- Politics; laws, decrees and speeches; military events; literary milestones; art and architecture; and miscellaneous, including such events as dates of marriages, natural disasters, fires, religious matters, sports and others. *Class No: 938(090)*

Biographies

[6725]

BOWDER, D., *ed*. **Who was who in the Roman world.** Oxford, Phaidon; New York, Cornell Univ. Press, 1980. 256p. 282 illus., maps, bibliog., geneal tables, index. £15.00. ISBN: 0714820490, UK; 0801413583, US.

More than 900 biographies, arranged A-Z according to whichever is best known, praenomen, nomen, or cognomen, covering the period 753BC-AD476, *i.e.* from the legendary date of the foundation of Rome to the collapse of the Roman Empire in the West. Entries end with a bibliographical reference either to an ancient source or to a modern book. Index to persons mentioned but without an entry p.232-235. Glossary p.236-242. Bibliography p.243-245. Maps and Stemmata p.246-252. Its greatest strength, reports *Choice*, v.18 no.8 April 1981: p.1078+1080, 'is the large number of entries on very minor figures'. *Class No: 938(092)*

[6726]

BROUGHTON, T.R.S. **Magistrates of the Roman Republic.** Atlanta, Ga., Scholars Press, 3v., 1986.

Originally published New York, American Philological Association (1951-52) and *Supplement* (1960).

1. *509BC-100BC.* xix,578p. ISBN 0891308121. Abbreviations (p.xvi-xix). Annual lists of magistrates and other officials (p.1-578). Data: ancient evidence regarding the name, office, date, and summary of activities in office. 2. *99BC-31BC.* ix,647p. 0891308113. Annual lists as in v.1 (p.1-428). Appendices: 1, Monetales - 2. Magistrates *etc.* of uncertain date (p.462-86) - 3. Supplementary list of Senators (p.487-98). Bibliography (p.499-523). Index of careers *i.e.* name and chronological list of offices (p.524-636). Note on chronology (p.637-9). 3. *Supplement.* vii,294p. Additions and corrections (p.1-225). Errata (p.227-35). Abbreviations (p.236-88). Bibliography (p.239-83). Concordance of names in the Index (v.2) and the relevant articles published in Pauly-Wissowa's *Reallexikon* since 1952 (p.284-94). This Supplement incorporates additional matter first printed in *Supplement of the magistrates of the Roman Republic* (1960). *Class No: 938(092)*

[6727]

GRANT, M.J. **The Roman emperors:** a biographical guide to the rulers of Imperial Rome. 31BC-AD476. London, Weidenfeld & Nicolson, 1996. xv,384p. illus., maps, geneal. tables, indexes. £14.95. $25.00. ISBN: 0297785559, UK; 0684183889, US.

First published 1985.

92 essays arranged in 9 dynastic sections outline the political and military events of each reign and provide a physical description of each emperor taken from contemporary coins and sculptures. Key to Latin terms p. 335-43. Index of Latin and Greek authors p.345-51. Index to maps and plans (with modern equivalents of place-names) p.353-67. 'An absolute must for every library' (*Choice*, v.23, no.5, January 1986, p.726). *Class No: 938(092)*

[6728]

JONES, A.H.M., *and others*. **The Prosopography of the Later Roman Empire.** Cambridge, Cambridge Univ. Press, 3v., 1971-92.

AD 260-395. 1971. xxii, 1152p. £150.00. ISBN 0521072336. 2. *AD 395-527.* 1980. 1324p. £175.00. 0521201594. 3. *AD 527-641.* 2v. 1992. xlv,1575p. £205. 0521201608.

Detailed information on the officials who ruled the later Roman Empire. The prosopography (A-Z, names), in v.1, p.1-994, gives brief biographies and cites sources (Flavius Stilicho, p.853-8). Fragmentary names and anonymi, p.997-1040; Fasti consulares, p.1041-1127; Stemmata (family trees); p.1128-47. Index to Fasti; index to consulares. Sources, p.xi-xx. A monumental specialized compilation, continuing *Prosopographia Imperii Romani* (1897-98) and complementing H. Marrou's *Prosopographie Chretienne*, and providing a complete secular biography of the Roman Empire.

See also A. Laniado's 'Some addenda to the Prosography of the Later Roman Empire Vol.II (395-527)', *Historia*, Bd.44. Heft 1, 1995, p.121-28. *Class No: 938(092)*

Ancient Africa

[6729]

FANTAR. **Carthage: la cité punique.** Tunis, Les Éditions de la Méditerranée, 1995. 127p. illus. (some col.), maps, bibliog. ISBN: 9973220196.

1. Plan: Carthage au IIe siècle avant J.C. - 2. La redécouverte de Carthage - 3. Les Phéniciens et la fondation - 4. La ville - 5. Les institutions politiques et administravies - 6. L' Économie et la Société - 8. Les dieux et les morts - 9. Les Lettres et les arts - 10. La survivance de Carthage. Chapter notes p.120-22. Chronology p.123. Bibliography p.124-25. Authoritative account by the Professor of History and Archaeology in the University of Tunis. *Class No: 939.7*

[6730]

LANCEL, S. **Carthage: a history.** Oxford, Blackwell, 1995. xvii,474p illus., maps, bibliogs., index. £19.95. ISBN: 1557864683.

First published as *Carthage* (Paris, Arthème Fayard, 1992).

Narrative history in 11 chronological and thematic chapters (*e.g.* 1. Founding of Carthage ... 3. Beginnings of Empire... 6. Religion - 7 Expansion into Africa), Chronological overview p.447-49. Bibliography (Mainly French-language sources) p.451-64. Additiona bibliographical notes for the English edition p.465-66. 'Should serve as the standard introduction to Punic Carthage for many years to come' (*Antiquity*, v.71, no.271. March 1997, p.218). *Class No: 939.7*

[6731]

PICARD, C.G. *and* PICARD, C. **Carthage:** a survey of Punic history and culture from its birth to the final tragedy. 4th rev. ed. London Sidgwick and Jackson, 1987. vi,362p. illus. (pl.), maps,. bibliog. index. £17.95. ISBN: 0283995327.

First published as *Le monde de Carthage* (Paris, 1956) and in English as *Carthage* (1964).

1. Carthage before the Magonids - 2. The Magonids - 3. Carthage under the oligarchy - 4. The first war against Rome - 5. The Barcid

...(contd.)
Revolution - 6. Hannibal - 7. The death throes of Carthage. Chronology p.5-14. Bibliography p.347-53. 52 plates. *Class No:* 939.7

[6732]
RAVEN, S. **Rome in Africa.** 3rd ed. London, Routledge, 1993. xxxiii,254p. illus., maps, bibliog., index. ISBN: 0415082617.
First published by Evans Brothers 1969; 2nd ed. Longman 1984.
Narrative history in 14 chapters with strong archaeological content. Chronology p.xix-xxv. Bibliography p.241-3. *Class No:* 939.7

Dictionaries

[6733]
Dictionnaire de la civilisation Phénicienne et Punique. Lipinski, E., *ed.* Paris, Brépois, 1992. xxii,502p.+16p. col.pl. illus., maps, tables, bibliogs. ISBN: 2503500331.
90 contributors. Generously illustrated encyclopedia of Phoenician and Carthaginian civilisation. Entries contain historical, cultural, religious, art and architectural, and linguistic information. Tables de Transcription p.xxii. 37 maps. *Class No:* 939.7(038)

Ancient North America

[6734]
BRAY, W. *and* FEEST, C., *eds.* **The Peoples of America.** Oxford, Basil Blackwell.
On same pattern as *The peoples of Europe (qv).* 1557862249; D'Altroy , T.N. *The Incas.* 1995. 0631176772; Kolata, A.L. *The Tiwanaku: Portrait of an Andean civilization.* 1993. 344p. 1557861838; and Snow, D. *The Iroquois.* 1994. 288p. 1557862257; Milanich, J.T. and Deagan, K. *The Timucua.* 1996. 288p. 1557864888; Smith, M.E. *The Aztecs.* 1996. 320p. 1557864969; Moore, J.H. *The Cheyenne.* 1996. 320p. 1557864845; Bawden, G. *The Moche.* 1996. 384p. 1557865205. *Class No:* 939.71-.73

[6735]
JENNINGS, J.D., *ed.* **Ancient North Americans.** San Francisco, W.H. Freeman, 1983. xii,642p. $29.95. ISBN: 0716714280.
12 chapters by different hands: 1. Changing directions in archaeological thought - 2. Origins - 3. Alaska and the Northwest Coast - 4. Pioneers. *Class No:* 939.71-.73

Ancient Central America

[6736]
DAVIES, N. **The Ancient kingdoms of Mexico.** London, Allen Lane, 1982. 272p. illus., maps, bibliog., index. £12.50. ISBN: 0713912456.
Covers the period 1500BC-AD1500 focussing on the Olmec, Teotihuacan, Toltec and Aztec civilizations. Popular work but useful for its Comparative chronology p.11; Principal Archaeological Sites of Mexico p.255-6; and Bibliography p.257-64. *Class No:* 939.728

Encyclopaedias

[6737]
BUNSON, S. **Encyclopedia of Mesoamerica.** New York, Facts On File, 1996, 336p. col.illus., col.maps. $40. £22.95. ISBN: 0816024022.
Entries varying in length from a brief paragraph to long articles relating to terminology, places, people, and events of significance in American-Indian cultures in the Mesoamerican regions of Mexico and Central America during the long period from the post-Ice Age to the Spanish arrival in the 16th century. *Class No:* 939.728(031)

Dictionaries

[6738]
PALKA, J.W. **Historical dictionary of Mesoamerica.** Lanham, MD., Scarecrow Press, 2000. 288p. bibliog. $59.50. (*Historical Dictionaries of Ancient Civilizations and Historical Eras no.2.*) ISBN: 0810837153.
Covers the major discoveries and findings of the diverse investigations throughout ancient Mesoamerica from the last 100 years. The results of previous and continuing research and explorations, plus recent interpretations of ancient cultures and new work at archaeological sites in Mesoamerica are summarized. Also included are information and insights on archaeological sites, material culture, social and economic organizations, religion and belief systems, and the social history of ancient Mesoamerica. The entries contain geographical, biographical, chronological, historical, and interpretive data that serve as a condensed and accessible resource of reference material on the general knowledge of the past in Mesoamerica. *Class No:* 939.728(038)

Ancient South America

[6739]
JENNINGS, J.D., *ed.* **Ancient South Americans.** San Francisco, W.H. Freeman, 1983. xi,414p. $29.95. ISBN: 0716714299.
1. Changing directions in archeological thought - 2. Mesoamerica - 2. The Palao-Indians - 4. The Northern Andes - 5. Central Andean civilization - 6. The Southern Andes - 7. Lowland South America and the Antilles - 8. Pre-Columbian transoceanic contacts. Glossary p.395-8. *Class No:* 939.8

Ancient Australasian Peoples

[6740]
BELLWOOD, P. *and* GLOVER, I., *eds.* **The Peoples of South-East Asia and the Pacific.** Oxford, Basil Blackwell, 1993-.
Hobart, A. *The Peoples of Bali.* 1996. 256p. 063117687x; Pelras, C. *The Bugis.* 1996; King, V.T. *The Peoples of Borneo.* 1993. 0631172211; Chandler, P. *The Khmers.* 1995. 0631175822; Kirch, P.V. *The Lapita peoples: ancestors of the Oceanic world. 1996.* 1557861129. Other volumes are in process of being published. *Class No:* 939.9

[6741]
BELLWOOD, P. **The Polynesians:** prehistory of an island people. Rev. ed. London, Thames and Hudson, 1987. 175p. illus., maps, bibliog., index, pbk. (*Ancient People and Places, no.92..*) ISBN: 0500274509.
First published 1978.
6 chapters: 1. Introduction (geography of Polynesia; European navigators; the influence of the Polynesians, theories before 1952) - 2. Culture - 3. Archaeological origins - 4. Tropical chiefdoms A.D.1200-1800 - 5. Into Southern Waters - 6. Achievements. Bibliography p.166-171. 107 illus. Analytical index. 'An excellent introduction to a fascinating theme' (*Geographical Journal,* v.146, no.1, March 1990, p.122-3). *Class No:* 939.9

Mediaeval & Modern History

[6742]
The New Cambridge modern history. Cambridge, Cambridge Univ. Press, 14v., 1957-79.
Reappraisal of the period covered by *Cambridge modern history* (13v. and atlas, 1902-26) omitting chapter bibliographies. These were eventually published subsequently: J. Roach, *A Bibliography of modern history* (1968) (*qv*).
1. *The Renaissance 1483-1520* edited by G.R. Potter. 1957. xxxvi, 532p. £55.00. ISBN 0521045414. 2nd ed. planned for 1991. 2. *The Reformation 1520-1559* edited by G.R. Elton. 2nd ed., 1990. 750p. £35.00. 0521345367. 3. *The Counter-Reformation and price revolution 1559-1610* edited by W.B. Wenham. 1968. xvi, 599p. £55.00. 0521045436. 4. *The Decline of Spain and the Thirty Years' War 1609-48/59* edited by J.P. Cooper. 1970. xxi, 832p. £75.00. 0521076188. 5. *The Ascendancy of France 1648-88* edited by F.L. Carsten. 1961. £65.00. 0521045444. 6. *The Rise of Great Britain and Russia 1685-1715/25* edited by J.S. Bromley. 1970. xxxiv, 947p. £75.00. 0521075246. 7. *The Old Régime 1713-63* edited by J.O. Lindsay. 1957. xx, 625p. £65.00. 0521045452. 8. *The American and French Revolutions 1763-93* edited by A. Goodwin. 1965. xxiii, 747p. £65.00. ISBN 0521045460. 9. *War and peace in an age of upheaval 1793-1830* edited by C.W. Crawley. 1965. xiv, 748p. £75.00. 0521045479. 10. *The Zenith of European power 1830-70* edited by J.P.T. Bury. 1960. xxii, 765p. £75.00. 0521045487. 11. *Material progress and world-wide problems 1870-1898* edited by F.H. Hinsley. 1962. xi, 743p. £75.00. 0521045495. 12. *The Shifting balance of world forces 1898-1945* edited by C.L. Mowat. 2nd ed. 1968. xxvii, 845p. £75.00. 0521045517. 13. *Companion volume* edited by P. Burke. 1979. vi, 378p. £45.00. 0521221285. 14 contributors. 12 overview essays on specific themes to complement v.6-12. *e.g.* 2. The environment and the economy ... 9. The scientific revolution ... 12. On the last 2,500 years in Western history, and some remarks on the coming 500. 14. *The Atlas* edited by H.C. Darby and H. Fullard. 1970. 319p. £65.00. 0521077087. *Class No:* 94

Bibliographies

[6743]
ROACH, J., *ed.* **A Bibliography of modern history.** Cambridge, Cambridge Univ. Press, 1968. xxiv,388p.
Bibliographical companion to *The New Cambridge modern history.*
The 6,040 entries (usually unannotated) are very largely the work of the *c.*200 contributors to the NCMH. 3 main sections: A. 1493-1648 (to be used with v.12-4 of NCMH) - B. 1648-1793 (with v.5-8) - C. 1793-1945 (with v.9-12). 195 sections and many itemised cross-references. Cites many published series 'and those books are noted which contain useful bibliographies' (*Introduction*). Main emphasis is

....(contd.)

on books in English mostly published prior to 1961; over 80% of them concern Europe, and 75%, Western Europe. Analytical subject-index. *Class No:* 94(01)

Encyclopaedias
[6744]

The Pimlico encyclopedia of the Middle Ages. Cantor, N.F., *ed.* London, Pimlico; New York, Viking, 1999., 464p. illus. (some col.), col. maps, geneal., tables., softcover. £16. $40. ISBN: 0712664076, UK; 0670100110, US.

US title: *Encyclopedia of the Middle Ages.*

600 A-Z cross-referenced entries plus 20 major essays relating to medieval history, religion, national heroes, military events, art and architecture, with glossaries and chronologies. Good first-stop and quick reference source. *Class No:* 94(031)

Dictionaries
[6745]

TOWNSON, D. The New Penguin dictionary of modern history. London, Penguin Books, 1994. 941p. £7.99, $13.95. ISBN: 0140512748.

Reference companion to the major political events, social, economic and ideological developments of the world. A-Z entries also include leading economists, industrialists and military leaders. 'Provides greater depth and a more interpretative treatment of people and events than ... the Hutchinson Dictionary of World History' (*Wilson Library Bulletin*, v.69, no.7, March 1995, p.84). *Class No:* 94(038)

Yearbooks & Directories
[6746]

The Annual register a record of world events, 1998. Day, A.J., *ed.* London, Keesings Worldwide, 1999. 608p., illus. (pl), tables, map, index. ISBN: 1886994218.

First edited in 1758 by Edmund Burke as *The Annual register: a review of public events at home and abroad for the year ...*

The story of the year, recorded by 92 expert contributors, in overview articles, covering every country in the world; the United Nations, the European Union, and other international bodies; social and economic trends; and science, the environment, religion, law, the arts, and sport. In addition, there is a 'quick reference' summary of key data for each country, text or summaries of the year's significant documents, obituaries of eminent men and women, and a chronological record of the principal events of the year. *Class No:* 94(058)

Maps & Atlases
[6747]

MAN, J. Atlas of the year 1000. London, Penguin, 1999. 144p. col.illus., col.maps, bibliog., index. £9.99. ISBN: 0140514198.

42 map features of world civilizations at the end of the 1st millenium A.D. A millenial glossary p.135-36. Bibliography p.137. 'The text is cumbrously. written and patchily researched, but it combines enduring entertainment with stylish design, crisp pictures, and clear, unambitious maps' (*The Times*, 66693, 9 December 1999, p.45). *Class No:* 94(084.3)

[6748]

The New Cambridge modern history. v.14. The Atlas. Darby, H.C. *and* Fullard, H. Cambridge, Cambridge Univ. Press, 1970. xxiv,319p. maps (some col.). £65.00. ISBN: 0521077087.

Supersedes *The Cambridge modern history atlas* (2nd ed., 1924).

288 pages of coloured maps; no text. Three groups: the first depicts exploration and political acquisition of parts of the world, plus achievement of independence, 1945-68; the second group covers wars and treaty settlements, from the Peasants' War of 1524-6 to World War II. The third group is of regional maps, each sub-group in chronological order. Well balanced: 15 areas are covered. 'Although it is designed to serve the need of readers of the *New Cambridge modern history*, the atlas is also intended to illustrate school or university courses on modern history' (*Geo Abstracts*, 1972/1, entry 72D/0321). 'One of the most informative and best historical atlases, but also one of the most compact and easiest to handle' (*Library Journal*, v.97, no.18, 15 April 1972, p.1386), giving fuller coverage than does Shepherd's *Historical atlas (qv)*. Page size, 20x28.5cm. *Class No:* 94(084.3)

[6749]

The Times atlas of the 20th century. Overy, R., *ed.* London, Times books, 1996. 239p. col.illus. col. maps, bibliog., index. £30. ISBN: 0723007667.

First published in the US as *Hammond atlas of the twentieth century* (Hammond, 1996. $39.95. ISBN 0843711485).

12 contributors. 93 chapters arranged in 6 chronological and thematic chapters: 1. End of the old world order - 2. The World between the Wars - 3. World at war - 4. Cold War - 5. Towards the new world order - 6. The Revolutionary century: themes. Chronology

....(contd.)

(5 regional timelines across the page) p.10-15. Bibliography p.214-15. Glossary (i.e. people, events, themes) p.217-26. 200+ full-colour maps. 'Should provide history buffs and students of other disciplines not only with engrossing reading but also with a basis for research about the vital events and issues of the twentieth century' (*Booklist*, v.93, no.8, 15 December 1996, p.748-49). *Class No:* 94(084.3)

Sound Recordings & Tapes
[6750]

HOWARTH, K. Oral history a handbook. Stroud, Glos., Sutton Publishing, 1998. ix,214p. illus. £25. ISBN: 0750917562.

Contents include techniques and preferred locations, UK and worldwide practices, ethical requirements, and the technologies involved. 'A more comprehensive volume on this subject would be hard to imagine' (*The Local Historian*, v.30, no.1, February 2000, p.67). *Class No:* 94(086.7)

[6751]

Oral history index: an international directory of oral history interviews. Wasserman, E.S., *ed.* Westport, Conn., Meckler, 1990. 434p. £90; $145. ISBN: 0887363490.

Over 30,000 oral historal transcripts from 400 institutions in US, Canada, UK and Israel principally arranged A-Z by name of person(s) interviewed. Data: interview date; subject content; and a coded reference to a second sequence of entries for institutions and collections. Compiled from questionnaires sent to 1,300 institutions. 'An immensely thorough basic guide which is primarily geared to the needs of biographers and family historians' (*Reference Reviews*, v,5, no.1, 1991, p.39-40). Supplements A. Smith's *Directory of oral history collections. Class No:* 94(086.7)

[6752]

YOW, V.R. Recording oral history a practical guide for social scientists. Thousand Oaks, California, and London, SAGE Publications, 1994. xi,284p. bibliogs., index. ISBN: 0803955782.

Researcher's guide to interviews (project preparation and techniques; legalities and ethics; interpersonal relationships; and to the varieties of oral history projects (Community Studies, Biography, and Family Research). Appendix B. Principles and standards of the Oral History Association. Each chapter ends with notes and lists of recommended reading. *Class No:* 94(086.7)

Bibliographies
[6753]

PERKS, R., *comp.* **Oral history:** an annotated bibliography. London, British Library National Sound Archive, 1990. xv,183p. index. pbk. £12.95. ISBN: 071230505x.

23132 numbered entries A-Z by author relating to books, pamphlets, periodicals, articles, catalogues, and published recordings. Coverage is comprehensive for UK and selective for elsewhere. *Class No:* 94(086.7)(01)

Yearbooks & Directories
[6754]

SMITH, A. Directory of oral history collections. Phoenix, Arizona, Oryx Press, 1988. 142p. indexes. $49.50; £33.65. ISBN: 0897743229.

Lists 476 repositories in 49 states and District of Columbia with entries arranged by state and city. Data: postal address, telephone, staff, size of collection, hours and access, finding aids, general and significant holdings. Described as a 'preliminary' edition, coverage is inevitably incomplete. An 'expanded and more comprehensive version is promised. *Class No:* 94(086.7)(058)

18th & 19th Centuries
[6755]

PALMER, A. An Encyclopaedia of Napoleon's Europe. London, Constable, 1998. xxiv,301p. maps, illus., bibliog, index. £20. ISBN 009478700x.

Previously published by Weidenfeld & Nicholson in 1984.

Encompasses Napoleon's battles and campaigns; leading military, naval, and political figures; the institutions of the consulate and Empire; and social, religious and economic themes. Chronology p.xv-xxiv. Bibliographical Note p.299-300. 5 maps. *Class No:* 94"17/18"

19th & 20th Centuries

Chronologies

[6756]

ILLIAMS, N. Chronology of the modern world 1901-1998. Oxford, Helicon, 1999. xi,1121p. indexes. £80. ISBN: 1859862845.

Year by year entries in 4 categories (1. politics, government, economics - 2. Science, technology and medicine - 3. Arts - 4. Society) and 25 special subjects. *Class No:* 94"18/19"(090)

20th Century

[6757]

OOK, C. *and* **STEVENSON, J. The Longman handbook of the modern world** international history and politics since 1945. London, Longman, 1998. ix,512p. maps, bibliogs., index. £46. ISBN: 0582304121.

1. Political history (7 regional chronologies of events) - 2. War and International Affairs (inc. principal international organizations and groupings, United Nations, nuclear development and arms control) - 3. Economic and Social (population, food production, energy) - 4. Biographies (c.200 key figures) - 5. Glossary (p.379-431) - 6. Topic bibliography (p.435-67): introductory works and 6 regional bibliographical essays, 5 maps. *Class No:* 94"19"

Dictionaries

[6758]

ROWNSTONE, D.M. *and* **FRANCK, I.M. Dictionary of 20th Century history.** New York, Prentice Hall, 1990. 444p. $24.95; £17.95. ISBN: 0132098830.

Almost 4,000 cross-referenced entries relating to key events (wars, revolutions, crimes and scandals *etc.*), world leaders, political and social movements and ideas, and scientific discoveries (BBC 12 lines; Prague Spring 91.; Watergate 62). 2 cols. x page. Pronounced US bias. *Class No:* 94"19"(038)

[6759]

ALMOVSKI, J. Oxford dictionary of twentieth-century world history. Oxford Univ. Press, 1997 vii,693p.. pbk., tables, maps. £7.99. $15.95. ISBN: 0192800167.

2,500 A-Z entries relating to major historical events, prominent personalities, and political movements. Particularly useful for concise histories, and name changes of newly independent countries emerging from decolonization and the disintegration of the Soviet *bloc*. Maps p.687-93. *Class No:* 94"19"(038)

[6760]

he Penguin dictionary of twentieth-century history 1900-1991. 4th ed. London, Penguin, 1992. ii,437p. pbk. £6.99. ISBN: 014052640.

1st ed. 1979; 3rd ed. 1990. Published in US as *Facts On File dictionary of twentieth-century history.*

Cross referenced guide to political, diplomatic, military, economic, and social and religious affairs. Entries of varying length (100-2000 words). 120 expanded and revised entries in this edition and 7 new entries (De Klerk, 2nd Gulf War, Intifada, Kohl, John Major, Saddam Hussein, Yeltsin). *Class No:* 94"19"(038)

Modern History—Developing Countries

Bibliographies

[6761]

ATHAM, A.J.H., *comp.* **Africa, Asia and South America since 1800. A bibliographical guide.** Manchester Univ. Press, 1995. xxxiii,259p. index. (*History And Related Disciplines Select Bibliographies.*) ISBN: 0719018773.

5000+ entries relating to material published in English and mostly published since 1945. Some citations are annotated. Complex arrangement in 4 sections: 1. General divided into 3 periods, 1800-1914, 1914-39, 1939 onwards each subdivided by Economy, Politics & Society. 2. Africa - 3. Asia - 4. South America each divided by Period, Region, and by Country. Author and title index p.234-59. Omissions and inconsistencies gave an unfavourable impression: 'this is a flawed and overpriced work which should never have been published in its present state' (*African Affairs,* vol.95, no.381, October 1996, p.608-609). *Class No:* 94-773(01)

Mediaeval & Modern History—Europe

[6762]

DUROSELLE, J-B. Europe: a history of its peoples. Mayne, R., *trans.* London, Viking, 1990. 423p. illus. (mostly col.), col. maps, tables, index. £25. ISBN: 0670829226.

Published simultaneously by Bertelsmann Lexikon Verlag; Librairie Academique Perrin (Fr); Aquilar El Pais (Sp); Lademann (Dk); Kosmos (Neths); Fabbri Bompiani (It); and Circulo de Leitores/Dom Quixote (Port).

1. What is Europe - 2. Prehistory - 3. The Celts - 4. Classical antiquity - 5. The first four centuries A.D. in the West - 6. The Germanic age - 7. Charlemagne: King of Europe? - 8. Europe under siege - 9. The heyday of Western Christianity (12th and 13th centuries) - 10. Towards a Europe of the States (14th and 15th centuries) - 11. Renaissance, Reformation and expansion - 12. Absolutism, liberties and cosmopolitanism - 13. Revolution and disillusion - 14. Napoleon: Europe by force - 15. Industrial Revolution - 16. Romanticism and the nations - 17. Road to European disaster (1871-1914) - 18. Europe destroys itself (1914-1945) - 19. Recovery and resurgent hopes. A single-volume history of Europe 'seen in overall European as opposed to national perspective' intended for students and general readers. The absence of a scholarly apparatus, apart from chapter chronologies, reduces its reference value. *Class No:* 940

[6763]

PEDERSEN, R.N. One Europe 100 nations. Clevedon, Avon, Channel View Books, 1992. 144p. col. illus., col. maps, bibliog. £14.95. ISBN: 1853591238.

Brief description of origins, history, minorities, linguistic struggle, political status for each of Europe's potential and *de facto* governing nations including Pomerania, Thuringia, Galicia, Castille, Normandy, Brittany, Cornwall, Shetland Is. *etc.* Col. illus. of flag and arms. Useful only for identifying current and historical 'minority' nations subsumed within nation-state borders. *Class No:* 940

[6764]

SCAMMELL, G.V. The World encompassed: the first European maritime empires.*c.*800-1650. London, Methuen; Berkeley, Univ. of California Press, 1982. xiv,538p. illus., maps, index. $47.50. ISBN: 0416762808, UK; 0520044223, US.

Covers an unfamiliar period: 800-1650, focussing in turn on the Norse, Hanse, Venetian, Genoese, Portuguese, Spanish, Dutch, French and English maritime ventures. Extensive bibliographical notes to each chapter further enhance a scholarly and well-researched book. *Class No:* 940

Dictionaries

[6765]

Encyclopedia of the Renaissance. Grendler, P.F., *ed.* New York, Charles Scribner's Sons, 6v., 1999. 3072p. illus. (some col.), maps, tables, bibliogs., index. $695. ISBN: 0684805146.

683 academic contributors. 1200 A-Z signed articles on culture, literature, humanism, religion, economics, politics, philosophy and history, and biographies of 600 leading figures and 26 families, surveying the entire cultural movement known as the Renaissance from 14th century Italy to 1650. Articles vary in length from 250 to 7,500 words each ending with a select bibliography, including modern editions of primary works and major secondary works. 750 illustrations, including colour inserts in all 6v., a year by year chronology, 30 maps, and a comprehensive index comprise the reference apparatus to these scholarly and luxurious volumes. Awarded the Dartmouth Medal 1999. 'Included in *Library Journal's* 'Best Reference Sources for 1999' list and selected as the Editor's choice for the best reference title 1999 in *Booklist/Reference Books Bulletin*. *Class No:* 940(038)

Maps & Atlases

[6766]

The Times atlas of European history. 2nd ed. London, Times Books, 1998. 206p. col.maps, bibliog., index. £25. ISBN: 0723006016.

1st ed. 1994.

Concentrates on mapping the frontiers and borders of European nations, states and empires at 46 key dates from 900BC onwards *e.g.* 732 The Arab advance ... 1530 The Hapsburg Ascendancy ... 1942 Hitler's Europe ... 1993 The Collapse of Communism). This edition concludes with a new section: 1997 The Aftermath of the Soviet Union. Each is supported by an accompanying historical text and 3-5 subsidiary maps focusing on the major historical events influencing the transition from one period to the next. Bibliography (p.192) of historical and thematic atlases and chronologically classified histories. *Class No:* 940(084.3)

Chronologies

[6767]

POWELL, J., *ed*. **Chronology of European history 15,000 BC to 1987.** Chicago & London, Fitzroy Dearborn, 2v., 1998. xxv,1835p. illus., maps, bibliogs., indexes. £175. ISBN: 1579580521.

175 academic contributors. 614 signed articles on significant occurrences in European history. Data and content: year of event set in context, capsule summary identifying its significance, date, locale, and a 1,000-1,500 word text, ending with bibliographies. Title, geographical, category of event, personal, and subject indexes. *Class No:* 940(090)

Mediaeval History—Europe

[6768]

The New Cambridge medieval history. Cambridge Univ. Press, 7v. in 8, 1995-2000.

The original *Cambridge Medieval History* was published between 1911 and 1936, with a new edition of Volume IV appearing in the 1960s. That famous series is now out of print, and is being replaced by *The New Cambridge Medieval History*.

V.1: c.500-700 edited by P. Fouracre. 2000. 0521362911.

V.2: c.700-c.900. Edited by R. McKitterick. 1995. 1056p. illus., maps. £75. 052136292x. 28 contributors. 30 chronological, regional and thematic chapters divided into 4 parts: 1. Political development - 2. Government and institutions - 3. Church and Society - 4. Culture and intellectual developments. *V.3: c.900-1024* ed. by T. Reuter, 1999. £65. 0521364477; *V.4(1): c.1024-1198.* 2000. £65. 0521414105 and *V.4(2): c.1025-1198* edited by D. Luscombe and J. Riley-Smith 2000. £65. 0521414113.

V.5: c.1198-c.1300 edited by D. Abulafia. 1998. 900p. 19p. maps. £65. 052136289x; . *V.6: c.1300-c.1415* ed. by M. Jones. 1999. 900p. 19 maps. £65. 0521362903; *V.7: v.1415-c.1500* edited by C. Allmand 1998. 1046p. 21 maps, 9 geneal tables. £65. $95. 0521382963. 32 chapters by independent hands in 4 sections: Government; Economics and social developments; Spiritual, cultural and artistic life; The Development of European states.

Forthcoming Volumes 1: *c.500-700.* Edited by P. Fouracre. 1999. 0521362911; 3: 0521364477; 4(1): *c.1024-1198.* (D. Luscombe). 1998. 0521414015; 4(2): *c.1024-1198* (D. Luscombe) 1998. 0521414113; 5: *c.1198-1300* (D. Abulafia) 1998. 052136289x; 6: *c.1300-1415* (M. Jones) 1997. 0521362903; 7: *c.1415-1500* (C. Allmand) 1997. 0521382963.

Written by leading international scholars and incorporating the very latest research, the *History* is the essential reference tool for anyone interested in the medieval world. *Class No:* 940.1

Bibliographies

[6769]

BAK, J.M. **Medieval narrative sources** : a chronological guide: (with a list of major letter collections). New York, Garland, 1987. xviii,117p., bibliog., index. $20. (*Garland reference library of the humanities, no.734.*) ISBN: 0824084403.

1001 collections deployed in 3 major chronological divisions: Early Middle Ages (to 900AD); Central Middle Ages (900-1300AD); Late Middle Ages (1300-1500AD). Data: Author/title; Date; Editions; Translations. Only sources for which there are printed editions are included. Major bibliography of medieval narrative sources p.xv-xviii. Author, regions and places indexes. *Class No:* 940.1(01)

[6770]

CROSBY, E.U., *and others*. **Medieval studies: a** bibliographical guide. New York, Garland Publishing, 1983. xxv,1131p., frontis. $109. ISBN: 0824091078.

9000 annotated entries relating to the history and culture of the Western European Middle Ages, Byzantium, and medieval Islamic civilization listed in 138 chapters - 1. History and historical method; 2. Historiography; 3. Historiography of the Middle Ages; 4. Modern historical writing; 7. Encyclopaedias and dictionaries; 10. Biography; 13. Guides to archives and libraries; 19. General medieval history; 22-37 geographical chapters; 46. Maritime history; 47. Travel and exploration; 123. Archaeology; 124. Chronology; 127. Geography; 129. Cartography; 130. Maps and atlases; 136. Genealogy; 177. Heraldry; 138. Serials. All entries are furnished with brief descriptions of subject matter and its importance in the field. Index of authors and editors p.1058-1127. Index of topics p.1129-1131. *Class No:* 940.1(01)

[6771]

International medieval bibliography. Leeds, School of History, Univ of Leeds, 1967- Annual, then 2pa.

V.27. Pt.2. Jul-Dec 1993. 1994. xxxiii,441p. has 5004 entries covering 952 journals and festschriften *etc.* on medieval topics AD450-1500 with some extensions to certain topics and areas. Arrangement general bibliography, general culture and history then by 61 A-Z topics *e.g.* Archaeology (general artifacts, sites), Genealogy, Heraldry, Historiography, Local history, subdivided by geographical areas. Works on Africa, the Near East and Oriental topics are only included when they bear directly on the study of medieval Europe. Author and general indexes.

International medieval bibliography on CD-ROM. Turnhout, Belgium. Brepols Publishers. 210,000 articles 1984-1993. Rolling programme to a comprehensive edition 1967-1997. *Class No:* 940.1(01)

[6772]

PAETOW, L.J. **A Guide to the study of medieval history.** Rev. ed prepared under the auspices of the Medieval Academy of America London, Kegan Paul, 1931. (Reprinted New York, Klaus, 1964) xix,643p.

First published 1917 (552)p.

Valuable guide to bibliographies, printed sources and secondary works for the history of medieval Europe and its Eastern neighbours. Pt.1. Numbered list of books arranged by subject under the headings Bibliography - Reference - Auxiliary Studies - Modern works - Collections of sources. Pts.2 & 3 arranged by topic, each containing an introduction, recommendations for reading, and a bibliography referring to pt.1. This edition adds material published 1917-1928 Revised and corrected edition (New York, Kraus Reprints, 1980 cxii,643p. 0527253456) has Errata (p.xxi-li) and an Addendum (p.liii-cxii) of *c.* 1100 titles published before 1930 but not in 1917 or 1931 editions. *Literature of medieval history 1930-1975: a supplement to Louis John Paetow's 'A guide to the study of medieval history* edited by G.C. Boyce (New York, Kraus International Publications, 5v. 1981. 2630p. $595.00 0527104620) follows the same format but with 55,000 references is some four times larger. 'A very valuable bibliography on medieval European history from 500 to 1500' (*Choice,* v.19,no.1, September 1981, p.45-6). *Class No:* 940.1(01)

[6773]

Repertorium fontium historiae Medii Aevi: primum ab A. Potthast, nunc cura collegii historicorum e pluribus nationibus emendatum et auctum. Rome, Istituto Storico Italiano per il Medio Evo, 1962-. v.1-(v.1-5, 1962-1984).

1. *Series collectionum* 2-5. *Fontes A-H.*

Sponsored by Istituto Storico per il Medio Aevo, Istituti di Archeologia, Storia e Storia dell'Arte in Roma, Medieval Academy of America, etc. V.1 gives contents of all the collections of narrative sources. V.2 is the first part of a detailed description of sources, A-Z (*c.*15,000 entries). The entry 'Abaelardus' (3 columns) has subheadings for manuscripts, medieval translations, editions, modern translations and commentaries. V.2 also includes a general list of sources (p.3-46) and list of journals cited (p.49-87). Designed to supersede A. Potthast's *Bibliotheca historica Medii Aevi/Wegweiser durch die Geschichtswerke des europäischen Mittelalters bis 1500* (2. verb. u. verm. Aufl. Berlin, Weber 1896. 2v. Reprinted 1955) - at present the fullest guide to printed sources (excluding records) for the history of medieval Europe, A.D.400-*c.*1500. *Class No:* 940.1(01)

Internet

[6774]

NetSERF: **the internet connection for medieval resources.** Harbin, B.C., *comp.* URL:http://itassrva.cpit.cua.edu/netserf/

Index to Internet medieval resources. 'A highly valuable resource for medieval historians, or for those interested in finding related Internet sites' (*Choice,* Supplement to v.36, August 1999, p.159). *Class No:* 940.1(01)(003.41)

Encyclopaedias

[6775]

BUNSON, M.E. **Encyclopedia of the Middle Ages.** New York, Facts On File, 1995. 498p. $45. ISBN: 0816024561.

A-Z cross-referenced entries for people, places and themes in medieval Europe and the Middle East. 'Readers will be better served by the 13-volume Dictionary of the Middle Ages' (*Choice,* v.33,no.8, April 1996, p.1282). *Class No:* 940.1(031)

[6776]

LETCHER, S. The Longman companion to Renaissance Europe, 1390-1530. Harlow, Longman, 2000. xiv,337p. maps, bibliog., index. £15.99. (*Longman Companions to History*.) ISBN: 0582298822.

Includes a chronology of events 1378-1534, brief profiles of the Popes of the period, a section on the Holy Roman Empire, 20 thematic sections (*e.g.*the church, commerce, libraries, printing, science), and a substantial bibliography. 'Can be added to reference library shelves with every confidence' (*Reference Reviews*, v.14, no.3, 2000, p.48-49). *Class No:* 940.1(031)

[6777]

OYN, H.R., *ed.* The Middle Ages: a concise encyclopaedia. London, Thames & Hudson, 1989. Distributed in US by Norton. 352p. illus., maps, bibliog. £24.00; $39.95. ISBN: 0500251037.

40 contributors. Nearly 100 cross-referenced A-Z entries including biographies (John of Gaunt: 17 lines and 2 refs.); broad themes *e.g.* chivalry (83 lines and 4 refs.), feudalism, heresy; wars and battles, artistic highlights, covering the period AD. 400-1500. Bibliographical note p.352. 250 illus. 'An accessible and valuable tool' (*Booklist*, v.86,no.2, 15 September 1989, p.207). *Class No:* 940.1(031)

[6778]

ZARMACH, P.E., *and others, eds.* Medieval Europe an encyclopedia. New York, Garland Publishing, 1998. lxiv, 882p. bibliogs., index. ISBN: 0824057864.

300 international academics contribute 700 signed entries relating to such themes as Old and Middle English, language and literature, music, liturgy, art history, architecture, law, and history. Varying in length from a line or two to several columns, the entries cover the period from the Anglo-Saxon settlement to the emergence of the Tudor Dynasty in 1485. *Class No:* 940.1(031)

Dictionaries

[6779]

AHLMUS, J. Dictionary of medieval civilization. New York, Macmillan Publishing Co., London, Collier Macmillan, 1984. viii, 700p. £52. ISBN: 0029078709.

6600 plus entries defining medieval terms and concepts. Topics covered include people, events, institutions etc., spanning the period AD300-1500. There is no bibliographical apparatus. 'An excellent source of brief, accurate information on things medieval' (*Wilson Library Bulletin*, v.59, no.2, October 1984, p.145. *Class No:* 940.1(038)

[6780]

TRAYER, J.R., *ed.* Dictionary of the Middle Ages. New York, Charles Scribner's Sons, 13v., 1982-1989. Distributed in UK by Macmillan. illus., maps. £780.00.

v.13 Index. 1989. 0684182793. Over 5000 commissioned articles, mostly from US and Canadian academics, cover all aspects of medieval life in Christendom and Islam. Entries range from 500 word definitions to critical essays of 10,000 words on major figures and topics. All are signed and end with bibliogs., and cross-references. More than 1000 illustrations, charts, and maps. Published under the auspices of the American Council of Learned Societies. The Dictionary receives a grant from the National Endowment for the Humanities. *Class No:* 940.1(038)

[6781]

OPHY, J.W., *ed.* The Holy Roman Empire: a dictionary handbook. Westport, Connecticut, Greenwood Press, 1980. xxvii,551p. maps,bibliog., index. £40.00; $50.95. ISBN: 0313214573.

Short signed essays with bibliographies appended on notable persons, places, terms, and important events, as well as significant topics in social, urban, economic, military, and women's history, from the time of Charlemagne to the Napoleonic dissolution in 1806. 32 contributors. 8 maps. Appendix A. The Holy Roman Emperors and their predecessor Kings p.501-502. B. Chronology p.503-504. Bibliography p.507-512. Indifferent review in *Choice*, v.18,no.8, April 1981, p.1080. *Class No:* 940.1(038)

[6782]

-ZOPHY, J., *ed.* An Annotated bibliography of the Holy Roman Empire. Westport, Connecticut, Greenwood Press, 1986. 398p. index. $65.00; £65.00. (*Bibliographies and Indexes in World History, no.3.*)

Over 3000 briefly annotated entries in 11 categories: 1. General historical surveys - 2. Constitutional and institutional history - 3. Emperors - 4. The Church - 5. The nobility - 6. Peasantry - 7. Economic and social history - 8. Towns and territories - 9. War and diplomacy - 10. Culture - 11. Reformation. 'Should serve as a valuable reference source for locating the most important scholarly works on any subject of German history during the period of the thousand-year Reich' (*German Studies Review*, v.10,no.1, February 1987, p.159-60). *Class No:* 940.1(01)

Maps & Atlases

[6783]

Atlas of medieval Europe. Mackay, A. *and* Ditchburn, D., *eds.* London, Routledge, 1997. ix,269p. maps, bibliog., index. £50. ISBN: 0415019230.

140+ maps cover the period from the fall of the Roman Empire through to the beginnings of the Renaissance. It comprehensively covers the areas within the broadest definition of Europe from the Atlantic coast to the Russian steppes. Each map approaches a separate issue or series of events in Medieval history, whilst a commentary locates it in its broader context. 'Although the short commentaries on the maps are useful, the maps themselves are cramped, often only half-page in size in black and white' (*Early Medieval Europe*, v.7,no.1, 1998, p.141). *Class No:* 940.1(084.3)

Atlantic Ocean

[6784]

FERNÁNDEZ-ARMESTO, F. Before Columbus exploration and colonisation from the Mediterranean to the Atlantic 1229-1492. London, Macmillan Education; Univ. of Pennsylvania Press, 1987. x,283p. maps, bibliog., index. £30.00. (*New Studies in Medieval History*.) ISBN: 0333403827, UK; 0812280830, US.

9 chapters: 1. The island conquests of the House of Barcelona - 2. The first 'Atlantic' Empire: Andalusia and its environs - 3. A Mediterranean land empire - 4. The Genose Mediterranean - 5. The rim of Africa - 6. Mapping the Eastern Atlantic - 7. The Atlantic crucible - 8. From the Canaries to the New World - 9. The mental horizon. References p.253-66. Bibliography p.267-75. A valuable work of research and synthesis in a somewhat neglected period. *Class No:* 940.1(261)

Crusades

[6785]

SETTON, K.M., *ed.* A History of the Crusades. Madison, Univ. of Wisconsin Press, 6v., 1969-1990. $40. each volume.

V.1-2 first published by Univ. of Pennsylvania Press 1955-1962.

1. *The first hundred years* edited by M.W. Baldwin, 1969. xxxi,707p. ISBN 0299048314. 2. *The later Crusades 1189-1311* edited by R.L. Wooff and H.W. Hazard. 2nd ed. 1969, xxii,859p. 0299048411. 3. *The fourteenth and fifteenth centuries* edited by H.W. Hazard. 1975. xxi,819p. 0299066703. 4. *The art and architecture of the Crusader states* edited by H.W. Hazard. 1977. xxvii,414+10p. 029906820x. 5. *The impact of the Crusades on the Near East* edited by N.P. Zacour and H.W. Hazard. 1985. xxii,599p. 0299091406. 6. *The impact of the Crusades on Europe* edited by N.P. Zacour and H.W. Hazard. 1990. xxiii,703p. 029910740x. V.5 has 10 chapters (*e.g.* 1. Arab culture in the twelfth century ... 2. Impact of the Crusades on Moslem lands ... 8. The Teutonic Knights in the Crusader states); gazetteer and notes on maps, p.519-552; and 13 maps V.4 carries 'Addenda and corrigenda' to v.1-4. V.6 has H.E. Mayer and J. McLellans' Select bibliography of the Crusades (p.511-644). This immense compilation includes A. General works, research aids, historiography - B. Narrative sources in many Western and Near Eastern languages - C. Secondary Works. Also Gazetteer and note on maps p.483-510. *Class No:* 940.1"1095-13"

Maps & Atlases

[6786]

The Atlas of the Crusades. Riley-Smith, J., *ed.* London, Times Books, 1990; New York, Facts on File, 1991. 192p. col. illus., col. maps, bibliog., index. £19.95, $40. ISBN: 0723003610, UK; 0816021864, US.

19 contributors. 22 narrative chapters arranged in 4 parts: 1. The way of God - 2. Defence of Christendom - 3. Crusading and the world of Chivalry - 4. The last crusaders. Chronology (in 3 cols: The East; Europe and North Africa; Background events) p.10-19. Glossary p.176-9. Bibliography p.173. History ranges from Urban II's. First crusade 1095 AD to the late eighteenth century. *Class No:* 940.1"1095-13"(084.3)

Renaissance

Encyclopaedias

[6787]

BERGIN, T.G. *and* SPEAKE, J., *eds.* Encyclopedia of the Renaissance. New York, Facts on File, 1987. London, B.T. Batsford Ltd. 1988. 454p., illus., geneal. tables, bibliog. £40. $45. ISBN: 0816013152, US; 0713459670, UK.

28 contributors. 2500 A-Z cross-referenced entries relating to individuals, issues and events in all fields of human endeavour in 14th-16th century Europe. Bibliography (in subject categories) p.433-440. Sparse chronological table p.441-454. 32 col. plates. 'Easily the best one-volume reference available' (*Choice*, v.25, no.8, April 1988, p.1219). *Class No:* 940.1"1095-1300"(031)

Maps & Atlases

[6788]

BLACK, C., *and others*. Atlas of the Renaissance. London, Cassell, 1993. 240p. col. illus., col. maps, bibliog., index. £20. ISBN: 0304343188.

11 contributors. Pt.1: The Heartland of the Renaissance (*i.e.* medieval Italy) - Renaissance and the wider world (Italy and Venice, Germany and the Low Countries. France, Spain and Portugal, England and Scotland). 38 special features (*e.g.* The Discovery of antiquity ... the printer-publisher ... New learning). Chronology p.8-9. Gazetteer p.230-33. Bibliography p.229. 42 maps. Authoritative, lavishly produced compendium. *Class No:* 940.1"1095-1300"(084.3)

Modern History—Europe (1492-)

Handbooks & Manuals

[6789]

COOK, C. and STEVENSON, J. The Longman handbook of modern European History 1763-1987. 3rd ed. London and New York, Longman, 1998. 530p. maps, bibliog., geneal tables, index. £28. $39.95. ISBN: 0582304164.

Quick reference guide organized in 7 sections: 1. Principal rulers and ministers - 2. Political events (chronology in 27 topics *e.g.* 19. Italian Fascism ... 23. Spain 1909-1939 ... 27. The movement for European unity) - 3. War, diplomacy and imperialism - 4. Economic and Social - 5. Biographies - 6. Glossary - 7. Topic Bibliography. Maps. Analytical index. Companion volume to *The Longman handbook of modern British history 1714-1987* (*q.v.*). 'An outstanding reference work, containing much information not available elsewhere in a single volume' (*Reference Reviews*, v.2, no.4, December 1988, p.224-5). *Class No:* 940.2(035)

Dictionaries

[6790]

TOWNLEY, E. Dictionary of 20th century European history. Chicago, Fitzroy Dearborn, 1999. 283p., maps. £20. ISBN: 1579581277.

First published in the UK by Hodder and Stoughton Educational as *The Complete A-Z 20th Century European History Handbook* (1997).

Most of the A-Z cross-referenced entries in this handbook/dictionary refer to people places, and events linked to, caused by, or related to the two world wars, 1914-1918 and 1939-1945, or to the Cold War, late 1940s-early 1990s. 18 maps. *Class No:* 940.2(038)

[6791]

WILLIAMS, E.N. The Penguin dictionary of English and European history, 1485-1789. London, Allen Lane, 1980. 509p. index. £5.99. ISBN: 0140510842.

Published in New York as *The Facts on File dictionary of European history 1485-1789* at $22.50.

'Follows the mainstream of political history without diverging too far into economics, the arts or science'. One third of the scholarly and substantial entries relate to English history. Extensive cross-references but no references to other sources. No bibliography. Analytical index p.469-509. *Class No:* 940.2(038)

Maps & Atlases

[6792]

BLACK, J. 'Mapping early modern Europe', *European Historical Quarterly*, v.25,no.3, July 1995, p.431-42.

Authoritative historiographic essay providing an overview of atlases produced in 10 European countries. *Class No:* 940.2(084.3)

[6793]

MAGOCSI, P.R. Historical atlas of East Central Europe. University of Toronto Press, 1994. $85. ISBN: 0802006078.

89 political and thematic maps with accompanying text covering from the early 5th century to January 1993. The atlas encompasses Poland, the Czech Republic, Slovakia, Hungary, Romania, Slovenia, Crotia, Bosnia-Herzegovina, Yugoslavia, Macedonia, Albania, Bulgaria, and Greece. Also included are the eastern parts of Germany (historic Mecklenburg, Brandenburg, Prussia, Saxony, and Lusatia), Bavaria, Austria, north-eastern Italy (historic Venetia), the lands of historic Poland-Lithuania (present-day Lithuania, Belarus, and Ukraine up to the Dnieper River), Moldova, and western Turkey. *Class No:* 940.2(084.3)

16th & 17th Centuries

Bibliographies

[6794]

CARTER, C.H. The Western European powers 1500-1700. London Hodder & Stoughton, 1971. 347p. index. ISBN: 0340126965.

1. The subject and the sources - 2. Archival materials - 3. Archive and archival collections: central repositories - 4. Public documents - ? Contemporary publications - 6. Code, cypher and security - ? Research in the diplomatic sources. England, France, Spain an Spanish Netherlands most closely studied.
Class No: 940.2"15/16"(01)

16th Century

Biographies

[6795]

Contemporaries of Erasmus: a biographical register of the Renaissanc and Reformation. Bietenholz, P. *and* Deutscher, T.B., *eds*. Toronte Buffalo/London, Univ. of Toronto Press, 3v., 1985-.

Companion volumes to the publisher's *Collected works of Erasmu* (1974-).

1: *A-E*. 1985. xii,462p. illus. $90. ISBN 0802025072. 2: *F-N* 1986. xii,490p. illus. $90. 0802025714. 3. *N-Z*. 1987. $9(0802025757. A biographical dictionary of identifiable persons from th second half of the 15th and the first half of the 16th century mentione in the writings of Erasmus - political leaders, religious figures, schola *etc.*, in effect forming a biographical reference source for most huma endeavours for the entire period. Entries are signed or initialled (v. has 122 contributors) and vary in length *e.g.* Emperor Charles V: 4 Martin Luther; 3½p.; Thomas Green, Vice Chancellor, Cambridg University, 1523-24,: 21 lines. Short or extended bibliographies a appended to entries as appropriate. *Class No:* 940.2"15"(092)

18th & 19th Centuries

[6796]

EMSLEY, C. Longman companion to Napoleonic Europe. Londor Longman, 1993. x,327p. maps, geneal. tables, index. £34. ISBN 0582072247.

Concise but authoritative guide to the Napoleonic age.
Class No: 940.2"17/18"

18th Century

Encyclopaedias

[6797]

The Blackwell companion to the Enlightenment. Yolton, J.W., ar *others, eds*. Oxford, Blackwell, 1991. x,581p. illus., bibliogs., inde. £60; $74. ISBN: 0631154035.

Over 100 academic contributors. Main focus is the period 1720-8 All facets of the period covered A-Z. Signed articles of varying lengt most with a select bibliography. An authoritative and comprehensi reference work. *Class No:* 940.2"17"(031)

19th Century

Bibliographies

[6798]

MEYER, J.A. An Annotated bibliography of the Napoleonic er recent publications, 1945-1985. Westport, Connecticut, Greenwoo Press, 1987. xvii,288p.index. $39.95; £45.00. (*Bibliographies a Indexes in World History*.)

1754 entries with indicative rather than critical annotations in chapters: 1. Research aids - 2. Printed primary sources - 3. Gener histories - 4. Napoleon - 5. Napoleon's family - 6. Personal lives France and the world - 8. The art of war on land - 9. Naval affairs 10. Supplement (1736-1754). Excludes journal articles. Intended as companion volume to O'Connelly's *Historical dictionary Napoleonic France 17990-1815*. 'A valuable current source for histo in the early 19th Century' (*Choice*, v.25,no.4, December 198 p.602). *Class No:* 940.2"18"(01)

World Wars 1 & 2

[6799]

British vessels lost at sea 1914-18 and 1939-45. Cambridge Patri Stephen, 1988. 304p. index. £14.95. ISBN: 1852601345.

Reprint of *Navy losses* and *Merchant shipping losses* (HMSO, 191 and *Ships of the Royal Navy: statement of losses during the Seco World War* and *British merchant vessels lost or damaged by ene action during Second World War* (HMSO, 1947). Under this title fi published in 2v., 1976-77.

Data: class, name, tonnage, date of completion, date of loss, h lost and where. *Class No:* 940.3+940.53

Bibliographies

[6800]

BIGHAM, R., *ed*. **Official histories** essays and bibliographies from around the world. Kansas State Univ. Press, 1970. xi, 644p. bibliogs. $12.00. ISBN: 0686208161.

Essays on American, British, Dutch, French, German, Indian, Italian, New Zealand, Norwegian, Polish, Russian and South African war histories and historical offices are all included.
Class No: 940.3+940.53(01)

World War 1

[6801]

FAYLE, C.E. Seaborne trade. London, John Murray, 3v. 1820-1924.
v.1 *The Cruiser period*. 1920. xvii, 442p. 2. *From the opening of the submarine campaign to the appointment of the shipping controller*. 1923. xv, 424p. 3. *The Period of unrestricted submarine warfare*. 1924. xx, 501p. Based on official documents. *Class No:* 940.3

[6802]

History of the Great War : based on official documents by direction of the Historical Section of The Committee of Imperial Defence. London, HMSO, 1922-1987.
Military Operations. East Africa August 1914 - September 1916 by C. Hordern. *Egypt and Palestine* (2v.). 1. *From the outbreak of war with Germany to June 1917* by G. Macmunn and C. Falls. 1928. xvii, 445p. 2. *From June 1917 to the end of war* by C. Falls. 1930. 395-748p. (*sic*). *France and Belgium* compiled by J.E. Edmonds (13v). *1914*. 1925. xxv, 548p. *1914* October to November, xxviii, 548p. *1915*. 1927. xliii, 433p. *1915*. 1928. xliv, 488p. *1916* 1932. xxxvi, 523p. *Appendices*. 1932. 232p. *1916 2nd July 1916 to the end of the Battle of the Somme* by W. Miles. 1938. xlv, 601p. *Maps and appendices*. 1935. x, 119p. *1917 The German retreat to the Hindenburg line and the Battle of Arras* by C. Falls. 1940. xxxix, 586p. *Appendices*. 1940. xi, 158p. V.2. *1917 The Battle of Cambrai* by W. Miles. 1948. xvi, 399p. *1918* v1. *The German offensive and its preliminaries*. 1935. xxx, 569p. *Appendices*. 1935. viii, 148p. 2.*The Continuation of the German offensive*. 1937. xxviii, 550p. 3. *May-July. The German offensives and the first Allied counter-offensive*. 1939. xxxii, 385p. 4. *26th September - 11th November. The Advance to victory*. 1947. xxix, 675p. 5. *September 26 - November 11. The Advance to victory*. 1947. xxix, 675p.
Italy, 1915-1919 by J. Edmonds and others. 1949. xxix, 450p. *Macedonia* (2v). by C. Falls. V.1. *From the outbreak of war to the Spring of 1917*. 1933. xvi, 409p. V.2. *From the Spring of 1917 to the end of the war*. 1935. xvi, 365p. *The Campaign in Mesopotamia 1914-1918* (4v). by F. Moberly. 1924-1927. vii, 402p.+Øiv, 581p.+Øiii, 460p.+Øiii, 447p. *Togoland and the Cameroons 1914-1916* by F. Moberly. 1931. xxv, 469p. *Gallipoli* (2v). by C.F. Aspinall-Oglander. V.1 *Inception of the campaign to May 1915*. 1929. xvii, 380p. 2. *May 1915 to the evacuation* 1932. xv, 517p. *Operations in Persia 1914-1919* by F.J. Moberly. 1987. xxii, 490p. ISBN 011290453x. *Transportation on the Western Front 1914-1918* by A.M. Henniker. 1937. xxxiv, 531p. *The Occupation of the Rhineland 1918-1939.* by J.E. Edmonds. 1987. xxv, 444p. ISBN 0112904548. *A history of the blockade of Germany and of the countries associated with her in the great war Austria-Hungary, Bulgaria, and Turkey 1914-1918* by A.C. Bell. xvi, 845p. *Class No:* 940.3

[6803]

HURD, A. The Merchant Navy. London, John Murray, 3v. 1921-1929. xiv, 473p.+Øviip., 464p.+Øix, 400p.
Based on official documents. *Class No:* 940.3

[6804]

RAFFIN, J. A Western Front companion 1914-1918 A-Z source to the battles, weapons, people, places, air combat. Stroud, Sutton Publishing. 224p. illus., maps. pbk. £10.99. ISBN: 075091520x.

A concise guide to every major battle; the armies; weapons and equipment; aircraft and airmen; decorations and military terms and a comprehensive gazetteer of all the important locations with outline descriptions of what can be seen now - memorials and monuments, commemoration plaques and war cemeteries. Details of local accommodation, transport, battlefield tours and maps are also given. *Class No:* 940.3

[6805]

Lloyd's war losses. The First World War Casualties to shipping through enemy causes 1914-1918. London, Lloyd's of London Press, 1990. viii,381 double pages, 383-404p. index. £75. ISBN: 1850443149.

A facsimile reprint of the original manuscript record held at the Guildhall Library, City of London.

Chronological listing of 6,927 British, allied and neutral merchant vessels destroyed, detained or captured by the Central Powers. Data: date, name of vessel, flag, tons gross, how sunk, voyage and cargo, summary (gross tonnage and how sunk). *Class No:* 940.3

[6806]

Naval operations. Corbett, J.S. *and* Newbolt, H. London, Longmans Green, 4v., 1920-1931.
V.1. To the Battle of the Falklands December 1914 by J.S. Corbett. 1920. xiv, 470p. V.2. by J.S. Corbett. 1921. xi, 382p. V.3 by J.S. Corbett. 1923. xiv, 417p. V.4 by H. Newbolt. 1928. xiii, 412p. V.5. by H. Newbolt. 1931. xx, 452p. All 5 vs. supplemented with independent boxes of maps. *Class No:* 940.3

[6807]

The War in the air: being the story of the part played in the Great War by the Royal Air Force. Raleigh, W., *ed.* *v.1 and* Jones, H.A., *ed.* *v.2-6.* Oxford, The Clarendon Press, 6v. and Appendices, 1922-1937.
V.4-5 have associated boxed maps. Appendix volume (1937) includes 46 documents *e.g.* List of squadrons Royal Flying Corps and Royal Air Force which served on the Western Front 1914-16 (p.130-141) and List of naval squadrons which served with the RFC and RAF ... (p.142-144). Based chiefly on the records of the Air Ministry. *Class No:* 940.3

Abbreviations & Symbols

[6808]

WILLIAMSON, H., *comp*. **A Dictionary of Great War abbreviations.** Harwich, Howard Williamson, 1999. (5 Hankin Avenue, Oakley Grange, Ramsey, Harwich, Essex, CI12 5HE). 228p. £7.50.

Includes 5000 terms given to British, Commonwealth, and German items used worldwide. *Class No:* 940.3(003)

Bibliographies

[6809]

ENSER, A.G.S. A Subject bibliography for the First World War. Books in English 1914-1987. 2nd ed. Aldershot, Hampshire, Gower, 1990. xi,412p. indexes. £45. ISBN: 0566056194.

First published by Andre Deutsch in 1979.

6800 entries drawn from standard bibliographical sources listed under 350 A-Z subject headings. Omits works of less than 40p., poetry, fiction, juvenile books, humour, Rolls of Honour, and publications of the War Graves Commission. Author, subject and titled books indexes. *Class No:* 940.3(01)

[6810]

FALLS, C. War books an annotated bibliography of the books about the Great War. Wyatt, R.J., *new introduction by*. London, Greenhill Books; Novato, California, Presidio Press, 1989. xx, 328p. index. £19.95. ISBN: 1853670405.

First published as *War books: a critical guide*. (Peter Davies, 1930).

Arranged in 7 categories :1. History; general - 2. History; formations and units - 3. History; foreign - 4. Reminiscences - 5. Reminiscences; foreign - 6. Fiction - 7. Fiction; foreign. This edition adds only 40 books. 'Will find an important place on the reference shelves of all students of Great War literature' *Antiquarian Book Monthly Review*, v.16, no.11, November 1989 p.430).
Class No: 940.3(01)

[6811]

SMITH, M.J. World War I in the air a bibliography and chronology. Metuchen, N.J., Scarecrow Press, 1977. xix,271p. illus., index. $27.50. ISBN: 0810809907.

2035 virtually unannotated items in a single A-Z by author or title sequence restricted to English language material. Chronology p.207-49. Appendix 1. List of WWI 'aces'. Subject index.
Class No: 940.3(01)

Encyclopaedias

[6812]

The European Powers and the first World War an encyclopedia. Tucker, S.C., *ed*. New York, Garland, 1996. 783p. maps, bibliogs., index. $95. ISBN: 0815303998.

94 contributors. 600 signed cross-referenced entries (350 biographical) cover major battles, weapon systems, tactics etc. Each entry is followed by further readings. 14 maps. 'It will provide a solid foundation of information for library reference sections' (*Booklist*, v.92,no.21, July 1996, p.1843-44). *Class No:* 940.3(031)

[6813]

HAYTHORNTHWAITE, P.J. The World War One sourcebook. London, Arms and Armour, 1992. 412p. illus., maps, tables, bibliog., index. £25. ISBN: 1854091026.

Encyclopedic work in 7 sections: 1. History of the war (*i.e.* a brief chronology) - 2. Weapons and tactics - 3. Review of all combatant states (nature of government and brief accounts of their armed forces) - 4. Biographies of important military and naval leaders - 5. Sources - 6. Miscellanea - 7. Glossary (of contemporary military terms and colloquialisms) p.387-402. *Class No:* 940.3(031)

Dictionaries

[6814]

HOGG, I.V. Historical dictionary of World War I. Lanham, MD., Scarecrow Press, 1998. xlii,267p. maps, bibliog. £47.50. (*Historical Dictionaries of War, Revolution and Civil Unrest, no.3.*) ISBN: 0810833727.

Chronology p.xvii-xx. Introduction (prewar alliances and crises, provocation and mobilisation) p.xxi-lii. Dictionary (campaigns and major battles, political leaders and military commanders, geographical locations, casualties etc.) p.1-198. Bibliography (introductory essay, thematic and campaign area sections A-Z). Each entry gives a basic overview of crucial and significant information. *Class No:* 940.3(038)

[6815]

POPE, S. *and* WHEAL, E-A. The Macmillan dictionary of the First World War. London, Macmillan, 1995. xxviii,561p. maps. £25. ISBN: 033361822x.

Published in US as *Dictionary of the First World War* (New York, St. Martin's Press, 1995. $40. ISBN 0312129319).

1,200 cross-referenced entries combining facts, narrative and analysis of campaigns, actions, forces engaged, theatres of war, fighters and commanders, tactics and strategies, politics and diplomacy etc. Chronology (day-by-day) p.523-34. 25 maps (p.537-51). 'Many reference works neglect operations in India, Asia and the Middle East, but the authors' coverage of these topics is impressive' (*Choice*, v.33,no.8, April 1996, p.1292). *Class No:* 940.3(038)

Maps & Atlases

[6816]

GILBERT, M. The Routledge atlas of the First World War. 3rd ed. London, Routledge, 1994. xxxiii,164p. maps, bibliog. £19.99. ISBN: 0415119324.

First published as *First World War atlas* (Weidenfeld and Nicolson, 1970).

'An introductory guide to as many aspects of the First World War as can reasonably be put in map form, naval, military, aerial, diplomatic, technical, economic, human'. 168 black and white outline maps (5 new to this edition). Bibliography p.xvii-xxvi. *Class No:* 940.3(084.3)

[6817]

LIVESEY, A. The Viking atlas of World War I. London, Viking, 1994. 192p. illus. (some col.), col.maps, bibliog., index. £20. ISBN: 0670853720.

Published in US as *The Historical atlas of World War I.* (New York, Holt, 1994. $45. 0805026517).

64 major campaigns and battles narrated and mapped in 5 annual illustrated sections 1914-1918 each beginning with a chronology. 100 x 4-colour maps. Bibliography p.190-91. Introduction outlines political and strategic backgrounds. *Class No:* 940.3(084.3)

Chronologies

[6818]

BURG, D.F. *and* PURCELL, L.E. Almanac of World War 1. Lexington, Univ. Press of Kentucky, 1998. xiv,320p. illus., maps, bibliog., index. ISBN: 0813120721.

Day-by-day diary of events in all areas of operations. Biographies p.243-84. Bibliography p.285-88. *Class No:* 940.3(090)

[6819]

GRAY, R. *and* ARGYLE, C. Chronicle of the First World War. New York and Oxford, Facts On File, 2v., 1990-91. £39.95 (set). ISBN: 0816025975, set.

1. *1914-1916.* 1990. 352p. maps, bibliog., tables, index. £21.95. ISBN 0816021392. Preliminary sections, 'Prelude to Sarajevo' p.8-9; 'Sarajevo to the Outbreak of War', p.9-10. Glossary (of abbreviations and First World War terminology) p.314-35. Bibliography p.309-13. 19 maps.

1917-1921. 1990. 383p. maps, bibliog., tables, index. £21.95. 0816025959. Supplementary material: Armistice Terms 11 Nov. 1918, p.264. Chronology: towards peace 1919-1921, p.265-78. The Peace process 1918-1923, p.279-80. Who's who in the First World War p.298-318. Glossary p.339-60. Bibliography p.334-38. 15 maps.

Definitive day-by-day outline of events, 28 July 1914 - 31 December 1916 and 1 January 1917 - 31 December 1918, presented in 9 vertical columns: 1. Western Front - 2. Eastern Front - 3. Southern Fronts - 4. Turkish Fronts - 5. African operations - 6. Sea war - 7. Air war - 8. International events - 9. Home Fronts. A minutely researched and definitive historical resource ... it will not easily be superseded' (*Reference Reviews*, v.6, no.1, 1992, p.47). *Class No:* 940.3(090)

[6820]

HERMAN, G. The Pivotal conflict a comprehensive chronology of the First World War, 1914-1919. Westport, Conn., Greenwood Press, 1992. xv,800p. ISBN: 0313227934.

Detailed chronology 28 June 1914 - 28 June 1919 in 3 subdivided columns: Military (Western, Eastern, Southern fronts and Colonial, Sea/Air); International-Diplomatic (Formal agreements, Conferences, Other contacts, Declarations); Domestic (Politics, Economic/Social, Cultural/Technological). Reproduced from typescript. *Class No:* 940.3(090)

Biographies

[6821]

The Cross of sacrifice. Jarvis, S.D. *and* Jarvis, D.B., *comps.* Reading Berks., Roberts Medals, 6v., 1993-.

1. *Officers who died in the service of British, Indian and East African regiments and corps 1914-1919.* 1993. 380p. £24.99. ISBN 1873058268.

2. *Officers who died of The Royal Navy, Royal Naval Reserve, Royal Naval Volunteer Reserve, Royal Marines, Royal Naval Air Service and Royal Air Force 1914-1919.* 1993. 165p. £24.99. 1873058314.

3. *Officers who died of British Commonwealth and Colonial Navies regiments and corps and air forces 1914-1919.* 1994. 171p. £24.99. 1873058365.

4. *Non-commissioned officers, men and women of the United Kingdom, Commonwealth and Empire who died in the services of the Royal Navy, Royal Marines, Royal Naval Air Service, Royal Flying Corps and the Royal Air Force 1914-21 including the Commonwealth navies and air forces.* 1996. 321p. £34.99. 1873058411.

5. *Officers, men and women of the Merchant Navy and Mercantile Fleet Auxiliary 1914-19.* £24.99. 187305412.

6. *Non-commissioned Officers and men of the Australian navy regiments and corps, and air force 1914-19.* £34.99. 1873058667.

Comprehensive A-Z listings of British officers and non commissioned officers who died in the service of their country identifying where they died and where commemorated. Data: name, rank, decorations, cause of death, date, unit, information from non official sources. All volumes include an appendix listing memorial and cemeteries mentioned in the text. *Class No:* 940.3(092)

[6822]

DAVIES, F. *and* MADDOCKS, G. Bloody red tabs general office casualities of the Great War 1914-1918 London, Leo Cooper, 1995. xii,225p. illus., bibliog. £17.95. ISBN: 0850524636.

Career and service biographical profiles of 78 British general officers killed and 146 wounded intended to nail the canard that they remained remote from the front line in the trench war on the Western Front. 4 chapters: 1. Chateaux Generals, the enduring myth and its origins - 2. Honourable exceptions - 3. Fatal casualties - 4. Wounded gassed and prisoners of war. Appendix 1. Cemetries where general officers are buried or commemorated (p.207-15) - 3. Bibliography (p.220-25) *Class No:* 940.3(092)

[6823]

FRANKS, N.L.R. Over the front a complete record of the fighter aces and units of the United States and French Air Services 1914-1918. London, Grub Street, 1992. 230p. illus., maps, tables, bibliog. £27.50. ISBN: 0948817542.

Biographies of American and French fighter pilots on the Western Front. Data: place and date of birth; previous military service; decorations; post-war career; citations received; full list of all claimed victims. Bibliography p.128. *Class No:* 940.3(092)

[6824]

HERWIG, H.H. *and* HEYMAN, N.M. Biographical dictionary of World War I. Westport, Connecticut, Greenwood Press, 1982. xiv, 624p. bibliog. £55.00. $67.95. ISBN: 0313213569.

Introduction (p.1-59) covers the origins of war, the Western front, the war in the East, the war at sea, the home front, and the Peace. Dictionary of biographical sketches p.61-365. Chronology p.367-376. Bibliography (p.395-406) lists works in 6 languages. Index. p.407-424. 'A model of its genre in both form and content and will likely become for all large libraries the standard reference work on the subject' (*RQ*, v.22, no.2, Winter 1982, p.196-197). *Class No:* 940.3(092)

[6825]

HOBSON, C., *comp.* Airman died in the Great War 1914-1918 The roll of honour of the British and Commonwealth Air Services of the First World War. Suffolk, J.B. Hayward, 1995. Distributed by Spink & Son (London). xxiv,466p. £45. ISBN: 0903754452.

Part 1: Biographical lists of 9,502 personnel (inc. 43 airwomen) (Royal Naval Air Service, Royal Flying Corps, Royal Air Force, Women's Royal Air Force, Australian Flying Corps) - 2. Chronological lists - 3. Unit lists. 10 Appendices (1918 order of battle statistics; aircraft types; ships; allocation of service numbers; casualty lists; cemeteries and memorials). 'This work is truly worthy of

....*(contd.)*

those Magnificent Men in their Flying Machines' (*Genealogists Magazine*, v.25,no.6, June 1996, p.239). Data: name, rank, unit, date of death and type of aircraft involved. *Class No:* 940.3(092)

[6826]
Officers died in the Great War 1914-19. Polstead, Suffolk, J.B. Hayward, 1988. 294p. £18.00. ISBN: 0903754401.

First published by HMSO 1919. Reprinted by J.L.R. Samson 1975. 34,000 casualties listed with rank, date of death, nature of casualty. Pt.1 Old and New Armies. Pt.2 Territorial Force. Pt.3 (new to this edition) Indian Army 1914-1920 listing a further 1400 officers killed in combat. Appendix 1. Regimental rolls - 2. List of deceased Territorial officers. *Class No:* 940.3(092)

[6827]
SHORES, C., *and others*. **Above the trenches** a complete record of the fighter aces and units of the British Empire Air Forces 1915-1920. London, Grub Street, 1990. 397p. maps, tables, ports. £35. ISBN: 0948817194.

Over 800 biographies of individual fighter scout pilots (place & date of birth, previous military service, and postwar career) and a full list of downed aircraft with date, time, type of aircraft flown, and source of information. Also brief squadron histories (p.30-43). Covers British, Canadian, Australian, New Zealand, South African and American fighter aces.

Above the trenches. Supplement. 1996. 62p.+12p. pl. ISBN 1898697396. £9.99. Includes new entrants plus amendments and additional information to pilots already recorded in the original text. *Class No:* 940.3(092)

[6828]
Soldiers died in the Great War 1914-19. Polstead, Suffolk, J.B. Hayward, 81v. 1988-89.

Originally published 1921.

Commemorates 635,000 soldiers listed A-Z by regiment or corps. Data: rank, place of birth, theatre of war, date and nature of casualty.

Soldiers died in the Great War 1914-19 on CD-ROM. Heathfield, E. Sussex, Naval & Military Press. £258. $330. System requirements: The *minimum* system requirement suggested to run this CD-ROM is a 486 PC, quad speed CD-ROM drive, 8MB of RAM, SVGA display (256 colours or more), 4Mb free hard disk space and Windows TM 3.1, Windows TM 95/98 or Windows TM NT. The *recommended* system is a Pentium PC with eight speed CD-ROM drive, 16Mb of RAM and a SVGA monitor. The CD-ROM can also be used on Apple Macintosh PowerPC's (200 MHz plus) and iMac running SoftWindows or Virtual PC.

Contains the complete set of all 81 volumes with software that allows searching of every element in each record. Searches can be executed for Regiments, Battalions, surnames, christian name(s), initial(s), born (town), born (country), enlisted (town), Enlisted (county), regimental number, rank, killed in action, died of wounds, died, theatre of war of death, date(s), supplementary notes.

Notes on presentation and installation, names, searches and results, responses and outputs, and output beyond the screen, can be found in R. Goring's review feature, *Family Tree Magazine*, v.10, no.1, November 1999, p.37-39. *Class No:* 940.3(092)

USA

Bibliographies

[6829]
The United States in the First World War: an encyclopedia. Venzon, A.C., *ed.* New York, Garland Press, 1995. 830p. bibliogs., maps. $95. ISBN: 0824070550.

200 US academic contributors. A-Z entries (mostly ranging from a column to a page in length) chronicle the biographical, economic, foreign relations, civil rights and women's, and military aspects of the US involvement in the First World War. Most articles include brief bibliographies. 6 maps. 'A solidly researched work recommended for public and academic libraries' (*Library Journal*, v.121,no.1, January 1996, p.92). *Class No:* 940.3(73)(01)

[6830]
WOODWARD, D.R. *and* MADDOX, R.F. **America and World War I** : a selected annotated bibliography of English-language sources. New York, Garland Publishing Inc., 1985. xvii, 368p. index. $49.00. (*Wars of the United States, 6.*)

2041 briefly annotated entries arranged in 8 sections: Reference works; Manuscripts, repositories and libraries; Origins and outbreak of war; Military aspects; Home front; Social and intellectual impact; Diplomacy; and The Peace Settlements. Chronology p.335-342. *Class No:* 940.3(73)(01)

Europe (From 1919)

Dictionaries

[6831]
STEVENSON, J., *ed.* **Macmillan dictionary of British and European history since 1914.** London, Macmillan, 1991. ix,437p. £35; $69.50. ISBN: 0333456254.

Published in US as *The Columbia Dictionary of European political history* (Columbia University Press, 1992. ISBN 0231078803).

1500 A-Z cross-referenced entries on the major events, individuals, topics, political groupings, and issues of the 20th century. Extra-European events are only recorded in terms of their significance to European affairs. Most entries have bibliographical references. *Class No:* 940.5(038)

[6832]
URWIN, D.W. **Dictionary of European history and politics 1945-1995.** London, Longman, 1996. v,423p. ISBN: 058225874x.

Includes the most significant events and issues, territories, national and international organisations, and the most prominent individuals of the post war period. *Class No:* 940.5(038)

World War 2

[6833]
BOOKMAN, J.T. *and* POWERS, S.T. **The March to Victory** a guide to World War II battles and battlefields from London to the Rhine. New York, Harper & Row, 1986. xi, 340p. illus., maps, ports, bibliog., index. $18.95. ISBN: 006015506x.

7 sections (The Battle of Britain and the bomber offensive; Normandy; The breakout from Normandy; Pursuit across France; Operation Market Garden (*i.e.* Arnhem); Battle of the Bulge; and Through the West Wall to the Rhine) describe the battlefields, the exploits of individuals and particular units, identify relics in the field, and locate museums and monuments. Appendix A. Museums (A-Z by country) p.312-320. Select bibliography p.321-326. Narrative and illustrations betray US origin. *Class No:* 940.53

[6834]
BROWN, D. **Warship losses of World War Two.** London, Arms And Armour, 1990. 256p. maps, indexes. ISBN: 0853688028.

A detailed record of over 1600 ships sunk or scuttled. Part 1. Chronology of warship losses (p.25-127) - 2. Summary of warship classes and particulars (A-Z by country); warship armament; theatres of war; statistical analysis. Indexes of principal battles and actions and ship losses p.238-9. *Class No:* 940.53

[6835]
CHORLEY, W.R. **Royal Air Force Bomber Commands losses or the Second World War.** Leicester, Midland Counties Publications, 4v., 192-96.

1. *Aircrew and crews lost during 1939-40.* 1992. 159p. £9.95. ISBN 0904597857.

2. *Aircraft and crew losses 1941.* 1993. 224p. £12.95. 0904597873.

3. *Aircraft and crew losses 1942.* 1993. 318p. £15.95. 090459789x.

4. *Aircraft and crew losses 1943.* 1996. 494p. £18.95. 0904597903.

Losses presented in date order. Data: unit, aircraft, type, circumstances of loss. Other information includes names of officers and men who evaded capture or escaped from prisoner of war camps. Meticulously researched. *Class No:* 940.53

[6836]
CRAVEN, W.F. *and* CATE, J.L., *eds.* **The Army Air Forces in World War II.** Chicago, The University of Chicago Press, 7v. 1948-1958. illus., maps.

1. *Plans and early operations from January 1939 to August 1942.* 1948. xxxi, 788p. 2. *Europe: Torch to Pointblank. August 1942 to December 1943.* 1949. xxi, 897p. 3. *Europe: Argument to V-E Day. January 1944 to May 1945.* 1951. xxxix, 948p. 4. *The Pacific: Guadalcanal to Saipan. August 1942 to July 1944.* 1950. xxxii, 825p. 5. *The Pacific. Matterhorn to Nagasaki. June 1944 to August 1945.* 1953. xxxviii, 878p. 6. *Men and planes.* 1955. xlvii, 808p. 7. *Services around the world* 1958. lii, 667p. Extensive chapter notes and analytical indexes. *Class No:* 940.53

[6837]
DETWILER, D.S., *ed.* **World War II German military studies** : a collection of 213 special reports on the Second World War prepared by Former officers of the Wehrmacht for the United States Army. New York, Garland Publishing Inc., 24v. 1980.

In 10 parts: Introduction and guide (Contents, German military historiography before 1945. Complete listing of German military studies held at the US National Archives in Washington). (v.1.); 2. European theater historical interrogations (v.2-3); 3. Command structure (v.4-6); 4. The OKW war diary (v.7-11); 5. The Western theater (v.12); 6. The Mediterranean theater (v.13-14); 7. The Eastern theater (v.15-19); 8. Diplomacy, strategy and military theory (v.20-21); 9. German military government (v.22); 10. Special topics (v.23). *Class No:* 940.53

[6838]

ELLIS, J. The World War II databook The essential facts and figures for all the combatants. London, Aurum Press, 1993. 315p. maps, tables, bibliog. £40. ISBN: 1854102540.

Detailed summary of facts and figures relating to the 26 main belligerent nations. 1. The war in maps (28) - 2. Command structure (8 tables) - 3. Orders of battle (combat divisions, campaigns) - 4. Table of organisation and equipment (A-Z by country) - 5. Strengths (military manpower, armour, airforces, navies) - 6. Casualties and losses - 7. Production - 8. Hardware. Bibliography p.311-15. 'Though it probably has less narrative drive than a Mayan telephone directory, it does at least attempt to present a fairly complete collection of the essential facts and figures' (*Preface*). *Class No:* 940.53

[6839]

FALCONER, J. The Bomber Command handbook. Stroud, Glos., Sutton Publishing, 1998. vii,280p. illus. bibliog., index. £25. ISBN: 0750918195.

11 chapters (*e.g.* 1. Organisation - 2. The men - 3. Aircraft ... 6. Tactics ... 9. Awards and medals - 10. The Commanders). Prologue: history of R.A.F. Bomber aircraft and overview of Bomber Command in 2nd World War. Epilogue reviews memorials in UK museums - 4. appendices: 1. War Diary 1939/45 - 2. Squadrons - 3. Airfields - 4. Orders of battle 1939, 1943, 1945. 'The index is adequate, the bibliography disappointing' but 'a well planned and ordered and commendably detailed handbook' (*Reference Reviews*, v.13, no.2, 1999, p.11-12). *Class No:* 940.53

[6840]

GREAT BRITAIN. Ministry of Defence. **Invasion Europe.** London, HM Stationery Office, 1994. Boxed set. £60. ISBN: 0117726591.

1. *The Campaign in North-West Europe June 1994-May 1945.* 87p. maps, tables, index. 2. *Invasion of the South of France. Operation 'Dragon' 15th August 1994.* 86p. 3. *Operation Neptune. Errata and Addenda.* 8p. sd. 4. *Invasion of the South of France/Campaign in NW Europe.* (map folder containing 16 plans). 5. *Operation Neptune* (map folder containing 14 plans). 'Written by naval officers who were versed in the art of naval operations, but were capable of synthesising the vast quantity of source material, they provide a combination of straightforward, readable narrative and close attention to detail which will be invaluable to researchers'. *Class No:* 940.53

[6841]

History of the Second World War. London, HMSO, 1949-. tables, charts, maps.

Certain volumes have been reprinted by Kraus-Thomson Organization Ltd.

United Kingdom. Military histories edited by Sir J.R.M. Butler. Grand strategy (6v.). Campaigns: The campaign in Norway - France and Flanders, 1939-40 - The Mediterranean and Middle East (6v.) - The war against Japan (5v.) - Victory in the West (2v.) - The defence of the United Kingdom - The war at sea (3v.) - The strategic air offensive against Germany 1939-1945 (4v.) - Civil affairs and military government (4v.).

United Kingdom. Civil series, edited by Sir K. Hancock. Introductory (4v., including Statistical digest of the war) - General series (16v.) - War production series (8v.).

United Kingdom. Medical series, Editor-in-chief, Sir A.S. McNalty Clinical volumes (3v.) - Fighting services: Royal Navy (2v.); Army (7v.); Royal Air Force (4v.) - Medical services in wars - Civilian services (4v.).

British Foreign Policy in the Second World War by L. Woodward (5v.).

British intelligence in the Second World War by F.H. Hinsley and others (5v. in 6, 1979-1990). V.1 ISBN 0116309334; v.2 0116309342; v.3 0116309350; v.4 *Security and counter-intelligence.* 1990. xii,408p. 0116309520; v.5 *Strategic deception.* 1990. 288p. 0116309547.

S.O.E. in France: an account of the work of the British Special Operations Executive in France 1940-1944 by M.R.D. Foot.

Sir J.R.M. Butler's 'The British Military Histories of the War of 1939-45' and Sir K. Hancock's 'British Civil Histories of the Second World War', p.511-14 and p.518-25, Robin Higham's *Official histories* (Kansas State University Library, 1970) offer interesting insights. *Class No:* 940.53

[6842]

Lloyd's war losses. The Second World War. London, Lloyd's, 2v., 1989-1991.

Facsimile reprint of the original typescript held at the Guildhall Library, City of London.

1. *British allied and neutral merchant vessels sunk or destroyed by war causes.* 1989. x,1053p. index. ISBN 1850442177. Chronological listing of 5411 vessels lost due to enemy action in 2 sequences: 1. Sunk or destroyed - 2. Captured. Data: date, name, tons gross, voyage, cargo, position, how sunk, personnel, remarks.

2. *Statistics showing monthly losses - Vessels posted at Lloyd's as missing or untraced - British allied and neutral merchant vessels seriously damaged by war causes - Naval craft lost - Vessels lost by mines or underwater explosions since the cessation of hostilities.* ...

....(contd.)

1991. ix,1925p. indexes. 1850444129.

'An enormous research tool for maritime libraries and those with significant collections devoted to the two world wars' (*Reference Reviews*, v.6, no.6, 1992, p.42). *Class No:* 940.53

[6843]

MASON, F.K. Battle over Britain a history of the German air assaults on Great Britain, 1917-18 and July-December 1940, and of the development of Britain's air defences between the World Wars. Bourne End, Bucks, Aston Publications, 1990-. 539p. illus., maps, tables, bibliog., index. £39.95. ISBN: 0946627150.

First published by McWhirter Twins Ltd. in 1969.

A monumental study of the Battle of Britain in 2 parts: 1. Preparation for battle (p.13-88) which includes an account of the German raids over Britain in the First World War and the history of the Royal Air Force and the Luftwaffe in the interwar years and 2. The Battle (p.89-398), the central narrative, which includes accurate day-by-day tables of Fighter Command and Luftwaffe losses. 13 Appendices: A. Fighter Command pilots and aircrew - B. Luftwaffe ditto - C. The fighting aircraft - D. Luftwaffe order of battle - E. British aircraft production and availability - F. Representative bomb damage - G. Victoria Cross and George Cross awards - H. German intelligence of the R.A.F. - I. Royal Navy losses in home waters 1 July-31 Oct 1940 - J. Bombing of British towns and cities - K. Ground defences - L. Air/Sea rescue services - M. Contemporary examination of German aircraft crashes. Bibliography p.524-6. Analytical index. *Class No:* 940.53

[6844]

MIDDLEBROOK, M. *and* **EVERITT, C. The Bomber Command war diaries** an operational reference book. Harmondsworth, Middlesex, Viking, 1985. 804p. illus., map, facsim., bibliog., index. ISBN: 0670801372.

Based on official Air Ministry documentation, and strictly limited to units flying under the operational control of RAF Bomber Command, these diaries record every single operation mounted. Pt.1 The Diaries are divided into 21 strategic, tactical or technical time-periods (*e.g.* 1. The Phoney War, 3 Sep 1939 to 8/9 April 1940 ... 21. Victory, 1 Jan 1945 - 7/8 May 1945). Data for each day/night: forces engaged, losses, actual damage, and descriptive notes. Pt.2 Operational Statistics (sorties and casualties) p.705-12. Pt.3 Squadrons' Second World War service, raids, sorties, losses, p.715-86. Sources and bibliography p.787-90. *Class No:* 940.53

[6845]

MITCHELL, W.H. *and* **SAWYER, L.A. The Empire ships** a record of British-built and acquired Merchant Ships during the Second World War. 2nd ed. London, Lloyd's of London Press, 1990. viii,504p. illus., bibliog., indexes. £38. ISBN: 1850442754.

First published 1965.

In 1939 a standard naming system was adopted by the Ministry of Shipping: all merchant ships built in Britain or acquired on government account would be given the prefix Empire to their name. These ships are listed here within general ship types and sublisted to every building yard. Data: yard number; gross tonnage; overall length, engine details; historical details (change of name and/or ownership); and launching/completion dates. Special section on Operation Overlord (Normandy landings). Bibliography p.487. *Class No:* 940.53

[6846]

Orders of battle: United Kingdom and colonial formations and units in the Second World War 1939-1945. Joslen, H.F., comp. London, HMSO, 2v. 1960. xii, 404p.+Ø, 405-628p. index.

9 Parts: 1. Divisions (with Appendix on composition and war establishment) - 2. Armoured, cavalry, tank, motor machine gun brigades - 3. Infantry brigades - 4. Parachute and air/landing brigades - 5. Colonial brigades - 6. Miscellaneous brigades - 7. GHQ, Army Group, Army and Corps troops - 8. British units ... in Indian formations - 9. British units in the colonies and Faroe Islands. Supplement: Formations and units engaged in The Battle of El Alamein 23 Oct. 1942 and The assault landings in Normandy 6-7 June 1944. Analytical index. No reference to the forces deployed by Commonwealth countries. Prepared for the Historical Section of the Cabinet Office. *Class No:* 940.53

[6847]

PLUMMER, R. The Ships that saved an army: a comprehensive record of the 1300 'little ships' of Dunkirk. Wellingborough, Northamptonshire, Patrick, Stephens, 1990. 240p. illus., bibliog., index. £17.99. ISBN: 1852602104.

Descriptive catalogue of all ships known to have been involved in Operation Dynamo, the evacuation of the British Expeditionary Force, and allied troops, from the beaches of Dunkirk, 26 May - 3rd June 1940. Bibliography p.235. *Class No:* 940.53

[6848]

OLMAR, N. *and* ALLEN, T.B. **America at war 1941-1945.** New York, Random, 1991. 940p. illus., maps, bibliog., index. $35. ISBN: 0394585305.

Encyclopedia in 2 parts: 1. Chronology 1 January 1941 - 19 December 1945 (48p.) - 2. A-Z War Guide consisting of 2400 cross-referenced entries (a few sentences to several pages) relating to political and military personalities, events, campaigns, battles, equipment, and social issues. 'Its currency and emphasis upon the American viewpoint make it a unique and useful work; (*Booklist*, v.88, no.10, 15 May 1992, p.980). *Class No:* 940.53

[6849]

READY, J.L. **World War Two nation by nation.** London, Arms and Armour Press, 1995. 344p. maps, bibliog., index. £18.99. ISBN: 1854092901.

How World War Two affected 170 nations A-Z. Data: useful information; status; government; population; ethnic make-up; religion; location; and narrative text. Glossary p.8. Bibliography p.324-29. *Class No:* 940.53

[6850]

SMITH, G. **The War at sea** Royal & Dominion Navy actions in World War 2. London, Ian Allan, 1989. 192p. illus., maps, bibliog., index. £19.95. ISBN: 0711017395.

Records details of all ship losses - when, where, and in what circumstances. Enemy ships sunk by R.N. and Dominion navies are also included. Background events and major warship losses indicated monthly in 4 war theatres: Atlantic; European waters, the Mediterranean, and Indian and Pacific Oceans. Maps p.180-7. Bibliography p.176. Analytical index. *Class No:* 940.53

[6851]

War with Japan. London, HMSO for Ministry of Defence (Navy), 6v. in 4, 1995. illus., bibliogs., indexes.

1. *Background to the war.* vii,154p. 2. *Defensive phase.* ix,287p. £60. ISBN 0117728187. 3. *The campaigns in the Solomons and New Guinea.* ix,297p. £50. 0117728195. 4. *The South-East Asia operations and Central Pacific advance.* viii,294p. 5. *The blockade of Japan.* xii,178p. £70. 0117728209. 6. *The advance to Japan.* x,341p. £55. 0117728217. Each volume has accompanying folder of maps. The full official version of the Allied campaign against Japan in the Second World War. *Class No:* 940.53

[6852]

WHITTAKER, L.B., *comp.* **Stand down:** orders of battle for the units of the Home Guard of the United Kingdom, November 1944. Newport, R. Westlake, 1990. 153p. ISBN: 1871167140.

Home guard units deployed in 7 formations: 1. General service battalions - 2. Sector organizations - 3. Anti-Aircraft regiments - 4. Light AA troops - 5. Transport columns - 6. Regimental affiliations - 7. HG. identity parade. Data: Battalion; Company; date mustered. *Class No:* 940.53

[6853]

YOUNG, J.M. **Britain's sea war:** a diary of ship losses 1939-1945. Wellingborough, Northamptonshire, Patrick Stephens, 1989. 288p. illus., index. £14.95. ISBN: 185260042x.

A day-by-day account of the Merchant Navy's losses 3 September 1939 to 14 September 1945 with details of each vessel's size, ownership, route and cargo, and loss of life. Index of ships p.246-88. *Class No:* 940.53

Bibliographies

[6854]

BAXTER, C. F. **The Normandy campaign 1944:** a selected bibliography. Westport, Conn., Greenwood Press, 1992. 184p. bibliog., index. £44.95. (*Bibliographies of Battles and Leaders, no.9.*) ISBN: 031328301x.

Following a brief historical background, part 2 lists 515 entries including bibliographies, guides, books, documents, dissertations, and journal articles, with an emphasis on English-language works. *Class No:* 940.53(01)

[6855]

BAXTER, C. F. **The War in North Africa 1940-1943** a selected bibliography. Westport, Conn., Greenwood Press, 1996. 119p. index. $49.95. (*Bibliographies of Battles and Leaders, no.16.*) ISBN: 0313291209.

1. Chronological historiography (including a chapter on important archive repositories) - 2. Bibliography of 504 mostly English-language items encompassing books, government publications, articles and dissertations mentioned in the historiography. *Class No:* 940.53(01)

[6856]

CONTROVICH, J.T. **The Central Pacific campaign,** 1943-1944: a bibliography. Westport, Conn., Meckler, 1990. 152p. index. $45.; £28. (*Meckler's Bibliographies of Battles and Leaders, no.2.*) ISBN: 0887363253.

1128 briefly annotated items arranged in 11 sub-divided sections: 1. Campaign narratives - 2. Reference works (atlases, bibliographies, research aids, newspaper indices) - 3. General histories - 4. Memoirs and biographies - 5/7. Gilbert Islands, Marshall Islands, Marianas operations - 8/11. Army Air Force, Army, Marine Corps and Naval unit histories. *Class No:* 940.53(01)

[6857]

ENSER, A.G.S. **A Subject bibliography of the Second World War** books in English 1939-1974. London, Deutsch, 1977. 592p. £29.50. ISBN: 0233967427.

Approximately 7000 unannotated entries Abyssinia-Zhukov. 'Omits, in general, works of less than 30 pages, poetry, fiction, juvenile literature, humour, cartoons and the publications of the War Graves Commission' (*Preface*). Cross-references. Author index; subject index (simply a list of the subject headings used). Decided British orientation; no annotations - in contrast to Bloomberg and Weber - unhelpful in selection. Compiled mainly from *British National Bibliography, Cumulative Book Index* and 'Whitaker' (*sic*). *Class No:* 940.53(01)

[6858]

—ENSER, A.G.S. A Subject bibliography of the Second World War and aftermath books in English 1975-1987. 2nd ed. Aldershot, Gower, 1990. 304p. index. £45. ISBN: 0566057360.

Supersedes *A subject bibliography of the Second World War: books in English 1975-1983* (1985). Incorporates more than 1500 new entries which are arranged under subject headings A-Z *e.g.* Aircraft carriers ... Hungary ... Stalin. *Class No:* 940.53(01)

[6859]

FUNK, A.L. **The Second World War** a select bibliography of books in English published since 1975. Claremont, Calif., Regina Books, 1985. xi, 210p. £22.30. ISBN: 0941690156.

2132 items closely classified in 5 sections: 1. General (*i.e.* bibliographies, research aids, collections of documents) - 2. International situation prior to the war - 3. The War - 4. Consequences of the war - 5. Nations at war. Prepared for the American Committee on the History of the Second World War on the occasion of the 16th International Congress of Historical Sciences, Stuttgart, August 1985. *Class No:* 940.53(01)

[6860]

PUFFER, R.L. **'The Day of infamy in print',** *Library Journal*, v.116, no.14, 1 September 1991, p.206-7.

New titles provoked by 50th anniversary of Pearl Harbour listed and briefly annotated in 5 categories: Pearl Harbour - Pacific battles and campaigns - Eyewitness accounts - Biographies - Reference. *Class No:* 940.53(01)

[6861]

SBREGA, J.J. **The War against Japan, 1941-1945** an annotated bibliography. New York, Garland, 1989. xxv,1050p. indexes. $95. (*Wars Of The United States, no.10.*) ISBN: 0842089405.

5259 annotated entries arranged in 6 main subdivided sections: 1. General works ('A. Reference works *i.e.* atlases; dictionaries; encyclopedias, almanacs, statistics; bibliographies; historiographies; chronologies; uniforms. B. General accounts. C. Documents and records. D. Military histories. E. East Asian histories) - 2. Diplomatic and political aspects - 3. Economic and legal - 4. Military aspects - 5. Religious - 6. Social and cultural. Appendix D: Chronology p.979-91. Author and subject indexes. 'Careful, often lengthy, occasionally brilliant annotations accompany each title ... thereby dramatically increasing the value of the work' (*Choice*, v.27,no.9, May 1990, p.1484). *Class No:* 940.53(01)

[6862]

SMITH, M.J. **World War II:** a bibliography of sources in English. Metuchen, New Jersey, Scarecrow Press, 4v. in 3, 1976. $72.50.

1. *The European theater.* 337p. $25.00. ISBN 0810808846. 2. *The Pacific theater.* 427p. $30.00. 0810809699. 3(1) *General works. Naval hardware and the All hands chronology (1941-1945).* 3(2) *Home fronts and special studies.* $40. 0810809702. 586p. 1976. Briefly annotated entries for books, monographs, periodical articles, government documents and dissertations, up to December 1973. Author and name index per volume and cumulated indexes in the final volume. 'Should be consulted widely in future' (*Library Journal*, 15 November 1976, p.2360).

V.3 Pt.1. *General works. Naval hardware ... and chronology* (1941-1945). *Class No:* 940.53(01)

[6863]

SMITH, M.J. **World War II at sea**: a bibliography of sources in English 1974-1989. Metuchen, N.J., Scarecrow Press, 1990. ix,304p. index. £24.35. ISBN: 0810822601.

3465 unannotated entries deployed in 4 heavily subdivided parts: 1. Reference/General works and Biography - 2. The European Theater (A. General Works, B-E. Regional and campaign subdivisions) - 3. The Pacific Theater (A. General Works; B. Japanese triumphant - C. Tide slowly turns - D. Island hopping - E. Allies triumphant) - 4. Home fronts and special studies. *Class No:* 940.53(01)

[6864]

SMITH, M.J. **World War II The European and Mediterranean theaters** : an annotated bibliography. New York, Garland Publishing Inc., 1984. xxiii, 450p. index. (*Wars of the United States*.) ISBN: 0824090136.

2827 entries arranged in 6 sections: Reference works; Special studies; The War in the air; The War on land; The War at sea; 16mm. documentary film guide, with extensive cross references. List of journals cited p.411-412. Preponderantly US sources. Favourably reviewed in *Choice*, v.22, no.6, February 1985, p.800. *Class No:* 940.53(01)

[6865]

WILSON, E. **Dangerous sky** a resource guide to the Battle of Britain. Westport, Conn., Greenwood Press, 1995. xxvii,128p. illus., maps, facsims., index. £58.50. (*Bibliographies of Battles and Leaders, no.14*.) ISBN: 0313282161. ISSN: 10567410.

Assembles the main sources published up to and including 1989 dealing with the battle. The guide provides information on how to conduct RAF research, and organises materials ranging from official documents through memoirs and biographies to secondary histories under major categories. Within each category, materials are cited in alphabetical order and short descriptive comments are provided. Access to material is augmented by an author index. *Class No:* 940.53(01)

Encyclopaedias

[6866]

CHANDLER, D. and COLLINS, J.L., eds. **The D-Day encyclopedia.** New York, Simon & Schuster; Oxford, Helicon, 1994. li,665p. illus., maps, bibliogs., index. £40. ISBN: 0091782651, UK.

141 academic and military contributors. 437 cross-referenced, profusely illustrated articles, all ending with short further readings, cover the period 6-18 June 1994. Guide to German military units p.605. Table of comparative ranks p.607. Glossary of acronyms, code names and special terms p.609-13. Analytical index. Authoritative and definitive reference work published to mark the 50th anniversary of Operation Overlord. *Class No:* 940.53(031)

[6867]

CHANT, C. **The Encyclopedia of code names of World War II.** London, Routledge & Kegan Paul, 1987. viii, 344p. £40.00. ISBN: 0710207182.

'Not so much as a complete listing ... but a summary of the more important strategic and operational codenames' (*Introduction*). Even so the 3000 entries arranged alphabetically include many given to some of the more obscure military operations. *Class No:* 940.53(031)

[6868]

DUNNIGAN, J.F. and NOFI, A.A. **The Pacific War encyclopedia.** New York, Facts On File, 2v., 1998. 704p. illus., maps, index. $125. ISBN: 0816034397.

Includes campaigns, ships and aircraft, equipment, weaponry, leading commanders, individual units, orders of battle, statistical data etc. A cyberlist includes relevant web sites and hyperlink resources on the Internet *Class No:* 940.53(031)

[6869]

The Oxford companion to the Second World War. Dear, I.C.B. and Foot, M.R.D., eds. Oxford Univ. Press, 1995. xxii,1343p. illus., maps (some col.), tables. ISBN: 0192141686.

Published in New York as *The Oxford companion to World War II* ISBN 0198662254.

144 contributors. Over 1,750 A-Z entries relating to grand strategy, politics, intelligence, weapons, battles, society, planning and tactics, individual actions, wartime leaders, and major country surveys. Includes German, Italian and Japanese perspectives M.R.D. Foot served as a wartime intelligence officer; I.C.B. Dear was a Royal Marine officer 1953-57. Published to mark the 50th anniversary of V.E. Day, May 1945. 'It will become the standard one-volume encyclopedia of World War II (*Choice*, v.33, no.4, December 1995, p.589). *Class No:* 940.53(031)

[6870]

PERRETT, B. *and* HOGG, I. **Encyclopedia of the Second World War.** Harlow, Essex, Longman, 1989. 447p. illus., maps, bibliog., index. £19.95. ISBN: 0582893283.

Over 3000 A-Z entries relating to battles and campaigns personalities, arms and equipment, codenames *etc*. Bibliography p.445-46. Over 400 contemporary photographs and 60 maps. The dustwrapper claim to be 'the ultimate reference book of the war verges on hyperbole. *Class No:* 940.53(031)

[6871]

The Simon and Schuster encyclopedia of World War II Parrish, T., ed. New York, Simon & Schuster, 1978. 767p. illus. maps, bibliog., index. softcover. ISBN: 0671242776.

47 contributors. 4000 A-Z cross referenced articles. Lengthie entries are signed. Glossary of terms and abbreviations p.703-07 Chronology: the war in synopsis p.708-15. Bibliography p.716-21 'For browsing general readers and war buffs; scholars will need mor depth' (*Choice*, v.'6, no.4, June 1979. p.512). *Class No:* 940.53(031

[6872]

ZABECKI, D.T. **World War II in Europe: an encyclopedia.** New York, Garland, 2v., 1999. 1920p. illus., maps, tables, bibliogs. indexes. $195. (*Military History of the United States Series, no.6.* ISBN: 0824070291.

1,400 signed entries, of varying length, on the war in Europe from US perspective, arranged A-Z within 6 major sections: 1. Social an political issues and events - 2. Leaders and individuals - 3. Units an organizations - 4. Weapons and equipment - 5. Strategy, tactics an operational techniques - 6. Battles, campaigns, and operations. Entrie end with short reading lists. Appendices: chronology, code names, an bibliography. Index of military units and a general index. 'A invaluable study of the Western half of the war and a worthy additio to reference collections in large public and academic libraries' (*Booklist*, v.95, no.21, July 1999, p.1975). *Class No:* 940.53(031)

Dictionaries

[6873]

WELLS, A.S. **The Historical dictionary of World War II: The Wa against Japan.** Lanham, MD., Scarecrow Press, 1999. 472p. bibliog. index. $75. ISBN: 0810836386.

586 entries relating to people, places, battles, weapons, logistics intelligence, propaganda etc. Ranges from the Japanese invasion o Manchuria in 1931 to the Chinese Civil Wars of the late 1940s 'Entries are necessarily concise, but the dictionary is abl complemented by a superb Pacific war overview essay, a chronology two appendixes, and an expansive bibliography ... from well-know facts to the obscure, this book provides a wealth of information making it a useful resource for research and reference work' (*Librar Journal*, v.124, no.19, 15 November 1999, p.62). *Class No:* 940.53(038)

[6874]

WHEAL, E-A., *and others*. **A Dictionary of the Second World War** London, Grafton Books, 1989. xv, 514p.+24p. of plates, illus., maps ports. £25.00. ISBN: 0246133910.

Analytical entries of the men and machines, battles and campaigns politics, events, the plans and accidents of global warfare in a singl sequence (Aachen-Zuiho). 7 Appendices, each a campaig chronology, p.524-41. Basically an Anglo-Saxon interpretation o events justified on the grounds that only Great Britain and the Unite States fought a world war. *Class No:* 940.53(038)

Quotations

[6875]

LANGER, H.J., *comp*. **World War II an encyclopedia of quotation** London, Fitzroy Dearborn, 1999. xv,449p. bibliog., indexes. £35 ISBN: 1579581587.

1554 quotations for 300+ individuals on various aspects of Worl War II arranged in 18 chapters (*e.g.* 1. War leaders - 2. Militar officers ... 5. Warriors ... 10. Historians and biographers ... 17. Wa lexicon). Appendix: quotations by category p.425-30. Bibliography p.431-38. 'Hauls in a kaleidoscopic collection of material, rangin from apocrypha, editorial cartoons, and war humour, to more tragi and horrifying entries' (*Reference Reviews*, vol.14, no.6, 1999, p.45 46). *Class No:* 940.53(082.2)

Maps & Atlases

[6876]

BADSEY, S., *ed*. **The Hutchinson atlas of World War II battle plan** before and after. Helicon, Oxford, 2000. 288p. maps. £27.50. ISBN 1859863191.

Divided into 7 groups of 3: Armoured blitzkriegs - Amphibiou landings - Slogging matches - Air Power - War at sea - Airborn Assaults - City Battles. 6,000-word introduction by the Editor - givin a strategic overview of the whole of the war, and placing the individua

....(contd.)

battles in context; in-depth essays on 21 battles, contrasting battle plans with their actual outcome; and 42 specially commissioned battle plans, as well as locator maps for every battle. *Class No:* 940.53(084.3)

[6877]

MAN, J. **The Penguin atlas of D-Day and the Normandy campaign.** London, Penguin Books, 1994. 143p. illus. (some col.), col. maps, bibliog., index. £17. ISBN: 014023859x.

62 Map features in 7 sections: 12. Overlord - 2. Assault from the air - 3. Walk-over at Utah, bloodshed at Omaha - 4. Gold, Juno and Sword - 5. Deadlock at Caen - 6. Breakthrough, break-out - 7. Falaise. Appendix 1. Military cemetries and monuments - 2. Allied and German Command Hierarchies. Chronology p.138-39. Codenames p.139. Bibliography and picture credits p.143.
Class No: 940.53(084.3)

[6878]

MESSENGER, C. **World War Two Chronological atlas** when, where, how and why. London, Bloomsbury; New York, Macmillan, 1989. 255p. £19.95. $32.50. ISBN: 0747502293, UK; 0025843915, US.

US title: *The chronological atlas of World War Two.*

13 chronological sections: 1. The legacy of the First World War ... 13. The Legacy (1945 to the present). Each double-page describes and maps a particular phase of the conflict in a continuous diary form. Over 200 col. maps. 'An excellent reference work for those who want a vivid and immediate grasp of the war' (*Booklist,* v.86, no.5, 1 November 1989, p.522). *Class No:* 940.53(084.3)

[6879]

PIMLOTT, J. **The Viking atlas of World War II.** London, Viking, 1995. 224p. col.illus., col.maps, bibliog., index. £20. ISBN: 0670853739.

Published in US as *The Historical Atlas of World War II* (New York, Henry Holt, 1995, 1995. $45. 0805039295).

85 map features grouped in 5 sections: The inter-war period - 2. The Axis ascendent - 3. Turning of the tide - 4. Allied offensives - 5. The Allies victorious. Chronology p.14-17. Bibliography p.224. Detailed chapter introductions ensure continuity. *Class No:* 940.53(084.3)

[6880]

PITT, B. *and* PITT, F. **Chronological atlas of World War II.** London, Macmillan, 1989. xi,178p. col. maps, bibliog., index.

Published in US by Summit Books as *The Month-by-month atlas of World War II.*

Double-page map and text spreads for each month of the war showing areas held by the original aggressors, Germany and Japan, with larger-scale detailed maps of current areas of conflict. Bibliography p.167. 'Both *The Times Atlas of the Second World War* and C. Messenger's *Chronological Atlas of World War Two* are preferable' (*Choice,* v.27, no.9, May 1990, p.1484).
Class No: 940.53(084.3)

[6881]

SMURTHWAITE, D. **The Pacific War atlas 1941-1945.** London, HMSO for the National Army Museum, 1996. 144p. illus. (some col.), maps. £22.50. ISBN: 0112905498.

Published in US by Facts On File (NY). ISBN 0876032866.

75 colour maps and accompanying text illustrate the ebb and flow of the war in the Pacific: battles, fleet movements, military and naval campaigns of the warring powers. *Class No:* 940.53(084.3)

[6882]

The Times atlas of the Second World War. Keegan, J., *ed.* London, Times Books, 1989. 254p. col. illus., col. maps, col. diagrs., bibliog., index. £27.50. ISBN: 0723003173.

13 contributors. 90 double-page geographic, thematic and chronological features (maps, text, illustrations) delineating every theatre of war. Military formations and units and key to map symbols p.13. Chronology (6 colour coded geographic bands) p.14-27. Bibliography p.208. Glossary p.209-19. 450 full-colour maps and major battle reconstructions. 150 photographic illustrations and diagrams. 'Conceived as a means of conveying to its users both the totality and complexity of the Second World War ... its coverage is not exclusively military' (*Introduction*). *Class No:* 940.53(084.3)

Chronologies

[6883]

Chronicle of the Second World War. Mercer, D., *ed.* London, Longman/Chronicle Communications, 1992. 791p. illus. (some col.), maps, diagrs., index. £29.95. ISBN: 0582075734.

Chronicle of events from the German invasion of Poland, 1 Sep 1939 to the Japanese surrender 2 Sep 1945 reported as if in a contemporary newspaper. On average 2 pages for each week of the war. Glossary p.670-1. 175 maps. Analytical index. 'Compares very favourably with other popular encyclopedic and chronological works of the 1939-45 war' (*Reference Reviews,* v.5, no.3, 1991, p.39-40).
Class No: 940.53(090)

[6884]

Chronology and index of the Second World War 1938-1945. Royal Institute of International Affairs, *comp.* Westport, Connecticut and London, Meckler, 1990. 448p. index. £50.00. ISBN: 088736568x.

First published 1947 as *Chronology of the Second World War.* Under current title published Reading, Newspaper Archive Developments 1975.

Period: 29 September 1938-24 October 1945. A day to day account of events. Analytical index. 'Of all the works published on the war, none has proved to be more useful' (*Preface to 1975 ed.*).
Class No: 940.53(090)

[6885]

GORALSKI, R. **World War II almanac 1931-1945** a political and military record. New York, Putnam, London, Hamish Hamilton, 1981. xii, 486p. illus., maps, bibliog. £9.95. $17.95. ISBN: 0399125485, US; 0241105730, UK.

A day by day chronology of military, political and diplomatic events beginning with the Japanese invasion of Manchuria in 1931 and ending with their surrender in September 1945. Men and arms (p.421-455) tabulates comparative ranks of all the major belligerents, their peak strengths, casualities, shipping losses, weaponry, military formations etc. Bibliography p.456-466. 'A fine reference source' (*Choice,* v. no. October 1981, p.220). *Class No:* 940.53(090)

[6886]

HUTCHISON, K.D. **World War II in the North Pacific** chronology and factbook. Westport, Conn., Greenwood Press, 1994. xviii,288p. illus., maps, bibliog., index. ISBN: 0313291306.

Detailed facts about the American, Japanese and Russian war in the Aleutian and Kurile Islands and adjacent areas. Bibliography p.275-79. *Class No:* 940.53(090)

[6887]

ROHWER, J. *and* HÜMMELCHEN, G. **Chronology of the war at sea 1939-1945** v.1 1939-1942: v.2 1943-1945. 2nd ed. London, Greenhill Books, 1992. xv, 288+Ø, 289-650p. illus. index. ISBN: 1853671177.

First published as *Chronik des Seekrieges 1939-1945* by Gerhard Stelling A.G. English edition substantially amplified and revised the orginal German language text.

A detailed chronology of World War II at sea. For a given date, subdivision into North Atlantic, South Atlantic, Baltic Sea, for each theatre of operations. Includes naval actions, fleet movements, convoys, naval air actions, and periodical assessments of overall situation. Preface (p.vii-xi) gives detail of German, British, Commonwealth, United States, Italy, USSR, Japanese and French documentary source material. Abbreviations and glossary p.xiii-xiv. Indexes of naval actions, convoys, personalities and ships' names. *Class No:* 940.53(090)

[6888]

SOMERVILLE, D. **World War II day by day.** Leicester, Magna Books, 1989. 320p. illus., maps, index. £22.95. ISBN: 1854220810.

Lavishly illustrated chronolgy and record of events. Begins June 1919 and ends June 1950 to cover events leading up to the war and the immediate post-war world. 400 illus. 50 maps. *Class No:* 940.53(090)

Biographies

[6889]

ANCELL, R.M. **The Biographical dictionary of World War II generals and flag officers: the U.S. Armed Forces.** Westport, Conn., Greenwood Press, 1996. 706p. bibliog., index. $95. ISBN: 0313295468.

2,400 A-Z biographical sketches in 6 chapters: Army, Army Air Force, National Guard, Navy, Marine Corps, Coast Guard. Data: place & date of birth; education; military career; decorations and awards; date and place of death (if applicable). *Class No:* 940.53(092)

[6890]

BOATNER, M.M. **The Biographical dictionary of World War II.** Presido, 1996. 733p. maps, bibliog. $50. ISBN: 0891415483.

1000+ A-Z cross-referenced entries for outstanding personalities ranging from 250 to 1000 words in length. Data: nationality, rank or position, dates of birth and death, biography, publications. 70-page glossary. 18-page bibliography. *Class No:* 940.53(092)

[6891]

KEEGAN, J. **Who's who in World War II.** New ed. London, Routledge, 1995. 182p. pbk. £10.99. ISBN: 0415118891.

First published Bison Books (1978).

300+ entries for major personalities of every country in every sphere of responsibility. *Class No:* 940.53(092)

[6892]

WYNN, K.G. **Men of the Battle of Britain** a who was who of the pilots and aircrew, British, Commonwealth and Allied, who flew with Royal Air Force Fighter Command July 10 to October 31 1940. Norwich, Gliddon Books, 1989. x,470p. ports., bibliog. £35. ISBN: 0947893156.

Short service biographies of 2,927 men awarded the Battle of Britain clasp to the 1939-1945 Star having flown at least one authorized operational sortie during the period stated. Data: Service number; rank; category; nationality; squadron(s). Squadron rolls p.453-66. Bibliography p.467-9. Glossary p.470. *Class No: 940.53(092)*

Archives

[6893]

CANTWELL, J.D. **The Second World War a guide to documents in the Public Record Office.** 2nd ed. London, HMSO, 1992. 233p. £10.95. (*Public Record Office Handbooks, no.15.*) ISBN: 011440254x.

First published 1972.

Revised edition of a guide issued to accompany the release of 2WW documents. 62 A-Z sections relating to government ministries or departments, indicating offices held by leading civil and military figures, describing the committee structure, and listing their records by registered file numbers. *Class No: 940.53(093.20)*

USA

[6894]

Federal records of World War II. Detroit, Gale Research Co., 2v., 1982. 2134p. $75.00. ISBN: 081030998x.

First published by US National Archives (1950).

V.1 *Civilian agencies* covers activities and records of over 100 agencies. V.2 *Military agencies* is a guide to the records of the departments of Interallied and Interservice Military Agencies, the War Department and the Army, the Naval Establishment and the Theatres of Operations. Name, acronym and analytical indexes. Official guide. *Class No: 940.53(093.20)(73)*

Europe

[6895]

HAESTRUP, J. **European resistance movements 1939-1945** a complete history. Westport, Connecticut and London, Meckler Books, 1981. 566p., bibliog., index. $65. ISBN: 0930466365.

Comprehensive account of the development of resistance movements in Europe 1939-1945 in 7 chapters: 1. Survey of problems - 2. Emergence and background - 3. Forms of civil disobedience - 4. Intelligence service - 5. The Home Front and fronts abroad - 6. Paramilitary forms of action - 7. Conclusion. *Class No: 940.53(4)*

Germany

[6896]

Germany and the Second World War. Oxford, Clarendon Press, 10v., 1990-.

First published as *Das Deutsche Reich und der Zweit Weltkrieg* (Stuttgart, Deutsche Verlags-Anstalt, 10v., 1979-).

1. Deist, W. and others. *The Build-up of German aggression.* 1990. xxviii,799p. tables, maps on endpapers, bibliog., index. £80. ISBN 019822866x. Glossary of German terms p.xxvii-xxviii. Bibliography p.733-88 (for the English edition has been supplemented by works published 1979-86). 2. Maier, K.A. and others *Germany's initial conquests in Europe,* 1991. xiv,444p. illus., bibliog., index. £65. 0198228856. Bibliography p.421-39. 3. Schreiber, G. and others. *The Mediterranean, South-East Europe and North Africa 1939-1941.* 820p. 39 maps. 1995. £85. 0198228848. 4., Boog, H. and others. *The Attack on the Soviet Union.* 1998. 1400p. 11 maps. £95. 0198228864. An intensively researched and well-documented cooperative but not necessary unanimous history by the staff of the Militärgeschictliches Forschungsamt examining the Second World War from the German point of view. 'This truly monumental volume is a triumph of research and scholarship ... a massive compilation of sources and indispensable map supplement' (*English Historical Review,* v.115, no.460, February 2000, p.166-68). *Class No: 940.53(430)*

Russia

Bibliographies

[6897]

PARRISH, M. **The USSR in World War II** : an annotated bibliography of books published in the Soviet Union, 1945-1975. With an addenda for the years 1975-1980. New York, Garland Publishing Inc., 2v., 1981. xxi, 308p.+vii, 309-906p. ISBN: 0824094859.

1521 entries in 5 parts: The military campaigns; the Soviet armed forces; Geographic areas of the USSR during the war; Subject divisions; Economic divisions. 'An attempt to organize, classify, and

....(contd.)

annotate the Soviet books, pamphlets, theses, pictorial collections etc., written since 1945 about the Great Patriotic War ... Not only books published in major cities but also from numerous provincial presses as well as dissertations are included' (*Preface*). Coverage does not extend from 1941 because of the disruption of publishing in the confusion of war and the unavailability of all but a fraction of wartime publications. 'Scholars interested in in-depth research will have to reach beyond this work' (*RQ*, v.21, no.1, Fall 1981, p.105). *Class No: 940.53(47)(01)*

Asia

[6898]

War in Asia and the Pacific. Detwiler, D.S. New York, Garland Publishing Inc., 15v. 1980.

1. *Introduction and guide.* Chapter 7 is Chronology of the Pacific War from Japanese point of view. 2. *Political background of the war.* 3. *Command, administration, and special operations.* 4-5. *The Naval armament program and naval operations.* 6-7. *The Southern Area.* 8-9. *China, Manchuria, and Korea.* 10-11. *Japan and the Soviet Union* 12. *Defense of the Homeland and end of the war.* 13-15. *The Sino-Japanese and Chinese civil wars.* Based on surviving documentation, supplemented by personal records, of investigation undertaken by the Japanese government after the surrender in 1945, translated into English, and now on file in the Department of the Army's Center of Military History in Washington. *Class No: 940.53(5)*

USA

[6899]

GREENFIELD, K.R., *ed.* **United States Army in World War 2.** Washington, Historical Division, Department of The Army, 58v., 1947-77.

Published in 11 series viz 1. The War Department - 2. Army ground forces- 3. Army service forces - 4. Western Hemisphere - 5. War in the Pacific - 6. China, Burma, India theater - 7. European theater of operations - 8. Mediterranean theater - 9. Middle East theater - 10. Technical services - 11. Special studies. Scholarly and extensive bibliographies, glossaries of abbreviations and code names, and analytical indexes enhance the reference value of this mammoth series.

K.R. Greenfield's 'Scholarship and the U.S. Army in World War II' p.551-552 and S. Conn's 'The Army's World War II history and related publications', p.553-564, Robin Higham's *Official histories* (Kansas State University Library, 1970) contain much useful information not easily available elsewhere. *Class No: 940.53(73)*

Commonwealth

[6900]

BUTLER, D. *and* LOW, D.A., *eds.* **Sovereigns and surrogates** constitutional Heads of State in the Commonwealth. London, Macmillan, 1991. 365p. bibliog., index. (*Cambridge Commonwealth Series.*) ISBN: 0333524438.

11 contributors. Primarily focuses on the constitutional powers and functions of the Governor-Generals or Presidents in 'those independent countries in the Commonwealth which have in large measure preserved the Westminster form of government, with executive power exercised by a Prime Minister and Cabinet answerable to the legislature, but with a Governor-General or President broadly carrying out the ceremonial and constitutional functions expected of the British sovereign'. Appendix 1. Constitutional Heads in the Commonwealth 1945-1990 p.331-54. Bibliography p.355-7. *Class No: 941-44*

[6901]

The Cambridge history of the British Empire. Cambridge, Cambridge Univ. Press, 8v., 1929-1988.

1: *The old Empire, from the beginnings to 1783.* 1929. 2: *Growth of the new Empire, 1783-1870.* 1940. 3: *The Empire-Commonwealth, 1870-1919;* edited by E.A. Benians. 1959. 4: *British India, 1497-1858;* edited by H.H. Dodwell. 1929. 5: *Indian Empire, 1858-1918, with chapters on the development of administration, 1818-1858;* edited by H.H. Dodwell, 1932. 6: *Canada and Newfoundland.* 1930. 7: pt.1: *Australia;* edited by E. Scott. Reissued 1988. xxv,759p. £35.00. ISBN 0521356210. 7: pt.2: *New Zealand* 1933. 8: *South Africa, Rhodesia and the Protectorates.* 2nd ed. 1963. Each volume carries some 20-30 chapters by specialists. The lengthy, valuable bibliography appended to each volume is divided into pt.1, Collections of MSS in public and private archives and official papers and publications, and pt.2, Other works. *Class No: 941-44*

[6902]

OXEY, M.P. The Commonwealth Secretariat and the contemporary Commonwealth. Basingstoke, Hampshire, Macmillan, 1989. ix,172p. bibliog., index. £33. (*Cambridge Commonwealth series*.) ISBN: 0333457285.

A 'down-to-earth' description of the activities conducted by the Secretariat itself or under its auspices: 1. The shape and character of the modern Commonwealth - 2. The Secretariat - 3. The office of Commonwealth Secretary-General - 4. Secretariat at work - 5. Cooperation in social and professional fields - 6. International affairs: the political dimensions - 7. Southern African problems - 8. Assessment. Appendix A: Commonwealth membership 1988. Chapter notes and references p.152-65. *Class No: 941-44*

[6903]

DROWER, G. Britain's dependent territories a fistful of islands. Aldershot, Dartmouth, 1992. 276p. maps, tables, bibliog., index. £32.50. ISBN: 1885212420.

Britain still retains the world's largest overseas empire, consisting mainly of islands in the Atlantic and Caribbean. This is an overview of recent political history in the various territories and their views regarding the imperial links. Bibliography p.241-71. 7 maps. *Class No: 941-44*

[6904]

McINTYRE, W.D. The Significance of the Commonwealth 1965-90. London, Macmillan, 1990. ix,305p. tables, index. £35. ISBN: 0333553160.

Review of the Commonwealth's structural and functional development and the main issues confronting it since the Secretariat was established in 1964. Not confined to political and constitutional issues, it extends to popular aspects of its activities like youth programmes, arts festivals and sport. Chapter notes p.270-91. *Class No: 941-44*

[6905]

The Oxford history of the British Empire. Oxford Univ. Press, 5v., 1998-99. maps, tables, bibliogs., indexes. £30 each volume.

1. *The Origins of Empire: British overseas enterprise to the close of the seventeenth century* ed. by N. Canny. 1998. xx,533p. ISBN 0198205627.
2. *The Eighteenth century* ed. by P.J. Marshall. 1998. xxi,639p. 0198205635.
3. *The Nineteenth century* ed. by A. Porter. 1999. xxii,774p. 0198205051.
4. *The Twentieth century* ed. by J.M. Brown and W.R. Louis. 1999. xxvi,773p. 0198205643. 31 chaps., each with bibliography, by independent hands. Chronology p.712-39. 22 maps.
5. *Historiography* ed. by R.W. Winks. 1999. xv,730p. 0198205664. 42 contributors. Series of historiographical essays (*e.g.* 2. First British Empire ... 18. Exploration and Empire ... 41. The Future of imperial history).

This major new assessment of the Empire takes full advantage of recent scholarship and the progressive opening of historical records. It offers specialist studies on every part of the world drawn into the imperial spheres of interest. 'A treasure trove of information, research and scholarship' (*Literary Review*, no.200, June 1999, p.41-42). *Class No: 941-44*

[6906]

STEWART, J. The British Empire: an encyclopedia of the Crown's holdings, 1493 through 1995. Jefferson, NC., McFarland, 1996. 384p. index. $65. ISBN: 078640177x.

Main text comprises A-Z sequence of individual territories, giving their geographical locations, descriptions, brief histories, and detailed listings of their native and administrative rulers and their years of office. *Class No: 941-44*

Bibliographies

[6907]

CATTERALL, P. 'The Empire, the Commonwealth and the Mandated Territories' *British history 1945-1987: an annotated bibliography* (*q.v.*).

'External relations', chapter 3 of *British history 1945-1987: an annotated bibliography* (1980) includes 1080 items listed in the following sub-divided sections: B. The Empire ... General - C. Empire and Commonwealth in Asia - D. Middle East - E. Sub-Saharan Africa - F. Caribbean - G. Australasia and the Pacific - H. Canada - I. Gibraltar and Malta - J. Atlantic and Antarctic (p.102-95). The aim of these sections 'has been to provide an extensive guide to the nature of the literature on the demission of power, both generally and area by area, and, where appropriate, on the continuation of Commonwealth relations' (*Preface*). *Class No: 941-44(01)*

[6908]

GIPSON, L.H. A Bibliographical guide to the history of the British Empire 1784-1776. New York, Knopf, 1969. 478p. (*The British Empire before the American Revolution, v.14*.)

Covers the constitutional, political, economic and some social aspects of British imperialism. Some entries are annotated; periodical articles are included. Overall arrangement is by geographical area, followed by bibliographical tools, printed source materials, secondary work, maps and cartographical aids. Index of authors and selected topics. More up-to-date and much more comprehensive than the bibliography in the *Cambridge history of the British Empire*, 'Probably the most ample bibliography on the topic at the present time' (*College and Research Libraries*, v.30, July 1969, p.379). V.1-13 comprise an encyclopaedic survey of the Empire during the period. *Class No: 941-44(01)*

[6909]

PALMEGIANO, E. The British Empire in the Victorian press 1832-1867. New York, Garland Publishing, 1986. 256p. indexes. $40.00. (*Themes in European Expansion*.) ISBN: 0824098021.

1. List of magazines published in London that dealt exclusively or extensively with imperial concerns - 2. Inventory of over 2000 articles from 50 general journals. *Class No: 941-44(01)*

Micromaterials

[6910]

Rhodes House Library Subject Catalogue. Cambridge and Alexandria, New York, Chadwyck-Healey, 1989. 105x148mm, 49 frame silver halide microfiche at a 24x reduction. Approx 540 microfiche with 132p. printed guide to the subject headings. £1600.00.

Entries for about 175,000 printed works 1760-1988, with references to archive material, arranged under 24 regional or country headings sub-divided where appropriate. A detailed subject arrangement (fully outlined in the printed guide) plus cross-references facilitate immediate access. A major reference guide and research tool for the study of Africa south of the Sahara, The Commonwealth (excluding South Asia), and the United States in history, politics, and government. Rhodes House Library, Oxford, is a dependent library of the Bodleian. *Class No: 941-44(01)(003.5)*

Dictionaries

[6911]

PALMER, A. Dictionary of the British Empire and Commonwealth. London, John Murray, 1996. xviii,395p. maps., bibliog., index. £25. ISBN: 0719556503.

650 A-Z entries relating to 'the political, cultural, religious, military and economic events that have shaped the transformation of a Victorian Empire into a world community of 51 sovereign states and 26 remaining dependencies'. 'Suffers from criteria of selection and length of treatment which are often baffingly perverse' (*Sunday Telegraph*, 17 March 1996., p.13). *Class No: 941-44(038)*

Maps & Atlases

[6912]

Atlas of the British Empire. Bayly, C.H., *ed*. London, Hamlyn, 1989. 256p. illus. (mostly col.), col.maps, index. £25.00. ISBN: 0600568318.

13 academic contributors. 41 chapters arranged in 4 sections: 1. Voyages and plantations 1500-1763 - 2. Age of free enterprise 1763-1860 - 3. Heydey of Empire 1860-1914 - 4. The World Wars 1914-1945 - 5. Retreat from Empire 1945 - the present. 39 col.maps. Lack of bibliography detracts from reference value. Condemned as a 'Coffee-table Book of the British Empire' in Royal Commonwealth Society *Library Notes*, new series, no.295, February 1990, p.7. *Class No: 941-44(084.3)*

Biographies

[6913]

ROYAL COMMONWEALTH SOCIETY. Biography catalogue of the Library of the Royal Commonwealth Society. Simpson, D.H. London, Royal Commonwealth Society, 1961. xxiii,511p. £7.50. ISBN: 0905067355.

'The aim has been to list all the Library's biographical material. Books published up to the autumn of 1960 and periodicals to the close of 1959 have been included' (*Preface*). Some 12,000 entries for over 6,500 individuals, embracing periodical articles and analytical entries from volumes of collective biography, as well as books and pamphlets. The main sequence, 'Individual biographies' (p.-388) is followed by 'Collective biography and country indexes' (p.388-431), 'Addenda' (p.433-5) and 'Supplementary list of authors' (p.441-511). 'The men and women included are in the main, those born in, or actively connected with, countries of the Commonwealth, and persons in the United Kingdom who have been of significance in Imperial affairs' (*Preface*). There are also numerous entries for explorers and travellers

....(contd.)

of many countries. Items asterisked represent books or periodicals destroyed by enemy action but inserted for their bibliographical value. Entries include full name, dates of birth and death and a brief description of the biographee; they indicate the presence of portraits and illustrations. Supplemented in v.7 of the RCS *Subject catalogue of the Royal Commonwealth Society* (Boston, Mass., G.K. Hall, 1971). *Class No: 941-44(092)*

Great Britain

[6914]

CANNON, J., *ed.* **The Oxford companion to British history.** Oxford Univ. Press, 1997. xii,1044p. maps, geneal. tables, index. £30.00. ISBN: 0198661762.

120 contributors 4,000+ initialled entries covering social, political, cultural, economic, military, scientific and feminist history, including legal and technical terms, newspapers and periodicals, counties, cathedrals, royal palaces etc. from 55BC to the present. Quick reference summaries and essay length overviews. Subject index arranged by headwords *e.g.* Commonwealth of Nations, exploration, First World War, landscape gardening. 12 maps. 6 geneal. tables. 'This is a useful desk guide through the basic facts, figures and fictions of British history for urgent seekers after truth and writers of essays and articles. For earnest browsers, the longer articles on general topics can be read for pleasure and disagreement as well as information'. (*The Times,* 1 December 1997). *Class No: 941.0*

[6915]

English historical documents. Douglas, D.C., *ed.* London, Eyre Methuen; New York, Oxford Univ. Press, 1953-. v.1-. diagrs. maps.

1. *c.500-1042* edited by D. Whitelock. 2nd ed., 1979. xxxii,960p. ISBN 0413324907. 2. *1042-1189* edited by D.C. Douglas and G.W. Greenaway. 2nd rev. ed., 1980. xxiv,1064p. £65. 0413325008. 3. *1189-1327* edited by H. Rothwell. 1975. xxiv,1032p. £65. 0413233006. 4. *1327-1485* edited by A.R. Myers. 1969. lxviii,1236p. £65. 0413233103. 5. *1485-1558* edited by C.H. Williams. 1967, xviii,1082p. £65. 0413233200. 6. *1558-1603* In preparation. 7. (1) *1603-1640*; (2) *1640-1660* In preparation. 8. *1660-1714* edited by A. Browning. 1953. xxxii, 966p. £65. 0413206505. 9. *American colonial documents to 1776* edited by Jensen. 1955. xxiv, 888p. £65. 0413206602. 10. *1714-1783* edited by D.B. Horn and M. Ransome. 1957. xxviii, 972p. £65. 0413233502. 11. *1783-1832* edited by A. Aspinall and E.A. Smith. 1959. xxx,992p. £65. 041323360x. 12. (1) *1833-1874* edited by G.M. Young and W.D. Handcock. 1956. xxiv,1018p. 12. (2) *1874-1914* edited by W.D. Handcock. 1977. xxiv,726p. £65. 0413233707.

Aims 'to make generally accessible a wide selection of the fundamental sources of English history' (*General preface,* v.12, pt.1). Each volume has a lengthy general introduction and a select bibliography; each of its parts has its own introduction and select bibliography. All documents (or selections from documents) are translated into English (as necessary), the text being well footnoted. V.12, pt.1 (12 parts has 269 items, including departmental and Royal Commission reports, *Times* leaders, legislation and statistical data. V.12, pt.2 (12 parts) covers such subjects as economic structure and development; religion and the churches; imperialism and foreign affairs; law penal system and courts; central and local government; education; poor law and problem of poverty; factories, health and housing; trade unions and socialism. *Class No: 941.0*

[6916]

HALLAM, E. *and* PRESCOTT, A., *eds.* **The British inheritance a treasury of historic documents.** London, The British Library, 1999. 160p. col. illus. £25. ISBN: 0712346376.

Displays in full colour over 250 key historical documents recording the defining moments of British history, ranging from a 13th century manuscript illustrating King Arthur's coronation to 20th century documents recording the influx of African immigrants. *Class No: 941.0*

[6917]

The Oxford history of England. Oxford, Clarendon Press, 1936-1981. £25.00 each volume.

1A: *Roman Britain* by P. Salway. 1981. ISBN 019821717x. This replaced the first part of *Roman Britain and the English settlements* by R.G. Collingwood and J.N.L. Myres, 2nd ed., 1937. 1B: *The English settlements* by J.N.L. Myers. £17.50. 2. *Anglo-Saxon England* by F.M. Stenton, 3rd ed. 1971. 0198217161. 3. *From Domesday Book to Magna Carta 1087-1216* by A.L. Poole, 2nd ed. 1955. 0198217072. 4. *The thirteenth century 1216-1307* by M. Powicke, 2nd ed. 1962. 0198217080. 5. *The fourteenth century 1307-1399* by M. McKisack. 1964. 0198217129. 6. *The fifteenth century 1399-1485* by E.F. Jacob. 1964. 0198217145. 7. *The earlier Tudors 1485-1558* by J.D. Mackie. 1964. 0198217064. 8. *The reign of Elizabeth 1558-1603* by J.B. Black. 2nd ed. 1959. 0198217013. 9. *The early Stuarts 1603-1660* by G. Davies. 2nd ed. 1959. 0198217048. 10. *The later Stuarts 1660-1714* by G. Clark. 2nd ed. 1956. 0198217021. 11. *The Whig supremacy 1714-1760* by B. Williams. 2nd ed. revised by C.H. Stuart 1962. 0198217102. 12. *The reign of George III 1760-1815* by J.S.

....(contd.)

Watson. 1964. 0198217137. 13. *The age of reform 1815-1870* by L. Woodward. 2nd ed. 1962. 0198217110. 14. *England 1870-1914* by R.C.K. Ensor. 1964. 0198217056. 15. *English history 1914-1945* by A.J.P. Taylor. 1965. 0198217153. *Consolidated index* edited by R. Raper 1991. vi,622p. 0198217862. Raper's 'Making the consolidated index of Oxford History of England', *The Indexer,* v.18, no.1, April 1992. p.1-2 is of interest.

Standard introduction to the periods concerned with valuable critical bibliographies. V.15, brilliantly and occasionally controversially written (see *Times Literary Supplement,* no.3329, 16 December 1965, p.1169-70, 'History Taylor-made'), has a lengthy bibliography in the form of a running commentary (p.602-39). *Class No: 941.0*

[6918]

—The New Oxford history of England. Oxford, Clarendon Press, 1989-.

Successor to the *Oxford history of England.* 'Each volume will set out an authoritative view of the present state of scholarship, presenting a distillation of the new knowledge built up by a half-century's research and publication of new sources...'

Volumes published: Langford, P. *A Polite and commercial people England 1727-1783.* 1989. xix,803p. illus. (incl.pl.), tables, bibliog., index. £25.00. ISBN 0198228287. 14 chapters. Chronology p.727-739. Bibliography (p.741-766) is in continuous narrative form and is subdivided into 20 thematic sections. Analytical index. Bartlett, D. *England under the Norman and Angevin kings 1075-1225.* 2000. xxx,772p. illus., maps, tables, indexes. £30. 0198227418. 12 chapters (*e.g.*Political patterns, Lordship and government). Chronology of political events p.693-94. Sources p.695-705. Hoppen, K.T. *The Mid-Victorian generation 1846-1886.* Williams, P. *The Later Tudors.* 1995. xxi,606p. illus., maps, bibliog., index. £25. 0198228201. 13 chronological and thematic chapters. Glossary p.540-42. Genealogical tables p.543-46. Chronology p.548-59. Bibliography p.561-80. *Class No: 941.0*

Bibliographies

[6919]

Bibliographical handbooks. Hecht, J.J., *general editor.* Cambridge, Cambridge Univ. Press, for the Conference on British Studies, 1968-.

Anglo-Norman England 1066-1154 by M. Altschul. 1969. *The High Middle Ages in England 1154-1377* by B. Wilkinson. 1978. *Late-medieval England 1377-1485* by D.J. Guth. 1976. *Tudor England 1485-1603* by M. Levine. 1968. *Restoration England 1660-1689* by W.L. Sachse. 1971. *Late Georgian and Regency England 1760-1837* by R.A. Smith. 1984. 0521255384. *Victorian England 1837-1901* by J.L. Altholz. 1970. *Modern England 1901-1984* by A.F. Havighurst. 1987. £25. 0521309743. First published as *Modern England 1901-1970* (1976). This volume has 2670 briefly annotated entries, some with references to further material. Numerous cross-refrences. 16 sections: 1. Bibliographies - 2. Catalogues, guides and handbooks - 3. General surveys - 4. Constitutional history - 5. Political history - 6. Foreign relations - 7. Social history - 8. Economic - 9. Labour - 10. Urban - 11. Agricultural - 12. Science and technology - 13. Military and naval - 14. Religious - 15. Fine arts - 16. Intellectual history. Index of authors, editors and translators. Subject range does not include literature *per se.* Many entries for periodical articles, as well as for biographies and other printed sources. Provides scholars and advanced students with handy guides to writings on each period, and also serves as a basis for research. *Class No: 941.0(01)*

[6920]

Bibliography of British history. Oxford, Clarendon Press, 1928-. Issued under the direction of the American Historical Association and the Royal Historical Society of Great Britain.

1. *A bibliography of English history to 1485* edited by E.B. Graves. 1975, xxiv,1103p. £60.00. ISBN 0198223919 (7,221 entries). Basically a revision of C. Gross' *Sources and literature of English history from the earliest times to about 1485* (London, Longmans, 2nd ed. 1915).

2. *Tudor period 1485-1603* edited by C. Read. 2nd ed. 1959. xxviii,624p. Reprinted Hassocks, Sussex, Harvester Press; Totowa, New Jersey, Rowan & Littlefield. 0855276843 (UK). 0847660745 (US) (6,543 entries). First published 1933.

3. *Stuart Period 1603-1714* edited by G. Davies and M.F. Keeler. 2nd ed., 1970. xxxv,734p. £60.00. 0198213719. (4,350 entries). First published 1928.

4. *The Eighteenth Century 1714-1789* edited by S. Pargellis and J.D. Medley. Harvester Press and Rowan and Littlefield. 1971. xxvi,642p. 0855271361 (UK) (4,558 entries).

5. *1789-1851* edited by L.M. Brown and I.R. Christie. 1977, xxxi,759p. £55.00. 0198223900. (4,782 entries).

6. *1851-1914* edited by H.J. Hanham. 1978. xxvii,1606p. £70.00. 019823897. (10,829 entries).

7. *1914-1989* edited by K. Robbins. 1996. xxxix,918p. 0198224966 (27,000+ entries).

Each volume has entries (mostly annotated) in sections, and usually with section introductions. V.7 has 12 sections: 1. General (bibliographies and other reference works) - 2. Constitutional and

..(contd.)

Political history - 3. Economy and Industry - 4. Society - 5. Religion and the Churches - 6. External Relations - 7. War and the Armed Services - 8. Transport - 9. Urban and Rural life - 10. Medicine and Health - 11. Education - 12. Culture, Recreation, Leisure, Sport. Alan Day's 'Birthpangs of a bibliography', *New Library World*, v.79, no.938, August 1978, p.154-7, is a brief account of this monumental and invaluable series. *Class No: 941.0(01)*

[6921]

ARDY, T.D. **Descriptive catalogue of materials relating to the history of Great Britain and Ireland to the end of the reign of Henry VII.** London, Longmans, 3v. in 4, 1862-71. (*The Rolls Series.*)
Vol. 1: *From the Roman period to the Norman invasion*, 2v. 1862. cxxxic,918p. Vol.2: *From AD1066 to AD1200*. 1865. civ,601p. Vol.3: *From AD1200 to AD1327*. 1871. cxxii,482p.

The documentary sources of early British history arranged chronologically by the year in which the latest event is recorded. 'If even major libraries understandably jib at the full cost of a full reprint edition of The Rolls Series they would be well advised to consider the purchase of these particular volumes ' (Day. A.E. *History: a reference handbook*, 1977,. Entry 210). *Class No: 941.0(01)*

[6922]

erum Britannicarum medii aevi scriptores or Chronicles and memorials of Great Britain and Ireland during the Middle Ages. London, Longmans Green, 253v., 1858-1911. (*The Rolls Series.*)
Reprinted by Kraus Reprints 1965.

Published under the direction of the Master of the Rolls these erudite volumes contain the primary sources of the history of Great Britain from the Roman invasion to the reign of Henry VIII. Editors were instructed to give the most correct text from a collation of the extant manuscripts, to introduce the text by describing their age and peculiarities, and to give a brief account of the life and time of the author. M.D. Knowles' presidential address to the Royal Historical Society (*Transactions of the RHS*, 5th series, v.11, 1961 p.137-59) reviews the preliminary moves leading to this monumental enterprise, the various editorial mishaps, and criticism of the series.
Class No: 941.0(01)

[6923]

oyal Historical Society. **Annual bibliography of British and Irish history.** Gee, A., *ed.* London, Harvester Wheatsheaf; since 1990 Oxford Univ. Press, 1976-. Annual.
Published for Royal Historical Society.

Comprehensive and authoritative survey of books and articles published in a calendar year. Arranged in 14 sub-divided sections: A. Collective volumes (Archives, Bibliography, Works of reference) - B. Long periods - C/I. by historical period - J. Medieval Wales - K. Scotland before the Union - L/M. Ireland - N. Empire & Commonwealth to-1783. P. Empire and Commonwealth post-1783. Each section is edited by a specialist in the period. Separate author, personal name, place, and subject indexes. *1998* v. (1999 405p. index. £55.) includes 2033 books, 3755 articles. 700+ journals scanned annually. *Class No: 941.0(01)*

[6924]

Writings on British History. London, Institute of Historical Research, annual.
1901-1933 (1968-70). 5v. in 7 (Williams Dawson): 1. *The auxiliary sciences and general works* - 2. *The Middle Ages* - 3. *The Tudor and Stuart periods* - 4. *The eighteenth century* - 5. *1815-1914. 1934-1945* (1937-60). 8v. (William Dawson). *1946-1948* (1973). (Inst. Hist. Res). *1949-1951* (1975). *1952-1954* (1975). *1955-1957* (1977). *1958-1959* (1977). *1960-1961* (1978). *1962-1964* (1979). *1965-1966* (1981). *1967-1968* (1982). *1969-1970* (1984). *1971-1972* (1985). *1973-1974* (1986).

The 1973-74 v. has sub-title: 'a bibliography of books and articles on the history of Great Britain from c.450AD to 1939 published during the year 1973-74 inclusive with appendix containing a select list of publications in these years on British history since 1939' (xix, 283p.). It has 5193 numbered entries, unannotated, but references to reviews are included. Over 400 journals scanned. Part 1. General works (Auxiliary sciences; Bibliographies and indexes; Archives and collections; Historiography, study and teaching; British history in general; English local history and topography; Wales and Monmouthshire; Scotland; Ireland; British Empire and Commonwealth; Genealogy and family history; Collected biography) - 2. Period histories (7 periods: Pre-conquest: Medieval; Tudor; Stuart; 18th century; 19th century; 20th century). Appendix: Select list of works published in the years 1973-74 on British history since 1939. Analytical index p.207-283. Slow progress is being made on the time-lag in publication. 'The *Writings* should be available, not only in every academic library, but also in every city and county reference library that claims to cater for serious historical study' (*History*, v.41, Feb-June-October 1956, p.361-363). *Class No: 941.0(01)*

CD-ROM

[6925]

The Royal Historical Society **bibliography on CD-ROM** The History of Britain, Ireland and the British overseas. Oxford University Press, 1998. £250 standard; £595 educational network. ISBN: 0192685732, standard; 019268650x, network.

Comprehensive database of references to books, articles and unpublished theses, taken from *Writings on British History* and the *Annual Bibliography of British and Irish History 1901-1992*. 'Students can search by author, title, or work, by subject or date of publication... They may also be combined to carry out complex queries in order to find a specific reference. Search results can be printed or exported to word package' (*Teaching History*, no.93, November 1998, p.47). *Class No: 941.0(01)(003.40)*

Encyclopaedias

[6926]

ARNOLD-BAKER, C. **The Companion to British history.** Tunbridge Wells, Kent, Longcross Press, 1996. ix,1386p. maps, geneal. tables. £48. ISBN: 0902378104.

c.13,500 well chosen and composed entries cover British history in 'the totality and interaction of its activities' and European and World history insofar it touched British history from 55BC. to 1996. Appendix A. English regnal years - B. Selected warlike events (p.1349-62) - C. Genealogies and diagrams (p.1363-86) 8 maps. In far more detail than *The History Today companion to British history* (*q.v.*), this is a tremendous achievement for a single author. 'Mr. Arnold-Baker's judgements are admirably free from prejudice, and his opinions are based on wide reading, experience and common sense' (*Daily Telegraph*, 22 February 1997, p.A3). *Class No: 941.0(031)*

[6927]

The Cambridge historical encyclopedia of Great Britain and Ireland. Haigh, C. Cambridge, Cambridge Univ. Press, 1985. 392p. illus. (some col.), maps (some col.), bibliog. £30. ISBN: 0521255597.

60 chapters contributed by academic historians arranged in 7 chronological sections: 1. Britons and Romans *c.*100 BC-AD 409 - 2. Saxons, Danes and Normans 409-1154 - 3. Medieval empire: England and her neighbours 1154-1450 - 4. Reformation and inflation 1450-1625 - 5. Disorder to stability: Britain and Ireland 1625-1783 - 6. Political reform and economic revolution 1783-1901 - 7. From imperial power to European partner 1901-1975. An overview of each chapter and marginal notes on events and personalities throughout justify the title. Who's Who (800 very brief biographical entries) p.338-373. Further readings (by chapter) p.374-376. Index p.377-391. 'As a work of ready reference it is not easy to find the limited information it contains, yet it is an indigestible read from cover to cover ... it essentially attempts too much in too small a space' (*British Book News*, December 1985, p.759-760). *Class No: 941.0(031)*

[6928]

GARDINER, J. *and* WEMBORN, N., *eds.* **The History Today companion to British history.** London, Collins and Brown, 1995. iii,840p. maps. £25. ISBN: 1855851784.

6 principal and other specialist contributors. Over 4,500 A-Z cross-referenced factual and interpretative entries, in double column pages for people, events, causes and issues covering political, social, economic, religious and cultural history of Britain from Roman invasion to 1979. 9 maps. *Class No: 941.0(031)*

[6929]

The Hutchinson illustrated encyclopedia of British History. Oxford, Helicon, 1999. xii,384p. illus. (inc. 22 col.pl.), maps, geneal. tables, bibliog. £14.99. ISBN: 1859862578.

21 contribs. 2,200+ A-Z entries relating to 'the people, events, and ideas that have shaped England, Scotland, Ireland, and Wales from prehistory to the present day'. 29 chronologies inc. Thematic Chronology of British and Irish history (p.366-79). 18 genealogies. 29 maps and battle plans. Bibliography (in 8 chronological periods) p.381-84. *Class No: 941.0(031)*

Dictionaries

[6930]

KENYON, J., *ed.* **A Dictionary of British history.** London, Secker & Warburg, 1987; New York, Stein and Day, 1983. viii, 415p. maps. geneal tables. £15. ISBN: 0436233088.

27 contributors. 3000 short A-Z entries relating to social and political events, foreign affairs, major cultural and scientific development, and prominent men and women of Britain and its overseas possessions, 55BC to AD1970. Chronology p.373-410. Genealogy of British monarchs p.411-415. *Class No: 941.0(038)*

[6931]

PANTON, K.J. *and* COWLARD, K.A. **Historical dictionary of the United Kingdom** Volume 1 England and the United Kingdom. Lanham, M.D., Scarecrow Press, 1997. xxix,700p. maps, bibliog. £75.05. (*European Historical Dictionaries, no.17.*) ISBN: 0810831503.

Chronologies (historical events, monarchs, governments) p.xiii-xxiv. Introduction (geography, shaping of the Kingdom, changing economy, social change, events since 1945) p.1-11. Dictionary p.13-537. Bibliography (in 14 subdivided form, historical period, and thematic sections) p.538-692. Appendix (entries in v.2) p.693-700. 5 maps. *Vol.2 Scotland, Wales, and Northern Ireland* 1998. 472p. maps, bibliog., £54. Not only does the second volume focus on the specifics of the individual economy, cultural traditions and history of each, but it investigates how they came together and interacted with each other under the umbrella of the U.K. The *Dictionary* begins with a chronology of the U.K. and a comprehensive introduction highlighting different aspects, issues and events that have impacted upon these three countries, including their attempts to preserve their own characters, and the turmoil that still exists. Entries include people, events, institutions, places and political, economic and cultural themes important to U.K. history. With maps, abbreviations and chronologies.
Class No: 941.0(038)

Maps & Atlases

[6932]

FALKUS, M. *and* GILLINGHAM, J., *eds.* **Historical atlas of Britain.** Rev. ed. London, Kingfisher Books, 1987. 223p. col. illus., col. maps. £19.95. ISBN: 0862722950.

First published London, Granada, 1981.

21 academic contributors. Arranged in 6 chronological chapters 4000 BC to the present day dealing with political changes and 2 chapters on social and economic developments. Chronology of world history p.216-217. Index p.218-223. 'Although much more expensive and ambitious than G.S.P. Freeman-Grenville's *Atlas of British History* (London 1879), it is a much superior work' (*Choice*, v.19, no.9, May 1982, p.1216). *Class No:* 941.0(084.3)

[6933]

GILBERT, M. **The Routledge atlas of British history** : from 54BC to the present day. 2nd ed. London, Routledge, 1994. 144p. maps. £19.99. ISBN: 0460861794.

First published by Weidenfeld & Nicolson 1968.

144 black and white outline political, war and conflict, trade and industry, religious, and social and economic maps (26 new to this edition) from The Celts in Britain by 50 BC to Public spending 1993-1994. *Class No:* 941.0(084.3)

[6934]

Historians' guide to early British maps: a guide to the location of pre-1900 maps of the British Isles preserved in the United Kingdom and Ireland. Wallis, H. *and* McConnel, A., *eds*. Cambridge Univ. Press for Royal Historical Society, 1995, ix,465p. bibliogs. (*Royal Historical Society Guides and Handbooks, no.18.*) ISBN: 0521551528.

First published in 1994 by Royal Historical Society and distributed by Boydell & Brewer Ltd.

Part 1: History and purpose of maps in 26 essays (*e.g.*General maps of GB and I. - Medieval maps - Cartobibliographies of county maps, local maps and town plans England and Wales ... Military surveys of GB c.1290-1700 ... Navigable waterways and railway maps ... Map collections). Part 2: The Repositories in England, Channel Islands and Isle of Man; Wales; Scotland; Northern Ireland; Ireland. Data: Address, Tel. No., Access, Indexes, Summary. 'As a guide to where to find maps and how to gain access to them this volume is of considerable value' (*Cartographic Journal*, v.33.no.1, June 1996, p.61-62). *Class No:* 941.0(084.3)

Chronologies

[6935]

CASTLEDEN, R. **Harrap's book of British dates** a comprehensive chronological dictionary of British dates from prehistoric times to the present day. London, Harrap, 1991. 446p. index. £14.95. ISBN: 0245603514.

Year by year entries with background information provide the dates for important political, dynastic, religious, and scientific events, which have shaped and influenced British traditions and culture.
Class No: 941.0(090)

[6936]

FRYDE, E.B., *and others*. **Handbook of British chronology.** 3rd ed. Cambridge Univ. Press (formerly Royal Historical Society) 1996. 608p. £30. (*R.H.S. Guides And Handbooks, no.2.*) ISBN: 052156350x. ISSN: 00804398.

First published in 1939 edited by F.M. Powicke; 2nd ed. (1961).

Lists of rulers, with style and significant dates, of officers of state, bishops, dukes, marquesses and earls; tables of parliament and councils. The 3rd ed. adds the names of Chancellors and Under-

....(contd.)

Treasurers of the Exchequer 1559-1713, First Secretaries of State 1962-1968, and Commanders-in-chief of land forces 1642-1904 Bibliographical guide to the lists of English office-holders p.xxiii xxxix. 'Clearly the editors have produced a most co-ordinated work c reference' (*Archives*, v.18, no.78). *Class No:* 941.0(090)

[6937]

Handbook of dates for students of English history. Cheney, C.R. *and* Jones, M., *revised by*. Rev. ed. Cambridge Univ. Press (formerl Royal Historical Society), 2000. xvii,246p. tables, bibliog., index £35. (*Royal Society Guides And Handbooks, no.4.*) ISBN 0521770955.

1st ed. 1945.

1. Reckonings of time (inc. Julian and Gregorian calendars) - 2 Rulers of England and regnal years - 3. List of Popes - 4. Saint's Day and Festivals used in dating - 5. Legal chronology - 6. The Roma calendar - 7. Celtic and Roman (Alexandrian) Easter Days - 8 Calendars for all possible dates of Easter - 9. Easter Days according t Old Style - 10. New Style - 11. The English calendar for 1752 - 12 Dates of adoption of the Gregorian calendar in Europe - 13. Th French Revolutionary calendar. Bibliography p.xiv-xvii.
Class No: 941.0(090)

[6938]

PALMER, A. *and* PALMER, V. **The Pimlico chronology of British history** from 250,000BC to the present. Updated ed. day. London Pimlico. 1996. 573p. maps, tables, index, pbk. £14. ISBN 0712673316.

First published in 1992 under the title *The Chronology of British history*.

Entries under various units of time (annually since 1855) o significant dates and events and key landmarks in arts and sciences scholarship, literature and drama, music, popular entertainment, an fashion. 50 lists (*e.g.* English and Scottish monarchs, prime ministers) 19 maps. *Class No:* 941.0(090)

Biographies

[6939]

Who's who in British history. Treasure, G.R., *ed.* London and Chicago, Fitzroy Dearborn, 2v., 1998. lxxxix,1392p. maps, bibliog. geneal. tables, index. £175. ISBN: 1884964907.

Previously published by Shepheard-Welwyn, 8v., 1988-1997.

10 contributors. Alphabetical list of entries p.xi-xx. Chronologica list p.xxi-xxiv. List of entries by category p.xxxv-liii. General reading list p.lv-lix. Chronology of events p.lxi-lxxvi. Glossary p.lxxvii lxxxiii. 2 maps. *Class No:* 941.0(092)

Government State Papers

[6940]

ELTON, G.R. **England 1200-1640.** Cambridge, Cambridge Univ. Press, 1976. 225p., index. (*The Sources Of History: Studies in The Use of Historical Evidence.*)

First published London, Hodder & Stoughton 1969.

Examines the range of material and sources available under 8 heads: 1. Narratives - 2. Official records; The State - 3. Official records; The church - 4. Official records; Lesser authorities - 5. Private materials - 6. The law - 7. Books and writings - 8. Non-documentary sources.
Class No: 941.0(093.200)

Jews

[6941]

JONES, P.F. **The Jews of Britain** a thousand years of history. Moreton-In-Marsh, Gloucestershire, Windrush Press, 1990. 208p. illus. £15.95. ISBN: 090007566x.

Traces the history of Britain's Jewish community from Roman times to the present. Marks the 700th anniversary of the expulsion of the Jews by Edward I. *Class No:* 941.0(=924)

[6942]

RUBINSTEIN, W.D. **A History of the Jews in the English speaking world: Great Britain.** London, Macmillan Press, 1996. viii,539p. bibliog., tables, index. £60. ISBN: 0333558332.

Major history expounding the thesis that the movement of the Jewish people to the English-speaking countries as one of the most central events of Jewish history in modern times. Extends from the Middle Ages to the modern period post-1945. Chapter notes p.435-521. Glossary of Hebrew and Yiddish terms p.522-23.
Class No: 941.0(=924)

Middle Ages

Bibliographies

[6943]

GRAVES, E.B., *ed.* A Bibliography of English history to 1485. Based on *The Sources and literature of English history from the earliest times to about 1485* by Charles Gross. Royal Historical Society, the American Historical Association and the Medieval Academy of America, *sponsor.* Oxford, Clarendon Press, 1975. xxiv, 1103p. £60. $135. ISBN: 0198223919.

C. Gross's *Sources and literature of English history, from the earliest times to about 1485* (2nd ed. London, Longmans Green, 1915, xxiv, 820p. (Reprinted Gloucester, Mass., Smith, 1952) was first published in 1900.

7,225 annotated entries. 'Basically a revision' of Gross (first published 1900; 2nd ed. 1915). Part 1: General works and auxiliary sciences - 2. Archives, source collections and modern narratives (section 7. Local history) - 3. From pre-history to Anglo-Saxon Conquest - 4. The Anglo-Saxon period - 5. From Normans to Tudors (section 13-23); 13. Chronicles and Royal biographies; 14. Law tracts; 15. Public administrative records; 16. Modern political narratives; 17. Military and naval history; 18. Land tenure and estates; 19. Agrarian society; 20. Urban society; 21. The church, 1066-1485; 22. Modern studies of the medieval English church; 23. Intellectual interests, 1066-1485). Index, p.937-1103. Section introductions. 'Like previous editions, it includes for the pre-Norman periods some fundamental studies on Welsh and Irish history' (*Preface*). The basic bibliography of the period. *Class No:* 941.0"01/14"(01)

[6944]

USILTON, L.W. The Kings of medieval England c.560-1485 a survey and research guide. Lanham, Md., Scarecrow Press, 1996. 115p. index. £28.05. ISBN: 0810831094.

Bibliography divided into 5 chronological chapters subdivided A-Z by author. 'The introductory sections to each chapter provide remarkably succinct, but balanced summaries of the lives, achievements and failures of the English kings during the Middle Ages' (*Reference Reviews*, v.11, no.2, 1997, p.46). *Class No:* 941.0"01/14"(01)

Institutions & Associations

[6945]

PINHORN, M., *comp.* Historical, archaeological and kindred societies in the United Kingdom: a list. Hulverstone Manor, Isle of Wight, Pinhorn, 1986. 105p. £10.00. ISBN: 901262226.

First published by Univ. of London Institute of Historical Research in 1965 (rev. ed. 1968) with S.E. Harcup as compiler.

An A-Z list giving date of foundation, number of members, permanent address or name and address of the Secretary, is indexed by a topographical list p.76-100. National Societies p.101-102. A 'Pinhorn history addresses - update service' has appeared in *Local History* (*qv*) from issue no.13, November/December 1986 onwards. *Class No:* 941.0:061:061.2

Roman & Anglo Saxon Period

[6946]

Anglo-Saxon England. Cambridge Univ. Press, 1972-. v.1-. Annual. illus. ISSN: 02636751.

No.24. *1995.* vii,358p. 052155845x. contains 10 articles and a Bibliography for 1994 (p.309-358) of all significant books, articles and reviews in any branch of Anglo-Saxon studies, arranged in 11 sections *e.g.* Palaeography, Diplomatic and Illumination ... History ... Archaeology. V.5 (1976), v.10 (1982) and v.15 (1986) contain detailed quinquennial indexes. *Class No:* 941.01

[6947]

ARNOLD, C.J. An Archaeology of the early Anglo-Saxon kingdoms. 2nd ed. London, Routledge, 1997. 280p. illus., tables, maps, bibliog., index. £50. ISBN: 0415153651.

1st ed. 1988.

Definitive study of the evolving social and political structure of Anglo-Saxon England 500-700 A.D. in the light of archaeological evidence including chapter 1. A history of early Anglo-Saxon archaeology. *Class No:* 941.01

[6948]

Britannia a history of Roman Britain. Frere, S. 3rd ed. extensively revised. London, Routledge & Kegan Paul, 1987. xvi, 423p.+32p. plates., illus., maps, bibliog., index. £25.00. ISBN: 0710212151.

1st ed. 1967; 2nd ed. 1978.

16 chapters *e.g.* 1. The background: the British Iron Age ... 6. The retreat from Scotland ... 14. Romanization of Britain ... 16. End of Roman Britain. Bibliography p.380-402. *Class No:* 941.01

[6949]

FRY, L.P.S. Roman Britain history and sites. Newton Abbot, Devon, David & Charles; Totowa, New Jersey, Barnes & Noble 1984. 560p. illus., maps, bibliog. £16. ISBN: 0715382675, UK; 0389204390, US.

17 chronological chapters (p.9-269) summarizing Roman involvement with Britain are followed by a gazetteer (p.274-520) of more than 1000 entries representing 'the great bulk (though not all) of the Roman sites in England, Wales and Scotland' arranged alphabetically by county and by region in Scotland. A large number of sites that are no longer visible are included. Notes (*i.e.* list of selected references relating to individual sites) p.527-543; glossary p.544-545; bibliography p.546-552; index of people and places p.553-558; subject index p.559-560. 'The gazetteer contains more entries than any similar compendium' (*Choice*, v.22, no.1, September 1984, p.166). *Class No:* 941.01

[6950]

SALWAY, P. Roman Britain. Oxford, Clarendon Press, 1981. xx+[xivp. maps], 824p. bibliog., index. £25.00. ISBN: 019821717x.

21 chapters in 5 parts: 1. The first Roman contacts - 2. The Roman conquest - 3. Imperial crisis and recovery - 4. Roman Britain and the fifth century world - 5. Britain under Roman rule. Appendices 1. Note on Roman names - 2. Roman Emperors from Augustus to Justinian - 3. Governors of the British provinces. Bibliography p.753-75, 'a review of sources in general, not a collection of references for individual statements in the text', is divided into the following sections: Ancient authors; The Roman Empire; Roman Britain: bibliographies and abstracts; Finds and excavations; Topography, regional and local surveys; Inscriptions; General works; Periodicals; Monuments and special subjects. *Class No:* 941.01

[6951]

WHITTOCK, M.J. The Origins of England 410-600. London, Croom Helm, 1986. xi,273p. index. £35.00. ISBN: 0709936796.

Presents the latest thinking on the literary sources, archaeology, and place name study in 4 heavily annotated chapters: 1. The coming of the English - 2. Romans and the English - 3. English Society - 4. The founding of the kingdoms. Appendix 1. King Lists/Genealogies (*i.e.*, a comparison of 2-3 sources for Bernicia, Deira, East Anglia, Essex, Kent, Lindsay, Mercia and Wessex (p.253-259). 2. The tribal heritage. 3. Early English Personal Names. *Class No:* 941.01

Bibliographies

[6952]

BONSER, W. An Anglo-Saxon and Celtic bibliography (450-1087). Oxford, Blackwell, 1957. xxvii,574p.

11,975 items, from 422 periodicals, collected works, etc. Closely classified. 1. General topics and historical source material - 2. Political history - 3. Local history - 4. Constitutional history and law - 5. Social and economic history - 6. Ecclesiastical history and religion - 7. Geography and place-names - 8. General culture - 9. Archaeology - 10. Numismatics and seals - 11. Epigraphy - 12. Art. A separate *Indices* volume provides author, subject, and topographical indexes. *Class No:* 941.01(01)

[6953]

BONSER, W. A Romano-British bibliography (55BC - AD449). Oxford, Blackwell, 2v., 1964.

9,370 items, closely classified; 15 classes and 666 subdivisions. Classes: 1. General topics - 2. History - 3. Army, fleet and defence - 4. Social and economic - 5. Religion - 6. Geography - 7. General archaeology - 8. Numismatics - 9. Art - 10-15. Regions of England, Scotland and Wales. 'Periodicals and collective works abstracted': 253 items. No annotations, but brief explanatory notes sometimes follow title, and presence of maps and plates is indicated. V.2 consists of indexes: author; subject; personal names; place-names (a) England, (b) Scotland (c) Wales and Monmouthshire. A valuable compilation for the period. *Class No:* 941.01(01)

[6954]

IRELAND, S. Roman Britain a sourcebook. London, Croom Helm, 1986. 266p. illus. maps. bibliog. ISBN: 070991315x.

Greek and Roman references to Britain translated into English and listed in 3 sequences: 1. The geography and people of Britain - 2. The political and military history - 3. Religion, commerce and society. Introduction (p.1-9) considers literary, epigraphic and numismatic evidence. Bibliography p.247-249. Index of literary sources p.250-253. Index of inscriptions P.254-256. General index. p.257-266. *Class No:* 941.01(01)

[6955]
KEYNES, S. **Anglo-Saxon history** a select bibliography. 2nd ed. Binghampton, NY., Center for Medieval and Early Renaissance Studies, State Univ. of New York, 1993. 73p. softcover.

c.3,000 unannotated entries in 18 thematic and chronological sections *e.g.* A. Textbooks and works of Reference - B. Primary source material .... D. Danish Kings of England (1016-1042) ... S. Anglo-Saxon scholarship. Designed for academics giving references in lectures and what to read for essays and dissertations. *Class No:* 941.01(01)

Encyclopaedias
[6956]
LAPIDGE, M., *and others, eds*. **The Blackwell encyclopaedia of Anglo-Saxon England.** Oxford, Blackwell, 1999. xviii,537p. illus.,maps, bibliogs. index. $99.95.

150 contributors. 700 A-Z signed articles relating to people, places, activities, and creations of the Anglo-Saxons. The articles are illustrated by maps, line-drawings and black and white photographs; the book is accompanied by a comprehensive table of the 'Rulers of the English, c.450-1066' and by a classified index of head-words (p.531-37) to facilitate across to the *Encyclopaedia* itself. 12 maps. *Choice* Outstanding Academic Title 1999. *Class No:* 941.01(031)

Handbooks & Manuals
[6957]
MAXFIELD, V.A., *ed*. **The Saxon shore** a handbook. University of Exeter, 1989. vi,178p. illus., maps, plans, bibliog. (*Exeter Studies in History, no.25.*) ISBN: 0859893308. ISSN: 02608626.

8 essays by independent hands present an up-to-date survey of the Saxon shore, its geographical setting, its forts and fleet. Gazetteer of sites p.113-64. Bibliography p.165-78. *Class No:* 941.01(035)

Maps & Atlases
[6958]
HILL, D. **An Atlas of Anglo-Saxon England.** Oxford, Blackwell, 1981. xi,180p. maps, chron. tables, bibliog. ISBN: 0631111816.

244 maps cover the physical, political, and economic geography of Anglo-Saxon England within the context of Viking Scandinavia, Iceland, and Western Europe. Bibliography p.167. Index locorum p.168-180. Favourably reviewed in *Antiquity*, v.57, no.219, March 1983, p.66-67. *Class No:* 941.01(084.3)

[6959]
JONES, B. *and* MATTINGLY, D. **An Atlas of Roman Britain.** Oxford, Blackwell Reference, 1990. x,341p. illus., maps, bibliog., index. £22.50. $49.94. ISBN: 0631137912.

Presents in cartographic form the whole corpus of knowledge of Romano - British studies: 1. Physical context - 2. Britain and the Roman geographers - 3. Britain before the conquest - 4. Conquest and garrisoning of Britain - 5. Development of the Provinces - 6. Economy - 7. Countryside - 8. Religion - 9. Devolution. Bibliography (by chapter) p.321-32. 273 maps. 'Perceptively abreast of the latest archaeological and literary discoveries' (*Choice*, v.28,no.9, May 1991, p.1546). *Class No:* 941.01(084.3)

Biographies
[6960]
BIRLEY, A.R. **The Fasti of Roman Britain.** Oxford, Clarendon Press, 1981. xii,476p. bibliog., index. ISBN: 0198148216.

Records the careers of almost 200 Romans who served in Britain either as governor or as a senior civil or military officer. Bibliography p.436-43. *Class No:* 941.01(092)

[6961]
WILLIAMS, A., *and others*. **A Biographical dictionary of Dark Age Britain** England, Scotland and Wales c.500-c.1050. London, Seaby, 1991. Distributed by Batsford. xlii,253p. geneal. tables, bibliog. ISBN: 1852640472.

Biographical sketches of varying length accompanied by a short list of references. Glossary p.viii-ix. Chronological tables p.x-xxiii. Genealogical and regnal tables p.xxiv-xlii. Consolidated list of references p.244-53. *Class No:* 941.01(092)

Government State Papers
Bibliographies
[6962]
SAWYER, P.H. **Anglo-Saxon charters:** an unannotated list and bibliography. London, Royal Historical Society, 1968. xiii,538p. £8.00. (*RHS Guides and Handbooks, no.8.*) ISBN: 0901050180.

Lists 1875 charters 'granting land or secular rights over land that purport to have been issued in England before the Norman Conquest

....(contd.)
(*Preface*). The first section lists chronologically the charters of which reasonably full texts have been preserved; the second lists charters los or only partly preserved. Data on each charter include MS source printed (with or without translation) form, plus comments Bibliography, p.1-25; list of manuscripts, (A-Z by locality or name) p.44-67. Detailed index of persons and places. A valuable tool for th researcher in this field. *Class No:* 941.01(093.200)(01)

Plantaganets
Encyclopaedias
[6963]
HALLAM, E. **The Plantagenet encyclopedia** an alphabetical guide to 400 years of English history. London, Weidenfeld and Nicolson, 1990 224p. col.illus., maps, geneal tables, bibliog., index. £14.95. ISBN 0297830031.

Over 1200 A-Z entries relating to prominent people, places and events from the origins of the House of Anjou to the Battle of Bosworth Field. Sumptuously illustated. Bibliography p.216-8. *Class No:* 941.03(031)

[6964]
SZARMACH, P.E., *and others, eds*. **Medieval England** an encyclopedia. New York, Garland, 1998. lxiv,882p. illus., maps bibliogs., index. £97. ISBN: 0824057864.

300+ UK and US academic contributors. 700+ signed articles each supported by a short bibliography, relating to all aspects of England in the Anglo-Saxon and post-Conquest periods Supplementary material lists of the Kings and Queens of England Alfred the Great to Henry VII, archbishops of Canterbury and York from St. Augustine to 1500, and Popes 590-1503. Glossaries of musical and architectural terms. 'Will surely remain a classic on its field for many years to come' (*Reference Reviews*, vol.12,no.7, 1998, p.45). *Class No:* 941.03(031)

Tudors
[6965]
O'DAY, R. **The Longman companion to the Tudor Age.** London Longman, 1995. x,336p. maps, geneal.tables, bibliog., index. £38. ISBN: 0582067251.

15 sections: 1. General chronological commentary 1485-1603 - 2. Ireland - 3. Rebellions: chronologies - 4. Ecclesiastical and religious developments - 5. World of learning - 6/7. Central government - 8. Local government ... 11. Biographical index - 12. Genealogical tables - 13. Tudor titles: who was who - 14. Glossary (p.251-88) - 15. Bibliography (p.291-311). 3 maps. *Class No:* 941.05

[6966]
POWELL, K. *and* COOK, C. **English historical facts 1485-1603.** London, Macmillan, 1977. vii,228p. £35.00. ISBN: 0333148886.

First published 1977.

Sourcebook of facts, figures and dates presented in 11 sections: 1. Crown and central government - 2. Parliament - 3. The judicature and the courts - 4. Local government - 5. The Church - 6. Education - 7. War, rebellion and diplomacy - 8. Scotland and Ireland - 9. Tudor economic legislation - 10. Population and growth of towns - 11. Tudor biographies. Bibliography p.221-8. No index. *Class No:* 941.05

Bibliographies
[6967]
RASOR, E.L. **The Spanish Armada of 1588** historiography and annotated bibliography. Westport, Conn., Greenwood Press, 1993. xviii,277p. index. (*Bibliographies of Battles and Leaders, no.10.*) ISBN: 0313283036.

1. Historiographical section (*i.e.* a series of thematic bibliographical essays - 2. Annotated bibliography (p.87-257) of 1114 entries. Chronology p.259-61. *Class No:* 941.05(01)

Dictionaries
[6968]
FRITZE, R., *ed*. **Historical dictionary of Tudor England 1485-1603.** Westport, Conn, Greenwood Press, 1991. xvii,594p. bibliog., index. $86. ISBN: 0313265984.

66 contributors. 295 signed cross-referenced entries (250-2,000 words in length) relating to the leading figures, events, laws, institutions, and specific topics (*e.g.* exploration) of the whole Tudor period. Entries end with lists of further readings. Chronology p.557-70. Bibliography p.571-80. One of *Library Journal's* 'Best reference books' 1991. *Class No:* 941.05(038)

[6969]

WAGNER, J.A. The Historical dictionary of the Elizabethan world: Britain, Ireland, Europe and America. Phoenix, Oryx Press, 1999. 432p. illus., maps, geneal. tables, bibliog., index. $65. ISBN: 1573562009.

500 cross-referenced A-Z entries relating to, *inter alia,* historians and antiquaries, international diplomacy and treaties, the royal line of succession, law and parliament, plots and rebellion, exploration and religion. Ancilliary material includes a chronology 1485-1603, listings of 16th century monarchs and popes, and selected web sites on subjects relating to the Tudor period. 'Offers a stylish well-composed look at a fascinating historical period. A good choice for academic and large public libraries' (*Booklist,* v.96, no.7, 1 December 1999, p.722+24). *Class No:* 941.05(038)

Stuarts

[6970]

COOK, C. *and* WROUGHTON, J. English historical facts 1603-1688. London, Macmillan, 1980. viii,231p., bibliog. £35. ISBN: 0333186346.

11 sections: 1. The monarchy - 2. Selected holders of major public offices - 3. Glossary of central government - 4. Biographies - 5. Parliament - 6. Local government - 7. The Church - 8. The armed forces - 9. Overseas trade and the colonies - 10. Education and learning - 11. Population and the towns. Bibliographical note p.230-1. Slated in *Choice,* v.18, no.10, May 1981, p.1232, for 'some extraordinary gaps' (*e.g.* nothing on Royal Navy, important buildings, agriculture, Scotland, Wales or Ireland). No index. *Class No:* 941.06

Dictionaries

[6971]

RITZE, R.H. *and* ROBISON, W.B., *eds.* Historical dictionary of Stuart England 1603-1689. Westport, Conn., Greenwood Press, 1996. xix,611p. bibliog., index. £85.50. ISBN: 0313283915.

80 contributors. 320 entries relating to leading personalites; the army and navy; constitutional and legal documents; wars and rebellions; and religious, social, economic, and cultural issues. Chronology p.559-77. Bibliography (17 form, chronological and thematic sections) p.579-92. *Class No:* 941.06(038)

[6972]

NEWMAN, P.R. Companion to the English Civil Wars. New York & Oxford, Facts on File, 1990. xxiv,192p. bibliog., maps. $29.95; £13.95. ISBN: 0816022372.

Over 1,000 A-Z cross-referenced entries (50-200 words) define and describe the events, persons, places, issues, and military terminology of the period 1642-1651. Chronology p.167-76. Bibliography p.177-80. 'The entries ... seek to stress the 'British' aspect of the wars, and to lay stress upon the Irish dimension' (*Preface*). *Class No:* 941.06(038)

Maps & Atlases

[6973]

BAKER, A. A Battlefield atlas of the English Civil War. London, Ian Allan Ltd., 1987. 128p., illus., maps, index. ISBN: 0711016542.

56 double-page map and text features on battles, actions and engagements, in date order, with 'enough detail to make the background to the battles and their effect on the war understandable'. *Class No:* 941.06(084.3)

Chronologies

[6974]

EMBERTON, W. The English Civil War day by day. Stroud, Gloucs., Alan Sutton, 1995. xxviii,228p. illus., map, bibliog., index. £19.99. ISBN: 0750909595.

Diary of English Civil War, recounting each day's events, with a full survey of major battles and an annual summary. Personalities p.xvii-xxvi. Bibliography p.217-20. *Class No:* 941.06(090)

Georgian & Regency Period

[6975]

COOK, C. *and* STEVENSON, J. British historical facts 1688-1760. London, Macmillan Press, 1988. x,252p. £38. ISBN: 0333172329.

14 sections: 1. The Monarchy - 2. Chronology - 3. Administration and political biographies - 4. Selected holders of public offices - 5. Parliament - 6. Elections - 7. Religion - 8. Treaties and diplomacy - 9. Armed forces - 10. Colonies - 11. Law and order - 12. Social developments - 13. The Economy and finance - 14. Local government. *Class No:* 941.07

[6976]

COOK, C. *and* STEVENSON, J. British historical facts 1760-1830. London, Macmillan, 1980. ix,197p. £35. ISBN: 0333215125.

15 sections: The monarchy - Ministries and administrations - Selected holders of public office - The peerage and Order of Knighthood - Parliaments and elections - Foreign affairs - The armed forces - The Empire and India - Radicalism, trade unions and political reform - Law and order - The press - Religion - Selected holders of local government office - The economy - Social developments. Sources stated; bibliographies appended to most sections. Appended bibliographical note, p.196-7. 'Seems destined to become the essential reference work for its period' (*British Book News,* July 1980, p.406-7). But no index. *Class No:* 941.07

Encyclopaedias

[6977]

NEWMAN, G., *ed.* Britain in the Hanoverian age 1714-1837 an encyclopedia. New York, Garland, 1997. xxiv,871p. illus., (ports), bibliog., index. £125. ISBN: 0815303963.

250 academic contributors. 1,100 cross-referenced signed entries in a single A-Z sequence relating to major events, key personalities, politics and government, wars, cities, the economy, scholarship, education, literature, and the arts. Guide to further research p.797-801. Analytical index p.811-71. *Class No:* 941.07(031)

Victorian Age

[6978]

COOK, C. *and* KEITH, B. British historical facts 1830-1900. London, Macmillan, 1975. xi, 279p. bibliog. £38. ISBN: 333132203.

17 chapters: 1. Ministries - 2. Political parties - 3. Parliament ... 5. Parliamentary reform ... 10. Armed services - 11. Education - 12. The Press - 13. Religion - 14. Population - 15. The economy - 16. Trade unions and the co-operative movement - 17. The British Empire. 'Bibliographical note', p.277-9. 'It lists almost all who held high political, judicial, military or administrative office in Britain between 1830 and 1900; and provides basic information about their institutions and the world in which they lived' (*Preface*). *Class No:* 941.08

[6979]

COOK, C. The Longman companion to Britain in the nineteenth century 1815-1914. Harlow, Longman, 1999. vii,359p. maps, bibliog., index. £44. ISBN: 0582279917.

Compendium of facts and figures arranged chronologically in 7 major sections: 1. Political history (chronology p.3-75, the monarchy, lists of principal ministers, cabinets and administrations, machinery of government etc.) - 2. Social and religious history - 3. Economic history - 4. Foreign Affairs, defence and the Empire - 5. 200 mini-biographies - 6. Glossary (p.289-313) - 7. Topic bibliography (21 sections). 4. Maps. *Class No:* 941.08

Bibliographies

[6980]

PROPAS, S.W. Victorian studies a research guide. New York, Garland, 1992. xxi,334p. index. $30. ISBN: 0824058402.

678 annotated entries relating to English-language reference works (books, microforms, periodicals, and databases) relating to all aspects of the Victorian period in Great Britain, Ireland, and the British Empire. Arranged under form and discipline headings. *Class No:* 941.08(01)

Encyclopaedias

[6981]

MITCHELL, S., *ed.* Victorian Britain: an encyclopedia. New York, Garland, 1988; London, St. James Press, 1991. xxi,986p. illus., bibliog., index. $125. ISBN: 0824015134, US; 1558621059, UK.

More than 400 signed articles cross-referenced covering persons, events, institutions, groups, and artifacts in Great Britain 1837-1901 are enhanced with individual authoritative bibliographies. Chronology p.xi-xxi. Research Materials for Victorian Studies p.887-93. Analytical index. 'Intended to serve as an overview and point of entry into the complex interdisciplinary field of Victorian studies' (*Preface*). *Class No:* 941.08(031)

Glossaries

[6982]

EVANS, E. The Complete A-Z 19th- and 20th- century British history handbook. London, Hodder and Stoughton Educational, 1995. iv,380p. maps, illus., index. softcover. ISBN: 0340673788.

Alphabetical glossary of the main individuals, events, themes, and issues of late modern British history intended for A and A/S level students. Eminently suitable for public library and sixth-form library quick reference shelves. *Class No:* 941.08(038.1)

20th Century

[6983]
COOK, C. *and* STEVENSON, J. **The Longman companion to Britain since 1945.** London, Longman, 1996. xii,324p. maps, bibliog., index. £38. ISBN: 0582070309.

Compendium of essential facts and figures arranged in 7 sections: Political, Social and Economic history - The wider world - Biographies (120+) - Glossary (p.243-94) - Topic bibliography (p.298-310). 2 maps. Analytical index. *Class No:* 941.082

[6984]
COOK, C. *and* STEVENSON, J. **The Longman handbook of modern British history 1714-1995.** 3rd ed. London, Longman, 1996. xi,418p., tables, geneal. tables, bibliog., index. £15.99. ISBN: 0582293049.

First published 1983. 2nd ed. 1988.

Essential facts and figures arranged in 7 sections: 1. Political history (political chronology, lists of principal ministers, British monarchs, *etc.*) - 2. Social - 3. Economic - 4. Foreign affairs and defence - 5. Biographies - 6. Glossary (p.308-325) - 7. Topic bibliographies (p.331-397). Intended for teachers, sixth form and undergraduate students. 'A remarkably compendious handbook' (*British Book News*, November 1983, p.715). *Class No:* 941.082

[6985]
MORGAN, K.O. **The People's peace:** British history 1945-1989. Oxford, Oxford Univ. Press, 1990. xiii,558p. illus., bibliog., index. £20. ISBN: 0198227647.

14 chapters assessing the course of recent British history arranged in 3 sections: 1. The era of advance 1945-1961 - 2. The years of retreat 1961-1979 - 3. Storm and stress 1979-1989. Bibliography p.517-32. 'The first major assessment of what can now be seen as a clearly definable area. It is an outstanding work: comprehensive, lucid and judicious' (*Sunday Times,* no.8,681, 6 January 1991. p.8.10). *Class No:* 941.082

[6986]
THORPE, A. **The Longman companion to Britain in the era of the two world wars, 1914-45.** London, Longman, 1994. xi,231p. tables, bibliogs., index. £32. (*Longman Companions to History*.) ISBN: 0582077710.

1-3. Political, Social, Economic history - 4. Foreign affairs, defence and the Empire - 5. Biographies - 6. Glossary (p.169-82) - 7. Topic bibliographies (p.185-220). Useful factbook for school, college and home use. *Class No:* 941.082

Bibliographies

[6987]
CATTERALL, P. **British history 1945-1987** an annotated bibliography. Oxford, Basil Blackwell for the Institute of Contemporary British History, 1990. xxxii,843p. indexes. £100. ISBN: 0631170499.

8644 entries record the significant literature on events between the 1945 and 1987 general elections. They are marshalled into 15 heavily sub-divided chapters: 1. General - 2. Political and constitutional history - 3. External relations - 4. Defence - 5. Legal system - 6. Religion - 7. Economic history - 8. Environmental history - 9. Social history - 10. Education - 11. Intellectual and cultural history - 12. Local history - 13. Wales - 14. Scotland - 15. Northern Ireland. Chapter 2 has 10 sub-categories (General; Histories of Post-war administrations; Constitution; Monarchy; Administration and central government; Parliament; Party history and political biography; Political thought; Electoral history; Pressure groups). Official publications, specialist articles from academic journals, bibliographies and databases are included. 'There can hardly be a research library in the country, or further afield for that matter, that will not need to order it despite its ton-up price' (*Reference Reviews*, v.5,no.3, 1991, p.41). *Reference Reviews* Best Generalist Reference Work 1991. *Class No:* 941.082(01)

Archives

[6988]
COOK, C. **Sources in British political history 1900-1951.** London, Macmillan, 6v., 1975-1985. £175. set. ISBN: 0333387899.

1. *A Guide to the archives of selected organizations and societies,* 1976. xiii, 330p. £33. ISBN 0333150368. 2. *A Guide to the papers of selected public servants*, 1976. xiii, 297p. £35. ISBN 0333150376. 3/4. *A Guide to the private papers of Members of Parliament,* 1977. xiv, 369p. £35. each. ISBNs 0333150384 and 0333191609. 5. *A Guide to the private papers of selected writers, intellectuals and publicists,* 1978. xiii, 221p. £35. ISBN 0333221249. 6. *First consolidated supplement,* 1985. x, 271p. £35. ISBN 0333265688. In 2 pts: 1. A Guide to the papers of organizations, societies, and pressure groups - 2. A Guide to the personal papers of private individuals. Appendix 1. A note on archival sources since 1931. 'A towering achievement of scholarship and a supremely useful bibliographical tool' (*TLS*, no.3821, 30 May 1975, p.809) on v.1.
Class No: 941.082(093.20)

Research Methods

[6989]
BUTLER, J. *and* GORST, A. **Modern British history** a guide to study and research. London, I.B. Tauris, 1997. x,310p. bibliogs., index. ISBN: 1860641032.

A practical guide for research students containing 16 essays by independent hands on research methodology (Historical writing, History: theory and practice, Public records, Archives, Libraries, Computer techniques for historical research) and on thematic studies (political, diplomatic, military, Imperial and Commonwealth, social, gender, economic, and business histories. *Class No:* 941.082:001.891

Scotland

[6990]
CAIRNEY, C.T. **Clans and families of Ireland and Scotland:** an ethnography of the Gael AD500-1750. Jefferson, North Carolina, McFarland & Co., 1989. xii, 210p. illustration, map, bibliog., index. £19.45. $25.95. ISBN: 0899503624.

1. The identity of the Gaels - 2. Gael society - 3. The coming of Gaeldom - 4. Kingdom of the Picts: Christianity, paganism and the making of Gaelic Scotland - 5. Tribal nomenclature - 6. The Cruithne - 7. The Ereinn - 8. The Laigin - 9. The Gaels - 10. The Vikings and Normans. Appendix 1. The Coats of arms (p.157-169) - 2. List of surnames (p.171-96). Bibliography p.197-203. Purpose: 'to provide in one volume an authoritative and comprehensive account of the Gaelic tribes and clans' (*Introduction*). *Class No:* 941.1

[6991]
CRAWFORD, B.C. **Scandinavian Scotland.** Leicester, Leicester Univ. Press; Atlantic Highlands, New Jersey, Humanities Press, 1987. xiv,274p. illus., maps, diagrs., bibliog., index. £30.00. ISBN: 0718511972, UK.

Introduction: Sources and evidence - 1. The geographical framework - 2/3. Chronological *c.*800-954; 975-1065 - 4. Linguistic - 5. Archaeological framework Pt.1: Settlement and economy - 6. Pt.2: Conversion and the organization of Christianity - 7. Literary framework: Norse society in the settlements. Chapter notes p.226-51. Bibliography p.252-63. *Class No:* 941.1

[6992]
GRANT, I.F. *and* CHEAPE, H. **Periods in Highland history.** London, Shepheard-Walwyn, 1987. xiii, 306p. illus. maps, index. £14.95. ISBN: 0856830577.

A structured history in 7 chronological periods. References p.289-99. *Class No:* 941.1

[6993]
MOODY, D. **Scottish towns** a guide for local historians. London, Batsford, 1992. 190p. illus., map, bibliog., index. £14.99. (*Batsford Local History Series*.) ISBN: 0713464976.

Outline history and topography of Scottish towns and a guide to source materials for local research. 5 chapters: 1. Introduction (visual and standard sources, mapping, and typology of towns) - 2. Story of a house - 3. Homes and suburbs - 4. Business - 5. The public town (civic facilities and services). Chapter notes p.135-56. Bibliography p.168-73. *Class No:* 941.1

[6994]
The New history of Scotland. Wormald, J., *ed.* London, Edward Arnold, later Edinburgh Univ. Press. maps, geneal tables, bibliogs., indexes.

1. *Warlords and holy men AD800-1000* by A.P. Smyth. 2. *Kingship and unity 1000-1306* by G.W.S. Barrow. 3. *Independence and nationhood 1306-1469* by A. Grant. 4. *Court, Kirk and community 1470-1625* by J. Wormald. 5. *Lordship to patronage 1603-1745* by R. Mitchison. 6. *Integration, enlightenment, and industrialization 1746-1832* by B. Lenman (rev. ed. 1992. 200p.pbk. £9.50. ISBN 0748603859). 7. *Industry and ethos 1832-1914* by S. Checkland and O. Checkland. 8. *No gods and precious few heroes 1914-1980* by C. Harvie (rev. ed. 1992. 192p. pbk. £9.50. 0748603875). Presents the latest research on Scottish history from the earliest period to the present day. *Class No:* 941.1

[6995]
SINCLAIR, C. **Tracing Scottish local history** a guide to local history research in the Scottish Record Office. Edinburgh, Scottish Record Office and HMSO, 1994. viii,167p. map, illus., facsims., bibliog., indexes. ISBN: 0114952310.

Authoritative survey of the primary source material held in the Scottish Record Office, arranged in 15 thematic sections (*e.g.* Houses and streets ... estates and farms ... ports ... sheriffdoms and counties ... businesses. A: Useful addresses p.153-56 - B. Useful books p.157-58. Indexes of classes and types of record, and of subjects. *Class No:* 941.1

[6996]
THOMSON, D.S., *ed*. **The Companion to Gaelic Scotland.** New ed.
Oxford, Blackwell, 1987. xx, 363p. illus., maps, bibliog., pbk. ISBN:
0631155783.
A-Z entries encompassing archaeology, history, geography,
language and place names, literature and music by 70 named
contributors, p.1-307. Chronology 55BC to 1975 p.309-311;
bibliography p.313-335; index p.337-363. 'A lasting source book for
students of Gaelic and Scotland' (*British Book News* March, 1984,
p.187-188). *Class No:* 941.1

Bibliographies

[6997]
ANDERSON, A.O. **Early sources of Scottish history** A.D. 500 to
1286. Stamford, Lincs., Paul Waters, 2v., 1990. clviii,805p. index.
Descriptive commentary on important documents in chronological
order. Bibliographical Supplement p.ix-xi. Bibliographical Notes p.xxi-
ci. Calendar Notes p.ciii-cvii. Orthographical Notes p.cix-cx. Tables
of the Succession of Kings p.cxi-cxiii. Index p.701-805.
Class No: 941.1(01)

[6998]
NICOLL, E.H., *ed*. **A Pictish panorama.** Belgavies, Angus, Pinkfoot
Press, 1995. xii,188p. bibliog., index. £30. ISBN: 1874012105.
Contents: 1. Summary articles by various hands on Pictish history,
language, place-names, art, and archaeology - 2. Bibliography of 800
items (2/3 published in last 40 years) A-Z x author and subject. List of
forthcoming publications appended. Subject index.
Class No: 941.1(01)

[6999]
OSBORNE, B.D., *ed*. **Scottish local studies resources** a directory of
publications from Scottish public libraries. 2nd ed. Motherwell,
Scottish Library Association, 1988. 63p. index. £3. ISBN:
0900649674.
First published 1986.
Details of 340 books and pamphlets in print issued by 35 libraries
arranged A-Z by local authority name. 'This publication promises
more than it achieves, but within its limits it contains much valuable
information' (*Reference Reviews*, v.2, no.3, September 1988, p.161).
Class No: 941.1(01)

Encyclopaedias & Dictionaries

[7000]
DONNACHIE, J. *and* HEWITT, G. **Companion to Scottish history:**
from the Reformation to the present. London, B.T. Batsford, 1989.
268p. illus., maps. £17.95; $27.50. ISBN: 0713457392.
Major events and personalities in essays ranging from less than 100
to more than 3000 words arranged A-Z but is 'neither a dictionary nor
an encyclopedia' (*Preface*). Selection of topics 'governed partly by the
relative historical importance of each entry and partly by the findings
of recent research.' 13 Appendices including 1. Chronological table
(p.217-23) ... 11. Principal surnames and territorial titles. 17 maps.
'Very well done and will be useful to laypeople and students interested
in modern Scottish history' (*Booklist*, v.86, no.22, August 1990,
p.2198++2200). *Class No:* 941.1(03)

[7001]
—DONNACHIE, I. *and* HEWITT, G. **The Companion to Scottish**
history (CD-ROM). Edinburgh, Dunedin Multimedia, 1996. Macintosh
38020 processor; PC 386/33; or Windows 3.1 processors.
'Based on a book published in 1989 ... the text has hardly been
altered, through the bibliographical references have been updated to
1996 ... There is a helpful guide to the use of the database, which is
not a complex one' (*Reference Reviews*, v.11, no.l3, 1997, p.41-42).
Class No: 941.1(03)

Encyclopaedias

[7002]
Collins encyclopedia of Scotland. Keay, J. *and* Keay, J., *eds*. London,
Harper Collins, 1994. xv,1046p. illus., maps, index. £40. ISBN:
0002550822.
125 contributors. 4,000 cross-referenced entries (with some subdivisions) cover all aspect of Scotland's past, people, art, industries,
environment, continuing traditions etc. Although in a single A-Z
sequence it effectively incorporates a biographical dictionary and a
gazetteer. 3 maps. Index p.1001-46. Appendix 1. Presbyterian
churches of Scotland - 2. House of Canmore to the House of Stewart -
3. To House of Hanover - 4. Kings of France, Scotland and England.
'Currently the best general information resource under one cover for
Scotland and things Scottish' (*Choice*, v.33,no.7, March 1996,
p.1090). *Class No:* 941.1(031)

Handbooks & Manuals

[7003]
MOODY, D. **Scottish local history:** an introductory guide. London,
B.T. Batsford, 1986. 178p. illus., bibliog., index. £17.95. ISBN:
071345220x.
1. Introduction (study and techniques) - 2. The Public Library and
its collections - 3. Archive offices and their records - 4. The individual
and the community - 5. Buildings - 6. Settlements (history of villages,
towns, and parishes) - 7. Writing and publishing results. Appendix.
Table of local government functions 1832-1975: a selective list p.146-
153. Bibliography p.154-169. Useful handbook filling a gap.
Class No: 941.1(035)

Dictionaries

[7004]
DONALDSON, G. *and* MORPETH, R.S. **A Dictionary of Scottish**
history. Edinburgh, John Donald Publishers, 1977. v, 234p. £5.50.
ISBN: 0859760189.
About 5,000 very brief entries. 'Mary, Queen of Scotland': nearly
½column. 'We have tried to be comprehensive with events, with
institutions (both civil and ecclesiastical) and with titles and offices'
(*Preface*). As to biographical notices, - hardly any limits at all.
Class No: 941.1(038)

Glossaries

[7005]
BURNESS, L.R. **A Scottish historian's glossary.** Aberdeen, Scottish
Family History Societies, 1997. 42p. map, index, pbk. £3. ISBN:
1874722129.
'A very useful reference booklet for local historians grappling with
Scottish church and legal documents' (*Local History Magazine*, no.67,
May/June 1998, p.19). *Class No:* 941.1(038.1)

Yearbooks & Directories

[7006]
COX, M. **Exploring Scottish history:** a directory of resource centres for
Scottish local history and national history of Scotland. Edinburgh,
Scottish Library Association and Scottish Local History Forum, 1992.
161p. £6.95. ISBN: 0900649798.
Guide to the collections and services of over 250 archive and record
offices. Data: hours, facilities, and other directory information. Index
of places. *Class No:* 941.1(058)

Maps & Atlases

[7007]
McNEILL, P.G.B. *and* McQUEEN, H.C. **Atlas of Scottish history to**
1707. Edinburgh, The Scottish Medievalists and the Department of
Geography, Univ. of Edinburgh, 1996. xviii,462p. maps. £30. ISBN:
0950390410.
Replaces McNeill and R. Nicholson's *An Historical atlas of Scotland
c.400-c.1600* (1975).
86 contributors. Map and text features arranged under 9 headings: 1.
Introduction (regional divisions ancient and modern) - 2/4. Roman
times to 1707 - 5. Administration - 6. Economic development ... 9.
Local and regional (Western and Northern Isles, Galloway, the
Borders, forest and burghs). 'Will be a vital tool to all with an interest
in the history of Scotland before the Union' (*Scottish Historical
Review*, v.77, no.1, (203), April 1998, p.96-97).
Class No: 941.1(084.3)

[7008]
MOORE, J.N. **The Maps of Glasgow** a history and cartobibliography.
Glasgow Univ. Library, 1996. ix,141p.+6p. col.pl. maps, bibliog.,
indexes. ISBN: 0852615558.
This well-documented study examines the maps and town plans
depicting Glasgow up to the first large scale O.S. maps which made
their appearance in 1865. Glossary p.viii. Bibliography p.1311-32.
Class No: 941.1(084.3)

Chronologies

[7009]
DUNBAR, A.H. **Scottish Kings** a revised chronology of Scottish history
1005 - 1625. With notices of the principal events, tables of regnal
years, pedigrees, calendars, etc. Edinburgh, David Douglas, 1899.
xv,420p. col. maps, tables, geneal., tables, bibliog., index.
The main part of this comprehensive handbook, 'Reigns of the
Scottish Kings' (p.1-279) contains particulars of the parentage, vital
records of each Sovereign with short notices of the principal events
during their reign followed by the names of contemporary Sovereigns
in England and France. 'An endeavour to settle the exact date of every
noteworthy event in Scottish history' (Preface). *Class No:* 941.1(090)

[7010]
OSBORNE, B.D. *and* ARMSTRONG, R. **Scottish dates.** Edinburgh, Birlinn, 1998(?). 160p. index. pbk. £6.99. $13.95. ISBN: 1874744408.

Essential information on pivotal moments, major personalities and absurd incidents in Scotland's varied and colourful history. Also a list of monarchs and a note on the Scottish capitals. *Class No:* 941.1(090)

Biographies

[7011]
DONALDSON, G. *and* MORPETH, R.S. **Who's who in Scottish history.** Oxford, Blackwell, 1973. xx, 254p. ports., index.

About 250 'Biographies of those who have figured prominently in political and ecclesiastical history, but special attention has been given to writers, scientists and others who contributed to the cultural development of Scotland' (E.G. Grant, Scotland, 1982. Entry 426). Glossary p.242-6. *Class No:* 941.1(092)

Orkney & Shetland

[7012]
SCHLEI, L.K. **The Shetland story.** London, B.H. Batsford, 1988. 273p. illus. (some col.), map, bibliog., index. £14.95. ISBN: 0713455128.

26 chapters *e.g.* 3. Early history ... 4. Norse times ... 5. In Scotland ... 6. In Britain ... 11. Place names ... 20. Scalloway - 21. Mainland - 22. The North Isles - 23. North Sea islands - 24. Atlantic Islands - 25. Fair Isle. Bibliography p.265-269. 16 col,. & 75 b/w plates. *Class No:* 941.12

[7013]
THOMSON, W.P.L. **History of Orkney.** Edinburgh, Mercat Press, 1987. xvi,321p. 16p. pl. illus., maps, geneal tables, bibliog., index. £14.95. ISBN: 0901824828.

28 chronological chapters *e.g.* 1. Pictish Orkney ... 14. Under Scottish rule ... 27. Twentieth century: a second farming revolution - 28. Twentieth century: war and peace. Glossary p.260-2. Chapter references p.263-90. Bibliography p.291-303. A scholarly and well-documented work. *Class No:* 941.12

Ireland

[7014]
HARTIGAN, M. **The History of the Irish in Britain.** London, Irish in Britain History Centre, 1986. 85p. index. sd. £2.50. ISBN: 0951094505.

Over 750 entries relating to history, sociology, demography, economic, politics and historical geography. Includes some unpublished theses and conference papers. *Class No:* 941.5

[7015]
A **New history of Ireland.** Moody, T.W., *and others.* Oxford, Clarendon Press, 10v., 1976-.

1. *Prehistoric and early Ireland* 2. *Medieval Ireland 1169-1534* edited by A. Cosgrove. 1987. xlviii, 982p.+42p. plates. £75.00. 0198217412. 3. *Early modern Ireland 1534-1691* edited by T.W. Moody and others. 1976. lxiii, 736p. £55.00. 0198217390. 4. *Eighteenth-century Ireland 1691-1800* edited by T.W. Moody and W.E. Vaughan. 1985. 914p. £70.00. ISBN 0198217420. 5. *Ireland under the Union 1. 1801-70* edited by W.E. Vaughan. 1988. lxv, 850p. £75.00. ISBN 0198217439. 6. *Ireland under the Union 2. 1870-1921* edited by W.E. Vaughan. 1996. 917p.+40p. illus. £96. 019821751x 7. *Ireland 1921-1984* And 3 Companion volumes: 8. *A chronology of Irish history to 1976* edited by T.W. Moody and others. 1987. xii, 591p. £60.00. ISBN 0198217447. 9. *Maps, genealogies, lists: a comprehensive guide to Irish history* edited by T.W. Moody and others. 1982. xii, 59'p. £95.00. ISBN 0198217455. 10. *Irish Historical Documents.* Authoritative large-scale, cooperative history to be completed in 10v. with some 70 contributors, published under the auspices of the Royal Irish Academy. T.W. Moody's 'A New History of Ireland' *Irish Historical Studies*, v.XVI, no.63, March 1969, p.1-17 outlines its genesis and planning. 'Over one hundred pages of bibliography reflect the depths of scholarship which have been dredged for this important work' (*Books Ireland*, no.200, December 1996, p.374) of vol.6. *Class No:* 941.5

Bibliographies

[7016]
CARTY, J. **Bibliography of Irish history 1870-1921.** Dublin, National Library of Ireland, 2v., 1936-40.

The first 2v. in a proposed series of bibliographies of Irish history. Entries are confined to publications in the collections of the National Library of Ireland, but they include books, rare pamphlets, parliamentary papers and other official publications, and articles in periodicals.

V.2, covering 1912-21, arranged by period, deals almost exclusively with political history; v.1, covering 1870-1911 (2,727 items), arranged

....(contd.)
by subject embraces political, economic, social, literary and ecclesiastical history, and as such serves as an excellent bibliography of Ireland for the period. *Class No:* 941.5(01)

[7017]
CULLEN, C. *and* HENCHY, M., *comps.* **Writings on Irish history 1987** incorporating addenda from previous years. Dublin, The Irish Committee of Historical Sciences and A New History of Ireland. 1991. x,73p. index. pbk. ISBN: 0950209740.

Printed in *Irish Historical Studies* 1936-1978. Published on microfiche 1979-83. Issued as a separate publication 1984 onwards.

Arranged in 9 sections: 1. General - 2. Prehistoric - 3. Fifth Century to 1169 - 4/8. Chronological periods - 9. Northern Ireland 1921-. Author index. *Class No:* 941.5(01)

[7018]
EDWARDS, R.W.D. *and* O'DOWD, M. **Sources for early modern Irish history 1534-1641.** Cambridge, Cambridge University Press, 1985. x, 222p. index. £30. (*The Sources of History.*) ISBN: 052125020x.

A critical guide to the written sources of Irish history in 8 chapters: 1. Irish civil central administration; 2. Irish civil local administration; 3. English and other central administrations and Ireland; 4. Irish ecclesiastical administration; 5. Contemporary accounts; 6. Maps and drawings; 7. Archival collections; and 8. Historiography. 'One of the main aims ... is to emphasise the need for historians to understand the administrative machinery which produced the documents they use'. Favourably received in *Irish Historical Studies*, v. xxv, no.99, May 1987, p.322-323. *Class No:* 941.5(01)

Internet

[7019]
Irish history on the Web. URL:http://wwwvms.utexas.edu/-jdana/irehist.html.

12 categories of links include general Irish history, Republican and Unionist history, Northern Ireland history, family web sites, and genealogy resources, presses and book shops, bibliographies, and other Irish history sites. 'Students at all levels will find this site interesting, easy to use, and very useful' (*Choice*, Supplement to v.,36, August 1999, p.170). *Class No:* 941.5(01)(003.41)

Encyclopaedias

[7020]
CONNOLLY, S.J., *ed.* **The Oxford companion to Irish history.** Oxford Univ. Press, 1998. xviii,618p. maps, bibliog., index. £25. ISBN: 0192116959.

87 specialist authors, mostly Irish academics. 1,800 cross-referenced A-Z initialled entries explore the history of Ireland and its peoples, from the earliest times to the late 20th century, and Ireland's impact on the modern world, combining concise definitions and factual information with analytical essays on general themes. 6 maps. Subject index p.613-18. 'The predictable entries are fine: the unpredictable are often fascinating' (*Sunday Times*, no.9056, 22 March 1998, sect 8, p.3). But 'many of the entries have the air of the British establishment peering across the Irish Sea and judging Ireland by British standards' (*Books Ireland*, no.215, September 1998, p.222-23). *Class No:* 941.5(031)

[7021]
NEWMAN, P.R. **Companion to Irish history 1603-1921** from the submission of Tyrone to Partition. Oxford & New York, Facts On File, 1991. xi,244p. maps, bibliog. £13.95. ISBN: 081602572x.

Compendium of cross-referenced A-Z entries relating to the personalities, organizations, policies, legislation, battles, philosophies, and beliefs which shaped Irish history. Appendices gives names of Viceroys of Ireland 1603-1921; Deputies in Ireland 1603-1880; and Chief Secretaries in Ireland 1603-1921. Chronology p.230-3. Bibliography p.234-6. 6 maps. *Class No:* 941.5(031)

Dictionaries

[7022]
HICKEY, D.J. *and* DOHERTY, J.E. **A Dictionary of Irish history 1800 - 1980.** Dublin. Gill & Macmillan, 1987. 615p. pbk. £12.95. ISBN: 0717115674.

First published in 1980 as *A Dictionary of Irish history since 1800*.
c. 2000 entries (100 - 3,000 words) covering all aspects of Irish history, not simply political topics. No bibliographies, but works are cited in text. Cross-references. 'An invaluable work of reference' (*British Book News*. April 1981, p.253). *Class No:* 941.5(038)

[7023]
HOMAS, C. *and* THOMAS, A. **Historical dictionary of Ireland.** Lanham, MD., Scarecrow Press, 1997 xliv, 263p. maps, bibliog. $99.50. £47.05. (*European Historical Dictionaries, no.20.*) ISBN: 081083300x.

Historical chronology p.xv-xliv. Introduction (physical features) p.1-14. Dictionary (politics, theatre, administrative divisions, historic events etc.) p.15-193. Appendix A. Viceroys and Lords Lieutenant - B. Chief Secretaries - C. Presidents of Ireland - D. Prime Ministers - E. Prime Ministers of Northern Ireland etc. Bibliography (under 41 form and thematic headings) p.207-262. 'It is ... difficult to give this work an unqualified recommendation as its genuine strengths are undermined by its organizational confusion and its selective modernity' (*Reference Reviews*, v.12, no.3, 1998, p.48-49). *Class No:* 941.5(038)

Maps & Atlases

[7024]
DUFFY, S., *ed.* **The Macmillan atlas of Irish history.** New York, Macmillan USA, 1997. 144p. col.illus., col.maps, index. $27.50. ISBN: 0028620119.

1st published in Dublin by Gill and Macmillan.

6 contributors. 49 double page map features exploring different themes forming the historical background to the major events that shaped Irish history arranged in 5 chronological periods: 1. Origins - 2. Conquest of Ireland - 3. Reformation to Restoration - 4. Splendour to famine - 5. Modern Ireland. Chronology p.132-35. Bibliography p.136-37. *Class No:* 941.5(084.3)

[7025]
Irish historic towns atlas. Andrews, J.H. *and* Simms, A., *eds.* Dublin, Royal Irish Academy, 1986-.

First published in fascicules 1986-.

1. *Kildare, Carrickfergus, Bandon, Kells, Mullingar and Athlone.* 1995. 46p. b/w maps, 6 col. maps, 88p. text. £IR.95. Maynooth. 1995. 12p. text, 8 maps, 2pl. £IR18. ISBN 0874045334. Core of the atlas comprises large-scale town plans showing differing modes of origin and subsequent growth phases of individual towns. 'When complete the Atlas will make available a series of carefully researched historical town plans for a substantial selection of Irish towns, representing various size categories, various regions of the country (both North and South), and various periods of origin and growth, with some bias in favour of the medieval period, but not excluding the estate towns, industrial towns, and resort towns characteristic of more modern times' (*Irish Geography* v.21, no.1, 1988, p.48-49). K.M. Davies' 'The Irish Historic Towns Atlas - a recentcomer to the European Towns Atlas scene', *Bulletin of Society of University Cartographers* v.21, no.2, 1988, p.61-5 is informative. *Class No:* 941.5(084.3)

Chronologies

[7026]
A Chronology of Irish history to 1976. Moody, T.W., *and others.* Oxford, Clarendon Press, 1982. xii, 591p. index. £60. (*A New History of Ireland.*) ISBN: 0198217447.

All dateable important events in the text of the *New history* are included along with others which do not find a place there, allowing the *Chronology* to stand as an independent reference work. Arranged in periods (each furnished with an introduction and glossary) corresponding with the primary divisions of the *New history* (*qv*). Analytical index p.473-591. *Class No:* 941.5(090)

[7027]
CREALEY, A.H. **An Irish almanac** notable events in Ireland from 1014 to the present. Mercier, 1993. 196p. pbk. ISBN: 1856350355.

A daily calendar with notes on events up to June 1992 that happened on that day with the relevant year. Mainly political events are listed but social, literary, academic, artistic, and legal events are also covered. List of centenaries falling due 1994-2003 are listed. *Class No:* 941.5(090)

[7028]
DOHERTY, J.E. *and* HICKEY, D.J. **A Chronology of Irish history since 1500.** Dublin, Gill and Macmillan, 1989. xiv,395p. index. ISBN: 0717116344.

Annalistic pattern: within each year the significant events of Irish life listed by date. In the case of particularly dramatic years (*e.g.* 1798 or 1919) there is an extended day by day account. For students and general readers. *Class No:* 941.5(090)

[7029]
O'DONNELL, J., *ed.* **Ireland the past twenty years: an illustrated chronology.** Dublin, Institute of Public Administration, 1986. 135p. illus. pbk. £4.95. ISBN: 0906980674.

Day by day record of events 1 June 1967 - 26 September 1986. 'Gives an impression of what has been going on in Irish society ... it lists events the media have seized on as important, as well as the many of the organizational changes the yearbook has recorded since it first appeared' (*Introduction*). Time-span: 1 January 1967 - 26 September 1986. *Class No:* 941.5(090)

Archives

[7030]
PROCHASKA, A. **Irish history from 1700:** a guide to sources in the Public Record Office. London, British Records Association, 1986. 96p. bibliog., index. pbk. £6.75. (*Archives and the user, 6.*) ISBN: 0900222077.

Introduction (location and availability of records in P.R.O. and an outline of British administration in Ireland) - Summary of classes of public records which contain material of relevance p.13-87. 'The documents in the PRO. in London constitute one of the largest collections within one institution of primary source material for the study of Ireland before 1900' (*Introduction*). *Class No:* 941.5(093.20)

Middle Ages

Bibliographies

[7031]
ASPLIN, P.W.A. **Medieval Ireland c.1170-1495** : a bibliography of secondary works. Dublin, Royal Irish Academy, 1971. xv, 139p.

721 entries, with brief, critical annotations; includes many periodical articles. 18 sections (1. Bibliographies, and guides - 2. Serials - 3. Essays, Festschiften - 4. Historical geography - 5. General history ... 10. History of literature - 11. History of science and technology ... 14. Archaeology - 15. Numismatics - 16. Seals - 17. Genealogy - 18. Heraldry.) Index. of authors, subjects, etc., p.17-39.

The first in a series of publications associated with the nine-volume *New history of Ireland* (*qv*). *Class No:* 941.5"01/14"(01)

[7032]
HUGHES, K. **Early Christian Ireland** introduction to the sources. Cambridge, Cambridge Univ. Press, 1976. 320p. (*The Sources of History.*)

First published London, The Sources of History Ltd; Ithaca, New York, Cornell Univ. Press, 1972.

9 footnoted chapters: 1. Archaeology - 2. Secular laws - 3. Ecclesiastical legislation - 4. The annals - 5. Secular literature - 6. Ecclesiastical learning - 7. Hagiography - 8. Art and architecture - 9. 11th and 12th century histories and compilations. Bibliography, p.302-15 (by chapters), brief index. *Class No:* 941.5"01/14"(01)

Irish Civil War

[7033]
HOPKINSON, M. **Green against green** the Irish Civil War. Dublin, Gill and Macmillan; New York, St. Martin's Press, 1988. xvi, 336p., illus. maps, bibliog., index. £30. $39.95. ISBN: 0717112020, UK; 0312024487, US.

37 chapters arranged in 6 periods: 1. 1912-1921 - 2. From the Treaty to the attack on the Four Courts - 3. The opening of the war - 4. The early civil war - 5. The War's end Jan-Apr. 1923 - 6. The post war period. Ch. notes p.277-316. Bibliography p.317-22. Analytical index. Definitive, scholarly, well-documented, and 'the best account yet and should be in all libraries' (*Choice*, v.26, no.9, May 1989, p.1576). *Class No:* 941.509

Biographies

[7034]
O'FARRELL, P. **Who's who in the Irish War of Independence and Civil War 1916-1923.** Dublin, Lilliput Press, 1997. xxiv,232p. map, bibliog., pbk. £9.99. ISBN: 1874675856.

First published as *Who's who in the Irish War of Independence 1916-1921* (Dublin, The Mercier Press, 1980).

Over 3,000 sketches of personalities involved in both sides of the conflicts. Lists of Irish Republican, non-combatant, and Crown dead; anti and pro-treaty casualties, and executions. Chronology p.xiii-xxiv. Bibliography p.228-32. 'Some entries are from reliable verbal sources' (*Introduction*). *Class No:* 941.509(092)

Northern Ireland

[7035]
BARDON, J. A History of Ulster. Belfast, Blackstaff Press, 1992. x,914p. maps, bibliog., index. £29.95. ISBN: 0856404667.

Comprehensive political, social and economic history in 15 chronological chapters (*e.g.* 1. Early Ulster c.7000 BC - AD 800 - 2. Viking raids and Norman invasion c.800-1300 ... 12. Wartime Ulster 1939-1945 ... 15. Direct rule 1972-1992). Chapter notes p.837-63. Bibliography p.865-78. 5 maps. Analytical index. 'A long awaited, definitive history of the Province' (*Books Ireland,* no.161, September 1992, p.162). *Class No:* 941.6

[7036]
COLLINS, P. Pathways to Ulster's past sources and resources for local studies. Belfast, Institute of Irish Studies, Queen's Univ., 1998. 160p. illus. maps, bibliog., index. pbk. £6.50. ISBN: 0853896933.

9 chapters: 1. Survey of local history and administrative units - 2/5. Records and sources - 6. Records by topic and theme - 7/9. Archives, Museums and Libraries. 'It is a great boon to have the mysteries of the myriad records, and House of the archives, museums and libraries in which they repose, so comprehensively elucidated within the covers of one paperback book' (*History Ireland,* v.7, no.2, Summer 1999, p.54). 'An essential work of reference for anyone interested in Irish history' (*Local History Magazine,* no.76, November/December 1999, p.22). *Class No:* 941.6

[7037]
QUEENS UNIVERSITY BELFAST. The Institute of Irish Studies. Ordnance Survey memoirs. Belfast, Institute of Irish Studies, Queens Univ. Belfast in association with The Royal Irish Academy, 1990-. 140p. illus., maps. £15.

1. *Parishes of County Armagh* (1990). 2. *Parishes of County Antrim: 1. South East Antrim covering present day Newtonabbey* (1990). 3. *Parishes of Co. Down: 1. South Down* (1990). 4. *Parishes of Co. Fermanagh: 1. Enniskillen* (1990).

'In the 1830s a major series of parish accounts or memoirs was commissioned to accompany the new Ordnance Survey maps. However, only the northern part of Ireland was covered before the scheme was dropped, and only one parish Memoir was published at the time. Now, 150 years later, it is planned that the Memoirs will be published in full' (*Publisher's advt.*). 'No other country in Europe has source material to equal the scope and detail of this most important series of texts' ('The publication of the O.S. Memoirs', *The Linen Hall Review,* v.7, no.1/2. Summer 1990, p.4-6). *Class No:* 941.6

[7038]
WICHERT, S. Northern Ireland since 1945. London, Longman, 1991. xiv,229p. maps, tables, bibliog., index. £21. (*The Postwar World.*) ISBN: 0582023912.

Narrative history in 8 chapters divided into 3 parts: 1,. 1921-1939: the roots of the problem - 2,. 1940-1968: the limits of modernization - 3. 1969-1989: the problems exposed. 4 maps. Bibliography p.204-10. *Class No:* 941.6

Encyclopaedias

[7039]
ELLIOTT, S. *and* FLACKES, W.D., *eds.* Conflict in Northern Ireland an encyclopedia. 5th ed. Santa Barbara, Calif., and Oxford, ABC-Clio, 1999. 744p. £37.50. ISBN: 0874369894.

First published in 1980 under the title *Northern Ireland: A Political Directory* this fifth edition has been completely revised and updated. Not available in the UK and Republic of Ireland.

This guide to the conflict in Northern Ireland during the thirty years of 'the troubles', 1968-1998, covers the various elements at home and abroad which have had an influence on the hostilities. It contains a chronology of major events (1921-1998), an alphabetical dictionary of people, parties, organizations, key places, and sections on election results, systems of government and the security system. *Class No:* 941.6(031)

Chronologies

[7040]
BEW, P. *and* GILLESPIE, G. Northern Ireland: a chronology of the Troubles 1968-1999. 2nd ed. Dublin, Gill and Macmillan, 1999. xxi,471p., maps, bibliog., index, pbk. £8.99. ISBN: 0717129268. 1st ed. 1993.

1000 individual dates recorded with 14 longer accounts (1-2p.) discussing the significance of major events, political initiatives, peace attempts etc. Bibliography p.409-415. 2 maps. 'Coverage is comprehensive and impeccably balanced' (*The Year in Reference* 1994, p.95-96). *Class No:* 941.6(090)

[7041]
LAUFER, D. 'Chronology of main events in Northern Ireland since 1969', p.393-401, *RUSI and Brassey's Defence Yearbook 1987* (London, Brassey's Defence Publishers, 1988. ISBN 0080336078).

From 21 April 1969 to 12 June 1986. *Class No:* 941.6(090)

Biographies

[7042]
McKITRICK, D., *and others, eds.* Lost lives the stories of the men women and children who died as a result of the Northern Ireland troubles. Edinburgh, Mainstream, 1999. 1630p. maps, tables, bibliog. indexes. £30. ISBN: 184018227x.

Chronicles 3637 fatalities in the period 1 June 1966 to 29 July 1999 - RUC officers, IRA volunteers, the young, the old, Protestants, Catholics, Loyalists, Republicans, in chronological order. Data: name, home, religion and short account of circumstances of death. Statistic p.1473-93. Glossary p.1495-1501. Bibliography p.1503-09. Victim index p.1513-47. General index p.1550-1630.

Walker, C. 'Book is memorial to Ulster's dead', *The Times,* October 1999, p.13) *Class No:* 941.6(092)

Eire

[7043]
SOMERVILLE-LARGE, P. Dublin: the first thousand years. Belfast, Appletree Pess, 1988. 330p. bibliog., index. £14.95. ISBN 0862812062.

14 chronological chapters (1. The Vikings AD837-1170 ... 12. Pos 1916). Bibliography p.299-304. 'A well-integrated body of historica research' (*Sunday Times,* no. 8575, 11 December 1988, p.G1.). *Class No:* 941.7

Bibliographies

[7044]
BOYLAN, H. This arrogant city. Dublin, A.A. Farmer, 1984. 75p.

Selective bibliography of books about Dublin and its history intended for the general reader. *Class No:* 941.7(01)

[7045]
NOLAN, W. Tracing the past: sources for local studies in the Republic of Ireland. Dublin, Geography Publications, 1982. x, 149p. illus. maps, bibliog., pbk. £4.50. ISBN: 0906602017.

Englarged and rewritten version of *Sources for local studies* (1977). 8 chapters - 1. The administrative framework - 2. Traces an sources before 1550 - 3/7. Sources: 1550-1650; 1650-1700; 1700 1800; 1800-1850; 1850-1900 - 9. Writing a local study - our nationa repositories. Extremely useful bibiliographical section (bibiliographies journals, articles on sources; chapter references; selective county bibliographies) p.123-146. Maps for local studies p.147-149. *Class No:* 941.7(01)

Encyclopaedias

[7046]
BENNETT, D. Encyclopaedia of Dublin. Dublin, Gill and Macmillan 1991. xiii,277p. illus., bibliog., index. £30. ISBN: 0717115992.

A-Z entries providing a complete portrait of the city, its origins and institutions, industry and commerce, streets and buildings, libraries and theatres, and eminent personalities. Celebrates Dublin as the Europea City of Culture. Bibliography p.275-7. *Class No:* 941.7(031)

Chronologies

[7047]
O'DONNELL, E.E. The Annals of Dublin. Dublin, Wolfhound Press 1987. 237p. illus., maps, charts, bibliog., index. £15.95. ISBN 0863271489.

An annotated and illustrated chronology celebrating Dublin's millenium in 29 chronological chapters: 1. Geological preamble ... 29 Modern Dublin. 13 appendices *e.g.* 1. Roll of the Honorary freedom of the city - 2. Some literary connections... 4. Dublin architects ... 6 Easter rising 1916. Bibliography p.224-8. *Class No:* 941.7(090)

Archives

[7048]
LESTER, D., *comp.* Irish research a guide to collections in North America, Ireland, and Great Britain. Westport, Conn., Greenwood Press, 1987. xvii,348p. index. £47.50. (*Bibliographies And Indexes In World History, no.9.*) ISBN: 0313246645.

792 entries listing libraries and repositories in US (A-Z by State); Canada (A-Z by Province); Ireland and Northern Ireland; and England and Wales (A-Z by County). Appendix A: Bookstores and bookdealers - B. Irish local newspapers. Data: A. Purpose of the organization - B General (Irish) collections - C. Special collections - D. Special services - E. Special rules (use of collections, hours, fees *etc.* - F. Special tips for researchers from the librarians. 'A research tool ... for any area of Irish research' (*Introduction*). but predominently for historical researchers. *Class No:* 941.7(093.20)

England & Wales—Local History

[7049]

ENDALL, S. **Dictionary of land surveyors and local map makers of Great Britain and Ireland 1530-1850** 2nd ed. London, The British Library, 2v., 1997. 312p.+578p. col.pl., refs., indexes. £75. ISBN: 0712345582, v.1; 0712345590, v.2; 0712345094, set.

V.1: *Historical guide to the use of the dictionary and indexes.* 312p. Outlines the history and development of surveying and map making and includes detail of surveyors and the making of estate and military maps. Separate indexes of surveyors, the areas in which they practised, the types of map they produced, and the places where they lived. V.2: *Dictionary.* 578p. 14,000 names of people known to have measured land, including 9,700 taken from preliminary lists published by Peter Eden. 'A great wealth of scholarly apparatus has been added in the form of references to more than 1500 published sources, to manuscript sources, and there are extensive cross-references between land surveyors in the main alphabetical list' (*Archives*, v.23, no.99, October 1998, p.186-7). *Class No:* 942.1/.9

[7050]

RISTOW, J., *comp.* **The Local historian's glossary and vade mecum.** 2nd ed. Department of Adult Education, Univ. of Nottingham, 1994. x,277p. illus., bibliog. ISBN: 1850410690.

First rate handbook that deserves a wide circulation. Glossary p.1-217. Regnal years 1066-1952 p.218-32. English currency before decimalisation p.233-40. Bibles p.241-44. Dates and meanings of named days p.245-50. Trades and occupations p.251-56. Weights and measures p.257-60. Latin words/phrases p.261-72. Roman numerals p.273. Old style dating p.274. Bibliography p.275-78. *Class No:* 942.1/.9

[7051]

The Darwen County Histories. Chichester, Sussex, Phillimore.

Hunter, J. *A History of Berkshire.* 1995. £14.95. ISBN 0850337291. Smith, B. and Ralph, E. *Bristol and Gloucestershire.* 1996. £15.99 - 9936. Reed, M. *Buckinghamshire.* 1993. £14.95 - 6376. Crosby *Cheshire.* 1966. - 9324. Rollinson, W. *Cumberland and Westermorland.* 1996. £15.95. 1860770096. Childs, J. *Derbyshire.* 1987. £12.99. - 6201. Staines, R. *Devon.* new edition in preparation. Cullingford, C.N. *Dorset.* 1999. £15.99. 1860770932. Edwards, A.C. *Essex.* 1994. £14.95. - 9154. Turner, B.C. *Hampshire.* 1978. £12.99. - 2540. West, J. and West, M. *Herefordshire.* 1985. £12.99. - 5701. Rook, T. *Hertfordshire.* 1997. £15.99. 1860770150. Wickes, M.J. *Huntingdonshire.* 1995. £14.95. - 9537.

Jessup, F. *Kent.* 1995. £14.95. - 9162. Crosby, A. *Lancashire.* 1998. £15.99. 1860770703. Millward, R. *Leicestershire and Rutland.* 1985. £12.99 - 3903. Bennett, S. *Lincolnshire.* 1999. £15.99. 1860770894. Martin, S.W. *Norfolk.* 1997. £15.99. 1860770142. Greenall, R. *Northamptonshire.* new edition in preparation. Kaye, D. *Nottinghamshire.* 1987. £12.99. - 6023. Jessup, M. *Oxfordshire.* new edition in preparation. Trinder, B. *Shropshire.* 1998. £15.99. 1860770363. Dunning, R. *Somerset.* 1983. £12.99. - 4616. Greenslade, M. and Stuart, D.G. *Staffordshire.* 1998. £15.99. 1860770711. Dymond, D. and Northeast, P. *Suffolk.* 1995. £14.95. - 9383. Brandon, P. *Surrey.* 1998. £15.99. 1860770312. Armstrong, J.R. *Sussex.* 1995. £14.99. - 9464. Slater, T. *Warwickshire.* 1997. £15.99. - 991x. Watkins, B.W. *Wiltshire.* £12.99. - 6929. Lloyd, D. *Worcestershire.* 1993. £14.95 - 6559. Rawnsley, S. and Singleton, F. *Yorkshire.* 1995. £14.95. - 9308.

'In contrast to *The Victoria history of the counties of England* the objective is to produce a concise and readable synopsis of the history of each county from prehistory to the present day'. Each volume has about 40,000 words of text and between 16 and 20 maps. 'All the authors show their ability to absorb local detail and recent research into a general narrative' (*Local Historian*, v.17, no.5, Febuary 1987, p.299). *Class No:* 942.1/.9

[7052]

Domesday Book. Morris, J., *ed.* Chichester, Sussex, Phillimore, 40v., 1975-86. maps, indexes. £826. With index volumes £600. All volumes priced individually. ISBN: 0850331285, set.

'The only uniform English translation ever made, in parallel text with the original Latin' (*Phillimore catalogue*). Only previous edition was printed in 1733 and then only of 1250 copies.

34 county volumes (5 counties in 2v.) and Boldon Book, a 12th century survey of Northumberland and Durham. Each volume has an introduction, glossary, maps, indexes and notes. Fundamental source material for local historians. *Class No:* 942.1/.9

[7053]

BATES, D. **A Bibliography of Domesday Book.** Woodbridge, Suffolk, The Boydell Press, 1987. xi, 166p. index. £25. $35. ISBN: 0851154336.

4684 briefly annotated items identifying place-names, interpreting terminology and statistics, and assessing how the record was made and its administrative and legal significance. In 3 pts: 1. General studies - 2. Local studies A-Z by historical counties - 3. Name and analytical subject index. Comprehensive in coverage 1886-1984; selective prior to 1856. *Class No:* 942.1/.9

[7054]

—Great Domesday. Williams, A., *Editor-in-chief.* Library ed. London & New York, Alecto Historical Editions (at the invitation of the Public Record Office), 1986-87. £3,000. ISBN: 094845900x.

1. Two linen bound cases containing the 413 folios of the manuscripts sewn into booklets. ISBN 0948459018 ISBN 0948459026. 2. Two linen bound cases containing translations divided into County booklets. ISBN 0948419034 ISBN 0948459042. 3. One linen bound case containing 33 loose leaf County maps to a scale of 3" to 1 mile and one complete map of Domesday England. ISBN 0948459050. 4. Two linen bound volumes of indices prepared by the University of California at Santa Barbara. ISBN 0948459069 ISBN 0948459077. Index v.1: *Index Nominum* contains 2 separate indices of persons: List of English landholders recorded in *DB* as owning property before the Conquest in 1066; and landholders at the time of the Domesday Survey in 1086. V.2 includes *Index Locorum* (all places mentioned in the manuscript) and *Index Rerum* (references to social, fiscal and judicial matters). 5. Optional: The UCSB Domesday data base on magnetic tape for those purchasers with access to a mainframe computer.

The County Edition, published in association with *The Daily Telegraph*, 1987-88, consists of 31 separately available county volumes. The *Telegraph Sunday Magazine*, no.468, 13 October 1985 carried 4 features and 3 boxed special items. *Class No:* 942.1/.9

[7055]

—HALLAM, E.M. **Domesday Book through nine centuries.** London, Thames and Hudson, 1986. 224p. illus., maps, index. £12.50. ISBN: 0500250979.

1. The making of D.B. - 2. The representation and uses of D.B. 1087-1272 - 3. D.B. as a working record 1672-1700 - 4. The ancient demesne and D.B. to 1833 - 5. D.B. in antiquarian and historical writing 1570-1800 - 6. D.B. since 1800. Some facts and figures p.8-9. Ch. notes p.177-98. Glossary p.218-9. Author is Assistant Keeper, Public Record Office. *Class No:* 942.1/.9

[7056]

—HINDE, T. **The Domesday Book: England's heritage then and now.** London, Hutchinson in association with the English Tourist Board, 1985. 351p. col. illus., col. maps, facsims., bibliog., index. £16.95. ISBN: 0091618304.

Introduction: The story of Domesday Book p.10-18. Descriptive gazetteer of 12000 places listed A-Z by their modern names under 37 historical (pre-1974) counties. Key to Domesday entries p.20-21. Glossary p.336-7. Major Domesday landholders p.338-42. Bibliography p.343-6. 143 colour and 62 black/white photographs. 322 drawings. Translations used are from Phillimore & Co.'s Domesday Book Series (*qv*). *Class No:* 942.1/.9

[7057]

—Index to Domesday Book. Dodgson, J. McN., *ed.* Chichester, Sussex, Phillimore, 3v., 1990.

Companion volumes to Phillimore's edition of Domesday Book. Part 1. *Places* by J.McN. Dodgson and J.J.N. Palmer. £50. ISBN 085033702x. Includes more than 16,000 place-names. Part 2. *Persons* by J.McN. Dodgson and J.J.N. Palmer. £50. 0850337038. More than 21,000 persons, personal names, surnames and titles. Part 3. *Subjects* by J.D. Foy. £50. 0850337046. Nearly 5,000 substantive items and many thousands of references. 'It will serve as a guide to historians at all levels, covering as it does every aspect of Domesday'.

'This great three-part index will indeed, *for the first time ever*, provide a comprehensive apparatus to meet the needs of serious study and historical research. It will be a guide to the new work made possible on local, manorial, county and national history; on agrarian, urban, ecclesiastical and legal history; on geography, topography and economics; on demography, ethnology and genealogy; and not least, on the origins and meanings of the place names and personal names in the Domesday Book.' (*Phillimore catalogue*). *Class No:* 942.1/.9

[7058]

EDWARDS, P. **Rural life guide to local records.** London, Batsford, 1993. 176p. illus. facsims., bibliog., index. £19.99. ISBN: 0713467878.

1. Government of rural England - 2. Village society - 3. Population trends - 4. Earning a living - 5. Peasant world - 6. Family and neighbourhood - 7. Rural housing. Chapter notes p.156-69. Bibliography p.170-2. Examination of types of records available to local historian. *Class No:* 942.1/.9

[7059]

GREEN, J.A. **English sheriffs to 1154.** London, HMSO, 1990. 106p. pbk. £17.50. ISBN: 0114402361.

Detailed critical list identifying and dating of sheriffs of all English counties before 1154. An introduction outlines the difficulties of using the original source material. *Class No:* 942.1/.9

[7060]

GUY, S., *comp.* **English local studies handbook** a guide to resources for each county including libraries, record offices, societies, journals and museums. University of Exeter Press, 1992. xiv,343p. maps. pbk. £6.95. ISBN: 0859893693.

Addresses and telephone numbers arranged by county together with location maps of the 'old' and 'new' counties. National societies and journals covering local history topics listed p.ix-xii. Useful directories and handbooks p.xiii-xiv. *Class No:* 942.1/.9

[7061]

MUMBY, L.M. Dates and time: a handbook for local historians. Salisbury, British Association for Local History, 1997. 86p. bibliog. £8. ISBN: 1860770746.

Originally intended to distil C.A. Cheyney's *Handbook of dates for students of English history (q.v.).*

Illustrates how historians can use older methods to ascribe dates to documents under scrutiny. 5 chapters (*e.g.* 2. Dating (relative and absolute dating, Christian dating, Easter and the Christian calendar, Saints' days and religious festivals) - 3. The Year and its divisions). 12 Appendices: 1. Regnal years - 2. Popes, bishops, abbots - 3. French Revolutionary calendar - 4/6. Chinese, Jewish and Muslim calendars. Notes and references p.83-84. Bibliography p.85-86. *Class No:* 942.1/.9

[7062]

A Regional history of England. Cunliffe, B. *and* Hey, D., *eds.* London, Longman, 1986-. illus.

10 regions each covered by two linked but independent volumes written by authors who have been actively involved in local research. The first relying on archaeological data covering the period up to 1000 AD; and the second extending the coverage to the present day. Higham, N. *The northern counties to AD 1000.* 1986. 404p. £25.00. ISBN 0582492750. McCord, N. and Thompson, R. *The northern counties from AD 1000.* Jones, G.D.B. *The Lancashire/Cheshire region to AD 1000.* Smith, J. *The Lancashire/Cheshire region from AD 1000.* Manby, T.G. *Yorkshire to AD 1000.* Hey, D *Yorkshire from AD 1000.* 1986. 360p. pbk. £11.50. 0582492122. Rowley, R.T. *The Severn Valley and West Midlands to AD 1000.* Rowlands, M.B. *The West Midlands from AD 1000* 1987. 464p. £26.00. 0582492157. Rowley, R.T. *The Welsh borders from AD 1000.* May, J. *The East Midlands to AD 1000.* Beckett, J.V. *The East Midlands from AD 1000.* 1988. 448p. £25.00. 0582492696. Miles, D. *The South Midlands and upper Thames to AD 1000.* Broad, J. *The South Midlands and upper Thames from AD 1000.* Rodwell, W.J. *The Eastern counties to AD 1000.* Holderness, B.A. *The Eastern counties from AD 1000.* Todd, M. *The South West to AD 1000.* 1987. 360p. £25.00. 0582492734. Coleman, B. and Higham, R.A. *The South West from AD 1000.* Cunliffe, B. *Wessex to AD 1000,* 0582492793. Bettey J.H. *Wessex from AD 1000.* 1986. 336p. £25.00. 0582492076. Drewett, P. *The South East to AD 1000.* 1988. 394p. £25.00. 0582492718. Brandon, P. and Short, B. *The South East from AD 1000.* 1989. 0582492467. 'The new Longman series ... is ambitious and deserves to succeed' (*Antiquity,* v.62, no.234, March 1988, p.194). *Class No:* 942.1/.9

[7063]

STUART, D. Manorial records. Chichester, Sussex, Phillimore, 1992. 160p. illus., facsims. £12.95. ISBN: 0850338212.

Structured manual and guide to the use of manorial records in the study of genealogy or local history. Explains the nature and Latin vocabulary in manorial court rolls, rentals and extents, accounts and custumals. *Class No:* 942.1/.9

[7064]

The Victoria history of the counties of England. London, Constable and St. Catherine Press; subsequently London, Oxford Univ. Press for the Institute of Historical Research, 1901-. illus. (pl.), maps. (Many volumes reprinted by Dawson (Folkestone, Kent).

General introduction (1970). xi,281p. £10. ISBN 0197227163. Contains a history of the project founded in 1899 and a bibliographical excursus *i.e.* a list of volumes published to date together with the names of their editors; year of publication; and contents lists for all volumes augmented with author and title indexes. *Supplement to the General Introduction* 1989. 64p. £10. ISBN 01972275 lists and indexes the further 50v. completed since 1970.

An indispensable series. Only Northumberland and Westmorland have still to be attempted. Each volume is by various hands and is heavily footnoted. General articles on each county usually occupy v.1-2 or v.1-3, with topography or history of parishes, boroughs and hundreds in later volumes. 'The history of each county will be complete in itself, beginning with the natural features and the flora and fauna, followed by the antiquities, pre-Roman and post-Roman; a translation and critical study of the Domesday Survey, and articles upon political, ecclesiastical, social and economic history; architecture, arts, industries, biography, folklore and sport' (*Introduction*). The evolution of *VCH* 'from Antiquarianism to professionalism' is traced in *Times literary supplement,* 13 November 1970, p.1327. Other useful commentaries include W.R. Powell's 'The Victoria History of the Counties of England', *Library Association Record,* v.59, no.8, August 1957, p.259-262; R.B. Pugh's 'The Victoria County Histories',

....(contd.)
History Today v.20, no.12, December 1970, p.885-887; and C.R.J. Currie's 'Victoria County History'. *The Historian,* no.8, Autumn 1985, p.16-18. See individual counties for more detailed entries. 019 ISBNs signify that volumes are available in the original edition; 07129s that only photographic facsimiles are in print.

C. Elrington's 'The Victoria County History' (*The Local Historian,* v.22, no.3, August 1992, p.128-37. map) looks at progress in recent years, at counties completed, ongoing, dormant, and not yet started. See also K. Tiller's 'The VCH: past, present and future', *Historian,* no.44, Summer 1994, p.17-19. *Class No:* 942.1/.9

[7065]

—**English county histories** A guide. Currie, C.R.J. *and* Lewis, C.P., *eds.* Stroud, Alan Sutton, 1994. xii,483p. ports., bibliog., index. £35. ISBN: 0750902892.

Published as a tribute to C.R. Elrington, retiring general editor of the *Victoria County History.*

Contents: Christopher Elrington and the VCH; Elrington: a bibliography; Historical introduction to county historiography; Architectural guides and inventories; and 41 chapter length studies, A-Z x County, sketching the development of research and writing each county's history. *Class No:* 942.1/.9

[7066]

—**LEWIS, C.** Particular places an introduction to English local history. London, The British Library, 1989. 84p. illus. (6 col.) pbk. £8.95. ISBN: 0712301755.

Publication coincided with the British Library exhibition to mark the 200th volume of the *Victoria County History.*

Coordinated overview of family, parish, urban and regional history and the interdependence of local and national history. Final section on the scope of *VCH* and its changes over the last 90 years. 'An extraordinarily rich piece of work. No local historian should be without it' (*Library Review,* v.39, no.1, 1990, p.63-64). *Class No:* 942.1/.9

[7067]

WEST, J. Town Records. Chichester, Sussex, Phillimore, 1983. xviii,366p. illus., maps, tables, bibliogs., index. £20.00. ISBN: 0850334721.

Essentially a gazetteer to local sources of information. 12 chapters: 1. The present state of the towns 1971-1981. (Includes tables with headings: Name of town; 1971 county; status; date incorporated; population; location of archives; 1981 county; district; status; population; location of archives) - 2. Origins of the towns A.D.60 - 1066 - 3. Boroughs in the Domesday Survey - 4. Medieval Borough charters - 5. Gild and Borough ordnances *c.*1066-1600 - 6. Town maps and plans - 7. The municipal Boroughs before 1835 - 8. Improvements and other Acts 1720-1835 - 9. Commercial directories 1763-1900 - 10. Provincial newspapers from 1690 - 11. The national censuses - 12. Photographs as evidence. Bibliography p.350. Chapter notes p.352-54. 23 plates. 'This book will endeavour to help the searcher, however unskilled, to find and use the essential records of his own town' (*Introduction*). *Class No:* 942.1/.9

[7068]

WHYBRA, J. A Lost English county Winchcombeshire in the tenth and eleventh centuries. Woodbridge, Suffolk, Boydell Press, 1990. ix,136p. maps, geneal. tables, bibliog., index. £35; $67. (*Studies in Anglo-Saxon History, no.1.*) ISBN: 0851155006.

The creation, development and demise of a vanished English shire. 11 chapters: 1. The English shire system - 2. Liber Wigorniensis: References to Winchcombeshire ... 10. England in the early eleventh century and the demise of W. - 11. W. lost and found. Bibliography p.134-6. *Class No:* 942.1/.9

Bibliographies of Bibliographies

[7069]

HUMPHREYS, A.L. A Handbook of county bibliography: being a bibliography of bibliographies relating to the counties and towns of Great Britain and Ireland. London, Dawson Pall Mall, 1974. x,501p.

First published London, Humphreys, 1917.

6,000 bibliographies, under counties A-Z; general works are followed by those on individual towns and villages. Includes manuscript and periodical sources. Full bibliographical details, with occasional brief annotations. Index (p.399-500) of authors, personal names, places and subjects, with full data under each entry as well as page references. *Class No:* 942.1/.9(009)

[7070]

LISTER, A. 'Bibliographies of the County Histories', *Antiquarian Book Monthly Review,* v.19, no.12, issue 224, December 1992, p.546-50.

Bibliographical history and survey. *Class No:* 942.1/.9(009)

Bibliographies

[7071]

ANDERSON, J.P. The Book of British topography: a classified catalogue of the topographical works in the library of the British Museum relating to Great Britain and Ireland. London, Satchell, 1881. xvi,472p.

Reprinted E.P. Publishing Ltd., 1976.

Nearly 14,000 entries, with full titles of works, but no annotations or pagination. Contents: Catalogues - General topography (including England and English counties A-Z) - Wales (general; regional; counties, A-Z) - Scotland (general; counties, A-Z) - Ireland (general; counties A-Z) - Addenda - Index of places and subjects. The 'General topography' section includes such topics as antiquities, directories, islands, railways and views. *Class No:* 942.1/.9(01)

[7072]

MAKEPEACE, C.E. 'Local history', p.144-83, *The Reference Sources Handbook* edited by P.W. Lea and A.E. Day (London, Library Association, 1996. xxxviii,446p. refs., index. ISBN 1856041778).

A critical running commentary on the various forms and types of local history material including bibliographies, records, archival sources, newspapers and periodicals, parliamentary papers, directories, genealogical research, census reports, place-names, biographical information, maps, and ephemera. *Class No:* 942.1/.9(01)

[7073]

MULLINS, E.L.C., comp. A Guide to the historical and archaeological publications of societies in England and Wales. 1901-1933. Compiled for the Institute of Historical Research. London, Athlone Press, 1968. xiii, 850p.

6,560 entries for books and periodical articles issued by more than 400 local and national societies in England and Wales, Isle of Man and Channel Islands. Listed A-Z (ranging from the Society of Glass Technology to the Friends Historical Society). Excellent detailed, analytical index, p.491-788; index of authors. Complements *Writings on British history*, which excludes publications of societies. *Class No:* 942.1/.9(01)

[7074]

Phillimore complete catalogue 1999-2000. Chichester, West Susex, Phillimore, 1999. 44p. col.illus., index. sd. gratis.

Full details of all Phillimore publications including the Darwen County Histories, The 'Past' Series, and Pictorial Histories. *Class No:* 942.1/.9(01)

[7075]

PORTER, S. Exploring urban history sources for local historians. London, Batsford, 1990. 160p. bibliog., index. £14.95. ISBN: 0713451378.

A comprehensive guide to finding and using the primary and secondary documentation resources available to local historians: 1. Antiquarian and historical background - 2. Site and layout - 3. Buildings - 4. Pre-modern population and society - 5. Population and society from 1800 - 6. Civic administration - 7. Government, Parliament and the Courts - 8. Culture and leisure. Chapter notes p.141-51. Bibliography p.152-3. *Class No:* 942.1/.9(01)

[7076]

RODGER, R. A Consolidated bibliography of urban history. Aldershot, Hants, Scolar Press, 1996. xxviii,791p.+873p. indexes. ISBN: 1859281133.

20,000 references to books and articles published 1971-1991 relating to the history of towns from classical times, arranged in 10 sections: 1. General - 2. Population - 3/5. Physical, Social and Economic structure - 6. Transport - 7. Politics and administration - 8. Planning and environment - 9. Culture - 10. Attitudes to towns and cities. Includes overseas urban areas. Data: author, title, place of publication, publisher, date, pagination. Index of place-names (indexed under country except for British and Irish towns) and author index. *Class No:* 942.1/.9(01)

[7077]

STEPHENS, W.B. Sources for English local history studies in the use of historical evidence. 2nd ed. Cambridge, Cambridge Univ. Press, 1981. xv, 342p. facsims., tables, index. £40. (*Sources of History*.) ISBN: 0521237637.

Revised and expanded edition of book of same title published by Manchester Univ. Press, in 1973.

9 chapters: 1. Introduction (146 footnotes, citing many of the sources) - 2. Population and social structure - 3. Local government and politics - 4. Poor relief, charities, prices and wages - 5. Industry, trade and communications - 6. Agriculture - 7. Education - 8. Religion - 9. Houses, housing, and health. Analytical index p.326-342. 'An indispensable research tool, both for beginners and scholars' (*British Book News*, January 1982, p.62). *Class No:* 942.1/.9(01)

[7078]

UPCOTT, W. A Bibliographical account of the principal works relating to English topography. East Ardsley, Wakefield, E.P. Publishing, 1978. ix,1576p.

First published R. & A. Taylor, 3v., 1818.

Section on general topographic works, followed by that on county histories, alphabetically arranged. Analyses rather less than 1500 works (J. Nichols' *The history and antiquities of the county of Leicester* (1795-1811. 4v. in 8) is allotted 43p., whereas J.P. Anderson's *The book of British topography* (1881) gives Nichols only 6 lines). 'Still an indispensable work of reference' (*British Book News*, July 1979, p.564). *Class No:* 942.1/.9(01)

Encyclopaedias

[7079]

HEY, D., ed. The Oxford companion to local and family history Oxford Univ. Press, 1996. x,517p. ISBN: 0019216886.

17 contributors. 2,000+ cross-referenced entries encompass definitions (abbey); types of document (fine rolls); significant books (William Owen's Book of Fairs); religious movements (Quakers); techniques (radio-carbon dating); legislation (Rose's Act 1812); local government legislation (Urban District Councils); historical and bibliographical essays (Welsh local and family history) *etc*. Scope: British Isles from prehistory to the present day, concentrating on the period following the Norman conquest. Appendix: addresses national and major county and local record offices (p.511-17). 'Stands apart by its breadth of coverage, currency, and size' (*Library Journal*, v.121,no.13, August 1996, p.64), but 'a more rigorous editorial stance would have been welcome' (*Journal of the Society of Archivists*, v.19,no.2, October 1998, p.249). *Class No:* 942.1/.9(031)

[7080]

RICHARDSON, J. The Local historian's encyclopaedia. 2nd ed. New Barnet, Herts., Historical Publications, 1986. 263p. illus., bibliogs., index. £13.95. ISBN: 095036567x.

First published 1974.

20 self contained sections covering all aspects of local history: Archives, documents and printed records p.54-99; Museums, libraries and county record offices p.108-114; Organizations and societies p.115-134; Genealogy p.135-140; Heraldry p.213-219;p Archaeology p.234-249. All sections end with a bibliography. *Class No:* 942.1/.9(031)

Handbooks & Manuals

[7081]

CAMPBELL-KEASE, J. A Companion to local history research. London, A & C Black, 1989. 384p. maps, illus., index. £15.95. ISBN: 0713631457.

33 chapters in 5 sections: 1. Outline history and sources for the local historians - 2. Basic record sources - 3. More detailed records by period - 4. Specialist topics, archives and collections (16 chapters) - 5. Writing a local history. Appendix 1. Publications of the Royal Commission on the Historical Monuments in England - 2. Status of the Victoria County History programme. Major study which 'identifies and describes the principal material available for the study of local history, indicates where it may be found, and set it against the broader framework of national, as well as regional events'. The author writes at length of his book in *Local History*, no.26, November 1989, p.11-13. *Class No:* 942.1/.9(035)

[7082]

FRIAR, S. The Batsford companion to local history. London, Batsford, 1991. 432p. maps, bibliog., index. £19.95. ISBN: 0713461810.

Over 2,000 cross-referenced A-Z entries ranging from brief definitions to short essays on major subjects covering such topics as architecture, education, genealogy, legal and ecclesiastical terms, place-names *etc*. *Class No:* 942.1/.9(035)

[7083]

GRIFFIN, J. and LOMAS, T. Exploring local history London, Teach Yourself Books, 1997 234p. illus., maps, bibliog., index. pbk. £7.99. ISBN: 0340669373.

12 chapters: 1. What should you read and why? - 2. Introduction to sources. 3-10 particular types of record *e.g.* 5. Home life ... 7. Occupations. 11. Case studies - 12. Making the best of hard work (organizing materials, the final product, how to get published). Glossary p.219-26. Reading list p.227-30. Useful addresses p.231. Enquiries into content, purpose, time, and problems of using each type of record. *Class No:* 942.1/.9(035)

[7084]

WINTERBOTHAM, D. *and* CROSBY, A. **The Local Studies library** a handbook for local historians. Salisbury, British Association for Local History, 1999, 120p. illus. £8.

An introduction to the use of local studies libraries and the types of material they hold in printed form, on microfilm, and on fiche. Also points the way to potential sources of information. *Class No:* 942.1/.9(035)

Glossaries

[7085]

STUART, D. **Latin for local and family historians.** Chichester, Phillimore, 1995. xii,130p. £13.95. ISBN: 0850339847.

In 2 sections: 1. A Latin grammar 2. Structure and vocabulary of church and manorial records, charters and deeds. 'Not only those who begin to study the primary sources of local or family history in their mature years but also the youthful postgraduate student embarking on research, who almost certainly has never studied Latin before, will find this book indispensable' (*Local Historian*, v.26,no.3, August 1996, p.178). *Class No:* 942.1/.9(038.1)

Yearbooks & Directories

[7086]

MAXTED, I., *comp*. **British national directories 1781-1819:** an index to places in the British Isles included in trade directories with general provincial coverage. Exeter, J. Maxted, 1989. vii,34p. map. A4 pbk. (*Exeter Working Papers in British Book Trade History. Special series, no.2*.) ISBN: 0951275216.

Listing by place p.1-23 (data: county, place, date code to one of 13 county based directories). County index p.24-31. 'Before the series of county based directories introduced by Pigot in 1820 there was a series of national directories, normally issued as supplements to London directories, which covered over one thousand places throughout the British Isles, the majority of which had no directory of their own. This index records the coverage in two tables, one in a single alphabetical sequence of places and the other arranged by county' (*Introduction*). *Class No:* 942.1/.9(058)

[7087]

NORTON, J.E. **Guide to the national and provincial directories of England and Wales** excluding London, published before 1856. London, Royal Historical Society, 1984. vii,241p. £12.00. (*RHS guides and handbooks, no.5*.) ISBN: 0861931025.

First published 1950. Complements *The London directories, 1677-1855*, by C.W.F. Goss (London, Archer, 1932, xi, 147p.).

878 numbered entries (English, national-chronologically arranged; English, local - by counties A-Z, then chronologically; Welsh chronologically; addenda). Locations are given for each directory. Excludes directories of particular trades or professions, but includes 'a number of histories and guide books to which directories have been added'. Index of authors, printers and publishers. General index. A valuable introduction deals with the origin and development of directories, authorship, methods of compilation and tests of reliability. *Class No:* 942.1/.9(058)

[7088]

SHAW, G., *and others*. **'Directories and the local historian'** *Local History Magazine*, no.44, May/June 1994, p.14-17; no.45, July/August 1994, p.10-14; no.46, September/October 1994,. p.12-17. illus., tables, maps.

Shaw, G. 'The evolution and availability of directories' (includes table of the general content of different directories). 2. Shaw, G. and Coles, T. 'Methods of compilation and the work of large-scale publishers'. 3. Shaw, G. and Alexander, A. 'Directories as sources in local history'. *Class No:* 942.1/.9(058)

Bibliographies

[7089]

ENSING, R.J. **Directories.** London, Wandsworth Historical Society, 1985. 32p. bibliog., sd. 0.75p. (*Guides to Local History Sources no.1*.) ISBN: 0905121015.

Of wide interest because of its historical examination of the *P.O. London Directory* and Kelly's Directories. *Class No:* 942.1/.9(058)(01)

[7090]

SHAW, G. *and* TIPPER, A. **British directories:** a bibliography and guide to directories published in England and Wales (1850-1950) and Scotland (1773-1950). 2nd ed. London, Mansell, 1996. xi,459p. illus., bibliog., index. £75. ISBN: 0720123291.

First edition published by Leicester Univ. Press in 1988. Extends coverage and complements (1) Goss, C.W.F. *The London directories 1677-1855* (1932) and Norton, J.E. *Guide to the national and provincial directories of England and Wales, excluding London* (1950).

1. Introduction and guide (evolution, different types, potential use in libraries) - 2. Bibliography (English, Welsh, Scottish directories and

....(contd.)

British directories of commerce, industry and trades) - 3. Library holdings and index. 2,200 titles arranged by county and then chronologically. Publishers, place, and subject indexes. 'To be revered for years to come by local, family and industrial historians, librarians, archivists and many others. An essential purchase for every large reference collection or historical research centre' (*Reference Reviews*, v.3,no.3, September 1989, p.139-40). *Class No:* 942.1/.9(058)(01)

Gazetteers

[7091]

Cassell's gazetteer of Britain and Ireland CD-ROM. Pawtucket, R.I. Quintin Publications, 1998. Adobe Acrobat format. This software included on CD-ROM for use with Windows. $39.95.

Originally published in printed form in 6v., 1900.

200,000+ geographical locations enhanced with illustrations and 60 maps. Data: location, population, distance by rail from London or Dublin, soil conditions, natural resources, goods manufactured, names of churches, monuments, and historical information. 'Since the data on the CD-ROM consists of scanned images only, you cannot cut-and-paste text ... to another document but you can print-out the displayed page' (*Family Tree Magazine*, v.15, no.6, April 1999, p.37). *Class No:* 942.1/.9(083.86)

Maps & Atlases

[7092]

ARMITAGE, G. *and* HALL, D. **A Brief guide to large scale Ordnance Survey maps of Great Britain in the Map Library.** London, The British Library, 1998. 13p. sd. gratis. (*Map Readers Guide, no.1*.)

Advises on how to trace and order the sheet(s) required of the 3 largest O.S. mapping series: 1:10,000; 1:2,500; and 1:1,250 in the British Library.

Similar Map Readers Guides of interest to local history researchers include (2) *A Brief guide to cartographic sources for rights of way evidence in England and Wales* and (3) *A Brief guide to cartographic sources for dating houses in England and Wales*. *Class No:* 942.1/.9(084.3)

[7093]

GREAT BRITAIN. Ordnance Survey. **Ordnance Survey Street Atlases.** Southampton, Ordnance Survey; London, George Philip 1988-. maps, indexes. £10.99, £12.99, or £14.99.

Ordnance Survey Street Atlases hardback edition.

Titles available: *Bedfordshire* 2000. *Berkshire* 1996. 180p.; *Birmingham & West Midlands; Bristol & Avon* 1995. 165p.; *Buckinghamshire* 1990. 239p.: *Cardiff, Swansea and Glamorgan* 1995.; *Cheshire; Derbyshire* 1998. 300p.; *Durham* 1996. 261p.; *Edinburgh and East Central Scotland* 1995. 258p.; *East Essex* 1990. 230p.; *North Essex; South Essex; West Essex* 1990. 220p.; *Glasgow and West Central Scotland* 1995. 290p.; *North Hampshire* 1991. 228p.: *South Hampshire* 1991, 230p.; *Hertfordshire* 1996. 204p.; *East Kent* 1997. 236p.; *West Kent* 1997. 227p.; *Lancashire* 1997. 289p.; *Leicestershire* 2000; *Greater Manchester* 1997. 240p.; *Merseyside* 1997. 129p.; *Nottinghamshire* 1994. 227p.; *Oxfordshire* 1997. 279p.; *Staffordshire* 1995. 320p.; *Surrey* 1996. 259p.; *East Sussex* 1988. 212p.; *West Sussex* 1988. 234p.; *Tyne & Wear* 1996. 150p.; *Warwickshire* 1992. 246p.; *South Yorkshire* 1996. 191p. *West Yorkshire* 1996. 250p.

All roads, streets and lanes, parks, woods, farms, bridleways and footpaths, Post Offices, schools and libraries, museums, government offices, hospitals, fire stations, ferry ports and harbours are clearly marked. Lists of towns, villages and rural localities are appended. Most are now coloured editions. *Class No:* 942.1/.9(084.3)

[7094]

—GREAT BRITAIN. Ordnance Survey. **Street atlas CD-ROMS.** Southamnpton, Ordnance Survey, 1997. IBM compatible PC with CD-ROM drive (double speed) 486 processor, 4Mb RAM, 15Mb hard disk space; Microsoft Windows 3.1

Hertfordshire ISBN 031900886x *Berkshire*. 0319008851. Bookmark facility provides rapid access to frequently used map areas. Rapid search facility by place names, locality and street names, District and Sector Postcodes, National Grid reference or Atlas page reference. Measure distances selected locations on each map layer. Facility to print out selected map images for personal reference only. *Class No:* 942.1/.9(084.3)

[7095]

HARRISON, K.C. **'Old county maps and their makers'** *Library Review*, v.44,no.4, 1995, p.36-41. bibliog.

Review of county atlases of the United Kingdom from 1579 to the 'railway' maps of the 19th century. *Class No:* 942.1/.9(084.3)

[7096]

HINDLE, B.P. **Maps for local historians.** London, Phillimore, 1998. xi,148p. maps. bibliog. index. £13.99. ISBN: 0850339340.

1st published as *Maps for local history* (Batsford, 1988).

Introduction. 6 chapters: 1. County maps - 2. Estate, enclosure and tithe maps - 3. Town plans - 4. Transport maps - 5. Ordnance Survey maps. Data and information: history of each type of map, description of sheet characteristics, the areas covered, content, detail and accuracy, how maps can be used, and their location. 'The changed emphasis of the title makes the book no less helpful to local historians - many of whom will find access to a copy' (*Local Historian*, v.29, no.3 August 1999, p.184-85). *Class No:* 942.1/.9(084.3)

[7097]

KAIN, R.J.P. *and* OLIVER, R.R. **The Tithe maps of England and Wales** a cartographic analyses and county-by-county catalogue. Cambridge Univ. Press, 1995. 873p. maps, illus., tables, index. £135. ISBN: 0521441919.

An informative introduction includes explanatory notes on tithes and tithe commutation; corn rent conversions; exemptions; tithe agreements and awards; apportioning tithe rent charges; boundaries; and tithe survey databases. A-Z county-by-county catalogue (p.29-707). Appendix 1. Tithe commissioners and local tithe agents - 2. Tithe district boundaries - 3. Tithemap-makers. Standard work of reference for years to come. 'A work of remarkable scholarship, a major contribution to the history of cartography, and the definitive guide to an immensely important national collection of maps' (*Geographical Journal*, v.162, no.3, November 1996, p.337). Awarded Library Association McColvin Medal for an outstanding reference work 1996. *Class No:* 942.1/.9(084.3)

[7098]

LOBEL, M.D., *ed.* **The British atlas of historic towns** to c.1520.

1. *Banbury, Caernarvon, Glasgow, Hereford, Nottingham, Reading, Salisbury* (London, Lovell-Johns, Cook, Hammond & Kell, 1969). 2. *Bristol, Cambridge, Coventry, Norwich* (London, Scolar Press, 1975). 3. *The City of London from prehistoric times to c.1520* (Oxford Univ. Press, 1989, 99p. £75. 0198229798). Published for the Historic Towns Trust these large format atlases present meticulously detailed colour maps, a textual commentary setting the towns in their historical context, and a gazetteer providing indispensable source material for known streets and buildings in the medieval period. *Class No:* 942.1/.9(084.3)

[7099]

Maps for local history. London, Public Record Office Publications, 1995. £8.95. ISBN: 1873162170.

'This detailed and helpful book explains the historical background, lists the information content (and indexes it: cottages, crop prices, factories, gas works, trees, the width of pavements, workhouses), and tells you how to find and use the records some of which are in county record offices. The value to family and local historians is obvious' (*Refer*, vol.11,no.3, Autumn 1995, p.14). *Class No:* 942.1/.9(084.3)

[7100]

OLIVER, R. **Ordnance Survey maps** a concise guide to historians. London, Charles Close Society, 1993. 192p. bibliog., index. £12.95. ISBN: 087059813x.

8 chapters: 1. Development of O.S. - 2. Scales and characteristics of O.S. maps ... 4. O.S. mapping of towns - 5. Counties ... 8. Bibliography (p.184-89) including a select list of O.S. maps for local history use. *Class No:* 942.1/.9(084.3)

[7101]

SMITH, D. **Maps and plans for the local historian and collector:** a guide to types of maps of the British Isles produced before 1914 valuable to local and other historians. London, B.T. Batsford, 1988. 240p. illus. (inc. 6 col. plates), facsims., bibliog., index. £19.95. ISBN: 0713451912.

Introduction and 20 chapters each with its own (sometimes extensive) bibliography: 1. Sources - 2. Documentation - 3. Parliamentary deposited plans and associated documents - 4. Estate plans - 5. Enclosure - 6. Title - 7. Regional maps - 8. Drainage - 9. County - 10. County divisions - 11. Military - 12. Ordnance Survey - 13. Transport and communications - 14. Marine charts - 15. Settlement plans - 16. Specialized urban plans - 17. Other parish plans - 18. London - 19. Industrial maps - 20. Themes and thematic maps. Notes p.211-220. Bibliography p.221. County bibliography p.223-5. Analytical index. *Class No:* 942.1/.9(084.3)

Bibliographies

[7102]

ARMITAGE, G. 'Cartobibliographies of city and town plans in England and Wales. A select list' *The Map Collector*, no.66, Spring 1994, p.42-47 and no.67, Summer 1994, p.33-40.

A-Z list with content annotation and a glossary of cartographical terms used. *Class No:* 942.1/.9(084.3)(01)

[7103]

ARMITAGE, G. 'County cartobibliographies of England and Wales: *a select list*' Map Collector, no.52, Autumn 1990, p.16-24 and no.73, Winter 1995, p.20-23.

1. General cartobibliography of British Isles. 2. English and Welsh counties A-Z. *Class No:* 942.1/.9(084.3)(01)

[7104]

SKELTON, R.A. **County atlases of the British Isles 1579-1859:** a bibliography. London, Carta Press, 1970. Reprinted by Dawsons, 1978. £20.00. ISBN: 0712908730.

Originally published in parts 1964-70.

124 county atlases, from Saxton to the Ordnance Survey, p.7-206; brief bibliographical descriptions and notes. Appendix B: 'Maps of parts of the British Isles in general atlases before 1650: a select list'; C: 'The London map-trade before 1700; with a biographical list of London map-publishers'. Indexes: Persons; Titles of atlases; Subjects. Page size, 25.5 x 18.6cm. Supersedes most of the first hundred pages of Chubb's *The printed maps in the atlases of Great Britain and Ireland, 1579-1870* (1927). *Class No:* 942.1/.9(084.3)(01)

[7105]

—HODSON, D., *comp.* County atlases of the British Isles: a bibliography. Welwyn, Hertfordshire, Tewin Press, 1984-89.

1. *Atlases published 1704 to 1742 and their subsequent editions.* 1984. xvi,200p. £20. ISBN 0950914908. 2. *Atlases published 1743 to 1763 and their subsequent editions.* 1989. xvi,193p. £30. 0950914916. Continues R.A. Skelton's *County atlases of the British Isles 1579-1850* which records works published 1579-1703. 'No reference library should be without these two volumes' (*Library Association Record*, v.92, no.9, September 1990, p.685). 3. *1764-1800.* London, The British Library, 1997. 256p. illus. £35. ISBN 0712345248. *Class No:* 942.1/.9(084.3)

Biographies

[7106]

KEATS-ROHAN, K.S.B. **Domesday people: a prosography of persons occurring in English documents 1066-1266.** Woodbridge, Suffolk, Boydell and Brewer, 1999. vii,563p. bibliogs., indexes. ISBN: 085115722x.

Wealth of information of men named in the Domesday Book. Former Anglo-Saxon landowners excluded; this is a prosography of post-Conquest England. 'No interested scholar could possibly neglect Keats-Rohan because she displays such an invaluable source of information from so wide a range of English and, above all, Continental sources' (*English Historical Review*, v.115, no.460, February 2000, p.174-75). *Class No:* 942.1/.9(092)

Official Records

Bibliographies

[7107]

EMMISON, F.G. *and* GRAY, I. **County records** (Quarter Sessions, Petty Sessions, Clerk of the Peace and Lieutenancy). 4th rev. ed. London, Historical Association, 1973. £3.20. (*Helps for Students of History, no.H62.*) ISBN: 0852781822.

First published 1948.

Confined to England and Wales. Sections: 1. Introduction - 2. Records of the Courts of Quarter Sessions and of Petty Sessions - 3. Other county records - 4. Topography and genealogy in county records. Appendix 1: Printed catalogues and transcripts of county records; 2. The County Record Office and the student (with addresses of repositories). Facilities. Selected records (types), p.29-32. *Class No:* 942.1/.9(093.2)(01)

Archives

[7108]

GIBSON, J. *and* PESKETT, P. **Record offices** how to find them. 7th ed. Birmingham, Federation of Family History Societies, 1996. 64p. maps. index. sd. £2.50. ISBN: 1860060285.

70 street maps indicating location of county and diocesan record offices. Routes from 'bus and railway stations and nearby carparks are indicated. *Class No:* 942.1/.9(093.20)

[7109]

MORTON, A. *and* DONALDSON, G. **British national archives and the local historian:** a guide to official record publications. London, The Historical Association, 1980. 52p. £1.60. (*Help for students of history, no.88.*) ISBN: 0852782365.

Descriptive guide in 2 parts: 1. Public Record Office publications (Chancery, Exchequer and Judicial records, state papers, and Treasury, Privy Council and Parliamentary archives) - 2. Scottish Record Office publications. *Class No:* 942.1/.9(093.20)

[7110]

RIDEN, P. **Record sources for local history.** London, B.T. Batsford, 1987. 253p. bibliog., index. £14.95. (*Batsford Local History Series.*) ISBN: 0713447265.

A guide to the main archival sources available to the local historian in 6 sections: 1. Records and Record Offices - 2. The Middle Ages - 3. Early modern central government and the local communities - 4. Modern local government - 5. The modern local government system - 6. Local material amongst the modern records of Central Government. Appendix 2: 'The division of records at the P.R.O.' (p.190-93), outlining the distribution of record groups between Kew and Chancery Lane is particularly useful. Chapter notes p.196-219. Bibliography p.220-243. *Class No:* 942.1/.9(093.20)

Bibliographies

[7111]

MULLINS, E.L.C. **Texts and calendars** : an analytical guide to serial publications. London, Royal Historical Society, 1958. xi, 674p. index. £8. (*RHS Guides and Handbooks, no.7.*) ISBN: 0901050148.

Covers texts and calendars for English and Welsh history issued by the various Record Commissions, the Public Record Office and local authorities and record societies. Parts: 1. Official bodies - 2. National bodies - 3. English local societies - 4. Welsh societies - 5. Addenda. Index. Invaluable in supplying complete lists of the publications of such bodies as the Camden Society, Harleian Society, English Place-Name Society, Rolls series, etc., with full subject index.

Texts and calendars: an analytical guide to serial publications 1957-1982. (1983). xi, 323p. ISBN 0861931009. More than 20 new series, notably the publications of the London and Suffolk Record Societies, along with *corrigenda* to the original work.

Texts and calendars since 1982. A Survey (electronic publication gratis on HMC Website http.//www.hnc.gov.uk/socs/).
Class No: 942.1/.9(093.20)(01)

London

[7112]

ATKINS, P.J. **The Directories of London 1677-1977.** London, Mansell, 1990. xii,732p. illus., bibliog., indexes. £60. ISBN: 0720120632.

Not so much a revision or update of C.W.F. Goss's *The London directories 1677-1855: a bibliography with notes on their origin and development* (1932) as a replacement work.

A magisterial guide to the history and development of printed London directories (directory types; history; compilation; and uses) together with a comprehensive bibliography (5800 items) and a list of the holdings of 65 libraries. Appendix: Bibliography of Directory titles (entries carry coded location guide) p.1-3. Title, publisher, and topographical indexes. 'Scholars, researchers and librarians - all will be grateful ... a fine example for future bibliographers to follow' (*Library Association Record,* v.92, no.8, August 1980. p.599). Library Association McColvin Medal commendation 1991. *Class No:* 942.1

[7113]

GREATER LONDON COUNCIL. **The Survey of London.** London, London County Council (then Athlone Press), 1900-.

Out of print volumes are being reprinted by AMS Press (New York). 1. *Bromley-by-Bow* (1900); 2, 4, 7, 11. *Chelsea* (1909-1927) v.7. £27.50. ISBN 048548027x; 3, 5. *St. Giles in the Fields* (1912-14); 6. *Hammersmith* (1915); 8. *St. Leonard, Shoreditch* (1922); 9. *St. Helen, Bishopgate* (1924); 10, 13, 14. *St. Margaret, Westminster* (1926-30); 12, 15. *All Hallows, Barking* (1929-34) v.15. £45. 0485482150; 16, 18, 20. *St. Martins-in-the-Fields* (1935-40); 17, 19, 21, 24. *St Pancras* (1936-52); 22. *St. Saviour and Christchurch, Southwark* (1950); 23, 26. *St. Mary, Lambeth* (1951-56); 25. *St. George the Martyr, Southwark* (1955) £35. 0485482258; 27. *Spitalfields and Mile End New Town* (1957); *Hackney,* pt.1 (1960) £35. 0485482282; 29-32. *St. James, Westminster* (5v., 1960-63) v.31-32 £65. 0485482312; 33-34. *St. Anne, Soho* (1966) £75. 0485482339; 35. *Theatre Royal, Drury Lane and the Royal Opera House, Covent Garden* (1970) £50. 0485482355; 36. *St. Paul, Covent Garden* (1970) £55. 0485482363; 37. *Northern Kensington* (1973) £55. 0485482371; 38. *The Museums area of South Kensington and Westminster* (1975) £60. 048548238x; 39-40. *The Grosvenor Estate* (1977-80) £55 and £70. 0485482398 and 0485482401; *Southern Kensington-Brompton* (1983) £55. 0485482241x; 42. *Southern Kensington-Kensington Square to Earls Court* (1986) £65. 0485482428. An historical survey of the administrative county of London. Each volume gives a detailed history of a parish, or part of a parish, with descriptions and illus. of historically important buildings. V.42 has 152p. plates, chapter references p.414-59, index p.461-502. *Class No:* 942.1

[7114]

SHEPPARD, F. **London: a history.** Oxford Univ. Press, 1998. 420p. illus., bibliog., index. £25. $30. ISBN: 0198229224.

1. Londinium - 2. From Londinium to the Chartered City of London 400 to 1500 - 3. Genesis of modern London 1530 to 1700 - 4. Augustan and Georgian London 1700 to 1830 - 5. Metropolitan and imperial London 1830 to 1914 - 6. The Uncertain Metropolis 1914 to 1997. The author was General Editor of the multi-volume *Survey of London,* 1954-1982. *Choice* Outstanding Academic Title 1999. *Class No:* 942.1

[7115]

The Victoria history of London including London without the Bars, Westminster and Southwark. London, Constable, 1909. £70.00. ISBN: 0712906053.

Reprinted by Dawsons Pall Mall 1974.

V.1 (all published) deals with pre-conquest London, and with ecclesiastical history down to modern times. *Class No:* 942.1

Bibliographies

[7116]

ADAMS, B. **London illustrated 1604-1951** a survey and index of topographical books and their plates. London, Library Association, 1983. xxxiii, 586p.+24p. plates. bibliog. £75. ISBN: 0853657343.

Catalogue (p.3-521) describes 238 books and sets of prints containing over 8000 plates illustrating London by means of line-engraving, etching or lithography. Detail includes notes on the volume's publishing history and its illustrations; transcription of the title page, its collation; and a checklist of its London plates. Chronological numbered list of books p.xxv-xxvii; list of illustrations p.xxix-xxx, topographical index p.523-556; index to artists, engravers, architects, authors, book titles, and select publishers p.557-562. Bibliography p.583-586. Absence of maps a surprising feature. 'A monumental task ... accomplished triumphantly' (*British Book News,* September 1983, p.541. *Class No:* 942.1(01)

[7117]

COHEN, B. **The Thames 1580-1980:** a general bibliography. London, Ben Cohen, 1985. [v], 335p. ISBN: 0951039105.

19 sections *e.g.* 1. Barrage, barrier, floods, drainage ... 2-3. Bridges ... 4. Docks, wharves, employment ... 5. Embankments ... 13. Navigation, tides, canals ... 15. River craft, transport, boat yards. No index on the advice of booksellers and librarians! Fills an undoubted gap. *Class No:* 942.1(01)

[7118]

CREATON, H., ed. **Bibliography of printed works on London history to 1939.** London, Library Association, 1994. xxxiii,896p. maps, indexes, £80. ISBN: 1856040747.

21,778 unannotated entries deployed in 96 sections grouped under 7 subject headings: 1. General - 2. Political, administrative and legal history - 3. Social - 4. Cultural - 5. Architectural history - 6. Medicine and public health - 7. Military, naval and air force history. Author and subject indexes p.609-809. Covers City of London and the area of the former Greater London Council.

The author is already actively collecting material published since 1990. *Class No:* 942.1(01)

[7119]

CREATON, H. **Sources for the history of London 1939-45** a guide and bibliography. London, British Records Association, 1998. xli,196p. bibliog. £12.50. (*Archives and the User Series, no.9.*) ISBN: 0900222123.

Two prong approach: the changing face of wartime London (civil defence, evacuation, and armed forces sources and records) and normal life (public opinion, work, law and order, education, health, and the arts). 'An exceptional guide to the location and use of historical sources, can scarcely be faulted, and will prove to be of great value to historians for many years to come' (*Archives,* v.24, no.101, October 1999, p.96). *Class No:* 942.1(01)

[7120]

MARCAN, P., comp. **Greater London local history directory and bibliography:** a borough by borough guide to local history organisations, their activities, and publications, 1983-1987. High Wycombe, Buckinghamshire, Peter Marcan Publications, 1988. iv, 83p. £15. ISBN: 0951028987.

Updates *London's local history* (1985).

Over 300 entries arranged within each borough in 8 categories: municipal collections and museums; historical and archaeological societies; community publishing projects and oral history groups; and amenity conservation societies, with separate sections on family history societies, of organizations spanning more than 1 borough and 'umbrella' organizations and record offices in adjacent counties. 'A valuable resource in local history libraries both in London and in other parts of the country. It will show researchers what is available and what work is being done in this popular and little-recorded field' (*Reference Reviews,* v.2, no.3, September 1988, p.162). *Greater London local history directory: a borough by borough guide ... (1988-*

...(contd.)
1992) 1993. 108p. index. 1871811082.

Supplemented by *Greater London history and heritage handbook* (London, Penter, 1999. £14.95). which has entries on museums, visitors, tourist and information centres, environmental associations, parks, cemeteries, and woods. *Class No:* 942.1(01)

[7121]
MARCAN, P., *and others, comps.* **London's local history:** an annotated catalogue of publications and resources issued by Greater London local authorities, local historical and archaeological societies, amenity societies and community publishing projects during the 1960s, 1970s and early 1980s with listings of local history collections, museums, societies, and notes on London wide historical societies and library collections. 2nd impression with corrections and amendments. High Wycombe, Buckinghamshire, Peter Marcan Publications, 1985. vi, 58p. pbk. £9.50. (*Public Library Resources Series.*) ISBN: 0950421162.

First published 1983. Supplemented by *Greater London local history directory and bibliography* (1988). *Class No:* 942.1(01)

Encyclopaedias

[7122]
The Book of London. Leapman, M., *ed.* London, Weidenfeld & Nicolson, 1989. 320p. illus. (many col.), maps, bibliog., index. £18. ISBN: 0297796240.

27 contributors. Every aspect of London's past and present is covered in this encyclopedic work arranged in 5 main parts and divided into 37 distinct sections: 1. The Growth of London (Londinium, Medieval London ... From the Great Fire to the Regency ... Twentieth-Century London, Chronology p.42) - 2. The Areas of London (*e.g.* The Thames, The City of London) - 3. A Place to live (*e.g.* Georgian terraces and Regency villas, Victorian houses for the masses, The growth of the suburbs) - 4. A Place to work - 5. A Place to enjoy (Theatre, Music ... A London Calendar). The Makers of London (architects and builders) p.302-6. Glossary of place names p.307. Bibliography p.308-10. *Class No:* 942.1(031)

[7123]
WEINREB, B. *and* HIBBERT, C. **The London encyclopaedia.** Rev. ed. London, Macmillan, 1993. xii,1060p. illus., indexes. £45. ISBN: 0333560280.

First published 1983.

164 contributors. Approximately 5000 cross-referenced entries form a complete portrait of the whole of Greater London: history, tradition, streets and buildings, people and events. 'An attractive and fascinating compilation' (*Reference Reviews*, v.2, no.2, June 1988, p.93-4). *Class No:* 942.1(031)

Dictionaries

[7124]
DICKENS, C. **Dicken's Dictionary of London 1888** an unconventional handbook. Moretonhampstead, Devon, Old House Books. 199? 272p. £10.99.

700+ detailed entries relating to London's principal buildings, churches, railway stations, theatres etc. *Class No:* 942.1(038)

Maps & Atlases

[7125]
The A to Z of ... London. maps, facsims., bibliog., indexes.

1. *A to Z of Elizabethan London* by A. Prockter and R. Taylor. London Topographical Society, 1979. 0902087150. Maps p.1-32. Place name index p.33-62. Bibliography p.xii. 2. *A to Z of Georgian London.* 1982. viii,88p. £16.00. 0902087169. Maps and atlas p.1-49. Place name index p.51-85. Bibliography p.viii. 3. *A to Z of Regency London.* Lympne Castle, Kent, Harry Margary, in association with Guildhall Library London, 1985. xvi,116p. £17.50. 090345136x. Atlas p.1-81. Index p.82-116. 4. *A to Z of Victorian London.* 1987. viii,140p. £19.50. 0903451394. Atlas p.1-120. Index p.121-140. Imaginative presentation of the street plans of London. *Class No:* 942.1(084.3)

[7126]
BARKER, F. *and* JACKSON, P. **The History of London in maps.** London, Barrie & Jenkins, 1990. 192p. illus. (some col.), maps (some col.). £19.95. ISBN: 0712636501.

A cartographical survey of 400 years of London's history with over 150 maps, paintings, engravings and photographs *etc.* *Class No:* 942.1(084.3)

[7127]
HYDE, R. **Ward maps of the City of London.** London Topographical Society, 1999. 84p. illus. £38. $45.

Descriptive catalogue of 110 ward maps tells the story of how these maps came to be made, their changing styles, the people who made them, and the development of the maps from attractive book illustrations to important tools of government. The City of London has been divided into words since the 12th century. *Class No:* 942.1(084.3)

[7128]
The Times London history atlas. Clout, H., *ed.* 2nd ed. London, Times Books, 1997. 192p. col. illus., col. maps, bibliog., index. £25. ISBN: 0723009058.

1st ed. 1991.

Traces growth of London from Roman period to present day: 1. Land under London (geology; River Thames) - 2/7. Roman, Anglo-Saxon and Norman, medieval, Tudor and Stuart, Georgian, and Victorian London - 8. Between the wars - 9. Post-war London - 10. London themes - 11. Places in London. 5 band thematic chronology p.12-17. Etymology of London place names p.172-7. Bibliography p.178-9. Magnificently produced. *Class No:* 942.1(084.3)

Bibliographies

[7129]
HOWGEGO, J. **Printed maps of London circa 1553 - 1850.** 2nd ed. Folkestone, Dawson, 1978. xv, 295p. illus. ports., maps (facsims.). £35.00. ISBN: 0712908218.

First published, 1964 (I.Dartington and J Howgego).

422 items with bibliographical notes. 40 locations, including Paris (Bibliothèque Nationale), Dublin, Leiden and Royal Library, Copenhagen. Valuable general introduction, p.1-34 (10 sections; *e.g.* 4. Pre-Fire map - names of London); 63 references. The catalogue (p.43-284) notes different editions. 'A select bibliography', p.35-36. Well produced. 'Every serious student of the history of the capital will consider the new edition an essential possession' (*Library Association Record*, v.81, no.5. May 1979, p.243). *Class No:* 942.1(084.3)(01)

Biographies

[7130]
GIBSON, P. **The Capital companion:** a street by street guide to London and its inhabitants. Exeter, Webb & Bower, 1985. 446p. illus. £12.95. ISBN: 0863500420.

1200 entries (780 biographies in a single A-Z sequence with 400 streets) relating to Central London *i.e.* a rectangle 4½miles x 3 miles centred on Leicester Square. A 'must' for tourists arriving at Heathrow or Gatwick intending to do London at the double. *Class No:* 942.1(092)

[7131]
SUMERAY, D. **Discovering London plaques.** Princes Risborough, Bucks, Shire Books, 1999. illus., indexes. ISBN: 0747803951.

Details of 1,500 plaques within the orbital M25 motorway, including brief biographical information of the people commemorated, erected not only by the former G.L.C. and by English Heritage, but also many erected by private individuals and by organizations and institutions. Indexes of professions, streets and postal areas,

Clive Frewin's 'Look out for signs of the times', *The Times* no.66659, 30 October 1999. Travel, p.29 is a half-page, illustrated review feature. *Class No:* 942.1(092)

[7132]
SYMONS, A. **Behind the blue plaques of London 1867-1994** the complete guide. London, Polo Publishing, 1994. 218p. indexes.

Data: descriptive entry at paragraph length for each individual commemorated; wording on plaque; and nearest Tube station. Indexes to places and occupations. *Class No:* 942.1(092)

Archives

Micromaterials

[7133]
Historical gazetteer of London before the Great Fire. Keene, D., *ed.* Cambridge and Alexandria, Virginia, Chadwyck-Healey.

Part 1. *Cheapside* by D. Keene and V. Harding. £195. 57 microfiche in a binder with printed introduction and 4 printed maps. A new series based on surviving documents recording London's development from 12th century onwards including deeds, rentals, accounts, surveys, livery company records, parish and monastic houses records. *Class No:* 942.1(093.20)(003.5)

Roman Times

[7134]

MERRIFIELD, R. **The Roman city of London.** London, Benn, 1965. 344p. illus. (inc.pl.), maps, plans, bibliog., index.

4 chapters: 1. Archaeology in the city of London - 2. Historical outline - 3. The topography of Roman London (p.81-154; 68 references) - 4. Visiting Roman London. Gazetteer (p.189-325: General; Wall; Gates; Bastions; including references to illus. and sources). Bibliography, p.327-32 (most important sources are asterisked). 140 plates; 'Intended for the general reader, including a guide for the visitor' (*Foreword*). 'The definitive work' (Dawe, D. *The city of London* (1972), p.25). His *Roman London* (London, Cassell, 1969, [12],212p. illus., maps, records finds in the 4 years subsequent to *The Roman city of London*. Bibliography, p.[11-12].
Class No: 942.1"0055-0449"

19th Century

Maps & Atlases

[7135]

HYDE, R. **Printed maps of Victorian London 1851-1900.** Folkestone, Kent, Dawson, 1975. xv,271p., illus., facsims., plans, maps, indexes. £25. ISBN: 0712906401.

General introduction (16 sections: 1. Maps of London in the year of the Great Exhibition ... 7. Thematic maps ... 13. 19th century atlases of London ... 16. Select bibliography, p.52-53) - 313 numbered entries (author; title; publisher; page size; scale; coverage; series or other features). 3 appendices (3. Aids to dating). Title and general indexes. Awarded the LA Besterman Medal for an outstanding bibliography/guide to the literature in 1975. *Class No:* 942.1"18"(084.3)

Middlesex

[7136]

The Victoria history of the county of Middlesex. London, Constable, (subsequently Oxford Univ. Press for the Institute of Historical Research), 1911-. v.1-9 (1911-1998). illus., maps. £40, £50, £50, £40, £40, £50, £60, £60, £60. £70. ISBN: 0197227139, v.1; 0712904484, v.2; 0712910344, v.3; 0197227279, v.4; 0197227422, v.5; 0197227503, v.6; 0197227562, v.7; 0197227627, v.8; 0197227724, v.9; 0197227821, v.10.

V.1-3 deal with the general history of Middlesex. V.1 contains articles on its physiography and prehistory, religious houses, etc., with a translation of the Middlesex Domesday. V.2 covers the history, industries and sport of the county and begins the topographical account continued in v.4-10. V.11. 274p. illus. 1998. 0197227910. £70. *Class No:* 942.19

Surrey

[7137]

The Victoria history of the county of Surrey. London, Constable, 1902-14, 4v. and Index. Reprinted Dawsons 1968. illus., maps. £50, £70, £70, £50. ISBN: 0712902368, v.1; 0712902376, v.2; 0712902384, v.3; 0712902392, v.4.

V.1 comprises the archaeology, Domesday survey, and natural history of Surrey. The various aspects of economic and social history are contained in v.2, and the topographical survey initiated. The last is completed in v.4 which has additional ch. on antiquities and civil history. *Class No:* 942.21

Kent

[7138]

The Victoria history of the county of Kent. London, Constable and St. Catherine's Press, 1908-32, v. 1-3 only. Reprinted Dawsons. illus., maps. £60, £50, £50. ISBN: 0712906061, v.1; 071290607x, v.2; 0712906088, v.3.

No topographical volumes for this county have been issued. The general introductory matter has been extended to more than the usual volumes to allow for the detailed survey of the county's maritime history and Roman remains. *Class No:* 942.23

Bibliographies

[7139]

BENNETT, G., *comp.* **The Kent bibliography** a finding list of Kent material in the public libraries of the County and of the adjoining London Boroughs. London, The Library Association, London & Home Counties Branch, 1977. ix, 452p. £11. ISBN: 0902119206.

About 10,000 entries, with 21 locations of repositories. One A-Z sequence of places, subjects, persons (*e.g.* Sir Winston Churchill). Data: author, title, date of publication, location. Includes much local government material. 'Should prove to be of major importance to scholars, researchers and librarians in the field of local studies' (*Library Review, v.28, Summer 1979, p.132*). Bergess, W. *The Kent*

....(contd.)
bibliography: supplement. 1981, vii, 368p. pbk. £9.50. ISBN 0902119303. Updates material to 31 December 1978 as reported by contributing libraries. List of repositories p.vii. *Class No:* 942.23(01)

[7140]

—BERGESS, W. Kent maps and plans in the libraries of Kent and the adjoining London Boroughs: a finding list. London, Library Association London and Home Counties Branch, 1992. viii,386p. indexes. £30. ISBN: 0902119346.

'Inevitably it suffers from the shortcomings of the catalogues from which information was abstracted [but] ... a very welcome addition to the field of local studies aids' (*Library Association Record*).
Class No: 942.23(01)

[7141]

Bibliotheca Cantiana or antiquarian Kentish books. Volume 1. Being an account of the published material, books, acts of parliament, maps and ephemera, relating to the County of Kent up to the year 1836. Chatham, Kent, John Hallewell Publications, 1980. 360p. index. ISBN: 0905540220.

Reprinted from the original edition of John Russell-Smith 1836.
Volumes covering the years 1836-1900 were reported to be in preparation. *Class No:* 942.23(01)

[7142]

GOULDEN, R. **Kent town guides 1763-1900** a bibliography. London, British Library, 1995. 136p. illus. £30. $55. ISBN: 0712303669.

This definitive bibliography of locally printed town guides includes publishers and publication dates together with essays on individual towns. 'Coverage is as complete as present knowledge permits' (*Reference Reviews*, v.10,no.5, 1996. p.40). *Class No:* 942.23(01)

Sussex

[7143]

The Victoria history of the county of Sussex. London, Constable and Oxford Univ. Press for the Institute of Historical Research, 1905-. V.1-4, 6 (pts.1-3), 7, 9 and Index v.1-4, 7 and 9 (1905-1987). £60, £60, £25, £30, £50, £50, £50, £40, £40, £25. ISBN: 0712905855, v.1; 0712905863, v.2; 0712905871, v.3; 071290588x, v.4; 0197227538, v.6 pt.2; 0197227678, v.6 pt.2; 0197227686, v.6 pt.3; 0712905898, v.7; 0712905901, v.9; 019722766x, Index.

The various aspects of the county's history and antiquities are surveyed in v.1-3. The topographical survey is commenced in v.3 and continues in the subsequent volumes. V5. Pt.1. 1997. 0197227813. *Class No:* 942.25

Bibliographies

[7144]

HOLLINGDALE, E.A., *comp.* **Sussex bibliography.** Lewes, East Sussex County Library, 1970-. pbk.

1975-76 (1978) £0.50. ISBN 0861470273. *1977* (1978) £0.40. 0900348623. *1978* (1979) £0.50. 0900348801. *1979* (1980) £0.60. 0900348879. Very useful bibliography. A sad loss if deceased. *Class No:* 942.25(01)

Maps & Atlases

[7145]

LESLIE, K. *and* SHORT, B., *eds.* **An Historical atlas of Sussex.** Chichester, West Sussex, Phillimore, 1999. 176p. maps (some col.). £25. ISBN: 1860771122.

70 map features, each including 1,000 words of text, ranging from prehistoric times, to 20th century commuting to work, via Saxon settlements and 17th century inns. Part of the local Millenium celebrations, this atlas is the result of a joint partnership between West and East Sussex county councils, Brighton and Hove Council, the Univ. of Sussex, and the Sussex Archaeological Society.
Class No: 942.25(084.3)

[7146]

STEER, F.W., *ed.* **A Catalogue of Sussex maps.** Lewes, Sussex Record Society, 2v., 1962-68. indexes.

1. *Estate and title award maps.* zxvi,240p. £5.00. ISBN 0900801077. 2. *Private estate maps.* vi,228p. About 2000 briefly annotated entries. *Class No:* 942.25(084.3)

Hampshire

[7147]

The Victoria history of Hampshire and the Isle of Wight. London, Constable, 1900-14. 5v. and index. Reprinted Dawsons. illus., maps. £60, £60, £60, £70, £70, £15. ISBN: 071290591x, v.1; 0712905928, v.2; 071290593, v.3; 071290594, v.4; 071290595, v.5; 0712905960, Index.

V.1 covers the county's archaeology, natural history, and Domesday

..*(contd.)*

survey. Religious history, education, and forestry are in v.2 which also commences the topography, concluded in v.5, along with the economic and general history of the region. Complete. *Class No:* 942.27

Berkshire

[7148]

he Victoria history of Berkshire. London, Constable and St. Catherine's Press, 1906-1927. 4v. and index. Reprinted London, Dawsons Pall Mall, 1972. illus., maps. £50, £40, £60, £60, £15. ISBN: 0712905278, v.1; 0712905286, v.2; 0712905294, v.3; 0712905308, v.4; 0712905316, Index.

V.1-2 are devoted to the introductory chapters on history and economic and social history. V.3-4 comprise the topographical survey. Complete. *Class No:* 942.29

Wiltshire

[7149]

he Victoria history of the county of Wiltshire. London, Oxford Univ. Press for the Institute of Historical Research, 1953-. Some volumes reprinted by Dawson. illus., maps. V.1(pt.2) £40; v.6 £50; v.7 £50; v.8 £40; v.9 £40; v.10 £40; v.11 £60; v.12 £60; v.13 £60.v.14 £60. v.15 £70. v.16 £70. ISBN: 019722735x, v.1 pt.2; 0712910328, v.6; 0712910360, v.7; 0197227104, v.8; 0197227368, v.9; 0197227406, v.10; 0197227511, v.11; 0197227597, v.12; 0197227694, v.13; 0197227791, v.14; 0197227856, v.15; 0197227937, v.16.

V.1 (pt.1) is largely an archaeological gazetteer; pt.2 covers archaeology and prehistory. V.2 is devoted to the Anglo-Saxon period and the Wiltshire Domesday which is treated in detail. V.3 covers ecclesiastical history. V.4 includes agriculture, industries, transport, forests, and sport. V.5-6 cover political history (*i.e.* city government from 1066 onwards and parliamentary representation) whilst v.7-16 are topographical. *Class No:* 942.31

Maps & Atlases

[7150]

rinted maps of Wiltshire 1787-1844 a selection of topographical, road and canal maps in facsimile. Chandler, J., *ed.* Trowbridge, Wiltshire Record Society, 1998. xxvii,268p. illus., facsims., maps, bibliog., index. £20. *Class No:* 942.31(084.3)

Dorset

[7151]

he Victoria history of the county of Dorset. London, Constable, 1908-. Reprinted Dawsons. illus., maps. £50, £25. ISBN: 0712906703, v.2; 019722718x, v.3.

V.2 covers the economic, political, religious and social history whilst v.3 contains a translation of the Dorset Domesday and Geld Rolls, plus commentary articles. *Class No:* 942.33

Channel Islands

[7152]

OCART, R. 'Guernsey: local history in an insular context', *Local Historian*, v.21, no.2, February 1991, p.20-3.

Running narrative review of sources for local history including the holdings of the Priaulx Library, the Island's Archive Service and the Société Guernesiaise. Major standard histories of Guernsey are also noted. *Class No:* 942.34

[7153]

ARR, L.J. A History of the Bailiwick of Guernsey the islanders' story. Chichester, Sussex, Phillimore, 1982. xvi,301p. illus. (pl.+col.pl.), maps on endpapers, bibliog., index. £15.00. ISBN: 0850334594.

67 short chapters deal with the religious, feudal, political, naval and military, and the social and economic aspects of Guernsey history. 18 appendices including lists of Lords of the Isles, Wardens and sub-wardens, Governors and Lieutenant Governors. Chronological table p.285-93. Bibliography p.xv-xvi. *Class No:* 942.34

[7154]

YVRET, M. *and* STEVENS, J. Balleine's history of Jersey. Rev. & enl. ed. Chichester, Sussex, Phillimore for La Société Jersiaise, 1981. xiv,306p. maps on endpapers. bibliog., index. £25.00. ISBN: 0850334136.

G.R. Balleine's *History of Jersey* first published 1950.

33 chronological chapters. Bibliography p.xiii-xiv. Sources (*i.e.*, chapter notes) p.279-295. 34 plates (12 col.). 2 maps. *Class No:* 942.34

Devonshire

[7155]

The New maritime history of Devon. London, Conway Press in association with the Univ. of Exeter. 2v. 1992. illus.

1. *From early times to the late eighteenth century.* 256p. £35. ISBN 0851776116. 2. *From the late eighteenth century to the present day.* 272p. £35. 0851776337. Topics include coastal geology and topography, ports and seafaring, fishing, overseas and coastal trade, shipbuilding and shipowning, cartography and navigation, exploration and colonisation, piracy and privateering, coastal fortification and naval strategy and, not least, the Navy and the establishment of Devonport Dockyard. *Class No:* 942.35

[7156]

The Victoria history of the County of Devon. London, Constable, 1906. v.1 only. Reprinted Dawson. illus., map. £65.00. ISBN: 0712906711.

This single volume comprises the archaeology, natural history, and feudal survey of the county. *Class No:* 942.35

Bibliographies

[7157]

HAMILTON-LEGGATT, P. The Dartmoor bibliography 1534-1991 including a 1992 supplement. Non fiction. Tiverton and Exeter, Devon Books in association with The Dartmoor National Park Authority, 1992. xii,367p. index. £25. ISBN: 0861148738.

Unannotated entries arranged by form: 1. Books, pamphlets & leaflets - 2. Articles. Appendix 1. Directories - 2. Theses - 3. Maps - 4. Local journals and magazines - 5. Local newspapers. Alphabetico-classified index p.277-359. Previous bibliographies p.viii. *Class No:* 942.35(01)

Maps & Atlases

[7158]

BATTEN, K. *and* BENNETT, F. The Printed maps of Devon county maps 1575-1837. Tiverton, Devon Books, 1996. xxvii,248p. map, facsims (some col.), bibliog., index. £45. ISBN: 0861149009.

Descriptive catalogue of 117 maps and their appearances in atlases. Introduction (first county maps, accuracy and scale, derivation and deviation, roads, longitude and latitude, coastline) p.ix-xv. Bibliography p.238. *Class No:* 942.35(084.3)

[7159]

KAIN, R. *and* RAVENHILL, W., *eds.* Historical atlas of South-West England. Univ. of Exeter Press, 1999. 584p. illus. (many col.), maps, diagrs. £55. ISBN: 0859894347.

58 academic contributors (geographers, archaeologists, historians). 395 maps convey the history of Devon and Cornwall from the beginning of human occupation to the present day. Pre-Medieval content arranged chronologically but thereafter structured thematically: political and military history, religion, education, agriculture, industry, transport, maritime activities, and tourism. *Class No:* 942.35(084.3)

[7160]

RAVENHILL, M.R. *and* ROWE, M.M., *eds.* Early Devon maps. Exeter, Friends of Devon Archives, Devon Record Office, 1999. £15.

25 maps, dating c.1550-1700, in reduced facsimile. Most of the originals are held at the Devon Record Office although others are in the Public Record Office, The British Library, and the Somerset Record Office. *Class No:* 942.35(084.3)

Cornwall

[7161]

The Victoria history of the county of Cornwall. London, Constable and St. Catherine's Press, 1902-24, v.1 and 2 (pts. 5 and 8) only. £75.00. ISBN: 071290672x.

V.1 Zoology and archaeology; pts. 5 and 8 of v.2 cover Romano-British antiquities and the Domesday survey respectively. *Class No:* 942.37

Scilly Isles

[7162]

BOWLEY, R.L. The Fortunate Islands the story of the Isles of Scilly. 8th ed. rev. and enl. St. Mary's, Bowley Publications, 1990. 224p. illus., map, bibliog., index. ISBN: 0900184280.

1st ed. by E.L. Bowley 1945; 7th ed. 1980.

Chronological and thematic history in 12 chapters: 1. Antiquity - 2. Lyonesse and King Arthur - 3. Romans, Saxons, and Vikings ... 9. Wrecks, lighthouses and lifeboats. Appendix 1. Place names and dialect - 2. Population and area - 3. Isles of Scilly (list) - 4. Governors - 5. Chronological survey p.194-9. Bibliography p.200-22. *Class No:* 942.371

Somerset
[7163]

The Victoria history of the county of Somerset. London, Constable and Oxford Univ. Press for the Institute of Historical Research, 5v., 1906-1985. V.1-3 reprinted by Dawsons Pall Mall. . £60, v.2 out of print; £40, £50, £50, £60. ISBN: 0197227805, v.6; 0712903755, v.1; 0197227392, v.3; 0197227473, v.4; 0197227643, v.5; 0197227805, v.6.

V.1-2 cover the archaeology, economic, natural and social history of Somerset. V.3-6 are topographical. *Class No: 942.38*

Gloucestershire
[7164]

The Victoria history of the county of Gloucester. London, Constable and Oxford Univ. Press for the Institute of Historical Research. 1907-. v.2, 4-8, 10-11. illus., maps. £50, £60, v.6 out of print; £50, £40, £40, £40. £70. ISBN: 0712905553, v.2; 0197227716, v.4; 0197227872, v.5; 0197227554, v.7; 0197227244, v.8; 0197227252, v.10; 0197227457, v.11.

V.2 covers the ecclesiastical, economic, industrial and sporting history of the county. V.4 recounts the history of the city of Gloucester whilst v. 5-8, 10-11, are topographical surveys. V.1 is in active preparation. *Class No: 942.41*

Monmouthshire
[7165]

BRADNEY, J.A. A History of Monmouthshire from the coming of the Normans down to the present time. London, Mitchell, Hughes and Clarke, 4v. in 12, 1906-1933.

Arranged according to Hundreds. *Class No: 942.43*

Maps & Atlases

Bibliographies
[7166]

Mapping of Monmouthshire: a descriptive catalogue of pre-Victorian maps of the county (now Gwent) from Saxton in 1577, with details of British atlases published during that period. Bristol, Regional Publications, 1985. £10.95. ISBN: 0906570182.
Class No: 942.43(084.3)(01)

Herefordshire
[7167]

The Victoria history of the county of Hereford. London, Constable, 1908. v.1 only. Reprinted Dawson. illus., map. £50. ISBN: 071290669x.

This single volume covers natural history, archaeology, the Domesday survey, political history and agriculture. Complete. *Class No: 942.44*

Shropshire
[7168]

The Victoria history of Shropshire. London, Constable and Oxford Univ. Press for the Institute of Historical Research, 1908-. v.1-4, 8, 10-11. illus., maps. £40, £40, £50, £60, £40, £50, £70. ISBN: 0712903070, v.1; 0197227295, v.2; 0197227309, v.3; 0197227759, v.4; 0197227317, v.8; 0197227899, v.10; 0197227635, v.11.

V.1 embraces the archaeology, Domesday survey, industries and natural history of the county. V.2 includes an index of the Shropshire Domesday in v.1 plus a general index to v.1-2. V.3 encompases county government, parliamentary representation; officers, seals and arms. V.4 is taken up with agriculture and v.8-11 are topographical. V.10. 1998. £70. 0197227899. *Class No: 942.45*

Staffordshire
[7169]

The Victoria history of the County of Stafford. London, Constable and Oxford Univ. Press for the Institute of Historical Research, 1908-. v.1-8, 17 and 20. illus., maps. £50, £40, £40, £50, £50, £50, v.8 out of print, £40, £60. £70. ISBN: 0712903089, v.1; 0197227155, v.2; 0197227325, v.3; 0712910387, v.4; 0712910395, v.5; 0197227333, v.6; 0197227864, v.7; 0197227783, v.14; 0197227430, v.17; 0197227651, v.20.

V.1 covers the county's natural history, archaeology and history. V.2 is mainly concerned with industrial history and v.3 with religious aspects. V.6 is devoted to agriculture and school histories and v.8 to the city of Stoke on Trent and the Borough of Newcastle under Lyme. V.4-5 and 20 are topographical. *Class No: 942.46*

Biographies
[7170]

STUART, D., *ed*. People of the Potteries a dictionary of local biography. Keele, Staffordshire, Department of Adult Education, Univ. of Keele, v.1., 1985. viii,9-250p. ISBN: 0903160234.

600 brief biographies of persons living in the 6 towns now comprising Stoke upon Trent 1760-1910 (Arnold Bennett 50 lines and 3 references). Appendix: The people of the Potteries and the struggle for Federation p.239-50. *Class No: 942.46(092)*

Worcestershire
[7171]

The Victoria history of the county of Worcester. London, Constable and St. Catherine's Press, 1901-1926, 4v. and index. Reprinted Dawsons Pall Mall. illus., maps. £40, £50, v.3 out of print, £70, £15. ISBN: 0712904794, v.1; 0712904808, v.2; 0712904824, v.4; 0712904840, Index.

The county's archaeology, Domesday survey and natural history are covered in v.1. V.2 deals with ecclesiastical and political history and begins the topography. V.4 concludes this last and also has chapters on economic and social history. *Class No: 942.47*

Warwickshire
[7172]

The Victoria history of the county of Warwick. London, Constable and Oxford Univ. Press for the Institute of Historical Research, 1904-69. 8v. and index. illus., maps. v.7 £40, v.8 £40. ISBN: 0197227082, v.7; 0197227341, v.8.

Archaeology, natural history and the Domesday survey are in v.1. V.2 comprises the economic, political, religious and social history of the county. The remaining volumes are topographical. V.7 deals with the growth of Birmingham and v.8 with the story of Coventry and Warwick. Complete. *Class No: 942.48*

Bibliographies
[7173]

LANE, J., *comp*. Warwickshire local history sources. Leamington Spa, History Sources, 1988. 112p. illus., maps, facsims., plans. pbk. ISBN: 095130500x.

1. Records and record offices in Warwickshire - 2. Apprenticeship and child labour - 3. Education - 4. Enclosure of Butlers Marston - 5. Friendly societies - 6. Medicine - 7. Old and new Poor Law - 8. Prisons - 9. Transport - 10. Urban and rural unrest - 11. Newspapers and directories - 12. Research notes. Poorly reproduced from typescript. *Class No: 942.48(01)*

Handbooks & Manuals
[7174]

BLIZZARD, A. *and* BAIRD, P. Five ways into Birmingham's past. Birmingham, Citypack Ltd., 1989. 60p. illus., facsims., bibliog., index. sd. ISBN: 1871837006.

5 sections each showing a different approach to Birmingham's local history. Reading; Visual; House; Family; and Oral plus methods of research, resources, and lists of Birmingham branch libraries, museums, and county record offices. Glossary p.5-9. *Class No: 942.48(035)*

Derbyshire
[7175]

The Victoria history of the county of Derby. London, Constable, 1905-07. 2v. Reprinted Dawson. illus., maps. £50, £50. ISBN: 0712904468, v.1; 0712904476, v.2.

These 2v. contain the natural history, archaeology, the Domesday survey, economic and political history, and ecclesiastical foundations of Derbyshire. There are no topographical volumes. *Class No: 942.51*

Maps & Atlases

Bibliographies
[7176]

NICHOLS, H. Local maps of Derbyshire to 1770: an inventory and introduction. Matlock, Derbyshire Library Service, 1980. xxi, 183p. bibliog., index. pbk. ISBN: 0903463091.

379 descriptive entries arranged A-Z by parish, urban district council or borough. Glossary p.172-5. Bibliography p.180-3. Index of surveyors p.176-9. *Class No: 942.51(084.3)(01)*

Nottinghamshire

[7177]

BECKETT, J., *ed*. **A Centenary history of Nottingham.** Manchester Univ. Press, 1997. xxv,.398p. illus., tables, bibliog., index. £50. ISBN: 0719040019.

22 contributors. 23 chapters organized in 4 pts: 1. Origins and the medieval town - 2. Early modern Nottingham - 3. Industrial Nottingham 1750 to 1914 - 4. Twentieth-century. Bibliography p.571-82. Chronological and thematic 'city biography'. *Class No:* 942.52

[7178]

The **Victoria history of the county of Nottingham.** London, Constable, 1906-10. v.1-2 only: Reprinted Dawson. illus., maps. £50, £50. ISBN: 0712904530, v.1; 0712904549, v.2.

These 2v. contain the introductory chapters on the various aspects of the county's economy and history. *Class No:* 942.52

Bibliographies

[7179]

DOBBIN, M., *comp*. **Nottinghamshire history and topography: a** select descriptive bibliography to 1980. 21 Mapperley Hall Drive, Nottingham, the compiler, 1983. ISBN: 0950862908.

533 items arranged chronologically for Nottinghamshire then for individual places A-Z. Literature, periodicals, poll books, biography and family history excluded. Author and subject indexes. No pagination. *Class No:* 942.52(01)

Maps & Atlases

[7180]

NICHOLS, H. **Local maps of Nottinghamshire to 1800: an inventory.** Nottingham, Nottinghamshire County Council Leisure Services. xii,162p. ISBN: 0900943068.

Data: date; scale; O.S. coordinates; brief description; and location. 'A very useful research tool for local historians' (*The Cartographical Journal*, v.25,no.2, December 1988, p.182). *Class No:* 942.52(084.3)

Lincolnshire

[7181]

History of Lincolnshire. Thirsk, J., *(later Barley, M.), eds*. Lincoln, Society for Lincolnshire History and Archaeology. 1970-. illus., maps, bibliog., index.

1. *Prehistoric Lincolnshire* by J. May. 1977. xix, 251p. ISBN 0902668005. 2. *Roman Lincolnshire* by J.B. Whitwell. 1970. xxv, 155p. 0902668013. 3. *Anglo-Saxon Lincolnshire* by D.A. Bullough. 4. *Land and people in medieval Lincolnshire* by G. Platts. 1985. xx, 340p. 090266803x. 5. *Church and society in medieval Lincolnshire* by D.M. Owen. 1971. xxii, 170p. 0902668048. 6. *Tudor Lincolnshire* by G.A.J. Hodgett. 1975. xvii, 212p. 0902668056. 7. *Seventeenth-century Lincolnshire* by C. Holmes. 1980. xv, 279p. 0902668064. 8. *The agricultural revolution in Lincolnshire* by T. H. Beastall. 1978. xii, 256p. 0902668072. 9. *The church and dissent in Lincolnshire* by M.R. Watts. 10. *Rural society and county government in nineteenth-century Lincolnshire* by R.J. Olney. 1979. xiv, 202p. 0902668099. 11. *Lincolnshire towns and industries 1700-1914.* 1982. xvi, 300p. 0902668102. 12. *Twentieth-century Lincolnshire* ed. by D.R. Mills. 1989. xvi, 401p. 0902669145 has 12-footnoted chapters, a bibliography (p.373-401) and an index. *Class No:* 942.53

[7182]

The **Victoria history of the county of Lincoln.** London, Constable, 1906. illus., maps. £65. ISBN: 071291045x.

Only v.2 has appeared. It concerns the ecclesiastical, economic, social and political history of the county. *Class No:* 942.53

Bibliographies

[7183]

SHORT, D.M., *comp*. **A Bibliography of printed items relating to the** city of Lincoln. Woodbridge, Suffolk, The Boydell Press for The Lincoln Record Society, 1990. xx, 540p. port. index. £19.95. (*The Lincoln Record Society, vol. 79.*) ISBN: 0901503525. ISSN: 02672634.

Based on Com's *Bibliotheca Lincolniensis* (1904).

4931 entries in 27 major (subdivided) sections: 1. Bibliography - 2. Natural history - 3. History - 4. Topography ... 15. Libraries - 16. Archives ... 23. Biographical - 24. Directories - 25. Almanacs. *Class No:* 942.53(01)

Maps & Atlases

[7184]

CARROLL, R.A. **The Printed maps of Lincolnshire 1576-1900** a carto-bibliography. With an appendix on road books 1675-1900. Woodbridge, Suffolk, The Lincoln Record Society/Boydell Press, 1996. xlvi,449p. index. illus. £35. (*Lincoln Record Society, no.84.*) ISBN: 0901503576, Boydell; 0901503575, LRS. ISSN: 02672634.

154 fully described and annotated entries in chronological order of publication. Data: serial no., name of engraver, date of issue, size. Notes on surveyor, engraver and publisher. Editor, imprint, scale, origin, and location of copies. Appendix 21 road books with similar information. Bibliography p.413-16. Excludes O.S. sheets from 1825. *Class No:* 942.53(084.3)

[7185]

An **Historical atlas of Lincolnshire.** Bennett, S. *and* Bennett, N., *eds*. Univ. of Hull Press, 1993. vi,159p. maps. bibliog. £14.95. ISBN: 0859586049.

34 contributors. 66 double page map features arranged in 4 groups: 1. Physical setting - 2. Early settlement and industry - 3. Medieval Lincolnshire - 4. From the 16th century. Further Information (*i.e.* chapter notes and bibliography) p.136-51. *Class No:* 942.53(084.3)

Leicestershire

[7186]

The **Victoria history of the county of Leicester.** London, Constable, St. Catherine's Press, and Oxford Univ. Press for the Institute of Historical Research, 1907-. 5v. V.1-3 reprinted by Dawsons. illus., maps. V.1 out of print, £40, £40, £70, v.5 out of print. ISBN: 0712903682, v.2; 0712903690, v.3; 0712910441, v.4.

V.1 comprises natural history, archaeology, ecclesiastical history, and the Domesday survey. Religious, political, and agrarian history are covered in v.2 whilst v.3 deals with industries, transport, population, education, and sport. V.4 is devoted to the city of Leicester and v.5 begins the county topographical sequence. *Class No:* 942.542

Maps & Atlases

[7187]

STRACHAN, A.J. **Atlas of Leicestershire.** 2nd ed. Leicester, Univ. of Leicester Community and Employment Research Unit, 1986. 71p. maps, diagr. ringbinder. £3.50.

1st ed. 1985.

71 maps showing administrative boundaries, historical setting, population, agriculture, contemporary statistics, nature reserves, Leicester, and county towns. For home, school and college use. *Class No:* 942.542(084.3)

Rutland

[7188]

The **Victoria history of the county of Rutland.** London, Constable, St. Catherine's Press and Oxford Univ. Press for the Institute of Historical Research, 1908-36, 2v. and index. illus., maps. £40, £40, £5.00. ISBN: 0712906614, v.1; 0712906622, v.2; 0197226612, Index.

Complete. V.1 covers natural history, archaeology, the Domesday survey, and various aspects of economic and social history. V.2 is purely topographical. *Class No:* 942.545

Northamptonshire

[7189]

The **Victoria history of the county of Northampton.** London, Constable, St. Catherine's Press, and Oxford Univ. Press for the Institute of Historical Research, 1902-37, v.1-4 only. Reprinted Dawson. illus., maps. £50, £70, £40, £40. ISBN: 0712904492, v.1; 0712904506, v.2; 0712904514, v.3; 0712904522, v.4.

The general chapters on antiquities, natural and social history are contained in v.1-2. The topographical survey commences in v.2. A genealogical volume was issued in 1906. *Class No:* 942.55

Huntingdonshire

[7190]

The **Victoria history of the county of Huntingdonshire.** London, St. Catherine Press and Institute of Historical Research, 3v. and index, 1926-1938.

The natural history, antiquities and religious history comprise v.1 whilst v.2 surveys the general and economic history of the county. The topographical chapters begin in v.2 and are concluded in v.3. *Class No:* 942.562

Maps & Atlases

[7191]

DICKINSON, P.G.M., *comp*. **Maps in the County Record Office, Huntingdon.** St. Ives, Imray, Lawrie, Norrie & Wilson, 1968. viii, 72p. map.

Maps of Huntingdonshire (county maps; parish maps - Miscellaneous maps) provincial; county; naval charts and plans; transport and communications maps; drainage; foreign; etc. Appendix A & B (B: list of Huntingdonshire maps in the Nottinghamshire Record Office). Index of cartographers. *Class No: 942.562(084.3)*

Bedfordshire

[7192]

The Victoria history of the county of Bedford. London, Constable, 1904-14. 3v. and index. Reprinted by Dawsons Pall Mall. illus., maps. £50, £50, £50, £15. ISBN: 0712905324, v.1; 9712905332, v.2; 0712905340, v.3; 0712905359, Index.

Complete. V.1 comprises natural history, archaeology, the Domesday survey, and ecclesiastical history and foundations. In v.2 is a review of the political, economic and agrarian history, and accounts of schools and sport. The topographical chapters, with emphasis on churches and manors, begin in v.2 and conclude in v.3.
Class No: 942.565

Maps & Atlases

[7193]

CHAMBERS, B. **Printed maps and town plans of Bedfordshire 1576-1900.** Bedford, Bedford Historical Record Society, 1983. 250p. illus., bibliog., index. (*Bedford Historical Record Society Publications, no.62*.) ISBN: 0851550444.

1. The mapping of Bedfordshire. Locations are given for most of the maps recorded. 2. Catalogue of county maps (p.27-206) and town plans (p.207-23). Bibliography p.25. *Class No: 942.565(084.3)*

Oxfordshire

[7194]

The Victoria history of the county of Oxford. London, Constable and Oxford Univ. Press for the Institute of Historical Research, 1899-. V.1-. V.1, 9-10 reprinted by Dawsons. illus., maps. £60, £60, v.3 out of print, £50, £60, v.6-8 out of print, £40, £40, £60. £70. ISBN: 0712904565, v.1; 0712910417, v.2; 0197227147, v.4; 0712910425, v.5; 0197227260, v.9; 0197227287, v.10; 0197227589, v.11; 0197227740, v.12; 0197227902, v.13.

Natural history, archaeology, the Domesday survey, political history, and education fill v.1. V.2 is devoted to religious history, industries and sport. The University takes up the whole of v.3 and v.4 is devoted to the city of Oxford. V.5-13 are occupied with the topographical survey. *Class No: 942.572*

Bibliographies

[7195]

CORDEAUX, E.H. *and* MERRY, D.H. **A Bibliography of printed works relating to Oxfordshire** (excluding the University and City of Oxford). Oxford, Clarendon Press, 1955. xv,411p.

Also issued by the Oxford Historical Society (new series, v.11. 1977. £18). Considered a model of its kind. Locations of books not in the Bodleian Library are indicated. *Supplementary volume.* 1981. xxvii,289p. includes *addenda, corrigenda* and other relevant items.

A Bibliography of printed works relating to the City of Oxford. 1976,. xiv, 377p. is arranged under 17 main headings *e.g.* History and topography; Heraldry; Biography; Directories, surveys, handbooks and almanacs. *Class No: 942.572(01)*

Encyclopaedias

[7196]

HIBBERT, C., *ed*. **The Encyclopaedia of Oxford.** London, Macmillan, 1988. xiii, 562p. illus., maps, bibliog., indexes. £30. ISBN: 033339917x.

100 contributors. 1020 unattributed, documented, cross-referenced entries on personages, places, buildings, institutions. 7 Appendices (Bishops; Mayors and Lord Mayors; MPs; Burgesses; Vice Chancellors; Chancellors; Presidents of the Union since 1900). Glossary p.533. Bibliography p.534-6. 250 drawings, prints and photographs. 'This book is the ideal point of reference for any information about Oxford' (*Reference Reviews*, v.3, no.2, June 1989, p.92). *Class No: 942.572(031)*

Buckinghamshire

[7197]

The Victoria history of the county of Buckingham. London, Constable and St. Catherine Press, 1905-28. 4v. and index. Reprinted Dawsons Pall Mall. illus., maps. £50, v.2 is out of print, £60, £60, £15. ISBN: 0712903704, v.1; 0712903720, v.3; 0712903739, v.4; 0712903747, Index.

V.1 covers the natural history, archaeology, ecclesiastical history, and the Domesday survey. V.2 deals with the economic and social history and initiates the topographical survey concluded in v.3-4. Complete. *Class No: 942.575*

Hertfordshire

[7198]

The Victoria history of the county of Hertford. London, Constable and Oxford Univ. Press for the Institute of Historical Research, 1902-37. 4v. and index. Reprinted Dawsons Pall Mall. illus., maps. £50, £60, £60, £60, £15. ISBN: 0712904571, v.1; 0712904476x, v.2; 0712904778, v.3; 0712904786, v.4; 0712904832, Index.

The topographical survey is contained in v.2-4. Antiquities, history and natural history spread over v.1, 2 and 4. A genealogical volume was published in 1907. Complete. *Class No: 942.58*

Maps & Atlases

[7199]

HODSON, D. **Printed maps of Hertfordshire.** Folkestone, Dawson, 1975. 251 p. maps, index. ISBN: 0712906215.

First published London, Map Collectors Circle, 5 pts., 1969-72. Parts: 1. 1577-1784(1969) - 2. 1785-1820 - 3. 1821-1860(1970) - 4. 1861 - 1885 (1971) - 5. 1886 - 1900, and supplement (1972). Detailed bibliographical descriptions; major locations (*e.g.* British Museum; RGS). Pt.5 concludes with a section on Ordnance Survey maps. 'This is as complete a catalogue as possible of the county maps of Hertfordshire printed before 1901' (*Introduction*. pt.1).
Class No: 942.58(084.3)

Cambridgeshire

[7200]

The Victoria history of the county of Cambridgeshire and the Isle of Ely. London, Oxford, Univ. Press for the Institute of Historical Research, 1938-. V.1-9 and index v. 1-4. illus., maps. £50. £50, £60, £40, £40, £40, £25, £60, £69, £10. ISBN: 0712902414, v.1; 071290242, v.2; 0712902430, v.3; 0712802449, v.4; 0197227171, v.5; 0197227465, v.6; 0197227481, v.7; 0197227570, v.8; 0197227732, v.9; 0197226973 Index.

V.1 comprises natural history and the Domesday survey. Archaeology is completed in v.2 which also covers ecclesiastical, economic, political and social history. V.3 is devoted to the city, colleges and university and V.7 to Roman Cambridgeshire. V.4-6, 7-9 are topographical. *Class No: 942.59*

Norfolk

[7201]

The Victoria history of the county of Norfolk. London, Constable, 1901-06. v.1-2 only. Reprinted Dawson. illus., maps. £40, £70. ISBN: 0712906452, v.1; 0712906460, v.2.

This series has never been completed. V.1 covers the natural history and archaeology of the county. The Domesday survey, art, political and religious history are in v.2. *Class No: 942.61*

Bibliographies

[7202]

DARROCH, E. *and* TAYLOR, B. **A Bibliography of Norfolk history.** Norwich, Univ. of East Anglia, 1975. xviii, 447p. £7.20. ISBN: 0902171097.

At head of title-page: 'Centre of East Anglian Studies'. 7,304 entries, unannotated. Sections (closely classified): Directories - Almanacks, annuals, handbooks - Newspapers - Geography - Guide books and descriptive works - History and archaeology - Politics and administration - Economic history - Religion - Culture and recreation - Art, architecture, monuments - Biography - Individual locations (including King's Lynn, Norwich, Yarmouth), p.196-422.
Class No: 942.61(01)

Maps & Atlases

[7203]
An Historical atlas of Norfolk. Wade-Martins, P., *ed*. 2nd ed. Norwich (?), Norfolk Museums Service in association with the Federation of Norfolk Historical and Archaeological Organizations, 1994. 207p. maps, bibliog., index. softcover. £11.95. ISBN: 0903101602.

61 contributors. 93 topical maps with explanatory text arranged in 7 sections: Physical setting - Early settlement - Medieval Norfolk - Later Norfolk - Communications - Industries - Twentieth century. 'In a sense this is a county history presented in a rather unusual form (*Introduction*). *Class No:* 942.61(084.3)

Suffolk

[7204]
The Victoria history of the county of Suffolk. London, Constable, 1907-11. v.1-2 only. Reprinted Dawson. illus., maps. £70, £50. ISBN: 0712906479, v.1; 0712906487, v.2.

General review of the county's antiquities, economy, and general history. No topographical chapters. *Class No:* 942.64

Bibliographies

[7205]
STEWARD, A.V., *comp*. A Suffolk bibliography. Ipswich, Suffolk Records Society, v.20, 1979 (distributed by Boydell Press). xxiii,453p. ISBN: 0851151159.

8,123 numbered entries. Directories, almanacs, annuals, handbooks, newspapers and periodicals - Geography, landscape and climate - Guide books and descriptive works - General and political history - Economic history and communications - Local government, social services, and justice - Religion - Social history, culture and recreation - Architecture - Biography, genealogy, and heraldry - Individual and family biography, A-Z (nos.2057-3511) - Localities, Action ... Yoxford (nos.3512-3812), with subject subdivisions. Index of authors, editors, publishers, sponsors and titles (for anonyma). *Class No:* 942.64(01)

Maps & Atlases

[7206]
YMOND, D. *and* MARTIN, E., *eds*. An Historical atlas of Suffolk. 2nd ed. Ipswich, Suffolk County Council Planning Department and Suffolk Institute of Archaeology and History, 1989. 160p. illus., maps (some col.), bibliog., index. ISBN: 0860551539.

1st ed. 1988.
27 contributors. 62 double-page text and map features in 8 sections: 1. Physical setting - 2. Administrative units - 3. Early settlement - 4. Medieval Suffolk - 5. Suffolk since 1550 - 6. Industries - 7. Urban growth - 8. Vernacular architecture. Further information (*i.e.* sources and bibliography) p.136-54. *Class No:* 942.64(084.3)

Essex

[7207]
The Victoria history of the county of Essex. London, Constable and Oxford Univ. Press for the Institute of Historical Research, 1903-. v.1-9. Bibliography 1959. *Bibliography: Supplement*. 1987. illus., maps. £75, £75, £60, £60, £40, £40, £50, £60, £40, £40. £70. ISBN: 0712907742, v.1; 0712907750, v.2; 0712907769, v.3; 0712907777, v.4; 0197227120, v.5; 0197227198, v.6; 0197227201, v.7; 019727721x, v.8; 0197227848, v.9; 0197227708, Bibliog. Supplt.

V.1-2 contain natural history, archaeology, and general history. V.3 is limited to Roman Essex. V.4-8 are topographical. The *Bibliography* volume and *Supplement* have 3 pts: 1. The county (subdivided) - 2. Biography and family history - 3. Places and regions.
Class No: 942.67

Maps & Atlases

[7208]
MASON, A.S. Essex on the map The 18th century land surveyors of Essex. Chelmsford, Essex Record Office, 1990. x,138p. illus. (a few col.), bibliogs. £14.95. ISBN: 0900360755.

Pt.1: Maps and surveying (purpose of estate maps; work of a land surveyor; references and notes) - 2. The Land Surveyors (1700-34, 1735-69, 1770-99). Data: maps responsible for and commentary. *Class No:* 942.67(084.3)

Cheshire

[7209]
The Victoria history of the county of Chester. London, Oxford Univ. Press for the Institute of Historical Research, 1979-. v.1-. v.1-3,5 illus., maps. £60, £50, £50, £70. ISBN: 0197227619, v.1; 019722749x, v.2; 0197227546, v.3; 0197227880, v.5.

V.1 includes physique, prehistory, Romans, Anglo-Saxons and Domesday. Administrative history, parliamentary representation, forests and population are in v.2 and v.3 covers the general ecclesiastical history of the county (including Chester Cathedral and medieval religious houses). V.5 *The City of Chester*. 1996.
Class No: 942.71

Archives

[7210]
KENNETT, A.M., *ed*. Archives and records of the City of Chester. Council of the City of Chester, 1985. 144p. index. ISBN: 0950833223.

1. Official records - 2. Public records - 3. Private records - 4. Access and facilities. *Class No:* 942.71(093.20)

Lancashire

[7211]
KIDD, A. Manchester. 2nd ed. Keele Univ. Press, 1996. 251p. illus., bibliog., index. (*Town & City Histories*.) ISBN: 185331028x. ISSN: 09526153.

1st ed. 1993.
11 well-documented chapters in 3 parts: Before the Industrial Revolution - 1. First industrial city 1780-1850. 2. Commercial metropolis 1850-1914. 3. Within living memory. Manchester since 1914. Bibliography p.233-38. *Class No:* 942.72

[7212]
The Victoria history of the county of Lancaster. London, Constable, 1906-14. 8v. Reprinted Dawsons. illus., maps, indexes. out of print.

V.1 covers archaeology, the feudal survey, and natural history. Economic, political, religious and social history are in v.2. The remaining volumes are topographical. Complete. V.2: ISBN 0712910549 and V.5 ISBN 0712910557 reprinted 1991. £75 each. *Class No:* 942.72

Bibliographies

[7213]
FISHWICK, H. The Lancashire Library: a bibliographical account of books on topography, biography, history, science and miscellaneous literature relating to the County Palatine; including an account of Lancashire tracts, pamphlets and sermons printed before 1720 ... London, George Routledge; Warrington, Percival Pearse, 1875. xi, 443p.

Reprinted London, S.R. Publishers, 1969. *Class No:* 942.72(01)

[7214]
HORROCKS, S., *ed*. Contributions towards a Lancashire bibliography. Manchester Joint Committee of the Lancashire Bibliography, 1968-.

1. *Lancashire directories 1684-1957*. 1968. vii, 78p. £1.50. 2. *Lancashire Acts of Parliament 1266-1957*. 1969. x, 350p. 3. *Lancashire business histories*. 1971. xii, 116p. 4. *Lancashire family histories pedigrees heraldry*. 1972. xi, 201p. 5. *Registers ... monumental inscriptions, names, wills*. 1973. xi, 162p. 6. *Lancashire history and topography. Historical periods Pre-Roman, Roman, Pre-Norman*. 1973. x, 130p. £1.50. 7. *Lancashire history. Historical periods; Norman, Plantagenet, Lancaster & York, Tudor*. 1974. x, 99p. £6.00. 8. *Lancashire history. Historical period: Stuart*. 1976. x, 122p. £1.50. 9. *Lancashire history. Historical period: Hanover*. 1978. xiv, 242p. £1.50. 10. Turner, P.R. comp. *Transport history. Railways*. 1981, xiv, 321p. £6.00. ISBN 0902217135. 11. *Manchester Ship Canal: a guide to historical sources*, edited by P. Hodson. 1985. £10.95. 0902217143. *Class No:* 942.72(01)

Yorkshire

[7215]
The Victoria history of the county of York. London, Constable, St. Catherine's Press, and Oxford Univ. Press for the Institute of Historical Research,1907-. illus., maps.

General series: 1. £60. ISBN 071296096; 2. £60. ISBN 071290610x; 3. £60. ISBN 0712906118; Index. 1925. £15. ISBN 0712906126. Complete. Introductory surveys for the whole county of the type normally to be found in the 1st two volumes of the Victoria histories.

East Riding: 1. *The city of Kingston-upon-Hull*, out of print; v.2-6 are topographical volumes. 2. £40. ISBN 0197227384; 3. £40. ISBN 0197227449; v.4 £50. 019722752x; v.5 £60. ISBN 0197227600; v.6 £60. ISBN 0197227767. V.7 is in active preparation. *North Riding* A complete topographical survey in 2v. Out of print. *Index* £70. ISBN

....(contd.)
0712903119.

The city of York covers the history from Roman times to 1959 as well as particular institutions and aspects of the city. £70. ISBN 0712910298. *Class No:* 942.74

Maps & Atlases
[7216]

NEAVE, S. *and* ELLIS, S., *eds*. **An Historical atlas of East Yorkshire.** Univ. of Hull Press, 1996. xi,160p. £18.75. ISBN: 0859586529.

23 contributors. Map and text features divided into 9 major groups: environment, archaeology, population and settlement, landownership and land use, trade and industry, communications, religion and social provision, riot and rebellion, administrative units. Notes and bibliography (by chapter) p.140-53. Place-name index p.154-7. East Riding parishes and townships in the mid-19th century p.158-60. Focuses mainly on pre-20th century topics. *Class No:* 942.74(084.3)

Bibliographies
[7217]

WHITAKER, H., *ed*. **A Descriptive list of the printed maps of Yorkshire and its Ridings, 1577-1900.** Leeds, Yorkshire Archaeological Society, 1971. 261p. illus.(pl.). £8.00. ISBN: 0902122088.

First published 1933.

This bibliography forms v.86, for 1933, of the Yorkshire Archaeological Society 'Record series'. The introduction gives a concise survey of the development of English cartography. The 706 items are chronologically arranged; detailed descriptive notes. Tabular index (name; date; title; dimensions; work in which map was issued; number); supplementary index of authors, engravers, printers and publishers. *Class No:* 942.74(084.3)(01)

Durham County
[7218]

The Victoria history of the county of Durham. London, Constable and St. Catherine's Press, 1905-28. v.1-3 only. Reprinted Dawson. illus., maps. £50 each volume. ISBN: 0712903046, v.1; 0712903054, v.2; 0712903062, v.3.

The general chapters on the various aspects of the county's history are in the first 2 volumes. V.3 is a topographical survey of the city of Durham. *Class No:* 942.81

Maps & Atlases
[7219]

An Historical atlas of County Durham. Durham County Local History Society, 1992. 88p. maps, bibliog., index. £6. ISBN: 0902958143.

41 double page map features on some important aspects of the county's past (*e.g.* 2. The land of Durham - 3/4 Prehistory ... 7. Place names and landscape - 8. Northumbria ... 29. Population in the 19th and 20th centuries). Bibliography p.85. *Class No:* 942.81(084.3)

Northumberland
[7220]

HIGHAM, N.J. **The Kingdom of Northumbria** AD 350-1100. Stroud, Alan Sutton, 1993. x,296p. illus. (mostly col.), maps (some col.), bibliog., index. £25. ISBN: 0862997305.

Examines the history and archaeology of Northumbria from its origins of Brigantia and the Roman province of Britannia Secunda to the end of the 11th century. Bibliography (by chapter) p.274-84). *Class No:* 942.82

[7221]

MARSDEN, J. **Northanhymbre saga** the history of the Anglo-Saxon kings of Northumbria. London, Kyle Cathie, 1992. 259p. illus., maps, geneal. table, bibliog. £18.99. ISBN: 1856260550.

History of Anglo-Saxon kingdom extending from the Humber to Firth of Forth c.547-764 based on Old English, Old Irish, Britonic-Welsh, and Latin documentary sources. Genealogies p.237-40. Chronology p.241-4. Bibliography p.245-50. 4 maps. *Class No:* 942.82

Cumberland
[7222]

CUMBRIAN ARCHIVE SERVICE. Cumbrian ancestors notes for genealogical searchers. 3rd ed. Carlisle, Cumbria County Council, 1996. 96p. including many left blank for notes, maps, tables, bibliog. ISBN: 0905404718.

1st ed. 1998; 2nd ed. 1993.

Identification of and guide to Cumbrian records of prime interest to family historians i.e. parish, probate, diocesan, Roman Catholic and

....(contd.)
Nonconformist, quarter session, and other records. Bibliography (general and local sources, types of record) p.48-52. Useful addresses p.53-55. Folded map of Church of England parishes in Cumbria inserted in pocket. *Class No:* 942.85

[7223]

The Victoria history of the county of Cumberland. London, Constable 1901-05, V.1-2 only. Reprinted Dawson. illus., maps. £50, £60 ISBN: 071290302x, v.1; 0712903038, v.2.

V.1 contains archaeology, natural history, and Domesday survey Ecclesiastical, economic, political, and sporting history are in v.2 There are no topographical chapters. *Class No:* 942.85

Isle of Man
[7224]

KINVIG, R.H. **The Isle of Man:** a social, cultural and political history 3rd ed. Liverpool, Liverpool Univ. Press, 1975. xv,198p.

First published as *A history of the Isle of Man* (1944).

13 chapters 1. The physical and human background - 2. The prehistory of man - 3. The early Christian period, 450-800 ... 11 Fiscal and political reform in the nineteenth century - 12. The structure of the Manx economy - 13. Modern times. Glossary of words found in Manx place-names, p.177-82. Bibliography, p.183-90 (by chapters) Detailed index. 50 plates. *Class No:* 942.89

Bibliographies
[7225]

CUBBON, W., *comp*. **A Bibliographical account of works relating to the Isle of Man,** with biographical memoranda and copious literary references. London, Oxford Univ. Press for the Manx Museum and Ancient Monuments Trustees, 2v., 1933-39. illus. index.

Systematically arranged. V.2 includes annotated lists of Manx periodicals, newspapers, directories, *etc*. *Class No:* 942.89(01)

Wales
[7226]

DAVIS, E. *and* HOWELLS, B., *eds*. **Pembrokeshire county history** Haverfordwest, Pembrokeshire Historical Society.

V.3 *Early modern Pembrokeshire 1536-1815* edited by B. Howells 1987. xx,482p. 0907158269. V.4 Modern Pembrokeshire 1815-1974 edited by E. Davies and D.W. Howell. 1993. xxii,521p. illus., maps tables, 0907158722. has 26 chapters (*e.g.* Social statistics and the economy - 2. Government and administration - 3. Military presence 4. Culture and recreation). *Class No:* 942.9

[7227]

The Histories of Wales series. Stevens, C., *ed*. Cardiff, Welsh Academic Press, 200-. c.2000p. c.£10.

The Rhondda 1860570267; *Cardiff* 1860570257; *Anglesey* 1860570283; *Merthyr Tudful* 1860570291; and *Pembrokeshire* 1860570305. A major new history series focusing on the counties valleys and cities of Wales. Each book is a concise and scholarly history of a particular Welsh region suited for students and academics and ademics yet written in an accessible manner so as to also appeal to the general reader. *Class No:* 942.9

[7228]

The History of Wales. Oxford, Clarendon Press; Univ. of Wales Press 6v., 1981-.

2. *Conquest, coexistence, and change: Wales 1063-1415* by R.R Davies. 1987. £40.00. ISBN 0198217323. 3. *Recovery, reorientation and reformation: Wales 1415-1642* by G. Williams. 1987. £40.00 019888217331. 4. *The foundation of modern Wales 1642-1780* by G.H. Jenkins. 1988. £40.00. 0198217734x. 6. *Rebirth of a nation Wales 1880-1980* by K.O. Morgan. 1981. £27.50. 0198217366. Major history of the Principality. *Class No:* 942.9

[7229]

HOWELL, R. **A History of Gwent.** Llandysul, Dyfed, Gomer, 1988 226p. illus., map, index. £5.95. ISBN: 0863833381.

Concise overview history in 32 chronological and thematic chapters (*e.g.* Earliest inhabitants ... Roman Gwent ... Early industrialization .. Myth of Monmouthshire ... Modern Gwent) and 3 Appendices (Arthurian Gwent - Castles - Seasonal traditions). Chapter notes. *Class No:* 942.9

[7230]

MAY, J. **A Chronicle of Welsh events.** Swansea, Christopher Davies 1994. 131p. pbk. £9.95. ISBN: 0715407236.

Chronology of the events, people, and politics that have shaped Wales 49AD-1993. *Class No:* 942.9

Bibliographies

[7231]
AVIES, J. 'What to read on the history of Wales before 1536,' *Local Historian*, v.17, no.5, February 1987, p.265-268 and 'What to read on the history of Wales since 1536', ibid, v.17, no.6, May 1987.

Literature surveys with consolidated lists of works mentioned A-Z by author. *Class No: 942.9(01)*

[7232]
ONES, P.H. A Bibliography of the history of Wales. Cardiff, University of Wales Press, 1989. Compiled for the History and Law Committee of the University of Wales Board of Celtic Studies. 75p. pbk. + 21 microfiche with a holder. £37.00. ISBN: 0708310370.

1st ed. 1931; 2nd ed. 1962 and 4 supplements 1962-1972.

Includes 22,000 items (5,400 in previous ed. and supplements). Now computerized so that it consists of 3 sets of microfiche (48 x reduction): main classified sequence, author-title index, and KWIC index to titles of records in the classified sequence. 'Without the help of the accompanying printed handbook both historians and librarians would have difficulty in getting to grips with the layout of various indexes. Indeed the handbook is essential, and provides a comprehensive and thorough guide to using the Bibliography and also, for those who are unacquainted with indexing methods, a good description of a Key Word in Context index... The editor has to be praised on the scope, accuracy detail and amount of material included'. (*Reference Reviews*, v.3, no.3, September 1989, p.137-8).

Class No: 942.9(01)

[7233]
Velsh history and its sources. Herbert, T. *and* Jones, G.E., *eds.* Cardiff, Univ. of Wales Press, 6v., 1988. illus., maps, bibliog., index.

Publication of an Open University in Wales project funded by a Welsh Office Research Development grant 1985-1988. Each volume contains 5-7 topics of crucial importance comprising an essay cross-referenced in detail to the sources on which that essay is based, and a discussion of the strengths and weaknesses of the documentary material. Titles: 1. *Edward I and Wales*. xxxvi, 158p. £7.95. ISBN 0708310125. 2. *Tudor Wales*. xxvi, 177p. £7.95. ISBN 0708309712. 3. *The remaking of Wales in the eighteenth century*. xxvi, 192p. £7.95. ISBN 0708310133. 4. *People and protest: Wales 1815-1880*. xxx, 215p. £7.95. ISBN 0708309887. 5. *Wales 1880-1914*. xxiv, 193p. £7.95. ISBN 0708309674. 6. *Wales between the wars*. xxiv, 296p. £9.95. ISBN 0708309895. *Class No: 942.9(01)*

[7234]
'elsh History Review Cylchgrawn Hanes Cymru. Cardiff, University of Wales Press for History and Law Committee of Board of Celtic Studies, 1960-.

Carries regular feature 'Articles relating to the history of Wales' published during a calendar year *e.g.* 1989 in v.15, no.4, December 1991, p.633-50. *Class No: 942.9(01)*

Maps & Atlases

[7235]
EES, W. An Historical atlas of Wales from early to modern times. 3rd. ed. London, Faber, 1977. vii,73p. 71pl. of maps.

First published Cardiff, the author, 1951.

71 line-maps illustrating various aspects of Welsh history (geological, political, ecclesiastical, social, economic, industrial and educational) from its origins to approximately the end of the 19th century, with adequate textual description. Various scales. Page size, 18.5x25cm. *Class No: 942.9(084.3)*

Biographies

[7236]
ISHER, D.C. Who's who in Welsh history. Swansea, Christopher Davies, 1997. 187p. bibliog. £12.99. ISBN: 0715407317.

Who's Who p.11-164. Families and Peerage p.168-85. Bibliography p.187. 'This is not a work of historical scholarship. It is a simple alphabetical index designed to aid the would-be student of Welsh history, or anyone with a passing interest in the subject' (*Introduction*). It is useful nevertheless, its scope is wide and it includes lesser known figures in Welsh history. *Class No: 942.9(092)*

Middle Ages

[7237]
AVIES, W. Wales in the early Middle Ages. Leicester, Leicester Univ. Press, 1982. xiv, 263p. illus., map, bibliog., index. (*Studies in the early history of Britain*.) ISBN: 0718511638.

A scholarly and well-documented account of Welsh history from the end of the Roman occupation to the beginning of the Norman Conquest in 7 chapters: 1. Land, landscape and environment - 2. Economy - 3. Social ties and social strata - 4. Secular politics - 5. Kings, law and order - 6. The Church - 7. Christianity and spirituality. An appendix on Source Material (p.198-218) examines records, laws,

....(contd.)
narrative sources, poems and stories, scholarly and liturgical writings, non-Welsh sources, place names, and the physical evidence. Chapter notes p.222-246. Bibliography p.247-254. *Class No: 942.9"01/14"*

[7238]
JACK, R.I. Medieval Wales. Cambridge, Cambridge Univ. Press, 1976. 255p. index. £19.50. (*Sources of History*.) ISBN: 0521214556.

9 chapters: 1. Literary sources - 2. The official records of Wales and their preservation - 3. The records of the English government - 4. Archives of individuals and corporations - 5. Ecclesiastical records - 6. The antiquaries - 7. Archaeology and numismatics - 8. Cartography and place-names - 9. Conclusions. Running commentary. Adequate cross-references. *Class No: 942.9"01/14"*

Caernarvonshire

[7239]
DODD, A.H. A History of Caernarvonshire 1284-1900. Wrexham, Bridge Books, 1990. 438p. illus., bibliogs., index. £14.95. ISBN: 1872424074.

First published Caernarvon, Caernarvonshire Historical Society, 1948.

15 chapters: 1. Making of the shire - 2. Tudor Caernarvonshire ... 13. Politics and religion (1780-1900) ... 15. Local government in the 19th century. Chapter bibliographies. *Class No: 942.92*

Denbighshire

Bibliographies

[7240]
DENBIGHSHIRE COUNTY LIBRARY. Bibliography of the county. Ruthin, Denbighshire County Library, 3v., 1935-7.

1: *Biographical sources*. 2: *Historical and topographical sources*. 3: *Denbighshire authors and their works*. A rev.ed. of pt.2 appeared in 1951 and a supplement, 1955-57 (56p.), in 1959 (Sections: list of periodicals; Denbighshire in general; towns, A-Z, with subdivisions). The three parts are easily the most comprehensive printed bibliography for any Welsh county and together constitute a remarkable tool for the study of Denbighshire local history. *Class No: 942.932(01)*

Cardiganshire

[7241]
Cardiganshire county history. Cardiff, Univ. of Wales Press on behalf of the Cardiganshire Antiquarian Society in association with the Royal Commission on the Ancient and Historical Monuments of Wales.

1. *From the earliest times to the coming of the Normans*. Edited by J.L. Davies and D.P. Kirby. 1994. xx,441p. illus (inc. 1 col. pl.), index. ISBN 0708311709. 15 contributors. In 2 pts. (Land and environment: Archeology and history). 13 thematic and chronological chapters. 3. *Cardiganshire in modern times*. Edited by G.H. Jenkins and I. Gwynedd. 1998. xvii,633p. £60. 0708314899. 'Both editions and contributors are to be congratulated on the extent to which the local historian and general reader will find valuable and digestible information on practically every facet of the country's history' (*English Historical Review*, v.115, no.460, February 2000, p.265-69). *Class No: 942.95*

Radnor

[7242]
GREGORY, D. Radnorshire a historical guide. Llanrwyst, Gwynedd, Gwag Carreg Gwalch, 1994. 166p. illus., maps. £4.50. ISBN: 0492642031.

1. Before 1066 - 2. 1066-1536 The Enemy at the Gate - 3. After 1536 - 4. Towns of Radnorshire. Index of place-names p.165-66. 17 maps. *Class No: 942.962*

Glamorgan

[7243]
Glamorgan county history. Williams, G., *ed.* Cardiff, Glamorgan County History Trust, 1936-. v.1-. illus., maps.

1. *Natural history* edited by W.M. Tattersall. 1936. (1971 reprint). xix, 444p. £15.00. ISBN 0904730026. 2. *Early Glamorgan prehistory and early history* edited by H.N. Savory. 1984. xx, 522p. £39.95. 0904730042. 3. *The Middle Ages* edited by T.B. Pugh. 1971. xix, 704p. £15.00. 090473000x. 4. *Early modern Glamorgan from the Act of Union of 1536 to the Industrial Revolution* edited by G. Williams. 1974. xviii, 717p. £15.00. 0904730018. 5. *Industrial Glamorgan from 1700-1970* edited by A.H. John and G. Williams. 1980. xiv, 671p. £35.00. 0904730034. *Glamorgan society 1780-1980* 1988. xv, 448p. £39.95. 0904730050. *Class No: 942.97*

Maps & Atlases

[7244]

THOMAS, H.M. A Catalogue of Glamorgan estate maps. Glamorgan Archives, 1992. x,134p. facsim maps and plans, bibliog., index. ISBN: 0905243250.

Introduction (p.1-34): historical background, Glamorgan estate maps, the surveyors *etc*. Map catalogue A-Z by Estate. Data: date, surveyor, physical format, scale, dimensions, contents. Bibliography p.127. *Class No:* 942.97(084.3)

Carmarthenshire

[7245]

LLOYD, J.E. A History of Carmarthenshire. Cardiff, London, 2v., 1937-39.

1. *From prehistoric times to the Act of Union (1536)*. xix, 374p. 2. *From the Act of Union (1536) to 1900*. xv, 548p. *Class No:* 942.98

Europe—Eastern

[7246]

HELD, J., *ed*. The Columbia history of Eastern Europe in the twentieth century. New York, Columbia Univ. Press, 1992. lxxii,435p. maps, bibliog., index. ISBN: 0231076967.

10 papers present overviews of the 20th century history of Eastern Europe and of Albania, Bulgaria, Czechoslovakia, East Germany, Hungary, Poland, Romania, and Yugoslavia. Chronology p.xi-lxix. Bibliography (p.405-16) includes non-English language material. 3 maps. *Class No:* 943/

Bibliographies

[7247]

GATES-COON, R., *comp*. Eastern Europe bibliography. Metuchen, NJ., Scarecrow Press, 1993. ix,175p. index. (*Scarecrow Area Bibliographies, no.2*.) ISBN: 0810827751.

1205 unannotated entries in 2 parts: General works (p.1-43) A-Z by country and A-Z by topic in Subject Bibliography (p.45-158) focussing on the history of non-Russian Eastern Europe. Author index. *Class No:* 943/(01)

Encyclopaedias

[7248]

Encyclopaedia of Eastern Europe frm the Congress of Vienna to the fall of communism Frucht, R., *ed*. New York, Garland Publishing, 2000. xiv,958p. bibliogs., index. £60. ISBN: 0815300921.

c.215 academic contributors. 8 major articles on Poland, Hungary, Romania, Bulgaria, the Czech Republic, Slovakia, Bulgaria, Albania, and European Russian form the cornerstones of this comprehensive encyclopedia and provide an introduction to the key events in their history over the last 200 years. The other signed cross-referenced entries deal with specific topics and themes: their geographical aspects, government, history, economy , culture, and the trends and ideas, external forces, and prominent individuals that have influenced the course of history. All entries end with reading lists. 14 unpaginated pages of maps are inserted between pages 472-473. *Class No:* 943/ (031)

Handbooks & Manuals

[7249]

Handbook of reconstruction in Eastern Europe and the Soviet Union. White, S., *ed*. Harlow, Essex, Longman Current Affairs, 1991. viii,407p. maps, tables, index. £75. ISBN: 0582085020.

11 contributors. Country profiles A-Z. Data: Detailed chronology of events 1989-1990; political and economic overviews; key economic factors; foreign economic relations; who's who of prominent personalities; and media. Key documents and election results are also included. *Class No:* 943/(035)

Dictionaries

[7250]

HELD, J. Dictionary of East European history since 1945. London, Mansell, 1994. x,509p. illus., map, index. £20. ISBN: 0720122384.

First published Westport, Conn., Greenwood Press 1994.c59.95. ISBN 0313265194.

Contents: Introductory essay comprising an overview of the regions' general characteristics prior to 1945. Then A-Z entries for major events, personalities, politics on country x country basis: Albania, Bulgaria, Czechoslovakia, Hungary, Poland, Romania, and Yugoslavia (by constitutent Republics). Each country begins with general information, map and chronology. *Class No:* 943/(038)

Maps & Atlases

[7251]

CRAMPTON, R. *and* CRAMPTON, B. Atlas of Eastern Europe in the twentieth century. London, Routledge, 1995. xvi,297p. illus. maps, tables, index. £55. ISBN: 0415066891.

129 maps and commentary marshalled in 7 sections: 1. Before th First World War - 2. First World War and Versailles peace settlement 3. Interwar years - 4. Second World War - 5. Eastern Europe unde Communist domination - 6. At the end of the Communist period - 7 End of Communist rule. Glossary of topographical names p.282-91 'The text is essentially useful and informative. Its quality is certainly far superior to that of the maps, raising the question whether th authors would not have served their readers better if they had remaine entirely with the means of communication which they are so clearly more at home'. (*The Times*, no.65759, 11 December 1996, p.36). *Class No:* 943/(084.3)

[7252]

HUPCHICK, D.P. *and* COX, H.E. A Concise historical atlas o Eastern Europe. New York, St. Martin's Press, 1996. 192p. col maps. $49.95. ISBN: 0132158939.

50 map features illustrating crucial periods in the history of Easter Europe from medieval times to the 20th century. *Class No:* 943/ (084.3)

[7253]

MAGOCSI, P.R. Historical atlas of East Central Europe. Univ. o Washington Press, 1994. xiii,218p., maps, tables, bibliog., index £49.99. (*A History of East Central Europe, no.1*.) ISBN: 0295972483.

Encompasses Poland, the Czech Republic, Slovakia, Hungary Romania, Slovenia, Croatia, Bosnia-Herzegovina, Yugoslavia Macedonia, Albania, Bulgaria, and Greece. Also included are th eastern parts of Germany (Historic Mecklenburg, Brandenburg Prussia, Saxony, and Lusatia). Bavaria, Austria, north-eastern Ital (historic Venetia), the lands of historic Poland-Lithuania (present-da; Lithuania, Belarus, and Ukraine up to the Dnieper River), Moldova and western Turkey, 400AD-1992.

The atlas is basically chronological in 4 sections: 1. Historical - 2 Geographical - 3. Thematic - 4. Others with 89 full-colour maps an accompanying text. Several maps illustrate the changing political an administrative boundaries at key historical dates and are intersperse with other maps that focus on similar changes within individua countries or specific areas. Thematic maps deal with such subjects a the economy, ecclesiastical structures, education and culture demography and ethnicity, and military affairs. Numerous tables an lists provide related statistical and demographic material. Bibliograph p.180-185. 'This volume is outstanding; dozens of sources have bee used in its preparation, and in terms of detail, accuracy and clarity it i unmatched' (*Library Association Record*, v.96,no.8, August 1994 p.451). *Class No:* 943/(084.3)

[7254]

SELLIER, A. *and* SELLIER, J. Atlas des peuples d'Europe Centrale new ed. Paris, Découverte, 1993. 192p. col.maps, tables, bibliog. index. ISBN: 2707120324.

First published 1992.

1. L'Europe Centrale (1000 years of history, language, and religion - 2. Vingt peuples (history in text and maps of the people of Finland Estonia, Latvia, Lithuania, Belorus, Ukraine, Poland, Czechoslovakia Hungary, Rumania, Yugoslavia, Bulgaria, Albania, and Greece. *Class No:* 943/(084.3)

20th Century

[7255]

Chronology of 20th-century Eastern European history Ference, G.C., *ed*. Detroit, Gale Reference, 1994. 530p. illus., maps bibliog., index. £46. ISBN: 0810388790.

Concise entries on 'the major political, economic and cultural event that have shaped the history of Eastern Europe from the turn of th century to the end of 1993' arranged in 9 sections: Albania, Bulgaria Czechoslovakia, East Germany, Hungary, Romania, Soviet Union Yugoslavia. 75 brief biographies of important historical figures. *Class No:* 943/"19"

Germany

[7256]

RICHIE, A. Faust's metropolis a history of Berlin. Londor HarperCollins, 1998. lx,1107p. illus., maps, index. £29.99. ISBN 0002158965.

Scholarly thematic and chronological narrative history in 18 chapte (*e.g.* 1. History, myth, and the birth of Berlin ... 6. Imperial Berlin . 11. Nazi Berlin ... 16. East Berlin ... 18. The New capital). Chapte notes p.859-1,071 include bibliographical references. *Class No:* 943./

[7257]
WEHLER, H-U. The German Empire 1871-1918. Leamington Spa, Warwickshire, Berg Publishers, 1985. [iii].293p. bibliog., index. £29.50. ISBN: 0907582222.

Translated from *Das Deutsche Kaiserreich 1871-1918* (Göttingen, Vandenhoeck u. Ruprecht, 6th ed., 1985).

Outstanding modern study. Chapter notes p.248-264 and an important bibliography p.264-290. *Class No:* 943.0

Encyclopaedias
[7258]
USE, D.K. *and* DOERR, J.C., *eds*. Modern Germany an encyclopedia of history, people and culture 1871-1990. New York, Garland, 2v., 1998. lii,1158p. illus., bibliog., index. £100; $195. ISBN: 0815305036.

c.400 contributors. 1300 entries presents 'information commonly accepted by most scholars rather than interpretations espoused by a specific school of specialists' (*Introduction*). Subject guide p.ix-xxiv. Chronology p.xxv-xxxvii. 'Every aspect of life and culture is covered in articles of generally very helpful lengths: long enough to avoid huge generalisations, short enough to impart relevant factual information with at least some approach to analysis and interpretation ... All are written to a consistent standard of clear and concise presentation of fact and essential background ... Each article also carries cross-references to related ones and a list of references suggested for further reading ... will be a very useful accession to any senior school, undergraduate or major reference collection' (*Reference Reviews*,v.12, no.7, 1998, p.49-50). *Class No:* 943.0(031)

Dictionaries
[7259]
EST, W. Dictionary of German history 1806-1945. London, George Prior, 1978. 189p. ISBN: 0860431088.

Entries A-Z for *c.*700 topics, with emphasis on the political angle and 20th century. Most articles have short bibliographical notes, covering writings published 1950-77. Cross-references. Intended as 'an aid to study, not as a substitute for it' (*Preface*). 'This is the first dictionary of modern German history in the English language' (*Library review*, Autumn 1979, p.193). 'A valuable reference book that should be in every undergraduate library' (*Choice*, v.16, no.4, June 1979, p.508). *Class No:* 943.0(038)

[7260]
HOMPSON, W., *and others*. Historical dictionary of Germany. Lanham, MD., Scarecrow Press, 1994. xvi,639p. illus., maps, bibliog. $62.50. (*European Historical Dictionaries, no.4*.) ISBN: 0810828693.

Introduction (people, geography, foreign and defence policies, integration problems) p.1-16. Chronology p.17-102. Dictionary (historical periods, significant people, places, events, institutions) p.105-514. Bibliography p.515-637. *Class No:* 943.0(038)

Maps & Atlases
[7261]
er grosse Bildatlas zur Deutschen Geschichte von Karl Dem Grossen biz zur Wiedervereinigung. München, Bertelsmann Lexicon Verlag, 1991. 296p.++ 32 col. pl. illus. (many col.), col. maps, bibliogs., index. ISBN: 3570065472.

16 contributors. Illustrated atlas in 21 chapters (*e.g.* 1. Germanen, Franken, Karolinger ... 10. Der Dreissigjährige Krieg ... 17. Nationalsozialismus in Deutschland ... 21. Die Bundesrepublik von den sechziger Jahren zur Wiedereinigung. *Class No:* 943.0(084.3)

[7262]
CHEUCH, M. Historischer Atlas Deutschland vom Frankenreich zur Wiedervereinigung in Karten, Bildern und Texten. [Historical atlas of Germany from the empire of the Franks to the second unification in maps, pictures and texts.] Wien und München, Christian Brandstätter, 1997. 255p. col.maps, illus. (mostly col.), bibliog., index. ISBN: 3854477066.

107 col. map features divided into 3 sections: 1. Deutsche Geschichte im Überblick (Roman times to progress towards European Union) - 2. Der Geschichte der Länder - 3. Frühere Länder des Reiches (Austria, Alsace Lorraine, Switzerland, Belgium and Luxembourg, Silesia etc.). Bibliography p.254-55. *Class No:* 943.0(084.3)

19th Century
Bibliographies
[7263]
BORN, K.E., *ed*. Bismarck-Bibliographie. Quellen and Literatur zur Geschichte Bismarcks und seiner Zeit. Köln & Berlin, G. Grotesche, 1966. 259p. ISBN: 3774500029.

About 4,000 entries in 18 sections: (5. Der Staatsmann (1862-1890), p.44-143 ... 1. Bismarck in der Kunst ... 17. Zeitungen und Zeitschriften Jahrbücher, Kalender, Mitteilungsblätter - 18. Literaturberichte, Bibliographen). Author index. *Class No:* 943.0"18"(01)

20th Century
[7264]
WEBB, A. Longman companion to Germany since 1945. London, Longman, 1998. xii,335p. maps, bibliog. £42. (*Longman Companions to History*.) ISBN: 0582307368.

Key facts and figures arranged in 13 sub-divided sections each comprising a chronology and explanatory text. Support apparatus includes biographies of politicians, statesmen, and other prominent figures. 'Equally at home in a public reference or academic library' (*Reference Reviews*, v.13, no.4, 1999, p.52-53). *Class No:* 943.0"19"

Bibliographies
[7265]
The Weimar Republic: a historical bibliography. Santa Barbara, California, and Oxford, ABC-Clio Information Services, 1984. xii,285p. indexes. (ABC-Clio Research Guide). £26.35. ISBN: 0874363780.

1035 abstracts of periodical articles published 1973-1982, culled from the *American History & Life* and *Historical Abstracts* databases, arranged in 9 sections: The Weimar Republic in historical context - The Beginnings of the Republic - Government, politics, and the economy - Weimar culture and society - The Jews of Weimar - Christianity in transition - The Growth of German communism - The Road to Nazi hegemony - The End of the Republic. A Subject Profile Index carries generic and specific index terms. 'Students of this very active field of scholarship will welcome the convenient repackaging of a decade's *Historical Abstracts*' (*Choice*, v.22,no.2, October 1984, p.255). *Class No:* 943.0"19"(01)

Dictionaries
[7266]
CARRINGTON-WINDO, T. *and* KOHL, K. A Dictionary of contemporary Germany. Chicago and London, Fitzroy Dearborn, 1996. vii,456p. bibliog. £35. ISBN: 1579581145.

1st published Hodder & Stoughton.

2000+ cross-referenced entries of varying length relating to institutions and personalities in German public life. Emphasis is on national and local government, education, the economy, and major commercial firms and industries. Bibliography (p.455-56) includes English and German-language works. *Class No:* 943.0"19"(038)

Maps & Atlases
[7267]
HILGEMANN, W. Atlas zur deutschen Zeitgeschichte 1918-1968. München, Piper, 1984. 208p. col. maps, tables, bibliog. ISBN: 3492024602.

103 geographical/historical features in 5 sections: 1. Ende des Kaiserreichs 1918 - 2. Weimarer Republik (1919-1933) - 3. Das Dritte Reich (1933-1945) - 4. Deutschland unter den Besatzungsmächten (1945-1949) - 5. Bundesrepublik Deutschland und Sowjetische Besatzungszone - DDR (1949-1968). Chronology p.194-208. Bibliography p.193. *Class No:* 943.0"19"(084.3)

Biographies
[7268]
BENZ, W. *and* GRAML, H., *eds*. Biographisches lexikon zur Weimarer Republik. München, Verlag, C.H. Beck, 1988. 392p. 49.80. ISBN: 3406329888.

59 contributors. Over 500 biographical sketches of prominent people 1918-1933 (Konrad Adenauer: 80 lines; Rosa Luxemburg: 61 lines). Die Regierungen der Weimarer Republik p.382-386. Politische Chronik p.387-392. *Class No:* 943.0"19"(092)

Nazi Germany

Bibliographies

[7269]

KEHR, H. *and* LANGMAID, J. **The Nazi era 1919-1945:** a select bibliography of published works from the early roots to 1980. London, Mansell Publishing Ltd., 1982. xvi,621p. index. £40.00. ISBN: 070211618x.

6523 works are listed, some with brief annotations, encompassing some 20 languages although preponderantly in English and German. Arrangement is in 9 parts each minutely divided and sub-divided to the point of confusion: 1. Reference books - 2. Nationalsozialistische Deutsche Arbeiterpartei - 3. From struggle to consolidation of power - 4. The Third Reich - 5. The criminal state - 6. Road to war - 7. World War II - 8. War crimes - 9. After the fall of the Third Reich. Analytical index p.529-561. 'Compiled with great scholarly care ... comprehensively covers the varied phenomena of Nazism ... this is a magnificent work' (*Choice*, v.20,no.4, December 1982, p.561). *Class No: 943.0"1933-1945"(01)*

[7270]

SNYDER, L.L., *ed.* **The Third Reich 1933-1945:** a bibliographical guide to German national socialism. New York, Garland Publishing Inc., 1987. 284p. index. $42.00. ISBN: 0824084632.

850 annotated entries grouped in 13 sections: 1. Documentary materials - 2. General - 3. Biography - 4. Politics and government - 5. Economics - 6. Social structure - 7. National Socialist culture - 8. Religion - 9. Psychological motivations - 10. Foreign policy - 11. Resistance movement - 12. Anti-semitism and the holocaust - 13. World War II. Cannot compare in coverage with H. Kehr's *The Nazi era* but 'recommended for undergraduate students beginning a research project' (*Choice*, v.25,no.5, January 1985, p.752). *Class No: 943.0"1933-1945"(01)*

[7271]

The Third Reich, 1933-1939: a historical bibliography. Santa Barbara, California and Oxford, ABC-Clio Information Services, 1984. xii,239p. indexes. £27.30. ISBN: 6874363799.

932 abstracts of journal articles printed 1973-1982 drawn from the publisher's renowned database. Arranged A-Z by author in 7 chapters: 1. Nazi Germany in historical context - 2. Domestic policies and politics - 3. Nazi foreign policy - 4. Culture and society in Hitler's Germany - 5. The crushing of German Jewry - 6. Christianity in crisis - 7. The Left under siege. The Subject Profile Index incorporates both generic and specific terms. *Class No: 943.0"1933-1945"(01)*

[7272]

—**The Third Reich at war:** a historical bibliography. Santa Barbara, California and Oxford, ABC-Clio Information Services. xii,270p. index. £27.30. ISBN: 0874363934.

Abstracts of 1061 journal articles, published 1973-1982, selected from the publisher's vast historical information database, assembled in 7 chapters: 1. Wartime Germany - 2. Trade and diplomacy - 3. Invasion and occupation of Poland - 4. At war with Western Europe - 5. Eastern and Southeastern Europe - 6. Russia - 7. The Holocaust. Author and subject indexes. *Class No: 943.0"1933-1945"(01)*

Encyclopaedias

[7273]

The Encyclopedia of the Third Reich. Zentner, C. *and* Bedürftig, F., *eds.* New York, Macmillan, 2v., 1991. 1120p. illus., bibliog., index. $175. ISBN: 0028975006.

Translated from *Das grosse Lexikon des Dritten Reiches* (1985).

40 contributors to this scholarly compendium of over 3,000 entries for events, people, culture, ideology, and almost every facet of Nazi Germany. 1,200 illustrations. 'The currently definitive reference source' (*Library Journal*, v.116,no.7, 15 April 1991, p.82). *Class No: 943.0"1933-1945"(031)*

[7274]

KIRK, T. **The Longman companion to Nazi Germany.** London, Longman, 1995. viii,277p. maps, tables, bibliog., index. £39. ISBN: 0582063760.

9 sections: 1. Politics and State: Weimar Republic and the rise of Nazism - 2. Third Reich - 3. Economy, society and culture 1918-1945 - 4. Diplomacy, rearmament and war 1918-1945 - 5. Anti-Semitism, racial politics and the Holocaust 1933-1945 - 6. Glossary (p.173-90) - 7. Biographies - 8. Bibliography (p.246-60) - 9. Sources (p.263-67). 5 maps. Analytical index. *Class No: 943.0"1933-1945"(031)*

Dictionaries

[7275]

TAYLOR, J. *and* SHAW, W. **A Dictionary of the Third Reich.** London, Grafton Books, 1987. Distributed in North America by St. Martin's Press. 401p. illus., maps, bibliog. £12.95. ISBN: 0246131780, UK; 0886873630, US.

Chronology p.11-20. A-Z of the Third Reich p.21-312. Military campaigns p.367-382. Selected quotations p.383-390. Bibliography

....(contd.)
p.391-392. For students and general readers. Cross-references Notwithstanding some idiosyncratic entries noticed *Reference Review* v,2,no.1, March 1988, p.35 reports that it is 'clearly based on a wealth of knowledge of the Third Reich'.

The Penguin dictionary of the Third Reich 1997. £8.99. ISBN 0140513892. *Class No: 943.0"1933-1945"(038)*

Maps & Atlases

[7276]

FREEMAN, M. **Atlas of Nazi Germany.** London, Longman, 1995. 248p. illus., maps, bibliog., index. pbk. £14.99. ISBN: 0582239249.

In 6 parts: 1. Rise of the Nazi party; 2. Adminstrative and political studies; 3. Society; 4. Population and economics; 5. The search for living space; the Third Reich at war; 6. The war machine. Reference p.191-192. Bibliographical guide p.195-196. Glossary p.193. 'This visual history will be very helpful to students up to the graduate level (*Choice*, v.25, no.8, April, 1988, p.1222). *Class No: 943.0"1933-1945"(084.3)*

[7277]

OVERY, R. **The Penguin historical atlas of the Third Reich.** London, Penguin Books, 1996. 143p. illus. (mostly col.), col.maps, tables, bibliog., index. £9.99. $16.95. ISBN: 0140513302.

40 map features grouped under 7 headings: 1. From war to the Third Reich 1918-1933 - 2. Establishing the dictatorship - 3. Foreign Policy in Germany 1933-1939 - 4. Expansion and war 1939-1945 - 5. German New Order - 6. German society and total war - 7. The aftermath. Timelines (4 colour coded columns across the page) German politics - War and foreign policy - Nazi movement - Society and economy p.116-21. Statistical appendix p.122-33. Bibliography p.134-36. *Class No: 943.0"1933-1945"(084.3)*

Chronologies

[7278]

EDELHEIT, H. *and* EDELHEIT, A.J. **A World in turmoil** a integrated chronology of the Holocaust and World War II. Westport, Conn., Greenwood Press, 1991. xiii,450p. bibliog., indexes. £67.50. (*Bibliographies and Indexes in World History, no. 22.*) ISBN 0313282188.

Concentrates on the most important political and diplomatic events primarily in Europe and the Middle East affecting world and Jewish history 30 January 1933 to 14 May 1958 (the date of the establishment of the State of Israel). Glossary p.385-403. Bibliography p.405-14. Name, place and subject indexes. *Class No: 943.0"1933-1945"(090)*

[7279]

HAUNER, M. **Hitler: a chronology of his life and time.** London, Macmillan Press, 1983. xi,221p., bibliog., index. £22.50. ISBN 0333309839.

Traces every known detail of Hitler's career with an itinerary of his movements on a daily basis and a chronological guide to his speeches and writings. Glossary p.ix. Bibliography p.204-5. *Class No: 943.0"1933-1945"(090)*

Biographies

[7280]

WISTRICH, R. **Who's who in Nazi Germany.** 2nd ed. London, Routledge, 1995. x,296p. ISBN: 0415127238.

First published by Weidenfeld & Nicolson 1982.

Nearly 350 biographies of individuals prominent or significant in Nazi Germany based on personal files, documentary material, press cuttings and historical works held in the Wiener Library. Glossary p.285-88. Bibliography p.290-96. 'Highly recommended for all institutions where history is taught' (*Choice*, v.20,no.8, April 1983, p.1116). *Class No: 943.0"1933-1945"(092)*

Jews

[7281]

EDELHEIT, A.J. *and* EDELHEIT, H. **History of the Holocaust** handbook and dictionary. Boulder, Colo., Westview Press, 1994. 542p. bibliog., index. $89.95. ISBN: 0813314119.

Part 1: Antecedents, Nazi totalitarian state, International response *i.e.* a history of European Jews in the Nazi era). Part 2: Holocaust glossary (300p.). Part 3: tables and graphs. *Class No: 943.0"1933-1945"(=924)*

[7282]

EPSTEIN, E.J. *and* ROSEN, P. **Dictionary of the Holocaust** biography, geography and terminology. Westport, CT., Greenwood Press, 1997. $49.95. ISBN: 031330355x.

2,000 entries relating to major personalities (victims, perpetrators, bystanders, collaborators, rescuers, physicians, industrialists) concentration and death camps, significant events etc. *Class No: 943.0"1933-1945"(=924)*

[7283]

ILBERT, M. The Holocaust : the Jewish tragedy. London, Collins, 1986. 959p. illus., maps, bibliog., index. £25. ISBN: 0002163055.

Definitive history in 41 chapters. Notes and sources p.831-96. 25 maps. Analytical index. *Class No:* 943.0"1933-1945"(=924)

Bibliographies

[7284]

AUPTMAN, R. *and* MOTIN, S.H., *comps*. The Holocaust: memories, research, reference. New York, Haworth Press, 1998. 320p. index. $49.95. ISBN: 0789003791.

Published simultaneously in *The Reference Librarian,* nos. 61/62, 1998.

30 contributors. 1. Memoirs (4 articles and poems) - 2. Research (10 articles) - 3. Reference (11 articles including M. Goldberg's 'Holocaust Autobiography'; A. Mirwis' 'Overlooked reference tools for researching the Holocaust'; and Judy Anderson's 'Expand reference resources: research the Holocaust through the Internet'. 'So much has been written about the Holocaust ... that a survey of this nature is extremely valuable' (*Library Association Record,* v.101, no.3, March 1999, p.171). *Class No:* 943.0"1933-1945"(=924)(01)

[7285]

ASKA, V. Nazism, resistance & holocaust in World War II. Metuchen, New Jersey, Scarecrow Press, 1985. xxii, 205p. £18.00. ISBN: 0810817713.

1907 numbered entries, some briefly annotated arranged in 13 chapters: 1. Jews and anti-Semitism - 2. Nazism - 3. Resistance - Women - 4. Jewish resistance - 5. Holocaust - 6. Holocaust - Women - 7. Women in hiding - 8. Pre-1945 knowledge of the Holocaust - 9. War crimes - 10. Art and photographs - 11. Philosophy and interpretation - 12. Literature - 13. Addenda. Not confined to Jews. *Class No:* 943.0"1933-1945"(=924)(01)

Encyclopaedias

[7286]

UTMAN, I., *ed*. Encyclopedia of the Holocaust. New York, Maxwell Macmillan, 4v., 1989. 1,1905p. illus., maps, bibliog., index. $335. ISBN: 0028960904, set; 0028971639, v.1; 0028971647, v.2; 0028971655, v.3; 0028971663, v.4.

950 signed and well-documented A-Z cross-referenced articles (most have reading lists of 2-12 items), contributed by 207 leading international scholars, cover all aspects of the Holocaust, including the history, politics and major figures of the Third Reich; the ideological roots of racism and anti-Semitism; Nazi medical practices and experiments; and the organization of genocide. Appendices include a glossary (p.1751); a detailed chronology 1920-1945 (p.1759); a list of major Jewish organizations in Germany 1893-1943; the structure of the Einsatzgruppen from June 1941; a summary of the Nuremburg Trial and subsequent trials with lists of defendants, and a country by country analysis of estimated Jewish losses in the Holocaust. V.4 has a detailed index. 'This wealth of information about one of the major events in the history of western civilization belongs in all public and academic libraries' (*Booklist,* v.86,no.13, 1 March 1990, p.1375+8). *Class No:* 943.0"1933-1945"(=924)(031)

Maps & Atlases

[7287]

ILBERT, M. Atlas of the Holocaust. 2nd rev. ed. London, Routledge, 1993. 282p. illus., maps, bibliog., index, pbk. £19.99. ISBN: 0460861719.

316 maps and accompanying text charting the destruction of the major Jewish communities in Europe from the anti-semitism of pre-war Germany onwards. *Class No:* 943.0"1933-1945"(=924)(084.3)

Federal Republic of Germany

[7288]

ARK, D.L. *and* GRESS, D.R. A History of West Germany. 2nd ed. Oxford, Blackwell, 2v., 1993. ISBN: 1557863237.

1st ed. 1989.

1. *From shadow to substance 1945-1963.* lvi,591p. illus., maps, bibliog., index. Bibliographic essay p.527-36. Documents and sources p.537-40. Bibliography p.541-66. Analytical index.

2. *Democracy and its discontents 1963-1991.* xvii,862p. Bibliographic essay p.798-808. Documents and sources p.809-12. Bibliography p.813-38. Analytical index. Exhaustive, scholarly and thoroughly researched history of post-World War 2 social, political and economic developments in West Germany. *Class No:* 943.01

German Democratic Republic

[7289]

OSMOND, J. German reunification a reference guide and commentary. Harlow, Essex, Longman, 1992. xviii,311p. tables, bibliog., maps, index. £45. ISBN: 0582096502.

Part 1: Revolution and reunification (including chronology of events 1989-92, p.3-14) - 2. Politics, economy and society - 3. Reference section (directory of German reunification *i.e.* political parties and movements, key figures and institutions; election results; economic indicators; texts of significant treaties). Bibliography p.197-302. Analytical index. Emphasis throughout is on the former East Germany. *Class No:* 943.02

Luxembourg

[7290]

NEWCOMER, J. The Grand Duchy of Luxembourg: the evolution of nationhood 963A.D. to 1983. Lanham, Maryland and London, Univ. Press of America in arrangement with Texas Christian Univ., 1984. xiii,343p. maps, bibliog., index. $25.50; £26.85. ISBN: 0819138452.

23 chapters. Despite dismissive appraisal in *Choice,* v.22,no.4 December 12984, p.605 this general history retains some value for its Bibliographic Essay p.319-327. *Class No:* 943.59

Dictionaries

[7291]

BARTEAU, H.C. Historical dictionary of Luxembourg. Lanham, Md., Scarecrow Press, 1996. xxvi,260p. illus., port, maps, bibliog. (*European Historical Dictionaries, no.14*.) ISBN: 0810831066.

Chronology p.xv-xxxiii. Introduction (geography, the people, religion, government and political parties, local government, education, history) p.1-23. Dictionary p.25-209. Appendix A. Rulers of Luxembourg - B. Ministers of State since 1948 - C. American units stationed in the Grand Duchy (WW1+WW2) - D. National hymn. Bibliography (in 31 thematic sections) p.221-60. 3 maps. *Class No:* 943.59(038)

Austria

[7292]

CARSTEN, F.L. The First Austrian republic 1918-1938 a study based on British and Austrian documents. Aldershot, Hampshire, Gower/ Maurice Temple Smith, 1986. 309p. map, bibliog., index. £28.00. ISBN: 0566051621.

10 chapters (5. last years of democratic government 1930-32 ... 7. Austria under Schuschnigg ... 9. The end of independence). Bibliography p.294-296. To a large extent based on reports from the British legation in Vienna. *Class No:* 943.6

[7293]

JELAVICH, B. Modern Austria empire and republic 1915-1986. Cambridge, Cambridge Univ. Press, 1986. xvii, 346p. illus. maps., bibliog. index. £39.50. ISBN: 0521316251.

7 chronological chapters concerned mainly with political history. Bibliography p.331-337. 'Her judgements of a host of complex and controversial issues are sensible and balanced' (*Choice* v.25, no.8, April 1988, p.1296). *Class No:* 943.6

[7294]

KANN, R.A. A History of the Hapsburg Empire 1526-1918. Los Angeles, Univ. of California Press, 1974. xiv, 646p. maps, index. $77.50. ISBN: 0520024087.

11 chapters (1. Towards the union of the Hapsburg lands ... 10. New beginnings; cultural trends from 1860 to 1918 - 11. Bibliographical essay, p.565-606: 1. The Hapsburg Empire: general works; 2. Literature on the history of the national groups: some running commentary). 4. appendices: 1. Population and nationality statistics - 2. The Austrian Hapsburg and Hapsburg-Lorraine rulers, from the middle of the 15th century to 1918 - 3. Chronology - 4. Maps. Analytical index, p.623-46. *Class No:* 943.6

[7295]

MACARTNEY, C.A. The Hapsburg Empire 1790-1918. London, Weidenfeld & Nicolson, 1971. xiv, 908p. maps, bibliog., index.

18 chapters (1. The monarchy in 1780 ... 5. The system at its zenith (1815-30)... 9. 1848 ... 15. Hungary under Dualism (p.687-731:1867-1903; 104 footnotes ... 18. The end of the monarchy). Many footnotes. 3 appendices (3. Place names). Bibliography (running commentary, by chapters), p.838-63. Analytical index. p.864-908. 6 maps. 'Has remained one of the best general works on the subject. A revised and shorter version is *The House of Austria; the later phase, 1790-1918* (Edinburgh, U.P., £10;£5). This contains much new material and 2 helpful maps' (*Annual bulletin of historical literature,* v.64; 1978. 1980. p.105). *Class No:* 943.6

Bibliographies

[7296]

Österreichische historische bibliographie/Austrian historical bibliography. Graz, Verlag Wolfgang Neugebauer; Santa Barbara, California, Clio Press, 1965-. Annual.

Lists the historical literature in Austrian periodicals or by Austrian publishers. The 1994v. (1995. 650p. 3853761305 has 5360 numbered entries. Sections: Reference works - Collections of essays - Auxiliary sciences - Austria - General and European history - Europe: nations - Non-European areas (by continent). Includes dissertations and festschriften. Author index. Five year indexes *1965-1969* (1974); *1970-1974* (1979); *1975-1979* (1983) 566p. 385376097x; 1980-1984 (1989. 793p. 3853760961); and 1985-1989 (1993. 3853760953).
Class No: 943.6(01)

[7297]

—Österreichische historische bibliographie. Ergänzungsheft 1. Liste der Zeitschriften/Austrian historical bibliography. Supplement 1. List of periodicals 1949-1979. (1980). Paulhart, H. *and* Paulhart, H., *eds.* 32p. sd. ISBN: 3853761003.
300 numbered entries. *Class No:* 943.6(01)

[7298]

—Österreichische historische bibliographie. Supplement 2. Information und Dokumentation auf dem Gebiet der Geschichte. (1985). Hödl, G., *and others.* 55p. ISBN: 3853760937. *Class No:* 943.6(01)

Dictionaries

[7299]

CSENDES, P. Historical dictionary of Vienna. Lanham, MD., Scarecrow Press, 1999. xxxv,258p. illus., maps, bibliog. $49.50. (*Historical Dictionaries of the Cities of the World, no.8.*) ISBN: 0810835622.
Chronology p.xvii-xxii. Introduction (early history, the Hapsburgs, two World Wars, postwar Vienna) p.xxiii-xxxv. Dictionary (education institutions, galleries, people, history, politics etc.) p.1-216. Bibliography (German and English language publications arranged under 8 form and thematic headings (*e.g.*bibliographies, encyclopedic works, history, guides and pictorial(s) p.217-51. Appendix 1. Holy Roman Emperors and rulers of Austria - 2. Mayors - 3. Statistical tables. *Class No:* 943.6(038)

[7300]

FICHTNER, P.S. Historical dictionary of Austria. Lanham, MD., Scarecrow Press, 1999. 432p. map, bibliography. $65. (*European Historical Dictionaries, no.36.*) ISBN: 0810836394.
Covers the country's Habsburg and pre-Habsburg legacy, its political and cultural elite, component provinces, and its leading cities, and includes a chronology, introduction, and bibliography.
Class No: 943.6(038)

Chronologies

[7301]

KLEINDEL, W. Österreich: Daten zur Geschichte und Kultur. Wien, Überreuter, 1978. 570p.
10,000 dates from prehistory to 1977. Includes abridged versions of treaties and other historical documents and a complete list of rulers. 'An unusual but extremely useful reference aid' (D. Salt and A.F. Radley. *Austria.* 1986. Entry 752). *Class No:* 943.6(090)

20th Century

Bibliographies

[7302]

MALINA, P. *and* SPANN, G. Bibliographie zur Österreichischen Zeitgeschichte 1918-1980. Wien, Verlag für Geschichte und Politik, 3v., 1980.
Handbooks, bibliographical references and general works on political, social and economic history are listed.
Class No: 943.6"19"(01)

Czech State

[7303]

SKILLING, H.G., *ed.* Czechoslovakia 1918-88. London, Macmillan in association with St. Anthony's College, Oxford, 1991. xv,232p. ISBN: 0333510828.
12 chapters by separate hands in 6 sections: 1. Triumph and tragedy of Czechoslovak leadership - 2. Independence achieved 3. Czechoslovakia in Europe - 4. The nationalities - 5. Political culture and economic change - 6. Literature: free, official and independent. 6 Appendices. Proceedings of a University of Toronto conference held 28-30 October 1988 to mark 70th anniversary of Czechoslovakia's independence. *Class No:* 943.7

Dictionaries

[730ₓ]

HOCHMAN, J. Historical dictionary of the Czech state. Lanham, MD., Scarecrow Press, 1998. xli,203p. illus., maps, bibliog. £43.7₀
(*European Historical Dictionaries, no.23.*) ISBN: 0810833387.
Chronology of Czech history p.xvii-xxxix. Introduction (geography, population, economy, transport and communications, political system p.1-15. Dictionary (principal, historical and political events, leading historical figures, universities, institutions) p.17-152. Bibliography (1 thematic sections) p.153-80. Appendix 1. List of Czech princes, kin; and presidents - 2. Text of Charter 77 - 3. Charter of fundamental rights and freedoms. *Class No:* 943.7(038)

20th Century

[730₈]

RENNER, H. A History of Czechoslovakia since 1945. London a₥ New York, Routledge, 1989. xi, 200p. bibliog., index. £25.00. ISBₙ 0415003636.
9 well-documented chronological chapters. Ch. notes p.162-9₁ Bibliogaphy p.193-6. *Class No:* 943.7"19"

Bibliographies

[730ₓ]

HEJZLAR, Z. *and* KUSIN, V.V. Czechoslovakia 1968-19₆₆ chronology, bibliography, annotation. New York, Garland, 197. 316p. ISBN: 0824010558.
Contents include Framework and lessons of the Prague Spring p.. 10; Chronicle p.13-148; Main documents in English translation p.15 154; Alexander Dubček in 1968-69 (a bibliography of speeche articles and interviews) p.157-163; Bibliography of Czech and Slova articles 1968-1970 p.182-257; Bibliography of books 1968-197 p.261-316. *Class No:* 943.7"19"(01)

[730ₓ]

PARRISH, M. The 1968 Czechoslovak crisis a bibliography 196₈ 1970. Santa Barbara, ABC Clio Press, 1971. v, 41p. index. softcove ISBN: 0874360757.
781 unannotated entries relating to books, pamphlets, journ₁ articles, newspapers *etc. Class No:* 943.7"19"(01)

Slovakia

Dictionaries

[730₈]

KIRSCHBAUM, S.J. Historical dictionary of Slovakia. Lanham MD., Scarecrow Press, 1999. lxxxvi,213p. maps, bibliog. (*European Historical Dictionaries, no.31.*) ISBN: 0810835061.
Chronology of Slovak history p.xxv-lv. Introduction (land an people, history, economy) p.lvii-lxxxvi. Dictionary (earlier politica status, history, politics, linguistic topics, associations and institution prominent individuals etc.) p.1-188 Appendix: ruler, king or head ₀ state on Slovak territory, p.189-93. Bibliography (general, histor₁ language and literature) p.195-211. 5 maps. *Class No:* 943.76(038)

Poland

[730₉]

The Cambridge history of Poland. Reddaway, W.F., *ed.* Cambridg₀ Cambridge Univ. Press, 2v., 1941-50.
1: *From the origins to Sobieski (to 1696).* 1950.
2: *From Augustus II to Pilsudski (1696-1935).* 1941.
The standard work in English; a co-operative effort still awaiting th volume of bibliography. *Class No:* 943.8

[731₀]

DAVIES, N. A History of Poland : God's playground. v.1. The origin to 1795. v.2 1795 to the present. Oxford, Clarendon Press; New Yorₖ Columbia Univ. Press, 1982. xxxiii, 605p.+Øxvii, 725p. illus. map diagrs., index. £27.50 $30.00 each. $120.00. ISBN: 0198225555, v.₁ 019822592x, v.2, UK; 0231053509, v.1; 0231053525, v.2, US.
V.1. - 18 chronological and thematic chapters in 2 sections: Th Origins to 1572 and The Life and death of the Polish - Lithuania republic 1569-1795. Chapter 1. 'Millenium: a thousand years ₐ history' is a superb review of Polish historiography. V.2. - 23 chapte in further 2 sections: Poland destroyed and reconstructed an Contemporary Poland since 1944. Bibliography v.2, p.680-684. *Class No:* 943.8

[7311]

IEYSZTOR, A., *and others*. A History of Poland. 2nd ed. Warsaw, PWN-Polish Scientific Publishers, 1980. Distributed by Hippocrene Books of New York. 668p. illus. maps, bibliog., index. $76.25. ISBN: 8301003928.

5 contributors. 4 parts (25 chapters, plus 'Conclusion'): Medieval Poland - The Commonwealth of gentry - Poland under foreign rule - Poland 1918-1939. Bibliography, p.727-40 (A. Bibliographical works; B. More important textbooks and synthetic works - C. Textbooks covering longer periods; D. History of various regions and towns). Chronological tables. Well illustrated. Non-analytical index, 42 maps. 'A reference work deserving a place alongside the *Cambridge history of Poland* (*Choice*, v.18, no.1, September 1980, p.148+150).
Class No: 943.8

Bibliographies

[7312]

KONSKI, W. Wartime Poland 1939-1945 a select annotated bibliography of books in English. Westport, CT., Greenwood Press, 1997. 128p. indexes. $65. £51.95. (*Bibliographies and Indexes in World History, no.45.*) ISBN: 0313300046.

Scope: Poland's role in Second World War in the broad international context *Class No:* 943.8(01)

Dictionaries

[7313]

OZDECKA-SANFORD, A. Historical dictionary of Warsaw. Lanham, MD, Scarecrow Press, 1997. £47.05. (*Historical Dictionaries of cities, no.3.*) ISBN: 0810832992.

Examines the history of this city from its foundations as a Lusation settlement in the fourth century B.C. to its establishment as the capital of the Kingdom of Poland in the 17th century, its period of major cultural development in the early 1800s, its rebuilding after the World Wars, and up to its current place in the world as a democratic capital city, concentrating on its political, intellectual and administrative life. A chronology highlights important dates in the historical development of Warsaw, with a listing of the Presidents of the city, two maps, lists of abbreviations and acronyms, a select bibliography, and notations on Polish spelling and usage. *Class No:* 943.8(038)

[7314]

ERSKI, G.J. Historical dictionary of Poland 966-1945. Westport, Conn., Greenwood Press, 1996. xviii,750p. maps, bibliog., index. $125. £100. ISBN: 0313260079.

2,000 entries for people, places, events, historical terms etc. 'Will become one of the most important reference works treating Poland' (*Choice*, v.34,no.1, September 1996, p.100+102). One of *Choice's* Outstanding Academic Books of 1996. *Class No:* 943.8(038)

[7315]

ANFORD, G. *and* GOZDECKA-SANFORD, A. Historical dictionary of Poland. Metuchen, NJ., Scarecrow Press, 1994. xxii,338p. map, bibliog. £42.75. (*European Historical Dictionaries, no.3.*) ISBN: 0810828189.

Dictionary (crucial persons, places, events, institutions *etc.*) p.25-232. Bibliography (19 sections) p.233-338. Chronology p.ix-xiii. Rulers of Poland p.xiv-xvii. *Class No:* 943.8(038)

Maps & Atlases

[7316]

OGONOWSKI, I.C. Poland a historical atlas. New York, Hippocrene Books, 1987. 322p. maps, col.coats of arms on endpapers, bibliog., index. $27.50. ISBN: 0870522825.

4 introductory historical essays. The main Atlas section (p.47-219) is arranged in 8 chronological periods: 1. Poland in western civilization 966-1986. 2. Hereditary monarchy c.840-1370. 3. Transition to constitutional monarchy 1370-1493. 4. Constitutional monarchy 1493-1569. 5. The first Polish Republic 1569-1795. 6. The century of partition 1795-1918. 7. The Second Polish Republic 1918-1945. 8. The Third Polish Republic 1944-present. Appendix (text, maps and charts) on Prehistory and language evolution p.227-60. Bibliography p.261. Multilingual glossary of place names p.265-7. Outline of Polish history p.269-95. Comprehensive and detailed maps supported by authoritative text. *Class No:* 943.8(084.3)

20th Century

Dictionaries

[7317]

VRÓBEL, P. Historical dictionary of Poland 1945-1996. Chicago and London, Fitzroy Dearborn, 1998. xx,423p. maps, bibliog., index. £50. ISBN: 1579580688.

Dictionary (political and religious leaders, events, political parties, dissidents and underground organizations, art and cultural affairs,

....(contd.)
armed forces, government bureaux, geographical features etc.) p.1-356. Chronology p.357-92. Bibliography p.393-7. 6 maps.
Class No: 943.8"19"(038)

Hungary

[7318]

A History of Hungary. Sugar, P.F., *and others, eds*. Bloomington and Indianopolis, Indiana Univ. Press; London, I.B. Tauris, 1990. xv,432p. illus., maps, bibliog., index. $35; £24.95. ISBN: 0253355788, US; 1850432864, UK.

Single-volume cooperative history (20 US, Canadian and Hungarian scholars) arranged in 21 chronological chapters e.g. 1. Hungary before the Hungarian conquest - 2. Prehistory ... 9. Principality of Transylvania ... 14. Dual Monarchy 1867-1890 ... 21. Contemporary Hungary 1956-1984 - Epilogue 1985-1990. Bibliography p.405-15. Analytical index. 'An outstanding collection that is due to become a standard work' (*Choice*, v,28, no.9, May 1991, p.1546).
Class No: 943.9

[7319]

HOENSCH, J.K. A History of modern Hungary 1867-1994. 2nd ed. London & New York, Longman, 1995. 416p. illus. maps, bibliog. index. pbk. £15.99. ISBN: 0582256496.

1st ed. 1988. First published as *Geschichte Ungarns 1867-1983* by Verlag W. Kohlhammer of Stuttgart.

Political, social and economic history in 6 chronological chapters. Chronology (5th century AD to 1983) p.285-293. Bibliography p.294-307. Author is Professor of Eastern European History in the University of the Saarland Saarbrucken. *Class No:* 943.9

Bibliographies

[7320]

TELEK, J. History of Hungary and the Hungarians 1848-1971 : a select bibliography. Toronto, Hungarian History Studies, 2v., 1980-1981. vii, 395p.+Øvi, 963p. index. ISBN: 0920984045, v.1; 0920984061, v.2.

V.1. first published in 1972 and reprinted with additons in 1980; v.2 first published in 1978.

4177 annotated entries in v.1; 9374 in v.2 arranged in 12 chapters (*e.g.* 4. Hungarian civilization and culture ... 10. After World War II ... 11. Foreign relations ... 12. Geography). Based on mongraphs held in the Univ. of Toronto library. *Class No:* 943.9(01)

[7321]

VÖLGYES, I. The Hungarian Soviet Republic 1919 an evaluation and a bibliography. Stanford, Calif., Hoover Institution Press, Stanford Univ., 1970. ix, 90p. ISBN: 817924310.

2 introductory chapters: A capsule history of the Hungarian Soviet Republic and The historiography of the HSR. Bibliography in 5 sections: 1. Bibliographies, documents, reference works - 2. General works - 3. Hungarian Soviet Republic - 4. Works of special scope - 5. Autobiographies etc. *Class No:* 943.9(01)

Dictionaries

[7322]

VÁRDY, S.B. Historical dictionary of Hungary. Lanham, MD., Scarecrow Press, 1997. xx,811p. maps, bibliog. $75. (*European Historical Dictionaries, no.18.*) ISBN: 0810832542.

Chronology p.1-40. Glossary of geographical terms p.41-46. Heads of State p.47-52. Hungary and the Hungarian past p.53-78. Dictionary (persons, places, important political, economic, social and cultural aspects, language, ethnic minorities, wars, battles) p.81-748. Bibliography (8 sub-divided form and thematic categories) p.749-811. *Class No:* 943.9(038)

France

[7323]

The Cambridge history of modern France. Cambridge, Cambridge Univ. Press; Paris Éditions de la Maison des Sciences de l'Homme, 8v. 1983-.

Each volume is a translation of a title or titles from the series *Nouvelle histoire de la France contemporaine* published by Éditions de Seuil of Paris 1972-.

1. *Restoration and reaction 1815-1848* by A. Jardin and A-J. Tudesq. 1983. xviii, 409p. £42.50. 0521252415 (UK). 2735100383 (Fr). 2. *The Republican experiment 1848-1852* by M. Agulhon. 1983. xiv, 211p. £27.50. 0521248299 (UK). 2735100286 (Fr). 3. *The Rise and Fall of the Second Empire 1852-1871* by A. Plessis. 1985. xvii, 193p. £27.50. 0521252423 (UK). 2735100758 (Fr). 4. *The Third Republic from its origins to the Great War 1871-1914* by J-M. Mayeur and M. Reberioux. 1984. xxi, 392p. £40.00. 0521249317 (UK). 2735100677 (Fr). 5. *The Decline of the Third Republic 1914-1938* by P. Bernard and H. Dubief 1985. xviii, 358p. £35.00. 0521252407 (UK). 2735100766 (Fr). 6. *From Munich to the Liberation 1938-1944*

....(contd.)

by J-P. Azema. 1984. xxxix, 294p. £30.00. 0521252377 (UK). 2735100782 (Fr). 7. *The Fourth Republic 1944-1958* by J-P. Rioux. 1987. xv, 531p. £40.00. 0521252385 (UK). 2735101665 (Fr).

Authors are either established historians or young scholars currently involved in the field. *Class No:* 944

[7324]
L'Almanach de Paris. Paris, Encyclopaedia Universalis, 2v., 1990. 336p. illus. 630F.
1. *Des origines à 1788.* ed. M. Fleury.
2. *De 1789 à nos jours* ed. J. Tulard.
'Une chronologie illustré par des documents d'époque. Toute d'histoire de Paris, tous les événements, tous les personnages et tous les lieux se trouvent rassemblés dans ces deux volumes' (*Livres de France*, n.122, Septembre 1990, p.56). *Class No:* 944

Bibliographies

[7325]
BARBIER, F. **Bibliographie de l'histoire de France.** Paris, Masson, 1987. 283p. Fr.160. ISBN: 2225808287.
Part 1. Bibliographie Générale: Chap 1. Notions (i.e. La recherche bibliographique and La recherche documentaire). Chap 2. L'historien et le travail en biblothèque. Part 2. Bibliographie de l'histoire générale: 3. Histoire générale. 4. Histoire des Religions.
Part 3. Bibliographie générale de l'histoire de France: 7. Manuels généraux et bibliographies d'ensemble. 8. L'accès au documents. 9. Sources legislatives et réglementaires. 10. L'accès aux documents: sources manuscrites. Part 4. Quelques domaines spécialisés. All entries are very briefly annotated. *Class No:* 944(01)

[7326]
CENTRE NATIONAL DE LA RECHERCHE SCIENTIFIQUE. Institut D'Histoire Moderne Et Contemporaine. **Bibliographie annuelle de l'histoire de France** du cinquième siècle à 1958. Sonnet, M. *and* Keriven, B., *eds.* Paris, Éditions du CNRS, 1956-. Annual. ISSN: 00676918.
Continues *Répertoire de l'histoire de France,* by P. Caron and H. Stein (années 1920/21-1930-31. Paris, Picard, 1923-38, 6v.), itself preceded by Répertoire méthodique de l'histoire moderne et contemporaine de la France pour l'année 1898-1912/12.
Année 1998 (1999). lxxxiii,958p. ISBN 227105673x has 12,458 entries. Systematic arrangement in 9 broad groups: 1. Manuels généraux et sciences auxiliares de l'histoire - 2. Histoire politique de la France - 3. Histoire des institutions - 4. Histoire économique - 5. Sociale - 6. Histoire religieuse - 7. La France outre-mer 8. Histoire de la civilization - 9. Histoire locale. Liste des périodiques dépouillés et des leurs abbréviations p.xvii-lxxx.Index Chronique p.683-721. Matières p.723-888. Table des noms d'auteurs p.889-958. *Class No:* 944(01)

[7327]
'Recent books and dissertations on French history', *French Historical Studies*, 1958-. Quarterly. ISSN: 00161071.
A regular feature since the first issue. Listed under 8 headings: 1. Bibliographical, reference and archival publications - 2. General and miscellaneous - 3. Ancient and medieval - 4. 1500 to 1774 - 5. the Revolutionary period and Napoleon - 6. 1815 to 1870 - 7. The Third Republic - 8. 1940 to the present. Since Fall 1987 the Bibliography has been available on 5.25 inch floppy disk prepared on IBM compatible computer (Wordperfect system). *Class No:* 944(01)

Micromaterials

[7328]
Bibliothèque Nationale Catalogue de l'histoire de France. Paris, Cambridge and Alexandria, Virginia, Chadwyck-Healey. 1988. 1500 positive silver halide 105 x 148 mm fiche at 24x reduction with printed guide subject index. £3500. ISBN: 2869760051.
Contents: Catalogue de l'histoire de France 1855-1895 (200,000 records) and unpublished card catalogues 1895-1987 (550,000 records) in 16 main sections: miscellaneous; historical periods; reigns; journals and publications; religion; constitutional; administrative; diplomatic; military history; manners and customs; archaeology; local; social; family history; biography; economic history. Printed subject index includes A-Z list of 500 subject terms with cross-references to the *Catalogue. Class No:* 944(01)(003.5)

Dictionaries

[7329]
FIERRO, A. **Historical dictionary of Paris.** Lanham, MD., Scarecrow Press, 1998. 392p. illus., maps, tables, bibliog. £64.60. (*Historical Dictionary of Cities, no.4.*) ISBN: 0810833182.
Chronology p.xv-xx. Introduction (Paris in France and Europe, history) p.1-20. Dictionary (400+ entries covering all important

....(contd.)

historical and current features of Paris) p.21-183. Bibliograph (subdivided by 9 major topics, including Americans in Paris) p.18. 235. Statistical appendixes p.237-243. 4 maps. *Class No:* 944(038)

[7330]
Historical dictionaries of French history. Westport, Connecticu Greenwood Press; London, Aldwych Press, 1985-1987. bibliogs indexes.
1. Scott, S.F. and Rothaus, B. *eds. Historical dictionary of th French Revolution 1789-1799.* 2v. 1985. xvii, 1143p. $95.00. ISB 0313211418, US. 0861720431, UK. 2. Connelly, O. ed. *Historic dictionary of Napoleonic France 1799-1815.* 1985. xiii, 586p. $65.0 £53.50. 0313213216, US. 0867120423, UK. 3. Newman, E.L. e *Historical dictionary of France from the 1815 Restoration to th Second Empire.* 2v., 1987. xvii, 1241p. $135.00. £115.0 0313227519, US. 0861720474, UK. 4. Echard, W.E. ed. *Historic dictionary of the French Second Empire 1952-1870.* 1985. xvi, 829 $87.50. £68.50. 0313211361, US. 086172044x, UK. 5. Hutton, P.F ed. *Historical dictionary of the Third French Republic 1870-1940.* 2v 1986. xvi, 1206p. $125.00. £115.00. 0313220880, US. 086172046 UK. 6. *World War II France: the Occupation, Vichy, and th Resistance, 1938-1946* ed. B.M. Gordon, 1998, 462p. £8 0313294216, US. 086172108x, UK. 7. *Historical dictionary of th French Fourth and Fifth Republics 1946-1991* edited by W. Northcut 1992. xv,527p. £68.; $85. 0313263566.
A multitude of contributors. Well-documented signed entries relatin to leading personalities, events, constitutional development chronologies *etc.* R.A. Jonces and D.A. Pinkney's 'The Greenwoo Press' historical dictionaries of French history', *French Historic Studies*, v.15, no.2, Fall 1987, p.345-57 subjects them to a detaile scrutiny. *Class No:* 944(038)

[7331]
RAYMOND, G. **Historical dictionary of France.** Lanham, MD Scarecrow Press, 1998. xxviii,347p. map. $55. (*European Historic Dictionaries, no.30.*) ISBN: 0810834677.
Monarchs and presidents p.xvii-xix. Chronology p.xxi-xxvii Introduction (territory and geography, people and nation, France Europe and the world) p.1-17. Dictionary (political parties an associations, historical figures and events the arts, treaties and wa etc.) p.19-283. Bibliography (arranged in 7 heavily sub-divide thematic categories p.285-345. *Class No:* 944(038)

Maps & Atlases

[7332]
Atlas historique de la France. Paris, Plon, 1985. 150p. col. maps tables. 185.00 F. £20.50. ISBN: 2259013171.
10 chapters: 1. Chronologie de l'histoire de France (p.8-39) - 2. L France avant la France - 3. Des Mérovingiens aux Capétiens - 4. L royaume de France - 5. La monarchie absolute et la fin de l'ancie régime - 6. Le xix siècle - 7. La France contemporaine - 8. La Franc en Europe - 9. Faits et chiffres - 10. Souverains, chefs d'État régimes. Closely integrated maps and text although mixture specially drawn maps for this publication and many maps from *Atla géneral Vidal-Lablache* is unsettling. *Class No:* 944(084.3)

[7333]
PINOL, J-L., *ed.* **Atlas historique des villes de France.** Paris Hachette, 1996. xv,318p. col.illus., col.maps, tables. ISBN 2012351921.
Part of the project, *Atlas historique des villes européennes*, of th Centre de Cultura Contemorània de Barcelona, supported b L'Universitat Politènica de Catlunya.
38 contributors. History of Paris, Rouen, Lille, Strasbourg, Lyon Marseille, Montpelier, Toulouse, Bordeaux, and Nante. Bibliograph and sources p.24. *Class No:* 944(084.3)

[7334]
SINCLAIR, S. **Atlas de géographie historique de la France et de l Gaulle** de la conquête césarienne à nos jours. Paris, Sedes, 1985 260p. maps, geneal. tables, bibliog., index. softcover. ISBN 2718122107.
13 chapters assembled in 3 parts: 1. Histoire - 2. Géographi administative et judiciare - 3. Géographie réligieuse. Bibliographi critique p.211-230. 'L'ouvrage couvre la quasi totalité de l'histoi nationale, dans tous ses aspects' (*Introduction*). *Class No:* 944(084.3

Middle Ages

Bibliographies

[7335]
SOCIÉTÉ DES HISTORIENS MÉDIÉVISTES D L'ENSEIGNEMENT SUPÉRIEUR. **Bibliographie de l'histoi médiévale en France (1965-1990).** Paris, Publications de la Sorbonne 1992. ii,486p. index. 190F. ISBN: 2859442146. ISSN: 02904500.
21 sections *e.g.* 1. Histoire des campagns médiévales en France - 2 Histoire urbaine en France Xe-XVe siècle ... 9. L'Archéologi

..(contd.)
médiévale ... 21. Vingt ans d'informatique en histoire médiévale. 'C'est un guide bibliographique commode, à l'usage des chercheurs, des bibliothèques et des amateurs d'histoire du Moyen-Age'.
Class No: 944"01/14"(01)

Encyclopaedias

[7336]
Medieval France an encyclopedia. Kibler, W.W. *and* Zinn, G.A., *eds.* New York, Garland Publishing, 1995. xxvi,1047p. illus., maps, bibliog., index. $95. (*Garland Encyclopedias of the Middle Ages, no.2.*) ISBN: 0824044444.
Over 200 contributors. Encompasses political, economic, social, religious, intellectual, literary, and artistic history of France from the early 5th century to the late 15th century. Cross-referenced entries range from 50 word ready references to 3000+ word essays on major institutions, writers and works, movements, and monuments, each with a selective bibliography appended. Lists of Kings, Counts, Dukes and Popes (with regnal dates) p.xi-xvi. Architectural, musical glossaries p.xvii-xix. Analytical index p.991-1047. *Class No:* 944"01/14"(031)

Dictionaries

[7337]
FAVIER, J. Dictionnaire de la France Médiévale. Paris, Fayard, 1993. 1016p. illus. (51 col.), maps, geneal. tables. F750.
5835 A-Z entries relating to people, events, movements, *etc.* of the period 600AD to 1500. 27 maps and plans. 19 genealogies.
Class No: 944"01/14"(038)

Maps & Atlases

[7338]
PARISSE, M. *and* LEURIDAN, J. Atlas de la France de l'an mil État de nos connaissances. Paris, Picard, 1994. 129p. col. maps, bibliogs., indexes. F350. ISBN: 2708404571.
20+ contributors. Divided into 12 regional areas each with 3 maps depicting Religious Communities, Fortified sites, and Economic and pre-urban aspects, and an extensive bibliography. Covers medieval period from the Carolingian period to Philip Augustus. Index of Latin names and French equivalents and a place-name index.
Class No: 944"01/14"(084.3)

17th Century

Dictionaries

[7339]
Dictionnaire du grand siècle. Bluche, F., *ed.* Paris, Fayard, 1990. 1640p. illus. (inc. 24 col. pl.), index. ISBN: 2213024251.
250 contributors. Short and long signed articles on the personalities, military, political, religious, and commercial history of the period from the accession of Henry IV to the death of his grandson Louis XIV *i.e.* 1589-1715. *Class No:* 944"16"(038)

18th & 19th Centuries

Dictionaries

[7340]
Dictionnaire Napoléon. Tulard, J., *ed.* New ed. Paris, Fayard, 1996. 1872p. illus.,(some col.), maps, tables. Fr950. ISBN: 2213020353.
1st ed. 1987.
Authoritative and comprehensive dictionary comprising 3628 entries by 228 contributors of 'tous les personnages marquants de la période 1800-1815' with the battles and grand themes (*e.g.* Armée; Musique militaire; Presse) of the Napoleonic era. *Class No:* 944"17/18"(038)

French Revolution

[7341]
DOYLE, W. The Oxford history of the French Revolution. Oxford, Clarendon Press, 1989. xi, 466p.+16p. of plates., illus., maps, ports., bibliog., index. £17.50. $29.95. ISBN: 0198227817.
Authoritative and reliable narrative covering the period from the accession of Louis XVI (1774) to Napoleon's triumph (1802). Notes p.426-33. Appendix 1. Chronology p.434-41. 2. The Revolutionary Calendar p.442-3. Bibliography p.444-8. Analytical index.
Class No: 944"1789-1799"

Bibliographies

[7342]
CALDWELL, R.J. The Era of the French Revolution a bibliography of the history of western civilization, 1789-1799. New York, Garland Publishing Inc., 2v, 1985. xvi, 609p.+611-1299p. $200.00. ISBN: 0824087941.
A monumental work containing 42,240 citations (many annotated) in 6 large sections: 1. General history in the French Revolutionary era - 2. The French Revolution 1787-1799 - 3. Biography - 4. Local history - 5. National history of Europe - 6. National history of the Americas. 'The present bibliography fulfills the need for a thorough catalogue of French Revolution history even though such a work cannot be absolutely comrprehensive.' (*Preface*). *Class No:* 944"1789-1799"(01)

[7343]
STEVANOVIC, B. 'French books', *Booklist,* v.86,no.11, 1 February 1990, p.1073-4.
62 briefly annotated titles A-Z by author of books published or reprinted in France to commemorate the bicentennial of the French Revolution. *Class No:* 944"1789-1799"(01)

Micromaterials

[7344]
Images of the French Revolution a comprehensive archive of 38,000 images. Paris, Bibliothèque Nationale; London, Pergamon Press, 1989. Videodisk (12"/30 cm. optical disk) compatible with all Laservision PAL or NTSC disk drives. £250.00. ISBN: 0080374174.
Images, drawn principally from the holdings of the Department of Engravings, are arranged in 7 sections: 1. Events of the Revolution - 2. Themes in culture & art - 3. Archives and documents - 4. The Revolution commemorated and celebrated - 5. The Revolution & 19th century polemic - 6. France at the end of the 18th century - 7. Revolution collections in the BN; The Videodisk. Supplied with a booklet comprising a general introduction; text of the summaries, and additonal information. Printed catalogue: v.1. contains an historical background to the BN's collections; subject listing; classsification guide; and bilingual (French/English) index. V.2-3 includes over 15,000 bibliographical notes. A software version is available £265.00. ISBN 0080374182. Videodisk and booklet + database with user manual and interface cable £565.00. ISBN 0080374190. Complete package: videodisk and booklet; 3v. printed catalogue; database and user mannual £655.00. ISBN 0080372473. *Class No:* 944"1789-1799"(01)(003.5)

[7345]
—The French Revolution research collection & videodisk. Lucas, C., *editor-in-chief.* Oxford, Pergamon Press, in cooperation with the Bibliothèque Nationale, Paris, 1989-92. 1,000,000p. on 105 x 148mm microfiche with a videodisk. £43,000.
Reproduces over 1 million pages of primary documentary material, mostly printed documents, but where necessary for a balance of coverage, a number of import manuscripts are included. 12 sections are organized in 2 parts. Part 1. Common core sections: 1. Newspapers edited by H. Gough (100,000p.) - 2. Memoirs & autobiographies ed. by C. Lucas (100,000p.) - 3. Basic printed collections ed. by C. Lucas (150,000p.) - 4. Bibliographical & research tools (20,000p). Part 2. Thematic sections: 5. Pre-revolutionary debate edited by J. Popkin and D. Van Kley (30,000p.) - 6. Political themes (Local government; Extra-parliamentary politics; Political authors) (160,000p.) - 7. Resistance to the Revolution ed. by R. Dupuy (100,000p.) - 8. Religion ed. by T. Tackett (100,000p.) - 9. The reorganization of society (The abolition of the corporate society and feudalism; The countryside; Towns and townspeople; Women & the family; Public Assistance) (125,000p.) - 10. The Economy (Policy, trade and finance; Agriculture; Industry & Technology) (100,000p.) - 11. War & the colonies (The Army and the Navy, The colonies) (65,000p.) - 12. Culture ed. by J. Leith (95,000p.). *Images of the French Revolution* (qv). *Class No:* 944"1789-1799"(01)(003.5)

Encyclopaedias

[7346]
JONES, C. The Longman companion to the French Revolution. London and New York, Longman, 1988. xiii, 473p. maps, geneal. table, bibliog., index. £40.00 $79.95. ISBN: 0582494184.
Compendious reference work organized in 13 sub-divided sections covering the period 1787-1799: 1. Political chronology - 2. Framework of government - 3. The Executive - 4. Structure of the Terror: the institutions of revolutionary government 1792-1795 - 5. International relations and war - 6. Politics - 7. Administration, justice and finance - 8. Religion and ideas - 9. Society and the economy - 10. Biographies (over 500 *dramatis personae* highlighting minor figures) - 11. Glossary of over 400 terms (p.401-424) - 12. The Revolutionary Calendar - 13. Bibliography (p.432-5). For all scholars, students and general readers requiring detailed factural data. *Class No:* 944"1789-1799"(031)

Dictionaries

[7347]

FURET, F. and OZOUF, M., eds. A Critical dictionary of the French Revolution. Cambridge, Massachusetts, Harvard Univ. Press, 1989. 1168p. illus., (some col.). $101.95. £67.95. ISBN: 0674177282.

99 essays A-Z by key words and themes under 5 major headings: Events - Actors - Institutions and creations - Ideas - Historians and commentators. François Furet is Professor of History and Social Thought in the Univ. of Chicago; Mona Ozouf is Director of Research at the Centre Nationale de la Recherche Scientifique. *Class No:* 944"1789-1799"(038)

[7348]

SOBOUL, A. Dictionnaire historique de la Révolution Française. Suratteau, J-R. and Gendron, F., eds. Paris, Presses Universitaires De France, 1989. xlvii,1132p. maps, bibliog., index. Fr495.00. ISBN: 2130425224.

English ed. *The French Revolution 1787-1799 from the storming of the Bastille to Napoleon.* London, Unwin Hyman, 1989. £30. ISBN 0044456107.

64 contributors offer over 1000 authoritative, well-documented and signed essays of varying length on the principal persons, places, events, and political ideologies of the Revolution (États-Généraux: 3p. 3refs.; Jean-Paul Marat: 4p., 8 refs.). Aperçu historiographique p.xv-xxxi. Bibliographie générale p.xxxiii-xxxvi. Tableau chronolgique synoptique p.xxxviii-xlvii. *Class No:* 944"1789-1799"(038)

Maps & Atlases

[7349]

Atlas de la Révolution Française. Paris, Éditions de l'École des Hautes Études en Sciences Sociales, 5v., 1987-89.

1. *Routes et communications* by G. Arbellot and others. 1987. 91p. FFr90. 2713208947. 2. *L'Enseignement 1760-1815* by D. Julia and others. 1987. 105p. FFr90. 2713208939. 3. *L'Armée et la guerre* edited by J.P. Bertrand and D. Reichel, 1989. 79p. 2713209277. 4. *Le Territoire (1): réalités et représentations* by D. Nordman and M.V. Ozouf-Marignier. 1989. 106p. FFr120. 2713209293. 5. *Le Territoire (2): les limites administratives.* 1989. 125p. FFr150. 2713209420. 6. *Les sociétés politiques.* by J. Boutier and others. 1992. 132p. 2713209676. 7. *Médecine et Santé* by J-P. Goubert and others. 1993. 83p. 2713209994. 8. *Population* by B. Lepetit and others. 1995. 2713211891. 9. *Religion.* by C. Langlois and others. 1996. 103p. FFr.120. National, regional and provincial maps supported by an explanatory text. 'A judicious blending of large-scale maps and 'close-ups' revealing the situation in this or that town, portion of territory, or sector of the national frontier' (*French History*, v.5, no.1, March 1991, p.118-9). *Class No:* 944"1789-1799"(084.3)

Biographies

[7350]

CARATINI, R. Dictionnaire des personages de la Révolution. Paris, LePré aux Clercs, 1988. xiv, 577p. illus. £23.85. ISBN: 2714422322.

3000 entries of French and foreign personalities of note and secondary importance caught up in the Revolution 1789-1795. Bibliography p.543-46. Chronology p.547-77. *Class No:* 944"1789-1799"(092)

[7351]

La Révolution Française Dictionnaire biographique. Manceron, C. and Manceron, A. Paris, Renaudot, 1989. 571p. Fr180. ISBN: 2877420086.

Definitive biographical details of all leading personalities and lesser known participants in all aspects of the Revolution. *Class No:* 944"1789-1799"(092)

19th & 20th Centuries

Bibliographies

[7352]

Bibliothèque Nationale Catalogue de la Troisième République 1870-1940. Amalvi, C., comp. Paris, Chadwyck-Healey France, 3v., 1990-91. 1800p. index. £240. ISBN: 2869760043.

V.1: *1871-1876;* v.2: *1877-1899;* v.3: *1900-1940* (includes a cumulated index of authors). 30,000 catalogue records relating to contemporary and retrospective works on French political, constitutional, colonial, religious and social history extracted from BN's *Catalogue de l'Histoire de France* (q.v.). A Four-page descriptive brochure is available. *Class No:* 944"18/19"(01)

19th Century

[7353]

CALDWELL, R.J. The Era of Napoleon a bibliography of the history of Western civilization 1799-1815. New York, Garland, 2v., 1991 xxi,1447p. $210. ISBN: 0824056442.

48,000 entries, some annotated, relating to books, periodicals, and dissertations. More than 50% cover France (French biography and local history account for some 14,000 entries). The majority of the items cited are non-English language works. Many of the chronological and thematic sections have introductions signalling the most valuable items. *Class No:* 944"18"

Dictionaries

[7354]

TULARD, J., ed. Dictionnaire du Second Empire. Paris, Fayard 1995. 1370p. illus. (some col.). Fr.850. ISBN: 2213592810.

188 contributors. 1910 articles on events and leading figures of the period of the Second Empire in the history of France (1852-70). *Class No:* 944"18"(038)

20th Century

Bibliographies

[7355]

EVLETH, D., comp. France under the German occupation, 1940 1944 an annotated bibliography. Westport, Conn., Greenwood Press 1991. xii,220p. indexes. £56.80. (*Bibliographies and Indexes in World History, no. 20.*) ISBN: 0313274746.

Selective annotated bibliography of printed works available in libraries, mainly related to metropolitan France, arranged in 7 heavily subdivided major sections: 1. The Vichy regime - 2. Daily life - 3 Collaboration - 4. The Resistance - 5. Position of the Communists - 6 Liberation - 7. The Purge. Guide to the Press under the Occupation p.193-4. Brief guide to the principal archives and libraries p.195-9. *Class No:* 944"19"(01)

Maps & Atlases

[7356]

BOUJU, P.M., and others. Atlas historique de la France contemporaine 1800-1965. Paris, Armand Colin, 1966. 234p., graphs, maps.

461 clearly-drawn maps and graphs (2-4 per page) in 8 chapters: 1. Le territoire national et l'administration - 2. La population - 3 Economique et financière - 4. Forces politiques et opinions publiques - 5. Forces et croyances religieuses - 6. L'enseignement et l'instruction - 7. Information, culture et loisirs - 8. Le français hors de France 'Orientation bibliographique', p.218-21. No index, but full contents-list. 'An extremely useful visual presentation of many aspects of French political, social, economic, religious and cultural life during the past 150 years' (*International Affairs*, v.43, no.4, October 1967, p.811). *Class No:* 944"19"(084.3)

Libraries

[7357]

McCRANK, L.J., ed. Bibliographical foundations of French historical studies. New York, Haworth Press, 1992. xii,243p. index. $29.95. (*Primary Sources and Original Works v.1, nos.1/2.*) ISBN: 1560241500. ISSN: 10428216.

Detailed information on bibliographic sources and institutions. 1. Bibliographic methods and French historical studies - 2. French archives and libraries - 3. Post-Revolution French bibliographic connections with the New World - 4. French Revolution of archives and libraries: from royal to national and from private to public institutions. Derived from selected papers presented at the annual conference of the Association of the Bibliography of History in conjunction with the American Historical Association, San Francisco, 1992. *Class No:* 944:061:026/027

Italy

[7358]

Longman history of Italy. Hay, D., ed. Harlow, Essex, Longman, 1980-. illus., tables, maps.

1. *Italy in the early Middle Ages 600-1216* by T.S. Brown. 2. *Italy in the age of Dante and Petrarch 1216-1380* by J. Larner. 1980. 3. *Italy in the age of the Renaissance 1380-1530* by D. Hay and J. Law. £19.95. ISBN 0582483581. 4. *Italy 1530-1630* by E. Cochrane. 1988. £19.95. ISBN 0582483646. 5. *Italy in the Age of Reason 1685-1789* by D. Carpanetto and G. Ricuperati. 1987. £19.95. ISBN 0582483387. 6. *Italy in the seventeenth century* by D. Sella - 7. *Italy in the age of the Risorgimento 1790-1870* by H. Hearder. ISBN 0582491460. 8. *Modern Italy 1871-1982* by M. Clark. 1985. ISBN 058248362x.

V.2 has 12 chapters, each with chapter notes (*e.g.* 8. The

....(contd.)
countryside, p.153-227, has 1¾p. of running bibliographical commentary, with 6 references. Scholarly. 'To appreciate this book fully, at least a basic knowledge of medieval history is required ... Maps and illustrations need to be used more imaginatively' (*British Book News*, January 1981, p.61-62, on v.2). *Class No:* 945.0

[7359]

Storia d'Italia. Torino, UTET, 1978-. bibliog., index.
Introduzione: L'Italia come problema storigraphico. 1979. ISBN 8802034311. 1. Delogu, P. and others. *Longobardi e Bizantini.* 1980. 8802035105. 2. *Il regno Italico.* 1978. 880202538x. 3. *Il mezzogiorno dai Bizantini a Federico II.* 1983. 8802038716. 4. *Comuni e signorie: instituzioni, società e lotte per l'egemonia.* 1981. 8802035687. 5. *Comuni e signorie: nell'Italia settentrionale.* 1986. 8802040362. 7(1) *Comuni e signorie: nell'Italia nordori éntale e centrale: Veneto, Emilia Romagna, Toscana.* 1987. 880204397. (2) *Lazio, Umbria e Marche, Luca.* 1987. 8802040389. 8(1) *Il Piemonte sabaudo: stato a territori in età moderna.* 1994. 8802046212. 8(2) *Il Piemonte sabaudo: Dal periodo napoleonico al Risorgimento* 1993. 8802047192. 9. *La Repubblica di Genova: nell'et moderna.* 1986. 8802025398. 10. *La Sardegna medioevale e moderna.* 1984. 8802039062. 11. *Il Duchato di Milano 1535-1796.* 1984. 8802038295. 12(1) *La Repubblica di Venezia nell'et à moderna: dalla guerra di Chiggia al 1517.* 1986. 8802040265. (2) *Dal 1517 alla fine della Repubblica.* 1992. 8802044988. 13(1) *Il granducato di Toscana; Medici.* 1982. 8802024510. (2) *Il granducato di Toscana.* 1997. 8802051577. (3) *Dagli 'anni francesci' all' Unità.* 8802047200. 14. *Lo stato pontificio de Martino V a Pio IX.* 1986. 8802025193. 15. *Il regno di Napoli 1266-1494.* 1992. 8802044996. 16. *La Sicilia dal Vespro all'Unit à d'Italia.* 1989. 8802042357. 17. *Ducati Padani Trento e Trieste.* 1979. 8802034737. 18(1) *L'Italia di Napoleone dalla Cisalpina al Regno.* 1986. 8802039550. 18(2) *Il regno Lombardo - Veneto.* 1987. 8802040435. 20. *Destra e sinistra da Cavour a Crispi.* 1982. 8802036578. 21. *La crisi di fine e l'età giolittiana.* 1982. 8802037582. 22. *La prima guerra mondiale e il fascismo.* 1995. 8802049475. 23. *La seconda guerra mondiale e la Repubblica.* 1984. 8802037957. 24. *La Rep*
Anneli II. Eli Ebrei in Italia (2v.) 1996-97. *Class No:* 945.0

Bibliographies
[7360]
Bibliografia storica nazionale. Roma and Bari, Laterza and Figli, 1942-. (Giunta Centrale Per Gli Studi Storici). Annual. L60,000. ISSN: 00852317.
Anni 45-46. 1983-1984. (xxxv,528p.) has 7711 numbered entries in 8 sections: A. Scienze ausiliare ... C. Preistoria e protohistoria ... G. Storia moderna 1871-1945 - H. Storia contemporanea 1946-1984. Annual bibliography of books and articles published in Italy and outstanding foreign publications, relating mainly to Italian history and related historical subjects. *Class No:* 945.0(01)

[7361]
COPPA, F.J. and ROBERTS, W. Modern Italian history an annotated bibliography. Westport, Conn., Greenwood Press, 1990. ix,226p. indexes. $45. £39.95. (*Bibliographies and Indexes in World History, no. 18.*) ISBN: 0313248125. ISSN: 07426852.
865 entries deployed in 7 sections: 1. General and reference works - 2. Monographic studies - 3. 18th century Italy - 4. The Risorgimento 1796 to 1861 - 5. Liberal Italy 1861 to 1922 - 6. Facist Italy 1922 to 1945 - 7. Italian Republic, 1945 to present. Author and subject indexes. 'A judiciously framed guide to recent Italian history' (*RQ*, Fall 1991, p.32). *Class No:* 945.0(01)

Dictionaries
[7362]
COPPA, F.J., ed. Dictionary of modern Italian history. Westport, Connecticut, Greenwood Press, 1985. xxvi, 496p. bibliogs., index. £62.25. $56.95. ISBN: 031322983x.
58 contributors survey 'the chief events, personalities, institutions, systems and problems of Italy from the eighteenth century to the present' in dictionary form. Longer entries end with bibliogaphical references. Appendix A. Chronology p.459-468. 'An excellent and much needed book' (*Choice*, v.23, no.4, December 1985, p.580). *Class No:* 945.0(038)

[7363]
GILBERT, M.P. and NILSSON, K.R. Historical dictionary of modern Italy. Lanham, MD., Scarecrow Press, 1999. xxxvi,463p. map, bibliog. $65. (*European Historical Dictionaries, no.34.*) ISBN: 0810835843.
Chronology p.xix-xxxvi. Introduction (geography and people, historical development, fascism, economy) p.1-22. Dictionary (political parties, leading figures, religion, soccer, associations and institutions etc.) p.23-383. Appendix 1. Royal heads of state - 2. Heads of government etc. since 1945 - 3. Economic statistics.

....(contd.)
Bibliography (divided into 7 major sections: 1. General histories - 2. Italy 1815-61. - 3. Liberal Italy - 4. Fascism - 5. First Italian republic - 6. Art, culture etc. - 7. Guide books) p.405-62. *Class No:* 945.0(038)

20th Century

Dictionaries
[7364]
CANNISTARO, P.V., ed. Historical dictionary of Fascist Italy. Westport, Connecticut, Greenwood Press, 1982. xxix, 657p. maps, index. £63.75. $76.95. ISBN: 0313213278.
56 contributing scholars provide mini-essays on political, military, diplomatic, economic, cultural, intellectual history. Biographical entries feature prominently and each entry ends with bibliographical references. Appendix A. Chronology p.579-582. J. Italian place-names altered during the Fascist regime p.607-630. 'The most comprehensive reference work on Italian fascism and a most welcome one' (*Choice*, v.20, no.5, January 1983. p.690). *Class No:* 945.0"19"(038)

Sicily
[7365]
FINLEY, M.I., and others. History of Sicily. London, Chatto & Windus, 1986. x,246p. 16p.plates, maps, bibliog., index. ISBN: 0701131551.
A much abridged and revised edition of M.I. Finley's *History of Sicily: ancient Siciliy to the Arab conquest;* D. Mack Smith's *History of Sicily: medieval Sicily 800-1713,* and Smith's *History of Sicily: modern Sicily after 1973* (1968).
Bibliography p.234-38. 'It is no reflection on the scholarly excellence of the original three volumes to say that this edition is likely to prove much more attractive and valuable to the more general reader' (*Geographical Journal,* v.154, no.1., March 1988, p.127). *Class No:* 945.082

Malta
[7366]
ABELA, J.S. Malta a panoramic history. San Gwann, Publisher's Enterprise Group, 1997. 248p.
'A very accessible overview history. Thirteen ages are identified and discussed in chronological order: they range from the age of the megabuilders to the age of world communications' (Boswell, D. and Beeley, B. *Malta,* World Bibliographical Series, 2nd ed. 1998, item no. 139). *Class No:* 945.82

[7367]
BLOUET, B. The Story of Malta. 5th ed. Malta, Progress Press, 1993. 253p. maps, tables, bibliog., index. pbk. £6.50. ISBN: 9990930325.
First published by Faber in 1967; 4th ed. in this format 1989.
1. Geographical setting - 2. Prehistory and antiquity - 3. Medieval Malta - 4. Knights of St. John and the Great Siege of Malta... 6. Malta and Britain - 7. Second World War - 8. Independence. Appendix 1. Grandmasters of the Order of St. John - 2. Governors, Presidents - 3. Prime Ministers. Bibliography (by chapter) p.229-44. *Class No:* 945.82

[7368]
GERADA-AZZOPARDI, E. Malta: an island republic. Boulogne. Editions Delroisse, 1980. 270p. col. illus., map, bibliog.
Sections: At the crossroads of destiny - History - Neolithic Malta - The temple builders of the Copper Age - The Bronze Age - The entrance of Malta into history - Medieval Malta - The Knights of St. John - The golden era of the Knights of Malta - The uprising against the French - The British period - Malta after the war. Sources and selected bibliography, p.266-7 (6 sections). Map of the Maltese Islands. *Class No:* 945.82

Dictionaries
[7369]
BERG, W.G. Historical dictionary of Malta. Lanham, Md, Scarecrow Press, 1995. xxii,163p. maps, bibliog. £38. (*European Historical Dictionaries, no.10.*) ISBN: 0810830183.
Dictionary (significant persons, places, events, institutions and contemporary issues) p.11-137. Bibliography (General, Culture, Economics, History, Society) p.139-63. Chronology p.p.xv-xxi. 5 maps. *Class No:* 945.82(038)

Spain

[7370]
BARD, R. Navarra: the durable kingdom. Reno, Univ. of Nevada Press, 1982. xiii,254p. geneal. table, bibliog., index. $22.95. (*The Basque Series*.) ISBN: 0874170737.

Outline history in 17 annotated chapters: 1. Prehistory: the mystery of the Basques ... 2. From Celts to Romans ... 8. Dynastic decline 1349 to 1517 ... 16. Into the twentieth century ... 17. The durable province. Appendix A. Rulers of the Kingdom of Navarra 818-1512. B. The Carlist succession to 1936. Bibliography p.230-240. Analytical index. 'A useful contribution ... but need continues for a longer, more thoroughly researched, and more thorough examination of Navarrese history in English' (*Choice*, v.20, no.7, March 1983, p.1044).
Class No: 946.0

[7371]
LYNCH, J., *ed.* A History of Spain. Oxford, Basil Blackwell, 14v., 1989-.

Castro, M.C.F.: *Iberia in prehistory.* 1995. 320p. 0631167843. Richardson, J.S. *The Romans in Spain.* 1996. 448p. 063117706x. Collins, R. *Visigothic Spain.* Collins, R. *Arab conquest of Spain 710-797.* 1989. 208p. £29.50. 0631159231. Collins, R. *Caliphs and Kings 798-1033.* 1997. 063117284x. Reilly, B. *Contest of Christian and Muslim Spain 1031-1157.* 1992. 272p. £40. 063116913x. Linehan, P. *Spain 1157-1300.* McKay, A. *Spain: centuries of crisis 1300-1474.* 1997. 0631152245. Edwards, J. *Spain of the Catholic monarchs 1474-1520.* 1997. 0631161651. Lynch, J. *Spain 1516-1598 From nation state to world empire.* 1991. 528p. £45. 0631176969. Lynch, J. *Hispanic world in crisis and change 1598-1700.* 1992. 464p. £45. 0631176977. Lynch, J. *Bourbon Spain 1700- 1808.* 1989. xiv,450p. £45. 0631145761. Blinkhorn, M. *Emergence of modern Spain.* Robinson, R. *Spain since 1939.* 1997. 0631156313.

Scholarly and well-documented multi-volume history 'designed to advance research and thinking on the subject as well as to represent its current state'. *Class No:* 946.0

[7372]
MENÉNDEZ PIDAL, R., *ed.* Historia de España. Madrid, Espasa-Calpe, 1935-. illus., ports., facsims, maps, bibliogs. ISBN: 8423948005, set.

1. *España Primitiva* 3v., 1952-1963: *España Prehistórica, Protohistórica, Preromana* - 2. *España Romana 218 A de JC - 414 de JC* 2v., 1982 - 3. *España Visigoda* 3v., 1991. 8423949958 and 8423949966 - 4/5. *España Musulmana (711-1031)* 2v. 1950-57.

6. *Los Comienzos de la Reconquista (711-1038).* 1956 - 7. *La España Christiana de los siglos VIII al XI.* 1980 - 8.1 *Los Reinos de Taifas.* 8.2 *El Retroceso Territorial de Al-Andalus. Almoravides y Almohades Siglos XI al XIII.* 1997. 8423989062. 9. *Reconquista y El Processo De Diferenciación Política (1035-1217).* 1998. 8423989089 10. *Los Reinos Christianos en los sigles XIX y XII.* 1992. 8423948129 - 11. *La Cultura del Románico Siglos XI al XIII.* 1995. 8423989011. 12. *La Baja edad media Peninsular Siglos XIII al XV.* 1996. 8423909046. 13. *La Expansión Peninsular y Mediterránea (c.1212 - c.1350).* 2v. 1990. 8423948153 and 8423948242. 14. *España Christiana crisis de la reconquista. Luchas civiles (c.1350-1410).* 1966. 16. *La Epoca del Gótico en la cultura Española (1220-1480).* - 17. *La España de los reyes católicos* 2v., 1968. 18. *La Época de los Descubrimentos y los Conquistas (1400-1500).* 1998. 8423989097.

19. *El siglo XVI.* 1989. 8423944827 - 20. *La España del Emperador Carlos V.* 3e. 1982. 8423948285 - 22. *Felipe II, El hombre y la politica.* 2v. 1955. 23. *La Crisis del siglo XVII.* 1989. 842394994x.

24. *La España de Felipe III.* 1979 - 25. *La España de Felipe IV. El Gobierno de la Monarquia, la crisis de 1640 y el fracaso de la hegemonia europea.* 1982. - 26. *El siglo del Quijote (1580-1650)* 2v., 1986. 28. *La Transición del Siglo XVII al XVIII.* 1993. 8423949982.

29. *La Época de los primeros Borbones.* 2v. 1985 - 31. *La Época de la ilustración.* 2v. 1987-88 - 32. *La España de Fernando VII,* 2nd ed. 1978 - 33. *Los Fundamentos de la España liberal (1834-1900).* 1997. 8423989070 - 34. *La era Isabelina y el sexenio democrático (1834-1874).* 1981 - 35. *Época del Romanticismo (1808-1874).* 2v. 1989.

37. *Los comienzos del siglo XX (1898-1931).* 1984. 38. *La España de Alfonso XIII* 2v. 39. *La Edad de plata de la cultura Española.* 2v. 1993. 8423949974.

41.1 *La Éupoca de Franco (1939-1975).* Política,$jército, Iglesia, Economa y Administracion. 1996.

A monumental history, planned to encompass 40 titles (many in 2v.), by various authorities. Some titles are reported to be 'in prepraration'; others are 'projected'. Critical chapter bibliographies and notes emphasise the scholarly value of this immense work.
Class No: 946.0

[7373]
PAYNE, S.G. The Franco regime 1936-1975. Madison, Univ. of Wisconsin Press, 1987. xvii,677p. illus., maps, biblilg., index. ISBN: 0229110702.

A chronological political history in 23 chapters ordered in 4 parts: 1. Origins - 2. The Civil War 1936-1939 - 2. The Dictadura 1939-1959 - 4. Developmentalism and decay 1959-1975. Chronology p.xv-xvii. Bibliography p.645-54. 5 maps. Analytical index. *Class No:* 946.0

[7374]
VALDEAVELLANO, L.G. de. Historia de España antigua y medieval. Madrid, Alianza Editoria, 3v., 1988. maps, bibliog., index. ISBN: 8420691003, set.

1. *De los orígenes al siglo X* viii,514p.+9p. maps. ISBN 842069097x. 2. *Del siglo X a las Navas de Tolosa.* 693p.+6p. maps. 8420690988. 3. *Castilla y Aragón en el siglo XIII.* 204p.+6p. geneal. tables. 8420690996. A work of considerable scholarship. V.1: has Bibliografía General p.29-41 and Fuentes p.43-104. *Class No:* 946.0

Bibliographies

[7375]
Indice histórico español: bibliografía histórica de España. Barcelona, Teide,1953-. v.1-. Publicación semestral del Centro de Estudios Históricos Internacionales, Facultad de Geografia e Historia Division 1. de Ciencias Humanes y Sociales, Universidad de Barcelona. ISSN: 05373522.

V.31, no.100 (1993) 347p. has 1780 abstracts from 97 contributors on many aspects of Spain and, more selectively, Hispanic America and elsewhere ordered in 7 regional sections: 1. Obras generales - 2. Historia de España - 3-5. Edad antigua, media, moderna y contemporanea - 6. América - 7. Otros territorios (Marruecos, Filipinas, Océania). Author index. *Class No:* 946.0(01)

Encyclopaedias

[7376]
Enciclopedia de historia de España. Artola, M., *ed.* Madrid, Alianza Editorial, 1988-1993. maps, bibliog. ISBN: 8420652946.

1. *Economía. Sociedad.* 1988. vi,7-715p. ISBN 8420652253. 2. *Instituciones. Políticas. Imperio.* 1988. 798p. 8420652261. 3. *Iglesia. Pensamiento. Cultura.* 1988. 552p. 842065227x. 4. *Diccionario biográfico.* 1991. 914p. 8420652407. 5. *Diccionario temático.* 1991. 1238p. 8420652415. 6. *Cronología. Mapas, Estadísticas.* 1993. 1241p. 8420652423. 7. *Fuentes Indice.* 1993. 853p. 8420652437.
Class No: 946.0(031)

[7377]
Gran enciclopedia de España. Zaragoza, Enciclopedia de España, 20v., 1990-. In progress. col. illus., col. maps. ISBN: 8487544010.

Historical perspective on the culture and people of Spain more suited to academic than to home use because of its 'small-size print, extensive use of abbreviations, and lack of subheadings that makes longer entries difficult to read' (*Booklist*, v.89, no.7, 1 Dec 1992, p.693).
Class No: 946.0(031)

Handbooks & Manuals

[7378]
BLEYE, P.A. Manual de historia de España. Novena edición, revisada por C.A. Molina. Madrid, Espasa-Calpe, 3v., 1963-1964. illus. bibliogs.

First published 1914; 6th ed. 1947.
Prehistoria. Edades antigua y media 1963. 1071p. 2. *Reyes católicos - Casa de Austria (1474-1700)* 1964. 1200p. 3. *Casa de Borbón (1700-1808). España contemporánea (1808-1955)* 1964. 1057p. V.1 has 45, v.2 has 38, and v.3 has 38 chapters, each with its own bibliography, and each divided into numbered topics.
Class No: 946.0(035)

Dictionaries

[7379]
BLEIBERG, G. Diccionario de historia de España. 2nd ed. corregida y aumentada. Madrid, Alianza, 3v., 1986. viii, 1358p.; 1179p.; v, 1207p. ISBN: 8420652989.

1st published. Ediciones de la Revista de Occident, 1952.
Signed articles A-Z. About 76 contributors. 'Arabismo (en España)'; p.289-93; numerous references in the text. Includes articles on Latin America and its Spanish connections ('Historiadores de América': v.2, p.373-9). Excludes living persons. V.3 includes as appendices a bibliography (p.1083-1111), plus a further bibliography for 1931-1968 (p.1113); chronology p.1115-92, and 24p. of outline maps.
'This is an excellent encyclopaedic dictionary, which also includes coverage of Spain's expansion in Europe and overseas' (G.J. Shields. *Spain*, 1985. Entry 131). *Class No:* 946.0(038)

[7380]
KERN, R.W. *and* DODGE, M.D., *eds.* Historical dictionary of modern Spain 1700-1988. Westport, Conn., Greenwood Press, 1990. xxvi,697p. maps, bibliog., index. £89.95. ISBN: 0313259712.

69 academics contribute well-documented, signed, cross-referenced A-Z entries offering quick reference information on political, governmental, diplomatic, institutional, cultural, social, and military historical material comprehending individuals, political concepts, parties and ideologies, armed forces personnel, geographical regions *etc.*, not easily available elsewhere. Chronology p.543-620.

....(contd.)
Bibliography (an introduction to the basic monographic literature) p.621-44. 6 maps. A major work of scholarship. *Class No:* 946.0(038)

[7381]
OLSON, J.S., *ed*. **Historical dictionary of the Spanish Empire.** Westport, Conn., Greenwood Press, 1992. x,705p. bibliog., index. $89.50. ISBN: 0313264139.
1,300 brief descriptive essays from 38 contributors on people, places, events, institutions, and historical developments in the Spanish Empire from the Castilians' first landing in the Canary Islands to the loss of Spanish Sahara in 1975. Appendix A. Chronology p.651-59. B. Colonial Viceroys 1535-1824 p.661-65. Bibliography p.667-78. *Class No:* 946.0(038)

[7382]
SMITH, A. **Historical dictionary of Spain.** Lanham, MD. Scarecrow Press, 1996. xxviii,435p. map, bibliog., tables. $69.50. (*European Historical Dictionaries, no.11*.) ISBN: 0810830809.
Chronology of modern Spanish history p.xvii-xxviii. Introduction (outline 19th and 20th century history) p.1-17. Dictionary p.19-360p. Appendices (population, election results etc.) p.363-69. Bibliography (Essay and under 23 heavily subdivided sections p.371-435. 3 maps. 'A sound piece of work containing a multitude of well-marshalled facts' (*International Journal of Iberian Studies*, v.11,no.3, 1998, p.190). *Class No:* 946.0(038)

Canary Islands

[7383]
TORRES, A.M. **Historia general de las Islas Canarias.** Las Palmas, Editora Regional Canaria, 6v., 1977-81. col.illus., maps, indexes.
'A definitive history of the Canary Islands first published 1893-1895 revised with numerous coloured plates, a volume of biographies, and indexes' (H.G.R. King. *Atlantic Ocean*, 1985. Entry 708). *Class No:* 946.0(649)

Middle Ages

Bibliographies

[7384]
FAULHABER, C.B. **Libros y bibliotecas en la España medieval: una bibliografia de fuentes impresas.** London, Grant & Culier, 1987. 213p. indexes, pbk. £18,00. (*Research Bibliographies and Checklists No.47*.) ISBN: 0729302660.
666 annotated entries: España; Corona de Aragon; Navarra; Corona de Castilla; Francia; Italia with geographical sub-divisions. Separate subject, chronological, toponymic, persons and modern scholarship indexes p.185-213. *Class No:* 946.0"01/14"(01)

[7385]
FERREIRO, A. **The Visigoths in Gaul and Spain AD 488-711 a bibliography.** Leiden, E.J. Brill, 1988. lxii, 822p. indexes. ISBN: 9004087931.
9096 unannotated entries in 17 sections: 1. Reference - 2. General studies - 3. Invasions - 4. Social - 5. Law - 6. Culture - 7. Palaeography - 8. Ecclesiastical - 9. Liturgy - 10. Patristics - 11. Isodore of Seville - 12. Archaeology - 13. Sueves - 14. Toulouse - 15. Other peoples - 16. Collected essays and Studia Honoraria - 17. Congresses. Abbvreviations (periodicals) p.xv-lxii. Author and subject indexes. *Class No:* 946.0"01/14"(01)

16th Century

[7386]
LOVETT, A.W. **Early Hapsburg Spain 1517-1598.** Oxford, Oxford Univ. Press, 1986. maps, geneal table, bibliogs., index. £25.00. ISBN: 0198221398.
Is especially valuable for its extensive bibliography p.305-340. *Class No:* 946.0"15"

18th Century

Bibliographies

[7387]
AGUILAR PINAL, F. **Bibliografia de Estudios sobre Carlos III y su epoca.** Madrid. Consejo Superior De Investigaciones Cientificas, 1988. xxiii,428p. index. ISBN: 8400069064.
8176 unannotated entries organized in 3 subdivided parts: 1. Historia politica y militar - 2. Historia economica y social - 3. Historia cultural y Cientifica (inc 4 exploraciones y viejes). *Class No:* 946.0"17"(01)

19th Century

Bibliographies

[7388]
DEL BURGO, J. **Bibliografia del Siglo XIX Guerras Carlistas luchas politicas.** 2nd ed. Pamplona, 1978. xxix,1072p. ISBN: 8423503429.
First published in 5v. 1953-1960.
Entries of books and articles relating to political history from the reign of Fernando VII to Alfonso Carlos de Bourbón y Austria-Este (1931-36) arranged A-Z by author and title. Subject guide to reigns, wars and other events covered p.xxvii-xxix. *Class No:* 946.0"18"(01)

20th Century

[7389]
The Spanish Civil War revolution and counter revolution. London, Harvester Wheatsheaf, 1991. xxxii,1074p. £50. ISBN: 074500763.
Massively researched and documented narrative history and analysis of Republican politics 1936-39. Acronyms p.xxiii-xxiv. Leading participants p.xxv-xxxii. Chapter notes p.745-935. Bibliography p.937-1018. 5 maps. Analytical index. *Class No:* 946.0"19"

Dictionaries

[7390]
CORTADA, J.W., *ed*. **Historical dictionary of the Spanish Civil War** 1936-1939. Westport, Connecticut, Greenwood Press, 1982. xxviii, 571p. maps, bibligo. $76.95. ISBN: 0313220549.
800 signed entries of varying length by 40 contributors on all aspects of the Civil War. Appendix A. Chronology 1930-1939; B. Military History; C. Civil War governments; D. Compendium of archives and libraries (A-Z by country) p.537-543; Selected bibliography of bibliographies p.544-546; Analytical index p.547-571. 'The long entries written by various experts and the inclusion of some rather unusual topics enhance the value of this reference tool' (*Choice* v.21, no.1, September 1983, p.62). *Class No:* 946.0"19"(038)

[7391]
RUBIO CABEZA, M. **Diccionario de la Guerra Civil Espanola.** Barcelona, Editorial Planeta, 2v., 1987. 819p. illus., ports., bibliog. ISBN: 8432058602, set; 8432058572, v.1; 8432058580, v.2.
Political, military, diplomatic events, organizations, institutions, individuals *etc*. in a single A-Z sequence. *Class No:* 946.0"19"(038)

Gibraltar

[7392]
DENNIS, P. **Gibraltar and its people.** Newton Abbot, Devon, David & Charles, 1990. 176p. illus., map, bibliog., index. £13.95. ISBN: 0715394932.
A narrative history with thematic chapters on Gibraltar's status as a British colony and a comparative scrutiny of other colonial enclaves. Appendix 1. Some notable dates (p.163-5) - 2. Article X of the Treaty of Utrecht. Bibliography p.169-71. *Class No:* 946.82

[7393]
JACKSON, W.G.F. **The Rock of the Gibraltarians: a history of Gibraltar.** London & Toronto, Associated Univ. Presses, 1987. 379p. illus., maps, bibliog., index. £30. ISBN: 0838632378.
17 well-documented chronological chapters setting Gibraltar's history in the context of world events. Notes p.339-357. Bibliography p.358-363. *Class No:* 946.82

[7394]
MORRIS, D.S. *and* HAIGH, R.H. **Britain, Spain and Gibraltar 1945-90 the eternal triangle.** London, Routledge, 1992. xii,180p. map, index. £35. ISBN: 0415071453.
Account of Gibraltar's post-war constitutional and political history and of its relations and negotiations with Spain. Chapter notes p.153-75. *Class No:* 946.82

Portugal

[7395]
BOXER, C.R. **The Portuguese seaborne empire 1415-1825.** 2nd ed. London, Carcanet in association with The Calouste Gulbenkian Foundation, 1991. xiv,426p. illus., maps, bibliog., index. ISBN: 0856359629.
First published Hutchinson, 1969.
A well-documented survey in 16 chapters. 6 appendices (*e.g.* 1: Outward-bound Portuguese East Indiamen. 1501-1800). Glossary p.386-91. Chapter bibliographies, p.392-413, with some annotations. Analytical index, p.415-26. 16 illus.; 7 maps. *Class No:* 946.9

[7396]

MATTOSO, J., *ed*. **Historia de Portugal**. Lisboa, Editorial Estampa, 1994-. ISBN: 9723309246, complete work.

1. *Antes de Portugal*. 565p. illus. (many col.), col.maps, col.tables, bibliog. ISBN 9723309203. Contents: Apresentaçâo Historiográfica Das Histórias de Portugal - 1. Introducâo geográfica - 2. O passado proto-histórico e Romano - 3. A i idado do ferro - 4. A Época Sueva e Visigótica - 5. O Garb-Al-Andaluz - 6. Portugal no reino Asturiano - Leonês. Bibliography p.563-65. *Class No: 946.9*

[7397]

OLIVEIRA MARQUES, A.H. de. **History of Portugal**. 2nd ed. New York and London, Columbia Univ. Press, 2v., 1976. illus., ports., maps, bibliog..

1. From Lusitania to Empire. 2. From Empire to Corporate State. 'The most important book on Portuguese history in English ... it concludes with a good and partially annotated bibliography' (P.T.H. Unwin. *Portugal*, 1987. Entry 174). *Class No: 946.9*

[7398]

SERRÃO, J. *and* OLIVEIRA MARQUES, A.D. de, *eds*. **Nova história de Portugal**. Lisboa, Editorial Presenca, 13v., 1986?-.

1. *Des origens a Romanização*. 2. *Islam e reconquista Christa*. 3. *Do condado Portucalense à crise do século XIV*. 4. *Portugal na crise dos séculos XIV e XV*. 5. *Descobrimentos e renascimento*. 6. *Da contra-reforma à restauração*. 7. *Da restaração ao auro do Brasil*. 8. *A crise do antigo regime*. 9. *A instauração do liberalismo*. 10. *A restauração*. 11. *Da monarquia para à républica*. 12. *O estado novo*.

V.11 (1991) 839p. tables. ISBN 9722314203 is in 16 thematic chapters. Fontes e bibliografia p.747-75. Indice dos mapas, gráficos e quadros p.777-81. Indice analitico p.783-827. *Class No: 946.9*

Bibliographies

[7399]

DE SILVA, D. **The Portuguese in Asia** an annotated bibliography on studies on Portuguese colonial history in Asia, 1498-c.1800. Zug, Switzerland, IDC AG, 1987. xxiv,313p. index. (*Bibliotheca Asiatic no.22*.) ISBN: 3300000068.

2773 entries in 9 main divisions: 1. Reference works - 2. Historiography - 3. Cartography - 4. Navigation - 5. Travel & Description - 6. Conquest, expansion and decline - 7. Religion - 8. Economic foundations - 9. Impact on Asian society. For the researcher. 1000 scarce titles from the *Bibliography* will be made available on microfiche - p.313. Correlation table of microfiche editions. 'An excellent and innovative work, admirably indexed and cross-referenced' (*Portuguese Studies*, No.4, 1988, p.238). *Class No: 946.9(01)*

Dictionaries

[7400]

SERRÃO, J., *ed*. **Dicionário de historia de Portugal**. 2nd ed. Porto, Livraria Figueirinhas, 6v. 1981. illus. maps, tables, bibliogs., index.

First published in 4v. by Iniciativas Editoriais of Lisbon 1963-71.

Subjects covered include political, legal and economic institutions; economic, social and technical history; cultural, ideological and religious movements; biographies; and articles on Portuguese literature, language, science and philosophy, archaeology, numismatics, palaeography and diplomatic. Longer signed entries include extensive bibliographies. *Class No: 946.9(038)*

[7401]

—SERRÃO, J. Pequeno dicionário de historia de Portugal. Porto, Figueirinhas, 1987. 654p. illus. maps. softcover.

First published by Iniciativas Editoriais 1976. *Class No: 946.9(038)*

[7402]

WHEELER, D.L. **Historical dictionary of Portugal**. Metuchen, NJ., Scarecrow Press, 1993. xxv,288p. maps. $37.95. (*European Historical Dictionaries, no.1*.) ISBN: 0810826968.

Chronology p.xv-xxv. Introduction (Physical features; population and emigration; history; society and economy) p.1-28. Dictionary p.29-183. Bibliography (28 form and thematic sections) p.184-283. Appendix A. Monarchs (1140-1910) - B. Presidents (1910-) - C. Prime Ministers (1932-). 2 maps. 'A useful first step, quick reference for the reader seeking information about Portugal's rich and eventful history' (*International Journal of Iberian Studies*, v.11,no.3, 1998, p.189-90). *Class No: 946.9(038)*

Chronologies

[7403]

SERRÃO, J. **Cronologia geral da historia de Portugal**. 5th ed. Lisboa, Livros Horizonte, 1956. 247p. index. pbk.

1st ed. 1971.

Descends from section bearing same title printed in v.4 *Dicionário de historia de Portugal* (1971). Stops at 1930. *Class No: 946.9(090)*

Middle Ages

Bibliographies

[7404]

OLIVEIRA MARQUES, A.H. de. **Guía do estudiante de historia medieval portuguesa**. 3rd ed. Lisboa, Editoria Estampa, 1988. 291p.

First published by Ediçes Cosmos 1964.

A running commentary in 8 chapters, covering bibliographies, atlases and dictionaries, handbooks, history auxiliaries, printed sources, archives and collections of manuscripts. *Class No: 946.9"01/14"(01)*

Contemporary

Bibliographies

[7405]

CHILCOTE, R.H., *comp*. **The Portuguese revolution of 25 April 1974**: annotated bibliography on the antecedents and aftermath/ Revolução Portuguesa de 25 de Abril de 1974: bibliografia anotada sombre os antecedentes e evolução posterior. Coimbra, Centro de Documentação 25 de Abril, Universidade de Coimbra, 1987. xv, 329p. indexes.

In 2 separate A-Z sequences: 1. Monographs and pamphlets (1116 entries) - 2. Periodical articles (1047 entries). Author and acronyms indexes. 'A later volume will include the listings for the third part, an annotated list of periodical titles, and part 4, a list of relevant organizations'. *Class No: 946.9"312"(01)*

[7406]

GALLAGHER, T. **Dictatorial Portugal** a bibliographical essay *Iberian Studies* v.9, no.1, Spring 1980, p.11-21.

Limited mainly to post-1974 writings. 106 references. *Class No: 946.9"312"(01)*

Russia

[7407]

Longman history of Russia. Shukman, H., *general ed*. Harlow, Essex, Longman, 7v., 1981-.

2. *Kievan Russia 850-1240* by D. Obolensky. 3. *The Crisis of medieval Russia 1200-1304* by J. Fennell. 1987. 296p. 4. *The Formation of Muscovy 1304-1613* by R.O. Crummey. 1987. xv, 275p. £22.00. 0582491525. 5. *The Making of Russian absolutism 1613-1801* by P. Dukes. 1982. viii, 197p. £22.00. 05824864x. 6. *Russia in the age of reaction and reform 1801-1881* by D. Saunders. 1983. 7. *Russia in the age of modernization and revolution 1881-1917* by Hans Rogger. 1983. viii, 323p. 8. *The Russian revolution 1917* by S. Smith. 9. *The Soviet Union 1917-1991* by M. McCauley, 2nd ed. 1993. 422p. £17.99. 0582013232. For student and non-specialist readership. Extensive bibliographies in all volumes.

1. *The Emergence of Rus 750-1200* by S. Franklin. 1996. 400p. £45. 058290901. *Class No: 947*

[7408]

PAXTON, J. **Encyclopedia of Russian history**: from the Christianization of Kiev to the breakup of the Soviet Union. Santa Barbara, Calif., and Oxford, ABC-Clio, 1993. 484p. maps, bibliog. $65. ISBN: 0874366909.

Much revised version of Paxton's *Companion to Russian history* (Batsford, 1983).

A-Z encyclopedia on post-Soviet Russia and the new sovereign states that were once republics of the Soviet Union. 2500 entries comprise this encyclopedia, gazetteer, atlas and chronology covering 100 years of history. 'This first-rate reference monograph will prove an invaluable asset for scholars' (*Library Journal*, v.118, no.21, December 1993. p.116). *Class No: 947*

[7409]

PAXTON, J. **The Longman companion to Imperial Russia 1682-1917**. London, Longman, 1996. 272p. maps, bibliog. £38. ISBN: 0582210526.

Political, military and diplomatic events; the arts, education and censorship; social and economic developments; religion; key biographies; glossary. *Class No: 947*

[7410]

SMITH, F., *ed*. **The Nationalities question in the post-Soviet states**. 2nd ed. London, Longman, 1996. xiv,524p. maps, tables, bibliog., index. ISBN: 058221808x.

First published as *The Nationalities question in the Soviet Union* (1990).

25 academic and professional contributors. 24 annotated chapters grouped in 7 parts: 1. Nationalities policy: from the Soviet Union to the post-Soviet states - 2. Russian Federation (Tatarstan, Northern minorities, Buryatiya) - 3. The Baltic states - 4. South-western borderlands (Ukraine, Belarus, Moldova) - 5. Transcaucasia (Armenia, Azerbaijan, Georgia) - 6. Muslim Central Asia (Kazakhstan, Uzbekistan, Turkmenistan, Tajikistan, Kyrgyzstan) - 7., The Diaspora

..(contd.)
Nationalities (Crimean Tatars. Volga Germans). Appendix 1: Ethnic and territorial claims of the post-Soviet states. Bibliography p.506-516. 9 maps. *Class No:* 947

[7411]
OLOVIEV, S.M. **History of Russia from earliest times.**
Orchard, G.E., *ed.* Gulf Breeze, Fl., Academic International Press, 50v. 1996-. $38. per volume.
Based on the 1959-1966 Moscow edition.
Classic work now available in English for the first time. 'Each volume is edited, translated and annotated by a scholar recognized as expert in the time and topic of the volume. All volumes feature scholarly introductory essays ... The new, extensive footnoting and indexing, notably the subject indexing which the Russian edition lacks, alone represent a unique, massive reference and research resource ... hitherto unavailable' (*advt.*). *Class No:* 947

[7412]
ERNADSKY, G., *and others, eds.* **A Source book for Russian history** from early times to 1917. New Haven, Connecticut, Yale Univ. Press, 3v., 1973.
1: *Early times to the late seventeenth century.* 352p.
2: *Peter the Great to Nicholas I.* 322p.
3: *Alexander II to the February Revolution.* 344p.
Praised in *TLS* (no.3705, 9 March 1973, p.260) for the careful translations of texts, informal notes and thoroughness of references. *Class No:* 947

Bibliographies

[7413]
CROWTHER, P.A., *ed.* **A Bibliography of works in English on early Russian history to 1800.** Oxford, Blackwell, 1969. xvii, 263p. indexes.
2,081 + 83 entries, in 20 sections (1. Bibliography - 2. Historiography - 3. General works - 4. The Slavs, Early Panslavism - 5. General history - 6. Diplomatic and foreign relations ... 19. Local and regional history - 20. Travel and description, contemporary accounts). Introductory sectional notes single out important items. Occasional annotations; references to reviews. Cross-references. Name and subject index.
A companion to David Shapiro's *A select bibliography of works in English on Russian history, 1801-1917* (Oxford, Blackwell, 1962. xii, [i], 106p.), which lists 1,070 books and articles in 21 sections, with evaluative sectional annotations and references to reviews. Covers all aspects of Russian history up to 1961, deliberately omitting more inclusive bibliographies and histories. Author index. *Class No:* 947(01)

[7414]
EGAN, D.R. *and* EGAN, M.A. **Russian autocrats from Ivan the Great to the fall of the Romanov dynasty** : an annotated bibliography of English language sources to 1985. Metuchen, New Jersey, Scarecrow Press, 1987. xxxv, 512p. $49.50. ISBN: 0810819589.
2082 descriptively annotated items, including popular and journalistic sources, on the 26 Czars who ruled Russia 1492-1917 arranged in 14 chronological sections for single or successive rulers. Chronology p.xxxv. Author and subject indexes. *Class No:* 947(01)

[7415]
FRAME, M., *comp.* **The Russian Revolution 1905-1921** a bibliographic guide to works in English. Westport, Conn., Greenwood Press, 1995. 308p. indexes. $79.50. ISBN: 031329559x.
Encompassing books, articles and doctoral theses, this guide is arranged by 24 broad categories subdivided by subject and date. 'A gem for researchers and students at all levels' (*Choice*, v.33,no.3, November 1995, p.434). *Class No:* 947(01)

[7416]
HORAK, S.M., *comp.* **Russia, the USSR and Eastern Europe.** A bibliographic guide to English language publications 1981-1985. Littleton, Colo., Libraries Unlimited, 1987. 273p. indexes. ISBN: 087287561x.
Follows the compiler's *Russia, The USSR ... 1964-1974.* (1978. 488p.) and *Russia, The USSR ... 1975-1980* (1982. 279p.) Updates P.L. Horecky's *Russia and Eastern Europe. A bibliographic guide to Western language publications* (Univ. of Chicago Press, 1965. 473p.).
Annotated entries (a total of 3673 in this and previous volumes) for the Russian Empire prior to 1917; the individual Soviet republics; and other Eastern *bloc* countries. *Class No:* 947(01)

[7417]
—BURGER, R.H. *and* SULLIVAN, H.F. **Eastern Europe** a bibliographical guide to English language publications 1986-1993 Englewood, Colo., Libraries Unlimited, 1995. xiii,254p. indexes. $67.50. ISBN: 1563080478.
Continues and expands S.M. Horak's *Russia, the USSR and Eastern Europe. A bibliographic guide to English language publications 1981-1985* (1986).
1008 descriptive annotated entries arranged in 9 national divisions Albania-Yugoslavia. Author and subject indexes. 'The annotations are the weakest featue of the book'. Gone are the gracefully written, authoritative evaluations of Horak's day, replaced by poorly-edited descriptive notes that draw far too heavily on quotations from the books themselves, and do little to help readers place a given work in a broader context' (*Choice*, v.33,no.10, June 1996, p.1612). *Class No:* 947(01)

[7418]
MAGOCSI, P.R. **Galicia:** a historical survey and bibliographic guide. Toronto, Univ. of Toronto Press in association with the Canadian Institute of Ukrainian Studies and the Harvard Ukrainian Research Institute, 1983. xix,299p. maps, index. ISBN: 0802024823.
1. Bibliographical and archival aids - 2. General studies - 3. Early history to 1340 - 4-9. Chronological periods to the present - 10. Minorities. An introduction to the basic historical problems of Galicia and a guide to the major published primary and secondary sources. More than 1000 notes and 3000 references. 'It is a meticulously researched, highly scholarly guide, prepared in the best tradition of bibliography' (*Choice*, v.21,no.6, February 1984, p.806). *Class No:* 947(01)

[7419]
PEARSON, R., *comp.* **Russia and Eastern Europe 1789-1985** a bibliographical guide. Manchester, Manchester Univ. Press, 1989. Distributed in North America by St. Martin's Press. xiii,210p. indexes. £40.00. (*History And Related Disciplines Select Bibliographies.*) ISBN: 0719017343.
5144 briefly annotated entries in 3 main sections: General; Nineteenth-century Russia and Eastern Europe; Twentieth-century Soviet Union... Subdivided A-Z by state and 16 subject headings *e.g.* Historiography ... National minorities ... War... Economy ... Tourist. Author index. Bibliographical details incomplete but a useful work nevertheless. *Class No:* 947(01)

[7420]
The Rise and fall of the Soviet Union a selected bibliography of sources in English. Edelheit, A.J. *and* Edelheit, H., *eds.* Westport, Conn., Greenwood Press, 1992. xviii,430p. indexes. $65. (*Bibliographies and Indexes in World History, no.27.*) ISBN: 0313286256. ISSN: 07426852.
2016 cross-referenced entries (some annotated) arranged in 12 chapters sub-divided into large thematic or chronological sections: 1. Reference works (Research guides; bibliographies; collections of primary sources) ... 3. Overviews of Soviet history (Historical overviews; Soviet political system; Social issues) ... 6. Stalinist Russia (Domestic policy; Foreign Policy to 1939; Terror) ... 12. Biographies and memoirs. Glossary p.345-52. Author/title and subject indexes. *Class No:* 947(01)

Encyclopaedias

[7421]
The Blackwell encyclopaedia of the Russian Revolution. Shukman, H., *ed.* Oxford, Blackwell Reference, 1988. xiv,418p., maps on endpapers, bibliogs., index. £45.00; $65.00. ISBN: 0631152385.
Part 1 consists of 128 cross-referenced, initialled articles, from 45 contributors, arranged in an approximate chronological sequence 1860-1921. Part 2 comprises 174 biographies, long enough to be useful, including Sir Robert Bruce Lockhart, Josef Pilsudski, John Reed, and Sidney Reilly. Short reading lists are appended to all Pt.1 articles and to many of the biographies. Designed as a reference source for students and teachers and for general readers interested in 20th century history. The editor is Director of the Russian and East European Centre, St. Anthony's College, Oxford. 'Unique as a reference source devoted to this topic' (*Booklist*,v.88,no.5, 1 November 1988, p.460). *Class No:* 947(031)

[7422]
The Modern encyclopaedia of Russian and Soviet history. Wieczynski, J., *ed.* Gulf Breeze, Florida, Academic International Press, 1976-.
55v. so far published: v. 1-46 (1976-1987) comprise the base set. Supplementary volumes 46-55. V.55. *Supplement Witchcraft in Russia - Zvenigord.* 1993. 274p. 0875690645 has signed articles, essays and bibliographes. Articles in English include translations from Russian sources (*e.g. Sovetskaya istoricheskaya entsiklopediya* as well as contributions by Western scholars. Coverage: persons, places, events and concepts relative to Russian/Soviet history.
Change of title to *The Modern Encyclopaedia of Russian, Soviet and*

....(contd.)

Eurasian History with v.56. *Index of entries and authors*. 1994. 57. *Index by topics*. 1994. 58. *Index by time periods*. 1994. 59. *Index to v.1-10* (Aachen, Conference of - Estonia, Soviet acquisition of). 1996. xvii,232p. 0875691811. *Supplement* edited by G.N. Rhyne. 1. 1995. 250p. 2. 1997. 251p. *Class No:* 947(031)

[7423]

SHAW, W. *and* PRYCE, D. **Encyclopedia of the USSR** 1905 to the present. Lenin to Gorbachev. London, Cassell, 1990. 351p. illus., maps, bibliog., index. £20. ISBN: 0304318183.

In 3 main parts: 1. Chronology of important dates and events, January 1905 to July 1990 (p.12-98) - 2. Encyclopedia *i.e.* political and economic background information arranged A-Z by topic (p.100-227) - 3. Biographies (p.230-318). Gazetteer of changed or alternative place-names p.329-30. Bibliography p.331-4. 8 maps. Useful compact guide for students and general readers. *Class No:* 947(031)

Dictionaries

[7424]

JACKSON, G. *and* DEVLIN, R., *eds*. **Dictionary of the Russian Revolution.** Westport, Connecticut, Greenwood Press, 1989. xviii,704p., maps, bibliog., indexes. $75. ISBN: 0313211310.

100 or so contributors. *c*.300 signed A-Z cross-referenced entries, 1/3 2000-4000 word essays, remainder shorter articles on the institutions, personalities and events of the Revolution. 'There is excellent coverage of the myriad committees, parties, interest groups, and other organizations that had a role in shaping the events of the period' (*Booklist*, v.86, no.4, 15 December 1989, p.422). *Class No:* 947(038)

[7425]

OLSON, J.S., *and others, eds*. **An Ethnohistorical dictionary of the Russian and Soviet Empires.** Westport, CT., Greenwood Press, 1994. 904p. bibliog., index. £99.95. ISBN: 0313274975.

'Focusing on ethnolinguistic groups rather than peoples with purely religious orientations, Olson provides entries on over 450 ethnic groups, with appropriate cross-references. Each entry concludes with references, and the volume includes a selected bibliography of English-language titles. The volume also includes a chronology, several appendices providing statistical information and an appendix essay on Islam in Russia and the Soviet Union' (*publishers catalogue*). *Class No:* 947(038)

[7426]

PUSHKAREV, S.G. **Dictionary of Russian historical terms** from the eleventh century to 1917. New Haven, Connecticut, Yale Univ. Press, 1970. xi, 199p.

A companion to *A source book for Russian history*. It aims 'to assist English-speaking readers to understand the specialized works on Russia' (*Preface*). The most important terms referring to social categories and political, military, educational and other institutions are supplied with brief historical sketches. 'A comprehensive reference work; more restricted but more scholarly than Paxton' (R. Pearson. *Russia and Eastern Europe*. 1989, Entry 1.128). *Class No:* 947(038)

[7427]

RAYMOND, R. *and* DUFFY, P. **Historical dictionary of Russia.** Lanham, MD., Scarecrow Press, 1998. xxxiv,405p. maps, bibliog £64.80. $72. (*European Historical Dictionaries, no.26*.) ISBN: 0810833573.

Introduction (overview of Russian history) p.i-iv. Dictionary (political leaders, major events, places, newspapers, cultural activities etc.) p.15-360. Bibliography (17 thematic categories) p.361-405. Appendix 1. Administrative divisions of the Russian republics - 2. Principal rivers, lakes and mountains. *Class No:* 947(038)

[7428]

WILSON, A. *and* BACHKATOV, N. **Russia revised** an alphabetical key to the Soviet collapse and the new republics. London, Deutsch, 1992. xii,258p. bibliog., index. £9.99. ISBN: 0233987673.

First published as *Les nouveaux Soviétiques de l'A à Z* (Paris, Cahmann-Lévy).

Pinpoints major developments up to the first months of 1992. A-Z sequence of persons, organizations, concepts and statistics, geographical entities, and political terminology *etc.* Bibliography p.248. Thematic index p.49-55. Both authors were newspaper correspondents in Moscow as the Soviet Union disintegrated. *Class No:* 947(038)

Maps & Atlases

[7429]

CHANNON, J. *and* HUDSON, R. **The Penguin historical atlas of Russia.** London, Penguin, 1995. 144p. col.illus., col.maps, bibliog., index. £13. $16.95. ISBN: 0140513264.

41 illustrated map features separated into 7 parts: 1. Origins of Russia - 2. From Tatars to Time of Troubles - 3. Muscovite to Imperial Russia - 4. Russia from the early 19th century - 5. Reform to

....(contd.)

Revolution. Timelines (4 colour coded columns across the page) p.8-13. Bibliography p.136. 60 colour maps. Fully catches Russia's turbulent history. *Class No:* 947(084.3)

[7430]

GILBERT, M. **Routledge atlas of Russian history.** 2nd ed. London, Routledge, 1993. v,197p. maps, bibliog., index. £25. ISBN: 0460861751.

First published as *Russian history atlas* (Weidenfeld & Nicolson, 1972).

161 pages of black and white outline maps arranged in 4 sections: 1. Ancient and early modern Russia (beginning with the Slavs 800BC) - 2. Imperial Russia - 3. Soviet Union - 4. End of Soviet Union. Bibliography (atlases, maps, reference works) p.162-6. Analytical index. *Class No:* 947(084.3)

[7431]

MILNER-GULLAND, R. *and* DEJEVSKY, N. **Atlas of Russia and the Soviet Union.** Oxford, Phaidon, 1989. 240p. illus. (some col.), col. maps, bibliog., index. £19.50. ISBN: 0714825492.

Narrative history in 3 major parts: 1. The geographical background - 2. The historical period - 3. Regions and republics of the Soviet Union (Belorussia; Moldavia and the Ukraine; The Baltic Republics; Transcaucasia; RSFSR; Central Asia). 24 special features *e.g.* Novgorod the Great ... Tolstoy the revolutionary ... Religion in the Soviet Union. Chronological table p. 8-9. The rulers of Russia and the Soviet Union p.10-11. Bibliography p.225-27. Glossary p.228-29. Gazetter p.232-34. *Class No:* 947(084.3)

Chronologies

[7432]

DE MOWBRAY, S.A. **Key facts in Soviet history:** a chronology of major events in Soviet history since 1917. Volume 1. 1917 to 22 June 1941. Boston, Massachusetts, G.K. Hall; London, Pinter in association with Spiers, 1990. 256p. bibliog., index. $40.00. Export $45.00. £65.00. ISBN: 0816118205, US; 0861870131, UK.

Emphasizes internal political developments. English terms provided for most Soviet organizations and the Library of Congress transliteration scheme is consistently followed. The bibliography lists all sources cited. Subsequent volumes will include newly revealed information. The final volume will be a cumulative index. *Class No:* 947(090)

Armenia

[7433]

CHAHIN, M. **The Kingdom of Armenia.** London, Croom Helm, 1987. 332p. 16p. plates. illus. maps, index. £40. $49.95. ISBN: 070994800x.

28 chapters (2 parts). 1. Uhartu - 2. Armenia. Main emphasis (2/3) is on Uhartu. Chronology of the ancient Near East p.iv-vii. Maps p.viii-xi. No bibliography. *Class No:* 947(479.25)

Maps & Atlases

[7434]

ARMEN, G. **Hayasdanee badmagan adias.** New York (?), Armenian National Education Committee, 1987. 51p. $29.

Historical maps of Armenia to the present day. *Class No:* 947(479.25)(084.3)

18th Century

Bibliographies

[7435]

CLENDENNING, P. *and* BARTLETT, R. **Eighteenth century Russia** : a select bibliography of works published since 1955. Newtonville, Massachusetts, Oriental Research Partners, 1981. x, 262p. index. $30.00. (*Russian Bibliography Series; no.3*.) ISBN: 0892501103.

270 entries, English, Russian, French and German material grouped in 14 sections: 1. Bibliography and reference - 2. Historiography and source studies - 3. General works - 4. Selections and collections of documents - 5. General history (by period) - 6. Political history - 7. Social and economic - 8. Diplomacy and international relations - 9. Military and naval - 10. Geography, demography, ethnology - 11. Individuals, biographies, memoirs - 12. Intellectual and cultural - 13. Religion - 14. Local and regional, national and ethnic minorities. For undergraduates and graduates embarking on research. *Class No:* 947"17"(01)

USSR

[7436]

OHDAN NAHAYLO *and* SWOBODA, V. **Soviet disunion** a history of the Nationalities Problem in the USSR. London, Hamish Hamilton, 1990. xvi,432p. illus., maps, bibliog., index. £20. ISBN: 0241125405.

History of the non-Russian nationalities in the Soviet Union since the Russian Revolution. 18 chaps: 1. Nations of the Russian Empire ... 3. 1919: Sovereign Soviet Republics - 4. Moslem nations ... 17. Crisis in the Empire - 18. Waiting for Gorbachev. Appendix (National structure of the USSR in early 1990 and The Union Republics) p.360-8. Chapter notes p.369-411. Bibliography p.412-7. 6 maps. *Class No:* 947.0

[7437]

ERVICE, R. **A History of twentieth-century Russia.** Harmondsworth, Allen Lane The Penguin Press, 1997. xxxiii,653p. illus., maps, index. £25. ISBN: 0713991488.

Taking advantage of the mass of documentation released to researchers since the break-up of the USSR, this scholarly work analyses the political, economic and social aspects of Soviet Russia 1917-1991, and the lingering vestiges of the Communist regime. *Class No:* 947.0

Baltic States

[7438]

IDEN, J. *and* SALMON, P. **The Baltic nations and Europe** Estonia, Latvia and Lithuania in the twentieth century. London, Longman, 1991. x,224p. maps, tables, bibliog., index. £19.99. ISBN: 0582082463.

Part 1 of this comprehensive account of the three Baltic Republics in the 20th century is a summary of their history from the Middle Ages to the First World War. Bibliographical essay (by chapter) p.193-9. 3 maps. *Class No:* 947.4

[7439]

IRBY, D. **Northern Europe in the early modern period** The Baltic World 1492-1772. London, Longman, 1990. xii,443p. maps, bibliog., index. $43.25. ISBN: 0582004101.

14 chapters in 4 parts: 1. The Baltic at the end of the Middle Ages - 2. The Livonian Wars - 3. Sweden as a great power - 4. Rise of Russia. Table of contemporary rulers in the Baltic lands 1500-1772 p.426-9. Glossary p.430-1. Bibliography p.405-15. 4 maps. Primarily conceived ... as a general introduction to the history and historical controversies of the Baltic region' (*Preface*). The first volume to appear in a sequence ... that explores the history of the Baltic World, and Northern Europe more generally. *Class No:* 947.4

[7440]

-KIRBY, D. **The Baltic world 1772-1993** Europe's northern periphery in an age of change. London, Longman, 1995. 480p. maps, bibliog., index. £46. ISBN: 058200408x.

Political and social historical narrative from the period of the French Revolution to the collapse of the Soviet Union. 'A model of fine writing and excellent scholarship, this volume should be found in every college and university library' *Choice,* v.33, no.1, September 1995, p.195-96). *Class No:* 947.4

Estonia

[7441]

RAUN, T.V. **Estonia and the Estonians.** Stanford, Calif., Hoover Institution, 1987. 313p. bibliog. index. $31.95. ISBN: 0817985115.

Thorough and extremely well documented history of Estonia. Extensive bibliography and glossary. 'In terms of scope, completeness of coverage, accuracy of scholarship, and readability, there are no other works in English that compare with this study' (*Choice,* v.25, no.4, December 1987, p.675). *Class No:* 947.42

Latvia

Dictionaries

[7442]

PLAKANS, A. **Historical dictionary of Latvia.** Lanham, MD., Scarecrow Press, 1997. xxvi,192p. map, bibliog. $34.50. (*European Historical Dictionaries, no.19.*) ISBN: 0810832925.

Chronology of Latvian history p.xiii-xxvi. Introduction (borders, physical features, Latvian-language culture, economic development, demographic changes) p.1-14. Dictionary (concentrates on today's problems and leaders plus German occupation, Russian and German domination, political events) p.15-161. Bibliography (general, culture, economy, history, juridical, politics, science). 'An important book towards making Latvian history accessible to non-Latvian readers' (*European History Quarterly,* v.29, no.2, April 1999, p.311-12). *Class No:* 947.43(038)

Lithuania

[7443]

VARDYS, V.S. *and* SEDAITIS, J. **Lithuania** the rebel nation. Boulder, Colo., Westview Press, 1996. 288p. illus., maps. $59.95. £44.50. (*Westview Series on the Post-Soviet Republics.*) ISBN: 0813383083.

Narrative history concentrating mainly on 20th century events: Lithuania's historical roots - Independence 1918-1940 ... Between the Kremlin and the West - Securing independence - New beginnings. *Class No:* 947.45

Dictionaries

[7444]

SUZIEDELIS, S. **Historical dictionary of Lithuania.** Lanham, Md, Scarecrow Press, 1997. xxxiv,352p. maps, bibliog. $47.50. (*European Historical Dictionaries, no.21.*) ISBN: 0810833352.

Maps p.xiii-xvi. Glossary p.xix-xx. Chronology of major events p.xxi-xxxiv. Introduction (land and people, government and economy, history) p.1-46. Dictionary (460+ entries) p.47-333. Bibliography (reference works, historical sources, historical studies, chronological and topical) p.335-72. Entries include historical figures and Jewish emigration and diaspora. *Class No:* 947.45(038)

Belarus

Dictionaries

[7445]

ZAPRUDNIK, J. **Historical dictionary of Belarus.** Lanham, MD., Scarecrow Press, 1998. xxxvii,298p. maps, bibliog. $55. (*European Historical Dictionaries, no.28.*) ISBN: 0810834499.

Historical chronology p.xxi-xxxvii. Introduction (geography, population, economy, independence) p.1-22. Dictionary (history, religion, culture, social policy, demography, events, institutions) p.23-228. Bibliography (in 24 sections) p.229-293. Appendix: Rulers of Belarus 860-1997 p.295-98. 2 maps. *Class No:* 947.6(038)

Ukraine

[7446]

CHIROVSKY, N.L. **An Introduction to Ukrainian history.** New York, Philosophical Library, 3v., 1981-86.

1. *Ancient and Kievan-Galician Ukraine-Rus'* 1981. 347p. 2. *The Lithuanian-Rus' Commonwealth, the Polish domination and the Cossak-Hetman state.* 1984. 400p. 3. *Nineteenth and Twentieth century Ukraine.* 1986. 517p. Ukrainian culture, economy, social structure, religion, literature music, theatre, as well as its political history is dealt with in this 3v. work. 'The most comprehensive coverage of Ukrainian history' (Wynar, B.S. *Ukraine,* 1990. Entry no.29). *Class No:* 947.7

[7447]

MAGOCSI, P.R. **A History of Ukraine.** Univ. of Toronto Press, 1996. 880p. maps, facsims, tables, bibliog., index. $90. ISBN: 0802008305.

10 sections of roughly 5 chapters each, it proceeds chronologically from the first millennium before the common era to the declaration of Ukranian independence in 1991. Each section provides a balanced discussion of political, economic, and cultural developments. Attempts to give judicious treatment as well to other peoples and cultures developed within the borders of Ukraine, including the Greeks of the Bosporan Kingdom, the Crimean Tatars, and the Poles, Russians, Germans, Jews, and Menonities, all of whom, form an essential part of Ukranian history. *Class No:* 947.7

[7448]

SUBTELNY, O. **Ukraine: a history.** 2nd ed. Toronto, Univ. of Toronto Press in association with the Canadian Institute of Ukrainian Studies, 1994. 700p. plates, illus., maps, bibliog., index. $60. ISBN: 0802005918.

1st ed. 1988.

28 ch. organized in 5 pts: 1. Kievian Rus' - 2. The Polish-Lithuanian period - 3. The Cossack era - 4. Ukraine under Imperial rule - 5. Twentieth-century Ukraine. Notes p.573-87. Glossary p.589-90. Bibliography p.591-620. 29 maps. Massive work of scholarship covering from the earliest period. 'No other one-volume English-language work can surpass this well-balanced survey' (*Choice,* v.26, no.11-12, July/August 1989. p.1890). *Class No:* 947.7

Maps & Atlases

[7449]

MAGOCSI, P.R. *and* MATTHEWS, G.J., *cartographer.* **Ukraine: a historical atlas.** Toronto, Univ. of Toronto Press, 1985. [64]p. maps. $40.00. ISBN: 0802032484.

24 maps and commentary with emphasis on politics and administrative changes but with geographical, military and cultural developments also represented *e.g.* 1. Geography of the Ukrainian lands ... 2. Ethnolinguistic setting ... 3. Greek colonies and the Steppe hinterland ... 24. The Ukrainian Soviet Socialist Republic since World

....(contd.)

War 2. 'An excellent supplement to historical textbooks illustrating complicated periods of Ukrainian history (*Choice*, v.24, no.5, January 1987, p.744). *Class No:* 947.7(084.3)

Georgia

[7450]

SUNY, R.G. **The Making of the Georgian nation.** London, I.B. Tauris, 1989. xviii,395p. maps, bibliog., index. ISBN: 1850431205.

14 chapters ordered in 3 parts: 1. The rise and fall of the Georgian monarchies - 2. Georgia in the Russian Empire - 3. Revolutionary and Soviet Georgia. Chapter notes p.325-80. Bibliography p.381-5. Glossary p.319-24. *Class No:* 947.922

Azerbaijan

Dictionaries

[7451]

SWIETOCHOWSKI, T. *and* COLLINS, B.C. **Historical dictionary of Azerbaijan.** Lanham, MD., Scarecrow Press, 1999. 160p. maps. bibliog. $40. (*Asian/Oceanian Historical Dictionaries, no. 31.*) ISBN: 0810835509.

Entries on persons, institutions and events, with some emphasis on recent periods, but with a view of the earliest history. There are other entries on the important aspects of the economy, society, religion and culture. Also useful are an introduction for context, and a helpful chronology. A select bibliography of works in English and other languages completes the volume. *Class No:* 947.924(038)

Armenia

[7452]

HOVANNISIAN, R.G., *ed.* **The Armenian people from ancient to modern times.** New York, St. Martin's Press, 2v., 1997. $49.98 each vol.

1. *The Dynastic periods: from antiquity to the fourteenth century.* xii,372p. maps, bibliog., index. 2. *Foreign dominion to statehood: the fifteenth century to the twentieth century.* xii,493p. maps, bibliog., index. Comprehensive history of the Armenian people, including the Armenian diaspora, from the earliest times to the formation of the Armenian Republic following the dissolution of the Soviet Union. Compiled by 16 US and other academics. 'The most dependable general history of the Armenians written in the English language' (*The International History Review*, v.20, no.4, December 1998, p.941-44). *Class No:* 947.925

[7453]

HOVANNISIAN, R.G. **The Republic of Armenia.** Berkeley, Univ. of California Press, 4v., 1995.

1. *The First Year 1918-1919. 1971.* 2. *From Versailles to London 1919-1920. 1982.* 3. *From London to Sèvres February-to August 1920.* xx,534p. $45. ISBN 0520088034. 4. *Between Crescent and Sickle: partition and Sovietization.* 488p. $45. 0520088042. Immensely detailed narrative history. Independence in 1991 gave the author access to important documents in Armenia's historical archives. 'Students of modern Armenian history are privileged to have such a monumental reference work at their disposal' (*Central Asian Survey*, v.17, no.3, September 1998, p.506-508). *Class No:* 947.925

Scandinavia

[7454]

SAWYER, P.H. **Kings and Vikings** Scandinavia and Europe AD700-1100. London and New York, Methuen, 1982. x,182p.+16p. plates. illus., map, bibliog., index. ISBN: 0416741800.

10 well-annotated chapters including 1. The age of the Vikings: an introductory outline and 3. Contemporary sources. Bibliography p.155-177. Analytical index. *Class No:* 948

Bibliographies

[7455]

OAKLEY, S.P., *comp.* **Scandinavian history 1520-1970** : a list of books and articles in English. London, Historical Association, 1984. 232p. (*Helps for Students of History, no.91.*) ISBN: 0852782683.

Arranged in chronological sections divided geographically and then by subject. 'A very userful partially annotated bibliography of works published from 1880-1980' (L.B. Sather. *Norway*. 1986. Entry 939). *Class No:* 948(01)

Dictionaries

[7456]

NORDSTROM, B.J. **Dictionary of Scandinavian history.** Westport Connecticut, Greenwood Press, 1986. xix, 703p. bibliog. index $75.00; £73.50. ISBN: 0313228876.

400 initialled entries contributed by 77 scholars cover the major events and personalities in the history of Denmark, Finland, Iceberg Norway and Sweden, with some information on Greenland and the Faroe Islands from A.D. 1000 to the present day. Entries on major topics open with a general introduction followed by a detailed study in some or all of the Nordic countries. 5 Appendices. Bibliography (p.661-663); Monarchs; Presidents; Prime ministers and governments and a chronology. Index p.685-703. 'Fills a serious gap in English language reference sources on the Scandinavian countries' (*Choice*, v.23, no. 10, June 1986, p.1519). *Class No:* 948(038)

Middle Ages

[7457]

PULSIANO, P., *ed.* **Medieval Scandinavia** an encyclopedia. New York, Garland, 1993. xix,768p. illus., maps, diagrs., bibliogs., index $95. ISBN: 0824047877.

Over 250 scholars contribute cross-referenced articles varying in length from 150-5000 words on all aspects of medieval Norden (*i.e.* Denmark, Finland, Iceland, Norway, and Sweden). *Class No:* 948"01/14"

Finland

[7458]

JUTIKKALA, E. *and* PIRINEN, K. **A History of Finland.** Sjöblom, P., *translator.* New and rev. ed. London, Heinemann, 1974. 253p.+3p. maps, bibliog., index.

First published 1968 by Praeger.

12 chapters: 1. The settlement of Finland begins - 2. Finland is drawn into the Western cultural sphere - 3. Finland in the Scandinavian Union - 4. From the Middle Ages to the modern era - 5. Finland as part of a great power ... 10. Independent Finland. *Class No:* 948.0

Dictionaries

[7459]

MAUDE, G. **Historical dictionary of Finland.** Lanham, MD., Scarecrow Press, 1995. xxiii,356p. map, bibliog. £54. (*European Historical Dictionaries, no.8.*) ISBN: 0810829959.

Heads of State p.xvii, Chronology p.xix-xxiii. Finland: an overview (physical, political and historical geography, politics, economy) p.14. Dictionary (society and institutions, political leaders, trade and exports, ethnic minorities) p.15-270. Bibliography (English language works on Finnish history, ethnology, geography current affairs etc.) p.271-356. *Class No:* 948.0(038)

Maps & Atlases

[7460]

Suomen historian Kartasto/Atlas of Finnish history. Jutikkala, E., *ed.* 2nd ed. Porvoo, Werner Söderström, 1959.

83 thematic maps with captions in Finnish and English. *Class No:* 948.0(084.3)

Vikings

[7461]

JONES, G. **A History of the Vikings.** 2nd ed. Oxford, Oxford Univ. Press, 1982. xvi,504p. illus. (inc.plates), maps. ISBN: 0192158821.

4 parts (14 chapters) 1. The Northern people to A.D.700 - 2. The Viking kingdom to the close of the tenth century - 3. The Viking movement overseas - 4. The Viking age ends (to 1066). Select bibliography p.431-444. Supplementary booklist in English 1984 p.430. *Class No:* 948.01

Maps & Atlases

[7462]

GRAHAM-CAMPBELL, J., *ed.* **Cultural atlas of the Viking World.** New York, Facts On File, 1994. 240p. col.illus., col.maps, bibliog., index. $45. £22.95. ISBN: 0816030049.

Map features arranged in 4 main parts: 1. Origins of the Vikings - 2. Viking Age Scandinavia - 3. Vikings overseas - 4. End of Viking World. 18 special features (*e.g.* Viking ships, Runes) and 22 Site features (York, Jarlshof, L'Anse Aux Meadows). Chronological table in 4 lateral columns across the double page (Scandinavia, Britain and Ireland, Continental Europe, North Atlantic) p.8-9. Glossary p.224-6. Bibliography (in 8 thematic/chronological sections) p.227-8. Gazetteer p.232-4. 29 maps. *Class No:* 948.01(084.3)

[7463]

AYWOOD, J. The Penguin historical atlas of the Vikings. London, Viking, 1995. 144p. illus. (mostly col.), col. maps, bibliog., index. £20. ISBN: 0670864633.

41 map features in 6 sections: 1. Origins - 2. Scandinavia in the Viking Age - 3. Viking raids - 4. North America sagas - 5. Vikings in the East - 6. Transformation of the Vikings. Kings and Rulers 800-1100 p.136-37. Bibliography p.138. *Class No:* 948.01(084.3)

Norway

[7464]

ERRY, T.K. A History of modern Norway 1814-1972. Rev. ed. London, Greenwood Press. 1979. xii, 503p. illus., maps, index. £24.75. ISBN: 0313214670.

13 chapters (1. Introductory; Norway in 1814 ... 5. The separation from Sweden, 1884-1905 ... 7. Norwegians abroad ... 12. War and recovery, 1939-1949 - 13. The latest age. Epilogue 1965-1972. Reference notes. Partly analytical index. Comprehensive. *Class No:* 948.1

Bibliographies

[7465]

Norwegian local history: a bibliography of material in the collections of the Memorial Library, University of Wisconsin - Madison. Hill, D.A., *ed.* Jefferson, North Carolina, McFarland, 1989. 144p. index. £26.25. ISBN: 0899503772.

c.1300 items including settlement books of individual places, directories, anniversary volumes *etc. Class No:* 948.1(01)

Maps & Atlases

[7466]

HAGEN, R.M., *with others*. Norsk historisk atlas. Oslo, J.W. Cappelens Forlag, 1980. 386p. maps. (*Norges Historie, no.15.*)

96p. of historical maps precede outlines of important topics in Norwegian history. *Class No:* 948.1(084.3)

Sweden

[7467]

SCOTT, F.D. Sweden the nations history. 2nd ed. Edwardsville, Southern Illinois Univ. Press, 1988. 688p. maps, bibliog. $45.00. ISBN: 0809315130.

'The most recent, complete and authoritative survey in English of Sweden's history' (L.B. Sather and A. Swanson. *Sweden*, 1987. Entry 147). *Class No:* 948.5

Bibliographies

[7468]

BRING, S.E. Bibliografisk handbok till Sveriges historia. Stockholm, Norstedt, 1934. xx,780p.

Bibliographical guide to Swedish history. Chapters on historical method, bibliographical aids in general, archives and libraries, publishing societies, historiography, etc.; then chapters on periods of Swedish history. The index occupies the last 110 pages. *Class No:* 948.5(01)

Dictionaries

[7469]

GOULD, D.E. Historical dictionary of Stockholm. Lanham, MD., Scarecrow Press, 1998. xxvii,257p. maps, bibliog. $64. (*European Historical Dictionaries.*) ISBN: 0810832380.

Chronology p.xv-xxvii. Introduction (geography, publishers, city management etc.) p.1-16. Dictionary (arts, music, leading historical figures, newspapers, military history etc.) p.17-189. Bibliography (17 categories) p.219-51. Appendix 1. Mayors - 2. Buildings - 3. Museums - 4. Sporting events - 5. Authors connected with Stockholm - 6. Art museums and galleries - 7. Miscellaneous statistics. 7p. of maps. *Class No:* 948.5(038)

[7470]

SCOBBIE, I. Historical dictionary of Sweden. xxiii,315p. map, bibliog. (*European Historical Dictionaries, no.7.*) ISBN: 0810829223.

Introduction (Sweden: an overview) p.1-24. Dictionary (Kings and nobles, politicians, economists, writers, political parties, newspapers, events *etc.*) p.25-243; Bibliography (11 sub-divided sections) p.244-310; Appendix 1. Swedish rulers p.311-12 - 2. B. Prime Ministers p.313-14. Chronology p.vii-xix. *Class No:* 948.5(038)

Denmark

[7471]

JONES, W.G. Denmark : a modern history. Rev. ed. London, Croom Helm, 1986. 248p. map. bibliog., index. £35.00. ISBN: 0709914687.

Previously published by Benn in 1970.

Chapter 1. Early history in brief (*c.*850-1814); remaining 8 chapters concerned with nineteenth and twentieth centuries. Appendix 1. The Faroe Islands (p.218-227). Appendix 2. Greenland (p.228-237). Bibliography p.238-240. This edition omits Appendix on Danish West Indies. *Class No:* 948.9

Dictionaries

[7472]

THOMAS, A.H. *and* **OAKLEY, S.P. Historical dictionary of Denmark.** Lanham, MD., Scarecrow Press, 1998. xxv,533p. illus., maps, bibliog. $65. (*European Historical Dictionaries, no.33.*) ISBN: 0810835444.

Chronology of Danish history p.xxi-xxv. Introduction (geography and people, history, Nordic Council and European Community, modern economy) p.1-21. Dictionary (monarchs, industries, politics, artists, social affairs, music and culture etc.) p.23-439. Bibliography (arranged in 8 major thematic sections) p.441-514. 7 Appendixes: 1. Danish monarchs - 2. Prime Ministers and Cabinets etc. 2 maps. *Class No:* 948.9(038)

Iceland

Dictionaries

[7473]

HÁLFDANARSON, G. Historical dictionary of Iceland. Lanham, MD., Scarecrow Press, 1997. xxiv,212p.+1p., map, bibliog. £38. (*European Historical Dictionaries, no.24.*) ISBN: 0810833522.

Chronology of Icelandic history p.xv-xxiv. Introduction (habitat, human and natural resources, history) p.1.-10. Dictionary (geographical features, ancient and modern literature, external affairs, events etc.) p.11-174. Bibliography (8 thematic sub-divisions) p.175-212. note on Icelandic language p.ix. *Class No:* 949.11(038)

Faeroe Islands

[7474]

JACKSON, A. The Faroes the faraway islands. London, Robert Hale, 1991. 223p. illus., maps, bibliog., index. ISBN: 070904304x.

19 chapters in 5 sections comprise this handbook for visitors: 1. Ancient past (556-1856) - 2. Traditional and recent past (1848-1948) - 3. Current political and social setting - 4. A tour through the islands - 5. Basic facts (Transport and accommodation; Chronology p.207-12; Glossary p.213-6; Bibliography p.217-8). This is by far the most comprehensive work in English. *Class No:* 949.12

[7475]

YOUNG, G.V.C. From the Vikings to the Reformation a chronicle of the Faroe Islands up to 1538. Douglas, Isle of Man, Shearwater Press, 1979. 184p. illus. £5.50. ISBN: 0904980200. *Class No:* 949.12

Netherlands

Bibliographies

[7476]

COOLHAAS, W. P. A Critical study of studies on Dutch colonial history. 2nd ed. rev. by G.J. Schutte. The Hague, Martinus Nijhoff, 1980. 264p. indexes. (*Koninklijk Institut voor Taal, Land-en Volkenkunde Bibligoraphical Series, no.4.*) ISBN: 9024723078.

1st ed. 1960. Enlarged from the author's 'Chronique de l'Histoire coloniale outre-mer neérlandaise' (*Revue d'histoire des colonies*, v.44, 1957, p.311-448).

6 main sections: 1. Archives - 2. Journals, institutes, university chairs - 3. Books of travel - 4. The area covered by the charter of the VOC (United East Indies Company) - 5. The Netherlands East Indies after 1795 - 6. The area covered by the charter of the Westindische Compagnie ... to the present day. Covers general works; sources; monographs; biographies, regional studies. 3 Indexes: by year, personal names, and placenames. 'An extremely useful and full bibliography covering all aspects of Dutch colonial history' (*Low Countries History Yearbook*, no.15, 1982, p.203). *Class No:* 949.2(01)

Dictionaries
[7477]
HUUSSEN, A.H. **Historical dictionary of the Netherlands**. Lanham, MD., Scarecrow Press, 1998. xxix,237p. maps, bibliog. £56.55. (*European Historical Dictionaries, no.32*.) ISBN: 0810835142.

Chronology p.xvii-xxix. Dictionary (towns, people, companies, historical figures, societies, political movements, science etc.) p.17-177. Appendix: Kings, Prime Ministers, provinces and capitals. Bibliography (arranged under 9 subject headings) p.181-235. 2 maps. *Class No:* 949.2(038)

Belgium

Dictionaries
[7478]
STALLAERTS, R. **Historical dictionary of Belgium**. Lanham, MD., Scarecrow Press, 1999. xxiv,302p. map, bibliog. $59.50. (*European Historical Dictionaries, no.35*.) ISBN: 0810836033.

Chronology p.xv-xviii. Introduction (history) p.1-16. Dictionary (historical and current events, laws, political parties and organizations, social institutions etc.) p.17-174. Appendix 1. Monarchs - 2. Governments since 1944 - 3. Economy. Bibliography (essay + 8 heavily sub-divided sections) p.186-302. 'Since those lacking Flemish will not be able to use more elaborate reference works like *Lexicon Geschiedenis van Nederland & Belgie*, ed. by Liek Mulder (Utrecht, 1994), this English-language dictionary is highly recommended' (*Choice*, v.37,no.5, January 2000, p.912). *Class No:* 949.3(038)

Switzerland
[7479]
LUCK, J.M. **A History of Switzerland** the first 100,000 years. Before the beginnings to the days of the present. Palo Alto, California, The Society for the Promotion of Science and Scholarship, 1985. xiv, 887p. illus., maps, tables, bibliog., index. $36.00. ISBN: 093066406x.

11 chronological heavily sub-divided chapters. Glossary p.846-7. Bibliography (425 items) p.849-59. 80p. plates. Analytical index. *Class No:* 949.4

[7480]
Nouvelle histoire de la Suisse et des Suisses. Lausanne, Editions Payot Lausanne, 3v., 1982-83. 368+304+328p. illus.

V.1: Introduction - L'Empreinte des anciennes civilisations - Les Racines de l'indépendance - L'Heure de la puissance. 1982. FS58. ISBN 2601003014. 2. Réformes, ruptures et croissances - Vie et mort de l'Ancient Régime - La Quête d'un état national 1983. FS58. 2601003022. 3. La Suisse des radicaux - Menace et repliement - Une course accélérée vers l'avenir. 1983. FS58. 2601003030. An authoritative cooperative history. A new single volume edition appeared in 1986 (1008p. illus. (some col.), indexes). FS98. 2601030178. *Class No:* 949.4

Greece
[7481]
CLOGG, R. **A Short history of modern Greece**. 2nd ed. Cambridge, Cambridge Univ., Press, 1986. viii, 242p. map. bibliog., index. £25.00. ISBN: 0521328373.

8 chapters (1. 'Waiting for the barbarians': the downfall of Byzantium, 1204-1453 ... 8. From authoritarianism to democracy, 1974-. Bibliography, 8. Cyprus). Analytical index. 'Greatly to be recommended ... An honest and authoritative attempt to be fair-minded' (TLS, No.4001, 23 November 1979, p.5). *Class No:* 949.5

[7482]
WOODHOUSE, C.M. **Modern Greece** : a short history. 4th ed. London, Faber, 1986. 344p. maps. bibliog., index. pbk. £4.95. ISBN: 0571138276.

First published in 1968 as *Story history of modern Greece*. 2nd edition under present title 1977.

12 chapters including 12. Trial of democracy 1977 - added for this edition. Bibliography (by chapters) p.325-329. 4 maps. *Class No:* 949.5

Dictionaries
[7483]
VEREMIS, T.M. *and* DRAGOUMIS, M. **Historical dictionary of Greece**. Metuchen, NJ., Scarecrow Press, 1995. xvii,258p. maps, bibliog. $32.50. (*European Historical Dictionaries, no.5*.) ISBN: 081082888x.

Concentrating on 19th and 20th century Greece the Dictionary (p.19-182) covers crucial persons, places, institutions, events, and historical, economic, social, religious and cultural issues. Bibliography: Books (1821-1993) and articles (1978-1993) p.183-243. Chronology p.p.ix-xvii. Appendices A-C Kings, Presidents and Prime Ministers - D. Basic data. 3 maps. *Class No:* 949.5(038)

Middle Ages
[7484]
CHEETHAM, N. **Medieval Greece**. New Haven and London, Yale Univ. Press, 1981. x, 341p. maps, general tables, bibliog., index. $40.00. £35.50. ISBN: 0300024215.

14 chronological chaps: 1. Death of ancient Hellas ... 14. Crete (1204-1669) cover an unfamiliar period for the general educated public. Note on sources p.302-305. Appendix: List of rulers p. Bibliography p.328-332. The author was a member of the Diplomatic Service in Greece for many years. *Class No:* 949.5"01/14"

Albania
[7485]
POLLO, S. *and* PUTO, A. **The History of Albania** from its origins to the present day. London, Routledge & Kegan Paul, 1981. xiii, 322p. ports., index. ISBN: 071000365x.

First published as *L'histoire de l'Albanie*, and written 'with the kind co-operation of the Historical Institute of the Science Academy of the People's Republic of Albania'.

12 chapters (1. Prehistoric and ancient times: the Illyrians ... 4. The age of Skanderkeg ... 6. The rebirth of the Albanian nation (1844-1912) ... 9. Albania under Zogu's regime - 10. The struggle against Fascism for national liberation (1939-) ... 12. Albania today. Bibliography, p.294-304 (Sources and documents; 2. Collected refeences; 3. Authors and studies), with occasional explanatory notes, 87 illus. The narrative goes up to 1970. A pioneer history, on Marxist orthodox lines. *The Times* review (18 July 1981, p.9) finds that 'the translation, plainly from a French version, is deplorably inept'. *Class No:* 949.65

Bibliographies
[7486]
DANIEL, O. **Albanie** une bibliographie historique. Paris, Éditions du Centre National de la Recherche Scientifique, 1985. 616p. Fr.335.00. ISBN: 2222032369.

Introduction (p.9-15) includes Une Albanie mythique; Le problème des sources d'étude; Les bibliographies de l'Albanie; and Nécessité d'une nouvelle bibliographie. 4380 unannotated entries in 4 large, subdivided sections: 1. Sources documentaires - 2. Études générales - 3. Sources historiques générales - 4. Histoire de l'Albanie. *Class No:* 949.65(01)

Dictionaries
[7487]
HUTCHINGS, R. **Historical dictionary of Albania**. Lanham. Md., Scarecrow Press, 1996. xvi,275p. bibliog. (*European Historical Dictionaries, no.12*.) ISBN: 0810831074.

Chronology p.xi-xvi. Introduction (background, history) p.1-10. Dictionary p.11-260. Bibliography (in 9 subdivided sections) p.261-75. 3 maps. *Class No:* 949.65(038)

Balkans
[7488]
BURDETT, A.L.P., *ed*. **The Historical boundaries between Bosnia, Croatia, Serbia** documents and maps 1815-1945. Farnham Common, Surrey, Archive Editions. 1995. 814p. maps (some col.). £395. (discounts to libraries). ISBN: 1852079657.

Background diplomatic and cartographic materials including Crown Copyright material and 24 maps. 'Will be of permanent value for Balkan scholars through the insights that flow from this valuable body of documentation' (*Geographical Journal*, v.163, no.1, March 1997, p.101). *Class No:* 949.7

[7489]
FINE, J.V.A. **The Early medieval Balkans** a critical survey from the sixth to the late twelfth century. Ann Arbor, Univ. of Michigan Press, 1983. xxvi, 336p. maps, bibliog., index. $34.50. ISBN: 0472100254.

Introduction - Balkan geography and society - 1. Historical background - 2. Slavic invasions - 3. Balkans in the eighth century - 4. Bulgaria in the ninth century - 5. Bulgaria under Symeon 893-927 - 6. Bulgaria after Symeon 927-1018 - 7. Dukla and the Central and Eastern Balkans from the death of Basil II 1025 to the 1180s - 8. Croatia and Dalmatia. Appendix: Medieval rulers. Glossaries (terms and peoples) p.299-308. Sources referred to in the text p.309-313. Bibliography p.315-18. Analytical index. *Class No:* 949.7

[7490]
—FINE, J.V.A. **The Late medieval Balkans** a critical survey from the late twelfth century to the Ottoman Conquest. Ann Arbor, Univ. of Michigan Press, 1987. xvi, 683p. bibliog., index. $39.95. ISBN: 0472100793.

10 chronological chapters covering 12th to early 15th centuries. Appendix: Medieval rulers. Glossary p.621-7. Sources referred to in text p.629-31. Bibliography p.633-43. Analytical index. *Class No:* 949.7

[7491]
JELAVICH, B. History of the Balkans. v.1. Eighteenth and nineteenth centuries. v.2. Twentieth century. Cambridge, Cambridge University Press, 1983. xiv, 407p.+Øi, 476p. illus., maps, bibliog., index. £42.00 each. ISBN: 0521252490, V.1; 0521254485, V.2.

Considers the history of the major Balkan nationalities - the Albanians, Bulgars, Croats, Greeks, Romanians, Serbs and Slovenes. An introdcution to v.1 presents the historical background up the beginning of the 18th century. Bibliography p.457-460 (v.2). 'This set can be highly recommended to undergraduate and graduate students, faculty, government experts, information services, and the general public' (*Choice*), v.21, no.6, February 1984, p.873). *Class No:* 949.7

[7492]
POULTON, H. The Balkans minorities and states in conflict. London, Minority Rights, 1991. x, 243p. maps, bibliog., index. ISBN: 1873194250.

Historical and current studies of ethnic conflicts in Yugoslavia, Bulgaria, Greece, and Albania. *Class No:* 949.7

Yugoslavia

[7493]
LAMPE, J.R. Yugoslavia as history twice there was a country Cambridge Univ. Press, 1996. xx, 421p. illus., maps, tables, bibliog., index. ISBN: 0521461227.

Narrative and analysis of the complex historical background preceding the break-up of Yugoslavia in the 1990s in 11 chronological chapters (*e.g.*1. Empires and fragmented borderlands 700 to 1800 ... 11. Ethnic politics and the end of Yugoslavia). Chapter notes p.357-92. Bibliography (of works in English and German) p.393-401. 12 maps. Scholarly narrative climaxing in Yugoslavia's disintegration. *Class No:* 949.71

[7494]
MAGAŠ, B. The Destruction of Yugoslavia tracking the break-up 1980-92. London, Verso 1993. xxv, 366p. map, table. ISBN: 0860913767.

5 parts: 1. The Kosovo watershed and its aftermath (1981-87) - 2. Interregnum (1980-88) - 3. Milošević assails the federal order (1988-89) - 4. Systemic Collapse (1990-91) - 5. War (Jun-Dec 1991). Political analysis, reportage, and personal reflection in chronological narrative. *Class No:* 949.71

[7495]
ROGEL, C. The Breakup of Yugoslavia and the war in Bosnia. Westport, CT., Greenwood Press, 1998. £31.95. (*Guides to Historic Events of the Twentieth Century.*) ISBN: 0313299188.

'One-stop ready reference guide to the breakup of Yugoslavia in 1991, the war in Bosnia, and the peace settlement. Combining narrative description, analytical essays, a timeline, biographical profiles, and the text of key primary documents ...' (*publisher's catalogue*). *Class No:* 949.71

[7496]
SINGLETON, F. A Short history of the Yugoslav peoples. Cambridge, Cambridge Univ. Press, 1985. xiv, 309p. maps, tables, bibliog. index. £22.50 $39.50. ISBN: 0521254787.

14 chapters (1. The lands of the South Slavs ... 3. The early Slav Kingdoms ... 4. The South Slavs under foreign rule ... 9. Yugoslavia and the Second World War ... 12. The 1960s - a decade of reform ... 14. Yugoslavia after Tito). Bibliography p.286-297. 8 tables, 4 maps. 'This book should be in every university, college, secondary school, and public library' (*Choice* v.23, no.4, December 1985, p.655). *Class No:* 949.71

Bibliographies

[7497]
STANKOVIĆ, D. *and* MOLTARIĆ, Z. Sovekska bibliografija o krizi u bivšoj Jugoslaviji. [World bibliography on the crisis in the former Yugoslavia.] Belgrade, Službeni glasnik, 1996. *Class No:* 949.71(01)

Encyclopaedias

[7498]
Conflict in the former Yugoslavia an encyclopedia. Allcock, J.B., *and others, eds.* Santa Barbara, Calif., and Oxford, ABC-Clio, 1998. xxxiv, 410p. illus., maps, bibliog., index. £39.95. ISBN: 0874369355.

500 cross-referenced A-Z entries from 27 contributors survey the origins, development, people, places, events, diplomacy and treaties relating to the turmoil following the break-up of the former Yugoslavia in the 1990s. Maps p.xiii-xxxiv. Bibliography p.345-50. Chronology p.351-88. Dayton Agreements p.389-91. *Class No:* 949.71(031)

Dictionaries

[7499]
SUSTER, Z. Historical dictionary of the Frederal Republic of Yugoslavia. Lanham, MD., Scarecrow Press, 1999. 432p. $65. (*European Historical Dictionaries, no.29.*) ISBN: 0810834669.

Rather than an exclusive history of the current Yugoslav state, this *Dictionary* a broad-based reference book of the cultural factors and events, people and institutions, that lent shape to Serbian and Yugoslav culture. An extensive chronology is included to provide a broad introduction. The Statistical Annex, places essential figures and data in one location. Additionally, a number of maps and tables illustrate the geography and provide a visual perspective of various entries, and the Federal Republic of Yugoslavia in general. Also included are usage notes on the Cyrillic alphabet and latinization of Serbian words. The book concludes with a comprehensive bibliography sub-divided by topic. *Class No:* 949.71(038)

Slovenia

Dictionaries

[7500]
PLUT-PREGELJ, L. *and* ROGEL, C. Historical dictionary of Slovenia. Lanham, Md., Scarecrow Press, 1996. xxxiii, 345p. maps, bibliog. $67. (*European Historical Dictionaries, no.13.*) ISBN: 0810831139.

Contents include a pronunciation guide, historical chronology (p.xix-xx), introduction, dictionary covering history, government, literature, art, education, women (p.7-303), and a 37-page thematically arranged bibliography (p.305-343). 6 maps. *Class No:* 949.712(038)

Croatia

Dictionaries

[7501]
STALLAERTS, R. *and* LAURENS, J. Historical dictionary of the Republic of Croatia. Metuchen, NJ., Scarecrow Press, 1995. xlii, 341p. maps, bibliog. (*European Historical Dictionaries, no.9.*) ISBN: 0810829911.

Chronology p.xvii-xlii. Introduction (outline history) p.1-17. Dictionary p.19-242. Bibliography (in 8 subdivided sections: 1. General - 2. Cultural - 3. Economic - 4. Historic - 5. Juridicial - 6. Political - 7. Scientific - 8. Social) p.243-340. 5 maps. *Class No:* 949.713(038)

Maps & Atlases

[7502]
BOBAN, L. Croatian borders 1918-1993. Zagreb, Croatian Academy of Sciences And Arts, 1993. 68p. col.maps, bibliog.

1st Croat ed. 1992. 2nd enlarged ed. 1992. This 1st English language edition is identical to 2nd Croat ed.

Conceived as a combination of a short history and a historical atlas. 3 levels of information in each section: a historical map, interpretation, and an account of the circumstances determining the map. In 8 sections: 1. States of the Slovenes, Croats and Serbs - 2. Kingdom - 3. 1922 Division into provinces - 4/5. Kingdom of Yugoslavia - 6. Banovina Hrvatska - 7. 1941 Occupation - 8. Yugoslavia after the Second World War Bibliography p.45. *Class No:* 949.713(084.3)

Kosovo

[7503]
MALCOLM, N. Kosovo a short history. Basingstoke, Macmillan, 1998. xxxvi, 492p. maps, bibliog., index. £20. ISBN: 0333666127.

Narrative history in 17 chapters (*e.g.* 5. Last years of medieval Serbian rule 1389/1455 ... 8. Austrian invasion and the great migration of the Serbs 1689/1690 ... 17. Kosovo after the death of Tito 1981/1997. Chapter notes p.357-427. Glossary p.428-30. Bibliography (including items in Western, Balkan and Eastern European languages) p.435-73. 8 maps. A well-documented and reliable history. *Class No:* 949.714

Bosnia

[7504]
MALCOLM, N. Bosnia. A short history. London, Macmillan, 1996. xxiv, 360p. maps, bibliog., index. £30. ISBN: 0333662156.

First published 1994.

Narrative history in 16 chronological and thematic chapters (*e.g.* 1. Races, myths and origins: Bosnia to 1180 ... 5. Islamicization of Bosnia ... 16. Destriction of Bosnia: 1992-1993. Glossary p.317-22. Chapter notes p.273-316. Bibliography (including items in Eastern and Western European languages) p.323-42. Epilogue: a short survey of events 1993-1995 p.253-71. *Class No:* 949.715

Dictionaries

[7505]

CUVALO, A. Historical dictionary of Bosnia and Herzegovina.
Lanham, Md., Scarecrow Press, 1997. lvi,353p. maps, bibliog.
£42.75, (*European Historical Dictionaries, no.25.*) ISBN:
0810833441.

Chronology p.xix-lvi. Introduction (territory, population; physical
features, history) p.1-50. Dictionary of leading historical figures,
crucial events, political institutions, newspaper and journals, religious
sects etc. p.51-251. Bibliography in 19 sub-divided sections p.255-
353. 4 maps. Emphasis is on current situation and recent past.
Class No: 949.715(038)

Macedonia

[7506]

PRIBICHEVICH, S. Macedonia : its people and history. Philadelphia,
Pennsylvania State Univ. Press, 1982. 270p. col. illus, maps, bibliog.,
index. $24.95 £19.05. ISBN: 0271003154.

Bibliography p.261-266. 'A lucid, brief account from antiquity to
the present ... For the person who is not familiar with Macedonia, this
is a very good introduction' (*Choice*, v.20, no.3, November 1982,
p.487). *Class No:* 949.717

Bibliographies

[7507]

WEAVER, S.M. 'Ancient and modern Macedonia' roots of the
'Macedonian Question'. *Choice*,,. v.35,no.4, December 1997, p.589-
99. bibliog.

Bibliographical essay including sections on modern histories,
reference sources, and Philip and Alexander. Bibliography p.598-99.
Class No: 949.717(01)

Dictionaries

[7508]

**GEORGIEVA, V. and KONECHNI, S. Historical dictionary of the
Republic of Macedonia.** Lanham, Md., Scarecrow Press, 1998.
xxvii,361p. map, bibliog. £47.05. (*European Historical Dictionaries,
no.22.*)

Introduction (background, history, economy) p.1-24. Dictionary
p.25-265. Bibliography (in 8 sub-divided sections) p.267-322. 4
Appendices: A. Political parties - B. Facts and Figures - C.
Macedonian geographical and personal names - D. Macedonian
Alphabet. Chronology p.viii-xxvii. 'A decidedly useful reference work
which omits nothing of any importance' (*Reference Reviews*,
v.13,no.1, 1999, p.46-47). *Class No:* 949.717(038)

Bulgaria

Dictionaries

[7509]

DETREZ, R. Historical dictionary of Bulgaria. Lanham, Md.,
Scarecrow Press, 1997. lvii,466p. bibliog. £71.25. (*European
Historical Dictionaries, no.16.*) ISBN: 0810831775.

Chronology of Bulgarian history p.xxix-xlix. Rulers of Bulgaria p.li-
liv. Introduction (geography, climate, population, history) p.1-16.
Dictionary p.17-363. Bibliography (8 heavily sub-divided sections)
p.365-466. 'Will be of immeasurable value for any library which
seriously pretends to encompass Balkan studies' (*Reference Reviews*,
v.12,no.4, 1998, p.46-7). *Class No:* 949.72(038)

Romania

[7510]

OTETEA, A., ed. A Concise history of Romania. London, Robert
Hale, 1985. 591p. illus., bibliog., index. £15.95. ISBN: 0709018657.

17 chapters based on *The history of the Romanian people* (1970).
Bibliog. p.559-566. *Class No:* 949.81

[7511]

PASCU, S. A History of Transylvania. Detroit, Wayne State Univ.
Press, 1982. xxiv,318p. illus., maps, bibliog., index. $89.70. ISBN:
0814317227.

Basis of the present work first published as *Voieodatul Transilvaniei*
(Cluj, Editura Dacia, 2v., 1972-79).

14 chapters e.g. 1. Pre-Roman Transylvania ... 2. Roman rule and
Daco-Roman civilization ... 5. The Transylvania Voivodate ... 7.
Turkish suzerainty ... 8. Under the Hapsburgs ... 14. Great Romania.
Bibliography p.298-311. *Class No:* 949.81

Dictionaries

[7512]

TREPTOW, K.W. and POPA, M. Historical dictionary of Romania.
Lanham, Md, Scarecrow Press, 1996. lxviii,310p. maps, bibliog.
(*European Historical Dictionaries, no.15.*)

Historical chronology p.xiii-xlvi. Rulers of Romania p.xlvii-lxv.
Introduction. Romania - a brief overview (Geography, Population,
History, Economy) p.1-20. Dictionary p.21-227. Bibliography p.229-
310. 2 maps. *Class No:* 949.81(038)

Moldova

Dictionaries

[7513]

BREZIANU, A. Historical dictionary of the Republic of Moldova.
Lanham, MD., Scarecrow Press, 2000. 336p. maps, bibliog. $60.
(*European Historical Dictionaries, no.37.*) ISBN: 081083734x.

The contributions of Moldovan scholars and journalists ensure that
the information represents the essence of the country. Complete with
maps, notes on spelling and pronunciation, abbreviations and
acronyms, and a chronology, this volume is a useful reference tool.
Class No: 949.83(038)

Asia

[7514]

Asian history on file. New York, Facts On File, 1995. 288p. maps,
timelines, diagrs., charts, index., looseleaf in binder. $155. ISBN:
081602975x.

1000+ maps etc. provide overview of Asian history from prehistoric
times to the present. Divided into 5 sections: 1. Prehistory - 2. South
Asia - 3. China region - 4. Japan and Korea - 5. Southeast Asia.
Extensive chronology. Matrix table of contents offer multiple access
points via chronological, topical or geographical entry points.
Class No: 95

[7515]

The Cambridge history of early Inner Asia. Sinor, D., ed.
Cambridge, Cambridge Univ. Press, 1990. x,518p. maps, bibliog.,
index. £45. ISBN: 0521243041.

1. The concept of Inner Asia - 2. Geographic setting - 3. Inner Asia
at the dawn of history - 4. Scythians and Sarmatians - 5. The Hsiung-
nu - 6. Indo-Europeans - 7. Hun period - 8. The Avars - 9. Peoples of
the Russian forest belt - 10. Peoples of the South Russian steppes - 11.
Establishment and dissolution of the Türk empire - 12. The Uighurs -
13. The Karakhanids and early Islam - 14. Early medieval Tibet - 15.
Forest people of Manchuria: Kitans and Jurchens. Bibliography p.424-
94. 'This volume is a splendid synthesis of narrative and analytical
history, and a definitive work of reference' (*Choice*, v.28,no.1,
September 1990, p.190). *Class No:* 95

[7516]

History of civilizations of Central Asia. Paris for Unesco, 6v., 1993-.

V.1: *The Dawn of civilization: earliest times to 700BC* edited by
A.H. Dani and V.M. Masson. 1993. 535p. illus., maps, biblig., index
£27. ISBN 9231027190. Appendix: A note on the meaning of the term
'Central Asia' (p.477-80). Chapter bibliographies, p.481-519).

V.2: The Development of sedentary and nomadic civilizations:
700BC to AD250. Edited by J. Harmatta and others. 1994. 573p.
illus., maps, bibliog., index. Chapter bibliographies p.494-508. 9
maps.

Cooperative history on a grand scale. Volumes still to be published
include 3. *The Crossroads of civilization AD250 to 750* - 4. *The Age of
achievement AD750 to the end of the fifteenth century* (in 2 parts) - 5.
Development in contrast: from the sixteenth to the eighteenth century -
6. *Towards contemporary civilization: from the beginning of the
nineteenth century to the present one.* *Class No:* 95

[7517]

MORGAN, D. The Mongols. Oxford & New York, Basil Blackwell,
1986. xv, 238p. illus., maps, geneal tables, bibliog. index. £15. (*The
Peoples of Europe.*) ISBN: 0631135561.

8 chapters: 1. The study of Mongol history - 2. Nomads of the
Steppe: Asia before Chingiz Khan - 3. Chingis Khan and the founding
of the Mongol empire - 4. Nature and institutions - 5. The Mongols in
China - 6. Expansion to the West - 7. The Mongols and Europe - 8.
What became of the Mongols? Bibliography p.207-218. Chronology
p.219-221. The author is Lecturer in the History of the Near and
Middle East at the School of Oriental and African Studies in the
University of London. *Class No:* 95

[7518]

ROGERS, M. and KNOX, R.J., eds. The Peoples of Asia. Oxford,
Basil Blackwell.

Harbans Mukhia. *The Mughals.* 1995. 288p. ISBN 0631185550;
Heywood, C. *The Turks.* 1997, 240p. 0631158979; Crossley, P.K.
The Manchus. 1997. 288p. 155786504. *Class No:* 95

Encyclopaedias

[7519]

Encyclopedia of Asian history. Embree, A.T., *editor in chief*. New York, Charles Scribner's Sons; London, Collier Macmillan, 4v., 1988. xiii, 528+538+516+478p. $325.00. £275.00. ISBN: 0684186195.

The history of the project is well told in D.C. Smith's 'The Encyclopedia of Asian history'. *Scholarly Publishing*, v.19, no.4, July 1988, p.202-209.

Covers all aspects of Asian civilization from the earliest period to the present. Excludes the Arabian peninsula, the Middle East and the Soviet Union except for the Central Asian republics. 1200 biographies of living and dead including Europeans closely involved with Asia. All entries are signed and most carry a bibliography. V4. includes list of entries p.319-356; Directory of (over 430) contributors p.357-371; synoptic outline; and an analytical index. Prepared under the auspices of the The Asia Society and intended 'to make available the highest level of contemporary scholarship on Asia to a nonspecialist audience'. 'An excellent overview of the subject ... large academic libraries will find it a must purchase, and others should consider it for its valuable scholarship and broad coverage' (*Booklist*, v.85, no.1, 1 September 1988, p.45). *Class No: 95(031)*

Handbooks & Manuals

[7520]

PHILIPS, C.H. Handbook of Oriental history. London, Dawsons Pall Mall, 1963. viii,265p. £5.00. (*Royal Historical Society Guides and Handbooks, no.6.*) ISBN: 0901050164.

First published London, Royal Historical Society, 1951.

5 sections (on the Near and Middle East, India and Pakistan, South-East Asia and the Archipelago, China and Japan, each by a specialist on the area). Each section gives guidance on: romanization of words; personal names; place-names; glossary of basic words; systems of dating; dynasties and rulers. A basic handbook for westerners embarking on studies relating to Oriental history. *Class No: 95(035)*

Maps & Atlases

[7521]

BARNES, I. and HUDSON, R. Historical atlas of Asia. Shirley, Derbys., Areadia Editions, 1998. 160p. col. illus., col. maps, bibliog., index. £36.95. ISBN: 1902305019.

First stop reference source, historical facts supported by maps, arranged in 6 sections: 1. Ancient civilizations - 2. Communications, commerce and culture - 3. Philosophies and empires - 4. Conquest, consolidation and decline - 5. Colonialism - 6. Asia today. Chronology p.150-52. Bibliography p.154-55. *Class No: 95(084.3)*

Asia—Far East

[7522]

BORTHWICK, M. Pacific century the emergence of modern Pacific Asia. Boulder, Colo., Westview Press; North Sydney, Allen & Unwin, 1992. xvii,590p. illus., maps, tables, bibliog., index. ISBN: 0813313724, US; 1863732802, Aust.

13 subdivided chapters *e.g.* 1. Dynasties, empires, and ages of commerce: Pacific Asia to the 19th century - 2. Seaborne barbarians: incursions by the West ... 10. China's long march to modernization - 11. Beyond the revolution: Indonesia and Vietnam - 12. Siberian salient - 13. Regional perspective. Bibliography p.547-54. Interdisciplinary study of Southeast and East Asian history. *Class No: 95.1/.2*

Islamic World

[7523]

The Cambridge history of Islam. Holt, P.M., *and others, eds.* Cambridge, Cambridge Univ. Press, 2v. in 4, 1970. illus.

1A: *The Central Islamic lands from pre-Islamic times to the First World War.* 1B: *The Central Islamic lands since 1918.* 2A: *The Indian sub-continent, South-East Asia, Africa and the Muslim West.* 2B: *Islam society and civilisation.* Aims 'to present the history of Islam as a whole cultural whole' (*Preface*). V.1 includes dynastic lists, a bibliography (p.737-50), glossary and detailed index (p.755-815). V.2 has a bibliography (p.891-905), glossary and equally lengthy index (p.911-66). 'Not at all conducive to continuous reading and yet not quite reference articles ... But ... will remain a standard work for many years to come' (*International Affairs*, v.47,no.4, October 1971, p.838-9). *Class No: 95.297*

[7524]

HITTI, P.K. History of the Arabs from earliest times to the present. 10th rev. ed. London, Macmillan, 1970. xxiv,822p. illus., maps, index.

6 parts (52 charts): 1. The pre-Islamic age - 2. The rise of Islam and the Caliphal State - 3. The Umayyad and the Abbasid Empires - 4. The Arabs in Europe; Spain and Sicily - 5. The last of the medieval Moslem states - 6. Ottoman rule and independence. No bibliography, but heavily footnoted. 21 maps. A standard text. *Class No: 95.297*

[7525]

HOURANI, A. A History of the Arab peoples. London, Faber; Cambridge, Mass., Harvard Univ. Press, 1991. xviii,551p. maps, geneal. tables, bibliog., indexes. £25; $24.95. ISBN: 0571133789, UK.

Full-scale narrative history of the Arabic-speaking parts of the Islamic world, from the rise of Islam to the present day, in 26 chapters arrayed in 5 sections: 1. The making of a world (7th-10th century) - 2. Arab Muslim societies (11-15th century) - 3. The Ottoman Age (16th-18th century) - 4. Age of European empires (1800-1939) - 5. Age of nation-states (1939). Chapter notes p.494-9. Bibliography p.500-29. 12 maps. 'In a masterly summational work, the whole story of the Arab peoples is laid out before us' (*Independent on Sunday*, 24 February 1991, Sunday Review section, p.22). *Class No: 95.297*

[7526]

HUMPHREYS, R.S. Islamic history a framework for enquiry. Rev. ed. London, Tauris, 1991. xiv,401p. bibliog., index. £14.95. ISBN: 1850433607.

First published Minneapolis, Bibliotheca Islamica, 1988.

12 chapters in 2 parts: 1. Sources and research tools (1. Reference works - 2. Sources: an analytical survey) - 2. Problems in Islamic history (3. Early historical tradition - 4. Modern historians ...). Bibliographic index p.311-94. 'A practical guide to the bibliography and research skills required for productive work in this area ... a useful overview of the current state of Islamic historiographical studies' (*Preface*) Concerned with Central Islamic Lands (*i.e.* Nile to Oxus region), North Africa and Spain. *Class No: 95.297*

[7527]

LAPIDUS, I.M. A History of Islamic societies. Cambridge, Cambridge Univ. Press, 1988. xxxi, 1002p. maps, tables, bibliog., index. £40.00. ISBN: 0521225523.

Prepared as a supplement to *Cambridge history of Islam* (2v., 1970) and intended for 'a broader readership'.

31 chapters in 3 parts: Pt.1. The origin of Islamic civilization: the Middle East from *c.*600 to *c.*1200 - 2. The worldwide diffusion of Islamic societies from the tenth to the nineteenth century - 3. The modern transformation: Muslim peoples in the nineteenth and twentieth centuries. Glossary p.918-28. Bibliography (by chapter) p.929-74. Analytical index. Primary emphasis is on 'the communal, religious, and political institutions ... rather than upon technologies and economies'. 'A brilliant *tour de force* which far from supplementing the Cambridge History bids fair to supplant it' (*History Today*, v.39, August 1989, p.53). *Class No: 95.297*

[7528]

The Muslim World: a historical survey. Bagley, F.R.C., *translated from the German by*. New York, Humanities Press; Leiden, E.J. Brill, 4v., 1960-81. bibliogs., indexes.

1. *The Age of the Caliphs* by B. Spuler. 1960. viii, 138p. 2. *The Mongol period* by B. Spuler. 1960. viii, 126p. 3. *The Last great Muslim empires.* 1969. x, 303p. 4. *Modern times.* 1981. x, 370p. V.4 has 7 chapters by various hands: 1. The Ottoman Empire 1774-1918 - 2. Turkey since the Armistice of Mudros - 3. Iran in the 19th and 20th centuries - 4. Central Asia under Russian rule - 5. Modern Afghanistan - 6. Arabian peninsula in the 19th century - 7. Short history of Indonesia. Chapter bibliographies. Indexes of personal names, geographical names and technical terms. *Class No: 95.297*

[7529]

NIZAMI, F.A., ed. History of the Islamic world. London, Macmillan in association with the Oxford Centre of Islamic Studies.

A new multi-volume history in 12v. is announced for publication over the next 5 years. Expected titles include 1. *The rise and spread of Islam 570AD to 661AD* - 2. *Umayyads and the early Abbasids* - 3. *The central lands to 1850* (to include the Mediterranean littoral and Southern Europe) - 4. *Africa* (excluding Egypt) - 5. *Central Asia* - 6. *The Ottomans* - 7. *Iran* - 8. *South Asia* - 9. *South-east Asia* - 10. *The modern Middle East* - 11. *Modern Europe and the Americas.* *Class No: 95.297*

[7530]

ROBINSON, F., *ed*. **The Cambridge illustrated history of the Islamic World.** Cambridge Univ. Press, 1996. xxiii,328p. illus. (many col.), maps (some col.), bibliog., index. £24.95. ISBN: 0521435102.

8 contributors. Pt.1. Narrative history: 1. Rise of Islam - 2. Emergence of Islamic world system 1000 to 1500 - 3. Age of Western expansion 1500 to 1800 - 4. Era of Western domination 1800 to the present. Pt.2. Thematic surveys: 5/8. Economy, Ordering, Transmission of knowledge, and Artistic expression in Muslim societies. Reference guide: Rulers of the Islamic world p.308-11; Glossary p.312; Bibliography (by chapter) p.313-18. Analytical index. Aim is to make Islamic world readily available to students and to the general reader. *Class No: 95.297*

[7531]

SAUVAGET, J. **Introduction to the history of the Muslim East** a bibliographical guide. 2nd ed. Berkeley and Los Angeles, Univ. of California Press, 1982. xxi, 252p. $35. ISBN: 0313234884.

Originally as *Introduction à l'histoire de l'Orient musulman* (1943; éd refondue. 1961).First published in English 1965.

Running commentary in 3pts: 1. The sources of Muslim history (chapters 1-9) - 2. Tools of research and general works (chapter 10: General information; 11: Special disciplines; 12. Dynastic series and tribal genealogies; 13: The main outlines of Muslim history) - 3. Historical bibliography (chapters 15-24). Index of names. Many references to periodical articles. *Class No: 95.297*

Dictionaries

[7532]

SHIMONI, Y., *ed*. **Political dictionary of the Arab World.** Jerusalem, The Jerusalem Publishing House; New York, Macmillan; London, Collier-Macmillan, 1987. 520p. maps. $50. £40. ISBN: 0029164222.

A revised and updated version of *Political dictionary of the Middle East in the twentieth century* (2nd ed., 1974).

About 500 A-Z informative essays and articles (up to 2000 words long) on the leading personalities, institutions, general issues, and political movements of the 20th century up to the mid-1980s. Excludes Cyprus, Turkey and Iran. *Class No: 95.297(038)*

Maps & Atlases

[7533]

An Historical atlas of Islam. Leiden, E.J. Brill, 1981. viii, 71p. maps, index. ISBN: 9004061169.

Forms part of *The Encyclopaedia of Islam*, new edition (*qv*).

73 coloured maps grouped in 9 sections: 1. The Early Muslim earth and sky - 2. The extension of the Muslim world - 3. Early Arabia - 4. The Near and Middle East - 5. Anatolia and the Balkans - 6. Muslim Spain - 7. North Africa - 8. India and the Indian seas - 9. The Far East. Index of place names p.58-70. Introduction carries bibliographical references. *Class No: 95.297(084.3)*

[7534]

HUSSAIN MENES. **Atlas of the history of Islam.** Cairo, Al-Zahraa for Arab Mass Media, 1987. 523p. col. maps, geneal tables, index. £40.50.

A comprehensive atlas of Islamic history in 213 full colour pages of maps, complemented by a history of all Muslim nations: 1. Introduction to Islamic geography and cartography - 2. Expansion of Islam - 3. Historical charts of Islam to 1985 - 4. The World before the rise of Islam - 5. The life and times of Prophet Mohammad - 6. Conquests of the first century of Islam - 7. Umayyad and Abbasid Caliphates - 8. North Africa and Al-Andalus (Moslem Iberia) - 9. Historical development of Arabia - 10. The eastern wing of the Islamic world - 11. Muslim India - 12. The Crusades - 13. Muslim activity in the Mediterranean - 14. The development of Egypt and Syria - 15. Egypt - 16. Islamic State of the Nile Valley (Egypt and Sudan) - 17. The Ottoman Empire - 18. The later development of Islam in Africa - 19. The economy. Routes of communication by earth and sea and pilgrimage - 20. Islam in modern times (including The Palestinian question). Apart from the Contents page the atlas is in Arabic throughout. The author is Professor of Islamic History in the University of Cairo. *Class No: 95.297(084.3)*

Chronologies

[7535]

JENKINS, E. **The Muslim diaspora** a comprehensive reference to the spread of Islam in Asia, Africa, Europe and the Americas. Volume 1, 570-1500. Jefferson, N.C., McFarland, 1999. xii,425p. bibliog., index. $75. £56.25. ISBN: 0786404310.

Chronicles the story of the Muslim diaspora from the birth of Muhammed in 570 of the Christian calendar to 1500 thus embracing the conquests of the Persian and Byzantine empires, the advance along the North African littoral, the crossing over to the Iberian peninsula, and the rise of Islam in India, China, and Indonesia. Annual entries record significant 'Muslim' events continent by continent and related historical events on a similar pattern. 10 Appendices (*e.g.* The Five

....(contd.)

Pillars of Islam ... C. Islamic Calendar ... H. Rulers of Muslim Spain ... I. Ottoman Empire - J. Muslim India) Bibliography p.359-61. Analytical index p.363-425. Thorough, detailed, well-researched, and an essential acquisition for Historical and Comparative Religion collections. *Class No: 95.297(090)*

Asia—Middle & Near East

[7536]

GRESH, A. *and* VIDAL, D. **The New A-Z of the Middle East.** Rev. ed. London, I.B. Tauris, 1999. 256p. maps, bibliog., index. pbk. £14.95. ISBN: 1860643264.

First published as *The A-Z of the Middle East* (Zed Books, 1987). Translation of *Les cent portes du Proche-Orient* (Paris, 1986).

Brief guide to people, countries, events, and movements, prominent in the political and economic development of the Middle East. Entries average two pages and contain description and analysis. Time span ranges from the break-up of the Ottoman Empire to the death of King Hussain of Jordan. 'Something rather more serious than a bluffer's guide while falling just short of being an encyclopaedia' (*The Independent*, no.1336, 26 January 1991, p.26). *Class No: 95.3/.6*

[7537]

—**An A-Z of the Middle East** a reference CD-ROM. Developer-Produces: Sindbad. Miniumum hadware required: For PC: 486 or Pentium processor; 12 Mb Ram (8Mb for Win 3.1); Windows 95/NT/3.1 or greater; card compatible with Sound Blaster; 4 x CD-Rom. For Mac: 68040 or Power PC processor; 8Mb Ram; 4 x CD-Rom drive. £19.99.

'The main option is "List of Entries", which contains an alphabetical rundown of major events, personalities and countries. It also has a search facility, which allows you to type in a key word and find all the pages in which it is mentioned. The only drawback is that you cannot narrow your search by typing in two terms - for example, "The Gaza Strip" and "violence" - which means it can take time sifting the pages, before finding what you want. (*The Times*, 9 September 1998, *Inter//face//*. p.10). *Class No: 95.3/.6*

[7538]

A History of the Near East. Holt, P.M., *ed*. London, Longman, 7v., 1986-. maps, bibliogs., tables, index.

A history of the region from the coming of Islam to the present day. Noteworthy for the excellent bibliographical surveys in each volume. *Titles* 1. *The Prophet and the age of Caliphates: the Islamic Near East from the sixth to the eleventh century* by Hugh Kennedy. 1986. 440p. £24.00. 0582493129. 2. *The Age of the Crusades: the Near East from the eleventh century to 1517* by P.M. Holt. 1986. xiii, 250p. £15.95. 058249303x. 3. *The Rise of the Ottoman Empire 1300-1574* by Colin Imber. 4. *The Decline of the Ottoman Empire 1574-1792* by R.C. Ropp. 5. *The Making of the modern Near East 1792-1923* by M.E. Yapp. 1987. xii, 404p. £25.00. 0582013666. 6. *The Near East since the First World War* by M.E. Yapp. 1990. £32. 0582495008. 7. *Medieval Persia 1040-1797* by David Morgan. 1988. x, 197. £17.95. 0582014832. *Class No: 95.3/.6*

[7539]

OVENDALE, R. **The Longman companion to the Middle East since 1914.** 2nd ed. London, Longman, 1998. x,413p. maps, bibliogs., index. £12.99. (*Longman Companions to History no.1*.) ISBN: 0582315557.

1st ed. 1992.

Comprehensive guide in 9 sections: 1. Annotated chronologies - 2. Biographies - 3. Treaties and alliances - 4. Religion & sects - 5. Rulers, political parties and movements (country by country) - 6. Glossary - 7. Economic & social data - 8. Maps - 9. Bibliographies. 'A comprehensive overview of a region which still shows no signs of stability or peace. No doubt within a very short time a third edition will be required' (*Reference Reviews*, v.13, no.1, 1999, p.47-48). *Class No: 95.3/.6*

[7540]

SASSON, J.M., *and others, eds*. **Civilizations of the ancient Near East.** New York, Scribner,. 4v., 1995. 2966p. illus., maps, bibliog., index. $449. ISBN: 0684192799.

189 essays from independent hands covering 4,000 years of history arranged in 11 broad sections: Ancient Near East in Western thought; environment; population; social institutions; economy and trade; technology and artistic production; religion and science; language, writing and literature; visual and performing arts; and retrospective essays. 46 maps. *Class No: 95.3/.6*

[7541]
SLUGLETT, P. *and* FAROUK-SLUGLETT, M., *eds*. The Times guide to the Middle East The Arab World and its neighbours. 3rd ed. London, Times Books. 1996. 349p. maps, index. pbk. £8.99. ISBN: 0813327881.

1st ed. 1991; 2nd ed. 1993.

13 contributors. 18 country and thematic chapters relating to Egypt, the Gulf States, Israel, Jordan, the Kurds, Lebanon, Libya, the Maghrib, the Palestinians, Saudi Arabia, Sudan, Syria, Yemen, oil in the Middle East, and Islam. An introduction supplies a historical and political overview from the fall of the Ottoman Empire to the Iraqi invasion of Kuwait. *Class No: 95.3/.6*

Bibliographies

[7542]
OLSON, W.J. Britain's elusive empire in the Middle East, 1900-1921: an annotated bibliography. New York, Garland Publishing Inc., 1982. xxvii, 404p. index. $61. (*Themes in European Expansion*.) ISBN: 0824092732.

Part 1 (p.1-68) is a magisterial survey of the international political and diplomatic background to 20th century British foreign policy in the Middle East. Part 2 comprises 664 extensively annotated entries (offering a critical analysis of their subject content) concerned with Empire and imperialism; international rivalry; Britain in the Middle East; Nationalism, westernization, Pan-Islam; and recent doctoral theses on the Middle East. 'There is probably no better introduction now available to the literature of the topics with which it deals' (*Choice*, v.20, no.1, September 1982, p.56). *Class No: 95.3/.6(01)*

[7543]
ORGILL, A. The 1990-91 Gulf War: crisis, conflict, aftermath. An annotated bibliography. London, Mansell, 1995. 228p. £40. ISBN: 0720121744.

1600 mostly annotated entries arranged in 16 chapters. Bibliographies and document collections - General works - Political and diplomatic background - Kuwait under occupation - Military campaign in general - Air campaign - Land campaign - Naval campaign - Weapons systems, vehicles and equipment - Biographies - Logistics - Intelligence - The war and the media - Political aftermath - Military lessons - Environmental consequences. Author/Subject index. Journal title index. *Class No: 95.3/.6(01)*

Dictionaries

[7544]
HIRO, D. Dictionary of the Middle East. London, Macmillan, 1996. xiii,367p. maps, index. £14.99. ISBN: 0333638433.

1000+ cross-referenced entries relating to the images, events, ideologies, natural resources, religious groups, organisations, historical places, wars, country profiles, international treaties and agreements, military leaders of Bahrain, Egypt, Iran, Iraq, Israel, Jordan, Kuwait, Lebanon, Oman, Palestine, Qatar, Saudi Arabia, Syria, United Arab Emirates, and Yemen. Selected as one of *Choices* Outstanding Academic Books of 1996. *Class No: 95.3/.6(038)*

Reviews & Abstracts

[7545]
The Middle East in conflict a historical bibliography. Santa Barbara, California and Oxford, ABC Clio Information Services, 1985. ix, 302p. indexes. $75. £58.05. (*Clio Bibliography Series, no.19*.) ISBN: 0874363810.

3,258 abstracts of articles published 1973-1982 drawn from the publisher's renowned historical database arranged in 9 sub-divided geographical and topical chapters: 1. General - 2. Political integration and cooperation - 3. International relations, aid, and trade - 4. The Middle East in the World Wars - 5. Intra-regional wars and conflicts - 6. North Africa - 7. The Fertile Crescent - 8. The Arabian Peninsula - 9. The Northern tier (Iran. Afghanistan. Pakistan). Subject Profile Index (SPIndex) and author index (p.213-97) offer generous access points. Some material could have been omitted without loss to overall subject coverage. *Class No: 95.3/.6(048)*

Crusades

[7546]
BOAS, A.J. Crusader archaeology the material culture of the Latin East. London, Routledge, 1999. 267p. illus., bibliog., index. $50. ISBN: 0415173612.

An overview of the archaeological evidence from recent excavations in Cyprus, Israel, Jordan, and Syria which lends substance to the historical record. 'An invaluable guide to the extensive material culture and society of Crusader times. In combining history and archaeology (with emphasis is this book on the latter), the author has succeeded in producing a study of fundamental importance' (*Choice*, v.37, no.7, March 2000, p.1348). *Class No: 95.3/.6"1095-13"*

20th Century

[7547]
MOSTYN, T. Major political events in Iran, Iraq and the Arabian peninsula 1945-1990. New York and Oxford, Facts on File, 1991. xii,308p. maps, bibliog., index. £14.95. ISBN: 0816021899.

Narrative chronology of major political, military, and economic events. The introduction carries a useful historical overview of Iran, Iraq, Saudi Arabia, Qatar, Bahrein, Oman, United Arab Emirates, and Yemen. Biographies p.268-84. Glossary p.285-89. Bibliography p.290-91. 10 maps. Analytical index. *Class No: 95.3/.6"19"*

Bibliographies

[7548]
GARDNER, J.A. The Iraq-Iran War: a bibliography. London, Mansell Publishing Ltd; Boston, G.K. Hall, 1988. xvi, 124p. index. £24.00. $56.00. ISBN: 0720118794, UK; 0816189978, US.

509 numbered and annotated entries in 7 chapters: 1. Introductory sources - 2. Background - 3. Iraq at war 1980-87 - 4. Domestic impact - 5. Foreign impact - 6. The conflict in the gulf - 7. The literature and films of war. Material in Arabic and Persian as well as Western and European languages is included. Author and title indexes. 'Highly recommended for larger political science collections and all Middle East collections' (*Choice*, v.26, no.10, June 1989, p.1661). *Class No: 95.3/.6"19"(01)*

Chronologies

[7549]
BEG, M.A.J. The Middle East in the twentieth century a chronology of events 1900-1993. London, Mansell, 1995. 640p. £60. ISBN: 0720122961.

Chronology of political, economic, social and religious events from the declining years of the Ottoman Empire to the Gulf War. Countries included are Bahrain, Egypt, Iran, Iraq, Jordan, Kuwait, Lebanon, Oman, Palestine and Israel, Qatar, Saudi Arabia, Syria, Turkey, the United Arab Emirates and Yemen. Two introductory chapters give an overview of events. *Class No: 95.3/.6"19"(090)*

Asia—South & South-East

[7550]
The Cambridge history of Southeast Asia. Tarling, N., *ed*. Cambridge, Cambridge Univ. Press, 2 vols., 1992.

1. *From early times to c.1800*. xv,655p. maps, bibliog. £55. ISBN 0521355052. 10 chapters: 1. The writing of Southeast Asian history; the remainder arranged in 2 chronological sections. 13 maps. 2. *The Nineteenth and twentieth centuries*. 704p. maps, bibliog., £55. 0521355052. 10 chapters in 2 sections: 1. From c.1800 to the 1930s - 2. World War II to the present. Bibliography (in 8 country and special topic sections) p.648-63. Cooperative history covering whole of mainland and island Southeast Asia from Burma to Indonesia. Thematic and regional rather than strictly national and chronological approach. Extensive bibliographical essays appended to all chapters. *Class No: 95.4/.0*

[7551]
HALL, D.G.E. A History of South-East Asia. 4th ed. London, Macmillan, 1981. xxx, 1070p. illus. maps, bibliog., index. ISBN: 0333241630.

First published 1955.

4 Parts: 1. To the beginning of the sixteenth century - 2. South-East Asia from the beginning of the sixteenth century to the end of the eighteenth - 3. The period of European territorial expansion - 4. Nationalism and the challenge to European domination. Appendix of dynastic lists with governors and governors-general p.954-986. Bibliography (12 sections) p.989-1039. 11 maps. *Class No: 95.4/.0*

Bibliographies

[7552]
DALBY, A. South-East Asia: a guide to reference material. Oxford, Hans Zell, 1993. 320p. index. £55. (*Regional Reference Guides, no.2*.) ISBN: 1873836007.

Annotated bibliography of reference material comprising 853 entries thematically arranged with regional subdivisions. Covers politics, religion, society, history, language, natural resources, geography, economics, and development. 'Should be used as a first step in any literature search and there is an excellent 50-page index to help in the process' (*Geographical Journal*, v.162, no.1, March 1996, p.87). *Class No: 95.4/.0(01)*

Maps & Atlases

[7553]

PLUVIER, J.M. **Historical atlas of South-East Asia.** Leiden, E.J. Brill, 1995. 83p.+64p. col. maps, bibliog., indexes. (*Handbook of Oriental Studies, vol.8.*) ISBN: 9004102388. ISSN: 01699571.

64 maps illustrating all stages of South-East Asian history: 1. S.E. Asia, physical - 2. Prehistory ... 63. Wars in Vietnam, Cambodia and East Timor - 64. S.E. Asia from 1910-1985. Introduction (p.7-52) provides brief backgrounds to the maps placing them in their historical context. Bibliography (by country) p.53-60. Jan M. Pluvier is Emeritus Professor of Modern Asian History in the Univ. of Amsterdam. 'Fills a long-standing need for students and scholars, who have lacked a comprehensive source for maps illustrating the historical development of the region' (*Choice*, v.34, no.5, January 1997, p.774).
Class No: 95.4/.0(084.3)

[7554]

SCHWARTZBERG, J.E., *with others eds.* **A Historical atlas of South Asia.** 2nd ed. New York, Oxford Univ. Press, 1992. xxxix, 369p. illus., maps, tables. £200. ISBN: 0195068696.

First published by Univ. of Chicago Press 1978.

149p. of maps (mostly coloured); 117p. of historical narrative, 'South Asia' extends from Afghanistan through the Indian subcontinent, to Burma. 14 sections of maps, including geopolitical, economic, social and cultural themes. (section 14; 'A geopolitical synopsis'; 60 small-scale maps). Bibliography of 38p. 48p. of index, photographs and diagrams. This edition includes 20p. of addenda and corrections. 'One of the very best atlases for any region of the world ... providing a distinctly *geographical* view of history' (*Bulletin*, Special Libraries Association, Geography and Map Division, no.118, December 1979, p.60, 61). *Class No: 95.4/.0(084.3)*

China

[7555]

Essays on the sources for Chinese history. Leslie, D.D., *and others, eds.* Canberra, Australian National Univ. Press, 1973. xii, 378p. bibliog., index. ISBN: 0708103987.

24 Western and Oriental academic contributors. *Contents* Archaeological studies in China; oracle bones; pre-Han literature; wooden documents; standard histories; comments on later standard histories; universal histories; local gazetteers; unofficial regional records; genealogical registers; legal sources; compilation and historical value of the Tao-tsang; Tun-huang manuscripts; Tibetan, Manchu, Arabic, Western, Jesuit and Russian sources; archives on modern China; Chinese newspapers; sources on Kuomintang and republican China, the history of the Chinese Communist Party, and the Chinese Peoples Republic; overseas Chinese; and lexicology as a primary source of material for the history of modern China. All except the last of these are accompanied by bibliographies. *Class No: 951*

[7556]

FAIRBANK, J.K. *and* TWITCHETT, D., *eds.* **The Cambridge history of China.** Cambridge, Cambridge Univ. Press, 1978-.

1. *The Ch'in and Han Empires 221BC-AD20.* 1986 xli,981p. £100. 0521243270. 2. *Sui and t'ang china 589-906 pt.1.* 1979, xx,850p. £100. 052124467., 6. *Alien regimes and border states 710-1368.* 1994. 816p. £80. 0521243319. 7. *The ming dynasty 1368-1644 pt.1.* 1988. xxv,976p. £100. 0521243327. 8. *The Ming Dynasty Pt.2. 1368-1644.* 1998. 1231p. £80. 0521243335. 10. *Late ch'ing 1800-1911. pt.1.* 1978. xvi,313p. £100. 0521214475. 11. *Late ch'ing 1800-1911 pt.2.* 1980. 754p. £100. 0521220297. 12. *Republican China 1912-1949 pt.1.* 1983. xviii,1002p. £100. 0521235413. 13. *Republican China 1912-1949 pt.2.* 1986. xix,1092p. £100. 0521243386. 14. *The people's republic pt.1. The emergence of revolutionary China 1949-1965.* 1987. xvii,722p. £90. 052124336x. 15. *The people's republic pt.2: revolutionaries within the Chinese revolution 1966-1982.* 1992. £95. 0521243378. All volumes have extensive bibliographies, most have bibliographical essays and all have a glossary. The maps have been prepared on the basis of the historical reconstruction of the most up-to-date historical atlas of China, the *Chung-kuo li-shih ti-t'u-chi (Shanghai 1975).* 'When the CHofC was first planned in 1966, the aim was to provide a substantial account of the history of China as a benchmark for the western history - reading public: an account of the current state of knowledge in six volumes. Since then the outpouring of current research, the application of new methods, and the extension of scholarship into new fields have further stimulated Chinese historical studies. This growth is indicated by the fact that the history has now become a planned 15 vols., but will still leave out such topics as the history of art and of literature, many aspects of economics and technology, and all the riches of local history' (*General Editor's Preface*). *Note* Eastman, L.E. and others. *The Nationalist era in China 1927-1949*

V.2, 4, 5, 9(1) and 9(2) are announced for publication in 1997. *Class No: 951*

[7557]

FRANCK, I.M. *and* BROWNSTONE, D.M. **The Silk Road:** a history. New York and Oxford, Facts On File Publications, 1987. 294p. maps,. bibliog., index. $24.95; £17.95. ISBN: 0816011222, UK.

Well documented popular history from primary and secondary sources of the 5000 mile route linking East and West from pre-classical times to the present. 5 maps including two on endpapers depicting the main and connecting routes in Roman-Han and Early T'ang and Muslim times. Bibliography p.281-291. *Class No: 951*

[7558]

GOODRICH, L.C. *and* FANG, C., *eds.* **Dictionary of Ming biography** 1368-1644. New York, The Ming Biographical History Project of the Association for Asian Studies; London, Columbia Univ. Press, 2v., 1976. 1050p. 830p. illus., maps, indexes. $170.00. ISBN: 0231030811, v.1; 023103833x, v.2; 0685620344, set.

Nearly 650 documented entries; 125 specialist contributors. Indexes of names, books and subjects. 'An indispensable acquisition for college and other specialized libraries;' (*Library Journal*, 1 June 1976, p.1275). *Class No: 951*

[7559]

HSU, I.C.Y. **The Rise of modern China.** 4th ed. New York, Oxford Univ. Press, 1990. xxxi,971p. illus., maps, bibliogs., index. £23. ISBN: 0195058674.

1st ed. 1970.

Narrative history conveying a primarily Chinese view of the evolution of modern China. 40 chapters ordered into 7 Chronological periods: 1. Persistence of traditional institutions 1600-1800 - 2. Foreign aggression and domestic rebellions 1800-1864 - 3. Self strengthening in an age of accelerrated foreign imperialism 1861-95 - 4. Reform and revolution 1898-1912 - 5. Ideological awakening and the wars of resistance 1917-45 - 6. Rise of the Chinese Peoples' Republic - 7. China after Mao. Reading list at the end of each chapter. 17 maps. Analytical index. *Class No: 951*

[7560]

O'NEIL, H.B. **Companion to Chinese history.** New York and Oxford, Facts on File Publications, 1987. x, 397p. maps. £13.95. (*Companions to History Series.*) ISBN: 087196841x.

Almost 1000 brief A-Z entries range from prehistory to 1985 with geographical and personal names well to the fore. Chronology (1506-1985) p.379-83. 14 b/w outline maps p.384-97. Brief bibliographies are appended to many of the entries. 'Useful to the western non-specialist who needs a guide to an unfamiliar civilization' (*Reference Reviews*, v.3, no.1, March 1989, p.42). *Class No: 951*

[7561]

WEI, B.P.T. **Shanghai:** crucible of modern China. Hong Kong, London, New York, Oxford Univ. Press, 1987. xvi, 299p. illus. (21 plates). maps on endpapers, bibliog. index. ISBN: 0195838319, UK; 0195838311, US.

14 chapters - 1. Shanghai before the coming of the foreigner - 2. The Opium War ... 5. The cosmopolitan city ... 13. The Nationalist era ... 14. Epilogue: Shanghai after 1945. Bibliography (inc. Sources in Chinese and Japanese) p.269-283. Glossary p.284-291. Analytical index. The author is an honorary lecturer in history and a research associate at the Centre of Asian Studies in the University of Hong Kong. *Class No: 951*

[7562]

WILKINSON, E. **Chinese history** a manual. Cambridge, Mass., Harvard Univ. Asia Center, 1998. Distributed by Harvard Univ. Press. 1068p., tables, indexes. ISBN: 0674123378.

This manual has 4 basic aims: to suggest solutions to basic problems encountered in researching Chinese history, to introduce the main primary and research tools, to give readers some sense of the variety and dangers of Chinese history, and to avoid a historical interpretations. Covering the Shang period to 1911 it considers the pre-Qin, literary, and other sources. *Class No: 951*

Bibliographies

[7563]

FRANKE, W. **An Introduction to the sources of Ming History.** Kuala Lumpur and Singapore, Univ. of Malaya Press, 1962. Distributed overseas by Oxford Univ. Press.

Enlarged and completely revised edition of *Preliminary notes on the important Chinese literary sources for the history of the Ming Dynasty (1365-1644)* published in the Studia Serica Monographs series by The Chinese Cultural Studies Research Institute, West China Union University, Chengtu (1948).

Introduction (the present state of research, some aspects of Ming historiography. The Veritable Records, transmission of works written by Ming authors). 9. Sections: 1. Works on the annalistic pattern - 2. Official and private historical compilations - 3. Biographical - 4. Notes dealing with historical subjects - 5. Memorials - 6. Political institutions - 7. Foreign affairs and military organizations - 8. Geography and local histories - 9. Economy and technology, encyclopaedias, collectanea.

...(contd.)
Author and title indexes. 'Not a bibliography of works which have been written, but an introduction to the available sources of Ming history' (*Foreword*). *Class No:* 951(01)

[7564]
HERVOUET, Y., *ed.* A Sung bibliography /Bibliographie des Sung. Hong Kong, Chinese Univ. Press, 1979. Distributed by Columbia Univ. Press. 598p.
The Sung dynasty: A.D.960-1279. 'A valuable research tool and as such belongs in all libraries equipped for research in traditional Chinese history and civilization' (*Choice*, v.16, no.8, October 1979, p.1000). *Class No:* 951(01)

[7565]
NATHAN, A.J. Modern China 1840-1972; : an introduction to sources and research aids. Ann Arbor, Univ. of Michigan Press, 1973. vi, 95p.
About 400 entries. Part 1: Research aids and libraries (1. Bibliographies ... 6. Biography and Elites). Part 2: Major types of primary sources (*e.g.* Chinese newspapers, radio and periodicals; government publications; diplomatic archives; Russian-language materials; materials on Taiwan). Includes many Chinese items. Author and title indexes. 'An inexpensive and valuable item for Asian studies collections' (*Library journal*, v.98, no.20, 15 November 1973, p.3365). *Class No:* 951(01)

Dictionaries

[7566]
DILLON, M. Dictionary of Chinese history. London, Cass, 1979. ix,240p. chron. table, map. £19.50. ISBN: 0714631078.
Aims 'to provide a quick and easy reference to the names and terms which occur most frequently in English-language works on China and which can be usefully explained in a few hundred words' (*Preface*). Entries cover the period from pre-history to the end of 1977. 'Mao Tse-tung': over 1p.; 'Congress of the Chinese Communist Party': nearly 2p. Cross-references. *Class No:* 951(038)

[7567]
JOHNSON, G.E. *and* PETERSON, G.D. Historical dictionary of Guangzhou (Canton) and Guangdong. Lanham, MD., Scarecrow Press, 1999. 320p. bibliog. $78. (*Historical Dictionary of Cities, no.6.*) ISBN: 0810835169.
A comprehensive, up-to-date dictionary of the geography, politics, and society of this premier city in south China and its surrounding province. The *Dictionary* focuses upon the contemporary history of Guangzhou and Guangdong. In two sections: the city of Guangzhou and the province of Guangdong. The dictionary is an alphabetical listing of the people, places, events and cultural activities significant to the modern history of Guangzhou and Guangdong. There is an introductory essay for each of the two sections to provide context for what follows. Two bibliographies follow the dictionary, primarily made up of English-language sources. *Class No:* 951(038)

[7568]
LEUNG, E. P-w., *ed.* Historical dictionary of revolutionary China 1839-1976. Westport, Conn., Greenwood Press, 1992. xvii,566p. map, bibliog., index. $85; £76.50. ISBN: 0313264570.
73 academic contributors. Dictionary consists of (c.270) short signed essays on events, ideas, personalities, battles, organizations *etc.* each with a list of references attached. Chronology p.495-519. Bibliography p.521-43. Glossary (of names in Roman and Chinese scripts) p.546-52. 'A major contribution to the meager collection of English-language reference materials' (*Choice*, v.30, no.2, October 1992, p.274). *Class No:* 951(038)

Maps & Atlases

[7569]
CHEN CHEN-SIANG. An Historical and cultural atlas of China. Tokyo, Hara Shobo, 1982. xx,190p. folded maps (some col.). Y29,600. ISBN: 4562012331.
First published in a single-sheet format by International House for China Studies 1975-79.
118 folded map sheets covering almost every aspect of Chinese life and culture. Each map is supplemented by an explanatory essay which may run into several pages. This is a Japanese-Chinese bilingual edition but there is a detailed English preface explaining the process of compiling the atlas and English legends to all the maps. *Class No:* 951(084.3)

Chronologies

[7570]
CHENG, J. A Chronology of the People's Republic of China 1949-1984. Beijing, Foreign Languages Press, 1986. 99p. sd. ISBN: 0835115666.
Briefly records most important political, economic, and cultural events. *Class No:* 951(090)

[7571]
CHENG, P.P. Chronology of the People's Republic of China 1970-1979. Metuchen, New Jersey, Scarecrow Press, 1986. vii,621p. bibliog., indexes. $55.00. ISBN: 0810817519.
10 annual chapters chronicling events on a daily basis as recorded in Chinese, Japanese, British, French and United States newspapers. Appendix A. Bibliographical sources p.569-570. Further reading p.571-572. 'Excellent for use as quick reference, to refresh reader memory, or to introduce the novice to the major events of the period' (*Choice*,v.24, no.10, June 1987, p.1599). Continues the same writer's *A Chronology of the People's Republic of China from October 1, 1949* (Totowa, New Jersey, Littlefield Adams, 1972). *Class No:* 951(090)

[7572]
DOLBY, W. Chronological tables of Chinese history. Edinburgh, Univ. of Edinburgh Department of Chinese, 1985. [59] leaves reproduced from typescript. pbk.
'This present work does not go into the finer points of cyclical locations or the pinpointing of months or days, but merely provides a broad run-through of the principal dynasties, rulers, by title and by personal names and surnames, and ruler's reign-periods' (*Preface*). Ranges 645BC-1911A.D. English and Chinese text.
Class No: 951(090)

[7573]
MACKERRAS, C. Modern China: a chronology from 1842 to the present. London, Thames & Hudson, 1982. 703p. maps, index. £22.50. ISBN: 0500250847.
Left hand pages chronicles major political or general incidents, military or civilian, domestic or foreign relations. Right hand pages divided into 6 categories: economy; official appointments, dismissals, resignations; cultural and social; publications; natural disasters; births and deaths. Introduction (p.7-20) describes the sources, lists general works, and specific topic chronologies. Glossary of titles and technical terms p.644-646. General index p.647-694. Geographical index p.695-703. 'Aims to present a classified and factually detailed chronology of modern China'. *Class No:* 951(090)

20th Century

Bibliographies

[7574]
Sino-Soviet conflict: a historical bibliography. Santa Barbara, California, and Oxford, ABC-Clio Information Services, 1985. xii, 190p. index. $40. £32.25. ISBN: 0317697544.
842 annotated entries covering the period 1914 onwards abstracted from the publisher's history database 1965-1982.
Class No: 951"19"(01)

Dictionaries

[7575]
SULLIVAN, L.R. *and* HEARST, N. Historical dictionary of the Peoples Republic of China 1949-1997. Lanham, MD., Scarecrow Press, 1998. xxxiv,277p. map, tables, bibliog. £53.20. (*Asian/Oceanian Historical Dictionaries, no.28.*) ISBN: 0810833492.
This has been a period marked by political turbulence and transformation but with substantial progress in economic growth, public health and social-economic infrastructure. The introduction to the *Dictionary* provides a brief history of the country during this time, which is marked by five distinct periods: economic reconstruction and political consolidation (1949-1957), The Great Leap Forward (1958-1965), The Great Proletarian Cultural Revolution (1966-1971), Late Maoism (1972-1977) and the era of reform and political crisis (from 1978-1996). *Class No:* 951"19"(038)

Hong Kong

[7576]
CAMERON, N. An Illustrated history of Hong Kong. Hong Kong, Oxford Univ. Press, 1991. iv,362p. illus (inc. col. pl.), maps, bibliog., index. £25; $39.95. ISBN: 0195849973.
Narrative history of 'British' Hong Kong in 24 chapters (*e.g.* 3. Treaty of Nanjing ... 10. Growth of Chinese institutions ... 20. Invasion and occupation (by Japan) ... 23. Growth on industrial giant). Chapter notes p.327-32. Bibliography p.342-5. Glossary p.346. 7 maps and on endpapers. 'The best overall history to date of the British Colony' (*Choice*, v.29, no.3, November 1991). *Class No:* 951.2317

[7577]
WELSH, F. A History of Hong Kong. London, Harper Collins, 1993. xv,624p.+ + 12p. pl. illus., maps, bibliog., index. ISBN: 0002158523.
Narrative history in 17 chapters. Appendix A: British governments and prominent Chinese (1830-1992) p.542-7 - B. Governors (1841-1992) p.548. Chapter notes p.549-75. Bibliography p.576-91. *Class No:* 951.2317

Dictionaries

[7578]

ROBERTS, E.V., *and others*. Historical dictionary of Hong Kong and Macau. Metuchen, NJ., Scarecrow Press, 1992. xlvii,357p. maps, bibliogs., tables. £44.50. (*Asian Historical Dictionaries, no.10*.) ISBN: 0810825740.

Introduction (History and politics of Hong Kong) p.xxi-xlvii. Dictionary p.1-225. Bibliography (introductory essay and then arranged in 12 section inc. History, Biographies and Company Histories, Newspapers and Periodicals, Bibliographies, and Statistics) p.227-59. Then similar pattern for Macau. 'Uneven depth and quality' (*Choice*, v.30,no.10, June 1993, p.1608). *Class No:* 951.2317(038)

Macau

[7579]

GUNN, G.C. Encountering Macau a Portuguese city-state on the periphery of China, 1575-1999. Boulder, Colo., Westview Press, 1996. 240p. illus., maps, bibliog., index. $54.95. £40.95. ISBN: 0813389704.

The shaping of Macau's history over 400 years in 10 chronological and thematic chapters: Macau and the world economy ... Sovereignty question ... Wartime Macau ... Toward 1999: Macau and China. *Class No:* 951.2318

Chronologies

[7580]

GOMES, L.G. Efemérides da história de Macau. [An Almanac of the history of Macau.] Macau, Notícias de Macau, 1954. 267p. (*Colecção Notícias de Macau, no.12*.)

'This chronological register of past events relating to the Portuguese in Asia is arranged by days of the month. Events included range from the late 16th century to 1950' (R.L. Edmonds. *Macau*, 1989. Entry 99). *Class No:* 951.2318(090)

Tibet

[7581]

GOLDSTEIN, M.C. A History of modern Tibet 1913-1951: the demise of the Lamaist state. Berkely, Univ. of California Press, 1989. xxxvi,898p. illus., maps, bibliog., index. ISBN: 0520061403.

A detailed history (21 chapters) in 2 parts: 1. Era of the 13th Dalai Lama and Reting 1913-1940 and 2. Era of the Taktra and the 14th Dalai Lama. Appendix A. Anglo-Chinese Convention of 1906 - B. Anglo-Russian Convention of 1907 - C. The Simla Agreements of 1914. Glossary of Tibetan terms p.843. Bibliography p.845-54. 11 maps. 'Examines what happended and why, and balances the traditional focus on international relations with an emphasis on the intricate web of internal affairs and events' (*Preface*). 'This book deserves high praise as the first attempt at an unbiased comprehensive account of Tibetan politics from 1913-1951', (*Journal of Asian studies*, v.49,no.4, November 1990, p.901). *Class No:* 951.5

[7582]

SMITH, W.W. A History of Tibet: nationalism and self-determination. Boulder, Colo., Westview Press, 1996. 800p. illus., maps, bibliog., index. $79.95. £59.50.

Narrative history in 14 chapters: Tibetan ethnic origins and relations with China - Tibetan Empire ... Invasion of Tibet ... Cultural revolution ... Tibet in international law. *Class No:* 951.5

Bibliographies

[7583]

CHAND, A. Tibet past and present a select bibliography with chronology of historical events 1660-1981. New Delhi, Sterling Publishers Pvt Ltd., 1982. Distributed in North America by Humanities Press. 257p. index. $24.50.

1. Introduction (to Tibetan history) p.1-67 - 2. Chronology p.68-108 - 3. Bibliography p.109-248. Arranged by subject with author index. 'This publication should not be inflicted upon anyone' (*Choice*, v.20,no.8, April 1983, p.1106). *Class No:* 951.5(01)

Encyclopaedias

[7584]

Encyclopaedia of Tibet. Sharma, S.K. *and* Sharma, S., *eds.* New Delhi, Anmol Publications, 7v., 1996. ISBN: 8174884130, set.

1. *History and geography of Tibet*. 260p. 8174884149. 2. *Travel and memoirs of Tibet*. 8174884157. 3. *Society and culture*. 285p. 8174884165. 4. *Religious heritage*. 258p. 8174884173. 5. *Dalai Lama and Tibet*, 245p. 8174884181. 6. *India and Tibet*, 241p. 817488419x. 7. *Tibet and the world*. 282p. 8174884203. Each v. arranged in a series of chronological chapters. *Class No:* 951.5(031)

Mongolia

[7585]

BAWDEN, C.R. The Modern history of Mongolia. 2nd rev. ed. London, Kegan Paul International, 1989. xiv,476p. 24p. pl. illus., maps, bibliog., index. pbk. ISBN: 0710303262.

First published London, Weidenfeld & Nicolson, 1968. In fact this 'revised' edition has the text of the 1st ed. reprinted without alteration. Only revision is the incoporation of a Supplementary bibliography p.455!.

Narrative in 9 chapters from loss of Mongol independence to post-Second World War achievements. Chapter notes p.439-47. Bibliographical note. p.451-4. *Class No:* 951.7

Dictionaries

[7586]

SANDERS, A.J.K. Historical dictionary of Mongolia. Lanham, MD, Scarecrow Press, 1996. xlix,317p. map, bibliog. £45.15. (*Asian Historical Dictionaries, no.19*.) ISBN: 0810830779.
Class No: 951.7(038)

Korea

[7587]

HAN, Woo-Keun. The History of Korea. 14th printing. Seoul, The Eul-Koo Publishing Co., 1983. xii, 551p. illus. (some col.) maps, geneal.tables, bibliog., index.

Authoritative history in 37 chapters covering the primitive, ancient, medieval, modern and contemporary periods. Bibliography (books and articles in Japanese, Korean and Western languages) p.516-527. Author is Professor of Korean History in Seoul National University. *Class No:* 951.9

[7588]

LEE, Ki-baik. A New history of Korea. Cambridge, Massachussetts, Harvard Univ. Press, 1984. xxii, 474p. illus. (some col.) maps, tables, bibliog., index. $25. ISBN: 0674615751.

First published in Korea as *Kuksa Sillon* (*A new history of our nation*) in 1961. Revised as *Han'guksa Sillon* (*A new history of Korea*) in 1967 and 1976.

Authoritative standard history in 16 chronological chapters subdivided into 73 sections: 1. The communal societies of prehistoric times ... 2. Walled-town states and confederated kingdoms ... 14. Nationalist stirrings and imperialist aggression ... 16. The beginnings of democracy. Bibliography p.395-413. Index-Glossary p.415-474. 'Supplements but by no means supersedes Woo-Keun Han's *The History of Korea*' (*Choice*, v.22, no.11-12, July-August 1985, p.1681). *Class No:* 951.9

Dictionaries

[7589]

PRATT, K. *and* RUTT, R. Korea. A Historical and cultural dictionary. Richmond, Surrey, Curzon, 1999. xx,568p. maps, bibliog., indexes. ISBN: 0700704647.

Designed as a quick access handbook providing factual information about events, people and topics in Korean history and culture. References to books and articles in Western languages where appropriate. Includes a chronological chart in East Asian history (China, Manchuria, Korea and Japan). Bibliography p.542. *Class No:* 951.9(038)

20th Century

[7590]

FARRAR-HOCKLEY, A. The British part in the Korean War. London, HMSO, 2v., 1990.

An official history consisting of chronological treatment of political and military events. 1. *A Distant obligation*. 1990. xxii,512p. illus., col. maps, bibliog. index. £50. ISBN 0116309539. Concerned with decision of the British government to commit military forces to the Korean War. Bibliography p.469-79. 2. *An Honourable discharge*. 1995. 550p. illus. 18 maps. £59. 011630958x. Describes the ebb and flow of fortunes on the battlefield and the parallel, sometimes consequential, political activities in the pursuit of a settlement. *Class No:* 951.9"19"

Bibliographies

[7591]

EDWARDS, P.M. The Korean War an annotated bibliography. Westport, Conn., Greenwood Press, 1998. x,346p. £63.50. (*Bibliographies and Indexes in Military Studies, no.20*.) ISBN: 0313303177.

2,205 briefly annotated citations, referring to books, periodical articles, government reports, captured North Korean documents, and other fugitive material, arranged under classified headings (*e.g.* history, military operations, media treatment, oral histories etc.). The

...*(contd.)*

compiler is Director of the Center for the Study of the Korean War, Independence, Missouri). 'A well-planned and well-researched annotated bibliography' (*Reference Reviews*, vol.12, no.7,. 1998, p.23-24). *Class No:* 951.9"19"(01)

[7592]
McFARLAND, K.D. The Korean War an annotated bibliography. New York, Garland, 1986. xxxiii, 463p. $70. £69. (*Wars of the United States, no.8.*) ISBN: 0824090683.

2311 English language entries paraded in 23 chapters *e.g.* 1. Reference works ... 7. US Army in Korea ... 12. The United Nations and the war ... 17. Peace negotiations and the armistice ... 19. Post-war Korea. Author and subject indexes. 'Because of its intelligent chapter arrangement, it may be used as an overview of any one of a score of war-related topics' (*Reference Books Bulletin 1986-1987*), p.155). *Class No:* 951.9"19"(01)

Encyclopaedias

[7593]
Encyclopedia of the Korean War a political, social, and military history. Tucker, S.C., *ed.* Oxford and Santa Barbara, Calif., ABC-Clio, 3v., 2000. 1240p. illus., maps, bibliog., index. $275. £175. ISBN: 1576070298.

100 civil and military contributors. Published on the 50th anniversary of the Korean War, this encyclopedia contains 600+ cross-referenced A-Z entries, many of which are based on research in Russian and Chinese archives, and covers all aspects of the War including pre- and postwar Korea. V.3 is devoted entirely to 85 primary source documents. A chronology of Korean history and a glossary complement the text. 20 maps. *Class No:* 951.9"19"(031)

[7594]
HOARE, J.E. *and* PARES, S. Conflict in Korea an encyclopedia. Oxford and Santa Barbara, Calif., ABC-Clio, 1999. 260p. $65. £37.50. (*Roots of Modern Conflict.*) ISBN: 0874369789.

A-Z cross-referenced entries, ranging from a short paragraph to 2 pages in length, related to the divisions among the people of the Korean peninsula, the war of 1950-53, and to subsequent events. Suitable for general reference libraries. *Class No:* 951.9"19"(031)

[7595]
SANDLER, S., *ed.* The Korean War: an encyclopedia. New York, Garland Press, 1996. 456p. maps, bibliog., index. $75. ISBN: 0824044452.

63 contributors. 142 A-Z entries relating to places, battles, leading individuals, logistics, naval, ground and air forces, strategy, and armistice negotiations. *Class No:* 951.9"19"(031)

Dictionaries

[7596]
MATRAY, J.I., *ed.* Historical dictionary of the Korean War. xxiii,626p. Westport, Conn., Greenwood Press, 1991. xxiii,626p. bibliogs. $85; £66.30. ISBN: 0313259240.

Series of signed mini-essays with their primary emphasis on political and diplomatic developments but with a substantial military element, each with brief biographies, describing the significant personalities, controversies, policy announcements, and combat operations. Appendix A. Statistical information - B. Summary of personnel changes - C. Chronology (p.559-74). Bibliography p.575-90. Analytical index. 20 maps. *Class No:* 951.9"19"(038)

Almanacs

[7597]
SUMMERS, H.G. Korean War almanac. New York and Oxford, Facts On File, 1990. xv,330p. illus., maps, bibliog., index. $24.95; £20. ISBN: 0816017379.

3 parts: 1. The setting (historical and geographical overviews) - 2. Chronology of events 25 Jun 1950 - 6 Sept 1953 - 3. The Korean War A-Z (375 entries of varying length relating to the people, battles, weapons, military units and key concepts of the war, some with cross-references and most with suggestions for further reading. 10 maps. Bibliography p.312-20. 'No rival in its chosen field' (*Reference Reviews*, v.4, no.3, 1990, p.31). *Class No:* 951.9"19"(059)

South Korea

Dictionaries

[7598]
NAHM, A.C. Historical dictionary of the Republic of Korea. Metuchen, N.J., Scarecrow Press, 1993. 272p. bibliog., maps. $39.50. (*Asian Historical Dictionaries, no.11.*) ISBN: 0810826038.

Chronology p.xxi-liii. Introduction (physical features, climate, history) p.1-55. Dictionary (domestic political and social events, foreign, economic and cultural development, biographers) p.57-206.

....*(contd.)*

Bibliography (under 9 sub-divided headings) p.207-63. 6 maps. 'Only marginally useful to Korean history scholars' (*Library Journal*, 15 June 1993. p.64). *Class No:* 951.95(038)

Japan

[7599]
The Cambridge history of Japan. Cambridge, Cambridge Univ. Press, 6v., 1989-1991.

1. Brown, D.M. *ed.* Ancient Japan. 1993. 650p. £80. 0521223520. 2. McCullough, W. and Shively D.H. *eds.* Heian Japan. 1999. 0521223539. 3. Kozo Yamamura *ed.* Medieval Japan. 1990. 734p. £85. 0521223547. 4. Hall, J.W. *ed.* Early modern Japan 1991. 976p. £88. 0521223555. 5. Jansen, M.B. *ed.* The Nineteenth century. 1989. 886p. £85. 0521223563. 6. Duus, P. *ed.* The Twentieth century. 1989. 836p. £85. 0521223571. Last volume has 14 chapters arranged in 4 pts: 1. Domestic politics - 2. External relations - 3. Economic development - 4. Social and intellectual change. Multi-volume cooperative history on the familiar Cambridge pattern providing a summary of the state of present knowledge of Japanese history for students and scholars. Supported by The Japan Foundation. *Class No:* 952

[7600]
NOUËT, N. The Shogun's city a history of Tokyo. Folkestone, Paul Norbury, 1990. nn 252p. illus., maps, index. £12.95. ISBN: 0904404617.

First published as *Histoire de Tokyo* (Paris, Presses, Universitaires de France, 1961).

Narrative history from Tokyo's earliest beginnings to the modern city surveying political, social and cultural developments. No bibliography in this English language edition. *Class No:* 952

Bibliographies

[7601]
BUNN, J.M. *and* ROBERTS, A.D.S., *comps.* A Union list of Japanese local histories in British libraries. Oxford, Bodleian Library, 1981. xvii,406p. pbk. £12.00. ISBN: 0900177837.

Resources of 6 libraries in 2 parts: 1. Histories referring to large geographical areas embracing more than 1 prefecture - 2. A-Z listing by single prefectures. Index of places and of obsolete place-names with their nearest modern equivalent. *Class No:* 952(01)

[7602]
DOWER, J.W. Japanese history and culture from ancient to modern times: seven basic bibliographies. Manchester, Manchester Univ. Press, 1986. vi,232p. £27.50; $34.50. ISBN: 0719019141, UK; 0910129207, US.

1. Ancient and medieval Japan - 2. Early modern and modern Japan 1600-1945 - 3. Japan abroad - 4. Japan and the crisis in Asia 1931-1945: primary materials in English - 5. Occupied Japan and the cold war in Asia - 6. Bibliographies and research guides - 7. Journals and other serial publications. Compiler holds the Joseph Naiman Endowed Chair in Japanese Studies, University of California. 'Dower's selection of English-language primary sources ... includes many unusual, elusive, but valuable sources' (*Choice*,v.24, no.11-12, July/August 1987,p.1674). *Class No:* 952(01)

[7603]
FUKUDA, N., *ed.* Japanese history: a guide to survey histories by period. Ann Arbor, Center for Japanese Studies, Univ. of Michigan, 1984. xix,120p. index. $12.00. ISBN: 093951219x.

Updates J.W. Hall's *Japanese history: a guide to Japanese reference and research materials* issued by the same publishers in 1954.

Almost 1000 annotated entries relating to books published 1955-1980 arranged by historical period with subject subdivisions: A. General history - B. Prehistory. Ancient history - C. Medieval - D. Early modern - E. Modern and Contemporary - F. Local history. Title index. *Class No:* 952(01)

[7604]
NAGAO, P.M., *comp.* Japanese local histories in the Library of Congress. Washington, Library of Congress, 1987. vii,324p. maps, bibliog., index. $29. ISBN: 0844405434.

2,848 entries including many works published under the auspices of prefectural, city, and village administrations. Arranged A-Z by romanized title (modified Hepburn system) and within 47 prefectures each preceded by a map. *Class No:* 952(01)

Encyclopaedias

[7605]

HUFFMAN, J.L., *ed*. **Modern Japan** an encyclopedia of history, culture and nationalism. New York, Garland Publishing, 1998. xxxiii,316p. illus., maps, bibliogs., index. ISBN: 0815325258.

103 academic contributors. Concentrating on the period since Commodore Perry's visit in the 1850's, this massive encyclopedia examines the historical events, the political leaders, and the societal pressures of Japan's recent past that affected its entry into the modern age. Japanese arts, religion, business, literature, and education also receive close attention. List of 30 subject headings (*e.g.* anti-nationalist activities, imperialism) p.xiii-xxi. Chronology (1853-) p.xxiii-xxvii. 2 maps. All major entries end with bibliographies. *Class No:* 952(031)

Dictionaries

[7606]

CYBRIWSKY, R. **Historical dictionary of Tokyo.** Lanham, MD., Scarecrow Press, 1997. 256p. bibliog. $49. (*Historical Dictionaries of Cities of the World, no.1.*) ISBN: 0810832348. *Class No:* 952(038)

[7607]

HUNTER, J. **Concise dictionary of modern Japanese history.** Berkeley, Univ. of California Press, 1984. xvi, 347p. map, index. $47.50. ISBN: 0520043901.

Information on the individuals and political, diplomatic and socioeconomic events, and institutions that have played a significant role in Japan's modern history 1853-1980. Aimed primarily at non-Japanese speakers, non-specialists, and undergraduate students. Japanese - English glossary of historical terms. 'The special virtue of Hunter ... is the reliable citation of additional accessible sources in English' (*Choice*, v.22, no.6, February 1985, p.795). *Class No:* 952(038)

[7608]

RÖPKE, J.M. **Historical dictionary of Osaka and Kyoto.** Lanham, MD., Scarecrow Press, 1999. xiii,273p. illus., maps, tables. $59.50. (*Historical Dictionaries of Cities of the World, no.9.*) ISBN: 081083622x.

Pt.1 Osaka. Chronology p.3-6. Introduction (administration, history, economy, transport, major districts etc.) p.7-24. Dictionary (local leaders, commerce, industry, education, religion etc.) p.27-106. Appendices (historical periods, population, foreign visitors, economic enterprises, postwar mayors and governors) p.107-111. Pt.2 Kyoto. Chronology p.115-22. Introduction p.123-41. Dictionary p.145-238. Appendices p.239-50. Bibliography p.251-71. *Class No:* 952(038)

Biographies

[7609]

ITASAKA, G. **100 Japanese you should know.** London, Kodansha Europe, 1999? 100p. £9.99. ISBN: 4770021593.

Single-page biographies of the key figures of Japanese history arranged in 8 chapters covering the emerging nation, development of culture, establishment of samurai government, surviving the troubled period, maintaining peace and security, opening up to modernisation, the two world wars and steering the nation in the aftermath. Bilingual. *Class No:* 952(092)

[7610]

IWAO, S., *ed*. **Biographical dictionary of Japanese history.** Tokyo, Kodansha International Ltd. in collaboration with the International Society of Educational Information, 1978. Distributed in North America by Harper & Row and by Phaidon in UK. 655p. maps, geneal tables, index. $39.50; £19.95. ISBN: 0870112740.

521 biographies. 4 Periods: Ancient; Medieval; Early Modern; Modern. Japanese characters follow transliterated form of name. 19 appendices (Imperial family lineage; regents; shoguns; institutions and terms). Bibliography p.580-618. 'Its utility for the reader who cannot use Japanese is limited' (*Journal of Asian Studies*, v.39,no.1, November 1979, p.183). *Class No:* 952(092)

Taiwan

Dictionaries

[7611]

COPPER, J.F. **Historical dictionary of Taiwan.** 2nd ed. Lanham, MD., Scarecrow Press, 1999. 368p. map. bibliog. $49.50. (*Asian/ Oceanian Historical Dictionaries, no.34.*) ISBN: 0810836653.

1st ed. 1993.

Provides detailed information on places, events, and people in Taiwan and explains the importance of each while relating most of Taiwan's identity as a nation or alternatively its ties to China. Also links Taiwan's history, society, economic growth, and politics to its status and importance in the world community. *Class No:* 952.9(038)

Saudi Arabia

[7612]

AL-FARSY, F. **Saudi Arabia** a case study in development. 4th ed. London, Routledge & Kegan Paul, 1986. 264p. illus., maps, tables, bibliog., index.

1st ed. 1978.

'An extremely valuable work providing an informative, fact-filled description of the structure of the Saudi government' (F.A. Clements. *Saudi Arabia*, 1988. Entry 669). *Class No:* 953.2

[7613]

KITCHEN, K.A. **'Ancient Arabia c.3000BC to 600AD: a fresh presentation of its chronology and history'** *Medieval History*, v.4, 1994. p.1-13 bibliog.

Historical profile of ancient Arabia. Bibliography p.10-13. *Class No:* 953.2

[7614]

VASSILIEV, A. **The History of Saudi Arabia.** London, Saqi Books, 1998. 576p. geneal. table, bibliog., index. ISBN: 0863569358.

Based on Arab texts and chronicles, accounts by European travellers, diplomats and scholars, and on official Saudi publications, this definitive work encompasses the transformation of Saudi society and politics over the past 250 years, the oil factor, and the Wahhabi religious reform movement. *Class No:* 953.2

Dictionaries

[7615]

PETERSON, J.E. **Historical dictionary of Saudi Arabia.** Metuchen, NJ., Scarecrow Press, 1993. xxii,245p. maps, bibliog. £34. (*Asian Historical Dictionaries, no.14.*) ISBN: 0810827808.

Dictionary (peoples, individuals, places, events and topical entries for economics, foreign affairs, government, history, military and defence *etc.*) p.1-187; Chronology p.189-206; Dynastic tables p.207-13. Bibliography (in 12 sub-divided sections) p.215-44. 3 maps. 'An accurate and detailed guide ... particularly useful as a rapid reference work for checking the persons and places which have played a major role in modern Saudi history' (*British Journal of Middle Eastern Studies*, v.25,no.2, November 1998, p.363). *Class No:* 953.2(038)

Yemen

[7616]

BIDWELL, R. **The Two Yemens.** London, Longman; Boulder, Colorado, Westview Press, 1983. xviii, 350p. map, bibliog., index. £31.50. ISEN: 0582783216, UK; 0865312958, US.

9 chronological chapters and postscript with a brief survey of pre-Islamic Yemen and subsequent emphasis on the post-war period. Bibliography p.338-342. 'A lucid and absorbing account' (*Geographical Journal*, v.153, no.1, March 1987, p.124). *Class No:* 953.3

Dictionaries

[7617]

BURROWES, R.D. **Historical dictionary of Yemen** Lanham, MD., Scarecrow Press, 1996. xvi,508p. maps, bibliog. £74.70. (*Asian Historical Dictionaries, no.17.*) ISBN: 0810829878.

North Yemen and South Yemen - the Yemen Arab Republic (YAR and the People's Democratic Republic of Yemen (PDRY), respectively - united to form the Republic of Yemen (ROY) in 1990. This volume the historical dictionary proper (p.55-432) as well as the lengthy descriptive essay (1-24) and detailed chronology (p.25-54), covers a great array of events, persons, institutions and other features of Yemen from ancient times to the short civil war that tested the ROY in mid 1994. Both parts of Yemen receive equal treatment over the many centuries before unification. Emphasis is upon the twentieth century Bibliography (in 17 thematic categories) p.438-507. *Class No:* 953.3(038)

Oman

[7618]

ALLEN, C.H. **Oman** the modernization of the Sultanate. Boulder Colorado, Westview Press; London, Croom Helm, 1987. xiii, 154p maps, bibliog., index. £30. (*Profiles: nations of the contemporary world.*) ISBN: 0813301254, US; 070995106x, UK.

9 chapters: 1. Land and people - 2. Ancient and medieval history 3. Oman's imperial age - 4. Imamate and Sultanate - 5. Challenges t unity - 6. Political development - 7. Economic and social developmen - 8. Oman and the world - 9. Oman to 2000. Bibliographic essa p.131-139. Glossary p.141-142. *Class No:* 953.5

Dictionaries

[7619]

ANTHONY, J.D., *and others*. **Historical and cultural dictionary of the Sultanate of Oman and the Emirates of Eastern Arabia.** Metuchen, N.J., Scarecrow Press, 1976. viii,136p. bibliog. (*Historical and Cultural Dictionaries of Asia, no.9.*)

Dictionary p.1-128. Bibliography p.129-36. Covers the area of al-Bahrayn, Qatar, United Arab Emirates, and Oman. *Class No: 953.5(038)*

Gulf States

[7620]

Bahrain through the ages. Abdullah bin Khalid al Khalifa *and* Rice, M., *eds*. London, Kegan Paul International, 1993. xiii,621p. index. ISBN: 071030272x.

37 papers presented originally at the historical sessions of the conference 'Bahrain Through the Ages' organized to mark the 200th anniversary of the arrival in the Bahrain islands of the Al-Khalifa family in 1783. Extensive chapter notes. Reference works on Bahrain p.78-97. *Class No: 953.6*

[7621]

Chronicle of progress. London, Trident Press, 1996. 432p. illus. (mostly col.), index. ISBN: 1900724030.

Annotated chronology and historical record of 25 years of economic, social, cultural, environmental development and UAE's international relations. *Class No: 953.6*

[7622]

GRAZ, L. The Turbulent Gulf. London, I.B. Tauris in association with The Gulf Centre for Strategic Studies, 1990. xi,312p. bibliog., index. ISBN: 185043199x.

Focuses on 'one or two salient aspects' of each of the Gulf States in turn. Chapter notes p.263-88. Bibliography p.299-302. The book was in the press when Iraq invaded Kuwait, 2 August 1990. *Class No: 953.6*

[7623]

POTTS, D.T. The Arabian Gulf in antiquity. Oxford, Clarendon Press, 2v., 1990. illus., map, tables, indexes. £45. each volume.

1. *From prehistory to the fall of the Achaemenid Empire.* xxviii,419p. ISBN 0198143907. 2. *From Alexander the Great to the coming of Islam.* xxii,369p. 0198143915. Comparative study of the archaeology and ancient history of the region. Heavily footnoted but lacks a consolidated bibliography. *Class No: 953.6*

[7624]

ZAHLAN, R.S. The Making of the modern Gulf states: Kuwait, Bahrain, Qatar, The United Arab Emirates and Oman. London, Unwin Hyman, 1989. ix,180p. illus., maps, index. pbk. ISBN: 0044452934.

Story of the formation, evolution from colonial dependency, and economic transformation. 10 chapters: 1. The Gulf in history - 2. Emergence of the Gulf states ... 10. International setting. *Class No: 953.6*

Dictionaries

[7625]

PECK, M. Historical dictionary of the Gulf (Arab) States. Lanham, MD, Scarecrow Press, 1997. xxvi,352p. bibliog. $45. ISBN: 0810832038.

Dictionary (p.1-225) covers all aspects of the culture and society of Bahrain, Kuwait, Oman, Qatar, and the United Arab Emirates, from prehistoric times to mid-1996. Bibliogaphy (with the emphasis on recently published works) is arranged in 10 sections (*e.g.* 1. Bibliography - 2. Official documents ... 4. General reference - 5. Biographies ... 7. History) p.227-311. *Class No: 953.6(038)*

Gulf War 1991

[7626]

SUMMERS, H.G. Persian Gulf War almanac. New York, Facts On File, 1995. 301p. illus., maps, bibliog., indexes. $35. ISBN: 0816028214.

200 A-Z entries relating to military units, major engagements, weapons, issues, and senior military personnel in the Iran-Iraq War of 1990-91. Each entry ends with references to further reading. Daily chronological record, a substantial bibliography, and subject and armaments indexes. *Class No: 953.60*

Encyclopaedias

[7627]

GROSSMAN, M. Encyclopedia of the Persian Gulf War. Santa Barbara, Calif. ABC Clio, 1995. xiii,522p. illus., maps, tables, bibliog., index. £34.95. ISBN: 0874366844.

A complete A-Z guide to the history, politics, people and weapons of the Gulf War, including theatres of operation, coalition and Iraqi forces, crucial diplomatic events, and significant documents. Chronology p.465-502. Bibliography p.503-512. 15 maps. *Class No: 953.60(031)*

Dictionaries

[7628]

NEWELL, C.R. Historical dictionary of the Persian Gulf War, 1990-1991. Lanham, MD., Scarecrow Press, 1998. 448p. maps, bibliog. $65. (*Historical dictionaries of War, Revolution and Civil Unrest, no.9.*) ISBN: 0810835118.

Includes 30-page introduction describing political developments leading to the war and a chronology of events. A-Z entries refer to leading personalities, events, places, and organizations involved in the war. *Class No: 953.60(038)*

Chronologies

[7629]

Gulf Crisis chronology. BBC World Service, *comp*. London, Longman Current Affairs, 1991. ix,454p. indexes. £65; $115. ISBN: 0582090059.

Day-to-day coverage of events in the Gulf conflict from the 2 August 1990 invasion of Kuwait by Iraq to the 3 March 1991 ceasefire. Name and subject indexes p.289-454. 'An invaluable tool for the study of the Gulf War which helps place closely spaced events in context' (*Choice*, v.29, no.11-12, July/August 1992, p.1656). *Class No: 953.60(090)*

United Arab Emirates

[7630]

PECK, M.C. The United Arab Emirates a venture in unity. Boulder, Colo., Westview Press; London, Croom Helm, 1986. xv,176p. illus., maps, tables, bibliog., index. (*Profiles/Nations of the Contemporary Middle East.*) ISBN: 0865311889, US; 0709940386, UK.

1. Land and people - 2. Historical background - 3. Society and culture - 4. Economy - 5. Domestic politics - 6. Regional and international arenas. Bibliography p.161-4. *Class No: 953.62*

[7631]

TARYAM, A.O. The establishment of the United Arab Emirates 1950-1985. London, Croom Helm, 1987. [vi], 290p. maps, index. £30. ISBN: 070994330x.

7 well-documented chapters: 1. Internal and External influences and their impact on the Arab Emirates 1950-60 - 2. Oil and the Change in British Policy - 3. The British Withdrawal Decision and Local, Regional and International Reactions - 4. The Dubai Agreement and Talks over the Proposed Nine-member Union - 5. Failure of Talks about the Nine-member Union and the Success of the Seven-member Union - 6. The Federation of the Emirates and the Conflict between the Constitutional Structure and Regional Authorities - 7. Evaluation of the Economic and Social Development in the United Arab Emirates. The Introduction (p.1-8) is a literature review of recent books and a list of sources. *Class No: 953.62*

Kuwait

[7632]

SCHOFIELD, R. Kuwait and Iraq: historical claims and territorial disputes. London: Royal Institute of International Affairs, 1991. 137p. maps, tables, bibliog., index. £9.75. ISBN: 0905031350.

A report compiled for the Middle East Programme of the Royal Institute of International Affairs.

Historical outline of Iraqi claims on Kuwaiti territory and of the international status of Kuwait since the 18th century. No bibliography but profuse footnotes and references. 10 maps. *Class No: 953.68*

India

[7633]

BASHAM, A.L., *ed*. A Cultural history of India. Oxford, Clarendon Press, 1984. xx,585p.+Øp. illus., tables, maps. £19.95. ISBN: 0195615204.

A new ed. of *Legacy of India* edited by G.T. Garratt (1937). First published under this title 1975.

28 contributors. 4 main parts (34 chapters): 1. The ancient heritage - 2. Age of Muslim dominance - 3. Challenge and response: the coming of the West - 4. India and the world outside. Footnotes. 'Books for further reading', p.507-17. Detailed, analytical index. Scholarly. *Class No: 954.0*

[7634]

BASHAM, A.L. **The Wonder that was India** a survey of the history and culture of the Indian sub-continent before the coming of the Muslims. 3rd rev. ed. London, Sidgwick & Jackson, 1967. xxi,568p. illus. (some col.), maps on endpapers, bibliog., index. ISBN: 0283354577.

10 chapters *e.g.* 2. Prehistory - 3. History of ancient and medieval empires - 4. Political life and thought. 10 Appendices including Cosmology and geography, the calendar, the alphabet and its pronunciation. Bibliography and references p.516-39. For the general reader. *Class No:* 954.0

[7635]

BENCE-JONES, M. **The Viceroys of India.** London, Constable, 1982. xv,343p. illus., ports., bibliog., index. ISBN: 0094638101.

15 chapters: 1. The office and the men before it ... 15. Wavell and Mountbatten. Source references p.317-33. Analytical index. Covers affairs of state, ceremonial, and social life. *Class No:* 954.0

[7636]

BHATTARCHARJEE, A. **A History of modern India.** Liverpool, Lucas Publications, 1988. 439p. 3p.plates. maps, geneal table, bibliog., index. ISBN: 1851800263.

Narrative history in 25 chapters *e.g.* 2. The later Mughals ... 14. The Sepoy mutiny of 1857 ... 19. The age of Mahatma Gandhi - 20. Final strides to freedom ... 25. Indo-Pak relations from independence to Tashkent. 5 Appendices: C. Important dates and events (p.416-22). Bibliography p.428-33. *Class No:* 954.0

[7637]

The Cambridge history of India. Rapson, E.J., *and others.* Cambridge, Cambridge Univ. Press, v.1, 3-6 and Supplementary volume, 1922-1953 (reprinted 1957-64). illus., maps, bibliogs., indexes.

1. *Ancient India.* 1922. xxii,684p. 2. Never published 'because the mansucript was allegedly destroyed upon the intervention of the British Government' (B.K. Gupta and D.S. Kharbas. *India,* 1984). 3. *Turks and Afghans.* 1928. xxxiii, 752p. 4. *Mughal period.* 1937. xxvii, 693p. 5. *British India 1497-1858.* 1929. xxii, 683p. 6. *The Indian Empire 1859-1918.* New ed. (Delhi, S. Chand & Co.), 1964. xxix, 759p. Supplementary volume: *The Indus civilization* by Sir Mortimer Wheeler (3rd ed. 1968. xi, 144p.) first published 1953. The new ed. of v.6 comprises 'The Indian Empire, with chapters on the development of administration, 1818-1858', edited by H.H. Dodwell, and 'The last phase, 1919-1947', by R.R. Sethi (19 chapters added to the original volume). V.5 contains 32 chapters by specialists; chapter bibliographies, p.609-53; chronological tables, p.613-8. Footnote references; no maps or illustrations. *Class No:* 954.0

[7638]

CORREIA-AFONSO, J. **Indo-Portuguese history:** sources and problems. Bombay, Oxford University Press, 1981. xii,201p. maps on endpapers, index. ISBN: 195612612.

Selected papers from the International Seminar on Indo-Portuguese history, Goa, 1978. These include Source material from the Goa archives; Indian history in the Cartorio des Jesuitas; The Portuguese Empire in India *c.*1550-1650; and some possible fields of research in the history of Portuguese India. *Class No:* 954.0

[7639]

MAJUMDAR, R.C., *and others.* **The History and culture of the Indian people.** Bombay, Bharatiya Vidya Bhavan, 11v., 1951-1978. maps, bibliogs.

1. *The Vedic age* (1951). 2. *The age of imperial unity* (1951). 3. *The classical age* (1954). 4. *The age of Imperial Kanauj* (1955). 5. *The struggle for Empire* (1957). 6. *The Delhi Sultanate* (1960). 7. *The Mughal Empire* (1974). 8. *The Maratha supremacy* (1977). 9-10. *British paramountcy and Indian Renaissance* (1963). 11. *Struggle for freedom* (2nd ed. 1978). Helps to bridge the gap in coverage of *The Cambridge history of India.* 75 contributors in all. Up-to-date bibliographies are appended to each volume. 'One of the most comprehensive studies of Indian history' (A.J. Mukherjee. *Guide to selected reference tools,* 1979. p.237). *Class No:* 954.0

[7640]

MOON, P. **The British conquest and dominion of India.** London, Duckworth, 1989. xi,1235p. illus., maps, bibliog., index. ISBN: 0715621696.

Outstanding narrative history in 77 chapters. Maps p.1199-1213. Glossary p.1214-15. Bibliography p.1216-18. Analytical index. *Class No:* 954.0

[7641]

The New Cambridge history of India. Johnson, G., ed. Cambridge Univ. Press, 30v., 1988-. Available in India through Foundation Books of New Delhi. bibliogs., maps.

The original *Cambridge history of India* (1922-1953) (*q.v.*) formulated a chronology for Indian history and described the administrative structures of government. This new series consists of 30 self-contained thematic volumes in 4 series.

1. *The Mughals and their contemporaries.* Pearson, M.N. *The*

....(contd.)

Portuguese in India. 1988. 202p. £30. 05212571312. 2. Stein, B. *Vijayanagara.* 1990. 170p. £30. 0521266939. 3. Beach, M.C. *Mughal and Rajput painting.* 1992. £50. 0521400279. 4. Asher, C.B. *Architecture of Mughal India.* 1992. £55. 5. Richards, J.F. *The Mughal Empire.* 1993. 344p. £30. 052125192. 6. Michell, G. *Architecture and art of Southern India.* 1995. 250p. £50. 0521441102. 7. Michel, G. and Zebrowski, M. *Architecture and art of the Deccan Sultanates.* 1999. 0521563216.

2. *Indian States and the transition to colonialism:* 1. Bayly, C.A. *Indian society and the making of British India.* 1988, 248p. £30. 0521250927. 2. Marshall, P.J. *Bengal: the British bridgehead.* 1988. 222p. £30. 0521253306. 3. Grewal, J.S. *The Sikhs of the Punjab.* 1991. 292p. £30. 0521268842. 4. Gordon, S. *The Marathas 1600-1878.* 1993. 224p. £30. 0521268834. 5. Prakash, O.M. European commercial enterprise in pre-colonial India. 1998. xviii,377p. maps. £35. 0521257581.

3. *The Indian Empire and the beginnings of modern society:* 1. Jones, K.W. *Socio-religious reform movements in British India.* 1990. £30. 0521249864. 2. Bose, S. *Peasant labour and colonial capital: rural Bengal since 1770.* 1993, 248p. £30. 0521266947. 3. Tomlinson, B.R. *The economy of modern India 1860-1970.* 1993. £30. 052136230x. 4. Metcalf, T.R. *Ideologies of the Raj* 1995. £30. 052139547x.

4. *The evolution of contemporary India:* 1. Brass, P.R. *The politics of India since independence.* 2nd ed. 1994. 400p. £40. 05214533623. 2. Forbes, G. *Women in modern India.* 1996. 300p. £30. 0521268125. 3. Bayley, S. *Caste, society and politics in India from the eighteenth century to the modern age.* 0521264340. 4. Ludden, D. *An Agrarian history of South Asia.* 1999. 0521364248.

'We do not expect the *New Cambridge History of India* to be the last world on the subject but an essential voice in a continuing discourse about it' (Johnson, G. The New Cambridge History of India', p.113-116, *South Asian Studies,* The British Library, 1986. *Class No:* 954.0

[7642]

WINK, A. **Al-Hind The Making of the Indo-Islamic world.** Leiden & Kinderhook (NY), E.J. Brill, 5v., 1990-. maps,bibliogs.

1. *Early medieval India and the expansion of Islam 7th-11th centuries.* 1990. viii,396p. Gld.165. US$82.50. ISBN 9004092498. 2. *The Slave Kings and the Islamic conquest of India 11th-13th centuries.* c.1997. xii,472p. 3. *Indo-Muslin society 14th-15th centuries.* c.1994. 4. *Imperial formations 16th-17th centuries.* c.1996. 5. *State and society in the eighteenth century.* c.1998. Encyclopedic work 'which aims to analyze the process of momentous and long-term change which came with the Islamization of the regions which the Arabs called AL-HIND, that is India and large parts of its Indianized hinterland' (*Publisher's brochure*). *Class No:* 954.0

[7643]

WOLPERT, S. **A New history of India.** 5th ed. New York, Oxford USA, 1997. xii,513p. maps, bibliog., index. £33.50. ISBN: 0195100301.

4th ed. 1993.

Narrative history for the student or interested general reader in 26 chapters. *e.g.* The Ecological setting - Aryan Age (1500-1000BC) - Impact of Islam (711-1556) - Indian nationalism (1885-1905) - From Janata Raj to Rajiv Raj - India today. Bibliography (by chapter) p.455-81. Glossary p.483-88. *Class No:* 954.0

Bibliographies

[7644]

SCHOLBERG, H. *and* DIVIEN, E. **Bibliographie des Français dans l'Inde.** Pondicherry, The Historical Society of Pondicherry, 1973. lxiv, 216p. maps, index.

1130 items organized in 32 lettered sections in 4 parts: 1. L'Exploration - 2. Le Commerce - 3. L'Histoire - 4. Les Français aux Indes. Historical writings on the French in India (Eng.) p.xxviii-xxxvi. Bibliographic research for a study of the French in India (Eng.) p.li-lxiv. Author, subject and title index. *Class No:* 954.0(01)

[7645]

SCHOLBERG, H. **Bibliography of Goa and the Portuguese in India.** New Delhi, Promilla & Co., 1982. xix,413p. illus. index. Rs300.

10 sections: 1. General works - 2. Bibliography and other sources - 3 History - 4. Biography - 5. Early historical accounts - 6. The people - 7. Government and politics - 8. Humanities - 9. Journals - 10 Religious life. Includes a supplement of 5 special papers on the sources for Indo-Portuguese history. Entries indicate location of copies in Indian or US academic libraries. *Class No:* 954.0(01)

[7646]

SEN, S.P., *ed*. **Sources of the history of India.** Calcutta, Institute of Historical Studies, 3v., 1978-80.

1. *Karnataka. Andhra Pradesh. Maharashtra. Goa* 2. *Rajasthan. Haryana. Meghalaya. Uttar Pradesh. Jammu and Kashmir.* 3. *Assam. Sikkim. Tamil Nadu.* 'A thorough description and analysis of archaeological, epigraphic, numismatic and written records covering ancient, medieval, and modern periods of regional and national history' (B.K. Gupta and D.S. Kharbas. *India* 1984. Entry 139). *Class No:* 954.0(01)

[7647]

SHARMA, S.R. **A Bibliography of Mughal India (1526-1707AD).** Bombay, Karnatka Publishing House, 1938. ix, 206p. index. Reprinted by Porcupine Press (Philadelphia, 1977).

Survey organized in 12 categories: 1. Original authorities - 2. Official records - 3. Official histories - 4. Royal autobiographies - 5. Non-official histories - 6. Provincial histories - 7. Biographies and memoirs - 8. Gazetteers - 9. Private letter books - 10. Administrative manuals - 11. Literary works - 12. Foreign works. Appendix 1. European travellers and their accounts ... 4. Original sources of Mughal India. *Class No:* 954.0(01)

Encyclopaedias

[7648]

India 2000 Reference encyclopedia. Columbia, MO., South Asia Books, 2v., 1995-99. variously paginated illus., maps, bibliogs.

Vol.1. London, Jaya Books. 1995. Edited by H. Myer. Variously paginated ISBN 1872374085. A. Profile (digest of useful up-to-date information - B. Perceptives (space, time and beyond) - C. National Symbols (flag, anthem etc.) - D. (democratic mixture and caste system) - E. Expression of India (major languages) - F. Religions (major and tribal) - G. Philosophy - H. History - I. Freedom movements - J. Lifestyles - K. Ancient concepts, sciences and systems - L. Coins... N. Archaeology - O. Architecture... Y. Luminaries (outstanding men and women) - Z. Wisdom of India. The encyclopedia was prepared by abridging and consolidating other previously published reference works.

Vol.2. Karnataka, Mermaid Centre and Indmark Publishing, 1999. Rs4,000. 8172090505. A. Physiography - B. Gazetteer... H/L. Northern, Central, Western, Southern and Eastern India - M. India in the world - N/R. India and Asia, Africa, America, Europe and Oceania... Y. Vision 2001... Z.

Vol.3. Forthcoming. *Class No:* 954.0(031)

[7649]

TAYLOR, P.J.O., *ed*. **A Companion to the Indian Mutiny of 1857.** New Delhi, Oxford Univ. Press India, 1996. 450p. illus. (some col.), bibliog., index. £32.50. ISBN: 0195638638.

1500 entries relating to events, incidents, battles, sites, military units, and to leading individuals. A glossary, chronology and an exhaustive bibliography supplement the text. *Class No:* 954.0(031)

Dictionaries

[7650]

DILGEER, H.S. **The Sikh reference book.** Edmonton, Alberta, The Sikh Educational Trust for the Sikh University Centre, Denmark, 1997. 719p. index.

1. Index - 2. Culture - 3. Literature about Sikhism - 4. Sikh polity - 5. Theology - 6. Sikh homeland (places and Gurdwaras) p.117-234 - 7. Dictionary of Sikh biography p.236-652 - 8. Chronology of Sikh history (1469-1996) p.653-719. This 'reference book' is essentially an Historical Dictionary in disguise. *Class No:* 954.0(038)

[7651]

MANSINGH, S. **Historical dictionary of India.** Lanham, Md., Scarecrow Press, 1996. xl,511p. maps, bibliog. £74.10. (*Asian Historical Dictionaries, no.20.*) ISBN: 0810830787.

A-Z entries relating India's significant persons, places, events, government, economy, culture and religion (p.23-453). Glossary p.xiii-xxi. Chronology p.xxiii-xxxiv. Maps p.xxxv-xl. Introduction (geographic setting, historical background) p.1-21. Bibliography (in 7 sub-divided sections) p.449-505. Appendix 1. Chief executives in British India - 2. Heads of State of independent India - 3. Prime Ministers. *Class No:* 954.0(038)

[7652]

MEHRA, P. **A Dictionary of modern Indian history 1707-1947.** Delhi, Oxford Univ. Press, 1985. xv, 823p. maps, bibliogs., index. Rs 250. £25. ISBN: 195615522.

400 compact essays, each concluding with a short bibliography, forming a succinct guide to men and affairs from the reign of Bhadur Shah I (1707-12), last of the Great Mughals, to independence. Glossary p.767-768. Select chronology, p.769-803. Governors-General and Viceroys of India. 1774-1947 p.805-807. 'The standard reference work in its field for many years to come' (*Reference Reviews* v.2, no.3, September 1988, p.163. *Class No:* 954.0(038)

Maps & Atlases

[7653]

IRFAN HABIB. **An Atlas of the Mughal Empire** political and economic maps with detailed notes, bibliography and index. Delhi, Oxford Univ. Press for Centre of Advanced Study in History, Aligarh Muslim University, 1982. 60p. maps, xvii, 102p.

32 political and 32 economic regional maps complemented by Notes (p.1-72) offering references to sources for every place, feature, or piece of information exhibited on the maps. Bibliography chronologically arranged within broad subdivisions p.73-77. 'A landmark in research into the pre-British period' (*Choice*, v.20, no.7, March 1983, p.956). *Class No:* 954.0(084.3)

Chronologies

[7654]

BHATTACHERJE, S.B. **Encyclopaedia of Indian events and dates.** New Delhi, Sterling Publishers Private Ltd., 1986. vi,456p.

A. Events by dates p.1-79. B. Events by years p.82-317. C. Dynasties of India p.319-357 (only relatively important rulers find a place). D. Analytical index p.358-456. Period covered is 4241 BC-AD1985. *Class No:* 954.0(090)

[7655]

BURGESS, J. **The Chronology of Indian history** medieval & modern. Delhi, Cosmo Publications, 1972. vi,483p. index.

Reprint of *The chronology of modern India, for four hundred years from the close of the fifteenth century, A.D. 1494-1894* (Edinburgh, Grant, 1913).

Detailed enumeration of events 1492-1894. *Class No:* 954.0(090)

[7656]

SHARMA, J.S. **India since the advent of the British** a descriptive chronology from 1600 to Oct.2, 1969. New Delhi, Chand, 1970. xxx,817p.

In 6 parts (1: 1600-1895 ... 6: 15 August 1947 to 2nd October 1969, by days, under months and years). Index (p.783-817) 'includes names of places, events, newspapers, some important books, subjects and other related information appearing in the text' (*Introduction*). *Class No:* 954.0(090)

Biographies

[7657]

BALRAJ SAGGAR. **Who's who in the history of the Punjab (1800-1849).** New Delhi, National Book Organisation, 1993. xxii,425p. bibliog., index. ISBN: 8185135606.

614 biographical profiles of personalities with a bearing on this crucial period in modern Indian history. Bibliography p.406-11. *Class No:* 954.0(092)

20th Century

[7658]

The Indian Annual Register: an annual digest of public affairs of India recording the nation's achievements each year in matters political, economic, industrial, educational, social etc. New Delhi, Gian Publishing House, 1990 -. tables, index. ISBN: 8121202132, set.

Reprint set covering 1919 - 47.

Slightly confused volume numbering system with each year being covered by 2v. *1923 v.1 Supplement* is in fact supplement to v.2. with index for v.1 and v.2. and *Supplement*. 1928 v.2. 516p. ISBN 8121202981 includes Chronicle of events, July-December 1928, p.1-8. *Class No:* 954.0"19"

Indian Ocean

[7659]

HALL, R. **Empires of the monsoon** a history of the Indian Ocean. London, HarperCollins, 1996. xxv,575p. illus., maps, bibliog., indexes. (£20..) ISBN: 0021159716.

Narrative history in 55 chapters arranged in 3 chronological parts: 1. A world apart - 2. The cannons of Christendom - 3. An enforced tutelage. Bibliography p.513-25. Commentary *i.e.* chapter notes) p.527-25. General and personal names indexes. A tightly controlled study. *Class No:* 954.026

Himalayan States

[7660]

SINGH, A.K.J. **Himalayan triangle** a historical survey of British India's relations with Tibet, Sikkim and Bhutan 1765-1950. London, The British Library, 1988. xii, 408p. bibliog., maps, index. £35. ISBN: 0712306307.

Well-documented examination of the complex diplomatic history of India's Himalayan frontier. Bibliography p.383-396 includes notes on archival sources in Bhutan, India, Sikkim and China. *Class No:* 954.13

[7661]

SUKHDEV SINGH CHARAK. History and culture of Himalayan states. New Delhi, Light and Life Publications, 1978-.

1-2. *Himachal Pradesh*. 1978-1979. 4-7. *Jamma Kingdom*. 1980-. Projected 15v. series on all facets of the history of Jamma and Kashmir, Himachal Pradash, Assam, Sikkim, Bhutan, and possibly Nepal. *Class No: 954.13*

Nepal

[7662]

RISHIKESH SHAHA. Modern Nepal: a political history 1769-1955. New Delhi. Manohar, 2v., 1990. ISBN: 8185425027, set.

1. *1769-1885*. ix,318p. map. bibliog., index. ISBN 8185425035. Chronology p.293-300. Bibliography p.301-10. 2. *1885-1955*. x,364p. bibliog., index. 8185425043. Chronology p.332-43. Bibliography p.344-53. Running account of political trends and developments in 17 well-documented chapters. Bibliographies include material in Western and Nepali languages. *Class No: 954.135*

Dictionaries

[7663]

HEDRICK, B.C. *and* HEDRICK, A.K. Historical and cultural dictionary of Nepal. Metuchen, New Jersey, Scarecrow Press, 1972. viii,198p. £24.00. (*Historical And Cultural Dictionaries of Asia, no.2.*) ISBN: 0810806495.

Entries, A-Z, on various aspects of Nepal's history, religion, art, administration, literature and society. Bibliography p.181-98. 'A curious combination of tourist-guide material and brief excursuses in more substantial and important subjects (*Library Journal*, v.98,no.5, 1 March 1973, p.728). *Class No: 954.135(038)*

Sri Lanka

[7664]

DE SILVA, C.R. *and* DE SILVA, D. The History of Ceylon (*c*.1500-1658) a historiographical and bibliographical survey, *Ceylon Journal of Historical and Social Studies*, ns. v.3, no.1, January-June 1973, p.52-77.

340 entries, some annotated. "Surveys the historical sources and writings related to the period of Portuguese rule in Sri Lanka' (V. Samaraweera. *Sri Lanka*, 1987. Entry 620). *Class No: 954.87*

[7665]

DE SILVA, K.M. A History of Sri Lanka. London, C. Hurst; Berkeley Univ. of California Press, 1981. xx,603p. illus., maps, bibliog., index. $49.50. ISBN: 0905838505, UK; 0520043200, US.

38 chronological chapters in 6 parts: 1. Ancient Sri Lanka - 2. The decline of the Sinhalese kingdom - 3. Sri Lanka and the Western powers - 4. Under British rule - 5. Sri Lanka in the twentieth century - 6. Independence and after. Sri Lanka's rulers: a chronological list p.565-573. Glossary p.574-6. Bibliography p.577-580. *Class No: 954.87*

Bibliographies

[7666]

DE SILVA, D. *and* DE SILVA, C.R. Sri Lanka since independence a reference guide to the literature. New Delhi, Navrang, 1992. viii,312p. R300 US $20. ISBN: 8170130883.

Classified bibliography of 2400 entries. The introduction which precedes the bibliography analyses the resources available for study in various fields of social science disciplines, evaluates the existing literature and highlights gaps. It also provides a list of Sri Lankan Libraries well-equipped in social science literature. The list of journals appended to the study gives the researcher an idea of the periodicals that publish on Sri Lankan affairs. *Class No: 954.87(01)*

Dictionaries

[7667]

SAMARASINGHE, S.W.R. de A. *and* SAMARASINGHE, V. Historical dictionary of Sri Lanka. Lanham, MD., Scarecrow Press, 1998. xliii,214p. maps, tables, bibliog. £36.60. (*Asian/Oceanian Historical Dictionaries, no.26.*)

Chronology of important events p.xv-xliii. Introduction (geography, population, history, independence) p.1-31. Dictionary (significant places, major events, Tamil War, crucial aspects of economy, culture and social affairs) p.33-138. Bibliography (under 7 subject headings) p.151-214. 2 maps. *Class No: 954.87(038)*

Pakistan

Bibliographies

[7668]

LONG, R.D. The Founding of Pakistan an annotated bibliography. Lanham, Md, Scarecrow Press, 1998. xv,327pp. indexes. £42.75. ISBN: 0810835576.

Select bibliography of 'the most renowned or most characteristic works' in the English language relating to the creation of Pakistan as an independent state arranged in 5 chapters: 1. Reference Works - 2. Political studies - 3. Provincial studies - 4. Mohammad Ali Jinnah - 5. Biographical studies. *Class No: 954.9(01)*

Dictionaries

[7669]

BURKI, S.J. Historical dictionary of Pakistan. Lanham, MD., Scarecrow Press, 1999. liii,403p. map, bibliog. $89.50. (*Asian Historical Dictionaries, no.33.*) ISBN: 0810836343.

Chronology (712-1999) p.xvii-liii. Introduction (arrival of Islam in India, demand for a separate state, history) p.1-29. Dictionary (political parties, historical events, principal personalities, economic plans, diplomatic relations, *etc.*) p.31-360. Bibliography (in 5 thematic sections) p.361-399. 'A very authoritative and readable source' (Choice, v.29, no.2, October 1992). *Class No: 954.9(038)*

Bangladesh

Dictionaries

[7670]

BAXTER, C. *and* RAHMAN, S. Historical dictionary of Bangladesh. 2nd ed. Lanham, MD., Scarecrow Press, 1996. xvii,284p. bibliog. £51.30. (*Historical Dictionaries of Asia, no.2.*) ISBN: 0810831872.

1st ed. 1989.

Introduction (geography, people, economy, history) p.1-26. Dictionary proper has c.500 entries (270 in 1st ed.) relating to leading political and cultural figures, events, places etc (p.27-163). Bibliography arranged under 12 subdivided subject headings (p.195-284). 'Overall a considerable amount of information is condensed into the concise easily-read dictionary entries' (*Reference Reviews*, v.11,no.4, 1997, p.38-39). *Class No: 954.93(038)*

Iran

[7671]

The Cambridge history of Iran. Cambridge, Cambridge Univ. Press, 7v., 1986-1991. illus., diagrs., tables, maps. ISBN: 0521451485, set.

1. *The Land of Iran* edited by W.B. Fisher. 1968. 804p. £85. ISBN 0521069351. 2. *The Median and Archaemenian periods* edited by I. Gershevitch. 1985. £90. 0521200911. 3. *The Seleucid, Parthian and Sasanid periods*, 2pts., edited by E. Yar-Shater. 1983. £80++£85. 0521246938 and 0521246998. 4. *From the Arab invasion to the Saljuqs* edited by R.N. Frye. 1975. 747p. £80. 0521200938. 5. *The Saljuq and Mongol periods* by J.A. Boyle. 1968. 778p. £80. 052106936x. 6. *The Timurid and Sefavid periods* edited by P. Jackson and L. Lockhart. 1986. 1120p. £95. 0521200946. 7. *From Nadir Shah to the Islamic Republic* edited by P. Avery and G.R.G. Hambly. 1989. £85. 0521200954. 8: Bibliography. All aspects of the religious, philosophical, political, economic, scientific and artistic elements in Iranian civilization are studied, with some emphasis on the geographical and ecological factors which have contributed to that civilization's special character. *Class No: 955*

Bibliographies

[7672]

HAMBLY, G.R.G. 'Continuities in the Iranian past since the 7th century C.E.', *Choice*, v.27, no.5, January 1990, p.744-52.

Bibliographical essay which considers *inter alia*, Historical writing; Turks and Mongols; Timurids and Safavids; Social history; and Journals and reference works. *Class No: 955(01)*

Dictionaries

[7673]

LORENTZ, J.H. Historical dictionary of Iran. Lanham, MD, Scarecrow Press, 1995. xxv,325p. maps, bibliog. £44.55. (*Asian Historical Dictionaries, no.16.*) ISBN: 0810829940.

Dictionary (political groups, constitution, organisations and companies, religious movements etc.) p.1-185. Chronology of Iranian History p.187-216. Bibliography (history, politics and government, Perso/Islamic political and social thought etc.) p.217-309. Appendix A. Basic facts - B. Provinces ... D. Text of U.N. Resolution 590 - E. Iranian statesmen 1787-1994. *Class No: 955(038)*

Gazetteers

[7674]
Historical gazetteer of Iran. Adamec, L.W., *ed*. Graz, Akademische Druck-u. Verlagsanstalt, 1976-.
   1. *Teharan and Northwestern Iran*. 1976. xvii, 734p.+200 unnumbered pages of maps. 2. *Meshad and Northeastern Iran*. 1981. xix, 708p.+188p. maps. 3201011592 ... 4. *Zahidan and Southern Iran*. x, 480p.+156p. maps. 3201014281. Each volume is arranged in 5 parts: Geographical and historical dictionary; glossary of geographical, historical and political terms; index of sub-tribes; map section. Based on formerly secret archival material compiled by the General Staff of British India during the 19th and early 20th centuries and updated from contemporary Iranian and western sources. 'Geographers will be pleased to have available the comprehensive map section ... they will equally regret that there is no adequate reference to the sources of these maps and that vital detail such as scale and date is omitted also. It would appear that the map section is a collection of sheets gathered from a variety of sources ... at an approximatel scale of 1:300,000' (*Geographical Journal*, v.144, no.1, March 1978, p.160-161). *Class No: 955(083.86)*

Kurdistan

[7675]
KREYENBROEK, P.G. *and* SPER, S., *eds*. The Kurds a contemporary overview. London, Routledge, 1992. xii,250p. tables, bibliog., index. ISBN: 0415072654.
   10 papers by different hands on the life and recent history of the Kurds in Iraq, Turkey, Iran, the Soviet Union, Syria, and Lebanon, and on Kurdish ethnicity, nationalism, and language. Chapter notes p.219-33. Bibliography p.234-41. *Class No: 955.6*

[7676]
McDOWALL, D. A Modern history of the Kurds. Rev. ed. London, I.B. Tauris, 2000. 504p. maps, index. pbk. £15.95. ISBN: 1860645356.
   1st ed. 1996.
   Arranged in 5 sub-divided Books: 1. Kurds in the age of tribe and empire - 2. Incorporating the Kurds - 3/5. Ethno-nationalism in Iran, Iraq, Turkey. Each chapter ends with a list of the main sources used. 4 maps. 'Arguably the first adequate in-depth study of modern Kurdish history' (*Journal of the Royal Asiatic Society*, v.7, no.1, April 1997, p.139). *etc.* This revised edition outlines regional developments of the last 10 years. *Class No: 955.6*

Byzantium

Handbooks & Manuals

[7677]
MAZAL, O. Handbuch der Byzantinistik. Graz, Akademische Druck-u. Verlagsanstalt, 1989. 279p. bibliog., index. ISBN: 320101432x.
   14 chapters: 1. Gegenstand und Aufgaben der Byzantinistik - 2. Die Geschichte der byzantinischen Studien ... 9. Die Geschichte der byzantinischen literatur ... 11. Die byzantinische Kunst. Liste der Kaiser p.209. Liste der Patriarchen p.210. Bibliography p.21-245. *Class No: 956+949.61(035)*

Dictionaries

[7678]
The Oxford dictionary of Byzantium. Kazhdan, A.P., *ed*. New York, Oxford Univ. Press, 3v., 1991. li,2232p. illus., geneal. tables, maps. $245. £200. ISBN: 0195046528.
   Over 5,500 initialled entries from 128 contributors relating to all aspects of Byzantine history and civilization from the 4th to the 15th century and covering all regions that at any time formed part of the Byzantine Empire or had significant connections with Byzantium. Average length of entries is 200 words although major thematic entries go up to 1,000 words. Most end with a list of bibliographic references. 24 maps. 'For its coverage and authority it will last for many years as the most significant reference item covering the whole vast field of Byzantine studies' (*Reference Reviews*, v.5,no.4, 1991, p.34-5). *Reference Reviews* Best Specialist Reference Work 1991. *Class No: 956+949.61(038)*

Biographies

[7679]
NICOL, D.M. A Biographical dictionary of the Byzantine Empire. London, Seaby, 1991. xxviii,156p. geneal., tables, bibliog., index. £18.50. ISBN: 1852640480.
   Brief biographies of 'most persons of note and influence in the East Roman or Byzantine Empire from the establishment of its capital at Constantinople in AD 330 to its conquest by the Ottoman Turks in 1453'. Chronology p.xiii-xv. Genealogical tables p.xvii-xxvii. References p.149-56. *Class No: 956+949.61(092)*

Turkey

[7680]
SHAW, S.J. *and* SHAW E.K. History of the Ottoman Empire and modern Turkey. Cambridge, Cambridge Univ. Press, 2v., 1977.
   1: *Empire of the Gazis: the rise and decline of the Ottoman Empire*, 1280-1808. xiii, 351p.
   2: *Reform, revolution and republic: the rise of modern Turkey*, V.1 has 2 parts: 1. Rise of the Ottoman Empire, 1280-1566; 2. Decentralisation and traditional reform in response to challenge. Bibliography: 'Ottoman history to 1808', p.302-24 (1. General histories - 2. Bibliographies - 3. General reference works - 4/11. Periods), with brief running commentary. Non-analytical index. V.2 is based on both Ottoman and European sources. 'Will remain an outstanding reference work ... excellent bibliographies at the end of each volume list all major works both in Turkish and English' (M. Güçlü. *Turkey*, 1981, Entry 674). *Class No: 956*

Bibliographies

[7681]
BODURGIL, A. Atatürk and Turkey a bibliography 1919-1938. Washington, Library of Congress, 1974. 74p.
   1338 entries for books and periodicals in Western languages on Kemal Atatürk (1881-1938). *Class No: 956(01)*

[7682]
—BODURGIL, A. Turkey, politics and government a bibliography 1938-1975. Washington, Library of Congress, 1976. vii,176p. indexes.
   2020 entries for books and articles. Sections: Reference sources - Bibliographies ... Relations with the Arab world and the Middle East - The Straights question. Periodical sources p.123-35.
   Class No: 956(01)

Dictionaries

[7683]
HEPER, M. Historical dictionary of Turkey. Metuchen, NJ., Scarecrow Press, 1994. xv,593p. maps, bibliog. £65.25. $72.50. (*European Historical Dictionaries, no.2*.) ISBN: 0810828170.
   Chronology (1261-1992) p.1-49; Rulers of Turkey (1299-1993) p.49-52; Introduction: Turkey: an overview (Geography and climate, Population, History, Economy, Society *etc.*) p.58-78; Dictionary of significant persons, places, and events and of important aspects of Turkish life p.79-320; Bibliography (12 sections) p.321-593. 'Immediately becomes the first stop source for most aspects of medieval and modern Turkish history' (*Reference Reviews*, v.9,no.7, 1995, p.47). *Class No: 956(038)*

Cyprus

[7684]
HILL, G. A History of Cyprus. Cambridge, Cambridge Univ. Press, 4v., 1972.
   1. To the conquest by Richard Lion Heart. xviii, 352p. 2. The Frankish period 1192-1432. xl, 496p. 3. The Frankish period 1432-1571. vi, 497-1198p. 4. The Ottoman period, the British colony. xxxi, 640p. 'With its footnote documentation and bibliographies in several languages, the work constitutes one of the most comprehensive and judicious bibliographical guides to Cyprus studies' (P.M. Kitromilides and M.L. Evriviades. *Cyprus*, 1982. Entry 135). *Class No: 956.43*

[7685]
PANTELI, S. A New history of Cyprus. London and The Hague, East-West Publications, 1984. x, 437p. £12.95. ISBN: 0856921270.
   14 chronological chapters 1. Cyprus through the centuries ... 4. 1914-1925 Cyprus becomes a British crown colony ... 14. Cyprus since 1960. 6 Appendices inc. a chronology, lists of British administrators, Ottoman sultans, Greek monarchs, Orthodox Archbishops of Cyprus. Bibliography p.423-430. Concentrates on 'the unexplored years between 1877 and 1950' (*Preface*). *Class No: 956.43*

Dictionaries

[7686]
PANTELI, S. Historical dictionary of Cyprus. Lanham, MD., Scarecrow Press, 1995. xxxi,223p. map, bibliog. £47.05. (*European Historical Dictionaries, no.6*.) ISBN: 0810829126.
   Chronology p.xiii-xxxi. Introduction (national overview) p.1-14. Dictionary (history, culture, economy, social affairs, political parties, institutions) p.15-147. Bibliography p.149-201. Articles in journals and periodicals p.203-212. Appendix 1. Lusignan rulers of Cyprus. 2. British personnel 1878-1960. Colonial Office Papers Housed at the Public Record Office, Kew Gardens p.219-23. *Class No: 956.43(038)*

Iraq

[7687]

MARR, P. The Modern history of Iraq. Boulder, Colorado, Westview Press; London, Longman, 1985. xviii, 382p. illus., maps, bibliog., index. £39. $49. ISBN: 0865311196, US; 0582782445, UK.

10 chronological and thematic chapters: 1. Legacy of the past ... 2. British mandate 1926-1932 ... 10. The Iran-Iraq war. Notes p.313-344. Bibliography p.343-353. Glossary p.355-359. 'A timely, comprehensive, and much-needed modern history of Iraq' (*Choice*, v.23, no.2, October 1985, p.349). *Class No:* 956.7

[7688]

ROUX, G. Ancient Iraq. 3rd ed. London, Penguin, 1992. xxii,547p. illus., maps, tables, index. £7.99. ISBN: 014012523x.

First published by George Allen & Unwin 1964.

Political, cultural, and socio-economic history of Mesopotamia to the Christian era. 25 chapters (*e.g.* 1. Geographical setting ... 9. Akkadians - 10. Great Kingdom of Ur... 19. Assyrian Empire ... 24. Splendour of Babylon). Bibliography and chapter notes p.433-97. Chronological tables p.500-15. 4 maps. *Class No:* 956.7

Syria

Dictionaries

[7689]

COMMINS, D. Historical dictionary of Syria. Lanham, MD, Scarecrow Press, 1996. xxxvi,299p. maps, bibliog. $49.50. (*Asian Historical Dictionaries, no.22.*) ISBN: 0810831767.

Chronology p.xix-xxxvi. Introduction (physical features, ancient history, Islamic period, modern era) p.1-14. Dictionary p.15-229. Bibliography (in 27 sections) p.235-99. *Class No:* 956.91(038)

Lebanon

[7690]

COBBAN, H. The Making of modern Lebanon. London, Hutchinson, 1985; Boulder, Colorado, Westview Press, 1986. 248p. illus., bibliog. index. (*The Making of the Middle East.*) ISBN: 0091607914, UK; 0813303079, US.

8 chronological chapters, the last 6 of which focus on events since 1920. Bibliography p.237-241. Analytical index. 'Cobban's well researched and clearly written history records with sensitivity and precision the stages of the development of the Lebanese entity, from the coming of the Ottoman Turks to the present' (*Choice*, v.23, no.6, February 1986, p.916). *Class No:* 956.93

Dictionaries

[7691]

AS'AD, Abukhalil. Historical dictionary of Lebanon. Lanham, Md., Scarecrow Press, 1998. xxiv,269p. maps, bibliog. £61.75 (*Asian Historical Dictionaries, no.30.*) ISBN: 0810833956.

Chronology p.xvii-xxi. Introduction (location and physical setting, population, culture and language, ethnicity, religion, historical profile) p.1-13. Dictionary (prominent figures, political parties and groups, political, social, religious institutions etc.) p.15-230. Bibliography (under 14 chronological and form headings) p.235-68. 2 maps 'Plugs an obvious gap ... will be a welcome addition to Middle East collections' (*Reference Reviews*, vol.12,no.7. 1998, p.51-52). *Class No:* 956.93(038)

Israel & Palestine

[7692]

ASALI, K.J., *ed*. Jerusalem in history. Buckhurst Hill, Essex, Scorpion Publishing, 1989. 295p. illus., map, bibliog., index.

9 constributors from 7 countries present an outline history 3000BC - 1987 A.D. 1. Bronze Age - 2. Jerusalem from 1000-63BC - 3. Rome and Byzantium - 4. Early Islamic period - 5. Crusader Jerusalem - 6. Ayyubids and Mamluks - 7. Ottomans - 8. Jerusalem in the 19th century - 9. The transformation of Jerusalem 1917-1987 A.D. Bibliography (by chapter) p.279-91. *Class No:* 956.94

[7693]

GIL, M. A History of Palestine 634-1099. Rev. ed. Cambridge, Cambridge Univ. Press, 1992. xxvi,968p. bibliog., index. ISBN: 0521404371.

First published in Hebrew by Tel Aviv University in 1983.

1. The Conquest - 2. Islam strikes roots - 3. Local population and the Muslims - 4. Economy - 5. Palestine from the beginning of Abbasid rule to the Fatimids - 6. Fatimid conquest - 7. The Christians - 8. Jewish population and its leadership - 9. Karaites and Samaritans - 10. Crusaders' conquest and the fate of Palestinian Jewry. Glossary of Hebrew and Arabic terms p.xxv-xxvi. Chronology p.893-61. Bibliographical index p.862-911. Based on extant sources of the period which are discussed in *Preface* (p.xii-xx). *Class No:* 956.94

[7694]

SACHAR, H.M. A History of Israel.

1. *From the rise of Zionism to our time* Oxford, Basil Blackwell, 1977. xix, 883, xlix p. bibliog., maps, index. 0613117870. 2. *From the aftermath of the Yom Kippur War* New York and Oxford, Oxford Univ. Press, 1987. xv, 319p. bibliog. maps, index. $19.95. £19.50. 0195043863. Extremely well-documented standard history with extensive bibliographies. *Class No:* 956.94

Bibliographies

[7695]

SHERMAN, J., *ed*. The Arab-Israeli conflict 1945-1971 a bibliography. New York, Garland Publishing Inc., 1978. xvii, 419p. illus., maps, index. $63. ISBN: 0824098293.

3694 English-language citations arranged on an annalistic pattern supported by bibliographical and supplementary notes. Author and subject indexes. *Class No:* 956.94(01)

Encyclopaedias

[7696]

An Historical encyclopedia of the Arab-Israeli conflict. Reich, B., *ed*. Westport, Conn., Greenwood Pres, 1996. 696p. maps, bibliogs. $99.50. ISBN: 031327374x.

Covers the important political, military and diplomatic events, places, people, groups, agreements, treaties, and issues that have marked the conflict since November 1947. *Class No:* 956.94(031)

Dictionaries

[7697]

NAZZALL, N.Y. *and* NAZZALL, L.A. Historical dictionary of Palestine. Lanham, MD., Scarecrow Press, 1997. xc,304p. maps, bibliog. (*Asian/Oceanian Historical Dictionaries, no.23.*) ISBN: 0810832399.

Chronology (very detailed 1980-) p.xix-xc. Introduction (West Bank and Gaza Strip, Israeli occupation, Palestinian - Jordanian relations, peace process, Palestinian National Authority, Oslo Two Agreement) p.1-20. Dictionary (significant persons, places, political/religious parties and movements) p.21-210. Bibliography p.211-90. Appendix A. Delcaration of Palestinian independence. B. Declaration of Principles. *Class No:* 956.94(038)

[7698]

REICH, B. Historical dictionary of Israel. Lanham, MD. Scarecrow Press, 1992. lxv,353p. tables, bibliog. (*Asian Historical Dictionaries, no.8.*) ISBN: 081082535x.

Chronology p.xi-xxix. Tables (presidents, prime ministers, ministers of foreign affairs, defense, finance, chiefs of staff) p.xxxi-xxxviii. Declaration of the Establishment of the State of Israel p.xxxix-xlii. Introduction (government, politics, geography, history) p.xliii-lxv. Dictionary (persons, places, events, universities, political parties etc.) p.1-284. Bibliography (10 thematic sub-divisions) p.287-351. *Class No:* 956.94(038)

Maps & Atlases

[7699]

CORRESPONDENTS OF THE New York Times. Israel: The historical atlas the story of Israel from ancient times to the modern nation. Gwertzman, B., *and others, eds*. New York, Macmillan USA, 1997. 208p. illus. (mostly col.), col.maps, index. $45. Can$63. ISBN: 0028619870.

8 chapters. (*e.g.* 1. The Ancient Land - 2. Struggle for statehood - 3. Young nation ... 6. The wars in Lebanon and at home ... 8. Hopes and fears). Nation builders, leaders who shaped Israel p.140-91. Israel Almanac (presidents, prime ministers, foreign and defense ministers etc.) p.192-95. Examines the political, military and social evolution of Israel on its 50th anniversary. *Class No:* 956.94(084.3)

[7700]

GILBERT, M. Jerusalem illustrated history atlas. Jerusalem, Steimatzky's Agency Ltd; London, the author with the Board of Deputies of British Jews; New York, Macmillan Publishing Inc., 1977(?). 128p. maps. illus., bibliog.

66 maps trace the city's history from Biblical times to the present day with special emphasis on developments over the last 150 years. Bibliography p.124-128. *Class No:* 956.94(084.3)

[7701]
GILBERT, M. The Routledge atlas of the Arab-Israeli conflict. 6th ed. London, Routledge, 1993. 152p. £25. ISBN: 041513630x.

First published as *The Arab-Israeli conflict: its history in maps* by Weidenfeld & Nicolson 1974.

146 clear maps with descriptive insets. In various periods: Prelude to conflict - The Jewish national home [1917-47] - The conflict intensifies - The State of Israel [1948-67] - After the Six Day War - The Yom Kippur War - Camp David and after. Covers before the Christian period to the 1990s. *Class No:* 956.94(084.3)

Jordan

[7702]
MA'AN ABU NOWAR. The History of the Hashemite Kingdom of Jordan. Vol.1 The creation and development of Transjordan: 1920-1929. Oxford, Ithaca Press for The Middle East Centre of St. Anthony's College Oxford, 1989. xiii,313p. illus., maps, bibliog., index. £24. (*St. Anthony's Middle East Monographs, no.21.*) ISBN: 0863721192.

Social, economic, political and legal history of Jordan in 9 chapters *e.g.* 2. Creation of Trans-Jordan - 3. From statelessness to mandate state ... 7. Independence under mandate. Bibliography p.252-9. *Class No:* 956.95

Dictionaries

[7703]
GUBSER, P. Historical dictionary of the Hashemite Kingdom of Jordan. Metuchen, N.J., Scarecrow Press, 1991. xxi,140p. maps, bibliog. £16.90. (*Asian Historical Dictionaries, no.4.*) ISBN: 0810824493.

Chronology p.xiii-xxi. Introduction (overview, geography and climate, people, history) p.1-14. Dictionary p.15-87. Bibliography p.89-140. 2 maps. *Class No:* 956.95(038)

Russia in Asia

[7704]
CHRISTIAN, D. A History of Russia, Central Asia and Mongolia. Oxford, Blackwell, 2v., 1999-. (*The Blackwell History of the World.*)

V.1: *Inner Eurasia from prehistory to the Mongol Empire.* 1998. xxiii,472p. illus., maps, bibliog., index. ISBN 0631183213. Inner Eurasia is defined as most of the former Soviet Union and Russia's huge territories in Siberia; Russia's former empire in Central Asia; China's Central Asian empire; and Mongolia, both the parts within China and those within the Mongolian People's Republic. This volume charts developments from the Old Stone Age, through changes under such peoples as the Scythians, the Huns and the Turks, to the emergence of an identifiable 'Rus' - the society from which modern Russian and Ukraine have evolved. *Class No:* 957

[7705]
STEPHAN, J.J. The Russian Far East a history. Stanford Univ. Press, 1994. Available in UK from Cambridge Univ. Press. xxiii,481p. illus., maps, bibliog., index. $49.50. £35. ISBN: 0804723117.

28 chapters (*e.g.* 1. Geography and prehistory ... 14. Civil War ... 16. Far Eastern Republic ... 23. Kolyma ... 28. Frontier ethos) with 11 appendices (A. Administrative chronology, p.305-309; D. Biographical notes, p.312-41; K. Glossary, p.349-54). Chapter notes p.355-414. Bibliography p.415-60. 10 maps. 'Incorporating a breathtaking range of source materials in Russian, Japanese, and Chinese as well as German, French, and English - but no archives - Stephan has wrought a tour de force' (*Russian History/Histoire Russe*, v.21,no.2, Summer 1994, p.232-34). *Class No:* 957

Siberia

[7706]
FORSYTH, J. A History of the peoples of Siberia Russia's North Asian colony 1581-1990. Cambridge, Cambridge Univ. Press, 1992. xx,455p. illus., maps, bibliog., index. ISBN: 0521403111.

Ethnohistory narrating and interpreting the gradual conquest and exploitation of Siberia and tracing the history of the Buryat Mongols, Yakuts, Tatars, Samoyeds, Tunguses, Chukchi, and other Siberian tribes. 17 Chronological chapters *e.g.* 1. Siberia discovered ... 5. Russia's North Asian colony ... 7. Expansion in the North Pacific ... 12. Native peoples ... 15. Soviet Siberia after 1941. 17. Siberia in the 1980s. *Class No:* 957.1

[7707]
WOOD, A., *ed*. The History of Siberia from Russian conquest to Revolution. London, Routledge, 1991. xiv,192p. £35. ISBN: 0415058732.

9 essays by separate hands *e.g.* 1. Siberia's role in Russian history ... 5. The Siberian native peoples before and after the Russian conquest - 6. Tsarist Russia in colonial America ... 9. Siberia in revolution and civil war. Glossary p.xi-xiv. No bibliography but extensive chapter notes and references. *Class No:* 957.1

Kazakhstan

[7708]
OLCOTT, M.B. The Kazakhs. Stanford, Calif., Hoover Institution Press, 1987. xxv,341p. maps, tables, bibliog., index. £25.75. (*Studies of Nationalities in the USSR.*) ISBN: 0817983813.

Historical narrative of The Kazakh Soviet Socialist Republic (now Kazakhstan) from the 15th century but highlighting contemporary political and economic problems. 11 chapters arranged in 3 parts: 1. Rise and fall of the Kazakh Khanate - 2. Kazakhs in Imperial Russia - 3. Revolutionary and Soviet Kazakhstan. 12 Appendices. Glossary p.277-82. Chapter notes p.283-308. Bibliography (inc. Russian language sources) p.309-34. *Class No:* 957.4

Uzbekistan

[7709]
ALLWORTH, E.A. The Modern Uzbeks from the fourteenth century to the present: a cultural history. Stanford, Calif., Hoover Institution Press, 1990. xiv,410p. illus., map, geneal., table, bibliog., index. (*Studies Of Nationalities In The USSR.*) ISBN: 0817987312.

18 chapters in 2 main divisions: 1. Bases of Uzbek group identity - 2. Conflict between old and new modernity (7. History ... 10. Politics - 11. Homeland ... 14. Genealogy). Chapter notes p.331-74. Bibliography p.375-94. Analytical index. Allworth is Professor of Turko-Soviet Studies in Columbia University. *Class No:* 957.51

[7710]
BURTON, A. The Bukharans a dynastic, diplomatic and commercial history 1550-1702. Richmond, Surrey, Curzon, 1997. xx,16p. pl., 664p. geneal tables, illus., maps, bibliog., index. ISBN: 0700704175.

15 chapters in 2 sections: History and Trade. Glossary p.xii-xvii. Abbreviations and tables of rulers p.xviii. Genealogical tables p.544-74. Bibliography (p.575-615) includes material in western and oriental languages. *Class No:* 957.51

[7711]
CRITCHLOW, J. Nationalism in Uzbekistan a Soviet Republic's road to sovereignty. Boulder, Colo., Westview Press, 1991. xviii,231p. map, tables, bibliog., index. pbk. ISBN: 0813384036.

11 well-documented chapters in 3 sections: 1. Rise of Uzbek nationalism - 2. Uzbek nationalism today - 3. Problems of sovereignty. Bibliography p.215-8. Analytical index. Critchlow is a fellow at the Russian Research Center, Harvard University. *Class No:* 957.51

Afghanistan

Dictionaries

[7712]
ADAMEC, L.W. Historical dictionary of Afghanistan. 2nd ed. Lanham, Md., Scarecrow Press, 1997. xiii,499p. map, bibliog. £55.10. (*Asian/Oceanian Historical Dictionaries, no 5.*) ISBN: 0810833123.

1st ed. 1991.

Introduction (historical summary) p.1-5. Dictionary (people, and events, geographical locations, religious and political groups, newspapers, wars and battles, educational institutions etc.) p.7-329. Chronology (2000BC-1987) p.331-428. Bibliography (in 7 sub-divided thematic sections) p.429-99. *Class No:* 958.1(038)

Myanmar

[7713]
TAYLOR, R.H. The State in Burma. London, C. Hurst; Honolulu, Hawaii Univ. Press, 1987. xvi,395p. maps, tables, bibliog., index. $32. ISBN: 1850650284.

The nature of the Burmese state at five different periods: 1. The pre-colonial state - 2. Rationalization of the state 1825-1942 - 3. Politics 1886 to 1942 - 4. Displacement of the state 1942 to 1962 - 5. Reasserting the state 1962 to 1987. Glossary p.xii-xiv. Bibliography p.373-86. 'Will become the unquestioned standard history of nineteenth and twentieth century Burmese history' (*Annual Bulletin of Historical Literature*, v.74, 1990, p.181). *Class No:* 959.1

Dictionaries

[7714]
BEČKA, J. Historical dictionary of Myanmar. Metuchen, NJ., Scarecrow Press, 1995. xxii,328p. map, bibliog. £47.50. (*Asian Historical Dictionaries, no.15.*) ISBN: 0810828405.

Guide to former and current names p.ix-x. Chronology p.xiv-xxi. Dictionary p.9-221. Bibliography in 8 sub-divided categories: General; Culture; Economy; History; Law and Constitution; Politics; Science; Society *etc.* First rate summary of individuals, movements, locations, prominent in Burmese history. *Class No:* 959.1(038)

Thailand

[7715]

TERWIEL, B.J. **A History of modern Thailand.** St. Lucia, Univ. of Queensland Press, 1983. xiv,379p. maps, bibliog., index. $29.95. (*History of Southeast Asia.*) ISBN: 0702218928.

10 chronological chapters. Glossary p.350-353. Bibliography p.354-369. Analytical index. 'A good contemporary introduction' (*Choice*, v.21,no.10, June 1984, p.1520). *Class No: 959.3*

[7716]

WYATT, D.K. **Thailand a short history.** New Haven, Connecticut, Yale Univ. Press 1983. xviii, 351p. illus., maps, bibliog., index. $35. ISBN: 0300030541.

10 chapters: 1. Beginnings of Tai history - 2. The Tai and the Classical Empires AD1000-1200 - 3. A Tai century 1200-1351 - 4. Ayudhya and its neighbors 1351-1569 - 5. The Empire of Ayudhya 1569-1767 - 6. The early Bangkok Empire 1767-1851 - 7. Mongkut and Chulalongkorn 1851-1910 - 8. Rise of elite nationalism 1910-1932 - 9. The military ascendant 1932-1957 - 10. Development and revolution 1957-1982. Appendix A. Kings of Sukhothai - B. Kings of Lan Na - C. Kings of Ayudhya, Thonburi and Bangkok - D. Prime Ministers of Thailand. Chapter notes p.315-19. Bibliography p.321-32. Analytical index. 'The discursive bibliography is the best available introduction to the historiography of Thailand in English and some other Western languages, and includes a guide to primary sources' (M. Watts. *Thailand*, 1986. Entry 229). *Class No: 959.3*

Dictionaries

[7717]

WIN, M.K. *and* SMITH, H.E. **Historical dictionary of Thailand.** Lanham, Md., Scarecrow Press, 1995. xlviii,297p. maps, bibliog. £44.90. (*Asian Historical Dictionaries, no.18.*) ISBN: 0810830647.

Dictionary encompassing history and culture, economy and society, politics and religion, and leading personalities, p.1-196. Bibliography in 7 sub-divided sections p.197-282. 11 Appendices. Chronology p.xix-xl. 2 maps. *Class No: 959.3(038)*

Malaysia

[7718]

ANDAYA, B.W. *and* ANDAYA, L.Y. **A History of Malaysia.** London, The Macmillan Press; New York, St. Martin's Press, 1982. xx,350p. maps,bibliog., index. £18.00. $30.00. (*Macmillan's Asian Histories.*) ISBN: 0333276728, UK; 0213381204, US.

Contents: Introduction: Environment and peoples - 1. Heritage of the past - 2. Melaka and its heirs - 3. Demise of the Malay entrepot state 1699-1819 - 4. A new world is created 1819-74 - 5. The making of British Malaya 1874-1919 - 6. The functioning of colonial society 1919-57 - 7. The forging of a nation 1957-80 - Conclusion: some themes in Malaysian history. Notes and further readings p.305-329. Glossary p.330-336. Analytical index. 'Beyond question the best general history of Malaysia in print' (*Choice*, v.20,nol.7, March 1983, p.1042). *Class No: 959.5*

Bibliographies

[7719]

HEUSSLER, R. **British Malaya.** a bibliographical and biographical compendium. New York, Garland Publishing Inc., 1981. xvii, 193p. $40. (*Themes in European Expansion.*) ISBN: 0824093690.

Part 1. Bibliographies (in 8 sections): 1. Bibliographies and directories - 2. History and social science - 3. British policy and administration - 4. Biography and autobiography - 5. Malay studies - 6. Immigrant peoples - 7. War, insurrection and terrorism - 8. Miscellaneous. Pt. 2. Biographies *i.e.* brief career details of family background and education of the personnel of the Malayan Civil Service from the assumption of Colonial Office responsibility in 1867 to the Japanese conquest in 1942. Author and subject indexes. 'An indispensable reference work for the historical collections of Southeast Asia' (*English Historical Review*, v.99, no.392, July 1984, p.657). *Class No: 959.5(01)*

Dictionaries

[7720]

KAUR, A. **Historical dictionary of Malaysia.** Metuchen, N.J., Scarecrow Press, 1993. xxvi,300p. maps, tables, bibliog. £37.50. (*Asian Historical Dictionaries, no.13.*) ISBN: 0810826291.

Political parties, historical events, legislative measures, leading political figures, economic affairs *etc.* in single A-Z sequence. Chronology p.xv-xxi. Dictionary p.23-157. Bibliography (form and subject divisions) p.158-262. Appendix 1-2. Rulers and Prime Ministers. Glossary p.299-300. 5 maps. *Class No: 959.5(038)*

Singapore

[7721]

CHEW, E.T. *and* LEE, E., *eds.* **A History of Singapore.** Singapore Oxford Univ. Press, 1991. xx,442p. illus., maps, tables, bibliog index. £27; $59. ISBN: 0195889177.

Issued under the auspices of the Southeast Asian Studies Program Institute of Southest Asian Studies, Singapore. It virtually supersede C.M. Turnbull's *A History of Singapore 1829-1975.* (Kuala Lumpur OUP., 2nd ed. 1977).

Cooperative history. 18 well-documented chapters arranged in sections: 1. Geography and early history - 2. Polity and econom under British rule to 1942 - 3. Under Japanese rule - 4. Transition t independence - 5. Securing of independence - 6. Social transformatio - 7. Foreign policy and domestic issues. Bibliography p.401-27. ' significant addition to Singapore's historiography' (*Journal Southeast Asian Studies*, v.23, no.1, March 1992, p.203-5). *Class No: 959.513*

Dictionaries

[7722]

MULLINER, K. *and* MULLINER, L.T. **Historical dictionary (Singapore.** Metuchen, N.J., Scarecrow Press, 1991. xxxii,251p maps, bibliog., index. (*Asian Historical Dictionaries, no.7.*) ISBN 081082504x.

Chronology p.xxi-xxxii. Overview (*i.e.* Geography - The People Economy - History) p.1-21. Dictionary (persons, localities, event ideologies *etc.*) p.23-164. Appendices (Heads of Governmen Cabinets, General Elections, Population, Distribution of Chines p.165-77. Bibliography p.179-238. 4 maps. *Class No: 959.513(038)*

Indo-China

[7723]

Major political events in Indo-China 1945-1990. New York an Oxford, Facts on File, 1991. xxvi,230p. maps, bibliog., index £13.95. ISBN: 0816023085.

Narrative chronology of major political, military, and economi events in Vietnam, Cambodia, and Laos. Historical perspective i Introduction (p.ix-xxvi). Biographies p.167-85. Glossary p.212-213 Bibliography p.214-17. 7 Maps. 28 Appendices. Analytical index. *Class No: 959.6/959.8*

Cambodia

[7724]

CHANDLER, D.P. **A History of Cambodia.** 2nd ed. Boulder Colorado, Westview Press, 1992. xvi, 237p. illus., map, bibliog index. £31.25. $35. ISBN: 0813309263.

First published 1983.

10 chronological chapters *e.g.* 2. The beginnings of Cambodia history - 3. Kingship and society at Angkor ... 8. Early stages of th French protectorate ... 10. Roads to independence and revolution. note on the names 'Cambodia' and 'Kampuchea' p.xv-xvi. Chapte notes p.197-218. Bibliographical essay p.219-222. Analytical inde 'The first scholarly general history of the country and its people t appear for more than half a century' (*Choice*, v.21, no.5, Januar 1984, p.748). *Class No: 959.6*

[7725]

CHANDLER, D.P. **The Tragedy of Cambodian history** politics, wa and revolution since 1945. New Haven, Yale Univ. Press, 1991 xiii,306p. illus., maps, bibliog., index. ISBN: 0300049196.

Sequel to *A History of Cambodia* (2nd ed. 1992) (*q.v.*).

8 chronological chapters cover the period 1945-79. Chapter note p.319-80. Bibliography p.381-7. 3 maps. Some overlap for 1945-5 with *A History of Cambodia* because of newly opened archival source 'A major contribution to Cambodian studies' (*Choice*, v.29, no.11-1 July-August 1992, p.1734). *Class No: 959.6*

Vietnam

Dictionaries

[7726]

DUICKER, W.J. **Historical dictionary of Vietnam.** 2nd ed. Lanham MD, Scarecrow Press, 1998. 512p. maps, tables, bibliog. £64.60 (*Asian/Oceanian Historical Dictionaries, no.27.*) ISBN: 0810821648. 1st ed. 1989.

Introduction (recent history) p.109. Dictionary (history partie economy, society, culture, foreign relations, prominent leaders) p.1 282. Bibliography (by form and topic categories) p.283-328. Append 1. Brief history of Vietnam - 2. Chronology of Vietnam history (p.33 345). Tables p.347-51. 4 maps. *Class No: 959.7(038)*

Vietnam War

[7727]

DAVIDSON, P.B. Vietnam at war: the history 1946-1975. Novato, California, Presidio Press; London, Sidgwick & Jackson, 1988. cxii, 838p. illus., maps, bibliog., index. $27.50. £16.95. ISBN: 0283997125, UK; 0891413065, US.

27 well-documented chapters: 2. The French campaign 1946-47 ... 11. Dien Bien Phu: a critique ... 18. The Tet offensive ... 26. Defeat - 27. Why we lost the war. Glossary p.795-818. Bibliography p.819-27. Analytical index. 'This fascinating book is the finest military history of the Vietnam War now available' (*Choice*, v.26 no.1 September 1988, p.217). *Class No: 959.70*

[7728]

SMITH, R.B. An International history of the Vietnam war. London, Macmillan, 4v., 1983-.

1. *Revolution versus containment, 1955-61.* 1983. xiii, 301p. £38. 0333242467. 2. *The struggle for South-East Asia, 1961-65.* 1985. xii, 492p. £38. 0333339576. 3. *The making of a limited war, 1965-66* 1991. xiv,490p. £38. 033339584. V.2 has 19 chapters organized in 5 chronological sections with a bibliography, notes, and index. The author is Reader in the History of South-East Asia, School of Oriental and African studies, University of London. 'Examples of modern historical writing at its best and inspire the confident expectation that the five volume work, when complete, will constitute a standard and indispensable historical record of the Vietnam War' (*International Affairs*, v.67,no.4, October 1991, p.803).

Forthcoming volumes: 4. *The Crippled giant 1967-70;* 5. *The Dénouement* 1970-75. *Class No: 959.70*

[7729]

STANTON, S.L. Vietnam order of battle. Washington, US News Books, 1981. xvii, 396p. illus., maps, tables, index. ISBN: 0891937005.

Brief but authoritative war accounts of all major units involved. 34 chapters deployed in 9 sections: 1. US Army organizations in Vietnam - 2. Major commands - 3. Divisions and separate infantry brigades - 4. Combat units - 5. Combat support units - 6. Service units - 7. Special warfare units - 8. Other US services - 9. Allies. 6 Appendices including US Army Medal of Honor recipients; Sources p.387-91; and Army badges and insignia in Vietnam. 31p. col. plates. *Class No: 959.70*

Micromaterials

[7730]

The History of the Vietnam War. Godstone, Surrey, UMI, 9 units, 1989 - 1991. Microfiche.

1. *Grand Strategy and general assessment of the Vietnam War.* 1989. 1,132 fiche (75,000p. documentary material). $3,415.00. In 3 major sections: General materials - Chronological materials - Insurgency warfare. Included is the US Department of Defense *United States - Vietnam relations 1945 - 1967,* better known as the 'Pentagon Papers'.

2. *General history of the Vietnam War.* 1989. 1,034 fiche. $3,715.00. Chronicles day-to-day routine military activity.

3. *Topical history of the Vietnam War.* 1989 1,500 fiche. $3,450.00. 15 chronologically arranged sections *e.g.* 1. Allied war participants - 2. Anti-war activity ... 4. Legal and legislative ... 14. War atrocities.

4. *Political settlement efforts.* 1990. 14 sections *e.g.* 3 - 12. Political settlement - 13. Ceasefire period - 14. Postwar.

5. *The National Liberation Front (Viet Cong).* 1990. 11 sections: 1. General studies . . . 7. Military activities - 8. Political struggle ... 11. Documentation.

6. *The Democratic Republic of Vietnam (North Vietnam).* 1990. 10 sections: 2. Government and politics/Communist Party ... 9. Communications and motivation.

7. *Republic of Vietnam (South Vietnam).*1991 Government and society 1956 - 1975 including a historical file with French colonial materials in 5 sections: 1. General - 2. History - 3. Chronological - 4. Education/intellectual - 5. Economic.

8. *Indochina (Cambodia and Laos)* 1991. 4 sections: 1. War in Cambodia - 2. War in Laos - 3. Ho Chi Min trail - 4. Indochinese Communist relations.

9. *The Asian Region during the Vietnam War.* 1991.

From the Indochina Archives at the Univ. of California, Berkeley. Includes 15,500 books, pamphlets and monographs; 6,000 newspaper and periodical articles. *Class No: 959.70(003.5)*

Bibliographies

[7731]

BURNS, R.D. *and* LEITENBERG, M. The Wars in Vietnam, Cambodia and Laos, 1945-1982: a bibliographic guide. Santa Barbara, California and Oxford, ABC-Clio Information Services, 1984. xxxii, 290p. maps, tables. (*War/Peace Bibliography Series*.) ISBN: 0874363101.

6200 entries in 9 chapters: 1. General reference aids - 2. Southeast Asia - 3. Vietnam: from the first to the third Indochina wars - 4.

....(contd.)

United States and the politics of intervention - 5. Congress, international law and negotiation - 6. Strategy, tactics and support efforts - 7. Combat operations - 8. The costs of war - 9. The war at home. Chronology p.xxix-xxxii. Glossary p.265-267. 'The most complete general bibliography on this topic currently available' (*Choice*, v.21, no.10, June 1984, p.1438). *Class No: 959.70(01)*

[7732]

PEAKE, L.A. The United States in the Vietnam War 1954-1975: a selected, annotated bibliography. New York, Garland Publishing Inc., 1986. xx, 406p. index. $49. (*Wars of the United States*.) ISBN: 0824089464.

1549 briefly annotated entries (some evaluative) grouped into 10 broad categories each divided into more specific topics: 1. General reference - 2. Southeast Asia - 3. Vietnam - 4. Vietnam and the US government - 5. The war - 6. American military experience in Vietnam - 7. The media war - 8. Literature, film, music and art - 9. Domestic impact - 10. Consequences. Chronology p.345-364. List of principal characters p.365-366. Glossary p.367-375. Intended for a broad audience: general readers, military buffs, collectors of militaria *etc*. *Class No: 959.70(01)*

[7733]

RUSCIO, A. La Première guerre d'Indochine (1945-1954). Bibliographie. Paris, Éditions L'Harmaltan, 1987. 286p. indexes. ISBN: 2858028311.

2356 unannotated entries relating to French, English, Vietnamese, Russian, Chinese and Japanese material. *Class No: 959.70(01)*

[7734]

SUGNET, C.L., *and others*. Vietnam War bibliography selected from Cornell University's John M. Echols Collection of Southeast Asia. Lexington, Massachusetts, D.C. Heath & Co., 1983. xiii,572p. $45.00. ISBN: 066906680x.

3 sections: 1. 3000 entries covering US involvement in Vietnam from the mid-1940s to 1975 listed alphabetically by title - 2. Name, subject and alternative title index p.461-563 - 3. Acronyms and cross-references p.565-572. The Echols Collection (1953-) is a national resource for Southeast Asian studies. 'The most comprehensive annotated guide to the literature of the vietnam War currently available' (*Choice*, v.21,no.6, February 1984, p.807-808). *Class No: 959.70(01)*

Encyclopaedias

[7735]

Encyclopedia of the Vietnam War a political, social and military history. Tucker, S.C., *ed*. Santa Barbara, Calif., and Oxford, ABC-Clio, 3v., 1998. lii,1196p. illus., maps, tables, bibliog., index. $275. £175. ISBN: 0874369835, set.

138 contributors. 980 cross-referenced entries relating to all aspects of the French and US. involvement in the Vietnam wars 1945-1954 and 1954-1975 including biographies of the leading personnel, orders of battle, weapons, strategy, domestic politics, and reviews of relevant drama, music, literature and films. All entries end with citations of further readings. V.3 includes 200 primary documents. Introduction: an overview of Vietnamese history (v.1: p.xxv-xxvii), 22 maps (v.1: p.xxxi-lii). Glossary (v.2: p.873-78). Bibliography (v.2: p.835-44). Chronology (v.2: p.845-71). Analytical index (v.3: p.1097-1196). 'A central resource for information and analysis' (*Library Journal*, v.123, no.20, December 1998, p.88+90). *Class No: 959.70(031)*

[7736]

KUTLER, S.I., *ed*. Encyclopedia of the Vietnam War. New York, Charles Scribners Sons, 1996. xxxiv,711p. illus., maps, bibliog., index. £86.50. ISBN: 0132769328.

54 contributors. 564 cross-referenced signed articles (50 to 5,000 words in length) on the people, places, military actions, policy, strategy and tactics, weapons, domestic politics, and the wider setting of the Vietnam War. Includes 10 major interpretative essays (*e.g.* Colonisation ... The Media and the War ... Prelude to US combat intervention). Chronology p.xxi-xxxii. Bibliographic guide (in 12 thematic sections) p.649-54. Paris Peace Accords p.657-78. Vietnam War Medal of Honor recipients p.679-83. 14 maps. 'An outstanding single-volume handbook on the history and personalities of the conflict' (*Library Journal*. v.122, no.1, January 1997, p.86). *Class No: 959.70(031)*

Dictionaries

[7737]

OLSON, J.S. Dictionary of the Vietnam War. Westport, Connecticut, Greenwood Press, 1988. viii, 584p. £53.25. $65. ISBN: 0313249431.

Brief descriptive entries on the personalities, legislation, military operations relating to US participation in the Vietnam War. Appendix D. Select bibliography p.525-46 - E. Chronology 1945-1975 p.547-60 - F. Maps p.561. Analytical index. *Class No: 959.70(038)*

Almanacs

[7738]

SUMMERS, H.G. **Vietnam War almanac.** New York and Oxford, Facts On File Publications, 1985. x, 414p. illus., maps, bibliog., index. £16.94. $24.95. ISBN: 081601017x.

3 pts: 1. The setting (introductory history from ancient times to 1959) - 2. Chronology of events in Vietnam and the United States - 3. The Vietnam War A-Z (500 entries relating to people, battles, weapons, controversial issues etc., some with cross-references and suggestions for further reading). Bibliography p.367-382. 21 maps. 'A thorough guide to the war' (*Reference Reviews*, v.2, no.3, September 1988, p.163). *Class No:* 959.70(059)

Maps & Atlases

[7739]

SUMMERS, H.G. **Historical atlas of the Vietnam War.** Boston, Houghton, 1996. 224p. illus., col. maps, index. $39.95. ISBN: 0395722232.

100x 4 colour-maps trace the geography, military strategy and tactics, and diplomatic history of the Vietnam conflict. *Class No:* 959.70(084.3)

Laos

[7740]

STUART-FOX, M. **A History of Laos.** Cambridge Univ. Press, 1997. xiii,253p. maps., bibliog., index. ISBN: 0521592356.

Narrative history, with strong emphasis on the modern period, in 6 chapters: 1. Kingdom of Lan Xang- 2. French Laos 1893-1945 - 3. Independence and unity 1945-1957 - 4. Neutrality subverted 1958-1964 - 5. War and revolution 1964-1975 - 6. The Lao Peoples Democratic Republic. Chronology p.x-xiii. Chapter notes p.209-31. Bibliography p.232-44. *Class No:* 959.8

Dictionaries

[7741]

STUART-FOX, M. *and* KOOYMAN, M. **Historical dictionary of Laos.** Metuchen, NJ., Scarecrow Press, 1992. xlix,258p. maps, tables, bibliog. £26.25. (*Asian Historical Dictionaries, no.6.*) ISBN: 0810824981.

Chronology p.xxv-xliv. Dictionary p.1-169. Bibliography (Historiographical introduction and 7 heavily subdivided sections: General; History; Politics and Government; Economy; Society; Culture; Newspapers/journals) p.170-239. 22 appendices. 9 maps. *Class No:* 959.8(038)

Africa

[7742]

African history on file. New York, Facts On File, 1994. 266p. maps, loose-leaf. $155. ISBN: 0816029105.

1000+ maps, timelines, diagrams and charts providing African history overview in 10 chronological and regional chapters: 1. Prehistory - 2. Nile kingdoms - 3/7. North, West, East, Central, and Southern Africa - 8. Exploration and colonialism - 9. Trade routes - 10. 20th century. Extensive chronology also included. *Class No:* 96

[7743]

The Cambridge history of Africa. Oliver, R. *and* Fage, J.D., *eds*. Cambridge Univ. Press. 8v., 1975-86. £619. set. ISBN: 0521334608, set.

1. Clark, J.D. *From the earliest times to c.500BC.* 1982. 1173p. £129.95. 052122215x. 2. Fage, J.D. *c.500BC to AD1050.* 1979. 858p. £119.95. 0521215927. 3. Oliver, R. *c.1050-c.1600.* 1977. 816p. £119.95. 0521209811. 4. Gray, R. *c.1600-c.1790.* 1975. 752p. £105. 0521204135. 5. Flint, J.F. *c.1790-c.1870.* 1977. £99.95. 0521207010. 6. Oliver, R. and Sanderson, G.N. *c.1870-1905.* 1985. 956p. £109.95. 0521228034. 7. Roberts, A. *c.1905-c.1940.* 1986. 1087p. £105. 0521225051. 8. Crowder, M. *c.1940-c.1975.* 1984. 1027p. £109.95. 0521224098.

History of the whole continent from prehistoric to post-colonial times. The approach is regional and the contributors offer a broad survey of the given area for the whole period covered by the volume. Each chapter includes a bibliography, bibliographical essay and maps when relevant. *Class No:* 96

[7744]

PHILLIPSON, D., *ed*. **The Peoples of Africa.** Oxford, Basil Blackwell. 1993-.

Beach, D. *The Shona.* 1993. 256p. 0631176780. Brett, M. and Fentress, E. *The Berbers.* 1996. 320p. 0631168524; Le May, G.H. *The Afrikaners.* 1995. 320p. 0631182047; Watterson, B. *The Egyptians.* 1996. 320p. 0631182721. McIntosh, R.J. *The People's of the Middle Niger;* Pankhurst, R. *The Ethiopians.* Other volumes are in preparation. *Class No:* 96

[7745]

Unesco General history of Africa. Paris, UNESCO; London, Heinemann Educational Books Ltd.; Berkeley, Univ. of California Press, 1981-. illus., maps, tables, bibliog. index.

1. *Methodology and African prehistory* edited by J. Ki-Zerbo. 1981 xxvii, 819p. 28 chaps. Bibliography p.753-800. 0435948075 (UK); 05200039122 (US) 9231017071 (Fr). 2. *Ancient civilizations of Africa* edited by G. Mokhtar. 1981. xvii, 804p. 29 chapters. Bibliography p.742-785. 0435948059 (UK); 0520039130 (US); 9231017084 (Fr). 3. *Africa from the seventh to the eleventh century* edited by M. El Fas and I. Hrbek. 1988. 869p. $45. ISBN 9231017098 (US). 4. *Africa from the twelfth century to the sixteenth century* edited by D.T. Niane. 1984. xxvii, 751p. 27 chaps. Bibliography p.692-733. 0435948105 (UK); 0520039157 (US); 9231017101 (Fr). 5. *Africa from the sixteenth to the eighteenth century* edited by B.A. Ogot. 6. *Africa in the nineteenth century until the 1880s* edited by J.F.A. Ajayi. 1989. 29 chapters. £18.00. ISBN 0435948121 (UK); 0520039173 (US); 9231017128 (Fr). 7. *Africa under colonial domination 1880-1935* edited by A.A. Boahen 1985. xxvii, 865p. 30 chapters. Bibliography p.815-844. ISBN 043594813x (UK); 0520039181 (US); 9231017136 (Fr). 8. *Africa since 1935* edited by A.A. Mazrui. 15 years in the planning this is a cooperative history on the grand scale. It reacts against what is seen as Euro-centred, warped ethno-history. Essential issues are the slave trade, colonisation, relations between sub-Sahara Africa and the Arab world, and decolonisation and nation building in an endeavour to highlight historical data allowing 'a clear picture of the evolution of the different peoples of Africa and their specific socio-cultural setting.' Each volume is edited by a native specialist, stressing cultural aspects and oral tradition and contains an important and extensive bibliographical essay. *Class No:* 96

Encyclopaedias

[7746]

DIAGRAM VISUAL INFORMATION. Encyclopedia of African peoples. New York and Oxford, Facts On File, 2000. 400p. illus., index. $55. ISBN: 0816040990.

4 major sections: 1. Peoples of Africa describing 200 major ethnic groups (*e.g.*Hausa, Maasi, Zulus) - 2. Culture and history (pictorial histories, ethnic distribution, and chronology of North, East, West, Central, and Southern Africa) - 3. Nations A-Z - 4. Biographies of 300+ Africans from antiquity to modern times. There is also a 9-page glossary in this compact but wide-ranging encyclopedia. *Class No:* 96(031)

[7747]

Encyclopedia of African peoples. The Diagram Group, *eds*. London, Fitzroy Dearborn, 2000. 500p. illus., index. £45. ISBN: 1579582672.

Sections include: Africa Today; The Peoples of Africa; Culture and History; The Nations of Africa; Biographies Past to Present; and a very useful glossary. *Class No:* 96(031)

[7748]

STEWART, J. **African states and rulers:** an encyclopaedia of native, colonial and independent states and rulers past and present. 2nd ed. Jefferson, N.C., McFarland, 1999. 420p. bibliog., tables, indexes. $45. ISBN: 0786406135.

1st ed. 1989.

A-Z entries to end of 1998. Data: official name of country; dates for that name; location; capital(s); other names known by; lists of rulers and their dates. New to this edition is an appendix table of all African states as they exist today with a list of their historical constituents and also a year-by-year chronology enabling the user to see at a glance events across the continent in a given year. Other charts list colonial powers and their African holdings and African nations 'dates of admission to the United Nations' (*Booklist*, v.96, no.12, 15 February 2000, p.1132). *Class No:* 96(031)

Dictionaries

[7749]

GRACE, J. *and* LAFFIN, J. **Fontana dictionary of Africa since 1960.** London, Fontana Press, 1991. xix,395p. map, bibliog. £7.99. ISBN: 0006862144.

Over 1,000 A-Z entries recording events, movements, and personalities significant in African history and politics. Chronology p.x-xiv. Bibliography p.vii-ix. *Class No:* 96(038)

[7750]

NUÑEZ, B. **Dictionary of Portuguese-African civilization.** Oxford, Hans Zell, 2v. 1992-96. £48 for each vol. ISBN: 0873836708, set.

1. *From discovery to independence.* 432p. bibliog. 0837836104. Over 3000 entries in v.1 identify historical and political events, social life and customs, geographical names, flora and fauna, organizations, literature, and culture in Portuguese Africa - Angola, Cape Verde, Guinea-Bissau, Mozambique, Sao Tome and Principe.

2. *From ancient kings to presidents.* 1996. 478p. bibliog., 187836651. 2,000 plus individual biographical sketches (inc. Africans, Europeans, Arabs). *Class No:* 96(038)

Maps & Atlases

[7751]
DE AJAYI, J.F. *and* **CROWDER, M.,** *eds.* **Historical atlas of Africa.** Harlow, Essex, Longman, 1985. 72p. maps + 72p. 22 plates. £66.00. ISBN: 058264335x.

72 maps of 3 types: event maps concerning historical events and locations of towns, battles, trade routes; process maps forming a visual interpretation of historical processes; and quantitative maps consisting of numerical data characterizing historical relationships. 'An invaluable and accurate source for ... the development of the continent during the last three thousand years' (*African Affairs* v.85,no.339, June 1986, p.301-302). M. Kwamena-Poh and others *African history in maps* (Longman, 1992. 76p. maps, index. ISBN 0582603315) has 36 two-colour map features covering major themes in African history. *Class No:* 96(084.3)

[7752]
REEMAN-GRENVILLE, G.S.P. The New atlas of African history. London, Macmillan; New York, Simon & Schuster, 1991. 144p. col. maps, index. £35; $65. ISBN: 0333559002, UK; 0136121519, US.

103 x two colour maps with commentaries provide an illustrated history of the African continent from prehistory to 1990 (e.g. 1. Africa-physical ... 4. Early Stone Age ... 9. Movements in Northern Africa between c.3500BC and c.500BC ... 67. European exploration ... 101. Principal languages ... 103. Vegetation). 'Suffers in comparison with Historical Atlas of Africa' (*Library Journal*). *Class No:* 96(084.3)

Chronologies

[7753]
REEMAN-GRENVILLE, G.S.P. Chronology of Afrian history. Oxford, Oxford University Press, 1973. xxii,312p.

Tabulates the principal events and dates in African history 1000BC-1971. 6 columns across the double page record the migration of peoples, dynasties, wars and treaties, and the emergence of modern states. *Class No:* 96(090)

Biographies

[7754]
IPSCHUTZ, M.R. *and* **RASMUSSEN, R.K. Dictionary of African historical biography.** 2nd ed. Berkeley, Calif, University of California Press, 1986. xiii, 328p. maps, bibliog., index. $40. ISBN: 0520051793.

First published by Aldine in 1978.

900 entries (57 new to this edition) mainly of political leaders from academically popular regions. Bibliography p.291-316. 'Essential for all academic libraries' (*Choice*, v.24, no.8, April 1987, p.1201-2). *Class No:* 96(092)

[7755]
Makers of modern Africa profiles in history. Bing, A., *ed.* 3rd ed. London, Africa Books Ltd. 1996. xvii,797p. ports., maps. £195. $295. (*Know Africa.*) ISBN: 0903274248. ISSN: 02611570.

1st ed. 1987; 2nd ed. 1991. Companion volume to *Africa today* and *Africa who's who* (qqv).

650 biographical sketches of eminent Africans now dead but who shaped the destiny of modern Africa. Includes Africans of European descent. Also 200 'living legends' (African élite alive today). *Class No:* 96(092)

19th Century

[7756]
GRIFFITHS, I. 'The Scramble for Africa: inherited political boundaries', *Geographical Journal*, v.152, no.2, July 1986, p.204-216. maps, bibliog.

Historical account of the problems resulting from the European partition of Africa following the Berlin Conference 1884-1885. *Class No:* 96"18"

Africa—North

[7757]
BUN-NASR, J.M. A History of the Magrib in the Islamic period. 3rd ed. Cambridge, Cambridge Univ. Press, 1987. xvi,455p. maps,bibliog., index. £40.00; $65.00. ISBN: 0521331846.

Supersedes the author's *A History of the Maghrib* (1971, 2e. 1975).

8 chronological chapters: 1. Introduction (land and people) - 2. Call of the minaret: the establishment of Islam in the Maghrib and Spain - 3. Under Berber dynasties - 4. Ottoman rule - 5. Morocco consolidates her national identity - 6. Age of aggressive European colonisation - 7. 1919 to independence - 8. Epilogue: after independence. Glossary p.xiii-xvi. Bibliography p.429-439. Analytical index. The history of the region now comprising Morocco, Tunisia, Algeria and Libya. 'There is not a better history of the Maghrib available in English' (*Choice*, v.25,no.8, April 1988, p.1299). *Class No:* 960/965

Tunisia

[7758]
PERKINS, K.J. Tunisia crossroads of the Islamic and European worlds. Boulder, Colorado, Westview Press; London, Croom Helm. 1986. xii,192p. illus., map, bibliog., index. $29.50. (*Profiles: Nations of the Contemporary Middle East.*) ISBN: 0865315914, US; 0709940505, UK.

12 chapters: 1. Land and people - 2. Pre-Islamic Tunisia - 3. Introduction of Islam and Arab rule - 4. Berber dynasties - 5. Ottoman and Husainid Tunisia ... 8. Tunisian Nationalist Movement ... 12. Foreign relations. Glossary of foreign words p.179-80. Bibliography p.181-3. *Class No:* 961.1

Dictionaries

[7759]
PERKINS, K.J. Historical dictionary of Tunisia. 2nd ed. Lanham, MD, Scarecrow Press, 1997. xxviii,310p. map, bibliog. £28.05. (*African Historical Dictionaries, no.45.*) ISBN: 0810832860.

1st ed. 1989.

Chronology p.xiii-xxii. Rulers of Tunisia (800-1996) p.xxiii-xxvi. Introduction: Tunisia: an overview p.1-11. Dictionary. (Islamic political movements and leaders, events, institutions, and places) p.13-196. Bibliography p.197-310. 'All those who are interested in Tunisia owe Perkins a debt for his fine contribution ... this volume is an enormously valuable work' (*Journal of African History*, v.40,no.2, 1999, p.347) *Class No:* 961.1(038)

Libya

Dictionaries

[7760]
ST. JOHN, R.B. Historical dictionary of Libya. 3rd ed. Lanham, MD, Scarecrow Press, 1998. xlix,451p. maps, bibliog. $75. (*African Historical Dictionaries, no.33.*) ISBN: 0810834952.

1st ed., compiled by L. Hahn (1981).

Chronology p.xxi-xlviii. Introduction (land and people, history, foreign affairs, economy etc. p.1-12. Dictionary (dynasties, political movements, geographical features, religion, oil), p.23-285. Bibliography (essays plus 8 sub-divided thematic categories) p.341-451. 2 maps. 'A judicious account of Libya's history and political development ... this is an historical dictionary of the highest quality and readers will be obliged for years to come for its precise and lucidly written entries' (*Middle East Studies Association Bulletin*, v.33, no.2, Winter 1999, p.285-86). *Class No:* 961.2(038)

Egypt

[7761]
PETRY, C.F., *ed.* **The Cambridge history of Egypt.** Cambridge Univ. Press. 2v., 1998.

1. *Islamic Egypt 641-1517* 800p. illus., maps, bibliog., index. £90. $120. ISBN 0521471370. Opens with a discussion of preceeding centuries and then proceeds chronologically according to the major dynasties. 'Will stand as a basic resource on Egypt for at least a generation' *Choice*, v.36, no.11/12, July/August 1999, p.1998).

2. *Modern Egypt, from 1517 to the end of the twentieth century.* 1998. 463p. illus., maps, bibliog., index. $100. 0521472113. 15 chronological and thematic chapters. 'An exceedingly valuable, comprehensive, and readable source for serious students and faculty interested in greater depth, more recent scholarship, and bibliographic reference' (*ibid*). *Class No:* 962.0

Dictionaries

[7762]
GOLDSCHMIDT, R. Historical dictionary of Egypt. 2nd ed. Metuchen, NJ., Scarecrow Press, 1994. xix,369p. maps, tables, bibliog. $42.50. (*African Historical Dictionaries, no.67.*) ISBN: 0810829495.

Replaces J.W. King's *Historical dictionary of Egypt* (1984).

Chronology p.xv-xix. Introduction (*i.e.* outline history), p.1-18. Dictionary p.19-310. Bibliography p.311-67. 'A well-done reference work, invaluable for understanding current events. Libraries should not discard the earlier edition; Goldschmidt supplements rather than supplants it' *Choice*, vol.32, no.9, May 1995, p.1428). *Class No:* 962.0(038)

Sudan

[7763]
DALY, M.W. **Imperial Sudan** The Anglo-Egyptian condominium 1934-
1956. Cambridge, Cambridge Univ. Press, 1991. xvi,471p. illus.,
map, bibliog., index. £55; $79.50. ISBN: 0521391636.

Follows Daly's *Empire on the Nile: The Anglo-Egyptian Sudan
1898-1934* (CUP, 1986).

12 chapters *e.g.* 3. Sudan in Anglo-Egyptian relations - 4.
Development of Sudanese nationalist politics 1934-90 ... 9. Path to
self-government. Glossary p.xv-xvi. Chapter notes p.402-49.
Bibliography p.450-7. 'Together, these two volumes provide a
comprehensive history of the Anglo-Egyptian condominium and should
represent the standard work on the subject for many years ... this book
is unmatched in studies of modern Sudan' (*The Middle East Journal*,
v.46, no.1, Winter 1992, p.98-9). *Class No: 962.4*

[7764]
HOLT, P.M. **A History of the Sudan:** from the coming of Islam to the
present day. 4th ed. London, Longman, 1988. x, 262p. maps,
bibliog., index, pbk. £7.95. ISBN: 0582004063.

First published 1961. 3rd ed. 1979.

16 chronological chapters arranged in 5 parts: 1. Before the Turko-
Egyptian conquest - 2. The Turko-Egyptian period - 3. The Mahdist
state 1881-98 - 4. The Anglo-Egyptian condominium 1899-1955 - 5.
The independent state. This edition extends coverage to 1986. Chapter
notes p.227-233. Bibliography p.243-250. 5 maps. Author is Professor
of Near and Middle East History in the University of London.
Class No: 962.4

[7765]
WOODWARD, P. **Sudan 1898-1989** the unstable state. Boulder, Colo.,
Lynne Rienner; London, Lester Crook Academic Publishing, 1990.
xiv,271p. map, bibliog., index. $35.

A political history in 6 chronological chapters: 1, Establishment of
the Condominium - 2. Condominium under pressure - 3.
Condominium to independence - 4. Nationalist generation in power
1956 to 1969 - 5. The Numeiri years - 6. A new beginning? 1985 to
1989. Glossary p.vii-viii. Chronology p.ix-xii. Chapter notes p.241-
59. Bibliography p.261-4. *Class No: 962.4*

Dictionaries

[7766]
FLUEHR-LOBBAN, C, *and others*. **Historical dictionary of The
Sudan.** 2nd ed. Metuchen, New Jersey, Scarecrow Press, 1992.
cvii,409p. illus., maps, bibliog. (*African Historical Dictionaries,
no.53.*) ISBN: 0810825473.

Substantially revised and expanded update of J.O. Voll's *Historical
dictionary of the Sudan* (1978).

Entries of varying length for historical events; social, religious, and
ethnic groups; political and cultural institutions, and geographical
locations and regions. Detailed chronology p.xix-lxx. Introduction
(geography, population and migration, history, present government
and economics) p.lxxi-xvii. Dictionary p.1-247. Bibliography (7
subject divisions) p.249-396. Appendix 1-4 rulers of Sudan.
Class No: 962.4(038)

Ethiopia

[7767]
MARCUS, H.G. **A History of Ethiopia.** Berkeley, Univ. of California
Press, 1994. xv,261p. illus., maps, bibliog., index. $35. ISBN:
0520081218.

14 narrative chapters (*e.g.* 1. Beginnings to 1270 ... 7. Defeat of
European imperialism to 1897 ... 9/12. Haile Sellasie to 1973 - 13.
The Revolution to 1977 - 14. Failure of the Revolution to 1991.
Glossary p.229-33. Bibliography p.235-46. Analytical index.
Class No: 963

Dictionaries

[7768]
PROUTY, C. *and* ROSENFELD, E. **Historical dictionary of Ethiopia
and Eritrea.** 2nd ed. Metuchen, NJ., Scarecrow Press, 1994.
xxvi,614p. maps, bibliog., index. £69.50. (*African Historical
Dictionaries, no.56.*) ISBN: 0810826631.

1st ed. as *Historical dictionary of Ethiopia* 1981.

Introduction (overview) p.xi-ix. Chronology p.xxi-xxiv. Dictionary
(Historical events, leading figures, religious and political movements,
international conferences, dynasties etc.) p.1-343. Bibliography in 20
thematic categories p.345-612. *Class No: 963(038)*

Eritrea

Dictionaries

[7769]
KILLION, T. **Historical dictionary of Eritrea.** Lanham, MD
Scarecrow Press, 1998. xli,535p. maps, bibliog. £58.50. $65. (*Africa
Historical Dictionaries, no 75.*) ISBN: 0810834375.

Chronology of Eritrean history p.xxiii-xli. Introduction (land
physical geography, population and ethnicity, historical overview
independence) p.1-23. Dictionary biographies of current leaders
struggle for independence, religious and ethnic groups, towns an
regions) p.25-449. Bibliography p.455-534. 4 maps. 'A most usefu
adjunct for those involved in Eritrean studies' (*African Affairs*, v.98
no.391, April 1999, p.253-54). *Class No: 963.5(038)*

Morocco

Dictionaries

[7770]
PARK, T.K. **Historical dictionary of Morocco.** New ed. Lanham, MD
Scarecrow Press, 1996. xxx,540p. maps, bibliog. £21. $20. (*Africa
Historical Dictionaries, no.71.*) ISBN: 0810830957.

1st ed. compiled by W. Spencer (1980).

Chronology p.xxi-xxx. Introduction (modern history) p.1-10
Dictionary (leading figures, places, political groups etc.) p.9-206
Appendix 1. Ruling chronology during Islamic era (p.207-16) - 2
Museums, libraries and archives (p.217-35) - 3. Maps (p.238-68)
Glossary (p.269-72). Massive bibliography in 25 sections (p.273-540)
Class No: 964(038)

Western Sahara

[7771]
DAMIS, J. **Conflict in Northwest Africa:** the Western Sahara dispute
Stanford, California, Hoover Institution Press, Stanford Univ., 1983
xviii, 196p. maps, tables, bibliog., index. (*Hoover Internationa
Studies.*) ISBN: 0817977813.

5 chapters: 1. The land and the people - 2. Parties to the conflict - 3
Evolution of the conflict - 4. Role of third parties - 5. Towards
resolution. Bibliography p.180-7. 'Aims to present a balanced an
concise analysis of the major factors and developments ... since 1975
(*Introduction*). *Class No: 964.8*

Dictionaries

[7772]
HODGES, T. *and* PAZZANITA, A.G. **Historical dictionary o
Western Sahara.** 2nd ed. Metuchen, New Jersey, Scarecrow Press
1994. lxxiii,560p. map. bibliog. $69.50. (*African Historica
Dictionaries, no.55.*) ISBN: 0810826615.

1st ed. 1982.

Chronology p.xv - lxxii. Dictionary p.21-472. Bibliography p.473
560. Tribes of Western Sahara p.561-64. *Class No: 964.8(038)*

Algeria

[7773]
AGERON, G.R. **Modern Algeria:** a history from 1830 to the present
London, Hurst, 1991. x,166p. maps, bibliog., index. £16.50. ISBN
1850650276.

First published as *Histoire de l'Algérie contemporaine*, 1964. 9th ed
1990.

9 chapters arranged in 5 main sections: 1. Under the military 1830
to 1870 - 2. Colonial Algeria 1870 to 1930 - 3. Will Algeria survive
(1930-1954) - 4. Algerian War - 5. Independent Algeria. Bibliography
p.145-60 is useful for French language sources. 'No other work i
English - or French for that matter - covers the period of French rul
in Algeria so satisfactorily' (*Journal of Imperial and Commonwealt
History*, v.20, no.3, September 1992, p.493-4). *Class No: 965*

Dictionaries

[7774]
HEGGOY, A.A. *and* NAYLOR, P.C. **Historical dictionary o
Algeria.** 2nd ed. Metuchen, New Jersey, Scarecrow Press, 1994
xxxix,443p. maps, bibliog., index. £57.50. (*African Historica
Dictionaries, no. 66.*) ISBN: 0810827484.

1st ed. 1981.

Introduction (Natural setting - Historical survey) p.1-42; Dictionary
(Events, Institutions, Economic, Social, Cultural aspects, Individuals
p.43-358; French governors in colonial Algeria p.359-61
Revolutionary organizations and National governments p.362-80
Name changes since independence p.381; Selective list newspaper
and journals p.382-86; Bibliography p.392-443. Glossary p. xxi-xxxiv
Chronology p.xxxv-xxxix. 9 maps. *Class No: 965(038)*

Africa—West

Maps & Atlases

[7775]

CATCHPOLE, B. *and* AKINJOGBIN, I.A. **A History of West Africa in maps and diagrams.** London, Collins Education, 1989. ix,150p. illus., maps, diagrs., index. ISBN: 00326520x.

100 double page features (map, illus., notes) arranged in 3 chronological sections: 1000-1800; 1800-1918; 1918 to the present day for students of the West African Examination Council's syllabus. *Class No:* 966(084.3)

Mauritania

Dictionaries

[7776]

PAZZANITA, A.G. **Historical dictionary of Mauritania.** Rev. ed. Lanham, MD, Scarecrow Press, 1996. xxx,314p. maps, tables, bibliog. (*African Historical Dictionaries, no.68.*) ISBN: 0810830957.

First published, compiled by A.G. Gerteiny (1981).

Chronology p.xxi-xxviii. Introduction (modern history) p.1-10. Dictionary (history, politics, geography, economics, culture etc.) p.11-295. Bibliography (5 sub-divided thematic categories) p.297-314. *Class No:* 966.12(038)

Mali

Dictionaries

[7777]

IMPERATO, P. J. **Historical dictionary of Mali.** 3rd ed. Lanham, Md. Scarecrow Press, 1996. lxxxv,362p. maps. bibliog. $87.50. (*African Historical Dictionaries, no.11.*) ISBN: 0810831287.

1st ed. 1977.

Chronology xix-lxvii. Dictionary p.23-253. Bibliography p.255-362. 6 maps. Tables (rulers and administration, population) p.lxix-lxxix. Introduction (early history, topography, river systems, climate etc.) p.1-21. *Class No:* 966.21(038)

Burkina Faso

Dictionaries

[7778]

McFARLAND, D.M. *and* RUPLEY, L. **Historical dictionary of Burkina Faso.** 2nd ed. Lanham, MD., Scarecrow Press, 1995. xxi,360p. maps, bibliog. $90. (*African Historical Dictionaries, no.74.*) ISBN: 0810834057.

1st ed. published in 1978 as *Historical Dictionary of Upper Volta (Haute Volta).* *Class No:* 966.25(038)

Niger

[7779]

FUGELSTAD, F. **A History of Niger.** Cambridge, Cambridge Univ. Press, 1984. viii, 275p. £20. $39.50. (*African Studies series.*) ISBN: 0521252687.

A descriptive and analytical account concentrating on the colonial period. 7 chapters: 1. Peoples and societies of Niger: early history to 1850 - 2. The revolutionary years 1850-1908 - 3. The decisive years 1908-22 - 4. Summing up and looking ahead - 5. The great silence: the classic period of colonial rule 1922-45 - 6. Towards a new order 1945-60 - 7. Conclusion. Notes p.193-241. Glossary p.242-243. Bibliography p.244-265. 'A significant piece of scholarship that ... raises important questions about the study of the colonial period' *Choice*, v.22, no.2, October 1984, p.325-326). *Class No:* 966.26

Dictionaries

[7780]

DECALO, S. **Historical dictionary of Niger.** 3rd ed. Lanham, MD, Scarecrow Press, 1997. xxxiii,488p. maps, tables, bibliog. $94.50. (*African Historical Dictionaries, no.20.*) ISBN: 0810831368.

1st ed. 1979; 2nd ed. 1989.

Recent political chronology p.xiii-xxi. Introduction (relief and climate, population, economy, history, politics) p.1-14. Dictionary (people and places, political parties, geography, government, industries) p.15-333. Bibliography (in 15 sub-divided categories) p.335-485. *Class No:* 966.26(038)

Senegal

Dictionaries

[7781]

CLARK, A.F. *and* PHILLIPS, L.C. **Historical dictionary of Senegal.** 2nd ed. Metuchen, NJ, Scarecrow Press, 1994. xii,353p. maps, bibliog. tables. $47.50. (*African Historical Dictionaries, no.65.*) ISBN: 0810827476.

1st ed. 1981.

Chronology of important events p.17-38. Dictionary (events, rulers, clerics, ethnic groups, themes) p.57-280. Bibliography in 18 sections under 6 headings (General works, Culture and society, Economics, History, Politics and Government, Science). p.281-353. 6 maps. 'Definitely a useful tool for scholars as well as the general public for the rich data it provides' (*International Journal of African Historical Studies,* v.29, no.1, 1996, p.159-61). *Class No:* 966.3(038)

Sierra Leone

[7782]

ALIE, J.A.D. **A New history of Sierra Leone.** London, Macmillan, 1990. xvii,300p. illus., maps, index. pbk. £6.95. ISBN: 0333519841.

Narrative survey of Sierra Leone's political, socio-cultural, and economic development in 12 chapters (*e.g.* 1. Land and people ... 3. Establishment and development of Sierra Leone colony ... 10. Transfer of power). Appendix 1. Governors of Sierra Leone ... 4. National anthem - 5. Flag - 6. Coat of arms - 7. Honours and awards. Chapter bibliographies. 16 maps. *Class No:* 966.4

Dictionaries

[7783]

FORAY, C.P. **Historical dictionary of Sierra Leone.** Metuchen, New Jersey, Scarecrow Press, 1977. lvii, 279p. maps, bibliog. £30. $28.50. (*African Historical Dictionaries, no.12.*) ISBN: 0810810352.

Chronology p.xiii-xxv. Dictionary p.1-236. Bibliography p.237-279. 4 maps. *Class No:* 966.4(038)

Gambia

Dictionaries

[7784]

HUGHES, A. *and* GAILEY, H.A. **Historical dictionary of The Gambia.** 3rd ed. Lanham, MD., Scarecrow Press, 1999. 240p. map, bibliog. $55. (*African Historical Dictionaries, no.79.*) ISBN: 0810836602.

1st ed. 1975.

Like its two predecessors, this edition looks at The Cambia;s history from precolonial times to the present. It includes entries on significant persons, places and events, institutions and parties, and various political, economic and social aspects. It provides a longer chronology, a more probing introduction, and expanded and additional entries. An extended bibliography takes into account new scholarship and publications. *Class No:* 966.51(038)

Guinea

Dictionaries

[7785]

IBRAHIMA BAH LALYA *and* O'TOOLE, T.E. **Historical dictionary of Guinea (Republic of Guinea/Conakry).** 3rd ed. Lanham, Md, Scarecrow Press, 1995. xlii,284p. map, bibliog., tables. (*African historical dictionaries, no.16.*) ISBN: 0810830655.

1st ed. 1978. 2nd ed. 1987.

Introduction (i.e. historical summary) p.1-14. Dictionary of people, institutions and events of importance to Guinea's history, economy and culture with emphasis on post-independence p.15-172. Bibliography divided into 14 subject sections p.177-279. Chronology p.xxi-xxxix *Class No:* 966.52(038)

Guinea-Bissau

Dictionaries

[7786]

LOBBAN, R. *and* MENDY, P.K. **Historical dictionary of the Republic of Guinea-Bissau.** 3rd ed. Lanham, MD., Scarecrow Press, 1997. xxiii,412p. maps, bibliog. $79. (*African Historical Dictionaries; no.22.*) ISBN: 0810832267.

1st ed. under the title of *Historical dictionary of the Republics of Guinea-Bissau and Cape Verde* (1979). 2nd ed. 1988.

Introduction (nomenclature, location and climate, history, slave-trade, colonialism) p.1-13. Chronology p.15-51. Maps p.52-63. Dictionary (significant persons, places, events, ethnic groups, political parties, government institutions etc.) p.65-318. Bibliography (13 thematic sections) p.319-81. *Class No:* 966.57(038)

Cape Verde Islands

Dictionaries

[7787]

LOBBAN, R. *and* LOPES, M. Historical dictionary of The Republic of Cape Verde. 3rd ed. Metuchen, New Jersey, Scarecrow Press, 1995. lxiii,336p. maps, bibliog. £44.55. $52. (*African Historical Dictionaries, no.62.*) ISBN: 0810829185.

First published as *Historical dictionary of the Republics of Guinea-Bissau and Cape Verde* in 1979.

Dictionary (major personalities, key events, institutions, locations, economic, health, social, political, cultural issues) p.12-221. Bibliography (in 20 thematic sections) p.225-314. Chronology p.xix-lii. 9 Appendices. 3 maps. *Class No:* 966.58(038)

Liberia

Dictionaries

[7788]

DUNN, D.E. *and* HOLSOE, S.E. Historical dictionary of Liberia. Metuchen, New Jersey, Scarecrow Press, 1985. xx, 274p. maps, bibliog., index. £22.50. $27.50. (*African Historical Dictionaries, no.38.*) ISBN: 0810817675.

Chronology p.xiii-xx. Dictionary p.15-192. Bibliography p.193-240. 7 maps. 'Far more scholarly than most of the Scarecrow volumes' (*Journal of African History*, 1982, no.3, p.468-9). *Class No:* 966.62(038)

Ivory Coast

Dictionaries

[7789]

MUNDT, R.J. Historical dictionary of the Côte D'Ivoire (The Ivory Coast). 2nd ed. Lanham, MD,, Scarecrow Press, 1998. xxxiv, 367p. map, tables, bibliog. £57. (*African Historical Dictionaries, no.41.*) ISBN: 0810830159.

First ed. published as *Historical dictionary of the Ivory Coast* (1987).

Chronology p.xix-xxiv. Introduction (location, climate, physical features, history) p.1-16. Dictionary (past and present leaders, places, trade unions, armed forces, social, political and economic issues etc.) p.17-179. Bibliography (in 8 sub-divided sections) p.181-365. 3 maps. *Class No:* 966.68(038)

Ghana

Dictionaries

[7790]

McFARLAND, D.M. *and* OWUSU-ANSAH, D. Historical dictionary of Ghana. 2nd ed. Metuchen, New Jersey, Scarecrow Press, 1995. lxxxviii,318p. maps, bibliog. £52.50. (*African Historical Dictionaries, no.63.*) ISBN: 0810829193.

1st ed. 1985.

Dictionary (including entries for major personalities, crucial events, essential institutions, economic, social, cultural issues, geographical features) p.1-255. Bibliography (arranged under 19 thematic headings) p.259-377. Chronology p.xix-lxxxviii. Appendix A. British administrators po.379-80 - B. Ghanaian leaders p.381. *Class No:* 966.7(038)

Togo

Dictionaries

[7791]

DECALO, S. Historical dictionary of Togo. 3rd ed. Lanham., Md, Scarecrow Press, 1996. xxvi,390p. maps, tables, bibliog. £79.80; $32.50. (*African Historical Dictionaries, no.9.*) ISBN: 0810830736.

1st ed. 1976. 2nd ed. 1987.

Political chronology p.xxiii. Dictionary p.13-294. Bibliography p.301-90. 'An essential reference tool' (*Booklist*, v.74, no.22, 15 July 1988, p.1758-1759). 3 maps. *Class No:* 966.8(038)

Benin

Dictionaries

[7792]

DECALO, S. Historical dictionary of Benin. 3rd ed. Lanham, Md. Scarecrow Press, 1995. xxxiii,564p. maps, tables, bibliog. $90. (*African Historical Dictionaries, no.61.*) ISBN: 0810829053.

1st ed. 1976 as *Historical dictionary of Dahomey (People's Republic of Benin)*.

Recent political chronology p.xi-xv. Introduction (an overview of Benin) p.1-17. Dictionary (leading figures of the economy, society,

....(contd.)

cultural activities, and the military, political parties and events etc. p.19-371. Bibliography (14 categories) p.374-564. 2 maps. *Class No:* 966.82(038)

Nigeria

[7793]

ISICHEI, E. A History of Nigeria. London, Longman, 1983. xix,517p illus, maps. bibliog. index. £19.95. ISBN: 0582643317.

20 meticulously documented thematic chapters with an emphasis on the pre-colonial period. Bibliography p.488-503. The author i Professor of History at the University of Jos. 'A highly original extensively researched and breathtakingly labor-intensive insight into the many millenia of Nigerian history' (*Africana Journal*, v.14, no.4 1987, p.338-40). *Class No:* 966.9

Dictionaries

[7794]

OYEWOLE, A. Historical dictionary of Nigeria. 2nd ed. Lanham MD., Scarecrow Press, 2000. 480p. maps, bibliog. £60.80. $64 (*African Historical Dictionaries, no.40.*) ISBN: 0810832623.

1st ed. 1987.

This second edition expands on information previously researched. I includes a chronology and a new bibliography by Thomas Ofcansky highlighting books and articles published in Nigeria about the country's security affairs. The author is Associate Professor of Politica Science at the Obafemi Awolowo University. *Class No:* 966.9(038)

Africa—East & Equatorial

[7795]

BIRMINGHAM, D. *and* MARTIN, P.M. History of Central Africa London, Longman, 2v., 1983. xii, 315p.+Ø, 432p. illus. maps bibliog., index. ISBN: 0582646731, v.1; 0582646758, v.2.

V1. concentrates on the culture and accomplishments of the native peoples of Central Africa before the European arrival. 7 chapters: 1 Society and economy before AD 1400 ... 3. The peoples of the fores ... 6. The Indian Ocean zone. Bibliographical essay p.278-296. V2 focusses on the colonial and post-colonial periods. 9. chapters: 1. The violence of Empire ... 2. Equatorial Africa under colonial rule ... 8 The Northern republics 1960-1980 ... 9. Settlers and liberators in the South. Bibliographical essay p.383-400. Analytical indexes. Devised for undergraduate students. *Class No:* 967

[7796]

LINIGER-GOUMAZ, M. Small is not always beautiful: the story of Equatorial Africa. London, C. Hurst, 1988. xx, 198p. maps, bibliog., index. £19.50. ISBN: 1850650233.

First published Rouen, Editions des Peuples Noir, 1986 under the title *Connaître la Guinée Équatoriale*.

7 Chapters: 1. Physical and human geography - 2. The colonial period - 3. Independence miscarried - 4. Demographic and cultural aspects of the Nguema era - 5. The Economy - 6. Present and future - 7. Conclusions. Bibliographical note p.170-174. Bibliography of post-independence publications p.175-9. *Class No:* 967

[7797]

LOW, D.A. *and* SMITH, A., *eds*. History of East Africa. Oxford, Clarendon Press, 3v., 1963-76. xiii,500p. li,766p. xii,691p. tables, maps, bibliogs.

1 [to 1898], edited by R. Oliver and G. Matthew. 1963. 2 [from 1890s to close of world War II], edited by V. Harlow and E.M. Chilver. 1965. 3 [1945-1963], edited by D.A. Low and Alison Smith. 1976. V.1 (12 chapters; 10 contributors) 'directly surveys results of original research' (*Prefatory note*). Bibliographies, p.457-80; analytical index. While conceding that it is an indispensable work of reference, the reviewer in *Commonwealth Journal* (v.6,no.5, October 1963, p.218) complains of uneveness of treatment and lack of general maps. V.3 (14 chapters, footnoted) has 40p. of statistical tables and a select bibliography in 4 sections. Analytical index, p.665-91). Studied from an African as well as a European standpoint. *Class No:* 967

[7798]

WILLS, A.J. An Introduction to the history of Central Africa Zambia, Malawi, Zimbabwe. 4th ed. Oxford, Oxford Univ. Press, 1985. xix, 556p. maps, tables, bibliog., index. £22.50. ISBN: 0198730756.

First published 1964.

12 chapters covering the area's pre-colonial history; the period of settlement and colonization; white-colonial rule; with substantial treatment of the two decades since Zambia's independence and Rhodesia's Unilateral Declaration of Independence. This latest edition adds chapters on the struggle for the liberation of Zimbabwe. Notes p.500-520. Bibliography p.521-533. Analytical index. *Class No:* 967

Bibliographies

[7799]

OFCANSKY, T.P. **British East Africa 1850-1963: an** annotated bibliography. New York, Garland Publishing, 1985. xxiii, 474p. index. $66. ISBN: 0824091647.

3089 annotated entries divided under 19 headings - East Africa, Kenya, Uganda, Tanganyika, Zanzibar and subject headings *e.g.* East African campaign (1914-18); Agriculture; Indian community; Mau-Mau revolt. *Journal of African History*, v.29, no.1, 1988, p.142-3, is not favourably impessed: ' a sad example of what can happen when bibliography is not taken seriously.' *Class No:* 967(01)

Cameroon

[7800]

TAMBI EYONGETAH MBUAGBAW. **A History of the Cameroon.** 2nd ed. Harlow, Essex, Longman, 1987. vii,151p. maps, index. pbk. ISBN: 0582585260.

First published 1974.

31 chronological chapters: 1. Geography and peoples - 2. The Carthaginian 'discovery' of Cameroon... 30. Cameroon under Ahidjo - 31. Cameroon and the 'New Deal'. 11 maps. Student textbook. *Class No:* 967.11

Dictionaries

[7801]

DE LANCEY, M.W. *and* MOKEBA, H.B. **Historical dictionary of the Republic of Cameroon.** 2nd ed. Metuchen, New Jersey, Scarecrow Press, 1990. xxii,297p. maps, bibliog. £28.15. (*African Historical Dictionaries, no.48.*) ISBN: 0810823705.

Replaces V.T. Le Vine and R.P. Nye's *Historical dictionary of Cameroon* (1974) the 1st volume in the African Historical Dictionaries series.

Chronology p.xv-xxii. Dictionary p.13-212. Bibliography p.213-97. *Class No:* 967.11(038)

Equatorial Guinea

Dictionaries

[7802]

LINIGER-GOUMAZ, M. **Historical dictionary of Equatorial Guinea.** 3rd ed. Lanham, MD., Scarecrow Press, 1999. 656p. bibliog. $115. (*African Historical Dictionaries, no.21.*) ISBN: 0810833948.

2nd ed. 1988.

Provides hard-to-find information on leading persons, places, events, political parties, and liberation movements before and after independence, expanding and improving upon the second edition. Historical entries go from prehistory to the present; with bibliography, chronology, and a list of abbreviations and acronyms. *Class No:* 967.18(038)

Gabon

Dictionaries

[7803]

GARDINIER, D.E. **Historical dictionary of Gabon.** 2nd ed. Metuchen, New Jersey, Scarecrow Press, 1994. 466p. maps, tables, bibliography. $59.50. (*African Historical Dictionaries, no.58.*) ISBN: 0810827689.

1st ed. 1981.

Chronology p.xiv-xx. Dictionary p.22-197. Bibliography p.198-254. 'Particularly useful are references following the dictionary entries to citations in the bibliography for further information' (*Choice*, v.19, no.9, May 1982, p.1215). *Class No:* 967.21(038)

Congo

Dictionaries

[7804]

DECALO, S., *and others*. **Historical dictionary of Congo.** 3rd ed. Lanham, Md., Scarecrow Press, 1996. xxxiv,378p. maps, tables, bibliog., £75.55. (*African Historical Dictionaries, no.69.*) ISBN: 0810831163.

Previous ed. published as *Historical dictionary of the People's Republic of the Congo* by V. Thompson and R. Adloff.

Recent chronology p.xiii-xx. Introduction (geography and resources, early history, colonial era, civilian era, Ngouabi era etc.) p.1-18. Dictionary p.19-315. Bibliography (in 13 thematic sections) p.317-78. 2 maps. *Class No:* 967.24(038)

Angola

Dictionaries

[7805]

BROADHEAD, S.H. **Historical dictionary of Angola.** 2nd ed. Metuchen, New Jersey, Scarecrow Press, 1992. 344p. maps, bibliog., tables, index. $45. (*African Historical Dictionaries, no.26.*) ISBN: 0810825325.

1st ed. by P.M. Martin published in 1980.

Chronology. Dictionary. Bibliography. 'A useful little book ... the select unannotated bibliography is most welcome as there had not been a general bibliography of Angola since 1912' (*Journal of African History*, v.22, no.4, 1981, p.578). *Class No:* 967.3(038)

Central African Republic

[7806]

KALCK, P. *and* O'TOOLE, T. **Historical dictionary of The Central African Republic.** 2nd ed. Metuchen, New Jersey, Scarecrow Press, 1992. 246p. map. bibliog. $34. (*African Historical Dictionaries, no.51.*) ISBN: 081082521x.

1st ed. 1980.

Heads of government p.xxi-xxiii. Chronology p.xxiv-xli. Dictionary p.1-135. Bibliography p.137-152. 5 maps. *Class No:* 967.41

Chad

Dictionaries

[7807]

DECALO, S. **Historical dictionary of Chad.** 3rd ed. Lanham, MD, Scarecrow Press, 1997. xlviii,601p. maps, tables, bibliog. £85.50. $95. (*African Historical Dictionaries, no.13.*) ISBN: 0810832534.

1st ed. 1976. 2nd ed. 1987.

Selected chronology p.xxxvii-xlviii. Introduction (land, people, history, economy, politics) p.1-23. Dictionary (persons, places, events, institutions, economy, society, culture, politics) p.25-457. Bibliography (in 14 categories (*e.g.* archaeology and prehistory, early explorations, history) p.458-601. 6 maps. 'An excellent point of departure for further study' (*The International Journal of African Studies*, v.31, no.2, 1998, p.486). *Class No:* 967.43(038)

Zaire

Dictionaries

[7808]

BOBB, F.S. **Historical dictionary of Democratic Republic of the Congo (Zaire).** Lanham, MD., Scarecrow Press, 1999. 632p., maps, tables, bibliog. $75. (*African Historical Dictionaries, no.76.*) ISBN: 0810835711.

First published as *Historical dictionary of Zaire* (1988).

Looks back at 30 years of Mobutu rule, nearly 40 years of independence, over a century of colonial rule, and even earlier kingdoms and groups that shared the territory. The care and effort which drove the creation of the earlier edition have been maintained in this revision. The *Dictionary* includes a useful introduction by the author, and is followed by a detailed bibliography. *Class No:* 967.5(038)

Burundi

Dictionaries

[7809]

EGGERS, E.K. **Historical dictionary of Burundi.** 2nd ed. Lanham, MD, Scarecrow Press, 1997. lxxvi,198p. map, bibliog. $38. (*African Historical Dictionaries, no.73.*) ISBN: 0810832615.

1st ed. by W. Weinstein 1976.

Chronology p.xxi-lxxvi. Introduction (overview) p.1-5. Dictionary (political parties, diplomatic agreements and foreign affairs, tribal and ethnic groups etc.) p.7-146. Bibliography (14 thematic sections) p.147-94. Appendix A. Kings of Burundi - B. Post-colonial Heads of State. *Class No:* 967.597(038)

Rwanda

Dictionaries

[7810]

DORSEY, L. **Historical dictionary of Rwanda.** Metuchen, NJ., Scarecrow Press, 1994. xvi,437p. map, bibliog. $55. (*African Historical Dictionaries, no.60.*) ISBN: 0810828200.

Historic overview (Geographical description and the economy; Ancient Rwanda; Colonial period; European rule to 1930; African and European reactions and post World War II; Movement towards

....(contd.)
independence; National period) p.1-35. Chronology p.36-162. Dictionary p.163-408. Bibliography p.409-37.
Class No: 967.5978(038)

Uganda

Bibliographies
[7811]
GERTZEL, C. **Uganda:** an annotated bibliography of source materials (with particular reference to the period since 1971 and up to 1988). London, Hans Zell, 1991. x,288p. index. £39; $90. ISBN: 0905450833.
2062 entries muster under 11 form and subject headings to provide a comprehensive guide to recent Ugandan history and politics. An extensive bibliographical essay (p.1-24) outlines how to use the Bibliography and introduces the sources available for research.
Class No: 967.61(01)

Dictionaries
[7812]
PIROUET, M.L. **Historical dictionary of Uganda.** Metuchen, NJ., Scarecrow Press, 1995. xlvii,533p. maps, bibliog. £56.25. (*African Historical Dictionaries, no.64.*) ISBN: 0810829207.
Introduction (geography, population, economy, history) p.1-20. Dictionary p.21-373. Bibliography (in 12 subdivided sections) p.374-533. Glossary p.xii. Chronology p.xl-xlv. 2 maps.
Class No: 967.61(038)

Kenya
[7813]
OCHIENG, W.R., *ed*. **A Modern history of Kenya 1895-1980.** London, Evans, 1989. v,259p. tables, bibliog., index. ISBN: 0237510820.
8 essays by independent hands each dealing with consecutive discrete periods: 1. Conquest state - 2. Establishment of colonial rule 1905-1920 ... 7. Independent Kenya 1963-1986. Published to coincide with 60th birthday of B.A. Ogot, Kenya's senior historian.
Class No: 967.62

[7814]
OCHIENG, W.R., *ed*. **Themes in Kenyan history.** Nairobi, Heinemann Kenya; London, James Currey; Athens, Ohio Univ. Press, 1990. vii,261p. map, bibliogs., index. pbk. £9.95. ISBN: 0852550731, UK; 0821409778, US.
16 contributors. Interdisciplinary exposition in 20 well-documented chapters *e.g.* Migrations and emergence of societies ... Urbanization ... Government ... Trade since early times ... Nationalism and decolonization ... Diplomacy and international relations.
Class No: 967.62

Dictionaries
[7815]
MAXON, R.M. *and* OFCANSKY, T.P. **Historical dictionary of Kenya.** 2nd ed. Lanham, MD, Scarecrow Press, 1999. xviii, 808p. map, bibliog. $110. £82.50. (*African Historical Dictionaries, no.77.*) ISBN: 0810836165.
1st ed. by B.A. Ogot published in 1987.
This new second edition of the Historical Dictionary of Kenya provides a ready reference to the history and culture of this complicated African nation. Entries cover the important people, places, events and culture of Kenya. The bibliography will serve both new and experienced researchers. Three appendices provide easy access to historical statistics, including the names and relevant dates of British Commissioners and Governors, Prime Ministers and Presidents, and economic data. *Class No:* 967.62(038)

Somalia
[7816]
LEWIS, J.M. **A Modern history of Somalia** nation and state in the Horn of Africa. London, Longman, 1980. ix, 279p. maps, index, pbk. £4.50. ISBN: 058264657x.
1st 8 chapters first published as *The modern history of Somaliland from nation to state* (Weidenfeld & Nicolson, 1965).
2 new chapters: 9. The Somali revolution 1969-76 - 10. Nationalism, ethnicity and revolution in the Horn of Africa, take the story up to 1978. Chapter notes p.256-272. 3 maps. Analytical index.
Class No: 967.7

Dictionaries
[7817]
CASTAGNO, M. **Historical dictionary of Somalia.** Metuchen, New Jersey, Scarecrow Press, 1975. xxviii, 213p. map. bibliog. £24. $24. (*African Historical Dictionaries, no.6.*) ISBN: 0810808307.
Chronology, p.xxiv-xxviii. Dictionary p.1-164. Bibliography p.165-213. *Class No:* 967.7(038)

Tanzania (Tanganyika)
[7818]
YEAGER, R. **Tanzania:** an African experiment. Boulder, Colorado, Westview Press; Aldershot, Hampshire, Gower, 1982. xii, 136p. illus., map, tables, bibliog., index. £18.50 $31.50. (*Profiles: Nations of Contemporary Africa.*) ISBN: 0891589236, US; 0566005549, UK.
7 chapters: 1. The origins of Tanzania - 2. The ecology of change - 3. The ambiguities of independence - 4. Towards Socialism and democracy - 5. Towards socialism and self-reliance - 6. International leadership and dependence - 7. Assessing the Tanzanian experiment. Bibliography p.127-130. 'Essential reading for all those interested in understanding the recent African past' (*Choice,* v.20, no.3, November 1982, p.483). *Class No:* 967.8

Bibliographies
[7819]
ROBERTS, A. '**A Bibliography of primary sources for Tanzania 1799-1899**', *Tanzania Notes and Records,* v.73, 1974, p.65-92.
424 items recorded-mostly 19th century travellers' accounts. 'A very useful and important compilation' (C. Darch. *Tanzania,* 1985. Entry 670). *Class No:* 967.8(01)

Dictionaries
[7820]
YEAGER, R. *and* OFCANSKY, T.P. **Historical dictionary of Tanzania.** 2nd ed. Lanham, MD, Scarecrow Press, 1997. xxxi, 331p. maps, bibliog. £30. $69. (*African Historical Dictionaries, no.72.*) ISBN: 0810832445.
1st ed. 1978.
Chronology p.xvi-xxxi. Introduction (historical overview) p.1-8. Dictionary (political, social, economic, cultural, historical events and developments) p.9-197. Bibliographies (in 23 form and thematic sections) p.201-291. *Class No:* 967.8(038)

Mozambique
[7821]
HENRIKSEN, T.H. **Mozambique:** a history. London, Rex Collings; Cape Town, David Philip, 1978. xi, 276p. maps, index. £13.50. ISBN: 0860360172.
2 Parts (10 chapters): 1. Invasions and empires - 2. Colonialism and nationalism. Chapter notes p.233-246. Emphasis on period after 1900.
Class No: 967.9

[7822]
História de Moçambique. Maputo, Departamento de História, Univ. Eduardo Mondlane, 4v., 1982 - .
1. 159p. 2. 336p. Imperialist aggression 1886-1930. 3. (Covers period 1930-1962) 4. História da luta Armada de Libertação Nacional. 'The first consistent attempt at a Marxist interpretation of Mozambiqan history, and highly recommended' (C. Darch. *Mozambique,* 1987. Entry 140). *Class No:* 967.9

Dictionaries
[7823]
AZEVEDO, M. **Historical dictionary of Mozambique.** Metuchen, NJ., Scarecrow Press, 1991. xxx,250p. map, tables, bibliog., index. £22.15. (*African Historical Dictionaries, no. 47.*) ISBN: 0810824132.
Brief essays on significant people, events, institutions, and places *etc.* in Mozambique's history. Introduction (location, climate, physical features, population, history) p.1-28. Dictionary p.19-131. Bibliography (in 12 sections) p.132-230. Chronology p.xiii-xxiii.
Class No: 967.9(038)

Africa—Southern
[7824]
OMER-COOPER, J.D. **History of Southern Africa.** London, James Currey; Portsmouth, New Hampshire, Heinemann Educational Books Inc., 1987. xiii, 298p. illus., maps, bibliog., index. £25. $20. ISBN: 0852550103, UK; 0435080105, US.
9 chapters: 1. The Khoisan people and Bantu-speaking settlement ... 4. The mass migration of the mfecane & the Great Trek ... 9. The three phases of apartheid. Appendix 1. The enclave states Lesotho, Swaziland and Botswana. 2. Namibia. Bibliography (by chapter) p.278-285. Analytical index. 'The most important theme is the

..(contd.)
historical explanation of that peculiar system of systematic racial discrimination, repression and exploitation known as apartheid'.
Class No: 968

Bibliographies

[7825]
HOMPSON, L., *and others*. **Southern African history before 1900** a select bibliography of articles. Stanford, California, Hoover Institution Press, Stanford Univ., 1971. xii, 102p. ISBN: 817924914.
1,136 unannotated items, in 26 main sections (1. Historiography and methodology - 2. Archives, bibliographies and other sources ... 4. Archaeology ... 10. The Bantu-speaking peoples of Southern Africa ... 20. The Transvaal, 1852-1899 ... 23. Rhodesia ... 24. The Indians - 25. British imperial policy in Southern Africa (nos. 1093-1133) - 26. German imperial policy in Southern Africa). Draws on 31 journals. 'This is a select bibliography, designed by historians for historians' (*Preface*). *Class No: 968(01)*

South Africa

[7826]
DAVENPORT, T.R.H. **South Africa** a modern history. 4th ed. London, Macmillan, 1991. xxv,662p. illus., maps, tables, bibliog., index. £35. ISBN: 0333550331.
1st ed. 1977; 3rd ed. 1987.
20 subdivided chapters in 3 parts: 1. Prelude to white dominion - 2. Consolidation of a White state - 3. Political economy of South Africa. This edition incorporates revised material on South African prehistory and focuses 'on the rapidly changing socio-economic and political scene since the mid-term crisis of P.W. Botha's Government'. Appendix: Heads of State 1652-1990 p.558-63. Bibliographical Notes (by chapter) p.568-613. *Class No: 968.0*

[7827]
LE MAY, G.H.L. **The Afrikaners** an historical interpretation. Oxford, Blackwell, 1995. 280p. index. ISBN: 0631182047.
A political history of the Afrikaner peoples from their arrival in southern Africa in 1652, up to the present day. The account covers the establishment of the Dutch East India trading post in the Cape, the Great Trek of the 1830s, the discovery of gold and diamonds in the Transvaal in the late nineteenth century, the Anglo-Boer War, the effects of the two World Wars and the democratic elections of 1994. *Class No: 968.0*

[7828]
Reader's Digest illustrated history of South Africa. Oakes, D., *ed.* 2nd ed. Cape Town, Reader's Digest, 1989. 485p. illus., maps, tables, bibliog., index.
1st ed. 1988.
Reliable history of South Africa. L.Witz and C. Hamiltons' 'Reaping the whirlwind'. *South African Historical Journal*, no.24, May 1991, p.185-202 explores some of the issues raised by the public demand for non-apartheid history, traces the circumstances which created the market for this particular title, and why it hs proved more successful than similar ventures. *Class No: 968.0*

Bibliographies

[7829]
MUSIKER, N. **South African history:** a bibliographical guide with special reference to territorial expansion and colonization. New York, Garland Publishing Inc., 1984. xxix, 297p. index. $84. (*Themes in European Expansion.*) ISBN: 0824091744.
1028 items, focussing on 'the fabric of South African history as the term is generally understood', with descriptive and evaluative annotations, drawn up in 18 chronological and geographical sections: 2. Travel and exploration ... 4. Cape general history ... 6. Zululand ... 12. South Africa 1910-1980. Author-title and subject-topographical indexes. *Class No: 968.0(01)*

[7830]
SCHOEMAN, K., *comp.* **Bibliography of the Orange Free State until 31 May 1910.** Cape Town, South African Library, 1984. xvi, 227p.
2500 titles covering historical, political, economic and cultural developments grouped in 17 sections (sub-divided) 1. Reference works ... 2A. Early history and archaeology ... 11. Local history. 'A thoroughly researched and valuable compilation' (*African Research and Documentation*, no.39, 1985, p.28). *Class No: 968.0(01)*

[7831]
SUTTIE, M-L. 'A select bibliography of South African history 1990-1993', *South African Historical Journal/Suid. Afrikaanse Joernaal*, no.31, November 1994, p.359-98.
Complements that published in November 1993 issue of *South African Historical Journal* and includes books which appeared in 1993. Unannotated bibliography arranged A-Z by author. *Class No: 968.0(01)*

Encyclopaedias

[7832]
EVANS, M.M. **Encyclopedia of the Boer War.** Oxford and Santa Barbara, Calif., ABC-Clio, 2000. 275p. illus., maps, bibliog., index. £44.95. ISBN: 1851093427.
A-Z reference work which covers all aspects of the Boer War including its origins, military strategy and tactics, the main battles and sieges, the principal political and military figures, weaponry and subjects such as the role of the railways, the treatment of the wounded, and the use of concentration camps. *Class No: 968.0(031)*

Dictionaries

[7833]
An Illustrated dictionary of South African history. Saunders, C.C., *ed.* Sandton, South Africa, Ibis Books, 1994. 283p. illus. (many col.), tables, bibliog., index.
25 contributors. Popular and attractive work encompassing political, economic, social, and art history. Bibliography p.273-74. *Class No: 968.0(038)*

[7834]
MUSIKER, N. *and* MUSIKER, R. **Historical dictionary of Greater Johannesburg.** Lanham, MD., Scarecrow Press, 1999. 544p. bibliog. $98.50. (*Historical Dictionaries of Cities, no.7.*) ISBN: 0810835207.
Includes information on the role of the original indigenous inhabitants of South Africa who occupied the area of the future city long before the first white settlers, and who, through their intensive labor on the gold mines, played a decisive role in the progress of Johannesburg. The present volume, besides covering the economic and political history of Johannesburg, also deals with cultural aspects of the city including architecture, art, music, and theatre. Generally, concentrates on recent material. *Class No: 968.0(038)*

[7835]
SAUNDERS, C. *and* SOUTHEY, N. **Historical dictionary of South Africa.** 2nd ed. Lanham, MD., Scarecrow Press, 1999. 592p. map, bibliog., indexes. $85. (*African Historical Dictionaries, no.78.*) ISBN: 0810813467.
1st ed. 1983. Published in South Africa as *A Dictionary of South African history* (Cape Town, David Philip. 1998. xxxiv, 198p. 0864864140).
Not only provides an update of the "new" South Africa, but expands on South Africa's complicated history as well, covering the period of British domination, problems with the Boers and the British, and the peopling of the region by Africans. Mary-Lynn Suttie of the Library of the University of South Africa has revised the bibliography for this edition. A comprehensive resource that covers history, politics, the economy, society and culture of the 'new' South Africa. *Class No: 968.0(038)*

[7836]
WORDEN, N. **A Concise dictionary of South African history.** Cape Town, Francolin, 1998. 173p. index. ISBN: 1868590364.
400+ cross-referenced entries covers the area that comprises the geographical territory of modern South Africa from the earliest evidence of human occupation to the democratic election of 1994. Entries spotlight the people, events, organizations, legislation, and broad themes that have influenced South Africa's politics, economy and social fabric. *Class No: 968.0(038)*

Botswana

Dictionaries

[7837]
MORTON, F., *and others*. **Historical dictionary of Botswana.** 3rd ed. Lanham, Md., Scarecrow Press, 1996. xxi,321p. bibliog. map. (*African Historical Dictionaries, no.70.*) ISBN: 0810831430.
First published as *Historical dictionary of the Republic of Botswama* (AHD.No.5). 2nd ed. as present title in 1990 (AHD no.40). Introduction (Country, People, History) p.1-7. Dictionary p.9-260. Chronology p.xvii-xxi. Bibliography (Bibliographies, Reference Works, and 5 specialised disciplinary studies) p.261-321. *Class No: 968.1(038)*

Swaziland

Dictionaries

[7838]
BOOTH, A.R. **Historical dictionary of Swaziland.** Lanham, MD., 2000. 456p. map. bibliog. $75. (*African Historical Dictionaries, no.80.*) ISBN: 0810837498.
There are entries on Swazi kings, queens, and others who played signifcant roles, and more that describe basic characteristics and customs. The colonial era is also clearly delineated, with entries on important figures, colonial secretaries, resident commissioners, missionaries, and concession-hunters. The contemporary history of

....*(contd.)*

Swaziland is also addressed, with entries on people, places, and events important to Swaziland's contemporary history. The considerable material provided in the dictionary is buttressed by a solid introduction, a chronology, and a substantial bibliography. *Class No:* 968.34(038)

Lesotho

Dictionaries

[7839]

HALIBURTON, G. **Historical dictionary of Lesotho.** Metuchen, New Jersey, Scarecrow Press, 1977. xxxv, 223p. maps, geneal. tables, bibliog. £24. $24. (*African Historical Dicitonaries, no.10.*) ISBN: 0810809931.

Chronology p.xii-xvii. Dictionary p.1-184. Bibliography p.185-223. 3 maps. *Class No:* 968.61(038)

Namibia

Dictionaries

[7840]

GROTPETER, J.J. **Historical dictionary of Namibia.** Metuchen, NJ., Scarecrow Press, 1994. xxxii,724p. map, bibliog. £89.50. (*African Historical Dictionaries, no.57.*) ISBN: 081082728x.

Chronology p.xvii-xxxi. Dictionary p.7-597. Appendices (elections and rulers) p.599-608. Bibliography arranged in 7 sub-divided sections (General; Cultural; Economic: Historic; Political; Scientific; Social) p.613-724. *Class No:* 968.8(038)

Zimbabwe

Dictionaries

[7841]

RASMUSSEN, R.K. *and* RUBERT, S.C. **Historical dictionary of Zimbabwe.** 3rd ed. Lanham, MD, Scarecrow Press, 2000. xxxviii,562p. maps, bibliog. $89.50 (*African Historical Dictionaries no.46.*) ISBN: 0810834715.

First published as *Historical dictionary of Rhodesia/Zimbabwe* (1979).

Zimbabwe has witnessed an incredible amount of history in the relatively short span of eighteen years. The new edition of this dictionary keeps abreast of the changes in the country. Hundreds of fresh entries cover new political leaders, changing government, cultural, and economic developments and scores of place name changes. There are also corrections to existing entries and an expanded bibliography. *Class No:* 968.91(038)

Zambia

Dictionaries

[7842]

GROTPETER, J.J., *and others*. **Historical dictionary of Zambia.** 2nd ed. Lanham, MD, Scarecrow Press, 1998. xxxv,570p. map, bibliog. £85.50. (*African Historical Dictionaries, no.19.*) ISBN: 081083345x.

1st ed. 1979.

Chronology p.xvii-xxxv. Introduction (recent history and politics) p.1-15. Dictionary (historical and political leaders, ethnic and linguistic groups, political parties, trade unions, religious bodies, places, and events) p.19-484. Bibliography (general, cultural, economic, historic, political, scientific, social sub-headings) p.485-570.
Class No: 968.94(038)

Malawi

Dictionaries

[7843]

CROSBY, C.A. **Historical dictionary of Malawi.** 2nd ed. Metuchen, New Jersey, Scarecrow Press, 1993. xxxv,202p. maps. bibliog. $35. (*African Historical Dictionaries, no.54.*) ISBN: 0810826283.

1st ed. 1980.

Chronology p.xi-xviii. Introduction (geography and climate, population, history etc.) p.xxi-xxxv. Dictionary p.1-118. Bibliography (in 8 subdivided sections) p.137-202. *Class No:* 968.97(038)

Madagascar

Dictionaries

[7844]

COVELL, M. **Historical dictionary of Madagascar.** Lanham, MD., Scarecrow Press, 1996. xlvi,356p. map, bibliog. £66.50. (*African Historical Dictionaries, no.50.*) ISBN: 0810829738.

The introduction summarises the history of the island, while the dictionary entries (p.17-256) cover the histories of the major ethnic groups and the most important pre-colonial political units. It includes entries on the important figures and events of the colonial period and nationalist movement, and on post-independence regimes. Chronology p.xvii-xlvi. Bibliography p.257-356. *Class No:* 969.1(038)

Comoro Islands

[7845]

NEWITT, M. **The Comoro Islands** struggle against dependency in the Indian Ocean. Boulder, Colorado, Westview Press; London, Gower, 1984. x, 144p. illus., map, bibliog, index. £19.50. $31.50. (*Profiles: nations of contemporary Africa.*) ISBN: 0865312923, US; 056600545x, UK.

Well documented overview of geography, history, politics, society, economy, and foreign relations. Bibliographical essay p.131-4. Analytical index. *Class No:* 969.41

Dictionaries

[7846]

OTTENHEIMER, M. *and* OTTENHEIMER, H. **Historical dictionary of the Comoro Islands.** Metuchen, NJ., Scarecrow Press, 1994. xviii,140p. map, bibliog. $69.50; £25. African Historical Dictionaries, no.59 ISBN: 0810828197.

Dictionary of events, leading figures, political and economic themes, ideologies etc. Includes chronology and 40-page bibliography. Lukewarm reception in *International Journal of African Studies*, v.29, no.1, 1996, p.138-39. *Class No:* 969.41(038)

Seychelles

[7847]

FRANDA, M. **The Seychelles:** unquiet islands. Boulder, Colorado, Westview Press; Aldershot, Hampshire, Gower, 1982. 140p. illus., maps, bibliog., index. £19.50. $28.50. (*Profiles. Nations of Contemporary Africa.*) ISBN: 0865312664, US; 90566005522, UK.

5 chapters (History, People, Politics, Economy, Change). Extensive chapter notes and Bibliography p.129. Despite some weaknesses, a limited bibliography, and an inadequate index, *Choice*, v.20, no.6, February 1983, p.873-874 concludes that 'there is no better modern introduction to the Seychelles'. *Class No:* 969.6

Mauritius

Dictionaries

[7848]

SELVON, S. **Historical dictionary of Mauritius.** 2nd ed. Metuchen, New Jersey, Scarecrow Press, 1991. xl,253p. maps, tables, bibliog. £26.25; $20.00. (*African Historical Dictionaries, no.49.*) ISBN: 0810824809.

First published (L. Riviere as author) 1982.

Introduction (geographical location and physical description, recent events etc.) p.vii-xv. Chronology p.xvii-xxv. Governors p.xxvii-xxix. Dictionary (history, ethnic and cultural strands, events, political parties etc.) p.1-205. Bibliography 16 categories including history, map collections, guidebooks) p.207-53. *Class No:* 969.82(038)

America

[7849]

FAGAN, B.F. **Kingdoms of gold, Kingdoms of jade** The Americas before Columbus. London, Thames and Hudson, 1991. 240p. illus. (some col.) maps, bibliog., index. £16.95. ISBN: 050005062.

Splendidly illustrated chronological narrative of rise and fall of American pre-Columbian civilizations. 14 chapters grouped in 5 parts: 1. Civilizations of 1492 - 2. First Americans - 3. Civilizations of ancient Mesoamerica - 4. Civilizations of the Andes - 5. Chiefdoms of North America. Bibliography (by chapter) p.230-4. *Class No:* 97

[7850]

INGERHUT, E.R. Who first discovered America? a critique of writings on pre-Columbian voyages. Claremont, California, Regina Books 1984. viii,147p. maps, bibliogs., index. $17.95. (*Guides to Historical Issues, no.1.*) ISBN: 0941690105.

Historiographic study in 9 chapters: Pt.1. The travelers: 1. Prehistoric and ancient Atlantic travelers - 2. Transatlantic contacts between medieval Europe and North America - 3. Norse expeditions to North America - 4/5. Transpacific contacts with America - 6. Sub-Sahara Africa connection with the New World. Pt.2 Transocean cultural diffusion vs. independent development. 7. Basic issues - 8. Biological evidence and claims of Pre-Columbian contact across the oceans - 9. Summary. Bibliographical sections list nearly 450 modern references. *Class No: 97*

Bibliographies
[7851]

Columbus literature guides.
1. Metz, A. 'Christopher Columbus: a selection guide to literature 1970-1989', *Reference Services Review*, v.19, no.4, 1991, p.21-44. 91 annotated entries arranged in 5 sub-divided parts: 1. European intellectual background - 2. Exploration - 3. Christopher Columbus - 4. Conquest and colonization - 5. Miscellaneous (Heraldry; Quincentennial).
2. Fialkoff, F. and De Candido, K. 'Rediscovering Columbus', *Library Journal*, v.116, no.13, August 1991, p.120-2. Literature review of books to be published in 1991 Fall season.
3. 'Dealing with Columbus', *Booklist*, v.88, no.4, 15 Oct 1991. p.369-80. 'A valid overview of how Columbus and his voyages have been read and misread over several centuries.
2. Shreve, J. 'Christopher Columbus: a bibliographic voyage', *Choice*, v.29, no.5, January 1992, p.703-11. Bibliographical essay assessing the books 'felt to have worth as potential additions to American collections arranged in 9 sections. Biographies - Language of Columbus - Family - Columbus' log and other writings - Toscanelli Letter - Landfall and other murky waters - Reference works - Other books - Poetry and fiction. Consolidated list of works cited p.709-11.
3. French and Spanish language material is considered in 'Les éditeurs sur les pas de Christophe Colomb', *Livres hebdo*, v.13, no.20, 17 Mai 1991, p.57-60. *Class No: 97(01)*

Encyclopaedias
[7852]

The Christopher Columbus encyclopedia. Bedini, S.A., *ed.* New York, Simon & Schuster, 1991; London, Macmillan, 2v., 1992. xxii,787p. illus., maps, ports. $175. £95. ISBN: 0131426621, US; 033358995, UK.

About 350 signed A-Z articles (350-10,000 words) from over 150 contributors on Columbus' life; the contemporary world (social, political, economic and cultural institutions of Europe, biographies of reigning monarchs); Pre-Columbian exploration and discovery; Science and technology of discovery; The New World (archaeology, settlements, natural history); and Post-Columbian exploration and discovery. Issues raised are discussed both from the indigenous and European viewpoint. Published to mark the quincentenary of Columbus' first voyage to America in 1492. 'Will remain a useful reference source long after the quincentenary is over' (*Booklist*, v.88, no.4, 15 Oct 1991, p.379). *Class No: 97(031)*

Maps & Atlases
[7853]

GREAT BRITAIN. Public Record Office. Maps and plans in the Public Record Office. America and West Indies. Penfold, P.A. London H.M. Stationery Office, 1975. xv,835p. £18.00. ISBN: 0114400539.

Inventory of 4,493 items, plus interpolations. 6 sections: 1. America, North America, Atlantic Ocean, Greenland - 2. Canada (nos. 143-1986) - 3. United States of America (nos.1987-2952) - 4. West Indies - 5. Mexico, Central America - 6. South America (nos.4081-446). Data: Title; date; description; nature (*e.g.* manuscript; slightly coloured); scale; compass indicator; location in PRO). Range is from large area maps to plans of buildings. Index of persons, 'but not of place-names and subjects of major interest' (*British Book News*, October 1975.p.698). *Class No: 97(084.3)*

Chronologies
[7854]

MORLEY, D.F. Wars of the Americas a chronology of armed conflict in the New World, 1492 to the present. Santa Barbara, Calif., and Oxford, ABC-Clio, 1998. xi,722p. illus., maps, bibliog., index. £34.95. ISBN: 0874368375.

Detailed narrative chronology of 86 wars, campaigns, disputes, incidents, raids and confrontations arranged in 8 parts: 1. Discovery and conquest (1492-1572) - 2. Seaborne Challengers (1526-1609) - 3.

....(contd.)
Rival outposts (1604-1659) - 4. Intercolonial friction (1660-1700) - 5. High tide of Empire (1700-1777) - 6. Independence (1775-1825) - 7. Nationhood (1872-1897) - 8. Pax Americana (1898-Present). Bibliography p.677-89. *Class No: 97(090)*

Amerindians, North
[7855]

The Cambridge history of the native peoples of the Americas. Cambridge Univ. Press. 3v. in 6, 1996-1999. ISBN: 0521344409, set.

V.1: *North America* in 2 pts. edited by B.G. Trigger and W.E. Washburn 1996. xix,564p.+xix,500p. illus., maps, indexes. ISBN 0521573920 (v.1); 0521573939 (v.2). £75. 15 chapters by 16 different hands (*e.g.* pt.1: 2. Native peoples in Euro-American historiography ... 6. Entertaining strangers: North America in the 16th century. pt.2: 9. The Great Plains from the arrival of the horse to 1885 ... 14. The Arctic from Norse contact to modern times.

V.2: *Mesoamerica.* in 2 pts. edited by R.E.W. Adams and M. MacLeod. Pt.1. 0521351650; Pt.2 0521652049. V.3 *South America* in 2 pts. edited by F. Salomon and S.B. Schwartz. 1999. xiv,1054p. and xiv, 976p. illus., maps, indexes. £120. $195. 0521630754 and 0521630762. Cooperative history slanted towards an idea-oriented approach. *Class No: 97(=97)*

America—North & Central
[7856]

Larousse dictionary of North American history. Min Lee, *ed.* Edinburgh, Larousse, 1994. 308p. £5.99. ISBN: 0752300059.

Mined from *Chambers dictionary of world history* (Edinburgh, Chambers, 1993).

'Simply presents the *Chambers* entries on Canada, Mexico and the United States plus a few additions that probably did not make the final selection for the Chambers volume' (*Reference Reviews*, vol.9,no.5, 1995, p.47). *Class No: 971/973*

[7857]

New American world a documentary history of North America to 1612. Quinn, D.B., *ed.* London, Macmillan, 5v., 1979. maps, bibliog., index. £295.00 boxed set. ISBN: 0333263839, set.

1. *America from concept to discovery. Early exploration of North America.* xxxvii,486p.+[70]p. ISBN 0333263847. 68 maps.
2. *Major Spanish searches in Eastern North America. The Franco-Spanish clash in Florida. The beginnings of Spanish Florida.* xxiv,594p.+[19]p. ISBN 0333263855. 19 maps.
3. *English plans for North America. The Roanoke voyages. New England ventures.* xxvi,494p.+[22]p. ISBN 0333263863. 25 maps.
4. *Newfoundlands from fishery to colony. Northwest Passage searches.* xxvi,454p.+[14]p. ISBN 03332638781. 16 maps.
5. *The extension of settlement in Florida, Virginia, and the Spanish southwest.* xxvi,490p.+[22]p. ISBN 0333263898. Bibliography p.513-28. Index p.531-72. 20 maps.

In all 851 documents in English or in English translation are printed with 148 maps. 'Must immediately become an indispensable tool for most libraries' (*TLS*, 2 May 1980). *Class No: 971/973*

Encyclopaedias
[7858]

COOKE, J.E., ed. Encyclopedia of the North American colonies. New York, Scribners, 3v., 1993. 865p. maps and charts, index. $320. ISBN: 0684192691.

274 essays cover the period from the late 10th century Norse settlements in Newfoundland to the establishment of the Dominion of Canada in 1867. V.3 contains a detailed and comprehensive index. 'A landmark reference work without equal' (*RQ*, v.33,no.4, Summer 1994, p.549-50). *Class No: 971/973(031)*

Maps & Atlases
[7859]

From sea charts to satellite images interpreting North American history through maps. Buisseret, D., *ed.* Chicago, Univ. of Chicago Press 1990. xvi,324p. illus. (some col.), maps, index. ISBN: 0226079929.

A collection of 12 essays, by 10 different hands: 1. European antecedents of New World maps - 2. Maps of the age of European exploration ... 7. City maps and plans - 8. North American county maps and atlases ... 10. Topographical surveys of the United States - 11. Twentieth-century highway maps. Glossary p.317-8. 'Each chapter begins with a general survey of the nature and history of the type of map in question, goes on to give eight or ten commentated examples ... of the way such maps can be used by historians, and concludes with a section on how to find this material' (*Preface*). *Class No: 971/973(084.3)*

[7860]

HAYES, D. **Historical atlas of the Pacific Northwest** maps of expoloration and discovery: British Columbia, Washington, Oregon, Alaska, Yukon Sasquatch, 1999. 208p. maps (many in col.), facsims., bibliog., index. $35. ISBN: 1570612153.

322 maps reproduced complemented by notes, details of sources, and a map catalogue combine 'to insure both a book of great beauty and a comprehensive record unlike any other on the Northwest' (*Choice*, v.37, no.6, February 2000, p.1156).
Class No: 971/973(084.3)

[7861]

HOMBERGER, E. **The Penguin historical atlas of North America.** London, Viking, 1995. 144p. illus. (many col.), col. maps, bibliog., index. £26. ISBN: 0670864625.

Timelines (40,000BC-1994) p.8-13. 42 map features in 6 sections: 1. First peoples - 2. European interest - 3. Making a nation - 4. Spanning a continent - 5. Urban people - 6. Imperial matters. Bibliography p.138. *Class No:* 971/973(084.3)

Biographies

Bibliographies

[7862]

People in history an index to US and Canadian biographies in history journals and dissertations. Kinnell, S., *ed.* Santa Barbara, California, and Oxford, ABC-Clio, 2v., 1988. $137.00; £103.75. ISBN: 0874364930, set.

Guide to biographical material relating to 6,000 individuals prominent in American history extracted from 737 journals on the ABC-Clio database. An extensive subject index allows access by a number of descriptors. *Class No:* 971/973(092)(01)

Canada

[7863]

Chronicle of Canada. Montreal, Chronicle Publications, 1990. 980p. col. illus., col. maps. £29.95. ISBN: 0920417176.

Concise popular newspaper style articles and datelines on Canadian history in 6 chronological sections: 1. New World BC 4.6 million to 1607 - 2. Foundations 1608 to 1763 - 3. Conquest and change 1764 to 1867 - 4. Nation building 1867 to 1913 -5. War and peace 1914 to 1945 - 6. Canada comes of age 1945 to 1989. *Class No:* 971

[7864]

Generations: A history of Canada's peoples. Toronto, McClelland & Stewart in association with the Multiculturalism Directorate, Department of the Secretary of State and the Canadian Government Publishing Centre, Supply and Services Canada, 1980-.

1. *An olive branch on the family tree. The Arabs in Canada.* by B. Abu-Laban. 1980. vii,259p. 2. *The Canadian odyssey, the Greek experience in Canada* by P.D. Chimbos. 1980. ix,176p. 3. *From fjiord to frontier. A history of the Norwegians in Canada.* by G. Loken. 1980. viii,264p. 4. *Struggle and hope: the Hungarian-Canadian experience.* by N.F. Dreisziger and others. 1982. viii,247p. 5. *A heritage in transition. Essays in the history of Ukranians in Canada.* by M.R. Lupul. 1982. viii,344p. 6. *For a better world: a history of the Croatians in Canada by A.W. Rasporich.* 1982. xiii,279p. 7. *From China to Canada. A history of the Chinese communities in Canada.* 1982. viii,369p. Readable histories of some of the many ethnic groups in contemporary Canada. *Class No:* 971

Bibliographies

[7865]

BEAULIEU, A., *and others.* **Guide d'Histoire du Canada.** Québec. Presses de l'Université Laval, 1969. xvi, 540p. (*Les Cahiers de l'Institut d'Histoire, no.13.*)

Based on A. Beaulieu's *Guide de l'etudiant en histoire du Canada.* Well-annotated entries for general reference works, MS and printed sources, maps and atlases, general, regional and specialised histories of Canada; historical auxiliary subjects; and relevant periodicals. *Class No:* 971(01)

[7866]

A Bibliography of Canadiana being items in the Metropolitan Toronto Library relating to the early history and development of Canada. Toronto, Metropolitan Toronto Library Board, 1934-.

V1. Staton, F.M. and Tremaine, M. eds., 1934. 828p. illus. 4646 numbered and annotated entries encompassing books, pamphlets and broadsides on Canada published 1534-1867. Author and selected subject indexes.

First supplement. Boyle, G.M. ed. 1959. 333p. A further 1640 entries.

Second supplement. Alston, S. ed. 1. *To 1800.* 2. *1801-1849.* 1985. 839p. 0887730299. Items 6800-8040 with Name, title, place of publication, printers, publishers, maps and plans, illustrations, and subject indexes. 3. *1850-1867.* 1985. 910p. 0887730299 Items 8041-

....(*contd.*)

9655. Bibliography p.27-34. Key to bibliographical sources p.19-25. *Second supplement* orders titles by imprint date, previously arrangement was by date of content significance. A bibliographical catalogue *par excellence* for researchers. *Class No:* 971(01)

[7867]

BOND, M.E. *and* CARON, M.M., *comps.* **Canadian reference sources:** an annotated bibliography: general reference works, history, humanities. Vancouver, Univ. of British Columbia Press/National Library of Canada, 1996. 1,076p., indexes. Can $225. ISBN: 077480565x.

Replaces D.E. Ryder's *Canadian reference sources* (Ottawa, Canadian Library Association, 2nd ed. 1981).

4,000 entries about Canada arranged according to subject, genre, document type, and geographical jurisdiction. Data: full biographical citation; ISBN/ISSN; descriptive annotation in English and French. 'Essential for all Canadiana, research and large public collections' (*Choice,* v.34, no.4, December 1996, p.586). Selected as one of *Choice's* Outstanding Academic Books of 1996. *Class No:* 971(01)

[7868]

GAGNON, P. **Essai de bibliographie Canadienne** inventaire d'une bibliothèque comprenant imprimés manuscrits, estampes etc. rélatifs à l'histoire du Canada et des pays adjacents avec des notes bibliographiques. New York, Irvington, 2v. vii, 711+462p. facsims. $90.00. ISBN: 0891977511, set; 0697000044, v.1; 0697000052, v.2.

V.1. originally published by the author 1895; v.2. by City of Montreal in 1913.

Definitive bibliography of Canadian history. V1. has 5018 items V2. *Collection Gagnon depuis 1895 à 1900 inclusivement, d'après les notes bibliographiques et le catalogue de l'auteur* is a supplement. *Class No:* 971(01)

[7869]

GOBBETT, B. *and* IRWIN, R. **Introducing Canada** An annotated bibliography of Canadian history in English. Lanham, Md., Scarecrow Press and Pasadena, Calif., Salem Press, 1998. 373p. indexes. £42.75. ISBN: 0810833832.

c.750 annotated entries arranged in 9 thematic sections: 1. General and reference works - 2. Political - 3. Economic - 4. Military - 5. Womens - 6. Immigrant - 7. Workers - 8. Intellectual - 9. Regional history. Each section opens with a historiographical review. Author, title and subject indexes. *Choice* Outstanding Academic Title 1999. *Class No:* 971(01)

[7870]

A Reader's guide to Canadian history. Toronto, University of Toronto Press, 2v., 1982.

V2, is a revision of Granatstein's *Canada since 1867: a bibliographic guide* (2nd ed., 1977).

1. *Beginnings to Confederation* edited by D.A. Muise. 1982. xv, 253p. index. $12.95. 0802064426. 2. *Confederation to the present* edited by J.L. Granatstein and P. Stevens. xiv, 329p. index. $13.95. 0802064906. A literature survey composed of 19 chronological, thematic and geographical chapters each beginning with a bibliographic essay followed by annotated lists of significant titles. 'An essential purchase for any library whose patrons have an interest in Canada' (*Choice,* v.20, no.5, January 1983, p.692). *Class No:* 971(01)

[7871]

SCHULTZ, J., *ed.* **Writing about Canada** a handbook for modern Canadian history. Scarborough, Ontario, Prentice-Hall Canada, 1990. xiii,282p. bibliogs., index. ISBN: 0139709304.

10 bibliographical essays by separate hands: 1. Writing about politics - 2. Economics - 3. Ideas - 4. Regions - 5. Rural life and agriculture - 6. Business - 7. Labour - 8. Women - 9. Ethnicity - 10. War. Each essay concludes with 'Endnotes' (*i.e.* bibliographical references). Appendix: Historiographical chronology p.251-61. Analytical index. *Class No:* 971(01)

[7872]

SMITH, D.L., *ed.* **The History of Canada** an annotated bibliography. Santa Barbara, Calif, and Oxford, ABC-Clio Information Services, 1983. xi, 325p. index. $55.00. £45.00. (*Clio Bibliography Series no.10.*) ISBN: 0874360471.

3362 abstracts of periodical literature 1973-1978 drawn from the *America History and Life* database grouped in 10 sections: 1. General Canadian history - 2. The natural setting - 3. The native peoples - 4. Pre-Columbian exploration and exploitation - 5. New France - 6. British North America 1763-1867 - 7. Emergent nationalism 1867-1914 - 8. Achievement of nationhood 1914-1945 - 9. The contemporary scene since 1945 - 10. Canada: regions. Subject and author indexes. Index to periodicals. *Class No:* 971(01)

[7873]

TAYLOR, M.B. *and* OWRAM, D., *eds*. **Canadian history. A readers guide**. Univ. of Toronto Press, 2v. 1994.

Replaces D.A. Muise, J.L. Granatstein, and P. Stevens *eds*. *A Reader's guide to Canadian history* (2v., 1982).

1. *Beginnings to Confederation*. 506p. $55. ISBN 0802050166. 2. *Confederation to the present*. 417p. $47.50. 0802028012. Selected critical literature guide, with an emphasis on the most recent scholarship, in 22 chronological, thematic, and geographical chapters. *Class No: 971(01)*

[7874]

THIBAULT, C., *comp*. **Bibliographia Canadiana**. Don Mills, Ontario, Longmans Canada, 1973. lxiv,795p.

25,568 unannotated entries, many for articles. 4 parts, with subdivisions: 1. Tools of research - 2. The French colonial régime - 3. British North America, 1713-1867 - 4. The Dominion of Canada, 1867-1967 (nos.12, 427-23, 485). Subject, name and locality index, in English and French. Sources, p.xiii-lxiv. 'Attempts to produce for scholars & students of Canadian history what the *Harvard Guide to American history* achieved for American studies' (*RQ*, v.14,no.1, Fall 1974, p.71). *Class No: 971(01)*

[7875]

WATERSTON, E., *and others, eds*. **The Travellers: Canada to 1900** an annotated bibliography of works published in English from 1577. Guelph, Ontario, Univ. of Guelph, 1989. 321p. illus. indexes. Can$49.00. ISBN: 0889551707.

Historical introduction. Over 700 items arranged in chronological order with author/title and subject indexes. *Class No: 971(01)*

Encyclopaedias

[7876]

STORY, N. **The Oxford companion to Canadian history and literature**. Toronto, Oxford Univ. Press, 1967. xx, 935p. maps, bibliog.

Parent volume contains *c*.1,900 articles (1,500 on Canadian history). Extensive bibliographies (*e.g.* 'Arcadia: bibliography': p.5-6; 'Rebellion of 1837: bibliography': p.699-700). 5 appendices (2. Governors General, etc.). List of titles referred to (title-date-author), p.866-935, *c*.6,000 entries. Important for entries on people, places, periodicals and societies of Canada. 'A very valuable reference tool' (*RQ*, v.7, no.4, Summer 1968, p.191).

W. Toye's *Supplement to the Oxford companion to Canadian history and literature* (1973) ISBN 0195402057 adds nearly 200 entries covering the period 1967-72. *Class No: 971(031)*

Dictionaries

[7877]

BERCUSON, D.J. *and* GRANATSTEIN, J.L. **The Collins dictionary of Canadian history** 1867 to the present. Toronto, Collins, 1988. xviii, 270p. illus. $24.95. ISBN: 0002177587.

Guide to the people, institutions, and events that have shaped Canada since Confederation in 1867. Timelines (political, social and economic, scientific and technical, artistic and cultural, and sport) p.x-xii. Long list of appendices *e.g.* Canada's Governors General, federal election results, *etc*. Sources p.269-70. 5 maps. *Class No: 971(038)*

[7878]

GOUGH, B. **Historical dictionary of Canada**. Lanham, MD., Scarecrow Press, 1999. 304p. $55. £41.25. ISBN: 081083541x.

In the initial historical overview found in the dictionary's introduction, Gough highlights Canada's geography, culture and history from its days as a European colony to NAFTA. He also includes the defined stages of Canada's self-perception, the four continuities of Canadian history, including its imperial connections, two founding European peoples, federal-provincial relations and the United States as Canada's neighbour. This handy reference to Canadian economics, history, government and colonisation studies includes a bibliography, maps and appendices of Canadian government leaders. *Class No: 971(038)*

Maps & Atlases

[7879]

Canada then and now maps of the nation's growth 1867-1982. Ottawa, Energy Mines and Resources Canada, nd. $5.95. (Canada). $7.15 (US and international).

3 maps showing Canada at the time of Confederation, the progressive evolution of provincial boundaries, and a modern map of Canada. Published to commemorate the repatriation of the constitution. There is also a French version: *Le Canada d'hier à aujourd'hui*. *Class No: 971(084.3)*

[7880]

Historical atlas of Canada. maps, bibliog. Univ. of Toronto Press, 3v., 1987-.

V.1: *From the beginning to 1800*. edited by R.C. Harris. 1987. xviii,198p. ISBN 0862024955. 69 two-page cartographic presentations, *i.e.* maps and closely integrated text, arranged in 6 sections: 1. Prehistory; 2. The Atlantic realm; 3. Inland expansion; 4. The St. Lawrence settlements; 5. The Northwest; 6. Canada in 1800, each introduced by a scholarly essay. Notes (including primary and secondary sources) p.179-198. 'A magisterial work of value to all interested in Canada, general and learned readers alike, and it is difficult to imagine that it could be even remotely paralleled in the future' (*Geographical Journal;* v.154,no.2, July 1988, p.295-296.

V.2: *The Land transformed 1800-1891* edited by R.L. Gentilcore. 1994. xxii,184p. $85. 0802034470. 58 map features. Pt.1. Extending the frontier: Settlement to mid-century - 2. Immigrant population - 3. Expanding economies. Pt.2: Building a nation: Canada to the end of the century - 4. Forging the links - 5. The people - 6. Economies in transition - 7. Urbanization and manufacturing - 8. A changing society.

V.3: *Addressing the twentieth century 1891-1961* edited by D. Kerr and D.W. Holdsworth, 1990. [xx],197p. $95. 0802034489. 66 map and text features: Canada 1891-1961: an overview (1. Canada in 1891 - 2. Territorial evolution - 3. Economic growth - 4. Population distribution) - Part 1. The great transformation 1891-1929 and Part 2. Crisis and response 1929-1961. 'The initiators and engineers of this project should be justly proud of their efforts: we should be most appreciative of their version' (*Cartographica*, v.28,no.2, Summer 1991, p.91-4).

Concise historical atlas of Canada edited by W.G. Dean and others. 1998. 228p. $85. 0802042031, 67 of the most important plates of the original volumes, organized thematically, with brief informative texts to accompany each map. *Class No: 971(084.3)*

Chronologies

[7881]

COOKE, A. *and* HOLLAND, C. **The Exploration of Northern Canada** 500 to 1920 a chronology. Toronto, The Arctic History Press, 1978. 549p.+25p., maps. ISBN: 0771022654.

First printed in *Polar Record*, May 1970-September 1973.

1. Chronology (p.11-348) with details of each voyage or expedition date, its nature, leader, and frequently other senior names, and its ship or sledge, the expedition's point of departure, dates of its duration, a succinct account, and references. 2. Roster of names (5000 entries). 3. Bibliography (p.449-505). Index. *Class No: 971(090)*

[7882]

The Fitzhenry Whiteside book of Canadian Facts and dates. Myers, J. *and* Musson, J., *comps*. 3rd ed. Markham, ON., Fitzhenry Whiteside, 1997. 905p. bibliog., indexes. ISBN: 1550411713.

10,000+ entries in a chronological listing of Canadian events from geological times to 1996. Covers military history, aboriginal affairs, arts and music, politics, events, customs, and personalities. *Class No: 971(090)*

[7883]

MYERS, J. **Canadian facts and dates**. Toronto, Fitzhenry and Whiteside, 1991. 404p. indexes. £24.95. ISBN: 1550410733.

7000 entry chronology of Canada from prehistoric beginnings to contemporary political, social and cultural events. Detailed general index and index of names. *Class No: 971(090)*

Official Records

[7884]

COOK, T. *and* WRIGHT, G.T. **Historical records of the Government of Canada** Documents historiques du governement du Canada. 2nd ed. Ottawa, Federal Archives Division, Public Archives of Canada, 1981. 84+88p. indexes, softcover. ISBN: 0662509935.

128 record groups (*e.g.* Governor-General's office; Royal Commissions; Public Archives of Canada) in numerical sequence p.9-76. New to this ed. are brief outlines of the principal functions and administrative background of each record group. Subject classification, p.77-80. Alphabetical index. Separate English and French sequences. 'This guide has been prepared to provide researchers and government officials with a concise description of the holdings of the Division' (*Preface*). *Class No: 971(093.2)*

Amerindians, North

Dictionaries

[7885]

'**Glossary of Indian tribal names**', *Dictionnary of Canadian biography*, v.1, 1966, p.12-16; v.2, 1969, p.xxvi-xxxix; v.3, 1974, p.xxxi-xliii and 'Glossary of native peoples', v.4, 1979, p.l-lvii.

'To assist the reader in identifying and locating geographically those

....*(contd.)*

tribes encountered by Europeans in the early exploration and development of Canada, but makes no claim to be a detailed and complete summary' (*v.1*). *Class No:* 971(=97)(038)

Canadian Provinces (History)

[7886]

COATES, K.S. *and* MORRISON, W.R. **Land of the midnight sun** a history of the Yukon. Edmonton, Alberta, Hurtig, 1988. vii,336p. illus., map, bibliog., index. $29.95. ISBN: 0888303319.

9 chronological chapters: 1,. The natives' Yukon - 2. The fur trade ... 8. War and upheaval 1939-1946 - 9. The new Yukon 1946-1987. Chapter notes p.300-19. Bibliography p.320-7. *Class No:* 971.1

[7887]

MORRISON, W.R. **True North** The Yukon and Northwest Territories. Don Mills, Ontario, Oxford Univ. Press Canada, 1998. 212p. illus. (some col.), maps, index. pbk £16.99. ISBN: 0195410459.

The history of the land and people of Subarctic Canada. *Class No:* 971.1

[7888]

PECK, M. **The Bitter with the sweet:** New Brunswick 1604-1984. Tantallon, Nova Scotia, Four East Publications, 1983. x, 174p. illus., maps. ISBN: 0969004184.

20 chapters arranged in 3 sections: Founders of the province; A developing society; and The second century. Chapter notes p.165-168. Bibliography p.169-172. 'Written for New Brunswick's Bicentennial year, this book tells the story of individuals and institutions that exemplify important aspects of the province's history' (*Acknowledgements*). *Class No:* 971.1

Bibliographies

[7889]

BISHOP, G.B. **Bibliography of Ontario history 1867-1976** cultural, economic, political, social. Toronto, Univ. of Toronto Press, 2v., 1980. A project of the Ontario Historical Studies Series for the Government of Ontario. xviii, 1760p. index. ISBN: 0802023592, set. ISSN: 03809188.

2nd ed. of *Ontario since 1867: a bibliography* (1974).

Lists 15,000 books, manuscripts, pamphlets, periodical articles with library locations.

Gervais, G. and others, eds. *The Bibliography of Ontario 1976-1986*. Toronto, Dundurn Press, 1989. xxxiv,605p. index. ISBN 1550020315. In 8 parts: 1. General - 2. Ontario before 1783 - 3. Economic history - 4. Social - 5. Political - 6. Military - 7. Culture and civilization - 8. Regional and local. Produced by the Institute of Northern Ontario Research and Development. *Class No:* 971.1(01)

[7890]

BRITISH COLUMBIA. Library of the Provincial Archives. **Dictionary catalogue of the Library.** Boston, Mass., G.K. Hall, 8v., 1971. $790.00 Export 955.00.

176,00 photolithographed catalogue cards, representing material on Western Canada, Alaska and Northwestern US. Classified under the Dewey Decimal System with Library of Congress subject headings. *Class No:* 971.1(01)

[7891]

Canadian local histories to 1950: a bibliography. Morley, W.F.E., *ed.* Toronto, Univ. of Toronto Press, 3v., 1967-78. illus., facsims., maps.

Sponsored by the Centennial Commission as a Centennial of Canadian Confederation Project under the Publications Assistance Programme.

1. *The Atlantic Provinces:* Newfoundland, Nova Scotia, New Brunswick, Prince Edward Island, by W.F.E. Morley. 1967. xx, [1], 137p. 2. *La province du Québec*, by A. Beaulieu and W.F.E. Morley. 1971. xxvii,408p. 3. *Ontario and the Canadian North*, by W.F.E. Morley. 1978. xxxii, 322p. V.3 has 2 parts (1. Ontario and regions; counties and districts; cities, towns and townships - 2. Canadian North; Hudson's Bay; Northern Territories; Yukon Territories). Sources, p.xxi-xxvii; locations: *c.*80 Canadian and 21 US libraries. Geographical and general indexes. 12 illus. and maps. *Class No:* 971.1(01)

[7892]

HALE, L.L. **Vancouver centennial bibliography:** a project of the Vancouver Historical Society. Vancouver, Vancouver Historical Society, 4v., 1986. xi, 1791p. ISBN: 0969237804, set; 0969237812, v.1; 0969237820, v.2; 0969237839, v.3; 0969237847, v.4.

1. Books, pamphlets and broadsides. 2. 15 sections based on format *e.g.* theses, articles, film and video productions. 3. Name and title index. 4. Subject and series index. 15090 unannotated entries taken from major libraries and archives in British Columbia, the National Library of Canada, and the Public Archives of Canada. Citations according to AACR2. Locations given. *Class No:* 971.1(01)

Maps & Atlases

[7893]

GENTILCORE, R.L. *and* HEAD, C.G. **Ontario's history in maps.** Toronto, Univ. of Toronto Press for the Ontario Historical Studies Series, 1984. xvii, 284p. maps (some col.), facsims., bibliog. ISBN: 0802034004.

268 maps illustrated and accompanied by text and notes. A cartobibliographical essay 'Sources for early maps on Ontario' (p.276-284) includes 106 references. No index but a detailed list of maps p.x-xiii. 'Our guiding principle has been to present maps as valuable documentary sources for the history of Ontario' (*Introduction*). *Class No:* 971.1(084.3)

Quebec

Bibliographies

[7894]

AUBIN, P. *and* CÔTÉ, L-M. **Bibliographie de l'histoire du Québec et du Canada** / Bibliography of the history of Quebec and Canada 1946-1965. Quebec, Institut Québécois De Recherche Sur la Culture. 2v.,1987. lxxvii,1396p. ISBN: 2892240980.

21,845 entries arranged in systematic classification of 6 divisions: General history; Prehistory; Ethnohistory; Exploration; Euro-Canada era; Demographic indexes and genealogies p.1-793. Classification tables p.xii-xiii. French and English indexes of terms used in systematic and analytic classification p.xxii-lxxvii. Analytic classification (subject index) p.797-1337. Classification by author (author index) p.1341-89. List of consulted periodicals (over 400) p.1393-6. Admirably controlled bibliography. Modelled on *Bibliographie annuelle de l'histoire de France*. This volume follows 2 previous volumes *1966-1975* and *1976-1980* (2nd ed. 1985. ISBN 2892240557) which contains 20,224 entries. *1981-1985* is in preparation. *Class No:* 971.4(01)

[7895]

Guide de l'histoire du Québec. Rouillard, J., *ed.* Montréal, Éditions du Méridien, 1991. 200p. Can$14.95. ISBN: 2894150520.

'Cette bibliographie est en fait un essai bibliographique dans lequel un groupe d'universitaires, d'historiens et de spécialistes des sciences humaines font un choix des meilleurs travaux ... Divisé selon les périodes traditionnelles entre le Régime français, le Régime brittanique et le Québec contemporain'. *Class No:* 971.4(01)

Chronologies

[7896]

PROVENCHER, J. **Chronologie du Québec.** Montréal, Les Éditions du Boréal, 1991. 240p. Can$22.95. ISBN: 2890524159.

Stretches from prehistory to 1980. Later political, social, and cultural events are set in North American and global context. *Class No:* 971.4(090)

Mexico

[7897]

COSIO VILLEGAS, D., *ed.* **Historia moderna de Mexico. 9v. in 10.** Mexico City, 1955-72.

1-3. *La republica restaurada.* 1. *La vida politica* (1955); 2. *La vida economica* (1955); 3. *La vida social* (1957). 4-9. *El porfiriato.* 4. *La vida social* (1957); 5-6. *La vida exterior* (1960-1963); 7. *La vida economica* (1965); 8-9. *La vida politica* (1970-1972). Review article of entire work: C.A. Hale's 'The Liberal impulse: Daniel Cosio Villegas and the Historia moderna de Mexico', *Hispanic American Historical Review*, v.54, no.3, August 1974, p.479-498. *See also* S.R. Ross' 'Cosio Villegas Historia moderna de Mexico', *ibid.*, v.46, no.3, August 1966, p.274-282. 'The most extensive and significant undertaking in Modern Mexican historiography' (Griffin, C.C. *Latin America*, Entry no.4160). *Class No:* 972

[7898]

MEYER, M.C., *and others, eds.* **The Course of Mexican history.** 6th ed. New York, OUP. USA, 1999. 794p. illus., maps, bibliog., index. $40. ISBN: 0195110005.

First published 1979.

45 chapters in 10 sections: 1. Pre-Columbian Mexico - 2. Spanish conquest ... 7. Modernization of Mexico 1876-1910 ... 10. The Revolution shifts gear: Mexico since 1940. Appendix: Mexican heads of state 1349-1988 p.i-iv. Chapter bibliographies. Select bibliography for those who read Spanish p.v-xix. Over 30 maps and charts. New to this edition: extended sections on historical background to Spanish conquistadores, society, religious and cultural history of Mexico. 'As a summary reference volume for the general reader it is superior to all others' (*Hispanic American Historical Review*, v.60,no.1, February 1980, p.99-101). *Class No:* 972

Encyclopaedias

[7899]

Encyclopedia of Mexico history, society and culture. Werner, M.S., *ed.*
London, Fitzroy Dearborn, 2v., 1997. xli,1749p. maps, bibliogs.
£175. ISBN: 1884964311.

350 academic contributors from 9 countries. 600 cross-referenced
entries of 2 kinds, longer surveys of primary themes, and
supplementary articles on specific events, leading figures and
institutions that played an important part in Mexican history.
Bibliographies cite items judged to be of most use to non-specialist
readers. *Choice* Outstanding Academic Book 1998.
Class No: 972(031)

Dictionaries

[7900]

BRIGGS, D.C. *and* ALISKY, M. Historical dictionary of Mexico.
Metuchen, New Jersey, Scarecrow Press, 1981. xiv,259,bibliog.
$24.00; £22.50. (*Latin American Historical Dictionaries, no.21.*)
ISBN: 0810813912.

Dictionary p.1-235. Bibliography p.237-259. 'A major
disappointment. Although it does contain much helpful material,
especially recent politics in Mexico, the book is weak on historical
data' (*Choice*, v.19,no.2, October 1981, p.218). *Class No:* 972(038)

[7901]

NELSON, G.E. *and* NELSON, M.B. Mexico A-Z an encyclopedic
dictionary of Mexico. Cuernevaca, Centro Para Retirados, 1975.
maps, bibliog.

Comprehensive historical and cultural dictionary from the earliest
times to the present. *Class No:* 972(038)

[7902]

VÁZQYEZ-GOMEZ, J. Dictionary of Mexican rulers 1325-1997.
Westport, CT., Greenwood Press, 1997. x,191p. bibliog., indexes.
ISBN: 0313300496.

Career and political profiles of successive rulers of Mexico: 1. The
Aztecs 1325-1524 - 2. Encounter, conquest and the Colonial Period
1502-1821. 3. From the War of Independence to the Díaz dictatorship
1810-1910. 4. Revolutions and modern Mexico 1910-1997. Glossary
p.143. Chronology p.159-65. Bibliography p.175-78.
Class No: 972(038)

Atlantic Ocean

[7903]

BUTEL, P. The Atlantic. London, Routledge, 1999. 336p. illus., maps,
bibliog., index. $65. ISBN: 0415106907.

Early sea legends and realities before the 15th century Portuguese
and Spanish voyages, geographers and explorers who shaped the
history and development of Atlantic navigation, are some of the themes
of this fluently written study. The bibliography list English and
French-language sources. *Class No:* 972.61

America—Central

Archives

[7904]

Research guide to Central America and the Caribbean. Grieb, K., *ed.*
Madison, Univ. of Wisconsin Press, 1985. xv,431p. $35.00; £42.
ISBN: 0299100502.

75 contributors. Divided between essays on the current state of
research and surveys of specific US library and archive resources. In 3
sections: Central America, the Caribbean, and English-speaking
Caribbean nations. 'A reference work of exceptional value' (*Bulletin of
Latin American Research*, v.6, no.1, 1987, p.116-7).
Class No: 972.8(093.20)

Guatemala

Dictionaries

[7905]

MOORE, R.C. Historical dictionary of Guatemala. Rev. ed.
Metuchen, New Jersey, Scarecrow Press, 1973. viii, 9-285p. bibliog.,
index. (*Latin American Historical Dictionaries, no.1.*) ISBN:
0810806045.

Dictionary p.9-242. Bibliography p.243-280. 'Many of the entries
on historical figures constitute the only information to be found on
them' (*Library Journal*, v.93, no.8, 15 April 1968, p.1618).
Class No: 972.81(038)

Honduras

Encyclopaedias

[7906]

ORTEGA, R.C. Enciclopedia histórica de Honduras obra fundamental
de información y consulta e imprescindible auxiliar pedagógico para
maestros ... [Historical encyclopedia of Honduras: a fundamental work
of information and reference and an indispensable teaching aid for
teachers...] Tegucigalpa, Graficentro Editores, 1988-. In process.

Fundamental information on the history and culture of Honduras
intended for student use. V.1 of this multi-volume work deals with the
pre-Columbian and Colonial periods. 'This is not really an
encyclopaedia and access to its contents is difficult for lack of an
index' (Howard-Reguindin, P.F. *Honduras*, 1992, Entry no.187).
Class No: 972.83(031)

Dictionaries

[7907]

MEYER, H.K. *and* MEYER, J.H. Historical dictionary of Honduras.
2nd ed. Metuchen, New Jersey, Scarecrow Press, 1994. xxvi,708p.
illus., maps, bibliog. $77.50. (*Latin American Historical Dictionaries,
no.25.*) ISBN: 0810828456.

1st ed. 1976.

4276 entries (1247 definitions and 2205 fuller entries, 824 cross-
references) including every municipio, office holders, heads of state,
US envoys since 1910, economic issues, places, events, and
institutions. Chronology p.xxi-xxvi. Dictionary p.1-688. Bibliography
arranged in 10 sub-divided sections p.689-708. 'An outstanding
volume, perhaps the best yet in Scarecrow's historical dictionaries
series' (*Choice* v.32, no.9, May 1995, p.1432).
Class No: 972.83(038)

El Salvador

Dictionaries

[7908]

FLEMION, P.F. Historical dictionary of El Salvador. Metuchen, New
Jersey, Scarecrow Press, 1972. vi,7-157p. bibliog. (*Latin American
Historical Dictionaries, no.5.*) ISBN: 0810804719.

Dictionary p.7-147. Bibliography p.149-57. *Class No:* 972.84(038)

[7909]

GARCÍA, M.A. Diccionario histórico-enciclopédico de la República
de El Salvador. San Salvador, Tipografiá del Diario Latino, 13v.,
1927-55.

V.1-13 A-Col. Largely a biographical dictionary although 'they
contain an enormous amount of information on Salvadoran and Central
American history' (R.L. Woodward. *El Salvador* 1990. Entry 636).
Class No: 972.84(038)

Nicaragua

Bibliographies

[7910]

ARGÜELLO, C.M. 'Bibliografía de Nicaragua' *Inter-American Review
of Bibliography*, v.4, 1954, p.9-22.

'A basic guide to the principal historical literature of Nicaragua in
Spanish' (R.L. Woodward. *Nicaragua*, 1983. Entry 148).
Class No: 972.85(01)

Dictionaries

[7911]

MEYER, H.K. Historical dictionary of Nicaragua. Metuchen, New
Jersey, Scarecrow Press, 1972. xiii,503p. illus., maps, bibliog. (*Latin
American Historical Dictionaries, no.6.*) ISBN: 0810804883.

Dictionary p.1-482. Bibliography p.483-99. List of maps p.500-3.
Class No: 972.85(038)

Costa Rica

[7912]

Historia general de Costa Rica. De la Cruz, V., *ed.* San José,
Euroamericana de Ediciones Costa Rica, 4v., 1988. illus., maps,
bibliog.

V.1: 459p. Geography of Costa Rica. V.2: 489p. Spanish
exploration and conquest in colonial period. Also archaeology. V.3:
623p. History: independence, federation (1821-38), to 1870. V.4:
663p. History : Liberal Republic (1870-1949). Supplement (65p.) of
Documents referring to independence. V.1-3 include biographical
inserts. A narrative rather than an interpretative history.
Class No: 972.86

Bibliographies

[7913]

JUNKINS, R.J. 'Historical sources in Costa Rica', *Latin American Research Review*, v.23, no.3, 1988, p.117-27.

Well-documented 'summary of the main domestic sources of material for studying the history of Costa Rica.' *Class No:* 972.86(01)

Dictionaries

[7914]

CREEDMAN, T.S. **Historical dictionary of Costa Rica.** 2nd ed. Metuchen, New Jersey, Scarecrow Press, 1991. xxii,338p. maps, bibliog. £31.90; $42.50. (*Latin American Historical Dictionaries, no.16.*) ISBN: 0810822156.

1st ed. 1977.

Chronology (1502-1990) p.xv-xxii. Dictionary (events, persons, cultural developments *etc.*) p.1-300. Bibliography p.301-38. 2 maps. *Class No:* 972.86(038)

Panama

Dictionaries

[7915]

HEDRICK, B.C. *and* HEDRICK, A.K. **Historical dictionary of Panama.** Metuchen, New Jersey, Scarecrow Press, 1970. vi,7-105p. bibliog. (*Latin American Historical Dictionaries, no.2.*) ISBN: 081080347x.

Dictionary p.7-100. Bibliography p.101-5. *Class No:* 972.87(038)

Caribbean

[7916]

UNESCO **general history of the Caribbean.** Basingstoke, Hants, Macmillan Caribbean and UNESCO publishing, 1997-.

Vol.3: *The Slave societies of the Caribbean* edited by F.W. Knight. 1997. xvi,379p. £40. ISBN 033365040. Topics treated include the slave economy, demographic changes, social study, slave resistance and control. 'Uninspiring and inadequate to the needs of Caribbean historians' (*Journal of Imperial and Commonwealth History*, v.27, no.3, September 1999, p.129-32). *Class No:* 972.9

[7917]

WILLIAMS, E. **From Columbus to Castro** the history of the Caribbean 1492-1949. London, Andre Deutsch, 1970; New York, Harper & Row, 1973. 576p. illus., tables, bibliog., index.

29 chapters: 26. Twentieth-century colonialism - 27. The colonial nationalist movement - 28. Castroism - 29. The future of the Caribbean. 'One of the most comprehensive studies' (R.A. Myers, *Dominica*, 1987. Entry 188). *Class No:* 972.9

Dictionaries

[7918]

LUX, W. **Historical dictionary of the British Caribbean.** Metuchen, New Jersey, Scarecrow Press, 1975. x,11-226p. bibliog. (*Latin American Historical Dictionaries, no.12.*) ISBN: 0810808471.

Dictionary in separate sections for Barbados, British Honduras (Belize), Guyana, Jamaica, Leeward Islands, Trinidad & Tobago, and Windward Islands. Bibliography p.251-66. *Class No:* 972.9(038)

Maps & Atlases

[7919]

ASHDOWN, P. **Caribbean history in maps.** London and New York, Longman, 1979. iv, 84p. maps, plans, index, pbk. $10.95. ISBN: 0582765412.

77 black-and-white maps, with commentary in margins. Covers the Caribbean region up to 1978. 15 sections: 1. General - 2. The Amerindian peoples - 3. European exploration and settlement - 4. Slavery and the plantation society - 5. European rivalry and changes of ownership - 6. Revolt and revolution - 7. Emancipation - 8. The decline of sugar - 9. Problems, 1834-1900 - 10. The USA in the Caribbean - 11. Economic distress and the rise of nationalism - 12. Regional co-operation; failure and success - 13. The West Indies in the 1970s - 14. West Indian heroes (p.53-58: *c.*100) - 15. The history of individual states (maps 68-77: Cuba; Hispànola; Puerto Rico; Jamaica; the Lesser Antilles; the Bahamas; Barbados, Trinidad; Belize; Guyana). For schools. *Class No:* 972.9(084.3)

18th Century

Biographies

[7920]

BURKHOLDER, M.A. **Biographical dictionary of Councilors of the Indies.** Westport, Connecticut, Greenwood Press, 1986. 224p. bibliog., index. $67.95. £59.95. ISBN: 0313240248.

172 biographies of men who served on the Council 1717-1808. Ancillary material includes archival abbreviations; a chronology of Spain and her colonies in the 18th century; and a glossary. The Council was the supreme judicial tribunal for Spain's colonial empire. *Class No:* 972.9"17"(092)

Cuba

[7921]

PÉREZ, L.A. **Cuba between reform and revolution.** New York, Oxford Univ. Press, 1988. xiv,504p. map, tables, bibliog., index. £20. (*Latin American Histories.*) ISBN: 0195045866.

Continuous narrative history in 12 chapters: 1. Geography and pre-Columbian peoples ... 10. Eclipse of old Cuba ... 12. Socialist Cuba. Political chronology p.382-99. The outstanding feature of this work is the extensive (22 sections) selective guide to the literature p.400-93. *Class No:* 972.91

Dictionaries

[7922]

SUCHLICKI, J. **Historical dictionary of Cuba.** Metuchen, New Jersey, Scarecrow Press, 1988. xxxvi, 368p. bibliog. $39.50; £29.65. (*Latin American Historical Dictionaries, no.22.*) ISBN: 0810820714.

Chronology p.xvii-xxxvi. Dictionary p.1-305. Bibliography p.306-59. 4. Appendices: 1. Country brief (geographical, economic and political data) - 2. Diplomatic relations - 4. Presidents of Cuba. 'The entries are informative, readable, and generally impartial ... particularly useful are the biographical entries for political leaders, painters, musicians, and writers' (*Booklist*, v.85,no.3, 1 October 1988, p.240-1). *Class No:* 972.91(038)

20th Century

Micromaterials

[7923]

The **Cuban missile crisis 1962.** Cambridge, Alexandria, Virginia and Paris, Chadwyck-Healey in cooperation with The National Security Archive, Washington D.C., 1990. 15,000p. government documentation on silver halide microfiche plus 2v. printed Guide. bibliogs, index. £2200.00. (*The Making of US Policy series no.4; Nuclear History series, no.1.*) ISBN: 0898870704.

Full history including Bay of Pigs episode; US secret war against the Castro regime; the Soviet deployment of Cuban based missiles; the US naval blockade; and US-USSR diplomacy. Documents are arranged in chronological order. Printed Guide in 2v.: 1. Name, organization and subject index - 2. Events chronology; glossaries of key individuals and organizations; chronological document bibliography; and a bibliography of secondary sources. Invaluable collection of primary source material. *Class No:* 972.91"19"(003.5)

Bibliographies

[7924]

PEREZ, L.A. **Historiography in the Revolution** a bibliography of Cuban Scholarship 1959-1979. New York, Garland Publishing, 1982. xxiv, 318p. indexes. $48.00. ISBN: 0824093291.

3,783 unannotated entries in 3 sub-divided parts: 1. General and 12 chronological sub-divisions ending with 1940-1952. - 2. 12 thematic classes *.e.g.* Women ... Communism in Cuba ... Bibliography ... Historiography and method - 3. Biographies. Almost entirely Spanish language material. 'An invaluable source' (*Library Journal*, 15 November 1982, p.2,164). *Class No:* 972.91"19"(01)

[7925]

PEREZ, L.A. **In the service of the Revolution** two decades of Cuban historiography 1959-1979, *Hispanic American Historical Review*, v.60, no.1, February 1980, p.78-89.

The politics of Republican historiography - Revisionists and revolutionaries - History at the barricades - The Past as solidarity. *Class No:* 972.91"19"(01)

Jamaica

[7926]
BLACK, C.V. The History of Jamaica. Harlow, Essex, Longman Caribbean, 1988. 176p. illus., maps, index. pbk. £4.10. ISBN: 0582038987.

First published Collins Educational 1958.

21 chronological chapters: 1. The first Jamaicans - 2. The discovery - 3. Jamaica under the Spaniards ... 21. Independent Jamaica. Important dates in the islands history p.7-8. *Class No: 972.92*

Dominican Republic

Dictionaries

[7927]
DOMINGUEZ, U.R. *and* LÉON, M.D. de, *comps*. Diccionario hisórico dominicano. Santo Domingo, Editora Universitara - USAD, 1986. 365p. illus., maps.

'A useful compilation of 2800 terms pertaining to the political and economic history of the Dominican Republic (K. Schoenhals: *Dominican Republic*, 1990. Entry 898). *Class No: 972.93(038)*

Haiti

Bibliographies

[7928]
LAWLESS, R. Haiti a research handbook. New York, Garland, 1990. ix,354p. indexes. $48. ISBN: 0824065433.

4 other contributors. 2040 unannotated items in 33 topical divisions each beginning with a short introductory essay: 1. Bibliographies - 2. General history - 3. Pre-history - 4. Colonial history - 5. Independence - 6. Post-independence (1820-1915) - 7. Occupation (1915-1934) - 8. Post-occupation (1934-1957) - 9. Duvalier era (1957-1986) - 10. Post-Duvalier (1986-.) ... 27. Migration. *Class No: 972.94(01)*

Dictionaries

[7929]
PERUSSE, R. Historical dictionary of Haiti. Metuchen, New Jersey, Scarecrow Press, 1977. xiv,124p. map, bibliog. (*Latin American Historical Dictionaries, no.15.*) ISBN: 0810810069.

Chronology p.xi-xiv. Dictionary p.1-106. Appendix: Haitian Chiefs of State p.107-8. Bibliographical Essay p.109-15. Bibliography p.116-24. *Class No: 972.94(038)*

Puerto Rico

Encyclopaedias

[7930]
FERNANDEZ, R., *and others, eds*. Puerto Rico past and present an encyclopedia., Westport, CT., Greenwood Press, 1998. 375p. bibliog., index. $59.95. ISBN: 031329822x.

Entries of varying length from a single paragraph to several pages, extend over a broad range of historical and contemporary issues and topics. 'The only recent and noteworthy English-language reference resource to focus solely on Puerto Rico and Puerto Ricans' (*Choice*, v.36, no.3, November 1998, p.489) *Choice* Outstanding Academic Book award 1998. *Class No: 972.95(031)*

Bahamas

[7931]
CRATON, M. A History of the Bahamas. 3rd ed. Waterloo, Ontario, San Salvador Press, 1986. 332p. maps, bibliog.

1st ed. 1962.

'The most authoritative general political history of the Bahamas' (P.G. Boultbee. *The Bahamas.*, 1989. Entry 255). *Class No: 972.96*

Bibliographies

[7932]
CASH, P., *and others*. Sources of Bahamian history. London, Macmillan Caribbean, 1991. xiii,374p. illus., drawings, map, bibliog., index. £5.95. ISBN: 0333437467.

32 chronological and thematic sections exploring contemporary written, pictorial and archaeological material in 6 divisions: 1. Peoples of the Bahamas - 2. American connection - 3. British connection - 5. African connection - 6. Colony of free people - 6. Decolonisation. List of references in text order p.343-65. Question and answer approach for use in schools and colleges. *Class No: 972.96(01)*

Bermuda

[7933]
ZUILL, W.S. The Story of Bermuda and her people. 2nd rev. ed. London, Macmillan Caribbean, 1987. xvi, 240p. illus. (inc. 4 col. plates), maps, bibliog., index. pbk. £5.95. ISBN: 0333341562.

First published 1973; 2nd ed. 1983.

4 Parts (23 chapters): 1. Pre-settlement Bermuda - 2. The Archipelago - 3. Story of the Bermuda people - 4. Modern Bermuda. Bibliography p.231-232. For students and the general reader. *Class No: 972.98*

Barbados

[7934]
BECKLES, H. McD. A History of Barbados: from Amerindian settlement to nation-state. Cambridge, Cambridge Univ. Press, 1990. xv,224p. illus., maps, tables, bibliog., index. £22.50; $37.50. ISBN: 0521353742.

Authoritative chronological narrative in 9 chapters: 1. The first Barbadians c.650-c.1540 - 2. English colonization 1625-1644 ... 9. Some post-independence trends. Chapter notes p.211-3. Bibliography p.214-9. 'A clear, competent, and comprehensive social history' (*Hispanic American Historical Review*, v.72, no.4, November 1992, p.601). *Class No: 972.986*

Bibliographies

[7935]
BOSTON PUBLIC LIBRARY. Bibliotheca Barbadiensis a catalog of materials relating to Barbados 1650-1860. Boston, Mass., Boston Public Library, 1968. 27p. indexes.

Printed books, pamphlets and manuscripts listed chronologically. Many rare items cited. *Class No: 972.986(01)*

[7936]
HANDLER, J.S. A Guide to source material for the study of Barbados history 1627-1834. Carbondale & Edwardsville, Southern Illinois Univ. Press; London and Amsterdam, Feffer & Simons, 1971. xvi, 205p. $12.50. ISBN: 0809304368.

5 sections (1. Printed books, pamphlets, broadsheets (5 periods) - 2. Parliamentary papers - 3. Newspapers - 4. Prints - 5. Manuscripts (p.121-82). 18 library locations for section 1.) A detailed inventory, with introductory note. Analytical index, p.183-205. An extremely useful bibliography ... by a leading Caribbean scholar' (R.B. Potter and G.M.S. Dunn. *Barbados*, 1987. Entry 940). *Class No: 972.986(01)*

Trinidad & Tobago

[7937]
BRERETON, B. A History of modern Trinidad 1783-1962. Kingston, Jamaica, Heinemann, 1982. x, 262p. illus., maps, bibliog., index, pbk. $15.00. £10.25. ISBN: 0435981161.

12 chronological chapters covering the period 1498-1962. Chronology of major events p.250-253. Bibliography p.255-258. For A-level and undergraduate use. The author is Senior Lecturer in History, University of the West Indies. *Class No: 972.987*

Dictionaries

[7938]
ANTHONY, M. Historical dictionary of Trinidad and Tobago. Lanham, MD., Scarecrow Press, 1997. xxx,670p. bibliog. £79.80. (*Latin American Historical Dictionaries, no.26.*) ISBN: 0810831732.

Chronology p.xx-xxx. Dictionary (major historical events, political parties, outstanding personalities, authors, companies) p.1-629. Bibliography (under 24 thematic sub-headings inc. historiography and cartography) p.633-70. *Class No: 972.987(038)*

Netherlands Antilles

Dictionaries

[7939]
GASTMANN, A. Historical dictionary of the French and Netherlands Antilles. Metuchen, New Jersey, Scarecrow Press, 1978. viii,162p. bibliog. $19.00; £19.00. (*Latin American Historical Dictionaries, no.18.*) ISBN: 0810811537.

Dictionary in 3 sections: General, French, Netherlands Antilles p.1-47. Bibliography (3 sections) p.149-62. *Class No: 972.988(038)*

Latin America

[7940]

The Cambridge history of Latin America. Bethell, L., *ed*. Cambridge, Cambridge Univ. Press, 11v. 1984-1998.

1-2. *Colonial Latin America* v.1: 1984. xx,645p. £89.95. ISBN 0521232236. V.2: 1984. xx,912p. £115. 0521245168. 3. *From independence to 1870.* 1985. xx,945p. £115. 0521232244. 4-5. *1870-1930* v.1: 1986. xiii,676p. £95. 0521232252. V.2: 1986. xviii,951p. £115. 0521245184. 7. *Latin America since 1830: Mexico, Central America and the Caribbean* 1990. 656p. £95. 05212451848. *Latin America since 1930. Spanish South America.* 1992. xiv,775p. £89.95. 0521266521. 6. *Latin America since 1930. Pt.1. Economy and society. 1994. 1120p. £65. 0521232260. Pt.2. Politics and society.* 1994. 800p. £65. 05214655467. 10. *Latin America since 1930: ideas, culture and society.* 1996. £70. 0521495946. 11. *Bibliographical essays.* 1995. £60. 0521395259. An important feature of the *History* has been the bibliographical essays accompanying each chapter which, with few exceptions, were contributed by the authors of the chapters. The essays survey the secondary literature on the history of Latin America: books, chapters in books, articles in a wide range of scholarly journals and noteworthy unpublished Ph.D. theses - mainly in English, Spanish and Portuguese, but to a lesser extent also in French and German. With the *History* nearing completion it was decided to bring together in a separate volume the bibliographical essays - revised, updated and in most cases expanded - from Volumes I to VIII (which were published between 1984 and 1994), along with several new essays that will eventually be published in Volumes IX and X. 'This work measures up to the standards of solid scholarship that characterize other multivolume Cambridge histories. The international contributors are all reputable specialists and present competent, up-to-date surveys' (*Choice*, v.23, no.9, May 1986, p.1446). *Class No: 972.99 (53424/0).* An important feature of the *History* has been the bibliographical essays accompanying each chapte *Class No: 972.99*

[7941]

Historia de España. Tuñón de Lara, M., *general editor*. Barcelona, Editorial Labor, 1983 and 1986. maps, tables, bibliog., indexes.

v.6 *América Hispánica (1492-1898)* by G. Céspedes del Castillo. 1983. 526p. 8433594265. 15 chapters in 4 parts: 1. La nueva frontera (1450-1550) - 2. Los reinos de las Indas (1550-1750) - 3. Las provincias de Ultramar (1750-1808) - 4. La desintegración de la Monarquia (1808-1898).

v.13. *Textos y documentos de la América Hispánica (1492-1898)* 1986. lxxxvi, 478p. 8433594478. Arranged according to v.6. *Class No: 972.99*

[7942]

PARRY, J.H., *ed*. **New Iberian world** a documentary history of the discovery and settlement of Latin America to the early seventeenth century. New York, Times Books and Hector & Rose, Toronto, Fitzhenry and Whiteside Ltd., 5v. 1984. 2912p. maps, bibliog., index. ISBN: 0812910702 (set).

1. *The Conquerors and the conquered* (Native societies, Iberian precedents. The formal structure of empire). xlix, 442p.+17p. maps. 081290710. General Introduction p.xxxix-xlviii. 2. *The Caribbean* (The Discovery of the New World, The Settlement of the West Indies, The Spanish Main). xxi, 552p.+16p. maps. 0812910729. 3. *Central America and Mexico* (The Isthmus, The Gulf of Honduras and the Gulf of Mexico 1503-1518, The invasion of central Mexico, Expansion from Mexico). xix, 582p.+18p. maps. 0812910737. 4. *The Andes* (The Discovery and conquest of Peru, Spanish Peru, The Northern Andes). xvii, 549p.+19p. maps. 0812910745. 5. *Coastlines, rivers and forests.* xvii, 572p. 0812910753. Maps p.461-498. Bibliography p.499-506. Index p.509-572. 494 documents 2/3 of them available in English for the first time. 110 plates and maps. Comprehensive index and subject index. The policy of the editors is to include 'small samples of all principal types of document that occur in the colonial archives and within each type to select documents for their significance.' Comments on the *Archivo de Indias* at Seville, and other notable collections, may be found in the General Introduction. All 5 v. include a useful glossary. 'Given its quality, this collection immediately becomes the standard source of translated documents for students, scholars, and general readers interested in the Americas in the 16th century' (*Choice*, v.22, no.5, January 1985, p.734-735). *Class No: 972.99*

[7943]

SKIDMORE, T.E. *and* **SMITH, P.H. Modern Latin America.** 3rd ed. New York, Oxford Univ. Press, 1992. xii,449p. illus., maps, tables, bibliog., index. ISBN: 0195076486.

1st ed. 1984; 2nd ed. 1989.

Authoritative survey of Latin American history with emphasis on 19th and 20th centuries. Chapter 1. The colonial foundations 1492-1880s - 2. Transformation of modern Latin America 1880s - 1990s, then individual chapters on Argentina, Chile, Brazil, Peru, Mexico, Cuba, The Caribbean, Central America, 11. Latin America, the United States and the World. and 12. What future for Latin America. Heads of State A-Z by country p.411-8. Further reading p.419-35 in narrative form by chapter. Analytical index. *Class No: 972.99*

Bibliographies

[7944]

The Cambridge history of Latin America v.11. Bibliographical Essays. Cambridge Univ. Press, 1995. 992p. maps. £60. (*Cambridge History of Latin America.*) ISBN: 0521395259.

Definitive bibliography of Latin America in the European area consisting of the bibliographical essays to be found in the *Cambridge History of Latin America (q.v.)* v.1-9. *Class No: 972.99(01)*

[7945]

COVINGTON, P.H., *and others eds*. **Latin America and the Caribbean** a critical guide to research sources. Westport, Conn., Greenwood Press, 1992. xvi,924p. bibliogs., indexes. $115; £103.50. (*Bibliographies and Indexes in Latin American and Caribbean Studies, no.2.*) ISBN: 0313264031.

49 US contributors. 5924 evaluative annotated entries arranged in 15 chapters (*e.g.* General - Anthropology - Art and Architecture - Data Bases ... Womens Studies) each comprising Essay and Bibliography (subdivided by country). Indispensable compendium of reference sources in US research libraries. *Class No: 972.99(01)*

[7946]

GRIFFIN, C.C. *and* **WARREN, J.B.,** *eds*. **Latin America:** a guide to the historical literature. Madison Univ. of Wisconsin Press, 1979. xxx, 700p. index. $35.00. ISBN: 0299082202.

First published Austin, Univ. of Texas Press, 1972.

7,087 annotated entries. 37 contributors. Includes material in Spanish and Portuguese. Some of the critical annotations are signed. 7 parts: 1. Reference - 2. General (including individual countries, A-Z) - 3. Background - 4. Colonial Latin America - 5. Independence - 6. Latin America since independence - 7. International relations since 1830. *Class No: 972.99(01)*

Encyclopaedias

[7947]

MARTIN, M.R. *and* **LOVETT, G.H. An Encyclopedia of Latin-American history.** Westport, Connecticut, Greenwood Press, 1981. vi, 384p. $35.00. £32.50. ISBN: 0313228817.

First published by Abelard-Schuman in 1956.

Political, economic and cultural development, including relations with Europe and North America, of all Latin American nations, from the earliest times, in dictionary form. Entries cover geographical features, government institutions, major wars and battles, and biographies of important figures. *Class No: 972.99(031)*

[7948]

TENENBAUM, B.A., *ed*. **Encyclopedia of Latin American history and culture.** New York, Charles Scribner's Sons, 5v., 1996. 2441p. illus., col. maps on endpapers, index. $449. ISBN: 0684192535.

832 contributors. 5287 articles (inc. 3,000 biographical) ranging from a single paragraph to several pages in length on history, politics, art, literature, warfare, gender, class, and economics. V.5 is an Appendix volume (696p.) comprising biographees divided into 22 groups and a subject index. 'Among the best reference books published this year' (*Library Journal*, v.121, no.12, July 1996. p.102). Selected as one of *Choice's* Outstanding Academic Books of 1996. *Class No: 972.99(031)*

Dictionaries

Amerindians, South

[7949]

OLSON, J.S. The Indians of Central and South America an ethnohistorical dictionary. Westport, Conn., Greenwood Press, 1991. xiii,515p. bibliog., index. $76. ISBN: 0313263876.

Cross-referenced entries provide social, demographic, and historical data on c.500 extant Amerindian tribes located south of Mexico with bibliographical citations. Appendix A. Tribal list by country (p.427-34) - B. Chronology of the conquest of Central and South America (p.435-50). Bibliography (by tribe) p.451-504. 'It has incorporated and updated information from a myriad of sources, filling a major void in Latin American research materials' (*Library Journal*, v.116, no.10, 1 June 1991, p.128). *Class No: 972.99(038)(=98)*

Maps & Atlases

[7950]

LOMBARDI, C.L., *and others*. **Latin American history** a teaching atlas. Madison and London, Univ. of Wisconsin Press, 1984. xvi, 104+39p. maps, bibliog., index. $22.50. £27.00. ISBN: 0299097102.

Maps are grouped in 3 sections: 1. Environment - 2. Colonial period (Iberian background; Amerindians; Discovery and conquest; Colonial governments; Trade; Independence of Spanish America) - 3. Modern period (Boundaries; International relations; Population; Economics and society). Bibliography p.xiv-xvi. 'A highly useful instrument of

....(contd.)
reference recommended to teachers and students alike' (*Bulletin of Latin Amrican Research*, v.4, 1985, p.89-90).
Class No: 972.99(084.3)

USA

[7951]
COOK, C. *and* WALLER, D. **The Longman handbook of modern American history 1763-1996.** London, Longman, 1998. xvi,451p. maps, tables, bibliog., index. (*Longman Handbooks to History*.) ISBN: 058208489x.
Notes, chronologies and statistics on 31 topics grouped in 4 sections: political history, social and religious history, economic history, and foreign policy and defence. Biographies p.260-95. Glossary p.299-366. Bibliography (in 19 topical sections) p.370-408. 6 maps. Appendix 1. US Constitution - 2. Bill of Rights. *Class No:* 973

[7952]
PARISH, P.J., *ed.* **Reader's guide to American history.** London & Chicago, Fitzroy Dearborn, 1997. xxxv,879p. bibliogs., indexes. £95. $125. ISBN: 1884964222.
234 UK and US academic contributors. 600 cross-referenced A-Z mini-biographical entries describing and assessing notable events, individuals, and broader themes and issues in US history. Thematic list (by 6 heavily sub-divided categories) p.xxi-xxxv. Booklist index p.789-837. General index p.839-62. Notes on advisers and contributors p.865-80. *Class No:* 973

CD-ROM

Bibliographies

[7953]
JUHL, B. **'Red, white, and Boolean** electronic resources for American history', *Choice*, v.35,no.8, April 1998. p.1313-26.
Bibliographical essay covering secondary literature (from indexes to electronic journals); reference sources (encyclopedias, biographies, almanacs, statistics); primary periodical literature etc. Bibliography p.1324-26. *Class No:* 973(003.40)(01)

Micromaterials

[7954]
SABIN, J. **Bibliotheca Americana** a dictionary of books relating to America from its discovery to the present time. Reading, Primary Source Media, Gale Group. Fiche. OCLC RETROCON records available. Machine-readable cataloguing on RLIN also available. £12,960 complete collection.
Slavery (1) Prior to 1850. 850 fiche. £2,050. (2) Post 1850. 983 fiche. £2,370; *Indians of North America.* 1723 fiche. £4,150; *Discovery and Exploration of the Americas.* 503 fiche. £1,210; *The Civil War.* 2,037 fiche. £4,910; *Immigration.* 230 fiche. £560. Printed guides accompany the collection. *Class No:* 973(003.5)

[7955]
Western American frontier history 1550-1900. Reading, Primary Source Material, Gale Group, 1999. Microfiche. 618 reels. £34,146.
A broad selection of printed sources relating to the discovery, exploration, settlement and development of the New World, from Mexico to the Arctic Ocean, and from the Mississippi River Valley and Hudson's Bay to the Pacific Ocean and the Bering Straits. Includes information on India/White relations, including missions, trade, government relations and Indian wars; Government and private exploration; Fur trade by land and sea; Manifest Destiny and the Oregon Question; and The Texas Revolution and the Mexican War. A printed guide accompanies the collection. *Class No:* 973(003.5)

Bibliographies

[7956]
BEERS, H.B. **Bibliographies in American history 1942-1978** a guide to materials for research. Woodbridge, Connecticut, Research Publications Inc., 2v., 1982. xviii, 512p.+Øii, 513-946p. index. $260.00. ISBN: 0892350385.
Continues *Bibliographies in American history* (1942).
11,784 entries grouped in 12 chapters, forming a comprehensive guide to bibliographic listings from the end of World War II to the late 1970s and covering the major areas of North and South American history - politics, economics, military, genealogy, and local history etc. V.2 is taken up with Chap.12. States, territories, possessions and dependencies listing archives and manuscripts, maps, newspapers etc. A-Z by state. *Class No:* 973(01)

[7957]
Bibliographic guide to North American history/ New York, G.K. Hall, 1978-. Annual.
1994 (1995). $335. ISBN 0783821948. Lists material catalogued by The Research Libraries of New York Public Library and the Library of Congress in a single A-Z sequence. 'Entries cover all aspects of United States and Canadian history, including Indians, the discovery of America and early exploration, Colonial history, the American Revolution, the War of 1812, the War with Mexico, slavery, Civil War, Spanish-American War, US local history, Canadian political and constitutional history, history of Canadian nationalities and races, Canadian provincial history, and the British and French periods' (G.K. Hall & Co. *Catalog of publications, 1979-1980*, p.127). Serves as an annual supplement to *United States Local History Catalog* (G.K. Hall, 1974). *Class No:* 973(01)

[7958]
BLAZEK, R. *and* PERRAULT. **United States history a selective guide to information sources.** Englewood, Colo., Libraries Unlimited, 1994. xxviii,411p. indexes. $55. ISBN: 0872879844.
947 annotated (85-250 words) entries dealing with library resources, bibliographic information and biographical sources in 7 sections: 1. Sources of general importance to US history - 2. Politics and government - 3. Diplomatic history and foreign affairs - 4. Military - 5. Social, cultural and intellectual - 6. Regional - 7. Economic history. Emphasis is on social history (421 entries) and coverage includes online databases and CD-ROM titles. *Class No:* 973(01)

[7959]
Harvard guide to American history. Freidel, F., *ed.* Cambridge, Mass., Harvard Univ. Press, 2v., 1974. xxx, 605p.+Øxvi, 609-1290p. ISBN: 0674375602.
1st ed. 1954 succeeded E. Channing and others' *Guide to the study and reading of American history* (Boston, Ginn, 1912).
V.1 has 4 parts (29 sections): 1. Research methods and materials (including unpublished primary sources; microform materials; reference works) - 2. Biographies and personal records. 3. Comprehensive and area histories - 4. Histories of special subjects (*e.g.* physical environment; economic history; intellectual history; the arts; pure and applied sciences), about 20,000 entries. No annotations, but each section has an introduction.
V.2 has 5 parts, arranged chronologically: 5. America, to 1789 - 6. United States, 1789-1860 - 7. Civil War and reconstruction - 8. Rise of industry and empire - 9. Twentieth century (p.927-1067). Cumulated index of names (p.107-1274) and subject index (p.1275-90; in small type). 'Remains the best single source for those studying the history of the US' (*RQ*, Spring 1975, v.14, no.3, p.261). *Class No:* 973(01)

[7960]
MAKOWER, J., *ed.* **The American history sourcebook.** Prentice Hall Press, 1988. 548p. illus., bibliog., indexes. $40.00. ISBN: 0130274917.
More than 3000 entries relating to museums, libraries, archives, photocollections, historical societies, and other sources of information on US history, politics, and culture. Data: location, telephone, hours, charges, areas of specialization, important holdings, and services. Key dates in American history p.403-427. An American history bibliography p.428-38. Organization and subject indexes. 'A worthwhile addition to reference collections in public, high school and academic libraries' (*Choice*, v.26, no.5, May 1989, p.1483). *Class No:* 973(01)

[7961]
MEIER, M.S., *comp.* **Bibliography of Mexican American history.** Westport, Connecticut, Greenwood Press, 1984. xiii, 500p. indexes. $40.95. ISBN: 031323776x.
A major work marshalling 4372 briefly annotated entries in 12 chronological, subject and bibliographical form chapters 'providing access to information necessary for a more sophisticated understanding of the Mexican American experience and its contribution to contemporary America' (*Preface*). 'A particular strength ... is the extensive list of obscure master theses and dissertations' (*Choice*, v.22, no.2, October 1984, p.250). *Class No:* 973(01)

[7962]
MERRIAM, L.A. *and* OBERLY, J.W. **United States history a** bibliography of the new writings on American history. Manchester Univ. Press, 1996. xi,227p. indexes. ISBN: 0719036887.
4,000+ entries relating to 'important and useful' English-language publications of the 1980s and early 1990s on American social and political history (2/3 books, 1/3 journal articles). Section 1. General historiography and methodology - 2/8. by chronological periods divided under 10 thematic sub-headings. 'A useful first-stop for undergraduates, graduate students, and higher education teachers' (*Choice*, v.34,no.2, October 1996, p.254). Selected as one of *Choice's* Outstanding Academic Books of 1996. *Class No:* 973(01)

[7963]

PARISH, P.J., *ed*. **Reader's guide to American history**. Chicago & London, Fitzroy Dearborn, 1998. xxxv,880p. bibliogs. index. £95. ISBN: 1884964222.

234 UK and US academics contribute 600 A-Z cross-referenced articles consisting of a bibliographical headnote listing the items to be covered (normally 6-12 books) and an essay 800-2000 words discussing the items related to the subject concerned, and concentrating on political, social and economic history. With courses in American history proliferating ... and the burgeoning interest in such areas as women's history. African and Native American history etc., this massive *Guide* can be recommended to all academic libraries supporting such courses' (*Reference Reviews*, v.12, no.2, 1998. p.45). *Class No:* 973(01)

[7964]

Writings on American history : a subject bibliography of articles 1962-1983/84. Washington and White Plains, New York, Kraus International Publications and the American Historical Association, 15v., 1974-1985. $685.00.

Succeeds the annual *Writings on American history* 1902-1960 (1930-72; various publishers). *Writings on American history 1961* filling the gap in 2v. 1979. $60.00. ISBN 0527982520. *Class No:* 973(01)

[7965]

—Writings on American history, 1962-73 a subject bibliography of books and monographs. White Plains, New York, Kraus International Publications and the American Historical Association, 10v., 1985. 6530p. index. $1300. ISBN: 0527982687.

Cites more than 50,000 books and monographs and is compiled from Library of Congress catalogue cards. V.1 includes sections on history and historians and a chronological classification. V.7(pt), v.8 and v.9(pt) comprise a geographical classification. The added emphasis on biography and genealogy in this set is reflected in the rest of v.9. V.10 is the index. *Class No:* 973(01)

Internet

[7966]

American and British history resources on the Internet. Nash, S.D. *and* Vincenti, W., *comps*. URL:http://www.libraries.rutgers.edu/rulib/socsci/hist/amhist.ht ml.

Arranged in 7 categories: 1. Reference - 2. History gateways and text sites - 3. Titles (by historic period) - 4. Archival and manuscripts guides - 5. Other Internet resources - 6. Library and publishers catalogues - 7. Resources available from Rutger's University. 'An excellent Internet resource for history research' (*Choice*, Supplement to v.36, August 1999, p.156). *Class No:* 973(01)(003.41)

Encyclopaedias

[7967]

FARAGHER, J.M., *ed*. **American Heritage encyclopedia of American history**. New York, Henry Holt, 1998. 1024p. illus. index. $45. ISBN: 0805044388.

125 contributors. 3,000 A-Z cross-referenced articles ranging from pre-colonial period to the 1990s on all aspects of US history including both traditional and new topics like American women, African-Americans and Native Americans. Appendices print text of the US Constitution, the Declaration of Independence, and a time-line of American history. *Choice* Outstanding Academic Title 1999. *Class No:* 973(031)

[7968]

GARRATY, J.A. **1001 things everyone should know about American history**. New York, Doubleday, 1989. 256p. illus. $19.95.

Divided into 8 parts relating to politics, ideas, people, presidents, literature and music, military affairs, and 'what'ses' (*i.e., what's new, what's old, what's great etc.*). 'Enough information is given to make this a useful reference source or simply a place to turn for diversion' (*Booklist*, v.85, no.16, 15 april 1989, p.1427). *Class No:* 973(031)

[7969]

MILNER, C.A., *and others, eds*. **The Oxford history of the American West**. New York, Oxford Univ. Press, 1994. xiii,872p. illus. (some col.), maps, tables. $39.95. £25. ISBN: 0195059689.

28 contributors. 23 chapters, each with a chronology and bibliographical essay, arranged in 4 sections: 1. Heritage: native peoples (28,000 BC-1821) - 2. Expansion (1804-1898) - 3. Transformation (1900-1992) - 4. Interpretation (visual and literary West, the popular myth etc.) (1810-1991). 17 maps. *Class No:* 973(031)

[7970]

MORRIS, J.B. *and* MORRIS, R.B., *eds*. **Encyclopedia of American history**. 7th ed. New York, HarperCollins, 1996. 1328p. $55. ISBN: 0062700553.

First published 1953.

4 parts: 1. Basic chronology, to 1975 - 2. Topical chronology (The expansion of the nation - Population, immigration and ethnic stock - Leading Supreme Court decisions - The American economy - Science, invention and technology - Thought and culture - Mass media) - 3. Notable American biographies (450 most influential Americans) p.961-1191 - 4. Structure of Federal Government (*e.g.*Presidents and their Cabinets ... The Constitution of the United States). 42 maps and charts. Analytical index. p.1193-1245. In this ed. more space is devoted to minorities, ethnic groups and women. *Class No:* 973(031)

[7971]

The New encyclopedia of the American West. Lamar, H.R., *ed*. New Haven, Yale Univ. Pres, 1998. xv,1324p. illus., maps, bibliogs., index. $60. ISBN: 0300070888.

Replaces Lamar's *The Readers encyclopedia of the American West* (1977).

300+ contributors. 2,400 initialled A-Z cross-referenced entries brimming with facts, figures, references, interpretations and explanations embracing the major events of America's expansion westwards from the colonial period onwards. 'Libraries with a Western collection or a strong interest in US history ... should buy it as *the* general encyclopedia on the West' (*Library Journal*, v.123, no.14, 1 September 1998, p.174-175. *Choce* Outstanding Academic Title 1999. *Class No:* 973(031)

[7972]

PHILLIPPS, C. *and* AXELROD, A., *eds*. **Encyclopedia of the American West**. Old Tappan, NJ., Macmillan, 4v., 1996. 1935p. illus., maps, bibliog., index. $375. ISBN: 0028974956.

1,700 + signed, cross-referenced articles of varying length, relating to people, places, features, organizations, and social customs that shaped the American West, covering the 23 states west of the Mississippi, including Alaska and Hawaii(!), from the 18th to the mid-20th century. 'Brings together a tremendous amount of condensed information - names, dates, trends, conflicts, heroes and villains' (*ARBA guide to biographical resources 1986-1997*, p.85). *Class No:* 973(031)

[7973]

The Reader's companion to American history. Foner, E. *and* Garraty, J., *eds*. Boston, Houghton Mifflin, 1991. xxii,1226p. tables, maps, index. $35; £24.95. ISBN: 0395513723.

400 contributors. Over 1000 A-Z, cross-referenced and signed entries, either giving essential information on specific topics, longer interpretative essays on broad issues, or biographies, relating to the political, economic, social and culture US history. Sponsored by the Society of American Historians. 'Informative and readable, an excellent combination of political, and social history' (*Booklist*, v.88, no.9, 1 January 1992, p.851-2). *Class No:* 973(031)

[7974]

ROLLER D.C. *and* TWYMAN, R.W., *eds*. **The Encyclopedia of Southern history**. Baton Rouge, Louisiana, Louisiana State Univ. Press, 1979. 1421p. tables, maps, bibligs., index. $90. ISBN: 0807105759.

1,100 contributors: *c.*2,900 signed articles. Encyclopedic, including biographies and detailed history of each state. ('South' is defined as 'all the states and the District of Columbia where slavery was legal in 1860' (p.1125).) Bibliographies are appended to most entries. 35 maps; 75 tables. 'The best and most accessible single reference to the American South' (*Library Journal*, v.105, no.7, 1 April 1980, p.842). *Class No:* 973(031)

Handbooks & Manuals

[7975]

PRUCHA, F.P. **Handbook for research in American history** a guide to bibliographies and other reference works. 2nd ed. Lincoln, Nebraska and London, Univ. of Nebraska Press, 1994. xiii,214p. index. $25. ISBN: 0803237014.

1st ed. 1987.

993 entries arranged in 20 form and subject chapters: 1. A revolution in access to research materials (microforms, online databases, CD-ROMs, Full text, The Internet) - 2. General guides to reference works ... 12. Oral History material ... 14. National Archives ... 17. Atlases, maps and geographical gazetteers ... 20. Picture sources. 'There are few similar guides to bibliographic sources of American history that present so much information for both beginners and researchers in such a manageable compass' (*Reference Reviews*, v.2, no.2, June 1988, p.89). *Class No:* 973(035)

[7976]
Webster's Guide to American history a chronological, geographical and biographical survey and compendium. Van Doren, C. *and* McHenry, R. Springfield, Massachusetts, Merriam, 1971. 1428p. illus., maps, index.

Part 1 (p.1-636): an illustrated chronology of events, 1492-1969, supported by *c*.1,000 quotations from primary sources. Part 2 (p.637-792) is a series of coloured and black-and-white maps, and statistical tables and charts, arranged by broad topics. Part 3 contains over 1,000 biographies of notable Americans. Index. 'Recommends itself for the home library or the student's personal reference shelf' (*College & Research Libraries,* v.32,no.4, July 1971, p.314). *Class No:* 973(035)

Dictionaries

[7977]
Dictionary of American history. New York, Scribner, 7v. & Index, 1976-77. 3344p. £500.00. ISBN: 0684138565.

First published 1940 (5v. & Index).

800 contributions; 7,200 signed entries, A-Z (Aachen ... Zwaanendael colony). Brief bibliographies (*e.g.* 'Alaska' (4 sections): 12 columns; 4 references; 'Mexican War (1846-1848)': 3½ columns. 3 references; 'Afro Americans': over 12 columns, 8 references; 'Antitrust laws ': 2½ cols., 5 references). Coverage of science and technology has been improved; lack of treatment of the arts is corrected (*e.g.* 'Theater': 9½ columns, 10 references); and coverage of native American Indians and Afro-Americans made more adequate, according to the *Preface*. No biographies. Index v. (xviii, 503p.) - *c*.90,000 entries. A standard, basic work. 'Most highly recommended' (*Library Journal,* v.102,no.13, July 1977, p.1480).
Concise dictionary of American history. Rev. ed. 1983, 1140p. $60.00. ISBN 0684173212. Adds new articles and revises others. 'A handy addition at reference desks far from the main set (*Choice,* v.20,no.11-12, July-August 1983, p.1572). *Class No:* 973(038)

[7978]
—Dictionary of American history. Supplement. Ferrell, R.H. *and* Hoff, J., *eds.* New York, Scribner, 2v., 1996. 383,409p. bibliog., index. $200. ISBN: 0684195798.

Updates and expands *Dictionary of American History* (7v. 1876-77). 340 contributors. 757 signed A-Z entries (469 new, the others replacing or updating original entries), most with bibliogs, ranging in length from less than a column to a little over 4 pages. 'Just as reliable a work as the master set and every library owning the original will definitely want to update it with these volumes' (*Booklist,* v.93, no.5, 1 November 1996, p.534). 'Can stand alone as a very useful dictionary of the recent history of America' (*Choice,* v.34,no.5, January 1997, p.768). *Class No:* 973(038)

[7979]
MEIER, M.S. *and* RIVERA, F. Dictionary of Mexican American history. Westport, Connecticut, Greenwood Press, 1981. xiii, 498p. maps, bibliog., index. $46.95. £34.50. ISBN: 0313212031.

28 contributors. All aspects of Mexican American history from the early 16th century are covered in entries of varying length some of which include suggestions for further reading. Appendix A. Bibliography p.377-383. B. Chronology (50,000 BC to 1980) p.385-395. C. Complete text of the Treaty of Guadalupe Hidalgo. D. Mexican American journals. 5 maps. Intended as a basic guide for undergraduates, librarians and scholars. *Class No:* 973(038)

[7980]
PURVIS, T.L. A Dictionary of American history. Oxford, Blackwell, 1995. viii,455p. £35. ISBN: 1557863989.

3,000 entries relating to all aspects of American life including histories of all states of the Union, biographies of leading figures, wars, the history of the American Indian peoples, and full coverage of political, constitutional and foreign affairs. *Class No:* 973(038)

Reviews & Abstracts

[7981]
America history and life article abstracts and citations of reviews and dissertations covering the United States and Canada. Santa Barbara, California, ABC Clio; Oxford, Clio Press, 1964-.

1954-1963 Abstracts of the world's periodical literature relating to the history of the United States and Canada included in *Historical Abstracts*. These were subsequently published as Vol.0 of *America history and life*. V. 1-10 (1964-1978) limited to abstracts. V. 11-25 (1979-1988) published in 4 parts: A. Articles, abstracts and citations (3 issues) - B. Index to book reviews (2 issues) - C. American history index (books, articles and dissertations) - D. Annual index. V.26- (1989-) 5 issues a year: issues 1-4 carry abstracts, reviews and dissertations, issue 5 is a cumulative annual index.

V.36. 1999 has 15,801 entries arranged in 6 parts subdivided under subject classification headings: 1. North America - 2. Canada - 3. United States national history to 1945 - 4. United States national history 1945 to present - 5. United States regional, state and local history (in 7 regional sub-divisions) - 6. History. The Humanities and

....(contd.)
Social Sciences (*e.g.* Archives, libraries, museums; General bibliography; Historiography; Tributes and Commemorations; Methodology; Sites, restoration and historical parks; Societies and meetings; Teaching and study of history). Subject, author, book and film title and reviewer indexes. Comprehensive worldwide coverage drawing upon more than 2000 journals in 45 languages. Cumulative quinquennial indexes are available: V.1-5 (1964-1968) £197.00; v.6-10 (1969-1973) £197.00; v.11-15 (1974-1978) £340.00; v.16-20 (1979-1983) £388.00. v.21-25 (1984-1988). v.26-30 (1989-1993). Falk, J.D. and Kinnell, S. *Searching America history and life and Historical abstracts on DIALOG,* rev. ed., 1987. 116p. (ABC-Clio Guides to Online Searching), £27.05. ISBN 0874360919. See also Bucknall, T. 'Searching Historical Abstracts and America: History And Life Online And On CD-ROM'. *Database,* v.15, no.4, August 1992, p.36-9. *Class No:* 973(048)

[7982]
—America history and life on disc. Sturgeon, A., *ed.* Santa Barbara, Calif., ABC-Clio, 197 Hardware: IBM PC/XT/AT or 100% compatible, 512 Kb memory (384K free), 20Mb hard drive. CD-ROM drive with appropriate controller card and interface cable (Hitachi, Philips, Sony, or any other CD-ROM drive with ISO 9660 compatible device driver) Operating System: MS-DOS 3.0 or higher.

Now with just one disc and a few simple keystrokes users can access more than 33 years' worth of historical information (Volumes 19-current), with over 218,000 journal articles, 104,000 book and media reviews, and over 40,000 dissertations on the history and culture of the United States and Canada.

BASIC SUBSCRIPTION Includes an initial CD-ROM disc with information from 1982 to present, plus two cumulative updates. Renewal includes three cumulative updates. EXPANDED SUBSCRIPTION Includes an intitial expanded Edition CD-ROM disc with retrospective information from 1974 to present, plus two cumulative updates. Renewal includes three cumulative updates. Updates will include additional older as well as current data. *Class No:* 973(048)

[7983]
—American history and life (Internet database). Speck, V. *and* Sturgeon, A., *eds.* Oxford and Santa Barbara, Calif., ABC-Clio, 1999. $6,800/network of 2-6 users.

'The electronic version includes in-process entries (abstract, subject terms, and chronologies not yet available) prior to inclusion in the print and CD-ROM products. The main menu screen allows searching by Keyword, Subject Terms, Author/Editor, Title/Translation, Language, Document Type, Journal Name, Publication Date, Time Period, and Entry Number, as well as a combination. The Subject Terms, Author/ Editor, Language, Document Type, Journal Name, and Time Period fields include browsable indexes. There are a number of options for displaying results, including sort order, showing a popup search progress window, and modifying the number of entries that will be displayed at one time. Several help screens are easily available and can be quickly printed along with a general User Guide. Language entries are extensive, including Catalan, Hopi, and Latin. Searching is similar to other resources, allowing truncation of titles, Boolean operators, and tagging and downloading of documents'. (Booklist, 1 November 1999, p.558+560). *Choice,* Outstanding Academic Title 1999. *Class No:* 973(048)

Almanacs

[7984]
The Almanac of American history. Schlesinger, A.M., *ed.* New York, G.P. Putnam, 1983. 623p. illus., maps, index. $24.95. ISBN: 0399128530.

5 sections each consisting of an introductory essay and an illustrated and annotated chronology: 1. Founding a nation 986-1787 - 2 Testing a union 1788-1865 - 3. Forging a nation 1866-1900 - 4. Expanding resources 1901-1945 - 5. Emerging as a world power 1946-. *Class No:* 973(059)

Quotations

[7985]
CONLIN, J.R. The Morrow book of quotations in American history. New York, Morrow, 1984. 346p. $15.95. ISBN: 0688020682.

Highly selective list. 'Because of the subject matter's broad appeal this will be more useful than many other specialized quotation books' (*Wilson Library Bulletin,* v.59, no.4, December 1984, p.292-3). *Class No:* 973(082.2)

Maps & Atlases

[7986]

Atlas of American frontiers. Stokie, Il., Rand McNally, 1992. 192p. col. illus., col. maps. $49.95. ISBN: 0528834932.

Photographic and cartographic history of the development of the United States from the early exploration to the opening of the West. Contents include 10 pages of historical maps drawn 1650-1930; maps illustrating significant historical concepts; and contemporary reference maps of present-day USA. *Class No: 973(084.3)*

[7987]

Atlas of American history. Jackson, K.T. 2nd ed. New York, Scribners, 1985. xv, 294p. maps. $55.00. ISBN: 0684184117.

First published 1943 edited by J.T. Adam.

The 1st ed. designed to accompany the *Dictionary of American history*, (1940 ed.), had 147 carefully drawn outline, black-and-white maps, arranged chronologically in 10 sections. The 1978 ed. adds 51 maps, mostly concerned with 20th-century developments. Index-gazetter (c.7,500 entries). The maps are lacking in detail, - 'uninspired and unimaginative' (*Choice*, v.15, no.7, September 1978, p.842). *Class No: 973(084.3)*

[7988]

Atlas of American history. Ferrell, R.H. *and* Natkiel, R. 3rd ed. New York and Oxford, Facts on File Publications, 1993. 192p. illus., (some col.), col. maps, facsims., col. plans. index. £19.95. ISBN: 0816028834.

First published 1987.

A useful single volume atlas of *c.*200 x 2 or 4 colour maps drawn in 1986-7 not too happily married to a superfluous illustrated history arranged in 6 chronological sections *e.g.* 1. The colonial era ... 5. The two World Wars ... 6. America in a divided world. 3 Map essays: Territorial expansion of the USA, Population; Presidential elections. 143 historical paintings, drawings and photographs. 'For the modern period the Facts on File atlas has much broader and more up-to-date coverage than its predecessors' (*Booklist*, v.84, no.13, 1 March 1988, p.1102). *Class No: 973(084.3)*

[7989]

GILBERT, M. Routledge atlas of American history. 3rd ed. London, Routledge, 1993. 148p. maps. £25. ISBN: 0415136237.

First published as *American history atlas* by Weidenfeld & Nicolson (1968).

138 black and white outline political, military, social history, transport, and economic maps (26 new to this edition) from Origins of settlement in America 50,000-1000 BC to Defence preparedness in space 1992-1993. *Class No: 973(084.3)*

[7990]

Historical atlas of the United States. Garrett, W., *ed.* 2nd ed. Washington, National Geographic Society, 1993. 288p. illus. (some col.), maps, diagrs., tables, facsims. $100. ISBN: 0870449702.

1st Centennial ed. 1988.

5 thematic chapters: 1. People - 2. Boundaries - 3. Economy - 4. Networks - 5. Communities alternate with 5 chronological chapters 1400-1990s. A heavy preponderance of text, 450 photographs, and 80 graphs over its 380 maps make this volume not so much an atlas as 'a pleasant, illustrated, popularized, brief US history' (*Choice*, v.26, no.9, May 1989, p.1496). Bibliography p.260-73. *Class No: 973(084.3)*

[7991]

Historical atlas series. Norman, Univ. of Oklahoma Press, 1976-. maps, bibliog., index.

Historical atlas of Arizona by H.P. Walker and D. Bufkin. 2nd ed., 1986. 137p. £19.95. ISBN 0806120231 *Arkansas* by G.T. Hanson and C.H. Moneyhon. 1989. 142,xxp. £27.95. 080611844x. *Kansas* by H.E. Socolofsky and H. Self. 2nd ed., 1989. 192p. 19.75. 0806121572. *Massachusetts* by R.W. Wilkie and J. Tager. 1990.160p. £42.95. 0870236970. *Oklahoma* by J.W. Morris and others, 3rd ed., 1987. 208p. £23.95. 0806119918. *Washington* by J. Scott and R. de Lorme. 1988. 200p. £27.95. 0806121084. *Texas* by A.R. Stephens and W. Homes. 1989. 160p. £19.75. 0806121580. *The American West* by W.A. Beck and Y.D. Haase. 1989. £23.75. 0806121939.

'Each atlas includes a physical description of the state, its exploration by Europeans, the history of its native population, its political history, and such other topics as economic development, transportation, agriculture, and education. With good reason, the earlier atlases have been favorably reviewed. They offer, in one volume, a concise historical, geographical, ethnographical, political, and economic overview and thus are handy reference books'. (*Choice*, v.27,no.5, January 1990, p.762+4). *Class No: 973(084.3)*

[7992]

McEVEDY, C. The Penguin atlas of North American history. Harmondsworth, Middlesex, Penguin, 1988. 112p. col.maps, index. pbk. £4.95; $6.95. ISBN: 0140511288.

Mixture of base map, used in 47 of the 57 maps depicted, and text commentary on left hand page to cover the period 20,000 BC to 1870 with a 1987 postscript. First fifth of the atlas is allocated to the pre-Columbian period. 'What this book demonstrates is that a good historical atlas of North America cannot be squeezed into an 8½-by-7 inch format' (*Booklist*, v.85,no.11, 1 February 1989, p.927). *Class No: 973(084.3)*

Bibliographies

[7993]

WHEAT, J.C. *and* **BRUN, C.F. Maps and charts published in America before 1800** a bibliography. rev. ed. London, Holland Press, 1979. 215p. maps. $125.00. ISBN: 0900470895.

915 maps, plus list of 552 books referred to. Arranged by region, then chronologically. Entries gives descriptions, map size and scale. Emphasis on USA. Very favourably reviewed in *RQ* (v.9, no.2, Winter 1969, p.181-2). *Class No: 973(084.3)(01)*

Chronologies

[7994]

The Peopling of America a timeline of events that helped shape our nation. Kullen, A.S., *comp.* Beltsville, MD, Americans All, 1994. 363p. $15.95.

Also published in a 2-vol. format dividing at the Civil War period ($9.95 each).

Unique parallel timelines in columns for Native, African, Asian European and Hispanic Americans plus the Americas and the World. *Class No: 973(090)*

[7995]

CARRUTH, G., ed. The Encyclopedia of American facts and dates. 10th ed. New York, HarperCollins, 1997. x,1096p. index. $45. ISBN: 0062701924.

Chronologically arranged, 4 columns across the double page: 1. Exploration and Settlement; Wars; Government; Civil Rights - 2. Publishing; Arts and Music; Popular Entertainment; Architecture; Theatre - 3. Business and Industry; Science; Education; Philosophy and Religion - 4. Sports; Social Issues and Crime; Folkways; Fashions; Holidays. 'As a ready reference tool this surely cannot be surpassed' (*Reference Reviews*, vol.12, no.6, 1998, p.50-51). *Class No: 973(090)*

[7996]

KASPI, A., ed. Great dates in United States history. New York, Facts On File, 1994. v,266p. maps, tables, index. ISBN: 0816025924.

30 chronological chapters, each reflecting a distinct time period, organised under various categories (*e.g.* politics and institutions, foreign policy, economy and society, civilization and culture). 10 maps. *Class No: 973(090)*

[7997]

URDANG, L., ed. The Timetables of American history. New York, Simon and Schuster, 1981. vi,470p. illus., index. ISBN: 0671252453.

Inspired by B. Grun's *The Timetables of history* (qv).

Chronology starting 1000A.D.; 1010A.D.; and yearly 1492-1980, in 4 columns across the double page: History and politics; The arts; Science and technology; Miscellaneous each sub-divided America and elsewhere. Index of 16,000 subjects and proper names. *Class No: 973(090)*

[7998]

The World almanac of the American West. Bowman, J.S., *ed.* New York, World Almanac, 1986. Distributed by Ballantine. 368p. illus. (some col.), index. $29.95. ISBN: 0886872731.

A descriptive chronology of events 1492-1985 recording the American movement westwards of the Appalachian Mountains, each year covered in 2-3 pages, with boxed biographies and short thematic essays. *Class No: 973(090)*

Hispanic Peoples

[7999]

KANELLOS, N. *and* **PÉREZ, C. Chronology of Hispanic-American history;** from pre-Columbian times to the present. Detroit, Gale, 1995. 427p. illus., bibliog., index. £46. ISBN: 0810392003.

Contents include regional histories; historical timelines and main chronology divided into 4 periods prehistory to 1995; and noteworthy events, themes, movements, biographies, and significant documents. *Class No: 973(090)(=60)*

Biographies

[8000]
Directory of American scholars Vol.1 History. Jaques Cattell Press. 8th ed. New York, R.R. Bowker, 1982. xi,924p. index. $90.00. ISBN: 0835214788.

Profiles approximately 11,000 scholars in all fields of historical study including art history, musicology, and archaeology. Data: primary discipline, education, honorary degrees, professional experience, membership of learned societies, honours and awards, research interest, publications. Geographic index p.859-924.
Class No: 973(092)

Women

[8001]
SCANLON, J. *and* **COSNER, S. American women historians** 1700s - 1900s: a biographical dictionary. Westport, Conn., Greenwood Press, 1996. 269p. bibliog., index. $75. ISBN: 0313296642.

200 historians entered. Data: family, education, career, publications, service to the profession, personal information, bibliography. Entries heavily weighted toward American history. *Class No:* 973(092)-0055.2

Jews

Bibliographies

[8002]
GUROCK, J.S. American Jewish history: a bibliographical guide. New York, Anti-Reformation League of B'nai B'rith, 1983. xxi,195p., bibliog., index, pbk. $6.95. ISBN: 088464037x.

Valuable introduction on the growth of American Jewish historiography p.xv-xxi. Pt.1. Bibliographical reviews of the Colonial and early national periods (1654-1850); the eras of German and East European immigration (1840-1924); the modern period; and on special topics. Pt.2. Future directions includes suggestions for further research. Bibliography p.121-171. Author and subject indexes.
Class No: 973(=924)(01)

Asian Races

[8003]
Japanese American history An A-Z reference from 1868 to the present. Niiya, B., *ed.* New York, Facts On File, 1993. 400p. illus., bibliog. $45. ISBN: 0816026807.

Produced under the auspices of the Japanese-American Museum, Los Angeles.

400+ profiles of individuals, organisations, events, and movements together with a chronology and historical overview. *Choice*, Outstanding Academic Book 1994. *Class No:* 973(=95)

Dictionaries

[8004]
HYUNG-CHAN KIM, *ed.* **Dictionary of Asian American history.** Westport, Connecticut, Greenwood Press, 1986. xv, 627p. bibliog., index. $65. ISBN: 0313237603.

13 contributors. Divided into 2 main sections: 1. 15 essays on the historical development of ethnic groups from Asian countries and Pacific Islands and their place in the American social order - 2. More than 800 dictionary entries encompassing all aspects of the history of Asian Americans in the US. Appendix A. Bibliography p.565-577. B. Chronology (1820-1985) p.580-602. 'An excellent one-volume dictionary' (*Reference Books Bulletin 1986-1987*, p.157).
Class No: 973(=95)(038)

Black Races

Chronologies

[8005]
HARLEY, S. The Timetables of African-American history: a chronology of the most important people and events in African-American history. New York, Simon & Schuster, 1995. 400p. ports., index. $35. ISBN: 0671795244.

Annalistic arrangement with historical events, important figures, and movements. 1492-1992, listed across the page under various headings (*e.g.* Education, Laws and Legal actions, Religion, Arts, Sciences). Detailed index. *Class No:* 973(=96)(090)

[8006]
HORNSBY, A. Chronology of African American history significant events and people from 1619 to the present. 2nd ed. Detroit, Gale Research, 1997. 500p. £46. ISBN: 0810385732.

Guide to the people, places and events significant to African American history. Includes details on important births and deaths, legislation and court decisions, rebellions and demonstrations, awards and honors, elections and appointments. Brief biographies on many noteworthy individuals are also included. *Class No:* 973(=96)(090)

Amerindians, North

Bibliographies

[8007]
HOXIE, F.E. *and* **MARKOWITZ, H. Native Americans** an annotated bibliography. Pasadena, Calif.; Englewood Cliffs, N.J., Salem Press, 1991. xiii,325p. index. $40. ISBN: 0893566705.

Over 1000 descriptive summaries of books mostly published in last 30 years relating to North American Indian history and anthropology. 4 Major sections: 1. General studies and reference works (by 8 culture areas) - 2. History (colonial America, US. and Canada 1776-1990) - 3. Culture areas subdivided by topic - 4. Contemporary life (family, religion, economic development, health/alcoholism, Indian law and government *etc.*). Author index. 'An excellent reference for both introductory and advanced students ... highly recommended for all academic libraries' (Choice, v.29, no.2). *Class No:* 973(=97)(01)

Encyclopaedias

[8008]
BRAUN, M. *and* **WALDMAN, C. Encyclopedia of native American tribes.** Rev. ed. New York and Oxford, Facts on File Publications, 1999. xiii, 293p. col. illus., col. maps, bibliog., index. $65.00 £18.95. ISBN: 0816039361.

1st ed. 1988.

The cultural and social historic record of more than 150 Indian tribes of North and Central America, arranged A-Z by tribe, covering location, migration, contact with Europeans, wars, and contemporary tribal affairs. Glossary p.265-273. Bibliography, grouped in 11 broad categories, p.275-278, lacks publication dates. 11 maps. 250 illustrations. 'As a work of reference this book should prove both useful and entertaining' (*Bulletin of Society of University Cartographers*, v.22, no.1, 1988, p.46-47). *Class No:* 973(=97)(031)

[8009]
Handbook of North American Indians. Washington, Smithsonian Institution, 1978-. illus., maps, bibliogs., index.

A planned 20v. 'encyclopedic summary of what is known about the prehistory, history, and cultures of the aboriginal peoples of North America who lived north of the urban civilizations of central Mexico' (*Preface*). 5. *Arctic*. 1984. 845p. $29.00 - 6. *Subarctic*. 1981. 853p. $25.00 - 7. *Northwest coast*. 1990. 777p. illus., maps, bibliog., index. $38. - 8. *California*. 1981. 800p. $25.00. 9. *Southwest*. 1979. 701p. $23.00 - 10. *Southwest*. 1983. 884p. $25.00 - 11. *Great Basin*. 1986. 868p. $27.00 - 12. 1998. 791p. illus., maps.c61. 01140495148. 15. *Northeast*. 1978. 924p. $27.00. V.9. *Southwest* has 50 contributors and 59 chapters including 1. Introduction - 2. History of archaeological research - 3. History of Ethnological research. Key to tribal territories map p.ix. Bibliography p.625-78. Volumes yet to be published: 1. *Introduction* - 2. *Indians in contemporary society* - 3. *Environment, origins, and population* - 4. *History of Indian-White relations* - 12. *Plateau* - 13. *Plains* - 14. *Southeast* - 16. *Technology and visual arts* - 17. *Languages* - 18/19. *Biographical dictionary* - 20. *Index*. *Class No:* 973(=97)(031)

[8010]
HOXIE, F.E., *ed.* **Encyclopedia of North American Indians** Native American history, culture, and life from Paleo-Indians to the present. Boston, Houghton, 1996. 756p. illus., maps. bibliog., index. $45. ISBN: 0395669219.

280 contributors. 400 (mostly) signed articles on Native American history, historical and contemporary biographies, statistical and directory information and essays on art, policy, law and religion, and cultural summaries. Over 100 tribes distinguished.
Class No: 973(=97)(031)

[8011]
PRITZKER, B.M. Native Americans an encyclopedia of history, culture, and peoples. Santa Barabra, Calif., and Oxford, ABC-Clio, 2v., 1998. xvii,868p. illus., maps, bibliog., index. $151. £89.95. ISBN: 0874368367.

Historical and modern data for all known Native American groups in the United States and Canada, listed A-Z within 10 geog-cultural areas including the Arctic and sub-Arctic. Data: tribal name; location; population; language; Historical information (inc. religion, government, customs, dwellings, diet, key technology, trade, arts, transport, war and weapons); and Contemporary information (government/reservations, economy, legal status, daily life). Glossary

....(contd.)

p.797-801. Bibliography (by chapter) p.803-805. 3 Appendices: 1. Canada Reserves and bands (name, linguistic group, affiliation, elections, population, no. reserves, key economic activities) - 2. Alaska native villages - 3. ANCSA village corporations. Analytical index. *Class No: 973(=97)(031)*

Handbooks & Manuals

[8012]

HEARD, J.N. Handbook of the American frontier: four centuries of Indian-White relationships. Metuchen, NJ., Scarecrow Press, 5v., 1987-. Distributed in UK by Shelwing Ltd. of Folkestone, Kent. (*Native American Resources Series, no.1.*)

1. *Southeastern Woodlands.* 1987. 2. *Northeastern Woodlands.* 1990. xi,403p. £31.90. 0810823241. Future volumes: will cover the Great Plains (v.3) and the Rocky Mountains, southwestern districts and the Pacific coast (v.4). V.5 will be a general index, choronology and bibliography.

Series of brief articles (up to 2p. in length with a few slightly longer), ending with source attributions, concerning American Indian tribes and leaders, explorers, traders, frontier settlers, soldiers, missionaries, mountain men, battles, massacres, forts, treaties, and other topics of interest in the history of the first 48 United States from the arrival of the earliest seafarers to the end of the Indian wars four hundred years later, arranged in 4 A-Z sequences. *Class No: 973(=97)(035)*

Maps & Atlases

[8013]

TANNER, H.H., *ed.* **Atlas of Great Lakes Indian history.** Norman, Univ. of Oklahoma Press for the Newberry Library, 1986. xv,224p. illus., maps, bibliog., index. $75.00; £62.00. ISBN: 0806115157.

33 newly researched colour maps of the Great Lakes region of the US and Canada, particularly of the Ohio Valley, depicting the movement of Indian communities 1640-1871. *e.g.* 6. The Iroquois Wars 1641-1701... 12. Distribution of Indian and white settlements *c.*1830. Bibliographic essay p.183-5. Bibliography p.187-208. *Class No: 973(=97)(084.3)*

[8014]

WALDMAN, C. Atlas of the North American Indian. New York and Oxford, Facts on File Publications, 2000. xi, 276p. illus., maps (mostly col.), bibliog., index. $45. ISBN: 0816039747.

Over 100 two-colour maps, together with complementary text cover the history, culture and location of the Indian people of Canada, the United States, and Central America. An appendix includes Chronology, Indian tribes of US and Canada with historical and contemporary locations; Federal and State Indian reservations, trust areas and native villages; Indian bands in Canada; Major Indian place-names in US and Canada; Museums, historical societies and archaeological sites; and a Bibliography. *Class No: 973(=97)(084.3)*

Chronologies

[8015]

Chronology of Native North American history from pre-Columbian times to the present. Champagne, D., *ed.* Detroit, Gale Research, 1994. 514p. illus., maps, bibliog., index. £46. ISBN: 0810391953.

Significant events arranged in a single chronological sequence in 3 sections: 50,000BC (advent of first native peoples over the Bering landbridge) to AD1492; 1500-1959; 1960-March 1994 (Indian Country Tourism Conference). Outline history of all North American peoples and a summary of important historical documents and legal cases are also included. *Class No: 973(=97)(090)*

Biographies

[8016]

WALDMAN, C. Who was who in Native American history: Indians and non-Indians from early contacts through 1900. New York and Oxford, Facts On File, 1990. vi,410p. illus., ports. £30. ISBN: 0816017972.

Over 1000 cross-referenced entries relating to Indian tribal leaders, medicine men, warrior chiefs, and army scouts and also to European explorers, statesmen, army officers, traders, artists and photographers, scholars and educators whose influence and policies affected native American history. Entry content: birth and death dates and concise biographies (John Cabot 29 lines ... Cochise 75 lines ... Buffalo Bill Cody 93 lines ... George Custer 112 lines ... Geronimo 132 lines). Appendix: Native Americans listed by tribe and non-Indians listed by occupation p.400-10. Restricted to North America. *Class No: 973(=97)(092)*

18th & 19th Centuries

Maps & Atlases

[8017]

WEXLER, A. Atlas of westward expansion. New York & Oxford, Facts On File, 1995. 240p. illus., maps. bibliog., index. $40. ISBN: 0816026602.

Maps 150 years of diplomatic, military and social events relating to the American expansion westwards from the Allegheny Mts to the Pacific. Appendix A. List of States and Territories entering the Union - B. Chronology 1750-1917. *Class No: 973"17/18"(084.3)*

18th Century

Maps & Atlases

[8018]

CAPPON, L.J., *and others.* **Atlas of early American history** the Revolutionary era 1760-1790. Princeton, New Jersey, Princeton Univ. Press for Newberry Library & Institute of Early American History & Culture, 1976. 157p. maps. $235.00. ISBN: 0691046344.

268 maps, mostly in colour, covering political, religious, cultural, economic, demographic and military aspects of the period, with explanatory text. Full index. Very favourably reviewed in *Library journal*, 15 November 1976, p.2357-8. *Class No: 973"17"(084.3)*

19th Century

Encyclopaedias

[8019]

Encyclopedia of the United States in the nineteenth century. New York, Charles Scribner's Sons, 3v., 2000. 1500p. illus., maps, tables, index. $325. ISBN: 0684805006.

600 A-Z articles explore all aspects of 19th-century history: population, politics and government, economy and work, society and culture, religion, social problems and reform, everyday life, and foreign policy. Includes an exhaustive year-by-year chronology and original documents. *Class No: 973"18"(031)*

Women

[8020]

WEATHERFORD, D.L. Milestones: a chronology of American women's history. New York, Facts On File, 1997. 400p. illus., bibliog., index. $45. ISBN: 0816032009.

Brief entries on the achievements of women in American Government, industry, the arts, education, and medicine in 10 chronological chapters 1492-1995. 'A complement to reference collections in public-libraries aiming for a thorough coverage of women's history' (*Library Journal*, v.122, no.6, 1 April 1997, p.86). *Class No: 973-0055.2*

Colonial Period

Bibliographies

[8021]

LYDON, J.G. Stuggle for empire a bibliography of the French and Indian War. New York, Garland, 1986. xxi,272p. indexes. $42. (*Wars Of The United States, no.7.*) ISBN: 0824090691.

1508 annotated English, French, and Spanish language items relating to the extension of the Europeon Seven Years War (1756-1763) to North America. 22 chapters in Topical (*e.g.* Military and Naval ... Indian relations ... Forts and topography) and Geographical divisions. Bibliographical references (items 1458-1508) p.245-53. *Class No: 973.02(01)*

Encyclopaedias

[8022]

FARAGHER, J.M., *ed.* **The Encylopedia of Colonial and Revolutionary America.** New York and Oxford, Facts on File, 1989. 448p. illus., maps, bibliogs., index. $50.00; £45.00. ISBN: 0816017441.

*c.*1500 entries of varying length cover political, military, social, economic and cultural aspects of the period (including French, Spanish and Russian America). About half the entries are biographical. Some longer entries are signed and carry bibliographies. *Class No: 973.02(031)*

War of Independence

Bibliographies

[8023]
BLANCO, R.L. **The War of the American Revolution** a selected annotated bibliography of published sources. New York, Garland, 1984 xxvii,654p. indexes. $56. (*Wars of the United States, no.1.*) ISBN: 082409171x.

3740 items in 14 sections: 1. Causes of the war - 2. Campaigns and battles - 3. American army ... 6. British army - 7. German troops ... 10. Diplomacy ... 14. Bibliographies. Periodicals cited p.xv-xxvii
Class No: 973.03(01)

[8024]
GEPHART, R.M. **Revolutionary America 1763-1789: a bibliography.** Washington, Library of Congress, 2v., 1984. (Distributed by Government Printing Office). xl,1672p. illus. on endpapers, index. $38. ISBN: 0844403598, v.1; 0844403792, v.2.

14110 annotated entries (encompassing over 20,000 titles) arranged in 12 chronological and thematic chapters (*e.g.* 1. Research aids ... 2. General studies: regional, state and local ... 10. The making of the Constitution ... 12. Biographies and personal primary sources) followed by an extensive essay, The Presentation and Publication of Documentary Sources on the American Revolution, p.1469-1671. 'This monumental work is absolutely essential' (*Choice*, v.22, no.1, September 1984, p.62). *Class No:* 973.03(01)

[8025]
SELBY, J.E. 'Revolutionary America: the historiography' *Magazine of History* v.8,no.4, Summer 1994. p.5-8.

Bibliographical essay fashioned on the premise 'that each generation writes its own history'. *Class No:* 973.03(01)

[8026]
SMITH, D.L., *ed.* **Era of the American Revolution: a bibliography.** Santa Barbara, California and Oxford, Clio Press, 1975. xiv,381p. (*Clio Bibliographical Series, no.4.*) ISBN: 0874361788.

1401 signed abstracts of articles published worldwide in 11 sections: 1. Interpreting the Revolution: the historical view - 2. General history: Lexington - Concord - 3. Participants - 4. Decade of controversy 1763-1775 - 5. The war for Rights: before the Declaration of Independence - 6. The war for independence - 7. The Revolution and the West - 8. The Loyalists - 9. The Confederation - 10. The Constitution - 11. Revolutionary society. Coverage is continued in *America: history and life. Class No:* 973.03(01)

[8027]
ZINK, S.D. 'Location and analysis of the historical publications produced by agencies of the United States Government during the era of the American Revolution Bicentennial 1974-1976', *Publishing History*, v.27, 1990, p.77-100.

489 publications are recorded: scholarly monographs; brief popular historical sketches; historical bibliographies; essays; lectures; memoirs; collections of documents; historical reference works and guides. Agencies covered include the Departments of the Interior, Defense, and Agriculture, Congress, and the Smithsonian Institution. *Class No:* 973.03(01)

Encyclopaedias

[8028]
The American Revolution an encyclopedia. Blanco, R.L., *ed.* New York, Garland, 2v., 1992. 1857p. maps, bibliogs. $175. (*Military History of the United States, no. 1.*) ISBN: 082405623x.

Over 130 specialist contributors. 800 entries consisting of short essays each with bibliographical references on the battles, campaigns and naval engagements, along with more than 400 biographical sketches of the leading American, British, French, German and Spanish commanders and prominent American and British statesmen. Coverage extends to Canada, the West Indies, and the waters of the Indian Ocean. A glossary explains contemporary terms. *Class No:* 973.03(031)

[8029]
The Blackwell encyclopedia of the American Revolution. Greene, J.P. and Pole, J.R., *eds.* Oxford, Blackwell, 1991. xvi,845p. illus., maps, bibliogs., index. £60; $49.95. ISBN: 1557582443.

75 full length articles by different hands exploring all aspects of the Revolution: 1. Context - 2/3. Themes and events - 4. External effects - 5. Internal effects - 6. Concepts - 7. Biographies. Chronology in 3 columns: 1. Political and legal events - 2. Military campaigns - 3. Scientific, cultural, educational, scientific and religious developments (p.794-827). Guides to further reading after every article. Analytical index. 'A very thorough compendium of recent scholarly thinking on this critical period' (*Booklist*, v.88, no.6, 15 November 1991, p.640). *Class No:* 973.03(031)

[8030]
BOATNER, M.M. **Encyclopedia of the American Revolution.** 3rd ed. Mechanasburg, PA., Stackpole Books, 1994. xx,1290p. maps, bibliog., index. $32.95. ISBN: 0811705781.

1st ed. 1966; 2nd ed. 1974.

Cross-referenced entries include 'Cover', *i.e.* summary articles of important and pervasive topics and shorter entries for the leading Revolutionary figures and key issues. 54 maps. Bibliography p.1253-73. Map index p.1275-87. *Class No:* 973.03(031)

Dictionaries

[8031]
MAYS, T.M. **Historical dictionary of the American Revolution.** Lanham, MD., Scarecrow Press, 1999. xxxvi,550p. maps, ports., bibliog. $125. (*Historical Dictionaries of Wars, Revolutions and Civil Unrest, no.7.*) ISBN: 0810834049. *Class No:* 973.03(038)

Maps & Atlases

[8032]
HARLEY, J.B., *and others.* **Mapping the American Revolutionary War.** Chicago and London, Univ. of Chicago Press, 1978. vii,187p., illus. maps, bibliog., index. $39.95. ISBN: 0226316319.

3 contemporary and 2 retrospective essays. Notes p.148-172. Bibliography p.173-182. 'Provides the final word on the subject' (*Geographical journal*, v.145, no.1, March 1979, p.146-147). *Class No:* 973.03(084.3)

[8033]
SYMONDS, C.L. **A Battlefield atlas of the American Revolution.** Annapolis, Maryland, The Nautical and Aviation Publishing Company of America. 1986. 110p. illus. maps. ISBN: 0933852533.

Part 1. Early campaignes - 2. The turning point - 3. A global war - 4. The war moves south. Epilogue: The world turned upside down. 41 double-page map/text features. Bibliography p.109-10. *Class No:* 973.03(084.3)

Biographies

[8034]
BOATNER, M.M. **Cassell's biographical dictionary of the American War of Independence 1763-1783.** London, Cassell, 1973. xviii,1287p., maps, diagrs., bibliog., index. ISBN: 0304292966.

Published in US as *Encyclopedia of the American Revolution.*

Nearly 2,000 cross-referenced entries providing the background and origins of the war; biographies (1/3 of total); and political issues and events. Bibliography p.1253-73. Index to maps p.1257-87. *Class No:* 973.03(092)

[8035]
PURCELL, L.E. **Who was who in the American Revolution.** New York and Oxford, Facts On File, 1993. 576p. illus., bibliog., index. $60; £39.95. ISBN: 0816021074.

Biographical sketches of 1500 British, loyalist, patriot, French, German, Polish and African Americans prominent in the war. *Class No:* 973.03(092)

Early Nineteenth Century, 1809-1845

Bibliographies

[8036]
SMITH, D.W. **The War of 1812** an annotated bibliography. New York, Garland, 1985. xxiv,340p. indexes. $61. (*Wars of the United States, no.3.*) ISBN: 0824089456.

1393 annotated entries in 9 sub-divided sections: 1. Bibliographies - 2. General histories - 3. Coming of the war - 4. Canadian-American theater - 5. War in the South - 6. British offensive 1814 - 7. War at sea - 8. Internal scene - 9. Peace. Chronology p.xix-xxiii. Author and subject indexes. *Class No:* 973.05(01)

Encyclopaedias

[8037]
HEIDLER, D.S. *and* HEIDLER, J.T., *eds.* **Encyclopedia of the War of 1812.** Santa Barbara, Calif., ABC-Clio, 1998. 636p. illus., maps, bibliogs., index. $95. £59.95. ISBN: 0874369681.

70 contributors. 500 cross-referenced short essays, each with a short bibliography, relating to the events of the war and its historical context. The Encyclopedia also contains the text of important documents such as the Embargo Act, the Rambouillet Decree, Macon's Bill No.2, and President James Madison's War Message of 1812, a chronology of political, military, and diplomatic maneuvres; a listing of the executive federal government officers during the Madison presidency; and a glossary of military, diplomatic, and nautical terms. 24 pages of maps. *Class No:* 973.05(031)

Mid Nineteenth Century, 1845-1861

Encyclopaedias

[8038]

CRAWFORD, M. **Encyclopedia of the Mexican-American War.** Oxford and Santa Barbara, Calif., ABC-Clio, 1999. 350p. illus., maps, bibliogs., index. $75. ISBN: 157607059x.

458 cross-referenced A-Z entries relating to civil and military leaders, battles and weapons, locations, political treaties, of varying length (from a single paragraph to 2 pages), all ending with a list of further readings. An extensive (25 pages) and wideranging bibliography includes Spanish-language items. 4 maps. *Class No:* 973.06(031)

American Civil War

[8039]

Battle chronicles of the Civil War. McPherson, J.M., *ed.* New York, Macmillan, 6v., 1989. illus., maps, bibliog., index. $299. ISBN: 0029206618.

40 contributors. A chronological military history: v.1-5 are each devoted to one year of the war 1861-65, with over 100 essays reprinted from the periodical, *Civil War Times Illustrated;* v.6 consists of essays on the Presidents of the Confederate and United States and their most renowned military leaders, a bibliography, and an index to the complete set. A 35-minute videotape is included. *Class No:* 973.07

[8040]

KATCHER, P. **The American Civil War source book.** London, Arms and Armour Press, 1992. 318p. illus., maps, bibliog., index. £24.95. ISBN: 1854091042.

Single-volume reference source in 10 sections: 1. Campaigns - 2. Weapons and the practice of war - 3. Military life - 4. Forces of the United States - 5. Forces of the Confederate States - 6. Militia of the individual states - 7. Biographies - 8. Sources (published, graphic arts, photography, videos) p.294-300 - 9. Miscellanea - 10. Glossary (p.309-11). Bibliography p.295-6. 10 maps. *Class No:* 973.07

Bibliographies

[8041]

EICHER, D.J. **The Civil War in books** an analytical bibliography. Univ. of Illinois, 1996. 403p. index. $39.95. ISBN: 0252022734.

6 contributors. Select list of 1,100 titles (from an estimated 50,000!) published 1865-1995 marshalled in 5 categories: 1. Battles and campaigns - 2/3. Confederate/Union biographies - 4. General works - 5. Unit histories. An appendix lists 54 Civil War bibliographies. *Class No:* 973.07(01)

[8042]

MURDOCK, E.C., *comp.* **The Civil War in the North** a selective annotated bibliography. New York, Garland, 1987. xx,761p. $58.00. (*Wars of the United States, no.9.*) ISBN: 0824089413.

5608 briefly annotated entries divided into 11 chapters: 1. Introduction (reference and general works) - 2. Government - 3. Army - 4. Navy - 5. Lincoln - 6. Biographies and personal accounts - 7. Soldier life - 8. The written word - 9. The Arts - 10. Minorities - 11. Special topics. Author and subject indexes. *Class No:* 973.07(01)

[8043]

NEVINS, A., *and others, eds.* **Civil War books** a critical bibliography. Wilmington, North Carolina, Broadfoot, 2v., 1984. ix, 278p.; ix, 326p. $50.00. ISBN: 0916107094.

First published Baton Rouge, Louisiana Univ. Press, 1967-69.

V.1: *c.*2,500 entries, with *c.*20-word evaluative annotations. 7 'categories': 1. Military aspects: Mobilization; organization; administration and supply - 2. Military aspects: Campaigns - 3. Military aspects: Soldier life - 4. Prisons and prisoners of war - 5. The negro - 6. The navies - 7. Diplomacy. Arranged by authors, A-Z, under categories. V.2 has entries for *c.*2,400 general works, biographies, and the government, politics, social and economic studies, state and local studies covering the Confederacy and the Union. Brief, evaluative annotations. Excludes periodical articles, dissertations, masters theses, pure literature. Author, title and subject index to both volumes, p.249-326. *Class No:* 973.07(01)

[8044]

WOODWORTH, S.E., *ed.* **The American Civil War** a handbook of literature and research. Westport, Conn., Greenwood Press, 1996. 677p. $99. ISBN: 0313290199.

47 bibliographic essays (10-20p. long) subdivided into 11 categories (*e.g.* General secondary sources ... International relations ... The Home Front) citing nearly 4,000 sources. An appendix lists 516 publishers and dealers of Civil War literature. *Class No:* 973.07(01)

Encyclopaedias

[8045]

NEELY, M.E. **The Abraham Lincoln encyclopedia.** New York, McGraw Hill, 1982. xii, 356p. illus., bibliogs. index. ISBN: 00700461457.

Entries for Lincoln's career, family, friends and enemies, the places he lived, events, his leading biographers, libraries with major Lincoln collections, societies *etc.* but not intended as a Civil War encyclopedia. 'Will become an indispensable reference source in every library' (*Choice*, v.19, no.7, March 1982, p.893-4). *Class No:* 973.07(031)

Maps & Atlases

[8046]

The Atlas of the Civil War. McPherson, J.M., *ed.* New York, Macmillan, 1994. 234p. illus., maps, bibliog., index. $40. ISBN: 0025790501.

200 maps arranged in 5 annual sections 1861-65 showing troop formations and units, physical features etc. 'Line clarity, color, and detailing are excellent. The photos could almost stand alone as a photographic essay of the war' (*Booklist*, v.91,no.17, May 1995, p.1592). *Class No:* 973.07(084.3)

[8047]

Atlas to accompany the official records of the Union and Confederate armies. Washington, General Printing Office, 1891-1895. 29p.+175 plates, col. maps, index.

Facsimile edition as *The Official military atlas of the Civil War* edited by G.B. Davis and others (Avenel, NJ., Grammercy Books, 1983) ISBN 0517415666.

Maps arranged in 4 sections: 1. Military operations in the field - 2. General topographic maps - 3. Military divisions and departments - 4. Miscellaneous (uniforms, ordnance, corps flags). Authorities *i.e.* contributors) p.11-15. *Class No:* 973.07(084.3)

[8048]

Civil War maps: an annotated list of maps and atlases in The Library of Congress. Stephenson, R.W., *comp.* 2nd ed. Washington, Library of Congress, 1989. 410p. maps (some col.), indexes. $46. ISBN: 0844405981.

Descriptive but not analytical guide to 2200 maps and 70++ atlases and sketch books. Data: author; title; publisher/printer; scale; and size. Indexes of (1) map title and (2) personal names (*i.e.* cartographers, engravers, lithographers, printers, publishers, surveyors). An introduction includes sections on pre-war, Union, Confederate maps *etc.* and gives information on the Union Army's Corps of Topographical Engineers and the Confederate Topographical Department. 'A unique and commendable reference work' (*Geographical Journal*, v.157., no.1, March 1991, p.96). *Class No:* 973.07(084.3)

Bibliographies

[8049]

A Guide to Civil War maps in the National Archives. Rev. ed. Washington, National Archives Publications, 1986. 140p. illus. $30.00. ISBN: 0911333363.

First published 1964.

Arranged in 2 parts: 1. a general guide to the 8000 maps in the Cartographic and Architectural Branch of the Archives - 2. a description of selected maps in greater detail. *Class No:* 973.07(084.3)(01)

Chronologies

[8050]

BOWMAN, J.S., *ed.* **American Civil War day by day.** New York, Facts On File, 1989. 224p., illus. (some col.), maps. £18.95. ISBN: 0816021813.

Pictorial chronology covering military history and also political, social and economic aspects of the war. 350 photographs. 13 maps. *Class No:* 973.07(090)

Biographies

[8051]

Biographical dictionary of the Union Northern leaders of the Civil War. Hubbell, J.T. *and* Geary, J.W., *eds.* Westport, Conn., Greenwood Press, 1995. 683p. $99.50. ISBN: 0313209200.

800 politicians and military leaders. Data: occupation or appointment, birth and death dates, education, career profile during and after the Civil War, together with source(s) of information. 'Researching individual leaders of the US Civil War has never been easy due to the large variety of possible sources. This biographical dictionary goes a long way toward solving this problem' (*ARBA Guide to Biographical Resources 1986-1997*, 1998, p.77). *Class No:* 973.07(092)

[8052]

BOATNER, M.M. Cassell's biographical dictionary of the American Civil War 1861-1865. London, Cassell, 1973. xvi, 974p. maps, bibliog.

First published New York, David McKay, 1959, as *The Civil War dictionary* (rev. ed. 1988) ISBN 081291726x.

Over 400 cross-referenced articles on campaigns, leading personnel, and political, social and economic events. Emphasis is on 'briefly covering the maximum number of important subjects rather than attempting a more detailed treatment of a smaller number of selected highspots' (*Introduction*). Sectional maps p.955-69. Bibliography p.970-74. *Class No:* 973.07(092)

[8053]

McPHERSON, J.M., *ed.* Encyclopedia of Civil War biographies. New York, M.E. Sharpe, 3v., 1999. 900p. illus., bibliog., index. $299. ISBN: 0765680211.

500+ Civil War biographies, mostly written in the late 19th and early 20th centuries, extracted from the *National Cyclopedia of American Biographies* (1888-1984). 'The benefits of this encyclopedia are the inclusion of many figures not represented elsewhere and the chance to see the Civil War through biography as it was written generations ago. Otherwise it is best to look elsewhere for biographical references' (*Library Journal,* v.125, no.4, 1 March 2000, p.74). *Class No:* 973.07(092)

[8054]

RITTER, C.F. *and* WAKELYN, J.L., *eds.* Leaders of the American Civil War a biographical and historiographical dictionary. Chicago and London, Fitzroy Dearborn, 1998. xxxiv,465p. index. £60. ISBN: 1579581129.

17 US academics contribute 47 biographical essays on civil and military leaders during the Civil War period (*e.g.*Jefferson Davis (9p.), Abraham Lincoln (13p.). and William Tecumseh Sherman (12p.). Each essay includes 'An evaluation of how historians have regarded these leaders and 'a chronological bibliography from the earliest works to the present' (*Preface*). *Class No:* 973.07(092)

[8055]

SIFAKIS, S. Who was who in the Civil War. New York and Oxford, Facts On File, 1988. ix,766p. illus., bibliog., index. $45.00; £25.00. ISBN: 0816010552.

Compendium of over 2500 concise biographies of the major military leaders (all 583 Union and 425 Confederate general officers) and leading political figures. Appendix A. Chronology p.742-46 - B. Officers receiving thanks of US Congress p.747. Bibliography p.748-49. 'An outstanding reference work' (*Booklist,*v.85,no.3, 1 October 1988, p.245.

Who was who in the Confederacy (1989. xi,324p. 0816022046) and *Who was who in the Union* (1989, ix,479p. 0816022038) were published in softcovers. *Class No:* 973.07(092)

Manuscripts & Incunabula

Bibliographies

[8056]

SELLERS, J.R., *comp.* Civil War manuscripts a guide to the collections in the Manuscript Division of the Library of Congress. Washington, Library of Congress, 1986. xvii,391p. ports., index. $20.00. ISBN: 0844403814.

Evolved from L.W. Dunlap's checklist *Civil War manuscripts* (1967).

1064 collections arranged A-Z by collection title. Data given: brief statement of identification; nature of collection; type of materials; content description; and finding aids. Analytical index. *Class No:* 973.07(093)(01)

Later Nineteenth Century, 1865-1901

Bibliographies

[8057]

VENZON, A.C. The Spanish-American War an annotated bibliography. New York, Garland, 1990. xi,255p., indexes. $40. (*Wars Of The United States, no.11.*) ISBN: 0824079744.

Select bibliography consisting of 1180 (mostly) annotated items written in English language and arranged in 17 sub-divided sections e.g. 1. General works ... 3. Biographies - 4. US Army - 5. US Navy ... 7. Cuba - 8. Philippines - 9. Puerto Rico. Also includes works on the Philippine-American War 1899-1902. Subject and author indexes. *Class No:* 973.08(01)

Dictionaries

[8058]

DYAL, D.H. Historical dictionary of the Spanish American War. Westport, CT., Greenwood Press, 1996. xii,378p. bibliog., index. ISBN: 0313288526.

Cross-referenced entries spotlight significant events, locations, bases, personnel, weapons and equipment, uniforms etc. Bibliography p.363-64. *Class No:* 973.08(038)

[8059]

TREFOUSSE, H.L. Historical dictionary of reconstruction. Westport, Conn., Greenwood Press, 1991. xii,284p. bibliog., index. $65. ISBN: 0313258627.

Nearly 250 A-Z cross-referenced articles (many over 1000 words) dealing with current research on major personalities, concepts and issues, relating to the period 1863-1877. At the end of each article there is a listing of the latest available literature. Chronology p.ix-xii. Bibliography p.263-6. 'A valuable addition to the historical reference literature of the US' (*Booklist,* v.88, no.7, 1 December 1991, p.721). *Class No:* 973.08(038)

20th Century

[8060]

RENSHAW, P. The Longman companion to America in the era of the two World Wars, 1910-1945. London, Longman, 1995. 256p. £36. ISBN: 0582091160.

Chronologies listing all the major events, both foreign and domestic; social and economic history, with many tables based on inaccessible data; scores of mini-biographies; listing of the major office holders; and maps. *Class No:* 973.09

Bibliographies

[8061]

KYVIG, D.E. *and* BLASIO, M.A. New day/New deal a bibliography of the great American depression 1929-1941. Westport, Connecticut, and London, Greenwood Press 1988. ix, 306p. index. $45.00. £40.50. (*Bibliographies and Indexes in American History.*) ISBN: 0313260273. ISSN: 07426828.

4600 unannotated English language items (1300 books, 2500 articles/essays, 800 discs) grouped in 44 subject categories arranged in 13 chapters e.g. 1. Overviews and general histories ... 2. Bibliography and historiography ... 5. The Hoover administration ... 6. The Roosevelt administration ... 13. After effects. *Class No:* 973.09(01)

Dictionaries

[8062]

Historical dictionary of the Progressive Era 1890-1920. Buenker, J.D. *and* Kantowicz, E.R., *eds.* Westport, Conn., Greenwood Press, 1988. ix,599p. bibliogs., indexes. $85; £73.10. ISBN: 0313243093.

197 contributors. Over 800 signed A-Z entries describing the most important people, events, organizations, legislation, and concepts of the period of study. Each entry ends with a brief bibliography. Chronology p.537-48. Name, title and subject indexes. 'An excellent, handy reference guide to one of the most important and certainly one of the most written-about eras of American history' (*Choice,* v.26, no.7, March 1990, p.1122++4). *Class No:* 973.09(038)

[8063]

HOCHMAN, S. *and* HOCHMAN, E. The Penguin dictionary of contemporary American history 1945 to the present. 3rd ed. New York, Penguin Reference Books, 1997. xiii,642p. index. pbk. £9.99. ISBN: 0140513728.

First published as *Yesterday and today* (McGraw Hill, 1979), 1st rev. ed. as *A Dictionary of contemporary American History* (Dutton Signet, 1993).

700+ cross-referenced A-Z entries relating to political, social and cultural events and trends that shaped America focusing on key people, events and issues. *Class No:* 973.09(038)

[8064]

OLSON, J.S. Historical dictionary of the 1920s from World War I to the New Deal, 1919-1933. Westport, Connecticut, Greenwood Press, 1988. Distributed in UK by Eurospan. xii, 420p. bibliog., index. $55.00. £49.50. ISBN: 0313256837.

Over 700 cross-referenced entries of varying length relating to personalities and political and social issues with suggestions for further reading. 'An asset for all reference collections and a useful handbook for students of twentieth-century American history' (*Booklist,* v.85, no.6, 15 November 1988, p.554). *Class No:* 973.09(038)

[8065]

OLSON, J.S., *ed*. **Historical dictionary of the 1960s.** Westport, CT., Greenwood Press, 1999., Distributed in UK by Eurospan. viii,548p. bibliog., index. £71.50. ISBN: 031329271x.

Dictionary (signed articles on broad range of topics, political, military, social, cultural, religious, economic, and diplomatic, in addition to short biographies of the decade's leading figures) p.1-491. Chronology of the 1960s p.493-506. Bibliography (in 20 thematic sections) p.507-526. Analytical index. *Class No:* 973.09(038)

[8066]

OLSON, J.S., *ed*. **Historical dictionary of the New Deal** From inauguration to preparation for war. Westport, Connecticut, Greenwood Press, 1985. viii, 611p. Bibliog. index. $67.95. ISBN: 0313238731.

50 contributors. Approximately 700 cross-referenced brief descriptive essays on the personalities, agencies, and legislation important to the New Deal 1933-1940. Appendix A. A New Deal chronology, 1933-1941 (p.553-561) - B. Bibliography (p.563-575) - C. New Deal Personnel (p.577-586) - D. Acronyms (p.587-588). 'The most comprehensive work of its kind yet published' (*Choice*, v.23, no.9, May 1986, p.1370). *Class No:* 973.09(038)

Amerindians, North

[8067]

DAVIS, M.B., *ed*. **Native America in the twentieth century: an encyclopedia.** New York, Garland Press, 1994. 787p. illus., charts, bibliogs., index. $95. ISBN: 0824048466.

300+ signed articles from 282 contributors including many on individual tribes in addition to longer overview essays on art, education, health *etc*. Each entry ends with an extensive bibliography. 'The diversity of expert voices - many of them native - and the scope of coverage of contemporary life in Native America make this an extremely valuable work' (*Choice*, v.32,no.6, February 1995, p.918). *Class No:* 973.09(=97)

Local Histories

[8068]

Atlas of historical county boundaries. New York, Charles Scribner's Sons. $130 each.

Alabama. ISBN 0133095681; *Delaware, Maryland, Washington DC*. ISBN 013366337x; *Florida*. ISBN 0133663299; *Illinois*. ISBN 0133664023; *Indiana*. IBSN 0133095509; *Iowa*. ISBN 0133663868; *Kentucky*. ISBN 0133095436; *Maine, Massachusetts, Connecticut, & Rhode Island*. ISBN 0130519472; *Michigan*. ISBN 0133663116; *Mississippi*. ISBN 0130519707; *New Hampshire and Vermont*. ISBN 0130519545. *New York*. ISBN 0130519626; *North Carolina*. ISBN 0133664694; *Ohio*. ISBN 0133663949; *South Carolina*. ISBN 0133663604; *Pennsylvania*. ISBN 0133155323; *Tennessee*. ISBN 0133664511. *Virginia, West Virginia*. ISBN 0133663450; *Wisconsin*. ISBN 0133663523. Details all changes in the boundaries and areas of the more than 3,000 U.S. counties, from colonial times to the 1990s. *Class No:* 974/979

[8069]

BURROWS, E.G. *and* WALLACE, M. **Gotham** a history of New York City to 1898. New York, Oxford Univ. Press, 1999. 1383p. illus., bibliog., indexes. $49.94. ISBN: 0195196348.

5 chronological sections: 1. Lenape County New Amsterdam - 2. British New York - 3. Mercantile town - 4. Emporium and manufacturing city - 5. Industrial center and corporate command post. 'Exceptional for its scope, reliability and authoritativeness' (*Choice*, v.36, no.8, April 1999, p.1515). *Class No:* 974/979

[8070]

RUSSO, D.J. **Keepers of our past** local historical writing in the United States 1820s-1930s. Westport, Conn., Greenwood Press, 1988. xiii,281p. bibliog., index. $39.951 £29.95. ISBN: 0313262365. ISSN: 00849219.

Traces the transition of local history from a favourite pursuit of local antiquarians to the province of academic historians in 4 stages: 1/2. Early, later antiquarians - 3. Formulaic local history (as a publishing venture, as an editorial project, as literature) - 4. Coming of the academics. Chapter notes p.215-54. Bibliography p.255-74. 'Recommended to Ph.D. candidates and professional historians researching and writing local history' (*Choice*, v.26, no.7, March 1989, p.1237). *Class No:* 974/979

Micromaterials

[8071]

County and regional histories and atlas. Reading, Primary Source Media (Gale Group), 1999. Microfilm. 660 reels. £33,000.

Encompass 8 states: California (97 titles); Illinois (361); Indiana (262); Michigan (325); New York (465); Ohio (305); Pennsylvania (283); and Wisconsin (158). Included in these sources are tables and

....(contd.)

lists of vital statistics, military service records, municipal and county officers, chronologies, portraits of individuals, and views of urban and rural life. *Class No:* 974/979(003.5)

Bibliographies

[8072]

FILBY, P.W. **A Bibliography of American county histories.** Baltimore, Genealogical Publishing Co. Inc., 1985. xiv, 449p. $24.95. ISBN: 0806311266.

Replaces Clarence S. Peterson's *Consolidated bibliography of county histories in fifty states* (1961).

Identifies all county histories of any consequence published before December 1984. Arranged alphabetically by state and then by county. No index. 'Libraries serving genealogists no longer can provide adequate reference service without it' (*RQ*, v.25, no.2, Winter 1985, p.252-253). *Class No:* 974/979(01)

[8073]

KAMINKOW, M.J., *ed*. **United States local histories in the Library of Congress** a bibliography. Randallstown, Maryland, Magna Carta Book Co., 5v., 1975. 4500p. $225.00. ISBN: 0910946175.

1: *Atlantic States, Maine to New York.*
2: *Atlantic States, New Jersey to Florida.*
3: *Middle West. Alaska, Hawaii.*
4: *The West.*
Supplement and Index.
Entries for the 50 states are arranged by Library of Congress call numbers in class F(DU, in the case of Hawaii). 'Material cannot be traced by author or title' (*RQ*, v.16, no.2, Winter 1976, p.188). *Class No:* 974/979(01)

[8074]

NEW YORK LIBRARY. The Research Libraries. Local History and Genealogy divison. **United States Local History Catalog.** Boston, Mass., G.K. Hall, 2v., 1974. (981p.) 2 reels. $165.00 (Export $200.00). ISBN: 0816112851.

Lists the separate bound monographs and serials cataloged in the Research Libraries' United States local history classification scheme. It is included in the *Dictionary Catalog of the Local History and Genealogy Division* of the New York Public Library but it may also be purchased and used independently by readers with particular interests in United States local history.

Supplemented annually by the *Bibliographic Guide to North American History*. *Class No:* 974/979(01)

[8075]

STEPHENS, W.B. **Sources for U.S. history** nineteenth-century communities. Cambridge, Cambridge Univ. Press, 1991. xviii,558p. £55. (*The Sources of History*.) ISBN: 0521353157.

1. Introduction (published, unpublished, and cartographic sources) - 2. Demography - 3. Ethnicity and race - 4/5. Land, settlement and farming - 6. Religion - 7. Local government, politics and organized labor - 8. Manufacturing, mining and business - 9. Maritime, communications, fur trade - 10. Education - 11. Poverty, health and crime. Series of detailed bibliographic essays on contemporary sources for research. *Class No:* 974/979(01)

Encyclopaedias

[8076]

The Encyclopedia of New York City. Jackson, K.T., *ed*. New Haven, Conn., Yale University Press; New York, New York Historical Society, 1995. xxi,1350p. illus., maps, tables, index. £40. ISBN: 0300055366.

4,300 signed entries by 680 contributors ranging in length from 26 to 6,000 words for overviews of large topics. Includes entries for individuals who have left a permanent mark on the city's history and culture, extant neighbourhoods, and institutions, ethnic groups, advertising agencies, newspapers, religious denominations etc. Its aim is 'to provide basic information and it is a place to begin research, not end it; those who seek further information are referred to other sources through bibliographic citations'. *Class No:* 974/979(031)

Yearbooks & Directories

Bibliographies

[8077]

City & State directories in print An annotated guide to over 4,500 State, City, and Local directories, rosters, guides, and lists of all kinds, covering: Arts and entertainments; Business & industry; Computers & telecommunications; Education; Government; Health and medicine; Law; Real Estate; Recreation; Science & technology; Social services; Travel; and many other topics. First Edition 1990-91. Towell, J.E. *and* Montney, C.B., *eds*. Detroit, Gale Research Inc. 1989. xix,966p. indexes. $145. ISBN: 0810318482. ISSN: 10438939.

Scope: 'general commercial and manufacturing directories; general

....(contd.)

and specialized lists of cultural institutions; directories of individual industries, trades and professions; rosters of professional and scientific societies; guides to events, accommodations, restaurants, and entertainments; and lists of community services. It also includes membership lists of special-interest groups of all kinds - political, recreational, cultural *etc.*; publications of government agencies listing their own activities or the programs supported by them; and a wide variety of lists and guides on other subjects' (*Introduction*). Arranged A-Z by State and US Territories. Subject, and title and keyword indexes. *Class No:* 974/979(058)(01)

Maps & Atlases

[8078]
HOMBERGER, E. The Historical atlas of New York City a visual celebration of nearly 400 years of New York City's history. New York, Henry Holt, 1994. 276p. col.illus., col.maps, bibliog., index. $45. ISBN: 0805026495.

8 chronological chapters profusely illustrated and mapped (*e.g.* 1. Hilly island - 2. Dutch New Amsterdam 1610-1664 - British New York 1664-1783 ... 8. Cultural capital 1945-1994). Chronology p.168-77. Biographical notes p.178-83. Bibliography p.184-6. Discovering New York, p.187. *Class No:* 974/979(084.3)

[8079]
LONG, J.H. Historical atlas and chronology of county boundaries 1788-1980. Boston, G.K. Hall, 4v., 1984. maps, plans, bibliogs.

1. *Delaware, Maryland, New Jersey, Pennsylvania.* 251p. Bibliography p.247-51. 2. *Illinois. Indiana. Ohio.* 321p. Bibliography p.317-21. 4. *Iowa, Missouri.* 375p. Bibliography p.371-5. 5. *Minnesota. North Dakota. South Dakota.* 479p. Bibliography p.475-9. Data: boundaries at international level down to counties; seats of government at each level; relevant coastlines; names of states. With boundary and regional maps and county chronologies. *Class No:* 974/979(084.3)

[8080]
NEWBERRY LIBRARY HISTORICAL BOUNDARY DATA FILE. Historical atlas and chronology of county boundaries 1788-1980. Boston, Mass, G.K. Hall, 5v., 1984. 1920p. maps, bibliogs. $475.00 (Export $720.00). ISBN: 081610431x, set.

1. *Delaware, Maryland, New Jersey, Pennsylvania.* ISBN 0816104492. 2. *Illinois, Indiana, Ohio.* ISBN 0816104506. 3. *Michigan and Wisconsin* ISBN 0816104514. 4. *Iowa and Missouri.* ISBN 0816104522. 5. *Minnesota, North Dakota, South Dakota.* ISBN 0816104530. Each is available separately at $99.00 (Export $108.00).

A compilation of maps and texts describing country and state boundary changes. Each volume includes a detailed history emphasizing major events and disputes affecting boundaries, a chronology of changes, and select bibliographies. *Class No:* 974/979(084.3)

Alaska

[8081]
NASKE, C-M. *and* SLOTNIK, H.E. Alaska a history of the 49th state. 2nd ed. Norman, Univ. of Oklahoma Press, 1987. xiv,349p. illus., maps, tables, bibliog., index. ISBN: 0806120991.

1st ed. Grand Rapids, Mich., W.B. Eerdman, 1979.

A well-documented historical narrative from early times with an emphasis on major developments in the 20th century. 15 chapters: 1. The Great Land and its peoples - 2. The early Russian period - 3. Russian naval rule and the sale of Alaska - 4. American purchase and settlement ... 8. Alaska's rocky road to Statehood - 9. Transition to statehood - 10. The State of Alaska ... 14. The oil boom. 8 Appendices: A. The Governors of Alaska ... D. Delegates to Congress. Chapter notes p.305-20. Bibliographical essay: the sources of Alaska's history p.321-35. Analytical index. *Class No:* 979.8

America—South

Bibliographies

[8082]
GOODMAN, E.J. The Exploration of South America: an annotated bibliography. New York, Garland Publishing, 1983. xx,174p. bibliog., index. $43.00. (*Themes in European expansion, no.4.*) ISBN: 0824091809.

915 briefly annotated items (some relating to Spanish and Portuguese language material) in 11 form, thematic, and chronological period sections. 'A strong recommendation to have the book in any library even if only slightly concerned with South America' (*Geographical Journal*, v.150, no.3, November 1984, p.383-4). *Class No:* 980(01)

Brazil

[8083]
BURNS, E.B. A History of Brazil. 2nd ed. New York, Columbia Univ. Press, 1990. x, 579p. illus., maps, bibliog., index. $32.50. ISBN: 0231047487.

First published 1970.

Standard single volume economic, social, cultural and political history. Chronology p.541-546. Glossary of Portuguese words used in text p.547-550. Bibliographical essay p.551-556. 6 maps. Analytical index. *Class No:* 981

[8084]
História geral da civilização Brasiliera. São Paulo, Diffel, 10v., 1960-83.

A Época Colonial. 1. *Do descobrimento à expansão territorial.* 1960. 2. *Administraçao, economia, sociedade.* 1977. *O Brasil Monárquico.* 1. *O processo de emancipação.* 1976. 2. *Dispersâo e unidade.* 1978. 3. *Reações e transações.* 1976. 4. *Declínio e queda do império.* 1982. 5. *Do império à República,* 3rd ed., 1983. *O Brasil Republicano.* 1. *Estrutura de poder e economica (1889-1930).* 1977. 2. *Sociedade e instituições (1889-1930).* 2nd ed., 1978. 3. *Sociedade e política (1930-1964).* 1981. Large scale cooperative history. *Class No:* 981

[8085]
Order and progress a political history of Brazil. Schneider, R.M. Boulder, Colo., Westview Press, 1991. xvii,486p. map, index. $55. ISBN: 0813310776.

10 chapters: 2. Monarchical Brazil ... 5. Quest for development and democracy 1946 to 1960 ... 7. The Military as ruler ... 10. Brazil faces the 1990s. Chapter notes p.388-466. List of Chief Executives of Republican Brazil p.467-8. 'A cogently written narrative that students of modern Brazil will find indispensable' (*Choice*, v.29, no.4, December 1991, p.652). *Class No:* 981

Bibliographies

[8086]
DUTRA, F.A. A Guide to the history of Brazil 1500-1822. Santa Barbara, California and Oxford, ABC-Clio, 1980. xxviii, 625p.

939 numbered entries in 26 sections (1. Bibliographies - 2. The Portuguese background - 3. The history of Brazil ... 26. The historiography of colonial Brazil, 1500-1822). Lengthy annotations. Entries include analyticals, periodical articles and dissertations. Glossary, p.591-601. Index of authors, editors, translators and illustrators. Index of 19th and 20th century authors cited in the text but not abstracted. Biographical index. 'Highly recommended for colleges and universities ... and for larger public libraries' (*Choice*, v.18, no.5, January 1981, p.634). *Class No:* 981(01)

Dictionaries

[8087]
Dicionário histórico-biográfico Brasileiro 1930-1983. Beloch, I. *and* Alves de Abreu, A., *eds.* Rio de Janeiro, Editora Forense - Universitária, 4v., 1984. xxxi, 3634p. bibliog.

Huge work (3 columns to the page) with 4,493 entries (3,741 biographies). Over 750 thematic articles deal with institutions; events; political concepts; constitutions; notorious laws and degrees. '*The* authoritative reference work on recent Brazilian history' (*Hispanic American Historical Review*, v.67, no.3, August 1987, p.545-546). *Class No:* 981(038)

[8088]
LEVINE, R.M. Historical dictionary of Brazil. Metuchen, New Jersey, Scarecrow Press, 1979. xi,297p. $24.00; £22.50. (*Latin American Historical Dictionaries no.19.*) ISBN: 0810811782.

Dictionary p.1-228. Bibliography p.229-97. Definitions 'treat not only people and events but Brazilian civilization in several dimensions'. 'A most helpful reference work' (S.V. Bryant. *Brazil.* 1985. Entry 145). *Class No:* 981(038)

Argentina

[8089]
ROCK, D. Argentina 1516-1982: from Spanish colonization to the Falklands War and Alphonsin. Los Angeles, Univ. of California Press, 1985. London, I.B. Tauris, 1986. xxix, 478p. illus., maps, bibliog., index. $40.00 £29.50. ISBN: 0520051890, US; 1850430861, UK.

'A standard work: undramatic but judicious and convincing' (*International Affairs*, v.62, no.4, Autumn 1986, p.717). *Class No:* 982

Falkland Islands

[8090]

AZPIRI, J.L.M. Historia completa de las Malvinas Tomos I-III. Buenos Aires, Editorial Oriente, 3v., 1966. maps, bibliog.

V.1: includes an 18-page chronology (1506-1966) a 49-page bibliography; V.2: 32 articles by independent hands; Vol.3: includes 176 official Argentine, British, Spanish and North American documents. 'A very thoroughly documented history of the Falkland Islands (Malvinas), though biased towards Argentina's territorial claims' (H.G.R. King, *Atlantic Ocean*. 1985. Entry 781).

Class No: 982.91

[8091]

BECK, P. The Falkland Islands as an international problem. London, Routledge, 1988. xii,211p. maps, tables, bibliog., index. £35. ISBN: 041500909x.

Extremely well-documented historical survey of the nature and development of the 170 year old dispute between Argentina and the United Kingdom. Extensive chapter notes. Bibliography p.197-205. 4 maps. 'Although the conflict itself is not covered in detail, subsequent developments are, and this is a useful compendium of events ... presented in a balanced way' (*British Bulletin of Latin America, the Caribbean, Portugal and Spain,* no.81, October 1989, p.34).

Class No: 982.91

[8092]

HOFFMAN, F.L. and HOFFMAN, O.M. Sovereignty in dispute: the Falklands/Malvinas 1493-1982. Boulder, Colorado, Westview Press, 1984. xiv, 194p. illus., maps, bibliog., index. $20.00 £22.00. (*Special studies on Latin America and the Caribbean.*)

An outline of the European discovery of the Falklands and a survey of the longstanding dispute between the United Kingdom and the Republic of Argentina in 12 chapters, 6 of which are devoted to events leading up to the war in the South Atlantic. Chronology, p.179-181. Bibliography p.182-185. *Class No:* 982.91

Bibliographies

[8093]

ORGILL, A. The Falklands War background, conflict, aftermath: an annotated bibliography. London, Mansell, 1993. xii,132p. £35. ISBN: 0720121302.

822 entries relating to mainly English and Spanish language books, document collections and journal articles in 6 sub-divided sections: Bibliographies; Sovereignty dispute; 1982 Crisis; Diplomatic and political aspects; 1982 War; Aftermath. *Class No:* 982.91(01)

[8094]

RASOR, E.L. The Falklands/Malvinas campaign a bibliography. Westport, Conn., Greenwood Press, 1992. xiii,196p. index. $45; £36.40. (*Bibliographies of Battles and Leaders, no.6.*) ISBN: 0313281513.

Part 1: Narrative and historiographical survey. 11 bibliographical essays (2. Sources - 3. Geography ... 5. Diplomacy - 6. The forces - 7. Operations ... 11. Research). Part 2: 554 annotated items, mostly English language material, including oral histories, official histories, pertinent journal and periodical articles, conference papers *etc.* but generally excluding popular magazines and newspapers. *Class No:* 982.91(01)

[8095]

REVELLO, J.T. Bibliografía de las Islas Malvinas, obras, mapas y documentos. Buenos Aires, Imprenta de la Universidad, 1953. 260p. maps. (*Universidad de Buenos Aires Facultad de Filosofía y Letras, Publicaciones del Instituto de Investigaciónes Historicas No.99.*)

1702 annotated entries in 3 subdivided sections: 1. Historia (bibliographies, general works, journal articles) - 2. Geografía (maps, descriptions, cartography) - 3. Catálogo de documentos editos. 'A comprehensive annotated bibliography ... with special reference to historical and geographical works before 1900. It includes a list of early maps including those in the Ministerio de Marina, Madrid' (H.G.R. King. *Atlantic Ocean*. 1985. Entry 768).

Updated by A.R. Geoghegen's 'Bibliografía de las Islas Malvinas; suplemento a la obra de José Torre Revello 1954-1975', *Historiografía,* v.2, 1974, p.165-212 which includes a further 95 items. *Class No:* 982.91(01)

Chile

[8096]

COLLIER, S. and SATER, W.F. A History of Chile, 1808-1994. Cambridge Univ. Press, 1996. xix,427p. maps, bibliog., index. ISBN: 0521560756.

Narrative history tracing Chile's political, economic, and social evolution in 13 chronological and thematic chapters (*e.g.* 1. Colonial foundations 1540-1810 ... 10. The industrial impulse 1930s-1960s ... 13. The Pinochet years). Glossary of Spanish terms p.391-93. Bibliography (thematic essays) p.399-409. 6 maps. Analytical index. *Class No:* 983

[8097]

ENCINA, F.A. and CASTEDO, L. Resumen de la historia de Chile 1535-1925. Santiago, Empresa Editora Zig-Zag, 4v., 1954-1982.

Encina's 20v. *Historia de Chile 1535-1891* completed in early 1950s. A 3v. abridgement was added to by Castedo who took the story up to 1935.

'The volume by Castedo is a major contribution to twentieth-century Chilean history' (H. Blakemore. *Chile*. 1988. Entry 102).

Class No: 983

Bibliographies

[8098]

BLAKEMORE, H. 'The Chilean Revolution of 1891 and its historiography'. *Hispanic American Historical Review,* v.45, no.3, August 1965, p.393-421.

'A seminal article' (H. Blakemore. *Chile*. 1988. Entry 620).

Class No: 983(01)

[8099]

SATER, W.F. 'A Survey of recent Chilean historiography 1965-1976' *Latin American Research Review,* v.14, no.2, 1979, p.55-88.

'An excellent and comprehensive survey ... omits no article or book' (H. Blakemore. *Chile*. 1988. Entry 618). *Class No:* 983(01)

Dictionaries

[8100]

BIZZARO, S. Historical dictionary of Chile. 2nd ed. Metuchen, New Jersey, Scarecrow Press, 1987. xv,583p. maps, bibliog. £41.25; $55.00. (*Latin American Historical Dictionaries, no.7.*) ISBN: 0810819643.

1st ed. 1972.

Dictionary p.1-534. Bibliography p.535-83. 'A global view of the history and politics of Chile emphasizing the contemporary period' (Introduction). 'A welcome version, updated and much enlarged' (H. Blakemore, *Chile*, 1988, Entry no.614). *Class No:* 983(038)

Bolivia

[8101]

KLEIN, H.S. Bolivia the evolution of a multi-ethnic society. New York, Oxford Univ. Press, 1982. xvii, 318p. maps, tables, bibliog., index. $29.95. (*Latin American Histories.*) ISBN: 0195030117.

9 chronological/thematic chapters: 1. Geography and pre-Columbian civilization ... 8. The National Revolution 1959-1964 ... 9. The emergence of a New Order 1964-1980. Political chronology p.270-274. Bolivian bibliographical essay p.275-293. 7 maps. Analytical index. 'Bolivia ... has lacked a modern historical survey in English. This excellent little volume takes care of the problem' (*Choice*, v.20, no.1, September 1982, p.164). *Class No:* 984

Dictionaries

[8102]

HEATH, D.B. Historical dictionary of Bolivia. Metuchen, New Jersey, Scarecrow Press, 1972. vi,324p. $15.00. (*Latin American Historical Dictionaries no.4.*)

About 2,000 very brief entries, covering people, places, events, institutions, etc. that have been important in the history of Bolivia and its antecedent, Alto Peru. 'Towards understanding Bolivia: a biblio essay', p.255-324. *Class No:* 984(038)

Peru

[8103]

Historia general de los Peruanos. 11th ed. Lima, Ediciones Peisa, 3v., 1988. illus., maps. ISBN: 9459968847, set.

1. Doig, F.K. *El Perú antiguo.* 783p. 38 chapters organized in 7 parts: 1. Conceptos preliminares - 2. Los primeros Peruanos - 3. Formacion de la alta cultura (2000BC-AD300) - 4. El apogeo cultural/ Artesanal (300-800) - 5. El fenomeno Tiahuanaco y Tiahuanaco-Huari (800-1200) - 6. Principales culturas tardias (1200-1438) - 7. El incanato (1220-1522). Bibliografia de arqueologia Peruana p.759-778.

2. Barrencha, R.P. and others. *El Perú virreinal.* 691p. Short studies in 6 parts: 1. Vision introductoria - 2. Los Incas de Vilcabamba - 3. Virreinato Peruano - 3/4. Aspectos sociologicos y costumbristas - 5. Indagaciones sombres - 6. Iconografia biografia de los Virreyos y Gobernadores 1535-1824 p.603-691.

3. Valárel, C.D. and others. *El Perú Republicano.* 722p.+[8]p. col. maps, 723-773p. 1. Tupac Amaru (Precursor de la Independencia) - 2. Emancipacion y republica hasta 1899-3. El Perú de 1900 a 1985 - 4. Indagaciones sombre El Perú Republicano - 5. Inconografia y biografia de los Presidentes del Perú. Apéndice: Mapas e información de los Departamentos del Peru p.723-73. *Class No:* 985

Bibliographies

[8104]
BARRENECHEA, R.P. Fuentes historicas peruanas. Lima, Instituto Raúl Porras Barrenechea, 1963. 601p.
'This classic bibliography of Peruvian history ... remains a standard work of reference for researchers' (J.R. Fisher, *Peru*, 1989. Entry 692). *Class No:* 985(01)

[8105]
BASADRE, J. Introducción a las bases documentales para la historia de la república del Perú, con algunas reflexiones. Lima, Villanueva, 3v., 1971. 1076p; 177p.
Follows compilers *Historia de la república de Perú 1822-1933.*
More than 170,000 items cited in v.1-2 with v.3 index. 'A monumental and indispensable work of reference' (J.R. Fisher. *Peru*, 1989. Entry 696). *Class No:* 985(01)

[8106]
TAURO, A. Bibliografia peruana de historia 1940-1953. Lima, 1953. 196p.
1214 annotated entries. 'It is indicative of the historiographical emphasis then in vogue that over 400 deal with the pre-hispanic and conquest period, 300 with the colonial era and only 150 with post independence; there is a separate section on local history' (J.R. Fisher. *Peru*, 1989, Entry 688). *Class No:* 985(01)

Dictionaries

[8107]
LISKY, M. Historical dictionary of Peru. Metuchen, New Jersey, Scarecrow Press, 1979. vi,157p. bibliog. $18.50. (*Latin American Historical Dictionaries, no.20.*) ISBN: 0810812355.
Dictionary p.9-116. Appendix A: Chronology of rulers of the Inca Empire p.119-20 - B. Departments of the Republic of Peru p.121-2. Bibliography p.132-57. *Class No:* 985(038)

Colombia

Dictionaries

[8108]
DAVIS, R.H. Historical dictionary of Colombia. Metuchen, New Jersey, Scarecrow Press, 2nd ed. 1993. xi,601p. (*Latin American Historical Dictionaries, no.23.*) ISBN: 0810809990.
1. A Chronology of Colombian history (10,450BC-1991) - 2. Dictionary of 1500+ entries - 3. A Bibliographical guide to Colombian history (7 sections). 'The accuracy and scholarly quality of the research encapsulated here ... are of the very highest order, making this extensive work indispensable for all Hispanic and Americanist libraries' (*Reference Reviews*, v.8,no.6, 1994, p.44-45). *Class No:* 986(038)

Ecuador

Bibliographies

[8109]
NORRIS, R.E. Guía bibliogáfia para el estudio de la historia ecuatoriana. Austin, Institute of Latin American Studies, Univ. of Texas, 1978. 295p. (*Guides and Bibliographies Series no.11.*)
4000 entries. 'The work is valuable ... for articles printed in Ecuadorian periodicals' (D. Corkhill. *Ecuador*. 1989. Entry 542). *Class No:* 986.6(01)

Dictionaries

[8110]
BORK, A.W. and MAIER, G. Historical dictionary of Ecuador. Metuchen, New Jersey, Scarecrow Press, 1973. x, 11-192p. bibliog. (*Latin American Historical Dictionaries, no.10.*) ISBN: 081080638x.
Dictionary p.11-160. 8 appendices. Bibliography p.175-92. *Class No:* 986.6(038)

Venezuela

[8111]
EWELL, J. Venezuela a century of change. Stanford, California, Stanford Univ. Press; London, C. Hurst & Co., 1984. xiii, 258p. maps, tables, bibliog., index. $27.50. £12.50. ISBN: 0804712131, US; 090583836x, UK.
7 chronological/thematic chapters covering the period 1890s to date. List of Presidents since 1871 p.228. Bibliography p.236-244. Glossary of Spanish terms p.245-247. Analytical index. 'A good general introduction to modern Venezuelan history' (*Bulletin of Latin American Research*, v.4, no.2, 1985, p.168-169). *Class No:* 987

Dictionaries

[8112]
RUDOLPH, D.K. and RUDOLPH, G.A. Historical dictionary of Venezuela. 2nd ed. Metuchen, New Jersey, Scarecrow Press, 1996. xxix,954p. map bibliog. $110. £104.50. (*Latin American Historical Dictionaries, no.3.*) ISBN: 0810830299.
1st ed. 1971.
Chronology p.xi-xxix. Dictionary (political administration; military, social, cultural, economic, ecclesiastical history) p.1-743. Bibliography (in 39 thematic categories) p.745-954. *Class No:* 987(038)

Guyana

20th Century

[8113]
MANLEY, R.H. Guyana emergent the post independence struggle for nondependent development. 2nd ed. Cambridge, Mass., Schenkman, 1982. ix, 176p. bibliog., index.
First published 1979.
8 chapters (1. The slave colony ... 8. Beyond the first post-independence decade). Chapter notes. This edition adds Epilogue, taking the story up to 1980, and adds a bibliography. *Class No:* 988.1"19"

Paraguay

[8114]
WARREN, H.G. Paraguay an informal history. Westport, Connecticut, Greenwood Press, 1982. xii, 393p. maps. bibliog. index. $48.50. ISBN: 0313236518.
Reprint of 1st ed. 1949 published by Univ. of Oklahoma Press.
Standard history in 20 chapters. Appendix: Governors, dictators, and presidents of Paraguay 1536-1941, p.355-8. Bibliographical essay p.359-68. 8 maps. 'Remains one of the best introductions to the history of Paraguay' (R.A. Nickson, *Paraguay*, 1987. Entry 81). *Class No:* 989.2

Dictionaries

[8115]
NICKSON, R.A. Historical dictionary of Paraguay. 2nd ed. Metuchen, New Jersey, Scarecrow Press, 1993. xxi,685p. maps, bibliog. $69.50; £69.50. (*Latin American Historical Dictionaries, no.24.*) ISBN: 0810826437.
Replaces C.J. Kolinski's *Historical Dictionary of Paraguay* (1973).
Over 1600 cross-referenced entries, 'an impressive range of persons, places, institutions, events, cultural topics, politics, administrations and geographical facts' (*Reference Reviews*, no.7, 1993, p.45-6). Chronology 1515-1989. Bibliography of 540 entries. 5 maps. *Class No:* 989.2(038)

Uruguay

Dictionaries

[8116]
WILLIS, J.L. Historical dictionary of Uruguay. Metuchen, New Jersey, Scarecrow Press, 1974. vii,275p. bibliog. $24.00. (*Latin American Historical Dictionaries, no.11.*) ISBN: 0810807661.
Dictionary p.1-260. Bibliography p.261-75. *Class No:* 989.9(038)

Australasia

Indonesia

[8117]
ABEYASKERE, S. Jakarta: a history. Rev. ed. Singapore, Oxford Univ. Press, 1987. xviii,298p.+16p. plates, illus., maps, index. softcover. ISBN: 0195889479.
General history of the city in 6 well-documented chapters (1. Company town: early origins to 1800... 4. Japanese occupation and the struggle for independence 1942-9... 6. Java under Sadikin and his successors 1966-1985). Glossary p.264-6. Bibliography p.267-84. 9 maps. This revised edition includes a new bibliography. *Class No:* 991

[8118]
RIKLEFS, M.C. A History of modern Indonesia: c.1300 to present. 2nd ed. London, The Macmillan Press, 1991. 340p. maps, bibliog., index. $18. (*Macmillan's Asian Histories.*) ISBN: 0333576896.
1st ed. 1981.
Comprehensive introductory text in 6 parts: 1. Emergence of the modern era (1300-1650) - 2. Struggles for hegemony (1630-1800) - 3. Creation of a colonial state (1800-1910) - 4. Emergence of the idea of Indonesia (1900-1942) - 5. Destruction of the colonial state (1942-50) - 6. Independent Indonesia. Bibliography p.292-307. Maps p.310-318. *Class No:* 991

[8119]

WESSELING, H.L. 'Dutch historiography on European Expansion since 1945', p.122-39, P.C. Emmer and H.L. Wesseling eds: *Reappraisals in Overseas History. Essays on post-war historiography about European expansion.* The Hague, Leiden Univ. Press-Nijhoff, 1979. 248p. ISBN: 906021447.

Historiographical survey on the history of Indonesia and Dutch colonial policies. *Class No:* 991

Dictionaries

[8120]

CRIBB, R. Historical dictionary of Indonesia. Metuchen, N.J., Scarecrow Press, 1992. lxxiv,663p. maps, bibliog. $72.50. (*Asian Historical Dictionnaires, no.9.*) ISBN: 0810825422.

Covers the entire area of the Republic of Indonesia *i.e.* Irian Jaya (Western New Guinea) and East Timor. Chronology p.xxxvii-lx. Maps p.lxii-lxxiv. Dictionary p.1-502. Bibliography p.549-661. Appendices list Governors-General Netherland East Indies, rulers of early states, Indonesian cabinets, Presidents *etc. Class No:* 991(038)

Chronologies

[8121]

TAYLOR, J.G. The Indonesian occupation of East Timor 1974-1989 a chronology. London, Catholic Institute for International Relations in association with the Refugee Studies Programme, Univ. of Oxford, 1990. iv,102p. illus., map, index. £14.99. ISBN: 1852870516.

An essential reference tool for events (727 listed) in this former Portuguese colony beginning 18 months before the Indonesian invasion, occupation, and annexation. From 1977 onwards events recorded include a source reference, usually an English-language publication, although some articles in translation from the Portuguese or Bahasa Indonesian are also to be found. *Class No:* 991(090)

Borneo

Bibliographies

[8122]

Borneo in history a catalogue of books in the Borneo collection of the University Library describing Borneo before 1960. Francis, S., *comp.* Brunei Darussalam, Universiti Brunei Darussalam, 1990. 70p. illus. typescript.

Annotated A-Z by author listing of all bound books and reports in the University Library's Borneo collection. *Class No:* 991.1(01)

Brunei

[8123]

SAUNDERS, G. A History of Brunei. Oxford Univ. Press South East Asia, 1994. 256p. illus. £17.95. ISBN: 9676530492.

The first full-length study of the Brunei Sultanate from earliest times to the present. Based on recent research and the writings of European and Bruneian scholars, it traces the history of the state and its line of rulers from their pre-Islamic origins up to the attainment of independence. *Class No:* 991.13

Dictionaries

[8124]

RAJIT SINGH, D.S. *and* SIDHU, J.S. Historical dictionary of Brunei Darrussalem. Lanham, MD., Scarecrow Press, 1997. xliv,178p. illus., maps, tables, bibliog. £60.80. (*Asian/Oceanian Historical Dictionaries, no 25.*) ISBN: 0810832763.

Chronology p.xxi-xxxiv. Introduction (location, climate, population, history, religion) p.1-31. Dictionary (politics, economy, foreign rule, government, past and present leaders) p.33-126. Bibliography (form and thematic sub-divisions) p.127-54. 5 Appendices inc. A. Genealogy of the Sultans 1363-1998. Glossary p.175-78. 10 maps. *Class No:* 991.13(038)

Philippines

Dictionaries

[8125]

GUILLERMO, A.R. *and* WIN, M.K. Historical dictionary of the Philippines. Lanham, MD., Scarecrow Press, 1997. xlii,362p. maps, bibliog. (*Asian/Oceanian Historical dictionaries, no.24.*) ISBN: 0810832437.

Replaces E.G. and J.M. Maring's *Historical and cultural dictionary of the Philippines* (1973).

Chronology of events p.xix-xl. Introduction (history, politics, economy) p.1-11. Dictionary (who, what and where - events, people and places) p.13-259. Bibliography (in 6 sub-divided sections) p.261-341. *Class No:* 991.4(038)

Oceania

[8126]

CAMPBELL, I.C. A History of the Pacific Islands. St. Lucia, Univ. o Queensland Press, 1990. 239p. maps, tables, bibliog., index. pbk ISBN: 0702222917.

First published Christchurch, Univ. of Canterbury Press, 1989.

Narrative history in 17 chapters of Polynesian, Melanesian Micronesian and European cultures and activities in the Pacific Ocean *e.g.* 1. The original inhabitants - 2. Austronesian colonization - 3 Polynesia: the age of European discovery ... 15. Attaining independence. Glossary p.229-31. Bibliography p.232-5. 8 maps. *Class No:* 993

[8127]

DENOON, D., *and others, eds.* The Cambridge history of the Pacific Islanders. Cambridge Univ. Press, 1997. xvii,518p. maps o endpapers, bibliog., index. £60. $79.95. ISBN: 0521441951.

20 international academic contributors. Part 1. The Pacific to 1941 1. Contending approaches - 2. Human settlement - 3. Pacific Edens? 4. Discovering outsiders... 8. Colonial administration. Part 2. Th Pacific since 1941: 9. The War in the Pacific - 10. A Nuclear Pacific ... 13. The End of insularity. All chapters end with a bibliographica essay. Glossary p.468-70. Bibliography (A-Z by author) p.471-93 Analytical index. 23 maps. 'Not strictly a work of reference [but] it i a bountiful cornucopia of reliable data' (*Reference Reviews*, v.13 no.5, 1999, p.52-53). 'Rather like those ancient Polynesian navigator and their much later European colleagues, this book sniffs the win and heads out into the open ocean questioning what lies beyond th horizon' (*Journal of Imperial and Commonwealth History.* v.27, no.3 September 1999, p.142-45). *Class No:* 993

[8128]

HOWE, K.R. Where the waves fall a new South Sea Islands history from first settlement to colonial rule. Sydney, Allen and Unwin Honolulu, Hawaii Univ. Press, 1984. xix,403p. illus., maps, bibliog. index. ISBN: 0868613436, Aust; 0824809211, US.

A thematic overview of the history of Polynesia and Islan Melanesia from c.50,000BC to colonial rule in the 19th century Chapter 16: Considering the new historiography. Chapter notes an references p.353-74. Bibliography p.375-92. *Class No:* 993

[8129]

SCARR, D. The History of the Pacific Islands kingdoms of the reefs South Melbourne, Macmillan, 1990. xi,426p. illus., maps, bibliog. index. $59.95. ISBN: 073290210x.

Narrative history in 20 chapters encompassing native cultura societies, local responses to European voyagers, the colonia experience, and postwar independence movements, 'from Micronesia to glimpses of New Zealand, and from Hawaii to Papua New Guinea' Chapter notes p.363-88. Bibliography p.389-415. 'No doubt that this i an ambitious and important work ... it will make a permanent scholarly mark' (*Pacific Affairs,* v.65, no.1, Spring 1992, p.137-8). *Class No:* 993

[8130]

SPATE, O.H.K. The Pacific since Magellan. Canberra, Australia National Univ. Press; London, Croom Helm, 3v. 1979-1988.

1. *The Spanish Lake.* 1979, xxiv,372p. £40.00. Chapter note p.293-354. illus. 25 maps. ISBN 0708107272 Aust. 070990049x UK 2. *Monopolists and freebooters.* 1983. xxi,426p. £35.00. Notes p.337 412. illus. 28 maps. 0708118445 Aust. 0709923716 UK. 3. *Paradis found and lost.* 1988. xxi,410p. £40.00. Notes p.325-95. illus. 2 maps. 0080344003 Aust. 0415025656 UK. Aim is 'to seek to explicat the process by which the greatest blank on the map became a nexus o global commercial and strategic relations' (*Preface to v.1*). 'A excellent survey of the scholarship about this area ... but the wor suffers seriously from lack of a bibliography' (*Choice,* v.27,no.1 September 1989, p.198). *Class No:* 993

Bibliographies

[8131]

KRAUSS, N.L.H. Bibliography of the Banks Islands, Wester Pacific. Honolulu, the author, 1971. 10p. sd.

152 annotated entries. *Class No:* 993(01)

[8132]

KRAUSS, N.L.H. Bibliography of the Line Islands, Central Pacific Honolulu, the author, 1970. 18p. index, sd.

317 entries A-Z by author with note on history of discovery an constitutional and administrative status. *Class No:* 993(01)

[8133]

KRAUSS, N.L.H. Bibliography of the Tokelau or Union Islands Central Pacific. Honolulu, the author, 1969. 11p. sd.

135 entries A-Z by author. With note on history of discovery an administrative and constitutional status. *Class No:* 993(01)

[8134]

KRAUSS, N.L.H. **Niué, South Pacific.** Honolulu, the author, 1970. 16p. sd.

206 entries A-Z by author with note on history of discovery and administrative and constitutional status. *Class No: 993(01)*

Dictionaries

[8135]

CRAIG, R.D. *and* KING, F.P., *eds.* **Historical dictionary of Oceania.** Westport, Connecticut, Greenwood Press, 1981. xxxv, 392p. maps, bibliog., index. $67.95. ISBN: 0313210608.

106 contributors and almost 500 entries cover the exploration, European settlement, and government of the islands of Melanesia, Micronesia and Polynesia. 7 Appendices (2. Historical chronology ... 3. Prehistoric settlements ... 4. European explorers). Bibliography p.373-375. 19 maps. *Class No: 993(038)*

[8136]

CRAIG, R.D. **Historical dictionary of Polynesia.** Metuchen, NJ., Scarecrow Press, 1993. xxvi,298p. map, bibliog. £37.50. (*Oceanian Historical Dictionaries, no.2.*) ISBN: 0810827069.

Chronology p.xiii-xxvi. Introduction (Pre-European history; European exploration; Western immigration; Colonial administration; Independence) p.1-12. Dictionary (inc. general island/nation entries) p.13-212. Bibliography (major publications since C.R.H. Taylor's *A Pacific bibliography* 1965) arranged in 15 sections: General - Cook Islands - Easter Island - French Polynesia - Hawai'i - New Zealand - Niue - Pitcairn - Samoa - Tokelau - Tonga - Tuvalu - Wallis and Futuna Islands. Appendix 1. Names of Polynesian Islands - 2. Rulers and administrators - 3. Summary guide 1991-92 (Island groups, population, area, political status). *Class No: 993(038)*

20th Century

[8137]

HINZ, E., *ed.* **Pacific Island battlegrounds of World War II** then and now. Honolulu, Bess Press, 1995. viii,104p. illus., (some col.). $29.95. ISBN: 1573060089.

'Essentially a collection of 13 succinct histories (to 1994) of islands significant in the Pacific War ... Pearl Harbor; Wake Island; Midway; Guadacanal; Tarawa; Marshall Islands; Rabaul; New Guinea; New Hebrides; Truk; Saipan; Guam; and Peteliu' (*Reference Reviews*, v.10,no.5, 1996, p.46). *Class No: 993"19"*

New Zealand

[8138]

OLSSEN, E. **A History of Otago.** Dunedin, John McIndoe Ltd., 1984. xvi, 270p. illus. (some col.), maps. ISBN: 0868680583.

Bibliographical note p.245. Index p.259-270. 'Attempts to explain the distinctive character of Otago's past'. *Class No: 993.1*

[8139]

RICE, G., *ed.* **Oxford history of New Zealand.** 2nd ed. Wellington, Oxford Univ. Press (NZ), 1993. xviii,755p. maps, tables, bibliog., index. Pbk. ISBN: 0195582578.

First published 1981 edited by W.H. Oliver and B.R. Williams. Single volume cooperative history (by 22 scholars) whose structure 'combines a broad chronological shape with a detailed thematic analysis' (*Introduction*). Chapter references p.607-64. Chapter bibliographies p.665-735. Glossary of Maori terms p.586-7. Analytical index. *Class No: 993.1*

Bibliographies

[8140]

WOOD, G.A. **Studying New Zealand history.** Dunedin, Univ. of Otago Press, 1992. 145p. index.

Research guide to reference works and bibliographies, periodicals and theses, national, regional and local sources, and newspapers, pamphlets and photographs. 'The organization of material is clear, the sections are well sign-posted and the information is comprehensive and detailed' (*New Zealand Geographer,* v.48, no.2, October 1992, p.92). *Class No: 993.1(01)*

Dictionaries

[8141]

JACKSON, K. *and* McROBIE, A. **Historical dictionary of New Zealand.** Lanham, Md. Scarecrow Press, 1996. xix,314p. maps, tables, bibliog. £51.30. (*Oceanian Historical Dictionaries, no.5.*) ISBN: 0810830868.

Glossary of Maori words p.xiii-xiv. Chronology p.1-33. 'NZ: a social and economic laboratory' p.35-53. Dictionary p.55-262. Bibliography (Essay and 12 divisions) p.263-308. 5 maps. *Class No: 993.1(038)*

Maps & Atlases

[8142]

McKINNON, M., *and others, eds.* **New Zealand historical atlas** ko papatuanuku e takoto nei. Auckland, David Bateman and Historical Branch, Department of Internal Affairs, 1997. 300p. col.illus., col. maps.

100 double page spreads (map, text, illustrations) each dealing with a separate topic. Time period ranges from geological times, to Maori settlement, European colonisation, to the 20th century. *Class No: 993.1(084.3)*

Chronologies

[8143]

The New Zealand book of events. Auckland, Reed Methuen, 1986. 448p. index. ISBN: 0474001237.

49 contributors. General reference source organized in 14 chapters: 1. The Maori - 2. European settlement - 3. Transport - 4. Communications - 5. Industries - 6. Trade, taxes and the economy - 7. The work force - 8. Government - 9. Law - 10. Defence - 11. Social development - 12. Science and environment - 13. Arts - 14. Disasters. Glossary of Maori words p.11. *Class No: 993.1(090)*

[8144]

REED, A.W., *comp.* **It happened in New Zealand:** a day-by-day illustrated chronology of famous and interesting events in New Zealand history from 1640 to 1971. Wellington, A.H. and A.W. Reed, 1973. 114p. illus., map, index. ISBN: 0589007602.

Factual unannotated chronology. Analytical index. *Class No: 993.1(090)*

Melanesia

[8145]

HOARE, M. **Norfolk Islands** an outline of its history 1774 - 1987. 4th ed. St. Lucia, Univ. of Queensland Press, 1988. xv11, 206p. illus. map. bibliog.., index. pbk.

1st ed. 1969.

Authoritative account in 4 pts; 1. European discovery, prehistory and 1st penal settlement (1774 - 1814) - 2. 2nd penal settlement (1825 - 1856) - 3. The Pitcairn Islanders and their descendants (1856 - 1945) - 4. The post war years. Chronology p. xiii - xvii. Bibliography p.175-93. *Class No: 993.2/.7*

Bibliographies

[8146]

KRAUSS, N.L.H. **Bibliography of the Santa Cruz Islands, Western Pacific.** Honolulu, the author, 1969. 8p. sd.

97 entries A-Z by author. Note on history of discovery and administrative and constitutional status. *Class No: 993.2/.7(01)*

[8147]

KRAUSS, N.L.H. **Bibliography of the Torres Islands, Southwest Pacific.** Honolulu, the author, 1971. 4p. sd.

47 unannotated entries. *Class No: 993.2/.7(01)*

Chronologies

[8148]

O'REILLY, P. 'Chronologique de Wallis et Futuna' *Journal de la Société des Océanistes*, v.19, 1963, p.12-45.

Summary of major political and economic events. *Class No: 993.2/.7(090)*

Australia

[8149]

Australian Ethnic Heritage Series. Gigler, M., *ed.* Melbourne, Australian Ethnic Press, 1983-.

A multi-volume series highlighting the background of the various national groups represented in Australia's population and their individual contributions to its history *e.g.* Prentis, M.D. *The Scottish in Australia.* 1987. 173p. illus., bibliog., index. A$16.00. 11 chapters. 3 Appendixes: 1. Governors and Governors General of Scottish birth or ancestry - 2. Premiers and Prime Ministers of Scottish birth or ancestry - 3. Scottish Christian names in Australia. Bibliography p.167-9.

Other titles: *The Afghans in Australia; The Americans; The Baltic peoples Lithuanians, Latvians, Estonians; The Czechs; The Cornish; The Dutch; The Germans; The Hungarians; The Italians; The Jews; The Lebanese; The Maltese; The Poles; The Scandinavians; The Spanish. Class No: 994*

[8150]

CANNON, M. **The Exploration of Australia.** Sydney, Reader's Digest, 1987. 304p. illus. (some col.), col.maps, bibliog., index. ISBN: 0864380364.

8 chronological and thematic chapters *e.g.* 1. Who really discovered the Great South Land? ... 8. The age of scientific expeditions ... 9. New technology revolutionises exploration. Chronology p.294-7. Bibliography p.298-299. Popular reference work at a high level of accomplishment. *Class No: 994*

[8151]

Chronicle of Australia. Farnborough, Chronicle Communications, 1993. 768p. illus. (some col.), col. maps, ports., index. £39.95. ISBN: 1872031889.

History of Australia in familiar 'Chronicle' format *i.e.* historical events reported as if contemporary newspapers. *Class No: 994*

[8152]

CLARK, C.M.H. **A History of Australia.** Melbourne, Melbourne Univ. Press, 6v., 1962-87. illus., tables, maps, indexes.

1. *From the earliest times to the age of Macquarie.* 1962. (new ed. 1977). xii, 422p. £25.00. ISBN 0522840056. 2. *New South Wales and Van Diemen's Land 1822-38.* 1968. xiii, 364p. £25.00. 0522838219. 3. *The Beginning of an Australian civilization 1824-51.* 1973. 491p. £25.00. 0522840544. 4. *The Earth abideth for ever 1851-88.* 1978. 427p. 0522841473. 5. *The People make laws 1888-1915.* 1981. 964p. 0522842232. 'The most comprehensive survey of our past' (Borchardt, D.H. *Australian bibliography* (1974), p.58). C.M.H. Clark is considered by many to be Australia's leading historian, though his strong and avowed bias against authoritarianism, the bourgeoisie, the church, the cult of heroes, and his fight against empty traditions have aroused much criticism' (*RSR*, v.7, no.2, April/June 1979, p.9). *Class No: 994*

[8153]

'The Cocos (Keeling) Islands', p.171-175, *Debrett's handbook of Australia and New Zealand* (2nd ed., 1984).

Outline history from early 19th century onwards. *Class No: 994*

[8154]

FITZGERALD, R. **From 1915 to the early 1980s:** a history of Queensland. St. Lucia (Queensland), Univ. of Queensland Press, 1984. xvii,653p. illus., maps. ISBN: 0702217344.

Part 1. From 1945 to 1957 Labor dominance. Part 2. 1957 to the early 1980s Conservative monopoly. Appendix. Queensland premiers 1859 to 1982 p.635-636. Index p.637-653. All chapters extensively footnoted and documented. *Class No: 994*

[8155]

—FITZGERALD, R. **From the Dreaming to 1915:** a history of Queensland. St. Lucia, Queensland, Univ. of Queensland Press, 1982. xviii,m354p. illus., maps. ISBN: 0702216348.

The theme is 'the effect of a particularly European idea of progress upon the land, the flora and fauna, the institutions, and the peoples of Queensland'. Part 1. The Dreamtime to 1859 investigates aboriginal culture and the European voyages of exploration and discovery. Part 2. 1859 to 1915 examines Queensland's development, and explores the growth of regionalism, and concludes with the politics of the period. Each chapter is heavily annotated. Index p.343-354. *Class No: 994*

[8156]

The Oxford history of Australia. Bolton, G., *ed.* Melbourne, Oxford University Press, 5v., 1986-92. maps, bibliogs., tables, indexes.

1. Murray, T. *Aboriginal Australia.* 2. Kociumbras, J. *Colonial Australia 1770-1860. possessions.* 1992. xv,397p. £25. 0195546105. 3. Kingston, B. *Glad confident morning.* 1988. xv,368p. 0195546113. 4. MacIntyre, S. *The succeeding age 1901-1942.* 1986. xx,399p. 0195546121. 5. Bolton, G. *1942-1988 The Middle Way.* 1990. xiv,334p. 019554613x. Chapter notes p.293-317. Bibliographic note p.320-1. 'A very solid contribution to the understanding of Australia's historical development' (*Choice*, v.27,no.2, October 1989, p.366+8). *Class No: 994*

[8157]

POWELL, A. **Far country** a short history of the Northern Territory. Melbourne, Melbourne Univ. Press, 1982. xii, 301p. illus., maps, bibliog., index. ISBN: 0522842569.

10 chronological chapters focussing on political and economic themes. Chapter notes p.245-269. Bibliography p.270-287. 'Should be extremely useful to both scholars and students' (*Choice*, v.20, no.11-12, July-August 1983, p.1644). *Class No: 994*

[8158]

ROBSON, L. **A History of Tasmania.** Melbourne, Oxford Univ. Press, 2v., 1983-91. $A.50. £38.

V.1 *Van Diemen's Land from the earliest times to 1855.* 1983. viii,632p. maps on endpapers, bibliog., index. $A50; £38. ISBN 0915543645. 24 chronological chapters. 3 Appendices: 1. Bibliography p.559-569 - B. Reference notes - C. Convicts on board the first and last transportation ships to Van Diemen's Land. 2. *Colony and state from 1856 to the 1980s.* 1991. 663p. bibliog., index. $A98.

.... *(contd.)*

0195530314. 'An essential acquisition for any collection supporting courses on Australia' (*Choice*, v.29, nos. 11-12, July/August 1992, p.1735). *Class No: 994*

[8159]

SCHILDER, G. **Australia unveiled** the share of the Dutch navigators in the discovery of Australia. Amsterdam, Theatrum Orbis Terrarum, 1976. xi, 419p. illus., maps, bibliog., indexes.

Survey with distinct cartographical emphasis of the Dutch discoveries of the Northern, Western and Southern coasts of Australia 1606-1644 in 26 chapters of text *e.g.* 3. Terra Australis: the development of geographical concept ... 7. The Dutch discovery of the fifth continent ... 26. Retrospect: a summary of Dutch discoveries in Australia to the time of Tasman. 3 chapters of maps p.239-419. Bibliography p.211-233. Name, ship and localities indexes. *Class No: 994*

[8160]

WILLIAMS, G. *and* FROST, A., *eds.* **Terra Australis to Australia.** Melbourne, Oxford Univ. Press in association with the Australian Academy of the Humanities, 1988. xviii, 242p. illus. (some col.), facsims., maps, index. $A95. £50. ISBN: 0195549082.

How European concepts of a southern continent emerged. In 6 chapters: 1. Terra Australis: theory and speculation - 2. Java la Grande: the enigma of the Dutch maps - 3. New Holland: the Dutch discoveries - 4. New Holland to New South Wales: the English approaches - 5. New South Wales: expectations and reality - 6. Australia: the emergence of a continent. Well documented. The Academy's contribution to the Bicentenary. *Class No: 994*

Bibliographies

[8161]

FEATHERSTONE, G.A. **A Bibliography of Victorian history.** Ascot Vale, Victoria, Red Rooster Press, 1986. xv,202p. *Class No: 994(01)*

[8162]

FERGUSON, J.A. **Bibliography of Australia.** Sydney and London, Angus and Robertson, 1941-1969. Canberra, National Library of Australia; Winchester, St. Paul's Bibliographies, 1986-. v.1-7 £32.00 each; v.8 £45.00. Set of 8v. £230.00.

1. *1784-1830* 1941. 2. *1831-1838* 1945. 3. *1839-1845* 1951. 4. *1846-1850* 1955. 5. *1851-1900 A-G* 1963. 6. *1851-1900 H-P* 1965. 7. *1851-1900 Q-Z* 1969. 8. *Addenda 1784-1850 (v.1-4)* 1986. x, 705p. index. 0642993076. A second *Addenda* volume will cover v.5-7.

Covers all printed matter relating to Australia, wherever published, in the period concerned. Arranged chronologically under year of publication, with author and anonymous title index. Covers books, pamphlets, broadsides, newspapers, periodicals and government publications. V.4 includes addenda to v.1-3 and it own index. Locations of items in ten Australian libraries and also the British Museum. 'Painstakingly compiled and spaciously and clearly set out' (*Times Literary Supplement* no.3333, 13 January 1966, p.29). *Class No: 994(01)*

[8163]

Index to journal articles on Australian history. Hogan, T., *and others eds.* Armidale, New South Wales, Univ. of New England Publishing Unit, 1976-. vii, 203p. ISBN: 0858341379.

3 sections: 1. List of journals indexed - 2. A-Z subject index - 3. 4,019 entries from 50 journals A-Z by author. Coverage to the end of 1973. The intention was to issue a supplement every 5 years.

Continued by Crittenden, V. and Thawley, J: *Index to journal articles on Australian history 1974-1978.* Kensington, NSW., Australia 1785-1988. A bicentennial History, 1981. 238p. $A6.75. 0949776033. Over 2000 entries including book reviews appearing in the indexed journals. 'This listing in effect constitutes a bibliography of the vast majority of Australian monographs which were received during those years' (*Introduction*).

Index to journal articles on Australian history for 1979. Kensington, Univ. of New South Wales, 1981. 90p. softcover. $A4.50, 0949776017. At this point it was decided to prepare an annual compilation for the years 1980-1988 and finally to cumulate them into a single Bicentennial volume. *Index to journal articles on Australian history for 1980. 1982. 161p. $A9.25. 0949776157. Index to journal articles on Australian history for 1981.* 1982. 110 0949776068. *Index to journal articles on Australian history for 1982,* North Balwyn, Victoria, Australian Reference Publications History Project, 1987. 186p. $A16. 0958787603. The 1983 volume was published in 1990.

Crittenden, V. and Borchardt, D. Index to journal articles on Australian history 1984-1988. North Balwyn, Vict., Australian Reference Publications, 1994. *Class No: 994(01)*

[8164]

JHNSTON, W.R. *and* ZERNER, M. **A Guide to the history of Queensland** a bibliographic survey of related resources in Queensland history. Brisbane, Library Board of Queensland, 1985. 241p. index. ISBN: 0724214917.

Reworked from W.R. Johnston's *A Bibliography of Queensland history* (1981).

6 sections: reference and general; Aborigines and early settlement; economic history; political and social; local. Author-title and subject indexes. For the general reader not the thesis writer. *Class No:* 994(01)

Internet

[8165]

ustralian history on the Internet. Wade, H., *comp.* URL:http://www.nla.au/oz/histsite.html.

Includes documentary sources on Australian history, Australian institutions holding historical collections, overseas sources, a list of online journals, historical resources of Australian universities, and appropriate Internet sources. 'Certainly the best organized Web-based resource of its kind on Australian history' (*Choice*, Supplement to v.36, August 1999, p.163). *Class No:* 994(01)(003.41)

Encyclopaedias

[8166]

ustralians a historical library. Broadway, New South Wales, Fairfax, Syme and Weldon; Cambridge, Cambridge Univ. Press, 11v., 1988. illus. tables, bibliog., index. A$695.00. £400.00 the set $495.00. ISBN: 0949288098, Australia; 052134073x, UK.

Cooperative history, 10 years in the making, involving 400 scholars and researchers, consisting of 5 history books, 5 reference works and a Guide and Index volume. *Titles:* 1. *Australians to 1788*; 2. *Australians 1838*; 3. *Australians 1888*; 4. *Australians 1938*; 5. *Australians from 1939.* Volumes 2-4 are instances of the distinctive 'slicing' method of writing history whereby single years are examined to explore every aspect of national life. Graeme Davison, an editor and contributor, expands on this in 'Slicing History. Nationhood And The Bicentennial', *History Today*, v.38. January 1988, p.25-32.

Reference Works: 6. *Australians: A historical atlas* (the first large-scale historical atlas of Australia). 7. *Australians: A historical dictionary.* xx, 462p. illus. index. A succinct overview of Australian history in 1233 entries encompassing historical episodes, concepts, institutions, industries, movements, achievements and failures and biography. 8. *Australians: Events and places.* xvi, 476p. col. illus. col. maps, index. 1. A chronology 1788-1984 accompanied by 2 'timeline' special features: Aboriginal Australia and European exploration to 1788. 2. A historical gazetteer and descriptive account of places that centres on their historical significance grouped in 32 regions. 9. *Australians: Historical statistics.* 17 chapters each with a brief introductory essay. 10. *Australians: A guide to sources.* xviii, 473p. 55 chapters in 10 sections: 1. The writing of Australian history ... 2. Archives ... 19. Genealogy ... 20. Biography. 11. *Australians. The Guide and Index.* 112p. Links the individual volume indexes and connects the more detailed information in individual volumes with the broader themes of Australian history. 'Prepared with great scholarly care from original sources ... can be recommended for public and academic libraries' (*Booklist*, v.85, no.2, 15 September 1988, p.128-130). *Class No:* 994(031)

[8167]

ustralia's yesterdays a look at our recent past. 3rd ed. Sydney, Reader's Digest, 1986. 360p. illus. (some col.), col. maps, index. £17.95. ISBN: 0949819980.

Pictorial encyclopedia. Part 1. Australia in the 20th century - 2. The passing years 1901-85 (historic events year by year) - 3. Makers of modern Australia (biographies of the Australians who made the news). Analytical index. *Class No:* 994(031)

[8168]

AVISON, G., *and others, eds.* **The Oxford companion to Australian history.** Melbourne, Oxford Univ. Press, 1998. xx,726p. maps (col. on endpapers). ISBN: 0195535979.

c.300 contributors. 1,600 signed cross-referenced A-Z entries, of between 100 to 2000 words, on events, persons, themes, topics, catchphrases, and allusions, cover the history of Australia from pre-colonial times to the present day. A particular attempt is made to show how Australian history has been interpreted at a time when Australia's national identity is being questioned. 9 full page maps. *Class No:* 994(031)

Dictionaries

[8169]

BASSETT, J. **The Concise Oxford dictionary of Australian history.** 2nd ed. Melbourne, Oxford Univ. Press, 1994. vii,341p. £8.95. 1st ed. 1986.

About 550 entries relating to the principal people, institutions, places, ideas, movements, events, documents and artefacts generally considered to be historically significant. But 'more suited to browsing or the pursuit of trivia' (*Choice*, v.25, no.5, January 1988, p.741).

Bassett's *The Oxford illustrated dictionary of Australian history* (1993. 304p. £27.50; *m49.95. 0195532430) is for general readers interested in Australian history. *Class No:* 994(038)

[8170]

DOCHERTY, J.C. **Historial dictionary of Australia.** 2nd ed. Lanham, MD, Scarecrow Press, 1999. xlii,425p. maps, bibliog. £61.75. (Asian/Oceanian Oceanian Historical Dictionaries, no.32.) ISBN: 0810835924.

1st ed. 1992.

Chronology p.xxi-xlii. Introduction (physical environment, historical setting, Australian society) p.1-19. Dictionary (history, contemporary social and political issues, trade and industry, biographies) p.21-262. Bibliography (in 45 form and thematic sections) p.263-373. Appendix 1. Governors General - 2. Prime Ministers - 3. Historical Statistics. 4 maps. *Class No:* 994(038)

[8171]

MURPHY, B. **Dictionary of Australian history.** Sydney, McGraw-Hill, 1982. 304p. illus., maps on endpapers, bibliog., index. ISBN: 0070729468.

350 cross-referenced entries describe significant events, issues and personalities. 'Designed primarily as a companion to a broader treatment of Australia's historical experience' (*Preface*). Bibliography p.291. 40 illus. *Class No:* 994(038)

Maps & Atlases

[8172]

Australians: a historical atlas. Camm, J.C.R. *and* McQuilton, J., *eds.* Broadway, NSW., Fairfax, Syme and Weldon, 1987. xiii,290p. illus. (mostly col.), col. maps, col. graphs, col. tables, index. ISBN: 0949288187.

Forms part of *Australians a historical library (q.v.).*

15 chapters with text, illustrations and maps closely integrated. *I. Place:* I. Environment - 2. Aboriginal landscapes - 3. European discovery and exploration - 4. Rural landscapes - 5. Urban - 6. Mining, manufacturing and transport. *II. People:* 7. Immigrant nations - 8. Life and death - 9. Religion and education - 10. Convicts, bushrangers, larrikins - 11. Australians and war - 12. Great Depression - 13. Government. *III. Landscapes:* 14. City - 15. Country. 'The atlas in its design, lay-out, cartography, photography and quality of reproduction, diagrams, printing and binding, is as nearly perfect as it is possible to imagine' (*Geographical Journal*, v.155,no.2, July 1989, p.290-1). *Class No:* 994(084.3)

[8173]

TERRY, T.M. **The Discovery of Australia** the charts and maps of the navigators and explorers. London, Hamish Hamilton, 1982. 159p. maps, facsims, bibliog., index. ISBN: 0241108632.

'The story of the discovery and exploration of Australia and the way in which the navigators' and explorers' knowledge and speculations were made available to the public through published maps' in 15 chapters of text and accompanying maps *e.g* 1. Terra incognita ... 3. First discoveries ... 9. The great expeditions ... 14. Across the desert ... 15. The changing map of Australia. Bibliography p.156. 85 plates. *Class No:* 994(084.3)

Chronologies

[8174]

BARKER, A. **When was that?** chronology of Australia. Sydney, John Ferguson, 1988. xii,562p. index. ISBN: 0949118184.

Guide to events in Australia's history from the beginnings of European settlement to its bicentenary in 1988. A mainline chronology of political and general events against precise dates is followed by separate lists dealing with architecture and building; science, technology, and discovery; arts and entertainment; books and writing; sport and recreation; statistics, social change and environment. Analytical index p.423-562. *Class No:* 994(090)

[8175]

Collins milestones in Australian history. Brown, R., *comp and* Appleton, R., *ed..* Sydney, Collins, 1986. x, 835p. ISBN: 0002165813.

An annalistic guide to significant events and achievements described as 'a kind of ready reckoner of Australian heritage, carefully arranged to provide quick accurate answers to those who, what, when and where questions.' 20,000 entries (60,000 facts) are listed under six headings: A. History, Politics, Economics, Law; B. Science, Technology, Transport, Discovery; C. Arts; D. Religion, Learning; E.

....(contd.)

Sport; F. *Historia dignum*. Each of these headings is allocated 1-2 columns for every year 1788-1984, two columns to the page. A comprehensive index p.743-835 is almost half as long as the 300,000 word text. Map of Australia on endpapers. *Class No:* 994(090)

[8176]

FRASER, B., *ed and* ATKINSON, A., *eds..* The Macquarie encyclopedia of Australian events. Sydney, Macquarie Library, 1997. 608p. illus.

36 contributors. 10,000 events that shaped Australia divided into 63 chapters arranged in 17 'ordered chronologies'. Entries contain background information and end with short reading lists. For students, teachers, journalists, businessmen *etc*. *Class No:* 994(090)

Biographies
[8177]

ELDER, B., *ed*. The A to Z of who's who in Australia's history. Brookevale, New South Wales, Child & Associates, 1987. 513p., illus., bibliog. ISBN: 0867773707.

Over 1000 brief biographies encompassing not only the country's major political, judicial and bureaucratic figures but also revolutionaries, movie stars, gold fossickers, and sporting heroes *etc*. (Sir Donald Bradman 42 lines, 2 illus.; Dame Nellie Melba 44 lines). Chronology of Australian history p.506-508. Bibliography p.513. *Class No:* 994(092)

Institutions & Associations
[8178]

REID, R. *and* REID, A. Into history: a guide to historical, genealogical, family history and heritage societies, groups and organisations in Australia. North Ryde, New South Wales, R.S. and A.F. Reid, 1988. various pagination (325p), index. softcover with spiral binding. ISBN: 0731627725.

Descriptive listings A-Z by State. Data: date established, aims and interests, activities, specific projects, memberships, meetings, publications, and research facilities. *Class No:* 994:061:061.2

Papua New Guinea
[8179]

WAIKO, J.D. A Short history of Papua New Guinea. Melbourne, Oxford Univ. Press, 1995. 288p. illus., maps, tables, index. pbk. £11.95. ISBN: 0195531647.

A concise book describing the quick and steady growth of the many small, isolated and self-sufficient societies that made up the fledgeling British Papua and German New Guinea colonies towards the end of the last century. The book traces how the British and German colonies grew and the effects that each administration had on health, religion, education and trade up to and beyond independence. *Class No:* 995

Dictionaries
[8180]

TURNER, A. Historical dictionary of Papua New Guinea. Metuchen, NJ., Scarecrow Press, 1994. xxviii,334p. maps, bibliog. £40.50. (*Oceanian Historical Dictionaries, no.4*.) ISBN: 0810828744.

Chronology p.xiii-xxviii. Introduction (history, European contacts) p.1-22. Dictionary (Economic and social developments, government, education, biographies, constitution) p.23-236. Bibliography (8 categories) p.241-323. 5 Appendices (rulers, leaders and government). 5 maps. *Class No:* 995(038)

Fiji
[8181]

SCARR, D. Fiji a short history. Sydney and London, George Allen & Unwin, 1984. xvi, 202p. illus., maps, bibliog., index. ISBN: 0868613118.

4 sections: 1. In the islands of Degai - 2. Search for stability 1865-1875 - 3. The multi-racial community 1875-1914 - 4. The makings of a nation. References p.178-188. Bibliography p. 189-195. Glossary p. xii, xiii. *Class No:* 996.11

Encyclopaedias
[8182]

The Cyclopedia of Fiji (illustrated); a complete historical and commercial review of Fiji.../a compendium of statistics and data concerning the Group never yet compiled or brought together in a single publication/descriptive and biographical facts, figures, and illustrations. Papakura, Central Auckland, R. McMillan, 1984. 332+4p.

Facsimile reprint of work first published in Sydney by McCarron

....(contd.)

Stewart in 1907.

Index to portraits of Fiji colonists p.330-332.
Class No: 996.11(031)

Samoa
[8183]

MASTERMAN, S. An Outline of Samoan history. Apia, Western Samoa, Commercial Printers Ltd., 1980. 79+23p.

17 chronological chapters *e.g.* 3. Samoa before 1830 ... 6. Growth of trade: the Germans in Samoa ... 7. US and Samoa ... 8. Great Britain, Australia and New Zealand in Samoa ... 16. Towards self government. 7. Appendices *e.g.* 6. Chronological history of Western Samoa p.13-23. Reproduced from author's typescript.
Class No: 996.13

Encyclopaedias
[8184]

Cyclopedia of Samoa, Tonga, Tahiti, and the Cook Islands (illustrated). A complete review of the history and traditions and the commercial development of the islands with statistics and data never before compiled in a single publication. Descriptive and biographical facts, figures and illustrations. Papakura, Central Auckland, R. McMillan, 1983. Various paginations, illus., maps.

Facsimile reprint of a work first published in Sydney by McCarron Stewart in 1907. *Class No:* 996.13(031)

Tuvalu
[8185]

LARACY, H., *ed*. Tuvalu a history. Institute of Pacific Studies and Extension Services, Univ. of South Pacific and Ministry of Social Services, Government of Tuvalu, 1983. 208p. illus., maps, bibliog. index.

17 contributors. 21 chapters in 4 parts: 1. Origin and culture - 2. Island traditions - 3. Fresh winds - 4. From Ellice to Tuvalu. Appendix A. Some important dates p.185-186. B. Some important facts p.187-189. Bibliography p.200-204. *Class No:* 996.14

Micronesia
[8186]

ROGERS, R.F. Destiny's landfall. A history of Guam. Honolulu, Univ. of Hawai'i Press, 1995. 380p. illus., maps, bibliog., index. $45. ISBN: 0824816161.

History of the Chamorro, the indigenous people of Guam, including the pre-European contact, Spanish and US Naval colonial rule, Second World War invasions, and their movement for independence. 'This is a fascinating and well-written work that will supersede Paul Cerano and Pedro Sanchez's outdated *Complete history of Guam* (1994)' (*Choice* v.35,no.5, January 1996, p.846). *Class No:* 996.5

Bibliographies
[8187]

KRAUSS, N.L.H. Bibliography of the Ocean Islands (Banaba) Western Pacific. Honolulu, the author, 1969. 7p. sd.

78 unannotated entries. *Class No:* 996.5(01)

[8188]

KRAUSS, N.L.H. Bibliography of The Phoenix Islands, Central Pacific. Honolulu, the author, 1970. 15p. sd. index.

230 entries A-Z by author. Also information on history of discovery and administrative and constitutional status. *Class No:* 996.5(01)

Guam

Dictionaries
[8189]

WUECH, W.L. *and* BALLENDORF, D.A. Historical dictionary of Guam and Micronesia. Metuchen, NJ., Scarecrow Press, 1994. xxxi,172p. maps, bibliog. $29.50. (*Oceanian Historical Dictionaries no.3*.) ISBN: 0810828588.

Chronology p.xv-xxii. Island names p.xxvii-xxxi. Dictionary p.1-133. Bibliography (10 subdivisions) p.135-71. 2 maps.
Class No: 996.72(038)

Kiribati

[8190]

MACDONALD, B. **Cinderellas of the empire** towards a history of Kiribati and Tuvalu. Canberra, Australian National Univ. Press, 1982. xx, 335p. maps, bibliog., index. ISBN: 0708116167.

14 chapters *e.g.* 1. The islands and their people ... 8. Rigidity and reforms: the Gilbert and Ellice Islands 1909-1941 ... Epilogue: From separation to independence. Notes p.227-296. Bibliography p.297-314. Traces history from early 19th century to late 1970s.
Class No: 996.82

Hawaii

[8191]

TABRAH, R. **Hawaii a bicentennial history.** New York, W.W. Norton; Nashville, American Association for State and Local History, 1980. xi, 233p.+18p. plates. maps, bibliog., index. $14.95. (*The States And The Nation Series*.) ISBN: 0393056805.

A popular history in 17 chronological chapters. Descriptive reading list p.225-6. 'One of the better histories in the series and one of the best about Hawaii in a long time' (*Choice*, v.18, no.5, January 1981, p.718). *Class No:* 996.9

Dictionaries

[8192]

CRAIG, R.D. **Historical dictionary of Honolulu and Hawai'i.** Lanham, MD., Scarecrow Press, Scarecrow Press, 1998. xlii,297p., illus., maps, bibliog., tables. $55. (*Historical Dictionaries of Cities, no.5*.) ISBN: 0810835134.

Chronology p.xvii-xlii. Introduction (history) p.1-35. Dictionary (persons, ethnic groups, places, institutions, religion, politics, economy) p.37-244. Bibliography (12 thematic sections) p.245-86. 6 Appendixes including Hawaian holidays and celebrations p.292-95. 2 maps. *Class No:* 996.9(038)

Biographies

[8193]

DAY, A.G. **A Biographical dictionary: historical makers of Hawaii.** Honolulu, Mutual Publishers, 1984. 174p.

Biographies of key figures in history of Hawaii.
Class No: 996.9(092)

Polar Regions

[8194]

KIRWAN, L.P. **The White road** a survey of Polar exploration. London, Hollis & Carter., 1959. x,374p. illus., maps, bibliog., index.

Published in US by W.W. Norton under title of *A history óf Polar exploration*.

24 chapters organized in 5 parts: 1. Age of discovery - 2. Age of exploration - 3. Age of adventure and research - 4. Heroic age - 5. Postscript to polar history. Bibliography p.355-64. Complete survey of Arctic and Antarctic exploration. *Class No:* 998/999

Manuscripts & Incunabula

Bibliographies

[8195]

HOLLAND, C., *ed*. **Manuscripts in the Scott Polar Research Institute Cambridge, England** a catalogue. New York, Garland, 1982. xii,815p. $121.00. ISBN: 0824093941.

Introduction gives details of the scope of SPRI's collection, a history of the catalogue, and of its organization and use. 6 indexes of Arctic and Antarctic exploration, whaling and sealing voyages p.742-815.
Class No: 998/999(093)(01)

Arctic

[8196]

VAUGHAN, R. **The Arctic:** a history. Stroud, Gloucs., Alan Sutton, 1994. ix,340p. illus., maps, tables, bibliog., index. £20. ISBN: 0750901772.

Well-researched, well-documented history of the lands and seas north of the Arctic Circle from their earliest occupation c.10,000BC to the present day encompassing the archeological record, the history of Arctic exploration, the exploitation of natural resources, and scientific research. Important bibliography p.290-324. 38 maps. *Class No:* 998

Bibliographies

[8197]

DAY, A.E. **Search for the Northwest Passage** an annotated bibliography. New York, Garland, 1986. xiv,632p. index. $78.00. (*Garland Reference Library Of Social Science, no.186*.) ISBN: 0824092880.

5160 entries arranged in 11 chapters: 1. Encyclopaedic works, maps and atlases *etc.* - 2. The search begins (1497-1553) - 3. Strait of Anian (1542-1677) - 4. Elizabethan/Stuart trading ventures (1566-1634) - 5. Hudson's Bay Company (1668-1791) - 6. Pacific search resumed (1761-1795) - 7. Royal Navy by land and sea (1815-1839) - 8. Sir John Franklin (1845-1848) - 9. Search for Franklin (1847-1880) - 10. The Passage navigated (1903-1984) - 11. Reference works. 'An excellent bibliographic source and a valuable addition to any reference collection' (*Association of Canadian Map Libraries And Archives Bulletin*, no.68, September 1988, p.25-26). *Class No:* 998(01)

[8198]

The North West Passage 1534-1859 a catalogue of an exhibition of books and manuscripts in the Toronto Public Library. Firth, E.G. Toronto, Baxter Publishing Co. in cooperation with the Toronto Public Library, 1963. [28]p. illus., maps on endpapers, facsims., index, pbk.

90 annotated entries in approximate chronological order of expedition or voyage. *Class No:* 998(01)

Greenland

[8199]

GAD, F. **The History of Greenland.** London, C. Hurst, 2v. 1970-1973. V.3 published in København by Nyt Nordisk Forlag (1982).

1. *Earliest times to 1700.* 1970. xiii, 350p. £30.00. ISBN 0900966238. 2. *1700-1782.* 1973. xviii, 446p. £35.00. 0900966572.

3. *1782-1808* V.1 ranges over 4,000 years in 9 chapters. Notes and references p.319-33; literature p.334-9; glossary p.340. V.2 deals with Greenland's connection with the Danes in 23 chapters. Note on source material p.430-2; glossary p.433-5. A third volume was to have covered Greenland until the end of the first decade of the 20th century but this has not so far appeared in English translation. 'This comprehensive, detailed and solidly documented history of Greenland from the first inhabitants to 1808' (K.E. Miller. *Denmark*, 1987. Entry 717). *Class No:* 998.8

Antarctic

[8200]

MARTIN, S. **A History of Antarctica.** Sydney, State Library of New South Wales Press, 272p. illus. $Aus.65. ISBN: 0731066014.

Covers the history of Antarctic exploration, discoverers and explorers, scientists, the evolution of the Antarctic Treaty, and subsequent events, 1960-1996. *Class No:* 999

[8201]

MICKLEBURGH, E. **Beyond the frozen sea** visions of Antarctica. London, Bodley Head, 1987. 256p. illus., (some col.), maps, bibliog., index. £15.00. ISBN: 0370310276.

4 chronological sections: 18th to late 20th century. Sources p.241-5. Further reading p.247-8. Analytical index. *Class No:* 999

Encyclopaedias

[8202]

STEWART, J. **Antarctica** an encyclopedia. Jefferson, N.C., McFarland, 2v., 1990. xxii,v,1193p. bibliog. $135. ISBN: 0899504701, set; 0899505597, v.1; 0899505988, v.2.

A-Z encyclopedia, with 15,000 cross-referenced entries on geographical features, expeditions, people, scientific subjects, and general interest items, with distinct historical and geographical bias. A Capsule history p.xv-xviii. Chronology (1502 to 1990) p.1133-60. Expeditions p.1161-70. Bibliography p.1173-93. A major work.
Class No: 999(031)

Maps & Atlases

[8203]

THOMSON, J.W. 'Which atlas? A guide to maps of Antarctica' *Cartographic Journal*, v.29,no.1, June 1992, pp.44-47. bibliog.

A survey of the Antarctic maps in 27 world atlases. Data: name of atlas, projection, date of edition/reprint, comment.
Class No: 999(084.3)

Chronologies

[8204]

HEADLAND, R.K., *comp*. **Chronological list of Antarctic expeditions** and related historical events. Cambridge, Cambridge Univ. Press, 1989. vii, 730p. illus., maps, bibliog., index. £65; $125. (*Studies in Polar Research*.) ISBN: 0521309034.

Based on B. Roberts' 'Chronological list of Antarctic expeditions', *Polar Record*, v.59, no.8, May 1958, p.97-134 and v.9, no.60, September 1958, p.191-239. Material in these lists had already appeared in the *Antarctic Pilot* (London, Hydrographic Department, 2nd ed., 1948).

Over 3,200 entries covering the period 700BC-1988 provide brief descriptions of events, names of individuals, ships, and source citations for each expedition. The region covered is the far south in general and Antarctica in particular. Bibliography p.604-21. 'An invaluable reference book for any investigation of Antarctic history' (*Choice*, v.28, no.1, September 1990, p.76++78). *Class No:* 999(090)

Author / Title Index

The index reference is to the running number given to each item. The running numbers are in one sequence throughout the volume and can be found at the top right-hand corner of the entry for each item.

This index is of authors and titles in one sequence. The names of the authors are printed in bold type. Where works are jointly authored, only the first name is indexed. All books and periodicals listed or mentioned in the text, except where cited as the source of review quotations or for purposes of comparison, are entered under the headings given. All entries in *Walford* have title entries in the index; where the main heading in *Walford* is under title, added entries to the index have usually been made for an editor or compiler.

Filing is word by word, with groups of initials counted as single words. Since *Walford* uses only initials and not forenames it may occasionally happen that titles by different authors with the same surname and initials are found grouped together.

The arrangement of entries under an author is alphabetically by title. To save space, most sub-titles have been omitted, and many lengthy titles have been shortened.

An Annotated bibliography of diaries printed in English 5761

An Annotated bibliography of exploration in Africa 5080

An Annotated bibliography of the Holy Roman Empire 6782

An Annotated bibliography of the Napoleonic era 6798

Annotated bibliography on clandestine employment 1882

Annotated bibliography on the economic history of India 2360

An Annotated critical bibliography of feminist criticism 4059

Annotated handbook of biblical quotations, verses and parables 479

An Annotated index of medieval women 5728

Annuaire administratif et judiciaire de Belgique 3339

Annuaire statistique 1239

Annuaire statistique de la Belgique 1255

Annuaire statistique de la France 1243

Annual abstract of statistics 1245

Annual abstract of statistics, 1999 1228

Annual bulletin of historical literature 83 6378

Annual bulletin of housing and building statistics for Europe 3258

Annual census of production reports ... 1970 - 2407

Annual economic report, 1991 2361

Annual Egyptological bibliography/ Bibliographie 4230

The Annual register 6746

Annual review of European Community affairs, 1992 2919

The Annual review of psychology 277

Annual review of sociology 1067

Annual survey of Commonwealth law, 1965-1977, v.1-13 2818

Annuario statistico italiano 1244

Anson, P.F.
The religious orders and congregations of Great Britain and Ireland 691

Anstruther, G.
The Seminary priests 744

The Antarctic 5058

The Antarctic Treaty regime 5056

Antarctica 5392, 5682, 8202

Antheume, B. and Bonnemaison, J.
Atlas des îles et états du Pacifique Sud 5374

Anthony, J.D.
Historical and cultural dictionary of the Sultanate of Oman and the Emirates of Eastern Arabia 7619

Anthony, M.
Historical dictionary of Trinidad and Tobago 7938

Anthony, P. and Arnold, J.
Costume: a general bibliography 3953

Anti-evolution 442

Anti-semitic propaganda 1507

Antigua and Barbuda 4915

The Antonine Wall 4417

Anuario estadístico de Cuba 1287

Anuario estadístico de España 1246

Anuario estadístico para América Latina y el Caribe ... Statistical year-book for Latin America and the Caribbean 1289

Anuário estatístico de Portugal = Statistical yearbook of Portugal 1247

Anuário estatístico do Brasil 1298

Anuarul statistic al României. Romanian statistical yearbook 1261

Aotearoa and New Zealand: a historical geography 5163

APAIS: Australian public affairs information service 974

The Apocrypha and Pseudepigrapha of the Old Testament in English ... 541

Appiah, K.A. and Gates, H.L.
Africana 4782

Appleby, B.L.
Elsevier's dictionary of commercial terms and phrases in five languages 2022

Appleton, G.
The Oxford book of prayer 657

Appleton, R. and Appleton, A.
The Cambridge dictionary of Australian places 5664

The Aquarian dictionary of festivals 4015

Arab education, 1956-78: a bibliography 3803

Arab Gulf States 5567

Arab history and the nation state 6434

Arab-Islamic biographical archive/Arabisch-Islamisches biographisches archiv 5890

The Arab-Israeli conflict 1945-1971 7695

Arab Republic of Egypt. Central Agency for Public Mobility and Statistics
Statistical yearbook, 1952-91 1279

The Arabian Gulf in antiquity 7623

Arabian personalities of the early twentieth century 5888

Arabic biographical dictionaries 5891

Arabic military dictionary 3380

ARBA guide to biographical dictionaries
ARBA guide to biographical resources 1986-1997 5710

ARBA guide to biographical resources 1986-1997 5710

Arbingast, S.A.
Atlas of Central America 5338

'The Archaeological and historical maps of the Ordnance Survey' 4268

Archaeological bibliography for Great Britain and Ireland 4259

Archaeological heritage management in the modern world 4368

Archaeological Mexico 4458

Archaeological site manual 4364

Archaeological survey of Ireland 4424

Archaeology 4208

The Archaeology handbook 4367

'Archaeology in Albania' 4303

Archaeology in Britain 4250

Archaeology in Central Europe 4246

'Archaeology in Turkey' 4318

The Archaeology of Africa 4321

The Archaeology of ancient China 4304

The Archaeology of ancient Israel 4234

The Archaeology of Anglo-Saxon England 4285

The Archaeology of boats and ships 4346

The Archaeology of Britain 4253

The Archaeology of Brittany, Normandy and the Channel Islands 4294

The Archaeology of early medieval Ireland 4277

'The Archaeology of industrial Wales' 4483

The Archaeology of Korea 4308

The Archaeology of mainland Southeast Asia 4320

The Archaeology of medieval England 4286

The Archaeology of Mesopotamia 4236

Archaeology of prehistoric Native America 4332

Archaeology of the British Isles 4385

Archaeology of the dreamtime 4345

An Archaeology of the early Anglo-Saxon kingdoms 6947

Archaeology of the land of the Bible 4233

The Archaeology of the New Testament 533

The Archaeology of the Welsh Marches 4288

The Archaeology of Ulster 4284

'Archaeology on the World Wide Web 4210

The Archaeology resource book 1992 4251

Archaeology under water 4353

Archaeology underwater 4351

Archäologische Bibliographie 4209

Archeological resource guide for Europe 4248

Archéologie de la France 4293

The Archeology of Northeast China 4307

'Archival resources for African studies in the United Kingdom 6564

The Archives: a guide to the National Archives Field Branches 6597

Archives and manuscript repositories in the USSR 6533

Archives and records of the City of Chester 7210

Archives biographiques Françaises. Deuxième Série/French biographical archive Series II/ Französisches biographisches archiv Neue Folge 5804

Archives biographiques Françaises/French biographical archive 5803

Archives biographiques Françaises jusqu'à 1999/French biographical archive to 1999 5805

'Archives', chapter 2, *Australians: a guide to sources* 6611

'Archives in Japan,' 6548

Archives in Russia 6531

Les Archives Nationales 6523

Archives New Zealand 6607

ArchivesUSA 6600

Archivio biografico Italiano sino al 1996/Italian biographical archive to 1996/Italienisches biographisches archiv bis 1996 5809

Archivo biográfico de España, Portugal e Iberoamérica 1960-1995/Spanish, Portuguese and Latin American biographical archive 1960-1995/Spanisches, Portugiesisches und Iberoamerikanisches archiv, 1960-1995 5814

Archivo biográfico de España, Portugal e Iberoamérica. Nueve serie/Spanish, Portuguese and Latin-American biographical archive. Series II 5816

Archivo biográfico de España, Portugal e Iberoamérica/Spanish, Portuguese and Latin American biographical archive 5813

Archivo biografico Italiano/Italian biographical archive 5808

Archivo biografico Italiano, nuova serie/Italian biographical archive. Series II 5810

ArchNet: WWW virtual library - archeology 4227

The Arctic 5052, 5683, 8196

Ardagh, J.
The Shell guide to Germany 5532

Area bibliography of China 4651

Arends, M.
Genealogy on CD-ROM 6097
Genealogy software guide 6010

Argentina 4977

Argentina 1516-1982: from Spanish colonization to the Falklands War and Alphonsin 8089

Argentine bibliography 4978

Argles, M.
British government publications in education during the 19th century 3787

Argles, M. and Vaughan, J.E.
British government publications concerning education during the 20th century 3786

Argüello, C.M.
'Bibliografía de Nicaragua' 7910

Argumentation and debate 1085

Ariès, P. and Duby, G.
A History of private life 1166

Aristotelian Society
A Synoptic index to the 'Proceedings of the Aristotelian Society...' 16

Aristotle: a bibliography 17

Ark, O.I.
English-Norwegian military dictionary 3377

Arksey, L.
American diaries 5942

Armed forces in Latin America 3419

Armed forces of the USSR 3412

Armen, G.
Hayasdanee badmagan adias 7434

Armenia 4621
The Armenian people from ancient to modern times 7452
The Armies of Britain, 1485-1980 3496
Armit, I.
Scotland's hidden history 4396
Armitage, G.
'Cartobibliographies of city and town plans in England and Wales. A select list' 7102
'County cartobibliographies of England and Wales: a select list' 7103
Armitage, G. and Hall, D.
A Brief guide to large scale Ordnance Survey maps of Great Britain in the Map Library 7092
Armorial families 6240
Armorial général 6231
Arms control and disarmament 2992
Arms control and disarmament, defense and military, international security and peace 2991
The Arms control, disarmament and military security dictionary 3003
Arms control fact book 2987
Arms, T.S. and Ridley, E.
World elections on file 1545
Armstrong, A.H.
The Cambridge history of later Greek and early medieval philosophy 107
Armstrong, C.J. and Fenton, R.R.
World databases in company information 2508
Armstrong, J. and Jones, S.
Business documents 2443
Armstrong, M.
A Handbook of personnel management 2627
The New manager's handbook 2606
The Army Air Forces in World War II 6836
Army badges and insignia of World War 2 3436-3437
The Army list. 1814- 3488
Army Museums Ogilby Trust
Index to British military costume prints, 1500-1914 3452
Army, navy and air force uniforms of the Warsaw Pact 3442
Armytage, W.H.G.
Four hundred years of English education 3792
Arndt, W.F. and Gingrich, F.W.
A Greek-English lexikon of the New Testament and other early Christian literature 536
Arnold-Baker, C.
The Companion to British history 6926
Arnold, C.J.
An Archaeology of the early Anglo-Saxon kingdoms 6947
Arnold, G.
Political and economic encyclopedia of Africa 1451
Third World Handbook 4522
Arnold, J.
A Handbook of costume 3960
Patterns of fashion 3961
The Royal houses of Europe 6314
Arnold, J. and Morris, D.
Monash biographical dictionary of 20th century Australia 5995
Arnstein, W.L.
Recent historians of Great Britain 6425
Arquelogia Brasileira 4337
The Art of heraldry 6232
The Arthurian bibliography 4173
An Arthurian dictionary 4176
The Arthurian handbook 4175
Arthurian legend and literature 4169
Arthurian literature in the Middle Ages 4177
The Arthurian material in the Chronicles 4172

Articles describing archives and mansucript collections in the United States 6602
Artola, M.
Enciclopedia de historia de España 7376
As'ad, Abukhalil
Historical dictionary of Lebanon 7691
Asali, K.J.
Jerusalem in history 7692
Ascoli, D.
A Companion to the British Army, 1660-1983 3504
Ashdown, P.
Caribbean history in maps 7919
Ashe, G.
Mythology of the British Isles 833
Ashford, N. and Davies, S.
A Dictionary of conservative and libertarian thought 82
Ashliman, D.L.
A Guide to folktales in the English language 4120
Ashmore, O.
The Industrial archaeology of North-west England 4477
Ashridge Management College
Management for the future: a bibliography 2597
Ashworth, G.
World minorities 1508
World minorities in the eighties 1509
Asia and Oceania 6544
Asia and Pacific: a directory of resources 4645
The Asian American almanac 4960
The Asian-American encyclopedia 4961
Asian & who's who international 5738
Asian economic handbook 2347
Asian history on file 7514
The Asian political dictionary 1441
Asiatic mythology 837
Aslib directory of information sources in the United Kingdom 1031
Aspects of maritime Scandinavia 4361
Asplin, P.W.A.
Medieval Ireland c.1170-1495 7031
Assassinations and executions 1537
Assessment of children's intelligence and special abilities 303
Association Des Géographes De Madagascar Tananarive
Atlas de Madagascar 5321
Association of African Universities
Directory of African universities 3945
Association of British Insurers
Insurance statistics, 1988-1992 3715
Association of British Market Research Companies
ABMRC handbook 2668
Association of British Theological and Philsophical Libraries
Bulletin .. 555
Association of Commonwealth Universities
Higher education in the United Kingdom, 1992-93 3933
Association of International Education, Japan
Japanese colleges and universities, 1989 3944
Association Suisse du Employés de Banque
Banking dictionary 2203
Aster, S.
British foreign policy, 1918-1945: a guide to research and research materials 1628
Aston, M. and Taylor, T.
The Atlas of archaeology 4222
Astrologer's handbook 197
Astrology 194
Astronomy for astrologers 190
Catalog .. 1885
Atatürk and Turkey 7681
Athenian officials 684-321 BC 6709

Atique Zafar Sheikh
'The National Archives of Pakistan' 6558
Atiya, A.S.
The Coptic encyclopedia 714
Atkin's encyclopaedia of court forms in civil proceedings 3191
Atkins, P.J.
The Directories of London 1677-1977 7112
Atkins, S.E.
Arms control and disarmament, defense and military, international security and peace 2991
Atkinson, A.
The Dictionary of famous Australians 5985
Atkinson, D.J. and Field, D.H.
New dictionary of Christian ethics and pastoral theology 620
Atkinson, S.D. and Hudson, J.
Women online 4050
Atlante Enciclopedico Touring 5393
Atlante stradale d'Italia 5239
Atlante tematico d'Italia 5240
The Atlantic 7903
The Atlantic Alliance 2982
Atlantic Ocean 4517
Atlas cantonal de Costa Rica 5339
Atlas cenedlaethol Cymru/National atlas of Wales 5218
Atlas Ceskoslovenské Socialistické Republiky 5225
Atlas de Belgique 5261
Atlas de Bolivia 5369
Atlas de Colombia 5372
Atlas de Cuba 5342
Atlas de France 5230-5231
Atlas de géographie historique de la France et de la Gaulle 7334
Atlas de la Côte d'Ivoire 5308
Atlas de la France de l'an mil 7338
Atlas de la France et de ses régions 5232
Atlas de la Haute-Volta 5303
Atlas de la nouvelle - Calédonie et Dépendences 5388
Atlas de la República Argentina 5366
Atlas de la Republica de Chile 5368
Atlas de la République Centrafricaine 5312
Atlas de la République Islamique de Mauritanie 5301
Atlas de la République Populaire du Congo 5311
Atlas de la Révolution Française 7349
Atlas de la Russie 5248
Atlas de Madagascar 5321
Atlas de Portugal 5244
Atlas de Tunisie 5298
Atlas de Venezuela 5373
Atlas del Desarrollo Territorial de La Argentina 5367
Atlas del Peru 5370
Atlas der Donauländer 5191
Atlas der Donauländer. Register 5192
Atlas der Republik Österreich 5224
Atlas der Schweiz 5263
Atlas des départements français d'Outre-mer 5233
Atlas des îles et états du Pacifique Sud 5374
Atlas des peuples d'Europe Centrale 7254
Atlas d'Iran 5286
Atlas du Luxembourg 5223
Atlas du Mali 5302
Atlas du Maroc 5300
Atlas du Niger 5304
Atlas du Senegal 5305
Atlas du Viêtnam 5292
Atlas et géographie de la France moderne 5145
Atlas for Guyana and Trinidad and Tobago 5347
Atlas geografico e historico del Peru 5371
Atlas grafico de España Aguilar 5241
Atlas historique de la France 7332

Atlas historique de la France contemporaine **7356**

Atlas historique des villes de France **7333**

Atlas nacional de Cuba/Natsional'nyi atlas Kuby **5343**

Atlas nacional de España **5243**

Atlas nacional de la Republica de Panama **5340**

Atlas nacional do Brasil **5365**

An Atlas of African affairs **4788**

Atlas of African prehistory **4325**

Atlas of American frontiers **7986**

Atlas of American history **7987-7988**

Atlas of American Indian affairs **5361**

Atlas of ancient America **4329**

Atlas of ancient Egypt **6656**

An Atlas of Anglo-Saxon England **6958**

The Atlas of archaeology **4222**

Atlas of Australia **5381**

Atlas of Belgium **5262**

The Atlas of Britain and Northern Ireland **5197**

Atlas of British Columbia **5329**

Atlas of British overseas expansion **5215**

Atlas of British politics **1429**

Atlas of British social and economic history since *c.*1700 **1167**

Atlas of Canada **5328**

Atlas of Central America **5338**

The Atlas of Central America and the Caribbean **5341**

Atlas of China **5268**

Atlas of classical archaeology **4240**

Atlas of Classical History **6697**

Atlas of Columbus and the great discoveries **5067**

Atlas of Communism **230**

Atlas of Danubian lands **5191**

Atlas of demographics **1355**

Atlas of early American history **8018**

Atlas of Eastern Europe in the twentieth century **7251**

An Atlas of EEC affairs **2943**

Atlas of global strategy **3485**

Atlas of Great Lakes Indian history **8013**

Atlas of Hawaii **5390**

Atlas of historical county boundaries **8068**

The Atlas of holy places and sacred sites **446**

An Atlas of India **5281**

Atlas of industrializing Britain, 1780-1914 **2309**

Atlas of Ireland **5212**

Atlas of Israel **5290**

Atlas of Jewish history **6669**

Atlas of Leicestershire **7187**

Atlas of maritime history **3534**

Atlas of medieval Europe **6783**

The Atlas of medieval man **6442**

Atlas of Mesopotamia **4319**

Atlas of Mexico **5336-5337**

Atlas of Micronesia **5389**

Atlas of military strategy **3495**

Atlas of modern Jewish history **6670**

Atlas of naval warfare **3533**

Atlas of Nazi Germany **7276**

The Atlas of Nepal in the modern world **5284**

Atlas of New Zealand boundaries **5379**

Atlas of Newfoundland and Labrador **5335**

The Atlas of North American exploration **5082**

Atlas of prehistoric Britain **4269**

An Atlas of Roman Britain **6959**

Atlas of Russia and the independent republics **5247**

Atlas of Russia and the post-Soviet republics **5246**

Atlas of Russia and the Soviet Union **7431**

Atlas of Saskatchewan **5333**

Atlas of Scottish history to 1707 **7007**

The Atlas of ship wreck & treasure **5113**

Atlas of Slovenia. 109 maps on the scale 1:50,000 and Slovenia in pictures and words **5264**

Atlas of South America **5364**

Atlas of South Australia **5382**

Atlas of Southeast Asia **4745**

An Atlas of territorial and border disputes **2948**

The Atlas of the Ancient World **6637**

Atlas of the ancient World CD-ROM **6639**

The Atlas of the Arab World geopolitics and society **5294**

Atlas of the Bible **481**

Atlas of the Biblical world **485**

Atlas of the British Empire **6912**

Atlas of the Christian church **674**

The Atlas of the Civil War **8046**

Atlas of the Commonwealth of the Bahamas **5346**

The Atlas of the Crusades **6786**

Atlas of the Greek and Roman world **6698**

Atlas of the Greek and Roman world in antiquity **6636**

Atlas of the history of Islam **7534**

Atlas of the Holocaust **7287**

Atlas of the Islamic world since 1500 **4768**

Atlas of the Lao P.D.R **5293**

Atlas of the Middle East **5278**

An Atlas of the Mughal Empire **7653**

Atlas of the North American Indian **8014**

Atlas of the People's Republic of China **5269**

Atlas of the Renaissance **6788**

Atlas of the Roman world **6722**

Atlas of the Slovak Socialist Republic **5226**

Atlas of the South Pacific **5181**

Atlas of the Third World **4526**

Atlas of the Union of South Africa **5317**

Atlas of the United Republic of Cameroon **5309**

Atlas of the world religions **424**

The Atlas of the world's worst natural disasters **5106**

Atlas of the year 1000 **6747**

Atlas of twentieth century world history **6453**

Atlas of Uganda **5313**

Atlas of Victoria **5383**

Atlas of westward expansion **8017**

An Atlas of world affairs **4514**

Atlas Ost-und Südosteuropa **5193**

Atlas over Danmark **5256**

Atlas Paris par arrondissements **5234**

Atlas Slovenije **5264**

Atlas SSR **5226**

Atlas to accompany the official records of the Union and Confederate armies **8047**

Atlas turístico de Portugal **5245**

Atlas van Nederland **5259**

Atlas van Nederland/Atlas of the Netherlands **5258**

Atlas zur deutschen Zeitgeschichte **7267**

Atlasul Republicii Socialiste România **5266**

Attila, Pók
  A Selected bibliography of modern historiography **6424**

Attwater, D.
  A Dictionary of Mary **593**
  A Dictionary of saints **605**
  The Lives of the saints **605**

Attwater, D. *and* **John, R.J.**
  Dictionary of saints **610**

Attwood, F.A. *and* **Stein, N.D.**
  De Paula's auditing **2592**

Aubin, P. *and* **Côté, L-M.**
  Bibliographie de l'histoire du Québec et du Canada **7894**

Aubrey, J.
  Monumenta Britannica **4376**

Auchterlonie, P.
  Arabic biographical dictionaries **5891**
  Introductory guide to Middle Eastern and Islamic bibliography **4685**

Auchterlonie, P. *(contd.)*
  Yemen **4694**

Audi, R.
  The Cambridge dictionary of philosophy **76**

'Audio-visual aids in education' **3839**

Audiovisual and microcomputer handbook **3835**

Aufstieg und Niedergang der Römischen Welt. Geschichte und Kultur Roms im Spiegel der neueren Forschung
  Rise and decline of the Roman world **6712**

August, E.R.
  Men's studies **1155**

Augustinian bibliography, 1970-1980 **19**

Augustus to Nero **6713**

Ausführliches Lexikon der griechischen und römischen Mythologie **845**

Austin-Broos, Diane J.
  Australian sociologies **1076**

Austral-Asian who's who **5986**

Australasia and South Pacific Islands bibliography **4996**

Australasian biographical archive/ Australasiatisches biographisches archiv **5973**

Australasian biographical index/Australasien biographischer index **5974**

Australia **5023**

Australia. Bureau of Statistics
  Year book Australia **1304**

Australia. Department of Foreign Affairs and Trade
  Documents on Australian foreign policy, 1937-1949 **1654**

Australia handbook **5667**

Australia road atlas **5384**

Australia unveiled **8159**

Australian and New Zealand legal abbreviations **2715**

Australian and New Zealand studies **5013**

Australian Antarctic bibliography **5057**

Australian dictionary of biography **5987**

The Australian economic review **2389**

The Australian encyclopaedia **5027**

Australian Ethnic Heritage Series **8149**

Australian history on the Internet **8165**

Australian maps **5386**

The Australian national flag **6357**

The Australian people **5028**

Australian sociologies **1076**

Australians **8166**

Australians: a historical atlas **8172**

Australia's national parks **5663**

Australia's yesterdays **8167**

Austria **4574**

Austria. Statistisches Zentralamt
  Statistisches Jahrbuch für die Republik Österreich **1240**

Austrian philosophy **109**

Author and subject catalogues of the Royal Navy Library **3536**

Author-title catalog **1760**

Authoritative guide to self-help resources in mental health **3675**

Author's guide to journals in law, criminal justice and criminology **2777**

Author's guide to journals in psychology, psychiatry & social work **282**

Authors of their own lives **1072**

The Autobiography of the working class **1903**

Automobile Association
  AA book of British towns **5451**
  AA book of British villages **5452**
  AA Great Britain road atlas 2000 **5194**
  AA guide to National Trust properties in Britain **5454**
  AA illustrated guide to Britain's coast **5456**
  AA illustrated guide to country towns and villages of Britain **5457**
  Baedeker guides **5421**

Beach, M.
A Subject bibliography of the history of American higher education **3905**

Beacham, W.
Beacham's guide to key lobbyists **1695**

Beacham's guide to key lobbyists **1695**

Beal, G.
The Independent book of anniversaries **6461**

Bean, R.
International labour statistics **1898**

Beattie, D.
Company administration handbook **2018, 2600**

Beauchamp, E.R. *and* Rubinger, R.
Education in Japan **3800**

Beaulieu, A.
Guide d'Histoire du Canada **7865**

Beaver, P.
Britain's modern Royal Navy **3557**
Encyclopaedia of the modern Royal Navy **3554**

Bechtel, W. *and* Graham, G
Companion to cognitive science **233**

Beck, C.
Political science thesaurus II **1463**

Beck, P.
The Falkland Islands as an international problem **8091**

Bečka, J.
Historical dictionary of Myanmar **7714**

Becker, L. *and* Becker, C.
Encyclopedia of ethics **354**

Becket, H.
The Dictionary of espionage **1664**

Beckett, J.
A Centenary history of Nottingham **7177**

Beckles, H. McD.
A History of Barbados **7934**

Bedini, S.A.
The Christopher Columbus encyclopedia **7852**

Beech, G.
Maps and plans in the Public Record Office. 4. Europe and Turkey **5190**

Beek, M.A.
Atlas of Mesopotamia **4319**

Beer, M.
History of British Socialism **213**

Beer, M. de
Who did what in South Africa **5901**

Beer, S.H.
Modern British politics **1713**

Beers, H.B.
Bibliographies in American history 1942-1978 **7956**

Before Columbus **6784**

Beg, M.A.J.
The Middle East in the twentieth century **7549**

Beginning your family history **6151**

Begley, D.F.
Handbook on Irish genealogy **6048**
Irish genealogy **6049**

Behind the blue plaques of London 1867-1994 **7132**

Behn, W.A.
Index Islamicus, 1665-1905 **4764**

Behrouz, K. *and* Ourmazdi, M.
Iran's who's who 1993 **5880**

Being religious, American style **432**

Beit-Hallahmi, B.
Psychoanalytic studies of religion **316**

Belanger, S.E.
Better said and clearly written **2562**

Belch, J.
Contemporary games **3844**

Belchem, J. *and* Price, R.
A Dictionary of nineteenth-century world history **6444**

Belford, R.
The Which? guide to Spain **5549**

Belgium **4631**

Belgium. Institut National de Statistique
Annuaire statistique de la Belgique **1255**

Belize **4886**

Belize handbook **5607**

Belkind, A.
Jean-Paul Sartre **48**

Bell, A.A. *and* Allis, J.B.
Resources in ancient philosophy **13**

Bell, D.
A Biographical dictionary of French political leaders since 1870 **1437**

Bell, D. *and* East, R.
Communist and Marxist parties of the world **1703**

Bell, G.M.
A Handlist of British diplomatic representation, 1509-1688 **3336**

Bell, P.
Victorian biography **5739**
Victorian women **5765**
Who was who in Edwardian Scotland **5768**

Bell, R.E.
Place-names in classical mythology: Greece **851**
Women in classical mythology **855**

Bellamy, J.M.
Yorkshire business histories **2467**

Bellamy, J.M. *and* Saville, J.
Dictionary of labour biography **1909**

Bellegarde-Smith, P.
Haiti **4905**

Bellwood, P.
Man's conquest of the Pacific **4229**
The Polynesians **6741**
Prehistory of the Indo-Malaysian archipelago **4340**

Bellwood, P. *and* Glover, I.
The Peoples of South-East Asia and the Pacific **6740**

Beloch, I. *and* Alves de Abreu, A.
Dicionário histórico-biográfico Brasileiro 1930-1983 **8087**

Bemis, S.F. *and* Griffin, G.G.
Guide to the diplomatic history of the United States, 1775-1921 **1650**

Benady, T.
Gibraltar guidebook **5550**

Bence-Jones, M.
The Viceroys of India **7635**

Bendall, S.
Dictionary of land surveyors and local map makers of Great Britain and Ireland 1530-1850 **7049**

Bender, B.
The Archaeology of Brittany, Normandy and the Channel Islands **4294**

Benedetto, R. *and* Guder, D.L. *and* McKim, D.K.
Historical dictionary of the reformed churches **775**

A Benedictine bibliography **663**

Benedictine monks of St. Augustine's Abbey, Ramsgate
The Book of Saints **602**

Benewick, R. *and* Green, P.
The Routledge dictionary of twentieth-century political thinkers **1473**

Benin **4827**

Benjamin, B.
Population statistics **1327**

Benjamin, L.T.
A History of American psychology in notes and news, 1883-1945 **295**

Bennett, B.M. *and* Scott, D.H.
Harper's encyclopedia of Bible life **451**

Bennett, D.
Encyclopaedia of Dublin **7046**

Bennett, G.
The Kent bibliography **7139**

Bennett, G. *and* Bennett, P.R.
Seychelles **4868**

Bennett, J. *and* Fawcett, J.
Industrial relations **1924**

Bennett, J. *and* Storey, R. *and* Tough, A.
Trade union and related records **1978**

Bennett, P.
The Typewriting dictionary **2567**

Bennett, P.R. *and* Bennett, G.J.
Mauritius **4870**

Bennett, R.
Dictionary of personnel and human resources management **2632**

Bennett, S. *and* Bennett, N.
An Historical atlas of Lincolnshire **7185**

Benningsen, A. *and* Wimbush, S.E.
Muslims of the Soviet empire **948**

Bentley, E.P.
Directory of family associations **6197**
The Genealogist's address book **6116**

Bentley, M.
Companion to historiography **6360, 6456**

Benvenisti, M. *and* Khayat, S.
The West Bank and Gaza atlas **5289**

Benz, W. *and* Graml, H.
Biographisches lexikon zur Weimarer Republik **7268**

Benzing, J.
Lutherbibliographie. Verzeichnis der gedruckten Schriften Martin Luthers bis zu dessen Tod.. **769**

Berardino, Angelo di
Encyclopedia of the Early Church **700**

Bercuson, D.J. *and* Granatstein, J.L.
The Collins dictionary of Canadian history **7877**

Bere, I. De la
Queen's orders of chivalry **6284**

Berens, D.
A Concise encyclopedia of Zimbabwe **4863**

Beresford, M.W. *and* Finberg, H.P.R.
English medieval boroughs **3304**

Berg, W.G.
Historical dictionary of Malta **7369**

Berger, A.S.
Lives and letters in American parapsychology **182**

Berger, A.S. *and* Berger, J.
The Encyclopedia of parapsychology and psychical research **178**

Berger, B.M. *and* Bendix, R.
Authors of their own lives **1072**

Bergess, W.
Kent maps and plans **7140**

Bergin, T.G. *and* Speake, J.
Encyclopedia of the Renaissance **6787**

Bergman, J.
Jehovah's Witnesses and kindred groups **803**

Berleant-Schiller, R.
Montserrat **4920**

Berleant-Schiller, R. *and* Lowes, S. *and* Benjamin, M.
Antigua and Barbuda **4915**

Berlin **4569**

Berman, D.
A History of atheism in Britain **439**

Berman, I.V.
The Talmud **931**

Bermuda **4928**

Bernal, J.
A History of Mexican archaeology **4334**

Bernard, Y *and* Colli, J.-C.
Dictionnaire économique et financier **1786**
Vocabulaire économique et financier **1787**
Wörterbuch der Wirtschaft und Finanzen.. **1788**

Berndt, J.
Rural sociology **1144**

A Bibliography of Christian worship **644**

A Bibliography of co-operative societies' histories **2005**

Bibliography of comparative adult education **3859**

Bibliography of costume **3955**

'Bibliography of current books on Christianity and politics, Christianity and the social order' **546**

A Bibliography of David Hume, and of Scottish philosophy **27**

A Bibliography of Domesday Book **7053**

Bibliography of education **3746**

A Bibliography of eighteenth century legal literature **2869**

A Bibliography of English history to 1485 **6943**

A Bibliography of English military books up to 1642 **3359**

Bibliography of ephemeral community information materials **3282**

Bibliography of European economic and social history **1851**

A Bibliography of Fiji, Tonga and Rotuma **5043**

A Bibliography of finance **2092**

The Bibliography of flags of foreign nations **6343**

A Bibliography of folklore, as contained in the first eighty years of the publications of the Folklore Society **4122**

A Bibliography of foreign and comparative law **2740**

Bibliography of genealogy and local history periodicals with union list of major US collections **6103**

A Bibliography of general histories of economics, 1692-1975 **1842**

A Bibliography of geographic thought **5059**

Bibliography of Geography **5118**

Bibliography of Goa and the Portuguese in India **7645**

A Bibliography of Greek New Testament manuscripts **523**

Bibliography of Hungarian legal literature, 1945-1980 **2839**

Bibliography of international geography congresses 1871-1976 **5150**

Bibliography of international law **2889**

A Bibliography of Iran **4727**

A Bibliography of Irish ethnology and folk tradition **4148**

Bibliography of Irish family history **6170**

Bibliography of Irish history 1870-1921 **7016**

Bibliography of Irish trials and other legal proceedings **3188**

Bibliography of Islamic Central Asia **4761**

Bibliography of Japanese education/ Bibliographie zum japanischen Erziehungswesen: postwar publications in Western languages **3801**

Bibliography of Jewish bibliographies **896**

A Bibliography of jurisprudence **2878**

A Bibliography of Ladakh **4709**

Bibliography of Latin American folklore **4159**

Bibliography of Libya 1970-1990 **4794**

The Bibliography of marketing research methods **2670**

Bibliography of Mexican American history **7961**

A Bibliography of military name lists **6105**

A Bibliography of modern history **6743**

Bibliography of monuments in the care of the Secretary of State for Scotland **4421**

A Bibliography of Mughal India (1526-1707AD) **7647**

Bibliography of nautical books, 2000 **3532**

Bibliography of Newfoundland **4882**

A Bibliography of Norfolk history **7202**

Bibliography of North African prehistory **4326**

Bibliography of official statistical yearbooks and bulletins **1210**

Bibliography of Ontario history 1867-1976 **7889**

A Bibliography of Parliamentary debates of Great Britain **3041**

Bibliography of periodicals on the quality of life **1893**

A Bibliography of philosophical bibliographies, edited and compiled by H. Guerry **2**

Bibliography of policy related education documents in selected countries in Africa, Asia, the Caribbean and the Pacific **3780**

A Bibliography of pre-Islamic Persia **4237**

'A Bibliography of primary sources for Tanzania 1799-1899' **7819**

A Bibliography of printed items relating to the city of Lincoln **7183**

Bibliography of printed works on London history to 1939 **7118**

A Bibliography of printed works relating to Oxfordshire **7195**

Bibliography of publications issued by Unesco or under its auspices (1946-1971) **2916**

Bibliography of published research of the World Employment Programme **1881**

Bibliography of published work on Irish foreign relations, 1921-78 **1629**

A Bibliography of Quaker literature, 1893-1967 **801**

A Bibliography of regimental histories of the British Army **3510**

A Bibliography of Rotuma **5042**

Bibliography of rural land economy and land ownership, 1900-1957 **1987**

A Bibliography of Salvation Army literature in English (1865-1987) **664**

'A Bibliography of Scottish economic history during the last decade: 1963-1970' **2315**

A Bibliography of Scottish education, 1872-1972 **3791**

A Bibliography of Scottish education before 1872 **3790**

A Bibliography of Shintoism **963**

A Bibliography of Shintoism of the Meiji, Taishô and Showâ eras **962**

A Bibliography of sources in Christianity and the arts **544**

Bibliography of South Asia **4704**

A Bibliography of studies in regional industrial development **2403**

Bibliography of Syrian archaelogical sites to 1980 **4453**

A Bibliography of the Anglo-Egyptian Sudan **4798**

The Bibliography of the Arab Middle East **4766**

Bibliography of the Banks Islands, Western Pacific **8131**

A Bibliography of the British Army, 1660-1914 **3498**

A Bibliography of the Caribbean **4895**

Bibliography of the Chartist movement, 1837-1976 **219**

Bibliography of the Continental Reformation **680**

Bibliography of the county **7240**

A Bibliography of the history of Wales **7232**

A Bibliography of the Inns of Court and Chancery **2797**

Bibliography of the international congresses of philosophy/Bibliographie der internationalen Philosophie Kongress, 1900-1978.. **147**

A Bibliography of the Iran-Irak borderland **4734**

Bibliography of the Line Islands, Central Pacific **8132**

A Bibliography of the Northern Territory **5025**

Bibliography of the Ocean Islands (Banaba), Western Pacific **8187**

Bibliography of the Orange Free State until 31 May 1910 **7830**

Bibliography of The Phoenix Islands **8188**

The Bibliography of the Reform, 1450-1648 **682**

A Bibliography of the Samaritans **3608**

Bibliography of the Santa Cruz Islands, Western Pacific **8146**

Bibliography of the Soviet social sciences, 1965-1975 **1039**

A Bibliography of the Sudan 1938-1958 **4799**

Bibliography of the Tokelau or Union Islands. Central Pacific **8133**

Bibliography of the Torres Islands, Southwest Pacific **8147**

Bibliography of Tristan da Cunha **4872**

A Bibliography of United States-Latin American relations since 1810 **1644**

A Bibliography of Victorian history **8161**

A Bibliography of Welsh hymnology **653**

A Bibliography of works in English on early Russian history to 1800 **7413**

Bibliography of works on Jewish history **6664**

Bibliography of works on John Stuart Mill **41**

'Bibliography on British and Irish legal history (works published after 1985)' **2799**

Bibliography on Holocaust literature **920-921**

Bibliography on international criminal law **3128**

Bibliography on international peacekeeping **2994**

Bibliography on Soviet intelligence and security services **1668, 3254**

Bibliography on urbanization in India, 1947 - 1976 **1142**

Biblioteca heraldica Magnae Britanniae **6236**

Bibliotheca Americana **7954**

Bibliotheca astrologica **193**

Bibliotheca Barbadiensis **7935**

Bibliotheca Cantiana **7141**

Bibliotheca Polynesia **5037**

Bibliotheca Sanctorum **601**

Bibliothèque Nationale Catalogue de la Troisième République 1870-1940 **7352**

Bibliothèque Nationale Catalogue de l'histoire de France **7328**

Biblgrafía de las Islas Malvinas, obras, mapas y documentos **8095**

The Bicentennial dictionary of Western Australians pre 1829-1888 **6202**

Bick, P.A.
Business ethics and responsibility **361**

Bickerman, E.J.
Chronology of the Ancient World **6640**

Bidwell, P.
Hadrian's Wall 1989-1999 **4431**

Bidwell, R.
Arabian personalities of the early twentieth century **5888**
The Two Yemens **7616**

Bidwell, R.L.
Guide to African ministers **3344**

Bienkowski, P. and **Millard, A.**
A Dictionary of the ancient Near East **6642**

Bier, J. A.
Reference map of Oceania: the Pacific islands of Micronesia, Polynesia, Melanesia **5182**

Bierbrier, M. L.
Historical dictionary of ancient Egypt **6654**

Bietenholz, P. and **Deutscher, T.B.**
Contemporaries of Erasmus **6795**

Bigelow, B.C.
Contemporary Black biography **5727**

Biger, E.
The Encyclopedia of international boundaries **5120**

Biggins, A.
Argentina **4977**

Bilancia, P.R.
Dictionary of Chinese law and government: Chinese-English **2852**

Bilboul, R.R. *and* **Kent, F.L.**
Retrospective index to theses of Great Britain and Ireland, 1917-1950 **1005**

Bilingual education **3732**

Bilingual guides to business and professional correspondence **2559**

Binark, L. *and* **Eren, H.**
World bibliography of translations of the meanings of the Holy Qur'an **935**

Bing, A.
Makers of modern Africa **7755**

Binks, G.
Visitors welcome **4365**

Binning, W.C. *and* **Esterly, L.E.** *and* **Stacic, P.A.**
Encyclopedia of American parties, campaigns and elections **1457**

Binns, D.
A Gypsy bibliography **4113**

Binns, M.
Guinea **4818**

Binns, M. *and* **Binns, T.**
Sierra Leone **4815**

Binstock, R.G.
Handbook of aging and the social sciences **1101**

Bio-Base 2000 Master Cumulation **5945**

Biografisch archief van de Benelux/Archives biographiques des Pays du Benelux. Biographical archive of the Benelux countries. Biographisches archiv der Benelux-länder **5736**

Biografisch index van de Benelux/Index biographique des Pays du Bénélux/ Biographical index of the Benelux countries/ Biographische index den Benelux-Länder **5737**

Biographic dictionary of Chinese Communism 1921-1965 **5861**

Biographical and bibliographical dictionary of the Christian Church **638**

Biographical archive of the Classical World/ Biographisches archiv der Antike **6700**

Biographical archive of the Soviet Union (1917-1991) **5823**

Biographical dictionaries and related works **5711**

A Biographical dictionary and analysis of China's Party leadership 1922-1988 **5866**

A Biographical dictionary: historical makers of Hawaii **8193**

Biographical dictionary of American business leaders **2484**

Biographical dictionary of American cults and sect leaders **713**

Biographical dictionary of American educators **3810**

Biographical dictionary of American labor **1986**

A Biographical dictionary of ancient Egypt **6658**

Biographical dictionary of Ancient Greek and Roman women **6702**

The Biographical dictionary of British feminists **4090-4091**

Biographical dictionary of British prime ministers **1424**

Biographical dictionary of British radicals in the seventeenth century **1749**

Biographical dictionary of Chinese women **5868**

A Biographical dictionary of contemporary Afghanistan **5886**

Biographical dictionary of Councilors of the Indies **7920**

A Biographical dictionary of Dark Age Britain **6961**

A Biographical dictionary of eminent Scotsmen **5769**

A Biographical dictionary of French political leaders since 1870 **1437**

Biographical dictionary of geography **5135**

The Biographical dictionary of Greater India **5879**

Biographical dictionary of Japanese history **7610**

Biographical dictionary of Latin American and Caribbean leaders **1741**

Biographical dictionary of Latin American historians and historiography **6436**

Biographical dictionary of Marxism **231**

Biographical dictionary of modern British radicals **1748**

Biographical dictionary of modern peace leaders **3014**

Biographical dictionary of Neo-Marxism **232**

Biographical dictionary of North American and European educationists **3809**

Biographical dictionary of psychology **289**

Biographical dictionary of Republican China **5860**

A Biographical dictionary of Scottish graduates **3942**

Biographical dictionary of social welfare in America **3630**

Biographical dictionary of the American Left **1744**

A Biographical dictionary of the British Colonial Service, 1939-1966 **1581**

A Biographical dictionary of the Byzantine Empire **7679**

Biographical dictionary of the Comintern **3233**

Biographical dictionary of the extreme right since 1890 **1715**

A Biographical dictionary of the former Soviet Union **5819**

Biographical dictionary of the Union **8051**

Biographical dictionary of World War I **6824**

The Biographical dictionary of World War II **6890**

The biographical dictionary of World War II generals and flag officers **3517**

The Biographical dictionary of World War II generals and flag officers: the U.S. Armed Forces **6889**

Biographical directory of the governors of the United States, 1789-1978 **3317**

Biographical directory of the governors of the United States, 1978-1983 **3318**

Biographical directory of the United States Congress, 1774-1989 **1688**

Biographical directory of the United States executive branch, 1774-1989 **3349**

Biographical encyclopedia of Pakistan 1996-97 **5878**

Biographical index of the Classical World **6701**

A Biographical register 1788-1939. Notes from the name index of the Australian Dictionary of Biography **5988**

Biographie nationale **5849**

Biographie nationale du pays de Luxembourg **5791**

Biographisch-Bibliographisches Kirchenlexikon **638**

Biographisches Handbuch der deutschsprachigen Emigration nach 1933/ International biographical dictionary of Central European emigrés, 1933-45 **1570**

Biographisches lexikon zur Weimarer Republik **7268**

Biography and genealogy master index **5943, 5946**

Biography catalogue of the Library **6913**

'Biography', chapter 20, *Australians: a guide to sources* **5998**

Biography database 1680-1830 **5703**

Biography index **5712**

Biography resource center **5707**

Birchenough, C.
History of elementary education in England and Wales, from 1800 to the present day **3794**

Birchfield, M.E.
Consolidated catalog of League of Nations publications **2905**

Bird, C.M. Peniston-
See
Peniston-Bird, C.M.$z100

Bird, K.W.
German naval history **3571**

Birds, J.
Secretarial administration **2019**

Birkett, P.
Checklist of parish registers **6218**

Birley, A.R.
The Fasti of Roman Britain **6960**

Birmingham, D. *and* **Martin, P.M.**
History of Central Africa **7795**

Birren, J.E. *and* **Schaie, K.W.**
Handbook of the psychology of aging **1102**

The Birth of prehistoric chronology **4225**

Birthplaces USA **5928**

Bischoff, B.
Latin palaeography **6613**

Bishop, G.B.
Bibliography of Ontario history 1867-1976 **7889**

Bishop, J.
'Newfoundland family records' **6186**

Bishop, P. *and* **Darton, M.**
The Encyclopedia of world faiths **394**

Bisignani, J.D.
Hawaii handbook. All Islands **5679**
Japan handbook **5563**

Bismarck-Bibliographie **7263**

Bissio, R.
The World guide 1999/1000 **4523**

The Bitter with the sweet: New Brunswick 1604-1984 **7888**

Bizzaro, S.
Historical dictionary of Chile **8100**

Bjersby, M.
'The Swedish National Register of Private Archives' **6541**

Bjorling, J.
The Church of God, Seventh Day **784**

Black Africa **4790**

Black American families, 1965-1984 **1126**

Black, C.
Atlas of the Renaissance **6788**

Black chronology **1133**

Black, C.V.
The History of Jamaica **7926**

The Black family in the United States **1127**

Black, G.F.
A Gypsy bibliography **4114**

The Black handbook **4771**

Black immigration and ethnicity in the United States **1573**

Black ivory **1585**

Black, J.
'Mapping early modern Europe' **6792**
Maps and history **6412**

Black, J. *and* **Porter, R.**
A Dictionary of eighteenth century world history **6443**

Black, J.L.
Origins, evolution, and nature of the Cold War **1655**

Black, M. *and* **Rowley, H.H.**
Peake's commentary on the Bible **512**

Black, R.
Angola **4837**

Black, R.D.C.
A Catalogue of pamphlets on economic subjects published between 1750 and 1900 **1752**

Black, S. *and* Sharpe, M.L.
  Practical public relations 2709
Black slavery in the Americas 1588
Blackburn, S.
  The Oxford dictionary of philosophy 77
Blackey, R.
  Modern revolutions and revolutionists 1522
Blackhurst, H.
  Africa bibliography 4775
Blackstock, P.W. *and* Schaf, F.L.
  Intelligence, espionage, counterespionage, and covert operations 1658
The Blackwell biographical dictionary of British political life in the twentieth century 1714
The Blackwell companion to the Enlightenment 6797
The Blackwell dictionary of cognitive psychology 234
The Blackwell dictionary of Evangelical biography 754
The Blackwell dictionary of historians 6392
The Blackwell dictionary of twentieth-century social thought 1060
The Blackwell encyclopaedia of Anglo-Saxon England 6956
The Blackwell encyclopaedia of political thought 1465
The Blackwell encyclopaedia of the Russian Revolution 7421
The Blackwell encyclopedia of industrial archaeology 4464
The Blackwell encyclopedia of modern Christian thought 553
The Blackwell encyclopedia of political institutions 1464
The Blackwell encyclopedia of the American Revolution 8029
The Blackwell guide to epistemology 347
The Blackwell guide to ethical theory 350
Blackwell, K. *and* Ruja, H.
  A Bibliography of Bertrand Russell 46
Blades, C.A.
  The International bibliography of health economics 3632
Blaiklock, E.M. *and* Harrison, R.K.
  The New international dictionary of Biblical archaeology 456
Blair, K.J.
  The History of American women's voluntary organizations, 1810-1960 3629
Blake, G.
  The Cambridge atlas of the Middle East and North Africa 5279
Blake, G.N. *and* Clark, A.N.
  Chisholm's handbook of commercial geography 2269
Blake, J. *and* Lawrence, P.
  The ABC of management 2608
Blakemore, H.
  Chile 4982
  'The Chilean Revolution of 1891 and its historiography' 8098
  South American economic handbook 2387
Blanchette, J.-F.
  'Une Bibliographie de la culture materielle traditionelle au Canada, 1965-1982/A Bibliography of folk material culture in Canada, 1965-1982' 4158
Blanco, R.L.
  The American Revolution 8028
  The War of the American Revolution 8023
Bland, D.S.
  A Bibliography of the Inns of Court and Chancery 2797
Blandford, L.A. *and* Evans, P.R.
  Supreme Court of the United States, 1789 - 1982 3207
Blank, Grant *and* McCartney, James L. *and* Brent, Edward E.
  New technology in sociology 1078

Blaug, M.
  Economics of education 3736
  Great economists before Keynes 1846
  Great economists since Keynes 1845
  Who's who in economics 1847
Blaustein, A.P.
  Independence documents of the world 2957
Blaustein, A.P. *and* Blaustein, E.B.
  Constitutions of dependencies and special sovereignties 3020
Blaustein, A.P. *and* Flanz, G.H.
  Constitutions of the countries of the world 3019
Blauvelt, E. *and* Durlacher, J.
  Sources of African and Middle Eastern economic information 2353, 2364
  Sources of Asian/Pacific economic information 2344
Blazek, R. *and* Perrault
  United States history a selective guide to information sources 7958
Bleaney, C.H.
  Iraq 4733
  Israel 4738
  Lebanon 4736
Bleeker, C.J. *and* Widengren, G.
  Historia religionum 425
Bleiberg, G.
  Diccionario de historia de España 7379
Bletzer, J.G.
  The Donning international encyclopedic psychic dictionary 174
Bleye, P.A.
  Manual de historia de España 7378
Bibliography of State bibliographies 1970-82 4954
Blishen, E.
  Blond's encyclopedia of education 3751
Bliss, A.M. *and* Rigg, J.A.
  Zambia 4865
Blizzard, A. *and* Baird, P.
  Five ways into Birmingham's past 7174
Bloch, A.P.
  Once a day 6672
Blombach-Schäfer, U.
  The New Europe 5189
Blondel, J.
  Government ministers in the contemporary world 3321
  The Organization of governments 3320
Blondel, J. *and* Walker, C.
  Directory of European political scientists 1409
Blond's encyclopedia of education 3751
Bloody red tabs 6822
Bloomfield, G.T.
  New Zealand 1302
Bloomfield, V.
  Commonwealth elections, 1945-1970 1562
Blouet, B.
  The Story of Malta 7367
Blouin, F.X.
  Vatican archives 6528
Bluche, F.
  Dictionnaire du grand siècle 7339
Blue Guide Wales 5530
Blue guides 5422
Blum, A.A.
  International handbook of industrial relations 1928
Blunden, C. *and* Elvin, M.
  Cultural atlas of China 4658
Boardman, J.
  Oxford history of the classical world 6686
Boas, A.J.
  Crusader archaeology 7546
Boase, F.
  Modern English biography 5779
Boatner, M.M.
  The Biographical dictionary of World War II 6890

Boatner, M.M. *(contd.)*
  Cassell's biographical dictionary of the American Civil War 8052
  Cassell's biographical dictionary of the American War of Independence 1763-1783 8034
  Encyclopedia of the American Revolution 8030
Boban, L.
  Croatian borders 1918-1993 7502
Bobb, F.S.
  Historical dictionary of Democratic Republic of the Congo (Zaire) 7808
Bochénski, I.M.
  Contemporary European philosophy 127
Bodensieck, J.H.
  The Encyclopedia of the Lutheran Church 768
Bodurgil, A.
  Atatürk and Turkey 7681
  Turkey, politics and government 7682
Boehm, E.H.
  Historical periodicals directory 6407
Boehm, K. *and* Lees-Spalding, J.
  The NatWest student book 2001 entry 3935
Boehn, M. von
  Modes and manners from the Middle Ages to the end of the eighteenth century 3971
Boehn, M. von *and* Fischel, O.
  Modes and manners of the nineteenth century 3972
Boff, K.R.
  Handbook of perception and human performance 308
Bogdanor, V.
  The Blackwell encyclopedia of political institutions 1464
Boggs, R.S.
  Bibliography of Latin American folklore 4159
Bogue, D.J.
  The Population of the United States 1351
Bohdan Nahaylo *and* Swoboda, V.
  Soviet disunion 7436
Bohlander, R.E.
  World explorers and discoverers 5075
Boia, L.
  Great historians from antiquity to 1800 6361
  Great historians of the modern age 6362
Boilard, S.D.
  Reinterpreting Russia 4608
Bold, A.
  Scotland's Kings and Queens. 6330
Bolivia 4983, 8101
Bolivia handbook 5648
Bollier, J.A.
  The Literature of theology 570
Bolton, G.
  The Oxford history of Australia 8156
Bolton, J.L.
  The Medieval English economy, 1150-1500 2312
The Bomber Command handbook 6839
The Bomber Command war diaries 6844
Bonapace, V. *and* Laureti, L.
  World geographical encyclopedia 5123
Bond, B.
  The First World War and British military history 6363
Bond, D.
  The Guinness guide to 20th-century fashion 3995
Bond, M.E. *and* Caron, M.M.
  Canadian reference sources 7867
Bond, M.F.
  Guide to the records of Parliament 3057
Bonine, M.E.
  Atlas of Mexico 5336
Bonkowske, J.A.
  The American flag 6353

Bonser, W.
An Anglo-Saxon and Celtic bibliography 6952
A Bibliography of folklore, as contained in the first eighty years of the publications of the Folklore Society 4122
A Prehistoric bibliography 4258
A Romano-British bibliography 6953
The Book of Australia 5031
Book of Biblical quotations 475
The Book of British topography 7071
The Book of Catholic quotations 736
Book of days 6462
The Book of Druidry 954
The Book of festivals 4017
The Book of goddesses and heroines 825
The Book of Jewish books 900
The Book of Kings: a royal genealogy 6316
The Book of London 7122
The Book of New Zealand women 5982
The Book of Orders and decorations 6277
The Book of public arms 6241
The Book of Saints 602
The Book of the States, 1998-99 3316
The Book of the World 5395
Book of world city rankings 3294
Book review index to social science periodicals 1007
Bookman, J.T. and Powers, S.T.
The March to Victory 6833
'Books: a review of ten years of books and articles on Hadrian's Wall' 4387
Books and periodicals on line 2009, 2717
Books on Buddhism 879
Books on Croatia and Croatians 4640
'Books on disability' 3669
Books on palaeography 6624
Boorman, H.L. and Howard, A.C.
Biographical dictionary of Republican China 5860
Booth, A.R.
Historical dictionary of Swaziland 7838
Bootle, R.
Directory of world stock exchanges 2241
Borchardt, C.F.A. and Vorster, W.S.
South African theological bibliography.. 590
Borchardt, D.H. and Francis, R.D.
How to find out in psychology 235
Borchardt, D.H. and Marshall, J.G.
'Biography', chapter 20, *Australians: a guide to sources* 5998
Border and territorial disputes 2947
Borgatta, E.F. and Borgatta, M.L.
Encyclopedia of sociology 1050
Boring, E.G.
A History of experimental psychology 299
Bork, A.W. and Maier, G.
Historical dictionary of Ecuador 8110
Born, K.E.
Bismarck-Bibliographie 7263
Borneo in history 8122
Borsa, I.
'Archives in Japan,' 6548
Borthwick, M.
Pacific century 7522
Bose, A.
Bibliography on urbanization in India, 1947 - 1976 1142
Bosnia. A short history 7504
Bossy, J.
The English Catholic Community, 1570-1850 741
Boston Public Library
Bibliotheca Barbadiensis 7935
Boswell, D. and Beeley, B.
Malta 4595
Boswick, S.
Guide to the universities of Europe 3931
Bosworth, C.E.
The New Islamic dynasties 6336

Botswana 4855
Botterweck, G.J. and Ringgren, H.
Theological dictionary of the Old Testament 520
Theologisches Wörterbuch zum Alten Testament 519
Bottomley, F.
The Church explorer's guide to symbols and their meaning 625
Bottomore, T.
A Dictionary of Marxist thought 220
Boucher, F.
20,000 years of fashion 3959
A History of costume in the West 3973
Boudon, R. and Bourricaud, F.
Dictionnaire critique de sociologie 1065
Bouju, P.M.
Atlas historique de la France contemporaine 7356
Boultbee, P.F.
Turks and Caicos Islands 4914
Boultbee, P.G.
The Bahamas 4912
Cayman Islands 4902
Boultbee, P.G. and Raine, D.F.
Bermuda 4928
Boulton, C.
Erskine May's Treatise on the law, privileges, proceedings and usage of Parliament 3044
Boulton, D'A.J.D.
Knights of the Crown 6262
Bound for Australia 6124
Bourne, S.
Ten London repositories 6181
Bourne, V.I.
History of ethics 356
Boustani, R. and Fargues, F.
The Atlas of the Arab World geopolitics and society 5294
Boutell, C.
Boutell's heraldry 6219
Boutell's heraldry 6219
Bouyer, L.
A History of Christian spirituality 630
Bowden, H.W.
Dictionary of American religious biography 711
Bowden, J.
Who's who in theology 589
Bowder, D.
Who was who in the Greek World 6708
Who was who in the Roman world 6725
Bowen, J.
A History of Western education 3781
Bowersock, G.
Late antiquity 6629
Bowker, J.
The Oxford dictionary of world religions 806
Bowley, R.L.
The Fortunate Islands 7162
Bowman, J.S.
American Civil War day by day 8050
The Cambridge dictionary of American biography 5921
Professional dissent 1523
The World almanac of the American West 7998
Bowman, L.W.
Mauritius 4869
Bowman, M.J. and Harris, D.J.
Multilateral treaties 2958
Bowring, R. and Kornicki, P.
The Cambridge encyclopedia of Japan 4675
Box, B.
Brazil handbook 5643
Boxer, C.R.
The Portuguese seaborne empire 1415-1825 7395

Boyce, M.
A History of Zoroastrianism 893
Zoroastrians 894
Boyd, A.
An Atlas of world affairs 4514
Boyd, K.
Chambers dictionary of world history 6393
Encyclopedia of historians and historical writing 6385
Boylan, H.
Dictionary of Irish biography 5773
This arrogant city 7044
Boyle, L.E.
A Survey of the Vatican archives 6527
The BP book of industrial archaeology 4467
Braby's maps of Southern Africa/Brabyse kaarte van Suidelike Afrika 5316
Bracher, K.D.
Age of ideologies 1407
Brackney, W.H.
The Baptists 778
Historical dictionary of the Baptists 781
BRAD/British rate and data 2699
Bradfield, N.
Costume in detail: women's dress, 1730-1930 4005
Bradley, J.E. and Muller, R.A.
Church history 672
Bradley, S.
Archives biographiques Françaises/French biographical archive 5803
Bradney, J.A.
A History of Monmouthshire 7165
Bradnock, R.
India 2001 5569
Bradnock, R. and Bradnock, R.
Sri Lanka handbook 5577
Bradnock, Robert and Bradnock, Roma
Goa handbook 5570
Indian Himalaya handbook 5571
South India handbook 5572
Bradt, H.
Madagascar 4867
Brady, A.
Women in Ireland 4093
Branch, A.E.
Dictionary of commercial terms 2418
Multilingual dictionary of commercial international trade and shipping terms 2419
Branch, A.E. and Hakmeh, J.A.
Dictionary of English-Arabic commercial, international trade and shipping terms 2421
Branchiard, M.
Dictionnaire économique et social: dictionnaire Thomas Suavet 1001
Brand, A.A. and Kinzie, L.A.
'A Comparison of online access to psychoanalytic literature' 240
Brand, D. and Durousset, M.
Dictionnaire thématique historie géographie 5166
Brand, J.
Brand's popular antiquities of Great Britain 4144
Brandon, S.G.F.
A Dictionary of comparative religion 402
Brandow, J.
Genealogies of Barbados families 6086
Brand's popular antiquities of Great Britain 4144
Brandt, E.R.
Germanic genealogy 6068
Branson, M.L.
The Reader's guide to the best evangelical books 545
Brasil obras de referência 1965-1998 4976
Brassey's armed services careers yearbook, 1987/88 3404
Brassey's battles 3462

British Library of Political and Economic
Science, at the London School of
Economics
International current awareness services/
ICAS 971
British Library. Science Reference and
Information Service
Business information 2047, 2513
Market research: a guide to British Library
holdings 2669
British Malaya 7719
British military uniforms from contemporary
pictures: Henry VII to the present day 3453
British monarchs 6321
British Museum dictionary of Ancient Egypt
6655
British national archives and the local historian
7109
British national directories 1781-1819 7086
British naval dress 3448
British naval history since 1815 3552
The British overseas 6030
British Parliamentary constituencies 3049
British Parliamentary election results, 1983-
1998 1554
British parliamentary lists, 1660-1800 3059
British parliamentary parties, 1742-1832, from
the fall of Walpole to the first Reform Act
1719
The British part in the Korean War 7590
British qualifications: a complete guide to
educational, technical, professional and
academic qualifications in Britain 3915
British rate and data 2699
British regional employment statistics, 1841-
1971 1906
The British secret services 1667
British social trends since 1900 1174
British sources of information: a subject guide
and bibliography 4539
British standard specification for codes for the
representation of names of counties and
similar areas 5489
British standards catalogue, 1993 3269
British Standards Institution
British standards catalogue, 1993 3269
Glossary of production planning and control
terms 2636
Glossary of terms used in metrology 3274
Glossary of terms used in work study and
organizational methods (O & M) 2549
Vocabulary of legal metrology 3273
British tax encyclopaedia 2152
British television advertising 2700
British V.C.s of World War Two 6293
British vessels lost at sea 1914-18 and 1939-45
6799
The British voter 1558
British warship names 3561
British weights and measures 3271
British women in the 20th century 4089
The British year book of international law,
1998 2898
Brittain, H.
The British budgetary system 2141
Brittin, M.
CD-ROM and online statistical databases
1193
Brivati, B.
The Contemporary history handbook 6455
Broadbent, K.A.
A Chinese-English dictionary of China's
rural economy 1823
Broadhead, S.H.
Historical dictionary of Angola 7805
Brock, C.
The Literature of political science 1378
Brockington, R.
A Concise dictionary of accounting and
finance 2575

Brockliss, L.
History of universities 3925
Brockman, N. C.
An African biographical dictionary 5893
Broekman, M.
Complete encyclopaedia of practical
palmistry 201
Bromell, A.
Tracing family history in New Zealand
6198, 6200
Tracing your family outside New Zealand
6199
Bromiley,, G.W
Evangelisches Kirchenlexikon 547
Bromiley, G.W.
The International standard Bible
encyclopedia 450
Theological dictionary of the New Testament
529
Brook, F.
The Industrial archaeology of the British
Isles 1. The West Midlands 4479
Brook, J.H.
Science and Religion 443
Brook, S.
The Oxford book of dreams 310
Brooke, I.
English costume.. 3989
Western European costume ... and its
relation to the theatre 3999
Brooke, J.L.
The Refiner's fire 794
Brooke-Little, J.P.
An Heraldic alphabet 6225
Brooke, M.Z. and Buckley, P.J.
Handbook of international trade 2487
Brooke-Taylor, D.
Guide to stamp duties 2153
Brooks, M.
Sources of free business information 2514
Brooks, M.J.
Sources of free business information 2048
Broster, E.J.
Glossary of applied management and
financial statistics 2112
Broughton, B.B.
Dictionary of medieval knighthood and
chivalry 4035-4036
Broughton, T.R.S.
Magistrates of the Roman Republic 6726
Brown, A.
The Cambridge encyclopedia of Russia and
the former Soviet Union 4611
Encyclopedia of the Ancient World 6634
Brown, A.C.S. and Dinsdale, W.A.
Spanish for insurance officials 3708
Brown, B.E.
Canadian business and economics 2373
Brown, C.
The New international dictionary of New
Testament theology 530
Brown, C.L. and Wheeler, J.O.
A Bibliography of geographic thought 5059
Brown, D.
The English labour movement, 1700-1951
1979
Warship losses of World War Two 6834
Brown, I. and Ampalavanar, R.
Malaysia 4751
Brown, J.S. and Kinnell, S.K.
American family history 6196
Brown, K. and O'Brien, J.
The Essential teachings of Buddhism 872
Brown, K.D.
A Social history of the Nonconformist
Ministry in England and Wales, 1800-
1930 776
Brown, M.
Films and videograms for managers 2624
Brown, M.P.
A Guide to Western historical scripts 6614

Brown, R.
Retirement made easy 1107
Brown, R. and Appleton, R.
Collins milestones in Australian history
8175
Brown, R.H.
Dictionary of marine insurance terms and
clauses 3699
Brown, S. and Collinson, D. and Wilkinson,
R.
Bibliographic dictionary of twentieth-century
philosophers 117
Brown, S.R.
Finding the source in sociology and
anthropology 1044
Brown, Y-Y.
Japanese studies 4669
Browning, W.R.F
A Dictionary of the Bible 457
Brownlie, I.
Basic documents on human rights 3098
Brownlie, I. and Crawford, J.
The British year book of international law,
1998 2898
Brownlie, L. and Burns, I.R.
African boundaries 2950
Brownrigg, R.
Who's who in the New Testament 534
Brownstone, D.M.
The VNR dictionary of business and finance
1799
Brownstone, D.M. and Franck, I.M.
Dictionary of 20th Century history 6758
Bruce, A.
A Bibliography of British military history
3499
Bruce, A.P.C.
A Bibliography of the British Army, 1660-
1914 3498
Bruce, A.P.C. and Cogar, W.B.
An Encyclopedia of naval history 3545
Brugel, L. van and Williams, R.H. and
Wood, B.
The Multilingual dictionary of real estate
1991
Bruhn, W. and Tilke, M.A.
A Pictorial history of costume 3974
Bruijn, R.K. de-
Area bibliography of Japan 4670
Brune, L.H.
Chronological history of United States
foreign relations, 1776-January 20 1981
1651
Brunei 5002
Brunei Darussalem in profile 5001
Brunel: the University of West London
Guide to the records of the Lord
Chancellor's Department 3058
Brunet, L.
Terminology of special education 3882
Brunet, R.
Atlas de la Russie 5248
Brunkow, R. de V.
Religion and society in North America 678
Bruno, F.J.
Dictionary of key words in psychology 272
The Family encyclopedia of child
psychology 300
Brunvand, J.H.
American folklore 4161
Bryan, C.D.B.
The National Geographic Society 5149
Buble, M.J.
Encyclopedia of the American Left 1742
Bubner, R.
Modern German philosophy 129
Buckland, C.E.
Dictionary of Indian biography 5873
Budapest 4582
Buddhism 878
A Buddhist Bible 875

The Buddhist directory 883
Buddhist Society
  The Buddhist directory 883
Buell, V.P.
  Handbook of modern marketing 2651
Buenker, J.D.
  Urban history 3308
Buenker, J.D. *and* Burckel, N.C.
  Immigration and ethnicity 1571
Buenker, J.D. *and* Kantowicz, E.R.
  Historical dictionary of the Progressive Era 8062
Bügd Nairamdakh Mongol Ard Uls ündesnii atlas 5274
Building a Judaica library collection 901
The Building societies facts file 2219
Building societies year book 2218
Buisseret, D.
  From sea charts to satellite images 7859
Bulfinch, T.
  Myths of Greece and Rome 843
Bulgaria 4641
Bulgaria. Natsionalen Statisticheski Institut
  Statisticheski godishnik = Statistical yearbook: Bulgaria 1260
Bull, M.J.
  Contemporary Italy 4590
Bullen, R. *and* Pelly, M.E.
  Documents on British policy overseas 1625
Bulletin .. 555
Bulletin analytique de documentation politique, économique et sociales contemporaines 1008
Bulletin bibliographique des études arthuriennes 4170
Bulletin of labour statistics 1900
Bulletin of the International Bureau of Education 3738
Bullinger, E.W.
  A Critical lexicon and concordance to the English and Greek New Testament 535
Bullock, A.
  The new Fontana dictionary of modern thought 85
Bullock, A. *and* Woodings, R.B.
  The Fontana biographical companion to modern thought 118
Bullolph, A.
  The Fashion book 3952
Bunch, A.
  Community information 3602
Bunch, A.J.
  Community information services 3603
  Sources of community information 3615
The Bundesbank 2213
Bunn, J.M. *and* Roberts, A.D.S.
  A Union list of Japanese local histories in British libraries 7601
Bunson, M.
  Encyclopedia of the Roman Empire 6718
Bunson, M.E.
  Encyclopedia of the Middle Ages 6775
Bunson, S.
  Encyclopedia of Mesoamerica 6737
Buranelli, V. *and* Buranelli, N.
  Spy/counterspy 1662
Burbridge, J.L.
  IFIP glossary of terms used in production control 2637
Burdett, A.
  Colonial related archive and manuscript collections in the UK 6515
Burdett, A.L.P.
  The Historical boundaries between Bosnia, Croatia, Serbia 7488
Burek, D.M.
  American wholesalers and distributors directory 2675
Burg, D.F. *and* Purcell, L.E.
  Almanac of World War 1 6818

Burger, R.H. *and* Sullivan, H.F.
  Eastern Europe 7417
Burgess, J.
  The Chronology of Indian history 7655
Burgess, N.
  How to find out about banking and investment 2191
Burgess, R.G.
  'Studying schooling' 3846
Burgess, S.M.
  Dictionary of Pentecostal and charismatic movements 702
Burial places
  Who's buried where in England 5513
Burke, J.
  The Dictionary of English law 2825
Burke, Sir J.B.
  A Genealogical history of the dormant, abeyant, forfeited, and extinct peerages of the British Empire 6273
  The General armory of England, Scotland, Ireland and Wales 6234
Burkert, W.
  Greek religion in the archaic and classical periods 847
Burke's American families with British ancestry 6189
Burke's family index 6267
Burke's genealogical and heraldic history of the landed gentry 6270
Burke's guide to the Royal Family 6322
Burke's Irish family records 6163
Burke's peerage and baronetage 6268
Burke's royal families of the world 6308
Burkett, R.K.
  The African-American biographical database 5956
Burkholder, M.A.
  Biographical dictionary of Councilors of the Indies 7920
Burki, S.J.
  Historical dictionary of Pakistan 7669
Burkina Faso 4810-4811
Burl, A.
  Great stone circles 4379
  A Guide to the stone circles of Britain, Ireland and Brittany 4377
  The Stone circles of the British Isles 4378
Burleigh, J.H.S.
  A Church history of Scotland 705
Burma 4747
Burness, L.R.
  A Scottish historian's glossary 7005
Burnett, C. *and* Dennis, M.
  Scotland's heraldic heritage 6242
Burnett, J.
  The Autobiography of the working class 1903
  A Social history of housing, 1815-1985 3262
Burns, E.
  Religious periodicals 411
Burns, E.B.
  A History of Brazil 8083
Burns, J.H.
  The Cambridge history of medieval political thought, c.350-1450 1479
  The Cambridge history of political thought, 1450-1700 1480
Burns, P.
  Butler's lives of the saints 604
Burns, R.
  Monuments of Syria 4452
Burns, R.D.
  Arms control and disarmament 2992
  Encyclopedia of arms control and disarmament 2999
  Guide to American foreign relations since 1700 1652

Burns, R.D. *and* Leitenberg, M.
  The Wars in Vietnam, Cambodia and Laos, 1945-1982 7731
Burns, T.S.
  A History of the Ostrogoths 6681
Burnstein, S.
  Directory of archives in Australia 6609
Buros, O.K.
  Personality tests and reviews.. 304
Burrington, F.A. How to find out about the social sciences 985
Burrowes, R.D.
  Historical dictionary of Yemen 7617
Burrows, E.G. *and* Wallace, M.
  Gotham 8069
Burston, D.
  An A-Z of careers and jobs 1953
Burton, A.
  The Bukharans 7710
  The National Trust guide to our industrial past 4469
Burton, W.C.
  Burton's legal thesaurus 2756
Burton's legal thesaurus 2756
Burundi 4842
Buse, D.K. *and* Doerr, J.C.
  Modern Germany 7258
Business acronyms 2008, 2506
Business and company databases, 1988 2046
Business and economics books, 1876-1983 2515
Business and economics books and serials in print, 1981 2516
Business briefing 2308
Business Chinese dictionary 2033
Business documents 2443
Business equipment digest 2555
Business ethics 358
Business ethics and responsibility 361
Business French dictionary 2030
Business German dictionary 2029
Business histories and biographies 2441
'Business history and biography' 2461
Business history of the world 2537
Business index 2012
Business information 1766, 2047, 2513, 2520
Business information alert 2013
'Business information needs in Scotland' 2055
Business information review 2535
Business information sources 1756, 2517
'Business information sources in Asia' 2058
Business law 3167
Business law terms 3159
Business-line finance 2089
Business master biography index 2483
Business organizations, agencies, and publications directory 2480
Business organizations, agencies and publications directory 2543
Business periodicals index 1753, 2533
Business publications index and abstracts 2534, 2616
Business serials of the US government 2063
Business statistics of the United States 2540
The Business who's who of Australia, 1983 2485
Bustros, G.
  Who's who in Lebanon 1999-2000 5883
Bustros, G.M.
  Who's who in the Arab World 1999-2000 5889
Butcher, T.
  'Public administration and policy studies' 3213
Bute, E.L. *and* Harmer, H.J.P.
  The Black handbook 4771
Butler, A.
  Butler's lives of the saints 604, 606
  Collins dictionary of dates 6464
  The Lives of the saints 605
  A New Guinea bibliography 4998

Butler, D. *and* Butler, G.
Twentieth-century British political facts, 1900-2000 **1426**

Butler, D. *and* Kavanagh, D.
The British general election 1997 **1556**

Butler, D. *and* Low, D.A.
Sovereigns and surrogates **6900**

Butler, D. *and* Trott, N.
British general elections since 1945 **1557**

Butler, P.
The Economist pocket Europe **1216**

Butler, W.E.
Russian law **2847**

Butler, W.E. *and* Nathanson, A.T.
Mongolian-English-Russian dictionary of legal terms and concepts **2747**

Butler's lives of patron saints **608**

Butler's lives of the saints **604, 606-607**

Butt, R.
A History of Parliament. V.1: The Middle ages **3050**

Butterworths company law handbook, 1993 **3168**

Butterworth's Editorial staff
Is it in force? 1993 **2802**

Butterworths law directory **3196**

Butterworth's Legal Editorial staff
Halsbury's Statutory Instruments **2821**

Butterworth's legal services directory, 1999 **2795**

Butterworth's orange tax handbook, 1993-94... inheritance tax, National Insurance contributions, stamp duties, value added tax **2155**

Butterworth's security dictionary **3251**

Butterworth's stamp duties guide **2157**

Butterworth's UK tax guide, 1993-94 **2159**

Butterworth's yellow tax handbook, 1993-94 **2154**

Buying a business **2504**

By appointment **2463**

Bybee, H.C. *and* L'Heureux, C.
Bibliography of Syrian archaelogical sites to 1980 **4453**

Byers, P.K.
Encyclopedia of world biography **5692**

Bynagle, H.E.
Philosophy **4**

Byrde, P.
Nineteenth century fashion **3994**

Byrne, P. *and* Houlden, L.
Companion encyclopedia of theology **574**

Byrne, P.R.
Women in American history **4102**

Byrne, P.R. *and* Ontiveros, S.R.
Women in the Third World **4084**

Cabinet government **3334**

Cabinet Office
The Civil Service year book, 1993 **3241**

Cabinet Office, Management and Personnel Office *and* Civil Service College
Plain figures **1305**

The Cabinet Office, to 1945 **3333**

Cahill, R.A.
Disasters at sea **5108**

Caiden, E.G.
American public administration **3224**

Cairney, C.T.
Clans and families of Ireland and Scotland **6990**

Calasibetta, C.M.
Fairchild's dictionary of fashion **4010**

Calder, J.D.
Intelligence, espionage and related topics **1659**

Calderini, S.
Mauretania **4807**

Caldwell, R.J.
The Era of Napoleon **7353**
The Era of the French Revolution **7342**

Calédonians **5983**

Calendars of charters and rolls in the manuscript collections of the British Library **6490**

California University. Institute of Governmental Studies Library
Subject catalog.. **3214**

Callan, G.O.
Dictionary of fashion and fashion designers **4009**

Callow, P.
Shaw's local government directory, 2000/2001 **3285**

Calvert, P.
Political and economic encyclopedia of South America and the Caribbean **1462**

Calvocoressi, P.
Who's who in the Bible **489**
World politics since 1945 **1413**

Cambodia **4756**

Cambodia handbook **5589**

The Cambridge ancient history **6630**

The Cambridge armorial **6235**

The Cambridge atlas of the Middle East and North Africa **5279**

The Cambridge Bible commentary on the New English Bible **513**

The Cambridge biographical encyclopedia **5685**

The Cambridge companion to Aquinas **207**

The Cambridge companion to Aristotle **70**

The Cambridge companion to Descartes **21**

The Cambridge companion to Freud **23**

The Cambridge companion to Kant **28**

The Cambridge companion to Marx **40**

The Cambridge companion to Sartre **50**

The Cambridge dictionary of American biography **5921**

The Cambridge dictionary of Australian places **5664**

The Cambridge dictionary of philosophy **76**

The Cambridge economic history of Europe **2273**

The Cambridge economic history of India **2358**

Cambridge-Eichborn German dictionary **1812**

The Cambridge encyclopedia of Africa **4784**

The Cambridge encyclopedia of archaeology **4212**

The Cambridge encyclopedia of Australia **5030**

The Cambridge encyclopedia of China **4652**

The Cambridge encyclopedia of India, Pakistan, Bangladesh, Sri Lanka, Nepal, Bhutan and the Maldives **4706**

The Cambridge encyclopedia of Japan **4675**

The Cambridge encyclopedia of Latin America and the Caribbean **4896**

The Cambridge encyclopedia of Russia and the former Soviet Union **4611**

The Cambridge encyclopedia of the Middle East and North Africa **4688**

The Cambridge gazetteer of the United States and Canada **5615**

The Cambridge guide to the historic places of Britain and Ireland **5470**

The Cambridge handbook of contemporary China **4656**

The Cambridge historical encyclopedia of Great Britain and Ireland **6927**

The Cambridge history of Africa **7743**

The Cambridge history of ancient China **6643**

The Cambridge history of British foreign policy, 1783-1919 **1623**

The Cambridge history of China **7556**

The Cambridge history of early Inner Asia **7515**

The Cambridge history of Egypt **7761**

The Cambridge history of Greek and Roman political thought **1476**

The Cambridge history of India **7637**

The Cambridge history of Iran **7671**

The Cambridge history of Islam **7523**

The Cambridge history of Japan **7599**

The Cambridge history of later Greek and early medieval philosophy **107**

The Cambridge history of later medieval philosophy **110**

The Cambridge history of Latin America **7940**

The Cambridge history of Latin America v.11. Bibliographical Essays **7944**

The Cambridge history of medieval political thought, *c.*350-1450 **1479**

The Cambridge history of modern France **7323**

The Cambridge history of Poland **7309**

The Cambridge history of political thought, 1450-1700 **1480**

The Cambridge history of renaissance philosophy **114**

The Cambridge history of Southeast Asia **7550**

The Cambridge history of the Bible **488**

The Cambridge history of the British Empire **6901**

The Cambridge history of the native peoples of the Americas **7855**

The Cambridge history of the Pacific Islanders **8127**

The Cambridge illustrated dictionary of British heritage **4543**

The Cambridge illustrated history of the Islamic World **7530**

The Cambridge Institute of Criminology: its background and scope **3146**

Cambridge Market Intelligence
Directory of European business **2449**

The Cambridge social history of Britain, 1750-1950 **1168**

Cambridge University. Institute of Criminology
Mafia **3158**

Cambridge University. Squire Law Library
Catalogue of international law **2887**
The Squire Law Library: law catalogue **2723**

Cameron, N.
An Illustrated history of Hong Kong **7576**

Cameron, R.
A Concise economic history of the world **1840**
Dictionary of Scottish church history and theology **676**

Cameron, S.
Caribbean Islands handbook 2001 **5609**
Cuba handbook **5611**
Dominican Republic handbook **5613**

Cameroon **4832-4833**

Camm, J.C.R. *and* McQuilton, J.
Australians: a historical atlas **8172**

Camp, A.J.
My ancestor was a migrant **6055**

Camp, R.A.
Mexican political biographies 1935-1993 **1683**
Who's who in Mexico today **5914**

Campbell, A.V.
A Dictionary of pastoral care **616**

Campbell, B.L. *and* Reynolds, R.
Marine badges and insignia of the world **3434**

Campbell, I.C.
A History of the Pacific Islands **8126**

Campbell-Kease, J.
A Companion to local history research **7081**

Campbell, M.J.
Manual of business library practice 2014, **2541**

Campbell, R.J.
The Routledge compendium of primary education **3855**

Canada **4876, 5604**

Canada: a portrait **4874**

The Cassell dictionary of the Napoleonic wars **3474**

Cassell English-Japanese business dictionary **2527**

Cassell historical atlases **6416**

Cassell's biographical dictionary of the American Civil War **8052**

Cassell's biographical dictionary of the American War of Independence 1763-1783 **8034**

Cassell's gazetteer of Britain and Ireland CD-ROM **7091**

Cassels, A.
Italian foreign policy, 1918-1945 **1635**

Castagno, A.J.
Book of Biblical quotations **475**

Castagno, M.
Historical dictionary of Somalia **7817**

Castle, T.
The Hodder book of Christian quotations **557**

Castle, T.C.
The New book of Christian quotations **558**

Castleden, R.
Harrap's book of British dates **6935**
Neolithic Britain **4381**

Castleman, D.
Navada handbook **5617**

A Catalog of files and microfilm of the German Foreign Ministry archives, 1920-1945 **1633**

Catalog of folklore, folklife and folk songs **4124**

Catalog of the Foreign Relations Library **1592**

Catalog of the Police Library **3242**

A Catalogue of British family histories **6144**

Catalogue of cartographic materials in the British Library 1975-1988 **5173**

Catalogue of Dr. Williams's Library **372**

Catalogue of European printed books, India Office Library **4712**

A Catalogue of Glamorgan estate maps **7244**

Catalogue of international law **2887**

Catalogue of library holdings **3670**

Catalogue of manuscripts of Australasia and the Pacific in the Mitchell Library Sydney **6605**

A Catalogue of pamphlets on economic subjects published between 1750 and 1900 **1752**

Catalogue of printed maps, charts and plans **5173**

Catalogue of publication **2276**

Catalogue of publications in print, 1994-95 **1883**

Catalogue of records, Scottish Industrial Archaeology Survey 1977-85 **4470**

A Catalogue of some labour records in Scotland and some Scots records outside Scotland **1914**

Catalogue of statistical materials of developing countries **1214**

A Catalogue of Sussex maps **7146**

Catalogue of the Colonial Office Library, London **1578**

Catalogue of the Foreign Office Library, 1926-1968 **1595**

Catalogue of the Goldsmiths' Library of economic literature **1767**

A Catalogue of the gypsy books collected by the late Robert Andrew Scott Macfie **4115**

Catalogue of the Howard League for Penal Reform **3149**

Catalogue of the Library **2736**

Catalogue of the library **5060**

Catalogue of the Library of the Society for Psychical Research **157**

Catalogue of the Library. Volume 3: Atlases and cartography **5177**

Catalogue of the Public Archives/Catalogue de la Bibliothèque des Archives Publiques **6578**

Catalogue of the Romany Collection **4117**

Catalogue of the Tavistock Joint Library **251**

The Catalogues of the Library of the Institute of Commonwealth Studies, University of London **4559**

Catastrophes and disasters **5107**

Catchpole, B. and Akinjogbin, I.A.
A History of West Africa in maps and diagrams **7775**

Catechism of the Catholic Church **720**

Cathedral libraries catalogue **767**

Catholic almanac, 1971- **721**

The Catholic directory for Scotland **742**

The Catholic directory of England and Wales **745**

Catholic education **3854**

The Catholic encyclopedia **730**

The Catholic fact book **722**

Catholic periodical and literature index **723**

Catholic religious orders **685**

Catholic University of America, editorial staff
New Catholic encyclopedia **729**

Catt, H.
'Diverse routes to electoral comprehension' **1544**

Catterall, P.
British history 1945-1987 **6987**
'The Empire, the Commonwealth and the Mandated Territories' **6907**

Causes of death **1357**

Cavalier, R.
Ethics in the history of Western philosophy **96**

Cavendish, R.
AA roadbook of Britain **5459**
Encyclopedia of the unexplained **158**
Man, myth and magic **159**

Cayman Islands **4902**

Cayman Islands yearbook and business directory 1990 **4903**

CD-Atlas de France **5237**

CD-ROM and online statistical databases **1193**

CD-ROM Encyclopedia of Japan **4677**

CD-ROM index
The National inventory of documentary sources in the United Kingdom and Ireland **6505**

CD-ROM Index to NIDS **6601**

Celtic folklore: Welsh and Manx **4152**

Census, 1991 **1333**

Census 1991 **1334**

Census data and analysis **1330**

Census of population, Northern Ireland, 1971 **1336**

Census of population of Ireland, 1991 **1342**

Census returns on microfilm. Directory to local holdings, 1841-1881 **1343**

A Census user's handbook **1316**

A Centenary guide to the publications of the Seldon Society **2798**

A Centenary history of Nottingham **7177**

The Center: a guide to genealogical research in the National Capital Area **6109**

Center for Southern Folklore Staff
American folklore films and video tapes **4165**

Center of Military History, United States Army
A Guide to the study and use of military history **3391**

The Central African Republic **4838**

Central African Republic **4839**

Central America & Mexico handbook 2001 **5606**

Central American economic handbook **2372**

Central and Equatorial Africa area bibliography **4778**

Central Council for Education and Training in Social Work
Glossary of abbreviations **3605**

Central European economic history from Waterloo to OPEC, 1815-1975 **1852**

Central Intelligence Agency
The World factbook 1998 **4492**

The Central Pacific campaign **6856**

Central Register and Clearing Houses Ltd.
NATFHE handbook of initial teacher training, 1996 **3902**

'The Central Register of Private Archives (CRPA) and the policy in the Netherlands regarding private archives' **6542**

Central Statistical Office
Annual abstract of statistics, 1999 **1228**
Economic trends **2306**
Financial statistics **2127**
Guide to the classification for overseas trade statistics **2427**
Monthly digest of statistics **1229**
Regional trends 30 **1230**

Centre de Terminologie de Bruxelles
Elsevier's dictionary of office automation in four languages **2553**

Centre for European Policy Studies
Annual review of European Community affairs, 1992 **2919**

Centre for Policy on Aging
CPA world directory of old age **1108**

Centre National De La Recherche Scientifique. Institut D'Histoire Moderne Et Contemporaine
Bibliographie annuelle de l'histoire de France **7326**

Centro di Studi Filosofici di Gallarate
Enciclopedia filosofica **62**

Centuries of darkness **6641**

A Century of diplomatic blue books, 1814-1914 **1620**

A Century of diplomatic blue books, 1914-1936 **1621**

A Century of serial publications in psychology, 1850-1950 **283**

Certoma, G.L.
The Italian legal system **2844**

Česky biografický archiv a Slovenský biografický archiv/Tschechisches und Slowakisches biographisches archiv/Czech and Slovakian biographical archive **5795**

Český biografický index a Slovenský biografický/Czech and Slovakian biographical index **5796**

Cevallos, E.E.
Puerto Rico **4909**

C.G. Jung and analytical psychology **323**

Chad **4840**

Chadwick, H.
Atlas of the Christian church **674**

Chadwick, H. and Chadwick, O.
Oxford history of the Christian Church **669**

Chadwick, O.
The Pelican history of the Church **667**

Chadwick, R.
Encyclopedia of applied ethics **353**

Chafetz, J. S.
Handbook of the sociology of gender **1079**

Chahin, M.
The Kingdom of Armenia **7433**

Chakrabarti, D.K.
Ancient Bangladesh **4317**

Chaliand, G. and Rageau, J-P.
A Strategic atlas **3484**

Challis, C.E.
A New history of the Royal Mint **2229**

Chaloner, W.H. and Richardson, R.C.
Bibliography of British economic and social history **2311**

Chamberlain, H.
Service lives remembered **6301**

Chamberlin, W.
Industrial relations in Germany, 1914-1939 **1940**

Chambers, B.
  Printed maps and town plans of Bedfordshire
    7193
Chambers biographical dictionary 5686
Chambers biographical dictionary of women
    5729
Chambers biographies on CD-ROM 5686
Chambers book of business quotations 2041
The Chambers book of business quotations
    2536
Chambers dictionary of beliefs and religions
    404
Chambers dictionary of world history 6393
Chambers, F.
  France 4585
  Guyana 4988
  Haiti 4906
  Paris 4586
  Trinidad and Tobago 4926
Chambers Scottish biographical dictionary
    5770
Chambers Scottish guides 5492
Chambers World gazetteer 5423
Chambliss, J.J.
  Philosophy of education 3752
Champagne, D.
  Chronology of Native North American
    history 8015
Champion, A.G. and Townsend, A.R.
  Contemporary Britain 5139
Champion, T.
  Prehistoric Europe 4242
Chan, V.
  Tibet handbook 5560
Chan, W.-T.
  An Outline and an annotated bibliography of
    Chinese philosophy 136
Chand, A.
  Tibet past and present 7583
Chandler, D. and Collins, J.L.
  The D-Day encyclopedia 6866
Chandler, D.G.
  Atlas of military strategy 3495
  Battles and battlescenes of World War Two
    3464
  Dictionary of the Napoleonic wars 3472
Chandler, D.P.
  A History of Cambodia 7724
  The Tragedy of Cambodian history 7725
Chandler, J.
  Printed maps of Wiltshire 1787-1844 7150
Chandler, K.
  Morris dancing 4150
  "Ribbons, bells and squeaking fiddles"
    4151
Chandler, M.J.
  A Guide to records in Barbados 6588
Chandler, P.
  An A-Z of employment law 1912
Chandler, R.
  Constitutional law dictionary 3017
Chandler, T.
  Four thousand years of urban growth 3297
Chang, Kwang-Chih
  The Archaeology of ancient China 4304
Chang Ying
  The Republic of China yearbook 1996 4684
The Channel Islands 4566
The Channel Islands an archaeological guide
    4287
Channon, J. and Hudson, R.
  The Penguin historical atlas of Russia 7429
Chant, C.
  The Encyclopedia of code names of World
    War II 6867
  Handbook of British regiments 3402
Chapin, J.
  The Book of Catholic quotations 736
Chapman, K.
  Investment statistics locator 2254

Chapman, M. and Wykes, C.
  Plain figures 1305
Chapman, M.B.
  Guide to the social services, 2000/2001
    3618
Chapman, M.D.
  Charities digest, 1991 3597
The Charities Acts handbook 3598
Charities and broadcasting 3594
Charities digest, 1991 3597
Charles, N. and James, J.
  The Rights of women 4083
Charles, R.H.
  The Apocrypha and Pseudepigrapha of the
    Old Testament in English ... 541
Charles Szladits' guide 2835
Charlesworth, J.H.
  The New Testament Apocrypha and
    Pseudepigrapha 542
  The Pseudepigraphia and modern research,
    with a supplement 543
Charlick, R.B.
  Niger 4812
Charny, I.W.
  Genocide 3134
Chartered Institute of Public Finance &
    Accountancy
  Glossary of audit terms 2594
Chartered Insurance Institute. Library
  Insurance reading list 3693
A Chartist's library 218
Chatfield, M. and Vandermeersch, R.
  The History of accounting 2573
Chaudesaigues-Deysine, A.E. and Dreuilhe,
    A.E.
  Dictionnaire anglais-français et lexique
    français-anglais des termes politiques,
    juridiques et économiques 1393
Checklist of parish registers 6218
Cheetham, N.
  Medieval Greece 7484
Chen Chen-siang
  An Historical and cultural atlas of China
    7569
Chen, V.
  The Economic conditions of East and
    Southeast Asia 2345
Cheney, C.R. and Jones, M.
  Handbook of dates for students of English
    history 6937
Cheng, J.
  A Chronology of the People's Republic of
    China 1949-1984 7570
Cheng, P.P.
  Chronology of the People's Republic of
    China 1970-1979 7571
Chesshyre, D.H.B. and Woodcock, T.
  Dictionary of British Arms 6239
Chesshyre, H. and Ailes, A.
  Heralds of today 6250
Chevrons 3459
Chew, E.T. and Lee, E.
  A History of Singapore 7721
Chichester, D. and Tobler, J.
  Christianity in South Africa 568
Chichester, H.M. and Burges-Short, G.
  The Records and badges of every regiment
    and corps in the British Army 3444
Chicorel index to abstracting and indexing
    services 973
The Chief sources of English legal history
    2831
Chilcote, R.H.
  The Portuguese revolution of 25 April 1974
    7405
Child development abstracts and bibliography
    301
Child, H. and Colles, D.
  Christian symbols, ancient and modern 622
Child labor 1899

Child psychology: behavior and development
    302
Child welfare training and practice 3684
Childhood information resources 3686
Children's costume in England, 1300-1900
    4011
Children's games in street and playground
    4187
Chile 4982
Chile handbook 5647
'The Chilean Revolution of 1891 and its
    historiography' 8098
China 4650
China: a provincial atlas 5270
China directory 1996 4657
China economic handbook 2350
China: facts and figures annual, 1999 1264
China. Financial & Economic Publishing
    House
  New China's population 1347
China off the beaten track 5558
China: politics and government 3341
China. State Statistical Bureau
  Statistical yearbook of China 1265
China statistical abstract, 1990 1266
China tax guide 2161
China urban statistics 1141
China's social statistics, 1986 1021
Chinese biographical databases 5863
Chinese biographical index 5865
The Chinese Communist movement, 1937-
    1949 1734
Chinese education and society 3799
A Chinese-English dictionary of China's rural
    economy 1823
A Chinese-English dictionary of Communist
    Chinese terminology 227
Chinese folk narratives 4154
Chinese genealogies at the Genealogical
    Society of Utah 6079
Chinese history 7562
Chinese law in English 2851
Chinese mythology 838
Chinese Sociology 1075
Chinese studies 4649
Chinesisches biographisches archiv/Chinese
    biographical archive 5864
Chirovsky, N.L.
  An Introduction to Ukrainian history 7446
Chisholm's handbook of commercial
    geography 2269
Chloros, A.G.
  Bibliographical guide to the law of the
    United Kingdom, the Channel Islands and
    the Isle of Man 2792
'Choosing a business database: the expert
    approach.' 2510
Chopra, P.M.
  Religions and communities of India 871
Chopra, P.N.
  The Gazetteer of India 4717
Chorley, W.R.
  Royal Air Force Bomber Commands losses
    or the Second World War 6835
Chorzempa, R.A.
  In search of Polish roots 6077
Choueiri, Y.M.
  Arab history and the nation state 6434
Christensen, D.E.
  Contemporary German philosophy, v.1-6,
    1982-87 130
Christian, D.
  A History of Russia, Central Asia and
    Mongolia 7704
Christian England 639
Christian periodical index 752
Christian pilgrimage in modern Western
    Europe 552
Christian symbols, ancient and modern 622
The Christian tradition 587
The Christian year 597

Christianity in a revolutionary age 559
Christianity in South Africa 568
Christianity in tropical Africa 567
Christienne, C.
French military aviation 3529
Christofory, C. and Thomas, E.
Luxembourg 4572
The Christopher Columbus encyclopedia 7852
Christophers, A.
An Index to nineteenth-century British educational biography 3797
Chronicle and memorials of Great Britain and Ireland
Rerum Britannicarum medii aevi scriptores 6922
Chronicle of Australia 8151
Chronicle of Canada 7863
Chronicle of parliamentary elections and development; 1 July 1986/30 June 1987 1547
Chronicle of progress 7621
Chronicle of the First World War 6819
Chronicle of the Roman Emperors 6715
Chronicle of the Royal Family 6323
Chronicle of the Second World War 6883
A Chronicle of Welsh events 7230
The Chronicle of Western fashion 3987
Chronicles of the Russian Tsars 6334
Chronological atlas of World War II 6880
Chronological dictionary of quotations 6410
Chronological history of United States foreign relations, 1776-January 20 1981 1651
Chronological list of Antarctic expeditions 8204
Chronological table of the Statutes, covering the legislation from 1235 to the end of 1990 2800
Chronological tables of Chinese history 7572
Chronologie du Québec 7896
Chronologies in New World archaeology 4330
'Chronologique de Wallis et Futuna' 8148
A Chronology and fact book of the United Nations, 1941-1991 2912
Chronology and index of the Second World War 1938-1945 6884
Chronology of 20th-century Eastern European history 7255
Chronology of Afrian history 7753
Chronology of African American history 8006
'The Chronology of colonization in New Zealand' 4341
A Chronology of conflict and revolution, 1945-1985 1519
Chronology of European history 15,000 BC to 1987 6767
Chronology of Hispanic-American history 7999
The Chronology of Indian history 7655
A Chronology of Irish history since 1500 7028
A Chronology of Irish history to 1976 7026
A Chronology of Islamic history, 570-1000 C.E 946
'Chronology of main events in Northern Ireland since 1969' 7041
Chronology of Native North American history 8015
A Chronology of post war British politics 1430
Chronology of the 20th century 6482
Chronology of the Ancient World 6640
Chronology of the Modern world 6463
Chronology of the modern world 1901-1998 6756
A Chronology of the People's Republic of China 1949-1984 7570
Chronology of the People's Republic of China 1970-1979 7571
Chronology of the war at sea 1939-1945 6887
Chronology of women worldwide 6483
Chronology of women's history 5732
Chronology of world history 6463, 6466

Chronology of world history CD-ROM 6481
Chua Sui Gim
'Guide to modern archives and manuscripts found in the UK relating to Brunei, Sabah and Sarawak,' 6606
Church court records 6139
The Church explorer's guide to symbols and their meaning 625
Church history 672
A Church history of Scotland 705
The Church of England year book, 1997 751
The Church of God, Seventh Day 784
The Church of Scotland year-book 771
Church vestments 648
Cinderellas of the empire 8190
Cipolla, C.M.
The Fontana economic history of Europe 2295
CIS/Index 3085
Cities of the United States 4953
Cities of the world 4503
City & State directories in print 8077
City directories of the United States 6193
The City directory, 1992 2129
City map library 5325
City profiles USA 1997 5618
City University. Business School
Working paper series, 1977- 2271
Civic and corporate heraldry 6237
Civic ceremonial 4032
Civil court practice 3200
The Civil Engineering Heritage Series 4474
Civil liberty 3112
The Civil Service today 3238
The Civil Service year book, 1993 3241
Civil War books 8043
The Civil War in books 8041
The Civil War in the North 8042
Civil War mansucripts 8056
Civil War maps 8048
Civilization of the Ancient Mediterranean. Greece and Rome 6688
Civilizations of the ancient Near East 7540
The Clan Almanac 6155
Clans and families of Ireland 6165
Clans and families of Ireland and Scotland 6990
The Clans and tartans of Scotland CD-ROM 6157
The Clans, septs and regiments of the Scottish Highlands 6160
Clapham, J.
The Bank of England 2214
Clapp, B.W.
Documents in English economic history: England from 1000 to 1760 2320
Documents in English economic history: England since 1760 2321
Claridge, A.
Rome 4373
Clarie, T.C.
Occult/paranormal bibliography 155
Clark, A.F. and Phillips, L.C.
Historical dictionary of Senegal 7781
Clark, C.M.H.
A History of Australia 8152
Clark, I.F.
Tale of the future 215
Clark, J.
Dictionary of insurance and finance terms 3700
History of the International 1701
Clark, J.D.
Atlas of African prehistory 4325
Clarke, B.R. and Neave, G.R.
The Encyclopedia of higher education 3924
Clarke, C.G.
Jamaica in maps 5344
Clarke, H.
The Archaeology of medieval England 4286

Clarke, J.
International dictionary of insurance and finance 3702
Clarke, J.D.
Gallantry medals and awards of the world 3429
Gallantry medals & awards of the world 6279
Clarke, J.L.
Sierra Leone in maps 5306
Clarke, P. B. and Linzey, Andrew
Dictionary of ethics, theology, and society 618
Clarke, P.B.
Finding out in education 3739
Clarke, R.A. and Matko, D.J.I.
Soviet economic facts, 1917-80 2337
Clarke, S. and Norton, M.
The Complete fundraising handbook 3588
Clason, W.E.
Elsevier's lexicon of international and national units 3267
The Classical foundations of modern historiography 6422
Classical mythology 849
Classical political economy 1774
'The Classical world' bibliography of philosophy, religion and rhetoric 15, 816
A Classified bibliography of literature on the Acts of the Apostles 540
Classified catalog of the ecumenical movement 641
The Classified catalogue of the Royal Institute of International Affairs for international relations, defence, diplomacy, international law, politics and economics.. 1599
Clay, K.
The School administrator's resource guide 3847
Clay, R.M.
The Mediaeval hospitals of England 3664
Clayton, D. and Jameson, J.
Bibliography of policy related education documents in selected countries in Africa, Asia, the Caribbean and the Pacific 3780
Clayton, P.
Guide to the archaeological sites of Britain 4382
A clearer sense of the census 1338
Cleave, G.E.
SCIMP/SCANP thesaurus 1772
Cleere, H.F.
Archaeological heritage management in the modern world 4368
Clegg, H.A.
A History of British trade unions since 1889 1975
Clegg, J.
Dictionary of social services 3611
Clegg, M.B.
Bibliography of genealogy and local history periodicals with union list of major US collections 6103
Clements, F.A.
Kuwait 4703
Oman 4696
Saudi Arabia 4693
United Arab Emirates 4698
Clements, M.N.
The Marketing glossary 2657
Clendenning, P. and Bartlett, R.
Eighteenth century Russia 7435
The Clerks of the Counties, 1360-1960 3314
Cleveland Public Library. John G. White Department
Catalog of folklore, folklife and folk songs 4124
Clews, J.A.
Malta year book 1999 4596
Clifton, C.S.
Encyclopedia of heresies and heretics 731

Corbin, J.
Find the law in the library **2875**
Cordasco, F.
Dictionary of American immigration history **1572**
Cordeaux, E.H. *and* Merry, D.H.
A Bibliography of printed works relating to Oxfordshire **7195**
Cordell, H.
Laos **4759**
Cordellier, S. *and* Poisson, E.
L'état de France **4583**
Cordesman, A.H. *and* Wagner, A.R.
The Lessons of modern war **3466**
Cordy, H.V.
The Multicultural dictionary of proverbs **4192**
Core collection: an author and subject guide, 1970/71- **2518**
Core list of books & journals in education **3741**
Coriden, J.
The Code of canon law **3212**
Corke, B.
Who's who in Latin America **1024**
Corkill, D.
Ecuador **4986**
Cornell, E.
ABTAPL union list of periodicals **412**
Cornell, T. *and* Matthews, J.
Atlas of the Roman world **6722**
Cornish, G.P.
Religious periodicals directory **413**
Cornwall, H.
The Industrial espionage handbook **3132**
The Corona Library **1579**
Corporate 500 **3600**
Corporate America **2478**
Corporate eponymy **2442**
Corpus Christianorum. Series Latina **699**
Correia-Afonso, J.
Indo-Portuguese history **7638**
Correspondents of the New York Times
Israel: The historical atlas **7699**
Corsica **4588**
Corsini, R.J.
Encyclopedia of psychology **256**
Corson, R.
Fashions in hair **4012**
Cortada, J.W.
A Bibliographic guide to Spanish diplomatic history, 1460-1977 **1636**
Historical dictionary of the Spanish Civil War **7390**
Cortés Conde, R. *and* Stein, S.J.
Latin America: a guide to economic history, 1830-1930 **2377**
Cory, K.B.
Tracing your Scottish ancestry **6042**
Cosio Villegas, D.
Historia moderna de Mexico. 9v. in 10 **7897**
Cossolotto, M.
The Almanac of European politics **1422**
Cosson, B.P.
The BP book of industrial archaeology **4467**
Costa Rica **4891**
Costa Rica handbook **5608**
Costume **3969**
Costume, 1066-1966 **3980**
Costume: a general bibliography **3953**
Costume cavalcade **3979**
Costume in detail: women's dress, 1730-1930 **4005**
Costume in the Western world **3964**
Costume index **3954**
Costume patterns and designs **3975**
Cotterell, A.
A Dictionary of world mythology **826**
The Illustrated encyclopedia of myths and legends **815**

Cotterell, A. *(contd.)*
The Penguin encyclopedia of Classical civilizations **6635**
The Pimlico dictionary of classical civilizations **6631**
Cottingham, J.
The Cambridge companion to Descartes **21**
Couch, M.
Education in Africa **3804**
Couling, S.
The Encyclopaedia Sinica **4653**
Coulson, J.
The Saints **609**
Coulter, E.
'Evolution of nuclear strategy in the United States' **3487**
Council for American Private Education (CAPE) Schools
Private schools of the United States **3852**
Council of Europe
People on the move **1568**
Council of Planning Librarians
CPL bibliographies **975**
Council of the Baptist Union of Great Britain
The Baptist Union directory **783**
Council on Foreign Relations, Inc., New York City
Catalog of the Foreign Relations Library **1592**
Councils and synods **764**
Councils, committees & boards **3232**
The Counties and regions of the United Kingdom **2304**
Counties USA 1997 **5620**
Countries and islands of the world **4513**
Countries of the world and their leaders, 1994 **3322**
Countries of the world encyclopedia **4502**
Country reports **2282**
Country studies **4504**
County and regional histories and atlas **8071**
County atlases of the British Isles **7105**
County atlases of the British Isles 1579-1859 **7104**
'County cartobibliographies of England and Wales: *a select list*' **7103**
County Court districts (England and Wales): index of place names **3205**
County records **7107**
Couper, A.
The Times atlas and encyclopaedia of the sea **5420**
The Course of Mexican history **7898**
Coutts, B.E.
Ethnics in American society **1513**
Covell, M.
Historical dictionary of Madagascar **7844**
Coveney, J.
Harrap's glossary of business management terms. German-English, English-German **2612**
Covill, L.
Germany's top 300 **2471**
Covington, P.H.
Latin America and the Caribbean **7945**
Cowan, I.B. *and* Easson, D.E.
Medieval religious houses: Scotland **688**
Cowitt, P.P.
World currency yearbook **2227**
Cowley, J.D.
A Bibliography of abridgements, digests, dictionaries and indexes of English law to the year 1800 **2832**
Cowley, R.
What about women? Information sources for women's studies **4073**
Cox, B.
South American handbook, 2001 **5641**
Cox, E.G.
A Reference guide to the literature of travel **5063**

Cox, J.
The Nation's memory: a pictorial guide to the Public Record Office **6493**
New to Kew? **6148**
Cox, J. *and* Colwell, S.
Never been here before? **6147**
Cox, M.
Exploring Scottish history **7006**
Coyle, J.M.
Women and aging **4100**
CPA world directory of old age **1108**
CPL bibliographies **975**
CRAC (Careers Research and Advisory Centre)
Graduate studies **3934**
Crafts, N. *and* Toniolo, G.
Economic growth in Europe since 1945 **1870**
Craig, E.
Routledge encyclopedia of philosophy **61**
Craig, R.D.
Dictionary of Polynesian mythology **841**
Historical dictionary of Honolulu and Hawai'i **8192**
Historical dictionary of Polynesia **8136**
Craig, R.D. *and* King, F.P.
Historical dictionary of Oceania **8135**
Craigie, J.
A Bibliography of Scottish education, 1872-1972 **3791**
A Bibliography of Scottish education before 1872 **3790**
Crampton, R. *and* Crampton, B.
Atlas of Eastern Europe in the twentieth century **7251**
Crampton, R.J.
Bulgaria **4641**
Crampton, W.
The Complete guide to flags **6339**
Crane, J.
French Guiana **4989**
Martinique **4916**
Craton, M.
A History of the Bahamas **7931**
Craven, W.F. *and* Cate, J.L.
The Army Air Forces in World War II **6836**
Crawford, A.
The Europa biographical dictionary of British women **5766**
'The Public Record Office' **6494**
Crawford, B.C.
Scandinavian Scotland **6991**
Crawford, M.
Encyclopedia of the Mexican-American War **8038**
Sources for ancient history **6632**
Creagh, O'M. *and* Humphris, E.M.
Distinguished Service Order, 1886-1923 **3433**
Crealey, A.H.
An Irish almanac **7027**
Creaton, H.
Bibliography of printed works on London history to 1939 **7118**
London **4565**
Sources for the history of London 1939-45 **7119**
Creedman, T.S.
Historical dictionary of Costa Rica **7914**
Creifelds, C.
Rechtswörterbuch **3162**
Cresswell, J. *and* Leinster, A.
The Hutchinson dictionary of business quotations **2039**
Crete **4643**
Crewe, I. *and* Fox, A.
British Parliamentary constituencies **3049**
Cribb, R.
Historical dictionary of Indonesia **8120**
Crim, K.
Abingdon dictionary of living religions **401**

Crime and criminal justice reference sources
 3126
Crime and punishment in America: a historical
 bibliography 3157
Crime and the elderly 1093
Crime dictionary 3154
Criminal ancestors 6175
Criminal justice abstracts 3121
Criminal justice periodical index 3117
Criminal law and criminology' 3130
Criminal statistics, England and Wales, 1992
 3125
Criminologica Foundation, the University of
 Leiden, and Joint Bureaus for Dutch Child
 Welfare (WIJN), Utrecht
 Criminology, penology & police science
 abstracts 3122
Criminological bibliographies 3147
Criminology and forensic sciences 3148
'Criminology and its literature' 3150
Criminology and the administration of criminal
 justice 3151
Criminology, penology & police science
 abstracts 3122
CRIS 1369
Critchlow, J.
 Nationalism in Uzbekistan 7711
A Critical dictionary of educational concepts
 3757
A Critical dictionary of Jungian analysis 328
A Critical dictionary of psychoanalysis 327
A Critical dictionary of the French Revolution
 7347
Critical guide to Catholic reference books 724
A Critical history of Western philosophy 125
A Critical lexicon and concordance to the
 English and Greek New Testament 535
A Critical study of studies on Dutch colonial
 history 7476
Croatia 4639
Crockford's clerical directory 756
The Cromwellian gazetteer 5466
Croner's care homes guide 3653
Croner's executive companion 2602
Cronologia geral da historia de Portugal 7403
Cropley, J.
 Directory of financial information sources
 2087
Crosby, C.A.
 Historical dictionary of Malawi 7843
Crosby, E.U.
 Medieval studies 6770
Cross, F.L. *and* Livingstone, E.A.
 The Oxford dictionary of the Christian
 Church 636
Cross, M.
 Bibliography of monuments in the care of
 the Secretary of State for Scotland 4421
Cross-national study of health systems -
 countries, world regions, and special
 problems 3633
The Cross of sacrifice 6821
Crossan, R. *and* Johnson, M.
 The Guide to international capital markets,
 1991 2179
Crossley, D.
 Post-medieval archaeology in Britain 4271
Croucher, M.
 Slavic studies 4533
Crow, B. *and* Thomas, A.
 Third World atlas 5184
Crowe, E.P.
 Genealogy online 6099
Crowl, P.A.
 The Intelligent traveller's guide to historic
 Scotland 5493
Crown, A.D.
 A Bibliography of the Samaritans 3608
Crowther, M.A.
 The Workhouse system, 1834-1929 3599

Crowther, P.A.
 A Bibliography of works in English on early
 Russian history to 1800 7413
Cruden, A.A.
 A Complete concordance to the Old and
 New Testament ... with ... a concordance
 to the Apocrypha 501
Crumb, L.N.
 The Oxford movement and its leaders 661
Crumlin-Pedersen, O.
 Aspects of maritime Scandinavia 4361
Crusader archaeology 7546
Crystal, J.
 Kuwait 4702
Csendes, P.
 Historical dictionary of Vienna 7299
A Dictionary of economic quotations 1839
Dictionary of genealogical sources in the
 Public Record Office 6062
Cuba 4899-4900
Cuba between reform and revolution 7921
Cuba. Dirección Central de Estadística
 Anuario estadístico de Cuba 1287
The Cuban missile crisis 1962 7923
Cubbon, W.
 A Bibliographical account of works relating
 to the Isle of Man 7225
Cucchi, L.
 'How to find Italian business information'
 2056
Cullen, C. *and* Henchy, M.
 Writings on Irish history 1987 7017
Cultural atlas of Africa 4789
Cultural atlas of China 4658
Cultural atlas of Japan 5275
Cultural atlas of Mesopotamia and the Ancient
 Near East 4451
Cultural atlas of Spain and Portugal 4598
Cultural atlas of the Viking World 7462
A Cultural history of India 7633
Cumbrian ancestors 7222
Cumbrian Archive Service
 Cumbrian ancestors 7222
Cumpston, J.
 Macquarie Islands 5022
Cunliffe, B.
 Iron Age communities in Britain 4252
Cunliffe, B. *and* Hey, D.
 A Regional history of England 7062
Cunnew, R.
 The Insurance sourcebook 3694
Cunningham, P.
 Local history of education in England and
 Wales 3795
Cunnington, C.W.
 A Dictionary of English costume. 900-1900
 3988
 English women's clothing in the nineteenth
 century 3991
Cunnington, C.W. *and* Cunnington, P.
 The History of underclothes 3976
Cunnington, P. *and* Buck, A.
 Children's costume in England, 1300-1900
 4011
The Currency options handbook 2225
Current accounting literature 2570
A Current bibliography of international law
 2888
Current biography 5687
Current biography cumulated index 1940-1995
 5689
Current biography on CD-ROM 5705
Current biography yearbook 5688
Current contents 976
Current index to journals in education 3767
Current international treaties 2959
Current law 2788
Current law index: multiple access to legal
 periodicals in print 2726
Current leaders of nations CD 1489
Current military and political literature 3360

Current publications by member societies
 6143
Current research in Britain: social sciences
 1037
Current research in management 2623
Current sociology .. 1043
Current Soviet leaders ... a cumulative guide to
 officials and notables in the USSR 3337
Current world affairs 3478
Currer-Briggs, N.
 Worldwide family history 6135
Currer-Briggs, N. *and* Gambier, R.
 Debrett's guide to tracing your family tree
 6149
 Huguenot ancestry 6073
Currie, C.R.J. *and* Lewis, C.P.
 English county histories 7065
Curtis, S.J. *and* Boultwood, M.E.A.
 A Short history of educational ideas 3826
Curtis, W.A.
 A History of creeds and confessions of faith
 in Christendom and beyond 615
Curzon, L.B.
 A Dictionary of law 2757
Cushing, H.G.
 Bibliography of costume 3955
The Customs and ceremonies of Britain 4014
The Cut of men's clothes, 1600-1900 4004
The Cut of women's clothes, 1600-1930 4007
Cutolo, V.O.
 Nuevo diccionario biográfico argentino
 (1750-1930) 5964
Cutter, C. *and* Oppenheim, M.F.
 Jewish reference sources 899
Cuvalo, A.
 Historical dictionary of Bosnia and
 Herzegovina 7505
CWLA's guide to adoption agencies 3687
Cybriwsky, R.
 Historical dictionary of Tokyo 7606
A Cyclopaedia of costume 3957
The Cyclopedia of Fiji (illustrated) 8182
Cyclopedia of Samoa, Tonga, Tahiti, and the
 Cook Islands 8184
Cyndi's list: a comprehensive list of 40,000
 genealogy sites on the Internet 6014
Cyndi's list of genealogy sites on the Internet
 6013
Cyprus 4731
Cyprus. Department of Statistics and
 Research
 Statistical abstract 1273
Czechoslovakia 4575
Czechoslovakia 1918-88 7303
Czechoslovakia 1968-1969 7306
The D-Day encyclopedia 6866
da Graça, J.
 Heads of state and government 3323
Daalder, H.
 Party systems in Denmark, Austria,
 Switzerland, the Netherlands and Belgium
 1709
Dahlmus, J.
 Dictionary of medieval civilization 6779
Daily law reports index 2794
The *Daily Telegraph* guide to working abroad
 1948
Dalby, A.
 South-East Asia 7552
Dalby, R.
 The Alaska guide 5639
Dale, S. *and* Carty, J.
 Finding out about continuing education
 3866
Dalton, B.
 Indonesia handbook 5654
Daly, M.
 Tonga 5044
Daly, M.W.
 Imperial Sudan 7763
 Sudan 4797

Damis, J.
  Conflict in Northwest Africa 7771
Danbury, E.
  Palaeography for historians 6615
Dancy, J. and Sosa, E.
  A Companion to epistemology 346
Dandekar, R.N.
  Vedic bibliography 862
D'Angelo, E.
  Developing a basic philosophy collection 5
Dangerous sky 6865
Daniel, O.
  Albanie 7486
D'Aniello, C.A.
  Teaching bibliographic skills in history 6381
Daniells, L.M.
  Business information sources 1756, 2517
Daniels, G.
  A Guide to the reports of the United States
    strategic bombing survey .. 3486
Daniels, M.
  Burundi 4842
  Côte D'Ivoire 4824
Danker, P.
  This is Greenland '99 5053
Danmark 1:100 000 topografisk atlas 5257
Dansk biografisk leksikon 5845
Darby, H.C. and Fullard, H.
  The New Cambridge modern history. v.14.
    The Atlas 6748
Darch, C.
  Mozambique 4850
  Tanzania 4849
Dark Age Britain 5472
Darnay, B.T. and DeMaggio, J.
  Subject directory of special libraries and
    information centers. v.1 Business,
    government and law libraries 1030
Darnborough, A. and Kinrade, D.
  Directory for disabled people 3673
  Directory for older people 1109
Darroch, E. and Taylor, B.
  A Bibliography of Norfolk history 7202
Darshan Singh Tatla and Talbot, I.
  Punjab 4710
The Dartmoor bibliography 1534-1991 7157
Darvill, T.
  Ancient monuments in the countryside 4433
The Darwen County Histories 7051
Dasgupta, S.
  A History of Indian philosophy 139
Data bases in the humanities and social
  sciences 972
Databasics 2596
Dates and time 7061
Dau, H.
  Bibliographie juristischer Festschriften und
    Festschriftenbeträge 2781
Davenport, T.R.H.
  South Africa 7826
Davey, G.B. and Seal, G.
  The Oxford companion to Australian folklore
    4166
David, R. and Brierley, J.E.C.
  Major legal systems of the world today
    2882
David, R. and David, A.E.
  A Biographical dictionary of ancient Egypt
    6658
Davids, L.E.
  Dictionary of banking and finance 2098
Davidson, G.
  A Dictionary of angels 595
Davidson, J.
  The Prehistory of New Zealand 4342
Davidson, L.K. and Dunn-Wood, M.
  Pilgrimages in the Middle Ages 633
Davidson, P.B.
  Vietnam at war 7727
Davidson, R.L.
  National directory of legal services 2865

Davidson, S. and Weil, R.L.
  Handbook of modern accounting 2574
Davies, B.L.
  Criminological bibliographies 3147
Davies, D.H.
  Zambia in maps 5319
Davies, G.
  Clwyd Library Service catalogue of the
    collection of Arthurian literature 4171
Davies, H.
  Worship and theology in England 564
Davies, J.
  'What to read on the history of Wales before
    1536,' 7231
Davies, J.G.
  A New dictionary of liturgy and worship
    646
Davies, K.
  Occupations, 93 1946
Davies, N.
  The Ancient kingdoms of Mexico 6736
  A History of Poland 7310
Davies, P.H.J.
  The British secret services 1667
Davies, R. and Rupp, G.
  A History of the Methodist Church in Great
    Britain 788
Davies, R.H.
  The Kingdom of Swaziland 4856
Davies, S. and Arduini, A.M.
  Manuale bilingue di corrispondinza e
    comunicazione commerciale. Italiane-
    Inglese 2566
Davies, W.
  Wales in the early Middle Ages 7237
Davies, W.V.
  Egypt and Africa 6645
Davis, B.
  An Introduction to Irish research 6046,
    6164
Davis, B.L.
  British army cloth insignia 3445
  British army uniforms and insignia of World
    War II 3451
  Flags of the Third Reich 6350
  United States army cloth insignia 3458
Davis, E. and Howells, B.
  Pembrokeshire county history 7226
Davis, G.V.
  South Africa 4854
Davis, L.
  Encyclopedia of natural disasters 5105
Davis, L.G.
  The Black family in the United States 1127
Davis, M.B.
  Native America in the twentieth century: an
    encyclopedia 8067
Davis, N.
  Afro-American reference 1128
Davis, R.H.
  Columbia 4985
  Historical dictionary of Colombia 8108
Davis, R.W.
  Historical abstracts on disc 6404
Davis, R.W. and Speck, V.
  Historical abstracts (Internet database) 6403
Davis, W.E.
  Resource guide to special education 3873
Davison, G.
  The Oxford companion to Australian history
    8168
Dawson, W. R. and Uphill, E. P. and
  Bierbrier, M. L.
  Who was who in Egyptology 4232
Day, A.
  England 4564
  The Falkland Islands 4980
  Political and economic dictionary of Eastern
    Europe 1716
  St. Helena, Ascension and Tristan da Cunha
    4871

Day, A.E.
  Discovery and exploration 5066
  Search for the Northwest Passage 8197
Day, A.G.
  A Biographical dictionary: historical makers
    of Hawaii 8193
Day, A.J.
  The Annual register 6746
  Border and territorial disputes 2947
  Government economic agencies of the world
    1869, 3229
  Peace movements of the world 3008
  Political parties of the world 1699
  State economic agencies of the world 3229
Day, J.
  A Guide to the industrial heritage of Avon
    and its borders 4480
  Oxford Bible atlas 483
Day, M. and Box, B.
  Rio & around handbook 5644
'The Day of infamy in print' 6860
De Conde, A.
  Encyclopedia of American foreign policy
    1653
De Courcy, A.
  A Guide to modern manners 4039
De Fiores, S. and Meo, S.
  Nuovo dizionaria di Mariologia 594
De Jong, F.J.
  Quadrilingual economics dictionary 1789
De La Bédoyère, G.
  The Finds of Roman Britain 4392
De La Chenaye-Desbois et Bodier, A.
  Dictionnaire de la Noblesse 6275
De la Cruz, V.
  Historia general de Costa Rica 7912
De Lancey, M.W.
  Somalia 4847
De Lancey, M.W. and Mokeba, H.B.
  Historical dictionary of the Republic of
    Cameroon 7801
de Lucca, J.L.
  Elsevier's dictionary of insurance and risk
    prevention in English, French, Spanish,
    German and Portuguese 3695
De Mente, B.L.
  Japan encyclopedia 4680
De Mowbray, S.A.
  Key facts in Soviet history 7432
De Munter, M. and Bauduin, C.
  Elsevier's fiscal and customs dictionary in
    five languages 2105
De Paula's auditing 2592
De Platt, L.
  Genealogical historical guide to Latin
    America 6123
De Randeck, J.H.
  Les plus anciennes familles du monde 6136
De Rietz, R.
  Bibliotheca Polynesia 5037
De Schutter, B. and Eliaerts, C.
  Bibliography on international criminal law
    3128
De Silva, C.R. and De Silva, D.
  The History of Ceylon (c.1500-1658) 7664
De Silva, D.
  The Portuguese in Asia 7399
De Silva, D. and De Silva, C.R.
  Sri Lanka since independence 7666
De Silva, K.M.
  A History of Sri Lanka 7665
De Smet, R.E.
  Atlas de Belgique 5261
De Sola, R.
  Crime dictionary 3154
De Souza, J.P. and Kulkarni, C.M.
  Historiography in Indian languages 6365
de Vries, A
  The Directory of jobs and careers abroad
    1950

istinguished Service Order, 1886-1923 **3433**

istinguished women of the twentieth century **5730**

he District Gazetteers of British India **5573**

Diverse routes to electoral comprehension' **1544**

Divorce in the 70s **1364**

Divorce in the United States, Canada and Great Britain **1363**

Dizionario biografico degli Italiani **5807**

Dizionario commerciale **1817**

Dizionario degli istituti di perfezione **686**

Dizionario giuridico. Law dictionary **2764**

Djibouti **4848**

Dmitrichev, T.F.
English-Russian dictionary on disarmament **3004**

Dobbin, M.
Nottinghamshire history and topography **7179**

Dobkin, U.S.
Handbook for the teaching of social studies **1077**

Dobler, D.W.
Purchasing and materials management **2645**

Dobson, C. and Payne, R.
The Dictionary of espionage **1665**

Docherty, J.C.
Historial dictionary of Australia **8170**
Historical dictionary of socialism **1697**

Dockrill, M.L.
The Collins atlas of twentieth century world history **6453**

Documentation juridique **2840**

The Documentation of colonial rule in Africa' **6566**

The Documentation of the European Communities **2926**

Documents in English economic history: England from 1000 to 1760 **2320**

Documents in English economic history: England since 1760 **2321**

Documents on Australian foreign policy, 1937-1949 **1654**

Documents on British foreign policy, 1919-1939 **1626**

Documents on British policy overseas **1625**

Documents on German foreign policy, 1918-1945 **1632**

Documents on international affairs, 1928-1963 **1614**

Dodd, A.H.
A History of Caernarvonshire 1284-1900 **7239**

Dodgshon, R.A. and Butlin, R.A.
An Historical geography of England and Wales **5156**

Dodgson, J. McN.
Index to Domesday Book **7057**

Dod's Parliamentary companion, 1999 **3054**

Dodson, A.M.
Monarchs of the Nile **6646**

Dogra, R.C.
Bhutan **4718**

Doherty, J.E. and Hickey, D.J.
A Chronology of Irish history since 1500 **7028**

Doherty, R. and Truesdale, D.
Irish winners of the Victoria Cross **6286**

Doing your own research **1026**

Dolby, W.
Chronological tables of Chinese history **7572**

Dolmens for the dead **4369**

Domesday Book **7052**

The Domesday Book **7056**

Domesday Book through nine centuries **7055**

Domesday people: a prosography of persons occurring in English documents 1066-1266 **7106**

Dominguez, U.R. and Léon, M.D. de
Diccionario histórico dominicano **7927**

Dominica **4921**

Dominican Republic **4904**

Dominican Republic handbook **5613**

Domschke, E. and Goyer, D.S.
The Handbook of national population censuses. V.1: Latin America and the Caribbean, North America and Oceania **1313**
The Handbook of national population censuses. V.2: Africa and Asia **1312**

Donaghy, P.J. and Laidler, J.
Dictionary of the language of financial reports **2118**

Donaghy, P.J. and Newton, M.T.
Spain: a guide to political and economic institutions **1438**

Donald, V.
How to choose a career **1947**

Donaldson, G.
Scottish church history **677**

Donaldson, G. and Morpeth, R.S.
A Dictionary of Scottish history **7004**
Who's who in Scottish history **7011**

Donnachie, I.
'Industrial archaeology in Australia' **4489**

Donnachie, I. and Hewitt, G.
The Companion to Scottish history (CD-ROM) **7001**

Donnachie, J.
'The industrial heritage of Australia and New Zealand' **4490**

Donnachie, J. and Hewitt, G.
Companion to Scottish history **7000**

The Donning international encyclopedic psychic dictionary **174**

Doolan, B.
Principles of Irish Law **2812**

Doolin, D. and Ridley, C.
A Chinese-English dictionary of Communist Chinese terminology **227**

Dophin, P.
The London Region **5143**

Dorgan, C.A.
Professional careers sourcebook **1958**
Small business sourcebook **2077**

Dorge, P.
Tibet handbook **5575**

Dorje, G.
Tibet handbook **5561**

Dorling, H. Taprell
Ribbons and medals **6280**

Dorling Kindersley atlas of world history **6413**

The Dorling Kindersley world reference atlas **5398**

Dorscheid, P.
Elsevier's dictionary of export financing **2497**

The Dorsey dictionary of American government and politics **3225**

Dorsey, L.
Historical dictionary of Rwanda **7810**

Dorson, R.M.
Handbook of American folklore **4162**

Doss, M.
Women's organizations **4103**

Dothan, T.
The Philistines and their material culture **6660**

Doucet, M.
Dictionnaire juridique et économique. Wörterbuch der Rechts .. **2748**

Doughan, D. and Sanchez, D.
Feminist periodicals, 1855-1984 **4072**

Douglas, A.
'Genealogical research in Canada' **6081**

Douglas, D.C.
English historical documents **6915**

Douglas, I.
Companion encyclopedia of geography **5061**

Douglas, J.D.
The Illustrated Bible dictionary **465**
The New international dictionary of the Christian Church **635**

Douglas, N. and Douglas, N.
Fiji handbook business and travel guide **5676**

Douglas, R.
The History of the Liberal Party, 1895-1970 **1726**

Doursther, H.
Dictionnaire universel des poids et mesures anciens et modernes **3268**

Dove, J.C.
Who's who in Germany: a biographical encyclopedia ... containing about 11,000 biographies of top-ranking decision makers, politicians and other leading personalities operating in the fields of business and finance, politics, science, the arts and entertainment **5786**

Dower, J.W.
Japanese history and culture from ancient to modern times: seven basic bibliographies **7602**

Downes, J. and Goodman, J.E.
Barron's finance and investment handbook **2166**

Downing, D.
An Atlas of territorial and border disputes **2948**

Doxey, M.P.
The Commonwealth Secretariat and the contemporary Commonwealth **6902**

Doyle, W.
The Oxford history of the French Revolution **7341**

Dr. Williams's Library, London
Catalogue .. **372**
Early Nonconformity, 1566-1800 **773**

Dragomir, V.
România: atlas rutier **5267**

Dragons can be defeated **6283**

Drake, M. and Finnegan, R.
Sources and methods for family and community historians **6138**

Draper, P.
The Scottish financial sector **2175**

Drazil, J.V.
Quantities and units of measurement **3263**

Dreams **309**

Dreams: a portal to the source **311**

Dreisprachiges Verzeichnis statistischer Fachausdrücke **1198**

Dreisprachiges Wörterbuch der Soziologie (Deutsch/Englisch/Französisch): ... Trilingual dictionary of sociology (German/English/French) **1062**

Dress in Anglo-Saxon England **3990**

Drewry, G.
'Judiciary and government' **2879**

Drewry, G. and Butcher, T.
The Civil Service today **3238**

Drexel, J.
The Facts On File encyclopedia of the 20th century **6448**

Drèze, J. and Sen, A.
The Political economy of hunger **1147-1148**

Driver, S.R.
International critical commentary on the Holy Scriptures **515**

Drodge, S.
Adult education **3861**

Dronke, P.
A History of twelfth-century Western philosophy **126**

Drost, H.
What's what and who's who in Europe **4527**

Eliade, M. *and* Coullardo, A.P.
The Eliade guide to world religions 386
Eliot, J.
Bali and the Eastern Isles handbook 5655
Indonesia handbook 5656
Laos handbook 5591
Myanmar (Burma) handbook 5584
Eliot, J. *and* Bickersteth, J.
Bangkok and the Beaches handbook 5585
Malaysia & Singapore handbook 5587
Singapore handbook 5588
Thailand handbook 5586
Elkins, D. *and* Elkins, T.H.
France 5146
Elling, R.H.
Cross-national study of health systems -
countries, world regions, and special
problems 3633
Ellington, H. *and* Harris, D.
Dictionary of instructional technology 3841
Elliot, J.M. *and* Elliot, R.R.
The Arms control, disarmament and military
security dictionary 3003
Elliott, J.K.
A Bibliography of Greek New Testament
manuscripts 523
Elliott, J.M. *and* Ali, S.R.
The State and local government political
dictionary 3315
Elliott, S. *and* Flackes, W.D.
Conflict in Northern Ireland 7039
Elliott, S.P.
A Reference guide to the United States
Supreme Court 3201
Ellis, A.
Philosophical books 9
Ellis, C.
A Collector's guide to the history and
uniform of Das Heer 3456
Ellis, J.
The Russian Orthodox Church 719
Ellis, J.T. *and* Trisco, R.
A Guide to American Catholic history 747
Ellis, P.B.
A Dictionary of Celtic mythology 955
A Dictionary of Irish mythology 834
A Guide to early Celtic remains in Britain
4384
Elon, M.
Jewish law 895
Elsevier's banking dictionary 2196
Elsevier's dictionary of commercial terms and
phrases in five languages 2022
Elsevier's dictionary of criminal science in
eight languages 3155
Elsevier's dictionary of export financing 2497
Elsevier's dictionary of financial terms in
English, German, Spanish, French, Italian
and Dutch 2109
Elsevier's dictionary of insurance and risk
prevention in English, French, Spanish,
German and Portuguese 3695
Elsevier's dictionary of office automation in
four languages 2553
Elsevier's dictionary of police and criminal law
3247
Elsevier's dictionary of the labour market
1889
Elsevier's fiscal and customs dictionary in five
languages 2105
Elsevier's lexicon of international and national
units 3267
Elsevier's lexicon of stock-market terms 2238
Elton, G.R.
England 1200-1640 6940
Modern historians on British history 1485-
1945 6426

Elvin, C.N.
A Hand-book of mottoes borne by the
nobility, gentry, cities, public companies,
etc. ... With Supplement by R. Pinches
6256
Elwell, W.A.
Evangelical dictionary of biblical theology
580
Evangelical dictionary of theology 581
Emberton, W.
The English Civil War day by day 6974
Emblems 6259
Embree, A.T.
Encyclopedia of Asian history 7519
Embree, L.
Encyclopedia of phenomenology 63
Emerson, W.K.
Chevrons 3459
Emery, A.
A-Z of British genealogical research 6028
Emigrants to Pennsylvania, 1641-1819 6094
'Emigration from Britain 6140
Emily Post's etiquette 4041
Eminent Filippines 5977
Eminent Indians who was who 1900-1980
5874
Emmison, F.G. *and* Gray, I.
County records 7107
The Empire ships 6845
'The Empire, the Commonwealth and the
Mandated Territories' 6907
Empires of the monsoon 7659
Employee relations bibliography and abstracts
1934
Employee relations bibliography and abstracts.
1989-. v.1-. Quarterly 1935
Employers' organizations of the world 1919
Employment gazette 1905
Emsley, C.
Longman companion to Napoleonic Europe
6796
Enayat, H.
Modern Islamic political thought 1478
Enciclopedia de historia de España 7376
Enciclopedia filosofica 62
Enciclopedia histórica de Honduras 7906
Encina, F.A. *and* Castedo, L.
Resumen de la historia de Chile 1535-1925
8097
Encountering Macau 7579
Encuyklopedia Warszawy 4579
The Encyclopaedia Africana dictionary of
African Biography 5894
Encyclopaedia Iranica 4729
Encyclopaedia Judaica 906
The Encyclopaedia of Aboriginal Australia.
Aboriginal and Torres Strait Islander history,
society and culture 5032
Encyclopaedia of Britain 4540
Encyclopaedia of Dublin 7046
Encyclopaedia of Eastern Europe 7248
The Encyclopaedia of historic places 5448
Encyclopaedia of Indian events and dates 7654
The Encyclopaedia of Islam 939
Encyclopaedia of modern British army
regiments 3502
Encyclopaedia of modern murder, 1962-82
3137
Encyclopaedia of murder 3136
An Encyclopaedia of Napoleon's Europe 6755
An Encyclopaedia of New Zealand 5011
An Encyclopaedia of occultism 176
The Encyclopaedia of Oxford 7196
An Encyclopaedia of Parliament 3076
An Encyclopaedia of philosophy 65
Encyclopaedia of religion and ethics 393
Encyclopaedia of religious quotations 418
Encyclopaedia of Soviet law 2848
Encyclopaedia of the laws of Scotland 2806
Encyclopaedia of the modern Royal Air Force
3527

Encyclopaedia of the modern Royal Navy
3554
Encyclopaedia of the modern territorial army
3503
Encyclopaedia of the social sciences 994
The Encyclopaedia of the United Nations and
international agreements 2909
Encyclopaedia of the Upanishads 864
Encyclopaedia of Tibet 7584
Encyclopaedia of underwater and maritime
archaeology 4350
Encyclopaedia of world crime, criminal justice,
criminology and law enforcement 3119
The Encyclopaedia Sinica 4653
An encyclopaedic dictionary of heraldry 6227
Encyclopedia Lituanica 4614
Encyclopedia of adolescence 1092
Encyclopedia of advertising 2689
Encyclopedia of aesthetics 149
Encyclopedia of Africa South of the Sahara
4783
Encyclopedia of African-American culture and
history 4963
Encyclopedia of African peoples 7747
The Encyclopedia of aging 1100
Encyclopedia of American biography 5947
Encyclopedia of American economic history
2379
The Encyclopedia of American facts and dates
7995
Encyclopedia of American family names 6195
Encyclopedia of American foreign policy 1653
Encyclopedia of American history 7970
The Encyclopedia of American intelligence and
espionage 1669
Encyclopedia of American parties, campaigns
and elections 1457
Encyclopedia of American religions 388-389
The Encyclopedia of apocalypticism 549
Encyclopedia of applied ethics 353
Encyclopedia of archaeology 4213
Encyclopedia of arms control and disarmament
2999
Encyclopedia of Asian history 7519
Encyclopedia of banking and finance 2097
Encyclopedia of Bible creatures 493
Encyclopedia of Biblical prophecy 499
Encyclopedia of Biblical theology 449
Encyclopedia of bilingualism and bilingual
education 3750
Encyclopedia of British battles 3461
Encyclopedia of business 2523
Encyclopedia of China 4654
The Encyclopedia of Christianity 547
Encyclopedia of Civil War biographies 8053
The Encyclopedia of code names of World
War II 6867
Encyclopedia of comparative education and
national systems of education 3724
Encyclopedia of conflicts, disputes and
flashpoints 1521
Encyclopedia of consumer brands 2667
Encyclopedia of crime and justice 3120
The Encyclopedia of dreams 314
Encyclopedia of early Christianity 550
The Encyclopedia of education 3754
Encyclopedia of educational research 3821
Encyclopedia of empiricism 64
The Encyclopedia of employment law and
practice 1911
Encyclopedia of ethics 354
Encyclopedia of European Community law
2928
Encyclopedia of fashion details 3956
The Encyclopedia of fashion from 1840 to the
1980s 4008
Encyclopedia of feminism 4065
Encyclopedia of financial services law 2169
The Encyclopedia of forensic science 2884
The Encyclopedia of forms and precedents
other than court forms 3190

The Encyclopedia of franchises and franchising 2686

Encyclopedia of Frontier biography 5925

Encyclopedia of geographical features in world history 5151

The Encyclopedia of ghosts and spirits 172-173

Encyclopedia of global industries 1897

Encyclopedia of gods 804, 820

Encyclopedia of government and politics 1482

Encyclopedia of governmental advisory organizations 3347

Encyclopedia of heads of states and governments, 1900 through 1945 1381

Encyclopedia of health information sources 3634

Encyclopedia of heresies and heretics 731

The Encyclopedia of higher education 3924

Encyclopedia of historians and historical writing 6385

Encyclopedia of human evolution and prehistory 4215

Encyclopedia of human rights 3097

Encyclopedia of human rights issues since 1945 3107

An Encyclopedia of Indian archaeology 4316

The Encyclopedia of international boundaries 5120

Encyclopedia of Japan 4681

The Encyclopedia of Jewish genealogy 6127

Encyclopedia of Jewish history 6666

The Encyclopedia of Judaism 907

An Encyclopedia of Latin-American history 7947

Encyclopedia of Latin American history and culture 7948

Encyclopedia of legal information sources 2860

The Encyclopedia of management 2598

The Encyclopedia of marriage, divorce and the family 1360

Encyclopedia of Mesoamerica 6737

Encyclopedia of Mexico 7899

The Encyclopedia of military history 3390

Encyclopedia of Mormonism 798

The Encyclopedia of myths and legends 819

Encyclopedia of nationalism 1502

The Encyclopedia of Native American biography 5957

The Encyclopedia of native American religions 810

Encyclopedia of native American tribes 8008

Encyclopedia of natural disasters 5105

An Encyclopedia of naval history 3545

Encyclopedia of New China 4655

The Encyclopedia of New York City 8076

Encyclopedia of Newfoundland and Labrador 4883

Encyclopedia of North American Indians 8010

Encyclopedia of occultism and parapsychology 161

The Encyclopedia of Papua and New Guinea 5036

The Encyclopedia of parapsychology and psychical research 178

Encyclopedia of phenomenology 63

The Encyclopedia of philosophy 67

The Encyclopedia of police science 3127

Encyclopedia of political economy 1777

The Encyclopedia of politics and religion 390

Encyclopedia of precolonial Africa 4324

Encyclopedia of psychology 256-257

Encyclopedia of public international law 2892

Encyclopedia of real estate terms 1990

The Encyclopedia of religion 392

Encyclopedia of religion and ethics 355

Encyclopedia of revolutions and revolutionaries 1525

Encyclopedia of Russian history 7408

Encyclopedia of school administration & supervision 3848

Encyclopedia of sleep and dreaming 312

Encyclopedia of social history 1162

Encyclopedia of social inventions 1157

Encyclopedia of social work 3626

Encyclopedia of sociology 1050

Encyclopedia of Southern culture 4949

The Encyclopedia of Southern history 7974

Encyclopedia of Soviet life 1731

Encyclopedia of special education 3876

The Encyclopedia of suicide 3143

Encyclopedia of terrorism and political violence 1538

Encyclopedia of the American Constitution 3025

Encyclopedia of the American judicial system 2864

Encyclopedia of the American Left 1742

Encyclopedia of the American religious experience 708

Encyclopedia of the American Revolution 8030

Encyclopedia of the American West 7972

Encyclopedia of the Ancient Greek world 6704

Encyclopedia of the Ancient World 6634

Encyclopedia of the archeology of Ancient Egypt 6652

Encyclopedia of the Boer War 7832

The Encyclopedia of the Chinese overseas 4516

Encyclopedia of the Early Church 700

Encyclopedia of the European Union 2927

The Encyclopedia of the First World 4499

An Encyclopedia of the history of classical archaeology 6690

Encyclopedia of the Holocaust 924, 7286

Encyclopedia of the human emotions 307

The Encyclopedia of the Irish in America 4950

The Encyclopedia of the Lutheran Church 768

Encyclopedia of the Mexican-American War 8038

Encyclopedia of the Middle Ages 6775

Encyclopedia of the modern British army 3507

Encyclopedia of the modern Middle East 4689

Encyclopedia of the North American colonies 7858

The Encyclopedia of the paranormal 166

Encyclopedia of the Persian Gulf War 7627

Encyclopedia of the Renaissance 6765, 6787

Encyclopedia of the Roman Empire 6718

Encyclopedia of the Second World 4534

Encyclopedia of the Second World War 6870

The Encyclopedia of the Third Reich 7273

Encyclopedia of the Third World 4521

Encyclopedia of the unexplained 158

The Encyclopedia of the United Nations and international relations 2908

Encyclopedia of the United States in the nineteenth century 8019

Encyclopedia of the United States in the twentieth century 4951

Encyclopedia of the USSR 7423

Encyclopedia of the Vatican and papacy 726

Encyclopedia of the Vietnam War 7735-7736

Encyclopedia of the War of 1812 8037

Encyclopedia of the world's air forces 3522

Encyclopedia of theology 576, 733

Encyclopedia of Transcendentalism 445

Encyclopedia of Ukraine 4618-4619

The Encyclopedia of unbelief 438

The Encyclopedia of witches and witchcraft 184

Encyclopedia of women and world religion 391

Encyclopedia of women's associations worldwide 4110

Encyclopedia of world biography 5692

Encyclopedia of world biography on CD-ROM 5694

Encyclopedia of world cities 4500

The Encyclopedia of world costume 3965

The Encyclopedia of world faiths 394

The Encyclopedia of world geography 5122

An Encyclopedia of world history 6358

Encyclopedia of world history 6386

The Encyclopedia of world Methodism 789

Encyclopedias, atlases, and dictionaries 5175

Encyclopedic dictionary of international law 2896

An encyclopedic dictionary of Marxism, socialism and Communism 1383

Encyclopedic dictionary of religion 728

Encyclopedic dictionary of Yoga 890

The Encyclopedic district gazetteers of India 5568

Encyclopedic handbook of cults in America 811

Encyclopédie du protestantisme 753

Encyclopédie du Québec 4879

The Encylopedia of Colonial and Revolutionary America 8022

Endruweit, G.
Dreisprachiges Wörterbuch der Soziologie (Deutsch/Englisch/Französisch): ... Trilingual dictionary of sociology (German/English/French) 1062

Engelsk-Amerikansk-Norsk, Norsk-Engelsk-Amerikansk... militaeir ordbok 3376

Engelstoft, P. and Dahl, S.
Dansk biografisk leksikon 5845

Engholm, C. and Grimes, S.
The Prentice-Hall directory of online business information 2502

England 4564

England 1200-1640 6940

England's undiscovered heritage 5518

Englebert, P.
Burkina Faso 4810

Englefield, D.
Printed records of the Parliament of Ireland, 1613-1800 3071

Englefield, D. and Drewry, G.
Information sources in politics and political science: worldwide 1370

Englisch-deutsches und deutsch-englisches Wörterbuch der Rechts und Geschäftssprache. Law dictionary: technical dictionary of the Anglo-American legal terminology, including commercial and statistical terms 2760

English, A.J.
Armed forces in Latin America 3419

English and Empire digest 2817

English-Arabic business dictionary 1822

English-Arabic dictionary of accounting and finance, with an Arabic-English glossary 2119

The English-Arabic dictionary of professional business terms 2032

The English Catholic Community, 1570-1850 741

The English ceremonial book 4033

English-Chinese glossaries, v.1-5 1004

The English Civil War day by day 6974

English costume.. 3989

English county histories 7065

English court hands AD1066-1500 6619

English cursive book hands 1250-1500 6620

The English festivals 4021

English folk-rhymes 4190

English, French, German, and Italian language materials relating to Greek law 2849

English genealogy 6058, 6060

English-German dictionary of marketing 2655

English, H.B. and English, A.C.
A Comprehensive dictionary of psychological and psychoanalytical terms 273

English Heritage book of ships and shipwrecks 4357

Gabrovska, S.
    European guide to social science information
        and documentation services **978**
Gad, F.
    The History of Greenland **8199**
'Gaelic law in early and medieval Ireland; a
    bibliography' **2811**
Gagnon, A-G.
    Québec **4881**
Gagnon, P.
    Essai de bibliographie Canadienne **7868**
Gaister, T.H.
    The New golden bough **814**
Gale, A.
    Historic shipwrecks **4356**
The Gale encyclopedia of Native American
    tribes **4970**
Galicia **7418**
Gall, T.L.
    Worldmark encyclopedia of the nations
        4501
    Worldmark encyclopedia of the States **4952**
Gallagher, T.
    Dictatorial Portugal **7406**
Gallantry medals and awards of the world
    3429
Gallantry medals & awards of the world **6279**
Gallaudet encyclopedia of deaf people and
    deafness **3679**
Galli, R.E.
    Guinea-Bissau **4821**
Gallia informations **4297**
Galloway, P.
    The Most illustrious Order **6287**
    The Order of the British Empire **6289**
    Royal service **6282**
The Gallup survey of Britain **1090**
The Gambia **4816**
Gamble, C.
    The Palaeolithic settlement of Europe **4244**
Gamble, D.P.
    The Gambia **4816**
Gander, T.
    Encyclopaedia of the modern Royal Air
        Force **3527**
    Encyclopedia of the modern British army
        3507
Gandy, M.
    'Tracing your Catholic ancestors in England
        6179
García, I.R.
    Diccionario de términos juridicos **2751**
García, M.A.
    Diccionario histórico-enciclopédico de la
        République de El Salvador **7909**
Gardiner, J. and Wemborn, N.
    The History Today companion to British
        history **6928**
Gardiner, V.
    The Channel Islands **4566**
Gardinier, D.E.
    Gabon **4835**
    Historical dictionary of Gabon **7803**
Gardner, D.E. and Smith, F.
    Genealogical research in England and Wales
        6056
Gardner, F.L.
    Bibliotheca astrologica **193**
Gardner, J.A.
    The Iraq-Iran War **7548**
Gardner, J.L.
    Reader's Digest atlas of the Bible **484**
Gardner, P.
    The Complete who's who in the Bible **490**
Garland, C.E.
    A Digest and index of tax cases .. **2160**
Garlick, K.B.
    Garlick's Methodist registry, 1983 **785**
Garlick's Methodist registry, 1983 **785**
Garneau, M.
    World directory of stock exchanges **2248**

Garner, B.A.
    A Dictionary of modern legal usage **2754**
Garner, J.F.
    Civic ceremonial **4032**
Garner, P.
    Financial management handbook **2100**
Garnett, K.
    Copinger and Skone James on copyright
        3179
Garraty, J.A.
    1001 things everyone should know about
        American history **7968**
Garraty, J.A. and Carnes, M.C.
    American national biography **5919**
Garraty, J.A. and Sternstein, J.L.
    Encyclopedia of American biography **5947**
Garrett, D. and Barbanell, E.
    Encyclopedia of empiricism **64**
Garrett, V.M.
    Mandarin squares **6306**
Garrett, W.
    Historical atlas of the United States **7990**
Gartside, L.
    Modern business correspondence **2550**
Gascoigne, B.
    Encyclopaedia of Britain **4540**
Gaskell, G.A.
    Dictionary of all Scriptures and myths **403**
Gastmann, A.
    Historical dictionary of the French and
        Netherlands Antilles **7939**
Gates-Coon, R.
    Eastern Europe bibliography **7247**
Gates, M-H.
    'Archaeology in Turkey' **4318**
Gateway to Japan **5564**
Gaunt, P.
    The Cromwellian gazetteer **5466**
Gaur, A.
    South Asian studies **4708**
Gaute, J.H.H. and Odell, R.
    New Murderer's who's who **3138**
Gavet-Imbert, M.
    Guinness book of explorers and exploration
        5062
Gay, W. and Pearson, M.
    The Nuclear arms race **2988**
Gaygill, H.
    A Kant dictionary **7**
Gayre of Gayre and Nigg, R.
    Heraldic standards and their ensigns **6221**
The Gazetteer of India **4717**
Gazetteer of Scotland **5495**
Gazetteer of the Falkland Islands Dependencies
    5646
Gazetteer of the Persian Gulf, Oman and
    Central Arabia **5566**
Gazetteers **5444**
Gazetteers of Canada **5602**
Geahigan, P.C. and Rose, R.F.
    Business serials of the US government **2063**
Geddes, C.L.
    Guide to reference books for Islamic studies
        936
Gee, A.
    Royal Historical Society. Annual
        bibliography of British and Irish history
        6923
Gee, P.
    Spicer and Pegler's book-keeping and
        accounts **2589**
Geelan, P.J.M. and Twitchett, D.C.
    Times atlas of China **5271**
Gehman, H.S.
    The New Westminster dictionary of the Bible
        459
Geiriadur termau archaeolog **4289**
Geisst, C.R.
    A Guide to financial institutions **2167**
    A Guide to the financial markets **2236**

Geldsetzer, L.
    Bibliography of the international congresses
        of philosophy/Bibliographie der
        internationalen Philosophie Kongress,
        1900-1978.. **147**
Genealogical and local history books in print
    6023
Genealogical archives: City Directories of the
    United States
    City directories of the United States **6193**
Genealogical archives online **6100**
Genealogical encyclopedia of the Colonial
    Americas **6080**
A Genealogical gazetteer of England **6061**
Genealogical historical guide to Latin America
    6123
A Genealogical history of the dormant,
    abeyant, forfeited, and extinct peerages of
    the British Empire **6273**
Genealogical Periodical Annual Index **6102**
Genealogical research directory 2000 **6020**
Genealogical research directory on CD-ROM
    1990-1999 **6021**
Genealogical research for Czech and Slovak
    Americans **6072**
'Genealogical research in Canada' **6081**
Genealogical research in England and Wales
    6056
Genealogical research in England's Public
    Record Office **6063**
The Genealogical services directory 2000
    6018
Genealogical sources in the United States of
    America **6118**
Genealogies in the Library of Congress **6024**
Genealogies of Barbados families **6086**
The Genealogist's address book **6116**
A Genealogist's bibliography **6059**
The Genealogist's virtual library **6012**
'Genealogy' **6207**
Genealogy for librarians **6040**
'Genealogy in Portugal' **6076**
Genealogy in the computer age **6098**
Genealogy on CD-ROM **6097**
Genealogy online **6099**
Genealogy software guide **6010**
Genealogy Sourcebook Series **6091**
General alphabetical index to the townlands
    and towns, parishes and baronies of Ireland
    6053
The General armory of England, Scotland,
    Ireland and Wales **6234**
General Assembly of Unitarian and Free
    Christian Churches
    Directory **791**
A General guide to the India Office Records
    6554
The General household survey **1169**
Generations: A history of Canada's peoples
    7864
The Genesis of modern process thought **8**
Genocide **3134**
Gentilcore, R.L. and Head, C.G.
    Ontario's history in maps **7893**
Geo abstracts **5127**
Geo-data **5432**
Geographers: bibliographical studies **5136**
Geographical abstracts. D **1159**
Geographical abstracts: human geography
    1068
Géographie de la Belgique **5147**
Geographie Deutschlands **5144**
Géographie et cartographie du Gabon **5310**
Geography and cartography **5119**
Geography in the Middle Ages **5131**
A Geography of the Third World **5137**
Geography since the Second World War **5134**
GeoKatalog **5176**
George, B.
    Jane's NATO handbook, 1991/92 **2984**

George, K.D.
Macmillan's mergers and acquisitions yearbook **2086**
Georgia in antiquity **6680**
Georgieva, V. and Konechni, S.
Historical dictionary of the Republic of Macedonia **7508**
Gephart, R.M.
Revolutionary America 1763-1789: a bibliography **8024**
Gerada-Azzopardi, E.
Malta: an island republic **7368**
Gerber, J.B.
Distinguished women of the twentieth century **5730**
Gerhan, D. R. and Wells, R.V.
A Retrospective biography of American demographic history from colonial times to 1983 **1356**
Gerholm, T. and Lithman, Y.G.
The New Islamic presence in Western Europe **947**
Gerlach, A.C.
The National atlas of the United States **5348**
The German army; 1933-45 **3407**
The German civil code, as amended to January 1, 1975 **2837**
The German Empire 1871-1918 **7257**
German-English, English-German military dictionary **3375**
German-English genealogical dictionary **6070**
German-English glossary of financial and economic terms **2116**
German foreign policy, 1890-1914, and colonial policy to 1914 **1630**
German foreign policy, 1918-1945 **1631**
German Institute for Economic Research
Handbook of the economy of the German Democratic Republic **2327**
German Knights of the Air 1914-1918 **6297**
German military history, 1648-1982 **3409**
German naval history **3571**
The German research companion **6184**
German reunification **7289**
German South West Africa **4860**
Germanic genealogy **6068**
Germany and the Second World War **6896**
Germany (Federal Republic). Statistisches Bundesamt
Statistisches Jahrbuch für die Bundesrepublik Deutschland **1238**
Germany's top 300 **2471**
Geron, L. and Pravda, A.
Who's who in Russia and the new states **5822**
Gertzel, C.
Uganda **7811**
Geschichte der altkirchlichen Literatur **679**
Gettings, F.
Dictionary of astrology **198**
Dictionary of demons **596**
Dictionary of occult, hermetic and alchemical sigils **165**
Ghana **4825**
Ghébali, V.Y. and Ghébali, C.
A Repertoire of League of Nations serial documents, 1919-1947 **2906**
Ghosh, A.
An Encyclopedia of Indian archaeology **4316**
Giannantonio, E.
Italian legal information network **2846**
Gibb, A.D.
Students glossary of Scottish legal terms **2804**
Gibb, H.A.R. and Kramer, J.H.
The Shorter encyclopedia of Islam **940**
Gibbney, H.J. and Smith, A.G.
A Biographical register 1788-1939. Notes from the name index of the Australian Dictionary of Biography **5988**

Gibbon, G.
Archaeology of prehistoric Native America **4332**
Gibbs, G.I.
Dictionary of gaming, modelling & simulation **3845**
Gibraltar **4604**
Gibraltar and its people **7392**
Gibraltar guidebook **5550**
Gibson, J. and Peskett, P.
Record offices **7108**
Gibson, J.S. and Nusberg, C.
International glossary of social gerontology **1104**
Gibson, J.S.W.
Census returns on microfilm. Directory to local holdings, 1841-1881 **1343**
Gibson, J.S.W. and Medlycott, M.
Local census listings, 1522-1930 **1344**
Gibson, P.
The Capital companion **7130**
Gide, C. and Rist, C.
A History of economic doctrines **1875**
Gieysztor, A.
A History of Poland **7311**
Gigler, M.
Australian Ethnic Heritage Series **8149**
Gil, M.
A History of Palestine 634-1099 **7693**
Gilbert, M.
Atlas of the Holocaust **7287**
The Holocaust **7283**
Jerusalem illustrated history atlas **7700**
Routledge atlas of American history **7989**
The Routledge atlas of British history **6933**
The Routledge atlas of Jewish history **6671**
Routledge atlas of Russian history **7430**
The Routledge atlas of the Arab-Israeli conflict **7701**
The Routledge atlas of the First World War **6816**
Gilbert, M.P. and Nilsson, K.R.
Historical dictionary of modern Italy **7363**
Gilbert, V.F. and Tatla, D.S.
Immigrants, minorities and race relations **1112**
Women's studies: a bibliography of dissertations, 1870-1982 **4058**
Gilbertson, G.
Harrap's German and English glossary of terms in international law **2897**
Gilissen, J.
Introduction bibliographique à l'histoire du droit et à l'ethnologie juridique/ Bibliographical introduction to legal history and ethnology **2782**
Gill, G.
The Rules of the Communist party of the Soviet Union **1732**
Gillen, M.
The Founders of Australia **5991**
Gillow, J.
A Literary and biographical history **740**
Gilmore, W.J.
Psychological enquiry **245**
Gilson, É.
History of Christian philosophy in the Middle Ages **111**
Ginger, A.F.
Human rights organizations and periodicals directory, 1993 **3102**
Gipson, L.H.
A Bibliographical guide to the history of the British Empire 1784-1776 **6908**
A Guide to manuscripts relating to the history of the British Empire 1748-1776 **6517**
Giraud, A.F.-S.
Diccionario comercial español-inglés, inglés-español. El secretario **2565**

Gisel, P.
Encyclopédie du protestantisme **753**
Glamorgan county history **7243**
Glanville, M.P.
Councils, committees & boards **3232**
The Glasgow encyclopedia **4547**
Glassé, C.
The Concise encyclopedia of Islam **938**
Glazier, I.A.
Migration from the Russian Empire **6191**
Glazier, M.
The Encyclopedia of the Irish in America **4950**
Glendinning, S.
The Edinburgh encyclopedia of continental philosophy **205**
Glickman, H.
Political leaders of contemporary Africa **1735**
A Global encyclopedia of historical writing **6391**
Global Explorer CD-ROM **5417**
Global links **4507**
Global terrorism **1535**
The Globe and Mail report on business **2476**
Glossaire de termes relatifs aux pratiques communicales restrictives/Glossary of terms relating to restrictive business practices **2083**
Glossaire des droits de l'homme **3103**
Glossario trilingue della proprietà industriale ... Trilingual glossary on industrial property **3176**
Glossary of abbreviations **3605**
Glossary of applied management and financial statistics **2112**
Glossary of audit terms **2594**
Glossary of Chinese political phrases **1395**
Glossary of educational technology terms **3842**
Glossary of fiscal terminology: French/Italian/ English/German/Dutch **2106**
'Glossary of Indian tribal names' **7885**
A Glossary of Islamic economics **1002**
Glossary of labour and the trade union movement **1888, 1968**
Glossary of mediaeval terms of business **1816**
Glossary of population and housing **1319**
Glossary of production planning and control terms **2636**
Glossary of public relations terms in seven languages (English-French-German-Spanish-Dutch-Finnish-Italian) **2714**
A Glossary of special education (children with special needs) **3881**
Glossary of terms in official statistics **1199**
A Glossary of terms used in heraldry **6229**
Glossary of terms used in metrology **3274**
Glossary of terms used in the management of quality control **2641**
Glossary of terms used in work study and organizational methods (O & M) **2549**
Glossary of the Third World **4525**
Glossary of training terms **1964**
Gluski, J.
Proverbs / Proverbes / Sprichwörter / Proverbi / Proverbios / Poslovity **4195**
Gnielinski, S. van
Liberia in maps **5307**
Goa handbook **5570**
Gobbett, B. and Irwin, R.
Introducing Canada **7869**
God pro and con **437**
Goddard, D.
A Buddhist Bible **875**
The Gods of the Celts **951**
Goehlert, R.U. and Fenton, S.M.
The Parliament of Great Britain **3040**
Goetzmann, W. H. and Williams, G.
The Atlas of North American exploration **5082**

Gokhale Institute of Politics and Economics *and* Indian Council of Social Science Research
  Annotated bibliography on the economic history of India **2360**
Gold **2221**
Gold, E.
  Maritime affairs **2951**
The Golden bough **813**
Goldenson, Robert M.
  Longman dictionary of psychology and psychiatry **263**
Goldschmidt, R.
  Historical dictionary of Egypt **7762**
Goldsmith, Devolvé et Associés
  Multilingual glossary of tax, financial and commercial terms **2107**
Goldstein, M.C.
  A History of modern Tibet **7581**
Goldstein, P.M.
  Copyright **3177**
Goldstone, H.P.
  Real estate/Bienes raíces **1995**
Gole, S.
  India within the Ganges **5283**
Golzen, G.
  The *Daily Telegraph* guide to working abroad **1948**
Gomes, L.G.
  Efemérides da história de Macau **7580**
Gomme, A.B.
  The Traditional games of England, Scotland and Ireland **4141**
The good retreat guide **444**
Goodall, B.
  The Facts on File dictionary of human geography **5167**
Goodall, F.
  A Bibliography of British business histories **2462**
Goode's world atlas **5399**
Goodin, R.E. *and* Klingemann, H.-D.
  A New handbook of political science **1376**
Goodin, R.E. *and* Pettit, P.
  A Companion to contemporary political philosophy **1466**
Goodman, A. *and* Cyprien, M.
  A Traveller's guide to early medieval Britain **5467**
Goodman, E.J.
  The Exploration of South America **8082**
Goodman, J. *and* Moncreiffe, Sir Ian
  Debrett's Royal Scotland **6329**
Goodman, M.J.
  Industrial tribunals: practice and procedure **1941**
Goodrich, L.C. *and* Fang, C.
  Dictionary of Ming biography **7558**
Goodrick, E.W. *and* Kohlenberger, J.P.
  The NIV complete concordance **502**
Goodwin, G.
  The Tavistock handbook and directory **2453**
Goralski, R.
  World War II almanac 1931-1945 **6885**
Gordon, A.E.
  Illustrated introduction to Latin epigraphy **6626**
Gordon, C.
  The Atlantic Alliance **2982**
Gordon, H.
  Dictionary of existentialism **206**
Gordon, L.L.
  British battles and medals **3401**
Gordon, P. *and* Aldrich, R.
  Biographical dictionary of North American and European educationists **3809**
Gordon, P. *and* Klug, F.
  Racism and discrimination in Britain **1120**
Gordon, P. *and* Lawton, D.
  A Guide to English educational terms **3760**

Gordon, S.
  The Encyclopedia of myths and legends **819**
  The Paranormal **154**
Gore-Booth, Lord
  Satow's guide to diplomatic practice **3351**
Goring, R.
  Chambers dictionary of beliefs and religions **404**
  Chambers Scottish biographical dictionary **5770**
Gorle, P.
  Handbook of national development plans **2397**
Gorman, G.E.
  'Concordances for Biblical studies' **537**
Gorman, G.E. *and* Gorman, L.
  Theological and religious reference materials **374**
Gorman, G.E. *and* Mahoney, M.
  Index to development studies literature **2394**
Gorman, G.E. *and* Mills, J.J.
  Fiji **5041**
Gorman, J.
  Banners bright **6258**
Gorman, R.A.
  Biographical dictionary of Marxism **231**
  Biographical dictionary of Neo-Marxism **232**
Gorsline, D.
  A History of fashion **3978**
Gorst, A.
  Modern British history **6989**
Gorton, R.A.
  Encyclopedia of school administration & supervision **3848**
Gorvin, I.
  Elections since 1945 **1546**
Gorzny, W.
  Deutscher Biographischer Index/German biographical index **5788**
  Deutsches biographisches archiv **5789**
Gorzny, W. *and* Van der Meer, W.
  Biografisch archief van de Benelux/Archives biographiques des Pays du Benelux. Biographical archive of the Benelux countries. Biographisches archiv der Benelux-länder **5736**
Goslinga, M.
  A Bibliography of the Caribbean **4895**
Gotham **8069**
Gotthold, J.J.
  Indian Ocean **4519**
Gottschalk, A.W.
  British industrial relations **1938**
Gough, B.
  Historical dictionary of Canada **7878**
Gouker, D.
  'Consumer information sources' **3173**
Gould, D.E.
  Historical dictionary of Stockholm **7469**
Goulden, R.
  Kent town guides 1763-1900 **7142**
Goulet, R.
  Dictionnaire des philosophies antiques **108**
The Government and politics of France **3077-3078**
Government Documents Round Table
  Directory of foreign document collections **1646**
Government finance statistics yearbook, 1992 **2137**
Government funding for United Kingdom business **2182**
Government ministers in the contemporary world **3321**
The Government of Northern Ireland, 1922-72 **3072**
Government publications. Sectional list 2. Revised May 1988: Education and science **3782**

Government publications. Sectional list 3, revised June 1988: Energy, trade and industry **2302**
Government publications. Sectional list 5, revised August 1991: Environment **3280**
Government publications. Sectional list 11, revised December 1988: Department of Health and Social Security **3649**
Government publications. Sectional list 21: Employment, health and safety. **1904**
Government publications. Sectional list 26, (revised September 1987): Home Office **3331**
Government publications. Sectional list 29, revised January 1992. Inland Revenue **2151**
Government publications. Sectional list 43, revised February 1992 **1988**
Government publications. Sectional list 44, revised January 1991: Treasury and Civil Service **3240**
Government publications. Sectional list 56: Office of Population Censuses and Surveys **1328**
Government publications. Sectional list 69, revised April 1987. Overseas affairs **1596**
Government publications. Sectional list 71: revised 1 June 1989. Scotland **3655**
Government reference books 92/93 **1500**
The Government Social Survey **1176**
Government statistics **1222**
Gower handbook of quality management **2643**
Goyer, D.S. *and* Draaijer, G.E.
  The Handbook of national population censuses. V.3: Europe **1314**
Gozdecka-Sanford, A.
  Historical dictionary of Warsaw **7313**
Grabois, A.
  The Illustrated encyclopedia of medieval civilization **6441**
Grace, J. *and* Laffin, J.
  Fontana dictionary of Africa since 1960 **7749**
Graduate studies **3934**
Grady, J. *and* Weale, M.
  British banking, 1960-85 **2211**
Graham, B.J. *and* Proudfoot, L.J.
  Historical geography of Ireland **5142**
Graham-Campbell, J.
  Cultural atlas of the Viking World **7462**
Graham-Campbell, J. *and* Batey, C.E.
  Vikings in Scotland **4402**
Graham, I.
  Encyclopedia of advertising **2689**
Graham, J
  Macmillan directory of global financial markets **2168**
Gran atlas de Carreteras España Portugal **5242**
Gran enciclopedia de España **7377**
La Gran enciyclopedia de Puerto Rico **4911**
Granberry, J.A.
  Bibliography of Bahaman prehistory **4335**
The Grand Duchy of Luxembourg **7290**
O Grande livro dos Portugueses **5817**
Grandes hombres de nuestria patria **5967**
Grandin, A.
  Bibliographie générale des sciences juridiques, politiques, économiques et sociales de 1800 à 1925/6 **979**
Grannum, G.
  Tracing your West Indian ancestors **6187**
Gransden, A.
  Historical writing in England **6429**
Grant, D.
  Business histories and biographies **2441**
Grant, I.F. *and* Cheape, H.
  Periods in Highland history **6992**
Grant, L.
  Civil liberty **3112**
Grant, M.
  A Guide to the Ancient World **6689**

Great Britain. Office of Population Census and Surveys *(contd.)*
Government publications. Sectional list 56: Office of Population Censuses and Surveys **1328**
Population projections ... [1985 -2001. England] **1335**

Great Britain. Office of Population Census and Surveys *and* **General Register Office for Scotland**
Guide to census reports: Great Britain, 1801-1966 **1329**

Great Britain. Office of Population Census and Surveys Census of 1981. England and Wales
Index of place names **5510**

Great Britain. Ordnance Survey
Ancient Britain (map) **4388**
Explorer maps **5199**
Landranger maps **5216**
Mapping index **5207**
Maps, atlases and guides. Catalogue 1999 **5205**
New Zealand touring atlas **5378**
The Ordnance Survey gazetteer of Great Britain **5468**
Ordnance Survey Street Atlases **7093**
Outdoor Leisure maps **5200**
Pathfinder maps **5201**
Roman Britain map **4394**
Street atlas CD-ROMs **7094**
Touring map Scotland **5210**

Great Britain. Overseas Development Administration
ABC of aid and development **2978**

Great Britain. Overseas Development Administration. Library Services
Public administration **3215**

Great Britain. Public Record Office
The Cabinet Office, to 1945 **3333**
Guide to the contents of the Public Record Office **6497**
Information for readers **6498**
Maps and plans in the Public Record Office 4. Europe and Turkey **5188**
Maps and plans in the Public Record Office. America and West Indies **7853**
Records of interest to social scientists, 1919-1939: Employment and unemployment **1910**
Records of interest to social scientists, 1919 to 1939 **1017**
Records of interest to social scientists: unemployment insurance 1911-1939 **1962, 3722**

Great Britain. Royal Commission on Historical Manuscripts
Accessions to repositories and records added to the National Register of Archives **6499**
Guide to the location of collections described in the Reports and Calendars series 1870-1980 **6502**
Record repositories in Great Britain **6500**
Surveys of historical manuscripts in the United Kingdom **6501**

Great Britain. Royal Commission on the Ancient And Historical Monuments In Wales
Inventories **4438**

Great Britain. Royal Commission on the Ancient and Historical Monuments of England
Inventories **4434**

Great Britain. Royal Commission on the Ancient and Historical Monuments of Scotland
Catalogue of records, Scottish Industrial Archaeology Survey 1977-85 **4470**
National Monuments Record of Scotland Jubilee **4411**
Reports and inventories **4410**

Great Britain. Scottish Office
Scottish abstract of statistics, 1998 **1232**

Great Britain. Scottish Record Office
Guide to the national archives of Scotland **6512**

Great Britain. Statutory Publications Office
The Public General Acts and General Synod Measures **2790**
Statutes in force **2801**

Great dates in United States history **7996**
Great Domesday **7054**
Great economists before Keynes **1846**
Great economists since Keynes **1845**
The Great goddesses of Egypt **831**
Great historians from antiquity to 1800 **6361**
Great historians of the modern age **6362**
Great Jewish quotations **916**
The Great journey **4327**
Great sieges of history **3467**
Great stone circles **4379**
Great thinkers of the Western world **122**
Great treasury of Western thought **93**
The Great Wall of China **6644**
The Great War **6128**

Greater London Council
The Survey of London **7113**
Greater London history and heritage handbook **7120**
Greater London local history directory and bibliography **7120**
The Greatness and decline of the Celts **952**

Greaves, M.A.
Education in British India, 1698-1947 **3802**

Greaves, R.L. *and* **Zaller, R.**
Biographical dictionary of British radicals in the seventeenth century **1749**

Greco, J. *and* **Sosa, E.**
The Blackwell guide to epistemology **347**
Greece **4635**
Greece and Rome at war **3465**

Greece. Ethnike Statistike Yperesia
Statistical yearbook of Greece **1258**
Greece in modern times **4634**
Greek biographical archive/Griechisches biographisches archiv **5855**
A Greek-English lexikon of the New Testament and other early Christian literature **536**
Greek historiography **6423**
Greek mythology **846**
Greek religion in the archaic and classical periods **847**
Green against green **7033**

Green, H.
Guide to the battlefields of Great Britain and Ireland **3470**

Green, J.
Maritime archaeology **4352**

Green, J.A.
English sheriffs to 1154 **7059**

Green, M.
The Gods of the Celts **951**

Green, M.L.
Dictionary of Celtic myth and legend **956**

Green, P.
Alexander to Actium **6685**

Green, R.
The Commonwealth yearbook 1999 **4561**

Green, W.C. *and* **Reeves, W.R.**
The Soviet military encyclopedia **3413**

Greenaway, D.
Companion to contemporary economic thought **1871**

Greenaway, D. *and* **Bleaney, M.** *and* **Stewart, I.**
A Guide to modern economics **1780**

Greenbert, B.
How to find out in psychiatry **330**

Greene, J.P.
Medieval monasteries **684**

Greene, J.P. *and* **Pole, J.R.**
The Blackwell encyclopedia of the American Revolution **8029**

Greener, M.
The Penguin business dictionary **2525**

Greenfield, G.M. *and* **Maram, S.L.**
Latin American labor organizations **1915**

Greenfield, K.R.
United States Army in World War 2 **6899**

Greenfield, L.R.
Encyclopedia of women's associations worldwide **4110**

Greenham, J.
Clans and families of Ireland **6165**

Greenhill, D. *and* **Morrison, J.**
The Archaeology of boats and ships **4346**
Greenland **5055, 5681**

Greenlaw, M.J. *and* **McIntosh, M.E.**
Educating the gifted **3874**

Greenstein, C.H.
Dictionary of logical terms and symbols **338**

Greenstein, D.L.
A Historian's guide to computing **6370**

Greenwald, D.
The Concise McGraw-Hill dictionary of modern economics **1802**
The McGraw-Hill dictionary of modern economics **1801**
The McGraw-Hill encyclopedia of economics **1776**

Greenwood, D.
Who's buried where in England **5513**

Greenwood, J.
Industrial archaeology and industrial history series **4475**

Greenwood, V.D.
The Researcher's guide to American genealogy **6112**

Gregg, J.R.
Gregg shorthand dictionary **2569**
Gregg shorthand dictionary **2569**

Gregory, D.
Radnorshire **7242**
Wales before 1066 **4439**

Gregory, R.L. *and* **Zangwill, O.L.**
The Oxford companion to the mind **262**

Gregory, R.W.
Anniversaries and holidays **4030**
Grenada **4924**

Grendler, P.F.
Encyclopedia of the Renaissance **6765**

Grenville, J.A.S.
The Major international treaties, 1914-1945 **2973**

Grenville, J.A.S. *and* **Wasserstein, B.**
The Major international treaties of the twentieth century **1615**
The Major international treaties since 1945 **2974**

Gresh, A. *and* **Vidal, D.**
The New A-Z of the Middle East **7536**

Greve, B.
Historical dictionary of the welfare state **1506**

Grey, A.
Aotearoa and New Zealand: a historical geography **5163**

Grey, I.
The Parliamentarians **1681**

Greyerz, K. von
Religion and society in early modern Europe, 1500-1800 **563**

Gribetz, J.
The Timelines of Jewish history **6673**

Grieb, K.
Research guide to Central America and the Caribbean **7904**
Griechische paläographie **6625**

Griffin, A.A.
A Brief guide to the sources for the study of Burma **6563**

Guttenplan, S.
A Companion to the philosophy of mind **72**
Guttman, D.
European American elderly **1097**
Guttman, S.A.
The Concordance to the Standard edition of the complete psychological works of Sigmund Freud **322**
Guttman, Samuel *and* Jones, Randall L. *and* Parrish, S.M.
Concordance to the standard edition of the complete psychological works of Sigmund Freud **237**
Guy, S.
English local studies handbook **7060**
Guyana **4988**
Guyana emergent **8113**
Guyer, P.
The Cambridge companion to Kant **28**
Gwertzman, B.
Israel: The historical atlas **7699**
Gwynn, A. *and* Hadcock, R.N.
Medieval religious houses: Ireland **689**
The Gypsies **4112**
Gypsies and travelling people **4116**
A Gypsy bibliography **4113-4114**
Haag, E.E.
Research guide for studies in infancy and childhood **3683**
Haas, M.
Basic documents of Asian regional organizations **2945**
Hacken, R.D.
Central European economic history from Waterloo to OPEC, 1815-1975 **1852**
Hackin, J.
Asiatic mythology **837**
Hadidian, D.Y.
Bibliography of British theological literature, 1850-1940 **569**
Hadjor, K.B.
Dictionary of Third World terms **4524**
Hadrian's Wall 1989-1999 **4431**
Haeffner, M.
The Dictionary of alchemy **189**
Haestrup, J.
European resistance movements 1939-1945 **6895**
Hagen, R.M.
Norsk historisk atlas **7466**
Hagger, A.J.
A Guide to Australian economic and social statistics **1303**
Haigh, C.
The Cambridge historical encyclopedia of Great Britain and Ireland **6927**
Haines, G.K. *and* Langbart, D.A.
Unlocking the files of the FBI **3255**
Haining, P.
A Dictionary of ghosts **175**
Haiti **4905-4906, 4908**
Haiti a research handbook **7928**
Hajnóczi, G.
Pannonia Hungarica Antiqua **4444**
Hakim, C.
Census data and analysis **1330**
The Hakluyt handbook **5099**
Hale, G.
The New source book for the disabled **3674**
Hale, L.L.
Vancouver centennial bibliography **7892**
Haleem, M.A.A. *and* Kay, E.
English-Arabic business dictionary **1822**
Hálfdanarson, G.
Historical dictionary of Iceland **7473**
Hálfdánarson, O.
Iceland road guide **5553**
Haliburton, G.
Historical dictionary of Lesotho **7839**
Halkon, P.
The Archaeology resource book 1992 **4251**

Hall, D.
International African bibliography **4779**
Hall, D.G.E.
Historians of South-East Asia **6433**
A History of South-East Asia **7551**
Hall, H.
A Select bibliography for the study, sources and literature of English mediaeval economic history **2323**
Hall, K.L.
A Comprehensive bibliography of American constitutional and legal history, 1896-1979 **3079**
The Oxford companion to the Supreme Court of the United States **3209**
Hall, N.V.
Tracing your family history in Australia **6206**
Hall, R.
Empires of the monsoon **7659**
Fifty years of Hume scholarship **26**
Hallam, E.
The Plantagenet encyclopedia **6963**
Hallam, E. *and* Prescott, A.
The British inheritance **6916**
Hallam, E.M.
Domesday Book through nine centuries **7055**
Hallewell, L.
'Latin American area librarianship **4932**
Hallam, C.N. *and* Lister, L.F.
White supremacy and its associated groups **1113**
Hallows, I.S.
Regiments and corps of the British Army **3506**
Halsey's Laws of England **2823**
Halsbury's Laws of England: a user's guide **2824**
Halsbury's Statutes of England and Wales **2791**
Halsbury's Statutory Instruments **2821**
Halsey, A.H.
British social trends since 1900 **1174**
Halsey, A.H. *and* Webb, J.
Twentieth-century British social trends **1175**
Halstead, J.P. *and* Porcari, S.
Modern European imperialism **1576**
Hambly, G.R.G.
'Continuities in the Iranian past since the 7th century C.E.' **7672**
Hambrick, M.
A Chartist's library **218**
Hamerton, D.N.
'Exploiting the publications of international organisations' **2900**
Hamilton-Edwards, G.
In search of Welsh ancestry **6067**
Hamilton-Leggatt, P.
The Dartmoor bibliography 1534-1991 **7157**
Hamilton, N.A.
Founders of modern nations **4515**
Hamilton, R.
Inca religion and customs **968**
Hamlin, A.
Historic monuments of Northern Ireland **4428**
Hamlin, A. *and* Lynn, C.
Pieces of the past **4282**
The Hammond atlas of the world with CD-ROM **5400**
Hammond, C.
Ricardian Britain **5469**
Hammond, N.G.L.
Atlas of the Greek and Roman world in antiquity **6636**
Hammond, T.T.
Soviet foreign relations and world Communism **1637**
Hammond, V.
Current research in management **2623**

Hampsher-Monk, I.
A History of modern political thought **1408**
Han, Woo-Keun
The History of Korea **7587**
Hanák, P.
'Short survey of recent literature on Hungarian economic history' **2329**
A Hand-book of mottoes borne by the nobility, gentry, cities, public companies, etc. ... With Supplement by R. Pinches **6256**
Hand, W.D.
Popular beliefs and superstitions **4163**
A Handbook for archival research in the USSR **6534**
Handbook for Biblical studies **472**
The Handbook for British and Irish archaeology **4263**
The Handbook for genealogists **6087**
Handbook for research in American history **7975**
Handbook for research students in the social sciences **1055**
Handbook for the teaching of social studies **1077**
Handbook for women travellers **5115**
Handbook of aging and the social sciences **1101**
Handbook of American folklore **4162**
A Handbook of archives and material on Pakistan's freedom struggle **6559**
The Handbook of British archaeology **4264**
Handbook of British chronology **6936**
Handbook of British regiments **3402**
Handbook of business information **1773**
The Handbook of Central Asia **4646**
Handbook of clinical sociology **1056**
A Handbook of costume **3960**
Handbook of counselling in Britain **292**
A Handbook of county bibliography **7069**
Handbook of dates for students of English history **6937**
Handbook of developmental psychology **260**
Handbook of family planning and reproductive healthcare **3665**
A Handbook of Greek mythology **850**
Handbook of human factors **2603**
Handbook of industrial relations **1929**
A Handbook of industrial relations practice **1927**
A Handbook of international human rights terminology **3100**
Handbook of international manpower market comparisons **1902**
Handbook of international trade **2487**
A Handbook of Irish folklore **4147**
A Handbook of Korea **4666**
A Handbook of Latin American and Caribbean national archives/Guia de los archivos nacionales de America Latino y el Caribe **6591**
Handbook of Latin American studies **4934**
Handbook of management **2604**
Handbook of management skills **2605**
Handbook of market leaders **2183**
Handbook of modern accounting **2574**
Handbook of modern marketing **2651**
Handbook of national development plans **2397**
The Handbook of national population censuses. V.1: Latin America and the Caribbean, North America and Oceania **1313**
The Handbook of national population censuses. V.2: Africa and Asia **1312**
The Handbook of national population censuses. V.3: Europe **1314**
Handbook of North American Indians **8009**
Handbook of Oriental history **7520**
Handbook of parapsychology **171**
Handbook of perception and human performance **308**
A Handbook of personnel management **2627**
Handbook of philosophical logic **343**

Handbook of psychological assessments **259**

Handbook of reconstruction in Eastern Europe and the Soviet Union **7249**

Handbook of research on social studies **3822**

Handbook of social psychology **261**

Handbook of sociology **1057**

Handbook of special education **3879-3880**

A Handbook of symbols in Christian art **624**

Handbook of the American frontier **8012**

Handbook of the economy of the German Democratic Republic **2327**

Handbook of the psychology of aging **1102**

Handbook of the Religious Society of Friends **802**

The Handbook of the SAS and elite forces **3497**

Handbook of the sociology of gender **1079**

Handbook of United States economic and financial indicators **2380**

The Handbook of Western philosophy **74**

Handbook of world commodity and stock exchanges **2243**

The Handbook of world stock and commodity exchanges **2237**

Handbook on Irish genealogy **6048**

Handbook on ocean politics and law **2952**

Handbook to the Islamic Middle East **4760**

Handbuch der Bibliographien zum Recht der Entwicklungsländer/Handbook of bibliographies on the laws of developing countries **2783**

Handbuch der Byzantinistik **7677**

Handbuch der Vorgeschichte **4216**

Handbuch zur deutschen Militärgeschichte, 1648-1939 **3408**

Handler, J.S.
A Guide to source material for the study of Barbados history 1627-1834 **7936**

Handley, C.S.
An Annotated bibliography of diaries printed in English **5761**

A Handlist of British diplomatic representation, 1509-1688 **3336**

A Handlist of parish registers **6216**

Handwriting in England and Wales **6616**

The Handwriting of English documents **6617**

Handy, R.
A History of the churches in the United States and Canada **709**

Hanham, H.J.
'Some neglected sources of biographical information: county biographical dictionaries 1890-1937' **5762**

Hannam, H.
'The Documentation of colonial rule in Africa' **6566**

Hansard's catalogue and breviate of Parliamentary Papers, 1696-1834 **3061**

Hansen, H.H.
Costume cavalcade **3979**

Hanson, D.G.
Dictionary of banking and finance **2198**

Hanson, F.A. and O'Reilly, P.
Bibliographie de Rapa, Polynésie Française **5038**

Hanson, J.L.
A Dictionary of economics and commerce **1803**

Hanson, T.
Directory of European Community and related databases **2923**

Hanson, W.S. and Slater, E.A.
Scottish archaeology **4273**

Hapsburg Empire
The Hapsburg Empire 1790-1918 **7295**
A History of the Hapsburg Empire **7294**

The Hapsburg Empire 1790-1918 **7295**

Harbin, B.C.
NetSERF: the internet connection for medieval resources **6774**

Harbison, P.
Guide to national and historic monuments of Ireland **4425**

Harbottle, T.B.
Dictionary of historical allusions **6396**

Hard, J.
Royal Navy language **3540**

Harding, L.
Dead countries of the nineteenth and twentieth centuries **5427**

Hardon, J.A.
Modern Catholic dictionary **735**

Hardy, G.J. and Robinson, J.S.
Subject guide to U.S. government reference sources **1501**

Hardy, T.D.
Descriptive catalogue of materials relating to the history of Great Britain and Ireland to the end of the reign of Henry VII **6921**

Hargreaves, G. and Wilson, P.
Dictionary of graphology **305**

Hargreaves-Mawdsley, W.N.
A History of academical dress in Europe **3912**
A History of legal dress in Europe **3189**

Harland, S.
The Educational grants directory, 1998/99 **3922**

Harley, J.B.
Mapping the American Revolutionary War **8032**

Harley, S.
The Timetables of African-American history **8005**

Harman, J.
Online information sources on social and community issues **3606**

Harmon, N.B.
The Encyclopedia of world Methodism **789**
The Interpreter's Bible **516**

Harmon, R.B.
Developing the library collection in political science **1372**

The Harper encyclopedia of military biography **3393**

Harper encyclopedia of military history...
The Encyclopedia of military history **3390**

Harper, P. and Fullerton, L.
Philippines handbook **5657**

The HarperCollins dictionary of American government and politics **3226**

The HarperCollins dictionary of religion **399**

The HarperCollins encyclopedia of Catholicism **727**

Harper's Bible commentary **514**

Harper's Bible dictionary **460**

Harper's encyclopedia of Bible life **451**

Harper's encyclopedia of mystical & paranormal experiences **160**

Harper's topical concordance **503**

Harrap's book of British dates **6935**

Harrap's book of business anecdotes **2038**

Harrap's business French-English dictionary **2031, 2531**

Harrap's business Italian dictionary. Italian-English **2532**

Harrap's English-Brazilian Portuguese business dictionary **1820**

Harrap's five-language business dictionary **2023**

Harrap's German and English glossary of terms in international law **2897**

Harrap's glossary of business management terms. German-English, English-German **2612**

Harrap's glossary of English and Spanish commercial and industrial terms **2420**

Harré, R. and Lamb, R.
The Dictionary of developmental and educational psychology **3830**

Harré, R. and Lamb, R. *(contd.)*
The Dictionary of personality and social psychology **274**

Harries, J.N.
Consumers: know your rights **3174**

Harrington, R.
Trouble-free travel **5088**

Harris, C.D.
Bibliography of Geography **5118**

Harris, D.E.
'Some notes on the industrial archaeology of South Africa' **4487**

Harris, D.J. and Shepherd, J.A.
An Index of British Treaties, 1101-1968 **2969**

Harris, G.
Central and Equatorial Africa area bibliography **4778**

Harris, G. and Diakonov, S.A.
Mapping Russia and its neighbours **5249**

Harris, J.C. and Friedman, J.P.
Barron's real estate handbook **2000**

Harris, M. and Billis, D.
Organizing voluntary agencies **3586**

Harris, M. and Harris, G.
Ancestry's concise genealogical dictionary **6016**

Harris, P.
Story of Scotland's flag **6348**

Harris, T.C.
Guide to parish registers deposited in the Greater London Record office **6215**

Harrison, A.
New sources of grants and aid for businessmen in the UK **2045**

Harrison, C.L.
Women in American history **4102**

Harrison, E.
Family history: a South African beginners' guide **6185**
Officials of royal commission of enquiry, 1870-1939 **3326**

Harrison, E.R.
A Digest and index of tax cases .. **2160**

Harrison, J.
An Economic history of modern Spain **2334**
'Spanish economic history from the restoration to the Franco regime **2333**

Harrison, J.F.C. and Thompson, D.
Bibliography of the Chartist movement, 1837-1976 **219**

Harrison, K.C.
'Old county maps and their makers' **7095**

Harrison, R.
The Warwick guide to British labour periodicals, 1790-1970 **1891**

Harrison, T.
Access to information in local government **3283**

Hart, G.
Dictionary of Egyptian gods and goddesses **832**
Dictionary of taxation **2158**
Pharaohs and pyramids **6647**

Hart, M.
World travel guide 1996/97 **5428**

Hart, N.A. and Stapleton, J.
The Marketing dictionary **2653**

Hartigan, M.
The History of the Irish in Britain **7014**

Hartley, J.M.
Guide to documents and manuscripts in the United Kingdom relating to Russia and the Soviet Union **6539**
The Study of Russian history from British archival sources **6538**

Hartman, T and Mitchell, J.
A World atlas of military history, 1945-1984 **3392**

Hartness, A.
Brasil obras de referência 1965-1998 **4976**

Hartz, F.R.
Prison librarianship 3145
Harvard guide to American history 7959
Harvard, J.
Bilingual guides to business and professional correspondence 2559
Harvard University. Graduate School of Business Administration. Baker Library
Author-title catalog 1760
Core collection: an author and subject guide, 1970/71- 2518
The Kress Library of Business and Economics. Catalogue 1763
Recent additions to Baker Library 1762
Subject catalog 1761
Harvard University. Law School. Library
Index to multilateral treaties 2964
Harvey, B.P.
An Introduction to Buddhism 873
Harvey, D.
Monuments to courage 6290
Harvey, J.M.
Statistics Africa 1278
Statistics America 1282
Statistics: Asia & Australia 1262
Statistics Europe 1215
Harvey, R.
Genealogy for librarians 6040
A Guide to genealogical sources in the Guildhall Library 6064
Harzfeld, L.A.
Periodical indexes in the social sciences and humanities 1010
Haselfoot, A.J.
The Batsford guide to the industrial archaeology of South-East England 4481
Haskins, G.
A Guide to small firms assistance in Europe 2081
Hasselbauer, K.J.
A Research guide to the health sciences 3635
Hastings, A.
A History of English Christianity, 1920-1985 565
Hastings, J.
A Dictionary of the Bible 461
Encyclopaedia of religion and ethics 393
Hastings, J
Encyclopedia of religion and ethics 355
Haswell-Smith, H.
The Scottish islands 5494
Hatch, J.M.
The American book of days 4031
Hatchments in Britain 6248
Hauner, M.
Hitler: a chronology of his life and time 7279
Hauptman, R. and Motin, S.H.
The Holocaust: memories, research, reference 7284
Hawai'i 5049
Hawaii a bicentennial history 8191
Hawaii a geography 5148
Hawaii fact and reference book 5048
Hawaii handbook. All Islands 5679
Hawgood, D.
Families on the Internet 6131
Hawkesworth, M. and Kogan, M.
Encyclopedia of government and politics 1482
Hawkings, D.T.
Bound for Australia 6124
Criminal ancestors 6175
Hawtrey, S.C. and Barclay, H.M.
Abraham and Hawtrey's parliamentary dictionary 3046
Hay, D.
Annalists and historians 6366
Longman history of Italy 7358

Hay, P.
Harrap's book of business anecdotes 2038
Hayasdanee badmagan adias 7434
Haycraft, F.W.
Degrees and hoods of the world's universities and colleges 3910
Hayden, A.J. and Newton, R.F.
British hymn writers and composers 656
Haydn, J.
Dictionary of dates and universal information 6469
Haydock, T.
Treasure trove 5103
Hayes, A.
Archaeology of the British Isles 4385
Hayes, D.
Historical atlas of the Pacific Northwest 7860
Hayes, J.H.
Dictionary of biblical interpretation 497
Hayes-McCoy, G.A.
A History of Irish flags from earliest times 6349
Hayes, S.V.
Who's who of Southern Africa 2000: an illustrated biographical record of prominent personalities in the Republic of South Africa, Botswana, Mauritius, Namibia, Swaziland, Zimbabwe, and neighbouring countries in South Africa 5900
Hayford, C.W.
China 4650
Haynes, J.E.
Communism and anti-Communism in the United States 221
Haynes, R.
The Society for Psychical Research, 1882-1982 168
Haythornthwaite, P.J.
The Napoleonic source book 3473
The World War One sourcebook 6813
Hayton, D. and Jones, C. and Ditchfield, G.M.
British parliamentary lists, 1660-1800 3059
Hayward, J.B.
British gallantry awards 3430
Hayward, P.H.C.
Jane's dictionary of military terms 3373
Haywood, J.
The Cassell atlas of world history 6415
Cassell historical atlases 6416
The Penguin historical atlas of the Vikings 7463
Haywood, P.
Bibliography of comparative adult education 3859
Haywood, P.G.
A Bibliography of adult teaching, psychology and research 3831
Hazell's guide to the judiciary and the courts 3198
The Bukharans 7710
Head-dress badges of the British Army 3447
Headland, R.
The Island of South Georgia 4979
South Georgia 4981
Headland, R.K.
Chronological list of Antarctic expeditions 8204
The Heads of religious houses 691
Heads of state and government 3323
Heald, G. and Wybrow, R.J.
The Gallup survey of Britain 1090
Heald, T.
By appointment 2463
Health advice for travellers 5087
Health and personal social service statistics for England, 1997 3656
Health and personal social services statistics for Wales, 1991 3657

The Health and safety at work directory, 1998/99 3643
Health education index 3650
Health service abstracts 3640
Heard, J.N.
Handbook of the American frontier 8012
Hearnshaw, L.S.
A Short history of British psychology, 1804-1940 291
Heath, D.B.
Historical dictionary of Bolivia 8102
Heathfield, D. and Russell, M.
Modern economics 1837
Hébert, J.
Travelling in tropical countries 5102
Hébridais 5984
Hecht, J.J.
Bibliographical handbooks 6919
Heckart, R.J.
'A Fresh look at the *Index to current urban documents* and the *Urban documents microfiche collection*'. 3310
Hector, L.C.
The Handwriting of English documents 6617
Hedrick, B.C. and Hedrick, A.K.
Historical and cultural dictionary of Nepal 7663
Historical dictionary of Panama 7915
Heere, W.P.
International bibliography of air law, 1900-1971 3184
Hegel bibliography 25
A Hegel dictionary 24
Heggie, G.F.
Canadian political parties, 1867-1968 1738
Heggoy, A.A. and Haar, J.M.
The Military in imperial history 3410
Heggoy, A.A. and Naylor, P.C.
Historical dictionary of Algeria 7774
Heichelheim, F.M.
An Ancient economic history 2274
A Heidegger dictionary 59
Heidler, D.S. and Heidler, J.T.
Encyclopedia of the War of 1812 8037
Heiliger, W.S.
Bibliography of the Soviet social sciences, 1965-1975 1039
Heinecken, M.T.
Encyclopedia of Bible creatures 493
Heinemann New Zealand atlas 5380
Heinl, R.D.
Dictionary of military and naval quotations 3387
Hejzlar, Z. and Kusin, V.V.
Czechoslovakia 1968-1969 7306
Helck, W. and Westendorf, W.
Lexikon der Ägyptologie 4231
Held, J.
The Columbia history of Eastern Europe in the twentieth century 7246
Dictionary of East European history since 1945 7250
Helferty, S. and Refaussé, R.
Directory of Irish archives 6514
Hellyer, R.
'The Archaeological and historical maps of the Ordnance Survey' 4268
Ordnance Survey small-scale maps. Indexes 1801-1998 5208
Helmer, D.
'Native American reference sources' 4972
Help yourself 1158
Helyer, P. and Swales, W.
Bibliography of Tristan da Cunha 4872
Hempstead, A.
Alberta and the Northwest Territories handbook 5603
Henderson, D.V.
Dragons can be defeated 6283

Henderson, G.
Maritime archaeology in Australia **4363**
Henderson, H. *and* Thompson, S.E.
Holidays, festivals, and celebrations of the World dictionary **6470**
Henderson, J. *and* Humphreys, F.
Audiovisual and microcomputer handbook **3835**
Henderson, M.
The Gabbitas, Truman & Thring guide to boarding schools and colleges, 1988/89 **3850**
Henige, D.
Serial bibliographies and abstracts in history **6405**
Henige, D.D.
Colonial governors **1575**
Henken, E.R.
Traditions of the Welsh saints **613**
Henriksen, P.
Det store Norges-Atlas **5254**
Henriksen, T.H.
Mozambique **7821**
Henry, B.
British television advertising **2700**
Henslin, J.M.
Homelessness **3680**
Heper, M.
Historical dictionary of Turkey **7683**
An Heraldic alphabet **6225**
Heraldic standards and their ensigns **6221**
Heraldry for the local historian and genealogist **6247**
Heraldry in the Royal Navy **3553**
Heraldry in the Vatican **6255**
Heraldry: sources, symbols and meaning **6222**
Heralds of England **6249**
Heralds of today **6250**
Herber, M.D.
Ancestral trails **6029**
Herbert, M.C. *and* McNeil, B.
Biography and genealogy master index **5943**
Herbert, P.M.
Burma **4747**
Herbert, T. *and* Jones, G.E.
Welsh history and its sources **7233**
Herbst, R.
Dictionary of commercial, financial and legal terms **1792**
Herculaneum: a guide to printed sources **4447**
Herd, M.
Who's who in Australia 2000 **5997**
Heritage: a visitors guide **5507**
Heritage in Wales **4440**
The Heritage of Australia **5666**
Herman, G.
The Pivotal conflict **6820**
Herman, K.
Women in particular **5960**
Herold, J.
Marketing and sales management **2648**
'Political science reference sources' **1373**
Herring, J.E.
School librarianship **3853**
Herring, M.Y.
Ethics and the professor **352**
Herron, N.L.
The Social sciences **986**
Hersen, M. *and* Bellack, A.S.
Dictionary of behavioral assessment techniques **332**
Herspring, D.R.
The Soviet High Command, 1967-1989 **3514**
Herstein, S.R. *and* Robbins, N.C.
United States of America **4943**
Hervouet, Y.
A Sung bibliography **7564**
Herwig, H.H. *and* Heyman, N.M.
Biographical dictionary of World War I **6824**

Hessayon, A.
A Patient's guide to the National Health Services **3660**
Hesslein, S.B.
Serials on aging **1106**
Heussler, R.
British Malaya **7719**
Hey, D.
The Oxford companion to local and family history **7079**
The Oxford dictionary of local and family history **6152**
The Oxford guide to family history **6132**
Heyel, C.
The Encyclopedia of management **2598**
Hibbert, C.
The Encyclopaedia of Oxford **7196**
Hickey, D.J. *and* Doherty, J.E.
A Dictionary of Irish history 1800 - 1980 **7022**
Hicks, P.
AA touring England **5511**
Hiden, J. *and* Salmon, P.
The Baltic nations and Europe **7438**
Hieronymussen, P.
Orders, medals and decorations of Britain and Europe in colour **6281**
Higgs, E.
A clearer sense of the census **1338**
Making sense of the census **1339**
Higham, C.
The Archaeology of mainland Southeast Asia **4320**
Higham, N.J.
The Kingdom of Northumbria **7220**
Higham, R.
A Guide to sources of US military history **3519**
A Guide to the sources of British military history **3406**
Official histories **6800**
'Higher education', 1980-85 **3891**
Higher education in developing nations **3897**
Higher education in international perspective **3889**
Higher education in the European Community **3899**
Higher education in the United Kingdom, 1992-93 **3933**
Higson, C.W.J.
Sources for the history of education **3775**
Hildenbrand, S.
Women's collections **4099**
Hildreth, S.S.
The A to Z of Wall Street: 2500 terms for the street smart investor **2258**
Hiler, H. *and* Hiler, M.
Bibliography of costume **3955**
Hilgard, E.R. *and* Bower, G.H.
Theories of learning **3825**
Hilgemann, W.
Atlas zur deutschen Zeitgeschichte **7267**
Hill, B.W.
British parliamentary parties, 1742-1832, from the fall of Walpole to the first Reform Act **1719**
The Growth of British parliamentary parties, 1689-1742 **1718**
Hill, D.
An Atlas of Anglo-Saxon England **6958**
Hill, D.A.
Norwegian local history **7465**
Hill, D.M.
'Local government' **3276**
Hill, E.
Guide to records in the National Archives relating to American Indians **6604**
Hill-forts of Britain **4386**
Hill, G.
A History of Cyprus **7684**

Hill, K.T.
Festivals USA **4025**
Hill, R.J.
The Soviet Union **2341**
Hill, R.L.
A Bibliography of the Anglo-Egyptian Sudan **4798**
Hillerbrand, H.J.
The Oxford encyclopedia of the Reformation **634**
Hills, P.J.
A Dictionary of education **3761**
Hillyer, N.
The New Bible dictionary **462**
Himalayan triangle **7660**
Himmelstrup, J. *and* Birket-Smith, K.
Søren Kierkegaard **32**
Hinde, T.
The Domesday Book **7056**
Hinding, A.
Women's history sources **4101**
Hindle, B.P.
Maps for local historians **7096**
Hindu mythology **869**
The Hindu world **868**
Hindustan yearbook and who's who 1999 **4715**
Hines, W.
'Bibliography on British and Irish legal history (works published after 1985)' **2799**
Hinnells, J.R.
Facts on File dictionary of religions **405**
A New dictionary of religions **400**
A New handbook of living religions **397**
The Penguin dictionary of religions **405**
Who's who of religions **427**
Hinshelwood, R.D.
A Dictionary of Kleinian thought **318**
Hintauer, S.
Canadian legal directory, 1987 **2858**
Hinton, J.
Labour and Socialism **1722**
Hints to exporters visiting.. **2281**
Hinz, E.
Pacific Island battlegrounds of World War II **8137**
Hiro, D.
Dictionary of the Middle East **7544**
Hirsch, E.
Facts about Israel 1998 **4737**
Hirschberger, J.
A Short history of Western philosophy **124**
Hirschfelder, A. *and* Montano, M.K. de
The Native American almanack **4967**
Hirschfolder, A. *and* Morin, P.
The Encyclopedia of native American religions **810**
The Hispanic American almanac **4956**
Hispanic American information directory **4957**
Histoire de la philosophie. Périod chrétienne **112**
Histoire de la population française **1186**
Histoire des relations internationales **1611**
Histoire et dictionnaire de Paris **4587**
Histoire générale du socialisme **211**
Histoire monetaire de la France, 1800-1980 **2130**
Historia completa de las Malvinas **8090**
Historia de España **7372, 7941**
Historia de España antigua y medieval **7374**
História de Moçambique **7822**
Historia de Portugal **7396**
Historia general de Costa Rica **7912**
Historia general de las Islas Canarias **7383**
Historia general de los Peruanos **8103**
História geral da civilização Brasiliera **8084**
Historia moderna de Mexico. 9v. in 10 **7897**
Historia religionum **425**
Historial dictionary of Australia **8170**
A Historian's guide to computing **6370**

Historical dictionary of the Korean War **7596**
Historical dictionary of the Netherlands **7477**
Historical dictionary of the New Deal **8066**
Historical dictionary of the Orthodox Church **718**
Historical dictionary of the Peoples Republic of China 1949-1997 **7575**
Historical dictionary of the Persian Gulf War, 1990-1991 **7628**
Historical dictionary of the Philippines **8125**
Historical dictionary of the Progressive Era **8062**
Historical dictionary of the reformed churches **775**
Historical dictionary of the Republic of Cameroon **7801**
Historical dictionary of The Republic of Cape Verde **7787**
Historical dictionary of the Republic of Croatia **7501**
Historical dictionary of the Republic of Guinea-Bissau **7786**
Historical dictionary of the Republic of Korea **7598**
Historical dictionary of the Republic of Macedonia **7508**
Historical dictionary of the Republic of Moldova **7513**
Historical dictionary of the Spanish American War **8058**
Historical dictionary of the Spanish Civil War **7390**
Historical dictionary of the Spanish Empire **7381**
Historical dictionary of The Sudan **7766**
Historical dictionary of the United States Air Force **3531**
Historical dictionary of the United States Navy **3585**
Historical dictionary of the welfare state **1506**
Historical dictionary of Togo **7791**
Historical dictionary of Tokyo **7606**
Historical dictionary of Trinidad and Tobago **7938**
Historical dictionary of Tudor England **6968**
Historical dictionary of Tunisia **7759**
Historical dictionary of Turkey **7683**
Historical dictionary of Uganda **7812**
Historical dictionary of Uruguay **8116**
Historical dictionary of Venezuela **8112**
Historical dictionary of Vienna **7299**
Historical dictionary of Vietnam **7726**
Historical dictionary of Warsaw **7313**
Historical dictionary of Western Sahara **7772**
The historical dictionary of world political geography **1388**
Historical dictionary of World War I **6814**
The Historical dictionary of World War II: The War against Japan **6873**
Historical dictionary of Yemen **7617**
Historical dictionary of Zambia **7842**
Historical dictionary of Zimbabwe **7841**
Historical directory of trade unions **1973**
The Historical encyclopedia of costumes **3958**
Historical encyclopedia of Honduras: a fundamental work of information and reference and an indispensable teaching aid for teachers.. **7906**
An Historical encyclopedia of the Arab-Israeli conflict **7696**
Historical gazetteer of Iran **7674**
Historical gazetteer of London before the Great Fire **7133**
An Historical geography of Europe **5152**
An Historical geography of France **5157**
Historical geography of Ireland **5142**
An Historical geography of modern Australia **5164**
An Historical geography of Scandinavia **5158**
Historical geography of the United States **5162**
A Historical guide to the United States **5622**

Historical periodicals directory **6407**
Historical record of the census of production, 1907-1970 **2406**
Historical records of the Government of Canada **7884**
'Historical sources in Costa Rica' **7913**
Historical statistics of Chile **1299**
Historical statistics of the United States: colonial times to 1970 **1297**
Historical writing in England **6429**
The Histories of Wales series **7227**
Historiography **6364, 6367**
Historiography in Indian languages **6365**
Historiography in the Revolution **7924**
The Historiography of Latin America **6437**
Historischer Atlas Deutschland **7262**
Historisches Wörterbuch der Philosophie **69**
History and culture of Himalayan states **7661**
The History and culture of the Indian people **7639**
The History highway **6374**
History in the Ordnance Map **5211**
History journals and serials **6409**
A History of academical dress in Europe **3912**
The History of accounting **2573**
A History of adult education **3863**
A History of African archaeology **4323**
The History of Albania **7485**
A History of American business **2066**
A History of American psychology in notes and news, 1883-1945 **295**
The History of American women's voluntary organizations, 1810-1960 **3629**
History of ancient geography **5132**
A History of ancient India **6678**
A History of ancient Israel **6661**
A History of Antarctica **8200**
The History of anti-Semitism **919**
A History of archaeological thought **4226**
The History of archaeology in Czechoslovakia **4291**
A History of astrology **199**
A History of atheism in Britain **439**
A History of Australia **8152**
A History of Barbados **7934**
A History of Brazil **8083**
A History of British industrial relations **1939**
History of British Socialism **213**
A History of British philosophy, to 1900 **128**
A History of British trade unionism **1976**
A History of British trade unions since 1889 **1975**
The History of British Universities, 1800-1969 **3939**
A History of Brunei **8123**
A History of Caernarvonshire 1284-1900 **7239**
A History of Cambodia **7724**
The History of Canada **7872**
A History of Carmarthenshire **7245**
History of Central Africa **7795**
The History of Ceylon (c.1500-1658) **7664**
A History of Chile, 1808-1994 **8096**
A History of Chinese philosophy **138**
History of Christian philosophy in the Middle Ages **111**
A History of Christian spirituality **630**
A History of Christianity **560**
A History of Christianity in India **566**
History of Christianity in the world **561**
History of civilizations of Central Asia **7516**
A History of costume in the West **3973**
A History of creeds and confessions of faith in Christendom and beyond **615**
A History of Cyprus **7684**
A History of Czechoslovakia since 1945 **7305**
History of East Africa **7797**
A History of ecclesiastical dress **647**
History of economic analysis **1878**
A History of economic doctrines **1875**
A History of economic thought **1876**

The History of economic thought and analysis **1877**
History of elementary education in England and Wales, from 1800 to the present day **3794**
A History of English Christianity, 1920-1985 **565**
A History of English criminal law and its administration from 1750 **3131**
A History of English law **2828**
History of ethics **356**
A History of Ethiopia **7767**
A History of experimental psychology **299**
A History of fashion **3978**
A History of Finland **7458**
A History of gold and money, 1450-1920 **2230**
A History of Greek philosophy **99**
The History of Greenland **8199**
A History of Gwent **7229**
A History of historical writing **6359**
A History of Hong Kong **7577**
History of humanity **6388**
A History of Hungary **7318**
History of Hungary and the Hungarians 1848-1971 **7320**
A History of Indian philosophy **139**
A History of Irish flags from earliest times **6349**
A History of Islamic philosophy **143**
A History of Islamic societies **945, 7527**
A History of Israel **7694**
The History of Jamaica **7926**
History of Jewish philosophy **918**
A History of Jewish philosophy in the Middle Ages **146**
The History of Korea **7587**
A History of Laos **7740**
A History of legal dress in Europe **3189**
History of Lincolnshire **7181**
The History of local government in England **3291**
A History of local government in the twentieth century **3287**
History of logic **344**
The History of London in maps **7126**
History of magic and experimental science **186**
A History of Malaysia **7718**
A History of Mexican archaeology **4334**
A History of modern British geography **5140**
The History of modern geography **5133**
A History of modern Hungary 1867-1994 **7319**
A History of modern India **7636**
A History of modern Indonesia **8118**
A History of modern Norway 1814-1972 **7464**
A History of modern political thought **1408**
History of modern psychology **286**
A History of modern Thailand **7715**
A History of modern Tibet **7581**
A History of modern Trinidad 1783-1962 **7937**
A History of Monmouthshire **7165**
A History of Niger **7779**
A History of Nigeria **7793**
History of Orkney **7013**
A History of Otago **8138**
A History of Palestine 634-1099 **7693**
The History of Parliament **3051**
History of Parliament, 1439-1509 **3052**
History of Parliament Trust
The History of Parliament **3051**
A History of Parliament. V.1: The Middle ages **3050**
The History of philosophy **95**
A History of philosophy **97, 106**
A History of Poland **7310-7311**
History of Polar exploration
The White road **8194**
A History of political theory **1477**

Holzman, D.
  Japanese religion and philosophy **961**
Homan, R.
  The Sociology of religion **375**
Homberger, E.
  The Historical atlas of New York City **8078**
Homelessness **3680-3681**
Homicide **3133**
Honduras **4887**
Hong Kong **4659**
Hong Kong, 1996 **4660**
Hong Kong atlas **5273**
Hong Kong. Census and Statistics Department
  Hong Kong monthly digest of statistics, 1978- **1267**
  Hong Kong monthly digest of statistics, 1978- **1267**
Honours and awards in the British Empire and Commonwealth **6291**
Hoogewoud, F.J.
  A Guide to libraries of Judaica and Hebraica in Europe **927**
Hoogvelt, A. *and* Puxty, A.
  Multinational enterprise **2072**
Hook, B. *and* Twitchett, D.
  The Cambridge encyclopedia of China **4652**
Hooke, N.
  Modern shipping disasters 1963-1987 **5110**
Hopcke, R.H.
  A Guided tour of the collected works of Jung **319**
Hopkins, D.J.
  Merriam-Webster's geographical dictionary **5436**
Hopkinson, M.
  Green against green **7033**
Hopwood, K.
  Ancient Greece and Rome **6687**
Horak, S.M.
  Eastern European national minorities, 1919-1980 **1512**
  Russia, the USSR and Eastern Europe **7416**
Horchler, G.F.
  Hungarian economic reforms **2328**
Horn, M.
  Scottish Office statistical publications **1233**
Hornblower, S.
  Greek historiography **6423**
Hornblower, S. *and* Spawforth, A.
  The Oxford companion to classical civilization **6691**
Horne, H.O.
  A History of savings banks **2217**
Horner, A.A.
  Population in Ireland **1340**
Hornsby, A.
  Chronology of African American history **8006**
Horowitz, L.
  A Bibliography of military name lists **6105**
Horrocks, S.
  Contributions towards a Lancashire bibliography **7214**
  Lancashire business histories **2469**
Horten, H.E.
  Export-import correspondence in four languages **2560**
Horton, D.
  The Encyclopaedia of Aboriginal Australia. Aboriginal and Torres Strait Islander history, society and culture **5032**
Horton, J.J.
  Yugoslavia **4637**
Horward, D.D.
  Napoleonic military history **3513**
Hoskins, J.W.
  Polish genealogy and heraldry **6006**
Hoskins, W.G. *and* Stamp, L.D.
  The Common lands of England and Wales **1997**

Hospital literature index **3661**
The Hospitals and health services yearbook .. **3646**
Houck, C.
  The Fashion encyclopedia **3962**
Houghton, D.H.
  The South African economy **2371**
Hounsell, D.
  Bibliographic and information services in education **3728**
  Bibliographic services in education **3726**
Hourani, R.
  A History of the Arab peoples **7525**
Hourcade, B.
  Atlas d'Iran **5286**
House, J.M.
  Military intelligence, 1870-1991 **3476**
The House magazine **3047**
House of Commons
  Manual of procedure in the public business **3037**
The House of Commons Library **1689**
The House of Lords **1678**
Housing **3256-3257**
Housing and construction statistics, 1982-1992, Great Britain **3261**
Housing and racial/ethnic minority status in the United States **1516**
A Housing bibliography **3259**
Housing year book, 1996 **3260**
Houston, J.E.
  Thesaurus of ERIC descriptors **3816**
Hovannisian, R.G.
  The Armenian people from ancient to modern times **7452**
  The Republic of Armenia **7453**
Hovet, T. *and* Trover, E.L.
  A Chronology and fact book of the United Nations, 1941-1991 **2912**
How Ireland is governed **3335**
How to choose a career **1947**
How to do business with Russians **2428**
How to find information 1992 **2663**
'How to find Italian business information' **2056**
How to find out about banking and investment **2191**
How to find out about the social sciences **985**
How to find out in psychiatry **330**
How to find out in psychology **235**
'How to find UK local statistics' **3286**
'How to find US business information' **2062**
How to interpret a birth chart **195**
How to organize information **2511**
How to set up & run your own business **2079**
How to start and run your own business **2080**
How to trace family history in Northern Ireland **6173**
How to trace your ancestors to Europe **6113**
How to trace your convict ancestors **6126**
How to use a law library **2725**
Howard, D.
  Directory of theatre resources **4001**
Howard League for Penal Reform. John Howard Library of Criminology and Penology
  Catalogue, 1963 **3149**
Howard-Reguindid, P.F.
  Honduras **4887**
The Howard University bibliography of African and Afro-American religious studies **967**
Howarth, K.
  Oral history **6750**
Howe, C. *and* Walker, K.R.
  The Foundations of the Chinese planned economy **2391**
Howe, K.R.
  Where the waves fall **8128**
Howell, R.
  A History of Gwent **7229**

Howells, C.
  The Cambridge companion to Sartre **50**
  Cyndi's list: a comprehensive list of 40,000 genealogy sites on the Internet **6014**
  Cyndi's list of genealogy sites on the Internet **6013**
Howells, J.G. *and* Osborn, M.L.
  A Reference companion to the history of abnormal psychology **246**
Howes, D.
  American women 1935-1940 **5959**
Howey, R.S.
  A Bibliography of general histories of economics, 1692-1975 **1842**
Howgego, J.
  Printed maps of London circa 1553 - 1850 **7129**
Howitt, Doran and Weinberger, Marvin, Inc.
  Databasics **2596**
Howlett, R.
  Hong Kong, 1996 **4660**
Hoxie, F.E.
  Encyclopedia of North American Indians **8010**
Hoxie, F.E. *and* Markowitz, H.
  Native Americans **8007**
Høyer, B.
  Groenlandica. Catalogue of Groenlandica collection in the National Library of Greenland **5054**
Hrsg.von Kurt Ranke [u.a.]
  Enzyklopädie des Märchens. Handwörterbuch zur historischen und vergleichenden Erzählforschung **4132**
Hsieh Chiao-min *and* Hsieh, J. K.
  China: a provincial atlas **5270**
Hsu, I.C.Y.
  The Rise of modern China **7559**
Hsüeh, C.-T.
  The Chinese Communist movement, 1937-1949 **1734**
Hubbard, L.S.
  Notable Americans **5930**
Hubbell, J.T. *and* Geary, J.W.
  Biographical dictionary of the Union **8051**
Huber, K.R.
  Women in Japanese society **4096**
Hubert, H.
  The Greatness and decline of the Celts **952**
  The Rise of the Celts **953**
Hübner, R.
  Who is Who in Österreich mit Südtiroltel **5794**
Hübscher, A.
  Schopenhauer-Bibliographie **52**
Hudland, M.F.
  Penguin shorter atlas of the Bible **482**
Hudson, A.H.
  Dictionary of commercial law **3160**
Hudson, G.L.
  Corsica **4588**
  Monaco **4589**
Hudson, K. *and* Nicholls, A.
  The Cambridge guide to the historic places of Britain and Ireland **5470**
Hudson, R.
  An Atlas of EEC affairs **2943**
Huellmantel, M.B.
  European business services directory **2450**
Huffman, J.L.
  Modern Japan **7605**
Hughes, A. *and* Gailey, H.A.
  Historical dictionary of The Gambia **7784**
Hughes, D.
  Lloyd's nautical year book, 1999 **3712**
Hughes, H.G.A.
  Samoa (American Samoa and Western Samoa, Samoans abroad) **5045**
Hughes, K.
  Early Christian Ireland **7032**

Hughes, S. *and* Reynolds, P.
Industrial archaeology of the Swansea region 4484
Huguenot ancestry 6073
Hultgren, A.J.
New Testament Christology 525
Human resources abstracts 1868
The Human resources glossary 2633
The Human resources management yearbook, 1993 2629
Human rights 3092-3093, 3096
Human rights bibliography 3094
Human rights directory 3104
Human rights directory: Latin America 3105
Human rights organizations and periodicals directory, 1993 3102
Human rights reports 3095
Human rights terminology in international law 3110
Human rights: the essential reference 3089
Human services in postrevolutionary Cuba 1190
Humana, C.
World human rights guide 3099
Humanities Reference Unit. University of Glasgow
The British biographical index 5760
Humby, M.
A Guide to the literature of education 3745
Hume, D.
A Bibliography of David Hume, and of Scottish philosophy 27
Hume, J.R.
Scotland's industrial past 4471
Humm, M.
An Annotated critical bibliography of feminist criticism 4059
The Dictionary of feminist theory 4049
Humphery-Smith, C.
The Cambridge armorial 6235
Humphery-Smith, C.R.
A Genealogist's bibliography 6059
'Genealogy in Portugal' 6076
The Phillimore atlas and index of parish registers 6213
Humphreys, A.L.
A Handbook of county bibliography 7069
Humphreys, C.A.
A Popular dictionary of Buddhism 880
Humphreys, N.K.
Historical dictionary of the International Monetary Fund 2184
Humphreys, R.S.
Islamic history 7526
A Hundred years of international relations 1610
A Hundred years of philosophy 103
Hungarian biographical Index/Magyar Életrajzi index 5800
Hungarian economic reforms 2328
The Hungarian Soviet Republic 1919 7321
Hungary 4581
Hungary. Essential facts and figures 4580
Hungary. Központi Statisztikai Hivatal
Magyar statisztikai evkönyv. Statistical yearbook 1242
Hunger in history 1149
Hunt, E.H.
British labour history, 1815-1914 1907
Hunt, T.C. *and* Carper, J.C.
Religious colleges and universities in America 3827
Hunter, J.
Concise dictionary of modern Japanese history 7607
Hunter, J. *and* Ralston, I.
The Archaeology of Britain 4253
Hunter, J.R.
Fair Isle 4274
Fair Isle. The archaeology of an island community 4406

Hunter, N.R.
Index to business reports 2036
Hunter, Rodney J.
Dictionary of pastoral care and counselling 619
Hunter, T.B.
The A to Z of international terrorist and counterterrorist organizations 1536
Huntington Free Library and Reading Room. New York
Dictionary catalog of the American Indian collections 1135
Hupchick, D.P. *and* Cox, H.E.
A Concise historical atlas of Eastern Europe 7252
Hupper, W.G.
An Index to English periodical literature on the Old Testament and ancient Near Eastern studies. V.I 474
Hurd, A.
The Merchant Navy 6803
Hurst, M.
Key treaties for the Great Powers, 1814-1914 2972
Huson, T. *and* Postlethwaite, T.N.
The International encyclopedia of education 3723
Hussain Menes
Atlas of the history of Islam 7534
Hustwit, J. *and* Webley, M.
Information in social welfare 3651
Hutchings, R.
Historical dictionary of Albania 7487
The Hutchinson atlas of World War II battle plans 6876
The Hutchinson chronology of world history 6472
The Hutchinson dictionary of biography 5696
The Hutchinson dictionary of business quotations 2039
The Hutchinson dictionary of world history 6397
The Hutchinson encyclopedia of Britain 1999 4541
The Hutchinson encyclopedia of Ireland 4553
The Hutchinson encyclopedia of modern political biography 1410
The Hutchinson guide to Britain 5471
The Hutchinson guide to the world 5429
The Hutchinson history reference suite 6375
The Hutchinson illustrated encyclopedia of British History 6929
Hutchinson, L.
Standard handbook for secretaries 2556
Hutchinson political systems of the world 1487
Hutchinson, T.P. *and* Ke, Y.
An Index to corrections, addenda, and comments that were published in statistical journals, 1970-1991 1192
Hutchinson, W.K.
American economic history 2385
History of economic analysis 1878
Hutchison, K.D.
World War II in the North Pacific 6886
Hutchison, P.
Central America & Mexico handbook 2001 5606
Hutton, R.
The Pagan religions 809
Huussen, A.H.
Historical dictionary of the Netherlands 7477
Huws, G. *and* Roberts, D.H.E.
Wales 4568
Hvass, S. *and* Storgaard, B.
Digging into the past 4300
Hvem er hvem 1994 5841
Hvem, Hva, hvor 4625
Hyamson, A.M.
Dictionary of universal biography 5714

Hyde, M.
Library and information services to business and industry 2067
Hyde, R.
Printed maps of Victorian London 1851-1900 7135
Ward maps of the City of London 7127
The hymn tune index: a census of English language hymn tunes in printed sources from 1535 to 1820 655
Hymns and tunes - an index 650
Hymns and tunes indexed 652
Hyung-Chan Kim
Dictionary of Asian American history 8004
IATG2 367
Ibrahima Bah Lalya *and* O'Toole, T.E.
Historical dictionary of Guinea (Republic of Guinea/Conakry) 7785
ICC Business Publications Ltd.
Macmillan's unquoted companies, 1994 2069
Iceland 4628
Iceland, Greenland and the Faroe Islands 5555
Iceland road guide 5553
Icelandic contemporaries 5847
Iconographie de l'art chrétien 623
Identifying tartans 6156
IFIP glossary of terms used in production control 2637
The IFR financial glossary 2108
Illsley, J.S.
An Indexed bibliography of underwater archaeology 4349
The Illustrated atlas of Jerusalem 5288
The Illustrated atlas of Jewish civilization 6667
The Illustrated Bible dictionary 465
Illustrated dictionary and concordance of the Bible 473
An Illustrated dictionary of South African history 7833
The Illustrated encyclopaedia of artillery 3490
Illustrated encyclopedia of dreams 313
The Illustrated encyclopedia of historical facts 6390
The Illustrated encyclopedia of medieval civilization 6441
The Illustrated encyclopedia of myths and legends 815
The Illustrated encyclopedia of New Zealand 5010
An Illustrated guide to the modern Soviet navy 3576
An Illustrated guide to the modern US Navy 3578
The Illustrated guide to the supernatural 162
An Illustrated history of Hong Kong 7576
The Illustrated history of Oxford University 3930
An Illustrated history of the R.A.F 3524
An Illustrated history of the world's religions 805
Illustrated introduction to Latin epigraphy 6626
The Illustrated who's who in mythology 830
ILO Thesaurus 1918
Images of the French Revolution 7344
IMF Bureau of Language Services
IMF glossary 1793
IMF glossary 1793
Imhof, E.
Atlas der Schweiz 5263
Immigrants, minorities and race relations 1112
Immigrants to the middle colonies 6095
Immigration and ethnicity 1571
Imperato, P. J.
Historical dictionary of Mali 7777
Imperato, P.J.
Mali 4808
Imperato, P.J. *and* Imperato, E.M.
Mali 1280

Italian genealogical records **6074**
Italian legal information network **2846**
The Italian legal system **2844**
Italian politics **1730**
Italy **4591**
Italy. Istituto Centrale di Statistica
Annuario statistico italiano **1244**
Itasaka, G.
100 Japanese you should know **7609**
Itzhak Ben
Who's who in Israel and Jewish personalities from all the world 1999 **5884**
Ivamy, E.R.H.
Dictionary of company law **3161**
Dictionary of insurance law **3717**
Mozley & Whiteley's law dictionary **2758**
Ivanovic, A.
Dictionary of marketing **2654**
English-German dictionary of marketing **2655**
Iwao, S.
Biographical dictionary of Japanese history **7610**
Jack, R.I.
Medieval Wales **7238**
Jackman, M.
The Macmillan book of business and economic quotations **1838**
Jackson, A.
The Faroes **7474**
Jackson, G. and Devlin, R.
Dictionary of the Russian Revolution **7424**
Jackson, G.M.
Women rulers throughout the ages **6337**
Jackson, K. and McRobie, A.
Historical dictionary of New Zealand **8141**
Jackson, K.T.
Atlas of American history **7987**
The Encyclopedia of New York City **8076**
Jackson, P.
British sources of information: a subject guide and bibliography **4539**
Jackson, R.
Dark Age Britain **5472**
Jackson, W.G.F.
The Rock of the Gibraltarians **7393**
Jacob, I.H. and Scott, R.
The Supreme Court practice 1999 **3203**
Jacob J.I.H., Sir
Atkin's encyclopaedia of court forms in civil proceedings **3191**
Jacobs, A. and Monk, J.
The Cambridge illustrated dictionary of British heritage **4543**
Jacobs, F.
Western European political parties **1710**
Jacobs, L.
The Jewish religion **909**
Jacobstein, J.M. and Mersky, R.M.
Fundamentals of legal research **2870**
Jaegwon, K. and Sosa, E.
A Companion to metaphysics **150**
Jaensch, D. and Teichmann, M.
Macmillan dictionary of Australian politics **1747**
Jain, H.C.
Indian legal materials **2853**
Jakarta: a history **8117**
Jamaica **4901**
Jamaica. Department of Statistics
Statistical yearbook of Jamaica **1288**
Jamaica handbook 2000 **5612**
Jamaica in maps **5344**
James, A.
Scottish roots **6154**
James, J.S.
Stroud's judicial dictionary of words and phrases **2746**
James, P.
Centuries of darkness **6641**

James, S.
A Dictionary of economic quotations **1839**
James, S. and Parker, R.
Collins dictionary of business quotations **2040**
James, S. and Stebbings, C.
A Dictionary of legal quotations **2779**
Jamieson, A.
Which subject? Which career? **1954**
Jamieson, D.
Singer and his critics **60**
Jammu and Kashmir
Jammu and Kashmir **4713**
Jammu and Kashmir **4713**
Jane's C31 systems **3477**
Jane's dictionary of military terms **3373**
Jane's dictionary of naval terms **3541**
Jane's NATO handbook, 1991/92 **2984**
Jane's pocket-book: armies of the world **3492**
Jane's world air forces **3521**
Jane's world armies **3491**
Janke, P. and Sim, R.
Guerrilla and terrorist organisations **1539**
Janosik, R.J.
Encyclopedia of the American judicial system **2864**
Japan **1861, 4674**
Japan: a bilingual atlas **5276**
Japan. Agency of Cultural Affairs
Japanese religion **964**
Japan an illustrated encyclopedia **4678**
Japan and the Japanese **4672**
Japan company handbook **2474**
Japan. Economic Planning Agency
Economic survey of Japan **2351**
Japan encyclopedia **4680**
Japan. Eyes on the country **4668**
Japan handbook **5563**
Japan marketing handbook **2666**
Japan statistical yearbook **1268**
Japan. Statistics Bureau. Management and Coordination Agency
Japan statistical yearbook **1268**
Japanese American history **8003**
Japanese biographical archive/Japanisches biographisches archiv **5871**
Japanese business language **2034**
Japanese business publications in English, 1987 **2059**
Japanese colleges and universities, 1989 **3944**
Japanese-English Buddhist dictionary **885**
The Japanese financial system **2131**
Japanese folk literature **4156**
Japanese history **7603**
Japanese history and culture from ancient to modern times: seven basic bibliographies **7602**
Japanese local histories **7604**
Japanese military history **3417**
Japanese political science **1443**
Japanese religion **964**
Japanese religion and philosophy **961**
Japanese studies **4669, 4673**
Jaques Cattell Press
Directory of American scholars Vol.1 History **8000**
Jarque, J.E.
Bibliographie générale des oeuvres et articles sur Pierre Teilhard de Chardin **55**
Jarrell, H.R.
International meditation bibliography, 1950-1982 **631**
International yoga bibliography, 1950-1980 **891**
Jarrett, D.
British naval dress **3448**
Jarvis, H.
Cambodia **4756**
Jarvis, P.
The International dictionary of adult education **3860**

Jarvis, S.D. and Jarvis, D.B.
The Cross of sacrifice **6821**
Jary, D. and Jary, J.
Collins dictionary of sociology **1061**
Jastrow, M.
Dictionary of the Targumin, the Talmud Babli and Yerushalmi, and the Midrashic literature **932**
Jay, A.
The Oxford dictionary of political quotations **1404**
Jean-Paul Sartre **48**
Jean-Paul Sartre and his critics **51**
Jee, S.
The World almanac of US politics, 1993-1995 **1459**
Jeffries, E.
The East German economy **2326**
Jeffries, J.
A Guide to the official publications of the European Communities **2924**
Jefkins, F.
Dictionary of advertising, direct response marketing and sales promotion **2691**
Jehovah's Witnesses and kindred groups **803**
Jelavich, B.
History of the Balkans. v.1. Eighteenth and nineteenth centuries. v.2. Twentieth century **7491**
Modern Austria **7293**
Jelks, E.B.
Historical dictionary of North American archaeology **4333**
Jellinek, D.
Official UK **1492**
Jenkins, E.H.
History of the French Navy, from its beginnnings to the present **3573**
Jenkinson, H.
The Later court hands in England **6618**
Jenner, M.
Scotland through the ages **4407**
Jennings, J.
Cabinet government **3334**
Jennings, J.D.
Ancient North Americans **6735**
Ancient South Americans **6739**
Jensen, J.
The Prehistory of Denmark **4301**
Jeremy, D.J.
Dictionary of business biography **2054, 2538**
Jerusalem illustrated history atlas **7700**
Jerusalem in history **7692**
Jerusalem, the Holy City **6665**
Jessop, T.E.
A Bibliography of David Hume, and of Scottish philosophy **27**
Jessup, J.E.
Balkan military history **3416**
A Chronology of conflict and revolution, 1945-1985 **1519**
Jessup, J.E. and Coakley, R.W.
A Guide to the study and use of military history **3391**
Jewish autobiographies and biographies **6005**
Jewish biographical archive. Series II **6676**
Jewish biographical index **6677**
Jewish-Christian relations: an annotated bibliography and resource guide **384**
The Jewish communities of the world **1132**
Jewish folklore **4167**
Jewish heritage in America **4959**
Jewish law **895**
Jewish mysticism **905**
Jewish reference sources **899**
The Jewish religion **909**
Jewish serials of the world **913**
The Jewish travel guide **914**
The Jewish world in modern times **923, 6663**
The Jewish yearbook **915**

Kannik, P.
Military uniforms in colour **3440**
A Kant dictionary **7**
Kant-Lexikon. Nachschlagewerk zu Kants
sämlichen Schriften, Briefen und
handschriftlichen Nachlass **30**
Kantautas, A. and Kantautas, F.
A Lithuanian bibliography **4613**
Kapsner, O.L.
A Benedictine bibliography **663**
Catholic religious orders **685**
Karasik, T.W.
Russia & Eurasia facts & figures annual
(formerly *USSR facts and figures annual*)
1248
Kari, Daven Michael
A Bibliography of sources in Christianity
and the arts **544**
Karkhanis, S.
Jewish heritage in America **4959**
Karni, R.S.
Directory of South-East Asian library
collections in the United Kingdom and
Western Europe **4746**
Karolle, B.G.
Atlas of Micronesia **5389**
Karpat, K.H.
Update on Turkish archives **6560**
Karpinski, L.M.
The Religious life of man **376**
Kaser, M.C. and Radice, E.A.
The Economic history of Eastern Europe,
1919-1975 **1855**
Kaspi, A.
Great dates in United States history **7996**
Kassis, H.E.
A Concordance of the Qur'an **934**
Kasten, S.
'Religion periodical indexes' **415**
Katcher, P.
The American Civil War source book **8040**
Katô, G.
Meiji taishô shôwa Shintô shoseki mokuroku
962
Shintô shoseki mokuroku **963**
Kauffman, J.W. and Hallahan, D.P.
Handbook of special education **3879**
Kauffmann, H.
Rechtswörterbuch **3162**
Kaur, A.
Historical dictionary of Malaysia **7720**
Kavass, I.I. and Sprudzs, A.
A Guide to the United States treaties in force
2971
Kay, B. and Bootman, C.
Who's who in Asia and the Pacific nations
5859
Kay, E.
International businessmen's who's who
2043
Kayyali, M.S.
Modern military dictionary **3381**
The Kazakhs **7708**
Kazhdan, A.P.
The Oxford dictionary of Byzantium **7678**
Kazmer, D.R. and Kazmer, Y.
Russian economic history **2340**
Kearley, T. and Fischer, W.
Charles Szladits' guide **2835**
Keatinge, R.W.
Peruvian prehistory **4338**
Keats-Rohan, K.S.B.
Domesday people: a prosography of persons
occurring in English documents 1066-
1266 **7106**
Keay, J.
The Royal Geographical Society history of
world exploration **5100**
Keay, J. and Keay, J.
Collins encyclopedia of Scotland **7002**

Keay, W.
Expedition guide **5089**
Keegan, J.
The Times atlas of the Second World War
6882
Who's who in World War II **6891**
World armies **3399**
Keegan, J. and Wheatcroft, A.
Who's who in military history **3394**
Keele, H.M. and Kiger, J.C.
Foundations **3601**
Keeler, M.F.
The Long Parliament, 1640-1641 **3060**
Keen, R.
'The Archaeology of industrial Wales' **4483**
Keene, D.
Historical gazetteer of London before the
Great Fire **7133**
Keepers of our past **8070**
Keeves, J.P.
Educational research, methodology, and
measurement **3811**
Kehr, H. and Langmaid, J.
The Nazi era 1919-1945 **7269**
Keightley, D.N.
The Origins of Chinese civilization **4306**
Keith-Lucas, B and Richards, P. G.
A History of local government in the
twentieth century **3287**
Kellas, J.G.
The Scottish political system **1727**
Kelly, D.H.
Women's education in the Third World -
3823
Kelly, J. and Marshall, B.
Atlas of New Zealand boundaries **5379**
Kelly, J.N.D.
Early Christian creeds **615**
The Oxford dictionary of Popes **748**
Kelly, M.
Encyclopedia of aesthetics **149**
Kelly, M.A.
Labor and industrial relations **1930**
Kelly, T.
A History of adult education **3863**
Kelly's **2006**
Kelly's United Kingdom exports
British exports, 1994 **2498**
Kemp, P.
The Admiralty regrets **3563**
Kemp, T.J.
The 1995 genealogy annual **6106**
The Genealogist's virtual library **6012**
'The Roots of genealogy collections' **6107**
Virtual roots **6015**
Vital records handbook **6025**
Kemp's property industry year book **2001**
Kenkyusha's English-Japanese dictionary of
trade and industry **1825**
Kennedy, C.H. and Rais, R.B.
Pakistan, 1995 **4722**
Kennedy, J.
Almanach de Gotha **6307**
Kennedy, J.R.
Library research guide to religion and
theology **378**
Kennedy, L. and Ollerenshaw, P.
An Economic history of Ulster, 1820-1940
2317
Kennedy, T.F.A.
A Descriptive atlas of the Pacific Islands
5183
Kennett, A.M.
Archives and records of the City of Chester
7210
Kenney, J.F.
The Sources for the early history of Ireland
706
Kennington, D.
Gypsies and travelling people **4116**
The Kent bibliography **7139**

Kent, G.O.
A Catalog of files and microfilm of the
German Foreign Ministry archives, 1920-
1945 **1633**
Kent maps and plans **7140**
Kent town guides 1763-1900 **7142**
Kenya **4845**
Kenya. Survey of Kenya
National Atlas of Kenya **5314**
Kenyon, J.
A Dictionary of British history **6930**
Kepars, I.
Australia **5023**
Tasmania **5024**
Keppie, L.
The Antonine Wall **4417**
Scotland's Roman remains **4423**
Kepple, R.J.
Reference works for theological research
571
Kern, R.W.
The Regions of Spain **4597**
Kern, R.W. and Dodge, M.D.
Historical dictionary of modern Spain **7380**
Kerr, N. and Kerr, M.
A Guide to Anglo-Saxon sites **5515**
A Guide to medieval sites in Britain **5473**
A Guide to Norman sites in Britain **5474**
Kerry, D.A. and Cornell, E.
A Guide to theological and religious studies
collections of Great Britain and Ireland
433
Kesler, J.
Theatre costume **3997**
Kettridge, J.O.
French-English and English-French
dictionary of commercial and financial
terms, phrases and practice **1811**
Key abstracts, business automation, 1989-
2546
Key British enterprises **2051**
Key facts in Soviet history **7432**
Key note guides **2042**
Key quotations in sociology **1070**
Key resources on teaching, learning,
curriculum and faculty development **3890**
Key to economic science **1831**
Key treaties for the Great Powers, 1814-1914
2972
Key words in education **3758**
Key words in international trade **2489**
Keyes, C.F.
Thailand **4748**
Keyguide to information sources in
archaeology **4211**
Keyguide to information sources in business
ethics **359**
Keyguide to information sources on the
international protection of human rights
3090
Keyguide to information sources on the Polar
and Cold Regions **5050**
Keynes, S.
Anglo-Saxon history **6955**
Keyser, D.J. and Sweetland, R. C.
Test critiques **336**
Khan, M.A.
A Glossary of Islamic economics **1002**
Kibbee, J.
American folklore **4160**
Kibler, W.W. and Zinn, G.A.
Medieval France an encyclopedia **7336**
Kidd, A.
Manchester **7211**
Kidd, C. and Williamson, D.
Debrett's peerage and baronetage 2000
6269
Kidd, S.
Dictionary of industrial security **3252**

Kiell, N.
Psychoanalysis, psychology and literature 247

Kies, C.
The Occult in the Western world 156

Kightly, C.
The Customs and ceremonies of Britain 4014

Killanin, Lord and Duignan, M.V.
Shell guide to Ireland 5506

Killick, A.
The Economies of East Africa 2368-2369

Killion, T.
Historical dictionary of Eritrea 7769

Killy, W. and Vierhaus, R.
Dictionary of German national biography 5784

Kim, E. and Ziring, L.
The Asian political dictionary 1441

Kimble, G.H.T.
Geography in the Middle Ages 5131

Kime's international law directory, 2000 3195

Kimmich, C.M.
German foreign policy, 1918-1945 1631

Kincade, W.H. and Hayner, P.B.
The Access resource guide 3013

Kindleberger, C.P.
A Financial history of Western Europe 2126

King, A. C.
British and Irish archaeology 4262

King, A.A.
The Rites of Eastern Christendom 716

King, D. and Ranck, S.
Papua New Guinea atlas 5387

King, H.G.R.
The Arctic 5052
Atlantic Ocean 4517

King, J.
Kingdoms of the Celts 6682
New Zealand handbook 5658

King, P. and Wintle, M.
The Netherlands 4629

King, R.
The New geography of European migrations 1569

The Kingdom of Armenia 7433
The Kingdom of Northumbria 7220
The Kingdom of Swaziland 4856
Kingdoms of Asia the Middle East and Africa 6310
Kingdoms of Europe 6320
Kingdoms of gold, Kingdoms of jade 7849
Kingdoms of the Celts 6682
Kings and Vikings 7454
The King's England 5516
The Kings of medieval England c.560-1485 6944

Kingston Publishers
Atlas of the Commonwealth of the Bahamas 5346

Kinloch, G.C.
Social stratification 1152

Kinnear, M.
The British voter 1558

Kinnell, S.
Bibliographies in history 6380
Historiography 6367
People in history 7862
People in world history 6420

Kinnell, S.K.
Communism in the world since 1945 222
Military history of the United States 3425

Kinvig, R.H.
The Isle of Man 7224

Kipling, A.L. and King, H.L.
Head-dress badges of the British Army 3447

Kipnis, R.
'Issues in Brazilian archaeology' 4336

Kipps, H.C.
Volunteerism: the directory of organizations, training, programs and publications 3628

Kirby, D.
The Baltic world 1772-1993 7440
Northern Europe in the early modern period 7439

Kirch, P.V.
Legacy of the landscape 4461

Kirchherr, E.C.
Place names of Africa 1935-1986 5592

Kirk, C.
People in plantations 1146

Kirk-Greene, A.H.M.
A Biographical dictionary of the British Colonial Service, 1939-1966 1581
Decolonization in British Africa 1582

Kirk, T.
The Longman companion to Nazi Germany 7274

Kirkland, F.
Order of Australia 1975-1995 6302

Kirkwood, C.
'Inter-institutional co-operation in the computer retrieval of information on private archives: the South African National Register of Manuscripts (NAREM)' 6575

Kirschbaum, E.
Lexikon der christlichen Ikonographie 626

Kirschbaum, S.J.
Historical dictionary of Slovakia 7308

Kirwan, F. and McGilvray, J.
Irish economic statistics 2316

Kirwan, L.P.
The White road 8194

Kish, G.
Bibliography of international geography congresses 1871-1976 5150
Economic atlas of the Soviet Union 2339

Kitchen, K.A.
'Ancient Arabia c.3000BC to 600AD: a fresh presentation of its chronology and history' 7613

Kitromilides, P.M. and Evriviades, M.L.
Cyprus 4731

Kittel, G. and Friedrich, G.
Theologisches Wörterbuch zum Neuen Testament 528

Klampner, G.H.
A Guide to the language of psychoanalysis 324

Klaus, H.
Banking dictionary 2202-2203

Klauser, T.
Reallexikon für Antike und Christentum. Sachwörterbuch 812

Klein, B.
Guide to American directories 2479

Klein, B.T.
Guide to American educational directories 3808
Reference encyclopedia of the American Indian 1136
The Reference encyclopedia of the American Indian 4971

Klein, D.W. and Clark, A.B.
Biographic dictionary of Chinese Communism 1921-1965 5861

Klein, H.S.
Bolivia 8101

Kleindel, W.
Österreich: Daten zur Geschichte und Kultur 7301

Kleinman, P.
World advertising review 2697

Klindt-Jensen, O.
A History of Scandinavian archaeology 4299

Knapp, S.D.
The Contemporary thesaurus of social science 1028

Knappert, J.
Indian mythology 840

Knappert, J. (contd.)
Pacific mythology 842

Kneale, W. and Kneale, M.
The Development of logic 345

Knight, M.G.
How to do business with Russians 2428

Knight, S. and Gann, R.
The Self-help guide 3620

Knights of the Crown 6262

Kniskern, N.V.
City profiles USA 1997 5618

Knötel, H. and Sieg, H.
Uniforms of the world 3439

Knötel, R.
Uniforms of the world 3439

Know how to find out about your rights 3114

Knowles, A.S.
The International encyclopedia of higher education 3892

Knowles, D.
Bare ruined choirs: the dissolution of the English monasteries 694
The Heads of religious houses 691
The Monastic order in England 692
The Religious orders in England 694

Knowles, D. and Hadcock, R.N.
Medieval religious houses 690

KnowUK 4538

Knox, W.
Scottish labour leaders, 1918-1939 1728

The Kodansha bilingual encyclopedia of Japan 4679

Kodansha encyclopedia of Japan 4676

Koek, K.E.
European consultants directory, 1991 2707

Kohlenberger, J.R.
The NRSV concordance unabridged 504

Kohler's dictionary for accountants 2577

Kohlick, G.
Digest of commercial laws of the world 3165

Kohls, S.
Dictionary of international economics 1795

Kolatch, A.J.
Great Jewish quotations 916

Komonchak, J.A.
The New dictionary of theology 582

Kompass 2007

Konczacki, Z.A. and Konczacki, J.
An Economic history of tropical Africa 2366

Kondo, S.
Japanese military history 3417

Kongelig dansk Hof- og Statskalender 3338

Koninklijke Vlaamse Academiën Van België
National biografisch woordenboek 5851

Konn, T.
Soviet studies guide 4610
'The Soviet Union' 2057

Korea 4665

Korea. A Historical and cultural dictionary 7589

Korea Annual 1996 4667

Korean biographical archive 5869

The Korean War 7591-7592

Korean War almanac 7597

The Korean War: an encyclopedia 7595

Koschnick, W.J.
Standard dictionary of the social sciences 999

Kosovo 7503

Kotz, S.
Russian-English/English-Russian glossary of statistical terms 1200

Kozicki, R.J.
International relations of South Asia, 1947-80 1639

Kraks blå bog 1996: 8149 biografier over nulevende danske, faerø og grønlandske maend og kvinder 5846

Kramme, U. *and* Muena, Z.U.
Český biografický index a Slovenský biografický/Czech and Slovakian biographical index **5796**
Südosteuropäisches biographisches archiv/ South-East European biographical archive **5856**
Ungarisches biographisches archiv/Magyar Életrajzi Archivum/Hungarian biographical archive **5799**

Krause, G. *and* Müller, G.
Theologische Realenzyklopädie **576**

Krauss, N.L.H.
Bibliography of the Banks Islands, Western Pacific **8131**
Bibliography of the Line Islands, Central Pacific **8132**
Bibliography of the Ocean Islands (Banaba), Western Pacific **8187**
Bibliography of The Phoenix Islands **8188**
Bibliography of the Santa Cruz Islands, Western Pacific **8146**
Bibliography of the Tokelau or Union Islands. Central Pacific **8133**
Bibliography of the Torres Islands, Southwest Pacific **8147**
Niué, South Pacific **8134**

Krausse, G.H. *and* Krausse, S.C.E.
Indonesia **4999**

Krausse, S.C. *and* Krausse, G.H.
Brunei **5002**

The Kress Library of Business and Economics. Catalogue **1763**

Kretzmann, N.
The Cambridge history of later medieval philosophy **110**

Kretzmann, N. *and* Stump, E.
The Cambridge companion to Aquinas **207**

Kreyenbroek, P.G. *and* Sper, S.
The Kurds **7675**

Krieger, J.
The Oxford companion to politics of the world **1366**

Kristal, L.
ABC of psychology **265**

Krug, S.E.
Psychware sourcebook **333**

Kruger, A.N.
Argumentation and debate **1085**

Kruskal, W.H. *and* Tanur, J.M.
International encyclopedia of statistics **1194**

Kruzel, J.
American military defense annual, 1987 **3422**

Kryszak, W.D.
The Small business index **2075**

Kto jest kim w Polsce **5829**

Kubijovyč, V.
Encyclopedia of Ukraine **4618**
Ukraine **4620**

Kubijovyč, V. *and* Shukovsky, A.
Encyclopedia of Ukraine **4619**

Kubursi, A.
The Economics of the Arabian Gulf **2356**

Kuka kukin oli/Who was who in Finland **5839**

Kuka kukin on Who's who in Finland.
Henkilötietoja nykypolven suomalaisista 1994 **5838**

Kulich, J.
Adult education in continental Europe **3865**

Kullen, A.S.
The Peopling of America **7994**

Kumar, S.
Yearbook on India's foreign policy, 1984-85 and 1985-86 **1640**

Kunhardt, U. von *and* Llistosella-Matzky, I.
Elsevier's dictionary of the labour market **1889**

Kuper, A. *and* Kuper, J.
The Social science encyclopedia **996**

Kuper, Adam *and* Kuper, J.
Social sciences encyclopedia **1053**

Kuppuram, G. *and* Kumudamani, G.
Marine archaeology **4347**

The Kurds **7675**

Kurian, G.
Atlas of the Third World **4526**
The World gazetteer of boundaries **5431**

Kurian, G. *and* Karch, J.
Encyclopedia of the Second World **4534**

Kurian, G.T.
The Encyclopedia of the First World **4499**
Encyclopedia of the Third World **4521**
Geo-data **5432**
Glossary of the Third World **4525**
New book of world rankings **1203**
Sourcebook of global statistics **1205**
World education encyclopedia **3777**
World encyclopedia of parliaments and legislatures **1672**
World encyclopedia of police forces and penal systems **3245**
Yearbook of American universities and colleges, 1986-1987 **3951**

Kurland, P. B. *and* Lerner, R.
The Founders' constitution **3022**

Kurtz, L.R.
Evaluating Chicago sociology **1058**

Kurucz, G.
Guide to documents and manuscripts in Great Britain relating to the Kingdom of Hungary **6521**

Kurzbiographien zur Geschichte der Juden 1918-1945 **5725**

Kurzweil, A. *and* Weiner, M.
The Encyclopedia of Jewish genealogy **6127**

Kutais, B.G. *and* Shohov, T.
Homelessness **3681**

Kutler, S.I.
Encyclopedia of the United States in the twentieth century **4951**
Encyclopedia of the Vietnam War **7736**

Kutzner, P.L.
World hunger **1151**

Kuwait **4702-4703**

Kuwait and Iraq **7632**

Kwamena-Poh, M. *African history in maps.*
Historical atlas of Africa **7751**

Kyvig, D.E. *and* Blasio, M.A.
New day/New deal **8061**

Labica, G. *and* Bensussan, G.
Dictionnaire critique du Marxisme **226**

Labor and industrial relations **1930**

Labor economics **1880**

Labor in America: a historical bibliography **1916**

Labor unions **1983**

Labordoc
International labour documentation (New series) **1890**

Labour and Socialism **1722**

Labour force statistics, 1970-1990 **1920**

Labour Party
Local government handbook, England and Wales **3290**

Labour people **1723**

Lacasa, N. R. *and* Bustamante, I. D. de
Diccionario de derecho, economia y politica **1790**

Lacey, A.R.
A Dictionary of philosophy **86**

Laclavère, G.
Atlas of the United Republic of Cameroon **5309**

Lacy, N.C.
The New Arthurian encyclopedia **4174**

Lacy, N.J. *and* Ashe, G. *and* Mancoff, D.N.
The Arthurian handbook **4175**

Lady behave **4043**

Laffin, J.
Brassey's battles **3462**

Laffin, J. *(contd.)*
British V.C.s of World War Two **6293**
A Western Front companion 1914-1918 **6804**

Lafollette, H.
The Blackwell guide to ethical theory **350**

Laguerre, M.S.
The Complete Haitiana **4907**

Laidlar, J.
Lisbon **4605**

Laine, M.
Bibliography of works on John Stuart Mill **41**

Laing, W.
Laing's review of private health care ... and directory of independent hospitals **3647**

Laing's review of private health care ... and directory of independent hospitals **3647**

Laitin, D.D. *and* Samatar, S.S.
Somalia **4846**

Lake, C.C. *and* Harper, P.C.
Public opinion polling **1088**

Lakos, A.
International negotiations: a bibliography **1597**
International terrorism **1528**
Terrorism, 1980-1990 **1529**

Lal, B.K.
Contemporary Indian philosophy **141**

Lalor, B.
Ultimate Dublin guide **5509**

Lamar, H.R.
The New encyclopedia of the American West **7971**

Lamb, M.
Directory of officials and organisations in China **3340**

Lambe, D.
Reference works on world religions **377**

Lambert, D.-C.
Dictionnaire français-anglais de l'économie monétaire **2117**

Lambert, E.
World of fashion **3970**

Lambert, H.
Directory of management consultants in the UK **2706**

Lambert, S.
Sessional Papers of the eighteenth century: George I and II **3063**
Sessional Papers of the eighteenth century: George III **3064**

Lamming, R. *and* Bessant, E.
Macmillan dictionary of business and management **2526**

Lamming, R. *and* Bessant, J.
Macmillan dictionary of business and management **2027**

Lampe, G.W.H.
A Patristic Greek lexicon **701**

Lampe, J.R.
Yugoslavia as history **7493**

Lancashire business histories **2469**

The Lancashire Library **7213**

Lancel, S.
Carthage: a history **6730**

Land of the midnight sun **7886**

Landranger maps **5216**

Landry, L.
Encyclopédie du Québec **4879**

Lane, E.
The Encyclopedia of forensic science **2884**

Lane, E. *and* Lane, J.
'Reference materials for the disabled' **3668**

Lane, J.
Warwickshire local history sources **7173**

Lane, J.-E.
Political data handbook **1406**

Lane, J.C.
America's military past **3424**

The Longman companion to America in the era of the two World Wars, 1910-1945 **8060**

The Longman companion to America, Russia, and the Cold War 1941-1998 **6447**

The Longman companion to Britain in the era of the two world wars, 1914-45 **6986**

The Longman companion to Britain in the nineteenth century 1815-1914 **6979**

The Longman companion to Britain since 1945 **6983**

Longman companion to Germany since 1945 **7264**

The Longman companion to Imperial Russia 1682-1917 **7409**

Longman companion to Napoleonic Europe **6796**

The Longman companion to Nazi Germany **7274**

The Longman companion to Renaissance Europe, 1390-1530 **6776**

The Longman companion to the French Revolution **7346**

The Longman companion to the Middle East since 1914 **7539**

The Longman companion to the Tudor Age **6965**

Longman dictionary of business English **2524**

Longman dictionary of psychology and psychiatry **263**

Longman directory of local authorities, 1993 **3284**

Longman guide to Bible quotations **477**

The Longman guide to sources in contemporary British history **6492**

The Longman guide to world affairs **4495**

The Longman handbook of modern American history 1763-1996 **7951**

The Longman handbook of modern British history 1714-1995 **6984**

The Longman handbook of modern European History 1763-1987 **6789**

The Longman handbook of the modern world **6757**

The Longman handbook of world history since 1914 **6449**

Longman history of Italy **7358**

Longman history of Russia **7407**

The Longman investment companion **2257**

Longstaff, T.R.W. *and* Thomas, P.A.
The Synoptic problems **572**

Loomis, R.S.
Arthurian literature in the Middle Ages **4177**

Loose, P.
The Company director **2505**

Lopez, M.D.
New York **4944**

Lopos, G.J.
Peterson's guide to certificate programs at American colleges and universities **3917**

Lord Hailsham
Halsbury's Laws of England **2823**

The Lore and language of school-children **4168**

Lorentz, J.H.
Historical dictionary of Iran **7673**

Lorie, J. *and* Sohanpaul, A.
The Traveller's handbook **5095**

Lorimer, J.G.
Gazetteer of the Persian Gulf, Oman and Central Arabia **5566**

Los Angeles handbook **5634**

Los Angeles Public Library
Catalog of the Police Library **3242**

Lossky, N.
Dictionary of the Ecumenical Movement **642**

A Lost English county **7068**

The Lost villages of Britain **4270**

Louda, J. *and* MacLagen, M.
Lines of succession **6315**

Loudon, N. *and* Glassier, A. *and* Gebbie, A.
Handbook of family planning and reproductive healthcare **3665**

Lovett, A.W.
Early Hapsburg Spain 1517-1598 **7386**

Lovett, R.W.
American economic and business history information sources .. **2065**

Low, C.
A roll of Australian arms **6254**

Low, D.A. *and* Smith, A.
History of East Africa **7797**

Lowe, E.A.
Codices Latini antiquiores **6627**

Lowe, J. D-H.
A Dictionary of military terms and military intelligence phrases: Chinese-English, English-Chinese **3382**

Lowndes, G.A.N.
The Silent social revolution **3793**

Loyn, H.R.
The Middle Ages **6777**

Lozano Irueste, J.M.
Diccionario bilingüe de economía y empresa **1819**

Luard, E.
A History of the United Nations **2914**

Lubetski, E. *and* Lubetski, M.
Building a Judaica library collection **901**

Lubitz, W.
Trotsky bibliography **223**

Lucas, C.
The French Revolution research collection & videodisk **7345**

Lucas, G.R.
The Genesis of modern process thought **8**

Luck, J.M.
A History of Switzerland **7479**

Ludlow, D.H.
Encyclopedia of Mormonism **798**

Ludwig Wittgenstein **58**

Lueker, E.L.
Lutheran cyclopedia **770**

Lumas, S.
The Dictionary of genealogy **6037**

Lumley, E.
Canadian who's who 1999 **5907**

Lundin, G.E. *and* Lundin, Anne H.
Contemporary religious ideas **371**

Lunn, K.
A Social history of British labour, 1870-1970 **1908**

Luntta, K.
Jamaica handbook 2000 **5612**

Luo Liang
Encyclopedia of New China **4655**

Lurker, M.
Dictionary of gods and goddesses, devils and demons **828**

Lutheran cyclopedia **770**

Lutherbibliographie. Verzeichnis der gedruckten Schriften Martin Luthers bis zu dessen Tod.. **769**

Lutz, J.M.
Protectionism **2417**

Lux, W.
Historical dictionary of the British Caribbean **7918**

Luxembourg **4572**

Luxembourg. Service Central de la Statistique et des études Économiques
Annuaire statistique **1239**

Weekly official intelligence **2252**

Lycett—Gregson D.C.
British defence directory **3405**

Lydon, J.G.
Stuggle for empire **8021**

Lynch, J.
A History of Spain **7371**

Lyndoe, E.
Everyman's astrology **196**

Lynskey, M.
Family trees **6133**

Lyon, D.J.
The Sailing Navy list **3565**

Lyttelton, M. *and* Forman, W.
The Romans, their gods and their beliefs **848**

Ma'an Abu Nowar
The History of the Hashemite Kingdom of Jordan **7702**

Mac Gréil, Mícheál
Prejudice and tolerance in Ireland **1177**

Mac Gréil, Mícheál *and* O'Kelly, Caroline
Prejudice in Ireland revisited **1178**

McArt, P.
Irish almanack and yearbook of facts 1999 **4550**

Macartney, C.A.
The Hapsburg Empire 1790-1918 **7295**

Macau **4661**

McAuley, M.
Soviet politics, 1917-1991 **1439**

McBrearty, J.C.
American labor history and comparative labor movements **1985**

McBride, F.
Iceland **4628**

McBrien, R. P.
The HarperCollins encyclopedia of Catholicism **727**

McCabe, J.P.
Critical guide to Catholic reference books **724**

MacCafferty, M.
Employment relations in the United Kingdom **1938**

McCarrick, E.M.
US constitution **3023**

McCarthy, J.M.
An International list of articles on the history of education **3776**

Pierre Teilhard de Chardin **57**

McCarthy, T.
The Irish roots guide **6047**

McCauley, M.
Who's who in Russia from 1900 **1495**

Who's who in Russia since 1900 **5818**

McClaughlin, T.
From shamrock to wattle **6125**

McClelland, R.
Directory of statistics in Canada, 1985- **1285**

McConnell, F.
Papua New Guinea **5035**

McCormick, E.J. *and* Ilgen, D.R.
Industrial and organizational psychology **2548**

McCrank, L.J.
Bibliographical foundations of French historical studies **7357**

McCullogh, V.
Pocket guide to the new City **2176**

McCutcheon, W.A.
The Industrial archaeology of Northern Ireland **4473**

Macdonald, B.
Cinderellas of the empire **8190**

Macdonald, C.
The Book of New Zealand women **5982**

Macdonald, J.
Great battles of the American Civil War **3475**

McDonald, M.R.
A Guide to Scottish industrial heritage **4472**

MacDonald, M.R.
The Storyteller's sourcebook **4129**

MacDonald, M.R. *and* Sturm, B.
The Storyteller's sourcebook, vol. 2 **4130**

Macdonald, R.
Dive **4358**

McPherson, J.M. *(contd.)*
Battle chronicles of the Civil War **8039**
Encyclopedia of Civil War biographies **8053**
The Macquarie encyclopedia of Australian
events **8176**
Macquarie Islands **5022**
Macquarrie, J. *and* Childers, J.F.
A New dictionary of Christian ethics **617**
McRae, W. *and* Jewell, J.
Montana handbook **5624**
McRedmond, L.
Modern Irish lives **5775**
McShane, P.
United Kingdom statistical sources **1226**
MacSorley, M.E.
Genealogical sources in the United States of
America **6118**
MacSween, A. *and* Sharp, M.
Prehistoric Scotland **4409**
Madagascar **4867**
Maddex, Robert L.
Constitutions of the world **3018**
Maddocks, G.
Bloody red tabs **6822**
Maddox, G.L.
The Encyclopedia of aging **1100**
Maddox, T.
Tests: a comprehensive reference.. **335**
Madge, D.
Directory of organisations in allied and
complementary health care **3642**
Madrid **4599**
Mafia **3158**
Magaš, B.
The Destruction of Yugoslavia **7494**
The Maghreb **4792**
Magill, F.N.
International encyclopedia of government
and politics **1483**
International encyclopedia of psychology
290
International encyclopedia of sociology
1052
Magill, F.N. *and* McGreal, I.P.
World philosophy **91**
Magistrates of the Roman Republic **6726**
Magna bibliotheca anglo-judaica **903**
Magocsi, P.R.
Carpatho-Rusyn studies **4532**
Galicia **7418**
Historical atlas of East Central Europe **7253**
A History of Ukraine **7447**
Ucrainica at the University of Toronto
Library **4616**
Magocsi, P.R. *and* Matthews, G.J.
Ukraine: a historical atlas **7449**
Magraw, R.
A History of the French working-class **1187**
Maguire, M.
Bibliography of published work on Irish
foreign relations, 1921-78 **1629**
Magyar statisztikai evkönyv. Statistical
yearbook **1242**
Magyarorsz ag nemzeti atlasza. National atlas
of Hungary **5227**
Magyarország autóatlasza **5228**
Mahoney, M.H.
Women in espionage **1666**
Mai, L.H.
Men and ideas in economics **1848**
Main economic indicators, 1965-. Monthly
2289
Mair, D. *and* Miller, A.
A Modern guide to economic thought **1872**
Maitron, J.
Dictionnaire biographique du mouvement
ouvrier français de 1789-1939 **1982**
Majama'al-lughat **1003**
Major companies of Europe, 1993/94 **2454**
Major companies of the Arab world, 1993/94
2475

Major companies of the Far East and
Australasia, 1993-94 **2473**
Major companies of the USA, 1989/90 **2481**
Major financial institutions of Europe, 1994
2172
The Major international treaties, 1914-1945
2973
The Major international treaties of the twentieth
century **1615**
The Major international treaties since 1945
2974
Major legal systems of the world today **2882**
Major political events in Indo-China 1945-1990
7723
Major political events in Iran, Iraq and the
Arabian peninsula 1945-1990 **7547**
Major stock markets of Europe **2249**
Majumdar, R.C.
The History and culture of the Indian people
7639
Makdisi, J.
'Islamic law bibliography' **2855**
Makepeace, C.E.
'Local history' **7072**
Maker, R.N.
Egypt **4796**
Makers of modern Africa **7755**
The Making of modern Africa a guide to
archives **6565**
The Making of modern Lebanon **7690**
The Making of the Georgian nation **7450**
The Making of the modern Gulf states **7624**
Making sense of English in psychology **297**
Making sense of the census **1339**
Makino, Y. *and* Miki, M.
Japan and the Japanese **4672**
Makower, J.
The American history sourcebook **7960**
The Map catalog **5358**
Malawi **4866**
Malaysia **4751**
Malaysia & Singapore handbook **5587**
Malaysia. Department of Statistics
Yearbook of statistics **1277**
Malaysian studies **4750**
Malcolm, N.
Bosnia. A short history **7504**
Kosovo **7503**
Mali **1280, 4808-4809**
Malina, P. *and* Spann, G.
Bibliographie zur Österreichischen
Zeitgeschichte 1918-1980 **7302**
Malinowski, S. *and* Abrams, G.H.J.
Notable native Americans **5958**
Malinowski, S. *and* Sheets, A.
The Gale encyclopedia of Native American
tribes **4970**
Mallan, C.
Belize handbook **5607**
Mallory, J.P. *and* McNeill, T.E.
The Archaeology of Ulster **4284**
Malta **4595, 7366**
Malta: an island republic **7368**
Malta. Central Office of Statistics
Annual abstract of statistics **1245**
Malta year book 1999 **4596**
Maltby, A.
The Government of Northern Ireland, 1922-
72 **3072**
Maltby, A. *and* Maltby, J.
Ireland in the nineteenth-century **3074**
Mamalakis, M.J.
Historical statistics of Chile **1299**
Man, J.
Atlas of the year 1000 **6747**
The Penguin atlas of D-Day and the
Normandy campaign **6877**
Man Mohan Sharma
An Introduction to the mountain kingdom of
Nepal **4719**
Man, myth and magic **159**

Management accounting **2578**
Management and accounting research **2591**
Management and marketing abstracts **2618**
Management bibliographies and reviews **2619**
Management contents, 1975- **1768**
Management dictionary **2613**
Management for the future: a bibliography
2597
Management information systems **2626**
Management media directory **2625**
The Manager's guide to competitive marketing
strategies **2652**
A Manager's guide to patents, trade marks &
copyright **3175**
Manceron, C. *and* Manceron, A.
La Révolution Française **7351**
Manchester **7211**
Manchester, A.H.
Sources of English legal history **2829**
Mancuso, J.
Mancuso's small business resource guide
2074
Mancuso's small business resource guide **2074**
Mandarin squares **6306**
Mander-Jones, P.
Manuscripts in the British Isles relating to
Australia, New Zealand and the Pacific
6487
Mandich, D.R. *and* Placek, J.A.
Russian heraldry and nobility **6253**
Manley, B.
The Penguin historical atlas of Ancient
Egypt **6657**
Manley, J.
Atlas of prehistoric Britain **4269**
Manley, R.H.
Guyana emergent **8113**
Mann, H.K.
The Lives of the Popes in the early Middle
Ages **749**
Mann, M.
Macmillan student encyclopedia of sociology
1051
Mannheim, I.
Jordan handbook **5582**
Mannheim, I. *and* Winter, D.
Jordan, Syria and Lebanon handbook **5580**
Manning, P.
Slavery and African life **1587**
Manning, T.D. *and* Walker, C.F.
British warship names **3561**
Manns, C. S. *and* Hal, J.
The hymn tune index: a census of English
language hymn tunes in printed sources
from 1535 to 1820 **655**
Manorial records **7063**
Manpower Services Commission. Training
Services
Glossary of training terms **1964**
Man's conquest of the Pacific **4229**
Manschreck, C.L.
History of Christianity in the world **561**
Manser, M.
Chambers book of business quotations **2041**
Manser, M.H.
The Chambers book of business quotations
2536
Mansergh, N.
The Commonwealth experience **1577**
Mansfield, A.D. *and* Mansfield, V.
The History of underclothes **3976**
Mansingh, S.
Historical dictionary of India **7651**
Manson, T.W.
A Companion to the Bible **496**
Manual de historia de España **7378**
Manual of business library practice **2014,
2541**
Manual of German law **2836**
Manual of law French **2762**
Manual of law librarianship **2744**

Manual of procedure in the public business
3037
Manual of the terminology of public
international law (peace) and international
organization: English-French-Spanish-
Russian 2894
A Manual on government finance statistics
2138
Manuale bilingue di corrispondinza e
comunicazione commerciale. Italiane-Inglese
2566
Manuel, E.A.
Dictionary of Philippine biography 5976
The Manuscript catalogue of the library ..
4563
Manuscript sources for British history 6506
Manuscripts and Government Records in the
United Kingdom and Ireland relating to
Canada 6580
Manuscripts in the British Isles relating to
Australia, New Zealand and the Pacific
6487
Manuscripts in the Scott Polar Research
Institute Cambridge, England 8195
Manuscripts relating to Commonwealth
Caribbean countries 6582
The Manx family tree 6065
Manx Museum And National Trust
The Ancient and historic monuments of the
Isle of Man 4436
The Map catalog 5358
Map librarianship 5170
Map of Wales 4441
Mapping index 5207
Mapping of Monmouthshire 7166
Mapping Russia and its neighbours 5249
Mapping the American Revolutionary War
8032
Mapping the UK 5206
Mapping time 6476
Maps and charts published in America before
1800 7993
Maps and history 6412
Maps and mapping of Africa 5295
Maps and plans for the local historian and
collector 7101
Maps and plans in the Public Record Office 3.
Africa 5296
Maps and plans in the Public Record Office 4.
Europe and Turkey 5188
Maps and plans in the Public Record Office. 4.
Europe and Turkey 5190
Maps and plans in the Public Record Office.
America and West Indies 7853
Maps, atlases and guides. Catalogue 1999
5205
Maps for family history 6176
Maps for local historians 7096
Maps for local history 7099
Maps in the County Record Office,
Huntingdon 7191
Maps of Africa 5297
The Maps of Canada 5334
The Maps of Glasgow 7008
Maqsood, R.
Petra: a traveller's guide 4454
Marcan, P.
Greater London local history directory and
bibliography 7120
London's local history 7121
The March to Victory 6833
Marcoux, Y.
'A National Register of Archives in mosaic
form: the Canadian example' 6581
Marcus, G.J.
A Naval history of England 3547
Marcus, H.G.
A History of Ethiopia 7767
Marcus, J.R.
The Concise dictionary of American Jewish
biography 5950

Marder, J.V.
British education thesaurus 3812
Marenbon, J.
Early medieval philosophy (480-1150) 102
Later medieval philosophy (1150-1350) 101
Marie J.-B.
Glossaire des droits de l'homme 3103
Marine archaeology 4347
Marine archaeology of Indian Ocean countries
4354
Marine badges and insignia of the world 3434
The Marine Conservation Society
The Readers' Digest good beach guide 1996
5481
Maritime affairs 2951
Maritime archaeology 4352
Maritime archaeology in Australia 4363
The Maritime political boundaries of the world
2949
Marius, R.
A Short guide to writing about history 6459
Marken, J.W.
Native American Bibliography Series 4968
Market economy and planned economy 1000
Market House Books
Encyclopedia of world history 6386
Market research: a guide to British Library
holdings 2669
Market research abstracts 2672
Market research: international directory of
published market research 2673
Marketing and sales management 2648
The Marketing dictionary 2653
Marketing + distribution abstracts 2658
The Marketing glossary 2657
The Marketing manager's yearbook 2665
Markets yearbook 2683
Marketsearch 2674
Markle, A. and Rinn, R.
Author's guide to journals in psychology,
psychiatry & social work 282
Marlin, J.T.
Book of world city rankings 3294
Marm, L.
Engelsk-Amerikansk-Norsk, Norsk-Engelsk-
Amerikansk... militaeir ordbok 3376
Marquis who's who
Who's who in America 2000 5933
Marquis who's who regional library 5926
Marr, D.G.
Vietnam 4758
Marr, L.J.
Guernsey people 5781
A History of the Bailiwick of Guernsey
7153
Marr, P.
The Modern history of Iraq 7687
Marriott, F.H.C.
A Dictionary of statistical terms 1195
Marsden, J.
Northanhymbre saga 7221
Marsden, P.
English Heritage book of ships and
shipwrecks 4357
Ships of the Port of London 4360
Marsh, A.
Concise encyclopedia of industrial relations
1931
Employee relations bibliography and
abstracts 1934
Employee relations bibliography and
abstracts. 1989-. v.1-. Quarterly 1935
Trade union handbook 1974
Marsh, A. and Ryan, V.
Historical directory of trade unions 1973
Marsh, D.
The Bundesbank 2213
Marsh, J.E.
The Financial 1000 2135
Marsh, J.H.
The Canadian encyclopaedia 4877

Marsh, S.B. and Bailey, J.B.
Terminology of business and company law
2021
Marshall, F.N.
The Asian-American encyclopedia 4961
Marshall, Gordon
The Concise Oxford dictionary of sociology
1048
Marshall, M.B.
Public finance 2140
Marshall, R.K.
Virgins and virago 4092
Marshall's Bible handbook 454
Marshallsay, D.
Ford list of British Parliamentary papers,
1974-1983, together with specialist
commentaries 3069
Marten, J.
Texas 4945
Martens, H.
EC direct 2941
Martin Buber and his critics 20
Martin, C.
Scotland's historic shipwrecks 4359
Martin, D.M.
Handbook of Latin American studies 4934
Martin, E.A.
A Dictionary of law 2745
Martin, G.H. and McIntyre, S.
A Bibliography of British and Irish municipal
history. v.1: General works 3303
Martin, G.H. and Spufford, P.
The Records of the nation 6508
Martin, G.J. and Armstrong, P.H.
Geographers: bibliographical studies 5136
Martin, J.
Heraldry in the Vatican 6255
Martin, K.C.
The Historical atlas of the United States
Congressional Districts, 1789-1983 3087
Martin, M.
1992 guide to grants for business 2181
The Almanac of women and minorities in
world politics 1511
Martin, M.R. and Lovett, G.H.
An Encyclopedia of Latin-American history
7947
Martin, M.S.
'New Zealand at 150' 5006
'The Other ocean: the discovery and
exploration of the Pacific' 5077
Martin, S.
A History of Antarctica 8200
Martin, S.B.
Worldwide franchise directory 2684
Martin, W.
Bertrand Russell 47
Martinique 4916
Martis, K.C.
The Historical atlas of political parties in the
United States Congress, 1787-1988 1743
Marwick, W.H.
'A Bibliography of Scottish economic history
during the last decade: 1963-1970' 2315
Marxist governments 1704
Masey, A.
Financial times guide: investment trusts
2255
Maskell, H.
'Electronic Egypt: *The shape of
archaeological knowledge on the Net*'
6651
Mason, A.S.
Essex on the map 7208
Mason, F.K.
Battle over Britain 6843
Mason, S.
The McGraw-Hill handbook of British
finance and trade 2101
Mass murder 3135
Massachusetts handbook 5630

Menos, D.
Arms control fact book **2987**
Men's studies **1155**
Mercatanti, A.S.
The Facts on File encyclopedia of world mythology and legend **821**
Mercer, D.
Chronicle of the Royal Family **6323**
Chronicle of the Second World War **6883**
Mercer, P.
Directory of British political organizations **1717**
The Merchant Navy **6803**
Měřička, V.
The Book of Orders and decorations **6277**
Merin, J. and Burdick, E.B.
International directory of theatre, dance and folk festivals **4018**
Merriam, L.A. and Oberly, J.W.
United States history **7962**
Merriam-Webster's biographical dictionary **5701**
Merriam-Webster's geographical dictionary **5436**
Merrifield, R.
The Roman city of London **7134**
Merrill, J.G.
A Current bibliography of international law **2888**
Merritt, A.J. and Richard, L.
Politics, economics and society in the two Germanies, 1945-75 **1185**
Merry, P.
Wellard's NHS handbook, 2000/2001 **3648**
Mersch, J.
Biographie nationale du pays de Luxembourg **5791**
Mersky, R.M.
Author's guide to journals in law, criminal justice and criminology **2777**
Messenger, C.
World War Two Chronological atlas **6878**
Messick, F.M.
Primary sources in European diplomacy, 1914-45 **1617**
Metford, J.C.J.
The Christian year **597**
Dictionary of Christian lore and legend **554**
Metherell, D. and Guthrie, P.
Scandinavian biographical archive/ Skandinavisches biographisches archiv **5836**
Method in ecumenical theology **640**
Methodist Union catalog: pre-1976 imprints **786**
Metra Consulting
Handbook of national development plans **2397**
Metzger, B.M.
Index to periodical literature on the Apostle Paul **600**
Metzger, B.M. and Coogan, M.D.
The Oxford companion to the Bible **455**
Mexican American biographies **5927**
Mexican autobiography **5916**
Mexican political biographies 1935-1993 **1683**
Mexico **4884**
Mexico A-Z **7901**
Meyer, H.K.
Historical dictionary of Nicaragua **7911**
Meyer, H.K. and Meyer, J.H.
Historical dictionary of Honduras **7907**
Meyer, J.A.
An Annotated bibliography of the Napoleonic era **6798**
Meyer, M.C.
The Course of Mexican history **7898**
Meyer, R.S.
Peace organizations, past and present **3006**
Meyerink, K.L.
Printed sources **6108**

Meyers, A.
'Reference sources on the US Constitution.' **3024**
Meyers, C.
Women and scripture **467**
Miatello, A.
Glossario trilingue della proprietà industriale ... Trilingual glossary on industrial property **3176**
Michelin Green tourist guides - France. Guides verts touristiques **5537**
Michelin regional maps - France **5235**
Mickleburgh, E.
Beyond the frozen sea **8201**
Mickler, M.L.
The Unification Church in America **793**
Mickolus, E.
The Literature of terrorism **1530**
Terrorism, 1980-1987 **1531**
Terrorism, 1988-1991 **1532**
Mickolus, E.F.
International terrorism in the 1980s **1542**
Mickolus, E.F. and Simmons, S.L.
Terrorism, 1992-1995 **1533**
Micronesia **5047**
Micronesia handbook **5678**
The Middle Ages **6777**
Middle East: a directory of resources **4687**
The Middle East and North Africa 2000 **4690**
The Middle East annual issues and events **4691**
Middle East economic handbook **2354**
The Middle East in conflict **7545**
The Middle East in the twentieth century **7549**
The Middle East: its oil, economics and investment policies **2132**
The Middle East political dictionary **1446**
The Middle East review: economic and business report, 1989 **2355**
Middlebrook, M. and Everitt, C.
The Bomber Command war diaries **6844**
Middleton, J.
Encyclopedia of Africa South of the Sahara **4783**
Miethe, T.L.
Augustinian bibliography, 1970-1980 **19**
Miethe, T.L. and Bourke, V.J.
Thomistic bibliography, 1940-1978 **54**
Migration from the Russian Empire **6191**
Miles, C.W.N.
Walmsley's rural estate management **1996**
Milestones: a chronology of American women's history **8020**
Miletich, J.J.
Retirement **1099**
Milewski, W.
Guide to the archives of the Polish Institute and Sikorski Museum **6540**
Militärgeschichtlichen Forschungsant durch Friedrich Forstmeier ... [et al]
Handbuch zur deutschen Militärgeschichte, 1648-1939 **3408**
The Military balance, 1993-94 **3396**
Military Eitzen.
German-English, English-German military dictionary **3375**
Military history of the United States **3425**
The Military in imperial history **3410**
Military intelligence, 1870-1991 **3476**
The Military-naval encyclopedia of Russia and the Soviet Union **3415**
Military uniforms in colour **3440**
Milkias, P.
Ethiopia **4800**
Millar, T.B.
Recent Australian historiography **6368**
Millard, P.
Trade associations and professional bodies **2425**
Miller, C.
Lobbying **1693**

Miller, D.
The Blackwell encyclopaedia of political thought **1465**
The World's navies **3538**
Miller, E.W.
'State atlases' **5359**
Miller, I.M.
Jobfile **1956**
Miller, J.
Dictionary of financial regulations, 1988/89 **2125**
Miller, J.C.
Slavery and slaving in world history **1584**
Miller, K.E.
Denmark **4627**
Greenland **5055**
Miller, M.S. and Miller, J.L.
Harper's encyclopedia of Bible life **451**
Miller, O.K.
Genealogical research for Czech and Slovak Americans **6072**
Miller, P.M. and Wilson, M.J.
A Dictionary of social science methods **1027**
Miller, R.
'The Literature of terrorism' **1534**
Miller, R.M. and Smith, J.D.
Dictionary of Afro-American slavery **1589**
Miller, T.B.
Current international treaties **2959**
Miller, W.C.
Minorities in America **1514**
Miller, W.C. and Vowell, F.N.
A Comprehensive bibliography for the study of American minorities **1129**
Million dollar directory **2070**
Mills, C.M.
A Bibliography of the Northern Territory **5025**
Mills, G.
Modern office management **2551**
Mills, W. and Speak, P.
Keyguide to information sources on the Polar and Cold Regions **5050**
Milner, C.A.
The Oxford history of the American West **7969**
Milner-Gulland, R. and Dejevsky, N.
Atlas of Russia and the Soviet Union **7431**
Milton, R.
The English ceremonial book **4033**
Min Lee
Larousse dictionary of North American history **7856**
Larousse dictionary of twentieth century history **6450**
Minary, R. and Moorman, C.
An Arthurian dictionary **4176**
Minchinton, W.
Guide to industrial archaeology sites in Britain **4468**
Mind your own local business **2015**
Minden, S. von
Chinese biographical index **5865**
Chinesisches biographisches archiv/Chinese biographical archive **5864**
Ministers of the Crown **3325**
Minnick, W.L.
Spies and provocateurs **1663**
Minorities in America **1514**
Minority organizations **1517**
Mir, M.
Dictionary of Qur'ānic terms and concepts **944**
Miscellanea bibliothecae Vaticanae **739**
Miskin, C.
Directory of law libraries in the British Isles **2873**
Library and information services for the legal profession **2871**

MIT dictionary of modern economics
The Macmillan dictionary of modern economics **1783**
The MIT encyclopedia of the cognitive sciences **254**
Mitchell, A.
The New Penguin guide to personal finance **1170**
Mitchell, A. *and* Ó Snodaigh, P.
Irish political documents, 1869-1916 **1432**
Irish political documents, 1916-1949 **1431**
Mitchell, B.
A New genealogical atlas of Ireland **6053**
The Mitchell Beazley world atlas of exploration **5068**
Mitchell, B.R.
British historical statistics **1231**
International historical statistics **1211**
International historical statistics: Africa, Asia and Oceania, 1750-1993 **1212**
International historical statistics: Europe, 1750-1993 **1213**
Mitchell, R.C. *and* Turner, H.W.
A Comprehensive bibliography of modern African religious movements **966**
Mitchell, S.
Victorian Britain **6981**
Mitchell, W.H. *and* Sawyer, L.A.
The Empire ships **6845**
Mitros, J.F.
Religions **379**
Mitsubishi Corporation
Japanese business language **2034**
Tatemae and honne **2035**
Modern Algeria **7773**
The Modern antiquarian **4383**
Modern Austria **7293**
Modern British history **6989**
Modern British politics **1713**
Modern business correspondence **2550**
Modern Catholic dictionary **735**
Modern China **7573**
Modern China 1840-1972 **7565**
A Modern companion to the European Community **2930**
Modern economics **1837**
The Modern encyclopaedia of Russian and Soviet history **7422**
Modern English biography **5779**
Modern European imperialism **1576**
Modern French philosophy **132**
Modern geography: an encyclopedic survey **5121**
Modern German philosophy **129**
Modern Germany **7258**
Modern Greece **7482**
A Modern guide to economic thought **1872**
Modern historians on British history 1485-1945 **6426**
The Modern history of Iraq **7687**
A Modern history of Kenya 1895-1980 **7813**
The Modern history of Mongolia **7585**
A Modern history of Somalia **7816**
A Modern history of the Kurds **7676**
Modern Ireland **4552**
Modern Irish lives **5775**
Modern Islamic political thought **1478**
Modern Italian history **7361**
Modern Japan **7605**
Modern Jewish morality **898**
Modern Latin America **7943**
Modern legal systems cyclopedia **3187**
Modern military dictionary **3381**
Modern Nepal **7662**
Modern office management **2551**
Modern political thought **1468**
Modern proverbs and proverbial sayings **4202**
Modern revolutions and revolutionists **1522**
Modern shipping disasters 1963-1987 **5110**
The Modern theologians **591**
The Modern Uzbeks **7709**

Modernity and tradition **4692**
Modes and manners from the Middle Ages to the end of the eighteenth century **3971**
Modes and manners of the nineteenth century **3972**
Moffat, D.
Economics dictionary **1804**
Mogano, M.
How to start and run your own business **2080**
Mohen, J-P.
The World of megaliths **4370**
Moir, M.
A General guide to the India Office Records **6554**
Moldenke, H.N. *and* Moldenke, A.L.
Plants of the Bible **494**
Moll, J.
Uniforms of the Royal Navy during the Napoleonic Wars **3449**
Moll, V.P.
St. Kitts-Nevis **4917**
Virgin Islands **4919**
Moller-Christensen, V. *and* Jorgensen, K.E.J.
Encyclopedia of Bible creatures **493**
Mollo, A. *and* Smith, D.
World army uniforms since 1939 **3441**
Molnár, E.
Hungary. Essential facts and figures **4580**
Molyneux, P.
Directory of European banking and financial associations **2206**
Momeni, J.A.
Demography of racial and ethnic minorities in the United States **1515**
Housing and racial/ethnic minority status in the United States **1516**
Momigliano, A.
The Classical foundations of modern historiography **6422**
Momsen, J.H.
St. Lucia **4918**
Monaco **4589**
Monaghan, P.
The Book of goddesses and heroines **825**
Monahan, P.
Guide to London docklands **5523**
The Monarchs of Scotland **6331**
Monarchs of the Nile **6646**
Monarchs, rulers, dynasties and kingdoms of the world **6311**
Monash biographical dictionary of 20th century Australia **5995**
The Monastic order in England **692**
Monasticon Anglicanum **693**
A Monetary history of the United Kingdom, 1870-1982 **2190**
Money **2226**
Money and banking in the U.K.: a history **2128**
Money, banking and macroeconomics: a guide to information sources **2095**
The Money book **2233**
The Money encyclopedia **2099**
Mongolia **4663**
Mongolian-English-Russian dictionary of legal terms and concepts **2747**
Mongolian Peoples Republic national atlas **5274**
The Mongols **7517**
Moniz, M.
Azores **4805**
Monro, I.S. *and* Cook, D.E.
Costume index **3954**
Monroe, W.S.
Bibliography of education **3746**
Montague-Smith, P.W.
The Royal line of succession **6325**
Montana handbook **5624**

Monte-Domecq, R.
Quien es quien en el Paraguay **5971**
Montgomery, H. *and* Cambray, P.G.
A Dictionary of political phrases and allusions **1403**
Montgomery-Massingberd, H.J.
Burke's family index **6267**
Burke's guide to the Royal Family **6322**
Burke's Irish family records **6163**
Monthly bibliography **990-991**
Monthly digest of statistics **1229**
Monthly index to the *Financial times*. **1770**
Montserrat **4920**
Monumenta Britannica **4376**
Monuments of Syria **4452**
Monuments to courage **6290**
Moody, D.
Scottish family history **6161**
Scottish local history **7003**
Scottish towns **6993**
Moody, T.W.
A Chronology of Irish history to 1976 **7026**
A New history of Ireland **7015**
Moon, P.
The British conquest and dominion of India **7640**
Moon, R. *and* Moon, V.
Discover Australia: national parks **5669**
Discover Australia: road guide **5670**
Moonan, W.
Martin Buber and his critics **20**
Moore, B.C.
A Dictionary of special education terms **3883**
Moore, B.E. *and* Fine, B.D.
Psychoanalystic terms and concepts **326**
Psychoanalytic terms and concepts **267**
Moore, G.H. *and* Moore, M.H.
International economic indicators **2288**
Moore, J.L.
Elections A to Z **1499**
Moore, J.N.
The Maps of Glasgow **7008**
Moore, R.C.
Historical dictionary of Guatemala **7905**
Moores & Rowlands orange tax guide
Butterworth's orange tax handbook, 1993-94... inheritance tax, National Insurance contributions, stamp duties, value added tax **2155**
Moores & Rowlands yellow tax guide
Butterworth's yellow tax handbook, 1993-94 **2154**
Mor, M *and* Rappaport, U.
Bibliography of works on Jewish history **6664**
Moran, K.
Hong Kong handbook including Macau and Guangzhou **5559**
Morby, G.
Know how to find out about your rights **3114**
Morby, J.E.
Dynasties of the world **6313**
More Irish families **6167**
More words of Wall Street: 2000 investment terms defined **2260**
Morford, M.P.O. *and* Lenardon, R.J.
Classical mythology **849**
Morgan, D.
The Mongols **7517**
Morgan, D.J.
The Official history of colonial development **1580**
Morgan, I.
The Holiday Which? guide to Greece and the Greek Islands **5556**
The Holiday Which? guide to Italy **5541**
Morgan, J.
Debrett's new guide to etiquette and modern manners **4040**

Morgan, J.R.
Hawaii a geography 5148
Morgan, K.O.
Labour people 1723
The People's peace 6985
Morkot, R.
The Penguin historical atlas of Ancient Greece 6706
Morley, D.F.
Wars of the Americas 7854
Morley, W.F.E.
Canadian local histories to 1950 7891
A Mormon bibliography, 1830-1930 796
Mormonism 799
Mormons and mormonism in the US government documents 795
Morocco 4803
Morocco handbook 5597
Morozov, V.
Who's who in Russia and the CIS Republics 5821
Morris, B.
Western concepts of the individual 238
Morris, D. and Morris, I.
Who was who in American politics 1746
Morris dancing 4150
Morris, D.S. and Haigh, R.H.
Britain, Spain and Gibraltar 1945-90 7394
Morris, J.
Domesday Book 7052
Morris, J.B. and Morris, R.B.
Encyclopedia of American history 7970
Morris, J.M. and Kearns, P.M.
Historical dictionary of the United States Navy 3585
Morris, N.J. and Dean, L.
Hawai'i 5049
Morrison, C.
An Analytical concordance to the Revised Standard Version of the New Testament 538
Morrison, D.G.
Black Africa 4790
Morrison, W.R.
True North 7887
The Morrow book of quotations in American history 7985
Mort, D.
The Counties and regions of the United Kingdom 2304
'How to find UK local statistics' 3286
Western European statistics 1217
Mort, D. and Wilkins, W.
Sources of unofficial UK statistics 1224
Mortensen, J.S.
Vem är det: Svensk biografisk handbok 1995 5844
Morton, A. and Donaldson, G.
British national archives and the local historian 7109
Morton, F.
Historical dictionary of Botswana 7837
Mosak, H.H. and Mosak, B.
A Bibliography of Adlerian psychology 306
Moser, M.J. and Zee, W.K.
China tax guide 2161
Mosley, C.
Burke's peerage and baronetage 6268
Moss, L.
The Government Social Survey 1176
Moss, M. and Moss, G.
Handbook for women travellers 5115
Mossman, J.
Current leaders of nations CD 1489
Holidays and anniversaries of the world 4028
The Most illustrious Order 6287
Mostecky, V.
Index to multilateral treaties 2964

Mostyn, T.
Major political events in Iran, Iraq and the Arabian peninsula 1945-1990 7547
Mostyn, T. and Hourani, A.
The Cambridge encyclopedia of the Middle East and North Africa 4688
Motif-index of folk-literature 4131
Mott, W.T.
Encyclopedia of Transcendentalism 445
Motta, G.
Dizionario commerciale 1817
Motteler, L.S.
Pacific island names 5653
Motyl, A.
Encyclopedia of nationalism 1502
Moule, T.
Biblioteca heraldica Magnae Britanniae 6236
Moulton, W.F. and Geden, A.S.
A Concordance to the Greek Testament 539
Mountner, T.
A Dictionary of philosophy 78
Mourre, M.
Dictionnaire encyclopédique d'histoire 6398
Il movimento operaio italiano: dizionario biografico, 1853-1943 1970
Mowat, M.
'Information sources on accountancy and finance' 2571
Moyles, R.G.
A Bibliography of Salvation Army literature in English (1865-1987) 664
Moys, E.M.
Manual of law librarianship 2744
Mozambique 4850, 7821
Mozley & Whiteley's law dictionary 2758
Mr. Charles Booth's inquiry 1182
Mucha, L.
The Orbis encyclopedia of flags and coats of arms 6344
Muckleroy, K.
Archaeology under water 4353
Muhammad Umar Kirmani
Biographical encyclopedia of Pakistan 1996-97 5878
Muir, R.
The Lost villages of Britain 4270
The National Trust guide to Dark Age and Medieval Britain 5476
Muir, R. and Welfare, H.
The National Trust guide to prehistoric and Roman Britain 5475
Mulhall, M.G.
The Dictionary of statistics 1196
Mulholland, J. and Jordan, A.
Victoria Cross bibliography 6296
Mullay, A.J.
Birthplaces USA 5928
British birthplaces 5750
The Edinburgh encyclopedia 4548
Müller, K.
Leibniz-Bibliographie 36
Leibniz-Bibliographie Bd. 2 37
Müller-Karpe, H.
Handbuch der Vorgeschichte 4216
Müller-Lutz, H.L.
Four-language insurance dictionaries 3697
Müller-Lutz, H.L. and Chidiac, J.S.
Insurance dictionary: English-French-Arabic, French-English-Arabic, Arabic-English-French 3698
Mulliner, K. and Mulliner, L.T.
Historical dictionary of Singapore 7722
Mullins, C.J.
A Guide to writing and publishing in the social and behavioral sciences 1025
Mullins, E.L.C.
A Guide to the historical and archaeological publications of societies in England and Wales. 1901-1933 7073
Texts and calendars 7111

Multi-lingual International Publishers Ltd. and Kay, E.
Arabic military dictionary 3380
The Multicultural dictionary of proverbs 4192
Multicultural education 3747
Multicultural education abstracts 3770
Multilateral treaties 2958
The Multilingual business handbook 2564
Multilingual commercial dictionary 1794
Multilingual dictionary of commercial international trade and shipping terms 2419
The Multilingual dictionary of real estate 1991
Multilingual glossary of abbreviations 2936
Multilingual glossary of tax, financial and commercial terms 2107
Multilingual law dictionary 2749
Multinational enterprise 2072
Multinational treaties deposited with the Secretary-General as at 31 December 1985 2961
Mumby, L.M.
Dates and time 7061
Mundo Lo, S. de
Index to Spanish American collective biography 5918
Mundt, R.J.
Historical dictionary of the Côte D'Ivoire (The Ivory Coast) 7789
The Municipal year book, 2000 3313
The Municipal year book and public services directory 3301
Munn, G. G.
Encyclopedia of banking and finance 2097
Munniksma, F.
International business dictionary in nine languages/... English/Esperanto/Deutsch/ Español/Français/Italiano/Nederlands/ Portuguese/ Svensk 1796
Munro, D.
Chambers World gazetteer 5423
The Oxford dictionary of the world 5449
The Scotia reference gazetteer of the Baltic States 5552
Munro, D. and Day, A.J.
A World record of major conflict areas 1520
Munro-Hay, S. and Pankhurst, R.
Ethiopia 4801
New Murderer's who's who 3138
Murdoch, H.
A Dictionary of Irish law 2813
Murdock, E.C.
The Civil War in the North 8042
Murphy, A.
Bolivia handbook 5648
Ecuador & Galápagos handbook 5651
Peru handbook 5649
Venezuela handbook 5652
Murphy, B.
Dictionary of Australian history 8171
Murphy, L.L. and Impara, J.C. and Plake, B.
Tests in print V 337
Murphy-O'Connor, J.
The Holy Land: an Oxford archaeological guide 4372
Murray, J.
Cultural atlas of Africa 4789
Musiker, N.
South African history 7829
Musiker, N. and Musiker, R.
Historical dictionary of Greater Johannesburg 7834
Musiker, R. and Musiker, N.
Southern African bibliography 4851
The Muslim diaspora 7535
The Muslim World: a historical survey 7528
Muslims of the Soviet empire 948
Musto, R.G.
The Peace tradition of the Catholic Church 725

Musty, J.
The Origins of the archaeological periodical 4221

Muthiah, S.
An Atlas of India 5281

Mwalimu, C.
'A Bibliographic essay of selected secondary sources on the common law and customary law of English speaking Sub-Saharan Africa' 2856

Mwiyeriwa, S.S.
'Developments in African archives' 6567

My ancestor was a migrant 6055

Mycenaean civilization 6703

Myers, Allen C.
The Eerdmans Bible dictionary 458

Myers, J.
Canadian facts and dates 7883

Myers, J. *and* Musson, J.
The Fitzhenry Whiteside book of Canadian Facts and dates 7882

Myers, R.A.
Dominica 4921
Ghana 4825
Nigeria 4829
A Resource guide to Dominica 1493-1986 4922

Mysticism 396

Myth, legend and romance 4149

Mythical and fabulous creatures 818

Mythologies of the world 817

Mythology of all races 822

Mythology of the British Isles 833

Myths and legends of the British Isles 4137

Myths of Greece and Rome 843

Naft, S *and* Sola, R.de
International conversion tables 3265

Nagao, P.M.
Japanese local histories 7604

Nagel, S.
Policy-studies handbook 1384

Nagy, L.
Bibliography of Hungarian legal literature, 1945-1980 2839

Nahm, A.C.
Historical dictionary of the Republic of Korea 7598

Nakamura, H.
Japanese-English Buddhist dictionary 885

Nally, M.
Glossary of public relations terms in seven languages (English-French-German-Spanish-Dutch-Finnish-Italian) 2714

Namibia 4859

Namibia handbook 5600

Naoki Mukoda
Emblems 6259

Napoleonic military history 3513

The Napoleonic source book 3473

Nappo, T.
Archives biographiques Françaises. Deuxième Série/French biographical archive Series II/Französisches biographisches archiv Neue Folge 5804
Indico biografico Italiano/Italienischer biographischer index/Italian biographical index 5811

Nappo, T. *and* Furlani, S.
Archivo biografico Italiano/Italian biographical archive 5808
Archivo biografico Italiano, nuova serie/Italian biographical archive. Series II 5810

Narasinham, J.
The Manx family tree 6065

Narkiewicz, O.
Eurocommunism, 1968-1986 224

Narodowy atlas Polski 5250

Nash, J.R.
Encyclopaedia of world crime, criminal justice, criminology and law enforcement 3119

Nash, S.D. *and* Vincenti, W.
American and British history resources on the Internet 7966

Naske, C-M. *and* Slotnik, H.E.
Alaska 8081

Nasr, Z.
The Dictionary of economics and commerce 1797

NATFHE handbook of initial teacher training, 1996 3902

Nathan, A.J.
Modern China 1840-1972 7565

Nathan, E.
'Archives', chapter 2, *Australians: a guide to sources* 6611

A Nation under siege 5529

National Academic Recognition Information Centre, British Council
International guide to qualifications in education 3914

The National accounts: a short guide 2146

National accounts of OECD countries, 1955/64- 2143

National and international tourism statistics, 1974-1985 2413

'The National archives in Turkey' 6560

'The National Archives of Pakistan' 6558

'National archives of Zimbabwe' 6577

National Atlas of Canada 5331

National atlas of Ethiopia 5299

National atlas of Hungary
Magyarorsz ag nemzeti atlasza. National atlas of Hungary 5227

National atlas of India 5282

National atlas of Jamaica 5345

The National atlas of Japan 5277

National Atlas of Kenya 5314

The National atlas of Malawi 5320

National atlas of South West Africa (Namibia) 5318

The National atlas of Sri Lanka 5285

National atlas of Sweden 5255

National atlas of the Democratic Republic of Afghanistan 5291

National atlas of The United Arab Emirates 5280

The National atlas of the United States 5348

National biografisch woordenboek 5851

National Centre for Christian Communities and Networks
Directory of Christian groups, communities and networks 662

National Council for Civil Liberties
Civil liberty 3112

The National Council for Research on Women
A Women's thesaurus 4108

National Council for Voluntary Organizations
Voluntary agencies directory 1997 3593

The National cyclopaedia of American biography 5929

National directory of legal services 2865

The National faculty directory 3950

National Geographic
Trip planner platinum 5635

'National Geographic' Atlas of the world 5401

National Geographic atlas of world history 6414

National Geographic desk reference 5116

National Geographic guide to America's hidden corners 5625

National Geographic index 1888-1988 5128

National Geographic maps on CD-ROM 5418

The National Geographic Society 5149

The National geographical dictionary of India 5574

National Geographic's guide to State Parks of the United States 5626

National health systems of the world 3631

National Historical Publications and Records Commission
Directory of archives and manuscript repositories in the United States 6595

National index of parish registers 6214

The National inventory of documentary sources in the United Kingdom and Ireland 6505

The National inventory of documentary sources in the United States 6596

National Library for the Handicapped Child
Catalogue of library holdings 3670

National Maritime Museum
The Commissioned sea officers of the Royal Navy, 1660-1815 3548

National Maritime Museum guide to maritime Britain 5486

National Monuments Record of Scotland Jubilee 4411

The National Register of Archives: an international perspective 6509

'A National Register of Archives in mosaic form: the Canadian example' 6581

'National Register of Archives (Scotland)' 6511

The National register of historic places 1984 5636

National register of historic places index 5637

National register of ship arrivals Australia and New Zealand 6204

National Technical Information Services
Directory of federal and state business assistance 2082

The National Trust guide to Dark Age and Medieval Britain 5476

The National Trust guide to Late Georgian and Victorian Britain 5485

The National Trust guide to late medieval and renaissance Britain 5479

The National Trust guide to our industrial past 4469

The National Trust guide to prehistoric and Roman Britain 5475

Nationalism in Uzbekistan 7711

The Nationalities question in the post-Soviet states 7410

The Nation's memory: a pictorial guide to the Public Record Office 6493

Native America in the twentieth century: an encyclopedia 8067

The Native American almanack 4967

Native American Bibliography Series 4968

'Native American reference sources' 4972

Native Americans 8007, 8011

The Native North American almanac 4966

NativeWeb 4498

NATO: a bibliography and resource guide 2983

NATO glossary of terms and definitions (English and French) 3378

Natoli, J. *and* Rusch, F.L.
Psychocriticism 249

Natural and supernatural 169

The Nature of women 4064

The NatWest student book 2001 entry 3935

Nauman, A.K.
A Handbook of Latin American and Caribbean national archives/Guia de los archivos nacionales de America Latino y el Caribe 6591

Naumann, St. E.
Dictionary of Asian philosophies 133

Nauru bibliography 5046

Navabpour, R.
Iran 4728

Navada handbook 5617

Naval and maritime history 3550

A Naval history of England 3547

Naval operations 6806

Newberry Library Historical Boundary Data File
Historical atlas and chronology of county boundaries 1788-1980 **8080**

Newby, E.
The Mitchell Beazley world atlas of exploration **5068**

Newcomer, J.
The Grand Duchy of Luxembourg **7290**

Newell, C.R.
Historical dictionary of the Persian Gulf War, 1990-1991 **7628**

Newell, V.J.
The Folklore of the British Isles **4139**

'Newfoundland family records' **6186**

Newham, G.
'Choosing a business database: the expert approach.' **2510**

Newitt, M.
The Comoro Islands **7845**

The Newly independent states of Eurasia **4741**

Newman, G.
Britain in the Hanoverian age 1714-1837 **6977**

Newman, K.
Dictionary of Ulster biography **5778**

Newman, L.
Hunger in history **1149**

Newman, O. and Foster, A.
European business rankings **2448**

Newman, P.
The New Palgrave dictionary of money and finance **1779**

Newman, P. and Milgate, M. and Eatwell, J.
The New Penguin dictionary of money and finance **2103**

Newman, P.C.
Debrett's illustrated guide to the Canadian establishment **5908**

Newman, P.R.
Companion to Irish history 1603-1921 **7021**
Companion to the English Civil Wars **6972**

Newson, T.
A Housing bibliography **3259**

Newton, D. and Kirkwood, J. and Lunn, S.
The FIAC directory of independent advice centres **3591**

Newton, M.
Mass murder **3135**

Newton, N.
The Shell guide to the islands of Britain **5490**

Newton, V.
Commonwealth Caribbean legal literature **2816**

Ngā Tāngata Taumata Rau **5979**

Nicaragua **4889-4890**

Nicholas, D.
Commodities futures trading **2416**
The Middle East: its oil, economics and investment policies **2132**

Nicholl, D. and Aschenbrenner
Contemporary European philosophy **127**

Nichols, A.
'Bibliography of current books on Christianity and politics, Christianity and the social order' **546**

Nichols, C.S.
Dictionary of national biography. Missing persons **5744**

Nichols, E.L.
Genealogy in the computer age **6098**

Nichols, H.
Local maps of Derbyshire to 1770 **7176**
Local maps of Nottinghamshire to 1800 **7180**

Nichols, R.
The Book of Druidry **954**

Nicholson, F.
Political and economic encyclopedia of Western Europe **1418**

Nicholson, N.L. and Sebert, L.M.
The Maps of Canada **5334**

Nickson, R.A.
Historical dictionary of Paraguay **8115**
Paraguay **4992**

Nicol, D.M.
A Biographical dictionary of the Byzantine Empire **7679**

Nicoll, E.H.
A Pictish panorama **6998**

Niger **4812-4813**

Nigeria **4829**

Nigeria: giant in the tropics **4828**

Nigeria in maps **4830**

Niiya, B.
Japanese American history **8003**

Nijhof, P.
'Industrial archaeology in the Netherlands' **4485**

Nilsen, R.
Honolulu-Waikiki handbook. The island of Oahu **5680**
South Korea handbook **5562**

Nineteenth century fashion **3994**

Nineteenth-century religious thought in the West **588**

Nippon **1269**

Nissel, M.
People count **1345**

Niué, South Pacific **8134**

The NIV complete concordance **502**

Nixon, J.W.
Glossary of terms in official statistics **1199**

Nizami, F.A.
History of the Islamic world **7529**

Nobari, N.S.
Books and periodicals on line **2009, 2717**

The Nobel Foundation **5724**

Nobel Prize winners **5719**

Noble, J.
Russia, Ukraine & Belarus **5551**

Noel, C.
Debrett's correct form **4046**

Noel, J.V.
Naval terms dictionary **3542**

Noffsinger, J.P.
World Ward I aviation **3523**

Nolan, C.J.
The Longman guide to world affairs **4495**

Nolan, M.L. and Nolan, S.
Christian pilgrimage in modern Western Europe **552**

Nolan, W.
Tracing the past **7045**

Nonconformist congregations in Great Britain **774**

Norback, C.T.
VGM's careers encyclopedia **1960**

Norcross, J.C.
Authoritative guide to self-help resources in mental health **3675**

Nordby, J.
Mongolia **4663**

Nordic Statistical Secretariat
Yearbook of Nordic statistics **1249**

Nordstrom, B.J.
Dictionary of Scandinavian history **7456**

Norfolk Islands **8145**

Norge biografisk leksikon **5842**

Norkett, P.
The Building societies facts file **2219**

The Normandy campaign 1944 **6854**

Norris, H.
Church vestments **648**

Norris, J.M.
History of the US Navy **3581**

Norris, R.E.
Guía bibliogáfia para el estudio de la historia ecuatoriana **8109**

Norsk historisk atlas **7466**

North American exploration **5081**

The North Atlantic Treaty Organisation **2981**

North of 50°: an atlas of Far Northern Ontario **5332**

The North West Passage 1534-1859 **8198**

Northal, G.F.
English folk-rhymes **4190**

Northanhymbre saga **7221**

Northcutt, W.
The Regions of France **4584**

Northedge, F.S. and Grieve, M.J.
A Hundred years of international relations **1610**

Northern business histories **2470**

Northern Crowns **6335**

Northern Europe in the early modern period **7439**

Northern Ireland
The Statutes revised, Northern Ireland, AD1226-1950 **2810**

Northern Ireland **4554-4555**

Northern Ireland; a census atlas **1341**

Northern Ireland: a chronology of the Troubles 1968-1999 **7040**

The Northern Ireland annual abstract of statistics, 1999 **1235**

Northern Ireland. General Register Office
Census of population, Northern Ireland, 1971 **1336**

Northern Ireland since 1945 **7038**

Northern labour history **1980**

Northern Territory dictionary of biography **5996**

Northumberland miners' banners **6260**

Norton, A.R.
NATO: a bibliography and resource guide **2983**

Norton, J.E.
Guide to the national and provincial directories of England and Wales **7087**

Norton-Kyshe, J.W.
The Dictionary of legal quotations **2827**

Norton, M.
A Guide to the benefits of charitable status **3595**

Norton, M. B. and Gerhardi, P.
The American Historical Association's Guide to historical literature **6377**

Norway **4624**

Norway. Statistisk Sentralbyra
Statistisk årbok/Statistical yearbook of Norway **1251**

Norwegian local history **7465**

Norwich, J.J.
Regions of Italy **5542**

Norwich, O.I.
Maps of Africa **5297**

Notable Americans **5930**

Notable Asian Americans **5952**

Notable British families 1600s-1990s **6266**

Notable Latino Americans **5948**

Notable native Americans **5958**

Notable women in American history **5962**

Notable women in world history **5735**

Notre Dame journal of formal logic **341**

Nottinghamshire history and topography **7179**

Nouët, N.
The Shogun's city **7600**

Nouvelle histoire de la Suisse et des Suisses **7480**

Nova história de Portugal **7398**

The NRSV concordance unabridged **504**

An Introduction to Ukrainian history **7446**

The Nuclear almanac: confronting the atom in war and peace **2989**

The Nuclear arms race **2988**

Nuevo diccionario biográfico argentino (1750-1930) **5964**

Nugent, N.
The European Community 1992 **2921**

The Nunavut handbook **5605**

Nuñez, B.
   Dictionary of Afro-Latin American civilization 4936
   Dictionary of Portuguese-African civilization 7750
Nunn, G.R.
   Asia and Oceania 6544
   Canada and Asia: a guide to archives and manuscripts 6545
Nuovo dizionaria di Mariologia 594
Nurcombe, V.J.
   International real estate valuation, investment and development 1989
Nurse, C.
   Argentina handbook 5645
   Chile handbook 5647
Nyaknno Osso
   Who's who in Nigeria 5898
Nyeko, B.
   Swaziland 4857
   Uganda 4844
N'Yeurt, A. De R.
   A Bibliography of Rotuma 5042
Ó Danachair, C.
   A Bibliography of Irish ethnology and folk tradition 4148
Ó Maoláin, C.
   Latin American political movements 1740
O Súilleabháin, S.
   A Handbook of Irish folklore 4147
Oakes, D.
   Reader's Digest illustrated history of South Africa 7828
Oakes, E.H. and Sheldon, K.E.
   A Guide to social science resources in women's studies 4055
Oakland, J.
   British civilization: an introduction 4536
Oakley, S.P.
   Scandinavian history 1520-1970 7455
Oberg, L.R.
   Human services in postrevolutionary Cuba 1190
Obin, A.
   Bibliography of nautical books, 2000 3532
O'Brien, J.W. and Wasserman, S.R.
   Statistics sources, 2000 1283
O'Brien, N.P.
   Education 3749
O'Brien, P. and Fabiano, E.
   Core list of books & journals in education 3741
O'Brien, P.K.
   Philip's atlas of world history 6418
The Occult in the Western world 156
Occult/paranormal bibliography 155
Occupations, 93 1946
Occupations of the people of Great Britain, 1801-1981 1952
Oceanic mythology 969
O'Cèirìn, K. and O'Cèirìn, C.
   Women of Ireland 5777
Ochieng, W.R.
   A Modern history of Kenya 1895-1980 7813
   Themes in Kenyan history 7814
Ochoa, G. and Corey, M.
   Fitzroy Dearborn guide to events of the 20th Century 6454
O'Clery, C.
   Phrases make history here: political quotations in Ireland, 1886-1987 1433
O'Connor, A.M.
   Urbanization in tropical Africa 3307
O'Connor, D.J.
   A Critical history of Western philosophy 125
O'Connor, K. and Epstein, L.
   Public interest law groups 3109

O'Day, R.
   'The History of women and the family' 4078
   The Longman companion to the Tudor Age 6965
O'Day, R. and Englander, D.
   Mr. Charles Booth's inquiry 1182
O'Dea, A.C.
   Bibliography of Newfoundland 4882
Odelain, O. and Séguineau, R.
   Dictionary of proper names and places in the Bible 468
O'Donnell, C.
   Ecclesia 575
O'Donnell, E.E.
   The Annals of Dublin 7047
O'Donnell, J.
   Ireland: a directory 2000 4557
   Ireland the past twenty years: an illustrated chronology 7029
O'Donnell, J.D.
   How Ireland is governed 3335
O'Donnell, T.S.
   World quality of life indicators 1163
OECD economic outlook 2284
OECD economic outlook - historical statistics, 1960-1989 2285
OECD economic surveys 2283
Of the hut I builded 4344
O'Farrell, P.
   Who's who in the Irish War of Independence and Civil War 1916-1923 7034
Ofcansky, T.P.
   British East Africa 1850-1963 7799
Office automation 2554
Office for National Statistics
   Social trends 1173
Office for National Statistics and Down, D.
   Family spending 1172
Office-holders in modern Britain 3328
Office of Population Censuses and Surveys
   Population trends 1332
Office of the Federal Register, National Archives and Records Service
   United States government manual, 1999-2000 3234
Officers died in the Great War 1914-19 6826
Official histories 6800
The Official history of colonial development 1580
The Official index to the *Financial times.* 1769
Official UK 1492
Official yearbook 1301
Officials of royal commission of enquiry, 1870-1939 3326
Officials of Royal Commissions of Inquiry, 1815-70 3329
Officials of the royal household 1660-1837 3330
Ofori, P.E.
   Christianity in tropical Africa 567
O'Hara, F.M. and Sicignano, R.
   Handbook of United States economic and financial indicators 2380
O'Hara, G.
   The Encyclopedia of fashion from 1840 to the 1980s 4008
O'Hara, P.A.
   Encyclopedia of political economy 1777
O'Higgins, P.
   Bibliography of Irish trials and other legal proceedings 3188
O'Higgins, P. and Partington, M.
   Social security law in Britain and Ireland 3721
Ohles, J.F.
   Biographical dictionary of American educators 3810
O'hOgain, D.
   Myth, legend and romance 4149

Oizon, R.
   Dictionnaire géographique de la France 5538
Oke, G.C.
   Oke's Magisterial formulist .. 3204
O'Kelly, M.J.
   Early Ireland 4278
Okely, J.
   The Traveller-gypsies 4118
Oke's Magisterial formulist .. 3204
Oko, A.S.
   The Spinoza bibliography 53
Okonski, W.
   Wartime Poland 1939-1945 7312
Olason, P.E.
   Islenzkar aeviskrár 5848
O'Laughlin, M.C.
   The Complete book for tracing your Irish ancestors 6052
Olcott, M.B.
   The Kazakhs 7708
'Old county maps and their makers' 7095
Old Testament abstracts 521
Oldfield, S.
   Collected biography of women in Britain 1550-1900 5767
O'Leary, J. and Cannon, T.
   'The Times' good universities guide 3937
Oliphant, M.
   The Atlas of the Ancient World 6637
Olivastri, V.
   Sicily 4592
Oliveira Marques, A.H. de
   Guía do estudiante de historia medieval portuguesa 7404
   History of Portugal 7397
Oliver, A.M.
   Hawaii fact and reference book 5048
Oliver, P.J. and Press, J.
   The Spicer and Oppenheim guide to securities markets around the world 2246
Oliver, R.
   Ordnance Survey maps 7100
Oliver, R. and Crowder, M.
   The Cambridge encyclopedia of Africa 4784
Oliver, R. and Fage, J.D.
   The Cambridge history of Africa 7743
Olney, R.J.
   Manuscript sources for British history 6506
Olsen, K.
   Chronology of women's history 5732
Olson, J.S.
   Dictionary of the Vietnam War 7737
   Dictionary of United States economic history 2383
   An Ethnohistorical dictionary of the Russian and Soviet Empires 7425
   Historical dictionary of the 1920s 8064
   Historical dictionary of the 1960s 8065
   Historical dictionary of the New Deal 8066
   Historical dictionary of the Spanish Empire 7381
   The Indians of Central and South America 7949
Olson, W.J.
   Britain's elusive empire in the Middle East, 1900-1921 7542
Olssen, E.
   A History of Otago 8138
Olsson, N.W.
   Tracing your Swedish ancestry 6078
Oman 4696, 7618
Oman '97 4695
Ó'Maoláin, C.
   The radical right 1707
O'Meara, M. and Patterson, K.
   World business directory 2447
Omer-Cooper, J.D.
   History of Southern Africa 7824
Omni gazetteer of the United States of America 5627

Parker, C.G.A.
Police and constabulary almanac 3249
Parker, D. *and* Parker, J.
A History of astrology 199
Parker's astrology 191
Parker, F. *and* Parker, B.J.
US higher education 3906
Parker G.
The Times compact atlas of world history 6419
Parker, G. *and* Parker, B.
A Dictionary of the European Communities 2934
Parker, J.
A Glossary of terms used in heraldry 6229
Parker, J.C.
Library service for genealogists 6122
Parker, M.St.J.
Britain's Kings & Queens 6326
Parker, N.
Charities and broadcasting 3594
Parker, R.H.
Macmillan dictionary of accounting 2579
Parker's astrology 191
Parkes, M.B.
English cursive book hands 1250-1500 6620
Parkinson, G.H.R.
An Encyclopaedia of philosophy 65
The Handbook of Western philosophy 74
Parks directory of the United States 5629
Parks, E.D.
Early English hymns 649
Parliament and government 1675
Parliament: functions, practice and procedures 1676
The Parliament of Great Britain 3040
The Parliamentarians 1681
The Parliamentary debates. Fifth series. House of Commons: official report 1909- 3034
The Parliamentary debates. Fifth series. House of Lords: official report, 1909- 3035
Parliamentary elections results in Ireland, 1801-1922 1560
Parliamentary elections results in Ireland, 1918-1992: Irish elections to Parliaments and Parliamentary assemblies at Westminster and Belfast, Dublin, Strasbourg 1561
The Parliaments of Scotland 3070
Parliaments of the world 3029
Parrinder, E.G.
A Dictionary of religious and spiritual quotations 421
Parrinder, G.
Africa's three religions 965
Dictionary of non-Christian religions 807
An Illustrated history of the world's religions 805
Parrish, M.
The 1968 Czechoslovak crisis 7307
The USSR in World War II 6897
Parrish, T.
The Simon and Schuster encyclopedia of World War II 6871
Parry, C.
The Consolidated treaty series, 1648-1918 2966
Encyclopedic dictionary of international law 2896
Parry, C. *and* Hopkins, C.
An Index of British Treaties, 1101-1968 2969
Parry, J.H.
New Iberian world 7942
Parry, M.
Chambers biographical dictionary 5686
Chambers biographical dictionary of women 5729
Parry, R.
Scottish political facts 1559
Particular places 7066

Partington, D.H.
The Middle East annual issues and events 4691
Partnow, E.
The New quotable woman 4074
Party systems in Denmark, Austria, Switzerland, the Netherlands and Belgium 1709
Pas, J.F.
Historical dictionary of Taoism 958
Pascu, S.
A History of Transylvania 7511
Paskins, B.
'Peace studies and disarmament.' 2996
Pass, C.
Collins dictionary of business 2020
Collins dictionary of economics 1806
Passenger and immigration lists bibliography. 1538-1900 6104
Passenger and immigration lists index 6089
Passenger and immigration lists index 1538-1940 6090
Passengers to America 6093
Passmore, J.A.
A Hundred years of philosophy 103
Recent philosophers 104
The Past today 5659
Pastor, Freiherr von L.
The History of the Popes, from the close of the Middle Ages 750
Paterson, L. *and* McCrone, D.
The Scottish government yearbook, 1992 3223
Pates, A.
The Education factbook 3784
Pathfinder maps 5201
Pathways to Ulster's past 7036
A Patient's guide to the National Health Services 3660
Patmore, E.
International handbook of aging 1103
A Patristic Greek lexicon 701
Patrology 696, 698
Patten, J.
English towns, 1500-1700 3306
Patterns of fashion 3961
Patterson, B. *and* Patterson, K.
New Zealand 5008
Patterson, S.
Royal insignia 6278
Patterson, S.C.
'Understanding the British Parliament' 1674
Pattie, T.S.
Astrology 194
Paul, J.B.
An Ordinary of arms contained in the Public Register of all arms and bearings in Scotland 6244
Paul J.B., Sir
The Scots peerage 6272
Paulhart, H. *and* Paulhart, H.
Österreichische historische bibliographie. Ergänzungsheft 1. Liste der Zeitschriften/ Austrian historical bibliography. Supplement 1. List of periodicals 1949-1979. (1980) 7297
Pauly, A.F. von *and* Wissowa, G.
Pauly's Real-Encyklopädie der classichen Altertumswissenschaft 6692
Pauly's Real-Encyklopädie der classichen Altertumswissenschaft 6692
Pawloski, B.M.
'Gaelic law in early and medieval Ireland; a bibliography' 2811
Paxton, J.
A Dictionary of the European Communities 2935
Encyclopedia of Russian history 7408
The Longman companion to Imperial Russia 1682-1917 7409
The Penguin encyclopedia of places 5437

Paxton, J. *(contd.)*
World legislatures 3030
Paxton, J. *and* Knappman, E.W.
The Fitzroy Dearborn calendar of world history 6465
Payne, J.B.
Encyclopedia of Biblical prophecy 499
Payne, S.G.
The Franco regime 7373
Pazzanita, A.G.
Historical dictionary of Mauritania 7776
The Maghreb 4792
Western Sahara 4804
PC Globe 5419
PC USA Version 2.0 5357
Peace and war 2990
The Peace Corps 2997
Peace information sources 2995
Peace movements of the world 3008
Peace organizations, past and present 3006
Peace research abstracts journal 3005
Peace resource book 3001
'Peace studies and disarmament.' 2996
The Peace tradition of the Catholic Church 725
The Peacetime army, 1900-1941 3518
Peacock, J.
20th century fashion 3996
The Chronicle of Western fashion 3987
Costume, 1066-1966 3980
Peacocke, C.A.B. *and* Scott, D.
A Selective bibliography of philosophical logic 339
Peake, A.G.
National register of ship arrivals Australia and New Zealand 6204
Peake, L.A.
The United States in the Vietnam War 1954-1975 7732
Peake's commentary on the Bible 512
Pearce, D.W.
The Macmillan dictionary of modern economics 1783
Pearce, N.
Britain 2000 4545
Pearson, C.
Conservation of maritime archaeological objects 4348
Pearson, J.D.
A Bibliography of pre-Islamic Persia 4237
Guide to documents and mansucrits in the British Isles relating to Africa 6568
A Guide to manuscripts and documents in the British Isles relating to South and South-East Asia 6552
South Asian bibliography 4705
Pearson, J.D. *and* Ashton, J.F.
Index Islamicus 1906-1955 4762
Pearson, J.E.
Oke's Magisterial formulist .. 3204
Pearson, R.
Russia and Eastern Europe 1789-1985 7419
Pearson, R.J.
Windows on the Japanese past 4310
Peaslee, A.J.
International governmental organizations: constitutional documents 2903
Peck, M.
The Bitter with the sweet: New Brunswick 1604-1984 7888
Historical dictionary of the Gulf (Arab) States 7625
Peck, M.C.
The United Arab Emirates 7630
Pedersen, R.N.
One Europe 100 nations 6763
Peedle, R.
Encyclopaedia of the modern territorial army 3503
Peerage creations 1689-1800 6265

Philosophy of education 3752

Phrases make history here: political quotations in Ireland, 1886-1987 1433

Picard, C.G. *and* Picard, C.
Carthage 6731

Picchi, F.
Economics and business 1818

Pick, F. *and* Sédillot, R.
All the monies of the world 2228

Pick, J.B.
Atlas of Mexico 5337

Picken, M.B.
A Dictionary of costume and fashion 3966
The Fashion dictionary 3967

Pickering, D.
The Cassell dictionary of proverbs 4197
Cassell dictionary of superstitions 4180

Pickford, C.B. *and* Last, R.
The Arthurian bibliography 4173

Pickford, N.
The Atlas of ship wreck & treasure 5113

Pickles, D.
The Government and politics of France 3077

Picknett, L.
The Encyclopedia of the paranormal 166

Picon, A. *and* Sloan, G.
PAIS subject headings 983

A Pictish panorama 6998

A Pictorial history of costume 3974

Picts 4415

Pieces of the past 4282

Pierre Teilhard de Chardin 56-57

Piggott, S. *and* Ritchie, G.
Scotland before history with a gazetteer of ancient monuments 4422

Pilgrimages 632

Pilgrimages in the Middle Ages 633

Pilling, S. *and* Kirby, D.
The International foundation directory 3592

Pillinger, D. *and* Staunton, A.
Victoria Cross locator 3432

Pimentel, R.P.
Diccionario biografico del Ecuador 5969

The Pimlico chronology of British history 6938

The Pimlico dictionary of classical civilizations 6631

The Pimlico encyclopedia of the Middle Ages 6744

Pimlott, J.
The Viking atlas of World War II 6879

Pinchemel, P.
France 5146

Pinches, J.H. *and* Pinches, R.V.
The Royal heraldry of England 6251

Pine, L.G.
The New extinct peerage 1184-1971 6274

Pines, P.
Reader's Digest travel guide USA 5631

Pinfold, J.
Tibet 4662

Pinfold, J.R.
African population census reports 1349

Pinhorn, M.
Historical, archaeological and kindred societies in the United Kingdom 6945

Pinol, J-L.
Atlas historique des villes de France 7333

Pirouet, M.L.
Historical dictionary of Uganda 7812

Pisier, G.
Bibliographie méthodique, analytique et critique de la Nouvelle - Calédonie 1955-1982 5016

The Pitman 2000 dictionary of English and shorthand 2568

Pitman business correspondence 2561

Pitman, L.
Russia/USSR 4609

Pitt, B. *and* Pitt, F.
Chronological atlas of World War II 6880

The Pivotal conflict 6820

Place-name changes since 1900 5440

Place-names in classical mythology: Greece 851

Place names of Africa 1935-1986 5592

Plain figures 1305

Plakans, A.
Historical dictionary of Latvia 7442

Planché, J.R.
A Cyclopaedia of costume 3957

Planhol, X. de
An Historical geography of France 5157

Plano, J.
Dictionary of political analysis 1471

Plano, J.C. *and* Greenberg, M.
The American political dictionary 3026

Plant, R.
Modern political thought 1468

The Plantagenet encyclopedia 6963

Plants of the Bible 494-495

Plato
Complete works 44

Plato and Socrates 43

Platt, C.
The Atlas of medieval man 6442
The National Trust guide to late medieval and renaissance Britain 5479
Travellers' guide to medieval England 5517

Platt, C.J.
Tax systems of Africa, Asia and Middle East 2147
Tax systems of Western Europe 2148

Plischke, E.
US foreign relations 1648

Plomp, T. *and* Ely, D.P.
International encyclopedia of educational technology 3725

Plummer, R.
The Ships that saved an army 6847

Les plus anciennes familles du monde 6136

Plut-Pregelj, L. *and* Rogel, C.
Historical dictionary of Slovenia 7500

Pluvier, J.M.
Historical atlas of South-East Asia 7553

PNG: a factbook on modern Papua New Guinea 5034

Pocket employer 2631

Pocket guide to the European Community 2931

Pocket guide to the new City 2176

Podell, D.K.
Thematic atlases for public, academic, and High School libraries 5178

Pogonowski, I.C.
Poland a historical atlas 7316

Pohl, R.
Handbook of the economy of the German Democratic Republic 2327

Poignant, R.
Oceanic mythology 969

Pokornowski, I.M. *and* Eicher, J.B. *and* Harris, M.F.
African dress II 3992

Polak, J.
Bibliographie maritime française depuis les temps les plus reculés jusquà 1914 3572

Poland 4578

Poland a historical atlas 7316

Poland. Glówny Ürzad Statystyczny
Rocznik statystyczny 1241

Polar and glaciological abstracts 5051

Polar regions atlas 5391

Polden, P.
Guide to the records of the Lord Chancellor's Department 3058

Polec: dictionary of politics and economics .. 1392

Polgár, L.
Bibliographie sur l'histoire de la Compagnie de Jésus 687

Poliakov, L.
The History of anti-Semitism 919

Police and constabulary almanac 3249

A Police bibliography 3244

Police dictionary and encyclopedia 3246

The Police of England and Wales 3250

Police science abstracts 3243

Policy-studies handbook 1384

'POLIS' in Parliament 1673

Polish Academy of Sciences. Institute of State and Law
Polish/English dictionary of legal terms 2768

Polish/English dictionary of legal terms 2768

Polish genealogy and heraldry 6006

Political and economic dictionary of Eastern Europe 1716

Political and economic encyclopedia of Africa 1451

Political and economic encyclopedia of South America and the Caribbean 1462

Political and economic encyclopedia of the Pacific 1382

Political and economic encyclopedia of the Soviet Union and Eastern Europe 1711

Political and economic encyclopedia of Western Europe 1418

Political and social science journals 1009

Political data handbook 1406

The Political dictionary of Israel 1448

A Political dictionary of the Arab world 1445

Political dictionary of the Arab World 7532

The Political economy of hunger 1147-1148

A Political economy of Uruguay since 1870 2388

Political geography in the twentieth century 1367

Political handbook of the world, 1999 1385

Political leaders in Black Africa 1453

Political leaders of contemporary Africa 1735

Political leaders of the contemporary Middle East and North Africa 3343

Political parties and elections in the French Fifth Republic 1729

Political parties of Asia and the Pacific 1733

Political parties of Europe 1708

Political parties of the Americas 1736

Political parties of the Americas, 1980s to 1990s, Canada, Latin America and the West Indies 1737

Political parties of the world 1699

Political quotations 1401

The political reference almanac 1999-2000 1415

Political risk yearbook 2037

Political science 1379

'Political science reference sources' 1373

Political science thesaurus II 1463

The Political system of the United States 3028

The Political systems of the Socialist States: an introduction to Marxist-Leninist regimes 1702

Political systems of the world 1486

Political thought since 1945 1475

Politics, economics and society in the two Germanies, 1945-75 1185

The politics of law making in China: institutions, processes and democratic prospects 2850

Pollard, G.S.
World poverty 1867

Pollard, P.
Colombia handbook 5650

Pollo, S. *and* Puto, A.
The History of Albania 7485

Pollock, N.J.
Nauru bibliography 5046

Polmar, N.
Guide to the Soviet Navy 3574
Polmar, N. and Allen, T.B.
America at war 1941-1945 6848
Polski indeks biograficzny/Polnischer
biographischer Index/Polish biographical
index 5833
Polski słownik biograficzny 5830
Polskie archiwum biograficzne/Polnisches
biographisches archiv/Polish biographical
archive 5832
Polskie archiwum biograficzne. Seria nova/
Polnisches biographisches archiv. Neue
folge/Polish biogoraphical archive. Series II
5834
Polynesia Melanesia Micronesia
A Pacific bibliography 4995
Polynesia - Tahiti
Bibliographie de la Tahiti et de la Polynésie
française 5039
The Polynesians 6741
Pompeii 4445
Poole, H.
Human rights: the essential reference 3089
Pope, B.H.
World defence forces, 1989 3354
Pope, R.
Atlas of British social and economic history
since c.1700 1167
Pope, S. and Robbins, K.
The Cassell dictionary of the Napoleonic
wars 3474
Pope, S. and Wheal, E-A.
The Macmillan dictionary of the First World
War 6815
Popplestone, J.A. and McPherson, M.W.
Dictionary of concepts in general psychology
266
Popular beliefs and superstitions 4163
A Popular dictionary of Buddhism 880
A Popular dictionary of Islam 942
A Popular dictionary of Sikhism 886
Popular fallacies 4181
Popular religious magazines of the United
States 431
Population 1323
The Population atlas of China 1348
Population bulletin of the United Nations 1322
Population Census Office of the State
Council of China and Institute of
Geography of the Chinese Academy of
Sciences
The Population atlas of China 1348
The Population history of England, 1541-1871
1325
Population in Ireland 1340
Population index 1309
'Population index' bibliography: cumulated
1969-1981 1310
Population information in nineteenth-century
census volumes 1353
Population information in twentieth-century
census volumes.. 1354
Population multilingual thesaurus .. 1320
The Population of the British colonies in
America before 1776 1352
The Population of the United States 1351
Population projections ... [1985 -2001.
England] 1335
Population statistics 1327
Population trends 1332
Porter, A.N.
Atlas of British overseas expansion 5215
Porter, G.
Encyclopedia of American economic history
2379
Porter, G.R.
The Progress of the nation in its various
social and economic relations 2313
Porter, S.
Exploring urban history 7075

Portrait of Britain 5480
Portugal 4606
Portugal. Instituto Nacional de Estatística
Anuário estatístico de Portugal = Statistical
yearbook of Portugal 1247
The Portuguese in Asia 7399
The Portuguese revolution of 25 April 1974
7405
The Portuguese seaborne empire 1415-1825
7395
Posner, J.L.
CWLA's guide to adoption agencies 3687
Pospielovsky, D.V.
A History of Soviet atheism in theory and
practice 440
Post-biblical saints art index 621
Post, E.P.
Emily Post's etiquette 4041
Post-Medieval Archaeology 4256
Post-medieval archaeology in Britain 4271
Postlethwaite, T.N.
Encyclopedia of comparative education and
national systems of education 3724
Potter, K.H.
Guide to Indian philosophy 142
Potter, R.B.
St. Vincent and the Grenadines 4923
Potter, R.B. and Dann, G.M.S.
Barbados 4925
Potts, A. and Jones, E.R.
Northern labour history 1980
Potts, D.
Zimbabwe 4862
Potts, D.T.
The Arabian Gulf in antiquity 7623
Poulson, B.W.
Economic history of the United States 2384
Poulton, H.
The Balkans 7492
Pounds, N.J.G.
An Historical geography of Europe 5152
Powell, A.
Far country 8157
Powell, G.
'The Exchange of archival information in
Australia' 6612
Powell, J.
Chronology of European history 15,000 BC
to 1987 6767
Powell, J.M.
An Historical geography of modern Australia
5164
Powell, K. and Cook, C.
English historical facts 1485-1603 6966
Powell, R.
AA guide to National Trust properties in
Britain 5454
Power, E.
Who owns what in world banking 2207
Powicke, F. M. and Emden, A.B.
The Universities of Europe in the Middle
Ages 3898
Poynting, J.
Resource guide to travel in the Caribbean
5610
Practical public relations 2709
Pratt, F.
Haiti 4908
Pratt, K. and Rutt, R.
Korea. A Historical and cultural dictionary
7589
Pre-Columbian contact with the Americas
across the oceans 5092
Prebble, G.H.
The Symbols, standards, flags and banners
of ancient and modern nations 6341
Prebish, C.S.
Historical dictionary of Buddhism 882
Precedence in England and Wales 6304
Predicasts F & S index Europe 2277
Predicasts F & S index international 2279

Predicasts F & S index United States 2278
The Prehistoric archaeology of Ireland 4279
The Prehistoric archaeology of the Aegean
4241
A Prehistoric bibliography 4258
Prehistoric Europe 4242
The Prehistoric exploration and colonisation of
the Pacific 4228
Prehistoric Orkney 4275
Prehistoric Scotland 4409
A Prehistory of Australia, New Guinea and
Sahul 4339
The Prehistory of Denmark 4301
The Prehistory of Germanic Europe 4245
Prehistory of Japan 4309
The Prehistory of New Zealand 4342
Prehistory of the Americas 4328
Prehistory of the Indo-Malaysian archipelago
4340
Prejudice and tolerance in Ireland 1177
Prejudice in Ireland revisited 1178
La Première guerre d'Indochine (1945-1954)
7733
Prentice, A.E.
Suicide 3141
The Prentice-Hall directory of online business
information 2502
Prescott, J.R.V.
The Maritime political boundaries of the
world 2949
Presidential elections since 1789 1564
The Presidential Medal of Freedom 6300
Presley, J.R.
A Directory of Islamic financial institutions
2134
Pressat, R.
The Dictionary of demography 1318
Pressnell, L.S. and Orbell, J.
A Guide to the historical records of British
banking 2212
Prest, A.R. and Barr, N.A.
Public finance in theory and practice 2142
Prest, J.
The Illustrated history of Oxford University
3930
Preston, S.H.
Causes of death 1357
Pretz, B.
Dictionary of military technological
abbreviations and acronyms 3356
Pribichevich, S.
Macedonia 7506
Price, V.J.
Register offices of births, deaths and
marriages in Great Britain and Northern
Ireland 6137
Prices and earnings around the globe 2415
Prickett, N.
The First thousand years 4343
Primary sources in European diplomacy, 1914-
45 1617
Primm, E.R.
Career discovering encyclopedia 1959
The Princeton encyclopaedia of classical sites
4239
Principles of Irish Law 2812
Printed maps and town plans of Bedfordshire
7193
The Printed maps of Devon 7158
Printed maps of Hertfordshire 7199
The Printed maps of Lincolnshire 1576-1900
7184
Printed maps of London circa 1553 - 1850
7129
Printed maps of Victorian London 1851-1900
7135
Printed maps of Wiltshire 1787-1844 7150
Printed records of the Parliament of Ireland,
1613-1800 3071
Printed sources 6108

Prischepenko, N.P.
Russian-English law dictionary **2767**
Prison librarianship **3145**
Pritchard, A.
Alchemy **188**
Pritchard, J.
The legal 500 **2796**
Pritchard, J.B.
The Times atlas of the Bible **487**
Pritzker, B.M.
Native Americans **8011**
Private schools of the United States **3852**
Prochaska, A.
History of the General Federation of Trade
Unions, 1899-1980 **1977**
Irish history from 1700 **7030**
Professional careers sourcebook **1958**
Professional dissent **1523**
The Progress of Afro-American women **4105**
The Progress of the nation in its various social
and economic relations **2313**
Prokurat, M. and Golitzin, A. and Peterson,
M.D.
Historical dictionary of the Orthodox Church
718
Prominent Hungarians, home and abroad **5798**
Propas, S.W.
Victorian studies **6980**
Property development and management into the
nineties **2002**
Pros and cons **1089**
The Prosopography of the Later Roman
Empire **6728**
Prospects directory **1957**
Protectionism **2417**
Prous, A.
Arquelogia Brasileira **4337**
Prouty, C. and Rosenfeld, E.
Historical dictionary of Ethiopia and Eritrea
7768
Proven, J. and Glogowski, M.P.
Management media directory **2625**
Provencher, J.
Chronologie du Québec **7896**
Proverbs / Proverbes / Sprichwörter / Proverbi
/ Proverbios / Poslovity **4195**
Proverbs, sentences and proverbial phrases,
from English writings mainly before 1500
4201
Provinces and provincial capitals of the world
5425
Provost, F.
Columbus, an annotated guide to the
scholarship on his life and writings 1750-
1988 **5091**
Prucha, F.P.
Atlas of American Indian affairs **5361**
A Bibliographical guide to the Indian-White
relations in the United States **1114**
Handbook for research in American history
7975
Indian-White relations in the United States
1115
Pryce-Jones, J.E.
Accounting in Scotland **2572**
The Pseudepigraphia and modern research,
with a supplement **543**
PsycBooks **279**
Psychiatry and the cults **435**
Psychoanalysis, psychology and literature **247**
Psychoanalystic terms and concepts **326**
Psychoanalytic studies of religion **316**
Psychoanalytic terms and concepts **267**
Psychocriticism **249**
Psychological abstracts **280**
Psychological bulletin **281**
Psychological enquiry **245**
The Psychological foundations of education
3829
Psychological index **250**
Psychological testing **334**

Psychology **242**
'Psychology' **253**
Psychology and theology in Western thought,
1672-1965 **252**
Psychology of religion **434**
Psychware sourcebook **333**
PsycINFO database **241**
Public administration **3215**
'Public administration and policy studies' **3213**
Public bodies, 1993 **3230**
Public finance **2140**
Public finance in theory and practice **2142**
The Public General Acts and General Synod
Measures **2790**
Public interest law groups **3109**
Public international law **2886, 2890**
Public opinion polling **1088**
Public opinion polls and survey research **1087**
Public Record Office
Making sense of the census **1339**
'The Public Record Office' **6494**
Public Record Office finding aids **6510**
The Public Record Office guide 1999. (to
microfiche ed.) **6507**
Public records and archives in classical Athens
6711
Public relations consultancy...Public relations
year book **2711**
Public relations handbook **2712**
The Public relations handbook **2713**
Publications **2303**
Published official sources of financial statistics
2123
Puckett, N.N.
Popular beliefs and superstitions **4163**
Puerto Rico **4909**
Puerto Rico past and present **4910, 7930**
Puffer, R.L.
'The Day of infamy in print' **6860**
Pullar, V.
Facts New Zealand **5005**
Pulsiano, P.
Medieval Scandinavia **7457**
The Pundits **5079**
Punjab **4710**
Purcell, L.E.
Who was who in the American Revolution
8035
Purchasing and materials management **2645**
Purvis, Canon J.S.
An Introduction to ecclesiastical records **765**
Purvis, J.D.
Jerusalem, the Holy City **6665**
Purvis, T.L.
A Dictionary of American history **7980**
Pusateri, C.J.
A History of American business **2066**
Pushkarev, S.G.
Dictionary of Russian historical terms **7426**
Pybus, V.
International directory of voluntary work
3614
Pycroft, C and Munslow, B.
Southern African annual review **4852**
Pye, M.
Macmillan dictionary of religion **406**
Qatar **4699**
Quadrilingual economics dictionary **1789**
Quah, S.R. and Quah, J.S.T.
Singapore **4754**
Quain, A.J.
The political reference almanac 1999-2000
1415
Quality assurance abstracts **3641**
Quality control and applied statistics **2644**
Quantities and units of measurement **3263**
Quarterly bulletin **1275**
Quarterly bulletin, 1968- **2362**
Quarterly strategic bibliography.
Current world affairs **3478**

Quasten, J.
Patrology **698**
Quebec
Encyclopédie du Québec **4879**
Québec **4881**
Quebec Office De La Langue Française
Terminologie de la gestion **2614**
Queens, Empresses, Grand Duchesses and
Regents **6317**
Queens University Belfast. The Institute of
Irish Studies
Ordnance Survey memoirs **7037**
Quemner, Th.A.
Dictionnaire juridique **2763**
Qui est qui en Belgique francophone 1985-
1989 **5852**
Quién es quién en América del Sur **5968**
Quien es quien en el Paraguay **5971**
Quinn, D.B.
The Hakluyt handbook **5099**
New American world **7857**
Quinn, P.L. and Taliaferro, C.
A Companion to the philosophy of religion
398
Quirke, S.
Who were the Pharaohs? **6649**
Raben, J. and Marks, G.
Data bases in the humanities and social
sciences **972**
Race and ethnic relations in Latin America and
the Caribbean **1125**
Rachlin, H.
The Money encyclopedia **2099**
Racinet, A.
The Historical encyclopedia of costumes
3958
Racism and discrimination in Britain **1120-**
1121
Rackham, P.
Jane's C31 systems **3477**
The radical right **1707**
Radice, B.
Who's who in the Ancient World **6699**
Radice, L.
Member of Parliament **3038**
Radnorshire **7242**
Radzinowicz, L.
The Cambridge Institute of Criminology: its
background and scope **3146**
A History of English criminal law and its
administration from 1750 **3131**
Radzinowicz, L. and Hood, R.G.
Criminology and the administration of
criminal justice **3151**
RAF **3525**
RAF records in the PRO **6496**
Rafique Akhtar
Pakistan year book 1993-94 **4725**
Ragazzini, G. and Gagliardelli, G.
Harrap's business Italian dictionary. Italian-
English **2532**
Rahman, H.U.
A Chronology of Islamic history, 570-1000
C.E **946**
Rahner, K.
Encyclopedia of theology **733**
Sacramentum mundi **732**
Rahner, K. and Vorgrimler, H.
Concise theological dictionary **583**
Rai, P.M.
Sikhism and the Sikhs **888**
Raimo, J.W.
Biographical directory of the governors of
the United States, 1978-1983 **3318**
Raistrick, D.
Lawyers' law books **2738**
Rajit Singh, D.S. and Sidhu, J.S.
Historical dictionary of Brunei Darrussalem
8124
Rake, A.
New African yearbook 1997-1998 **4786**

A Reference guide to the literature of travel 5063

A Reference guide to the United States Supreme Court 3201

Reference guide to United States military history 3423

'Reference materials for the disabled' 3668

Reference sources in history 6457

Reference sources in social work 3607

'Reference sources on the US Constitution.' 3024

Reference Wales 4567

Reference works for theological research 571

Reference works on world religions 377

The Refiner's fire 794

Regazzi, J.J. and Hines, T.C.
A Guide to indexed periodicals in religion 417

Regents of nations 1485, 6478

Regimental badges 3446

Regiments and corps of the British Army 3506

Regiments of the Empire 3512

A Regional history of England 7062

Regional trends 30 1230

The Regions of France 4584

Regions of France 5539

Regions of Italy 5542

The Regions of Spain 4597

Regions of Spain 5548

The Register of chartered psychologists 284

Register of defunct companies 2245

Register of periodicals in the ILO library 1892

Register of ships of the U.S. Navy, 1775-1990: major combatants 3580

The Register of the George Cross 6294

The Register of the Victoria Cross 6295

Register offices of births, deaths and marriages in Great Britain and Northern Ireland 6137

Registered Nursing Home Association: reference book, 1990/91 3652

Registrum sacrum Anglicanum 763

Reich, B.
Historical dictionary of Israel 7698
An Historical encyclopedia of the Arab-Israeli conflict 7696
Political leaders of the contemporary Middle East and North Africa 3343

Reich, B. and Goldberg, D.H.
The Political dictionary of Israel 1448

Reichert, H.W. and Schlecta, K.
International Nietzsche bibliography 42

Reid, B.J.
'Higher education', 1980-85 3891

Reid, C.D.
'Business information needs in Scotland' 2055

Reid, J.M.H. and Rowley, H.H.
Atlas of the Bible 481

Reid, J.P.
Genealogical research in England's Public Record Office 6063

Reid, R. and Reid, A.
Into history 8178

Reinhold, Gerd and Lamneck, S. and Recker, Helga
Soziologie-Lexicon 1049

Reinterpreting Russia 4608

Reiss, E.
Arthurian legend and literature 4169

Relations in records 6208

Religion and society in early modern Europe, 1500-1800 563

Religion and society in North America 678

Religion in contemporary Japan 959

Die Religion in Geschichte und Gegenwart 395

Religion in today's world 366

Religion index one: periodicals 380

Religion index two: multi-author works 381

Religion journals and serials 414

'Religion periodical indexes' 415

Religions 379

Religions and communities of India 871

The Religions of the Roman Empire 844

Religious and theological abstracts 408

Religious bibliographies in serial literature 410

Religious bodies in the United States 710

Religious books in print 382

Religious colleges and universities in America 3827

Religious information sources 383

The Religious life of man 376

Religious orders and congregations of Great Britain and Ireland 691

The Religious orders in England 694

Religious periodicals 411

Religious periodicals directory 413

Religious periodicals of the United States 416

Religious Society of Friends
Handbook of the Religious Society of Friends 802

Religious studies review 409

Remington, R.A.
The International relations of Eastern Europe 1619

Renfrew, C. and Bahn, P.
Archaeology 4208

Rengger, N.
Treaties and alliances of the world 1616

Renner, H.
A History of Czechoslovakia since 1945 7305

Renner, R. and Sachs, R.
Wirtschaftssprache/Economic terminology 1814

Renouvin, P.
Histoire des relations internationales 1611

Renshaw, P.
The Longman companion to America in the era of the two World Wars, 1910-1945 8060

Renstrom, P.G. and Rogers, C.B.
The Electoral politics dictionary 1565

Répertoire bibliographique de la philosophie 12

Répertoire bibliographique de Saint Augustin, 1950-1960 18

A Repertoire of League of Nations serial documents, 1919-1947 2906

Repertorium fontium historiae Medii Aevi 6773

Report of the Committee appointed ... under the chairmanship of Lord Robbins. 1961-1963 3903

[Report on the Civil Service] 3239

Reports and inventories 4410

Reports of the European Communities, 1952-1977: an index to authors and chairmen 2937

The Republic of Armenia 7453

The Republic of China yearbook 1996 4684

Rerum Britannicarum medii aevi scriptores 6922

Research catalogue 5117

Research guide for psychology 248

Research guide for studies in infancy and childhood 3683

Research guide to Central America and the Caribbean 7904

Research guide to central party and government meetings in China, 1949-1986 3237

Research guide to philosophy 14

A Research guide to the health sciences 3635

Research in ritual studies 645

Research index 2438

Research into higher education abstracts 3894

The Research Libraries of the New York Public Library and the Library of Congress
Bibliographic guide to psychology 243

Research on foreign students and international study 3731

Research on suicide 3140

The Researcher's guide to American genealogy 6112

Researcher's guide to archives and regional history sources 6594

A Researcher's guide to sources on Soviet social history in the 1930s 1019

Researching family history in Wales 6182

Researching local charities 3589

A Resource guide to Dominica 1493-1986 4922

Resource guide to special education 3873

Resource guide to travel in South America 5642

Resource guide to travel in Sub-Saharan Africa 5593

Resource guide to travel in the Caribbean 5610

Resources for middle childhood 3685

Resources in ancient philosophy 13

Resources in education (RIE), 1975-. v.10, no.1- 3807

Resumen de la historia de Chile 1535-1925 8097

Retail directory of the UK 2685

Retail trade international 2678

Retailing in the European single market, 1993 2679

Retirement 1099

Retirement made easy 1107

A Retrospective biography of American demographic history from colonial times to 1983 1356

Retrospective index to theses of Great Britain and Ireland, 1917-1950 1005

Returning to work 3869

Reuter, P.
Introduction to the law of treaties 2962

Reuter's glossary of international financial and economic terms 1807

Revello, J.T.
Bibliografía de las Islas Malvinas, obras, mapas y documentos 8095

'Reversals, ironies, hegemonies. Notes on the contemporary historiography of modern China' 6430

Review of educational research 3819

Reviews of United Kingdom statistical sources 1225

Reviews of United Kingdom statistical sources: v.20: Religion 423

La Révolution Française 7351

La Révolution Française à travers les archives 6525

Revolutionary America 1763-1789: a bibliography 8024

'Revolutionary America: the historiography' 8025

Revolutionary and dissident movements 1518

Revue d'histoire ecclésiastique 671

Rew, J. and Sturge, C.
Macmillan directory of Lloyds of London 3714

Reynard, K.W. and Reynard, J.M.E.
Aslib directory of information sources in the United Kingdom 1031

Reynolds, C.R. and Fletcher-Janzen, E.
Concise encyclopedia of special education 3877
Encyclopedia of special education 3876

Reynolds, F.E.
Guide to Buddhist religion 876

Reynolds, S.
An Introduction to the history of English medieval towns 3305

Rhind, D.
A Census user's handbook 1316

Rhodes House Library Subject Catalogue 6910

The Roman world 6719
Romania 4642
România: atlas rutier 5267
Romania. Comisa Nationala Pentru Statistica
　Anuarul statistic al României. Romanian
　　statistical yearbook 1261
A Romano-British bibliography 6953
The Romans in Cologne and Lower Germany
　4443
The Romans, their gods and their beliefs 848
Rome 4373
Rome in Africa 6732
Rome in the fourth century 6716
Romer, J.-C.
　Le Dictionnaire encyclopédique militaire
　　soviétique 3366
Room, A.
　Corporate eponymy 2442
　Place-name changes since 1900 5440
Roper, F.W. and Boorkman, J.A.
　Introduction to reference sources in the
　　health sciences 3637
Roper, G.
　The Bibliography of the Arab Middle East
　　4766
Roper, G.J. and Bleaney, C.H.
　Index Islamicus 4763
　Index Islamicus on CD-ROM 4765
Röpke, J.M.
　Historical dictionary of Osaka and Kyoto
　　7608
Roscher, W.H.
　Ausführliches Lexikon der griechischen und
　　römischen Mythologie 845
Rose, H.J.
　A Handbook of Greek mythology 850
Rosenberg, J.
　'American family history' 6194
Rosenberg, J.M.
　Dictionary of banking and financial services
　　2114
　Dictionary of business and management
　　2610
　Dictionary of investing 2180
　McGraw-Hill dictionary of business
　　acronyms 2507
　McGraw-Hill dictionary of Wall Street
　　acronyms 2234
Rosenberg, M.B. and Bergstrom, L.V.
　Women and society 4061
Rosenberg, P.M. and Durr, W.T.
　The Urban information thesaurus 1140
Rosenblatt, J.T.
　Who's who in world Jewry 5726
Rosie, G.
　The Directory of international terrorism
　　1540
Rosignoli, G.
　Air Force badges and insignia of World War
　　2 3435
　Army badges and insignia of World War 2
　　3436-3437
Ross, A. and Cyprien, M.
　A Traveller's guide to Celtic Britain 5484
Ross, J. A.
　Family planning and child survival 3667
Ross, J.A.
　International encyclopedia of population
　　1315
Ross, S.
　The Monarchs of Scotland 6331
Ross,, S.T.
　French military history, 1661-1799 3411
Rossi, E.E. and McCrea, B.P.
　The European political dictionary 1419
Rossi, E.E. and Plano, J.C.
　Latin America: a political dictionary 1456
Rossi, J.
　The Gulag handbook 3144
Rostow, W.W.
　Theorists of economic growth 1873

Roth, C.
　Magna bibliotheca anglo-judaica 903
Roth, C. and Wigoder, G.
　Encyclopaedia Judaica 906
Rothberg School for Overseas Students of
the Hebrew University
　International bibliography of Jewish history
　　and thought 922
Rothermund, D.
　An Economic history of India 2359
The Rough guide to travel online 5442
The Rough Guides 5441
Rouillard, J.
　Guide de l'histoire du Québec 7895
Rouse, R. and Neill, S.C.
　A History of the ecumenical movement 643
The Rousseau dictionary 45
Routh, G.
　Occupations of the people of Great Britain,
　　1801-1981 1952
Routledge atlas of American history 7989
The Routledge atlas of British history 6933
The Routledge atlas of Classical History 6696
The Routledge atlas of Jewish history 6671
Routledge atlas of Russian history 7430
The Routledge atlas of the Arab-Israeli conflict
　7701
The Routledge atlas of the First World War
　6816
The Routledge compendium of primary
　education 3855
The Routledge critical dictionary of global
　economics 1782
Routledge dictionary of economics 1785
The Routledge dictionary of twentieth-century
　political thinkers 1473
Routledge encyclopedia of philosophy 61
Roux, G.
　Ancient Iraq 7688
Rowat, D.C.
　International handbook on local government
　　reorganization 3278
Rowe, C. and Schofield, M.
　The Cambridge history of Greek and Roman
　　political thought 1476
Rowe, D.J.
　Northern business histories 2470
Rowe, H.
　A Guide to the records of Bermuda 6589
Rowe, K.E.
　Methodist Union catalog: pre-1976 imprints
　　786
Rowland, I.
　Timor 5004
Rowlands, J. and Rowlands, S.
　Welsh family history 6183
Rowley, E.E.
　The Financial system today 2102
Rowley, H.H.
　A Companion to the Bible 496
　Dictionary of Bible place names 480
Rowntree, D.
　A Dictionary of education 3764
Roy, A.K. and Gidwani, N.N.
　A Dictionary of Indology 4714
Royal Air Force Bomber Commands losses or
　the Second World War 6835
Royal Commonwealth Society
　Biography catalogue of the Library 6913
　The Manuscript catalogue of the library ..
　　4563
　Subject catalogue of the Library of the Royal
　　Empire Society 4560
Royal families 6309
The Royal Geographical Society history of
　world exploration 5100
The Royal heraldry of England 6251
Royal Historical Society. Annual bibliography
　of British and Irish history 6923
The Royal Historical Society bibliography on
　CD-ROM 6925

The Royal houses of Europe 6314
Royal insignia 6278
Royal Institute of International Affairs
　Chronology and index of the Second World
　　War 1938-1945 6884
　Documents on international affairs, 1928-
　　1963 1614
　Survey of international affairs, 1920/23-66
　　1612
Royal Institute of International Affairs.
Library
　The Classified catalogue of the Royal
　　Institute of International Affairs for
　　international relations, defence,
　　diplomacy, international law, politics and
　　economics.. 1599
　Index to periodical articles, 1950-1964 ..
　　1600
　Index to periodical articles, 1965-1972 ..
　　1601
　Index to periodical articles, 1979-1989 1602
The Royal line of succession 6325
The Royal Mail direct mail handbook 2687
The Royal Marines - a pictorial history, 1664-
　1988 3567
Royal National Institute for the Blind.
Reference Library
　Works on blindness and associated subjects
　　3678
The Royal Navy 3558
The Royal Navy day by day 3566
The Royal Navy in World War Two 3537
Royal Navy language 3540
Royal orders 6284
Royal service 6282
Royal tombs of England 6333
Royal United Services Institute for Defence
Studies
　R.U.S.I. and Brassey's defence yearbook,
　　1991 3385
Royle, T.
　A Dictionary of military quotations 3386
Ruben, D.H.
　Philosophy journals and serials 92
Rubin, H.W.
　Dictionary of insurance terms 3703
Rubin, J.
　Antarctica 5682
Rubinstein, W.D.
　A History of the Jews in the English
　　speaking world: Great Britain 6942
Rubio Cabeza, M.
　Diccionario de la Guerra Civil Espanola
　　7391
Ruble, B.A. and Teeter, M.J.
　A Scholars' guide to humanities and social
　　sciences in the Soviet Union and the Baltic
　　States 1020
Ruck, A.
　The Holiday Which? guide to France 5535
Rudolph, D.K. and Rudolph, G.A.
　Historical dictionary of Venezuela 8112
Ruitenberg, G.N.W.
　'The Central Register of Private Archives
　　(CRPA) and the policy in the Netherlands
　　regarding private archives' 6542
The Rules of the Communist party of the
　Soviet Union 1732
Ruokonen, K. and Miyakawa, T.
　Japan 1861
Ruokonen, K and Rinne, B.
　Economic and business libraries in
　　Scandinavia 1860
Rural life guide to local records 7058
Rural sociology 1144
Ruscio, A.
　La Première guerre d'Indochine (1945-1954)
　　7733
Rush, M.
　Parliament and government 1675

R.U.S.I. and Brassey's defence yearbook, 1991 **3385**

Russell, B.
History of Western philosophy **105**

Russell, J.B.
A History of witchcraft throughout the ages **185**

Russia and Eastern Europe 1789-1985 **7419**

Russia & Eurasia facts & figures annual (formerly *USSR facts and figures annual*) **1248**

Russia revised **7428**

Russia, the USSR and Eastern Europe **7416**

Russia, Ukraine & Belarus **5551**

Russian autocrats from Ivan the Great to the fall of the Romanov dynasty **7414**

Russian biographical archive/Russisches biographisches archiv **5824**

Russian economic history **2340**

The Russian Empire and the Soviet Union **6532**

Russian-English/English-Russian glossary of statistical terms **1200**

Russian-English law dictionary **2767**

Russian-English military dictionary **3379**

The Russian Far East **7705**

Russian heraldry and nobility **6253**

Russian law **2847**

The Russian Orthodox Church **719**

Russian philosophical terminology **88**

Russian psychology **293**

The Russian Revolution 1905-1921 **7415**

Russo, D.J.
Keepers of our past **8070**

Rust, V.D.
Education in East and West Germany **3798**

Rutherford, D.
Routledge dictionary of economics **1785**

Ruud, I.M.
Women and Judaism **4106**

Ruvigny and Raineval, 9th Marquis of
The Titled Nobility of Europe **6318**

Rwanda **4843**

Ryan, B.
The Women's movement **4062**

Ryan, F.J.
Company information online **2436**

Ryan, J.G.
A Guide to tracing your Dublin ancestors **6054**
Irish records **6168**

Ryan, Liam
Social dimensions of Irish Catholicism **1180**

Ryan, M.
Contemporary Soviet society **1074**

Ryan, M. *and* Prentice, R.
Social trends in contemporary Russia **1188**

Ryan, P.
The Encyclopedia of Papua and New Guinea **5036**

Ryan, R.B.
The Second Fleet convicts **5993**

Ryan, R.J.
The Third Fleet convicts **5994**

Ryans, C.C.
International business reference sources **2016**

Rycroft, C.
A Critical dictionary of psychoanalysis **327**

Rydlewska-Szewczykowa, D. *and* Zaczkiewiczowa, J.
Slownik prawniczy polsko-angielski/Polish-English dictionary of legal terms **2769**

Ryken, L. *and* Wilhoit, J. C. *and* Longman III, T.
Dictionary of biblical imagery **470**

Ryskamp, G.R.
Finding your Hispanic roots **6120**

Saba & Co
The English-Arabic dictionary of professional business terms **2032**

Sabin, J.
Bibliotheca Americana **7954**

Sabine, G.H.
A History of political theory **1477**

Sabiq, J.
Majama'al-lughat **1003**

Sachar, H.M.
A History of Israel **7694**

Sachar, J.S.
Asian & who's who international **5738**

Sachs, D.
EUDISED R & D bulletin, no.1,1976-.
Quarterly **3820**

Sachwörterbuch der Geschichte Deutschlands und der deutscher Arbeiterbewegung **1981**

Sacks, D.
Encyclopedia of the Ancient Greek world **6704**

Sacramentum mundi **732**

Sacred books of the Buddhists **874**

The Sacred books of the East **859**

The Sacred books of the Hindus **861**

Sader, M. *and* Lewis, A.
Encyclopedias, atlases, and dictionaries **5175**

Sadikali, M.
Butterworth's yellow tax handbook, 1993-94 **2154**

Sadler, J.D.
Families in transition **1080**

Saffroy, G.
Bibliographie généalogique, héraldique et nobilaire de la France **6007**

Safire, W.
Safire's political dictionary **1390**
Safire's political dictionary **1390**

Saga of the American flag
The American flag **6353**

Sage family studies abstracts, 1979- **1160**

Sage public administration abstracts **3222**

Sage race relations abstracts **1119**

Sage urban studies abstracts **3295**

Saha, S.
Dictionary of human rights advocacy organizations in Africa **3108**

Saich, T.
China: politics and government **3341**

The Sailing Navy list **3565**

Sainsbury, A.B.
The Royal Navy day by day **3566**

St. James guide to biography **5716**

St. John, R.B.
Historical dictionary of Libya **7760**

St. Kitts-Nevis **4917**

St. Lucia **4918**

Saint Marc, M.
Histoire monetaire de la France, 1800-1980 **2130**

St. Vincent and the Grenadines **4923**

Sainthood in the middle ages **614**

The Saints **609**

Saints and their attributes **598**

Sainty, J.
A List of English law officers, King's Counsel and holders of patents of procedure **2830**

Sainty, J.C.
Office-holders in modern Britain **3328**
Peerage creations 1689-1800 **6265**

Sakala, C.
Women in South Asia: A guide to resources **4097**

Sakoian, F. *and* Acker, L.S.
Astrologer's handbook **197**

Salda, A.C.M.
The International Monetary Fund **2222**

Saliba, J.A.
Psychiatry and the cults **435**

Sallnow, J. *and* John, A.
An Electoral atlas of Europe, 1968-1981 **1551**

Salt, D. *and* Radley, A.F.
Austria **4574**

Salvat, B
L'Encyclopédie de la Polynésie **5040**

The Salvation Army year book **665**

Salvendy, G.
Handbook of human factors **2603**

Salway, P.
Roman Britain **6950**

Salzman, J.
American studies **4946-4947**
Encyclopedia of African-American culture and history **4963**

Samarasinghe, S.W.R. de A. *and* Samarasinghe, V.
Historical dictionary of Sri Lanka **7667**

Samaraweera, V.
Sri Lanka **4721**

Samoa (American Samoa and Western Samoa, Samoans abroad) **5045**

Samuels, A.
A Critical dictionary of Jungian analysis **328**

San Marino **4593**

Sandahl, P. *and* deBea, L.
Dictionnaire politique et diplomatique **1394**

Sandall, R. *and* Wiggins, A.R. *and* Coutts, F.
The History of the Salvation Army **666**

Sanders, A.J.K.
Historical dictionary of Mongolia **7586**

Sandhu, J.
Directory of non-medical research relating to handicapped people, 1987 **3676**

Sandison, A.
Tracing ancestors in Shetland **6044**

Sandler, S.
The Korean War: an encyclopedia **7595**

Sanford, G. *and* Gozdecka-Sanford, A.
Historical dictionary of Poland **7315**
Poland **4578**

Santoro, C.M.
A World directory of criminological institutes **3124**

São Tomé and Príncipe **4831**

SarDesai, D.R.
Vietnam **4757**

Sargent, D.
The National Register of Archives: an international perspective **6509**
The National Register of Archives: an international perspective **6511, 6530, 6541-6542, 6575, 6581, 6612, 7831**

Sargent, L.T.
British and American utopian literature, 1516-1985 **348**

Sarkar, S.
Hindustan yearbook and who's who 1999 **4715**

Sárközi, M.
Budapest **4582**

Sartre, J.-P.
Les Écrits de Sartre. Chronologie, bibliographie commentée **49**
Jean-Paul Sartre **48**

Sasson, J.M.
Civilizations of the ancient Near East **7540**

Sater, W.F.
'A Survey of recent Chilean historiography 1965-1976' **8099**

Sather, L.B.
Norway **4624**

Sather, L.B. *and* Swanson, A.
Sweden **4626**

Sather, T. *and* Hutton, W.
Pros and cons **1089**

Satow's guide to diplomatic practice **3351**

Sattler, J.M.
Assessment of children's intelligence and special abilities **303**

Saudi Arabia **4693, 7612**

Saunders, C. and Southey, N.
Historical dictionary of South Africa 7835

Saunders, C.C.
An Illustrated dictionary of South African history 7833

Saunders, G.
A History of Brunei 8123

Saunders, J.B.
Words and phrases legally defined 2755

Saunders, M. and Scott, M.
Directory of national voluntary organisations in Scotland 3623

Sauvaget, J.
Introduction to the history of the Muslim East 7531

Sawinski, D.M. and Mason, W.H.
Encyclopedia of global industries 1897

Sawyer, P. and Fraser, J.
Bridges 1183

Sawyer, P.H.
Anglo-Saxon charters 6962
Kings and Vikings 7454
The Saxon shore 6957

Sayegh, K.S.
Housing 3257

Sayer, M.J.
'The Scope of Burke's Landed Gentry' 6271

Sayers, R.S.
The Bank of England, 1891-1944 2216

Sbrega, J.J.
The War against Japan, 1941-1945 6861

Scaffer, J.
Historical dictionary of the cooperative movement 2004

Scammell, G.V.
The World encompassed 6764

Scandinavian biographical archive/ Skandinavisches biographisches archiv 5836

Scandinavian biographical index/ Skandinavischer biographischer index 5837

Scandinavian history 1520-1970 7455

Scandinavian mythology 836

Scandinavian Scotland 6991

Scanlon, J. and Cosner, S.
American women historians 8001

Scarborough, W.
A Collection of Chinese proverbs 4205

Scarlett, C.
Road atlas of Indonesia 5375

Scarr, D.
Fiji a short history 8181
The History of the Pacific Islands 8129

Scarre, C.
Ancient France 6,000-2,000 BC 4296
Chronicle of the Roman Emperors 6715
The Seventy wonders of the ancient world 6633
The Times of archaeology of the world 4223

Scarrett, D.
Sources of property market information 2003

Schaefer, C.K.
The Center: a guide to genealogical research in the National Capital Area 6109
Genealogical encyclopedia of the Colonial Americas 6080
The Great War 6128
Guide to naturalization records of the United States 6092
Instant information on the Internet 6031, 6101

Schäfers, B.
The State of Germany atlas 5221

Scharf, T. and Balin, M.
Dictionary of development economics 2399

Scharf, T. and Shetty, M.C.
Dictionary of development banking 2197

Scheduled ancient monuments 4418

Schei, L.K. and Moberg, G.
The Faroe Islands 5554

Scheiman, D.L. and Slonim, M.
Resources for middle childhood 3685

Scheina, R.L.
Latin America: a naval history, 1810-1985 3577

Schellinger, P.E.
St. James guide to biography 5716

Scheub, H.
A Dictionary of African mythology 857

Scheuch, M.
Historischer Atlas Deutschland 7262

Scheven, Y.
Bibliographies for African studies 1987-1993 4774

Schevichaven, H.D.J. van
English inn signs 2702

Schilder, G.
Australia unveiled 8159

Schlei, L.K.
The Shetland story 7012

Schleiffer, H. and Crandall, R.
Index to economic history essays in Festschriften, 1900-1950 1843

Schlesinger, A.M.
The Almanac of American history 7984

Schlessinger, B.S.
The Basic business library 2017, 2521

Schlessinger, B.S. and Schlessinger, J.H.
The Who's who of Nobel Prize winners 1901-1995 5721

Schmatz, George-Marie
La sociologie de la Chine 1075

Schmidt, G.W. and Singson, K.P.
The Awards almanac 3918

Schmidt, M.
Economic reforms in the People's Republic of China since 1979 2349

Schmitt, C.B.
The Cambridge history of renaissance philosophy 114

Schmitthoff, C.M.
The Export trade 2501
Palmer's company law 3170

Schmittroth, L.
Statistical record of women worldwide 4075

Schmuck, H.
Biographical archive of the Classical World/ Biographisches archiv der Antike 6700
Biographical index of the Classical World 6701
Jüdisches biographisches archiv/Jewish biographical archive 6675

Schnädelbach, H.
Philosophy in Germany, 1831-1933 131

Schneider, G.
Exegetical dictionary of the New Testament 527

Schneider, R.M.
Order and progress 8085

Schoeffler, O.E. and Gale, W.
Esquire's encyclopedia of 20th century men's fashions 4003

Schoeman, K.
Bibliography of the Orange Free State until 31 May 1910 7830

Schoeman, S. and Schoeman, E.
Namibia 4859

Schoenhals, K.
Dominican Republic 4904
Grenada 4924
Netherlands Antilles and Aruba 4927

Schofield, R.
Kuwait and Iraq 7632

A Scholar's guide to geographical writing on the American and Canadian past 5161

A Scholars' guide to humanities and social sciences in the Soviet Union and the Baltic States 1020

Scholar's guide to intelligence literature 1660

Scholarships abroad 3919

Scholberg, H.
Bibliography of Goa and the Portuguese in India 7645
The Biographical dictionary of Greater India 5879
The District Gazetteers of British India 5573

Scholberg, H. and Divien, E.
Bibliographie des Français dans l'Inde 7644

Scholfield, G.H.
A Dictionary of New Zealand biography 5980

Schonberg Center for Research in Black Culture
The New York Public Library African American desk reference 4964

The School administrator's resource guide 3847

School librarianship 3853

School organization and management abstracts 3849

Schooley, H.
Conflicts in Central America 1645

Schopenhauer-Bibliographie 52

Schraeder, P.J.
Djibouti 4848

Schramm, L.
The Israel year book and almanac 1999 4739

Schubart, W.
Griechische paläographie 6625

Schultz, D.P. and Schultz, S.E.
History of modern psychology 286

Schultz, J.
Writing about Canada 7871

Schultze, S.
Population information in nineteenth-century census volumes 1353
Population information in twentieth-century census volumes.. 1354

Schulz, A.
International and regional politics in the Middle East and North Africa 1641

Schumacher, S. and Woerner, G.
The Rider encyclopedia of Eastern philosophy and religion 858

Schürer, K. and Anderson, S.J.
A Guide to historical datafiles held in machine-readable form 6373

Schutz, H.
The Prehistory of Germanic Europe 4245

Schwartz, B.
China off the beaten track 5558

Schwartz, R.A.
The Cold War reference guide 1657

Schwartzberg, J.E.
A Historical atlas of South Asia 7554

Schwartzkopf, R.B.
'State atlases from the eighties' 5360

Schwarz, U. and Hadik, L.
Strategic terminology 3483

Schwarzkopf, L.
Government reference books 92/93 1500

Schwertner, S.M.
IATG2 367

Science and Religion 443

SCIMP: European index of management periodicals 1771

SCIMP/SCANP thesaurus 1772

SCIMP [Selective cooperative index of management periodicals] 2620

Scobbie, I.
Historical dictionary of Sweden 7470

SCOLMA directory of Libraries and special collections on Africa in the UK and in Europe 4787

'The Scope of Burke's Landed Gentry' 6271

The Scotia reference gazetteer of the Baltic States 5552

Scotland 4546

Scotland and her tartans 6153

Scotland: archaeology and early history **4276**

Scotland BC **4416**

Scotland before history with a gazetteer of ancient monuments **4422**

Scotland. Parliament
The Acts of the Parliaments of Scotland, 1424-1707 **2809**

Scotland through the ages **4407**

Scotland's heraldic heritage **6242**

Scotland's hidden history **4396**

Scotland's historic shipwrecks **4359**

Scotland's industrial past **4471**

Scotland's Kings and Queens **6330**

Scotland's regions **3288**

Scotland's Roman remains **4423**

The Scots and Parliament **1494**

Scots heraldry **6243**

The Scots peerage **6272**

Scott, B.K.C.
Dictionary of military abbreviations **3357**

Scott, D.L.
Wall Street words **2259**

Scott, F.D.
Sweden **7467**

Scott, H.F. *and* **Scott, W.F.**
Armed forces of the USSR **3412**

Scott, I.
Hong Kong **4659**

Scott, J.W.
A Synoptic index to the 'Proceedings of the Aristotelian Society...' **16**

Scott-Roberts, F.
Macmillan directory of international asset managers **2264**

Scottish abstract of statistics, 1998 **1232**

Scottish archaeology **4273**

Scottish burgh and county heraldry **6245**

Scottish church history **677**

Scottish civic heraldry **6246**

Scottish clans & tartans **6162**

Scottish current law year book ... 1948- **2805**

Scottish dates **7010**

Scottish economic bulletin **2314**

Scottish family histories **6158**

Scottish family history **6161**

The Scottish financial sector **2175**

The Scottish government yearbook, 1992 **3223**

A Scottish historian's glossary **7005**

Scottish historical guides **5496**

The Scottish islands **5494**

The Scottish jurists **2880**

Scottish Kings **7009**

Scottish labour leaders, 1918-1939 **1728**

The Scottish law directory, 2000 **3199**

The Scottish legal system **2803**

Scottish local history **7003**

Scottish local studies resources **6999**

Scottish military dress **3455**

Scottish Office
Scottish economic bulletin **2314**

Scottish Office statistical publications **1233**

Scottish political facts **1559**

The Scottish political system **1727**

Scottish roots **6154**

Scottish texts and calendars **6513**

Scottish towns **6993**

'The Scramble for Africa: inherited political boundaries' **7756**

Screen, J.E.O.
Finland **4623**

The Scribner encyclopedia of American lives **5931**

Scrivener, D. *and* **Sheehan, M.**
Bibliography of arms control verification **3361**

Scrivener, R.S.
USSR economic handbook **2336**

Scruton, R.
A Dictionary of political thought **1474**
A Short history of modern philosophy **115**
Thinkers of the new Left **209**

Seaborne trade **6801**

Seager, J. *and* **Olson, A.**
Women in the world **4076**

Search for the Northwest Passage **8197**

Searing, S.E. *and* **Goetsch, L.**
Introduction to library research in women's studies **4109**

Seaton, A.
The German army; 1933-45 **3407**

Sebba, G.
Bibliographia Cartesiana **22**

Seccombe, I.J.
Jordan **4740**
Syria **4735**

The Second Fleet convicts **5993**

The Second World War **6859**

The Second World War a guide to documents in the Public Record Office **6893**

The Secret wars **1661**

Secretarial administration **2019**

Seeberg, E.S.
Dictionary of archaeology: English, German, Norwegian **4220**

Segal, G.
Political and economic encyclopedia of the Pacific **1382**
The World affairs companion **4496**

Segall, A.
Guide to Jewish archives **6562**

Seide, K.
A Dictionary of arbitration and its terms **3194**

Seingry, G.-F.
Euro who's who **1490**

Selby, J.E.
'Revolutionary America: the historiography' **8025**

Seldon, A. *and* **Pennance, F.G.**
Everyman's dictionary of economics **1808**

Seldon Society
A Centenary guide to the publications of the Seldon Society **2798**

Select bibliographies on aging **1098**

A Select bibliography for the study, sources and literature of English mediaeval economic history **2323**

A Select bibliography of adult continuing education in Great Britain, including works published to the end of the year 1981 **3867**

'Select bibliography of genealogical research aids published by the National Archives and Records Administration' **6110**

A Select bibliography of modern economic theory, 1870-1929 **1874**

'A select bibliography of South African history 1990-1993' **7831**

Select list of British Parliamentary Papers, 1833-1899 **3065**

A Select list of reports of enquiries of the Irish Dáil and Senate, 1922-1972 **3075**

A Selected and annotated bibliography of American naval history **3583**

Selected and annotated bibliography of youth, youth work and provision for youth **3690**

A Selected bibliography of modern historiography **6424**

Selected list of UK theses and dissertations in management studies **2615**

Selected references to literature on marine expeditions, 1700-1960 **5093**

A Selected vocabulary of financial terms **2113**

A Selective bibliography of philosophical logic **339**

A Selective bibliography on Kant **29**

Selective cooperative index of management periodicals **2620**

The Self-help guide **3620**

Seligman, E.R.A.
Encyclopaedia of the social sciences **994**

Selkirk, A.
The Riches of British archaeology **4257**

Sell, K.D.
Divorce in the 70s **1364**

Sell, K.D. *and* **Sell, B.H.**
Divorce in the United States, Canada and Great Britain **1363**

Sellers, J.R.
Civil War mansucripts **8056**

Sellier, A. *and* **Sellier, J.**
Atlas des peuples d'Europe Centrale **7254**

Selvon, S.
Historical dictionary of Mauritius **7848**

Selwyn, N.
Dictionary of employment law **1913**

The Seminary priests **744**

Sen, S.P.
Sources of the history of India **7646**

Senegal **4814**

Senior, M.
The Illustrated who's who in mythology **830**

Serial bibliographies and abstracts in history **6405**

Serial publications in the British Parliamentary Papers, 1900-1968 **3048**

Serials on aging **1106**

Serrão, J.
Cronologia geral da historia de Portugal **7403**
Dicionário de historia de Portugal **7400**
Pequeno dicionário de historia de Portugal **7401**

Serrão, J. *and* **Oliveira Marques, A.D. de**
Nova história de Portugal **7398**

Service, A. *and* **Bradbery, J.**
The Standing stones of Europe **4375**

Service lives remembered **6301**

Service, R.
A History of twentieth-century Russia **7437**

Sessional information digest. 1991-92 **1680**

Sessional Papers of the eighteenth century: George I and II **3063**

Sessional Papers of the eighteenth century: George III **3064**

Seton, R.
The Indian Mutiny 1857-58 **6555**

Settlers of the Old Empire **6174**

Setton, K.M.
A History of the Crusades **6785**

The Seventy wonders of the ancient world **6633**

Seychelles **4868**

The Seychelles **7847**

Seymour, A. *and* **Seymour, E.**
Dictionary of Guyanese biography **5970**

Seymour-Smith, C.
Macmillan dictionary of anthropology **1064**

Seymour, W.
Battles in Britain **3469**
Great sieges of history **3467**

Shackleton on the law and practice of meetings **3235**

Shadbolt, M.
Reader's Digest guide to New Zealand **5660**

Shafritz, J.M.
Almanac of modern terrorism **1541**
The Dorsey dictionary of American government and politics **3225**
The Facts on File dictionary of military science **3374**
The Facts on File dictionary of public administration **3219**
The HarperCollins dictionary of American government and politics **3226**
The international encyclopedia of public policy and administration **3217**
War on words **3388**

Shaikh, F.
Islam and Islamic groups **933**

Shamir, I. *and* **Shavit, S.**
Encyclopedia of Jewish history **6666**

Shanghai **7561**

Shanks, D.
Guide to bibliographies on education 3729
Shannon, G.W.B.
'Folk literature and children' 4127
Shannon, M.O.
Irish Republic 4556
Modern Ireland 4552
Northern Ireland 4555
Shannon, R.
The age of Salisbury, 1881-1902 1720
Shap Working Party on World Religions in Education
Festivals in world religions 4019
Shapero, F.R.
Oxford dictionary of American legal quotations 2780
The Shaping of America 5160
Sharma, J.S.
India since the advent of the British 7656
The National geographical dictionary of India 5574
Sharma, S.K. and Sharma, S.
Encyclopaedia of Tibet 7584
Sharma, S.R.
A Bibliography of Mughal India (1526-1707AD) 7647
Sharp, M.
A Traveller's guide to saints in Europe 612
Shaver, J.
Handbook of research on social studies 3822
Shaw, C.S.
Cape Verde 4822
São Tomé and Príncipe 4831
Shaw, G.
British directories as sources in historical geography 5154
'Directories and the local historian' 7088
Shaw, G. and Tipper, A.
British directories 7090
Shaw, G.W.
Academical dress of British and Irish universities 3913
Shaw, I. and Jameson, R.
A Dictionary of archaeology 4218
Shaw, I. and Nicholson, P.T.
British Museum dictionary of Ancient Egypt 6655
Shaw, J.
The Bateman concise encyclopaedia of Australia 5029
Shaw, S.J. and Shaw E.K.
History of the Ottoman Empire and modern Turkey 7680
Shaw, T.
The Archaeology of Africa 4321
Shaw, W. and Pryce, D.
Encyclopedia of the USSR 7423
Shaw's directory of courts in the United Kingdom 3206
Shaw's local government directory, 2000/2001 3285
Shearer, B.F. and Shearer, B.S.
State names, seals, flags and symbols 6356
Shearer, B.S. and Shearer, B.F.
Periodical literature on United States cities 3292
Shearman, I.
Shackleton on the law and practice of meetings 3235
Sheehan, S. and Levy, P.
Ireland handbook 5505
Sheimo, S.
International encyclopedia of the stock market 2235
Sheldon, Joseph K.
Rediscovery of creation 573
Shell, D.
The House of Lords 1678
The Shell guide to Germany 5532
Shell guide to Ireland 5506

The Shell guide to the islands of Britain 5490
Shemanski, F.
A Guide to fairs and festivals in the United States 4026
Shepard, L.A.
Encyclopedia of occultism and parapsychology 161
Sheppard, F.
London: a history 7114
Sherman, J.
The Arab-Israeli conflict 1945-1971 7695
Sherman, M.D.
Orthodox Judaism in America 926
Shermis, M.
Jewish-Christian relations: an annotated bibliography and resource guide 384
Sherratt, A.
The Cambridge encyclopedia of archaeology 4212
Sherrill, R.
Why they call it politics: a guide to America's government 1684
The Shetland story 7012
Shield and crest 6220
Shields, G.
Madrid 4599
Shields, G.J.
Gibraltar 4604
Spain 4600
Shields, S.L.
The Latter Day Saint churches 797
Shimoni, Y.
A Political dictionary of the Arab world 1445
Political dictionary of the Arab World 7532
Shinar, P.
Essai de bibliographie sélective et annotée sur l'Islam 949
Shintô shoseki mokuroku 963
Shipley, D. and Peplow, M.
England's undiscovered heritage 5518
Shipps, J.
Mormonism 799
Ships and shipwrecks of the Americas 4362
Ships of the Port of London 4360
Ships of the Royal Navy 3559-3560
The Ships that saved an army 6847
Shipwreck index of the British Isles 5114
The Shogun's city 7600
Shores, C.
Above the trenches 6827
Short book reviews 1306
Short, D.
Czechoslovakia 4575
Short, D.M.
A Bibliography of printed items relating to the city of Lincoln 7183
A Short guide to writing about history 6459
A Short history of British psychology, 1804-1940 291
A Short history of educational ideas 3826
A Short history of electoral systems in Western Europe 1552
A Short history of medieval philosophy 113
A Short history of modern Greece 7481
A Short history of modern philosophy 115
A Short history of Papua New Guinea 8179
A Short history of sociological thought 1071
A Short history of the Catholic Church 737
A Short history of the Labour Party 1724
A Short history of the Liberal Party, 1900-88 1725
A Short history of Western philosophy 124
'Short survey of recent literature on Hungarian economic history' 2329
Shorter Cambridge-Eichborn German dictionary 1813
The Shorter encyclopedia of Islam 940
Showalter, D.E.
German military history, 1648-1982 3409

Showers, V.
World facts and figures 1209, 5443
Shrader, C.R.
Reference guide to United States military history 3423
Shukman, H.
The Blackwell encyclopaedia of the Russian Revolution 7421
Longman history of Russia 7407
Shulman, F.J.
Japan 4674
Shunami, S.
Bibliography of Jewish bibliographies 896
Siani-Davies, P. and Siani-Davies, M.
Romania 4642
SIBD, 92-93 2472
Siberia and the Soviet Far East 4742
Sichel, B. and Sichel, W.
Economic journals and serials 1835
Sicily 4592
Sickinger, J.P.
Public records and archives in classical Athens 6711
Siddiqi, M. N.
Contemporary literature on Islamic economics 2363
Siddons, M.P.
The Development of Welsh heraldry 6252
Siegal, J.G.
The McGraw-Hill pocket guide to business finance 2607
Siegman, G.
Awards, honors, and prizes 5723
World of winners 5722
Sierra, C.
'Censo-guía de Archivos Españoles' 6530
Sierra Leone 4815
Sierra Leone in maps 5306
Sifakis, S.
Who was who in the Civil War 8055
Sigler, J.
International handbook of race and race relations 1117
Sigma 1219
Sigmund Freud's writings: a comprehensive bibliography 321
The Significance of the Commonwealth 1965-90 6904
The Sikh reference book 7650
Sikhism and the Sikhs 888
The Sikhs: their religious beliefs and practices 887
The Silent social revolution 3793
Siliday, G.L.
History of the family and kinship 1153
The Silk Road 7557
Sill, G.G.
A Handbook of symbols in Christian art 624
Sill, M. and Kirkby, J.
The Atlas of Nepal in the modern world 5284
Sills, D.L.
International encyclopedia of the social sciences 995
International encyclopedia of the social sciences. v.18: Biographical supplement 1016
Sills, D.L. and Merton, R.
The Macmillan book of social science quotations 1013
The Silver bough 4020
Silver, D.A.
Who's who in venture capital 2267
Silverstone, P.H.
Directory of the world's capital ships 3544
Simmler, O.
World directory of administrative libraries 3228
Simmonds, K.R.
Encyclopedia of European Community law 2928

Stutley, M. *and* Stutley, J.
A Dictionary of Hinduism **867**

A Subject bibliography for the First World War **6809**

A Subject bibliography of the history of American higher education **3905**

A Subject bibliography of the Second World War **6857**

A Subject bibliography of the Second World War and aftermath **6858**

Subject catalog. [California University. Institute of Governmental Studies Library] **3214**

Subject catalog. [Harvard University. Graduate School of Business Administration. Baker Library] **1761**

Subject catalogue of the House of Commons Parliamentary papers, 1801-1900 **3043**

Subject catalogue of the Library of the Royal Empire Society **4560**

Subject directory of special libraries and information centers. v.1 Business, government and law libraries **1030**

Subject guide to U.S. government reference sources **1501**

Subrahmanian, N.S.
Encyclopaedia of the Upanishads **864**

Subtelny, O.
Ukraine: a history **7448**

Subterranean Lisbon **4449**

Suchlicki, J.
Historical dictionary of Cuba **7922**

Sudan **4797**

Sudan 1898-1989 **7765**

Südosteuropäisches biographisches archiv/ South-East European biographical archive **5856**

A Suffolk bibliography **7205**

Sugar, P.F.
A History of Hungary **7318**

Sugnet, C.L.
Vietnam War bibliography **7734**

Suicide **3139, 3141**

Suicide and the elderly **3142**

Sukhdev Singh Charak
History and culture of Himalayan states **7661**

Sullivan, B.M.
Historical dictionary of Hinduism **870**

Sullivan, L.R. *and* Hearst, N.
Historical dictionary of the Peoples Republic of China 1949-1997 **7575**

Summary bibliography of the history of the universities of Great Britain and Ireland up to 1800 **3938**

Summer jobs abroad **1951**

Summers, H.G.
Historical atlas of the Vietnam War **7739**
Korean War almanac **7597**
Persian Gulf War almanac **7626**
Vietnam War almanac **7738**

Summers, P.
Hatchments in Britain **6248**

Sunday telegraph business finance directory, 1987 **2173**

Sundiata, I.K.
Equatorial Guinea **4817**

A Sung bibliography **7564**

Suny, R.G.
The Making of the Georgian nation **7450**

Suomen historian Kartasto/Atlas of Finnish history **7460**

Suomen Kartasto/Atlas of Finland/Atlas över Finland **5253**

Suomen tilastollinen vuosikirja **1250**

Supplementary service to European taxation **2150**

Supreme Court of the United States, 1789 - 1982 **3207**

The Supreme Court practice 1999 **3203**

Suratteau, J-R. *and* Gendron, F.
Dictionnaire historique de la Révolution Française **7348**

Surdam, W.
Bibliography of Asian studies **4644**

Suriname **4990**

Survey guide to Spanish archives **6530**

Survey of British research in audio-visual aids, 1945-71 **3838**

Survey of current business **2382**

Survey of international affairs, 1920/23-66 **1612**

Survey of Israel
Atlas of Israel **5290**

The Survey of London **7113**

'A Survey of recent Chilean historiography 1965-1976' **8099**

A Survey of the Vatican archives **6527**

Surveys of historical manuscripts in the United Kingdom **6501**

Sussex bibliography **7144**

Suster, Z.
Historical dictionary of the Frederal Republic of Yugoslavia **7499**

Sutcliffe, J.M.
A Dictionary of religious education **3828**

Sutherland, S.
Macmillan dictionary of psychology **269**
The World's religions **365**

Suttie, M-L.
'A select bibliography of South African history 1990-1993' **7831**

Sutton, S.C.
A Guide to the India Office Library **6556**

Sutton, W.
The Currency options handbook **2225**

Suziedelis, S.
Historical dictionary of Lithuania **7444**

Sužiedélis, S. *and* Vesaitis, A.
Encyclopedia Lituanica **4614**

Suzuki, Y
The Japanese financial system **2131**

Svensk-engelsk fackordbok **1815**

Svenskt biografiskt lexikon **5843**

Swain, T.
Aboriginal religions in Australia **970**

Swann, B. *and* Turnbull, M.
Records of interest to social scientists, 1919-1939: Employment and unemployment **1910**

Swaziland **4857**

Sweden **4626, 7467**

Sweden. Statistiska Centralbyrån
Statistisk arsbok för Sverige **1252**

The Swedish economy **2343**

'The Swedish National Register of Private Archives' **6541**

Sweetland, R. C. *and* Keyser, D.J.
Tests: a comprehensive reference.. **335**

Sweetman, J.
American naval history **3549**
A Dictionary of European land battles **3463**

Swietochowski, T. *and* Collins, B.C.
Historical dictionary of Azerbaijan **7451**

Swingewood, A.
A Short history of sociological thought **1071**

Swinscoe, A.
The British flag **6347**

Switzerland **4632**

Switzerland. Eidgenössisches Statistisches Amt
Statistisches Jahrbuch der Schweiz/Annuaire statistiques de la Suisse **1256**

Sworakowski, W.S.
The Communist International and its front organizations **1638**

Sykes, E.
Everyman's dictionary of non-classicial mythology **829**

Sykes, W.
Directory of social research organisations in the United Kingdom **1036**

Sylvester, C.
Zimbabwe **4861**

Symbole und Zeremoniell in deutschen Striekräften vom 18. bis zum. 20. Jahrhundert **3457**

The Symbols, standards, flags and banners of ancient and modern nations **6341**

Symonds, C.L.
A Battlefield atlas of the American Revolution **8033**

Symons, A.
Behind the blue plaques of London 1867-1994 **7132**

A Synoptic index to the 'Proceedings of the Aristotelian Society...' **16**

The Synoptic problems **572**

Syria **4735**

Systematic glossary, English-French-Spanish-Russian, of selected economic and social terms **1784**

Systematic glossary of the terminology of statistical methods **1307**

Syvret, M. *and* Stevens, J.
Balleine's history of Jersey **7154**

Szajkowski, B.
Encyclopedia of conflicts, disputes and flashpoints **1521**
Marxist governments **1704**

Szarmach, P.E.
Medieval England **6964**
Medieval Europe **6778**

Szladits, C.
A Bibliography of foreign and comparative law **2740**
Guide to foreign legal materials, French, German, Swiss **2787**

Szladits, C. *and* Germain, C.M.
Guide to foreign legal materials: French **2842**

Szucs, L. *and* Luebking, S.H.
The Archives: a guide to the National Archives Field Branches **6597**

Szucs, L.D. *and* Luebking, S.H.
The Source **6115**

Tabex encyclopedia Zimbabwe **4864**

Tabrah, R.
Hawaii a bicentennial history **8191**

Tabula Imperii Romani: Iudea. Palaestina **6662**

Tahiti - Polynesia handbook **5674**

Tahitiens **6001**

Taiwan **4682-4683**

Taking up a franchise **2681**

Talbert, R.J.A.
Atlas of Classical History **6697**

Talbot, A.M. *and* Talbot, W.J.
Atlas of the Union of South Africa **5317**

Talbot, R.
Atlas of the Greek and Roman world **6698**

Tale of the future **215**

Tale type- and motif-indexes **4121**

Talking philosophy: a wordbook **1**

The Talmud **931**

Talocci, M.
Guide to the flags of the world **6342**

Tambi Eyongetah Mbuagbaw
A History of the Cameroon **7800**

Tamsma, R.
The Netherlands in 50 maps **5260**

Tanner, H.H.
Atlas of Great Lakes Indian history **8013**

Tanner, M.S.
The politics of law making in China: institutions, processes and democratic prospects **2850**

Tanner, N.
Conciliorum Oecumenicorum decreta **668**

Tanzania **4849, 7818**

Tapsell, R.F.
Monarchs, rulers, dynasties and kingdoms of the world 6311

Tardiff, J.C. and Mabunda, L.M.
Dictionary of Hispanic biography 6003

Tarling, N.
The Cambridge history of Southeast Asia 7550

Tarver, A.
Church court records 6139

Taryam, A.O.
The establishment of the United Arab Emirates 1950-1985 7631

Tasmania 5024

Tatemae and honne 2035

Tattersall, I.
Encyclopedia of human evolution and prehistory 4215

Tauro, A.
Bibliografia peruana de historia 1940-1953 8106

Taussig, L.
Resource guide to travel in Sub-Saharan Africa 5593

The Tavistock handbook and directory 2453

Tavistock Joint Library. London
Catalogue of the Tavistock Joint Library 251

Tax systems of Africa, Asia and Middle East 2147

Tax systems of Western Europe 2148

Taylor, A. and Whiting, B.J.
A Dictionary of American proverbs and proverbial phrases, 1820-1880 4206

Taylor, B.
Andorra 4602
Society and economy in early modern Europe, 1450-1789 1854

Taylor, C.R.H.
A Pacific bibliography 4995

Taylor, D.
Pakistan 4723

Taylor, J. and Shaw, W.
A Dictionary of the Third Reich 7275

Taylor, J.G.
The Indonesian occupation of East Timor 1974-1989 8121

Taylor, M.
Thomas Cook world atlas of travel 5070

Taylor, M. and Presley, F.
Community work in the UK, 1982-1986 3619

Taylor, M.B. and Owram, D.
Canadian history. A readers guide 7873

Taylor, M.J.H.
Encyclopedia of the world's air forces 3522

Taylor, N.
Computers in genealogy beginners hand book 6011

Taylor, P.J.
Political geography in the twentieth century 1367

Taylor, P.J.O.
A Companion to the Indian Mutiny of 1857 7649

Taylor, R.E. and Meighan, C.W.
Chronologies in New World archaeology 4330

Taylor, R.H.
The State in Burma 7713

Teaching bibliographic skills in history 6381

Technical education abstracts from British sources 1965

Teed, P.
Dictionary of twentieth-century history (1914-1990) 6452

Teichler, U. and Voss, F.
Bibliography of Japanese education/ Bibliographie zum japanischen Erziehungswesen: postwar publications in Western languages 3801

Teilhard de Chardin, P.
Bibliographie générale des oeuvres et articles sur Pierre Teilhard de Chardin 55

Telek, J.
History of Hungary and the Hungarians 1848-1971 7320

Television and ethics 362

Telford, T.A.
Chinese genealogies at the Genealogical Society of Utah 6079

Temperley, H. and Penson, L.M.
A Century of diplomatic blue books, 1814-1914 1620
A Century of diplomatic blue books, 1914-1936 1621

Temperley, N.
The hymn tune index: a census of English language hymn tunes in printed sources from 1535 to 1820 655

Temperton, P.
A Guide to UK monetary policy 2189

Temporini, H. and Haase, W.
Rise and decline of the Roman world 6712

Ten London repositories 6181

Tenney, M. and Barabas, S.
The Zondervan pictorial encyclopedia of the Bible 452

Tepper, M.
Emigrants to Pennsylvania, 1641-1819 6094
Immigrants to the middle colonies 6095
New World immigrants 6096
Passengers to America 6093

Termau archifau/Archive terms 6485

Termau cyfraith/Welsh terms .. 2770

Terminologie de la gestion 2614

Terminologie de la sécurité sociale .. 3719

Terminologie économique 1791

Terminologie le la société anonyme européenne/Terminology of the European company 2439

Terminology of business and company law 2021

Terminology of human rights 3101

Terminology of management and financial accountancy 2590

Terminology of special education 3882

Terra Australis to Australia 8160

The Territories of the Russian Federation 4607

Terrorism, 1980-1987 1531

Terrorism, 1980-1990 1529

Terrorism, 1988-1991 1532

Terrorism, 1992-1995 1533

Terrorism: current readings 1527

Terry, M.R.
Historical dictionary of the United States Air Force 3531

Terry, T.M.
The Discovery of Australia 8173

Terwiel, B.J.
A History of modern Thailand 7715

Test critiques 336

Tester, J.
A History of Western astrology 200

Testimony 236

Tests: a comprehensive reference.. 335

Tests in print V 337

Texas 4945

Texas University. Population Research Center
International population census bibliography 1311

Texts and calendars 7111

Thackeray, A. and Jones, M.
The FIAC directory of independent advice centres 3617

Thackrah, J.R.
Encyclopedia of terrorism and political violence 1538

Thailand 4748-4749

Thailand: a handbook of historical statistics 1276

Thailand a short history 7716

Thailand handbook 5586

Thakurdas, H. and Thakurdas, L.
Dictionary of psychiatry. Revised by Betty Thakurdas 331

The Thames 1580-1980 7117

Thaper, B.K.
Recent archaeological discoveries in India 4315

Thawley, J.
Australasia and South Pacific Islands bibliography 4996

Thawley, J. and Gauci, S.
Bibliographies on the Australian aborigines 5033

The Diagram Group
Encyclopedia of African peoples 7747

The Nationalities question in the Soviet Union 7410

Theatre costume 3997

Thematic atlases for public, academic, and High School libraries 5178

Themes in Kenyan history 7814

Theological and religious bibliographies 385

Theological and religious reference materials 374

Theological book review. October 1988- 585

Theological dictionary of the New Testament 529

Theological dictionary of the Old Testament 520

A Theological word book of the Bible 469

Theologische Literaturzeitung. Monatsschrift für das gesamte Gebiet der Theologie und Religionswissenschaft 556

Theologische Realenzyklopädie 576

Theologisches Wörterbuch zum Alten Testament 519

Theologisches Wörterbuch zum Neuen Testament 528

Theories of learning 3825

Theorists of economic growth 1873

Thernstrom, S.
Harvard encyclopedia of American ethnic groups 1131

Thesaurus of archaeological site types 4435

Thesaurus of ERIC descriptors 3816

Thesaurus of individual development terms 2401

Thesaurus of psychological index terms 298

Thesaurus of vocational training 3814

Thibault, C.
Bibliographia Canadiana 7874

Thinkers of the new Left 209

Thinkers of the twentieth century 120

The Third Fleet convicts 5994

The Third Reich, 1933-1939 7271

The Third Reich 1933-1945 7270

The Third Reich at war 7272

Third World 4521, 4526

Third World atlas 5184

Third World directory 2292

Third World economic handbook 1850

Third World Handbook 4522

Third World political organizations 1416

Third World resource directory 1994-1995 1164

Thirsk, J.
History of Lincolnshire 7181

This arrogant city 7044

This day in religion 4027

This is Greenland '99 5053

Thode, E.
Address book for Germanic genealogy 6071
German-English genealogical dictionary 6070

Thole, B.L.L.M.
Elsevier's lexicon of stock-market terms 2238

Thomas, A.H. and Oakley, S.P.
Historical dictionary of Denmark 7472

Towns
See
    Automobile Association$zAA Great
    Britain town plans
Townsend, J.
   Women in developing countries 4086
Townsend, P.
   Burke's genealogical and heraldic history of
   the landed gentry 6270
Townson, D.
   The New Penguin dictionary of modern
   history 6745
Toynbee, J.M.C.
   Roman historical portraits 6721
Tracey, W.R.
   The Human resources glossary 2633
Tracing ancestors in Shetland 6044
Tracing family history in New Zealand 6198,
   6200
Tracing Scottish local history 6995
Tracing the past 7045
Tracing your ancestors in Northern Ireland
   6171
Tracing your ancestors in the Public Record
   Office 6019
'Tracing your Catholic ancestors in England
   6179
Tracing your family history in Australia 6206
Tracing your family outside New Zealand
   6199
Tracing your family tree 6145
Tracing your Irish ancestors 6051
Tracing your Scottish ancestors 6041
Tracing your Scottish ancestry 6042
Tracing your Swedish ancestry 6078
Tracing your West Indian ancestors 6187
Trade associations and professional bodies
   2425
Trade contacts in China 2493
Trade union and related records 1978
Trade Union Congress. Library
   List of current trade union periodicals 1969
Trade union handbook 1974
Trade unions of the world 1967
Traditional Chinese folktales 4155
The Traditional games of England, Scotland
   and Ireland 4141
Traditions of the Welsh saints 613
The Tragedy of Cambodian history 7725
Trager, J.
   The People's chronology 6477
Training and development organizations
   directory 1917
The Training directory 1966
Tranter, N. *and* Cyprien, M.
   A Traveller's guide to the Scotland of Robert
   the Bruce 5497
Trask, D.F.
   A Bibliography of United States-Latin
   American relations since 1810 1644
Trask, W.R.
   Yoga 889
Trattner, W.I.
   Biographical dictionary of social welfare in
   America 3630
Trattner, W.L. *and* Achenbaum, W.A.
   Social welfare in America 3625
Travel and tourism data 2412
Travel legend and lore 5094
Travel trade gazette directory 2410
The Traveler's sourcebook 5632
The Traveller-gypsies 4118
The Travellers: Canada to 1900 7875
The Travellers' dictionary of quotations 5096
A Traveller's guide to Celtic Britain 5484
A Traveller's guide to early medieval Britain
   5467
Travellers' guide to medieval England 5517
A Traveller's guide to Roman Britain 5477
A Traveller's guide to saints in Europe 612

A Traveller's guide to the Scotland of Robert
   the Bruce 5497
The Traveller's handbook 5095
The Traveller's key to ancient Egypt 6650
Travelling in tropical countries 5102
Treadwell, T.C. *and* Wood, A.C.
   German Knights of the Air 1914-1918 6297
The Treasure Act 1996 4430
Treasure chest for teachers 3833
Treasure, G.R.
   Who's who in British history 6939
Treasure trove 5103
Treaties and alliances of the world 1616
A Treatise on heraldry, British and foreign
   6224
Treaty series 2975
Treaty series, 1892- 2968
Treaty series: treaties and international
   agreements registered or filed and recorded
   with the Secretariat of the United Nations ...
   1946/47- 2960
Trefousse, H.L.
   Historical dictionary of reconstruction 8059
'Trekking Australia and New Zealand' 5662
Treky, T.H.
   Dictionary of insurance terms. In English
   and Arabic 3709
Treml, V.G. *and* Hardt, J.P.
   Soviet economic statistics 2338
Treptow, K.W. *and* Popa, M.
   Historical dictionary of Romania 7512
Treviño, A.J.
   The Sociology of law 2741
Trigger, B.G.
   A History of archaeological thought 4226
Triggs, G.D.
   The Antarctic Treaty regime 5056
Trinder, B.
   The Blackwell encyclopedia of industrial
   archaeology 4464
Trinidad and Tobago 4926
Trinkle, D.A.
   The History highway 6374
   Writing, teaching and researching history in
   the electronic age 6460
Trip planner platinum 5635
Tripp, E.
   Dictionary of classical mythology 854
Trotsky: a bibliography 225
Trotsky bibliography 223
Trott, L. *and* Smith, D.C.
   Mafia 3158
Trouble-free travel 5088
True North 7887
Truhart, P.
   Historical dictionary of states 6400
   Regents of nations 1485, 6478
Truman, N.
   Historic costuming 4000
Truschel, L.W.
   German South West Africa 4860
Truscott, S. *and* García, M.
   A Dictionary of contemporary Spain 4601
Trzyna, T.C.
   International peace directory 3007
   Population 1323
Tseng, H.P.
   The Law schools of the world 2876
Tsouris, P.G.
   Warriers' words: a quotation book 3389
Tsuboi Kiyotari
   Recent archaeological discoveries in Japan
   4311
Tsuneta Yano Memorial Society
   Nippon 1269
Tucker, S.C.
   Encyclopedia of the Korean War 7593
   Encyclopedia of the Vietnam War 7735
   The European Powers and the first World
   War 6812

Tuckerman, N. *and* Dunnan, N. *and* Aher, J.
   The Amy Vanderbilt complete book of
   etiquette 4042
Tudor, J.
   Macmillan directory of business information
   sources 2522, 2545
   Macmillan directory of UK business
   information sources 2052
Tulard, J.
   Dictionnaire du Second Empire 7354
   Dictionnaire Napoléon 7340
Tully, C.
   The A-Z guide for lightweight travellers
   5090
Tunisia 4793, 7758
Tunisia handbook with Western Libya 5594
Tuñón de Lara, M.
   Historia de España 7941
The Turbulent Gulf 7622
Turkey 4730, 5579
Turkey. Devlet Istatistik Enstitüsü
   Türkiye istatistik yıllığı. Statistical yearbook
   of Turkey 1272
Turkey, politics and government 7682
Türkisches biographisches archiv/Turkish
   biographical archive 5882
Türkiye atlası/Atlas of Turkey 5287
Türkiye istatistik yıllığı. Statistical yearbook of
   Turkey 1272
Turks and Caicos Islands 4914
Turner, A.
   A Bibliography of Quaker literature, 1893-
   1967 801
   Historical dictionary of Papua New Guinea
   8180
Turner, B.
   The Statesman's year-book 4508
Turner, C.A.
   Directory of foreign document collections
   1646
Turner-Evans, H.
   A Bibliography of Welsh hymnology 653
Turner, N.
   Handbook for Biblical studies 472
Turner, R.W.
   Thinkers of the twentieth century 120
Turner, V.
   Ancient Shetland 4420
Turnock, D.
   Eastern Europe an historical geography
   1815-1945 5153
Tuson, P.
   Sources for Middle East studies 6549
Tuttle, A.C.
   'The Strategic defense initiative' 3480
Tuttle, L.
   Encyclopedia of feminism 4065
Tuvalu 8185
Twentieth-century American historians 6438
Twentieth-century Britain 4542
Twentieth-century British political facts, 1900-
   2000 1426
Twentieth-century British social trends 1175
Twentieth-century shapers of American popular
   religion 428
Twentieth century warriors 3428
Twentieth-century world history 6445
The Two Yemens 7616
The Typewriting dictionary 2567
Tyrrell, C.
   The Parents' guide to independent schools
   3856
Tyson, G.F.
   A Guide to manuscript sources in United
   States and West Indian depositories
   relating to the British West Indies during
   the era of the American Revolution 6583
Ucrainica at the University of Toronto Library
   4616
Udaondo, E.
   Diccionario biográfico argentino 5965

The Victoria history of the county of Lancaster 7212

The Victoria history of the county of Leicester 7186

The Victoria history of the county of Lincoln 7182

The Victoria history of the county of Middlesex 7136

The Victoria history of the county of Norfolk 7201

The Victoria history of the county of Northampton 7189

The Victoria history of the county of Nottingham 7178

The Victoria history of the county of Oxford 7194

The Victoria history of the county of Rutland 7188

The Victoria history of the county of Somerset 7163

The Victoria history of the County of Stafford 7169

The Victoria history of the county of Suffolk 7204

The Victoria history of the county of Surrey 7137

The Victoria history of the county of Sussex 7143

The Victoria history of the county of Warwick 7172

The Victoria history of the county of Wiltshire 7149

The Victoria history of the county of Worcester 7171

The Victoria history of the county of York 7215

Victorian biography 5739

Victorian Britain 6981

Victorian science and religion 441

Victorian studies 6980

Victorian women 5765

Vienna 4573

Viet, J.
Thesaurus of individual development terms 2401
Thesaurus of vocational training 3814

Viet, J. and Slype, G.van
EUDISED; multilingual thesaurus 3813

Vietnam 4757-4758

Vietnam at war 7727

Vietnam handbook 5590

Vietnam order of battle 7729

Vietnam War almanac 7738

Vietnam War bibliography 7734

Viking age Denmark 4302

The Viking atlas of World War I 6817

The Viking atlas of World War II 6879

Vikings in Scotland 4402

Vilar, P.
A History of gold and money, 1450-1920 2230

Village studies 1145

Villarel, H.K.
Eminent Filippines 5977

Viller, M.
Dictionnaire de spiritualité, ascétique et mystique, doctrine et histoire 628

Vincent, M. and Stradling, R.A.
Cultural atlas of Spain and Portugal 4598

Vincie, J.F. and Rathbauer-Vincie, M.
C.G. Jung and analytical psychology 323

Virgin Islands 4919

Virginia handbook 5633

Virgins and virago 4092

Virtual roots 6015

Viscount Dunedin
Encyclopaedia of the laws of Scotland 2806

The Visible past 4238

The Visigoths in Gaul and Spain AD 488-711 7385

Visitors welcome 4365

A Visual history of costume 3982

Vital records handbook 6025

Vital Records Index British Isles (1538-1888) 6039

Vital statistics on American politics 1687

Vitaver, P.R.
Quién es quién en América del Sur 5968

Vives, J.V.
An Economic history of Spain 2335

The VNR dictionary of business and finance 1799

Vocabulaire-atlas héraldique en six langues 6233

Vocabulaire économique et financier 1787

Vocabulary of legal metrology 3273

Vocational rehabilitation and the employment of the disabled 3671

Vocational training: glossarium 1963

Vogel, Joseph O. and Vogel, Jean
Encyclopedia of precolonial Africa 4324

Vogel, R.
A Breviate of British diplomatic blue books, 1919-1939 1622

Volborth, C.A. von
The Art of heraldry 6232

Völgyes, I.
The Hungarian Soviet Republic 1919 7321

Voluntary agencies directory 1997 3593

Volunteerism: the directory of organizations, training, programs and publications 3628

Vomende, R.
Criminology and forensic sciences 3148

von Elbe, J.
The Romans in Cologne and Lower Germany 4443

von Elbe, J. and von Elbe, D.
Roman Germany 4442

Vose, C.E.
A Guide to library resources in political science: American government 3345

Vronskaya, J. and Chuguev, V.
A Biographical dictionary of the former Soviet Union 5819

Wacher, J.
The Roman world 6719

Waddell, D.A.G.
Venezuela 4987

Waddell, J.
The Prehistoric archaeology of Ireland 4279

Wade, H.
Australian history on the Internet 8165

Wade-Martins, P.
An Historical atlas of Norfolk 7203

Wagenhauser, B.
Resource guide to travel in South America 5642

Waggoner, B.A. and Waggoner, G.R.
Universities in the Caribbean region - 3947

Wagner, A.
Heralds of England 6249

Wagner, G.
An Exegetical bibliography of the New Testament 526

Wagner, J.A.
The Historical dictionary of the Elizabethan world 6969

Wagner, Sir Anthony
English genealogy 6058

Waiko, J.D.
A Short history of Papua New Guinea 8179

Wainwright, M. and Locke, T.
The Which? guide to Yorkshire and the Peak District 5519

Wainwright, M.D. and Matthews, N.
A Guide to Western manuscripts and documents in the British Isles relating to South and South East Asia 6551

Wakefield,, G.S.
A Dictionary of Christian spirituality 629

Walch, T.
Our family, our town 6192

Walden, G.R.
Public opinion polls and survey research 1087

Waldman, C.
Atlas of the North American Indian 8014
Encyclopedia of native American tribes 8008
Who was who in Native American history 8016
Who was who in world exploration 5074

Waldman, H.
The Dictionary of SDI 3482

Waldram, G.N.
Civic ceremonial 4032

Waldron, A.
The Great Wall of China 6644

Wales 4568

Wales before 1066 4439

Wales in the early Middle Ages 7237

Wales Tourist Board map 5531

The Wales yearbook, 2000 1436

Walicki, A.
A History of Russian thought 214

Walker, B.
The Hindu world 868

Walker, B.M.
Parliamentary elections results in Ireland, 1801-1922 1560

Walker, D.
The Pundits 5079

Walker, D.M.
A Legal history of Scotland 2807
The Oxford companion to law 2743
The Scottish jurists 2880
The Scottish legal system 2803

Walker, R.
Government funding for United Kingdom business 2182

Walker, R.C.S.
A Selective bibliography on Kant 29

Walker, T.W.
Nicaragua 4889

Wall Street words 2259

Wallace, C.D.
Foreign direct investment and the multinational enterprise 2178

Wallace, J.
East Germany 4571

Wallace, W.
Berlin 4569

Wallach, J.L.
Israeli military history 3418

Waller, P. and Rowett, J.
Chronology of the 20th century 6482

Waller, R.
Atlas of British politics 1429

Waller, R. and Criddle, B.
The Almanac of British politics 1428

Wallis, H. and McConnel, A.
Historians' guide to early British maps 6934

Walmesley, J.
Dictionary of international finance 2115

Walmsley, K.
Butterworths company law handbook, 1993 3168

Walmsley's rural estate management 1996

Walne, P.
Dictionary of archival terminology. Dictionnaire de terminologie archivistique 6484
A Guide to manuscript sources for the history of Latin America and the Caribbean in the British Isles 6593

Walsh, D. and Poole, A.
A Dictionary of criminology 3156

Walsh, J.
Crime and criminal justice reference sources 3126

Walsh, K. and King, A.
Handbook of international manpower market comparisons 1902

Walsh, K. and Pearson, R.
UK labour market guide **1886**

Walsh, M.
Butler's lives of patron saints **608**
Butler's lives of the saints **607**

Walsh, M.J.
Religious bibliographies in serial literature **410**
Vatican City State **4594**

Walsh, R.M. and Birkin, S.J.
Job satisfaction and motivation **1926**

Walter, C.
Winners **5720**

Walters, D.
Chinese mythology **838**

Walters, F.P.
A History of the League of Nations **2907**

Walton, F.
The Encyclopedia of employment law and practice **1911**

Walton, J.
The National Trust guide to Late Georgian and Victorian Britain **5485**

Walton R., Sir
The Encyclopedia of forms and precedents other than court forms **3190**

Walvin, J.
Black ivory **1585**

Wang, J.C.
Handbook on ocean politics and law **2952**

Wang, M.C.
Handbook of special education **3880**

Wang, R.T.
Area bibliography of China **4651**

The War against Japan, 1941-1945 **6861**
The War at sea **6850**
War books **6810**
War in Asia and the Pacific **6898**
The War in North Africa 1940-1943 **6855**
The War in the air: being the story of the part played in the Great War by the Royal Air Force **6807**
The War of 1812 **8036**
The War of the American Revolution **8023**
War on words **3388**
War with Japan **6851**

Ward A.W., Sir and Gooch, G.P.
The Cambridge history of British foreign policy, 1783-1919 **1623**
Ward maps of the City of London **7127**

Ward, P.
A Dictionary of common fallacies **4182**

Ward, R.E. and Watanabe, H.
Japanese political science **1443**

Ward, S.
A-Z of meetings **3236**

Warde, A.
Contemporary British society **1073**
Ward's business directory of US private and public companies, 1994 **2482**

Ware, T.
The Orthodox Church **717**
Warfare in the classical world **3364**

Warner, M.
The International encyclopedia of business & management **2599**

Warner, O.
Battle honours of the Royal Navy **3569**

Warnes, D.
Chronicles of the Russian Tsars **6334**

Warren, C.
Personnel administration manual **1887**

Warren, H.G.
Paraguay an informal history **8114**

Warren, M.A.
The Nature of women **4064**

Warren, P. and Hankey, V.
Aegean Bronze Age chronology **6707**
Warriors' words: a quotation book **3389**

Warry, J.
Warfare in the classical world **3364**

The Wars in Vietnam, Cambodia and Laos, 1945-1982 **7731**
Wars of the Americas **7854**
Warship losses of World War Two **6834**
Wartime Poland 1939-1945 **7312**

Warwick, E.
Early American dress **3993**
The Warwick guide to British labour periodicals, 1790-1970 **1891**

Warwick Statistics Service
The Counties and regions of the United Kingdom **2304**
Warwickshire local history sources **7173**
Washington information directory, 1993-94 **3346**
Washington's representatives .. **1696**

Wasserman, E.S.
Oral history index **6751**

Wasserman, P.
Encyclopedia of health information sources **3634**
Festivals sourcebook **4024**

Wasserman, P. and Kennington, A.E.
Ethnic information sources in the United States **1130**

Wasserman, S. and O'Brien, J.W.
Law and legal information directory **2866**

Wastenson, L.
National atlas of Sweden **5255**

Waterston, E.
The Travellers: Canada to 1900 **7875**

Watson, D.
A Dictionary of mind and spirit **167**

Watson, J.
Bibliography of ephemeral community information materials **3282**

Watson, M.H.
Disasters at sea **5111**

Watson, R.I.
'Psychology' **253**

Watt, D.C.
'United States documentary resources for the study of British foreign policy, 1919-1939' **1627**

Watt, D.E.R.
A Biographical dictionary of Scottish graduates **3942**

Watts, D.
The West Indies **5159**

Waugh, N.
The Cut of men's clothes, 1600-1900 **4004**
The Cut of women's clothes, 1600-1930 **4007**

Way, G. and Squire, R.
Collins Scottish clan and family encyclopedia **6159**
We the people **1131**

Weatherford, D.L.
Milestones: a chronology of American women's history **8020**

Weatherill, S. and Beaumont, P.
EC law **3021**

Weaver, S.M.
'Ancient and modern Macedonia' **7507**

Webb, A.
Compendium of Irish biography **5776**
Longman companion to Germany since 1945 **7264**

Webb, A.D.
The New dictionary of statistics **1197**

Webb, H.B. and Collier, R.
Butterworth's stamp duties guide **2157**

Webb, W.
Sources of information in the social sciences **993**
Webster's American military biographies **3427**
Webster's Guide to American history **7976**
Webster's new world illustrated encyclopedic dictionary of real estate **1994**
Webster's secretarial handbook **2557**

Wedberg, A.
A History of philosophy **106**

Wedeck, H.E.
Dictionary of gypsy life and lore **4119**

Wedgewood, J.C.
History of Parliament, 1439-1509 **3052**

Weekes, R.V.
The World of Islam **941**
Weekly information bulletin **1679**
Weekly law reports **2820**

Weeks, A.L.
Brassey's Soviet and communist quotations **229**

Weeks, G.
Family directory **1161**

Weeks, J.
Jane's pocket-book: armies of the world **3492**

Wehler, H-U.
The German Empire 1871-1918 **7257**

Wei, B.P.T.
Shanghai **7561**

Wei-Chin Lee
Taiwan **4683**

Wei, K.T.
Women in China **4095**

Weigall, D.
Britain and the world, 1815-1986 **1605**

Weightman, A.E.
Heraldry in the Royal Navy **3553**
The Weights and measures of England **3270**

Weigley, R.F.
The Age of battles **3468**

Weihs, J.
Facts about Canada **4875**
The Weimar Republic **7265**

Weinberg, J.R.
A Short history of medieval philosophy **113**

Weinberg, M.
World racism and related inhumanities **1116**

Weinreb, B. and Hibbert, C.
The London encyclopaedia **7123**

Weir, A.
Britain's Royal Families **6327**
Early Ireland **4427**

Weir, K.
Los Angeles handbook **5634**

Welch, J.M.
Free bank letters as sources of economic and financial information **2192**
Welcome to Historic Scotland **4405**
Welfare, poverty and development in Latin America **1191**
Wellard's NHS handbook, 2000/2001 **3648**

Wells, A.S.
The Historical dictionary of World War II: The War against Japan **6873**

Wells, R.V.
The Population of the British colonies in America before 1776 **1352**

Welsby, P.A.
A History of the Church of England, 1945-1980 **755**

Welsh, B.W.W. and Butorin, P.
Dictionary of development **1849**
Welsh economic trends/Tueddiadau'r economi, 1992 **2324**

Welsh, F.
A History of Hong Kong **7577**
Welsh family history **6183**
Welsh folk customs **4153**
Welsh genealogies AD300-1400 **6066**
Welsh history and its sources **7233**
Welsh History Review **7234**
Welsh nation builders **5783**

Welsh Office
Health and personal social services statistics for Wales, 1991 **3657**
Welsh economic trends/Tueddiadau'r economi, 1992 **2324**

Who's who in Ancient Egypt **6659**

Who's who in Asia and the Pacific nations **5859**

Who's who in Asian and Australasian politics **1442**

Who's who in Australia 2000 **5997**

Who's who in British economics **1856**

Who's who in British history **6939**

Who's who in Canada 1999 **5911**

Who's who in China 1918-1950 **5862**

Who's who in Church history **675**

Who's who in classical mythology **856**

Who's who in economics **1847**

Who's who in espionage
The Dictionary of espionage **1665**

Who's who in European business **2451**

Who's who in European politics **1421, 3324**

Who's who in fashion **3983-3984**

Who's who in Fiji **6002**

Who's who in finance and industry, 1992-1993 **2177**

Who's who in France 1996-1997 **5802**

Who's who in Germany: a biographical encyclopedia ... containing about 11,000 biographies of top-ranking decision makers, politicians and other leading personalities operating in the fields of business and finance, politics, science, the arts and entertainment **5786**

Who's who in international affairs **1613**

Who's who in international banking **2187**

Who's who in Israel and Jewish personalities from all the world 1999 **5884**

Who's who in Japan 1991-92 **5870**

Who's who in Japanese Government, 1988/89 **1497**

Who's who in Jewish history after the period of the Old Testament **6674**

Who's who in Latin America **1024**

Who's who in Lebanon 1999-2000 **5883**

Who's who in Mexico today **5914**

Who's who in military history **3394**

Who's who in Nazi Germany **7280**

Who's who in New Zealand **5981**

Who's who in Nigeria **5898**

Who's who in Pacific navigation **5078**

Who's who in Poland **5831**

Who's who in Polish America **5936**

Who's who in religion **712**

Who's who in Russia **5820**

Who's who in Russia and the CIS Republics **5821**

Who's who in Russia and the new states **5822**

Who's who in Russia from 1900 **1495**

Who's who in Russia since 1900 **5818**

Who's who in Scandinavia **5835**

Who's who in Scotland 1998 **5772**

Who's who in Scottish history **7011**

Who's who in South African politics **1454**

Who's who in Spain 1996 **5812**

Who's who in Switzerland **5854**

Who's who in the Ancient Near East **6679**

Who's who in the Ancient World **6699**

Who's who in the Arab World 1999-2000 **5889**

Who's who in the Bible **489**

Who's who in the Channel Islands 1987 **5780**

Who's who in the City, 1993 **2174**

Who's who in the Greek world **6710**

Who's who in the history of the Punjab (1800-1849) **7657**

Who's who in the Irish War of Independence and Civil War 1916-1923 **7034**

Who's who in the New Testament **534**

Who's who in the Old Testament **522**

Who's who in the People's Republic of China **5867**

Who's who in the Socialist countries of Europe **1712**

Who's who in the world 2000 Millenium edition **5702**

Who's who in theology **589**

Who's who in Uganda 1993-94 **5899**

Who's who in venture capital **2267**

Who's who in Welsh history **7236**

Who's who in world insurance **3710**

Who's who in world Jewry **5726**

Who's who in World War II **6891**

Who's who in Zimbabwe **5905**

Who's who of American women 2000-2001 **5961**

Who's who of Australian women **6000**

Who's who of British Members of Parliament **3053**

The Who's who of Nobel Prize winners 1901-1995 **5721**

Who's who of religions **427**

Who's who of Southern Africa 2000: an illustrated biographical record of prominent personalities in the Republic of South Africa, Botswana, Mauritius, Namibia, Swaziland, Zimbabwe, and neighbouring countries in South Africa **5900**

Who's who of women in world politics **1411**

Who's who Sarawak 1985-86 **5975**

Why they call it politics: a guide to America's government **1684**

Whybra, J.
A Lost English county **7068**

Whyte, D.
A Dictionary of Scottish emigrants to Canada before Confederation **6082**

Whyte, J.D. and Whyte, K.
Exploring Scotland's historic landscapes **5499**

Whyte, J.D. and Whyte, K.H.
Sources for Scottish historical geography **5155**

Wichert, S.
Northern Ireland since 1945 **7038**

Wick, R.L. and Mood, T.A.
ARBA guide to biographical resources 1986-1997 **5710**

Wicks, P.
'Audio-visual aids in education' **3839**

Widdows, R.
Philip's world handbook **5438**

Wie is wie in Vlaanderen 1985-1989 **5853**

Wieczynski, J.
The Modern encyclopaedia of Russian and Soviet history **7422**

Wiener, F
Army, navy and air force uniforms of the Warsaw Pact **3442**

Wiener, P.P.
Dictionary of the history of ideas **66, 79**

Wierzbianski, B.
Who's who in Polish America **5936**

Wigoder, G.
Dictionary of Jewish biography **925, 6004**
The Encyclopedia of Judaism **907**
Everyman's Judaica **908**
Illustrated dictionary and concordance of the Bible **473**

Wiktor, C.L.
Canadian bibliography of international law **2891**

Wilcocks, J.
Countries and islands of the world **4513**

Wilcox, R.T.
The Dictionary of costume **3968**

Wilczynski, J.
An encyclopedic dictionary of Marxism, socialism and Communism **1383**

Wilding, N. and Laundy, P.
An Encyclopaedia of Parliament **3076**

Wile, A.N.
CRIS **1369**

Wilgus, A.C.
The Historiography of Latin America **6437**

Wilkins, W.J.
Hindu mythology **869**

Wilkinson, E.
Chinese history **7562**

Wilkinson, F.
Badges of the British Army **3450**

Wilkinson, P. and Stewart, A.M.
Contemporary research on terrorism **1526**

Willcox, W.F.
International migrations **1567**

Williams, A.
A Biographical dictionary of Dark Age Britain **6961**
Great Domesday **7054**

Williams, A.E.
Termau archifau/Archive terms **6485**

Williams, C.J. and Watts-Williams, J.
Cofrestri plwyf Cymru/Parish registers of Wales **6217**

Williams, D.
A Dictionary of Japanese financial terms **2120**

Williams, D. and Muirhead, G.
Northumberland miners' banners **6260**

Williams, D.B.
Zaire **4841**

Williams, D.W.
Reader's Digest you and your rights **3113**

Williams, E.
From Columbus to Castro **7917**

Williams, E.L. and Brown, C.F.
The Howard University bibliography of African and Afro-American religious studies **967**

Williams, E.N.
The Penguin dictionary of English and European history, 1485-1789 **6791**

Williams, G.
Glamorgan county history **7243**
Learning the law **2822**
Third World political organizations **1416**

Williams, G. and Frost, A.
Terra Australis to Australia **8160**

Williams, G.L.
Papal genealogy **6075**

Williams, J.
Digest of Welsh historical statistics **1236**

Williams, J. Ll.
Geiriadur termau archaeolog **4289**

Williams, J.B.
A Guide to the printed materials for English social and economic history. 1750-1850 **2322**

Williams, J.F.
A Manager's guide to patents, trade marks & copyright **3175**

Williams, L.
Who's who in the City, 1993 **2174**

Williams, L.J.
Digest of Welsh historical statistics, 1974-1996 **1237**

Williams, N.
Chronology of the Expanding world **6463**
Chronology of the modern world 1901-1998 **6756**

Williams, P.
A Glossary of special education (children with special needs) **3881**

Williamson, D.
Brewer's British royalty **6328**
Debrett's guide to heraldry and regalia **6261**
Debrett's Kings and Queens of Britain **6324**
Debrett's Kings and Queens of Europe **6319**

Williamson, G.K.
The Longman investment companion **2257**

Williamson, H.
A Dictionary of Great War abbreviations **6808**

Willis, J.L.
Historical dictionary of Uruguay **8116**

Willmann-Institut, München-Wein. Leitung der Herausgabe: Heinrich Rombach
Lexikon der Pädagogik **3755**

Wright, P. *and* Coutts, B.E.
Belize **4886**
Wright, V.
The Government and politics of France **3078**
Wrigley, C.
A History of British industrial relations **1939**
Wrigley, E.A. *and* Schofield, R.S.
The Population history of England, 1541-1871 **1325**
Writing about Canada **7871**
'Writing Scotland's history **6427**
Writing, teaching and researching history in the electronic age **6460**
Writings on African archives **6570**
Writings on American history **7964**
Writings on American history, 1962-73 **7965**
Writings on British History **6924**
Writings on Irish history 1987 **7017**
Written in blood **2883**
Wróbel, P.
Historical dictionary of Poland 1945-1996 **7317**
Wuech, W.L. *and* Ballendorf, D.A.
Historical dictionary of Guam and Micronesia **8189**
Wurman, R.S.
US atlas **5353**
Wuthnow, R.
The Encyclopedia of politics and religion **390**
Wyatt, D.K.
Thailand a short history **7716**
Wyatt, R.J.
War books **6810**
Wybrow, R.J.
Britain speaks out, 1937-87 **1091**
Wynar, B.S.
Ukraine **4617**
Wynar, L.R.
Guide to reference materials in political science **1377**
Wynn, K.G.
Men of the Battle of Britain **6892**
Wypyski, E.M.
Legal periodicals in English **2776**
Xydis, D.P.
International governmental organizations: constitutional documents **2903**
Yakan, M.Z.
Almanac of African peoples and nations **4772**
Yale, D.E.C. *and* Baker, J.H.
A Centenary guide to the publications of the Seldon Society **2798**
Yang Dan
Atlas of the People's Republic of China **5269**
Yapp, P.
The Travellers' dictionary of quotations **5096**
Yarshater, E.
Encyclopaedia Iranica **4729**
Yarwood, D.
Costume in the Western world **3964**
The Encyclopedia of world costume **3965**
Yassif, E.
Jewish folklore **4167**
Ydegaard, T.
Greenland **5681**
Yeager, G.M.
Bolivia **4983**
Yeager, R.
Tanzania **7818**
Yeager, R. *and* Ofcansky, T.P.
Historical dictionary of Tanzania **7820**
Year book, 1987-88 **2986**
Year book Australia **1304**
Year book of social policy in Britain.
Social policy review, 1999 **1171**

Yearbook of American universities and colleges, 1986-1987 **3951**
Yearbook of English festivals **4022**
Yearbook of European law, 1981- **2784**
Yearbook of labour statistics, 1993 **1901**
Yearbook of national accounts statistics, 1990 **2144**
Yearbook of Nordic statistics **1249**
Yearbook of statistics **1277**
Yearbook on human rights **3106**
Yearbook on India's foreign policy, 1984-85 and 1985-86 **1640**
Yearbook on international Communist affairs: parties and political movements, 1991 **1706**
Yemen **4694**
Yeo, G.
The British overseas **6030**
Yin-Lien C. Chin
Traditional Chinese folktales **4155**
Yoga **889**
Yoga dictionary **892**
Yolton, J.S. *and* Yolton, J.W.
John Locke: a reference guide **39**
Yolton, J.W.
The Blackwell companion to the Enlightenment **6797**
Yoo, Y.
Books on Buddhism **879**
Buddhism **878**
Yoram Tsafrir
Tabula Imperii Romani: Iudea. Palaestina **6662**
York, H.E.
Political science **1379**
Yorkshire business histories **2467**
Young, A.
Albania **4636**
Young, G.V.C.
From the Vikings to the Reformation **7475**
Young, J.
A Dictionary of ships of the Royal Navy of the Second World War **3562**
Young, J.D.
Socialism and the English working class **1921**
Socialism since 1889 **212**
Young, J.M.
Britain's sea war **6853**
Young, J.W.
The Longman companion to America, Russia, and the Cold War 1941-1998 **6447**
Young, M.D.
The Parliaments of Scotland **3070**
Young, M.L.
The American dictionary of campaigns and elections **1566**
Young people now **3691**
Young, R.
Young's analytical concordance to the Bible **508**
Young, R.J.
French foreign policy, 1918-1945 **1634**
Young, S.
Encyclopedia of women and world religion **391**
Young, T.M.
Afro-American genealogy sourcebook **6111**
Young's analytical concordance to the Bible **508**
Youngs, F.A.
Guide to the local administrative units of England **3275**
Youth movements of the world **3689**
Yow, V.R.
Recording oral history **6752**
Ypersele, J. van *and* Koeune, J.-C.
The European monetary system **2139**
Yrigoyen, C. *and* Warrick, S.G.
Historical dictionary of Methodism **787**

Yu, D.C. *and* Thompson, L.G.
Guide to Chinese religion **957**
Yugoslavia **4637**
Yugoslavia as history **7493**
Yugoslavia. Savezni Zavod za Statistiku
Statisticki godisnjak FNRJ **1259**
Yurdan, M.
Irish family history **6169**
Zabecki, D.T.
World War II in Europe: an encyclopedia **6872**
Zagorin, J.S.
Bibliography of books and articles on international commercial arbitration **3192**
Zahlan, R.S.
The Making of the modern Gulf states **7624**
Zahn, H.L.
Wörterbuch für das Bank- und Börsenwesen. Deutsch-Englisch, Englisch-Deutsch. Dictionary of banking and stock trading **2201**
Zaidner, M.
The Jewish travel guide **914**
Zaire **4841**
Zambia **4865**
Zambia in maps **5319**
Zamponi, L.F.
Niger **4813**
Zarach, S.
British business history **1858**
Debrett's bibliography of business history **2460**
Zeitschrift für die neutestamentliche Wissenschaft **532**
Zell, H.M. *and* Lomer, C.
The African studies companion **4773**
Zemtsov, I.
Encyclopedia of Soviet life **1731**
Zen Buddhism **877**
Zentner, C. *and* Bedürftig, F.
The Encyclopedia of the Third Reich **7273**
Zetter, L.
Vachers biographical guide, 1990 **3056**
Zhao Xilin
Tourist atlas of China **5272**
Zheltov, L.M. *and* Kniazev, V.S.
Anglo-russkii i russko-angliiskii slovar po morskomu pravu/English-Russian and Russian-English law of the sea dictionary **2956**
Zia, H. *and* Gall, S.B.
Notable Asian Americans **5952**
Ziegler, E.B.
Folklore **4125**
Zimbabwe **4861-4862**
Zimbabwe. Central Statistical Office
Statistical yearbook of Zimbabwe, **1281**
Zink, S.D.
'Location and analysis of the historical publications produced by agencies of the United States Government during the era of the American Revolution Bicentennial 1974-1976' **8027**
Ziring, L.
The Middle East political dictionary **1446**
Ziring, L *and* Plano, J.C. *and* Olton, R.
International relations **1606**
Zito, D.R. *and* Zito, G.V.
A Guide to research in gerontology: strategies and resources **1111**
Znapierowski, A.
The World encyclopedia of flags **6345**
Zohary, M.
Plants of the Bible **495**
Zolar's encyclopaedia of omens, signs and superstitions **4178**
The Zondervan pictorial encyclopedia of the Bible **452**
Zonhoven, L.M.J.
Annual Egyptological bibliography/ Bibliographie **4230**

Subject Index

The index reference is to the running number given to each item. The running numbers are in one sequence throughout the volume and can be found at the top right-hand corner of the entry for each item.

The index is computer generated, thus terms for the index have been largely derived from the headings and sub-headings used throughout *Walford*, but many other entries have been added, including synonyms, inverted headings, and cross-references. Some form headings such as 'Bibliographies', 'Dictionaries', etc., are omitted as leading to too great a bulk.

The arrangement of the index is alphabetical and filing is word by word, with groups of initials counted as single words. Under each main heading printed in bold type in the index will be found a resumé of all the subject terms used under that heading and the numbers of the items to which they refer. Similarly, under each narrower sub-heading there is a list of terms used. Where the term in the index needs to be qualified by the broader term of which it is a sub-division, then the broader term is given in square brackets, *e.g.* **Japan** [Buddhism] or [Statistics].

Germany (History) *(contd.)*
Nazi Germany
Jews
Maps & Atlases **7287**
Maps & Atlases **7276-7277**
Germany, Federal Republic of
See
Federal Republic of Germany
Ghana
Bibliographies **4825**
[Area Studies] **4825**
Ghana (History)
Dictionaries **7790**
Gibraltar **5550**
Bibliographies **4604**
[Area Studies] **4604**
Glamorgan (History)
Maps & Atlases **7244**
Goa **7645**
Goblins
Bibliographies **4183-4184**
Dictionaries **4185-4186**
Goths **6684**
Government (Politics) **1481**
Biographies **1485**
China
Yearbooks & Directories **1496**
Democracy
Dictionaries **1506**
Dictatorships **1502**
Encyclopaedias **1482-1483**
EU
Yearbooks & Directories **1490**
Fascism **1503-1505**
Great Britain
EU
Handbooks & Manuals **1493**
Handbooks & Manuals **1491-1492**
Japan
Biographies **1497**
Russia
Yearbooks & Directories **1495**
Scotland
Histories **1494**
USA **1498-1499**
Bibliographies of Bibliographies **1500-1501**
Worldwide **1486**
Biographies **1489**
Yearbooks & Directories **1487-1488**
Yearbooks & Directories **1484**
Government Bodies
Great Britain **3230-3231**
Yearbooks & Directories **3232**
Russia
Biographies **3233**
USA
Handbooks & Manuals **3234**
Worldwide **3229**
Government, Central **3319**
Africa **3344**
Asia—Near East **3343**
Belgium **3339**
China **3340-3341**
Denmark **3338**
Eire **3335**
England **3336**
Europe **3324**
Great Britain **3325-3330**
Bibliographies **3331**
Histories **3333-3334**
Yearbooks & Directories **3332**
India **3342**
Russia **3337**
USA
Bibliographies **3345**
Biographies **3349**
Yearbooks & Directories **3346-3348**
Worldwide **3320**
Yearbooks & Directories **3321-3323**
Government, Local **3275**

Government, Local *(contd.)*
Bibliographies **3276-3277**
Counties
England & Wales
Histories **3314**
USA
Biographies **3317-3318**
Dictionaries **3315**
Yearbooks & Directories **3316**
England
Histories **3291**
England & Wales
Handbooks & Manuals **3289-3290**
Europe—Western **3279**
Great Britain
Bibliographies **3280-3282**
Handbooks & Manuals **3283**
Histories **3287**
Tables & Data Books
Bibliographies **3286**
Yearbooks & Directories **3284-3285**
Handbooks & Manuals **3278**
Information Services
Great Britain **3293**
Scotland **3288**
Urban Areas (Towns & Cities) **3294**
Africa
Bibliographies **3307**
England **3304-3306**
Europe
Histories **3298**
Europe—Western
Histories **3299**
Great Britain
Histories **3302-3303**
Reviews & Abstracts **3300**
Yearbooks & Directories **3301**
Histories **3297**
Reviews & Abstracts **3295**
USA
Bibliographies **3308-3311**
Reviews & Abstracts **3312**
Yearbooks & Directories **3313**
Yearbooks & Directories **3296**
USA
Bibliographies **3292**
Grants (Further & Higher Education) **3918-3921**
Great Britain
Yearbooks & Directories **3922**
USA
Yearbooks & Directories **3923**
Great Britain (History) **6990-6996, 7014-7015, 7035-7038, 7043, 7049-7068, 7226-7230, 7246, 7256-7257, 7290, 7292-7295, 7303, 7309-7311, 7318-7319, 7323-7324, 7358-7359, 7365-7368, 7370-7374, 7392-7398, 7407-7412, 7436-7441, 7443, 7446-7448, 7450, 7452-7454, 7479-7482, 7485, 7488-7496, 7503-7504, 7506, 7510-7511**
20th Century **6983-6986**
Archives **6988**
Bibliographies **6987**
Research Methods **6989**
Azerbaijan
Dictionaries **7451**
Bibliographies **6919-6924**
CD-ROM **6925**
Biographies **6939**
Chronologies **6935-6938**
Dictionaries **6930-6931**
Encyclopaedias **6926-6929**
Georgian & Regency Period **6975-6976**
Encyclopaedias **6977**
Government State Papers **6940**
Institutions & Associations **6945**
Jews **6941-6942**
Maps & Atlases **6932-6934**
Middle Ages

Great Britain (History) *(contd.)*
Middle Ages
Bibliographies **6943-6944**
Moldova
Dictionaries **7513**
Plantagenets
Encyclopaedias **6963-6964**
Roman & Anglo Saxon Period **6946-6951**
Bibliographies **6952-6955**
Biographies **6960-6961**
Encyclopaedias **6956**
Government State Papers
Bibliographies **6962**
Handbooks & Manuals **6957**
Maps & Atlases **6958-6959**
Stuarts **6970**
Chronologies **6974**
Dictionaries **6971-6972**
Maps & Atlases **6973**
Tudors **6965-6966**
Bibliographies **6967**
Dictionaries **6968-6969**
Victorian Age **6978-6979**
Bibliographies **6980**
Encyclopaedias **6981**
Glossaries **6982**
Greece **5556**
Bibliographies **2849, 4634-4635**
Micromaterials **5855**
[Area Studies] **4634-4635**
[Biography] **5855**
[Law] **2849**
[Statistics] **1258**
Greece (Ancient History)
Archives **6711**
Bibliographies **6703**
Biographies **6708-6710**
Chronologies **6707**
Encyclopaedias **6704**
Handbooks & Manuals **6705**
Maps & Atlases **6706**
Greece (History)
Dictionaries **7483**
Middle Ages **7484**
Greece, Ancient **6423, 6625**
Bibliographies
Internet **4241**
Greece & Rome (Ancient History) **6685-6686**
Bibliographies **6687**
Biographies **6699**
Micromaterials **6700-6701**
Women **6702**
Dictionaries **6694-6695**
Encyclopaedias **6688-6693**
Maps & Atlases **6696-6697**
Internet **6698**
Greece & Rome, Ancient **15, 107-108, 4238-4239, 4355, 4520, 6422**
Maps & Atlases **4240**
Greenland **5681**
Bibliographies **5054-5055**
[Area Studies] **5053-5055**
Grenada
Bibliographies **4924**
[Area Studies] **4924**
Guam (History)
Dictionaries **8189**
Guatemala
Bibliographies **4885**
[Area Studies] **4885**
Guatemala (History)
Dictionaries **7905**
Guernsey **7153**
Guide Books
See
Gazetteers & Guide Books
Guinea
Bibliographies **4818-4819**
[Area Studies] **4817-4819**
Guinea (History)
Dictionaries **7785**

Online and Database Services Index

The index reference is to the running number given to each item. The running numbers are in one sequence throughout the volume and can be found at the top right hand corner of the entry for each item. This index is of authors and titles in one sequence. The names of authors are printed in bold type. Filing is word by word with groups of initials counted as single words.

The titles appearing in this index have been published as electronic databases. The databases are available on subscription as online database services, as websites or in CD-ROM or disk formats. An indication of the names of some of the hosts from whom the online databases are available is given in the text.